Massachusetts Juvenile Delinquency and Child Welfare Law Sourcebook & Citator

2020 EDITION

Hon. Peter M. Coyne

Amy M. Karp

Wendy Wolf

MCLE
NEW ENGLAND
Keep raising the bar.®

2200163B17

Printed in the United States of America

This publication should be cited: Hon. Peter M. Coyne, Amy M. Karp, Esq., and Wendy Wolf, Esq., *Massachusetts Juvenile Delinquency and Child Welfare Law Sourcebook & Citator 2020* (MCLE, Inc. 2019).

ISSN: 1553-4499
ISBN: 1-68345-191-0

Massachusetts Continuing Legal Education, Inc.
Ten Winter Place, Boston, MA 02108-4751
800-966-6253 | Fax 617-482-9498 | www.mcle.org

Dedication

When we are caught up in the daily grind of preparing cases, meeting with clients, and appearing in court, it is easy to overlook the compelling work that is done on a daily basis in the Juvenile and Probate and Family Courts of the Commonwealth. It is important from time to time to step back and reflect on this. When one does so, the reflection is of the vast number of lawyers, probation officers, clerks, social workers, court clinicians, support staff, law clerks, court officers, and judges who day in and day out truly do God's work—repairing families when it is possible, protecting and saving children when it is not, and prosecuting and defending children while keeping in mind the important goal of rehabilitation. For these individuals' commitment to this most compelling work, we dedicate this book to them.

Acknowledgments

First and foremost, we express our sincere gratitude to past coeditor, the Honorable Stephen M. Limon, for his dedication and many contributions to the sourcebook. We wish him the very best in his retirement. We also offer thanks to MCLE for its continuing support and to our colleagues at the Juvenile Court and the Committee for Public Counsel Services Children and Family Law Division and Youth Advocacy Division.

Hon. Peter M. Coyne
Amy M. Karp
Wendy Wolf

MCLE Press benefits greatly from the attorneys and judges who serve as volunteer editors, commentators, and authors for our books. Their willingness to share their time and expertise is an integral part of our continuing effort to educate Massachusetts attorneys and help to enhance the quality of legal services provided to the public.

For their shared vision for this publication and its previous editions, and for their valuable guidance on the most useful primary sources to be included as its content, MCLE thanks the coeditors, the Honorable Peter M. Coyne, Amy M. Karp, and Wendy Wolf. Their many contributions are greatly appreciated.

We also offer our acknowledgment of past coeditors, the Honorable Stephen M. Limon and the Honorable R. Marc Kantrowitz (both now retired), and the following persons and entities for their assistance and contributions to the book both this year and in past years: the Children's Law Center, the Administrative Office of the Juvenile Court, the Boston Juvenile Court Clinic, and Dr. Virginia Merritt.

Additionally, we would like to acknowledge the hard work of MCLE staff members in producing this book on an annual basis.

On behalf of Jack Reilly, Publisher, Maryanne G. Jensen, Editor-in-Chief, and the MCLE Board of Trustees, our appreciation extends to all whose talent and hard work helped create and revise this valuable publication.

Alexis J. LeBlanc
Publications Attorney
December 2019

About the Editors

HON. PETER M. COYNE is an associate justice of the Suffolk County Juvenile Court in Boston. Formerly, he was an assistant clerk magistrate of the Suffolk County Juvenile Court, and before that was a practitioner specializing in the area of juvenile law, accepting civil and delinquency appointments at the Suffolk County Juvenile Court. Judge Coyne is a graduate of the University of Massachusetts Amherst (B.A.), Northeastern University (M.S.), and Suffolk University Law School (J.D.). He is an adjunct professor in the Sociology Department at Suffolk University.

AMY M. KARP is the training director for the Children and Family Law Division of the Committee for Public Counsel Services in Boston. She is a graduate of Cornell University and Harvard Law School. She joined the Children and Family Law Program in 1995 as a staff attorney. From 1990 to 1995, she was in private practice. Ms. Karp has served on a number of boards and committees addressing issues related to children and families, including the Massachusetts Appleseed Center for Law and Justice, the Massachusetts Children's Justice Act Task Force, the Massachusetts Court Improvement Program Steering Committee, and the Task Force on Children Affected by Domestic Violence. As training director for the Children and Family Law Division, Ms. Karp develops training programs and resources for trial and appellate attorneys appointed to represent children and indigent parents in state intervention cases. She has served as cochair for a number of multidisciplinary conferences, including the Children's Justice Act Conference and MCLE's annual Juvenile Delinquency and Child Welfare Law Conference.

WENDY WOLF is the director of training for the Youth Advocacy Division (YAD) of the Committee for Public Counsel Services in Boston. She has been a trial attorney with CPCS since 1985. She began her practice representing adults accused of felonies and was a supervising attorney in the Cambridge office of CPCS. In 1996, she joined the Youth Advocacy Project as the supervising attorney. In 2002, Ms. Wolf started the Juvenile Defense Network, which has evolved into the YAD training unit. She is a codirector of the New England Juvenile Defender Center and a 2007 recipient of the Massachusetts Bar Association Access to Justice Defender Award. Ms. Wolf earned her B.S. in social work from the University of Vermont and her J.D. from Suffolk University Law School.

Editorial Note

This sourcebook features the text of primary sources in their "official" versions, which may include typographical irregularities. Rather than inserting "[sic]" or editing the primary source text, MCLE has made the editorial decision to leave such irregularities untouched; in this way the information provided by the sourcebook may stay true to the original text, free from editorial overlay.

Contents

Electronic Materials Download

All of the content of this book is available for download as a PDF file from the MCLE website. **You must be signed into the account used to purchase this book to access the downloadable ebook**.

To download the ebook, go to

www.mcle.org/forms

and enter Forms Download Code (case sensitive):

JUnnSSPB

This code applies only to the 2020 Edition of the *Massachusetts Juvenile Delinquency and Child Welfare Law Sourcebook & Citator.* You may download the ebook in PDF format, and may return to the download page anytime while this edition remains in print.

Use Note:

The ebook is an electronic version of the content as it appears in the book—there is no interactive software that deletes information or fills in blank lines in the forms included in the book. For court forms and other standardized forms, be sure to check with the original source to obtain the most recent version and any special instructions.

If you have any questions or problems accessing your ebook download, please contact MCLE's Customer Service at **customerserv-ice@mcle.org** or by phone at 1-800-966-6253

PART 1

Selected Statutes

Chapter 6. Criminal Record Information

§ 172. Maintenance of criminal offender record information in electronic format; accessibility via world wide web; eligibility for access to database; use and dissemination criminal offender record information

[Amended by 2010 Mass. Acts c. 256, § 21, effective May 4, 2012; 2014 Mass. Acts c. 284, § 2, effective Aug. 13, 2014; 2015 Mass. Acts c. 10, § 3, effective Mar. 31, 2015; 2016 Mass. Acts c. 187, § 1, effective Nov. 3, 2016; 2017 Mass. Acts c. 110, § 3, effective Nov. 3, 2017; 2018 Mass. Acts c. 69, § 6, effective Apr. 13, 2018; 2018 Mass. Acts c. 202, § 1, effective date per § 26.]

(a) The department shall maintain criminal offender record information in a database, which shall exist in an electronic format and be accessible via the world wide web. Except as provided otherwise in this chapter, access to the database shall be limited as follows:

(1) Criminal justice agencies may obtain all criminal offender record information, including sealed records, for the actual performance of their criminal justice duties. Licensing authorities, as defined in section 121 of chapter 140, may obtain all criminal offender record information, including sealed records, for the purpose of firearms licensing in accordance with sections 121 to 131P, inclusive, of chapter 140. The criminal record review board may obtain all criminal offender record information, including sealed records, for the actual performance of its duties.

(2) A requestor authorized or required by statute, regulation or accreditation requirement to obtain criminal offender record information other than that available under clause (3) may obtain such information to the extent and for the purposes authorized to comply with said statute, regulation or accreditation requirement.

(3) A requestor or the requestor's legally designated representative may obtain criminal offender record information for any of the following purposes: (i) to evaluate current and prospective employees including full-time, part-time, contract, internship employees or volunteers; (ii) to evaluate applicants for rental or lease of housing; (iii) to evaluate volunteers for services; and (iv) to evaluate applicants for a professional or occupational license issued by a state or municipal entity. Criminal offender record information made available under this section shall be limited to the following: (i) felony convictions or findings of not guilty by reason of insanity for 10 years following the disposition thereof, including termination of any period of incarceration or custody, (ii) misdemeanor convictions for 5 years following the disposition thereof, including termination of any period of incarceration or custody, and (iii) pending criminal charges, which shall include cases that have been continued without a finding until such time as the case is dismissed pursuant to section 18 of chapter 278; provided, however, that prior misdemeanor and felony conviction records shall be available for the entire period that the subject's last available conviction record is available under this section; and provided further, that a violation of section 7 of chapter 209A and a violation of section 9 of chapter 258E shall be treated as a felony for purposes of this section.

(4) Any member of the general public may upon written request to the department and in accordance with regulations established by the department obtain the following criminal offender record information on a subject: (i) convictions or findings of not guilty by reason of insanity for any felony punishable by a term of imprisonment of 5 years or more, for 10 years following the disposition thereof, including termination of any period of incarceration or custody; (ii) information indicating custody status and placement within the correction system for an individual who has been convicted of any offense and sentenced to any term of imprisonment, and at the time of the request: is serving a sentence of probation or incarceration, or is under the custody of the parole board; (iii) felony convictions or findings of not guilty by reason of insanity for 2 years following the disposition thereof, including any period of incarceration or custody; and (iv) misdemeanor convictions for 1 year following the disposition thereof, including any period of incarceration or custody.

(5) A subject who seeks to obtain his own criminal offender record information and the subject's legally designated representative may obtain all criminal offender record information from the department pertaining to the subject under section 175.

(6) The commissioner may provide access to criminal offender record information to persons other than those entitled to obtain access under this section, if the commissioner finds that such dissemination to such requestor serves the public interest. Upon such a finding, the commissioner shall also determine the extent of access to criminal offender record information necessary to sustain the public interest. The commissioner shall make an annual report to the governor and file a copy of the report with the state secretary, the attorney general, the clerk of the house of representatives and the clerk of the senate documenting all access provided under this paragraph, without inclusion of identifying data on a subject. The annual report shall be available to the public upon request.

(7) Housing authorities operating pursuant to chapter 121B may obtain from the department conviction and pending criminal offender record information for the sole purpose of evaluating applications for housing owned by such housing authority, in order to further the protection and well-being of tenants of such housing authorities.

1

(8) The department of telecommunications and cable and the department of public utilities may obtain from the department all available criminal offender record information for the purpose of screening applicants for motor bus driver certificates and applicants who regularly transport school age children or students under chapter 71B in the course of their job duties. The department of public1 telecommunications and cable and the department of public utilities shall not disseminate such information for any purpose other than to further the protection of children.

(9) The department of children and families and the department of youth services may obtain from the department data permitted under section 172B.

(10) A person providing services in a home or community-based setting for any elderly person or disabled person or who will have direct or indirect contact with such elderly or disabled person or access to such person's files may obtain from the department data permitted under section 172C.

(11) The IV-D agency as set forth in chapter 119A may obtain from the department data permitted under section 172D and section 14 of chapter 119A.

(12) A long-term care facility, as defined in section 72W of chapter 111, an assisted living residence as defined in section 1 of chapter 19D, and any continuing care facility as defined in section 1 of chapter 40D may obtain from the department data permitted under section 172E.

(13) The department of early education and care and adoption and foster placement agencies licensed by the department may obtain from the department data permitted under section 172F.

(14) Operators of camps for children may obtain from the department data permitted under section 172G.

(15) An entity or organization primarily engaged in providing activities or programs to children 18 years of age or younger that accepts volunteers may obtain from the department data permitted under section 172H.

(16) School committees or superintendents that have contracted with taxicab companies to provide for the transportation of pupils pursuant to section 7A of chapter 71 may obtain from the department data permitted under section 172I.

(17) The commissioner of banks may obtain from the department data permitted under section 172J, section 3 of chapter 255E and section 3 of chapter 255F.

(18) A children's camp or school that plans to employ a person or accept a volunteer for a climbing wall or challenge course program may obtain from the department data permitted under section 172K.

(19) A victim of a crime, a witness or a family member of a homicide victim, as defined in section 1 of chapter 258B, may obtain from the department data permitted under section 178A.

(20) The motor vehicle insurance merit rating board may obtain from the department data permitted under section 57A of chapter 6C.

(21) The department of early education and care, or its designee, may obtain from the department data permitted under sections 6 and 8 of chapter 15D.

(22) The district attorney may obtain from the department data permitted under section 2A of chapter 38.

(23) A school committee and superintendent of any city, town or regional school district and the principal, by whatever title the position be known, of a public or accredited private school of any city, town or regional school district, may obtain from the department data permitted under section 38R of chapter 71.

(24) The Massachusetts Port Authority may obtain from the department data permitted under section 61 of chapter 90.

(25) The department of children and families may obtain from the department data permitted under section 26A of chapter 119, section 3B of chapter 210.

(26) The state racing commission may obtain from the department data permitted under section 9A of chapter 128A.

(27) A court, office of jury commissioner, and the clerk of court or assistant clerk may obtain from the department data permitted under section 33 of chapter 234A.

(28) The pension fraud unit within the public employee retirement administration commission may obtain from the department data permitted under section 1 of chapter 338 of the acts of 1990.

(29) Special education school programs approved under chapter 71B may obtain from the department all criminal offender record information provided for in paragraph (3) of subsection (a).

(30) The department shall configure the database to allow for the exchange, dissemination, distribution and direct connection of the criminal record information system to criminal record information systems in other states and relevant federal agencies including the Federal Bureau of Investigation and Immigration and Customs Enforcement that utilize fingerprint or iris scanning and similar databases.

(31) Navigator organizations certified by the commonwealth health insurance connector authority under 42 U.S.C. § 18031(i) may obtain from the department data permitted under section 172L.

(31) A person licensed pursuant to section 122 of chapter 140 may obtain from the department data permitted under section 172L.

(32) A person licensed pursuant to section 122 of chapter 140 may obtain from the department data permitted under section 172M.

(33) The department of public utilities and its departments or divisions may obtain from the department all available criminal offender record information, as defined in section 167, to determine the suitability of an applicant to obtain a transportation network driver certificate pursuant to chapter 159A½. Information obtained pursuant to this section shall not be disseminated for any purpose other than to further public protection and safety.

(b) Notwithstanding the foregoing, convictions for murder, voluntary manslaughter, involuntary manslaughter, and sex offenses as defined in section 178C of chapter 6 that are punishable by a term of incarceration in state prison shall remain in the database permanently and shall be available to all requestors listed in paragraphs (1) through (3), inclusive, of subsection (a) unless sealed under section 100A of chapter 276.

(c) The department shall specify the information that a requestor shall provide to query the database, including, but not limited to, the subject's name, date of birth and the last 4 digits of the subject's social security number; provided, however, that a member of the public accessing information under paragraph (4) of subsection (a) shall not be required to provide the last four digits of the subject's social security number. To obtain criminal offender record information concerning a subject pursuant to subsection (a)(2) or (a)(3), the requestor must certify under the penalties of perjury that the requestor is an authorized designee of a qualifying entity, that the request is for a purpose authorized under subsection (a)(2) or (a)(3), and that the subject has signed an acknowledgement form authorizing the requestor to obtain the subject's criminal offender record information. The requestor must also certify that he has verified the identity of the subject by reviewing a form of government-issued identification. Each requestor shall maintain acknowledgement forms for a period of 1 year from the date the request is submitted. Such forms shall be subject to audit by the department. The department may establish rules or regulations imposing other requirements or affirmative obligations upon requestors as a condition of obtaining access to the database; provided, however, that such additional rules and regulations are not in conflict with the state and federal Fair Credit Reporting Acts.

In connection with any decision regarding employment, volunteer opportunities, housing or professional licensing, a person in possession of an applicant's criminal offender record information shall provide the applicant with the criminal history record in the person's possession, whether obtained from the department or any other source, (a) prior to questioning the applicant about his criminal history and (b) if the person makes a decision adverse to the applicant on the basis of his criminal history; provided, however, that if the person has provided the applicant with a copy of his criminal offender record information prior to questioning the person is not required to provide the information a second time in connection with an adverse decision based on this information. Failure to provide such criminal history information to the individual in accordance with this section may subject the offending person to investigation, hearing and sanctions by the board.

(d) Except as authorized by this section, it shall be unlawful to request or require a person to provide a copy of his criminal offender record information. Violation of this subsection is punishable by the penalties set forth in section 178.

(e) No employer or person relying on volunteers shall be liable for negligent hiring practices by reason of relying solely on criminal offender record information received from the department and not performing additional criminal history background checks, unless required to do so by law; provided, however, that the employer made an employment decision within 90 days of obtaining the criminal offender record information and maintained and followed policies and procedures for verification of the subject's identifying information consistent with the requirements set forth in this section and in the department's regulations.

No employer shall be liable for discriminatory employment practices for the failure to hire a person on the basis of criminal offender record information that contains erroneous information requested and received from the department, if the employer would not have been liable if the information had been accurate; provided, however, that the employer made an employment decision within 90 days of obtaining the criminal offender record information and maintained and followed policies and procedures for verification of the individual's information consistent with the requirements set forth in this section and the department's regulations.

Neither the board nor the department shall be liable in any civil or criminal action by reason of any criminal offender record information or self-audit log that is disseminated by the board, including any information that is false, inaccurate or incorrect because it was erroneously entered by the court or the office of the commissioner of probation.

(f) A requestor shall not disseminate criminal offender record information except upon request by a subject; provided, however, that a requestor may share criminal offender record information with individuals within the requesting entity that have a need to know the contents of the criminal offender record information to serve the purpose for which the information was obtained; and provided further, that upon request, a requestor shall share criminal offender record information with the government entities charged with overseeing, supervising, or regulating them. A requestor shall maintain a secondary dissemination log for a period of one year following the dissemination of a subject's criminal offender record information. The log shall include the following information: (i) name of subject; (ii) date of birth of the subject; (iii) date of the dissemination; (iv) name of person to whom it was disseminated; and (v) the purpose for the dissemination. The secondary dissemination log shall be subject to audit by the department.

Unless otherwise provided by law or court order, a requestor shall not maintain a copy, electronic or otherwise, of requested criminal offender record information obtained from the department for more than 7 years from the last date of employment, volunteer service or residency or from the date of the final decision of the requestor regarding the subject.

(g) The department shall maintain a log of all queries that shall indicate the name of the requestor, the name of the subject, the date of the query, and the certified purpose of the query. A self-audit may be requested for no fee once every 90 days. The commissioner may impose a fee in an amount as determined by the secretary of public safety and security, for self-audit requests made more than once every 90 days. Upon request, the commissioner may transmit the self-audit electronically. Further, if funding is available and technology reasonably allows, the department shall establish a mechanism that will notify a subject, or an advocate or agent designated by the subject, by electronic mail or other communication mechanism whenever a query is made regarding the subject. The self-audit log and query log shall not be considered a public record.

(h) Notwithstanding the provisions of this section, the motor vehicle insurance merit rating board may disseminate information concerning convictions of automobile law violations as defined in section 1 of chapter 90C, or information concerning a charge of operating a motor vehicle while under the influence of intoxicating liquor that results in assignment to a driver alcohol program as described in section 24D of chapter 90, directly or indirectly, to an insurance company doing motor vehicle insurance business within the commonwealth, or to such insurance company's agents, independent contractors or policyholders to be used exclusively for motor vehicle insurance purposes.

(i) Notwithstanding any other provisions of this section, information indicating custody status and placement within the correction system shall be available to any person upon request; provided, however that no information shall be disclosed that identifies family members, friends, medical or psychological history, or any other personal information unless such information is directly relevant to such release or custody placement decision, and no information shall be provided if its release would violate any other provisions of state or federal law.

(j) The parole board, subject to sections 130 and 154 of chapter 127, the department of correction, a county correctional authority or a probation officer with the approval of a justice of the appropriate division of the trial court may, in its discretion, make available a summary, which may include references to criminal offender record information or evaluative information, concerning a decision to release an individual on a permanent or temporary basis, to deny such release, or to change the individual's custody status.

(k) Notwithstanding any other provision of this section or any other general or special law to the contrary, members of the public who are in fear of an offender may obtain from the department advance notification of the temporary or permanent release of an offender from custody, including but not limited to expiration of a sentence, furlough, parole, work release or educational release. An individual seeking access to advance notification shall verify by a written declaration under the penalties of perjury that the individual is in fear of the offender and that advance notification is warranted for physical safety reasons.

(l) Any individual or entity that receives or obtains criminal offender record information from any source in violation of sections 168 through 175 of this chapter, whether directly or through an intermediary, shall not collect, store, disseminate, or use such criminal offender record information in any manner or for any purpose.

(m) Notwithstanding this section or chapter 66A, the following shall be public records: (1) police daily logs, arrest registers, or other similar records compiled chronologically; (2) chronologically maintained court records of public judicial proceedings; (3) published records of public court or administrative proceedings, and of public judicial administrative or legislative proceedings; and (4) decisions of the parole board as provided in section 130 of chapter 127.

(n) The commissioner, upon the advice of the board, shall promulgate rules and regulations to carry out the provisions of this section.

(o) Notwithstanding any other provision of this section or any other general or special law to the contrary, all gaming service employees shall be required to register with the investigations and enforcement bureau established in section 6 of chapter 23K but the Massachusetts gaming commission may, in its discretion, exempt certain gaming service employees by job position from the registration requirement. The commission and the bureau may require a gaming service employee to produce any information deemed necessary.

§ 172B. Children and families department; youth services department; available information

[Amended by 2008 Mass. Acts c. 176, § 8, effective July 8, 2008.]

Notwithstanding any provision of section one hundred seventy-two of this chapter or of any other provision of law, the following information shall be available to the department of children and families and the department of youth services, upon request, for the purpose of evaluating any and all foster homes and adoptive homes, whether with public or private agencies, in order to further the protection of children: conviction data, arrest data, sealed record data, and juvenile arrest or conviction data. The department of children and families and the department of youth services shall not make, and shall prohibit, any dissemination of such information, for any purpose other than as set forth herein.

§ 175. Right of subject to inspect criminal offender record information; correction of inaccurate or incomplete information; procedure; restrictions

[Amended by 2010 Mass. Acts c. 256, § 35, effective May 4, 2012.]

A subject shall have the right to inspect, and if practicable, obtain a copy of all criminal offender record information from the department that refers to the subject. The commissioner shall publish and furnish, upon request, guidelines for individuals on how to correct inaccurate or incomplete information. Subject to appropriation, the department shall provide assistance to individuals that have requested assistance to correct inaccurate or incomplete criminal offender record information. Such assistance shall include but not be limited to cooperation with appropriate entities to correct, modify or appropriately supplement criminal offender record information that has been determined to be inaccurate or incomplete. If criminal offender record information is corrected by the office of the commissioner of probation or the courts, any corrections made by such commissioner or court shall be transmitted forthwith to the department and the department's database shall reflect the corrected criminal offender record information.

Requestors shall prescribe reasonable hours and places for subjects to inspect their criminal offender record information under subsection (f) of section 172 and shall impose such additional restrictions as are reasonably necessary both to ensure the record's security and to verify the identities of those who seek to inspect them.

§ 178C. Definitions

[Amended by 1999 Mass. Acts c. 74, § 2, effective Sept. 10, 1999; 2003 Mass. Acts c. 77, §§ 1–3, effective Sept. 30, 2003; 2006 Mass. Acts c. 139, §§ 5–6, effective July 1, 2006; 2010 Mass. Acts c. 256, § 38, effective Nov. 4, 2010; 2011 Mass. Acts c. 178, §§ 1–3, effective Nov. 21, 2011; 2018 Mass. Acts c. 219, § 1, effective Nov. 7, 2018.]

As used in sections 178C to 178P, inclusive, the following words shall have the following meanings:

"Agency", an agency, department, board, commission or entity within the executive or judicial branch, excluding the committee for public counsel services, which has custody of, supervision of or responsibility for a sex offender as defined in accordance with this chapter, including an individual participating in a program of any such agency, whether such program is conducted under a contract with a private entity or otherwise. Each agency shall be responsible for the identification of such individuals within its custody, supervision or responsibility. Notwithstanding any general or special law to the contrary, each such agency shall be certified to receive criminal offender record information maintained by the department for the purpose of identifying such individuals.

"Employment", includes employment that is full-time or part-time for a period of time exceeding 14 days or for an aggregate period of time exceeding 30 days during any calendar year, whether compensated or uncompensated.

"Institution of higher learning", a post secondary institution.

"Mental abnormality", a congenital or acquired condition of a person that affects the emotional or volitional capacity of such person in a manner that predisposes that person to the commission of criminal sexual acts to a degree that makes such person a menace to the health and safety of other persons.

"Predatory", an act directed at a stranger or person with whom a relationship has been established, promoted or utilized for the primary purpose of victimization.

"Secondary addresses," the addresses of all places where a sex offender lives, abides, lodges, or resides for a period of 14 or more days in the aggregate during any calendar year and which is not a sex offender's primary address; or a place where a sex offender routinely lives, abides, lodges, or resides for a period of 4 or more consecutive or nonconsecutive days in any month and which is not a sex offender's permanent address, including any out-of-state address.

"Sentencing court", the court that sentenced a sex offender for the most recent sexually violent offense or sex offense or the superior court if such sentencing occurred in another jurisdiction or the sex offender registry board to the extent permitted by federal law and established by the board's regulations.

"Sex offender", a person who resides, has secondary addresses, works, or attends an institution of higher learning in the commonwealth and who has been convicted of a sex offense or who has been adjudicated as a youthful offender or as a delinquent juvenile by reason of a sex offense or a person released from incarceration or parole or probation supervision or custody with the department of youth services for such a conviction or adjudication or a person who has been adjudicated a sexually dangerous person under section 14 of chapter 123A, as in force at the time of adjudication, or a person released from civil commitment pursuant to section 9 of said chapter 123A, whichever last occurs, on or after August 1, 1981.

"Sex offender registry", the collected information and data that is received by the department pursuant to sections 178C to 178P, inclusive, as such information and data is modified or amended by the sex offender registry board or a court of competent jurisdiction pursuant to said sections 178C to 178P, inclusive.

"Sex offense", an indecent assault and battery on a child under 14 under section 13B of chapter 265; indecent assault and battery on a mentally retarded person under section 13F of said chapter 265; indecent assault and battery on a person age 14 or over under section 13H of said chapter 265; rape under section 22 of said chapter 265; rape of a child under 16 with force under section 22A of said chapter 265; rape and abuse of a child under section 23 of said chapter 265; assault with intent to commit rape under section 24 of said chapter 265; assault of a child with intent to commit rape under section 24B of said chapter 265; kidnapping of a child under section 26 of said chapter 265; enticing a child under the age of 16 for the purposes of committing a crime under section 26C of said chapter 265; enticing a child under 18 via electronic communication to engage in prostitution, human trafficking or commercial sexual activity under section 26D of said chapter 265; trafficking of persons for sexual servitude under section 50 of said chapter 265; a second or subsequent violation of human trafficking for sexual servitude under section 52 of chapter 265 enticing away a person for prostitution or sexual intercourse under section 2 of chapter 272; drugging persons for sexual intercourse under section 3 of said chapter 272; inducing a minor into prostitution under section 4A of said chapter 272; living off or sharing earnings of a minor prostitute under section 4B of said chapter 272; second and subsequent adjudication or conviction for open and gross lewdness and lascivious behavior under section 16 of said chapter 272, but excluding a first or single adjudication as a delinquent juvenile before August 1, 1992; incestuous marriage or intercourse under section 17 of said chapter 272; disseminating to a minor matter harmful to a minor under section 28 of said chapter 272; posing or exhibiting a child in a state of nudity under section 29A of said chapter 272; dissemination of visual material of a child in a state of nudity or sexual conduct under section 29B of said chapter 272; possession of child pornography under section 29C of said chapter 272; unnatural and lascivious acts with a child under 16 under section 35A of said chapter 272; engaging in sexual contact with an animal under section 77C of said chapter 272; aggravated rape under section 39 of chapter 277; and any attempt to commit a violation of any of the aforementioned sections pursuant to section 6 of chapter 274 or a like violation of the laws of another state, the United States or a military, territorial or Indian tribal authority.

"Sex offense involving a child", an indecent assault and battery on a child under 14 under section 13B of chapter 265; rape of a child under 16 with force under section 22A of said chapter 265; rape and abuse of a child under section 23 of said chapter 265; assault of a child with intent to commit rape under section 24B of said chapter 265; kidnapping of a child under the age of 16 under section 26 of said chapter 265; enticing a child under the age of 16 for the purposes of committing a crime under section 26C of said chapter 265; enticing a child under 18 via electronic communication to engage in prostitution, human trafficking or commercial sexual activity under section 26D of said chapter 265; trafficking of persons for sexual servitude upon a person under 18 years of age under subsection (b) of section 50 of said chapter 265; inducing a minor into prostitution under section 4A of chapter 272; living off or sharing earnings of a minor prostitute under section 4B of said chapter 272; disseminating to a minor matter harmful to a minor under section 28 of said chapter 272; posing or exhibiting a child in a state of nudity under section 29A of said chapter 272; dissemination of visual material of a child in a state of nudity or sexual conduct under section 29B of said chapter 272; unnatural and lascivious acts with a child under 16 under section 35A of said chapter 272; aggravated rape under section 39 of chapter 277; and any attempt to commit a violation of any of the aforementioned sections pursuant to section 6 of chapter 274 or a like violation of the laws of another state, the United States or a military, territorial or Indian tribal authority.

"Sexually violent offense", indecent assault and battery on a child under 14 under section 13B of chapter 265; indecent assault and battery on a mentally retarded person under section 13F of said chapter 265; rape under section 22 of said chapter 265; rape of a child under 16 with force under section 22A of said chapter 265; assault with intent to commit rape under section 24 of said chapter 265; assault of a child with intent to commit rape under section 24B of said chapter 265; enticing a child under 18 via electronic communication to engage in prostitution, human trafficking or commercial sexual activity under section 26D of said chapter 265; trafficking of persons for sexual servitude under section 50 of chapter 265; a second or subsequent violation of human trafficking for sexual servitude under section 52 of chapter 265; drugging persons for sexual intercourse under section 3 of chapter 272; unnatural and lascivious acts with a child under 16 under section 35A of said chapter 272; aggravated rape under section 39 of chapter 277; and any attempt to commit a violation of any of the aforementioned sections pursuant to section 6 of chapter 274 or a like violation of the law of another state, the United States or a military, territorial or Indian tribal authority, or any other offense that the sex offender registry board determines to be a sexually violent offense pursuant to the Jacob Wetterling Crimes Against Children and Sexually Violent Offender Registration Act, 42 U.S.C. § 14071.

"Sexually violent predator", a person who has been convicted of a sexually violent offense or who has been adjudicated as a youthful offender or as a delinquent juvenile by reason of a sexually violent offense, or a person released from incarceration, parole, probation supervision or commitment under chapter 123A or custody with the department of youth services for such a conviction or adjudication, whichever last occurs, on or after August 1, 1981, and who suffers from a mental abnormality or personality disorder that makes such person likely to engage in predatory sexually violent offenses.

§ 178D. Sex offender registry

[Amended by 1999 Mass. Acts c. 74, § 2, effective Sept. 10, 1999; 2003 Mass. Acts c. 77, § 4, effective Sept. 30, 2003; 2003 Mass. Acts c. 140, § 5, effective Nov. 26, 2003; 2006 Mass. Acts c. 139, §§ 7–8, effective July 1, 2006; 2010 Mass. Acts c. 256, § 39, effective Nov. 4, 2010; 2013 Mass. Acts c. 38, § 7, effective July 1, 2013.]

The sex offender registry board, known as the board, in cooperation with the department, shall establish and maintain a central computerized registry of all sex offenders required to register pursuant to sections 178C to 178P, inclusive, known as the sex offender registry. The sex offender registry shall be updated based on information made available to the board, including information acquired pursuant to the registration provisions of said sections 178C to 178P, inclusive. The file on each sex offender required to register pursuant to said sections 178C to 178P, inclusive, shall include the following information, hereinafter referred to as registration data:

(a) the sex offender's name, aliases used, date and place of birth, sex, race, height, weight, eye and hair color, social security number, home address, any secondary addresses and work address and, if the sex offender works at or attends an institution of higher learning, the name and address of the institution;

(b) a photograph and set of fingerprints;

(c) a description of the offense for which the sex offender was convicted or adjudicated, the city or town where the offense occurred, the date of conviction or adjudication and the sentence imposed;

(d) any other information which may be useful in assessing the risk of the sex offender to reoffend; and

(e) any other information which may be useful in identifying the sex offender.

Notwithstanding sections 178C to 178P, inclusive, or any other general or special law to the contrary and in addition to any responsibility otherwise imposed upon the board, the board shall make the sex offender information contained in the sex offender registry, delineated below in subsections (i) to (viii), inclusive, available for inspection by the general public in the form of a comprehensive database published on the internet, known as the "sex offender internet database"; provided, however, that no registration data relating to a sex offender given a level 1 designation by the board under section 178K shall be published in the sex offender internet database but may be disseminated by the board as otherwise permitted by said sections 178C to 178P, inclusive; and provided further, that the board shall keep confidential and shall not publish in the sex offender internet database any information relating to requests for registration data under sections 178I and 178J:

(i) the name of the sex offender;

(ii) the offender's home address and any secondary addresses;

(iii) the offender's work address;

(iv) the offense for which the offender was convicted or adjudicated and the date of the conviction or adjudication;

(v) the sex offender's age, sex, race, height, weight, eye and hair color;

(vi) a photograph of the sex offender, if available;

(vii) whether the sex offender has been designated a sexually violent predator; and

(viii) whether the offender is in compliance with the registration obligations of sections 178C to 178P, inclusive.

All information provided to the general public through the sex offender internet database shall include a warning regarding the criminal penalties for use of sex offender registry information to commit a crime or to engage in illegal discrimination or harassment of an offender and the punishment for threatening to commit a crime under section 4 of chapter 275. The sex offender internet database shall be updated regularly, based on information available to the board and shall be open to searches by the public at any time without charge or subscription. The board shall promulgate rules and regulations to implement, update and maintain such a sex offender internet database, to ensure the accuracy, integrity and security of information contained therein, to ensure the prompt and complete removal of registration data for persons whose duty to register has terminated or expired under section 178G, 178L or 178M or any other law and to protect against the inaccurate, improper or inadvertent publication of registration data on the internet.

The board shall develop standardized registration and verification forms, which shall include registration data as required pursuant to sections 178C to 178P. The board shall make blank copies of such forms available to all agencies having custody of sex offenders and all city and town police departments; provided, however, that the board shall determine the format for the collection and dissemination of registration data, which may include the electronic transmission of data. Records maintained in the sex offender registry shall be open to any law enforcement agency in the commonwealth, the United States or any other state. The board shall promulgate rules and regulations to implement the provisions of sections 178C to 178P, inclusive. Such rules and regulations shall include provisions which may permit police departments located in a city or town that is divided into more than one zip code to disseminate information pursuant to the provisions of section 178J categorized by zip code and to disseminate such information limited to one or more zip codes if the request for such dissemination is so qualified; provided, however, that for the city of Boston dissemination of information may be limited to one or more police districts.

The board may promulgate regulations further defining in a manner consistent with maintaining or establishing eligibility for federal funding pursuant to the Jacob Wetterling Crimes Against Children and Sexually Violent Offender Registration Act, 42 U.S.C. § 14071, the eligibility of sex offenders to be relieved of the obligation to register, including but not limited to, regulations limiting motions under subsection (e) of section 178E, section 178G and relief from registration pursuant to paragraph (d) of subsection (2) of section 178K.

§ 178E. Transmission of registration data to criminal history systems board, police departments, and FBI

[Amended by 1999 Mass. Acts c. 74, § 2, effective Sept. 10, 1999; 2003 Mass. Acts c. 77, §§ 5–11, effective Sept. 30, 2003; 2003 Mass. Acts c. 140, §§ 6–11, effective Nov. 26, 2003; 2006 Mass. Acts c. 139, §§ 9–20, effective July 1, 2006; 2006 Mass. Acts c. 303, § 1, effective Dec. 20, 2006.]

(a) Within 5 days of receiving upon sentence any sex offender required to register under sections 178C to 178Q, inclusive, the agency which has custody of the sex offender, including the department of correction, the department of youth services and each of the houses of correction, shall transmit to the board said sex offender's registration data, which shall include identifying factors, anticipated future residence, any anticipated secondary addresses, offense history, documentation of any treatment received for a mental abnormality, the official version of any sex offenses, the mittimus, any prior incarceration history, and the projected maximum release date and the earliest possible release date for the sex offender. All custodial agencies shall inform the board immediately of any transfers of sex offenders so that there may be contact with the offender throughout the classification process. The bureau shall classify such a sex offender at least 10 days before the offender's earliest possible release date. The board shall promptly transmit the registration data to the police departments in the municipalities where the sex offender intends to live, maintain any secondary address and work and where the offense was committed and to the Federal Bureau of Investigation. The sex offender shall be informed by, and shall acknowledge in writing to, the agency which has custody of the sex offender of the duty to register in the commonwealth and in any state where he resides, is employed, carries on a vocation or is a student, to verify registration information, to give notice of change of address or intended change of address within the commonwealth or in another state and the penalties for failure to do so and for giving false registration information, and of his right to submit to the board, according to section 178L, documentary evidence relative to his risk of reoffense, the degree of dangerousness posed to the public and of his duty to register under this section. If such sex offender is a juvenile at the time of such notification, notification shall also be mailed to such sex offender's legal guardian or agency having custody of the juvenile in the absence of a legal guardian and his most recent attorney of record. The agency shall transmit such acknowledgment to the board within ten days of receipt of such acknowledgment. Not later than two days before his release from custody, a sex offender shall register by mailing to the board on a form approved by the board and signed under the pains and penalties of perjury, the sex offender's name, date of birth, home address or intended home address, any secondary addresses or intended secondary addresses, work address or intended work address and, if the sex offender is or intends to become a part-time or full-time employee of an institution of higher learning, the name and address of the institution, and, if the sex offender is or intends to become a part-time or full-time student of an institution of higher learning, the name and address of the institution. No sex offender shall be released from custody unless such registration has been filled out, signed, and mailed to the board.

(b) An agency that has supervision of a sex offender required to register pursuant to sections 178C to 178P, inclusive, on probation or parole shall, within five days of assuming supervision of such sex offender, transmit to the board such sex offender's registration data which, for purposes of this paragraph, shall include identifying factors, residential address or anticipated future residence, secondary addresses or anticipated secondary addresses, work address, offense history, documentation of any sex offender treatment, and documentation of any treatment received for a mental abnormality. The agency shall also report any changes of address of any sex offender required to register pursuant to said sections 178E to 178P, inclusive, within its jurisdiction to the board. The board shall promptly transmit the registration data to the police departments in the municipalities where such sex offender intends to live and work and where the offense was committed and to the Federal Bureau of Investigation. The sex offender shall be informed by, and shall acknowledge in writing to, the agency which has custody of the sex offender of the duty to register in the commonwealth and in any state where he resides, has any secondary addresses, is employed, carries on a vocation, or is a student, to verify registration information and to give notice of change of address, or any secondary addresses or intended change of address within the commonwealth or in another state and the penalties for failure to do so and for giving false registration information, and of his right to submit to the board, according to section 178L, documentary evidence relative to his risk of reoffense, the degree of dangerousness posed to the public and his duty to register under this section. If such sex offender is a juvenile at the time of such notification, notification shall also be mailed to such sex offender's legal guardian or agency having custody of the juvenile in the absence of a legal guardian, and his most recent attorney of record. A sex offender shall, within two days of receiving such notice, register by mailing to the board on a form approved by the board and signed under the pains and penalties of perjury, the sex offender's name, date of birth, home address or intended home address, any secondary addresses or intended secondary addresses, work address or intended work address and, if the sex offender is or intends to become a part-time or full-time employee of an institution of higher learning, the name and address of the institution, and, if the sex offender is or intends to become a part-time or full-time student of an institution of higher learning, the name and address of the institution.

(c) Any court which enters a conviction for a sex offense or adjudication as a youthful offender or as a delinquent juvenile by reason of a sex offense, but does not impose a sentence of confinement of 90 days or more to be served immediately shall inform the sex offender and require the sex offender to acknowledge, in writing, his duty to register in the commonwealth and in any state where he resides, is employed, carries on a vocation, or is a student, to verify registration information and to give notice of change of address or intended change of address within the commonwealth or in another state and the penalties for failure to do so and for giving false registration information, and of his right to submit to the board, according to section 178L, documentary evidence relative to his risk of reoffense, the degree of dangerousness posed to the public and of his duty to register under this section. If such sex offender is a juvenile at the time of such adjudication, the legal guardian or agency having custody of the juvenile and his most recent attorney of record shall also be required to acknowledge, in writing, such information. The court shall cause such sex offender's registration data which, for purposes of this paragraph, shall include identifying factors, anticipated future residence, any anticipated secondary addresses, offense history and documentation of any treatment received for a mental abnormality to be transmitted to the board within five days of sentencing. The board shall promptly transmit the registration data to the police departments in the municipalities where such sex offender intends to live and work and where the offense was committed and to the Federal Bureau of Investigation. A sex offender shall, within two days of receiving such notice or of release from confinement, whichever is later, register by mailing to the board on a form approved by the board and signed under the pains and penalties of perjury, the sex offender's name, date of birth, home address or intended home address, any secondary addresses or intended secondary addresses, work address or intended work address and, if the sex offender is or intends to become a part-time or full-time employee of an institution of higher learning, the name and address of the institution, and, if the sex offender is or intends to become a part-time or full-time student of an institution of higher learning, the name and address of the institution.

(d) Any court which accepts a plea for a sex offense shall inform the sex offender prior to acceptance and require the sex offender to acknowledge, in writing, that such plea may result in such sex offender being subject to the provisions of sections 178C to 178P, inclusive. Failure to so inform the sex offender shall not be grounds to vacate or invalidate the plea.

(e) Upon written motion of the commonwealth, a court which enters a conviction or adjudication of delinquent or as a youthful offender may, at the time of sentencing, having determined that the circumstances of the offense in conjunction with the offender's criminal history does not indicate a risk of reoffense or a danger to the public, find that a sex offender shall not be required to register under sections 178C to 178P, inclusive. Such motion by the commonwealth shall state the reasons for such motion with specificity. The court may not make such a finding if the sex offender has been determined to be a sexually violent predator; has been convicted of two or more sex offenses defined as sex offenses pursuant to the Jacob Wetterling Crimes Against Children and Sexually Violent Offender Registration Act, 42 U.S.C. section 14071, committed on different occasions; has been convicted of a sex offense involving a child or a sexually violent offense; or if the sex offender is otherwise subject to minimum or lifetime registration requirements as determined by the board pursuant to section 178D.

(f) In the case of a sex offender who has been convicted of a sex offense or adjudicated as a youthful offender or as a delinquent juvenile by reason of a sex offense, on or after December 12, 1999, and who has not been sentenced to immediate confinement, the court shall, within 14 days of sentencing, determine whether the circumstances of the offense in conjunction with the offender's criminal history indicate that the sex offender does not pose a risk of reoffense or a danger to the public. If the court so determines, the court shall relieve such sex offender of the obligation to register under sections 178C to 178P, inclusive. The court may not make such a determination or finding if the sex offender has been determined to be a sexually violent predator; has been convicted of two or more sex offenses defined as sex offenses pursuant to the Jacob Wetterling Crimes Against Children and Sexually Violent Offender Registration Act, 42 U.S.C. section 14071, committed on different occasions; has been convicted of a sex offense involving a child or a sexually violent offense; or if the sex offender is otherwise subject to minimum or lifetime registration requirements as determined by the board pursuant to section 178D.

(g) A sex offender who moves into the commonwealth from another jurisdiction shall, within two days of moving into the commonwealth, register by mailing to the board on a form approved by the board and signed under the pains and penalties of perjury, the sex offender's name, date of birth, home address or intended home address, any secondary addresses or intended secondary addresses, work address or intended work address and, if the sex offender is or intends to become a part-time or full-time employee of an institution of higher learning, the name and address of the institution, and, if the sex offender is or intends to become a part-time or full-time student of an institution of higher learning, the name and address of the institution. The board shall transmit the registration data to the police department in the municipality where such sex offender intends to live and work and, if the sex offender intends to work at or become a student at an institution of higher learning, to the police departments in the municipalities where the sex offender will work or attend such institution and shall transmit the same to the Federal Bureau of Investigation.

(h) A sex offender required to register pursuant to sections 178C to 178P, inclusive, who intends to move to a different city or town within the commonwealth shall, not later than ten days prior to establishing such new residence, register by mailing to the board on a form approved by the board and signed under the pains and penalties of perjury, the sex offender's name, date of birth, home address or intended home address, any secondary addresses or intended secondary addresses, work address or intended work address and, if the sex offender is or intends to become a part-time or full-time employee of an institution of higher learning, the name and address of the institution, and, if the sex offender is or intends to become a part-time or full-time student of an institution of higher learning, the name and address of the institution. The board shall transmit notice of such change of address to all the police departments in the municipalities where the offense was committed, where the sex offender last registered and where the sex offender intends to live or attend an institution of higher learning and shall transmit the same to the Federal Bureau of Investigation. A sex offender required to register pursuant to said sections 178C to 178P, inclusive, who intends to change his address within a city or town shall notify the board in writing not later than ten days prior to establishing such new residence. The board shall transmit notice of the change of address to the police departments within such city or town, in the municipality where the offense was committed and to the Federal Bureau of Investigation.

(i) A sex offender required to register pursuant to sections 178C to 178P, inclusive, who intends to move out of the commonwealth shall notify the board not later than ten days before leaving the commonwealth. The board shall transmit notice of the change of address to the police departments in the municipalities where such sex offender last registered, where the offense was committed and to the Federal Bureau of Investigation. The board shall notify such sex offender of the duty to register in the new jurisdiction and shall forward a copy of his registration data to the appropriate law enforcement agency in such new jurisdiction.

(j) A sex offender required to register pursuant to sections 178C to 178P, inclusive, who intends to change his work address shall notify the board in writing not later than ten days prior to establishing the new work address. The board shall transmit notice of the change of address and, if the sex offender is or intends to become employed part-time or full-time at an institution of higher learning, the name and address of the institution to the police department in the municipalities where such sex offender previously worked, where such sex offender intends to work, where such sex offender resides or intends to reside, and where the offense was committed. The board shall transmit notice of the change of address to the Federal Bureau of Investigation.

(k) The registrar of motor vehicles shall inform a person applying for or renewing a license to operate a motor vehicle that he has a duty to register with the board if such person is a sex offender, pursuant to regulations established by the board.

(l) Except as hereinbefore provided, a sex offender residing or working in the commonwealth or working at or attending an institution of higher learning in the commonwealth shall, within ten days of the effective date of this section, register by mailing to the board on a form approved by the board and signed under the pains and penalties of perjury, the sex offender's name, date of birth, home address or intended home address, any secondary addresses or intended secondary addresses, work address or intended work address and, if the sex offender is or intends to become a part-time or full-time employee of an institution of higher learning, the name and address of the institution, and, if the sex offender is or intends to become a part-time or full-time student of an institution of higher learning, the name and address of the institution. The board shall promptly transmit the registration data to the police departments where the sex offender intends to live and work, where the offense was committed and, if the sex offender intends to work at or become a student at an institution of higher learning, to the police departments in the municipalities where the sex offender will work or attend such institution and to the Federal Bureau of Investigation. The board shall send written notification of the requirements of sections 178C to 178P, inclusive, to the last known address of all sex offenders residing in the commonwealth who, prior to the effective date of this section, have been released from all custody and supervision. If any such sex offender is a juvenile at the time of such notification, notification shall also be mailed to such sex offender's legal guardian or the agency having custody of the juvenile in the absence of a legal guardian and his most recent attorney of record.

(m) Upon registering, verifying registration information, or giving notice of change of address or intended change of address under this section, a sex offender shall provide independent written verification of the address at which he is registered or, if changing address, will be registered.

(n) Registration data received by the board and disseminated to law enforcement pursuant to this section shall not be disseminated to the public except in accordance with sections 178D, 178I, 178J, and 178K.

(o) A sex offender who plans to work at or attend an institution of higher learning part-time or full-time in the commonwealth shall, within 10 days prior to commencing employment or enrollment in classes at an institution of higher learning, register by mailing to the board on a form approved by the board and signed under the pains and penalties of perjury, the sex offender's name, date of birth, home address or intended home address, any secondary addresses or intended secondary addresses, work address or intended work address, and the name and address of the institution of higher learning. The board shall transmit notice of such change of address to all police departments in the municipalities where the sex offender plans to work at or attend an institution of higher learning and shall transmit the same to the Federal Bureau of Investigation.

(p) A sex offender required to register pursuant to section 178C to 178P, inclusive, who intends to transfer from the institution of higher learning he is attending or stop attending shall notify the board in writing not later than 10 days before leaving the present institution of higher learning and shall provide the board with the name and address of the new institution of higher learning, if applicable. The board shall transmit notice of any such change of address to all police departments in the municipalities where the sex offender previously attended an institution of higher learning and, if applicable, to the police department in the municipality where the sex offender plans to attend an institution of higher learning. The board shall transmit notice of any change of address for the institution of higher learning to the Federal Bureau of Investigation.

(q) Any nonresident person enrolled on a full-time or part-time basis, in any public or private education institution in the commonwealth, including any secondary school, trade or professional institution, shall register with the board if such person is required to register as a sex offender in the state in which he resides. Such student shall, within 10 days of attending such institution, register by mailing to the board on a form approved by the board and signed under the pains and penalties of perjury, the student's name, date of birth, home address, any secondary addresses, and the name and address of the educational institution he is attending.

NOTE Section 178E(f). *Commonwealth v. Samuel S.*, 476 Mass. 497 (2017), "sentenced to immediate confinement" does not include a commitment to the Department of Youth Services on a delinquency or youthful offender case. Juveniles committed to the Department of Youth Services can be relieved from sex offender registration under Sections 178C–178P.

§ 178F. Verification of registration data; annual mailing to board

[Amended by 1999 Mass. Acts c. 74, § 2, effective Sept. 10, 1999; 2003 Mass. Acts c. 77, §§ 12–14, effective Sept. 30, 2003; 2006 Mass. Acts c. 139, §§ 21–22, effective July 1, 2006; 2006 Mass. Acts c. 303, § 2, effective Dec. 20, 2006; 2010 Mass. Acts c. 256, § 40, effective Nov. 4, 2010.]

Except as provided in section 178F½ for a sex offender finally classified by the board as a level 2 or a level 3 sex offender, a sex offender required to register pursuant to sections 178C to 178P, inclusive, shall annually verify that the registration data on file with the board remains true and accurate by mailing to the board on a form approved by the board and signed under the pains and penalties of perjury, the sex offender's name, date of birth, home address or intended home address, any secondary addresses or intended secondary addresses, work address or intended work address and, if the sex offender is or intends to become a part-time or full-time employee of an institution of higher learning, the name and address of said institution and, if the sex offender is a part-time or full-time student at an institution of higher learning or intends to become a part-time or full-time student of an institution of higher learning, the name and address of said institution of higher learning. A homeless sex offender shall verify registration data every 30 days with the board by mailing to the board on a form approved by the board and signed under the pains and penalties of perjury the sex offender's name, date of birth, home address, any secondary addresses, and work address. A homeless shelter receiving state funding shall cooperate in providing information in the possession of or known to such shelter, when a request for information is made to such shelter by the board; provided, however, that such request for information shall be limited to that which is necessary to verify an offender's registration data or a sex offender's whereabouts. A shelter that violates the provisions of this paragraph shall be punished by a fine of $100 a day for each day that such shelter continues to violate the provisions of this paragraph. In addition, in each subsequent year during the month of birth of any sex offender required to register, the board shall mail a nonforwardable verification form to the last reported address of such sex offender. If such sex offender is a juvenile at the time of such notification, notification shall also be mailed to such sex offender's legal guardian or the agency having custody of the juvenile in the absence of a legal guardian and his most recent attorney of record. Such sex offender shall, within five days of receipt, sign the verification form under the penalties of perjury and mail it back to the board. The board shall periodically, and at least annually, send written notice to a city or town police department regarding any sex offender required to register whose last known address was in such city or town or who gave notice of his intent to move to or is otherwise believed to live or work or attend an institution of higher learning in such city or town, but who has failed to register or verify registration information as required.

The board shall examine through electronic transfer of information the tax returns, wage reports, child support enforcement records, papers, or other documents on file with the commissioner of revenue or any other entity within the executive branch when there is reason to believe a sex offender required to register has not so registered in accordance with this chapter or where the address of such sex offender cannot be verified through other means; provided, however, that nothing herein shall be construed to authorize the disclosure, directly or indirectly, of any information other than the address of such sex offender.

§ 178F½. Verification of registration data; personal appearance at local police department

[Added by 1999 Mass. Acts c. 74, § 2, effective Sept. 10, 1999. Amended by 2003 Mass. Acts c. 74, § 2, effective Sept. 30, 2003; 2003 Mass. Acts c. 140, § 12, effective Nov. 26, 2003; 2006 Mass. Acts c. 139, §§ 23–25, effective July 1, 2006; 2006 Mass. Acts c. 303, § 3, effective Dec. 20, 2006; 2010 Mass. Acts c. 256, § 41, effective Nov. 4, 2010; 2013 Mass. Acts c. 63, effective Aug. 7, 2013.]

An incarcerated sex offender finally classified by the board as a level 2 or level 3 sex offender who is required to register under sections 178C to 178P, inclusive, shall appear in person within 2 days of release from the custody of an agency, including the department of correction, the department of youth services or any of the houses of correction, at the local police department in the city or town in which the sex offender lives, or if the sex offender does not reside in the commonwealth, in the city or town in the commonwealth in which the sex offender has a secondary address, works or attends an institution of higher learning, to register; but no such obligation to register in person shall arise where the pertinent address is the same as that provided to the board by the offender before his release under subsection (a) of section 178E. The sex offender shall be informed by, and shall acknowledge in writing to, the agency that has custody of the sex offender of the duty to comply with this section. A sex offender who is finally classified by the board as a level 2 or level 3 offender and who is required to register under said sections 178C to 178P, inclusive, shall appear in person annually at the local police department in the city or town in which the sex offender lives or, if the sex offender does not reside in the commonwealth, in the city or town in the commonwealth in which the sex offender has a secondary address, works or attends an institution of higher learning, to verify that the registration data on file remains true and accurate. At such time, the sex offender's photograph and fingerprints shall be updated. Such sex offender who has been determined to be a sexually violent predator under paragraph (c) of subsection (2) of section 178K shall also appear in person at such police department every 45 days to verify under the pains and penalties of perjury that the registration data on file remains true and accurate. A homeless sex offender shall appear in person at such police station every 30 days to verify that the registration data on file remains true and accurate. A homeless shelter receiving state funding shall cooperate in providing information in the possession of or known to such shelter, when a request for information is made to such shelter by the board or such local police department; provided, however, that such request for information shall be limited to that which is necessary to verify an offender's registration data or a sex offender's whereabouts. A shelter that violates the provisions of this paragraph shall be punished by a fine of $100 a day for each day that such shelter continues to violate the provisions of this paragraph. In addition, in each subsequent year during the month of birth of any sex offender required to register, the board shall mail a nonforwardable verification form to the last reported address of such sex offender. If such sex offender is a juvenile at the time of such notification, notification shall also be mailed to such sex offender's legal guardian or the agency having custody of the juvenile in the absence of a legal guardian and his most recent attorney of record. Such sex offender shall, within five days of receipt, sign the verification form under the penalties of perjury and register in person at the police department in the municipality in which such sex offender lives, or if such sex offender does not reside in the commonwealth, in the city or town in which such sex offender has a secondary address, works, or attends an institution of higher learning. The board shall periodically, and at least annually, send written notice to a city or town police department regarding any sex offender required to register whose last known address was in such city or town or who gave notice of his intent to move to or is otherwise believed to live or work in such city or town, but who has failed to register or verify registration information as required. A sex offender finally classified as a level 2 or level 3 offender shall also comply with the provisions of paragraphs (g) to (j), inclusive, of section 178E, but the offender shall give the required notice in person at the police department in the city or town where such sex offender resides, or if such sex offender does not reside in the commonwealth, in the city or town in which such sex offender has a secondary address, works or attends an institution of higher learning.

The board shall examine through electronic transfer of information the tax returns, wage reports, child support enforcement records, papers, or other documents on file with the commissioner of revenue or any other entity within the executive branch when there is reason to believe a sex offender required to register has not so registered in accordance with this chapter or where the address of such sex offender cannot be verified through other means; provided, however, that nothing herein shall be construed to authorize the disclosure, directly or indirectly, of any information other than the address of such sex offender, except as otherwise provided by sections 178C to 178P, inclusive.

§ 178F¾. Homeless sex offenders

[Added by 2010 Mass. Acts c. 256, § 42, effective Nov. 4, 2010.]

A homeless sex offender shall wear a global positioning system device, or any comparable device, administered by the commissioner of probation.

§ 178G. Termination of obligation to register

[Amended by 1999 Mass. Acts c. 74, § 2, effective Sept. 10, 1999; 2003 Mass. Acts c. 77, § 16, effective Sept. 30, 2003.]

The duty of a sex offender required to register pursuant to this chapter and to comply with the requirements hereof shall, unless sooner terminated by the board under section 178L, end 20 years after such sex offender has been convicted or adjudicated or has been released from all custody or supervision, whichever last occurs, unless such sex offender was convicted of two or more sex

1

offenses defined as sex offenses pursuant to the Jacob Wetterling Crimes Against Children and Sexually Violent Offender Registration Act, 42 U.S.C. § 14071, committed on different occasions, has been convicted of a sexually violent offense; has been determined by the sentencing court to be a sexually violent predator, or if such sex offender is otherwise subject to lifetime registration requirements as determined by the board pursuant to section 178D, in which cases the duty to register shall never be terminated. A person required to register with the sex offender registry board may make an application to said board to terminate the obligation upon proof, by clear and convincing evidence, that the person has not committed a sex offense within ten years following conviction, adjudication or release from all custody or supervision, whichever is later, and is not likely to pose a danger to the safety of others. For so long as such sex offender is under a duty to register in the commonwealth or in any other state where the offender resides or would be under such a duty if residing in the commonwealth, such sex offender shall not be entitled to relief under the provisions of section 100A or 100B of chapter 276.

§ 178H. Failure to register, to verify registration information or to provide change of address notice; false information; penalties

[Amended by 1999 Mass. Acts c. 74, § 2, effective Sept. 10, 1999; 2006 Mass. Acts c. 139, §§ 27–29, effective July 1, 2006; 2006 Mass. Acts c. 303, §§ 4–5, effective Dec. 20, 2006; 2010 Mass. Acts c. 267, §§ 4-6, effective Nov. 5, 2010.]

(a) A sex offender required to register pursuant to this chapter who knowingly: (i) fails to register; (ii) fails to verify registration information; (iii) fails to provide notice of a change of address; or (iv) who knowingly provides false information shall be punished in accordance with this section.

(1) A first conviction under this subsection shall be punished by imprisonment for not less than six months and not more than two and one-half years in a house of correction nor more than five years in a state prison or by a fine of not more than $1,000 or by both such fine and imprisonment.

A person convicted under this paragraph, who has been adjudicated or convicted of any of the offenses set forth in sections 13B, 13B½, 13B¾, 13F, 22A, 22B, 22C, 23, 24B, and 26 of chapter 265 or for conspiracy to commit any of these offenses, or as an accessory thereto, or a like violation of the laws of another state, the United States or a military, territorial or Indian tribal authority shall, in addition to the term of imprisonment authorized by this section, be punished by a term of community parole supervision for life, to be served under the jurisdiction of the parole board, as set forth in section 133D of said chapter 127. The sentence of community parole supervision for life shall commence immediately upon the expiration of the term of imprisonment imposed upon such person by the court or upon such person's release from probation or parole supervision or upon the expiration of a continuance without a finding or upon discharge from commitment to the treatment center pursuant to section 9 of chapter 123A, whichever first occurs.

(2) A second and subsequent conviction under this subsection shall be punished by imprisonment in the state prison for not less than five years.

Any person convicted under this paragraph who is a level 2 or level 3 offender shall, in addition to the term of imprisonment authorized by this paragraph, be punished by a term of community parole supervision for life, to be served under the jurisdiction of the parole board, as set forth in said section 133D of said chapter 127. The sentence of community parole supervision for life shall commence immediately upon the expiration of the term of imprisonment imposed upon such person by the court or upon such person's release from probation or parole supervision or upon the expiration of a continuance without a finding or upon discharge from commitment to the treatment center pursuant to section 9 of chapter 123A, whichever first occurs.

(3) Any person convicted under this subsection who is a level 2 or level 3 sex offender shall, in addition to the term of imprisonment authorized by this subsection, be subject to community parole supervision for life, to be served under the jurisdiction of the parole board, as set forth in section 133D of chapter 127. The sentence of community parole supervision for life shall commence immediately upon the expiration of the term of imprisonment imposed upon such person by the court or upon such person's release from any post-release supervision or upon the expiration of a continuance without a finding or upon discharge from commitment to the treatment center under section 9 of chapter 123A, whichever first occurs.

(b) Violations of this section may be prosecuted and punished in any county where the offender knowingly (i) fails to register; (ii) fails to verify registration information; (iii) fails to provide notice of a change of address; or (iv) knowingly provides false information.

§ 178I. Requests for sex offender registration information

[Amended by 1999 Mass. Acts c. 74, § 2, effective Sept. 10, 1999.]

Any person who is 18 years of age or older and who states that he is requesting sex offender registry information for his own protection or for the protection of a child under the age of 18 or another person for whom the requesting person has responsibility, care, or custody shall receive at no cost from the board a report to the extent available pursuant to sections 178C to 178P, inclusive, which indicates whether an individual identified by name, date of birth, or sufficient personal identifying characteristics is a sex offender with an obligation to register pursuant to this chapter, the offenses for which he was convicted or adjudicated and the dates of such convictions or adjudications. Any records of inquiry shall be kept confidential, except that the records may be disseminated to assist or defend in a criminal prosecution.

Information about an offender shall be made available pursuant to this section only if the offender is a sex offender who has been finally classified by the board as a level 2 or level 3 sex offender.

All reports to persons making inquiries shall include a warning regarding the criminal penalties for use of sex offender registry information to commit a crime or to engage in illegal discrimination or harassment of an offender and the punishment for threatening to commit a crime under section 4 of chapter 275.

The board shall not release information identifying the victim by name, address, or relation to the offender.

§ 178J. Procedures for making request for sex offender registry information; information disseminated

[Amended by 1999 Mass. Acts c. 74, § 2, effective Sept. 10, 1999; 2003 Mass. Acts c. 77, §§ 17, 18(c); 2006 Mass. Acts c. 139, §§ 5–6, effective July 1, 2006; 2008 Mass. Acts c. 215, § 2, effective July 31, 2008.]

(a) A person who requests sex offender registry information shall:

(1) be 18 years of age or older;

(2) appear in person at a city or town police station and present proper identification;

(3) require sex offender registry information for his own protection or for the protection of a child under the age of 18 or another person for whom such inquirer has responsibility, care or custody, and so state; and

(4) complete and sign a record of inquiry, designed by the board, which shall include the following information: the name and address of the person making the inquiry, the person or geographic area or street which is the subject of the inquiry, the reason for the inquiry, and the date and time of the inquiry.

Such records of inquiries shall include a warning regarding the criminal penalties for use of sex offender registry information to commit a crime or to engage in illegal discrimination or harassment of an offender and the punishment for threatening to commit a crime under the provisions of section 4 of chapter 275. Such records of inquiries shall state, before the signature of the inquirer, as follows: "I understand that the sex offender registry information disclosed to me is intended for my own protection or for the protection of a child under the age of 18 or another person for whom I have responsibility, care, or custody." Such records of inquiries shall be kept confidential, except that such records may be disseminated to assist in a criminal prosecution.

(b) The person making the inquiry may either:

(1) identify a specific individual by name or provide personal identifying information sufficient to allow the police to identify the subject of the inquiry; or

(2) inquire whether any sex offenders live, work, or attend an institution of higher learning within the same city or town at a specific address including, but not limited to, a residential address, a business address, school, after-school program, child care center, playground, recreational area, or other identified address and inquire in another city or town whether any sex offenders live, work, or attend an institution of higher learning within that city or town, upon a reasonable showing that the sex offender registry information is requested for his own protection or for the protection of a child under the age of 18 or another person for whom the inquirer has responsibility, care, or custody; or

(3) inquire whether any sex offenders live, work, or attend an institution of higher learning on a specific street within the city or town in which such inquiry is made.

(c) If the search of the sex offender registry results in the identification of a sex offender required to register pursuant to this chapter who has been finally classified by the board as a level 2 or level 3 offender under section 178K, the police shall disseminate to the person making the inquiry:

(1) the name of the sex offender;

(2) the home address and any secondary address if located in the areas described in clause (2) or (3) of subsection (b);

(3) the work address if located in the areas described in said clause (2) or (3) of said subsection (b);

(4) the offense for which he was convicted or adjudicated and the dates of such conviction or adjudication;

(5) the sex offender's age, sex, race, height, weight, eye and hair color; and

(6) a photograph of the sex offender, if available;

(7) the name and address of the institution of higher learning where the sex offender works or is enrolled as a student, if located in the areas described in clause (2) or (3) of subsection (b).

The police shall not release information identifying the victim by name, address, or the victim's relation to the offender.

§ 178K. Sex offender registry board

[Amended by 1999 Mass. Acts c. 74, § 2, effective Sept. 10, 1999; 2003 Mass. Acts c. 77, §§ 19–22, effective Sept. 30, 2003; 2003 Mass. Acts c. 140, § 13, effective Nov. 26, 2003; 2004 Mass. Acts c. 149, § 13(b), effective July 1, 2004; 2006 Mass. Acts c. 139, §§ 29–31, effective July 1, 2006; 2006 Mass. Acts c. 303, § 6, effective Dec. 20, 2006; 2008 Mass. Acts c. 176, § 9, effective July 8, 2008; 2010 Mass. Acts c. 256, § 43, effective Nov. 4, 2010; 2013 Mass. Acts c. 38, §§ 9, 10, effective July 1, 2013.]

(1) There shall be, in the executive office of public safety and security, a sex offender registry board which shall consist of seven members who shall be appointed by the governor for terms of six years, with the exception of the chairman, and who shall devote their full time during business hours to their official duties. The board shall include one person with experience and knowledge in the field of criminal justice who shall act as chairman; at least two licensed psychologists or psychiatrists with special expertise in the assessment and evaluation of sex offenders and who have knowledge of the forensic mental health system; at least one licensed psychologist or psychiatrist with special expertise in the assessment and evaluation of sex offenders, including juvenile sex offenders and who has knowledge of the forensic mental health system; at least two persons who have at least five years of training and experience in probation, parole or corrections; and at least one person who has expertise or experience with victims of sexual abuse. Members shall be compensated at a reasonable rate subject to approval of the secretary of administration and finance.

The chairman shall be appointed by and serve at the pleasure of the governor and shall be the executive and administrative head of the sex offender registry board, shall have the authority and responsibility for directing assignments of members of said board and shall be the appointing and removing authority for members of said board's staff. In the case of the absence or disability of the chairman, the governor may designate one of the members to act as chairman during such absence or disability. The chairman shall, subject to appropriation, establish such staff positions and employ such administrative, research, technical, legal, clerical, and other personnel and consultants as may be necessary to perform the duties of said board. Such staff positions shall not be subject to section 9A of chapter 30 or chapter 31.

The governor shall fill any vacancy for the unexpired term. As long as there are four sitting members, a vacancy shall not impair the right of the remaining members to exercise the powers of the board.

The sex offender registry board shall promulgate guidelines for determining the level of risk of reoffense and the degree of dangerousness posed to the public or for relief from the obligation to register and shall provide for three levels of notification depending on such risk of reoffense and the degree of dangerousness posed to the public; apply the guidelines to assess the risk level of particular offenders; develop guidelines for use by city and town police departments in disseminating sex offender registry information; devise a plan, in cooperation with state and local law enforcement authorities and other appropriate agencies, to locate and verify the current addresses of sex offenders including, subject to appropriation, entering into contracts or interagency agreements for such purposes; and conduct hearings as provided in section 178L. The attorney general and the chief counsel of the committee for public counsel services, or their designees, shall assist in the development of such guidelines. Factors relevant to the risk of reoffense shall include, but not be limited to, the following:

(a) criminal history factors indicative of a high risk of reoffense and degree of dangerousness posed to the public, including:

(i) whether the sex offender has a mental abnormality;

(ii) whether the sex offender's conduct is characterized by repetitive and compulsive behavior;

(iii) whether the sex offender was an adult who committed a sex offense on a child;

(iv) the age of the sex offender at the time of the commission of the first sex offense;

(v) whether the sex offender has been adjudicated to be a sexually dangerous person pursuant to section 14 of chapter 123A or is a person released from civil commitment pursuant to section 9 of said chapter 123A; and

(vi) whether the sex offender served the maximum term of incarceration;

(b) other criminal history factors to be considered in determining risk and degree of dangerousness, including:

(i) the relationship between the sex offender and the victim;

(ii) whether the offense involved the use of a weapon, violence, or infliction of bodily injury;

(iii) the number, date and nature of prior offenses;

(c) conditions of release that minimize risk of reoffense and degree of dangerousness posed to the public, including whether the sex offender is under probation or parole supervision, whether such sex offender is receiving counseling, therapy or treatment and whether such sex offender is residing in a home situation that provides guidance and supervision, including sex offender-specific treatment in a community-based residential program;

(d) physical conditions that minimize risk of reoffense including, but not limited to, debilitating illness;

(e) whether the sex offender was a juvenile when he committed the offense, his response to treatment and subsequent criminal history;

(f) whether psychological or psychiatric profiles indicate a risk of recidivism;

(g) the sex offender's history of alcohol or substance abuse;

(h) the sex offender's participation in sex offender treatment and counseling while incarcerated or while on probation or parole and his response to such treatment or counseling;

(i) recent behavior, including behavior while incarcerated or while supervised on probation or parole;

(j) recent threats against persons or expressions of intent to commit additional offenses;

(k) review of any victim impact statement; and

(l) review of any materials submitted by the sex offender, his attorney or others on behalf of such offender.

(2) The guidelines shall provide for three levels of notification depending on the degree of risk of reoffense and the degree of dangerousness posed to the public by the sex offender or for relief from the obligation to register:

(a) Where the board determines that the risk of reoffense is low and the degree of dangerousness posed to the public is not such that a public safety interest is served by public availability, it shall give a level 1 designation to the sex offender. In such case, the board shall transmit the registration data and designation to the police departments in the municipalities where such sex offender lives and works and attends an institution of higher learning or, if in custody, intends to live and work and attend an institution of higher learning upon release and where the offense was committed and to the Federal Bureau of Investigation. The police shall not disseminate information to the general public identifying the sex offender where the board has classified the individual as a level 1 sex offender. The police and the board may, however, release such information identifying such sex offender to the department of correction, any county correctional facility, the department of youth services, the department of children and families, the parole board, the department of probation and the department of mental health, all city and town police departments and the Federal Bureau of Investigation.

(b) Where the board determines that the risk of reoffense is moderate and the degree of dangerousness posed to the public is such that a public safety interest is served by public availability of registration information, it shall give a level 2 designation to the sex offender. In such case, the board shall transmit the registration data and designation to the police departments in the municipalities where the sex offender lives and works and attends an institution of higher learning or, if in custody, intends to live and work and attend an institution of higher learning upon release and where the offense was committed and to the Federal Bureau of Investigation. The public shall have access to the information regarding a level 2 offender in accordance with the provisions of sections 178D, 178I and 178J. The sex offender shall be required to register and to verify registration information pursuant to section 178F½.

(c) Where the board determines that the risk of reoffense is high and the degree of dangerousness posed to the public is such that a substantial public safety interest is served by active dissemination, it shall give a level 3 designation to the sex offender. In such case, the board shall transmit the registration data and designation to the police departments in the municipalities where the sex offender lives and works and attends an institution of higher learning or, if in custody, intends to live and work and attend an institution of higher learning upon release and where the offense was committed and to the Federal Bureau of Investigation. A level 3 community notification plan shall require the police department to notify organizations in the community which are likely to encounter such sex offender and individual members of the public who are likely to encounter such sex offender. The sex offender shall be required to register and to verify registration information pursuant to section 178F½. Neighboring police districts shall share sex offender registration information of level 3 offenders and may inform the residents of their municipality of a sex offender they are likely to encounter who resides in an adjacent city or town. The police or the board shall actively disseminate in such time and manner as such police department or board deems reasonably necessary the following information:

(i) the name of the sex offender;

(ii) the offender's home address;

(iii) the offender's work address;

(iv) the offense for which the offender was convicted or adjudicated and the date of the conviction or adjudication;

(v) the sex offender's age, sex, race, height, weight, eye and hair color; and

(vi) a photograph of the sex offender, if available; provided, that such active dissemination may include publication of such information on the internet by the police department at such time and in such manner as the police or the board deem reasonably necessary; and provided further that the police or the board shall not release information identifying the victim by name, address, or relation to the sex offender. All notices to the community shall include a warning regarding the criminal penalties for use of sex offender registry information to commit a crime or to engage in illegal discrimination or harassment of an offender and the punishment for threatening to commit a crime under section 4 of chapter 275; and

(vii) the name and address of the institution of higher learning that the sex offender is attending.

The public shall have access to the information regarding a level 3 offender in accordance with sections 178D, 178I, and 178J.

If the board, in finally giving an offender a level 3 classification, also concludes that such sex offender should be designated a sexually violent predator, the board shall transmit a report to the sentencing court explaining the board's reasons for so recommending, including specific identification of the sexually violent offense committed by such sex offender and the mental abnormality from which he suffers. The report shall not be subject to judicial review under section 178M. Upon receipt from the board of a report recommending that a sex offender be designated a sexually violent predator, the sentencing court, after giving such sex offender an opportunity to be heard and informing the sex offender of his right to have counsel appointed, if he is deemed to be indigent in accordance with section 2 of chapter 211D, shall determine, by a preponderance of the evidence, whether such sex offender is a sexually violent predator. An attorney employed or retained by the board may make an appearance, subject to section 3 of chapter 12, to defend the board's recommendation. The board shall be notified of the determination. A determination that a sex offender should not be designated a sexually violent predator shall not invalidate such sex offender's classification. Where the sentencing court determines that such sex offender is a sexually violent predator, dissemination of the sexually violent predator's registration data shall be in accordance with a level 3 community notification plan; provided, however, that such dissemination shall include such sex offender's designation as a sexually violent predator.

(d) The board may, upon making specific written findings that the circumstances of the offense in conjunction with the offender's criminal history do not indicate a risk of reoffense or a danger to the public and the reasons therefor, relieve such sex offender of any further obligation to register, shall remove such sex offender's registration information from the registry and shall so notify the police departments where said sex offender lives and works or if in custody intends to live and work upon release, and where the offense was committed and the Federal Bureau of Investigation. In making such determination the board shall consider factors, including but not limited to, the presence or absence of any physical harm caused by the offense and whether the offense involved consensual conduct between adults. The burden of proof shall be on the offender to prove he comes within the provisions of this subsection. The provisions of this subsection shall not apply if a sex offender has been determined to be a sexually violent predator; if a sex offender has been convicted of two or more sex offenses defined as sex offenses pursuant to the Jacob Wetterling Crimes Against Children and Sexually Violent Offender Registration Act, 42 U.S.C. § 14071, committed on different occasions; or has been convicted of a sexually violent offense. The provisions of this subsection shall also not apply if a sex offender has been convicted of a sex offense involving a child or a sexually violent offense, and such offender has not already registered pursuant to this chapter for at least ten years, or if the sex offender is otherwise subject to lifetime or minimum registration requirements as determined by the board pursuant to section 178D.

(3) The sex offender registry board shall make a determination regarding the level of risk of reoffense and the degree of dangerousness posed to the public of each sex offender listed in said sex offender registry and shall give immediate priority to those offenders who have been convicted of a sex offense involving a child or convicted or adjudicated as a delinquent juvenile or as a youthful offender by reason of a sexually violent offense or of a sex offense of indecent assault and battery upon a mentally retarded person pursuant to section 13F of chapter 265, and who have not been sentenced to incarceration for at least 90 days, followed, in order of priority, by those sex offenders who (1) have been released from incarceration within the past 12 months, (2) are currently on parole or probation supervision, and (3) are scheduled to be released from incarceration within six months. All agencies shall cooperate in providing files to the sex offender registry board and any information the sex offender registry board deems useful in providing notice under sections 178C to 178P, inclusive, and in assessing the risk of reoffense and the degree of dangerousness posed to the public by the sex offender. All agencies from which registration data, including data within the control of providers under contract to such agencies, is requested by the sex offender registry board shall make such data available to said board immediately upon request. Failure to comply in good faith with such a request within 30 days shall be punishable by a fine of not more than $1,000 per day.

(4) The sex offender registry board, in cooperation with the executive office of public safety and security, and with the consultation of the offices of the district attorneys, the department of probation, the department of children and families and the Massachusetts Chiefs of Police Association Incorporated, shall establish and maintain a system of procedures for the ongoing sharing of information that may be relevant to the board's determination or reevaluation of a sex offender's level designation among the board, the offices of the district attorneys and any department, agency or office of the commonwealth that reports, investigates or otherwise has access to potentially relevant information, including, but not limited to, the department of youth services, the department of children and families, the department of mental health, the department of developmental services, the department of correction, the department of probation, the department of early education and care, the department of public health and the office of the child advocate.

The board shall promulgate any rules or regulations necessary to establish, update and maintain this system including, but not limited to, the frequency of updates, measures to ensure the comprehensiveness, clarity and effectiveness of information, and metrics to determine what information may be relevant. When sharing information through this system, all members shall have discretion to delay sharing information where it is reasonably believed that disclosure would compromise or impede an investigation or prosecution or would cause harm to a victim.

(5) The sex offender registry board shall have access to any information that is determined to be relevant to the board's determination or reevaluation of a sex offender's level designation, as defined in subsection (4), through the system of procedures established in said subsection (4).

§ 178L. Recommended classifications; notification; evidentiary hearings; right to counsel

[Added by 1999 Mass. Acts c. 74, § 2, effective Sept. 10, 1999; 2013 Mass. Acts c. 38, § 11, effective July 1, 2013.]

(1) Upon review of any information useful in assessing the risk of reoffense and the degree of dangerousness posed to the public by the sex offender, including materials described in the board guidelines and any materials submitted by the sex offender, the board shall prepare a recommended classification of each offender. Such recommendation may be made by board staff members upon written approval by one board member; provided, however, that if the sex offender was a juvenile at the time of the offense, written approval must be given by a board member who is a licensed psychologist or psychiatrist with special expertise in the assessment and evaluation of juvenile sex offenders.

(a) Not less than 60 days prior to the release or parole of a sex offender from custody or incarceration, the board shall notify the sex offender of his right to submit to the board documentary evidence relative to his risk of reoffense and the degree of dangerousness posed to the public and his duty to register according to the provisions of section 178E. If the sex offender is a juvenile at the time of such notification, notification shall also be mailed to the sex offender's legal guardian or agency having custody of the juvenile in the absence of a legal guardian and his most recent attorney of record. Such sex offender may submit such evidence to the board within 30 days of receiving such notice from the board. Upon a reasonable showing, the board may extend the time in which such sex offender may submit such documentary evidence. Upon reviewing such evidence, the board shall promptly notify the sex offender of the board's recommended sex offender classification, his duty to register, if any, his right to petition the board to request an evidentiary hearing to challenge such classification and duty, his right to retain counsel to represent him at such hearing and his right to have counsel appointed for him if he is found to be indigent as determined by the board using the standards under chapter 211D; provided, however, that such indigent offender may also apply for and the board may grant payment of fees for an expert witness in any case where the board in its classification proceeding intends to rely on the testimony or report of an expert witness prepared specifically for the purposes of the classification proceeding. Such sex offender shall petition the board for such hearing within 20 days of receiving such notice. The board shall conduct such hearing in a reasonable time according to the provisions of subsection (2). The failure timely to petition the board for such hearing shall result in a waiver of such right and the registration requirements, if any, and the board's recommended classification shall become final.

(b) The district attorney for the county where such sex offender was prosecuted may, within ten days of a conviction or adjudication of a sexually violent offense, file a motion with the board to make an expedited recommended classification upon a showing that such sex offender poses a grave risk of imminent reoffense. If the petition is granted, the board shall make such recommendation within ten days of the expiration of the time to submit documentary evidence. If the petition is not granted, the board shall make such recommended classification as otherwise provided in this section.

(c) In the case of any sex offender not in custody, upon receiving registration data from the agency, the police department at which the sex offender registered, the sentencing court or by any other means, the board shall promptly notify the sex offender of his right to submit to the board documentary evidence relative to his risk of reoffense and the degree of dangerousness posed to the public and his duty to register, if any, according to section 178E. If such sex offender is a juvenile at the time of such notification, notification shall also be mailed to such sex offender's legal guardian or agency having custody of the juvenile in the absence of a legal guardian and his most recent attorney of record. Such sex offender may submit such evidence to the board within 30 days of receiving such notice from the board. Upon a reasonable showing, the board may extend the time in which a sex offender may submit such documentary evidence. Upon reviewing such evidence, the board shall promptly notify such sex offender of the board's recommended sex offender classification, his duty to register, if any, and his right to petition the board to request an evidentiary hearing to challenge such classification and duty, his right to retain counsel to represent him at such hearing and his right to have counsel appointed for him if he is found to be indigent as determined by the board using the standards under chapter 211D; provided, however, that such indigent offender may also apply for and the board may grant payment of fees for an expert witness in any case where the board in its classification proceeding intends to rely on the testimony or report of an expert witness prepared specifically for the purposes of the classification proceeding. Such sex offender shall petition the board for such hearing within 20 days of receiving such notice. The board shall conduct such hearing in a reasonable time according to the provisions of subsection (2). The failure timely to petition the board for such hearing shall result in a waiver of such right and the registration requirements, if any, and the board's recommended classification shall become final.

(2) If an offender requests a hearing in accordance with subsection (1), the chair may appoint a member, a panel of three board members or a hearing officer to conduct the hearing, according to the standard rules of adjudicatory procedure or other rules which the board may promulgate, and to determine by a preponderance of evidence such sex offender's duty to register and final classification. The board shall inform offenders requesting a hearing under the provisions of subsection (1) of their right to have counsel appointed if a sex offender is deemed to be indigent as determined by the board using the standards under chapter 211D. If the sex offender does not so request a hearing, the recommended classification and determination of duty to register shall become the board's final classification and determination and shall not be subject to judicial review. All offenders who are juveniles at the time of notification shall be represented by counsel at the hearing.

(3) The board may, on its own initiative or upon written request by a police department or district attorney, seek to reclassify any registered and finally classified sex offender in the event that new information, which is relevant to a determination of a risk of re-offense or degree of dangerousness, is received. The board shall promulgate regulations defining such new information and establishing the procedures relative to a reclassification hearing held for this purpose; provided that (i) the hearing is conducted according to the standard rules of adjudicatory procedure or other rules which the board may promulgate, (ii) the hearing is conducted in a reasonable time, and (iii) the sex offender is provided prompt notice of the hearing, which includes: the new information that led the board to seek reclassification of the offender, the offender's right to challenge the reclassification, the offender's right to submit to the board documentary evidence relative to his risk of reoffense and the degree of dangerousness posed to the public, the offender's right to retain counsel for the hearing, and the offender's right to have counsel appointed if the offender is indigent, as determined by the board using the standards in chapter 211D. An indigent offender may also apply for and the board may grant payment of fees for an expert witness in any case in which the board intends to rely on the testimony or report of an expert witness prepared specifically for the purposes of the reclassification proceeding. The failure of the offender to attend the hearing may result in a waiver of the offender's rights and the board's recommended reclassification becoming final.

All offenders who are juveniles at the time of notification shall be represented by counsel at the hearing and notification shall also be mailed to the sex offender's legal guardian or agency having custody of the juvenile in the absence of a legal guardian and the offender's most recent attorney of record.

§ 178M. Judicial review of board's final classification and registration requirements; confidential proceedings and records

[Amended by 1999 Mass. Acts c. 74, § 2, effective Sept. 10, 1999; 2013 Mass. Acts c. 38, § 12, effective July 1, 2013.]

An offender may seek judicial review, in accordance with section 14 of chapter 30A, of the board's final classification, reclassification and registration requirements. The court shall, if requested, appoint counsel to represent the sex offender in the proceedings if such sex offender is deemed indigent in accordance with section 2 of chapter 211D. An attorney employed or retained by the board may make an appearance, subject to section 3 of chapter 12, to defend the board's decision. The court shall reach its final decision within 60 days of such sex offender's petition for review. The court shall keep proceedings conducted pursuant to this paragraph and records from such proceedings confidential and such proceedings and records shall be impounded, but the filing of an action under this section shall not stay the effect of the board's final classification.

§ 178N. Misuse of information; penalties

[Amended by 1999 Mass. Acts c. 74, § 2, effective Sept. 10, 1999.]

Information contained in the sex offender registry shall not be used to commit a crime against a sex offender or to engage in illegal discrimination or harassment of an offender. Any person who uses information disclosed pursuant to the provisions of sections 178C to 178P, inclusive, for such purpose shall be punished by not more than two and one-half years in a house of correction or by a fine of not more than $1,000 or by both such fine and imprisonment.

§ 178O. Liability of police officials and public employees

[Amended by 1999 Mass. Acts c. 74, § 2, effective Sept. 10, 1999, and 2003 Mass. Acts c. 140, § 14, effective Nov. 26, 2003.]

Police officials and other public employees acting in good faith shall not be liable in a civil or criminal proceeding for any dissemination of sex offender registry information or for any publication on the internet under section 178D or other act or omission pursuant to the provisions of sections 178C to 178P, inclusive.

§ 178P. Failure to comply with registration requirements; warrantless arrests

[Amended by 1999 Mass. Acts c. 74, § 2, effective Sept. 10, 1999; 2013 Mass. Acts c. 63, effective Aug. 7, 2013.]

Whenever a police officer has probable cause to believe that a sex offender has failed to comply with the registration requirements of sections 178C to 178P, inclusive, such officer shall have the right to arrest such sex offender without a warrant and to keep such sex offender in custody.

Whenever a police officer, district attorney or agent, employee or representative of the executive office of health and human services has information indicating that a sex offender is at risk to reoffend, the police department, district attorney or, to the extent permitted by federal law, the executive office of health and human services agent, employee or representative shall forward that information to the board; but a police department or district attorney shall not forward information to the board that the police department or district attorney believes will compromise an ongoing investigation. The board, after consulting the executive office of health and human services, shall adopt regulations to provide specific guidance concerning the type and location of information that might indicate that a sex offender is at risk to reoffend and the circumstances that require disclosure.

§ 178Q. Sex offender registry fee

[Added by 2003 Mass. Acts c. 26, § 12, effective July 1, 2003; 2010 Mass. Acts c. 112, § 3, effective May 22, 2010.]

The sex offender registry board shall assess upon every sex offender a sex offender registration fee of $75, hereinafter referred to as a sex offender registry fee. Said offender shall pay said sex offender registry fee upon his initial registration as a sex offender and annually thereafter on the anniversary of said registration; provided, however, that no such fee shall be assessed or collected until the offender has either (1) waived his right to petition for an evidentiary hearing to challenge his duty to register as a sex offender as set forth in section 178L or (2) has completely exhausted the legal remedies made available to him to so challenge said duty to register pursuant to sections 178L and 178M and has not prevailed in his attempt to eliminate said duty. A sex offender's duty to pay the fee established by this section shall only terminate upon the termination of said offender's duty to register as a sex offender as set forth in section 178G.

The sex offender registry board may waive payment of said sex offender registry fee if it determines that such payment would constitute an undue hardship on said person or his family due to limited income, employment status, or any other relevant factor. Any such waiver so granted shall be in effect only during the period of time that said person is determined to be unable to pay the sex offender registry fee. The sex offender registry board shall establish procedures relative to the collection and waiver of such fee by regulation. Said sex offender registry fee shall be collected and retained by the sex offender registry board. The sex offender registry board shall account for all such fees received and report said fees annually to the secretary of administration and finance and the house and senate committees on ways and means.

Chapter 6A. Executive Offices

§ 16R. Geographically-based interagency review team for disabled children who qualify for services from multiple agencies

[Amended by 2018 Mass. Acts c. 208, § 2, effective Aug. 9, 2018.]

There shall be geographically-based interagency review teams to collaborate on complex cases when a child, which shall include a person under the age of 22 who is disabled or has special needs, may qualify for services from multiple state agencies consisting, as determined by the needs of the individual child, of representatives selected from agencies within the executive office of health and human services, the department of early education and care, and the department of elementary and secondary education. If appropriate and if proper consent has been provided, representatives of local education agencies and juvenile probation shall be invited to participate. Such a child may be referred to the team by a state agency, the juvenile court or the child's parent or guardian. The teams, after hearing from the parents or guardian of the child, relevant agencies and service providers, and reviewing relevant materials, shall determine which services, including case management services, are appropriate for the child and who shall provide those services. If the team is unable to reach a consensus decision, the matter shall be referred to the regional directors of the respective agencies for resolution. The regional directors shall meet within 10 business days of the referral and shall issue their decision within 3 business days thereafter. If the regional directors are unable to resolve the case and the disagreement involves matters solely within the purview of the executive office of health and human services, the team shall notify the secretary of health and human services who shall render a decision within 30 days of the notice.

If, after 14 days from the date that the team determines which services a child is eligible for, the team is unable to reach a consensus on the responsibility of payment, and the child is unable to access those services because of disagreement about responsibility for payment among state agencies and local education agencies, the child advocate shall be notified and shall have the authority to impose a binding temporary cost share agreement on those state agencies and local education agencies. The cost share agreement shall remain in effect until the child advocate is informed in writing of a permanent cost share or payment agreement having been implemented or until the child no longer qualifies for the services.

If the parent or guardian of the child disputes the decision of the team or the secretary, the parent or guardian may file an appeal with the division of administrative law appeals, established under section 4H of chapter 7, which shall conduct an adjudicatory proceeding and order any necessary relief consistent with state or federal law.

Nothing in this section shall be construed to entitle a child to services to which the child would be otherwise ineligible under applicable agency statutes or regulations.

Notwithstanding chapters 66A, 112 and 119 or any other law related to the confidentiality of personal data, the teams, the secretary and the division of administrative law appeals shall have access to and may discuss materials related to the case while the case is under review once the parent or guardian has consented in writing and those having access agree in writing to keep the materials confidential. Once the review is complete, all materials shall be returned to the originating source.

The secretary of health and human services, the commissioner of elementary and secondary education and the commissioner of early education and care shall jointly promulgate regulations to effectuate the purposes of this section.

The secretary of health and human services shall publish an annual report by February 15 summarizing the cases reviewed by the teams in the previous year, the length of time spent at each stage and their final resolution. The report shall be provided to the child advocate.

Nothing in this section shall limit the rights of parents or children under chapter 71B, the federal Individuals with Disabilities Education Act, 20 U.S.C. 1400 et seq., or Section 504 of the Rehabilitation Act of 1973, 29 U.S.C. 794 et seq.

§ 16W. Commission for the study and making of recommendations relative to services for unaccompanied homeless youth

[Added by 2014 Mass. Acts c. 450, effective Apr. 6, 2015.]

(a) As used in this section and section 16X, the following words shall have the following meanings unless the context clearly requires otherwise:

"Fixed, regular nighttime residence", a dwelling at which a person resides on a regular basis that provides safe shelter, sufficient for meeting both the physical and psychological needs typically met in home environments; provided, however, that "fixed, regular nighttime residence" shall not include: (i) a publicly or privately-operated institutional shelter designed to provide temporary

1

living accommodations; (ii) transitional housing; (iii) temporary placement with a peer, friend or family member who has not offered a permanent residence, residential lease or temporary lodging for more than 30 days; or (iv) a public or private place not designed for or ordinarily used as a regular sleeping accommodation for human beings.

"Unaccompanied homeless youth", a person 24 years of age or younger who is not in the physical custody or care of a parent or legal guardian and who lacks a fixed, regular nighttime residence; provided, however, that "unaccompanied homeless youth" shall not include a person incarcerated or otherwise detained under federal or state law.

(b) There shall be a commission within the executive office of health and human services for the purpose of studying and making recommendations relative to services for unaccompanied homeless youth, with the goal of providing a comprehensive and effective response to the unique needs of this population. The focus of the commission's work shall include, but not be limited to: (i) an analysis of the barriers to serving unaccompanied homeless youth who are gay, lesbian, bisexual or transgender; (ii) an analysis of the barriers to serving unaccompanied youth under 18 years of age; (iii) an assessment of the impact of mandated reporting requirements on unaccompanied homeless youths' access to services; (iv) the commonwealth's ability to identify and connect with unaccompanied homeless youth; and (v) recommendations to reduce identified barriers to serving this population. The commission, in formulating its recommendations, shall take into account the best practices and policies in other states and jurisdictions.

The commission shall include: the secretary of health and human services or a designee, who shall serve as chair; the commissioner of children and families or a designee; the commissioner of elementary and secondary education or a designee; the commissioner of public health or a designee; the commissioner of mental health or a designee; the director of Medicaid or a designee; the commissioner of transitional assistance or a designee; the undersecretary for housing and community development or a designee; the commissioner of youth services or a designee; the senate and house chairs of the joint committee on children, families and persons with disabilities; 1 member of the senate; 1 member of the house of representatives; 1 member who shall be appointed by the house minority leader; 1 member who shall be appointed by the senate minority leader; 3 youths who have experienced homelessness who shall be appointed by the office of the child advocate; 3 direct service providers who work with unaccompanied homeless youths who shall be appointed by the governor; and 1 representative from each of the following organizations: the Massachusetts Coalition for the Homeless, Inc.; the Massachusetts Task Force on Youth Aging Out of DCF Care; the Massachusetts Appleseed Center for Law and Justice, Inc.; MassEquality Org, the Campaign for Equality, Inc.; the Massachusetts Housing and Shelter Alliance, Inc.; the Massachusetts Transgender Political Coalition, Inc. and the Boston Alliance of Gay, Lesbian, Bisexual and Transgender Youth. Nongovernmental members shall serve for 2-year terms and may be reappointed.

The commission shall submit an annual report by December 31 to the governor, the clerks of the house of representatives and the senate, the joint committee on children, families and persons with disabilities and the office of the child advocate. The report shall include, but not be limited to, the commission's findings and any recommendations for regulatory or legislative action, with a timeline for implementation, cost estimates and finance mechanisms, and shall detail the extent of homelessness among unaccompanied homeless youth in the commonwealth and the progress made toward implementing the commission's recommendations and any other efforts to address the needs of this population.

§ 16X. Contracts to provide housing and support services for unaccompanied homeless youths

[Added by 2014 Mass. Acts c. 450, effective Apr. 6, 2015.]

(a) Subject to appropriation or third party reimbursement, the executive office of health and human services shall enter into performance-based contracts with organizations and agencies to provide housing and support services to address the needs of unaccompanied homeless youths in urban, suburban and rural areas. In entering into such contracts, the executive office of health and human services shall take into consideration the recommendations of the commission on unaccompanied homeless youth established in section 16W on identifying, connecting and serving unaccompanied homeless youth, in general, and unaccompanied homeless youth under the age of 18 and youth who are lesbian, gay, bisexual or transgender, in particular. Contracts authorized in this section shall include housing services for unaccompanied homeless youth which may include, but shall not be limited to: emergency shelter; kinship home placements; short-term housing; and transition to independent living programs. Programs shall provide any such unaccompanied homeless youth with stable out-of-home placement, help to reunite any such youth with the youth's parent or legal guardian if family reunification is in the youth's best interest and help to create educational and residential stability. Additional support services may include, but shall not be limited to: individual, family and group counseling; access to medical, dental and mental health care; education and employment services; case management, advocacy and referral services; independent living skills training; and provision of basic needs.

(b) The executive office of health and human services shall monitor organizations awarded contracts under this section to ensure that appropriate and high-quality services are being delivered to unaccompanied homeless youth and shall collect common data and outcome measures from these organizations and agencies. Data collected from the organizations and agencies, the incidence of unaccompanied youth homelessness in the commonwealth and the status of and any change in housing, residential stability, educational stability and outcomes and well-being of unaccompanied homeless youth shall be included in the annual report of the special commission on unaccompanied homeless youth pursuant to section 16W.

Chapter 18B. Department of Children and Families

§ 1. Establishment

[Amended by 2008 Mass. Acts c. 176, § 25, effective July 8, 2008.]

There shall be a department of children and families, in this chapter called the department.

§ 2. Services enumerated

[Amended by 2008 Mass. Acts c. 176, § 26, effective July 8, 2008.]

The department shall provide and administer a comprehensive child welfare program for children and families, including the following services:

(1) casework or counseling, including services to families, foster families or individuals;

(2) protective services for children;

(3) legal services for families, children or individuals who are clients of the department;

(4) adoption services;

(5) information and referral services;

(6) foster family care for children and specialized foster family care for children with special needs;

(7) residential care for children with special needs who are not suited for foster family care or specialized foster family care;

(8) informal education and group activities;

(9) training in parenthood and home management for parents, foster parents and prospective parents;

(10) family services intended to prevent the need for foster care and services to children in foster care;

(11) temporary residential programs providing counseling and supportive assistance for families in transition and their children who, because of domestic violence, homelessness, or other situations, require temporary shelter and assistance;

(12) camping services;

(13) information and referral services;

(14) services for families and individuals in emergency and transitional housing;

(15) comprehensive youth development services;

(16) access to and coordination of medical, dental and mental health services for children in foster care whose families are receiving services from other state agencies; and

(17) child care placements for children whose families have an open case with the department.

§ 3. Functions of department; area-based service programs

[Amended by 2008 Mass. Acts c. 176, § 26, effective July 8, 2008.]

(a) The department shall provide comprehensive, area-based child welfare services. These services shall be organized by regions and areas consistent with those established by the secretary of health and human services under section 16 of chapter 6A.

(b) In order that the area-based services be adapted, organized and coordinated to meet the needs of certain population groups, the department shall provide programs for:

(1) families and children which shall, among other objectives, serve to assist, strengthen and encourage family life for the care and protection of children, assist and encourage the use by any family of all available resources to this end, and provide substitute care of children only when preventive services have failed and the family itself, or the resources needed and provided to the family, cannot insure the integrity of the family and the necessary care and protection to guarantee the rights of any child to sound health and normal physical, mental, spiritual and moral development; and

(2) other population groups which require special adaptation of the services provided because of special needs.

(c) The department shall:

(1) formulate the policies, procedures and rules necessary for the full and efficient implementation of programs authorized by the laws of the commonwealth and federal laws in the area of services for children and families;

(2) administer the services, funds and personnel necessary for these programs throughout the commonwealth;

(3) establish and enforce high standards of service and strive to elevate such standards;

(4) provide the range of services on a fair, just and equitable basis to all people in need of such services;

(5) collaborate with other departments of the commonwealth and with voluntary or private agencies or organizations to assure efficient and high-quality social and educational services for persons who are unable, for social or economic reasons, to provide such services for themselves;

(6) study the social and economic problems in the commonwealth and make recommendations to the appropriate branches and agencies of government, including the office of the child advocate, for broadening and improving the scope and quality of child welfare services; and

(7) recruit and retain foster care and pre-adoption parents sufficient for the needs of children serviced by the department, including expanded efforts through education of the public.

§ 4. Payment for services

Subject to appropriation, services of the department shall not be denied to any person because of such person's financial assets or income; provided, however, that the department shall establish a schedule of fees for services which may vary with the ability of the recipient of such services to pay therefor.

The department shall develop regulations defining standards of need and priorities for the allocation of social services; such regulations may not deny any category of social services to any person on the basis of such person's financial assets or income, except with regard to any category of social service which, prior to July twenty-second, nineteen hundred and seventy-eight, could have been denied to a person on the basis of such person's financial assets or income.

§ 6A. Foster care review unit; director

[Amended by 2008 Mass. Acts c. 176, §§ 29–31, effective July 8, 2008; 2010 Mass. Acts c. 359, §§ 9–10, effective Jan. 3, 2011.]

The commissioner shall appoint a foster care review director who shall establish an independent foster care review unit within the department. The director shall appoint, subject to the approval of the commissioner, the members of the unit who shall be employees of the department, shall devote their full time exclusively to case reviews and shall convene and conduct administrative case reviews of the status of each child in the care of the department and young adults who remain under the responsibility of the department pursuant to subsection (f) of section 23 of chapter 119, at least once every 6 months. The reviews shall be performed by panels consisting of 1 member of the unit and 2 other persons, at least 1 of whom shall not be an employee of the department and represent to the maximum extent feasible the various socioeconomic, racial and ethnic groups served by the panel. No panel member shall be the social worker with direct case responsibility for the child or young adult whose case is being reviewed or the immediate supervisor of the social worker. Such reviews shall be held at convenient locations throughout the commonwealth and shall be chaired by the member of the panel from the unit. Panel members shall have sufficient experience or training to enable them to make recommendations.

The purpose of the case review shall be to determine: (a) the necessity and appropriateness of the child's continued placement; (b) the extent of the parties' compliance with a written plan which has been developed between the department or its agent, the child's parents, and the child, where appropriate, and which states actions which must be undertaken within specified time limits by all parties to achieve identified service goals; (c) the extent of progress which has been made toward alleviating or mitigating the causes necessitating the child's placement; and (d) a projected date by which the child may likely be returned to his parents or guardian, or placed for adoption, or have a guardian appointed other than the department or its agent, or live permanently with kin or another permanent planned living arrangement.

The department shall promulgate regulations for the conduct of case reviews. The regulations shall include, but not be limited to, standards for the conduct of the reviews; for the initial and ongoing training of the members of the unit and of the panels; for the participation by the social worker with direct case responsibility for the child, the child's parents, the child, where appropriate, and such other persons whose participation may be helpful; for adequate notice to all participants of the time and place of the review; for a written report of the panel's determinations and recommendations; for an appeal to the commissioner of children and families, or his designee, by the social worker, the parents, or the child aggrieved by the panel's determinations and recommendations. The decision by said commissioner or his designee shall be final.

Administrative case reviews shall not be subject to chapter 30A; provided, however, that nothing in this section shall prevent the exercise of any right of review a party may have pursuant to any other provisions of law.

The director of the unit shall submit an annual report to the governor, the child advocate and the joint committee on children, families and persons with disabilities on the performance of the unit. The report shall contain: an analysis and evaluation of the foster care review system and recommendations, if any, for its improvement; the total number of children in the care of the department or its agents during the previous fiscal year; the number of children who were in its care for more than 6 months; the number of reviews conducted; the number of children returned to their parents or guardian; the number of children for whom guardians, other than the department or its agent, were appointed; the number of children released for adoption; and the number of children adopted.

§ 18. Trust funds; investment deposits; expenditures

The commissioner may receive funds in trust for the use of children born out of wedlock or other persons under the care or supervision of the department. The commissioner shall deposit such funds in savings banks in the commonwealth or in savings accounts in trust companies or national banks therein, or in paid-up shares and accounts of and in co-operative banks, or may use said funds to purchase share accounts of federal savings and loan associations located in the commonwealth and, when necessary, make expenditures from said funds for the benefit of or on behalf of the ward. All such funds received by the commissioner under this section shall be deposited in interest bearing accounts.

§ 19. Unclaimed money of former wards; annual pay over to state treasurer; disposition

Annually on or before November thirtieth, the commissioner shall pay to the state treasurer all unclaimed money held by the department for the benefit of any former ward of the department whose whereabouts is then unknown and has been unknown for seven years subsequent to his coming of age. At the time of so paying over any such money, the commissioner shall certify to the comptroller the amount of such money then held for the benefit of each former ward, his full name, age, if known, and last known address, the names of his parents, if known, and such further information as the commissioner deems relevant, and said comptroller shall make and keep a record thereof.

The state treasurer may receive from the commissioner the unclaimed money paid over under this section and shall hold it as a separate fund. Upon certificate of the comptroller that a claim thereto satisfactory to him shall have been established and approved in writing by the attorney general, the state treasurer shall pay to any former ward, or to his guardian or conservator in case of his mental or other legal disability, or to his legal representatives in case of his death, the amount of money held for his benefit and paid over to the state treasurer under this section, without any accumulations accruing thereto after such payment, out of the principal of the fund in which the money so claimed was held as aforesaid. The said funds, if in cash, shall be invested safely by the state treasurer, or, if in securities he may hold them in their original form or, upon the approval of the governor sell them and reinvest the proceeds in securities which are legal investments for the commonwealth sinking funds. He shall be held responsible for the faithful management of said trust funds in the same manner as for other funds held by him in his official capacity.

§ 21. Adoption subsidy program

The department shall establish an adoption subsidy program for the purpose of facilitating the adoption of children with special needs who are in substitute care and who would not otherwise be placed in an appropriate adoptive home or be adopted. The department acting under such program shall take into consideration the circumstances of the adopting parents and the needs of the child being adopted and the department shall determine the amount to be paid by the department to the adoptive parents.

The department shall promulgate regulations to implement the provisions of this section.

§ 22. Adoption and medical assistance for interstate children; interstate compacts

[Amended by 2008 Mass. Acts c. 176, § 44, effective July 8, 2008.]

As used in this section, unless the context clearly requires otherwise, the following terms shall have the following meanings:

"Adoption assistance state", the state that is a signatory to an adoption assistance agreement in a particular case.

"State", a state of the United States, the District of Columbia, the commonwealth of Puerto Rico, the Virgin Islands, Guam, the commonwealth of the Northern Mariana Islands or a territory or possession of or administered by the United States.

"Residence state", the state in which the child is a resident by virtue of the residence of the adoptive parents.

The department, with the concurrence of the department of transitional assistance may develop, participate in the development of, negotiate and enter into one or more interstate compacts on behalf of the commonwealth with other states to implement one or more of the following purposes: for the protection of children on behalf of whom adoption assistance is being provided by the department; and to provide procedures for adoption assistance payments and medical payments for interstate children. When so entered into, and for so long as it shall remain in force, such a compact shall have the force and effect of law.

A compact entered into pursuant to the provisions of this section shall have: a provision making it available for joinder by all states; a provision for withdrawal from the compact upon written notice to the parties, but with a period of one year between the date of such notice and the effective date of such withdrawal; a requirement that the protection afforded by or pursuant to the compact continue in force for the duration of the adoption assistance and be applicable to all children and their adoptive parents who, on the effective date of the withdrawal, are receiving adoption assistance from a party state other than the one in which they are resident and have their principal place of abode; a requirement that each instance of adoption assistance to which the compact applies be covered by an adoption assistance agreement, in writing, between the adoptive parents and the state child welfare agency of the state which undertakes to provide the adoption assistance and that any such agreement be expressly for the benefit of the adopted child and enforceable by the adoptive parents and the state agency providing the adoption assistance; and such other provisions as may be appropriate to implement the proper administration of the compact.

A child with special needs who is a resident of the commonwealth and who is the subject of an adoption assistance agreement with another state, shall be entitled to receive a medical assistance identification from the commonwealth, upon the filing, in the department of transitional assistance, of a certified copy of the adoption assistance agreement obtained from the adoption assignment state. In accordance with regulations of the department, the adoptive parents shall be required, at least annually, to show that the agreement is still in force or has been renewed.

The department of transitional assistance shall consider the holder of a medical assistance identification pursuant to this section as any other holder of a medical assistance identification under the laws of the commonwealth and shall process and make payment on claims on account of that holder in the same manner and pursuant to the same conditions and procedures as set forth for other recipients of medical assistance.

Whoever submits any claim for payment or reimbursement for services or benefits, pursuant to this section or the making of any statement in connection therewith, which claim or statement the maker knows or should know to be false, misleading or fraudulent shall be guilty of perjury and subject to criminal and civil liability under the laws of the commonwealth.

The provisions of this section shall apply only to medical assistance for children under adoption assistance agreements from states that have entered into a compact with the commonwealth under which such other state provides medical assistance to children with special needs under adoption assistance agreements made in the commonwealth. All other children entitled to medical assistance, pursuant to adoption assistance agreements entered into by the commonwealth shall be eligible to receive such medical assistance in accordance with the laws and procedures relative thereto.

Consistent with federal law, the department, pursuant to the provisions of this section, and any compact entered into hereunder, shall include in any state plan made pursuant to the Adoption Assistance and Child Welfare Act of 1980, Public Law 96-272, Titles IV-E and XIX of the United States Social Security Act and any other applicable federal laws, the provision of adoption assistance and medical assistance for which the federal government pays some or all of the cost. Said department shall apply for and administer all relevant federal aid, in accordance with law.

§ 23. Annual reporting requirement

[Text of section 23 as added by 2008 Mass. Acts c. 176, § 45, effective July 8, 2008.]

The commissioner shall report annually on September 1 on the number of children placed in residential care by region and the cost of care and treatment provided to those children. The information reported for each region shall include, but not be limited to: (i) the age and gender of the children; (ii) the reasons for placement; (iii) the intensity, frequency and type of services provided to each child; (iv) the length of each placement; and (v) the disposition of the child's case at the end of the residential placement, including whether the child was returned to the child's family or placed in other care within the community. The report shall also include the cost of residential placement by region and any other information necessary for the evaluation of the operation of state-funded residential homes. The report shall be filed with the clerks of the senate and the house, the senate and house committees on ways and means, the joint committee on children, families and persons with disabilities, the office of the child advocate, and the governor.

Contact of parent or guardian for child receiving inpatient psychiatric services

[Text of Section 23 as added by 2008 Mass. Acts c. 321, § 8, effective Nov. 18, 2008.]

If the department has care and custody of a child receiving inpatient psychiatric services, the department shall contact the child's parents or guardians, as appropriate, and a member of the child's treatment team within 3 business days of the hospitalization, shall maintain weekly contact with them until the child is discharged, and shall immediately begin discharge planning, with the priority of returning the child to his home or to a community placement. Not later than 5 business days after being notified that continued hospitalization is no longer clinically appropriate, the department shall determine the appropriate type of placement for the child and shall immediately initiate the placement referrals. The department shall document its activities in assisting with discharge placement, including identification of available resources for home-based, community or alternative residential placements, and the barriers, if any, to discharge to the most clinically-appropriate setting. If the initial placement shall not be deemed to be the most clinically-appropriate, the department shall continue to seek an appropriate placement. Not longer than 30 days after being notified that continued hospitalization is no longer clinically appropriate, the department shall refer the child to the interagency review team established pursuant to section 16R of chapter 6A. The department shall submit a monthly report to the secretary of health and human services detailing the activities undertaken pursuant to this section, including the length of time required to place each such child in a clinically appropriate post-discharge setting.

NOTE 2008 Mass. Acts c. 321, § 8 states that "chapter 18B is hereby further amended by adding the following Section . . ." Accordingly, two different provisions have been designated as Section 23.

§ 24. Semi-annual report

[Added by 2008 Mass. Acts c. 176, § 45, effective July 8, 2008.]

The commissioner shall report semi-annually on: (i) the status of high-risk children and the department's efforts to identify such children and address their needs for child protection; (ii) the status of racial disproportionality and disparity of the department's client population and its efforts, including the use of culturally competent staffing, resources and practices, to reduce overrepresentation of children of color in the child welfare system; (iii) the status of the department's procurement of services; and (iv) the status of children who, due to their age, are transitioning out of the child welfare system. The reports shall be filed with the clerks of the senate and the house, the senate and house committees on ways and means, the joint committee on children, families and persons with disabilities, the office of the child advocate, and the governor.

§ 25. Multiple 51A reports; quarterly report

[Added by 2008 Mass. Acts c. 176, § 45, effective July 8, 2008.]

In addition to the immediate notification required under subsection (n) of section 7, the commissioner shall report quarterly on the total number of cases of multiple 51A reports reviewed by the department under subsection (r) of section 51B of chapter 119, the types of those cases, and their resolutions. The report shall be filed with the governor, the clerks of the senate and the house, the joint committee on children, families and persons with disabilities, and the child advocate.

Chapter 18C. Office of the Child Advocate

§ 1. Definitions

[Added by 2008 Mass. Acts c. 176, § 46, effective July 8, 2008. Amended by 2016 Mass. Acts c. 133, § 21, effective July 1, 2016.]

As used in this chapter, the following words shall have the following meanings unless the context clearly requires otherwise:

"Advisory council", the child advocate advisory council established in section 4.

"Child advocate", the child advocate appointed under section 3.

"Critical incident", (i) a fatality, near fatality or serious bodily or emotional injury of a child who is in the custody of or receiving services from an executive agency or a constituent agency; or (ii) circumstances which result in a reasonable belief that an executive agency or a constituent agency failed in its duty to protect a child and, as a result, the child was at imminent risk of, or suffered serious bodily or emotional injury or death.

"Department", the department of children and families.

"Executive agency", a state agency within the office of the governor, including the executive office of education, the executive office of public safety and security, executive office of health and human services, and their constituent agencies, the Massachusetts interagency council on housing and homelessness and the executive office of housing and economic development.

"Office", the office of the child advocate.

"Serious bodily or emotional injury", an injury which involves a substantial risk of death, extreme physical pain, protracted and obvious disfigurement or protracted loss or impairment of the function of a bodily member, organ or mental faculty or emotional distress.

§ 2. Establishment

[Added by 2008 Mass. Acts c. 176, § 46, effective July 8, 2008. Amended by 2016 Mass. Acts c. 133, §§ 22–23, effective July 1, 2016; 2018 Mass. Acts c. 208, §§ 13, 14, effective Aug. 9, 2018.]

There shall be an office of the child advocate which shall be independent of any supervision or control by any executive agency. The office shall:

(a) ensure that children involved with an executive agency, in particular, children served by the child welfare or juvenile justice systems, receive timely, safe and effective services;

(b) ensure that children placed in the care of the commonwealth or receiving services under the supervision of an executive agency in any public or private facility shall receive humane and dignified treatment at all times, with full respect for the child's personal dignity, right to privacy, and right to a free and appropriate education in accordance with state and federal law;

(c) examine, on a system-wide basis, the care and services that executive agencies provide children;

(d) advise the public and those at the highest levels of state government about how the commonwealth may improve its services to and for children and their families; and

(e) impose temporary cost share agreements, as necessary pursuant to section 16R of chapter 6A to ensure children's timely access to services.

The office shall act to investigate and ensure that the highest quality of services and supports are provided to safeguard the health, safety and well-being of all children receiving services. The office shall examine systemic issues related to the provision of services to children and provide recommendations to improve the quality of those services in order to give each child the opportunity to live a full and productive life.

§ 3. Child advocate

[Added by 2008 Mass. Acts c. 176, § 46, effective July 8, 2008. Amended by 2016 Mass. Acts c. 162, § 1, effective July 1, 2016.]

The office of the child advocate shall be under the direction of the child advocate. The child advocate shall be the administrative head of the office and shall devote full-time to the duties of the office. The child advocate shall be appointed by a majority vote of the attorney general, the state auditor and the governor from a list of 3 nominees submitted by a nominating committee to recommend a child advocate. The nominating committee shall consist of: the secretary of health and human services; the commissioner of children and families; the commissioner of youth services; the commissioner of mental health; the executive director of the child abuse prevention board; a pediatrician experienced in treating victims of child abuse who shall be designated by the Massachusetts chapter of the American Academy of Pediatrics; a child psychiatrist who shall be designated by the Massachusetts Psychiatric Society, Inc.; a child psychologist who shall be designated by The Massachusetts Psychological Association, Inc.; a representative from the Massachusetts Association for Mental Health, Inc.; a representative of an organization that advocates on behalf of children at risk of abuse who shall be designated by the Children's League of Massachusetts, Inc.; an attorney experienced in care and protection cases who shall be designated by the Massachusetts Bar Association; a social worker who shall be designated by the Massachusetts chapter of the National Association of Social Workers, Inc.; a person with experience in the juvenile justice system who shall be designated by the chief justice of the juvenile court department and a representative of organized labor who shall be designated by the president of a collective bargaining unit that represents social workers. The work of the nominating committee shall be coordinated by the executive office of health and human services.

Any person appointed to the position of child advocate shall be selected without regard to political affiliation and on the basis of integrity and demonstrated ability in child welfare, juvenile justice, auditing, law, management analysis, public administration and investigation or criminal justice administration. The child advocate may, subject to appropriation, appoint such other personnel as the child advocate deems necessary for the efficient management of the office.

The child advocate shall serve for a term of 5 years. In case of a vacancy in the position of the child advocate, a successor shall be appointed in the same manner for the remainder of the unexpired term. No person shall be appointed as child advocate for more than 2 full terms.

The child advocate may be removed from office for cause by a majority vote of the attorney general, the state auditor and the governor. Such cause may include substantial neglect of duty, gross misconduct or conviction of a crime. The cause for removal of the child advocate shall be stated in writing and shall be sent to the clerks of the senate and house of representatives and to the governor at the time of removal and shall be a public document.

§ 4. Child advocate advisory council

[Added by 2008 Mass. Acts c. 176, § 46, effective July 8, 2008. Amended by Mass. Acts c. 451, § 25, effective June 30, 2009; 2010 Mass. Acts c. 256, § 48, effective Nov. 4, 2010; 2016 Mass. Acts c. 133, §§ 25–27, effective July 1, 2016.]

There shall be a 25-member child advocate advisory council. The advisory council shall consist of the child advocate, who shall serve as chair, the secretary of health and human services, the secretary of public safety and security, the secretary of education, the commissioner of the department of criminal justice information services, the undersecretary of criminal justice from the executive office of public safety and security, the commissioner of early education and care, the commissioner of elementary and secondary education, the commissioner of mental health, the commissioner of developmental services, the commissioner of public health, the commissioner of children and families, the commissioner for the deaf and hard of hearing, the commissioner for the blind, the commissioner of transitional assistance, the commissioner of youth services, the deputy commissioner of the child support enforcement division within the department of revenue, the president of the Massachusetts District Attorneys Association, the commissioner of probation, the chief counsel of the committee for public counsel services, the chief justice of the superior court department, the chief justice of the juvenile court department, the chief justice of the probate and family court department, the executive director of the child abuse prevention board, and 3 persons appointed by the governor.

The child advocate shall meet with the advisory council at least annually and shall present to the advisory council the annual goals of the office and its plans for monitoring the work, including the continuing quality improvement, of the child service agencies and the identification of any critical gaps and issues relating to interagency collaboration. The child advocate may consult with or request the assistance of members of the advisory council with respect to the duties and responsibilities of the office; provided however, that any request for assistance shall not place requirements on any member of the council to fulfill the request.

The advisory council shall annually set the salary of the child advocate; provided, however, that such salary shall not exceed 90 per cent of the salary of the chief justice of the supreme judicial court.

§ 5. Child advocate investigative and reporting functions

[Added by 2008 Mass. Acts c. 176, § 46, effective July 8, 2008. Amended by 2016 Mass. Acts c. 133, §§ 28–31, effective July 1, 2016.]

(a) An executive agency shall inform the child advocate as soon as practicable when a critical incident has occurred. The child advocate may conduct an investigation of the critical incident or may review an executive agency's investigation of a critical incident. When the child advocate conducts his own investigation, he shall determine: (1) the factual circumstances surrounding the critical incident; (2) whether an agency's activities or services provided to a child and his family were adequate and appropriate and in accordance with agency polic[i]es and state and federal law; and (3) whether the agency's policies, regulations, training or delivery of services or state law can be improved.

(b) Before investigating any critical incident, the child advocate shall determine whether an executive or law enforcement agency is already conducting an investigation. If a law enforcement agency is conducting an investigation, the child advocate shall, when appropriate, defer to that agency or may conduct his own investigation. The child advocate shall coordinate efforts to minimize the impact on the child, family or employees of the agency involved, unless he determines such coordination would impede his investigation. If an executive agency is conducting an investigation, the child advocate may defer to that investigation or may conduct his own investigation. The child advocate may coordinate efforts to minimize the impact on the child, family or employees of the agency involved. In every instance, the child advocate shall notify the head of the relevant agency of his involvement before beginning any investigation.

(c) The child advocate shall receive complaints relative to the provision of services to children by an executive agency and shall review and monitor the complaints that reasonably cause him to believe that a child may be in need of assistance and to ensure that the complaint is resolved. If the complaint is not resolved by the relevant executive agency within a reasonable period of time in light of the circumstances, if the resolution is determined to be unsatisfactory to the child advocate, or if the complaint reasonably causes the child advocate to believe that a child may be in need of immediate assistance, the child advocate may conduct an investigation and upon completion of the investigation, the child advocate may provide relevant information in the form of a report to any relevant agencies and request a meeting, if necessary, to review the investigation and accompanying report.

(d) The child advocate shall receive complaints from children in the care of the commonwealth and assist such children in resolving problems and concerns associated with their placement, plans for life-long adult connections and independent living, and decisions regarding custody of persons aged between 18 and 22, including ensuring that relevant executive agencies have been alerted to the complaint and facilitating intra-agency cooperation, if appropriate. For the purposes of this section, the office shall develop procedures to ensure appropriate responses to the concerns of youth in foster care.

(e) The child advocate shall periodically review, report and make recommendations, as appropriate, with respect to systemwide improvements that may increase the effectiveness of the care and services provided to children and their families and suggested legislative and regulatory changes including, but not limited to, a review of the programs and procedures established by the department to provide and administer a comprehensive child welfare program under section 2 of chapter 18B.

(f) The child advocate shall perform oversight functions to ensure that agencies serving children are fulfilling their obligations in the most effective and efficient manner.

(g) The child advocate shall undertake activities designed to educate the public regarding the services of the office and of the mission of the executive agencies in providing services to children and families.

(h) The child advocate shall be authorized to apply for, and accept on behalf of the commonwealth, federal, local or private grants, bequests, gifts or contributions for the purpose of carrying out the functions of the office.

§ 6. Access to facilities and records; release of information

[Added by 2008 Mass. Acts c. 176, § 46, effective July 8, 2008. Amended by 2011 Mass. Acts c. 68, § 28, effective July 1, 2011; 2016 Mass. Acts c. 133, § 32, effective July 1, 2016.]

The child advocate or his designee shall have access at any and all reasonable times to any facility, residence, program, or portion thereof, that is operated, licensed or funded by an executive agency, and shall have unrestricted access to all electronic information systems records, reports, materials and employees in order to better understand the needs of children in the custody of the commonwealth or who are receiving services from an executive agency. The child advocate shall have access to relevant records held by the clerk of the juvenile court and the clerk of the probate and family court, including the right to inspect and copy, without cost. The child advocate shall be bound by any limitations on the use or release of information imposed by law upon the party furnishing such information, except as provided in subsection (e) of section 12.

§ 7. Hearings; subpoenas

[Added by 2008 Mass. Acts c. 176, § 46, effective July 8, 2008.]

The child advocate may request the attendance and testimony of witnesses and the production of documents, papers, books, records, reports, reviews, recommendations, correspondence, data and other evidence that the child advocate reasonably believes is relevant. If a request is denied, the child advocate shall have the power to issue a subpoena for witnesses and the production of documents and any other data and evidence that the child advocate reasonably believes is relevant.

If any person to whom a subpoena is issued fails to appear or, having appeared, refuses to give testimony or fails to produce the evidence required, the child advocate may apply to the Suffolk county superior court to issue an order to compel the testimony and production of documents of any such witnesses. A failure to obey the order may be punished as contempt.

The district attorney may seek injunctive relief in Suffolk county superior court to defer a subpoena issued by the child advocate.

§ 8. Protection for reporters

[Added by 2008 Mass. Acts c. 176, § 46, effective July 8, 2008.]

No discriminatory or retaliatory action shall be taken against any person who communicates with or provides information to the office. Any person who knowingly or willfully discriminates or retaliates against such a person shall be liable to such person for treble damages, costs and attorney's fees.

1

§ 9. Internal procedures

[Added by 2008 Mass. Acts c. 176, § 46, effective July 8, 2008.]

The child advocate shall develop internal procedures appropriate for the effective performance of his duties.

The child advocate may, subject to chapter 30A, adopt, amend or repeal such rules and regulations as are deemed necessary to carry out the functions of the office.

§ 10. Reporting requirement

[Added by 2008 Mass. Acts c. 176, § 46, effective July 8, 2008. Amended by 2016 Mass. Acts c. 133, § 33, effective July 1, 2016.]

The child advocate shall report annually to the governor, the president of the senate, the speaker of the house, the senate and the house committees on ways and means, and the chairs of the joint committee on children, families and persons with disabilities on the activities of the office, including an analysis of the delivery of service to children, activities undertaken to implement subsection (d) of section 5, recommendations for changes in agency procedures which would enable the commonwealth to better provide services to and for children and their families and priorities for implementation of those changes to services. The report shall be made public.

§ 11. Examination of systemwide responses to child abuse and neglect

[Added by 2008 Mass. Acts c. 176, § 46, effective July 8, 2008. Amended by 2016 Mass. Acts c. 133, § 34, effective July 1, 2016.]

The child advocate, in consultation with the advisory council, may from time to time, examine systemwide responses to child abuse and neglect, including related mental health, substance use and domestic violence issues, and shall file a report on any such examination with the governor, the clerks of the senate and house of representatives, the senate and house committees on ways and means and the joint committee on children, families and persons with disabilities. The child advocate's examination may include, without limitation, racial disproportionality and disparity, truancy and runaways, mandated reporting, screening of child abuse and neglect reports, social worker qualifications and caseloads, law enforcement involvement, health service needs, including behavioral health needs, of children at risk, criminal offender record information reviews, administrative and cost requirements, federal funding for child welfare purposes and the effectiveness of child abuse laws. The child advocate may seek advice broadly from individuals with expertise in child welfare in preparing a report under this section.

§ 12. Information obtained by the office of the child advocate

[Added by 2008 Mass. Acts c. 176, § 46, effective July 8, 2008. Amended by 2016 Mass. Acts c. 133, § 35, effective July 1, 2016.]

The following provisions apply to information and records obtained, reviewed or maintained by the child advocate:

(a) Notwithstanding chapter 66A, section 70 of chapter 111, section 11 of chapter 111B, section 18 of chapter 111E, sections 51E and 51F of chapter 119, chapter 112, chapter 123, or sections 20B, 20J, or 20K of chapter 233 to the contrary, the disclosure of information to the office of the child advocate pursuant to this chapter shall not be prohibited. Any information considered to be confidential under the aforementioned sections shall be submitted for the child advocate's review upon the determination of the child advocate that the review of said information is necessary. The child advocate shall ensure that no information submitted for his review is disseminated to parties outside the office, except when disclosure may be necessary to enable the child advocate to perform the child advocate's duties. Under no circumstances shall the child advocate or any employee of the office violate the confidentiality provisions set forth in the aforementioned statutes, except as authorized under subsection (e).

(b) Any and all information and records acquired by the child advocate in the exercise of the office's purpose and duties under this chapter shall be confidential and exempt from disclosure under chapter 66 and clause Twenty-sixth of section 7 of chapter 4.

(c) Information, documents and records of the child advocate and his office shall not be subject to subpoena, discovery or introduction into evidence in any civil or criminal proceeding; provided, however, that information, documents and records otherwise available from any other source shall not be immune from subpoena, discovery or introduction into evidence through these sources solely because they were presented during the child advocate's investigation or maintained by the office of the child advocate.

(d) Statistical compilations of data which do not contain any information that would permit the identification of any person may be disclosed to the public.

(e) The restrictions of this section shall not preclude the child advocate from sharing with the governor, the attorney general, a district attorney, a secretary, an agency commissioner or other agency personnel, or the chairs of the joint committee on children, families and persons with disabilities, the report of, or the results of, a critical incident investigation involving that agency. Any executive or legislative branch employees who receive or read such a document shall be bound by the confidentiality requirements of this section.

§ 13. Immunity from suit

[Added by 2008 Mass. Acts c. 176, § 46, effective July 8, 2008.]

No person employed by or contracted by or volunteering for the office shall be subject to suit directly, derivatively or by way of contribution or indemnification for any civil damages under the laws of the commonwealth resulting from any act or omission performed during or in connection with the discharge of his duties within the scope of his employment or appointment, unless such act or failure to act was committed with gross negligence, maliciously, or in bad faith.

Chapter 27. Department of Correction

§ 4. Parole board; members; appointment and term; chairman; powers and duties; salaries

[Amended by 2014 Mass. Acts c. 189, § 1, effective July 25, 2014.]

There shall be in the department, but not subject to its jurisdiction, a parole board, consisting of seven members, 1 of whom shall at all times have experience in forensic psychology, to be appointed by the governor, with the advice and consent of the council, for terms of five years. The governor may, with the advice and consent of the council, remove members from the board for cause, upon a written certification of such cause; provided, that such member shall have the right to notice and the opportunity for a public hearing before the council relative to such removal.

Whenever a vacancy occurs in the membership of the board the governor may appoint a panel of 9 persons consisting of the administrative justice for the superior court department, the president of the state parole officers association, 1 person chosen from a list of 3 nominees submitted by the Massachusetts District Attorneys Association, 1 person chosen from a list of 3 nominees submitted by the committee for public counsel services, 1 person chosen from a list of 3 nominees submitted by the Prisoners' Legal Services and 1 member from local law enforcement, the chairman of the advisory committee on correction, the president of the Massachusetts bar association or his designee, and the secretary of the executive office of public safety who shall serve as chairman of said panel. Said panel shall submit to the governor, within sixty days of the establishment of said panel, a list of not less than six nor more than nine persons, or not more than twelve persons in the event there should be two or more vacancies to fill, who are qualified by knowledge, education or experience in the administration of criminal justice or in the behavioral sciences as hereinafter provided. Such persons shall be graduates of an accredited four-year college or university and shall have had at least five years of training and experience in one or more of the following fields:— parole, probation, corrections, law, law enforcement, psychology, psychiatry, sociology and social work; provided, however, that the panel may, by unanimous vote, submit the name of a person who has demonstrated exceptional qualifications and aptitude for carrying out the duties required of a parole board member, if such person substantially, although not precisely, meets the above qualifications. At least 1 person on said list shall be a professional with not less than 5 years of experience and training in adolescent development and psychology, and shall be selected from a list of proposed nominees provided by the following organizations: the Massachusetts Chapter of the American Academy of Pediatrics, Inc.; the New England Council of Child and Adolescent Psychiatry, Inc.; the Massachusetts Psychological Association, Inc.; and the Massachusetts Psychiatric Society, Inc. The list of names of such persons for each vacancy shall include one or more of the following, insofar as it is possible to select such persons who are willing and able to fill promptly the existing vacancy or vacancies:— an attorney admitted to practice in Massachusetts, a psychiatrist who is a member in good standing of the American Psychiatric Association, a victim witness advocate; provided, that such victim representative is otherwise qualified as provided for above, a psychologist certified by the Massachusetts Board of Certification in Psychology, Inc., and a member of the Massachusetts parole staff. If the governor does not appoint a panel as aforesaid any vacancy on said board shall be filled by the appointment of a member who possesses the qualifications as hereinbefore provided.

The governor shall designate one of the members as chairman, said member to serve as chairman at the will of the governor. The chairman shall be the executive and administrative head of said board, shall have the authority and responsibility of directing assignments of members of said board and shall be the appointing and removing authority for parole agents and other members of the parole staff. In the case of the absence or disability of the chairman, the governor may designate one of the members to act as chairman during such absence or disability.

The positions of chairman and each of the other members shall be classified in accordance with section forty-five of chapter thirty and the salaries shall be determined in accordance with section forty-six C of said chapter thirty. Members shall devote full time to their duties, and no member shall hold any other salaried public office or engage in any activity which is in violation of any law or which interferes or conflicts with his full time service as a member during his incumbency.

Chapter 30A. State Administrative Procedure

§ 10. Adjudicatory proceedings; appeals

In conducting adjudicatory proceedings, as defined in this chapter, agencies shall afford all parties an opportunity for full and fair hearing. Unless otherwise provided by any law, agencies may (1) place on any party the responsibility of requesting a hearing if the agency notifies him in writing of his right to a hearing and of his responsibility to request the hearing; (2) make informal disposition of any adjudicatory proceeding by stipulation, agreed settlement, consent order or default; (3) limit the issues to be heard or vary the procedures prescribed by section eleven, if the parties agree to such limitation or variation; and (4) allow any person showing that he may be substantially and specifically affected by the proceeding to intervene as a party in the whole or any portion of the proceeding, and allow any other interested person to participate by presentation of argument orally or in writing, or for any other limited purpose, as the agency may order.

When a party to an adjudicatory proceeding has the opportunity, by provision of any law or by regulation, to obtain more than one agency hearing on the same question, whether before the same agency or before different agencies, it shall be sufficient if the last hearing available to the party complies with the requirements of this chapter, and the earlier hearings need not so comply.

When a party has the opportunity to obtain an agency hearing, followed by one or more appeals before the same agency or before different agencies, such appeals being limited to the record made at the hearing, the appeal procedure need not comply with any requirement of this chapter for the conduct of adjudicatory proceedings except paragraphs (7) and (8) of section eleven.

When, under a provision of any law, a hearing is required only upon direction of an agency or upon request made in accordance with such provision by a person entitled to make such request, the requirements of this chapter governing the conduct of adjudicatory proceedings shall not apply unless and until such direction or request is in fact made.

§ 11. Adjudicatory proceedings; additional requirements

In addition to other requirements imposed by law and subject to the provisions of section ten, agencies shall conduct adjudicatory proceedings in compliance with the following requirements:

(1) Reasonable notice of the hearing shall be accorded all parties and shall include statements of the time and place of the hearing. Parties shall have sufficient notice of the issues involved to afford them reasonable opportunity to prepare and present evidence and argument. If the issues cannot be fully stated in advance of the hearing, they shall be fully stated as soon as practicable. In all cases of delayed statement, or where subsequent amendment of the issues is necessary, sufficient time shall be allowed after full statement or amendment to afford all parties reasonable opportunity to prepare and present evidence and argument respecting the issues.

(2) Unless otherwise provided by any law, agencies need not observe the rules of evidence observed by courts, but shall observe the rules of privilege recognized by law. Evidence may be admitted and given probative effect only if it is the kind of evidence on which reasonable persons are accustomed to rely in the conduct of serious affairs. Agencies may exclude unduly repetitious evidence, whether offered on direct examination or cross-examination of witnesses.

(3) Every party shall have the right to call and examine witnesses, to introduce exhibits, to cross-examine witnesses who testify, and to submit rebuttal evidence.

(4) All evidence, including any records, investigation reports, and documents in the possession of the agency of which it desires to avail itself as evidence in making a decision, shall be offered and made a part of the record in the proceeding, and no other factual information or evidence shall be considered, except as provided in paragraph (5) of this section. Documentary evidence may be received in evidence in the form of copies or excerpts, or by incorporation by reference.

(5) Agencies may take notice of any fact which may be judicially noticed by the courts, and in addition, may take notice of general, technical or scientific facts within their specialized knowledge. Parties shall be notified of the material so noticed, and they shall be afforded an opportunity to contest the facts so noticed. Agencies may utilize their experience, technical competence,

and specialized knowledge in the evaluation of the evidence presented to them.

(6) Agencies shall make available an official record, which shall include testimony and exhibits, and which may be in narrative form, but the agency need not arrange to transcribe shorthand notes or sound recordings unless requested by a party. If so requested, the agency may, unless otherwise provided by any law, require the party to pay the reasonable costs of the transcript before the agency makes the transcript available to the party.

(7) If a majority of the officials of the agency who are to render the final decision have neither heard nor read the evidence, such decision, if adverse to any party other than the agency, shall be made only after (a) a tentative or proposed decision is delivered or mailed to the parties containing a statement of reasons and including determination of each issue of fact or law necessary to the tentative or proposed decision; and (b) an opportunity is afforded each party adversely affected to file objections and to present argument, either orally or in writing as the agency may order, to a majority of the officials who are to render the final decision. The agency may by regulation provide that, unless parties make written request in advance for the tentative or proposed decision, the agency shall not be bound to comply with the procedures of this paragraph.

(8) Every agency decision shall be in writing or stated in the record. The decision shall be accompanied by a statement of reasons for the decision, including determination of each issue of fact or law necessary to the decision, unless the General Laws provide that the agency need not prepare such statement in the absence of a timely request to do so. Parties to the proceeding shall be notified in person or by mail of the decision; of their rights to review or appeal the decision within the agency or before the courts, as the case may be; and of the time limits on their rights to review or appeal. A copy of the decision and of the statement of reasons, if prepared, shall be delivered or mailed upon request to each party and to his attorney of record.

§ 12. Adjudicatory proceedings; subpoenas

In conducting adjudicatory proceedings, agencies shall issue, vacate, modify and enforce subpoenas in accordance with the following provisions:

(1) Agencies shall have the power to issue subpoenas requiring the attendance and testimony of witnesses and the production of any evidence, including books, records, correspondence or documents, relating to any matter in question in the proceeding. Agencies may administer oaths and affirmations, examine witnesses, and receive evidence. The power to issue subpoenas may be exercised by any member of the agency or by any person or persons designated by the agency for such purpose.

(2) The agency may prescribe the form of subpoena, but it shall adhere, in so far as practicable, to the form used in civil cases before the courts. Witnesses shall be summoned in the same manner as witnesses in civil cases before the courts, unless another manner is provided by any law. Witnesses summoned shall be paid the same fees for attendance and travel as in civil cases before the courts, unless otherwise provided by any law.

(3) Any party to an adjudicatory proceeding shall be entitled as of right to the issue of subpoenas in the name of the agency conducting the proceeding. The party may have such subpoenas issued by a notary public or justice of the peace, or he may make written application to the agency, which shall forthwith issue the subpoenas requested. However issued, the subpoena shall show on its face the name and address of the party at whose request the subpoena was issued. Unless otherwise provided by any law, the agency need not pay fees for attendance and travel to witnesses summoned by a party.

(4) Any witness summoned may petition the agency to vacate or modify a subpoena issued in its name. The agency shall give prompt notice to the party, if any, who requested issuance of the subpoena. After such investigation as the agency considers appropriate it may grant the petition in whole or part upon a finding that the testimony, or the evidence whose production is required, does not relate with reasonable directness to any matter in question, or that a subpoena for the attendance of a witness or the production of evidence is unreasonable or oppressive, or has not been issued a reasonable period in advance of the time when the evidence is requested.

(5) Upon the failure of any person to comply with a subpoena issued in the name of the agency and not revoked or modified by the agency as provided in this section, any justice of the superior court, upon application by the agency or by the party who requested that the subpoena be issued, may in his discretion issue an order requiring the attendance of such person before the agency and the giving of testimony or production of evidence. Any person failing to obey the court's order may be punished by the court for contempt.

§ 14. Judicial review

[Amended by 2015 Mass. Acts c. 108, effective Oct. 27, 2015.]

Except so far as any provision of law expressly precludes judicial review, any person or appointing authority aggrieved by a final decision of any agency in an adjudicatory proceeding, whether such decision is affirmative or negative in form, shall be entitled to a judicial review thereof, as follows:

Where a statutory form of judicial review or appeal is provided such statutory form shall govern in all respects, except as to standards for review. The standards for review shall be those set forth in paragraph (7) of this section, except so far as statutes provide for review by trial de novo. Insofar as the statutory form of judicial review or appeal is silent as to procedures provided in this section, the provisions of this section shall govern such procedures.

Where no statutory form of judicial review or appeal is provided, judicial review shall be obtained by means of a civil action, as follows:

(1) Proceedings for judicial review of an agency decision shall be instituted in the superior court for the county (a) where the plaintiffs or any of them reside or have their principal place of business within the commonwealth, or (b) where the agency has its principal office, or (c) of Suffolk. The court may grant a change of venue upon good cause shown. The action shall, except as otherwise provided by law, be commenced in the court within thirty days after receipt of notice of the final decision of the agency or if a petition for rehearing has been timely filed with the agency, within thirty days after receipt of notice of agency denial of such petition for rehearing. Upon application made within the thirty-day period or any extension thereof, the court may for good cause shown extend the time.

(2) Service shall be made upon the agency and each party to the agency proceeding in accordance with the Massachusetts Rules of Civil Procedure governing service of process. For the purpose of such service the agency upon request shall certify to the plaintiff the names and addresses of all such parties as disclosed by its records, and service upon parties so certified shall be sufficient. All parties to the proceeding before the agency shall have the right to intervene in the proceeding for review. The court may in its discretion permit other interested persons to intervene.

(3) The commencement of an action shall not operate as a stay of enforcement of the agency decision, but the agency may stay enforcement, and the reviewing court may order a stay upon such terms as it considers proper. Notwithstanding the foregoing, if the sex offender registry board issues a stay of a final classification in a sex offender registry board proceeding, then such stay shall be for not more than 60 days but if a court issues a stay of a final classification in a court appeal held pursuant to section 178M of chapter 6, then such hearing shall be expedited and such stay

shall be for not more than 60 days, without written findings and good cause shown.

(4) The agency shall, by way of answer, file in the court the original or a certified copy of the record of the proceeding under review. The record shall consist of (a) the entire proceedings, or (b) such portions thereof as the agency and the parties may stipulate, or (c) a statement of the case agreed to by the agency and the parties. The expense of preparing the record may be assessed as part of the costs in the case, and the court may, regardless of the outcome of the case, assess any one unreasonably refusing to stipulate to Limit the record, for the additional expenses of preparation caused by such refusal. The court may require or permit subsequent corrections or additions to the record when deemed desirable.

(5) The review shall be conducted by the court without a jury and shall be confined to the record, except that in cases of alleged irregularities in procedure before the agency, not shown in the record, testimony thereon may be taken in the court.

(6) If application is made to the court for leave to present additional evidence, and it is shown to the satisfaction of the court that the additional evidence is material to the issues in the case, and that there was good reason for failure to present it in the proceeding before the agency, the court may order that the additional evidence be taken before the agency upon such conditions as the court deems proper. The agency may modify its findings and decision by reason of such additional evidence and shall file with the reviewing court, to become part of the record, the additional evidence, together with any modified or new findings or decision.

(7) The court may affirm the decision of the agency, or remand the matter for further proceedings before the agency; or the court may set aside or modify the decision, or compel any action unlawfully withheld or unreasonably delayed, if it determines that the substantial rights of any party may have been prejudiced because the agency decision is:

(a) In violation of constitutional provisions; or

(b) In excess of the statutory authority or jurisdiction of the agency; or

(c) Based upon an error of law; or

(d) Made upon unlawful procedure; or

(e) Unsupported by substantial evidence; or

(f) Unwarranted by facts found by the court on the record as submitted or as amplified under paragraph (6) of this section, in those instances where the court is constitutionally required to make independent findings of fact; or

(g) Arbitrary or capricious, an abuse of discretion, or otherwise not in accordance with law.

The court shall make the foregoing determinations upon consideration of the entire record, or such portions of the record as may be cited by the parties. The court shall give due weight to the experience, technical competence, and specialized knowledge of the agency, as well as to the discretionary authority conferred upon it.

If the court finds that the action of the appointing authority in discharging, removing, suspending, laying off, lowering in rank or compensation or abolishing his position, or the action of the commission confirming the action taken by the appointing authority, was not justified, the employee shall be reinstated in his office or position without loss of compensation and the court shall assess reasonable costs against the employer.

§ 15. Supreme judicial court and appeals court; concurrent jurisdiction

The supreme judicial court and the appeals court shall have concurrent jurisdiction to review any proceedings had, determinations made, and orders or judgments entered in the superior court pursuant to section fourteen. The supreme judicial court or the appeals court, subject to the provisions of section thirteen of chapter two hundred and eleven A, may by rule vary the procedure authorized or required for such review upon a finding that the review by the court will thereby be made more simple, speedy and effective.

Chapter 71. Public Schools

§ 37H. Policies relative to conduct of teachers or students; student handbooks

[Amended by 2008 Mass. Acts c. 386, § 1, effective Mar. 16, 2009; 2008 Mass. Acts c. 451, § 50, effective Jan. 5, 2009; 2010 Mass. Acts c. 92, § 4, effective May 3, 2010; 2012 Mass. Acts c. 222, § 1, effective July 1, 2014.]

The superintendent of every school district shall publish the district's policies pertaining to the conduct of teachers and students. Said policies shall prohibit the use of any tobacco products within the school buildings, the school facilities or on the school grounds or on school buses by any individual, including school personnel. Said policies shall further restrict operators of school buses and personal motor vehicles, including students, faculty, staff and visitors, from idling such vehicles on school grounds, consistent with section 16B of chapter 90 and regulations adopted pursuant thereto and by the department. The policies shall also prohibit bullying as defined in section 37O and shall include the student-related sections of the bullying prevention and intervention plan required by said section 37O. Copies of these policies shall be provided to any person upon request and without cost by the principal of every school within the district.

Each school district's policies pertaining to the conduct of students shall include the following: disciplinary proceedings, including procedures assuring due process; standards and procedures for suspension and expulsion of students; procedures pertaining to discipline of students with special needs; standards and procedures to assure school building security and safety of students and school personnel, and the disciplinary measures to be taken in cases involving the possession or use of illegal substances or weapons, the use of force, vandalism, or violation of other student's civil rights. Codes of discipline, as well as procedures used to develop such codes shall be filed with the department of education for informational purposes only.

In each school building containing the grades nine to twelve, inclusive, the principal, in consultation with the school council, shall prepare and distribute to each student a student handbook setting forth the rules pertaining to the conduct of students. The student handbook shall include an age-appropriate summary of the student-related sections of the bullying prevention and intervention plan required by section 37O. The school council shall review the student handbook each spring to consider changes in disciplinary policy to take effect in September of the following school year, but may consider policy changes at any time. The annual review shall cover all areas of student conduct, including but not limited to those outlined in this section.

Notwithstanding any general or special law to the contrary, all student handbooks shall contain the following provisions:

(a) Any student who is found on school premises or at school-sponsored or school-related events, including athletic games, in possession of a dangerous weapon, including, but not limited to, a gun or a knife; or a controlled substance as defined in chapter ninety-four C, including, but not limited to, marijuana, cocaine, and heroin, may be subject to expulsion from the school or school district by the principal.

1

(b) Any student who assaults a principal, assistant principal, teacher, teacher's aide or other educational staff on school premises or at school-sponsored or school-related events, including athletic games, may be subject to expulsion from the school or school district by the principal.

(c) Any student who is charged with a violation of either paragraph (a) or (b) shall be notified in writing of an opportunity for a hearing; provided, however, that the student may have representation, along with the opportunity to present evidence and witnesses at said hearing before the principal.

After said hearing, a principal may, in his discretion, decide to suspend rather than expel a student who has been determined by the principal to have violated either paragraph (a) or (b).

(d) Any student who has been expelled from a school district pursuant to these provisions shall have the right to appeal to the superintendent. The expelled student shall have ten days from the date of the expulsion in which to notify the superintendent of his appeal. The student has the right to counsel at a hearing before the superintendent. The subject matter of the appeal shall not be limited solely to a factual determination of whether the student has violated any provisions of this section.

(e) Any school district that suspends or expels a student under this section shall continue to provide educational services to the student during the period of suspension or expulsion, under section 21 of chapter 76. If the student moves to another district during the period of suspension or expulsion, the new district of residence shall either admit the student to its schools or provide educational services to the student in an education service plan, under section 21 of chapter 76.

(f) Districts shall report to the department of elementary and secondary education the specific reasons for all suspensions and expulsions, regardless of duration or type, in a manner and form established by the commissioner. The department of elementary and secondary education shall use its existing data collection tools to obtain this information from districts and shall modify those tools, as necessary, to obtain the information. On an annual basis, the department of elementary and secondary education shall make district level de-identified data and analysis, including the total number of days each student is excluded during the school year, available to the public online in a machine readable format. This report shall include district level data disaggregated by student status and categories established by the commissioner.

(g) Under the regulations promulgated by the department, for each school that suspends or expels a significant number of students for more than 10 cumulative days in a school year, the commissioner shall investigate and, as appropriate, shall recommend models that incorporate intermediary steps prior to the use of suspension or expulsion. The results of the analysis shall be publicly reported at the school district level.

§ 37H½. Delinquency complaint against student; suspension; hearing; expulsion upon conviction; appeal

[Amended by 2012 Mass. Acts c. 222, § 2, effective July 1, 2014.]

Notwithstanding the provisions of section eighty-four and sections sixteen and seventeen of chapter seventy-six:

(1) Upon the issuance of a criminal complaint charging a student with a felony or upon the issuance of a felony delinquency complaint against a student, the principal or headmaster of a school in which the student is enrolled may suspend such student for a period of time determined appropriate by said principal or headmaster if said principal or headmaster determines that the student's continued presence in school would have a substantial detrimental effect on the general welfare of the school. The student shall receive written notification of the charges and the reasons for such suspension prior to such suspension taking effect. The student shall also receive written notification of his right to appeal and the process for appealing such suspension; provided, however, that such suspension shall remain in effect prior to any appeal hearing conducted by the superintendent.

The student shall have the right to appeal the suspension to the superintendent. The student shall notify the superintendent in writing of his request for an appeal no later than five calendar days following the effective date of the suspension. The superintendent shall hold a hearing with the student and the student's parent or guardian within three calendar days of the student's request for an appeal. At the bearing, the student shall have the right to present oral and written testimony on his behalf, and shall have the right to counsel. The superintendent shall have the authority to overturn or alter the decision of the principal or headmaster, including recommending an alternate educational program for the student. The superintendent shall render a decision on the appeal within five calendar days of the hearing. Such decision shall be the final decision of the city, town or regional school district with regard to the suspension.

(2) Upon a student being convicted of a felony or upon an adjudication or admission in court of guilt with respect to such a felony or felony delinquency, the principal or headmaster of a school in which the student is enrolled may expel said student if such principal or headmaster determines that the student's continued presence in school would have a substantial detrimental effect on the general welfare of the school. The student shall receive written notification of the charges and reasons for such expulsion prior to such expulsion taking effect. The student shall also receive written notification of his right to appeal and the process for appealing such expulsion; provided, however, that the expulsion shall remain in effect prior to any appeal hearing conducted by the superintendent.

The student shall have the right to appeal the expulsion to the superintendent. The student shall notify the superintendent, in writing, of his request for an appeal no later than five calendar days following the effective date of the expulsion. The superintendent shall hold a hearing with the student and the student's parent or guardian within three calendar days of the expulsion. At the hearing, the student shall have the right to present oral and written testimony on his behalf, and shall have the right to counsel. The superintendent shall have the authority to overturn or alter the decision of the principal or headmaster, including recommending an alternate educational program for the student. The superintendent shall render a decision on the appeal within five calendar days of the hearing. Such decision shall be the final decision of the city, town or regional school district with regard to the expulsion.

Any school district that suspends or expels a student under this section shall continue to provide educational services to the student during the period of suspension or expulsion, under section 21 of chapter 76. If the student moves to another district during the period of suspension or expulsion, the new district of residence shall either admit the student to its schools or provide educational services to the student under an education service plan, under section 21 of chapter 76.

§ 37H¾. Suspension or expulsion on grounds other than those set forth in Secs. 37 or 37H½

[Added by 2012 Mass. Acts c. 222, § 3, effective July 1, 2014.]

(a) This section shall govern the suspension and expulsion of students enrolled in a public school in the commonwealth who are not charged with a violation of subsections (a) or (b) of section 37H or with a felony under section 37H½.

(b) Any principal, headmaster, superintendent or other person acting as a decision-maker at a student meeting or hearing, when deciding the consequences for the student, shall exercise discretion; consider ways to re-engage the student in the learning process; and avoid using expulsion as a consequence until other remedies and consequences have been employed.

(c) For any suspension or expulsion under this section, the principal or headmaster of a school in which the student is enrolled, or a designee, shall provide, to the student and to the parent or guardian of the student, notice of the charges and the reason for the suspension or expulsion in English and in the primary language spoken in the home of the student. The student shall receive the written notification and shall have the opportunity to meet with the principal or headmaster, or a designee, to discuss the charges and reasons for the suspension or expulsion prior to the suspension or expulsion taking effect. The principal or headmaster, or a designee, shall ensure that the parent or guardian of the student is included in the meeting, provided that such meeting may take place without the parent or guardian only if the principal or headmaster, or a designee, can document reasonable efforts to include the parent or guardian in that meeting. The department shall promulgate rules and regulations that address a principal's duties under this subsection and procedures for including parents in student exclusion meetings, hearings or interviews under this subsection.

(d) If a decision is made to suspend or expel the student after the meeting, the principal or headmaster, or a designee, shall update the notification for the suspension or expulsion to reflect the meeting with the student. If a student has been suspended or expelled for more than 10 school days for a single infraction or for more than 10 school days cumulatively for multiple infractions in any school year, the student and the parent or guardian of the student shall also receive, at the time of the suspension or expulsion decision, written notification of a right to appeal and the process for appealing the suspension or expulsion in English and in the primary language spoken in the home of the student; provided, however, that the suspension or expulsion shall remain in effect prior to any appeal hearing. The principal or headmaster or a designee shall notify the superintendent in writing, including, but not limited to, by electronic means, of any out-of-school suspension imposed on a student enrolled in kindergarten through grade 3 prior to such suspension taking effect. That notification shall describe the student's alleged misconduct and the reasons for suspending the student out-of-school. For the purposes of this section, the term "out-of-school suspension" shall mean a disciplinary action imposed by school officials to remove a student from participation in school activities for 1 day or more.

(e) A student who has been suspended or expelled from school for more than 10 school days for a single infraction or for more than 10 school days cumulatively for multiple infractions in any school year shall have the right to appeal the suspension or expulsion to the superintendent. The student or a parent or guardian of the student shall notify the superintendent in writing of a request for an appeal not later than 5 calendar days following the effective date of the suspension or expulsion; provided, that a student and a parent or guardian of the student may request, and if so requested, shall be granted an extension of up to 7 calendar days. The superintendent or a designee shall hold a hearing with the student and the parent or guardian of the student within 3 school days of the student's request for an appeal; provided that a student or a parent or guardian of the student may request and, if so requested, shall be granted an extension of up to 7 calendar days; provided further, that the superintendent, or a designee, may proceed with a hearing without a parent or guardian of the student if the superintendent, or a designee, makes a good faith effort to include the parent or guardian. At the hearing, the student shall have the right to present oral and written testimony, cross-examine witnesses and shall have the right to counsel. The superintendent shall render a decision on the appeal in writing within 5 calendar days of the hearing. That decision shall be the final decision of the school district with regard to the suspension or expulsion.

(f) No student shall be suspended or expelled from a school or school district for a time period that exceeds 90 school days, beginning the first day the student is removed from an assigned school building.

Chapter 71B. Children with Special Needs

§ 1. Definitions

[Amended by 2000 Mass. Acts c. 159, §§ 149–152, effective Jan. 1, 2001; 2006 Mass. Acts c. 176, § 64, effective July 8, 2008; 2008 Mass. Acts c. 451, § 52, effective June 30, 2009.]

The following words as used in this chapter shall, have the following meanings, unless the context clearly requires otherwise:

"Department", the department of education.

"Free appropriate public education", special education and related services as consistent with the provisions set for in the 20 U.S.C. § 1400 et seq., its accompanying regulations, and which meet the education standards established by statute or established by regulations promulgated by the board of education.

"Least restrictive environment", the educational placement that assures that, to the maximum extent appropriate, children with disabilities, including children in public or private institutions or other care facilities, are educated with children who are not disabled, and special classes, separate schooling or other removal of children with disabilities from the regular educational environment occurs only when the nature or severity of the disability of a child is such that education in regular classes with the use of supplementary aids and services, cannot be achieved satisfactorily.

"Regular education", the school program and pupil assignment which normally leads to college preparatory or technical education or to a career;

"School age child", any person of ages three through twenty-one who has not attained a high school diploma or its equivalent.

"School age child with special needs", a school age child who, because of a disability consisting of a developmental delay or an intellectual, sensory, neurological, emotional, communication, physical, specific learning or health impairment or combination thereof, is unable to progress effectively in regular education and requires special education services in order to successfully develop the child's individual educational potential; provided, however,

1

that no child shall be determined to be a student with special needs solely because the child's behavior violates the school's disciplinary code; and provided, further, that use of the word disability in this section shall not be used to provide a basis for labeling or stigmatizing the child or defining the needs of the child, and shall in no way limit the services, programs, and integration opportunities provided to such child.

"School age child with a disability", a school age child in a public or non-public school setting who, because of a disability consisting of a developmental delay or any intellectual, sensory, neurological, emotional, communication, physical, specific learning or health impairment or combination thereof, is unable to progress effectively in regular education and requires special education services, including a school age child who requires only a related service or related services if said service or services are required to ensure access of the child with a disability to the general education curriculum. The term "specific learning impairment" shall be defined pursuant to 24 C.F.R. § 300.7 (c)(10), the definition of specific learning disability contained in federal regulations implementing the Individual with Disabilities Education Act in effect on January 1, 2000. The term "emotional impairment" shall be defined pursuant to 34 C.F.R. § 300.7 (c)(4), the definition of "emotional disturbance" contained in federal regulations implementing the Individual with Disabilities Education Act in effect on January 1, 2000. No child shall be determined to be a student with a disability solely because such child's behavior violates the school's disciplinary code and no child shall be determined to be a student with a disability solely because such child shall have failed the statewide assessment tests authorized pursuant to section 11 of chapter 69. The use of the word disability in this section shall not be used to provide a basis for labeling or stigmatizing the child or defining the needs of the child and shall in no way limit the services, programs, and integration opportunities provided to such child.

"School age child requiring special education", a child with a disability who requires special education as determined in accordance with the provisions of this chapter and the regulations set forth by the board.

"Special education", educational programs and assignments including, special classes and programs or services designed to develop the educational potential of children with disabilities including, but not limited to, educational placements of children by school committees, the departments of public health, mental health, developmental services, youth services and children and families in accordance with the provisions of this chapter and the regulations set forth by the board.

§ 2. Regulations; special education programs; pre-school level admission to programs; assignment of child

[Amended by 2000 Mass. Acts c. 159, §§ 153–155, effective Jan. 1, 2001; 2002 Mass. Acts c. 184, § 81, effective July 1, 2002; 2008 Mass. Acts c. 176, § 65, effective July 8, 2008; 2008 Mass. Acts c. 285, effective Nov. 4, 2008; 2008 Mass. Acts c. 451, § 53, effective June 30, 2009.]

The board shall promulgate, jointly with the departments of mental health, developmental services, public health, children and families and youth services, the Massachusetts commission for the blind and the commission for the deaf and hard of hearing, regulations regarding educational programs for children with disabilities including, but not limited to a definition of disability which definition shall emphasize a thorough, narrative description of each child's development potential so as to minimize the possibility of stigmatization and to assure a free and appropriate public education in the least restrictive environment of a child with a disability. The definition shall be sufficiently flexible to include children with multiple disabilities.

Prior to referral of a school age child for evaluation under the provisions of this chapter, the principal of the child's school shall ensure that all efforts have been made to meet such child's needs within the regular education program. Such efforts may include, but not be limited to: modifying the regular education program, the curriculum, teaching strategies, reading instruction, environments or materials, the use of support services, the use of consultative services and building-based student and teacher support and assistance teams to meet the child's needs in the regular education classroom. Such efforts and their results shall be documented and placed in the child's school record but they shall not be construed to limit or condition the right to refer a school age child for an evaluation under the provisions of this chapter. The principal of each school shall implement the district's curriculum accommodation plan created under section 38Q½ of chapter 71 in developing strategies for serving children with diverse learning styles within the regular classroom. The principal of each school may designate one professional staff person in the curriculum accommodation plan required in said section 38Q½ of chapter 71 to coordinate services, support and resources designed to meet each child's needs within regular education.

Children receiving or requiring special education shall be entitled to participate in any of the following programs: (1) additional direct or indirect instruction consultation service, materials, equipment or aid provided children or their regular classroom teachers which directly benefits children requiring special education; (2) supplementary individual or small group instruction or treatment in conjunction with a regular classroom program; (3) integrated programs in which children are assigned to special resource classrooms but attend regular classes to the extent that they are able to function therein; (4) full-time special class teaching in a public school building; (5) teaching at home; (6) full-time teaching in a special day school or other day facility; (7) teaching at a hospital; (8) teaching at a short or long-term residential school; (9) occupational or preoccupational training in conjunction with the regular occupational training program in a public school; (10) occupational and pre-occupational training in conjunction with full-time special class teaching in a public school building, at home, in a special day school or other day facility, hospital or short or long-term residential school; and (11) any combination or modification of these programs or other programs, services or experimental provisions which obtain the prior approval of the department. Children in public schools shall be entitled to teaching at home and in the hospital if the child's physician determines the child will have to remain at home or in a hospital for more than 14 school days in any school year. Children in non-public schools shall be entitled to home and hospital services when deemed eligible under this chapter. An expedited evaluation, which shall be limited to a child's physician statement unless there is a clear indication of the need or unless the parents request additional evaluations, shall be conducted and services provided to eligible students by the school district within 15 calendar days of the school district's receipt of the child's physician statement.

Admission to such programs on the pre-school level at an earlier age than at which schooling is ordinarily provided shall be regulated by the department in conjunction with the departments of public health, mental health and developmental services and shall be restricted to children with substantial disabilities who are judged by said departments to require such programming.

No child shall be assigned to a special education class unless it is first determined by an evaluation of the child's disability and the particular special education program that the child is likely to benefit from such program; periodically thereafter, and in no event less often than annually the child and his program shall be reevaluated to determine whether said child is benefiting from said program in accordance with the procedures set forth in section three. In the event that said program is not benefiting the child and that another program may benefit the child more, or said program has benefited the child sufficiently to permit re-assignment, the child shall be reassigned, and in the event of consistent failure of a program to benefit children there assigned, the program shall be abolished or altered.

Beginning age 14 or sooner if determined appropriate by an individualized education program team, school age children with disabilities shall be entitled to transition services and measurable postsecondary goals, as provided under the federal Individual Disabilities with Education Act, 20 USC sec. 1400, et sec.

§ 3. Identification of school age children with a disability; diagnosis of disability; proposal of program; evaluations and assessments of child and program

[Amended by 2002 Mass. Acts c. 184, § 83, effective July 1, 2002; 2003 Mass. Acts c. 26, § 214, effective July 1, 2003; 2006 Mass. Acts c. 57, effective July 6, 2006; 2008 Mass. Acts c. 176, § 66, effective July 8, 2008; 2008 Mass. Acts c. 451 § 54, effective June 30, 2009; 2010 Mass. Acts c. 92, §§ 7–8, effective May 3, 2010; 2010 Mass. Acts c. 131, § 54, effective July 1, 2010; 2013 Mass. Acts c. 140, effective Feb. 18, 2014.]

In accordance with the regulations, guidelines and directives of the department issued jointly with the departments of mental health, developmental services, public health, youth services, and the commission for the blind and the commission for the deaf and hard of hearing and with assistance of the department, the school committee of every city, town or school district shall identify the school age children residing therein who have a disability, as defined in section 2, diagnose and evaluate the needs of such children, propose a special education program to meet those needs, provide or arrange for the provision of such special education program, maintain a record of such identification, diagnosis, proposal and program actually provided and make such reports as the department may require. Until proven otherwise, every child shall be presumed to be appropriately assigned to a regular education program and presumed not to be a school age child with a disability or a school age child requiring special education.

The department shall take all steps necessary to monitor and enforce compliance with this section no less than every three years, including but not limited to investigations, on-site visits and public hearings, and shall provide assistance in planning and implementing any necessary corrective actions to ensure that no school committee provides special education services to a child pursuant to this chapter unless an evaluation conducted pursuant to this section determines that the child has a disability, as defined in section 1. The department shall further take any and all steps necessary to monitor and enforce compliance with all other provisions of this chapter, including but not limited to the requirement that school committees educate children in the least restrictive environment, as defined in section 1. The department shall also ensure that teachers and administrators are fully informed about their responsibilities for implementing the provisions of this chapter and are provided with technical assistance and training necessary to assist them in such effort.

No school committee shall refuse a school age child with a disability admission to or continued attendance in public school without the prior written approval of the department, and without complying with state and federal requirements for disciplining students with disabilities, where applicable. During the pendency of administrative or judicial proceedings, a court of competent jurisdiction shall have the authority to change a child's educational placement, including removing the child from school, in any circumstances when the school committee shows that the child's behavior poses a substantial likelihood of injury to himself or others; provided, however, that the foregoing shall not be construed to abrogate any authority concerning discipline for such a child which is available to a school committee under said regulations and procedures or any other law. No child who is so refused or removed shall be denied an alternative form of education approved by the department, as provided for in section 10, through a tutoring program at home, through enrollment in an institution operated by a state agency, or through any other program which is approved for the child by the department.

No child shall be placed in a special education program without prior consultation, evaluation, reevaluation, and consent as set forth and implemented by regulations promulgated by the department.

Within five days after the referral of a child enrolled in a regular education program by a school official, parent or guardian, judicial officer, social worker, family physician, or person having custody of the child for purposes of determining whether such child requires special education, the school committee shall notify the parents or guardians of such child in writing in the primary language of the home of such referral, the evaluation procedure to be followed, and the child's right to an independent evaluation at clinics or facilities approved by the department under regulations adopted jointly by the department and the departments of mental health, developmental services and public health and the right to appeal from any evaluation, first to the department, and then to the courts; provided, however, that a school district shall not be required to refer a child for an evaluation solely because the child presents a risk of or fails to be promoted at the end of the school year; and provided further, that a school district shall not be required to refer a child for an evaluation solely because such child failed the statewide assessment tests authorized pursuant to section1I of chapter 69.

Within thirty days after said notification the school committee shall provide an evaluation as hereinafter defined. The parents or guardians of such child shall be consulted about the content of such evaluation and the evaluators being used. Said evaluation shall include an assessment of the child's current educational status by a representative of the local school department, an assessment by a classroom teacher who has dealt with the child in the classroom, a complete medical assessment by a physician, an assessment by a psychologist, an assessment by a nurse, social worker, or a guidance or adjustment counselor of the general home situation and pertinent family history factors; and assessments by such specialists as may be required in accordance with the diagnosis including when necessary, but not limited to an assessment by a neurologist, an audiologist, an ophthalmologist, a specialist competent in speech, language and perceptual factors and a psychiatrist. Whenever the evaluation of the Individualized Education Program team indicates that the child has a disability that affects social skills development or that the child is vulnerable to bullying, harassment or teasing because of the child's disability, the Individualized Education Program shall address the skills and proficiencies needed to avoid and respond to bullying, harassment or teasing. Whenever an evaluation indicates that a child is blind, as defined in section one hundred and thirty-six of chapter six, said evaluation shall also include an assessment of the appropriateness of Braille instruction for the child. Such assessment shall include (i) the child's efficiency in reading and writing print as compared with children who do not have a disability; (ii) the child's stamina in using print before fatigue occurs; (iii) the child's prognosis for further sight loss; and (iv) the child's present competence in Braille and a detailed explanation as to whether instruction is appropriate, conducted by a certified teacher of students with visual impairments. Any such instruction found to be essential to meet such child's disability shall be available at a frequency and duration sufficient to meet fully the educational needs of the child. Braille instruction may be used in combination with other special education services appropriate to the child's educational needs. Whenever an evaluation indicates that a child has a disability on the autism spectrum, which includes autistic disorder, Asperger's disorder, pervasive developmental disorder not otherwise specified, childhood disintegrative disorder, or Rhett's Syndrome, as defined in the most recent edition of the Diagnostic and Statistical

Manual of the American Psychiatric Association, the Individualized Education Program (IEP) team, as defined by regulations of the department, shall consider and shall specifically address the following: the verbal and nonverbal communication needs of the child; the need to develop social interaction skills and proficiencies; the skills and proficiencies needed to avoid and respond to bullying, harassment or teasing; the needs resulting from the child's unusual responses to sensory experiences; the needs resulting from resistance to environmental change or change in daily routines; the needs resulting from engagement in repetitive activities and stereotyped movements; the need for any positive behavioral interventions, strategies, and supports to address any behavioral difficulties resulting from autism spectrum disorder; and other needs resulting from the child's disability that impact progress in the general curriculum, including social and emotional development. A child's Individualized Education Program, as defined in 20 USC § 1401 (14), shall include a statement of measurable annual goals, including academic and functional goals, and a description of benchmarks or short-term objectives.

The department jointly with the departments of mental health, developmental services and public health shall issue regulations to specify qualifications for persons assessing said child.

These departments through their joint regulations may define circumstances under which the requirement of any or all of these assessments may be waived so long as an evaluation appropriate to the educational needs of the child is provided. Those persons assessing said child shall maintain a complete and specific record of diagnostic procedures attempted and their results, the conclusions reached, the suggested courses of special education best suited to the child's educational needs, and the specific benefits expected from such action. A suggested special education program may include family guidance or counseling services. When the suggested course of study is other than regular education those persons assessing said child shall present a method of monitoring the benefits of such special education and conditions that would indicate that the child should return to regular classes, and a comparison of expected outcomes in regular class placement.

If a child with a disability requires special education and related services in accordance with the provisions of the federal Individuals with Disabilities Education Act of 1975, the provisions of this chapter, and federal and state regulations promulgated pursuant thereto, such services shall be made available.

Upon completion of said evaluation, the child's parents may obtain an independent evaluation at school committee expense, from child evaluation clinics or facilities approved by the department jointly with the departments of mental health, mental retardation and public health, provided that the school committee may initiate within five school working days of the request, a hearing with the bureau of special education appeals to show that its evaluation is appropriate, in accordance with the provisions of the Individuals with Disabilities Education Act and regulations promulgated pursuant thereto; provided, however, that the parents may choose, on a voluntary basis, to share the costs of the independent evaluation with the school committee pursuant to a sliding fee scale established in regulations issued by the department pursuant to this section, in which case the school committee shall pay its share of the costs in accordance with the scale; provided, that, if the child's family income does not exceed 400 per cent of the federal poverty level established by the United States department of health and human services, parents shall pay no cost; provided, however, that the secretary of health and human services under section 2A of chapter 118G shall establish rates for educational assessments conducted or performed by psychologists and other trained certified educational personnel notwithstanding the provisions of any general or special law or rule or regulation to the contrary. A parent may obtain an independent evaluation at private expense from any specialist.

The written record and clinical history from both the evaluation provided by the school committee and independent evaluation, if any, shall be made available to the parents, guardians, or persons with custody of the child. Separate instructions, limited to the information required for adequate care of the child, shall be distributed only to those persons directly concerned with the care of the child. Otherwise said records shall be confidential.

The department may hold hearings through the bureau of special education appeals regarding said evaluation, said hearings to be held in accordance with the provisions of chapter thirty A. The parents, guardians, or persons with custody may refuse the education program suggested by the initial evaluation and request said hearing by the department into the evaluation of the child and the appropriate education program. The hearing officer shall order such educational placement and services as he deems appropriate and consistent with this chapter to assure the child receives a free and appropriate public education in the least restrictive environment; provided, however, that a presumption shall exist to direct such placement to the regular educational environment. The hearing officer may determine, in accordance with the rules, regulations and policies of the respective agencies, that services shall be provided by the department of children and families, the department of mental retardation, the department of mental health, the department of public health, or any other state agency or program, in addition to the program and related services to be provided by the school committee. Such order may provide for: the placement or services requested by the school committee, the placement or services requested by the parent, either of those placements or services with modifications, or such alternative programs or services as may be required to assure such development of such child. Said parents, guardians or persons with custody may either consent to or reject such placement, program or services. If rejected, and the program desired by the parents, guardian or person with custody is a regular education program, the department and the local school committee shall provide the child with the educational program chosen by the parent, guardian or persons with custody except where such placement would seriously endanger the health or safety of the child, substantially disrupt the program for other students or, if the child is currently placed in a special education program, deny the child a free appropriate public education. In such circumstances the local school committee may proceed to the superior court with jurisdiction over the residence of the child to make such showing. Said court upon such showing shall be authorized to place the child in an appropriate education program.

At any time, school committees and parents, guardians, or persons with custody of a student may voluntarily agree to seek resolution of any dispute through mediation provided by the bureau of special education appeals, provided, that the mediation process may not be used to deny or delay a parent's right to a due process hearing or to delay or deny any other rights afforded under this chapter and the federal Individuals with Disabilities Education Act of 1975, as so amended and shall be scheduled as soon as practicable after such agreement.

If the parents, guardians or persons with custody reject the educational placement recommended by the department and desire a program other than a regular education program, they may proceed to the superior court with jurisdiction over the residence of the child and said court shall be authorized to order the placement of the child in an appropriate education program.

During the course of the evaluations, assessments, or hearings provided for above, a child shall be placed in a regular education program unless such placement endangers the health or safety of the child or substantially disrupts such education program for other children. No parent or guardian of any child placed in a special education program shall be required to perform duties not required of a parent or guardian of a child in a regular school program.

The educational progress of any child placed in a special education program shall be reviewed at least annually as set forth above. If such evaluation suggests that the initial evaluation was in error or that a different program or medical treatment would now benefit the child more, appropriate reassignment or alteration in treatment shall be recommended to the parents, guardians or persons having custody of the child. If the evaluation of the special education program shows that said program does not provide educational benefit to the child in the least restrictive environment, then such child shall be reassigned. If the evaluation shows that the child no longer needs special education services, the team shall recommend that the child no longer be considered a school age child with disabilities for the purposes of this chapter.

Evaluations and assessments of children and special education programs shall remain confidential and be used solely for the administration of special education in the commonwealth, including, but not limited to, inspection by the department and regional and state advisory councils to insure that every special education program does benefit the children there assigned. The school committee of any city, town, or school district shall establish a parent advisory council on special education. Membership shall be offered to all parents of children with disabilities and other interested parties. The parent advisory council duties shall include but not be limited to: advising the school committee on matters that pertain to the education and safety of students with disabilities; meeting regularly with school officials to participate in the planning, development, and evaluation of the school committee's special education programs. The parent advisory council shall establish by-laws regarding officers and operational procedures. In the course of its duties under this section, the parent advisory council shall receive assistance from the school committee without charge, upon reasonable notice, and subject to the availability of staff and resources.

If a student's individual education plan necessitates special education services in a day or residential facility or an educational collaborative, the IEP team shall consider whether the child requires special education services and supports to promote the student's transition to placement in a less restrictive program. If the student requires such services, then the IEP shall include a statement of any special education services and supports necessary to promote the child's transition to placement in a less restrictive program.

§ 5. Costs or obligations; payment; budget

[Amended by 2000 Mass. Acts c. 159, § 170, effective Jan. 1, 2001.]

Any school committee which provides or arranges for the provision of special education pursuant to the provisions of section three shall pay for such special education personnel, materials and equipment, tuition, room and board, transportation, rent and consultant services as are necessary for the provision of special education; provided, however, that the school committee shall not be obligated to pay for health care goods or services to the extent that such goods or services constitute medically necessary treatment for disease, illness, injury, or bodily dysfunction which would be covered by a third party payor but for a school-aged child's eligibility for such goods and services under this chapter; provided, further, that the determination of medical necessity shall be made by the third party payor under its standard program of utilization review, that the school-aged child with a disability or his parent or guardian if he is a minor shall have the right to freedom of choice in the selection of the provider of health care goods and services, and that the provider of health care goods and services does not have a direct or indirect financial relationship to the school committee; and provided, further, that school committees may accept payment for health care goods and services provided by certified school committee employees from third party payors other than the program of medical care and assistance established under chapter one hundred and eighteen E except as provided under section seventy-two of chapter forty-four. Where no such third party payor is available, school committees are not relieved of their responsibilities under this chapter.

Notwithstanding the provisions of section 27C of chapter 29 or any other general or special law to the contrary, if a child with a disability for whom a school committee currently provides or arranges for the provision of special education in an approved private day or residential school placement, including placement in a pediatric nursing home pursuant to the provisions of section 3, or his parent or guardian moves to a different school district on or after July 1 of any fiscal year, such school committee of the former community of residence shall pay the approved budgeted costs, including necessary transportation costs, of such day or residential placement, including placement in a pediatric nursing home, of such child for the balance of such fiscal year; provided, however, that if such move occurs between April 1 and June 30, such school committee of the former community of residence shall pay such costs for the balance of the fiscal year in which the move occurred as well as for the subsequent fiscal year. The school committee of the new community of residence shall assume all responsibilities for reviewing the child's progress, monitoring the effectiveness of the placement, and reevaluating the child's needs from the date of new residence; provided, however, that during the period when the financial obligation of the former community of residence for such day or residential placement continues pursuant to this section, the school committee of such new community of residence shall provide the school committee of the former community of residence with notice of any such review, monitoring, and reevaluation, and an opportunity to participate; and provided, further, that the school committee of such new community of residence shall be financially responsive for any increase, and the obligation of the school committee of such former community of residence shall be reduced by any decrease, in the costs of such day or residential placement during such period which results from any such review, monitoring or reevaluation.

A school committee which incurs costs or obligations under the provision of this section shall include within its annual budget an amount of money to comply with said provisions. Said amount shall be added to the annual budget appropriation for school purposes in each city or town for the support of public schools for the purposes of, and enforceable pursuant to, section thirty-four of chapter seventy-one, notwithstanding any general or special laws or charter provisions which limit the amount of money that may be appropriated in any city or town for school purposes.

§ 6. Assignment of children to classes; annual report; equal educational opportunities; prima facie denial; hearings; injunctive or other relief

[Amended by 2000 Mass. Acts c. 159, § 173, effective July 1, 2000.]

School committees shall annually report to the department, pursuant to regulations promulgated by the department, the assignment by sex, national origin, economic status, race and religion, of children by age level to special education classes and the distribution of children residing in the district by sex, national origin, economic status, race and religion of children by age level. Within any school district if in any special education program there is a pattern of assignment throughout the district on the basis of sex, national origin, economic status, race or religion of the students which is substantially disproportionate from the distribution, the department shall notify such school district of its prima facie denial of equal educational opportunities. The department shall hold public hearings to investigate into such prima facie denial, at which hearings the local school district shall show that such disproportion is necessary to promote a compelling education interest of the children affected and of the commonwealth. If the local school district fails to make such showing, a denial of equal educational opportunities shall be declared by the department and it shall order said district to submit a plan to eliminate such denial to be effective for the school year immediately following such declaration and order. If in the view of the department the plan submitted is inadequate, or if implementation of said plan proves inadequate, the department may request the attorney general to proceed to the superior court for all necessary injunctive and other relief. If such prima facie denial has continued without elimination for a period of two consecutive years in any school district, any person residing in such school district may bring suit in the superior court of his residence to determine whether there is such adequate justification for the prima facie denial, and in the event there is not, to obtain the necessary and appropriate injunctive or other relief.

§ 7. Tests for selection of children for referral, diagnosis, or evaluation

[Amended by 2000 Mass. Acts c. 159, § 174, effective July 1, 2000.]

No results of standardized or local tests of ability, aptitude, attitude, affect, achievement, or aspiration may be used exclusively in the selection of children for referral, diagnosis, or evaluation. Such tests shall be approved by the department in accordance with regulations issued by the board to insure that they are as free as possible from cultural and linguistic bias or, wherever necessary, separately evaluated with reference to the linguistic and cultural groups to which the child belongs.

§ 8. Transportation to and from school

[Amended by 2000 Mass. Acts c. 159, § 175, effective Jan. 1, 2001; 2010 Mass. Acts c. 188, § 60, effective Oct. 25, 2010.]

If a school age child with a disability attends a school approved by the department within or without the city or town of residence of the parent or guardian, the school committee of the town where the child resides may be required by the department to provide transportation once each day including weekends where applicable to and from such school while the child is in attendance. The city or town providing transportation under this section shall be reimbursed according to the provisions of section fourteen.

A school committee may adopt a program to reimburse parents who voluntarily choose to transport their disabled child to a school approved by the department that is located outside of the city or town of residence of the parent or guardian. The reimbursement program may utilize rates in excess of the standard state mileage reimbursement amounts and may be based on a mileage, daily or weekly rate. Committees choosing to utilize this option shall be able to demonstrate that parental reimbursements represent a cost savings compared to other modes of available transportation. An eligible parent shall not be required to participate in the program.

§ 10. Referral of children to institutions within or without the commonwealth on annual renewal basis upon request; requisites; expenses and cost

[Amended by 2000 Mass. Acts c. 159, §§ 178–179, effective Jan. 1, 2001; 2006 Mass. Acts c. 176, § 68, effective July 8, 2008; 2008 Mass. Acts c. 451, § 56, effective June 30, 2009.]

The department may, on an annual renewal basis, upon the request of the parents or guardians and the recommendations of a local school committee refer children requiring special education to any institution within or without the commonwealth which offers curriculum, instruction and facilities which are appropriate to the child's disability and which are approved by the department under regulations prescribed by the departments of education, mental health, developmental services and public health. The curriculum at such an institution shall for approval be equivalent, insofar as the department deems feasible, to the curriculum for children of comparable age and ability in the public schools of the commonwealth. Notwithstanding the foregoing, the department shall give preference to programs that are offered within the child's school district and if no such program is available, to programs offered within the commonwealth. Placement in another state shall be made only when no public or private facility which can provide the services in the student's individualized education plan, consistent with requirements of state and federal law, is available in the commonwealth; but no child in an out of state placement as of June 1, 2000 shall be required to transfer to a facility located within the commonwealth unless the transfer is in accordance with the child's individualized education plan and is not based solely upon this section.

Before acting on said request, the department shall determine the nature and extent of a child's disability, and shall require the local school committee to prepare and submit plans detailing the time needed to establish facilities adequate for children with a disability in the city, town or school district where the child resides, and shall ascertain whether adequate facilities and instruction programs are available or when adequate facilities can be made available in the city, town or school district where the child with a disability resides. Until adequate facilities can be made available, such child shall be placed in the most adequate program available as determined by the department. The department shall further define by regulation the circumstances in which it shall be directly responsible for the placement of children in such special education programs, and by standards available to the public determine the methods and order of such placements; provided, however, that no child shall be denied access to any program operated by the department of mental health, developmental services, public health or children and families to which in the judgment of the operating department the child should be admitted.

The expenses of the instruction and support actually rendered or furnished to such children with disabilities, including their necessary traveling expenses, whether daily or otherwise, but not exceeding ordinary and reasonable compensation therefor, may be paid by the commonwealth; but the department shall issue regulations jointly with the departments of mental health, developmental services, public health, youth services and children and families defining the circumstances in which the commonwealth shall bear all or part of such cost, the circumstances in which school committees shall be required to bear part or all of such cost, and the circumstances in which a parent or guardian may be required to reimburse the commonwealth for part or all of such cost; provided, however, that in no event shall the cost to the school committee for placement under this section be less than the average per pupil cost for pupils of comparable age within the city, town or school district; and provided, further, that in determining the cost to the parent or guardian, if any, no charge shall be made for any educational cost but only for support and care. In determining the cost to the parent or guardian the department shall apply criteria which take into account relative ability to pay.

The department shall direct and supervise the education of all such children, and the commissioner of education shall state in his annual report their number, the cost of their instruction and support, the manner in which the money appropriated therefor has been expended, to what extent reimbursed and such other information as he deems important.

The board of education shall not limit the rights of a school district to conduct unannounced visits to any private school in which the district has placed any students pursuant to this chapter.

Nothing contained herein shall affect the continued authority of the departments of mental health, developmental services and public health over all non-educational programs and all treatment for residents or patients in institutions under their control.

§ 11. Repealed

[Repealed by 1991 Mass. Acts c. 138, § 144.]

§ 11A. Incarcerated children with a disability; special education

[Amended by 2000 Mass. Acts c. 159, § 180, effective Jan. 1, 2001.]

The department of education shall provide special education to school aged children with a disability who are incarcerated in county houses of correction.

§ 12. School departments; establishment; administration; staff; operation; expenditures; costs of education

[Amended by 2000 Mass. Acts c. 159, § 181, effective Jan. 1, 2001; 2005 Mass. Acts c. 6, § 8, effective Feb. 24, 2005; 2008 Mass. Acts c. 451, § 57, effective June 30, 2009.]

The department shall establish and maintain a school department for school-age children in each institution under the control of the departments of mental health, developmental services, public health and youth services which provides support and care for resident children with a disability, acting jointly with the department which has control over the particular institution; provided, however, that appropriations for the administration of said school departments shall be administered by the department of education.

Each such school department shall be administered by a director, appointed jointly by the commissioner of education and the superintendent of said institution.

Each such school department shall have such staff as the department and the department which administers the institution involved deem appropriate.

Such school departments shall operate pursuant to regulations established jointly by the department and the department which administers said institution. Nothing contained herein shall affect the continued authority of departments operating such institutions over all non-educational programs and all treatment for residents or patients in institutions under their control.

The director and staff of such school departments shall be employees of the department of education, which shall assume the costs of all aspects of the educational programs in such departments. Said school departments may operate twelve months of the year. Nothing contained herein shall operate to remove from employment any educational personnel already employed by any institution now under the administration of the department of mental health, developmental services, public health or youth services, or to reduce their salaries or other employee benefits.

The per capita expenditure on education programs in such school departments shall be equivalent to or higher than the average expenditure for special education programs in the public schools of the commonwealth less the average transportation costs. Said average expenditure shall be computed annually by the department of education.

The city, town or regional school district in which each school-age child in any institution described in this section would normally be eligible to attend school and the city, town, or regional school district in which each day student admitted to an institution under the control of the department of public health and receiving educational services from the department of education would normally be eligible to attend school shall pay to the commonwealth the costs of the education of that child in the school department of that institution in an amount determined according to the regulations issued under section 10. The payment for each such child shall not be less than its average per pupil cost for pupils of comparable age within the city, town or regional school district. The amount due the commonwealth each year shall be deducted from the annual distribution to said city, town or regional school district pursuant to section 20 of chapter 59.

§ 12A. Definitions applicable to Secs. 12A to 12C

For the purposes of sections twelve A to twelve C, inclusive, the following words shall have the following meanings:

"Disabled person", a person who is unable to engage in substantial gainful activity by reason of medically determinable physical or mental impairment which can be expected to result in death or be of at least twelve months' duration; provided, however, that such impairment is of such severity that such individual is unable to do his previous work, if any, and, considering his age, education, and work experience, cannot engage in substantial gainful activity.

"Education authority", the school committee or other education provider responsible for the provision of special education pursuant to the provisions of this chapter.

"Habilitative services", services directed toward the alleviation of limitations on major life activities of a disabled person, including diagnosis, evaluation, treatment, personal care, daycare, respite care, home care, residential care, group care in a community residence, special living arrangements, training, education, sheltered employment, supported work, recreation, counseling, protective and social services, legal services, information and referral services, and transportation services.

"Major life activity", self-care, including personal hygiene, dressing and eating; communication and language skills, including reception and expression; learning; mobility; capacity for independent living; and economic self-sufficiency.

"Substantial gainful activity", the performance of a task for at least twenty hours per week for which a disabled person receives compensation either in currency or in-kind; provided, however, that such activity shall not include sheltered workshops, supported work, occupational therapy or any other work activity supported by the federal, state, or local governments for the purpose of assisting such disabled person to participate in such activity.

"Transitional plan", a plan for a program of habilitative services for disabled person whose entitlement to services under special education programs has terminated or will terminate as a result of such person's graduation from high school or attainment of age twenty-two.

§ 12B. Bureau of transitional planning; transitional advisory committee; establishment

[Amended by 2006 Mass. Acts c. 176, § 69, effective July 8, 2008; 2008 Mass. Acts c. 451, § 58, effective June 30, 2009; 2011 Mass. Acts c. 3, § 110, effective Mar. 27, 2011.]

There shall be within the executive office of human services a bureau of transitional planning. There is also hereby established within the executive office of human services a committee, to be known as the transitional advisory committee, which shall meet on a regular and periodic basis for the purpose of reviewing and approving transitional plans for disabled persons whose entitlement to services under special education programs has terminated or will terminate within two years. The committee shall consist of the secretary of the executive office of human services who shall be chairman, or his designee, and one representative from each of the following agencies: the executive office of labor and workforce development, the department of mental health, the department of developmental services, the department of children and families, the department of transitional assistance, the department of public health, the Massachusetts rehabilitation commission, the Massachusetts office of deafness, the Massachusetts commission for the blind and the department of education. Said representatives shall be designated by the executive secretary, commissioner or department head whose agency they shall represent. The committee shall adopt rules and procedures governing its proceedings. Members of the committee shall not be compensated for service on said committee.

§ 12C. Continuing habilitative services; eligibility; transitional plan; rules and regulations

[Amended by 2000 Mass. Acts c. 159, §§ 182–183, effective Jan. 1, 2001.]

A disabled person who has been receiving special education under the provisions of this chapter shall be eligible, subject to appropriation, upon graduation from high school or upon attaining the age of twenty-two, whichever occurs first, to receive habilitative services in the manner hereinafter provided. The education authority which is responsible for the education of a person with a disability shall, with the consent of such person or his parent or guardian, at least two years before such person attains the age of twenty-two or at least two years before such person's graduation, whichever first occurs, determine whether such person may need continuing habilitative services and notify the bureau of transitional planning of the name and address of such person, the record of the special education services being provided to such person, and the expected date of termination of such services. Within thirty days of such notification, said bureau will begin to prepare a case file on such person consisting of all available information relevant to the questions of whether such person is a disabled person within the meaning of section twelve A and which habilitative services may be necessary or appropriate to assist such person in realizing his potential for self-sufficiency in major life activities. The education authority shall, with the consent of such person or his parent or guardian, provide said bureau with copies of relevant portions of record of such person, which shall be included in such person's case file. Said bureau shall also provide an opportunity for the submission by or on behalf of such person, of information relative to such person's disability, and all information so provided shall be included in such person's case file.

If at the time of said notification to said bureau, such person has been determined to be eligible for disability benefits under Title II or Title XVI of the United States Social Security Act, such person shall be deemed to be a disabled person within the meaning of section twelve A, and said bureau shall make a preliminary determination of the agency or agencies which shall develop a transitional plan for such person. If at such time such person has not been determined to be eligible for such benefits, said bureau shall refer such person to the Massachusetts rehabilitation commission for a determination whether he is a disabled person within the meaning of section twelve A. As a condition of such referral, said bureau may require that an application be submitted forthwith on behalf of such person for such benefits.

With respect to each such person referred to it under the preceding paragraph, the Massachusetts rehabilitation commission shall provide written notice to said bureau and to such person or his parent or guardian of its determination whether such person is a disabled person. If such person is determined by the commission to be disabled, then his case file shall be referred to said bureau for the preliminary determination of the agency or agencies which shall develop a transitional plan. In addition to any appeal rights under Titles II and XVI of the Social Security Act, a finding by the commission that such person is not disabled may be appealed by requesting review by the secretary of health and human services within sixty days after the date of issuance of the commission's determination. The secretary shall approve, disapprove, or remand to said commission for further consideration any such request within ninety days of its receipt by said secretary.

Upon receipt of a case file of a disabled person said bureau shall make a preliminary determination of the agency which shall develop a transitional plan for such individual.

If such preliminary determination is approved by the transitional advisory committee, such agency shall, in accordance with its usual planning procedures, except as modified by the provisions of this section, in cooperation with said bureau, and such person, develop a transitional plan for such person. The parent or guardian may participate in the development of the transitional plan unless such participation is objected to by the disabled person. Said transitional plan shall include, but not be limited to, the following information: the habilitative services found by the committee to be necessary or appropriate to assist such person in realizing his potential for self-sufficiency in major life activities; the agencies responsible for the provision of such services; the location in the least restrictive environment at which such services will be provided; and the expected duration for the provision of such services. Each transitional plan shall be submitted to the transitional advisory committee for its approval no later than six months prior to the date each disabled person attains age twenty-two or graduates, whichever occurs first. The committee shall meet at least once a month for the purpose of Considering the approval of such transitional plans.

Said committee shall provide the person and his parent or guardian with a written copy of an approved transitional plan developed for such person. If the plan calls for the provision of services by an agency in the executive office of health and human services or on the department of labor and workforce development, the secretary and director shall also be provided with a copy of the plan. The secretary and director shall each review the portion of such plan which calls for the provision of services by an agency within his executive office or department and may, after consultation with such agency and written notification to such person or his parent or guardian, make such modifications to such portion of such plan as are necessary or appropriate. Any plan which has not been so modified by said secretary or director within 60 days of its submission to said secretary or director shall be deemed to be approved in the form submitted.

After a transitional plan for a disabled person has been approved and after said individual attains the age of twenty-two or graduates, whichever first occurs, habilitative services shall be provided to such person in accordance with the transitional plan. The secretary of health and human services shall promulgate rules and regulations for the modification, extension, termination, or appeal of the transitional plan by such person, his parent or guardian, or any agency responsible for the provision of services pursuant to such plan.

§ 13. Repealed

[Repealed by 1986 Mass. Acts c. 599, § 27.]

§ 13A. Repealed

[Repealed by 1978 Mass. Acts c. 367, § 70J.]

§ 15. Repealed

[Repealed by 1983 Mass. Acts c. 688, § 2.]

2005 Mass. Acts Chapter 107. An act relative to federal reimbursement for services for children with autism

Be it enacted by the Senate and House of Representatives in General Court assembled, and by the authority of the same, as follows:

The secretary of health and human services shall, within 3 months of the effective date of this act, apply to the federal Centers for Medicare & Medicaid Services for a home and community-based services waiver under section 1915(c) of the federal Social Security Act, 42 U.S.C. section 1396(n), to allow eligible children with autism spectrum disorder to receive waiver services to support the children in their homes and communities.

The waiver application shall provide services for children with autism spectrum disorder who are institutionalized or at risk of institutionalization. Autism spectrum disorder includes the following disorders as defined in the Diagnostic and Statistical Manual of Mental Disorders, fourth edition (DSM-IV-TR, 2000): autistic disorder, Asperger's disorder, pervasive developmental disorder not otherwise specified, childhood disintegrative disorder, and Rett's disorder.

The waiver application shall include intensive in-home intervention services for children with autism spectrum disorder, and any other services determined appropriate to support children with autism spectrum disorder in their homes and communities.

The waiver application shall specify the required credentials for the providers of services covered by the waiver, including credentials required for supervisors of direct care providers and credentials required for direct care providers.

The waiver application shall ensure that the process and procedures for applying for waiver services are fully accessible to families of children with autism spectrum disorder who are from linguistically and culturally diverse communities.

Services under the waiver shall be coordinated with services provided by school committees under chapters 71B and 111G of the General Laws. This section shall not affect or limit a school district's ability to obtain Medicaid reimbursement for school-related health services, or affect or limit a school district's responsibility to provide all services, including home-based services, required pursuant to said chapter 71B, 20 U.S.C. section 1400 to 1487, inclusive, and 29 U.S.C. section 794.

On January 15, 2006, and every year thereafter, the secretary of health and human services shall file a report with the clerk of the house of representatives who shall forward the same to the joint committees on education and health care financing on the status of the waiver application and on the operation of waiver, once obtained. The report on the operation of the waiver shall include, but not be limited to, a description of the number of children receiving services under the waiver, the race and primary language of the children served and their families, the types of services provided, and any available information pertaining to impact and effectiveness of the waiver.

Approved Oct. 5, 2005; effective Jan. 6, 2006.

Chapter 76. School Attendance

§ 2. Duties of parents; penalty

Every person in control of a child described in section one shall cause him to attend school as therein required, and, if he fails so to do for seven day sessions or fourteen half day sessions within any period of six months, he shall, on complaint by a supervisor of attendance, be punished by a fine of not more than twenty dollars. No physical or mental condition capable of correction, or rendering the child a fit subject for special instruction at public charge in institutions other than public day schools, shall avail as a defense unless it appears that the defendant has employed all reasonable measures for the correction of the condition and the suitable instruction of the child. The Boston juvenile court shall have jurisdiction within the territorial limits described in section fifty-seven of chapter two hundred and eighteen of complaints hereunder. The Worcester juvenile court shall have jurisdiction, concurrent with the central district court of Worcester, of complaints hereunder. The Springfield juvenile court shall have jurisdiction, concurrent with the district court of Springfield, of complaints hereunder. The Bristol county juvenile court shall have jurisdiction, concurrent with all of the district courts of Bristol county, of complaints hereunder, and the presiding judge of said court shall establish hearing dates on a circuit basis to be held in such respective courts. Complaints hereunder brought in other district courts shall be heard in the juvenile sessions thereof.

Chapter 90. Motor Vehicles and Aircraft

§ 10. Operation of motor vehicle without license; members of armed forces; nonresidents; suspension or revocation of license

[Amended by 2018 Mass. Acts c. 154, §§ 35–36, effective July 1, 2018.]

No person under sixteen years of age shall operate a motor vehicle upon any way. No other person shall so operate unless licensed by the registrar unless he possesses a receipt issued under section eight for persons licensed in another state or country or unless he possesses a valid learner's permit issued under section eight B, except as is otherwise herein provided or unless he is the spouse of a member of the armed forces of the United States who is accompanying such member on military or naval assignment to this commonwealth and who has a valid operator's license issued by another state, or unless he is on active duty in the armed forces of the United States and has in his possession a license to operate motor vehicles issued by the state where he is domiciled, or unless he is a member of the armed forces of the United States returning from active duty outside the United States, and has in his possession a license to operate motor vehicles issued by said armed forces in a foreign country, but in such case for a period of not more than forty-five days after his return. The motor vehicle of a nonresident may be operated on the ways of the commonwealth in accordance with section three by its owner or by any nonresident operator without a license from the registrar if the nonresident operator is duly licensed under the laws of the state or country where such vehicle is registered and has such license on his person or in the vehicle in some easily accessible place. Subject to the provisions of section three, a nonresident who holds a license under the laws of the state or country in which he resides may operate any motor vehicle of a type which he is licensed to operate under said license, duly registered in this commonwealth or in any state or country; provided, that he has the license on his person or in the vehicle in some easily accessible place, and that, as finally determined by the registrar, his state or country prescribes and enforces standards of fitness for operations of motor vehicles substantially as high as those prescribed and enforced by this commonwealth. The nonresident shall have in their possession a valid international driver's permit, or a document containing a photo and an English translation that substantially corresponds to an international driving permit, that shall be used solely to properly identify the individual appearing on the license for the purpose of enforcing this section if no English translation appears on the front or back of the license that the nonresident is required to have in possession at all times while operating a motor vehicle.

Notwithstanding the foregoing provisions, no person shall operate on the ways of the commonwealth any motor vehicle, whether registered in this commonwealth or elsewhere, if the registrar shall have suspended or revoked any license to operate motor vehicles issued to him under this chapter, or shall have suspended his right to operate such vehicles, and such license or right has not been restored or a new license to operate motor vehicles has not been issued to him. Operation of a motor vehicle in violation of this paragraph shall be subject to the same penalties as provided in section twenty-three for operation after suspension or revocation and before restoration or issuance of a new license or the restoration of the right to operate.

§ 22½. Suspension of right to operate based upon violation of Sec. 32E of chapter 94C

[Added by 2016 Mass. Acts c. 64, § 2, effective Mar. 30. 2016.]

The registrar shall suspend, without a hearing, the license or right to operate of a person who is convicted of a violation of subsection (b), (c) or (c½) of section 32E of chapter 94C or adjudged a delinquent child by reason of having violated said subsection (b),

1 (c) or (c½) of said section 32E of said chapter 94C; provided, however, that the period of such suspension shall not exceed 5 years from the date of conviction; and provided further, that the person may, after the completion of any time served, apply for and shall be granted a hearing before the registrar to request the issuance of a new license for employment or educational purposes or for any other hardship purpose for the balance of the license suspension. The registrar may issue such license under such terms or conditions as the registrar may prescribe. If the registrar denies the applicant's request for a hardship license, the registrar shall issue written findings supporting the denial.

§ 24. Driving while under influence of intoxicating liquor, etc.; second and subsequent offenses; punishment; treatment programs; reckless and unauthorized driving; failure to stop after collision

[Amended by 2002 Mass. Acts c. 52, § 2; 2002 Mass. Acts c. 302, §§ 1–4; 2003 Mass. Acts c. 28, §§ 1–7; 2005 Mass. Acts c. 122, § 3, effective Oct. 28, 2005; 2005 Mass. Acts c. 122, §§ 6–8, effective Jan. 1, 2006; 2006 Mass. Acts c. 428, § 13, effective Jan. 3, 2007; 2008 Mass. Acts c. 182, § 45, effective July 1, 2008; 2008 Mass. Acts c. 302, §§ 14, 15, effective July 1, 2008; 2010 Mass. Acts c. 155, § 11, effective Sept. 30, 2010; 2010 Mass. Acts c. 256, § 63, effective Nov. 4, 2010; 2012 Mass. Acts c. 139, §§ 97–100, effective July 1, 2012, effective date of 2012 Mass. Acts c. 139, § 97 extended to July 1, 2013 by 2012 Mass. Acts c. 239, § 49; 2013 Mass. Acts c. 38, § 80, effective Mar. 1, 2014; 2018 Mass. Acts c. 69, §§ 32–33, effective Apr. 13, 2018.]

(1)(a)(1) Whoever, upon any way or in any place to which the public has a right of access, or upon any way or in any place to which members of the public have access as invitees or licensees, operates a motor vehicle with a percentage, by weight, of alcohol in their blood of eight one-hundredths or greater, or while under the influence of intoxicating liquor, or of marijuana, narcotic drugs, depressants or stimulant substances, all as defined in section one of chapter ninety-four C, or while under the influence from smelling or inhaling the fumes of any substance having the property of releasing toxic vapors as defined in section 18 of chapter 270 shall be punished by a fine of not less than five hundred nor more than five thousand dollars or by imprisonment for not more than two and one-half years, or both such fine and imprisonment.

There shall be an assessment of $250 against a person who is convicted of, is placed on probation for, or is granted a continuance without a finding for or otherwise pleads guilty to or admits to a finding of sufficient facts of operating a motor vehicle while under the influence of intoxicating liquor, marijuana, narcotic drugs, depressants or stimulant substances under this section; provided, however, that but $187.50 of the amount collected under this assessment shall be deposited monthly by the court with the state treasurer for who shall deposit it into the Head Injury Treatment Services Trust Fund, and the remaining amount of the assessment shall be credited to the General Fund. The assessment shall not be subject to reduction or waiver by the court for any reason.

There shall be an assessment of $50 against a person who is convicted, placed on probation or granted a continuance without a finding or who otherwise pleads guilty to or admits to a finding of sufficient facts for operating a motor vehicle while under the influence of intoxicating liquor or under the influence of marihuana, narcotic drugs, depressants or stimulant substances, all as defined by section 1 of chapter 94C, pursuant to this section or section 24D or 24E or subsection (a) or (b) of section 24G or section 24L. The assessment shall not be subject to waiver by the court for any reason. If a person against whom a fine is assessed is sentenced to a correctional facility and the assessment has not been paid, the court shall note the assessment on the mittimus. The monies collected pursuant to the fees established by this paragraph shall be transmitted monthly by the courts to the state treasurer who shall then deposit, invest and transfer the monies, from time to time, into the Victims of Drunk Driving Trust Fund established in section 66 of chapter 10. The monies shall then be administered, pursuant to said section 66 of said chapter 10, by the victim and witness assistance board for the purposes set forth in said section 66. Fees paid by an individual into the Victims of Drunk Driving Trust Fund pursuant to this section shall be in addition to, and not in lieu of, any other fee imposed by the court pursuant to this chapter or any other chapter. The administrative office of the trial court shall file a report detailing the amount of funds imposed and collected pursuant to this section to the house and senate committees on ways and means and to the victim and witness assistance board not later than August 15 of each calendar year.

If the defendant has been previously convicted or assigned to an alcohol or controlled substance education, treatment, or rehabilitation program by a court of the commonwealth or any other jurisdiction because of a like violation preceding the date of the commission of the offense for which he has been convicted, the defendant shall be punished by a fine of not less than six hundred nor more than ten thousand dollars and by imprisonment for not less than sixty days nor more than two and one-half years; provided, however, that the sentence imposed upon such person shall not be reduced to less than thirty days, nor suspended, nor shall any such person be eligible for probation, parole, or furlough or receive any deduction from his sentence for good conduct until such person has served thirty days of such sentence; provided, further, that the commissioner of correction may, on the recommendation of the warden, superintendent, or other person in charge of a correctional institution, or the administrator of a county correctional institution, grant to an offender committed under this subdivision a temporary release in the custody of an officer of such institution for the following purposes only: to attend the funeral of a relative; to visit a critically ill relative; to obtain emergency medical or psychiatric services unavailable at said institution; to engage in employment pursuant to a work release program; or for the purposes of an aftercare program designed to support the recovery of an offender who has completed an alcohol or controlled substance education, treatment or rehabilitation program operated by the department of correction; and provided, further, that the defendant may serve all or part of such thirty day sentence to the extent such resources are available in a correctional facility specifically designated by the department of correction for the incarceration and rehabilitation of drinking drivers.

If the defendant has been previously convicted or assigned to an alcohol or controlled substance education, treatment, or rehabilitation program by a court of the commonwealth, or any other jurisdiction because of a like offense two times preceding the date of the commission of the offense for which he has been convicted, the defendant shall be punished by a fine of not less than one thousand nor more than fifteen thousand dollars and by imprisonment for not less than one hundred and eighty days nor more than two and one-half years or by a fine of not less than one thousand nor more than fifteen thousand dollars and by imprisonment in the state prison for not less than two and one-half years nor more than five years; provided, however, that the sentence imposed upon such person shall not be reduced to less than one hundred and fifty days, nor suspended, nor shall any such person be eligible for probation, parole, or furlough or receive any deduction from his sentence for good conduct until he shall have served one hundred and fifty days of such sentence; provided, further, that the commissioner of correction may, on the recommendation of the warden, superintendent, or other person in charge of a correctional institution, or the administrator of a county correctional institution, grant to an offender committed under this subdivision a temporary release in the custody of an officer of such institution for the following purposes only: to attend the funeral of a relative, to visit a critically ill relative; to obtain emergency medical or psychiatric services unavailable at said institution; to engage in employment pursuant to a work release program; or for the purposes of an aftercare program designed to support the recovery of an offender who has completed an alcohol or controlled substance education, treatment or rehabilitation program operated by the department of correction; and provided, further, that the defendant may serve all or part of such one hundred and fifty days sentence to the extent such resources are available in a correctional facility specifically designated by the department of correction for the incarceration and rehabilitation of drinking drivers.

If the defendant has been previously convicted or assigned to an alcohol or controlled substance education, treatment, or rehabilitation program by a court of the commonwealth or any other jurisdiction because of a like offense three times preceding the date of the commission of the offense for which he has been convicted the defendant shall be punished by a fine of not less than one thousand five hundred nor more than twenty-five thousand dollars and by imprisonment for not less than two years nor more than two and one-half years, or by a fine of not less than one thousand five hundred nor more than twenty-five thousand dollars and by imprisonment in the state prison for not less than two and one-half years nor more than five years; provided, however, that the sentence imposed upon such person shall not be reduced to less than twelve months, nor suspended, nor shall any such person be eligible for probation, parole, or furlough or receive any deduction from his sentence for good conduct until such person has served twelve months of such sentence; provided, further, that the commissioner of correction may, on the recommendation of the warden, superintendent, or other person in charge of a correctional institution, or the administrator of a county correctional institution, grant to an offender committed under this subdivision a temporary release in the custody of an officer of such institution for the following purposes only: to attend the funeral of a relative; to visit a critically ill relative; to obtain emergency medical or psychiatric services unavailable at said institution; to engage in employment pursuant to a work release program; or for the purposes of an aftercare program designed to support the recovery of an offender who has completed an alcohol or controlled substance education, treatment or rehabilitation program operated by the department of correction; and provided, further, that the defendant may serve all or part of such twelve months sentence to the extent that resources are available in a correctional facility specifically designated by the department of correction for the incarceration and rehabilitation of drinking drivers.

If the defendant has been previously convicted or assigned to an alcohol or controlled substance education, treatment or rehabilitation program by a court of the commonwealth or any other jurisdiction because of a like offense 4 times preceding the date of the commission of the offense for which the defendant has been convicted, the defendant shall be punished by a fine of not less than $2,000 nor more than $50,000 and by imprisonment for not less than 2 and one-half years or by a fine of not less than $2,000 nor more than $50,000 and by imprisonment in the state prison for not less than 2 and one-half years nor more than 5 years; provided, however, that the sentence imposed upon such person shall not be reduced to less than 24 months, nor suspended, nor shall any such person be eligible for probation, parole, or furlough or receive any deduction from his or her sentence for good conduct until he or she shall have served 24 months of such sentence; provided, further, that the commissioner of correction may, on the recommendation of the warden, superintendent, or other person in charge of a correctional institution, or the administrator of a county correctional institution, grant to an offender committed under this subdivision a temporary release in the custody of an officer of such institution for the following purposes only: to attend the funeral of a relative; to visit a critically ill relative; to obtain emergency medical or psychiatric services unavailable at said institution; to engage in employment pursuant to a work release program; or for the purposes of an aftercare program designed to support the recovery of an offender who has completed an alcohol or controlled substance education, treatment or rehabilitation program operated by the department of correction; and provided further, that the defendant may serve all or part of such 24 months sentence, to the extent that resources are available, in a correctional facility specifically designated by the department of correction for the incarceration and rehabilitation of drinking drivers.

If the defendant has been previously convicted or assigned to an alcohol or controlled substance education, treatment or rehabilitation program by a court of the commonwealth or any other jurisdiction because of a like offense 5 times preceding the date of the commission of the offense for which the defendant has been convicted, the defendant shall be punished by a fine of not less than $2,000 nor more than $50,000 and by imprisonment for not less than 2 and one-half years or by a fine of not less than $2,000 nor more than $50,000 and by imprisonment in the state prison for not less than 2 and one-half years nor more than 5 years; provided, however, that the sentence imposed upon such person shall not be reduced to less than 24 months, nor suspended, nor shall any such person be eligible for probation, parole or furlough or receive any deduction from his or her sentence for good conduct until he or she shall have served 24 months of such sentence; provided further, that the commissioner of correction may, on the recommendation of the warden, superintendent, or other person in charge of a correctional institution, or the administrator of a county correctional institution, grant to an offender committed under this subdivision a temporary release in the custody of an officer of such institution for the following purposes only: to attend the funeral of a relative; to visit a critically ill relative; to obtain emergency medical or psychiatric services unavailable at said institution; to engage in employment pursuant to a work release program; or for the purposes of an aftercare program designed to support the recovery of an offender who has completed an alcohol or controlled substance education, treatment or rehabilitation program operated by the department of correction; and provided further, that the defendant may serve all or part of such 24 months sentence, to the extent that resources are available, in a correctional facility specifically designated by the department of correction for the incarceration and rehabilitation of drinking drivers.

If the defendant has been previously convicted or assigned to an alcohol or controlled substance education, treatment or rehabilitation program by a court of the commonwealth or any other jurisdiction because of a like offense 6 times preceding the date of the commission of the offense for which defendant has been convicted, the defendant shall be punished by a fine of not less than $2,000 nor more than $50,000 and by imprisonment in the state prison for not less than 3 and one-half years nor more than 8 years; provided, however, that the sentence imposed upon such person shall not be reduced to less than 36 months, nor suspended, nor shall any such person be eligible for probation, parole or furlough or receive any deduction from his or her sentence for good conduct until he or she shall have served 36 months of such sentence; provided further, that the commissioner of correction may, on the recommendation of the warden, superintendent, or other person in charge of a correctional institution, or the administrator of a county correctional institution, grant to an offender committed under this subdivision a temporary release in the custody of an officer of such institution for the following purposes only: to attend the funeral of a relative; to visit a critically ill relative; to obtain emergency medical or psychiatric services unavailable at said institution; to engage in employment pursuant to a work release program; or for the purposes of an aftercare program designed to support the recovery of an offender who has completed an alcohol or controlled substance education, treatment or rehabilitation program operated by the department of correction; and provided further, that the defendant

1

may serve all or part of such 36 months sentence, to the extent that resources are available, in a correctional facility specifically designated by the department of correction for the incarceration and rehabilitation of drinking drivers.

If the defendant has been previously convicted or assigned to an alcohol or controlled substance education, treatment or rehabilitation program by a court of the commonwealth or any other jurisdiction because of a like offense 7 times preceding the date of the commission of the offense for which the defendant has been convicted, the defendant shall be punished by a fine of not less than $2,000 nor more than $50,000 and by imprisonment in the state prison for not less than 3 and one-half years nor more than 8 years; provided, however, that the sentence imposed upon such person shall not be reduced to less than 36 months, nor suspended, nor shall any such person be eligible for probation, parole or furlough or receive any deduction from his or her sentence for good conduct until he or she shall have served 36 months of such sentence; provided further, that the commissioner of correction may, on the recommendation of the warden, superintendent or other person in charge of a correctional institution, or the administrator of a county correctional institution, grant to an offender committed under this subdivision a temporary release in the custody of an officer of such institution for the following purposes only: to attend the funeral of a relative; to visit a critically ill relative; to obtain emergency medical or psychiatric services unavailable at said institution; to engage in employment pursuant to a work release program; or for the purposes of an aftercare program designed to support the recovery of an offender who has completed an alcohol or controlled substance education, treatment or rehabilitation program operated by the department of correction; and provided further, that the defendant may serve all or part of such 36 months sentence, to the extent that resources are available, in a correctional facility specifically designated by the department of correction for the incarceration and rehabilitation of drinking drivers.

If the defendant has been previously convicted or assigned to an alcohol or controlled substance education, treatment or rehabilitation program by a court of the commonwealth or any other jurisdiction because of a like offense 8 or more times preceding the date of the commission of the offense for which the defendant has been convicted, the defendant shall be punished by a fine of not less than $2,000 nor more than $50,000 and by imprisonment in the state prison for not less than 4 and one-half years nor more than 10 years; provided, however, that the sentence imposed upon such person shall not be reduced to less than 48 months, nor suspended, nor shall any such person be eligible for probation, parole or furlough or receive any deduction from his or her sentence for good conduct until he or she shall have served 48 months of such sentence; provided further, that the commissioner of correction may, on the recommendation of the warden, superintendent, or other person in charge of a correctional institution, or the administrator of a county correctional institution, grant to an offender committed under this subdivision a temporary release in the custody of an officer of such institution for the following purposes only: to attend the funeral of a relative; to visit a critically ill relative; to obtain emergency medical or psychiatric services unavailable at said institution; to engage in employment pursuant to a work release program; or for the purposes of an aftercare program designed to support the recovery of an offender who has completed an alcohol or controlled substance education, treatment or rehabilitation program operated by the department of correction; and provided further, that the defendant may serve all or part of such 48 months sentence, to the extent that resources are available, in a correctional facility specifically designated by the department of correction for the incarceration and rehabilitation of drinking drivers.

A prosecution commenced under the provisions of this subparagraph shall not be placed on file or continued without a finding except for dispositions under section twenty-four D. No trial shall be commenced on a complaint alleging a violation of this subparagraph, nor shall any plea be accepted on such complaint, nor shall the prosecution on such complaint be transferred to another division of the district court or to a jury-of-six session, until the court receives a report from the commissioner of probation pertaining to the defendant's record, if any, of prior convictions of such violations or of assignment to an alcohol or controlled substance education, treatment, or rehabilitation program because of a like offense; provided, however, that the provisions of this paragraph shall not justify the postponement of any such trial or of the acceptance of any such plea for more than five working days after the date of the defendant's arraignment. The commissioner of probation shall give priority to requests for such records.

At any time before the commencement of a trial or acceptance of a plea on a complaint alleging a violation of this subparagraph, the prosecutor may apply for the issuance of a new complaint pursuant to section thirty-five A of chapter two hundred and eighteen alleging a violation of this subparagraph and one or more prior like violations. If such application is made, upon motion of the prosecutor, the court shall stay further proceedings on the original complaint pending the determination of the application for the new complaint. If a new complaint is issued, the court shall dismiss the original complaint and order that further proceedings on the new complaint be postponed until the defendant has had sufficient time to prepare a defense.

If a defendant waives right to a jury trial pursuant to section twenty-six A of chapter two hundred and eighteen on a complaint under this subdivision he shall be deemed to have waived his right to a jury trial on all elements of said complaint.

(2) Except as provided in subparagraph (4) the provisions of section eighty-seven of chapter two hundred and seventy-six shall not apply to any person charged with a violation of subparagraph (1) and if said person has been convicted of or assigned to an alcohol or controlled substance education, treatment or rehabilitation program because of a like offense by a court of the commonwealth or any other jurisdiction preceding the commission of the offense with which he is charged.

(3) Notwithstanding the provisions of section six A of chapter two hundred and seventy-nine, the court may order that a defendant convicted of a violation of subparagraph (1) be imprisoned only on designated weekends, evenings or holidays; provided, however, that the provisions of this subparagraph shall apply only to a defendant who has not been convicted previously of such violation or assigned to an alcohol or controlled substance education, treatment or rehabilitation program preceding the date of the commission of the offense for which he has been convicted.(4) Notwithstanding the provisions of subparagraphs (1) and (2), a judge, before imposing a sentence on a defendant who pleads guilty to or is found guilty of a violation of subparagraph (1) and who has not been convicted or assigned to an alcohol or controlled substance education, treatment or rehabilitation program by a court of the commonwealth or any other jurisdiction because of a like offense two or more times of the date of the commission of the offense for which he has been convicted, shall receive a report from the probation department of a copy of the defendant's driving record, the criminal record of the defendant, if any, and such information as may be available as to the defendant's use of alcohol and may, upon a written finding that appropriate and adequate treatment is available to the defendant and the defendant would benefit from such treatment and that the safety of the public would not be endangered, with the defendant's consent place a defendant on probation for two years; provided, however, that a condition for such probation shall be that the defendant be confined for no less than fourteen days in a residential alcohol treatment program and to participate in an out patient counseling program designed for

such offenders as provided or sanctioned by the division of alcoholism, pursuant to regulations to be promulgated by said division in consultation with the department of correction and with the approval of the secretary of health and human services or at any other facility so sanctioned or regulated as may be established by the commonwealth or any political subdivision thereof for the purpose of alcohol or drug treatment or rehabilitation, and comply with all conditions of said residential alcohol treatment program. Such condition of probation shall specify a date before which such residential alcohol treatment program shall be attended and completed.

Failure of the defendant to comply with said conditions and any other terms of probation as imposed under this section shall be reported forthwith to the court and proceedings under the provisions of section three of chapter two hundred and seventy-nine shall be commenced. In such proceedings, such defendant shall be taken before the court and if the court finds that he has failed to attend or complete the residential alcohol treatment program before the date specified in the conditions of probation, the court shall forthwith specify a second date before which such defendant shall attend or complete such program, and unless such defendant shows extraordinary and compelling reasons for such failure, shall forthwith sentence him to imprisonment for not less than two days; provided, however, that such sentence shall not be reduced to less than two days, nor suspended, nor shall such person be eligible for furlough or receive any reduction from his sentence for good conduct until such person has served two days of such sentence; and provided, further, that the commissioner of correction may, on the recommendation of the warden, superintendent, or other person in charge of a correctional institution, or of the administrator of a county correctional institution, grant to an offender committed under this subdivision a temporary release in the custody of an officer of such institution for the following purposes only: to attend the funeral of a relative; to visit a critically ill relative; to obtain emergency medical or psychiatric services unavailable at said institution; or to engage in employment pursuant to a work release program. If such defendant fails to attend or complete the residential alcohol treatment program before the second date specified by the court, further proceedings pursuant to said section three of said chapter two hundred and seventy-nine shall be commenced, and the court shall forthwith sentence the defendant to imprisonment for not less than thirty days as provided in subparagraph (1) for such a defendant.

The defendant shall pay for the cost of the services provided by the residential alcohol treatment program; provided, however, that no person shall be excluded from said programs for inability to pay; and provided, further, that such person files with the court, an affidavit of indigency or inability to pay and that investigation by the probation officer confirms such indigency or establishes that payment of such fee would cause a grave and serious hardship to such individual or to the family of such individual, and that the court enters a written finding thereof. In lieu of waiver of the entire amount of said fee, the court may direct such individual to make partial or installment payments of the cost of said program.

(b) A conviction of a violation of subparagraph (1) of paragraph (a) shall revoke the license or right to operate of the person so convicted unless such person has not been convicted of or assigned to an alcohol or controlled substance education, treatment or rehabilitation program because of a like offense by a court of the commonwealth or any other jurisdiction preceding the date of the commission of the offense for which he has been convicted, and said person qualifies for disposition under section twenty-four D and has consented to probation as provided for in said section twenty-four D; provided, however, that no appeal, motion for new trial or exceptions shall operate to stay the revocation of the license or the right to operate. Such revoked license shall immediately be surrendered to the prosecuting officer who shall forward the same to the registrar. The court shall report immediately any revocation, under this section, of a license or right to operate to the registrar and to the police department of the municipality in which the defendant is domiciled. Notwithstanding the provisions of section twenty-two, the revocation, reinstatement or issuance of a license or right to operate by reason of a violation of paragraph (a) shall be controlled by the provisions of this section and sections twenty-four D and twenty-four E.

(c) (1) Where the license or right to operate has been revoked under section twenty-four D or twenty-four E, or revoked under paragraph (b) and such person has not been convicted of a like offense or has not been assigned to an alcohol or controlled substance education, treatment or rehabilitation program because of a like offense by a court of the commonwealth or any other jurisdiction preceding the date of the commission of the offense for which he has been convicted, the registrar shall not restore the license or reinstate the right to operate to such person unless the prosecution of such person has been terminated in favor of the defendant, until one year after the date of conviction; provided, however, that such person may, after the expiration of three months from the date of conviction, apply for and shall be granted a hearing before the registrar for the purpose of requesting the issuance of a new license for employment or educational purposes, which license shall be effective for not more than an identical twelve hour period every day on the grounds of hardship and a showing by the person that the causes of the present and past violations have been dealt with or brought under control, and the registrar may, in his discretion, issue such license under such terms and conditions as he deems appropriate and necessary; and provided, further, that such person may, after the expiration of six months from the date of conviction, apply for and shall be granted a hearing before the registrar for the purpose of requesting the issuance of a new license on a limited basis on the grounds of hardship and a showing by the person that the causes of the present and past violations have been dealt with or brought under control and the registrar may, in his discretion, issue such a license under such terms and conditions as he deems appropriate and necessary.

(2) Where the license or the right to operate of a person has been revoked under paragraph (b) and such person has been previously convicted of or assigned to an alcohol or controlled substance education, treatment or rehabilitation program by a court of the commonwealth or any other jurisdiction because of a like violation preceding the date of the commission of the offense for which such person has been convicted, the registrar shall not restore the license or reinstate the right to operate of such person unless the prosecution of such person has been terminated in favor of the defendant, until two years after the date of the conviction; provided, however, that such person may, after the expiration of 1 year from the date of conviction, apply for and shall be granted a hearing before the registrar for the purpose of requesting the issuance of a new license for employment or education purposes, which license shall be effective for not more than an identical twelve hour period every day on the grounds of hardship and a showing by the person that the causes of the present and past violations have been dealt with or brought under control and that such person shall have successfully completed the residential treatment program in subparagraph (4) of paragraph (a) of subdivision (1), or such treatment program mandated by section twenty-four D, and the registrar may, in his discretion, issue such license under such terms and conditions as he deems appropriate and necessary; and provided, further, that such person may, after the expiration of 18 months from the date of conviction, apply for and shall be granted a hearing before the registrar for the purpose of requesting the issuance of a new license on a limited basis on the grounds of hardship and a showing by the person that the causes of the present and past violations have been dealt with or brought under control

and the registrar may, in his discretion, issue such a license under such terms and conditions as he deems appropriate and necessary. A mandatory restriction on a hardship license granted by the registrar under this subparagraph shall be that such person have an ignition interlock device installed on each vehicle owned, each vehicle leased and each vehicle operated by the licensee for the duration of the hardship license.

(3) Where the license or right to operate of any person has been revoked under paragraph (b) and such person has been previously convicted or assigned to an alcohol or controlled substance education, treatment or rehabilitation program because of a like offense by a court of the commonwealth or any other jurisdiction two times preceding the date of the commission of the crime for which he has been convicted or where the license or right to operate has been revoked pursuant to section twenty-three due to a violation of said section due to a prior revocation under paragraph (b) or under section twenty-four D or twenty-four E, the registrar shall not restore the license or reinstate the right to operate to such person, unless the prosecution of such person has terminated in favor of the defendant, until eight years after the date of conviction; provided however, that such person may, after the expiration of two years from the date of the conviction, apply for and shall be granted a hearing before the registrar for the purpose of requesting the issuance of a new license for employment or education purposes, which license shall be effective for not more than an identical twelve hour period every day, on the grounds of hardship and a showing by the person that the causes of the present and past violations have been dealt with or brought under control and the registrar may, in his discretion, issue such license under such terms and conditions as he deems appropriate and necessary; and provided, further, that such person may, after the expiration of four years from the date of conviction, apply for and shall be granted a hearing before the registrar for the purpose of requesting the issuance of a new license on a limited basis on the grounds of hardship and a showing by the person that the causes of the present and past violations have been dealt with or brought under control and the registrar may, in his discretion, issue such a license under such terms and conditions as he deems appropriate and necessary. A mandatory restriction on a hardship license granted by the registrar under this subparagraph shall be that such person have an ignition interlock device installed on each vehicle owned, each vehicle leased and each vehicle operated by the licensee for the duration of the hardship license.

(3½) Where the license or the right to operate of a person has been revoked under paragraph (b) and such person has been previously convicted of or assigned to an alcohol or controlled substance education, treatment or rehabilitation program by a court of the commonwealth or any other jurisdiction because of a like violation three times preceding the date of the commission of the offense for which such person has been convicted, the registrar shall not restore the license or reinstate the right to operate of such person unless the prosecution of such person has been terminated in favor of the defendant, until ten years after the date of the conviction; provided, however, that such person may, after the expiration of five years from the date of the conviction, apply for and shall be granted a hearing before the registrar for the purpose of requesting the issuance of a new license for employment or education purposes which license shall be effective for an identical twelve hour period every day on the grounds of hardship and a showing by the person that the causes of the present and past violations have been dealt with or brought under control and the registrar may, in his discretion, issue such license under such terms and conditions as he deems appropriate and necessary; and provided, further, that such person may, after the expiration of eight years from the date of conviction, apply for and shall be granted a hearing before the registrar for the purpose of requesting the issuance of a new license on a limited basis on the grounds of hardship and a showing by the person that the causes of the present and past violations have been dealt with or brought under control and the registrar may, in his discretion, issue such a license under the terms and conditions as he deems appropriate and necessary. A mandatory restriction on a hardship license granted by the registrar under this subparagraph shall be that such person have an ignition interlock device installed on each vehicle owned, each vehicle leased and each vehicle operated by the licensee for the duration of the hardship license.

(3¾) Where the license or the right to operate of a person has been revoked under paragraph (b) and such person has been previously convicted of or assigned to an alcohol or controlled substance education, treatment or rehabilitation program by a court of the commonwealth or any other jurisdiction because of a like violation four or more times preceding the date of the commission of the offense for which such person has been convicted, such person's license or right to operate a motor vehicle shall be revoked for the life of such person, and such person shall not be granted a hearing before the registrar for the purpose of requesting the issuance of a new license on a limited basis on the grounds of hardship; provided, however, that such license shall be restored or such right to operate shall be reinstated if the prosecution of such person has been terminated in favor of such person. An aggrieved party may appeal, in accordance with the provisions of chapter thirty A, from any order of the registrar of motor vehicles under the provisions of this section.

(4) In any prosecution commenced pursuant to this section, introduction into evidence of a prior conviction or a prior finding of sufficient facts by either certified attested copies of original court papers, or certified attested copies of the defendant's biographical and informational data from records of the department of probation, any jail or house of corrections, the department of correction, or the registry, shall be prima facie evidence that the defendant before the court had been convicted previously or assigned to an alcohol or controlled substance education, treatment, or rehabilitation program by a court of the commonwealth or any other jurisdiction. Such documentation shall be self-authenticating and admissible, after the commonwealth has established the defendant's guilt on the primary offense, as evidence in any court of the commonwealth to prove the defendant's commission of any prior convictions described therein. The commonwealth shall not be required to introduce any additional corrob[or]ating evidence, nor live witness testimony to establish the validity of such prior convictions.

(d) For the purposes of subdivision (1) of this section, a person shall be deemed to have been convicted if he pleaded guilty or admits to a finding of sufficient facts or was found or adjudged guilty by a court of competent jurisdiction, whether or not he was placed on probation without sentence or under a suspended sentence or the case was placed on file, and a license may be revoked under paragraph (b) hereof notwithstanding the pendency of a prosecution upon appeal or otherwise after such a conviction. Where there has been more than one conviction in the same prosecution, the date of the first conviction shall be deemed to be the date of conviction under paragraph (c) hereof.

(e) In any prosecution for a violation of paragraph (a), evidence of the percentage, by weight, of alcohol in the defendant's blood at the time of the alleged offense, as shown by chemical test or analysis of his blood or as indicated by a chemical test or analysis of his breath, shall be admissible and deemed relevant to the determination of the question of whether such defendant was at such time under the influence of intoxicating liquor; provided, however, that if such test or analysis was made by or at the direction of a police officer, it was made with the consent of the defendant, the results thereof were made available to him upon his request and the defendant was afforded a reasonable opportunity, at his request and at his expense, to have another such test or analysis made by a person or physician selected by him; and provided, further, that blood shall not be withdrawn from any party for the purpose of such test or analysis except by a physician, registered nurse or certified medical technician. Evidence that the defendant failed or refused to consent to such test or analysis shall not be admissible against him in a civil or criminal proceeding, but shall be admissible in any action by the registrar under paragraph (f) or in any proceedings provided for in section twenty-four N. If such evidence is that such percentage was five one-hundredths or less, there shall be a permissible inference that such defendant was not under the influence of intoxicating liquor, and he shall be released from custody forthwith, but the officer who placed him under arrest shall not be liable for false arrest if such police officer had reasonable grounds to believe that the person arrested had been operating a motor vehicle upon any such way or place while under the influence of intoxicating liquor; provided, however, that in an instance where a defendant is under the age of twenty-one and such evidence is that the percentage, by weight, of alcohol in the defendant's blood is two one-hundredths or greater, the officer who placed him under arrest shall, in accordance with subparagraph (2) of paragraph (f), suspend such defendant's license or permit and take all other actions directed therein, if such evidence is that such percentage was more than five one-hundredths but less than eight one-hundredths there shall be no permissible inference. A certificate, signed and sworn to, by a chemist of the department of the state police or by a chemist of a laboratory certified by the department of public health, which contains the results of an analysis made by such chemist of the percentage of alcohol in such blood shall be prima facie evidence of the percentage of alcohol in such blood.

(f) (1) Whoever operates a motor vehicle upon any way or in any place to which the public has right to access, or upon any way or in any place to which the public has access as invitees or licensees, shall be deemed to have consented to submit to a chemical test or analysis of his breath or blood in the event that he is arrested for operating a motor vehicle while under the influence of intoxicating liquor; provided, however, that no such person shall be deemed to have consented to a blood test unless such person has been brought for treatment to a medical facility licensed under the provisions of section 51 of chapter 111, and provided, further, that no person who is afflicted with hemophilia, diabetes or any other condition requiring the use of anticoagulants shall be deemed to have consented to a withdrawal of blood. Such test shall be administered at the direction of a police officer, as defined in section 1 of chapter 90C, having reasonable grounds to believe that the person arrested has been operating a motor vehicle upon such way or place while under the influence of intoxicating liquor. If the person arrested refuses to submit to such test or analysis, after having been informed that his license or permit to operate motor vehicles or right to operate motor vehicles in the commonwealth shall be suspended for a period of at least 180 days and up to a lifetime loss, for such refusal, no such test or analysis shall be made and he shall have his license or right to operate suspended in accordance with this paragraph for a period of 180 days; provided, however, that any person who is under the age of 21 years or who has been previously convicted of a violation under this section, subsection (a) of section 24G, operating a motor vehicle with a percentage by weight of blood alcohol of eight one-hundredths or greater, or while under the influence of intoxicating liquor in violation of subsection (b) of said section 24G, section 24L or subsection (a) of section 8 of chapter 90B, section 8A or 8B of said chapter 90B, or section 13½ of chapter 265 or a like violation by a court of any other jurisdiction or assigned to an alcohol or controlled substance education, treatment or rehabilitation program by a court of the commonwealth or any other jurisdiction for a like offense shall have his license or right to operate suspended forthwith for a period of 3 years for such refusal; provided, further, that any person previously convicted of, or assigned to a program for, 2 such violations shall have the person's license or right to operate suspended forthwith for a period of 5 years for such refusal; and provided, further, that a person previously convicted of, or assigned to a program for, 3 or more such violations shall have the person's license or right to operate suspended forthwith for life based upon such refusal. If a person refuses to submit to any such test or analysis after having been convicted of a violation of section 24L, the re[g]istrar shall suspend his license or right to operate for 10 years. If a person refuses to submit to any such test or analysis after having been convicted of a violation of subsection (a) of section 24G, operating a motor vehicle with a percentage by weight of blood alcohol of eight one-hundredths or greater, or while under the influence of intoxicating liquor in violation of subsection (b) of said section 24G, or section 13½ of chapter 265, the registrar shall revoke his license or right to operate for life. If a person refuses to take a test under this paragraph, the police officer shall:

(i) immediately, on behalf of the registrar, take custody of such person's license or right to operate issued by the commonwealth;

(ii) provide to each person who refuses such test, on behalf of the registrar, a written notification of suspension in a format approved by the registrar; and

(iii) impound the vehicle being driven by the operator and arrange for the vehicle to be impounded for a period of 12 hours after the operator's refusal, with the costs for the towing, storage and maintenance of the vehicle to be borne by the operator.

The police officer before whom such refusal was made shall, within 24 hours, prepare a report of such refusal. Each report shall be made in a format approved by the registrar and shall be made under the penalties of perjury by the police officer before whom such refusal was made. Each report shall set forth the grounds for the officer's belief that the person arrested had been operating a motor vehicle on a way or place while under the influence of intoxicating liquor, and shall state that such person had refused to submit to a chemical test or analysis when requested by the officer to do so, such refusal having been witnessed by another person other than the defendant. Each report shall identify the police officer who requested the chemical test or analysis and the other person witnessing the refusal. Each report shall be sent forthwith to the registrar along with a copy of the notice of intent to suspend in a form, including electronic or otherwise, that the registrar deems appropriate. A license or right to operate which has been confiscated pursuant to this subparagraph shall be forwarded to the registrar forthwith. The report shall constitute prima facie evidence of the facts set forth therein at any administrative hearing regarding the suspension specified in this section.

The suspension of a license or right to operate shall become effective immediately upon receipt of the notification of suspension from the police officer. A suspension for a refusal of either a chemical test or analysis of breath or blood shall run consecutively and not concurrently, both as to any additional suspension periods arising from the same incident, and as to each other.

No license or right to operate shall be restored under any circumstances and no restricted or hardship permits shall be issued during the suspension period imposed by this paragraph; provided, however, that the defendant may immediately, upon the entry of a not guilty finding or dismissal of all charges under this section, section 24G, section 24L, or section 13½ of chapter 265, and in the absence of any other alcohol related charges pending against said defendant, apply for and be immediately granted a hearing before the court which took final action on the charges for the purpose of requesting the restoration of said license. At said hearing, there shall be a rebuttable presumption that said license be restored, unless the commonwealth shall establish, by a fair preponderance of the evidence, that restoration of said license would likely endanger the public safety. In all such instances, the court shall issue written findings of fact with its decision.

(2) If a person's blood alcohol percentage is not less than eight one-hundredths or the person is under twenty-one years of age and his blood alcohol percentage is not less than two one-hundredths, such police officer shall do the following:

(i) immediately and on behalf of the registrar take custody of such person's drivers license or permit issued by the commonwealth;

(ii) provide to each person who refuses the test, on behalf of the registrar, a written notification of suspension, in a format approved by the registrar; and

(iii) immediately report action taken under this paragraph to the registrar. Each report shall be made in a format approved by the registrar and shall be made under the penalties of perjury by the police officer. Each report shall set forth the grounds for the officer's belief that the person arrested has been operating a motor vehicle on any way or place while under the influence of intoxicating liquor and that the person's blood alcohol percentage was not less than .08 or that the person was under 21 years of age at the time of the arrest and whose blood alcohol percentage was not less than .02. The report shall indicate that the person was administered a test or analysis, that the operator administering the test or analysis was trained and certified in the administration of the test or analysis, that the test was performed in accordance with the regulations and standards promulgated by the secretary of public safety, that the equipment used for the test was regularly serviced and maintained and that the person administering the test had every reason to believe the equipment was functioning properly at the time the test was administered. Each report shall be sent forthwith to the registrar along with a copy of the notice of intent to suspend, in a form, including electronic or otherwise, that the registrar deems appropriate. A license or right to operate confiscated under this clause shall be forwarded to the registrar forthwith.

The license suspension shall become effective immediately upon receipt by the offender of the notice of intent to suspend from a police officer. The license to operate a motor vehicle shall remain suspended until the disposition of the offense for which the person is being prosecuted, but in no event shall such suspension pursuant to this subparagraph exceed 30 days.

In any instance where a defendant is under the age of twenty-one years and such evidence is that the percentage, by weight, of alcohol in the defendant's blood is two one-hundredths or greater and upon the failure of any police officer pursuant to this subparagraph, to suspend or take custody of the driver's license or permit issued by the commonwealth, and, in the absence of a complaint alleging a violation of paragraph (a) of subdivision (1) or a violation of section twenty-four G or twenty-four L, the registrar shall administratively suspend the defendant's license or right to operate a motor vehicle upon receipt of a report from the police officer who administered such chemical test or analysis of the defendant's blood pursuant to subparagraph (1). Each such report shall be made on a form approved by the registrar and shall be sworn to under the penalties of perjury by such police officer. Each such report shall set forth the grounds for the officer's belief that the person arrested had been operating a motor vehicle on a way or place while under the influence of intoxicating liquor and that such person was under twenty-one years of age at the time of the arrest and whose blood alcohol percentage was two one-hundredths or greater. Such report shall also state that the person was administered such a test or analysis, that the operator administering the test or analysis was trained and certified in the administration of such test, that the test was performed in accordance with the regulations and standards promulgated by the secretary of public safety, that the equipment used for such test was regularly serviced and maintained, and that the person administering the test had every reason to believe that the equipment was functioning properly at the time the test was administered. Each such report shall be endorsed by the police chief as defined in section one of chapter ninety C, or by the person authorized by him, and shall be sent to the registrar along with the confiscated license or permit not later than ten days from the date that such chemical test or analysis of the defendant's blood was administered. The license to operate a motor vehicle shall thereupon be suspended in accordance with section twenty-four P.

(g) Any person whose license, permit or right to operate has been suspended under subparagraph (1) of paragraph (f) shall, within fifteen days of suspension, be entitled to a hearing before the registrar which shall be limited to the following issues: (i) did the police officer have reasonable grounds to believe that such person had been operating a motor vehicle while under the influence of intoxicating liquor upon any way or in any place to which members of the public have a right of access or upon any way to which members of the public have a right of access as invitees or licensees, (ii) was such person placed under arrest, and (iii) did such person refuse to submit to such test or analysis. If, after such hearing, the registrar finds on any one of the said issues in the negative, the registrar shall forthwith reinstate such license, permit or right to operate. The registrar shall create and preserve a record at said hearing for judicial review. Within thirty days of the issuance of the final determination by the registrar following a hearing under this paragraph, a person aggrieved by the determination shall have the right to file a petition in the district court for the judicial district in which the offense occurred for judicial review. The filing of a petition for judicial review shall not stay the revocation or suspension. The filing of a petition for judicial review shall be had as soon as possible following the submission of said request, but not later than thirty days following the submission thereof. Review by the court shall be on the record established at the hearing before the registrar. If the court finds that the department exceeded its constitutional or statutory authority, made an erroneous interpretation of the law, acted in an arbitrary and capricious manner, or made a determination which is unsupported by the evidence in the record, the court may reverse the registrar's determination.

Any person whose license or right to operate has been suspended pursuant to subparagraph (2) of paragraph (f) on the basis of chemical analysis of his breath may within ten days of such suspension request a hearing and upon such request shall be entitled to a hearing before the court in which the underlying charges are pending or if the individual is under the age of twenty-one and there are no pending charges, in the district court having jurisdiction where the arrest occurred, which hearing shall be limited to the following issue; whether a blood test administered pursuant to paragraph (e) within a reasonable period of time after such chemical analysis of his breath, shows that the percentage, by weight, of alcohol in such person's blood was less than eight one-hundredths or, relative to such person under the age of twenty-one was less than two one-hundredths. If the court finds that such a blood test shows that such percentage was less than eight one-hundredths or, relative to such person under the age of twenty-one, that such percentage was less than two one-hundredths, the court shall restore such person's license, permit or right to operate and shall direct the prosecuting officer to forthwith notify the department of criminal justice information services and the registrar of such restoration.

(h) Any person convicted of a violation of subparagraph (1) of paragraph (a) that involves operating a motor vehicle while under the influence of marihuana, narcotic drugs, depressants or stimulant substances, all as defined in section one of chapter ninety-four C, or while under the influence from smelling or inhaling the fumes of any substance having the property of releasing toxic vapors as defined in section 18 of chapter 270, may, as part of the disposition in the case, be ordered to participate in a driver education program or a drug treatment or drug rehabilitation program, or any combination of said programs. The court shall set such financial and other terms for the participation of the defendant as it deems appropriate.

(2)(a) Whoever upon any way or in any place to which the public has a right of access, or any place to which members of the public have access as invitees or licensees, operates a motor vehicle recklessly, or operates such a vehicle negligently so that the lives or safety of the public might be endangered, or upon a bet or wager or in a race, or whoever operates a motor vehicle for the purpose of making a record and thereby violates any provision of section seventeen or any regulation under section eighteen, or whoever without stopping and making known his name, residence and the register number of his motor vehicle goes away after knowingly colliding with or otherwise causing injury to any other vehicle or property, or whoever loans or knowingly permits his license or learner's permit to operate motor vehicles to be used by any person, or whoever makes false statements in an application for such a license or learner's permit, or whoever knowingly makes any false statement in an application for registration of a motor vehicle or whoever while operating a motor vehicle in violation of section 8M, 12A or 13B, such violation proved beyond a reasonable doubt, is the proximate cause of injury to any other person, vehicle or property by operating said motor vehicle negligently so that the lives or safety of the public might be endangered, shall be punished by a fine of not less than twenty dollars nor more than two hundred dollars or by imprisonment for not less than two weeks nor more than two years, or both; and whoever uses a motor vehicle without authority knowing that such use is unauthorized shall, for the first offense be punished by a fine of not less than fifty dollars nor more than five hundred dollars or by imprisonment for not less than thirty days nor more than two years, or both, and for a second offense by imprisonment in the state prison for not more than five years or in a house of correction for not less than thirty days nor more than two and one half years, or by a fine of not more than one thousand dollars, or by both such fine and imprisonment; and whoever is found guilty of a third or subsequent offense of such use without authority committed within five years of the earliest of his two most recent prior offenses shall be punished by a fine of not less than two hundred dollars nor more than one thousand dollars or by imprisonment for not less than six months nor more than two and one half years in a house of correction or for not less than two and one half years nor more than five years in the state prison or by both fine and imprisonment. A summons may be issued instead of a warrant for arrest upon a complaint for a violation of any provision of this paragraph if in the judgment of the court or justice receiving the complaint there is reason to believe that the defendant will appear upon a summons.

There shall be an assessment of $250 against a person who, by a court of the commonwealth, is convicted of, is placed on probation for or is granted a continuance without a finding for or otherwise pleads guilty to or admits to a finding of sufficient facts of operating a motor vehicle negligently so that the lives or safety of the public might be endangered under this section, but $250 of the $250 collected under this assessment shall be deposited monthly by the court with the state treasurer, who shall deposit it in the Head Injury Treatment Services Trust Fund, and the remaining amount of the assessment shall be credited to the General Fund. The assessment shall not be subject to reduction or waiver by the court for any reason.

(a½)(1) Whoever operates a motor vehicle upon any way or in any place to which the public has right of access, or upon any way or in any place to which members of the public shall have access as invitees or licensees, and without stopping and making known his name, residence and the registration number of his motor vehicle, goes away after knowingly colliding with or otherwise causing injury to any person not resulting in the death of any person, shall be punished by imprisonment for not less than six months nor more than two years and by a fine of not less than five hundred dollars nor more than one thousand dollars.

(2) Whoever operates a motor vehicle upon any way or in any place to which the public has a right of access or upon any way or in any place to which members of the public shall have access as invitees or licensees and without stopping and making known his name, residence and the registration number of his motor vehicle, goes away to avoid prosecution or evade apprehension after knowingly colliding with or otherwise causing injury to any person shall, if the injuries result in the death of a person, be punished by imprisonment in the state prison for not less than two and one-half years nor more than ten years and by a fine of not less than one thousand dollars nor more than five thousand dollars or by imprisonment in a jail or house of correction for not less than one year nor more than two and one-half years and by a fine of not less than one thousand dollars nor more than five thousand dollars. The sentence imposed upon such person shall not be reduced to less than one year, nor suspended, nor shall any person convicted under this paragraph be eligible for probation, parole, or furlough or receive any deduction from his sentence until such person has served at least one year of such sentence; provided, however, that the commissioner of correction may on the recommendation of the warden, superintendent or other person in charge of a correctional institution, or the administrator of a county correctional institution, grant to an offender committed under this paragraph, a temporary release in the custody of an officer of such institution for the following purposes only: to attend the funeral of a relative; to visit a critically ill relative; to obtain emergency medical or psychiatric services unavailable at said institution or to engage in employment pursuant to a work release program.

(3) Prosecutions commenced under subparagraph (1) or (2) shall not be continued without a finding nor placed on file.

(b) A conviction of a violation of paragraph (a) or paragraph (a½) of subdivision (2) of this section shall be reported forthwith by the court or magistrate to the registrar, who may in any event, and shall unless the court or magistrate recommends otherwise, revoke immediately the license or right to operate of the person so convicted, and no appeal, motion for new trial or exceptions shall operate to stay the revocation of the license or right to operate. If it appears by the records of the registrar that the person so convicted is the owner of a motor vehicle or has exclusive control of any motor vehicle as a manufacturer or dealer or otherwise, the registrar may revoke the certificate of registration of any or all motor vehicles so owned or exclusively controlled.

(c) The registrar, after having revoked the license or right to operate of any person under paragraph (b), in his discretion may issue a new license or reinstate the right to operate to him, if the prosecution has terminated in favor of the defendant. In addition, the registrar may, after an investigation or upon hearing, issue a new license or reinstate the right to operate to a person convicted in any court for a violation of any provision of paragraph (a) or (a½) of subdivision (2); provided, however, that no new license or right to operate shall be issued by the registrar to: (i) any person convicted of a violation of subparagraph (1) of paragraph (a½) until one year after the date of revocation following his conviction if for a first offense, or until two years after the date of revocation following any subsequent conviction; (ii) any person convicted of a violation of subparagraph (2) of paragraph (a½) until three years after the date of revocation following his conviction if for a first offense or until ten years after the date of revocation following any subsequent conviction; (iii) any person convicted, under paragraph (a) of using a motor vehicle knowing that such use is unauthorized, until one year after the date of revocation following his conviction if for a first offense or until three years after the date of revocation following any subsequent conviction; and (iv) any person convicted

1

of any other provision of paragraph (a) until sixty days after the date of his original conviction if for a first offense or one year after the date of revocation following any subsequent conviction within a period of three years. Notwithstanding the forgoing, a person holding a junior operator's license who is convicted of operating a motor vehicle recklessly or negligently under paragraph (a) shall not be eligible for license reinstatement until 180 days after the date of his original conviction for a first offense or 1 year after the date of revocation following a subsequent conviction within a period of 3 years. The registrar, after investigation, may at any time rescind the revocation of a license or right to operate revoked because of a conviction of operating a motor vehicle upon any way or in any place to which the public has a right of access or any place to which members of the public have access as invitees or licensees negligently so that the lives or safety of the public might be endangered. The provisions of this paragraph shall apply in the same manner to juveniles adjudicated under the provisions of section fifty-eight B of chapter one hundred and nineteen.

(3) The prosecution of any person for the violation of any provision of this section, if a subsequent offence, shall not, unless the interests of justice require such disposition, be placed on file or otherwise disposed of except by trial, judgment and sentence according to the regular course of criminal proceedings; and such a prosecution shall be otherwise disposed of only on motion in writing stating specifically the reasons therefor and verified by affidavits if facts are relied upon. If the court or magistrate certifies in writing that he is satisfied that the reasons relied upon are sufficient and that the interests of justice require the allowance of the motion, the motion shall be allowed and the certificate shall be filed in the case. A copy of the motion and certificate shall be sent by the court or magistrate forthwith to the registrar.

(4) In any prosecution commenced pursuant to this section, introduction into evidence of a prior conviction or prior finding of sufficient facts by either original court papers or certified attested copy of original court papers, accompanied by a certified attested copy of the biographical and informational data from official probation office records, shall be prima facie evidence that a defendant has been convicted previously or assigned to an alcohol or controlled substance education, treatment, or rehabilitation program because of a like offense by a court of the commonwealth one or more times preceding the date of commission of the offense for which said defendant is being prosecuted.

§ 24½. Ignition interlock device license restriction; revocation of license for failure to install or maintain device; revocation of license for attempt to operate motor vehicle with elevated blood alcohol level

[Added by 2005 Mass. Acts c. 122, § 13, effective Jan. 1, 2006.]

No person whose license has been suspended in the commonwealth or any other jurisdiction by reason of: an assignment to an alcohol or controlled substance education, treatment or rehabilitation program; or a conviction for violating paragraph (a) of subdivision (1) of section 24, subsection (a) of section 24G, operating a motor vehicle with a percentage by weight of blood alcohol of eight one-hundredths or greater, or while under the influence of intoxicating liquor in violation of subsection (b) of said section 24G, section 24L, section 13½ of chapter 265, subsection (a) of section 8 of chapter 90B, section 8A or 8B of chapter 90B or, in the case of another jurisdiction, for any like offense, shall be issued a new license or right to operate or have his license or right to operate restored if he has previously been so assigned or convicted, unless a certified ignition interlock device has been installed on each vehicle owned, each vehicle leased and each vehicle operated by that person as a precondition to the issuance of a new license or right to operate or the restoration of such person's license or right to operate. A certified ignition interlock device shall be installed on all vehicles owned, leased and operated by the licensee for a period of 2 years and person restricted by a certified ignition interlock device shall have such device inspected, maintained and monitored in accordance with such regulations as the registrar shall promulgate. The registrar may, after hearing, revoke for an extended period or for life, the license of whoever removes such device or fails to have it inspected, maintained or monitored on at least 2 occasions during the period of the restricted license or right to operate if the licensee has operated or attempted to operate a vehicle with a blood alcohol level that caused the certified ignition interlock device to prohibit a vehicle from starting on at least 2 occasions or that recorded a blood alcohol level in excess of .02 on at least 2 occasions. A person aggrieved by a decision of the registrar pursuant to this section may file an appeal in the superior court of the trial court department. If the court determines that the registrar abused his discretion, the court may vacate the suspension or revocation of a license or right to operate or reduce the period of suspension or revocation as ordered by the registrar.

NOTE Pursuant to 2005 Mass. Acts c. 122, § 21, approved on October 28, 2005, any assignment to an alcohol or controlled substance education, treatment, or rehabilitation program or conviction rendered before the effective date of this act shall be considered a previous assignment or conviction for the purposes of this act.

Chapter 94C. Controlled Substances Act

§ 32. Class A controlled substances; unlawful manufacture, distribution, dispensing or possession with intent to manufacture, etc.

[Amended by 2010 Mass. Acts c. 256, § 67, effective May 4, 2012; 2012 Mass. Acts c. 192, § 12, effective Aug. 2, 2012.]

(a) Any person who knowingly or intentionally manufactures, distributes, dispenses, or possesses with intent to manufacture, distribute or dispense a controlled substance in Class A of section thirty-one shall be punished by imprisonment in the state prison for not more than ten years or in a jail or house of correction for not more than two and one-half years or by a fine of not less than one thousand nor more than ten thousand dollars, or by both such fine and imprisonment.

(b) Any person convicted of violating this section after one or more prior convictions of manufacturing, distributing, dispensing or possessing with the intent to manufacture, distribute, or dispense a controlled substance as defined by section thirty-one of this chapter under this or any prior law of this jurisdiction or of any offense of any other jurisdiction, federal, state, or territorial, which is the same as or necessarily includes the elements of said offense shall be punished by a term of imprisonment in the state prison for not less than 3½ nor more than fifteen years. No sentence imposed under the provisions of this section shall be for less than a mandatory minimum term of imprisonment of 3½ years and a fine of not less than two thousand and five hundred nor more than twenty-five thousand dollars may be imposed but not in lieu of the mandatory minimum 3½ year term of imprisonment, as established herein.

(c) Any person serving a mandatory minimum sentence for violating any provision of this section shall be eligible for parole after serving one-half of the maximum term of the sentence if the sentence is to the house of correction, except that such person shall not be eligible for parole upon a finding of any 1 of the following aggravating circumstances:

(i) the defendant used violence or threats of violence or possessed a firearm, rifle, shotgun, machine gun or a weapon described in paragraph (b) of section 10 of chapter 269, or induced another participant to do so, during the commission of the offense;

(ii) the defendant engaged in a course of conduct whereby he directed the activities of another who committed any felony in violation of chapter 94C; or

(iii) the offense was committed during the commission or attempted commission of a violation of section 32F or section 32K of chapter 94C.

A condition of such parole may be enhanced supervision; provided, however, that such enhanced supervision may, at the discretion of the parole board, include, but shall not be limited to, the wearing of a global positioning satellite tracking device or any comparable device, which shall be administered by the board at all times for the length of the parole.

§ 32A. Class B controlled substances; unlawful manufacture, distribution, dispensing or possession with intent to manufacture, etc.

[Amended by 2010 Mass. Acts c. 256, § 68, effective Nov. 4, 2010; 2012 Mass. Acts c. 192, §§ 13–14, effective Aug. 2, 2012; 2018 Mass. Acts c. 69, § 47, effective Apr. 13, 2018.]

(a) Any person who knowingly or intentionally manufactures, distributes, dispenses or possesses with intent to manufacture, distribute or dispense a controlled substance in Class B of section 31 shall be punished by imprisonment in the state prison for not more than 10 years, or in a jail or house of correction for not more than 2½ years, or by a fine of not less than $1,000 nor more than $10,000, or both such fine and imprisonment.

(b) Any person convicted of violating this section after 1 or more prior convictions of manufacturing, distributing, dispensing or possessing with the intent to manufacture, distribute or dispense a controlled substance as defined by section 31 under this or any other prior law of this jurisdiction or of any offense of any other jurisdiction, federal, state or territorial, which is the same as or necessarily includes the elements of said offense shall be punished by a term of imprisonment in the state prison for not more than 10 years, by a term of imprisonment in the state prison for not more than 10 years and by a fine of not less than $2,500 and not more than $25,000, or by a fine of not more than $25,000.

(c) Any person who knowingly or intentionally manufactures, distributes, dispenses or possesses with intent to manufacture, distribute or dispense phencyclidine or a controlled substance defined in clause (4) of paragraph (a) or in clause (2) of paragraph (c) of Class B of section 31 shall be punished by a term of imprisonment in the state prison for not more than 10 years, a term of imprisonment in the state prison for not more than 10 years and a fine of not less than $1,000 and not more than $10,000, by imprisonment in a jail or house of correction for not more than 2½ years, by imprisonment in a jail or house of correction for not more than 2½ years and a fine of not less than $1,000 and not more than $10,000, or by a fine of not more than $10,000.

(d) Any person convicted of violating the provisions of subsection (c) after 1 or more prior convictions of manufacturing, distributing, dispensing or possessing with the intent to manufacture, distribute, or dispense a controlled substance, as defined in section 31 or of any offense of any other jurisdiction, either federal, state or territorial, which is the same as or necessarily includes, the elements of said offense, shall be punished by a term of imprisonment in the state prison for not more than 15 years, a term of imprisonment in the state prison for not more than 15 years and a fine of not less than $2,500 nor more than $25,000 or a fine of not more than $25,000.

§ 32B. Class C controlled substances; unlawful manufacturer, distribution, dispensing or possession with intent to manufacture, etc.

[Amended by 2010 Mass. Acts c. 256, § 69, effective Nov. 4, 2010; 2012 Mass. Acts c. 192, §§ 15–16, effective Aug. 2, 2012; 2018 Mass. Acts c. 69, § 47, effective Apr. 13, 2018.]

(a) Any person who knowingly or intentionally manufactures, distributes, dispenses or possesses with intent to manufacture, distribute, or dispense a controlled substance in Class C of section 31 shall be imprisoned in state prison for not more than 5 years or in a jail or house of correction for not more than 2½ years, or by a fine of not less than $500 nor more than $5,000, or both such fine and imprisonment.

(b) Any person convicted of violating this section after 1 or more prior convictions of manufacturing, distributing, dispensing or possessing with the intent to manufacture, distribute or dispense a controlled substance as defined by section 31 under this or any prior law of this jurisdiction or of any offense of any other jurisdiction, federal, state or territorial, which is the same as or necessarily includes the elements of said offense shall be punished by a term of imprisonment in the state prison for not more than 10 years, a term of imprisonment in the state prison for not more than 10 years and a fine of not less than $1,000 nor more than $10,000, a term of imprisonment in a jail or house of correction for not more than 2½ years, a term of imprisonment in a jail or house of correction for not more than 2½ years and a fine of not less than $1,000 nor more than $10,000, or a fine of not more than $10,000.

§ 32C. Class D controlled substances; unlawful manufacture, distribution, dispensing, cultivation or possession with intent to manufacture, etc.

[Amended by 2018 Mass. Acts c. 69, § 48, effective Apr. 13, 2018.]

(a) Any person who knowingly or intentionally manufactures, distributes, dispenses or cultivates, or possesses with intent to manufacture, distribute, dispense or cultivate a controlled substance in Class D of section thirty-one shall be imprisoned in a jail or house of correction for not more than two years or by a fine of not less than five hundred nor more than five thousand dollars, or both such fine and imprisonment.

(b) Any person convicted of violating this section after one or more prior convictions of manufacturing, distributing, dispensing, cultivating or possessing with intent to manufacture, distribute, dispense or cultivate a controlled substance as defined by section thirty-one under this or any prior law of this jurisdiction or of any offense of any other jurisdiction, federal, state, or territorial, which is the same as or necessarily includes the elements of said offense shall be punished by a term of imprisonment in a jail or house of correction for not more than two and one-half years, or by a fine of not less than one thousand nor more than ten thousand dollars, or both such fine and imprisonment.

§ 32D. Class E controlled substances; unlawful manufacture, distribution, dispensing, or possession with intent to manufacture, etc.

(a) Any person who knowingly or intentionally manufactures, distributes, dispenses, or possesses with intent to manufacture, distribute, or dispense a controlled substance in Class E of section thirty-one shall be imprisoned in a jail or house of correction for not more than nine months, or by a fine of not less than two hundred and fifty nor more than two thousand and five hundred dollars, or both such fine and imprisonment.

(b) Any person convicted of violating this section after one or more prior convictions of manufacturing, distributing, dispensing or possessing with the intent to manufacture, distribute or dispense a controlled substance as defined by section thirty-one under this or any prior law of this jurisdiction or of any offense of any other jurisdiction, federal, state, or territorial which is the same as or necessarily includes the elements of said offense shall be punished by a term of imprisonment in a jail or house of correction for not more than one and one-half years, or by a fine of not less than five hundred nor more than five thousand dollars, or both such fine and imprisonment.

§ 32E. Trafficking in marihuana, cocaine, heroin, synthetic opioids, morphine, opium, etc.

[Amended by 2010 Mass. Acts c. 256, § 70, effective Nov. 4, 2010; 2012 Mass. Acts c. 139, § 102, effective July 1, 2012; 2012 Mass. Acts c. 192, §§ 17–27, effective Aug. 2, 2012; 2014 Mass. Acts c. 154, §§ 134–135, effective July 15, 2014; 2015 Mass. Acts c. 136, effective Feb. 22, 2016; 2018 Mass. Acts c. 69, §§ 49–51, effective Apr. 13, 2018.]

(a) Any person who traffics in marihuana by knowingly or intentionally manufacturing, distributing, dispensing, or cultivating or possessing with intent to manufacture, distribute, dispense, or cultivate, or by bringing into the commonwealth a net weight of fifty pounds or more of marihuana or a net weight of fifty pounds or more of any mixture containing marihuana shall, if the net weight of marihuana or any mixture thereof is:

(1) Fifty pounds or more, but less than one hundred pounds, be punished by a term of imprisonment in the state prison for not less than two and one-half nor more than fifteen years or by imprisonment in a jail or house of correction for not less than one nor more than two and one-half years. No sentence imposed under the provisions of this section shall be for less than a mandatory minimum term of imprisonment of one year and a fine of not less than five hundred nor more than ten thousand dollars may be imposed but not in lieu of the mandatory minimum one year term of imprisonment, as established herein.

(2) One hundred pounds or more, but less than two thousand pounds, be punished by a term of imprisonment in the state prison for not less than 2 nor more than fifteen years. No sentence imposed under the provisions of this section shall be for less than a mandatory minimum term of imprisonment of 2 years and a fine of not less than two thousand and five hundred nor more than twenty-five thousand dollars may be imposed but not in lieu of the mandatory minimum term of imprisonment, as established herein.

(3) Two thousand pounds or more, but less than ten thousand pounds, be punished by a term of imprisonment in the state prison for not less than 3½ nor more than fifteen years. No sentence imposed under the provisions of this section shall be for less than a mandatory minimum term of imprisonment of 3½ years and a fine of not less than five thousand nor more than fifty thousand dollars may be imposed but not in lieu of the mandatory minimum term of imprisonment, as established herein.

(4) Ten thousand pounds or more, be punished by a term of imprisonment in the state prison for not less than 8 nor more than fifteen years. No sentence imposed under the provisions of this section shall be for less than a mandatory minimum term of imprisonment of 8 years and a fine of not less than twenty thousand nor more than two hundred thousand dollars may be imposed but not in lieu of the mandatory minimum term of imprisonment, as established herein.

(b) Any person who traffics in a controlled substance defined in clause (4) of paragraph (a) or in clause (3) of paragraph (c) of Class B of section thirty-one by knowingly or intentionally manufacturing, distributing or dispensing or possessing with intent to manufacture, distribute or dispense or by bringing into the commonwealth a net weight of 18 grams or more of a controlled substance as so defined, or a net weight of 18 grams or more of any mixture containing a controlled substance as so defined shall, if the net weight of a controlled substance as so defined, or any mixture thereof is:—

(1) Eighteen grams or more but less than 36 grams, be punished by a term of imprisonment in the state prison for not less than 2 nor more than 15 years. No sentence imposed under this clause shall be for less than a minimum term of imprisonment of 2 years, and a fine of not less $2,500 nor more than $25,000 may be imposed but not in lieu of the mandatory minimum term of imprisonment, as established herein.

(2) Thirty-six grams or more, but less than 100 grams, be punished by a term of imprisonment in the state prison for not less than 3½ nor more than 20 years. No sentence imposed under this clause shall be for less than a mandatory minimum term of imprisonment of 3½ years, and a fine of not less than $5,000 nor more than $50,000 may be imposed but not in lieu of the mandatory minimum term of imprisonment, as established herein.

(3) One hundred grams or more, but less than two hundred grams, be punished by a term of imprisonment in the state prison for not less than 8 nor more than twenty years. No sentence imposed under the provisions of this clause shall be for less than a mandatory minimum term of imprisonment of 8 years and a fine of not less than ten thousand nor more than one hundred thousand dollars may be imposed but not in lieu of the mandatory minimum term of imprisonment, as established herein.

(4) Two hundred grams or more, be punished by a term of imprisonment in the state prison for not less than 12 nor more than twenty years. No sentence imposed under the provisions of this clause shall be for less than a mandatory minimum term of imprisonment of 12 years and a fine of not less than fifty thousand nor more than five hundred thousand dollars may be imposed but not in lieu of the mandatory minimum term of imprisonment, as established herein.

(c) Any person who traffics in heroin or any salt thereof, a controlled substance defined in paragraph (d) of Class A of section 31, morphine or any salt thereof, opium or any derivative thereof by knowingly or intentionally manufacturing, distributing or dispensing or possessing with intent to manufacture, distribute, or dispense or by bringing into the commonwealth a net weight of 18 grams or more of heroin or any salt thereof, a controlled substance defined in paragraph (d) of Class A of section 31, morphine or any salt thereof, opium or any derivative thereof or a net weight of fourteen grams or more of any mixture containing heroin or any salt thereof, a controlled substance defined in paragraph (d) of Class A of section 31, morphine or any salt thereof, opium or any derivative thereof shall, if the net weight of heroin or any salt thereof, a controlled substance defined in paragraph (d) of Class A of section 31, morphine or any salt thereof, opium or any derivative thereof or any mixture thereof is:

(1) Eighteen grams or more but less than 36 grams, be punished by a term of imprisonment in the state prison for not less than 3½ nor more than 30 years. No sentence imposed under this clause shall be for less than a mandatory minimum term of imprisonment of 3½ years, and a fine of not less than $5,000 nor more than $50,000 may be imposed but not in lieu of the mandatory minimum term of imprisonment, as established herein.

(2) Thirty-six grams or more but less than 100 grams, be punished by a term of imprisonment in the state prison for not less than 5 nor more than 30 years. No sentence imposed under this clause shall be for less than a mandatory minimum term of imprisonment of 5 years, and a fine of not less than $5,000 nor more than $50,000 may be imposed, but not in lieu of the mandatory minimum term of imprisonment, as established herein.

(3) One hundred grams or more but less than two hundred grams, be punished by a term of imprisonment in the state prison for not less than 8 nor more than 30 years. No sentence imposed under the provisions of this clause shall be for less than the mandatory minimum term of imprisonment of 8 years, and a fine of not less than ten thousand nor more than one hundred thousand dollars may be imposed but not in lieu of the mandatory minimum term of imprisonment, as established therein.

(4) Two hundred grams or more, be punished by a term of imprisonment in the state prison for not less than 12 nor more than 30 years. No sentence imposed under the provisions of this clause shall be for less than a mandatory minimum term of imprisonment of 12 years and a fine of not less than fifty thousand nor more than five hundred thousand dollars may be imposed but not in lieu of the mandatory minimum term of imprisonment, as established therein.

(c½) Any person who trafficks in fentanyl or any derivative of fentanyl by knowingly or intentionally manufacturing, distributing, dispensing or possessing with intent to manufacture, distribute or dispense or by bringing into the commonwealth a net weight of 10 grams or more of fentanyl or any derivative of fentanyl, or a net weight of 10 grams or more of any mixture containing fentanyl or any derivative of fentanyl, shall be punished by a term of imprisonment in state prison for not less than 3 and one half nor more than 20 years. No sentence imposed under the provisions of this subsection shall be for less than a mandatory minimum term of imprisonment of 3 and one-half years.

(c¾) Any person who trafficks in carfentanil, including without limitation, any derivative of carfentanil by knowingly or intentionally manufacturing, distributing, dispensing or possessing with intent to manufacture, distribute or dispense or by bringing into the commonwealth carfentanil or any derivative of carfentanil, any mixture containing carfentanil or a derivative of carfentanil, provided, that such person had specific knowledge that such mixture contained carfentanil or any derivative of carfentanil, shall be punished by a term of imprisonment in state prison for not less than 3 and one-half nor more than 20 years. No sentence imposed pursuant to this subsection shall be for less than a mandatory minimum term of imprisonment of 3 and one-half years.

(d) Any person serving a mandatory minimum sentence for violating this section shall be eligible for parole after serving one-half of the maximum term of the sentence if the sentence is to the house of correction, except that such person shall not be eligible for parole upon a finding of any 1 of the following aggravating circumstances:

(i) the defendant used violence or threats of violence or possessed a firearm, rifle, shotgun, machine gun or a weapon described in paragraph (b) of section 10 of chapter 269, or induced another participant to do so, during the commission of the offense;

(ii) the defendant engaged in a course of conduct whereby he directed the activities of another others [sic] who committed any felony in violation of chapter 94C; or

(iii) the offense was committed during the commission or attempted commission of a violation of section 32F or section 32K of chapter 94C.

A condition of such parole may be enhanced supervision; provided, however, that such enhanced supervision may, at the discretion of the parole board, include, but shall not be limited to, the wearing of a global positioning satellite tracking device or any comparable device, which shall be administered by the board at all times for the length of the parole.

§ 32F. Unlawful manufacture, distribution, dispensing or possession with intent to manufacture, etc. of controlled substances in classes A to C to minors

(a) Any person who knowingly or intentionally manufactures, distributes, dispenses, or possesses with intent to manufacture, distribute, or dispense a controlled substance in Class A of section thirty-one to a person under the age of eighteen years shall be punished by a term of imprisonment in the state prison for not less than five nor more than fifteen years. No sentence imposed under the provisions of this section shall be for less than a mandatory minimum term of imprisonment of five years and a fine of not less than one thousand nor more than twenty-five thousand dollars may be imposed but not in lieu of the mandatory minimum term of imprisonment, as established herein.

(b) Any person who knowingly or intentionally manufactures, distributes, dispenses, or possesses with intent to manufacture, distribute, or dispense a controlled substance in Class B of section thirty-one to a person under the age of eighteen years shall be punished by a term of imprisonment in the state prison for not less than three nor more than fifteen years. No sentence imposed under the provisions of this section shall be for less than a mandatory minimum term of imprisonment of three years and a fine of not less than one thousand nor more than twenty-five thousand dollars may be imposed but not in lieu of the mandatory minimum term of imprisonment, as established herein.

(c) Any person who knowingly or intentionally manufactures, distributes, dispenses, or possesses with intent to manufacture, distribute, or dispense a controlled substance in Class C of section thirty-one to a person under the age of eighteen years shall be punished by a term of imprisonment in the state prison for not less than two and one-half nor more than fifteen years or in a jail or house of correction for not less than two nor more than two and one-half years. No sentence imposed under the provisions of this section shall be for less than a mandatory minimum term of imprisonment of two years and a fine of not less than one thousand nor more than twenty-five thousand dollars may be imposed but not in lieu of the mandatory minimum two year term of imprisonment, as established herein.

(d) Any person who knowingly or intentionally manufactures, distributes, dispenses, or possesses with intent to manufacture, distribute or dispense a controlled substance as defined in clause (4) of paragraph (a) of class B of section thirty-one, to a person under the age of eighteen years shall be punished by a term of imprisonment in the state prison for not less than five nor more than fifteen years. No sentence imposed under the provisions of this section shall be for less than a minimum term of imprisonment of five years, and a fine of not less than one thousand nor more than twenty-five thousand dollars may be imposed but not in lieu of the mandatory minimum term of imprisonment, as established herein.

§ 32G. Counterfeit substances; unlawful creation, distribution, dispensing or possession with intent to distribute or dispense

Any person who knowingly or intentionally creates, distributes, dispenses or possesses with intent to distribute or dispense a counterfeit substance shall be punished by imprisonment in a jail or house of correction for not more than one year or by a fine of not less than two hundred and fifty nor more than two thousand and five hundred dollars, or both such fine and imprisonment.

§ 32H. Prosecutions not to be continued or placed on file; suspension or reduction of sentence; eligibility for parole, etc.

[Amended by 2010 Mass. Acts c. 256, § 71, effective Nov. 4, 2010; 2012 Mass. Acts c. 192, §§ 28–29, effective Aug. 2, 2012; 2013 Mass. Acts c. 84, § 4, effective Sept. 18, 2013; 2018 Mass. Acts c. 69, §§ 52–54, effective Apr. 13, 2018; 2018 Mass. Acts c. 72, §§ 1–2, effective Jan. 13, 2019.]

A prosecution commenced under paragraph (b) of section thirty-two, paragraphs (b), (c) and (d) of section thirty-two A, paragraph (b) of section thirty-two B, sections thirty-two E thirty-two F and thirty-two J shall not be placed on file or continued without a finding, and the sentence imposed upon a person convicted of violating paragraph (b) of section 32 or sections 32E, 32F or 32J shall not be reduced to less than the mandatory minimum term of imprisonment as established in said section, nor shall any sentence of imprisonment imposed upon any person be suspended or reduced until such person shall have served said mandatory minimum term of imprisonment.

A person convicted of violating paragraph (b) of section 32 or sections 32E, 32F or 32J shall not, until he shall have served the mandatory minimum term of imprisonment established in said sections, be eligible for probation, furlough, work release or receive any deduction from his sentence for good conduct under sections 129C and 129D of chapter 127, except as authorized pursuant to section 32H½, nor shall he be eligible for parole except as authorized pursuant to subsection (c) of Section 32 or subsection (d) of section 32E section 32H½; provided, however, that the commissioner of correction, on the recommendation of the warden, superintendent or other person in charge of the correctional institution, or a sheriff, on the recommendation of the administrator of a county correctional institution, may grant to said offender a temporary release, subject to the rules and regulations of the institution and under the direction, control and supervision of the officers thereof for the following purposes: (1) to attend the funeral of a relative, to visit a critically ill relative, to obtain emergency medical or psychiatric services unavailable at said institution; (2) to participate in education, training, or employment programs established under section 48 of chapter 127; (3) to participate in a program to provide services under section 49B or 49C of chapter 127; or (4) to engage in employment under a work release program under sections 49, 49A, 86F or 86G of chapter 127. Section 87 of chapter 276 shall not apply to any person, 18 years of age or older, charged with a violation of said sections, or to any child between age 14 and 18, so charged by indictment under section 54 of chapter 119.

§ 32H½. Good behavior deductions from sentence after serving mandatory minimum term of imprisonment; eligibility; parole; work release

[Added by 2018 Mass. Acts c. 72, § 3, effective Jan. 13, 2019; 2018 Mass. Acts c. 273, § 37, effective Jan. 13, 2019.]

(a) As used in this section, the words "ineligible offender" shall shall mean a person sentenced to a mandatory minimum term of imprisonment in the state prison upon conviction for: (i) violating section 32, subsections (c), (c½) or (c¾) of section 32E, section 32F or section 32K; or (ii) violating this chapter upon a finding of 1 of the following aggravating circumstances: (A) the person used violence or threats of violence or possessed a firearm, rifle, shotgun, machine gun or a weapon described in subsection (b) of section 10 of chapter 269, or induced another participant to do so, during the commission of the offense; (B) the person engaged in a course of conduct whereby such person directed the activities of another who committed a felony in violation of this chapter; or (C) the offense was committed during the commission or attempted commission of a violation of section 32F or 32K.

(b) No person serving a mandatory minimum term of imprisonment in the state prison for violating any provision of this chapter as set forth in section 32H shall be eligible for deductions from his sentence for good conduct under subsection (b) of section 129D of chapter 127 until he shall have served such mandatory minimum term of imprisonment. Any person serving a mandatory minimum term of imprisonment in the state prison for violating any provision of this chapter as set forth in section 32H shall be eligible for deductions from his sentence for good conduct under subsection (d) of section 129D of chapter 127, except that an ineligible offender serving such a mandatory minimum term shall not be eligible for such deductions until the ineligible offender shall have served such mandatory minimum term of imprisonment.

(c) Notwithstanding subsection (i) of section 130B of chapter 127, any person serving a mandatory minimum term of imprisonment for violating any provision of this chapter set forth in section 32H shall be eligible for a parole permit pursuant to section 130B of chapter 127 on the date determined under subsection (a) of said section 130B, except that an ineligible offender shall not be eligible for such a permit until the ineligible offender shall have served such mandatory minimum term of imprisonment.

(d) Any person serving a mandatory minimum term of imprisonment in the state prison for violating any provision of this chapter set forth in section 32H shall be eligible for work release, except that an ineligible offender serving such a mandatory minimum term shall not be eligible for work release until such ineligible offender has served such mandatory minimum term of imprisonment.

§ 32J. Controlled substances violations in, on, or near school property or public parks or playgrounds

[Amended by 2010 Mass. Acts c. 256, § 72, effective Nov. 4, 2010; 2012 Mass. Acts c. 192, §§ 30–31, effective Aug. 2, 2012; 2018 Mass. Acts c. 69, § 57, effective Apr. 13, 2018.]

Any person who violates the provisions of section 32, 32A, 32B, 32C, 32D, 32E, 32F or 32I while in, on or within 300 feet of the real property comprising a public or private accredited preschool, accredited headstart facility, elementary, vocational or secondary school if the violation occurs between 5:00a.m. and midnight, whether or not in session, or within 100 feet of a public park or playground and who during the commission of the offense: (i) used violence or threats of violence or possessed a firearm, rifle, shotgun, machine gun or a weapon described in paragraph (b) of section 10 of chapter 269, or induced another participant to do so during the commission of the offense; or (ii) engaged in a course of conduct whereby the person directed the activities of another person who committed any felony in violation of this chapter; or (iii) committed or attempted to commit a violation of section 32F or section 32K shall be punished by a term of imprisonment in the state prison for not less than 2½ nor more than 15 years or by imprisonment in a jail or house of correction for not less than 2 nor more than 2½ years. No sentence imposed pursuant to this section shall be for less than a mandatory minimum term of imprisonment of 2 years. A fine of not less than $1,000 nor more than $10,000 may be imposed but not in lieu of the mandatory minimum 2 year term of imprisonment as established herein. In accordance with section 8A of chapter 279 such sentence shall begin from and after the expiration of the sentence for violation of section 32, 32A, 32B, 32C, 32D, 32E, 32F or 32I.

Lack of knowledge of school boundaries shall not be a defense to any person who violates this section.

§ 34. Unlawful possession of particular controlled substances, including heroin and marihuana; lawful possessing, storing, analyzing, processing and testing of medical marijuana and medical marijuana-infused products by laboratories exception

[Amended by 2008 Mass. Acts c. 387, § 5, effective Dec. 4, 2008; 2015 Mass. Acts c. 46, § 90, effective July 1, 2015.]

No person knowingly or intentionally shall possess a controlled substance unless such substance was obtained directly, or pursuant to a valid prescription or order, from a practitioner while acting in the course of his professional practice, or except as otherwise authorized by the provisions of this chapter. Except as provided in Section 32L of this Chapter or as hereinafter provided, any person who violates this section shall be punished by imprisonment for not more than one year or by a fine of not more than one thousand dollars, or by both such fine and imprisonment. Any person who violates this section by possessing heroin shall for the first offense be punished by imprisonment in a house of correction for not more than two years or by a fine of not more than two thousand dollars, or both, and for a second or subsequent offense shall be punished by imprisonment in the state prison for not less than two and one-half years nor more than five years or by a fine of not more than five thousand dollars and imprisonment in a jail or house of correction for not more than two and one-half years. Any person who violates this section by possession of more than one ounce of marihuana or a controlled substance in Class E of section thirty-one shall be punished by imprisonment in a house of correction for not more than six months or a fine of five hundred dollars, or both. Except for an offense involving a controlled substance in Class E of section thirty-one, whoever violates the provisions of this section after one or more convictions of a violation of this section or of a felony under any other provisions of this chapter, or of a corresponding provision of earlier law relating to the sale or manufacture of a narcotic drug as defined in said earlier law, shall be punished by imprisonment in a house of correction for not more than two years or by a fine of not more than two thousand dollars, or both.

If any person who is charged with a violation of this section has not previously been convicted of a violation of any provision of this chapter or other provision of prior law relative to narcotic drugs or harmful drugs as defined in said prior law, or of a felony under the laws of any state or of the United States relating to such drugs, has had his case continued without a finding to a certain date, or has been convicted and placed on probation, and if, during the period of said continuance or of said probation, such person does not violate any of the conditions of said continuance or said probation, then upon the expiration of such period the court may dismiss the proceedings against him, and may order sealed all official records relating to his arrest, indictment, conviction, probation, continuance or discharge pursuant to this section; provided, however, that departmental records which are not public records, maintained by police and other law enforcement agencies, shall not be sealed; and provided further, that such a record shall be maintained in a separate file by the department of probation solely for the purpose of use by the courts in determining whether or not in subsequent proceedings such person qualifies under this section. The record maintained by the department of probation shall contain only identifying information concerning the person and a statement that he has had his record sealed pursuant to the provisions of this section. Any conviction, the record of which has been sealed under this section, shall not be deemed a conviction for purposes of any disqualification or for any other purpose. No person as to whom such sealing has been ordered shall be held thereafter under any provision of any law to be guilty of perjury or otherwise giving a false statement by reason of his failure to recite or acknowledge such arrest, indictment, conviction, dismissal, continuance, sealing, or any other related court proceeding, in response to any inquiry made of him for any purpose.

Notwithstanding any other penalty provision of this section, any person who is convicted for the first time under this section for the possession of marihuana or a controlled substance in Class E and who has not previously been convicted of any offense pursuant to the provisions of this chapter, or any provision of prior law relating to narcotic drugs or harmful drugs as defined in said prior law shall be placed on probation unless such person does not consent thereto, or unless the court files a written memorandum stating the reasons for not so doing. Upon successful completion of said probation, the case shall be dismissed and records shall be sealed.

It shall be a prima facie defense to a charge of possession of marihuana under this section that the defendant is a patient certified to participate in a therapeutic research program described in chapter ninety-four D, and possessed the marihuana for personal use pursuant to such program.

Notwithstanding any general or special law to the contrary, a laboratory may possess, store, analyze, process and test medical marijuana and medical marijuana-infused products; provided, however, that such laboratory shall do so in accordance with the department's regulations and written guidelines governing procedures for quality control and testing of products for potential contaminants.

§ 36. Protective custody of children found present where controlled substances are unlawfully kept or possessed

[Amended by 2013 Mass. Acts c. 84, § 6, effective Sept. 18, 2013.]

Notwithstanding the provisions of section thirty-five, if a police officer finds a child present where said officer finds a substance which he reasonably believes to be a controlled substance listed in Class A, B, or C of section thirty-one kept or possessed in violation of any provision of this chapter, and if the police officer reasonably believes that the child has not reached his eighteenth birthday and that the child knew of the presence of such controlled substance, the police officer may lawfully take such child into protective custody for a period not to exceed four hours. Persons having custody of a child under this section shall make reasonable efforts to notify the child's parent or guardian or other person having lawful custody. Such persons shall be considered to be acting in the conduct of their official duties and shall not be held criminally or civilly liable for such acts. A child detained pursuant to the provisions of this section shall not be considered to have been arrested or to have a criminal record for any purpose; however, only a departmental record of custody shall be made by the officer indicating the circumstances of custody. The procedures and processes provided by this section for the care, protection, and custody of children are not exclusive but are in addition to all others provided by law.

§ 40. Conspiracy

Whoever conspires with another person to violate any provision of this chapter shall be punished by imprisonment or fine, or both, which punishment shall not exceed the maximum punishment prescribed for the offense, the commission of which was the object of the conspiracy.

§ 41. Arrest without warrant

A police officer shall have the authority to arrest without a warrant:

(a) any person committing in his presence any offense set forth in this chapter;

(b) any person who he has probable cause to believe has committed or is committing a felony set forth under the provisions of this chapter; or

(c) any person who he has probable cause to believe has committed or is committing a violation of the provisions of sections twenty-seven, thirty-two, thirty-two A, thirty-two B, thirty-two C, thirty-two D, thirty-two E, thirty-two F, thirty-three, thirty-four, thirty-five, thirty-seven and forty.

§ 44. Violations of Sec. 34; acquittal, dismissal or indictment nol prossed; sealing of records

If any person is found not guilty of the violation of any provision of section thirty-four or if a complaint against him is dismissed or an indictment nol prossed for a violation of said section, the court shall order all official records relating to his arrest, indictment, con-

1

viction, continuance or discharge to be sealed; provided, however, that departmental records maintained by police and other law enforcement agencies which are not public records shall not be sealed.

No person as to whom such sealing has been ordered shall be held thereafter under any provision of any law to be guilty of perjury or otherwise making a false statement by reason of his failure to recite or acknowledge such arrest, indictment, disposition, sealing or any other related court proceeding, in response to any inquiry made of him for any purpose.

§ 45. Photographing and fingerprinting of persons charged with felony

Any person arrested for or charged with the criminal violation of any provision of this chapter which constitutes a felony may at the time of arrest or as soon thereafter as is practicable be photographed and fingerprinted according to the system of the state bureau of identification, and upon conviction any such fingerprints and photographs shall be made a part of permanent records of the police department of the municipality where the arrest took place, and without delay two copies of the fingerprints and photographs shall be forwarded, with such other description as may be required and a written history of the offense, to the state bureau of identification.

Chapter 94G. Regulation of the Use and Distribution of Marijuana Not Medically Prescribed

§ 13. Penalties

[Added by 2016 Mass. Acts c. 334, § 5, effective Dec. 15, 2016; 2017 Mass. Acts c. 55, § 38, effective July 28, 2017, § 39, effective upon execution of transfer agreement between Dep't of Pub. Health & Mass. Cannabis Control Comm'n or on Dec. 31, 2018, whichever occurs first.]

(a) Restrictions on personal cultivation. No person shall cultivate or process marijuana plants pursuant to section 8 of this chapter if the plants are visible from a public place without the use of binoculars, aircraft or other optical aids or cultivate or process marijuana plants outside of an area that is equipped with a lock or other security device. A person who violates this subsection shall be punished by a civil penalty of not more than $300 and forfeiture of the marijuana, but shall not be subject to any other form of criminal or civil punishment or disqualification solely for this conduct.

(b) Restrictions on personal possession. No person shall possess more than 1 ounce of marijuana or marijuana products within the person's place of residence pursuant to section 8 of this chapter unless the marijuana and marijuana products are secured by a lock. A person who violates this subsection shall be punished by a civil penalty of not more than $100 and forfeiture of the marijuana.

(c) Restrictions on public consumption of marijuana. No person shall consume marijuana in a public place or smoke marijuana where smoking tobacco is prohibited. A person who violates this subsection shall be punished by a civil penalty of not more than $100. This subsection shall not apply to a person who consumes marijuana or marijuana products in a designated area of a marijuana establishment located in a city or town that has voted to allow consumption on the premises where sold and shall not be construed to limit the medical use of marijuana.

(d) Possession of marijuana in motor vehicles. No person shall, upon any way or in any place to which the public has a right of access, or upon any way or in any place to which members of the public have access as invitees or licensees, possess an open container of marijuana or marijuana products in the passenger area of any motor vehicle. A person who violates this subjection shall be punished by a civil penalty of not more than $500. For purposes of this section, "open container" shall mean that the package containing marijuana or marijuana products has its seal broken or from which the contents have been partially removed or consumed and "passenger area'' shall mean the area designed to seat the driver and passengers while the motor vehicle is in operation and any area that is readily accessible to the driver or passenger while in a seated position; provided however that the passenger area shall not include a motor vehicle's trunk, locked glove compartment or the living quarters of a house coach or house trailer, or if a motor vehicle is not equipped with a trunk, the area behind the last upright seat or an area not normally occupied by the driver or passenger.

(e) Possession or cultivation of excess marijuana. Notwithstanding chapter 94C of the General Laws and until the import or export of marijuana to or from the commonwealth is not prohibited by federal law, a person who is at least 21 years of age and who cultivates more than 6 but not more than 12 marijuana plants or who possesses an amount of marijuana outside of his or her place of residence having a weight of more than 1 ounce but not more than 2 ounces shall be subject only to a civil penalty of not more than $100 and forfeiture of the marijuana not allowed by section 8 of this chapter, but shall not be subject to any other form of criminal or civil punishment or disqualification solely for this conduct.

(f) Procurement of marijuana by a person under 21 years of age. A person under 21 years of age, except a qualifying patient holding a valid registration card for the medical use of marijuana, who purchases or attempts to purchase marijuana, marijuana products or marijuana accessories, or makes arrangements with any person to purchase or in any way procure marijuana, marijuana products or marijuana accessories, or who willfully misrepresents such person's age, or in any way alters, defaces or otherwise falsifies identification offered as proof of age, with the intent of purchasing marijuana, marijuana products or marijuana accessories, shall be punished by a civil penalty of not more than $100 and shall complete a drug awareness program established pursuant to section 32M of chapter 94C of the General Laws. The parents or legal guardian of any offender under the age of 18 shall be notified in accordance with section 32N of chapter 94C of the General Laws and the failure within 1 year of the offense of such an offender to complete a drug awareness program may be a basis for delinquency proceedings for persons under the age of 17 at the time of the person's offense.

(g) Enforcement. Civil penalties imposed pursuant to this section shall be enforced by utilizing the non-criminal disposition procedures provided in section 32N of chapter 94C of the General Laws.

(h) Notwithstanding chapter 94C, a person less than 21 years of age, except a qualifying patient holding a valid registration card for the medical use of marijuana, who cultivates not more than 12 marijuana plants shall be punished by a civil penalty of not more than $100 and shall complete a drug awareness program established pursuant to section 32M of chapter 94C. If that person is less than 18 years of age, the parent or legal guardian of that person shall be notified in accordance with section 32N of said chapter 94C. If a person is less than 17 years of age at the time of the offense and fails to complete a drug awareness program not later than 1 year after the offense, that person may be subject to delinquency proceedings.

(i) Whoever furnishes marijuana, marijuana products or marijuana accessories to a person less than 21 years of age, either for the person's own use or for the use of the person's parent or another person shall be punished by a fine of not more than $2,000 or by imprisonment for not more than 1 year or both such fine and imprisonment.

For the purposes of this subsection, "furnish" shall mean to knowingly or intentionally supply, give or provide to or allow a person less than 21 years of age, except for the children and grandchildren of the person being charged, to possess marijuana, marijuana products or marijuana accessories on premises or property owned or controlled by the person charged.

This subsection shall not apply to the sale, delivery or furnishing of medical marijuana pursuant to chapter 94I.

Chapter 111. Public Health

§ 9. Inspectors, analysts and chemists; appointment; removal; power and authority; interference with

In the performance of the duties relative to the sale of drugs and food the commissioner may appoint and remove inspectors, analysts and chemists. Such inspectors shall, in addition to the powers given by sections one hundred and twenty-one to one hundred and twenty-three, inclusive, of chapter ninety-four, have the same power and authority relative to drugs, fish, food and milk as is given inspectors of milk by sections thirty-five and sixty of said chapter. Such inspectors shall, in the enforcement of laws relative to controlled substances as defined in section one of chapter ninety-four C, have all the powers and authority of police officers and constables except the power to serve civil process. Inspectors assigned to investigate violations of laws relative to controlled substances as defined in section one of chapter ninety-four C may at the request of the commissioner carry revolvers, billies, clubs, handcuffs and any other paraphernalia necessary for their protection and the enforcement of such laws. Whoever hinders, obstructs or in any way interferes with any such inspector, analyst or chemist in the performance of his official duty shall for the first offense be punished by a fine of not more than fifty dollars, and for a subsequent offense by a fine of not more than one hundred dollars.

§ 10. Repealed

[Repealed by 1989 Mass. Acts c. 610, § 2.]

§§ 11–13. Repealed

[Repealed by 2012 Mass. Acts c. 139, § 107, effective July 1, 2012.]

§ 70. Records of hospitals or clinics; custody; inspection; copies; fees

[Amended by 2000 Mass. Acts c. 54, § 5; 2003 Mass. Acts c. 135, § 1, effective July 1, 2004; 2008 Mass. Acts c. 305, §§ 12–13, effective Aug. 10, 2008.]

Hospitals or clinics subject to licensure by the department of public health or supported in whole or in part by the commonwealth, shall keep records of the treatment of the cases under their care including the medical history and nurses' notes and, in the case of a patient brought to a hospital by an ambulance service licensed pursuant to chapter 111C, a copy of the call summary set forth in paragraph (15) of subsection (b) of section 3 of said chapter 111C. These records may be handwritten, printed, typed or in electronic digital media or converted to electronic digital media as originally created by such hospital or clinic, by the photographic or microphotographic process, or any combination thereof. The hospital or clinic may destroy records only after the applicable retention period has elapsed and after notifying the department of public health, in accordance with its regulations, that the records will be destroyed. The department, through its regulations, shall establish an appropriate notification process. On the notice of privacy practices distributed to its patients, a hospital or clinic shall provide: (i) information concerning the provisions of this section and (ii) the hospital or clinic's records termination policy. Such records shall be in the custody of the hospital or clinic. Section ten of chapter sixty-six shall not apply to such records; provided, however, that such records and similar records kept by the hospital or clinic, except a hospital or clinic under the control of the department of mental health, may be inspected by the patient to whom they relate, the patient's attorney upon delivery of a written authorization from said patient, the duly appointed executor or administrator of the deceased person's estate or the attorney for such executor or administrator upon delivery of a written authorization from such executor or administrator, and a copy shall be furnished upon the payment of a reasonable fee, which for the purposes of this section shall mean a base charge of not more than $15 for each request for a hospital or clinic medical record; a per page charge of not more than $0.50 for each of the first 100 pages of a hospital or clinic medical record that is copied per request; and not more than $0.25 per page for each page in excess of 100 pages of a hospital or clinic medical record that is copied per request, except that no fee shall be charged to any applicant, beneficiary or individual representing said applicant or beneficiary for furnishing a record if the record is requested for the purpose of supporting a claim or appeal under any provision of the Social Security Act or any federal or state financial needs-based benefit program; and provided, further, that upon proper judicial order, whether in connection with pending judicial proceedings or otherwise, or, except in the case of records of hospitals under the control of the department of mental health, upon order of the head of the state department which issues the license or of the head of the state department having jurisdiction or control of such hospital or clinic, and in compliance with the terms of said order, and, in the case of a hospital or clinic under the control of the department of mental health, when the commissioner of mental health determines that a disclosure would be in the best interest of a patient as provided in the rules and regulations promulgated by the commissioner, such records may be inspected and copies furnished on payment of a reasonable fee, except that no fee shall be charged to any applicant, beneficiary or individual representing said applicant or beneficiary for furnishing a record if the record is requested for the purpose of supporting a claim or appeal under any provision of the Social Security Act or any federal or state financial needs-based benefit program. A health care provider shall furnish a health record requested pursuant to a claim or appeal under any provision of the Social Security Act or any federal or state financial needs-based benefit program within thirty days of the request. Any person for whom no fee shall be charged shall present reasonable documentation at the time of such records request that the purpose of said request is to support a claim or appeal under any provision of the Social Security Act or any federal or state financial needs-based benefit program. Notwithstanding the foregoing, a hospital or clinic served with a subpoena for such records of any party named in that proceeding as shown by the case caption appearing on the subpoena, shall deliver certified copies of the subpoenaed records in its custody to the court or place of hearing designated on the subpoena. Any such record or any part or portion thereof may be destroyed 20 years after the discharge or the final treatment therein of the patient to whom it relates.

In the event of the transfer of ownership of a hospital, an institution for unwed mothers or a clinic, all medical records of the same shall be maintained by the new owner as if there were no change in ownership. In the event of the permanent closing of a hospital, an institution for unwed mothers or a clinic, such hospital, institution or clinic shall arrange for preservation of such medical records for the time required herein.

The term "record" as used herein shall not include within its meaning the records or proceedings of medical peer review committees as defined in section one.

The reasonable fee under this section may be adjusted to reflect the consumer price index for medical care services, such that the base amount and the per page charge shall be increased by the proportional consumer price index in effect as of October of the calendar year in which the request is made, rounded to the nearest dollar. A hospital or clinic may also charge an additional fee to cover the cost of postage, other priority mailing and preparation of an explanation or summary of the hospital or clinic medical record if so requested.

§ 70F. HTLV-III test; confidentiality; informed consent

[Amended by 2012 Mass. Acts c. 84, effective July 26, 2012.]

A facility, as defined in section 70E, physician or health care provider shall not (1) test any person for the presence of the HIV antibody or antigen without first obtaining that person's verbal informed consent; (2) disclose the results of such test to any person other than the subject of the test without first obtaining the subject's written informed consent; or (3) identify the subject of such tests to any person without first obtaining the subject's written informed consent. A written consent form shall state the purpose for which the information is being requested and shall be distinguished from written consent for the release of any other medical information.

No employer shall require HIV antibody or antigen tests as a condition for employment.

Whoever violates this section shall be considered to have violated section 2 of chapter 93A.

For the purpose of this section "written informed consent" shall mean a written consent form for each requested release of the results of an individual's HIV antibody or antigen test or for the release of medical records containing such information.

It shall not be a violation of this section for any physician, health care provider, health care institution or laboratory to report information to the department of public health under chapter 111 or chapter 111D and regulations promulgated thereunder. No physician, health care provider, health care institution or laboratory required to report shall be liable in any civil or criminal action by reason of any such report.

This section shall not apply to premortem and postmortem serological testing for purposes of donation under chapter 113A.

Chapter 111E. Drug Rehabilitation

§ 9A. Incapacitated person; protective custody

[Added by 2016 Mass. Acts c. 161, effective July 1, 2016.]

For purposes of this section, "incapacitated" shall mean the condition of a person who, by reason of the consumption of a controlled substance or toxic vapor or other substance other than alcohol is: (i) unconscious; (ii) in need of medical attention; (iii) likely to suffer or cause physical harm or damage property; or (iv) disorderly.

Any person who is incapacitated may be placed into protective custody by a police officer without the person's consent for the purpose of immediately transporting the person to an acute care hospital or satellite emergency facility as defined in section 51½ of chapter 111 or otherwise immediately obtaining appropriate emergency medical treatment. For the purposes of this section, to determine whether or not a person is incapacitated, a police officer may request the person to submit to reasonable tests of coordination, coherency of speech and breath. A police officer may place the person into protective custody when such tests or other information or observations indicate that the person is incapacitated. Whenever a police officer places into protective custody a person under the age of 18 in accordance with this section, the police officer shall notify the parent or guardian of that person forthwith.

A person may not be held in protective custody against the person's will beyond the time required to complete the person's immediate transport to an acute care hospital or satellite emergency facility as defined in section 51½ of chapter 111, or to otherwise immediately obtain appropriate emergency medical treatment.

A police officer acting in accordance with this section may use such force as is reasonably necessary to carry out the officer's authorized responsibilities. If the police officer reasonably believes that there may be a risk to the safety of the incapacitated person, the safety of the officer or the safety of other persons present, the police officer may search the person and the immediate surroundings of the person placed into protective custody but only to the extent necessary to discover and seize any items or weapons which may pose a danger. Any item taken shall be inventoried and, unless the item is contraband or otherwise unlawfully possessed, shall be returned to the person when the person is no longer incapacitated.

A person placed under protective custody in accordance with this section shall not be considered to have been arrested or to have been charged with any crime. An entry of custody shall be made indicating the date, time, place of custody, the name of the assisting officer and the name of the officer in charge. No such entry shall be treated as an arrest or criminal record for any purpose.

§ 10. Defendant charged with drug offense; request for examination; stay of proceedings; report of findings; assignment; hearing; discharge or transfer; quarterly reports; juveniles; review

[Amended by 2018 Mass. Acts c. 69, §§ 64–67, effective July 12, 2018.]

Any defendant who is charged with a drug offense shall, upon being brought before the court on such charge, be informed that he is entitled to request an examination to determine whether or not he is a drug dependent person who would benefit by treatment, and that if he chooses to exercise such right he must do so in writing within five days of being so informed.

If the defendant requests such an examination, the court may in its discretion determine that the defendant is a drug dependent person, who would benefit by treatment, without ordering the examination. In such event, the court shall inform the defendant that he may request assignment to a drug treatment facility, and advise him of the consequences of assignment and that if he is so assigned the court proceedings shall be stayed for the term of such assignment.

The court proceedings shall be stayed for the period during which a request made under this section is under consideration by the court. If the defendant requests an examination, the court shall, unless the court has already determined that the defendant is a drug dependent person, appoint an addiction specialist to conduct the examination at an appropriate location designated by it. In no event shall the request for such an examination or any statement made by the defendant during the course of the examination, or any finding of the an addiction specialist be admissible against the defendant in any court proceedings.

The an addiction specialist shall report his findings in writing to the court within five days after the completion of the examination, stating the facts upon which the findings are based and the reasons therefor.

If the defendant is also charged with a violation of any law other than a drug offense, the stay of the court proceedings may be vacated by the court upon the report of the addiction specialist, whereupon the report shall be considered upon disposition of the charges in accordance with sections eleven and twelve, and the remaining provisions of this chapter shall not apply. If the defendant is charged with a drug offense only and if the addiction specialist reports that the defendant is a drug dependent person who would benefit by treatment, the court shall inform the defendant that he may request assignment to a drug treatment facility, and advise him of the consequences of the assignment and that if he is so assigned the court proceedings shall be stayed for the term of such assignment.

If the defendant requests assignment and if the court determines that he is a drug dependent person who would benefit from treatment the court may stay the court proceedings and assign him to a drug treatment facility.

An order assigning a person under this section shall specify the period of assignment, which shall not exceed eighteen months or the period of time equal to the maximum sentence he could have received had he been found guilty of every count alleged in the complaint or indictment whichever is shorter.

In determining whether or not to grant a request for assignment under this section, the court shall consider the report, the past criminal record of the defendant, the availability of adequate and appropriate treatment at a facility, the nature of the offense with which the defendant is charged including, but not limited to, whether the offense charged is that of a sale or sale to a minor, and any other relevant evidence.

In the event that the defendant requests assignment and if the court determines that the defendant is a drug dependent person who would benefit by treatment, and the defendant is charged for the first time with a drug offense not involving the sale or manufacture of dependency related drugs, and there are no continuances outstanding with respect to the defendant pursuant to this section, the court shall order that the defendant be assigned to a drug treatment facility without consideration of any other factors.

Before such assignment, the court shall consult with the facility or the division, to determine that adequate and appropriate treatment is available.

If the defendant requests assignment, and if the court determines that the defendant is a drug dependent person who would benefit by treatment, and the defendant is charged for the first time with a drug offense not involving the sale or manufacture of dependency related drugs, and there are no continuances outstanding with respect to the defendant pursuant to this section, and adequate and appropriate treatment at a facility is not available, the stay of court proceedings shall remain in effect until such time as adequate and appropriate treatment at a facility is available.

In all other cases, an assignment order shall not be made unless, after consultation with the facility or the division, the court determines that adequate and appropriate treatment is available, provided, however, that the court may in its discretion order that the stay of court proceedings remain outstanding until such time as adequate and appropriate treatment is available.

In the event that the stay of the court proceedings remains in effect for the reason that adequate and appropriate treatment at a facility is not available, the issue of the availability of adequate and appropriate treatment at a facility may be reopened at any time by the court on its own motion, or on motion by the prosecutor, or the defendant.

In no event shall any defendant be assigned pursuant to this section unless the defendant consents in writing to the terms of the assignment order.

If the addiction specialist reports that the person is not a drug dependent person who would benefit by treatment, the defendant shall be entitled to request a hearing to determine whether or not he is a drug dependent person who would benefit by treatment. The court may on its own motion, or shall, upon request of the defendant or his counsel, appoint an independent addiction specialist to examine the defendant and testify at the hearing. If the court determines that the defendant is a drug dependent person who would benefit by treatment, the procedures and standards applicable to a defendant who is determined by the court, following the report of the first examining addiction specialist to be a drug dependent person who would benefit by treatment, shall apply to the defendant.

If the court does not assign the defendant to a facility, the stay of the court proceedings shall be vacated.

At any time during the term of assignment the administrator may transfer any inpatient, to an outpatient program if he finds that the patient is a proper subject for an outpatient program; provided, however, that the administrator may retransfer the patient to an inpatient program if he finds that the person is not suitable for outpatient treatment, and provided further that immediately upon such transfer the administrator shall notify in writing the assigning court and the director of such transfer.

Any patient assigned under this section may apply in writing to the assigning court for discharge or transfer either from inpatient or outpatient treatment or from one facility to another; provided, however, that not more than one such application may be made in any three-month period. Upon receipt of an application for discharge or transfer, the court shall give written notice to the patient of his right to a hearing and to be represented by counsel at the hearing.

Within ten days of the receipt by the court of an application for discharge, the administrator and an independent addiction specialist, designated by the court to make an examination of the patient shall report to the court as to whether or not the patient would benefit from further treatment at a facility. If the court determines that the patient would no longer so benefit, the patient's application for discharge shall be granted. If the court does not so determine, said application shall be denied.

Within ten days of the receipt by the court of an application for transfer, the administrator shall report to the court as to whether the patient is a proper subject for the transfer for which he has made application. If the court determines that the patient is a proper subject for the transfer, the patient's application for transfer shall be granted and the assigning court shall be so notified. If the court does not so determine, said application shall be denied.

Throughout the period of assignment at a facility pursuant to this section, the administrator of said facility shall provide quarterly written reports on the progress being made in treatment by the defendant to the assigning court. Failure to comply may be grounds for suspension of the facility's license. At the end of the assignment period, or when the patient is discharged by the administrator, or when the patient prematurely terminates treatment at a facility, whichever occurs first, the administrator shall notify in writing the assigning court and the director of such termination, and further shall state the reasons for such termination, including whether the defendant successfully completed the treatment program.

In reaching its determination of whether or not the defendant successfully completed the treatment program, the court shall consider, but shall not be limited to, whether the defendant cooperated with the administrator and complied with the terms and conditions imposed on him during his assignment. If the report states that the defendant successfully completed the treatment program, or if the defendant completes the term of treatment ordered by the court, the court shall dismiss the charges pending against the defendant. If the report does not so state, or if the defendant does not complete the term of treatment ordered by the court, then, based on the report and any other relevant evidence, the court may take such action as it deems appropriate, including the dismissal of the charges or the revocation of the stay of the court proceedings.

As to any defendant determined by the court pursuant to this section to be a drug dependent person who would benefit by treatment, concerning whom the court does not order assignment in lieu of prosecution, the court may in the event that such person is convicted of the criminal charges, order that he be afforded treatment pursuant to either section eleven or twelve. The provisions of this chapter shall apply to juveniles in the same manner and under the same terms and conditions as adults; provided that no juvenile shall be committed to a facility without the consent of his parents or guardian.

The provisions of this section shall apply to proceedings in the superior court provided, however, that no defendant who has been examined for his drug dependency pursuant to this section in a district court shall have the right to a new examination if his case is bound over or appealed to the superior court; provided, however, that a superior court judge may, in his discretion, grant a second such drug examination.

During any stays authorized by this section, the court may in its discretion place the defendant in the care of a probation officer until he is accepted at a facility. For the purposes of this section, the term "facility" shall include federal facilities. The provisions of this section shall not apply to a person charged with violating sections thirty-two to thirty-two G, inclusive, of chapter ninety-four C of the General Laws.

§ 11. Defendant charged with other than drug offense; request for examination; evidence; report; treatment; consent; hearing; order

[Amended by 2018 Mass. Acts c. 69, §§ 68–70, effective July 12, 2018.]

Any person found guilty of a violation of any law other than a drug offense, who prior to disposition of the charge, states that he is a drug dependent person, and requests an examination shall be examined by an addiction specialist to determine whether or not he is a drug dependent person who is a drug addict who would benefit by treatment or a drug dependent person who is not a drug addict but who would benefit by treatment.

If the defendant has previously been examined, pursuant to a request for an examination made in accordance with section ten, the report of the addiction specialist who conducted the examination shall serve at the examination provided for under this section.

The examination shall be conducted at any appropriate location upon appropriate order of the court. In no event shall the request for such examination or any statement made by the defendant during the course of the examination or any finding of the addiction specialist be admissible against the defendant in any criminal proceeding. The addiction specialist shall report in writing to the court within five days after the completion of the examination, stating the facts upon which the report is based and the reasons therefor.

If the report states that the defendant is a drug dependent person who would benefit by treatment, and if the court orders that the defendant be confined to a jail, house of correction, prison, or other correctional institution, the court may further order that the defendant be afforded treatment at a penal facility for the whole or any part of the term of imprisonment; provided, however, that the court shall determine the term of treatment to be afforded with the advice of the administrator of the penal facility; and provided, further, that the court shall not order that the defendant be afforded treatment at a penal facility unless the defendant consents to the order in writing. The administrator may terminate treatment of the defendant at such time as he determines the defendant will no longer benefit by treatment.

If the report states that the defendant is not a drug dependent person who would benefit by treatment, the defendant shall be entitled to request a hearing on whether or not he is a drug dependent person who would benefit by treatment. If the court determines that he is a drug dependent person who would benefit by treatment and if the court orders that the defendant be confined to a jail, house of correction, prison, or other correctional institution, the court may order that the defendant be afforded treatment at a penal facility in accordance with the standards and procedures set forth in this section.

If the court does not order that the defendant be confined to a jail, house of correction, prison, or other correctional institution, the court may order that the defendant be afforded treatment pursuant to section twelve.

§ 12. Probation of drug dependent persons; treatment; urinalysis program; reports

[Amended by 2014 Mass. Acts c. 165, § 147, effective June 1, 2015.]

Any court may, in placing on probation a defendant who is a drug dependent person who would benefit by treatment impose as a condition of probation that the defendant receive treatment in a facility as an inpatient or outpatient; provided, however, that the court shall not impose such a condition of probation unless, after consulting with the facility, it determines that adequate and appropriate treatment is available. The defendant shall receive treatment at the facility for so long as the administrator of the facility deems that the defendant will benefit by treatment, but in no event shall he receive treatment at the facility for a period longer than the period of probation ordered by the court. A periodic program of urinalysis may be employed as a condition of probation to determine the drug free status of the probationer. The cost of the administration of such program shall be borne by the commonwealth. If the court requires as a condition of probation that the defendant shall reside in alcohol and drug free housing, the judge issuing the order shall require the probation officer to refer the defendant only to alcohol and drug free housing certified pursuant to section 18A of chapter 17 and the probation officer shall require the defendant to reside in housing so certified in order to satisfy such condition if such certified housing is available. If at any time during the period of treatment the defendant does not cooperate with the administrator or the probation officer, or does not conduct himself in accordance with the order or conditions of his probation, the administrator or the probation officer may make a report thereon to the court which placed him on probation, which may consider such conduct as a breach of probation.

Throughout the period of probation at a facility pursuant to this section, the administrator of said facility shall provide quarterly written reports on the progress being made in treatment by the defendant to the defendant's probation officer.

§ 13. Juveniles and youthful offenders; examination; admission; inpatient or outpatient treatment; report; department of youth services; jurisdiction

The division shall accept for referral juveniles and youthful offenders referred to the division by the department of youth services. Application by the department of youth services for such referral shall be made to the director.

Upon receipt by the director of a request for referral from the youth service board, he shall, unless the person has been examined pursuant to section ten, designate a psychiatrist or, if in the discretion of the director it is impracticable to do so, a physician, to make an examination of the person to be referred to determine whether or not he is a drug dependent person who would benefit by treatment. The psychiatrist or physician shall report his findings in writing to the director after the completion of the examination, stating the facts upon which the findings are based and the reasons therefor.

If the director finds that the person is a drug dependent person who would benefit by treatment and that adequate treatment is available at an appropriate facility, he may recommend to the department of youth services that the person be admitted to the facility as an inpatient or an outpatient.

In determining whether to admit to a facility a person who is reported to be a drug dependent person who would benefit by treatment, the director shall consider the past record of treatment if any, afforded the person at a facility, and whether or not the person complied with the terms of any prior admission.

If the director decides to admit to a facility a juvenile or youthful offender pursuant to this section, he shall recommend to the department of youth services the period deemed necessary to accomplish adequate and appropriate treatment but in no case shall the period exceed one year. The director shall also notify the department of youth services of the unaware of the treatment to be afforded and the facility to which the person will be admitted. If the department of youth services consents in writing to admission to the facility, to the nature of the treatment to be afforded, and to the period deemed necessary to accomplish treatment, the person shall be admitted to the facility.

If the director decides that the referral to the division is to be refused because the juvenile or youthful offender is not a drug dependent person who would benefit by treatment or because adequate treatment is not available at an appropriate facility, he shall make known in writing to the department of youth services the basis for this decision.

The referral to the division shall terminate at the conclusion of the period of treatment to which the department of youth services consents, or upon a determination by the director that the juvenile or youthful offender will no longer benefit by treatment, whichever first occurs. If the director determines before the conclusion of the period of treatment to which the department of youth services consents that the juvenile or youthful offender will no longer benefit by treatment, he shall make known in writing to the department of youth services the basis for his decision.

Juveniles and youthful offenders referred to the division pursuant to this section shall remain subject to the jurisdiction and control of the department of youth services for all purposes, including, but not limited to, discharge and release; provided, however, that the treatment to be afforded the juvenile and youthful offenders referred to the division shall be within the jurisdiction and control of the division. In no event, however, shall a juvenile or youthful offender be referred for a period longer than the period during which he is subject to the jurisdiction and control of the department of youth services.

§ 13A. Children referred by department of children and families or juvenile court; examination; report; treatment; jurisdiction

[Amended by 2008 Mass. Acts c. 176, § 78, effective July 8, 2008; 2018 Mass. Acts c. 69, § 71, effective July 12, 2018.]

The division shall, in accordance with this section, accept for referral children determined to be in need of services under section 39G of chapter 119 and referred to the division by the department of children and families, hereinafter referred to as the department, or by the juvenile court. Such referral shall be made to the director of the division.

Upon receipt by the director of a request for referral he may, unless the child has been examined pursuant to section ten, designate a qualified addiction specialist to make an examination of the child to determine whether or not he is a drug dependent child who would benefit from treatment.

The addiction specialist designated shall report his findings in writing to the director stating the facts upon which the findings are based and the reasons therefore, and said report shall be kept confidential by the division and shall not be disclosed to any person, other than the department or the court, without the written approval of the child or his parent or legal guardian.

If the director finds that the child is a drug dependent person who would benefit from treatment and that adequate treatment is available at an appropriate drug treatment facility, he may recommend to the department or the court that the child be admitted to the facility on an inpatient or an outpatient basis.

The director may also recommend to the department or the juvenile court the period of time necessary to accomplish adequate and appropriate treatment, not to exceed one year; the nature of the treatment to be afforded and the facility to which the child could be admitted. If the department or court determines that admission to the facility, the nature of the treatment to be afforded and the period deemed necessary to accomplish treatment are appropriate and the child and his parent or legal guardian agree to the treatment, the child may, subject to the availability of funds appropriated for that purpose, be admitted to the facility for such treatment. Said determination shall be provided in writing.

If the director decides that referral to the division is inappropriate because the child is not a drug dependent person who would benefit by treatment or because adequate treatment is not available at an appropriate facility, he shall make known in writing to said department or said court the basis for this decision.

The referral to the division shall terminate at the conclusion of the period of treatment to which the department or the court consents, or upon a determination by the director that the child will no longer benefit by treatment, whichever first occurs. If the director determines before the conclusion of such period of treatment that the child will no longer benefit by treatment, he shall make known in writing to the department or the court the basis for his decision.

Children in need of services referred to the division pursuant to this section shall remain subject to the jurisdiction and control of the department or the court for all purposes, including, but not limited to, discharge and release; provided, however, that the treatment to be afforded the child in need of services referred to the division shall be within the jurisdiction and control of the division. In no event, however, shall a child in need of services be referred for a period longer than the period during which he is subject to the jurisdiction and control of the department or the court.

Chapter 112. Registration of Certain Professions and Occupations

§ 12E. Drug dependent minors; consent to medical care; liability for payment; records

A minor twelve years of age or older who is found to be drug dependent by two or more physicians may give his consent to the furnishing of hospital and medical care related to the diagnosis or treatment of such drug dependency. Such consent shall not be subject to disaffirmance because of minority. The consent of the parent or legal guardian of such minor shall not be necessary to authorize hospital and medical care related to such drug dependency and, notwithstanding any provision of section fifty-four of chapter one hundred and twenty-three to the contrary, such parent or legal guardian shall not be liable for the payment of any care rendered pursuant to this section. Records shall be kept of such care. The provisions of this section shall not apply to methadone maintenance therapy.

§ 12E½. Drug or alcohol overdose of minor

[Added by 2012 Mass. Acts c. 244, § 10, effective Jan. 1, 2013; 2017 Mass. Acts c. 47, § 49, effective July 1, 2017 per § 153.]

The department of public health shall produce a pamphlet with contact information for its bureau of substance addiction services, including its telephone helpline number, and with information on the benefits and availability of addiction treatment and on the prevention of overdoses. A physician, nurse practitioner or hospital that treats a person under 18 years of age for a drug or alcohol overdose, as defined by regulations of the department, shall: (i) notify the minor's parent, legal guardian or other person having custody or control of a minor child of the overdose as part of the discharge planning process; (ii) provide the pamphlet to the parent, legal guardian or other person having custody or control of a minor child and to the minor child; and (iii) provide access to a social worker, if available.

The department shall promulgate regulations to ensure that the notification provisions of this section are applied in a manner consistent with the federal Health Insurance Portability and Accountability Act.

§ 12F. Emergency treatment of minors

No physician, dentist or hospital shall be held liable for damages for failure to obtain consent of a parent, legal guardian, or other person having custody or control of a minor child, or of the spouse of a patient, to emergency examination and treatment, including blood transfusions, when delay in treatment will endanger the life, limb, or mental well-being of the patient.

Any minor may give consent to his medical or dental care at the time such care is sought if (i) he is married, widowed, divorced; or (ii) he is the parent of a child, in which case he may also give consent to medical or dental care of the child; or (iii) he is a member of any of the armed forces; or (iv) she is pregnant or believes herself to be pregnant; or (v) he is living separate and apart from his parent or legal guardian, and is managing his own financial affairs; or (vi) he reasonably believes himself to be suffering from or to have come in contact with any disease defined as dangerous to the public health pursuant to section six of chapter one hundred and eleven; provided, however, that such minor may only consent to care which relates to the diagnosis or treatment of such disease.

Consent shall not be granted under subparagraphs (ii) through (vi), inclusive, for abortion or sterilization.

Consent given under this section shall not be subject to later disaffirmance because of minority. The consent of the parent or legal guardian shall not be required to authorize such care and, notwithstanding any other provisions of law, such parent or legal guardian shall not be liable for the payment for any care rendered pursuant to this section unless such parent or legal guardian has expressly agreed to pay for such care.

No physician or dentist, nor any hospital, clinic or infirmary shall be liable, civilly and criminally, for not obtaining the consent of the parent or legal guardian to render medical or dental care to a minor, if, at the time such care was rendered, such person or facility: (i) relied in good faith upon the representations of such minor that he is legally able to consent to such treatment under this section; or (ii) relied in good faith upon the representations of such minor that he is over eighteen years of age.

All information and records kept in connection with the medical or dental care of a minor who consents thereto in accordance with this section shall be confidential between the minor and the physician or dentist, and shall not be released except upon the written consent of the minor or a proper judicial order. When the physician or dentist attending a minor reasonably believes the condition of said minor to be so serious that his life or limb is endangered, the physician or dentist shall notify the parents, legal guardian or foster parents of said condition and shall inform the minor of said notification.

§ 12S. Consent to abortion; form; persons less than eighteen years of age

No physician may perform an abortion upon a pregnant woman without first obtaining her written informed consent. The commissioner of public health shall prescribe a form for physicians to use in obtaining such consent. This form shall be written in a manner designed to permit a person unfamiliar with medical terminology to understand its purpose and content, and shall include the following information: a description of the stage of development of the unborn child; the type of procedure which the physician intends to use to perform the abortion; and the possible complications associated with the use of the procedure and with the performance of the abortion itself; the availability of alternatives to abortion; and a statement that, under the law of the commonwealth, a person's refusal to undergo an abortion does not constitute grounds for the denial of public assistance. A pregnant woman seeking an abortion shall sign the consent form described above at least twenty-four hours in advance of the time for which the abortion is scheduled, except in an emergency requiring immediate action. She shall then return it to the physician performing the abortion who shall maintain it in his files and destroy it seven years after the date upon which the abortion is performed.

The said consent form and any other forms, transcript of evidence, or written findings and conclusions of a court, shall be confidential and may not be released to any person except by the pregnant woman's written informed consent or by a proper judicial order, other than to the pregnant woman herself to whom such documents relate, the operating physician, or any person whose consent is required pursuant to this section, or under the law. If a pregnant woman is less than eighteen years of age and has not married, a physician shall not perform an abortion upon her unless he first obtains both the consent of the pregnant woman and that of her parents, except as hereinafter provided. In deciding whether to grant such consent, a pregnant woman's parents shall consider only their child's best interests. If one of the pregnant woman's parents has died or is unavailable to the physician within a reasonable time and in a reasonable manner, consent of the remaining parent shall be sufficient. If both parents have died or are otherwise unavailable to the physician within a reasonable time and in a reasonable manner, consent of the pregnant woman's guardian or guardians shall be sufficient. If the pregnant woman's parents are divorced, consent of the parent having custody shall be sufficient. If a pregnant woman less than eighteen years of age has not maintained and if one or both of her parents or guardians refuse to consent to the performance of an abortion, or if she elects not to seek the consent of one or both of her parents or guardians, a judge of the superior court department of the trial court shall, upon petition, or motion, and after an appropriate hearing, authorize a physician to perform the abortion if said judge determines that the pregnant woman is mature and capable of giving informed consent to the proposed abortion or, if said judge determines that she is not mature, that the performance of an abortion upon her would be in her best interests. A pregnant woman less than eighteen years of age may participate in proceedings in the superior court department of the trial court on her own behalf, and the court may appoint a guardian ad litem for her. The court shall, however, advise her that she has a right to court appointed counsel, and shall, upon her request, provide her with such counsel. Proceedings in the superior court department of the trial court under this section shall be confidential and shall be given such precedence over other pending matters that the court may reach a decision promptly and without delay so as to serve the best interests of the pregnant woman. A judge of the superior court department of the trial court who conducts proceedings under this section shall make in writing specific factual findings and legal conclusions supporting his decision and shall order a record of the evidence to be maintained including his own findings and conclusions.

Nothing in this section is intended to abolish or limit any common law rights of persons other than those whose rights it governs for the purpose of any civil action or any action for injunctive relief under section twelve U.

§ 12FF. Immunity of person administering naloxone or other opioid antagonist to person experiencing opiate-related overdose
[Added by 2016 Mass. Acts c. 52, § 37, effective Mar. 14, 2016.]

Any person who, in good faith, attempts to render emergency care by administering naloxone or any other opioid antagonist, as defined in section 19B of chapter 94C, to a person reasonably believed to be experiencing an opiate-related overdose, shall not be liable for acts or omissions resulting from the attempt to render this emergency care; provided, however, that this section shall not apply to acts of gross negligence or willful or wanton misconduct.

§ 129A. Psychologists; confidential communications
[Amended by 2000 Mass. Acts c. 348, effective Mar. 1, 2001.]

All communications between a licensed psychologist and the individuals with whom the psychologist engages in the practice of psychology are confidential. At the initiation of the professional relationship the psychologist shall inform the patient of the following limitations to the confidentiality of their communications. No psychologist, colleague, agent or employee of any psychologist, whether professional, clerical, academic or therapeutic, shall disclose any information acquired or revealed in the course of or in connection with the performance of the psychologist's professional services, including the fact, circumstances, findings or records of such services, except under the following circumstances: (a) pursuant to the provisions of section twenty B of chapter two hundred and thirty-three or any other law; (b) upon express, written consent of the patient; (c) upon the need to disclose information which protects the rights and safety of others if:

(1) the patient presents a clear and present danger to himself and refuses explicitly or by his behavior to voluntarily accept further appropriate treatment. In such circumstances, where the psychologist has a reasonable basis to believe that a patient can be committed to a hospital pursuant to chapter one hundred and twenty-three, he shall have a duty to seek said commitment. The psychologist may also contact members of the patient's family or other individuals if in the psychologist's opinion, it would assist in protecting the safety of the patient; or

(2) the patient has communicated to the psychologist an explicit threat to kill or inflict serious bodily injury upon a reasonably identified person and the patient has the apparent intent and ability to carry out the threat. In such circumstances the psychologist shall have a duty to take reasonable precautions. A psychologist shall be deemed to have taken reasonable precautions if said psychologist makes reasonable efforts to take one or more of the following actions:

(a) communicates a threat of death or serious bodily injury to a reasonably identified person;

(b) notifies an appropriate law enforcement agency in the vicinity where the patient or any potential victim resides;

(c) arranges for the patient to be hospitalized voluntarily;

(d) takes appropriate steps to initiate proceedings for involuntary hospitalization pursuant to law.

(3) the patient has a history of physical violence which is known to the psychologist and the psychologist has a reasonable basis to believe that there is a clear and present danger that the patient will attempt to kill or inflict serious bodily injury upon a reasonably identified person. In such circumstances the psychologist shall have a duty to take reasonable precautions. A psychologist shall be deemed to have taken reasonable precautions if said psychologist makes reasonable efforts to take one or more of the following actions:

(a) communicates a threat of death or serious bodily injury to the reasonably identified person;

(b) notifies an appropriate law enforcement agency in the vicinity where the patient or any potential victim resides;

(c) arranges for his patient to be hospitalized voluntarily;

(d) takes appropriate steps to initiate proceedings for involuntary hospitalization pursuant to law.

(4) nothing contained herein shall require a psychologist to take any action which, in the exercise of reasonable professional judgment, would endanger himself or increase the danger to a potential victim or victims.

(5) the psychologist shall only disclose that information which is essential in order to protect the rights and safety of others.

(d) in order to collect amounts owed by the patient for professional services rendered by the psychologist or his employees; provided, however, that the psychologist may only disclose the nature of services provided, the dates of services, the amount due for services and other relevant financial information; provided, further, that if the patient raises as a defense to said action substantive assertions concerning the competence of the psychologist or the quality of the services provided, the psychologist may disclose whatever information is necessary to rebut such assertions; or

(e) in such other situations as shall be defined in the rules and regulations of the board.

No provision of this section shall be construed to prevent a nonprofit hospital service or medical service corporation from inspecting and copying, in the ordinary course of determining eligibility for or entitlement to benefits, any and all records relating to diagnosis, treatment or other services provided to any person, including a minor or incompetent, for which coverage, benefit or reimbursement is claimed, so long as the policy or certificate under which the claim is made provides that such access to such records is permitted. No provision of this section shall be construed to prevent access to any such records in connection with any coordination of benefits, subrogation, workers' compensation, peer review, utilization review or benefit management procedures applied and implemented in good faith.

§ 135. Definitions applicable to Secs. 135 to 135B

As used in this section and sections one hundred and thirty-five A and one hundred and thirty-five B the following words shall have the following meanings, unless the context clearly indicates otherwise:—

"Client", a person with whom a social worker has established a social worker-client relationship.

"Communications", includes conversations, correspondence, actions and occurrences regardless of the client's awareness of such conversations, correspondence, actions and occurrences and any records, memoranda or notes of the foregoing.

"Reasonable precautions", reasonable efforts to take one or more of the following actions as would be taken by a reasonably prudent social worker under the same or similar circumstances:

(a) communicates a threat of death or serious bodily injury to any reasonably identified victim or victims;

(b) notifies an appropriate law enforcement agency in the vicinity where the client or any potential victim resides;

(c) arranges for the client to be hospitalized voluntarily; or

(d) takes appropriate steps, within the legal scope of social work practice, to initiate proceedings for involuntary hospitalization.

§ 135A. Social workers; confidential communications; exceptions

All communications between a social worker licensed pursuant to the provisions of section one hundred and thirty-two or a social worker employed in a state, county or municipal governmental agency, and a client are confidential. During the initial phase of the professional relationship, such social worker shall inform the client of such confidential communications and the limitations thereto as set forth in this section and section one hundred and thirty-five B, in accordance with sound professional practice.

No such social worker, colleague, agent or employee of any social worker, whether professional, clerical, academic or therapeutic, shall disclose any information acquired or revealed in the course of or in connection with the performance of the social worker's professional services, including the fact, circumstances, findings or records of such services, except under the following circumstances:

(a) pursuant to the provisions of this section and section one hundred and thirty-five B or any other law;

(b) upon express, written consent of such client or, in the event of a client incompetent to consent, of a guardian appointed to act in the client's behalf;

(c) upon the need to disclose that information which is necessary to protect the safety of the client or others if

(1) the client presents a clear and present danger to himself and refuses explicitly to voluntarily accept further appropriate treatment. In such circumstances, where the social worker has a reasonable basis to believe that a client can be committed to a hospital pursuant to section twelve of chapter one hundred and twenty-three, the social worker shall take appropriate steps within the legal scope of social work practice, to initiate proceedings for involuntary hospitalization. The social worker may also contact members of the client's family or other individuals if in the social worker's opinion, it would assist in protecting the safety of the client;

(2) the client has communicated to the social worker an explicit threat to kill or inflict serious bodily injury upon a reasonably identified victim or victims and the client has the apparent intent and ability to carry out the threat or has a history of physical violence which is known to the social worker and the social worker has a reasonable basis to believe that there is a clear and present danger that the client will attempt to kill or inflict serious bodily injury against a reasonably identified victim or victims. In either of such circumstances, any duty owed by a social worker to warn or in any other way protect a potential victim or victims shall be discharged if the social worker takes reasonable precautions. No cause of action shall lie against, nor shall legal liability be imposed against, a social worker for failure to warn or in any other way protect a potential victim or victims, unless the social worker fails to take such reasonable precautions. Nothing in this paragraph shall require a social worker to take any actions which, in the exercise of reasonable professional judgment, would endanger such social worker or increase the danger to a potential victim or victims;

(d) in order to collect amounts owed by the client for professional services rendered by the social worker or his employees; provided, however, that the social worker may disclose only the nature of services provided, the dates of services, the amount due for services and other relevant financial information; and, provided, further, that if the client raises as a defense to said action substantive assertions concerning the competence of the social worker or the quality of the services provided, the social worker may disclose whatever information is necessary to rebut such assertions;

(e) to initiate a proceeding under paragraph C of section twenty-three or section twenty-four of chapter one hundred and nineteen, or section three of chapter two hundred and ten or to give testimony in connection therewith;

[There is no clause (f).]

(g) where the social worker has acquired the information while acting as an elder protective services worker for a designated protective services agency as defined in section fourteen of chapter nineteen A and has acquired the information while conducting an assessment in accordance with section eighteen of said chapter nineteen A;

(h) where the social worker has acquired the information while conducting an investigation pursuant to subsections (b) and (c) of section four or section five of chapter nineteen C;

(i) in the case of marital therapy, family therapy or consultation in contemplation of such therapy, with the written consent of each adult patient participant.

The provision of information acquired by a social worker from a client to any insurance company, nonprofit hospital service corporation, medical service corporation or health maintenance organization or to a board established pursuant to section twelve of chapter one hundred and twenty-six B, pertaining to the administration or provision of benefits, including utilization review or peer review, provided for expenses arising from the out-patient diagnosis or treatment or both, of mental or nervous conditions, shall not constitute a waiver or breach of any right to which said client is otherwise entitled under this section.

No provision of this section shall be construed to prevent a nonprofit hospital service or medical service corporation from inspecting and copying, in the ordinary course of determining eligibility for or entitlement to benefits, any and all records relating to diagnosis, treatment or other services provided to any person, including a minor or incompetent, for which coverage, benefit or reimbursement is claimed, so long as the policy or certificate under which the claim is made provides that such access to such records is permitted. No provision of this section shall be construed to prevent access to any such records in connection with any coordination of benefits, subrogation, workers' compensation, peer review, utilization review or benefit management procedures applied and implemented in good faith.

§ 135B. Social workers; confidential communications; testimonial privilege

Except as hereinafter provided, in any court proceeding and in any proceeding preliminary thereto and in legislative and administrative proceedings, a client shall have the privilege of refusing to disclose and of preventing a witness from disclosing, any communication, wherever made, between said client and a social worker licensed pursuant to the provisions of section one hundred and thirty-two of chapter one hundred and twelve, or a social worker employed in a state, county or municipal governmental agency, relative to the diagnosis or treatment of the client's mental or emotional condition.

If a client is incompetent to exercise or waive such privilege, a guardian shall be appointed to act in the client's behalf under this section. A previously appointed guardian shall be authorized to so act.

Upon the exercise of the privilege granted by this section, the judge or presiding officer shall instruct the jury that no adverse inference may be drawn therefrom.

The privilege granted hereunder shall not apply to any of the following communications:

(a) If a social worker, in the course of making a diagnosis or treating the client, determines that the client is in need of treatment in a hospital for mental or emotional illness or that there is a threat of eminently dangerous activity by the client against himself or another person, and on the basis of such determination discloses such communication either for the purpose of placing or retaining the client in such hospital; provided, however, that the provisions of this section shall continue in effect after the client is in said hospital, or placing the client under arrest or under the supervision of law enforcement authorities;

(b) If a judge finds that the client, after having been informed that the communications would not be privileged, has made communications to a social worker in the course of a psychiatric examination ordered by the court; provided, however, that such communications shall be admissible only on issues involving the client's mental or emotional condition but not as a confession or admission of guilt;

(c) In any proceeding, except one involving child custody, adoption or adoption consent, in which the client introduces his mental or emotional condition as an element of his claim or defense, and the judge or presiding officer finds that it is more important to the interests of justice that the communication be disclosed than that the relationship between the client and the social worker be protected;

(d) In any proceeding after the death of a client in which his mental or emotional condition is introduced by any party claiming or defending through or as a beneficiary of the client as an element of the claim or defense, and the judge or presiding officer finds that it is more important to the interests of justice that the communication be disclosed than that the relationship between client and social worker be protected;

(e) In the initiation of proceedings under paragraph C of section twenty-three or under section twenty-four of chapter one hundred and nineteen, or section three of chapter two hundred and ten or to give testimony in connection therewith;

(f) In any proceeding whereby the social worker has acquired the information while conducting an investigation pursuant to section fifty-one B of chapter one hundred and nineteen;

(g) In any other case involving child custody, adoption or the dispensing with the need for consent to adoption in which, upon a hearing in chambers, the judge, in the exercise of his discretion, determines that the social worker has evidence bearing significantly on the client's ability to provide suitable care or custody, and that it is more important to the welfare of the child that the communication be disclosed than that the relationship between client and social worker be protected; provided, however, that in such case of adoption or the dispensing with the need for consent to adoption, a judge shall determine that the client has been informed that such communication would not be privileged; or

(h) In any proceeding brought by the client against the social worker and in any malpractice, criminal or license revocation proceeding in which disclosure is necessary or relevant to the claim or defense of the social worker.

§ 163. Registration of allied mental health and human services professionals; definitions applicable to Secs. 163 to 172

As used in sections one hundred and sixty-three to one hundred and seventy-two, inclusive, the following words shall, unless the context clearly requires otherwise, have the following meanings:

"Allied mental health and human services professional", a licensed marriage and family therapist, a licensed rehabilitation counselor, a licensed educational psychologist or a licensed mental health counselor.

"Licensed marriage and family therapist", a person licensed or eligible for licensure under section one hundred and sixty-five.

"Practice of marriage and family therapy", the rendering of professional services to individuals, family groups, couples or organizations, either public or private for compensation, monetary or otherwise. Said professional services shall include applying principles, methods and therapeutic techniques for the purpose of reasoning emotional conflicts, modifying perceptions and behavior, enhancing communications and understanding among all family members and the prevention of family and individual crisis. Individual marriage and family therapists may also engage in psychotherapy of a nonmedical nature with appropriate referrals to psychiatric resources and research and teaching in the overall field of human development and interpersonal relationships.

"Licensed rehabilitation counselor", a person licensed or eligible for licensure under Section one hundred and sixty-five.

"Practice of rehabilitation counseling", the rendering of professional services for compensation, monetary or otherwise. These professional services would include the application of principles, methods and techniques of the rehabilitation counseling profession such as client assessment, job analysis, vocational assessment, counseling and job development for the purpose of maximizing or restoring the capacities of physically or mentally handicapped individuals for self-sufficiency and independent living including vocational and social functioning and creating those conditions favorable to this goal. The practice of rehabilitation counseling involves the following objectives: assisting individuals in the coordination of appropriate services; counseling with individuals, families or groups; serving an advocacy role with communities or groups toward the provision or implementation of rehabilitation services; research and teaching in the field of rehabilitation counselor education.

"Licensed mental health counselor", a person licensed or eligible for licensure under section one hundred and sixty-five.

"Practice of mental health counseling", the rendering of professional services to individuals, families or groups for compensation, monetary or otherwise. These professional services include: applying the principles, methods and theories of counseling, human development, learning theory, group and family dynamics, the etiology of mental illness and dysfunctional behavior and psychotherapeutic techniques to define goals and develop treatment plans aimed toward the prevention, treatment and resolution of mental and emotional dysfunction and intra or interpersonal disorders in all persons irrespective of diagnosis. The practice of mental health counseling shall include, but not be limited to, diagnosis and treatment, counseling and psychotherapy, of a nonmedical nature of mental and emotional disorders and the psychoeducational techniques aimed at prevention of such disorders and consultations to individuals, couples, families, groups, organizations and communities.

Practice of mental health counseling in independent practice with individuals diagnosed with psychosis may be undertaken by a licensed mental health counselor: (a) who is licensed under section 165 on or after March 1, 1992; or (b) who was licensed prior to March 1, 1992 and who meets the certification criteria for independent practice with individuals diagnosed with psychosis as established by the board of registration of allied mental health and human services professions.

"Licensed educational psychologist", a person licensed or eligible for licensure under Section one hundred and sixty-five of this chapter and who has been certified as a school psychologist by the Massachusetts department of education; provided, however, that an educational psychologist shall not perform in private practice any of the services for which he is licensed for any student in a school system by which such educational psychologist is employed and provided, further, that an educational psychologist who violates this provision shall have his license suspended for a period to be determined by the board pursuant to the provisions of section one hundred and sixty-nine.

"Practice of educational psychology", the rendering of professional services to individuals, groups, organizations or the public for compensation, monetary or otherwise.

Such professional services include: applying psychological principles, methods and procedures in the delivery of services to individuals, groups, families, educational institutions and staff and community agencies for the purpose of promoting mental health and facilitating learning. Such services may be preventative, developmental or remedial and include psychological and psychoeducational assessment, therapeutic intervention, program planning and evaluation, research, teaching in the field of educational psychology, consultation and referral to other psychiatric, psychological, medical and educational resources when necessary.

"Advertise", includes, but is not limited to, distributing or causing to be distributed any card, sign or device to any person; or the causing, permitting or allowing of any sign or marking on or in any building or structure, or in any newspaper or magazine or in any directory, or on radio or television, or by the use of any other means designed to secure public attention.

"Use a title or description of", means to hold oneself out to the public as having a particular status by means of statements on signs, mailboxes, address plates, stationery, announcement, calling cards or other instruments of professional identification.

"Board", the Massachusetts board of registration of allied mental health and human services professions.

"Recognized educational institution", any educational institution which grants a bachelor's, master's, or doctor's degree and which is recognized by the board, or by a nationally or regionally recognized educational or professional accrediting organization; provided, however, that such institution is also approved by the United States Department of Education.

"Approved Continuing Education", continuing education such as research and training programs, college and university courses, in service training programs, seminars and conferences designed to maintain and enhance the skills of allied mental health and human services professionals and which are recognized by the board.

§ 172. Allied mental health and human services professionals; confidential communications; waiver

Any communication between an allied mental health or human services professional and a client shall be deemed to be confidential. Said privilege shall be subject to waiver only in the following circumstances:

(a) where the allied mental health and human services professional is a party defendant to a civil, criminal or disciplinary action arising from such practice in which case the waiver shall be limited to that action;

(b) where the client is a defendant in a criminal proceeding and the use of the privilege would violate the defendant's right to compulsory process and right to present testimony and witnesses in his own behalf,

(c) when the communication reveals the contemplation or commission of a crime or a harmful act; and

(d) where a client agrees to the waiver, or in circumstances where more than one person in a family is receiving therapy, where each such family member agrees to the waiver.

The provisions of this section shall not be construed to prevent third party reimburser from inspecting and copying, in the ordinary course of determining eligibility for or entitlement to benefits, any and all records relating to diagnosis, treatment or other services provided to any person, including a minor or incompetent, for which coverage, benefit or reimbursement is claimed, so long as the policy or certificate under which the claim is made provides that such access to such records is permitted. The provisions of this section shall not be construed to prevent access to any such records pursuant to any peer review or utilization review procedures applied and implemented in good faith.

§ 172A. Allied mental heatlh and human service professionals; privilege against disclosures in court, legislative or administrative proceedings; exercise or waiver of privilege by guardian; scope of privilege

[Added by 2007 Mass. Acts c. 142, effective Jan. 23, 2008.]

(a) Except as hereinafter provided, in a court proceeding, in a proceeding preliminary thereto or in a legislative or administrative proceeding, a client of a mental health counselor who is licensed pursuant to the provisions of section 165 or employed in a state, county or municipal government agency shall have the privilege of refusing to disclose and of preventing a witness from disclosing any communication relative to the diagnosis or treatment of the client's mental or emotional condition, wherever made, between the client and the mental health counselor.

(b) If a client is incompetent to exercise or waive the privilege, a guardian shall be appointed to act on the client's behalf under this section. A previously appointed guardian shall be authorized to so act. Upon the exercise of the privilege granted by this section, the judge or presiding officer shall instruct the jury that no adverse inference may be drawn therefrom.

(c) The privilege granted by this section shall not apply to the following communications:

(1) if a mental health counselor, in the course of his diagnosis or treatment of the client, determines that the client is in need of treatment in a hospital for mental or emotional illness or that there is a threat of imminently dangerous activity by the patient against himself or another person and, on the basis of that determination, discloses the communication either for the purpose of placing or retaining the client in the hospital; but, this section shall continue in effect after the patient is in the hospital or placed under arrest or under the supervision of law enforcement authorities;

(2) if a judge finds that the client, after having been informed that a communication would not be privileged, has made a communication to a mental health counselor in the course of a psychiatric examination ordered by the court; but, the communication shall be admissible only on issues involving the patient's mental or emotional condition but not as a confession or admission of guilt;

(3) in a proceeding, except one involving child custody, in which the client introduces his mental or emotional condition as an element of his claim or defense and the judge or presiding officer finds that it is more important to the interests of justice that the communication be disclosed than that the relationship between client and mental health counselor be protected;

(4) in a proceeding after the death of a client in which his mental or emotional condition is introduced by any party claiming or defending through or as beneficiary of the patient as an element of the claim or the defense and the judge or presiding officer finds that it is more important to the interests of justice that the communication be disclosed than that the relationship between client and mental health counselor be protected;

(5) in the initiation of proceedings under paragraph C of section 23 of chapter 119 or under section 24 of said chapter 119 or section 3 of chapter 210 or to give testimony in connection therewith;

(6) in a proceeding whereby the mental health counselor has acquired the information while conducting an investigation pursuant to section 51B of chapter 119;

(7) in a case involving child custody, adoption or the dispensing with the need for consent to adoption where, upon hearing in chambers, the judge exercises his discretion to determine that the mental health counselor has evidence bearing significantly on the client's ability to provide suitable care or custody and it is more important to the welfare of the child that the communication be disclosed than that the relationship between the client and the mental health counselor be protected; but, in the case of adoption or the dispensing with the need for consent to adoption, a judge shall determine that the client has been informed that the communication should not be privileged; or

(8) if in a proceeding brought by the client against the mental health counselor, and in any malpractice, criminal or license revocation proceeding, in which disclosure is necessary or relevant to the claim or defense of the mental health counselor.

Chapter 119. Protection and Care of Children and Proceedings Against Them

§ 1. Declaration of policy; purpose

[Amended by 2008 Mass. Acts c. 176, § 82, effective July 8, 2008.]

It is hereby declared to be the policy of this commonwealth to direct its efforts, first, to the strengthening and encouragement of family life for the care and protection of children; to assist and encourage the use by any family of all available resources to this end; and to provide substitute care of children only when the family itself or the resources available to the family are unable to provide the necessary care and protection to insure the rights of any child to sound health and normal physical, mental, spiritual and moral development.

The purpose of this chapter is to insure that the children of the commonwealth are protected against the harmful effects resulting from the absence, inability, inadequacy or destructive behavior of parents or parent substitutes, and to assure good substitute parental care in the event of the absence, temporary or permanent inability or unfitness of parents to provide care and protection for their children.

The health and safety of the child shall be of paramount concern and shall include the long-term well-being of the child.

1

In all matters and decisions by the department of children and families, the policy of the department, as applied to children in its care and protection or children who receive its services, shall be to define best interests of the child as that which shall include, but not be limited to, considerations of precipitating factors and previous conditions leading to any decisions made in proceedings related to the past, current and future status of the child, the current state of the factors and conditions together with an assessment of the likelihood of their amelioration or elimination; the child's fitness, readiness, abilities and developmental levels; the particulars of the service plan designed to meet the needs of the child within the child's current placement whether with the child's family or in a substitute care placement and whether such service plan is used by the department or presented to the courts with written documentation; and the effectiveness, suitability and adequacy of the services provided and of placement decisions, including the progress of the child or children therein. The department's considerations of appropriate services and placement decisions shall be made in a timely manner in order to facilitate permanency planning for the child.

In all department proceedings that affect the child's past, current and future placements and status, when determining the best interests of the child, there shall be a presumption of competency that a child who has attained the age of 12 is able to offer statements on the child's own behalf and shall be provided with timely opportunities and access to offer such statements, which shall be considered by the department if the child is capable and willing. In all matters relative to the care and protection of a child, the ability, fitness and capacity of the child shall be considered in all department proceedings.

For purposes of this section, the words "all department proceedings" shall include departmental hearings and proceedings but shall not include a court proceeding even when the department is a party.

§§ 2–20. Repealed

[Repealed by 1972 Mass. Acts c. 785, § 6.]

§ 21. Definitions applicable to Secs. 21 to 51H

[Amended by 2008 Mass. Acts c. 176, § 83, effective July 8, 2008: 2008 Mass. Acts c. 215, §§ 63–64A, 90 effective July 8, 2008; 2010 Mass. Acts c. 359, § 18, effective Jan. 3, 2011; 2011 Mass. Acts c. 178, §§ 6–8, effective Nov. 21, 2011; 2012 Mass. Acts c. 240, effective Nov. 5, 2012; 2013 Mass. Acts c. 3, § 5B, effective Feb. 15, 2013; 2018 Mass. Acts c. 219, § 6, effective Nov. 7, 2018.]

As used in sections 21 to 51H, inclusive, the following words shall have the following meanings, unless the context clearly otherwise requires:

"51A report", a report filed with the department under section 51A that details suspected child abuse or neglect.

"Advocate", an employee of a governmental or nongovernmental organization or entity providing appropriate services, or a similar employee of the department of children and families who has been trained to work and advocate for the needs of sexually exploited children.

"Appropriate services", the assessment, planning and care provided by a state agency or nongovernmental organization or entity, through congregate care facilities, whether publicly or privately funded, emergency residential assessment services, family-based foster care or the community, including food, clothing, medical care, counseling and appropriate crisis intervention services, provided: (i) that such agency, organization or entity has expertise in providing services to sexually exploited children or children who are otherwise human trafficking victims; and (ii) that such services are provided in accordance with such regulations that the department of children and families may adopt or the policies of such department.

"Child", a person under the age of 18.

"Child advocate", the child advocate appointed under chapter 18C.

"Child requiring assistance", a child between the ages of 6 and 18 who: (i) repeatedly runs away from the home of the child's parent, legal guardian or custodian; (ii) repeatedly fails to obey the lawful and reasonable commands of the child's parent, legal guardian or custodian, thereby interfering with their ability to adequately care for and protect the child; (iii) repeatedly fails to obey the lawful and reasonable regulations of the child's school; (iv) is habitually truant; or (v) is a sexually exploited child.

"Commissioner", the commissioner of children and families.

"Custody", the power to: (1) determine a child's place of abode, medical care and education; (2) control visits to a child; and (3) consent to enlistments, marriages and other contracts otherwise requiring parental consent. If a parent or guardian objects to the carrying out of any power conferred by this paragraph, that parent or guardian may take application to the committing court and the court shall review and make an order on the matter.

"Department", the department of children and families.

"Family requiring assistance", a parent, guardian, custodian, sibling and any relative or caretaker responsible for a child requiring assistance.

"Habitually truant", a school-aged child, not excused from attendance under the lawful and reasonable regulations of such child's school, who willfully fails to attend school for more than 8 school days in a quarter.

"Mandated reporter", a person who is: (i) a physician, medical intern, hospital personnel engaged in the examination, care or treatment of persons, medical examiner, psychologist, emergency medical technician, dentist, nurse, chiropractor, podiatrist, optometrist, osteopath, allied mental health and human services professional licensed under section 165 of chapter 112, drug and alcoholism counselor, psychiatrist or clinical social worker; (ii) a public or private school teacher, educational administrator, guidance or family counselor, child care worker, person paid to care for or work with a child in any public or private facility, or home or program funded by the commonwealth or licensed under chapter 15D that provides child care or residential services to children or that provides the services of child care resource and referral agencies, voucher management agencies or family child care systems or child care food programs, licensor of the department of early education and care or school attendance officer; (iii) a probation officer, clerk-magistrate of a district court, parole officer, social worker, foster parent, firefighter, police officer or animal control officer; (iv) a priest, rabbi, clergy member, ordained or licensed minister, leader of any church or religious body, accredited Christian Science practitioner, person performing official duties on behalf of a church or religious body that are recognized as the duties of a priest, rabbi, clergy, ordained or licensed minister, leader of any church or religious body, accredited Christian Science practitioner, or person employed by a church or religious body to supervise, educate, coach, train or counsel a child on a regular basis; (v) in charge of a medical or other public or private institution, school or facility or that person's designated agent; or (vi) the child advocate.

"Parent", a mother or father, unless another relative has been designated as a parent as defined in section 1 of chapter 118 for the purposes of receiving benefits from the department of transitional assistance.

"Relative", the father or mother of a child; a stepfather, stepmother, stepbrother, stepsister, or any blood relative of a child, including those of the half blood, except cousins who are more distantly related than first cousins; any adoptive relative of equal propinquity to the foregoing; or a spouse of any such persons.

"Serious bodily injury", bodily injury which involves a substantial risk of death, extreme physical pain, protracted and obvious disfigurement or protracted loss or impairment of the function of a bodily member, organ or mental faculty.

"Sexually exploited child", any person under the age of 18 who has been subjected to sexual exploitation because such person: (1) is the victim of the crime of sexual servitude pursuant to section 50 of chapter 265 or is the victim of the crime of sex trafficking as defined in 22 United States Code 7105; (2) engages, agrees to engage or offers to engage in sexual conduct with another person in return for a fee, in violation of subsection (a) of section 53A of chapter 272, or in exchange for food, shelter, clothing, education or care; (3) is a victim of the crime, whether or not prosecuted, of inducing a minor into prostitution under by section 4A of chapter 272; or (4) engages in common night walking or common streetwalking under section 53 of chapter 272.

"Young adult", a person between the ages of 18 and 22.

§ 21A. Admissibility of evidence; qualified experts

[Added by 2008 Mass. Acts c. 176, § 83, effective July 8, 2008; amended by 2008 Mass. Acts c. 215, §§ 64B, 90, effective July 8, 2008.]

Evidence in proceedings under sections 21 to 51H, inclusive, shall be admissible according to the rules of the common law and the General Laws and may include reports to the court by any person who has made an investigation of the facts relating to the welfare of the child and is qualified as an expert according to the rules of the common law or by statute or is an agent of the department or of an approved charitable corporation or agency substantially engaged in the foster care or protection of children. Such person may file with the court in a proceeding under said sections 21 to 51H, inclusive, a full report of all facts obtained as a result of such investigation. The person reporting may be called as a witness by any party for examination as to the statements made in the report. Such examination shall be conducted as though it were on cross-examination. Evidence may include testimony of foster parents or pre-adoptive parents concerning the welfare of a child if such child has been in the care of the foster or pre-adoptive parents for 6 months or more, and may include the testimony of the child if the court determines that the child is competent and willing, after consultation with counsel, if any, to testify.

§ 22. Visitation of family foster homes; removal of child; discharge of child to parent or legal guardian

[Amended by 2008 Mass. Acts c. 176, § 83, effective July 8, 2008.]

An agent of the department shall visit each family foster home, not supervised and approved by a licensed placement agency, at least once a year and may be authorized by the department to remove a child to its care if, in its judgment, the welfare of the child or its protection from neglect or abuse so require. An agent who is refused entry or hindered in the removal of such child may make complaint, on oath, to a justice of the court having jurisdiction, who may thereupon issue a warrant authorizing the agent to obtain sufficient aid and, at any reasonable time, enter the building designated, and any part thereof, to investigate the treatment and condition of a child found there and to remove the child as herein provided. The department shall take the child temporarily into its care, immediately notify the child's parent or legal guardian and, upon request, discharge the child to a parent or legal guardian. If the parent or legal guardian is unable or refuses to make suitable provisions for the child, the department shall make lawful provisions for the child's care under section 23 or 24.

§ 23. Responsibility of department to provide foster care for children; placement with relatives; funeral expenses; child profile form; extension of support of child until 22 years of age; assignment of support rights; assistance to foster care families

[Amended by 2002 Mass. Acts c. 371, § 1; 2005 Mass. Acts c. 163, § 40; 2008 Mass. Acts c. 176, § 83, effective July 8, 2008; 2008 Mass. Acts c. 451, § 82, effective June 30, 2009; 2010 Mass. Acts c. 131, § 86, effective July 1, 2010; 2010 Mass. Acts c. 359, § 19, effective Jan. 3, 2011; 2017 Mass. Acts c. 110, § 15, effective Nov. 3, 2017.]

(a) The department shall have the responsibility, including financial responsibility, for providing foster care for children through its own resources or by use of appropriate voluntary agencies, according to the rules and regulations of the department, in the following instances:

(1) If a child, parent, guardian, or any person acting on behalf of a child, applies for foster care, the department may accept a child who, in the judgment of the department, is in need of foster care. Such acceptance shall entail no abrogation of parental rights or responsibilities, but the department may accept from parents a temporary delegation of certain rights and responsibilities necessary to provide the foster care for a period of time under conditions agreed upon by both and terminable by either. If the department determines that continued placement beyond 6 months is required for reasons unrelated to parental unfitness and the parent consents to continued placement, the department may file a petition for care and responsibility in the probate court on behalf of a child accepted into foster care. At the initial hearing on the petition, the court shall determine whether continued placement with the department is in the child's best interests and shall issue its determination, including its rationale, in written form. The allowance of the petition shall not abrogate a parent's right to make decisions on behalf of the child, but the department may accept from the parent a temporary delegation of certain rights and responsibilities necessary to continue to provide foster care for the child under conditions agreed upon by both and terminable by either. Notwithstanding any general or special law to the contrary, a permanency hearing shall be held within 60 days of the transfer of responsibility by order of the probate court or within 12 months of initial placement into foster care with the department, whichever date is later. The hearing shall be conducted as provided in section 29B.

(2) If a parent or parents apply for voluntary surrender of custody of a child for purposes of giving consent to adoption, the department may accept the child following the procedure described in clause (1).

(3) If a child is without proper guardianship due to death, unavailability, incapacity or unfitness of a parent or guardian or with the consent of a parent or parents, the department may seek, and shall accept, an order of the probate court granting responsibility for the child to the department. Such responsibility shall include the right to: (i) determine the child's abode, medical care and education; (ii) control visits to the child; (iii) consent to enlistments, marriages and other contracts requiring parental consent; and (iv) consent to adoption only when it is expressly included in an order of the court. In making an order, the probate court shall consider section 29C and shall make the written certification and determinations required by said section 29C. If a child is in the care of the department of mental health or the department of developmental services, the responsibility for the child as described in this section and all rights therein contained shall continue in the department. If a person with mental retardation who has been declared mentally incompetent was the responsibility of the department prior to reaching the age of 18, the department shall continue to exercise responsibility for that person until that person is declared to be no longer legally incompetent.

(4) The department shall accept on commitment from the juvenile court any child declared in need of foster care under section 26 or declared to be a child in need of services under section 39G.

(5) Any child who is left in any place and who is seemingly without a parent or legal guardian available shall be immediately reported to the department, which shall proceed to arrange care for that child temporarily and shall forthwith cause search to be made for that child's parent or guardian. If a parent or guardian cannot be located or is unable or refuses to make suitable provision for the child, the department shall make such lawful provision it deems in the best interest of that child as provided under this chapter.

(6) If the department has in its care a child whose parent or parents have consented to the child's adoption and the department has been unable to place that child in an adoptive home within 60 days of receipt of the consent, the department shall so notify all children's foster care agencies in the commonwealth licensed to place children for adoption. The notice shall request that each such agency attempt to find an adoptive home for such child. If 1 of the agencies locates an adoptive home for this child, the department shall cooperate with the agency in the placement of the child in this home and in the supervision of the placement during the 1 year waiting period. Any person in whose home a child has been placed by the department shall also be informed by the department if the child has become eligible for adoption, and this person may request consideration as a prospective adoptive parent.

(7) A temporary shelter care facility program or a group care facility, licensed under chapter 15D, may provide temporary shelter for a 72-hour period to a child without parental consent, if the child's welfare would be endangered if such shelter were not immediately provided. At the expiration of the 72-hour period, the licensee shall: (i) secure the consent of a parent or guardian to continued custody and care; (ii) refer the child to the department for custody and care; or (iii) refuse to provide continued care and custody to the child.

(b) The department shall develop guidelines and standards for the placement of children in foster care. The guidelines and standards shall be reviewed by the executive office of health and human services and the child advocate.

(c) Whenever the department places a child in foster care, the department shall immediately commence a search to locate any relative of the child, including the parents of siblings who have custody of the siblings, or other adult person who has played a significant positive role in that child's life in order to determine whether the child may appropriately be placed with that relative or person if, in the judgment of the department, that placement would be in the best interest of the child.

The department shall also seek to identify any minor sibling or half-sibling of the child and attempt to place these children in the same foster family if, in the judgment of the department, that placement would be in the best interests of the children.

(d) The department may pay to a funeral establishment a sum not to exceed $1,100 for the funeral and final disposition of a child in its care if there are insufficient resources to pay for the cost of such funeral and final disposition. The commonwealth shall have the right of reimbursement from whatever resources may exist in the estate of the child.

(e) If a child is placed in or transferred to a foster home, a completed child profile form shall precede or accompany the child to the foster home. In the case of an emergency placement, the department, the department of youth services, the department of mental health, other departments of the commonwealth responsible for the placement of foster children, or a placement agency shall immediately provide a brief verbal or written statement describing the child's outstanding problem behaviors and mental and emotional problems and shall provide the child profile form within 10 days to the foster parents.

The department shall develop a child profile form to be used by all other departments of the commonwealth or placement agencies that shall contain the child profile and any other relevant information necessary to the care, well-being, protection and parenting of the child by the foster parents, including, but not be limited to: (i) a history of the child's previous placements and reasons for placement changes; (ii) a history of the child's problem behaviors and mental and emotional problems; (iii) educational status and school related problem behaviors; and (iv) any other necessary psychological, educational, medical or health information.

The child profile form shall immediately be prepared by the department of the commonwealth which is granted care and custody of the child at the time such care and custody is granted.

(f) The department shall offer to continue its responsibility to any young adult who is under the custody, care, or responsibility of the department including, but not limited to, those persons who meet any of the criteria set forth in 42 USC § 675(8)(B)(iv): (i) for the purposes of specific educational or rehabilitative programs, or (ii) to promote and support that person in fully developing and fulfilling that person's potential to be a participating citizen of the commonwealth under conditions agreed upon by both the department and that person. The department's continued responsibility for such persons is contingent upon the express written consent of the person or their guardian unless: (i) before reaching the age of 18, the person had an intellectual disability and was declared mentally incompetent under clause (3) of subsection (a) while under the responsibility of the department; or (ii) the person is under the responsibility of the department pursuant to section 5-305 of chapter 190B. The purposes and conditions of such responsibility may be reviewed and revised or terminated by either the person or the department; provided, however, that within 90 days before the termination of such responsibility, the department shall provide the person with assistance and support in developing a transition plan which fulfills the requirements of 42 USC § 675(5)(H). If after termination the person requests that the department renew its responsibility therefor, the department shall make every reasonable attempt to provide a program of support which is acceptable to the person and which permits the department to renew its responsibility; provided, however, that the department may require the person to meet 1 of the criteria set forth in 42 USC § 675(8)(B)(iv). If the department renews its responsibility, all other provisions of this subsection shall apply. The department shall report annually to the child advocate, the senate and house chairs of the joint committee on children, families and persons with disabilities and the chairs of the senate and house committees on ways and means on the number of persons it serves and declines to serve under this subsection.

(g) The department shall obtain and provide to the IV-D agency, as set forth in chapter 119A, an assignment of support rights on behalf of each child receiving foster care maintenance payments under Title IV, Part E, of the Social Security Act. The department shall be subrogated to the rights of each such child and shall obtain and provide to the IV-D agency information that may be reasonably necessary to enforce the department's right including, but not limited to, the following information: the child's name, date of birth, place of birth, Social Security number, address and benefit level and, if known, each parent's name, date of birth, place of birth, Social Security number, most recent address and most recent employer. The department shall immediately notify the IV-D agency when a child whose rights to support are subrogated no longer receives foster care maintenance payments under said Title IV, Part E, of the Social Security Act.

(h) The department shall, subject to appropriation, provide assistance to foster care families which includes maintenance payments at the daily rate recommended and periodically adjusted by the United States Department of Agriculture. The department shall periodically review the level of assistance including maintenance payments provided to adoptive and guardianship families and may, subject to appropriation, and consistent with federal law and policy, adjust such assistance as warranted by the financial circumstances of the family, the needs of the child or the rate of inflation.

The department shall report annually on September 1, to the senate and house committees on ways and means and the joint committee on children, families and persons with disabilities on the amounts expended to provide to foster care, adoptive and guardianship families financial and other assistance including, but not limited to, payments to provide for the care of children.

(i) The department, in consultation with the executive office of public safety and security, shall work with the department of state police and municipal police departments to ensure that adequate efforts are being made to identify and to provide for the immediate protection, care and custody of the minor children of a person arrested or placed in custody by police officers in the performance of their official duties.

§ 23A. Children born to inmates of correctional institutions or jails; care and custody

Any child born to an inmate of the Massachusetts Correctional Institution, Framingham, or of the Industrial School for Girls at Lancaster, or of a jail or a house of correction, shall be accepted by the department, and any child whose mother is committed to the Massachusetts Correctional Institution, Framingham, to a jail or a house of correction, or to the custody of the youth service board, may be accepted by the department. Thereupon the department in consultation with the commissioner of correction or the chairman of the youth service board shall make such provision at said place of commitment or elsewhere for the care of said child as may seem to be for the best interests of said child.

§ 23B. Services to unwed mothers

The department may, through its own resources or the resources of other appropriate agencies, provide services to mothers bearing children out of wedlock.

§ 24. Procedure to commit child to custody or other disposition; notice and summons; emergency order transferring custody; investigation; abandoned children

[Amended by 2008 Mass. Acts c. 176, § 84, effective July 8, 2008 and 2008 Mass. Acts c. 215, §§ 64C, 90, effective July 8, 2008.]

A person may petition under oath the juvenile court alleging on behalf of a child within its jurisdiction that the child: (a) is without necessary and proper physical or educational care and discipline; (b) is growing up under conditions or circumstances damaging to the child's sound character development; (c) lacks proper attention of the parent, guardian with care and custody or custodian; or (d) has a parent, guardian or custodian who is unwilling, incompetent or unavailable to provide any such care, discipline or attention.

The court may issue a precept to bring the child before the court, and shall issue a notice to the department and summonses to both parents of the child to show cause why the child should not be committed to the custody of the department or why any other appropriate order should not be made. A petition under this section may be brought in the judicial district where the child is located or where the parent, guardian with care and custody or custodian is domiciled. The summonses shall include notice that the court may dispense with the right of the parents to notice of or consent to the adoption, custody or guardianship or any other disposition of the child named therein if it finds that the child is in need of care and protection and that the best interests of the child would be served by any such disposition. Notice shall be by personal service upon the parent. If the identity or whereabouts of a parent is unknown, the petitioner shall cause notice in a form prescribed by the court to be served upon such parent by publication once in each of 3 successive weeks in any newspaper as the court may order. If no parent can be found after reasonable search, a summons shall be issued to the child's legal guardian, if any, known to reside within the commonwealth and, if none, to the person with whom such child last resided, if known.

If the court is satisfied after the petitioner testifies under oath that there is reasonable cause to believe that: (i) the child is suffering from serious abuse or neglect or is in immediate danger of serious abuse or neglect; and (ii) that immediate removal of the child is necessary to protect the child from serious abuse or neglect, the court may issue an emergency order transferring custody of the child for up to 72 hours to the department or to a licensed child care agency or individual described in subclause (ii) of clause (2) of subsection (b) of section 26.

Upon entry of the order, notice to appear before the court shall be given to either parents, both parents, a guardian with care and custody or another custodian. At that time, the court shall determine whether temporary custody shall continue beyond 72 hours until a hearing on the merits of the petition for care and protection is concluded before the court. The court shall also consider the provisions of section 29C and shall make the written certification and determinations required by said section 29C.

Upon the issuance of the precept and order of notice, the court shall appoint a person qualified under section 21A to investigate the conditions affecting the child and to make a report under oath to the court, which shall be attached to the petition and be a part of the record.

If the child is alleged to be abandoned, as defined in section 3 of chapter 210, hearings on the petition under section 26 shall be expedited. If the parents or guardians consent, a child may be committed to the department under this section without a hearing or notice.

§ 25. Hearing; custody of child

[Amended by 2008 Mass. Acts c. 176, § 84, effective July 8, 2008.]

The petition under section 24 may be heard on the merits when a child is taken into custody and brought before the court or may be continued to a time fixed for hearing. Pending the hearing on the merits, the court may allow the child to be placed in the care of some suitable person or licensed agency providing foster care for children or may commit the child to the custody of the department. If the court commits a child to the custody of the department, the court shall consider the provisions of section 29C and shall make the written certification and determinations required by said section 29C.

§ 26. Procedure at hearing; order of commitment; petition to dispense with parental consent to adoption; reimbursement of commonwealth; petition for review

[Amended by 2008 Mass. Acts c. 176, § 84, effective July 8, 2008 and 2008 Mass. Acts c. 215, §§ 64D, 90, effective July 8, 2008.]

(a) If the child is identified by the court and it appears that the precept and summonses have been duly and legally served, that notice has been issued to the department and the report of the person qualified under section 21A is received, the court may excuse the child from the hearing and shall proceed to hear the evidence.

(b) If the court finds the allegations in the petition proved within the meaning of this chapter, it may adjudge that the child is in need of care and protection. In making such adjudication, the health and safety of the child shall be of paramount concern. If the child is adjudged to be in need of care and protection, the court may commit the child to the custody of the department until he becomes an adult or until, in the opinion of the department, the object of his commitment has been accomplished, whichever occurs first; and the court shall consider the provisions of section 29C and shall make the written certification and determinations required by said section 29C. The court also may make any other appropriate order, including conditions and limitations, about the care and custody of the child as may be in the child's best interest including, but not limited to, any 1 or more of the following:

(1) It may permit the child to remain with a parent, guardian or other custodian, and may require supervision as directed by the court for the care and protection of the child.

(2) It may transfer temporary or permanent legal custody to:

(i) any person, including the child's parent, who, after study by a probation officer or other person or agency designated by the court, is found by the court to be qualified to give care to the child;

(ii) any agency or other private organization licensed or otherwise authorized by law to receive and provide care for the child; or

(iii) the department of children and families.

(3) It may order appropriate physical care including medical or dental care.

(4) It may dispense with the need for consent of any person named in section 2 of chapter 210 to the adoption, custody, guardianship or other disposition of the child named therein.

In determining whether such an order should be made, the standards set forth in section 3 of said chapter 210 concerning an order to dispense with the need for consent to adoption of a child shall be applied. If the child who is the subject of the petition is under the age of 12, and if the court adjudicates the child to be in need of care and protection under this section, the court shall enter an order dispensing with the need for consent to adoption upon finding that the best interests of the child, as defined in paragraph (c) of said section 3 of said chapter 210, will be served thereby. The entry of such an order shall have the effect of terminating the rights of a person named therein to receive notice of or to consent to any legal proceeding affecting the custody, guardianship, adoption or other disposition of the child named therein.

The department shall file a petition or a motion to amend a petition to dispense with parental consent to adoption, custody, guardianship or other disposition of the child if: (i) the child has been abandoned; (ii) the parent has been convicted by a court of competent jurisdiction of the murder or voluntary manslaughter of another child of such parent, of aiding, abetting, attempting, conspiring or soliciting to commit such murder or voluntary manslaughter or of an assault constituting a felony which resulted in serious bodily injury to the child or to another child of such parent; or (iii) the child has been in foster care in the custody of the state for 15 of the immediately preceding 22 months. Under this paragraph, a child shall be considered to have entered foster care on the earlier of: (a) the date of the first judicial finding, under section 24 or this section, that the child has been subjected to abuse or neglect; or (b) the date that is 60 days after the date on which the child is removed from the home. The department shall concurrently identify, recruit, process and approve a qualified family for adoption.

The department need not file such a motion or petition to dispense with parental consent to the adoption, custody, guardianship or other disposition of the child if the child is being cared for by a relative or the department has documented in the case plan a compelling reason for determining that such a petition would not be in the best interests of the child or that the family of the child has not been provided, consistent with the time period in the case plan, such services as the department deems necessary for the safe return of the child to the child's home if reasonable efforts as set forth in section 29C are required to be made with respect to the child.

Notwithstanding the foregoing, the following circumstances shall constitute grounds for dispensing with the need for consent to adoption, custody, guardianship or other disposition of the child: (i) the child has been abandoned; or (ii) the parent has been convicted by a court of competent jurisdiction of the murder or voluntary manslaughter of another child of such parent, of aiding, abetting, attempting, conspiring or soliciting to commit such murder or voluntary manslaughter or of an assault constituting a felony which resulted in serious bodily injury to the child or to another child of the parent.

(5) The court may order the parents or parent of said child to reimburse the commonwealth or other agency for care in appropriate cases.

(c) On any petition filed in any court under this section, the department or the parents, person having legal custody, probation officer or guardian of a child or the counsel or guardian ad litem for a child may petition the court not more than once every 6 months for a review and redetermination of the current needs of such child whose case has come before the court, except that any person against whom a decree to dispense with consent to adoption has been entered under clause (4) of subsection (b) shall not have such right of petition for review and redetermination. Unless the court enters written findings setting forth specific extraordinary circumstances that require continued intervention by the court, the court shall enter a final order of adjudication and permanent disposition, not later than 15 months after the date the case was first filed in court. The date by which a final order of adjudication and permanent disposition shall be entered may be extended once for a period not to exceed 3 months and only if the court makes a written finding that the parent has made consistent and goal-oriented progress likely to lead to the child's return to the parent's care and custody. Findings in support of such final order of adjudication and permanent disposition shall be made in writing within a reasonable time of the court's order. The court shall not lose jurisdiction over the petition by reason of its failure to enter a final order and the findings in support thereof within the time set forth in this paragraph.

§ 26A. Registration of interest for foster care placement; criminal record review; fingerprint-based checks; grounds for rejection

[Amended by 2008 Mass. Acts c. 176, § 84, effective July 8, 2008; 2014 Mass. Acts c. 165, § 152, effective July 15, 2014; 2015 Mass. Acts c. 63, effective Aug. 5, 2015.]

(a) As part of the department's licensing and background record check process, the department shall conduct fingerprint-based checks of the state and national criminal history databases for all applicants filing a request to become adoptive or foster parents as authorized by 42 U.S.C. § 16962. All household members age 15 or older of any applicants filing a request to become adoptive or foster parents shall be subject to a fingerprint-based check of the state and national criminal history databases as authorized by Public Law 92-544. Only authorized department staff may receive the results of checks of state and national databases under said Public Law 92-544 and shall not further disseminate the results except as authorized under said Public Law 92-544. When the department obtains the results of checks of state and national criminal history databases, it shall treat the information according to sections 167 to 178, inclusive, of chapter 6 and the regulations thereunder regarding criminal offender record information.

(b) Fingerprints, as referenced in subsection (a), shall be submitted to the identification section of the department of state police for a state criminal history check and forwarded to the Federal Bureau of Investigation for a national criminal history check according to the policies and procedures established by the state identification section and by the department of criminal justice information services. Fingerprint submissions may be retained by the Federal Bureau of Investigation, the state identification section and the department of criminal justice information services to assist the department in its review of suitability for initial or continued approval of pre-adoptive or foster parents. Pursuant to 42 U.S.C. § 16962, the department of criminal justice information services may disseminate the results of a state and national criminal history check to authorized department of children and families staff to determine the suitability of adoptive and foster parent applicants. Pursuant to Public Law 92-544, the department of criminal justice information services may disseminate the results of a state and national criminal history check to authorized department of children and families staff to determine the suitability of the household members age 15 or older of adoptive and foster parent applicants. If the department of children and families receives information from a fingerprint-based check that does not include a final disposition or is otherwise incomplete, the department may request that an applicant provide additional information to assist the department in determining the suitability of the individual for approval.

(c) The department shall, subject to appropriation and the approval of the secretary of administration and finance, pay all fees required to operate and administer the fingerprint-based criminal background check system established in this section. The secretary of administration and finance, in consultation with the secretary of public safety and the commissioner, shall determine the appropriate fees necessary to offset the costs of the program. Any fees required for fingerprinting activity pursuant to this section shall be deposited into the Fingerprint-Based Background Check Trust Fund established by section 2HHHH of chapter 29.

(d) The department shall also obtain from the sex offender registry board all available sex offender registry information associated with the address of all persons filing a registration of interest for pre-adoptive or foster care placement and their household members age 15 or older.

(e) The department shall promulgate regulations requiring: (i) applicants filing a request to become adoptive or foster parents to be subject to a fingerprint-based check of the state and national criminal history databases pursuant to 42 U.S.C. § 16962; (ii) the household members age 15 or older of any applicants, to be subject to a fingerprint-based check of the state and national criminal history databases pursuant to Public Law 92-544; and (iii) applicants and their household members age 15 or older to be subject to a sexual offender registry information check pursuant to sections 178I and 178J of chapter 6. The regulations shall incorporate all fees associated with conducting fingerprint-based checks under said 42 U.S.C. § 16962 and said Public Law 92-544 as set by the department.

(f) If a record check pursuant to this section reveals a state felony conviction for: (1) assault and battery upon a child under section 13J of chapter 265; (2) assault with intent to rape under section 24 of chapter 265; (3) forcible rape of a child or assault with intent to rape a child under sections 22A, 22B, 22C, 23, or 24B of chapter 265; (4) rape and abuse of a child aggravated by age under section 23A of chapter 265; (5) rape and abuse of a child by previous offenders under section 23B of chapter 265; (6) posing or exhibiting a child under section 29A of chapter 272; (7) incest under section 17 of chapter 272; (8) indecent assault and battery under sections 13B, 13F or 13H of chapter 265; (9) inducing a minor into prostitution under section 4A of chapter 272; (10) murder under section 1 of chapter 265; (11) rape under section 22 of chapter 265; (12) unnatural acts with a child under 16 under section 35A of chapter 272; (13) enticement of a child under 18 to engage in prostitution under section 26D of chapter 265; or (14) human trafficking under sections 50 to 53, inclusive, of chapter 265 or similar conviction under the law of another state, the United States or a military, territorial or Native American tribal authority and a court of competent jurisdiction has determined that the felony was committed, the department shall reject the request for foster care placement, adoption or kinship care.

(g) If a record check pursuant to this section reveals a felony conviction under state, federal or a military, territorial or Native American tribal authority law for physical assault, battery or a drug-related offense and a court of competent jurisdiction has determined that the felony was committed in the past 5 years, the department shall reject the request for foster care placement, adoption or kinship care.

(h) If an applicant for foster care placement, adoption or kinship care was convicted for a crime other than those included in subsections (f) and (g), the department shall consider the following factors in making its decision whether to approve the request for foster care placement, adoption or kinship care: (1) the type of crime; (2) the number of crimes; (3) the nature of the offenses; (4) the age of the individual at the time of conviction; (5) the length of time that has elapsed since the last conviction; (6) the relationship of the crime and the capacity to care for children; (7) the current and future needs of the child to be placed and the probable effect that the misdemeanor would have on the applicant's ability to fulfill those needs; (8) the relationship between the individual and the child in question; (9) evidence of rehabilitation; and (10) opinions of community members concerning the individual in question. Prior to the approval of any such application, the department shall require screening and a written opinion by a mental health or criminal justice professional that the individual does not pose a risk of harm to the child.

§ 26B. Grandparents' and siblings' rights to visitation; appeal of decision to deny visitation

[Added by 2008 Mass. Acts c. 176, § 84, effective July 8, 2008.]

(a) Whenever a child is placed in family foster care, the court and the department shall ensure that a grandparent of a child who is in the department's care or is the subject of a petition under this chapter shall, upon that grandparent's request, have access to reasonable visitation and that the department establish a schedule for that visitation, unless it is determined by the court or the department that grandparent visitation is not in the child's best interests. In determining the best interests of the child, the court or the department shall consider the goal of the service plan and the relationship between the grandparent and the child's parents or legal guardian. Upon recommendation by the department or on its own accord, the court may establish reasonable conditions governing grandparent visitation, including requiring that the grandparent be restrained from revealing the whereabouts of the child's placement.

A grandparent of a child who is placed with the department voluntarily under clause (1) of subsection (a) of section 23 or placed in the custody of the department under an adoption surrender under section 2 of chapter 210, who is denied grandparent visitation by the department, may appeal through the department's fair hearing process. A grandparent may appeal the decision reached through the department's fair hearing process by filing a petition in the probate and family court for grandparent visitation. That grandparent shall have the right to court review by trial de novo.

A grandparent of a child who is the subject of a petition under this chapter and placed in the custody of the department may file a petition for visitation in the court which has committed the child to the custody of the department.

(b) The court or the department shall, whenever reasonable and practical and based upon a determination of the best interests of the child, ensure that children placed in foster care shall have access to and visitation with siblings in other foster or pre-adoptive homes or in the homes of parents or extended family members throughout the period of placement in the care and custody of the department, or after such placements, if the children or their siblings are separated through adoption or long-term or short-term placements in foster care.

The court or the department shall determine, at the time of the initial placements wherein children and their siblings are separated through placements in foster, pre-adoptive or adoptive care, that sibling visitation rights be implemented through a schedule of visitations or supervised visitations, to be arranged and monitored through the appropriate public or private agency, and with the participation of the foster, pre-adoptive or adoptive parents, or extended family members, and the child, if reasonable, and other parties who are relevant to the preservation of sibling relationships and visitation rights.

A child in foster care or sibling of a child placed voluntarily under clause (1) of subsection (a) of section 23 or under an adoption surrender under section 2 of chapter 210, who are denied visitation rights by the department, may appeal through the department's fair hearing process. The child or sibling may appeal the decision reached through the department's fair hearing process by filing a petition in the probate and family court for visitation. That child or sibling shall have the right to court review by trial de novo.

For children in the custody of the department pursuant to petition under this chapter, a child, sibling, parent, legal guardian or the department may file a petition for sibling visitation in the court committing the child to the custody of the department.

Periodic reviews shall evaluate the effectiveness and appropriateness of sibling visitations.

Any child over 12 years of age may request visitation with siblings who have been separated and placed in care or have been adopted in a foster or adoptive home other than where the child resides.

(c) A parent: (i) against whom a decree to dispense with consent to adoption has been entered under clause 4 of subsection (b) of section 26 or section 3 of chapter 210 or (ii) who has signed a voluntary adoption surrender under section 2 of chapter 210 shall not have the rights provided under this section as to the child who is the subject of that decree or surrender.

(d) A child, parent, guardian, grandparent or the department may appeal a decision or order of the trial court to the appeals court under this section if such person or the department is a party thereto. The claim of appeal shall be filed in the office of the clerk or register of the trial court within 30 days following the court's decision or order. Thereafter, the appeal shall be governed by the Massachusetts Rules of Appellate Procedure.

NOTE "Whether a court has jurisdiction in particular cases brought under G.L. c. 119, § 26B(b), [turns] on whether, by virtue of State intervention, siblings were placed in different homes and thereby separated from one another, and not on whether, at the time a child petitions for visitation, siblings are in particular types of custodial arrangements." *Care & Protection of Jamison*, 467 Mass. 269, 279 (2014) (holding that Juvenile Court has jurisdiction over sibling visitation where petitioning child is in custody of Department of Children and Families and siblings are wards subject to a guardianship established in the Probate and Family Court).

§ 26C. Summary of foster care providers' employment

[Added by 2008 Mass. Acts c. 176, § 84, effective July 8, 2008.]

The department shall provide all children's foster care agencies acting as agents of the department and that employ foster care providers, a summary of the record of any such foster care provider's employment as a foster care provider as compiled by the department. Said summary shall include names and contacts of all other agencies that employed such person as a foster care provider, the tenure of each such employment as a foster care provider, the reasons for ending each such employment, and any other information the department deems relevant and necessary to determine the employee's fitness to continue to be employed as a foster care provider. The department shall require any foster care agency that employs foster care providers and with which it contracts to supply the information included in such summary to the department and maintain this information in a database. The department shall consult the department of early education and care if necessary to facilitate the collection of this information.

§ 27. Appeals; procedure; notice of right of appeal; time limits

A child, parent, guardian or person appearing in behalf of such child, or the department, may appeal from the adjudication of the court and from any order of commitment made as a result of the adjudication under the provisions of section twenty-six to the appeals court. The trial justice entering the adjudication or order of commitment shall, prior to said adjudication, or within ten days thereafter, file detailed findings of fact and conclusions of law. Pending the appeal, the child may be committed to the custody of the department or placed in the care of some suitable person or licensed children's foster care agency. The district court or juvenile court where the order of adjudication was entered shall retain jurisdiction to and may enter any order for the needs of the child. The court shall notify the child, parent, guardian or person appearing in behalf of such child of the right of appeal at the time of adjudication and also at the time of commitment.

The claim of appeal under this section shall be filed in the office of the clerk of the said division of the district court department or the division of the juvenile court department within 30 days of the entry of the adjudication or order of commitment by the court. The completion of said appeal shall be governed by the Massachusetts rules of appellate procedure.

§ 28. Orders for payment of support; who may bring action; expiration of order or judgment

[Amended by 2008 Mass. Acts c. 176, § 85, effective July 8, 2008; 2011 Mass. Acts c. 93, § 18, effective July 1, 2012; 2019 Mass. Acts c. 34, § 5, effective July 8, 2019.]

(a) During the pendency of an action brought pursuant to section 24, temporary orders providing for the support of a child may be entered. The court may thereafter enter a judgment against the party chargeable with support. Any order of support entered under this section shall conform to and be enforced under section 12 of chapter 119A.

(b) Actions under this section to establish support of a child may be commenced by a parent, whether a minor or not; by the child; by the child's guardian, next of kin or other person standing in a parental relationship to the child; by the authorized agent of the department of children and families or any agency licensed under chapter 15D if the child is in its custody or is or was a recipient of any type of public assistance by the IV-D agency as set forth in chapter 119A on behalf of the department of transitional assistance, the department of children and families, the division of medical assistance, or any other public assistance program of the commonwealth. In the event that someone other than the IV-D agency commences the action, if the parent or child is or was a recipient of any type of public assistance, the court shall notify the IV-D agency of the pendency of the action and the IV-D agency shall be permitted to intervene in the action.

(c) An order, or judgment of support under this section, may be entered notwithstanding the default of the person chargeable with support or his failure to appear personally.

(d) In determining the amount of current support to be paid, the court shall apply the child support guidelines established by the chief justice of the trial court, or, in the absence of such standards, shall consider the factors set forth in section 32 of chapter 209.

(e) The person chargeable with support shall comply with this order, or judgment until it is dismissed or expires. When an action brought under section 24 is dismissed or a final order of commitment is entered, the order or judgment of support shall expire 6 months after the judgment of dismissal or final order of commitment. At the time of the dismissal or final order of commitment, the court shall notify the parties and the IV-D agency, as set forth in chapter 119A, of the expiration date of the support order or judgment.

§ 29. Counsel for child; appointment

[Amended by 2008 Mass. Acts c. 176, § 85, effective July 8, 2008; 2010 Mass. Acts c. 239, § 38; 2010 Mass. Acts c. 359, § 20, effective Jan. 3, 2011.]

The following persons shall have and shall be informed of the right to counsel, and the court shall appoint counsel for all such persons if the person is not able to retain counsel: (i) an adult who is under the responsibility of the department under clause (1) of subsection (a) of section 23; (ii) a child who is before the court under clauses (1) and (3) of said subsection (a) of said section 23, sections 24 to 27, inclusive, or section 29B; (iii) a child in a custody proceeding where the department or a licensed placement agency is a party; and (iv) any young adult to whom subsection (f) of section 23 applies.

Whenever the department or a licensed child placement agency is a party to child custody proceedings, the parent, guardian or custodian of the child, or a parent or guardian of an adult who is the responsibility of the department under clause (3) of subsection (a) of section 23: (i) shall have and be informed of the right to counsel at all such hearings, including proceedings under sections 5-201, 5-204 or 5-206 of chapter 190B, and that the court shall appoint counsel if the parent, guardian or custodian is financially unable to retain counsel; and (ii) shall have and be informed of the right to a service plan or case plan for the child and the child's family, or an adult who is the responsibility of the department under clause (3) of subsection (a) of section 23, which complies with applicable state and federal laws and regulations for these plans. Any young adult to whom subsection (f) of section 23 applies is also entitled to such service plan or case plan. The probate and family court and the juvenile court departments of the trial court shall establish procedures for: (i) notifying the parent, guardian or custodian of these rights; and (ii) appointing counsel for an indigent parent, guardian or custodian within 14 days of a licensed child placement agency filing or appearing as a party in any such action. The department or agency shall provide a copy of the service or case plan to the parent, guardian or custodian of the child or of an adult who is the responsibility of the department under clause (3) of subsection (a) of section 23, or to an adult who is the responsibility of the department under clause (3) of subsection (a) of section 23 or section 5-305 of chapter 190B, or any young adult to whom subsection (f) of section 23 applies and to the attorneys for all parties appearing in the proceeding within 45 days of the department or agency filing an appearance in such proceeding. Thereafter, any party may have the original or changed plan introduced as evidence, and with the consent of all parties the plan shall be filed with the court. Notwithstanding this section, the court may make such temporary orders as may be necessary to protect the adult who is under the responsibility of the department under clause (3) of subsection (a) of section 23 or the child and society.

The department, upon its request, shall be represented by the district attorney for the district in which the case is being heard.

§ 29A. Legal fees of minors in criminal proceedings; liability of parents

[Amended by 2003 Mass. Acts c. 26, § 168, effective July 1, 2003.]

The parents of an unemancipated minor shall be liable for such reasonable legal fees and expenses of an attorney representing the minor in criminal proceedings. Except where the parent is the alleged victim, the court shall determine whether the parent or guardian of an unemancipated minor is indigent. If the parent or guardian is not determined to be indigent, the court shall assess a $300 fee against the parent or guardian to pay for the cost of any attorney that is supplied by the committee for public counsel services or assigned to represent the minor by the court and paid out of public funds in the criminal proceedings. If the parent is determined to be indigent but is still able to contribute toward the payment of some of the costs, the court shall order the parent to pay a reasonable amount toward the cost of appointed counsel. This section shall not apply to a parent who, as a result of decree of a court of competent jurisdiction, does not have custody of the minor.

§ 29B. Determination of future status of committed children; orders; appeals

[Amended by 2008 Mass. Acts c. 4, §§ 1–2, effective Jan. 11, 2008; 2008 Mass. Acts c. 176, § 86; 2010 Mass. Acts c. 359, § 21, effective Jan. 3, 2011; 2011 Mass. Acts c. 93, § 19, effective July 1, 2012.]

(a) Except as provided in subsection (d), within 12 months of the original commitment, grant of custody or transfer of responsibility of a child to the department by a court of competent jurisdiction and not less than every 12 months thereafter while the child remains in the care of the department, the committing court shall conduct a permanency hearing, in accordance with rules established by the chief justice of the trial court, to determine and periodically review thereafter the permanency plan for the child. The plan shall address whether and, if applicable, when: (i) the child will be returned to the parent; (ii) the child will be placed for adoption and the steps the department will take to free the child for adoption; (iii) the child will be referred for legal guardianship; (iv) the child will be placed in permanent care with relatives; or (v) the child will be placed in another permanent planned living arrangement. The department shall file a permanency plan prior to a permanency hearing that shall address the above placement alternatives. The court shall consult with the child in an age-appropriate manner about the permanency plan developed for the child.

(b) The committing court shall continue to hold annual permanency hearings as described in subsection (a) for young adults to whom subsection (f) of section 23 applies. The young adult shall be entitled to counsel under section 29.

(c) If a child or a young adult is not to be returned to the child or young adult's parents, the permanency plan shall consider in-state and out-of-state placement options. In the case of a child placed in foster care outside the state in which the home of the parents of the child is located or a young adult in an out-of-state placement, the permanency plan shall also address whether the out-of-state placement continues to be appropriate and in the best interests of the child or young adult. In the case of a child who has attained age 16 or any young adult, the permanency plan shall also address the services needed to assist the child or young adult in making the transition from foster care to independent living; provided, however, that the court shall consult with the child or young adult in an age-appropriate manner about the permanency plan. If a person in the custody of or under the responsibility of the department has attained the age of 17 years and 9 months, the permanency plan shall also address the status of and the topics of the transition plan required under 42 USC § 675(5)(H); provided, however, that the court shall retain jurisdiction until it finds, after a hearing at which the person is present unless the person chooses otherwise, that a satisfactory transition plan has been provided for the person.

(d) In conducting a permanency hearing, the court may make any appropriate order as may be in the child or the young adult's best interests including, but not limited to, orders with respect to care or custody. At the same time, the court shall consider the provisions of section 29C, and shall make the written certification and determinations required by said section 29C. The health and safety of the child or young adult shall be of paramount, but not exclusive, concern.

The permanency hearing for a child or young adult shall be held within 30 days of a hearing at which a court determines that reasonable efforts to preserve and reunify families are not required pursuant to section 29C. The court may, however, make such determination at the time of the permanency hearing.

If continuation of reasonable efforts to return a child or young adult safely to the child or young adult's parent or guardian are found to be inconsistent with the permanency plan for the child or young adult or if reasonable efforts are not required pursuant to section 29C, or in the case of any young adult to whom subsection (f) of section 23 applies, the department shall make reasonable efforts to place the child or young adult in a timely manner in accordance with the permanency plan including, if appropriate, through an interstate placement, and to complete whatever steps are necessary to finalize the permanent placement of the child or young adult. In subsequent permanency hearings held on behalf of the child or young adult, the court shall determine whether the department has made such efforts in accordance with section 29C.

(e) A child, parent of a child, guardian, young adult, or the department may appeal to the appeals court from the determination or order of the trial court. The claim of appeal shall be filed in the office of the clerk or register of the trial court within 30 days following the court's determination or order. Thereafter, the appeal shall be governed by the Massachusetts Rules of Appellate Procedure.

1

The scope of appellate review shall be limited to abuse of judicial discretion.

§ 29C. Judicial certification of need to remove child from home

[Amended by 2002 Mass. Acts c. 371, § 2, effective Feb. 18, 2003; amended by 2008 Mass. Acts c. 176, § 87, effective July 8, 2008; 2010 Mass. Acts c. 359, § 22, effective Jan. 3, 2011.]

If a court of competent jurisdiction commits, grants custody or transfers responsibility for a child to the department or its agent, the court shall certify that the continuation of the child in his home is contrary to his best interests and shall determine whether the department or its agent, as appropriate, has made reasonable efforts prior to the placement of a child with the department to prevent or eliminate the need for removal from the home; but, if a child has been placed voluntarily with the department by the parent under clause (1) of subsection (a) of section 23 and the parent consents to continued placement under a petition filed under said clause (1) or clause (2) of said subsection (a) of said section 23, the court shall determine at an initial hearing only whether continued placement is in the child's best interests. Except as provided herein, if a court has previously committed, granted custody or transferred responsibility for a child to the department or its agent, the court shall determine not less than annually whether the department or its agent has made reasonable efforts to make it possible for the child to return safely to his parent or guardian. In making any determination, the health and safety of the child shall be of paramount concern.

If a young adult continues under the responsibility of the department pursuant to subsection (f) of section 23, the committing court shall continue to annually determine whether the department or the department's agent has made reasonable efforts to achieve the permanent plan approved by the court under section 29B.

Reasonable efforts by the department prior to removal of a child from the home or to return the child to a parent or guardian shall not be required if the court finds that: (i) the child has been abandoned as defined in section 3 of chapter 210; (ii) the parent's consent to adoption of a sibling of the child was dispensed with under section 26 or under said section 3 of said chapter 210, or the parent's rights were involuntarily terminated in a case involving a sibling of the child; (iii) the parent has been convicted of 1 of the following crimes by a court of competent jurisdiction: (a) murder or voluntary manslaughter of another child of the parent or aiding, abetting, attempting, conspiring or soliciting to commit such a murder or voluntary manslaughter; or (b) an assault constituting a felony which resulted in serious bodily injury to the child or another child of the parent; or (iv) a parent has subjected the child to aggravated circumstances consisting of murder of another parent of the child in the presence of the child or by subjecting the child or other children in the home to sexual abuse or exploitation or severe or repetitive conduct of a physically or emotionally abusive nature. For the purposes of this section, conduct of an "emotionally abusive nature" shall mean any conduct causing an impairment to or disorder of the intellectual or psychological capacity of a child as evidenced by observable and substantial reduction in the child's ability to function within a normal range of performance and behavior.

If a court has determined at a permanency hearing convened under section 29B, that reasonable efforts to safely return the child to his parent or guardian are inconsistent with the permanency plan for the child or if a court has determined that reasonable efforts are not required as set forth herein, the court shall determine at least annually thereafter whether the department has made reasonable efforts to place the child in a timely manner in accordance with the permanency plan determined and reviewed under section 29B.

The court shall make the certification and determinations required under this section in written form, which shall include the basis for the certification and determinations. A determination by the court that reasonable efforts were not made shall not preclude the court from making any appropriate order conducive to the child's best interest.

§ 29D. Notice of hearing

The department shall provide notice of hearings held under sections 26, 29B and 39G to a foster parent, pre-adoptive parent or relative providing care for the child who is the subject of the petition and shall inform the foster parent, pre-adoptive parent or relative of his right to attend the hearing and to be heard. Nothing in this provision shall be construed to provide that such foster parent, pre-adoptive parent or relative shall be made a party to the proceeding.

§§ 30–31. Repealed

[Repealed by 1961 Mass. Acts c. 396, § 5.]

§ 32. Placement of children in private families; early and periodic screening; diagnostic and treatment standards; individualized health care plan

[Amended by 2008 Mass. Acts c. 176, § 88, effective July 8, 2008.]

Children in the care or custody of the department shall be placed in private families; provided, that any child who upon examination is found to be in need of special care, treatment or education may, if it is found by the department to be in the best interest of the child, be placed in a public or private institution or school, the primary purpose of which is the special care, treatment or education of children. The reasons for the placement of any such child shall be entered in the records of the department.

The department shall insure that every foster child upon entry into the foster care system shall be screened and evaluated under the early and periodic screening, diagnostic and treatment standards established by Title XIX of the Social Security Act, unless the child has been screened and evaluated within 30 days prior to his entry into the system.

A medically needy child who is in foster care, whether specialized or other type of care as provided by the department or its agents, may not be placed in another foster home or other placement without an individualized health care plan that is unique to the child's health care needs; provided, however, that in an emergency due to abuse or neglect, the child may be removed without a plan. The plan shall include, but not be limited to: a description of the specific health care needs of the child and specific treatment and services necessary to meet those needs; identification of health care agencies or personnel or other professionals who may conduct transitional training on the child's health care needs for the subsequent foster parents or other placement or the family to whom the child will return. The department shall also provide to the subsequent foster parents or other placement or to the family to whom the child will return information on health care resources available and health care and other personnel whose services are required by the child.

§ 33. Placement of children in family home care

In placing a child in family home care, the department, or any private charitable or child-care agency, shall consider all factors relevant to the child's physical, mental and moral health.

§ 33B. Placement in family home care of juvenile who has or may have committed a sexual offense or arson

[Amended by 2011 Mass. Acts c. 68, § 91, effective July 1, 2011.]

At the time of placing a child in family home care, but in any event no later tha[n] five working days following such placement, the department or any other child-care agency shall determine whether the child has been adjudicated delinquent for a sexual offense or the commission of arson, or has admitted to such behavior, or is the subject of a documented or substantiated report of such behavior. If the department or other agency determines that the child has been so adjudicated, admitted, or found to have engaged in such behavior, it shall immediately refer the child to a qualified diagnostician for evaluation and assessment, including a risk management assessment of the child and a recommendation as to the type of appropriate and safe placement for the child. Such evaluation and assessment shall be completed within not more than ten working days from referral by the department or agency. No delay beyond the time periods in this section by the department shall in itself give rise to any claim of negligence or any other claim for damages. For the purposes of this section, a qualified diagnostician shall mean an individual who possesses specialized training and experience in the evaluation and treatment of sexually abusive youth or arsonists, as appropriate. Pending completion of such evaluation, the department or agency may place the child in an interim setting that is able to provide appropriate safety and security in light of the known risks posed by the child. Such risks shall be disclosed to the caretaker, including an interim safety plan to be implemented by the caretaker.

If the diagnostician recommends that the placement, including situations in which the child remains at home, should have adequate sex offender or arson specific risk management procedures, the department or agency responsible for placing the child shall prepare and implement a plan to address the safety of the child and other children in the home or residence, and to address the safety of the children in the immediate neighborhood. Such plan must include notification to all adults responsible for supervising the child in the home or residence of the child's behavioral history, including adjudications, if any, and education of all persons living in the home or residence about the known risks attendant to the child's behavior and methods of preventing such behavior, and provision for appropriate treatment for the child who is being placed. Where the department or agency makes a referral of such child to a foster home, residential facility, other agencies or organizations, or individuals for the purpose of receiving custodial services, the department or agency shall disclose the child's behavioral history, including adjudications, if any, to the designated recipient of the referral, prior to placement or at referral. All state agencies that use the assessment for safe and appropriate placement instrument shall: (i) consult with relevant experts to revise the instrument based on evidence-based practice; (ii) create a process for keeping the instrument current with evolving best practice standards; and (iii) ensure that all relevant staff are informed about the instrument and have appropriate training in how to make referrals and incorporate results from the instrument into their case management and treatment planning. The Massachusetts Adolescent Sex Offender Coalition and the Juvenile Firesetters Coalition shall provide training staff in partnership with the department on the revised and updated assessment for safe and appropriate placement instrument.

§ 34. Transportation of children in patrol wagons

A child involved in any proceeding shall not be transported in a patrol wagon from his home or from any other place to any court or institution, but if a conveyance is necessary shall convey him in such other suitable vehicle as shall be provided or designated by the department. Violation of this section shall be punished by a fine of not less than twenty-five nor more than fifty dollars or by imprisonment for not more than three months.

§ 35. Furnishing parent or guardian information as to child; permission to visit; petition; notice

If the parent or guardian of a child placed in charge of any person, association or public or private institution by any state department, town board, or by any public or private corporation or body of persons authorized by law to so place children, or if one of the next of kin of an orphan so placed in charge and without guardian, is not, upon request, informed by such department, board, corporation or body of persons where the child is, the probate court for the county where such child has his legal residence may, upon petition of such parent, guardian or next of kin, and upon notice, if in its opinion the welfare of the child and the public interest will not be injured thereby, require such department, board, corporation or body of persons to give the information and permit the parent, guardian or next of kin to visit the child at such times and under such conditions as the court orders; and the court may revise its order or make new orders or decrees as the welfare of the child and the public interest may require. No court shall make an order providing visitation rights to a parent who has been convicted of murder in the first degree of the other parent of the child who is the subject of the order, unless such child is of suitable age to signify his assent and assents to such order; provided, further, that until such order is issued, no person shall visit, with the child present, a parent who has been convicted of murder in the first degree of the other parent of the child without the consent of the child's custodian or legal guardian.

§ 36. Bringing child into commonwealth with view to adoption, custody or care; permit; application; bond

No person or institution shall bring or cause to be brought into the commonwealth, or receive therein, from any other state, province or country, any child for the purpose of placing or boarding, or of procuring the placing or boarding of such child, in a family or home within the commonwealth, with a view to adoption, guardianship, custody or care by any person other than one related to him by blood or marriage, without first obtaining a permit therefor from the department. Such a permit shall not issue until a written application therefor has been filed with the department on forms by it prepared, containing such information relative to such child as the department may require, accompanied by an individual or blanket bond running to the commonwealth in such penal sum and with such surety or sureties as the department may approve, conditioned on the following:— (1) that all statements contained in such an application are true in substantial particulars; (2) that any such child becoming a public charge during his minority shall be removed from the state not later than thirty days after notice from the department; (3) that such child shall be removed from the state immediately upon his release from any penal or reformatory institution or training school to which he has been committed, within three years of his arrival within the state, for juvenile delinquency or crime; (4) that such child shall be placed or boarded under such agreement as will secure to him a proper home and surroundings, and as will render his custodian responsible for his proper care, education and training, under adequate supervision and subject to annual visitation by an agent; and (5) that such reports relative to the child shall be made to the department as it may require. In case of a breach of any condition of such a bond, the attorney general, upon request of the department, shall put the bond in suit, and the commonwealth or any city or town thereof shall be reimbursed from the proceeds for any expense incurred by reason of a breach of any such condition. Violation of this section shall be punished by a fine of not more than one hundred dollars or by imprisonment for not more than six months, or both.

§ 37. Rules and regulations of department

The department shall make rules and regulations concerning the administration of its duties.

§ 38. Closed hearings; publication of names

[Amended by 2008 Mass. Acts c. 176, § 89, effective July 8, 2008.]

All hearings under sections 1 to 38A, inclusive, except those related to court orders to not resuscitate or to withdraw life-sustaining medical treatment for children in the custody of the department under a care and protection order, shall be closed to the general public. It shall be unlawful to publish the names of persons before the court in any closed hearing.

§ 38A. Petitions for order to not resuscitate or to withdraw life-sustaining treatment; required recommendations; appeals

[Added by 2008 Mass. Acts c. 176, § 89, effective July 8, 2008.]

In any proceedings related to court orders to not resuscitate or to withdraw life-sustaining medical treatment, the department or the party petitioning for the order shall require: (i) a written opinion from the child's treating physician, (ii) a written recommendation from the ethics committee of the hospital at which the child is a patient, and (iii) a written second opinion from a physician who is certified in the same medical specialty as the child's treating physician and who is not affiliated with the hospital at which the child is a patient. The department or the party petitioning for the order shall submit these documents to the court. The commissioner shall determine and make the department's recommendation to the court. The court shall also seek a recommendation from the child's parent or guardian. The court shall appoint a guardian ad litem to make a recommendation to the court on behalf of the child. Any appeal made under this section shall be an interlocutory appeal.

§ 39. Abandonment of infant under age of ten

Whoever abandons an infant under the age of ten within or without any building, or, being its parent, or being under a legal duty to care for it, and having made a contract for its board or maintenance, absconds or fails to perform such contract, and for four weeks after such absconding or breach of his contract, if of sufficient physical and mental ability, neglects to visit or remove such infant or notify the department of his inability to support such infant, shall be punished by imprisonment in a jail or house of correction for not more than two years; or, if the infant dies by reason of such abandonment, by imprisonment in a jail or house of correction for not more than two and one half years or in the state prison for not more than five years.

§ 39½. Placement of a newborn into foster care

[Added by 2004 Mass. Acts c. 227, § 1, effective Oct. 28, 2004. Amended by 2007 Mass. Acts c. 86, § 1, effective Nov. 4, 2007; 2008 Mass. Acts c. 176, §§ 90–91, effective July 8, 2008.]

Subject to appropriation, the department of children and families shall accept for placement into foster care any newborn infant 7 days of age or less that is voluntarily placed with a hospital, police department or manned fire station, hereinafter "designated facility" by a parent of said newborn infant. Such a voluntary placement under this section shall not constitute, in an of itself, an automatic termination of parental rights or an abrogation of the parental rights or responsibilities but shall, for purposes of authorizing the department to initiate a petition to terminate parental rights under chapter 210, be presumed to be an abandonment of the newborn infant that has been so placed.

Voluntary abandonment of a newborn infant 7 days of age or younger to an appropriate person at a hospital, police department or manned fire station shall not by itself constitute either a finding of abuse or neglect or a violation of any criminal statu[t]e for child abuse or neglect or for abandonment. If child abuse or neglect, that is not based solely on the newborn infant having been left in the hospital, police department or manned fire station is suspected, hospital, police or fire department personnel who are mandated reporters under section 51A shall report the abuse or neglect.

The designated facility receiving a newborn infant shall immediately notify the department of the placement of the newborn infant at the facility. Upon receipt of such notice, the department shall take immediate custody of the newborn infant and shall initiate all actions authorized by law to achieve the safety and permanent placement of the newborn infant in a manner that is consistent with the best interests of the child.

The person accepting a newborn infant at a designated facility shall make every effort to solicit the following information from the parent placing the newborn infant: (1) the name of the newborn infant; (2) the name and address of the parent placing the newborn infant; (3) the location of the newborn infant's birthplace; (4) information relative to the newborn infant's medical history and his or her biological family's medical history, if available; and (5) and any other information that might reasonably assist the department or the court in current or future determinations of the best interests of the child, including whether the parent or guardian plans on returning to seek future custody of the child. The person receiving the newborn infant shall encourage the parent to provide the information but the parent shall not be required to provide such information.

The department shall develop and implement a public information program to inform the general public of the provisions of this section, teen pregnancy prevention programs and adoption information. The department shall also work in conjunction with other departments and agencies of the commonwealth and the Massachusetts Hospital Association relative to development of the program. The program may include, but not be limited to, educational and informational materials in print, audio video, electronic and other media, public service announcements and advertisements and the establishment of a toll-free hotline.

For purposes of this section only, the following term shall be defined in the following manner unless the context shall clearly indicate a different meaning or intent:— "hospital", a hospital that is licensed under section 51 of chapter 111, or operated by the teaching hospital of the University of Massachusetts Medical School.

The department shall explore the possibility of expending funds received from the United States Department of Health and Human Services pursuant to the Promoting Safe and Stable Families Program, as most recently amended by the Promoting Safe and Stable Families of 2001, in order to implement the public information program required by this section and to alleviate the burden said information program may have on the department's appropriation from the commonwealth. When implementing its public information program, the department shall prioritize those areas of the commonwealth that have been identified by the department of public health as having the highest teen pregnancy rates.

The department of children and families, in conjunction with a designee of the juvenile court, the probate and family court, the center for adoption research at the University of Massachusetts, Massachusetts Families for Kids, Massachusetts Children's Trust Fund, Massachusetts Society for the Prevention of Cruelty to Children, Alliance on Teen Pregnancy and the department of early care and education, shall report every 2 years on the overall effectiveness of the program of voluntary placement of newborn infants established pursuant to this section. The report shall include, but not be limited to, the following: (1) an analysis of this section's effectiveness in decreasing the number of newborns that are abandoned in an unsafe manner in the commonwealth; (2) the department's success or failure in permanently placing in the adoption process any newborn placed with a designated facility pursuant to this section; (3) the average length of time that newborns remain in foster care after being so placed; (4) any issues arising from the termination of parental rights following the placement of a newborn pursuant to this section; (5) the success or failure of any public information campaign implemented by the department pursuant to this section; (6) any increased administrative burdens that may be placed upon any department or agency of the commonwealth as a result of this section; (7) issues with regard to the eligibility of any newborn infant placed pursuant to this section for federal entitlements such as foster care or adoption subsidies under Title IV-E of the United States Social Security Act or any other applicable federal law; and (8) the frequency or infrequency with which a parent placing a newborn at a designated facility supplies the facility with the information sought by the facility pursuant to the fourth paragraph of this section and any negative effects the lack of medical or background information on the child or parents may have had on facilitating the temporary or permanent placement of the child through the foster care or adoption process. The report, including any legislative recommendations, shall be submitted to the joint committee on children, families and persons with disabilities and the house and senate committees on ways and means on or before December 1, 2008 and not later than December 1 of each even numbered year thereafter.

§§ 39A–39C. Repealed

[Repealed by 1973 Mass. Acts c. 107, § 6.]

§ 39D. Visitation rights to certain grandparents of unmarried minor children

If the parents of an unmarried minor child are divorced, married but living apart, under a temporary order or judgment of separate support, or if either or both parents are deceased, or if said unmarried minor child was born out of wedlock whose paternity has been adjudicated by a court of competent jurisdiction or whose father has signed an acknowledgement of paternity, and the parents do not reside together, the grandparents of such minor child may be granted reasonable visitation rights to the minor child during his minority by the probate and family court department of the trial court upon a written finding that such visitation rights would be in the best interest of the said minor child; provided, however, that such adjudication of paternity or acknowledgment of paternity shall not be required in order to proceed under this section where maternal grandparents are seeking such visitation rights. No such visitation rights shall be granted if said minor child has been adopted by a person other than a stepparent of such child and any visitation rights granted pursuant to this section prior to such adoption of the said minor child shall be terminated upon such adoption without any further action of the court.

A petition for grandparents visitation authorized under this section shall, where applicable, be filed in the county within the commonwealth in which the divorce or separate support complaint or the complaint to establish paternity was filed. If the divorce, separate support or paternity judgment was entered without the commonwealth but the child presently resides within the commonwealth, said petition may be filed in the county where the child resides.

NOTE Grandparent visitation rights statute was not unconstitutional on due process or equal protection challenges as applied to a maternal grandparent of a child living in a disrupted family with the child's mother. *Blixt v. Blixt*, 437 Mass. 649 (2002).

CRA

§ 39E. Petitions seeking determination that child requires assistance; jurisdiction; standing

[Amended by 2008 Mass. Acts c. 176, § 92, effective July 8, 2008; 2012 Mass. Acts c. 240, §§ 5–12, effective Nov. 5, 2012.]

The divisions of the juvenile court department may receive and hear requests for assistance stating there is a child requiring assistance or a family requiring assistance as defined in section twenty-one, in accordance with the provisions of this section and of sections thirty-nine F to thirty-nine I, inclusive. Proceedings pursuant to sections thirty-nine E to thirty-nine I, inclusive, shall not be deemed criminal proceedings and any record of these proceedings, including the filing of an application for assistance and creation of a docket, shall not be entered in the criminal offender record information system. Notwithstanding any general or special law to the contrary, no record pertaining to the child involved in the proceedings shall be maintained or remain active after the application for assistance is dismissed. The identity and record of any child for which an application for assistance is filed shall not be submitted to the department of criminal justice information services, criminal offender record information system, court activity record index or any other criminal record information system. Proceedings under sections 39E to 39I, inclusive, shall be confidential and not open to the public. The jurisdiction of the Boston juvenile court for the subject matter of this section shall extend to the territorial limits of Suffolk county.

A parent, legal guardian, or custodian of a child having custody of such child, may initiate an application for assistance in one of said courts stating that said child repeatedly runs away from the home of said parent or guardian or repeatedly runs away from the home of said parent or guardian or persistently refuses to obey the lawful and reasonable commands of said parent or guardian resulting in said parent's or guardian's inability to adequately care for and protect said child.

A school district may initiate an application for assistance in said court stating that said child is not excused from attendance in accordance with the lawful and reasonable regulations of such child's school, has willfully failed to attend school for more than 8 school days in a quarter or repeatedly fails to obey the lawful and reasonable regulations of the child's school. The application for assistance shall also state whether or not the child and the child's family have participated in the truancy prevention program, if one is available, and a statement of the specific steps taken under the truancy prevention program to prevent the child's truancy; and if the application for assistance states that a child has repeatedly failed to obey the lawful and reasonable regulations of the school, a statement of the specific steps taken by the school to improve the child's conduct.

When an application for assistance is presented to the clerk for filing, the clerk shall inform the petitioner that the petitioner may delay filing the request and choose to have the child and the child's family referred to a family resource center, community-based services program or other entity designated by the secretary of health and human services to provide community-based services in the juvenile court district where the child resides and return to court at a later time to file an application for assistance, if needed. The clerk shall prepare, publish and disseminate to each petitioner educational material relative to available family resource centers, community-based services programs and other entities designated by the secretary of health and human services. If the petitioner is a parent, legal guardian or custodian the clerk shall provide to the petitioner informational materials, prepared by the court that explain the court process and shall include the types of orders that the court may issue and the possibility of changes in the custody of the child and may include an explanation of the services available through the court process, including language translation services and the manner in which those services are delivered.

Whenever an application for assistance is initiated, the clerk shall set a date for a hearing as soon as possible, but not later than 15 days after the request is presented to the clerk for filing, to determine whether assistance is needed, shall notify the child of such hearing and shall request the chief probation officer or a designee to conduct an immediate inquiry to determine whether in the officer's opinion the best interest of the child require that assistance be given. The court shall hold a hearing in which it shall receive the recommendation of the probation officer and shall either (i) decline to accept the application for assistance because there is no probable cause to believe that the child and family are in need of assistance; (ii) decline to accept the application for assistance because it finds that the interests of the child would best be served by informal assistance, in which case the court shall, with the consent of the child and the child's parents or guardian, refer the child to a probation officer for assistance; or (iii) accept the application for assistance and schedule a fact-finding hearing. If the child is brought in on custodial protection, the court shall accept an application for assistance unless one has already been filed, and the court shall immediately request the probation officer promptly to make like inquiry and thereafter report to the court the probation officer's recommendation as to whether the interests of the child can best be served by informal assistance without a fact-finding hearing. Upon receiving such recommendation, the court may hold a hearing and shall decide whether to proceed with a fact-finding hearing or to refer the child to the care of a probation officer for assistance.

When an application for assistance is dismissed under this section, the court shall enter an order directing expungement of any records of the request and related proceedings maintained by the clerk, the court, the department of criminal justice information services, the court activity record index and the probation department that directly pertain to the application for assistance.

Whenever a child is referred to a probation officer for assistance, such officer may: refer the child to an appropriate public or private organization or person for psychiatric, psychological, educational, occupational, medical, dental or social services; and may conduct conferences with the child and the child's family to effect adjustments or agreements which are calculated to resolve the situation which formed the basis of the application for assistance and which will eliminate the need for a fact finding hearing. During the pendency of such referrals or conferences, neither the child nor the child's parents may be compelled to appear at any conferences, produce any papers or visit any place. However, if the child or the child's parents fail to participate in good faith in the referrals or conferences arranged by the probation officer, the probation officer shall so certify in writing, and the clerk shall accept the application for assistance if one has not already been accepted and shall set a date for a fact finding hearing. The judge who conducted the hearing on the acceptance of the application for assistance shall not preside at any subsequent hearing. Conferences and referrals arranged under this section may extend for a period not to exceed 90 days from the date that the application for assistance was initially filed, unless the parent and child voluntarily agree in writing to a continuation of such conferences or referrals for an additional period not to exceed 90 days from the expiration of the original period. Upon the expiration of the initial 90 day period, or of such additional 90 day period, the application for assistance, if any, shall be dismissed and the child and his parents discharged from any further obligation to participate in such conferences and referrals, or an application for assistance shall, if not already accepted, be accepted and a date set for a fact-finding hearing. No statements made by a child or by any other person during the period of inquiries, conferences or referrals may be used against the child at any subsequent hearing to determine that the child requires assistance, but such statements may be received by the court after the fact finding hearing for the purpose of disposition.

The commissioner of probation shall establish a system to collect data on all requests for assistance made and how they are resolved under sections 39E to 39I, inclusive. Said system shall maintain the privacy of clients served, assist the court in addressing the needs of the population to be served and collect information related to: the racial and ethnic identity of the child; the insurance status and coverage of clients served; the length of time a child is receiving assistance from a probation officer, including the time prior to and subsequent to the filing of an application for assistance; the identity of any public or private organization to whom a probation officer has referred a child or family for services; and any other information that may assist the commissioner and the court in evaluating the availability and effectiveness of services for children who are the subjects of requests for assistance under this section. The probation officer shall gather information concerning each child and family referred to the officer including, but not limited to, insurance status and coverage and other information that may assist the commissioner of probation and the court in evaluating the availability and effectiveness of services for children who are the subjects of requests for assistance under this section.

Upon the filing of an application for assistance under this section, the court may issue a summons, to which a copy of the application for assistance shall be attached, requiring the child named in such application to appear before said court at the time set forth in the summons. If such child fails to obey the summons, said court may issue a warrant reciting the substance of the petition and requiring the officer to whom it is directed forthwith to take and bring such child before said court. Notice of the hearing shall be given to the department of children and families and the department of youth services.

Where the court summons such child, the court shall in addition issue a summons to both parents of the child, if both parents are known to reside in the commonwealth, or to one parent if only one is known to reside within the commonwealth, or, if there is no parent residing in the commonwealth, then to the parent having custody or to the lawful guardian of such child. Said summons shall require the person served to appear at a time and place stated therein at a hearing to determine whether or not such child is in need of assistance.

Unless service of the summons required by this section is waived in writing, such summons shall be served by the constable or police officer, either by delivering it personally to the person to whom addressed, or by leaving it with a person of proper age to receive the same, at the place of residence or business of such person, and said constable or police officer shall immediately make return to the court of the time and manner of service.

§ 39F. Right to counsel; determination of indigency; assessment of costs

[Amended by 2003 Mass. Acts c. 26, § 169; 2012 Mass. Acts c. 240, §§ 13–15, effective Nov. 5, 2012.]

When an application for assistance stating the a [sic] child and family are in need of assistance is initiated the child shall be informed that he has a right to counsel at all hearings, and if said child is not able to retain counsel, the court shall appoint counsel for said child. The clerk shall cause a copy of the application for assistance and notice of the time and place of the any scheduled hearing or proceeding to be delivered to counsel at the time of appointment. When the application for assistance is filed, each parent, legal guardian or custodian of the child shall be informed of the right to be heard in any proceeding under sections 39E to 39I, inclusive, involving the child and that a parent or legal guardian has the right to counsel at any hearing or proceeding regarding custody of such child. If said parent or legal guardian is indigent, the court shall appoint counsel for said parent or legal guardian. The court shall determine whether the parent or guardian of a child stated to require assistance is indigent. If the court determines that the parent or guardian is not indigent, the court shall assess a $300 fee against the parent or guardian to pay for the cost of appointed counsel. If the parent is determined to be indigent but is still able to contribute toward the payment of some of said costs, the court shall order the parent to pay a reasonable amount toward the cost of appointed counsel.

§ 39G. Hearing; determination of child requiring assistance

[Amended by 2008 Mass. Acts c. 176, § 93, effective July 8, 2008; 2012 Mass. Acts c. 240, §§ 16–23, effective Nov. 5, 2012.]

At any hearing to determine whether a child and family require assistance, said child and the child's attorney shall be present and the parent, legal guardian or custodian shall be given an opportunity to be heard. The petitioner and any party may file a motion to dismiss the request for assistance at any time prior to a hearing to determine the disposition of a request for assistance. The judge, upon a filing of a motion to dismiss, may order that the request for assistance be dismissed upon a showing that the dismissal is in the best interests of the child or if all parties agree to the dismissal. A probation officer may at any time recommend to the court that the request for assistance be dismissed upon a showing that dismissal is in the best interests of the child.

Upon making a finding that a child requires assistance after a fact finding hearing, the court shall convene and may participate in a conference of the probation officer who conducted the preliminary inquiry, a representative from a family resource center or other community-based services program, if involved with the family, the petitioner, a representative from the child's school, the child's parent, legal guardian or custodian, the child and the child's attorney, a representative of the department of children and families, if involved with the family, and any other person who may be helpful in determining the most effective assistance available to be offered to the child and family. The probation officer shall present written recommendations and other persons at the conference may present written recommendations to the court to advise the court on appropriate treatment and services for the child and family, appropriate placement for the child, and appropriate conditions and limitations of such placement.

At the conference and subsequent hearing on disposition, the child and the child's attorney shall be present and the parents, legal guardian or custodian, and the child and petitioner shall be given an opportunity to be heard. The court may receive evidence as to the best disposition from all persons who participate in the conference and any other person who may be helpful in determining an appropriate disposition.

If the court finds the statements in the application for assistance have been proved at the hearing beyond a reasonable doubt, it may determine the child to be in need of assistance. Upon making such determination, the court, taking into consideration the physical and emotional welfare of the child, may make any of the following orders of disposition:

(a) subject to any conditions and limitations the court may prescribe, including provision for medical, psychological, psychiatric, educational, occupational and social services, and for supervision by a court clinic or by any public or private organization providing counseling or guidance services, permit the child to remain with his parents, legal guardian or custodian;

(b) subject to such conditions and limitations as the court may prescribe, including, but no limited to provisions for those services described in clause (a), place the child in the care of any of the following:

(1) a relative, probation officer, or other adult individual who, after inquiry by the probation officer or other person or agency designated by the court, is found to be qualified to receive and care for the child; (2) a private charitable or childcare agency or other private organization, licensed or otherwise authorized by law to receive and provide care for such children; or (3) a private organization which, after inquiry by the probation officer or other person or agency designated by the court, is found to be qualified to receive and care for the child; or

(c) subject to the provisions of sections 32 and 33 and with such conditions and limitations as the court may recommend, place the child in the custody of the department of children and families. At the same time, the court shall consider the provisions of section 29C and shall make the written certification and determinations required by said section 29C. The department shall give due consideration to the recommendations of the court. The department may not refuse out-of-home placement of a child if the placement is recommended by the court provided that the court has made the written certification and determinations required by said section 29C. The department shall direct the type and length of such out-of-home placement. The department shall give due consideration to the requests of the child that the child be placed outside the home of a parent or guardian where there is a history of abuse and neglect in the home by the parent or guardian.

If the family or child are directed by the court to participate in treatment or services which are eligible for coverage by an insurance plan or other third-party payer, payment for such services shall not be denied if the treatment or services otherwise meet the criteria for coverage.

A child who is the subject of an application for assistance may not be confined in shackles or similar restraints or in a court lockup facility in connection with any proceedings under sections 39E to 39I,inclusive. A child who is the subject of an application for assistance shall not be placed in a locked facility or any facility designated or operated for juveniles who are alleged to be delinquent or who have been adjudicated delinquent. Such child may, however, be placed in a facility which operates as a group home to provide therapeutic care for juveniles, regardless of whether juveniles adjudicated delinquent are also provided care in such facility.

Any order of disposition pursuant to this section shall continue in force for not more than 120 days; provided, however, that the court which entered the order may, after a hearing, extend its duration for up to 3 additional periods, each such period not to exceed 90 days if the court finds that the purposes of the order have not been accomplished and that such extension would be reasonable likely to further those purposes.

No order shall continue in effect after the eighteenth birthday of a child named in an application for assistance authorized to be filed by a parent, a legal guardian or custodian or a police officer or after the sixteenth birthday of a child named in a petition authorized to be filed by a school district.

§ 39H. Custodial protection of child; notification to juvenile court; temporary placement; bail; detention; limitations; right of appeal

[Amended by 2008 Mass. Acts c. 176, § 94, effective July 8, 2008; 2008 Mass. Acts c. 215, § 65, effective July 31, 2008; 2012 Mass. Acts c. 240, §§ 24–30, effective Nov. 5, 2012.]

A child may be taken into custodial protection for engaging in the behavior described in the definition of "Child requiring assistance" in section 21, only if such child has failed to obey a summons issued pursuant to section thirty-nine E, or if the law enforcement officer initiating such custodial protection has probable cause to believe that such child has run away from the home of his parents or guardian and will not respond to a summons.

After a law enforcement officer has taken a child into custodial protection, the officer shall immediately notify the parent, other person legally responsible for the child's care or the person with whom the child is domiciled, that such child is under the custodial protection of the officer and a representative of the department of children and families, if the law enforcement officer has reason to believe that the child is or has been in the care or custody of such department, and shall inquire into the case.

The law enforcement officer, in consultation with the probation officer, shall then immediately make all reasonable diversion efforts so that such child is delivered to the following types of placements, and in the following order of preference:

(i) to one of the child's parents, or to the child's guardian or other responsible person known to the child, or to the child's legal custodian including the department of children and families or the child's foster home upon the written promise, without surety, of the person to whose custody the child is released that such parent, guardian, person or custodian will bring the child to the court on the next court date;

(ii) forthwith and with all reasonable speed take the child directly and without first being taken to the police station house, to a temporary shelter facility licensed or approved by the department of early education and care, a shelter home approved by a temporary shelter facility licensed or approved by said department of early education and care or a family foster care home approved by

1

a placement agency licensed or approved by said department of early education and care; or

(iii) take the child directly to the juvenile court in which the act providing the reason to take the child into custodial protection occurred if the officer affirms on the record that the officer attempted to exercise the options identified in clauses (i) and (ii), was unable to exercise these options and the reasons for such inability.

A child in custodial protection may not be confined in shackles or similar restraints or in a court lockup facility in connection with any proceedings under sections 39E to 39I, inclusive. A child who is the subject of an application for assistance shall not be placed in a locked facility or a facility designated or operated for juveniles who are alleged to be delinquent or who have been adjudicated delinquent. Such child may, however, be placed in a facility which operates as a group home to provide therapeutic care for juveniles, regardless of whether juveniles adjudicated delinquent are also provided care in such facility.

Notwithstanding the foregoing requirements for placement, any such child who is taken into custodial protection shall, if necessary, to be taken to a medical facility for treatment or observation.

If the court finds that a child stated to require assistance by reason of repeatedly refusing to obey the lawful and reasonable commands of such child's parents, legal guardian or custodian or is likely not to appear at the fact finding or disposition hearing, the court may order the child to be released upon such terms and conditions as it determines to be reasonable or, if the standards below are met, may place the child in the temporary custody of the department of children and families. The court shall not order the child to be placed in the custody of the department of youth services. Prior to the court granting temporary custody to the department of children and families, the court shall make a written certification and determination that it is contrary to the best interests of the child for the child to be in the child's home or current placement and that the department of children and families has made reasonable efforts to prevent removal of the child from the child's home or the existing circumstances indicate that there is an immediate risk of harm or neglect which precludes the provision of preventative services as an alternative to removal. An order placing a child with the department under this section shall be valid for not more than 15 days upon which the child and the child's parents, legal guardians or custodians, represented by counsel, shall be brought again before the court for a hearing on whether such order should be continued for another 15 day period based on the preponderance of the evidence. If the court decides to continue said order, it shall note in writing the detailed reasons for its decision; provided, however that no child shall be placed with the department under this section for more than 45 days.

§ 39I. Appeals

[Amended by 2012 Mass. Acts c. 240, § 31, effective Nov. 5, 2012; 2013 Mass. Acts c. 118, § 10, effective Oct. 29, 2013.]

A child, parent, legal guardian or custodian may appeal from any order or determination, whether final or not final, made under sections 39E to 39H, inclusive. Pending the appeal, the juvenile court shall retain jurisdiction and may enter any order under this chapter to meet the needs of the child. Notwithstanding any general or special law to the contrary, the appeal shall be to a single justice of the appeals court under section 118 of chapter 231 and shall proceed in accordance with the procedures governing petitions to a single justice.

§ 39J. Repealed

[Repealed by 2012 Mass. Acts c. 240, § 32, effective Nov. 5, 2012.]

§ 39K. Child welfare service needs of sexually exploited children

[Added by 2011 Mass. Acts c. 178, § 9, effective Feb. 19, 2012.]

(a) Notwithstanding any general or special law to the contrary, the department of children and families, in collaboration with the department of mental health and other appropriate state agencies, shall: (i) provide for the child welfare services needs of sexually exploited children including, but not limited to, services for sexually-exploited children residing in the commonwealth at the time they are taken into custody by law enforcement or are identified by the department as sexually-exploited children, for the duration of any legal or administrative proceeding in which they are either the complaining witness, defendant or the subject child; and (ii) provide appropriate services to a child reasonably believed to be a sexually exploited child in order to safeguard the child's welfare. If a child reasonably believed to be a sexually exploited child declines services or is unable or unwilling to participate in the services offered, the department or any person may file a care and protection petition under section 24. Sexually exploited children shall have access to an advocate. The advocate or a member of the multi-disciplinary service team established under section 51D shall accompany the child to all court appearances and may serve as a liaison between the service providers and the court.

(b) The services that shall be provided under this section shall be available to all sexually exploited children, whether they are accessed voluntarily, through a court proceeding under this section or through a referral, which may be made by any person.

(c) In determining the need for and capacity of the services that may be provided under this section, the department of children and families shall recognize that sexually exploited youth have separate and distinct service needs according to gender and appropriate services shall be made available while ensuring that an appropriate continuum of services exists.

(d) The commissioner of the department may, subject to appropriation, contract with nongovernmental organizations or entities with experience working with sexually exploited children to train law enforcement officials likely to encounter sexually exploited children in the course of their law enforcement duties. The training shall include, but not be limited to, awareness and compliance with the provisions of this section, identification of, access to, and the provision of services for sexually-exploited children and any other services the department deems necessary.

(e) The department may apply to the victim and witness assistance board for grants from the Victims of Human Trafficking Trust Fund, established in section 66A of chapter 10,, grants from the United States Department of Justice's Office of Juvenile Justice and Delinquency Prevention or any other federal agency, or grants from any other private source to fund the law enforcement training and services for sexually-exploited children.

(f) The department shall adopt regulations to carry out this section.

§ 39L. Children in violation of prohibition against common night walking or streetwalking; petition for care and protection; appointment of guardian ad litem; stay of juvenile delinquency or criminal proceedings; failure of child to comply with requirements

[Added by 2011 Mass. Acts c. 178, § 9, effective Feb. 19, 2012.]

(a) Before or after arraignment in any juvenile delinquency or criminal proceeding against a sexually exploited child alleging that such juvenile or such defendant violated the prohibition against common night walking or common streetwalking under section 53 of chapter 272 or the provisions of subsection (a) of section 53A of said chapter 272, there shall be a presumption that a care and protection petition on behalf of such child, or a child in need of services petition under section 39E, shall be filed. Any person, including the juvenile, may file a care and protection petition on behalf of such child, including a petition for emergency commitment under section 24, or a parent or a police officer may file a child in need of services petition under section 39E.

(b) The court may appoint a guardian ad litem and shall hold a hearing on such petition. The court may allow a reasonable delay in the proceedings, including any arraignment, to consider the petition. The necessary findings of fact to support the court's decision shall be reduced to writing and made part of the court record.

(c) Upon a motion by a party to the juvenile delinquency or criminal proceeding or by a guardian ad litem, unless the district attorney or the attorney general objects, and upon a finding that a child alleged to be a juvenile delinquent by reason of violating section 53 of chapter 272 or subsection (a) of section 53A of said chapter 272 is a child in need of care and protection or a child in need of services, the court shall, if arraignment has not yet occurred, indefinitely stay arraignment and place the proceeding on file. If the court finds that the child has failed to substantially comply with the requirements of services or that the child's welfare or safety so requires, the court may remove the proceeding from file, arraign the child and restore the delinquency or criminal complaint to the docket for trial or further proceedings in accordance with the regular course of such proceedings. If arraignment has already occurred, unless the district attorney or the attorney general objects, the court shall place the child on pretrial probation under section 87 of chapter 276. If appropriate, the conditions of such probation shall include, but not be limited to, requiring the child to substantially comply with all lawful orders of the court, including orders relating to any care and protection or child in need of services proceeding, and the child shall also comply with the guidance and services of the department or any designated non-governmental service provider. If the child fails to substantially comply with the conditions of probation or if the child's welfare or safety so requires, the court may in its discretion restore the delinquency or criminal complaint to the docket for trial or further proceedings in accordance with the regular course of such proceedings.

§§ 40–51. Repealed

[Repealed by 1954 Mass. Acts c. 646, § 1.]

§ 51A. Reporting of suspected abuse or neglect

[Amended by 2002 Mass. Acts c. 107, §§ 1–5; 2008 Mass. Acts c. 176, §§ 95–97, effective July 8, 2008; 2008 Mass. Acts c. 176, § 97, effective Jan. 1, 2010; 2011 Mass. Acts c. 178, § 10, effective Nov. 21, 2011.]

(a) A mandated reporter who, in his professional capacity, has reasonable cause to believe that a child is suffering physical or emotional injury resulting from: (i) abuse inflicted upon him which causes harm or substantial risk of harm to the child's health or welfare, including sexual abuse; (ii) neglect, including malnutrition; (iii) physical dependence upon an addictive drug at birth, shall immediately communicate with the department orally and, within 48 hours, shall file a written report with the department detailing the suspected abuse or neglect; or (iv) being a sexually exploited child; or (v) being a human trafficking victim as defined by section 20M of chapter 233.

If a mandated reporter is a member of the staff of a medical or other public or private institution, school or facility, the mandated reporter may instead notify the person or designated agent in charge of such institution, school or facility who shall become responsible for notifying the department in the manner required by this section.

A mandated reporter may, in addition to filing a report under this section, contact local law enforcement authorities or the child advocate about the suspected abuse or neglect.

(b) For the purpose of reporting under this section, hospital personnel may have photographs taken of the areas of trauma visible on the child without the consent of the child's parents or guardians. These photographs or copies thereof shall be sent to the department with the report.

If hospital personnel collect physical evidence of abuse or neglect of the child, the local district attorney, local law enforcement authorities, and the department shall be immediately notified. The physical evidence shall be processed immediately so that the department may make an informed determination within the time limits in section 51B. If there is a delay in processing, the department shall seek a waiver under subsection (d) of section 51B.

(c) Notwithstanding subsection (g), whoever violates this section shall be punished by a fine of not more than $1,000. Whoever knowingly and willfully files a frivolous report of child abuse or neglect under this section shall be punished by: (i) a fine of not more than $2,000 for the first offense; (ii) imprisonment in a house of correction for not more than 6 months and a fine of not more than $2,000 for the second offense; and (iii) imprisonment in a house of correction for not more than 2½ years and a fine of not more than $2,000 for the third and subsequent offenses.

Any mandated reporter who has knowledge of child abuse or neglect that resulted in serious bodily injury to or death of a child and willfully fails to report such abuse or neglect shall be punished by a fine of up to $5,000 or imprisonment in the house of correction for not more than 2½ years or by both such fine and imprisonment; and, upon a guilty finding or a continuance without a finding, the court shall notify any appropriate professional licensing authority of the mandated reporter's violation of this paragraph.

(d) A report filed under this section shall contain: (i) the names and addresses of the child and the child's parents or other person responsible for the child's care, if known; (ii) the child's age; (iii) the child's sex; (iv) the nature and extent of the child's injuries, abuse, maltreatment or neglect, including any evidence of prior injuries, abuse, maltreatment or neglect; (v) the circumstances under which the person required to report first became aware of the child's injuries, abuse, maltreatment or neglect; (vi) whatever action, if any, was taken to treat, shelter or otherwise assist the child; (vii) the name of the person or persons making the report; (viii) any other information that the person reporting believes might be helpful in establishing the cause of the injuries; (ix) the identity of the person or persons responsible for the neglect or injuries; and (x) other information required by the department.

(e) A mandated reporter who has reasonable cause to believe that a child has died as a result of any of the conditions listed in subsection (a) shall report the death to the district attorney for the county in which the death occurred and the office of the chief medical examiner as required by clause (16) of section 3 of chapter 38. Any person who fails to file a report under this subsection shall be punished by a fine of not more than $1,000.

(f) Any person may file a report under this section if that person has reasonable cause to believe that a child is suffering from or has died as a result of abuse or neglect.

(g) No mandated reporter shall be liable in any civil or criminal action for filing a report under this section or for contacting local law enforcement authorities or the child advocate, if the report or contact was made in good faith, was not frivolous, and the reporter did not cause the abuse or neglect. No other person filing a report under this section shall be liable in any civil or criminal action by reason of the report if it was made in good faith and if that person did not perpetrate or inflict the reported abuse or cause the reported neglect. Any person filing a report under this section may be liable in a civil or criminal action if the department or a district attorney determines that the person filing the report may have perpetrated or inflicted the abuse or caused the neglect.

(h) No employer shall discharge, discriminate or retaliate against a mandated reporter who, in good faith, files a report under this section, testifies or is about to testify in any proceeding involving child abuse or neglect. Any employer who discharges, discriminates or retaliates against that mandated reporter shall be liable to the mandated reporter for treble damages, costs and attorney's fees.

(i) Within 30 days of receiving a report from a mandated reporter, the department shall notify the mandated reporter, in writing, of its determination of the nature, extent and cause or causes of the injuries to the child and the services that the department intends to provide to the child or the child's family.

(j) Any privilege relating to confidential communications, established by sections 135 to 135B, inclusive, of chapter 112 or by sections 20A and 20B of chapter 233, shall not prohibit the filing of a report under this section or a care and protection petition under section 24, except that a priest, rabbi, clergy member, ordained or licensed minister, leader of a church or religious body or accredited Christian Science practitioner need not report information solely gained in a confession or similarly confidential communication in other religious faiths. Nothing in the general laws shall modify or limit the duty of a priest, rabbi, clergy member, ordained or licensed minister, leader of a church or religious body or accredited Christian Science practitioner to report suspected child abuse or neglect under this section when the priest, rabbi, clergy member, ordained or licensed minister, leader of a church or religious body or accredited Christian Science practitioner is acting in some other capacity that would otherwise make him a mandated reporter.

(k) A mandated reporter who is professionally licensed by the commonwealth shall complete training to recognize and report suspected child abuse or neglect.

NOTE 1 2002 Mass. Acts c. 107 § 5, effective May 3, 2002, provides: Any individual mentioned in section 51A of chapter 119 of the General Laws, as amended by section 2 of this act, who was not previously subject to said section 51A and who on the effective date of this act has reasonable cause to believe that a child under the age of 18 years is or was being injured as set forth in section 51A, except if this belief is based solely on information exempt from reporting under section 4 of this act, shall make the reports required by said section 51A to the department of social services within 30_days after the effective date of this act. If on the effective date of this act, the alleged victim is no longer under the age of 18 years, the individual required by this section to report shall instead make a report to the office of the district attorney for the district where the alleged abuse occurred within 30 days after the effective date of this act and shall notify the alleged victim in writing of this report.

Reports required by this section shall be subject to the penalties provided in said Section 51A.

NOTE 2 The reporting requirement under G.L. c. 119, § 51A does not create the kind of regulatory nexus that could justify treating the reporting party as a state actor for purposes of 42 U.S.C.S. § 1983, Civil Rights. *Brown v. Newberger*, 291 F.3d 89 (1st Cir. 2002).

§ 51B. Investigation of report of abuse under Sec. 51A

[Amended by 2008 Mass. Acts c. 176, § 98, effective July 8, 2008; 2008 Mass. Acts c. 451, § 83, effective June 30, 2009; 2010 Mass. Acts c. 267, § 13; 2011 Mass. Acts c. 178, §§ 11–12, effective Nov. 21, 2011.]

(a) Upon receipt of a report filed under section 51A, the department shall investigate the suspected child abuse or neglect, provide a written evaluation of the household of the child, including the parents and home environment and make a written determination relative to the safety of and risk posed to the child and whether the suspected child abuse or neglect is substantiated. The department shall immediately report to the district attorney and local law enforcement authorities, a sexually exploited child or a child who is otherwise a human trafficking victim, regardless of whether the child is living with a parent, guardian or other caretaker.

(b) The investigation shall include: (i) a home visit at which the child is viewed, if appropriate; (ii) a determination of the nature, extent and cause or causes of the injuries; (iii) the identity of the person or persons responsible therefore; (iv) the name, age and condition of other children in the same household; (v) an evaluation of the parents and the home environment; and (vi) all other pertinent facts or matters. The department shall coordinate with other agencies to make all reasonable efforts to minimize the number of interviews of any potential victim of child abuse or neglect. Upon completion of the investigation and evaluation, the department shall make a written determination relative to: (i) the safety of the child and risk of physical or emotional injury to that child and the safety of and risk thereto of any other children in the household; and (ii) whether the suspected child abuse or neglect is substantiated.

(c) If the department has reasonable cause to believe a child's health or safety is in immediate danger from abuse or neglect, the department shall take a child into immediate temporary custody if it has reasonable cause to believe that the removal is necessary to protect the child from abuse or neglect. The investigation and evaluation shall commence within 2 hours of initial contact and an interim report with an initial determination regarding the child's safety and custody shall be completed as soon as possible but not more than 24 hours after initial contact. The final report required under this section shall be complete within 5 business days of initial contact. If a child is taken into immediate temporary custody, the department shall make a written report stating the reasons for such removal and shall file a care and protection petition under section 24 on the next court day.

(d) If the department does not have reasonable cause to believe that a child's health or safety is in immediate danger from abuse or neglect, the investigation and evaluation shall commence within 2 business days of initial contact and a determination shall be made within 15 business days, unless a waiver has been approved by the area director or requested by law enforcement.

(e) Notwithstanding subsection (c), whenever the department has reasonable cause to believe that removal is necessary to protect a child from abuse or neglect, it shall take the child into immediate temporary custody. If a child is taken into immediate temporary custody, the department shall make a written report stating the reasons for such removal and shall file a care and protection petition under section 24 on the next court day.

(f) If a child named in a report filed under section 51A is in an out-of-home placement and the suspected child abuse or neglect is substantiated, the department shall notify his parents that such report was filed and has been substantiated by the department. If the child died or suffered serious bodily injury, the department shall notify the parents, including the biological parents, if the department determines that such notification is in the best interest of the child or of another child in the same placement. The department shall consult with these parents in decisions about removal or further placement. These notifications and consultations shall not be required if the commissioner determines that such notifications or consultations are not appropriate or in the best interests of a child.

(g) The department shall offer appropriate services to the family of any child which it has reasonable cause to believe is suffering from any of the conditions described in the report to prevent further injury to the child, to safeguard his welfare, and to preserve and stabilize family life whenever possible. If the family declines or is unable to accept or to participate in the offered services, the department or any person may file a care and protection petition under section 24.

(h) The department shall file in the central registry, established under section 51F, a written report containing information sufficient to identify each child whose name is reported under this section or section 51A. A notation shall be sent to the central registry whenever further reports on each such child are filed with the department. If the department determines during the initial screening period of an investigation that a report filed under section 51A is frivolous, or other absolute determination that abuse or neglect has not taken place, such report shall be declared as "allegation invalid". If a report is declared "allegation invalid", the name of the child, or identifying characteristics relating to the child, or the names of his parents or guardian or any other person relevant to the report, shall not be placed in the central registry or in any other computerized program utilized in the department.

(i) The department may purchase and utilize such protective services of private and voluntary agencies as it determines necessary.

(j) The department shall adopt regulations to implement the sections 51A to 51F, inclusive.

(k) The department shall notify and shall transmit copies of substantiated 51A reports and its written evaluations and written determinations under subsection (a) or (b) to the district attorney for the county in which the child resides and for the county in which the suspected abuse or neglect occurred, and to the local law enforcement authorities in the city or town in which the child resides and in the city or town in which the suspected abuse or neglect occurred when the department has reasonable cause to believe that 1 of the conditions listed below resulted from abuse or neglect.

The department shall immediately report to the district attorney and local law enforcement authorities listed above when early evidence indicates there is reasonable cause to believe that one of the conditions listed below resulted from abuse or neglect:

(1) a child has died or has suffered brain damage, loss or substantial impairment of a bodily function or organ, substantial disfigurement, or serious physical injury including, but not limited to, a fracture of any bone, a severe burn, an impairment of any organ or an injury requiring the child to be placed on life-support systems;

(2) a child has been sexually assaulted, which shall include a violation of section 13B, 13B½, 13B¾, 13H, 22, 22A, 22B, 22C, 23, 23A, 24 or 24B of chapter 265;

(3) a child has been sexually exploited, which shall include a violation of section 4A, 4B or 29A of said chapter 272; or is a sexually exploited child or a child who is otherwise a human trafficking victim; or

(4) any other disclosure of physical abuse involving physical evidence which may be destroyed, any current disclosure by a child of sexual assault, or the presence of physical evidence of sexual assault.

Within 45 days of the notification under the first paragraph, the department shall further notify the district attorney of a service plan, if any, developed for such child and his family.

No provision of chapter 66A, sections 135 to 135B, inclusive, of chapter 112, or sections 51E and 51F of this chapter relating to confidential data or confidential communications shall prohibit the department from making such notifications or from providing to the district attorney or local law enforcement authorities any information obtained under this section. No person providing notification or information to a district attorney or local law enforcement authorities under this section shall be liable in any civil or criminal action by reason of such action. Nothing herein shall be construed to prevent the department from notifying a district attorney relative to any incident reported to the department under section 51A or to limit the prosecutorial power of a district attorney.

(l) If the department substantiates a report alleging that abuse or neglect occurred at a facility approved, owned, operated or funded, in whole or in part, by the department of elementary and secondary education, the department of early education and care, the department of mental health, the department of developmental services, the department of public health or the department of youth services, the department shall notify the office of the child advocate and the affected department, in writing, by transmitting a copy of the report filed under section 51A and the department's written evaluation and written determination.

If the department is aware of a licensing violation in any such facility, the department shall immediately notify the affected department.

No provision of chapter 66A, sections 135 to 135B, inclusive, of chapter 112, or sections 51E and 51F, or any other provision of law shall prohibit: (i) the department from transmitting copies of reports filed under section 51A or its written evaluations and written determinations to the office of the child advocate or the affected departments; (ii) the department, the office of the child advocate and the affected departments from coordinating activities and sharing information for the purposes of this section or for investigating a licensing violation; or (iii) the department's employees from testifying at administrative hearings held by the affected department in connection with a licensing violation.

(m) Notwithstanding any privilege created by statute or common law relating to confidential communications or any statute prohibiting the disclosure of information but subject to subsection (j) of section 51A, a mandated reporter shall answer questions and provide information posed by the department relating to an investigation conducted under this section, whether or not that person filed the 51A report being investigated. A statutory or common law privilege shall not preclude the admission of any such information in any civil proceeding concerning abuse or neglect of a child, placement or custody of a child.

(n) No person required to provide such information under this section or permitted to disclose information under section 5A of chapter 119A shall be liable in any civil or criminal action for providing such information.

(o) No employer shall discharge, discriminate or retaliate against a mandated reporter who, in good faith, provides such information, testifies or is about to testify in any proceeding involving child abuse or neglect unless such person perpetrated or inflicted such abuse or neglect. Any employer who discharges, discriminates or retaliates against such a person shall be liable to such person for treble damages, costs and attorney's fees.

(p) If the department determines that a 51A report is not substantiated, the department shall notify in writing any and all sources or recipients of information in connection with the investigation that the report of abuse or neglect has not been substantiated, unless the target of the investigation requests that such notification not occur.

(q) The department and the private agencies under contract with it, shall conduct periodic and regular training and education to caseworkers, screeners of 51A reports, and administrators of the department and the agencies regarding their duties and obligations under section 51A and 51B.

(r) There shall be a review by a regional clinical review team when 3 or more 51A reports involving separate incidents have been filed on any child in a family within 3 months and a review by an area clinical review team when 3 or more 51A reports involving separate incidents have been filed on any child in a family within 1 year.

NOTE 2008 Mass. Acts c. 176, § 135, effective July 8, 2008, provides:

(a) Notwithstanding section 51B of chapter 119 of the General Laws or any other general or special law to the contrary and consistent with any relevant collective bargaining agreement, the department of children and families may establish a pilot program of family engagement in child welfare practice. The department shall select 4 to 8 area offices in which to implement the pilot program. Each office shall then be divided into a control group and a differential response group, with each group using social worker teams based on caseload standards recommended by the Child Welfare League of America, Inc.

(b) The differential response group shall use a local unified entry point for (i) requests for voluntary services filed under section 23 of chapter 119 of the General Laws, (ii) court referrals, including those for children in need of services filed under section 39E of said chapter 119, and (iii) reports of suspected child abuse or neglect filed under section 51A of said chapter 119.

Upon entry of any such request, referral or report, the department shall have a period of initial engagement during which the request, referral or report shall be evaluated and a differential response, if any, shall be determined; but if the department has reasonable cause to believe the child's health or safety is in immediate danger from abuse or neglect, the department shall also view the child, conduct a safety assessment, and take any steps necessary to ensure the safety of the child. A rapid initial engagement for the latter circumstances shall commence within 2 hours and shall be completed within 36 hours; all other initial engagements shall be completed within 3 business days. The department shall determine whether the request, referral or report is appropriate for response and, if so, which differential response is appropriate: a protective response, a support and stabilization response or a community resource response.

A protective response shall be required if the department determines that the child has been or is at risk of serious harm. The protective response shall be conducted pursuant to said section 51B, except that the investigation shall be completed within 15 business days of the differential response determination unless a waiver has been approved by the area director or requested by law enforcement.

A support and stabilization response shall require department contact with the child's family within 2 business days of the differential response determination and an initial assessment of the family within 30 business days of the determination. Such a response shall include at least 3 department visits with the child's family and may include the immediate provision of services.

A community resource response shall consist of providing information about and referral to community-based services. Such a response shall not include an investigation or a family assessment by the department.

After the completion of a protective response or a support and stabilization response and based on a family assessment, the department may determine that sustained engagement with the child's family is necessary. During sustained engagement, family assessments shall be conducted every 6 months until the department terminates its sustained engagement.

The differential response group shall use (i) evidence-based safety and risk assessment tools, (ii) family assessments, (iii) resource and service planning activities, and (iv) culturally competent staffing, resources and practices.

(c) The pilot program shall include an independent evaluation, including the impact on children and families, the effect on racial disproportionality and disparity, the associated costs, any recommendations for statewide implementation, and shall survey children, families, and staff involved with the pilot program.

(d) The department shall report the results of the evaluation and legislative recommendations, if appropriate, no later than 1 year after pilot program is established. The report shall be filed with the clerks of the house and the senate, the house and senate committees on ways and means, the committee on children, families and persons with disabilities, the speaker of the house, the president of the senate and the governor.

§ 51C. Custody of injured child pending transfer to department or hearing

If a parent or other person requests the release from a hospital of a child reported pursuant to section fifty-one A, the presiding judge of the juvenile court of the judicial district in which such hospital is located may, if he believes such release would be detrimental to the child's health or safety, authorize the hospital and the attending physician, by any means of communication, to keep such a child in the hospital until custody is transferred to the department or until a hearing may be held relative to the care and custody of such child.

Any other physician treating a child reported pursuant to section fifty-one A may be so authorized by the court to keep such child in his custody until such time as the custody of the child has been transferred to the department or until a hearing may be held relative to the care and custody of such child.

§ 51D. Powers and duties of area directors; multi-disciplinary service teams

[Amended by 2008 Mass. Acts c. 176, § 99, effective July 8, 2008; 2011 Mass. Acts c. 178, §§ 13–14, effective Nov. 21, 2011; 2011 Mass. Acts c. 178, §§ 13–14, effective Feb. 19, 2012.]

Each area director of the department shall be responsible for implementing subsection (k) of section 51B.

Each area director shall, in cooperation with the appropriate district attorney, establish 1 or more multi-disciplinary service teams to review the provision of services to the children and families who are the subject of 51A reports that meet the conditions of subsection (k).

Each team shall consist of the department's caseworker for the particular case, 1 representative of the appropriate district attorney, and at least 1 other member appointed by the area director who is not an employee of either office. The additional member shall have training and experience in the fields of child welfare or criminal justice and, as far as practicable, be involved with the provision of services to these families. No members of a team shall receive any compensation, or in the case of a state employee, any additional compensation, for service on the team.

For 51A reports specifically involving a sexually exploited child or a child who is otherwise a human trafficking victim, the multi-disciplinary service team may consist of a team of professionals trained or otherwise experienced and qualified to assess the needs of sexually exploited children or children who are otherwise human trafficking victims including, but not limited to, a police officer, as defined by section 1 of chapter 90C, or other person designated by a police chief, as defined in said section 1 of said chapter 90C, an employee of the department of children and families, a representative of the appropriate district attorney, a social service provider, a medical professional or a mental health professional.

The team shall review and monitor the service plan developed by the department under subsection (g) of section 51B. The team shall evaluate the effectiveness of the service plan in protecting the child from further abuse or neglect. The team shall make recommendations regarding amendments to the service plan, the advisability of prosecuting members of the family, and the possibility of utilizing diversionary alternatives. If the team finds that services required under such plan are not provided to the family, the case shall be referred to the commissioner.

The team shall have full access to the service plan and any personal data known to the department which is directly related to the implementation of the plan, notwithstanding sections 51E and 51F, chapter 66A, and section 135 of chapter 112. The members of the team shall be considered to be employees of the department for purposes of protecting the confidentiality of the data and the data shall be utilized solely to carry out the provisions of this section; provided, however, that the team may report to the district attorney if the family has failed to participate in the plan.

For 51B reports specifically involving a sexually exploited child, the purpose of the multi-disciplinary service team shall be to determine whether the child has been sexually exploited or is otherwise a human trafficking victim and to recommend a plan for services to the department that may include, but shall not be limited to, shelter or placement, mental health and medical care needs and other social services.

Each area director shall file a monthly report with the commissioner regarding the activities in the area which have occurred in the previous month pursuant to this section. The report shall be written on a form prescribed by the commissioner and shall include, but not be limited to, the number of cases reported under said subsection (k) of said section 51B, the activities of the teams, the availability of services described in the service plans, and the number of family members that are subject of the reports that have been prosecuted. The commissioner, after deleting all personal identifying information, shall combine these area reports into a monthly report that shall be filed with the secretary of health and human services, each district attorney, the joint committee on children, families and persons with disabilities, and the house and senate committees on ways and means.

§ 51E. Reports of injured children; files; confidentiality; penalties

[Amended by 2008 Mass. Acts c. 3, §§ 1, 2, effective Jan. 11, 2008; 2008 Mass. Acts c. 176, § 100, effective July 8, 2008.]

The department shall maintain a file of the written reports prepared under this section and sections 51A to 51D, inclusive. These written reports shall be confidential. Upon request and with the approval of the commissioner, copies of written reports of initial investigations may be provided to: (i) the child's parent, guardian, or counsel, (ii) the reporting person or agency, (iii) the appropriate review board, (iv) a child welfare agency of another state for the purpose of assisting that agency in determining whether to approve a prospective foster or adoptive parent, or (v) a social worker assigned to the case. No such report shall be made available to any persons other than those specified in this section without the written and informed consent of the child's parent or guardian, the written approval of the commissioner, or an order of a court of competent jurisdiction. Pursuant to chapter 18C, the child advocate shall have access to these reports.

A child welfare agency of another state may, upon request, and upon the approval of the commissioner, receive a copy of the written report of the initial investigation if the agency has a need for such information in order to carry out its responsibilities under law to protect children from abuse and neglect.

The name and all other identifying information relating to any child, or to his parents or guardian, shall be removed from said reports 1 year after the department determines that the allegation of serious physical or emotional injury resulting from abuse or neglect cannot be substantiated, or, if said allegations are substantiated, when the child reaches the age of 18, or 1 year after the date of termination of services to the child or his family, whichever date occurs last; provided, however, that the department may retain information on unsubstantiated reports to assist in future risk and safety assessments of children and families and may release said information to the child welfare agencies of other states upon request of said child welfare agency for the purpose of assisting said child welfare agency in determining whether to approve a prospective foster or adoptive parent.

Any person who permits any information in the files to be released to persons other than those specified in this section shall be punished by a fine of not more than $1,000 or by imprisonment for not more than 2½ years, or both.

§ 51F. Central registry of information; confidentiality; penalties

[Amended by 2008 Mass. Acts c. 3, § 3, effective Jan. 11, 2008; 2008 Mass. Acts c. 176, § 100, effective July 8, 2008.]

The department shall maintain a central registry of information sufficient to identify children whose names are reported under sections 51A to 51B. Data and information relating to individual cases in the central registry shall be confidential and shall be made available only with the approval of the commissioner or upon court order; provided, however, that the department, upon request, may release this data and information to a child welfare agency of another state for the purpose of assisting that agency in determining whether to approve a prospective foster or adoptive parent. The commissioner shall establish rules and regulations governing the availability of such data and information. Pursuant to chapter 18C, the child advocate shall have access to the information in the registry.

A child welfare agency of another state may, upon request, and upon the approval of the commissioner, receive information from the central registry if the agency has a need for such information in order to carry out its responsibilities under law to protect children from abuse and neglect.

The name and all other identifying characteristics relating to any child which is contained in the central registry, or to his parents or guardian, shall be removed 1 year after the department determines, after investigation, that the allegation of serious physical or emotional injury resulting from abuse or neglect cannot be substantiated or, if said allegations are substantiated, when the child reaches the age of 18, or 1 year after the date of termination of services to the child or his family, whichever date occurs last. If the department determines during the initial screening period of an investigation that said report under section 51A is frivolous, or other absolute determination that abuse or neglect has not taken place, then said report shall be declared as "allegation invalid". If such reports are declared "allegation invalid", the name of the child, or identifying characteristics relating to the child, or the names of his parents or guardian or any other person relevant to the report, shall not be placed in the central registry, nor under any other computerized program utilized in the department. Nothing in this section shall prevent the department from keeping information on unsubstantiated reports to assist in future risk and safety assessments of children and families.

Any person employed in the central registry who permits the data and information stored in the registry to be released without authorization to persons other than those specified in the rules and regulations shall be punished by a fine of not more than $1,000 or by imprisonment for not more than 2½ years, or both.

§ 51G. Severability; Secs. 51A–51F

Sections fifty-one A to fifty-one F, inclusive, are severable and the invalidity of any of said sections shall not affect the continuing validity of any other of said sections.

§ 51H. Protective alerts; transport of child to another state or country

[Added by 2008 Mass. Acts c. 176, § 101, effective July 8, 2008.]

Notwithstanding any general or special law to the contrary, the department may send to, or receive from, any other state or country a protective alert containing any information about a child related to a substantiated report of child abuse or neglect if the department reasonably believes that the child has been or will be transported to another state or country.

DELINQUENT CHILDREN

§ 52. Definitions

[Amended by 2013 Mass. Acts c. 84, § 7, effective Sept. 18, 2013; 2018 Mass. Acts c. 69, § 72, effective July 12, 2018.]

The following words as used in the following sections shall, except as otherwise specifically provided, have the following meanings:

"Court", a division of the juvenile court department.

"Delinquent child", a child between 12 and 18 years of age who commits any offense against a law of the commonwealth; provided, however, that such offense shall not include a civil infraction, a violation of any municipal ordinance or town by-law or a first offense of a misdemeanor for which the punishment is a fine, imprisonment in a jail or house of correction for not more than 6 months or both such fine and imprisonment.

"Probation officer", a probation officer or assistant probation officer of the court having jurisdiction of the pending case.

"Punishment as is provided by law", any sentence which may be imposed upon an adult by a justice of the district court or superior court.

"Youthful offender", a person who is subject to an adult or juvenile sentence for having committed, while between the ages of fourteen and 18, an offense against a law of the commonwealth which, if he were an adult, would be punishable by imprisonment in the state prison, and (a) has previously been committed to the department of youth services, or (b) has committed an offense which involves the infliction or threat of serious bodily harm in violation of law, or (c) has committed a violation of paragraph (a), (c) or (d) of section ten or section ten E of chapter two hundred and sixty-nine; provided that, nothing in this clause shall allow for less than the imposition of the mandatory commitment periods provided in section fifty-eight of chapter one hundred and nineteen.

§ 53. Liberal construction; nature of proceedings against children

Sections fifty-two to sixty-three, inclusive, shall be liberally construed so that the care, custody and discipline of the children brought before the court shall approximate as nearly as possible that which they should receive from their parents, and that, as far as practicable, they shall be treated, not as criminals, but as children in need of aid, encouragement and guidance. Proceedings against children under said sections shall not be deemed criminal proceedings.

§ 54. Complaint; examination of complainant; indictment; summons; warrant

[Amended by 2013 Mass. Acts c. 84, § 8, effective Sept. 18, 2013; 2018 Mass. Acts. c. 69, §§ 73, effective July 12, 2018, § 74, effective July 1, 2019.]

If complaint is made to any court that a child between 12 and 18 years of age is a delinquent child, said court shall examine, on oath, the complainant and the witnesses, if any, produced by him, and shall reduce the complaint to writing, and cause it to be subscribed by the complainant.

An application for such complaint submitted to the juvenile court by a police department against a child arrested for a felony offense shall be accompanied by an offense-based tracking number. The failure to include the arrestee's offense-based tracking number shall not preclude the issuance of a complaint where there is otherwise a valid application submitted by a police department against a child. If a complaint is issued based on an application for a complaint for a felony submitted by a police department against a child that did not include the child's offense-based tracking number, the prosecutor shall submit the offense-based tracking number of the child to the court to be included in the case file.

The commonwealth may proceed by complaint in juvenile court or in a juvenile session of a district court, as the case may be, or by indictment as provided by chapter two hundred and seventy-seven, if a person is alleged to have committed an offense against a law of the commonwealth while between the ages of fourteen and 18 which, if he were an adult, would be punishable by imprisonment in the state prison, and the person has previously been committed to the department of youth services, or the offense involves the infliction or threat of serious bodily harm in violation of law or the person has committed a violation of paragraph (a), (c) or (d) of section ten or section ten E of chapter two hundred and sixty-nine. The court shall proceed on the complaint or the indictment, as the case may be, in accordance with sections fifty-five to seventy-two, inclusive. Complaints and indictments brought against persons for such offenses, and for other criminal offenses properly joined under Massachusetts Rules of Criminal Procedure 9 (a) (1), shall be brought in accordance with the usual course and manner of criminal proceedings.

NOTE 1 2013 amendment extending the Juvenile Court's jurisdiction to persons age seventeen at the time of committing an offense is not retroactive to cases "begun and pending before September 18, 2013," the act's effective date. *Watts v. Commonwealth*, 468 Mass. 49 (2014).

NOTE 2 The Commonwealth may proceed by complaint against a juvenile even if the Grand Jury has returned a no bill. *Commonwealth v. Dale D.*, 431 Mass. 757, 761 (2000).

NOTE 3 "The juvenile's position of authority [uncle; babysitter], age difference between the juvenile [15] and the victim [6], and the vulnerability of the victim are sufficient to support a youthful offender indictment under [G.L. c. 265, 23, statutory rape]." *Commonwealth v. Clint C.*, 430 Mass. 219, 226 (1999). The Supreme Judicial Court also indicated that "absent an error of law, a judge may not dismiss an indictment brought under G.L. c. 119, § 54." *Commonwealth v. Clint C.*, 430 Mass. at 224. *See also N.M. v. Commonwealth*, 478 Mass. 89 (2017) (when considering whether the element of threat or serious bodily injury has been established the inquiry is "fact intensive").

§ 54A. Delinquent children; diversion of child to program of community supervision or other rehabilitative services

A juvenile court shall have jurisdiction to divert from further court processing a child who is subject to the jurisdiction of the juvenile court as the result of an application for complaint brought pursuant to section 54. The court may divert a child to a program as defined in section 1 of chapter 276A.

(b) A child complained of as a delinquent child may, upon the request of the child, undergo an assessment prior to arraignment to enable the judge to consider the suitability of the child for diversion. If a child chooses to request a continuance for the purpose of such an assessment, the child shall notify the judge prior to arraignment. Upon receipt of such notification, the judge may grant a 14-day continuance. The department of probation may conduct such assessment prior to arraignment to assist the judge in making that decision. If the judge determines it is appropriate, a determination of eligibility by the personnel of a program may substitute for an assessment. If a case is continued pursuant to this subsection, the child shall not be arraigned and an entry shall not be made into the criminal offender record information system until a judge issues an order to resume the ordinary processing of a delinquency proceeding. A judge may order diversion without first ordering an assessment in any case in which the court finds that sufficient information is available without an assessment.

(c)(1) After the completion of the assessment, the probation officer or, where applicable, the director of a program to which the child has been referred shall submit to the court and to the counsel for the child a recommendation as to whether the child would benefit from diversion.

Upon receipt of the recommendation, the judge shall provide an opportunity for both the commonwealth and counsel for the child to be heard regarding diversion of the child. The judge shall then make a final determination as to the eligibility of the child for diversion. The proceedings of a child who is found eligible for diversion shall be stayed for 90 days unless the judge determines that the interest of justice would best be served by a lesser period of time or unless extended under subsection (f).

(2) A stay of proceedings shall not be granted under this section unless the child consents in writing to the terms and conditions of the stay of proceedings and knowingly executes a waiver of the child's right to a speedy trial on a form approved by the chief justice of the juvenile court department. Consent shall be given only upon the advice of counsel.

(3) The following shall not be admissible against the child in any proceedings: (i) a request for assessment; (ii) a decision by the child not to enter a program; (iii) a determination by probation or by a program that the child would not benefit from diversion; and (iv) any statement made by the child or the child's family during the course of assessment. Any consent by a child to a stay of proceedings or any act done or statement made in fulfillment of the terms and conditions of a stay of proceedings shall not be admissible as an admission, implied or otherwise, against the child if the stay of proceedings was terminated and proceedings were resumed on the original complaint. A statement or other disclosure or a record thereof made by a child during the course of assessment or during the stay of proceedings shall not be disclosed at any time to a commonwealth or other law enforcement officer in connection with the investigation or prosecution of any charges against the child or a codefendant.

(4) If a child is found eligible for diversion pursuant to this section, the child shall not be arraigned and an entry shall not be made into the criminal offender record information system unless a judge issues an order to resume the ordinary processing of a delinquency proceeding. If a child is found eligible pursuant to this section, the eligibility shall not be considered an issuance of a criminal complaint for the purposes of section 37H½ of chapter 71.

(d) A district attorney may divert any child for whom there is probable cause to issue a complaint, either before or after the assessment procedure set forth in subsection (b), with or without the permission of the court and without regard to the limitations in subsection (g). A district attorney who diverts a case pursuant to this subsection may request a report from a program regarding the child's status in and completion of the program.

(e) If during the stay of proceedings a child is charged with a subsequent offense, a judge in the court that entered the stay of proceedings may issue such process as is necessary to bring the child before the court. When the child is brought before the court, the judge shall afford the child an opportunity to be heard. If the judge finds probable cause to believe that the child has committed a subsequent offense, the judge may order that the stay of proceedings be terminated and that the commonwealth be permitted to proceed on the original complaint as provided by law.

(f)(1) Upon the expiration of the initial 90-day stay of proceedings, the probation officer or the program director shall submit to the court a report indicating the successful completion of diversion by the child or recommending an extension of the stay of proceedings for not more than an additional 90 days so that the child may complete the diversion program successfully.

(2) If the probation officer or the program director indicates the successful completion of diversion by a child, the judge may dismiss the original complaint pending against the child. If the report recommends an extension of the stay of proceedings, the judge may, on the basis of the report and any other relevant evidence, take such action as the judge deems appropriate, including the dismissal of the complaint, the granting of an extension of the stay of proceedings or the resumption of proceedings.

(3) If the conditions of diversion have not been met, the child's attorney shall be notified prior to the termination of the child from diversion and the judge may grant an extension to the stay of proceedings if the child provides good cause for failing to comply with the conditions of diversion.

(4) If the judge dismisses a complaint under this subsection, the court shall, unless the child objects, enter an order directing expungement of any records of the complaint and related proceedings maintained by the clerk, the court, the department of criminal justice information services and the court activity record index.

(g) A child otherwise eligible for diversion pursuant to this section shall not be eligible for diversion if the child is indicted as a youthful offender or if the child is charged with a violation of 1 or more of the offenses enumerated in the second sentence of section 70C of chapter 277, other than the offenses in subsection (a) of section 13A of chapter 265 and sections 13A and 13C of chapter 268, or if the defendant is charged with an offense for which a penalty of incarceration greater than 5 years may be imposed or for which there is a minimum term penalty of incarceration or which may not be continued without a finding or placed on file. Diversion of juvenile court charges under this chapter shall not preclude a subsequent indictment on the same charges in superior court.

§ 55. Summoning of parent or guardian

If a child has been summoned to appear or is brought before such court upon a warrant, as provided in section fifty-four, a summons shall be issued to at least one of its parents, if either of them is known to reside within the commonwealth, and, if there is no such parent, then to its lawful guardian, if there is one known to be so resident, and if not, then to the person with whom such child resides, if known. Said summons shall require the person served to appear at a time and place stated therein, and show cause why such child should not be adjudged a delinquent child and why it is not in such child's best interest that he be removed from his home and whether reasonable efforts were made to prevent or eliminate the need for removal from his home. If there is no such parent, guardian or person who can be summoned as aforesaid, the court may appoint a suitable person to act for such child. A parent, guardian or person with whom such child resides who is summoned to appear before the court to show cause why such child shall not be adjudged a delinquent child by reason of having committed the offense of willful or malicious destruction or wanton destruction of property, in violation of the provisions of section one hundred and twenty-seven or one hundred and twenty-seven A of chapter two hundred and sixty-six, and who willfully fails to so appear shall be punished by a fine of not less than two hundred nor more than three hundred dollars.

If such child is summoned, the time for appearance fixed in the summons to a parent, guardian or other person, as herein provided, shall, when practicable, be that fixed for the appearance of said child.

A summons required by this and said section fifty-four, unless service thereof is waived in writing, shall be served by a constable or police officer, by delivering it personally to the person to whom addressed, or by leaving it with a person of proper age to receive the same, at the place of residence or business of such person; and said constable or officer shall immediately make return to the court of the time and manner of the service.

If the court shall be of the opinion that the interests of the child require the attendance at any proceedings of an agent of the department of youth services and shall request such attendance by reasonable notice to the commissioner of youth services, such agent shall attend to protect the interests of said child.

§ 55A. Jury trials; discovery orders; jury-waived trials; appointment of stenographer

Trial of a child complained of as a delinquent child or indicted as a youthful offender in a division of the juvenile court department shall be by a jury, unless the child files a written waiver and consent to be tried by the court without a jury. Such waiver shall not be received unless the child is represented by counsel or has filed, through his parent or guardian, a written waiver of counsel. No decision on such waiver shall be received until after the completion of a pretrial conference and a hearing on the results of such conference and until after the disposition of any pretrial discovery motions and compliance with any order of the court pursuant to said motions. Such waiver shall be filed in accordance with the provisions of section six of chapter two hundred and sixty-three; provided, however, that defense counsel shall execute a certificate signed by said counsel indicating that he has made all the necessary explanations and determinations regarding such waiver. The form of such certificates shall be prescribed by the chief justice for the juvenile court department.

In the juvenile court department upon the motion of a child consistent with criminal procedure, or upon the court's own motion, the judge shall issue an order of discovery requiring the prosecutor to provide in writing any information to which the child is entitled and also requiring that the child be permitted to discover, inspect, and copy any material and relevant evidence, documents, statements or persons, or reports of physical or mental examinations of any person or of scientific tests or experiments, within the possession, custody, or control of the prosecutor or persons under his direction and control. Upon motion of the child the judge shall order the production by the commonwealth of the names and addresses of the prospective witnesses and the production by the probation department of the record of prior convictions of any such witnesses. The commonwealth shall be entitled to reciprocal discovery as set forth in Rule 14 (a) (1) (3) of the Massachusetts Rules of Criminal Procedure.

Trial by jury in the juvenile court department shall be in those jury sessions designated in accordance with section fifty-six. Where the child has properly filed a waiver and consented to be tried without a jury, as hereinbefore provided, trial shall proceed in accordance with the provisions of law applicable to jury-waived trials in the superior court; provided, however, that at the option of the child, the trial may be before a judge who has not rejected an agreed upon recommendation or disposition request made by the child pursuant to the provisions of section fifty-five B. Review in such cases may be had directly by the appeals court, by appeal, report or otherwise in the same manner provided for trials of criminal cases in the superior court.

The justice presiding over such jury-waived trial in the juvenile court department shall have and exercise all of the powers which a justice sitting in the superior court department has and may exercise in the trial and disposition of criminal cases including the power to report questions of law to the appeals court.

The justice presiding at such jury-waived session in the juvenile court department shall, upon the request of the child, appoint a stenographer; provided, however, that where the child claims indigence, such appointment is determined to be reasonably necessary in accordance with the provisions of sections twenty-seven A to twenty-seven G, inclusive, of chapter two hundred and sixty-one. Such stenographer shall be sworn, and shall take stenographic notes of all the testimony given at the trial, and shall provide the parties thereto with a transcript of his notes or any part thereof taken at the trial or hearing for which he shall be paid by the party requesting it at the rate fixed by the chief justice of the juvenile court department; provided, however, that such rate shall not exceed the rate provided pursuant to section eighty-eight of chapter two hundred and twenty-one. Said chief justice may make regulations not inconsistent with law relative to the assignments, duties and services of stenographers appointed for sessions in his department and any other matter relative to stenographers. The compensation and expenses of a stenographer shall be paid by the commonwealth.

The request for the appointment of a stenographer to preserve the testimony at a trial in the juvenile court department shall be given to the clerk of the court by the child in writing no later than forty-eight hours prior to the proceeding for which the stenographer has been requested. The child shall file with such request an affidavit of indigence and request for payment by the commonwealth of the cost of the transcript and the court shall hold a hearing on such request prior to appointing a stenographer, in those cases where the child alleges that he will be unable to pay said cost. Said hearing shall be governed by the provisions of sections twenty-seven A to twenty-seven G, inclusive, of chapter two hundred and sixty-one, and the cost of such transcript shall be considered an extra cost as provided therein. If the court is unable, for any reason, to provide a stenographer, the proceedings may be recorded by electronic means. The original recording of proceedings in the juvenile court department made with a recording device under the exclusive control of the court shall be the official record of such proceedings. Said record or a copy of all or a part thereof, certified by the presiding justice or his designee, to be an accurate electronic reproduction of said record or part thereof, or a typewritten transcript of all or part of said record or copy thereof, certified to be accurate by the court or by the preparer of said transcript, or stipulated to by the parties, shall be admissible in any court as evidence of testimony given wherever proof of such testimony is otherwise competent. The child may request payment by the commonwealth of the cost of said transcript subject to the same provisions regarding a transcript of a stenographer as provided hereinbefore.

§ 55B. Plea; disposition request; pretrial motions

[Amended by 2010 Mass. Acts c. 267, §§ 14–16; 2011 Mass. Acts c. 178, § 15, effective Nov. 21, 2011.]

A child who is before the juvenile court on a delinquency complaint or an indictment within the court's jurisdiction shall plead not delinquent, or that he should not be adjudged as a youthful offender, as the case may be. Such plea shall be submitted by the child and acted upon by the court; provided, however, that a child with whom the commonwealth cannot reach agreement for a recommended disposition shall be allowed to tender a plea together with a request for a specific disposition. Such request may include any disposition or dispositional terms within the court's jurisdiction, including, unless otherwise prohibited by law, a disposition request that a finding not be entered, but rather the case be continued without a finding to a specific date thereupon to be dismissed, such continuance conditioned upon compliance with specific terms and conditions or that the child be placed on probation pursuant to the provisions of section 57; provided, however, that a complaint alleging a child to be a delinquent child by reason of having violated the provisions of section 13B, 13B½, 13B¾, section 22A, 22B, 22C or section 23, 23A, 23B or section 50 of chapter 265 shall not be placed on file or continued without a finding. If a plea, with an agreed upon recommendation or with a disposition request by the child, is tendered, the court shall inform the child that it will not impose a disposition that exceeds the terms of the agreed upon recommendation or the disposition request by the child, whichever is applicable, without giving the child the right to withdraw the plea.

Notwithstanding the foregoing requirements, if a child attempts to enter a plea or statement consisting of an admission of facts sufficient for a finding of delinquency or adjudication as a youthful offender, or some similar statement, such admission shall be deemed a tender of plea for purposes of the procedures set forth in this section.

Any pretrial motion filed in a delinquency case or case in which the commonwealth has proceeded by indictment pending in the juvenile court and decided before entry of the child's decision on waiver of the right to jury trial shall not be refiled or reheard thereafter, except in the discretion of the court as substantial justice requires. Any such pretrial motion not filed or filed but not decided prior to entry of the child's decision on waiver of the right to jury trial may be filed thereafter but not later than twenty-one days after entry of said decision on waiver of the right to jury trial, except for good cause shown.

§ 56. Adjournments; jury sessions; appointment of stenographer

Hearings upon cases arising under sections fifty-two to eighty-four, inclusive, may be adjourned from time to time; provided however, that no adjournment shall exceed fifteen days at any one time against the objection of the child. Section thirty-five of chapter two hundred and seventy-six relative to recognizance in cases continued shall apply to cases arising under sections fifty-two to eighty-four, inclusive.

(a) Every division of the juvenile court department shall be authorized to hold jury sessions for the purpose of conducting jury trials of cases commenced in the several courts of offenses over which the juvenile courts have original jurisdiction.

(b) The chief justice for the juvenile court department shall designate at least one division in each county or an adjoining county for the purpose of conducting jury trials.

The chief justice of the juvenile court department may also designate one or more divisions in each county for the purpose of conducting jury-waived trials of cases commenced in any court of said county consistent with the requirements of the proper administration of justice.

(c) A child in any division of the juvenile court who waives his right to jury trial as provided in section fifty-five A shall be provided a jury-waived trial in the same division.

A child in any division of the juvenile court who does not waive his right to jury trial as provided in section fifty-five A shall be provided a jury trial in a jury session in the same division if such session has been established in said division. If such session has not been so established, the child shall be provided a jury trial in a jury session in an adjoining county as designated by the clerk in the division where the case is pending. In cases where the child declines to waive the right to jury trial, the clerk shall forthwith transfer the case for trial in the appropriate jury session. Such transfer shall be governed by procedures to be established by the chief justice for the juvenile court department.

(d) The justice presiding over a jury session shall have and exercise all the powers and duties which a justice sitting in the superior court department has and may exercise in the trial and disposition of criminal cases including the power to report questions of law to the appeals court. No justice so sitting shall act in a case in which he has sat or held an inquest or otherwise taken part in any proceeding therein.

(e) Trials by jury shall proceed in accordance with the provisions of law applicable to trials by jury in the superior court. The commonwealth shall be entitled to as many challenges as equal the whole number to which all the children in the case are entitled. Trial by jury shall be by juries of six persons, except that in cases where the commonwealth has proceeded by indictment, said child shall be entitled to a jury of twelve.

(f) For the jury sessions, jurors shall be provided by the office of the jury commissioner in accordance with the provisions of chapter two hundred and thirty-four A.

(g) The district attorney for the district in which the alleged offense or offenses occurred shall appear for the commonwealth in the trial of all cases in which the right to jury trial has not been waived and may appear in any other case. The chief justice for the juvenile court department shall arrange for the sittings of the jury sessions and shall assign justices thereto, to the end that speedy trials may be provided. Review may be had directly by the appeals court, by appeal, report or otherwise in the same manner provided for trials of criminal cases in the superior court. A claim of trial by jury under this section may be withdrawn before trial, in which event trial and disposition of the case shall be by a justice in a jury session sitting without a jury.

(h) The justice presiding at such session in the juvenile court department shall, upon request of the child, appoint a stenographer in accordance with section fifty-five A herein.

The request for the appointment of a stenographer to preserve the testimony at a trial in the juvenile court department shall be given to the clerk of the court by the child in writing no later than forty-eight hours prior to the proceeding for which the stenographer has been requested. The child shall file with such request an affidavit of indigence and request for payment by the commonwealth of the cost of the transcript and the court shall hold a hearing on such request prior to appointing a stenographer, in those cases where the child alleges that he will be unable to pay said cost. Said hearing shall be governed by the provisions of sections twenty-seven A to twenty-seven G, inclusive, of chapter two hundred and sixty-one, and the cost of such transcript shall be considered an extra cost as provided therein. If the court is unable, for any reason, to provide a stenographer, the proceedings may be recorded by electronic means. The original recording of proceedings in the juvenile court department made with a recording device under the exclusive control of the court shall be the official record of such proceedings. Said record or a copy of all or a part thereof, certified by the presiding justice or his designee, to be an accurate electronic reproduction of said record or part thereof, or a typewritten transcript of all or part of said record or copy thereof, certified to be accurate by the court or by the preparer of said transcript, or stipulated to by the parties, shall be admissible in any court as evidence of testimony given wherever proof of such testimony is otherwise competent. The child may request payment by the commonwealth of the cost of said transcript subject to the same provisions regarding a transcript of a stenographer as provided hereinbefore.

§ 57. Investigation by probation officer; record of performance; reports

Every case of a delinquent child shall be investigated by the probation officer, who shall make a report regarding the character of such child, his school record, home surroundings and the previous complaints against him, if any. In every case involving a child attending a special class authorized by law, he shall secure from the bureau of special education a record of performance of said child. He shall be present in court at the trial of the case, and furnish the court with such information and assistance as shall be required. At the end of the probation period of a child who has been placed on probation, the officer in whose care he has been shall make a report as to his conduct during such period.

§ 58. Adjudication as delinquent child or youthful offender

[Amended by 2010 Mass. Acts c. 267, §§ 17-19; 2011 Mass. Acts c. 178, § 16, effective Nov. 21, 2011; 2013 Mass. Acts c. 84, §§ 9–11, effective Sept. 18, 2013.]

At the hearing of a complaint against a child the court shall hear the testimony of any witnesses who appear and take such evidence relative to the case as shall be produced. If the allegations against a child are proved beyond a reasonable doubt, he may be adjudged a delinquent child, or in lieu thereof, the court may continue the case without a finding and, with the consent of the child and at least one of the child's parents or guardians, place said child on probation; provided, however, that any such probation may be imposed until such child reaches age eighteen or age nineteen in the case of a child whose case is disposed of after he has attained his eighteenth birthday or age 20 in the case of a child whose case is disposed of after he has attained his nineteenth birthday; provided further, that a complaint alleging a child to be a delinquent child by reason of having violated the provisions of section 13B, 13B½, 13B¾, section 22A, 22B, 22C, 23, 23A, section 23B or section 50 of chapter 265 shall not be placed on file or continued without a finding. Said probation may include a requirement, subject to agreement by the child and at least one of the child's parents or guardians, that the child do work or participate in activities of a type and for a period of time deemed appropriate by the court.

If a child is adjudicated a delinquent child on a complaint, the court may place the case on file or may place the child in the care of a probation officer for such time and on such conditions as it deems appropriate or may commit him to the custody of the department of youth services, but the probationary or commitment period shall not be for a period longer than until such child attains the age of eighteen, or nineteen in the case of a child whose case is disposed of after he has attained his eighteenth birthday or age 20 in the case of a child whose case is disposed of after he has attained his nineteenth birthday.

If a child is adjudicated a youthful offender on an indictment, the court may sentence him to such punishment as is provided by law for the offense. The court shall make a written finding, stating its reasons therefor, that the present and long-term public safety would be best protected by:

(a) a sentence provided by law; or

(b) a combination sentence which shall be a commitment to the department of youth services until he reaches the age of twenty one, and an adult sentence to a house of correction or to the state prison as is provided by law for the offense. The adult sentence shall be suspended pending successful completion of a term of probation, which shall include, but not be limited to, the successful completion of the aforementioned commitment to the department of youth services. Any juvenile receiving a combination sentence shall be under the sole custody and control of the department of youth services unless or until discharged by the department or until the age of twenty-one, whichever occurs first, and thereafter under the supervision of the juvenile court probation department until the age of twenty-one and thereafter by the adult probation department; provided, however, that in no event shall the aggregate sentence imposed on the combination sentence exceed the maximum adult sentence provided by law; or

(c) a commitment to the department of youth services until he reaches the age of twenty-one.

In making such determination the court shall conduct a sentencing recommendation hearing to determine the sentence by which the present and long-term public safety would be best protected. At such hearing, the court shall consider, but not be limited to, the following factors: the nature, circumstances and seriousness of the offense; victim impact statement; a report by a probation officer concerning the history of the youthful offender; the youthful offender's court and delinquency records; the success or lack of success of any past treatment or delinquency dispositions regarding the youthful offender; the nature of services available through the juvenile justice system; the youthful offender's age and maturity; and the likelihood of avoiding future criminal conduct. In addition, the court may consider any other factors it deems relevant to disposition. No such sentence shall be imposed until a presentence investigation report has been filed by the probation department and made available to the parties no less than seven days prior to sentencing.

A youthful offender who is sentenced as is provided by law either to a state prison or to a house of correction but who has not yet reached his eighteenth birthday shall be held in a youthful offender unit separate from the general population of adult prisoners; provided, however, that such youthful offender shall be classified at a facility other than the reception and diagnostic center at the Massachusetts Correctional Institution, Concord, and shall not be held at the Massachusetts Correctional Institution, Cedar Junction, prior to his eighteenth birthday.

If it is alleged in the complaint upon which the child is so adjudged that a penal law of the commonwealth, a city ordinance or a town by-law has been violated, the court may commit such child to the custody of the commissioner of youth services and authorize him to place such child in the charge of any person, and, if at any time thereafter the child proves unmanageable, to transfer such child to that facility which in the opinion of said commissioner, after study, will best serve the needs of the child. The department of youth services shall provide for the maintenance, in whole or part, of any child so placed in the charge of any person.

Notwithstanding any other provisions of this chapter, a person adjudicated a delinquent child by reason of a violation of paragraph (a), (c) or (d) of section ten or section ten E of chapter two hundred and sixty-nine, shall be committed to the custody of the commissioner of youth services who shall place such child in the custody of a facility supported by the commonwealth for the care, custody and training of such delinquent children for a period of at least one hundred and eighty days or until such child attains his eighteenth birthday, or his nineteenth birthday in the case of a child whose case is disposed of after he has attained his eighteenth birthday whichever first occurs, provided, however, that said period of time shall not be reduced or suspended.

Upon the second or subsequent violation of said paragraph (a), (c) or (d) of said section ten or ten E of said chapter two hundred and sixty-nine, the commissioner of youth services shall place such child in the custody of a facility supported by the commonwealth for the care, custody and training of such delinquent child for not less than one year; provided, however, that said period of time shall not be reduced or suspended.

The court may make an order for payment by the child's parents or guardian from the child's property, or by any other person responsible for the care and support of said child; to the institution, department, division, organization or person furnishing care and support at times to be stated in an order by the court of sums not exceeding the cost of said support after ability to pay has been determined by the court; provided, however, that no order for the payment of money shall be entered until the person by whom payments are to be made shall have been summoned before the court and given an opportunity to be heard. The court may from time to time, upon petition by, or notice to the person ordered to pay such sums of money, revise or alter such order or make a new order, as the circumstances may require.

The court may commit such delinquent child to the department of youth services, but it shall not commit such child to any institution supported by the commonwealth for the custody, care and training of delinquent children or juvenile offenders.

Except in cases in which the child has attained the age of majority, whenever a court of competent jurisdiction adjudicates a child as delinquent and commits the child to the department of youth services, the court, in order to comply with the requirements contained in the federal Adoption Assistance and Child Welfare Act of 1980 and any amendments thereto, shall receive evidence in order to determine whether continuation of the child in his home is contrary to his best interest, and whether reasonable efforts were made prior to the commitment of the child to the department, to prevent or eliminate the need for removal from his home; or whether an emergency situation existed making such efforts impossible. No such determination shall be made unless the parent or guardian of the delinquent shall have been summoned before the court and, if present, given an opportunity to be heard. The court, in its discretion, may make its determinations concerning said best interest and reasonable efforts in written form, but in the absence of a written determination to the contrary, it shall be presumed that the court did find that continuation of the child in his home was contrary to his best interest and that reasonable efforts to prevent or eliminate the need for removal of the child from his home did occur. Nothing in this section shall diminish the department's responsibility to prevent delinquent acts and to protect the public safety.

NOTE *See Commonwealth v. Magnus M.*, 461 Mass. 459 (2012) (allowing for CWOF after jury trial).

§ 58A. Repealed

[Repealed by 1948 Mass. Acts c. 310, § 5.]

§ 58B. Commitment of delinquent child

If, under the provisions of section fifty-eight, a child is adjudged a delinquent child by reason of having violated any statute, by-law, ordinance or regulation relating to the operation of motor vehicles, the court may place the case on file, or may place the child in the care of a probation officer, or may commit him to the custody of the department of youth services, as provided in section fifty-eight, and may require restitution as provided in section sixty-two; and in addition to or in lieu of such disposition, the court may impose upon such child a fine not exceeding the amount of the fine authorized for the violation of such statute, by-law, ordinance or regulation. Any fine imposed under the authority of this section shall be collected, recovered and paid over in the manner provided by chapters two hundred and seventy-nine and two hundred and eighty; provided, however, that if any child shall neglect, fail or refuse to pay a fine imposed under this section, he may be arrested upon order of the court and brought before the court, which may thereupon place him in the care of a probation officer or commit him to the custody of the department of youth services; but no such child shall be committed to any jail, house of correction, or correctional institution of the commonwealth. The provisions of sections sixty and sixty A shall apply to any case disposed of under this section; provided, however, that the court shall provide the registrar of motor vehicles with an abstract of every such adjudication and disposition in the manner provided by section twenty-seven of chapter ninety; and provided, further, that such adjudication and disposition shall be admissible as evidence in any proceeding for the revocation or restoration of the child's license or right to operate a motor vehicle and for the cancellation of a motor vehicle insurance policy covering the vehicle operated by such child, and in any action of tort arising out of the negligent operation of a motor vehicle by said child, to the same extent that such evidence would be admissible if said child were an adult.

§ 59. Violation of terms of probation

If a child has been placed in care of a probation officer, said officer, at any time before the final disposition of the case, may arrest such child without a warrant and take him before the court, or the court may issue a warrant for his arrest. When such child is before the court, it may make any disposition of the case which it might have made before said child was placed on probation, or may continue or extend the period of probation.

§ 60. Admissibility of adjudication in subsequent proceeding; disqualification for public service

An adjudication of any child as a delinquent child under sections fifty-two to fifty-nine, inclusive, or any disposition thereunder of any child so adjudicated, or any evidence given in any case arising against any child under said sections fifty-two to fifty-nine, or any records in cases arising against any child under said sections fifty-two to fifty-nine shall not be received in evidence or used against such child for any purpose in any proceedings in any court except in subsequent delinquency or criminal proceedings against the same person; nor shall such adjudication or disposition or evidence operate to disqualify a child in any future examination, appointment, or application for public service under the government either of the commonwealth or of any political subdivision thereof; provided, however, that adjudication of delinquency by reason of the child having committed an offense against the commonwealth may be used for impeachment purposes in subsequent delinquency or criminal proceedings in the same manner and to the same extent as prior criminal convictions.

§ 60A. Inspection of records in youthful offender and delinquency cases

[Amended by 2013 Mass. Acts c. 84, §§ 12–13, effective Sept. 18, 2013.]

The records of a youthful offender proceeding conducted pursuant to an indictment shall be open to public inspection in the same manner and to the same extent as adult criminal court records. All other records of the court in cases of delinquency arising under sections fifty-two to fifty-nine, inclusive, shall be withheld from public inspection except with the consent of a justice of such court; provided, however, that such records shall be open, at all reasonable times, to inspection by the child proceeded against, his parents, guardian or attorney; provided further, that nothing herein shall be construed to provide access to privileged or confidential communications and information; and provided further, that said protections shall be construed to include information and communications entered at the indictment.

Notwithstanding the provisions of this section, the name of a child shall be made available to the public by the probation officer without such consent if the child is: alleged to have committed an offense while between his fourteenth and eighteenth birthdays; and has previously been adjudicated delinquent on at least two occasions for acts which would have been punishable by imprisonment in the state prison if such child had been age 18 or older; and is charged with delinquency by reason of an act which would be punishable by imprisonment in the state prison if such child were age 18 or older.

§ 61. Repealed

[Repealed by 1996 Mass. Acts c. 200, § 7.]

§ 62. Restitution or reparation by child to injured person

If, in adjudging a person a delinquent child, the court finds, as an element of such delinquency, that he has committed an act involving liability in a civil action, and such delinquent child is placed on probation, the court may require, as a condition thereof, that he shall make restitution or reparation to the injured person to such an extent and in such sum as the court determines. If the payment is not made at once, it shall be made to the probation officer, who shall give a receipt therefor, keep a record of the payment, pay the money to said injured person, and keep on file his receipt therefor.

NOTE Court did not abuse its discretion in ordering a juvenile who admitted to "tagging" several properties to pay restitution to the victims under G.L. c. 119, § 62, because 1) the prosecution provided adequate documentation concerning the amount of damage the juvenile caused; and 2) the juvenile offered no evidence that due to his age—twelve—he was unable to make any payments. *Commonwealth v. Avram A.*, 83 Mass. App. Ct. 208, *review or reh'g denied*, 464 Mass. 1108 (2013).

"[A] judge must consider a defendant's ability to pay, and may not impose a longer period of probation or extend the length of probation because of a defendant's limited ability to pay restitution." *Commonwealth v. Henry*, 475 Mass. 117, 118 (2016). The judge must also determine "the actual economic loss causally connected to the defendant's crime." *Commonwealth v. Henry*, 475 Mass. at 121. The judge must determine what the length of probation is before the determination of whether the defendant has the ability to pay the restitution.

§ 63. Inducing or abetting delinquency of child

Any person who shall be found to have caused, induced, abetted, or encouraged or contributed toward the waywardness or delinquency of a child, or to have acted in any way tending to cause or induce such waywardness or delinquency, may be punished by a fine of not more than five hundred dollars or by imprisonment of not more than one year, or both. The court may release on probation under section eighty-seven of chapter two hundred and seventy-six, subject to such orders as it may make as to future conduct tending to cause, induce or contribute to such delinquency, or it may suspend sentence under section one of chapter two hundred and seventy-nine, or before trial, with the defendant's consent, it may allow the defendant to enter into a recognizance, in such penal sum as the court may fix, conditioned to comply with such terms as the court may order for the promotion of the future welfare of the child, and the said case may then be placed on file. The provisions for recognizance in section fifty-six shall be applicable to cases arising hereunder. The divisions of the juvenile court department shall, within their respective territorial limits, have exclusive jurisdiction over complaints alleging violations of this section.

§ 63A. Inducing or abetting child to violate court order or custody arrangement

[Added by 2008 Mass. Acts c. 176, § 102, effective July 8, 2008; 2013 Mass. Acts c. 84, § 14, effective Sept. 18, 2013.]

Whoever is 19 years of age or older and: (i) knowingly and willfully aids or abets a child under the age of 18, to violate an order of a juvenile court; or (ii) knowingly and willfully conceals or harbors a child who has taken flight from the custody of the court, a parent, a legal guardian, the department of children and families or the department of youth services shall be punished by a fine of not more than $500 or by imprisonment in the house of correction for not more than 1 year, or by both such fine and imprisonment.

It shall be a defense to a violation of clause (ii) if the defendant concealed or harbored a child in the reasonable good faith belief that the child would be at risk of physical or sexual abuse if the child returned to his custodial residence, unless the defendant concealed or harbored such child with intent to abuse the child or if the defendant committed abuse on that child.

The court may release on probation under section 87 of chapter 276, subject to such orders as it may make as to future conduct tending to cause, induce or contribute to a person's status as a child in need of services or delinquency, or it may suspend sentence under section 1 of chapter 279, or before trial, with the defendant's consent, it may allow the defendant to enter into a recognizance, in such penal sum as the court may fix, conditioned to comply with such terms as the court may order for the promotion of the future welfare of the child, and the case may then be placed on file. The provisions for recognizance in section 56 of chapter 276 shall be applicable to cases arising hereunder.

The divisions of the juvenile court department shall, within their respective territorial limits, have exclusive jurisdiction over complaints alleging a violation of this section.

§ 64. Powers of commissioner of probation; annual report

The commissioner of probation may supervise the probation work for wayward and delinquent children, and make necessary inquiries in regard to the same, and in his annual report may make such recommendations as he considers advisable for the improvement of methods of dealing with such children.

PROVISIONS COMMON TO ALL PROCEEDINGS AGAINST CHILDREN

§ 65. Juvenile sessions; presence of minors; exclusion of public

[Amended by 2013 Mass. Acts c. 84, § 15, effective Sept. 18, 2013.]

Courts shall designate suitable times for the hearing of cases of children under 18 years of age, which shall be called the juvenile session, for which a separate docket and record shall be kept. Said session shall be separate from that for the trial of criminal cases, shall not, except as otherwise expressly provided, be held in conjunction with other business of the court, and shall be held in rooms not used for criminal trials; and in places where no separate juvenile courtroom is provided, hearings, so far as possible, shall be held in chambers. The court shall exclude the general public from juvenile sessions admitting only such persons as may have a direct interest in the case, except in cases where the commonwealth has proceeded by indictment. A complaint under section sixty-three may be heard in such juvenile session.

§ 66. Detention of child in police station; commitment to jail, house of correction or state farm

[Amended by 2013 Mass. Acts c. 84, § 16, effective Sept. 18, 2013.]

Except as otherwise provided in section sixty-seven and in section twelve of chapter one hundred and twenty, no child under 18 years of age shall be detained by the police in a lockup, police station or house of detention pending arraignment, examination or trial by the court. No child under 18 years of age shall be committed by the court to a jail or house of correction or to the state farm, pending further examination or trial by the court or pending any continuance of his case or, except as otherwise provided in sections fifty-two through eighty-four upon adjudication as a youthful offender.

§ 67. Notice of arrest of child to probation officer and parent or guardian; detention

[Amended by 2013 Mass. Acts c. 84, § 17, effective Sept. 18, 2013; 2018 Mass. Acts c. 69, § 76, effective July 12, 2018.]

(a) Whenever a child between 12 and 18 years of age is arrested with or without a warrant, as provided by law, and the court or courts having jurisdiction over the offense are not in session, the officer in charge shall immediately notify at least 1 of the child's parents, or, if there is no parent, the guardian or custodian with whom the child resides or if the child is in the custody and care of the department, the department of children and families. Pending such notice, such child shall be detained pursuant to subsection (c).

(b) Upon the acceptance by the officer in charge of the police station or town lockup of the written promise of the parent, guardian, custodian or representative of the department of children and families to be responsible for the presence of the child in court at the time and place when the child is ordered to appear, the child shall be released to the person giving such promise; provided, however, that if the arresting officer requests in writing that a child between 14 and 18 years of age be detained, and if the court issuing a warrant for the arrest of a child between 14 and 18 years of age directs in the warrant that the child shall be held in safekeeping pending the child's appearance in court, the child shall be detained in a police station, town lockup, a place of temporary custody commonly referred to as a detention home of the department of youth services or any other home approved by the department of youth services pending the child's appearance in court; provided further, that in the event any child is so detained, the officer in charge of the police station or town lockup shall notify the parents, guardian, custodian or representative of the department of children and families of the detention of the child. Nothing contained in this section shall prevent the admitting of such child to bail in accordance with law.

(c) No child between 14 and 18 years of age shall be detained in a police station or town lockup pursuant to subsection (a) or (b) unless the detention facilities for children at the police station or town lockup have received the approval in writing of the commissioner of youth services. The department of youth services shall make inspection at least annually of police stations and town lockups where children are detained. If no approved detention facility exists in a city or town, the city or town may contract with an adjacent city or town for the use of approved detention facilities to prevent children who are detained from coming in contact with adult prisoners. A separate and distinct place shall be provided in police stations, town lockups or places of detention for such children. Nothing in this section shall permit a child between 14 and 18 years of age to be detained in a jail or house of correction.

(d) When a child is arrested who is in the care and custody of the department of children and families, the officer in charge of the police station or town lockup where the child has been taken shall immediately contact the department's emergency hotline and notify the on-call worker of the child's arrest. The on-call worker shall notify the social worker assigned to the child's case who shall make arrangement for the child's release as soon as practicable if it has been determined that the child will not be detained.

§ 68. Commitment of children held for examination or trial

[Amended by 2013 Mass. Acts c. 84, § 18, effective Sept. 18, 2013; 2018 Mass. Acts c. 69, § 77, effective July 12, 2018.]

A child who has attained the age of 12 but not yet attained the age of 18 held by the court for further examination, trial or continuance, or for indictment and trial, if unable to furnish bail, shall be committed by the court to the care of the department of youth services or to a probation officer, a parent, guardian, or other responsible person who shall provide for his safekeeping; provided, however, that the appearance of the child at such examination or trial, shall be the responsibility of the court for which he is being held in safekeeping.

The court may recommend that a child who has attained the age of fourteen and who is committed to the care of the department shall be held in a secure detention facility if the court further determines that the child (a) is a fugitive from another jurisdiction on a delinquency petition; or (b) is charged with an offense for which the commonwealth may proceed by indictment in accordance with the provisions of section fifty-four; provided, however, that such child is already detained or on conditional release in conjunction with another delinquency proceeding, or has demonstrated a recent record of willful failure to appear at juvenile court proceedings, or has demonstrated a recent record of violent conduct resulting in physical injury to others.

The court shall forward such recommendation and the reasons therefor, in writing, to the department. Such recommendation shall not be binding upon the department, but if the department chooses not to comply with such recommendation, the department shall inform the court within two business days.

The department may provide special foster homes, and places of temporary custody commonly referred to as detention homes of the department of youth services for the care, maintenance and safekeeping of such children who may be committed by the court to said department under this section; provided, however, that no more than five such children shall be detained in any such special foster home at any one time.

A child between 12 and 18 years of age so committed by the court to the department to await further examination or trial by the court, shall be returned thereto within fifteen days after the date of the order of such commitment, and final disposition of the case shall thereupon be made by adjudication or otherwise, unless, in the opinion of the court, the interest of the child and the public otherwise require.

The provisions of section twenty-four of chapter two hundred and twelve, relative to the precedence of cases of persons actually confined in prison and awaiting trial, shall apply to children held in detention facilities of the department of youth services under this section.

Said probation officer shall have the same authority, rights and powers in relation to a child committed to his care under this section, and in relation to a child released to him as provided in section sixty-seven, as he would have if he were surety on the recognizance of such child.

A person who at the time of the offense had attained the age of fourteen but had not attained the age of 18, and who is charged with murder in the first or second degree and is held by the superior court for trial or continuance, or for indictment and trial, if unable to furnish bail, shall be committed by the court to the custody of the sheriff of the county in which the court is situated; provided, however, that the appearance of the person at such examination or trial shall be the responsibility of the court for which he is being held in safekeeping.

§ 68A. Diagnostic study by department of youth services; report and recommendations

[Amended by 2013 Mass. Acts c. 84, § 19, effective Sept. 18, 2013; 2018 Mass. Acts c. 69, § 78, effective July 12, 2018.]

A child between 12 and 18 years of age, held by the court for further examination, trial or continuance, or for indictment and trial, may at the discretion of the court be referred to the department of youth services, any court clinic, or the department of mental health, with its consent, and with the consent of the parents or guardian, for diagnostic study on an inpatient or outpatient basis; and, upon completion of such study, the department of youth services, court clinic or department of mental health, as the case may be, shall forward a report and recommendations to the court. In default of bail, any such child may be committed by the court to the department of youth services for a period not to exceed thirty days while undergoing diagnostic study. At the expiration of such period, such child shall be returned to the court, together with the report and recommendations to the department of youth services.

§ 68B. Special foster homes; detention homes; transfer of child

[Amended by 2009 Mass. Acts c. 166, § 29A, effective Nov. 24, 2009.]

The department of youth services may use or provide special foster homes and places of temporary custody commonly referred to as detention homes, at various places in the commonwealth which shall be completely separate from any police station, town lockup or jail, and which shall be used solely for the temporary care, custody and study of children committed to the care of the department of youth services. Nothing in this section shall prevent the department from using or providing alternative placements and employing alternative measures which, in its discretion, will reasonably assure the appearance of the children before the court.

§ 68C. Diagnostic services by department of youth services

The department of youth services shall maintain and provide diagnostic services for the purpose of providing the diagnostic studies and making the reports and recommendations provided for under section sixty-eight A, and the department may provide offices and facilities for such diagnostic services, at such places in the commonwealth as will best serve the needs of the several courts.

§ 69. Information and reports of superintendents of schools and teachers relating to conduct of child awaiting examination or trial

The superintendent of the public schools in any town, any teacher therein, and any person in charge of a private school, or any teacher therein, shall furnish to any court from time to time any information and reports requested by any justice thereof relating to the attendance, conduct and standing of any pupil enrolled in such school, if said pupil is at the time awaiting examination or trial by the court or is under the supervision of the court.

§ 69A. Information of probation officers, police and school authorities

When a person has been committed to the department of youth services, the court, the probation officers, and other public and police authorities, the school authorities, and other public officials shall make available to said department all pertinent information in their possession in respect to the case.

§ 70. Summoning of parent or guardian during case

[Amended by 2013 Mass. Acts c. 84, § 20, effective Sept. 18, 2013.]

At any time during the pendency of any case before a court or trial justice against a child under 18 years of age, whether pending adjudication or during continuances or probation or after the case has been taken from the files, the court or trial justice may summon any parent or guardian of said child, or any person with whom the child resides, in the manner provided in section fifty-five.

§ 71. Failure to appear on summons; capias

If any person to whom a summons is issued under the preceding section or section forty-two or fifty-five fails to appear in response to such summons, the court issuing the summons may issue a capias to compel the attendance of such person, and such capias shall be issued and served in the same manner as a capias to compel the attendance of witnesses who have failed to appear on a subpoena issued in behalf of the commonwealth in a criminal case.

§ 72. Continuance of jurisdiction of courts in juvenile sessions

[Amended by 2013 Mass. Acts c. 84, §§ 21–22A, effective Sept. 18, 2013; 2014 Mass. Acts c. 165, § 153, effective July 15, 2014.]

(a) The divisions of the juvenile court department shall continue to have jurisdiction over children who attain their eighteenth birthday pending final adjudication of their cases, including all remands and retrials following appeals from their cases, or during continuances or probation, or after their cases have been placed on file, or for any other proceeding arising out of their cases. Except as provided in subsection (b), nothing herein shall authorize the commitment of a person to the department of youth services after he has attained his twentieth birthday.

If a child commits an offense prior to his eighteenth birthday, and is not apprehended until between such child's eighteenth and nineteenth birthday, the court shall deal with such child in the same manner as if he has not attained his eighteenth birthday, and all provisions and rights applicable to a child under 18 shall apply to such child.

(b) If the commonwealth has proceeded by indictment, the divisions of the juvenile court department shall continue to have jurisdiction over such persons who attain their eighteenth birthday pending the final adjudication of their cases, including all remands and retrials following appeals from their cases, or pending the determination allowed under section 58, or during continuances or probation, or after their cases have been placed on file, or for any other proceeding arising out of their cases. Nothing herein shall authorize the commitment of a youthful offender to the department of youth services after he has attained his twenty-first birthday.

§ 72A. Proceedings upon apprehension after nineteenth birthday

[Amended by 2013 Mass. Acts c. 84, § 23, effective Sept. 18, 2013.]

If a person commits an offense or violation prior to his eighteenth birthday, and is not apprehended until after his nineteenth birthday, the court, after a hearing, shall determine whether there is probable cause to believe that said person committed the offense charged, and shall, in its discretion, either order that the person be discharged, if satisfied that such discharge is consistent with the protection of the public; or, if the court is of the opinion that the interests of the public require that such person be tried for such offense or violation instead of being discharged, the court shall dismiss the delinquency complaint and cause a criminal complaint to be issued. The case shall thereafter proceed according to the usual course of criminal proceedings and in accordance with the provisions of section thirty of chapter two hundred and eighteen and section eighteen of chapter two hundred and seventy-eight. Said hearing shall be held prior to, and separate from, any trial on the merits of the charges alleged.

§ 72B. Persons between the ages of fourteen and eighteen convicted of murder; penalties

[Amended by 2013 Mass. Acts c. 84, §§ 24–24A, effective Sept. 18, 2013; 2014 Mass. Acts c. 189, § 2, effective July 25, 2014.]

If a person is found guilty of murder in the first degree committed on or after his fourteenth birthday and before his eighteenth birthday under the provisions of section one of chapter two hundred and sixty-five, the superior court shall commit the person to such punishment as is provided by law for the offense.

If a person is found guilty of murder in the second degree committed on or after his fourteenth birthday and before his eighteenth birthday under the provisions of section one of chapter two hundred and sixty-five, the superior court shall commit the person to such punishment as is provided by law. Said person shall be eligible for parole under section one hundred and thirty-three A of chapter one hundred and twenty-seven when such person has served fifteen years of said confinement. Thereafter said person shall be subject to the provisions of law governing the granting of parole permits by the parole board.

The superior court shall not suspend the commitment of a person found guilty of murder in the first or second degree, nor shall the provisions of section one hundred and twenty-nine C or one hundred and twenty-nine D of chapter one hundred and twenty-seven apply to such commitment. In all cases where a person is alleged to have violated section one of chapter two hundred and sixty-five, the person shall have the right to an indictment proceeding under section four of chapter two hundred and sixty-three.

A person who is found guilty of murder and is sentenced to a state prison but who has not yet reached his eighteenth birthday shall be held in a youthful offender unit separate from the general population of adult prisoners; provided, however, that such person shall be classified at a facility other than the reception and diagnostic center at the Massachusetts Correctional Institution, Concord, and shall not be held at the Massachusetts Correctional Institution, Cedar Junction, prior to his eighteenth birthday.

The department of correction shall not limit access to programming and treatment including, but not limited to, education, substance abuse, anger management and vocational training for youthful offenders, as defined in section 52, solely because of their crimes or the duration of their incarcerations. If the youthful offender qualifies for placement in a minimum security correctional facility based on objective measures determined by the department, the placement shall not be categorically barred based on a life sentence.

If a defendant is not found guilty of murder in the first or second degree, but is found guilty of a lesser included offense or a criminal offense properly joined under Massachusetts Rules of Criminal Procedure 9(a)(1), then the superior court shall make its disposition in accordance with section fifty-eight.

CRIMINAL PROCEEDINGS

§ 73. Repealed

[Repealed by 1964 Mass. Acts c. 308, § 5.]

§ 74. Limitations on criminal proceedings against children

[Amended by 2013 Mass. Acts c. 84, §§ 25–26, effective Sept. 18, 2013.]

Except as hereinafter provided and as provided in sections fifty-two to eighty-four, inclusive, no criminal proceeding shall be begun against any person who prior to his eighteenth birthday commits an offense against the laws of the commonwealth or who violates any city ordinance or town by-law, provided, however, that a criminal complaint alleging violation of any city ordinance or town by-law regulating the operation of motor vehicles, which is not capable of being judicially heard and determined as a civil motor vehicle infraction pursuant to the provisions of chapter ninety C may issue against a child between sixteen and 18 years of age without first proceeding against him as a delinquent child.

The juvenile court shall not have jurisdiction over a person who had at the time of the offense attained the age of fourteen but not yet attained the age of 18 who is charged with committing murder in the first or second degree. Complaints and indictments brought against persons for such offenses, and for other criminal offenses properly joined under Massachusetts Rules of Criminal Procedure 9 (a) (1), shall be brought in accordance with the usual course and manner of criminal proceedings.

§ 75. Repealed

[Repealed by 1975 Mass. Acts c. 840, § 2A.]

§§ 76–82. Repealed

[Repealed by 1964 Mass. Acts c. 208, § 5.]

§ 83. Repealed

[Repealed by 1996 Mass. Acts c. 200, § 16.]

§ 84. Warrant of commitment to department of youth services

[Amended by 2013 Mass. Acts c. 84, § 27, effective Sept. 18, 2013; 2018 Mass. Acts c. 69, § 79, effective July 12, 2018.]

Whenever a person is committed to the department of youth services by a court under section fifty-six, fifty-eight or eighty-three, a warrant of commitment shall be issued in substance as follows:—

THE COMMONWEALTH OF MASSACHUSETTS

(COUNTY) ss.

To the Sheriff of the County of _____ or his Deputy, or any Constable or Police Officer in said County, and to the Department of Youth Services at

GREETING:

Whereas, (name of person committed) of _____ in the county of _____ a boy (or girl) between twelve and eighteen (or nineteen) years of age, has this day been brought before the _____ court of _____ by virtue of a summons (or warrant) issued to (against) him (or her) on the complaint Of _____ of _____ in the county of _____ who therein, upon oath, says that said defendant, at _____ in the county of _____ on the _____ day of _____ in the year one thousand nine hundred and _____ was guilty of _____ as is more fully alleged in said complaint.

And after hearing all matters and things concerning the same, and all persons entitled thereto having been summoned and notified of the pendency of said complaint, as required by law, it is adjudged by said court that said defendant is delinquent and that he (or she) is of the age of _____ years and _____ months, and is a suitable subject for commitment to the custody of the department of youth services, and that his (or her) moral welfare and best interest and the good of society require that he (or she) should be sent thereto for diagnosis, treatment and training;, and said court shall also find that reasonable efforts were made to prevent or eliminate the need for the defendant's removal from his home or that an emergency situation made such efforts impossible and it is thereupon ordered by said court that said defendant stand committed to the custody of the department of youth services during his (or her) minority, or until he (or she) be discharged according to law.

You are therefore hereby required, in the name of the Commonwealth of Massachusetts, to take said defendant and him (or her) carry to the department of youth services and him (or her) deliver to the (designated officer) thereof, together with an attested copy thereof, and thereafterward forthwith to return this warrant with your doings thereon into said court.

And you, the department of youth services, are alike required to receive said defendant into your custody, and him (or her) safely keep for diagnosis, treatment, instruction and training until the expiration of said term of his (or her) minority, or he (or she) be discharged according to law.

Witness _____ at said _____ this _____ day of _____ in the year one thousand nine hundred and _____

Clerk.

A true copy.

(Constable of _____)

Attest: (Sheriff of _____)

No variance from said form shall be considered material if it sufficiently appears upon the face thereof that the person is committed by the court in the exercise of the powers conferred by this chapter. The warrant may be executed by any officer qualified to serve civil or criminal process in the county where the case is heard. Accompanying the warrant, the court or magistrate shall transmit to the designated officer of the department of youth services, by the officer serving it, a statement of the substance of the complaint and testimony given in the case, and such other particulars relative to the person committed as can be ascertained.

§ 86. Use of restraints during court proceedings

[Added by 2018 Mass. Acts c. 69, § 80, effective July 12, 2018.]

(a) For the purposes of this section, the following words shall, unless the context clearly requires otherwise, have the following meanings—

"Juvenile", (1) a person appearing before a division of the juvenile court department who is (i) subject to a delinquency proceeding, (ii) a child requiring assistance or (iii) a child in a care and protection proceeding or (2) a person under the age of 21 in a youthful offender proceeding.

"Restraints", a device that limits voluntary physical movement of an individual, including leg irons and shackles, which have been approved by the trial court department.

(b) A juvenile shall not be placed in restraints during court proceedings and any restraints shall be removed prior to the appearance of a juvenile before the court at any stage of a proceeding unless the justice presiding in the courtroom issues an order and makes specific findings on the record that: (i) restraints are necessary because there is reason to believe that a juvenile presents an immediate and credible risk of escape that cannot be curtailed by other means; (ii) a juvenile poses a threat to the juvenile's own safety or to the safety of others; or (iii) restraints are reasonably necessary to maintain order in the courtroom.

(c) The court officer charged with custody of a juvenile shall report any security concern to the presiding justice. On the issue of courtroom or courthouse security, the presiding justice may receive information from the court officer charged with custody of a juvenile, a probation officer or any other source determined by the court to be credible.

The authority to use restraints shall reside solely within the discretion of the presiding justice at the time that a juvenile appears before the court. A juvenile court justice shall not impose a blanket policy to maintain restraints on all juveniles or a specific category of juveniles who appear before the court.

§ 87. Placement of juvenile in secure detention facility or secure correctional facility or in any institution in which juvenile has contact with adult inmates

[Added by 2018 Mass. Acts c. 69, § 80, effective July 12, 2018.]

(a) The department of youth services and the department of correction shall not place in a secure detention facility or secure correctional facility any juvenile who has: (1) been charged with or who has committed an offense that would not be criminal if committed by an adult, except juveniles who are held in accordance with the interstate compact on juveniles, as enacted by the commonwealth; (2) not been charged with any offense; or (3) been alleged to be dependent on the court, neglected or abused.

(b) The department of youth services and the department of correction shall not detain or confine any juvenile identified subsection (a) or any juvenile alleged to be or found to be delinquent in any institution in which they have contact with adult inmates; and shall require that individuals employed by the department of youth services or the department of corrections who work with both juveniles and adult inmates be trained and certified to work with juveniles by the department of youth services.

The department of youth services and the department of correction shall promulgate regulations and policies for the implementation, administration and enforcement of this section and maintain adequate records to ensure compliance with this section.

§ 88. Participation in community-based restorative justice program

[Added by 2018 Mass. Acts c. 69, § 80, effective July 12, 2018.]

A child against whom a complaint is brought pursuant to this chapter may participate in a community-based restorative justice program pursuant to chapter 276B.

§ 89. Juvenile justice policy and data board

[Added by 2018 Mass. Acts c. 69, § 80, effective July 12, 2018.]

(a) As used in this section the following words shall, unless the context clearly requires otherwise, have the following meanings:—

"Alternative lock-up program", a facility or program that provides for the physical care and custody of a juvenile being held by a criminal justice agency after an arrest and before an arraignment, including a program provided by the police or municipal, county or state government, as well as any contractor, vendor or service-provider working with such agencies.

"Child advocate", the child advocate appointed pursuant to section 3 of chapter 18C.

"Contact", any action or decision by criminal justice agencies or by any other official of the commonwealth or private service provider under contract or other agreement with the commonwealth, involving a juvenile at any stage of the juvenile justice system which causes such juvenile to enter or exit the juvenile justice system or which will change the custodial status, liberty, case processing or status of the juvenile within the juvenile justice system.

"Criminal justice agencies", agencies at all levels of government which perform as their principal function, activities relating to: (a) crime prevention, including research or the sponsorship of research; (b) the apprehension, prosecution, adjudication, incarceration or rehabilitation of criminal offenders; or (c) the collection, storage, dissemination or usage of criminal offender record information.

"Juvenile", a child under the age of 18; provided, however, that the term juvenile shall include a person under the age of 22 if

1

the person remains within the jurisdiction of the juvenile court or juvenile justice system and a child between the ages of 14 to 18, inclusive, who is charged with first or second degree murder pursuant to section 74.

"Office", the office of the child advocate.

"Racial or ethnic category", the socio-cultural racial and ethnic category of an individual as categorized in a manner that is consistent with the categories established and utilized by the federal Office of Juvenile Justice and Delinquency Prevention.

"Type of crime", the category of crime consistent with the categories established and utilized by the National Incident-Based Reporting System.

(b) There shall be a juvenile justice policy and data board, referred to in this section as the board. The board shall evaluate policies and procedures related to the juvenile justice system, examine the feasibility of the child advocate collecting and disseminating data regarding juvenile contact with criminal justice agencies and study the implementation of any statutory changes to the juvenile justice system.

The board shall consist of 21 members, 1 of whom shall be a member of the house of representatives appointed by the speaker of the house of representatives; 1 member of the house of representatives to be appointed by the minority leader of the house; 1 of whom shall be a member of the senate appointed by the president of the senate; 1 member of the senate to be appointed by the senate minority leader; 1 of whom shall be the child advocate, who shall serve as chair; 1 of whom shall be the chief justice of the juvenile court or a designee; 1 of whom shall be the commissioner of probation or a designee; 1 of whom shall be the commissioner of youth services or a designee; 1 of whom shall be the commissioner of children and families or a designee; 1 of whom shall be the commissioner of mental health or a designee; 1 of whom shall be the commissioner of public health or a designee; 1 of whom shall be the secretary of education or a designee; 1 of whom shall be the chief counsel of the committee for public counsel services or a designee; 1 of whom shall be the president of the Massachusetts District Attorneys Association or a designee; 1 of whom shall be the chair of the Massachusetts juvenile justice advisory committee or a designee; and 6 of whom shall be appointed by the governor, provided that: 1 of whom shall be from a list provided by Citizens for Juvenile Justice, Inc., 1 of whom shall be from a list provided by the Children's League of Massachusetts, Inc., 1 of whom shall be from a list provided by the Massachusetts Chiefs of Police Association Incorporated, 2 of whom shall be parents whose children have been subject to juvenile court jurisdiction and 1 of whom shall have experience or expertise related to the design and implementation of state administrative data systems. Members of the board shall serve without compensation.

The board shall analyze and make a recommendation on the feasibility of the child advocate creating and annually updating an instrument to record aggregate statistical data for every contact a juvenile has with: (i) criminal justice agencies; (ii) any contractor, vendor or service-provider working with said agencies; and (iii) any alternative lock-up programs. The data to be recorded on the instrument shall include, without limitation, age, gender, racial or ethnic category and type of crime. The recommendation shall include a study of the feasibility of all offices and departments subject to this section using the instrument to record a juvenile's contact. The board shall determine the best practices for departments to submit data to the child advocate.

The board shall submit its findings and recommendations relative to data collection by the child advocate by June 30, 2019 to the clerks of the house and the senate, who shall forward the report to the chairs of the house committee on ways and means, the senate committee on ways and means, and the joint committee on the judiciary.

The board shall annually report to the governor, the house and senate chairs of the joint committee on the judiciary, the house and senate chairs of the joint committee on public safety and homeland security and the chief justice of the trial court regarding the following:

(1) any statutory changes concerning the juvenile justice system that the board recommends to: (i) improve public safety, (ii) promote the best interests of children and young adults who are under the jurisdiction, supervision, care or custody of the juvenile court, the commissioner of youth services or the commissioner of children and families; (iii) improve transparency and accountability with respect to state-funded services for children and young adults in the juvenile justice system with an emphasis on goals identified by the committee for community-based programs and facility-based interventions; (iv) promote the efficient sharing of information between the executive branch and the judicial branch to ensure the regular collection and reporting of recidivism data; and (v) promote public welfare and public safety outcomes related to the juvenile justice system;

(2) an analysis of the capacities and limitations of the data systems and networks used to collect and report state and local juvenile caseload and outcome data. The analysis shall include, without limitation, the following: (i) a review of the relevant data systems, studies and models from the commonwealth and other states; (ii) identification of changes or upgrades to current data collection processes to remove inefficiencies, track and monitor state agency and court-involved juveniles and facilitate the coordination of information sharing between relevant agencies and the courts including without limitation, data that is required to be reported under federal law or for purposes of securing federal funding; (iii) the identification and evaluation of any gender, racial and ethnic disparities within the juvenile justice system and recommendations regarding ways to reduce such disparities; (iv) recommendations for the creation of a web-based statewide information center to make relevant juvenile justice information on operations, caseloads, dispositions and outcomes available in a user-friendly, query-based format for stakeholders and members of the public, including a feasibility assessment of implementing such system; (v) a plan for improving the current juvenile justice reporting requirements, including streamlining and consolidating current requirements without impacting data collection and including a detailed analysis of the information technology and other resources necessary to implement improved data collection; (vi) any other matters which the board determines may improve the collection and interagency coordination of juvenile justice data;

(3) the impact of any statutory change that expands or alters the jurisdiction or functioning of the juvenile court, as measured by the following: (i) any change in the average age of children and young adults involved in the juvenile justice system; (ii) the types of services used by designated age groups and the outcomes of those services; (iii) the types of delinquent acts or criminal offenses that children and young adults have been charged with since the enactment and implementation of such statutory change; (iv) the gaps in services identified by the committee with respect to children and young adults involved in the juvenile justice system, including, but not limited to, young adults who have attained the age of 18 after being involved in the juvenile justice system, and recommendations to address such gaps in services; and (v) the strengths and barriers identified by the board that support or impede the educational needs of children and young adults in the juvenile justice system, with specific recommendations for reforms;

(4) the quality and accessibility of diversion programs available to juveniles;

(5) an assessment of the system of community-based services for children and juveniles who are under the supervision, care or custody of the department of youth services or the juvenile court;

(6) an assessment of the number of juveniles who, after being or while under the supervision or custody of the department of children and families, are adjudicated delinquent or as a youthful offender; and

(7) an assessment of the overlap between the juvenile justice system and the mental health care system for children.

The board shall establish a timeframe for review and reporting regarding the responsibilities outlined in this section. Each report submitted by the board shall include specific recommendations to improve outcomes and a timeline by which specific tasks or outcomes shall be achieved.

Appendix to Chapter 119. Interstate Compact on the Placement of Children

§ 2-1. Form and contents

A compact is hereby entered into with all jurisdictions legally joining therein in substantially the following form:—

INTERSTATE COMPACT ON THE
PLACEMENT OF CHILDREN

Article I. Purpose and policy

It is the purpose and policy of the party states to co-operate with each other in the interstate placement of children to the end that:

(a) Each child requiring placement shall receive the maximum opportunity to be placed in a suitable environment and with persons or institutions having appropriate qualifications and facilities to provide a necessary and desirable degree and type of care.

(b) The appropriate authorities in a state where a child is to be placed may have full opportunity to ascertain the circumstances of the proposed placement, thereby promoting full compliance with applicable requirements for the protection of the child.

(c) The proper authorities of the state from which the placement is made may obtain the most complete information on the basis of which to evaluate a projected placement before it is made.

(d) Appropriate jurisdictional arrangements for the care of children will be promoted.

Article II. Definitions

As used in this compact:

(a) "Child" means a person who, by reason of minority, is legally subject to parental guardianship or similar control.

(b) "Sending agency" means a party state, officer or employee thereof; a subdivision of a party state, or officer or employee thereof; a court of a party state; a person, corporation, association, charitable agency or other entity which sends, brings or causes to be sent or brought any child to another party state.

(c) "Receiving state" means the state to which a child is sent, brought or caused to be sent or brought, whether by public authorities or private persons or agencies, and whether for placement with state or local public authorities or for placement with private agencies or persons.

(d) "Placement" means the arrangement for the care of a child in a family free or boarding home or in a child-caring agency or institution but does not include any institution caring for the mentally ill, mentally defective or epileptic or any institution primarily educational in character, and any hospital or other medical facility.

Article III. Conditions for placement

(a) No sending agency shall send, bring or cause to be sent or brought into any other party state any child for placement in foster care or as a preliminary to a possible adoption unless the sending agency shall comply with each and every requirement set forth in this article and with the applicable laws of the receiving state governing the placement of children therein.

(b) Prior to sending, bringing or causing any child to be sent or brought into a receiving state for placement in foster care or as a preliminary to a possible adoption, the sending agency shall furnish the appropriate public authorities in the receiving state written notice of the intention to send, bring or place the child in the receiving state. The notice shall contain:

(1) The name, date and place of birth of the child.

(2) The identity and address or addresses of the parents or legal guardian.

(3) The name and address of the person, agency or institution to or with which the sending agency proposes to send, bring or place the child.

(4) A full statement of the reasons for such proposed action and evidence of the authority pursuant to which the placement is proposed to be made.

(c) Any public officer or agency in a receiving state which is in receipt of a notice pursuant to paragraph (b) of this article may request of the sending agency, or any other appropriate officer or agency of or in the sending agency's state, and shall be entitled to receive therefrom, such supporting or additional information as it may deem necessary under the circumstances to carry out the purpose and policy of this compact.

(d) The child shall not be sent, brought or caused to be sent or brought into the receiving state until the appropriate public authorities in the receiving state shall notify the sending agency, in writing, to the effect that the proposed placement does not appear to be contrary to the interests of the child.

Article IV. Penalty for illegal placement

The sending, bringing or causing to be sent or brought into any receiving state of a child in violation of the terms of this compact shall constitute a violation of the laws respecting the placement of children of both the state in which the sending agency is located or from which it sends or brings the child and of the receiving state. Such violation may be punished or subjected to penalty in either jurisdiction in accordance with its laws. In addition to liability for any such punishment or penalty, any such violation shall constitute full and sufficient grounds for the suspension or revocation of any license, permit or other legal authorization held by the sending agency which empowers or allows it to place or care for children.

Article V. Retention of jurisdiction

(a) The sending agency shall retain jurisdiction over the child sufficient to determine all matters in relation to the custody, supervision, care, treatment and disposition of the child which it would have had if the child had remained in the sending agency's state, until the child is adopted, reaches majority, becomes self-supporting or is discharged with the concurrence of the appropriate authority in the receiving state. Such jurisdiction shall also include the power to effect or cause the return of the child or its transfer to another location and custody pursuant to law. The sending agency shall continue to have financial responsibility for support and maintenance of the child during the period of the placement. Nothing contained herein shall defeat a claim of jurisdiction by a receiving state sufficient to deal with an act of delinquency or crime committed therein.

(b) When the sending agency is a public agency, it may enter into an agreement with an authorized public or private agency in the receiving state providing for the performance of one or more services in respect of such case by the latter as agent for the sending agency.

(c) Nothing in this compact shall be construed to prevent a private charitable agency authorized to place children in the receiving state from performing services or acting as agent in that state for a private charitable agency of the sending state; nor to prevent the agency in the receiving state from discharging financial responsibility for the support and maintenance of a child who has been placed on behalf of the sending agency without relieving the responsibility set forth in paragraph (a) hereof.

Article VI. Institutional care of delinquent children

A child adjudicated delinquent may be placed in an institution in another party jurisdiction pursuant to this compact, but no such placement shall be made unless the child is given a court hearing on notice to the parent or guardian with opportunity to be heard, prior to his being sent to such other party jurisdiction for institutional care and the court finds that:

1. Equivalent facilities for the child are not available in the sending agency's jurisdiction; and
2. Institutional care in the other jurisdiction is in the best interest of the child and will not produce undue hardship.

Article VII. Compact administrator

The executive head of each jurisdiction party to this compact shall designate an officer who shall be general coordinator of activities under this compact in his jurisdiction and who, acting jointly with like officers of other party jurisdictions, shall have power to promulgate rules and regulations to carry out more effectively the terms and provisions of this compact.

Article VIII. Limitations

This compact shall not apply to:

(a) The sending or bringing of a child into a receiving state by his parent, step-parent, grandparent, adult brother or sister, adult uncle or aunt, or his guardian and leaving the child with any such relative or non-agency guardian in the receiving state.

(b) Any placement, sending or bringing of a child into a receiving state pursuant to any other interstate compact to which both the state from which the child is sent or brought and the receiving state are party, or to any other agreement between said states which has the force of law.

Article IX. Enactment and withdrawal

This compact shall be open to joinder by any state, territory or possession of the United States, the District of Columbia, the Commonwealth of Puerto Rico, and, with the consent of Congress, the Government of Canada or any province thereof. It shall become effective with respect to any such jurisdiction when such jurisdiction has enacted the same into law. Withdrawal from this compact shall be by the enactment of a statute repealing the same, but shall not take effect until two years after the effective date of such statute and until written notice of the withdrawal has been given by the withdrawing state to the governor of each other party jurisdiction. Withdrawal of a party state shall not affect the rights, duties and obligations under this compact of any sending agency therein with respect to a placement made prior to the effective date of withdrawal.

Article X. Construction and severability

The provisions of this compact shall be liberally construed to effectuate the purposes thereof. The provisions of this compact shall be severable and if any phrase, clause, sentence or provision of this compact is declared to be contrary to the constitution of any party state or of the United States or the applicability thereof to any government, agency, person or circumstances is held invalid, the validity of the remainder of this compact and the applicability thereof to any government, agency, person or circumstance shall not be affected thereby. If this compact shall be held contrary to the constitution of any state party thereto, the compact shall remain in full force and effect as to the remaining states and in full force and effect as to the state affected as to all severable matters.

§ 2-2. Construction

The provisions of section thirty-six of chapter one hundred and nineteen of the General Laws shall not apply to a public sending agency of, or in, another state party to said compact.

§ 2-3. Financial responsibility

Financial responsibility for any child placed pursuant to the provisions of the interstate compact on the placement of children shall be determined in accordance with the provisions of Article V thereof in the first instance. However, in the event of partial or complete default of performance thereunder, the provisions of said section thirty-six also may be invoked.

§ 2-4. Appropriate authority in the receiving state defined

As used in Articles III (b) and V (a) of the interstate compact on the placement of children, the phrase "appropriate authority in the receiving state" with reference to the Commonwealth of Massachusetts shall mean the state department of public welfare.

§ 2-5. Officers and agencies; power to enter into agreements; financial obligations

The officers and agencies of the commonwealth and its political subdivisions having authority to place children are hereby empowered to enter into agreements with appropriate officers or agencies of or in other party states pursuant to Article V (b) of the interstate compact on the placement of children. Any such agreement which contains a financial commitment or imposes a financial obligation on the commonwealth or a political subdivision or agency thereof shall not be binding unless it has the approval in writing of the commissioner of administration in the case of the commonwealth and of the chief local fiscal officer in the case of a political subdivision thereof.

§ 2-6. Requirements for visitation, inspection or supervision of children, homes or institutions in another party state

Any requirements for visitation, inspection or supervision of children, homes, institutions or other agencies in another party state which may apply under sections fourteen, fifteen and sixteen of said chapter one hundred and nineteen, shall be deemed to be met if performed pursuant to an agreement entered into by appropriate officers or agencies of the commonwealth or a political subdivision thereof as contemplated by Article V (b) of the interstate compact on the placement of children.

§ 2-7. Jurisdiction of courts to place delinquent children

Any court having jurisdiction to place delinquent children may place a delinquent child in an institution of or in another state pursuant to Article VI of the interstate compact on the placement of children, and shall retain jurisdiction as provided in Article V thereof.

§ 2-8. Executive head, defined

As used in Article VII of the interstate compact on the placement of children, the term "executive head" means the governor.

Interstate Compact on the Placement of Children (ICPC) Regulations

NOTE The following regulations were promulgated by the Association of Administrators of the Interstate Compact on the Placement of Children (AAICPC). They are available at https://aphsa.org/AAICPC/AAICPC/ICPC_Regulations.aspx.

Regulation No. 1. Conversion of intrastate placement into interstate placement; relocation of family units

Regulation No. 1 as first effective May 1, 1973, amended April 1999, is repealed and is replaced by the following:

The following regulation was amended by the Association of Administrators of the Interstate Compact on the Placement of Children on April 18, 2010, and is declared to be effective as amended as of October 1, 2010.

1. A placement initially intrastate in character becomes an interstate placement subject to the Interstate Compact on the Placement of Children (ICPC) if the child's principal place of abode is moved to another state, except as set forth herein.

2. Intent: This Regulation addresses the request for approval for placement of a child in an approved placement resource in the receiving state where the sending state has already approved the placement in the sending state and the resource now desires to move to the receiving state. The intent of Regulation 1 is to ensure that an already safe and stable placement made by a sending agency in the sending state will continue if the child is relocated to the receiving state. Additionally, it is the intent of this Regulation for supervision of the placement to be uninterrupted, for the family to comply with the requirements of the receiving state, and for both states to comply with all applicable state and federal laws, rules and regulations.

3. Applicability to Relocation: This Regulation shall apply to relocation of a child and the placement resource where supervision is ongoing. A request for a home study solely for the purpose of a periodic assessment of the placement where there is no on-going supervision shall not be governed by this regulation and shall be a matter of courtesy between the states. Nothing shall prohibit a sending state from contracting privately for a periodic assessment of the placement.

4. Applicability to Temporary Relocation: If a child is brought into the receiving state by an approved placement resource for a period of ninety (90) days or less and remains with the approved placement resource, approval of the receiving state is not required. Either the sending or receiving state may request approval of the placement, and, if the request is made, the sending and receiving states shall take the necessary action to process the request if the sending and receiving states agree to do so.

Supervision by the receiving state is not required for a temporary relocation of ninety (90) days or fewer; however, pursuant to section 422(b)(17) of the Social Security Act 422 U.S.C. 622, supervision by the sending agency is required. Supervision may be provided as a courtesy to the sending state. If supervision is requested, the sending state shall provide a Form 100B and the information required in Section 5(b) below.

If a child is brought into the receiving state by an approved placement resource for a temporary placement in excess of ninety (90) days or if the temporary relocation will recur, full compliance with this regulation is required.

The public child placing agency in the sending state is responsible to take action to ensure the ongoing safety of a child placed in a receiving state pursuant to an approved placement under Article III(d) of the ICPC, including return of the child to the sending state as soon as possible when return is requested by the receiving state.

5. Provisional Approval:

(a) In any instance where the decision to relocate into another state is made or it is intended to send or bring the child to the receiving state, or the child and existing family unit have already been sent or brought into the receiving state, an ICPC-100A and its supporting documentation shall be prepared immediately upon the making of the decision, processed within five (5) business days by the sending agency's state compact administrator and transmitted to the receiving state compact administrator with notice of the intended placement date. The sending agency's state compact administrator shall request that the receiving state respond to the case within five (5) business days of receipt of the request and with due regard for the desired time for the child to be sent or brought to the receiving state. If the family unit and child are already present in the receiving state, the receiving state's compact administrator shall determine within five (5) business days of receipt of the 100A and complete home study request packet whether provisional approval shall be granted and provide the decision in writing to the sending state compact administrator by facsimile, mail, overnight mail or electronic transmission, if acceptable.

(b) The documentation provided with a request for prompt handling shall include:

A form ICPC-100A fully completed.

A form 100B if the child is already present in the receiving state

A copy of the court order pursuant to which the sending agency has authority to place the child or, if authority does not derive from a court order, a statement of the basis on which the sending agency has authority to place the child and documentation that supervision is on-going.

A case history for the child, including custodial and social history, chronology of court involvement, social dynamics and a description of any special needs of the child.

In any instance where the sending state has required licensure, certification or approval, a copy of the most recent license, certificate or approval of the qualification of the placement resource(s) and/or their home showing the status of the placement resource(s), as qualified placement resource(s).

A copy of the most recent home study of the placement resource(s) and any updates thereof.

Copies of the progress reports on the family unit for the last six months and the most recent judicial review court report and court order completed in the sending state.

A copy of the child's case/services/permanency plan and any supplements to that plan, if the child has been in care long enough for such a plan to be required.

An explanation of the current status of the child's Title IV-E eligibility under the Federal Social Security Act.

(c) Requests for prompt handling shall be as provided in paragraph 5(a) hereof. Some or all documents may be communicated by express mail or any other recognized method for expedited communication, including electronic transmission, if acceptable. The receiving state shall recognize and give effect to any such expedited transmission of an ICPC-100A and/or supporting documentation, provided that it is legible and appears to be a complete representation of the original. However, the receiving state may request and shall be entitled to receive originals or duly certified copies if it considers them necessary for a legally sufficient record under its laws.

(d) In an instance where a placement resource(s) holds a current license, certificate or approval from the sending state evidencing qualification as a foster parent or other placement resource, the receiving state shall give effect to such license, certificate or approval as sufficient to support a determination of qualification pursuant to Article III(d) of the ICPC, unless the receiving state compact administrator has substantial evidence that the license, certificate, or approval is expired or otherwise not valid. If the receiving state requires licensure as a condition of placement approval, or the receiving state compact administrator determines that the license, certificate, or approval from the sending state has expired or otherwise is not valid, both the sending state and the placement resource shall state in writing that the placement resource will become licensed in the receiving state.

(e) The receiving state shall recognize and give effect to evidence that the placement resource has satisfactorily completed required training for foster parents or other parent training. Such recognition and effect shall be given if:

the training program is shown to be substantially equivalent to training offered for the same purpose in the receiving state; and the evidence submitted is in the form of an official certificate or document identifying the training.

6. Initial Home Study Report:

(a) Pursuant to the Safe and Timely Interstate Placement of Foster Children Act of 2006, within sixty (60) days after receiving a home study request, the receiving state shall directly or by contract conduct, complete, and return a report to the sending state on the results of the study of the home environment for purposes of assessing the safety and suitability of the child remaining in the home. The report shall address the extent to which placement in the home would meet the needs of the child. In the event the parts of the home study involving the education and training of the placement resource remain incomplete, the report shall reference such items by including a prospective date of completion.

(b) Approval of the request may be conditioned upon compliance by the placement resource with any licensing or education requirement in the receiving state. If such condition is placed upon approval, a reasonable date for compliance with the education or licensing requirement shall be set forth in the documentation granting approval.

7. Final Approval or Denial:

(a) Pursuant to Article III(d), final approval or denial of the placement resource request shall be provided by the receiving state compact administrator as soon as practical but no later than one-hundred and eighty days (180) days from receipt of the initial home study request.

(b) If necessary or helpful to meet time requirements, the receiving state may communicate its determination pursuant to Article III(d) to the sending agency and the sending agency's state compact administrator by "FAX" or other means of facsimile transmission or electronic transmission, if acceptable. However, this may not be done before the receiving state compact administrator has actually recorded the determination on the ICPC-100A. The written notice (the completed ICPC-100A) shall be mailed, sent electronically, if acceptable, or otherwise sent promptly to meet Article III(d) written notice requirements.

8. Nothing in this regulation shall be construed to alter the obligation of a receiving state to supervise and report on the placement; nor to alter the requirement that the placement resource(s) comply with the licensing and other applicable laws of the receiving state after arrival therein.

9. A favorable determination made by a receiving state pursuant to Article III(d) of the ICPC and this regulation means that the receiving state is making such determination on the basis of the best evidence available to it in accordance with the requirements of paragraph 5(a) of this regulation and does not relieve any placement resource or other entity of the obligation to comply with the laws of the receiving state as promptly as possible after arrival of the child in the receiving state.

10. The receiving state may decline to provide a favorable determination pursuant to Article III(d) of the Compact if the receiving state compact administrator finds that the child's needs cannot be met under the circumstances of the proposed relocation or until the compact administrator has the documentation identified in subparagraph 5(b) hereof.

11. If it is subsequently determined by the receiving state Compact Administrator that the placement in the receiving state appears to be contrary to the best interest of the child, the receiving state shall notify the sending agency that approval is no longer given and the sending state shall arrange to return the child or make an alternative placement as provided in Article V(a) of the ICPC.

12. Supervision:

Within thirty (30) days of the receiving state compact administrator being notified by the sending state compact administrator or by the placement resource that the placement resource and the child have arrived in the receiving state, the appropriate personnel of the receiving state shall visit the child and the placement resource in the home to ascertain conditions and progress toward compliance with applicable federal and state laws and requirements of the receiving state. Subsequent supervision must include face-to-face visits with the child at least once each month. A majority of visits must occur in the child's home. Face-to-face visits must be performed by a Child Welfare Caseworker in the receiving state. Such supervision visits shall continue until supervision is terminated by the sending state. Concurrence of the receiving state compact administrator for termination of supervision should be sought by the sending state prior to termination. Reports of supervision visits shall be provided to the sending state in accordance with applicable federal laws and as set forth elsewhere in these regulations.

The public child placing agency in the sending state is responsible to take action to ensure the ongoing safety of a child placed in a receiving state pursuant to an approved placement under Article III(d) of the ICPC, including return of the child to the sending state as soon as possible when return is requested by the receiving state.

13. Words and phrases used in this regulation have the same meanings as in the Compact, unless the context clearly requires another meaning.

14. This regulation is adopted pursuant to Article VII of the Interstate Compact on the Placement of Children by action of the Association of Administrators of the Interstate Compact on the Placement of Children at its annual meeting of April 2010.

Regulation No. 2. Public court jurisdiction cases: placements for public adoption or foster care in family settings and/or with parents, relatives

The following regulation, adopted by the Association of Administrators of the Interstate Compact on the Placement of Children, is declared to be in effect on and after October 1, 2011. Words and phrases used in this regulation have the same meanings as in the Compact, unless the context clearly requires another meaning. If a court or other competent authority invokes the Compact, the court or other competent authority is obligated to comply with Article V (Retention of Jurisdiction) of the Compact.

1. Intent of Regulation No. 2: The intent of this regulation is to provide at the request of a sending agency, a home study and placement decision by a receiving state for the proposed placement of a child with a proposed caregiver who falls into the category of: placement for public adoption, or foster care and/or with parents, or relatives.

2. Regulation No. 2 does apply to cases involving children who are under the jurisdiction of a court for abuse, neglect or dependency, as a result of action taken by a child welfare agency: The court has the authority to determine supervision, custody and placement of the child or has delegated said authority to the child welfare agency, and the child is being considered for placement in another state.

(a) Children not yet placed with prospective placement resource: This Regulation covers consideration of a placement resource where the child has not yet been placed in the home. ICPC Regulation No. 7 Expedited Home Study can be used instead of Regulation No. 2 for this category when requirements are met for an expedited home study request.

(b) Change of status for children who have already been placed with ICPC approval: This regulation is used when requesting a new home study on the current approved placement resource. This might include an upgrade from unlicensed relative to licensed foster home or to adoption home placement category (see Regulation No. 3 section 2(a) Types of Placement Categories).

(c) Child already placed without ICPC approval, except when the child has relocated with the caregiver to the receiving state pursuant to Regulation 1: When a child has been placed in a receiving state prior to ICPC approval, the case is considered a violation of ICPC and the placement is made with the sending state bearing full liability and responsibility for the safety of the child. The receiving state may request immediate removal of the child until the receiving state has made a decision per ICPC. The receiving state is permitted to proceed, but not required to proceed with the home study/ICPC decision process, as long as the child is placed in violation of ICPC. The receiving state may choose to open the case for ICPC courtesy supervision but is not required to do so, as is required under ICPC Regulation No. 1 Relocation of Family Unit Cases.

3. Placements made without ICPC protection: Regulation No. 2 does not apply to:

(a) A placement with a parent from whom the child was not removed: When the court places the child with a parent from whom the child was not removed, and the court has no evidence that the parent is unfit, does not seek any evidence from the receiving state that the parent is either fit or unfit, and the court relinquishes jurisdiction over the child immediately upon placement with the parent, the receiving state shall have no responsibility for supervision or monitoring for the court having made the placement.

(b) Sending court makes parent placement with courtesy check: When a sending court/agency seeks an independent (not ICPC-related) courtesy check for placement with a parent from whom the child was not removed, the responsibility for credentials and quality of the courtesy check rests directly with the sending court/agency and the person or party in the receiving state who agree to conduct the courtesy check without invoking the protection of the ICPC home study process. This would not prohibit a sending state from requesting an ICPC.

4. Definitions and placement categories: (See Regulation No. 3)

5. Sending state case documentation required with ICPC-100A request: The documentation provided with a request for prompt handling shall be current and shall include:

(a) A Form ICPC-100A fully completed.

(b) A Form ICPC-100B if the child is already placed without prior approval in the receiving state. The receiving state is not obligated to provide supervision until the placement has been approved with an ICPC-100A signed by the receiving state ICPC office, unless provisional approval has been granted.

(c) A copy of the current court order pursuant to which the sending agency has authority to place the child or, if authority does not derive from a court order, a statement of the basis on which the sending agency has authority to place the child and documentation that supervision is on-going.

(d) Signed statement required from assigned sending agency case manager:

- confirming the potential placement resource is interested in being a placement resource for the child and is willing to cooperate with the ICPC process.
- including the name and correct physical and mailing address of the placement resource and all available telephone numbers and other contact information for the potential placement resource.
- describing the number and type of bedrooms in the home of the placement resource to accommodate the child under consideration and the number of people, including children, who will be residing in the home.
- confirming the potential placement resource acknowledges that he/she has sufficient financial resources or will access financial resources to feed, clothe, and care for the child, including child care, if needed.
- that the placement resource acknowledges that a criminal records and child abuse history check will be completed for any persons residing in the home required to be screened under the law of the receiving state.

(e) A current case history for the child, including custodial and social history, chronology of court involvement, social dynamics and a description of any special needs of the child.

(f) Any child previously placed with placement resource in sending state: If the placement resource had any child placed with them in the sending state previously, the sending agency shall provide all relevant information regarding said placement to the receiving state, if available.

(g) Service (case) Plan: A copy of the child's case/service/permanency plan and any supplements to that plan, if the child has been in care long enough for a permanency plan to be required.

(h) Title IV-E Eligibility verification: An explanation of the current status of the child's Title IV-E eligibility under the Federal Social Security Act and Title IV-E documentation, if available. Documentation must be provided before placement is approved.

(i) Financial/Medical Plan: A detailed plan of the proposed method for support of the child and provision of medical services.

(j) A copy of the child's Social Security card or official document verifying correct Social Security Number, if available, and a copy of the child's birth certificate, if available.

6. Methods for transmission of documents: Some or all documents may be communicated by express mail or any other recognized method for expedited communication, including FAX and/or electronic transmission, if acceptable by both sending and receiving state. The receiving state shall recognize and give effect to any such expedited transmission of an ICPC-100A and/or supporting documentation, provided that it is legible and appears to be a complete representation of the original. However, the receiving state may request and shall be entitled to receive originals or duly certified copies of any legal documents if it considers them necessary for a legally sufficient record under its laws. All such transmissions must be sent in compliance with state laws and/or regulations related to the protection of confidentiality.

7. Safe and Timely Interstate Home Study Report to be completed within sixty (60) calendar days. This report is not equivalent to a placement decision.

(a) Timeframe for completion of Safe and Timely Interstate Home Study Report: As quickly as possible, but not more than sixty (60) calendar days after receiving a home study request, the receiving state shall, directly or by contract, complete a study of the home environment for purposes of assessing the safety and suitability of the child being placed in the home. The receiving state shall return to the sending state a report on the results of the home study that shall address the extent to which placement in the home would meet the needs of the child. This report may, or may not, include a decision approving or denying permission to place the child. In the event the parts of the home study involving the education and training of the placement resource remain incomplete, the report shall reference such items by including an anticipated date of completion.

(b) Receiving state placement decision may be postponed: If the receiving state cannot provide a decision regarding approval or denial of the placement at the time of the safe and timely home study report, the receiving state should provide the reason for delay and an anticipated date for a decision regarding the request. Reasons for delay may be such factors as receiving state requires all relatives to be licensed as a foster home therefore ICPC office cannot approve an unlicensed relative placement request until the family has met licensing requirements. If such condition must be met before approval, a reasonable date for compliance shall be set forth in the receiving state transmittal accompanying the initial home study, if possible.

8. Decision by receiving state to approve or deny placement resource (100A).

(a) Timeframe for final decision: Final approval or denial of the placement resource request shall be provided by receiving state

Compact Administrator in the form of a signed ICPC-100A, as soon as practical but no later than one hundred and eighty (180) calendar days from receipt of the initial home study request. This six (6)-month window is to accommodate licensure and/or other receiving state requirements applicable to foster or adoption home study requests.

(b) Expedited communication of decision: If necessary or helpful to meet time requirements, the receiving state ICPC office may communicate its determination pursuant to Article III(d) to the sending agency's state Compact Administrator by FAX or other means of facsimile transmission or electronic transmission, if acceptable to both receiving and sending state. However, this may not be done before the receiving state Compact Administrator has actually recorded the determination on the ICPC-100A. The written notice (the completed ICPC-100A) shall be mailed, sent electronically, if acceptable, or otherwise sent promptly to meet Article III(d) written notice requirements. The receiving state home study local agency shall not send the home study and/or recommendation directly to the sending state local agency without approval from the sending and receiving state ICPC offices.

(c) Authority of receiving state to make final decision: The authority of the receiving state is limited to the approval or denial of the placement resource. The receiving state may decline to provide a favorable determination pursuant to Article III(d) of the Compact if the receiving state Compact Administrator finds that based on the home study, the proposed caregiver would be unable to meet the individual needs of the child, including the child's safety, permanency, health, well-being, and mental, emotional and physical development.

(d) Authority of sending court/placing agency: When the receiving state has approved a placement resource, the sending court/placing agency has the final authority to determine whether to use the approved placement resource in the receiving state. The receiving state ICPC-100A approval expires six months from the date the 100A was signed by receiving state.

9. Reconsideration of an ICPC denial: (requested by the sending ICPC Office)

(a) Sending state may request reconsideration of the denial within 90 days from the date 100A denying placement is signed by receiving state. The request can be with or without a new home study, see items 9(a)(1) and 9(a)(2) below. After 90 days there is nothing that precludes the sending state from requesting a new home study.

Request reconsideration without a new home study: The sending ICPC office can request that the receiving state ICPC office reconsider the denial of placement of the child with the placement resource. If the receiving state ICPC office chooses to overturn the denial it can be based on review of the evidence presented by the sending ICPC office and any other new information deemed appropriate. A new 100A giving an approval without a new home study will be signed.

Request new home study re-examining reasons for original denial: A sending ICPC office may send a new ICPC home study request if the reason for denial has been corrected; i.e., move to new residence with adequate bedrooms. The receiving state ICPC office is not obligated to activate the new home study request, but it may agree to proceed with a new home study to reconsider the denial decision if it believes the reasons for denial have been corrected. This regulation shall not conflict with any appeal process otherwise available in the receiving state.

(b) Receiving state decision to reverse a prior denied placement: The receiving state ICPC office has 60 days from the date formal request to reconsider denial has been received from the sending state ICPC office. If the receiving state ICPC administrator decides to change the prior decision denying the placement, an ICPC transmittal letter and the new 100A shall be signed reflecting the new decision.

10. Return of child to sending state/Receiving state requests to return child to sending state:

(a) Request to return child to sending state at time of ICPC denial of placement: If the child is already residing in the receiving state with the proposed caregiver at the time of the above decision, and the receiving state Compact Administrator has denied the placement based on 8(c) then the receiving state Compact Administrator may request the sending state to arrange for the return of the child as soon as possible or propose an alternative placement in the receiving state as provided in Article V(a) of the ICPC. That alternative placement resource must be approved by the receiving state before placement is made. Return of the child shall occur within five (5) working days from the date of notice for removal unless otherwise agreed upon between the sending and receiving state ICPC offices.

(b) Request to return child to sending state after receiving state ICPC had previously approved placement: Following approval and placement of the child, if the receiving state Compact Administrator determines that the placement no longer meets the individual needs of the child, including the child's safety, permanency, health, well-being, and mental, emotional, and physical development, then the receiving state Compact Administrator may request that the sending state arrange for the return of the child as soon as possible or propose an alternative placement in the receiving state as provided in Article V(a) of the ICPC. That alternative placement resource must be approved by the receiving state before placement is made. Return of the child shall occur within five (5) working days from the date of notice for removal unless otherwise agreed upon between the sending and receiving state ICPC offices.

The receiving state request for removal may be withdrawn if the sending state arranges services to resolve the reason for the requested removal and the receiving and the sending state Compact Administrators mutually agree to the plan.

11. Supervision for approved placement should be conducted in accordance with ICPC Regulation No. 11.

12. Words and phrases used in this regulation have the same meanings as in the Compact, unless the context clearly requires another meaning.

13. This regulation is adopted pursuant to Article VII of the Interstate Compact on the Placement of Children by action of the Association of Administrators of the Interstate Compact on the Placement of Children at its annual meeting, April 30–May 1, 2011.

Regulation No. 3. Definitions and placement categories: applicability and exemptions

This Regulation No. 3 is adopted pursuant to Article VII of the Interstate Compact on the Placement of Children.

This Regulation No. 3 as first effective July 2, 2001, was amended by the Association of Administrators of the Interstate Compact on the Placement of children on May 1, 2011 and is declared to be effective as of October 1, 2011.

1. Intent of Regulation No. 3: To provide guidance in navigating the ICPC regulations and to assist its users in understanding which interstate placements are governed by, and which are exempt from, the ICPC.

(a) Nothing in this regulation shall be construed to alter the obligation of a receiving state to supervise and report on the placement; nor to alter the requirement that the placement resource(s) comply with the licensing and other applicable laws of the receiving state after placement of the child in the receiving state.

(b) Age restrictions: The ICPC Articles and Regulations do not specify an age restriction at time of placement, but rather use the broad definition of "child." The sending state law may permit the extension of juvenile court jurisdiction and foster care maintenance payments to eligible youth up to age 21. Consistent with Article V, such youth should be served under ICPC if requested by the sending agency and with concurrence of the receiving state.

2. Placement categories requiring compliance with ICPC: Placement of a child requires compliance with the Compact if such placement is made under one of the following four types of placement categories:

(a) Four types of placement categories: Adoptions: Placement preliminary to an adoption (independent, private or public adoptions)

Licensed or approved foster homes (placement with related or unrelated caregivers)

Placements with parents and relatives when a parent or relative is not making the placement as defined in Article VIII (a) "Limitations"

Group homes/residential placement of all children, including adjudicated delinquents in institutions in other states as defined in Article VI and Regulation No. 4.

(b) Court involvement and court jurisdiction legal status: The above placement categories may involve placement by persons and/or agencies that at the time of placement may not have any court involvement (i.e., private/independent adoptions and residential placements). Where there is court jurisdiction with an open court case for dependency, abandonment, abuse and/or neglect, the case is considered a public court jurisdiction case, which requires compliance with ICPC Article III (see Regulations No. 1, No. 2, No. 7 and No. 11) note exemption for selected "parent" cases as described below in Section 3, "cases that are exempt from ICPC regulations. In most public court jurisdiction cases the court has taken guardianship and legal custody away from the "offending" caregiver and has given it to a third party at the time placement of the child is made with an alternative caregiver. However, in select cases identified below, the sending court may not have taken guardianship or legal custody away from the parent/guardian, when the ICPC-100A requesting permission to place is sent to the receiving state. Those cases are identified on the ICPC-100A with the legal status of "court jurisdiction only" as explained below.

(c) Court jurisdiction only: The sending court has an open abuse, neglect or dependency case that establishes court jurisdiction with the authority to supervise, remove and/or place the child. Although the child is not in the guardianship/custody of an agency or the court at the time of completing ICPC-100A, the agency or the court may choose to exert legal authority to supervise and or remove and place the child and therefore is the sending agency. As the sending agency/court it would have specified legal responsibilities per ICPC Article V, including the possible removal of the child if placement in the receiving state disrupts or the receiving state requests removal of the child. There are several possible situations where "court jurisdiction only" might be checked as the "legal status" on the ICPC-100A:

Residential placement (Regulation No. 4): The court has jurisdiction, but in some situations, such as with some probation (delinquent) cases, guardianship remains with the parent/relative, but the court/sending agency is seeking approval to place in a receiving state residential treatment program, and has authority to order placement and removal.

Contingency/concurrent request in cases where removal may become necessary (Regulations No. 2 or No. 7): The child may be in the custody of the offending parent or relative while the public agency tries to bring the family into compliance with court orders and or agency service (case) plan. (Some states call this an order of "protective supervision" or "show cause.") The court may have requested an ICPC home study on a possible alternative caregiver in a receiving state. It is understood at time of placement the court would have guardianship/legal custody and Article V would be binding.

Parent/relative relocated to receiving state (Regulation No. 1): If the sending court selects to invoke ICPC Article V and to retain court jurisdiction even though the family/relative has legal guardianship/custody and has moved to the receiving state, then the sending court may request a home study on the parent/relative who has moved with the child to the receiving state. By invoking ICPC the sending court is bound under Article V. If the receiving state determines the placement to be contrary to the interests of the child, the sending court must order removal of the child and their return to the sending state or utilize an alternative approved placement resource in the receiving state. The ICPC-100A must be signed by the sending judge or authorized agent of the public agency on behalf of the sending court in keeping with ICPC Article V.

3. Placements made without ICPC protection:

(a) A placement with a parent from whom the child was not removed: When the court places the child with a parent from whom the child was not removed, and the court has no evidence that the parent is unfit, does not seek any evidence from the receiving state that the parent is either fit or unfit, and the court relinquishes jurisdiction over the child immediately upon placement with the parent. Receiving state shall have no responsibility for supervision or monitoring for the court having made the placement.

(b) Sending court makes parent placement with courtesy check: When a sending court/agency seeks an independent (not ICPC related) courtesy check for placement with a parent from whom the child was not removed, the responsibility for credentials and quality of the "courtesy check" rests directly with the sending court/agency and the person or party in the receiving state who agree to conduct the "courtesy" check without invoking the protection of the ICPC home study process. This would not prohibit a sending state from requesting an ICPC.

(c) Placements made by private individuals with legal rights to place: Pursuant to Article VIII (a), this Compact does not apply to the sending or bringing of a child into a receiving state by the child's parent, stepparent, grandparent, adult brother or sister, adult uncle or aunt, or the child's non-agency guardian and leaving the child with any such parent, relative or non-agency guardian in the receiving state, provided that such person who brings, sends, or causes a child to be sent or brought to a receiving state is a person whose full legal right to plan for the child: (1) has been established by law at a time prior to initiation of the placement arrangement, and (2) has not been voluntarily terminated, or diminished or severed by the action or order of any court.

(d) Placements handled in divorce, paternity or probate courts: The compact does not apply in court cases of paternity, divorce, custody, and probate pursuant to which or in situations where children are being placed with parents or relatives or non-relatives.

(e) Placement of children pursuant to any other Compact: Pursuant to Article VIII (b), the Compact does not apply to any placement, sending or bringing of a child into a receiving state pursuant to any other interstate Compact to which both the state from which the child is sent or brought and the receiving state are party, or to any other agreement between said states which has the force of law.

4. Definitions: The purpose of this section is to provide clarification of commonly used terms in ICPC. Some of these words and definitions can also be found in the Interstate Compact on the Placement of Children, ICPC Regulations, Interstate Compact on Juveniles, and federal statutes and regulations.

(Note: source of definition is identified right after the word prior to the actual definition.)

1. Adoption: the method provided by state law that establishes the legal relationship of parent and child between persons who are not so related by birth or some other legal determination, with the same mutual rights and obligations that exist between children and their birth parents. This relationship can only be termed adoption

after the legal process is complete (see categories or types of ICPC adoptions below).

2. Adoption categories:

(a) Independent adoption: adoptions arranged by a birth parent, attorney, other intermediary, adoption facilitator or other person or entity as defined by state law.

(b) Private agency adoption: an adoption arranged by a licensed agency whether domestic or international that has been given legal custody or responsibility for the child including the right to place the child for adoption.

(c) Public adoption: Adoptions for public court jurisdiction cases.

3. Adoption home study: (definition listed under "home studies")

4. Adjudicated delinquent: a person found to have committed an offense that, if committed by an adult, would be a criminal offense.

5. Adjudicated status offender: a person found to have committed an offense that would not be a criminal offense if committed by an adult.

6. Age of majority: the legally defined age at which a person is considered an adult with all the attendant rights and responsibilities of adulthood. The age of majority is defined by state laws, which vary by state and is used in Article V, ". . . reaches majority, becomes self-supporting or is discharged with the concurrence of the appropriate authority in the receiving state" (see definition below of "child" as it appears in Article II).

7. Approved placement: the receiving state Compact Administrator has determined that "the proposed placement does not appear to be contrary to the interests of the child."

8. Boarding home: as used in Article II (d) of the ICPC, means the home of a relative or unrelated individual whether or not the placement recipient receives compensation for care or maintenance of the child, foster care payments, or any other payments or reimbursements on account of the child's being in the home of the placement recipient (has same meaning as family free).

9. Case history: an organized record concerning an individual, their family and environment that includes social, medical, psychological and educational history and any other additional information that may be useful in determining appropriate placement.

10. Case plan: (see "service plan" definition)

11. Central Compact office: the office that receives ICPC placement referrals from sending states and sends ICPC placement referrals to receiving states. In states that have one central Compact office that services the entire state, the term "central Compact office" has the same meaning as "central state Compact office" as described in Regulation No. 5 of the ICPC. In states in which ICPC placement referrals are sent directly to receiving states and received directly from sending states by more than one county or other regional area within the state, the "central Compact office" is the office within each separate county or other region that sends and receives ICPC placement referrals.

12. Certification: to attest, declare or swear to before a judge or notary public.

13. Child: a person, who by reason of minority, is legally subject to parental guardianship or similar control.

14. Child welfare caseworker: a person assigned to manage the cases of dependency children who are in the custody of a public child welfare agency and may include private contract providers of the responsible state agency.

15. Concurrence to discharge: is when the receiving ICPC office gives the sending agency written permission to terminate supervision and relinquish jurisdiction of its case pursuant to Article V leaving the custody, supervision and care of the child with the placement resource.

16. Concurrence: is when the receiving and sending Compact Administrator agree to a specific action pursuant to ICPC, i.e., decision as to providers.

17. Conditions for placement: as established by Article III apply to any placement as defined in Article II(d) and regulations adopted by action of the Association of Administrators of the Interstate Compact on the Placement of Children.

18. Courtesy: consent or agreement between states to provide a service that is not required by ICPC.

19. Courtesy check: Process that does not involve the ICPC, used by a sending court to check the home of a parent from whom the child was not removed.

20. Court jurisdiction only cases: The sending court has an open abuse, neglect or dependency case that establishes court jurisdiction with the authority to supervise and/or remove and place the child for whom the court has not taken guardianship or legal custody.

21. Custody: (see physical custody, see legal custody)

22. Emancipation: the point at which a minor becomes self-supporting, assumes adult responsibility for his or her welfare, and is no longer under the care of his or her parents or child placing agency, by operation of law or court order.

23. Emergency placement: a temporary placement of 30 days or less in duration.

24. Family free: as used in Article II (d) of the ICPC means the home of a relative or unrelated individual whether or not the placement recipient receives compensation for care or maintenance of the child, foster care payments, or any other payments or reimbursements on account of the child's being in the home of the placement recipient (has same meaning as boarding home).

25. Family unit: a group of individuals living in one household.

26. Foster care: If 24-hour-a-day care is provided by the child's parent(s) by reason of a court-ordered placement (and not by virtue of the parent-child relationship), the care is foster care. In addition to the federal definition (45 C.F.R. § 1355.20 "Definitions") this includes 24-hour substitute care for children placed away from their parents or guardians and for whom the state agency has placement and care responsibility. This includes, but is not limited to, placements in foster family homes, foster homes of relatives, group homes, emergency shelters, residential facilities, child care institutions and pre-adoptive homes. A child is in foster care in accordance with this definition regardless of whether the foster care facility is licensed and payments are made by the state or local agency for the care of the child, whether adoption subsidy payments are being made prior to the finalization of an adoption, or whether there is federal matching of any payments that are made.

27. Foster home study: (see definition under home studies)

28. Foster parent: a person, including a relative or non-relative, licensed to provide a home for orphaned, abused, neglected, delinquent or disabled children, usually with the approval of the government or a social service agency.

29. Guardian [see ICPC Regulation No. 10 section 1(a)]: a public or private agency, organization or institution that holds a valid and effective permanent appointment from a court of competent jurisdiction to have custody and control of a child, to plan for the child, and to do all other things for or on behalf of a child for which a parent would have authority and responsibility for doing so by virtue of an unrestricted parent-child relationship. An appointment is permanent for the purposes of this paragraph if the appointment would allow the guardianship to endure until the child's age of majority without any court review, subsequent to the appointment, of the care that the guardian provides or the status of other permanency planning that the guardian has a professional obligation to carry out.

30. Home Study (see Safe and Timely Interstate Placement of Foster Children Act of 2006): an evaluation of a home environment conducted in accordance with applicable requirements of the state in which the home is located, to determine whether a proposed placement of a child would meet the individual needs of the

child, including the child's safety, permanency, health, well-being, and mental, emotional and physical development.

(a) Adoption home study: a home study conducted for the purpose of placing a child for adoption with a placement resource. The adoption home study is the assessment and evaluation of a prospective adoptive parent(s).

(b) Foster home study: a home study conducted for the purpose of placing a child with a placement resource who is required to be licensed or approved in accordance with federal and/or receiving state law.

(c) Interstate home study (see Federal Safe and Timely Act): a home study conducted by a state at the request of another state, to facilitate an adoptive or foster care placement in the state of a child in foster care under the responsibility of the state [see foster care definition(s)].

(d) Parent home study: applies to the home study conducted by the receiving state to determine whether a parent placement meets the standards as set forth by the requirements of the receiving state.

(e) Relative home study: a home study conducted for the purpose of placing a child with a relative. Such a home study may or may not require the same level of screening as required for a foster home study or an adoptive home study depending upon the applicable law and/or requirements of the receiving state.

(f) Non-relative home study: a home study conducted for the purpose of placing a child with a non-relative of the child. Such a home study may or may not require the same level of screening as required for a foster home study or an adoptive home study depending upon the applicable law and/or requirements of the receiving state.

(g) Safe and Timely Interstate Home Study Report (see Federal Safe and Timely Act): an interstate home study report completed by a state if the state provides to the state that requested the study, within 60 days after receipt of the request, a report on the results of the study. The preceding sentence shall not be construed to require the state to have completed, within the 60-day period, the parts of the home study involving the education and training of the prospective foster or adoptive parents.

31. ICPC: The Interstate Compact on the Placement of Children is a Compact between states and parties pursuant to law, to ensure protection and services to children who are placed across state lines.

32. Independent adoption entity: any individual authorized in the sending state to place children for adoption other than a state, county or licensed private agency. This could include courts, private attorneys and birth parents.

33. Intrastate: existing or occurring within a state.

34. Interstate: involving, connecting or existing between two or more states.

35. Interstate home study: (see definition under Home studies)

36. Jurisdiction: the established authority of a court to determine all matters in relation to the custody, supervision, care and disposition of a child.

37. Legal custody: court-ordered or statutory right and responsibility to care for a child either temporarily or permanently.

38. Legal guardianship (see 45 C.F.R. § 1355.20 "Definitions"): a judicially created relationship between child and caretaker that is intended to be permanent and self-sustaining as evidenced by the transfer to the caretaker of the following parental rights with respect to the child: protection, education, care and control of the person, custody of the person, and decision-making. The term legal guardian means the caretaker in such a relationship.

39. Legal risk placement (legal risk adoption): a placement made preliminarily to an adoption where the prospective adoptive parents acknowledge in writing that a child can be ordered returned to the sending state or the birth mother's state of residence, if different from the sending state, and a final decree of adoption shall not be entered in any jurisdiction until all required consents or termination of parental rights are obtained or are dispensed with in accordance with applicable law.

40. Member state: a state that has enacted this Compact (see also definition of state).

41. Non-agency guardian [see ICPC Regulation No. 10 section 1(b)]: an individual holding a currently valid appointment from a court of competent jurisdiction to have all of the authority and responsibility of a guardian as defined in ICPC Regulation No. 10 section 1(a).

42. Non-custodial parent: a person who, at the time of the commencement of court proceedings in the sending state, does not have sole legal custody of the child or physical custody of a child.

43. Non-offending parent: the parent who is not the subject of allegations or findings of child abuse or neglect.

44. Non-relative: a person not connected to the child by blood, marriage or adoption, or otherwise defined by the sending or receiving state.

45. Parent: a biological, adoptive parent or legal guardian as determined by applicable state law and is responsible for the care, custody and control of a child or upon whom there is legal duty for such care.

46. Parent home study: (see definition under home studies)

47. Physical custody: Person or entity with whom the child is placed on a day-to-day basis.

48. Placement (see ICPC Article II (d) "Definitions"): the arrangement for the care of a child in a family free, in a boarding home or in a child-caring agency or institution, but does not include any institution caring for the mentally ill, mentally defective or epileptic, or any institution primarily educational in character, and any hospital or other medical facility.

49. Placement resource: the person(s) or facility with whom the child has been or may be placed by a parent or legal custodian; or, placed by the court of jurisdiction in the sending state; or, for whom placement is sought in the receiving state.

50. Progress report: (see "supervision report" definition)

51. Provisional approval: an initial decision by the receiving state that the placement is approved subject to receipt of required additional information before final approval is granted.

52. Provisional denial: the receiving state cannot approve a provisional placement pending a more comprehensive home study or assessment process due to issues that need to be resolved.

53. Provisional placement: a determination made in the receiving state that the proposed placement is safe and suitable and, to the extent allowable, the receiving state has temporarily waived its standards or requirements otherwise applicable to prospective foster or adoptive parents so as to not delay the placement. Completion of the receiving state requirements regarding training for prospective foster or adoptive parents shall not delay an otherwise safe and suitable placement.

54. Public child-placing agency: any government child welfare agency or child protection agency or a private entity under contract with such an agency, regardless of whether they act on behalf of a state, county, municipality or other governmental unit and which facilitates, causes or is involved in the placement of a child from one state to another.

55. Receiving state (see ICPC Article II (c) "Definitions"): the state to which a child is sent, brought or caused to be sent or brought, whether by public authorities or private persons or agencies, and whether for placement with state or local public authorities or for placement with private agencies or persons.

56. Relative: a birth or adoptive brother, sister, stepparent, stepbrother, stepsister, uncle, aunt, first cousin, niece, nephew, as well as relatives of half blood or marriage and those denoted by the prefixes of grand and great, including grandparent or great

grandparent, or as defined in state statute for the purpose of foster and or adoptive placements.

57. Non-relative: a person not connected to the child by blood, marriage or adoption.

58. Relative home study: (see definition under home studies)

59. Relocation: the movement of a child or family from one state to another.

60. Residential facility or residential treatment center or group home: a facility providing a level of 24-hour, supervised care that is beyond what is needed for assessment or treatment of an acute condition. For purposes of the Compact, residential facilities do not include institutions primarily educational in character, hospitals or other medical facilities (as used in Regulation 4, they are defined by the receiving state).

61. Return: the bringing or sending back of a child to the state from which they came.

62. Sending agency: (see ICPC Article II (b) "Definitions"): a party state, officer or employee thereof; a subdivision of a party state, or officer or employee thereof; a court of a party state; a person, corporation, association, charitable agency or other entity having legal authority over a child who sends, brings, or causes to be sent or brought any child to another party state.

63. Sending state: the state where the sending agency is located, or the state in which the court holds exclusive jurisdiction over a child, which causes, permits or enables the child to be sent to another state.

64. Service (case) plan: a comprehensive individualized program of action for a child and his/her family establishing specific goals and objectives and deadlines for meeting these goals and objectives.

65. State: a state of the United States, the District of Columbia, the Commonwealth of Puerto Rico, the U.S. Virgin Islands, Guam, American Samoa, the Northern Marianas Islands, and any other territory of the United States.

66. State court: a judicial body of a state that is vested by law with responsibility for adjudicating cases involving abuse, neglect, deprivation, delinquency or status offenses of individuals who have not attained the age of eighteen (18) or as otherwise defined by state law.

67. Stepparent: a man or woman married to a parent of a child at the time of the intended placement or as otherwise defined by the sending and/or receiving state laws, rules and/or regulations.

68. Supervision: monitoring of the child and the child's living situation by the receiving state after a child has been placed in a receiving state pursuant to a provisional approval or an approved placement under Article III(d) of the ICPC or pursuant to a child's relocation to a receiving state in accordance with Regulation No. 1 of the ICPC.

69. Supervision report: provided by the supervising case worker in the receiving state; a written assessment of a child's current placement, school performance and health and medical status, a description of any unmet needs and a recommendation regarding continuation of the placement.

70. Timely Interstate Home Study: (see definition under home studies)

71. Visit: as defined in Regulation No. 9.

Regulation No. 4. Residential placement

Regulation No. 4, as adopted by the Association of Administrators of the Interstate Compact on the Placement of Children on April 20, 1983, was readopted in 1999 and amended in 2001, and is replaced by the following:

The following regulation, adopted by the Association of Administrators of the Interstate Compact on the Placement of Children, is declared to be in effect on and after October 1, 2012. Words and phrases used in this regulation have the same meaning as in the Compact, unless the context clearly requires another meaning. If a court or other competent authority invokes the Compact, the court or other competent authority is obligated to comply with Article V (Retention of Jurisdiction) of the Compact.

1. Intent of this Regulation: It is the intent of Regulation No. 4 to provide for the protection and safety of children being placed in a residential facility in another state. Residential facility is further defined in Section 3 below.

(a) Approval by receiving state prior to placement: Approval prior to placement is required for the protection of the child and the sending agency making the placement. Sending agency includes the parent, guardian, court, or agency ultimately responsible for the planning, financing, and placement of the child as designated in section I of the form 100A. (See Article II(b) or Regulation 3, Section 4. (62) for full definition of sending agency.)

(b) Monitoring residential facility while child is placed: While children are placed in the receiving state, the receiving state ICPC office shall keep a record of all children currently placed at the residential facility through the ICPC process. The receiving state ICPC office shall notify the sending state ICPC office of any significant change of status at the residential facility that may be "contrary to the interests of the child" (Article III(d) or may place the safety of the child at risk of which the receiving state ICPC office becomes aware.

(c) Prevent children from being abandoned in receiving state: Once the sending agency makes a residential facility placement, the sending agency remains obligated under Article V to retain jurisdiction and responsibility for the child while the child remains in the receiving state until the child becomes independent, self-supporting, or the case is closed in concurrence with both the receiving and sending state ICPC offices. The role of the sending and receiving state ICPC offices is to promote compliance with Article V that children are not physically or financially abandoned in a receiving state.

2. Categories of children: This regulation applies to cases involving children who are being placed in a residential facility by the sending agency, regardless of whether the child is under the jurisdiction of a court for delinquency, abuse, neglect, or dependency, or as a result of action taken by a child welfare agency.

Age restrictions: (Regulation No. 3 Section 1(b)) The ICPC articles and regulations do not specify an age restriction at time of placement, but rather use the broad definition of "child." The sending state law may permit the extension of juvenile court jurisdiction and foster care maintenance payments to eligible youth up to age 21. Consistent with Article V, such youth should be served under ICPC if requested by the sending agency and with concurrence of the receiving state.

(a) Delinquent Child: Placement by a sending agency involving a delinquent child must comply with Article VI, Institutional Care of Delinquent Children, which reads as follows: "A child adjudicated delinquent may be placed in an institution in another party jurisdiction pursuant to this compact but no such placement shall be made unless the child is given a court hearing on notice to the parent or guardian with the opportunity to be heard prior to his being sent to such other party jurisdiction for institutional care and the court finds that:

(1) Equivalent facilities for the child are not available in the sending agency's jurisdiction; and

(2) Institutional care in the other jurisdiction is in the best interest of the child and will not produce undue hardship." (Hardship may apply to the child and his/her family.)

(b) A child not yet placed in a residential facility in another state: The primary application of this regulation is to request approval to place prior to placement at the residential facility.

(c) Change of status for a child: A new ICPC 100A and documents listed in Section 5 are required for a child who has been placed with prior ICPC approval, but now needs to move to a residential facility in this or another state, other than the child's state of origin.

(d) Child already placed without ICPC approval: For the safety and protection of all involved, placement in a residential facility should not occur until after the receiving state has approved the placement pursuant to Article III (d). When a child has been placed in a receiving state prior to ICPC approval, the case is considered a violation of ICPC, and the placement is made with the sending agency and residential facility remaining liable and responsible for the safety of the child. The receiving state may request immediate removal of the child until the receiving state has made a decision per ICPC, in addition to any other remedies available under Article IV. The receiving state is permitted to proceed with the residential facility request for approval, but is not required to proceed as long as the child is placed in violation of ICPC.

3. Definition of "Residential Facility" covered by this regulation:

(a) Definition in ICPC Regulation No. 3 Section 4.(60) Residential facility or residential treatment center or group home: a facility providing a level of 24-hour, supervised care that is beyond what is needed for assessment or treatment of an acute condition. For purposes of the compact, residential facilities do not include institutions primarily educational in character, hospitals, or other medical facilities (as used in Regulation 4, they are defined by the receiving state). Residential facilities may also be called by other names in the receiving state, such as those listed under "Type of Care Requested on the ICPC 100A: Group Home Care, Residential Treatment Center, Child Caring Institution, and Institutional Care (Article VI), Adjudicated Delinquent."

(b) The type of license, if any, held by an institution is evidence of its character but does not determine the need for compliance with ICPC. Whether an institution is either generally exempt from the need to comply with the Interstate Compact on the Placement of Children or exempt in a particular instance is to be determined by the services it actually provides or offers to provide. In making any such determinations, the criteria set forth in this regulation shall be applied.

(c) The type of funding source or sources used to defray the costs of treatment or other services does not determine whether the Interstate Compact on the Placement of Children applies.

4. Definition of institutional facilities not covered by this regulation: In determining whether the sending or bringing of a child to another state is exempt from the provisions of the Interstate Compact on the Placement of Children by reason of the exemption for various classes of institutions in Article II(d), the following concepts and terms shall have the following meanings:

(a) "Primarily educational institution" means an institution that operates one or more programs that can be offered in satisfaction of compulsory school attendance laws, in which the primary purpose of accepting children is to meet their educational needs; and the educational institution does not do one or more of the following. (Conditions below would require compliance with this Regulation.)

(1) accepts responsibility for children during the entire year;

(2) provide or hold itself out as providing child care constituting nurture sufficient to substitute for parental supervision and control or foster care;

(3) provide any other services to children, except for those customarily regarded as extracurricular or co-curricular school activities, pupil support services, and those services necessary to make it possible for the children to be maintained on a 24-hour residential basis in the aforementioned school program or programs.

(b) "Hospital or other medical facility" means an institution for the acutely ill that discharges its patients when they are no longer acutely ill, which does not provide or hold itself out as providing child care in substitution for parental care or foster care, and in which a child is placed for the primary purpose of treating an acute medical problem.

(c) "Institution for the mentally ill or mentally defective" minors means a facility that is responsible for treatment of acute conditions, both psychiatric and medical, as well as such custodial care as is necessary for the treatment of such acute conditions of the minors who are either voluntarily committed or involuntarily committed by a court of competent jurisdiction to reside in it. Developmentally disabled has the same meaning as the phrase "mentally defective."

(d) Outpatient Services: If the treatment and care and other services are entirely out-patient in character, an institution for the mentally ill or developmentally disabled may accept a child for treatment and care without complying with ICPC.

5. Sending state case documentation for Residential Facility Request: The documentation provided with a request for prompt handling shall be current and shall include:

(a) Form ICPC-100A fully completed (required for all residential facility requests).

(b) Form ICPC-100B required for all residential facility requests, if the child is already placed without prior approval in the receiving state.

(c) Court or other authority to place the child:

(1) Delinquent child—a copy of the court order indicating the child has been adjudicated delinquent stating that equivalent facilities are not available in the sending agency's jurisdiction and that institutional care in the receiving state is in the best interest of the child and will not produce undue hardship. (See Article VI or Section 2.A above.)

(2) Public agency child—For public court jurisdiction cases, the current court order is required indicating the sending agency has authority to place the child or, if authority does not derive from a court order, a written legal document executed in accordance with the laws of the sending state that provides the basis for which the sending agency has authority to place the child and documentation that supervision is on-going or a copy of the voluntary placement agreement, as defined in Section 472(f)(2) of the Social Security Act executed by the sending agency and the child's parent or guardian.

(3) Child in the custody of a relative or legal guardian—a current court order or legal document is required indicating the sending agency has the authority to place the child.

(4) Parent placement (no court involvement)—The 100A is required and must be signed by the sending agency with the box checked under legal status indicating the parent has custody or guardianship and any additional documents required by the sending or receiving state.

(d) Letter of acceptance from the residential facility: For some receiving states this is a mandatory document for all placement requests, including those submitted by a parent or guardian. It provides the receiving state ICPC office with indication that the residential facility has screened the child as an appropriate placement for their facility.

(e) A current case history for the child: (optional for placements requested under 5. (c) (3) and (4)), including custodial and social history, chronology of court involvement, social dynamics and a description of any special needs of the child.

(f) Service (case) plan: (optional for placements requested under 5.C(3) and (4))—A copy of the child's case or service or permanency plan and any supplements to that plan, if the child has been in care long enough for a permanency plan to be required.

(g) Financial and medical plan: A written description of the responsibility for payment of the cost of placement of the child in the facility, including the name and address of the person or entity that will be making the payment and the person or entity who will be otherwise financially responsible for the child. It is expected that the medical coverage will be arranged and confirmed between the sending agency and the residential facility prior to the placement.

(h) Title IV-E eligibility verification: (not required for parent placements)—An explanation of the current status of the child's Title IV-E eligibility under the Federal Social Security Act and Title IV-E documentation, if available. Documentation must be provided before placement is approved.

(i) Placement Disruption Agreement: Some states may require a signed Placement Disruption Agreement indicating who will be responsible for the return of the child to the sending state if the child disrupts or a request is made for the child's removal and return to the sending state.

6. Methods for transmission of documents: Some or all documents may be communicated by express mail or any other recognized method for expedited communication, including FAX and electronic transmission, if acceptable by both the sending and the receiving state. The receiving state shall recognize and give effect to any such expedited transmission of an ICPC-100A and supporting documentation, provided that it is legible and appears to be a complete representation of the original. However, the receiving state may request and shall be entitled to receive originals or duly certified copies of any legal documents if it considers them necessary for a legally sufficient record under its laws. All such transmissions must be sent in compliance with state laws and regulations related to the protection of confidentiality.

7. Decision by receiving state to approve or deny placement resource (100A).

(a) Receiving state decision process: The receiving state ICPC office reviews the child specific information and the current status of the residential facility. The receiving state ICPC office approves or denies the placement based on a determination that "the proposed placement does not appear to be contrary to the interests of the child" (ICPC Article III(d)). The ICPC office may as part of its review process verify that the residential facility is properly licensed and not under an investigation by law enforcement, child protection, or licensing staff for unfit conditions or illegal activities that might place the child at risk of harm.

(1) Receiving state ICPC office may check to make sure the child is an appropriate match for the category of residential facility program.

(2) Receiving state ICPC office may check with the residential facility program to ensure that the request to place the child has been fully reviewed and officially accepted before ICPC approval is granted.

(b) Time frame for final decision: Final approval or denial of the placement resource request shall be provided by the receiving state compact administrator in the form of a signed ICPC 100A as soon as practical, but no later than three (3) business days from receipt of the complete request by the receiving state ICPC office. It is recognized that some state ICPC offices must obtain clearances from child protection, residential facility licensing and law enforcement before giving approval for a residential facility placement.

(c) Expedited communication of decision: If necessary or helpful to meet time requirements, the receiving state ICPC office may communicate its determination pursuant to Article III(d) to the sending agency's state Compact Administrator by FAX or other means of electronic transmission, if acceptable to both receiving and sending state. However, this may not be done before the receiving state Compact Administrator has actually recorded the determination on the ICPC 100A. The written notice (the completed ICPC100A) shall be mailed, sent electronically, if acceptable, or otherwise sent promptly to meet Article III(d) written notice requirements.

(d) Authority of receiving state to make final decision: The authority of the receiving state is limited to the approval or denial of the placement resource. The receiving state may approve or deny the placement resource if the receiving state Compact Administrator finds based upon the review of the child specific information and on the review of the current status of the residential facility, "the proposed placement does not appear to be contrary to the interests of the child." (ICPC Article III.(d))

(e) Emergency Residential Facility Placement Temporary Decision: Occasionally residential facility placements need to be made on an emergency basis. In those limited cases, sending and receiving state offices may, with mutual agreement, proceed to authorize emergency placement approval. Such emergency placement decision must be made within one business day or other mutually agreed timeframe, based upon receipt by the receiving state of the ICPC-100A request and any other document required by the receiving state to consider such emergency placement; e.g., a financial medical plan and a copy of a court order or other authority to make the placement. If emergency placement approval is temporarily granted, the formal ICPC placement approval will not be final until there has been full compliance with Sections 5 and 7 of this regulation.

8. Authority of sending agency: When the receiving state has approved a placement resource, the sending agency has the final authority to determine whether to use the approved placement resource in the receiving state. The receiving state ICPC-100A approval for placement in a residential facility expires thirty calendar days from the date the 100A was signed by the receiving state. The thirty (30) calendar day timeframe can be extended upon mutual agreement between the sending and receiving state ICPC offices.

9. Submission of ICPC-100B: Upon determination by the sending agency to use the approved resource, the sending agency is responsible for filing an ICPC-100B Notice of Placement with the Sending State ICPC office within three (3) business days of the actual placement. That notice is to be submitted to the receiving state ICPC office, who is to forward the ICPC-100B to the residential facility within five (5) business days of receipt of the ICPC-100B.

10. Supervision Expectations:

(a) Residential Facility: The residential facility is viewed as the agency responsible for the 24-hour care of a child away from the child's parental home. In that capacity the residential facility is responsible for the supervision, protection, safety, and well-being of the child. The sending agency making the placement is expected to enter into an agreement with the residential facility as to the program plan or expected level of supervision and treatment and the frequency and nature of any written progress or treatment reports.

(b) Receiving state local child welfare workers and probation staff are not expected to provide any monitoring or supervision of children placed in residential facility programs. The one exception are those children who may become involved in an incident or allegation occurring in the receiving state that may involve the receiving state law enforcement, probation, child protection or, ultimately, the receiving state court.

(c) "Sending" agency making placement: The frequency and nature of monitoring visits by the sending agency or individual making the placement are determined by the sending agency in accordance with applicable laws.

11. Return of child to sending state at the request of receiving state:

(a) Request to return child to sending state at time of ICPC denial of placement: If the child is already placed in the receiving state residential facility at the time of the decision, and the receiving state Compact Administrator has denied the placement, then the receiving state Compact Administrator may request the sending state ICPC office to facilitate with the sending agency for the return of the child as soon as possible or propose an alternative placement in the receiving state as provided in Article V(a) of the ICPC. The alternative placement resource must be approved by the receiving state before placement is made. Return of the child shall occur within five (5) business days from the date of notice for removal unless otherwise agreed upon between the sending and receiving state ICPC offices.

(b) Request to return child to sending state after receiving state ICPC had previously approved placement: Following approval and placement of the child in the residential facility, if the receiving state Compact Administrator determines that the placement "appears to be contrary to the interests of the child," then the receiving state Compact Administrator may request that the sending state ICPC office facilitate with the sending agency for the return of the child as soon as possible or propose an alternative placement in the receiving state as provided in Article V(a) of the ICPC. That alternative placement resource must be approved by the receiving state before placement is made. Return of the child shall occur within five (5) business days from the date of notice for removal, unless otherwise agreed upon between the sending and receiving state ICPC offices.

The receiving state ICPC office's request for removal may be withdrawn if the sending agency arranges services to resolve the reason for the requested removal and the receiving and the sending state Compact Administrators mutually agree to the plan.

12. Words and phrases used in this regulation have the same meanings as in the Compact, unless the context clearly requires another meaning.

13. This regulation was amended pursuant to Article VII of the Interstate Compact on the Placement of Children by action of the Association of Administrators of the Interstate Compact on the Placement of Children at its annual meeting May 4 through 7, 2012; such amendment was approved on May 5, 2012 and is effective as of October 1, 2012.

Regulation No. 5. Central state compact office

Regulation No. 5 ("Central State Compact Office"), as first effective April 1982, amended as of April 1999 and April 2002, is amended to read as follows:

1. It shall be the responsibility of each state party to the Interstate Compact on the Placement of Children to establish a procedure by which all Compact referrals from and to the state shall be made through a central state compact office. For those states that have decentralized specific activities regarding Compact referrals from the central state compact office to a county, local office, or designated agency, the county, local office, or designated agency shall have the same authority and responsibility with respect to those specific activities regarding Compact referrals as if it were the central state compact office. The Compact office shall also be a resource for inquiries into requirements for placements into the state for children who come under the purview of this Compact.

2. The Association of Administrators of the Interstate Compact on the Placement of Children deems certain appointments of officers who are general coordinators of activities under the Compact in the party states to have been made by the executive heads of states in each instance wherein such an appointment is made by a state official who has authority delegated by the executive head of the state to make such an appointment. Delegated authority to make the appointments described above in this paragraph will be sufficient if it is either: specifically described in the applicable state's documents that establish or control the appointment or employment of the state's officers or employees; a responsibility of the official who has the delegated authority that is customary and accepted in the applicable state; or consistent with the personnel policies or practices of the applicable state. Any general coordinator of activities under the Compact who is or was appointed in compliance with this paragraph is deemed to be appointed by the executive head of the applicable jurisdiction regardless of whether the appointment preceded or followed the adoption of this paragraph. No person within an agency so designated by the appropriate authority in a state to make recommendations for or against placement of a child, as evidenced by signing Form 100A, shall also conduct the home study upon which such recommendation is made.

3. Words and phrases used in this regulation have the same meaning as in the Compact, unless the context clearly requires another meaning.

4. This regulation was amended pursuant to Article VII of the Interstate Compact on the Placement of Children by action of the Association of Administrators of the Interstate Compact on the Placement of Children at its annual meeting May 4 through 7, 2012; such amendment was approved on May 5, 2012 and is effective as of July 1, 2012.

Regulation No. 6. Permission to place child: time limitations, reapplication

The following regulation, originally adopted in 1991 by the Association of Administrators of the Interstate Compact on the Placement of Children, is amended in 2001 and declared to be in effect, as amended, on and after July 2, 2001.

1. Permission to place a child given pursuant to Article III (d) of the Interstate Compact on the Placement of Children shall be valid and sufficient to authorize the making of the placement identified in the written document ICPC-100A, by which the permission is given for a period of six (6) months commencing on the date when the receiving state compact administrator or his duly authorized representative signs the aforesaid ICPC-100A.

2. If the placement authorized to be made as described in Paragraph 1. of this Regulation is not made within the six (6) months allowed therein, the sending agency may reapply. Upon such reapplication, the receiving state may require the updating of documents submitted on the previous application, but shall not require a new home study unless the laws of the receiving state provide that the previously submitted home study is too old to be currently valid.

3. If a foster care license, institutional license or other license, permit or certificate held by the proposed placement recipient is still valid and in force, or if the proposed placement recipient continues to hold an appropriate license, permit or certificate, the receiving state shall not require that a new license, permit or certificate be obtained in order to qualify the proposed placement recipient to receive the child in placement.

4. Upon a reapplication by the sending agency, the receiving state shall determine whether the needs or condition of the child have changed since it initially authorized the placement to be made. The receiving state may deny the placement if it finds that the proposed placement is contrary to the interests of the child.

5. Words and phrases used in this regulation have the same meanings as in the Compact, unless the context clearly requires another meaning.

6. This regulation was readopted pursuant to Article VII of the Interstate Compact on the Placement of Children by action of the Association of Administrators of the Interstate Compact on the Placement of Children at its annual meeting of April 1999; it is amended pursuant to Article VII of the Interstate Compact on the Placement of Children by action of the Association of Administrators of the Interstate Compact on the Placement of Children at its annual meeting of April 29 through May 2, 2001, was approved May 2, 2001, and is effective in such amended form as of July 2, 2001.

Regulation No. 7. Expedited placement decision

The following regulation adopted by the Association of Administrators of the Interstate Compact on the Placement of Children as Regulation No. 7, Priority Placement, as first adopted in 1996, is amended to read as follows:

2. This regulation shall hereafter be denoted as Regulation No. 7 for Expedited Placement Decision.

3. Intent of Regulation No. 7: The intent of this regulation is to expedite ICPC approval or denial by a receiving state for the placement of a child with a parent, stepparent, grandparent, adult uncle or aunt, adult brother or sister, or the child's guardian, and to:

(a) Help protect the safety of children while minimizing the potential trauma to children caused by interim or multiple placements while ICPC approval to place with a parent or relative is being sought through a more comprehensive home study process.

(b) Provide the sending state court and/or sending agency with expedited approval or denial. An expedited denial would underscore the urgency for the sending state to explore alternative placement resources.

4. This regulation shall not apply if:

(a) the child has already been placed in violation of the ICPC in the receiving state, unless a visit has been approved in writing by the receiving state Compact Administrator and a subsequent order entered by the sending state court authorizing the visit with a fixed return date in accordance with Regulation No. 9.

(b) the intention of the sending state is for licensed or approved foster care or adoption. In the event the intended placement [must be parent, stepparent, grandparent, adult aunt or uncle, adult brother or sister, or guardian as per Article VIII(a)] is already licensed or approved in the receiving state at the time of the request, such licensing or approval would not preclude application of this regulation.

(c) the court places the child with a parent from whom the child was not removed, the court has no evidence the parent is unfit, does not seek any evidence from the receiving state the parent is either fit or unfit, and the court relinquishes jurisdiction over the child immediately upon placement with the parent.

5. Criteria required before Regulation No. 7 can be requested: Cases involving a child who is under the jurisdiction of a court as a result of action taken by a child welfare agency, the court has the authority to determine custody and placement of the child or has delegated said authority to the child welfare agency, the child is no longer in the home of the parent from whom the child was removed, and the child is being considered for placement in another state with a parent, stepparent, grandparent, adult uncle or aunt, adult brother or sister, or the child's guardian, must meet at least one of the following criteria in order to be considered a Regulation No. 7 case:

(a) unexpected dependency due to a sudden or recent incarceration, incapacitation or death of a parent or guardian. Incapacitation means a parent or guardian is unable to care for a child due to a medical, mental or physical condition of a parent or guardian, or

(b) the child sought to be placed is four years of age or younger, including older siblings sought to be placed with the same proposed placement resource; or

(c) the court finds that any child in the sibling group sought to be placed has a substantial relationship with the proposed placement resource. Substantial relationship means the proposed placement has a familial or mentoring role with the child, has spent more than cursory time with the child, and has established more than a minimal bond with the child; or

(d) the child is currently in an emergency placement.

6. Provisional approval or denial:

(a) Upon request of the sending agency and agreement of the receiving state to make a provisional determination, the receiving state may, but is not required to, provide provisional approval or denial for the child to be placed with a parent or relative, including a request for licensed placement if the receiving state has a separate licensing process available to relatives that includes waiver of non-safety issues.

Upon receipt of the documentation set forth in Section 7 below, the receiving state shall expedite provisional determination of the appropriateness of the proposed placement resource by:

1. performing a physical "walk through" by the receiving state's caseworker of the prospective placement's home to assess the residence for risks and appropriateness for placement of the child,

2. searching the receiving state's child protective services data base for prior reports/investigations on the prospective placement as required by the receiving state for emergency placement of a child in its custody,

3. performing a local criminal background check on the prospective placement,

4. undertaking other determinations as agreed upon by the sending and receiving state Compact Administrators, and

providing a provisional written report to the receiving state Compact Administrator as to the appropriateness of the proposed placement.

(b) A request by a sending state for a determination for provisional approval or denial shall be made by execution of an Order of Compliance by the sending state court that includes the required findings for a Regulation No. 7 request and a request for provisional approval or denial.

(c) Determination made under a request for provisional approval or denial shall be completed within seven (7) calendar days of receipt of the completed request packet by the receiving state Compact Administrator. A provisional approval or denial shall be communicated to the sending state Compact Administrator by the receiving state Compact Administrator in writing. This communication shall not include the signed Form 100A until the final decision is made pursuant to Section 9 below.

(d) Provisional placement, if approved, shall continue pending a final approval or denial of the placement by the receiving state or until the receiving state requires the return of the child to the sending state pursuant to paragraph 12 of this regulation.

(e) If provisional approval is given for placement with a parent from whom the child was not removed, the court in the sending state may direct its agency to request concurrence from the sending and receiving state Compact Administrators to place the child with the parent and relinquish jurisdiction over the child after final approval is given. If such concurrence is not given, the sending agency shall retain jurisdiction over the child as otherwise provided under Article V of the ICPC.

(f) A provisional denial means that the receiving state cannot approve a provisional placement pending the more comprehensive home study or assessment process due to issues that need to be resolved.

7. Sending agency steps before sending court enters Regulation No. 7 Order of Compliance: In order for a placement resource to be considered for an ICPC expedited placement decision by a receiving state, the sending agency shall take the following minimum steps prior to submitting a request for an ICPC expedited placement decision:

(a) Obtain either a signed statement of interest from the potential placement resource or a written statement from the assigned case manager in the sending state that following a conversation with the potential placement resource, the potential placement resource confirms appropriateness for the ICPC expedited placement decision process. Such statement shall include the following regarding the potential placement resource:

1. s/he is interested in being a placement resource for the child and is willing to cooperate with the ICPC process.

2. s/he fits the definition of parent, stepparent, grandparent, adult brother or sister, adult aunt or uncle, or his or her guardian, under Article VIII(a) of the ICPC.

3. the name and correct address of the placement resource, all available telephone numbers and other contact information for the potential placement resource, and the date of birth and social security number of all adults in the home.

4. a detail of the number and type of rooms in the residence of the placement resource to accommodate the child under consideration and the number of people, including children, who will be residing in the home.

5. s/he has financial resources or will access financial resources to feed, clothe and care for the child.

6. if required due to age and/or needs of the child, the plan for child care, and how it will be paid for.

7. s/he acknowledges that a criminal records and child abuse history check will be completed on any persons residing in the home required to be screened under the law of the receiving state and that, to the best knowledge of the placement resource, no one residing in the home has a criminal history or child abuse history that would prohibit the placement.

8. whether a request is being made for concurrence to relinquish jurisdiction if placement is sought with a parent from whom the child was not removed.

(b) The sending agency shall submit to the sending state court:

1. the signed written statement noted in 7a, above, and

2. a statement that based upon current information known to the sending agency, that it is unaware of any fact that would prohibit the child being placed with the placement resource and that it has completed and is prepared to send all required paperwork to the sending state ICPC office, including the ICPC-100A and ICPC Form 101.

8. Sending state court orders: The sending state court shall enter an order consistent with the Form Order for Expedited Placement Decision adopted with this modification of Regulation No. 7 subject to any additions or deletions required by federal law or the law of the sending state. The order shall set forth the factual basis for a finding that Regulation No. 7 applies to the child in question, whether the request includes a request for a provisional approval of the prospective placement and a factual basis for the request. The order must also require completion by the sending agency of ICPC Form 101 for the expedited request.

9. Time frames and methods for processing of ICPC expedited placement decision:

(a) Expedited transmissions: The transmission of any documentation, request for information under paragraph 10, or decisions made under this regulation shall be by overnight mail, facsimile transmission, or any other recognized method for expedited communication, including electronic transmission, if acceptable. The receiving state shall recognize and give effect to any such expedited transmission of an ICPC-100A and/or supporting documentation provided it is legible and appears to be a complete representation of the original. However, the receiving state may request and shall be entitled to receive originals or duly certified copies if it considers them necessary for a legally sufficient record under its laws. Any state Compact Administrator may waive any requirement for the form of transmission of original documents in the event he or she is confident in the authenticity of the forms and documents provided.

(b) Sending state court orders to the sending state agency: The sending state court shall send a copy of its signed order of compliance to the sending state agency within two (2) business days of the hearing or consideration of the request. The order shall include the name, mailing address, e-mail address, telephone number and FAX number of the clerk of court or a designated court administrator of the sending state court exercising jurisdiction over the child.

(c) Sending agency sends ICPC request to sending state ICPC office: The sending state court shall direct the sending agency to transmit to the sending state Compact Administrator within three (3) business days of receipt of the signed Order of Compliance, a completed ICPC-100A and Form 101, the statement required under Paragraph 7 above and supporting documentation pursuant to ICPC Article III.

(d) Sending State ICPC office sends ICPC Request to Receiving State ICPC office: Within two (2) business days after receipt of a complete Regulation 7 request, the sending state Compact Administrator shall transmit the complete request for the assessment and for any provisional placement to the receiving state Compact Administrator. The request shall include a copy of the Order of Compliance rendered in the sending state.

(e) Timeframe for receiving state ICPC office to render expedited placement decision: no later than twenty (20) business days from the date that the forms and materials are received by the receiving state Compact Administrator, the receiving state Compact Administrator shall make his or her determination pursuant to Article III(d) of the ICPC and shall send the completed 100-A to the sending state Compact Administrator by expedited transmission.

(f) Timeframe for receiving state ICPC office to send request packet to receiving local agency: The receiving state Compact Administrator shall send the request packet to the local agency in the receiving state for completion within two (2) business days of receipt of the completed packet from the sending state Compact Administrator.

(g) Timeframe for receiving state local agency to return completed home study to central office: The local agency in the receiving state shall return the completed home study to the receiving state Compact Administrator within fifteen (15) business days (including date of receipt) of receipt of the packet from the receiving state Compact Administrator.

(h) Timeframe for receiving state ICPC Compact Administrator to return completed home study to sending state: Upon completion of the decision process under the timeframes in this regulation, the receiving state Compact Administrator shall provide a written report, a 100A approving or denying the placement, and a transmittal of that determination to the sending state Compact Administrator as soon as possible, but no later than three (3) business days after receipt of the packet from the receiving state local agency and no more than twenty (20) business days from the initial date that the complete documentation and forms were received by the receiving state Compact Administrator from the sending state Compact Administrator.

10. Recourse if sending or receiving state determines documentation is insufficient:

(a) In the event the sending state Compact Administrator finds that the ICPC request documentation is substantially insufficient, s/he shall specify to the sending agency what additional information is needed and request such information from the sending agency.

(b) In the event the receiving state Compact Administrator finds that the ICPC request documentation is substantially insufficient, he or she shall specify what additional information is needed and request such information from the sending state Compact Administrator. Until receipt of the requested information from the sending state Compact Administrator, the receiving state is not required to continue with the assessment process.

(c) In the event the receiving state Compact Administrator finds that the ICPC request documentation is lacking needed information but is otherwise sufficient, s/he she shall specify what additional information is needed and request such information from the sending state Compact Administrator. If a provisional placement is being pursued, the provisional placement evaluation process shall continue while the requested information is located and provided.

(d) Failure by a Compact Administrator in either the sending state or the receiving state to make a request for additional documentation or information under this paragraph within two (2) business days of receipt of the ICPC request and accompanying documentation by him or her shall raise a presumption that the sending agency has met its requirements under the ICPC and this regulation.

11. Failure of receiving state ICPC office or local agency to comply with ICPC Regulation No. 7: Upon receipt of the Regulation No. 7 request, if the receiving state Compact Administrator determines that it will not be possible to meet the timeframes for the Regulation No. 7 request, whether or not a provisional request is made, the receiving state Compact Administrator shall notify the sending state Compact Administrator as soon as practical and set forth the receiving state's intentions in completing the request, including an estimated time for completion or consideration of the request as a regular ICPC request. Such information shall also be transmitted to the sending agency by the sending state Compact Administrator for it to consider other possible alternatives available to it.

If the receiving state Compact Administrator and/or local state agency in the receiving state fail(s) to complete action for the expedited placement request as prescribed in this regulation within the time period allowed, the receiving state shall be deemed to be out of compliance with this regulation and the ICPC. If there appears to be a lack of compliance, the sending state court that sought the provisional placement and expedited placement decision may so inform an appropriate court in the receiving state, provide that court with copies of relevant documentation and court orders entered in the case, and request assistance. Within its jurisdiction and authority, the requested court may render such assistance, including the holding of hearings, taking of evidence, and the making of appropriate orders, for the purpose of obtaining compliance with this regulation and the ICPC.

12. Removal of a child: Following any approval and placement of the child, if the receiving state Compact Administrator determines that the placement no longer meets the individual needs of the child, including the child's safety, permanency, health, well-being, and mental, emotional, and physical development, then the receiving state Compact Administrator may request the sending state Compact Administrator arrange for the immediate return of the child or make alternative placement as provided in Article V (a) of the ICPC. The receiving state request for removal may be withdrawn if the sending state arranges services to resolve the reason for the requested removal and the receiving and sending state Compact Administrators mutually agree to the plan. If no agreement is reached, the sending state shall expedite return of the child to the sending state within five (5) business days unless otherwise agreed in writing between the sending and receiving state Compact Administrators.

13. This regulation as first effective October 1, 1996, and readopted pursuant to Article VII of the Interstate Compact on the Placement of Children by action of the Association of Administrators of the Interstate Compact on the Placement of Children at its annual meeting of April 1999, is amended pursuant to Article VII of the Interstate Compact on the Placement of Children by action of the Association of Administrators of the Interstate Compact on the Placement of Children at its annual meeting of May 1, 2011; the regulation, as amended was approved on May 1, 2011 and is effective as of October 1, 2011.

Regulation No. 8. Change of placement purpose

1. An ICPC-100B should be prepared and sent in accordance with its accompanying instructions whenever there is a change of purpose in an existing placement, e.g., from foster care to preadoption even though the placement recipient remains the same. However, when a receiving state or a sending state requests a new ICPC-100A in such a case, it should be provided by the sending agency and transmitted in accordance with usual procedures for processing of ICPC-100As.

2. Words and phrases used in this regulation have the same meanings as in the Compact, unless the context clearly requires another meaning.

3. This regulation is effective on and after April 30, 2000, pursuant to Article VII of the Interstate Compact on the Placement of Children by action of the Association of Administrators of the Interstate Compact on the Placement of Children at its annual meeting of April 30–May 3, 2000.

Regulation No. 9. Definition of a visit

Regulation No. 9 ("Definition of a Visit"), as first adopted in 1999, is amended to read as follows:

1. A visit is not a placement within the meaning of the Interstate Compact on the Placement of Children (ICPC). Visits and placements are distinguished on the basis of purpose, duration, and the intention of the person or agency with responsibility for planning for the child as to the child's place of abode.

2. The purpose of a visit is to provide the child with a social or cultural experience of short duration, such as a stay in a camp or with a friend or relative who has not assumed legal responsibility for providing child care services.

3. It is understood that a visit for twenty-four (24) hours or longer will necessarily involve the provision of some services in the nature of child care by the person or persons with whom the child is staying. The provision of these services will not, of itself, alter the character of the stay as a visit.

4. If the child's stay is intended to be for no longer than thirty (30) days and if the purpose is as described in Paragraph 2, it will be presumed that the circumstances constitute a visit rather than a placement.

5. A stay or proposed stay of longer than thirty (30) days is a placement or proposed placement, except that a stay of longer duration may be considered a visit if it begins and ends within the period of a child's vacation from school as ascertained from the academic calendar of the school. A visit may not be extended or renewed in a manner which causes or will cause it to exceed thirty (30) days or the school vacation period, as the case may be. If a stay does not from the outset have an express terminal date, or if its duration is not clear from the circumstances, it shall be considered a placement or proposed placement and not a visit.

6. A request for a home study or supervision made by the person or agency which sends or proposes to send a child on a visit and that is pending at the time that the visit is proposed will establish a rebuttable presumption that the intent of the stay or proposed stay is not a visit.

7. A visit as defined in this regulation is not subject to the Interstate Compact on the Placement of Children.

8. Words and phrases used in this regulation have the same meanings as in the Compact, unless the context clearly requires another meaning.

9. This regulation was first adopted as a resolution effective April 26, 1983; was promulgated as a regulation as of April 1999; and is amended by the Compact Administrators, acting jointly and pursuant to Article VII of the Interstate Compact on the Placement of Children, at their annual meeting of April 2002, with such amendments effective after June 27, 2002.

Regulation No. 10. Guardians

Regulation No. 10 ("Guardians"), as first adopted in 1999, is amended to read as follows:

1. Guardian Defined.

As used in the Interstate Compact on the Placement of Children (ICPC) and in this Regulation:

(a) "Guardian" means a public or private agency, organization or institution which holds a valid and effective permanent appointment from a court of competent jurisdiction to have custody and control of a child, to plan for the child, and to do all other things for or on behalf of a child which a parent would have authority and responsibility for doing by virtue of an unrestricted parent-child relationship. An appointment is permanent for the purposes of this paragraph if the appointment would allow the guardianship to endure until the child's age of majority without any court review, subsequent to the appointment, of the care that the guardian provides or the status of other permanency planning which the guardian has a professional obligation to carry out. Guardian also means an individual who is a non-agency guardian as defined in subparagraph (b) hereof.

(b) "Nonagency guardian" means an individual holding a currently valid appointment from a court of competent jurisdiction to have all of the authority and responsibility of a guardian as defined in subparagraph (a) hereof.

2. Prospective Adoptive Parents Not Guardians.

An individual with whom a child is placed as a preliminary to a possible adoption cannot be considered a non-agency guardian of the child, for the purpose of determining applicability of ICPC to the placement, unless the individual would qualify as a lawful recipient of a placement of the child without having to comply with ICPC as provided in Article VIII (a) thereof.

3. Effect of Guardianship on ICPC Placements.

(a) An interstate placement of a child with a nonagency guardian, whose appointment to the guardianship existed prior to consideration of the making of the placement, is not subject to ICPC if the sending agency is the child's parent, stepparent, grandparent, adult brother or sister, or adult uncle or aunt.

(b) An appropriate court of the sending agency's state must continue its jurisdiction over a non-exempt placement until applicability of ICPC to the placement is terminated in accordance with Article V (a) of ICPC.

4. Permanency Status of Guardianship.

(a) A state agency may pursue a guardianship to achieve a permanent placement for a child in the child welfare system, as required by federal or state law. In the case of a child who is already placed in a receiving state in compliance with ICPC, appointment of the placement recipient as guardian by the sending state court is grounds to terminate the applicability of the ICPC when the sending and receiving state compact administrators concur on the termination pursuant to Article V (a). In such an instance, the court which appointed the guardian may continue its jurisdiction if it is maintainable under another applicable law.

(b) If, subsequent to the making of an interstate placement pursuant to ICPC, a court of the receiving state appoints a nonagency guardian for the child, such appointment shall be construed as a request that the sending agency and the receiving state concur in the discontinuance of the application of ICPC to the placement. Upon concurrence of the sending and receiving states, the sending agency and an appropriate court of the sending state shall close the ICPC aspects of the case and the jurisdiction of the sending agency pursuant to Article V (a) of ICPC shall be dismissed.

5. Guardian Appointed by Parent.

If the statutes of a jurisdiction so provide, a parent who is chronically ill or near death may appoint a guardian for his or her children, which guardianship shall take effect on the death or mental incapacitation of the parent. A nonagency guardian so appointed shall be deemed a nonagency guardian as that term is used in Article VIII (a) of ICPC, provided that such nonagency guardian has all of the powers and responsibilities that a parent would have by virtue of an unrestricted parent-child relationship. A placement with a nonagency guardian as described in this paragraph shall be effective for the purposes of ICPC without court appointment or confirmation unless the statute pursuant to which it is made otherwise provides and if there is compliance with procedures required by the statute. However, the parent must be physically present in the jurisdiction having the statute at the time that he or she makes the appointment or expressly submits to the jurisdiction of the appointing court.

6. Other Definitions of Guardianship Unaffected.

The definitions of "guardian" and "nonagency guardian" contained in this regulation shall not be construed to affect the meaning or applicability of any other definitions of "guardian" or "nonagency guardian" when employed for purposes or to circumstances not having a bearing on placements proposed to be made or made pursuant to ICPC.

7. Words and phrases used in this regulation have the same meanings as in the Compact, unless the context clearly requires another meaning.

8. This regulation was first promulgated in April 1999; it is amended by the Compact Administrators, acting jointly and pursuant to Article VII of the Interstate Compact on the Placement of Children, at their annual meeting of April 2002, with such amendments effective after June 27, 2002.

Regulation No. 11. Responsibility of states to supervise children

The following regulation was adopted by the Association of Administrators of the Interstate Compact on the Placement of Children on April 18, 2010 and is declared to be in effect on and after October 1, 2010.

1. Words and phrases used in this regulation have the same meanings as those ascribed to them in the Interstate Compact on the Placement of Children (ICPC). A word or phrase not defined in the ICPC shall have the same meaning ascribed to it in common usage.

2. Definitions:

(a) "Central Compact Office" means the office that receives ICPC placement referrals from sending states and sends ICPC placement referrals to receiving states. In states that have one central compact office that services the entire state, the term "central compact office" has the same meaning as "central state compact office" as described in Regulation 5 of the ICPC. In states in which ICPC placement referrals are sent directly to receiving states and received directly from sending states by more than one county or other regional area within the state, the "central compact office" is the office within each separate county or other region that sends and receives ICPC placement referrals.

(b) "Child Welfare Caseworker" means a person assigned to manage the cases of dependency children who are in the custody or under the supervision of a public child welfare agency.

(c) "Public Child Placing Agency" means any government child welfare agency or child protection agency or a private entity under contract with such an agency, regardless of whether they act on behalf of a state, county, municipality or other governmental unit and which facilitates, causes or is involved in the placement of a child from one state to another.

(d) "Supervision" means monitoring of the child and the child's living situation by the receiving state after a child has been placed in a receiving state pursuant to an approved placement under Article III(d) of the ICPC or pursuant to a child's relocation to a receiving state in accordance with Regulation 1 of the ICPC.

3. A receiving state must supervise a child placed pursuant to an approved placement under Article III(d) of the Interstate Compact on the Placement of Children (ICPC) if supervision is requested by the sending state, and;

(a)the sending agency is a public child placing agency, and

(b)the agency that completed the home study for placement of the child in the receiving state is a public child placing agency, and

(c)the child's placement is not in a residential treatment center or a group home.

4. Supervision must begin when the child is placed in the receiving state pursuant to an approved placement under Article III(d) of the ICPC and the receiving state has received a form 100B from the sending state indicating the date of the child's placement. Supervision can and should begin prior to receipt of the form 100B if the receiving state has been informed by other means

1

that the child has been placed pursuant to an approved placement under Article III(d) of the ICPC.

5. (a) Supervision must continue until: the child reaches the age of majority or is legally emancipated; or the child's adoption is finalized; or legal custody of the child is granted to a caregiver or a parent and jurisdiction is terminated by the sending state; or the child no longer resides at the home approved for placement of the child pursuant to Article III(d) of the ICPC; or jurisdiction over the child is terminated by the sending state; or legal guardianship of the child is granted to the child's caregiver in the receiving state; or the sending state requests in writing that supervision be discontinued, and the receiving state concurs.

(b)Supervision of a child in a receiving state may continue, notwithstanding the occurrence of one of the events listed above in 5(a)(1–7), by mutual agreement of the sending and receiving state's central compact offices.

6. Supervision must include face-to-face visits with the child at least once each month and beginning no later than 30 days from the date on which the child is placed, or 30 days from the date on which the receiving state is notified of the child's placement, if notification occurs after placement. A majority of visits must occur in the child's home. Face-to-face visits must be performed by a Child Welfare Caseworker in the receiving state. The purpose of face-to-face visits is to help ensure the on-going safety and well being of the child and to gather relevant information to include in written reports back to the Public Child Placing Agency in the sending state. If significant issues of concern are identified during a face-to-face visit or at any time during a child's placement, the receiving state shall promptly notify the central compact office in the sending state in writing.

7. The Child Welfare Caseworker assigned to supervise a child placed in the receiving state shall complete a written supervision report at least once every ninety (90) days following the date of the receipt of the form 100B by the receiving state's central compact office notifying the receiving state of the child's placement in the receiving state. Completed reports shall be sent to the central compact office in the sending state from the central compact office in the receiving state. At a minimum such reports shall include the following:

(a) Date and location of each face-to-face contact with the child since the last supervision report was completed.

(b) A summary of the child's current circumstances, including a statement regarding the on-going safety and well-being of the child.

(c) If the child is attending school, a summary of the child's academic performance along with copies of any available report cards, education-related evaluations or Individual Education Program (IEP) documents.

(d) A summary of the child's current health status, including mental health, the dates of any health-related appointments that have occurred since the last supervision report was completed, the identity of any health providers seen, and copies of any available health-related evaluations, reports or other pertinent records.

(e) An assessment of the current placement and caretakers (e.g., physical condition of the home, caretaker's commitment to child, current status of caretaker and family, any changes in family composition, health, financial situation, work, legal involvement, social relationships; child care arrangements).

(f) A description of any unmet needs and any recommendations for meeting identified needs.

(g) If applicable, the supervising caseworker's recommendation regarding continuation of the placement, return of legal custody to a parent or parents with whom the child is residing and termination of the sending state's jurisdiction, finalization of adoption by the child's current caretakers or the granting of legal guardianship to the child's current caretakers.

8. (a) The receiving state shall respond to any report of abuse or neglect of a child placed in the receiving state pursuant to an approved placement under Article III(d) of the ICPC and will respond in the same manner as it would to a report of abuse or neglect of any other child residing in the receiving state.

(b) If the receiving state determines that a child must be removed from his or her home in order to be safe, and it is not possible for the child placing agency in the sending state to move the child at the time that the receiving state makes this determination, the receiving state shall place the child in a safe and appropriate setting in the receiving state. The receiving state shall promptly notify the sending state if a child is moved to another home or other substitute care facility.

(c) The receiving state shall notify the central compact office in the sending state of any report of child abuse or neglect of a child placed in the receiving state pursuant to an approved placement under Article III(d) of the ICPC, regardless of whether or not the report is substantiated. Notification of the central compact office in the sending state will occur as soon as possible after such a report is received.

(d) It is the responsibility of the public child placing agency in the sending state to take action to ensure the ongoing safety of a child placed in a receiving state pursuant to an approved placement under Article III(d) of the ICPC, including return of the child to the sending state as soon as possible when return is requested by the receiving state.

(e) Pursuant to Article V of the ICPC, it is the responsibility of the public child placing agency in the sending state to take timely action to relieve the receiving state of any financial burden the receiving state has incurred as a result of placing a child into substitute care after removing the child from an unsafe home in which the child was previously placed by the public child placing agency in the sending state pursuant to Article III(d) of the ICPC.

9. (a) The child placing agency in the sending state is responsible for case planning for any child placed in a receiving state by the child placing agency in the sending state pursuant to an approved placement under Article III(d) of the ICPC.

(b) The child placing agency in the sending state is responsible for the ongoing safety and well-being of any child placed in a receiving state by the child placing agency in the sending state pursuant to an approved placement under Article III(d) of the ICPC and is responsible for meeting any identified needs of the child that are not being met by other available means.

(c) The receiving state shall be responsible to assist the sending state in locating appropriate resources for the child and/or the placement resource.

(d) The receiving state shall notify the central compact office in the sending state in writing of any unmet needs of a child placed in the receiving state pursuant to an approved placement under Article III(d) of the ICPC.

(e) If the child's needs continue to be unmet after the notification described in (d) above has occurred, the receiving state may require the child placing agency in the sending state to return the child to the sending state. Before requiring the return of the child to the sending state, the receiving state shall take into consideration the negative impact on the child that may result from being removed from his or her home in the receiving state and shall weigh the potential for such negative impact against the potential benefits to the child of being returned to the sending state. Notwithstanding the requirement to consider the potential for such negative impact, the receiving state has sole discretion in determining whether or not to require return of a child to the sending state.

Regulation No. 12. Private/independent adoptions

The following regulation, as adopted by the Association of Administrators of the Interstate Compact on the Placement of

Children, is declared to be in effect on and after October 1, 2012. Words and phrases used in this regulation have the same meanings as in the Compact, unless the context clearly requires another meaning. If a court or other competent authority invokes the Compact, the court or other competent authority is obligated to comply with Article V (Retention of Jurisdiction) of the Compact.

1. Definitions:

(a) "Adoption" is the method provided by state law that establishes the legal relationship of parent and child between persons who are not so related by birth or some other legal determination, with the same mutual rights and obligations that exist between children and their birth parents. This relationship can only be termed "adoption" after the legal process for adoption finalization is complete.

(b) "Adoption Home Study" is a home study conducted for the purpose of placing a child for adoption with a placement resource. The adoption home study is the assessment and evaluation of a potential adoptive parent.

(c) "Adoption Facilitator" is an individual that is not licensed or approved by a state as an adoption agency, child-placing agency, or attorney, and who is engaged in the matching of birth parents with adoptive parents.

(d) "Independent Adoption" is an adoption arranged by a birth parent or other person or entity as designated, defined, and authorized by the laws of the applicable state or states, to take custody of and to place children for adoption.

(e) "Independent Adoption Entity" is any individual or entity authorized by the law of the applicable state or states to take custody of and to place children for adoption and to place children for adoption other than a state, county, or licensed private agency.

(f) "Intermediary" is any person or entity who is not an Independent Adoption Entity as defined above, but who acts for or between any parent and any prospective parent, or acts on behalf of either, in connection with the placement of the parent's child born in one state, for adoption by a prospective parent in a different state.

(g) "Legal Risk Placement" means a placement made preliminary to an adoption where the prospective adoptive parents acknowledge in writing that a child can be ordered returned to the sending state or the birth mother's state of residence, if different from the sending state, and a final decree of adoption shall not be entered in any jurisdiction until all required consents or termination of parental rights are obtained or are dispensed with in accordance with applicable law.

(h) "Legal Risk Medical Statement" is an acknowledgment by the prospective adoptive parents that known physical, emotional, or other relevant history of the child has been disclosed.

(i) "Private Agency" is a licensed or state approved agency whether domestic or international that has been given legal authority to place a child for adoption.

(j) "Private Agency Adoption" is an adoption arranged by a licensed or approved agency whether domestic or international that has been given legal custody or responsibility for the child including the right to place the child for adoption.

2. Intent of Regulation No. 12: The intent of this regulation is to provide guidance and ICPC requirements for the processing of private agency or independent adoptions. The ICPC process exists to ensure protection and services to children and families involved in executing adoptions across state lines and to ensure that the placement is in compliance with all applicable requirements. It is further the intent of Regulation No. 12 for the sending agency to comply with each and every requirement set forth in Article III of the ICPC that governs the placement of children therein.

3. Application of Regulation No. 12: This regulation applies to children being placed for private adoption or independent adoption whether being placed by a private agency or by an Independent Adoption Entity, as defined herein, or with the assistance of an Intermediary, as defined herein, and as in compliance with the other articles and regulations.

4. Conditions for placement as stated in ICPC Article III: Prior to sending, bringing, or causing any child to be sent or brought into a receiving state for placement in foster care or as a preliminary to a possible adoption, the sending agency shall furnish the appropriate public authorities in the receiving state written notice of the intention to send, bring, or place the child in the receiving state. The notice shall contain:

(a) The name, date, and place of birth of the child.

(b) The identity and address or addresses of the parents or legal guardian. If the identity or address of a birth parent and/or legal parent is not provided, an explanation as to why it has not been provided shall be included to the extent that it is consistent with the laws of the applicable state.

(c) The name and address of the person, agency, or institution to or with which the sending agency proposes to send, bring, or place the child.

(d) A full statement of the reasons for such proposed action and evidence of the authority pursuant to which the placement is proposed to be made.

Compliance with this requirement may be met by submission of the documentation required under Section 6 below.

5. Legal and financial responsibility during placement: For placement of a child by a private agency for independent adoption, the private agency shall be:

(a) Legally responsible for the child, including return of the child to the sending state if the adoption does not occur during the period of placement.

(b) Financially responsible for the child absent a contractual agreement to the contrary or a statement by the prospective adoptive parent or parents that they will assume financial responsibility.

6. Sending agency or party case documentation required with ICPC-100A private agency/independent adoption request:

(a) For placement by a private agency or independent entity, the required content to accompany a request packet for approval shall include all of the following:

(1) ICPC-100A: Form requesting ICPC approval to make placement;

(2) Cover letter: A request for approval signed by the person requesting approval identifying the child, birth parent(s), the prospective adoptive parent(s), a statement as to how the match was made, name of the intermediary, if any, and the name of the supervising agency and address;

(3) Consent or relinquishment: signed by the parents in accordance with the law of the sending state, and, if requested by the receiving state, in accordance with the laws of the receiving state. If a parent is permitted and elects to follow the laws of a state other than his or her state of residence, then he or she should specifically waive, in writing, the laws of his or her state of residence and acknowledge that he or she has a right to sign a consent under the law of his or her state of residence. The packet shall contain a statement detailing how the rights of all parents shall be legally addressed;

(4) Certification by a licensed attorney or authorized agent of a private adoption agency or independent entity that the consent or relinquishment is in compliance with the applicable laws of the sending state, or where requested, the laws of the receiving state;

(5) Verification of compliance with Indian Child Welfare Act (25 U.S.C. 1901, et. seq.);

(6) Legal risk acknowledgement signed by the prospective adoptive parents, if applicable in either the sending or receiving state;

(7) Statement of authority: A copy of the current court order pursuant to which the sending agency has authority to place the child or, if the authority does not derive from a court order, a

statement of the basis on which the sending agency has authority to place the child and documentation that supervision is on-going;

(8) Current case history for the child, including custodial and social history, chronology of court involvement, social dynamics, education information (if applicable), and a description of any special needs of the child. If an infant, at a minimum, a copy of the medical records of the birth and hospital discharge summary for the child, if the child has been discharged;

(9) Foster home license: If the receiving state placement resource previously lived in the sending state and that state has required licensure, certification, or approval, a copy of the most recent license, certificate, or approval of the qualification of the placement resource(s) and/or their home showing the status of the placement resource as a qualified placement resource, if available. If the receiving state placement resource was previously licensed, certified, or approved as a foster or adoptive parent in the sending state and such license, certificate, or approval was involuntarily revoked, a statement of when such revocation occurred and the reasons for such revocation;

(10) Adoptive home study or approval: A copy of the most recent adoption home study or approval of the prospective adoptive family must be provided, including, in accordance with the law of the receiving state, verification of compliance with federal and state background clearances, including FBI fingerprint and Child Abuse/Neglect clearances and Sex Offender Registry clearance, a copy of any court order approving the adoptive home (if entered), and a statement by the person or entity that the home is approved or a revised current home study update if the home study is more than 12 months old;

(11) A copy of the Order of Appointment of Legal Guardian, if applicable;

(12) Affidavit of Expenses, if applicable; and

(13) Copy of sending agency's license or certification, if applicable;

(14) Biological parents' information—social history, medical history, ethnic background, reasons for adoption plan, and circumstances of proposed placement. If the child was previously adopted, the adoptive parents shall provide the information set forth in this section for the biological parents, if available;

(15) A written statement from the person or entity that will be providing post-placement supervision (may be included in adoption home study) acknowledging the obligation to provide post-placement supervision; and

(16) Authority for the prospective adoptive parents to provide medical care, if applicable.

(b) If a home study is completed by a licensed private agency in the receiving state, the sending state shall not impose any additional requirements to complete the home study that are not required by the receiving state unless the adoption is finalized in the sending state.

7. Authorization to travel: Additional documents may be requested

(a) Except as set forth herein, the child shall not be sent, brought, or caused to be sent or brought into the receiving state until the appropriate public authorities in the receiving state shall notify the sending agency, in writing, to the effect that the proposed placement does not appear to be contrary to the interests of the child. Art. III(d).

(b) The sending and receiving state ICPC office may request additional information or documents prior to finalization of an approved placement. Travel by the prospective adoptive parents into the receiving state with the child shall not occur until the required content of the request packet for approval has been submitted, received and reviewed by the sending and receiving ICPC offices and approval to travel has been given, provided, however, a receiving state may, at its sole discretion, approve travel while awaiting provision of additional documentation requested.

8. Approval by the receiving state ICPC office: A provisional or final approval for placement must be obtained in writing from the receiving state ICPC office in accordance with the Interstate Compact on the Placement of Children. A signed Form 100A must be provided by the receiving state if the writing was in any other form. In any event, approval or denial must be given within three (3) business days of the receipt of the completed packet by the receiving state Compact Administrator.

9. Upon placement of a child by the sending agency following approval by the receiving state Compact Administrator, the sending agency shall, within five (5) business days of placement of the child, submit a completed 100B form confirming placement to the sending state Compact Administrator. Upon finalization of the adoption, if the sending agency is a private adoption agency, the private adoption agency shall provide to the sending state Compact Administrator a copy of the final judgment of adoption together with a 100B form for closure, which shall then be sent to the receiving state Compact Administrator within thirty (30) business days of entry of judgment. Upon finalization of an independent adoption, the sending agency or entity shall provide a copy of the final judgment of adoption together with a 100B form for closure within thirty (30) business days of entry of judgment to the sending state Compact Administrator who shall then send it to the receiving state Compact Administrator.

10. Notification if child placed in violation of Article III: A child placed into the receiving state prior to a decision for placement constitutes a violation of Article III and the laws respecting the placement of children of both states; subject to liability cited in Article IV. Penalty for Illegal Placement. All parties to the placement arrangements, including prospective resource parents, the sending agency, private licensed child-placing agency or legal counsel are responsible for notifying the appropriate ICPC authorities in both states of the circumstances and to coordinate action to provide for the safety and well-being of the child pending further action. If a child has been placed in the receiving state in violation of Article III, a Form 100B indicating the date the child was placed in the prospective adoptive home, together with items listed in Section 6 above, shall then be filed with the sending state Compact Administrator who shall forward them to the receiving state's Compact Administrator. If all required documents are provided, the sending state and the receiving state shall give due and appropriate consideration to placement as permitted under the sending and receiving state laws.

11. This regulation is adopted pursuant to Article VII of the Interstate Compact on the Placement of Children by action of the Association of Administrators of the Interstate Compact on the Placement of Children at its annual meeting May 4 through 7, 2012; such adoption was approved on May 6, 2012 and is effective as of October 1, 2012.

Chapter 119A. Child Support Enforcement

§ 12. Support orders; enforcement; arrearages; assignment of wages; notice and hearing; order

[Amended by 2003 Mass. Acts c. 9, §§ 11–35, effective Apr. 1, 2003; 2019 Mass. Acts c. 34, §§ 6–13, effective July 8, 2019.]

(a) Each judgment or order for support issued pursuant to section 28 of chapter 119 and chapters 207, 208, 209, 209A and 209C, or received, entered or registered pursuant to chapter 209D shall conform to and shall be enforced according to this section. Each such judgment or order for support shall include a provision for immediate withholding of income, as provided in paragraph (6) of subsection (b); provided, however, that such order for income withholding may be suspended, pursuant to subsection (c). Each such judgment or order for support shall also include an order for health care coverage, as provided in paragraph (5) of subsection (b). Each outstanding order for support which is reviewed, modified or otherwise brought before the court pursuant to any of said chapters or pursuant to section eighteen A of chapter two hundred and seventy-three shall be amended so as to conform to and shall thereafter be enforced in accordance with the provisions of this section.

(b)(1) Each judgment or order for support to which this section applies shall be made payable to the IV-D agency on behalf of each obligee who applies for or is a recipient of IV-D services. Until September 30, 1998, if the obligee is not a recipient of public assistance or has not signed an application for IV-D services, the judgment or order if to be paid by withholding of income of the obligor, shall be made payable on behalf of the obligee to an entity designated by the commissioner of revenue or the court unless the obligor and obligee agree that payment shall be made either directly to the obligee or in some other manner. Such entity shall deduct a fee as determined by the commissioner prior to forwarding payments to the obligee.

(2) All judgments and orders of support entered in the commonwealth on or after October 1, 1998, in which support is ordered to be paid by withholding of income of the obligor, shall be made payable to the IV-D agency on behalf of the obligee; but any judgment or order of support which is solely for alimony or spousal support shall be made payable to the obligee.

(3) In all other cases in which support is payable by withholding income of the obligor, including cases not receiving IV-D services, payment of income withholding pursuant to such judgment or order for support shall be paid, on and after October 1, 1998, to the IV-D agency on behalf of the obligee, notwithstanding the payee specified in the order, provided that a party or the employer notifies the IV-D agency of the amount to be withheld, including any amount to be withheld toward payment of arrearages, and provides the IV-D agency with the identifying information required by paragraph (5) of subsection (b) and a copy of the most recent order or notice of income withholding; but any order of support payable by withholding income of the obligor which is solely for alimony or spousal support shall be paid to the obligee.

(4) With respect to any case in which support to be paid by withholding income is or becomes payable to the IV-D agency on behalf of the obligee under this section and such support payment was previously made payable to the obligee or another entity, the IV-D agency upon receipt of the case shall execute an order to make payments under the income withholding order payable to the IV-D agency, and shall so notify the employer, the obligor, and the obligee; provided, however, that if insufficient information identifying the obligee and the obligor has been provided to the IV-D agency, the IV-D agency shall return to the employer or other source of periodic income any payment received and shall direct such employer or other source of periodic income to provide information identifying the obligor and obligee prior to transmitting additional payments to the IV-D agency; and provided further that the IV-D agency shall not be liable to such obligor or obligee for not transmitting the payments to the obligee.

G.L. c. 119A, § 12. Support orders; enforcement; arrearages;

(5) (A) A judgment or order shall include: (i) the name and address of the obligor; (ii) the name, address and federal employer identification number of the obligor's employer; and (iii) such other information as the IV-D agency requires to assist it in collecting support payments. With respect to an order for income withholding made payable to the IV-D agency, the issuing court shall provide to the IV-D agency: (i) a copy of the judgment or order for support and the order for income withholding; (ii) the address of the obligee; (iii) the date of birth of the child; and (iv) such other information as the IV-D agency requires to assist it in collecting support payments; provided, however, that such information need not be included in the order for income withholding.

(B) Each such judgment or order shall also include a provision for health care coverage for the child in accordance with this section and may require the obligor to pay an amount toward the obligee's cost of health care coverage or toward uninsured medical expenses on behalf of the child. The court shall enter an order that requires the obligor or the obligee to provide health care coverage if such coverage is available at reasonable cost and accessible to the child. If the court determines that an order for health care coverage is not in the best interest of the child or creates an undue hardship for the obligor or the obligee, then the court shall enter written findings.

(C) If the child is enrolled in MassHealth, an equivalent program in another state pursuant to 42 U.S.C. 1397aa et seq. or 42 U.S.C. 1396a et seq. or an equivalent program in another state that is substantially similar to the program established in chapter 118E, the court shall order the obligee to maintain such coverage as long as the child remains eligible; provided, however, that the court may also order the obligor to enroll the child in private health insurance if: (i) private health insurance is available to the obligor at reasonable cost and accessible to the child; (ii) enrollment in the insurance is in the best interest of the child; and (iii) enrollment in the insurance will not create an undue hardship for the obligor or the obligee.

(D) If health care coverage pursuant to this section is not available to the obligor or the obligee at the time the order is entered, the court shall order the parties to notify the IV-D agency if such coverage becomes available. For the purposes of this section: (i) health care coverage shall be deemed reasonable in cost if the cost to the party ordered to provide health care coverage does not exceed 5 per cent of the gross income of the party; (ii) health care coverage shall be deemed accessible to the child if covered services are available within 15 miles of the child's primary residence; (iii) health care coverage includes private health insurance available through employment, union affiliation or otherwise, and public health coverage administered by the Title XIX agency; and (iv) private health insurance shall be deemed not available at reasonable cost to an obligor or obligee whose gross income does not exceed 150 per cent of the federal poverty guidelines for the family size or who receives MassHealth on behalf of the obligor, the obligee or the child.

(E) If the IV-D agency is responsible for enforcing the order, the court shall order the obligor and the obligee to notify the IV-D agency of any changes in the availability and terms of health care coverage. If the obligor is required to provide health care coverage for a child of the obligor's through an employment-related health plan and if the IV-D agency has the name and address of the employer, the IV-D agency shall transfer the national medical support notice, as required by Title IV, Part D of the federal Social Security Act, to the employer notifying the employer to enroll the child in a health care plan provided by the employer for which the obligor is eligible. If the obligee is required to provide health care coverage, the IV-D agency may transmit such national medical support notice to the employer of the obligee and the provisions of this section with respect to the notice shall apply to such obligee and such employer. The notice may be transmitted to the employer by any method, including paper, facsimile, magnetic tape or other electronic means.

(6) Each such judgment or order shall include a provision under which a portion of the obligor's income as defined in section 1-A, shall be withheld, except as expressly limited by law, in an amount sufficient to comply with the support order. Each such judgment or order shall also include a provision that any income withholding be sufficient to reduce any arrearage of support that accrues under the order or accrued prior to entry of the order by increasing income withholding by twenty-five per cent until such arrearage is paid off. No current order shall be reduced in order to pay off an arrearage.

This section shall not affect the availability of any method for collecting an arrearage. In any case with an outstanding support order under this chapter in which no order of income withholding has been executed, said IV-D agency shall execute an order, by any reasonable means, including by electronic means, to withhold income, without the need for judicial or administrative hearing, and this section shall apply; provided, however, that the IV-D agency shall notify the obligor that the withholding has commenced and of the procedures to follow under section 17 if the obligor wishes to contest such withholding on the grounds that the withholding or the amount withheld is improper due to mistake of fact. If on the basis of mistake of fact, the obligor contests the income withholding or contests the withholding of the employee share of premiums for health care coverage, the employer shall initiate and continue the withholding until the employer receives notice from the IV-D agency, the court or an administrative agency of competent jurisdiction to terminate the income withholding or the withholding of the employee share of premiums for health care coverage.

(c) Any withholding of income shall take effect immediately when the obligor is found in violation or contempt of an order of support. Income withholding shall also take effect immediately, without the necessity of any judicial or administrative hearing, in all other cases, unless the court or the hearing officer finds good cause exists to order that the income withholding be suspended and makes written findings in support of suspension or unless the obligor and the obligee agree in writing that payment shall be made directly to the obligee. Such written findings shall include a determination by the court that immediate income withholding would not be in the best interests of the child and the reasons therefor and, in the case of a modification of a support order, shall include proof of timely payments made in compliance with the existing order. Before the hearing regarding the suspension of such income withholding, the court shall inform the obligor that under the provisions of subsections (d) and (e), such income withholding, even if suspended, will take effect without any further hearing if an arrearage accrues as described in paragraph (1) or (2), and that a hearing will be available as provided in said subsections (d) and (e).

In the event that income withholding is suspended in the first instance, it shall take effect immediately:—

(1) when a total arrearage amounting to the support owing for a fourteen-day period has accrued; or

(2) in cases where payment is to be made once per month, fourteen days after a payment is missed, or, if no payment is missed, fourteen days after an arrearage amounting to one-half the amount of support owing for one month has accrued; or

(3) at the request of the obligor or the obligee.

Income withholding pursuant to this section shall terminate when the underlying support obligation terminates and all arrears are paid. With respect to a case receiving IV-D services, when an obligor changes employers or other source of periodic income, the obligor shall promptly notify his subsequent employer or other source of periodic income of his child support order and the IV-D agency of his subsequent employment or other source of periodic income and within 2 business days of receipt of the information, the IV-D agency shall transfer the income withholding order or the national medical support notice or both to the subsequent employer or other source of periodic income. With respect to a case receiving IV-D services, the IV-D agency shall transfer the income withholding order, the national medical support notice, or both, to the obligor's employer or other source of periodic income within 2 business days of the entry of the obligor's employment information in the wage reporting system as set forth in chapter 62E. With respect to a case receiving IV-D services, if an income withholding order or order for health care coverage is in effect under this section but cannot be executed because the obligor has no employer or other source of periodic income, said agency shall send the income withholding order or national medical support notice or both, together with notice of the provisions of subsection (f), to an employer or other source of periodic income who later employs or pays the obligor as soon as the new such employment or other source of periodic income is ascertained.

(d) With respect to a case receiving IV-D services or where an obligee applies for child support services from the IV-D agency, when the IV-D agency determines on its own information or on account of a claim in writing under the penalties of perjury that an arrearage has accrued, it shall immediately send the notice on income withholding increased by 25 per cent to the obligor's employer or other source of periodic income as specified in subsection (f) and shall send a notice to the obligor that he may, within 15 days from the date the notice is sent submit a request in writing for a hearing as to whether the income withholding should be further suspended. With respect to all other case, an obligee making a claim that an arrearage has accrued shall make the claim in writing under the penalties of perjury to the court that entered the order and the court may order that the withholding be increased by 25 per cent. The notice to the obligor shall also specify the amount to be withheld, and the procedure and grounds for further suspending the income withholding or appealing the amount of any arrearage alleged to be owed. Such notice to the obligor shall set forth that the income withholding order applies to the obligor's subsequent employers or other sources of periodic income and that the obligor is bound to notify said agency immediately when his employment or other source of periodic income changes or be subject to possible punishment for civil contempt of court or other enforcement remedies under this chapter. When the agency ascertains that an obligor has failed to comply with a judgment or order for health care coverage and health care coverage is available to the obligor at reasonable cost and accessible to the child, the IV-D agency shall send notice of the judgment or national medical support notice to the employer or to a provider of health care coverage together with notice of the provisions of subsection (f). The judgment or order shall operate to enroll the child as fully and completely as if the obligor had executed a document authorizing the enrollment and, upon receipt of notice of the judgment or order from the IV-D agency, the employer or provider of health care coverage shall enroll such child, notwithstanding the employee's failure to sign or submit an application for enrollment for health care coverage and without regard to any restrictions on enrollment periods. The employer or provider of health care shall not refuse to enroll the child on the grounds stated in subsection (m). The obligor or obligee may contest or seek a modification of an order for health care coverage on the grounds that the coverage: (i) is no longer available to the obligor at reasonable cost; (ii) is no longer accessible to the child; (iii) is no longer in the best interest of the child; or (iv) creates an undue hardship for the moving party; provided, however, that the moving party shall bear the burden of proving that the coverage: (i) is no longer available to the moving party at reasonable cost; (ii) is no longer accessible to the child; (iii) is no longer in the best interest of the child; or (iv) creates an undue hardship for the moving party; and provided further, that the provider of health care coverage shall maintain coverage for the child under the order pending a modification of the order.

(e)(1) If the obligor contests income withholding, he shall, in a case receiving IV-D services, request an administrative review under section 17, or, in all other cases, seek judicial review from the court that entered the order. If at the hearing the obligor establishes that no arrearage satisfying the requirements of clause (1) or (2) of subsection (c) existed at the time notice was given or at any time thereafter, or that he is not the person owing such arrearage, the court or hearing officer may order that such income withholding order be suspended until such an arrearage does accrue. A suspension shall not be ordered upon any other grounds, including the fact that an arrearage satisfying said clause (1) or (2) does not exist at the time of the hearing if such an arrearage existed at the time when the notice was mailed or any time thereafter.

If the court or hearing officer orders that income withholding be suspended, upon notice to the IV-D agency, said agency shall promptly notify the employer or other source of periodic income.

(2) The obligor may also request a hearing, under the same procedure and with the same notice as set forth in paragraph (1), if he contends that the payment of arrears at the rate of twenty-five per cent of the face amount of the child support order is excessive or that the total arrears owing is incorrect. If it is determined that payment of the arrearage at the rate of twenty-five percent of the support order creates an undue hardship upon the obligor or that the withholding would exceed the maximum amount permitted by the Consumer Credit Protection Act, 15 U.S.C. § 1673(b), the rate at which such arrearage must be paid shall be reduced to a rate that is fair and reasonable considering the circumstances of the parties and the best interests of the child. If the court or hearing officer determines at the hearing that the total amount of arrears calculated is erroneous, he shall reduce the amount calculated to correct the amount.

(f) The IV-D agency shall send notice of the income withholding order and the national medical support notice to the employer or other source of periodic income at the time required by this section. The notice of income withholding and the national medical support notice sent to the employer or other source of periodic income shall contain notice, of this subsection, and shall also state the amount to be withheld and that such amount shall be made payable to the IV-D agency on behalf of the obligee and sent to the state disbursement unit as provided in section 5 and shall not exceed the limit on the obligors income set by the Consumer Credit Protection Act, 15 U.S.C. § 1673(b).

(1) The employer or other source of periodic income may deduct from said earnings or income a sum not exceeding one dollar per pay period as reimbursement for costs incurred, and may submit to said agency one check covering all its employees or recipients of periodic income whose income is withheld along with a statement enumerating the obligation of each employee or recipient of periodic income and amount paid.

(2) The employer may not discipline, suspend or discharge an employee, or refuse to hire any individual because of an income withholding order issued pursuant to this section or because of any obligation such income withholding imposes against the employer. Any employer who violates this section shall be liable in a civil action, action for contempt or other appropriate proceeding to such employee or individual for all wages and employment benefits lost by the employee or individual from the time of the unlawful discipline, suspension, refusal to hire or discharge to the period of reinstatement, and an additional penalty of up to $1,000.

(3)(A) If an employer or other source of periodic income fails to comply with an order of income withholding executed pursuant to this section the court may, on its own motion or upon report of the IV-D agency or other administrative agency of competent jurisdiction, or upon the motion or complaint of any party to the order of income withholding, summon the employer or other source of periodic income to appear in court and show cause why he should not be held in civil contempt for failure to obey said order. Said employer or other source of periodic income shall also be liable to the obligee in a civil action, action for contempt, or other appropriate proceeding for the full amount of the income that the employer or other source of periodic income failed to withhold or remit, and shall also be liable for a civil penalty equal to that amount or in the amount of $500, whichever is greater, payable to the IV-D agency or to the moving or complaining party. A finding by the court, by an administrative agency of competent jurisdiction, or by the IV-D agency that the employer or other source of periodic income has failed or neglected to comply with an income withholding order executed pursuant to this section shall be prima facie evidence of the liability of such employer in such proceeding.

(B) With respect to a case receiving IV-D services, upon a finding by the IV-D agency that the employer or other source of periodic income has failed to withhold, or has withheld and failed to remit, any amount required to be withheld and remitted under this section, the IV-D agency may notify the employer or other source of periodic income of its obligation to withhold and remit pursuant to the income withholding order. Any subsequent failure to withhold and remit after the IV-D agency has sent said notice, or any failure to remit within 30 days an amount that has been withheld, shall result in an assessment by the IV-D agency against the employer or other source of periodic income of the amount subject to withholding and a penalty equal to that amount or in the amount of $500, whichever is greater. Such employer or other source of periodic income shall have 30 days from the date of the assessment to pay the amount due to the IV-D agency under the assessment and the penalty, or to request an administrative hearing by the IV-D agency to review the assessment.

(C) In any action pursuant to subparagraphs (A) or (B), the following defenses may be raised by the entity alleged to have failed to withhold or remit support pursuant to the income withholding order:

(i) said entity withheld and remitted the amount required by the order;

(ii) said entity was not a source of periodic income to the obligor during the period of alleged non-compliance;

(iii) no order to withhold support was in effect during the period of alleged non-compliance; or

(iv) said entity had no notice of an order to withhold support during the period of alleged non-compliance.

(D) Any amount assessed under subparagraph (A) by a court in a case receiving IV-D services, and any amount assessed by the IV-D agency under subparagraph (B), shall be collected and enforced by any means authorized under this chapter for the enforcement and collection of support. Any penalty imposed under this paragraph shall not be credited against the support liability. Any employer or other source of periodic income who contests an assessment confirmed by the IV-D agency after an administrative hearing pursuant to subparagraph (B) may, after exhaustion of administrative remedies, seek judicial review pursuant to section 17 of this chapter.

(4) This order shall have priority over all other orders of assignment income withholding, attachment, liens, executions and other legal process, from whatever source, notwithstanding any other provision of law.

(5) As provided in subsection (b), the employer or other source of periodic income shall send the amount required by the income withholding order to the IV-D agency within three business days of the date the employee or recipient of periodic income is paid, and shall furnish such identifying information as the I-VD agency may require, including name, telephone number and employer identification number of the employer or other source of income, and the names, addresses, and social security numbers of the obligor and, if known, of the obligee, and the amount of support attributable to each obligor and obligee. With respect to income

1

withholding orders issued by a court or agency of competent jurisdiction of another state and sent pursuant to section 5-501 of chapter 209D, the employer or other source of periodic income shall send the amount required by the income withholding order to the state disbursement unit in such other state and shall comply with the procedural rules governing income withholding for the state where the employee or other recipient of periodic income works or receives such income.

(6) The income withholding shall begin on the first payment of income that occurs more than three days after the employer or other source of periodic income receives notice of the income withholding and shall continue until the employee leaves that employment, the recipient of periodic income no longer receives periodic income from that source, or the employer or other source of periodic income is notified by said agency that the income withholding should be terminated.

(7) With respect to a case receiving IV-D services, if the employee leaves the employment, the employer shall be responsible to notify said IV-D agency of his departure and his subsequent employer, if known, or his subsequent source of periodic income, including pension or retirement payments, if known, prior to the time that the next payment to said agency is due and, if a recipient of periodic income no longer is to receive periodic income from a source of such income, that source shall notify the IV-D agency of the termination of his receipt of periodic income from that source and, if known, his subsequent source of periodic income, prior to the time that the next payment to said agency is due. Any subsequent employer or other source of periodic income of the obligor shall, upon notice of an income withholding order or upon receipt of a national medical support notice, or both, comply with the provisions of this section.(h) Each obligor making payments to the IV-D agency under this section shall be provided a notice describing the procedure for withholding income, including the factors triggering income withholding under subsection (c), the obligor's duty to report changes in employment, address, and other identifying information as required under section 4(c). Such notice may be provided at the time that the support order is entered.

(i) When the obligor is self-employed, income withholding shall be ordered in compliance with subsection (b) and such self-employed obligor shall be subject to the same penalties provided in this section for failure to comply with income withholding to which any other employer is subject. When income withholding cannot be obtained because the obligor has insufficient periodic income subject to attachment, the court may require that the obligor post a bond in an amount sufficient to secure the obligation of support.

(j) Obligations may also be enforced in accordance with the provisions of section six.

(k) Upon receipt of the national medical support notice or upon application of the employee pursuant to the order for health care coverage, the employer shall enroll the child in the health care plan. The national medical support notice shall have the same effect as an enrollment application signed by the employee and shall operate to enroll the child in the health care plan. The employer shall comply with the requirements of the national medical support notice as set forth in the instructions incorporated into the notice. If health care coverage is provided by the obligor, the employer or the provider of health care coverage shall furnish the obligee with such information as may be necessary for the child to obtain benefits through the plan and shall permit the obligee or, with the approval of the obligee, the provider of medical services to submit claims for covered services without the approval of the obligor. A claim submitted in accordance with this subsection shall be payable, as appropriate, directly to the obligee, to the provider of medical services or, if the individual has assigned the individual's rights to medical support pursuant to Title XIX of the federal Social Security Act, to the division of medical assistance. If the division of medical assistance has been assigned the rights of an individual covered for health benefits from the provider of health care coverage and eligible for medical assistance under said Title XIX, the provider of health care coverage shall apply to the division the same requirements applicable to an agent or assignee of any other individual so covered.

(l) If the employee is eligible for family coverage, the employer and the provider of health care coverage shall permit the employee to enroll, under the coverage, any child who is eligible for such coverage without regard to any enrollment season restrictions. If the employee is enrolled in a family health care plan but fails to make application to obtain coverage of a child, the employer and the provider of health care coverage shall enroll such child under the coverage upon application by such child's other parent, by the division of medical assistance or upon receipt of the national medical support notice from the IV-D agency. An employer or a provider of health care coverage shall not eliminate family coverage for a child enrolled pursuant to this section unless the employer or provider of health care, coverage is provided satisfactory written evidence that the health care order is no longer in effect or that the child is or will be enrolled in a comparable plan, effective no later than the effective date that such coverage is eliminated, through another provider of health care coverage or, in the case of an employer, the employer has eliminated family health care coverage for all of its employees. An employer shall withhold from an obligors compensation the obligors share, if any, of premiums for health care coverage and shall pay such share of premiums to the provider of health care coverage unless federal regulations promulgated pursuant to Title XIX of the Social Security Act permit the employer to withhold less than the obligors share of such premiums; provided, however, that the amount so withheld may not exceed the maximum amount permitted to be withheld under the Consumer Credit Protection Act, 15 U.S.C. § 1673 (b). The IV-D agency shall promptly notify the employer when there is no longer an order for medical support in effect.

(m) A provider of health care coverage shall not deny enrollment to a child under the health coverage of the child's parent on the ground that such child was born out of wedlock, that such child is not claimed as a dependent on the parent's federal income tax return or that such child does not reside with the parent or within the area served by the provider of health care coverage or that such child receives benefits or is eligible to receive benefits under any plan administered by the division of medical assistance or by the department of public health. An employer or provider of health care coverage who, upon notice of a health care order, fails without reasonable cause to enroll a child in a health care plan shall be liable in a civil action, action for contempt, or other appropriate proceeding for the full amount of the medical costs incurred and for attorneys' fees. A finding by the IV-D agency or by a court or administrative agency of competent jurisdiction that an employer or provider of health care coverage has failed without reasonable cause to enroll a child in a health care plan shall be prima facie evidence of such liability.

§ 13. Support payments or installments; judgment by operation of law; retroactive modification; application

[Amended by 2011 Mass. Acts c. 93, § 22, effective July 1, 2012.]

(a) Any payment or installment of support under any child support order issued by any court of this commonwealth or by a court or agency of competent jurisdiction of any other state shall be on or after the date it is due, a judgment by operation of law, with the full force, effect, and attributes of a judgment of this commonwealth including the ability to be enforced; shall be entitled as a judgment to full faith and credit; and a judicial or administrative action to enforce said judgment may be commenced at any time; provided that said judgment shall not be subject to retroactive modification except with respect to any period during which there is pending a complaint for modification, but only from the date that notice of such complaint has been given, either directly or through the appropriate agent, to the obligee or, where the obligee is the plaintiff, to the obligor.

(b) After a judgment pursuant to chapters two hundred and eight, two hundred and nine or two hundred and nine C, an agreement between parents that provides for the support of a minor child shall not be enforceable to bar a modification of the amount of support due on behalf of the minor child unless the court finds all of the following: 1) that the agreement survives the original judgment and has independent legal significance; 2) that the agreement was fair and reasonable and free from fraud and coercion at the time of the judgment; 3) that the provisions for support of the minor child continue to be fair and reasonable considering the child support guidelines and the circumstances of the parties and the child; and 4) that enforcement of the agreement is in the best interests of the child.

(c) In any proceeding to establish or modify an amount of child support, the child support guidelines promulgated by the chief justice of the trial court shall apply. There shall be a rebuttable presumption that the amount of the order which would result from the application of the guidelines is the appropriate amount of child support to be ordered. If, after taking into consideration the best interests of the child, the court determines that a party has overcome such presumption, the court shall make specific written findings indicating the amount of the order that would result from application of the guidelines, that the guidelines amount would be unjust or inappropriate under the circumstances; the specific facts of the case which justify departure from the guidelines and that such departure is consistent with the best interests of the child.

(d) The provisions of this section shall apply to all actions for establishment, modification or enforcement of a judgment or order for child support pursuant to or adjudicated under the provisions of chapters one hundred and nineteen, 119A, two hundred and seven, two hundred and eight, two hundred and nine, two hundred and nine A, two hundred and nine C and two hundred and nine D.

Chapter 120. Department of Youth Services and Massachusetts Training Schools

Section

§ 1. Corporate status of department of youth services; holding and investing trust funds

The department of youth services shall be a corporation for the purpose of taking, holding and investing in trust for the commonwealth, subject to section fifteen of chapter ten, any grant or devise of land or any gift or bequest made at any time for the use of any institution of which said department has the management, government and care, and it shall succeed to and retain the rights, powers and duties formerly held or acquired by the division of youth service and by the youth service board, except as otherwise provided in said section fifteen and in this chapter.

§ 2. Management, government and care of industrial schools; employment of expert personnel by director

The department of youth services shall have the management, government and care of the Lyman school for boys at Westborough, the industrial school for girls at Lancaster, the industrial school for boys at Shirley, and of all other institutions, except correctional institutions of the commonwealth, supported by the commonwealth for the custody, diagnosis, care and training of delinquent or wayward children or habitual truants or habitual absentees or habitual school offenders or juvenile offenders. The department of youth services shall have control of the land and buildings of said schools. To carry out its duties under this chapter, the commissioner shall authorize the employment within the limits of the amount appropriated therefore, such medical, dental, psychiatric, psychological, social work, legal, investigative and other expert personnel, including experts in the fields of fiscal affairs, research and planning, and personnel administration and training, superintendents, field representatives, supervisory, clerical and other employees as he shall deem necessary, and shall prescribe their duties. Physicians, dentists and psychiatrists employed hereunder shall not be subject to the provisions of chapter thirty-one or section nine A of chapter thirty.

§ 2A. Repealed

[Repealed by 1969 Mass. Acts c. 838, § 29.]

§ 3. Appointment of superintendents, chaplains and physicians

The commissioner of youth services shall from time to time appoint a superintendent, chaplains and a physician of each of said schools and institutions, and shall, in accordance with law appoint all other officers and employees required at said schools and institutions and shall prescribe their duties.

1

§ 4. Rules and regulations; by-laws

The commissioner of youth services shall establish rules, regulations, and by-laws for the government of each institution and shall see that its affairs are conducted according to law and to such rules, regulations, and by-laws; but the purpose thereof and of all education, employment, training, discipline, recreation and other activities carried on in the institutions shall be to restore and build up the self-respect and self-reliance of the children lodged therein and to qualify them for good citizenship and honorable employment.

§ 4A. Repealed

[Repealed by 1969 Mass. Acts c. 838, § 32.]

§ 5. Examination and study of children committed; re-examinations; records; discharge

(a) When a person has been committed to the department of youth services, it shall, under rules established by it, forthwith examine and study him and investigate all pertinent circumstances of his life and behavior.

(b) The department of youth services shall make periodic reexamination of all persons within its control. These examinations may be made as frequently as the department considers desirable, and shall be made with respect to every person at intervals not exceeding one year.

(c) The department of youth services shall keep written records of all examinations and of the conclusions based thereon, and of all orders concerning the disposition or treatment of every person subject to its control.

(d) Failure of the department of youth services to examine a person committed to it, or to reexamine him within one year of a previous examination, shall not of itself entitle the person to discharge from the control of the department, but shall entitle him to petition the committing court for an order of discharge, and the court shall discharge him unless the department upon due notice satisfies the court of the necessity for further control.

(e) Within eighteen months of the original commitment of a child to the department by a court of competent jurisdiction, and periodically thereafter, the committing court shall reconvene upon petition of the department, in accordance with rules established by the chief administrative judge of the trial court, to determine the future status of the child as to whether or not it is in the child's best interests to be returned to his home. All such determinations shall indicate whether, after the departmental placement of the child, reasonable efforts were made to make it possible for the child to return to his home.

§ 6. Liberty under supervision; confinement; reconfinement; revocation or modification of order; discharge

When a person has been committed to the department of youth services, it may after an objective consideration of all available information—

(a) Permit him his liberty under supervision and upon such conditions as it believes conducive to law-abiding conduct; or—

(b) Order his confinement under such conditions as it believes best designed for the protection of the public; or—

(c) Order reconfinement or renewed release as often as conditions indicate to be desirable; or—

(d) Revoke or modify any order, except an order of final discharge, as often as conditions indicate to be desirable; or—

(e) Discharge him from control with notice to the court, except as provided in section twelve, when it is satisfied that such discharge is consistent with the protection of the public.

§ 6A. Correction of socially harmful tendencies

As a means of correcting the socially harmful tendencies of a person committed to it, the department of youth services may—

(a) Require participation by him in vocational, physical, educational, and correctional training and activities.

(b) Require such modes of life and conduct as seem best adapted to fit him for return to full liberty without danger to the public.

(c) Provide such medical or psychiatric treatment as is necessary.

§ 7. Powers and duties of superintendent

The superintendent of each school or other institution, with the subordinate officers, shall have general charge of and be responsible for the welfare and custody of the children lodged therein, and for carrying out the rehabilitative program prescribed by the commissioner of youth services. He shall be a constant resident at the school, and, under the direction of the commissioner of youth services, shall seek to establish relationships and to organize ways of life that will meet the moral, physical, emotional, intellectual and social needs of the children under his care as those needs would be met in adequate homes.

§ 8. Bond and accounts of superintendents; accounting to commissioner of youth services

Each superintendent shall before entering upon his duties give bond to the commonwealth, with sureties approved by the governor and council, in such sum as the comptroller may prescribe, conditioned that he shall faithfully perform all his duties and account for all money received by him as superintendent. The bond shall be filed in the office of the state treasurer. Each superintendent shall have charge of all the property of the institution within the precincts thereof. He shall keep accounts of all his receipts and expenditures, and of all property entrusted to him, showing the income and expenses of the institution; and shall account to the commissioner of youth services, in such manner as said commissioner may require, for all money received by him. His books and all documents relative to the school shall at all times be open to the inspection of the commissioner of youth services.

§ 9. Rogers fund

The superintendent of the industrial school for girls, under the direction of the commissioner of youth services, shall purchase books with the income and profits and according to the terms of the donation of Henry B. Rogers.

§ 10. Use of public or private facilities, institutions and agencies; control; inspection; acceptance and control of delinquent children; effect of placement of person in or release from institution or control by department

(a) For the purpose of carrying out its duties and effectuating the decisions of the department of youth services with respect to the classification, placement for training and treatment, transfer, release under supervision and discharge of persons committed to the department the commissioner of youth services is authorized to make use of law enforcement, detention, supervisory, medical, educational, correctional, segregative, and other facilities, institutions and agencies, whether public or private, within the commonwealth wherever feasible, otherwise outside the commonwealth; provided however, that the department shall not transfer custody of any person who was committed to the department by a juvenile court or district court juvenile session and who is under eighteen to a penal institution. The commissioner of youth services may enter into agreements with the appropriate private or public officials for separate care and special treatment in existing institutions of persons committed to the department. In cases where a person has been adjudicated a delinquent for a violation of section one of chapter two hundred and sixty-five, the commissioner of youth services may, with the concurrence of the commissioner of correction, transfer the custody of said child to the department of correction, provided that such person has reached his eighteenth birthday.

At least twice annually, the commissioner of youth services with the assistance of the executive secretary to the advisory committee shall be responsible for convening and programming a meeting of a youth services coordinating council composed of the commissioners of public health, mental health, education, transitional assistance, corrections, and probation, and the commissioner of administration and finance or their designees. The youth services coordinating council shall meet for the purposes of providing for the coordination and mutual assistance in the carrying out and evaluation of all the programs relating to youth services in the commonwealth. Said council shall jointly prescribe and from time to time amend rules and recommendations of their various departments for the aforementioned purposes.

(b) Nothing herein shall be construed as giving the department of youth services control over existing facilities, institutions or agencies other than those listed in section two, or as requiring such facilities, institutions or agencies to service said department inconsistently with their functions, or with the authority of their officers, or with the laws and regulations governing their activities, or as giving said department power to make use of any private institution or agency without its consent, or to pay a private institution or agency for services which a public institution or agency is willing and able to perform.

(c) Public institutions and agencies are hereby required to accept and care for delinquent children or convicted persons sent to them by the department in the same manner as they would be required to do had such persons been committed thereto by a juvenile court, district court, superior court or probate court.

(d) The department is hereby given the right and shall be required periodically to inspect all public and all private institutions and agencies whose facilities it is using. Every institution and agency, whether public or private, is required to afford the department reasonable opportunity to examine or consult with persons committed to the department who are for the time being in the custody of the institution or agency.

(e) Placement of a person by the department in any institution or agency not operated by the department or the release of such person from such an institution or agency shall not terminate the control of the department over such person. No person placed in such institution or under such an agency may be released by the institution or agency without the approval of the department.

§ 10A. Repealed

[Repealed by 1949 Mass. Acts c. 593, § 2.]

§ 10B. Involuntary room confinement prohibited

[Added by 2018 Mass. Acts c. 69, § 82, effective Apr. 13, 2018.]

A person detained by and committed to the department of youth services shall not be placed in involuntary room confinement as a punishment, harassment or consequence for noncompliance or in retaliation for any conduct.

§ 11. Places for detention and diagnosis; treatment and training facilities; facilities to aid persons given conditional releases; forest or farm school camps

[Amended by 2003 Mass. Acts c. 26, § 365, effective July 1, 2003.]

When funds are available for the purpose, the commissioner of youth services may (a) establish and operate places for detention and diagnosis of all persons committed to the department; (b) establish and operate additional treatment and training facilities necessary to classify and segregate and handle delinquents, youthful offenders and juvenile offenders of different ages, habits and mental and physical condition according to their needs; (c) establish facilities to aid persons given conditional release or discharged by the department to find employment and to lead a law-abiding existence, and shall establish, on land under the control of the department of environmental management or upon other sites approved by the commissioner of conservation and recreation, forest or farm school camps to which children placed in the care of the department of youth services may be sent for such education and training as may be deemed best for their readjustment, the work projects of which may be assigned in farming or reforestation, maintenance and development of state forests and recreational areas as may be approved by the commissioner of conservation and recreation.

§ 12. Parole; placing custody in home or family; notice to police authority; supervising agents; notice to commissioner of transitional assistance; resumption of custody

[Amended by 2010 Mass. Acts c. 267, §§ 20–22, effective Nov. 5, 2010.]

The department may direct release under supervision at any time, and may place children in its custody in their usual homes or in any situation or family that has been approved by the department; provided, however, that if the child has been committed to the department of youth services for murder in the first or second degree, as defined by section one of chapter two hundred and sixty-five; or manslaughter, as defined by section thirteen of said chapter two hundred and sixty-five; or rape, as defined by section twenty-two or section twenty-two A of said chapter two hundred and sixty-five; or aggravated rape of a child under 16 with force, under section 22B of said chapter 265; or a repeat offense, under section 22C of said chapter 265; or kidnapping, as defined by section twenty-five of said chapter two hundred and sixty-five; or aggravated rape and abuse of a child, under section 23A of said chapter 265; or a repeat offense, under section 23B of said chapter 265; or indecent assault and battery on a child under the age of fourteen years, as defined by section thirteen B of said chapter two hundred and sixty-five; or aggravated indecent assault and battery on a child under the age of 14, under section 13B½ of said chapter 265; or a repeat offense, under section 13B¾ of said chapter 265; or assault on a child under the age of sixteen with intent to commit a rape, as defined by section twenty-four B of said chapter two hundred and sixty-five; or unnatural and lascivious acts with a child under the age of sixteen, as defined by section thirty-five A of chapter two hundred and seventy-two; then the department shall notify the police authority, of the city or town of which such child is a resident and as the police authority of the city or town where the offense occurred, of the intention to place such child in his usual home. Such notification shall occur at least seven days prior to the placement of any such child in his usual home. The commissioner of youth services may, subject to appropriation, employ agents for investigating places and for visiting and supervising children, and may provide for the maintenance, in whole or in part, of any child so placed in the charge of any person. Immediately on placing children in families or homes, the commissioner of youth services shall notify the commissioner of transitional assistance of the name of each child so placed and of the name and residence of the person to whose care he is entrusted. The department may at any time, until the expiration of the period of commitment, resume the care and custody of any child released under supervision. The department shall place children in families or homes of the religious belief of such children, but if this be impracticable, then due regard shall be had to the locality, and, if practicable, the home shall be such that the children shall have the opportunity to attend religious worship of their own belief.

§ 13. Escape; breach of parole; arrest; detention

The department may issue a warrant for the arrest of any person committed to it who has escaped from a facility or who has been released on parole and broken the conditions thereof. Such person may be arrested with or without such warrant by a police officer, sheriff, deputy sheriff, constable or person employed or authorized by the department and may be kept in custody in a suitable place and there detained until such person may be returned to the custody of the department.

1

§ 13A. Compensation for property damage caused by inmates; notice of damage; claim; filing

Upon written request of the department, there shall be paid out of the state treasury, from such funds as may be available therefor, to any person determined by the attorney general to be entitled to compensation for damage to his property caused by the act of any inmate of the Lyman school for boys at Westborough, the industrial school for girls at Lancaster, the industrial school for boys at Shirley, the department of youth services reception center at Westborough or any other institution of which the department has management, government and care under the provisions of section two while escaping therefrom, such sum as the attorney general shall determine to be just and reasonable and as the governor and council shall approve; provided, that written notice of said damage and claim for compensation therefor be filed with the department within one year next after the date on which such damage occurred.

§ 14. Applications for new commitments for mentally ill, developmentally disabled or sexually dangerous persons

Whenever the department finds that any person committed to it is mentally ill, within the meaning of chapter one hundred and twenty-three, developmentally disabled or a sexually dangerous person, within the meaning of chapter one hundred and twenty-three A, or a potential psychotic as defined and determined by the assistant commissioner of the bureau of clinical services, the department may make application to the proper court for a new commitment to the appropriate agency in accordance with law.

§ 15. Transfers from Massachusetts reformatory and reformatory for women

[Amended by 2013 Mass. Acts c. 84, § 28, effective Sept. 18, 2013.]

With the consent of the department, the commissioner of correction may transfer to the care of the department any boy under 18 sentenced to the Massachusetts reformatory, or any girl under 18 sentenced to the reformatory for women, for such disposition as in the opinion of the department, after study, will best serve the needs of the boy or girl and best protect the interests of the public.

§ 16. Discharge

[Amended by 2016 Mass. Acts c. 70, § 6, effective Apr. 1, 2016.]

Every person committed to the department until the age of 18 as a delinquent child, if not already discharged, shall be discharged upon reaching the person's eighteenth birthday. Every person committed to the department until the age of 19 as a delinquent child, if not already discharged, shall be discharged upon reaching the person's nineteenth birthday. Every person committed to the department until the age of 20 as a delinquent child, if not already discharged, shall be discharged upon reaching the person's twentieth birthday. Every person committed to the department until the age of 21 as a youthful offender, if not already discharged, shall be discharged upon reaching the person's twenty-first birthday. The department may continue to have responsibility for any person provided for in this chapter under 22 years of age for the purposes of specific educational or rehabilitative programs, under conditions agreed upon by both the department and such persons and terminable by either. Such services must be offered prior to the person's discharge date as provided herein; however, a person may request and the department shall consider any such request for the services described, for up to 90 days after the person's effective date of discharge, even where the person has previously declined services or services were terminated for non-compliance, and may reach an agreement with the person, terminable by either, to provide the services described herein until such person attains the age of 22.

§ 17. Procedure when discharge deemed dangerous; control beyond age limit; order; application; statement of facts; review of order

Whenever the department is of the opinion that discharge of a person from its control at the age limit stated in section sixteen would be physically dangerous to the public, the department shall make an order directing that the person remain subject to its control beyond the period and shall make application to the committing court for a review of that order by the court. The order and application may be made at any time prior to the date of discharge stated in said section sixteen. The application shall be accompanied by a written statement of the facts upon which the department bases its opinion that discharge from its control at the time stated would be physically dangerous to the public, but no such application shall be dismissed nor shall the order be discharged, merely because of its form or an asserted insufficiency of its allegations; every order shall be reviewed upon its merits.

NOTE The Supreme Judicial Court declared that the standard for an extension order under this section does not comport with substantive due process requirements of the Fourteenth Amendment and is unconstitutionally vague. *See Kenniston v. Dep't of Youth Servs.*, 453 Mass. 179 (2009).

§ 18. Notice of application for review of order; hearing; appointment of counsel; court order

If the department applies to the court for review of an order as provided in section seventeen, the court shall notify the person whose liberty is involved, and if he or she be not sui juris, his parent or guardian (if such person can be reached and if not the court shall appoint a person to act in the place of the parent or guardian), of the application, and shall afford him an opportunity to appear in court with the aid of counsel and of process to compel attendance of witnesses and production of evidence. When he is unable to provide his own counsel, the court shall appoint counsel to represent him. Said proceedings shall be conducted according to the provisions of sections fifty-five A, fifty-five B and fifty-six of chapter one hundred and nineteen.

If after a full hearing the court is of the opinion that discharge of the person to whom the court order applies would be physically dangerous to the public, the court shall confirm the order of the department. If the court is of opinion that discharge of the person from continued control of the department would not be physically dangerous to the public, the court shall disapprove the order of the department and shall order the person to be discharged from its control.

NOTE The Supreme Judicial Court declared that the standard for an extension order under this section does not comport with substantive due process requirements of the Fourteenth Amendment and is unconstitutionally vague. *See Kenniston v. Dep't of Youth Servs.*, 453 Mass. 179 (2009).

§ 19. Control continued upon court confirmation of department order; power to transfer custody of persons eighteen or older

When an order of the department is confirmed as provided in section eighteen, the control of the department over the person shall continue, subject to the provisions of this chapter; provided, however, unless the person is previously discharged in accordance with section six (e), the department shall discharge the person upon his twenty-first birthday. The department shall have the power, in order to protect children and adolescents, to transfer the custody of any person eighteen years of age or older to the department of correction for placement in an appropriate institution.

NOTE The Supreme Judicial Court declared that the standard for an extension order under this section does not comport with substantive due process requirements of the Fourteenth Amendment and is unconstitutionally vague. *See Kenniston v. Dep't of Youth Servs.*, 453 Mass. 179 (2009).

§ 20. Repealed

[Repealed by 1996 Mass. Acts c. 200, § 22.]

§ 21. Effect of commitment on application for public service; discharge; restoration of civil rights; records; inspection; consent; evidence in other proceedings

[Amended by 2013 Mass. Acts c. 84, § 29, effective Sept. 18, 2013.]

Commitment to the care of the department of a delinquent child or youthful offender shall not operate to disqualify said child in any future examination, appointment or application for public service under the government either of the commonwealth or of any political subdivision thereof

Whenever a person committed to the department by a court upon conviction of a crime is discharged from its control such discharge shall, when so ordered by the department, restore such person to all civil rights and shall have the effect of setting aside the conviction. The conviction of such a person shall not operate to disqualify him for any future examination, appointment or application for public service under the government either of the commonwealth or of any political subdivision thereof.

The records of commitment to the department shall be withheld from public inspection except with the consent of the department, but such records concerning any child who at the time of commitment was between seven and 18 years of age shall be open, at all reasonable times, to the inspection of the child, his or her parent or parents, guardian or attorney, or any of them. A commitment to the department shall not be received in evidence or used in any way in any proceeding in any court except in subsequent proceedings for waywardness or delinquency against the same child, and except in imposing sentence in any criminal proceeding against the same person.

§ 22. Inquiry into effectiveness of methods; information; annual report; contents

The department shall conduct continuing inquiry into the effectiveness of the treatment methods it employs in seeking the reformation of juvenile and youthful offenders. To this end the department shall obtain from the commissioner of probation all court record information on its wards compiled subsequent to their discharge from the jurisdiction of the department, and with the cooperation of the commissioner of probation tabulate and analyze these data so that they may be used to evaluate the relative merits of methods of treatment. The results of such studies shall be made available to the public in each annual report of the department. The department shall make an annual report to the governor and to the general court containing, in addition to other matters required by law, a statement of the number of persons committed to the department during the preceding fiscal year and of the disposition made of such persons and of all other persons under its supervision during said year. The report shall include such inventories as the institutions under the department's supervision are required by law to make, a statement of the condition and needs of the facilities under its supervision, and of the progress made towards an integrated rehabilitory system capable of giving the most effective individual treatment for rehabilitation. The report shall include such recommendations for legislation as the department may wish to make.

§ 23. Power of department to act as guardian of children

[Amended by 2000 Mass. Acts c. 236, § 17.]

The department may act as guardian for a child under 18 years of age in its charge who has neither parent living, or of whom neither parent can be located, and for whom no guardian has been appointed. In such instances, the department may act with all the power and authority conferred by chapter 201, except that once a guardian is appointed, the powers herein conferred shall cease. The department may, without need for parent or guardian approval, serve as the fully authorized representative of a child in its charge not living with his parents or guardian for the purpose of completing and submitting an application on the child's behalf to the division of medical assistance for benefits or assistance under chapter 118E or to the department of transitional assistance for benefits or assistance which said department is authorized to provide under chapter 18.

§ 23A. Disposition of unclaimed money held for former ward; records

Annually on or before November thirtieth, the department shall pay to the state treasurer all unclaimed money held by it for the benefit of any former ward of the department whose whereabouts are then unknown to it and have been unknown for seven years subsequent to his becoming of age. At the time of so paying over any such money, the department shall certify to the comptroller the amount of such money then held for the benefit of each former ward, his full name, age, if known, and last known address, the names of his parents, if known, and such further information as it deems relevant; and said comptroller shall make and keep a record thereof.

§ 24. Expenditure of gifts

The department may expend any money given for the purpose in erecting houses or other buildings on the land of the commonwealth at Lancaster, for increasing the accommodation and facilities of the industrial school, if the plans therefor are first approved by the bureau of building construction.

§ 25. Children committed by United States courts

The provisions of this chapter relative to commitment to the care of the department shall extend to boys and girls committed by authority of the courts or magistrates of the United States.

§ 26. Escape or attempt to escape; aiding or assisting child in escape

Whoever escapes, or attempts to escape from the department or aids or assists a child in the custody of the department to escape or attempt to escape shall be punished by a fine of not more than five hundred dollars or by imprisonment for not more than two years.

NOTE "The fact that [DYS] has a wide range of facilities available for placements does not render Section 26 vague. The defendant was committed to [DYS], not to a facility. The essence of that commitment was the creation of a custodial relationship between the defendant and [DYS]. The meaning of the word 'escape' as appearing in Section 26 is its ordinary meaning, i.e., absenting oneself from custody without permission. . . . The proscribed conduct simply is escape from [DYS], not from any particular facility of [DYS]." *Commonwealth v. Carrion*, 431 Mass. 44, 46 (2000) (citations and quotations marks omitted).

Chapter 123. Mental Health

§ 1. Definitions

The following words as used in this section and sections two to thirty-seven, inclusive, shall, unless the context otherwise requires, have the following meanings:

"Commissioner", the commissioner of mental health.

"Department", the department of mental health.

"Dependent funds", those funds which a resident is unable to manage or spend himself as determined by the periodic review.

"District court", the district court within the jurisdiction of which a facility is located.

"Facility", a public or private facility for the care and treatment of mentally ill persons, except for the Bridgewater State Hospital.

"Fiduciary", any guardian, conservator, trustee, representative payee as appointed by a federal agency, or other person who receives or maintains funds on behalf of another.

"Funds", all cash, checks, negotiable instruments or other income or liquid personal property, and governmental and private pensions and payments, including payments pursuant to a Social Security Administration program.

"Independent funds", those funds which a resident is able to manage or spend himself as determined by the periodic review.

"Licensed mental health professional", any person who holds himself out to the general public as one providing mental health services and who is required pursuant to such practice to obtain a license from the commonwealth.

"Likelihood of serious harm", (1) a substantial risk of physical harm to the person himself as manifested by evidence of, threats of, or attempts at, suicide or serious bodily harm; (2) a substantial risk of physical harm to other persons as manifested by evidence of homicidal or other violent behavior or evidence that others are placed in reasonable fear of violent behavior and serious physical harm to them; or (3) a very substantial risk of physical impairment or injury to the person himself as manifested by evidence that such person's judgment is so affected that he is unable to protect himself in the community and that reasonable provision for his protection is not available in the community.

"Patient", any person with whom a licensed mental health professional has established a mental health professional-patient relationship.

"Psychiatric nurse", a nurse licensed pursuant to section seventy-four of chapter one hundred and twelve who specializes in mental health or psychiatric nursing.

"Psychiatrist", a physician licensed pursuant to section two of chapter one hundred and twelve who specializes in the practice of psychiatry.

"Psychologist", an individual licensed pursuant to section one hundred and eighteen to one hundred and twenty-nine, inclusive, of chapter one hundred and twelve.

"Qualified physician", a physician who is licensed pursuant to section two of chapter one hundred and twelve who is designated by and who meets qualifications required by the regulations of the department; provided that different qualifications may be established for different purposes of this chapter. A qualified physician need not be an employee of the department or of any facility of the department.

"Qualified psychiatric nurse mental health clinical specialist", a psychiatric nurse mental health clinical specialist authorized to practice as such under regulations promulgated pursuant to the provisions of section eighty B of chapter one hundred and twelve who is designated by and meets qualifications required by the regulations of the department, provided that different qualifications may be established for different purposes of this chapter. A qualified psychiatric nurse mental health clinical specialist need not be an employee of the department or of any facility of the department.

"Qualified psychologist", a psychologist who is licensed pursuant to sections one hundred and eighteen to one hundred and twenty-nine, inclusive, of chapter one hundred and twelve who is designated by and who meets qualifications required by the regulations of the department, provided that different qualifications may be established for different purposes of this chapter. A qualified psychologist need not be an employee of the department or of any facility of the department.

"Reasonable precautions", any licensed mental health professional shall be deemed to have taken reasonable precautions, as that term is used in section thirty-six B, if such professional makes reasonable efforts to take one or more of the following actions as would be taken by a reasonably prudent member of his profession under the same or similar circumstances:—

(a) communicates a threat of death or serious bodily injury to the reasonably identified victim or victims;

(b) notifies an appropriate law enforcement agency in the vicinity where the patient or any potential victim resides;

(c) arranges for the patient to be hospitalized voluntarily;

(d) takes appropriate steps, within the legal scope of practice of his profession, to initiate proceedings for involuntary hospitalization.

"Restraint", bodily physical force, mechanical devices, chemicals, confinement in a place of seclusion other than the placement of an inpatient or resident in his room for the night, or any other means which unreasonably limit freedom of movement.

"Social worker", an individual licensed pursuant to sections one hundred and thirty to one hundred and thirty-two, inclusive, of chapter one hundred and twelve.

"Superintendent", the superintendent or other head of a public or private facility.

§ 5. Commitment or retention hearings; right to counsel; medical examination; notice

Whenever the provisions of this chapter require that a hearing be conducted in any court for the commitment or further retention of a person to a facility or to the Bridgewater state hospital or for medical treatment including treatment with antipsychotic medication, it shall be held as hereinafter provided. Such person shall have the right to be represented by counsel and shall have the right to present independent testimony. The court shall appoint counsel for such person whom it finds to be indigent and who is not represented by counsel, unless such person refuses the appointment of counsel. The court may provide an independent medical examination for such indigent person upon request of his counsel or upon his request if he is not represented by counsel. The person shall be allowed not less than two days after the appearance of his counsel in which to prepare his case and a hearing shall be conducted forthwith after such period unless counsel requests a delay. Notice of the time and place of hearing shall be furnished by the court to the department, the person, his counsel, and his nearest relative or guardian. The court may hold the hearing at the facility or said hospital.

§ 6. Retention of persons; validity of orders; hearing

(a) No person shall be retained at a facility or at the Bridgewater state hospital except under the provisions of paragraph (a) of section ten, the provisions of paragraphs (a), (b), and (c) of section twelve, section thirteen, paragraph (e) of section sixteen and section thirty-five or except under a court order or except during the pendency of a petition for commitment or to the pendency of a request under section fourteen. A court order of commitment to a facility or to the Bridgewater state hospital shall be valid for the period stipulated in this chapter or, if no such period is so stipulated, for one year. A petition for the commitment of a person may not be issued except as authorized under the provisions of this chapter.

(b) Following the filing of a petition for a commitment to a facility or to the Bridgewater state hospital, a hearing shall be held unless waived in writing by the person after consultation with his counsel. In the event the hearing is waived, the person may request a hearing for good cause shown at any time during the period of commitment.

§ 7. Commitment and retention of dangerous persons; petition; notice; hearing

[Amended by 2002 Mass. Acts c. 127, effective Aug. 28, 2002; 2004 Mass. Acts c. 410, § 1, effective Mar. 1, 2005.]

(a) The superintendent of a facility may petition the district court or the division of the juvenile court department in whose jurisdiction the facility is located for the commitment to said facility and retention of any patient at said facility whom said superintendent determines that the failure to hospitalize would create a likelihood of serious harm by reason of mental illness.

(b) The medical director of the Bridgewater state hospital, the commissioner of mental health, or with the approval of the commissioner of mental health, the superintendent of a facility, may petition the district court or the division of the juvenile court department in whose jurisdiction the facility or hospital is located for the commitment to the Bridgewater state hospital of any male patient at said facility or hospital when it is determined that the failure to hospitalize in strict security would create a likelihood of serious harm by reason of mental illness.

(c) Whenever a court receives a petition filed under any provisions of this chapter for an order of commitment of a person to a facility or to the Bridgewater state hospital, such court shall notify the person, and his nearest relative or guardian, of the receipt of such petition and of the date a hearing on such petition is to be held. The hearing on a petition brought for commitment pursuant to paragraph (e) of section 15, and sections 16 and 18, or for a subsequent commitment pursuant to paragraph (d) of section 8 shall be commenced within 14 days of the filing of the petition, unless a delay is requested by the person or his counsel. For all other persons, the hearing shall be commenced within 5 days of the filing of the petition, unless a delay is requested by the person or his counsel. The periods of time prescribed or allowed under the provisions of this section shall be computed pursuant to Rule 6 of the Massachusetts Rules of Civil Procedure.

§ 8. Proceedings to commit dangerous persons; notice; hearing; orders; jurisdiction

(a) After a hearing, unless such hearing is waived in writing, the district court or the division of the juvenile court department shall not order the commitment of a person at a facility or shall not renew such order unless it finds after a hearing that (1) such person is mentally ill, and (2) the discharge of such person from a facility would create a likelihood of serious harm.

(b) After hearing, unless such hearing is waived in writing, the district court or the division of the juvenile court department shall not order the commitment of a person at the Bridgewater state hospital or shall not renew such order unless it finds that (1) such person is mentally ill; (2) such person is not a proper subject for commitment to any facility of the department; and (3) the failure to retain such person in strict custody would create a likelihood of serious harm. If the court is unable to make the findings required by this paragraph, but makes the findings required by paragraph (a), the court shall order the commitment of the person to a facility designated by the department.

(c) The court shall render its decision on the petition within ten days of the completion of the hearing, provided, that for reasons stated in writing by the court, the administrative justice for the district court department may extend said ten day period.

(d) The first order of commitment of a person under this section shall be valid for a period of six months and all subsequent commitments shall be valid for a period of one year; provided that if such commitments occur at the expiration of a commitment under any other section of this chapter, other than a commitment for observation, the first order of commitment shall be valid for a period of one year; and provided further, that the first order of commitment to the Bridgewater state hospital of a person under commitment to a facility shall be valid for a period of six months. If no hearing is held before the expiration of the six months commitment, the court may not recommit the person without a hearing.

(e) In the event that the hearing is waived and on the basis of a petition filed under the authority of this chapter showing that a person is mentally ill and that the discharge of the person from a facility would create a likelihood of serious harm, the district court or the division of the juvenile court department which has jurisdiction over the commitment of the person may order the commitment of the person to such facility.

(f) In the event that the hearing is waived and on the basis of a petition filed under the authority of this chapter showing that a person is mentally ill, that the person is not a proper subject for commitment to any facility of the department and that the failure to retain said person in strict security would create a likelihood of serious harm, the district court or the division of the juvenile court department which has jurisdiction over a facility, or the Brockton district court if a person is retained in the Bridgewater state hospital, may order the commitment of the person to said hospital.

§ 8B. Treatment of committed persons with antipsychotic medication; petition; notice; hearing; guardian

(a) With respect to any patient who is the subject of a petition for a commitment or an order of a commitment for care and treatment under the provisions of sections seven, eight, fifteen, sixteen or eighteen, the superintendent of a facility or medical director of the Bridgewater state hospital may further petition the district court or the division of the juvenile court department in whose jurisdiction the facility is located (i) to adjudicate the patient incapable of making informed decisions about proposed medical treatment, (ii) to authorize, by an adjudication of substituted judgment, treatment with antipsychotic medications, and (iii) to authorize according to the applicable legal standards such other medical treatment as may be necessary for the treatment of mental illness.

(b) A petition filed under this section shall be separate from any pending petition for commitment and shall not be heard or otherwise considered by the court unless the court has first issued an order of commitment on the pending petition for commitment.

(c) Whenever a court receives a petition filed under the provisions of this section, such court shall notify the person, and his nearest relative or guardian of the receipt of such petition and of the date a hearing on such petition is to be held. The hearing shall be commenced within fourteen days of the filing of the petition unless a delay is requested by the person or his counsel, provided that the commencement of such hearing shall not be delayed beyond the date of the hearing on the commitment petition if the petition was filed concurrently with a petition for commitment.

(d) After a hearing on the petition regarding antipsychotic medication treatment the court shall not authorize medical treatment unless it (i) specifically finds that the person is incapable of making informed decisions concerning the proposed medical treatment, (ii) upon application of the legal substituted judgment standard, specifically finds that the patient would accept such treatment if competent, and (iii) specifically approves and authorizes a written substituted judgment treatment plan. The court may base its findings exclusively upon affidavits and other documentary evidence if it (i) determines, after careful inquiry and upon representations of counsel, that there are not contested issues of fact and (ii) includes in its findings the reasons that oral testimony was not required.

(e) The court may delegate to a guardian who has been duly appointed by a court of competent jurisdiction the authority to monitor the antipsychotic medication treatment process to ensure that an antipsychotic medication treatment plan is followed, provided such a guardian is readily available for such purpose. Approval of a treatment plan shall not be withheld, however, because such a guardian is not available to perform such monitoring. In such circumstances, the court shall monitor the treatment process to ensure that the treatment plan is followed.

(f) Any authorization for treatment that is ordered pursuant to the provisions of this section shall expire at the same time as the expiration of the order of commitment that was in effect when the authorization for treatment was ordered; provided that subsequent authorizations may be ordered and any party may at any time petition the court for modification of a medical treatment authorization that has been ordered pursuant to the standards and procedures established in this section.

(g) An adjudication of competency or incompetency with respect to treatment for mental illness by a court pursuant to this section shall be binding upon the juvenile court department in any subsequent guardianship proceedings only with respect to matters which were the subject of the district court or juvenile court department adjudication.

(h) Any privilege established by section one hundred and thirty-five of chapter one hundred and twelve or by section twenty B of chapter two hundred and thirty-three, relating to confidential communications, shall not prohibit the filing of reports or affidavits, or the giving of testimony, pursuant to this section, for the purpose of obtaining treatment of a patient, provided that such patient has been informed prior to making such communications that they may be used for such purpose and has waived the privilege.

§ 9. Review of matters of law; application for discharge; notice; hearing

(a) Matters of law arising in commitment hearings, antipsychotic medication hearings or incompetency for trial proceedings in a district court may be reviewed by the appellate division of the district courts in the same manner as the civil cases generally.

(b) Any person may make written application to a justice of superior court at any time and in any county, stating that he believes or has reason to believe that a person named in such application is retained in a facility or the Bridgewater state hospital, who should no longer be so retained, or that a person named in such application is the subject of a medical treatment order issued by a district court or a division of the juvenile court department and should not be so treated, giving the names of all persons interested in his confinement or medical treatment and requesting his discharge or other relief. The justice within seven days thereof shall order notice of the time and place for hearing to be given to the superintendent or medical director and to such other persons as he considers proper; and such hearing shall be given promptly before a justice of the superior court in any county. The justice shall appoint an attorney to represent any applicant whom he finds to be indigent. The alleged mentally ill person may be brought before the justice at the hearing upon a writ of habeas corpus, upon a request approved by the justice. Pending the decision of the court such person may be retained in the custody of the superintendent or medical director. If the justice decides that the person is not mentally ill or that failure to retain the person in a facility or the Bridgewater state hospital would not create a likelihood of serious harm; has not engaged in repeated and recent incidents of serious self-destructive behavior or assaultive behavior as an inpatient at a facility or an inmate of a place of detention; can be properly treated in any other facility licensed, operated or regulated by the department, said person shall be discharged. If the justice decides that a patient at the Bridgewater state hospital does not require strict security, he shall be transferred to a facility. If the justice decides that a person who is the subject of a medical treatment order issued by a district court or a division of the juvenile court department pursuant to section eight B should not be treated, the justice shall issue an appropriate order modifying or vacating such order and, where such previous order is modified, the court shall monitor said modified order by means of a guardian or otherwise as provided in paragraph (e) of section eight B.

§ 10. Voluntary admissions; consultation with attorney; discharge; outpatients; veterans

(a) Pursuant to departmental regulations on admission procedures, the superintendent may receive and retain on a voluntary basis any person providing the person is in need of care and treatment and providing the admitting facility is suitable for such care and treatment. The application may be made (1) by a person who has attained the age of sixteen, (2) by a parent or guardian of a person on behalf of a person under the age of eighteen years, and (3) by the guardian of a person on behalf of a person under his guardianship. Prior to accepting an application for a voluntary admission, the superintendent shall afford the person making the application the opportunity for consultation with an attorney, or with a person who is working under the supervision of an attorney, concerning the legal effect of a voluntary admission. The superintendent may discharge any person admitted under the provisions of this paragraph at any time he deems such discharge in the best interest of such person, provided, however, that if a parent or guardian made the application for admission, fourteen days' notice shall be given to such parent or guardian prior to such discharge.

(b) Pursuant to departmental regulations, the superintendent of a facility may treat persons as outpatients providing application for outpatient treatment is made in accordance with the application provisions of paragraph (a). The superintendent may, in the best interest of the person, discontinue the outpatient treatment of a person at any time.

(c) The chief officer of any facility of the Veterans Administration within the commonwealth may admit eligible veterans under the provisions of this chapter and thereupon shall be vested with the same powers as the department has under this chapter with respect to retention or discharge.

§ 11. Voluntary admissions; withdrawal; notice; examination; retention

[Amended by 2000 Mass. Acts c. 249, § 3.]

Any person retained in a facility under the provisions of paragraph (a) of section ten shall be free to leave such facility at any time, and any parent or guardian who requested the admission of such person may withdraw such person at any time, upon giving written notice to the superintendent. The superintendent may restrict the right to leave or withdraw to normal working hours and weekdays and, in his discretion, may require persons or the parents or guardians of persons to give three days written notice of their intention to leave or withdraw. Where persons or their parents or guardians are required to give three days notice of intention to leave or withdraw, an examination of such persons may be conducted to determine their clinical progress, their suitability for discharge and to investigate other aspects of their case including their legal competency and their family, home or community situation in the interest of discharging them from the facility. Such persons may be retained at the facility beyond the expiration of the three day notice period if, prior to the expiration of the said three day notice period, the superintendent files with the district court a petition for the commitment of such person at the said facility. Before accepting an application for voluntary admission where the superintendent may require three days written notice of intention to leave or withdraw, the admitting or treating physician shall assess the person's capacity to understand that: (i) the person is agreeing to stay or remain at the hospital; (ii) the person is agreeing to accept treatment; (iii) the person is required to provide the facility with three days written advance notice of the person's intention to leave the facility; and (iv) the facility may petition a court for an extended commitment of the person and that he may be held at the facility until the petition is heard by the court. If the physician determines that the person lacks the capacity to understand these facts and consequences of hospitalization, the application shall not be accepted.

§ 12. Emergency restraint and hospitalization of persons posing risk of serious harm by reason of mental illness

[Amended by 2004 Mass. Acts c. 410, § 2, effective Mar. 1, 2005; 2010 Mass. Acts c. 278, § 1, effective Nov. 7, 2010.]

(a) Any physician who is licensed pursuant to section 2 of chapter 112 or qualified psychiatric nurse mental health clinical specialist authorized to practice as such under regulations promulgated pursuant to the provisions of section 80B of said chapter 112 or a qualified psychologist licensed pursuant to sections 118 to 129, inclusive, of said chapter 112, or a licensed independent clinical social worker licensed pursuant to sections 130 to 137, inclusive, of chapter 112 who, after examining a person, has reason to believe that failure to hospitalize such person would create a likelihood of serious harm by reason of mental illness may restrain or authorize the restraint of such person and apply for the hospitalization of such person for a 3-day period at a public facility or at a private facility authorized for such purposes by the department. If an examination is not possible because of the emergency nature of the case and because of the refusal of the person to consent to such examination, the physician, qualified psychologist, qualified psychiatric nurse mental health clinical specialist or licensed independent clinical social worker on the basis of the facts and circumstances may determine that hospitalization is necessary and may apply therefore. In an emergency situation, if a physician, qualified psychologist, qualified psychiatric nurse mental health clinical specialist or licensed independent clinical social worker is not available, a police officer, who believes that failure to hospitalize a person would create a likelihood of serious harm by reason of mental illness may restrain such person and apply for the hospitalization of such person for a 3-day period at a public facility or a private facility authorized for such purpose by the department. An application for hospitalization shall state the reasons for the restraint of such person and any other relevant information which may assist the admitting physician or physicians. Whenever practicable, prior to transporting such person, the applicant shall telephone or otherwise communicate with a facility to describe the circumstances and known clinical history and to determine whether the facility is the proper facility to receive such person and also to give notice of any restraint to be used and to determine whether such restraint is necessary.

(b) Only if the application for hospitalization under the provisions of this section is made by a physician specifically designated to have the authority to admit to a facility in accordance with the regulations of the department, shall such person be admitted to the facility immediately after his reception. If the application is made by someone other than a designated physician, such person shall be given a psychiatric examination by a designated physician immediately after his reception at such facility. If the physician determines that failure to hospitalize such person would create a likelihood of serious harm by reason of mental illness he may admit such person to the facility for care and treatment.

Upon admission of a person under the provisions of this subsection, the facility shall inform the person that it shall, upon such person's request, notify the committee for public counsel services of the name and location of the person admitted. Said committee for public counsel services shall forthwith appoint an attorney who shall meet with the person. If the appointed attorney determines that the person voluntarily and knowingly waives the right to be represented, or is presently represented or will be represented by another attorney, the appointed attorney shall so notify said committee for public counsel services, which shall withdraw the appointment.

Any person admitted under the provisions of this subsection, who has reason to believe that such admission is the result of an abuse or misuse of the provisions of this subsection, may request, or request through counsel an emergency hearing in the district court in whose jurisdiction the facility is located, and unless a delay is requested by the person or through counsel, the district court shall hold such hearing on the day the request is filed with the court or not later than the next business day.

(c) No person shall be admitted to a facility under the provisions of this section unless he, or his parent or legal guardian in his behalf, is given an opportunity to apply for voluntary admission under the provisions of paragraph (a) of section ten and unless he, or such parent or legal guardian has been informed (1) that he has a right to such voluntary admission, and (2) that the period of hospitalization under the provisions of this section cannot exceed three days. At any time during such period of hospitalization, the superintendent may discharge such person if he determines that such person is not in need of care and treatment.

(d) A person shall be discharged at the end of the three-day period unless the superintendent applies for a commitment under the provisions of sections seven and eight of this chapter or the person remains on a voluntary status.

(e) Any person may make application to a district court justice or a justice of the juvenile court department for a three day commitment to a facility of a mentally ill person whom the failure to confine would cause a likelihood of serious harm. The court shall appoint counsel to represent said person. After hearing such evidence as he may consider sufficient, a district court justice or a justice of the juvenile court department may issue a warrant for the apprehension and appearance before him of the alleged mentally ill person, if in his judgment the condition or conduct of such person makes such action necessary or proper. Following apprehension, the court shall have the person examined by a physician designated to have the authority to admit to a facility or examined by a qualified psychologist in accordance with the regulations of the department. If said physician or qualified psychologist reports that the failure to hospitalize the person would create a likelihood of serious harm by reason of mental illness, the court may order the person committed to a facility for a period not to exceed three days, but the superintendent may discharge him at any time within the three day period. The periods of time prescribed or allowed under the provisions of this section shall be computed pursuant to Rule 6 of the Massachusetts Rules of Civil Procedure.

§ 15. Competence to stand trial or criminal responsibility; examination; period of observation; reports; hearing; commitment; delinquents

[Amended by 2000 Mass. Acts c. 357.]

(a) Whenever a court of competent jurisdiction doubts whether a defendant in a criminal case is competent to stand trial or is criminally responsible by reason of mental illness or mental defect, it may at any stage of the proceedings after the return of an indictment or the issuance of a criminal complaint against the defendant, order an examination of such defendant to be conducted by one or more qualified physicians or one or more qualified psychologists. Whenever practicable, examinations shall be conducted at the court house or place of detention where the person is being held. When an examination is ordered, the court shall instruct the examining physician or psychologist in the law for determining mental competence to stand trial and criminal responsibility.

(b) After the examination described in paragraph (a), the court may order that the person be hospitalized at a facility or, if such person is a male and appears to require strict security, at the Bridgewater state hospital, for a period not to exceed twenty days for observation and further examination, if the court has reason to believe that such observation and further examination are necessary in order to determine whether mental illness or mental defect have so affected a person that he is not competent to stand trial or not criminally responsible for the crime or crimes with which he has been charged. Copies of the complaints or indictments and the physician's or psychologist's report under paragraph (a) shall be delivered to the facility or said hospital with the person. If, before the expiration of such twenty day period, an examining qualified physician or an examining qualified psychologist believes that observation for more than twenty days is necessary, he shall so notify the court and shall request in writing an extension of the twenty day period, specifying the reason or reasons for which such further observation is necessary. Upon the receipt of such request, the court may extend said observation period, but in no event shall the period exceed forty days from the date of the initial court order of hospitalization; provided, however, if the person requests continued care and treatment during the pendency of the criminal proceedings against him and the superintendent or medical director agrees to provide such care and treatment, the court may order the further hospitalization of such person at the facility or the Bridgewater state hospital.

(c) At the conclusion of the examination or the observation period, the examining physician or psychologist shall forthwith give to the court written signed reports of their findings, including the clinical findings bearing on the issue of competence to stand trial or criminal responsibility. Such reports shall also contain an opinion, supported by clinical findings, as to whether the defendant is in need of treatment and care offered by the department.

(d) If on the basis of such reports the court is satisfied that the defendant is competent to stand trial, the case shall continue according to the usual course of criminal proceedings; otherwise the court shall hold a hearing on whether the defendant is competent to stand trial; provided that at any time before trial any party to the case may request a hearing on whether the defendant is competent to stand trial. A finding of incompetency shall require a preponderance of the evidence. If the defendant is found incompetent to stand trial, trial of the case shall be stayed until such time as the defendant becomes competent to stand trial, unless the case is dismissed.

(e) After a finding of guilty on a criminal charge, and prior to sentencing, the court may order a psychiatric or other clinical examination and, after such examination, it may also order a period of observation in a facility, or at the Bridgewater state hospital if the court determines that strict security is required and if such person is male. The purpose of such observation or examination shall be to aid the court in sentencing. Such period of observation or examination shall not exceed forty days. During such period of observation, the superintendent or medical director may petition the court for commitment of such person. The court, after imposing sentence on said person, may hear the petition as provided in section eighteen, and if the court makes necessary findings as set forth in section eight, it may in its discretion commit the person to a facility or the Bridgewater state hospital. Such order of commitment shall be valid for a period of six months. All subsequent proceedings for commitment shall take place under the provisions of said section eighteen in the district court which has jurisdiction of the facility or hospital. A person committed to a facility or Bridgewater state hospital pursuant to this section shall have said time credited against the sentence imposed as provided in paragraph (c) of said section eighteen.

(f) In like manner to the proceedings under paragraphs (a), (b), (c), and (e) of this section, a court may order a psychiatric or psychological examination or a period of observation for an alleged delinquent in a facility to aid the court in its disposition. Such period shall not exceed forty days.

§ 16. Hospitalization of persons incompetent to stand trial or not guilty by reason of mental illness; examination period; commitment; hearing; restrictions; dismissal of criminal charges

[Amended by 2014 Mass. Acts c. 46, § 108, effective July 17, 2015; 2015 Mass. Acts c. 112, effective Oct. 30, 2015.]

(a) The court having jurisdiction over the criminal proceedings may order that a person who has been found incompetent to stand trial or not guilty by reason of mental illness or mental defect in such proceedings be hospitalized at a facility for a period of forty days for observation and examination; provided that, if the defendant is a male and if the court determines that the failure to retain him in strict security would create a likelihood of serious harm by reason of mental illness, or other mental defect, it may order such hospitalization at the Bridgewater state hospital; and provided, further, that the combined periods of hospitalization under the provisions of this section and paragraph (b) of section fifteen shall not exceed fifty days.

(b) During the period of observation of a person believed to be incompetent to stand trial or within sixty days after a person is found to be incompetent to stand trial or not guilty of any crime by reason of mental illness or other mental defect, the district attorney, the superintendent of a facility or the medical director of the Bridgewater state hospital may petition the court having jurisdiction of the criminal case for the commitment of the person to a facility or to the Bridgewater state hospital. However, the petition for the commitment of an untried defendant shall be heard only if the defendant is found incompetent to stand trial, or if the criminal charges are dismissed after commitment. If the court makes the findings required by paragraph (a) of section eight it shall order the person committed to a facility; if the court makes the findings required by paragraph (b) of section eight, it shall order the commitment of the person to the Bridgewater state hospital; otherwise the petition shall be dismissed and the person discharged. An order of commitment under the provisions of this paragraph shall be valid for six months. In the event a period of hospitalization under the provisions of paragraph (a) has expired, or in the event no such period of examination has been ordered, the court may order the temporary detention of such person in a jail, house of correction, facility or the Bridgewater state hospital until such time as the findings required by this paragraph are made or a determination is made that such findings cannot be made.

(c) After the expiration of a commitment under paragraph (b) of this section, a person may be committed for additional one year periods under the provisions of sections seven and eight of this chapter, but no untried defendant shall be so committed unless in addition to the findings required by sections seven and eight the court also finds said defendant is incompetent to stand trial. If the person is not found incompetent, the court shall notify the court with jurisdiction of the criminal charges, which court shall thereupon order the defendant returned to its custody for the resumption of criminal proceedings. All subsequent proceedings for the further commitment of a person committed under this section shall be in the court which has jurisdiction of the facility or hospital.

(d) The district attorney for the district within which the alleged crime or crimes occurred shall be notified of any hearing conducted for a person under the provisions of this section or any subsequent hearing for such person conducted under the provisions of this chapter relative to the commitment of the mentally ill and shall have the right to be heard at such hearings.

(e) Any person committed to a facility under the provisions of this section may be restricted in his movements to the buildings and grounds of the facility at which he is committed by the court which ordered the commitment. If such restrictions are ordered, they shall not be removed except with the approval of the court. If the superintendent seeks removal or modification of such restriction, the superintendent shall notify the district attorney who has or had jurisdiction of the relevant criminal case. If, after the superintendent communicates the superintendent's intention to remove or modify such restriction in writing to the court and the district attorney who has or had jurisdiction of the relevant criminal case, neither the court nor the district attorney makes written objection to such removal or modification within 14 days of receipt of the notice, such restriction shall be removed by the superintendent. If the superintendent or medical director of the Bridgewater state hospital intends to discharge a person committed under this section or at the end of a period of commitment intends not to petition for his further commitment, he shall notify the court and district attorney which have or had jurisdiction of the criminal case. Within thirty days of the receipt of such notice, the district attorney may petition for commitment under the provisions of paragraph (c). During such thirty day period, the person shall be held at the facility or hospital. This paragraph shall not apply to persons originally committed after a finding of incompetence to stand trial whose criminal charges have been dismissed.

(f) If a person is found incompetent to stand trial, the court shall send notice to the department of correction which shall compute the date of the expiration of the period of time equal to the time of imprisonment which the person would have had to serve prior to becoming eligible for parole if he had been convicted of the most serious crime with which he was charged in court and sentenced to the maximum sentence he could have received, if so convicted. For purposes of the computation of parole eligibility, the minimum sentence shall be regarded as one half of the maximum sentence potential sentence. Where applicable, the provisions of sections one hundred and twenty-nine, one hundred and twenty-nine A, one hundred and twenty-nine B, and one hundred and twenty-nine C of chapter one hundred and twenty-seven shall be applied to reduce such period of time. On the final date of such period, the court shall dismiss the criminal charges against such person, or the court in the interest of justice may dismiss the criminal charges against such person prior to the expiration of such period.

§ 17. Periodic review of incompetence to stand trial; petition; hearing; continued treatment; defense to charges; release

(a) The periodic review of a person found incompetent to stand trial shall include a clinical opinion with regard to the person's competence to stand trial, which opinion shall be noted in writing on the patient's record. If any person found incompetent to stand trial is determined by the superintendent of the facility or the medical director of the Bridgewater state hospital to be no longer incompetent, the superintendent or medical director shall notify the court, which shall without delay hold a hearing on the person's competency to stand trial. Any person found incompetent to stand trial may at any time petition the court for a hearing on his competency. Whenever a hearing is held and the court finds that the person is competent to stand trial, his commitment, if any, to a facility or to the Bridgewater state hospital shall be terminated and he shall be returned to the custody of the court for trial. However, if the person requests continued care and treatment during the pendency of the criminal proceedings against him and the superintendent or medical director agrees to provide such care and treatment, the court may order the further hospitalization of such person at the facility or the Bridgewater state hospital.

(b) If either a person or counsel of a person who has been found to be incompetent to stand trial believes that he can establish a defense of not guilty to the charges pending against the person other than the defense of not guilty by reason of mental illness or mental defect, he may request an opportunity to offer a defense thereto on the merits before the court which has criminal jurisdiction. The court may require counsel for the defendant to support the request by affidavit or other evidence. If the court in its discretion grants such a request, the evidence of the defendant and of the commonwealth shall be heard by the court sitting without a jury. If after hearing such petition the court finds a lack of substantial evidence to support a conviction it shall dismiss the indictment or other charges or find them defective or insufficient and order the release of the defendant from criminal custody.

(c) Notwithstanding any finding of incompetence to stand trial under the provisions of this chapter, the court having jurisdiction may, at any appropriate stage of the criminal proceedings, allow a defendant to be released with or without bail.

§ 18. Hospitalization of mentally ill prisoners; examination; reports; hearing; commitment; voluntary admission; reduction of sentence; discharge

(a) If the person in charge of any place of detention within the commonwealth has reason to believe that a person confined therein is in need of hospitalization by reason of mental illness at a facility of the department or at the Bridgewater state hospital, he shall cause such prisoner to be examined at such place of detention by a physician or psychologist, designated by the department as qualified to perform such examination. Said physician or psychologist shall report the results of the examination to the district court which has jurisdiction over the place of detention or, if the prisoner is awaiting trial, to the court which has jurisdiction of the criminal case. Such report shall include an opinion, with reasons therefore, as to whether such hospitalization is actually required. The court which receives such report may order the prisoner to be taken to a facility or, if a male, to the Bridgewater state hospital to be received for examination and observation for a period not to exceed thirty days. After completion of such examination and observation, a written report shall be sent to such court and to the person in charge of the place of detention. Such report shall be signed by the physician or psychologist conducting such examination, and shall contain an evaluation, supported by clinical findings, of whether the prisoner is in need of further treatment and care at a facility or, if a male, the Bridgewater state hospital by reason of mental illness. The person in charge of the place of detention shall have the same right as a superintendent of a facility and the medical director of the Bridgewater state hospital to file a petition with the court which received the results of the examination for the commitment of the person to a facility or to the Bridgewater state hospital; provided, however, that, notwithstanding the court's failure, after an initial hearing or after any subsequent hearing, to make a finding required for commitment to the Bridgewater state hospital, the prisoner shall be confined at said hospital if the findings required for commitment to a facility are made and if the commissioner of correction certifies to the court that confinement of the prisoner at said hospital is necessary to insure his continued retention in custody. An initial court order of commitment issued subject to the provisions of this section shall be valid for a six-month period, and all subsequent commitments during the term of the sentence shall take place under the provisions of sections seven and eight and shall be valid for one year.

(b) Notwithstanding any contrary provision of general or special law, a prisoner who is retained in any place of detention within the commonwealth and who is in need of care and treatment in a facility may, with the approval of the person in charge of such place of detention apply for voluntary admission under the provisions of paragraph (a) of section ten.

(c) At the commencement of hospitalization under the provisions of paragraph (a) or paragraph (b) the department of correction shall enter in the patient record of such prisoner the date of the expiration of the sentence of the prisoner. Where applicable, the provisions of sections one hundred and twenty-nine, one hundred and twenty-nine A, one hundred and twenty-nine B and one hundred and twenty-nine C of chapter one hundred and twenty-seven may be applied to reduce such sentence, and on such date the prisoner shall be discharged; provided, however, that if the superintendent or other head of a facility or the medical director of the Bridgewater state hospital determines that the discharge of the prisoner committed subject to the provisions of paragraph (a) would create a likelihood of serious harm by reason of mental illness, he shall petition the district court having jurisdiction over the facility prior to the date of expiration to order the commitment of such person to a facility or to the Bridgewater state hospital under the provisions of this chapter other than paragraph (a); and provided, further, that any prisoner resident in a facility subject to the provisions of paragraph (b) shall be free to leave such facility subject to the provisions of section eleven.

(d) In the event the provisions of this chapter require the release of a prisoner from a facility or from the Bridgewater state hospital prior to the date of expiration of his sentence calculated under the provisions of paragraph (c), such prisoner shall be forthwith returned to the place of detention from which he was transferred to such facility or to said hospital.

§ 19. Parties or witnesses; determination of mental condition

In order to determine the mental condition of any party or witness before any court of the commonwealth, the presiding judge may, in his discretion, request the department to assign a qualified physician or psychologist, who, if assigned shall make such examinations as the judge may deem necessary.

§ 33. Expenses of apprehension, examination, hearing, commitment or delivery; certification; audit; payment; fees

[Amended by 2012 Mass. Acts c. 224, § 137, effective Nov. 4, 2012.]

All necessary expenses attending the apprehension, examination, hearing, commitment or delivery of a mentally ill person, or an alleged alcoholic shall be allowed and certified by the judge if said person is committed pursuant to this chapter, and presented as often as once a year to the comptroller, who shall examine and audit the same. Necessary expenses attending the apprehension, examination or hearing of any person sought to be committed pursuant to this chapter but not so committed shall be so presented, examined and audited if they have been allowed in the discretion of the judge and certified by him. All expenses certified, examined and audited as provided in this section shall be paid by the commonwealth. If application is made for the commitment of a person whose expenses and support are not to be paid by the commonwealth, said expenses shall be paid by the applicant or by a person in his behalf. The compensation of the physicians and officers taking part in the commitment or admission of persons to facilities in accordance with this chapter shall be as follows: The fee for each physician making an authorized mental examination and for making a written report thereon to the court, or for making a medical certificate, shall be twenty-five dollars, and twenty cents for each mile traveled one way or such other rates as may be set by the executive office of health and human services or governmental unit designated by the executive office. Any physician required to appear before a judge or justice in any commitment proceedings, in which such physician has made an examination, shall receive a fee of twenty-five dollars, and twenty cents for each mile traveled one way for such appearance before the court, or such other rate as may be set by the executive office of health and human services or governmental unit designated by the executive office. The fees for officers servicing process shall be the same as are allowed by law in like cases.

§ 35. Commitment of alcoholics or substance abusers

[Amended by 2010 Mass. Acts c. 292, effective Nov. 8, 2010; 2011 Mass. Acts c. 142, § 18, effective July 1, 2012; 2014 Mass. Acts c. 165, § 155, effective July 15, 2014; 2014 Mass. Acts c. 284, § 15, effective Jan. 1, 2015; 2015 Mass. Acts c. 8, effective Apr. 24, 2016; 2016 Mass. Acts c. 52, § 40, effective Mar. 14, 2016; 2017 Mass. Acts c. 47, §§ 56–57, effective July 1, 2017 per § 153; 2018 Mass. Acts c. 208, §§ 72–74, effective Aug. 9, 2018.]

For the purposes of this section the following terms shall, unless the context clearly requires otherwise, have the following meanings:

"Alcohol use disorder", the chronic or habitual consumption of alcoholic beverages by a person to the extent that (1) such use substantially injures the person's health or substantially interferes with the person's social or economic functioning, or (2) the person has lost the power of self-control over the use of such beverages.

"Facility", a public or private facility that provides care and treatment for a person with an alcohol or substance use disorder.

"Substance use disorder", the chronic or habitual consumption or ingestion of controlled substances or intentional inhalation of toxic vapors by a person to the extent that: (i) such use substantially injures the person's health or substantially interferes with the person's social or economic functioning; or (ii) the person has lost the power of self-control over the use of such controlled substances or toxic vapors.

Any police officer, physician, spouse, blood relative, guardian or court official may petition in writing any district court or any division of the juvenile court department for an order of commitment of a person whom he has reason to believe has an alcohol or substance use disorder. Upon receipt of a petition for an order of commitment of a person and any sworn statements the court may request from the petitioner, the court shall immediately schedule a hearing on the petition and shall cause a summons and a copy of the application to be served upon the person in the manner provided by section twenty-five of chapter two hundred and seventy-six. In the event of the person's failure to appear at the time summoned, the court may issue a warrant for the person's arrest. Upon presentation of such a petition, if there are reasonable grounds to believe that such person will not appear and that any further delay in the proceedings would present an immediate danger to the physical well-being of the respondent, said court may issue a warrant for the apprehension and appearance of such person before it. If such person is not immediately presented before a judge of the district court, the warrant shall continue day after day for up to 5 consecutive days, excluding Saturdays, Sundays and legal holidays, or until such time as the person is presented to the court, whichever is sooner; provided, however that an arrest on such warrant shall not be made unless the person may be presented immediately before a judge of the district court. The person shall have the right to be represented by legal counsel and may present independent expert or other testimony. If the court finds the person indigent, it shall immediately appoint counsel. The court shall order examination by a qualified physician, a qualified psychologist or a qualified social worker.

If, after a hearing which shall include expert testimony and may include other evidence, the court finds that such person is an individual with an alcohol or substance use disorder and there is a likelihood of serious harm as a result of the person's alcohol or substance use disorder, the court may order such person to be committed for a period not to exceed 90 days to a facility designated by the department of public health, followed by the availability of case management services provided by the department of public health for up to 1 year; provided, that a review of the necessity of the commitment shall take place by the superintendent on days 30, 45, 60 and 75 as long as the commitment continues. A person so committed may be released prior to the expiration of the period of commitment upon written determination by the superintendent of the facility that release of that person will not result in a likelihood of serious harm; provided, that the superintendent shall provide timely notification to the committing court and, if consent is obtained from the committed person, to the petitioner; provided further, that the superintendent shall request such consent from all committed persons. Such commitment shall be for the purpose of inpatient care for the treatment of an alcohol or substance use disorder in a facility licensed or approved by the department of public health or the department of mental health. Subsequent to the issuance of a commitment order, the superintendent of a facility may authorize the transfer of a patient to a different facility for continuing treatment; provided, that the superintendent shall timely notification of the transfer to the committing court and, if consent is obtained from the committed person, to the petitioner; provided further, that the superintendent shall request such consent from all committed persons.

If the department of public health informs the court that there are no suitable facilities available for treatment licensed or approved by the department of public health or the department of mental health, or if the court makes a specific finding that the only appropriate setting for treatment for the person is a secure facility, then the person may be committed to: (i) a secure facility for women approved by the department of public health or the department of mental health, if a female; or (ii) the Massachusetts correctional institution at Bridgewater or other such facility as designated by the commissioner of correction, if a male; provided, however, that any person so committed shall be housed and treated separately from persons currently serving a criminal sentence. The person shall, upon release, be encouraged to consent to further treatment and shall be allowed voluntarily to remain in the facility for such purpose. The department of public health shall maintain a roster of public and private facilities available, together with the number of beds currently available and the level of security at each facility, for the care and treatment of alcohol use disorder and substance use disorder and shall make the roster available to the trial court.

A facility used for commitment under this section for a person found to be a person with a substance use disorder shall maintain or provide for the capacity to possess, dispense and administer all drugs approved by the federal Food and Drug Administration for use in opioid agonist treatment, including partial agonist treatment, and opioid antagonist treatment for opioid use disorder and shall make such treatment available to any person for whom such treatment is medically appropriate.

Annually, not later than February 1, the commissioner shall report on whether a facility other than the Massachusetts correctional institution at Bridgewater is being used for treatment of males under the previous paragraph and the number of persons so committed to such a facility in the previous year. The report shall be provided to the clerks of the senate and house of representatives, the chairs of the joint committee on public safety and homeland security and the chairs of the joint committee on the judiciary.

Nothing in this section shall preclude a facility, including the Massachusetts correctional institution at Bridgewater or such other facility as may be designated by the commissioner of correction, from treating persons on a voluntary basis.

The court, in its order, shall specify whether such commitment is based upon a finding that the person is a person with an alcohol use disorder, substance use disorder, or both. The court, upon ordering the commitment of a person found to be a person with an alcohol use disorder or substance use disorder pursuant to this section, shall transmit the person's name and nonclinical identifying information, including the person's social security number and date of birth, to the department of criminal justice information services. The court shall notify the person that such person is prohibited from being issued a firearm identification card pursuant to section 129B of chapter 140 or a license to carry pursuant to sections 131 and 131F of said chapter 140 unless a petition for relief pursuant to this section is subsequently granted.

After 5 years from the date of commitment, a person found to be a person with an alcohol use disorder or substance use disorder and committed pursuant to this section may file a petition for relief with the court that ordered the commitment requesting that the court restore the person's ability to possess a firearm, rifle or shotgun. The court may grant the relief sought in accordance with the principles of due process if the circumstances regarding the person's disqualifying condition and the person's record and reputation are determined to be such that: (i) the person is not likely to act in a manner that is dangerous to public safety; and (ii) the granting of relief would not be contrary to the public interest. In making the determination, the court may consider evidence from a licensed physician or clinical psychologist that the person is no longer suffering from the disease or condition that caused the disability or that the disease or condition has been successfully treated for a period of 3 consecutive years.

If the court grants a petition for relief pursuant to this section, the clerk shall provide notice immediately by forwarding a certified copy of the order for relief to the department of criminal justice information services, who shall transmit the order, pursuant to paragraph (h) of section 167A of chapter 6, to the attorney general of the United States to be included in the National Instant Criminal Background Check System.

A person whose petition for relief is denied may appeal to the appellate division of the district court for a de novo review of the denial.

§ 36B. Duty to warn patient's potential victims; cause of action

(1) There shall be no duty owed by a licensed mental health professional to take reasonable precautions to warn or in any other way protect a potential victim or victims of said professional's patient, and no cause of action imposed against a licensed mental health professional for failure to warn or in any other way protect a potential victim or victims of such professional's patient unless: (a) the patient has communicated to the licensed mental health professional an explicit threat to kill or inflict serious bodily injury upon a reasonably identified victim or victims and the patient has the apparent intent and ability to carry out the threat, and the licensed mental health professional fails to take reasonable precautions as that term is defined in section one; or (b) the patient has a history of physical violence which is known to the licensed mental health professional and the licensed mental health professional has a reasonable basis to believe that there is a clear and present danger that the patient will attempt to kill or inflict serious bodily injury against a reasonably identified victim or victims and the licensed mental health professional fails to take reasonable precautions as that term is defined by said section one. Nothing in this paragraph shall be construed to require a mental health professional to take any action which, in the exercise of reasonable professional judgment, would endanger such mental health professional or increase the danger to potential victim or victims.

(2) Whenever a licensed mental health professional takes reasonable precautions, as that term is defined in section one of chapter one hundred and twenty-three, no cause of action by the patient shall lie against the licensed mental health professional for disclosure of otherwise confidential communications.

Chapter 127. Officers and Inmates of Penal and Reformatory Institutions; Paroles and Pardons

§ 133A. Eligibility for parole; notice and hearing; parole permits; revision of terms and conditions; revocation; arrest

[Amended by 2014 Mass. Acts c. 189, § 3, effective July 25, 2014; 2018 Mass. Acts c. 69, § 98, effective Apr. 13, 2018.]

1

Every prisoner who is serving a sentence for life in a correctional institution of the commonwealth, except prisoners confined to the hospital at the Massachusetts Correctional Institution, Bridgewater, except prisoners serving a life sentence for murder in the first degree who had attained the age of 18 years at the time of the murder and except prisoners serving more than 1 life sentence arising out of separate and distinct incidents that occurred at different times, where the second offense occurred subsequent to the first conviction, shall be eligible for parole at the expiration of the minimum term fixed by the court under section 24 of chapter 279. The parole board shall, within 60 days before the expiration of such minimum term, conduct a public hearing before the full membership unless a member of the board is determined to be unavailable as provided in this section. Notwithstanding the previous sentence, the board may postpone a hearing until 30 days before the expiration of such minimum term, if the interests of justice so require and upon publishing written findings of the necessity for such postponement. For the purposes of this section, the term unavailable shall mean that a board member has a conflict of interest to the extent that he cannot render a fair and impartial decision or that the appearance of a board member would be unduly burdensome because of illness, incapacitation, or other circumstance. Whether a member is unavailable for the purposes of this section shall be determined by the chair. Board members shall appear unless said chair determines them to be unavailable. Under no circumstances shall a parole hearing proceed pursuant to this section unless a majority of the board is present at the public hearing. Unless a board member is unavailable due to a conflict of interest, any board member who was not present at the public hearing shall review the record of the public hearing and shall vote in the matter.

Said board shall at least thirty days before such hearing notify in writing the attorney general, the district attorney in whose district sentence was imposed, the chief of police or head of the organized police department of the municipality in which the crime was committed and the victims of the crime for which sentence was imposed, and said officials and victims may appear in person or be represented or make written recommendations to the board, but failure of any or all of said officials to appear or make recommendations shall not delay the paroling procedure; provided, however, that no hearing shall take place until the parole board has certified in writing that it has complied with the notification requirements of this paragraph, a copy of which shall be included in the record of such proceeding; and provided further, that this paragraph shall also apply to any parole hearing for an applicant who was convicted of a crime listed in clause (i) of subsection (b) of section 25 of chapter 279 and sentenced and committed to prison for 5 or more years for such crime and does not show that a pardon has been issued for the crime.

After such hearing the parole board may, by a vote of two-thirds of its members, grant to such prisoner a parole permit to be at liberty upon such terms and conditions as it may prescribe for the unexpired term of his sentence. If such permit is not granted, the parole board shall, at least once in each ensuing five year period, consider carefully and thoroughly the merits of each such case on the question of releasing such prisoner on parole, and may, by a vote of two-thirds of its members, grant such parole permit.

Such terms and conditions may be revised, altered and amended, and may be revoked, by the parole board at any time. The violation by the holder of such permit or any of its terms or conditions, or of any law of the commonwealth, may render such permit void, and thereupon, or if such permit has been revoked, the parole board may order his arrest and his return to prison, in accordance with the provisions of section one hundred and forty-nine.

If a prisoner is indigent and is serving a life sentence for an offense that was committed before the prisoner reached 18 years of age, the prisoner shall have the right to have appointed counsel at the parole hearing and shall have the right to funds for experts pursuant to chapter 261.

§ 133C. Representation of deceased victims at hearing by family members

[Amended by 2014 Mass. Acts c. 189, § 4, effective July 25, 2014.]

The family members of a deceased victim may represent the victim at any parole hearing for a prisoner serving a sentence for a crime which resulted in the death of such victim or for a crime for which a prisoner is serving a sentence for life in a correctional institution of the commonwealth, except prisoners serving a life sentence for murder in the first degree who had attained the age of 18 years at the time of the murder and prisoners confined to the hospital at the Massachusetts Correctional Institution, Bridgewater. For the purposes of this section, family members shall include: parent, stepparent or guardian of the victim, spouse or person with whom the victim lived and in a relationship similar to marriage, child, stepchild, grandchild, grandparent, sibling, aunt, uncle, niece, nephew and guardian of the minor child or stepchild of the victim.

Chapter 138. Alcoholic Liquors

§ 34A. Persons under twenty-one years; purchase or attempt to purchase alcoholic beverages

Any person under twenty-one years of age who purchases or attempts to purchase alcoholic beverages or alcohol, or makes arrangements with any person to purchase or in any way procure such beverages, or who willfully misrepresents his age, or in any way alters, defaces or otherwise falsifies his identification offered as proof of age, with the intent of purchasing alcoholic beverages, either for his own use or for the use of any other person shall be punished by a fine of three hundred dollars and whoever knowingly makes a false statement as to the age of a person who is under twenty-one years of age in order to procure a sale or delivery of such beverages or alcohol to such person under twenty-one years of age, either for the use of the person under twenty-one years of age or for the use of some other person, and whoever induces a person under twenty-one years of age to make a false statement as to his age in order to procure a sale or delivery of such beverages or alcohol to such person under twenty-one years of age, shall be punished by a fine of three hundred dollars. A conviction of a violation of this section shall be reported forthwith to the registrar of motor vehicles by the court. Upon receipt of such notice the registrar shall thereupon suspend for 180 days the defendant's license or right to operate a motor vehicle.

The commission shall prepare and distribute to business establishments which sell, serve or otherwise dispense alcohol or alcoholic beverages to the general public, posters to be displayed therein in a conspicuous place. Said posters shall contain a summary and explanation of this section.

§ 34C. Persons under twenty-one years of age; operation of motor vehicles containing alcoholic beverages

Whoever, being under twenty-one years of age and not accompanied by a parent or legal guardian, knowingly possesses, transports or carries on his person, any alcohol or alcoholic beverages, shall be punished by a fine of not more than fifty dollars for the first offense and not more than one hundred and fifty dollars for a second or subsequent offense; provided, however, that this section shall not apply to a person between the ages of eighteen and twenty-one who knowingly possesses, transports or carries on his person, alcohol or alcoholic beverages in the course of his employment. A police officer may arrest without a warrant any person who violates this section. A conviction of a violation of this section shall be reported forthwith to the registrar of motor vehicles by the court, and said registrar shall thereupon suspend for a period of ninety days the license of such person to operate a motor vehicle.

§ 36. Analysis of alcoholic beverages by department of public health

[Amended by 2012 Mass. Acts c. 139, § 123, effective July 1, 2012.]

The analyst or assistant analyst of the department of state police shall upon request make, free of charge, an analysis of all alcoholic beverages sent to it by the licensing authorities or by police officers or other officers authorized by law to make seizures of alcoholic beverages, if the department is satisfied that the analysis requested is to be used in connection with the enforcement of the laws of the commonwealth. The said department shall return to such police or other officers, as soon as may be, a certificate, signed by the analyst or assistant analyst making such analysis, of the percentage of alcohol which such samples of beverages contain, and, if the commission so requests, of the composition and quality of such beverages as shown by the samples submitted. Such certificate shall be prima facie evidence of the composition and quality of the alcoholic beverages to which it relates, and the court may take judicial notice of the signature of the analyst or the assistant analyst, and of the fact that he is such.

§ 37. Certificate accompanying sample of beverages to be analyzed; contents

[Amended by 2012 Mass. Acts c. 139, § 124, effective July 1, 2012.]

A certificate shall accompany each sample of beverages sent for analysis by an officer to the department of state police stating from whom the beverages were seized, the date of the seizure and the name and residence of the officer who seized said beverages. Said department shall note upon said certificate the date of the receipt and the analysis of said alcoholic beverages and the percentage of the alcohol or the composition and quality of said beverages, as the case may be, as required by section thirty-six on a form prescribed by said department of state police.

Chapter 140. Licenses

§ 1. "Licensing authorities" defined

"Licensing authorities", as used in this chapter, unless a contrary meaning is required by the context shall mean the boards in Boston and other cities which by special statutes or city charters have the power to issue licenses for inn holders or common victuallers, licensing boards appointed under section four of chapter one hundred and thirty-eight in cities which at the municipal election next preceding the first day of January, nineteen hundred and twenty-five, voted to authorize the granting of licenses for the sale of certain nonintoxicating beverages and also in cities wherein by special statutes said boards are vested with all the powers and duties exercised by licensing boards in cities that vote to grant such licenses, the aldermen in all other cities and the selectmen in towns.

§ 121A. Identification of firearms; certificate by ballistics expert as prima facie evidence

A certificate by a ballistics expert of the department of the state police or of the city of Boston of the result of an examination made by him of an item furnished him by any police officer, signed and sworn to by such expert, shall be prima facie evidence of his findings as to whether or not the item furnished is a firearm, rifle, shotgun, machine gun, sawed off shotgun or ammunition, as defined by section one hundred and twenty-one, provided that in order to qualify as an expert under this section he shall have previously qualified as an expert in a court proceeding.

Chapter 190B. Massachusetts Uniform Probate Code

NOTE Selected sections of Article V of the Massachusetts Uniform Probate Code are included here. For the complete text of Article V, see this part's Additional Materials.

Part 1: General Provisions and Definitions

§ 5-106. Appointment of counsel; guardian ad litem

[Added by 2008 Mass. Acts c. 521, § 9, effective July 1, 2009. Amended by 2012 Mass. Acts c. 140, § 27, effective July 8, 2012.]

(a) After filing of a petition for appointment of a guardian, conservator or other protective order, if the ward, incapacitated person or person to be protected or someone on his behalf requests appointment of counsel; or if the court determines at any time in the proceeding that the interests of the ward, incapacitated person or person to be protected are or may be inadequately represented, the court shall appoint an attorney to represent the person, giving consideration to the choice of the person if 14 or more years of age. If the ward, incapacitated person or person to be protected has adequate resources, his counsel shall be compensated from the estate, unless the court shall order that such compensation be paid by the petitioner. Counsel for any indigent ward, incapacitated person or person to be protected shall be compensated by the commonwealth or the petitioner as the court may order. This section shall not be interpreted to abridge or limit the right of any ward, incapacitated person or person to be protected to retain counsel of his own choice and to prosecute or defend a petition under this article.

(b) The court may appoint as guardian ad litem, an individual or any public or charitable agency to investigate the condition of the ward, incapacitated person or person to be protected and make appropriate recommendations to the court.

(c) The incapacitated person or person to be protected is entitled to be present at any hearing in person. A ward, if 14 or more years of age, is entitled to be present at any hearing in person unless the court, upon written findings, determines that the best interest of the ward will not be served thereby. The person is entitled to be represented by counsel, to present evidence, to cross-examine witnesses, including any physician or other qualified person and any guardian ad litem. The issue may be determined at a closed hearing if the person or counsel for the person so requests.

(d) Any person may apply for permission to provide information in the proceeding and the court may grant the request, with or without hearing, upon determining that the best interest of the person to be protected will be served thereby. The court may attach appropriate conditions to the permission.

Part 2: Guardians of Minors

§ 5-201. Appointment and status of guardian of minor

[Added by 2008 Mass. Acts c. 521, § 9, effective July 1, 2009.]

A person may become a guardian of a minor by appointment by parent or guardian or upon appointment by the court. The guardianship status continues until terminated, without regard to the location from time to time of the guardian or minor ward. The district or juvenile court may appoint guardians of minors if the person who is the subject of the petition is a minor and there is a proceeding before such district or juvenile court and shall have continuing jurisdiction over resignation, removal, reporting, and other proceedings related to the guardianship.

§ 5-202. Parental or guardian appointment of guardian for minor

[Added by 2008 Mass. Acts c. 521, § 9, effective July 1, 2009.]

(a) A parent, by will or other writing signed by the parent and attested by at least 2 witnesses, may appoint a guardian for any minor child the parent has or may have in the future, may revoke or amend the appointment, and may specify any desired limitations on the powers to be granted to the guardian.

(b) A guardian, by will or other writing signed by the guardian and attested by at least 2 witnesses, may appoint a guardian for any minor child for whom the guardian serves, may revoke or amend the appointment, and may specify any desired limitations on the powers to be granted to the guardian.

(c) Upon petition of an appointing parent or guardian, upon finding that the appointing parent or guardian will likely become unable to care for the minor within 2 years or less, and after notice as provided in section 5-206(b), the court, before the appointment becomes effective, may confirm the parent's or guardian's selection of a guardian and terminate the rights of others under section 5-203.

(d) Subject to section 5-203, the appointment of a guardian becomes effective on the first to occur of the appointing parent's or guardian's death, an adjudication that the parent or guardian is an incapacitated person, or a written determination by a physician who has examined the parent or guardian that the parent or guardian is no longer able to care for the minor unless the minor is in the care or custody of a person other than a parent pursuant to sections 24, 25, 26 and 39G of chapter 119, chapter 201; or section 3 of chapter 210.

(e) Within 30 days after the appointment becomes effective, a guardian shall:

(1) file a notice of acceptance of appointment and a copy of the will or other nominating instrument with the court of the county in which the will was or could be probated or, in the case of another nominating instrument, with the court of the county in which the minor resides; and

(2) unless the appointment was previously confirmed by the court, petition the court for confirmation of the appointment, giving notice in the manner provided in section 5-206(b).

(f) The parental appointment of a guardian shall not supersede the parental rights of either parent. If both parents are dead or have been adjudged incapacitated persons, an appointment by the last parent who dies or was adjudged incapacitated has priority.

(g) The powers of a guardian who timely complies with the requirements of subsection (e) relate back to give acts by the guardian which are of benefit to the minor and which occurred on or after the date the guardian was eligible to file an acceptance of office the same effect as those which occurred after the filing.

(h) The authority of a guardian appointed under this section terminates upon the first to occur of the appointment of a guardian by the court, the revocation of the appointment by the appointing parent or guardian, or the filing of an objection pursuant to section 5-203.

§ 5-203. Objection by minor fourteen or older to parental appointment

[Added by 2008 Mass. Acts c. 521, § 9, effective July 1, 2009.]

Except where the court has previously confirmed a nominee under section 5-202(c),

(i) a minor 14 or more years of age who is the subject of a parental appointment,

(ii) the other parent, if that parent's parental rights have not been terminated, or

(iii) a person other than a parent having care or custody of the minor or with whom the minor has resided during the 60 preceding days, excluding a foster parent may prevent the appointment or cause it to terminate by filing in the court in which the appointing instrument is filed a written objection to the appointment before it is accepted or within 30 days after receiving notice of its acceptance. An objection may be withdrawn. An objection shall not preclude appointment of the nominee by the court in a proper proceeding of the parental nominee or any other suitable person. The court may treat the filing of an objection as a petition for the appointment of a temporary guardian, and proceed accordingly.

§ 5-204. Court appointment of guardian of minor; conditions for appointment; temporary guardian

[Added by 2008 Mass. Acts c. 521, § 9, effective July 1, 2009. Amended by 2012 Mass. Acts c. 140, § 29, effective July 8, 2012.]

(a) The court may appoint a guardian for a minor if (i) the minor's parents are deceased or incapacitated, (ii) the parents consent, (iii) the parents' parental rights have been terminated, (iv) the parents have signed a voluntary surrender, or (v) the court finds the parents, jointly, or the surviving parent, to be unavailable or unfit to have custody. A guardian appointed pursuant to section 5-202 whose appointment has not been prevented or nullified under section 5-203 has priority over any guardian who may be appointed by the court, but the court may proceed with another appointment upon a finding that the parental nominee has failed to accept the appointment within 30 days after notice of the guardianship proceeding.

(b) While a petition for appointment of a guardian is pending, if a minor has no guardian, and the court finds that following the procedures of this article will likely result in substantial harm to the health, safety or welfare of the minor occurring prior to the return date, and no other person appears to have authority to act in the circumstances, on appropriate motion, the court may appoint a temporary guardian who may exercise those powers granted in the order. A motion for appointment of a temporary guardian shall state the nature of the circumstances requiring appointment, the particular harm sought to be avoided, and the actions which will be necessary by the temporary guardian to avoid the occurrence of the harm. Such motion shall be accompanied by an affidavit containing facts supporting the statements and requests in the motion. The appointment of a temporary guardian for a minor may occur even though the conditions described in subsection (a) have not been established. The appointment may be for a period of up to 90 days except that upon a finding of extraordinary circumstances set forth in its order, the court may order an appointment for a longer period to a date certain. The court may for good cause shown extend the appointment for additional 90 day periods.

(c) If an appointed guardian is not effectively performing duties and the court further finds that the welfare of the minor requires immediate action, it may appoint, with or without notice, a special guardian for the minor having the powers of a general guardian, except as limited in the letters of appointment. The authority of any guardian previously appointed is suspended as long as a special guardian has authority. The appointment may be for a period of up to 90 days except that upon a finding of extraordinary circumstances set forth in its order the court may order an appointment for a longer period to a date certain. The court may for good cause shown extend the appointment for additional 90 day periods.

(d) The petitioner shall give written notice 7 days prior to any hearing for the appointment of a temporary guardian in hand to the minor if 14 or more years of age and by delivery or by mail to all persons named in the petition for appointment of guardian. A certificate that such notice has been given, setting forth the names and addresses of those to whom notice has been given, shall be prima facie evidence thereof.

(e) If the court determines that an immediate emergency situation exists which requires the immediate appointment of a temporary guardian, it may shorten or waive the notice requirements in whole or in part and grant the motion, provided, however, that prior notice shall be given to the minor, if the minor is 14 or more years of age, as the court may order and post-appointment notice of any appointment is given to the minor and those named in the petition for appointment of guardian stating further that any such person may move to vacate the order of the court or request that the court take any other appropriate action on the matter, and on said motion to vacate. The court shall hear said motion as a de novo matter, as expeditiously as possible. A certificate stating that such notice has been given shall be filed with the court within 7 days following the appointment. Upon failure to file such certificate the court may on its own motion vacate said order.

(f) In the event that any person to whom notice is required is of parts unknown, such notice shall be delivered or mailed to that person's last known address, and the fact of such delivery or mailing shall be recited in the certificate of notice.

§ 5-205. Reserved

§ 5-206. Procedure for court appointment of guardian of minor
[Added by 2008 Mass. Acts c. 521, § 9, effective July 1, 2009. Amended by 2012 Mass. Acts c. 140, § 30, effective July 8, 2012.]

(a) A minor 14 or more years of age or any person interested in the welfare of the minor may petition for appointment of a guardian.

(b) After the filing of a petition, notice shall be given in the manner prescribed by section 1-401 by the petitioner to:

(1) the minor, if the minor is 14 or more years of age and is not the petitioner;

(2) any person who has been awarded care or custody of the minor by a court of competent jurisdiction, whom is alleged to have had the principal care or custody of the minor or with whom the minor has resided during the 60 days preceding the filing of the petition, excluding foster parents;

(3) any living parent of the minor, excluding a parent whose parental rights have been terminated or a parent who has signed a voluntary surrender, or, if none, brothers and sisters, or, if none, heirs apparent or presumptive;

(4) the spouse if the minor is married;

(5) any person nominated as guardian by the minor if the minor has attained 14 years of age;

(6) any parental or guardian appointee whose appointment has not been prevented or terminated under section 5-203;

(7) any guardian or conservator currently acting for the minor in the commonwealth or elsewhere; and

(8) the United States veterans administration or its successor if the minor is entitled to any benefit, estate or income paid or payable by or through said administration or its successors.

(c) Upon hearing, if the court finds that a qualified person seeks appointment, venue is proper, the required notices have been given, the conditions of section 5-204(a) have been met, and the welfare and best interest of the minor will be served by the requested appointment, it shall make the appointment and issue letters. In other cases, the court may dismiss the proceedings or make any other disposition of the matter that will serve the best interest of the minor.

§ 5-207. Court appointment of guardian of minor; qualifications; priority of minor's nominee
[Added by 2008 Mass. Acts c. 521, § 9, effective July 1, 2009.]

(a) The court may appoint as guardian any person whose appointment would be in the best interest of the minor. The court shall appoint a person nominated by the minor, if the minor is 14 or more years of age, unless the court finds the appointment contrary to the best interest of the minor.

(b) In the interest of developing self-reliance of a ward or for other good cause, the court, at the time of appointment or later, on its own motion or on motion of the minor ward or other interested person, may limit the powers of a guardian otherwise granted by this article and thereby create a limited guardianship. Any limitation on the statutory power of a guardian of a minor shall be endorsed on the guardian's letters or, in the case of a guardian by parental appointment, shall be reflected in letters that are issued at the time any limitation is imposed. Following the same procedure, additional powers may be granted or existing powers may be withdrawn.

§ 5-208. Bond; consent to service by acceptance of appointment; notice
[Added by 2008 Mass. Acts c. 521, § 9, effective July 1, 2009.]

(a) Prior to receiving letters, a guardian shall accept appointment by filing a bond conditioned upon faithful discharge of all duties of the trust according to law and containing a statement of acceptance of the duties of the office. By accepting a parental or court appointment as guardian, a guardian submits personally to the jurisdiction of the court in any proceeding relating to the guardianship that may be instituted by any interested person. The petitioner shall cause notice of any proceeding to be delivered or mailed to the guardian at the guardian's address listed in the court records and to the address then known to the petitioner.

(b) A surety shall be required on the bond of a guardian of a minor unless the court determines that it is in the best interest of the minor to waive the surety or to require additional sureties.

(c) The requirements and provisions of section 5-411 apply to guardians appointed under this part.

§ 5-209. Powers, duties, rights and immunities of guardian of minor; limitations
[Added by 2008 Mass. Acts c. 521, § 9, effective July 1, 2009.]

(a) A guardian of a ward has the powers and responsibilities of a parent regarding the ward's support, care, education, health and welfare. A guardian shall act at all times in the ward's best interest and exercise reasonable care, diligence and prudence.

(b) In particular and without qualifying the foregoing, a guardian of a ward or incapacitated person shall:

(1) if consistent with the terms of any order by a court of competent jurisdiction take custody of the person of the ward or incapacitated person and establish his place of abode within or without the commonwealth;

(2) become or remain personally acquainted with the ward or incapacitated person and maintain sufficient contact with the person to know of his capacities, limitations, needs, opportunities, and physical and mental health;

(3) take reasonable care of the personal effects and commence protective proceedings if necessary to protect other property of the ward or incapacitated person;

(4) apply any available money of the ward or incapacitated person to his current needs for support, care, education health and welfare; provided that if any person has a legal duty to support a minor and has sufficient funds, the minor's funds are not to be used to discharge the legal obligation of support without prior order of the court unless the court determines that the minor's funds may be used for support;

(5) conserve any excess money of the person for his future needs, but if a conservator has been appointed for the estate of the ward or incapacitated person, the guardian, at least quarterly, shall pay to the conservator money of the ward or incapacitated person to be conserved for his future needs; and

(6) report the condition of the ward or protected person and of his estate that has been subject to the guardian's possession or control, as ordered by the court on petition of any person interested in the respondent's welfare or as required by court rule, but not less than annually.

(c) A guardian of a ward or incapacitated person may:

(1) apply for and receive money for the support of the ward or incapacitated person otherwise payable to his parent, guardian, or custodian for his support under the terms of any statutory benefit or insurance system or any private contract, devise, trust, conservatorship, or custodianship;

(2) if no conservator for the estate of the ward or incapacitated person has been appointed, institute proceedings, including administrative proceedings, or take other appropriate action to compel the performance by any person of a duty to support the ward or incapacitated person or to pay sums for his benefit;

(3) if consistent with the terms of any order by a court of competent jurisdiction and sections 5-306A and 5-309, consent to medical or other professional care, treatment, or advice for the ward or incapacitated person without liability by reason of the consent for injury to the ward or incapacitated person resulting from the negligence or acts of third persons unless a parent would have been liable in the circumstances;

(4) consent or refuse to consent to the marriage, divorce or adoption of the ward or incapacitated person;

(5) if reasonable under all of the circumstances, delegate to the ward or incapacitated person certain responsibilities for decisions affecting his well-being; and

(6) utilize the services of agencies and individuals to provide necessary and desirable social and protective services of different types appropriate to such person including, but not limited to, counseling services, advocacy services, legal services, and other aid as the guardian deems to be in the interest of such person.

(d) guardian is entitled to reasonable compensation for services as guardian and to reimbursement for room, board and clothing personally provided to the ward or incapacitated person, but only as approved by order of the court and only from the person's estate. If a conservator, other than the guardian or one who is affiliated with the guardian, has been appointed for the estate of the person, reasonable compensation and reimbursement to the guardian may be approved and paid by the conservator without order of the court controlling the guardian.

(e) A guardian need not use the guardian's personal funds for the ward or incapacitated person's expenses. A guardian is not liable to a third person for acts of the respondent solely by reason of the relationship.

§ 5-210. Termination of appointment of guardian; general

[Added by 2008 Mass. Acts c. 521, § 9, effective July 1, 2009.]

A guardian's authority and responsibility terminates upon the death, resignation, or removal of the guardian or upon the minor's death, adoption, marriage, or attainment of majority, but termination shall not affect the guardian's liability for prior acts or the obligation to account for funds and assets of the ward. Resignation of a guardian shall not terminate the guardianship until it has been approved by the court. A parental appointment under an informally probated will is voided if the will is later denied probate in a formal proceeding.

§ 5-211. Reserved

§ 5-212. Resignation, removal, and other post-appointment proceedings

[Added by 2008 Mass. Acts c. 521, § 9, effective July 1, 2009.]

(a) Any person interested in the welfare of a ward or the ward, if 14 or more years of age, may petition for removal of a guardian on the ground that removal would be in the best interest of the ward or for any other order that is in the best interest of the ward. A guardian may petition for permission to resign. A petition for removal or for permission to resign may, but need not, include a request for appointment of a successor guardian.

(b) Notice of hearing on a petition for an order subsequent to appointment of a guardian shall be given to the ward, the guardian, the parents of the ward, provided that the parental rights have not been terminated or a voluntary surrender has not been signed, and any other person as ordered by the court.

(c) After notice and hearing on a petition for removal or for permission to resign, the court may terminate the guardianship and make any further order that may be appropriate, including appointment of a successor guardian.

Part 3: Guardians of Incapacitated Persons

§ 5-306A. Substituted judgment

[Added by 2008 Mass. Acts c. 521, § 9, effective July 1, 2009. Amended by 2012 Mass. Acts c. 140, §§ 37–40, effective July 8, 2012.]

(a) No guardian, temporary guardian or special guardian of a minor or an incapacitated person shall have the authority to consent to treatment for which substituted judgment determination may be required, provided that the court shall authorize such treatment when it (i) specifically finds using the substituted judgment standard that the person, if not incapacitated, would consent to such treatment and (ii) specifically approves and authorizes a treatment plan and endorses said plan in its order or decree. The court shall not authorize such treatment plan except after a hearing for the purpose of which counsel shall be provided for any indigent minor or incapacitated person. Said hearing shall be held as soon as is practicable; provided, however, that if the petitioner requests a temporary order on the grounds that the welfare of the minor or person alleged to be incapacitated requires an immediate authorization of treatment, the court shall act on such request in accordance with the procedures set forth in section 5-308. When approving and authorizing an antipsychotic medication treatment plan by order or decree, the court shall consider the testimony or affidavit of a licensed physician or certified psychiatric nurse clinical specialist regarding such plan.

(b) The court may delegate to a guardian the authority to monitor the treatment process to ensure that a treatment plan is followed, provided a guardian is readily available for such purpose. Approval of a treatment plan shall not be withheld, however, because a guardian is not available to serve as monitor. In such circumstances, the court shall appoint a suitable person to monitor the treatment process to ensure that the treatment plan is followed. Reasonable expense incurred in such monitoring may be paid out of the estate of such person, by the petitioner, or, subject to appropriation, by the commonwealth, as may be determined by the court.

(c) Each order authorizing a treatment plan pursuant to this section shall provide for periodic review at least annually to determine whether the minor's or incapacitated person's condition and circumstances have substantially changed such that, if competent, the minor or incapacitated person would no longer consent to the treatment authorized therein. Each such order shall further provide for an expiration date beyond which the authority to provide treatment thereunder shall, if not extended by the court, terminate.

(d) A minor 14 or more years of age or an incapacitated person shall be required to attend any hearing relative to authority to consent to treatment for which a substituted judgment determination is required, unless the court finds that there exist extraordinary circumstances requiring the absence of the minor or incapacitated person in which event the attendance of his counsel shall suffice; provided that the court may base its findings exclusively upon affidavits and other documentary evidence if it (1) determines after careful inquiry and upon representations of counsel, that there are no contested issues of fact and (2) includes in its findings the reason that oral testimony was not required.

(e) Any privilege established by section 135A of chapter 112 or by section 20B of chapter 233 relating to confidential communications shall not prohibit the filing of reports or affidavits, or the giving of testimony, pursuant to this part, for the purposes of obtaining treatment of a person alleged to be incapacitated; provided, however, that such person has been informed prior to making such communication that they may be used for such purpose and has waived the privilege.

Chapter 201F. Caregiver Authorization Affidavits

Section

§ 1. Definitions

[Added by 2008 Mass. Acts c. 511, effective Apr. 14, 2009.]

As used in this chapter the following words shall have the following meanings, unless the context clearly indicates otherwise:—

"Authorizing party", a parent, legal guardian or legal custodian who authorizes a caregiver to act under a caregiver authorization affidavit.

"Caregiver", an adult with whom a minor resides.

"Caregiver authorization affidavit", an affidavit prepared pursuant to this chapter that authorizes a designated caregiver to act relative to a minor's education and health care.

"Parental rights and responsibilities", rights and responsibilities of a parent, legal guardian or legal custodian under state or federal law or court order.

§ 2. Caregiver authorization to exercise parental rights and responsibilities; education and health care

[Added by 2008 Mass. Acts c. 511, effective Apr. 14, 2009.]

A parent, legal guardian or legal custodian of a minor, by a caregiver authorization affidavit, may authorize a designated caregiver to exercise certain concurrent parental rights and responsibilities relative to a designated minor's education and health care, as described in section 3. If a conflicting decision is made under these concurrent rights and responsibilities, the decision of the authorizing party shall supersede the decision of the caregiver.

The caregiver authorization affidavit shall only authorize those rights and responsibilities that the authorizing party possesses and shall not divest the authorizing party of his rights or responsibilities.

The authorizing party shall not use a caregiver authorization affidavit to circumvent any state or federal law, solely for the purposes of attendance at a particular school, or to re-confer rights to a caregiver from whom those rights have been removed by a court of law.

§ 3. Caregiver rights and responsibilities

[Added by 2008 Mass. Acts c. 511, § 1, effective Apr. 14, 2009.]

Under a caregiver authorization affidavit, a caregiver may:

(1) consent to medical, surgical, dental, developmental, mental health or other treatment for the minor under the supervision or upon the advice of a health care professional licensed to practice in the commonwealth;

(2) exercise parental rights to obtain records and other information with regard to health care services and insurance provided to the minor; and

(3) make educational decisions on behalf of the minor and in all other ways stand in for the authorizing party with respect to federal, state and district educational policy, including, but not limited to, accessing the minor's educational records, representing the minor in enrollment, disciplinary, curricular, special education or other educational matters, signing permission slips for school activities and any other decision that facilitates the minor's educational experience.

§ 4. Reliance on caregiver authorization and affidavit

[Added by 2008 Mass. Acts c. 511, effective Apr. 14, 2009.]

A person who relies on a caregiver authorization affidavit that is consistent with the requirements of this chapter has no obligation to make any further inquiry or investigation and shall not incur any criminal or civil liability or be subject to professional discipline for doing so, unless he knows facts contrary to the affidavit or knows that an authorizing party has made a decision to supersede the caregiver's decision. Nothing in this chapter shall relieve a person from liability arising from other provisions of the law.

§ 5. Contents of affidavit

[Added by 2008 Mass. Acts c. 511, effective Apr. 14, 2009.]

The caregiver authorization affidavit shall include the following information:—

(1) the name, address and telephone number of the parent, legal guardian or legal custodian;

(2) the name, address and telephone number of the caregiver;

(3) the name and date of birth of the minor;

(4) the relationship of the caregiver to the minor;

(5) a statement by the authorizing party that there are no court orders in effect that would prohibit him from exercising or conferring the rights and responsibilities that he seeks to confer upon the caregiver;

(6) a statement of the authority being conferred and of any prohibitions; and

(7) a statement that the affidavit is not for the purposes of circumventing any state or federal law, for the purposes of attendance at a particular school, or to re-confer rights to a caregiver from whom those rights have been removed by a court of law.

The affidavit shall be signed under the pains and penalties of perjury by the authorizing party in the presence of 2 adult witnesses, neither of whom may be the caregiver and the affidavit shall be notarized. The affidavit also shall be signed by the caregiver, who shall attest to being an adult with whom the minor resides.

The caregiver authorization affidavit may be valid for up to 2 years and may be reauthorized. The authorizing party may reauthorize, amend or revoke the caregiver authorization affidavit by notifying the caregiver in writing. The authorizing party shall provide the amended affidavit or revocation to all parties to whom he has provided the original affidavit. The caregiver shall provide the amended affidavit or revocation to all parties to whom he has provided the original affidavit prior to further exercising any rights or responsibilities under the affidavit.

§ 6. Form of affidavit

[Added by 2008 Mass. Acts c. 511, effective Apr. 14, 2009.]

The caregiver authorization affidavit shall be substantially in the following form, except that the use of alternative language consistent with the statute shall not be precluded:

Caregiver Education and Health Care Authorization Affidavit

I. What this form enables: A parent, legal guardian or legal custodian of a minor, by this affidavit, may authorize a designated caregiver, who is an adult with whom the minor child resides, to exercise certain concurrent parental rights and responsibilities relative to a designated minor's education and health care. If a conflicting decision is made under these concurrent rights and responsibilities, the decision of the authorizing party shall supersede the decision of the caregiver.

The caregiver authorization affidavit shall only authorize those rights and responsibilities that the authorizing party possesses and shall not divest the authorizing party of his rights or responsibilities.

Under a caregiver authorization affidavit, a caregiver may:

(1) consent to medical, surgical, dental, developmental, mental health or other treatment for the minor under the supervision or upon the advice of a health care professional licensed to practice in the commonwealth;

(2) exercise parental rights to obtain records and other information with regard to health care services and insurance provided to the minor; and

(3) make educational decisions on behalf of the minor and in all other ways stand in for the authorizing party with respect to federal, state and district educational policy, including, but not limited to, accessing the minor's educational records, representing the minor in enrollment, disciplinary, curricular, special education or other educational matters, signing permission slips for school activities and any other decision that facilitates the minor's educational experience.

II. Steps to authorize caregiver rights and responsibilities:

1. AUTHORIZING PARTY

I, [name of authorizing party], residing at [address of authorizing party] am the parent/legal guardian/legal custodian of the minor child(ren) listed below.

I, [name of parent or legal guardian or legal custodian], do hereby authorize [name of caregiver], residing at [address of caregiver], to exercise concurrently the rights and responsibilities, except those prohibited below, that I possess relative to the education and health care of the minor child(ren) listed:

Minor Child's Name	Date of Birth
____________________	____________________
____________________	____________________
____________________	____________________

The caregiver may NOT:

(Please list specifically any education or health care rights and responsibilities that you do NOT wish to confer upon the caregiver.)

There are no court orders in effect that would prohibit me from exercising or conferring the rights and responsibilities that I wish to confer upon the caregiver. *(If you are the legal guardian or custodian, attach the court order.)*

I am not using this affidavit to circumvent any state or federal law, for the purposes of attendance at a particular school, or to re-confer rights to a caregiver from whom those rights have been removed by a court of law.

I confer these rights and responsibilities freely and knowingly in order to provide for the child(ren) and not as a result of pressure, threats or payments by any person or agency.

I understand that, if the affidavit is amended or revoked, I must provide the amended affidavit or revocation to all parties to whom I have provided this affidavit.

This document shall remain in effect until [enter date up to 2 years hence] or until I notify the caregiver in writing that I have amended or revoked it.

I hereby affirm that the above statements are true, under pains and penalties of perjury.

Signature:

Printed name:

Telephone number:

2. WITNESSES TO AUTHORIZING PARTY SIGNATURE

(To be signed by persons over the age of 18 who are not the designated caregiver.)

Witness No. 1 signature:

Witness No. 1 printed name and address:

Witness No. 2 signature:

Witness No. 2 printed name and address:

3. NOTARIZATION OF AUTHORIZING PARTY SIGNATURE

On this [date] before me, the undersigned notary public, personally appeared [name of authorizing party], proved to me through satisfactory evidence of identification, which was [driver's license, etc.], to be the person whose name is signed on the preceding document, and swore under the pains and penalties of perjury that the foregoing statements are true.

Signature and seal of notary:

Printed name of notary:

My commission expires:

4. CAREGIVER ACKNOWLEDGEMENT

I, [name of caregiver], am at least 18 years of age and the child(ren) currently reside with me at [address of caregiver]. I am [relationship to the minor].

I understand that I may, without obtaining further consent from a parent, legal custodian or legal guardian of the child(ren), exercise concurrent rights and responsibilities relative to the education and health care of the child(ren), except those rights and responsibilities prohibited above. However, I may not knowingly make a decision that conflicts with the decision of the child(ren)'s parent, legal guardian or legal custodian.

I understand that, if the affidavit is amended or revoked, I must provide the amended affidavit or revocation to all parties to whom I have provided this affidavit prior to further exercising any rights or responsibilities under the affidavit.

I hereby affirm that the above statements are true, under pains and penalties of perjury.

Signature of caregiver:

Printed name:

Telephone Number:

III. Explanations: This caregiver authorization affidavit is pursuant to chapter 201F of the General Laws. A dispute arising hereunder shall be the exclusive jurisdiction of the probate courts pursuant to section 3 of chapter 215 of the General Laws.

A person who relies on a caregiver authorization affidavit that is consistent with the requirements of said chapter 201F has no obligation to make any further inquiry or investigation and shall not incur any criminal or civil liability or be subject to professional discipline for doing so, unless he knows facts contrary to the affidavit or knows that an authorizing party has made a decision to supersede the caregiver's decision. The reliance on the affidavit shall not relieve a person from liability arising from other provisions of the law.

Chapter 209A. Abuse Prevention

Section

§ 1. Definitions

As used in this chapter the following words shall have the following meanings:

"Abuse", the occurrence of one or more of the following acts between family or household members:

(a) attempting to cause or causing physical harm;

(b) placing another in fear of imminent serious physical harm;

(c) causing another to engage involuntarily in sexual relations by force, threat or duress.

"Court", the superior, probate and family, district or Boston municipal court departments of the trial court, except when the petitioner is in a dating relationship when "Court" shall mean district, probate, or Boston municipal courts.

"Family or household members", persons who:

(a) are or were married to one another;

(b) are or were residing together in the same household;

(c) are or were related by blood or marriage;

(d) having a child in common regardless of whether they have ever married or lived together; or

(e) are or have been in a substantive dating or engagement relationship, which shall be adjudged by district, probate or Boston municipal courts consideration of the following factors:

(1) the length of time of the relationship; (2) the type of relationship; (3) the frequency of interaction between the parties; and (4) if the relationship has been terminated by either person, the length of time elapsed since the termination of the relationship.

"Law officer", any officer authorized to serve criminal process.

"Vacate order", court order to leave and remain away from a premises and surrendering forthwith any keys to said premises to the plaintiff. The defendant shall not damage any of the plaintiff's belongings or those of any other occupant and shall not shut off or cause to be shut off any utilities or mail delivery to the plaintiff. In the case where the premises designated in the vacate order is a residence, so long as the plaintiff is living at said residence, the defendant shall not interfere in any way with the plaintiff's right to possess such residence, except by order or judgment of a court of competent jurisdiction pursuant to appropriate civil eviction proceedings, a petition to partition real estate, or a proceeding to divide marital property. A vacate order may include in its scope a household, a multiple family dwelling and the plaintiff's workplace. When issuing an order to vacate the plaintiff's workplace, the presiding justice must consider whether the plaintiff and defendant work in the same location or for the same employer.

"Protection order issued by another jurisdiction", any injunction or other order issued by a court of another state, territory or possession of the United States, the Commonwealth of Puerto Rico, or the District of Columbia, or tribal court that is issued for the purpose of preventing violent or threatening acts or harassment against, or contact or communication with or physical proximity to another person, including temporary and final orders issued by civil and criminal courts filed by or on behalf of a person seeking protection.

§ 2. Abuse prevention proceedings; venue

Proceedings under this chapter shall be filed, heard and determined in the superior court department or the Boston municipal court department or respective divisions of the probate and family or district court departments having venue over the plaintiff's residence. If the plaintiff has left a residence or household to avoid abuse, such plaintiff shall have the option of commencing an action in the court having venue over such prior residence or household, or in the court having venue over the present residence or household.

§ 3. Remedies; period of relief

[Amended by 2000 Mass. Acts c. 236, §§ 22–23; 2002 Mass. Acts c. 184, § 113; 2014 Mass. Acts c. 260, §§ 12–13, effective Aug. 8, 2014.]

A person suffering from abuse from an adult or minor family or household member may file a complaint in the court requesting protection from such abuse, including, but not limited to, the following orders:

(a) ordering the defendant to refrain from abusing the plaintiff, whether the defendant is an adult or minor;

(b) ordering the defendant to refrain from contacting the plaintiff, unless authorized by the court, whether the defendant is an adult or minor;

(c) ordering the defendant to vacate forthwith and remain away from the household, multiple family dwelling, and workplace. Notwithstanding the provisions of section thirty-four B of chapter two hundred and eight, an order to vacate shall be for a fixed period of time, not to exceed one year, at the expiration of which time the court may extend any such order upon motion of the plaintiff, with notice to the defendant, for such additional time as it deems necessary to protect the plaintiff from abuse;

(d) awarding the plaintiff temporary custody of a minor child; provided, however, that in any case brought in the probate and family court a finding by such court by a preponderance of the evidence that a pattern or serious incident of abuse, as defined in section 31A of chapter 208, toward a parent or child has occurred shall create a rebuttable presumption that it is not in the best interests of the child to be placed in sole custody, shared legal custody or shared physical custody with the abusive parent. Such presumption may be rebutted by a preponderance of the evidence that such custody award is in the best interests of the child. For the purposes of this section, an "abusive parent" shall mean a parent who has committed a pattern of abuse or a serious incident of abuse.

For the purposes of this section, the issuance of an order or orders under chapter 209A shall not in and of itself constitute a pattern or serious incident of abuse; nor shall an order or orders entered ex parte under said chapter 209A be admissible to show whether a pattern or serious incident of abuse has in fact occurred; provided, however, that an order or orders entered ex parte under said chapter 209A may be admissible for other purposes as the court may determine, other than showing whether a pattern or serious incident of abuse has in fact occurred; provided further, that the underlying facts upon which an order or orders under said chapter 209A was based may also form the basis for a finding by the probate and family court that a pattern or serious incident of abuse has occurred.

1

If the court finds that a pattern or serious incident of abuse has occurred and issues a temporary or permanent custody order, the court shall within 90 days enter written findings of fact as to the effects of the abuse on the child, which findings demonstrate that such order is in the furtherance of the child's best interests and provides for the safety and well-being of the child.

If ordering visitation to the abusive parent, the court shall provide for the safety and well-being of the child and the safety of the abused parent. The court may consider:

(a) ordering an exchange of the child to occur in a protected setting or in the presence of an appropriate third party;

(b) ordering visitation supervised by an appropriate third party, visitation center or agency;

(c) ordering the abusive parent to attend and complete, to the satisfaction of the court, a certified batterer's treatment program as a condition of visitation;

(d) ordering the abusive parent to abstain from possession or consumption of alcohol or controlled substances during the visitation and for 24 hours preceding visitation;

(e) ordering the abusive parent to pay the costs of supervised visitation;

(f) prohibiting overnight visitation;

(g) requiring a bond from the abusive parent for the return and safety of the child;

(h) ordering an investigation or appointment of a guardian ad litem or attorney for the child; and

(i) imposing any other condition that is deemed necessary to provide for the safety and well-being of the child and the safety of the abused parent.

Nothing in this section shall be construed to affect the right of the parties to a hearing under the rules of domestic relations procedure or to affect the discretion of the probate and family court in the conduct of such hearing;

(e) ordering the defendant to pay temporary support for the plaintiff or any child in the plaintiff's custody or both, when the defendant has a legal obligation to support such a person. In determining the amount to be paid, the court shall apply the standards established in the child support guidelines. Each judgment or order of support which is issued, reviewed or modified pursuant to this chapter shall conform to and shall be enforced in accordance with the provisions of section 12 of chapter 119A;

(f) ordering the defendant to pay the person abused monetary compensation for the losses suffered as a direct result of such abuse. Compensatory losses shall include, but not be limited to, loss of earnings or support, costs for restoring utilities, out-of-pocket losses for injuries sustained, replacement costs for locks or personal property removed or destroyed, medical and moving expenses and reasonable attorney's fees;

(g) ordering information in the case record to be impounded in accordance with court rule;

(h) ordering the defendant to refrain from abusing or contacting the plaintiff's child, or child in plaintiff's care or custody, unless authorized by the court;

(i) the judge may recommend to the defendant that the defendant attend a batterer's intervention program that is certified by the department of public health.

No filing fee shall be charged for the filing of the complaint. Neither the plaintiff nor the plaintiff's attorney shall be charged for certified copies of any orders entered by the court, or any copies of the file reasonably required for future court action or as a result of the loss or destruction of plaintiff's copies.

Any relief granted by the court shall be for a fixed period of time not to exceed one year. Every order shall on its face state the time and date the order is to expire and shall include the date and time that the matter will again be heard. If the plaintiff appears at the court at the date and time the order is to expire, the court shall determine whether or not to extend the order for any additional time reasonably necessary to protect the plaintiff or to enter a permanent order. When the expiration date stated on the order is on a weekend day or holiday, or a date when the court is closed to business, the order shall not expire until the next date that the court is open to business. The plaintiff may appear on such next court business day at the time designated by the order to request that the order be extended. The court may also extend the order upon motion of the plaintiff, for such additional time as it deems necessary to protect from abuse the plaintiff or any child in the plaintiff's care or custody. The fact that abuse has not occurred during the pendency of an order shall not, in itself, constitute sufficient ground for denying or failing to extend the order, of allowing an order to expire or be vacated, or for refusing to issue a new order.

The court may modify its order at any subsequent time upon motion by either party. When the plaintiff's address is inaccessible to the defendant as provided in section 8 of this chapter and the defendant has filed a motion to modify the court's order, the court shall be responsible for notifying the plaintiff. In no event shall the court disclose any such inaccessible address.

No order under this chapter shall in any manner affect title to real property.

No court shall compel parties to mediate any aspect of their case. Although the court may refer the case to the family service office of the probation department or victim/witness advocates for information gathering purposes, the court shall not compel the parties to meet together in such information gathering sessions.

A court shall not deny any complaint filed under this chapter solely because it was not filed within a particular time period after the last alleged incident of abuse.

A court may issue a mutual restraining order or mutual no-contact order pursuant to any abuse prevention action only if the court has made specific written findings of fact. The court shall then provide a detailed order, sufficiently specific to apprise any law officer as to which party has violated the order, if the parties are in or appear to be in violation of the order.

Any action commenced under the provisions of this chapter shall not preclude any other civil or criminal remedies. A party filing a complaint under this chapter shall be required to disclose any prior or pending actions involving the parties for divorce, annulment, paternity, custody or support, guardianship, separate support or legal separation, or abuse prevention.

If there is a prior or pending custody support order from the probate and family court department of the trial court, an order issued in the superior, district or Boston municipal court departments of the trial court pursuant to this chapter may include any relief available pursuant to this chapter including orders for custody or support; provided, however, that upon issuing an order for custody or support, the superior, district or Boston municipal court shall provide a copy of the order to the probate and family court department of the trial court that issued the prior or pending custody or support order immediately; provided further, that such order for custody or support shall be for a fixed period of time, not to exceed 30 days; and provided further, that such order may be superseded by a subsequent custody or support order issued by the probate and family court department, which shall retain final jurisdiction over any custody or support order. This section shall not be interpreted to mean that superior, district or Boston municipal court judges are prohibited or discouraged from ordering all other necessary relief or issuing the custody and support provisions of orders pursuant to this chapter for the full duration permitted under subsection (c).

If the parties to a proceeding under this chapter are parties in a subsequent proceeding in the probate and family court department for divorce, annulment, paternity, custody or support, guardianship or separate support, any custody or support order or judgment issued in the subsequent proceeding shall supersede any prior custody or support order under this chapter.

§ 3A. Nature of proceedings and availability of other criminal proceedings; information required to be given to complainant upon filing

Upon the filing of a complaint under this chapter, a complainant shall be informed that the proceedings hereunder are civil in nature and that violations of orders issued hereunder are criminal in nature. Further, a complainant shall be given information prepared by the appropriate district attorney's office that other criminal proceedings may be available and such complainant shall be instructed by such district attorney's office relative to the procedures required to initiate criminal proceedings including, but not limited to, a complaint for a violation of section forty-three of chapter two hundred and sixty-five. Whenever possible, a complainant shall be provided with such information in the complainant's native language.

§ 3B. Order for suspension and surrender of firearms license; surrender of firearms; petition for review; hearing

Upon issuance of a temporary or emergency order under section four or five of this chapter, the court shall, if the plaintiff demonstrates a substantial likelihood of immediate danger of abuse, order the immediate suspension and surrender of any license to carry firearms and or firearms identification card which the defendant may hold and order the defendant to surrender all firearms, rifles, shotguns, machine guns and ammunition which he then controls, owns or possesses in accordance with the provisions of this chapter and any license to carry firearms or firearms identification cards which the defendant may hold shall be surrendered to the appropriate law enforcement officials in accordance with the provisions of this chapter and, said law enforcement official may store, transfer or otherwise dispose of any such weapon in accordance with the provisions of section 129D of chapter 140; provided however, that nothing herein shall authorize the transfer of any weapons surrendered by the defendant to anyone other than a licensed dealer. Notice of such suspension and ordered surrender shall be appended to the copy of abuse prevention order served on the defendant pursuant to section seven. Law enforcement officials, upon the service of said orders, shall immediately take possession of all firearms, rifles, shotguns, machine guns, ammunition, any license to carry firearms and any firearms identification cards in the control, ownership, or possession of said defendant. Any violation of such orders shall be punishable by a fine of not more than five thousand dollars, or by imprisonment for not more than two and one-half years in a house of correction, or by both such fine and imprisonment.

Any defendant aggrieved by an order of surrender or suspension as described in the first sentence of this section may petition the court which issued such suspension or surrender order for a review of such action and such petition shall be heard no later than ten court business days after the receipt of the notice of the petition by the court. If said license to carry firearms or firearms identification card has been suspended upon the issuance of an order issued pursuant to section four or five, said petition may be heard contemporaneously with the hearing specified in the second sentence of the second paragraph of section four. Upon the filing of an affidavit by the defendant that a firearm, rifle, shotgun, machine gun or ammunition is required in the performance of the defendant's employment, and upon a request for an expedited hearing, the court shall order said hearing within two business days of receipt of such affidavit and request but only on the issue of surrender and suspension pursuant to this section.

§ 3C. Continuation or modification of order for surrender or suspension

[Bracketed text stricken by 2014 Mass. Acts c. 284, § 71, effective Jan. 1, 2021.]

Upon the continuation or modification of an order issued pursuant to section 4 or upon petition for review as described in section 3B, the court shall also order or continue to order the immediate suspension and surrender of a defendants license to carry firearms[, including a Class A or Class B license,] and firearms identification card and the surrender of all firearms, rifles, shotguns, machine guns or ammunition which such defendant then controls, owns or possesses if the court makes a determination that the return of such license to carry firearms[, including a Class A or Class B license,] and firearm identification card or firearms, rifles, shotguns, machine guns or ammunition presents a likelihood of abuse to the plaintiff. A suspension and surrender order issued pursuant to this section shall continue so long as the restraining order to which it relates is in effect; and, any law enforcement official to whom such weapon is surrendered may store, transfer or otherwise dispose of any such weapon in accordance with the provisions of section 129D of chapter 140; provided, however, that nothing herein shall authorize the transfer of any weapons surrendered by the defendant to anyone other than a licensed dealer. Any violation of such order shall be punishable by a fine of not more than $5,000 or by imprisonment for not more than two and one-half years in a house of correction or by both such fine and imprisonment.

§ 3D. Transmission of report to department of criminal justice information services after issuance of order for suspension or surrender pursuant to Secs. 3B or 3C

[Added by 2014 Mass. Acts c. 284, § 72, effective Jan. 1, 2015.]

Upon an order for suspension or surrender issued pursuant to sections 3B or 3C, the court shall transmit a report containing the defendant's name and identifying information and a statement describing the defendant's alleged conduct and relationship to the plaintiff to the department of criminal justice information services. Upon the expiration, cancellation or revocation of the order, the court shall transmit a report containing the defendant's name and identifying information, a statement describing the defendant's alleged conduct and relationship to the plaintiff and an explanation that the order is no longer current or valid to the department of criminal justice information services who shall transmit the report, pursuant to paragraph (h) of section 167A of chapter 6, to the attorney general of the United States to be included in the National Instant Criminal Background Check System.

§ 4. Temporary orders; notice; hearing

Upon the filing of a complaint under this chapter, the court may enter such temporary orders as it deems necessary to protect a plaintiff from abuse, including relief as provided in section three. Such relief shall not be contingent upon the filing of a complaint for divorce, separate support, or paternity action.

If the plaintiff demonstrates a substantial likelihood of immediate danger of abuse, the court may enter such temporary relief orders without notice as it deems necessary to protect the plaintiff from abuse and shall immediately thereafter notify the defendant that the temporary orders have been issued. The court shall give the defendant an opportunity to be heard on the question of continuing the temporary order and of granting other relief as requested by the plaintiff no later than ten court business days after such orders are entered.

Notice shall be made by the appropriate law enforcement agency as provided in section seven.

If the defendant does not appear at such subsequent hearing, the temporary orders shall continue in effect without further order of the court.

§ 5. Granting of relief when court closed; relief granted by telephone; certification

[Amended by 2011 Mass. Acts c. 93, § 40, effective July 1, 2012.]

When the court is closed for business or the plaintiff is unable to appear in court because of severe hardship due to the plaintiff's physical condition, any justice of the superior, probate and family, district or Boston municipal court departments may grant relief to the plaintiff as provided under section four if the plaintiff demonstrates a substantial likelihood of immediate danger of abuse. In the discretion of the justice, such relief may be granted and communicated by telephone to an officer or employee of an appropriate law enforcement agency, who shall record such order on a form of order promulgated for such use by the chief justice of the trial court and shall deliver a copy of such order on the next court day to the clerk-magistrate of the court having venue and jurisdiction over the matter. If relief has been granted without the filing of a complaint pursuant to this section of this chapter, then the plaintiff shall appear in court on the next available business day to file said complaint. If the plaintiff in such a case is unable to appear in court without severe hardship due to the plaintiff's physical condition, then a representative may appear in court on the plaintiff's behalf and file the requisite complaint with an affidavit setting forth the circumstances preventing the plaintiff from appearing personally. Notice to the plaintiff and defendant and an opportunity for the defendant to be heard shall be given as provided in said section four.

Any order issued under this section and any documentation in support thereof shall be certified on the next court day by the clerk-magistrate or register of the court issuing such order to the court having venue and jurisdiction over the matter. Such certification to the court shall have the effect of commencing proceedings under this chapter and invoking the other provisions of this chapter but shall not be deemed necessary for an emergency order issued under this section to take effect.

§ 5A. Protection order issued by another jurisdiction; enforcement; filing; presumption of validity

Any protection order issued by another jurisdiction, as defined in section one, shall be given full faith and credit throughout the commonwealth and enforced as if it were issued in the commonwealth for as long as the order is in effect in the issuing jurisdiction.

A person entitled to protection under a protection order issued by another jurisdiction may file such order in the superior court department or the Boston municipal court department or any division of the probate and family or district court departments by filing with the court a certified copy of such order which shall be entered into the statewide domestic violence record keeping system established pursuant to the provisions of section seven of chapter one hundred and eighty-eight of the acts of nineteen hundred and ninety-two and maintained by the office of the commissioner of probation. Such person shall swear under oath in an affidavit, to the best of such person's knowledge, that such order is presently in effect as written. Upon request by a law enforcement agency, the register or clerk of such court shall provide a certified copy of the protection order issued by the other jurisdiction.

A law enforcement officer may presume the validity of, and enforce in accordance with section six, a copy of a protection order issued by another jurisdiction which has been provided to the law enforcement officer by any source; provided, however, that the officer is also provided with a statement by the person protected by the order that such order remains in effect. Law enforcement officers may rely on such statement by the person protected by such order.

§ 6. Powers of police; civil liability; victim's right to copy of incident report; notice of release of arrested persons; no-contact orders

[Amended by 2010 Mass. Acts c. 256, § 103, effective Nov. 4, 2010.]

Whenever any law officer has reason to believe that a family or household member has been abused or is in danger of being abused, such officer shall use all reasonable means to prevent further abuse. The officer shall take, but not be limited to the following action:

(1) remain on the scene of where said abuse occurred or was in danger of occurring as long as the officer has reason to believe that at least one of the parties involved would be in immediate physical danger without the presence of a law officer. This shall include, but not be limited to remaining in the dwelling for a reasonable period of time;

(2) assist the abused person in obtaining medical treatment necessitated by an assault, which may include driving the victim to the emergency room of the nearest hospital, or arranging for appropriate transportation to a health care facility, notwithstanding any law to the contrary;

(3) assist the abused person in locating and getting to a safe place; including but not limited to a designated meeting place for a shelter or a family member's or friend's residence. The officer shall consider the victim's preference in this regard and what is reasonable under all the circumstances;

(4) give such person immediate and adequate notice of his or her rights. Such notice shall consist of handing said person a copy of the statement which follows below and reading the same to said person. Where said person's native language is not English, the statement shall be then provided in said person's native language whenever possible.

"You have the right to appear at the Superior, Probate and Family, District or Boston Municipal Court, if you reside within the appropriate jurisdiction, and file a complaint requesting any of the following applicable orders: (a) an order restraining your attacker from abusing you; (b) an order directing your attacker to leave your household, building or workplace; (c) an order awarding you custody of a minor child; (d) an order directing your attacker to pay support for you or any minor child in your custody, if the attacker has a legal obligation of support; and (e) an order directing your attacker to pay you for losses suffered as a result of abuse, including medical and moving expenses, loss of earnings or support, costs for restoring utilities and replacing locks, reasonable attorney's fees and other out-of-pocket losses for injuries and property damage sustained.

For an emergency on weekends, holidays, or weeknights the police will refer you to a justice of the superior, probate and family, district, or Boston municipal court departments.

You have the right to go to the appropriate district court or the Boston municipal court and seek a criminal complaint for threats, assault and battery, assault with a deadly weapon, assault with intent to kill or other related offenses.

If you are in need of medical treatment, you have the right to request that an officer present drive you to the nearest hospital or otherwise assist you in obtaining medical treatment.

If you believe that police protection is needed for your physical safety, you have the right to request that the officer present remain at the scene until you and your children can leave or until your safety is otherwise ensured. You may also request that the officer assist you in locating and taking you to a safe place, including but not limited to a designated meeting place for a shelter or a family member's or a friend's residence, or a similar place of safety.

You may request a copy of the police incident report at no cost from the police department."

The officer shall leave a copy of the foregoing statement with such person before leaving the scene or premises.

(5) assist such person by activating the emergency judicial system when the court is closed for business;

(6) inform the victim that the abuser will be eligible for bail and may be promptly released; and

(7) arrest any person a law officer witnesses or has probable cause to believe has violated a temporary or permanent vacate, restraining, or no-contact order or judgment issued pursuant to section eighteen, thirty-four B or thirty-four C of chapter two hundred and eight, section thirty-two of chapter two hundred and nine, section three, three B, three C, four or five of this chapter, or sections fifteen or twenty of chapter two hundred and nine C or similar protection order issued by another jurisdiction. When there are no vacate, restraining, or no-contact orders or judgments in effect, arrest shall be the preferred response whenever an officer witnesses or has probable cause to believe that a person:

(a) has committed a felony;

(b) has committed a misdemeanor involving abuse as defined in section one of this chapter;

(c) has committed an assault and battery in violation of section thirteen A of chapter two hundred and sixty-five.

The safety of the victim and any involved children shall be paramount in any decision to arrest. Any officer arresting both parties must submit a detailed, written report in addition to an incident report, setting forth the grounds for dual arrest.

No law officer investigating an incident of domestic violence shall threaten, suggest, or otherwise indicate the arrest of all parties for the purpose of discouraging requests for law enforcement intervention by any party.

No law officer shall be held liable in any civil action regarding personal injury or injury to property brought by any party to a domestic violence incident for an arrest based on probable cause when such officer acted reasonably and in good faith and in compliance with this chapter and the statewide policy as established by the secretary of public safety.

Whenever any law officer investigates an incident of domestic violence, the officer shall immediately file a written incident report in accordance with the standards of the officer's law enforcement agency and, wherever possible, in the form of the National Incident-Based Reporting System, as defined by the Federal Bureau of Investigation. The latter information may be submitted voluntarily by the local police on a monthly basis to the crime reporting unit of the department of criminal justice information services.

The victim shall be provided a copy of the full incident report at no cost upon request to the appropriate law enforcement department.

When a judge or other person authorized to take bail bails any person arrested under the provisions of this chapter, he shall make reasonable efforts to inform the victim of such release prior to or at the time of said release.

When any person charged with or arrested for a crime involving abuse under this chapter is released from custody, the court or the emergency response judge shall issue, upon the request of the victim, a written no-contact order prohibiting the person charged or arrested from having any contact with the victim and shall use all reasonable means to notify the victim immediately of release from custody. The victim shall be given at no cost a certified copy of the no-contact order.

§ 7. Abuse prevention orders; domestic violence record search; service of order; enforcement; violations

[Amended by 2006 Mass. Acts c. 418, § 1, effective Apr. 3, 2007; 2014 Mass. Acts c. 260, §§ 14–15, effective Aug. 8, 2014.]

When considering a complaint filed under this chapter, a judge shall cause a search to be made of the records contained within the statewide domestic violence record keeping system maintained by the office of the commissioner of probation and shall review the resulting data to determine whether the named defendant has a civil or criminal record involving domestic or other violence. Upon receipt of information that an outstanding warrant exists against the named defendant, a judge shall order that the appropriate law enforcement officials be notified and shall order that any information regarding the defendant's most recent whereabouts shall be forwarded to such officials. In all instances where an outstanding warrant exists, a judge shall make a finding, based upon all of the circumstances, as to whether an imminent threat of bodily injury exists to the petitioner. In all instances where such an imminent threat of bodily injury is found to exist, the judge shall notify the appropriate law enforcement officials of such finding and such officials shall take all necessary actions to execute any such outstanding warrant as soon as is practicable.

Whenever the court orders under sections eighteen, thirty-four B, and thirty-four C of chapter two hundred and eight, section thirty-two of chapter two hundred and nine, sections three, four and five of this chapter, or sections fifteen and twenty of chapter two hundred and nine C, the defendant to vacate, refrain from abusing the plaintiff or to have no contact with the plaintiff or the plaintiff's minor child, the register or clerk-magistrate shall transmit two certified copies of each such order and one copy of the complaint and summons forthwith to the appropriate law enforcement agency which, unless otherwise ordered by the court, shall serve one copy of each order upon the defendant, together with a copy of the complaint, order and summons and notice of any suspension or surrender ordered pursuant to section three B of this chapter. Law enforcement agencies shall establish adequate procedures to ensure that, when effecting service upon a defendant pursuant to this paragraph, a law enforcement officer shall, to the extent practicable: (i) fully inform the defendant of the contents of the order and the available penalties for any violation of an order or terms thereof and (ii) provide the defendant with informational resources, including, but not limited to, a list of certified batterer intervention programs, substance abuse counseling, alcohol abuse counseling and financial counseling programs located within or near the court's jurisdiction. The law enforcement agency shall promptly make its return of service to the court.

Law enforcement officers shall use every reasonable means to enforce such abuse prevention orders. Law enforcement agencies shall establish procedures adequate to insure that an officer on the scene of an alleged violation of such order may be informed of the existence and terms of such order. The court shall notify the appropriate law enforcement agency in writing whenever any such order is vacated and shall direct the agency to destroy all record of such vacated order and such agency shall comply with that directive.

Each abuse prevention order issued shall contain the following statement: VIOLATION OF THIS ORDER IS A CRIMINAL OFFENSE.

Any violation of such order or a protection order issued by another jurisdiction shall be punishable by a fine of not more than five thousand dollars, or by imprisonment for not more than two and one-half years in a house of correction, or by both such fine and imprisonment. In addition to, but not in lieu of, the forgoing penalties and any other sentence, fee or assessment, including the victim witness assessment in section 8 of chapter 258B, the court shall order persons convicted of a crime under this statute to pay a fine of $25 that shall be transmitted to the treasurer for deposit into the General Fund. For any violation of such order, or as a condition of a continuance without a finding, the court shall order the defendant to complete a certified batterer's intervention program unless, upon good cause shown, the court issues specific written findings describing the reasons that batterer's intervention should not be ordered or unless the batterer's intervention program determines that the defendant is not suitable for intervention. The court shall not order substance abuse or anger management treatment or any other form of treatment as a substitute for certified batterer's intervention. If a defendant ordered to undergo treatment has received a suspended sentence, the original sentence shall be reimposed if the defendant fails to participate in said program as required by the terms of his probation. If the court determines that the violation was in retaliation for the defendant being reported by the plaintiff to the department of revenue for failure to pay child support payments or for the establishment of paternity, the defendant shall be punished by a fine of not less than one thousand dollars and not more than ten thousand dollars and by imprisonment for not less than sixty days; provided, however, that the sentence shall not be suspended, nor shall any such person be eligible for probation, parole, or furlough or receive any deduction from his sentence for good conduct until he shall have served sixty days of such sentence.

When a defendant has been ordered to participate in a treatment program pursuant to this section, the defendant shall be required to regularly attend a certified or provisionally certified batterer's treatment program. To the extent permitted by professional requirements of confidentiality, said program shall communicate with local battered women's programs for the purpose of protecting the victim's safety. Additionally, it shall specify the defendant's attendance requirements and keep the probation department informed of whether the defendant is in compliance.

In addition to, but not in lieu of, such orders for treatment, if the defendant has a substance abuse problem, the court may order appropriate treatment for such problem. All ordered treatment shall last until the end of the probationary period or until the treatment program decides to discharge the defendant, whichever comes first. When the defendant is not in compliance with the terms of probation, the court shall hold a revocation of probation hearing. To the extent possible, the defendant shall be responsible for paying all costs for court ordered treatment.

Where a defendant has been found in violation of an abuse prevention order under this chapter or a protection order issued by another jurisdiction, the court may, in addition to the penalties provided for in this section after conviction, as an alternative to incarceration and, as a condition of probation, prohibit contact with the victim through the establishment of court defined geographic exclusion zones including, but not limited to, the areas in and around the complainant's residence, place of employment, and the complainant's child's school, and order that the defendant to wear a global positioning satellite tracking device designed to transmit and record the defendant's location data. If the defendant enters a court defined exclusion zone, the defendant's location data shall be immediately transmitted to the complainant, and to the police, through an appropriate means including, but not limited to, the telephone, an electronic beeper or a paging device. The global positioning satellite device and its tracking shall be administered by the department of probation. If a court finds that the defendant has entered a geographic exclusion zone, it shall revoke his probation and the defendant shall be fined, imprisoned or both as provided in this section. Based on the defendant's ability to pay, the court may also order him to pay the monthly costs or portion thereof for monitoring through the global positioning satellite tracking system.

In each instance where there is a violation of an abuse prevention order or a protection order issued by another jurisdiction, the court may order the defendant to pay the plaintiff for all damages including, but not limited to, cost for shelter or emergency housing, loss of earnings or support, out-of-pocket losses for injuries sustained or property damaged, medical expenses, moving expenses, cost for obtaining an unlisted telephone number, and reasonable attorney's fees.

Any such violation may be enforced in the superior, the district or Boston municipal court departments. Criminal remedies provided herein are not exclusive and do not preclude any other available civil or criminal remedies. The superior, probate and family, district and Boston municipal court departments may each enforce by civil contempt procedure a violation of its own court order.

The provisions of section eight of chapter one hundred and thirty-six shall not apply to any order, complaint or summons issued pursuant to this section.

§ 8. Confidentiality of records

[Amended by 2000 Mass. Acts c. 236, § 24.]

The records of cases arising out of an action brought under the provisions of this chapter where the plaintiff or defendant is a minor shall be withheld from public inspection except by order of the court; provided, that such records shall be open, at all reasonable times, to the inspection of the minor, said minor's parent, guardian, attorney, and to the plaintiff and the plaintiff's attorney, or any of them.

The plaintiff's residential address, residential telephone number and workplace name, address and telephone number, contained within the court records of cases arising out of an action brought by a plaintiff under the provisions of this chapter, shall be confidential and withheld from public inspection, except by order of the court, except that the plaintiff's residential address and workplace address shall appear on the court order and accessible to the defendant and the defendant's attorney unless the plaintiff specifically requests that this information be withheld from the order. All confidential portions of the records shall be accessible at all reasonable times to the plaintiff and plaintiff's attorney, to others specifically authorized by the plaintiff to obtain such information, and to prosecutors, victim-witness advocates as defined in section 1 of chapter 258B, domestic violence victim's counselors as defined in section 20K of chapter 233, sexual assault counselors as defined in section 20J of chapter 233, and law enforcement officers, if such access is necessary in the performance of their duties. The provisions of this paragraph shall apply to any protection order issued by another jurisdiction, as defined in section 1, that is filed with a court of the commonwealth pursuant to section 5A. Such confidential portions of the court records shall not be deemed to be public records under the provisions of clause twenty-sixth of section 7 of chapter 4.

§ 9. Form of complaint; promulgation

The administrative justices of the superior court, probate and family court, district court, and the Boston municipal court departments shall jointly promulgate a form of complaint for use under this chapter which shall be in such form and language to permit a plaintiff to prepare and file such complaint pro se.

§ 10. Assessments against persons referred to certified batterers' treatment program as condition of probation

[Amended by 2018 Mass. Acts c. 69, § 105, effective Apr. 13, 2018.]

The court shall impose an assessment of three hundred and fifty dollars against any person who has been referred to a certified batterers' treatment program as a condition of probation. Said assessment shall be in addition to the cost of the treatment program. In the discretion of the court, said assessment may be reduced or waived when the court finds that the person is indigent or that payment of the assessment would cause substantial financial hardship to the person or the person's immediate family or the person's dependents. Assessments made pursuant to this section shall be in addition to any other fines, assessments, or restitution imposed in any disposition. All funds collected by the court pursuant to this section shall be transmitted monthly to the state treasurer, who shall deposit said funds in the General Fund.

§ 11. Possession, care and control of domesticated animal owned by persons involved in certain protective orders; notice to law enforcement upon finding of imminent threat to household member or animal

[Added by 2012 Mass. Acts c. 193, § 50, effective Oct. 31, 2012.]

(a) Whenever the court issues a temporary or permanent vacate, stay away, restraining or no contact order or a judgment under section 18, 34B or 34C of chapter 208, or under section 32 of chapter 209, or under section 3, 4 or 5 of this chapter, or under section 15 or 20 of chapter 209C, or under section 3 to 7, inclusive, of chapter 258E or a temporary restraining order or preliminary or permanent injunction relative to a domestic relations, child custody, domestic abuse or abuse prevention proceeding, the court may order the possession, care and control of any domesticated animal owned, possessed, leased, kept or held by either party or a minor child residing in the household to the plaintiff or petitioner. The court may order the defendant to refrain from abusing, threatening, taking, interfering with, transferring, encumbering, concealing, harming or otherwise disposing of such animal.

(b) A party to any proceeding listed in subsection (a) may petition the court for an order authorized by said subsection (a).

(c) Whenever the court issues a warrant for a violation of a temporary or permanent vacate, stay away, restraining or no contact order or a judgment issued under section 18, 34B or 34C of chapter 208, or under section 32 of chapter 209, or under section 3, 4 or 5 of this chapter, or under section 15 or 20 of chapter 209C, or section 3 to 7, inclusive, of chapter 258E or otherwise becomes aware that an outstanding warrant for such a violation has been issued against a person before the court, the judge may make a finding, based upon the totality of the circumstances, as to whether there exists an imminent threat of bodily injury to any party to such judgment or the petitioner of any such protective order, a member of the petitioner's family or household or to a domesticated animal belonging to the petitioner or to a member of the petitioner's family or household. If the court makes a finding that such an imminent threat of bodily injury to a person or domesticated animal exists, the court shall notify the appropriate law enforcement officials of such finding and the law enforcement officials shall take all necessary actions to execute any such outstanding warrant as soon as is practicable.

Chapter 209B. Massachusetts Child Custody Jurisdiction Act

§ 1. Definitions

As used in this chapter the following words, unless the context requires otherwise, shall have the following meanings:—

"Contestant", a person who claims a legal right to custody or visitation with respect to a child;

"Custody determination", any court order, instruction or judgment, whether temporary or final, providing for the custody of or visitation rights with a child; it shall not be deemed to include any order or judgment concerning other child-related matters except to the extent such order of judgment contains a custody determination as above-stated;

"Custody proceeding", includes proceedings in which a custody determination is one of several issues presented for resolution, such as an action for divorce or separation, guardianship, and care and protection;

"Judgment" or "Custody judgment", a custody determination made in a custody proceeding, and includes an initial judgment and a modification judgment;

"Home state", the state in which the child immediately preceding the date of commencement of the custody proceeding resided with his parents, a parent, or a person acting as parent, for at least 6 consecutive months, and in the case of a child less than 6 months old the state in which the child lived from birth with any of the persons mentioned. Periods of temporary absence of any of the named persons are counted as part of the 6-month or other period;

"Initial judgment", the first custody determination concerning a particular child;

"Modification judgment", a custody determination which modifies or replaces a prior custody determination, whether made by the court which rendered the prior determination or by another court;

"Physical custody", actual possession and control of a child;

"Person acting as parent", a person other than a parent who has physical custody of a child and who has either been awarded custody of a child or claims a legal right to custody and includes an authorized social service agency exercising legal or physical custody of a child; and

"Parent", a biological, foster, or adoptive parent whose parental rights have not previously been terminated;

"State", any state, territory, or possession of the United States, the Commonwealth of Puerto Rico, and the District of Columbia.

§ 2. Child custody jurisdiction

(a) Any court which is competent to decide child custody matters has jurisdiction to make a custody determination by initial or modification judgment if:

(1) the commonwealth (i) is the home state of the child on the commencement of the custody proceeding, or (ii) had been the child's home state within six months before the date of the commencement of the proceeding and the child is absent from the commonwealth because of his or her removal or retention by a person claiming his or her custody or for other reasons, and a parent or person acting as parent continues to reside in the commonwealth; or

(2) it appears that no other state would have jurisdiction under paragraph (1) and it is in the best interest of the child that a court of the commonwealth assume jurisdiction because (i) the child and his or her parents, or the child and at least one contestant, have a significant connection with the commonwealth, and (ii) there is available in the commonwealth substantial evidence concerning the child's present or future care, protection, training, and personal relationships; or

(3) the child is physically present in the commonwealth and (i) the child has been abandoned or (ii) it is necessary in an emergency to protect the child from abuse or neglect or for other good cause shown, provided that in the event that jurisdictional prerequisites are not established pursuant to any other paragraph of this subsection and a court of another state shall be entitled to assert jurisdiction under any other subparagraph of this paragraph then a court exercising jurisdiction pursuant to this clause of paragraph (3) may do so only by entering such temporary order or orders as it deems necessary unless the court of the other state has declined to exercise jurisdiction, has stayed its proceedings or has otherwise deferred to the jurisdiction of a court of the commonwealth; or

(4) (i) it appears that no other state would have jurisdiction under prerequisites substantially in accordance with paragraph (1), (2) or (3), or another state has declined to exercise jurisdiction on the ground that the commonwealth is the more appropriate forum

1

to determine the custody of the child, and (ii) it is in the best interest of the child that a court of the commonwealth assume jurisdiction.

(b) Except under subparagraphs (3) and (4) of paragraph (a), physical presence in the commonwealth of the child or of the child and one of the contestants, is not alone sufficient to confer jurisdiction on a court of the commonwealth to make a custody determination.

(c) Physical presence of the child, while desirable, is not a prerequisite for jurisdiction to make a custody determination.

(d) A court of the commonwealth shall not exercise jurisdiction in any custody proceeding commenced during the pendency of a proceeding in a court of another state where such court of that state is exercising jurisdiction consistently with the provisions of this section for the purpose of making a custody determination, except in accordance with paragraph (3) of subsection (a), unless the court of the other state shall decline jurisdiction pursuant to paragraph (4) of subsection (a) or shall stay its proceedings or otherwise defer to the jurisdiction of a court of the commonwealth.

(e) If a court of another state has made a custody determination in substantial conformity with this chapter, a court of the commonwealth shall not modify that determination unless (1) it appears to the court of the commonwealth that the court which made the custody determination does not now have jurisdiction under jurisdictional prerequisites substantially in accordance with this chapter or that such court has declined to assume jurisdiction to modify its determination and (2) a court of the commonwealth now has jurisdiction pursuant to this chapter.

§ 3. Affidavits; contents; amendment; examination under oath; disclosure of addresses

(a) Every party in any custody proceeding shall state in an affidavit which shall be filed together with his first pleading the following information:

(1) the child's present address of residence;

(2) each address at which the child has resided during the two years immediately prior to the filing of the instant custody proceeding;

(3) the names and, if known, the current residential addresses or, if unknown, the last and usual residential addresses, of all persons who have been parties to any custody proceedings involving the child during the said two-year period, other than any person whose rights have been terminated in any parental rights termination proceeding, and any other persons who, according to the knowledge and belief of the affiant, claim a legal right to the custody or physical possession of the child; and

(4) whether or not the party knows of or has participated in any prior custody proceeding involving the child in the commonwealth or in any other jurisdiction and the nature of his participation, as party, witness, or in any other capacity, in such prior proceeding.

(b) Unless the same have already been filed by another party, every party in any custody proceeding shall attach to the affidavit a certified copy of each pleading and of any determination entered in any custody proceeding he knows of or has participated in involving the child in the commonwealth or in any other jurisdiction.

(c) The court may examine any one or more of the parties under oath concerning the information required to be furnished under this section and concerning other matters pertinent to any jurisdictional or other issues before the court.

(d) Each party shall amend the affidavit at any time after filing to inform the court of any custody proceeding filed in any jurisdiction after the date of filing of the instant custody proceeding of which the affiant becomes aware after filing the affidavit and shall further amend the affidavit to include the names and addresses, in conformity with paragraph (3) of subsection (a), of any person of whom the affiant becomes aware after filing the affidavit who claims a legal right to the custody or physical possession of the child.

(e) Notwithstanding the provisions of this section, a court may waive disclosure of the present or prior address of the child or of a contestant when such waiver is necessary to protect the child or the contestant from physical or emotional abuse. Application for an order waiving disclosure under this paragraph shall be made upon such notice as the court shall prescribe. The court shall waive disclosure whenever the present or prior address of the child or of a contestant is a shelter for battered persons and their dependent children. The reasons for waiver of any disclosure requirement of this section shall be stated by the court in the record of the custody proceeding.

(f) The court may impose sanctions against any party who fails to act in conformity with this section without leave of court granted for good cause shown.

§ 4. Parties; joinder; service of process

(a) After examination of the pleadings, affidavits, certified copies of the documentation relative to other custody proceedings and such oral testimony as it may require, the court shall determine the proper parties to the custody proceeding.

(b) During the pendency of the proceeding, the court may require the joinder of additional parties and in that event, the court shall specify that such additional parties be served with process in accordance with section five or six, as applicable, or that they be otherwise notified in such manner as the court shall determine.

§ 5. Notice and opportunity to be heard; proper parties

(a) Reasonable notice in conformity with section six and an opportunity to be heard shall be given to the contestants, to any parent whose parental rights have not been previously terminated, to any person acting as parent, and to any other persons designated proper parties by the court pursuant to section four, provided that in the event a court of the commonwealth assumes jurisdiction pursuant to clause (ii) of paragraph (3) of subsection (a) of section two, then the court may waive such notice requirement for such period as may be allowed under applicable court rules.

(b) Any notice shall include the nature of the action, copies of all pleadings filed with the court, and the statement that any person so notified may apply to the court concerning allocation of the costs of those reasonable and necessary expenses to be incurred in connection with the custody proceeding in accordance with applicable sections of this chapter.

§ 6. Notice; nonresidents; proof of service

(a) Notice to a person in the commonwealth shall be given in accordance with the applicable Massachusetts rules of court or in such other manner as is prescribed by law.

(b) Notice required for the exercise of jurisdiction over a person outside the commonwealth shall be given in accordance with the applicable Massachusetts Rules of Court or statute or, in the discretion of the court, in the manner prescribed by the law of the place in which the service is made concerning service of process in an action of its court of general jurisdiction, provided, however, that in no event shall notice under this paragraph be served, mailed, delivered or last published less than twenty days before any custody determination is made in this state, other than a determination made pursuant to clause (ii) of paragraph (3) of subsection (a) of section two.

(c) Proof of service outside the commonwealth may be made by affidavit of the individual who made the service, in accordance with the applicable law or the Massachusetts rules of court, in accordance with the order pursuant to which the service is made, or, in the discretion of the court, otherwise in accordance with the law of the place in which the service is made.

(d) Notice is not required to be given to a contestant who submits to the jurisdiction of the court.

§ 7. Jurisdiction; determination of appropriate forum; factors

(a) A court which has jurisdiction pursuant to section two may decline to exercise its jurisdiction at any time prior to making a custody determination upon finding that its assumption of jurisdiction would be (i) violative of the purposes of this chapter; or (ii) would be based upon the illegal or otherwise wrongful conduct of a party; or (iii) would constitute an inconvenient forum and that a court of another state would constitute a more convenient forum.

(b) A court may decline jurisdiction for any of the reasons set forth in paragraph (a) upon motion of a party or of any representative of the child entitled to appear before the court or upon the court's own motion.

(c) In order to determine whether it is the appropriate forum, a court of the commonwealth may, in its discretion, at any time during the pendency of the custody proceeding, communicate and exchange information with a court or courts of any other relevant jurisdiction.

(d) For the purposes of this section, a court may consider the following factors:

(1) whether another state is or recently was the child's home state;

(2) whether another state has a closer connection with the child and his family or with the child and one or more of the contestants;

(3) whether more substantial evidence concerning the child's present or future care, protection, training, and personal relationships is available or whether such evidence is more readily available in another state;

(4) whether the parties have agreed on another forum which is not less appropriate; and

(5) whether the exercise of jurisdiction by a court of the commonwealth would contravene any of the purposes of this chapter.

(e) If a court shall find that a court of another jurisdiction is or may be a more appropriate forum under the terms of this chapter for the adjudication of the custody proceeding, it may do one or more of the following:

(1) dismiss the proceeding with or without prejudice;

(2) vacate any order or judgment already entered;

(3) stay the proceeding upon condition that a custody proceeding be initiated or prosecuted in another state in a timely manner or upon any other condition that the court might deem just;

(4) retain jurisdiction over any action to which the custody proceeding is incident, while declining to render a custody determination;

(5) enter such temporary order or orders as may be required, in the court's discretion, pursuant to clause (ii) of paragraph (3) of section two;

(6) assess any or all of the costs of the custody proceeding in this state, having due regard for the purposes of this chapter, including the reasonable travel and other expenses of any party and his or her witnesses, the reasonable attorneys' fees of any party, the costs of the court's communications and information exchanges with other courts and the fees and costs of any person entitled to appear before the court as the representative of a child;

(7) assess sanctions against any party whom the court finds has engaged in illegal or otherwise wrongful conduct;

(8) enter any other order or judgment which may be meet and just under the circumstances of the case.

(f) A court shall communicate to the court of any other relevant jurisdiction any determination or finding made pursuant to this section.

§ 8. Personal appearance before court; expenses

(a) The court may order any party to the proceeding who is in the commonwealth to appear personally before the court. If that party has physical custody of the child the court may order that he or she appear personally with the child.

(b) If a party to the proceeding whose presence is desired by the court is outside the commonwealth with or without the child, the court may order that the notice given under section five include a statement directing the party to appear personally with or without the child and declaring that failure to appear may result in a decision adverse to that party.

(c) If a party to the proceeding who is outside the commonwealth is directed to appear under paragraph (b) or desires to appear personally before the court with or without the child, the court may require another party to pay to the clerk or register of the court travel and other necessary expenses of the party so appearing and of the child if this is just and proper under the circumstances.

§ 9. Testimony of witnesses outside state

In addition to other procedural devices available to a party, any party to the proceeding or a guardian ad litem or other representative of the child may adduce testimony of witnesses, including parties and the child, by deposition or otherwise, in another state. The court on its own motion may direct that the testimony of a person be taken in another state and may prescribe the manner in which and the terms upon which the testimony shall be taken.

§ 10. Foreign courts; evidentiary hearings; transfer of information; orders to appear within state; expenses

(a) A court of the commonwealth may request the appropriate court of another state to hold a hearing to adduce evidence, to order a party to produce or give evidence under other procedures of that state, or to have an investigation made with respect to the custody of a child involved in proceedings pending in the court of the commonwealth; and to forward to the court of the commonwealth certified copies of the transcript of the record of the hearing, the evidence otherwise adduced, or any investigation prepared in compliance with the request. The cost of these services may be assessed against the parties.

(b) A court of the commonwealth may request the appropriate court of another state to order a party to custody proceedings pending in the court of the commonwealth to appear in the proceedings, and if that party has physical custody of the child, to appear with the child. The request may state that travel and other reasonable and necessary expenses of the party and of the child whose appearance is desired may be assessed against another party or may otherwise be paid.

§ 11. Custody proceedings in foreign courts; evidentiary hearings within state; transfer of information; orders to appear in foreign court; expenses

(a) Upon request of the court of another state the courts of the commonwealth which are competent to hear custody matters may order a person in the commonwealth to appear at a hearing to adduce evidence or to produce or give evidence under other procedures available in the commonwealth or may order investigations to be made for use in a custody proceeding in another state. A certified copy of the transcript of the record of the hearing or the evidence otherwise adduced and of any investigation shall be forwarded by the clerk or register of the court to the requesting court.

(b) Upon request of the court of another state a competent court of the commonwealth may order a person in the commonwealth to appear alone or with the child in a custody proceeding in another state. The court may condition compliance with the request upon assurance by the other state, that travel and other necessary expenses will be advanced or reimbursed.

Notwithstanding any provision of this chapter to the contrary, no child shall be ordered or compelled to appear or attend such proceeding in another state when, after a hearing a judge makes a finding that there is probable cause to believe that such child may be placed in jeopardy or exposed to risk of mental or physical harm by such return to said other state.

§ 12. Custody judgment of foreign state; filing within state; enforcement of judgment within state; expenses

(a) A certified copy of a custody judgment of another state may be filed in the office of the clerk or register of any court of competent jurisdiction in the commonwealth. The clerk or register shall treat the judgment in the same manner as a custody judgment of a court of the commonwealth. A custody judgment so filed has the same effect and shall be enforced in like manner as a custody judgment rendered by a court of the commonwealth.

(b) A person violating a custody judgment of another state the violation of which makes it necessary to enforce the judgment in the commonwealth may be required to pay the reasonable and necessary travel, witness and other expenses, including attorneys' fees, incurred by the party entitled to custody of the child.

§ 13. Preservation of record; time; copies

In any custody proceeding in the commonwealth the court shall preserve the pleadings, orders and judgments and any record that has been made of its hearings, investigations and other pertinent documents until the child reaches eighteen years of age. Upon appropriate request of the court of another state and receipt of payment therefor the court shall forward to the other court certified copies of any or all of such documents.

§ 14. International custody determinations; recognition

To the extent that the legal institutions of other nations have rendered custody determinations in substantial conformity with the provisions of this chapter, the courts of the commonwealth shall grant due recognition to such determinations.

Chapter 209C. Children Born Out of Wedlock

Section

§ 1. Declaration of purpose; definition; responsibility for support of children born out of wedlock

Children born to parents who are not married to each other shall be entitled to the same rights and protections of the law as all other children. It is the purpose of this chapter to establish a means for such children either to be acknowledged by their parents voluntarily or, on complaint by one or the other of their parents or such other person or agency as is authorized to file a complaint by section five, to have an acknowledgment or adjudication of their paternity, to have an order for their support and to have a declaration relative to their custody or visitation rights ordered by a court of competent jurisdiction. For the purpose of this chapter, the term "child born out of wedlock" shall refer to any child born to a man and woman who are not married to each other and shall include a child who was conceived and born to parents who are not married to each other but who subsequently intermarry and whose paternity has not been acknowledged by word or deed or whose paternity has not been adjudicated by a court of competent jurisdiction; and a child born to parents who are not married to each other whose paternity has been adjudicated by a court of competent jurisdiction, including an adjudication in a proceeding pursuant to this chapter or prior law. Every person is responsible for the support of his child born out of wedlock from its birth up to the age of eighteen, or, where such child is domiciled in the home of a parent and principally dependent upon said parent for maintenance, to age twenty-one. Each person charged with support under this section shall be required to furnish support according to his financial ability and earning capacity pursuant to the provisions of this chapter.

§ 2. Paternity; acknowledgment or adjudication

Paternity may be established by filing with the court, the clerk of the city or town where the child was born or the registrar of vital records and statistics an acknowledgment of parentage executed by both parents pursuant to section 11 or pursuant to an action to establish paternity filed pursuant to this chapter; provided, however, that if a judgment or finding of paternity has been issued by a court or administrative agency of competent jurisdiction under the law of another state or foreign country or if both parents executed a voluntary acknowledgment of parentage in accordance with the law of another state or foreign country, such judgment, finding or voluntary acknowledgment shall be accorded full faith and credit and paternity shall not be relitigated. Upon receipt of an acknowledgment of paternity, the clerk of such city or town shall forward the original acknowledgment to said registrar as provided in chapter 46. Upon receipt of an acknowledgment of parentage or upon an adjudication of paternity under this chapter, the court shall transmit to the registrar of vital records and statistics a certified copy of the acknowledgment or order establishing paternity, together with such statistical information as said registrar may require, upon such form and in such format as designated by said registrar, which shall include the name, residence, date of birth, place of birth and social security number of each of the parties and the child, the sex of the child, and such additional information as the commissioner of public health deems useful for statistical and research purposes. Actions to establish support obligations or for custody or visitation rights may also be filed pursuant to this chapter.

§ 3. Paternity and support actions; jurisdiction; enforcement of prior orders or judgments; juvenile court commitment proceedings; parents convicted of first degree murder

[Amended by 2014 Mass. Acts c. 260, § 16, effective Aug. 8, 2014.]

(a) The district, Boston municipal and the probate and family court departments of the trial court shall have concurrent jurisdiction over complaints to establish paternity or support and the registration of voluntary acknowledgments of parentage; provided, however, that the district and Boston municipal court departments shall have no jurisdiction of custody or visitation matters under this chapter. Complaints to establish paternity or support or for voluntary acknowledgments of parentage which also include a request for an order relative to custody or visitation shall be filed only in the probate and family court department. No court shall make an order providing visitation rights to any parent who has been convicted of murder in the first degree of the other parent of the child who is the subject of the order, unless such child is of suitable age to signify his assent and assents to such order; provided, further, that until such order is issued, no person shall visit, with the child present, a parent who has been convicted of murder in the first degree of the other parent of the child without the consent of the child's custodian or legal guardian. No court shall make an order providing visitation rights to a parent who was convicted of rape, under sections 22 to 23B, inclusive, of chapter 265 or section 2, 3, 4 or 17 of chapter 272, and is seeking to obtain visitation with the child who was conceived during the commission of that rape, unless the judge determines that such child is of suitable age to signify the child's assent and the child assents to such order and that assent is in the best interest of the child; provided, however, that a court may make an order providing visitation rights to a parent convicted of rape under section 23 of said chapter 265, if (i) visitation is in the best interest of the child and (ii) either the other parent of the child conceived during the commission of that rape has reached the age of 18 and said parent consents to such visitation or the judge makes an independent determination that visitation is in the best interest of the child.

(b) Any party to an action for paternity or support which is pending or was previously adjudicated by the district or Boston municipal court departments who seeks an order relative to custody or visitation may, after the adjudication or voluntary acknowledgment of paternity and entry of an order or judgment for support, file an action in the probate and family court department in the county where the child resides to determine custody or visitation. The filing of the action in the probate and family court shall act to transfer the case from the district court or the Boston municipal court department to the probate and family court department. The register of probate shall make entry in the docket that the case shall thereafter be heard only in the probate and family court department. The party seeking transfer shall notify the parties, the district court or the Boston municipal court and, if applicable, the IV-D agency as set forth in chapter 119A that the action has been transferred to the probate and family court department. The clerk magistrate of the district court or the Boston municipal court shall make entry in the docket of such transfer.

(c) The juvenile court department shall have concurrent jurisdiction to adjudicate paternity and support and to accept registration of voluntary acknowledgments of parentage under this chapter, provided that actions brought under this chapter are joined or consolidated with actions brought under section twenty-four of chapter one hundred and nineteen and, provided further, that the action under section twenty-four of chapter one hundred and nineteen is initiated before the filing of a complaint under this chapter.

(d) Any action pursuant to this chapter that is pending or was previously adjudicated in the district court or Boston municipal court departments may be transferred by any party or by the IV-D agency as set forth in chapter 119A to the probate and family court department in the county where the child resides or, if the child does not reside in the commonwealth and a court of the commonwealth has jurisdiction under chapter 209D, in the county where one of the parents resides. An action shall be transferred upon the filing of the following documents with the probate and family court:— (1) a copy of the complaint; (2) a copy of the order of the district court or Boston municipal court, if any; (3) a copy of the findings of the court, if any; (4) a copy of the financial statements submitted by the parties, if any; (5) a copy of the worksheet used to calculate the amount of the child support order pursuant to the child support guidelines, if any; and (6) a copy of the docket maintained by the district court or the Boston municipal court, if any. Once transferred, the order of the district court or the Boston municipal court shall have the same force and effect, and shall be subject to the same procedures and defenses as an order of the probate and family court and may be enforced or modified in the same manner available to enforce or modify any judgment or order of the probate and family court. Transfer of an order pursuant to this section shall not limit the use of any enforcement remedy, whether judicial or administrative, that may be available and the probate and family court shall preserve all arrears that have accrued pursuant to the order of the district or Boston municipal court departments.

(e) An order or judgment for support entered in the juvenile court department shall remain in full force and effect and shall be enforced in the division of the juvenile court department in which the original order or judgment of support was entered during the pendency of an action pursuant to section twenty-four of chapter one hundred and nineteen. Six months after the dismissal or final order of commitment pursuant to section twenty-four of chapter one hundred and nineteen, the order or judgment of support shall expire. At the time of such dismissal or final order of commitment, the clerk-magistrate shall notify the parties and the IV-D agency, as set forth in chapter one hundred and nineteen A, of the date of expiration of the support order or judgment. If, before the expiration of the order or judgment of support, any of the parties or said IV-D agency files an action for support in the Boston municipal court department or the appropriate division of the district or probate and family court departments, the prior order or judgment shall be transferred to that court department and shall remain in full force and effect and shall be enforced and modified in said court department.

§ 4. Venue; service

[Amended by 2005 Mass. Acts c. 163, § 48, effective Dec. 8, 2005.]

Actions under this chapter to establish paternity, support, custody or visitation of a child shall be filed in the judicial district or county in which the child and 1 of the parents lives and if neither of the parents lives in the same judicial district or county as the child then the complaint shall be filed in the judicial district or county where the child lives; but, if the parents have been parties to a prior action under this chapter and that action has not been dismissed, a subsequent action under this chapter may be filed in the judicial district or county where the earlier action was filed.

The fact that the child was conceived, was born, or lives outside the commonwealth does not bar a proceeding to establish paternity pursuant to this chapter. Service of the complaint shall be made in accordance with applicable rules of court. In addition to those otherwise authorized to serve civil process, any officer authorized under the laws of the commonwealth to serve criminal process may serve any process under this chapter.

§ 5. Persons entitled to maintain actions or execute voluntary acknowledgment of parentage; parties

[Amended by 2008 Mass. Acts c. 176, § 110, effective July 8, 2008; 2008 Mass. Acts c. 215, § 78, effective July 31, 2008.]

(a) Complaints under this chapter to establish paternity, support, visitation or custody of a child may be commenced by the mother, whether a minor or not; by a person presumed to be or alleging himself to be the father, whether a minor or not; by the child, whether a minor or not; by the child's guardian, next of kin, or other person standing in a parental relation to the child; by the parent or personal representative of the mother if the mother has died or has abandoned the child; by the parent or personal representative of the father if the father has died; by the authorized agent of the department of children and families or any agency licensed under chapter 15D provided that the child is in their custody; or, if the child is or was a recipient of any type of public assistance, by the IV-D agency as set forth in chapter 119A on behalf of the department of transitional assistance, the department of children and families, the division of medical assistance or any other public assistance program of the commonwealth; provided, however, that

1

if the mother of the child was or is married and the child's birth occurs during the marriage or within three hundred days of its termination by death, annulment or divorce, complaints to establish paternity under this chapter may not be filed by a person presumed to be or alleging himself to be the father unless he is or was the mother's husband at the time of the child's birth or conception.

(b) Voluntary acknowledgments of parentage may be executed by the mother and the putative father, whether either or both is a minor, and may be registered pursuant to section 11 only if the signatures of the mother and the father are notarized. If the mother of the child was or is married and the child's birth occurs during the marriage or within 300 days of its termination by divorce, a voluntary acknowledgment of parentage naming the putative father may be executed by the mother and the putative father only if the mother and the person who was the spouse of the mother at the time of the child's birth or conception sign an affidavit denying that the spouse is the father of the child; provided, however, that where the marriage has been terminated by annulment or by the death of either spouse, paternity of the putative father may only be established by filing a complaint to establish paternity as provided in this chapter. A mother and a putative father signing a voluntary acknowledgment of parentage at the hospital or thereafter at the office of the city or town clerk as part of the birth registration process pursuant to section 3C of chapter 46, with the department of transitional assistance, with the IV-D agency set forth in chapter 119A, with any agency designated by the federal Secretary of Health and Human Services or with any official of a court shall receive notice orally, or through the use of video or audio equipment, and in writing of alternatives to signing the acknowledgment, including the availability of genetic marker testing, as well as the benefits and responsibilities with respect to child support, custody and visitation that may arise from signing the acknowledgment, and subsequently filing the acknowledgment with the court or with the registrar of vital records and statistics as provided in this chapter.

(c) Any agency or person living with such child who is actually furnishing support to the child or, if the child who is the subject of an action under this chapter is a recipient of public assistance, the department of transitional assistance, shall be made a party to any action for paternity or support under this chapter.

(d) The IV-D agency as set forth in chapter 119A on behalf of the department of transitional assistance, the department of children and families, the division of medical assistance or any other public assistance program may not file complaints solely for custody or visitation, but shall be permitted to file actions for paternity or support; provided, however, that said IV-D agency shall be permitted to maintain an action for paternity or support even if issues related to custody or visitation are raised.

(e) In actions under this chapter relative to custody or visitation, the child, if the child is fourteen years of age or older, shall be made a party to such action.

§ 6. Presumption of paternity; mandatory joinder

(a) In all actions under this chapter a man is presumed to be the father of a child and must be joined as a party if:

(1) he is or has been married to the mother and the child was born during the marriage, or within three hundred days after the marriage was terminated by death, annulment or divorce; or

(2) before the child's birth, he married or attempted to marry the mother by a marriage solemnized in apparent compliance with law, although the attempted marriage is or could be declared invalid, and the child was born during the attempted marriage or within three hundred days after its termination; or

(3) after the child's birth, he married or attempted to marry the mother by a marriage solemnized in apparent compliance with law, although the attempted marriage is or could be declared invalid, and

(i) he agreed to support the child under a written voluntary promise, or

(ii) he has engaged in any other conduct which can be construed as an acknowledgment of paternity; or

(4) while the child is under the age of majority, he, jointly with the mother, received the child into their home and openly held out the child as their child; or

(5) he has acknowledged paternity in a parental responsibility claim as provided in section four A of chapter two hundred and ten and the mother, having received actual notice thereof, has failed within a reasonable time, to object thereto; or

(6) with respect to a child born before April 13, 1994, with his consent and the consent of the child's mother, he is named as the child's father on the birth certificate as provided in section one of chapter forty-six.

(b) Notwithstanding the provisions of subsection (a), a husband or former husband shall not be required to be joined as a party if nonpaternity of the child has previously been adjudicated in a proceeding between the husband and the mother of such child in a court or administrative agency of competent jurisdiction.

(c) Notice to a party joined as herein provided shall be sufficient if the summons is mailed to the last known address by a form of mail requiring a receipt and, if actual notice shall not be made as aforesaid, by publishing a copy of the notice once in each of three successive weeks in a newspaper designated by the court.

§ 7. Representation in paternity actions; appointment of counsel; burden of proof

Actions under this chapter shall be civil actions. The IV-D agency, as set forth in chapter one hundred and nineteen A, may appear on behalf of a plaintiff in an action to establish paternity. In actions in which custody or visitation are contested, court may appoint counsel to represent either party whenever the interests of justice require.

The burden of proof in proceedings under this chapter to establish paternity shall be by clear and convincing evidence.

§ 8. Judgment of paternity; age of father; notice

[Amended by 2008 Mass. Acts c. 176, § 111, effective July 8, 2008.]

On complaint to establish paternity, the court shall make a judgment establishing or not establishing paternity which shall be determinative for all purposes. Upon default of the defendant or his failure to personally appear, the court shall make a judgment establishing paternity if a showing is made that the complaint was served in accordance with the applicable rules of court and that the mother or putative father submits that sexual intercourse between the parties occurred during the probable period of conception. For good cause shown, the court may set aside an entry of default and, if a judgment has been entered, may likewise set it aside in accordance with rule 60 (b) of the Massachusetts Rules of Domestic Relations Procedure. The age of the person alleged to be the father or mother in any action under this chapter, including a filing of a voluntary acknowledgment of parentage, shall not be a bar to the establishment of paternity or entry of a support order pursuant to section nine. If the child or the mother on behalf of the child is a recipient of public assistance and if the department of transitional assistance, the department of children and families, the division of medical assistance or any other public assistance program has not been made a party as required by section five, the court shall notify the IV-D agency as set forth in chapter 119A of the judgment. If the judgment is at variance with the child's birth certificate, the court shall order that a new birth certificate be issued under section thirteen of chapter forty-six.

§ 9. Judgment or order for support; health insurance; financial statement; determination of amount; notice

[Amended by 2008 Mass. Acts c. 176, § 112, effective July 8, 2008; 2011 Mass.

Acts c. 93, § 41; 2012 Mass. Acts c. 244, § 219, effective Nov. 4, 2012; 2019 Mass. Acts c. 34, §§ 20, 21, effective July 8, 2019.]

(a) If the court finds that a parent is chargeable with the support of a child, the court shall make an order in accordance with subsection (c) requiring a parent to pay weekly or at other fixed periods a sum for and toward the current support and maintenance of such child. The court may make appropriate orders of maintenance, support and education for any child who has attained age eighteen but who has not attained age twenty-one, who is domiciled in the home of a parent and is principally dependent upon said parent for maintenance. The court may make appropriate orders of maintenance, support and education for any child who has attained age twenty-one but who has not attained age twenty-three if such child is domiciled in the home of a parent, and is principally dependent upon said parent for maintenance due to the enrollment of such child in an educational program, excluding educational costs beyond an undergraduate degree. Upon the petition of a party, the court shall also order past support for the period from the birth of the child to the entry of the order, taking into consideration the parent's ability to pay under subsection (c) and any support provided by the parent during such period. An order or judgment of support pursuant to this chapter shall be entered notwithstanding the default of the defendant or his failure to appear personally upon a showing that notice was served in accordance with the applicable rules of court. For good cause shown, the court may set aside an entry of default and, if a judgment has been entered, may likewise set it aside in accordance with rule 60(b) of the Massachusetts Rules of Domestic Relations Procedure. An order may be entered requiring a parent chargeable with support to reimburse the mother or the department of transitional assistance or the office of Medicaid or the executive office of health and human services for medical expenses attributable to the child or associated with childbirth or resulting from the pregnancy.

If the court makes an order or judgment for maintenance or support of a child, the court shall require either parent to provide health care coverage for the child if such coverage is available at reasonable cost and accessible to the child. The court may require the obligor to pay an amount toward the obligee's cost of health care coverage or toward uninsured medical expenses on behalf of the child. If the court determines that an order for health care coverage is not in the best interest of the child or creates an undue hardship for either parent, the court shall enter written findings.

If the child is enrolled in MassHealth, an equivalent program in another state pursuant to 42 U.S.C. 1397aa et seq. or 42 U.S.C. 1396a et seq. or an equivalent program in another state that is substantially similar to the program established in chapter 118E, the court shall order the obligee to maintain coverage as long as the child remains eligible; provided, however, that the court may also order the obligor to enroll the child in private health insurance if: (i) private health insurance is available to the obligor at reasonable cost and accessible to the child; (ii) enrollment in the insurance is in the best interest of the child; and (iii) enrollment in the insurance will not create an undue hardship for the obligor or the obligee.

If the IV-D agency under chapter 119A is responsible for enforcing the order, the court shall order the parents to notify the IV-D agency of any changes in the availability and terms of health care coverage. For the purposes of this section: (i) health care coverage shall be deemed reasonable in cost if the cost to the party ordered to provide health care coverage does not exceed 5 per cent of the gross income of the party; (ii) health care coverage shall be deemed accessible to the child if covered services are available within 15 miles of the child's primary residence; (iii) health care coverage includes private health insurance available through employment, union affiliation or otherwise, and public health coverage administered by the Title XIX agency; and (iv) private health insurance shall be deemed not available at reasonable cost to an obligor or obligee whose gross income does not exceed 150 per cent of the federal poverty guidelines for the family size or who receives MassHealth on behalf of the obligor, the obligee or the child.

(b) Upon demand by either party, including the department of transitional assistance, the other party shall be compelled to provide a financial statement, except that the department of transitional assistance shall not be compelled to provide a financial statement for a recipient of public assistance, and, provided further, if no party makes such a demand, the court may require a financial statement of each party.

(c) In determining the amount of the child support obligation or in approving the agreement of the parties, the court shall apply the child support guidelines promulgated by the chief justice for administration and management. There shall be a rebuttable presumption that the amount resulting from application of the guidelines is the appropriate amount of child support to be ordered. If, after taking into consideration the best interests of the child, the court determines that a party has overcome such presumption, the court shall make specific written findings indicating the amount of the order that would result from application of the guidelines; that the guidelines amount would be unjust or inappropriate under the circumstances; the specific facts of the case which justify departure from the guidelines; and that such departure is consistent with the best interests of the child. In the event that no child support guidelines are in effect, the court shall make such order as is in the best interests of the child, taking into consideration the financial ability and earning capacity of the parents of the child.

(d) It shall not be a defense that the parent from whom support is sought has ceased to have custody or the right to custody of a minor child for whom support is sought, or that the custodial parent is interfering with the other parent's right of visitation.

(e) If the child on whose behalf an order of support is sought is a recipient of benefits pursuant to chapter 117, 118 or 119 and the department of transitional assistance, the department of children and families, the division of medical assistance or any other public assistance program has not been made a party as required by section 5, the court shall notify the IV-D agency of the order or judgment of support.

(f) In determining the amount to be paid, the court, in addition to applying the standards established by the chief justice of the trial court, shall determine whether the obligor is responsible for the maintenance or support of any other children of the obligor even if a court order for such maintenance or support does not exist. If the court determines that such responsibility does, in fact, exist and that such obligor is fulfilling such responsibility, such court shall take into consideration such responsibility in setting the amount to be paid under the current order for maintenance or support.

§ 10. Award of custody; criteria

[Amended by 2014 Mass. Acts c. 260, § 17, effective Aug. 8, 2014.]

(a) Upon or after an adjudication or voluntary acknowledgment of paternity, the court may award custody to the mother or the father or to them jointly or to another suitable person as hereafter further specified as may be appropriate in the best interests of the child.

In awarding custody to one of the parents, the court shall, to the extent possible, preserve the relationship between the child and the primary caretaker parent. The court shall also consider where and with whom the child has resided within the six months immediately preceding proceedings pursuant to this chapter and whether one or both of the parents has established a personal and parental relationship with the child or has exercised parental responsibility in the best interests of the child.

In awarding the parents joint custody, the court shall do so only if the parents have entered into an agreement pursuant to section eleven or the court finds that the parents have successfully exercised joint responsibility for the child prior to the commencement of proceedings pursuant to this chapter and have the ability to communicate and plan with each other concerning the child's best interests.

(b) Prior to or in the absence of an adjudication or voluntary acknowledgment of paternity, the mother shall have custody of a child born out of wedlock. In the absence of an order or judgment of a probate and family court relative to custody, the mother shall continue to have custody of a child after an adjudication of paternity or voluntary acknowledgment of parentage.

(c) If either parent is dead, unfit or unavailable or relinquishes care of the child or abandons the child and the other parent is fit to have custody, that parent shall be entitled to custody.

(d) If a person who is not a parent of the child requests custody, the court may order custody to that person if it is in the best interests of the child and if the written consent of both parents or the surviving parent is filed with the court. Such custody may also be ordered if it is in the best interests of the child and if both parents or the surviving parent are unfit to have custody or if one is unfit and the other files his written consent in court.

(e) In issuing any temporary or permanent custody order, the probate and family court shall consider evidence of past or present abuse toward a parent or child as a factor contrary to the best interest of the child. For the purposes of this section, "abuse" shall mean the occurrence of one or more of the following acts between a parent and the other parent or between a parent and child: (a) attempting to cause or causing bodily injury; or (b) placing another in reasonable fear of imminent bodily injury. "Serious incident of abuse" shall mean the occurrence of one or more of the following acts between a parent and the other parent or between a parent and child: (a) attempting to cause or causing serious bodily injury; (b) placing another in reasonable fear of imminent serious bodily injury; or (c) causing another to engage involuntarily in sexual relations by force, threat or duress. For purposes of this section, "bodily injury" and "serious bodily injury" shall have the same meanings as provided in section 13K of chapter 265. For the purposes of this section, if the child was conceived during the commission of a rape and the parent was convicted of said rape, under sections 22 to 23B, inclusive, of chapter 265 or section 2, 3, 4 or 17 of chapter 272, said conviction shall be conclusive evidence of a serious incident of abuse by the convicted parent.

A probate and family court's finding by a preponderance of the evidence, that a pattern or serious incident of abuse has occurred shall create a rebuttable presumption that it is not in the best interests of the child to be placed in sole custody, shared legal custody, or shared physical custody with the abusive parent. Such presumption may be rebutted by a preponderance of the evidence that such custody award is in the best interests of the child. For the purposes of this section, an "abusive parent" shall mean a parent who has committed a pattern of abuse or a serious incident of abuse.

For the purposes of this section, the issuance of an order or orders under chapter 209A shall not in and of itself constitute a pattern or serious incident of abuse; nor shall an order or orders entered ex parte under said chapter 209A be admissible to show whether a pattern or serious incident of abuse has in fact occurred; provided, however, that an order or orders entered ex parte under said chapter 209A may be admissible for other purposes as the court may determine, other than showing whether a pattern or serious incident of abuse has in fact occurred; provided further, that the underlying facts upon which an order or orders under said chapter 209A was based may also form the basis for a finding by the probate and family court that a pattern or serious incident of abuse has occurred.

If the court finds that a pattern or serious incident of abuse has occurred and issues a temporary or permanent custody order, the court shall within 90 days enter written findings of fact as to the effects of the abuse on the child, which findings demonstrate that such order is in the furtherance of the child's best interests and provides for the safety and well-being of the child.

If ordering visitation to the abusive parent the court shall provide for the safety and well-being of the child, and the safety of the abused parent. The court may consider:

(a) ordering an exchange of the child to occur in a protected setting or in the presence of an appropriate third party;

(b) ordering visitation supervised by an appropriate third party, visitation center or agency;

(c) ordering the abusive parent to attend and complete, to the satisfaction of the court, a certified batterer's treatment program as a condition of visitation;

(d) ordering the abusive parent to abstain from possession or consumption of alcohol or controlled substances during the visitation and for 24 hours preceding visitation;

(e) ordering the abusive parent to pay the costs of supervised visitation;

(f) prohibiting overnight visitation;

(g) requiring a bond from the abusive parent for the return and safety of the child;

(h) ordering an investigation or appointment of a guardian ad litem or attorney for the child; and

(i) imposing any other condition that is deemed necessary to provide for the safety and well-being of the child and the safety of the abused parent.

Nothing in this section shall be construed to affect the right of the parties to a hearing under the rules of domestic relations procedure or to affect the discretion of the probate and family court in the conduct of such hearing.

§ 11. Acknowledgment of paternity; approval; parental agreements regarding custody, support and visitation

[Amended by 2008 Mass. Acts c. 176, § 113, effective July 8, 2008.]

(a) A written voluntary acknowledgment of parentage executed jointly by the putative father, whether a minor or not, and the mother of the child, whether a minor or not, and filed with the registrar of vital records and statistics or with the court shall be recognized as a sufficient basis for seeking an order of support, visitation or custody with respect to the child without further proceedings to establish paternity, and no judicial proceeding shall be required or permitted to ratify an acknowledgment that has not been challenged pursuant to this section. A report, prepared on an electronic system of birth registration approved by the commissioner of public health and indicating that an acknowledgment pursuant to this chapter has been executed in accordance with section 3C of chapter 46 and filed with the registrar of vital records and statistics, shall be presumed to be a sufficient basis for seeking an order of support, visitation or custody without further proceedings to establish paternity. The voluntary acknowledgment shall be attested to before a notary public and shall have the legal effect as provided in this section. Unless either signatory rescinds the acknowledgment within 60 days of the date of signing as provided in this section, the acknowledgment shall establish paternity as of the date it has been signed by such putative father and mother and shall have the same force and effect as a judgment of paternity, subject to challenge within one year only on the basis of fraud, duress or material mistake of fact; provided, however, that if, prior to the expiration of the 60-day period, the signatory is a party to an administrative or judicial proceeding related to the child, including a proceeding to establish child support, visitation or custody, and fails to rescind the acknowledgment at the time of such proceeding, the acknowledgment shall thereafter have the same force and effect as a judgment, subject to challenge only as provided in this section. The person seeking to rescind the acknowledgment shall, within 60 days of signing the acknowledgment, file a petition in the probate and family court in the county in which the child and one of the parents resides seeking to rescind the acknowledgment, with notice to the other parent. If neither of the parents lives in the same county as the child, then such complaint shall be filed in the county where the child lives. If the child whose paternity is challenged is a recipient of public assistance and the department of transitional assistance, the department of children and families, the division of medical assistance or any other public assistance program has not been made a party, or if the child is receiving child support enforcement services from the IV-D agency pursuant to chapter 119A, the court shall notify the IV-D agency. The person seeking to rescind the acknowledgment shall bear the burden of proof in such proceeding. The responsibilities of a signatory arising from the acknowledgment shall not be suspended during the pendency of such challenge unless the court so orders for good cause shown. If either party rescinds the acknowledgment in a timely fashion, the court shall order genetic marker testing and proceed to adjudicate paternity or nonpaternity in accordance with this chapter; provided, however, that the rescinded acknowledgment shall constitute the proper showing required for an order to submit to such testing; and provided further, that the rescinded acknowledgment shall be admissible as evidence of the putative father's paternity and shall serve as sufficient basis for admitting the report of the results of genetic marker tests. Upon adjudication of nonpaternity, the court shall instruct the registrar of vital records and statistics as provided in section 13 of chapter 46 to amend the birth record of the child in accordance with the order of the court.

(b) If a mother and father execute a voluntary acknowledgment of parentage as provided in (a), they may also make agreements regarding custody, support and visitation. Such agreements may be filed with any court with jurisdiction pursuant to this chapter; provided, that any such agreement which includes issues of custody or visitation must be filed with a division of the probate and family court department in the judicial district or county in which the child and one of the parents lives. Such agreements, if filed with and approved by the court shall have the same force and effect as a judgment of the court; provided, however, that the court shall have the same power to investigate the facts regarding custody, support and visitation prior to entering an order relative to those issues as it would have if no agreement had been filed; and provided further, that an agreement regarding custody and visitation shall be approved only if the court finds it to be in the best interests of the child.

(c) Voluntary acknowledgments and agreements made pursuant to this chapter shall be acknowledged in the presence of a notary public and shall include the residence addresses and social security numbers of each of the parents, the residence address of the child and, if available, the social security number of the child.

(d) A voluntary acknowledgment of parentage taken outside of the commonwealth shall be valid for the purposes of this section if it was taken in accordance with the laws of the state or the country where it was executed.

§ 12. Trial; exclusion of public

In actions under this chapter, the trial shall be by the court without a jury. In an action to establish paternity, the court shall, upon request of any party, exclude the general public from the room where the trial is held and may admit only persons directly interested in the case, including officers of the court and witnesses.

§ 13. Inspection of paternity documents; segregation of records

[Amended by 2008 Mass. Acts c. 176, § 114, effective July 8, 2008.]

In an action to establish paternity or in which paternity of a child is an issue, all complaints, pleadings, papers, documents or reports filed in connection therewith, docket entries in the permanent docket and record books shall be segregated and unavailable for inspection only if the judge of the court where such records are kept, for good cause shown, so orders or the person alleged to be the father is adjudicated not to be the father of the child; provided, however, that the child, the child's mother, the person adjudicated to be the father and the department of transitional assistance, the department of children and families, the division of medical assistance or any other public assistance program and the IV-D agency as set forth in chapter 119A, when the child who is or was the subject of the complaint is a recipient of public assistance or the attorney for any of them, and the department of children and families, when the child who is or was the subject of the complaint is within the care and protection of the department of children and families, is the subject of a petition for such care or protection pursuant to chapter 119 or is the subject of a petition to dispense with consent for adoption pursuant to subsection (b) of section 3 of chapter 210, shall have access to and the right to obtain copies of the papers, docket books and judgments in actions pursuant to this chapter. For good cause shown, which may be made ex parte or upon credible evidence, parties may file a complaint without the address, and the court shall impound a party's address by excluding it from the complaint and from all other court documents and testimony, and shall ensure that the address is kept confidential from each other party except the IV-D agency as set forth in chapter 119A.

§ 14. Complaints brought prior to birth

An action to establish paternity of a child may be instituted during pregnancy of the mother but shall only be filed by the mother or her representative or by the IV-D agency as set forth in chapter 119A on behalf of the mother. In the case of any complaint brought prior to the birth of the child, no final judgment on the issue of paternity shall be made until after the birth of the child; provided, however, that the court may order temporary support or health care coverage.

§ 15. Temporary orders; enforcement; information required to be given to petitioner; domestic violence record search

At any time pursuant to an action under this chapter, the court may upon motion of any party or on its own motion issue a temporary order or final judgment including a vacate, restraining or no-contact order to protect a party or child. Any such order or judgment, including a custody provision if issued by a probate court, shall be served as specified under sections four and seven of chapter two hundred and nine A and shall contain the following statement: VIOLATION OF THIS ORDER IS A CRIMINAL OFFENSE. Criminal violations of such orders shall be enforced pursuant to section seven of chapter two hundred and nine A.

The court may, in like manner, upon motion of any party or of a next friend on behalf of the child, and upon notice to the other parties, enter temporary orders providing for the support of the child or relative to the care and custody of the child or visitation rights with the child in accordance with the provisions of sections nine and ten.

All orders entered pursuant to this section, unless modified or revoked pursuant to section twenty or twenty-three of chapter two hundred and nine C, shall continue in force and be incorporated in the final judgment. Violations of any order or judgment may be punished as contempt.

Upon the filing of a request for an order to protect a party or a child under the provisions of the first paragraph of this section, a petitioner shall be informed that proceedings hereunder are civil in nature and that violations of orders issued hereunder are criminal in nature. Further, a petitioner shall be given information prepared by the appropriate district attorney's office that other criminal proceedings may be available and such petitioner shall be instructed by such district attorney's office relative to the procedures required to initiate criminal proceedings including, but not limited to, a complaint for a violation of section forty-three of chapter two hundred and sixty-five. Whenever possible, a petitioner shall be provided with such information in the petitioner's native language.

1

When considering a request for relief pursuant to this section, a judge shall cause a search to be made of the records contained within the statewide domestic violence record keeping system maintained by the office of the commissioner of probation and shall review the resulting data to determine whether the named defendant has a civil or criminal record involving domestic or other violence. Upon receipt of information that an outstanding warrant exists against the named defendant, a judge shall order that the appropriate law enforcement officials be notified and shall order that any information regarding the defendant's most recent whereabouts shall be forwarded to such officials. In all instances where an outstanding warrant exists, a judge shall make a finding, based upon all of the circumstances, as to whether an imminent threat of bodily injury exists to the petitioner. In all instances where such an imminent threat of bodily injury is found to exist, the judge shall notify the appropriate law enforcement officials of such finding and such officials shall take all necessary actions to execute any such outstanding warrant as soon as is practicable.

§ 16. Competency to testify; refusal to testify; immunity; contempt; admissibility of evidence

[Amended by 2005 Mass. Acts c. 163, § 49; 2008 Mass. Acts c. 176, § 115, effective July 8, 2008.]

(a) Both the plaintiff and the defendant are competent to testify in proceedings hereunder.

(b) Upon refusal of a witness, including a party, to testify under oath and produce evidence, the court may order such witness or party to testify under oath and produce evidence concerning all relevant facts. If a witness or party refuses to answer on the ground that the testimony may be self-incriminating, the court may draw an adverse inference from such refusal.

(c) In an action pursuant to this chapter, the mother and the man alleged to be the father shall be competent to testify and no privilege or disqualification created under chapter two hundred and thirty-three shall prohibit testimony by a spouse or former spouse which is otherwise competent. If the mother is or was married, both she and her husband or her former husband may testify to non-access and parentage of the child.

(d) In an action to establish paternity, testimony relating to sexual access to the mother by an unidentified man at any time or by an identified man at any time other than the probable time of conception of the child is inadmissible in evidence unless offered by the mother.

(e) In an action to establish paternity, the court may view the mother, the child, and the putative father to note any resemblance among the parties notwithstanding the absence of expert testimony.

(f) Copies; of bills for genetic marker tests and for prenatal and postnatal health care of the mother and child, furnished to the adverse party at least ten days before trial, shall be admissible in evidence to prove the amount of the charges billed and that the charges were reasonable, necessary and customary. Nothing in this section shall be construed to limit the right of any party to the action or the IV-D agency to summon, at its own expense, a physician, agent of a hospital or other individual for the purpose of examination with respect to such bills or to rebut the contents thereof or for any other purpose to limit the right of a party or the IV-D agency to summon any other person to testify in respect to such bills or for any other purpose.

(g) All other evidence relevant to the issue of paternity of the child, custody of a child or support of a child shall also be admissible.

(h) In an action pursuant to this chapter where the rights to support of a party have been subrogated to the commonwealth pursuant to chapters 18, 119, or 118E, or Title IV, Parts A or E, or Title XIX of the Social Security Act, or any other public assistance program as required by federal or state law, the court shall proceed to establish orders pursuant to this chapter, notwithstanding the failure of the party to attend a hearing, upon a showing that written notice of the hearing was provided to the party by first class mail to the most recent residential address that the party has provided to the department of transitional assistance, the department of children and families or the division of medical assistance. For good cause shown, the court may set aside an entry of default and, if an order or judgment has been entered, may likewise set aside such order or judgment in accordance with rule 60(b) of the rules of domestic relations procedure.

(i) In an action pursuant to this chapter in a case receiving IV-D services, the court shall, upon good cause shown and upon verification of identity satisfactory to the court, permit a party to testify in an action pursuant to this chapter by telephone; and upon a showing that a party is incarcerated, permit the party to submit testimony by affidavit.

§ 17. Blood or genetic marker tests; affidavit; admissibility of evidence; costs

In an action under this chapter to establish paternity of a child born out of wedlock, the court shall, on motion of a party and upon a proper showing except as provided in this section, order the mother, the child and the putative father to submit to one or more genetic marker tests of a type generally acknowledged as reliable and performed by a laboratory approved by an accreditation body designated by the federal Secretary of Health and Human Services pursuant to Title IV, Part D of the Social Security Act. An affidavit by the mother or the putative father alleging that sexual intercourse between the mother and the putative father occurred during the probable period of conception shall be sufficient to establish a proper showing. If during the probable period of conception, the mother was married to someone other than the putative father, the court may order genetic marker tests only after notice pursuant to subsection (c) of section 6 to the spouse or former spouse. The court or the IV-D agency as provided in section 3A of chapter 119A may, order any person properly made a party under this chapter to submit to such testing. Unless a party objects in writing to the test results upon notice of the hearing date or within thirty days prior to the hearing, whichever is shorter, the report of the results of genetic marker tests, including a statistical probability of the putative father's paternity based upon such tests, shall be admissible in evidence without the need for laying a foundation or other proof of authenticity or accuracy; provided, further, that such report shall not be considered as evidence of the occurrence of intercourse between the mother and the putative father; and provided, however, that such report shall not be admissible absent sufficient evidence of intercourse between the mother and the putative father during the period of probable conception. If such report indicates a statistical probability of paternity of ninety-seven percent or greater, there shall be a rebuttable presumption that the putative father is the father of such child and, upon motion of any party or on its own motion, the court shall issue a temporary order of support. If the report of the results of genetic marker tests or an expert's analysis of inherited characteristics is disputed, the court may then order that an additional test be made at the same laboratory or different laboratory at the expense of the party requesting additional testing. Verified documentation of the chain of custody of genetic marker or other specimens is competent evidence to establish such chain of custody. The fact that any party refuses to submit to a genetic marker test shall be admissible and the court may draw an adverse inference from such refusal. The cost of making any tests ordered pursuant to this section shall, in the first instance, be chargeable against the party making the motion. The court in its discretion may order the costs of such testing to be apportioned among the parties provided, however, the court may not direct the IV-D agency as set forth in chapter 119A to pay for such tests, unless said IV-D agency is the moving party and provided further, that if the putative father is found to be the father, the court shall order the putative father to reimburse the IV-D agency or the other party. Payment for the costs of such tests shall be considered a necessary expense and if any party chargeable with the costs of the genetic marker tests is indigent as provided in section twenty-seven A of chapter two hundred and sixty-one, the court may direct payment of such costs by the commonwealth regardless of the type of tests requested by the moving party.

§ 18. Judgments or orders of support; enforcement

Each judgment or order of support which is issued, reviewed or modified pursuant to this chapter shall conform to and shall be enforced in accordance with the provisions of chapter one hundred and nineteen A.

§ 19. Judgment or temporary order of support; enforcement

A judgment of support issued in conclusion of a proceeding under this chapter or a temporary support order issued under this chapter may be enforced with one or more of the following methods:

(1) contempt in accordance with sections thirty-four and thirty-four A of chapter two hundred and fifteen;

(2) execution of the judgment;

(3) attachment of or lien against property;

(4) trustee process, in accordance with the provisions of chapter two hundred and forty-six;

(5) equitable actions to reach and apply for the enforcement of judgments; and

(6) any other civil remedy available for the enforcement of judgments or for the enforcement of support or custody orders entered under chapter two hundred and eight, and two hundred and nine, or received, entered or registered pursuant to chapter two hundred and nine D, including any remedy available under chapter 119A.

§ 20. Modification of judgments; jurisdiction

[Amended by 2011 Mass. Acts c. 93, § 42, effective July 1, 2012.]

A court with original jurisdiction pursuant to section three has continuing jurisdiction, upon a complaint filed by a person or agency entitled to file original actions, to modify judgments of support, custody or visitation; provided however, that no modification concerning custody or visitation shall be granted unless the court finds that a substantial change in the circumstances of the parties or the child has occurred and finds modification to be in the child's best interests. Except as restricted by section twenty-three, the court may also modify a judgment to protect a party or child. In furtherance of the public policy that dependent children be maintained as completely as possible from the resources of their parents and upon a complaint filed after a judgment of support, orders of maintenance and for support of minor children shall be modified if there is an inconsistency between the amount of the existing order and the amount that would result from application of the child support guidelines promulgated by the chief justice of the trial court or if there is a need to provide for the health care coverage of the child. A modification to provide for the health care coverage of the child shall be entered whether or not a modification in the amount of child support is necessary. There shall be a rebuttable presumption that the amount of the order which would result from the application of the guidelines is the appropriate amount of child support to be ordered. If, after taking into consideration the best interests of the child, the court determines that a party has overcome the presumption, the court shall make specific written findings indicating the amount of the order that would result from application of the guidelines; that the guidelines amount would be unjust or inappropriate under the circumstances; the specific facts of the case which justify departure from the guidelines; and that such departure is consistent with the best interests of the child. The order shall be modified accordingly unless the inconsistency between the amount of the existing order and the amount of the order that would result from application of the guidelines is due to the fact that the amount of the existing order resulted from a rebuttal of the guidelines and that there has been no change in the circumstances which resulted in such rebuttal; provided, however, that even if the specific facts that justified departure from the guidelines upon entry of the original order remain in effect, the order shall be modified in accordance with the guidelines unless the court finds that the guidelines amount would be unjust or inappropriate under the circumstances and that the existing order is consistent with the best interests of the child. A modification of child support may enter notwithstanding an agreement of the parents that has independent legal significance. For cases being enforced by the IV-D agency as set forth in chapter 119A, a support order may also be modified in accordance with section 3B of said chapter 119A.

§ 21. Action to determine mother and child relationship

Any interested party may bring an action to determine the existence of a mother and child relationship. Insofar as practicable, the provisions of this chapter applicable to establishing paternity shall apply.

§ 22. Proceedings barred under this chapter

(a) A decree or judgment entered on a petition filed pursuant to sections three or six of chapter two hundred and ten shall be a bar to a proceeding under this chapter.

(b) A proceeding under chapter two hundred and seven, two hundred and eight, two hundred and nine, two hundred and seventy-three, or two hundred and nine D shall not be a bar to any proceeding under this chapter. An action brought under this chapter may be consolidated with an action brought under chapters two hundred and seven, two hundred and eight, two hundred and nine or two hundred and nine D if both actions are pending in the same department of the trial court.

(c) If an action under chapter two hundred and seven, two hundred and eight, or two hundred and nine, is filed after the commencement of proceedings or after a judgment under this chapter, any order or judgment for support of a child issued in the annulment, divorce or separate support proceedings shall supersede any prior order or judgment for support of the same child under this chapter; and any assignment made under this chapter shall be superseded by an assignment made in the divorce, separate support, or annulment proceeding; provided, however, that nothing herein shall prevent the court in such annulment, separate support or divorce proceeding from entering an order or judgment enforcing any previous support order or judgment for support under this chapter which has not been paid, consistent with the provisions of section nine.

(d) No proceeding hereunder shall be barred by a prior finding or adjudication under any repealed sections of chapter two hundred and seventy-three or by the fact that a child was born prior to the effective date of this chapter.

§ 23. Intermarriage of parents; jurisdiction

[Amended by 2005 Mass. Acts c. 163, § 50, effective Dec. 8, 2005.]

(a) If, after adjudication of paternity or voluntary acknowledgment of parentage, the parents of the child intermarry, any order or judgments of the court relative to support, custody, visitation and restraint on personal liberty shall be null and void, except as to any support arrearage which is owed to the commonwealth as reimbursement for public assistance and which accrued before the date that the parents intermarry and the court shall have no continuing jurisdiction over the parties under this chapter.

(b) If, after proceedings are commenced but before an adjudication of paternity is issued, the parents intermarry, the court may adjudicate paternity hereunder but shall have no other jurisdiction over the child or the parents under this chapter.

(c) An action under this chapter may be commenced after the intermarriage of the parents of the child only to determine paternity.

§ 24. Forms

The administrative justices of the district, Boston municipal and the probate and family court department of the trial court shall jointly promulgate forms for complaints, agreements and registrations of parentage for use under this chapter, which shall be in such form and language to permit a person to prepare and file such forms pro se.

Chapter 210. Adoption of Children and Change of Names

§ 1. Nature of adoption; exercise of court powers

[Amended by 2008 Mass. Acts c. 176, § 116, effective July 8, 2008.]

A person of full age may petition the probate court in the county where he resides for leave to adopt as his child another person younger than himself, unless such other person is his or her wife or husband, or brother, sister, uncle or aunt, of the whole or half blood. A minor may likewise petition, or join in the petition of his or her wife or husband, for the adoption of a natural child of one of the parties. If the petitioner has a husband or wife living, competent to join in the petition, such husband or wife shall join therein, and upon adoption the child shall in law be the child of both; provided, however, that the prayer of the petition may be granted although the spouse of the petitioner is not a party to the petition if the court finds: (i) the failure of the spouse to join in the petition or to consent to the adoption is excused by reason of prolonged unexplained absence, legal separation, prolonged separation, incapacity or circumstances constituting an unreasonable withholding of consent; (ii) the husband and wife are not in the process of an ongoing divorce; and (iii) the granting of the petition is in the best interests of the child. If a person not an inhabitant of this commonwealth desires to adopt a child residing here, the petition may be made to the probate court in the county where the child resides.

The district or juvenile court may, if it appears necessary or convenient, exercise the powers authorized by this chapter, but only in respect to a pending proceeding before such district or juvenile court.

§ 2. Written consent of certain persons; form of consent

[Amended by 2008 Mass. Acts c. 176, § 117, effective July 8, 2008.]

A decree of adoption shall not be made, except as provided in this chapter, without the written consent of the child to be adopted, if above the age of twelve; of the child's spouse, if any; of the lawful parents, who may be previous adoptive parents, or surviving parent; or of the mother only if the child was born out of wedlock and not previously adopted. A person whose consent is hereby required shall not be prevented from being the adoptive parent.

Such written consent shall be executed no sooner than the fourth calendar day after the date of birth of the child to be adopted. It shall be attested and subscribed before a notary public in the presence of two competent witnesses, one of whom shall be selected by said person. The agency or person receiving custody shall act as guardian of the child until such time as a court of competent jurisdiction appoints a guardian or grants a petition for adoption. Execution of such consent shall be carried out in a manner which shall preserve privacy and confidentiality. A copy of said consent shall be filed with the department of children and families. A consent executed in accordance with the provisions of this section shall be final and irrevocable from date of execution.

The form of such consent shall be as follows:—

I, as the (relationship) of (name of child), age _____, of the _____ sex, born in (place of birth), on (date of birth), do hereby voluntarily and unconditionally surrender (child) to the care and custody of (agency or person receiving custody) for the purpose of adoption or such other disposition as may be made by a court of competent jurisdiction. I waive notice of any legal proceeding affecting the custody, guardianship, adoption or other disposition of (child).

I UNDERSTAND THAT THIS SURRENDER IS FINAL AND CANNOT BE REVOKED.

/s/ (person giving consent)

On this _____ day of _____ (insert year), before me personally came and appeared and in my presence duly executed the foregoing instrument, and (he, she) acknowledged to me that (he, she) executed the same as (his, her) free act and deed, fully cognizant of its irrevocability.

Date

State of

Notary Public _____

County of

Signed by (name of person giving consent) as (his, her) freely executed consent in the presence of each of us, and of each other, who thereafter have hereunto signed our names as witnesses.

/s/ _____

Address _____

/s/ _____

Address _____

Any surrender given outside of the commonwealth shall be valid for the purpose of this section if it was taken in accordance with laws of the state or the country where it was executed.

If an agency or person receiving a child born out of wedlock for purposes of a subsequent adoption receives from the child's mother an executed consent form as prescribed by this chapter, and no person has acknowledged paternity of the child in accordance with chapter two hundred and nine C or has been adjudicated the father of the child by any court of competent jurisdiction, then the person or agency shall request that the mother voluntarily provide a sworn written statement, executed before a notary and in the presence of two competent witnesses, one of whom shall be selected by the mother, that identifies the child's father and his current or last known address. Any such statement shall be used solely for the purpose of notifying the person named as the father of the status of the child.

§ 2A. Decree of adoption; entry; conditions precedent

[Amended by 2008 Mass. Acts c. 176, § 118, effective July 8, 2008.]

No decree of adoption shall be entered for the adoption of a child below the age of fourteen until one of the following conditions has been met:

(A) The child sought to be adopted has been placed with the petitioners for adoption by the department of children and families or by an agency authorized by said department for such purpose, or

(B) The petitioner is a blood relative of the child sought to be adopted, or

(C) The petitioner is a step-parent of the child sought to be adopted, or

(D) The petitioner was nominated in the will of a deceased natural parent of the child as a guardian or an adoptive parent, or

(E) The petition for adoption has been approved in writing by the department of children and families or by an agency authorized by said department. Any petitioner aggrieved by the refusal of the department or of an agency to approve such petition after being requested to do so, may appeal such refusal to the probate court in which the petition for adoption is pending, which court shall make final determination as to the allowance or dismissal of the petition.

§ 2B. Adoption decrees; mandatory language

Every decree of adoption entered by the court shall include the words "This adoption is final and irrevocable."

§ 3. Dispensing with required consent in certain cases

[Amended by 2008 Mass. Acts c. 176, § 119, effective July 8, 2008; 2011 Mass. Acts c. 93, § 43, effective July 1, 2012.]

(a) Whenever a petition for adoption is filed by a person having the care or custody of a child, the consent of the persons named in section 2, other than that of the child, shall not be required if:— (i) the person to be adopted is 18 years of age or older; or (ii) the court hearing the petition finds that the allowance of the petition is in the best interests of the child pursuant to paragraph (c).

(b) The department of children and families or a licensed child care agency may commence a proceeding, independent of a petition for adoption, in the probate court in Suffolk county or in any other county in which the department or agency maintains an office, to dispense with the need for consent of any person named in section 2 to adoption of the child in the care or custody of the department or agency. Notice of such proceeding shall be given to such person in a manner prescribed by the court. The court shall appoint counsel to represent the child in the proceeding unless the petition is not contested by any party. The court shall issue a decree dispensing with the need for consent or notice of any petition for adoption, custody, guardianship or other disposition of the child named therein, if it finds that the best interests of the child as provided in paragraph (c) will be served by the decree. Pending a hearing on the merits of a petition filed under this paragraph, temporary custody may be awarded to the petitioner. The entry of such decree shall have the effect of terminating the rights of a person named therein to receive notice of or to consent to any legal proceeding affecting the custody, guardianship, adoption or other disposition of the child named therein. The department shall provide notice of the hearing on the merits to any foster parent, pre-adoptive parent or relative providing care for the child informing the foster parent, pre-adoptive parent or relative of his right to attend the hearing and be heard. The provisions of this paragraph shall not be construed to require that a foster parent, pre-adoptive parent or relative be made a party to the proceeding.

A petition brought pursuant to this paragraph may be filed and a decree entered notwithstanding the pendency of a petition brought under chapter 119 or chapter 201 regarding the same child. The chief justice of the trial court may, pursuant to the provisions of section 9 of chapter 211B, assign a justice from any department of the trial court to sit as a justice in any other department or departments of the trial court and hear simultaneously a petition filed under this paragraph and any other pending case or cases involving custody or adoption of the same child. A temporary or permanent custody decree shall not be a requirement to the filing of such petition.

A juvenile court or a district court shall enter a decree dispensing with the need for consent of any person named in section 2 to the adoption of a child named in a petition filed pursuant to section 24 of chapter 119 in such court upon a finding that such child is in need of care and protection pursuant to section 26 of said chapter 119 and that the best interests of the child as defined in paragraph (c) will be served by such decree. The entry of such decree shall have the effect of terminating the rights of a person named therein to receive notice of or to consent to any legal proceeding affecting the custody, guardianship, adoption or other disposition of the child named therein. Facts may be set forth either in the care and protection petition filed pursuant to said section 24 of said chapter 119 or upon a motion made in the course of a care and protection proceeding, alleging that the allowance of the petition or motion is in the best interests of the child.

The department of children and families shall file a petition or, in the alternative, a motion to amend a petition pending pursuant to section 26 of chapter 119 to dispense with parental consent to adoption, custody, guardianship or other disposition of the child under the following circumstances: (i) the child has been abandoned; (ii) the parent has been convicted by a court of competent jurisdiction of the murder or voluntary manslaughter of another child of such parent, of aiding, abetting, attempting, conspiring or soliciting to commit such murder or voluntary manslaughter or of any assault constituting a felony which results in serious bodily injury to the child or to another child of the parent; or (iii) the child has been in foster care in the custody of the commonwealth for 15 of the immediately preceding 22 months. For the purposes of this paragraph, a child shall be considered to have entered foster care on the earlier of: (a) the date of the first judicial finding, pursuant to section 24 or section 26 of chapter 119, that the child has been subjected to abuse or neglect; or (b) the date that is 60 days after the date on which the child is removed from the home. For the purposes of this paragraph, "serious bodily injury" shall mean bodily injury which involves a substantial risk of death, extreme physical pain, protracted and obvious disfigurement or protracted loss or impairment of the function of a bodily member, organ or mental faculty.

The department shall concurrently identify, recruit, process and approve a qualified family for adoption.

The department need not file a motion or petition to dispense with parental consent to the adoption, custody, guardianship or other disposition of the child, or, where the child is the subject of a pending petition pursuant to section 26 of chapter 119, a motion to amend the petition to dispense with parental consent to the adoption, custody, guardianship or other disposition of the child, if the child is being cared for by a relative or the department has documented in the case plan a compelling reason for determining that such a petition would not be in the best interests of the child or that the family of the child has not been provided, consistent with the time period in the case plan, such services as the department deems necessary for the safe return of the child to the child's home if reasonable efforts as set forth in section 29C of said chapter 119 are required to be made with respect to the child.

(c) In determining whether the best interests of the child will be served by granting a petition for adoption without requiring certain consent as permitted under paragraph (a), the court shall consider the ability, capacity, fitness and readiness of the child's parents or other person named in section 2 to assume parental responsibility and shall also consider the ability, capacity, fitness and readiness of the petitioners under said paragraph (a) to assume such responsibilities. In making the determination, the health and safety of the child shall be of paramount, but not exclusive, concern.

In determining whether the best interests of the child will be served by issuing a decree dispensing with the need for consent as permitted under paragraph (b), the court shall consider the ability, capacity, fitness and readiness of the child's parents or other person named in section 2 to assume parental responsibility, and shall also consider the plan proposed by the department or other agency initiating the petition. In making the determination, the health and safety of the child shall be of paramount, but not exclusive, concern.

In considering the fitness of the child's parent or other person named in section 2, the court shall consider, without limitation, the following factors:

(i) the child has been abandoned;

(ii) the child or another member of the immediate family of the child has been abused or neglected as a result of the acts or omissions of one or both parents, the parents were offered or received services intended to correct the circumstances which led to the abuse or neglect and refused, or were unable to utilize such services on a regular and consistent basis so that a substantial danger of abuse or neglect continues to exist, or have utilized such services on a regular and consistent basis without effectuating a substantial and material or permanent change in the circumstances which led to the abuse or neglect;

(iii) a court of competent jurisdiction has transferred custody of the child from the child's parents to the department, the placement has lasted for at least six months and the parents have not maintained significant and meaningful contact with the child during the previous six months nor have they, on a regular and consistent basis, accepted or productively utilized services intended to correct the circumstances;

(iv) the child is four years of age or older, a court of competent jurisdiction has transferred custody of the child from the child's parents to the department and custody has remained with the department for at least 12 of the immediately preceding 15 months and the child cannot be returned to the custody of the parents at the end of such 15-month period; provided, however, that the parents were offered or received services intended to correct the circumstances and refused or were unable to utilize such services on a regular and consistent basis;

(v) the child is younger than four years of age, a court of competent jurisdiction has transferred custody of the child from the child's parents to the department and custody has remained with the department for at least 6 of the immediately preceding 12 months and the child cannot be returned to the custody of the parents at the end of such 12-month period; provided, however, that the parents were offered or received services intended to correct the circumstances and refused or were unable to utilize such services on a regular and consistent basis;

(vi) the parent, without excuse, fails to provide proper care or custody for the child and there is a reasonable expectation that the parent will not be able to provide proper care or custody within a reasonable time considering the age of the child provided that the parents were offered or received services intended to correct the circumstances and refused or were unable to utilize such services on a regular and consistent basis;

(vii) because of the lengthy absence of the parent or the parent's inability to meet the needs of the child, the child has formed a strong, positive bond with his substitute caretaker, the bond has existed for a substantial portion of the child's life, the forced removal of the child from the caretaker would likely cause serious psychological harm to the child and the parent lacks the capacity to meet the special needs of the child upon removal;

(viii) a lack of effort by a parent or other person named in section 2 to remedy conditions which create a risk of harm due to abuse or neglect of the child;

(ix) severe or repetitive conduct of a physically, emotionally or sexually abusive or neglectful nature toward the child or toward another child in the home;

(x) the willful failure to visit the child where the child is not in the custody of the parent or other person named in section 2;

(xi) the willful failure to support the child where the child is not in the custody of the parent or other person named in section 2. Failure to support shall mean that the parent or other person has failed to make a material contribution to the child's care when the contribution has been requested by the department or ordered by the court;

(xii) a condition which is reasonably likely to continue for a prolonged, indeterminate period, such as alcohol or drug addiction, mental deficiency or mental illness, and the condition makes the parent or other person named in section 2 unlikely to provide minimally acceptable care of the child;

(xiii) the conviction of a parent or other person named in section 2 of a felony that the court finds is of such a nature that the child will be deprived of a stable home for a period of years. Incarceration in and of itself shall not be grounds for termination of parental rights; or

(xiv) whether or not there has been a prior pattern of parental neglect or misconduct or an assault constituting a felony which resulted in serious bodily injury to the child and a likelihood of future harm to the child based on such prior pattern or assault.

For the purposes of this section "abandoned" shall mean being left without any provision for support and without any person responsible to maintain care, custody and control because the whereabouts of the person responsible therefor is unknown and reasonable efforts to locate the person have been unsuccessful. A brief and temporary absence from the home without intent to abandon the child shall not constitute abandonment.

Hearings on petitions to dispense with consent to adoption that allege that a child has been abandoned shall be scheduled and heard on an expedited basis. Notwithstanding the foregoing, the following circumstances shall constitute grounds for dispensing with the need for consent to adoption, custody, guardianship or other disposition of the child: (i) the child has been abandoned; (ii) the parent has been convicted by a court of competent jurisdiction of the murder or voluntary manslaughter of another child of such parent, of aiding, abetting, attempting, conspiring or soliciting to commit such murder or voluntary manslaughter or of an assault constituting a felony which resulted in serious bodily injury to the child or to another child of the parent. For the purposes of this section, "serious bodily injury" shall mean bodily injury which involves a substantial risk of death, extreme physical pain, protracted and obvious disfigurement or protracted loss or impairment of the function of a bodily member, organ or mental faculty.

(d) Nothing in this section shall be construed to prohibit the petitioner and a birth parent from entering into an agreement for post-termination contact or communication. The court issuing the termination decree under this section shall have jurisdiction to resolve matters concerning the agreement. Such agreement shall become null and void upon the entry of an adoption or guardianship decree.

Notwithstanding the existence of any agreement for post-termination or post-adoption contact or communication, the decree entered under this section shall be final.

Nothing in this section shall be construed to prohibit a birth parent who has entered into a post-termination agreement from entering into an agreement for post-adoption contact or communication pursuant to section 6C once an adoptive family has been identified.

§ 3A. Repealed
[Repealed by 1972 Mass. Acts c. 800, § 3.]

§ 3B. Registration of interest for pre-adoptive or adoptive placement; criminal record review
When deciding whether to approve or reject a registration of interest for pre-adoptive or adoptive placement, the department shall conduct a review of any misdemeanor offense discovered through a criminal offender record information search conducted pursuant to section 172B of chapter 6 in order to assist the department in accurately evaluating whether the mere existence of the offense has a substantial effect on the applicant's current or future ability to assume and carry out the responsibilities of an adoptive or pre-adoptive parent in such a manner that the rights of the child to sound health and normal physical, mental, spiritual and moral development are insured. The review shall include, but need not be limited to, a review of the following: the time that has elapsed between the date of the offense and the filing of the registration of interest, the seriousness and specific circumstances of the offense, the number and nature of other offenses, the age of the offender at the time of the offense, the findings and recommendations of the family resource worker assigned by the department to discuss the facts surrounding the misdemeanor with the applicant, the recommendations given to the family resource worker by personal or employment references chosen by the applicant or received otherwise, the current and future needs of the child to be placed or adopted and the probable effect that the misdemeanor would have on the applicant's ability to fulfill those needs, any reports or recommendations received by the department from the applicant's parole or probation officer should one have been assigned, a copy of the police report pertaining to the offense in question if obtainable within a reasonable period of time or discussions with a police officer familiar with the facts surrounding the offense and, unless inappropriate, discussions with the child to be placed regarding his current and past relationship with the applicant. Nothing in this section shall be construed to affect the discretion of the department to approve or reject the registration of interest for adoptive or pre-adoptive placement.

§ 4. Notice
[Amended by 2008 Mass. Acts c. 176, § 120, effective July 8, 2008.]

If the written consent required by section two is not submitted to the court with the petition, the court shall, except where the court under section three has determined that such consent and notice is not required, order notice by personal service upon the parties of an order of notice, in such form as shall be prescribed under section thirty of chapter two hundred and fifteen, or, if the parties are not found within this commonwealth, by publication of said order of notice once in each of three successive weeks in such newspaper as the court orders, the last publication to be seven days at least before the time appointed for the hearing, and the court may require additional notice and consent. But if such child is of unknown parentage and is a foundling, publication as herein set forth shall not be required; but notice of the petition shall be given to the department of children and families.

§ 4A. Fathers of children born out of wedlock; adoption rights
[Amended by 2008 Mass. Acts c. 176, § 121, effective July 8, 2008.]

Whenever the mother of a child born out of wedlock has surrendered the child in accordance with section two, or whenever the right of such mother to withhold consent for adoption has been terminated in accordance with section three, notice of such surrender or termination and a right to petition for adoption shall be afforded to any person who, prior to such surrender or termination, has filed a declaration seeking to assert the responsibilities of fatherhood, hereinafter called a parental responsibility claim, or has been adjudicated the father of the child, except when a decree has been issued pursuant to section three dispensing with the need of consent of said father. The paternal responsibility claim shall be filed with the department of children and families, hereinafter called the department, on a form prescribed by the department. The department shall provide the person filing with evidence of the filing within five days and shall at the same time, send notice of the filing to such mother by registered mail at her address as stated on the paternal responsibility claim or to such other address as the department determines to be correct after making every reasonable effort to locate such mother. Such filing shall constitute an acknowledgment and admission of paternity.

Upon request of any person or agency receiving a child for the purpose of adoption, the department shall examine all paternal responsibility claims filed with it and shall within five days provide an affidavit to such person or agency stating whether or not there has been a paternal responsibility claim filed with respect to such child. If such a paternal responsibility claim has been filed, the department shall, notify the person claiming paternity by registered mail, at the address stated on said paternal responsibility claim, that the child is in the care of a licensed placement agency which is planning for the adoption of the child. A copy of the notice shall be sent to the person or agency requesting the affidavit. The person claiming paternity may within thirty days from the date of mailing of said notice by the department file a petition for adoption or custody of such child in the probate court of the county where the agency is located. If he fails to do so, he shall not be entitled to notice of any subsequent proceeding concerning custody, guardianship, or adoption of the child. The court shall consider the case as expeditiously as possible, and, without regard to other potential adoptive parents, shall allow the petition of the person claiming paternity if it finds that such adoption or custody is in the child's best interest and if it finds that such person is the father of the child. The court on its own motion may order the production of any evidence to determine if the petitioner is the father of the child. Any such petition shall be subject to clause (E) of section two A. Any costs incurred for the temporary care of the child pending the hearing on the petition of the person claiming paternity shall be borne by said person.

No other petition for adoption shall be allowed without proof of compliance with this section.

§ 5. Failure to object after notice; proceedings
If, after such notice, a person whose consent is required does not appear and object to the adoption, the court may act upon the petition without his consent, subject to his right of appeal, or it may appoint a guardian ad litem with power to give or withhold consent.

§ 5A. Children under fourteen; adoption; regulations; removals
[Amended by 2008 Mass. Acts c. 176, § 122, effective July 8, 2008.]

Upon the filing of a petition for adoption of a child under the age of fourteen, notice shall be given to the department of children and families which shall make appropriate inquiry to determine the condition and antecedents of the child for the purpose of ascertaining whether he is a proper subject for adoption and to determine whether the petitioners and their home are suitable for the proper rearing of the child. The department shall submit to the court not later than thirty days after receipt of such notice such written report as will give the court full knowledge as to the desirability of the proposed adoption. In any petition for adoption the department shall submit to the court verification that the adoptee is not registered with the federal register for missing children and the central register. If the report of the department is not submitted to the court within said thirty days, upon motion of the petitioner, seven days notice of which shall be given to the department by service in hand or by certified mail, return receipt requested, the court shall, if the court finds that the department has made substantial progress but has not completed the report due to circumstances

1

beyond the department's control, grant the department up to an additional thirty days in which to complete the report and if the court does not so find, the court shall appoint any charitable corporation organized under general or special laws of the commonwealth for the purpose of engaging in the care of children and principally so engaged to conduct such inquiry, and the report thereof shall have the same force and effect as a report of the department. The court may require such further investigation and report by the department as may be necessary. All reports submitted hereunder shall be filed separate and apart from the other papers in the case, and shall not at any time be open to inspection except by the parties and their attorneys, unless the court, for good cause shown, shall otherwise order. No decree shall be made upon such a petition until such report has been received, nor until the child shall have resided for not less than six months in the home of the petitioner; provided, that for good cause shown the court may, in its discretion, waive the requirement of residence. This section shall not apply in the case of a petition for adoption presented, sponsored or recommended by any charitable corporation organized under general or special laws of the commonwealth for the purpose of engaging in the care of children and principally so engaged; provided, however, that such petitions shall be accompanied by a written report from said charitable corporation, which report shall be of the same force and effect as a report of the department of children and families; and further provided, that no decree shall be made upon such a petition in the case of a child who has resided for less than six months in the home of the petitioner, except that, for good cause shown, the court may, in its discretion, waive the. requirement of residence. Whenever the requirement of residence in the home of the petitioner is waived under this section, the probate judge shall file a memorandum setting forth the facts upon which such waiver was based.

At any time after the report has been filed, the court after notice and hearing shall order the removal of the child from the proposed adoption home if, in the opinion of the court, such removal is in the best interests of the child. If such removal is ordered, the court shall appoint a guardian who shall be a relative of the child, a person designated by the department of children and families or an agency licensed by the department to have custody of the child, with authority to provide for his future care.

The court may waive the provisions of this section in the case of a petition for the adoption of a child of one of the parties petitioning for said adoption.

§ 5B. Adoptive custody; factors considered; request for religious designation

In making orders for adoption, the judge shall consider the need of the child for loving and responsible parental care and all factors relevant to the physical, mental and moral health of the child.

If, at the time of surrender of the child for adoptive custody, the parent or parents of said child requested a religious designation for the child, the court may grant a petition for adoption of the child only to a person or persons of the religious designation so requested, unless a placement for adoptive custody based on such request would not have been in the best interests of the child. If a request for religious designation is not given effect, such reasons in support of such determination shall be made a part of the records of the proceedings.

§ 5C. Inspection of pleadings, reports, etc.; docket book

All petitions for adoption, all reports submitted thereunder and all pleadings, papers or documents filed in connection therewith, docket entries in the permanent docket and record books shall not be available for inspection, unless a judge of probate of the county where such records are kept, for good cause shown, shall otherwise order. Such petitions, reports, pleadings, papers, documents and permanent docket and record books shall be segregated. A separate permanent docket book shall be provided for all such entries. This section shall apply to the index of the court of all such entries, a separate index of which shall be provided.

§ 5D. Release of information concerning adoption

[Amended by 2008 Mass. Acts c. 215, § 79, effective July 31, 2008.]

(a) A placement agency, as defined in section 1A of chapter fifteen, holding records relating to an adopted person, the biological parents of an adopted person or the adoptive parents of an adopted person shall:

(1) release to such adopted person, if he has reached the age of eighteen years, upon his written request, information about his biological parents which will not identify or tend to lead to the identification of the biological parents or their present or former locations.

(2) release to a biological parent of an adopted person, upon the biological parent's written request, information about such adopted person which will not reveal or tend to reveal his identity after adoption or his present or former locations, and which will not tend to lead to his identity after adoption or present or former locations.

(3) release to an adoptive parent, if the adopted person is under the age of eighteen years, upon the adoptive parent's written request, information about the adopted person and his biological parents which will not identify or tend to lead to the identification of the biological parents or their present or former locations.

Such information shall include such nonidentifying information which the agency holds concerning the medical, ethnic, socio-economic, and educational circumstances of the person. The agency, in its discretion, shall further release such nonidentifying information concerning the circumstances under which the adopted person became available for adoption as it deems to be in the best interest of the person so requesting.

(b) If a placement agency, as defined in section nine of chapter twenty-eight A, has received written permission from a biological parent of an adopted person to release the identity of the biological parent to the adopted person and the said agency has received written permission from the adopted person, or written permission from the adoptive parents if the adoptive person is under the age of twenty-one, to release the identity after adoption of the adopted person to the biological parent, then the agency shall release the identity of the adopted person to the biological parent and the identity of the biological parent to the adopted person; provided, however, that if the biological parent is surviving, that he or she has given written consent at least thirty days before the release of said identifying information. The term "biological parent", as used in this subsection, shall mean a biological mother, or a father named on the birth certificate of the adopted person filed in court with the adoption papers, or a man who has signed, as father, an adoption surrender filed in court with the adoption papers.

(c) Information released to a person pursuant to paragraphs (a) and (b) shall be provided in writing if such person so requests.

(d) Such placement agency shall:

(1) release to the biological parent of an adopted person, upon the biological parent's written request, any personal data, as defined in section one of chapter sixty-six A, which it holds relating to the biological parent.

(2) release to an adoptive parent, upon his written request, any personal data, as defined in section one of chapter sixty-six A, which it holds relating to the adoptive parent.

(3) in making any disclosure of information pursuant to this paragraph, the agency shall remove personal identifiers relating to a third person. No agency shall rely on any exception contained in clause Twenty-sixth of section seven of chapter four to withhold personal data otherwise accessible under this paragraph.

(e) All other adoption records held by such placement agency shall be confidential and shall not be released.

§ 5E. Department of children and families adoption report

[Amended by 2008 Mass. Acts c. 176, § 123, effective July 8, 2008.]

The department of children and families shall submit a report detailing the number and nature, as defined jointly by department and the University of Massachusetts center for adoption research and policy in Worcester, of adoptions processed by the department during each calendar quarter to be filed with said center on the first day of each calendar quarter.

§ 6. Decree of court; force and effect; private hearings

[Amended by 2008 Mass. Acts c. 176, § 124, effective July 8, 2008.]

If the court is satisfied of the identity and relations of the persons, and that the petitioner is of sufficient ability to bring up the child and provide suitable support and education for it, and that the child should be adopted, it shall make a decree, by which, except as regards succession to property, all rights, duties and other legal consequences of the natural relation of child and parent shall thereafter exist between the child and the petitioner and his kindred, and such rights, duties and legal consequences shall, except as regards marriage, incest or cohabitation, terminate between the child so adopted and his natural parents and kindred or any previous adopting parent; but such decree shall not place the adopting parent or adopted child in any relation to any person, except each other, different from that before existing as regards marriage, or as regards rape, incest or other sexual crime committed by either or both. The court may also decree such change of name as the petitioner may request. If the person so adopted is of full age, he shall not be freed by such decree from the obligations imposed by section six of chapter one hundred and seventeen and section twenty of chapter two hundred and seventy-three.

In evaluating whether a petitioner is of sufficient ability to provide suitable support for the child, the court shall give consideration to assurances by the department of children and families that it will provide an adoption subsidy for the child.

No decree shall be made under this section until there has been filed in the court a statement, signed and sworn to by the petitioner, or petitioners, setting forth the date of birth and place of residence of each adopting parent and such other facts relating to each such parent as would be required by section thirteen of chapter forty-six for the correction of the record of the birth of the person sought to be adopted, and also a copy of the birth record of such person; provided, that in case such person has been previously adopted, either a copy of the record of his birth amended to conform to the previous decree of adoption or a copy of such decree may be so filed; and, provided further, that the filing of any such copy may be dispensed with if the judge is satisfied that it cannot be obtained.

Every decree of adoption entered by the court shall include the words "This adoption is final and irrevocable."

The probate judge may determine that the hearing on any adoption petition shall be held in chambers. He shall, on the request of any party to an adoption proceeding, hold the hearing thereon in chambers, except that if said petition is contested, the consent of the other party or parties shall be required. No person shall be allowed to be present at any such hearing unless his presence is necessary either as a party or as a witness, and the probate judge shall exclude the general public from the hearing.

§ 6A. Certificates of adoption

The court shall forthwith, following the making of a decree of adoption, issue to the petitioner, or petitioners, a certificate of adoption setting forth all the facts relating to the adopting parent, or parents, as appearing in the statement required to be filed by section six, the name of, and all other facts relating to, the person adopted, as appearing in any copy of birth record or decree of adoption filed as required by said section, the name of the court making such decree and the date thereof, and, if such decree authorizes a change in the name of the person adopted, his name as so changed; provided, that if such person has been born out of wedlock, the name, or names, of, and all other facts relating to, his natural parent, or parents, shall be omitted from such certificate.

Certificates under this section shall be made on forms furnished by the commissioner of public health, and shall provide for the indicating thereon by the adopting parent, or parents, as to whether or not a correction of the record of the birth of the person adopted is desired; and, in case such desire is so indicated, the court shall forthwith send a certified copy of such certificate to the clerk of the city or town where such person was born.

If either of the parents who have adopted a child so request, the register of probate shall issue a special certificate of adoption upon which the original or prior name of the child and the names of its natural parents shall not appear.

§ 6B. Adoption nunc pro tunc

In the event that either of the petitioning adopting parents to a petition for adoption, which has been filed with the probate court, should die prior to the entry of a decree of adoption, the probate court may enter a decree within three months following the date of death nunc pro tunc to the date of the filing of the adoption petition. Said decree shall have all of the effect of a decree of adoption as to both petitioners and the person adopted as provided for in section seven.

§ 6C. Post-adoption contact or communication

[Amended by 2008 Mass. Acts c. 176, § 125, effective July 8, 2008.]

(a) Prior to the entry of an adoption decree, prospective adoptive parents and a birth parent may enter into an agreement for post-adoption contact or communication between or among a minor to be adopted, the prospective adoptive parents and the birth parents. Such agreement may be approved by the court issuing the termination decree under section 3; provided, however, that an agreement under this section shall be finally approved by the court issuing the adoption decree. Any breach, modification or invalidation of the agreement, or any part of it, shall not affect the validity of the adoption. The adoption shall be final.

(b) The court shall approve an agreement for post-adoption contact or communication if the court finds that such agreement:

(i) is in the best interests of the child;

(ii) contains terms that are fair and reasonable; and

(iii) has been entered knowingly and voluntarily by all parties to the agreement. This requirement may be satisfied by an affidavit executed by all parties, either jointly or separately, that is filed with the court. The affidavit shall state that the agreement is entered into knowingly and voluntarily and is not the product of coercion or duress. The court may hear testimony from the parties to the agreement.

(c) To be approved by the court, an agreement for post-adoption contact or communication shall contain the following statements:

(i) This agreement is entered into pursuant to the provisions of section 6C of chapter 210 of the General Laws.

(ii) Any breach, modification or invalidation of the agreement or any part of it shall not affect the validity of the adoption. The adoption shall be final.

(iii) The parties acknowledge that either the birth or adoptive parents who have entered into the agreement have the right to seek enforcement as set forth in section 6D of chapter 210 of the General Laws.

(iv) The parties have not relied on any representations other than those contained in this agreement.

The agreement shall be signed by the parties and acknowledged before a notary public as the free act and deed of the parties. If the child is above the age of 12, the agreement shall contain the written consent of the child. If the child is in the custody of the department of children and families, the agreement shall contain the written approval of the department and the attorney for the child. If the child is in the custody of a licensed child care agency, the agreement shall contain the written approval of the agency.

(d) To be enforceable, an agreement for post-adoption contact or communication shall be: (i) in writing; (ii) approved by the court prior to the date for entry of the adoption decree; and (iii) incorporated but not merged into the adoption decree, and shall survive as an independent contract.

(e) An agreement under this section need not disclose the identity of the parties to be enforceable; but if an identity is not disclosed, the unidentified person shall designate an agent for the purpose of service of process.

(f) An agreement for post-adoption contact or communication shall cease to be enforceable on the date the adopted person turns 18 years of age.

§ 6D. Enforcement of agreement

A party to a court-approved agreement for post-adoption contact or communication may seek to enforce the agreement by commencing a civil action for specific performance. A court order for specific performance of the terms of a post-adoption contact agreement shall be the sole remedy for breach of an agreement.

In such proceedings, parties shall not be entitled to the appointment of counsel; provided, however, that the court may appoint a guardian ad litem to represent the interests of the child.

In an enforcement proceeding, the court may modify the terms of the agreement if the court finds that there has been a material and substantial change in circumstances and the modification is necessary in the best interests of the child. A court-imposed modification of a previously approved agreement may limit, restrict, condition or decrease contact between the birth parents and the child but in no event shall a court-imposed modification serve to expand, enlarge or increase the amount of contact between the birth parents and the child or place new obligations on adoptive parents.

If the court finds that an action brought under this section was wholly insubstantial, frivolous and not advanced in good faith in accordance with the provisions of section 6F of chapter 231, the court may award attorney's fees to all prevailing parties.

Nothing in the agreement shall preclude a party seeking to enforce an agreement for post-adoption contact or communication from utilizing child welfare mediation or permanency mediation before, or in addition to, the commencement of a civil action for specific enforcement. All proceedings conducted under this section shall be closed to the public and confidential and papers shall be segregated in accordance with section 5D.

§ 6E. Decisions of adoptive parent on behalf of child

Nothing contained in sections 6C and 6D shall be construed to abrogate the right of an adoptive parent to make decisions on behalf of his child.

§ 7. Repealed

[Repealed by 2012 Mass. Acts c. 140, § 57, effective July 8, 2012.]

§ 8. Repealed

[Repealed by 2012 Mass. Acts c. 140, § 58, effective July 8, 2012.]

§ 9. Succession to property; right of child adopted in foreign state

A person adopted in another state or country, in accordance with the laws thereof, shall upon proof of such fact be entitled in this commonwealth to the same rights of succession to property by grant, trust settlement, entail, devise, bequest, or by intestacy as he would have had if he had been adopted in the commonwealth.

§ 10. Second adoption; effect

If the child has been previously adopted, all the legal consequences of the former decree shall, upon a subsequent adoption, determine, except so far as any interest in property may have vested in the adopted child, and a decree to that effect shall be entered on the records of the court.

§ 11. Appeals

The supreme judicial court may allow a parent, who, upon a petition for adoption, had no notice of the proceedings before the decree and had neither waived notice in accordance with section two nor been the subject of a decree dispensing with need for notice in accordance with section three, to appeal therefrom within one hundred and twenty days after actual notice thereof.

§ 11A. Adoption services offered by certain persons or agencies; penalty

[Amended by 2008 Mass. Acts c. 176, § 126, effective July 8, 2008; 2008 Mass. Acts c. 215, § 80, effective July 31, 2008.]

Any person or entity other than a duly authorized agent or employee of the department of children and families or a child care or placement agency licensed under the provisions of chapter 15D, who causes to be published in the commonwealth an advertisement or notice of children offered or wanted for adoption, or in any way offers to place, locate or dispose of children offered or wanted for adoption, or who holds himself out in any way as being able to place, locate or dispose of children for adoption shall be punished by a fine of not less than one hundred nor more than one thousand dollars. Any such person who shall accept payment in the form of money or other consideration in return for placing a child for adoption shall be punished by a fine of not less than five thousand and not more than thirty thousand dollars, or by imprisonment in jail or house of correction for not more than two and one-half years or in the state prison for not more than five years, or both.

CHANGE OF NAMES

§ 12. Petitions for change of name

A petition for the change of name of a person may be heard by the probate court in the county where the petitioner resides. The change of name of a person shall be granted unless such change is inconsistent with public interests.

§ 13. Notice and certificate; decree; entry; conditions precedent

The court shall, before decreeing a change of name, request a report from the commissioner of probation on the person filing the petition and, except for good cause shown, require public notice of the petition to be given and any person may be heard thereon, and, upon entry of a decree, the name as established thereby shall be the legal name of the petitioner, and the register may issue a certificate, under the seal of the court, of the name as so established.

No decree shall be entered, however, until there has been filed in the court a copy of the birth record of the person whose name is sought to be changed and, in case such person's name has previously been changed by decree of court or at marriage pursuant to section one D of chapter forty-six, either a copy of the record of his birth amended to conform to the previous decree changing his name, a copy of such decree, or a copy of the record of marriage; provided, that the filing of any such copy may be dispensed with if the judge is satisfied that it cannot be obtained.

§ 14. Annual return of changes

Each register of probate shall annually, in December, make a return to the commissioner of public health and the commissioner of probation of all changes of name made in his court.

1

Chapter 211. Supreme Judicial Court

§ 3. Superintendence of inferior courts; power to issue writs and process

[Amended by 2011 Mass. Acts c. 93, § 46, effective July 1, 2012.]

The supreme judicial court shall have general superintendence of all courts of inferior jurisdiction to correct and prevent errors and abuses therein if no other remedy is expressly provided; and it may issue all writs and processes to such courts and to corporations and individuals which may be necessary to the furtherance of justice and to the regular execution of the laws.

In addition to the foregoing, the justices of the supreme judicial court shall also have general superintendence of the administration of all courts of inferior jurisdiction, including, without limitation, the prompt hearing and disposition of matters pending therein, and the functions set forth in section 3C; and it may issue such writs, summonses and other processes and such orders, directions and rules as may be necessary or desirable for the furtherance of justice, the regular execution of the laws, the improvement of the administration of such courts, and the securing of their proper and efficient administration; provided, however, that general superintendence shall not include the authority to supersede any general or special law unless the supreme judicial court, acting under its original or appellate jurisdiction finds such law to be unconstitutional in any case or controversy. Nothing herein contained shall affect existing law governing the selection of officers of the courts, or limit the existing authority of the officers thereof to appoint administrative personnel.

Chapter 211B. Trial Court of the Commonwealth

§ 10. Chief justice and deputy court administrators; powers and duties

[Amended by 2011 Mass. Acts c. 93, § 52, effective July 1, 2012.]

Subject to the superintendence authority of the supreme judicial court as provided in section 3 of chapter 211, the chief justice and the deputy court administrator shall be responsible for the operation of their department, its clerks, other officers and employees subject to section 99 of chapter 276 and the appropriate collective bargaining agreement. To achieve sound operation of their department they shall have the following powers, authority and responsibilities, and shall allocate between themselves and the deputy court administrator primary responsibility for each in a manner that conforms to the division of responsibilities between the chief justice of the trial court and the court administrator under sections 9 and 9A of chapter 211B; provided, however, that any power specifically assigned to the chief justice in the subsections that follow shall be performed by the chief justice alone:

(i) the power to appoint, discipline, evaluate, transfer and define the duties of all non-judicial personnel within their department including special masters, court reporters, law clerks, temporary clerks and other support personnel consistent with the provisions of section 8 and 10A; provided, however, that they shall not have the power to appoint non-judicial personnel serving in the office of a clerk, recorder or register, but shall have the authority to discipline said clerks, recorders and registers and all other personnel in the offices of said clerks, recorders or registers, upon the raising of any dispute between a first justice and a clerk, recorder or register. Any person aggrieved by any decision of a chief justice or deputy court administrator under this paragraph may appeal such decision to the chief justice of the trial court; provided, further, that no person holding a commission as a clerk of court, whether elected or appointed, a register of probate or a recorder shall be assigned under the provisions of this paragraph outside the department, division or court to which he is elected or appointed without his consent. Any clerk aggrieved by any transfer or assignment of himself or personnel of his office under this paragraph shall appeal to the court administrator who shall forthwith hear and determine the matter;

(ii) the chief justice shall have the power to assign or to transfer justices appointed to his department of the trial court to any particular court within that department for such period or periods of time as the chief justice deems necessary; the chief justice shall also have the power to appoint regional justices and to define their duties. Any justice aggrieved by an order of the chief justice assigning or transferring him to a particular court other than that to which he was appointed, may appeal the assignment or transfer to the chief justice of the trial court who shall forthwith determine the matter;

(iii) the authority, prior to making assignments or transfers referred to in paragraph (ii) of this section, to ascertain, if they so desire, the respective preferences of the justices as to which court or courts, if any, they wish to be assigned or transferred.

(iv) the power to suspend any particular session in any court within their department; the power to move sessions so that the availability of court personnel is consistent with the needs of individual courts; and to make such periodic adjustments in the scheduling and locations of court sessions as are deemed necessary for the proper administration of justice;

(v) the chief justice shall have the power to transfer cases and matters from a court to any other court within his department, to consolidate cases;

(vi) notwithstanding any general or special law to the contrary, when necessary to ensure the proper administration of justice, transfer employees of their department to serve where needed; impose discipline on such officers and employees, including dismissal and suspension with or without pay; provided, however, that they may, upon reasonable notice, temporarily transfer nonjudicial personnel within their department, divisions and places for holding court, and in no event shall any such transfer be more than a reasonable distance from the place where such personnel is employed unless the employee so transferred shall consent thereto; provided, further, that such transfer of the employee shall not be for more than 90 days, but such transfer may be extended for 3 consecutive 90 day periods, provided that notice is given to the house and senate committees on ways and means upon each extension, including the employee's position, duties, and reason for the transfer, but such transfer shall not exceed 360 consecutive days. The first justice of the court to where the employee is transferred shall provide the first justice of the court to where the employee is permanently assigned with appropriate personnel records and records of activities, including records necessary for the payment of compensation; and provided, however, that this provision shall not apply to a clerk or clerk-magistrate, whether elected or appointed by the governor, register of probate or recorder;

(vii) the authority to visit any court within their department;

(viii) the authority to call conferences of any or all of the justices within their department;

(ix) the responsibility to compile a comprehensive written report of the operation of their department of the trial court at the conclusion of each fiscal year, and shall deliver said report together with recommendations to the chief justice of the trial court and the court administrator on or before October 15 of the ensuing fiscal year. They shall make such additional reports as may from time to time be required by the chief justice of the trial court or the court administrator;

(x) the responsibility to perform such further administrative duties as may from time to time be assigned by the chief justice of the trial court or the court administrator;

(xi) the responsibility, annually, to prepare and submit to the court administrator a budget estimate, in detail, for the ordinary maintenance of their department of the trial court, and all revenue therefrom, as provided in clause (5) of the first paragraph of section 3 of chapter 29. Said budget estimate shall include judicial salaries and the salaries of employees within said department and shall include estimates of all sums which the commonwealth is obligated to pay under the provisions of chapter 29A;

(xii) the authority, upon receipt of an appropriated sum, to administer that appropriation;

(xiii) the responsibility for the administrative management of the personnel, staff services and business of their departments, including financial administration and budget preparation, record-keeping, information systems and statistical controls, purchasing, planning, construction, case flow management, assignments of sittings of the justices of their respective departments, including justices not appointed thereto but assigned, for the time being therein. They may delegate their responsibilities and powers hereunder and as otherwise provided by law to a justice, regional justice, first justice, court officer, clerk, or any employee of their department, for such period of time and with such limitations as he may impose, whenever in their opinion such delegation of authority will expedite the judicial business of the department; provided, however, that in the exercise or delegation of their powers, they shall in all cases act in a manner consistent with the policies and procedures established by the court administrator and the chief justice of the trial court;

(xiv) the power to set the days and hours during which courts within their department shall be open for business;

(xv) the chief justice shall have the responsibility to sit and perform judicial duties, within his department, during the course of the calendar year;

(xvi) the chief justice shall have the power to discipline any justice assigned or appointed to his department who refuses or fails to comply with any order concerning the performance of his duties as justice or any other lawful order of the chief justice or deputy court administrator of his department; provided, however, that the chief justice shall also have the power to require any justice assigned or appointed to his department to participate in a judicial enhancement program in response to any action of such justice which brings the judiciary into disrepute, which lowers the public confidence in the judiciary or which impedes the administration of justice. A justice who is disciplined by the chief justice may appeal the imposition of discipline to the chief justice of the trial court. Any justice aggrieved by decision of the chief justice of the trial court may appeal said decision to the supreme judicial court. Consistent with the provisions of chapter 211C, all proceedings, documents, and other matters relating to such discipline shall at all times be confidential and not open to the public unless the justice appealing the disciplinary action agrees that the same shall not be confidential, or unless the supreme judicial court determines that it is in the public interest for any such proceeding, document, or other matter relating to such discipline to be made public. All disciplinary action imposed by a chief justice, whether consensual or not, shall be reported to the supreme judicial court by the chief justice; and

(xvii) the power, notwithstanding any law to the contrary, to transfer cases between courts consistent with the efficient distribution of caseload and workload within said department;

The chief justice and deputy court administrator shall likewise allocate between themselves in a manner on which they agree and subject to the approval of the chief justice of the trial court and the court administrator, the powers assigned to the chief justice pursuant to section 6 of chapter 29A; sections 4 5, 9, 10, 11, 14, and section 16 of chapter 185C; section 13 of said chapter 211B; section 19 of chapter 212; sections 23, 23A, 23C, 28, 29, 29A, 29B, 29C, 29D, 29E, 29F, 29G, 29H, 29I, 29J, 29K, 29L and section 42 of chapter 217; sections 9, 15, 19D, 43E, 58, 67 and section 70 of chapter 218; section 6 of chapter 220; sections 62B, 91 and section 99 of chapter 221; section 1B of chapter 279 or any other general or special law that are not inherently judicial in nature.

The chief justice and deputy court administrator shall be provided with suitable offices.

Chapter 211D. Committee for Public Counsel Services

Section

§ 1. Committee for public counsel services; establishment

[Amended by 2011 Mass. Acts c. 68, § 112, effective July 1, 2011; 2018 Mass. Acts c. 24, § 3, effective Feb. 16, 2018.]

There shall be a committee for public counsel services, hereinafter referred to as the committee, to plan, oversee, and coordinate the delivery of criminal and certain noncriminal legal services by salaried public counsel, bar advocate and other assigned counsel programs and private attorneys serving on a per case basis. The committee shall consist of 15 persons: 2 of whom shall be appointed by the governor; 2 of whom shall be appointed by the president of the senate; 2 of whom shall be appointed by the speaker of the house of representatives; and 9 of whom shall be appointed by the justices of the supreme judicial court, 1 of whom shall have experience as a public defender, 1 of whom shall have experience as a private bar advocate, 1of whom shall have criminal appellate experience, 1 shall have a background in public administration and public finance, and 1 of whom shall be a current or former dean or faculty member of a law school. The court shall request and give appropriate consideration to nominees for the 9 positions from the Massachusetts Bar Association, county bar associations, the Boston Bar Association and other appropriate bar groups including, but not limited to, the Massachusetts Black Lawyers' Association, Inc., Women's Bar Association of Massachusetts, Inc., and the Massachusetts Association of Women Lawyers, Inc.

All members of the committee shall have a strong commitment to quality representation in indigent defense matters or have significant experience with issues related to indigent defense. The committee shall not include presently serving judges, elected state, county or local officials, district attorneys, state or local law enforcement officials or public defenders employed by the commonwealth. The term of office of each member of the committee shall be 4 years. Members of the committee may be removed for cause by the justices of the supreme judicial court. Vacancies shall be filled by the appointing authority that made the initial appointment to the unexpired term of the appointee within 60 days of the occurrence of the vacancy. An appointee shall continue in office beyond the expiration date of the appointee's term until a successor in office has been appointed and qualified. No member shall receive any compensation for service on the committee, but each member shall be reimbursed for actual expenses incurred in attending the committee meetings.

Chapter 268A shall apply to all members, officers and employees of the committee, except that the committee may provide representation or enter into a contract pursuant to section 3 or section 6, although a member of the committee may have an interest or involvement in any such matter if such interest and involvement is disclosed in advance to the other members of the committee and recorded in the minutes of the committee; provided, however, that no member having an interest or involvement in any contract under section 3 may participate in any particular matter, as defined in section 1 of chapter 268A, relating to such contract.

§ 2. Indigency; definition, standards and procedures for determination

[Amended by 2011 Mass. Acts c. 68, § 112, effective July 1, 2011.]

The committee for public counsel services shall establish a definition of "indigency" for the purposes of this chapter and uniform standards and procedures for the determination by the courts of the commonwealth that: (1) a person is indigent and is unable to obtain counsel or (2) a person is indigent, but has the ability to pay a reduced fee for the appointment of counsel. The definition and standards, and any amendments thereto, shall be subject to the approval of the supreme judicial court and shall be used by the courts of the commonwealth in determining assignment of cases to the committee pursuant to section 5. In the formulation of the definition, standards and procedures, the committee shall utilize: (1) the reporting system operated by the commissioner of transitional assistance for the purpose of verifying financial eligibility of participants in state or federally funded programs; (2) the accessibility of income data available from the department of revenue; and (3) verifying material assets through the registry of motor vehicles.

§ 2½. Repealed

[Repealed by 2011 Mass. Acts c. 68, §112; see Section 2A below for new provision.]

§ 2A. Verification of claim of indigency; waiver by claimant allowing access to information; reassessments following appointment of counsel; reporting

[Replaced former Section 2A: 2011 Mass. Acts c.68, § 112, effective July 1, 2011; amended by 2011 Mass. Acts c. 142, § 22, effective Oct. 27, 2011; 2012 Mass. Acts c. 139, §§ 135–137, effective July 1, 2012; 2018 Mass. Acts c. 69, § 107, effective Apr. 13, 2018.]

(a) A person claiming indigency under section 2 shall execute a waiver authorizing the court's chief probation officer, or the officer's designee, to obtain the person's wage, tax and asset information from the department of revenue, department of transitional assistance and the registry of motor vehicles that the court may find useful in verifying the person's claim of indigency. The waiver shall authorize the chief probation officer, or the officer's designee, to conduct any further reassessment required by this section.

(b) It shall be the responsibility of the chief probation officer assigned to each court to ensure that a person claiming to be indigent meets the definition of indigency under section 2. A person seeking the appointment of counsel shall be interviewed by the chief probation officer or the officer's designee prior to the appointment of counsel. The person conducting the interview shall explain to the person seeking appointment of counsel: (1) the definition of indigency; (2) the process used to verify the person's information with other state agencies; and (3) the penalties for misrepresenting financial information in applying for the appointment of counsel. The officer or the officer's designee conducting the interview shall prepare a written indigency intake report that shall record the results of the interview and state a recommendation on whether or not the person seeking appointment of counsel is indigent. The person seeking appointment of counsel and the officer or the officer's designee conducting the interview shall sign the indigency intake report. In signing the report, the person seeking appointment of counsel shall certify under the pains and penalties of perjury that the information contained therein is true and that the person has not concealed any information relevant to the person's financial status. All statements contained in the report shall be deemed material statements. The completed report shall be presented to a judge who may adopt or reject the recommendations in the report, either in whole or in part.

(c) Appointment of counsel by a court shall, at all times, be subject to verification of indigency by the chief probation officer assigned to each court. The chief probation officer or the officer's designee shall, within 7 business days of appointment of counsel, complete a final report of the financial circumstances of the person for whom counsel was appointed containing wage, tax and asset information. In preparing the final report, the chief probation officer or the officer's designee shall access, through electronic sharing of information pursuant to a memorandum of understanding, wage, tax and asset information in the possession of the department of revenue and the department of transitional assistance, and any other information relevant to the verification of indigency in the possession of the registry of motor vehicles. These departments shall provide this information to the chief probation officer or the officer's designee upon request. The chief probation officer or the officer's designee shall sign the final report, certifying that the person for whom counsel was appointed either continues to meet or no longer meets the definition of indigency. Thereafter, the report shall be filed with the case papers and shall be presented to the judge presiding at the person's next court appearance; provided, however, that if a person for whom counsel was appointed is found to not meet the definition of indigency, a court appearance shall be scheduled as soon as feasible prior to the person's next court appearance if the next court appearance is more than 2 weeks from the date the final report is completed. If, upon receipt of the report, a judge finds that the person for whom counsel was appointed no longer meets the definition of indigency, the judge shall revoke the appointment of counsel and allow such person a reasonable continuance to obtain new counsel.

Not later than 6 months after the appointment of counsel, and every 6 months thereafter, the chief probation officer or the officer's designee shall conduct a further reassessment of the financial circumstances of the person for whom counsel was appointed to ensure that the person continues to meet the definition of indigency. The chief probation officer or the officer's designee shall prepare, sign and file a written report certifying that the person either continues to meet, or no longer meets, the definition of indigency.

Upon request of the department of children and families, the commissioner of probation shall provide to the department a copy of a person's indigency intake form, final assessment of financial circumstances, and any report certifying that the person either continues to meet or no longer meets the definition of indigency prepared by the chief probation officer in accordance with this section. The department shall only use these forms, assessments and reports for the purpose of completing eligibility determinations under Title IV-E of the Social Security Act. The commissioner of probation and the commissioner of children and families shall jointly determine the process by which the department of children and families shall obtain and maintain these forms, assessments and reports. The department of children and families shall not disseminate, and shall prohibit dissemination of, such information for any purpose other than those set forth in this paragraph.

(d) If a criminal defendant is charged with a second or further offense while continuing to be represented by court-appointed counsel for a previously charged offense, the court in its discretion shall determine whether any further determination of indigency, other than the bi-annual reassessments required by the defendant's representation for the first offense, need be undertaken. Upon completion of a reassessment, the chief probation officer shall prepare a written report of the officer's findings. The chief probation officer or the officer's designee shall sign the report, certifying that the defendant either continues to meet or no longer meets the definition of indigency. The report shall be filed with the case papers and shall be presented to the judge presiding at the defendant's next court appearance. If, upon receipt of the report, a judge finds that the defendant no longer meets the definition of indigency, the judge shall revoke the appointment of counsel and allow the defendant a reasonable continuance to obtain new counsel.

(e) If the court finds that a person has materially misrepresented or omitted information concerning the person's property or assets for purposes of determining indigency and that the person does not meet the definition of indigency, the court shall immediately terminate any assignment or appointment of counsel made under this chapter and shall assess costs of not less than $1,000 against the person.

(f) Except for a person under 18 years of age, a person provided counsel under this chapter shall be assessed a counsel fee of $150, which the court may waive only upon a determination from officer's data verification process that the person is unable to pay such $150 within 180 days. If, upon the biannual reassessment of the person's indigency, the court concludes that the person is able to pay the $150 counsel fee of which the person obtained a waiver, the court shall revoke the waiver and reimpose the $150 counsel fee. The fee shall be in addition to any reduced fee required pursuant to section 2.

(g) The court may authorize a person for whom counsel was appointed to perform community service in lieu of payment of the counsel fee. A person seeking to work off a counsel fee in community service shall perform 10 hours of community service, in a community service program administered by the administrative office of the trial court, for each $100 owed in legal counsel fees, which may be prorated. Notwithstanding any general or special law to the contrary, a court proceeding shall not be terminated and the person shall not be discharged if the person owes any portion of the legal counsel fee imposed by this section. The clerk shall not release any bail posted on such court proceeding until the legal counsel fee is satisfied in accordance with this chapter.

(h) The clerk of the court shall, within 60 days of appointment of counsel, report to the department of revenue, the department of transitional assistance and the registry of motor vehicles the amount of any legal counsel fee owed by the person for whom counsel was appointed under this chapter. The department of revenue shall intercept payment of such fee from tax refunds due to persons who owe all or a portion of such fee. The registry of motor vehicles shall not issue or renew a person's driver's license or motor vehicle registration for any vehicle subsequently purchased by such person until it receives notification from the clerk of the court that the fee has been collected or worked off in community service.

(i) The office of the commissioner of probation shall submit quarterly reports to the house and senate committees on ways and means that shall include, but not be limited to: (a) the number of individuals claiming indigency who are determined to be indigent; (b) the number of individuals claiming indigency who are determined not to be indigent; (c) the number of individuals found to have misrepresented wage, tax or asset information; (d) the number of individuals found to no longer qualify for appointment of counsel upon any re-assessment of indigency required by this section; (e) the total number of times an indigent misrepresentation fee was collected and the aggregate amount of indigent misrepresentation fees collected; (f) the total number of times indigent counsel fees were collected and waived and the aggregate amount of indigent counsel fees collected and waived; (g) the average indigent counsel fee that each court division collects; (h) the total number of times an indigent but able to contribute fee was collected and waived and the aggregate amount of indigent but able to contribute fees collected and waived; (i) the highest and lowest indigent but able to contribute fee collected in each court division; (j) the number of cases in which community service in lieu of indigent counsel fees was performed; and (k) other pertinent information to ascertain the effectiveness of indigency verification procedures. The information within such reports shall be delineated by court division, and delineated further by month.

§ 2B. Legal counsel for criminal defendant charged with misdemeanor or municipal ordinance violation

[Added by 2011 Mass. Acts c. 68, § 112, effective July 1, 2011.]

A person charged with a misdemeanor or a violation of a municipal ordinance or bylaw, on motion of the commonwealth, the person or on the court's own motion, shall not be appointed counsel if the judge, at arraignment, informs such person on the record that, if the person is convicted of such offense, the person's sentence shall not include any period of incarceration. For good cause, that judge or another judge of the same court may later revoke such determination on the record and appoint counsel, and on the request such counsel shall be entitled to a continuance to conduct any necessary discovery and to prepare adequately for trial. Any such determination or revocation by a judge shall be endorsed upon the docket of the case.

§ 3. Accepting of gifts, grants or contributions; contracts

Said committee may accept gifts, grants or contributions from any source, whether public or private, and may enter into contracts to provide or receive services with any federal, state, county or municipal entity, with any group or individual, whether profit or nonprofit, or with any nonprofit or voluntary charitable group, corporation, association or organization, including any bar association or bar advocate group.

§ 4. Rules and regulations; annual report; training; rotating appointment mechanism

[Amended by 2012 Mass. Acts c. 244, § 13, effective Jan. 1, 2013; 2017 Mass. Acts c. 47, § 84, effective July 1, 2017.]

Said committee shall adopt such rules and regulations as may be necessary for the conduct of its affairs and may from time to time amend or revise the same. The committee shall prepare an annual report which shall be a public document. The committee shall establish standards and guidelines for the training, qualification and removal of counsel in the public and private counsel divisions who accept its appointments, and shall provide pre-service and in-service training for both private counsel who accept assignments and salaried public counsel. The committee may establish a rotating appointment mechanism that will encourage open access among attorneys participating within the private counsel division.

The committee, in consultation with the bureau of substance addiction services within the department of public health, shall provide substance abuse training to attorneys that helps attorneys identify substance abuse treatment resources for persons charged with or convicted of a crime or adjudicated delinquent who could benefit from those resources.

§ 5. Appointment or assignment of counsel

Said committee shall establish, supervise and maintain a system for the appointment or assignment of counsel at any stage of a proceeding, either criminal or noncriminal in nature, provided, however, that the laws of the commonwealth or the rules of the supreme judicial court require that a person in such proceeding be represented by counsel; and, provided further, that such person is unable to obtain counsel by reason of his indigency. The committee may also establish a system for the provision of counsel in any prearraignment procedure. A justice or associate justice shall assign a case to the committee, as hereinafter provided, after receiving from the probation officer a written report containing the probation officer's opinion as to the defendant's ability to pay for counsel, based on the standards and procedures provided for in section two.

§ 6. Public defender and private counsel divisions; duties

[Amended by 2004 Mass. Acts c. 149, § 193, effective July 1, 2004; 2011 Mass. Acts c. 68, § 113, effective July 1, 2011.]

(a) In carrying out its duties as prescribed in section 5, the committee shall utilize its staff of attorneys, which shall be known hereafter as the public defender division. The division shall include a unit to be known as the Roxbury defenders unit, which shall represent clients as assigned pursuant to this chapter in the Roxbury division of the district court department. The public defender division shall be assigned to represent indigent defendants in all criminal cases, except that: (i) the public defender division shall not be assigned to represent more than 1 defendant in any matter before any court on the same case or arising out of the same incident; (ii) the public defender division shall not be assigned to represent a defendant in any case in which there is a conflict of interest with any of its clients; (iii) notwithstanding any general or special law to the contrary, the public defender division shall be assigned in any civil or criminal matter described in subsection (b) if the chief counsel determines in writing that insufficient numbers of qualified attorneys are available for assignment by the private counsel division.

(b) In carrying out its duties as prescribed in section 5, the committee shall establish, supervise and maintain a system for the appointment of private counsel, hereafter called the private counsel division, which shall include a children and family law program and a mental health unit. The committee shall enter into contractual agreements with any state, county or local bar association or voluntary charitable group, corporation or association, including bar advocate groups, for the purpose of providing such counsel. The committee may also contract with such other organized groups of attorneys as may be formed to afford representation to indigent defendants and may appoint and compensate private attorneys, on a case-by-case basis, as counsel for indigents entitled to representation. No individual, member or participant in a group, corporation or association with whom the committee may contract under this paragraph shall be considered to be or have any rights as a state employee.

The private counsel division shall be assigned for all persons accused of crimes entitled to counsel who, through their inability to pay for counsel, shall have counsel appointed to them, but who, pursuant to subsection (a) shall not be represented by the public counsel division.

The private counsel division shall also be assigned to represent persons in such other proceedings as the chief counsel shall determine to be necessary.

§ 6A. Establishment of children and family law program; utilization of certified private counsel

[Amended by 2011 Mass. Acts c. 68, § 113, effective July 1, 2011.]

In carrying out its duties as prescribed in sections 5 and 6, the committee shall establish a children and family law program which shall, upon the court's appointment, provide representation to indigent persons in children and family law cases. Nothing herein shall be construed to limit the system as established in sections 5 and 6, whereby the court appoints certified private counsel to represent children and parents in the majority of children and family law cases.

§ 6B. Payment of counsel

[Added by 2004 Mass. Acts c. 149, § 194, effective July 1, 2004.]

Not more than 1 counsel assigned or appointed under section 5, 6 or 6A shall be paid for representation of a party in civil proceedings pending in any trial court under paragraph C of section 23, section 24 or 29B or sections 39E to 39I, inclusive, of chapter 119 or section 3 of chapter 210. The chief counsel of the committee for public counsel services may permit an exception to this provision in extraordinary circumstances, such as the pendency of separate actions in distant counties on behalf of a client.

§ 7. Repealed

[Repealed by 2011 Mass. Acts c. 68, § 114, effective July 1, 2011.]

§ 8. Assignment of case of indigent accused of murder

Upon a determination by a court that a person accused of murder in the first or second degree is indigent, the chief counsel or his designee may assign the case to either the public defender division or the private counsel division, subject to the approval of the justice making the determination of indigency.

§ 9. Division standards

The committee shall establish standards for the public defender division and the private counsel division which shall include but not be limited to:

(a) vertical or continuous representation at the pre-trial and trial stages by the attorney either assigned or appointed, whenever possible;

(b) required participation by each attorney in an approved course of training in the fundamentals of criminal trial practice, unless the attorney has a level of ability which makes such participation unnecessary;

(c) specified caseload limitation levels;

(d) investigative services;

(e) a method for the provision of social services or social service referrals;

(f) availability of expert witnesses to participating counsel;

(g) clerical assistance, interview facilities, and the availability of a law library and model forms to participating counsel; and

(h) adequate supervision provided by experienced attorneys who shall be available to less experienced attorneys.

(i) qualifications for vendors for the services provided in clauses (d), (e) and (f) and a range of rates payable for said services, taking into consideration the rates, qualifications and history of performance; provided, however, that such ranges may be exceeded with approval of the court. Payment of such costs and fees shall be in accordance with the provisions of section twenty-seven A to G, inclusive, of chapter two hundred and sixty-one.

§ 10. Committee monitoring of standards compliance; review of client complaints

The committee shall monitor and evaluate compliance with the standards and the performance of counsel in its divisions in order to insure competent representation of defendants in all courts of the commonwealth and shall establish a procedure for the review and disposition of client complaints. The committee shall also establish procedures whereby comments on the standard of performance of counsel in its divisions may be submitted by the justice hearing a particular matter.

§ 11. Compensation rates; limitation on annual billable hours payable; limitation on new appointments

[Amended by 2005 Mass. Acts c. 54, § 2, effective July 1, 2005; 2008 Mass. Acts c. 182, § 69, effective July 1, 2008; 2011 Mass. Acts c. 68, § 115, effective July 1, 2011; 2015 Mass. Acts c. 46, § 119, effective July 1, 2016; 2016 Mass. Acts c. 133, § 119, effective July 1, 2016; 2018 Mass. Acts c. 154, §§ 49, 50, effective July 1, 2018.]

(a) The rates of compensation payable to all counsel, who are appointed or assigned to represent indigents within the private counsel division of the committee in accordance with the provisions of paragraph (b) of section 6, shall, subject to appropriation, be as follows: for homicide cases the rate of compensation shall be $100 per hour; for superior court non-homicide cases, including sexually dangerous person cases, the rate of compensation shall be $68 per hour; for district court cases and children in need of services cases the rate of compensation shall be $53 per hour; for children and family law cases and care and protection cases the rate of compensation shall be $55 per hour; for sex offender registry cases and mental health cases the rate of compensation shall be $53 per hour. These rates of compensation shall be reviewed periodically at public hearings held by the committee at appropriate locations throughout the state, and notice shall be given to all state, county and local bar associations and other interested groups, of such hearings by letter and publication in advance of such hearings. This periodic review shall take place not less than once every 3 years.

(b) The committee shall set an annual cap on billable hours not in excess of 1,650 hours. Counsel appointed or assigned to represent indigents within the private counsel division shall not be paid for any time billed in excess of the annual limit of billable hours. It shall be the responsibility of private counsel to manage their billable hours.

(c) Any counsel who is appointed or assigned to represent indigents within the private counsel division, except any counsel appointed or assigned to represent indigents within the private counsel division in a homicide case, shall be prohibited from accepting any new appointment or assignment to represent indigents after that counsel has billed 1,350 billable hours during any fiscal year.

(d) Notwithstanding the billable hour limitations in subsections (c) and (d), the chief counsel may waive the annual cap on billable hours for private counsel appointed or assigned to the children and family law cases and the care and protection cases if the chief counsel finds that: (i) there is limited availability of qualified counsel in that practice area; (ii) shifting the services to private counsel would result in cost efficiencies; or (iii) shifting the service to private counsel would improve the quality of service; provided, however, that counsel appointed or assigned to such cases within the private counsel division shall not be paid for any time billed in excess of 1,800 billable hours. It shall be the responsibility of private counsel to manage their billable hours.

§ 12. Private counsel compensation; audit and oversight department; submission of invoices for payment

[Amended by 2002 Mass. Acts c. 184, § 117, effective July 1, 2002; 2009 Mass. Acts c. 27, § 88, effective July 1, 2009; 2011 Mass. Acts c. 68, § 116, effective July 1, 2011.]

(a) The committee shall establish policies and procedures to provide fair compensation to private counsel and vendors, which shall include a remedy for an attorney aggrieved by the amount of payment. The committee shall also establish an audit and oversight department to monitor billing and private attorney and vendor compensation. All private attorney invoices shall be processed for payment within 30 days of receipt by the chief counsel, excluding any bills held for review or audit. Bills shall be submitted to the committee within 60 days of the conclusion of a case or, if the case is pending at the end of the fiscal year, within 30 days after the end of such fiscal year. The amount of payment for invoices received by the chief counsel more than 60 days but less than 90 days after the final disposition of the case or more than 30 days but less than 60 days after the end of the fiscal year shall be reduced by 10 per cent. Bills submitted after such date need not be processed for payment within 30 days. For all bills not submitted to the committee within 90 days after the conclusion of a case or, if the case is pending at the end of the fiscal year, within 60 days after the end of the fiscal year, those bills so submitted after such date shall not be processed for payment; provided, however, that the chief counsel may authorize the payment of such bills, either in whole or in part, upon a determination that the delay was due to extraordinary circumstances beyond the control of the attorney.

(b) Bills shall be submitted to the committee for services provided under sections 27A to 27G, inclusive, of chapter 261 within 60 days of the last date of service or, if the case is pending at the end of the fiscal year, within 30 days after the end of such fiscal year. The amount of payment for invoices received by the chief counsel more than 60 days but less than 90 days after the last date of service or more than 30 days but less than 60 days after the end of the fiscal year shall be reduced by 10 per cent. For all bills not submitted to the committee within 90 days after the last date of service or, if the case is pending at the end of the fiscal year, within 60 days after the end of the fiscal year, those bills so submitted after such date shall not be processed for payment; provided, however, that the chief counsel may authorize the payment of such bills either in whole or in part upon a determination that the delay was due to extraordinary circumstances beyond the control of the vendor.

(c) The committee may further prescribe such policies and procedures for payment as it deems appropriate; provided, however, that the committee may impose interest and penalties, where appropriate, upon overpayment of the private attorney bills recovered from private attorneys and upon overpayment of vendor bills recovered from vendors.

§ 13. Chief counsel; deputies; staff; compensation

The committee shall appoint a chief counsel, whose responsibilities and duties shall be defined by the committee and shall include, but not be limited to, the overall supervision of the workings of the various divisions of the committee. The committee shall further appoint two deputy chief counsel, with duties defined by the committee, one of whom shall supervise the public defender division, and the other shall supervise the private counsel division. The committee shall also prescribe the procedures for the appointment of all legal and nonlegal staff of the public defender division and for the procurement of office space as may be required. The chief counsel shall authorize the certification of all payments under section twenty-seven G of chapter two hundred and sixty-one and section twenty of chapter twenty-nine. All legal and nonlegal staff of the public counsel division shall be full time and shall devote their entire time during ordinary business hours to their duties and shall neither directly or indirectly engage in the private practice of law. The chief counsel and deputy chief counsels shall likewise devote full time to their duties. The chief counsel, deputy chief counsels and all legal and non-legal staff of the committee, including staff attorneys hired under subparagraphs (a) and (b) of section 6 but not including persons described in the fourth sentence of said subparagraph (b) of said section 6, shall be considered public employees for purposes of chapter 258. The chief counsel shall be paid a salary comparable to the salary paid to a district attorney. The salaries of the deputy chief counsels shall be established by the committee. All other legal staff of the public defender division shall be paid at salaries comparable to the salary paid to an attorney employed in a district attorney's office.

The counsel and other employees appointed by the committee shall not be subject to the provisions of chapter thirty-one.

§ 14. Repealed

[Repealed by 2011 Mass. Acts c. 68, § 117, effective July 1, 2011.]

§ 15. Community advisory board; Roxbury community; consultation

The committee shall consult regularly with a community advisory board appointed by the committee to represent the greater Roxbury community. Members of the community advisory board shall not receive compensation or reimbursement for expenses.

§ 16. Appointment of counsel for indigents subject to sex offender registry classification system

The committee shall establish, supervise and maintain a system for the appointment of counsel for the provision of legal services for indigents subject to the sex offender registry classification system and resulting appeals pursuant to sections 178C to 178P, inclusive, of chapter 6.

COUNSEL ASSESSMENT/CONTRIBUTION FEE *CARE AND PROTECTION CASES ONLY* *(G.L. c. 119, §24)*	DOCKET NO.	MASSACHUSETTS TRIAL COURT JUVENILE COURT DEPARTMENT
CARE AND PROTECTION OF:		DIVISION
COUNSEL ASSESSMENT FEE (c.211D, §2A¶2) Required when counsel is appointed for any person.		
Name	☐ **$150** **Date Payment Due:**	☐ Waived-Defendant Found Unable to Pay ☐ 15 hours Community Serv Ordered (10 hrs of community service may be ordered for every $100 owed)
Name	☐ **$150** **Date Payment Due:**	☐ Waived-Defendant Found Unable to Pay ☐ 15 hours Community Serv Ordered
Name	☐ **$150** **Date Payment Due:**	☐ Waived-Defendant Found Unable to Pay ☐ 15 hours Community Serv Ordered
Name	☐ **$150** **Date Payment Due:**	☐ Waived-Defendant Found Unable to Pay ☐ 15 hours Community Serv Ordered
Name(s) of child(ren)	☐ **$150** **Date Payment Due:**	☐ Waived-Defendant Found Unable to Pay
COUNSEL CONTRIBUTION FEE (c.211D §2; SJC RULE 3:10[10][C]) "Reasonable amount" required toward cost of counsel (in addition to Counsel Fee) when counsel appointed for a person who is indigent but able to contribute.		
Name	☐ **$** **Date Payment Due:**	
Name	☐ **$** **Date Payment Due:**	
COMMENTS, ADDITIONAL FINDINGS, INSTRUCTIONS OR ORDERS:		
DATE:	SIGNATURE OF JUDGE:	

JC FEE1A (7/01/2004)

1

INDIGENCY DETERMINATION FOR PURPOSES OF OBTAINING COURT APPOINTED COUNSEL
G.L. c. 211D, §2 1/2
(EFFECTIVE 7/1/2004)

CHILD/DEFENDANT/ RESPONDENT hereinafter "Defendant"	**CHIEF PROBATION OFFICER/ DESIGNEE (ACPO, PO)**	**CHIEF PROBATION OFFICER ONLY**	**JUDGE**	**CLERK-MAGISTRATE**
1. Execute waiver authorizing probation to obtain information from DOR, DTA, DMA & RMV. 2. Review indigency intake form with PO. 3. Certify Intake Report by signing under pains and penalties of perjury that information contained in the report is true and accurate and that he/she has not concealed any information relevant to his/her financial status. 4. Pay counsel fee within 60 days if assessed by court or perform community service as ordered.	**Initial Request for Appointment of Counsel** 1. Interview defendant requesting counsel 2. Explain the following: a) definition of indigency, b) process used to verify information with other state agencies, c) consequences of misrepresenting financial information in applying for the appt of counsel, d) appt is subject to verification of indigency by CPO assigned to court. 3. Obtain waiver 4. Prepare written Indigency Intake Report that contains results of interview and	1. It is the responsibility of the Chief Probation Officer assigned to each to ensure that a defendant claiming to be indigent meets the definition of indigency under section 2 of 211D. 2. Appointment of counsel is at all times subject to verification of indigency by Chief Probation Officer. 3. Sixty (60) days after the appointment of counsel, the Chief Probation Officer shall prepare a written report of initial reassessment, and sign certifying that the defendant meets the definition of indigency. The CPO may not designate this duty the PO.	1. Review PO's written intake report and determine whether to adopt or reject recommendation in whole or in part. 2. Assess $150 fee if defendant is determined to be indigent and counsel is appointed. Judge should order counsel fee to be paid within 60 days. 3. Judge may waive fee if the court finds that defendant is unable to pay the fee. 15 hours of community service may be ordered. 4. Review written reassessment and bi-annual reassessment at next court date and make determination whether defendant continues to remain indigent.	1. If counsel fee is assessed, the Clerk-Magistrate shall notify DOR, DTA, DMA, RMV if the defendant respondent does not pay the fee within 60 days of assessment. 2. Notify DOR, DTA, DMA, RMV if counsel fee is paid after notice of non-payment has been sent. [DOR shall intercept the fee from tax refunds, DTA and DMA shall deduct the fee in weekly or monthly increments from the benefit payments, RMV shall place a lien upon the title of any motor vehicle owed by the defendant in whole or in part. The lien shall be released only upon notification from the clerk magistrate that the debt has been collected or worked off in community service.]

INDIGENCY DETERMINATION FOR PURPOSES OF OBTAINING COURT APPOINTED COUNSEL-PG3
(EFFECTIVE 7/1/2004)

CHILD/DEFENDANT/ RESPONDENT	**CHIEF PROBATION OFFICER/ DESIGNEE (ACPO, PO)**	**CHIEF PROBATION OFFICER ONLY**	**JUDGE**	**CLERK-MAGISTRATE**
	2. Prepare written report of findings and submit to CPO for signature certifying that the defendant continues to meet or does not meet the definition of indigence. 3. File written report in the clerk's office for filing in the case papers. The report shall be submitted to the judge at the defendant's next court appearance. **Six Months after the Appt of Counsel (four months after the reassessment) and every six months thereafter.** 1. Conduct reassessment of person's financial circumstances to ensure that he/she continues to meet the definition of indigency. 2. Prepare and sign written reassessment report certifying that the defendant meets or continues to meet the definition of indigency. Arrange community service as ordered by the judge.		7. Judge shall not terminate or discharge a criminal matter until if any portion of the legal fee is unpaid or community service has not been completed. 8. If defendant commits a second offense while another case is pending, the judge in his/her discretion may require probation to conduct another reassessment in addition to the 60 day reassessment and biannual reassessment prior to assessing an additional $150 counsel fee.	

Chapter 211F. Office of Community Corrections

§ 3. Sentence to community corrections program; duration; conditions; eligibility

(a) Any court exercising jurisdiction is authorized to sentence any eligible offender to a community corrections program; provided, however, that the court designate the duration of the sentence of imprisonment that otherwise would have been imposed.

(b) The court may dictate the duration and conditions of the sentence in a community corrections program for any period of time consistent with existing law.

(c) A sentence to a community corrections program shall be imposed as a condition of probation consistent with chapters two hundred and seventy-six and two hundred and seventy-six A. The court may modify the sentence of an offender serving a sentence in a community corrections program in the same manner as if the offender had been placed on probation.

(d) The commissioner shall develop interim standards for the eligibility of offenders for community corrections, taking into consideration the following factors:

(1) the nature and circumstances of the offense;

(2) the offender's mental state at the time of the offense;

(3) the relationship, if any, between the offender and victim;

(4) the nature and degree of the harm caused by the offense;

(5) the community view of the gravity of the offense;

(6) the public concern generated by the offense;

(7) the age of the offender;

(8) the deterrent effect a particular sentence may have on the commission of the offense by others;

(9) the current incidence of the offense in the community and in the commonwealth as a whole;

(10) the role of the offender in cases involving multiple offenders;

(11) the mental and emotional condition of the offender;

(12) the offender's physical condition;

(13) the offender's family ties and responsibilities;

(14) the offender's community ties;

(15) the offender's degree of dependence upon criminal activity for a livelihood;

(16) the offender's character and personal history;

(17) the offender's amenability to correction, treatment, or supervision;

(18) the offender's past criminal history, including convictions, acquittals, guilty pleas, pleas of nolo contendere, dismissals and matters continued without a finding;

(19) the offender's arrest record;

(20) the offender's past history of violence.

No offender shall be eligible for sentencing to a community corrections program who is:

(1) convicted of a crime that results in serious bodily harm or death to another person, excluding offenses in which negligence was the primary element,

(2) convicted of rape, attempted rape, or sexual assault, or

(3) convicted of a crime involving the use of a firearm.

Chapter 215. Probate Courts

§ 6. Equity jurisdiction

The probate and family court department shall have original and concurrent jurisdiction with the supreme judicial court and the superior court department of all cases and matters of equity cognizable under the general principles of equity jurisprudence and, with reference thereto, shall be courts of general equity jurisdiction, except that the superior court department shall have exclusive original jurisdiction of all actions in which injunctive relief is sought in any matter growing out of a labor dispute as defined in section twenty C of chapter one hundred and forty-nine.

Probate courts shall also have jurisdiction concurrent with the supreme judicial and superior courts, of all cases and matters in which equitable relief is sought relative to: (i) the administration of the estates of deceased persons; (ii) wills, including questions arising under section twenty of chapter one hundred and ninety-one; (iii) trusts created by will or other written instrument; (iv) cases involving in any way the estate of a deceased person or the property of an absentee whereof a receiver has been appointed under chapter two hundred or the property of a person under guardianship or conservatorship; (v) trusts created by parol or constructive or resulting trusts; (vi) all matters relative to guardianship or conservatorship; and (vii) actions such as one described in clause (11) of section three of chapter two hundred and fourteen and of all other matters of which they now have or may hereafter be given jurisdiction. They shall also have jurisdiction to grant equitable relief to enforce foreign judgments for support of a wife or of a wife and minor children against a husband who is a resident or inhabitant of this commonwealth, upon an action by the wife commenced in the county of which the husband is a resident or inhabitant. They shall, after the divorce judgment has become absolute, also have concurrent jurisdiction to grant equitable relief in controversies over property between persons who have been divorced. They shall also have jurisdiction of an action by an administrator, executor, guardian, conservator, receiver appointed as aforesaid or trustee under a will to enjoin for a reasonable period of time the foreclosure, otherwise than by open and peaceable entry, of a mortgage on real estate, or the foreclosure of a mortgage on personal property, which real estate or personal property is included in the estate or trust being administered by such fiduciary, if in the opinion of the court the proper administration of the estate or trust would be hindered by such foreclosure. They shall also have jurisdiction, concurrent with the superior court, of proceedings in which equitable relief is sought under sections seven to twelve, inclusive, of chapter one hundred and seventeen and section twenty-six of chapter one hundred and twenty-three.

Notwithstanding any contrary or inconsistent provisions of the General Laws, procedure in cases in the probate court within the jurisdiction granted by this section shall be governed by the Massachusetts Rules of Civil Procedure.

§ 22. Effect of appeal; interlocutory orders

After an appeal has been claimed and filed in the registry of probate, all proceedings in pursuance of the act appealed from shall, except as otherwise expressly provided, be stayed until the determination thereof by the supreme judicial court or appeals court, but if, upon such appeal, such act is affirmed, it shall there after be of full force and validity. An appeal from an interlocutory order, judgment or decree, however, shall not suspend proceedings under the same pending the appeal, except as otherwise expressly provided by law.

§ 56A. Investigations

Any judge of a probate court may appoint a guardian ad litem to investigate the facts of any proceeding pending in said court relating to or involving questions as to the care, custody or maintenance of minor children and as to any matter involving domestic relations except those for the investigation of which provision is

1

made by section sixteen of chapter two hundred and eight. Said guardian ad litem shall, before final judgment or decree in such proceeding, report in writing to the court the results of the investigation, and such report shall be open to inspection to all the parties in such proceeding or their attorneys. The compensation shall be fixed by the court and shall be paid by the commonwealth, together with any expense approved by the court, upon certificate by the judge to the state treasurer. The state police, local police and probation officers shall assist the guardian ad litem so appointed, upon his request.

Chapter 218. District Courts

§ 58. Justices and clerks; assignment; salaries; vacation and sick leave; interpreters

[Amended by 2006 Mass. Acts c. 164, § 6, effective Jan. 1, 2006; 2007 Mass. Acts c. 61, §§ 25, 26, effective July 1, 2007; 2011 Mass. Acts c. 93, §§ 88–90, effective July 1, 2012; 2018 Mass. Acts c. 154, § 51, effective July 1, 2018.]

The Suffolk county division of the juvenile court department shall consist of seven justices, the Middlesex county division shall consist of six justices, the Worcester county division shall consist of four justices, the Franklin and Hampshire counties division shall consist of one justice, the Bristol county division shall consist of three justices, the Essex county division shall consist of four justices, the Norfolk county division shall consist of two justices, the Plymouth county division shall consist of three justices, the Barnstable county and town of Plymouth division shall consist of one justice, and the Berkshire and Hampden counties division shall consist of four justices, all of whom shall be members of the bar. There shall be 5 associate justices of the trial court appointed for the juvenile court department who shall be and perform the duties of circuit justices in the following counties, and when so assigned, they shall receive from the commonwealth the expenses incurred by them: three justices in the Worcester, Franklin and Hampshire, Berkshire, and Hampden county divisions, and three justices in the Suffolk, Barnstable and town of Plymouth, Plymouth, Norfolk, Middlesex, Essex, and Bristol county divisions. The chief justice of the district court department may, upon request of the chief justice of the juvenile court department, assign a special justice who is not serving full-time under the provisions of section six A from the district court department to sit in any court of the juvenile court department. The chief justice of the juvenile court department shall have the power to define the duties of said first justices, and shall appoint, from among the justices of the juvenile court department, a first justice for each of the divisions within said department; provided, that appropriate consideration shall be given to seniority, length of service at that particular division, and managerial ability. Each first justice so appointed shall serve as the first justice of that particular division for a five-year term, and shall be eligible to be reappointed for additional five-year terms at that particular division. Any first justice may be removed from his position as first justice by the chief justice of the juvenile court department; provided, however, that any such removal is not for arbitrary or capricious reasons. Any first justice who is removed from his position as first justice by the chief justice of the juvenile court department may appeal the removal to the chief justice of the trial court, who shall hear and determine the matter.

Citations, orders of notice, writs, executions and all other processes issued by the clerk of each division shall bear the teste of the first justice thereof. The first justice shall be the administrative head of his division; provided, however, that the clerks shall have responsibility for the internal administration of his office, including the selection, appointment, and management of personnel, staff services and record keeping. A first justice or a clerk of the court may submit any dispute that arises between said first justice and said clerk concerning the management and administration of the office of the clerk, the duties, powers and obligations of the clerk, or a member of their staff, or the interpretation of the personnel standards provided for under section eight of chapter two hundred and eleven B, to the chief justice of the department. Any person aggrieved by a decision of a chief justice under this paragraph may appeal said decision to the chief justice of the trial court, who shall, within thirty days, hear and determine the matter.

In the case of the absence, death or removal of a clerk of a division of the juvenile court department, or a vacancy in the position of clerk for any other reason, the chief justice of the juvenile court department may appoint a temporary clerk, to act until the clerk resumes his duties, or until the vacancy is filled. The clerk of the court shall appoint assistant clerks and support personnel in his division, with all of such appointments subject to approval by the court administrator with respect to personnel standards as provided in section eight of chapter two hundred and eleven B. In the case of the absence, death or removal of an assistant clerk of a division of the juvenile court department, or a vacancy in the position of assistant clerk for any other reason, the clerk may appoint a temporary assistant clerk, to act until such assistant clerk resumes his duties, or until the vacancy is filled.

Each division shall have a clerk, who shall be appointed by the governor, with the advice and consent of the council and who shall hold office during good behavior, subject, however, to retirement under the provisions of any applicable general or special law relative to retirement systems. The Suffolk county division held at Boston shall have a first assistant clerk and said division shall have eleven assistant clerks; the Barnstable county division held at Plymouth shall have a first assistant clerk and said division shall have two assistant clerks; the Bristol county division shall have a first assistant clerk and five assistant clerks; the Franklin and Hampshire counties division shall have an assistant clerk; the Essex county division shall have a first assistant clerk and 3 assistant clerks; the Berkshire and Hampden counties division held at North Adams shall have an assistant clerk; the Hampden division held at Springfield shall have an assistant clerk; the Middlesex county division shall have a first assistant clerk and 8 assistant clerks; the Norfolk county division held at Quincy shall have four assistant clerks; the Plymouth county division shall have a first assistant clerk and two assistant clerks; and the Worcester county division shall have a first assistant clerk and two assistant clerks. Said first assistant clerks and assistant clerks shall be appointed by the clerks of said courts, with all such appointments subject to approval by the court administrator with respect to personnel standards promulgated under section 8 of chapter 211B.

The salaries of the clerks in the juvenile court department shall be 81.57 per cent of the salary of the chief justice of said department and shall be paid, subject to appropriation, by the commonwealth. The salaries of the first assistant clerks in said department and the salary of the assistant clerk in charge of the appeals session shall be eighty-three and one-half percent of the salary of the clerks of said court and shall be paid, subject to appropriation, by the commonwealth. The salaries of the assistant clerks in said department shall be seventy-seven percent of the salary of said clerks and shall be paid, subject to appropriation, by the commonwealth.

The clerks and assistant clerks of the juvenile court department shall devote their entire time during ordinary business hours to their respective duties and shall not, directly or indirectly, engage in the practice of law.

Each clerk and assistant clerk of the juvenile court department appointed to such position prior to January first, nineteen hundred and eighty-seven and serving continuously in such position thereafter shall be entitled to thirty days vacation and thirty days sick leave in each calendar year. Each such clerk and assistant clerk may accumulate vacation leave and sick leave not used in any such year; provided, however, that the number of vacation days so accumulated shall not exceed sixty and the total amount of sick leave shall not exceed one hundred and eighty days; and provided, further, that no additional such days shall be accumulated on or after said January first except in accordance with the policies and procedures established by the court administrator pursuant to section eight of chapter two hundred and eleven B. Any other clerk and assistant clerk of said department shall be entitled to vacation leave and sick leave in accordance with the policies and procedures established by the court administrator pursuant to said section eight.

The first justice of each division of the juvenile court department may, with the approval of the chief justice of the trial court, appoint such official interpreters, or enter into service contracts for telephone-based interpretation services, as he may deem necessary for the sessions of his division. Any such interpreter shall hold his position at the pleasure of said first justice, and shall render such additional services as said first justice may require. Said first justice shall forthwith discharge any such interpreter who is found by him to have requested or received, directly or indirectly, any gratuity, bonus or fee in connection with any case pending or in the course of preparation for presentation to any court. Other interpreters may be employed by the first justice when the services of the official interpreter are not available.

§ 59. Powers; duties and procedure; jurisdiction

Except as otherwise provided by law, the divisions of the juvenile court department shall have and exercise, within their respective jurisdictions, the same powers, duties, and procedure as the divisions of the district court department; and all laws relating to district courts or municipal courts in their respective counties or officials thereof or proceedings therein, shall, so far as applicable, apply to said divisions of the juvenile court department.

The divisions of the juvenile court department shall also have jurisdiction in equity concurrent with the supreme judicial court and with the superior court department in all cases and matters arising under the provisions of chapters 119 and 210.

Chapter 231. Pleading and Practice in Civil Proceedings

§ 118. Temporary appellate relief from interlocutory orders; appeals to appeals court or supreme judicial court

[Amended by 2012 Mass. Acts c. 240, § 33, effective Nov. 5, 2012.]

A party aggrieved by an interlocutory order of a trial court justice in the superior court department, the housing court department, the land court department, the juvenile court department or the probate and family court department may file, within thirty days of the entry of such order, a petition in the appropriate appellate court seeking relief from such order. A single justice of the appellate court may, in his discretion, grant the same relief as an appellate court is authorized to grant pending an appeal under section one hundred and seventeen. If the petition is filed with respect to a discovery order and is denied, the single justice may, after such hearing as the single justice in his discretion deems appropriate, require the petitioning party or the attorney advising the petition or both of them to pay to the party who opposed the petition the reasonable expenses incurred in opposing the petition, including attorney's fees, unless the court finds that the filing of the petition was substantially justified or that other circumstances make an award of expenses unjust.

A party aggrieved by an interlocutory order of a trial court justice in the superior court department, the housing court department, the land court department or the probate and family court department, granting, continuing, modifying, refusing or dissolving a preliminary injunction, or refusing to dissolve a preliminary injunction, or a party aggrieved by an interlocutory order of a single justice of the appellate court granting a petition for relief from such an order, may appeal therefrom to the appeals court or, subject to the provisions of section ten of chapter two hundred and eleven A, to the supreme judicial court, which shall affirm, modify, vacate, set aside, reverse the order or remand the cause and direct the entry of such appropriate order as may be just under the circumstances. An appeal under this paragraph shall be taken within thirty days of the date of the entry of the interlocutory order and in accordance with the Massachusetts rules of appellate procedure. Pursuant to action taken by the appellate court the cause shall be remanded to the trial court for further proceedings.

The filing of a petition hereunder shall not suspend the execution of the order which is the subject of the petition, except as otherwise ordered by a single justice of the appellate court.

Chapter 233. Witnesses, Evidence

Section	
1	Issuance of summonses for witnesses
2	Service of summons
3	Witness fees; payment or tender
4	Liability for nonattendance
5	Penalty for nonattendance; contempt
6	Warrant for nonattendance witness
20	Competency of witnesses; husband and wife; criminal defendant; parent and child
20A	Privileged communications; communications with clergymen
20B	Privileged communications; patients and psychotherapists; exceptions
20C	Immunity from prosecution; privilege against self-incrimination
20J	Sexual assault; confidential communications with sexual assault counselor; disclosure; discovery
20K	Domestic violence victims' counselors
20L	Confidentiality of domestic violence victim's program and rape crisis center locations
20M	Disclosure of confidential communication regarding human trafficking victim by caseworker
20N	Disclosure of social worker home address and service of process procedures
22	Cross-examination of adverse party; corporation's agent as adverse party
23	Impeachment of party's own witness
23C	Work product of mediator confidential; confidential communications; exception; mediator defined
23E	Alternative procedures for determining competency of witness with intellectual disability
23F	Admissibility of past physical, sexual or psychological abuse of defendant
24	Depositions in civil cases authorized
24A	Medial witnesses
25	Grounds for deposition
26	Notice of taking deposition
27	Persons on whom notice may be served
28	Mode of service
29	Verbal notice; waiver of notice, etc.
30	Oath and examination of deponent
31	Order of examination
32	Mode of taking deposition
33	Certification of deposition
34	Delivery and preservation of deposition
35	Exclusion of deposition
36	Objections to deposition
37	Use of deposition in second action
38	Compelling giving of deposition; place
39	Place of taking deposition of nonresident found within Commonwealth
40	Rules for taking depositions

§ 1. Issuance of summonses for witnesses

A clerk of a court of record, a notary public or a justice of the peace may issue summonses for witnesses in all cases pending before courts, magistrates, auditors, referees, arbitrators or other persons authorized to examine witnesses, and at all hearings upon applications for complaints wherein a person may be charged with the commission of a crime; but a notary public or a justice of the peace shall not issue summonses for witnesses in criminal cases except upon request of the attorney general, district attorney or other person who acts in the case in behalf of the commonwealth or of the defendant. If the summons is issued at the request of the defendant that fact shall be stated therein. The summons shall be in the form heretofore adopted and commonly used, but may be altered from time to time like other writs.

§ 2. Service of summons

Such summons may be served in any county by an officer qualified to serve civil process or by a disinterested person by exhibiting and reading it to the witness, by giving him a copy thereof or by leaving such copy at his place of abode.

§ 3. Witness fees; payment or tender

No person shall be required to attend as a witness in a civil case or for the defendant in a criminal case except a person summonsed to attend as a witness for an indigent defendant in a criminal case, unless the legal fees for one day's attendance and for travel to and from the place where he is required to attend are paid or tendered to him.

§ 4. Liability for nonattendance

If a person who has been duly summoned and required to attend as a witness under the preceding sections or section thirty-seven of chapter two hundred and eighteen fails, without a sufficient excuse, to attend, he shall be liable to the aggrieved party in tort for all damages caused by such failure.

§ 5. Penalty for nonattendance; contempt

Such failure to attend as a witness before a court, justice of the peace, master in chancery, master or auditor appointed by a court, or the county commissioners, shall also be a contempt of the court, and may be punished, in case of such failure to attend as a witness in a criminal prosecution, by a fine of not more than two hundred dollars or by imprisonment for not more than one month or both, or, in case of any other such failure to attend as aforesaid, by a fine of not more than twenty dollars.

§ 6. Warrant for nonattending witness

The court, justice, master in chancery, master, auditor or county commissioners may in such case issue a warrant to bring such witness before them to answer for the contempt, and also to testify in the case in which he was summoned.

§ 20. Competency of witnesses; husband and wife; criminal defendant; parent and child

[Amended by 2018 Mass. Acts c. 69, § 111, effective Apr. 13, 2018.]

Any person of sufficient understanding, although a party, may testify in any proceeding, civil or criminal, in court or before a person who has authority to receive evidence, except as follows:

First, Except in a proceeding arising out of or involving a contract made by a married woman with her husband, a proceeding under chapter two hundred and nine D and in a prosecution begun under sections one to ten, inclusive, of chapter two hundred and seventy-three, any criminal proceeding in which one spouse is a defendant alleged to have committed a crime against the other spouse or to have violated a temporary or permanent vacate, restraining, or no-contact order or judgment issued pursuant to section eighteen, thirty-four B or thirty-four C of chapter two hundred and eight, section thirty-two of chapter two hundred and nine, section three, three B, three C, four, or five of chapter two hundred and nine A, or sections fifteen or twenty of chapter two hundred and nine C, or a similar protection order issued by another jurisdiction, obtained by the other spouse, and except in a proceeding involving abuse of a person under the age of eighteen, including incest, neither husband nor wife shall testify as to private conversations with the other.

Second, Except as otherwise provided in section seven of chapter two hundred and seventy-three and except in any proceeding relating to child abuse, including incest, neither husband nor wife shall be compelled to testify in the trial of an indictment, complaint or other criminal proceeding against the other.

Third, The defendant in the trial of an indictment, complaint or other criminal proceeding shall, at his own request, but not otherwise, be allowed to testify; but his neglect or refusal to testify shall not create any presumption against him.

Fourth, A parent shall not testify against the parent's minor child and a minor child shall not testify against the child's parent in a proceeding before an inquest, grand jury, trial of an indictment or complaint or any other criminal, delinquency or youthful offender proceeding in which the victim in the proceeding is not a family member and does not reside in the family household; provided, however, that for the purposes of this clause, "parent" shall mean the biological or adoptive parent, stepparent, legal guardian or other person who has the right to act in loco parentis for the child; provided further, that in a case in which the victim is a family member and resides in the family household, the parent shall not testify as to any communication with the minor child that was for the purpose of seeking advice regarding the child's legal rights.

§ 20A. Privileged communications; communications with clergymen

A priest, rabbi or ordained or licensed minister of any church or an accredited Christian Science practitioner shall not without the consent of the person making the confession, be allowed to disclose a confession made to him in his professional character, in the course of discipline enjoined by the rules or practice of the religious body to which he belongs; nor shall a priest, rabbi or ordained or licensed minister of any church or an accredited Christian Science practitioner testify as to any communication made to him by any person in seeking religious or spiritual advice or comfort, or as to his advice given thereon in the course of his professional duties or in his professional character, without the consent of such person.

§ 20B. Privileged communications; patients and psychotherapists; exceptions

The following words as used in this section shall have the following meanings:—

"Patient", a person who, during the course of diagnosis or treatment, communicates with a psychotherapist;

"Psychotherapist", a person licensed to practice medicine, who devotes a substantial portion of his time to the practice of psychiatry. "Psychotherapist" shall also include a person who is licensed as a psychologist by the board of registration of psychologists; a graduate of, or student enrolled in, a doctoral degree program in psychology at a recognized educational institution as that term is defined in section 118, who is working under the supervision of a licensed psychologist; or a person who is a registered nurse licensed by the board of registration in nursing whose certificate of registration has been endorsed authorizing the practice of professional nursing in an expanded role as a psychiatric nurse mental health clinical specialist, pursuant to the provisions of section eighty B of chapter one hundred and twelve.

"Communications" includes conversations, correspondence, actions and occurrences relating to diagnosis or treatment before, during or after institutionalization, regardless of the patient's awareness of such conversations, correspondence, actions and occurrences, and any records, memoranda or notes of the foregoing.

Except as hereinafter provided, in any court proceeding and in any proceeding preliminary thereto and in legislative and administrative proceedings, a patient shall have the privilege of refusing to disclose, and of preventing a witness from disclosing, any communication, wherever made, between said patient and a psychotherapist relative to the diagnosis or treatment of the patient's mental or emotional condition. This privilege shall apply to patients engaged with a psychotherapist in marital therapy, family therapy, or consultation in contemplation of such therapy.

If a patient is incompetent to exercise or waive such privilege, a guardian shall be appointed to act in his behalf under this section A previously appointed guardian shall be authorized to so act.

Upon the exercise of the privilege granted by this section, the judge or presiding officer shall instruct the jury that no adverse inference may be drawn therefrom.

The privilege granted hereunder shall not apply to any of the following communications:

(a) If a psychotherapist in the course of his diagnosis or treatment of the patient, determines that the patient is in need of treatment in a hospital for mental or emotional illness or that there is a threat of imminently dangerous activity by the patient against himself or another person, and on the basis of such determination discloses such communication either for the purpose of placing or retaining the patient in such hospital, provided however that the provisions of this section shall continue in effect after the patient is in said hospital, or placing the patient under arrest or under the supervision of law enforcement authorities.

(b) If a judge finds that the patient, after having been informed that the communications would not be privileged, has made communications to a psychotherapist in the course of a psychiatric examination ordered by the court, provided that such communications shall be admissible only on issues involving the patient's mental or emotional condition but not as a confession or admission of guilt.

(c) In any proceeding, except one involving child custody, adoption or adoption consent, in which the patient introduces his mental or emotional condition as an element of his claim or defense, and the judge or presiding officer finds that it is more important to the interests of justice that the communication be disclosed than that the relationship between patient and psychotherapist be protected.

(d) In any proceeding after the death of a patient in which his mental or emotional condition is introduced by any party claiming or defending through or as a beneficiary of the patient as an element of the claim or defense, and the judge or presiding officer finds that it is more important to the interests of justice that the communication be disclosed than that the relationship between patient and psychotherapist be protected.

(e) In any case involving child custody, adoption or the dispensing with the need for consent to adoption in which, upon a hearing in chambers, the judge, in the exercise of his discretion, determines that the psychotherapist has evidence bearing significantly on the patient's ability to provide suitable care or custody, and that it is more important to the welfare of the child that the communication be disclosed than that the relationship between patient and psychotherapist be protected; provided, however, that in such cases of adoption or the dispensing with the need for consent to adoption, a judge shall determine that the patient has been informed that such communication would not be privileged.

(f) In any proceeding brought by the patient against the psychotherapist, and in any malpractice, criminal or license revocation proceeding, in which disclosure is necessary or relevant to the claim or defense of the psychotherapist.

The provision of information acquired by a psychotherapist relative to the diagnosis or treatment of a patient's emotional condition, to any insurance company, nonprofit hospital service corporation, medical service corporation, or health maintenance organization, or to a board established pursuant to section twelve of chapter one hundred and seventy-six B, pertaining to the administration or provision of benefits, including utilization review or peer review, for expenses arising from the out-patient diagnosis or treatment, or both, of mental or nervous conditions, shall not constitute a waiver or breach of any right to which said patient is otherwise entitled under this section and section thirty-six B of chapter one hundred and twenty-three.

§ 20C. Immunity from prosecution; privilege against self-incrimination

In any investigation or proceeding before a grand jury, or in a criminal proceeding in the supreme judicial court, appeals court or superior court involving any offense listed in section 20D, a witness shall not be excused from testifying or from producing books, papers or other evidence on the ground that the testimony or evidence required of him may tend to incriminate him or subject him to a penalty or forfeiture, if he has been granted immunity with respect to the transactions, matters or things concerning which he is compelled, after having claimed his privilege against self-incrimination, to testify or produce evidence by a justice of the supreme judicial court, appeals court or superior court, as provided in section 20E.

§ 20J. Sexual assault; confidential communications with sexual assault counselor; disclosure; discovery

As used in this section the following words, unless the context clearly requires otherwise, shall have the following meaning:—

"Rape crisis center", any office, institution or center offering assistance to victims of sexual assault and the families of such victims through crisis intervention, medical and legal counseling.

"Sexual assault counselor", a person who is employed by or is a volunteer in a rape crisis center, has undergone thirty-five hours of training, who reports to and is under the direct control and supervision of a licensed social worker, nurse, psychiatrist, psychologist or psychotherapist and whose primary purpose is the rendering of advice, counseling or assistance to victims of sexual assault.

"Victim", a person who has suffered a sexual assault and who consults a sexual assault counselor for the purpose of securing advice, counseling or assistance concerning a mental, physical or emotional condition caused by such sexual assault.

"Confidential communication", information transmitted in confidence by and between a victim of sexual assault and a sexual assault counselor by a means which does not disclose the information to a person other than a person present for the benefit of the victim, or to those to whom disclosure of such information is reasonably necessary to the counseling and assisting of such victim. The term includes all information received by the sexual assault counselor which arises out of and in the course of such counseling and assisting, including, but not limited to reports, records, working papers or memoranda.

A sexual assault counselor shall not disclose such confidential communication, without the prior written consent of the victim; provided, however, that nothing in this chapter shall be construed to limit the defendant's right of cross-examination of such counselor in a civil or criminal proceeding if such counselor testifies with such written consent.

Such confidential communications shall not be subject to discovery and shall be inadmissible in any criminal or civil proceeding without the prior written consent of the victim to whom the report, record, working paper or memorandum relates.

§ 20K. Domestic violence victims' counselors; confidential communications

As used in this section the following words shall unless the context clearly requires otherwise have the following meanings:—

"Abuse", causing or attempting to cause physical harm; placing another in fear of imminent physical harm; causing another to engage in sexual relations against his will by force, threat of force, or coercion.

"Confidential communication", information transmitted in confidence by and between a victim and a domestic violence victims' counselor by a means which does not disclose the information to a person other than a person present for the benefit of the victim, or to those to whom disclosure of such information is reasonably necessary to the counseling and assisting of such victim. The term includes all information received by the domestic violence victims' counselor which arises out of and in the course of such counseling and assisting, including, but not limited to, reports, records, working papers, or memoranda.

"Domestic violence victims' counselor", a person who is employed or volunteers in a domestic violence victims' program, who has undergone a minimum of twenty-five hours of training and who reports to and is under the direct control and supervision of a direct service supervisor of a domestic violence victims' program, and whose primary purpose is the rendering of advice, counseling or assistance to victims of abuse.

"Domestic violence victims' program", any refuge, shelter, office, safe home, institution or center established for the purpose of offering assistance to victims of abuse through crisis intervention, medical, legal or support counseling.

"Victim", a person who has suffered abuse and who consults a domestic violence victims' counselor for the purpose of securing advice, counseling or assistance concerning a mental, physical or emotional condition caused by such abuse.

A domestic violence victims' counselor shall not disclose such confidential communication without the prior written consent of the victim, except as hereinafter provided. Such confidential communication shall not be subject to discovery in any civil, legislative or administrative proceeding without the prior written consent of the victim to whom such confidential communication relates. In criminal actions such confidential communication shall be subject to discovery and shall be admissible as evidence but only to the extent of information contained therein which is exculpatory in relation to the defendant; provided, however, that the court shall first examine such confidential communication and shall determine whether or not such exculpatory information is therein contained before allowing such discovery or the introduction of such evidence.

§ 20L. Confidentiality of domestic violence victims' program and rape crisis center locations

The location and street address of all domestic violence victims' programs, as defined in section twenty K and rape crisis centers, as defined in section twenty J, shall be absolutely confidential and shall not be required to be revealed in any criminal or civil proceeding.

§ 20M. Human trafficking victim caseworker

[Added by 2011 Mass. Acts c. 178, § 17, effective Nov. 21, 2011.]

(a) As used in this section, the following words shall, unless the context clearly requires otherwise, have the following meanings:—

"Confidential communication", information transmitted in confidence by and between a victim and a victim's caseworker by a means which does not disclose the information to a person other than a person present for the benefit of the victim, or to those to whom disclosure of such information is reasonably necessary to the counseling and assisting of such victim. The term confidential communication shall include all information received by a victim's caseworker which arises out of and in the course of such counseling and assisting including, but not limited to, reports, records, working papers or memoranda.

"Human trafficking victim" or "victim", a person who is subjected to the conduct prohibited under sections 50 or 51 of chapter 265.

"Human trafficking victims' caseworker," a person who is employed by or volunteers with a program serving human trafficking victims, who has undergone a minimum of 25 hours of training and who reports to and is under the direct control and supervision of a direct service supervisor of a human trafficking victim program, and whose primary purpose is the rendering of advice, counseling or assistance to human trafficking victims.

"Human trafficking victims' program", any refuge, shelter, office, safe house, institution or center established for the purpose of offering assistance to human trafficking victims through crisis intervention, medical, legal or support counseling.

(b) A human trafficking victims' caseworker shall not disclose any confidential communication without the prior written consent of the victim, or the victim's guardian in the case of a child, except as hereinafter provided. Such confidential communication shall not be subject to discovery in any civil, legislative or administrative proceeding without the prior written consent of the victim, or victim's guardian in the case of a child, to whom such confidential communication relates. In criminal actions such confidential communication shall be subject to discovery and shall be admissible as evidence but only to the extent of information contained therein which is exculpatory in relation to the defendant; provided, however, that the court shall first examine such confidential communication and shall determine whether or not such exculpatory information is contained in the communication before allowing such discovery or the introduction of such evidence.

(c) During the initial meeting between a caseworker and victim, the caseworker shall inform the human trafficking victim and any guardian thereof of the confidentiality of communications between a caseworker and victim and the limitations thereto.

§ 20N. Disclosure of social worker home address and service of process procedures

[Added by 2015 Mass. Acts c. 46, § 126, effective July 17, 2015.]

(a) No court shall permit or require the disclosure of the home address or personal telephone number of a social worker employed by the department of children and families; and no witness shall be required to disclose such social worker's home address or personal telephone number in any court proceeding or in any proceeding preliminary thereto or in any documents filed with the court, except as otherwise ordered by the court, for good cause shown; provided, however, that an order of the court shall include, if possible, conditions to limit the disclosure of any such address or phone number so as to protect the privacy and safety of the social worker.

(b) Service of process, summons or subpoena upon a department of children and families social worker in any court proceeding and in any proceeding preliminary thereto shall be made upon the agency employing the social worker and in accordance with the Massachusetts Rules of Civil Procedure or the Massachusetts Rules of Criminal Procedure governing any such service of process, summons or subpoena. For the purpose of making such service, the employing agency, upon request, shall certify to the summoning party the name and work address of any such social worker as disclosed by its records, and a summoning party may serve the social worker at the work address so certified.

§ 22. Cross-examination of adverse party; corporation's agent as adverse party

A party who calls the adverse party as a witness shall be allowed to cross-examine him. In case the adverse party is a corporation, an officer or agent thereof, so called as a witness, shall be deemed such an adverse party for the purposes of this section.

§ 23. Impeachment of party's own witness

The party who produces a witness shall not impeach his credit by evidence of bad character, but may contradict him by other evidence, and may also prove that he has made at other times statements inconsistent with his present testimony; but before proof of such inconsistent statements is given, the circumstances thereof sufficient to designate the particular occasion shall be mentioned to the witness, and he shall be asked if he has made such statements, and, if so, shall be allowed to explain them.

§ 23C. Work product of mediator confidential; confidential communications; exception; mediator defined

All memoranda, and other work product prepared by a mediator and a mediator's case files shall be confidential and not subject to disclosure in any judicial or administrative proceeding involving any of the parties to any mediation to which such materials apply. Any communication made in the course of and relating to the subject matter of any mediation and which is made in the presence of such mediator by any participant, mediator or other person shall be a confidential communication and not subject to disclosure in any judicial or administrative proceeding; provided, however, that the provisions of this section shall not apply to the mediation of labor disputes.

For the purposes of this section a "mediator" shall mean a person not a party to a dispute who enters into a written agreement with the parties to assist them in resolving their disputes and has completed at least thirty hours of training in mediation and who either has four years of professional experience as a mediator or is accountable to a dispute resolution organization which has been in existence for at least three years or one who has been appointed to mediate by a judicial or governmental body.

§ 23E. Alternative procedures for determining competency of witness with intellectual disability

[Amended by 2010 Mass. Acts c. 239, §§ 68–70, effective Nov. 2, 2010.]

(a) For the purposes of this section, the following words shall have the following meanings, unless the context clearly requires otherwise:

"Witnesses with an intellectual disability", a witness in a proceeding whom the presiding justice has found after hearing, as provided in paragraph (1) of subsection (b), to have an intellectual disability.

"Intellectual disability", substantial limitations in present functioning manifesting before age eighteen and characterized by significantly subaverage intellectual functioning, existing concurrently with related limitations in two or more of the following applicable skill areas: communication, self-help, home living, social skills, community use, self-direction, health and safety, functional academics, leisure and work.

(b)(1) In any judicial proceeding in which a witness with an intellectual disability will testify, the court, on its own motion or on motion of the proponent of the witness with an intellectual disability and after hearing on the witness's competency to testify, may order the use of alternative procedures for taking testimony of the witness with an intellectual disability; provided, however, that the court finds at the time of the order, by clear and convincing evidence in the case of a criminal proceeding, and by a preponderance of the evidence in the case of a noncriminal proceeding, that the witness with an intellectual disability is likely, as a result of submitting to usual procedures for determining competency or as a result of testifying in open court, as the case may be, (i) to suffer severe psychological or emotional trauma; or (ii) to suffer a temporary loss of or regression in cognitive or behavioral functioning or communicative abilities, such that his ability to testify will be significantly impaired. If the court so finds, the court may order the use of alternative procedures for determining competency to testify or for taking testimony of the witness with an intellectual disability including, but not limited to, the following:

(i) permitting a person familiar to the witness, such as a family member, clinician, counselor, social worker or friend, to sit near or next to such witness;

(ii) permitting the witness with mental retardation to testify in court but off the witness stand; provided, however, that if the proceeding is a bench proceeding, testimony may be taken at another location within the courthouse but outside the courtroom; and, provided further, that if the proceeding is a jury trial, testimony may be taken on videotape out of the presence of the jury or in a location chosen by the court or by agreement of the parties; or

(iii) combining alternative procedures provided in clauses (i) and (ii).

(c) When the proceedings are not criminal or juvenile delinquency related, testimony taken by videotape pursuant to an order under paragraph (1) of subsection (b) shall be taken in the presence of the judge, counsel for all parties and such other persons as the court may allow. Counsel shall be given the opportunity to examine or cross-examine the witness with mental retardation to the same extent as he would be permitted if ordinary procedures had been followed.

(d) When the proceedings are criminal or juvenile delinquency related, the defendant shall have the right to be present during the taking of the testimony, to have an unobstructed view of the

1

witness with an intellectual disability, and to have the witness's view of the defendant be unobstructed.

(e) If the court orders that the testimony of the witness with an intellectual disability be videotaped out of the presence of the jury, the videotape shall be shown in court to the jury in the presence of the judge, the parties and the parties' counsel. The videotape shall be marked as an exhibit and retained by the court as part of the record of the case.

(f) Testimony taken by alternative procedures authorized by this section shall be admissible as substantive evidence to the same extent as in lieu of live testimony by the witness in any proceeding in which such testimony is taken.

(g) The witness requesting that testimony be taken by videotape shall bear the responsibility of producing an acceptable videotape of the testimony. The commonwealth shall reimburse such witness for reasonable costs of producing such videotape. Each party shall be afforded an opportunity to view the recording before it is shown in the courtroom.

(h) The fact that the witness with an intellectual disability has been found in a court proceeding to be incompetent to make informed decisions of a personal, medical or financial nature or that he is under a guardianship or conservatorship shall not preclude such witness from testifying if he is found to be competent to testify and shall not preclude a determination of competency to testify.

(i) A witness shall not be denied the benefit of appropriate alternative procedures provided by this section and the court shall allow such additional time or continuances to permit application of such procedures.

(j) A person with expertise in persons with an intellectual disability may be called by the proponent of the witness to testify in all relevant matters, including the competency determination of such witness.

(k) Nothing in this section shall be construed to prohibit a court from using other appropriate means consistent with this section and any other general or special law and with the defendant's rights to accomplish the purpose of this section.

§ 24. Depositions in civil cases authorized

Depositions may be taken as provided in this chapter to be used only in those proceedings in the land court and probate court which are not governed by the Massachusetts Rules of Civil Procedure. The provisions of this section and of sections twenty-five through forty-five, inclusive, of this chapter, shall not apply to civil actions governed by said rules, or by the District-Municipal Courts Rules of Civil Procedure.

§ 24A. Medical witnesses

At trial of a civil matter in the district court department of the trial court, the justice may order, or, upon the request of a party, authorize the taking of a deposition of the testimony of a medical witness. Said deposition shall be taken for use as medical evidence only, and shall be admissible in whole or in part in a proceeding before said district court department. The expense for stenographic service in connection with the taking of such deposition shall be paid by the party requesting that such witness be deposed, or whose witness is ordered to be deposed; provided, however, that if the judgment entered by the district court justice is in favor of the plaintiff, the cost of such stenographic expense shall be added to such judgment and shall be paid by the insurer, if the defendant has insurance, or by the defendant, if he does not have such insurance.

§ 25. Grounds for deposition

If a witness or party whose testimony is wanted in a civil cause or proceeding pending in the commonwealth lives more than thirty miles from the place of trial, or is about to go out of the commonwealth and not to return in time for the trial, or is so ill, aged or infirm as to make it probable that he will not be able to attend at the trial, his deposition may be taken.

§ 26. Notice of taking deposition

After service of process in an action, or after a submission to arbitrators or referees, either party may apply to a justice of the peace or a notary public, who shall issue a notice to the adverse party to appear and propose interrogatories before said justice or any other justice of the peace or before said notary or any other notary public at the time and place appointed for taking the deposition.

§ 27. Persons on whom notice may be served

The notice may be served on the adverse party, his agent or attorney, and if there are several plaintiffs or defendants, on any of them.

§ 28. Mode of service

The notice shall be served by delivering an attested copy thereof to the person to be notified, or by leaving such copy at his place of abode, not less than twenty-four hours before the time appointed for taking the deposition, and also allowing not less time than at the rate of one day, Sundays excluded, for every twenty miles' travel to the place appointed.

§ 29. Verbal notice; waiver of notice, etc.

The justice or notary who takes the deposition may give a verbal instead of the written notice. If the adverse party or his attorney in writing waives notice, or if the defendant does not enter his appearance in the action within the time required by law, no notice shall be required.

§ 30. Oath and examination of deponent

The deponent shall be sworn or affirmed to testify the truth, the whole truth and nothing but the truth, relative to the cause for which the deposition is taken. The deponent shall then be examined by the justice or notary, and may be examined by the parties, and the testimony may be taken in writing or by any recording device, including an electronic device, which will accurately preserve such testimony.

§ 31. Order of examination

The party producing the deponent shall be allowed first to examine him, either upon verbal or written interrogatories, on all the points which he considers material; the adverse party may then examine him in like manner, after which either party may propose further interrogatories.

§ 32. Mode of taking deposition

The deposition shall be written by the justice or notary or deponent or by a disinterested person in the presence and under the direction of the justice or notary, shall be carefully read to or by the deponent, and then subscribed by him.

§ 33. Certification of deposition

The justice or notary shall annex to the deposition a certificate of the time and manner of taking it, the person at whose request and the cause in which it was taken, the reason for taking it and that the adverse party attended, or if he did not attend what notice was given to him.

§ 34. Delivery and preservation of deposition

The deposition shall be delivered by the justice or notary to the court, arbitrators, referees or other persons before whom the cause is pending, or shall be enclosed and sealed by him and directed to it or them, and shall remain sealed until opened by it or them.

§ 35. Exclusion of deposition

The court may exclude the deposition if it finds that the adverse party failed without fault to attend the taking thereof, and shall exclude it if it finds that the reason for taking it, or other sufficient cause for its use, no longer exists.

§ 36. Objections to deposition

Objections to the competency or credibility of the deponent and to the admissibility of any questions asked of or answers made by him may be made when the deposition is produced in the same manner as if he were personally examined as a witness at the trial; but if a deposition is taken upon written interrogatories annexed to a commission, all objections to an interrogatory shall be made before the commission issues, and unless the interrogatory is withdrawn shall be noted in the deposition, otherwise they shall not be allowed.

§ 37. Use of deposition in second action

If a plaintiff discontinues his action or becomes nonsuit, and another action is afterward commenced for the same cause between the same parties or their respective representatives, depositions lawfully taken for the first action may be used in the second in the same manner and subject to the same conditions and objections as if originally taken for the second action, if the deposition was duly filed in the court in which the first action was pending and has remained in the custody of the court from the termination of the first action until the commencement of the second.

§ 38. Compelling giving of deposition; place

A person may be summoned and compelled to give his deposition at a place within twenty miles of his place of abode, in like manner and under the same penalties as are provided for a witness before a court.

§ 39. Place of taking deposition of nonresident found within commonwealth

A person not a resident of but found within the commonwealth may be summoned and compelled to give his deposition at any place within ten miles of the place at which the summons is served upon him, in like manner and under the same penalties as he may be summoned and compelled to attend as a witness before a court.

§ 40. Rules for taking depositions

The courts may make rules regulating the game and manner of opening, filing and safe keeping of depositions, and the taking and use thereof.

§ 41. Taking deposition outside commonwealth

The deposition of a person without the commonwealth may be taken under a commission issued to one or more competent persons in another state or country by the court in which the cause is pending, or it may be taken before a commissioner appointed by the governor for that purpose, and in either case the deposition may be used in the same manner and subject to the same conditions and objections as if it had been taken in the commonwealth.

§ 42. Written interrogatories; notice to adverse party; production of documents

Unless the court otherwise orders, a deposition taken before commissioners shall be taken upon written interrogatories, which shall be filed in the clerk's office and notice thereof given to the adverse party or his attorney, and upon cross interrogatories, if any are filed by him. But if the defendant does not enter his appearance in the action within the time required by law, no notice to him shall be required. The court may in any case order depositions to be taken before commissioners, in the manner provided by law for taking the depositions of witnesses within the commonwealth in actions at law, or in such manner as the court orders, and in such cases shall determine what notice shall be given to the adverse party, his agent or attorney, and the manner of service thereof, may authorize the taking of depositions of witnesses not specifically named in the commission, and may limit the extent of the inquiry. The court may order the production before the commissioner of any books, instruments or papers relative to any matter in issue.

§ 43. Rules for taking depositions outside of commonwealth

The courts may make rules for the issuing of commissions, the filing of interrogatories and all other matters relative to depositions taken without the commonwealth.

§ 44. Foreign depositions obtained contrary to statute

Depositions and affidavits taken without the commonwealth in any manner other than is provided in the three preceding sections, if taken before a notary public or other person authorized by the laws of any other state or country to take depositions, may be admitted or rejected in the discretion of the court; but such deposition or affidavit shall not be admitted unless the court finds that the adverse party had sufficient notice of the taking thereof and an opportunity to cross-examine the witness, or that from the circumstances of the case it was impossible to give him such notice.

§ 45. Deposition for use in another state

A person may be summoned and compelled, in like manner and under the same penalties as are provided for a witness before a court, to give his deposition in a cause pending in a court of any other state or government. Such deposition may be taken before a justice of the peace or a notary public in the commonwealth, or before a commissioner appointed under the authority of the state or government in which the action is pending. If the deposition is taken before such commissioner, the witness may be summoned and compelled to appear before him by process from a justice of the peace or a notary public in the commonwealth.

§ 46. Application to take deposition to perpetuate testimony

If a person desires to perpetuate his own testimony or the testimony of another person, he shall apply in writing to two of the peace or notaries public, or a justice of the peace and a notary public, one of whom shall be an attorney at law, requesting them to take his deposition or the deposition of the person whose testimony he desires to perpetuate, and stating briefly and substantially his title, claim or interest in or to the subject relative to which he desires the evidence perpetuated, the names of all other persons interested or supposed to be interested therein and the name of the witness proposed to be examined.

§ 47. Notice of taking deposition; compelling testimony

The justices or notaries shall thereupon cause notice of the time and place appointed for taking the deposition to be given to all persons named in said statement as interested in the case, in the manner provided in sections twenty-six to twenty-nine, inclusive; and if in the opinion of the justices or notaries no sufficient provision is made by law for giving notice to parties adversely interested, they shall cause such reasonable notice to be given as they consider proper. A person may be summoned and compelled to give a deposition in perpetuation of his testimony in like manner and under the same penalties as are provided for a witness before a court.

§ 48. Objections to taking deposition; procedure

If at the time and place so appointed a witness or a person interested appears and objects, the justices or notaries shall not take the deposition unless upon hearing the parties they shall find that such testimony may be material to the petitioner and, except when the witness himself is petitioner, that it is not sought for the purpose of discovery or of using it in an action then pending or thereafter to be brought against said witness, and that the petitioner is in danger of losing the same before it can be taken in any action wherein his right, title, interest or claim can be tried. In all cases the petitioner, his agent or attorney shall, at the request of such witness or of a person interested, be examined on oath relative to his reasons for taking the deposition.

§ 49. Mode of taking deposition

The deponent shall be sworn and examined, and his deposition shall be written, read and subscribed in the manner provided in sections thirty to thirty-two, inclusive; and the justices or notaries shall sign and annex thereto a certificate of the name of the person at whose request it was taken, the names of all persons who were notified to attend, of all who attended the taking thereof, of the time and manner of taking it, and that it was taken for the purpose of perpetuating the testimony therein.

§ 50. Recording deposition

The deposition, the certificate and the application of the petitioner shall, within ninety days after the taking of the deposition, be recorded in the registry of deeds in the county or district where the land lies, if the deposition relates to land; otherwise, in the county or district where the parties or some of them reside.

§ 51. Use of deposition in action

If, at the time of taking such deposition or afterward, and the action is pending between the petitioner and the persons named in his application or any of those who were notified as aforesaid, or any persons claiming under any of said persons, relative to the title, claim or interest set forth in the application, the deposition or a certified copy of it from the registry of deeds may be used in such action in the same manner and subject to the same conditions and objections as if it had been originally taken therefor.

§ 52. Perpetuation of testimony of nonresidents

Depositions to perpetuate the testimony of persons living without the commonwealth may be taken without the commonwealth upon a commission issued by the supreme judicial or the superior court.

§ 53. Application to perpetuate testimony of nonresidents

The person who desires to take such deposition shall file in either of said courts the application provided for in section forty-six; and if the subject of the proposed deposition relates to land within the commonwealth, a copy of the application with the statement therein shall be filed in the registry of deeds for the county or district where the land or any part thereof lies; otherwise, in the registry of deeds for the county or district where the parties or some of them reside.

§ 54. Notice of taking deposition

The court shall order notice of such application and statement to be served on all the persons named therein as adversely interested, and living within the commonwealth, fourteen days at least before the time therein appointed for hearing the parties, and shall order reasonable notice to be given to such persons living without the commonwealth.

§ 55. Issuance of commission

If, upon hearing the parties who appear, the court finds that there is sufficient cause for taking the deposition, it shall issue a commission therefor in like manner as for taking a deposition to be used in a cause pending in the same court.

§ 56. Written interrogatories

The deposition shall be taken upon written interrogatories filed by the applicant, and cross interrogatories, if any are filed by any party adversely interested, and it shall be taken and returned substantially in the same manner as d taken to be used in a cause pending in the same court.

§ 57. Rules for perpetuation of testimony of witnesses without commonwealth

The supreme judicial court may make rules for taking depositions to perpetuate the testimony of witnesses without the commonwealth, taken under a commission from the supreme judicial or the superior court, and for filing or recording them.

§ 58. Use of deposition

Depositions to perpetuate the testimony of witnesses which are taken without the commonwealth under this chapter may be used in like manner as if taken within the commonwealth.

§ 59. Perpetuation of testimony for use against all persons

Depositions to perpetuate the testimony of witnesses within or without the commonwealth, so that they may be evidence against all persons, may, after public notice, be taken upon a commission issued by the supreme judicial court or the superior court.

§ 60. Application for deposition

The person who desires to have such deposition taken may apply to either of said courts in the manner provided in section fifty-three, and the proceedings thereon shall be the same as are provided in sections fifty-four to fifty-six, inclusive.

§ 61. Naming persons interested; notice of taking deposition

The court shall, in addition to the proceedings before provided, require the applicant, upon oath or otherwise, in its discretion, to state the names of all persons known or supposed to be interested in the subject matter of the application, and shall in the commission direct the commissioner or commissioners to publish in such newspaper within or without the commonwealth, or both, or in such other manner, as the court orders, such notice of the time and place of taking such deposition and of the subject matter thereof as the court approves. Such notice shall be addressed by name to all persons who are known or supposed to be interested in the subject matter of the application, and generally to all others, and shall state that they may attend and propose cross interrogatories to the witness. The court may require additional personal notice of the time and place of taking and of the subject matter of such deposition to be given to such persons and in such manner as it orders.

§ 62. Recording deposition

After such deposition has been taken, it shall be returned to the court by whose order the commission issued, which, if the deposition is found to have been taken according to law and the directions contained in the commission, shall order it to be recorded within thirty days after the date of the order in the registry of deeds, in the manner provided in section fifty.

§ 63. Use of deposition against any person

A deposition taken and recorded under the provisions of the four preceding sections, or a certified copy thereof from the registry of deeds, may be used by the person at whose request it was taken, or by any person who claims under him, against any person whatever, in any action or process wherein is brought in question the title, claim or interest set forth in the statement upon which the commission was founded, in the same manner, and subject to the same conditions and objections, as if it had been originally taken for said action or process.

§ 68. Proof of signature

A signature to an attested instrument or writing, except a will, may be proved in the same manner as if it were not attested.

§ 69. Records of courts of other states or United States

The records and judicial proceedings of a court of another state or of the United States shall be admissible in evidence in this commonwealth, if authenticated by the attestation of the clerk or other officer who has charge of the records of such court under its seal.

§ 70. Judicial notice of foreign law

The courts shall take judicial notice of the law of the United States or of any state, territory or dependency thereof or of a foreign country whenever the same shall be material.

§ 73. Foreign oaths and affidavits

All oaths and affidavits administered or taken by a notary public, duly commissioned and qualified by authority of any other state or government within the jurisdiction for which he is commissioned, and certified under his official seal, shall be as effectual in this commonwealth as if administered or taken and certified by a justice of the peace therein.

§ 75. Admissibility of printed copies of acts of legislative and administrative bodies

The printed copies of all statutes, acts and resolves of the commonwealth, public or private, which are published under its authority, and copies of the ordinances of a city, the by-laws of a town or of the rules and regulations of a board of aldermen, if attested by the clerk of such city or town, shall be admitted as sufficient evidence thereof in all courts of law and on all occasions. Printed copies of rules and regulations purporting to be issued by authority of any department, commission, board or officer of the commonwealth or of any city or town having authority to adopt them, or printed copies of any city ordinances or town by-laws, or printed copies of the United States Code Annotated or the United States Code Service and all federal regulations, and the titles, chapters, subchapters, parts and sections thereof shall be admitted without certification or attestation, but, if their genuineness is questioned, the court shall require such certification or attestation thereof as it deems necessary.

§ 76. Admissibility of authenticated records of governmental departments

[Amended by 2008 Mass. Acts c. 522 § 42, effective Apr. 15, 2009.]

Copies of books, papers, documents and records in any department of the commonwealth or of any city or town, authenticated by the attestation of the officer who has charge of the same, shall be competent evidence in all cases equally with the originals thereof; provided, that, except in the case of books, papers, documents and records of the department of public utilities or the department of telecommunications and cable in matters relating to common carriers, and of the registry of motor vehicles, the genuineness of the signature of such officer shall be attested by the secretary of the commonwealth under its seal or by the clerk of such city or town, as the case may be.

§ 78. Entry, writing or record made in regular course of business; impeachment

An entry in an account kept in a book or by a card system or by any other system of keeping accounts, or a writing or record, whether in the form of an entry in a book or otherwise, made as a memorandum or record of any act, transaction, occurrence or event, shall not be inadmissible in any civil or criminal proceeding as evidence of the facts therein stated because it is transcribed or because it is hearsay or self-serving, if the court finds that the entry, writing or record was made in good faith in the regular course of business and before the beginning of the civil or criminal proceeding aforesaid and that it was the regular course of such business to make such memorandum or record at the time of such act, transaction, occurrence or event or within a reasonable time thereafter. For the purposes hereof, the word "business", in addition to its ordinary meaning, shall include profession, occupation and calling of every kind. The court, in its discretion, before admitting such entry, writing or record in evidence, may, to such extent as it deems practicable or desirable, but to no greater extent than the law required before April eleventh, nineteen hundred and thirteen, require the party offering the same to produce and offer in evidence the original entry, writing, document or account or any other form which the entry, writing or record offered or the facts therein stated were transcribed or taken, and to call as his witness any person who made the entry, writing or record offered or the original or any other entry, writing, document or account from which the entry, writing or record offered or the facts therein stated were transcribed or taken, or who has personal knowledge of the facts stated in the entry, writing or record offered. When any such entry, writing or record is admitted, all other circumstances of the making thereof, including lack of personal knowledge by the entrant or maker, may be shown to affect its weight and when such entry, writing or record is admitted in a criminal proceeding all questions of fact which must be determined by the court as the basis for the admissibility of the evidence involved shall be submitted to the jury, if a jury trial is had for its final determination.

§ 79. Records and copies of records of hospitals and certain institutions; admissibility in evidence

Records kept by hospitals, dispensaries or clinics, and sanatoria under section seventy of chapter one hundred and eleven shall be admissible, and records which the court finds are required to be kept by the laws of any other state or territory, or the District of Columbia, or by the laws and regulations of the United States of America pertaining to the department of national defense and the veterans administration, by hospitals, dispensaries or clinics, and sanatoria similarly conducted or operated or which, being incorporated, offer treatment free of charge, may be admitted by the court, in its discretion, as evidence in the courts of the commonwealth so far as such records relate to the treatment and medical history of such cases and the court may, in its discretion, admit copies of such records, if certified by the persons in custody thereof to be true and complete; but nothing therein contained shall be admissible as evidence which has reference to the question of liability. Copies of photographic or microphotographic records so kept by hospitals, dispensaries or clinics, or sanatoria, when duly certified by the person in charge of the hospital, dispensary or clinic, or sanatorium, shall be admitted in evidence equally with the original photographs or microphotographs.

A record kept by any hospital, dispensary or clinic, or sanatorium under section seventy of chapter one hundred and eleven which is required to be produced in court by any party shall be certified by the affidavit of the person in custody thereof to be a true and complete record, and shall be delivered by such hospital, dispensary or clinic, or sanatorium to the clerk of such court, who shall keep the same in his custody until its production is called for at the trial or hearing by the party requiring the said record. Such record, so certified and delivered shall be deemed to be sufficiently identified to be admissible in evidence if admissible in all other respects. The party requiring the production of said record and, in the discretion of the court, any other party may examine said record in the custody of the clerk at any time before it is produced in court. The clerk upon completion of such trial or hearing shall notify such hospital that said record is no longer required and will be returned to the hospital by certified mail unless an authorized representative of the hospital calls for the same at the office of said clerk within seven days of said notice.

§ 79A. Certified copies of public and private records

Copies of public records, of records described in sections five, seven and sixteen, respectively, of chapter sixty-six, and of records of banks, trust companies, insurance companies and hospitals, whether or not such records or copies are made by the photographic or microphotographic process, shall, when duly certified by the person in charge thereof, be admitted in evidence equally with the originals.

§ 79B. Fact statements published for persons in particular occupation

Statements of facts of general interest to persons engaged in an occupation contained in a list, register, periodical, book or other compilation, issued to the public, shall, in the discretion of the court, if the court finds that the compilation is published for the use of persons engaged in that occupation and commonly is used and relied upon by them, be admissible in civil cases as evidence of the truth of any fact so stated.

§ 79C. Statements of fact or opinion in scientific publication; notice of intention to use

Statements of facts or opinions on a subject of science or art contained in a published treatise, periodical, book or pamphlet shall, in so far as the court shall find that the said statements are relevant and that the writer of such statements is recognized in his profession or calling as an expert on the subject, be admissible in actions of contract or tort for malpractice, error or mistake against physicians, surgeons, dentists, optometrists, hospitals and sanitaria, as evidence tending to prove said facts or as opinion evidence; provided, however, that the party intending to offer as evidence any such statements shall, not less than thirty days before the trial of the action, give the adverse party or his attorney notice of such intention, stating the name of the writer of the statements, the title of the treatise, periodical, book or pamphlet in which they are contained, the date of publication of the same, the name of the publisher of the same, and wherever possible or practicable the page or pages of the same on which the said statements appear.

§ 79D. Photographic copies of newspaper in library; prints from photographic film

Copies of any newspaper, or part thereof made by the photographic or microphotographic process deposited in any public library or a library of any college or university located in the commonwealth, shall, when duly certified by the person in charge thereof, be admitted in evidence equally with the originals.

A print, whether enlarged or not, from any photographic film, including any photographic plate, microphotographic film, photostatic negative or reproduction of any original record, document, instrument, plan, book or paper destroyed, lost or for any reason unavailable after such film was taken, shall be admissible in evidence in all instances that the original record, document, instrument, plan, book or paper might have been admitted in evidence, and shall have the full force and effect of said original if it is proved that (a) such reproduction was made in the regular course of any business and that it was the regular course of any such business to make such reproductions; (b) said photographic film, microphotographic, photostatic or similar reproduction was taken in order to keep a permanent record of the original; and (c) the said original was subsequently destroyed, lost or is unavailable.

§ 79E. Reproductions of public or business records

If any business, institution, member of a profession or calling, or any department or agency of government, in the regular course of business or activity, has kept or recorded any memorandum, writing entry, print, representation or combination thereof of any act, transaction, occurrence or event, and in the regular course of business has caused any or all of the same to be recorded, copied or reproduced by any photographic, photostatic, microfilm, microcard, miniature photographic or other process which accurately reproduces or forms a durable medium for so reproducing the original, the original may be destroyed in the regular course of business unless its preservation is required by law. Such reproduction, when satisfactorily identified, shall be as admissible in evidence as the original itself in any judicial or administrative proceeding whether the original is in existence or not and an enlargement or facsimile of such reproduction shall be likewise admissible in evidence if the original reproduction is in existence and available for inspection under direction of the court. The introduction of a reproduced record, enlargement or facsimile, shall not preclude admission of the original.

§ 79G. Medical and hospital services; evidence

In any proceeding commenced in any court, commission or agency, an itemized bill and reports, including hospital medical records, relating to medical, dental, hospital services, prescriptions, or orthopedic appliances rendered to or prescribed for a person injured, or any report of any examination of said injured person, including, but not limited to hospital medical records subscribed and sworn to under the penalties of perjury by the physician, dentist, authorized agent of a hospital or health maintenance organization rendering such services or by the pharmacist or retailer of orthopedic appliances, shall be admissible as evidence of the fair and reasonable charge for such services or the necessity of such services or treatments, the diagnosis of said physician or dentist, the prognosis of such physician or dentist, the opinion of such physician or dentist as to proximate cause of the condition so diagnosed, the opinion of such physician or dentist as to disability or incapacity, if any, proximately resulting from the condition so diagnosed; provided, however, that written notice of the intention to offer such bill or report as such evidence, together with a copy thereof has been given to the opposing party or parties, or to his or their attorneys, by mailing the same by certified mail, return receipt requested, not less than ten days before the introduction of same into evidence, and that an affidavit of such notice and the return receipt is filed with the clerk of the court, agency or commission forthwith after said receipt has been returned. Nothing contained in this section shall be construed to limit the right of any party to the action to summon, at his own expense, such physician, dentist, pharmacist, retailer of orthopedic appliances or agent of such hospital or health maintenance organization or the records of such hospital or health maintenance organization for the purpose of cross examination with respect to such bill, record and report or to rebut the contents thereof, or for any other purpose, nor to limit the right of any party to the action or proceeding to summon any other person to testify in respect to such bill, record or report or for any other purpose.

The words "physician" and "dentist" shall not include any person who is not licensed to practice as such under the laws of the jurisdiction within which such services were rendered, but shall include chiropodists, chiropractors, optometrists, osteopaths, physical therapists, podiatrists, psychologists and other medical personnel licensed to practice under the laws of the jurisdiction within which such services were rendered.

The word "hospital" shall mean any hospital required to keep records under section seventy of chapter one hundred and eleven, or which is in any way licensed or regulated by the laws of any other state, or by the laws and regulations of the United States of America, including hospitals of the Veterans Administration or similar type institutions, whether incorporated or not.

The words "health maintenance organization" shall have the same meaning as defined in section one of chapter one hundred and seventy-six G.

§ 79J. Business records required to be produced in court; certification, admissibility and inspection; copies

A record kept by any business which is required to be produced in court by any party shall be certified by the affidavit of the person in custody thereof to be a true and complete record and shall be delivered by such business to the clerk of such court who shall keep the same in his custody until its production is called for at the trial or hearing by the party requiring the said record. Such record, so certified and delivered shall be deemed to be sufficiently identified to be admissible in evidence if admissible in all other respects. The party requiring the production of said record and, in the discretion of the court, any other party may examine said record in the custody of the clerk at any time before it is produced in court. The clerk upon completion of such trial or hearing shall notify such business that said record is no longer required and will be returned by mail unless an authorized representative of the business calls for the same at the office of said clerk within seven days of said notice.

A copy of such record made by the photographic process may be delivered to the clerk of such court in place of the original and, if certified as hereinbefore provided, shall be admitted in evidence equally with the original.

§ 79K. Duplicate of computer data file or program file; admissibility

A duplicate of a computer data file or program file shall be admissible in evidence as the original itself unless (1) a genuine question is raised as to the authenticity of the original or (2) in the circumstances it would be unfair to admit the duplicate in lieu of the original.

For the purposes of this section, if data is stored in a computer or similar device, any printout or other output readable by sight, shown to reflect the data accurately, shall be an original.

A "duplicate of a computer data file or program file" shall mean a file produced by the same impression as the original, or from the same matrix, or by mechanical or electronic recording, in the normal way such a duplicate is produced on a computer, or by other equivalent techniques that accurately reproduce the original.

§ 80. Transcripts from stenographic notes

Transcripts from stenographic notes duly taken under authority of law in any court proceeding by a stenographer duly appointed for the purpose and sworn, when verified by the certificate of such stenographer, shall be admissible as evidence of testimony given whenever proof of such testimony is otherwise competent.

§ 81. Criminal proceedings; out-of-court statements describing sexual contact; admissibility

(a) An out-of-court statement of a child under the age of ten describing an act of sexual contact performed on or with the child, the circumstances under which it occurred, or which identifies the perpetrator shall be admissible as substantive evidence in any criminal proceeding; provided, however, that the statement is offered as evidence of a material fact and is more probative on the point for which it is offered than any other evidence which the proponent can procure through reasonable efforts; the person to whom the statement was made or who heard the child make the statement testifies; the judge finds pursuant to subsection (b) that the child is unavailable as a witness; and the judge finds pursuant to subsection (c) that the statement is reliable.

(b) The proponent of such statement shall demonstrate a diligent and good faith effort to produce the child and shall bear the burden of showing unavailability. A finding of unavailability shall be supported by specific findings on the record, describing facts with particularity, demonstrating that:

(1) the child is unable to be present or to testify because of death or physical or mental illness or infirmity; or

(2) by a ruling of the court, the child is exempt on the ground of privilege from testifying concerning the subject matter of such statement; or

(3) the child testifies to a lack of memory of the subject matter of such statement; or

(4) the child is absent from the hearing and the proponent of such statement has been unable to procure the attendance of the child by process or by other reasonable means; or

(5) the court finds, based upon expert testimony from a treating psychiatrist, psychologist, or clinician, that testifying would be likely to cause severe psychological or emotional trauma to the child; or

(6) the child is not competent to testify.

(c) If a finding of unavailability is made, the out-of-court statement shall be admitted if the judge further finds: (1) after holding a separate hearing, that such statement was made under oath, that it was accurately recorded and preserved, and there was sufficient opportunity to cross-examine; or (2) after holding a separate hearing and, where practicable and where not inconsistent with the best interests of the child, meeting with the child, that such statement was made under circumstances inherently demonstrating a special guarantee of reliability.

For the purposes of finding circumstances demonstrating reliability pursuant to clause (2) of subsection (c), a judge may consider whether the relator documented the child witness's statement, and shall consider the following factors:

(i) the clarity of the statement, meaning, the child's capacity to observe, remember, and give expression to that which such child has seen, heard, or experienced; provided, however, that a finding under this clause shall be supported by expert testimony from a treating psychiatrist, psychologist, or clinician;

(ii) the time, content and circumstances of the statement;

(iii) the child's sincerity and ability to appreciate the consequences of such statement.

(d) An out-of-court statement which is admissible by common law or by statute shall remain admissible notwithstanding the provisions of this section.

§ 82. Civil proceedings; out-of-court statements describing sexual contact; admissibility

(a) The out-of-court statements of a child under the age of ten describing any act of sexual contact performed on or with the child, the circumstances under which it occurred, or which identifies the perpetrator shall be admissible as substantive evidence in any civil proceeding, except proceedings brought under subparagraph C of section twenty-three or section twenty-four of chapter one hundred and nineteen; provided, however, that such statement is offered as evidence of a material fact and is more probative on the point for which it is offered than any other evidence which the proponent can procure through reasonable efforts; the person to whom such statement was made or who heard the child make such statement testifies; the judge finds pursuant to subsection (b) that the child is unavailable as a witness; and the judge finds pursuant to subsection (c) that such statement is reliable.

(b) The proponent of such statement shall demonstrate a diligent and good faith effort to produce the child and shall bear the burden of showing unavailability. A finding of unavailability shall be supported by specific findings on the record, describing facts with particularity, demonstrating that:

(1) the child is unable to be present or to testify because of death or existing physical or mental illness or infirmity; or

(2) by a ruling of the court, the child is exempt on the ground of privilege from testifying concerning the subject matter of such statement; or

(3) the child testifies to a lack of memory of the subject matter of such statement; or

(4) the child is absent from the hearing and the proponent of such statement has been unable to procure the attendance of the child by process or by other reasonable means; or

(5) the court finds, based upon expert testimony from a treating psychiatrist, psychologist, or clinician, that testifying would be likely to cause severe psychological or emotional trauma to the child; or

(6) the child is not competent to testify.

(c) If a finding of unavailability is made, the out-of-court statement shall be admitted if the judge further statement was made under oath, that it was accurately recorded and preserved, and there was sufficient opportunity to cross-examine; or (2) after holding a separate hearing and, where practicable and where not inconsistent with the best interests of the child, meeting with the child, that such statement was made under circumstances inherently demonstrating a special guarantee of reliability.

For the purposes of finding circumstances demonstrating reliability pursuant to clause (2) of subsection (c) a judge may consider whether the relator documented the child witness's statement, and shall consider the following factors:

(i) the clarity of the statement, meaning, the child's capacity to observe, remember, and give expression to that which such child has seen, heard, or experienced; provided, however, that a finding under this clause shall be supported by expert testimony from a treating psychiatrist, psychologist, or clinician;

(ii) the time, content and circumstances of the statement;

(iii) the existence of corroborative evidence of the substance of the statement regarding the abuse including either the act, the circumstances, or the identity of the perpetrator;

(iv) the child's sincerity and ability to appreciate the consequences of the statement.

(d) An out-of-court statement admissible by common law or by statute shall remain admissible notwithstanding the provisions of this section.

§ 83. Custody hearings; out-of-court statements describing sexual contact; admissibility

(a) Any out-of-court statements of a child under the age of ten describing any act of sexual contact performed on or with the child, the circumstances under which it occurred, or which identifies the perpetrator offered in an action brought under subparagraph C of section twenty-three or section twenty-four of chapter one hundred and nineteen shall be admissible; provided, however that the person to whom the statement was made, or who heard the child make the statement testifies, and the judge finds that the statement is offered as evidence of a material fact and is more probative on the point for which it is offered than any other evidence which the proponent can procure through reasonable effort.

(b) An out-of-court statement admissible by common law or by statute shall remain admissible notwithstanding the provisions of this section.

Chapter 234A. Office of the Jury Commissioner of the Commonwealth

§ 27A. Questioning of summoned juror

[Added by 2016 Mass. Acts c. 36, § 2, effective May 10, 2016.]

After a summons has been received by a juror, no person shall, except as otherwise provided by law, question any juror so summoned for the purpose of obtaining information as to the juror's background in connection with the juror's jury duty.

§ 67A. Examination of jurors

[Added by 2016 Mass. Acts c. 36, § 4, effective May 10, 2016.]

Upon motion of either party, the court shall, or the parties or their attorneys may under the direction of the court, examine on oath a person who is called as a juror, to learn whether the juror related to either party or has any interest in the case, or has expressed or formed an opinion, or is sensible of any bias or prejudice. The objecting party may introduce other competent evidence in support of the objection. If the court finds that the juror does not stand indifferent in the case, another juror shall be called in. In a criminal case such examination shall include questions designed to learn whether such juror understands that a defendant is presumed innocent until proven guilty, that the commonwealth has the burden of proving guilt beyond a reasonable doubt, and that the defendant need not present evidence on the defendant's behalf. If the court finds that such juror does not so understand, another juror shall be called in.

To determine whether a juror stands indifferent in the case, if it appears that, as a result of the impact of considerations which may cause a decision to be made in whole or in part upon issues extraneous to the case, including, but not limited to, community attitudes, possible exposure to potentially prejudicial material or possible preconceived opinions toward the credibility of certain classes of persons, the juror may not stand indifferent, the court shall, or the parties or their attorneys may, with the permission and under the direction of the court, examine the juror specifically with respect to such considerations, attitudes, exposure, opinions or any other matters which may cause a decision to be made in whole or in part upon issues extraneous to the issues in the case. Such examination may include a brief statement of the facts of the case, to the extent the facts are appropriate and relevant to the issue of such examination and shall be conducted individually and outside the presence of other persons about to be called as jurors or already called.

§ 67D. Voir dire procedures

[Added by 2016 Mass. Acts c. 36, § 4, effective May 10, 2016.]

Notwithstanding section 67A, the following procedures shall govern in all criminal and civil superior court jury trials:

(1) In addition to whatever jury voir dire of the jury venire is conducted by the court, the court shall permit, upon the request of any party's attorney or a self-represented party, the party's attorney or self-represented party to conduct an oral examination of the prospective jurors at the discretion of the court.

(2) The court may impose reasonable limitations upon the questions and the time allowed during such examination, including, but not limited to, requiring pre-approval of the questions.

(3) In criminal cases involving multiple defendants, the commonwealth shall be entitled to the same amount of time as that to which all defendants together are entitled.

(4) The court may promulgate rules to implement this section, including, but not limited to, providing consistent policies, practices and procedures relating to the process of jury voir dire.

Chapter 258E. Harassment Prevention Orders

§ 1. Definitions

[Added by 2010 Mass. Acts c. 23, effective May 10, 2010.]

As used in this chapter the following words shall, unless the context clearly requires otherwise, have the following meanings:—

"Abuse", attempting to cause or causing physical harm to another or placing another in fear of imminent serious physical harm.

"Harassment", (i) 3 or more acts of willful and malicious conduct aimed at a specific person committed with the intent to cause fear, intimidation, abuse or damage to property and that does in fact cause fear, intimidation, abuse or damage to property; or (ii) an act that: (A) by force, threat or duress causes another to involuntarily engage in sexual relations; or (B) constitutes a violation of section 13B, 13F, 13H, 22, 22A, 23, 24, 24B, 26C, 43 or 43A of chapter 265 or section 3 of chapter 272.

"Court", the district or Boston municipal court, the superior court or the juvenile court departments of the trial court.

"Law officer", any officer authorized to serve criminal process.

"Malicious", characterized by cruelty, hostility or revenge.

"Protection order issued by another jurisdiction", an injunction or other order issued by a court of another state, territory or possession of the United States, the Commonwealth of Puerto Rico, or the District of Columbia, or a tribal court that is issued for the purpose of preventing violent or threatening acts, abuse or harassment against, or contact or communication with or physical proximity to another person, including temporary and final orders issued by civil and criminal courts filed by or on behalf of a person seeking protection.

§ 2. Jurisdiction

[Added by 2010 Mass. Acts c. 23, effective May 10, 2010; stricken & replaced by 2010 Mass. Acts c. 112, § 29, effective May 22, 2010; amended by 2014 Mass. Acts c. 284, § 74, effective Aug. 11, 2014.]

Proceedings under this chapter shall be filed, heard and determined in the superior court department or the respective divisions of the district court department or the Boston municipal court department having venue over the plaintiff's residence. The juvenile court department shall have exclusive jurisdiction of proceedings under this chapter in which the defendant is under the age of 18. Such proceedings shall be filed, heard and determined in the division of the juvenile court department having venue over the plaintiff's residence.

§ 3. Filing of complaint; impoundment; filing fee; expiration of order; modification of order; time for filing; nonexclusivity of remedy

[Added by 2010 Mass. Acts c. 23, effective May 10, 2010; amended by 2010 Mass. Acts c. 112, § 30, effective May 22, 2010.]

(a) A person suffering from harassment may file a complaint in the appropriate court requesting protection from such harassment. A person may petition the court under this chapter for an order that the defendant:

(i) refrain from abusing or harassing the plaintiff, whether the defendant is an adult or minor;

(ii) refrain from contacting the plaintiff, unless authorized by the court, whether the defendant is an adult or minor;

(iii) remain away from the plaintiff's household or workplace, whether the defendant is an adult or minor; and

(iv) pay the plaintiff monetary compensation for the losses suffered as a direct result of the harassment; provided, however, that compensatory damages shall include, but shall not be limited to, loss of earnings, out-of-pocket losses for injuries sustained or property damaged, cost of replacement of locks, medical expenses, cost for obtaining an unlisted phone number and reasonable attorney's fees.

(b) The court may order that information in the case record be impounded in accordance with court rule.

(c) No filing fee shall be charged for the filing of the complaint. The plaintiff shall not be charged for certified copies of any orders entered by the court, or any copies of the file reasonably required for future court action or as a result of the loss or destruction of plaintiff's copies.

(d) Any relief granted by the court shall not extend for a period exceeding 1 year. Every order shall, on its face, state the time and date the order is to expire and shall include the date and time that the matter will again be heard. If the plaintiff appears at the court at the date and time the order is to expire, the court shall determine whether or not to extend the order for any additional time reasonably necessary to protect the plaintiff or to enter a permanent order. When the expiration date stated on the order is on a date when the court is closed to business, the order shall not expire until the next date that the court is open to business. The plaintiff may appear on such next court business day at the time designated by the order to request that the order be extended. The court may also extend the order upon motion of the plaintiff, for such additional time as it deems necessary to protect the plaintiff from harassment. The fact that harassment has not occurred during the pendency of an order shall not, in itself, constitute sufficient ground for denying or failing to extend the order, or allowing an order to expire or be vacated or for refusing to issue a new order.

(e) The court may modify its order at any subsequent time upon motion by either party; provided, however, that the non-moving party shall receive sufficient notice and opportunity to be heard on said modification. When the plaintiff's address is inaccessible to the defendant as provided in section 10 and the defendant has filed a motion to modify the court's order, the court shall be responsible for notifying the plaintiff. In no event shall the court disclose any such inaccessible address.

(f) The court shall not deny any complaint filed under this chapter solely because it was not filed within a particular time period after the last alleged incident of harassment.

(g) An action commenced under this chapter shall not preclude any other civil or criminal remedies. A party filing a complaint under this chapter shall be required to disclose any prior or pending actions involving the parties; including, but not limited to, court actions, administrative proceedings and disciplinary hearings.

§ 4. Notice of nature of proceedings and availability of other criminal proceedings

[Added by 2010 Mass. Acts c. 23, effective May 10, 2010.]

Upon the filing of a complaint under this chapter, a complainant shall be informed that the proceedings hereunder are civil in nature and that violations of orders issued hereunder are criminal in nature. Further, a complainant shall be given information prepared by the appropriate district attorney's office that other criminal proceedings may be available and such complainant shall be instructed by such district attorney's office relative to the procedures required to initiate criminal proceedings including, but not limited to, a complaint for a violation of section 13B, 13F, 13H, 22, 22A, 23, 24, 24B, 26C, 43 and 43A of chapter 265 or section 3 of chapter 272. Whenever possible, a complainant shall be provided with such information in the complainant's native language.

§ 5. Temporary orders

[Added by 2010 Mass. Acts c. 23, § 5, effective May 10, 2010.]

Upon the filing of a complaint under this chapter, the court may enter such temporary orders as it deems necessary to protect a plaintiff from harassment, including relief as provided in section 3.

If the plaintiff demonstrates a substantial likelihood of imme diate danger of harassment, the court may enter such temporary relief orders without notice as it deems necessary to protect the plaintiff from harassment and shall immediately thereafter notify the defendant that the temporary orders have been issued. The court shall give the defendant an opportunity to be heard on the question of continuing the temporary order and of granting other relief as requested by the plaintiff not later than 10 court business days after such orders are entered.

Notice shall be made by the appropriate law enforcement agency as provided in section 9.

1

If the defendant does not appear at such subsequent hearing, the temporary orders shall continue in effect without further order of the court.

§ 6. Granting of relief without filing of complaint

[Added by 2010 Mass. Acts c. 23, § 6, effective May 10, 2010; amended by 2011 Mass. Acts c. 93, § 113, effective July 1, 2012.]

When the court is closed for business or the plaintiff is unable to appear in court because of severe hardship due to the plaintiff's physical condition, the court may grant relief to the plaintiff as provided under section 5 if the plaintiff demonstrates a substantial likelihood of immediate danger of harassment. In the discretion of the justice, such relief may be granted and communicated by telephone to an officer or employee of an appropriate law enforcement agency, who shall record such order on a form of order promulgated for such use by the chief justice of the trial court and shall deliver a copy of such order on the next court day to the clerk or clerk-magistrate of the court having venue and jurisdiction over the matter. If relief has been granted without the filing of a complaint pursuant to this section, the plaintiff shall appear in court on the next available business day to file a complaint. If the plaintiff in such a case is unable to appear in court without severe hardship due to the plaintiff's physical condition, a representative may appear in court, on the plaintiff's behalf and file the requisite complaint with an affidavit setting forth the circumstances preventing the plaintiff from appearing personally. Notice to the plaintiff and defendant and an opportunity for the defendant to be heard shall be given as provided in said section 5.

Any order issued under this section and any documentation in support thereof shall be certified on the next court day by the clerk or clerk-magistrate of the court issuing such order to the court having venue and jurisdiction over the matter. Such certification to the court shall have the effect of commencing proceedings under this chapter and invoking the other provisions of this chapter but shall not be deemed necessary for an emergency order issued under this section to take effect.

§ 7. Enforcement of protection order issued by another jurisdiction

[Added by 2010 Mass. Acts c. 23, effective May 10, 2010.]

Any protection order issued by another jurisdiction shall be given full faith and credit throughout the commonwealth and enforced as if it were issued in the commonwealth for as long as the order is in effect in the issuing jurisdiction.

A person entitled to protection under a protection order issued by another jurisdiction may file such order with the appropriate court by filing with the court a certified copy of such order. Such person shall swear under oath in an affidavit, to the best of such person's knowledge, that such order is presently in effect as written. Upon request by a law enforcement agency, the clerk or clerk-magistrate of such court shall provide a certified copy of the protection order issued by the other jurisdiction.

A law officer may presume the validity of, and enforce in accordance with section 8, a copy of a protection order issued by another jurisdiction which has been provided to the law officer by any source; provided, however, that the officer is also provided with a statement by the person protected by the order that such order remains in effect. Law officers may rely on such statement by the person protected by such order.

§ 8. Law officer emergency response to prevent further abuse or harassment

[Added by 2010 Mass. Acts c. 23, effective May 10, 2010; stricken & replaced by 2010 Mass. Acts c. 112, § 31, effective May 22, 2010.]

Whenever a law officer has reason to believe that a person has been abused or harassed or is in danger of being abused or harassed, such officer shall use all reasonable means to prevent further abuse or harassment. Law officers shall make every reasonable effort to do the following as part of the emergency response:

(1) assess the immediate physical danger to the victim and provide assistance reasonably intended to mitigate the safety risk;

(2) if there is observable injury to the victim or if the victim is complaining of injury, encourage the victim to seek medical attention and arrange for medical assistance or request an ambulance for transport to a hospital;

(3) if a sexual assault has occurred, notify the victim that there are time-sensitive medical or forensic options that may be available, encourage the victim to seek medical attention and arrange for medical assistance or request an ambulance for transport to a hospital;

(4) provide the victim with referrals to local resources that may assist the victim in locating and getting to a safe place; and

(5) provide adequate notice to the victim of his rights including, but not limited to, obtaining a harassment prevention order; provided, however, that the notice shall consist of providing the victim with a copy of the following statement before the officer leaves the scene or premises and after reading the statement to the victim; provided further, that if the victim's native language is not English, the statement shall be then provided in the victim's native language whenever possible:

"You have the right to appear at the Superior, Juvenile (only if the attacker is under 17), District or Boston Municipal Court, if you reside within the appropriate jurisdiction, and file a complaint requesting any of the following applicable orders: (i) an order restraining your attacker from harassing or abusing you; (ii) an order directing your attacker to refrain from contacting you; (iii) an order directing your attacker to stay away from your home and your workplace; (iv) an order directing your attacker to pay you for losses suffered as a result of the harassment or abuse, including loss of earnings, out-of-pocket losses for injuries sustained or property damaged, costs of replacement of locks, medical expenses, cost for obtaining an unlisted phone number, and reasonable attorneys' fees.

For an emergency on weekends, holidays or weeknights, the police will assist you in activating the emergency response system so that you may file a complaint and request a harassment prevention order.

You have the right to go to the appropriate court and apply for a criminal complaint for sexual assault, threats, criminal stalking, criminal harassment, assault and battery, assault with a deadly weapon, assault with intent to kill or other related offenses.

If you are in need of medical treatment, you have the right to request that an officer present drive you to the nearest hospital or otherwise assist you in obtaining medical treatment.

If you believe that police protection is needed for your physical safety, you have the right to request that the officer present remain at the scene until you can leave or until your safety is otherwise ensured. You may also request that the officer assist you in locating and taking you to a safe place including, but not limited to, a designated meeting place for a shelter or a family member's or a friend's residence or a similar place of safety.

You may request and obtain a copy of the police incident report at no cost from the police department.";

(6) assist the victim by activating the emergency judicial system when the court is closed for business;

(7) inform the victim that the abuser will be eligible for bail and may be promptly released; and

(8) arrest any person that a law officer witnessed or has probable cause to believe violated a temporary or permanent vacate, restraining, stay-away or no-contact order or judgment issued under this chapter or similar protection order issued by another jurisdiction; provided, however, that if there are no vacate, restraining, stay-away or no-contact orders or judgments in effect, arresting the person shall be the preferred response if the law officer witnessed

or has probable cause to believe that a person: (i) has committed a felony; (ii) has committed a misdemeanor involving harassment or abuse as defined in section 1; or (iii) has committed an assault and battery in violation of section 13A of chapter 265; provided further, that the safety of the victim shall be paramount in any decision to arrest; and provided further, that if a law officer arrests both parties, the law officer shall submit a detailed, written report in addition to an incident report, setting forth the grounds for arresting both parties.

No law officer shall be held liable in a civil action for personal injury or property damage brought by a party to an incident of abuse or for an arrest based on probable cause when such officer acted reasonably and in good faith and in compliance with this chapter.

Whenever a law officer investigates an incident of harassment, the officer shall immediately file a written incident report in accordance with the standards of the law officer's law enforcement agency and, wherever possible, in the form of the National Incident-Based Reporting System, as defined by the Federal Bureau of Investigation. The latter information may be submitted voluntarily by the local police on a monthly basis to the crime reporting unit of the state police crime reporting unit established in section 32 of chapter 22C.

The victim shall be provided with a copy of the full incident report at no cost upon request to the appropriate law enforcement department.

When a judge or other person authorized to take bail bails any person arrested under this chapter, reasonable efforts shall be made to inform the victim of such release prior to or at the time of the release. When any person charged with or arrested for a crime involving harassment under this chapter is released from custody, the court or the emergency response judge shall issue, upon the request of the victim, a written no-contact order or stay-away order prohibiting the person charged or arrested from having any contact with the victim and shall use all reasonable means to notify the victim immediately of release from custody. The victim shall be provided, at no cost, with a certified copy of the no-contact or stay-away order.

§ 9. Review of filing of records within court activity record information system and statewide domestic violence recordkeeping system; execution of outstanding warrants; service upon defendant; order for payment of damages

[Added by 2010 Mass. Acts c. 23, § 9, effective May 10, 2010.]

When considering a complaint filed under this chapter, the court shall order a review of the records contained within the court activity record information system and the statewide domestic violence recordkeeping system, as provided in chapter 188 of the acts of 1992 and maintained by the commissioner of probation, and shall review the resulting data to determine whether the named defendant has a civil or criminal record involving violent crimes or abuse. Upon receipt of information that an outstanding warrant exists against the named defendant, a judge shall order that the appropriate law enforcement officials be notified and shall order that any information regarding the defendant's most recent whereabouts shall be forwarded to such officials. In all instances in which an outstanding warrant exists, the court shall make a finding, based upon all of the circumstances, as to whether an imminent threat of bodily injury exists to the petitioner. In all instances in which such an imminent threat of bodily injury is found to exist, the judge shall notify the appropriate law enforcement officials of such finding and such officials shall take all necessary actions to execute any such outstanding warrant as soon as is practicable.

Whenever the court orders that the defendant refrain from harassing the plaintiff or have no contact with the plaintiff under section 3, 5 or 6, the clerk or clerk-magistrate shall transmit: (i) to the office of the commissioner of probation information for filing in the court activity record information system or the statewide domestic violence recordkeeping system as provided in said chapter 188 of the acts of 1992 or in a recordkeeping system created by the commissioner of probation to record the issuance of, or violation of, prevention orders issued pursuant to this chapter; and (ii) 2 certified copies of each such order and 1 copy of the complaint and summons forthwith to the appropriate law enforcement agency which, unless otherwise ordered by the court, shall serve 1 copy of each order upon the defendant, together with a copy of the complaint and order and summons. The law enforcement agency shall promptly make its return of service to the court. The commissioner of probation may develop and implement a statewide harassment prevention order recordkeeping system.

Law officers shall use every reasonable means to enforce such harassment prevention orders. Law enforcement agencies shall establish procedures adequate to ensure that an officer on the scene of an alleged violation of such order may be informed of the existence and terms of such order. The court shall notify the appropriate law enforcement agency in writing whenever any such order is vacated and shall direct the agency to destroy all record of such vacated order and such agency shall comply with that directive.

Each harassment prevention order issued shall contain the following statement: VIOLATION OF THIS ORDER IS A CRIMINAL OFFENSE.

Any violation of such order or a protection order issued by another jurisdiction shall be punishable by a fine of not more than $5,000, or by imprisonment for not more than 2½ years in a house of correction, or both. In addition to, but not in lieu of, the foregoing penalties and any other sentence, fee or assessment, including the victim witness assessment in section 8 of chapter 258B, the court shall order persons convicted of a violation of such an order to pay a fine of $25 that shall be transmitted to the treasurer for deposit into the General Fund. For any violation of such order, the court may order the defendant to complete an appropriate treatment program based on the offense.

In each instance in which there is a violation of a harassment prevention order or a protection order issued by another jurisdiction, the court may order the defendant to pay the plaintiff for all damages including, but not limited to, loss of earnings, out-of-pocket losses for injuries sustained or property damaged, cost of replacement locks, medical expenses, cost for obtaining an unlisted telephone number and reasonable attorney's fees.

Any such violation may be enforced by the court. Criminal remedies provided herein are not exclusive and do not preclude any other available civil or criminal remedies. The court may enforce by civil contempt procedure a violation of its own court order.

Section 8 of chapter 136 shall not apply to any order, complaint or summons issued pursuant to this section.

§ 10. Confidentiality of records

[Added by 2010 Mass. Acts c. 23, § 10, effective May 10, 2010.]

The records of cases arising out of an action brought under this chapter in which the plaintiff or defendant is a minor shall be withheld from public inspection except by order of the court; provided, however, that such records shall be open, at all reasonable times, to the inspection of the minor, such minor's parent, guardian and attorney and to the plaintiff and the plaintiff's attorney.

The plaintiff's residential address, residential telephone number and workplace name, address and telephone number, contained within the court records of cases arising out of an action brought by a plaintiff under this chapter, shall be confidential and withheld from public inspection, except by order of the court; provided, however, that the plaintiff's residential address and workplace address shall appear on the court order and be accessible to the defendant and the defendant's attorney unless the plaintiff specifically requests that this information be withheld from the order. All confidential portions of the records shall be accessible at all reasonable times to the plaintiff and plaintiff's attorney, to others specifically authorized by the plaintiff to obtain such information and to prosecutors, victim-witness advocates as defined in section 1 of chapter 258B, sexual assault counselors as defined in section 20J of chapter 233 and law officers, if such access is necessary in the performance of their duties. This paragraph shall apply to any protection order issued by another jurisdiction filed with a court of the commonwealth pursuant to section 7. Such confidential portions of the court records shall not be deemed to be public records under clause Twenty-sixth of section 7 of chapter 4.

§ 11. Adoption of suitable form of complaint

[Added by 2010 Mass. Acts c. 23, § 11, effective May 10, 2010; amended by 2011 Mass. Acts c. 93, § 114, effective July 1, 2012.]

The chief justice of the trial court shall adopt a form of complaint for use under this chapter which shall be in such form and language to permit a plaintiff to prepare and file such complaint pro se.

§ 12. Assessment against persons referred to treatment program as condition of probation

[Added by 2010 Mass. Acts c. 23, § 12, effective May 10, 2010.]

The court shall impose an assessment of $350 against any person who has been referred to a treatment program as a condition of probation. Such assessment shall be in addition to the cost of the treatment program. In the discretion of the court, such assessment may be reduced or waived if the court finds that such person is indigent or that payment of the assessment would cause the person, or the dependents of such person, severe financial hardship. Assessments made pursuant to this section shall be in addition to any other fines, assessments or restitution imposed in any disposition. All funds collected by the court pursuant to this section shall be transmitted monthly to the state treasurer, who shall deposit such funds into the General Fund.

Chapter 261. Costs in Civil Actions

§ 27A. Definitions applicable to Secs. 27A–27G

As used in sections twenty-seven A to twenty-seven G, inclusive, the following words shall have the following meanings:

"Indigent", (a) a person who receives public assistance under aid to families with dependent children, program of emergency aid for elderly and disabled residents or veterans' benefits programs or who receives assistance under Title XVI of the Social Security Act or the medicaid program, 42 U.S.C.A. 1396, et seq.; (b), a person whose income, after taxes, is 125 per cent or less of the current poverty threshold established annually by the Community Services Administration pursuant to section 625 of the Economic Opportunity Act, as amended; or (c) a person who is unable to pay the fees and costs of the proceeding in which he, is involved or is unable to do so without depriving himself or his dependents of the necessities of life, including food, shelter and clothing, but in inmate, shall not be adjudged indigent pursuant to section 27C unless the inmate has complied with the procedures set forth in section 29 and the court finds that the inmate is incapable of making payments under the plans forth in said section 29.

"Fees and costs", fees and costs shall not include attorneys' fees.

"Normal fees and costs", the fees and costs a party normally is required to pay in order to prosecute or defend the particular type of proceeding in which he is involved shall include, but not be limited to, the following: in all civil cases, filing or entry fees, including the surcharges required by section four C of chapter two hundred and sixty-two; fees and related costs for service of process, including publications of a citation when publication is ordered; fees and costs for the issuance or service of a subpoena and witness fees for trial or deposition; jury trial fees; removal fees; costs assessed in a bill of costs; in equity, fees for the issuance of an injunction, restraining order, writ or other process; in the probate and family court department, fees for an amendment of record.

"Extra fees and costs", the fees and costs, in addition to those a party is normally required to pay in order to prosecute or defend his case, which result when a party employs or responds to a procedure not necessarily required in the particular type of proceeding in which he is involved. They shall include, but not necessarily be limited to, the cost of transcribing a deposition, expert assistance and appeal bonds and appeal bond premiums.

"Clerk", the clerk or an assistant clerk or the register or an assistant register.

"Inmate", a person committed to, held by or in the custody of the department of correction or a state, county or federal correctional facility or the treatment center under chapter 123A.

§ 27B. Affidavit of indigency; waiver, substitution or state payment of fees or costs; supplementary affidavits

Upon or after commencing or answering to any civil, criminal or juvenile proceeding or appeal in any court, including but not limited to civil actions, proceedings for divorce or separate support, summary and supplementary processes, and proceedings upon petitions to vacate, for review or, upon appeal in a criminal case, any party may file with the clerk an affidavit of indigency and request for waiver, substitution or payment by the commonwealth of fees and costs upon a form prescribed by the chief justice of the supreme judicial court and in accordance with the standards set forth in sections twenty-seven C to twenty-seven F, inclusive, and sworn to under oath by the affiant.

An indigent party may subsequently file one or more supplementary affidavits requesting the waiver, substitution or payment by the commonwealth of fees and costs not previously granted at any time while the case is still pending in the original court or elsewhere.

§ 27C. Granting requests for waiver, substitution or state payment

[Amended by 2011 Mass. Acts c. 68, § 120, effective July 1, 2011.]

(1) If the affidavit is filed with the complaint or other paper initiating the proceeding, the clerk shall receive the complaint or other paper for filing and proceed as if all regular filing fees had been paid. Such filing shall be conditional until either (a) the affidavit is granted or (b) if the affidavit is denied, the payment of necessary and regular filing fees is made within five days of the denial of the affidavit, or such further time as the court may allow, or within five days of the denial of any appeal relating to the affidavit, whichever is later.

(2) If the affidavit appears regular and complete on its face and indicates that the affiant is indigent, as defined in section twenty-seven A, and requests a waiver, substitution or payment by the commonwealth, of normal fees and costs, the clerk shall grant such request forthwith without hearing and without the necessity of appearance of any party or counsel.

(3) If the affidavit does not appear to satisfy the condition of paragraph (2), the clerk or register shall forthwith bring the affidavit

to the attention of the justice or judge, as the case may be. The justice or judge may grant such request forthwith or may have the clerk or register notify the affiant that a hearing will be held on the affidavit within five days. If it appears at the hearing that there is a serious question as to the affiant's indigency, as defined in section twenty-seven A, then before making a finding of indigency, the court shall consider the following facts with respect to the applicant as of the time of hearing, in the immediate past and with respect to the immediate future; his age, education, training, physical and mental ability and number of dependents; gross and net income; regular and extraordinary expense, if any; assets and liabilities; whether or not he is a recipient of public assistance and for what purposes; and any other facts which are relevant to the applicant's ability to pay court costs.

(4) If the court makes a finding of indigency, it shall not deny any request with respect to normal fees and costs, and it shall not deny any request with respect to extra fees and costs if it finds the document, service or object is reasonably necessary to assure the applicant as effective a prosecution, defense or appeal as he would have if he were financially able to pay. The court shall not deny any request without first holding a hearing thereon; and if there is an appeal pursuant to section twenty-seven D following a denial, the court shall, within three days, set forth its written findings and reasons justifying such denial, which document shall be part of the record on appeal.

(5) The clerk of each court shall conspicuously post in the part of his office open to the public a notice informing the public in plain language of the availability of waiver, substitution or payment by the commonwealth of fees and costs for indigent persons.

(6) If the court makes a finding that the applicant could reasonably pay part of the normal fees and costs or extra fees and costs, the court may assess a reasonable partial payment towards said fees or costs and a date by which same is to be paid by the applicant. The court shall not order partial payment without first holding a hearing thereon, and if there is an appeal pursuant to section 27D following such an order, the court shall, within 3 days, set forth its written findings and reasons justifying the order of partial payment, which document shall be part of the record on appeal.

§ 27D. Appeal; notice; record; speedy hearing; stay of proceedings; decision final

[Amended by 2004 Mass. Acts c. 252, § 20, effective Aug. 9, 2004; applicable as provided by 2004 Mass. Acts c. 252, § 23.]

In any case where the court denies a request for waiver, substitution or payment by the commonwealth of fees and costs, pursuant to section twenty-seven C or any other provision of law, the applicant may take an appeal as hereafter provided. If the matter arises in the superior, the land, the probate or the housing court departments, the appeal shall be to a single justice of the appeals court at the next sitting thereof. If the matter arises in the juvenile court department, the appeal shall be to the superior court sitting in the nearest county or in Suffolk county. If the matter arises in the district court or Boston municipal court departments, the appeal shall be to the appellate division. Upon being notified of the denial the applicant shall also be advised of his right of appeal, and he shall have seven days thereafter to file a notice of appeal with the clerk or register. Upon receipt of notice of appeal timely filed the clerk or register shall forthwith notify the judge or justice, who shall within three days set forth his written findings and reasons as provided in paragraph (4) of section twenty-seven C. The court denying the request may, with or without motion, stay proceedings pending appeal or issue any other order or process to preserve the rights of the parties pending the appeal. The clerk or register shall then forward the affidavit and request, the court's findings and reasons for denial and any other documents on file relevant to the appeal, to the clerk of the court deciding the appeal, who, upon receipt thereof, shall refer the matter to the court for speedy decision and shall promptly notify the applicant of such decision. The court deciding the appeal may enter a stay or revoke an existing stay or other order, and its decision shall be final with respect to such request.

§ 27E. Repayment; deductions from judgment or settlement; notice; procedure

Any party on whose behalf any fees or costs have been waived or paid by the commonwealth pursuant to sections twenty-seven C or twenty-seven F, or both, shall repay the total amount thereof to the clerk or register of the court if said party shall have recovered, as a result of the proceeding in which said fees or costs were waived or paid, an amount in excess of three times the total amount of said fees and costs. In any case in which any fees or costs have been so waived or paid, the court, upon the waiver or payment of any such fees or costs shall notify all parties of the total amount of said fees and costs to date and that any money judgment or settlement in favor of the party for whom said fees or costs were waived or paid which exceeds three times the total amount thereof shall be deposited with the clerk or register of the court in the following manner. Any party obligated to pay any judgment or settlement exceeding three times the total amount of said fees and costs, or any portion of such a judgment or settlement shall pay to the clerk or register the total amount of said fees or costs, or if more than one party is so obligated, his proportional share thereof, and deduct the same from such judgment or settlement. The clerk or register shall notify all parties when the total amount of fees and costs has been so reimbursed. When said notification is received by the party obligated to pay such judgment or settlement or portion thereof, or if no such notification is received after the expiration of thirty days after the payment by said party of such fees or costs or his share thereof, said party shall promptly forward the remainder of the judgment or settlement to the party entitled to it. This procedure shall not be construed to excuse any person on whose behalf any fees or costs have been waived or paid from the obligation to repay the same as provided in this section.

§ 27F. Substitute documents, services or objects at less cost; court order

The court may, upon its own motion or that of any party, order that the document, service or object for which a normal or extra fee or cost would be charged shall be provided by an alternative means at lower or no cost, if the substitute thereby provided is substantially equivalent and the provision thereof does not materially impair the rights of any party. In any such order the court may direct payment by the commonwealth of the cost of any substitute to the same extent that the court would but for this section have ordered payment by the commonwealth for the document, service or object in question.

§ 27G. Payment procedure; public record; report of expenditures

[Amended by 2011 Mass. Acts c. 93, § 115, effective July 1, 2012.]

The clerk shall receive from any indigent party or his attorney all bills and vouchers for any document, service or object rendered to said party for which an order for payment by the commonwealth has been issued, and shall transmit said bills and vouchers and an attested copy of said order to the office of the court administrator, who shall make prompt payment thereon.

The office of the court administrator shall keep a record of all payments or waivers made pursuant to this section and of all repayments made pursuant to section twenty-seven E, including therein the name of the party, his attorney if any, the names and addresses of the person or persons to whom payment is made, the dates each was rendered to the party and the charge for each, and the dates payment was made by the office of the court administrator. This record shall be a public record.

The office of the court administrator shall on or before December first of each year make a written report to the general court indicating the amounts and purposes of all expenditures under sections twenty-seven A to twenty-seven G, inclusive, and making such recommendations for change in the law as he deems necessary.

Chapter 265. Crimes Against the Person

§ 1. Murder

Murder committed with deliberately premeditated malice aforethought, or with extreme atrocity or cruelty, or in the commission or attempted commission of a crime punishable with death or imprisonment for life, is murder in the first degree. Murder which does not appear to be in the first degree is murder in the second degree. Petit treason shall be prosecuted and punished as murder. The degree of murder shall be found by the jury.

§ 2. Punishment for murder; parole; executive clemency

[Amended by 2014 Mass. Acts c. 189, § 5, effective July 25, 2014.]

(a) Except as provided in subsection (b), any person who is found guilty of murder in the first degree shall be punished by imprisonment in the state prison for life and shall not be eligible for parole pursuant to section 133A of chapter 127.

(b) Any person who is found guilty of murder in the first degree who committed the offense on or after the person's fourteenth birthday and before the person's eighteenth birthday shall be punished by imprisonment in the state prison for life and shall be eligible for parole after the term of years fixed by the court pursuant to section 24 of chapter 279.

(c) Any person who is found guilty of murder in the second degree shall be punished by imprisonment in the state prison for life and shall be eligible for parole after the term of years fixed by the court pursuant to section 24 of chapter 279.

(d) Any person whose sentence for murder is commuted by the governor and council pursuant to section 152 of chapter 127 shall thereafter be subject to the laws governing parole.

NOTE 1 Previously, Section 2 provided for mandatory life imprisonment without parole for first-degree murder without regard to the defendant's age. Such punishment was held unconstitutional as applied to juveniles under age eighteen at the time of the offense in *Miller v. Alabama*, 567 U.S. 460 (2012). The 2014 amendments to Section 2 were made in response to the Supreme Judicial Court's decisions in *Diatchenko v. Commonwealth*, 387 Mass. 718 (2013) and *Commonwealth v. Brown*, 466 Mass. 676 (2013).

NOTE 2 Per 2014 Mass. Acts c. 189, § 8, this provision applies "only to a person who commits a murder after the effective date of this act"—July 25, 2014.

NOTE 3 Per 2014 Mass. Acts c. 189, § 7: "There shall be a commission to study and determine the usefulness and practicality of creating a developmental evaluation process for all cases of first degree murder committed by a juvenile. For the purposes of this section, a juvenile shall mean a person between the ages of 14 and 18. The evaluation process shall determine the developmental progress and abilities of the juvenile offender at the time of sentencing and parole eligibility and the parole board shall utilize the evaluation process for future parole decisions regarding the juvenile offender. In making recommendations, the commission shall establish factors to analyze in determining the developmental progress of a juvenile offender. The commission shall consist of: the secretary of public safety and security or a designee, who shall serve as chair; the executive director of the Massachusetts office of victim assistance or a designee; the commissioner of mental health or a designee; the chief justice of the trial court or a designee; the chief justice of the juvenile court department or a designee; the chief counsel for the committee for public counsel services or a designee; the president of the Massachusetts District Attorneys Association or a designee; 2 members of the senate, 1 of whom shall be appointed by the minority leader of the senate; 2 members of the house of representatives, 1 of whom shall be appointed by the minority leader of the house of representatives; and at least 2 people who specialize in child psychology and mental development, who shall be appointed by the governor. The commission shall submit its report and findings, along with any drafts of legislation, to the house and senate committees on ways and means, the joint committee on the judiciary and the clerks of the senate and the house of representatives by December 31, 2014."

§ 13. Manslaughter

[Amended by 2010 Mass. Acts c. 160, § 5, effective July 15, 2010.]

Whoever commits manslaughter shall, except as hereinafter provided, be punished by imprisonment in the state prison for not more than twenty years or by a fine of not more than one thousand dollars and imprisonment in jail or a house of correction for not more than two and one half years. Whoever commits manslaughter while violating the provisions of sections 102 to 102C, inclusive, of chapter 266 shall be imprisoned in the state prison for life or for any term of years.

§ 13½. Manslaughter while operating a motor vehicle; punishment

[Added by 2005 Mass. Acts c. 122, § 20, effective Oct. 28, 2005.]

Whoever commits manslaughter while operating a motor vehicle in violation of paragraph (a) of subdivision (1) of section 24 of chapter 90 or section 8A of chapter 90B, shall be punished by imprisonment in the state prison for not less than 5 years and not more than 20 years, and by a fine of not more than $25,000. The sentence of imprisonment imposed upon such person shall not be reduced to less than 2½ years, nor suspended, nor shall any such person be eligible for probation, parole or furlough or receive a deduction from his sentence for good conduct until he shall have served 2½ years of such sentence. The commissioner of correction may, on the recommendation of the warden, superintendent or other person in charge of a correctional institution, or of the administrator of a county correctional institution, grant to an offender committed under this section a temporary release in the custody of an officer of such institution for the following purposes only: to attend the funeral of a relative; to visit a critically ill relative; to obtain emergency medical or psychiatric services unavailable at said institution; or to engage in employment pursuant to a work release program. Upon receipt of notice of a conviction under this section, the registrar may suspend the license or right to operate of such person for any extended period up to life, provided that such suspension be at least a 15 year period. A person aggrieved by a decision of the registrar pursuant to this section may file an appeal in the superior court of the trial court department. If the court determines that the registrar abused his discretion, the court may vacate the suspension or revocation of a license or right to operate and reduce the period of suspension or revocation as ordered by the registrar, but in no event may the reduced period of suspension be for less than 15 years.

§ 13A. Assault or assault and battery; punishment

[Amended by 2002 Mass. Acts c. 35, § 1.]

(a) Whoever commits an assault or an assault and battery upon another shall be punished by imprisonment for not more than 2½ years in a house of correction or by a fine of not more than $1,000.

A summons may be issued instead of a warrant for the arrest of any person upon a complaint for a violation of any provision of this subsection if in the judgment of the court or justice receiving the complaint there is reason to believe that he will appear upon a summons.

(b) Whoever commits an assault or an assault and battery:

(i) upon another and by such assault and battery causes serious bodily injury;

(ii) upon another who is pregnant at the time of such assault and battery, knowing or having reason to know that the person is pregnant; or

(iii) upon another who he knows has an outstanding temporary or permanent vacate, restraining or no contact order or judgment issued pursuant to section 18, section 34B or 34C of chapter 208, section 32 of chapter 209, section 3, 4 or 5 of chapter 209A, or section 15 or 20 of chapter 209C, in effect against him at the time of such assault or assault and battery; shall be punished by imprisonment in the state prison for not more than 5 years or in the house of correction for not more than 2½ years, or by a fine of not more than $5,000, or by both such fine and imprisonment.

(c) For the purposes of this section, "serious bodily injury" shall mean bodily injury that results in a permanent disfigurement, loss or impairment of a bodily function, limb or organ, or a substantial risk of death.

§ 13B. Indecent assault and battery on child under fourteen

[Amended by 2008 Mass. Acts c. 205, § 1 effective Oct. 22, 2008.]

Whoever commits an indecent assault and battery on a child under the age of 14 shall be punished by imprisonment in the state prison for not more than 10 years, or by imprisonment in the house of correction for not more than 2½ years. A prosecution commenced under this section shall neither be continued without a finding nor placed on file.

In a prosecution under this section, a child under the age of 14 years shall be deemed incapable of consenting to any conduct of the defendant for which such defendant is being prosecuted.

§ 13B½. Aggravated indecent assault and battery on child under fourteen

[Added by 2008 Mass. Acts c. 205, § 1, effective Oct. 22, 2008.]

Whoever commits an indecent assault and battery on a child under the age of 14 and:

(a) the indecent assault and battery was committed during the commission or attempted commission of the following offenses:—(1) armed burglary as set forth in section 14 of chapter 266; (2) unarmed burglary as set forth in section 15 of said chapter 266; (3) breaking and entering as set forth in section 16 of said chapter 266; (4) entering without breaking as set forth in section 17 of said chapter 266; (5) breaking and entering into a dwelling house as set forth in section 18 of said chapter 266; (6) kidnapping as set forth in section 26 of chapter 265; (7) armed robbery as set forth in section 17 of said chapter 265; (8) unarmed robbery as set forth in section 19 of said chapter 265; (9) assault and battery with a dangerous weapon or assault with a dangerous weapon, as set forth in sections 15A and 15B of said chapter 265; (10) home invasion as set forth in section 18C of said chapter 265; or (11) posing or exhibiting child in state of nudity or sexual conduct as set forth in section 29A of chapter 272; or

(b) at the time of commission of said indecent assault and battery, the defendant was a mandated reporter as is defined in section 21 of chapter 119, shall be punished by imprisonment in the state prison for life or for any term of years, but not less than 10 years. The sentence imposed on such person shall not be reduced to less than 10 years, or suspended, nor shall any person convicted under this section be eligible for probation, parole, work release, or furlough or receive any deduction from his sentence for good conduct until he shall have served 10 years of such sentence. Prosecutions commenced under this section shall neither be continued without a finding nor placed on file.

In a prosecution under this section, a child under the age of 14 years shall be deemed incapable of consenting to any conduct of the defendant for which such defendant is being prosecuted.

§ 13B¾. Indecent assault and battery on child under fourteen, subsequent offense

[Added by 2008 Mass. Acts c. 205, § 1, effective Oct. 22, 2008.]

Whoever commits an indecent assault and battery on a child under the age of 14 and has been previously convicted of or adjudicated delinquent or as a youthful offender for: indecent assault and battery on a child under 14 as set forth in section 13B; aggravated indecent assault and battery on a child under 14 as set forth in section 13B½; indecent assault and battery on a person 14 or older as set forth in section 13H; assault of a child with intent to commit rape as set forth in section 24B; rape of a child with force as set forth in section 22A; aggravated rape of a child with force as set forth in section 22B; rape and abuse of a child as set forth in section 23; aggravated rape and abuse of a child as set forth in section 23A; rape as set forth in section 22 or; a like violation of the laws of another state, the United States or a military, territorial or Indian tribal authority, shall be punished by imprisonment in the state prison for life or for any term of years, but not less than 15 years. The sentence imposed on such person shall not be reduced to less than 15 years, or suspended, nor shall any person convicted under this section be eligible for probation, parole, work release or furlough or receive any deduction from his sentence for good conduct until he shall have served 15 years of such sentence. Prosecutions commenced under this section shall neither be continued without a finding nor placed on file.

In any prosecution commenced pursuant to this section, introduction into evidence of a prior adjudication or conviction or a prior finding of sufficient facts by either certified attested copies of original court papers, or certified attested copies of the defendant's biographical and informational data from records of the department of probation, any jail or house of correction or the department of correction shall be prima facie evidence that the defendant before the court had been convicted previously by a court of the commonwealth or any other jurisdiction. Such documentation shall be self-authenticating and admissible, after the commonwealth has established the defendant's guilt on the primary offense, as evidence in any court of the commonwealth to prove the defendant's commission of any prior conviction described therein. The commonwealth shall not be required to introduce any additional corroborating evidence or live witness testimony to establish the validity of such prior conviction.

§ 13C. Assault and battery in order to collect loan

Whoever commits an assault and battery upon another for the purpose of collecting a loan shall for the first offense be punished by imprisonment in the state prison for not less than three nor more than five years or by imprisonment for not more than two and one half years in a jail or house of correction; and for a second or subsequent offense, by imprisonment in the state prison for not less than five nor more than ten years. Except in the case of a conviction for the first offense for violation of this section, the imposition or execution of the sentence shall not be suspended and no probation or parole shall be granted until the minimum imprisonment herein provided for the offense shall have been served.

§ 13D. Assault and battery upon certain public servants

[Amended by 2014 Mass. Acts c. 165, § 177, effective July 15, 2014; 2014 Mass. Acts c. 284, § 75, effective Jan. 1, 2015.]

Whoever commits an assault and battery upon any public employee when such person is engaged in the performance of his duties at the time of such assault and battery, shall be punished by imprisonment for not less than ninety days nor more than two and one-half years in a house of correction or by a fine of not less than five hundred nor more than five thousand dollars. Whoever commits an offense under this section and which includes an attempt to disarm a police officer in the performance of the officer's duties shall be punished by imprisonment in the state prison for not more than 10 years or by a fine of not more than $1,000 and imprisonment in a jail or house of correction for not more than 2½ years.

An officer authorized to make arrests may arrest any person upon probable cause and without a warrant if the person has committed an offense under this section upon a public employee when the public employee was operating a public transit vehicle and the officer may keep the person in custody during which period the officer shall seek the issuance of a complaint and request a bail determination with all reasonable promptness.

§ 13D½. Injury to firefighter

Whoever commits an offense set forth in section one, two, five or seven of chapter two hundred and sixty-six where said offense results in injury to a firefighter in the performance of his duty, shall be punished by imprisonment in the state prison for not more than ten years, or by a fine of not more than one thousand dollars and imprisonment in a jail or house of correction for not more than two and one-half years.

§ 13F. Indecent assault and battery on person with intellectual disability; assault and battery

[Amended by 2010 Mass. Acts c. 239, § 72, effective Nov. 2, 2010.]

Whoever commits an indecent assault and battery on a person with an intellectual disability knowing such person to have an intellectual disability shall for the first offense be punished by imprisonment in the state prison for not less than five years or not more than ten years; and for a second or subsequent offense, by imprisonment in the state prison for not less than ten years. Except in the case of a conviction for the first offense for violation of this section, the imposition or execution of the sentence shall not be suspended, and no probation or parole shall be granted until the minimum imprisonment herein provided for the offense shall have been served. This section shall not apply to the commission of an indecent assault and battery by a person with an intellectual disability upon another person with an intellectual disability.

Whoever commits an assault and battery on a person with an intellectual disability knowing such person to have an intellectual disability shall for the first offense be punished by imprisonment in a house of correction for not more than two and one-half years or by imprisonment in the state prison for not more than five years; and, for a second or subsequent offense, by imprisonment in the state prison for not more than ten years. This section shall not apply to the commission of an assault and battery by a mentally retarded person upon another mentally retarded person.

§ 13H. Indecent assault and battery on child of fourteen, elder person, or person with disability

[Amended by 2004 Mass. Acts c. 501, § 2.]

Whoever commits an indecent assault and battery on a person who has attained age fourteen shall be punished by imprisonment in the state prison for not more than five years, or by imprisonment for not more than two and one-half years in a jail or house of correction.

Whoever commits an indecent assault and battery on an elder or person with a disability, as defined in section 13K, shall be punished by imprisonment in the state prison for not more than 10 years, or by imprisonment in the house of correction for not more than 2½ years, and whoever commits a second or subsequent such offense shall be punished by imprisonment in the state prison for not more than 20 years. A prosecution commenced under this paragraph shall not be placed on file nor continued without a finding.

§ 13I. Assault or assault and battery on emergency medical technician, ambulance operator, or ambulance attendant or health care provider

[Amended by 2010 Mass. Acts c. 151, effective July 2, 2010.]

Whoever commits an assault or assault and battery on an emergency medical technician, an ambulance operator, an ambulance attendant, or a health care provider as defined in chapter 111, while the technician, operator, attendant or provider is treating or transporting a person in the line of duty shall be punished by imprisonment in the house of correction for not less than 90 days nor more than 2 and one-half years or by a fine of not less than $500 nor more than $5,000, or both.

§ 13J. Assault and battery of a child; liability of person having custody

(a) For the purposes of this section, the following words shall, unless the context indicates otherwise, have the following meanings:

"Bodily injury", substantial impairment of the physical condition including any burn, fracture of any bone, subdural hematoma, injury to any internal organ, any injury which occurs as the result of repeated harm to any bodily function or organ including human skin or any physical condition which substantially imperils a child's health or welfare.

"Child", any person under fourteen years of age.

"Person having care and custody", a parent, guardian, employee of a home or institution or any other person with equivalent supervision or care of a child, whether the supervision is temporary or permanent.

"Substantial bodily injury", bodily injury which creates a permanent disfigurement, protracted loss or impairment of a function of a body member, limb or organ, or substantial risk of death.

(b) Whoever commits an assault and battery upon a child and by such assault and battery causes bodily injury shall be punished by imprisonment in the state prison for not more than five years or imprisonment in the house of correction for not more than two and one-half years.

Whoever commits an assault and battery upon a child and by such assault and battery causes substantial bodily injury shall be punished by imprisonment in the state prison for not more than fifteen years or imprisonment in the house of correction for not more than two and one-half years.

Whoever, having care and custody of a child, wantonly or recklessly permits bodily injury to such child or wantonly or recklessly permits another to commit an assault and battery upon such child, which assault and battery causes bodily injury, shall be punished by imprisonment for not more than two and one-half years in the house of correction.

Whoever, having care and custody of a child, wantonly or recklessly permits substantial bodily injury to such child or wantonly or recklessly permits another to commit an assault and battery upon such child, which assault and battery causes substantial bodily injury, shall be punished by imprisonment in the state prison for not more than five years, or by imprisonment in a jail or house of correction for not more than two and one-half years.

§ 13K. Assault, abuse, neglect or financial exploitation of elderly or disabled persons

[Amended by 2004 Mass. Acts c. 501, §§ 3–8.]

(a) For the purpose of this section the following words shall, unless the context requires otherwise, have the following meanings:—

"Abuse", physical contact which either harms or creates a substantial likelihood of harm.

"Bodily injury", substantial impairment of the physical condition, including, but not limited to, any burn, fracture of any bone, subdural hematoma, injury to any internal organ, or any injury which occurs as the result of repeated harm to any bodily function or organ, including human skin.

"Caretaker", a person with responsibility for the care of an elder or person with a disability, which responsibility may arise as the result of a family relationship, or by a fiduciary duty imposed by law, or by a voluntary or contractual duty undertaken on behalf of such elder or person with a disability. A person may be found to be a caretaker under this section only if a reasonable person would believe that such person's failure to fulfill such responsibility would adversely affect the physical health of such elder or person with a disability. Minor children and adults adjudicated incompetent by a court of law may not be deemed to be caretakers under this section.

(i) "Responsibility arising from a family relationship", it may be inferred that a husband, wife, son, daughter, brother, sister, or other relative of an elder or person with a disability is a caretaker if the person has provided primary and substantial assistance for the physical care of the elder or person with a disability as would lead a reasonable person to believe that failure to provide such care would adversely affect the physical health of the elder or person with a disability.

(ii) "Responsibility arising from a fiduciary duty imposed by law", it may be inferred that the following persons are caretakers of an elder or person with a disability to the extent that they are legally required to apply the assets of the estate of the elder or person with a disability to provide the necessities essential for the physical health of the elder or person with a disability: (i) a guardian of the person or assets of an elder or person with a disability; (ii) the conservator of an elder or person with a disability, appointed by the probate court pursuant to chapter two hundred and one; and (iii) an attorney-in-fact holding a power of attorney or durable power of attorney pursuant to chapter two hundred and one B.

(iii) "Responsibility arising from a contractual duty", it may be inferred that a person who receives monetary or personal benefit or gain as a result of a bargained-for agreement to be responsible for providing primary and substantial assistance for the care of an elder or person with a disability is a caretaker.

(iv) "Responsibility arising out of the voluntary assumption of the duties of caretaker", it may be inferred that a person who has voluntarily assumed responsibility for providing primary and substantial assistance for the physical care of an elder or person with a disability is a caretaker if the person's conduct would lead a reasonable person to believe that failure to provide such care would adversely affect the physical health of the elder or person with a disability, and at least one of the following criteria is met: (i) the person is living in the household of the elder or person with a disability, or present in the household on a regular basis; or (ii) the person would have reason to believe, as a result of the actions, statements or behavior of the elder or person with a disability, that he is being relied upon for providing primary and substantial assistance for care.

"Elder", a person sixty years of age or older.

"Mistreatment", the use of medications or treatments, isolation, or physical or chemical restraints which harms or creates a substantial likelihood of harm.

"Neglect", the failure to provide treatment or services necessary to maintain health and safety and which either harms or creates a substantial likelihood of harm.

"Person with disability", a person with a permanent or long-term physical or mental impairment that prevents or restricts the individual's ability to provide for his or her own care or protection.

"Serious bodily injury", bodily injury which results in a permanent disfigurement, protracted loss or impairment of a bodily function, limb or organ, or substantial risk of death.

(a½) Whoever commits an assault and battery upon an elder or person with a disability shall be punished by imprisonment in the state prison for not more than 3 years or by imprisonment in a house of correction for not more than 2½ years, or by a fine of not more than $1,000, or both such fine and imprisonment.

(b) Whoever commits an assault and battery upon an elder or person with a disability and by such assault and battery causes bodily injury shall be punished by imprisonment in the state prison for not more than five years or in the house of correction for not more than two and one-half years or by a fine of not more than one thousand dollars or by both such fine and imprisonment.

1

(c) Whoever commits an assault and battery upon an elder or person with a disability and by such assault and battery causes serious bodily injury shall be punished by imprisonment in the state prison for not more than ten years or in the house of correction for not more than two and one-half years or by a fine of not more than five thousand dollars or by both such fine and imprisonment.

(d) Whoever, being a caretaker of an elder or person with a disability, wantonly or recklessly permits bodily injury to such elder or person with a disability, or wantonly or recklessly permits another to commit an assault and battery upon such elder or person with a disability which assault and battery causes bodily injury, shall be punished by imprisonment in the state prison for not more than five years or in the house of correction for not more than two and one-half years or by a fine of not more than five thousand dollars or by both such fine and imprisonment.

(d½) Whoever, being a caretaker of an elder or person with a disability, wantonly or recklessly commits or permits another to commit abuse, neglect or mistreatment upon such elder or person with a disability, shall be punished by imprisonment in the state prison for not more than 3 years, or imprisonment in the house of correction for not more than 2½ years, or by a fine of not more than $5,000, or by both such fine and imprisonment.

(e) Whoever, being a caretaker of an elder or person with a disability, wantonly or recklessly permits serious bodily injury to such elder or person with a disability, or wantonly or recklessly permits another to commit an assault and battery upon such elder or person with a disability which assault and battery causes serious bodily injury, shall be punished by imprisonment in the state prison for not more than ten years or by imprisonment in the house of correction for not more than two and one-half years or by a fine of not more than ten thousand dollars or by both such fine and imprisonment.

(f) Conduct shall not be construed to be wanton or reckless conduct under this section if directed by a competent elder or person with a disability, or for the sole reason that, in lieu of medical treatment, an elder or person with a disability is being furnished or relies upon treatment by spiritual means through prayer if such treatment is in accordance with the tenets and practices of the established religious tradition of such elder or person with a disability, and is provided at the direction of such elder or person with a disability, who shall be competent, or pursuant to the direction of a person who is properly designated a health care proxy under chapter two hundred and one D.

§ 13M. Assault and battery on a family or household member

[Added by 2008 Mass. Acts c. 534, effective Jan. 16, 2009; 2014 Mass. Acts c. 260, § 23, effective Aug. 8, 2014.]

(a) Whoever commits an assault or assault and battery on a family or household member shall be punished by imprisonment in the house of correction for not more than 2½ years or by a fine of not more than $5,000, or both such fine and imprisonment.

(b) Whoever is convicted of a second or subsequent offense of assault or assault and battery on a family or household member shall be punished by imprisonment in the house of correction for not more than 2½ years or by imprisonment in the state prison for not more than 5 years.

(c) For the purposes of this section, "family or household member" shall mean persons who (i) are or were married to one another, (ii) have a child in common regardless of whether they have ever married or lived together or (iii) are or have been in a substantive dating or engagement relationship; provided, that the trier of fact shall determine whether a relationship is substantive by considering the following factors: the length of time of the relationship; the type of relationship; the frequency of interaction between the parties; whether the relationship was terminated by either person; and the length of time elapsed since the termination of the relationship.

(d) For any violation of this section, or as a condition of a continuance without a finding, the court shall order the defendant to complete a certified batterer's intervention program unless, upon good cause shown, the court issues specific written findings describing the reasons that batterer's intervention should not be ordered or unless the batterer's intervention program determines that the defendant is not suitable for intervention.

§ 13N. Misdemeanor involving use or attempted use of physical force or threatened use of deadly weapon against household or family member; reporting to department of criminal justice information services

[Added by 2014 Mass. Acts c. 284, § 76, effective Jan. 1, 2015.]

Upon entry of a conviction for any misdemeanor offense that has as an element the use or attempted use of physical force or the threatened use of a deadly weapon the court shall determine whether the victim or intended victim was a family or household member, as defined in section 1 of chapter 209A, of the defendant. If the victim or intended victim was a family or household member of the defendant, the court shall enter the offense, the chapter, section and subsection, if any, of the offense and the relationship of the defendant to the victim or intended victim upon the records and this entry shall be forwarded to the department of criminal justice information services for inclusion in the criminal justice information system and to provide the attorney general of the United States with information required or permitted under federal law to be included in the National Instant Criminal Background Check System or any successor system maintained to conduct background checks for firearm sales or licensing.

§ 14. Mayhem

Whoever, with malicious intent to maim or disfigure, cuts out or maims the tongue, puts out or destroys an eye, cuts or tears off an ear, cuts, slits or mutilates the nose or lip, or cuts off or disables a limb or member, of another person, and whoever is privy to such intent, or is present and aids in the commission of such crime, or whoever, with intent to maim of disfigure, assaults another person with a dangerous weapon, substance or chemical, and by such assault disfigures, cripples or inflicts serious or permanent physical injury upon such person, and whoever is privy to such intent, or is present and aids in the commission of such crime, shall be punished by imprisonment in the state prison for not more than twenty years or by a fine of not more than one thousand dollars and imprisonment in jail for not more than two and one half years.

§ 15. Assault; intent to murder or maim

Whoever assaults another with intent to commit murder, or to maim or disfigure his person in any way described in the preceding section, shall be punished by imprisonment in the state prison for not more than ten years or by a fine of not more than one thousand dollars and imprisonment in jail for not more than two and one half years.

§ 15A. Assault and battery by means of dangerous weapon

[Amended by 2002 Mass. Acts c. 35, § 2; 2014 Mass. Acts c. 284, §§ 77–78, effective Aug. 11, 2014.]

(a) Whoever commits assault and battery upon a person sixty years or older by means of a dangerous weapon shall be punished by imprisonment in the state prison for not more than ten years or by a fine of not more than one thousand dollars or imprisonment in jail for not more than two and one-half years.

Whoever, after having been convicted of the crime of assault and battery upon a person sixty years or older, by means of a dangerous weapon, commits a second or subsequent such crime, shall be punished by imprisonment for not less than two years. Said sentence shall not be reduced until two years of said sentence have been served nor shall the person convicted be eligible for probation, parole, furlough, work release or receive any deduction from his sentence for good conduct until he shall have served two years of such sentence; provided, however, that the commissioner of correction may, on the recommendation of the warden, superintendent, or other person in charge of a correctional institution, or the administrator of a county correctional institution, grant to said offender a temporary release in the custody of an officer of such institution for the following purposes only: to attend the funeral of next of kin or spouse; to visit a critically ill close relative or spouse; or to obtain emergency medical services unavailable at said institution. The provisions of section eighty-seven of chapter two hundred and seventy-six relating to the power of the court to place certain offenders on probation shall not apply to any person 18 years of age or over charged with a violation of this subsection.

(b) Whoever commits an assault and battery upon another by means of a dangerous weapon shall be punished by imprisonment in the state prison for not more than 10 years or in the house of correction for not more than 2½ years, or by a fine of not more than $5,000, or by both such fine and imprisonment.

(c) Whoever:

(i) by means of a dangerous weapon, commits an assault and battery upon another and by such assault and battery causes serious bodily injury;

(ii) by means of a dangerous weapon, commits an assault and battery upon another who is pregnant at the time of such assault and battery, knowing or having reason to know that the person is pregnant;

(iii) by means of a dangerous weapon, commits an assault and battery upon another who he knows has an outstanding temporary or permanent vacate, restraining or no contact order or judgment issued pursuant to section 18, section 34B or section 34C of chapter 208, section 32 of chapter 209, section 3, 4 or 5 of chapter 209A, or section 15 or 20 of chapter 209C, in effect against him at the time of such assault and battery; or

(iv) is 18 years of age or older and, by means of a dangerous weapon, commits an assault and battery upon a child under the age of 14; shall be punished by imprisonment in the state prison for not more than 15 years or in the house of correction for not more than 2½ years, or by a fine of not more than $10,000, or by both such fine and imprisonment.

(d) For the purposes of this section, "serious bodily injury" shall mean bodily injury which results in a permanent disfigurement, loss or impairment of a bodily function, limb or organ, or a substantial risk of death.

§ 15B. Assault by means of dangerous weapon

[Amended by 2014 Mass. Acts c. 284, § 79, effective Aug. 11, 2014.]

(a) Whoever, by means of a dangerous weapon, commits an assault upon a person sixty years or older, shall be punished by imprisonment in the state prison for not more than five years or by a fine of not more than one thousand dollars or imprisonment in jail for not more than two and one-half years.

Whoever, after having been convicted of the crime of assault upon a person sixty years or older, by means of a dangerous weapon, commits a second or subsequent such crime, shall be punished by imprisonment for not less than two years. Said sentence shall not be reduced until one year of said sentence has been served nor shall the person convicted be eligible for probation, parole, furlough, work release or receive any deduction from his sentence for good conduct until he shall have served one year of such sentence; provided, however, that the commissioner of correction may, on the recommendation of the warden, superintendent, or other person in charge of a correctional institution, or the administrator of a county correctional institution, grant to said offender a temporary release in the custody of an officer of such institution for the following purposes only: to attend the funeral of next of kin or spouse; to visit a critically ill close relative or spouse; or to obtain emergency medical services unavailable at said institution. The provisions of section eighty-seven of chapter two hundred and seventy-six relative to the power of the court to place certain offenders on probation shall not apply to any person 18 years of age or over charged with a violation of this subsection.

For the purposes of prosecution, a conviction obtained under subsection (a) of section fifteen A or paragraph (a) of section 18 shall count as a prior criminal conviction for the purpose of prosecution and sentencing as a second or subsequent conviction.

(b) Whoever, by means of a dangerous weapon, commits an assault upon another shall be punished by imprisonment in the state prison for not more than five years or by a fine of not more than one thousand dollars or imprisonment in jail for not more than two and one-half years.

§ 15C. Assault by means of hypodermic syringe or needle; assault and battery by means of hypodermic syringe or needle

(a) Whoever commits an assault upon another, by means of a hypodermic syringe, hypodermic needle, or any instrument adapted for the administration of controlled or other substances by injection, shall be punished by imprisonment in the state prison for not more than 10 years or in the house of correction for not more than 2½ years, or by a fine of not more than $1,000, or by both such fine and imprisonment.

(b) Whoever commits an assault and battery upon another, by means of a hypodermic syringe, hypodermic needle, or any instrument adapted for the administration of controlled or other substances by injection, shall be punished by imprisonment in the state prison for not more than 15 years or in the house of correction for not more than 2½ years, or by a fine of not more than $5,000, or by both such fine and imprisonment.

§ 15D. Strangling or suffocating another person

[Added by 2014 Mass. Acts c. 260, § 24, effective Aug. 8, 2014.]

(a) For the purposes of this section the following words shall have the following meanings, unless the context clearly indicates otherwise:

"Serious bodily injury", bodily injury that results in a permanent disfigurement, loss or impairment of a bodily function, limb or organ or creates a substantial risk of death.

"Strangulation", the intentional interference of the normal breathing or circulation of blood by applying substantial pressure on the throat or neck of another.

"Suffocation", the intentional interference of the normal breathing or circulation of blood by blocking the nose or mouth of another.

(b) Whoever strangles or suffocates another person shall be punished by imprisonment in state prison for not more than 5 years or in the house of correction for not more than 2½ years, or by a fine of not more than $5,000, or by both such fine and imprisonment.

(c) Whoever: (i) strangles or suffocates another person and by such strangulation or suffocation causes serious bodily injury; (ii) strangles or suffocates another person, who is pregnant at the time of such strangulation or suffocation, knowing or having reason to know that the person is pregnant; (iii) is convicted of strangling or suffocating another person after having been previously convicted of the crime of strangling or suffocating another person under this section, or of a like offense in another state or the United States or a military, territorial or Indian tribal authority; or (iv) strangles or suffocates another person, with knowledge that the individual has an outstanding temporary or permanent vacate, restraining or no contact order or judgment issued under sections 18 or 34B of chapter 208, section 32 of chapter 209, sections 3, 4 or 5 of chapter 209A or sections 15 or 20 of chapter 209C, in effect against such person at the time the offense is committed, shall be punished by imprisonment in state prison for not more than 10 years, or in the house of correction for not more than 2½ years, and by a fine of not more than $10,000.

(d) For any violation of this section, or as a condition of a continuance without a finding, the court shall order the defendant to complete a certified batterer's intervention program unless, upon good cause shown, the court issues specific written findings describing the reasons that batterer's intervention should not be ordered or unless the batterer's intervention program determines that the defendant is not suitable for intervention.

§ 15E. Assault and battery by discharging firearm

[Added by 2014 Mass. Acts c. 284, § 80, effective Jan. 1, 2015.]

(a) Whoever commits an assault and battery upon another by discharging a firearm, large capacity weapon, rifle, shotgun, sawed-off shotgun or machine gun, as defined in section 121 of chapter 140, shall be punished by imprisonment in the state prison for not more than 20 years or by imprisonment in the house of correction for not more than 2½ years or by a fine of not more than $10,000, or by both such fine and imprisonment.

§ 15F. Attempted assault and battery by discharging firearm

[Added by 2014 Mass. Acts c. 284, § 80, effective Jan. 1, 2015.]

(a) Whoever attempts to commit an assault and battery upon another by means of discharging a firearm, large capacity weapon, rifle, shotgun, sawed-off shotgun or machine gun, as defined in section 121 of chapter 140, shall be punished by imprisonment in the state prison for not more than 15 years or by imprisonment in the house of correction for not more than 2½ years or by a fine of not more than $10,000, or by both such fine and imprisonment.

§ 17. Armed robbery

Whoever, being armed with a dangerous weapon, assaults another and robs, steals or takes from his person money or other property which may be the subject of larceny shall be punished by imprisonment in the state prison for life or for any term of years; provided, however, that any person who commits any offence described herein while masked or disguised or while having his features artificially distorted shall, for the first offence be sentenced to imprisonment for not less than five years and for any subsequent offence for not less than ten years. Whoever commits any offense described herein while armed with a firearm, shotgun, rifle, machine gun or assault weapon shall be punished by imprisonment in the state prison for not less than five years. Any person who commits a subsequent offense while armed with a firearm, shotgun, rifle, machine gun or assault weapon shall be punished by imprisonment in the state prison for not less than 15 years.

§ 18. Armed assault with intent to rob or murder

[Amended by 2014 Mass. Acts c. 284, § 81, effective Aug. 11, 2014.]

(a) Whoever, being armed with a dangerous weapon, assaults a person sixty years or older with intent to rob or murder shall be punished by imprisonment in the state prison for not more than twenty years. Whoever commits any offense described herein while armed with a firearm, shotgun, rifle, machine gun or assault weapon shall be punished by imprisonment in the state prison for not less than ten years.

Whoever, after having been convicted of the crime of assault upon a person sixty years or older with intent to rob or murder while being armed with a dangerous weapon, commits a second or subsequent such crime, shall be punished by imprisonment for not less than two years. Said sentence shall not be reduced until two years of said sentence have been served nor shall the person convicted be eligible for probation, parole, furlough, work release or receive any deduction from his sentence for good conduct until he shall have served two years of such sentence; provided, however, that the commissioner of correction may, on the recommendation of the warden, superintendent, or other person in charge of a correctional institution, or the administrator of a county correctional institution, grant to said offender a temporary release in the custody of an officer of such institution for the following purposes only: to attend the funeral of next of kin or spouse; to visit a critically ill close relative or spouse; or to obtain emergency medical services unavailable at said institution. The provisions of section eighty-seven of chapter two hundred and seventy-six relating to the power of the court to place certain offenders on probation shall not apply to any person 18 years of age or over charged with a violation of this subsection. Whoever, after having been convicted of the crime of assault upon a person 60 years or older with intent to rob or murder while armed with a firearm, shotgun, rifle, machine gun or assault weapon commits a second or subsequent such crime shall be punished by imprisonment in the state prison for not less than 20 years.

(b) Whoever, being armed with a dangerous weapon, assaults another with intent to rob or murder shall be punished by imprisonment in the state prison for not more than twenty years. Whoever, being armed with a firearm, shotgun, rifle, machine gun or assault weapon assaults another with intent to rob or murder shall be punished by imprisonment in state prison for not less than five years and not more than 20 years.

§ 18A. Armed assault in dwelling house

Whoever, being armed with a dangerous weapon, enters a dwelling house and while therein assaults another with intent to commit a felony shall be punished by imprisonment in the state prison for life, or for a term of not less than ten years. No person imprisoned under this paragraph shall be eligible for parole in less than five years.

Whoever, being armed with a dangerous weapon defined as a firearm, shotgun, rifle or assault weapon, enters a dwelling house and while therein assaults another with intent to commit a felony shall be punished by imprisonment in the state prison for a term of not less than ten years. Such person shall not be eligible for parole prior to the expiration of ten years.

§ 18B. Use of firearms while committing a felony

[Amended by 2014 Mass. Acts c. 284, § 82, effective Aug. 11, 2014.]

Whoever, while in the commission of or the attempted commission of an offense which may be punished by imprisonment in the state prison, has in his possession or under his control a firearm, rifle or shotgun shall, in addition to the penalty for such offense, be punished by imprisonment in the state prison for not less than five years; provided, however, that if such firearm, rifle or shotgun is a large capacity weapon, as defined in section 121 of chapter 140, or if such person, while in the commission or attempted commission of such offense, has in his possession or under his control a machine gun, as defined in said section 121, such person shall be punished by imprisonment in the state prison for not less than ten years. Whoever has committed an offense which may be punished by imprisonment in the state prison and had in his possession or under his control a firearm, rifle or shotgun including, but not limited to, a large capacity weapon or machine gun and who thereafter, while in the commission or the attempted commission of a second or subsequent offense which may be punished by imprisonment in the state prison, has in his possession or under his control a firearm, rifle or shotgun shall, in addition to the penalty for such offense, be punished by imprisonment in the state prison for not less than 20 years; provided, however, that if such firearm, rifle or shotgun is a large capacity semiautomatic weapon or if such person, while in the commission or attempted commission of such offense, has in his possession or under his control a machine gun, such person shall be punished by imprisonment in the state prison for not less than 25 years.

A sentence imposed under this section for a second or subsequent offense shall not be reduced nor suspended, nor shall any person convicted under this section be eligible for probation, parole, furlough or work release or receive any deduction from his sentence for good conduct until he shall have served the minimum term of such additional sentence; provided, however, that the commissioner of correction may, on the recommendation of the warden, superintendent or other person in charge of a correctional institution or the administrator of a county correctional institution, grant to such offender a temporary release in the custody of an officer of such institution for the following purposes only: (i) to attend the funeral of a spouse or next of kin; (ii) to visit a critically ill close relative or spouse; or (iii) to obtain emergency medical services unavailable at such institution. Prosecutions commenced under this section shall neither be continued without a finding nor placed on file. The provisions of section 87 of chapter 276 relative to the power of the court to place certain offenders on probation shall not apply to any person 18 years of age or over charged with a violation of this section.

§ 18C. Home invasion

[Amended by 2004 Mass. Acts c. 150, § 17, effective Sept. 29, 2004.]

Whoever knowingly enters the dwelling place of another knowing or having reason to know that one or more persons are present within or knowingly enters the dwelling place of another and remains in such dwelling place knowing or having reason to know that one or more persons are present within while armed with a dangerous weapon, uses force or threatens the imminent use of force upon any person within such dwelling place whether or not injury occurs, or intentionally causes any injury to any person within such dwelling place shall be punished by imprisonment in the state prison for life or for any term of not less than twenty years.

§ 19. Unarmed robbery

[Amended by 2014 Mass. Acts c. 284, § 83, effective Aug. 11, 2014.]

(a) Whoever, not being armed with a dangerous weapon, by force and violence, or by assault and putting in fear, robs, steals or takes from the person of a person sixty years or older, or from his immediate control, money or other property which may be the subject of larceny, shall be punished by imprisonment in the state prison for life or for any term of years.

Whoever, after having been convicted of said crime, commits a second or subsequent such crime, shall be punished by imprisonment for not less than two years. Said sentence shall not be reduced until two years of said sentence have been served nor shall the person convicted be eligible for probation, parole, furlough, work release or receive any deduction from his sentence for good conduct until he shall have served two years of such sentence; provided, however, that the commissioner of correction may, on the recommendation of the warden, superintendent, or other person in charge of a correctional institution, or the administrator of a county correctional institution, grant to said offender a temporary release in the custody of an officer of such institution for the following purposes only: to attend the funeral of next of kin or spouse; to visit a critically ill close relative or spouse; or to obtain emergency medical services unavailable at said institution. The provisions of section eighty-seven of chapter two hundred and seventy-six relative to the power of the court to place certain offenders on probation shall not apply to any person 18 years of age or over charged with a violation of this subsection.

(b) Whoever, not being armed with a dangerous weapon, by force and violence, or by assault and putting in fear, robs, steals or takes from the person of another, or from his immediate control, money or other property which may be the subject of larceny, shall be punished by imprisonment in the state prison for life or for any term of years.

§ 20. Assault with intent to rob

Whoever, not being armed with a dangerous weapon, assaults another with force and violence and with intent to rob or steal shall be punished by imprisonment in the state prison for not more than ten years.

§ 21A. Carjacking

[Amended by 2014 Mass. Acts c. 284, § 84, effective Jan. 1, 2015.]

Whoever, with intent to steal a motor vehicle, assaults, confines, maims or puts any person in fear for the purpose of stealing a motor vehicle shall, whether he succeeds or fails in the perpetration of stealing the motor vehicle be punished by imprisonment in the state prison for not more than fifteen years or in a jail or house of correction for not more than two and one-half years and a fine of not less than one thousand nor more than fifteen thousand dollars; provided, however, that any person who commits any offense described herein while being armed with a dangerous weapon shall be punished by imprisonment in the state prison for not more than twenty years or in a jail or house of correction for not less than one year nor more than two and one-half years and a fine of not less than five nor more than fifteen thousand dollars. Whoever commits any offense described in this section while armed with a firearm, rifle, shotgun, machine gun or assault weapon, shall be punished by imprisonment in the state prison for not less than 7 years.

§ 22. Aggravated rape; rape

(a) Whoever has sexual intercourse or unnatural sexual intercourse with a person, and compels such person to submit by force and against his will, or compels such person to submit by threat of bodily injury and if either such sexual intercourse or unnatural sexual intercourse results in or is committed with acts resulting in serious bodily injury, or is committed by a joint enterprise, or is committed during the commission or attempted commission of an offense defined in section fifteen A, fifteen B, seventeen, nineteen or twenty-six of this chapter, section fourteen, fifteen, sixteen, seventeen or eighteen of chapter two hundred and sixty-six or section ten of chapter two hundred and sixty-nine shall be punished by imprisonment in the state prison for life or for any term of years.

Whoever commits any offense described in this section while being armed with a firearm, rifle, shotgun, machine-gun or assault weapon, shall be punished by imprisonment in the state prison for not less than ten years. Whoever commits a second or subsequent such offense shall be punished by imprisonment in the state prison for life or for any term of years, but not less than 15 years.

No person serving a sentence for a second or subsequent such offense shall be eligible for furlough, temporary release, or education, training or employment programs established outside a correctional facility until such person shall have served two-thirds of such minimum sentence or if such person has two or more sentences to be served otherwise than concurrently, two-thirds of the aggregate of the minimum terms of such several sentences.

(b) Whoever has sexual intercourse or unnatural sexual intercourse with a person and compels such person to submit by force and against his will, or compels such person to submit by threat of bodily injury, shall be punished by imprisonment in the state prison for not more than twenty years; and whoever commits a second or subsequent such offense shall be punished by imprisonment in the state prison for life or for any term or years.

No person serving a sentence for a second or subsequent such offense shall be eligible for furlough, temporary release, or education, training or employment programs established outside a correctional facility until such person shall have served two-thirds of such minimum sentence or if such person has two or more sentences to be served otherwise than concurrently, two-thirds of the aggregate of the minimum terms of such several sentences.

For the purposes of prosecution, the offense described in subsection (b) shall be a lesser included offense to that described in subsection (a).

§ 22A. Rape of a child under sixteen

[Amended by 2008 Mass. Acts c. 205, § 2, effective Oct. 22, 2008.]

Whoever has sexual intercourse or unnatural sexual intercourse with a child under 16, and compels such child to submit by force and against his will or compels such child to submit by threat of bodily injury, shall be punished by imprisonment in the state prison for life or for any term of years. A prosecution commenced under this section shall neither be continued without a finding nor placed on file.

§ 22B. Aggravated rape of a child under sixteen

[Added by 2008 Mass. Acts c. 205, § 2, effective Oct. 22, 2008.]

Whoever has sexual intercourse or unnatural sexual intercourse with a child under 16, and compels such child to submit by force and against his will or compels such child to submit by threat of bodily injury and:

(a) the sexual intercourse or unnatural sexual intercourse is committed during the commission or attempted commission of any of the following offenses: (1) armed burglary as set forth in section 14 of chapter 266; (2) unarmed burglary as set forth in section 15 of said chapter 266; (3) breaking and entering as set forth in section 16 of said chapter 266; (4) entering without breaking as set forth in section 17 of said chapter 266; (5) breaking and entering into a dwelling house as set forth in section 18 of said chapter 266; (6) kidnapping as set forth in section 26 of chapter 265; (7) armed robbery as set forth in section 17 of said chapter 265; (8) unarmed robbery as set forth in section 19 of said chapter 265; (9) assault and battery with a dangerous weapon or assault with a dangerous weapon as set forth in sections 15A and 15B of said chapter 265; (10) home invasion as set forth in section 18C of said chapter 265; or (11) posing or exhibiting child in state of nudity or sexual conduct as set forth in section 29A of chapter 272;

(b) the sexual intercourse or unnatural sexual intercourse results in, or is committed by means of an act or acts resulting in, substantial bodily injury as defined in section 13J;

(c) the sexual intercourse or unnatural sexual intercourse is committed while the victim is tied, bound or gagged;

(d) the sexual intercourse or unnatural sexual intercourse is committed after the defendant administered, or caused to be administered, alcohol or a controlled substance by injection, inhalation, ingestion, or any other means to the victim without the victim's consent;

(e) the sexual intercourse or unnatural sexual intercourse is committed by a joint enterprise; or

(f) the sexual intercourse or unnatural sexual intercourse was committed in a manner in which the victim could contract a sexually transmitted disease or infection of which the defendant knew or should have known he was a carrier, shall be punished by imprisonment in the state prison for life or for any term of years, but not less than 15 years. The sentence imposed on such person shall not be reduced to less than 15 years, or suspended, nor shall any person convicted under this section be eligible for probation, parole, work release or furlough or receive any deduction from his sentence for good conduct until he shall have served 15 years of such sentence. Prosecutions commenced under this section shall neither be continued without a finding nor placed on file. Whoever has sexual intercourse or unnatural sexual intercourse with a child under 16, and compels such child to submit by force and against his will or compels such child to submit by threat of bodily injury, shall be punished by imprisonment in the state prison for life or for any term of years. A prosecution commenced under this section shall neither be continued without a finding nor placed on file.

§ 22C. Aggravated rape of a child under sixteen by certain previously convicted offenders

[Added by 2008 Mass. Acts c. 205, § 2, effective Oct. 22, 2008.]

Whoever has sexual intercourse or unnatural sexual intercourse with a child under 16, and compels such child to submit by force and against his will or compels such child to submit by threat of bodily injury, and has been previously convicted of or adjudicated delinquent or as a youthful offender for: indecent assault and battery on a child under 14 as set forth in section 13B; aggravated indecent assault and battery on a child under 14 as set forth in section 13B½; indecent assault and battery on a person 14 or older as set forth in section 13H; assault of a child with intent to commit rape as set forth in section 24B; rape of a child with force as set forth in section 22A; aggravated rape of a child with force as set forth in section 22B; rape and abuse of a child as set forth in section 23; aggravated rape and abuse of a child as set forth in section 23A; rape as set forth in section 22; or a like violation of the laws of another state, the United States or a military, territorial or Indian tribal authority, shall be punished by imprisonment in the state prison for life or for any term of years, but not less than 20 years. The sentence imposed on such person shall not be reduced to less than 20 years, or suspended, nor shall any person convicted under this section be eligible for probation, parole, work release or furlough or receive any deduction from his sentence for good conduct until he shall have served 20 years of such sentence. Prosecutions commenced under this section shall neither be continued without a finding nor placed on file.

In any prosecution commenced pursuant to this section, introduction into evidence of a prior adjudication or conviction or a prior finding of sufficient facts by either certified attested copies of original court papers, or certified attested copies of the defendant's biographical and informational data from records of the department of probation, any jail or house of correction or the department of correction, shall be prima facie evidence that the defendant before the court has been convicted previously by a court of the commonwealth or any other jurisdiction. Such documentation shall be self-authenticating and admissible, after the commonwealth has established the defendant's guilt on the primary offense, as evidence in any court of the commonwealth to prove the defendant's commission of any prior conviction described therein. The commonwealth shall not be required to introduce any additional corroborating evidence or live witness testimony to establish the validity of such prior conviction.

§ 23. Statutory rape

[Amended by 2008 Mass. Acts c. 205, § 2, effective Oct. 22, 2008.]

Whoever unlawfully has sexual intercourse or unnatural sexual intercourse, and abuses a child under 16 years of age, shall be punished by imprisonment in the state prison for life or for any term of years or, except as otherwise provided, for any term in a jail or house of correction. A prosecution commenced under this section shall neither be continued without a finding nor placed on file.

§ 23A. Aggravated statutory rape

[Added by 2008 Mass. Acts c. 205, § 2, effective Oct. 22, 2008.]

Whoever unlawfully has sexual intercourse or unnatural sexual intercourse, and abuses a child under 16 years of age and:

(a) there exists more than a 5 year age difference between the defendant and the victim and the victim is under 12 years of age;

(b) there exists more than a 10 year age difference between the defendant and the victim where the victim is between the age of 12 and 16 years of age; or

(c) at the time of such intercourse, was a mandated reporter as defined in section 21 of chapter 119, shall be punished by imprisonment in the state prison for life or for any term of years, but not less than 10 years. The sentence imposed on such person shall not be reduced to less than 10 years, or suspended, nor shall any person convicted under this section be eligible for probation, parole, work release, or furlough or receive any deduction from his sentence for good conduct until he shall have served 10 years of such sentence. Prosecutions commenced under this section shall neither be continued without a finding nor placed on file.

§ 23B. Statutory rape, subsequent offense

[Added by 2008 Mass. Acts c. 205, § 2, effective Oct. 22, 2008.]

Whoever unlawfully has sexual intercourse or unnatural sexual intercourse, and abuses a child under 16 years of age and has been previously convicted of or adjudicated delinquent or as a youthful offender for: indecent assault and battery on a child under 14 under section 13B; aggravated indecent assault and battery on a child under 14 under section 13B½; indecent assault and battery on a person 14 or older under section 13H; assault of a child with intent to commit rape under section 24B; rape of a child with force under section 22A; aggravated rape of a child with force under section 22B; rape and abuse of a child under section 23; aggravated rape and abuse of a child under section 23A; rape under section 22; or a like violation of the laws of another state, the United States or a military, territorial or Indian tribal authority, shall be punished by imprisonment in the state prison for life or for any term of years, but not less than 15 years. The sentence imposed on such person shall not be reduced to less than 15 years, or suspended, nor shall any person convicted under this section be eligible for probation, parole, work release, or furlough or receive any deduction from his sentence for good conduct until he shall have served 15 years of such sentence. Prosecutions commenced under this section shall neither be continued without a finding nor placed on file.

In any prosecution commenced pursuant to this section, introduction into evidence of a prior adjudication or conviction or a prior finding of sufficient facts by either certified attested copies of original court papers, or certified attested copies of the defendant's biographical and informational data from records of the department of probation, any jail or house of correction or the department of correction, shall be prima facie evidence that the defendant before the court has been convicted previously by a court of the commonwealth or any other jurisdiction. Such documentation shall be self-authenticating and admissible, after the commonwealth has established the defendant's guilt on the primary offense, as evidence in any court of the commonwealth to prove the defendant's commission of any prior conviction described therein. The commonwealth shall not be required to introduce any additional corroborating evidence or live witness testimony to establish the validity of such prior conviction.

§ 24. Assault with intent to commit rape

Whoever assaults a person with intent to commit a rape shall be punished by imprisonment in the state prison for not more than twenty years or by imprisonment in a jail or house of correction for not more than two and one-half years; and whoever commits a second or subsequent such offense shall be punished by imprisonment in the state prison for life or for any term of years. Whoever commits any offense described in this section while armed with a firearm, rifle, shotgun, machine gun or assault weapon shall be punished by imprisonment in the state prison for not less than five years. Whoever commits a second or subsequent such offense shall be punished by imprisonment in the state prison for life or for any term of years, but not less than 20 years.

No person serving a sentence for a second or subsequent such offense shall be eligible for furlough, temporary release, or education, training or employment programs established outside a correctional facility until such person shall have served two-thirds of such minimum sentence or if such person has two or more sentences to be served otherwise than concurrently, two-thirds of the aggregate of the minimum terms of such several sentences.

§ 24A. Venue

[Amended by 2010 Mass. Acts c. 267, §§ 55-57, effective Nov. 5, 2010.]

If, in connection with the alleged commission of a crime described in section thirteen B, 13B½, 13B¾, thirteen F, thirteen H, twenty-two, twenty-two A, 22B, 22C, twenty-three, 23A, 23B, twenty-four or twenty-four B of this chapter or in section five of chapter two hundred and seventy-two, the person against whom said crime is alleged to have been committed has been conveyed from one county or judicial district into another, said crime may be alleged to have been committed, and may be prosecuted and punished, in the county or judicial district where committed or from which such person was so conveyed.

§ 24B. Assault of child with intent to commit rape

Whoever assaults a child under sixteen with intent to commit a rape, as defined in section thirty-nine of chapter two hundred and seventy-seven, shall be punished by imprisonment in the state prison for life or for any term of years; and whoever over the age of eighteen commits a subsequent such offense shall be punished by imprisonment in the state prison for life or for any term of years but not less than five years.

Whoever commits any offense described in this section while being armed with a firearm, rifle, shotgun, machine gun or assault weapon shall be punished by imprisonment in the state prison for life or for any term of years, but not less than ten years. Whoever over the age of 18 commits a second or subsequent such offense shall be punished by imprisonment in the state prison for life or for any term of years, but not less than 15 years.

§ 24C. Victim's name; confidentiality

[Amended by 2010 Mass. Acts c. 267, §§ 58–60, effective Nov. 5, 2010; 2011 Mass. Acts c. 178, § 21, effective Nov. 21, 2011.]

That portion of the records of a court or any police department of the commonwealth or any of its political subdivisions, which contains the name of the victim in an arrest, investigation or complaint for rape or assault with intent to rape under section thirteen B, 13B½, 13B¾, twenty-two, twenty-two A, 22B, 22C, twenty-three, 23A, 23B, twenty-four or twenty-four B, inclusive, of chapter two hundred and sixty-five, or an arrest, investigation or complaint for trafficking of persons under section 50 of said chapter 265, shall be withheld from public inspection, except with the consent of a justice of such court where the complaint or indictment is or would be prosecuted.

Said portion of such court record or police record shall not be deemed to be a public record under the provisions of section seven of chapter four.

Except as otherwise provided in this section, it shall be unlawful to publish, disseminate or otherwise disclose the name of any individual identified as an alleged victim of any of the offenses described in the first paragraph. A violation of this section shall be punishable by a fine of not less than two thousand five hundred dollars nor more than ten thousand dollars.

§ 25. Attempted extortion

Whoever, verbally or by a written or printed communication, maliciously threatens to accuse another of a crime or offence, or by a verbal or written or printed communication maliciously threatens an injury to the person or property of another, or any police officer or person having the powers of a police officer, or any officer, or employee of any licensing authority who verbally or by written or printed communication maliciously and unlawfully uses or threatens to use against another the power or authority vested in him, with intent thereby to extort money or any pecuniary advantage, or with intent to compel any person to do any act against his will, shall be punished by imprisonment in the state prison for not more than fifteen years, or in the house of correction for not more than two and one half years, or by a fine of not more than five thousand dollars, or both.

§ 26. Kidnapping

[Amended by 2010 Mass. Acts c. 267, § 61, effective Nov. 4, 2010.]

Whoever, without lawful authority, forcibly or secretly confines or imprisons another person within this commonwealth against his will, or forcibly carries or sends such person out of this commonwealth, or forcibly seizes and confines or inveigles or kidnaps another person, with intent either to cause him to be secretly confined or imprisoned in this commonwealth against his will, or to cause him to be sent out of this commonwealth against his will or in any way held to service against his will, shall be punished by imprisonment in the state prison for not more than ten years or by a fine of not more than one thousand dollars and imprisonment in jail for not more than two years. Whoever commits any offence described in this section with the intent to extort money or other valuable thing thereby shall be punished by imprisonment in the state prison for life or for any term of years.

Whoever commits any offense described in this section while armed with a firearm, rifle, shotgun, machine gun or assault weapon shall be punished by imprisonment in the state prison for not less than ten years or in the house of correction for not more than two and one-half years. The provisions of the preceding sentence shall not apply to the parent of a child under 18 years of age who takes custody of such child. Whoever commits such offense described in this section while being armed with a firearm, rifle, shotgun, machine gun or assault weapon with the intent to extort money or other valuable thing thereby shall be punished by imprisonment in the state prison for life or for any term of years but not less than 20 years.

Whoever commits any offense described in this section while armed with a dangerous weapon and inflicts serious bodily injury thereby upon another person or who sexually assaults such person shall be punished by imprisonment in the state prison for not less than 25 years. For purposes of this paragraph the term "serious bodily injury" shall mean bodily injury which results in a permanent disfigurement, protracted loss or impairment of a bodily function, limb or organ or substantial risk of death. For purposes of this paragraph, the term "sexual assault" shall mean the commission of any act set forth in sections 13B, 13B½, 13B¾, 13F, 13H, 22, 22A, 22B, 23, 23A, 23B, 24 or 24B.

Whoever, without lawful authority, forcibly or secretly confines or imprisons a child under the age of 16 within the commonwealth against his will or forcibly carries or sends such person out of the commonwealth or forcibly seizes and confines or inveigles or kidnaps a child under the age of 16 with the intent either to cause him to be secretly confined or imprisoned in the commonwealth against his will or to cause him to be sent out of the commonwealth against his will or in any way held to service against his will, shall be punished by imprisonment in the state prison for not more than 15 years. The provisions of the preceding sentence shall not apply to the parent of a child under 16 years of age who takes custody of such child.

NOTE A 12-year-old child falls within the "tender years doctrine" and cannot consent, as a matter of law, to leaving the custody of his or her parent or legal guardian. The doctrine holds that "a child of tender years is incapable of assenting to forcible removal from the legal custody of his or her parents." *Commonwealth v. Colon*, 431 Mass. 188, 191 (2000) (citation and quotation marks omitted).

§ 26A. Kidnapping of minor by relative

Whoever, being a relative of a child less than eighteen years old, without lawful authority, holds or intends to hold such a child permanently or for a protracted period, or takes or entices such a child from his lawful custodian, or takes or entices from lawful custody any incompetent person or other person entrusted by authority of law to the custody of another person or institution shall be punished by imprisonment in the house of correction for not more than one year or by a fine of up to one thousand dollars, or both. Whoever commits any offense described in this section by taking or holding said child outside the commonwealth or under circumstances which expose the person taken or enticed from lawful custody to a risk which endangers his safety shall be punished by a fine of not more than five thousand dollars, or by imprisonment in the state prison for not more than five years, or by both such fine and imprisonment.

§ 26B. Drugging persons for kidnapping

Whoever applies, administers to or causes to be taken by a person any drug, matter or thing with intent to stupefy or overpower such person so as to, without lawful authority, forcibly or secretly confine or imprison another person within the commonwealth against his will or to forcibly carry or send such person out of the commonwealth, or to forcibly seize and confine or inveigle or kidnap such person with intent to cause him to be secretly confined or imprisoned in the commonwealth against his will, or to cause him to be sent out of the commonwealth against his will or in any way held to service against his will, shall be punished by imprisonment in the state prison for life or for any term of years not less than ten years. Whoever violates the provisions of this section with the intent to extort money or other valuable thing thereby shall be punished by imprisonment in the state prison for life or for any term of years not less than 15 years.

§ 26C. Definition of "entice"; enticement of child under age 16; punishment

[Added by 2002 Mass. Acts c. 385, § 3, effective Feb. 25, 2003; 2010 Mass. Acts c. 267, §§ 62–64, effective Nov. 5, 2010.]

(a) As used in this section, the term "entice" shall mean to lure, induce, persuade, tempt, incite, solicit, coax or invite.

(b) Any one who entices a child under the age of 16, or someone he believes to be a child under the age of 16, to enter, exit or remain within any vehicle, dwelling, building, or other outdoor space with the intent that he or another person will violate section 13B, 13B½, 13B¾, 13F, 13H, 22, 22A, 22B, 22C, 23, 23A, 23B, 24 or 24B of chapter 265, section 4A, 16, 28, 29, 29A, 29B, 29C, 35A, 53 or 53A of chapter 272, or any offense that has as an element the use or attempted use of force, shall be punished by imprisonment in the state prison for not more than 5 years, or in the house of correction for not more than 2 years, or by both imprisonment and a fine of not more than $5,000.

§ 27. Kidnapping venue

A crime described in section twenty-six may be tried in the county where committed or in any county in or to which the person so seized, inveigled or kidnapped is confined, held, carried or brought; and upon the trial of any such crime, the consent thereto of the person so seized, inveigled, kidnapped or confined shall not be a defense unless the jury finds that such consent was not obtained by fraud or extorted by duress or threats.

§ 27A. Kidnapping of minor by relative; venue

A crime described in section twenty-six A may be tried in the county where committed or in a county in or to which the person so taken or enticed is held, carried to, or brought.

§ 28. Poison

Whoever mingles poison with food, drink or medicine with intent to kill or injure another person, or willfully poisons any spring, well or reservoir of water with such intent, shall be punished by imprisonment in the state prison for life or for any term of years.

§ 29. Assault with intent to commit felony

Whoever assaults another with intent to commit a felony shall, if the punishment of such assault is not hereinbefore provided, be punished by imprisonment in the state prison for not more than ten years or by a fine of not more than one thousand dollars and imprisonment in jail for not more than two and one half years.

§ 32. Glass; throwing in public streets and beaches

Whoever throws or drops glass on a public way, or on or near a bathing beach, or on a public way, sidewalk or reservation in the immediate neighborhood of a bathing beach, shall be punished by a fine of not more than one hundred dollars or by imprisonment for not more than one month.

§ 37. Violations of constitutional rights

No person, whether or not acting under color of law, shall by force or threat of force, willfully injure, intimidate or interfere with, or attempt to injure, intimidate or interfere with, or oppress or threaten any other person in the free exercise or enjoyment of any right or privilege secured to him by the constitution or laws of the commonwealth or by the constitution or laws of the United States. Any person convicted of violating this provision shall be fined not more than one thousand dollars or imprisoned not more than one year or both; and if bodily injury results, shall be punished by a fine of not more than ten thousand dollars or by imprisonment for not more than ten years, or both.

§ 39. Assault or battery for purpose of intimidation; due to race, etc.

[Amended by 2011 Mass. Acts c. 93, § 117, effective July 1, 2012; 2011 Mass. Acts c. 199, § 8, effective July 1, 2012.]

(a) Whoever commits an assault or a battery upon a person or damages the real or personal property of a person with the intent to intimidate such person because of such person's race, color, religion, national origin, sexual orientation, gender identity or disability shall be punished by a fine of not more than five thousand dollars or by imprisonment in a house of correction for not more than two and one-half years, or by both such fine and imprisonment. The court may also order restitution to the victim in any amount up to three times the value of property damage sustained by the owners of such property. For the purposes of this section, the term "disability" shall have the same meaning as "handicap" as defined in subsection 17 of section one of chapter one hundred and fifty-one B; provided, however, that for purposes of this section, the term "disability" shall not include any condition primarily resulting from the use of alcohol or a controlled substance as defined in section one of chapter ninety-four C.

(b) Whoever commits a battery in violation of this section and which results in bodily injury shall be punished by a fine of not more than ten thousand dollars or by imprisonment in the state prison for not more than five years, or by both such fine and imprisonment. Whoever commits any offense described in this subsection while armed with a firearm, rifle, shotgun, machine gun or assault weapon shall be punished by imprisonment in the state prison for not more than ten years or in the house of correction for not more than two and one-half years. For purposes of this section, "bodily injury" shall mean substantial impairment of the physical condition, including, but not limited to, any burn, fracture of any bone, subdural hematoma, injury to any internal organ, or any injury which occurs as the result of repeated harm to any bodily function or organ, including human skin.

There shall be a surcharge of one hundred dollars on a fine assessed against a defendant convicted of a violation of this section; provided, however, that moneys from such surcharge shall be delivered forthwith to the treasurer of the commonwealth and deposited in the Diversity Awareness Education Trust Fund established under the provisions of section thirty-nine Q of chapter ten. In the case of convictions for multiple offenses, said surcharge shall be assessed for each such conviction.

A person convicted under the provisions of this section shall complete a diversity awareness program designed by the secretary of the executive office of public safety in consultation with the Massachusetts commission against discrimination and approved by the chief justice of the trial court. A person so convicted shall complete such program prior to release from incarceration or prior to completion of the terms of probation, whichever is applicable.

§ 43. Stalking

[Amended by 2010 Mass. Acts c. 92, § 9, effective May 3, 2010; 2014 Mass. Acts c. 284, § 85, effective Aug. 11, 2014.]

(a) Whoever (1) willfully and maliciously engages in a knowing pattern of conduct or series of acts over a period of time directed at a specific person which seriously alarms or annoys that person and would cause a reasonable person to suffer substantial emotional distress, and (2) makes a threat with the intent to place the person in imminent fear of death or bodily injury, shall be guilty of the crime of stalking and shall be punished by imprisonment in the state prison for not more than 5 years or by a fine of not more than $1,000, or imprisonment in the house of correction for not more than 2½ years or by both such fine and imprisonment. The conduct, acts or threats described in this subsection shall include, but not be limited to, conduct, acts or threats conducted by mail or by use of a telephonic or telecommunication device or electronic communication device including, but not limited to, any device that transfers signs, signals, writing, images, sounds, data, or intelligence of any nature transmitted in whole or in part by a wire, radio, electromagnetic, photo-electronic or photo-optical system, including, but not limited to, electronic mail, internet communications, instant messages or facsimile communications.

(b) Whoever commits the crime of stalking in violation of a temporary or permanent vacate, restraining, or no-contact order or judgment issued pursuant to sections eighteen, thirty-four B, or thirty-four C of chapter two hundred and eight; or section thirty-two of chapter two hundred and nine; or sections three, four, or five of chapter two hundred and nine A; or sections fifteen or twenty of chapter two hundred and nine C or a protection order issued by another jurisdiction; or a temporary restraining order or preliminary or permanent injunction issued by the superior court, shall be punished by imprisonment in a jail or the state prison for not less than one year and not more than five years. No sentence imposed under the provisions of this subsection shall be less than a mandatory minimum term of imprisonment of one year.

A prosecution commenced hereunder shall not be placed on file or continued without a finding, and the sentence imposed upon a person convicted of violating any provision of this subsection shall not be reduced to less than the mandatory minimum term of imprisonment as established herein, nor shall said sentence of imprisonment imposed upon any person be suspended or reduced until such person shall have served said mandatory term of imprisonment.

A person convicted of violating any provision of this subsection shall not, until he shall have served the mandatory minimum term of imprisonment established herein, be eligible for probation, parole, furlough, work release or receive any deduction from his sentence for good conduct under sections one hundred and twenty-nine, one hundred and twenty-nine C and one hundred and twenty-nine D of chapter one hundred and twenty-seven; provided, however, that the commissioner of correction may, on the recommendation of the warden, superintendent, or other person in charge of a correctional institution, grant to said offender a temporary release in the custody of an officer of such institution for the following purposes only: to attend the funeral of next of kin or spouse; to visit a critically ill close relative or spouse; or to obtain emergency medical services unavailable at said institution. The provisions of section eighty-seven of chapter two hundred and seventy-six relating to the power of the court to place certain offenders on probation shall not apply to any person 18 years of age or over charged with a violation of this subsection. The provisions of section thirty-one of chapter two hundred and seventy-nine shall not apply to any person convicted of violating any provision of this subsection.

(c) Whoever, after having been convicted of the crime of stalking, commits a second or subsequent such crime shall be punished by imprisonment in a jail or the state prison for not less than two years and not more than ten years. No sentence imposed under

1

the provisions of this subsection shall be less than a mandatory minimum term of imprisonment of two years.

A prosecution commenced hereunder shall not be placed on file or continued without a finding, and the sentence imposed upon a person convicted of violating any provision of this subsection shall not be reduced to less than the mandatory minimum term of imprisonment as established herein, nor shall said sentence of imprisonment imposed upon any person be suspended or reduced until such person shall have served said mandatory term of imprisonment.

A person convicted of violating any provision of this subsection shall not, until he shall have served the mandatory minimum term of imprisonment established herein, be eligible for probation, parole, furlough, work release or receive any deduction from his sentence for good conduct under sections one hundred and twenty-nine, one hundred and twenty-nine C and one hundred and twenty-nine D of chapter one hundred and twenty-seven; provided, however, that the commissioner of correction may, on the recommendation of the warden, superintendent, or other person in charge of a correctional institution, grant to said offender a temporary release in the custody of an officer of such institution for the following purposes only: to attend the funeral of next of kin or spouse; to visit a critically ill close relative or spouse; or to obtain emergency medical services unavailable at said institution. The provisions of section eighty-seven of chapter two hundred and seventy-six relating to the power of the court to place certain offenders on probation shall not apply to any person 18 years of age or over charged with a violation of this subsection. The provisions of section thirty-one of chapter two hundred and seventy-nine shall not apply to any person convicted of violating any provision of this section.

§ 43A. Criminal harassment; punishment

[Amended by 2010 Mass. Acts c. 92, § 10, effective May 3, 2010.]

(a) Whoever willfully and maliciously engages in a knowing pattern of conduct or series of acts over a period of time directed at a specific person, which seriously alarms that person and would cause a reasonable person to suffer substantial emotional distress, shall be guilty of the crime of criminal harassment and shall be punished by imprisonment in a house of correction for not more than 2½ years or by a fine of not more than $1,000, or by both such fine and imprisonment. The conduct or acts described in this paragraph shall include, but not be limited to, conduct or acts conducted by mail or by use of a telephonic or telecommunication device including, but not limited to, any device that transfers signs, signals, writing, images, sounds, data or intelligence of any nature transmitted in whole or in part by a wire, radio, electromagnetic, photo-electronic or photo-optical system, including, but not limited to, electronic mail, internet communications, instant messages or facsimile communications.

(b) Whoever, after having been convicted of the crime of criminal harassment, commits a second or subsequent such crime, or whoever commits the crime of criminal harassment having previously been convicted of a violation of section 43, shall be punished by imprisonment in a house of correction for not more than two and one-half years or by imprisonment in the state prison for not more than ten years.

§ 44. Assault and battery on child to join gang

Whoever commits an assault and battery on a child under the age of eighteen for the purpose of causing or coercing such child to join or participate in a criminal conspiracy in violation of section seven of chapter two hundred and seventy-four, including but not limited to a criminal street gang or other organization of three or more persons which has a common name, identifying sign or symbol and whose members individually or collectively engage in criminal activity, shall, for the first offense, be punished by imprisonment in the state prison for not less than three nor more than five years or by imprisonment in the house of correction for not more than two and one-half years; and for a second or subsequent offense by imprisonment in the state prison for not less than five nor more than ten years.

§ 47. Global positioning system device to be worn by certain sex offender probationers

[Added by 2006 Mass. Acts c. 303, § 8, effective Dec. 20, 2006.]

Any person who is placed on probation for any offense listed within the definition of "sex offense," a "sex offense involving a child," or a "sexually violent offense," as defined in section 178C of chapter 6, shall, as a requirement of any term of probation, wear a global positioning system device, or any comparable device, administered by the commissioner of probation, at all times for the length of his probation for any such offense. The commissioner of probation, in addition to any other conditions, shall establish defined geographic exclusion zones including, but not limited to, the areas in and around the victim's residence, place of employment and school and other areas defined to minimize the probationer's contact with children, if applicable. If the probationer enters an excluded zone, as defined by the terms of his probation, the probationer's location data shall be immediately transmitted to the police department in the municipality wherein the violation occurred and the commissioner of probation, by telephone, electronic beeper, paging device or other appropriate means. If the commissioner or the probationer's probation officer has probable cause to believe that the probationer has violated this term of his probation, the commissioner or the probationer's probation officer shall arrest the probationer pursuant to section 3 of chapter 279. Otherwise, the commissioner shall cause a notice of surrender to be issued to such probationer.

The fees incurred by installing, maintaining and operating the global positioning system device, or comparable device, shall be paid by the probationer. If an offender establishes his inability to pay such fees, the court may waive them.

NOTE *See Commonwealth v. Samuel S.*, 476 Mass. 497 (2017); *Commonwealth v. Hanson H.*, 464 Mass. 807 (2013) (mandatory imposition of GPS does not apply to juveniles adjudicated delinquent of a sex offense and placed on probation).

§ 49. Definitions applicable to Secs. 50 to 51

[Added by 2011 Mass. Acts c. 178, § 23, effective Nov. 21, 2011.]

As used in sections 50 to 51, inclusive, the following words shall, unless the context clearly requires otherwise, have the following meanings:

"Commercial sexual activity", any sexual act on account of which anything of value is given, promised to or received by any person.

"Financial harm", a detrimental position in relation to wealth, property or other monetary benefits that occurs as a result of another person's illegal act including, but not limited to, extortion under by section 25, a violation of section 49 of chapter 271 or illegal employment contracts.

"Forced services", services performed or provided by a person that are obtained or maintained by another person who: (i) causes or threatens to cause serious harm to any person; (ii) physically restrains or threatens to physically restrain another person; (iii) abuses or threatens to abuse the law or legal process; (iv) knowingly destroys, conceals, removes, confiscates or possesses any actual or purported passport or other immigration document, or any other actual or purported government identification document, of another person; (v) engages in extortion under section 25; or (vi) causes or threatens to cause financial harm to any person.

"Services", acts performed by a person under the supervision of or for the benefit of another including, but not limited to, commercial sexual activity and sexually-explicit performances.

"Sexually-explicit performance", an unlawful live or public act or show intended to arouse or satisfy the sexual desires or appeal to the prurient interests of patrons.

§ 50. Trafficking of persons for sexual servitude; persons under 18; trafficking by business entities; penalties; tort actions by victims

[Added by 2011 Mass. Acts c. 178, § 23, effective Nov. 21, 2011.]

(a) Whoever knowingly: (i) subjects, or attempts to subject, or recruits, entices, harbors, transports, provides or obtains by any means, or attempts to recruit, entice, harbor, transport, provide or obtain by any means, another person to engage in commercial sexual activity, a sexually-explicit performance or the production of unlawful pornography in violation of chapter 272, or causes a person to engage in commercial sexual activity, a sexually-explicit performance or the production of unlawful pornography in violation of said chapter 272; or (ii) benefits, financially or by receiving anything of value, as a result of a violation of clause (i), shall be guilty of the crime of trafficking of persons for sexual servitude and shall be punished by imprisonment in the state prison for not less than 5 years but not more than 20 years and by a fine of not more than $25,000. Such sentence shall not be reduced to less than 5 years, or suspended, nor shall any person convicted under this section be eligible for probation, parole, work release or furlough or receive any deduction from his sentence for good conduct until he shall have served 5 years of such sentence. No prosecution commenced under this section shall be continued without a finding or placed on file.

(b) Whoever commits the crime of trafficking of persons for sexual servitude upon a person under 18 years of age shall be punished by imprisonment in the state prison for life or for any term of years, but not less than 5 years. No person convicted under this subsection shall be eligible for probation, parole, work release or furlough or receive any deduction from his sentence for good conduct until he shall have served 5 years of such sentence.

(c) A business entity that commits trafficking of persons for sexual servitude shall be punished by a fine of not more than $1,000,000.

(d) A victim of subsection (a) may bring an action in tort in the superior court in any county wherein a violation of subsection (a) occurred, where the plaintiff resides or where the defendant resides or has a place of business. Any business entity that knowingly aids or is a joint venturer in trafficking of persons for sexual servitude shall be civilly liable for an offense under this section.

§ 51. Trafficking of persons to forced servitude; victims under 18; trafficking by business entities; penalties; tort actions by victims

[Added by 2011 Mass. Acts c. 178, § 23, effective Nov. 21, 2011.]

(a) Whoever knowingly: (i) subjects, or attempts to subject, another person to forced services, or recruits, entices, harbors, transports, provides or obtains by any means, or attempts to recruit, entice, harbor, transport, provide or obtain by any means, another person, intending or knowing that such person will be subjected to forced services; or (ii) benefits, financially or by receiving anything of value, as a result of a violation of clause (i), shall be guilty of trafficking of persons for forced services and shall be punished by imprisonment in the state prison for not less than 5 years but not more than 20 years and by a fine of not more than $25,000. Such sentence shall not be reduced to less than 5 years, or suspended, nor shall any person convicted under this section be eligible for probation, parole, work release or furlough or receive any deduction from his sentence for good conduct until he shall have served 5 years of such sentence. No prosecution commenced under this section shall be continued without a finding or placed on file.

(b) Whoever commits the crime of trafficking of persons for forced services upon a person under 18 years of age shall be punished by imprisonment in the state prison for life or for any term of years, but not less than 5 years. No person convicted under this subsection shall be eligible for probation, parole, work release or furlough or receive any deduction from his sentence for good conduct until he shall have served 5 years of such sentence.

(c) A business entity that commits trafficking of persons for forced labor services shall be punished by a fine of not more than $1,000,000.

(d) A victim of subsection (a) may bring an action in tort in the superior court in any county wherein a violation of subsection (a) occurred, where the plaintiff resides or where the defendant resides or has a place of business. Any business entity that knowingly aids or is a joint venturer in trafficking of person for forced labor or services shall be civilly liable for an offense under this section.

§ 52. Subsequent violations of Sec. 50 or 51; penalties; evidence of prior adjudication or conviction

[Added by 2011 Mass. Acts c. 178, § 23, effective Nov. 21, 2011.]

(a) Whoever, after having been convicted of or adjudicated delinquent by reason of a violation of section 50 or 51, commits a second or subsequent violation of either section 50 or 51, shall be punished by imprisonment in the state prison for life or for any term of years, but not less than 10 years. Such sentence shall not be reduced to less than 10 years, or suspended, nor shall any person convicted under this section be eligible for probation, parole, work release or furlough or receive any deduction from his sentence for good conduct until he shall have served 10 years of such sentence. No prosecutions commenced under this section shall be continued without a finding or placed on file.

(b) In any prosecution commenced pursuant to this section, introduction into evidence of a prior adjudication or conviction or a prior finding of sufficient facts by either certified attested copies of original court papers, or certified attested copies of the defendant's biographical and informational data from records of the department of probation, any jail or house of correction or the department of correction, shall be prima facie evidence that the defendant before the court has been convicted previously by a court of the commonwealth or any other jurisdiction. Such documentation shall be self-authenticating and admissible, after the commonwealth has established the defendant's guilt on the primary offense, as evidence in any court of the commonwealth to prove the defendant's prior conviction described therein. The commonwealth shall not be required to introduce any additional corroborating evidence or live witness testimony to establish the validity of such prior conviction.

§ 53. Organ trafficking, victims under 18, penalties

[Added by 2011 Mass. Acts c. 178, § 23, effective Nov. 21, 2011.]

(a) Whoever: (i) recruits, entices, harbors, transports, delivers or obtains by any means, another person, intending or knowing that an organ, tissue or other body part of such person will be removed for sale, against such person's will; or (ii) knowingly receives anything of value, directly or indirectly as a result of a violation of clause (i) shall be guilty of organ trafficking and punished by imprisonment in the state prison for not more than 15 years or by a fine of not more than $50,000, or both.

(b) Whoever commits the crime of organ trafficking upon a person under 18 years of age shall be punished by imprisonment in the state prison for 5 years. Such sentence shall not be reduced to less than 5 years, or suspended, nor shall any person convicted under this subsection be eligible for probation, parole, work release, or furlough or receive any deduction from such sentence for good conduct until having served 5 years of such sentence.

§ 54. Transmittal of fines to state treasurer

[Added by 2011 Mass. Acts c. 178, § 23, effective Nov. 21, 2011.]

The court shall transmit fines collected pursuant to sections 50 and 51 to the state treasurer. The treasurer shall deposit such fines into the Victims of Human Trafficking Trust Fund established in section 66A of chapter 10.

1

§ 55. Forfeiture of funds use to facilitate violation of Sec. 50 or 51; victim restitution

[Added by 2011 Mass. Acts c. 178, § 23, effective Nov. 21, 2011.]

All monies furnished or intended to be furnished by any person in exchange for forced labor or services or sexual servitude, and all monies used or intended to be used to facilitate any violation of section 50 or 51 shall be subject to forfeiture to the commonwealth and shall be made available by the court to any victim ordered restitution by the court pursuant to section 3 of chapter 258B.

§ 56. Property subject to forfeiture resulting from violations of Secs. 50 or 51; procedure; exceptions; records; preliminary orders for seizure; referral to office of seized property management; homestead exemptions; recording of certificate of fact of final judgment

[Added by 2011 Mass. Acts c. 178, § 23, effective Nov. 21, 2011.]

(a) The following property shall be subject to forfeiture to the commonwealth and all property rights therein shall be in the commonwealth:

(i) all conveyances, including aircraft, vehicles or vessels used, or intended for use, to transport, conceal or otherwise facilitate a violation of section 50 or 51;

(ii) all books, records and research, including microfilm, tapes and data which are used, or intended for use, in violation of section 50 or 51;

(iii) all negotiable instruments, securities or other things of value furnished or intended to be furnished by any person in exchange for forced labor or services or sexual servitude, all proceeds traceable to such an exchange, including real estate and any other thing of value, and all negotiable instruments and securities used or intended to be used to facilitate any violation of section 50 or 51; and

(iv) all real property, including any right, title and interest in the whole of any lot or tract of land and any appurtenances or improvements thereto, which is used in any manner or part to commit or to facilitate any violation of section 50 or 51.

No forfeiture under this section shall extinguish a perfected security interest held by a creditor in a conveyance or in any real property at the time of the filing of the forfeiture action.

(b) Property subject to forfeiture pursuant to clauses (i) to (iv), inclusive, of subsection (a) shall, upon motion of the attorney general or district attorney, be declared forfeit by any court having jurisdiction over said property or having final jurisdiction over any related criminal proceeding brought under this section.

(c) The court shall order forfeiture of all conveyances and real property subject to forfeiture under this section, except as follows:

(i) no conveyance used by any person as a common carrier in the transaction of business as a common carrier shall be forfeited unless it shall appear that the owner or other person in charge of such conveyance was a consenting party or privy to a violation of section 50 or 51;

(ii) no conveyance shall be forfeited by reason of any act or omission established by the owner thereof to have been committed or omitted by any person other than such owner while such conveyance was unlawfully in the possession of a person other than the owner in violation of the criminal laws of the United States, of the commonwealth or of any state; and

(iii) no conveyance or real property shall be subject to forfeiture unless the owner thereof knew or should have known that such conveyance or real property was used in violation of section 50 or 51.

(d) A district attorney or the attorney general may petition the superior court in the name of the commonwealth in the nature of a proceeding in rem to order forfeiture of a conveyance, real property or other things of value subject to forfeiture under subsection (a). Such petition shall be filed in the court having jurisdiction over the conveyance, real property or other things of value or having final jurisdiction over any related criminal proceeding brought under section 50 or 51. In all such suits in which the property is claimed by any person, other than the commonwealth, the commonwealth shall have the burden of proving to the court the existence of probable cause to institute the action, and any such claimant shall then have the burden of proving that the property is not forfeitable pursuant to subsection (c). The owner of the conveyance or real property, or other person claiming thereunder, shall have the burden of proof as to all exceptions set forth in subsections (c) and (j). The court shall order the commonwealth to give notice by certified or registered mail to the owner of the conveyance, real property or other things of value and to such other persons as appear to have an interest therein, and the court shall promptly, but not less than 2 weeks after notice, hold a hearing on the petition. Upon the motion of the owner of the conveyance, real property or other things of value, the court may continue the hearing on the petition pending the outcome of any criminal trial related to the violation of sections 50 or 51. At such hearing, the court shall hear evidence and make conclusions of law, and shall thereupon issue a final order from which the parties shall have a right of appeal. In all such suits in which a final order results in a forfeiture, the final order shall provide for disposition of the conveyance, real property or any other thing of value by the commonwealth or any subdivision thereof in any manner not prohibited by law, including official use by an authorized law enforcement or other public agency, or sale at public auction or by competitive bidding. The proceeds of any such sale shall be used to pay the reasonable expenses of the forfeiture proceedings, seizure, storage, maintenance of custody, advertising and notice and the balance thereof shall be distributed as further provided in this section.

(e) The final order of the court shall be deposited into the Victims of Human Trafficking Trust Fund established in section 66A of chapter 10.

(f) Any officer, department, or agency having custody of any property subject to forfeiture under this section or having disposed of the property shall keep and maintain full and complete records showing from whom it received the property, under what authority it held or received or disposed of said property, to whom it delivered the property, the date and manner of disposition of the property, and the exact kinds, quantities and forms of the property. The records shall be open to inspection by all federal and state officers charged with enforcement of federal and state human trafficking laws. Persons making final disposition of the property under court order shall report, under oath, to the court the exact circumstances of such disposition.

(g) During the pendency of the proceedings, the court may issue at the request of the commonwealth ex parte any preliminary order or process as is necessary to seize or secure the property for which forfeiture is sought and to provide for its custody including, but not limited to: an order that the commonwealth remove the property if possible and safeguard it in a secure location in a reasonable fashion; that monies be deposited in an interest-bearing escrow account; and that a substitute custodian be appointed to manage such property. Property taken or detained under this section shall not be repleviable, but once seized shall be deemed to be lawfully in the custody of the commonwealth pending forfeiture, subject only to the orders and decrees of the court having jurisdiction thereof. Process for seizure of the property shall issue only upon a showing of probable cause, and the application therefore and the issuance, execution and return thereof shall be subject to chapter 276, so far as applicable.

(h) A district attorney or the attorney general may refer any real property, and any furnishings, equipment and related personal property located therein, for which seizure is sought, to the division of capital asset management and maintenance office of seized property management, established under section 47 of chapter 94C. The office of seized property management shall preserve and manage the property in a reasonable fashion and dispose of the property upon a judgment ordering forfeiture, and to enter into contracts to preserve, manage and dispose of the property. The office of seized property management may receive initial funding from the special law enforcement trust funds of the attorney general and each district attorney under paragraph (f) and shall subsequently be funded by a portion of the proceeds of each sale of such managed property to the extent provided as payment of reasonable expenses in paragraph (d).

(i) The owner of any real property which is the principal domicile of the immediate family of the owner and which is subject to forfeiture under this section may file a petition for homestead exemption with the court having jurisdiction over such forfeiture. The court may, in its discretion, allow the petition exempting from forfeiture an amount allowed under section 1 of chapter 188. The value of the balance of the principal domicile, if any, shall be forfeited as provided in this section. Such homestead exemption may be acquired on only 1 principal domicile for the benefit of the immediate family of the owner.

(j) A forfeiture proceeding affecting the title to real property or the use and occupation thereof or the buildings thereon shall not have any effect except against the parties thereto and persons having actual notice thereof, until a memorandum containing the names of the parties to such proceeding, the name of the town wherein the affected real property lies, and a description of the real property sufficiently accurate for identification is recorded in the registry of deeds for the county or district wherein the real property lies. At any time after a judgment on the merits, or after the discontinuance, dismissal or other final disposition is recorded by the court having jurisdiction over such matter, the clerk of such court shall issue a certificate of the fact of such judgment, discontinuance, dismissal or other final disposition, and such certificate shall be recorded in the registry in which the original memorandum recorded pursuant to this section was filed.

§ 57. Victim of human trafficking as affirmative defense to charges of common night walking or common streetwalking

[Added by 2011 Mass. Acts c. 178, § 23, effective Nov. 21, 2011.]

In any prosecution or juvenile delinquency proceeding of a person who is a human trafficking victim, as defined by section 20M of chapter 233, it shall be an affirmative defense to charges of engaging in common night walking or common streetwalking in violation of section 53 of chapter 272 and to a violation of section 53A of said chapter 272 that, while a human trafficking victim, such person was under duress or coerced into committing the offenses for which such person is being prosecuted or against whom juvenile delinquency proceedings have commenced.

§ 58. Possession of deceptive weapon device during commission of violent crime

[Added by 2014 Mass. Acts c. 284, § 86, effective Aug. 11, 2014.]

Any person who is in possession of a deceptive weapon device as defined in section 121 of chapter 140 during the commission of a violent crime as defined in said section 121 of said chapter 140 shall be deemed to be armed and shall be punishable by penalties set forth in this chapter.

Chapter 266. Crimes Against Property

§ 1. Arson (dwelling)

Whoever willfully and maliciously sets fire to, burns, or causes to be burned, or whoever aids, counsels or procures the burning of, a dwelling house, or a building adjoining or adjacent to a dwelling house, or a building by the burning whereof a dwelling house is burned, whether such dwelling house or other building is the property of himself or another and whether the same is occupied or unoccupied, shall be punished by imprisonment in the state prison for not more than twenty years, or by imprisonment in a jail or house of correction for not more than two and one half years, or by a fine of not more than ten thousand dollars, or by both such fine and imprisonment. The words "dwelling house", as used in this section, shall mean and include all buildings used as dwellings such as apartment houses, tenement houses, hotels, boarding houses, dormitories, hospitals, institutions, sanatoria, or other buildings where persons are domiciled.

§ 2. Arson (building)

Whoever willfully and maliciously sets fire to, burns, or causes to be burned, or whoever aids, counsels or procures the burning of, a meeting house, church, court house, town house, college, academy, jail or other building which has been erected for public use, or a banking house, warehouse, store, manufactory, mill, barn, stable, shop, outhouse or other building, or an office building, lumber yard, ship, vessel, street car or railway car, or a bridge, lock, dam, flume, tank, or any building or structure or contents thereof, not included or described in the preceding section, whether the same is the property of himself or of another and whether occupied, unoccupied or vacant, shall be punished by imprisonment in the state prison for not more than ten years, or by imprisonment in a jail or house of correction for not more than two and one half years.

§ 5. Arson (wood and other property)

Whoever willfully and maliciously sets fire to, or burns or otherwise destroys or injures by burning, or causes to be burned or otherwise so destroyed or injured, or whoever aids, counsels or procures the burning of, a pile or parcel of wood, boards, timber or other lumber, or any fence, bars or gate, or a stack of grain, hay or other vegetable product, or any vegetable product severed from the soil and not stacked, or any standing tree, grain, grass or other standing product of the soil, or the soil itself, or any personal property of whatsoever class or character exceeding a value of twenty-five dollars, of another, or any boat motor vehicle as defined in section one of chapter ninety, or other conveyance, whether of himself or another, shall be punished by imprisonment in the state prison for not more than three years, or by a fine of not more than five hundred dollars and imprisonment in a jail or house of correction for not more than one year.

§ 5A. Attempted arson

Whoever willfully and maliciously attempts to set fire to, or attempts to burn, or aids, counsels or assists in such an attempt to set fire to or burn, any of the buildings, structures or property mentioned in the foregoing sections, or whoever commits any act preliminary thereto or in furtherance thereof, shall be punished by imprisonment in the state prison for not more than ten years, or by imprisonment in a jail or house of correction for not more than two and one half years or by a fine of not more than one thousand dollars.

The placing or distributing of any flammable, explosive or combustible material or substance or any device in or against any building, structure or property mentioned in the foregoing sections in an arrangement or preparation with intent eventually to willfully and maliciously set fire to or burn such building, structure or property, or to procure the setting fire to or burning of the same shall, for the purposes of this section, constitute an attempt to burn such building, structure or property.

§ 7. Woods; wanton or reckless injury or destruction by fire

Whoever by wantonly or recklessly setting fire to any material, or by increasing a fire already set, causes injury to, or the destruction of, any growing or standing wood of another shall be punished by a fine of not more than one thousand dollars or by imprisonment for not more than two years.

§ 8. Injury by fire; negligent use

Whoever, not being a tenant thereof, sets or increases a fire upon land of another whereby the property of another is injured, or whoever negligently or willfully suffers any fire upon his own land to extend beyond the limits thereof whereby the woods or property of another are injured, shall be punished by a fine of not more than one thousand dollars or by imprisonment for not more than two years, and the town where such fire occurred may recover in an action of tort, brought within two years after the cause of action accrues, against any such person the expense of extinguishing such fire.

§ 14. Burglary; armed assault on occupants

Whoever breaks and enters a dwelling house in the night time, with intent to commit a felony, or whoever, after having entered with such intent, breaks such dwelling house in the night time, any person being then lawfully therein, and the offender being armed with a dangerous weapon at the time of such breaking or entry, or so arming himself in such house, or making an actual assault on a person lawfully therein, shall be punished by imprisonment in the state prison for life or for any term of not less than ten years.

Whoever commits any offense described in this section while armed with a firearm, rifle, shotgun, machine gun or assault weapon shall be punished by imprisonment in the state prison for life or for any term of years, but not less than 15 years. Whoever commits a subsequent such offense shall be punished by imprisonment in the state prison for life or for any term of years, but not less than 20 years.

The sentence imposed upon a person who, after being convicted of any offence mentioned in this section, commits the like offence, or any other of the offences therein mentioned, shall not be suspended, nor shall he be placed on probation.

§ 15. Burglary; unarmed

Whoever breaks and enters a dwelling house in the night time, with the intent mentioned in the preceding section, or, having entered with such intent, breaks such dwelling house in the night time, the offender not being armed, nor arming himself in such house, with a dangerous weapon, nor making an assault upon a person lawfully therein, shall be punished by imprisonment in the state prison for not more than twenty years and, if he shall have been previously convicted of any crime named in this or the preceding section, for not less than five years.

§ 16. Breaking and entering building

Whoever, in the night time, breaks and enters a building, ship, vessel or vehicle, with intent to commit a felony, or who attempts to or does break, burn, blow up or otherwise injures or destroys a safe, vault or other depository of money, bonds or other valuables in any building, vehicle or place, with intent to commit a larceny or felony, whether he succeeds or fails in the perpetration of such larceny or felony, shall be punished by imprisonment in the state prison for not more than twenty years or in a jail or house of correction for not more than two and one-half years.

§ 16A. Building, vessel or vehicle; breaking and entering with intent to commit misdemeanor

Whoever in the nighttime or daytime breaks and enters a building, ship, vessel or vehicle with intent to commit a misdemeanor shall be punished by a fine of not more than two hundred dollars or by imprisonment for not more than six months, or both.

§ 17. Entering without breaking at night; breaking and entering in day time

[Amended by 2014 Mass. Acts c. 284, § 87, effective Jan. 1, 2015.]

Whoever, in the night time, enters without breaking, or breaks and enters in the day time, a building, ship, vessel, or vehicle, with intent to commit a felony, the owner or any other person lawfully therein being put in fear, shall be punished by imprisonment in the state prison for not more than ten years. Whoever commits any offense described in this section while armed with a firearm, rifle, shotgun, machine gun or assault weapon shall be punished by imprisonment in the state prison for not less than 7 years or in the house of correction for not less than 2 years nor more than 2½ years.

§ 18. Dwelling house; entry at night; breaking and entering in day time

[Amended by 2014 Mass. Acts c. 284, § 88, effective Jan. 1, 2015.]

Whoever, in the night time, enters a dwelling house without breaking, or breaks and enters in the day time a building, ship or motor vehicle or vessel, with intent to commit a felony, no person lawfully therein being put in fear, shall be punished by imprisonment in the state prison for not more than ten years or by a fine of not more than five hundred dollars and imprisonment in jail for not more than two years. Whoever commits any offense described in this section while armed with a firearm, rifle, shotgun, machine gun or assault weapon shall be punished by imprisonment in the state prison for not less than 7 years or by imprisonment in the house of correction for not less than 2 years nor more than 2½ years.

§ 18A. Entering dwelling house by false pretenses; intent to commit felony; larceny; punishment

Whoever enters a dwelling house by false pretenses, without breaking and with the intent to commit a felony, no person lawfully therein being put in fear, or whoever enters a dwelling house by false pretenses, without breaking and, after having entered, commits a larceny, as defined by section 30, no person lawfully therein being put in fear, shall be punished by imprisonment in the state prison for not more than ten years or by a fine of not more than $5,000 and imprisonment in a house of correction for not more than two years, or by both such fine and imprisonment.

§ 25. Larceny from the person

(a) Whoever commits larceny by stealing from the person of a person sixty-five years or older shall be punished by imprisonment in the state prison for not more than five years or in jail for not more than two and one-half years.

Whoever, after having been convicted of said crime commits a second or subsequent such crime, shall be punished by imprisonment for not less than two years. Said sentence shall not be reduced until one year of said sentence has been served nor shall the person convicted be eligible for probation, parole, furlough, work release or receive any deduction from his sentence for good conduct until he shall have served one year of such sentence; provided, however, that the commissioner of correction may, on the recommendation of the warden, superintendent, or other person in charge of a correctional institution, or the administrator of a county correctional institution, grant to said offender a temporary release in the custody of an officer of such institution for the following purposes only: to attend the funeral of next of kin or spouse; to visit a critically ill close relative or spouse; or to obtain emergency medical services unavailable at said institution. The provisions of section eighty-seven of chapter two hundred and seventy-six relating to the power of the court to place certain offenders on probation shall not apply to any person seventeen years of age or over charged with a violation of this subsection.

(b) Whoever commits larceny by stealing from the person of another shall be punished by imprisonment in the state prison for not more than five years or in jail for not more than two and one-half years.

§ 28. Motor vehicle theft

(a) Whoever steals a motor vehicle or trailer, whoever maliciously damages a motor vehicle or trailer, whoever buys, receives, possesses, conceals, or obtains control of a motor vehicle or trailer, knowing or having reason to know the same to have been stolen, or whoever takes a motor vehicle without the authority of the owner and steals from it any of its parts or accessories, shall be punished by imprisonment in the state prison for not more than fifteen years or by imprisonment in a jail or house of correction for not more than two and one-half years or by a fine of not more than fifteen thousand dollars, or by both such fine and imprisonment.

Evidence that an identifying number or numbers of a motor vehicle or trailer or part thereof has been intentionally and maliciously removed, defaced, altered, changed, destroyed, obliterated, or mutilated, shall be prima facie evidence that the defendant knew or had reason to know that the motor vehicle, or trailer or part thereof had been stolen.

A prosecution commenced under this subdivision shall not be placed on file or continued without a finding and the sentence imposed upon a person convicted of violating this subdivision for a second or subsequent offense shall not be reduced to less than one year imprisonment, nor shall any sentence imposed upon any person be suspended, or reduced, until such person shall have served one year of such sentence if convicted of a second or subsequent such offense.

A person convicted of a second or subsequent offense of violating the provisions of this subdivision shall not be eligible for probation, parole, furlough or work release; provided, however that the commissioner of correction may, on the recommendation of warden, superintendent, or other person in charge of a correctional institution, or the administrator of a county correctional institution, to said offender a temporary release in the custody of an officer of such institution for the following purposes: to attend the funeral of next of kin or spouse; to visit a critically ill close relative or spouse; or to obtain emergency medical services unavailable at said institution.

(b) Whoever conceals any motor vehicle or trailer thief knowing him to be such, shall be punished by imprisonment for not more than ten years or by imprisonment in jail or house of correction for not more than two and one-half years or by a fine of not more than five thousand dollars, or both.

(c) A conviction of a violation of this section or any adjudication that a person is a delinquent child by reason thereof shall be reported forthwith by the court or magistrate to the registrar of motor vehicles who shall revoke immediately the license to operate motor vehicles or the right to operate motor vehicles of the person so convicted or adjudged, and no appeal, motion for new trial or exceptions shall operate to stay the revocation of such license or right to operate. The registrar of motor vehicles after having revoked the license or right to operate of any such person so convicted or adjudged shall issue a new license or reinstate such right to operate, if the prosecution of such person is finally terminated in his favor; otherwise, no new license shall be issued nor shall such right to operate be reinstated until one year after the date of revocation following his original conviction or adjudication if for a first offense, or until five years after the date of revocation following any subsequent conviction or adjudication.

§ 29. Statement concerning theft; recovery of vehicles; restitution

Whenever a motor vehicle is stolen or misappropriated, the owner of record shall sign and submit to the appropriate police authority a statement under the penalties of perjury on a form containing such information relating to the theft or misappropriation of the vehicle as is prescribed by the registrar of motor vehicles.

Whenever a stolen or misappropriated motor vehicle is recovered by a police officer or other law enforcement officer, the police department shall notify the registry of motor vehicles, the owner of record and the storage facility if any, as soon as possible after the identity of the owner is determined. Such notification may be made by letter, telephone call or personal visit to the owner and shall include information as to the location of the recovered vehicle. In the event the vehicle is placed in a garage or other storage facility, the owner of said facility shall lose his lien for the reasonable charges for storage and towing unless he notifies the owner of record of the vehicle by certified mail and return receipt requested within five days of the date of said recovery or his actual knowledge of the identity of the owner of record. Said notice shall contain the information on the location of the vehicle and the amount of charge due on said vehicle.

The court shall, after a defendant is convicted of a violation of subsection (a) of section twenty-eight, conduct an evidentiary hearing to ascertain the extent of the damages or financial loss suffered as a result of the defendant's crime. A person found guilty of violating subsection (a) of section twenty-eight shall in all cases, upon conviction, in addition to any other punishment, be ordered to make restitution to the insurer for any financial loss sustained as a result of the commission of the crime; provided, however, that restitution shall not be ordered to a party whom the court determines to be aggrieved without that party's consent. restitution shall be imposed in addition to incarceration or fine, and not in lieu thereof; provided, however, the court shall consider the defendant's present and future ability to pay in its determinations regarding a fine; provided, further, that whenever possible subject to the constraints of this paragraph and the first paragraph of said subsection (a) of section twenty-eight the amount of a fine imposed for a violation of said subsection (a) of section twenty-eight shall equal twice the amount of damages or financial loss suffered as a result of the defendant's crime.

In determining the amount, time and method of payment of restitution, the court shall consider the financial resources of the defendant and the burden restitution will impose on the defendant. Upon a real or impending change in financial circumstances, a defendant ordered to pay restitution may petition the court for a modification of the amount, time or method of payment of restitution. If the court finds that because of any such change the payment of restitution will impose an undue financial hardship on the defendant or his family, the court may modify the amount, time or method of payment, but may not grant complete remission from payment of restitution.

If a defendant who is required to make restitution defaults in any payment of restitution or installment thereof the court shall hold him in contempt unless said defendant has made a good faith effort to pay such restitution. If said defendant has made a good faith effort to pay such restitution, the court may modify the amount, time or method of payment, but may not grant complete remission from payment of restitution.

§ 30. Larceny

(1) Whoever steals, or with intent to defraud obtains by a false pretence, or whoever unlawfully, and with intent to steal or embezzle, converts, or secretes with intent to convert, the property of another as defined in this section, whether such property is or is not in his possession at the time of such conversion or secreting, shall be guilty of larceny, and shall, if the property stolen is a firearm, as defined in section one hundred and twenty-one of chapter one hundred and forty, or, if the value of the property stolen exceeds two hundred and fifty dollars, be punished by imprisonment in the state prison for not more than five years, or by a fine of not more than twenty-five thousand dollars and imprisonment in jail for not more than two years; or, if the value of the property stolen, other than a firearm as so defined, does not exceed two hundred and fifty dollars, shall be punished by imprisonment in jail for not more than one year or by a fine of not more than three hundred dollars; or, if the property was stolen from the conveyance of a common carrier or of a person carrying on an express business, shall be punished for the first offence by imprisonment for not less than six months nor more than two and one half years, or by a fine of not less than fifty nor more than six hundred, dollars, or both, and for a subsequent offence, by imprisonment for not less than eighteen months nor more than two and one half years, or by a fine of not less than one hundred and fifty nor more than six hundred dollars, or both.

(2) The term "property", as used in the section, shall include money, personal chattels, a bank note, bond, promissory note, bill of exchange or other bill, order or certificate, a book of accounts for or concerning money or goods due or to become due or to be delivered, a deed or writing containing a conveyance of land, any valuable contract in force, a receipt, release or defeasance, a writ, process, certificate of title or duplicate certificate issued under chapter one hundred and eighty-five, a public record, anything which is of the realty or is annexed thereto, a security deposit received pursuant to section fifteen B of chapter one hundred and eighty-six, electronically processed or stored data, either tangible or intangible, data while in transit, telecommunications services, and any domesticated animal, including dogs, or a beast or bird which is ordinarily kept in confinement.

(3) The stealing of real property may be a larceny from one or more tenants, sole, joint or in common, in fee, for life or years, at will or sufferance, mortgagors or mortgagees, in possession of the same, or who may have an action of tort against the offender for trespass upon the property, but not from one having only the use or custody thereof. The larceny may be from a wife in possession, if she is authorized by law to hold such property as if sole, otherwise her occupation may be the possession of the husband. If such property which was of a person deceased is stolen, it may be a larceny from any one or more heirs, devisees, reversioners, remaindermen or others, who have a right upon such decease to take possession, but not having entered, as A would be after entry. The larceny may be from a person whose name is unknown, if it would be such if the property stolen were personal, and may be committed by those who have only the use or custody of the property, but not by a person against whom no action of tort could be maintained for acts like those constituting the larceny.

(4) Whoever steals, or with intent to defraud obtains by a false pretense, or whoever unlawfully, and with intent to steal or embezzle, converts, secretes, unlawfully takes, carries away, conceals or copies with intent to convert any trade secret of another, regardless of value, whether such trade secret is or is not in his possession at the time of such conversion or secreting, shall be guilty of larceny, and shall be punished by imprisonment in the state prison for not more than five years, or by a fine of not more than twenty-five thousand dollars and imprisonment in jail for not more than two years. The term "trade secret' as used in this paragraph means and includes anything tangible or intangible or electronically kept or stored, which constitutes, represents, evidences or records a secret scientific, technical, merchandising, production or management information, design, process, procedure, formula, invention or improvement.

(5) Whoever steals or with intent to defraud obtains by a false pretense, or whoever unlawfully, and with intent to steal or embezzle, converts, or secretes with intent to convert, the property of another, sixty years of age or older, or of a person with a disability as defined in section thirteen K of chapter two hundred and sixty-five, whether such property is or is not in his possession at the time of such conversion or secreting, shall be guilty of larceny, and shall, if the value of the property exceeds two hundred and fifty dollars, be punished by imprisonment in the state prison for not more than ten years or in the house of correction for not more than two and one-half years, or by a fine of not more than fifty thousand dollars or by both such fine and imprisonment; or if the value of the property does not exceed two hundred and fifty dollars, shall be punished by imprisonment in the house of correction for not more than two and one-half years or by a fine of not more than one thousand dollars or by both such fine and imprisonment. The court may order, regardless of the value of the property, restitution to be paid to the victim commensurate with the value of the property.

§ 30A. Shoplifting

Any person who intentionally takes possession of, carries away, transfers or causes to be carried away or transferred, any merchandise displayed, held, stored or offered for sale by any store or other retail mercantile establishment with the intention of depriving the merchant of the possession, use of benefit of such merchandise or converting the same to the use of such person without paying to the merchant the value thereof; or any person who intentionally conceals upon his person or otherwise any merchandise offered for sale by any store or other retail mercantile establishment with the intention of depriving the merchant of proceeds, use or benefit of such merchandise or converting the same to the use of such person without paying to the merchant the value thereof or any person who intentionally alters, transfers or removes any label, price tag or marking indicia of value or any other markings which aid in determining value affixed to any merchandise displayed, held, stored or offered for sale by any store or other retail mercantile establishment and to attempt to purchase such merchandise personally or in consort with another at less than the full retail value with the intention of depriving the merchant of all or some part of the retail value thereof; or any person who intentionally transfers any merchandise displayed, held, stored or offered for sale by any store or other retail mercantile establishment from the container in or on which the same shall be displayed to any other container with intent to deprive the merchant of all or some part of the retail value thereof; or any person who intentionally records a value for the merchandise which is less than the actual retail value with the intention of depriving the merchant of the full retail value thereof; or any person who intentionally removes a shopping cart from the premises of a store or other retail mercantile establishment, without the consent of the merchant given at the time of such removal, with the intention of permanently depriving the merchant of the possession, use or benefit of such cart; and where the retail value of the goods obtained is less than one hundred dollars, shall be punished for a first offense by a fine not to exceed two hundred and fifty dollars, for a second offense by a fine of not less than one hundred nor more than five hundred dollars and for a third or subsequent offense by a fine of not more than five hundred dollars or imprisonment in a jail for not more than two years, or by both such fine and imprisonment. Where the retail value of the goods obtained equals or exceeds one hundred dollars, any violation of this section shall be punished by a fine of not more than one thousand dollars or by imprisonment in the house of correction for not more than town and one-half years, or by both such fine and imprisonment.

If the retail value of the goods obtained is less than one hundred dollars, this section shall apply to the exclusion of section thirty.

Law enforcement officers may arrest without warrant any person he has probable cause for believing has committed the offense of shoplifting as defined in this section. The statement of a merchant or his employee or agent that a person has violated a provision of this section shall constitute probable cause for arrest by any law enforcement officer authorized to make an arrest in such jurisdiction.

§ 30B. Distribution or possession of theft detection shielding device

[Added by 2014 Mass. Acts c. 451, § 2, effective Apr. 6, 2015.]

(a) A person shall be guilty of unlawful distribution of a theft detection shielding device if the person knowingly manufactures, sells, offers for sale or distributes a laminated or coated bag or other device intended to shield merchandise from detection by an electronic or magnetic theft detector.

(b) A person shall be guilty of unlawful possession of a theft detection shielding device if the person, with the intent to commit, aid or abet a theft, knowingly possesses a laminated or coated bag or device intended to shield merchandise from detection by an electronic or magnetic theft detector.

(c) A person shall be guilty of unlawful possession of a theft detection device deactivator or remover if the person knowingly possesses any tool or device designed or adapted to either: (i) allow the deactivation of a theft detection device, with the intent to use such tool or device to deactivate a theft detection device on merchandise without the permission of the merchant or person owning or lawfully holding said merchandise; or (ii) allow the removal of a theft detection device from merchandise, with the intent to use such tool or device to remove a theft detection device from merchandise without the permission of the merchant or person owning or lawfully holding said merchandise.

(d) A person shall be guilty of unlawful distribution of a theft detection device deactivator or remover if the person knowingly manufacturers, sells, offers for sale or distributes a tool or device designed or adapted to allow the deactivation of a theft detection device or to allow the removal of a theft detection device from merchandise, without the permission of the merchant or person owning or lawfully holding said merchandise.

(e) A person shall be guilty of unlawful deactivation or removal of a theft detection device if the person intentionally deactivates or removes a theft detection device from merchandise prior to purchase, in a retail establishment, with the intent to steal said merchandise.

(f) A violation of this section shall be punished by imprisonment in a house of correction for not more than 2½ years or by imprisonment in the state prison for not more than 5 years or by a fine of not more than $25,000, or by both such fine and imprisonment.

§ 30C. Counterfeiting of retail sales or return receipt or price ticket

[Added by 2014 Mass. Acts c. 451, § 2, effective Apr. 6, 2015.]

A person who, with intent to cheat or defraud a retailer, possesses, uses, utters, transfers, makes, alters, counterfeits or reproduces a retail sales or return receipt, price ticket or universal product code label shall be punished by imprisonment in a house of correction for not more than 2½ years or by imprisonment in the state prison for not more than 5 years or by a fine of not more than $10,000, or by both such fine and imprisonment.

§ 30D. Organized retail crime

[Added by 2014 Mass. Acts c. 451, § 2, effective Apr. 6, 2015.]

(a) For purposes of this section, "retail merchandise" shall mean 1 or more items of tangible personal property displayed, held, stored or offered for sale in a retail establishment.

(b) A person commits an organized retail crime if the person, acting in concert with 2 or more persons and within a 180 day period steals, embezzles or obtains by fraud, false pretense or other illegal means retail merchandise valued at more than $2,500 to resell or otherwise reenter such retail merchandise into commerce; provided, that a series of thefts from 1 or more mercantile establishments may be aggregated; provided further, that said person may be prosecuted in any county where a theft from a mercantile establishment occurred.

A violation of this subsection shall be punished by imprisonment in a state prison for not more than 10 years.

(c) A person commits an aggravated organized retail crime if the person, acting in concert with 2 or more persons and within a 180 day period, steals, embezzles or obtains by fraud, false pretense or other illegal means retail merchandise valued at more than $10,000 to resell or otherwise reenter such retail merchandise into commerce; provided, that a series of thefts from 1 or more mercantile establishments may be aggregated; provided further, that said person may be prosecuted in any county where a theft from a mercantile establishment occurred.

A violation of this subsection shall be punished by imprisonment in a state prison for not more than 15 years.

(d) A person shall be a leader of an organized retail theft enterprise if the person conspires with others as an organizer, supervisor, financier or manager, to commit an organized retail crime or an aggravated organized retail crime. A leader of organized retail crime may be punished by a fine of not more than $250,000 or 5 times the retail value of the merchandise seized at the time of the arrest, whichever is greater, or imprisonment in state prison for not more than 20 years, or both such fine and imprisonment.

§ 37. Fraudulent checks, etc.; drawing or uttering

Whoever, with intent to defraud, makes, draws, utters or delivers any check, draft or order for the payment of money upon any bank or other depositary, with knowledge that the maker or drawer has not sufficient funds or credit at such bank or other depositary for the payment of such instrument, although no express representation

1

is made in reference thereto, shall be guilty of attempted larceny, and if money or property or services are obtained thereby shall be guilty of larceny. As against the maker or drawer thereof, the making, drawing, uttering or delivery of such a check, draft or order, payment of which is refused by the drawee, shall be prima facie evidence of intent to defraud and of knowledge of insufficient funds in, or credit with, such bank or other depositary, unless the maker or drawer shall have paid the holder thereof the amount due thereon, together with all costs and protest fees, within two days after receiving notice that such check, draft or order has not been paid by the drawee. The word "credit", as used herein, shall be construed to mean an arrangement or understanding with the bank or depositary for the payment of such check, draft or order.

§ 37A. Misuse of credit cards; definitions

As used in sections thirty-seven A to thirty-seven C, inclusive, the following words shall have the following meanings, unless the context otherwise requires:

"Cardholder", the person named on the face of a credit card to whom. or for whose benefit the credit card is issued by an issuer.

"Credit card", any instrument or device, whether known as a credit card, credit plate, or by any other name, issued with or without fee by an issuer for the use of the cardholder in obtaining money, goods, services or anything else of value on credit.

"Expired credit card", a credit card which is no longer valid because the term shown on its face has elapsed.

"Falsely embosses", completion of a credit card, without the authorization of the named issuer, by adding any of the matter, other than the signature of the cardholder, which an issuer requires to appear on the credit card before it can be used by a cardholder.

"Falsely makes", making or drawing, in whole or in part, a device or instrument which purports to be the credit card of a named issuer but which is not such a credit card because the issuer did not authorize the making or drawing, or altering a credit card which was validly issued.

"Incomplete credit card", a credit card that does not contain all of the matter that must be stamped, embossed, imprinted or written on said card other than the signature, as required by the issuer before it can be used by a cardholder.

"Issuer", the business organization or financial institution which issues a credit card or his duly authorized agent.

"Receives" or "receiving", acquiring possession or control or accepting as security for a loan.

"Revoked credit card", a credit card which is no longer valid because permission to use it has been suspended or terminated by the issuer.

§ 37B. Misuse of credit cards; penalties; multiple possession, presumption; arrest

Whoever with intent to defraud, (a) makes or causes to be made, either directly or indirectly, any false statement as to a material fact in writing, knowing it to be false and with intent that A be relied on, respecting his identity or that of any other person, or his financial condition or that of any other person, for the purpose of procuring the issuance of a credit card, or (b) takes a credit card from the person, possession, custody or control of another without the cardholder's consent by any conduct which would constitute larceny, or who, with knowledge that it has been so taken, receives the credit card with intent to use it or to sell it, or to transfer k to a person other than the issuer or cardholder, or (e) receives a credit card that he knows to have been lost, mislaid, or delivered under a mistake as to the identity or address of the cardholder, and who retains possession with intent to use it or to sell it or to transfer it to a person other than the issuer or the cardholder, or (d) being a person other than the issuer or his authorized agent, sells a credit card, or buys a credit card from a person other than the issuer or his authorized agent, or (e) being a person other than the cardholder or a person authorized by him, signs a credit card, or (f) uses, for the purpose of obtaining money, goods, services or anything else of value, a credit card obtained or retained in violation of clauses (b) to (e), inclusive, or a credit card which he knows is forged, expired or revoked, where the value of money, goods or services obtained in violation of this section is not in excess of two hundred and fifty dollars, or (g) obtains money, goods, services or anything else of value by representing without the consent of the cardholder that he is said cardholder or by representing that he is the holder of a card and such card has not in fact been issued, where the value of money, goods or services obtained is not in excess of two hundred and fifty dollars, (h) being a person authorized by an issuer to furnish money, goods, services or anything else of value upon presentation of a credit card by the cardholder, or any agent or employees of such person, furnishes money, goods, services or anything else of value upon presentation of a credit card which he knows was obtained or retained in violation of clauses (b) to (e), inclusive, or a credit card which he knows is forged, expired or revoked where the value of the goods or services obtained is not in excess of two hundred and fifty dollars, or 6) being a person who is authorized by an issuer to furnish money, goods, or services or anything else of value upon presentation of a credit card by the cardholder, or any agent or employee of such person, fails to furnish money, goods, services or anything else of value which he represents in writing to the issuer that he has furnished, and the difference between the value of all money, goods, services and anything else of value actually furnished and the value represented to the issuer to have been furnished does not exceed two hundred and fifty dollars, or (j) receives money, goods, services or anything else of value obtained in violation of clauses (f) to (i), inclusive, or (k) makes a false statement in reporting a credit card to be lost or stolen, shall be punished by a fine of not more than five hundred dollars or by imprisonment in a jail or house of correction for not more than one year or both.

Whoever has in his possession or under his control stolen credit cards issued in the names of four or more other persons shall be presumed to have violated clause (b).

Whoever is discovered by a police officer in the act of violating this section, while such officer is lawfully at or within the place where such violation occurs, may be arrested without a warrant by such police officer.

§ 37C. Fraudulent use of credit cards to obtain money, goods or services; false embossment of credit cards, multiple possession, presumption; arrest

Whoever, with intent to defraud, (a) obtains control over a credit card as security for debt, or (b) receives a credit card which he knows was taken or retained under circumstances which constitute credit card theft or a violation of clauses (a) or (d) of section thirty-seven B or clause (a) of this section, or (c) falsely makes or falsely embosses a purported credit card or utters such a credit card, or (d) obtains money, goods, services or anything else of value by use of a credit card obtained or retained in violation of clauses (b) to (e), inclusive, of section thirty-seven B, or by use of a credit card which he knows is forged, expired or revoked, where the value of the money, goods or services obtained in violation of this section is in excess of two hundred and fifty dollars, or (e) obtains money, goods or services or anything else of value by representing without the consent of the cardholder that he is said cardholder or by representing that he is the holder of a card and such card has not in fact been issued, where the value of money, goods or services obtained in violation of this section is in excess of two hundred and fifty dollars, or (f) being a person authorized by an issuer to furnish money, goods, services or anything else of value upon presentation of a credit card which he knows was obtained in violation of subsections (b) to (e), inclusive, of section thirty-seven B, or a credit card which he knows is forged, expired or revoked, when the value of the money, goods or services obtained is in excess of two hundred and fifty dollars, or (g) being a person authorized by an issuer to furnish money, goods, services or anything else of value upon presentation of a credit card by the cardholder or any agent or employee of such person, fails to furnish money, goods or services or anything else of value which he represents in writing to the issuer that he has furnished, and the difference between the value of all money, goods, services and anything else of value actually furnished and the value represented to the issuer to have been furnished exceeds two hundred and fifty dollars, or (h) receives money, goods, services or anything else of value obtained in violation of subsections (f) or (g) of section thirty-seven B, or (i) possesses one or more incomplete credit cards, intending to complete them without the consent of the issuer, or 6) possesses, with knowledge of its character, machinery, plates or any other contrivance designed to reproduce instruments purporting to be the credit cards of an issuer who has not consented to the preparation of such credit cards, shall be punished by a fine of not more than two thousand dollars, or by imprisonment in a jail or house of correction for not more than two and one half years or in the state prison for not more than five years, or by both such fine and imprisonment.

Whoever has in his possession or under his control four or more credit cards which are falsely embossed shall be presumed to have violated clause (c).

Whoever is discovered by a police officer in the act of violating this section, while such officer is lawfully at or within the place where such violation occurs, may be arrested without a warrant by such police officer.

§ 41. Larceny of bicycles; second conviction

Whoever is convicted of a second offence of the larceny of a bicycle shall, if the value of the bicycle stolen exceeds ten dollars, be punished by imprisonment in the state prison for not more than five years or by a fine of not more than two hundred dollars or by imprisonment in jail for not more than two years.

§ 49. Possession of burglarious tools

Whoever makes or mends, or begins to make or mend, or knowingly has in his possession, an engine, machine, tool or implement adapted and designed for cutting through, forcing or breaking open a building, room, vault, safe or other depository, in order to steal therefrom money or other property, or to commit any other crime, knowing the same to be adapted and designed for the purpose aforesaid, with intent to use or employ or allow the same to be used or employed for such purpose, or whoever knowingly has in his possession a master key designed to fit more than one motor vehicle, with intent to use or employ the same to steal a motor vehicle or other property therefrom, shall be punished by imprisonment in the state prison for not more than ten years or by a fine of not more than one thousand dollars and imprisonment in jail for not more than two and one half years.

§ 60. Stolen goods; buying or receiving

[Added by 2014 Mass. Acts c. 451, § 3, effective Apr. 6, 2015.]

Whoever buys, receives or aids in the concealment of stolen or embezzled property, knowing it to have been stolen or embezzled, or whoever with intent to defraud buys, receives or aids in the concealment of property, knowing it to have been obtained from a person by false pretense of carrying on a business in the ordinary course of trade or whoever obtains or exerts control over property in the custody of any law enforcement agency, or any individual acting on behalf of a law enforcement agency, which is explicitly represented to such person by any law enforcement officer or any individual acting on behalf of a law enforcement agency as being stolen and who intends to deprive its rightful owner permanently of the use and enjoyment of said property shall be punished as follows: if the value of such property does not exceed $250, for a first offense by imprisonment in the house of correction for not more than 2½ years or by a fine of not more than $1,000; if the value of such property does not exceed $250, for a second or subsequent offense by imprisonment in the house of correction for not more than 2½ years or by imprisonment in the state prison for not more than 5 years or by a fine of not more than $5,000 or by both such fine and imprisonment; or if the value of such property exceeds $250 by imprisonment in the house of correction for not more than 2½ years or by imprisonment in the state prison for not more than 5 years or by a fine of not more than $5,000 or by both such fine and imprisonment.

It shall not be a defense that the property was obtained by means other than through the commission of a theft offense if the property was explicitly represented to the accused as having been obtained through the commission of a theft offense.

§ 75. Obtaining property by trick

Whoever, by a game, device, sleight of hand, pretended fortune telling or by any trick or other means by the use of cards or other implements or instruments, fraudulently obtains from another person property of any description shall be punished as in the case of larceny of property of like value.

§ 101. Definitions related to Secs. 101–102D

[Amended by 2010 Mass. Acts c. 160, § 6, effective July 15, 2010.]

For the purposes of sections 101 to 102D, inclusive, the following terms shall have the following meanings, unless otherwise clearly required:—

"Ammunition", cartridges or cartridge cases, primers (igniter), bullets or propellant powder designed for use in any weapon utilizing a propellant including, but not limited to, ammunition produced by or for the military for national defense and security.

"Biological weapon", any microorganism, virus, infectious substance or biological product that may be engineered as a result of biotechnology, or any naturally occurring or bioengineered component of any such microorganism, virus, infectious substance or biological product, except if intended for a purpose not prohibited under this chapter or chapter 265, specifically prepared in a manner to cause death, disease or other biological malfunction in a human, animal, plant or another living organism, deterioration of food, water, equipment supplies or material of any kind, or deleterious alteration of the environment.

"Black powder", a compound or mixture of sulfur, charcoal and an alkali nitrate including, but not limited to, potassium or sodium nitrate.

"Chemical weapon", (i) a toxic chemical or substance, including the precursors to any toxic chemical or substance; and (ii) ammunition or a device designed to cause death or bodily harm by means of the release of a toxic chemical or substance.

"Delivery system", any equipment designed or adapted for use in connection with the deployment of chemical, biological or nuclear weapons.

"Denial of access", contamination to an area, including any structures thereon, which poses a health risk to humans, animals or plants and which precludes the safe use of such area until the contaminant becomes inactive, decays or is removed.

"Destructive or incendiary device or substance", an explosive, article or device designed or adapted to cause physical harm to persons or property by means of fire, explosion, deflagration or detonation and consisting of substance capable of being ignited, whether or not contrived to ignite or explode automatically.

"Element", a substance that is made entirely from 1 type of atom.

"Explosive", any element, compound or mixture that is manufactured, designed or used to produce an explosion and that contains an oxidizer, fuel or other ingredient, in such proportion, quantity or packing that an ignition by fire, friction, concussion, percussion or detonation of the element or of any part of the compound or mixture may cause such a sudden generation of highly heated gases that the resultant gaseous pressures, release of heat or fragmentation is capable of producing destructive effects on contiguous objects or of destroying life or causing bodily harm including, but not limited to, all material which is classified as division 1.1, 1.2, 1.3, 1.4, 1.5 or 1.6 explosives by the United States Department of Transportation or listed pursuant to 18 U.S.C. 841(d) and 27 C.F.R. 555.23. Explosive shall not include a pyrotechnic, small arms ammunition, small arms ammunition primers, smokeless powder weighing less than 50 pounds and black powder weighing less than 5 pounds, unless possessed or used for an illegal purpose.

"Hoax explosive", "hoax destructive or incendiary device or substance" or "hoax chemical, biological or nuclear weapon", any device, article or substance that would cause a person to reasonably believe that such device, article or substance is: (i) an explosive; (ii) a destructive or incendiary device or substance; or (iii) a chemical, biological or nuclear weapon, harmful radioactive substance or poison capable of causing bodily injury which is actually an inoperable facsimile.

"Nuclear weapon", a device designed for the purpose of causing bodily injury, death or denial of access through the release of radiation or radiological material either by propagation of nuclear fission or by means of any other energy source.

"Oxidizer", a substance that yields oxygen readily to stimulate the combustion of organic matter or other fuel.

"Pyrotechnic", any commercially manufactured combustible or explosive composition or manufactured article designed and prepared for the purpose of producing an audible effect or a visible display and regulated by chapter 148 including, but not limited to: (i) fireworks, firecrackers; (ii) flares, fuses and torpedoes, so-called, and similar signaling devices.

"Small arms ammunition", any shotgun, rifle, pistol, or revolver cartridge, and cartridges for propellant-actuated power devices and industrial guns.

"Smokeless powder", a rapid-burning solid material containing nitrocellulose used as a propellant.

§ 102. Possession or control of incendiary device or material; possession of hoax device or material; penalty

[Amended by 2010 Mass. Acts c. 160, § 6, effective July 15, 2010.]

(a) Whoever, without lawful authority, has in his possession or under his control:

(i) any substance, material, article, explosive or ingredient which, alone or in combination, could be used to make a destructive or incendiary device or substance and who intends to make a destructive or incendiary device or substance; or

(ii) any substance, material, article, explosive or ingredient which, alone or in combination, could be used to make a chemical, biological or nuclear weapon and who intends to make a chemical, biological or nuclear weapon, shall be punished by imprisonment in the house of correction for not more than 2 and one-half years or in state prison for not less than 5 years nor more than 10 years or by a fine of not more than $25,000, or by both such fine and imprisonment. It shall not be a defense to a violation of this subsection that the defendant did not possess or have under his control every substance, material, article, explosive or ingredient, or combination thereof, required to make a complete and functional destructive or incendiary device or substance or chemical, biological or nuclear weapon.

(b) Whoever, without lawful authority, has in his possession or uses or places, or causes another to knowingly or unknowingly possess, use or place, any hoax explosive, hoax destructive or incendiary device or substance or any hoax chemical, biological or nuclear weapon, with the intent that such hoax explosive, device or substance or weapon be used to cause anxiety, unrest, fear or personal discomfort to any person or group of persons, shall be punished by imprisonment in the house of correction for not more than 2 and one-half years or by imprisonment in the state prison for not more than 5 years or by a fine of not more than $10,000, or by both such fine and imprisonment.

(c) Whoever, without lawful authority, has in his possession or under his control any explosive or any destructive or incendiary device or substance shall be punished by imprisonment for not more than 2 and one-half years in the house of correction or for not less than 10 years nor more than 20 years in the state prison or by a fine of not more than $25,000, or by both such fine and imprisonment.

§ 102A. Throwing, secreting, launching or placing of incendiary device; intent; punishment

[Amended by 2010 Mass. Acts c. 160, § 6, effective July 15, 2010.]

Whoever, without lawful authority, secretes, throws, launches or otherwise places an explosive or a destructive or incendiary device or substance with the intent: (i) to cause fear, panic or apprehension in any person; or (ii) to ignite, explode or discharge such explosive or such destructive or incendiary device or substance; or (iii) to release or discharge any chemical, biological or nuclear weapon, shall be punished by imprisonment for not more than 2 and one-half years in the house of correction or for not less than 10 years nor more than 25 years in the state prison or by a fine of not more than $25,000, or by both such fine and imprisonment.

§ 102A½. Repealed

[Repealed by 2010 Mass. Acts c. 160, § 6.]

§ 102B. Malicious explosion

[Amended by 2010 Mass. Acts c. 160, § 6, effective July 15, 2010.]

Whoever, without lawful authority, willfully discharges, ignites or explodes any destructive or incendiary device or substance shall be punished by imprisonment in the state prison by not less than 15 years nor more than 25 years or by a fine of $50,000 or by both such fine and imprisonment.

§ 102C. Biological, chemical or nuclear weapon or delivery system; possession; punishment

[Amended by 2010 Mass. Acts c. 160, § 6, effective July 15, 2010; 2010 Mass. Acts c. 359, § 33, effective Oct. 15, 2010.]

Whoever, without lawful authority, knowingly develops, produces, stockpiles, acquires, transports, possesses, controls, places, secretes or uses any biological, chemical or nuclear weapon or delivery system, with the intent to cause death, bodily injury or property damage, shall be punished by imprisonment in the house of correction for not more than 2 and one-half years or by imprisonment in the state prison for not more than 25 years or by a fine of not more than $50,000, or by both such fine and imprisonment.

§ 102D. Notice of seizure of explosive or incendiary device resulting from a violation of Secs. 102–102C; restitution

[Added by 2010 Mass. Acts c. 160, § 6, effective July 15, 2010.]

(a) Notice of the seizure of an explosive, destructive or incendiary device or substance, any weapon or the component parts thereof, in violation of any provision of section 102 to 102C, inclusive, shall be sent forthwith to the state fire marshal by the officer who made such seizure. The marshal may, in his sole discretion, render safe or direct any other official to assist him in rendering safe any item so seized, if such item cannot be safely kept pending trial. Upon final conviction of such person, such explosive, device, substance or weapon, or component parts thereof, shall be adjudged forfeited to the commonwealth and be disposed of by the marshal or his authorized representative.

(b) Upon conviction for a violation of sections 102 to 102C, inclusive, the court shall conduct a hearing to ascertain the extent of costs incurred, damages and financial loss suffered by local, county or state public safety agencies and the amount of property damage caused as a result of the violation of this section, if any. A person found guilty of violating sections 102 to 102C, inclusive, shall, in all cases, in addition to any other punishment, be ordered to make restitution to the local, county or state government for any costs incurred, damages and financial loss sustained as a result of the commission of such offense. Restitution shall be imposed in addition to incarceration or fine; provided, however, that the court shall consider the defendant's present and future ability to pay in its determinations regarding a fine. In determining the amount, time and method of payment of restitution, the court shall consider the financial resources of the defendant and the burden restitution will impose on the defendant.

§ 120. Entry upon private property after being forbidden as trespass; prima facie evidence; penalties; arrest; tenants or occupants excepted

Whoever, without right enters or remains in or upon the dwelling house, buildings, boats or improved or enclosed land, wharf, or pier of another, or enters or remains in a school bus, as defined in section 1 of chapter 90, after having been forbidden so to do by the person who has lawful control of said premises, whether directly or by notice posted thereon, or in violation of a court order pursuant to section thirty-four B of chapter two hundred and eight or section three or four of chapter two hundred and nine A, shall be punished by a fine of not more than one hundred dollars or by imprisonment for not more than thirty days or both such fine and imprisonment. Proof that a court has given notice of such a court order to the alleged offender shall be prima facie evidence that the notice requirement of this section has been met. A person who is found committing such trespass may be arrested by a sheriff, deputy sheriff, constable or police officer and kept in custody in a convenient place, not more than twenty-four hours, Sunday excepted, until a complaint can be made against him for the offence, and he be taken upon a warrant issued upon such complaint.

This section shall not apply to tenants or occupants of residential premises who, having rightfully entered said premises at the commencement of the tenancy or occupancy, remain therein after such tenancy or occupancy has been or is alleged to have been terminated. The owner or landlord of said premises may recover possession thereof only through appropriate civil proceedings.

§ 120E½. Reproductive health care facilities

[Amended by 2007 Mass. Acts c. 155, §§ 1–2, effective Nov. 13, 2007; 2014 Mass. Acts c. 197, effective July 30, 2014.]

(a) As used in this section, the following words shall have the following meanings unless the context clearly requires otherwise:

"Driveway", an entry from a public street to a public or private parking area used by a reproductive health care facility.

"Entrance", a door to a reproductive health care facility that directly abuts the public sidewalk; provided, however, that if the door does not directly abut the public sidewalk, the "entrance" shall be the point at which the public sidewalk intersects with a pathway leading to the door.

"Impede", to obstruct, block, detain or render passage impossible, unsafe or unreasonably difficult.

"Law enforcement official", a duly authorized member of a law enforcement agency, including a member of a municipal, metropolitan or state police department, sheriffs or deputy sheriffs.

"Reproductive health care facility", a place, other than within or upon the grounds of a hospital, where abortions are offered or performed including, but not limited to, the building, grounds and driveway of the facility and a parking lot in which the facility has an ownership or leasehold interest.

(b) A law enforcement official may order the immediate withdrawal of 1 or more individuals who have on that day substantially impeded access to or departure from an entrance or driveway to a reproductive health care facility. A withdrawal order issued pursuant to this section shall be in writing and shall include the following statements: (i) the individual or individuals have substantially impeded access to or departure from the reproductive health care facility; (ii) the individual or individuals so ordered shall, under the penalty of arrest and prosecution, immediately withdraw and cease to stand or be located within at least 25 feet of an entrance or driveway to the reproductive health care facility; and (iii) the order shall remain in place for 8 hours or until the close of business of the reproductive health facility, whichever is earlier. This subsection shall apply during the business hours of a reproductive health care facility. This subsection shall also apply only if the 25-foot boundary is clearly marked and subsections (a) through (c), inclusive, of this section are posted outside of the reproductive health care facility.

(c) A person who fails to comply with a withdrawal order pursuant to subsection (b) shall be punished, for the first offense, by a fine of not more than $500 or not more than 3 months in a jail or house of correction or by both such fine and imprisonment and, for each subsequent offense, by a fine of not less than $500 nor more than $5,000 or not more than 2½ years in a jail or house of correction or by both such fine and imprisonment.

(d) A person who, by force, physical act or threat of force, intentionally injures or intimidates or attempts to injure or intimidate a person who attempts to access or depart from a reproductive health care facility shall be punished, for the first offense, by a fine of not more than $2,000 or not more than 1 year in a jail or house of correction or by both such fine and imprisonment and, for each subsequent offense, by a fine of not less than $10,000 nor more than $50,000 or not more than 2½ years in a jail or house of correction or not more than 5 years in a state prison or by both such fine and imprisonment. For the purpose of this subsection, "intimidate" shall mean to place a person in reasonable apprehension of bodily harm to that person or another.

(e) A person who impedes a person's access to or departure from a reproductive health care facility with the intent to interfere with that person's ability to provide, support the provision of or obtain services at the reproductive health care facility shall be punished, for the first offense, by a fine of not more than $1,000 or not more than 6 months in a jail or house of correction or by both such fine and imprisonment and, for each subsequent offense, by a fine of not less than $5,000 nor more than $25,000 or not more than 2½ years in a jail or house of correction or not more than 5 years in the state prison or by both such fine and imprisonment.

(f) A person who knowingly impedes or attempts to impede a person or a vehicle attempting to access or depart from a reproductive health care facility shall be punished, for the first offense, by a fine of not more than $500 or not more than 3 months in a jail or house of correction or by both such fine and imprisonment and, for each subsequent offense, by a fine of not less than $1,000 nor more than $5,000 or not more than 2½ years in a jail or house of correction or by both such fine and imprisonment.

(g) A person who recklessly interferes with the operation of a vehicle that attempts to enter, exit or park at a reproductive health care facility shall be punished, for the first offense, by a fine of not more than $500 or not more than 3 months in a jail or house of correction or by both such fine and imprisonment and, for each subsequent offense, by a fine of not less than $1,000 nor more than $5,000 or not more than 2½ years in a jail or house of correction or by both such fine and imprisonment.

(h) A person who fails to comply with a withdrawal order pursuant to said subsection (b) or who is found in violation of subsection (c), (d), (e), (f) or (g) may be arrested without a warrant by a law enforcement official.

(i) If a person or entity fails to comply with a withdrawal order pursuant to subsection (b) or who is found in violation of subsection (c), (d), (e), (f) or (g), an aggrieved person or entity or the attorney general or both may commence a civil action. The civil action shall be commenced either in the superior court for the county in which the conduct complained of occurred or in the superior court for the county in which the person or entity complained of resides or has a principal place of business.

(j) In an action pursuant to subsection (i), a court may award as remedies: (1) temporary, preliminary and permanent injunctive relief; (2) compensatory and punitive damages; and (3) costs, attorneys' fees and expert witness fees. In an action brought by the attorney general pursuant to subsection (i), the court may also award civil penalties against each defendant in an amount not exceeding: (A) $5,000 for a nonviolent violation and $7,500 for other first violations; and (B) $7,500 for a subsequent nonviolent violation and $12,500 for any other subsequent violation.

(k) A violation of an injunction entered by a court in an action brought pursuant to subsection (i) shall be a criminal offense under section 11J of chapter 12.

§ 126B. Walls, signs, gravestones, etc.; penalty for "tagging"

Whoever sprays or applies paint or places a sticker upon a building, wall, fence, sign, tablet, gravestone, monument or other object or thing on a public way or adjoined to it, or in public view, or on private property, such person known or commonly known as "taggers" and such conduct or activity known or commonly known as "tagging", or other words or phrases associated to such persons, conduct or activity, and either as an individual or in a group, joins together with said group, with the intent to deface, mar, damage, mark or destroy such property, shall be punished by imprisonment in a house of correction for not more than two years or by a fine of not less than fifteen hundred dollars or not more than three times the value of such damage to the property so defaced, marked, marred, damaged or destroyed, whichever is greater, or both fine and imprisonment and shall also be required to pay for the removal or obliteration of such "tagging" or to obliterate such "tagging"; provided, however that when a fine is levied pursuant to the value of the property marred, defaced, marked, damaged or destroyed or where the cost of removal or obliteration is assessed the court shall, after conviction, conduct an evidentiary hearing to ascertain the value of the property so defaced, marked, marred, damaged or destroyed or to ascertain the cost of the removal or obliteration. A police officer may arrest any person for commission of the offenses prohibited by this section without a warrant if said police officer has probable cause to believe that said person has committed the offenses prohibited by this section.

Upon conviction for said offense the individual's driver[']s license shall be suspended for one year. If the individual convicted of defacing or vandalizing the real or personal property of another is under the age of sixteen then one year shall be added to the minimum age eligibility for driving.

§ 127. Personalty; malicious or wanton injuries

Whoever destroys or injures the personal property, dwelling house or building of another in any manner or by any means not particularly described or mentioned in this chapter shall, if such destruction or injury is wilful and malicious, be punished by imprisonment in the state prison for not more than ten years or by a fine of three thousand dollars or three times the value of the property so destroyed or injured, whichever is greater and imprisonment in jail for not more than two and one-half years; or if such destruction or injury is wanton, shall be punished by a fine of fifteen hundred dollars or three times the value of the property so destroyed or injured, whichever is greater, or by imprisonment for not more than two and one-half years; if the value of the property so destroyed or injured is not alleged to exceed two hundred and fifty dollars, the punishment shall be by a fine of three times the value of the damage or injury to such property or by imprisonment for not more than two and one-half months; provided, however, that where a fine is levied pursuant to the value of the property destroyed or injured, the court shall, after conviction, conduct an evidentiary hearing to ascertain the value of the property so destroyed or injured. The words "personal property", as used in this section, shall also include electronically processed or stored data, either tangible or intangible, and data while in transit.

§ 127B. Actions for civil rights violations; liability

Any person incurring injury to his person or damage or loss to his property as a result of conduct in violation of section one hundred and twenty-seven A or of section thirty-nine of chapter two hundred and sixty-five shall have a civil action to secure injunctive relief, special and general damages, reasonable attorney fees and costs against the person whose conduct has violated said section one hundred and twenty-seven A of this chapter or of section thirty-nine of chapter two hundred and sixty-five. In any such action the burden of proof shall be the same as in other civil actions for similar relief.

Notwithstanding any other provision of law to the contrary, the parent or legal guardian of an unemancipated minor child shall be liable for any judgment rendered against such minor under the provisions of this section.

Chapter 267. Forgery and Crimes Against the Currency

§ 1. False or forged records, certificates, returns, attestations and other writings

Whoever, with intent to injure or defraud, falsely makes, alters, forges or counterfeits a public record, or a certificate, return or attestation of a clerk or register of a court, public register, notary public, justice of the peace, town clerk or any other public officer, in relation to a matter wherein such certificate, return or attestation may be received as legal proof; or a charter, deed, will, testament, bond or writing obligatory, power of attorney, policy of insurance, bill of lading, bill of exchange or promissory note; or an order, acquittance or discharge for money or other property or a credit card or an instrument described as a United States Dollar Traveller's Check or Cheque, purchased from a bank or other financially responsible institution, the purpose of which is a source of ready money on cashing the instrument without identification other than the signature of the purchaser; or an acceptance of a bill of exchange, or an endorsement or assignment of a bill of exchange or promissory note for the payment of money; or an accountable receipt for money, goods or other property; or a stock certificate, or any evidence or muniment of title to property; or a certificate of title, duplicate certificate of title, certificate issued in place of a duplicate certificate, the registration book, entry book, or any indexes provided for by chapter one hundred and eighty-five, or the docket of the recorder; shall be punished by imprisonment in the state prison for not more than ten years or in jail for not more than two years.

§ 5. Uttering false or forged records, deeds or other writings

Whoever, with intent to injure or defraud, utters and publishes as true a false, forged or altered record, deed, instrument or other writing mentioned in the four preceding sections, knowing the same to be false, forged or altered, shall be punished by imprisonment in the state prison for not more than ten years or in jail for not more than two years.

Chapter 268. Crimes Against Public Justice

§ 1. Perjury

[Amended by 2006 Mass. Acts c. 48, § 2, effective Mar. 30, 2006.]

Whoever, being lawfully required to depose the truth in a judicial proceeding or in a proceeding in a course of justice, willfully swears or affirms falsely in a matter material to the issue or point in question, or whoever, being required by law to take an oath or affirmation, willfully swears or affirms falsely in a matter relative to which such oath or affirmation is required, shall be guilty of perjury. Whoever commits perjury on the trial of an indictment for a capital crime shall be punished by imprisonment in the state prison for life or for any term of years, and whoever commits perjury in any other case shall be punished by imprisonment in the state prison for not more than twenty years or by a fine of not more than one thousand dollars or by imprisonment in jail for not more than two and one half years, or by both such fine and imprisonment in jail.

An indictment or complaint for violation of this section alleging that, in any proceedings before or ancillary to any court or grand jury proceedings relating to an indictment or complaint for the commission of a violent crime, as defined in section 121 of chapter 140, the defendant under oath has knowingly made 2 or more declarations, which are inconsistent to the degree that 1 of them is necessarily false, need not specify which declaration is false if: (1) each declaration was material to the point in question and (2) each declaration was made within the period of the statute of limitations for the offense charged under this section. In any prosecution under this section, the falsity of a declaration set forth in the indictment or complaint shall be established sufficient for conviction by proof that the defendant, while under oath, made irreconcilably contradictory declarations material to the point in question. If, in the same continuous court or grand jury proceeding in which a declaration is made, the person making the declaration admits to such declaration to be false, such admission shall bar prosecution under this section if, at the time the admission is made, the declaration has not substantially affected the proceeding, or it has not become manifest that such falsity has been or will be exposed. It shall be a defense to an indictment or complaint made pursuant to this section that the defendant, at the time he made each declaration, believed each such declaration to be true or its falsity was the result of a good faith mistake or error.

§ 2. Subornation of perjury

Whoever is guilty of subornation of perjury, by procuring another person to commit perjury, shall be punished as for perjury.

§ 3. Attempt to procure another to commit perjury

Whoever attempts to incite or procure another person to commit perjury, although no perjury is committed, shall be punished by imprisonment in the state prison for not more than five years or in jail for not more than one year.

§ 4. Testimony creating presumption of perjury; commitment; recognizance; witnesses bound over; notice to district attorney

If it appears to a court of record that a party or a witness who has been legally sworn and examined, or has made an affidavit, in any proceeding in a court or course of justice has so testified as to create a reasonable presumption that he has committed perjury therein, the court may forthwith commit him or may require him to recognize with sureties for his appearance to answer to an indictment for perjury; and thereupon the witnesses to establish such perjury may, if present, be bound over to the superior court, and notice of the proceedings shall forthwith be given to the district attorney.

§ 13B. Intimidation of witnesses, jurors and persons furnishing information in connection with criminal proceedings

[Amended by 2006 Mass. Acts c. 48, § 3, effective Mar. 30, 2006; 2010 Mass. Acts c. 92, § 11, effective May 3, 2010; 2010 Mass. Acts c. 256, § 120, effective Nov. 4, 2010; 2018 Mass. Acts c. 69, § 155, effective Apr. 13, 2018.]

(a) As used in this section, the following words shall have the following meanings unless the context clearly requires otherwise:—

"Investigator", an individual or group of individuals lawfully authorized by a department or agency of the federal government or any political subdivision thereof or a department or agency of the commonwealth or any political subdivision thereof to conduct or engage in an investigation of, prosecution for, or defense of a violation of the laws of the United States or of the commonwealth in the course of such individual's or group's official duties.

"Harass", to engage in an act directed at a specific person or group of persons that seriously alarms or annoys such person or group of persons and would cause a reasonable person or group of persons to suffer substantial emotional distress including, but not limited to, an act conducted by mail or by use of a telephonic or telecommunication device or electronic communication device including, but not limited to, a device that transfers signs, signals, writing, images, sounds, data or intelligence of any nature, transmitted in whole or in part by a wire, radio, electromagnetic, photo-electronic or photo-optical system including, but not limited to, electronic mail, internet communications, instant messages and facsimile communications.

(b) Whoever willfully, either directly or indirectly: (i) threatens, attempts or causes physical, emotional or economic injury or property damage to; (ii) conveys a gift, offer or promise of anything of value to; or (iii) misleads, intimidates or harasses another person who is a: (A) witness or potential witness; (B) person who is or was aware of information, records, documents or objects that relate to a violation of a criminal law or a violation of conditions of probation, parole, bail or other court order; (C) judge, juror, grand juror, attorney, victim witness advocate, police officer, correction officer, federal agent, investigator, clerk, court officer, court reporter, court interpreter, probation officer or parole officer; (D) person who is or was attending or a person who had made known an intention to attend a proceeding described in this section; or (E) family member of a person described in this section, with the intent to or with reckless disregard for the fact that it may; (1) impede, obstruct, delay, prevent or otherwise interfere with: a criminal investigation at any stage, a grand jury proceeding, a dangerousness hearing, a motion hearing, a trial or other criminal proceeding of any type or a parole hearing, parole violation proceeding or probation violation proceeding; or an administrative hearing or a probate or family court proceeding, juvenile proceeding, housing proceeding, land proceeding, clerk's hearing, court-ordered mediation or any other civil proceeding of any type; or (2) punish, harm or otherwise retaliate against any such person described in this section for such person or such person's family member's participation in any of the proceedings described in this section, shall be punished by imprisonment in the state prison for not more than 10 years or by imprisonment in the house of correction for not more than 2 ½ years or by a fine of not less than $1,000 or more than $5,000 or by both such fine and imprisonment. If the proceeding in which the misconduct is directed at is the investigation or prosecution of a crime punishable by life imprisonment or the parole of a person convicted of a crime punishable by life imprisonment, such person shall be punished by imprisonment in the state prison for not more than 20 years or by imprisonment in the house of corrections for not more than 2 ½ years or by a fine of not more than $10,000 or by both such fine and imprisonment.

(c) A prosecution under this section may be brought in the county in which the criminal investigation, trial or other proceeding was being conducted or took place or in the county in which the alleged conduct constituting the offense occurred.

§ 14B. Witnesses at criminal proceedings; discharge, etc., from employment

Any person who is a victim of a crime upon which an accusatory instrument is based, or is subpoenaed to attend a criminal action as a witness and who notifies his employer of such subpoena prior to the day of his attendance, shall not be subject to discharge or penalty by said employer on account of his absence from employment by reason of such witness service. An employer shall not subject an employee to discharge or penalty or the threat of discharge or penalty on account of the absence of such employee from employment by reason of his attendance as a witness at a criminal action. An employer who violates the provisions of this section shall be punished by a fine of not more than two hundred dollars or by imprisonment for not more than one month, or both such fine and imprisonment.

§ 15. Aiding escape from a correctional institution or jail; rescue

Whoever conveys into a correctional institution of the commonwealth or into a jail, house of correction, house of reformation or like place of confinement, a disguise, instrument, tool, weapon or other thing which is adapted or useful to aid a prisoner in making his escape, with intent to aid the escape of a prisoner, or whoever, by any means, aids or assists such prisoner in endeavoring to escape therefrom, whether such escape is effected or attempted or not, and whoever forcibly or fraudulently rescues or attempts to rescue a prisoner held in custody upon a conviction or charge of crime, shall, if the person whose escape or rescue was effected or intended is a convict under sentence to the state prison or is charged with a felony, be punished by a fine of not more than five hundred dollars or by imprisonment in the state prison for not more than ten years; but if he is a convict under sentence to any other of said institutions, by imprisonment in the state prison for not more than seven years; and if he is charged with a misdemeanor, then by a fine of not more than five hundred dollars or by imprisonment in jail for not more than two years.

§ 15A. Escape from city or town jails; penalties

Whoever, after lawfully being placed in custody in a jail of a city or town, escapes from any such jail shall be punished by imprisonment in a jail or house of correction for not more than two and one-half years, or by a fine of not more than five hundred dollars, or both.

§ 16. Escape or attempt to escape, or failure to return from temporary release or furlough

[Amended by 2010 Mass. Acts c. 256, § 121, effective Nov. 4, 2010.]

A prisoner of any penal institution including a prisoner who is held in custody for a court appearance or a person committed under the provisions of section five or six of chapter one hundred and twenty-three A to a treatment center or branch thereof described in sections two and four of said chapter one hundred and twenty-three A, or a prisoner committed to any jail or correctional institution under a lawful order of a court, who escapes or attempts to escape from any such institution or from land appurtenant thereto, or from any courthouse or from land appurtenant thereto or from the custody of any officer thereof while being conveyed to or from said institution, center or branch, or who knowingly disables or attempts to disable or defeat electronic monitoring of the prisoner, or fails to return from any temporary release from said institution under the provisions of section ninety A of chapter one hundred and twenty-seven, or fails to return from any temporary release from said institution, center or branch, may be pursued and recaptured and shall be punished by imprisonment in the state prison for not more than ten years or by imprisonment in a jail or house of correction for not more than two and one-half years.

§ 17. Aiding escape from officer or person having custody

Whoever aids or assists a prisoner in escaping or attempting to escape from an officer or person who has the lawful custody of such prisoner shall be punished by a fine of not more than five hundred dollars or by imprisonment for not more than two years.

§ 32. Interference or tampering with police or fire signal systems, or motorist highway emergency aid call boxes; false alarms or calls

Whoever opens a signal box connected with a police signal system for the purpose of giving, or causing to be given, a false alarm, or interferes in any way with such box by breaking, cutting, injuring or defacing the same; or whoever, without authority, opens, tampers or meddles with such box, or with any part or parts thereof, or with the police signal wires, or with anything connected therewith, or with such purpose, wantonly and without cause tampers or meddles with a signal box connected with a fire signal system or with any part or thing connected therewith, shall be subject to immediate arrest and shall be punished by a fine of not less than five hundred nor more than one thousand dollars, or by imprisonment for not more than two years, or both.

Whoever opens a motorist highway emergency aid call box on any state highway connected with a highway emergency signal system for the purpose of giving or causing to be given a false call for aid, or interferes in any way with such box by breaking, cutting, injuring or defacing the same; or, without authority, opens, tampers or meddles with such box, or with any part or parts thereof or with anything connected therewith, or, with such purpose, wantonly and without cause tampers or meddles with a motorist highway emergency aid call box or with any part or thing connected therewith, shall be punished by a fine of not less than one hundred dollars nor more than five hundred dollars.

§ 32B. Resisting arrest

(a) A person commits the crime of resisting arrest if he knowingly prevents or attempts to prevent a police officer, acting under color of his official authority, from effecting an arrest of the actor or another, by:

(1) using or threatening to use physical force or violence against the police officer or another; or

(2) using any other means which creates a substantial risk of causing bodily injury to such police officer or another.

(b) It shall not be a defense to a prosecution under this section that the police officer was attempting to make an arrest which was unlawful, if he was acting under color of his official authority, and in attempting to make the arrest he was not resorting to unreasonable or excessive force giving rise to the right of self-defense. A police officer acts under the color of his official authority when, in the regular course of assigned duties, he is called upon to make, and does make, a judgment in good faith based upon surrounding facts and circumstances that an arrest should be made by him.

(c) The term "police officer" as used in this section shall mean a police officer in uniform or, if out of uniform, one who has identified himself by exhibiting his credentials as such police officer while attempting such arrest.

(d) Whoever violates this section shall be punished by imprisonment in a jail or house of correction for not more than two and one-half years or a fine of not more than five hundred dollars, or both.

§ 34A. Furnishing false name or social security number to law enforcement officer or official; penalty; restitution

[Amended by 2018 Mass. Acts c. 69, § 156, effective Apr. 13, 2018.]

Whoever knowingly and willfully furnishes a false name, Social Security number, date of birth, home address, mailing address or phone number, or other information as may be requested for the purposes of establishing the person's identity, to a law enforcement officer or law enforcement official following an arrest shall be punished by a fine of not more than $1,000 or by imprisonment in a house of correction for not more than 1 year or by both such fine and imprisonment. Such sentence shall run from and after any sentence imposed as a result of the underlying offense. The court may order that restitution be paid to persons whose identity has been assumed and who have suffered monetary losses as a result of a violation of this section.

§ 40. Reports of crimes to law enforcement officials

Whoever knows that another person is a victim of aggravated rape, rape, murder, manslaughter or armed robbery and is at the scene of said crime shall, to the extent that said person can do so without danger or peril to himself or others, report said crime to an appropriate law enforcement official as soon as reasonably practicable. Any person who violates this section shall be punished by a fine of not less than five hundred nor more than two thousand and five hundred dollars.

Chapter 269. Crimes Against Public Peace

§ 10. Carrying dangerous weapons; possession of machine gun or sawed-off shotguns

[Amended by 2006 Mass. Acts c. 48, §§ 5–7, effective Mar. 30, 2006; 2014 Mass. Acts c. 284, §§ 89, 92, effective Aug. 11, 2014; 2014 Mass. Acts c. 284, § 90, effective Jan. 1, 2015. Bracketed text in subsection (m) stricken by 2014 Mass. Acts c. 284, § 91, effective Jan. 1, 2021.]

(a) Whoever, except as provided or exempted by statute, knowingly has in his possession; or knowingly has under his control in a vehicle; a firearm, loaded or unloaded, as defined in section one hundred and twenty-one of chapter one hundred and forty without either:

(1) being present in or on his residence or place of business; or

(2) having in effect a license to carry firearms issued under section one hundred and thirty-one of chapter one hundred and forty; or

(3) having in effect a license to carry firearms issued under section one hundred and thirty-one F of chapter one hundred and forty; or

(4) having complied with the provisions of sections one hundred and twenty-nine C and one hundred and thirty-one G of chapter one hundred and forty; or

(5) having complied as to possession of an air rifle or BB gun with the requirements imposed by section twelve B; and whoever knowingly has in his possession; or knowingly has under control in a vehicle; a rifle or shotgun, loaded or unloaded, without either:

(1) being present in or on his residence or place of business; or

(2) having in effect a license to carry firearms issued under section one hundred and thirty-one of chapter one hundred and forty; or

(3) having in effect a license to carry firearms issued under section one hundred and thirty-one F of chapter one hundred and forty; or

(4) having in effect a firearms identification card issued under section one hundred and twenty-nine B of chapter one hundred and forty; or

(5) having complied with the requirements imposed by section one hundred and twenty-nine C of chapter one hundred and forty upon ownership or possession of rifles and shotguns; or

(6) having complied as to possession of an air rifle or BB gun: with the requirements imposed by section twelve B; shall be punished by imprisonment in the state prison for not less than two and one half years nor more than five years, or for not less than 18 months nor more than two and one half years in a jail or house of correction. The sentence imposed on such person shall not be reduced to less than 18 months, nor suspended, nor shall any person convicted under this subsection be eligible for probation, parole, work release, or furlough or receive any deduction from his sentence for good conduct until he shall have served 18 months of such sentence; provided, however, that the commissioner of correction may on the recommendation of the warden, superintendent, or other person in charge of a correctional institution, grant to an offender committed under this subsection a temporary release in the custody of an officer of such institution for the following purposes only: to attend the funeral of a relative; to visit a critically ill relative; or to obtain emergency medical or psychiatric service unavailable at said institution. Prosecutions commenced under this subsection shall neither be continued without a finding nor placed on file.

No person having in effect a license to carry firearms for any purpose, issued under section one hundred and thirty-one or section one hundred and thirty-one F of chapter one hundred and forty shall be deemed to be in violation of this section.

The provisions of section eighty-seven of chapter two hundred and seventy-six shall not apply to any person 18 years of age or older, charged with a violation of this subsection, or to any child between ages fourteen and 18 so charged, if the court is of the opinion that the interests of the public require that he should be tried as an adult for such offense instead of being dealt with as a child.

The provisions of this subsection shall not affect the licensing requirements of section one hundred and twenty-nine C of chapter one hundred and forty which require every person not otherwise duly licensed or exempted to have been issued a firearms identification card in order to possess a firearm, rifle or shotgun in his residence or place of business.

(b) Whoever, except as provided by law, carries on his person, or carries on his person or under his control in a vehicle, any stiletto, dagger or a device or case which enables a knife with a locking blade to be drawn at a locked position, any ballistic knife, or any knife with a detachable blade capable of being propelled by any mechanism, dirk knife, any knife having a double-edged blade, or a switch knife, or any knife having an automatic spring release device by which the blade is released from the handle, having a blade of over one and one-half inches, or a slung shot, blowgun, blackjack, metallic knuckles or knuckles of any substance which could be put to the same use with the same or similar effect as metallic knuckles, nunchaku, zoobow, also known as klackers or kung fu sticks, or any similar weapon consisting of two sticks of wood, plastic or metal connected at one end by a length of rope, chain, wire or leather, a shuriken or any similar pointed starlike object intended to injure a person when thrown, or any armband, made with leather which has metallic spikes, points or studs or any similar device made from any other substance or a cestus or similar material weighted with metal or other substance and worn on the hand, or a manrikigusari or similar length of chain having weighted ends; or whoever, when arrested upon a warrant for an alleged crime, or when arrested while committing a breach or disturbance of the public peace, is armed with or has on his person, or has on his person or under his control in a vehicle, a billy or other dangerous weapon other than those herein mentioned and those mentioned in paragraph (a), shall be punished by imprisonment for not less than two and one-half years nor more than five years in the state prison, or for not less than six months nor more than two and one-half years in a jail or house of correction, except that if the court finds that the defendant has not been previously convicted of a felony, he may be punished by a fine of not more than fifty dollars or by imprisonment for not more than two and one-half years in a jail or house of correction.

(c) Whoever, except as provided by law, possesses a machine gun, as defined in section one hundred and twenty-one of chapter one hundred and forty, without permission under section one hundred and thirty-one of said chapter one hundred and forty; or whoever owns, possesses or carries on his person, or carries on his person or under his control in a vehicle, a sawed-off shotgun, as defined in said section one hundred and twenty-one of said chapter one hundred and forty, shall be punished by imprisonment in the state prison for life, or for any term of years provided that any sentence imposed under the provisions of this paragraph shall be subject to the minimum requirements of paragraph (a).

(d) Whoever, after having been convicted of any of the offenses set forth in paragraph (a), (b) or (c) commits a like offense or any other of the said offenses, shall be punished by imprisonment in the state prison for not less than five years nor more than seven years; for a third such offense, by imprisonment in the state prison for not less than seven years nor more than ten years; and for a fourth such offense, by imprisonment in the state prison for not less than ten years nor more than fifteen years. The sentence imposed upon a person, who after a conviction of an offense under paragraph (a), (b) or (c) commits the same or a like offense, shall not be suspended, nor shall any person so sentenced be eligible for probation or receive any deduction from his sentence for good conduct.

(e) Upon conviction of a violation of this section, the firearm or other article shall, unless otherwise ordered by the court, be confiscated by the commonwealth. The firearm or article so confiscated shall, by the authority of the written order of the court be forwarded by common carrier to the colonel of the state police, who, upon receipt of the same, shall notify said court or justice thereof. Said colonel may sell or destroy the same, except that any firearm which may not be lawfully sold in the commonwealth shall be destroyed, and in the case of a sale, after paying the cost of forwarding the article, shall pay over the net proceeds to the commonwealth.

(f) The court shall, if the firearm or other article was lost by or stolen from the person lawfully in possession of it, order its return to such person.

(g) Whoever, within this commonwealth, produces for sale, delivers or causes to be delivered, orders for delivery, sells or offers for sale, or fails to keep records regarding, any rifle or shotgun without complying with the requirement of a serial number, as provided in section one hundred and twenty-nine B of chapter one hundred and forty, shall for the first offense be punished by confinement in a jail or house of correction for not more than two and one-half years, or by a fine of not more than five hundred dollars.

(h)(1) Whoever owns, possesses or transfers a firearm, rifle, shotgun or ammunition without complying with the provisions of section 129C of chapter 140 shall be punished by imprisonment in a jail or house of correction for not more than 2 years or by a fine of not more than $500.Whoever commits a second or subsequent violation of this paragraph shall be punished by imprisonment in a house of correction for not more than 2 years or by a fine of not more than $1,000, or both. Any officer authorized to make arrests may arrest without a warrant any person whom the officer has probable cause to believe has violated this paragraph.

(2) Any person who leaves a firearm, rifle, shotgun or ammunition unattended with the intent to transfer possession of such firearm, rifle, shotgun or ammunition to any person not licensed under section 129C of chapter 140 or section 131 of chapter 140 for the purpose of committing a crime or concealing a crime shall be punished by imprisonment in a house of correction for not more than 2 years or in state prison for not more than 5 years.

(i) Whoever knowingly fails to deliver or surrender a revoked or suspended license to carry or possess firearms or machine guns issued under the provisions of section one hundred and thirty-one or one hundred and thirty-one F of chapter one hundred and forty, or firearm identification card, or receipt for the fee for such card, or a firearm, rifle, shotgun or machine gun, as provided in section one hundred and twenty-nine D of chapter one hundred and forty, unless an appeal is pending, shall be punished by imprisonment in a jail or house of correction for not more than two and one-half years or by a fine of not more than one thousand dollars.

(j) For the purposes of this paragraph, "firearm" shall mean any pistol, revolver, rifle or smoothbore arm from which a shot, bullet or pellet can be discharged.

Whoever, not being a law enforcement officer and notwithstanding any license obtained by the person pursuant to chapter 140, carries on the person a firearm, loaded or unloaded, or other dangerous weapon in any building or on the grounds of any elementary or secondary school, college or university without the written authorization of the board or officer in charge of the elementary or secondary school, college or university shall be punished by a fine of not more than $1,000 or by imprisonment for not more than 2 years or both. A law enforcement officer may arrest without a warrant and detain a person found carrying a firearm in violation of this paragraph.

Any officer in charge of an elementary or secondary school, college or university or any faculty member or administrative officer of an elementary or secondary school, college or university that fails to report a violation of this paragraph shall be guilty of a misdemeanor and punished by a fine of not more than $500.

[There is no paragraph (k).]

(l) The provisions of this section shall be fully applicable to any person proceeded against under section seventy-five of chapter one hundred and nineteen and convicted under section eighty-three of chapter one hundred and nineteen, provided, however, that nothing contained in this section shall impair, impede, or affect the power granted any court by chapter one hundred and nineteen to adjudicate a person a delinquent child, including the power so granted under section eighty-three of said chapter one hundred and nineteen.

(m) Notwithstanding the provisions of paragraph (a) or (h), any person not exempted by statute who knowingly has in his possession, or knowingly has under his control in a vehicle, a large capacity weapon or large capacity feeding device therefor who does not possess a valid [Class A or Class B] license to carry firearms issued under section 131 or 131F of chapter 140, except as permitted or otherwise provided under this section or chapter 140, shall be punished by imprisonment in a state prison for not less than two and one-half years nor more than ten years. The possession of a valid firearm identification card issued under section 129B shall not be a defense for a violation of this subsection; provided, however, that any such person charged with violating this paragraph and holding a valid firearm identification card shall not be subject to any mandatory minimum sentence imposed by this paragraph. The sentence imposed upon such person shall not be reduced to less than one year, nor suspended, nor shall any person convicted under this subsection be eligible for probation, parole, furlough, work release or receive any deduction from his sentence for good conduct until he shall have served such minimum term of such sentence; provided, however, that the commissioner of correction may, on the recommendation of the warden, superintendent or other person in charge of a correctional institution or the administrator of a county correctional institution, grant to such offender a temporary release in the custody of an officer of such institution for the following purposes only: (i) to attend the funeral of a spouse or next of kin; (ii) to visit a critically ill close relative or spouse; or (iii) to obtain emergency medical services unavailable at such institution. Prosecutions commenced under this subsection shall neither be continued without a finding nor placed on file. The provisions of section 87 of chapter 276 relative to the power of the court to place certain offenders on probation shall not apply to any person 18 years of age or over charged with a violation of this section.

The provisions of this paragraph shall not apply to the possession of a large capacity weapon or large capacity feeding device by (i) any officer, agent or employee of the commonwealth or any other state or the United States, including any federal, state or local law enforcement personnel; (ii) any member of the military or other service of any state or the United States; (iii) any duly authorized law enforcement officer, agent or employee of any municipality of the commonwealth; (iv) any federal, state or local historical society, museum or institutional collection open to the public; provided, however, that any such person described in clauses (i) to (iii), inclusive, is authorized by a competent authority to acquire, possess or carry a large capacity semiautomatic weapon and is acting within the scope of his duties; or (v) any gunsmith duly licensed under the applicable federal law.

(n) Whoever violates paragraph (a) or paragraph (c), by means of a loaded firearm, loaded sawed off shotgun or loaded machine gun shall be further punished by imprisonment in the house of correction for not more than a years, which sentence shall begin from and after the expiration of the sentence for the violation of paragraph (a) or paragraph (c).

(o) For purposes of this section, "loaded" shall mean that ammunition is contained in the weapon or within a feeding device attached thereto.

For purposes of this section, "ammunition" shall mean cartridges or cartridge cases, primers (igniter), bullets or propellant powder designed for use in any firearm, rifle or shotgun.

§ 10G. Violations of Sec. 10 by persons previously convicted of violent crimes or serious drug offenses; punishment

[Amended by 2014 Mass. Acts c. 284, § 95, effective Aug. 22, 2014.]

(a) Whoever, having been previously convicted of a violent crime or of a serious drug offense, both as defined herein, violates the provisions of paragraph (a), (c) or (h) of section 10 shall be punished by imprisonment in the state prison for not less than three years nor more than 15 years.

(b) Whoever, having been previously convicted of two violent crimes, or two serious drug offenses or one violent crime and one serious drug offense, arising from separate incidences, violates the provisions of said paragraph (a), (c) or (h) of said section 10 shall be punished by imprisonment in the state prison for not less than ten years nor more than 15 years.

(c) Whoever, having been previously convicted of three violent crimes or three serious drug offenses, or any combination thereof totaling three, arising from separate incidences, violates the provisions of said paragraph (a), (c) or (h) of said section 10 shall be punished by imprisonment in the state prison for not less than 15 years nor more than 20 years.

(d) The sentences imposed upon such persons shall not be reduced to less than the minimum, nor suspended, nor shall persons convicted under this section be eligible for probation, parole, furlough, work release or receive any deduction from such sentence for good conduct until such person shall have served the minimum number of years of such sentence; provided, however, that the commissioner of correction may, on the recommendation of the warden, superintendent or other person in charge of a correctional institution or the administrator of a county correctional institution, grant to such offender a temporary release in the custody of an officer of such institution for the following purposes only: (i) to attend the funeral of a spouse or next of kin; (ii) to visit a critically ill close relative or spouse; or (iii) to obtain emergency medical services unavailable at such institution. Prosecutions commenced under this section shall neither be continued without a finding nor placed on file. The provisions of section 87 of chapter 276 relative to the power of the court to place certain offenders on probation shall not apply to any person 18 years of age or over charged with a violation of this section.

(e) For the purposes of this section, "violent crime" shall have the meaning set forth in section 121 of chapter 140. For the purposes of this section, "serious drug offense" shall mean an offense under the federal Controlled Substances Act, 21 U.S.C. 801, et seq., the federal Controlled Substances Import and Export Act, 21 U.S.C. 951, et seq. or the federal Maritime Drug Law Enforcement Act, 46 U.S.C. App. 1901, et seq. for which a maximum term of imprisonment for ten years or more is prescribed by law, or an offense under chapter 94C involving the manufacture, distribution or possession with intent to manufacture or distribute a controlled substance, as defined in section 1 of said chapter 94C, for which a maximum term of ten years or more is prescribed by law.

NOTE "Violent crime" is defined in G.L. c. 140, § 121.

§ 11A. Definitions

For the purposes of this section and sections eleven B, eleven C and eleven D, the following words shall have the following meanings:—

"Firearm", a firearm as defined in section one hundred and twenty-one of chapter one hundred and forty, or a rifle or shotgun.

"Serial number", the number stamped or placed upon a firearm by the manufacturer in the original process of manufacture.

"Identification number", the number stamped or placed upon a firearm by the colonel of the state police under authority of section eleven D.

§ 11B. Possession or control of firearm with serial or identification number removed or mutilated while committing or attempting a felony; destruction

Whoever, while in the commission or attempted commission of a felony, has in his possession or under his control a firearm the serial number or identification number of which has been removed, defaced, altered, obliterated or mutilated in any manner shall be punished by imprisonment in the state prison for not less than two and one half nor more than five years, or in a jail or house of correction for not less than six months nor more than two and one half years. Upon a conviction of a violation of this section, said firearm or other article, by the authority of the written order of the court, shall be forwarded to the colonel of the state police, who shall cause said weapon to be destroyed.

§ 11C. Removal or mutilation of serial or identification numbers of firearms; receiving such firearm; possession or control as evidence; destruction

Whoever, by himself or another, removes, defaces, alters, obliterates or mutilates in any manner the serial number or identification number of a firearm, or in any way participates therein, and whoever receives a firearm with knowledge that its serial number or identification number has been removed, defaced, altered, obliterated or mutilated in any manner, shall be punished by a fine of not more than two hundred dollars or by imprisonment for not less than one month nor more than two and one half years. Possession or control of a firearm the serial number or identification number of which has been removed, defaced, altered, obliterated or mutilated in any manner shall be prima facie evidence that the person having such possession or control is guilty of a violation of this section; but such prima facie evidence may be rebutted by evidence that such person had no knowledge whatever that such number had been removed, defaced, altered, obliterated or mutilated, or by evidence that he had no guilty knowledge thereof. Upon a conviction of a violation of this section said firearm or other article shall be forwarded, by the authority of the written order of the court, to the colonel of the state police, who shall cause said firearm or other article to be destroyed.

§ 12. Sale of knives and similar weapons

Whoever manufactures or causes to be manufactured, or sells or exposes for sale, an instrument or weapon of the kind usually known as a dirk knife, a switch knife or any knife having an automatic spring release device by which the blade is released from the handle, having a blade of over one and one-half inches or a device or case which enables a knife with a locking blade to be drawn at a locked position, any ballistic knife, or any knife with a detachable blade capable of being propelled by any mechanism, slung shot, sling shot, bean blower, sword cane, pistol cane, bludgeon, blackjack, nunchaku, zoobow, also known as klackers or kung fu sticks, or any similar weapon consisting of two sticks of wood, plastic or metal connected at one end by a length of rope, chain, wire or leather, a shuriken or any similar pointed starlike object intended to injure a person when thrown, or a manrikigusari or similar length of chain having weighted ends; or metallic knuckles or knuckles of any other substance which could be put to the same use and with the same or similar effect as metallic knuckles, shall be punished by a fine of not less than fifty nor more than one thousand dollars or by imprisonment for not more than six months; provided, however, that sling shots may be manufactured and sold to clubs or associations conducting sporting events where such sling shots are used.

§ 12A. Selling or furnishing BB gun to minor

Whoever sells to a minor under the age of eighteen or whoever, not being the parent, guardian or adult teacher or instructor, furnishes to a minor under the age of eighteen an air rifle or so-called BB gun, shall be punished by a fine of not less than fifty nor more than two hundred dollars or by imprisonment for not more than six months.

§ 12B. Possession or shooting of BB gun by minor under 18

No minor under the age of eighteen shall have an air rifle or so-called BB gun in his possession while in any place to which the public has a right of access unless he is accompanied by an adult or unless he is the holder of a sporting or hunting license and has on his person a permit from the chief of police of the town in which he resides granting him the right of such possession. No person shall discharge a BB shot, pellet or other object from an air rifle or so-called BB gun into, from or across any street, alley, public way or railroad or railway right of way, and no minor under the age of eighteen shall discharge a BB shot, pellet or other object from an air rifle or BB gun unless he is accompanied by an adult or is the holder of a sporting or hunting license. Whoever violates this section shall be punished by a fine of not more than one hundred dollars, and the air rifle or BB gun or other weapon shall be confiscated. Upon a conviction of a violation of this section the air rifle or BB gun or other weapon shall, by the written authority of the court, be forwarded to the colonel of the state police, who may dispose of said article in the same manner as prescribed in section ten.

§ 12C. Repealed

§ 12D. Carrying a loaded rifle or shotgun on a public way

[Amended by 2005 Mass. Acts c. 137, effective Nov. 22, 2005.]

(a) Except as exempted or provided by law, no person shall carry on his person on any public way a loaded rifle or shotgun having cartridges or shells in either the magazine or chamber thereof. For purposes of this section, "loaded shotgun or loaded rifle" shall mean any shotgun or rifle having ammunition in either the magazine or chamber thereof, such ammunition including a live cartridge, primer (igniter), bullet or propellant powder designed for use in any firearm, rifle or shotgun and, in the case of a muzzle loading or black powder shotgun or rifle, containing powder in the flash pan, a percussion cap and shot or ball; but the term "loaded shotgun or loaded rifle" shall not include a shotgun or rifle loaded with a blank cartridge, which contains no projectile within such blank or within the bore or chamber of such shotgun or rifle.

Whoever violates the provisions of this subsection shall be punished by a fine of not less than $500 nor more than $5,000 or by imprisonment in the house of correction for not more than two years, or by both such fine and imprisonment, and may be arrested without a warrant; provided, however, that if such rifle or shotgun is a large capacity weapon, as defined in section 121 of chapter 140, such person shall be punished by a fine of not less than $1,000 nor more than $10,000 or by imprisonment for not less than one year nor more than ten years, or by both such fine and imprisonment, and may be arrested without a warrant.

(b) Except as exempted or provided by law, no person shall carry on his person on any public way an unloaded rifle or shotgun, unless such rifle or shotgun is enclosed in a case.

Whoever violates the provisions of this subsection shall be punished by a fine of not less than $100 nor more than $1,000, and may be arrested without a warrant; provided, however, that if such unloaded rifle or shotgun is a large capacity weapon and is carried simultaneously with a fully or partially loaded large capacity feeding device, such person shall be punished by a fine of not less than $1,000 nor more than $10,000 or by imprisonment for not less than one year nor more than ten years, or by both such fine and imprisonment, and may be arrested without a warrant.

This subsection shall not apply to drills, parades, military reenactments or other commemorative ceremonies, color guards or memorial service firing squads, so-called, as permitted by law.

(c) Upon a conviction of a violation of any provision of this section, such rifle or shotgun shall be confiscated by the commonwealth and, upon written order of the court, such weapon shall be forwarded to the colonel of the state police, who may dispose of such weapon in the manner prescribed in section 10.

(d) The provisions of this section shall not apply to the carrying of a loaded or unloaded rifle or shotgun on a public way by (i) any officer, agent or employee of the commonwealth or any other state or the United States, including any federal, state or local law

1

enforcement personnel; (ii) any member of the military or other service of any state or the United States, including members of the national guard, reserves and junior reserve officer training corps; (iii) any duly authorized law enforcement officer, agent or employee of any municipality of the commonwealth; provided, however, that any such person described in clauses (i) to (iii), inclusive, shall be authorized by a competent authority to so carry a loaded or unloaded rifle or shotgun on a public way and such person is acting within the scope of his duties or training; or (iv) a person who is lawfully engaged in hunting and is the holder of a valid hunting or sporting license issued pursuant to chapter 131. This section shall not apply to the operation of a shooting gallery, licensed and defined under the provisions of section 56A of chapter 140, nor to persons using the same.

§ 12E. Discharge of a firearm within 500 feet of a dwelling or other building in use; exceptions

Whoever discharges a firearm as defined in section one hundred and twenty-one of chapter one hundred and forty, a rifle or shotgun within five hundred feet of a dwelling or other building in use, except with the consent of the owner or legal occupant thereof, shall be punished by a fine of not less than fifty nor more than one hundred dollars or by imprisonment in a jail or house of correction for not more than three months, or both. The provisions of this section shall not apply to (a) the lawful defense of life and property; (b) any law enforcement officer acting in the discharge of his duties; (e) persons using underground or indoor target or test ranges with the consent of the owner or legal occupant thereof; (d) persons using outdoor skeet, trap, target or test ranges with the consent of the owner or legal occupant of the land on which the range is established; (e) persons using shooting galleries, licensed and defined under the provisions of section fifty-six A of chapter one hundred and forty; and (f) the discharge of blank cartridges for theatrical, athlete, ceremonial, firing squad, or other purposes in accordance with section thirty-nine of chapter one hundred and forty-eight.

§ 13. False alarms of fire

Whoever, without reasonable cause, by outcry or the ringing of bells, or otherwise, makes or circulates or causes to be made or circulated a false alarm of fire shall be punished by a fine of not less than one hundred dollars nor more than five hundred dollars, or by imprisonment in a jail or house of correction for not more than one year.

§ 13A. False reports to police officers

Whoever intentionally and knowingly makes or causes to be made a false report of a crime to police officers shall be punished by a fine of not less than one hundred nor more than five hundred dollars or by imprisonment in a jail or house of correction for not more than one year, or both.

§ 14A. Annoying telephone calls or electronic communication

[Amended by 2010 Mass. Acts c. 92, § 12, effective May 3, 2010.]

Whoever telephones another person or contacts another person by electronic communication, or causes a person to be telephoned or contacted by electronic communication, repeatedly, for the sole purpose of harassing, annoying or molesting the person or the person's family, whether or not conversation ensues, or whoever telephones or contacts a person repeatedly by electronic communication and uses indecent or obscene language to the person, shall be punished by a fine of not more than $500 or by imprisonment for not more than 3 months, or by both such a fine and imprisonment.

For purposes of this section, "electronic communication" shall include, but not be limited to, any transfer of signs, signals, writing, images, sounds, data or intelligence of any nature transmitted in whole or in part by a wire, radio, electromagnetic, photoelectronic or photo-optical system.

§ 14B. False reports to emergency response services provider

[Added by 2008 Mass. Acts c. 223, § 16, effective July 31, 2008; 2018 Mass. Acts c. 69, § 158, effective Apr. 13, 2018.]

As used in this section, the following words shall have the following meanings:—

"Emergency response services provider", a police department, fire department, emergency medical service provider, PSAP, public safety department, private safety department or other public safety agency.

"PSAP", a facility assigned the responsibility of receiving 911 calls and, as appropriate, directly dispatching emergency response services or transferring or relaying emergency 911 calls to other public or private safety agencies or other PSAPs.

"Silent call", a call or other communication made to a PSAP in which the initiating party fails to provide information regarding his or her identity or location or the nature of the emergency. The initiating party shall not be considered to have provided any information that is automatically transmitted by a communication device or network upon connection with a PSAP including, but not be limited to, automatic location information and automatic number information.

(a) Whoever willfully and maliciously communicates with a PSAP, or causes a communication to be made to a PSAP, which communication transmits information which the person knows or has reason to know is false and which results in the dispatch of emergency services to a nonexistent emergency or to the wrong location of an actual emergency; or (b) whoever willfully and maliciously, makes or causes to be made 3 or more silent calls to any PSAP and thereby causes emergency services to be dispatched 3 or more times shall be punished by imprisonment in the house of correction for not more than 2½ years or by a fine of not more than $1,000. Whoever commits a second or subsequent violation of this section shall be punished by imprisonment in the house of correction for not more than 2½ years or by imprisonment in the state prison for not more than 10 years or by a fine of not more than $5,000 dollars, or by both such fine and imprisonment.

(b) Upon any conviction under this section, the court shall conduct a hearing to ascertain the extent of costs incurred, and damages and financial loss sustained by any emergency response services provider as a result of the violation and shall order the defendant to make restitution to the emergency response services provider or providers for any such costs, damages or loss. The court shall consider the defendant's present and future ability to pay restitution in its determinations relative to the imposition of a fine. In determining the amount, time and method of payment of restitution, the court shall consider the defendant's employment status, earning ability, financial resources, living expenses, dependents and any special circumstances that may have bearing on their ability to pay. The court may waive restitution or modify the amount, time or method of payment if such restitution payment would cause a substantial financial hardship to the defendant or the defendant's immediate family or the defendant's dependents.

Chapter 272. Crimes Against Chastity, Morality, Decency and Good Order

§ 16. Open and gross lewdness and lascivious behavior

A man or woman, married or unmarried, who is guilty of open and gross lewdness and lascivious behavior, shall be punished by imprisonment in the state prison for not more than three years or in jail for not more than two years or by a fine of not more than three hundred dollars.

§ 29C. Knowing purchase or possession of visual material of child depicted in sexual conduct; punishment

[Added by 1997 Mass. Acts c. 181, § 2.]

Whoever knowingly purchases or possesses a negative, slide, book, magazine, film, videotape, photograph or other similar visual reproduction, or depiction by computer, of any child whom the person knows or reasonably should know to be under the age of 18 years of age and such child is:

(i) actually or by simulation engaged in any act of sexual intercourse with any person or animal;

(ii) actually or by simulation engaged in any act of sexual contact involving the sex organs of the child and the mouth, anus or sex organs of the child and the sex organs of another person or animal;

(iii) actually or by simulation engaged in any act of masturbation;

(iv) actually or by simulation portrayed as being the object of, or otherwise engaged in, any act of lewd fondling, touching, or caressing involving another person or animal;

(v) actually or by simulation engaged in any act of excretion or urination within a sexual context;

(vi) actually or by simulation portrayed or depicted as bound, fettered, or subject to sadistic, masochistic, or sadomasochistic abuse in any sexual context; or

(vii) depicted or portrayed in any pose, posture or setting involving a lewd exhibition of the unclothed genitals, pubic area, buttocks or, if such person is female, a fully or partially developed breast of the child; with knowledge of the nature or content thereof shall be punished by imprisonment in the state prison for not more than five years or in a jail or house of correction for not more than two and one-half years or by a fine of not less than $1,000 nor more than $10,000, or by both such fine and imprisonment for the first offense, not less than five years in a state prison or by a fine of not less than $5,000 nor more than $20,000, or by both such fine and imprisonment for the second offense, not less than 10 years in a state prison or by a fine of not less than $10,000 nor more than $30,000, or by both such fine and imprisonment for the third and subsequent offenses.

A prosecution commenced under this section shall not be continued without a finding nor placed on file.

The provisions of this section shall not apply to a law enforcement officer, licensed physician, licensed psychologist, attorney or officer of the court who is in possession of such materials in the lawful performance of his official duty. Nor shall the provisions of this section apply to an employee of a bona fide enterprise, the purpose of which enterprise is to filter or otherwise restrict access to such materials, who possesses examples of computer depictions of such material for the purposes of furthering the legitimate goals of such enterprise.

§ 35. Unnatural and lascivious acts

Whoever commits any unnatural and lascivious act with another person shall be punished by a fine of not less than one hundred nor more than one thousand dollars or by imprisonment in the state prison for not more than five years or in jail or the house of correction for not more than two and one half years.

§ 35A. Unnatural and lascivious acts with child under 16

Whoever commits any unnatural and lascivious act with a child under the age of sixteen shall be punished by a fine of not less than one hundred dollars nor more than one thousand dollars or by imprisonment in the state prison for not more than five years or in jail or the house of correction for not more than two and one half years, and whoever over the age of eighteen commits a second or subsequent such offence shall be sentenced to imprisonment in the state prison for a term of not less than five years.

§ 40. Disturbance of schools or assemblies

[Amended by 2018 Mass. Acts c. 69, § 159, effective Apr. 13, 2018.]

Whoever willfully interrupts or disturbs an assembly of people meeting for a lawful purpose shall be punished by imprisonment for not more than 1 month or by a fine of not more than $50; provided, however, that an elementary or secondary student shall not be adjudged a delinquent child for an alleged violation of this section for such conduct within school buildings or on school grounds or in the course of school-related events.

§ 42B. Disturbance of military funeral service; penalty

[Added by 2014 Mass. Acts c. 62, § 26, effective July 2, 2014.]

Whoever willfully pickets, loiters or otherwise creates a disturbance within 500 feet of a funeral home, church, temple, burial or other building where military funeral services are being held, shall be punished by a fine of not more than $2,000 or by imprisonment for not more than 2 years in a house of correction, or both.

§ 53. Disorderly conduct, prostitution, etc.

[Amended by 2009 Mass. Acts c. 27, § 98, effective July 1, 2009; 2014 Mass. Acts c. 417, effective Mar. 24, 2015; 2018 Mass. Acts c. 69, § 160, effective Apr. 13, 2018.]

(a) Common night walkers, common street walkers, both male and female, persons who with offensive and disorderly acts or language accost or annoy another person, lewd, wanton and lascivious persons in speech or behavior, keepers of noisy and disorderly houses, and persons guilty of indecent exposure shall be punished by imprisonment in a jail or house of correction for not more than 6 months, or by a fine of not more than $200, or by both such fine and imprisonment.

(b) Disorderly persons and disturbers of the peace shall, for a first offense, be punished by a fine of not more than $150. For a second or subsequent offense, disorderly persons and disturbers of the peace shall be punished by imprisonment in a jail or house of correction for not more than 6 months or by a fine of not more than $200 or by both such fine and imprisonment; provided, however, that an elementary or secondary school student shall not be adjudged a delinquent child for a violation of this subsection for such conduct within school buildings or on school grounds or in the course of school-related events.

§ 53A. Engaging in sexual conduct for a fee

[Amended by 2006 Mass. Acts c. 363, effective Feb. 14, 2007; 2006 Mass. Acts c. 434, § 1, effective Apr. 3, 2007; 2011 Mass. Acts c. 178, § 25, effective Nov. 21, 2011.]

(a) Whoever engages, agrees to engage or offers to engage in sexual conduct with another person in return for a fee, shall be punished by imprisonment in the house of correction for not more than 1 year or by a fine of not more than $500, or by both such imprisonment and fine, whether such sexual conduct occurs or not.

(b) Whoever pays, agrees to pay or offers to pay another person to engage in sexual conduct, or to agree to engage in sexual conduct with another person, shall be punished by imprisonment in the house of correction for not more than 2 and one-half years or by a fine of not less than $1,000 and not more than $5,000, or by both such imprisonment and fine, whether such sexual conduct occurs or not.

(c) Whoever pays, agrees to pay or offers to pay any person with the intent to engage in sexual conduct with a child under the age of 18, or whoever is paid, agrees to pay or agrees that a third person be paid in return for aiding a person who intends to engage in sexual conduct with a child under the age of 18, shall be punished by imprisonment in the state prison for not more than 10 years, or in the house of correction for not more than 2 and one-half years and by a fine of not less than $3,000 and not more than $10,000, or by both such imprisonment and fine, whether such sexual conduct occurs or not; provided, however, that a prosecution commenced under this section shall not be continued without a finding or placed on file.

§ 73. Tombs, graves, memorials, trees, plants; injuring, removing

[Amended by 2004 Mass. Acts c. 117, effective Aug. 26, 2004; 2015 Mass. Acts c. 130–31, effective Feb. 21, 2016.]

Whoever willfully destroys, mutilates, defaces, injures or removes a tomb, monument, gravestone, American flag, veteran's grave marker, metal plaque, veteran's commemorative flag holder, commemorative flag holder representing service in a police or fire department, veteran's flag holder that commemorates a particular war, conflict or period of service or flag, or other structure or thing which is placed or designed for a memorial of the dead, or a fence railing, curb or other thing which is intended for the protection or ornament of a structure or thing before mentioned or of an enclosure for the burial of the dead, or willfully removes, destroys, mutilates, cuts, breaks or injures a tree, shrub or plant placed or being within such enclosure, or wantonly or maliciously disturbs the contents of a tomb or a grave, shall be punished by imprisonment in the state prison for not more than five years or by imprisonment in the jail or house of correction for not more than two and one-half years and by a fine of not more than five thousand dollars. In addition, the court shall order any person convicted of an offense pursuant to this section to pay restitution to the owner of the property that was damaged, destroyed, mutilated, defaced, injured or removed.

§ 73B. Sale of or attempt to sell stolen commemorative grave marker; receipt, retention or disposal of stolen commemorative grave marker

[Added by 2015 Mass. Acts c. 129, effective Feb. 21, 2016.]

(a) For purposes of this section, "commemorative grave marker" shall mean a grave marker, headstone, monument, structure, medallion or other object designed to commemorate the grave of a veteran, police officer or firefighter.

(b) Whoever sells or attempts to sell a commemorative grave marker that has been stolen and the person knows or should know the commemorative grave marker to be stolen, shall be punished by a fine of not more than $5,000 for a first offense and for a second or subsequent offense by imprisonment in a state prison for not more than 5 years or by imprisonment in a jail or house of correction for not more than 2½ years and by a fine of not more than $5,000.

(c) Whoever receives, retains or disposes of a commemorative grave marker that the person knows or should know to be stolen, shall be punished by a fine of not more than $5,000; provided, however, that no such penalty shall be imposed upon: (i) a person who receives or retains the commemorative grave marker with the intent to return it to a cemetery, a member of law enforcement, a member of a fire department, a member of the department of veterans' services, a non-profit veterans' services group or a veterans' agent of a city or town; or (ii) a person who in fact disposes of the commemorative grave marker by returning it to a cemetery, a member of law enforcement, a member of a fire department, a member of the department of veterans' services, a nonprofit veterans' services group or a veterans' agent of a city or town.

§ 77. Cruelty to animals

[Amended by 2004 Mass. Acts c. 319, § 4, effective Nov. 17, 2004; 2006 Mass. Acts c. 434, § 1, effective Apr. 3, 2007; 2012 Mass. Acts c. 193, § 49, effective Oct. 31, 2012; 2014 Mass. Acts c. 293, §§ 3–4, effective Nov. 18, 2014; 2018 Mass. Acts c. 219, § 22, effective Nov. 7, 2018.]

Whoever overdrives, overloads, drives when overloaded, overworks, tortures, torments, deprives of necessary sustenance, cruelly beats, mutilates or kills an animal, or causes or procures an animal to be overdriven, overloaded, driven when overloaded, overworked, tortured, tormented, deprived of necessary sustenance, cruelly beaten, mutilated or killed; and whoever uses in a cruel or inhuman manner in a race, game, or contest, or in training therefor, as lure or bait a live animal, except an animal if used as lure or bait in fishing; and whoever, having the charge or custody of an animal, either as owner or otherwise, inflicts unnecessary cruelty upon it, or unnecessarily fails to provide it with proper food, drink, shelter, sanitary environment, or protection from the weather, and whoever, as owner, possessor, or person having the charge or custody of an animal, cruelly drives or works it when unfit for labor, or willfully abandons it, or carries it or causes it to be carried in or upon a vehicle, or otherwise, in an unnecessarily cruel or inhuman manner or in a way and manner which might endanger the animal carried thereon, or knowingly and willfully authorizes or permits it to be subjected to unnecessary torture, suffering or cruelty of any kind shall be punished by imprisonment in the state prison for not more than7 years in state prison or imprisonment in the house of correction for not more than 2½ years or by a fine of not more than $5,000 or by both fine and imprisonment; provided, however, that a second or subsequent offense shall be punished by imprisonment in the state prison for not more than 10 years or by a fine of not more than $10,000 or by both such fine and imprisonment. Notwithstanding section 26 of chapter 218 or any other general or special law to the contrary, the district courts and the divisions of the Boston municipal court department shall have original jurisdiction, concurrent with the superior court, of a violation of this section.

In addition to any other penalty provided by law, upon conviction for any violation of this section or of sections 77A, 77C, 78, 78A, 79A, 79B, 80A, 80B, 80C, 80D, 80E, 80E ½ , 80F, 86, 86A, 86B or 94 the defendant shall forfeit to the custody of any society, incorporated under the laws of the commonwealth for the prevention of cruelty to animals or for the care and protection of homeless or suffering animals, the animal whose treatment was the basis of such conviction.

A person convicted of a crime of cruelty to an animal shall be prohibited from working in any capacity that requires such person to be in contact with an animal, including a commercial boarding or training establishment, shelter, animal control facility, pet shop, grooming facility, commercial breeder service, veterinary hospital or clinic or animal welfare society or other nonprofit organization incorporated for the purpose of providing for and promoting the welfare, protection and humane treatment of animals.

Chapter 274. Felonies, Accessories and Attempts to Commit Crimes

§ 1. Felonies and misdemeanors

A crime punishable by death or imprisonment in the state prison is a felony. All other crimes are misdemeanors.

§ 2. Accessory before the fact

Whoever aids in the commission of a felony, or is accessory thereto before the fact by counseling, hiring or otherwise procuring such felony to be committed, shall be punished in the manner provided for the punishment of the principal felon.

§ 3. Prosecution venue

Whoever counsels, hires or otherwise procures a felony to be committed may be indicted and convicted as an accessory before the fact, either with the principal felon or after his conviction; or may be indicted and convicted of the substantive felony, whether the principal felon has or has not been convicted, or is or is not amenable to justice; and in the last mentioned case may be punished in the same manner as if convicted of being an accessory before the fact. An accessory to a felony before the fact may be indicted, tried and punished in the same county where the principal felon might be indicted and tried, although the counselling, hiring or procuring the commission of such felony was committed within or without the commonwealth or on the high seas.

§ 4. Accessory after the fact

Whoever, after the commission of a felony, harbors, conceals, maintains or assists the principal felon or accessory before the fact, or gives such offender any other aid, knowing that he has committed a felony or has been accessory thereto before the fact, with intent that he shall avoid or escape detention, arrest, trial or punishment, shall be an accessory after the fact, and, except as otherwise provided, be punished by imprisonment in the state prison for not more than seven years or in jail for not more than two and one half years or by a fine of not more than one thousand dollars. The fact that the defendant is the husband or wife, or by consanguinity, affinity or adoption, the parent or grandparent, child or grandchild, brother or sister of the offender, shall be a defense to a prosecution under this section. If such a defendant testifies solely as to the existence of such relationship, he shall not be subject to cross examination on any other subject matter, nor shall his criminal record, if any, except for perjury or subornation of perjury, be admissible to impeach his credibility.

§ 5. Venue

An accessory to a felony after the fact may be indicted, convicted and punished, whether the principal felon has or has not been previously convicted, or is or is not amenable to justice, either in the county where he became an accessory or in the county where the principal felony was committed.

§ 6. Attempt to commit crimes

Whoever attempts to commit a crime by doing any act toward its commission, but fails in its perpetration, or is intercepted or prevented in its perpetration, shall, except as otherwise provided, be punished as follows:

First, by imprisonment in the state prison for not more than ten years, if he attempts to commit a crime punishable with death.

Second, by imprisonment in the state prison for not more than five years or in a jail or house of correction for not more than two and one half years, if he attempts to commit a crime, except any larceny under section thirty of chapter two hundred and sixty-six, punishable by imprisonment in the state prison for life or for five years or more.

Third, by imprisonment in a jail or house of correction for not more than one year or by a fine of not more than three hundred dollars, if he attempts to commit a crime, except any larceny under said section thirty, punishable by imprisonment in the state prison for less than five years or by imprisonment in a jail or house of correction or by a fine.

Fourth, by imprisonment in a jail or house of correction for not more than two and one half years or by a fine, or by both such fine and imprisonment, if he attempts to commit any larceny punishable under said section thirty.

§ 7. Conspiracy

Any person who commits the crime of conspiracy shall be punished as follows:

First, if the purpose of the conspiracy or any of the means for achieving the purpose of the conspiracy is a felony punishable by death or imprisonment for life, by a fine of not more than ten thousand dollars or by imprisonment in the state prison for not more than twenty years or in jail for not more than two and one half years, or by both such fine and imprisonment.

Second, if clause first does not apply and the purpose of the conspiracy or any of the means for achieving the purpose of the conspiracy is a felony punishable by imprisonment in the state prison for a maximum period exceeding ten years, by a fine of not more than ten thousand dollars or by imprisonment in the state prison for not more than ten years or in jail for not more than two and one half years, or by both such fine and imprisonment.

Third, if clauses first and second do not apply and the purpose of the conspiracy or any of the means for achieving the purpose of the conspiracy is a felony punishable by imprisonment in the state prison for not more than ten years, by a fine of not more than five thousand dollars or by imprisonment in the state prison for not more than five years or in jail for not more than two and one half years, or by both such fine and imprisonment.

Fourth, if clauses first through third do not apply and the purpose of the conspiracy or any of the means for achieving the purpose of the conspiracy is a crime, by a fine of not more than two thousand dollars or by imprisonment in jail for not more than two and one half years, or both.

If a person is convicted of a crime of conspiracy for which crime the penalty is expressly set forth in any other section of the General Laws, the provisions of this section shall not apply to said crime and the penalty therefor shall be imposed pursuant to the provisions of such other section.

Chapter 275. Proceedings to Prevent Crimes

§ 2. Threats

If complaint is made to any such court or justice that a person has threatened to commit a crime against the person or property of another, such court or justice shall examine the complainant and any witnesses who may be produced, on oath, reduce the complaint to writing and cause it to be subscribed by the complainant.

§ 4. Punishment

If the person complained of is convicted, he may be punished by a fine of not more than one hundred dollars or by imprisonment for not more than six months. Instead of imposing sentence, the court or justice may order the person complained of to enter into a recognizance, with sufficient sureties, in such sum as the court or justice orders, to keep the peace toward all the people of the commonwealth, and especially toward the person requiring such security, for such term, not exceeding six months, as the court or justice may order. The court or justice may, for good cause, revoke such order or reduce the amount of the recognizance, or order that it be taken without surety.

Chapter 276. Search Warrants, Rewards, Fugitives from Justice, Arrest, Examination, Commitment and Bail; Probation Officers and Board of Probation

§ 1. Complaint; warrant for designated property or articles; search incident to arrest; documentary evidence subject to privilege

A court or justice authorized to issue warrants in criminal cases may, upon complaint on oath that the complainant believes that any of the property or articles hereinafter named are concealed in a house, place, vessel or vehicle or in the possession of a person anywhere within the commonwealth and territorial waters thereof, if satisfied that there is probable cause for such belief issue a warrant identifying the property and naming or describing the person or place to be searched and commanding the person seeking such warrant to search for the following property or articles:

First, property or articles stolen, embezzled or obtained by false pretenses, or otherwise obtained in the commission of a crime;

Second, property or articles which are intended for use, or which are or have been used, as a means or instrumentality of committing a crime, including, but not in limitation of the foregoing, any property or article worn, carried or otherwise used, changed or marked in the preparation for or perpetration of or concealment of a crime;

Third, property or articles the possession or control of which is unlawful, or which are possessed or controlled for an unlawful purpose; except property subject to search and seizure under sections forty-two through fifty-six, inclusive, of chapter one hundred and thirty-eight;

Fourth, the dead body of a human being.

Fifth, the body of a living person for whom a current arrest warrant is outstanding.

A search conducted incident to an arrest may be made only for the purposes of seizing fruits, instrumentalities, contraband and other evidence of the crime for which the arrest has been made, in order to prevent its destruction or concealment; and removing any weapons that the arrestee might use to resist arrest or effect his escape. Property seized as a result of a search in violation of the provisions of this paragraph shall not be admissible in evidence in criminal proceedings.

The word "property", as used in this section shall include books, papers, documents, records and any other tangible objects.

Nothing in this section shall be construed to abrogate, impair or limit powers of search and seizure granted under other provisions of the General Laws or under the common law.

Notwithstanding the foregoing provisions of this section, no search and seizure without a warrant shall be conducted, and no search warrant shall issue for any documentary evidence in the possession of a lawyer, psychotherapist, or a clergyman, including an accredited Christian Science practitioner, who is known or may reasonably be assumed to have a relationship with any other person which relationship is the subject of a testimonial privilege, unless, in addition to the other requirements of this section, a justice is satisfied that there is probable cause to believe that the documentary evidence will be destroyed, secreted, or lost in the event a search warrant does not issue. Nothing in this paragraph shall impair or affect the ability, pursuant to otherwise applicable law, to search or seize without a warrant or to issue a warrant for the search or seizure of any documentary evidence where there is probable cause to believe that the lawyer, psychotherapist, or clergyman in possession of such documentary evidence has committed, is committing, or is about to commit a crime. For purposes of this paragraph, "documentary evidence" includes, but is not limited to, writings, documents, blueprints, drawings, photographs, computer printouts, microfilms, X-rays, files, diagrams, ledgers, books, tapes, audio and video recordings, films or papers of any type or description.

§ 1B. Definitions

[Added by 2008 Mass. Acts c. 205, § 4, effective Oct. 22, 2008.]

(a) As used in this section, the following words shall have the following meanings:—

"Adverse result", occurs when notification of the existence of a search warrant results in:—

(1) danger to the life or physical safety of an individual;

(2) a flight from prosecution;

(3) the destruction of or tampering with evidence;

(4) the intimidation of a potential witness or witnesses; or

(5) serious jeopardy to an investigation or undue delay of a trial.

"Electronic communication services", shall be construed in accordance with sections 2701 to 2711 Title 18, of the United States Code. This definition shall not apply to corporations that do not provide electronic communication services to the general public.

"Foreign corporation", any corporation or other entity that makes a contract or engages in a terms of service agreement with a resident of the commonwealth to be performed in whole or in part by either party in the commonwealth. The making of the contract or terms of service agreement shall be considered to be the agreement of the foreign corporation that a search warrant or subpoena which has been properly served on it has the same legal force and effect as if served personally within the commonwealth.

"Massachusetts corporation", any corporation or other entity that is subject to chapter 155 or chapter 156B.

"Properly served", delivery of a search warrant or subpoena by hand, by United States mail, by commercial delivery service, by facsimile or by any other manner to any officer of a corporation or its general manager in the commonwealth, to any natural person designated by it as agent for the service of process, or if such corporation has designated a corporate agent, to any person named in the latest certificate filed pursuant to section 15.03 of chapter 156D.

"Remote computing services", shall be construed in accordance with sections 2701 to 2711, inclusive, of Title 18, of the United States Code. This definition shall not apply to corporations that do not provide those services to the general public.

1

"Subpoena", a grand jury or trial subpoena issued in the course of a criminal proceeding or an administrative subpoena issued pursuant to section 17B of chapter 271.

(b) A court or justice authorized to issue warrants in criminal cases may, upon complaint on oath that the complainant believes that any of the records hereinafter named are actually or constructively possessed by a foreign corporation that provides electronic communication services or remote computing services, if satisfied that probable cause has been established for such belief, issue a warrant identifying those records to be searched for and commanding the person seeking such warrant to properly serve the warrant upon the foreign corporation:—

(1) those records which would reveal the identity of a customer using those services;

(2) data stored by or on behalf of a customer;

(3) records of a customer's usage of those services;

(4) records of the source of communications sent to or the recipient or destination of communications sent from a customer; or

(5) the content of those communications stored by an electronic communication or remote commuting service.

(c) The following provisions shall apply to any search warrant issued pursuant to this section and to any subpoena issued in the course of a criminal investigation or proceeding directed to a foreign corporation that provides electronic communication services or remote computing services:

(1) when properly served with a search warrant issued by any court of the commonwealth or justice pursuant to this section or a subpoena, a foreign corporation subject to this section shall provide all records sought pursuant to that warrant or subpoena within 14 days of receipt, including those records maintained or located outside the commonwealth;

(2) if the applicant makes a showing and the court or justice finds that failure to produce records within less than 14 days would cause an adverse result, a warrant may require production of records within less than 14 days;

(3) a court or justice may reasonably extend the time required for production of the records upon finding that the foreign corporation has shown good cause for that extension and that an extension of time would not cause an adverse result;

(4) a foreign corporation seeking to quash a warrant or subpoena served on it pursuant to this section shall seek relief from the court that issued the warrant or the court which has jurisdiction over the subpoena within the time required for production of records pursuant to this section. The court shall hear and decide such motion not later than 14 days after the motion is filed;

(5) in the case of an administrative subpoena issued by the attorney general, the superior court of Suffolk county shall have jurisdiction and in the case of an administrative subpoena issued by a district attorney, the superior court in any county in which the district attorney maintains an office shall have jurisdiction; and

(6) the foreign corporation shall verify the authenticity of records that it produces by providing an affidavit from the person in custody of those records certifying that they are true and complete.

(d) A Massachusetts corporation that provides electronic communication services or remote computing services, when served with a warrant or subpoena issued by another state to produce records that would reveal the identity of the customers using those services, data stored by, or on behalf of the customer, the customer's usage of those services, the recipient or destination of communications sent to or from those customers, or the content of those communications, shall produce those records as if that warrant or subpoena had been issued under the law of the commonwealth.

(e) No cause of action shall lie against any foreign or Massachusetts corporation subject to this section, its officers, employees, agents or other persons for providing records, information, facilities or assistance in accordance with the terms of a warrant or subpoena issued pursuant to this section. A search conducted incident to an arrest may be made only for the purposes of seizing fruits, instrumentalities, contraband and other evidence of the crime for which the arrest has been made, in order to prevent its destruction or concealment; and removing any weapons that the arrestee might use to resist arrest or effect his escape. Property seized as a result of a search in violation of the provisions of this paragraph shall not be admissible in evidence in criminal proceedings.

§ 2. Requisites of warrant

Search warrants shall designate and describe the building, house, place, vessel or vehicle to be searched and shall particularly describe the property or articles to be searched for. They shall be substantially in the form prescribed in section two A of this chapter and shall be directed to the sheriff or his deputy or to a constable or police officer, commanding him to search in the daytime, or if the warrant so directs, in the nighttime, the building, house, place, vessel or vehicle where the property or articles for which he is required to search are believed to be concealed, and to bring such property or articles when found, and the persons in whose possession they are found, before a court having jurisdiction.

§ 2A. Form of warrant

The warrant shall be in substantially the following form:

THE COMMONWEALTH OF MASSACHUSETTS

(COUNTY), ss. (NAME) COURT.

To the Sheriffs of our several counties, or their deputies, any State Police Officer, or any Constable or Police Officer of any city or town, within our said Commonwealth.

Proof by affidavit having been made this day before (name of person authorized to issue warrant) by (names of person or persons whose affidavits have been taken) that there is probable cause for believing that (certain property has been stolen, embezzled, or obtained by false pretenses; certain property is intended for use or has been used as the means of committing a crime; certain property has been concealed to prevent a crime from being discovered; certain property is unlawfully possessed or kept or concealed for an unlawful purpose).

We therefore command you in the daytime (or at any time of the day or night to make an immediate search of (identify premises) (occupied by A. B.) and (of the person of A. B.) and of any person present who may be found to have such property in his possession or under his control or to whom such property may have been delivered, for the following property:

(description of property)

and if you find any such property or any part thereof to bring it and the persons in whose possession A is found before (court having jurisdiction) at (name of court and location).

Dated at (city or town) this _____ day of _____ (insert year).

Clerk.

§ 2B. Affidavit in support of application for warrant; contents and form

A person seeking a search warrant shall appear personally before a court or justice authorized to issue search warrants in criminal cases and shall give an affidavit in substantially the form hereinafter prescribed. Such affidavit shall contain the facts, information, and circumstances upon which such person relies to establish sufficient grounds for the issuance of the warrant. The person issuing the warrant shall retain the affidavit and shall deliver it within three days after the issuance of the warrant to the court to which the warrant is returnable. Upon the return of said warrant the affidavit shall be attached to A and shall be filed therewith, and it shall not be a public document until the warrant is returned.

The affidavit in support of the application for a search warrant shall be in substantially the following form:

THE COMMONWEALTH OF MASSACHUSETTS

(COUNTY), ss. (NAME) COURT.
______, (insert year).

I, (name of applicant) being duly sworn, depose and say:

1. I am (describe position, assignment, office, etc.).

2. I have information, based upon (describe source, facts indicating reliability of source and nature of information; if based on personal knowledge and belief, so state).

3. Based upon the foregoing reliable information (and upon my personal knowledge) there is probable cause to believe that the property hereinafter described (has been stolen, or is being concealed, etc.) and may be found (in the possession of A. B. or any other person) at premises (identify).

4. The property for which I seek the issuance of a search warrant is the following: (here describe the property as particularly as possible).

Wherefore, I respectfully request that the court issue a warrant and order of seizure, authorizing the search of (identify premises and the persons to be searched) and directing that if such property or evidence or any part thereof be found that it be seized and brought before the court; together with such other and further relief that the court may deem proper.

_____ Name.

Then personally appeared the above named _____ and made oath that the foregoing affidavit by him subscribed is true.

Before me this _____ day of _____, (insert year).

Justice or Special Justice,

Clerk or Assistant Clerk of the _____ Court.

§ 2C. Manner of issuing warrants; application of Secs. 2, 2A–2B

Search warrants issued pursuant to section two hundred and thirteen of chapter ninety-four, sections twenty and twenty-five of chapter one hundred and ten, section ten of chapter one hundred and thirty, shall be issued in the manner provided in sections two, two A and two B, in so far as they are applicable.

§ 3. Seizure, custody and disposition of articles; exceptions

If an officer in the execution of a search warrant finds property or articles therein described, he shall seize and safely keep them, under the direction of the court or justice, so long as necessary to permit them to be produced or used as evidence in any trial. As soon as may be, thereafter, all property seized under clause First of section one shall be restored to the owners thereof and all other property seized in execution of a search warrant shall be disposed of as the court or justice orders and may be forfeited and either sold or destroyed, as the public interest requires, in the discretion of the court or justice, except:

(a) Diseased animals or carcasses thereof, or any tainted, diseased, corrupt, decayed or unwholesome meat, fish, vegetables, produce, fruit or provisions of any kind, or the meat of any calf killed when less than two weeks old, or any product thereof kept or concealed with intent to kill, sell or offer the same for sale for food, shall be destroyed or disposed of in accordance with section one hundred and forty-six of chapter ninety-four by the board of health or by an officer designated by the court or justice; and diseased animals found to have been kept or concealed in a particular building, place or enclosure shall be destroyed or disposed of by the division of animal health and department of food and agriculture without compensation to the owners thereof.

(b) Rifles, shotguns, pistols, knives or other dangerous weapons which have been found to have been kept, concealed or used unlawfully or for an unlawful purpose shall be forfeited to the commonwealth and delivered forthwith to the colonel of the state police for destruction or preservation in the discretion of the colonel of the state police.

(c) Money seized under clause Third of section one shall be forfeited and paid over to the state treasurer.

(d) Any property, including money seized under section one, the forfeiture and disposition of which is specified in any general or special law shall be disposed of in accordance therewith.

§ 3A. Time for return of warrant

Every officer to whom a warrant to search is issued shall return the same to the court by which it was issued as soon as it has been served and in any event not later than seven days from the date of issuance thereof, with a return of his doings thereon; provided, however, that a justice of the superior court may at any time receive complaints and issue search warrants returnable in seven days before a district court named in such warrant and in that event the officer shall make his return to such district court as directed.

§ 56A. Written ruling that abuse is alleged when judge releases, discharges, or admits to bail any person

[Added by 2014 Mass. Acts c. 260, § 30, effective Aug. 8, 2014.]

Before a judge of the superior court, district court or Boston municipal court releases, discharges or admits to bail any person arrested and charged with a crime against the person or property of another, the judicial officer shall inquire of the commonwealth as to whether abuse, as defined in section 1 of chapter 209A, is alleged to have occurred immediately prior to or in conjunction with the crime for which the person was arrested and charged. The commonwealth shall file a preliminary written statement if it is alleged that abuse has so occurred. The judicial officer shall make a written ruling that abuse is alleged in connection with the charged offense. Such preliminary written statement shall be maintained within the statewide domestic violence record keeping system. Such preliminary written statement shall not be considered criminal offender record information or public records and shall not be open for public inspection. Such preliminary written statement shall not be admissible in any investigation or proceeding before a grand jury or court of the commonwealth related to the crime for which the person was brought before the court.

If the defendant has been found not guilty by the court or jury, or a no bill has been returned by the grand jury or a finding of no probable cause has been made by the court, the court shall remove the preliminary written statement from the statewide domestic violence record keeping system; provided however, that a dismissal shall not be eligible for removal from the statewide domestic record keeping system.

Nothing in this section shall be construed as modifying or limiting the presumption of innocence.

§ 58. Bail

[Amended by 2006 Mass. Acts c. 48, § 8, effective Mar. 30, 2006; 2014 Mass. Acts c. 260, § 32, effective Aug. 8, 2014; 2018 Mass. Acts c. 69, §§ 170, 171, 173, effective Apr. 13, 2018; 2018 Mass. Acts c. 69, § 172, effective July 12, 2018.]

A justice or a clerk or assistant clerk of the district court, a bail commissioner or master in chancery, in accordance with the applicable provisions of section fifty-seven, shall, when a person is held under arrest or committed either with or without a warrant for an offense other than an offense punishable by death, or, upon the motion of the commonwealth, for an offense enumerated in section fifty-eight A or for any offense on which a warrant of arrest has been issued by the superior court, hold a hearing in which the defendant and his counsel, if any, may participate and inquire into the case and shall admit such person to bail on his personal recognizance without surety unless said justice, clerk or assistant clerk, bail commissioner or master in chancery determines, in the exercise of his discretion, that such a release will not reasonably assure the appearance of the person before the court. Except in cases where the person is determined to pose a danger to the safety of any other person or the community under section 58A, bail shall be set in an amount no higher than what would reasonably assure

1

the appearance of the person before the court after taking into account the person's financial resources; provided, however, that a higher than affordable bail may be set if neither alternative nonfinancial conditions nor a bail amount which the person could likely afford would adequately assure the person's appearance before the court. In his determination under this section as to whether release will reasonably assure the appearance of the person before the court, said justice, clerk or assistant clerk, bail commissioner or master in chancery shall, on the basis of any information which he can reasonably obtain, take into account the nature and circumstances of the offense charged, the potential penalty the person faces, the person's family ties, financial resources and financial ability to give bail, employment record and history of mental illness, his reputation and the length of residence in the community, his record of convictions, if any, any illegal drug distribution or present drug dependency, any flight to avoid prosecution or fraudulent use of an alias or false identification, any failure to appear at any court proceeding to answer to an offense, whether the person is on bail pending adjudication of a prior charge, whether the acts alleged involve abuse as defined in section one of chapter two hundred and nine A, or violation of a temporary or permanent order issued pursuant to sections eighteen or thirty-four B of chapter two hundred and eight, section thirty-two of chapter two hundred and nine, sections three, four or five of chapter two hundred and nine A, or sections fifteen or twenty of chapter two hundred and nine C, whether the person has any history of orders issued against him pursuant to the aforesaid sections, whether he is on probation, parole, or other release pending completion of sentence for any conviction, and whether he is on release pending sentence or appeal for any conviction. The person authorized to admit the person to bail shall provide as an explicit condition of release for any person admitted to bail pursuant to this section or section fifty-seven that, should said person be charged with a crime during the period of his release, his bail may be revoked in accordance with the third paragraph of this section. If the justice or clerk or assistant clerk of the district court, the bail commissioner or master in chancery determines that a cash bail is required, the person shall be allowed to provide an equivalent amount in a surety company bond. If the justice or clerk or assistant clerk of the district court, the bail commissioner or master in chancery determines it to be necessary, the defendant may be ordered to abide by specified restrictions on personal associations or conduct including, but not limited to, avoiding all contact with an alleged victim of the crime and any potential witness or witnesses who may testify concerning the offense, as a condition of release.

If bail is set at an amount that is likely to result in the person's long-term pretrial detention because he or she lacks the financial resources to post said amount, an authorized person setting bail must provide written or orally recorded findings of fact and a statement of reasons as to why, under the relevant circumstances, neither alternative nonfinancial conditions nor a bail amount that the person can afford will reasonably assure his or her appearance before the court, and further, must explain how the bail amount was calculated after taking the person's financial resources into account and why the commonwealth's interest in bail or a financial obligation outweighs the potential adverse impact on the person, their immediate family or dependents resulting from pretrial detention.

Except where prohibited by section 57, for any violation of an order issued pursuant to section 18 or 34B of chapter 208, section 32 of chapter 209, section 3, 4 or 5 of 209A or section 15 or 20 of chapter 209C or any act that would constitute abuse, as defined in section 1 of said chapter 209A, or a violation of sections 13M or 15D of chapter 265, a person arrested, who has attained the age of 18 years, shall not be admitted to bail sooner than 6 hours after arrest, except by a judge in open court. Any person authorized to take bail for such violation may impose conditions on a person's release in order to ensure the appearance of the person before the court and the safety of the alleged victim, any other individual or the community; provided, however, that the person authorized to take bail shall, prior to admitting the person to bail, modifying an existing order of bail or imposing such conditions, have immediate access to all pending and prior criminal offender record information, board of probation records and police and incident reports related to the person detained, upon oral, telephonic, facsimile or electronic mail request, to the extent practicable.

The person shall, prior to admittance to bail, with or without conditions, be provided with informational resources related to domestic violence by the person admitting the arrestee to bail, which shall include, but is not limited to, a list of certified batterer intervention programs located within or near the court's jurisdiction. If the defendant is released on bail from the place of detention, a reasonable attempt shall be made to notify the victim of the defendant's release by the arresting police department. If the defendant is released on bail by order of a court, a reasonable attempt shall be made to notify the victim of the defendant's release by the district attorney.

The commonwealth shall be the only party permitted to move for arraignment, within 3 hours of a complaint being signed by a magistrate or a magistrate's designee, for a person charged with violation of said sections 18 or 34B of said chapter 208, said section 32 of chapter 209, said sections 3, 4 or 5 of said chapter 209A or said sections 15 or 20 of said chapter 209C or was a violation of said sections 13M or 15D of said chapter 265.

A person, before being released on personal recognizance without surety, shall be informed by the person authorized to admit such person to bail of the penalties provided by section eighty-two A if he fails without sufficient excuse to appear at the specified time and place in accordance with the terms of his recognizance. A person authorized to take bail may charge the fees authorized by section twenty-four of chapter two hundred and sixty-two, if he goes to the place of detention of the person to make a determination provided for in this section although said person is released on his personal recognizance without surety. Said fees shall not be charged by any clerk or assistant clerk of a district court during regular working hours.

A person aforesaid charged with an offense and not released on his personal recognizance without surety by a clerk or assistant clerk of the district court, a bail commissioner or master in chancery shall forthwith be brought before the next session of the district court for a review of the order to recognize in accordance with the standards set forth in the first paragraph of this section. The court shall provide as an explicit condition of release for any person admitted to bail pursuant to this section or section fifty-seven that should said person be charged with a crime during the period of his release, his bail may be revoked in accordance with this paragraph and the court shall enter in writing on the court docket that the person was so informed and the docket shall constitute prima facie evidence that the person was so informed. If a person is on release pending the adjudication of a prior charge, and the court before which the person is charged with committing a subsequent offense after a hearing at which the person shall have the right to be represented by counsel, finds probable cause to believe that the person has committed a crime during said period of release, the court shall then determine, in the exercise of its discretion, whether the release of said person will seriously endanger any person or the community. In making said determination, the court shall consider the gravity, nature and circumstances of the offenses charged, the person's record of convictions, if any, and whether said charges or convictions are for offenses involving the use or threat of physical force or violence against any person, whether the person is on probation, parole or other release pending completion of sentence for any conviction, whether he is on release pending sentence or appeal for any conviction, the person's mental condition, and any illegal drug distribution or present drug dependency. If the court determines that the release of said person will seriously endanger any person or the community and that the detention of the person is necessary to reasonably assure the safety of any person or the community, the court may revoke bail on the prior charge and may order said person held without bail pending the adjudication of said prior charge, for a period not to exceed sixty days. The hearing shall be held upon the person's first appearance before the court before which the person is charged with committing an offense while on release pending adjudication of a prior charge, unless that person, or the attorney for the commonwealth, seeks and the court allows, a continuance because a witness or document is not immediately available. Except for good cause, a continuance on motion of the person shall not exceed seven days and on motion of the attorney for the commonwealth may not exceed three business days. During such continuance, the person may be detained consistent with the provisions of this section. Said order shall state in writing the reasons therefor and shall be reviewed by the court upon the acquittal of the person, or the dismissal of, any of the cases involved. A person so held shall be brought to trial as soon as reasonably possible. A person aggrieved by the denial of a district court justice to admit him to bail on his personal recognizance without surety may petition the superior court for a review of the order of the recognizance and the justice of the district court shall thereupon immediately notify such person of his right to file a petition for review in the superior court. When a petition for review is filed in the district court or with the detaining authority subsequent to petitioner's district court appearance, the clerk of the district court or the detaining authority, as the case may be, shall immediately notify by telephone, the clerk and probation officer of the district court, the district attorney for the district in which the district court is located, the prosecuting officer, the petitioner's counsel, if any, and the clerk of courts of the county to which the petition is to be transmitted. The clerk of the district court, upon the filing of a petition for review, either in the district court or with the detaining authority, shall forthwith transmit the petition for review, a copy of the complaint and of the record of the court, including the appearance of the attorney, if any is entered, and a summary of the court's reasons for denying the release of the defendant on his personal recognizance without surety to the superior court for the county in which the district court is located, if a justice thereof is then sitting, or to the superior court of the nearest county in which a justice is then sitting; the probation officer of the district court shall transmit forthwith to the probation officer of the superior court, copies of all records of the probation office of said district court pertaining to the petitioner, including the petitioner's record of prior convictions, if any, as currently verified by inquiry of the commissioner of probation. The district court or the detaining authority, as the case may be, shall cause any petitioner in its custody to be brought before the said superior court on the same day the petition shall have been filed, unless the district court or the detaining authority shall determine that such appearance and hearing on the petition cannot practically take place before the adjournment of the sitting of said superior court for that day and in which event, the petitioner shall be caused to be brought before said court for such hearing during the morning of the next business day of the sitting of said superior court. The district court is authorized to order any officer authorized to execute criminal process to transfer the petitioner and any papers herein above described from the district court or the detaining authority to the superior court, and to coordinate the transfer of the petitioner and the papers by such officer. The petition for review shall constitute authority in the person or officer having custody of the petitioner to transport the petitioner to said superior court without the issuance of any writ or other legal process, provided, however, that any district or superior court is authorized to issue a writ of habeas corpus for the appearance forthwith of the petitioner before the superior court.

The superior court shall in accordance with the standards set forth in the first paragraph of this section, hear the petition for review as speedily as practicable and except for unusual circumstances, on the same day the petition is filed; provided, however, that the court may continue the hearing to the next business day if the required records and other necessary information are not available. The justice of the superior court may, after a hearing on the petition for review, order that the petitioner be released on bail on his personal recognizance without surety, or, in his discretion, to reasonably assure the effective administration of justice, make any other order of bail or recognizance or remand the petitioner in accordance with the terms of the process by which he was ordered committed by the district court.

If a defendant has posted bail in the district court and has subsequently been arraigned in the superior court for the same offense, the superior court clerk shall notify the district court clerk holding the defendant's bail of such arraignment. Upon such notification, the amount of any bail bond posted by a defendant in the district court shall be carried over to a bail bond required by the superior court. The superior court justices' discretion in setting the amount of bail shall not be affected by the provisions of this paragraph.

Except where the defendant has defaulted on his recognizance or has been surrendered by a probation officer, an order of bail or recognizance shall not be revoked, revised or amended by the district court, because the defendant has been bound over to the superior court; provided, however, that if any court, in its discretion, finds that changed circumstances or other factors not previously known or considered, make the order of bail or recognizance ineffective to reasonably assure the appearance of said defendant before the court, the court may make a further order of bail, either by increasing the amount of the recognizance or requiring sufficient surety or both, which order will not revoke the order of bail or recognizance previously in force and effect. The court may also review such changed circumstances or other factors not previously known or considered in accordance with the third paragraph of this section.

The chief justice of the district court department and the chief justice of the Boston municipal court department shall prescribe forms for use in their respective courts, for the purpose of notifying a defendant of his right to file a petition for review in the superior court, forms for a petition for review and forms for the implementation of any other procedural requirements. The clerk of courts shall forthwith notify the district court of all orders or judgments of the superior court on petitions for review. Costs or expenses of services and transportation under this section shall be ordered paid in the amount determined by the superior court out of the state treasury.

For an offense enumerated in section fifty-eight A, and upon the motion of an attorney for the commonwealth for an order of pretrial detention or imposition of conditions of release based on dangerousness, a justice of the district or superior court shall hold a hearing pursuant to the provisions of subsection (4) of said section fifty-eight A and shall admit such person to bail on his personal recognizance without surety or subject to conditions of release unless said justice, determines, in the exercise of his discretion, that such release will endanger the safety of any other person or the community.

Participation in a community corrections program pursuant to chapter 211F may be ordered by the court, in lieu of bail, or as a condition of release; provided, however, that the defendant shall consent to such participation.

NOTE "[W]e conclude that in setting the amount of bail, whether under G.L. c. 276, § 57 or § 58, a judge must consider a defendant's financial resources, but is not required to set bail in an amount the

1

defendant can afford if other relevant considerations weigh more heavily than the defendant's ability to provide the necessary security for his appearance at trial. Where, based on the judge's consideration of all the circumstances, including the record of defaults and other factors relevant to the likelihood of the defendant's appearance for trial, neither alternative nonfinancial conditions nor a bail amount the defendant can afford will adequately assure his appearance for trial, the judge may set bail at a higher amount, but no higher than necessary to ensure the defendant's appearance for trial." *Brangan v. Commonwealth*, 477 Mass. 691, 693 (2017). See also *A Juvenile v. Commonwealth*, 480 Mass. 1012 (2018), where the juvenile was in DCF custody and on the run and was held on unaffordable bail. The Supreme Judicial Court held that given the fact that the child was in the custody of DCF and had been a runaway for months, there was no reasonable alternative to assure the defendant's appearing in court other than setting a bail he cannot post. The court reiterated the holding in *Brangan*: "where a bail determination is likely to lead to pretrial detention, a judge making that determination must consider alternative nonfinancial conditions and must make findings in connection with the decision. Those findings should demonstrate that a judge has engaged in fair and meaningful consideration of reasonable alternatives relevant to the circumstances of the case such that a reviewing court can be satisfied that the requirements detailed in Brangan have been met." *A Juvenile v. Commonwealth*, 480 Mass. at 1014. In *A Juvenile*, the court stated that the record must show that "reasonable nonfinancial conditions were not discussed or considered by the judges below." *A Juvenile v. Commonwealth*, 480 Mass. at 1014.

§ 58A. Dangerousness hearing

[Amended by 2010 Mass. Acts c. 256, § 125, effective Nov. 4, 2010; 2014 Mass. Acts c. 260, §§ 33–38, effective Aug. 8, 2014; 2014 Mass. Acts c. 284, § 97, effective Jan. 1, 2015; 2018 Mass. Acts c. 69, §§ 174–76, effective Apr. 13, 2018; 2018 Mass. Acts c. 219, § 30, effective Nov. 7, 2018.]

(1) The commonwealth may move, based on dangerousness, for an order of pretrial detention or release on conditions for a felony offense that has as an element of the offense the use, attempted use or threatened use of physical force against the person of another or any other felony that, by its nature, involves a substantial risk that physical force against the person of another may result, including the crimes of burglary and arson whether or not a person has been placed at risk thereof, or a violation of an order pursuant to section 18, 34B or 34C of chapter 208, section 32 of chapter 209, section 3, 4 or 5 of chapter 209 A or section 15 or 20 of chapter 209C, or arrested and charged with a misdemeanor or felony involving abuse as defined in section 1 of said chapter 209A or while an order of protection issued under said chapter 209A was in effect against such person, an offense for which a mandatory minimum term of 3 years or more is prescribed in chapter 94C, arrested and charged with a violation of section 13B of chapter 268 or a charge of a third or subsequent violation of section 24 of chapter 90 within 10 years of the previous conviction for such violation, or convicted of a violent crime as defined in said section 121 of said chapter 140 for which a term of imprisonment was served and arrested and charged with a second or subsequent offense of felony possession of a weapon or machine gun as defined in section 121 of chapter 140, or arrested and charged with a violation of paragraph (a), (c) or (m) of section 10 of chapter 269, section 112 of chapter 266 or section 77 or 94 of chapter 272; provided, however, that the commonwealth may not move for an order of detention under this section based on possession of a large capacity feeding device without simultaneous possession of a large capacity weapon; or arrested and charged with a violation of section 10G of said chapter 269.

(2) Upon the appearance before a superior court or district court judge of an individual charged with an offense listed in subsection (1) and upon the motion of the commonwealth, the judicial officer shall hold a hearing pursuant to subsection (4) issue an order that, pending trial, the individual shall either be released on personal recognizance without surety; released on conditions of release as set forth herein; or detained under subsection (3).

If the judicial officer determines that personal recognizance will not reasonably assure the appearance of the person as required or will endanger the safety of any other person or the community, such judicial officer shall order the pretrial release of the person--

(A) subject to the condition that the person not commit a federal, state or local crime during the period of release; and

(B) subject to the least restrictive further condition, or combination of conditions, that such judicial officer determines will reasonably assure the appearance of the person as required and the safety of any other person and the community that the person--

(i) remain in the custody of a designated person, who agrees to assume supervision and to report any violation of a release condition to the court, if the designated person is able reasonably to assure the judicial officer that the person will appear as required and will not pose a danger to the safety of any other person or the community;

(ii) maintain employment, or, if unemployed, actively seek employment;

(iii) maintain or commence an educational program;

(iv) abide by specified restrictions on personal associations, place of abode or travel;

(v) avoid all contact with an alleged victim of the crime and with any potential witness or witnesses who may testify concerning the offense;

(vi) report on a regular basis to a designated law enforcement agency, pretrial service agency, or other agency;

(vii) comply with a specified curfew;

(viii) refrain from possessing a firearm, destructive device, or other dangerous weapon;

(ix) refrain from excessive use of alcohol, or any use of a narcotic drug or other controlled substance, without a prescription by a licensed medical practitioner;

(x) undergo available medical, psychological, or psychiatric treatment, including treatment for drug or alcohol dependency and remain in a specified institution if required for that purpose;

(xi) execute an agreement to forfeit upon failing to appear as required, property of a sufficient unencumbered value, including money, as is reasonably necessary to assure the appearance of the person as required, and shall provide the court with proof of ownership and the value of the property along with information regarding existing encumbrances as the judicial officer may require;

(xii) execute a bail bond with solvent sureties; who will execute an agreement to forfeit in such amount as is reasonably necessary to assure appearance of the person as required and shall provide the court with information regarding the value of the assets and liabilities of the surety if other than an approved surety and the nature and extent of encumbrances against the surety's property; such surety shall have a net worth which shall have sufficient unencumbered value to pay the amount of the bail bond;

(xiii) return to custody for specified hours following release for employment, schooling, or other limited purposes; and

(xiv) satisfy any other condition that is reasonably necessary to assure the appearance of the person as required and to assure the safety of any other person and the community.

The judicial officer may not impose a financial condition that results in the pretrial detention of the person.

The judicial officer may at any time amend the order to impose additional or different conditions of release.

Participation in a community corrections program pursuant to chapter 211F may be ordered by the court or as a condition of release; provided, however, that the defendant shall consent to such participation.

(3) If, after a hearing pursuant to the provisions of subsection (4), the district or superior court justice finds by clear and convincing evidence that no conditions of release will reasonably assure the safety of any other person or the community, said justice shall order the detention of the person prior to trial. A person detained under this subsection shall be brought to a trial as soon as reasonably

possible, but in absence of good cause, the person so held shall not be detained for a period exceeding 120 days by the district court or for a period exceeding 180 days by the superior court excluding any period of delay as defined in Massachusetts Rules of Criminal Procedure Rule 36(b)(2). A justice may not impose a financial condition under this section that results in the pretrial detention of the person. Nothing in this section shall be interpreted as limiting the imposition of a financial condition upon the person to reasonably assure his appearance before the courts.

(4) When a person is held under arrest for an offense listed in subsection (1) and upon a motion by the commonwealth, the judge shall hold a hearing to determine whether conditions of release will reasonably assure the safety of any other person or the community.

The hearing shall be held immediately upon the person's first appearance before the court unless that person, or the attorney for the commonwealth, seeks a continuance. Except for good cause, a continuance on motion of the person may not exceed seven days, and a continuance on motion of the attorney for the commonwealth may not exceed three business days. During a continuance, the individual shall be detained upon a showing that there existed probable cause to arrest the person. At the hearing, such person shall have the right to be represented by counsel, and, if financially unable to retain adequate representation, to have counsel appointed. The person shall be afforded an opportunity to testify, to present witnesses, to cross-examine witnesses who appear at the hearing, and to present information. Prior to the summons of an alleged victim, or a member of the alleged victim's family, to appear as a witness at the hearing, the person shall demonstrate to the court a good faith basis for the person's reasonable belief that the testimony from the witness will be material and relevant to support a conclusion that there are conditions of release that will reasonably assure the safety of any other person or the community. The rules concerning admissibility of evidence in criminal trials shall not apply to the presentation and consideration of information at the hearing and the judge shall consider hearsay contained in a police report or the statement of an alleged victim or witness. The facts the judge uses to support findings pursuant to subsection (3), that no conditions will reasonably assure the safety of any other person or the community, shall be supported by clear and convincing evidence. In a detention order issued pursuant to the provisions of said subsection (3) the judge shall (a) include written findings of fact and a written statement of the reasons for the detention; (b) direct that the person be committed to custody or confinement in a corrections facility separate, to the extent practicable, from persons awaiting or serving sentence or being held in custody pending appeal; and (c) direct that the person be afforded reasonable opportunity for private consultation with his counsel. The person may be detained pending completion of the hearing. The hearing may be reopened by the judge, at any time before trial, or upon a motion of the commonwealth or the person detained if the judge finds that: (i) information exists that was not known at the time of the hearing or that there has been a change in circumstances and (ii) that such information or change in circumstances has a material bearing on the issue of whether there are conditions of release that will reasonably assure the safety of any other person or the community.

(5) In his determination as to whether there are conditions of release that will reasonably assure the safety of any other individual or the community, said justice, shall, on the basis of any information which he can reasonably obtain, take into account the nature and seriousness of the danger posed to any person or the community that would result by the person's release, the nature and circumstances of the offense charged, the potential penalty the person faces, the person's family ties, employment record and history of mental illness, his reputation, the risk that the person will obstruct or attempt to obstruct justice or threaten, injure or intimidate or attempt to threaten, injure or intimidate a prospective witness or juror, his record of convictions, if any, any illegal drug distribution or present drug dependency, whether the person is on bail pending adjudication of a prior charge, whether the acts alleged involve abuse as defined in section one of chapter two hundred and nine A, or violation of a temporary or permanent order issued pursuant to section eighteen or thirty-four B of chapter two hundred and eight, section thirty-two of chapter two hundred and nine, sections three, four or five of chapter two hundred and nine A, or sections fifteen or twenty of chapter two hundred and nine C, whether the person has any history of orders issued against him pursuant to the aforesaid sections, whether he is on probation, parole or other release pending completion of sentence for any conviction and whether he is on release pending sentence or appeal for any conviction; provided, however, that if the person who has attained the age of 18 years is held under arrest for a violation of an order issued pursuant to section 18 or 34B of chapter 208, section 32 of chapter 209, section 3, 4 or 5 of chapter 209A or section 15 or 20 of chapter 209C or any act that would constitute abuse, as defined in section 1 of said chapter 209A, or a violation of sections 13M or 15D of chapter 265, said justice shall make a written determination as to the considerations required by this subsection which shall be filed in the domestic violence record keeping system.

(6) Nothing in this section shall be construed as modifying or limiting the presumption of innocence.

(7) A person aggrieved by the denial of a district court justice to admit him to bail on his personal recognizance with or without surety may petition the superior court for a review of the order of the recognizance and the justice of the district court shall thereupon immediately notify such person of his right to file a petition for review in the superior court. When a petition for review is filed in the district court or with the detaining authority subsequent to petitioner's district court appearance, the clerk of the district court or the detaining authority, as the case may be, shall immediately notify by telephone, the clerk and probation officer of the district court, the district attorney for the district in which the district court is located, the prosecuting officer, the petitioner's counsel, if any, and the clerk of courts of the county to which the petition is to be transmitted. The clerk of the district court, upon the filing of a petition for review, either in the district court or with the detaining authority, shall forthwith transmit the petition for review, a copy of the complaint and the record of the court, including the appearance of the attorney, if any is entered, and a summary of the court's reasons for denying the release of the defendant on his personal recognizance with or without surety to the superior court for the county in which the district court is located, if a justice thereof is then sitting, or to the superior court of the nearest county in which a justice is then sitting; the probation officer of the district court shall transmit forthwith to the probation officer of the superior court, copies of all records of the probation office of said district court pertaining to the petitioner, including the petitioner's record of prior convictions, if any, as currently verified by inquiry of the commissioner of probation. The district court or the detaining authority, as the case may be, shall cause any petitioner in its custody to be brought before the said superior court within two business days of the petition having been filed. The district court is authorized to order any officer authorized to execute criminal process to transfer the petitioner and any papers herein above described from the district court or the detaining authority to the superior court, and to coordinate the transfer of the petitioner and the papers by such officer. The petition for review shall constitute authority in the person or officer having custody of the petitioner to transport the petitioner to said superior court without the issuance of any writ or other legal process; provided, however, that any district or superior court is authorized to issue a writ of habeas corpus for the appearance forthwith of the petitioner before the superior court.

The superior court shall in accordance with the standards set forth in section fifty-eight A, hear the petition for review under section fifty-eight A as speedily as practicable and in any event within five business days of the filing of the petition. The justice of the superior court hearing the review may consider the record below which the commonwealth and the person may supplement. The justice of the superior court may, after a hearing on the petition for review, order that the petitioner be released on bail on his personal recognizance without surety, or, in his discretion, to reasonably assure the effective administration of justice, make any other order of bail or recognizance or remand the petitioner in accordance with the terms of the process by which he was ordered committed by the district court.

(8) If after a hearing under subsection (4) detention under subsection (3) is ordered or pretrial release subject to conditions under subsection (2) is ordered, then: (A) the clerk shall immediately notify the probation officer of the order; and (B) the order of detention under subsection (3) or order of pretrial release subject to conditions under subsection (2) shall be recorded in (i) the defendant's criminal record as compiled by the commissioner of probation under section 100 and (ii) the domestic violence record keeping system.

NOTE 1 *Commonwealth v. Diggs/Soto*, 475 Mass. 79 (2016), is the first case interpreting the language "held under arrest" in § 58A(4). In this case the court stated: "where a criminal defendant has been arrested or is subject to an outstanding arrest warrant for an enumerated offense, the defendant may be subject to pretrial detention under G.L. c. 276, § 58A(4), even if the defendant is not held in custody following the arrest, so long as the dangerousness hearing takes place 'immediately upon the person's first appearance before the court.'" *Commonwealth v. Diggs/Soto*, 475 Mass. at 80.

NOTE 2 Section 58A(1)'s residual clause ("any other felony that, by its nature, involves a substantial risk that physical force against the person of another may result") was held unconstitutional in *Scione v. Commonwealth*, 428 Mass. 225 (2019). The court stated: "the language in the residual clause of § 58A is unconstitutionally vague under art. 12, and therefore § 23A cannot qualify as a predicate offense pursuant to it." *Scione v. Commonwealth*, 428 Mass. at 232.

§ 58B. Revocation of release

[Amended by 2006 Mass. Acts c. 48, § 9, effective Mar. 30, 2006; 2014 Mass. Acts c. 260, § 38, effective Aug. 8, 2014.]

A person who has been released after a hearing pursuant to sections 42A, 58, 58A or 87 and who has violated a condition of his release, shall be subject to a revocation of release and an order of detention. The judicial officer shall enter an order of revocation and detention if after a hearing the judicial officer finds (1) that there is probable cause to believe that the person has committed a federal or state crime while on release, or clear and convincing evidence that the person has violated any other condition of release; and (2) the judicial officer finds that there are no conditions of release that will reasonably assure the person will not pose a danger to the safety of any other person or the community; or the person is unlikely to abide by any condition or combination of conditions of release.

If there is probable cause to believe that, while on release, the person committed a federal felony or an offense described in clause (1), a rebuttable presumption arises that no condition or combination of conditions will assure that the person will not pose a danger to the safety of any other person or the community. If the judicial officer finds that there are conditions of release that will assure that the person will not pose a danger to the safety of any other person or the community, and that the person will abide by such conditions, the judicial officer shall treat the person in accordance with the provisions of this section and may amend the conditions of release accordingly. Upon the person's first appearance before the judicial officer in the court which will conduct proceedings for revocation of an order of release under this section, the hearing concerning revocation shall be held immediately unless that person or the attorney for the commonwealth seeks a continuance. During a continuance the person shall be detained without bail unless the judicial officer finds that there are conditions of release that will reasonably assure that the person will not pose a danger to the safety of any other person or the community and that the person will abide by conditions of release. If the person is detained without bail, except for good cause, a continuance on motion of the person shall not exceed seven days, a continuance on motion of the attorney for the commonwealth or probation shall not exceed three business days. A person detained under this subsection, shall be brought to trial as soon as reasonably possible, but in the absence of good cause, a person so held shall not be detained for a period exceeding ninety days excluding any period of delay as defined in Massachusetts Rules of Criminal Procedure Rule 36(b)(2).

§ 71. Default on recognizance

If a person under recognizance to appear and answer or to prosecute an appeal in a criminal case fails to appear according to his recognizance, and if a person under recognizance to testify in a criminal prosecution fails to perform the condition of his recognizance, his default shall be recorded, his obligation and that of his sureties forfeited, and process issued against them or such of them as the prosecuting officer directs; but in such suit no costs shall be taxed for travel. No such process shall issue in cases where bank books, bonds or money have been deposited at the time of such recognizance.

§ 82A. Failure to appear in court after release on bail or recognizance; penalty

A person who is released by court order or other lawful authority on bail or recognizance on condition that he will appear personally at a specified time and place and who fails without sufficient excuse to so appear shall be punished by a fine of not more than one thousand dollars or by imprisonment in a house of correction for not more than one year, or both, in the case of a misdemeanor, and by a fine of not more than fifty thousand dollars and imprisonment in a state prison for not more than five years, or a house of correction for not more than two and one-half years, or by fine and imprisonment, in the case of a felony.

A term of imprisonment imposed under this section shall be consecutive to any other sentence of imprisonment for the offense for which the prisoner failed to appear.

§ 85. Probation officers

Each person who receives an appointment as a probation officer shall, within six months of the date of his appointment, attend a basic orientation training course conducted by the commissioner of probation pursuant to section ninety-nine. All probation officers shall attend at least every three years an in-service training course pursuant to this section. In addition to the other duties imposed upon him, each probation officer shall, as the court may direct, inquire into the nature of every criminal case brought before the court under the appointment of which he acts, and inform the court, so far as is possible, whether the defendant has previously been convicted of crime and in the case of a criminal prosecution before said court charging a person with an offense punishable by imprisonment for more than one year the probation officer shall in any event present to the court such information as the commissioner of probation has in his possession relative to prior criminal prosecutions, if any, of such person and to the disposition of each such prosecution, and all other available information relative thereto, before such person is admitted to bail in court and also before disposition of the case against him by sentence, or placing on file or probation. Such record of the probation officer presented to the court shall not contain as part thereof any information of prior criminal prosecutions, if any, of the defendant wherein the defendant was found not guilty by the court or jury in said prior criminal prosecution. Prior to the aforesaid disposition such record of the probation officer shall be made available to the defendant and his counsel for inspection. When it comes to the knowledge of a probation officer that the defendant in a criminal case before his court charged with an offense punishable by imprisonment is then on probation in another court or is then at liberty on parole or on a permit to be at liberty, such probation officer shall forthwith certify the fact of the presence of the defendant before his court to the probation officer of such other court or the parole authorities granting or issuing such parole or permit to be at liberty, as the case may be. He may recommend to the justice of his own court that any person convicted be placed on probation. He shall perform such other duties as the court requires. He shall keep full records of all cases investigated by him or placed in his care by the court, and of all duties performed by him. Every person released upon probation shall be given by the probation officer a written statement of the terms and conditions of the release.

§ 87. Placing certain persons in care of probation officer

[Amended by 2010 Mass. Acts c. 267, § 66, effective Nov. 5, 2010; 2011 Mass. Acts c. 178, § 26, effective Nov. 21, 2011; 2013 Mass. Acts c. 84, § 30A, effective Sept. 18, 2013.]

The superior court, any district court and any juvenile court may place on probation in the care of its probation officer any person before it charged with an offense or a crime for such time and upon such conditions as it deems proper, with the defendant's consent, before trial and before a plea of guilty, or in any case after a finding or verdict of guilty; provided, that, in the case of any child under the age of 18 placed upon probation by the superior court, he may be placed in the care of a probation officer of any district court or of any juvenile court, within the judicial district of which such child resides; and provided further, that no person convicted under section twenty-two A, 22B, 22C, 24B or subsection (b) of section 50 of chapter two hundred and sixty-five or section thirty-five A of chapter two hundred and seventy-two shall, if it appears that he has previously been convicted under said sections and was eighteen years of age or older at the time of committing the offense for which he was so convicted, be released on parole or probation prior to the completion of five years of his sentence.

§ 87A. Conditions of probation; probation fees

[Amended by 2002 Mass. Acts c. 300, § 13 and 2003 Mass. Acts c. 26, § 510, effective July 1, 2003; 2009 Mass. Acts c. 27, §§ 99, 100, effective July 1, 2009; 2014 Mass. Acts c. 165, § 179, effective June 1, 2015; 2016 Mass. Acts c. 133, § 121, effective July 1, 2016; 2018 Mass. Acts c. 69, §§ 180–182, effective Apr. 13, 2018.]

The conditions of probation imposed by a court upon a person pursuant to section eighty-seven of this chapter, section fifty-eight of chapter one hundred and nineteen or section one or section one A of chapter two hundred and seventy-nine, may include, but shall not be limited to, participation by said person in specified rehabilitative programs or performance by said person of specified community service work for a stated period of time. If the court requires as a condition of probation that the defendant reside in alcohol and drug free housing within the commonwealth, the judge issuing the order shall require the probation officer to refer the defendant only to alcohol and drug free housing certified under section 18A of chapter 17 and the probation officer shall require the defendant to reside in such certified housing in order to satisfy such condition. If accredited alcohol and drug free housing is not available, the judge issuing the order may permit the probation officer to refer the person placed on supervised probation to alcohol and substance free housing that is available and that, in the judge's discretion, appropriately supports the recovery goals of the person. If the court imposes as a condition of probation that the person reside in alcohol and drug free housing in another state, the judge issuing the order may permit the probation officer to refer the person to alcohol and drug free housing that, in the judge's discretion, appropriately supports the recovery goals of the person. No person placed on probation shall be found to have violated a condition of probation: (i) solely on the basis of possession or use of a controlled substance that has been lawfully dispensed pursuant to a valid prescription to that person by a health professional registered to prescribe a controlled substance pursuant to chapter 94C and acting within the lawful scope of the health professional's practice; or (ii) solely on the basis of possession or use of medical marijuana obtained in compliance with and in quantities consistent with applicable state regulations if that person received a written certification from a healthcare professional for the use of medical marijuana to treat a debilitating medical condition and the person possesses a valid medical marijuana registration card and if the quantity in the person's possession is not greater than the amount recommended in the healthcare professional's written certification. If a person is required to submit a DNA sample pursuant to chapter 22E, such submittal and compliance with chapter 22E shall be required as a condition of probation.

The court shall assess upon every person placed on supervised probation, including all persons placed on probation for offenses under section 24 of chapter 90, a monthly probation supervision fee, hereinafter referred to as "probation fee", in the amount of $60 per month. Said person shall pay said probation fee once each month during such time as said person remains on supervised probation. The court shall assess upon every person placed on administrative supervised probation a monthly administrative probation supervision fee, hereinafter referred to as "administrative probation fee", in the amount of $45 per month. Said person shall pay said administrative probation fee once each month during such time as said person remains on administrative supervised probation. Notwithstanding the foregoing, said fees shall not be assessed upon any person accused or convicted of a violation of section 1 or 15 of chapter 273, where compliance with an order of support for a spouse or minor child is a condition of probation.

The court shall not assess said monthly probation fee or said administrative probation fee upon any person placed on supervised probation or administrative supervised probation after release from prison or a house of correction for said person's first 6 months of such probation. Either or both of said fees shall be assessed after the first 6 months of such probation unless otherwise waived by the court pursuant to this section.

The court may waive payment of either or both of said fees if it determines after a hearing that such payment would impose a substantial financial hardship on the person, the person's immediate family or dependents. Following the hearing and upon a finding of hardship, the court may require any such person to perform unpaid community service work at a public or nonprofit agency or facility, monitored by the probation department, for not more than 4 hours per month in lieu of payment of a probation fee. A waiver shall be in effect only during the period of time that a person is unable to pay the monthly probation fee.

The court may waive payment of either or both of said fees in whole or in part if said person is assessed payment of restitution. In such cases, said fees may be waived only to the extent and during the period that restitution is paid in an amount equivalent to said fee.

Said probation fee shall be collected by the several probation offices of the trial court and transmitted to the state treasurer for deposit into the General Fund. The state treasurer shall account for all such fees received and report said fees annually, itemized by court division, to the house and senate committees on ways and means.

The court shall also assess upon every person placed on supervised probation, including all persons placed on probation for offenses under section 24 of chapter 90, a monthly probationers' victim services surcharge, hereinafter referred to as "victim services surcharge", in the amount of $5 per month. Said person shall pay said victim services surcharge once each month during such time as said person remains on supervised probation. The court shall assess upon every person placed on administrative supervised probation a monthly administrative probationer's victim services surcharge, hereinafter referred to as "administrative victim services surcharge" in the amount of $5 per month.

Said person shall pay said administrative victim services surcharge once each month during such time as said person remains on administrative supervised probation. Notwithstanding the foregoing, said fees shall not be assessed upon any person accused or convicted of a violation of section 1 or 15 of chapter 273, where compliance with an order of support for a spouse or minor child is a condition of probation.

The court may waive payment of either or both of said fees if it has determined, after a hearing, that the payment would impose a substantial financial hardship on the person, the person's immediate family or dependents. A waiver shall be in effect only during the period of time that the person is unable to pay the monthly probation fee.

Said probation fee shall be collected by the several probation offices of the trial court and shall be transmitted to the state treasurer for deposit into the General Fund of the commonwealth. The state treasurer shall account for all such fees received and report said fees annually, itemized by court division, to the house and senate committees on ways and means.

Notwithstanding this section or any other general or special law to the contrary, no fee or surcharge required pursuant to this section shall be assessed upon any person placed on probation while under the age of 18.

§ 91. Power of probation officers appointed by Boston juvenile court to serve process

Probation officers appointed by the Boston juvenile court may serve such process as may be directed to them by the court.

§ 92. Restitution or reparation to injured person through probation officer

If a person is placed on probation upon condition that he make restitution or reparation to the person injured by him in the commission of his offence, and payment is not made at once, the court may order that it shall be made to the probation officer, who shall give receipts for and keep record of all payments made to him, pay the money to the person injured and keep his receipt therefor, and notify the clerk of the court whenever the full amount of the money is received or paid in accordance with such order or with any modification thereof.

§ 92A. Restitution in cases involving motor vehicle theft or fraudulent claims

[Amended by 2018 Mass. Acts c. 69, § 184, effective Apr. 18, 2018.]

A person found guilty of violating the provisions of sections twenty-seven, twenty-eight, one hundred and eleven B and one hundred and thirty-nine of chapter two hundred and sixty-six shall, in all cases, upon conviction, in addition to any other punishment, be ordered to make restitution to any person whom the court deems appropriate for any financial loss sustained by the victim of his crime, his dependents or an insurer as a result of the commission of the crime. The term "financial loss" shall be interpreted to include but shall not be limited to, loss of earnings, out-of-pocket expenses, and replacement costs. Losses due to pain and suffering are not financial loss. Restitution shall be interpreted to include monetary reimbursement, work or service, or a combination thereof, provided to any person, organization, corporation, or governmental entity, the court determines, has suffered said damage or financial loss, or to perform such work or service for any other person, organization, corporation or governmental entity as the court may determine. Restitution shall be imposed in addition to incarceration or fine, but not in lieu thereof. In an extraordinary case such as indigency, the court may determine that the interests of the victim and justice would not be served by ordering restitution. In such a case, the court shall make and enter specific written findings on the record concerning the extraordinary circumstances presented which militated against the imposition of restitution.

The court shall, after conviction, conduct an evidentiary hearing to ascertain the extent of the damages or financial loss suffered as a result of the defendant's crime. The court may then determine the amount and method of restitution. In so determining, the court shall consider the financial resources of the defendant and the burden restitution will impose on the defendant. The defendant's present and future ability to make such restitution shall be considered.

A defendant ordered to make restitution may petition the court for remission from any payment of restitution or from any unpaid portion thereof. If the court finds that the payment of restitution due will cause a substantial financial hardship to the defendant, the defendant's immediate family or the defendant's dependents, the court may grant remission from any payment of restitution, or modify the amount, time or method of payment.

If a defendant who is required to make restitution defaults in any payment of restitution or installment thereof, the court may hold him in contempt unless said defendant has made a good faith effort to make restitution. If the defendant has made a good faith effort to make restitution, the court may, upon motion of the defendant, modify the order requiring restitution by:

(a) providing for additional time to make any payment in restitution;

(b) reducing the amount of any payment in restitution or installment thereof;

(c) granting a remission from any payment of restitution or part thereof.

Restitution shall not be authorized to a party whom the court determines to be aggrieved, without that party's consent.

§ 100. Detailed reports of probation work; records; accessibility of information

[Amended by 2010 Mass. Acts c. 256, §§ 126–127, effective Nov. 10, 2012.]

Every probation officer, or the chief or senior probation officer of a court having more than one probation officer, shall transmit to the commissioner of probation, in such form and at such times as he shall require, detailed reports regarding the work of probation in the court, and the commissioner of correction, the penal institutions commissioner of Boston and the county commissioners of counties other than Suffolk shall transmit to the commissioner, as aforesaid, detailed and complete records relative to all paroles and permits to be at liberty granted or issued by them, respectively, to the revoking of the same and to the length of time served on each sentence to imprisonment by each prisoner so released specifying the institution where each such sentence was served; and under the direction of the commissioner a record shall be kept of all such cases as the commissioner may require for the information of the justices and probation officers. Police officials shall co-operate with the commissioner and the probation officers in obtaining and reporting information concerning persons on probation. The information so obtained and recorded shall not be regarded as public records and shall not be open for public inspection but shall be accessible to the justices and probation officers of the courts, to the police commissioner for the city of Boston, to all chiefs of police and city marshals, and to such departments of the state and local governments as the commissioner may determine. Upon payment of a fee of three dollars for each search, such records shall be accessible to such departments of the federal government and to such educational and charitable corporations and institutions as the commissioner may determine. The commissioner of correction and the department of youth services shall at all times give to the commissioner and the probation officers such information as may be obtained from the records concerning prisoners under sentence or who have been released. The commissioner may use systems operated by the department of criminal justice information services, pursuant to sections one hundred sixty-seven to one hundred seventy-eight, inclusive, of chapter six, for any record-keeping lawfully required by him provided that such records remain subject to the regulations of said department.

§ 100A. Requests to seal files; conditions; application of section; effect of sealing of records

[Amended by 2010 Mass. Acts c. 256, §§ 128–130, effective May 4, 2012; 2018 Mass. Acts c. 69, §§ 186–192, effective Oct. 13, 2018.]

Any person having a record of criminal court appearances and dispositions in the commonwealth on file with the office of the commissioner of probation may, on a form furnished by the commissioner and signed under the penalties of perjury, request that the commissioner seal the file. The commissioner shall comply with the request provided that: (1) the person's court appearance and court disposition records, including any period of incarceration or custody for any misdemeanor record to be sealed occurred not less than 3 years before the request; (2) the person's court appearance and court disposition records, including any period of incarceration or custody for any felony record to be sealed occurred not less than 7 years before the request; (3) the person had not been found guilty of any criminal offense within the commonwealth in the case of a misdemeanor, 3 years before the request, and in the case of a felony, 7 years before request, except motor vehicle offenses in which the penalty does not exceed a fine of $50; (4) the form includes a statement by the petitioner that he has not been convicted of any criminal offense in any other state, United States possession or in a court of federal jurisdiction, except such motor vehicle offenses, as aforesaid, and has not been imprisoned in any state or county in the case of a misdemeanor, within the preceding 3 years, and in the case of a felony, within the preceding 7 years; and (5) the person's record does not include convictions of offenses other than those to which this section applies. This section shall apply to court appearances and dispositions of all offenses; provided, however, that this section shall not apply in case of convictions for violations of sections 121 to 131H, inclusive, of chapter 140 or for violations of chapter 268 or chapter 268A, except for convictions for resisting arrest.

In carrying out the provisions of this section, notwithstanding any laws to the contrary:

1. Any recorded offense which was a felony when committed and has since become a misdemeanor shall be treated as a misdemeanor.

2. Any recorded offense which is no longer a crime shall be eligible for sealing forthwith, except in cases where the elements of the offense continue to be a crime under a different designation.

3. In determining the period for eligibility, any subsequently recorded offenses for which the dispositions are "not guilty", "dismissed for want of prosecution", "dismissed at request of complainant", "nol prossed", or "no bill" shall not be held to interrupt the running of the required period for eligibility.

4. If it cannot be ascertained that a recorded offense was a felony when committed said offense shall be treated as a misdemeanor.

5. Any violation of section 7 of chapter 209A or section 9 of chapter 258E shall be treated as a felony.

6. Sex offenses, as defined in section 178C of chapter 6, shall not be eligible for sealing for 15 years following their disposition, including termination of supervision, probation or any period of incarceration, or for so long as the offender is under a duty to register in the commonwealth or in any other state where the offender resides or would be under such a duty if residing in the commonwealth, whichever is longer; provided, however, that any sex offender who has at any time been classified as a level 2 or level 3 sex offender, pursuant to section 178K of chapter 6, shall not be eligible for sealing of sex offenses.

When records of criminal appearances and criminal dispositions are sealed by the commissioner in his files, he shall notify forthwith the clerk and the probation officer of the courts in which the convictions or dispositions have occurred, or other entries have been made, of such sealing, and said clerks and probation officers likewise shall seal records of the same proceedings in their files.

Such sealed records shall not operate to disqualify a person in any examination, appointment or application for public service in the service of the commonwealth or of any political subdivision thereof; nor shall such sealed records be admissible in evidence or used in any way in any court proceedings or hearings before any boards or commissions, except in imposing sentence in subsequent criminal proceedings, and except that in any proceedings under sections 1 to 39I, inclusive, of chapter 119, sections 2 to 5, inclusive, of chapter 201, chapters 208, 209, 209A, 209B, 209C, or sections 1 to 11A, inclusive, of chapter 210, a party having reasonable cause to believe that information in a sealed criminal record of another party may be relevant to (1) an issue of custody or visitation of a child, (2) abuse, as defined in section 1 of chapter 209A or (3) the safety of any person may upon motion seek to introduce the sealed record into evidence. The judge shall first review such records in camera and determine those records that are potentially relevant and admissible. The judge shall then conduct a closed hearing on the admissibility of those records determined to be potentially admissible; provided, however, that such records shall not be discussed in open court and, if admitted, shall be impounded and made available only to the parties, their attorneys and court personnel who have a demonstrated need to receive them.

An application used to screen applicants for employment, housing or an occupational or professional license which seeks information concerning prior arrests or convictions of the applicant shall include the following statement: "An applicant for employment or for housing or an occupational or professional license with a sealed record on file with the commissioner of probation may answer 'no record' with respect to an inquiry herein relative to prior arrests, criminal court appearances or convictions. An applicant for employment or for housing or an occupational or professional license with a sealed record on file with the commissioner of probation may answer 'no record' to an inquiry herein relative to prior arrests or criminal court appearances. In addition, any applicant for employment or for housing or an occupational or professional license may answer 'no record' with respect to any inquiry relative to prior arrests, court appearances and adjudications in all cases of delinquency or as a child in need of services which did not result in a complaint transferred to the superior court for criminal prosecution." The attorney general may enforce the provisions of this paragraph by a suit in equity commenced in the superior court.

The commissioner, in response to inquiries by authorized persons other than any law enforcement agency, any court, or any appointing authority, shall in the case of a sealed record or in the case of court appearances and adjudications in a case of delinquency or the case of a child in need of services which did not result in a complaint transferred to the superior court for criminal prosecution, report that no record exists.

§ 100B. Requests to seal delinquency files or records; conditions; sealing by commissioner; notice for compliance; effect of sealing; limited disclosure

Any person having a record of entries of a delinquency court appearance in the commonwealth on file in the office of the commissioner of probation may, on a form furnished by the commissioner, signed under the penalties of perjury, request that the

1

commissioner seal such file. The commissioner shall comply with such request provided (1) that any court appearance or disposition including court supervision, probation, commitment or parole, the records for which are to be sealed, terminated not less than three years prior to said request; (2) that said person has not been adjudicated delinquent or found guilty of any criminal offense within the commonwealth in the three years preceding such request, except motor vehicle offenses in which the penalty does not exceed a fine of fifty dollars nor been imprisoned under sentence or committed as a delinquent within the commonwealth within the preceding three years; and (3) said form includes a statement by the petitioner that he has not been adjudicated delinquent or found guilty of any criminal offense in any other state, United States possession or in a court of federal jurisdiction, except such motor vehicle offenses as aforesaid, and has not been imprisoned under sentence or committed as a delinquent in any state or county within the preceding three years.

When records of delinquency appearances and delinquency dispositions are sealed by the commissioner in his files, the commissioner shall notify forthwith the clerk and the probation officer of the courts in which the adjudications or dispositions have occurred, or other entries have been made, and the department of youth services of such sealing, and said clerks, probation officers, and department of youth services likewise shall seal records of the same proceedings in their files.

Such sealed records of a person shall not operate to disqualify a person in any future examination, appointment or application for public service under the government of the commonwealth or of any political subdivision thereof; nor shall such sealed records be admissible in evidence or used in any way in any court proceedings or hearings before any boards of commissioners, except in imposing sentence for subsequent offenses in delinquency or criminal proceedings.

Notwithstanding any other provision to the contrary, the commissioner shall report such sealed delinquency record to inquiring police and court agencies only as "sealed delinquency record over three years old" and to other authorized persons who may inquire as "no record". The information contained in said sealed delinquency record shall be made available to a judge or probation officer who affirms that such person, whose record has been sealed, has been adjudicated a delinquent or has pleaded guilty or has been found guilty of and is awaiting sentence for a crime committed subsequent to sealing of such record. Said information shall be used only for the purpose of consideration in imposing sentence.

NOTE Because of the existence of the statutory scheme contained in G.L. c. 276, §§ 100A and B, the Juvenile Court does not have discretion to order the commissioner of probation to expunge a juvenile's delinquency record. *Commonwealth v. Gavin G.*, 437 Mass. 470 (2002). *Cf. Police Comm'r of Boston v. Mun. Court of Dorchester Dist.*, 374 Mass. 640 (1978).

§ 100C. Sealing of records or files in certain criminal cases; effect upon employment reports; enforcement

[Amended by 2010 Mass. Acts c. 256, § 131–132, effective May 4, 2012; 2018 Mass. Acts c. 69, §§ 193–194, effective Oct. 13, 2018.]

In any criminal case wherein the defendant has been found not guilty by the court or jury, or a no bill has been returned by the grand jury, or a finding of no probable cause has been made by the court, the commissioner of probation shall seal said court appearance and disposition recorded in his files and the clerk and the probation officers of the courts in which the proceedings occurred or were initiated shall likewise seal the records of the proceedings in their files. The provisions of this paragraph shall not apply if the defendant makes a written request to the commissioner not to seal the records of the proceedings.

In any criminal case wherein a nolle prosequi has been entered, or a dismissal has been entered by the court, and it appears to the court that substantial justice would best be served, the court shall direct the clerk to seal the records of the proceedings in his files. The clerk shall forthwith notify the commissioner of probation and the probation officer of the courts in which the proceedings occurred or were initiated who shall likewise seal the records of the proceedings in their files.

Such sealed records shall not operate to disqualify a person in any examination, appointment or application for public employment in the service of the commonwealth or of any political subdivision thereof.

An application used to screen applicants for employment, housing or an occupational or professional license which seeks information concerning prior arrests or convictions of the applicant shall include in addition to the statement required under section one hundred A the following statement: "An applicant for employment, housing or an occupational or professional license with a sealed record on file with the commissioner of probation may answer 'no record' with respect to an inquiry herein relative to prior arrests or criminal court appearances." The attorney general may enforce the provisions of this section by a suit in equity commenced in the superior court.

The commissioner or the clerk of courts in any district or superior court or the Boston municipal court, in response to inquiries by authorized persons other than any law enforcement agency or any court, shall in the case of a sealed record report that no record exists. After a finding or verdict of guilty on a subsequent offense such sealed record shall be made available to the probation officer and the same, with the exception of a not guilty, a no bill, or a no probable cause, shall be made available to the court.

Chapter 277. Indictments and Proceedings Before Trial

§ 20. Time and place of commission of crime

The time and place of the commission of the crime need not be alleged unless it is an essential element thereof. The allegation of time in the caption shall, unless otherwise stated, be considered as an allegation that the act was committed before the finding of the indictment after it became a crime, and within the period of limitations. The name of the county and court in the caption shall, unless otherwise stated, be considered as an allegation that the act was committed within the territorial jurisdiction of the court. All allegations of the indictment shall, unless otherwise stated, be considered to refer to the same time and place.

§ 21. Means

The means by which a crime is committed need not be alleged in the indictment unless an essential element of the crime.

§ 24. Description of value or price

The value or price of property need not be stated, unless an essential element of the crime. If the nature, degree or punishment of a crime depends upon the fact that the property exceeds or does not exceed a certain value, it may be described, as the case may be, of more than that value, or of not more than that value.

§ 25. Description of ownership

If an indictment for a crime involving the commission or attempted commission of an injury to property describes the property with sufficient certainty in other respects to identify the act, it need not allege the name of the owner.

§ 26. Description of public place

If one element of the criminality of an act is its commission in a public place, and if such place is not more particularly defined in the statute, the act may be alleged generally to have been committed "in a public place".

§ 33. Unnecessary and immaterial allegations

Presumptions and conclusions of law, matters of which judicial notice is taken and allegations not required to be proved need not be alleged. An indictment shall not be considered defective or insufficient because it omits to allege that the crime was committed, or the act was done "traitorously", "feloniously", "burglariously", "willfully", "maliciously", "negligently", "unlawfully" or otherwise similarly to describe the crime, unless such description is an element of the crime charged, or because it omits to allege that the crime was committed or done with "force and arms", or "against the peace", or against the form of the statute or statutes, or against a by-law, ordinance, order, rule or regulation of any public authority, or because it omits to state or misstates the title, occupation, estate or degree of the defendant or of any other person named in the indictment, or of the name of the county, city, town or place of his residence, unless such omission or misstatement tends to the prejudice of the defendant, or by reason of describing a fine or forfeiture as enuring to the use of the commonwealth instead of to the use of the county, city or town, or by reason of any misstatement as to the appropriation of any fine or forfeiture, or by reason of its failure to allege or recite a special statute or a bylaw or ordinance of a city or town or order of the mayor and aldermen or selectmen or rules or regulations of any public board of officers.

§ 34. Immaterial defects

An indictment shall not be dismissed or be considered defective or insufficient if it is sufficient to enable the defendant to understand the charge and to prepare his defense; nor shall A be considered defective or insufficient for lack of any description or information which might be obtained by requiring a bill of particulars.

§ 35. Variance; prejudice

A defendant shall not be acquitted on the ground of variance between the allegations and proof if the essential elements of the crime are correctly stated, unless he is thereby prejudiced in his defense. He shall not be acquitted by reason of an immaterial misnomer of a third party, an immaterial mistake in the description of property or the ownership thereof, failure to prove unnecessary allegations in the description of the crime or any other immaterial mistake in the indictment.

§ 38. Allegations, bill of particulars, presumption and proof in prosecutions involving controlled substances

In a prosecution under any provision of chapter ninety-four C, for unlawfully manufacturing, dispensing or distributing a controlled substance in violation of any provision of said chapter, it shall be sufficient to allege that the defendant did unlawfully manufacture, dispense or distribute, as the case may be, such alleged substance, without any further allegations, without naming the person to whom it dispensed or distributed, or quantity of the substance; but the defendant shall be entitled to a bill of particulars. In such a prosecution, a defendant relying upon a prescription, written order, receipt, registration, appointment or authority, or exemption as a defense or justification shall prove the same, and until he has proved A the presumption shall be that he is not so justified or authorized.

§ 47A. Defenses or objections

In a criminal case, any defense or objection based upon defects in the institution of the prosecution or in the complaint or indictment, other than a failure to show jurisdiction in the court or to charge an offense, shall only be raised prior to trial and only by a motion in conformity with the requirements of the Massachusetts Rules of Criminal Procedure. The failure to raise any such defense or objection by motion prior to trial shall constitute a waiver thereof but a judge or special magistrate may, for cause shown, grant relief from such waiver. A defense or objection based upon a failure to show jurisdiction in the court or the failure to charge an offense may be raised by motion to dismiss prior to trial, but shall be noticed by the court at any time.

§ 63. Limitations of criminal prosecutions

[Amended by 2006 Mass. Acts c. 303, § 9, effective Dec. 20, 2006; 2010 Mass. Acts c. 267, §§ 67–69, effective Nov. 5, 2010; 2011 Mass. Acts c. 178, §§ 27–29, effective Nov. 21, 2011.]

An indictment for murder may be found at any time after the death of the person alleged to have been murdered. An indictment or complaint for an offense set forth in section 13B, 13B½, 13B¾, 13F, 13L, 22A, 22B, 22C, 23, 23A, 23B, 24B or subsection (b) of section 50 of chapter 265, for conspiracy to commit any of these offenses, as an accessory thereto, or any 1 or more of them may be found and filed at any time after the date of the commission of such offense; but any indictment or complaint found and filed more than 27 years after the date of commission of such offense shall be supported by independent evidence that corroborates the victims allegation. Such independent evidence shall be admissible during trial and shall not consist exclusively of the opinions of mental health professionals. An indictment for an offense set forth in sections 22, 24 or subsection (a) of section 50 of chapter 265, or for conspiracy to commit either of these offenses or as an accessory thereto or any 1 or more of them may be found and filed within 15 years of the date of commission of such offense. An indictment for an offense set forth in sections 17, 18, 19 and 21 of said chapter 265 or section 17 of chapter 272, for conspiracy to commit any such crime, as an accessory thereto, or any 1 or more of them may be found and filed within 10 years after the date of commission of such offense. An indictment for any other crime shall be found and filed within 6 years after such crime has been committed. Any period during which the defendant is not usually and publicly a resident within the commonwealth shall be excluded in determining the time limited.

Notwithstanding the first paragraph, if a victim of a crime set forth in section 13B, 13F, 13H, 22, 22A, 23, 24B, 26A or 50 of chapter 265, or section 1, 2, 3, 4, 4A, 4B, 5, 6, 7, 8, 12, 13, 17, 26, 28, 29A, 29B, 33, 34, 35 or 35A of chapter 272 is under the age of 16 at the time the crime is committed, the period of limitation for prosecution shall not commence until the victim has reached the age of 16 or the violation is reported to a law enforcement agency, whichever occurs earlier.

§ 70. Recognizance of witnesses

A justice of a court of record may at any time order a witness for the commonwealth in a criminal case or in a case under sections fifty-two to sixty-four, inclusive, of chapter one hundred and nineteen, pending in such court to recognize, with or without sureties, to appear and testify at the next or any succeeding sitting of said court, and may issue a warrant to bring such witness before him to recognize as aforesaid; but a witness unable to procure sureties shall not on that account be committed to jail except in cases of felony.

§ 70B. Placing cases on file; statement of reasons

Except as otherwise provided by law, a criminal case shall not be placed on file, on motion of a district attorney or assistant district attorney, unless such motion is accompanied by a written statement of the reasons for such disposition, signed by the district attorney or assistant district attorney, which shall be filed with the pleadings, and also accompanied by a statement of any previous criminal record of the accused.

§ 70C. Civil infractions

[Amended by 2005 Mass. Acts c. 54, § 3, effective July 29, 2005; 2010 Mass. Acts c. 267, §§ 70–71, effective Nov. 5, 2010; 2018 Mass. Acts c. 273, § 24, effective Oct. 23, 2018.]

Upon oral motion by the commonwealth or the defendant at arraignment or pretrial conference, or upon the court's own motion at any time, the court may, unless the commonwealth objects, in writing, stating the reasons for such objection, treat a violation of a municipal ordinance, or by-law or a misdemeanor offense as a civil infraction. This section shall not apply to the offenses in sections 22F, 24, 24D, 24G, 24L and 24N of chapter 90, sections 8, 8A and 8B of chapter 90B, sections 34, 36, 39, 51A, 51E, 51F, 55, 63 and 63A of chapter 119, chapter 119A, chapter 209, chapter 209A, chapter 265, section 25 of chapter 266, sections 1, 2, 3, 6, 6A, 6B, 8B, 13, 13A, 13B, 13C, 14, 14B, 15, 15A, 16, 17, 18, 19, 20, 23, 28, 31 and 36 of chapter 268, chapter 268A, sections 10, 10A, 10C, 10D, 10E, 11B, 11C, 11E, 12, 12A, 12B, 12D and 12E of chapter 269 and sections 1, 2, 3, 4, 4A, 4B, 6, 7, 8, 12, 13, 16, 28, 29A and 29B of chapter 272. If a motion to proceed civilly is allowed, the court shall not appoint counsel. If counsel has already been appointed, the court shall revoke the appointment. A person complained of for such civil infraction shall be adjudicated responsible upon such finding by the court and shall not be sentenced to any term of incarceration. The commonwealth shall maintain a copy of all objections filed under this section and shall report the number of such objections, delineated by divisions of the district court, every 6 months to the house and senate committees on ways and means.

When the court has treated a violation of a municipal ordinance or by-law or a misdemeanor offense as a civil infraction under this section and the ordinance, by-law or misdemeanor in question does not set forth a civil fine as a possible penalty, the court may impose a fine of not more than $5,000. An adjudication of responsibility shall neither be used in the calculation of second and subsequent offenses under any chapter, nor as the basis for the revocation of parole or of a probation surrender. An adjudication of responsibility under this section may include an order of restitution.

Chapter 278. Trials and Proceedings Before Judgment

§ 6A. Testimony concerning ownership in cases involving motor vehicle theft or fraudulent claims; preservation of testimony

At the arraignment of a defendant charged with violating the provisions of sections twenty-seven A, twenty-eight, twenty-nine, one hundred and eleven A and one hundred and thirty-nine of chapter two hundred and sixty-six, the court shall, upon a showing of need by the commonwealth, and after granting adequate time to defense counsel to consult with the defendant, allow testimony from the owner or person in control of such vehicle, solely on the issue of ownership and unauthorized use, and such testimony shall be taken and preserved and shall be admissible at trial.

In the prosecution of a person charged with violating the provisions of sections twenty-seven A, twenty-eight, twenty-eight A, twenty-nine, one hundred and eleven A and one hundred and thirty-nine of chapter two hundred and sixty-six, the court shall order, as a condition of granting a continuance, that the testimony of a witness then present in court be taken and preserved for subsequent use at trial or any other proceeding. The witness shall be examined in open court by the party on whose behalf he is present and the adverse party shall have the right to cross-examination. The expenses of taking and preserving the testimony shall be assessed as costs against the party requesting the continuance.

§ 7. Burden to prove license or admission to practice as attorney at law

A defendant in a criminal prosecution, relying for his justification upon a license, appointment, admission to practice as an attorney at law, or authority, shall prove the same; and, until so proved, the presumption shall be that he is not so authorized.

§ 9. Proof of ownership of property

In the prosecution of crimes which relate to or affect real or personal estate, it shall be sufficient, and shall not be a variance, if it is proved on the trial that, at the time when the crime was committed, either the actual or constructive possession or the general or special property in the whole or any part of such real or personal estate was in the person or community alleged to be the owner thereof.

§ 10. Night time; definition

If a crime is alleged to have been committed in the night time, night time shall be deemed the time between one hour after sunset on one day and one hour before sunrise on the next day; and the time of sunset and sunrise shall be ascertained according to mean time in the place where the crime was committed.

§ 11. Directed verdict; setting aside verdict, new trial or finding of guilty of included offense

If a motion for a directed verdict of not guilty is denied and the case is submitted to the jury and a verdict of guilty is returned, the judge may on a renewed motion for a directed verdict of not guilty pursuant to the Massachusetts Rules of Criminal Procedure set aside the verdict and order a new trial, or order the entry of a finding of guilty of any offense included in the offense charged in the indictment or complaint.

§ 16D. Child witness testimony; videotaping or transmission by simultaneous electronic means in certain cases

[Amended by 2010 Mass. Acts c. 267, §§ 72–74, effective Nov. 5, 2010; 2011 Mass. Acts c. 178, § 30, effective Feb. 19, 2012.]

(a) For the purposes of this section, the following words shall have the following meanings:—

"Child witness", a person who is under the age of fifteen years and who is alleged to have been a victim of, or a witness to an alleged violation of section thirteen B, 13B½, 13B¾, thirteen F, thirteen H, twenty-two, twenty-two A, 22B, 22C, twenty-three, 23A, 23B, twenty-four, 24B or 50 of chapter two hundred and sixty-five, or section two, three, four, four A, four B, five, six, seven, eight, twelve, thirteen, sixteen, seventeen, twenty-four, twenty-eight, twenty-nine, twenty-nine A, twenty-nine B, thirty-three, thirty-four or thirty-five A of chapter two hundred and seventy-two.

"Simultaneous electronic means", Any device capable of projecting a live visual and aural transmission such as closed-circuit television.

(b)(1) At any time after the issuance of a complaint or indictment alleging an offense punished by any of the statutes listed herein, the court on its own motion or on motion of the proponent of a child witness, and after a hearing, may order the use of a suitable alternative procedure for taking the testimony of the child witness, in proceedings pursuant to said complaint or indictment, provided that the court finds by a preponderance of the evidence at the time of the order that the child witness is likely to suffer psychological or emotional trauma as a result of testifying in open court, as a result of testifying in the presence of the defendant, or as a result of both testifying in open court and testifying in the presence of the defendant. If the court orders the use of a suitable alternative for taking the testimony of a child witness pursuant to this section, the court shall make and enter specific findings upon the record describing with particularity the reasons for such order.

(2) An order issued under paragraph (1) shall provide that the testimony of the child witness be recorded on videotape or film to be shown in court at a later time or that the testimony be transmitted to the courtroom by simultaneous electronic means.

(3) Testimony taken by an alternative procedure pursuant to an order issued under paragraph (1) shall be taken in the presence of the judge, the prosecutor, defense counsel and such other persons as the court may allow. The defendant shall also have the right to be present unless the court's order under paragraph (1) is based wholly or in part upon a finding that the child witness is likely to suffer trauma as a result of testifying in the presence of the defendant. If the order is based on such a finding, the testimony of the child witness shall not be taken in the presence of the defendant except as provided in paragraph (4).

(4) Testimony taken by an alternative procedure pursuant to an order issued under paragraph (1) shall be taken in a suitable setting outside the courtroom, except that an order based only on a finding that the child witness is likely to suffer trauma as a result of testifying in the presence of the defendant may provide that the testimony be taken in a suitable setting inside the courtroom in a manner so that the child witness is not able to see or hear the defendant.

(5) When testimony is taken by an alternative procedure pursuant to an order issued under paragraph (1), counsel shall be given the opportunity to examine or cross-examine the child witness to the same extent as would be permitted at trial, and the defendant shall be able to see and hear the child witness and to have constant private communication with defense counsel.

(6) The film, videotape or transmission of testimony taken by an alternative procedure pursuant to an order issued under paragraph (1) shall be admissible as substantive evidence to the same extent as and in lieu of live testimony by the child witness in any proceeding for which the order is issued or in any related criminal proceeding against the same defendant when consistent with the interests of justice, provided that such an order is entered or re-entered based on current findings at the time when or within a reasonable time before the film, videotape or transmission is offered into evidence. Subsequent testimony of a child witness in any such proceeding shall also be taken by a suitable alternative procedure pursuant to this section.

(7) Whenever pursuant to an order issued under paragraph (1), testimony is recorded on videotape or film or is transmitted to the courtroom by simultaneous electronic means, the court shall ensure that:

(a) The recording or transmitting equipment is capable of making an accurate recording or transmission and is operated by a competent operator;

(b) The recording or transmission is in color and the witness is visible at all times;

(c) Every voice on the recording or transmission is audible and identified;

(d) The courtroom is equipped with monitors which permit the jury and others present in the courtroom to see and hear the recording or transmission;

(e) In the case of recorded testimony, the recording is accurate and has not been altered;

(f) In the case of recorded testimony, each party is afforded the opportunity to view the recording before it is shown in the courtroom.

(8) Nothing in this section shall be deemed to prohibit the court from using other appropriate means, consistent with this section and other laws and with the defendant's rights, to protect a child witness from trauma during a court proceeding.

§ 16F. Expedited trials of sex crimes involving minor children as victims or witnesses; continuance; impact statement

In any criminal proceeding involving an alleged sex crime perpetrated upon a minor child, or in which a minor child is expected to testify as a witness to a sex crime, the court shall, in order to minimize stress on such child, take action to expedite trial and give precedence to the case over any other case; provided, however, that nothing in this section shall be construed to mean that trial shall be expedited if it is not in the best interests of the child.

When a motion or a request for a continuance is made the prosecutor shall file an impact statement which specifies whether the commonwealth agrees to the request for continuance, whether the child or the child's representative agrees to such request, and the effect, if any, the granting of the continuance will have on the child. In ruling on any motion or request for continuance or other delay, the court shall consider and give weight to any possible adverse impact that a delay or continuance may have on the child. Prior to issuing an order on a motion for continuance or delay, the court shall make written findings of fact concerning the impact on the child of continuing or delaying the case.

§ 18. Pleas of not guilty, guilty or nolo contendere; requests for specific disposition; pretrial motions

A defendant who is before the Boston municipal court or a district court or a district court sitting in a juvenile session or a juvenile court on a criminal offense within the court's final jurisdiction shall plead not guilty or guilty, or with the consent of the court, nolo contendere. Such plea of guilty shall be submitted by the defendant and acted upon by the court; provided, however, that a defendant with whom the commonwealth cannot reach agreement for a recommended disposition shall be allowed to tender a plea of guilty together with a request for a specific disposition. Such request may include any disposition or dispositional terms within the court's jurisdiction, including, unless otherwise prohibited by law, a dispositional request that a guilty finding not be entered, but rather the case be continued without a finding to a specific date thereupon to be dismissed, such continuance conditioned upon compliance with specific terms and conditions or that the defendant be placed on probation pursuant to the provisions of section eighty-seven of chapter two hundred and seventy-six. If such a plea, with an agreed upon recommendation or with a dispositional request by the defendant, is tendered, the court shall inform the defendant that it will not impose a disposition that exceeds the terms of the agreed upon recommendation or the dispositional request by the defendant, whichever is applicable, without giving the defendant the right to withdraw the plea.

If a defendant, notwithstanding the requirements set forth hereinbefore, attempts to enter a plea or statement consisting of an admission of facts sufficient for finding of guilt, or some similar statement, such admission shall be deemed a tender of a plea of guilty for purposes of the procedures set forth in this section.

Any pretrial motion filed in a criminal case pending in the Boston municipal court or district court or a district court sitting in a juvenile session or a juvenile court and decided before entry of defendant's decision on waiver of the right to jury trial shall not be refiled or reheard thereafter, except in the discretion of the court as substantial justice requires. Any such pretrial motion not filed or filed but not decided prior to entry of the defendant's decision on waiver of the right to jury trial may be filed thereafter but not later than twenty-one days after entry of said decision on waiver of the right to jury trial, except for good cause shown.

§ 28. Appeal to supreme judicial court

A defendant aggrieved by a judgment of the district court or of the superior court in any criminal proceeding may appeal therefrom to the supreme judicial court.

§ 28E. Appeals by commonwealth

An appeal may be taken by and on behalf of the commonwealth by the attorney general or a district attorney from the district court to the appeals court in all criminal cases and in all delinquency cases from a decision, order or judgment of the court (1) allowing a motion to dismiss an indictment or complaint, (2) allowing a motion to suppress evidence, or (3) denying a motion to transfer pursuant to section sixty-one of chapter one hundred and nineteen.

An appeal may be taken by and on behalf of the commonwealth by the attorney general or a district attorney from the superior court to the supreme judicial court in all criminal cases from a decision, order or judgment of the court (1) allowing a motion to dismiss an indictment or complaint, or (2) allowing a motion for appropriate relief under the Massachusetts Rules of Criminal Procedure.

An application for an appeal from a decision, order or judgment of the superior court determining a motion to suppress evidence prior to trial may be filed in the supreme judicial court by a defendant or by and on behalf of the commonwealth by the attorney general or a district attorney. If such application is denied, or if such application is granted but the interlocutory appeal is heard by a single justice, the determination of the motion to suppress evidence shall be open to review by the full court after trial in the same manner and to the same extent as determinations of such motions not appealed under the interlocutory procedure herein authorized.

Rules of practice and procedure with respect to appeals authorized by this section shall be the same as those applicable to criminal appeals under the Massachusetts Rules of Appellate Procedure.

§ 29D. Conviction upon plea of guilty, nolo contendere or an admission to sufficient facts; motion to vacate

[Prior language of this section stricken and replaced by 2004 Mass. Acts c. 225, § 1, effective Oct. 27, 2004.]

The court shall not accept a plea of guilty, a plea of nolo contendere, or an admission to sufficient facts from any defendant in any criminal proceeding unless the court advises such defendant of the following: "If you are not a citizen of the United States, you are hereby advised that the acceptance by this court of your plea of guilty, plea of nolo contendere, or admission to sufficient facts may have consequences of deportation, exclusion from admission to the United States, or denial of naturalization, pursuant to the laws of the United States." The court shall advise such defendant during every plea colloquy at which the defendant is proffering a plea of guilty, a plea of nolo contendere, or an admission to sufficient facts. The defendant shall not be required at the time of the plea to disclose to the court his legal status in the United States.

If the court fails so to advise the defendant, and he later at any time shows that his plea and conviction may have or has had one of the enumerated consequences, even if the defendant has already been deported from the United States, the court, on the defendant's motion, shall vacate the judgment, and permit the defendant to withdraw the plea of guilty, plea of nolo contendere, or admission of sufficient facts, and enter a plea of not guilty. Absent an official record or a contemporaneously written record kept in the court file that the court provided the advisement as prescribed in this section, including but not limited to a docket sheet that accurately reflects that the warning was given as required by this section, the defendant shall be presumed not to have received advisement. An advisement previously or subsequently provided the defendant during another plea colloquy shall not satisfy the advisement required by this section, nor shall it be used to presume the defendant understood the plea of guilty, or admission to sufficient facts he seeks to vacate would have the consequence of deportation, exclusion from admission to the United States, or denial of naturalization.

NOTE This amended section applies "to pleas of guilty, pleas of nolo contendere and admissions to sufficient facts which occur on or after [October 27, 2004]. *See* 2004 Mass. Acts c. 225, § 2.

Chapter 278A. Post Conviction Access to Forensic and Scientific Analysis

§ 1. Definitions

[Added by 2012 Mass. Acts c. 38, effective May 17, 2012.]

As used in this chapter, the following words shall, unless the context clearly requires otherwise, have the following meanings:-

"Analysis", the process by which a forensic or scientific technique is applied to evidence or biological material to identify the perpetrator of a crime.

"Biological material", a sexual assault forensic examination kit, semen, blood, saliva, hair, skin tissue or other identified biological substance.

"Conviction", a verdict or finding of guilty, a plea of guilty, a plea of nolo contendere or an adjudication of delinquency as a juvenile entered by the trial court.

"Exhaustive testing", analysis of a particular item of evidence or biological material that precludes replicate analysis of the evidence or biological material.

"Factually innocent", a person convicted of a criminal offense who did not commit that offense.

"Governmental entity", an official body of the commonwealth, or of a county, city or town within the commonwealth.

"Identity", the moving party's identity as the perpetrator of the offense for which the moving party was convicted in the underlying case.

"Moving party", a person who files a motion under this chapter.

"Post conviction", indicates any time after which a conviction has been entered.

"Prosecuting attorney", the district attorney for the district in which the moving party was convicted or the attorney general of the commonwealth.

"Replicate analysis", the duplication of an analysis performed on a particular item of evidence or biological material.

"Underlying case", the trial court proceedings that resulted in the conviction of the moving party.

"Victim", any natural person who suffered direct or threatened physical, emotional or financial harm as the result of the commission or attempted commission of the crime or delinquency case that is the subject of the underlying case; "victim" shall also include the parent, guardian, legal representative or administrator or executor of the estate of such person if that person is a minor, incompetent or deceased.

§ 2. Persons who may file motion

[Added by 2012 Mass. Acts c. 38, effective May 17, 2012.]

A person may file a motion for forensic or scientific analysis under this chapter if that person: (1) has been convicted of a criminal offense in a court of the commonwealth; (2) is incarcerated in a state prison, house of correction, is on parole or probation or whose liberty has been otherwise restrained as the result of a conviction; and (3) asserts factual innocence of the crime for which the person has been convicted.

This chapter shall not be construed to prohibit the performance of forensic or scientific analysis under any other circumstances, including by agreement between the person convicted of a criminal offense and the prosecuting attorney.

§ 3. Filing and content of motion

[Added by 2012 Mass. Acts c. 38, effective May 17, 2012.]

(a) A person seeking relief under this chapter shall file a motion in the court in which the conviction was entered, using the same caption and docket number as identified the underlying case.

(b) The motion shall include the following information, and when relevant, shall include specific references to the record in the underlying case or to affidavits that are filed in support of the motion that are signed by a person with personal knowledge of the factual basis of the motion:

(1) the name and a description of the requested forensic or scientific analysis;

(2) information demonstrating that the requested analysis is admissible as evidence in courts of the commonwealth;

(3) a description of the evidence or biological material that the moving party seeks to have analyzed or tested, including its location and chain of custody if known;

(4) information demonstrating that the analysis has the potential to result in evidence that is material to the moving party's identification as the perpetrator of the crime in the underlying case; and

(5) information demonstrating that the evidence or biological material has not been subjected to the requested analysis because:

(i) the requested analysis had not yet been developed at the time of the conviction;

(ii) the results of the requested analysis were not admissible in the courts of the commonwealth at the time of the conviction;

(iii) the moving party and the moving party's attorney were not aware of and did not have reason to be aware of the existence of the evidence or biological material at the time of the underlying case and conviction;

(iv) the moving party's attorney in the underlying case was aware at the time of the conviction of the existence of the evidence or biological material, the results of the requested analysis were admissible as evidence in courts of the commonwealth, a reasonably effective attorney would have sought the analysis and either the moving party's attorney failed to seek the analysis or the judge denied the request; or

(v) the evidence or biological material was otherwise unavailable at the time of the conviction.

(c) If the moving party is unable to include for filing with the motion any of the items or information described in subsection (b), or if the moving party lacks items or information necessary to establish any of the factors listed in subsection (b) of section 7, the moving party shall include a description of efforts made to obtain such items and information and may move for discovery of such items or information from the prosecuting attorney or any third party.

(d) The moving party shall file with the motion an affidavit stating that the moving party is factually innocent of the offense of conviction and that the requested forensic or scientific analysis will support the claim of innocence. A person who pleaded guilty or nolo contendere in the underlying case may file a motion. The court shall not find that identity was not or could not have been a material issue in the underlying case because of the plea. A person who is alleged to have, or admits to having, made a statement that is or could be incriminating may file a motion under this chapter. The court shall not find that identity was not or should not have been a material issue in the underlying case because the moving party made, or is alleged to have made, an incriminating statement. If the moving party entered a plea of guilty or nolo contendere to the offense of conviction or made an incriminating statement, the moving party shall state in the affidavit that the claim of factual innocence is made notwithstanding the plea or incriminating statement.

(e) The court shall expediously review all motions filed and shall dismiss, without prejudice, any such motion without a hearing if the court determines, based on the information contained in the motion, that the motion does not meet the requirements set forth in this section. The prosecuting attorney may provide a response to the motion, to assist the court in considering whether the motion meets the requirement under this section. The court shall notify the moving party and the prosecuting attorney as to whether the motion is sufficient to proceed under this chapter or is dismissed.

§ 4. Service of copy of motion on prosecuting attorney; Response

[Added by 2012 Mass. Acts c. 38, effective May 17, 2012.]

(a) The moving party shall file a motion under section 3 with the court that adjudicated the underlying case and shall serve a copy of the motion on the prosecuting attorney.

(b) If the motion is not dismissed by the court under subsection (e) of section 3, the prosecuting attorney shall file a response with the court within 60 days after the date upon which the court issues notice under said subsection (e) of said section 3, and shall simultaneously serve the response on the moving party. The prosecuting attorney may request additional time in which to file the response, which the court may grant for good cause shown.

(c) The prosecuting attorney's response shall include any specific legal or factual objections that the prosecuting attorney has to the requested analysis.

§ 5. Counsel

[Added by 2012 Mass. Acts c. 38, effective May 17, 2012.]

The court may assign or appoint counsel to represent a moving party who meets the definition of indigency under section 2 of chapter 211D in the preparation and presentation of motions filed under this chapter.

§ 6. Hearing

[Added by 2012 Mass. Acts c. 38, effective May 17, 2012.]

(a) The court shall order a hearing on the motion if the motion meets the requirements of section 3. The moving party shall be present for the hearing unless the moving party waives the party's presence at the hearing.

(b) The judge who conducted the trial or accepted the moving party's plea of guilty or nolo contendere in the underlying case shall conduct the hearing if possible.

§ 7. Grounds for allowance of motion

[Added by 2012 Mass. Acts c. 38, effective May 17, 2012.]

(a) After reviewing the motion, the prosecuting attorney's response and after holding a hearing, the court shall state findings of fact and conclusions of law on the record, or shall make written findings of fact and conclusions of law that support the decision to allow or deny a motion brought under section 3.

(b) The court shall allow the requested forensic or scientific analysis if each of the following has been demonstrated by a preponderance of the evidence:

(1) that the evidence or biological material exists;

(2) that the evidence or biological material has been subject to a chain of custody that is sufficient to establish that it has not deteriorated, been substituted, tampered with, replaced, handled or altered such that the results of the requested analysis would lack any probative value;

(3) that the evidence or biological material has not been subjected to the requested analysis for any of the reasons in clauses (i) to (v), inclusive, of paragraph (5) of subsection (b) of section 3;

(4) that the requested analysis has the potential to result in evidence that is material to the moving party's identification as the perpetrator of the crime in the underlying case;

(5) that the purpose of the motion is not the obstruction of justice or delay; and

(6) that the results of the particular type of analysis being requested have been found to be admissible in courts of the commonwealth.

(c) The court on motion of any party, after notice to the opposing party and any third party from whom discovery is sought, and an opportunity to be heard, may authorize such discovery as provided for under Rule 30(c)(4) of the Massachusetts Rules of Criminal Procedure, from either party or any third party as is deemed appropriate, subject to appropriate protective orders or an order to the party seeking discovery to produce reciprocal discovery.

Such discovery may include items and biological materials from third parties, provided the party seeking discovery demonstrates that analysis of these items or biological material will, by a preponderance of the evidence, provide evidence material to the identification of a perpetrator of the crime.

If, in response to a motion made under subsection (c) of section 3, the court finds good cause for the moving party's inability to obtain items or information required under subsection (b) of said section 3 and subsection (b) of section 7, the court may order discovery to assist the moving party in identifying the location and condition of evidence or biological material that was obtained in relation to the underlying case, regardless of whether it was introduced at trial or would be admissible. The court, when considering such discovery requests, shall not require the establishment of a prima facie case for relief under Rule 30 of the Massachusetts Rules of Criminal Procedure.

§ 8. Conditions; forensic services provider

[Added by 2012 Mass. Acts c. 38, effective May 17, 2012; amended by 2014 Mass. Acts c. 165, effective July 15, 2014.]

(a) In allowing a motion under section 3, the court shall specify conditions on the analysis, including, but not limited to, the transportation, handling and return of evidence or biological materials, to protect the integrity of the evidence or biological material and the analysis.

(b) The prosecuting attorney and the moving party shall agree on a forensic services provider accredited by an accreditation body that is a signatory to the International Laboratory Accreditation Cooperation Mutual Recognition Agreement and offers forensic laboratory accreditation services to conduct the analysis, which, except in the case of exhaustive testing, may include the forensic and technology center of the state police crime laboratory or the Boston police department crime laboratory units.

(c) If the prosecuting attorney and the moving party are unable to agree on a forensic services provider, the prosecuting attorney and the moving party shall submit to the court a list of not more than 3 forensic services providers who are accredited by an accreditation body that is a signatory to the International Laboratory Accreditation Cooperation Mutual Recognition Agreement and offers forensic laboratory accreditation services and have the capability to perform the requested analysis. The court shall select a forensic services provider from either list. For purposes of this section, "laboratory" shall refer to the forensic services provider selected under this subsection or subsection (b).

(d) The laboratory shall give equal access to its personnel, opinions, conclusions, reports and other documentation to the prosecuting attorney and the moving party.

(e) The laboratory shall retain and maintain the integrity of a sufficient portion of the evidence or biological material for replicate analysis. If, after initial examination of the evidence or biological material, but before the actual analysis, the laboratory determines that there is insufficient material for replicate analysis, it shall simultaneously notify in writing the prosecuting attorney, the moving party and the court. Exhaustive testing shall not occur except by specific order of the court. In the event that exhaustive testing is so authorized, upon request of either party, the court shall make such orders to ensure that representatives of the moving party and the prosecuting attorney have the opportunity to observe the analysis, unless such observation is inconsistent with the practices or protocols of the laboratory conducting the analysis.

(f) The moving party shall cooperate with the laboratory. At the laboratory's or the prosecuting attorney's request and upon court order, the moving party shall provide biological samples to the laboratory or to law enforcement personnel. If the moving party unreasonably fails to cooperate with such orders, the court may deny the motion with prejudice.

§ 9. Timing of analysis

[Added by 2012 Mass. Acts c. 38, effective May 17, 2012.]

Upon allowance of a motion under section 3, analysis shall take place as soon as practicable.

§ 10. Costs of analysis

[Added by 2012 Mass. Acts c. 38, effective May 17, 2012.]

The costs of the analysis shall be paid:

(1) by the moving party if the moving party does not meet the definition of indigency under section 2 of chapter 211D and has sufficient means to make such payment; (2) if the moving party meets the definition of indigency under said section 2 of said chapter 211D, as an extra fee or cost under sections 27A through 27G, inclusive, of chapter 261; or (3) if a person is indigent, but has the ability to pay a reduced fee as defined under said section 2 of said chapter 211D, by the moving party to the maximum feasible amount possible given the financial resources of the moving party as the court deems equitable.

§ 11. Interference with sentence

[Added by 2012 Mass. Acts c. 38, effective May 17, 2012.]

Proceedings under this chapter shall not stay or otherwise interfere with a term of incarceration, parole, probation or other sentence imposed.

§ 12. Analysis results

[Added by 2012 Mass. Acts c. 38, effective May 17, 2012.]

(a) The results of the analysis shall be simultaneously disclosed to the moving party, the prosecuting attorney and the court.

(b) The court shall, at the request of a party or on its own initiative, order production of the underlying laboratory data, documents and notes.

§ 13. Inconclusive analysis

[Added by 2012 Mass. Acts c. 38, effective May 17, 2012.]

If the analysis is inconclusive, the court may order any additional analysis requested if the court concludes that the requirements of subsection (b) of section 7 are met.

§ 14. Notification of victim

[Added by 2012 Mass. Acts c. 38, effective May 17, 2012.]

(a) If a motion is filed under section 3, the prosecuting attorney shall notify the victim of the crime in the underlying case.

(b) The prosecuting attorney shall notify the victim if the court allows a motion for forensic or scientific analysis and, if the victim is notified of the allowance of the motion, shall promptly notify the victim of the result of the analysis.

§ 15. Waiver of right to file motion

[Added by 2012 Mass. Acts c. 38, effective May 17, 2012.]

The right to file a motion under this chapter shall not be waived. This prohibition of any waiver includes, but is not limited to, any stated or unstated waiver that is or is alleged to be part of any agreement or understanding related to any plea of guilty or of nolo contendere or to any sentencing or appellate proceeding or to any correctional placement or conditions.

§ 16. Retention and preservation of evidence or biological material by governmental entities

[Added by 2012 Mass. Acts c. 38, effective May 17, 2012.]

(a) Any governmental entity that is in possession of evidence or biological material that is collected for its potential evidentiary value during the investigation of a crime, the prosecution of which results in a conviction, shall retain such evidence or biological material for the period of time that a person remains in the custody of the commonwealth or under parole or probation supervision in connection with that crime, without regard to whether the evidence or biological material was introduced at trial. Each governmental entity shall retain all such evidence or biological material in a manner that is reasonably designed to preserve the evidence and biological material and to prevent its destruction or deterioration. The evidence or biological material need not be preserved if it is to be returned to a third party or if it is of such a size, bulk or physical character as to render retention impracticable.

(b) The director of the crime laboratory within the department of state police, in consultation with the forensic sciences advisory board established by section 184A of chapter 6, shall promulgate regulations governing the retention and preservation of evidence or biological material by any governmental entity. The regulations shall include standards for maintaining the integrity of the materials over time, the designation of officials at each governmental entity with custodial responsibility and requirements for contemporaneously recorded documentation of individuals having and obtaining custody of any evidence or biological material.

§ 17. Liability

[Added by 2012 Mass. Acts c. 38, effective May 17, 2012.]

(a) Governmental officials and employees acting in good faith shall not be liable in a civil or criminal proceeding for any act under this chapter.

(b) If a governmental entity responsible for the preservation of evidence or biological material engages in willful or wanton misconduct or gross negligence, which results in the deterioration or destruction of evidence or biological material so that a laboratory is unable to perform adequate or proper analysis, that entity shall be subject to proceedings for contempt.

(c) Nothing in this chapter shall create any cause of action for damages against the commonwealth or any of its subdivisions or officers, employees, agents or subdivisions, except as provided in this section.

§ 18. Appeals

[Added by 2012 Mass. Acts c. 38, effective May 17, 2012.]

An order allowing or denying a motion for forensic or scientific analysis filed under this chapter shall be a final and appealable order. If the moving party appeals an order denying a motion for forensic or scientific analysis the moving party shall file a notice of appeal with the court within 30 days after the entry of the judgment.

Chapter 279. Judgment and Execution

§ 1. Suspension of execution; payment of fine, etc.; revocation of suspension; exceptions

[Amended by 2010 Mass. Acts c. 256, § 134, effective Nov. 4, 2010; 2018 Mass. Acts c. 69, § 206, effective Apr. 13, 2018.]

When a person convicted before a court is sentenced to imprisonment, the court may direct that the execution of the sentence, or any part thereof, be suspended and that he be placed on probation for such time and on such terms and conditions as it shall fix. When a person so convicted is sentenced to pay a fine and to stand committed until it is paid, the court may direct that the execution of the sentence, or any part thereof, be suspended for such time as it shall fix and in its discretion that he be placed on probation on condition that he pay the fine within such time. If the fine does not exceed two hundred dollars and the court finds that the defendant is unable to pay it when imposed, the execution of the sentence shall be suspended and he may in its discretion be placed on probation, unless the court shall find that he will probably default, or that such suspension will be detrimental to the interests of the public. If he is committed for nonpayment of a fine, the order of commitment shall contain a recital of the findings of the court on which suspension is refused. The fine shall be paid in one payment, or in part payments, to the probation officer, and when fully paid the order of commitment shall be void. The probation officer shall give a receipt for every payment so made, shall keep a record of the same, shall pay the fine, or all sums received in part payment thereof, to the sheriff if such fine is imposed in the superior court, or to the clerk of the court if such fine is imposed in the district court, at the end of the period of probation or any extension thereof, and shall keep on file the sheriff's or clerk's receipt therefor. If during or at the end of said period the probation officer shall report that the fine is in whole or in part unpaid, and in his opinion the person is unwilling or unable to pay it, the court may either extend said period, place the case on file or revoke the suspension of the execution of the sentence. When such suspension is revoked, in a case where the fine has been paid in part, the defendant may be committed for default in payment of the balance.

The provisions of this section shall not permit the suspension of the execution of the sentence of a person convicted of a crime punishable by death or imprisonment for life. In granting probation under this section, the court shall include in its terms and conditions of probation that the person convicted shall pay any child support due under a support order, as defined in section 1A of chapter 119A, including payment toward any arrearage of support that accrues or has accrued or compliance with any payment plan between the person convicted and the IV-D agency as set forth in said chapter 119A.

When a person is sentenced by a court upon conviction of any crime, he shall be informed by the probation department on a form provided by the department of criminal justice information services that he will have a criminal record that may be accessible to the public under certain conditions, and of his rights pertaining thereto, as provided in sections one hundred and sixty-seven through one hundred and seventy-eight of chapter six.

When a person is sentenced to pay a fine of any amount or is assessed fines, fees, costs, civil penalties or other expenses at disposition of a case, the court shall inform that person that: (i) nonpayment of the fines, fees, costs, civil penalties or expenses may result in commitment to a correctional facility; (ii) payment must be made by a date certain; (iii) failure to appear at such date certain or failure to make the payment may result in the issuance of a default; and (iv) if an inability to pay exists as the result of a change in financial circumstances or for any other reason, the person has a right to address the court if the person alleges that such assessed fines, fees, costs, civil penalties or other expenses would cause a substantial financial hardship to the person, the person's immediate family or the person's dependents.

§ 2. Suspension of execution of orders of commitment to Massachusetts reformatory, etc.

In all cases the execution of orders of commitment to any training school or reformatory, however named, the department of youth services, or the department of public welfare may be suspended, and such suspension continued or revoked, in the same manner and with the same effect as the execution of sentences in criminal cases.

§ 3. Arrest without warrant of person on probation; warrant for arrest of persons already imprisoned; application for disposition

[Amended by 2004 Mass. Acts c. 65, § 27, effective Apr. 5, 2004.]

At any time before final disposition of the case of a person placed under probation supervision or in the custody or care of a probation officer, the probation officer may arrest him without a warrant and take him before the court, or the court may issue a warrant for his arrest. When taken before the court, it may, if he has not been sentenced, sentence him or make any other lawful disposition of the case, and if he has been sentenced, it may continue or revoke the suspension of the execution of his sentence; provided however, that in all cases where the probationer is served with notice of surrender and at least one of the underlying crimes for which he is on probation is a felony, then the probation officer shall provide a duplicate copy of the notice of surrender to the district attorney, and the court shall provide to the district attorney the opportunity to be heard and present evidence at the surrender hearing. If such suspension is revoked, the sentence shall be in full force and effect. If a warrant has been issued by the court for the arrest of such a person and he is a prisoner in any correctional institution, jail or house of correction, the commissioner of correction, the sheriff, master or keeper of said house of correction, or in Suffolk county, the penal institutions commissioner of the city of Boston, as the case may be, having such prisoner under his supervision or control, upon receiving notice of such warrant, shall notify such prisoner that he has the right to apply to the court for prompt disposition thereof. Such an application shall be in writing and given or sent by such prisoner to the commissioner of correction, or such sheriff, master, keeper, or penal institutions commissioner, who shall promptly forward it to the court from which the warrant issued, by certified mail, together with a certificate of said commissioner of correction, sheriff, master, keeper, or penal institutions commissioner, stating (a) the term of commitment under which such prisoner is being held, (b) the amount of time served, (c) the amount of time remaining to be served, (d) the amount of good time earned, (e) the time of parole eligibility of such prisoner, and (f) any decisions of the board of parole relating to such prisoner. Said commissioner of correction, sheriff, master, keeper, or penal institutions commissioner shall notify the appropriate district attorney by certified mail of such application to the court. Any such prisoner shall, within six months after such application is received by the court, be brought into court for sentencing or other lawful disposition of his case as hereinbefore provided.

In no case where a provision of this chapter provides for a finding, disposition or other order to be made by the court, or for a warrant to be issued, shall such be made or issued by any person other than a justice, special justice or other person exercising the powers of a magistrate.

Notwithstanding any restriction in the preceding paragraph, if a probation officer has probable cause to believe that a person placed under probation supervision or in the custody or care of a probation officer pursuant to sections 42A, 58A or 87 of chapter 276 or any other statute that allows the court to set conditions of release, has violated the conditions set by the court, the probation officer may arrest the probationer or may issue a warrant for the temporary custody of the probationer for a period not to exceed 72 hours or until the next sitting, of the court, during which period the probation officer shall arrange for the appearance of the probationer before the court pursuant to the first paragraph of this section. Such warrant shall constitute sufficient authority to a probation officer and to the superintendent, jailer, or any other person in charge of any jail, house of correction, lockup, or place of detention to whom it is exhibited, to hold in temporary custody the probationer detained pursuant thereto.

§ 3A. Motion of district attorney for sentence

Not later than seven days after a plea of guilty or after a verdict of guilty and in any event before adjournment of the sitting at which such plea or verdict has been taken and recorded in a case of felony wherein no question of law has been reported for decision by the supreme judicial court, the district attorney shall move for sentence; provided, that nothing herein shall preclude the district attorney from again making such a motion in any case where the imposition of sentence is delayed under section forty-seven.

§ 4. Imposition of sentence; stay of execution

Sentence shall be imposed upon conviction of a crime, regardless of whether an appeal has been taken, except as otherwise provided in section sixty-one in case of a conviction of a capital crime.

If sentence is imposed upon conviction of a crime punishable by death, the justice imposing the sentence shall at the same time stay the execution of the sentence, such stay to be effective until revoked by the superior court department of the trial which is hereby granted full powers of revocation in the premises. The clerk of such court shall, forthwith upon the revocation by the court of any such stay of execution of sentence, certify that said stay has been revoked and cause said certificate to be served upon the superintendent of the state prison, or the officer performing his duties, by any officer qualified to serve criminal process; and the officer serving the same shall forthwith make due return of service to the clerk.

§ 4B. Notice to victim of sentencing proceedings; oral or written statements

Before disposition in any case where a defendant has been found guilty of any felony or any crime against the person or crime where physical injury to a person results, excluding any crime for which a sentence of death may be imposed, and which involves an identified victim whose whereabouts are known, the district attorney shall give the victim actual notice of the time and place of sentencing and of the victim's right to make a statement to the court, orally or in writing at the victim's option, as to the impact of the crime and as to a recommended sentence. Before disposition, the court shall allow any victim who elects to make such an oral statement the opportunity to do so in the presence of the defendant. Before disposition, the district attorney shall file any such written statement with the court and shall make it available to the defendant.

If the victim is unable to make an oral or written statement because of his mental, emotional, or physical incapacity or his age, his attorney or a designated family member shall be provided the notice and the opportunity to make a statement prescribed in this paragraph.

Before said disposition the office of the district attorney shall cause to be prepared a written statement as to the impact of the crime on the victim, which shall be filed with the court as part of the presentence report and made available to the defendant. The statement shall include the following: (1) the name of the victim; (2) documentation of the net financial loss, if any, suffered by the victim or a family member as a result of the crime; (3) in cases where the crime has had an impact on the victim's personal welfare or family relationship or has had a psychological impact on the victim or his family, a statement of such impact.

The court shall allow the defendant to have the opportunity to rebut the victim's oral or written statement and the district attorney's written statement if the court decides to rely upon such statements or parts thereof in imposing sentence.

No sentence shall be invalidated because of failure to comply with the provisions of this section. This section shall not be construed to create any cause of action or any right of appeal on behalf of any person.

§ 5. Sentence if no punishment is provided by statute

If no punishment for a crime is provided by statute, the court shall impose such sentence, according to the nature of the crime, as conforms to the common usage and practice in the commonwealth. If a person is convicted of a misdemeanor punishable by imprisonment, he may, unless otherwise expressly provided, be sentenced to imprisonment either in the jail or in the house of correction.

§ 24. Indeterminate sentence to state prison

[Amended by 2014 Mass. Acts c. 189, § 6, effective July 25, 2014.]

If a convict is sentenced to the state prison, except as an habitual criminal, the court shall not fix the term of imprisonment, but shall fix a maximum and a minimum term for which he may be imprisoned. The maximum term shall not be longer than the longest term fixed by law for the punishment of the crime of which he has be convicted, and the minimum term shall be a term set by the court, except that, where an alternative sentence to a house of correction is permitted for the offense, a minimum state prison term may not be less than one year. In the case of a sentence to life imprisonment, except in the case of a sentence for murder in the first degree, and in the case of multiple life sentences arising out of separate and distinct incidents that occurred at different times, where the second offense occurred subsequent to the first conviction, the court shall fix a minimum term which shall be not less than 15 years nor more than 25 years.

In the case of a sentence of life imprisonment for murder in the first degree committed by a person on or after the person's fourteenth birthday and before the person's eighteenth birthday, the court shall fix a minimum term of not less than 20 years nor more than 30 years; provided, however, that in the case of a sentence of life imprisonment for murder in the first degree with extreme atrocity or cruelty committed by a person on or after the person's fourteenth birthday and before the person's eighteenth birthday, the court shall fix a minimum term of 30 years; and provided further, that in the case of a sentence of life imprisonment for murder in the first degree with deliberately premeditated malice aforethought committed by a person on or after the person's fourteenth birthday and before the person's eighteenth birthday, the court shall fix a minimum term of not less than 25 years nor more than 30 years.

Chapter 280. Fines and Forfeitures

§ 6B. Criminal assessments

[Amended by 2013 Mass. Acts c. 84, § 33, effective Sept. 18, 2013; 2018 Mass. Acts c. 69, § 209, effective Apr. 13, 2018.]

The court shall impose an assessment of not less than thirty-five dollars nor more than one hundred dollars against any person who has attained the age of 18 years and who is convicted of a misdemeanor or against whom a finding of sufficient facts for a conviction is made on a complaint charging a misdemeanor under sections thirty-two C, thirty-two D, and thirty-two G and thirty-five of chapter ninety-four C. The court shall impose an assessment of not less than one hundred and fifty dollars nor more than five hundred dollars against any person who is convicted of a felony or against whom a finding of sufficient facts for a conviction is made on a complaint charging a felony under sections thirty-two, thirty-two A, thirty-two B, thirty-two E, thirty-two F and thirty-four of chapter ninety-four C. When multiple criminal offenses arising from a single incident are charged, the total assessment shall not exceed five hundred dollars. The court or justice may waive all or any part of said assessment upon a finding that such payment would cause a substantial financial hardship to the person, the person's immediate family or the person's dependents.

All such assessments made shall be collected by the court and shall be transmitted monthly to the state treasurer. The assessment from any conviction which is subsequently overturned on appeal shall be refunded by the court to the person whose conviction is overturned. Said court shall deduct such funds from the assessments transmitted to the state treasurer. Assessments pursuant to this section shall be in addition to any other fines or restitution imposed in any disposition.

Additional Materials

Note: The following materials are available in the eBook version of this Sourcebook. See the Electronic Download page at the front of this book for instructions on downloading a copy of the eBook.

Massachusetts Uniform Probate Code Article V, G.L. c. 190B, §§ 5-101 to 5-507, Protection of Persons Under Disability and Their Property

PART 2

Selected Court Rules and Standards

Massachusetts Rules of Criminal Procedure

[Effective July 1, 1979.]

Rule 1. Title; Scope

[Applicable to cases initiated (by indictment or complaint) on or after Sept. 7, 2004. Amended effective Sept. 7, 2004.]

(a) Title. These rules may be known and cited as the Massachusetts Rules of Criminal Procedure. (Mass. R. Crim. P.)

(b) Scope. These rules govern the procedure in all criminal proceedings in the District Court, in all criminal proceedings in the Superior Court, in all delinquency and youthful offender proceedings in the Juvenile Court, District Court and Superior Court consistent with the General Laws, and in proceedings for post-conviction relief.

Rule 2. Purpose; Construction; Definition of Terms

[Applicable to District Court and Superior Court. Amended effective July 1, 1986.]

(a) Purpose; Construction. These rules are intended to provide for the just determination of every criminal proceeding. They shall be construed to secure simplicity in procedure, fairness in administration, and the elimination of expense and delay.

(1) Words or phrases importing the singular number may extend and be applied to several persons or things, words importing the plural number may include the singular, and words importing the masculine gender may include the feminine and neuter.

(2) When in these rules reference is made to a subdivision of a rule, that reference is to that subdivision and to any subdivisions thereof.

(b) Definition of Terms. In construing these rules the following words and phrases shall have the following meanings unless a contrary intent clearly appears from the context in which they are used:

(1) "Indigent" means any defendant who is unable to procure counsel with his funds as defined in Supreme Judicial Court Rule 3:10.

(2) "Indigent but able to contribute" means any defendant who is unable to procure counsel with his funds but is able to contribute funds for the cost of counsel as defined in Supreme Judicial Court Rule 3:10.

(3) "Capital Crime" means a charge of murder in the first degree.

(4) "Commonwealth" includes the prosecuting office or agency and all officers or agents responsible thereto.

(5) "Court" includes a judge, special magistrate, or clerk.

(6) "District Attorney" or "Attorney General" include assistant district attorneys or assistant attorneys general and other attorneys specially appointed to aid in the prosecution of a case.

(7) "District Court" includes all divisions of the District Court Department of the Trial Court, the Boston Municipal Court Department of the Trial Court, and the Juvenile Court Department of the Trial Court, or sessions thereof for holding court.

(8) "Interested Person" includes the adverse party, a co-defendant, and a witness who is to be deposed.

(9) "Judge" includes a judge of a court or one properly assigned to a court or a special magistrate when in the performance of those duties imposed and authorized by these rules.

(10) "Juvenile Court" means a division of the Juvenile Court Department of the Trial Court, or a session thereof for holding court.

(11) "Mailing" means the use of regular mail and shall not require registered or certified mail.

(12) "Prosecuting Attorney" means the attorney general or assistant attorneys general, district attorney, assistant district attorneys, special assistant district attorneys, or legal assistants to the district attorney, or other attorneys specially appointed to aid in the prosecution of a case.

(13) "Prosecutor" means any prosecuting attorney or prosecuting officer, and shall include a city solicitor, a police prosecutor, or a law student approved for practice pursuant to and acting as authorized by the rules of the Supreme Judicial Court.

(14) "Related Offense" means one of two or more offenses which are based on the same criminal conduct or episode or arise out of a course of criminal conduct or series of criminal episodes connected together or constituting parts of a single scheme or plan.

(15) "Return Day" means the day upon which a defendant is ordered by summons to first appear or, if under arrest, does first appear before a court to answer to the charges against him, whichever is earlier.

(16) "Special Magistrate" means any person who is appointed

2

pursuant to, and empowered to administer those functions authorized by, rule forty-seven of these rules.

(17) "Summons" means

(A) criminal process issued to a person requiring him to appear at a stated time and place to answer to criminal charges; or

(B) process issued to a person requiring him to appear at a stated time and place to give testimony in a criminal proceeding; or

(C) process issued to a person requiring him to appear and produce at a stated time and place books, designated papers, documents, or other objects for use in a criminal proceeding.

(18) "Superior Court" means the Superior Court Department of the Trial Court, or a session thereof for holding court.

Rule 3. Complaint and Indictment; Waiver of Indictment

[Applicable to District Court and Superior Court. Amended effective Sept. 7, 2004.]

(a) Commencement of Criminal Proceeding. A criminal proceeding shall be commenced in the District Court by a complaint and in the Superior Court by an indictment, except that if a defendant is charged in the District Court with a crime as to which the defendant has the right to be proceeded against by indictment and the defendant has waived the right to an indictment pursuant to subdivision (c), the Commonwealth may proceed in the Superior Court upon the complaint.

(b) Right to Indictment. A defendant charged with an offense punishable by imprisonment in state prison shall have the right to be proceeded against by indictment except when the offense charged is within the concurrent jurisdiction of the District and Superior Courts and the District Court retains jurisdiction.

(c) Waiver of Indictment.

(1) *Right to Waive Indictment.* A defendant charged in a District Court with an offense as to which the defendant has the right to be proceeded against by indictment shall have the right, except when the offense charged is a capital crime, to waive indictment, unless the Commonwealth proceeds by indictment pursuant to subdivision (e) of this rule.

(2) *Procedure for Waiving Indictment.* The defendant may waive the right to be proceeded against by indictment by filing a written waiver of that right in the District Court prior to the determination to bind the case over to the Superior Court for trial. The District Court may for cause shown grant relief from that waiver. After the determination by the District Court to bind the case over to the Superior Court for trial, the defendant may waive the right to be proceeded against by indictment by filing a written waiver of that right, with the consent of the prosecutor, in the Superior Court.

(d) Transmission of Papers. If the defendant is bound over to the Superior Court for trial after a finding of probable cause or after the defendant waives a probable cause hearing, the clerk of the District Court shall transmit to the clerk of the Superior Court a copy of the complaint and of the record; the original recognizances; a list of the witnesses; a statement of the expenses and the appearance of the attorney for the defendant, if any is entered; the waiver of the right to be proceeded against by indictment, if any is executed; the pretrial conference report, if any has been filed; and the report of the department of mental health as to the mental condition of the defendant, if such report has been filed under the provisions of the General Laws.

(e) Indictment after Waiver. Notwithstanding the defendant's waiver of the right to be proceeded against by indictment, the prosecuting attorney may proceed by indictment.

(f) Probable Cause Hearing. Defendants charged in a District Court with an offense as to which they have the right to be proceeded against by indictment and defendants charged in a District Court with an offense within the concurrent jurisdiction of the District and Superior Courts for which the District Court will not retain jurisdiction, have the right to a probable cause hearing, unless an indictment has been returned for the same offense. If the District Court finds that there is probable cause to believe that the defendant committed the crime or crimes alleged in the complaint, the court shall bind the defendant over to the Superior Court. If the District Court finds that there is no probable cause to believe that the defendant committed the crime or crimes alleged in the complaint, the court shall dismiss the complaint.

(g) The Complaint Process.

(1) *Procedure for Obtaining a Complaint.* Any person having knowledge, whether first hand or not, of the facts constituting the offense for which the complaint is sought may be a complainant. The complainant shall convey to the court the facts constituting the basis for the complaint. The complainant's account shall be either reduced to writing or recorded. The complainant shall sign the complaint under oath, before an appropriate judicial officer.

(2) *Probable Cause Requirement.* The appropriate judicial officer shall not authorize a complaint unless the information presented by the complainant establishes probable cause to believe that the person against whom the complaint is sought committed an offense.

Rule 3.1. Determination of Probable Cause for Detention

[Applicable to District Court and Superior Court. Added effective Sept. 7, 2004.]

(a) No person shall be held in custody more than twenty-four hours following an arrest, absent exigent circumstances, unless:

(i) a warrant or other judicial process authorizes the person's detention,

(ii) a complaint has been authorized under Rule 3(g), or

(iii) a determination of probable cause for detention has been made pursuant to subsection (b).

(b) A determination of probable cause for detention shall be made by an appropriate judicial officer. The appropriate officer shall consider any information presented by the police, whether or not known at the time of arrest. The police shall present the information under oath or affirmation, or under the pains and penalties of perjury. The police may present the information orally, in person or by any other means, or in writing. If presented in writing, the information may be transmitted to the appropriate judicial officer by facsimile transmission or by electronic mail or by such other electronic means as may be found acceptable by the court. The determination of probable cause for detention shall be an ex parte proceeding. The person arrested has no right to appear, either in person or by counsel.

(c) Where subsection (a) requires a determination of probable cause for detention, the police shall present the information necessary to obtain such determination to the appropriate judicial officer as soon as reasonably possible after the arrest, but no later than twenty-four hours after arrest, absent exigent circumstances.

(d) The judicial officer shall promptly reduce to writing his or her determination as to probable cause and notify the police. A copy of the written determination shall be transmitted to the police, by facsimile transmission or other means, as soon as possible.

(e) The judicial officer shall apply the same standard in making the determination of probable cause for detention as in deciding whether an arrest warrant should issue. If the judicial officer determines that there is probable cause to believe the person arrested committed an offense, the judicial officer shall make a written determination of his or her decision which shall be filed with the record of the case together with all the written information submitted by police.

(f) If there is no probable cause to believe that the person arrested committed an offense, the judicial officer shall order the person's prompt release from custody. The order and a written determination of the judicial officer shall be filed in the District Court having jurisdiction over the location of the arrest, together with all the written information submitted by police. These documents shall be filed separately from the records of criminal and delinquency cases, but shall be public records.

Rule 4. Form and Contents of Complaint or Indictment; Amendment

[Applicable to District Court and Superior Court.]

(a) Contents of Indictment or Complaint. An indictment and a complaint shall contain a caption as provided by law, together with a plain, concise description of the act which constitutes the crime or an appropriate legal term descriptive thereof.

(b) Subscription of Application for Issuance of Process. An application for issuance of process may be subscribed by the arresting officer, the police chief, or any police officer within the jurisdiction of a crime, a prosecutor, or a private person.

(c) Indictment Based Upon Secondary Evidence. An indictment shall not be dismissed on the grounds that the evidence presented before the grand jury consisted in whole or in part of the record from the defendant's probable cause hearing or that other hearsay evidence was presented before the grand jury.

(d) Amendment. Upon his own motion or the written motion of either party, a judge may allow amendment of the form of a complaint or indictment if such amendment would not prejudice the defendant or the Commonwealth.

Rule 5. The Grand Jury

[Applicable to Superior Court. Amended effective Sept. 7, 2004.]

(a) Summoning Grand Juries. As prescribed by law, the appropriate number of jurors shall be summoned in the manner and at the time required, from among whom the court shall select not more than twenty-three grand jurors to serve in said court as long as and at those specific times required by law, or as required by the court.

The regular grand jury shall be called upon and directed to sit by the Chief Justice of the Superior Court Department whenever within his or her discretion the conduct of regular criminal business and timely prosecution within a particular county so dictate. Notwithstanding the foregoing, special grand juries shall be summoned in the manner prescribed by the General Laws.

(b) Foreman, Foreman Pro Tem; Clerk, Clerk Pro Tem. After the grand jurors have been impanelled they shall retire and elect one of their number as foreperson. The foreperson and the prosecuting attorney shall have the power to administer oaths and affirmations to witnesses who appear to testify before the grand jury, and the foreperson shall, under his or her hand, return to the court a list of all witnesses sworn before the grand jury during the sitting. If the foreperson is unable to serve for any part of the period the grand jurors are required to serve, a foreperson pro tem shall be elected in the same manner as provided herein for election of the foreperson. The foreperson pro tem shall serve until the foreperson returns or for the remainder of the term if the foreperson is unable to return. The grand jury may also appoint one of their number as clerk to be charged with keeping a record of their proceedings, and, if the grand jury so directs, to deliver such record to the attorney general or district attorney. If the clerk is unable to serve for any part of the period the grand jurors are required to serve, a clerk pro tem may be appointed.

(c) Who May Be Present. Attorneys for the Commonwealth who are necessary or convenient to the presentation of the evidence, the witness under examination, the attorney for the witness, and such other persons who are necessary or convenient to the presentation of the evidence may be present while the grand jury is in session. The attorney for the witness shall make no objections or arguments or otherwise address the grand jury or the prosecuting attorney. No witness may refuse to appear because of unavailability of counsel for that witness.

(d) Secrecy of Proceedings and Disclosures. The judge may direct that an indictment be kept secret until after arrest. In such an instance, the clerk shall seal the indictment and no person may disclose the finding of the indictment except as is necessary for the issuance and execution of a warrant. A person performing an official function in relation to the grand jury may not disclose matters occurring before the grand jury except in the performance of his official duties or when specifically directed to do so by the court. No obligation of secrecy may be imposed upon any person except in accordance with law.

(e) Finding and Return of Indictment. An indictment may be found only upon the concurrence of twelve or more jurors. The indictment shall be returned by the grand jury to a judge in open court.

2

(f) No Bill; Discharge of Defendant. The grand jury shall during its session make a daily return to the court of all cases as to which it has determined not to present an indictment against an accused. Each such complaint shall be endorsed "no bill" and shall be filed with the court.

If upon the filing of a no bill the accused is held on process, he shall be discharged unless held on other process.

(g) Deliberation. The prosecuting attorney shall not be present during deliberation and voting except at the request of the grand jury.

(h) Discharge. A grand jury shall serve until the first sitting of the next authorized grand jury unless it is discharged sooner by the court or unless its service is extended to complete an investigation then in progress.

Rule 6. Summons to Appear; Arrest Warrant

[Applicable to District Court and Superior Court.]

(a) Issuance of Process.

(1) *Summons.* A defendant not under arrest or otherwise in custody shall, except as provided in subdivision (a)(2) of this rule, be notified of the criminal proceedings against him and of the date of the return day by means of a summons. A copy of the complaint or indictment shall accompany the summons. If the accused is a juvenile, a summons and copy of the complaint or indictment shall also be served upon the parent or legal guardian of the juvenile or upon the person with whom the juvenile resides. Such notice shall also advise the defendant to report in person to the probation department before the return day.

(2) *Warrant.* The District Court may authorize the issuance of a warrant in any case except where the accused is a juvenile less than twelve years of age. Upon the return of an indictment against a defendant, the Superior Court may authorize the issuance of a warrant. The decision to issue a warrant may be based upon the representation of a prosecutor made to the court that the defendant may not appear unless arrested. If a defendant fails to appear in response to a summons or for any reason is not amenable to service, the prosecutor may request that a warrant issue or may resummon the defendant.

(b) Form.

(1) *Warrant.* An arrest warrant issued pursuant to this rule shall be signed by the official issuing it and shall contain the name of the defendant or, if his name is unknown, any name or description by which he can be identified with reasonable certainty. The warrant shall recite the substance of the offense charged in the complaint or indictment. It shall command that the defendant be arrested and brought before the court.

(2) *Summons.* A summons shall be in the same form as a warrant except that it shall summon the defendant to appear before the court at a stated time and place.

(c) Service or Execution; Return.

(1) *By Whom.* A summons may be served in the manner provided by subdivision (c)(3) of this rule by any person authorized by the General Laws to serve criminal process. A warrant shall be directed to and executed by an officer authorized by the General Laws to serve criminal process.

(2) *Territorial Limits.* A summons may be served or a warrant executed at any place within the Commonwealth.

(3) *Manner.* A summons shall be served upon a defendant by delivering a copy to him personally, or by leaving it at his dwelling house or usual place of abode with some person of suitable age and discretion then residing therein, or by mailing it to the defendant's last known address. A warrant shall be executed by the arrest of the defendant. The officer need not have the warrant in his possession at the time of the arrest, but upon request he shall show the warrant to the defendant as soon as possible. If the officer does not have the warrant in his possession at the time of the arrest, he shall then inform the defendant that a warrant has issued and of the offense charged, but if the officer does not then know of the offense charged, he shall inform the defendant thereof within a reasonable time after arrest.

(4) *Return.* On or before the return day, the person to whom a summons was delivered for service shall make return thereof to the issuing court. The clerk shall maintain a list of those summonses returned unserved which shall include a statement of the efforts made by the person to whom the summonses were delivered for service to serve them. If a summons is mailed pursuant to subdivision (c)(3) of this rule and returned, the clerk shall record that fact upon the list. The officer executing a warrant shall make return thereof to the issuing court. At the request of the prosecutor any unexecuted warrant shall be returned to the issuing court and may be cancelled by that court upon its own motion or upon the motion of the prosecutor. At the request of the prosecutor made at any time while a complaint or an indictment is pending, a summons returned unserved or a warrant returned unexecuted and not cancelled may be delivered to an authorized person for service or execution.

(d) Default.

(1) *Costs.* A judge may order that expenses incurred as a result of the entry of a default against a defendant are to be assessed as costs against the defendant.

(2) *Preservation of Testimony.* If counsel for a defendant is present upon the entry of a default against the defendant and if the judge finds that to require the attendance at a later time of a witness then present in court would constitute a hardship upon the witness because of age, infirmity, illness, profession or other sufficient reason, the judge may order that the testimony of the witness be taken and preserved for subsequent use at trial or any other proceeding. The witness shall be examined in open court by the party on whose behalf he is present and the adverse party shall have the right of cross-examination. The expense of taking and preserving the testimony may be assessed as costs against the defendant.

Rule 7. Initial Appearance and Arraignment

[Amended effective June 1, 2012.]

(a) Time of Arraignment; Probation Interview; Indigency and Bail Reports

(1) ***Upon Arrest or Summons.*** A defendant who has been arrested and is not released shall be brought for arraignment before a court if then in session; and if not, at its next session. A defendant who receives a summons or who has been arrested but is thereupon released shall be ordered to appear before the court for arraignment on a date certain.

(2) ***Arrest of a Juvenile.*** Upon the arrest of a juvenile, the arresting officer shall notify the parent or guardian of the juvenile and the probation office.

(3) ***Probation Interview.*** On the day of the arraignment, the probation department shall interview the defendant; the probation department shall report to the court the pertinent information reasonably necessary to determine the issues of bail and indigency.

(b) Arraignment Procedure.

(1) ***Notice; Plea; and Bail.*** The court shall:

(A) read the charges to the defendant in open court, except that the reading of the charges in open court may be waived by the defendant if he or she is represented by counsel;

(B) enter the defendant's plea to the charges;

(C) inform the defendant of all warnings and advisories required by law; and,

(D) determine the conditions of the defendant's release, if any.

(2) ***Appointment of Counsel.*** If the court finds that the defendant is indigent or indigent but able to contribute and has not knowingly waived the right to counsel under the procedures established in Supreme Judicial Court Rule 3:10, the Committee for Public Counsel Services shall be assigned to provide representation for the defendant.

(3) ***Provision of Criminal Record; Preservation of Evidence.*** The court shall ensure that at or before arraignment, (i) a copy of the defendant's criminal record, if any, as compiled by the Commissioner of Probation is provided to the defense and to the prosecution, and (ii) the parties are afforded an opportunity to move for the preservation of evidence pursuant to Rule 14(a)(1)(E).

(4) ***Order Scheduling Pretrial Proceedings.*** At a District Court arraignment on a complaint which is outside of the District Court's final jurisdiction or on which jurisdiction is declined, the court shall schedule the case for a probable cause hearing. In all other District and Superior Court cases the court shall issue an order at arraignment requiring the prosecuting attorney and defense counsel to (1) engage in a pretrial conference on a date certain, and (2) appear at a pretrial hearing on a specified subsequent date.

(c) Appearance of Counsel.

(1) ***Filing.*** An appearance shall be entered by the attorney for the defendant and the prosecuting attorney on or before the arraignment. The appearance may be entered either by personally appearing before the clerk or by submitting an appearance slip, which shall include the name, Board of Bar Overseers number, address, and telephone number of the attorney. An attorney appearing on behalf of an organization shall also file with the court proof of the attorney's authorization to represent the organization.

(2) ***Effect; Withdrawal.*** An appearance shall be in the name of the attorney who files the appearance and shall constitute a representation that the attorney shall represent the defendant for trial or plea or shall prosecute the case, except that, if at the arraignment such a representation cannot be made and no contrary legal restriction applies, (1) the court may permit an appearance to be entered by an attorney to represent the defendant or prosecute the case for such time as the court may order, and (2) the court shall permit an appearance in the name of the prosecuting agency, which shall constitute representations that the agency will prosecute the case, will ensure that throughout the duration of the appearance a prosecutor is assigned to the case, and upon request of the court or a party will identify the prosecutor assigned to the case. If the attorney who files an appearance for the defendant on or before the arraignment wishes to withdraw the appearance, he or she may do so within fourteen days of the arraignment, provided that the attorney who shall represent the defendant at trial files an appearance simultaneously with such withdrawal; thereafter no appearance shall be withdrawn without permission of the court. The appearance of the prosecuting officer shall be withdrawn only with permission of the court.

(3) ***Notice.*** A copy of all appearances and withdrawals of appearance shall be filed and shall be served upon the adverse party pursuant to Rule 32.

Rule 8. Assignment of Counsel

[Applicable to District Court and Superior Court. Amended effective July 1, 1986.]

If a defendant charged with a crime for which a sentence of imprisonment or commitment to the custody of the Department of Youth Services may be imposed initially appears in any court without counsel, the judge shall follow the procedures established in G.L. c. 211D and in Supreme Judicial Court Rule 3:10.

Rule 9. Joinder of Offenses or Defendants

[Applicable to District Court and Superior Court.]

(a) Joinder of Offenses.

(1) *Related Offenses.* Two or more offenses are related offenses if they are based on the same criminal conduct or episode or arise out of a course of criminal conduct or series of criminal episodes connected together or constituting parts of a single scheme or plan.

(2) *Joinder of Related Offenses in Complaint or Indictment.* If two or more related offenses are of the same or similar character, they may be charged in the same indictment or complaint, with each offense stated in a separate count.

(3) *Joinder of Related Offenses for Trial.* If a defendant is charged with two or more related offenses, either party may move for joinder of such charges. The trial judge shall join the charges for trial unless he determines that joinder is not in the best interests of justice.

(4) *Joinder of Unrelated Offenses.* Upon the written motion of a defendant, or with his written consent, the trial judge may join for trial two or more charges of unrelated offenses upon a showing that failure to try the charges together would constitute harassment or unduly consume the time or resources of the parties. The trial judge shall join the charges for trial unless he determines that joinder is not in the best interests of justice.

(b) Joinder of Defendants. Two or more defendants may be joined in the same indictment or complaint if the charges against them arise out of the same criminal conduct or episode or out of a course of criminal conduct or series of criminal episodes so connected as to constitute parts of a single scheme, plan, conspiracy or joint enterprise. The defendants may be charged separately or together in one or more counts; all of the defendants need not be charged in each count.

(c) Consolidation of Offenses or Defendants on Motion of Court. The trial judge may order two or more indictments or complaints to be tried together if the offenses and the defendants, if more than one, could have been joined in a single indictment or complaint. The procedure shall be the same as if the prosecution were under a single indictment or complaint.

(d) Relief from Prejudicial Joinder.

(1) *In General.* If it appears that a joinder of offenses or of defendants is not in the best interests of justice, the judge may upon his own motion or the motion of either party order an election of separate trials of counts, grant a severance of defendants, or provide whatever other relief justice may require.

(2) *Motion by the Defendant.* A motion of the defendant for relief from prejudicial joinder shall be in writing and made before trial and shall be supported by an affidavit setting forth the grounds upon which any alleged prejudice rests, except that a motion for severance may be made before or at the close of all the evidence if based upon a ground not previously known.

(e) Conspiracy. An indictment or complaint for conspiracy to commit a substantive offense shall not be tried simultaneously with an indictment or complaint for the commission of the substantive offense, unless the defendant moves for joinder of such charges pursuant to subdivision (a) of this rule.

Rule 10. Continuances

[Applicable to District Court and Superior Court. Amended effective Dec. 1, 1997.]

(a) Continuances.

(1) After a case has been entered upon the trial calendar, a continuance shall be granted only when based upon cause and only when necessary to insure that the interests of justice are served.

(2) The factors, among others, which a judge shall consider in determining whether to grant a continuance in any case are:

(A) Whether the failure to grant a continuance in the proceeding would be likely to make a continuation of the proceeding impossible, or result in a miscarriage of justice.

(B) Whether the case taken as a whole is so unusual or so complex, because of the number of defendants or the nature of the prosecution or otherwise, that it is unreasonable to expect adequate preparation of the case at the time it is scheduled for trial.

(C) Whether the overall caseload of defense counsel routinely prohibits his making scheduled appearances, whether there has been a failure of diligent preparation by a party, and whether there has been a failure by a party to use due diligence to obtain available witnesses.

(3) An attorney who is to be otherwise engaged in a trial, evidentiary hearing, or appellate argument so as to require a continuance shall notify the court and the adverse party or the attorney for the adverse party of such conflicting engagement not less than twenty-four hours before the scheduled appearance, or within such other time as is reasonable under the circumstances.

(4) A motion for a continuance may include a request that the court rule on the motion without a hearing. If such a motion is filed at least three court days prior to the scheduled appearance or trial date and indicates that all parties have agreed to the continuance, the court shall, prior to the scheduled date, rule on the motion without a hearing unless it deems a hearing to be necessary. In any other case, the court may in its discretion rule on a continuance motion without a hearing, provided that all parties have had an adequate opportunity to file an opposition to the motion. If the court continues the case without a hearing, defendant's counsel shall inform the defendant of the revised date. Any motion filed pursuant to this subdivision shall provide one or more proposed continuance dates and state all supporting grounds, and any factual allegations shall be supported by affidavit.

(b) Assessment of Costs. When a continuance is granted upon the motion of either the Commonwealth or the defendant without adequate notice to the adverse party, causing the adverse party to incur unnecessary expenses, a judge may in his discretion assess those expenses as costs against the party or counsel requesting the continuance.

(c) Preservation of Testimony. A judge may order as a condition upon the granting of a continuance that the testimony of a witness then present in court be taken and preserved for subsequent use at trial or any other proceeding. The witness shall be examined in open court by the party on whose behalf he is present and the adverse party shall have the right of cross-examination. The expense of taking and preserving the testimony shall be assessed as costs against the party requesting the continuance.

Rule 11. Pretrial Conference and Pretrial Hearing

[Amended effective Sept. 7, 2004.]

(a) The Pretrial Conference.

At arraignment, except on a complaint regarding which the court will not exercise final jurisdiction, the court shall order the prosecuting attorney and defense counsel to attend a pretrial conference on a date certain to consider such matters as will promote a fair and expeditious disposition of the case. The defendant shall be available for attendance at the pretrial conference. The court may require the conference to be held at court under the supervision of a judge or clerk-magistrate.

(1) *Conference Agenda.* Among those issues to be discussed at the pretrial conference are:

(A) Discovery and all other matters which, absent agreement of the parties, must be raised by pretrial motion. All motions which cannot be agreed upon shall be filed pursuant to Rule 13(d).

(B) Whether the case can be disposed of without a trial.

(C) If the case is to be tried, (i) the setting of a proposed trial date which shall be subject to the approval of the court and which when fixed by the court shall not be changed without express permission of the court; (ii) the probable length of trial; (iii) the availability of necessary witnesses; and (iv) whether issues of fact can be resolved by stipulation.

(2) *Conference Report.*

2

(A) Filing. A conference report, subscribed by the prosecuting attorney and counsel for the defendant, and when necessary to waive constitutional rights or when the report contains stipulations as to material facts, by the defendant, shall be filed with the clerk of the court pursuant to subdivision (b)(2)(i). The conference report shall contain a statement of those matters upon which the parties have reached agreement, including any stipulations of fact, and a statement of those matters upon which the parties could not agree which are to be the subject of pretrial motions. Agreements reduced to writing in the conference report shall be binding on the parties and shall control the subsequent course of the proceeding.

(B) Failure to File. If a party fails to participate in a pretrial conference or to cooperate in the filing of a conference report, the adverse party shall notify the clerk of such failure. If a conference report is not filed and a party does not appear at the pretrial hearing, no request of that party for a continuance of the trial date as scheduled shall be granted and no pretrial motion of that party shall be permitted to be filed, except by leave of court for cause shown. If the parties fail to file a conference report or do not appear at the pretrial hearing, the case shall be presumed to be ready for trial and shall be scheduled for trial at the earliest possible time. The parties shall be subject to such other sanctions as the judge may impose.

(b) The Pretrial Hearing.

At arraignment, except on a complaint regarding which the court will not exercise final jurisdiction, the court shall order the prosecuting attorney and defense counsel to appear before the court on a date certain for a pretrial hearing. The defendant shall be available for attendance at the hearing. The pretrial hearing may include the following events:

(1) *Tender of Plea.* The defendant may tender a plea, admission, or other requested disposition, with or without the agreement of the prosecutor.

(2) *Pretrial Matters.* Unless the court declines jurisdiction over the case or disposes of the case at the pretrial hearing, the pretrial hearing shall include the following events:

(i) Filing of Pretrial Conference Report. The prosecuting attorney and defense counsel shall file the pretrial conference report with the clerk of court.

(ii) Discovery and Pretrial Motions. The court shall hear all discovery motions pending at the time of the pretrial hearing. Other pending pretrial motions may be heard at the pretrial hearing, continued to a specified date for hearing, or transmitted for hearing and resolution by the trial session.

(iii) Compliance and Trial Assignment. The court shall determine whether the pretrial conference report is complete, all discovery matters have been resolved, and compliance with discovery orders has been accomplished. If so, the court shall obtain the defendant's decision on waiver of the right to a jury trial, and assign a trial date or trial assignment date. If completion of either the pretrial conference report or discovery is still pending, the court shall schedule and order the parties to appear for a compliance hearing pursuant to Rule 11(c) unless the aggrieved party waives the right to a compliance hearing.

(iv) The court may issue such additional orders as will promote the fair, speedy, and orderly disposition of the case.

(c) Compliance Hearing.

A compliance hearing ordered pursuant to Rule 11(b)(2)(iii) shall be limited to the following court actions:

(1) determining whether the pretrial conference report and discovery are complete and, if necessary, hearing and deciding discovery motions and ordering appropriate sanctions for noncompliance;

(2) receiving and acting on a tender of plea or admission; and

(3) if the pretrial conference report and discovery are complete, obtaining the defendant's decision on waiver of the right to a jury trial, and scheduling the trial date or trial assignment date.

Rule 12. Pleas and Plea Agreements

[Applicable to District Court and Superior Court. Amended effective Jan. 1, 1987; Sept. 7, 2004; May 11, 2015; Sept. 1, 2019.]

(a) Pleas in General.

(1) *Pleas That May Be Entered and by Whom.* A defendant may plead not guilty, or guilty, or with the consent of the judge, nolo contendere, to any crime with which the defendant has been charged and over which the court has jurisdiction. A plea of guilty or nolo contendere shall be received only from the defendant personally except pursuant to the provisions of Rule 18(b). Pleas shall be received in open court and the proceedings shall be recorded. If a defendant refuses to plead or if the judge refuses to accept a plea of guilty or nolo contendere, a plea of not guilty shall be entered.

(2) *Admission to Sufficient Facts.* In a District Court, a defendant may, after a plea of not guilty, admit to sufficient facts to warrant a finding of guilty.

(3) *Acceptance of Plea of Guilty, a Plea of Nolo Contendere, or an Admission to Sufficient Facts.* A judge may accept a plea of guilty or a plea of nolo contendere or an admission to sufficient facts only after first determining that it is made voluntarily with an understanding of the nature of the charge and the consequences of the plea or admission. A judge may refuse to accept a plea of guilty or a plea of nolo contendere or an admission to sufficient facts.

(b) Plea Discussions; Pleas Without Plea Agreement and With Plea Agreement.

(1) *In General.* The defendant may tender a guilty plea, a plea of nolo contendere, or an admission to sufficient facts to warrant a finding of guilty without entering into a plea agreement with the prosecutor. Alternatively, if the defendant intends to tender a plea of guilty or an admission to sufficient facts, the prosecutor and the defendant may enter into a plea agreement pursuant to Rule 12(b)(5).

(2) *Plea Discussions.* The judge may participate in plea discussions at the request of one or both of the parties if the discussions are recorded and made part of the record.

(3) *Inquiry as to the Existence of a Plea Agreement.* After being informed that a defendant intends to plead guilty or to admit to sufficient facts, the judge shall inquire as to the existence of a plea agreement.

(4) *Pleas Without an Agreement.* If the defendant intends to plead guilty or nolo contendere or to admit to sufficient facts and there is no agreement under Rule 12(b)(5), the judge shall follow the procedures set forth in Rule 12(c).

(5) *Pleas Conditioned Upon an Agreement.* The defendant may enter into a plea agreement with the prosecutor if the defendant intends to plead guilty or admit to sufficient facts but not if the defendant intends to plead nolo contendere.

(A) A plea agreement may specify both that the parties agree on a specific sentence, including the length of any term of probation, and that the prosecutor will make one or more of the following charge concessions: amend an indictment or complaint; dismiss, reduce, or partially dismiss charges; not seek an indictment; or not bring other charges. The judge shall follow the procedures set forth in Rule 12(d) when the parties enter into a plea agreement that includes both an agreement to a specific sentence and a charge concession. If the judge accepts the plea agreement and the defendant's plea, Rule 12(d) requires the judge to sentence the defendant according to the terms of the plea agreement.

(B) When the plea is conditioned on a plea agreement other than one described in Rule 12(b)(5)(A), the judge shall follow the procedures set forth in Rule 12(c).

(6) *Pleas Reserving Appellate Review.* With the written agreement of the prosecutor, the defendant may tender a plea of guilty or an admission to sufficient facts while reserving the right to appeal any ruling or rulings that would, if reversed, render the Commonwealth's case not viable on one or more charges. The written agreement must specify the ruling or rulings that may be appealed,

and must state that reversal of the ruling or rulings would render the Commonwealth's case not viable on one or more specified charges. The judge, in an exercise of discretion, may refuse to accept a plea of guilty or an admission to sufficient facts reserving the right to appeal. If the defendant prevails in whole or in part on appeal, the defendant may withdraw the guilty plea or the admission to sufficient facts on any of the specified charges. If the defendant withdraws the guilty plea or the admission to sufficient facts, the judge shall dismiss the complaint or indictment on those charges, unless the prosecutor shows good cause to do otherwise. The appeal shall be governed by the Massachusetts Rules of Appellate Procedure, provided that a notice of appeal is filed within thirty days of the acceptance of the plea.

(c) Procedure If No Plea Agreement or If Plea Agreement Does Not Include Both a Specific Sentence and a Charge Concession.

(1) *Disclosure of the Terms of Any Plea Agreement.* If the parties have entered into a plea described in Rule 12(b)(5)(B), the parties shall disclose the terms of that agreement on the record in open court unless the judge for good cause allows the parties to disclose the terms of the plea agreement in camera on the record.

(2) *Tender of Plea.* The defendant's plea or admission shall be tendered to the judge.

(3) *Colloquy.* The judge shall:

(A) Provide notice to the defendant of the consequences of a plea. The judge shall inform the defendant:

(i) that by a plea of guilty or nolo contendere, or an admission to sufficient facts, the defendant waives the right to trial with or without a jury, the right to confrontation of witnesses, the right to be presumed innocent until proved guilty beyond a reasonable doubt, and the privilege against self-incrimination;

(ii) of the maximum possible sentence on the charge, and, if applicable,

(a) any different or additional punishment based upon subsequent offense provisions of the General Laws;

(b) that the defendant may be subject to adjudication as a sexually dangerous person and required to register as a sex offender;

(c) the mandatory minimum sentence on the charge; and

(d) that a conviction or plea of guilty for an offense listed in G.L. c. 279, § 25(b) implicates the habitual offender statute, and that upon conviction or plea of guilty for the third or subsequent of said offenses: (1) the defendant may be imprisoned in the state prison for the maximum term provided by law for such third or subsequent offense; (2) no sentence may be reduced or suspended; and (3) the defendant may be ineligible for probation, parole, work release or furlough, or to receive any deduction in sentence for good conduct;

(iii) of the following potential immigration consequences of the plea:

(a) that, if the defendant is not a citizen of the United States, the guilty plea, plea of nolo contendere, or admission may have the consequence of deportation, exclusion of admission, or denial of naturalization; and

(b) that, if the offense to which the defendant is pleading guilty, nolo contendere, or admitting to sufficient facts is under federal law one that presumptively mandates removal from the United States and federal officials decide to seek removal, it is practically inevitable that this conviction would result in deportation, exclusion from admission, or denial of naturalization under the laws of the United States.

(B) Factual basis for the charge. The prosecutor shall present the factual basis of the charge.

(C) Rights of Victims and Witnesses of Crimes. If applicable, the judge shall inquire of the prosecutor as to compliance with the requirements of G.L. c. 258B, Rights of Victims and Witnesses of Crimes. At any time prior to imposing sentence, the judge shall give any person entitled under G.L. c. 258B to make an oral and/or written victim impact statement the opportunity to do so.

(4) *Disposition Requests.*

(A) When there is no agreed-upon recommendation as to sentence. The judge shall give both parties the opportunity to recommend a sentence to the judge. In the District Court, the judge shall inform the defendant that the disposition imposed will not exceed the terms of the defendant's request without first giving the defendant the right to withdraw the plea. In the Superior Court, the judge shall inform the defendant that the disposition imposed will not exceed the terms of the prosecutor's recommendation without first giving the defendant the right to withdraw the plea. At any time prior to accepting the plea or admission, the judge may continue the hearing on the judge's own motion to ensure that the judge has been provided with, and has had an opportunity to consider, all of the facts pertinent to a determination of a just disposition in the case.

(B) Where there is an agreed-upon recommendation as to disposition. The judge shall inform the defendant that the sentence imposed will not exceed the terms of the agreement without first giving the defendant the right to withdraw the plea. At any time prior to accepting the plea or admission, the judge may continue the hearing on the judge's own motion to ensure that the judge has been provided with, and has had an opportunity to consider, all of the facts pertinent to a determination of a just disposition in the case.

(5) *Findings of Judge; Acceptance of Plea.* The judge shall inquire whether the defendant still wishes to plead guilty or nolo contendere or admit to sufficient facts. If so, the judge will then make findings as to whether the plea or admission is knowing and voluntary, and whether there is an adequate factual basis for the charge. The defendant's failure to acknowledge all aspects of the factual basis shall not preclude a judge from accepting a guilty plea or admission. At the conclusion of the hearing, the judge shall accept or reject the tendered plea or admission.

(6) *Sentencing.* After acceptance of a plea of guilty or nolo contendere or an admission, the judge shall sentence the defendant.

(A) Conditions of Probation. If the judge's disposition includes a term of probation, the judge, with the assistance of probation where appropriate and after considering the recommendations of the parties, shall impose appropriate conditions of probation.

(B) Intent to Impose Sentence Exceeding Requested Disposition. In District Court, if the judge decides to impose a sentence that will exceed the defendant's request for disposition under Rule 12(c)(4)(A) or the parties' request for disposition under Rule 12(c)(4)(B), the judge shall, on the record, advise the defendant of that intent and shall afford the defendant the opportunity to withdraw the plea or admission. In Superior Court, if the judge decides to impose a sentence that will exceed the prosecutor's request for disposition under Rule 12(c)(4)(A) or the parties' request for disposition under Rule 12(c)(4)(B), the judge shall, on the record, advise the defendant of that intent and shall afford the defendant the opportunity to withdraw the plea or admission. In both District and Superior Court, the judge may indicate to the parties what sentence the judge would impose.

(d) Procedure If Plea Agreement Includes Both a Specific Sentence and a Charge Concession.

(1) *Disclosure of the Terms of the Plea Agreement.* The parties shall disclose the terms of the plea agreement on the record in open court unless the judge for good cause allows the parties to disclose the terms of the plea agreement in camera on the record.

(2) *Tender of Plea.* The defendant's plea or admission shall be tendered to the judge.

(3) *Colloquy.* The judge shall:

(A) Provide notice to the defendant of the consequences of a plea. The judge shall inform the defendant:

(i) that by a plea of guilty or an admission to sufficient facts, the defendant waives the right to trial with or without a jury, the right to confrontation of witnesses, the right to be presumed innocent until proved guilty beyond a reasonable doubt, and the privilege against self-incrimination;

(ii) of the maximum possible sentence on the charge, and, if applicable,

2

(a) any different or additional punishment based upon subsequent offense provisions of the General Laws;

(b) that the defendant may be subject to adjudication as a sexually dangerous person and required to register as a sex offender;

(c) the mandatory minimum sentence on the charge; and

(d) that a conviction or plea of guilty for an offense listed in G.L. c. 279, § 25(b) implicates the habitual offender statute, and that upon conviction or plea of guilty for the third or subsequent of said offenses: (1) the defendant may be imprisoned in the state prison for the maximum term provided by law for such third or subsequent offense; (2) no sentence may be reduced or suspended; and (3) the defendant may be ineligible for probation, parole, work release or furlough, or to receive any deduction in sentence for good conduct;

(iii) of the following potential immigration consequences of the plea:

(a) that, if the defendant is not a citizen of the United States, the guilty plea or admission may have the consequence of deportation, exclusion from admission, or denial of naturalization; and

(b) that, if the offense to which the defendant is pleading guilty or admitting to sufficient facts is under federal law one that presumptively mandates removal from the United States and federal officials decide to seek removal, it is practically inevitable that this conviction would result in deportation, exclusion from admission, or denial of naturalization under the laws of the United States.

(B) Factual basis for the charge. The prosecutor shall present the factual basis of the charge.

(C) Rights of Victims and Witnesses of Crimes. If applicable, the judge shall inquire of the prosecutor as to compliance with the requirements of G.L. c. 258B, Rights of Victims and Witnesses of Crimes. The judge shall give any person entitled under G.L. c. 258B to make an oral and/or written victim impact statement the opportunity to do so.

(4) *Review; Acceptance or Rejection of Plea Agreement.* The judge must accept or reject the plea agreement before the judge accepts a guilty plea or admission. The judge should not accept a plea agreement without considering whether the proposed disposition is just. At any time prior to the acceptance or rejection of the plea agreement, the judge may continue the plea hearing on the judge's own motion to ensure that the judge has been provided with, and has had an opportunity to consider, all of the facts pertinent to a determination whether the plea agreement provides for a just disposition in the case.

(A) Accepted Plea Agreement. If the judge accepts the plea agreement, the judge shall inform the defendant that the judge will impose the sentence, including the length of any term of probation, provided in the plea agreement.

(B) Rejected Plea Agreement. If the judge rejects the plea agreement, the judge shall, on the record and in open court (or, for good cause, in camera on the record):

(i) inform the parties that the judge rejects the plea agreement, but the judge may indicate to the parties what sentence the judge would impose or what additional information the judge will require before the judge may make this determination;

(ii) allow either party to withdraw from the plea agreement; and

(iii) allow the defendant to withdraw his or her plea or admission.

(5) *Findings of Judge as to Plea Agreement and Plea; Acceptance of Plea.* If the judge has accepted the plea agreement, the judge shall inquire whether the defendant still wishes to plead guilty or admit to sufficient facts. If so, the judge will then make findings as to whether the plea agreement and plea or admission are knowing, voluntary, and supported by an adequate factual basis. The defendant's failure to acknowledge all aspects of the factual basis shall not preclude a judge from accepting a guilty plea or admission. At the conclusion of the hearing, the judge shall accept or reject the tendered plea or admission.

(6) *Sentencing.* After accepting the plea agreement and the plea or admission, the judge shall impose sentence according to the terms of the plea agreement. If the plea agreement includes a term of probation, the judge, with the assistance of probation where appropriate and after considering the recommendations of the parties, shall impose appropriate conditions of probation.

(e) Availability of Criminal Record and Presentence Report.

Prior to sentencing under Rule 12(c)(6) or to the judge's decision to accept or reject a plea agreement under Rule 12(d)(4), the judge, prosecutor, and counsel for the defendant shall have an opportunity to review the defendant's criminal record and any report of the presentence investigation as described in Rule 28(d)(2). In extraordinary cases, the judge may except from disclosure to the parties parts of the report which are not relevant to a proper sentence, diagnostic opinion which might seriously disrupt a program of rehabilitation, sources of information obtained upon a promise of confidentiality, or any other information which, if disclosed, might result in harm, physical or otherwise, to the defendant or other persons. If the report is not made fully available, the portions thereof which are not disclosed shall not be relied upon in determining sentence. No party may make any copy of the presentence report.

(f) Inadmissibility of Pleas, Offers of Pleas, and Related Statements.

Except as otherwise provided in this subdivision, evidence of a plea of guilty, or a plea of nolo contendere, or an admission, or of an offer to plead guilty or nolo contendere or an admission to the crime charged or any other crime, later withdrawn, or statements made in connection with, and relevant to, any of the foregoing pleas or offers, is not admissible in any civil or criminal proceedings against the person who made the plea or offer. However, evidence of a statement made in connection with, and relevant to, a plea of guilty, later withdrawn, or a plea of nolo contendere, or an admission or an offer to plead guilty or nolo contendere or an admission to the crime charged or any other crime, is admissible in a criminal proceeding for perjury if the statement was made by the defendant under oath, on the record, and in the presence of counsel, if any.

Reporter's Notes (2019). Subdivision (b)(6) is added in response to a referral in *Commonwealth v. Gomez*, 480 Mass. 240 (2018), requesting that the Committee propose a rule providing for conditional guilty pleas in Massachusetts. Like the federal rules and the rules of many states, it enables a defendant to enter a plea reserving a right to appeal (commonly called a "conditional plea"). Under this rule, a defendant may, with the prosecutor's agreement, plead guilty (or in District or Juvenile Courts admit to sufficient facts), appeal a ruling the defendant believes is erroneous and, if successful on appeal, withdraw the plea (or the admission to sufficient facts) and presumptively obtain dismissal of the charge. A guilty plea or admission to sufficient facts reserving appellate review of a specified ruling or rulings may be tendered under either Mass. R. Crim. P. 12(c) or 12(d). In all respects other than reserving the right to appeal, this subdivision works no change in existing rules governing pleas, sentencing, or appeal.

A guilty plea, voluntarily and intelligently made, ordinarily "waives all nonjurisdictional defects." *Commonwealth v. Cabrera*, 449 Mass. 825, 830 (2007) (citing *Garvin v. Commonwealth*, 351 Mass. 661, 663–664 (1967)). Adverse rulings thus cannot be appealed, even by a defendant who might otherwise plead guilty, without the time and expense of a trial. As the Supreme Judicial Court recognized in *Commonwealth v. Gomez*, 480 Mass. 240 (2018), the Federal Rules of Criminal Procedure and the law of most states permit defendants to enter a guilty plea conditioned on the right to appeal a specified ruling of the court. *See, e.g.*, Fed. R. Crim. P. 11(a)(2). In *Gomez*, the Court exercised its superintendence authority under G.L. c. 211, § 3 to authorize conditional guilty pleas provided the Commonwealth and the court agreed, and the defendant specified the ruling on which appellate review was sought. *Gomez, supra* at 252. This subdivision implements *Gomez* by permitting guilty pleas or admissions to sufficient facts in which the defendant reserves for appellate review one or more rulings.

This procedure facilitates plea bargaining and conserves judicial resources. These savings are greatest when the rulings reserved for appeal effectively dispose of the case; thus, the procedure requires that the Commonwealth agree that reversal of the ruling subject to appeal would render its case on the specified charge or charges not viable. While most conditional pleas involve legally dispositive rulings, even certain non-dispositive rulings can be subject to conditional pleas. *See Gomez*, 480 Mass. at 252. The rule thus extends to situations in which, should the reserved ruling be reversed, the Commonwealth would choose not to proceed because the case would no longer be viable for prosecution. The viability standard also appears in S.J.C. Order regarding Applications to a Single Justice Pursuant to Mass. R. Crim. P. 15(a)(2) (June 8, 2016) (applications for interlocutory appeal by the Commonwealth must include a "statement whether the Commonwealth has a viable case without the suppressed evidence, and the strength of that case, if viable").

This rule requires the parties to specify, by written agreement, the ruling or rulings reserved for appeal, and the charge or charges that would presumptively be dismissed if the defendant prevails on appeal and chooses to withdraw the guilty plea or admission to sufficient facts. The ruling or rulings should be identified by stating the name of the motion or pleading ruled upon, the date of the ruling or rulings, and the judge who issued the ruling. The charge or charges should be identified by reference to the complaint and offense or count of the indictment. The written agreement should be filed with the court and become part of the record for appeal. A guilty plea or admission to sufficient facts reserving appellate review of a specified ruling or rulings may be tendered under either Mass. R. Crim. P. 12(c) or 12(d). As with any guilty plea, the judge has discretion to refuse to accept a plea reserving appellate review. *See* Mass. R. Crim. P. 12(a)(3). While a plea that does not result in a conviction would ordinarily not merit appeal, in special circumstances the collateral consequences of even a continuance without a finding may warrant a defendant pursuing an appeal. *See, e.g., Commonwealth v. Henry*, 88 Mass. App. Ct. 446 (2015) (admission to sufficient facts and continuance without a finding equivalent to a guilty plea in evaluating immigration consequences, citing *Commonwealth v. Grannum*, 457 Mass. 128, 130 n.4 (2010)); *Burke v. Bd. of Appeal on Motor Vehicle Liability Policies and Bonds*, 90 Mass. App. Ct. 203, *rev. denied* 476 Mass. 1101 (2016) (admission to sufficient facts in connection with continuance without a finding on first offense operating under the influence could qualify as a conviction for purposes of lifetime revocation of driver's license pursuant to G.L. c. 90 § 24(1)(d)). The process for taking appellate review of the specified ruling or rulings is governed by the Massachusetts Rules of Appellate Procedure, provided that the notice of appeal is filed within thirty days of the acceptance of the plea.

If the defendant prevails in whole or in part on appeal, the defendant has the choice whether to withdraw the guilty plea, or the admission to sufficient facts, on the specified charge or charges. If the defendant elects to withdraw the plea or admission, dismissal of the specified charge or charges, which the Commonwealth previously agreed would not be viable should the defendant prevail on appeal, is presumptively appropriate. In cases in which, for example, the defendant prevails on appeal in part (e.g., the appellate court suppresses some but not all the evidence which the defendant sought to exclude), the Commonwealth has an opportunity to show good cause that the court should not dismiss the charge or charges. If the judge does not intend to dismiss the specified charge or charges, the judge should indicate that intention to the defendant before the defendant withdraws the guilty plea or admission to sufficient facts.

Appellate relief for the defendant may necessitate re-sentencing. As when a conviction or sentencing provision is vacated, in the normal course the trial judge has an opportunity to reassess the sentence given the remaining convictions and sentencing options. *Commonwealth v. Sallop*, 472 Mass. 568, 570 (2015); *Commonwealth v. Kruah*, 47 Mass. App. Ct. 341, 348 (1999); *Commonwealth v. Clermy*, 37 Mass. App. Ct. 774, 779, *aff'd*, 421 Mass. 325 (1995).

NOTE See http://masscases.com/cases/sjc/480/480mass240.html for the complete text of *Commonwealth v. Gomez*, 480 Mass. 240 (2018). See this Part's Additional Materials for a copy of Juvenile Court Form JV-170—Written Agreement Between the Parties Pursuant to a Conditional Tender of Plea Mass. R. Crim. P. 12(b)(6). The form is also available at https://www.mass.gov/lists/juvenile-court-forms.

Rule 13. Pretrial Motions

[Applicable to District Court and Superior Court. Amended effective Sept. 7, 2004.]

(a) In General.

(1) *Requirement of Writing and Signature; Waiver.* A pretrial motion shall be in writing and signed by the party making the motion or the attorney for that party. Pretrial motions shall be filed within the time allowed by subdivision (d) of this rule.

2

(2) *Grounds and Affidavit.* A pretrial motion shall state the grounds on which it is based and shall include in separately numbered paragraphs all reasons, defenses, or objections then available, which shall be set forth with particularity. If there are multiple charges, a motion filed pursuant to this rule shall specify the particular charge to which it applies. Grounds not stated which reasonably could have been known at the time a motion is filed shall be deemed to have been waived, but a judge for cause shown may grant relief from such waiver. In addition, an affidavit detailing all facts relied upon in support of the motion and signed by a person with personal knowledge of the factual basis of the motion shall be attached.

(3) *Service and Notice.* A copy of any pretrial motion and supporting affidavits shall be served on all parties or their attorneys pursuant to Rule 32 at the time the originals are filed. Opposing affidavits shall be served not later than one day before the hearing. For cause shown the requirements of this subdivision (3) may be waived by the court.

(4) *Memoranda of Law.* The judge or special magistrate may require the filing of a memorandum of law, in such form and within such time as he may direct, as a condition precedent to a hearing on a motion or interlocutory matter. No motion to suppress evidence, other than evidence seized during a warrantless search, and no motion to dismiss may be filed unless accompanied by a memorandum of law, except when otherwise ordered by the judge or special magistrate.

(5) *Renewal.* Upon a showing that substantial justice requires, the judge or special magistrate may permit a pretrial motion which has been heard and denied to be renewed.

(b) Bill of Particulars.

(1) *Motion.* Within the time provided for the filing of pretrial motions by this rule or within such other time as the judge may allow, a defendant may request or the court upon its own motion may order that the prosecution file a statement of such particulars as may be necessary to give both the defendant and the court reasonable notice of the crime charged, including time, place, manner, or means.

(2) *Amendment.* If at trial there exists a material variance between the evidence and bill of particulars, the judge may order the bill of particulars amended or may grant such other relief as justice requires.

(c) Motion to Dismiss or to Grant Appropriate Relief.

(1) All defenses available to a defendant by plea, other than not guilty, shall only be raised by a motion to dismiss or by a motion to grant appropriate relief.

(2) A defense or objection which is capable of determination without trial of the general issue shall be raised before trial by motion.

(d) Filing. Only pretrial motions the subject matter of which could not be agreed upon at the pretrial conference shall be filed with the court.

(1) *Discovery Motions.* Any discovery motions shall be filed prior to the conclusion of the pretrial hearing, or thereafter for good cause shown. A discovery motion filed after the conclusion of the pretrial hearing shall be heard and considered only if (A) the discovery sought could not reasonably have been requested or heard prior to the conclusion of the pretrial hearing, (B) the discovery is sought by the Commonwealth, and the Commonwealth could not reasonably provide all discovery due to the defense prior

to the conclusion of the pretrial hearing, or (C) other good cause exists to warrant consideration of the motion.

(2) *Non-Discovery Pretrial Motions.* A pretrial motion which does not seek discovery shall be filed before the assignment of a trial date pursuant to Rule 11(b) or (c) or within 21 days thereafter, unless the court permits later filing for good cause shown.

(e) Hearing on Motions. The parties shall have a right to a hearing on a pretrial motion. The opposing party shall be afforded an adequate opportunity to prepare and submit a memorandum of law prior to the hearing.

(1) *Discovery Motions.* All pending discovery motions shall be heard and decided prior to the defendant's election of a jury or jury-waived trial. Any discovery matters pending at the time of the pretrial hearing or the compliance hearing shall be heard at that hearing. Discovery motions filed pursuant to subdivision (d)(1) after the defendant's election shall be heard and decided expeditiously.

(2) *Non-Discovery Pretrial Motions.* A non-discovery motion filed prior to the pretrial hearing may be heard at the pretrial hearing, at a hearing scheduled to address the motion, or at the trial session. A non-discovery motion filed at or after the pretrial hearing shall be heard at the next scheduled court date unless otherwise ordered.

(3) Within seven days after the filing of a motion, or if the motion is transmitted to the trial session within seven days after the transmittal, the clerk or judge shall assign a date for hearing the motion, but the judge or special magistrate for cause shown may entertain such motion at any time before trial. If the parties have agreed to a mutually convenient time for the hearing of a pretrial motion, the clerk shall mark up the motion for hearing at that time subject to the approval of the court. The clerk shall notify the parties of the time set for hearing the motion.

Rule 14. Pretrial Discovery

[Applicable to cases initiated (by indictment or complaint) on or after Sept. 7, 2004. Amended effective Apr. 1, 2009; Sept. 17, 2012; Jan. 1, 2016.]

(a) Procedures for Discovery.

(1) *Automatic Discovery.*

(A) Mandatory Discovery for the Defendant. The prosecution shall disclose to the defense, and permit the defense to discover, inspect and copy, each of the following items and information at or prior to the pretrial conference, provided it is relevant to the case and is in the possession, custody or control of the prosecutor, persons under the prosecutor's direction and control, or persons who have participated in investigating or evaluating the case and either regularly report to the prosecutor's office or have done so in the case:

(i) Any written or recorded statements, and the substance of any oral statements, made by the defendant or a co-defendant.

(ii) The grand jury minutes, and the written or recorded statements of a person who has testified before a grand jury.

(iii) Any facts of an exculpatory nature.

(iv) The names, addresses, and dates of birth of the Commonwealth's prospective witnesses other than law enforcement witnesses. The Commonwealth shall also provide this information to the Probation Department.

(v) The names and business addresses of prospective law enforcement witnesses.

(vi) Intended expert opinion evidence, other than evidence that pertains to the defendant's criminal responsibility and is subject to subdivision (b)(2). Such discovery shall include the identity, current curriculum vitae, and list of publications of each intended expert witness, and all reports prepared by the expert that pertain to the case.

(vii) Material and relevant police reports, photographs, tangible objects, all intended exhibits, reports of physical examinations of any person or of scientific tests or experiments, and statements of persons the party intends to call as witnesses.

(viii) A summary of identification procedures, and all statements made in the presence of or by an identifying witness that are relevant to the issue of identity or to the fairness or accuracy of the identification procedures.

(ix) Disclosure of all promises, rewards or inducements made to witnesses the party intends to present at trial.

(B) Reciprocal Discovery for the Prosecution. Following the Commonwealth's delivery of all discovery required pursuant to subdivision (a)(1)(A) or court order, and on or before a date agreed to between the parties, or in the absence of such agreement a date ordered by the court, the defendant shall disclose to the prosecution and permit the Commonwealth to discover, inspect, and copy any material and relevant evidence discoverable under subdivision (a)(1)(A)(vi), (vii), and (ix) which the defendant intends to offer at trial, including the names, addresses, dates of birth, and statements of those persons whom the defendant intends to call as witnesses at trial.

(C) Stay of Automatic Discovery; Sanctions. Subdivisions (a)(1)(A) and (a)(1)(B) shall have the force and effect of a court order, and failure to provide discovery pursuant to them may result in application of any sanctions permitted for non-compliance with a court order under subdivision 14(c). However, if in the judgment of either party good cause exists for declining to make any of the disclosures set forth above, it may move for a protective order pursuant to subdivision (a)(6) and production of the item shall be stayed pending a ruling by the court.

(D) Record of Convictions of the Defendant, Codefendants, and Prosecution Witnesses. At arraignment the court shall order the Probation Department to deliver to the parties the record of prior complaints, indictments and dispositions of all defendants and of all witnesses identified pursuant to subdivisions (a)(1)(A)(iv) within 5 days of the Commonwealth's notification to the Department of the names and addresses of its witnesses.

(E) Notice and Preservation of Evidence. (i) Upon receipt of information that any item described in subparagraph (a)(1)(A)(i)–(viii) exists, except that it is not within the possession, custody or control of the prosecution, persons under its direction and control, or persons who have participated in investigating or evaluating the case and either regularly report to the prosecutor's office or have done so in the case, the prosecution shall notify the defendant of the existence of the item and all information known to the prosecutor concerning the item's location and the identity of any persons possessing it. (ii) At any time, a party may move for an order to any individual, agency or other entity in possession, custody or control of items pertaining to the case, requiring that such items be preserved for a specified period of time. The court shall hear and rule upon the motion expeditiously. The court may modify or vacate such an order upon a showing that preservation of particular evidence will create significant hardship, on condition that the probative value of said evidence is preserved by a specified alternative means.

(2) Motions for Discovery. The defendant may move, and following its filing of the Certificate of Compliance the Commonwealth may move, for discovery of other material and relevant evidence not required by subdivision (a)(1) within the time allowed by Rule 13(d)(1).

(3) Certificate of Compliance. When a party has provided all discovery required by this rule or by court order, it shall file with the court a Certificate of Compliance. The certificate shall state that, to the best of its knowledge and after reasonable inquiry, the party has disclosed and made available all items subject to discovery other than reports of experts, and shall identify each item provided. If further discovery is subsequently provided, a supplemental certificate shall be filed with the court identifying the additional items provided.

(4) Continuing Duty. If either the defense or the prosecution subsequently learns of additional material which it would have been under a duty to disclose or produce pursuant to any provisions of this rule at the time of a previous discovery order, it shall

promptly notify the other party of its acquisition of such additional material and shall disclose the material in the same manner as required for initial discovery under this rule.

(5) Work Product. This rule does not authorize discovery by a party of those portions of records, reports, correspondence, memoranda, or internal documents of the adverse party which are only the legal research, opinions, theories, or conclusions of the adverse party or its attorney and legal staff, or of statements of a defendant, signed or unsigned, made to the attorney for the defendant or the attorney's legal staff.

(6) Protective Orders. Upon a sufficient showing, the judge may at any time order that the discovery or inspection be denied, restricted, or deferred, or make such other order as is appropriate. The judge may alter the time requirements of this rule. The judge may, for cause shown, grant discovery to a defendant on the condition that the material to be discovered be available only to counsel for the defendant. This provision does not alter the allocation of the burden of proof with regard to the matter at issue, including privilege.

(7) Amendment of Discovery Orders. Upon motion of either party made subsequent to an order of the judge pursuant to this rule, the judge may alter or amend the previous order or orders as the interests of justice may require. The judge may, for cause shown, affirm a prior order granting discovery to a defendant upon the additional condition that the material to be discovered be available only to counsel for the defendant.

(8) A party may waive the right to discovery of an item, or to discovery of the item within the time provided in this Rule. The parties may agree to reduce or enlarge the items subject to discovery pursuant to subsections (a)(1)(A) and (a)(1)(B). Any such waiver or agreement shall be in writing and signed by the waiving party or the parties to the agreement, shall identify the specific items included, and shall be served upon all the parties.

(b) Special Procedures.

(1) *Notice of Alibi.*

(A) Notice by Defendant. The judge may, upon written motion of the Commonwealth filed pursuant to subdivision (a)(2) of this rule, stating the time, date, and place at which the alleged offense was committed, order that the defendant serve upon the prosecutor a written notice, signed by the defendant, of his or her intention to offer a defense of alibi. The notice by the defendant shall state the specific place or places at which the defendant claims to have been at the time of the alleged offense and the names and addresses of the witnesses upon whom the defense intends to rely to establish the alibi.

(B) Disclosure of Information and Witness. Within seven days of service of the defendant's notice of alibi, the Commonwealth shall serve upon the defendant a written notice stating the names and addresses of witnesses upon whom the prosecutor intends to rely to establish the defendant's presence at the scene of the alleged offense and any other witnesses to be relied on to rebut testimony of any of the defendant's alibi witnesses.

(C) Continuing Duty to Disclose. If prior to or during trial a party learns of an additional witness whose identity, if known, should have been included in the information furnished under subdivision (b)(1)(A) or (B), that party shall promptly notify the adverse party or its attorney of the existence and identity of the additional witness.

(D) Failure to Comply. Upon the failure of either party to comply with the requirements of this rule, the judge may exclude the testimony of any undisclosed witness offered by such party as to the defendant's absence from or presence at the scene of the alleged offense. This rule shall not limit the right of the defendant to testify.

(E) Exceptions. For cause shown, the judge may grant an exception to any of the requirements of subdivisions (b)(1)(A) through (D) of this rule.

(F) Inadmissibility of Withdrawn Alibi. Evidence of an intention to rely upon an alibi defense, later withdrawn, or of statements made in connection with that intention, is not admissible in any civil or criminal proceeding against the person who gave notice of that intention.

(2) *Mental Health Issues.*

(A) Notice. If a defendant intends at trial to raise as an issue his or her mental condition at the time of the alleged crime, or if the defendant intends to introduce expert testimony on the defendant's mental condition at any stage of the proceeding, the defendant shall, within the time provided for the filing of pretrial motions by Rule 13(d)(2) or at such later time as the judge may allow, notify the prosecutor in writing of such intention. The notice shall state:

(i) whether the defendant intends to offer testimony of expert witnesses on the issue of the defendant's mental condition at the time of the alleged crime or at another specified time;

(ii) the names and addresses of expert witnesses whom the defendant expects to call; and

(iii) whether those expert witnesses intend to rely in whole or in part on statements of the defendant as to his or her mental condition.

The defendant shall file a copy of the notice with the clerk. The judge may for cause shown allow late filing of the notice, grant additional time to the parties to prepare for trial, or make such other order as may be appropriate.

(B) Examination. If the notice of the defendant or subsequent inquiry by the judge or developments in the case indicate that statements of the defendant as to his or her mental condition will be relied upon by a defendant's expert witness, the court, on its own motion or on motion of the prosecutor, may order the defendant to submit to an examination consistent with the provisions of the General Laws and subject to the following terms and conditions:

(i) The examination shall include such physical, psychiatric, and psychological tests as the court-appointed examiner (examiner) deems necessary to form an opinion as to the mental condition of the defendant at the relevant time. No examination based on statements of the defendant may be conducted unless the judge has found that (a) the defendant then intends to offer into evidence expert testimony based on his or her own statements or (b) there is a reasonable likelihood that the defendant will offer that evidence.

(ii) No statement, confession, or admission, or other evidence of or obtained from the defendant during the course of the examination, except evidence derived solely from physical examinations or tests, may be revealed to the prosecution or anyone acting on its behalf unless so ordered by the judge.

(iii) The examiner shall file with the court a written report as to the mental condition of the defendant at the relevant time.

Unless the parties mutually agree to an earlier time of disclosure, the examiner's report shall be sealed and shall not be made available to the parties unless (a) the judge determines that the report contains no matter, information, or evidence which is based upon statements of the defendant as to his or her mental condition at the relevant time or which is otherwise within the scope of the privilege against self-incrimination; or (b) the defendant files a motion requesting that the report be made available to the parties; or (c) after the defendant expresses the clear intent to raise as an issue his or her mental condition, the judge is satisfied that (1) the defendant intends to testify, or (2) the defendant intends to offer expert testimony based in whole or in part on statements made by the defendant as to his or her mental condition at the relevant time.

At the time the report of the examiner is disclosed to the parties, the defendant shall provide the Commonwealth with a report of the defense psychiatric or psychological expert(s) as to the mental condition of the defendant at the relevant time.

The reports of both parties' experts must include a written summary of the expert's expected testimony that fully describes: the defendant's history and present symptoms; any physical, psychiatric, and psychological tests relevant to the expert's opinion regarding the issue of mental condition and their results; any oral or written statements made by the defendant relevant to the issue of the mental condition for which the defendant was evaluated; the expert's opinions as to the defendant's mental condition, including the bases and reasons for these opinions; and the witness's qualifications.

If these reports contain both privileged and nonprivileged matter, the court may, if feasible, at such time as it deems appropriate prior to full disclosure of the reports to the parties, make available to the parties the nonprivileged portions.

(iv) If a defendant refuses to submit to an examination ordered pursuant to and subject to the terms and conditions of this rule, the court may prescribe such remedies as it deems warranted by the circumstances, which may include exclusion of the testimony of any expert witness offered by the defense on the issue of the defendant's mental condition or the admission of evidence of the refusal of the defendant to submit to examination.

(C) Discovery for the purpose of a court-ordered examination under Rule 14(b)(2)(B).

(i) If the judge orders the defendant to submit to an examination under Rule 14(b)(2)(B), the defendant shall, within fourteen days of the court's designation of the examiner, make available to the examiner the following:

(a) All mental health records concerning the defendant, whether psychological, psychiatric, or counseling, in defense counsel's possession;

(b) All medical records concerning the defendant in defense counsel's possession; and

(c) All raw data from any tests or assessments administered to the defendant by the defendant's expert or at the request of the defendant's expert.

(ii) The defendant's duty of production set forth in Rule 14(b)(2)(C)(i) shall continue beyond the defendant's initial production during the fourteen-day period and shall apply to any such mental health or medical record(s) thereafter obtained by defense counsel and to any raw data thereafter obtained from any tests or assessments administered to the defendant by the defendant's expert or at the request of the defendant's expert.

(iii) In addition to the records provided under Rule 14(b)(2)(C)(i) and (ii), the examiner may request records from any person or entity by filing with the court under seal, in such form as the Court may prescribe, a writing that identifies the requested records and states the reason(s) for the request. The examiner shall not disclose the request to the prosecutor without either leave of court or agreement of the defendant.

Upon receipt of the examiner's request, the court shall issue a copy of the request to the defendant and shall notify the prosecutor that the examiner has filed a sealed request for records pursuant to Rule 14(b)(2)(C)(iii). Within thirty days of the court's issuance to the defendant of the examiner's request, or within such other time as the judge may allow, the defendant shall file in writing any objection that the defendant may have to the production of any of the material that the examiner has requested. The judge may hold an ex parte hearing on the defendant's objections and may, in the judge's discretion, hear from the examiner. Records of such hearing shall be sealed until the report of the examiner is disclosed to the parties under Rule 14(b)(2)(B)(iii), at which point the records related to the examiner's request, including the records of any hearing, shall be released to the parties unless the court, in its discretion, determines that it would be unfairly prejudicial to the defendant to do so.

If the judge grants any part of the examiner's request, the judge shall indicate on the form prescribed by the Court the particular records to which the examiner may have access, and the clerk shall subpoena the indicated record(s). The clerk shall notify the examiner and the defendant when the requested record(s) are delivered to the clerk's office and shall make the record(s) available to the examiner and the defendant for examination and copying, subject to a protective order under the same terms as govern disclosure of reports under Rule 14(b)(2)(B)(iii). The clerk's office shall maintain these records under seal except as provided herein. If the judge denies the examiner's request, the judge shall notify the examiner, the defendant, and the prosecutor of the denial.

(iv) Upon completion of the court-ordered examination, the examiner shall make available to the defendant all raw data from any tests or assessments administered to the defendant by the Commonwealth's examiner or at the request of the Commonwealth's examiner.

(D) Additional discovery. Upon a showing of necessity, the Commonwealth and the defendant may move for other material and relevant evidence relating to the defendant's mental condition.

(3) *Notice of Other Defenses.* If a defendant intends to rely upon a defense based upon a license, claim of authority or ownership, or exemption, the defendant shall, within the time provided for the filing of pretrial motions by Rule 13(d)(2) or at such later time as the judge may direct, notify the prosecutor in writing of such intention and file a copy of such notice with the clerk. If there is a failure to comply with the requirements of this subdivision, a license, claim of authority or ownership, or exemption may not be relied upon as a defense. The judge may for cause shown allow a late filing of the notice or grant additional time to the parties to prepare for trial or make such other order as may be appropriate.

(4) *Self Defense and First Aggressor.*

(A) Notice by Defendant. If a defendant intends to raise a claim of self defense and to introduce evidence of the alleged victim's specific acts of violence to support an allegation that he or she was the first aggressor, the defendant shall no later than 21 days after the pretrial hearing or at such other time as the judge may direct for good cause, notify the prosecutor in writing of such intention. The notice shall include a brief description of each such act, together with the location and date to the extent practicable, and the names, addresses and dates of birth of the witnesses the defendant intends to call to provide evidence of each such act. The defendant shall file a copy of such notice with the clerk.

(B) Reciprocal Disclosure by the Commonwealth. No later than 30 days after receipt of the defendant's notice, or at such other time as the judge may direct for good cause, the Commonwealth shall serve upon the defendant a written notice of any rebuttal evidence the Commonwealth intends to introduce, including a brief description of such evidence together with the names of the witnesses the Commonwealth intends to call, the addresses and dates of birth of other than law enforcement witnesses and the business address of law enforcement witnesses.

(C) Continuing Duty to Disclose. If prior to or during trial a party learns of additional evidence that, if known, should have been included in the information furnished under subdivision (b)(4)(A) or (B), that party shall promptly notify the adverse party or its attorney of such evidence.

(D) Failure to Comply. Upon the failure of either party to comply with the requirements of this rule, the judge may exclude the evidence offered by such party on the issue of the identity of the first aggressor.

(c) Sanctions for Noncompliance.

(1) *Relief for Nondisclosure.* For failure to comply with any discovery order issued or imposed pursuant to this rule, the court may make a further order for discovery, grant a continuance, or enter such other order as it deems just under the circumstances.

(2) *Exclusion of Evidence.* The court may in its discretion exclude evidence for noncompliance with a discovery order issued or imposed pursuant to this rule. Testimony of the defendant and evidence concerning the defense of lack of criminal responsibility which is otherwise admissible cannot be excluded except as provided by subdivision (b)(2) of this rule.

(d) Definition.

The term "statement", as used in this rule, means:

(1) a writing made, signed, or by a person having percipient knowledge of relevant facts and which contains such facts, other than drafts or notes that have been incorporated into a subsequent draft or final report; or

(2) a written, stenographic, mechanical, electrical, or other recording, or transcription thereof, which is a substantially verbatim recital of an oral declaration except that a computer assisted real time translation, or its functional equivalent, made to assist a deaf or hearing impaired person, that is not transcribed or permanently saved in electronic form, shall not be considered a statement.

Reporter's Notes (2015).

(2015) Rule 12(b)(2)(C)

Rule 14(b)(2)(C) discovery for the purpose of a court-ordered examination under Rule 14(b)(2)(B)

In *Commonwealth v. Hanright*, 465 Mass. 639, 648 (2013), the Supreme Judicial Court held that, when a judge orders a defendant under Rule 14(b)(2)(B) to submit to a forensic mental evaluation, the judge may also require the defendant to disclose to the court-appointed examiner ("Commonwealth's examiner" or "examiner") treatment records necessary to conduct that forensic evaluation. Rule 14(b)(2)(C) sets out the scope and sequence of that disclosure and the procedure by which it is implemented. Under the rule, both experts—the Commonwealth's examiner and the defendant's expert—must be given equal access to the information they collectively deem necessary to conduct an effective forensic examination and produce a competent report. The rule achieves this result, without involving the prosecutor, through a reciprocal discovery process that makes available to each expert (1) the defendant's pertinent medical and mental-health records and (2) the raw data from tests or assessments of the defendant administered during the course of the experts' respective examinations of the defendant. By ensuring that the experts are working from a common, comprehensive set of records and objective, test-generated data, the rule advances the reliability and fairness of the examinations and the ensuing reports, and it promotes efficiency in the examination process.

Rule 14(b)(2)(C)(i)

Rule 14(b)(2)(C)(i) outlines the defendant's disclosure obligation. The rule requires that the defendant make available to the Commonwealth's examiner, within 14 days of the examiner's appointment, three categories of information: (a) the defendant's mental-health records, broadly defined, that are possessed by defense counsel, (b) the defendant's medical records that are possessed by defense counsel, and (c) the raw data from any tests or assessments administered to the defendant in the course of the defense expert's examination of the defendant. This discovery obligation is intended to provide equal and full access for both parties to the defendant's pertinent mental-health and medical history at the time each expert is conducting his or her examination of the defendant. Full discovery of pertinent source material at this point, when the examiners are forming their respective opinions concerning the defendant's mental health without yet having access to the opinions of the other, promotes the truth-seeking function of the trial, *see Hanright*, 465 Mass. at 644–645, while making the examination process more efficient.

In defining the scope of the mental-health and medical records to be produced as those possessed by defense counsel, the rule intends as wide a reach as is reasonably possible, covering every such record that the defense collected in the course of considering whether to assert this defense. At this point in the process, the defendant has waived any privilege that might preclude producing his statements and records to the Commonwealth's examiner, *see Hanright*, 465 Mass. 2 at 645–648, and the rule means to give both experts access to every record reasonably available, relying on the experts independently to decide which records are relevant to the inquiry. If, in examining the defendant and the records that the defendant produced, the Commonwealth's examiner identifies a mental-health or medical record that the defense overlooked, or chose not to collect, and thus did not produce, Rule 14(b)(2)(C)(iii), discussed below, provides for a process by which the examiner can seek that record. Any such records would, under the rule, be available to both experts.

The raw testing data that Rule 14(b)(2)(C)(i) requires the defendant to produce consists of objective, uninterpreted test results, for example, multiple-choice, bubble outputs from a psychological test with quantification on various scales. As discussed below, Rule 14(b)(2)(C)(iv) requires the same disclosure from the Commonwealth's examiner. The intent is to provide both experts with all of the relevant, objective testing data available at the time each writes his or her report, thus avoiding the need for supplemental reports or evaluations that consider pertinent testing data first revealed in the other expert's report. Not only would the necessity of such supplemental reports or evaluations extend the examination process, but these reports would necessarily be written after reviewing the opposing expert's report, thus putting in question the independence of this supplemental evaluation of these testing data. The rule's discovery obligation reaches only raw testing data; it does not apply to the defense expert's work product, such as notes interpreting this raw testing data or notes relating to a clinical interview of the defendant. This mandatory disclosure of raw testing data generated by the experts during the course of their respective examinations works no unfair advantage to either side. The discovery obligation is mutual. As with defendant's mental-health and medical records, the raw data resulting from tests administered to the defendant are essential to determining the defendant's mental-health at the time in question, and all of these data must be considered by both examiners if their respective reports are to serve their truth-seeking function. Finally, the test results will ultimately be released with the final reports under Rule 14(b)(2)(B)(iii); the only question Rule 14(b)(2)(C)(i) & (iv) address is the timing of that release.

2

Rule 14(b)(2)(C)(ii)

As noted, Rule 14(b)(2)(C)(i) requires the defendant to produce the mental-health and medical records and raw testing data within 14 days after the judge appoints the Commonwealth examiner. Under Rule 14(b)(2)(C)(ii), the defendant's duty to disclose records and raw testing data continues throughout the examination period provided under Rule 14(b)(2)(B). If the defendant discovers records or raw testing data that was subject to production under Rule 14(b)(2)(C)(i) but was not produced, those records or data must be produced as soon as they are discovered. Moreover, if subsequent to the initial production under Rule 14(b)(2)(C)(i) defense counsel obtains records covered by the rule or the defense expert generates test data covered by the rule, Rule 14(b)(2)(C)(ii) requires that these materials be promptly produced to the Commonwealth's examiner.

Rule 14(b)(2)(C)(iii)

As noted, this subsection anticipates the possibility that the Commonwealth's examiner will learn of additional medical or mental-health records that he or she believes necessary to conducting a professionally competent examination. For example, a record provided by the defendant, or a comment by the defendant during the court-ordered examination, might refer to an earlier hospitalization of the defendant for which the defendant did not produce records. If the examiner concludes that there is a reasonable possibility that such records exist and should be reviewed, Rule 14(b)(2)(C)(iii) provides for a procedure by which the examiner can file with the court a prescribed form under seal identifying the requested records (with as much specificity as circumstances reasonably permit) and stating the reason(s) for the request. Because at this point the court has yet to find sufficient evidence of privilege waiver by the defendant to permit the prosecutor's involvement in the examination process, see Rule 14(b)(2)(B)(iii), under Rule 14(b)(2)(C)(iii), the examiner may not inform the prosecutor of the document request or its contents, absent permission from either the defense or the court.

Upon receiving the sealed request, the court must issue a copy to the defendant, notifying the Commonwealth only that a sealed request for additional records has been filed. The defendant has 30 days to file ex parte a written objection to the requested production. If the defendant timely files such an objection, the judge has the discretion to hold an ex parte hearing on it, including, again in the judge's discretion, permitting the Commonwealth's examiner to participate. If the judge grants any part of the examiner's request, the judge must inform the clerk to which records the examiner may have access, and the clerk must then subpoena those records. When the records arrive at the clerk's office, the clerk must notify the examiner and the defendant of the records' availability for examination and copying, subject to a protective order forbidding their disclosure to the prosecutor unless the judge determines that the conditions set forth in Rule 14(b)(2)(B)(iii) for permitting prosecutorial access to the examiners' reports are met. The clerk's office must maintain the records under seal.

When the report of the Commonwealth's examiner is disclosed to the parties under Rule 14(b)(2)(B)(iii), the records related to the examiner's Rule 14(b)(2)(C)(iii) request for additional records shall also be released to the parties, subject to the judge's narrow discretion to forbid such release. At this point in the process, the defendant has effectively waived any claim of privilege concerning evidence relating to the mental-health defense. *See Hanright*, 465 Mass. at 645–647. The only reason for withholding from the prosecutor information concerning the examiner's request for additional records would presumably be a concern that information there set forth would have little or no relevance to the mental-health defense and would cause unfair prejudice to the defendant in conducting the mental-health defense, a balancing of interests with which judges are quite familiar. As is so with the release of the examiners' reports and supporting records, the release of records relating to a request for additional records would be confined to the parties; these records would remain sealed to the public. Granting the prosecutor access to the records relating to a denial of an examiner's request for records would not only permit full communication between the prosecutor and the examiner in preparing for trial, but it would also allow the Commonwealth to weigh the possibility, however remote, of seeking appellate review of the denial.

2

Rule 14(b)(2)(C)(iv)

As noted above, once the Commonwealth's examiner completes his or her examination of the defendant, the examiner must disclose to the defendant all raw data from any tests or assessments that the examiner conducted or requested. This ensures full reciprocity between the parties. Presumably, the only mental-health or medical records available to the examiner would be those provided by the defendant or produced in response to a court order under Rule 14(b)(2)(C)(iii), making any reciprocal discovery of such records unnecessary. The production of raw testing data by the court-ordered examiner would result in both experts having full access to the same records and raw testing data before they complete and file their respective reports.

Reporter's Notes (2012). In 2012, Rule 14 was amended in several respects. These revisions are discussed below.

Subdivision (b)(2). Mental health issues. This amendment responds to the Supreme Judicial Court's expansion of the Blaisdell procedure to analogous situations such as defenses based on an inability to form the requisite intent for an element of the crime, *see Commonwealth v. Dias*, 431 Mass. 822, 829 (2000), on an inability to premeditate, *see Commonwealth v. Contos*, 435 Mass. 19, 24 n.7 (2001), and where the defendant places at issue his or her mental ability voluntarily to waive Miranda rights, *see Commonwealth v. Ostrander*, 441 Mass. 344, 352 (2004). In addition, the Court has indicated in dicta that the same would hold true in the case of a defense based on battered woman syndrome, *see Ostrander*, 441 Mass. at 355 (2004).

There are two different dimensions to the problem that this subsection addresses. One concerns giving notice to the Commonwealth of a complex issue that the prosecutor otherwise would have no reason to expect to litigate. The other deals with redressing the unfairness of allowing a defense expert to testify based on statements obtained from the defendant without giving the prosecution an opportunity to obtain equivalent access for its expert.

The proposed amendment addresses the first concern by expanding the scope of the notice provision beyond the context of Blaisdell to include all mental health defenses. A mental health defense is one that places in issue the defendant's mental condition at the time of the alleged crime, based on a claim that some mental disease or defect or psychological impairment, such as battered woman syndrome, affected the defendant's cognitive ability. These are complex issues for which the prosecutor should have time to prepare, whether an expert testifies for the defense or not. As used in this subsection, the term "mental health defense" does not include a claim that the defendant's cognitive ability was affected by intoxication, an issue that arises more frequently and does not present the same level of complexity as do the former examples.

The proposed amendment addresses the second concern by requiring notice whenever the defendant intends to rely on expert testimony concerning the defendant's mental condition at any stage of the process on any issue, whether it related to culpability, competency or because it concerns the admission of evidence. Thus, for example, if the defendant intends to introduce expert testimony in support of a claim that a confession was not voluntary, as in *Ostrander*, the notice would specify that the witness would testify as to the defendant's mental condition at the time of the confession. If it appears that the expert will rely on statements of the defendant as to his or her mental condition, then the judge may order the defendant to submit to an examination pursuant to subsection 14(b)(2)(B).

Subdivision (b)(2)(B)(i). The proposed amendment deletes "physiological tests" from those that may be included in a court-ordered examination. This deletion is not intended to work any substantive change to the rule but rather to eliminate a superfluous term. Under the rule, "physical tests" is meant to include "physiological tests," including but not limited to neurological tests and examinations such as magnetic resonance imaging (MRI) and positron emission tomography (PET) scans.

Subdivision (b)(2)(B)(iii). The Rule applies not only to experts who are psychiatrists, but to psychologists as well.

The regime for disclosure of expert reports has been amended in light of *Commonwealth v. Sliech-Brodeur*, 457 Mass. 300 (2010). The timing of the release of the Commonwealth's expert's report was altered only to make clear that the parties can agree on its disclosure at a time earlier than previously set out in the Rule. *See Sliech-Brodeur*, 457 Mass. at 325 n.34 (2010). As required by *Sliech-Brodeur*, defense experts as well as the prosecution's must prepare and disclose reports. In order to avoid infringing on the defendant's privilege against self incrimination, the defense expert's report is released to the prosecution at the same time that the defendant receives the report of the Commonwealth's expert. The Rule also has been amended to address the timing of the exchange of reports. The latest date of exchange would be when the defendant expresses a "clear intent" to rely on mental impairment as an issue in the case, relying in part on the defendant's statements or testimony. This will often occur at the final pretrial conference or comparable event. The Rule attempts to avoid the delay and inconvenience of disclosing the reports only after the defendant's expert offers testimony on direct examination. Finally, the rule as amended makes clear the judge's discretion to review any expert report filed with and sealed by the court, and, if feasible and appropriate, to release to the parties any unprivileged material contained in the report prior to the report's full disclosure to the parties.

Once the reports have been released to the parties, they may be shared with the respective experts for each side.

The Rule has been amended to require more detail in the content of the report that both prosecution and defense experts must file. This portion of the Rule is patterned after 18 U.S.C.S. § 4247(c). In one major respect, however, the Rule goes beyond the federal model by requiring the report to contain a complete account of the statements of the defendant that are relevant to the issue of his or her mental condition. This includes both statements relating to the underlying incident as well as any statements prior to or following it that are relevant to the defendant's mental condition. If the examiner considered written statements of the defendant, the report should contain the relevant portions. If the examiner considered oral statements of the defendant, the report should include the substance of what the defendant said that bears on the question of his or her mental condition. In reporting on the defendant's statements, examiners should not withhold relevant evidence contrary to their own position.

The protection of the work product doctrine and the principle that notes or preliminary drafts are not discoverable if they are incorporated into a final report, applicable elsewhere in the discovery regime that Rule 14 establishes, apply as well in this context.

Subdivision (b)(2)(C). This provision gives trial judges the flexibility to require the parties to provide additional discovery beyond the information contained in the notice that the defendant must give and the reports that the experts must file. It is a very limited grant of discretion and should be reserved for cases presenting discovery issues that are out of the ordinary. In this respect, it is more restrictive than the analogous discovery provision in Rule 14(a)(2).

Subdivision (b)(4). Self Defense and First Aggressor. This amendment implements the discovery obligation created by *Commonwealth v. Adjutant*, 443 Mass. 649 (2005). The procedure it mandates applies only to situations such as those in *Adjutant*, where the defendant intends to rely on self defense claiming that the victim was the first aggressor. The notice procedure established in this amendment does not apply to other instances where prior violent conduct by the victim may be admissible, such as where the defendant intends to introduce evidence of a violent act by the victim of which he or she was aware at the time of the incident that is the subject of the criminal case before the court. *See Commonwealth v. Fontes*, 396 Mass. 733, 735–36 (1986). However, in a case where the defendant wishes to introduce evidence of an act of prior violence by the victim to support a claim based on both *Adjutant* and *Fontes*, the notice provision of this subsection would apply.

Beyond notice of an intent to raise the issue of prior violent acts by the alleged victim as it bears on the identity of the first aggressor, the amendment also requires the defendant to provide specific information about each incident. Where the defendant lacks specific details as to the time and place of a prior incident, the notice should contain as much information as is available, subject to a continuing duty to supplement the notice as counsel becomes aware of further facts.

The reciprocal obligation on the Commonwealth extends to all evidence that it intends to introduce to rebut the defendant's claim that the victim was the first aggressor. This may concern the victim's role in the incidents of prior violence upon which the defendant may rely, or any other evidence the Commonwealth may introduce in rebuttal.

Nothing in this amendment is intended to derogate from the discovery obligations of Rule 14(a)(1)(A)–(B) concerning physical evidence or documents that either party may rely on with respect to prior acts of violence by the victim.

This subsection does not affect the ultimate decision the judge must make on the admissibility of the evidence contained in the defendant's notice, or of any rebuttal evidence the prosecution might offer. The rule does contemplate, however, that failure to provide notice in advance may bar a party from offering evidence that might otherwise be admissible.

Subdivision (d). Definition. In 2012, Rule 23 was eliminated because the 2004 revision of Rule 14 largely made it irrelevant. Almost all of the statements that Rule 23 required a party to produce after a witness testified were made part of the automatic pretrial discovery mechanism of Rule 14. Because a small class of statements covered by Rule 23 was not included in the definition of a statement in the 2004 revision of Rule 14(d), an amendment to this subsection was made. The amendment brings within the confines of Rule 14 the remaining class of statements that were subject to the discovery provision of the former Rule 23.

Section 14(d)(1) was amended to include not only writings made by a witness, but also writings made by another and signed or otherwise adopted by the witness. A person otherwise adopts a statement when he or she approves it or accepts it as accurate. *See, e.g., Smith v. United States*, 31 F.3d 1294, 1301 (4th Cir. 1994) ("[n]otes taken by prosecutors and other government agents during a pretrial interview of a witness may qualify as a 'statement' . . . if the witness has reviewed them in their entirety—either by reading them himself or by having them read back to him—and formally and unambiguously approved them—either orally or in writing—as an accurate record of what he said during the interview.")

Section 14(d)(2) was amended to remove the requirement that a witness's statement has been recorded contemporaneously. This is an issue that will only be relevant with respect to written accounts of what the witness said, since by their nature stenographic, mechanical, electrical or other means of recordings must be made contemporaneously. With respect to written accounts, Rule 14(d) includes substantially verbatim statements of a witness that are contained in a document written by someone else, whether the document consists solely of the witness's statement or the witness's statements appear only in part of the document. In the latter case, only that portion of the document that consists of the substantially verbatim account of the witness's statement must be produced. This provision is intended only to require the production of statements that can "fairly be deemed to reflect fully and without distortion" what the witness said. *See Palermo v. United States*, 360 U.S. 343, 352-53 (1959); *United States v. Hodges*, 556 F.2d 366 (5th Cir. 1977) *cert. den.* 434 US 1016 (1978) (that investigators' notes contained occasional verbatim recitation of phrases used by the person interviewed did not make such notes discoverable).

Rule 15. Interlocutory Appeal

[Applicable to District Court and Superior Court. Amended effective July 1, 1986, Apr. 14, 1995, Mar. 1, 1996; Aug. 1, 2016; Mar. 1, 2017.]

(a) Right of Interlocutory Appeal.

(1) *Right of Appeal Where Pretrial Motion to Dismiss or for Appropriate Relief Granted.* The Commonwealth shall have the right to appeal to the Appeals Court a decision by a judge granting a motion to dismiss a complaint or indictment or a motion for appropriate relief made pursuant to the provisions of Rule 13(c).

(2) *Right of Appeal Where Motion to Suppress Evidence Determined.* A defendant or the Commonwealth shall have the right and opportunity to apply to a single justice of the Supreme Judicial Court, in the form and manner prescribed by a standing order of that court, for leave to appeal an order determining a motion to suppress evidence prior to trial. If the single justice determines that the administration of justice would be facilitated, the justice may grant that leave and may hear the appeal or may order it to the full Supreme Judicial Court or to the Appeals Court for determination.

(3) *Right of Appeal Where Delinquency Defendant Discharged.* The Commonwealth shall have the right to appeal to the Appeals Court a decision by a judge discharging a person pursuant to G.L. c. 119, § 72A.

(4) *Probable Cause Hearings.* No interlocutory appeal or report may be taken of matters arising out of a probable cause hearing.

(b) Procedural Requirements.

(1) *Time for Filing Appeal.* An appeal under Rule 15(a)(1) shall be taken by filing a notice of appeal in the trial court within thirty days of the date of entry of the order being appealed. An application for leave to appeal under Rule 15(a)(2) shall be made by filing within thirty days of the date of entry of the order being appealed, or such additional time as either the trial judge or the single justice of the Supreme Judicial Court shall order, (a) a notice of appeal in the trial court, and (b) an application to the single justice of the Supreme Judicial Court for leave to appeal.

(2) *Record.* The record for an interlocutory appeal shall be defined and assembled pursuant to Massachusetts Rule of Appellate Procedure 8.

(3) *Findings.* The judge shall make all findings of fact relevant to the appeal or the application for leave to appeal within the period specified in Rule 15(b)(1) for filing the notice of appeal.

(c) Determination of Motions. Any motion the determination of which may be appealed pursuant to this rule shall be decided by the judge before the defendant is placed in jeopardy under established rules of law.

(d) Costs Upon Appeal. If an appeal or application therefor is taken by the Commonwealth, the appellate court, upon the written motion of the defendant supported by affidavit, shall determine and approve the payment to the defendant of his or her costs of appeal together with reasonable attorney's fees to be paid on the order of the trial court upon the entry of the rescript or the denial of the application.

(e) Stay of the Proceedings. If the trial court issues an order which is subject to the interlocutory procedures herein, the trial of the case shall be stayed and the defendant shall not be placed in jeopardy until interlocutory review has been waived or the period specified in Rule 15(b)(1) for instituting interlocutory procedures has expired. If an appeal is taken or an application for leave to appeal is granted, the trial shall be stayed pending the entry of a rescript from or an order of the appellate court. If an appeal or application therefor is taken by the Commonwealth, the defendant may be released on personal recognizance during the pendency of the appeal.

Reporter's Notes (2016). The 2016 amendments to Rule 15 respond to the Supreme Judicial Court's decision in *Commonwealth v. Jordan*, 469 Mass. 134 (2014), a case in which the Commonwealth sought interlocutory review of a suppression order through a late-filed notice of appeal and application for leave to appeal. In agreeing to consider the appeal in spite of the late filings, the Court acknowledged that the procedures governing the timeliness of such appeals lacked clarity, *id.* at 145, a problem that the Court addressed by announcing specific procedures prospectively applicable to Rule 15 filings seeking leave to appeal suppression orders. *Id.* at 147–148. In addition to this clarification of Rule 15 filing procedures, the Court expressed concern that then-Rule 15(b)(1)'s ten-day filing period for such appeals might be insufficient. *Id.* at 149–150. As discussed below, amended Rule 15 implements the procedural framework mandated in *Jordan* and expands to thirty days the time for filing a notice of appeal and an application for leave to appeal from an order determining a motion to suppress evidence. Amended Rule 15 also includes non-substantive changes that clarify its mandate and update it to reflect current law.

Rule 15(a)(1) Right of Appeal Where Pretrial Motion to Dismiss or for Appropriate Relief Granted. Amended Rule 15(a)(1) reflects longstanding case law, making it clear that the Appeals Court is the court to which the Commonwealth may appeal the allowance of a motion to dismiss or of a motion for appropriate relief other than to suppress evidence. *See Commonwealth v. Friend*, 393 Mass. 310, 314 (1984) (Commonwealth's appeal from allowance of a motion to dismiss must be to the Appeals Court).

Rule 15(a)(2) Right of Appeal Where Motion to Suppress Evidence Determined. Amended Rule 15(a)(2) implements the late-filing procedures mandated by the Supreme Judicial Court in *Commonwealth v. Jordan*, 469 Mass. 134 (2014) for interlocutory appeals of an order determining a motion to suppress. Former Rule 15(a)(2) did not specify what showing an applicant for such relief must make concerning the timeliness of the necessary filings, hampering the efforts of single justices to be consistent in addressing the threshold issue of whether the notice of appeal and application for leave to appeal were timely filed and, if not, whether they should nevertheless be considered. *See Jordan*, 469 Mass. at 145 (acknowledging a "lack of clarity" in the single justices' application of procedural rules governing timeliness of Rule 15(a)(2) filings).

Amended Rule 15(a)(2) cures this deficiency, incorporating by reference the Supreme Judicial Court's standing order prescribing with specificity the form and manner for making an application to a single justice for leave to appeal a suppression order. This standing order, Supreme Judicial Court Order Regarding Applications to A Single Justice Pursuant to Mass. R. Crim. P. 15(a)(2) (2016), in effect codifies *Jordan*'s procedural framework for addressing timeliness issues, including a requirement that an application for leave to appeal a suppression order contain an affirmative representation that the application and notice to appeal are, or are not, timely under Rule 15(b)(1). If the appeal or application is untimely, the standing order requires that the application be accompanied by a motion to enlarge time for filing, supported by an affidavit providing "in meaningful detail the reasons for the delay." *See* Supreme Judicial Court Order Regarding Applications to A Single Justice Pursuant to Mass. R. Crim. P. 15(a)(2), § (a)(7) (2016). *See also Commonwealth v. Jordan*, 469 Mass. 134, 147–148 (2014) (setting out 2 "Rule 15 procedure in future cases").

The purpose of this provision is to permit the single justice to whom the application is made to decide (1) whether the application satisfies Rule 15's timing requirements, and, if it does not, (2) whether the application should nevertheless be considered, before proceeding to the merits of the application and, if appropriate, the appeal. This threshold determination by the single justice is intended to be final, foreclosing further consideration of this procedural issue by the full court or the Appeals Court if the single justice refers the appeal to either for determination. *See Jordan*, 469 Mass. at 148 (2014).

Rule 15(a)(3) Right of Appeal Where Transfer of Delinquency Proceeding is Denied. Rule 15(a)(3), permitting the Commonwealth to appeal a judge's denial of a requested transfer of a delinquency proceeding to Superior or District Court for criminal prosecution, is deleted. G.L. c. 119, § 61, which provided for such transfers, was repealed, making Rule 15(a)(3) obsolete. This section is reserved for possible amendment to reflect current law.

Rule 15(b)(1) Time for Filing Appeal. Rule 15(b)(1), as amended, increases the time to file a notice of appeal and an application for leave to appeal a suppression order to thirty days, clarifying that the starting point for that time period is the date that the order being appealed is entered by the lower court. This filing period is meant to balance the need for adequate time to consider and prepare an application for interlocutory review of a suppression order against the potential for unnecessary, widespread delays in resolving the many criminal cases which involve suppression orders. Thirty days, the filing period applicable to other interlocutory appeals under Rule 15 and presumptively applicable to all appeals in criminal cases, *see* Rule 4(b), Mass. R. A. P., as amended, 431 Mass. 1601 (2000), should ordinarily suffice. However, if in a particular case a party can demonstrate with specificity that thirty days is insufficient, the rule provides for leave to seek additional time from either the trial judge or single justice. If there is a timely motion to reconsider the suppression order in question, the thirty-day time period for filing an application for interlocutory review does not commence until the trial court enters its order deciding the motion to reconsider. *See Jordan*, 469 Mass. at 147 n.24.

The SJC's standing order incorporated in amended Rule 15(a)(2) provides that the party opposing interlocutory appeal of the suppression order may file a memorandum in opposition to that application within fourteen days after the application for leave to appeal is entered. Supreme Judicial Court Order Regarding Applications to A Single Justice Pursuant to Mass. R. Crim. P. 15(a)(2), § (c) (2016). The order further permits the single justice to extend or shorten the time to file such opposition and provides that a party deciding not to file an opposition must serve notice of that intention within the time allowed for filing the opposition. *Id.*

Rule 15(b)(2) Record; Rule 15(b)(3) Findings. Rule 15(b)(2) and Rule 15(b)(3) contain the provisions of former Rule 15(b)(2), renumbered to separate former Rule 15(b)(2) into two parts, Rule 15(b)(2) providing for definition and assembly of the record and Rule 15(b)(3) requiring timely findings by the trial judge.

Rule 16. Dismissal by the Prosecution

[Applicable to District Court and Superior Court.]

(a) Entry of a Nolle Prosequi. A prosecuting attorney may enter a nolle prosequi of pending charges at any time prior to the pronouncement of sentence. A nolle prosequi shall be accompanied by a written statement, signed by the prosecuting attorney, setting forth the reasons for that disposition.

(b) Entry of Nolle Prosequi During Trial. After jeopardy attaches, a nolle prosequi entered without the consent of the defendant shall have the effect of an acquittal of the charges contained in the nolle prosequi.

Rule 17. Summonses for Witnesses

[Applicable to District Court and Superior Court.]

(a) Summons.

(1) *For Attendance of Witness; Form; Issuance.* A summons shall be issued by the clerk or any person so authorized by the General Laws. It shall state the name of the court and the title, if any, of the proceeding and shall command each person to whom it is directed to attend and give testimony at the time and place specified therein.

(2) *For Production of Documentary Evidence and of Objects.* A summons may also command the person to whom it is directed to produce the books, papers, documents, or other objects designated therein. The court on motion may quash or modify the summons if compliance would be unreasonable or oppressive or if the summons is being used to subvert the provisions of Rule 14. The court may direct that books, papers, documents, or objects designated in the summons be produced before the court within a reasonable time prior to the trial or prior to the time when they are to be offered in evidence and may upon their production permit the books, papers, documents, objects, or portions thereof to be inspected and copied by the parties and their attorneys if authorized by law.

(b) Defendants Unable to Pay. At any time upon the written ex parte application of a defendant which shows that the presence of a named witness is necessary to an adequate defense and that the defendant is unable to pay the fees of that witness, the court shall order the issuance of an indigent's summons. The witness so summoned shall be paid in accordance with the provisions of subdivision (c) of this rule. If the court so orders, the costs incurred shall be assessed to the defendant in accordance with the General Laws or the provisions of these rules.

(c) Payment of Witnesses. Expenses incurred by a witness summoned on behalf of a defendant determined to be indigent under this rule as well as expenses incurred by a witness summoned on behalf of the Commonwealth, as such expenses are determined in accordance with the General Laws, shall be paid after the witness certifies in a writing filed with the court the amount of his travel and attendance.

(d) Service.

(1) *By Whom; Manner.* A summons may be served by any person authorized to serve a summons in a civil action or to serve criminal process. A summons shall be served upon a witness by delivering a copy to him personally, by leaving it at his dwelling house or usual place of abode with some person of suitable age and discretion then residing therein, or by mailing to the witness' last known address.

(2) *Place of Service.*

(A) Within the Commonwealth. A summons requiring the attendance of a witness at a hearing or a trial may be served at any place within the Commonwealth.

(B) Outside the Commonwealth or Abroad. A summons directed to a witness outside the Commonwealth or abroad shall issue and be served in a manner consistent with the General Laws.

(3) *Return.* The person serving a summons pursuant to this rule shall make a return of service to the court.

(e) **Failure to Appear.** If a person served with a summons pursuant to this rule fails to appear at the time and place specified therein and the court determines that such person did receive actual notice to appear, a warrant may issue to bring that person before the court.

Rule 18. Presence of Defendant

[Applicable to District Court and Superior Court.]

(a) Presence of Defendant. In any prosecution for crime the defendant shall be entitled to be present at all critical stages of the proceedings.

(1) *Defendant Absenting Himself.* If a defendant is present at the beginning of a trial and thereafter absents himself without cause or without leave of court, the trial may proceed to a conclusion in all respects except the imposition of sentence as though the defendant were still present.

(2) *Waiver of Presence in Misdemeanor Cases.* A person prosecuted for a misdemeanor may at his own request, with leave of court, be excused from attendance if represented by counsel or an agent authorized by law and may be excused from attendance without leave of court if so authorized by the General Laws.

(3) *Presence Not Required.* A defendant need not be present at a revision or revocation of sentence pursuant to Rule 29 or at any proceeding where evidence is not to be taken.

(b) Presence of Corporation. A corporation may appear by a duly authorized agent for the purposes of this rule.

Rule 19. Trial by Jury or by the Court

[Applicable to Superior Court and jury sessions of District Court.]

(a) General. A case in which the defendant has the right to be tried by a jury shall be so tried unless the defendant waives a jury trial in writing with the approval of the court and files the waiver with the clerk, in which instance he shall be tried by the court instead of by a jury. If there is more than one defendant, all must waive the right to trial by jury, and if they do not so waive, there must be a jury trial unless the court in its discretion severs the cases. The court may refuse to approve such a waiver for any good and sufficient reason provided that such refusal is given in open court and on the record.

(b) Less Than a Full Jury. If after jeopardy attaches there is at any time during the progress of a trial less than a full jury remaining, a defendant may waive his right to be tried by a full jury and request trial by the remaining jurors by signing a written waiver which shall be filed with the court. If there is more than one defendant, all must sign and file a waiver unless the court in its discretion severs the cases.

Rule 20. Trial Jurors

[Applicable to Superior Court and jury sessions of District Court.]

(a) Motion for Appropriate Relief. Either party may challenge the array by a motion for appropriate relief pursuant to Rule 13(c). A challenge to the array shall be made only on the ground that the prospective jurors were not selected or drawn according to law. Challenges to the array shall be made and decided before any individual juror is examined unless otherwise ordered by the court. A challenge to the array shall be in writing supported by affidavit and shall specify the facts constituting the ground of the challenge. Challenges to the array shall be tried by the court and may in the discretion of the court be decided on the basis of the affidavit filed with the challenge. Upon the hearing of a challenge to the array, a witness may be examined on oath by the court and may be so examined by either party. If the challenge to the array is sustained, the court shall discharge the panel.

(b) Challenge for Cause.

(1) *Examination of Juror.* The court shall, or upon motion, the parties or their attorneys may under the direction of the court, examine on oath a person who is called as a juror in a case to learn whether he is related to either party, has any interest in the case, has expressed or formed an opinion, or is sensible of any bias or prejudice. The objecting party may, with the approval of the court, introduce other competent evidence in support of the objection.

(2) *Examination Upon Extraneous Issues.* The court shall examine or cause a juror to be examined upon issues extraneous to the case if it appears that the juror's impartiality may have been affected by the extraneous issues. The examination may include a brief statement of the facts of the case, to the extent the facts are appropriate and relevant to the issues of such examination, and shall be conducted individually and outside the presence of other persons about to be called or already called as jurors.

(3) *Challenge of Juror.* Either party may challenge an individual prospective juror before the juror is sworn to try the case. The court may for cause shown permit a challenge to be made after the juror is sworn but before any evidence is presented. When a juror is challenged for cause, the ground of the challenge shall be stated. A challenge of a prospective juror and the statement of the grounds thereof may be made at the bench. The court shall determine the validity of each such challenge.

(c) Peremptory Challenges.

(1) *Number of Challenges.* Upon the trial of an indictment for a crime punishable by imprisonment for life, each defendant shall be entitled to twelve peremptory challenges of the jurors called to try the case; in any other criminal case tried before a jury of twelve, each defendant shall be entitled to four peremptory challenges; and in a case tried before a jury of six, each defendant shall be entitled to two peremptory challenges. Each defendant in a trial of an indictment for a crime punishable by imprisonment for life in which additional jurors are impaneled under subdivision (d) of this rule shall be entitled to one additional peremptory challenge for each additional juror. Each defendant in a case in which several indictments or complaints are consolidated for trial shall be entitled to no more peremptory challenges than the greatest number to which he would have been entitled upon trial of any one of the indictments or complaints alone. In every criminal case the Commonwealth shall be entitled to as many peremptory challenges as equal the whole number to which all the defendants in the case are entitled.

(2) *Time of Challenge.* Peremptory challenges shall be made before the jurors are sworn and may be made after the determination that a person called to serve as a juror stands indifferent in the case.

(d) Alternate Jurors.

(1) *Impanelling Jury With Alternate Jurors.* If a jury trial is likely to be protracted, the judge may impanel a jury of not more than sixteen members and the court shall have jurisdiction to try the case with that jury.

(2) *Selection of Twelve Jurors.* If at the time of the final submission of the case to the jury more than twelve members of the jury who have heard the whole case are alive and not incapacitated or disqualified, the judge shall direct the clerk to place the names of all the remaining jurors except the foreman in a box and draw the names of a sufficient number to reduce the jury to twelve members. Those jurors whose names are drawn shall not be discharged, but shall be known as alternate jurors and shall be kept separate and apart from the other jurors in some convenient place, subject to the same rules and regulations as the other jurors, until the jury has agreed upon a verdict or has been otherwise discharged.

(3) *Disabled Juror:* Selection of Alternate. If, at any time after the final submission of the case by the court to the jury but before the jury has agreed on a verdict, a juror dies, becomes ill, or is unable to perform his duty for any other cause, the judge may order him to be discharged and shall direct the clerk to place the names of all the remaining alternate jurors in a box and draw the name of an alternate who shall take the place of the discharged juror on the jury, which shall renew its deliberations with the alternate juror.

(e) Regulation and Separation of Jurors.

(1) *Sequestration.* After the jurors have been sworn they shall hear the case as a body and, within the discretion of the trial judge, may be sequestered.

(2) *After Submission of the Cause.* Unless the jurors have been sequestered for the duration of the trial, the judge after the final submission of the case, may order that the jurors be permitted to separate for a definite time to be fixed by the judge and then reconvene in the courtroom before retiring for consideration of their verdict.

(3) *After Commencement of Deliberations.* After final submission of the case to the jury and after deliberations have commenced, the judge may allow the jurors, under proper instructions, to separate for a definite time to be fixed by the judge and to reconvene in the courtroom before retiring for further deliberation of their verdict.

Rule 21. Sequestration of Witnesses

[Applicable to District Court and Superior Court.]

Upon his own motion or the motion of either party, the judge may, prior to or during the examination of a witness, order any witness or witnesses other than the defendant to be excluded from the courtroom.

Rule 22. Objections

[Applicable to Superior Court and jury sessions of District Court.]

Exceptions to rulings or orders of the court are unnecessary and for all purposes for which an exception has heretofore been necessary, it is sufficient that a party, at the time the ruling or order of the court is made or sought, makes known to the court the action which he desires the court to take or his objection to the action of the court, but if a party has no opportunity to object to a ruling or order, the absence of an objection does not thereafter prejudice him.

If a party objects to a ruling or order of the court, he may state the precise legal grounds of his objection, but he shall not argue or further discuss such grounds unless the court calls upon him for such argument or discussion.

Rule 23. Stipulations

[Previous Rule 23 removed effective Sept. 17, 2012; new rule added effective July 1, 2015.]

(a) Essential Elements. Any stipulation to an essential element of a charged offense entered by the parties before or during trial shall be in writing and signed by the prosecutor, the defendant, and defense counsel. Any such stipulation shall be read to the jury before the close of the Commonwealth's case and may be introduced into evidence.

(b) Other Stipulations. Any other stipulation shall be placed on the record before the close of evidence and may be read or otherwise communicated to the jury or introduced into evidence in the discretion of the court.

Rule 24. Opening Statements; Arguments; Instructions to Jury

[Applicable to Superior Court and jury sessions of District Court.]

(a) Opening and Closing Statements; Arguments.

(1) *Order of Presentation.* The Commonwealth shall present its opening statement first. The defendant may present an opening statement of his defense after the opening statement of the Commonwealth or after the close of the Commonwealth's evidence. The defendant shall present his closing argument first.

(2) *Time Limitation.* Counsel for each party shall be allowed fifteen minutes for an opening statement and thirty minutes for argument; but before the opening or the argument commences, the judge on motion or sua sponte, may reasonably reduce or extend the time.

(b) Instructions to Jury; Objection. At the close of the evidence or at such earlier time during the trial as the judge reasonably directs, any party may file written requests that the judge instruct the jury on the law as set forth in the requests. The judge shall inform counsel of his proposed action upon requests prior to their arguments to the jury. No party may assign as error the giving or the failure to give an instruction unless he objects thereto before the jury retires to consider its verdict, specifying the matter to which he objects and the grounds of his objection. Upon request, reasonable time shall be given to each party to object to the charge before the jury retires. Where either party wishes to object to the charge or to request additional instructions, the objection or the request shall be made out of the hearing of the jury, or where appropriate, out of the presence of the jury.

Rule 25. Motion for Required Finding of Not Guilty

[Applicable to District Court and Superior Court. Amended effective July 1, 1983, Apr. 14, 1995.]

(a) Entry by Court. The judge on motion of a defendant or on his own motion shall enter a finding of not guilty of the offense charged in an indictment or complaint or any part thereof after the evidence on either side is closed if the evidence is insufficient as a matter of law to sustain a conviction on the charge. If a defendant's motion for a required finding of not guilty is made at the close of the Commonwealth's evidence, it shall be ruled upon at that time. If the motion is denied or allowed only in part by the judge, the defendant may offer evidence in his defense without having reserved that right.

(b) Jury Trials.

(1) *Reservation of Decision on Motion.* If a motion for a required finding of not guilty is made at the close of all the evidence, the judge may reserve decision on the motion, submit the case to the jury, and decide the motion before the jury returns a verdict, after the jury returns a verdict of guilty, or after the jury is discharged without having returned a verdict.

(2) *Motion After Discharge of Jury.* If the motion is denied and the case is submitted to the jury, the motion may be renewed within five days after the jury is discharged and may include in the alternative a motion for a new trial. If a verdict of guilty is returned, the judge may on motion set aside the verdict and order a new trial, or order the entry of a finding of not guilty, or order the entry of a finding of guilty of any offense included in the offense charged in the indictment or complaint.

(c) Appeal.

(1) *Right of Appeal Where Motion for Relief Under Subdivision (b) Is Allowed After a Jury Verdict of Guilty.* The Commonwealth shall have the right to appeal to the appropriate appellate court a decision of a judge granting relief under the provisions of subdivisions (b)(1) and (2) of this rule on a motion for required finding of not guilty after the jury has returned a verdict of guilty or on an order for the entry of a finding of guilt of any offense included in the offense charged in the indictment or complaint.

(2) *Costs Upon Appeal.* If an appeal or application therefor is taken by the Commonwealth, the appellate court, upon the written motion of the defendant supported by affidavit, may determine and approve the payment to the defendant of his costs of appeal together with reasonable attorney's fees, if any, to be paid on the order of the trial court upon the entry of the rescript or the denial of the application.

Rule 26. Requests for Rulings

[Applicable to jury-waived trials in District Court and Superior Court.]

Requests for rulings in the trial of a case shall be in writing and shall be presented to the court before the beginning of closing arguments, unless consent of the court is given to present requests later.

Rule 27. Verdict

[Applicable to jury trials in District Court and Superior Court.]

(a) Return. The verdict shall be unanimous. It shall be a general verdict returned by the jury to the judge in open court. The jury shall file a verdict slip with the clerk upon the return of the verdict.

(b) Several Offenses or Defendants. If there are two or more offenses or defendants tried together, the jury may, with the consent of the judge at any time during its deliberations return or be required by the judge to return a verdict or verdicts with respect to the defendants or charges as to which a verdict has been reached; and thereafter the jury may in the discretion of the judge resume deliberation. The judge may declare a mistrial as to any charges upon which the jury cannot agree upon a verdict; provided, however, that the judge may first require the jury to return verdicts on those charges upon which the jury can agree and direct that such verdicts be received and recorded.

(c) Special Questions. The trial judge may submit special questions to the jury.

(d) Poll of Jury. When a verdict is returned and before the verdict is recorded, the jury may be polled in the discretion of the judge. If after the poll there is not a unanimous concurrence, the jury may be directed to retire for further deliberations or may be discharged.

Rule 28. Judgment

[Applicable to District Court and Superior Court. Amended effective Apr. 1, 2009.]

(a) Judgment. If the defendant has been determined to be guilty, a verdict or finding of guilty shall be rendered, or if he has been determined to be not guilty, a verdict or finding of not guilty shall be rendered, in open court, and shall be entered on the court's docket.

(b) Imposition of Sentence. After a verdict, finding, or plea of guilty, or a plea of nolo contendere, or an admission to sufficient facts, the defendant shall have the right to be sentenced without unreasonable delay. Pending sentence the court may commit the defendant or continue or alter the bail as provided by law. Before imposing sentence the court shall afford the defendant or his counsel an opportunity to speak on behalf of the defendant and to present any information in mitigation of punishment.

(c) Notification of Right to Appeal. After a judgment of guilty is entered, the court shall advise the defendant of his right to appeal. In the District Court, upon the request of the defendant, the clerk of the court shall prepare and file forthwith a notice of appeal.

(d) Presentence Investigation.

(1) *Criminal Record.* The probation officer shall inquire into the nature of every criminal case or juvenile complaint brought before the court and report to the court information concerning all prior criminal prosecutions or juvenile complaints, if any, and the disposition of each such prosecution, except where the defendant was found not guilty. Such information is to be presented before a defendant is admitted to bail in court, and also before disposition of the case against him.

(2) *Report.* The report of the presentence investigation shall contain any prior criminal or juvenile prosecution record of the defendant, but shall not contain any information relating to criminal or juvenile prosecutions in which the defendant was found not guilty. In addition, the report shall include such other available information as may be helpful to the court in the disposition of the case.

(3) *Availability to Parties.* Prior to the disposition the presentence report shall be made available to the prosecutor and counsel for the defendant for inspection. In extraordinary cases, the judge may except from disclosure parts of the report which are not relevant to a proper sentence, diagnostic opinion which might seriously disrupt a program of rehabilitation, sources of information obtained upon a promise of confidentiality, or any other information which, if disclosed, might result in harm, physical or otherwise, to the defendant or other persons. If the report is not made fully available, the portions thereof which are not disclosed shall not be relied upon in determining sentence. No party may make any copy of the presentence report.

(e) Filing. The court may file a case after a guilty verdict or finding without imposing a sentence if the defendant and the Commonwealth both consent. With the consent of both parties, the judge may specify a time limit beyond which the case may not be removed from the file, and may specify any events that may cause the case to be removed from the file. The defendant shall file a written consent with the court as to both the filing of the case and any time limit or events regarding removal from the file. Prior to accepting the defendant's consent, the court shall inform the defendant on the record in open court:

(i) that the defendant has a right to request sentencing on any or all filed case(s) at any time;

(ii) that subject to any time limit imposed by the court, the prosecutor may request that the case be removed from the file and sentence imposed if a related conviction or sentence is reversed or vacated or upon the prosecutor's establishing by a preponderance of the evidence either that the defendant committed a new criminal offense or that an event occurred on which the continued filing of the case was expressly made contingent by the court; and

(iii) that if the case is removed from the file the defendant may be sentenced on the case. In sentencing the defendant after the removal of a case from the file, the court shall consider the over-all scheme of punishment employed by the original sentencing judge.

Rule 29. Revision or Revocation of Sentence

[Applicable to District Court and Superior Court. Amended effective Sept. 1, 2016.]

(a) Revision or Revocation.

(1) *Illegal Sentences.* The trial judge, upon the judge's own motion, or the written motion of the prosecutor, filed within sixty days after imposition of a sentence, may revise or revoke such sentence if the judge determines that any part of the sentence was illegal.

(2) *Unjust Sentences.* The trial judge, upon the judge's own motion, or the written motion of a defendant, filed within sixty days after the imposition of a sentence or within sixty days after issuance of a rescript by an appellate court on direct review, may, upon such terms and conditions as the judge shall order, revise or revoke such sentence if it appears that justice may not have been done.

(b) Affidavits. If a party files a motion pursuant to this rule, the party shall file and serve, and the other party may file and serve, affidavits in support of their respective positions. The judge may deny a motion filed pursuant to this rule on the basis of facts alleged in the affidavits without further hearing.

(c) Notice. The moving party shall serve the other party with a copy of any motion and affidavit filed pursuant to this rule. If the judge orders that a hearing be held on the motion, the court shall give the parties reasonable notice of the time set for the hearing.

(d) Place of Hearing. A motion filed pursuant to this rule may be heard by the trial judge wherever the judge is then sitting.

(e) Appeal. An appeal from a final order under this rule may be taken to the Appeals Court, or the Supreme Judicial Court in an appropriate case, by either party.

Reporter's Notes (2016). This amendment to Rule 29 is intended to fill a gap in the Rules of Criminal Procedure identified by the Supreme Judicial Court in *Commonwealth v. Selavka*, 469 Mass. 502 (2014), in which the Court upheld the Commonwealth's authority to move to correct an illegal sentence. After noting that neither former Rule 29(a) nor Rule 30(a) permitted a Commonwealth motion to revise or revoke an illegal sentence, the Court concluded that "rule 29(a), with its sixty-day time frame, is the proper vehicle by which the Commonwealth may challenge illegal sentences." *Selavka*, 469 Mass. at 508. This amendment to Rule 29 permits the Commonwealth to seek such relief.

Rule 29(a) Revision or Revocation.

Rule 29(a)(1), Illegal Sentences, provides that, within 60 days after a trial judge imposes a sentence, either the Commonwealth or the judge may move to revise or revoke that sentence if any part of the sentence is illegal. While Rule 29(a) has long authorized a trial judge to increase a sentence under Rule 29(a), either because the sentence imposed is illegal or, on reflection, unjust, *see Commonwealth v. Aldoupolis*, 386 Mass. 260, 268–270 (1982), former Rule 29 did not authorize the Commonwealth to seek revision or revocation of a sentence for any purpose. *See Selavka*, 469 Mass. at 506. Rule 29(a)(1) makes it clear that the judge's authority to correct an illegal sentence remains unchanged, but the rule further permits the Commonwealth to seek such relief. This narrow provision for a Commonwealth motion to revise or revoke a sentence is intentionally limited to correcting an illegal sentence; it does not permit a motion to increase a legal sentence that the prosecutor considers to be legal but unduly lenient.

Rule 29(a)(1)'s authority to challenge an illegal sentence within 60 days of sentencing is limited to the Commonwealth and the trial judge for two reasons. First, the defendant is already authorized to file such a motion. Rule 29(a)(2), Unjust Sentences, leaves unchanged the defendant's right to challenge a sentence "if it appears that justice may not have been done," which includes a sentence imposing punishment not permitted by law. *See Selavka*, 469 Mass. 508 n.7. Quite apart from Rule 29(a), Rule 30(a) gives the defendant the right to challenge an illegal sentence at any time.

Second, a successful prosecution or judicial motion to revise or revoke an illegal sentence that is too lenient would result in additional punishment, which, if unduly belated, would implicate the defendant's double-jeopardy interest in sentence finality even though the original sentence was illegal. *See Selavka*, 469 Mass. at 509. The Court in *Selavka* concluded that limiting the potential for such upward adjustment of an illegal sentence to Rule 29(a)'s 60-day timeframe marks a reasonable balance between a defendant's interest in sentence finality and society's interest in enforcement of the sentencing laws. *Selavka*, 469 Mass. at 508. Rule 29(a)(1) thus provides for a 60-day time limit for the Commonwealth to file a motion seeking, or for the judge to initiate consideration of, the revision or revocation of an illegal sentence. After that, any motion to revise or revoke an illegal sentence must come from the defendant under Rule 30(a), which would raise no double-jeopardy problems.

Rule 29(a)(1) includes revocation as a potential remedy for an illegal sentence that is too lenient, in part because that sentence might have been the result of a guilty plea from which the defendant could have withdrawn had the sentence been more harsh than it was. *See* Rule 12(c)(4) (permitting defendant to withdraw (1) from a District-Court plea if the judge intends to impose a sentence in excess of defendant's request and (2) from a Superior-Court plea if the judge intends to sentence in excess of either the agreed recommendation or the prosecutor's recommendation); Rule 12(d)(4) (requiring a judge who accepts a plea agreement providing for both a charge concession and a specific sentence to impose the agreed sentence and permitting the defendant to withdraw if the judge rejects the plea agreement); former Rule 12(c)(2) (permitting defendant to withdraw (1) from a District-Court plea if the judge intends to impose a sentence in excess of defendant's request and (2) from a Superior-Court plea if the judge intends to sentence in excess of an agreed recommendation on which the plea was contingent). At the very least, such a case would require resentencing, with the defendant presumably having the right to withdraw the plea if Rule 12 would have afforded that right at the plea hearing and initial sentencing. *See Selavka*, 469 Mass. at 514–515.

Rule 29(a)(2), Unjust Sentences, clarifies former Rule 29(a)'s provision for filing a motion to revise or revoke an unjust sentence following appellate review.

First, the rule makes clear that, other than the imposition of sentence, the only event that triggers the sixty-day period to file a Rule 29(a)(2) motion is the appellate court's issuance of the rescript in a case on direct review. If the conviction is affirmed, the issuance of the rescript marks the point at which the conviction becomes final, *see Foxworth v. St. Amand*, 457 Mass. 200, 206 (2010), making it an appropriate time for filing a motion to revise or revoke the sentence based on that conviction. Although on its face the rule does not limit such motions to cases in which the conviction is affirmed, as a practical matter, a conviction's reversal would result in vacation of the sentence, leaving nothing to revise or revoke.

Pegging the beginning of the sixty-day filing period to the rescript's issuance permits a defendant whose conviction is affirmed by the Appeals Court to seek either rehearing or further appellate review without impinging on the time period for filing a motion to revise and revoke. Rule of Appellate Procedure 23 requires the Appeals Court, after deciding an appeal and mailing the decision to the parties, to wait twenty-eight days before issuing the rescript, *see* Mass. R.A.P. 23, thereby affording the parties time to file for rehearing or further review. *See* Mass. R.A.P. 27 (petition for rehearing to be filed within fourteen days of decision); Mass. R.A.P. 27.1 (application for further review to be filed within twenty days of decision). If either is granted, the rescript's issuance is stayed pending disposition of that proceeding. *See* Mass. R.A.P. 23. Finally, the appellate court's issuance of the rescript, finalizing a conviction which is affirmed, is a procedural event of which the defendant would surely be aware and thus a fair time for the sixty-day filing period to begin. The amendment eliminates the uncertainty caused by basing the time period on the trial court's receipt of the rescript, which was subject to the vagaries of mail delivery and clerical document processing.

Second, by confining the extension of the sixty-day filing period to cases on direct review, Rule 29(a)(2) clarifies the reach of its predecessor. Former Rule 29(a) did not specify whether a rescript on appellate review of a collateral attack on a sentence would allow a Rule 29 motion, though the Appeals Court found in an unpublished opinion that it would not. *Commonwealth v. White*, No. 08-P-766, 74 Mass. App. Ct. 1115, 2009 Mass. App. Unpub. LEXIS 788, at *3–*6 (Mass. App. Ct. June 4, 2009). The rule's purpose is to permit the trial judge to revise or revoke a sentence that, based on the facts existing at the time of sentencing, appears in retrospect to have been unjust. *See Commonwealth v. Rodriguez*, 461 Mass. 256, 260 (2012); *Commonwealth v. DeJesus*, 440 Mass. 147, 152 (2003). This purpose is best served if the sentence review prompted by the motion occurs reasonably soon after the sentence's imposition. *See Commonwealth v. Barclay*, 424 Mass. 377, 380 (1997) (holding Rule 29 motion must be decided within reasonable time of its filing); *Commonwealth v. Layne*, 386 Mass. 291, 295–296 (1982) (noting that, with "the passage of time from the date of sentencing, it becomes increasingly difficult for a trial judge to make the determination called for by [then Rule 29(a)] without improperly considering postsentencing events"). Rule 29(a)(2) accordingly limits the filing time to sixty days from the imposition of sentence or from the issuance of the rescript in any direct appeal, the latter filing period commencing as soon as the conviction becomes final. The former rule's provision permitting filing within sixty days of any appellate court order or judgment "denying review of, or having the effect of upholding, a judgment of conviction" has been deleted as being either redundant (if the order or judgment in question is part of the rescript concluding a direct appeal), or not sufficiently clear.

Finally, Rule 29(a)(2) achieves gender neutrality.

Rule 29(b) Affidavits

Rule 29(b), Affidavits, is amended to accommodate the Commonwealth's narrow authority to file a motion to revise or revoke an illegal sentence under the rule, authorizing both parties to file appropriate affidavits in that event. Consistent with Rule 18(a)(3), the amended rule further provides that the judge may deny a motion filed under Rule 29(a) without a hearing, based solely on the affidavits. Mass. R. Cr. P. 18(a)(3), Presence [of Defendant] Not Required, 378 Mass. 887 (1979) ("A defendant need not be present at a revision or revocation of sentence pursuant to Rule 29 or at any proceeding where evidence is not to be taken)." However, any revision or revocation of a sentence under Rule 29, whether because the sentence imposed is illegal or unjust, must be predicated on a hearing. *See* E.B. Cypher, Revise or Revoke of Sentence Hearings, 30A Criminal Practice and Procedure, § 30:27 (4th ed. Mar. 2015). *See also Thompson v. United States*, 495 F.2d 1304, 1307 (1st Cir. 1974) (vacating post-trial sentence imposed in absentia to correct an illegal sentence, holding defendant must be present for resentencing; cited by Reporter's Notes to Mass. R. Cr. P. 18(a), Presence of Defendant, as example of sentencing requiring defendant's presence). Although the defendant does not have the right to present evidence at this hearing, *see Commonwealth v. Coggins*, 324 Mass. 552, 556–557, *cert. denied*, 338 U.S. 881 (1949), he or she has the right to be present and to be heard. *See Aldoupolis v. Commonwealth*, 386 Mass. 260, 275–276 (1982); E.B. Cypher, Presence of the Defendant at the [Rule 29] Hearing, 30B Criminal Practice and Procedure, § 41:12 (4th ed. Mar. 2015). Further, any victim(s) covered by G.L. c. 258B, Rights of Victims and Witnesses of Crime, may present a victim-impact statement at such a hearing. *See Commonwealth v. Doucette*, 81 Mass. App. Ct. 740, 742, *rev. denied*, 463 Mass. 1103 (2012) (upholding judge's discretion under G.L. c. 258B, § 3(p) to permit victims to be heard on Rule 30(a) motion for a new trial, adding that "[t]he victim's family was also entitled [under the statute] to make a victim impact statement at sentencing or disposition").

Rule 29(c) Notice—(d) Place of Hearing

Rule 29(c), Notice, and Rule 29(d), Place of Hearing, are amended (1) to recognize the Commonwealth's narrow authority to file a motion to revise or revoke an illegal sentence, and (2) to achieve gender neutrality.

Rule 29(e) Appeal

Rule 29(e) provides that either party may appeal from a final order under the rule. This provision clarifies that the Commonwealth may appeal a denial of its motion to revise or revoke an illegal sentence. Prior to Rule 29(e), a defendant's right to appeal the denial of a motion to revise or revoke a sentence was well established, *see Commonwealth v. Richards*, 44 Mass. App. Ct. 478, 481 (1998), as was the Commonwealth's right to appeal the allowance of such a motion. *See Commonwealth v. Cowan*, 422 Mass. 546, 547 (1996) (recognizing Commonwealth's right under G.L. c. 211, § 3 to appeal District Court allowance of Rule 29 motion); *Commonwealth v. Amirault*, 415 Mass. 112, 115 (1993) (same under G.L. c. 278, § 28E for Superior Court motion). In contrast, while the Commonwealth had the right to move to correct an illegal sentence and presumably the attendant right to appeal the denial of such a motion, *see Commonwealth v. Selavka*, 469 Mass. 502, 507 & n.6 (2014), its avenue for pursuing that appeal was not clear. *Id.* Rule 29(e) cures that deficiency.

Rule 30. Post Conviction Relief

[Amended effective Oct. 1, 2001.]

(a) Unlawful Restraint. Any person who is imprisoned or whose liberty is restrained pursuant to a criminal conviction may at any time, as of right, file a written motion requesting the trial judge to release him or to correct the sentence then being served upon the ground that his confinement or restraint was imposed in violation of the Constitution or laws of the United States or of the Commonwealth of Massachusetts.

(b) New Trial. The trial judge upon motion in writing may grant a new trial at any time if it appears that justice may not have been done. Upon the motion the trial judge shall make such findings of fact as are necessary to resolve the defendant's allegations of error of law.

(c) Post Conviction Procedure.

(1) *Service and Notice.* The moving party shall serve the office of the prosecutor who represented the Commonwealth in the trial court with a copy of any motion filed under this rule.

(2) *Waiver.* All grounds for relief claimed by a defendant under subdivisions (a) and (b) of this rule shall be raised by the defendant in his original or amended motion. Any grounds not so raised are waived unless the judge in the exercise of his discretion permits them to be raised in a subsequent motion, or unless such grounds could not reasonably have been raised in the original or amended motion.

(3) *Affidavits.* Each moving party shall file and serve and parties opposing a motion may file and serve affidavits where appropriate in support of his respective position. The judge may rule on the issue or issues presented by such motion on the basis of the facts alleged in the affidavits without further hearing if no substantial issue is raised by the motion or affidavits.

(4) *Discovery.* Where affidavits filed by the moving party under subdivision (c)(3) establish a prima facie case for relief, the judge on motion of any party, after notice to the opposing party and an opportunity to be heard, may authorize such discovery as is deemed appropriate, subject to appropriate protective order.

(5) *Counsel.* The judge in the exercise of discretion may assign or appoint counsel in accordance with the provisions of these rules to represent a defendant in the preparation and presentation of motions filed under subdivisions (a) and (b) of this rule. The court, after notice to the Commonwealth and an opportunity to be heard, may also exercise discretion to allow the defendant costs associated with the preparation and presentation of a motion under this rule.

(6) *Presence of Moving Party.* A judge may entertain and determine a motion under subdivisions (a) and (b) of this rule without requiring the presence of the moving party at the hearing.

(7) *Place and Time of Hearing.* All motions under subdivisions (a) and (b) of this rule may be heard by the trial judge wherever he is then sitting. The parties shall have at least 30 days notice of any hearing unless the judge determines that good cause exists to order the hearing held sooner.

(8) *Appeal.* An appeal from a final order under this rule may be taken to the Appeals Court, or to the Supreme Judicial Court in an appropriate case, by either party.

(A) If an appeal is taken, the defendant shall not be discharged from custody pending final decision upon the appeal; provided, however, that the defendant may, in the discretion of the judge, be admitted to bail pending decision of the appeal.

(B) If an appeal or application therefor is taken by the Commonwealth, upon written motion supported by affidavit, the Appeals Court or the Supreme Judicial Court may determine and approve payment to the defendant of his costs of appeal together with reasonable attorney's fees, if any, to be paid on the order of the trial court after entry of the rescript or the denial of the application. If the final order grants relief other than a discharge from custody, the trial court or the court in which the appeal is pending may, upon application by the Commonwealth, in its discretion, and upon such conditions as it deems just, stay the execution of the order pending final determination of the matter.

(9) *Appeal Under G.L. c. 278, § 33E.* If an appeal or application for leave to appeal is taken by the Commonwealth under the provisions of Chapter 278, Section 33E, upon written notice supported by affidavit, the Supreme Judicial Court may determine and approve payment to the defendant of his costs of appeal together with reasonable attorney's fees to be paid on order of the trial court after entry of the rescript or the denial of the application.

Rule 31. Stay of Execution; Relief Pending Review

[Amended effective Oct. 1, 2009.]

(a) Imprisonment. If a sentence of imprisonment is imposed upon conviction of a crime, the entry of an appeal shall not stay the execution of the sentence unless the judge imposing it or, pursuant to Mass. R. App. P. 6, a single justice of the court that will hear the appeal, determines in the exercise of discretion that execution of said sentence shall be stayed pending the determination of the appeal. If execution of a sentence of imprisonment is stayed, the judge or justice may at that time make an order relative to the custody of the defendant or for admitting the defendant to bail.

(b) If the application for a stay of execution of sentence is allowed, the order allowing the stay may state the grounds upon which the stay may be revoked and, in any event, shall state that upon release by the appellate court of the rescript affirming the conviction, stay of execution automatically expires unless extended by the appellate court. Any defendant so released shall provide prompt written notice to the clerk of the trial court regarding the defendant's current address and promptly notify the clerk in writing of any change thereof. The clerk shall notify the appellate court that will hear the appeal that a stay of execution of sentence has been allowed. At any time after the stay expires, the Commonwealth may move in the trial court to execute the sentence. The court shall schedule a prompt hearing and issue notice thereof to the defendant unless the prosecutor requests, for good cause shown, that a warrant shall issue.

(c) Fine. If a reservation, filing, or entry of an appeal is made following a sentence to pay a fine or fine and costs, the sentence shall be stayed by the judge imposing it or by a single justice of the court that will hear the appeal if there is a diligent perfection of appeal.

(d) Probation or Suspended Sentence. An order placing a defendant on probation or suspending a sentence may be stayed if an appeal is taken.

Rule 32. Filing and Service of Papers

[Applicable to District Court and Superior Court. Amended effective Feb. 1, 2017.]

(a) Service: When Required. Written motions other than those which are heard ex parte, written notices, and similar papers shall be served upon each of the parties.

(b) Service: How Made. Whenever under these rules or by order of court service is required or permitted to be made upon a party represented by an attorney, service shall be made upon the attorney, unless service upon the party himself is ordered by the court. Service upon the attorney or upon a party shall be made in the manner provided for in civil actions.

(c) Notice of Orders and Judgments. If upon the entry of a judgment or order made on a written motion either or both of the parties are not present in court, the clerk shall immediately mail to the absent party or parties a notice of that entry and shall record the mailing in the docket.

(d) Filing. Papers required to be served shall be filed with the court. Papers shall be filed in the manner provided for in civil actions.

(e) Additional Time After Service by Mail. Whenever a party has the right or is required to do an act within a prescribed period after the service of a notice or other paper upon him and the notice or other paper is served upon him by mail, three days shall be added to the prescribed period.

(f) Protection of Personal Identifying Information. Publicly accessible documents filed with the court shall conform to Supreme Judicial Court Rule 1:24, Protection of Personal Identifying Information in Publicly Accessible Court Documents.

Rule 33. Counsel for Defendants Indigent and Indigent but Able to Contribute

[Applicable to District Court and Superior Court. Amended effective July 1, 1986.]

The assignment of counsel for defendants determined to be indigent or indigent but able to contribute shall be governed by the provisions of G.L. c. 211D and Supreme Judicial Court Rule 3:10.

Rule 34. Report

[Amended effective Sept. 7, 2004.]

If, prior to trial, or, with the consent of the defendant, after conviction of the defendant, a question of law arises which the trial judge determines is so important or doubtful as to require the decision of the Appeals Court, the judge may report the case so far as necessary to present the question of law arising therein. If the case is reported prior to trial, the case shall be continued for trial to await the decision of the Appeals Court.

Rule 35. Depositions to Perpetuate Testimony

[Applicable to District Court and Superior Court.]

(a) General Applicability. Whenever due to exceptional circumstances, and after a showing of materiality and relevance, it is deemed to be in the interest of justice that the testimony of a prospective witness of the defendant or the Commonwealth be taken and preserved, the judge may at any time after the filing of a complaint or return of an indictment, upon his own motion or the motion of either party with notice to all interested persons, order that the testimony of the witness be taken by deposition and that any designated book, paper, document, record, recording, or other material not privileged be produced at the same time and place. If a witness is committed for failure to give bail to appear to testify at a trial or hearing, the judge may direct that his deposition be taken. A copy of a deposition ordered upon the judge's own motion shall be transmitted to the court by the person administering the deposition. In determining a motion filed pursuant to this rule, the judge may order a hearing or may determine whether exceptional circumstances exist and the materiality and relevance of the testimony on the basis of the supporting affidavit.

(b) Summonses. An order to take a deposition shall authorize the issuance by the clerk of summonses pursuant to Rule 17 for the persons and objects named or described in such order. A witness whose deposition is to be taken may be required to attend at any place designated by the trial court, taking into account the convenience of the witness and the parties.

(c) Notice of Taking of Deposition. The party on whose motion a deposition is to be taken shall give all interested persons reasonable written notice of the time and place for the taking of the deposition. If a defendant is in custody, the officer having custody of the defendant shall be notified by the court of the time and place set for the taking of the deposition and shall produce the defendant at that time and place and keep him in the presence of the witness during the taking of the deposition. A defendant not in custody shall have the right to be present at the taking of a deposition, but his failure to appear after notice and without cause shall constitute a waiver of the right to be present and of all objections based upon that right.

(d) Payment of Expenses. Whenever a deposition is taken upon motion of the Commonwealth, the court shall direct that the reasonable expenses of travel and subsistence of the defendant and his counsel and the witness be paid for by the Commonwealth. Expenses for a deposition taken upon motion of a defendant may be assessed to the defendant to be paid forthwith or in such other manner as the judge may determine.

(e) Scope of Examination. Subject to such additional conditions as the judge may specify and except as otherwise provided in these rules, the taking of depositions in criminal cases shall be in the manner provided for in civil actions. The scope and manner of examination and cross-examination at the taking of the deposition shall be such as would be allowed in the trial itself.

(f) Objections to Deposition Testimony. Objections to deposition testimony or evidence or parts thereof and the grounds for the objections shall be stated at the time of the taking of the deposition.

(g) Admissibility. At a trial or upon any hearing, a part or all of a deposition, so far as it is otherwise admissible under the law of evidence, may be used as substantive evidence if the judge finds that the deponent is unavailable or if the deponent gives testimony at the trial or hearing which is inconsistent with his deposition. Any deposition may be used by any party for the purpose of contradicting or impeaching the testimony of the deponent as a witness. "Unavailable" as a witness includes situations in which the deponent:

(1) is exempt by a ruling of the judge on the ground of privilege from testifying concerning the subject matter of his deposition;

(2) persists in refusing to testify concerning the subject matter of his deposition despite an order of the judge to do so;

(3) lacks memory of the subject matter of his deposition;

(4) is unable to be present or to testify at the trial or hearing because of death or physical or mental illness or infirmity;

(5) is absent from the trial or hearing and the proponent of the deposition has been unable to procure the deponent's attendance by process or other reasonable means; or

(6) is absent from the trial or hearing and his testimony was ordered taken and preserved pursuant to Rule 6(d)(2).

A deponent is not unavailable as a witness if his exemption, refusal, claim of lack of memory, inability, or absence is due to the procurement or wrongdoing of the proponent of his deposition for the purpose of preventing the deponent from attending or testifying.

(h) Notice.

(1) *District Court.* All interested parties shall be given reasonable notice by the clerk of the time set for hearing motions filed under this rule.

(2) *Superior Court.* The moving party shall notify all interested parties of the time set for hearing motions filed under this rule at least seven days prior to the hearing.

(i) Deposition by Agreement Not Precluded. Nothing in this rule shall preclude the taking of a deposition, orally or upon written questions, by agreement of the parties with the consent of the judge.

Rule 36. Case Management

[Applicable to District Court and Superior Court. Amended effective Mar. 1, 1996.]

(a) General Provisions.

(1) *Order of Priorities.* The trial of defendants in custody awaiting trial and defendants whose pretrial liberty is reasonably believed to present unusual risks to society shall be given preference over other criminal cases.

(2) *Function of the Court.*

(A) District Court. The court shall determine the sequence of the trial calendar.

(B) Superior Court. The court shall determine the sequence of the trial calendar after cases are selected for prosecution by the district attorney.

(b) Standards of a Speedy Trial. The time limitations in this subdivision shall apply to all defendants as to whom the return day is on or after the effective date of these rules. Defendants arraigned prior to the effective date of these rules shall be tried within twenty-four months after such effective date.

(1) *Time Limits.* A defendant, except as provided by subdivision (d)(3) of this rule, shall be brought to trial within the following time periods, as extended by subdivision (b)(2) of this rule:

(A) During the first twelve-month period following the effective date of this rule, a defendant shall be tried within twenty-four months after the return day in the court in which the case is awaiting trial.

(B) During the second such twelve-month period, a defendant shall be tried within eighteen months after the return day in the court in which the case is awaiting trial.

(C) During the third and all successive such twelve-month periods, a defendant shall be tried within twelve months after the return day in the court in which the case is awaiting trial.

(D) If a retrial of the defendant is ordered, the trial shall commence within one year after the date the action occasioning the retrial becomes final, as extended by subdivision (b)(2) of this rule. The order of an appellate court requiring a retrial is final upon the issuance by the appellate court of the rescript. In the event that the clerk of the appellate court fails to issue the rescript within the time provided for in Massachusetts Rule of Appellate Procedure 23, retrial shall commence within one year after the date when the rescript should have issued.

If a defendant is not brought to trial within the time limits of this subdivision, as extended by subdivision (b)(2), he shall be entitled upon motion to a dismissal of the charges.

(2) *Excluded Periods.* The following periods shall be excluded in computing the time within which the trial of any offense must commence:

(A) Any period of delay resulting from other proceedings concerning the defendant, including, but not limited to:

(i) delay resulting from an examination of the defendant, and hearing on, his mental competency, or physical incapacity;

(ii) delay resulting from a stay of the proceedings due to an examination or treatment of the defendant pursuant to section 47 of chapter 123 of the General Laws;

(iii) delay resulting from a trial with respect to other charges against the defendant, which period shall run from the commencement of such other trial until fourteen days after an acquittal or imposition of sentence;

(iv) delay resulting from interlocutory appeals;

(v) delay resulting from hearings on pretrial motions;

(vi) delay resulting from proceedings relating to transfer to or from other divisions or counties pursuant to Rule 37;

(vii) delay reasonably attributable to any period, not to exceed thirty days, during which any proceeding concerning the defendant is actually under advisement.

(B) Any period of delay resulting from the absence or unavailability of the defendant or an essential witness. A defendant or an essential witness shall be considered absent when his whereabouts are unknown and he is attempting to avoid apprehension or prosecution or his whereabouts cannot be determined by due diligence. A defendant or an essential witness shall be considered unavailable whenever his whereabouts are known but his presence for trial cannot be obtained by due diligence or he resists appearing at or being returned for trial.

(C) Any period of delay resulting from the fact that the defendant is mentally incompetent or physically unable to stand trial.

(D) If the complaint or indictment is dismissed by the prosecution and thereafter a charge is filed against the defendant for the same or a related offense, any period of delay from the date the charge was dismissed to the date the time limitation would commence to run as to the subsequent charge.

(E) A reasonable period of delay when the defendant is joined for trial with a codefendant as to whom the time for trial has not run and there is no cause for granting a severance.

(F) Any period of delay resulting from a continuance granted by a judge on his own motion or at the request of the defendant or his counsel or at the request of the prosecutor, if the judge granted the continuance on the basis of his findings that the ends of justice served by taking such action outweighed the best interests of the public and the defendant in a speedy trial. No period of delay resulting from a continuance granted by the court in accordance with this paragraph shall be excludable under this subdivision unless the judge sets forth in the record of the case, either orally or in writing, his reasons for finding that the ends of justice served by the granting of the continuance outweigh the best interests of the public and the defendant in a speedy trial.

(G) Any period of time between the day on which a defendant or his counsel and the prosecuting attorney agree in writing that the defendant will plead guilty or nolo contendere to the charges and such time as the judge accepts or rejects the plea arrangement.

(H) Any period of time between the day on which the defendant enters a plea of guilty and such time as an order of the judge permitting the withdrawal of the plea becomes final.

(3) *Computation of Time Limits.* In computing any time limit other than an excluded period, the day of the act or event which causes a designated period of time to begin to run shall not be included. Computation of an excluded period shall include both the first and the last day of the excludable act or event.

(c) Dismissal for Prejudicial Delay. Notwithstanding the fact that a defendant is not entitled to a dismissal under subdivision (b) of this rule, a defendant shall upon motion be entitled to a dismissal where the judge after an examination and consideration of all attendant circumstances determines that: (1) the conduct of the prosecuting attorney in bringing the defendant to trial has been unreasonably lacking in diligence and (2) this conduct on the part of the prosecuting attorney has resulted in prejudice to the defendant.

(d) Special Procedures: Persons Serving Term of Imprisonment.

(1) *General Provisions.* A person serving a term of imprisonment either within or without the prosecuting jurisdiction is entitled to all safeguards afforded him under subdivisions (a), (b), and (c) of this rule in the conduct of any criminal proceeding, subject to the limitations stated herein.

(2) *Persons Detained Within the Commonwealth.* Any person who is detained within the Commonwealth upon the unexecuted portion of a sentence imposed pursuant to a criminal proceeding is entitled to be tried upon any untried indictment or complaint pending against him in any court in this Commonwealth within the time prescribed by subdivision (b) of this rule.

(3) *Persons Detained Outside the Commonwealth.* Any person who is detained outside the Commonwealth upon the unexecuted portion of a sentence imposed pursuant to a criminal proceeding, and against whom an untried indictment or complaint is pending within the Commonwealth shall, subsequent to the filing of a detainer, be notified by the prosecutor by mail of such charges and of his right to demand a speedy trial. If the defendant pursuant to such notification does demand trial, the person having custody shall so certify to the prosecutor, who shall promptly seek to obtain the presence of the defendant for trial. If the prosecutor has unreasonably delayed (A) in causing a detainer to be filed with the official having custody of the defendant, or (B) in seeking to obtain the defendant's presence for trial, and the defendant has been prejudiced thereby, the pending charges against the defendant shall be dismissed.

(e) Effect of a Dismissal. A dismissal of any charge ordered pursuant to any provision of this rule shall apply to all related offenses.

(f) Case Status Reports.

(1) *District Court.* The First Justice of each division of the District Court shall be advised periodically by the clerk of the status of all cases which have been pending in that court for six months or longer. The report shall be transmitted to the Administrative Justice for the District Court Department.

(2) *Superior Court.* The Administrative Justice for the Superior Court Department shall be notified by the clerk for each county of the status of all cases which have been pending in that court for six months or longer within the following time periods:

(A) for the first twelve-month period following the effective date of this rule, sixty days after the last day of a sitting;

(B) for the second such twelve-month period, forty-five days after the last day of a sitting;

(C) for the third and all successive such twelve-month periods, thirty days after the last day of a sitting.

Such notice shall include the number of the case, the name of the defendant, the offense charged, the name of defense counsel, if any, and the name of the prosecutor.

NOTE *Commonwealth v. Taylor*, 469 Mass. 516, 518 (2014) ("[T]he time it takes to resolve a rule 14 motion brought to compel mandatory discovery should not, as at present, automatically be excluded from the speedy trial calculus. Instead, the judge who hears such a motion must determine on a case-by-case basis whether delays resulting from its resolution fairly should count towards the Commonwealth's twelve-month timeline.").

Rule 37. Transfer of Cases

[Applicable to District Court and Superior Court.]

(a) Transfer for Plea and Sentence.

(1) *District Court.* A defendant against whom a complaint is pending and who appears in District Court, whether under arrest or pursuant to a summons, and against whom a complaint is pending in a division other than that in which he appears, may state in writing that he wishes to plead guilty or nolo contendere, to waive trial in the division in which the other complaint is pending, and to consent to disposition of the case in the division in which he appears. The District Court in which the defendant appears may order that the other complaint be transferred for disposition, subject to the written approval of the prosecutor in each division.

(2) *Superior Court.* A defendant against whom a complaint or indictment is pending and who appears in Superior Court, whether under arrest or pursuant to a summons, and against whom a complaint or indictment is pending in a county other than that in which he appears, may state in writing that he wishes to plead guilty or nolo contendere, to waive trial in the county in which the other complaint or indictment is pending, and to consent to disposition of the case in the county in which he appears. The Superior Court in which the defendant appears may order that the other complaint or indictment be transferred for disposition, subject to the written approval of the prosecuting attorney in each county.

(3) *Effect of Not Guilty Pleas.* If after a proceeding has been transferred pursuant to subdivision (a) of this rule the defendant pleads not guilty, the clerk shall return the papers transmitted pursuant to subdivision (c) of this rule to the court in which the prosecution was commenced, and the proceeding shall be restored to the docket of that court.

(b) Transfer for Trial.

(1) *Transfer for Prejudice.* A judge upon his own motion or the motion of a defendant or the Commonwealth made prior to trial may order the transfer of a case to another division or county for trial if the court is satisfied that there exists in the community where the prosecution is pending so great a prejudice against the defendant that he may not there obtain a fair and impartial trial.

(2) *Transfer of Other Cases.* A judge, upon motion of a defendant made pursuant to subdivision (3) or (4) of Rule 9(a), and after taking into account the convenience of the court, the parties, and their witnesses, may with the written approval of the prosecuting attorney in each division or county order the transfer and consolidation for trial of any or all charges pending against the defendant in the several divisions or counties of the Commonwealth.

(c) Proceedings on Transfer. Upon receipt of the defendant's statement and the written approval of the prosecutor required by this rule, the clerk of the court in which a complaint or indictment is pending shall transfer the papers in the case and any bail taken to the clerk of the court to which the case is transferred. The clerk of the transferee court shall make immediate entry of the case upon the docket of that court and shall so notify the clerk of the transferor court so that the case may be closed on the docket of that court. The prosecution shall continue in the transferee court.

Rule 38. Disability of Judge

[Applicable to Superior Court and jury sessions of District Court.]

(a) During Trial. If by reason of death, sickness, or other disability the judge before whom a jury trial has commenced is unable to proceed with the trial, any other judge of that court or properly assigned to that court, upon certifying in writing that he has familiarized himself with the record of the trial, may proceed with and finish the trial.

(b) Receipt of Verdict. Any judge of a court or any judge properly assigned to that court may receive a verdict of the jury.

(c) After Verdict or Finding of Guilt. If by reason of absence, unavailability, death, sickness, or other disability the judge before whom the defendant has been tried is unable to perform the duties to be performed by the judge after a verdict or finding of guilt, any other judge of that court or properly assigned to that court may perform those duties; but if the other judge is satisfied that he cannot perform those duties because he did not preside at the trial or for any other reason, he may, in his discretion or upon motion of the defendant, order a new trial.

Rule 39. Records of Foreign Proceedings and Notice of Foreign Law

[Applicable to District Court and Superior Court.]

(a) Records of Courts of Other States or of the United States. The records and judicial proceedings of a court of another state or of the United States shall be competent evidence in this Commonwealth if authenticated by the attestation of the clerk or other officer who has charge of the records of such court under its seal.

(b) Notice of Foreign Law. The court shall upon request take judicial notice of the law of the United States or of any state, territory, or dependency thereof or of a foreign country whenever it shall be material.

Rule 40. Proof of Official Records

[Applicable to District Court and Superior Court.]

(a) Authentication.

(1) *Domestic.* An official record kept within the Commonwealth, or an entry therein, when admissible for any purpose, may be evidenced by an official publication thereof or by a copy attested by the officer having legal custody of the record, or by his deputy. If the record is kept in any other state, district, commonwealth, territory or insular possession of the United States, or within the Panama Canal Zone or the Trust Territory of the Pacific Islands, any such copy shall be accompanied by a certificate that such custodial officer has the custody. This certificate may be made by a judge of a court of record of the district or political subdivision in which the record is kept, authenticated by the seal of the court, or may be made by any public officer having a seal of office and having official duties in the district or political subdivision in which the record is kept, authenticated by the seal of his office.

(2) *Foreign.* A foreign official record, or an entry therein, when admissible for any purpose, may be evidenced by an official publication thereof, or a copy thereof, attested by a person authorized to make the attestation, and accompanied by a final certification as to the genuineness of the signature and official position (i) of the attesting person, or (ii) of any foreign official whose certificate of genuineness of signature and official position relates to the attestation or is in a chain of certificates of genuineness of signature and official position relating to the attestation. A final certification may be made by a secretary of embassy or legation, consul general, consul, vice consul, or consular agent of the United States, or a diplomatic or consular official of the foreign country assigned or accredited to the United States. If reasonable opportunity has been given to all parties to investigate the authenticity and accuracy of the documents, the court may, for good cause shown, (i) admit an attested copy without final certification, or (ii) permit the foreign official record to be evidenced by an attested summary with or without a final certification.

(b) Lack of Record. A written statement that after diligent search no record or entry of a specified tenor is found to exist in the records designated by the statement, authenticated as provided in subdivision (a)(1) of this rule in the case of a domestic record, or complying with the requirements of subdivision (a)(2) of this rule for a summary in the case of a foreign record, is admissible as evidence that the records contain no such record or entry.

(c) Other Proof. This rule does not prevent the proof, by any other method authorized by law, of the existence of, or the lack of, an official record, or of entry, or lack of entry therein.

Rule 41. Interpreters and Experts

[Applicable to District Court and Superior Court.]

The judge may appoint an interpreter or expert if justice so requires and may determine the reasonable compensation for such services and direct payment therefor.

Rule 42. Clerical Mistakes

[Applicable to District Court and Superior Court.]

Clerical mistakes in judgments, orders, or other parts of the record and errors therein arising from oversight or omission may be corrected by the court at any time of its own initiative or on the motion of any party and after such notice, if any, as the court orders. During the pendency of an appeal, such mistakes may be corrected before the appeal is docketed in the appellate court, and thereafter while the appeal is pending may be corrected with leave of the appellate court.

Rule 43. Summary Contempt Proceedings

[Applicable to District Court and Superior Court. Amended effective Jan. 1, 2014.]

(a) When Warranted. A criminal contempt may be punished summarily when

(1) summary punishment is necessary to maintain order in the courtroom;

(2) the contemptuous conduct occurred in the presence of, and was witnessed by, the presiding judge;

(3) the presiding judge enters a preliminary finding at the time of the contemptuous conduct that a criminal contempt occurred; and

(4) the punishment for each contempt does not exceed three months imprisonment and a fine of $2,000.

(b) Procedure.

(1) Upon making a preliminary finding that a criminal contempt occurred, the presiding judge shall give the alleged contemnor notice of the charges and shall hold a hearing to provide at least a summary opportunity for the alleged contemnor to produce evidence and argument relevant to guilt or punishment. For good cause shown, the presiding judge may continue the hearing to enable the contemnor to obtain counsel or evidence.

(2) The presiding judge may order the alleged contemnor held, subject to bail and/or conditions of release, pending the hearing provided for in subsection (b)(1) if the judge finds it necessary to maintain order in the courtroom or to assure the alleged contemnor's appearance.

(3) (i) If, after the hearing provided for in subsection (b)(1), the presiding judge determines that summary contempt is not appropriate because the appropriate punishment for the alleged contempt exceeds three months imprisonment and a fine of $2,000, the judge shall refer the alleged contemnor for prosecution under Rule 44. If necessary to maintain order in the courtroom or to assure the alleged contemnor's appearance, the judge may order the alleged contemnor held, subject to bail and/or conditions of release, for a reasonable period of time, not to exceed 15 days absent good cause shown, pending the issuance of a complaint or indictment under Rule 44(a).

(ii) If, after the hearing, the presiding judge determines that summary contempt is not appropriate because one or more of the requirements in subsection (a)(1), (a)(2), or (a)(3) is not satisfied, or for another reason, the judge shall discharge the alleged contemnor. The judge, in his or her discretion, may refer the matter to the government for investigation and possible prosecution, and nothing in this subsection shall preclude such investigation or prosecution, whether undertaken in response to the judge's referral or independently.

(iii) If, after the hearing, the presiding judge determines that summary contempt is appropriate, the judge shall make a finding on the record of summary contempt, setting forth the facts upon which that finding is based. The court shall further announce a judgment of summary contempt in open court, enter that judgment on the court's docket, and notify the contemnor of the right to appeal. The judge may defer sentencing, or the execution of any sentence, where the interests of orderly courtroom procedure and substantial justice require. If necessary to maintain order in the courtroom or to assure the contemnor's appearance, the judge may order the contemnor held, subject to bail and/or conditions of release, pending sentencing.

(c) Appeal. A contemnor may appeal a judgment of summary contempt to the Appeals Court.

Reporter's Notes (2014). This amendment to Rule 43 is intended to clarify the procedures by which a judge can impose summary punishment for criminal contempt or, alternatively, refer an alleged contemnor for prosecution by complaint or indictment under Rule 44. *See Vizcaino v. Commonwealth*, 462 Mass. 266, 279 n.11 (2012) (suggesting a need for clarification in the operation of Rule 43). Amended Rule 43 resolves ambiguities concerning the prerequisites for summary punishment of contempt and the procedural steps in a summary-contempt proceeding. Further, amended Rule 43(b) explicitly recognizes discretionary authority that judges have presumably enjoyed in summary contempt proceedings, principally the common-law authority to hold an accused contemnor if necessary to maintain courtroom order or to assure his or her appearance at any subsequent proceeding. The amended rule also increases the maximum fine permitted from $500 to $2,000.

Rule 43(a) When Warranted

Amended Rule 43(a), like its predecessor, provides for the four conditions necessary to warrant summary punishment for contempt. Such punishment must be necessary to maintain courtroom order; the contemptuous conduct must occur in the presence of and be witnessed by the judge; the judge must enter a finding of contempt at the time it occurs; and the punishment cannot exceed three months' imprisonment and a fine of $2,000. As discussed below, amended Rule 43(a)(3) clarifies an ambiguity in former Rule 43(a), the amended rule expressly providing that this threshold, contemporaneous finding of contempt be preliminary. As such, it gives notice to the alleged contemnor of the charges, but it is subject to reconsideration after affording the alleged contemnor an opportunity to be heard as required under Rule 43(b)(1).

Former Rule 43(a)(2) referred to the threshold, contemporaneous finding as a "judgment of contempt," leading to possible confusion between it and the final "judgment of contempt" which, under former Rule 43(b), the judge could make only after "giv[ing] the contemnor notice of the charges and at least a summary opportunity to adduce evidence or argument relevant to guilt or punishment." Mass. R. Crim. P. 43, 378 Mass. 919 (1979). *See Vizcaino v. Commonwealth*, 462 Mass. 266, 276 (2012) (holding that an opportunity to be heard followed by entry of the judgment on docket are necessary predicates to a Rule 43 judgment of summary contempt); *Commonwealth v. Segal*, 401 Mass. 95, 99-100 (1987) (same). Amended Rule 43(a)(3) makes it clear that the judge's threshold, contemporaneous finding of contempt is preliminary. While the Supreme Judicial Court had read former Rule 43(a)(2) to provide that this preliminary "judgment of contempt" be written, see *Vizcaino v. Commonwealth*, 462 Mass. 266, 272 & n.7 (2012) (interpreting Rule 43(a)'s contemporaneity requirement to permit reasonable, minor delays in preparing Rule 43(a)(2)'s written judgment of contempt), amended Rule 43(a)(2) neither provides nor contemplates that the preliminary finding of contempt be written. Such a requirement seems unnecessary given that the judge's finding is in open court and presumably subject to transcription if necessary. Moreover, requiring a written finding could delay both the alleged contemnor's opportunity to be heard and the trial in which the contemptuous conduct occurred. Finally, as noted, the amended rule increases the maximum fine for summary contempt from $500 to $2,000, an increase that partially accounts for the inflation that has occurred since the rule's adoption in 1979. This maximum fine is well within the punishment that may be imposed without implicating the Sixth Amendment right to a jury trial. *See Blanton v. City of N. Las Vegas, Nev.*, 489 U.S. 538, 544–45 (1989) (holding no Sixth Amendment right to jury trial for offense the maximum punishment for which was six months imprisonment and $1,000 fine, noting the possible fine was "well below" the $5,000 federal benchmark utilized in identifying petty offenses that can be tried without a jury); *Furtado v. Furtado*, 380 Mass. 137, 142 n.5 (1980) (noting Supreme Judicial Court has not interpreted article 12 to impose a stricter jury-trial requirement).

2

Rule 43(b) Procedure

As did former Rule 43(b), amended Rule 43(b)(1) provides that, following the preliminary finding of contempt under Rule 43(a)(3), the judge must conduct a hearing, affording the accused contemnor at least a summary opportunity to produce evidence and/or argument relevant to guilt or punishment. The amended rule further gives the judge discretion, for good cause shown, to continue the hearing so that the accused contemnor can obtain evidence or counsel.

Rule 43(b)(2) authorizes the judge to hold the accused contemnor, subject to bail and/or conditions of release, pending the summary-contempt hearing if necessary to maintain courtroom order or to assure the contemnor's appearance. Judges presumably had such common-law authority under former Rule 43, *see In re Terry*, 128 U.S, 289, 307–13 (1888) (recognizing longstanding judicial authority to apprehend, commit, and summarily punish one who engages in contemptuous conduct in the judge's presence); see also G.L. c. 276, § 57 (authorizing justices of the superior and district courts to admit a committed prisoner to bail upon finding that such release will reasonably assure the prisoner's future appearance before the court), but the amended rule makes it explicit.

Amended Rule 43(b)(3) sets out the respective procedures for the three possible results of the Rule 43(b)(1) hearing.

First, under Rule 43(b)(3)(i), if the judge determines that summary contempt is not appropriate because the accused contemnor deserves greater punishment than that permitted for summary contempt, the judge must refer the alleged contemnor for prosecution by complaint or indictment under Rule 44. In that event, if necessary to maintain courtroom order or the appearance of the accused, the rule recognizes the judge's common-law authority to hold the alleged contemnor subject to bail and/or conditions of release for up to 15 days, extendable for 3 good cause shown, pending issuance of the contempt complaint or indictment under Rule 44(a). Although the judge has wide discretion in determining what constitutes good cause to extend the 15-day limitation, it would ordinarily include a superior court referral in which there is no grand jury in session during that 15-day period.

Second, Rule 43(b)(3)(ii) covers the case in which, after considering the facts and arguments presented in the summary-contempt hearing, the judge decides for whatever reason that summary contempt is not appropriate. This possibility, although inferable under former Rule 43(b), is here explicit. Under Rule 43(b)(3)(ii), such a decision to forgo further proceedings and to discharge the alleged contemnor does not bar the alleged contemnor's prosecution for the alleged contempt. The rule explicitly provides that, in spite of this termination of summary-contempt proceedings, the judge has discretion to refer the matter to the government for investigation and possible prosecution, and that, even in the absence of such a judicial referral, the government may investigate and prosecute the alleged contempt. *Cf. Vizcaino*, 462 Mass. at 274–75 (holding that, where judge had not entered summary contempt judgment on the court's docket as required by Rule 43(b), further prosecution for nonsummary contempt under Rule 44 not barred by double jeopardy).

Third, Rule 43(b)(3)(iii) sets out the procedure if, after the hearing, the judge decides that summary punishment for the contempt is appropriate. The judge must make a finding of summary contempt on the record, setting out the facts on which it is based. Unlike former Rule 43(b), this finding need not be written; a transcript of the factual finding provides an adequate record for purposes of appeal. The rule further provides that, as in any criminal conviction, the court must announce the summary-contempt judgment in open court, enter the judgment on the docket, and notify the contemnor of the right to appeal. See Mass. R. Crim. P. 28(a), 378 Mass. 898 (1979). As did former Rule 43(b), Rule 43(b)(3)(iii) allows the judge discretion to defer summary-contempt sentencing or its execution where orderly courtroom procedure and substantial justice require. Although the rule does not explicitly limit the purpose or length of such sentence deferral, as was so under former Rule 43(b), it ordinarily would be reserved for cases of summary contempt by one of the parties or lawyers in the trial, see *Taylor v. Hayes*, 418 U.S. 488, 497–98 (1974), and imposition or execution of sentence would be deferred until after the trial is completed. The rule further permits the judge, if necessary, to order the contemnor held, subject to bail and/or conditions of release, pending sentencing.

Rule 43(c), providing for the right of appeal to the Appeals Court, remains in substance unchanged.

Rule 44. Contempt

[Applicable to District Court and Superior Court.]

(a) Nature of the Proceedings. All criminal contempts not adjudicated pursuant to Rule 43 shall be prosecuted by means of complaint, unless the prosecutor elects to proceed by indictment. Except as otherwise provided by these rules, the case shall proceed as a criminal case in the court in which the contempt is alleged to have been committed.

(b) Special Provisions for District Court. The District Court shall have jurisdiction to try all contempts committed therein except those prosecuted by indictment. Whenever a contemnor asserts his right to a jury trial in District Court, the trial shall be held before a jury in District Court. The contemnor's only right of appeal shall be to the Appeals Court.

(c) Disqualification of the Judge. The contempt charges shall be heard by a judge other than the trial judge whenever the nature of the alleged contemptuous conduct is such as is likely to affect the trial judge's impartiality.

Rule 45. Removal of the Disruptive Defendant

[Applicable to District Court and Superior Court.]

(a) Removal of Defendant. Upon the direction of the trial judge, a defendant may be removed from the courtroom during his trial when his conduct has become so disruptive that the trial cannot proceed in an orderly manner. Gagging or shackling may be employed if the trial judge has found such restraint reasonably necessary to maintain order. If the trial judge orders such restraint, he shall enter into the record of the case the reasons therefor. Whenever physical restraint of a defendant or witness occurs in the presence of the jury trying the case, or whenever the defendant is removed, the judge, at the request of the defendant, shall instruct the jury that such restraint or removal is not to be considered in assessing the proof and determining guilt.

(b) Defendant's Rights After Removal. A defendant once removed shall be required to be present in the court building while the trial is in progress. At the time of his removal he shall be advised that he has the right to be returned to the courtroom upon his request and assurances of good behavior. Notwithstanding the failure of a defendant to request to be returned to the courtroom, he shall be returned to the courtroom, at appropriate intervals in the absence of the jury, and shall be advised in open court that he will be permitted to remain upon the giving of assurances of good behavior.

Rule 46. Time

[Applicable to District Court and Superior Court.]

(a) Computation. In computing any period of time prescribed or allowed by these rules, by order of court, or by any applicable statute or rule, the day of the act, event, or default after which the designated period of time begins to run shall not be included. The last day of the period so computed shall be included, unless it is a Saturday, a Sunday, or a legal holiday, in which event the period runs until the end of the next day which is not a Saturday, a Sunday, or a legal holiday. When the period of time prescribed or allowed is less than seven days, intermediate Saturdays, Sundays, and legal holidays shall be excluded in the computation. As used in this rule, "legal holiday" includes any day appointed as a holiday by the President or the Congress of the United States or so designated by the laws of the Commonwealth.

(b) Enlargement. When by these rules or by a notice given thereunder or by order or rule of court an act is required or allowed to be done at or within a specified time, the court for cause shown may at any time in its discretion (1) with or without motion or notice order the period enlarged if a request therefor is made before the expiration of the period originally prescribed or as extended by a previous order; or (2) upon motion made after the expiration of the specified period permit the act to be done where the failure to act was the result of excusable neglect; or (3) permit the act to be done by stipulation of the parties; but the court may not extend the time for taking any action under Rules 25 and 29 except to the extent and under the conditions stated therein.

(c) For Motions, Affidavits in Superior Court. A written motion, other than one which may be heard ex parte, and notice of the hearing thereof shall be served on all interested parties not later than seven days prior to the hearing unless a different period is fixed by these rules or by order of the court. For cause shown, such an order may issue upon an ex parte application. When a motion is supported by affidavit, the affidavit shall be served with the motion. Opposing affidavits shall be served not later than one day before the hearing, unless the court permits them to be served at a later time.

Rule 47. Special Magistrates

[Applicable to Superior Court.]

The Justices of the Superior Court may appoint special magistrates to preside over criminal proceedings in the Superior Court. Such special magistrates shall have the powers to preside at arraignments, to set bail, to assign counsel, to supervise pretrial conferences, to mark up pretrial motions for hearing, to make findings and report those findings and other issues to the presiding justice or Administrative Justice, and to perform such other duties as may be authorized by order of the Superior Court. The doings of special magistrates shall be endorsed upon the record of the case. Special magistrates shall be compensated in the same manner as is provided by the General Laws for the compensation of masters in civil cases.

Rule 48. Sanctions

[Applicable to District Court and Superior Court.]

A willful violation by counsel of the provisions of these rules or of an order issued pursuant to these rules shall subject counsel to such sanctions as the court shall deem appropriate, including citation for contempt or the imposition of costs or a fine.

Selected Massachusetts Rules of Civil Procedure

Rule 1. Scope of Rules

[Amended effective July 1, 1974; Jan. 1, 1980; Jan. 1, 1982; July 1, 1996; June 1, 2007, Mar. 1, 2008; Aug. 1, 2016.]

These rules govern the procedure before a single justice of the Supreme Judicial Court or of the Appeals Court, and in the following departments of the Trial Court: the Superior Court, the Housing Court the Probate and Family Court in proceedings seeking equitable relief, the Juvenile Court in proceedings seeking equitable relief, in the Land Court, in the District Court and in the Boston Municipal Court, in all suits of a civil nature whether cognizable as cases at law or in equity, with the exceptions stated in Rule 81. They should be construed, administered, and employed by the court and the parties to secure the just, speedy, and inexpensive determination of every action and proceeding.

As used in these rules the following terms shall be deemed to have the following meanings:

"Superior Court" shall mean the Superior Court Department of the Trial Court, or a session thereof for holding court.

"Housing Court" shall mean a division of the Housing Court Department of the Trial Court, or a session thereof for holding court.

"Probate Court" shall mean a division of the Probate and Family Court Department of the Trial Court, or a session thereof for holding court.

"Land Court" shall mean the Land Court Department of the Trial Court, or a session thereof for holding court.

"District Court" or "Municipal Court" shall mean a division of the District Court Department of the Trial Court, or a session thereof for holding court; except when the context means something to the contrary, said words shall include the Boston Municipal Court Department.

"Municipal Court of the City of Boston" or "Boston Municipal Court" shall mean a division of the Boston Municipal Court Department of the Trial Court, or a session thereof for holding court.

"Juvenile Court" shall mean the Juvenile Court Department of the Trial Court, or a session thereof for holding court.

Reporter's Notes (2016). The amendment to Rule 1, adopted from the Federal Rules of Civil Procedure, changed the second sentence of the first paragraph so that it reads: "They [the Massachusetts Rules of Civil Procedure] should be construed, administered, and employed by the court and the parties to secure the just, speedy, and inexpensive determination of every action and proceeding."

The purpose of the change was to acknowledge that both the court and the parties have the obligation to employ the rules for the purposes set forth.

Rule 24. Intervention

(a) Intervention of Right. Upon timely application anyone shall be permitted to intervene in an action: (1) when a statute of the Commonwealth confers an unconditional right to intervene or (2) when the applicant claims an interest relating to the property or transaction which is the subject of the action and he is so situated that the disposition of the action may as a practical matter impair or impede his ability to protect that interest, unless the applicant's interest is adequately represented by existing parties.

(b) Permissive Intervention. Upon timely application anyone may be permitted to intervene in an action: (1) when a statute of the Commonwealth confers a conditional right to intervene; or (2) when an applicant's claim or defense and the main action have a question of law or fact in common. When a party to an action relies for ground of claim or defense upon any statute or executive order administered by a federal or state governmental officer or agency or upon any regulation, order, requirement, or agreement issued or made pursuant to the statute or executive order, the officer or agency upon timely application may be permitted to intervene in the action. In exercising its discretion the court shall consider whether the intervention will unduly delay or prejudice the adjudication of the rights of the original parties.

(c) Procedure. A person desiring to intervene shall serve a motion to intervene upon the parties as provided in Rule 5. The motion shall state the grounds therefor and shall be accompanied by a pleading setting forth the claim or defense for which intervention is sought.

(d) Intervention by the Attorney General. When the constitutionality of an act of the legislature or the constitutionality or validity of an ordinance of any city or the by-law of any town is drawn in question in any action to which the Commonwealth or an officer, agency, or employee thereof is not a party, the party asserting the unconstitutionality of the act or the unconstitutionality or invalidity of the ordinance or by-law shall notify the attorney general within sufficient time to afford him an opportunity to intervene.

Rule 26. General Provisions Governing Discovery

[Amended effective Jan. 1, 1981; July 1, 1996; Apr. 1, 2008; Jan. 1, 2014; July 1, 2016; Sept. 1, 2017.]

(a) Discovery Methods. Parties may obtain discovery by one or more of the following methods except as otherwise provided in Rule 30(a) and Rule 30A(a), (b): depositions upon oral examination or written questions; written interrogatories; production of documents or things or permission to enter upon land or other property, for inspection and other purposes; physical and mental examinations; and requests for admission. Unless the court orders otherwise, or unless otherwise provided in these rules, the frequency of use of these methods is not limited.

(b) Scope of Discovery. Unless otherwise limited by order of the court in accordance with these rules, the scope of discovery is as follows:

(1) *In General.* Parties may obtain discovery regarding any matter, not privileged, which is relevant to the subject matter involved in the pending action, whether it relates to the claim or defense of the party seeking discovery or to the claim or defense of any other party, including the existence, description, nature, custody, condition and location of any books, documents, or other tangible things and the identity and location of persons having knowledge of any discoverable matter. It is not ground for objection that the information sought will be inadmissible at the trial if the information sought appears reasonably calculated to lead to the discovery of admissible evidence.

(2) *Insurance Agreements.* A party may obtain discovery of the existence and contents of any insurance agreement under which any person carrying on an insurance business may be liable to satisfy part or all of a judgment which may be entered in the action or to indemnify or reimburse for payments made to satisfy the judgment. Information concerning the insurance agreement is not by reason of disclosure admissible in evidence at trial. For purposes of this paragraph, an application for insurance shall not be treated as part of an insurance agreement.

(3) *Trial Preparation: Materials.* Subject to the provisions of subdivision (b)(4) of this rule, a party may obtain discovery of documents and tangible things otherwise discoverable under subdivision (b)(1) of this rule and prepared in anticipation of litigation or for trial by or for another party or by or for that other party's representative (including his attorney, consultant, surety, indemnitor, insurer, or agent) only upon a showing that the party seeking discovery has substantial need of the materials in the preparation of his case and that he is unable without undue hardship to obtain the substantial equivalent of the materials by other means. In ordering discovery of such materials when the required showing has been made, the court shall protect against disclosure of the mental impressions, conclusions, opinions, or legal theories of an attorney or other representative of a party concerning the litigation.

A party may obtain without the required showing a statement concerning the action or its subject matter previously made by that party. Upon request, a person not a party may obtain without the required showing a statement concerning the action or its subject matter previously made by that person. If the request is refused, the person may move for a court order. The provisions of Rule 37(a)(4) apply to the award of expenses incurred in relation to the motion. For purposes of this paragraph, a statement previously made is (A) a written statement signed or otherwise adopted or approved by the person making it, or (B) a stenographic, mechanical, electrical, or other recording, or a transcription thereof, which is a substantially verbatim recital of an oral statement by the person making it and contemporaneously recorded.

(4) *Trial Preparation: Experts.* Discovery of facts known and opinions held by experts, otherwise discoverable under the provisions of subdivision (b)(1) of this rule and acquired or developed in anticipation of litigation or for trial, may be obtained only as follows:

(A) (i) A party may through interrogatories require any other party to identify each person whom the other party expects to call as an expert witness at trial, to state the subject matter on which the expert is expected to testify, and to state the substance of the facts and opinions to which the expert is expected to testify and a summary of the grounds for each opinion. (ii) Upon motion, the court may order further discovery by other means, subject to such restrictions as to scope and such provisions, pursuant to subdivision (b)(4)(C) of this rule, concerning fees and expenses as the court may deem appropriate.

(B) A party may discover facts known or opinions held by an expert who has been retained or specially employed by another party in anticipation of litigation or preparation for trial and who is not expected to be called as a witness at trial, only as provided in Rule 35(b) or upon a showing of exceptional circumstances under which it is impracticable for the party seeking discovery to obtain facts or opinions on the same subject by other means.

(C) Unless manifest injustice would result, (i) the court shall require that the party seeking discovery pay the expert a reasonable fee for time spent in responding to discovery under subdivisions (b)(4)(A)(ii) and (b)(4)(B) of this rule; and (ii) with respect to discovery obtained under subdivision (b)(4)(A)(ii) of this rule the court may require, and with respect to discovery obtained under subdivision (b)(4)(B) of this rule the court shall require, the party seeking discovery to pay the other party a fair portion of the fees and expenses reasonably incurred by the latter party in obtaining facts and opinions from the expert.

(5) *Claims of Privilege or Protection of Trial Preparation Materials.*

(A) Information Withheld. When a party withholds information otherwise discoverable under these rules by claiming that it is privileged or subject to protection as trial preparation material, the party must:

(i) expressly make the claim; and

(ii) describe the nature of the documents, communications, or tangible things not produced or disclosed—and do so in a manner that, without revealing information itself privileged or protected, will enable other parties to assess the claim.

The court, upon motion, may order the withholding party to provide such additional information as is necessary to assess the claim of privilege.

(B) Information mistakenly produced; claim of privilege. If information produced in discovery is subject to a claim of privilege or of protection as trial-preparation material, the party making the claim may notify any party that received the information of the claim and the basis for it. After being notified, a party shall promptly return, sequester, or destroy the specified information and any copies it has; shall not use or disclose the information until the claim is resolved; shall take reasonable steps to retrieve the information if the party disclosed it before being notified; and may promptly present the information to the court under Trial Court Rule VIII, Uniform Rules on Impoundment Procedure, for a determination of the claim. The producing party shall preserve the information until the claim is resolved.

In resolving any such claim, the court should determine whether:

(i) the disclosure was inadvertent;

(ii) the holder of the privilege or protection took reasonable steps to prevent disclosure; and

(iii) the holder promptly took reasonable steps to rectify the error

(C) Effect of a ruling. If the court, following such procedure, or pursuant to an order under Rule 26(f)(3), upholds the privilege or protection in a written order, the disclosure shall not be deemed a waiver in the matter before the court or in any other proceeding.

(c) Protective Orders. Upon motion by a party or by the person from whom discovery is sought, and for good cause shown, the court in which the action is pending or alternatively, on matters relating to a deposition, the court in the county or judicial district, as the case may be, where the deposition is to be taken may make any order which justice requires to protect a party or person from annoyance, embarrassment, oppression, or undue burden or expense, including one or more of the following: (1) that the discovery not be had; (2) that the discovery may be had only on specified terms and conditions, including a designation of the time, place, or manner; or the sharing of costs; (3) that the discovery may be had only by a method of discovery other than that selected by the party seeking discovery; (4) that certain matters not be inquired into, or that the scope of the discovery be limited to certain matters; (5) that discovery be conducted with no one present except persons designated by the court; (6) that a deposition after being sealed be opened only by order of the court; (7) that a trade secret or other confidential research, development, or commercial information not be disclosed or be disclosed only in a designated way; (8) that the parties simultaneously file specified documents or information enclosed in sealed envelopes to be opened as directed by the court.

Factors bearing on the decision whether discovery imposes an undue burden or expense may include the following:

(1) whether it is possible to obtain the information from some other source that is more convenient or less burdensome or expensive;

(2) whether the discovery sought is unreasonably cumulative or duplicative; and

(3) whether the likely burden or expense of the proposed discovery outweighs the likely benefit of its receipt, taking into account the parties' relative access to the information, the amount in controversy, the resources of the parties, the importance of the issues, and the importance of the requested discovery in resolving the issues.

If the motion for a protective order is denied in whole or in part, the court may, on such terms and conditions as are just, order that any party or person provide or permit discovery. The provisions of Rule 37(a)(4) apply to the award of expenses incurred in relation to the motion.

(d) Sequence and Timing of Discovery. Unless the court upon motion, for the convenience of parties and witnesses and in the interests of justice, orders otherwise, methods of discovery may be used in any sequence and the fact that a party is conducting discovery, whether by deposition or otherwise, shall not operate to delay any other party's discovery.

(e) Supplementation of Responses. A party who has responded to a request for discovery with a response that was complete when made is under no duty to supplement his response to include information thereafter acquired, except as follows:

(1) A party is under a duty seasonably to supplement his response with respect to any question directly addressed to (A) the identity and location of persons having knowledge of discoverable matters, and (B) the identity of each person expected to be called as an expert witness at trial, the subject matter on which he is expected to testify, and the substance of his testimony.

(2) A party is under a duty seasonably to amend a prior response if he obtains information upon the basis of which (A) he knows that the response was incorrect when made, or (B) he knows that the response though correct when made is no longer true and the circumstances are such that a failure to amend the response is in substance a knowing concealment.

(3) A duty to supplement responses may be imposed by order of the court, agreement of the parties, or at any time prior to trial through new requests for supplementation of prior responses.

(f) Electronically Stored Information.

(1) *Definition.*

"Inaccessible electronically stored information" means electronically stored information from sources that the party identifies as not reasonably accessible because of undue burden or cost.

2

(2) *Electronically Stored Information Conferences.*

(A) Conference as of right. Upon the written request of any party made no later than 90 days after the service of the first responsive pleading by any defendant, the parties shall confer regarding electronically stored information. Such request shall be served on each party that has appeared, but it shall not be filed with the court. The conference shall be held as soon as practicable but no later than 30 days from the date of service of the request.

(B) Conference by agreement of the parties. At any time more than 90 days after the service of the first responsive pleading, any party may serve on each party that has appeared a request that all parties confer regarding electronically stored information. Such request shall not be filed with the court. If within 30 days after the request all parties do not agree to confer, any party may move that the court conduct a conference pursuant to Rule 16 regarding electronically stored information.

(C) Purpose of electronically stored information conference among the parties. The purpose of an electronically stored information conference is for the parties to develop a plan relating to the discovery of electronically stored information. Within 14 days after such conference the parties shall file with the court the plan and a statement concerning any issues upon which the parties cannot agree. At any electronically stored information conference the parties shall discuss:

(i) any issues relating to preservation of discoverable information;

(ii) the form in which each type of the information will be produced;

(iii) what metadata, if any, shall be produced;

(iv) the time within which the information will be produced;

(v) the method for asserting or preserving claims of privilege or of protection of trial preparation materials, including whether such claims may be asserted after production;

(vi) the method for asserting or preserving confidential and proprietary status of information either of a party or a person not a party to the proceeding;

(vii) whether allocation among the parties of the expense of production is appropriate, and,

(viii) any other issue related to the discovery of electronically stored information.

(3) *Electronically Stored Information Orders.* The court may enter an order governing the discovery of electronically stored information pursuant to any plan referred to in subparagraph (2)(C), or following a Rule 16 conference, or upon motion of a party or stipulation of the parties, or sua sponte, after notice to the parties. Any such order may address:

(A) whether discovery of the information is reasonably likely to be sought in the proceeding;

(B) preservation of the information;

(C) the form in which each type of the information is to be produced;

(D) what metadata, if any, shall be produced;

(E) the time within which the information is to be produced;

(F) the permissible scope of discovery of the information;

(G) the method for asserting or preserving claims of privilege or of protection of the information as trial-preparation material after production;

(H) the method for asserting or preserving confidentiality and the proprietary status of information relating to a party or a person not a party to the proceeding;

(I) allocation of the expense of production; and

(J) any other issue relating to the discovery of the information.

(4) *Limitations on Electronically Stored Information Discovery.*

2

(A) A party may object to the discovery of inaccessible electronically stored information, and any such objection shall specify the reason that such discovery is inaccessible.

(B) On motion to compel or for a protective order relating to the discovery of electronically stored information, a party claiming inaccessibility bears the burden of showing inaccessibility.

(C) The court may order discovery of inaccessible electronically stored information if the party requesting discovery shows that the likely benefit of its receipt outweighs the likely burden of its production, taking into account the amount in controversy, the resources of the parties, the importance of the issues, and the importance of the requested discovery in resolving the issues.

(D) The court may set conditions for the discovery of inaccessible electronically stored information, including allocation of the expense of discovery.

(E) The court may limit the frequency or extent of electronically stored information discovery, even from an accessible source, in the interests of justice. Factors bearing on this decision include the following:

(i) whether it is possible to obtain the information from some other source that is more convenient or less burdensome or expensive;

(ii) whether the discovery sought is unreasonably cumulative or duplicative;

(iii) whether the party seeking discovery has had ample opportunity by discovery in the proceeding to obtain the information sought; or

(iv) whether the likely burden or expense of the proposed discovery outweighs the likely benefit.

Reporter's Notes (2016). At the request of the Rules Committee of the Supreme Judicial Court, the Standing Advisory Committee on the Massachusetts Rules of Civil and Appellate Procedure ("Standing Advisory Committee") considered possible changes to the Massachusetts discovery rules that were based on amendments to the federal discovery rules. The proposed amendments to the Massachusetts discovery rules were intended to address the burdens of discovery that have been the subject of significant debate across the country over the past few years.

There were three proposed changes involving the Massachusetts discovery rules, all taken from amendments to the federal discovery rules.

The first proposed change to Rule 26(b) would have involved the scope of discovery by deleting the language that discovery must be "relevant to the subject matter involved" in the action. The proposal would have added in place of the deleted language that discovery must be relevant to a party's claim or defense. This language was drawn from a 2000 amendment to Rule 26 of the Federal Rules of Civil Procedure refining the scope of discovery.

The second proposed change to Rule 26(b) would have adopted the principle of proportionality for discovery requests—i.e., discovery should be "proportional to the needs of the case." This proposed amendment would have adopted the principle of proportionality as set forth in amendments to the Federal Rules of Civil Procedure that were effective in 2015. The proposed rule listed the factors that were to be taken into account in determining whether a discovery request was proportional to the needs of a case: "the importance of the issues at stake in the action, the amount in controversy, the parties' relative access to relevant information, the parties' resources, the importance of the discovery in resolving the issues, and whether the burden or expense of the proposed discovery outweighs its likely benefit."

The third proposed change would have deleted the language in Rule 26(b)(1) that "[i]t is not ground for objection that the information sought will be inadmissible at the trial if the information sought appears reasonably calculated to lead to the discovery of admissible evidence." In its place, the proposal would have added language that information "need not be admissible in evidence to be discoverable."

The Standing Advisory Committee reviewed the many comments submitted by both lawyers and judges after the proposal was published for public comment and voted not to recommend to the Supreme Judicial Court adoption of the three changes to the discovery rules. The comments reflected significant opposition to the proposed changes and described them as unnecessary and inadvisable at the present time. The principal objection to the amendments by the Standing Advisory Committee was based on the perception by many Committee members of drawbacks and unintended consequences of imposing the federal changes on the Massachusetts trial courts, as well as the newness of the federal changes. Most Committee members were in favor of a "wait and see" approach that would allow review of how the federal amendments affect litigants and civil litigation prior to considering whether similar amendments should be adopted in Massachusetts.

The Standing Advisory Committee also prepared draft language for consideration by the Supreme Judicial Court that alluded to proportionality in discovery, not in the context of the scope of discovery, but in the context of a court's decision to grant a protective order involving discovery under Rule 26(c). The Standing Advisory Committee referred to this as "compromise" language in the event that the Supreme Judicial Court did not accept the Standing Advisory Committee's recommendation not to change the Massachusetts discovery rules, at least until there is sufficient experience under the federal amendments. It is this compromise language that the Supreme Judicial Court adopted in 2016.

The amendment to the protective order language of Rule 26(c) lists factors similar to those that are relevant to a court's decision to limit the discovery of electronically stored information under Rule 26(f)(4)(E). These factors are:

(1) whether it is possible to obtain the information from some other source that is more convenient or less burdensome or expensive;

(2) whether the discovery sought is unreasonably cumulative or duplicative; and

(3) whether the likely burden or expense of the proposed discovery outweighs the likely benefit of its receipt, taking into account the parties' relative access to the information, the amount in controversy, the resources of the parties, the importance of the issues, and the importance of the requested discovery in resolving the issues.

Under Rule 26(f)(4)(E)(iii), a relevant factor in limiting electronic discovery is "whether the party seeking discovery has had ample opportunity by discovery in the proceeding to obtain the information sought." This factor has been omitted from the listing of factors in the 2016 amendment to Rule 26(c).

The addition of these factors to Rule 26(c) should not result in any significant change to Massachusetts practice. The amendment confirms the existing authority of a trial judge in determining whether to grant a protective order.

Reporter's Notes (2014). The 2014 amendments relating to electronically stored information have resulted in changes to Rule 26(b) and (f).

Rule 26(b).

The existing paragraph that had constituted Rule 26(b)(5) ("Claims of Privilege or Protection of Trial Preparation Materials: Privilege Log") was designated as 26(b)(5)(A), with no changes made to the text. Simultaneously, new provisions were added that have been designated as 26(b)(5)(B) and (C) to deal with information that was mistakenly produced in discovery and subject to a claim of privilege or protection.

The provisions of the first paragraph of Rule 26(b)(5)(B) were adapted from Rule 26(b)(5)(B) of the Federal Rules of Civil Procedure. The provisions of the second paragraph of Rule 26(b)(5)(B) and Rule 26(b)(5)(C) were adapted from Rule 502 of the Federal Rules of Evidence. The language addresses concerns that have been raised about inadvertent waiver of a privilege or claim of protection for trial-preparation material that may result from production of materials in connection with discovery. The problem has become particularly acute in light of the increased likelihood that privileged and protected material can easily be inadvertently produced in discovery where the materials are embedded in voluminous material in electronic format that has been turned over in discovery. But the language of the rule is not restricted to privilege or protection in connection with electronically stored information.

The Standing Advisory Committee decided that an appropriate place to add "clawback" provisions to the Massachusetts Rules was in Rule 26(b)(5), which prior to the 2014 amendment, dealt with privilege and privilege logs. A simultaneous amendment to Mass. R. Civ. P. 16 in 2014 also added this topic to the list of items to be discussed at a pretrial conference.

The Comment to Rule 9 of the Uniform Rules Relating to the Discovery of Electronically Stored Information aptly summarizes the scope of the problem as follows: "The risk of privilege waiver and the work necessary to avoid it add to the costs and delay of discovery. When the review is of electronically stored information, the risk of waiver and the time and effort to avoid it can increase substantially because of the volume of electronically stored information and the difficulty of ensuring that all information to be produced has in fact been reviewed. This rule provides a procedure for a party to assert a claim of privilege or trial-preparation material protection after information is produced in discovery and, if the claim is contested, permits any party that received the information to present the matter to the court for resolution . . . ."

The Massachusetts version of the "clawback" rule provides that a party may present the information to the court for resolution pursuant to the provisions of the Uniform Rules on Impoundment Procedure, Trial Court Rule VIII. The cognate language in the federal rules uses "under seal" terminology that the Standing Advisory Committee thought to be less appropriate under Massachusetts practice.

Although Rule 26(b)(5)(B) sets forth a "clawback" provision, there is nothing in the rule that precludes the parties from modifying the procedures set forth in the rule to deal with information within the scope of a privilege or protection.

The language of Rule 26(b)(5)(C) provides that if the procedure is used and a court enters a written order upholding the privilege or protection, "the disclosure shall not be deemed a waiver in the matter before the court or in any other proceeding." Such an order is necessary to avoid a waiver of privilege or protection as to non-parties.

Rule 26(c).

Rule 26(c) includes a listing of types of protective orders that a court may enter. Item (2) in the list provides for an order that discovery "be had only on specified terms and conditions, including a designation of the time, place, or manner; or the sharing of costs." The reference to "manner" would, for example, permit an order that discovery be provided on a compact disc. The reference to "sharing of costs" makes clear that the court may order sharing of costs in light of the expenses associated with electronic discovery.

Rule 26(f).

Rule 26(f) is new and deals with conferences regarding electronically stored information.

The definition set forth in Rule 26(f)(1) that the term "inaccessible electronically stored information" is "electronically stored information from sources that the party identifies as not reasonably accessible because of undue burden or cost" is taken from Federal Rule 26(b)(2)(B).

Unlike the Federal Rules of Civil Procedure and the Uniform Rules Relating to the Discovery of Electronically Stored Information, the Massachusetts version of Rule 26(f) does not require a conference between the parties as a matter of course (sometimes referred to as a "meet and confer" conference, although a telephonic conference may be permissible). The Massachusetts version, on the contrary, is a recognition that courts in Massachusetts may not necessarily be set up to provide in all instances a right to a conference with the judge as a matter of course in all litigation at the early stages of litigation.

The approach taken by Rule 26(f), however, recognizes that a conference between the parties at the early stages of litigation will often be helpful where there may be discovery of electronically stored information. Thus, the Massachusetts rule has been drafted to encourage a meaningful conference between the parties to deal with electronically stored information.

The Massachusetts version is an attempt to foster communication between counsel on issues of electronic discovery in a court environment that is not set up, as is the case in the federal courts, to provide individual conferences or individual court management of litigation in all instances. A similar approach that did not adopt the federal model in full can be seen in the "Guidelines For State Trial Courts Regarding Discovery of Electronically-Stored Information," approved by the Conference of Chief Justices, August 2006. See generally, Guideline 3 and the Comments that accompany Guideline 3.

Conference as of right. Under Rule 26(f)(2)(A), a party has a right to demand a conference with the other party by serving a written request for a conference "no later than 90 days after the service of the first responsive pleading" of a defendant. The term "pleading" as used in this rule is intended to reflect the definition of "pleading" as set forth in Rule 7(a). Thus, an answer of a defendant would be a pleading that would trigger the right to serve a request for a conference, whereas a motion to dismiss would not. The rule specifically provides that the request for a conference not be filed with the clerk's office, in an attempt not to overburden an already-beleaguered court system with additional filings. The conference must be held no later than thirty days from the date a party served the request.

Although the rule itself does not define the term "conference," the parties should not feel that they are required to meet in person. A conference by telephone or through electronic communication is satisfactory.

Conference by agreement. If there has been no request for a conference as of right within the 90-day period, Rule 26(f)(2)(B) allows a party to request a conference at a later point. Such a request should not be filed with the clerk's office. If the other parties to the case do not agree to such a conference, a party desiring a conference may move that the court conduct a conference under the provisions of Rule 16 to deal with matters relating to electronically stored information.

Purpose of conference; plan. Rule 26(f)(2)(C) sets forth the purpose of the conference, whether occurring as of right or by agreement of the parties—to develop a plan that relates to discovery of electronically stored information. The rule sets forth a variety of topics that must be discussed at the conference, adapted in part from Rule 3 of the Uniform Rules Relating to the Discovery of Electronically Stored Information.

2

The parties must discuss at the conference the preservation of electronically stored information (see item (i), "any issues relating to preservation of discoverable information"). Given the practice that exists in many organizations of deleting or disposing of electronic files after a set period of time, discussion of preservation may serve to avoid later disputes about the availability and expense of retrieving electronic information.

The language of the rule makes specific reference to the production of metadata as a subject to be discussed at the conference (see item (iii),"what metadata, if any, shall be produced"). Specific reference to metadata has also been added to the rule regarding a court order governing electronically stored information (Rule 26(f)(3)).

The parties may also want to address at the conference details regarding how the responding party accesses electronically stored information. This may aid the requesting party in formulating or refining discovery requests involving electronically stored information.

Within fourteen days after the conference, the parties must file with the court a plan that deals with electronically stored information. If the parties are not able to agree on certain issues, they shall file a statement so indicating. The parties must submit a plan to the court whether there was a conference as of right or by agreement, or by order of the court.

Electronically stored information orders. The language of Rule 26(f)(3) provides a court with discretion to enter an order relating to electronically stored information and sets forth the matters that may be addressed in such an order. These matters are drawn in part from Rule 4 of the Uniform Rules Relating to the Discovery of Electronically Stored Information.

A court may enter an order after the parties have filed a plan, or upon motion or stipulation of the parties, or sua sponte. A court order may be entered whether or not the parties have conferred. If the parties have agreed about the method to assert or preserve a claim of privilege or protection (Rule 26(f)(3)(F)), the court order may so state.

Limitations on electronically stored information discovery. Rule 26(f)(4) is drawn from Rule 8 of the Uniform Rules Relating to the Discovery of Electronically Stored Information. It provides considerations for a judge to limit discovery of electronically stored information and to allocate the costs involved. Rule 26(f)(4) applies regardless of whether the parties have had a conference or not.

The philosophy behind Rule 26(f)(4) is similar to that of Federal Rule 26(b)(2)(B), reflecting a two-tiered approach to electronic discovery. Upon request, electronic discovery shall be produced, unless limited under Rule 26(f)(4)(E). However, a party believing that electronically stored information is "inaccessible" (as defined in Rule 26(f)(1)) may object to the discovery. In the event that there is a motion to compel the discovery, or a motion for protective order, the court will then determine whether to order the discovery. See Rule 26(f)(4)(C).

Rule 27. Depositions Before Action or Pending Appeal

[Amended effective July 1, 1996; July 1, 2009.]

(a) Before Action.

(1) *Petition.* A person who desires to perpetuate his own testimony or that of another person regarding any matter that may be cognizable in any court where these rules apply may file a verified petition in the Superior Court in the county or District Court in the judicial district, as the case may be, of the residence of any expected adverse party. The petition shall be entitled in the name of the petitioner and shall show: 1, that the petitioner expects to be a party to an action cognizable in a court where these rules apply but is presently unable to bring it or cause it to be brought, 2, the subject matter of the expected action and his interest therein, 3, the facts which he desires to establish by the proposed testimony and his reasons for desiring to perpetuate it, 4, the names or a description of the persons he expects will be adverse parties and their addresses so far as known, and 5, the names and addresses of the persons to be examined and the substance of the testimony which he expects to elicit from each, and shall ask for an order authorizing the petitioner to take the depositions of the persons to be examined named in the petition, for the purpose of perpetuating their testimony.

(2) *Notice and Service.* The petitioner shall thereafter serve a notice upon each person named in the petition as an expected adverse party, together with a copy of the petition, stating that the petitioner will apply to the court, at a time and place named therein, for the order described in the petition. At least 20 days before the date of hearing the notice shall be served either within or without the Commonwealth in the manner provided in Rule 4 for service of summons; but if such service cannot with due diligence be made upon any expected adverse party named in the petition, the court may make such order as is just for service by publication or otherwise, and shall appoint, for persons not served in the manner provided in Rule 4, an attorney who shall represent them, and, in case they are not otherwise represented, shall cross-examine the deponent. If any expected adverse party is a minor or incompetent, or an incapacitated person as defined in G.L. c. 190B the provisions of Rule 17(b) apply.

(3) *Order and Examination.* If the court is satisfied that the perpetuation of the testimony may prevent a failure or delay of justice, it shall make an order designating or describing the persons whose depositions may be taken and specifying the subject matter of the examination and whether the depositions shall be taken upon oral examination or written interrogatories. The depositions may then be taken in accordance with these rules; and the court may make orders of the character provided for by Rules 34 and 35. For the purpose of applying these rules to depositions for perpetuating testimony, each reference therein to the court in which the action is pending shall be deemed to refer to the court in which the petition for such deposition was filed.

(4) *Use of Deposition.* If a deposition to perpetuate testimony is taken under these rules or if, although not so taken, it would be admissible in evidence in the courts of the Commonwealth, it may be used in any action involving the same subject matter subsequently brought in such a court, in accordance with the provisions of Rule 32(a).

(b) Pending Appeal. If an appeal has been taken from a judgment of a court of this Commonwealth or before the taking of an appeal if the time therefor has not expired, the court in which the judgment was rendered may allow the taking of the depositions of witnesses to perpetuate their testimony for use in the event of further proceedings in that court. In such case the party who desires to perpetuate the testimony may make a motion in that court for leave to take the depositions, upon the same notice and service thereof as if the action was pending in that court. The motion shall show (1) the names and addresses of persons to be examined and the substance of the testimony which he expects to elicit from each; (2) the reasons for perpetuating their testimony. If the court finds that the perpetuation of the testimony is proper to avoid a failure or delay of justice, it may make an order allowing the depositions to be taken and may make orders of the character provided for by Rules 34 and 35, and thereupon the depositions may be taken and used in the same manner and under the same conditions as are prescribed in these rules for depositions taken in pending actions.

(c) Perpetuation by Action. This rule does not limit the power of a court to entertain an action to perpetuate testimony.

Rule 28. Persons Before Whom Depositions May Be Taken

[Amended effective Jan. 1, 1982.]

(a) Within the United States. Within the United States or within a territory or insular possession subject to the jurisdiction of the United States, depositions shall be taken before an officer authorized to administer oaths by the laws of the United States or of the place where the examination is held, or before a person appointed by the court in which the action is pending. A person so appointed has power to administer oaths and take testimony. The term officer as used in Rules 30, 31 and 32 includes a person appointed by the court or designated by the parties under Rule 29.

(b) In Foreign Countries. In a foreign country, depositions may be taken (1) on notice before a person authorized to administer oaths in the place in which the examination is held, either by the law thereof or by the laws of the United States, or (2) before a person commissioned by the court, and a person so commissioned shall have the power by virtue of his commission to administer any necessary oath and take testimony, or (3) pursuant to a letter rogatory. A commission or a letter rogatory shall be issued on application and notice and on terms that are just and appropriate. It is not requisite to the issuance of a commission or a letter rogatory that the taking of the deposition in any other manner is impracticable or inconvenient; and both a commission and a letter rogatory may be issued in proper cases. A notice or commission may designate the person before whom the deposition is to be taken either by name or descriptive title. A letter rogatory may be addressed "To the Appropriate Authority in [here name the country]." Evidence obtained in response to a letter rogatory need not be excluded merely for the reason that it is not a verbatim transcript or that the testimony was not taken under oath or for any similar departure from the requirements for depositions taken within the United States under these rules.

(c) Disqualification for Interest. No deposition shall be taken before a person who is a relative or employee or attorney or counsel of any of the parties, or is a relative or employee of such attorney or counsel, or is financially interested in the action.

Rule 29. Stipulations Regarding Discovery Procedure

Unless the court orders otherwise, the parties may by written stipulation (1) provide that depositions may be taken before any person, at any time or place, upon any notice, and in any manner and when so taken may be used like other depositions; and (2) modify the procedures provided by these rules for other methods of discovery.

Rule 30. Depositions Upon Oral Examination

[Amended effective Jan. 1, 1981; Jan. 1, 1982; July 1, 1982; Mar. 1, 1989; July 1, 1996; Nov. 2, 1998; Sept. 1, 2017.]

(a) When Depositions May Be Taken. After commencement of the action, any party may take the testimony of any person, including a party, by deposition upon oral examination. Leave of court, granted with or without notice, must be obtained only if: (i) the plaintiff seeks to take a deposition prior to the expiration of 30 days after service of the summons and complaint upon any defendant or service made under Rule 4(e) (except that leave is not required (1) if a defendant has served a notice of taking deposition or otherwise sought discovery, or (2) if special notice is given as provided in subdivision (b)(2) of this rule); (ii) there is no reasonable likelihood that recovery will exceed $5,000 if the plaintiff prevails; (iii) the action is pending in the Superior Court and there has been a trial in a District Court before a transfer; (iv) there has been a hearing before a master; or (v) the relief sought is the custody of minor children, divorce, affirmance or annulment of marriage, separate support, or any like relief. The attendance of witnesses may be compelled by subpoena as provided in Rule 45. The deposition of a person confined in prison may be taken only by leave of court on such terms as the court prescribes.

(b) Notice of Examination: General Requirements; Special Notice; Non-Stenographic Recording; Production of Documents and Things; Deposition of Organization.

(1) A party desiring to take the deposition of any person upon oral examination shall give at least seven days' notice in writing to every other party to the action. The notice shall state the time and place for taking the deposition and the name and address of each person to be examined, if known, and, if the name is not known, a general description sufficient to identify him or the particular class or group to which he belongs. If a subpoena duces tecum is to be served on the person to be examined, the designation of the materials

to be produced as set forth in the subpoena shall be attached to or included in the notice.

(2) Leave of court is not required for the taking of a deposition by plaintiff if the notice (A) states that the person to be examined is about to go out of the county where the action is pending and more than 100 miles from the place of trial, or is about to go out of the United States, or is bound on a voyage abroad, and will be unavailable for examination unless his deposition is taken before expiration of the 30-day period, and (B) sets forth facts to support the statement. The plaintiff's attorney shall sign the notice, and his signature constitutes a certification by him that to the best of his knowledge, information, and belief the statement and supporting facts are true. The sanctions provided by Rule 11 are applicable to the certification.

If a party shows that when he was served with notice under this subdivision (b)(2) he was unable through the exercise of diligence to obtain counsel to represent him at the taking of the deposition, the deposition may not be used against him.

(3) The court may for cause shown enlarge or shorten the time for taking the deposition.

(4) Any oral deposition may be recorded by (i) stenographic or (ii) stenographic and audio-visual means. If the deposition is recorded by stenographic and audio-visual means, the parties shall comply with the provisions of Mass.R.Civ.P. 30 and 30A. With prior notice to the deponent and other parties, any party may designate another method for recording the testimony in addition to that specified in the original notice. Except as otherwise provided by this rule, the rules governing the practice and procedure in depositions and discovery shall apply. The party choosing to have the testimony recorded by stenographic and audio-visual means shall bear the entire cost of the audio-visual recording, except that each party shall bear the cost for a copy of the audio-visual recording and the stenographic record. By leave of court upon motion with notice and an opportunity to be heard in opposition, or by stipulation in writing of all parties, a party taking an oral deposition may have the testimony recorded by other than stenographic or stenographic and audio-visual means. The stipulation or order shall designate the person before whom the deposition shall be taken, the manner of recording, preserving and filing the deposition, and may include other provisions to assure that the recorded testimony will be accurate and trustworthy. A party may arrange to have a stenographic transcription made at his own expense. Any objections under subdivision (c), any changes made by the witness, his signature identifying the deposition as his own or the statement of the officer that is required if the witness does not sign, as provided in subdivision (e), and the certification of the officer required by subdivision (f) shall be set forth in a writing to accompany a deposition recorded by non-stenographic means. In any event, however, where testimony is to be recorded by audio-visual means, the provisions of Rule 30A shall apply.

(5) The notice to a party deponent may be accompanied by a request made in compliance with Rule 34 for the production of documents and tangible things at the taking of the deposition. The procedure of Rule 34 shall apply to the request and, notwithstanding the provisions of subdivision (b)(1) of this Rule, the party making the request shall give at least 30 days' notice in writing to every other party to the action. The court may on motion with or without notice allow a shorter or longer time.

(6) A party may in his notice and in a subpoena name as the deponent a public or private corporation or a partnership or association or governmental agency and describe with reasonable particularity the matters on which examination is requested. The organization so named shall designate one or more officers, directors, or managing agents, or other persons who consent to testify on its behalf, and may set forth, for each person designated, the matters on which he will testify. A subpoena shall advise a non-party organization of its duty to make such a designation. The persons so designated shall testify as to matters known or reasonably available to the organization. This subdivision (b)(6) does not preclude taking a deposition by any other procedure authorized in these rules.

(7) By leave of court upon motion with notice and an opportunity to be heard in opposition, or by stipulation in writing of all parties, a deposition may be taken by telephone. For the purpose of this rule and Rules 28(a), 37(a)(1), 37(b)(1) and 45(d), a deposition taken by telephone is taken in the county and at the place where the deponent is to answer questions propounded to him.

(c) Examination and Cross-Examination; Record of Examination; Oath; Objections. Examination and cross-examination of witnesses may proceed as permitted at the trial under the provisions of Rule 43(b). The officer before whom the deposition is to be taken shall put the witness on oath and shall personally, or by someone acting under the officer's direction and in the officer's presence, record the testimony of the witness. The testimony shall be taken stenographically or by voice writing or recorded by any other means ordered in accordance with subdivision (b)(4) of this rule. If requested by one of the parties, the testimony shall be transcribed. In lieu of participating in the oral examination, parties may serve written questions in a sealed envelope on the party taking the deposition and such party shall transmit them to the officer, who shall propound them to the witness and record the answers verbatim.

All objections made at the time of the examination to the qualifications of the officer taking the deposition, or to the manner of taking it, or to the evidence presented, or to the conduct of any party, and any other objection to the proceedings, shall be noted by the officer upon the deposition; but the examination shall proceed. Any objection to testimony during a deposition shall be stated concisely and in a non-argumentative and non-suggestive manner. Testimony to which objection is made shall be taken subject to the objections. Counsel for a witness or a party may not instruct a deponent not to answer except where necessary to assert or preserve a privilege or protection against disclosure, to enforce a limitation on evidence directed by the court or stipulated in writing by the parties, or to terminate the deposition and present a motion to the court pursuant to Rules 30(d) or 37(d).

(d) Motion to Terminate or Limit Examination. At any time during the taking of the deposition, on motion of any party or of the deponent and upon a showing that the examination is being conducted in bad faith or in such manner as unreasonably to annoy, embarrass, or oppress the deponent or party, the court in which the action is pending or the court in the county or judicial district, as the case may be, where the deposition is being taken may order the officer conducting the examination to cease forthwith from taking the deposition, or may limit the scope and manner of the taking of the deposition as provided in Rule 26(c). If the order made terminates the examination, it shall be resumed thereafter only upon the order of the court in which the action is pending. Upon demand of the objecting party or deponent, the taking of the deposition shall be suspended for the time necessary to make a motion for an order. The provisions of Rule 37(a)(4) apply to the award of expenses incurred in relation to the motion.

(e) Submission to Witness; Changes; Signing. When the testimony is fully transcribed the deposition transcript and any audio-visual recording thereof shall be submitted to the witness for examination and the deposition transcript shall be read to or by the witness, unless such examination and reading are waived by the witness and by the parties. Any changes in form or substance which the witness desires to make shall be entered upon the deposition transcript by the officer with a statement of the reasons given by the witness for making them. The deposition transcript shall then be signed by the witness, unless the parties by stipulation waive the signing or the witness is ill or cannot be found or refuses to sign. If the deposition transcript is not signed by the witness within 30 days of its submission to him, the officer shall sign it and state on the record the fact of the waiver or of the illness or absence of the witness or the fact of the refusal to sign together with the reason, if any, given therefor; and the deposition transcript may then be used as fully as though signed, unless on a motion to suppress under Rule 32(d)(4) the court holds that the reasons given for the refusal to sign require rejection of the deposition in whole or in part.

(f) Certification and Delivery by Officer; Exhibits; Copies; Notice of Receipt.

(1) The officer shall certify on the deposition transcript that the witness was duly sworn by him and that the deposition transcript is a true record of the testimony given by the witness. Unless otherwise ordered by the court generally or in a specific case or stipulated by the parties, he shall then securely seal the deposition transcript in an envelope endorsed with the title of the action and marked "Deposition of [here insert name of witness]" and shall promptly deliver or send it to the party taking the deposition.

Documents and things produced for inspection during the examination of the witness, shall, upon the request of a party, be marked for identification and annexed to the deposition transcript and may be inspected and copied by any party, except that if the person producing the material desires to retain them he may (A) offer copies to be marked for identification and annexed to the deposition and to serve thereafter as originals if he affords to all parties fair opportunity to verify the copies by comparison with the originals, or (B) offer the originals to be marked for identification, after giving to each party an opportunity to inspect and copy them, in which event the materials may then be used in the same manner as if annexed to the deposition. Any party may move for an order that the original be annexed to and returned with the deposition transcript to the court, pending final disposition of the case.

(2) Upon payment of reasonable charges therefor, the officer shall furnish a copy of the deposition transcript to any party or to the deponent.

(3) The party taking the deposition shall give prompt notice of its receipt to all other parties.

(g) Failure to Attend or to Serve Subpoena; Expenses.

(1) If the party giving the notice of the taking of a deposition fails to attend and proceed therewith and another party attends in person or by attorney pursuant to the notice, the court may order the party giving the notice to pay to such other party the amount of the reasonable expenses incurred by him and his attorney in so attending, including reasonable attorney's fees.

(2) If the party giving the notice of the taking of a deposition of a witness fails to serve a subpoena upon him and the witness because of such failure does not attend, and if another party attends in person or by attorney because he expects the deposition of that witness to be taken, the court may order the party giving the notice to pay to such other party the amount of the reasonable expenses incurred by him and his attorney in so attending, including reasonable attorney's fees.

Rule 30A. Audiovisual Depositions and Audiovisual Evidence

[Amended effective Jan. 1, 1981; Jan. 1, 1985; Jan. 1, 1990; Sept. 1, 2017.]

(a) Authorization of Audio-Visual Depositions. Any oral deposition may be recorded by stenographic and audio-visual means by complying with the provisions of this rule. Except as otherwise provided by this rule, the rules governing the practice and procedure in depositions and discovery shall apply. At the taking of any such deposition, unless the parties otherwise stipulate, or the court for good cause otherwise orders, there shall also be prepared a simultaneous stenographic record of the deposition. The party choosing to have the testimony recorded by audio-visual means shall bear the entire cost of the audio-visual recording, except that each party shall bear the cost for a copy of the audio-visual recording and the stenographic record.

(b) Notice. Every notice for the taking of an audio-visual deposition and the subpoena for attendance at that deposition shall state that it is to be recorded by audio-visual means and the name and address of the person whose deposition is to be taken. If the operator is an employee of the attorney choosing the audio-visual recording, the notice shall so indicate.

(c) Procedure. The party taking the audio-visual deposition shall be responsible for assuring that the necessary equipment for making an audio-visual recording of the deposition is present at the time the deposition is taken.

The following procedure shall be observed in recording an audio-visual deposition:

(1) *Opening of Deposition.* The deposition shall begin with an oral or written statement on camera which includes:

(i) the operator's name and business address;

(ii) the name and address of the operator's employer;

(iii) the date, time and place of the deposition;

(iv) the caption of the case;

(v) the name of the witness-deponent;

(vi) the name of the party on whose behalf the deposition is being taken; and

(vii) any stipulation by the parties.

The opening statement, if oral, shall be made by the operator, unless counsel agree that one of counsel will make the statement.

(2) *Counsel.* Counsel shall identify themselves on camera by stating their names, their addresses, and the names of the parties or persons for whom they appear at the deposition, and nothing more.

(3) *Oath.* The officer before whom the deposition is taken shall then identify himself and swear or affirm the witness on camera.

(4) *Multiple Units.* When the length of the deposition requires the use of more than one recording unit, the end of each recording unit and the beginning of each succeeding recording unit shall be announced on camera by the operator.

(5) *Closing of Deposition.* At the conclusion of the deposition, a statement shall be made on camera that the deposition is concluded. A statement may be made on camera setting forth any stipulation made by counsel concerning the custody of the audio-visual recording and exhibits and other pertinent matters.

(6) *Index.* The deposition shall be timed by a digital clock on camera which shall show continually each hour, minute and second of each recording unit of the deposition, or otherwise suitably indexed by a time generator. The date(s) on which the deposition is taken shall be shown.

(7) *Objections.* An objection shall be made as in the case of depositions taken solely by stenographic means.

(8) *Interruption of Recording.* No party shall be entitled to cause the operator to interrupt or halt the recording of the audio-visual deposition without the assent of all other parties present.

(9) *Submission to Witness; Changes; Signing.* Unless the parties have stipulated that a simultaneous stenographic record of the deposition not be prepared, the provisions of Rule 30(e) shall apply to the stenographic record of the deposition.

(10) *Certification.* The operator before whom the audio-visual deposition is taken shall attach to the original audio-visual recording a certificate stating that the audio-visual recording is a true record of the testimony given by the witness.

(d) Recording Officer; Use of Camera; Copies. The operator before whom an audio-visual deposition is taken shall be subject to the provisions enumerated in Rule 28(a)–(c).

During the taking of the audio-visual deposition, the operator shall assure that the audio-visual recording records the witness in a standard fashion at all times during the deposition, unless all counsel agree otherwise, or unless on motion before the court, the court directs otherwise. In no event shall the operator use, or permit the use of, audio-visual recording techniques to vary the view which is being recorded for presentation in the courtroom unless agreed upon or ordered by the court as recited above. As an exception to the foregoing, the operator shall, at the request of the attorney questioning the witness, cause a close-up view of a deposition exhibit or visual aid to be taken while the witness is being questioned concerning the exhibit.

Upon the request of any of the parties, the officer shall provide, at the cost of the party making the request, a copy of the deposition transcript in the form of an audio-visual recording or a written transcription.

(e) Custody; Filing; Notice of Filing. Unless the parties have otherwise stipulated, the officer shall take custody of each recording unit upon its completion and shall retain custody of all completed units throughout the deposition. When a deposition is to be completed on another day, the officer shall also take custody of any uncompleted recording unit during the interval.

(f) Inspection and Release of Audio-Visual Recordings. Except upon order of the court and upon such terms as may be provided, the audio-visual recordings on file with the clerk of the court in which the action is pending shall not be available for inspection or viewing after their filing and prior to their use at the trial of the case or their disposition in accordance with this rule. The clerk may release the audio-visual recording to the operator taking the deposition, without an order of court, for the purpose of preparing a copy at the request of a party as provided in subdivisions (a) and (d) of this rule.

(g) Rulings on Objections; Editing of Recording. If any party has any objections to the audio-visual deposition which would otherwise be made at trial, pursuant to Rule 32(b), such objections shall if practicable, be submitted to the trial judge prior to commencement of the trial or hearing for the purpose of obtaining rulings on such objections. An audio copy of the sound track or the transcript may be submitted in lieu of the audio-visual recording for this purpose. For the purpose of ruling on the objections, the trial judge may view the entire audio-visual recording, or view only those parts of the audio-visual recording pertinent to the objections made, or he may listen to an audio recording submitted in lieu of the audio-visual recording, or he may read the transcript. The trial judge shall, if practicable, rule on the objections prior to the commencement of the trial or hearing and shall return the recording to the party who took the audio-visual deposition, with notice to all parties of his rulings and of his instructions as to editing. The editing shall reflect the rulings of the trial judge and shall then remove all references to the objections. After making a copy of the audio-visual recording, the officer shall cause said copy to be edited in accordance with the court's instructions. He shall then cause both the original audio-visual recording and the edited version thereof, each clearly identified, to be returned to the trial judge for use during the trial or hearing. The original audio-visual recording shall be preserved intact and unaltered.

(h) Transcribing of Audio Portion; Marking for Identification. At a trial or hearing, that part of the audio portion of an audio-visual deposition which is offered in evidence and admitted, or which is excluded on objection, shall be transcribed in the same manner as the testimony of other witnesses. Both the original unedited audio-visual recording and the edited version shall be marked for identification.

(i) Use of Audio-Visual Deposition and Responsibility for Assuring Necessary Equipment at Time of Use. An audio-visual deposition may be used for any purpose and under any circumstances in which a stenographic deposition may be used.

The party desiring to use the audio-visual deposition for any purpose shall be responsible for assuring that the necessary equipment for playing the audio-visual recording back is available when the audio-visual deposition is to be used. When an audio-visual deposition is used during a hearing, a trial, or any other court proceeding, the party first using such audio-visual deposition in whole or in part shall assure the availability of the same or comparable audio-video playback equipment to any other party for such other party's use in further showing such audio-visual deposition during the hearing, the trial, or other court proceeding or at any rehearing, recess, or continuation thereof.

(j) Discrepancy Between Audio-Visual Recording and Stenographic Transcript. Upon the claim of a party that a discrepancy exists between the audio-visual recording and the stenographic transcript, the trial judge shall determine: (i) whether such discrepancy reasonably appears; and (ii) whether the relevant part of the audio-visual recording is intelligible. If the relevant part of the audio-visual recording is not intelligible, the stenographic transcript controls. If the relevant part of the audio-visual recording is intelligible and the trial judge rules that a discrepancy reasonably appears, the jury, in a jury action, shall determine from the audio-visual recording the deponent's testimony. The trial judge, in his discretion, may permit the jury to be aided in its determination by the stenographic transcript.

(k) Evidence by Audio-Visual Recording.

(1) *Authorization of Audio-Visual Testimony or Other Evidence.* Upon motion with notice and an opportunity to be heard, or by stipulation of all parties approved by the court, or upon the court's motion, the court may order, in the interest of justice and with due regard to the importance of presenting the testimony of witnesses orally in open court, that all or part of the testimony, and such other evidence as may be appropriate, may be presented at trial by audiovisual means. The provisions of Rule 30A shall govern such audio-visual recordings.

(2) *Introduction as Evidence.* Notwithstanding Rule 30A(i) or Rule 32(a)(3), but subject to rulings on objections pursuant to Rule 30A(k)(3), any party may introduce any such audio-visual recording, that has been authorized under Rule 30A(k)(1), at trial if the court finds its introduction to be in the interest of justice.

(3) *Objections.* Before such audio-visual recording is admitted at trial, the trial judge shall rule upon any objection to any portion thereof and the recording shall be edited to reflect the rulings. The objections shall be presented to the trial judge and the editing to reflect the rulings shall be accomplished, each in accordance with the provisions of Rule 30A(g).

(4) *Part of the Record; Not an Exhibit.* Any portion of the audio-visual recording so introduced shall be part of the record, and subject to the provisions of Rule 30A(h), but not an exhibit.

(l) Costs. The reasonable expense of recording, editing, and using an audio-visual deposition may be taxed as costs, pursuant to the provisions of Rule 54(e).

(m) Audio-Visual Depositions of Treating Physicians and Expert Witnesses for Use at Trial.

(1) *Authorization and Definitions.* Unless the court upon motion orders otherwise, any party intending to call a treating physician or expert witness at trial as that party's own witness may take the oral deposition of any such treating physician or expert witness by audio-visual means for the purpose of its being used as evidence at trial in lieu of oral testimony. Such depositions shall be known as "audio-visual expert witness depositions for trial." This rule 30A(m) does not apply to another party's treating physician or expert, discovery from whom is subject to the provisions of Rule 26(b)(4)(A) or 26(b)(4)(B). A "treating physician" is a physician who has provided medical treatment to a party or other person involved in the lawsuit, and who will be questioned about such treatment and matters related thereto. An "expert witness" is a person qualified as an expert by knowledge, skill, experience, training, or education to testify in the form of an opinion or otherwise.

(2) *Timing, Curriculum Vitae, and Report.* Except by leave of court, a notice for the taking of an audio-visual expert witness deposition for trial shall not be served (i) sooner than six (6)

2

months after the action has been commenced, and (ii) until thirty (30) days after a written report of that witness has been furnished to all parties. Such report shall contain a curriculum vitae of that witness, shall cover the subjects described in, Rule 26(b)(4)(A)(i) and, in the case of a treating physician, a description of the treatment and its costs. Any party may move for further discovery of that witness, to take place prior to the audio-visual expert witness deposition for trial, in accordance with Rule 26(b)(4)(A)(ii).

(3) *Notice; Opposition.* In addition to the requirements of rule 30A(b), every notice for the taking of an audio-visual expert witness deposition for trial shall state that it is to be recorded by audio-visual means with the purpose of its being used as evidence at trial in lieu of oral testimony. Any motion in opposition to the taking of an audio-visual expert witness deposition for trial must be filed within fourteen (14) days of receipt of the notice or on or before the specified time for taking of the audio-visual expert witness deposition for trial, if such time is less than fourteen (14) days from receipt of the notice. The audio-visual expert witness deposition shall not occur until the court rules on the motion opposing the deposition.

(4) *Ruling on Objections; Editing of Recording.* When an audio-visual expert witness deposition for trial is taken, all evidential objections shall, to the extent practicable, be made during the course of the deposition. If any party has made objections during the course of the audio-visual expert witness deposition for trial, or has any objections to such deposition which would otherwise be made at trial, pursuant to Rule 32(b), such objections shall be filed with the trial judge or a motion judge, if the trial judge has not yet been designated, no later than twenty-one (21) days before the commencement of the trial. Objections not so submitted shall be deemed waived, except to the extent that events at the trial, which could not have reasonably been foreseen by the objecting party, necessitate an objection at trial. The nonobjecting party shall file a response to the submissions by the objecting party within fourteen (14) days of the receipt of the objecting party's submissions. Failure to respond to an objection shall constitute a waiver with respect thereto. The party making the objection shall be responsible for providing the judge with a stenographic record of the deposition, unless it is already on file at the court, and, if the judge requests, with the audiovisual recording or an audio copy of the sound track. For the purpose of ruling on the objections, the judge may utilize the entire stenographic record, audiovisual recording, or audio recording, or those portions that are pertinent to the objections made. The judge shall rule on the objections prior to the commencement of trial or hearing and give notice to all parties of the rulings and instructions as to editing. The editing shall reflect the rulings of the judge and shall remove all references to the objections. The operator shall cause a copy of the audio-visual recording to be edited in accordance with the court's instructions. The operator shall then cause copies of the edited version thereof to be delivered to the parties who ordered them, and to the court, if so instructed by the court. The stenographic record, and the original audio-visual recording and the edited version thereof, if any, shall be preserved intact and unaltered.

(5) *Use at Trial.* Unless the court upon motion orders otherwise, an audio-visual expert witness deposition for trial may be used by any party for any purpose and under any circumstances in which a stenographic deposition may be used and, in addition, may be used at trial in lieu of oral testimony whether or not such witness is available to testify.

(6) *Applicability of Rule 30A(a)-(l).* Except as altered by Rule 30(A)(m), the provisions of rule 30A(a)-(l) shall apply to audio-visual expert witness depositions for trial.

Rule 31. Depositions of Witnesses Upon Written Questions

[Amended effective Mar. 1, 1989.]

(a) Serving Questions; Notice. After commencement of the action, any party may take the testimony of any person, including a party, by deposition upon written questions. The attendance of witnesses may be compelled by the use of subpoena as provided in Rule 45. The deposition of a person confined in prison may be taken only by leave of court on such terms as the court prescribes.

A party desiring to take a deposition upon written questions shall serve them upon every other party with a notice stating (1) the name and address of the person who is to answer them, if known, and if the name is not known, a general description sufficient to identify him or the particular class or group to which he belongs, and (2) the name or descriptive title and address of the officer before whom the deposition is to be taken. A deposition upon written questions may be taken of a public or private corporation or a partnership or association or governmental agency in accordance with the provisions of Rule 30(b)(6).

Within 30 days after the notice and written questions are served, a party may serve cross questions upon all other parties. Within 10 days after being served with cross questions, a party may serve redirect questions upon all other parties. Within 10 days after being served with redirect questions, a party may serve recross questions upon all other parties. The court may for cause shown enlarge or shorten the time.

(b) Officer to Take Responses and Prepare Record. A copy of the notice and copies of all questions served shall be delivered by the party taking the deposition to the officer designated in the notice, who shall proceed promptly, in the manner provided by Rule 30(c), (e), and (f), to take the testimony of the witness in response to the questions and to prepare, certify, and deliver or send the deposition to the party taking the deposition, attaching thereto the copy of the notice and questions received by him.

(c) Notice of Receipt. When the deposition is received the party taking it shall promptly give notice thereof to all other parties.

Rule 32. Use of Depositions in Court Proceedings

[Amended effective Jan. 1, 1982; July 1, 1984.]

(a) Use of Depositions. At the trial or upon the hearing of a motion or an interlocutory proceeding, any part or all of a deposition, so far as admissible under the rules of evidence applied as though the witness were then present and testifying, may be used against any party who was present or represented at the taking of the deposition or who had due notice thereof, in accordance with any one of the following provisions:

(1) Any deposition may be used by any party for the purpose of contradicting or impeaching the testimony of deponent as a witness.

(2) The deposition of a party or of any one who at the time of taking the deposition was an officer, director, or managing agent, or a person designated under Rule 30(b)(6) or 31(a) to testify on behalf of a public or private corporation, partnership or association or governmental agency which is a party may be used by an adverse party for any purpose.

(3) The deposition of a witness, whether or not a party, may be used by any party for any purpose if the court finds: (A) that the witness is dead; or (B) that the witness is out of the Commonwealth, unless it appears that the absence of the witness was procured by the party offering the deposition; or (C) that the witness is unable to attend or testify because of age, sickness, infirmity, or imprisonment; or (D) that the party offering the deposition has been unable to procure the attendance of the witness by subpoena; or (E) upon application and notice, that such exceptional circumstances exist as to make it desirable, in the interest of justice and with due regard to the importance of presenting the testimony of witnesses orally in open court, to allow the deposition to be used.

(4) If only part of a deposition is offered in evidence by a party, an adverse party may require him to introduce any other part which ought in fairness to be considered with the part introduced, and any party may introduce any other parts.

Substitution of parties pursuant to Rule 25 does not affect the right to use depositions previously taken; and when an action has been brought in any court of the United States or of any state and another action involving the same subject matter is afterward brought between the same parties or their representatives or successors in interest, all depositions lawfully taken and duly filed in the former action may be used in the latter as if originally taken therefor.

(b) Objections to Admissibility. Subject to the provisions of Rules 28(b) and subdivision (d)(3) of this rule, objection may be made at the trial or hearing to receiving in evidence any deposition or part thereof for any reason which would require the exclusion of the evidence if the witness were then present and testifying.

(c) Effect of Taking or Using Depositions. A party does not make a person his own witness for any purpose by taking his deposition. The introduction in evidence of the deposition or any part thereof for any purpose other than that of contradicting or impeaching the deponent makes the deponent the witness of the party introducing the deposition, but this shall not apply to the use by an adverse party of a deposition under subdivision (a)(2) of this rule. At the trial or hearing any party may rebut any relevant evidence contained in a deposition whether introduced by him or by any other party.

(d) Effect of Errors and Irregularities in Depositions.

(1) As to Notice. All errors and irregularities in the notice for taking a deposition are waived unless written objection is promptly served upon the party giving the notice.

(2) As to Disqualification of Officer. Objection to taking a deposition because of disqualification of the officer before whom it is to be taken is waived unless made before the taking of the deposition begins or as soon thereafter as the disqualification becomes known or could be discovered with reasonable diligence.

(3) As to Taking of Deposition.

(A) Objections to the competency of a witness or to the competency, relevancy, or materiality of testimony are not waived by failure to make them before or during the taking of the deposition, unless the ground of the objection is one which might have been obviated or removed if presented at that time.

(B) Errors and irregularities occurring at the oral examination in the manner of taking the deposition, in the form of the questions or answers, in the oath or affirmation, or in the conduct of parties, and errors of any kind which might be obviated, removed, or cured if promptly presented, are waived unless seasonable objection thereto is made at the taking of the deposition.

(C) Objections to the form of written questions submitted under Rule 31 are waived unless served in writing upon the party propounding them within the time allowed for serving the succeeding cross or other questions and within 5 days after service of the last questions authorized.

(4) As to Completion and Return of Deposition. Errors and irregularities in the manner in which the testimony is transcribed or the deposition is prepared, signed, certified, sealed, indorsed, transmitted, filed, or otherwise dealt with by the officer under Rules 30 and 31 are waived unless a motion to suppress the deposition or some part thereof is made with reasonable promptness after such defect is, or with due diligence might have been, ascertained.

Rule 33. Interrogatories to Parties

[Amended effective July 1, 1974; Jan. 1, 1976; Jan. 1, 1982; May 1, 2002; Aug. 1, 2009.]

(a) Availability: Procedures for Use.

(1) *In General.* Any party may serve upon any other party written interrogatories to be answered by the party served or, if the party served is a public or private corporation or a partnership or association or governmental agency, by any officer or agent, who shall furnish such information as is available to the party. Interrogatories may, without leave of court, be served upon the plaintiff after commencement of the action and upon any other party with or after service of the summons and complaint upon that party.

(2) *Number.* No party shall serve upon any other party as of right more than thirty interrogatories, including interrogatories subsidiary or incidental to, or dependent upon, other interrogatories, and however the same may be grouped or combined; but the interrogatories may be served in two or more sets, as long as the total number of interrogatories served does not exceed thirty. The court on motion for good cause shown may allow service of additional interrogatories; or the party interrogated, subject to Rule 29, may agree to such service. All interrogatories shall be numbered consecutively.

2

(3) *Answers; Final Request for Answers.* Each interrogatory shall be answered separately and fully in writing under the penalties of perjury, unless it is objected to, in which event the reasons for objection shall be stated in lieu of the answer; each answer or objection shall be preceded by the interrogatory to which it responds. The answers are to be signed by the person making them, the objections by the person or attorney making them. The party upon whom the interrogatories have been served shall serve answers and objections, if any, within 45 days after the service of the interrogatories. The court may, on motion with or without notice, specify a shorter or longer time. Unless otherwise specified, further answers to interrogatories shall be filed within 30 days of the entry of the order to answer further. The interrogating party may move for an order under Rule 37(a) with respect to any objection to or other failure to answer an interrogatory. Alternatively, for failure to serve timely answers or objections to interrogatories (or further answers, as the case may be), the interrogating party may serve a final request for answers, specifying the failure. The final request for answers shall state that the interrogating party may apply for final judgment for relief or dismissal pursuant to paragraph 4 in the event that answers or objections are not timely received. The party upon whom the interrogatories have been served shall serve the answers or objections either within 30 days from the date of service of the final request or prior to the filing of an application for a final judgment for relief or dismissal, whichever is later.

(4) *Application for Final Judgment; Affidavit.* In the event that answers or objections have not been received and after the expiration of 40 days from the date of service of the final request for answers, or such further time as the parties may agree upon in writing or the court may allow, the interrogating party may file a written application for entry of final judgment for relief or dismissal. The period of time set forth in the previous sentence shall be deemed to include the three day period allowed pursuant to Rule 6(d). The application must be accompanied by a copy of the final request for answers and an affidavit containing the following information:

a. the date and manner in which interrogatories were served on the party against whom relief is sought;

b. the fact that the 45-day time period for service of answers or objections has expired, and no answers have been received;

c. the date and manner in which the final request for answers was served;

d. the fact that the 40-day time period for answers or objections after a final request for answers has expired, and that no answers or objections have been received; and

e. that the party now applies for final judgment for relief or dismissal.

(5) *Motion to Extend.* The pendency of a motion to extend any time hereunder, unless the motion be assented to, or heard within 30 days of filing, shall not stay the entry of any judgment.

(6) *Entry of Judgment.* Upon receipt of the application for final judgment and only if accompanied by a copy of the final request for answers and by the required affidavit as set forth above, the clerk shall enter an appropriate judgment, subject to the provisions

of Rules 54(b), 54(c), 55(b)(1), 55(b)(2) (final sentence), 55(b)(4) and 55(c).

(b) Scope: Use at Trial. Interrogatories may relate to any matters which can be inquired into under Rule 26(b), and the answers may be used to the extent permitted by the rules of evidence.

An interrogatory otherwise proper is not necessarily objectionable merely because an answer to the interrogatory involves an opinion or contention that relates to fact or the application of law to fact, but the court may order that such an interrogatory need not be answered until after designated discovery has been completed, or until a pretrial conference, or other later time.

(c) Option to Produce Business Records. Where the answer to an interrogatory may be derived or ascertained from the business records of the party upon whom the interrogatory has been served or from an examination, audit or inspection of such business records, including a compilation, abstract or summary thereof, and the burden of deriving or ascertaining the answer is substantially the same for the party serving the interrogatory as for the party served, it is a sufficient answer to such interrogatory to specify the records from which the answer may be derived or ascertained and to afford to the party serving the interrogatory reasonable opportunity to examine, audit or inspect such records and to make copies, compilations, abstracts or summaries. A specification shall be in sufficient detail to permit the interrogating party to locate and to identify, as readily as can the party served, the records from which the answer may be ascertained.

Rule 34. Producing Documents, Electronically Stored Information, and Tangible Things, or Entering Onto Land, for Inspection and Other Purposes

[Amended effective Jan. 1, 1982; Jan. 1, 2014; Aug. 1, 2016.]

(a) **In General.** A party may serve on any other party a request within the scope of Rule 26(b):

(1) to produce and permit the requesting party or its representative to inspect, copy, test, or sample the following items in the responding party's possession, custody, or control:

(A) any designated documents or electronically stored information—including writings, drawings, graphs, charts, photographs, sound recordings, images and other data or data compilations—stored in any medium from which information can be obtained either directly or, if necessary, after translation by the responding party into a reasonably usable form; or

(B) any designated tangible things; or

(2) to permit entry onto designated land or other property possessed or controlled by the responding party, so that the requesting party may inspect, measure, survey, photograph, test, or sample the property or any designated object or operation on it.

(b) **Procedure.**

(1) *Contents of the Request.* The request may, without leave of court, be served upon the plaintiff after commencement of the action and upon any other party with or after service of the summons and complaint upon that party. The request shall set forth the items to be inspected either by individual item or by category, and describe each item and category with reasonable particularity. The request shall specify a reasonable time, place, and manner of making the inspection and performing the related acts, and it may specify the form in which electronically stored information is to be produced.

(2) *Responses and Objections.*

(A) In General. The party upon whom the request is served shall serve a written response within 30 days after the service of the request, except that a defendant may serve a response within 45 days after service of the summons and complaint upon that defendant. The court may allow a shorter or longer time. The response shall state, with respect to each item or category, that inspection and related activities will be permitted as requested, unless the request is objected to, in which event the reasons for objection shall be stated. If objection is made to part of an item or category, the part shall be specified. The party submitting the request may move for an order under Rule 37(a) with respect to any objection to or other failure to respond to the request or any part thereof, or any failure to permit inspection as requested.

(B) Responding to a request for production of electronically stored information. The response may state an objection to a requested form for producing electronically stored information. If the responding party objects to a requested form—or if no form was specified in the request—the party shall state the form or forms it intends to use.

(C) Producing the documents or electronically stored information. Unless otherwise stipulated or ordered by the court, these procedures apply to producing documents or electronically stored information:

(i) A party shall produce documents as they are kept in the usual course of business or shall organize and label them to correspond to the categories in the request;

(ii) The producing party may produce copies of the documents, including by electronic means, provided that, if requested, the producing party affords all parties a fair opportunity to verify the copies by comparison with the originals.

(iii) If a request does not specify a form for producing electronically stored information, a party shall produce it in a form or forms in which it is ordinarily maintained or in a reasonably usable form or forms; and

(iv) A party need not produce the same electronically stored information in more than one form.

(c) **Persons Not Parties.**

(1) This rule does not preclude an independent action against a person not a party for production of documents and things and permission to enter upon land.

(2) As provided in Rule 45, a nonparty may be compelled to produce documents and tangible things or to permit an inspection.

Reporter's Notes (2016). Rule 34 was amended in 2016 to recognize the common practice of producing copies of documents rather than permitting inspection of the originals (Rule 34(b)(2)(C)(ii)). This amendment reflects a similar amendment to the Federal Rules of Civil Procedure effective in 2015.

The 2016 amendment further states that upon request, the producing party shall provide "all parties a fair opportunity to verify the copies by comparison with the originals." This language, which is not part of the Federal Rules, reinforces the requesting party's right to inspect the original documents under the existing language of Rule 34(a). To the extent that producing the original is deemed unduly burdensome or expensive, the producing party may seek a protective order under Rule 26(c). Such an order may restrict access to the original document, or may allow access upon payment of costs associated with production of the original. Rule 34(c) was also amended to add a cross-reference to Rule 45 (Rule 34(c)(2)). Rule 45 had been amended in 2015 to allow a "documents only" subpoena against a nonparty (Rule 45(d)).

Reporter's Notes (2014). The 2014 amendments to Rule 34 were part of a series of amendments concerning discovery of electronically stored information. For background, see the 2014 Reporter's Notes to Rule 26.

The title to Rule 34 has been changed to add a reference to "electronically stored information." The title to Rule 34 is now consistent with the title to Rule 34 of the Federal Rules of Civil Procedure.

The 2014 amendments made some stylistic changes in Rule 34(a) so as to conform the rule to the format set forth in Rule 34(a) of the Federal Rules of Civil Procedure. In addition, the phrase "or electronically stored information" has been added to Rule 34(a)(1)(A), also in conformity with the cognate federal rule.

Formatting and stylistic changes have been made in Rule 34(b), again modeled after Rule 34(b) of the Federal Rules of Civil Procedure, but no substantive changes were intended. Language has been added to Rule 34(b)(1) to the effect that a request for production "may specify the form in which electronically stored information is to be produced."

Rule 34(b)(2)(B) and (C), modeled after Federal Rule 34(b)(2)(D) and (E), have been added to deal with responding to a request for production of electronically stored information and the important aspect of the form for producing such information.

Issues surrounding the production of electronically stored information, including the format for production, should be discussed by the parties in their conference regarding electronically stored information, if there is one. See Rule 26(f)(2).

Rule 35. Physical and Mental Examination of Persons

(a) Order for Examination. When the mental or physical condition (including the blood group) of a party, or of a person in the custody or under the legal control of a party, is in controversy, the court in which the action is pending may order the party to submit to a physical or mental examination by a physician or to produce for examination the person in his custody or legal control. The order may be made only on motion for good cause shown and upon notice to the person to be examined and to all parties and shall specify the time, place, manner, conditions, and scope of the examination and the person or persons by whom it is to be made.

(b) Report of Examining Physician.

(1) If requested by the party against whom an order is made under Rule 35(a) or the person examined, the party causing the examination to be made shall deliver to him a copy of a detailed written report of the examining physician setting out his findings, including results of all tests made, diagnoses and conclusions, together with like reports of all earlier examinations of the same condition. After delivery the party causing the examination shall be entitled upon request to receive from the party against whom the order is made a like report of any examination, previously or thereafter made, of the same condition, unless, in the case of a report of examination of a person not a party, the party shows that he is unable to obtain it. The court on motion may make an order against a party requiring delivery of a report on such terms as are just, and if a physician fails or refuses to make a report the court may exclude his testimony if offered at the trial.

(2) By requesting and obtaining a report of the examination so ordered or by taking the deposition of the examiner, the party examined waives any privilege he may have in that action or any other involving the same controversy, regarding the testimony of every other person who has examined or may thereafter examine him in respect of the same mental or physical condition; but he does not otherwise waive his right to object at the trial to the introduction into evidence of the report or any part thereof.

(3) This subdivision applies to examinations made by agreement of the parties, unless the agreement expressly provides otherwise. This subdivision does not preclude discovery of a report of an examining physician or the taking of a deposition of the physician in accordance with the provisions of any other rule.

Rule 36. Requests for Admission

(a) Request for Admission. A party may serve upon any other party a written request for admission, for purposes of the pending action, only, of the truth of any matters within the scope of Rule 26(b) set forth in the request that relate to statements or opinions of fact or of the application of law to fact, including the genuineness of any documents described in the request. Copies of documents shall be served with the request unless they have been or are otherwise furnished or made available for inspection and copying. The request may, without leave of court, be served upon the plaintiff after commencement of the action and upon any other party with or after service of the summons and complaint upon that party.

Each matter of which an admission is requested shall be separately set forth. The matter is admitted unless, within 30 days after service of the request, or within such shorter or longer time as the court may allow, the party to whom the request is directed serves upon the party requesting the admission either (1) a written statement signed by the party under the penalties of perjury specifically (i) denying the matter or (ii) setting forth in detail why the answering party cannot truthfully admit or deny the matter; or (2) a written objection addressed to the matter, signed by the party or his attorney, but, unless the court shortens the time, a defendant shall not be required to serve answers or objections before the expiration of 45 days after service of the summons and complaint upon him. If objection is made, the reasons therefor shall be stated. A denial shall fairly meet the substance of the requested admission, and when good faith requires that a party qualify his answer or deny only a part of the matter of which an admission is requested, he shall specify so much of it as is true and qualify or deny the remainder. An answering party may not give lack of information or knowledge as a reason for failure to admit or deny unless he states that he has made reasonable inquiry and that the information known or readily obtainable by him is insufficient to enable him to admit or deny. A party who considers that a matter of which an admission has been requested presents a genuine issue for trial may not, on that ground alone, object to the request; he may, subject to the provisions of Rule 37(c), deny the matter or set forth reasons why he cannot admit or deny it. Each admission, denial, objection, or statement shall be preceded by the request to which it responds.

The party who has requested the admissions may move to determine the sufficiency of the answers or objections. Unless the court determines that an objection is justified, it shall order that an answer be served. If the court determines that an answer does not comply with the requirements of this rule, it may order either that the matter is admitted or that an amended answer be served. The court may, in lieu of these orders, determine that final disposition of the request be made at a pre-trial conference or at a designated time prior to trial. The provisions of Rule 37(a)(4) apply to the award of expenses incurred in relation to the motion.

(b) Effect of Admission. Any matter admitted under this rule is conclusively established unless the court on motion permits withdrawal or amendment of the admission. Subject to the provisions of Rule 16 governing amendment of a pre-trial order, the court may permit withdrawal or amendment when the presentation of the merits of the action will be subserved thereby and the party who obtained the admission fails to satisfy the court that withdrawal or amendment will prejudice him in maintaining his action or defense on the merits. Any admission made by a party under this rule is for the purpose of the pending action only and is not an admission by him for any other purpose nor may it be used against him in any other proceeding.

Rule 37. Failure to Make Discovery: Sanctions

[Amended effective July 1, 1974; Jan. 1, 1984; May 1, 1984; July 1, 1996; Jan. 1, 2014.]

(a) Motion for Order Compelling Discovery. Upon reasonable notice to other parties and all persons affected thereby, a party may apply for an order compelling discovery as follows:

(1) *Appropriate Court.* An application for an order to a party may be made to the court in which the action is pending, or on matters relating to a deposition, to the court in the county or judicial district, as the case may be, where the deposition is being taken. An application for an order to a deponent who is not a party shall be made to the court in the county or judicial district, as the case may be, where the deposition is being taken.

(2) *Motion.* If a deponent fails to answer a question propounded or submitted under Rules 30 or 31, or a corporation or other entity fails to make a designation under Rule 30(b)(6) or 31(a), or a party fails to answer an interrogatory submitted under Rule 33, or if a party, in response to a request for inspection submitted under Rule 34, fails to respond that inspection will be permitted as requested or fails to permit inspection as requested, the discovering party may move for an order compelling an answer or a designation or an order compelling inspection in accordance with the request. When taking a deposition on oral examination, the proponent of the question may complete or adjourn the examination before he applies for an order. If the court denies the motion in

2

whole or in part, it may make such protective order as it would have been empowered to make on a motion made pursuant to Rule 26(c).

(3) *Evasive or Incomplete Answer.* For purposes of this subdivision an evasive or incomplete answer is to be treated as a failure to answer.

(4) *Award of Expenses of Motion.* If the motion is granted, the court may, after opportunity for hearing, require the party or deponent whose conduct necessitated the motion or the party or attorney advising such conduct or both of them to pay to the moving party the reasonable expenses incurred in obtaining the order, including attorney's fees, unless the court finds that the opposition to the motion was substantially justified or that other circumstances make an award of expenses unjust.

If the motion is denied, the court may, after opportunity for hearing, require the moving party or the attorney advising the motion or both of them to pay to the party or deponent who opposed the motion the reasonable expenses incurred in opposing the motion, including attorney's fees, unless the court finds that the making of the motion was substantially justified or that other circumstances make an award of expenses unjust.

If the motion is granted in part and denied in part, the court may apportion the reasonable expenses incurred in relation to the motion among the parties and persons in a just manner.

(b) Failure to Comply With Order.

(1) *Sanctions by Court in County or District Where Deposition is Taken.* If a deponent fails to be sworn or to answer a question after being directed to do so by the court in the county or judicial district, as the case may be, in which the deposition is being taken, the failure may be considered a contempt of that court.

(2) *Sanctions by Court in Which Action is Pending.* If a party or an officer, director, or managing agent of a party or a person designated under Rule 30(b)(6) or 31(a) to testify on behalf of a party fails to obey an order to provide or permit discovery, including an order made under subdivision (a) of this rule or Rule 35, the court in which the action is pending may make such orders in regard to the failure as are just, and among others the following:

(A) An order that the matters regarding which the order was made or any other designated facts shall be taken to be established for the purposes of the action in accordance with the claim of the party obtaining the order;

(B) An order refusing to allow the disobedient party to support or oppose designated claims or defenses, or prohibiting him from introducing designated matters in evidence;

(C) An order striking out pleadings or parts thereof, or staying further proceedings until the order is obeyed, or dismissing the action or proceeding or any part thereof, or rendering a judgment by default against the disobedient party;

(D) In lieu of any of the foregoing orders or in addition thereto, an order treating as a contempt of court the failure to obey any orders except an order to submit to a physical or mental examination;

(E) Where a party has failed to comply with an order under Rule 35(a) requiring him to produce another for examination, such orders as are listed in paragraphs (A), (B), and (C) of this subdivision, unless the party failing to comply shows that he is unable to produce such person for examination.

In lieu of any of the foregoing orders or in addition thereto, the court may require the party failing to obey the order or the attorney advising him or both to pay the reasonable expenses, including attorney's fees, caused by the failure.

(c) Expenses on Failure to Admit. If a party fails to admit the genuineness of any documents or the truth of any matters as requested under Rule 36, and if the party requesting the admissions thereafter proves the genuineness of the document or the truth of the matter, he may apply to the court for an order requiring the other party to pay him the reasonable expenses incurred in making that proof, including reasonable attorney's fees. The court shall make the order unless it finds that (1) the request was held objectionable pursuant to Rule 36(a), or (2) the admission sought was of no substantial importance, or (3) the party failing to admit had reasonable grounds to believe that he might prevail on the matter, or (4) there was other good reason for the failure to admit.

(d) Failure of Party to Attend at Own Deposition or Serve Answers to Interrogatories or Respond to Request for Inspection. If a party or an officer, director, or a managing agent of a party or a person designated under Rule 30(b)(6) or 31(a) to testify on behalf of a party willfully fails (1) to appear before the officer who is to take his deposition, after being served with a proper notice, or (2) to serve answers or objections to interrogatories submitted under Rule 33, after proper service of the interrogatories, or (3) to serve a written response to a request for inspection submitted under Rule 34, after proper service of the request, the court in which the action is pending on motion may make such orders in regard to the failure as are just, and among others it may take any action authorized under paragraphs (A), (B), and (C) of subdivision (b)(2) of this rule. In lieu of any order or in addition thereto, the court may require the party failing to act or the attorney advising him or both to pay the reasonable expenses, including attorney's fees, caused by the failure.

The failure to act described in this subdivision may not be excused on the ground that the discovery sought is objectionable unless the party failing to act has applied for a protective order as provided by Rule 26(c).

(e) Expenses Against Commonwealth. Except to the extent permitted by statute, expenses and fees may not be awarded against the Commonwealth under this rule.

(f) Failure to Provide Electronically Stored Information. Absent exceptional circumstances, a court may not impose sanctions on a party for failing to produce electronically stored information lost as a result of the routine, good-faith operation of an electronic information system.

Reporter's Notes (2014). The 2014 amendments to Rule 37 were part of a series of amendments concerning discovery of electronically stored information. For background, see the 2014 Reporter's Notes to Rule 26.

These amendments added section (f) to Rule 37. This section establishes a "safe harbor" provision that will preclude imposition of sanctions where electronically stored information "is lost as a result of the routine, good-faith operation of an electronic information system." It is taken from Rule 37(e) of the Federal Rules of Civil Procedure and Rule 5 of the Uniform Rules Relating to the Discovery of Electronically Stored Information.

The 2014 amendment to Rule 37, as well as the other amendments to the discovery rules regarding electronically stored information, was not intended to change any existing law in Massachusetts on the obligation to preserve evidence when litigation is reasonably anticipated or has commenced. A duty to preserve may exist as a matter of common law, statutory law, or by reason of a court order.

The following comment from the 2006 Advisory Committee Notes to Federal Rule 37 is equally applicable in Massachusetts:

> The good faith requirement of Rule 37(f) means that a party is not permitted to exploit the routine operation of an information system to thwart discovery obligations by allowing that operation to continue in order to destroy specific stored information that it is required to preserve. When a party is under a duty to preserve information because of pending or reasonably anticipated litigation, intervention in the routine operation of an information system is one aspect of what is often called a "litigation hold."

Rule 52. Findings by the Court

[Amended effective July 1, 1996; Mar. 1, 2008.]

(a) Courts Other Than District Court: Effect. In all actions tried upon the facts without a jury, the court shall find the facts specially and state separately its conclusions of law thereon, and judgment shall be entered pursuant to Rule 58. Requests for findings are not necessary for purposes of review. Findings of fact shall not be set aside unless clearly erroneous, and due regard shall be given to the opportunity of the trial court to judge of the credibility of the witnesses. The findings of a master, to the extent that the court adopts them, shall be considered as the findings of the court. If an opinion or memorandum of decision is filed, it will be sufficient if the findings of fact and conclusions of law appear therein. Findings of fact and conclusions of law are unnecessary on decisions of motions under Rules 12 or 56 or any other motion except as provided in Rule 41(b)(2).

(b) Courts Other Than District Court: Amendment. Upon motion of a party made not later than 10 days after entry of judgment the court may amend its findings or make additional findings and may amend the judgment accordingly. The motion may be made with a motion for a new trial pursuant to Rule 59. When findings of fact are made in actions tried by the court without a jury, the question of the sufficiency of the evidence to support the findings may thereafter be raised whether or not the party raising the question has made in the trial court an objection to such findings or has made a motion to amend them or a motion for judgment.

(c) District Court: Effect. In all actions tried upon the facts without a jury, except as otherwise provided in Rule 65.3, the court shall find the facts specially and state separately its conclusions of law thereon, provided that any party submits before the beginning of any closing arguments proposed findings of fact and rulings of law. Upon request made before the beginning of any closing arguments, such party shall have the right to submit supplemental proposed findings of fact and rulings of law within three days. Each proposed finding of fact and ruling of law should be set forth concisely in a separately numbered paragraph covering one subject. Judgment shall be entered pursuant to Rule 58. Findings of fact shall not be set aside unless clearly erroneous, and due regard shall be given to the opportunity of the trial court to judge the credibility of the witnesses. If an opinion or memorandum of decision is filed, it will be sufficient if the findings of fact and conclusions of law appear therein. Findings of fact and conclusions of law are unnecessary on decisions of motions under Rules 12 or 56 or any other motion except as provided in Rule 41(b)(2).

(d) District Court: Amendment. Upon motion of a party made not later than 10 days after entry of judgment, or upon its own initiative not later than 10 days after entry of judgment, the court may amend its findings, if any, or make additional findings and may amend the judgment accordingly. The motion may be made with a motion for a new trial pursuant to Rule 59.

Rule 59. New Trials: Amendment of Judgments

(a) Grounds. A new trial may be granted to all or any of the parties and on all or part of the issues (1) in an action in which there has been a trial by jury, for any of the reasons for which new trials have heretofore been granted in actions at law in the courts of the Commonwealth; and (2) in an action tried without a jury, for any of the reasons for which rehearings have heretofore been granted in suits in equity in the courts of the Commonwealth. A new trial shall not be granted solely on the ground that the damages are excessive until the prevailing party has first been given an opportunity to remit so much thereof as the court adjudges is excessive. A new trial shall not be granted solely on the ground that the damages are inadequate until the defendant has first been given an opportunity to accept an addition to the verdict of such amount as the court adjudges reasonable. On a motion for a new trial in an action tried without a jury, the court may open the judgment if one has been entered, take additional testimony, amend findings of fact and conclusions of law or make new findings and conclusions, and direct the entry of a new judgment.

(b) Time for Motion. A motion for a new trial shall be served not later than 10 days after the entry of judgment.

(c) Time for Serving Affidavits. When a motion for new trial is based upon affidavits they shall be served with the motion. The opposing party has 10 days after such service within which to serve opposing affidavits, which period may be extended for an additional period not exceeding 20 days either by the court for good cause shown or by the parties by written stipulation. The court may permit reply affidavits.

(d) On Initiative of Court. Not later than 10 days after entry of judgment the court of its own initiative may order a new trial for any reason for which it might have granted a new trial on motion of a party. After giving the parties notice and an opportunity to be heard on the matter, the court may grant a motion for a new trial, timely served, for a reason not stated in the motion. In either case, the court shall specify in the order the grounds therefor.

(e) Motion to Alter or Amend a Judgment. A motion to alter or amend the judgment shall be served not later than 10 days after entry of the judgment.

Rule 60. Relief from Judgment or Order

(a) Clerical Mistakes. Clerical mistakes in judgments, orders or other parts of the record and errors therein arising from oversight or omission may be corrected by the court at any time of its own initiative or on the motion of any party and after such notice, if any, as the court orders. During the pendency of an appeal, such mistakes may be so corrected before the appeal is docketed in the appellate court, and thereafter while the appeal is pending may be so corrected with leave of the appellate court.

(b) Mistake; Inadvertence; Excusable Neglect; Newly Discovered Evidence; Fraud, etc. On motion and upon such terms as are just, the court may relieve a party or his legal representative from a final judgment, order, or proceeding for the following reasons: (1) mistake, inadvertence, surprise, or excusable neglect; (2) newly discovered evidence which by due diligence could not have been discovered in time to move for a new trial under Rule 59(b); (3) fraud (whether heretofore denominated intrinsic or extrinsic), misrepresentation, or other misconduct of an adverse party; (4) the judgment is void; (5) the judgment has been satisfied, released, or discharged, or a prior judgment upon which it is based has been reversed or otherwise vacated, or it is no longer equitable that the judgment should have prospective application; or (6) any other reason justifying relief from the operation of the judgment. The motion shall be made within a reasonable time, and for reasons (1), (2), and (3) not more than one year after the judgment, order or proceeding was entered or taken. A motion under this subdivision (b) does not affect the finality of a judgment or suspend its operation. This rule does not limit the power of a court to entertain an independent action to relieve a party from a judgment, order, or proceeding, or to set aside a judgment for fraud upon the court. Writs of review, of error, of audita querela, and petitions to vacate judgment are abolished, and the procedure for obtaining any relief from a judgment shall be by motion as prescribed in these rules or by an independent action.

Reporter's Notes (2013). The 1973 Reporter's Notes to Rule 60, second paragraph state in part: ". . . [B]ecause a Rule 60(b) motion does not affect the finality of the judgment, it does not toll the time for taking an appeal." In 2013, however, an amendment to Rule 4(a) of the Massachusetts Rules of Appellate Procedure provided that a Rule 60 motion, if served within ten days after entry of judgment, tolls the time period to claim an appeal.

The 2013 amendment to Mass. R.A.P. 4(a) was intended to address the confusion that sometimes arose when a post-judgment motion, denominated a motion for "reconsideration," was served within ten days after entry of judgment. Since the text of the Massachusetts Rules of Civil Procedure does not refer to motions for reconsideration, a motion for reconsideration, if served within ten days of judgment, could have been treated as a motion under Rule 59 (for new trial or to alter or amend judgment) or as a motion under Rule 60(b) (for relief from judgment). If treated as a Rule 59 motion, the motion for reconsideration would have operated to toll the time period to claim an appeal. If treated as a Rule 60(b) motion, the motion for reconsideration would not have served to toll the time period to claim an appeal. Mass. R.A.P. 4(a), as it existed prior to the 2013 amendment. The 2013 amendment to Mass. R.A.P. 4(a) eliminates this potential for confusion by tolling the time period to claim an appeal where a post-judgment motion for reconsideration is served within ten days after entry of judgment.

See 2013 Reporter's Notes to Mass. R.A.P. 4(a).

Rule 61. Harmless Error

No error in either the admission or the exclusion of evidence and no error or defect in any ruling or order or in anything done or omitted by the court or by any of the parties is ground for granting a new trial or for setting aside a verdict or for vacating, modifying or otherwise disturbing a judgment or order, unless refusal to take such action appears to the court inconsistent with substantial justice. The court at every stage of the proceeding must disregard any error or defect in the proceeding which does not affect the substantial rights of the parties.

Massachusetts Supreme Judicial Court

Selected Rules of the Supreme Judicial Court

Chapter One: General Rules

Rule 1:07. Fee Generating Appointments and the Maintenance of Appointment Dockets in All Courts

[Pursuant to an order dated Mar. 28, 2000, the effective date of this rule for the Land Court Department is June 5, 2000. Pursuant to orders dated Mar. 28, 2000, and June 28, 2000, the effective date of this rule for the Probate and Family Court Department is July 3, 2000, for Categories A through C; Dec. 4, 2000, for Categories D through H; and May 7, 2001, for Categories I through BB.]
[Amended effective Jan. 1, 1989; July 1, 1999; Apr. 3, 2000.]

NOTE See List of Categories supplied by the Supreme Judicial Court for fiscal year 2019 following Rule 1:07.

Preamble. The Justices understand the importance of allowing judges the flexibility of selecting appointees based on the particular expertise needed in a given case. In recognition of the necessity to safeguard judicial discretion, a waiver from the requirement of successive appointments has been included in Rule 1:07. In making an appointment, a judge may select a qualified person who is not on the list or who is not next in order on the list by making a brief notation of the reasons for the selection.

The goal of this rule is to assure that all fee-generating appointments made by the courts of the Commonwealth are made on a fair and impartial basis with equal opportunity and access for all qualified candidates for appointments. The Justices have concluded that the fairest way to accomplish this goal, and at the same time avoid favoritism or the appearance of favoritism, is by requiring each court to create lists of qualified candidates and then generally make appointments from those lists in rotation or sequential order.

(1) Annual Publication. At the beginning of each fiscal year, the chief justice of each Trial Court department and the chief justices of the appellate courts shall submit to the Chief Justice for Administration and Management (CJAM) a listing of the types of fee-generating appointments made in their department or court and the qualifications for those appointments. The CJAM shall compile the listings into a unified report which shall be published annually by the CJAM. The report shall include a description of the educational, professional, and other qualifications required for each type of appointment. The report shall state the method by which a person may apply to be considered for each particular type of appointment. It shall also include a statement that appointments of counsel for indigent defendants in criminal matters and for parties in certain non-criminal matters are governed by the Committee for Public Counsel Services (CPCS). An address and telephone number for interested persons to receive information on CPCS appointments shall be included in the report. This annual publication shall be accompanied by a statement from the Supreme Judicial Court that the appointments in the report are open to all qualified persons without regard to race, sex, religion, national origin, disability, age, sexual orientation or socioeconomic status.

(2) Court Lists. Every individual court making fee-generating appointments shall maintain a list of persons eligible for each type of appointment made by the court. The list shall be generated by the court or, where applicable, by CPCS. All court-generated lists shall be open to all qualified candidates and shall not be restricted to a fixed number of candidates. The method for removing individuals from a list shall be the responsibility of

CPCS, in the case of CPCS-generated lists, and of the CJAM, in the case of court-generated lists. The lists shall be public.

(3) Successive Appointments. Each court appointment shall be made from the list maintained pursuant to section (2) of this rule, except as otherwise provided in section (4). Appointments from the list shall be made successively, except that, if an appointment is not made in successive order, the judge (or other person) making the appointment shall provide a brief written statement of reasons for not following the order of the list. For appointees compensated by CPCS, such written statement shall be kept by the Clerk, Register or Recorder in a separate file marked "CPCS appointments." A judge may direct that an appointment made successively from the list be entered administratively by the clerk, register, or recorder.

(4) Persons Not On List. If a judge appoints a person not on the list maintained pursuant to section (2), the judge (or other person) making the appointment shall provide a brief written statement of reasons for not appointing from the list.

(5) Appointment Docket. All clerks, registers, and recorders, for trial and appellate courts, shall establish and maintain, currently indexed, as part of the public records of the court open during regular business hours to public inspection, an appointment docket with respect to the appointment by the court of each fee-generating appointment, excluding appointees compensated by CPCS. The appointment dockets shall include the following:

(a) guardian ad litem,

(b) investigator appointed pursuant to G.L. c. 208, § 16,

(c) appraiser in any estate estimated to have gross assets in excess of $100,000,

(d) commissioner to sell real estate,

(e) appellate court conference counsel,

(f) master or special master,

(g) counsel in any civil matter,

(h) monitor for the administration of antipsychotic medications,

(i) investigator in care and protection proceedings,

(j) title examiner,

(k) administrator, trustee, guardian, conservator, or receiver, whose appointment was not prayed for by name in a petition, pleading, or written motion, and any guardian or conservator who is an attorney, social worker or other social service professional unrelated to the ward by blood or marriage,

(l) any other fee-generating appointment not compensated by CPCS and not otherwise excluded by this section. The appointment of a guardian ad litem to serve process under G.L. c. 215, § 56B, shall not be entered on the appointment docket. The appointment of an executor, administrator, trustee, guardian, conservator or receiver shall not be entered on the appointment docket except as required by section (5)(k). Appointments shall be entered on the appointment docket regardless of the anticipated source, if any, of payment to the appointee.

(6) Data Collection. Such docket shall contain at a minimum the following:

(a) the docket number and, if the case file is available for public inspection or if access to the information is not otherwise prohibited, the name of the case,

(b) the date of the appointment,

(c) the name of the appointee,

(d) the position to which appointed,

(e) by whom the appointment was made,

(f) a notation if the appointment was not made successively from the court's list or if the appointee was a person not on the list, and

(g) the amount of any payment received and the source thereof (party, estate, or Commonwealth) or whether payment was waived or declined.

(7) Payments. No payment shall be made or received on account of any appointment required to be recorded in the appointment docket until a statement under the penalties of perjury, certifying the services provided, amount of payment, and itemization of expenses, is filed with the clerk, register, or recorder, to be placed with the papers in the case. No person holding an appointment required to be recorded in the appointment docket under section (5) of this rule shall make any payment to himself or herself until such payment is approved by the court.

(8) Compliance. Each appointment made under this rule shall include language on the document of appointment itself that section (7) of this rule must be complied with. After July 1, 2000, no person whose appointment is subject to this rule shall accept reappointment unless he or she has filed a certification that all fee reports for payments received in the previous fiscal year have been filed.

(9) Implementation. The CJAM shall promulgate, subject to the approval of the Supreme Judicial Court, such uniform practices as are necessary to implement this rule.

(10) Alternative Dispute Resolution Exclusion. The provisions of this rule are not applicable to fee-generating appointments made pursuant to Rule 1:18, Uniform Rules on Dispute Resolution.

Fee Generating Categories
Probate and Family Court Department
Fiscal Year 2019
(Available at http://www.mass.gov/courts/docs/feegen.pdf)

A **Counsel in Mental Health Cases**
Substituted Judgment and *Rogers* cases
G.L. c. 190B, § 5-306A(a)
Counsel for incapacitated person or person to be protected, if above age of minority
G.L. c. 190B, §§ 5-106(a), 5-309(g)
Council for principal in health care proxy proceedings
G.L. c. 201D, §§ 6, 17
Counsel for elderly person in protective services action
G.L. c. 19A, § 20
Counsel for disabled person in protective services action
G.L. c. 19C, § 7

B **Counsel for ward, minor incapacitated person or minor person to be protected**
G.L. c. 190B, § 5-106(a)

BP **Counsel for parent in petition to appoint guardian of minor, petition for removal of guardian of minor, petition for parental access in guardianship of minor proceeding**
G.L. c. 190, § 5, Part 2
Guardianship of V.V., 470 Mass. 590, 592 (2015)
L.B. v. Chief Justice of the Probate and Family Court Department, 474 Mass. 231, 242 (2016)
Counsel for guardian in petition for removal of guardian of minor
Guardianship of K.N., 475 Mass. 762 (2017)

C **Counsel for child or parent**
G.L. c. 119, §§ 23(a)(1), 23(a)(3), 29, 29B
G.L. c. 210, § 3
Dept. of Public Welfare v. J.K.B., 379 Mass. 1 (1979); *Balboni v. Balboni*, 39 Mass. App. Ct. 210 (1995)
Counsel for child or parent in contested, private adoption
G.L. c. 210, § 6 cases *Adoption of Meaghan*, 461 Mass. 1006 (2012)

D **Guardian ad litem or next friend**
For minor, protected person, incapacitated person or person not ascertained or not in being, in a formal proceeding involving trusts or estates of decedents, minors, protected persons, or incapacitated persons, and in judicial supervised settlements, G.L. c. 190B, § 1-404(a)

2

Guardian ad litem—Notice
For spouse, heir at law or devisee who is an incapacitated or protected person or a minor, in a probate or appointment proceeding, unless the spouse, heir or devisee is under conservatorship or, if not under conservatorship, is under guardianship by someone other than the petitioner or is represented by someone other than the petitioner, G.L. c. 190B, § 1-404(d), G.L. c. 203A, § 3
Guardian ad litem—Account,
G.L. c. 190B, § 5-418(d)
Guardian ad litem—Trust,
G.L. c. 203E, § 305
Trustee, G.L. c. 203, § 4; G.L. c. 203E, § 414(b), § 704(c)(3), § 704(d)
Trustee for animal trust, G.L. c. 203E, § 408(e)
Person to enforce animal trust, G.L. c. 203E, § 408(f)
Person to enforce non-charitable trust without ascertainable beneficiary,
G.L. c. 203E, § 409(2)

E **Guardian ad litem**
Evaluator—custody/parenting time/adoption issue G.L. c. 215, § 56A

F **Guardian ad litem**
Investigator—domestic relations or custody/parenting time/adoption case, G.L. c. 215, § 56A
Guardian ad litem or next friend G.L. c. 190B, §§ 1-404, 5-106(b)
For attorneys only:
Guardian for incompetent divorce defendant, G.L. c. 208, § 15
Counsel
In divorce action to investigate or to investigate and defend, G.L. c. 208, § 16
Guardian ad litem
To commence contempt action, G.L. c. 215, § 56B
Guardian ad litem/next friend
To exercise or waive privileges in nonstate intervention cases

G **Guardian ad litem/next friend**
For actions involving state intervention pursuant to G.L. c. 119, § 29 or G.L. c. 210, § 3
To exercise or waive privileges—*Adoption of Diane*, 400 Mass. 196 (1987); G.L. c. 112, § 135B; G.L. c. 233, § 20B
For a minor parent signing an adoption surrender—*Adoption of Thomas*, 408 Mass. 446 (1990)

H **Monitor of treatment process**
G.L. c. 190B, § 5-306A(b)

I **Guardian ad litem for elderly or disabled person in protective services action**
Counsel for non-indigent elderly or disabled person in protective services action
For elderly person in protective services action, G.L. c. 19A, § 20
For disabled person in protective services action, G.L. c. 19C, § 7

J **Guardian ad litem/next friend**
Interest in real property, G.L. c. 190B, § 1-404
Alienation of land, G.L. c. 183, § 50
Partition of land, G.L. c. 241, § 9
Commissioner
Partition of land, G.L. c. 241, § 12

K **Guardian ad litem**
To investigate condition of incapacitated person or person to be protected, G.L. c. 190B, § 5-106(b)

L **Guardian ad litem**
To investigate condition of ward, G.L. c. 190B, § 5-106(b)

M **Guardian ad litem**
Temporary Guardianship—withholding medical treatment *Matter of Spring*, 380 Mass. 629 (1980),
G.L. c. 190B, §§ 5-306A, 5-308

N **Guardian ad litem**
Child Performers, G.L. c. 231, § 85P½(d)(4)

O **Physician, Certified Psychiatric Nurse Clinical Specialist or Licensed Psychologist**
Expert in mental illness, Mass. R. Civ. P. 35, Mass. R. Dom. Rel. P. 35
G.L. c. 190B, § 5-303(e)

P **Guardian of Minor**
G.L. c. 190B, §§ 5-201, 5-204, 5-207

Q **Guardian**
For an incapacitated person, G.L. c. 190B, §§ 5-305, 5-308

R **Conservator**
G.L. c. 190B, §§ 5-407, 5-409, 5-412A
Receiver for absentee's property
G.L. c. 200, § 5

S **Master**
Mass. R. Civ. P. 53; Mass. R. Dom. Rel. P. 53; G.L. c. 221, § 57

T **Special Master**
To perform specific acts—Mass. R. Civ. P. 70, Mass. R. Dom. Rel. P. 70

U **Discovery Master**
Mass. R. Dom. Rel. P. 26(j)

V **Parenting Coordinator**

W **Counsel**
For defendant in criminal contempt action, G.L. c. 211D, § 6(b)(ii)

X **Counsel**
(Military Attorney) for person in armed forces, Servicemembers Civil Relief Act, 50 U.S.C. Apps. § 501 et seq. *United States v. Henagan*, 552 F. Supp. 350 (M.D. Ala. N.D. 1982)

Y **Special Process Server**
G.L. c. 215, § 34A

Z **Stenographer**
Supplemental Probate and Family Court Rule 18

AA **Visitation Supervisor**

BB **Transcriber**

Rule 1:15. Impoundment Procedure

[Applicable to the Supreme Judicial Court and Appeals Court. Adopted effective Jan. 1, 1988. Amended effective Oct. 1, 2015.]

Section 1. Requests for Impoundment in the First Instance.

(a) Supreme Judicial Court.

(i) As used herein, "impoundment" shall mean the act of keeping some or all of the papers, documents, or exhibits, or portions thereof, in a case separate and unavailable for public inspection.

(ii) Requests for impoundment in proceedings in the Supreme Judicial Court shall be made by written motion describing with particularity the information sought to be impounded and the period of time for which impoundment is sought, and demonstrating good cause for the impoundment. The motion shall be accompanied by an affidavit in support thereof.

(iii) An order of impoundment may be entered by the court for good cause shown and in accordance with applicable law. In determining good cause, the court shall consider the nature of the parties and the controversy, the type of information and the privacy interests involved, the extent of community interest, the reason(s) for the request, and any other relevant factors.

(iv) Upon filing of the motion to impound and accompanying affidavit, the motion, affidavit, and the information sought to be impounded shall be treated by the court as temporarily impounded pending a ruling on the motion. Subsequent to the ruling on the motion, the motion, affidavit, and any impoundment order shall be part of the public docket and not impounded unless otherwise ordered by the court. If the motion is denied, the information sought to be impounded shall be part of the public docket.

(v) Hearings, if any, on requests under this rule shall be scheduled at the discretion of the court.

(vi) Upon entry of an order of impoundment, the Clerk of the Supreme Judicial Court or his or her assistants shall make a notation in the docket indicating what material has been impounded. All impounded material shall be kept separate from other papers in the case and shall not be available for public inspection. Such impounded material shall be available to the court, the attorneys of record, the parties to the case, and the clerk, unless otherwise ordered by the court.

(b) Appeals Court. Requests for impoundment in proceedings in the Appeals Court shall be governed by the provisions of Trial Court Rule VIII with the following exceptions: (i) the term "clerk" shall mean the Clerk of the Appeals Court and his or her assistants; and (ii) the Appeals Court or a single justice thereof has discretion to enter, either sua sponte or upon motion, any order relating to impoundment without holding a hearing.

Section 2. Maintaining Confidentiality of Previously Impounded Material in Cases on Appeal.

(a) Duties of Trial Court Clerks. When an appeal has been taken in a case in which material has been impounded, the clerk of the trial court shall notify the clerk of the appellate court, in writing, at the time of the transmission of the record that material was impounded by the trial court. Such notification shall specify those papers, documents or exhibits, or portions thereof, which were impounded below and shall include a copy of the order of impoundment, if any, or a reference to other authority for the impoundment.

(b) Duties of Appellate Court Clerk. Unless otherwise ordered by the appellate court, or otherwise provided in the trial court order of impoundment, material impounded in the trial court shall remain impounded in the appellate courts and material impounded in the Appeals Court shall remain impounded in the Supreme Judicial Court. The clerk shall keep all impounded material separate from other papers in the case and unavailable for public inspection. Such impounded material shall be available to the court, the attorneys of record, the parties to the case and the clerk, unless otherwise ordered by the court.

(c) Duties of the Parties. When an appeal has been taken in a case in which material has been impounded, the parties shall protect the confidentiality of the impounded material. Unless it is necessary to do so, the parties shall not include impounded information in briefs and appendices filed with the court. If material filed with the court contains impounded information, the parties shall so notify the clerk and shall identify the impounded material, which shall be unavailable for public inspection. The appellate court, a single justice, or the clerk thereof may require any party filing a document containing impounded information to file a redacted copy of the document that the appellate court may make available for public inspection.

During oral argument in public sessions the parties shall not disclose impounded material, provided that in cases where such disclosure is necessary the parties shall notify the clerk in advance and, in appropriate cases, shall make such disclosures in a manner that protects the confidentiality of the parties.

Rule 1:18. Uniform Rules on Dispute Resolution

[See this part's Additional Materials for text.]

Chapter Two: Rules for the Regulation of Practice Before the Single Justice of the Supreme Judicial Court

Rule 2:01. Fixing Time for Pleadings and Proceedings

[Applicable to all cases.]

The court in its discretion may order or permit pleadings to be filed, or any act to be done, at other times than are provided in these rules.

Whenever in the progress of any case it becomes necessary that a pleading be filed or other step taken so that the case may proceed, and the matter is not covered by any provision of statute or rule, the court may fix the time for the filing of such pleading or make any other appropriate order.

Rule 2:02. Form and Indorsement of Papers

[Applicable to all cases. See SJC Rule 1:08.]

All papers filed in the county court shall be legibly typed with double spacing. The page shall be eight and three-eighths or eight and one-half inches in width and ten and three-fourths or eleven inches in height. The left hand margin shall be not less than one and three-fourths inches. The right hand margin shall be not less than one inch. Documents shall be bound at the left side only. They shall be filed unfolded except applications for admission to the bar.

All information required by S.J.C. Rule 1:08 shall be indorsed on the paper before filing in the clerk's office.

In case of failure to comply with this rule, the court may entertain a motion to strike such paper from the files, and may allow such motion to strike or deny it upon terms against the party at fault.

Rule 2:03. Appearances

[Applicable to criminal cases.]

The name, address, and business telephone number of the attorney for every party, or of the party if no attorney appears for him, shall be entered upon the docket as they appear upon the paper or papers constituting the appearance, or some paper transmitted to the clerk therewith. Where no address of the attorney or party, as the case may be, appears upon the docket, notice to such party may be given by posting the same publicly in the clerk's office or in a room, hall or passage adjacent thereto. The clerk upon request shall post the same.

A substitution of attorneys or change of address or telephone number shall be entered by the clerk upon the docket on written request filed in the particular case. The court and the parties, until such substitution or change is entered, and thereafter until the parties have notice thereof, may rely on action by, and notice to, any attorney previously appearing, and on notice at an address previously entered.

Any appearance shall constitute a general appearance unless the purposes thereof are specified in writing.

Rule 2:04. Giving of Notice

[Applicable to criminal cases.]

A notice to a party required by or given in pursuing of these rules, or any statute relative to procedure not requiring a different notice, shall be in writing, and except as otherwise permitted by Rule 2:03, shall be given to such party or his attorney or any of his attorneys by delivering the same personally to him or by mailing the same, postage prepaid, to him at his business address or the address entered under Rule 2:03.

An affidavit of the person giving the notice shall be evidence thereof.

This rule shall not apply to original process or notice to bring a party before the court.

The words "registered mail" in these rules shall include "certified mail."

Rule 2:05. Time for Pleadings and Proceedings When Last Day for Performance Falls on Saturday, Sunday, or a Legal Holiday

[Applicable to criminal cases.]

When the day or the last day for the performance of any act authorized or required by these rules or by any order of the court falls on Saturday, Sunday, or a legal holiday, the act may be performed on the next succeeding business day, unless a contrary intent appears.

Rule 2:06. Eliminating Requirements for Verification by Oath or Affirmation

[Applicable to criminal cases.]

No written statement in any proceeding in this court required to be verified by affidavit shall be required to be verified by oath or affirmation if it contains or is verified by a written declaration that it is made under the penalties of perjury.

Rule 2:07. Hearings Before Single Justice. Notice

[Applicable to civil cases.]

When any party desires a hearing before a single justice, except at a sitting of the court held in Suffolk County, he may apply to a justice to appoint a time and place for the hearing; and when such time and place have been appointed, notice shall be given in accordance with the Massachusetts Rules of Civil Procedure (see, e.g., Rule 5 of Mass.R.Civ.P.) or the Massachusetts Rules of Appellate Procedure, where applicable (see, e.g., Rule 1[b], 13, and 15[c] of Mass. R.A.P., and S.J.C. Rule 2:20). But this rule shall not prevent a party from obtaining a temporary restraining order, or a dissolution of the same or of an injunction, or other order, upon a shorter notice, or without notice, if the court shall think the same reasonable. And cases may be heard by consent of parties, and the permission of the court, without such notice.

Rule 2:08. Jury Issues

[Applicable to criminal cases.]

Whenever it is necessary or proper to have any fact tried and determined by a jury, the court will direct an issue for that purpose, to be framed by the parties, containing a distinct affirmation and denial of the points in question, or in such form as the court shall order, and the issue thus framed and joined shall be submitted to a jury together with such part of the answers, depositions, and other proceedings in the cause as the court shall direct.

Rule 2:09. Copies to Adverse Parties

[Applicable to criminal cases.]

When any pleading or motion is filed after the bill, complaint or petition, or when any bill of particulars or specifications or answers to interrogatories are filed, a copy thereof shall be given not later than the day of filing to each of the adverse parties in the manner provided for notice by Rule 2:04.

In case of failure to comply with this rule, the court may entertain a motion to strike such paper from the files, and may allow such motion to strike or deny it upon terms against the party at fault.

Rule 2:10. Money Paid into Court

[Applicable to civil cases.]

Money paid into court shall be in the custody of the clerk, whose duty it shall be to receive it when paid under the authority of law or rule or order of the court. He shall pay it as directed by the court, but money paid into court upon tender, or otherwise for the present and unconditional use of a party, shall be paid, on request, without special order, with any interest which has accrued thereon, to such party, at whose risk it shall be from the time when it is paid into court. Money payable to a party may be paid to his attorney of record.

No interest shall be deemed to accrue on any sum less in amount than the minimum on which interest is payable in the depositary in which the money is deposited.

Rule 2:11. Hearings upon Motions Grounded upon Facts

[Applicable to criminal cases.]

The court need not hear any motion, or opposition thereto, grounded on facts, unless the facts are verified by affidavit, or apparent upon the record and files, or are agreed and stated in writing signed by the attorneys for the parties interested.

Rule 2:12. Postponement for Want of Evidence

[Applicable to criminal cases.]

The court need not entertain any motion for postponement, grounded on the want of material testimony, unless supported by an affidavit, which shall state (1) the name, and, if known, the residence, of the witness whose testimony is wanted, (2) the particular testimony which he is expected to give, with the grounds of such expectation, and (3) the endeavors and means that have been used to procure his attendance or deposition; to the end that the court may judge whether due diligence has been used for that purpose. The party objecting to the postponement shall not be allowed to contradict the statement of what the absent witness is expected to testify, but may disprove any other fact stated in such affidavit. Such motion will not ordinarily be granted if the adverse party will admit that the absent witness would, if present, testify as stated in the affidavit, and will agree that the same shall be received and considered as evidence at the trial or hearing, as though the witness were present and so testified; and such agreement shall be in writing, upon the affidavit, and signed by such adverse party of his attorney. The same rule shall apply, mutates mutandis, when the motion is grounded on the want of any material document, thing or other evidence. In all cases the granting or denial of a motion for postponement shall be discretionary, whether the foregoing provisions have been complied with or not.

Rule 2:13. Special Masters and Commissioners

[Applicable to all cases]

The full court may designate special masters and commissioners to deal with specified cases or with such matters as may be referred to them by a written order of a single justice or of the full court. The acts of any such special master and commissioner, when confirmed or approved, by a single justice or by the full court, as the case may be, shall have all the force and effect of a decision by a single justice or by the full court.

Rule 2:14. Writ of Protection

[Applicable to all cases.]

A writ of protection shall issue only upon the application of the person for whom the writ of protection is to be issued, or some person in his behalf, and upon order of the court, and then only in case it is made to appear to the court, by affidavit and any other evidence that the court may require, (1) that the application is made in good faith and for the purpose of enabling such person to attend this court as a party or witness in some specified case pending, (2) if such person is a party, that such case has not been brought collusively to enable him to obtain a writ of protection, and (3) if such person is a witness, that he has not been required to attend as a witness by his own request or procurement to enable him to obtain a writ of protection.

Rule 2:15. Objections

[See Mass. R. Civ. P. 46.]

(1) Civil Cases. Objections to evidence in civil cases shall be decided without argument, unless the presiding judge calls upon the parties to state the grounds upon which the evidence is offered or objected to.

(2) Criminal Cases. Exceptions to rulings or orders of the court in criminal cases are unnecessary and for all purposes for which an exception has heretofore been necessary, it is sufficient that a party, at the time the ruling or order of the court is made or sought, makes known to the court the action which he desires the court to take or his objection to the action of the court, but if a party has no opportunity to object to a ruling or order, the absence of an objection does not thereafter prejudice him.

If a party objects to a ruling or order of the court, he may state the precise legal grounds of his objection, but he shall not argue or further discuss such grounds unless the court calls upon him for such argument or discussion.

Objections to any opinion, ruling, direction or judgment made in the absence of counsel shall be taken by a writing filed with the clerk within three days after receipt from the clerk of notice thereof.

Rule 2:16. Requests for Rulings

[Applicable to all cases.]

Requests for rulings, when appropriate, shall be made in writing before the closing arguments unless special leave is given to present further requests later.

Rule 2:17. Time for Arguments

[Applicable to criminal cases.]

All arguments shall be limited to one-half hour on each side unless, for good cause shown, the court shall allow further time; and, when more than one counsel are to be heard on the same side, the time may be divided between them as they may elect.

Rule 2:18. Order of Business. Single Justice Sittings

[Amended effective Oct. 2, 1995; Jan. 1, 1997; July 1, 2002.]

The justice designated to hear matters within the jurisdiction of a single justice at Boston will hear such matters once each week, except in the weeks in which his or her attendance with the full court is required during consultation or argument, and except as the number of cases to be heard does not require sitting. The sitting shall be on Wednesday unless the single justice otherwise directs. A weekly list for hearing in Boston will be made up on which cases from any county may be set down, either by order of the court or by joint request of the counsel, the hearing of which cases shall be subject to the discretion of the court. Matters to be heard before a single justice will be heard in Boston unless the full court or the single justice shall otherwise order. The single justice in his or her discretion may set any matter for hearing in any place within the Commonwealth.

Rule 2:19. Reviews of Orders of Department of Public Utilities

[Applicable to proceedings to review orders, etc., of the Department of Public Utilities.]

So far as the Massachusetts Rules of Civil Procedure are applicable, they shall govern proceedings brought under the provision of G.L. c. 25, § 5, or acts in amendment thereof.

Unless the interests of justice plainly require, no stay of any order of the department of public utilities shall be ordered except after notice to the Attorney General or the commissioners of the department.

An order of the department fixing the rates, fares, charges, or prices for service furnished by a person or corporation under its jurisdiction shall not be stayed unless provision be made by the party applying for such stay by bond or other security for the repayment, in the event the order is finally sustained, of so much of rates, fares, charges, or prices collected, while such stay is in effect, as is in excess of those fixed in the order.

Rule 2:20. Appeals from Decisions of Appellate Tax Board

Interlocutory matters arising in appeals from the decisions of the Appellate Tax Board and questions of final disposition thereof when further proceedings appear unnecessary may be presented to a single justice, who may after notice hear and determine the same both as to questions of law and of fact or reserve and report the case.

Rule 2:21. Appeal from Single Justice Denial of Relief on Interlocutory Ruling

[Applicable to civil and criminal cases. Adopted effective Nov. 15, 1995, amended effective June 1, 2001.]

(1) When a single justice denies relief from a challenged interlocutory ruling in the trial court and does not report the denial of relief to the full court, the party denied relief may appeal the single justice's ruling to the full court. Unless the court otherwise orders, the notice of appeal shall be filed with the Clerk of the Supreme Judicial Court for Suffolk County within seven days of the entry of the judgment appealed from. Unless the single justice or the full court orders otherwise, neither the trial nor the interlocutory ruling in the trial court shall be stayed.

(2) The appeal shall be presented to the full court on the papers filed in the single justice session, including any memorandum of decision. Nine copies of the record appendix must be filed in the Office of the clerk for the Supreme Judicial Court for the commonwealth within fourteen days after the date on which the appeal is docketed in the full Supreme Judicial Court. The record appendix shall be accompanied by eight copies of a memorandum of not more than ten pages, double-spaced, in which the appellant must set forth the reasons why review of the trial court decision cannot adequately be obtained on appeal from any final adverse judgment in the trial court or by other available means. No response from the prevailing party shall be filed, unless requested by the court.

(3) This rule shall not apply to interlocutory appeals governed by Rule 15 of the Massachusetts Rules of Criminal Procedure.

(4) The full court will consider the appeal on the papers submitted pursuant to this rule, unless it otherwise orders.

Rule 2:22. Petitions under G.L. c. 211, § 3

[Applicable to civil and criminal cases. Adopted effective May 13, 1996.]

Any petition seeking to invoke the general superintendency power of the court pursuant to G.L. c. 211, § 3, shall name as respondents and make service upon all parties to the proceeding before the lower court, including in criminal cases the Commonwealth through the District Attorney or Attorney General as appropriate. When the lower court is named as a respondent, service upon the lower court shall be made in accordance with Rule 4(d)(3) of the Rules of Civil Procedure by delivering a copy to the clerk of the lower court and to the Boston office of the Attorney General. Unless otherwise ordered by the single justice, the lower court shall thereafter be treated as a nominal party which may, but need not, appear and be heard.

Chapter Three: Ethical Requirements and Rules Concerning the Practice of Law

Rule 3:10. Assignment of Counsel

[Applicable to all courts. Amended effective Oct. 1, 1993; Nov. 1, 2016.]

Section 1. Definitions. The following definitions apply in this rule:

(a) *Available funds*—A party's liquid assets and disposable net monthly income calculated after providing for the party's bail obligations. A party's available funds shall include the liquid assets and disposable net monthly income of the party's spouse (or person in substantially the same relationship), provided that person lives in the same residence as the party and contributes substantially towards the household's basic living costs, unless that person has an adverse interest in the proceeding (e.g. is the victim, complainant, or petitioning party, is a prospective prosecution witness, or, in a civil matter, is a party) or unless the inclusion of the income of the party's spouse would be contrary to the interests of justice.

(b) *Basic living costs*—The average monthly amount spent for reasonable payments toward living costs, such as shelter, food, utilities, health care, transportation, clothing, education, child care, alimony and child support payments, and payments and interest on loans for such living costs.

(c) *Child welfare proceeding*—Where the party is a juvenile, a care and protection proceeding, termination of parental rights proceeding, child requiring assistance proceeding, adoption, guardianship of a minor, or permanency hearing. Where the party is a young adult, a permanency hearing.

(d) *Contribution fee*—A fee imposed by a judge pursuant to Section 10 on a party who has been determined to be indigent but able to contribute. The contribution fee shall not include the indigent counsel fee, but shall be an amount above and beyond the indigent counsel fee that the party is able to pay without substantial financial hardship for the cost of any attorney appointed to represent the party.

(e) *Disposable net monthly income*—The income remaining each month after deducting income taxes, social security and Medicare taxes, ordinary retirement contributions, union dues, and basic living costs.

(f) *Income*—Salary, wages, interest, dividends, rental income, and other earnings and regular cash payments, such as amounts received from pensions, annuities, social security, alimony, and child support. Irregular or infrequent income (e.g., earnings from day labor, seasonal, or on-call work) that a party can reasonably be expected to receive shall count as income under this rule. Irregular or infrequent income that cannot reasonably be anticipated to continue shall not count as income.

(g) *Indigency verification process*—The attempt by probation to verify a claim of indigency, in accordance with G.L. c. 211D, § 2A(c), by a party or, where appropriate, a parent or guardian, by accessing wage, tax, and asset information in the possession of the Department of Revenue, information regarding benefits received from the Department of Transitional Assistance, and any information relevant to the determination of indigency in the possession of the Registry of Motor Vehicles.

(h) *Indigent*—A party who is:

(i) receiving one of the following types of public assistance: Transitional Aid to Families with Dependent Children (TAFDC), Emergency Aid to Elderly, Disabled and Children (EAEDC), need-based veterans' benefits, Supplemental Nutrition Assistance Program (SNAP) benefits, Refugee Cash Assistance, or SSI State Supplemental Program;

(ii) receiving an annual income, after taxes, of one hundred twenty-five percent or less of the current poverty guidelines referred to in G.L. c. 261, § 27A(b);

(iii) (1) residing in a tuberculosis treatment center, a mental health facility or a facility for individuals with intellectual or developmental disabilities, including the Bridgewater State Hospital and Massachusetts Treatment Center; or (2) the subject of a proceeding regarding admission or commitment to such a center or facility, a proceeding to make a substituted judgment determination concerning treatment, a proceeding under G.L. c. 190B, § 5-309(g) to admit to a nursing facility defined in G.L. c. 190B, § 5-101(15), or a civil commitment proceeding under G.L. c. 123, § 35; provided, however, that when the judge has reason to believe that the party is not indigent, a determination of indigency shall be made in accordance with Section 5 and other applicable provisions of this rule; or

(iv) a juvenile, a child who is in the care or custody of the Department of Children and Families, or a young adult provided, however, that when a judge has reason to believe that the juvenile or young adult is not indigent, a determination of indigency shall be made in accordance with Section 5 and other applicable provisions of this rule.

(i) *Indigent but able to contribute*—A party who:

(i) has an annual income, after taxes, of more than one hundred twenty five percent and less than two hundred fifty percent of the current poverty guidelines referred to in G.L. c. 261, § 27A(b), or

(ii) (1) is charged with a felony solely within the jurisdiction of the Superior Court or is the parent, guardian, or custodian of a juvenile or young adult who is the subject of a child welfare proceeding, subject to the exception in Section 6A for a parent or guardian who has had custody of the juvenile removed by a court of competent jurisdiction, or who has an interest adverse to the juvenile or young adult, and (2) has an annual income, after taxes, of more than two hundred fifty percent of the current poverty guidelines referred to in G.L. c. 261, § 27A(b); and (3) whose available funds are insufficient to pay the anticipated cost of counsel for this representation, but are sufficient to pay part of that cost. The anticipated cost of counsel shall be the cost of retaining private counsel for, as applicable, the defense of a felony charge within the jurisdiction of the Superior Court, or a child welfare proceeding, as estimated and published from time to time by the Committee for Public Counsel Services; or

(iii) is over the age of eighteen and is claimed as a dependent for tax purposes by a parent or guardian who is not indigent.

(j) *Indigent counsel fee*—A fee assessed on a person provided counsel pursuant to G.L. c. 211D, § 2A(f).

(k) *Intake report*—The report provided to the judge by probation regarding the party's or, where appropriate, the party's parents' or guardians', responses to biographical and financial questions asked by probation.

(l) *Juvenile*—A child under the age of 18 who is the subject of a child welfare proceeding or a delinquency or youthful offender proceeding.

(m) *Juvenile legal fee*—The fee assessed on a parent or guardian to pay for the cost of any attorney appointed to represent a party under the age of 18. The fee shall not exceed the fee set forth in G.L. c. 119, § 29A or G.L. c. 119, § 39F.

(n) *Liquid assets*—Cash, savings accounts, bank accounts, stocks, bonds, certificates of deposit, equity in real estate, and equity in a motor vehicle or other tangible property, provided that any equity in real or personal property is reasonably convertible to cash. Any motor vehicle necessary to maintain employment, including travel to and from the party's employment, shall not be considered a liquid asset. Expenses associated with the liquidation of assets, including penalties for early withdrawal and tax burdens, shall not be included as available funds.

(o) *Party*—Any person who may be entitled to the appointment of counsel in relation to any court proceeding on the basis of indigency under the law of the Commonwealth.

(p) *Probation*—The Office of the Commissioner of Probation or any member of its staff.

(q) *Young adult*—A person between the ages of 18 and 22 who is the subject of a child welfare proceeding.

Section 2. Advice as to Right to Counsel.

If any party to a proceeding appears in court without counsel where the party has a right to be represented by counsel under the law of the Commonwealth, the judge shall advise the party or, if the party is a juvenile, the party and a parent or legal guardian, where appropriate, that: (a) the party may be entitled to the appointment of counsel at public expense; and (b) the Committee for Public Counsel Services will provide counsel to the party at no cost or at a reduced cost if the court finds that the party wants but cannot afford counsel.

Section 3. Waiver of Counsel.

If the party elects to proceed without counsel, the party shall sign a written waiver and the judge shall certify in writing that the party executed the waiver in the judge's presence after the judge informed the party of the right of counsel. If the party elects to proceed without counsel but refuses to sign the written waiver, the judge shall so certify in writing.

Before allowing a waiver of counsel, the judge, after conducting a colloquy with the party, shall make written findings that the party is competent to waive counsel and that the party has knowingly and voluntarily elected to proceed without counsel.

Section 4. Standby Counsel.

Notwithstanding a party's waiver of counsel, where the interests of justice so require, the judge may assign standby counsel to assist the party in the course of the proceedings regardless of whether the party is indigent.

Section 5. Determination of Indigency Status.

(a) If the party requests appointment of counsel, or if counsel is appointed under Section 6 or 6A of this rule, or if the judge for any reason finds that the party has not knowingly and voluntarily elected to proceed without counsel, probation shall provide the judge with an intake report. Probation shall attempt to verify the self-reported information on the intake report through the indigency verification process.

(b) Unless the party is a juvenile, or is a person over eighteen who is claimed as a dependent for tax purposes, probation shall make a recommendation as to the indigency of the party. Where the party is a juvenile, probation shall make a recommendation as to the indigency of the parents or guardian in accordance with Sections 1, 6 and 6A of this rule and G.L. c. 119, § 29A and 39F. Where a person over eighteen is claimed as a dependent for tax purposes, probation shall make a recommendation as to the indigency of the parents or guardian.

(c) After reviewing the intake report and recommendation and questioning the party, as appropriate, the judge shall make a determination that:

(i) the party is indigent,

(ii) the party is indigent but able to contribute, or

(iii) the party is not indigent.

The clerk shall enter the judge's determination on the court docket.

(d) In order to determine a party's current financial status, the judge shall evaluate (1) the party's income in the current calendar quarter (i.e., January-March, April-June, July-September, October-December), and (2) the party's income in the three preceding calendar quarters.

(e) Any party seeking appointment of counsel shall bear the burden of proving indigency by a preponderance of the evidence.

(f) Even where a party meets or fails to meet the definitions of "indigent" or "indigent but able to contribute," the judge retains the discretion to determine that the interests of justice require a different determination based on the party's available funds in relation to the party's basic living costs, or special circumstances, or both. A judge may consider, for example, receipt of Medicaid benefits as one factor in assessing whether the interests of justice would require a different determination. Where a judge exercises this discretion, the judge shall set forth on the record the reason for doing so.

Section 6. Assignment of Counsel/Notice of Assignment.

If under Section 5 the judge finds that a party is indigent or indigent but able to contribute, the judge shall assign the Committee for Public Counsel Services to provide representation for the party, unless exceptional circumstances, supported by written findings, necessitate a different procedure that is consistent with G.L. c. 211D and the rules of the Supreme Judicial Court. The clerk or register shall promptly notify the party of the assignment of counsel.

If a judge has determined that a party is not indigent, and the party after a reasonable time has not waived counsel, procured counsel, or petitioned for the appointment of counsel on the ground that, despite reasonable efforts, the party has been unable to afford the cost of counsel, the case may be ordered to proceed without appointed counsel. In proceedings where there is an entitlement to the appointment of counsel pursuant to General Laws, chapter 111, §§ 94C and 94G, chapter 123, chapter 123A, and chapter 190B, the judge shall appoint counsel immediately upon the filing of a petition and entry of any requisite findings. If, before the hearing, the judge determines that the party is not indigent, assigned counsel may be dismissed, and the party shall be advised to retain private counsel without delay; provided, however, that the judge shall authorize the continued services of appointed counsel at public expense where the interests of justice so require. The interests of justice may require such appointment if, for example, the party is incompetent to obtain counsel, unable to access funds, or unable to retain counsel. If, after the hearing has commenced, the judge determines that the party is not indigent, appointed counsel shall continue to represent the party and the judge may order the party to reimburse the Commonwealth for the cost of counsel.

Section 6A. Assignment of Counsel for Juveniles.

All juveniles, regardless of the financial status of their parents or guardians, shall be entitled to the appointment of counsel. Unless the juvenile is represented by retained private counsel, the judge shall assign the Committee for Public Counsel Services to represent the juvenile in accordance with Section 6. If the juvenile is provided with appointed counsel and the judge determines that the juvenile's parent or legal guardian is not indigent, the judge shall assess the juvenile legal fee against the parent or guardian as payment toward the cost of counsel supplied by the Committee for Public Counsel Services. If the parent or guardian is determined to be indigent but able to contribute, the court shall order the parent or guardian to pay a reasonable amount toward the cost of appointed counsel, provided that the amount shall not exceed the juvenile legal fee and shall not cause substantial financial hardship. This section shall not apply to a parent or guardian who has had custody of the juvenile removed by a court of competent jurisdiction, or who has an interest adverse to the juvenile. The failure of a juvenile's parent or guardian to pay any fee assessed under this Section shall not be grounds for withholding or revoking the juvenile's appointed counsel.

Section 7. Review of Indigency Determination.

(a) The judge may review indigency status at any stage of a proceeding if information regarding a change in financial circumstances is obtained by probation through the indigency verification process or from some other source, including the party.

(b) There shall be a right to an evidentiary hearing to reconsider the judge's findings and determination as to the party's entitlement to appointed counsel. The judge shall schedule the evidentiary hearing promptly after it is requested. If requested by the party, the judge shall appoint counsel to represent the party at the evidentiary hearing. Before the hearing, the judge shall provide the party with a copy of probation's intake report and recommendation described in Section 5(a) and any records in the court's possession relating to the party's financial status. The judge may issue any protective orders needed to protect the privacy of the party or any third parties. The party shall have the opportunity to introduce any relevant evidence and to call witnesses to testify. The party shall bear the burden of proving indigency by a preponderance of the evidence. At the conclusion of the hearing, the judge shall make written findings regarding whether the party is entitled to appointed counsel. These findings shall be part of the case record and maintained in the official file of the case.

Section 8. Inadmissibility of Information Obtained from a party.

(a) No information provided by a party pursuant to this rule may be used in any proceeding against the party except in a prosecution for perjury or contempt committed in providing such information or at an evidentiary hearing conducted under Section 7(b).

(b) No party shall be asked or required to provide any information regarding his or her immigration or citizenship status as part of intake, indigency determination, or verification.

Section 9. Counsel for parties who are indigent or indigent but able to contribute.

(a) *Appearance of Counsel.* Counsel assigned by the Committee for Public Counsel Services to represent a party pursuant to this rule shall file an appearance within forty-eight hours after receipt of notification of the assignment.

(b) *Withdrawal of Appearance.* If counsel assigned by the Committee for Public Counsel Services has filed an appearance and is unable or unwilling to represent a party, counsel shall move to withdraw the appearance. If the judge allows the motion for withdrawal, the clerk or register shall immediately notify the Committee for Public Counsel Services to make a new assignment of counsel.

2

Section 10. Contribution toward Cost of Counsel.

(a) If a judge determines that a party is indigent, the judge may not order, require, or solicit the party to make any payment toward the cost of counsel, except for an indigent counsel fee. The indigent counsel fee shall be waived where a judge, after the indigency verification process, determines that the party is unable without substantial financial hardship to pay the indigent counsel fee within 180 days. Where the indigent counsel fee is not waived, the judge may authorize the party to perform community service in lieu of payment of the indigent counsel fee in accordance with G.L. c. 211D, § 2A(g). The clerk shall enter the judge's determination on the court docket.

(b) If a judge determines that a party is indigent but able to contribute, the judge shall order the party to pay the indigent counsel fee plus a contribution fee based on the financial circumstances of the party, provided that the amount of the contribution fee shall not cause substantial financial hardship. The party shall be given an opportunity to be heard and to present information, including witness affidavits or testimony, regarding whether the contribution fee would cause substantial financial hardship.

(c) If a party over the age of eighteen is determined to be indigent but able to contribute under Section 1(h)(iii) because the party is claimed as a dependent for tax purposes by a parent or guardian who is not indigent, the contribution fee shall be based on the financial circumstances of the parent or guardian. The parent or guardian shall be solely responsible for paying any contribution fee assessed under this subsection.

Section 11. Collection of Fees and Contributions.

(a) All payments toward the cost of counsel, including the indigent counsel fee, the contribution fee, and the juvenile legal fee, shall be made to the office of the clerk of court and shall be deposited with the State Treasurer in accordance with law.

(b) The clerk shall inform the judge at each court event for a case whether the party has failed to pay an indigent counsel fee or contribution fee. If the party has failed to pay an indigent counsel fee or contribution fee within sixty days of appointment of counsel, the clerk, unless otherwise ordered by the judge, shall report the unpaid amount to the Department of Revenue, the Department of Transitional Assistance, and the Registry of Motor Vehicles as required by G.L. c. 211D, § 2A.

(c) The failure of a party, parent, or guardian to pay an indigent counsel fee, a contribution fee, or a juvenile legal fee shall not be grounds for withholding or revoking appointed counsel.

(d) Probation shall not be responsible for monitoring or enforcing payment of any indigent counsel fee, contribution fee, or juvenile legal fee.

(e) No party may be subject to incarceration for failing to pay an indigent counsel fee or a contribution fee.

Supreme Judicial Court Standards on Substance Abuse

Supreme Judicial Court Statement

[Adopted Mar. 30, 1995.]

On March 1, 1995, acting on the advice of its Substance Abuse Task Force, the Supreme Judicial Court adopted the following system-wide policy designed to enhance the judiciary's response to the impact of substance abuse on the courts of the Commonwealth.

Every judge in the Commonwealth should attempt to identify and appropriately respond to the indication of substance abuse by any party appearing before him or her in a court of the Commonwealth, where substance abuse is a factor in behavior related to the case. At every stage of the adjudicatory process, courts should provide access to substance abuse information and to referrals for screening, assessment and treatment for substance abuse.

INTRODUCTION

Definition. For purposes of these standards, substance abuse is defined as chronic or habitual ingestion of drugs or alcohol to the extent that (i) such use substantially injures a person's heath or substantially interferes with his or her social or economic functioning, or (ii) a person has lost the power of self-control over the use of drugs or alcohol. It is a chronic, relapsing disorder requiring ongoing rather than episodic intervention. It is predictable, progressive, symptomatic, and treatable.

As used in these standards, "substance abuse" includes abuse of alcohol as well as other legal and illegal drugs, the term "party" means both a party to a civil case and a defendant or convicted or convicted offender in a criminal case, and the term "court" means the court as an institution, including judges, clerks, probation officers, and other court personnel.

Effectiveness of Court-ordered Treatment. A key premise of these standards is that treatment is effective.[1] Court-mandated substance abuse treatment programs have been convincingly demonstrated to work.[2] Furthermore, research reveals that motivation improves as treatment progresses, and that abusers who are coerced into treatment fare just as well as, if not better than, those who enter into treatment voluntarily.[3] In fact, most substance abusers enter treatment not voluntarily, but rather because they are forced by such factors as a family intervention, pressure from a spouse, or the insistence of an employer or co-worker. Voluntary participation is rare, since denial is a symptom of the disease of substance abuse. One goal of treatment is for the substance abuser to recover to the degree that he or she takes responsibility for his or her behavior. Treatment does not always work the first or even the second time, so that relapse should not be a cause for giving up on a substance abuser. In fact, strategies to prevent and address relapse are critical to the effectiveness of treatment. (See Standard XIII with respect to relapse prevention.)

[1] *"Drug and alcohol dependence are treatable medical illnesses", A. Thomas McClellan, Charles P. O'Brien, Norman Hoffman, and Herbert D. Kleber, Is Drug Dependence A Treatable Medical Illness: A Review of Recent Research, supported by grants from the Department of Veterans Affairs, National Institute on Drug Abuse, and Robert Wood Johnson Foundation, p. 30, 1998.*

[2] *See for example, Corbett & Petersilia, "A Review of Research for Practitioners," Federal Probation, vol. 58, no. 1, March 1994.*

[3] *Singer, Amy, Effective Treatment for Drug-Involved Offender's: A Review and Synthesis for Judges and Other Court Personnel, produced by Education Development Center, Inc., 55 Chapel St., Newton, MA 02160, p. 144 (May 1992).*

Purpose. The following standards are intended to provide guidance in the implementation of the Supreme Judicial Court Policy Statement on Substance Abuse. They present a single orientation with which the judicial branch, including judges and all court personnel, can work together with prosecutors, the defense bar, corrections officials, and public and private treatment providers to address the problem of substance abuse which pervades the court system's caseload. Statistics from the Office of the Commissioner of Probation show that abuse of alcohol and other drugs is a factor in close to 80% of probation cases classified under the risk/need system. In civil cases, substance abuse is frequently cited as a significant factor in requests for orders of protection, civil commitments, CHINS petitions, eviction, divorce proceedings, contract dispute, custody, and child visitation and support cases. The standards contain recommended steps, consistent with public safety, for courts to take in responding effectively to substance abuse. The steps are stated broadly in order to leave room for each court to tailor implementation to local needs. The standards are intended not to create any new authority or power in the courts, but rather to encourage judges to use their existing authority to respond effectively to substance abuse, consistent with rules of evidence and other statutory, procedural and constitutional provisions.

Implementation of the steps contained in the standards will promote public safety, provide access to treatment, protect due process, reduce recidivism, ensure offender accountability, and maintain a responsible and productive world environment for court personnel. By embracing them, the courts will become leaders in the Commonwealth's efforts to stop the abuse of all addictive substances—alcohol and other drugs—and to curtail related criminal activities and social dysfunction. Public safety will be enhanced, because offenders who succeed in treatment are much less likely to re-offend. Substance abusers will be directed toward treatment, recovery, and more productive lives. Public funds will be saved, since treatment is significantly less expensive than incarceration.[4]

[4] *Treatment Works: The Tragic Cost of Undervaluing Treatment in the Drug War—A Review of 15 Years of Research Findings on Alcohol and Other Drug Abuse Treatment Outcomes, published by NASADAD (National Association of State Alcohol and Drug Abuse Directors), March 1990, p. 25.*

While much substance abuse treatment is provided in the community, there are some offenders, even among those suffering from substance abuse, who are so violent and anti-social that public safety demands incarceration. In these situations, treatment is not a substitute for incarceration. Public safety in the Commonwealth will be enhanced, however, by making treatment available to offenders while they are incarcerated.

Standard I. Judge as Leader in Court's Response to Substance Abuse

Every judge should become well informed about the problem of substance abuse and the process of recovery, and should serve as a leader in the court's efforts to address substance abuse. Judges should be aware of substance abuse, alert to its occurrence, and prepared to use their authority to take action when it is present.

COMMENTARY

Judges should have a general knowledge of the nature of substance abuse, the recovery process, various treatment methods, and payment mechanisms for substance abuse treatment, including MassHealth, private insurance, the Department of Public Heath, and the Office of Community Corrections. Judges should encourage and enable courthouse staff to obtain substance abuse training appropriate to their respective positions. Judges should be aware of all options for ordering treatment (as provided in the Commentary to Standard V) and be active in ensuring that courts have strategies in place to address cases involving substance abuse. Judges should engage in continuing dialogue with the probation department in order to maintain up-to-date information about treatment options available to the court, keeping in mind limitations on ex parte communications in specific cases. See Supreme Judicial Court Rule 3:09, Code of Judicial Conduct, Canon 3(A)(4).

Although some judges believe that responding to substance abuse is not part of a judge's role, judges who do not take advantage of opportunities to promote recovery of substance abusers are missing the chance to respond to an important societal need which absorbs an inordinate amount of the court's time. Responding appropriately to substance abuse does not convert the courts into a social service agency, or require judges to ignore the other issues in a case. Instead, an effective substance abuse strategy is one element, with many others, of the courts' central mission of resolving disputes and dispensing justice. The practices of screening for substance abuse, assessing treatment needs, referring parties to substance abuse treatment, and monitoring their progress in treatment, as recommended in these standards, will address the underlying cause of the problems presented in many cases. These practices will thus help to ensure that cases are actually resolved with finality, and that the same problems, caused by the same, recurring substance abuse, do not reappear. In criminal cases, moreover, these practices will promote public safety and contribute to reducing recidivism. By assuming leadership of the courts' response to substance abuse, judges will help to ensure its effectiveness and enhance the administration of justice.

Standard II. Courthouse as Information and Referral Center

Since substance abuse is a factor in a large percentage of criminal and family cases, the courthouse should serve as a substance abuse information and referral resource center. Substance abuse information and referral services should be available to every party at every stage of every case.

COMMENTARY

Written information about substance abuse and the availability of treatment should be made available in the courthouse, given to anyone who requests it, and distributed by court staff. Information about substance abuse can be disseminated through a display of pamphlets and brochures in the courthouse lobby, or at the clerk's or register's counter, the probation or family service offices, the court clinic, the child care center, the victim/witness office, or the law library. The Probation Department should obtain information suitable for distribution from the Department of Public Health and other sources.

Standard III. Access to Continuing Education

The court should provide all court personnel with access to continuing education about substance abuse and should encourage court personnel to avail themselves of educational opportunities inside and outside the court system.

COMMENTARY

All court personnel should understand the problem of substance abuse. Substance abuse education is fundamental to such understanding. The more understanding court personnel have of this disorder, the more effective they can be in successfully responding to the issue. Education may be provided through the Supreme Judicial Court Standing Committee on Substance Abuse, the Office of the Commissioner of Probation, the Bureau of Substance Abuse Services of the Department of Public Health, the Judicial Institute of the Trial Court, the Flaschner Judicial Institute, the Human Resources Department of the Administrative Office of the Trial Court, and other educational groups. Training should include basic substance abuse education, including information on treatment options and the recovery process, information on research regarding effective substance abuse treatment programs, planning sessions to develop strategies to improve the processing of cases involving substance abuse in each court, and specialized information and skills to meet the professional needs of certain employee groups. Continuing education should include updated information on these topics.

Standard IV. Probation Department Responsibilities

The probation department in every court should be responsible for identifying substance abuse, conducting substance abuse screening, performing or arranging and overseeing substance abuse assessments, ensuring that judges are informed about substance abuse assessment results, arranging for appropriate treatment placements, and monitoring compliance with treatment orders. The probation department should be available to perform these functions at any stage of a case.

COMMENTARY

If a court is to respond effectively to substance abuse when it is a factor in a case, it is critical that every probation officer have training and competence in the field of substance abuse. Probation officers should be immediately available to assist judges in identifying substance abuse issues, conducting screenings, performing or referring parties for substance abuse assessments or for appropriate treatment where advisable, and monitoring compliance with treatment orders.

In addition to training and competence in the field of substance abuse, probation officers should understand mental health issues and the impact of mental illness on the capacity to engage in the substance abuse recovery process. See Commentary to Standard VIII for suggestions about referrals to court clinics or outside vendors for substance abuse assessments in certain cases involving mental illness. Probation officers should also be knowledgeable about payment mechanisms for substance abuse testing and treatment, including MassHealth, private insurance, the Department of Public Health, and the Office of Community Corrections.

The Commissioner of Probation should set standards for ensuring that probation office receive necessary training in the field of substance abuse and should assume responsibility for ensuring that qualified probation officers are in fact available at each court to assist judges with substance abuse issues. Insofar as possible, probation officers should receive training sufficient to qualify them to conduct substance abuse assessments as provided in Standard VIII, and should be available to conduct such assessments.

Probation officers should be available to assist the court with substance abuse issues at all stages of a matter, including pretrial proceedings, even before probation is imposed.

Standard V. Ordering Treatment

Judges should be familiar with the options available at each stage of every case to provide access and make referrals to treatment for substance abuse, as defined in the Introduction, and to order treatment for substance abuse. Every court in every Trial Court department should make use of existing options for providing access and making referrals to treatment, if appropriate, and ordering treatment in appropriate circumstances. A list of options is provided in the Commentary.

COMMENTARY

The court should use its authority to direct a reluctant party into treatment for substance abuse in appropriate situations. Substance abuse can be treated effectively, and involuntary participants in treatment do recover. (See introduction.) Court involvement creates a crisis in a person's life, and courts are uniquely situated to take advantage of the crisis by directing the person toward treatment. A timely response to the individual's crisis is most likely to lead to success in treatment. The court's authority should be used to order treatment or impose treatment conditions only when substance abuse is a factor in behavior related to the case, and the treatment ordered should be proportional to the underlying behavior. Judges are encouraged to consider information provided by the victim when fashioning treatment orders in criminal cases.

There are many occasions under the law when a treatment order is appropriate.

Adult Criminal Cases. Criminal proceedings afford several opportunities to use the court's authority to coerce a criminal defendant into substance abuse treatment and to motivate the defendant to comply with any treatment orders.

1. Pretrial

- At the pre-trial stage, the court may, with the defendant's consent, place the defendant on probation and make alcohol or drug treatment and testing a condition of that probation. G.L. c. 276, § 87.
- G.L. c. 111E, § 10 lays out procedures at the time of arraignment for offering a defendant charged with a drug offense the opportunity to be evaluated for "drug dependency." If the court determines that the defendant is a "drug dependent or drug addicted" person, the court can assign the defendant to a drug treatment facility with the treatment provider's consent, and eventually dismiss the charges.
- District courts may reestablish a pre-trial diversion program, which may have as a component alcohol or drug treatment. G.L. c. 276A, §§ 1–9. If a defendant completes the diversion program, the case is usually dismissed.
- In cases involving certain crimes, the Commonwealth may move on the grounds of the defendant's dangerousness for pre-trial petition or release on conditions under G.L. c. 276, § 58A. In these cases, a judge may, depending on findings, decide to hold a defendant without bail pending trial, release the defendant on personal recognizance, or release the defendant under certain conditions, which may include refraining from the use of alcohol or drugs and undergoing drug treatment for drug or alcohol dependency. G.L. c. 276, § 58A.
- In cases involving actual or potential physical harm to a family or household member, the judge may set any terms in lieu of or in addition to personal recognizance that will insure the safety of the person suffering or threatened with abuse and will prevent its recurrence. G.L. c. 276, § 42A. Substance abuse treatment can be one of those conditions.
- If it is appropriate to hold a defendant in custody in lieu of bail, the judge is encouraged to ask probation to provide information to the jail or house of correction regarding any defendant's apparent substance abuse. See also Standard X.

2. Pre-Sentencing

After a finding of guilty and prior to sentencing a defendant, a judge may order a substance abuse assessment of the defendant to aid in sentencing. This can be especially helpful where the relationship between mental health and drug addiction issues needs to be clarified. G.L. c. 123, § 15(e).

The judge may always postpone sentencing to enable the probation departed to prepare a pre-sentence report which details the defendant's substance abuse history, including treatment needs and prior or current or current efforts to seek treatment. Mass. Rules of Criminal Procedure, Rule 28(d)(2).

After an admission to sufficient facts and a court-imposed continuance without a finding, probation can be conditioned upon compliance with specific terms and conditions, such as substance abuse treatment. G.L. c. 278, § 18.

3. Sentencing

At sentencing, the judge may suspend any part of a sentence to a House of Correction under any conditions it might set, including treatment. G.L. c. 279, §§ 1, 1A. The sentencing of defendants charged with first and second offenses involving operating motor vehicles under the influence of alcohol or drugs creates opportunities for court ordered treatment which are explicitly prescribed by statute. G.L. c. 90, § 24 et seq. In sentencing defendants involved in family or household abuse situations, the court has explicit authority to order substance abuse treatment, including residential treatment. G.L. c. 276, § 42A.

Any defendant who is found guilty of any type of offense may inform the court that he or she is a "drug dependent person who is in need of treatment." If this is confirmed, the court may order that the defendant be afforded substance abuse treatment at any facility in which he or she may be incarcerated. G.L. c. 111E, § 11. (See Standard X.) The court has broad discretion in setting conditions of probation for any defendant. G.L. c. 276, §§ 87, 87A. This may include attendance at a drug treatment program. The court may also order a drug dependent defendant to a treatment facility as a condition of probation. G.L. c. 111E, § 12.

When structuring a sentence for a defendant who is a substance abuser, the judge should keep in mind that substance abuse is a disease of relapse, and try to fashion a sentence which leaves room for the application of escalating sanctions for non-compliance with specific conditions of probation. Straight probation with strict conditions provides the greatest flexibility to respond to relapse. When the defendant is convicted of more than one charge, the judge can also lay a foundation for the application of escalating sanctions for non-compliance, by imposing a combination of different sanctions for the different charges—e.g., a committed sentence to the House of Correction followed by probation, probation concurrent with or on and after a committed sentence, a combination of straight probation with probation conditions, or different lengths of suspended sentences on and after one another.

4. Probation Violation Hearing

Probation violation and modification hearings present valuable opportunities for mandating substance abuse treatment. When a probationer is before the court for a probation violation, the court may order a new assessment, initial treatment, or intensified treatment as an alternative to incarceration. A court may modify conditions of probation as a matter of common law. *Buckley v. Quincy Division of the District Court*, 395 Mass. 815 (1985). However, a court may not impose only part of a formerly suspended sentence as a means of coercion. G.L. c. 279, § 3; *Comm. v. Holmgren*, 421 Mass 224 (1995). The use of straight probation and the imposition of suspended sentences of different lengths, as recommended under paragraph 3 above, however, gives the judge the flexibility at the time of a violation hearing to apply gradually escalating sanctions for non-compliance. Sometimes, it is necessary for the judge to revoke probation in order to protect public safety.

Civil Commitments. The District, Juvenile, or Boston Municipal Court may hear requests for the civil commitment of alcoholics and substance abusers upon the written application of certain petitioners (police officer, physician, spouse, blood relative, guardian or court official). G.L. c. 123, § 35. The judge may order a person committed for up to 30 days upon a finding, based on competent medical testimony, that the person is an alcoholic or a substance abuser and that there is a likelihood of serious harm as a result of his or her alcoholism or substance abuse. These civil commitments may occur at any time during the pendency of a criminal case, including at arraignment, and should also be considered in other situations. Citizens who come to court looking for help with a family member with a substance abuse problem should be informed about community treatment resources or, if there appears to be a likelihood of serious harm, should be informed about a petition for a § 35 commitment.

Juvenile Cases. The Juvenile Courts and juvenile sessions of the District Courts also have options to order treatment for juveniles and parents in various types of cases.

1. Delinquency

In delinquency and youthful offender cases, the judge may order substance abuse assessment and treatment as a condition of probation for a juvenile adjudicated delinquent or a youthful offender. G.L. c. 119, § 58. With the defendant's consent, probation or diversion may be ordered even before adjudication. G.L. c. 276, § 87; G.L. c. 276A. If a juvenile is ordered committed as a delinquent to the custody of the Department of Youth Services (DYS), then DYS is responsible for finding suitable treatment services. In such a case, the court should make specific recommendations to DYS regarding substance abuse treatment.

2. Children In Need of Service

"Children in need of service" (CHINS), which includes runaways, truants, and stubborn children, may be placed in the custody of the Department of Social Services (DSS) with a request by the judge that treatment be provided. G.L. c. l19, § 39H. After adjudication as a CHINS, a juvenile may be committed to the custody of DSS with the same request by the judge for substance abuse treatment. Another disposition is to allow the child to remain in the custody of his or her parents, on the condition that he or she comply with the substance abuse treatment ordered by the court. Any such order must be made as a condition of custody only. The judge may not directly order the child to engage in substance abuse treatment. See *Matter of Vincent,* 408 Mass. 527 (1990).

3. Care and Protection

Care and protection cases present a strategic opportunity for court intervention with substance abusing parents, keeping in mind the best interests of the children. G.L. c. 119, § 51A et seq. If the judge believes substance abuse may be a factor, the judge should advise the respondent parent(s)/guardian that failure to comply with substance abuse treatment will be considered as a factor in making the ultimate determination of parental unfitness or of termination of parental rights. However, the fact that the judge did not advise the parent(s)/guardian of the ramifications of fai1ure to comply with substance abuse treatment does not prevent the judge from considering substance abuse in making an ultimate determination of parental unfitness or termination of parental rights.

Domestic Relations Cases. Probate and Family Court cases routinely involve substance abuse issues. These cases may involve divorce or paternity-related custody or visitation disputes under G.L. c. 208 and c. 209C, petitions to dispense with parents' rights to consent to adoption under G.L. c. 210, guardianship of minors under G.L. c. 201, or applications for orders of protection under G.L. c. 209A. The judge should identify substance abuse early in any case involving children, provide for an assessment of the parent's treatment needs, refer the parent to an appropriate substance abuse treatment provider in order to address the problem, monitor the parent's progress in treatment through interim hearings, and manage the case by bringing it back periodically to determine progress and adjust visitations accordingly. Faced with the loss of custody of a child, a substance abusing parent is likely to be receptive to treatment.

In domestic relations cases, either a party or a probation officer (family service officer in the Probate and Family Court) can best inform the judge of substance abuse issues. The judge may also direct a family service officer to investigate a family situation and submit a report to the judge. As part of that report, the family service officer can assess the validity and severity of any substance abuse allegations and make recommendations to the court regarding custody, visitation, and treatment for the substance abuser.

Abuse Petitions. The court should take special precautions when dealing with orders of protection under G.L. c. 209A. When dealing with a batterer who is also a substance abuser, treatment for substance abuse should precede or be in conjunction with batterer's treatment or the batterer's treatment will be ineffective. Therefore, in cases involving batterers who are also substance abusers, the judge should order substance abuse treatment as well as a certified batterer's program. The Standards on Judicial Practice, Abuse Prevention Guidelines, Guideline 6.01 state in part "In addition to including in the order terms necessary to ensure the safety of the plaintiff, the judge or court personnel may recommend and refer the parties to appropriate agencies for victims of violence and certified batterers' programs. Among these may be counseling for substance abuse."

Standard VI. Indications of Substance Abuse

All judges and court personnel should look for indications of substance abuse that may be a factor related to a case before the court.

COMMENTARY

Indications of Substance Abuse in Criminal and Delinquency Cases

There can be at least seven sources of information which suggest that substance abuse may be a factor related to the case.

1. The **offense title.** Any criminal offense can involve substance abuse. For some offenses, however, substance abuse generally appears more likely—a drug or alcohol related offense, disorderly conduct, disturbing the peace, assault and battery, malicious destruction of property, leaving the scene of an accident, breaking and entering, larceny, prostitution, and shoplifting.

2. The **actual allegations.** The statement that an offense was committed while the defendant was under the influence of drugs or alcohol or was otherwise related to substance abuse may appear in the information provided by the District Attorney, such as the police report, or in the clerk's file, among allegations presented at the hearing on an application for a criminal complaint.

3. The **criminal record.** In general a history of offenses which probably involve substance abuse may be discerned from a defendant's criminal record. Even a first offense, however, may merit inquiry regarding substance abuse.

4. Abuse prevention order. In cases when an order against domestic violence is sought in connection with the criminal complaint or has been issues previously, the affidavit in support of the application may allege substance abuse or reveal facts suggesting substance abuse.

5. A party's **demeanor or physical appearance.** Substance abuse may be indicated if the party appears agitated, glassy-eyed, unkempt, or unsteady, or if the party smells of alcohol. Judges and other court personnel should be aware, however, that slurring of speech or tremors can also be symptoms of neurological or metabolic illnesses.

6. A party may **identify himself or herself** as a substance abuser, and request referral to a detoxification center or treatment program.

7. The **victim** of a crime, the police officer, a family member, or others may provide information about an offender's substance abuse.

Indications of Substance Abuse in Civil Cases. In cases involving divorce or paternity-related custody, termination of parental rights, guardianship of minors, or applications for restraining orders under G.L. c. 209A, factors similar to those listed for criminal cases may indicate that substance abuse is involved. In addition, substance abuse may be present if the parents are alleged to have left children unattended or to have frequently left children with friends or neighbors while staying out late, or if parents are charged with a criminal offense. In other kinds of cases, substance abuse may be indicated by sudden or persistent financial difficulties.

Determination That Substance Abuse Is a Factor. Judges and court personnel should be alert to other interpretations of the indications listed. Counsel may wish to be heard on the issue of whether substance abuse is a factor in the case.

Standard VII. Screening

If there is an indication that substance abuse is a factor in a case, at the earliest stage and at any stage, the court is encouraged to use tools for prompt screening. Screening is a mechanism for rapid initial determination whether it is appropriate for a person to undergo a substance abuse assessment (as provided in Standard VIII) or to participate in a treatment program. In performing screening, courts should observe applicable constitutional and statutory safeguards, including the right to counsel and the privilege against self-incrimination.

COMMENTARY

The purpose of screening is to provide the court rapidly with information regarding any drug or alcohol factor in a case. Screening results usually provide a sufficient clinical basis for a court order directing a person to appear for a substance abuse assessment (as provided in Standard VIII) and to undergo treatment, but in some cases the judge may prefer to refer the person for a substance abuse assessment before ordering treatment. The probation department is responsible for conducting screening and recommending whether a substance abuse assessment is appropriate.

Screening is the first stage of the diagnostic process, but an assessment is necessary for full and clear understanding of a party's substance abuse. Screeners look for possible abuse of alcohol or other drug; primary substance used, if any; symptoms of acute mental health problems, signs of acute intoxication or withdrawal; other medical problems, particularly infectious diseases such as HIV/AIDS or tuberculosis; motivation or readiness for treatment; criminal history; prior involvement in treatment; and use of psychotropic medication.

Judges and other court personnel should be aware that a defendant or party who is shaking or suffering from flu-like symptoms may need detoxification, a medical intervention to manage withdrawal symptoms caused by abstinence from alcohol or drugs. Since such withdrawal can cause very serious medical problems, and can be life threatening in the case of alcohol, the judge should initiate an appropriate response, such as directing the probation department to refer the person to a treatment facility or, if involuntary commitment is necessary, initiating a commitment for detoxification pursuant to G.L. c. 123, § 35. If the person is remanded to the House of Correction, the mittimus should make a clear statement concerning the need for detoxification.

Even if a screening cannot be performed, courts should consider the indications of substance abuse to the extent allowed by law.

Standard VIII. Assessments

When the court has determined as a result of a screening that substance abuse is a factor in the case and has issued or is considering a court order of substance abuse treatment, a substance abuse assessment should be conducted under the direction of the probation department, in order to determine which form of treatment will be most appropriate and effective.

COMMENTARY

The purpose of this standard is to assure that court-ordered treatment will be based on comprehensive information regarding a party's drug or alcohol abuse. An assessment should be done and considered by the court at each stage of a case when the court is considering a change in a party's status. An assessment is an in-depth process to determine a person's specific treatment needs, which takes much longer than a screening. An assessment is an evaluation performed under the direction of the probation department by a qualified clinician or other qualified substance abuse professional. In general, the probation department should refer parties to treatment providers for substance abuse assessments, but some probation officers have the requisite training and experience to conduct substance abuse assessments. Probation officers should be alert to mental health problems which compound substance abuse problems, and, in cases involving poor mental illness in addition to substance abuse, the probation department should use the court clinic or an outside vendor with mental health expertise to conduct the assessment. The treatment provider to which the party is eventually referred should always conduct its own clinical assessment, in order to confirm that the referral is appropriate, design a treatment plan, and engage the party in the treatment.

A court-ordered substance abuse assessment should determine whether and to what extent a party is using substances, evaluate the party's suitability for treatment, determine whether and what treatment is appropriate, and establish the degree of risk to the community due to the substance abuse of a defendant or convicted offender in a criminal case. If treatment is appropriate, the assessment should result in a recommendation for treatment appropriate to the party's needs, for a specific time in a designated residential facility or community placement, with proposed monitoring requirements. The assessment should include information regarding any insurance coverage available to the party, including coverage, or eligibility for coverage, by the Massachusetts Medical Assistance program. The assessment should consider all available, relevant information regarding the party, including, where applicable, substance abuse history; mental health history; other areas of psychosocial history and functioning, such as medical and health status, employment and job status, social and family relationships; educational status; legal status (current case and other pending or active cases); treatment history, including responses to and compliance with treatment, prior experience with self help recovery groups, motivation or readiness for treatment; resources and limitations affecting ability to participate in treatment; learning or other developmental disabilities, and family history of mental health and substance abuse disorders.

Standard IX. Treatment Matching

Court-ordered treatment should match the party's treatment needs, and should be selected on the basis of expert information about what type of treatment will work best for the party, with full consideration of public safety.

COMMENTARY

Court-ordered treatment should be based on the court-ordered assessment and the treatment recommendation resulting from the assessment, including the manner of payment for the treatment recommended. The treatment recommendation should address the party's needs, if any, for educational assistance, psychological or psychiatric services, vocational services, and social skills training. If an assessment is conducted before the issuance of the treatment order, the probation department, with the judge's approval, should make all relevant information and recommendations available to the court, the parties, and their attorneys, within a reasonable time prior to the issuance of a treatment order. See Massachusetts Rules of Criminal Procedure 28(d)(3) regarding access to presentence reports. The objective of matching treatment to the party's treatment needs is to match the intensity of the intervention to the severity of the substance abuse problem. It involves consideration not only of the individual qualities addressed by the assessment, including the severity of the dependency and the support structures available to the person through family, work, school, and peers, but also of the latest available information about the effectiveness of treatment programs. Appropriate matching, using only those resources and restrictions called for by the substance abuser's problem, greatly enhances the effectiveness of treatment, is essential in addressing relapse and reducing recidivism, and promotes the efficient use of resources.

Self-help recovery groups, such as Alcoholics Anonymous or Narcotics Anonymous, are typically part of a good, comprehensive treatment plan. For example, if a treatment program slot is not immediately available, the judge may order that the party abstain from alcohol or drugs (as provided in Standard XI) and suggest that he or she should participate in a self-help recovery program in order to comply with the abstinence order. Such participation can be a valuable interim action. Participation in a self-help recovery group can also be an essential adjunct to treatment and a means of sustaining recovery. The judge should allow the party the option of attending either AA/NA meetings or other daily self-help recovery meetings that do not conflict with his or her religious beliefs.

Standard X. Recommendation to Correctional Authorities

Criminal courts should indicate to correctional authorities on the mittimus when a defendant has a substance abuse problem, to assist in classifying the inmate and addressing treatment needs. Judges are encouraged to recommend a particular treatment program or a particular institution on the mittimus. Courts should also provide correctional authorities with the results of court ordered assessments and any other relevant information that will assist in the classification of the inmate.

COMMENTARY

The purpose of this standard to encourage courts to make recommendations directly on the defendant's mittimus to the sheriff's department or Department of Correction in an effort to provide correctional authorities with information about a defendant's substance abuse problem and to promote the placement of a defendant in an appropriate substance abuse treatment program operated by correctional authorities. Since most defendants are released eventually, public safety is served and recidivism is less likely when treatment is provided in the institution. Judges and probation officers should familiarize themselves with treatment programs in jails and prisons, including eligibility requirements, and, if possible, waiting lists, in order to recommend a particular treatment program or institution on the mittimus. Whenever possible, judges and probation officers are encouraged to obtain personal knowledge about available treatment programs. This knowledge will not only inform sentencing decisions, but also will permit judges to explain sentences more accurately to the public. This standard will also help to expedite the classification of offenders held without bail or sentenced to short terms of incarceration.

The Office of the Commissioner of Probation, in consultation with the Standing Committee on Substance Abuse, should develop, distribute, and maintain a directory of substance abuse treatment programs run by correctional institutions that includes each program's address, contact person and title, eligibility requirements, duration, process of referral, treatment method, and program capacity. The directory of institutional treatment programs should be organized by regions. The Office of the Commissioner of Probation may combine the directory of institutional treatment programs with the directory of community treatment providers recommended in Standard XV.

One way of assuring that correctional authorities are alerted to substance abuse issues would be to add a check-off box for substance abusers to the mittimus form.

Standard XI. Mandatory Abstinence

Every court order which sets substance abuse conditions should prohibit all use of alcohol and illicit drugs for the duration of the order.

COMMENTARY

Some substance abusers erroneously believe that they can use alcohol or drugs in moderation without adverse consequences. Overwhelming clinical evidence demonstrates that the use of alcohol while in recovery from drug addiction, or the use of drugs while in recovery from alcohol addiction, is a clear indication that the substance abuser is not yet in recovery or has failed in recovery.[5]

[5] *"Abstinence from alcohol and other drugs is the recommended goal for all drug addiction treatment." Terence T. Gorski, John M. Kelley, and Lisa Havens, Relapse Prevention and the Substance Abusing Offender: An Executive Briefing, p. 12. Technical Assistance Publication Series, Number 8, Center for Substance Abuse Treatment, Substance Abuse and Mental Health Services, Public Health Service, U.S. Department of Health and Human Services, 1993, 1995. "Recovery involves . . . abstaining from alcohol and other drugs." Relapse and Recovery, p. 12, Massachusetts Probation Service, 1998.*

Accordingly, once the judge has concluded that a party's substance abuse is a factor in the case, in supervising criminal and civil cases and in establishing court ordered substance abuse conditions, the judge should specifically and unambiguously prohibit the party from all use of alcohol and illicit drugs and the abuse of prescribed drugs. Compliance with such a prohibition order should be enforced through the drug testing called for in Standard XII.

Standard XII. Monitoring Compliance

Every court should intensely monitor compliance with court-imposed treatment conditions. Tools available should include drug testing, verification of attendance at counseling sessions and self-help recovery meetings, and communication with treatment providers. Tools for monitoring compliance, such as drug testing and breathalyzers, should be available in every courthouse and drug testing results should be made available to the court as quickly as possible. The court should inform every person who is subject to court ordered treatment conditions that non-compliance with the conditions will have consequences and the court should directly and expeditiously address any non-compliance.

COMMENTARY

The probation department should monitor compliance by means of drug and alcohol testing, verification of attendance at self-help recovery meetings, frequent progress reports from the treatment provider, and, wherever possible, day and nighttime visits at the person's home, school, place of work, or treatment provider. In order to facilitate such monitoring, the probation department should obtain the person's signed consent to provide the treatment provider with relevant information in the person's probation case file, such as the person's criminal record and treatment history.[6] (See also Standard XIV, Commentary, first paragraph.) The benefits of compliance and the consequences of non-compliance with drug or alcohol testing and treatment—such as modification of the conditions of probation or probation revocation—should be clearly and emphatically made known to the party. Positive tests, failure to submit to tests, and failure to attend counseling sessions or self-help recovery meeting are serious matters and should be addressed promptly by the court. See Standard XIII for further suggestions about how to address non-compliance using graduated sanctions or consequences.

[6] *See Standards for Certain Office Procedures for the Probation Offices of the Superior Court Department, Probate and Family Court Department, District Court Department, Boston Municipal Court Department and the Juvenile Court Department, Commissioner of Probation, Standard 5:05.*

Conversely, if a party is complying with treatment conditions, positive reinforcement is also a valuable aid to recovery.

Standard XIII. Relapse

Every court should implement strategies to prevent relapse of a substance abuser who is in recovery and be prepared to address relapse. The strategies should include a plan for imposing graduated sanctions or consequences. The court should inform every party that relapse will have consequences.

COMMENTARY

Relapse is a stalling or slowing of a person's recovery process, when a person's unmet needs lead to stress and recovery difficulties. Relapse is not an event, but a process, in which the stress keeps building and the person becomes increasingly isolated, confused, and overwhelmed. Without an intervention, the person will often return to substance abuse. Often a relapse means that a person has reached an impasse in his or her recovery, sometimes called a "stuck point." The processes of relapse and recovery are intimately related to one another. The process of relapse can be interrupted by making a needed intervention, such as the responses noted below, which may resolve the person's recovery problems.

Relapse prevention techniques can provide people with an understanding of their own relapse warning signs, to that they will know when their recovery is in trouble and that they need to address their problems immediately.

Recovery is a lengthy process, and substance abuse cannot be "cured" any more than other chronic disease, such as diabetes, hypertension, or asthma, can be cured.[7] People can, however, be taught to manage their substance abuse by remaining abstinent and following recovery principles. It is just as important to understand relapse and to support behavior change as it is to enforce treatment conditions vigilantly and supervise people closely. See Commentary to Standard XIV, sixth paragraph, for the suggestion that courts should refer parties only to treatment providers which offer comprehensive relapse prevention services.

[7] *See McClellan et al., Is Drug Dependence a Treatable Illness, op. cit., p. 26–31.*

It is of vital importance that courts understand relapse, anticipate relapse, be prepared to deal with it, and respond to it promptly The appropriate response to a relapse must be fashioned based on each person's individual needs, history of substance abuse, and previously utilized treatment modalities. Graduated responses are generally appropriate, including ordering or increasing drug testing, increasing frequency of attendance at outpatient or day treatment services or recovery meetings, increased supervision, and ordering in-patient detoxification or residential placement. In some cases, an offender's behavior or uncooperative attitude will present such a clear or immediate threat to public safety that probation revocation and incarceration are the only appropriate responses.

Standard XIV. Standards for Treatment Providers

Courts should order substance abuse treatment through providers licensed by the Department of Public Health (DPH) to treat substance abuse, licensed by the Department of Mental Health (DMH) to treat mental illness, jointly licensed by DPH and DMH to treat both substance abuse and mental illness, or approved by the Probation Department or the Office of Community Corrections as qualified to provide substance abuse treatment. Subject to established rules of confidentiality, the Probation Department should require providers to communicate regularly and candidly with the court regarding a party's compliance with court-ordered behavior and treatment.

COMMENTARY

The Commissioner of Probation and the Office of Community Corrections should promulgate criteria for courts to use in selecting treatment providers to receive court referrals. These criteria should not apply to self help recovery groups such as Alcoholics Anonymous or Narcotics Anonymous. Referrals to providers should not involve even the appearance of a conflict of interest. The criteria for treatment providers should include at least the following.

1) As a condition of court-ordered treatment, the provider should require the party to sign a release authoring the provider to disclose information to the probation department about the party's progress in treatment and compliance with treatment orders. The release should state how much and what kind of information is to be disclosed, but the release should not be unlimited; it should not call for the disclosure of all confidential communications between the party and the treatment provider. This release should be in addition to the consent kept in the files of the Probation Department under Standard XII, and, in a criminal case, neither the consent nor the release should be rescinded during the period of probation supervisor. See 42 CFR Ch. 1, Subpart C, § 2.35(c).

2) The provider's treatment staff should be available to consult with the Probation Department to the extent allowed by the terms of the release.

3) The provider should submit periodic, written progress reports to the probation officer which disclose the party's attendance record, compliance with treatment orders, and any drug testing results, and should submit a written report in case of any non-compliance.

4) The provider should notify the probation department immediately with respect to any serious non-compliance, including any positive drug tests of the party.

5) The provider should furnish the court with a final discharge report when the party completes the treatment. The reason for the discharge should be dearly documented.

6) The provider's treatment protocol should include comprehensive relapse prevention services delivered according to a model of proven effectiveness.

Standard XV. Treatment Directory

To assist in the identification of treatment resources, the Commissioner of Probation, in consultation with the Department of Public Health, should maintain an updated directory of treatment providers.[8] The directory should include each treatment provider's phone number, address contact person and title, eligibility requirements, accepted payment methods, hours of operation, process of referral, treatment method, and procedures with respect to relapse. The directory should include services for a diverse population.

[8] *Such a directory is called for by Standards 10:01, 10:02, and 10:03 of the Commissioner of Probation's Standards for Supervision for Probate Offices of the Superior Court Department, District Court Department, Boston Municipal Court Department and the Juvenile Court Department.*

COMMENTARY

The purpose of the directory is to provide the courts with information facilitating access to comprehensive and current drug and alcohol treatment resources and services available in each community in Massachusetts. Only treatment providers which satisfy the criteria promulgated under Standard XIV should be included in the directory.

The directory should be divided into regions and the communities within each region. Probation departments in each region should compile the information on resources and services in the communities within the region. The Office of the Commissioner of Probation should update the directory at least annually. If a provider is not in compliance with the criteria established by the probation department under Standard XIV, the provider should be removed from the directory. The Office of the Commissioner of Probation may combine the directory of community treatment providers with the directory of institutional treatment programs recommended in the Commentary to Standard X.

Judges should become familiar with the resources included in the directory. Whenever possible, judges and probation officers are encouraged to make site visits to treatment providers to gain a better understanding of available treatment services to foster stronger community collaboration between the various courts and their treatment providers.

Standard XVI. Community Resources

Every court should identify the specific resources available in the community for the treatment of substance abuse, and establish and maintain relationships with local treatment providers. If services for a diverse population are not available in the community, the court should determine where such services are available and develop and maintain relationships with the providers of those services.[9]

[9] *Identification of Community Resources is called for by Standards 10:04 and 10:05 of the Commissioner of Probation's Standards for Supervision for Probate Offices of the Superior Court Department, District Court Department, Boston Municipal Court Department and the Juvenile Court Department.*

2

COMMENTARY

In each court, the effectiveness of the substance abuse strategy will depend in large measure on knowledge of treatment resources in the local community and the cultivation of relationships with various providers. Often, for example, the ability to find a bed at an in-patient facility springs from the personal knowledge of a judge or probation officer about the facility and its personnel. The judge and the probation officer, therefore, should acquire a thorough understanding of treatment providers in the local community and should be aware of the meeting times and places in the community for self-help recovery groups such as Alcoholics Anonymous (AA) and Narcotics Anonymous (NA). The directory developed pursuant to Standard XV should be used as a resource for identifying facilities to serve a diverse population.

Standard XVII. Communication and Collaboration Within Court and With Community

All court staff, treatment providers, prosecutors, police, defense counsel, correctional authorities, and the media should communicate clearly with one another on substance abuse issues. The first, regional administrative, or chief justice, as applicable, of each court should promote communication and collaboration on substance abuse issues within the court, as well as between. the court and the community.

COMMENTARY

A relationship with the community is critical to ensuring the success of every court's response to substance abuse. It is important that the defense bar and assistant district attorneys understand that the clients and the community are the beneficiaries of the courts' actions with respect to substance abuse. Police should be encouraged to attend and, if possible, be part of the faculty in any court sponsored training program. The local bar association should be encouraged to take part in a public meeting where the courts' substance abuse policy is explained. Probation officers should meet with treatment providers, in order to form collegial relationships and facilitate appropriate referrals. Of course, all court personnel should avoid creating any actual or apparent conflict of interest through their relationships with the providers. The business community and the schools have important roles to play in providing recovering substance abusers with jobs and education. Community-based operations, including the faith community, can help to foster communication between the courts and the public regarding the courts' response to substance abuse services available in the community and the community's particular problems. The media should be made aware of the court's approach to substance abuse, and court leaders should consult with the court system's Public Information Office about outreach to the media concerning new initiatives and success stories. One way of forming and enhancing these community relationships is to establish an advisory committee for a court or group of courts as a forum for communication between the courts and the community. The community corrections advisory boards required by G.L. c. 211F, § 6 and the Substance Abuse Leadership Teams formed during the Judicial Institute substance abuse training programs may also contribute to communication and collaboration on substance abuse issues within the courts and between the courts and the community.

Standard XVIII. Use of Courthouse for Recovery and Education Sessions

The justices who have administrative responsibility for courthouses are encouraged to seek permission from the Chief Justice for Administration and Management of the Trial Court to authorize access to the court buildings for court-referred recovery meetings, counseling sessions, and substance abuse education group meetings, in order to ensure that security and other issues are addressed. All courts are encouraged to refer defendants to such meetings and sessions in the court building.

COMMENTARY

Many courts already offer space for counseling, recovery meetings, and education groups for parties referred by the court. For example, Alcoholics Anonymous or Rational Recovery meetings are held at a number of courts. While most of these courthouse meetings occur in the evenings, several courts hold daily lunchtime AA meetings in the courthouse. Narcotics Anonymous meetings occur regularly in a few courts, while other courts accommodate drug education and drug prevention programs.

Substance abusers benefit psychologically when they enter the court as part of a group of self-respecting, recovering addicts helping one another. The courthouse changes from a place of shame and loss of control over one's life to one of strength and hope. This effect is magnified if court personnel, such as probation officers and judges, attend these meetings to give those in recovery some positive feedback concerning their success in staying away from alcohol or drugs.

Additionally, the courts are usually centrally located and easily accessible to the local community by public transportation. This can be an important factor in facilitating attendance.

Any group wishing to conduct courthouse meetings must seek permission from the Chief Justice for Administration and Management, in order to ensure that security and other issues are addressed.

Standard XIX. Substance Abuse Within Courts.

The court system should respond to substance abuse among judges, clerks, court personnel, and lawyers. The response should include the creation of opportunities to receive referrals for treatment and the recognition by disciplinary authorities that required participation in treatment can be an appropriate condition of discipline.

COMMENTARY

The people who work in the court system are part of society, and hence are vulnerable to the disease of substance abuse. Justice will be better administered if the court system responds to this problem among its own personnel. The efforts of the judiciary to address substance abuse when it is a factor in cases will have far greater credibility and will be far more effective if the court system addresses the issue when it affects people who work within it. Personal policies throughout the court system should include standards for addressing the problem of substance abuse. The Trial Court Personnel Policies and Procedures Manual, the Appellate Courts' Personnel Policies, the Commission on Judicial Conduct, the Committee on Professional Responsibility for Clerks of the Courts, and the Board of Bar Overseers should take substance abuse into account in employment policies and disciplinary remedies. A judges' group within Lawyers Concerned for Lawyers is a valuable resource.

Standard XX. Substance Abuse Among Attorneys

Any judge or clerk-magistrate who believes that substance abuse is a factor in the professional performance of an attorney appearing before him or her should refer the attorney to a lawyers' assistance program, or, if the performance amounts to professional misconduct, report the misconduct to the Board of Bar Overseers. If the issue of professional performance arises in connection with an imminent proceeding in an active matter, the judge or clerk should make inquiries and, if necessary, postpone the proceeding.

COMMENTARY

The most extensive lawyers' assistance program is Lawyers Concerned for Lawyers, a group of lawyers and judges who stand ready, willing, and able to assist other lawyers and judges who have problems with alcoholism and addiction. A judge who becomes aware of unprofessional conduct by a lawyer is required to "initiate appropriate investigate or disciplinary measures." See SJC Rule 3:09, Canon 3(B)(3)(b). If the attorney was assigned the case by the Committee for Public Counsel Services (CPCS), the court should notify CPCS, pursuant to G.L. c. 211D, § 10. The Board of Bar Overseers is bound by specific rules regarding what to do with an alcoholic or addicted lawyer. See SJC Rule 4:01, § 13, pars. 2, 3, 4, 5, and 6, which address the response by the Board of Bar Overseers to the issue of incapacity of a lawyer.

Guidelines for Developing Proposed Findings of Fact and Rulings of Law in Child Welfare Cases

[Dated Fall 2001.]

Supreme Judicial Court

Committee on Delay in Child Welfare Cases

Comprehensive and well written proposed findings of fact and rulings of law greatly assist in the just adjudication of petitions brought pursuant to G.L. c. 119, §§ 24 and 26, and G.L. c. 210, § 3 (colloquially known as "care and protection" and "termination of parental rights" cases, and collectively referred to in these guidelines as "child welfare cases"). The following guidelines and model outline have been developed and endorsed by the Supreme Judicial Court's Committee on Delay in Child Welfare Cases. They are intended to assist trial counsel in child welfare cases in preparing proposed findings of fact and rulings of law.

General Guidelines

1. In every contested child welfare case (unless the court otherwise instructs), the attorneys representing the parties at trial should submit comprehensive proposed findings of fact and rulings of law to the presiding judge under a timeline to be established by the court.

2. The parties' proposed findings and rulings should be composed in short, numbered paragraphs grouped under subheadings such as those set forth in the Outline section below. Each paragraph should deal with only one set of related facts or one proposition of law.

Guidelines for Drafting Proposed Findings of Fact

1. Within each topical area, the numbered paragraphs should follow an orderly progression. In the proposed findings of fact section, the information will usually be presented in chronological order. However, in some subsections it may be more appropriate to organize information according to a thematic design (e.g., child by child).

2. Proposed findings of fact should be specific and detailed, particularly in the areas most central to the party's theory of the case.

3. An attorney should propose only findings that are supported by the evidence or reasonable inferences therefrom. Every proposed fact should be followed by a reference to the supporting evidence or to any stipulated facts. There should be a cite to the trial exhibits or trial transcript whenever possible. If a transcript is not available sufficiently in advance of the due date of the proposed findings, then the attorney should identify the witness who testified to each fact and give the date of that testimony.

4. Where there is conflicting or disputed evidence concerning particular factual matters, it is advisable to include proposed credibility findings that articulate why certain testimony or evidence should be credited and conflicting evidence rejected.

Guidelines for Drafting Proposed Conclusions of Law

1. In drafting proposed rulings of law, the attorney should articulate his or her theory of the case and set forth the legal analysis that supports the client's position, with citations to supporting legal authority, including pinpoint citations to the page of a case on which the relevant material appears.

2. Proposed rulings of law should be carefully tailored to the legal issues actually raised in the case and should apply the law to the particular facts of the case.

3. Well established propositions of law common to many child welfare cases should be stated succinctly, without significant elaboration, and should be followed by a citation to the leading case(s) on point. Avoid the use of string citations and boilerplate formulations of the general law in this area.

Model Outline of Proposed Findings of Fact

Each topic area should be addressed unless it is plainly irrelevant to a particular case. It is recommended that either the proposed findings as a whole follow a logical, generally chronological order, or that the findings be divided into subsections by subject matter (e.g., findings concerning each parent or child where more than one parent or child is involved), with all of the findings contained within each subsection laid out in some logical (e.g., chronological) fashion.

I. Introductory Paragraph Concerning the Child(ren) and Parent(s)

Identify the parties, including the child(ren) who are the subject of the proceedings, by name (including any alias) and date (and place, if known) of birth. Specify the child(ren)'s age(s) at the time of trial. Also identify other immediate family members who are not parties before the court. Describe the legal relationships among the members of the immediate family (e.g., specify if legal or putative parent, full or half-sibling). If paternity has been adjudicated, enter the date of adjudication or the date a voluntary acknowledgment of paternity was executed.

II. Procedural History of the Case

Use the docket sheets to capture information regarding all significant procedural steps in this case and any related cases. Include, for example, the date the petition was filed; the names and dates of appointment of counsel and any court investigator or guardian ad litem; and the date(s) of trial. Specify the date and manner of service of process for each respondent. Set forth the substance of any preliminary court rulings, motions in limine, and significant evidentiary rulings. Lay out the procedural history of any past legal actions, including dates, courts, and docket numbers; findings of fact, if any; and prior determinations.

III. List of Exhibits and Witnesses

List all exhibits, trial witnesses, and stipulated facts. Where applicable, specify whether exhibits were redacted or admitted for a limited purpose only. The witness list should identify each witness by name and by title (e.g., guardian ad litem) or relationship to the child (e.g., mother). For expert witnesses, provide licensure information (e.g., LICSW) or area of expertise (e.g., child psychiatrist).

IV. The Facts of the Particular Case

A. History of the Period Prior to DSS Involvement

1. If the child(ren) resided with the parent(s) prior to DSS involvement, specify the duration (giving dates); location, including a description of the surroundings; and amount of daily contact between parent(s) and child(ren).

2. Identify other relevant persons in the child(ren)'s life (especially the noncustodial parent, siblings and extended family) and describe the amount of contact and activities engaged in together. Incorporate evidence regarding the child(ren)'s development, including their health history (both physical and mental/emotional); educational history; and social adjustment.

3. Describe the parent(s)' circumstances, including their health history (both physical and mental/emotional); economic circumstances; employment history; and marital information (such as dates of marriage, separation, and divorce); and relationship with each other and with other partners or spouses, if relevant.

B. History of the Family's Involvement with DSS Prior to Filing of the Petition

Include details of evidence regarding the events immediately preceding the filing of the petition, including the dates and circumstances of any 51A reports and 51B investigations, voluntary agreements for custody, or parental surrenders.

C. Evidence Regarding Reasonable Efforts, Services Offered, and Parental Utilization of Services

Describe evidence of any services offered to the parent(s) and the child. State the evidence of the parent(s)' and DSS's compliance or lack of compliance with any service plan. Discuss any evidence of the parent(s)' course of treatment, if applicable, and of the prognosis for the parent's rehabilitation. Indicate if a court has determined that no reasonable efforts are required to reunite the child(ren) with their parent(s).

D. Evidence Regarding Each Parent

Set forth the relevant evidence regarding the ability, capacity, fitness, and readiness of the parent(s) to assume or resume parental responsibilities. Parties supporting the petition should, in particular, describe any evidence of the parent(s)' abuse or neglect of the child (specify by date, incident, and person making observation).

Parties supporting the petition should pay particular attention to any evidence of an adverse impact on the child of any alleged unfitness of the parent(s). Parties opposing the petition should show why evidence of unfitness is incredible, insignificant, stale, or without negative impact on the child and should propose findings to show change, good parenting, a positive parent-child relationship, and the ability to provide a stable physical and emotional home environment.

E. Evidence Regarding Each Child

Describe the child(ren)'s behavior, as well as present emotional and physical health. Specify any educational, developmental, or intellectual challenges. Evidence of the child(ren)'s medical needs should also be set forth here. Include evidence concerning: (a) the parent(s)' ability to meet the child's special needs; (b) the effect on child(ren) of terminating or maintaining their relationship with their parent(s), foster or pre-adoptive parents, and/or siblings, relatives, or other significant persons; and (c) the wishes of the child(ren) regarding reunification, curtailment or continuation of contact with parent(s), and/or adoption, if appropriate.

F. Evidence Regarding the Child's Substitute Care Placement History

Provide dates and specify types of placement. Explain changes, if any, and the reasons therefor. If applicable, include information concerning any foster care review meetings and DSS permanency planning conferences, assuming evidence of such is introduced at trial. Parties should discuss any evidence of the child's behavior while in substitute care and/or evidence of any bonds formed with a substitute caretaker, whether the child will suffer harm if the placement is changed, and whether the child's parent has the capacity to meet the child's needs upon removal from substitute care.

G. Evidence Regarding Visitation

Include information concerning the dates, frequency, and location of visitation; any efforts by the parent(s) to obtain or increase visitation; parent(s)' and DSS's compliance or noncompliance with the visitation schedule; activities undertaken and person(s) present during visits; response of child(ren) before, during, and after visits. Also include information concerning any contacts between child(ren) and siblings or other relatives and any nonvisitation contacts (e.g., telephone, letters, cards, school or medical-related contacts) between the child(ren) and the parent(s).

H. Summary of Evidence Pertaining to the Fourteen Factors Set Forth in G.L. c. 210, § 3(c) *(if applicable)*

I. Evidence Regarding the DSS Plan for the Child(ren) and Any Alternative Plan(s) Offered by the Other Parties *(if applicable)*

Summarize the evidence regarding DSS's efforts to implement a permanent plan for the child(ren) and/or any evidence supporting or opposing the feasibility of a plan other than that propounded by the petitioner. Summarize the evidence that demonstrates that DSS's plan or any other plan(s) proposed at trial is or is not in the best interest of the child. It is not enough to assert the conclusion that the plan serves the child's best interests. The attorney should propose a series of specific findings that discuss the various factors demonstrating the merit or lack of merit of the plan(s) in question. Also summarize any evidence concerning the timetable for implementation of the plan(s) and the nature and effect of any anticipated delay, change of schedule, or obstacles to implementation.

J. Evidence Regarding the Advisability and/or Feasibility of Post-Adoption Contact

Set forth evidence of any existing personal relationship between parent and child(ren) (or, if relevant, between child(ren) and siblings), or the degree of dissociation; evidence that demonstrates the significance of the existing bond, or lack thereof; and evidence, if any, showing that terminating the relationship would be harmful to the child or that continued contact is currently in the best interests of the child.

V. Conclusions of Law

In the proposed rulings of law section, threshold legal issues and procedural issues should be addressed first, followed by the core legal issues implicated in the case, and then any subsidiary legal issues. Where applicable, the so-called "fourteen factors" set forth in G.L. c. 210, § 3(c), should be dealt with in numerical order, with a brief statement noting the inapplicability of those factors not implicated in the case. This section should conclude with an identification of those factors that lead to the ultimate conclusion and the remedy sought.

VI. Proposed Order

State with specificity the relief your client seeks, including, if appropriate, an alternative form of relief. A draft Order should be included with your submission.

Massachusetts Appeals Court

Selected Rules of the Massachusetts Appeals Court

Rule 2:01. Practice Before a Single Justice

[General. Amended effective Feb. 27, 1975.]

Any matter which is within the jurisdiction of this court, whether originally entered or transferred to this court under the provisions of G.L. c. 211, § 4A, and which might otherwise be disposed of by a single justice of the Supreme Judicial Court, shall be filed with the clerk of this court and shall be heard and determined by a single justice of this court in accordance with the same rules, practices and procedures which would govern if the same matters were heard and determined by a single justice of the Supreme Judicial Court. The Massachusetts Rules of Civil or Appellate Procedure shall apply to any matter which would be subject thereto if it were being heard and determined by a single justice of the Supreme Judicial Court; and any other matter shall be heard and determined in accordance with the rules, practices and procedures of the Supreme Judicial Court which would be applicable thereto if it were being heard and determined by a single justice of that court.

A determination of any of the foregoing matters by a single justice of this court may be reviewed by a panel of other justices of this court in the same manner and to the same extent that the determination of a like matter by a single justice of the Supreme Judicial Court may be reviewed by the full court of the Supreme Judicial Court. As to such review in civil matters, see paragraphs (a) and (b) of Rule 1 of the Massachusetts Rules of Appellate Procedure.

Rule 2:02. Review Under Rule 15(c) of the Massachusetts Rules of Appellate Procedure

[Applicable to civil cases. Adopted effective Feb. 27, 1975.]

The review of the action of a single justice which is afforded by the last sentence of paragraph (c) of Rule 15 of the Massachusetts Rules of Appellate Procedure shall be by a panel of other justices of this court, shall be claimed by an appeal to such a panel, and shall be prosecuted in the same manner as if the single justice were the "lower court" within the meaning of paragraph (c) of Rule 1 of said Rules. See paragraphs (a) and (b) of Rule 1 of said Rules.

Rule 2:03. Special Masters and Commissioners

[Applicable to all cases. Adopted effective May 5, 1976.]

A majority of the justices of this court may designate special masters and commissioners to deal with specified cases or with such matters as may be referred to them by a written order of a single justice or of a panel of the justices. The acts of such special master and commissioner, when confirmed or approved by a single justice or by a panel of the justices, as the case may be, shall have all the force and effect of a decision by a single justice or by a panel of the Justices.

Standing Order Concerning Petitions to the Single Justice Pursuant to G.L. c. 231, § 118 (First Paragraph)

[Adopted effective Sept. 1, 1989, with strict enforcement delayed until Mar. 1, 1990. Amended effective Jan. 1, 2002; June 1, 2011; Oct. 1, 2015; Nov. 1, 2016; Sept. 1, 2018.]

(a) Contents of Petition for Relief; Form. A petition for relief pursuant to G.L. c. 231, § 118 (first paragraph), or Rule 12(a) of the Uniform Rules on Impoundment procedure, shall include, in the following order:

(1) a request for review, which shall state briefly the nature of the order or action of the trial court from which review is sought, the entry date of such order or action, and the name of the judge who entered it;

(2) a statement of the issues of law raised by the petition;

(3) a statement as to whether a party has filed, served, or intends to file a motion for reconsideration in the trial court;

(4) a statement of the specific relief requested; and

(5) an addendum containing a copy of the order or action of the trial court (a draft order for the single justice may be attached).

References to the parties in the petition shall be by designation of the party in the trial court (e.g., "plaintiff," "defendant," "third-party defendant," etc.). The petition shall not exceed five pages of text compliant with Mass.R.A.P. 20[a][1]–[3] without leave of the court.

(b) Supporting Memorandum of Law and Record Appendix. The petition shall, unless otherwise ordered, be accompanied by a memorandum of law (not to exceed fifteen pages of text compliant with Mass.R.A.P. 20[a][1]–[3] unless leave of the court has been obtained) in support of the petitioner's position, with citations to appropriate authorities and a statement addressing why relief is appropriate. The argument shall make reference to those portions of the record which are directly relevant to the issues raised by the petition. Relevant portions of the record shall be filed as a record appendix, and include a current copy of the trial court docket entries and all relevant papers filed in the trial court, including those filed by the other party or parties. The record appendix shall be consecutively numbered starting with the cover or first page as page 1 followed by a table of contents that lists each document contained therein and the page on which it appears. Only those pleadings, exhibits, and papers which were before the trial court when the order appealed from was entered, and which are necessary for an adjudication of the issues raised, may be submitted.

(c) Opposition; Form. Within seven days (ten days if the petitioner's certificate of service required under [d] hereof shows service by first-class mail) after the filing of the petition, or such other time as the court may direct, the other party or parties to the case may, but need not, file and serve an opposition thereto (not to exceed fifteen pages of text compliant with Mass.R.A.P. 20[a][1]–[3] unless leave of court has been obtained) setting forth reasons why the petition should not be granted. The opposition shall not restate matters contained in the petition unless the opposing party is dissatisfied with the statement thereof contained in the petition. The opposition may be accompanied by a supplemental record appendix containing such additional portions of the record as were before the trial court and are necessary for adjudication, and which the petitioner failed to include in its record appendix.

2

(d) Filing; Service. The petition, memorandum, record appendix, and any subsequently filed opposition and supplemental record appendix, shall be filed electronically if the filing party is represented by counsel. Self-represented litigants may file electronically, or may file a single paper original or duplicate in the office of the Clerk of the Appeals Court. Any document required to be e-filed may be filed on paper upon allowance of a motion to waive the e-filing requirement, preferably filed in advance or with the document. The motion must contain a showing of undue hardship, significant prejudice, exigency, or other good cause.

Whether filed electronically or on paper, all filings shall include a certificate of service on all other parties in the case, including the service and filing of a copy in the appropriate trial court clerk's office from which the matter arose. The certificate of service shall set forth the name, address, email address, and telephone number of counsel or other persons upon whom service has been made, and specify the date and manner of service. The certificate of service shall identify the name of each party represented by counsel and specify the counsel who represents each party.

Service may be personal, by first class mail, or electronically with the consent of the person served. Personal service includes delivery of the copy to a clerk or other responsible person at the office of counsel. Service by first class mail is complete on mailing. Registration for and use of the electronic filing system constitutes consent to electronic service, and such service is complete upon e-filing.

(e) Impounded or Confidential Information. In any case in which the trial court entered an order impounding, sealing, or excluding from public access all or any portion of the trial court records, or there is material or information in a party's petition, addendum, opposition, or any appendix that is automatically impounded or deemed confidential by statute or court rule, the parties shall comply with Mass.R.A.P. 16(d), 16(m), and 18(g). The parties shall comply with Supreme Judicial Court Rule 1:24, Protection of Personal Identifying Information in Publicly Accessible Court Documents in all filings to the Appeals Court.

(f) Hearing. The single justice has discretion to determine whether a hearing shall be held.

Massachusetts Rules of Appellate Procedure

[Amended effective Mar. 1, 2019.]

Rule

Rule 1. Scope of Rules: Definitions

(a) Scope and Construction of Rules. These rules govern procedure in appeals to an appellate court. They shall be construed, administered, and employed to secure the just, speedy, and inexpensive determination of appeals. They shall be construed in conjunction with the rules and standing orders of the appellate courts.

(b) Rules Not to Affect Jurisdiction. These rules shall not be construed to extend or limit the jurisdiction, as established by law, of the Supreme Judicial Court or the Appeals Court.

(c) Definitions. As used in these rules, unless the context clearly indicates otherwise: "appeal" means an appeal to an appellate court and supersedes any procedure other than reservation and report by which matters have heretofore been brought before an appellate court for review.

"appellate court" means the full Supreme Judicial Court, the full Appeals Court, or a statutory quorum of either, as the case may be, whichever court is exercising jurisdiction over the case at bar.

"child welfare case" means any case that is before a court of competent jurisdiction pursuant to G.L. c. 119, §§ 21–39J; G.L. c. 190B regarding guardianship of minors; or G.L. c. 210, §§ 1–11.

"clerk" means "clerk," "register," "recorder," and their respective assistants or deputies;

"clerk of the appellate division" means the clerk of the trial court from which the action was reported to the appellate division.

"decision" means, when referring to an appellate court, the court's written opinion, memorandum and order pursuant to Appeals Court Rule 1:28, or other final adjudicative order in the case.

"first class mail or its equivalent" means (1) use of the United States Postal Service through first class postage or other class of mail that is at least as expeditious, postage prepaid or (2) dispatch to a third-party commercial carrier for delivery within 3 days. Registration or certification shall not be required unless specifically stated to be necessary.

"indigent party" means a person who is a party to a legal proceeding and whom a court has determined meets the statutory criteria to obtain waiver, reduction, or payment of certain fees and costs incident to civil and criminal litigation, including appeals in that proceeding.

"lower court" means the single justice, court, appellate division, board, commission, or other body whose decision is the subject of a direct appeal to an appellate court; for the purpose of Rule 9, the term includes any member of the lower court.

"party" means a person or entity appearing in a case, including an appeal. In the context of performing any act under these rules, a party means counsel, where a party is represented by counsel, and, when a party is not represented by counsel, it means the selfrepresented litigant.

"rescript" means the appellate court's order, direction, or mandate to the lower court disposing of the appeal.

"single justice" means a single justice of whichever appellate court is exercising jurisdiction over the case at bar.

"transmission" or "transmit" means the sending or conveying of a document or court record through a medium authorized by the court or these rules, and may include, but is not limited to, first class mail or its equivalent, electronic filing, electronic mail, facsimile, or electronic file share.

(d) Construction. Words or phrases importing the singular number may extend and be applied to several persons or things, and words importing the plural number may include the singular.

Rule 2. Suspension of Rules

In the interest of expediting decision, or for other good cause shown, the appellate court or a single justice may, except as otherwise provided in Rule 14(b), suspend the requirements or provisions of any of these rules in a particular case, on such reasonable terms as the court or the single justice may order, on application of a party or on its own motion and may order proceedings in accordance with its direction.

Rule 3. Appeal—How Taken

(a) Filing the Notice of Appeal.

(1) An appeal permitted by law from a lower court shall be taken by filing a notice of appeal with the clerk of the lower court within the time allowed by Rule 4, with service upon all parties. Failure of an appellant to take any step other than the timely filing of a notice of appeal shall not affect the validity of the appeal, but shall be ground only for such action as the appellate court deems appropriate, which may include dismissal of the appeal.

(2) A party need not claim an appeal from an interlocutory order to preserve the party's right to have such order reviewed upon appeal from the final judgment; but for all purposes for which an appeal from an interlocutory order has heretofore been necessary, it is sufficient that the party comply with the requirement of Massachusetts Rule of Civil Procedure 46 or Massachusetts Rule of Criminal Procedure 22, whichever was applicable to the trial of the case in the lower court.

(b) Appeals by Multiple Parties. If 2 or more persons are entitled to appeal from a judgment, decree, adjudication, order, or part thereof of a lower court and their interests are such as to make joinder practicable, they may file a joint notice of appeal, or may join in appeal after filing separate timely notices of appeal.

(c) Content of the Notice of Appeal.

(1) Content of the Notice of Appeal, Generally. The notice of appeal shall specify the party or parties taking the appeal and shall, in civil cases, designate the judgment, decree, adjudication, order, or part thereof appealed from.

(2) Content of the Notice of Appeal in Child Welfare Cases. In child welfare cases, the notice of appeal and any request for a transcript, if required, shall be signed by the person or persons, or by counsel for the entity, taking the appeal; however, if the appellant is a minor, the notice and request shall be signed by the minor's counsel. A notice of appeal that is not so signed shall not be accepted for filing by the clerk.

(d) Service of the Notice of Appeal. The clerk of the lower court shall serve notice of the filing of a notice of appeal by transmitting a copy thereof to counsel of record for each party other than the appellant, or, if a party is not represented by counsel, to the party. The clerk shall note on each copy served the date on which the notice of appeal was filed. Failure of the clerk to serve notice shall not affect the validity of the appeal. Service shall be sufficient notwithstanding the death of a party or counsel. The clerk shall note in the docket the names of the persons to whom copies are transmitted, and the date of transmission.

(e) Change of Counsel on Appeal in Criminal and Certain Non-criminal Cases. If the defendant in a criminal case, or any party in any other proceeding, excluding child welfare cases, in which counsel is required to be made available to such party pursuant to Supreme Judicial Court Rule 3:10, was represented by counsel at trial, the trial court counsel shall continue to represent that party on appeal until an appearance is filed by substitute counsel, if such assignment of counsel is made by the Committee for Public Counsel Services. In such proceedings, assigned trial court counsel shall, no later than the day on which the notice of appeal is filed, notify the Committee for Public Counsel Services that appellate counsel should be assigned. Assigned appellate counsel shall promptly file a notice of appearance in the trial court, following which trial court counsel may file a notice of withdrawal.

(f) Appointment of Appellate Counsel in Child Welfare Cases.

(1) Subject to the provisions of Rule 10(d), any party to a child welfare case in which counsel was appointed pursuant to Supreme Judicial Court Rule 3:10 and who was represented by counsel at trial shall continue to be represented by that counsel on appeal until either the lower court has appointed counsel for appellate purposes and an appearance has been filed by appellate counsel or the lower court has denied a motion to appoint counsel for appellate purposes.

(2) Lower court counsel shall, on the day upon which the signed notice of appeal is filed, file, and request a hearing on, a motion to allow reasonable costs associated with the appeal in the lower court. At the same time, if lower court counsel is not appellate certified by the Committee for Public Counsel Services, counsel shall also file, and request a hearing on, a motion to appoint counsel for appellate purposes in the lower court. Subject to the provisions of Supreme Judicial Court Rule 3:10, § 7, lower court counsel shall continue to represent the party at all lower court proceedings.

(3) If the motion to appoint counsel for appellate purposes is allowed, the Committee for Public Counsel Services shall be assigned to provide representation according to the procedures established in Supreme Judicial Court Rule 3:10.

(4) If counsel has not filed a motion to withdraw appearance in the lower court, or counsel has filed a motion to withdraw but the motion has not been allowed by the lower court prior to the date that the lower court transmits to the appellate court the notice of assembly of the record pursuant to Rule 9, lower court counsel will be designated as counsel in the appellate court. Any motion to withdraw filed thereafter shall comply with Rule 10(d).

Rule 4. Appeal—When Taken

(a) Appeals in Civil Cases.

(1) In a civil case, unless otherwise provided by statute, the notice of appeal required by Rule 3 shall be filed with the clerk of the lower court within 30 days of the date of the entry of the judgment, decree, appealable order, or adjudication appealed from, but if the Commonwealth or an officer or agency thereof is a party, the notice of appeal may be filed by any party within 60 days of such entry, except in child welfare cases, in which the notice of appeal shall be filed within 30 days from the date of the entry of the judgment, decree, appealable order, or adjudication. If a notice of appeal is mistakenly filed in an appellate court, the clerk of such appellate court shall note the date on which it was received and transmit it to the clerk of the lower court from which the appeal was taken and it shall be deemed filed in such lower court on the date so noted. If a timely notice of appeal is filed by a party, any other party may file a notice of appeal within 14 days of the date on which the first notice of appeal was filed, or within the time otherwise prescribed by this rule, whichever period last expires.

(2) If a motion is made or served in a timely manner under the Massachusetts Rules of Civil Procedure and filed with the lower court by any party, the time to file an appeal runs for all parties from the entry of the order disposing of the last remaining motion:

(A) for judgment under Rule 50(b);

(B) under Rule 52(b) to amend or make additional findings of fact, whether or not an alteration of the judgment would be required if the motion is granted;

(C) to alter or amend a judgment under Rule 59 or for relief from judgment under Rule 60(b), however titled, but only if either motion is served within 10 days after entry of judgment; or

(D) under Rule 59 for a new trial.

(3) A notice of appeal filed before the disposition of any timely motion listed in Rule 4(a)(2) shall have no effect. A new notice of appeal must be filed within the prescribed time measured from the entry of the order disposing of the last such remaining motion.

(b) Appeals in Criminal Cases.

(1) In a criminal case, unless otherwise provided by statute or court rule, the notice of appeal required by Rule 3 shall be filed with the clerk of the lower court within 30 days after entry of the judgment, appealable order, or adjudication appealed from, or entry of a notice of appeal by the Commonwealth, or the imposition of sentence, whichever comes last.

(2) The running of the time for filing a notice of appeal shall be terminated as to the moving party by a motion for a new trial pursuant to Massachusetts Rules of Criminal Procedure 25(b)(2) and 30 filed in the lower court within 30 days after the verdict or finding of guilt or within 30 days after imposition of sentence, and the full time fixed by this rule shall commence to run and shall be computed from the date of entry of an order denying such motion.

(c) Extension of Time for Filing Notice of Appeal. Upon a showing of excusable neglect, the lower court may extend the time for filing the notice of appeal or notice of cross appeal by any party for a period not to exceed 30 days from the expiration of the time otherwise prescribed by this rule. Such an extension may be granted before or after the time otherwise prescribed by this rule has expired; but if a request for an extension is made after such time has expired, it shall be made by motion with service upon all other parties.

(d) Appeal by a Self-Represented Party Confined in an Institution. If an institution has a system designed for legal mail, a self-represented party confined there must use that system to receive the benefit of this rule. If such party files a notice of appeal in either a civil or criminal case, the notice is timely if deposited in the institution's internal mail system on or before the last day for filing and is accompanied by a signed certificate in compliance with Rule 13(a)(1)(B) setting out the date of deposit. If the notice of appeal is not received by the last day for filing, the certificate shall give rise to a presumption of timely filing provided it shows compliance with this rule.

Failure to attach the certificate shall not of itself render the notice of appeal invalid or untimely, and the lower court may permit the later filing of a certificate. If such party files the first notice of appeal in a civil case under Rule 4(d), the 14-day period provided in Rule 4(a)(1) for another party to file a notice of appeal runs from the date when the lower court enters the first notice.

Rule 5. Report of a Case for Determination

A report of a case for determination by an appellate court shall for all purposes under these rules be taken as the equivalent of a notice of appeal. Whenever a case or any part of it is reported after decision or verdict, the aggrieved party (as designated by the lower court) shall be treated as the appellant. Whenever a case or any part of it is reported without decision or verdict, the plaintiff in a civil action or the defendant in a criminal case shall be treated as the appellant. The clerk of the lower court shall serve notice of the filing of the report by transmitting a copy thereof to each party.

Rule 6. Stay or Injunction Pending Appeal

(a) Civil Cases.

(1) Stay Must Ordinarily Be Sought in the First Instance in Lower Court; Motion for Stay in Appellate Court. In civil cases, an application for a stay of the judgment or order of a lower court pending appeal, or for approval of a bond under Rule 6 (a)(2), or for an order suspending, modifying, restoring, or granting an injunction during the pendency of an appeal must ordinarily be made in the first instance in the lower court. A motion for such relief may be made to the appellate court or to a single justice, but the motion shall show that application to the lower court for the relief sought is not practicable, or that the lower court has denied an

application, or has failed to afford the relief which the applicant requested, with the reasons given by the lower court for its action. The motion shall also show the reasons for the relief requested and the facts relied upon, and if the facts are subject to dispute, the motion shall be supported by affidavits or other statements signed under the penalties of perjury or copies thereof. With the motion shall be filed such parts of the record as are relevant. Reasonable notice of the motion shall be given to all parties. The motion shall be filed with the clerk of the appellate court to which the appeal is being taken. If the court is the Supreme Judicial Court, the motion shall be filed with the clerk of the Supreme Judicial Court for Suffolk County.

(2) Stay May Be Conditioned Upon Giving of Bond; Proceedings Against Sureties. Relief available in the appellate court under this rule may be conditioned upon the filing of a bond or other appropriate security in the lower court. If security is given in the form of a bond or stipulation or other undertaking with 1 or more sureties, each surety thereby shall submit to the jurisdiction of the lower court and irrevocably appoint the clerk of the lower court as an authorized agent upon whom any documents affecting liability on the bond or undertaking may be served. A surety's liability may be entered against the surety on motion in the lower court without the necessity of an independent action. The motion and such notice of the motion as the lower court prescribes may be served on the clerk of the lower court, who shall forthwith mail copies to the sureties if their addresses are known.

(3) Terms. Relief available in the appellate court under this rule, or denial of such relief, may be conditioned on such reasonable terms as the appellate court or single justice may impose. For failure to observe such terms, the appellate court or single justice may make such further order as it or the single justice deems just and appropriate.

(b) Criminal Cases. A motion for a stay of execution of a sentence shall be governed by Rule 6(b) and by Massachusetts Rule of Criminal Procedure 31.

(1) Stay Must Ordinarily Be Sought in the First Instance in Lower Court; Motion for Stay in Appellate Court. In criminal cases, an application for a stay of execution of a sentence pending appeal must ordinarily be made in the first instance in the lower court. A motion for such relief may be made to the single justice of the appellate court to which the appeal is being taken, but the motion shall show that application to the lower court for the relief sought is not practicable, or that the lower court has previously denied an application for a stay or has failed to afford the relief which the applicant requested with the reasons given by the lower court for its action. The motion shall also show the reasons for the relief requested and the facts relied upon, and if the facts are subject to dispute, the motion shall be supported by affidavits or other statements signed under the penalties of perjury or copies thereof. With the motion shall be filed such parts of the record as are relevant. The motion shall be filed with the clerk of the appellate court to which the appeal is being taken. If the court is the Supreme Judicial Court, the motion shall be filed with the clerk of the Supreme Judicial Court for Suffolk County.

(2) Reasonable Notice. Reasonable notice of the motion for a stay shall be given to the Commonwealth.

(A) If the motion is filed prior to the docketing of the appeal in an appellate court, the time for response shall be governed by Rule 15.

(B) After an appeal has been docketed pursuant to Rule 10(a)(2), (i) if the motion is filed at least 30 days prior to the date the appellant's brief is due, the time for a response shall be governed by Rule 15; or (ii) if the motion is filed at any other time, the Commonwealth shall have 30 days to respond.

(C) A single justice may shorten or extend the time for responding to any motion authorized by this rule.

(3) Appealability of Single Justice Order; Finality. An order by the single justice allowing or denying an application for a stay may be appealed to the appellate court in which the appeal is pending. An order by the appellate court in which the appeal is pending, allowing or denying an application for a stay, shall be final.

(4) Revocation of Stay Pending Appeal. If a defendant fails at any time to take any measure necessary for the hearing of an appeal or report, a stay of execution of a sentence may, on motion of the Commonwealth, be revoked.

(5) Expiration of Stay. Upon the release of the decision by the appellate court of a judgment affirming the conviction, the stay of execution of the sentence automatically expires, unless extended by the appellate court.

(6) Notice of Expiration of Stay. Upon release of a decision affirming the conviction, the clerk of the appellate court shall notify the clerk of the lower court and the parties that the conviction has been affirmed and that therefore, the stay of execution of the sentence has automatically expired.

Rule 7. Disability of a Member of the Lower Court

If a judge whose decision has been appealed to the appellate court becomes unable to participate further, then any other judge of or assigned to the lower court may be substituted.

Rule 8. The Record on Appeal

(a) Definition. The record on appeal shall consist of the documents and exhibits on file, the transcript of the proceedings, if any, and the docket entries.

(b) Producing the Transcript of Proceedings.

(1) Cases Other than Child Welfare Cases.

(A) Transcript Orders and Certifications. For those proceedings relevant to the appeal that were recorded by a court reporter, the appellant shall order a transcript of those proceedings within 14 days of filing the notice of appeal in accordance with procedures set by the Chief Justice of the Trial Court, unless the appellant certifies to the clerk (i) that no lower court proceedings are relevant to the appeal or (ii) that the transcript is on file with the court. For those proceedings relevant to the appeal that were electronically recorded, the appellant shall request the transmission of the audio recording of those proceedings and order the transcription of those proceedings within 14 days of filing the notice of appeal in accordance with procedures set by the Chief Justice of the Trial Court, unless the appellant certifies to the clerk (i) that no lower court proceedings are relevant to the appeal or (ii) that the transcript of all proceedings relevant to the appeal is on file with the court. The appellant shall at the same time file a copy of the transcript orders or certifications with the clerk and serve a copy on all other parties. Within 14 days of service of the appellant's transcript orders or certifications, any other party may order a transcript of additional proceedings in accordance with procedures set by the Chief Justice of the Trial Court. Such party shall at the same time file a copy of the transcript order with the clerk and serve a copy on all other parties.

(B) Stipulation that Transcript is Unnecessary. To the extent consistent with the appellant's duty to provide an adequate record to the appellate court, the parties may stipulate that the transcription of some or all of the proceedings relevant to the appeal is unnecessary to the adjudication of the appeal, in which case the appellant need order only the transcript of the proceedings, if any, that the parties agree are necessary to the adjudication of the appeal. The parties shall file the stipulation with the clerk within 14 days of the filing of the notice of appeal.

(C) Costs of Transcription. In any criminal case and in a civil case in which the appellant is entitled to have counsel made available pursuant to Supreme Judicial Court Rule 3:10, the Commonwealth shall pay for the cost of providing the transcript of all proceedings relevant to the appeal, including those designated by the appellee, to the lower court clerk. In all other cases, unless ordered otherwise by the lower court, the appellant shall pay for such costs. If the parties cannot agree on which proceedings are relevant to the appeal, the lower court shall settle the matter upon motion. Payment, if required, for copies of the transcript for the parties shall be governed by procedures set by the Chief Justice of the Trial Court.

(2) Child Welfare Cases. Upon the filing of a notice of appeal, unless the parties file a stipulation designating the parts of the proceedings which need not be transcribed or a statement of intent to proceed under Rule 8(d), the clerk of the lower court shall order, within 14 days and in accordance with procedures set by the Chief Justice of the Trial Court, a transcript of the proceedings relevant to the appeal and shall serve a copy of the transcript order on the parties.

(3) Delivery of the Transcript. Upon completion, the transcriber shall deliver the transcript to the clerk of the lower court in accordance with procedures set by the Chief Justice of the Trial Court. The delivery of transcripts to the parties shall be governed by procedures set by the Chief Justice of the Trial Court. Upon receipt of all of the transcripts ordered by the parties, the clerk shall notify all parties within 14 days that the transcripts have been received.

(c) Statement of the Proceedings When No Report or Transcript is Available. If no report of the evidence or proceedings at a hearing or trial was made and a transcript is unavailable, the appellant shall file a motion to reconstruct the record within 14 days of the filing of the notice of appeal. The parties shall confer and reconstruct the record. Within such time as the lower court shall allow, the appellant shall file a proposed statement of the proceedings. Within 14 days of service of the proposed statement, any other party may file objections or proposed amendments or additions. The lower court shall promptly settle any disputes and approve a statement of the proceedings for inclusion in the record on appeal.

(d) Agreed Statement as the Record on Appeal. If the parties intend to submit an agreed statement as the record on appeal in lieu of the procedures set forth in Rule 8(a)–(c), the parties shall notify the clerk in writing within 14 days of the filing of the notice of appeal. Within 28 days of the filing of the notice to the clerk, the parties shall submit to the lower court an agreed statement of the record on appeal containing such information as is necessary for consideration of the appeal. If the statement conforms to the truth, the lower court shall approve the statement, along with any additions the lower court considers useful to the appellate court.

(e) Correction or Modification of the Record.

(1) Omissions. If anything material is omitted from the record, the parties may supply it by stipulation and submit the stipulation for the approval of the lower court. If the parties are unable to agree, the lower court on motion shall settle the dispute and add to the record on appeal. On motion of the parties or on its own motion, the appellate court or a single justice may direct that any omission be rectified.

(2) Corrections. If any part of the record on appeal fails to accord with what occurred in the lower court, the parties may correct the record by stipulation and submit the stipulation for the approval of the lower court. If the parties are unable to agree, the lower court on motion shall settle any disputes and conform the record to the truth. On motion of the parties or on its own motion, the appellate court or a single justice may direct that any part of the record be corrected.

(3) Inaudible Recording. If portions of the proceedings cannot be transcribed because they are unintelligible, the parties shall promptly use reasonable efforts to stipulate to their content, and shall submit any such stipulation for the approval of the lower court. If the parties are unable to agree, the lower court shall settle the dispute on motion.

Rule 9. Assembly of the Record; Reproduction of Exhibits; Notice of Assembly; and Transmission of Documents from the Lower Court

(a) Assembly.

(1) Upon the filing of a notice of appeal, the clerk of the lower court shall promptly review the file and ensure the accuracy of the docket entries and that all documents are properly numbered in order of filing or identified with reasonable specificity. The clerk shall prepare a list of all exhibits filed in the lower court and ensure that all exhibits are properly numbered and labeled. The clerk shall maintain the file until the final disposition of the appeal, unless otherwise ordered by a judge.

(2) The lower court or the appellate court or a single justice thereof may order the record to be assembled, and the appellate court or a single justice thereof may order the appeal to be docketed, at any time.

(b) Exhibits. The lower court shall make such orders as it deems necessary for the preservation of exhibits, and shall not transmit any exhibit to the appellate court unless pursuant to an order of the appellate court or a justice thereof. The parties may reproduce exhibits for inclusion in the record appendix insofar as necessary to their appeal, pursuant to Rule 18.

(c) Impounded materials. When an appeal has been taken in a case in which material has been impounded, the clerk of the lower court shall provide written notification to the appellate court clerk that material was impounded by the lower court when notice of the assembled record is transmitted. Such notification shall specify the materials or portions thereof which were impounded below and shall include a copy of the order of impoundment, if any, or a reference to other authority for the impoundment. Unless otherwise ordered by the appellate court, or otherwise provided in the lower court order of impoundment, material impounded in the lower court shall remain impounded in the appellate courts.

(d) Appellant's Obligation.

(1) In General. In a civil or criminal case, upon request by the clerk of the lower court, a party shall forthwith perform any act reasonably necessary to enable the clerk to assemble the record.

(2) Civil Cases. Notwithstanding any other obligation which these rules may impose, but excepting electronically recorded proceedings governed by Rule 8(b)(1), each appellant in a civil case shall, within 14 days after filing a notice of appeal, deliver to the clerk of the lower court either

(A) a transcript or those portions of the transcript of the lower court proceedings which the appellant deems necessary for determination of the appeal,

(B) a signed statement certifying that the appellant has ordered such portions, or

(C) a signed statement certifying that the appellant has not ordered and does not intend to order the transcript or any portion thereof.

(3) Denial of Motion for Post-Conviction Relief in a Criminal Case. Excepting an appellant in a criminal case in which the defendant was convicted of murder in the first degree, and notwithstanding any other obligation these rules may impose, after the direct appeal, each appellant in a criminal case in which the appeal concerns the denial of a motion for post-conviction relief shall, within 14 days after filing a notice of appeal, deliver to the clerk of the lower court an electronically formatted transcript of the lower court proceedings related to the appellant's underlying conviction or a statement that such a transcript may not be obtained with due diligence, is not relevant, or has been ordered and not yet produced. In lieu of a copy of the transcript, the appellant may file with the clerk of the lower court a certification that a copy of the transcript is available in the appellate court. The certification shall include the appellate court docket number of the case in which the transcript is available. The clerk of the lower court shall transmit the transcript

of the lower court proceedings or the certification to the appellate court when notice of the assembled record is transmitted.

(e) Duty of Clerk; Transmission.

(1) Unless otherwise ordered by the lower court or the appellate court or a single justice thereof pursuant to Rule 9(a)(2), the clerk of the lower court shall complete the assembly of the record and transmit notice of the assembled record to the parties and the clerk of the appellate court either:

(A) within 21 days from the later of

(i) the clerk's receipt of the transcript of proceedings, if any, in the lower court; or (ii) the clerk's receipt of notice from the appellant that no transcript will be ordered; or (iii) the expiration of the time for filing any other notice of appeal after the filing of a first notice of appeal pursuant to Rule 4(a); or

(B) if the parties notify the clerk of their intent to file an agreed statement as to the record on appeal pursuant to Rule 8(d), within 21 days of the lower court's approval of the statement.

(2) The notice of assembly transmitted to the appellate court shall be accompanied by the following:

(A) a completed appellate court entry statement;

(B) a copy of the notice of assembly issued to the parties;

(C) a copy of the notice(s) of appeal;

(D) a copy of the docket entries;

(E) the written notification regarding impounded materials as required by Rule 9(c);

(F) a list of all the exhibits; and,

(G) in criminal cases, any electronically formatted transcript, if a transcript is necessary for the appeal.

(3) In case of an order to transmit, transmission shall be effected when the clerk of the lower court mails or otherwise forwards a copy of the notice of assembly and other information as required in this rule to the clerk of the appellate court.

(4) The clerk of the lower court shall indicate, by endorsement on the face of the notice of assembly, the date upon which it is transmitted to the appellate court.

Rule 10. Docketing the Appeal

(a) Docketing the Appeal.

(1) Civil Cases.

(A) Within 14 days after receiving from the clerk of the lower court the notice of assembly of the record, each appellant, including each cross-appellant and each appellant in a joint appeal, shall pay to the clerk of the appellate court the docket fee required by law or request waiver of the fee, and the clerk shall thereupon enter the appeal of such appellant or cross-appellant upon the docket. If an appellant is authorized to prosecute the appeal without payment of fees, the clerk shall enter the appeal upon the docket at the written request of a party.

(B) When payment or request for waiver is made by first class mail or its equivalent, it shall be deemed timely if accompanied by a certificate attesting that the day of mailing was within 14 days of receipt of the notice of assembly.

(2) Criminal Cases. Upon receipt of the notice of assembly of the record, pursuant to Rule 9(e), the clerk of the appellate court shall enter the appeal upon the docket.

(3) In General. Upon docketing of the appeal, the clerk shall serve written notice thereof upon each party and the clerk of the lower court. Upon motion, the lower court or a single justice of the appellate court may, for cause shown, enlarge the time for docketing the appeal or permit the appeal to be docketed out of time. An appeal shall be docketed under the title given to the action in the lower court, with the appellant identified as such, but if such title does not contain the name of the appellant, then the party's name, unless permitted to proceed under a pseudonym, identified as appellant, shall be added to the title.

(4) Certain Constitutional Claims. Within 14 days after the docketing of any civil appeal that draws into question the constitutionality of an act of the legislature, if neither the Commonwealth nor an officer, agency, or employee thereof is a party to the appeal, the party asserting the unconstitutionality of the act shall notify the attorney general of such challenge. If such a question becomes apparent to a party after the 14-day period has expired, the party shall immediately notify the attorney general. Such notice shall be given either in writing or by use of any electronic method the attorney general may designate for this purpose.

(5) Consolidated Appeals. Appeals may be consolidated by order of the appellate court upon its own motion or upon motion of a party, on such terms as the court may order.

(6) Joint Appeal. Upon entry of an appeal pursuant to Rule 10(a)(1) or 10(a)(2), parties who have filed a joint notice of appeal shall proceed on appeal as a single appellant, unless upon motion the appellate court grants leave to proceed separately.

(7) Cross Appeals. If a cross appeal is filed, the party who files a notice of appeal first is the appellant for the purposes of these Rules. If notices are filed on the same day, the plaintiff in the proceeding below is the appellant. These designations may be modified by the parties' agreement, filed with the appellate court, or by court order.

(b) Filing. The clerk of the appellate court shall file upon receipt any part of the record or any document authorized to be filed in lieu of the record under any provision of Rule 9, following timely docketing of the appeal. The clerk shall immediately give notice to all parties of the date of each such filing.

(c) Dismissal for Failure of Appellant in a Civil Case to Comply With Rule 9(d) or Rule 10(a). If any appellant in a civil case shall fail to comply with Rule 9(d) or Rule 10(a)(1), the lower court may, on motion with notice by any appellee, dismiss the appeal, but only upon a finding of inexcusable neglect; otherwise, the court shall enlarge the appellant's time for taking the required action. If, prior to the lower court's hearing such motion for noncompliance with Rule 9(d), the appellant shall have cured the noncompliance, the appellant's compliance shall be deemed timely.

(d) Withdrawal of Counsel. In all cases, any counsel who does not intend to continue representing a client on appeal, for any reason, should file a motion to withdraw his or her appearance in the lower court as soon as is practicable. After an appeal has been docketed in an appellate court, any motion to withdraw appearance of counsel shall be filed with the appellate court. The motion shall include a certificate of service in compliance with Rule 13, which shows service upon all parties to the appeal, including those represented by counsel filing the motion, at the party's or parties' last known address.

Rule 11. Direct Appellate Review

(a) Application; When Filed; Grounds. An appeal within the concurrent appellate jurisdiction of the Appeals Court and Supreme Judicial Court shall be docketed in the Appeals Court before a party may apply to the Supreme Judicial Court for direct appellate review. Within 21 days after the docketing of an appeal in the Appeals Court, any party to the case (or 2 or more parties jointly) may apply in writing to the Supreme Judicial Court for direct appellate review, provided the questions presented by the appeal are (1) questions of first impression or novel questions of law which should be submitted for final determination to the Supreme Judicial Court; (2) questions of law concerning the Constitution of the Commonwealth or questions concerning the Constitution of the United States which have been raised in a court of the Commonwealth; or (3) questions of such public interest that justice requires a final determination by the full Supreme Judicial Court.

(b) Contents of Application; Form. The application for direct appellate review shall contain, in the following order: (1) a request for direct appellate review; (2) a statement of prior proceedings in the case; (3) a short statement of facts relevant to the appeal; (4) a statement of the issues of law raised by the appeal, together with a statement indicating whether the issues were raised and properly preserved in the lower court; (5) a brief argument thereon (consisting of not more than either 10 pages of text in monospaced font or 2,000 words in proportional font, as defined in Rule 20(a)(4)(B)) including appropriate authorities, in support of the applicant's position on such issues; and (6) a statement of reasons why direct appellate review is appropriate. A copy of the docket entries shall be appended to the application. The applicant shall also append a copy of any written decision, memorandum, findings, rulings, or report of the lower court relevant to the appeal. The application shall comply with the requirements of Rule 20(a), and shall contain a certification of such compliance, including a statement of how compliance with the foregoing length limit was ascertained, as specified in Rule 16(k).

(c) Response; Form. Within 14 days after the filing of the application, any other party to the case may, but need not, file and serve a response thereto (consisting of not more than either 10 pages of text in monospace font or 2,000 words in proportional font, as defined in Rule 20(a)(4)(B)) setting forth reasons why the application should or should not be granted. The response shall not restate matters described in Rule 11(b)(2) and (3) unless the party is dissatisfied with the statement thereof contained in the application. The response shall comply with the requirements of Rule 20(a), and shall contain a certification of such compliance, including a statement of how compliance with the foregoing length limit was ascertained, as specified in Rule 16(k). A response may be filed in a different form as permitted by the court.

(d) Filing; Service. One copy of the application and of each response shall be filed in the office of the clerk of the full Supreme Judicial Court. Filing and service of the application and of any response shall comply with Rule 13.

(e) Effect of Application Upon Appeal. The filing of an application for direct appellate review shall not extend the time for filing briefs or doing any other act required to be done under these rules.

(f) Vote of Direct Appellate Review; Certification. If any 2 justices of the Supreme Judicial Court vote for direct appellate review, or if a majority of the justices of the Appeals Court shall certify that direct appellate review is in the public interest, an order allowing the application (or transferring the appeal sua sponte) or the certificate, as the case may be, shall be transmitted to the clerk of the Appeals Court with notice to the lower court. The clerk of the Appeals Court shall forthwith transmit to the clerk of the full Supreme Judicial Court all documents filed in the case.

(g) Cases Transferred for Direct Review; Time for Serving and Filing Briefs. In any appeal transferred to the full Supreme Judicial Court from the Appeals Court:

(1) If at the time of transfer all parties have served and filed briefs in the Appeals Court, no further briefs may be filed by the parties except that a reply brief may be served and filed on or before the last date allowable had the case not been transferred, or within 14 days after the date on which the appeal is docketed in the full Supreme Judicial Court, whichever is later.

(2) If at the time of transfer only the appellant's brief has been served and filed in the Appeals Court the appellant may, but need not, serve and file an amended brief within 21 days after the date on which the appeal is docketed in the full Supreme Judicial Court. The appellee shall serve and file a brief within 30 days after service of any amended brief of the appellant, or within 50 days after the date on which the appeal is docketed in the full Supreme Judicial Court, whichever is later.

(3) Service and filing of a reply brief shall comply with Rule 19.

(4) If at the time of transfer to the full Supreme Judicial Court no party to the appeal has served or filed a brief, the appellant shall serve and file a brief within 21 days after the date on which the appeal is docketed in the full Supreme Judicial Court or within 40 days after the date on which the appeal was docketed in the Appeals Court, whichever is later.

Rule 11.1. Transfer from Supreme Judicial Court

In the case of a direct appeal to the Supreme Judicial Court, except as to any appeal concerning a conviction of murder in the first degree, within 14 days after the appeal has been docketed, or such further time as a single justice upon motion for cause shown may allow, any party may serve and file a motion to transfer the appeal to the Appeals Court. The motion (a) shall not exceed either 5 pages of text in monospaced font or 1,000 words in proportional font, as defined in Rule 20(a)(4)(B); (b) shall succinctly specify the grounds for transfer; and (c) shall conform to Rules 13, 14, 15, and 20(b). Within 7 days after filing of the motion, any other party may serve and file a response to the transfer. The response (a) shall not exceed either 5 pages of text in monospaced font or 1,000 words in proportional font, as defined in Rule 20(a)(4)(B); (b) shall succinctly specify the reasons why transfer should or should not be granted; and (c) shall conform to Rules 13, 14, 15, and 20(b).

Rule 12. Proceedings Involving an Indigent Party

(a) Leave to Proceed on Appeal as an Indigent Party from Lower Court to Appellate Court. Either a lower court or the appellate court or a single justice thereof, for cause shown and after reasonable notice, may authorize an appeal to be prosecuted by an indigent party, upon such reasonable terms as such court or justice may prescribe.

(b) Form of Briefs, Appendices, and Other Documents. Parties allowed to proceed as indigent may upon motion and with leave of the appellate court or a single justice thereof, file and serve a reduced number of copies of briefs, appendices, and other documents than otherwise required by these rules.

Rule 13. Filing and Service

(a) Filing. Documents required or permitted to be filed in the appellate court shall be filed with the clerk.

(1) Filing Generally. Except as provided in Rule 13(a)(2), filing may be accomplished in hand, through any electronic means provided by the clerk or by first class mail or its equivalent, addressed to the clerk, but filing shall not be timely unless the documents are received by the clerk within the time fixed for filing, except that briefs and appendices shall be docketed on the date of receipt and shall be deemed timely filed if

(A) received within the time fixed for filing, or

(B) when filed by first class mail or its equivalent, they are accompanied by a certificate attesting that the day of mailing was within the time fixed for filing. If a motion requests relief which may be granted by a single justice, the justice may permit the motion to be filed, in which event the justice shall note thereon the date of filing and shall thereafter transmit it to the clerk.

(2) Documents Filed by a Self-Represented Party Confined in an Institution. If an institution has a system designed for legal mail, a self-represented party confined in an institution must use that system to receive the benefit of this rule. A document other than a notice of appeal filed by such party is timely if it is deposited in the institution's internal mail system on or before the last day for filing and is accompanied by a signed certificate in compliance with Rule 13(a)(1)(B) setting out the date of deposit. If the document is not received by the last day for filing, the certificate shall give rise to a presumption of timely filing provided it shows compliance with this rule. Failure to attach the certificate shall not of itself render the document invalid or untimely, and the appellate court may permit the later filing of a certificate. The time period for the opposing party to file any response to the document runs from the date when the appellate court dockets the document.

(b) Service of All Documents Required. Copies of all documents filed by any party shall, at or before the time of filing, be served by a party on all other parties to the appeal or review.

(c) Manner of Service. Service may be personal or by first class mail or its equivalent. Personal service includes delivery of the copy to the party's mailing address. Service by first class mail or its equivalent is complete on mailing. Service may also be completed electronically with the consent of the party being served.

(d) Certificate of Service of All Documents Other than Briefs and Appendices.

(1) Requirement. Documents presented for filing, other than a brief or appendix, shall contain a certificate of service. A certificate of service may appear on or be affixed to the document filed. The clerk may permit documents to be filed without a certificate of service but shall require such certificate to be filed promptly thereafter.

(2) Contents. A certificate of service shall be in the form of a statement certifying

(A) the date and manner of service;

(B) the name, mailing address, and, if known, electronic address of the person(s) served; and

(C) the printed and signed name, Board of Bar Overseers (BBO) number, if any, mailing and electronic addresses, and telephone number of the person who made service, and if that person is affiliated with a firm or office, the office name.

(e) Certificate of Service of Briefs and Appendices.

(1) Requirement. Briefs and appendices presented for filing shall be accompanied by a certificate of service. The certificate of service shall appear as a part of the brief being filed as required in Rule 16(a)(15).

(2) Contents. The certificate of service shall be in the form of a certification that includes

(A) the name of the court and the number of the case;

(B) the title of the case;

(C) the title of the brief;

(D) the party on whose behalf service was made;

(E) the printed and signed name, Board of Bar Overseers (BBO) number, if any, mailing and electronic addresses, and telephone number of the person who made service, and, if that person is affiliated with a firm or office, the office name;

(F) the name and mailing address and, if known, electronic address of the person(s) served; and

(G) the date and manner of service.

Rule 14. Computation and Extension of Time

(a) Computation of Time. In computing any period of time prescribed by these rules, by order of court, or by any applicable statute, the day of the act, event, or default after which the designated period of time begins to run shall not be included. The last day of the period shall be included, unless it is a Saturday, Sunday, or a legal holiday, in which event the period shall extend until the end of the next day which is not a Saturday, Sunday, or legal holiday. When the period of time prescribed or allowed is less than 7 days, intermediate Saturdays, Sundays, and legal holidays shall be excluded in the computation. As used in this rule "legal holiday" means those days specified in G.L. c. 4, § 7 and any other day appointed as a holiday by the President or the Congress of the United States or so designated by the laws of the Commonwealth.

(b) Enlargement of Time. The appellate court or a single justice of the appellate court in which the appeal will be, or is, docketed for good cause shown may upon motion enlarge the time prescribed by these rules or by its order for doing any act, or may permit an act to be done after the expiration of such time; but neither the appellate court nor a single justice may enlarge the time for filing a notice of appeal beyond 1 year from the date of entry of the judgment or order sought to be reviewed, or, in a criminal case, from the date of the verdict or finding of guilt or the date of imposition of sentence, whichever date is later.

(c) Additional Time After Service by First Class Mail or Its Equivalent. Whenever a party is required or permitted to do an act within a prescribed period after service of a document upon the party and the document is served by first class mail or its equivalent, 3 days shall be added to the prescribed period.

Rule 15. Motions

(a) Content of Motions; Response; Reply. Unless another form is elsewhere prescribed by these rules, an application for an order or other relief shall be made by filing a motion for such order or relief with proof of service upon all other parties. The motion shall comply with Rule 20(b)(2) and shall contain or be accompanied by any matter required by a specific provision of these rules governing such a motion, shall state with particularity the grounds on which it is based, shall set forth the order or relief sought, and, if known, should state whether the motion is assented to, or that no other party is in opposition, or if any party intends to file an opposition or other response.

If a motion is supported by briefs, affidavits, or other documents, they shall be served and filed with the motion. Any party may file a response to a motion other than for a procedural order (for which see Rule 15(b)) within 7 days after service of the motion, but motions authorized by Rule 6 may be acted upon after reasonable notice, and the appellate court or a single justice may shorten or extend the time for responding to any motion.

(b) Determination of Motions for Procedural Orders. Notwithstanding the provisions of the preceding paragraph as to motions generally, motions for procedural orders, including any motion under Rule 14(b), may be acted upon at any time, without awaiting a response thereto. Any party adversely affected by such action may request reconsideration, vacation, or modification of such action.

(c) Power of a Single Justice to Entertain Motions. In addition to the authority expressly conferred by these rules or by law, a single justice may entertain and may grant or deny any request for relief which under these rules may properly be sought by motion, except that a single justice may not dismiss or otherwise determine an appeal or other proceeding, and except that the appellate court may provide by order or rule that any motion or class of motions shall be acted upon by the appellate court. The action of a single justice may be reviewed by the appellate court.

(d) Motions for New Trial in Capital Cases. After the docketing of an appeal in a "capital case" as defined in G.L. c. 278, § 33E, and until the issuance of a rescript by the appellate court, any motion for a new trial pursuant to Massachusetts Rule of Criminal Procedure 30 shall be filed in the appellate court and may be remitted to the trial judge for hearing and determination at such time as the appellate court may direct.

Rule 16. Briefs

(a) Brief of the Appellant. The brief of the appellant shall be formatted and paginated as provided in Rule 20(a)(4), and contain under appropriate headings and in the order here indicated:

(1) Cover. The cover of the brief shall contain the information identified in Rule 20(a)(6)(B).

(2) Corporate Disclosure Statement. A corporate disclosure statement, if required pursuant to Supreme Judicial Court Rule 1:21, shall be contained within the brief.

(3) Table of Contents. The table of contents shall list each section of the brief, including the headings and subheadings of each section, and the page on which they begin.

(4) Table of Authorities. The table of authorities shall list each case, statute, rule, and other authority cited in the brief, with references to each page on which it is cited. The authorities shall be listed alphabetically or numerically, as applicable.

(5) Statement of Issues. The statement of issues shall concisely and particularly describe each issue presented for review.

(6) Statement of Case. The statement of the case shall briefly describe the nature of the appeal, the procedural history relevant to the issues presented for review, with page references to the record appendix or transcript in accordance with Rule 16(e), and the disposition of these issues by the lower court.

(7) Statement of Facts. The statement of the facts shall describe the facts relevant to the issues presented for review, but need not repeat items otherwise included in the statement of the case, and each statement of fact shall be supported by page references to the record appendix or transcript in accordance with Rule 16(e).

(8) Summary of Argument. In a brief with more than 20 pages of argument, or more than 4,500 words if produced in a proportionally spaced font, there shall be a summary of the argument that contains a succinct, clear, and accurate statement of the arguments made in the body of the brief, which must not merely repeat the argument headings, and is to include page references to where in the body of the brief each argument is made.

(9) Argument. The argument shall contain:

(A) the contentions of the appellant with respect to the issues presented, and the reasons therefor, with citations to the authorities and parts of the record on which the appellant relies. The appellate court need not pass upon questions or issues not argued in the brief; and

(B) for each issue, a concise statement of the applicable standard of review (which may appear in the discussion of the issue or under a separate heading placed before the discussion of the issues).

(10) Request for Attorney's Fees and Costs. Any request for appellate attorney's fees and costs must be included in the brief, with a citation to the authority therefor.

(11) Conclusion. The brief shall contain a short conclusion stating the precise relief sought.

(12) Signature Block. The signature block shall contain

(A) the printed and signed name(s), Board of Bar Overseers (BBO) number(s), if any, mailing and electronic addresses, and telephone number(s) of the person(s) who prepared the brief, and, if any individual counsel is affiliated with a firm or office, the office name; and

(B) the date of signing.

(13) Addendum. An addendum, contained within the brief, shall consist of the following:

(A) a table of contents listing each item contained therein and the page on which it begins;

(B) any appealed judgment or order (including any written opinion, memorandum of decision, or findings of fact and conclusions thereon relating to an issue raised on appeal, including a typed version of any pertinent handwritten or oral endorsement, notation, findings, or order made by the lower court);

(C) copies of constitutional provisions, statutes, rules, regulations, or relevant parts thereof, as in effect at the relevant time, consideration of which is required for determination of the issues presented;

(D) a copy of any unpublished decision cited in the brief; and

(E) in a case where geographical facts are of importance, unless appropriate plans are reproduced in the printed record or record appendix, an outline plan (preferably based on exhibits in evidence). This outline plan should be suitable for reproduction on one 1 page of the printed law reports.

(14) Certificate of Compliance. The certification required by Rule 16(k) shall be contained within the brief.

(15) Certificate of Service. The certificate of service required by Rule 13(e) shall be contained within the brief.

(b) Brief of the Appellee. The brief of the appellee shall conform to the requirements of Rule 16(a), except as follows:

(1) Statements of the Issues, Case, Facts, and Standard(s) of Review. Statements of the issues, of the case, of the facts, and of the applicable standard(s) of review need not be made unless the appellee is dissatisfied with the statements of the appellant.

(2) Argument. The argument shall contain the contentions of the appellee with respect to the issues presented, and the reasons therefor, with citations to the authorities and parts of the record on which the appellee relies.

(3) Addendum. The addendum shall include copies of items required by Rule 16(a)(13) insofar as pertinent to the issues argued by the appellee, even if included in the addendum of the appellant.

(c) Appellant's Reply Brief. The appellant may file a reply brief responding to the appellee's argument. No new issues shall be raised in the reply brief. No further briefs may be filed except with leave of the appellate court or a single justice. The reply brief shall comply with the requirements of Rule 16(a)(1), (3), (4), (9), and (11)–(15).

(d) References in Briefs to Parties. Parties will be expected in their briefs and oral arguments to keep to a minimum references to parties by such designations as "appellant" and "appellee." It promotes clarity to use the designations used in the lower court, or the actual names of the parties, or descriptive terms such as "the employee," "the injured person," "the taxpayer," "the landlord," etc. If the name of a party has been impounded or has been made confidential by statute, rule, or court order, the party shall preserve confidentiality in briefs and oral arguments.

(e) References in Briefs to the Record. Any factual statement in a brief shall be supported by a citation to the volume number(s) and page number(s) at which it appears in an appendix, and if not contained in an appendix, to the volume number(s) and page number(s) at which it appears in the transcript(s) or exhibits volume(s). Only clear abbreviations may be used, for example RAII/55 (meaning Record Appendix volume II at page 55) or TRIII/231-232 (meaning Transcript volume III at pages 231–232). Any record material cited in a brief must be reproduced in an appendix or transcript or exhibit volume. Any record material cited in a brief that is included in the addendum should also include a citation to the addendum. If reference is made to evidence the admissibility of which is in controversy, reference shall be made to the pages of the appendix or of the transcript at which the evidence was identified, offered, and received or rejected.

(f) Reserved.

(g) Massachusetts Citations. Citations to Massachusetts decisions, statutes, and regulations shall be made only to the official report of the decision or to the official publication containing the statute or regulation, if any. References to decisions should include, in addition to the page at which the decision begins, a page reference to the particular material therein upon which reliance is placed, and the year of the decision.

(h) Length of Briefs in Cases Other than Cross Appeals. In any case other than a cross appeal, the length of briefs shall comply with Rule 20(a)(2).

(i) Briefs in Cases Involving Cross Appeals. In a cross appeal,

(1) the length of briefs shall comply with Rule 20(a)(3);

(2) the appellee's principal and response brief shall contain the issues and argument involved in the appellee's appeal as well as the answer to the brief of the appellant;

(3) the appellee may file a reply brief responding to the appellant's argument as to the issues presented by the cross appeal; and

(4) except with leave of the appellate court or a single justice, an appellee that has crossappealed may file only a single brief in reply to the responses of multiple appellants to the issues presented by the cross appeal.

(j) Briefs in Cases Involving Multiple Appellants or Appellees. In cases involving more than one appellant or appellee, including cases consolidated for purposes of the appeal per Rule 10(a)(5),

2

(1) any number of either may join in a single brief or reply brief, provided appropriate notice is given to the clerk and other parties;

(2) any appellant or appellee may adopt by reference any part of the brief of another; and

(3) except with leave of the appellate court or a single justice, an appellee may file only a single brief in response to multiple appellant briefs, and an appellant may file only a single brief in reply to multiple appellee briefs.

(k) Required Certification; Non-complying Briefs. The last page of each brief shall include a certification by the party that the brief complies with the rules of court that pertain to the filing of briefs, including, but not limited to: Rule 16(a)(13) (addendum); Rule 16(e) (references to the record); Rule 18 (appendix to the briefs); Rule 20 (form and length of briefs, appendices, and other documents); and Rule 21 (redaction). The certification shall specify how compliance with the applicable length limit of Rule 20 was ascertained, by stating either (1) the name, size, and number of characters per inch of the monospaced font used and the number of non-excluded pages, or (2) the name and size of the proportionally spaced font used, the number of nonexcluded words, and the name and version of the word-processing program used. A brief not complying with these rules (including a brief that does not contain a certification) may be struck from the files by the appellate court or a single justice.

(l) Citation of Supplemental Authorities. When pertinent and significant authorities come to the attention of a party after the party's brief has been filed, or after oral argument but before decision, a party may promptly advise the clerk of the court, by letter setting forth the citations. There shall be a reference either to the page of the brief or to a point argued orally to which the citations pertain, but the letter shall without argument state the reasons for the supplemental citations. Any response shall be made promptly and shall be similarly limited. Filing and service of any letter pursuant to this paragraph shall comply with Rule 13.

(m) References to Impounded Material. Upon the filing of any brief or other document containing references to matters that are impounded or have been made confidential by statute, rule, or order, the party shall file a written notice with the clerk, with a copy to all parties, so indicating. Wherever possible, the party shall not disclose impounded material. Where it is necessary to include impounded material in a brief, the cover of the brief shall clearly indicate that impounded information is included therein.

(n) Amendment of Brief. On motion for good cause, the court may grant leave for a party to file an amended brief. The motion shall describe the nature and reason for the amendment. The party shall file with the motion the amended brief marked as such on the front page or cover. Except as the court otherwise orders, the filing of an amended brief has no effect on any filing deadlines.

Rule 17. Brief of an Amicus Curiae

(a) General. A brief of an amicus curiae may be filed only (1) by leave of the appellate court or a single justice granted on motion or (2) when solicited by the appellate court, except that leave shall not be required when the brief is presented by the Commonwealth or its officer or agency. The brief may be conditionally filed with the motion for leave. A motion for leave shall identify the interest of the applicant and shall state the reasons why a brief of an amicus curiae is desirable.

(b) Timing. In all cases, an amicus curiae shall file its brief no later than 21 days before the date of oral argument for that case unless the appellate court or a single justice for cause shown shall grant leave for later filing. Any party may request leave from the appellate court or a single justice to file a response to a brief filed by an amicus curiae.

(c) Cover, Length, and Content. An amicus brief must comply with Rule 20. In addition to the requirements of Rule 20, the cover must identify the party or parties supported and indicate whether the brief supports affirmance or reversal or neither. An amicus brief need not comply with all the requirements of Rule 16, but must include the following:

(1) if the amicus curiae is a corporation, a disclosure statement like that required of parties by Supreme Judicial Court Rule 1:21;

(2) a table of contents with page references, in accord with Rule 16(a)(3);

(3) a table of authorities, in accord with Rule 16(a)(4);

(4) a concise statement of the identity of the amicus curiae and its interest in the case;

(5) unless the brief is presented by the Commonwealth or its officer or agency, a declaration that indicates whether

(A) a party or a party's counsel authored the brief in whole or in part;

(B) a party or a party's counsel contributed money that was intended to fund preparing or submitting the brief;

(C) a person or entity—other than the amicus curiae, its members, or its counsel—contributed money that was intended to fund preparing or submitting the brief and, if so, identifying each such person or entity; and

(D) the amicus curiae or its counsel represents or has represented one of the parties to the present appeal in another proceeding involving similar issues, or was a party or represented a party in a proceeding or legal transaction that is at issue in the present appeal, and, if so, identifying the proceeding or transaction, its relevance to the present appeal, and the parties involved;

(6) a summary of argument, in accord with Rule 16(a)(8), if the argument is more than 20 pages in length or more than 4,500 words if produced in a proportionally spaced font;

(7) an argument, which need not include a statement of the applicable standard of review;

(8) a signature block, in accord with Rule 16(a)(12);

(9) a certificate stating that the brief complies with the requirements of this rule and Rule 20 and specifying how compliance with the length limit of Rule 20(a)(3)(E) was ascertained, by stating either (A) the name, size, and number of characters per inch of the monospaced font used and the number of non-excluded pages, or (B) the name and size of the proportionally spaced font used, the number of non-excluded words, and the name and version of the word-processing program used; and

(10) a certificate of service, in accord with Rule 13(e).

A brief not complying with these rules (including a brief that does not contain a certification) may be struck from the files by the appellate court or a single justice.

(d) Filing. The same number of copies of the brief of an amicus curiae shall be filed with the clerk and served on each party as required by Rule 19(d).

(e) Oral argument. A motion of an amicus curiae to participate in the oral argument will be granted only for good cause.

Rule 18. Appendix to the Briefs: Contents, Cost, Filing, and Service

(a) Duty of Appellant to Prepare and File; Content of Appendix; Time for Filing; Number of Copies. The appellant shall prepare and file an appendix to the briefs which shall be separately bound. The parties are cautioned that, under Rule 9, the lower court does not ordinarily transmit the entire record to the appellate court. Therefore, the appendix or appendices must include the items specified in this rule.

(1) Requirements in Civil and Criminal Cases.

(A) The appendix shall contain, in the order hereinafter provided: (i) a cover that conforms substantially to Rules 20(a)(5)(A) and (a)(6). (ii) a table of contents, listing the parts of the record reproduced therein, and including a detailed listing of exhibits, affidavits, and other documents associated with those parts, with references to the pages of the appendix at which each begins; (iii) the docket entries in the lower court proceedings; (iv) any order of impoundment or confidentiality from the lower court; and (v) in chronological order of filing in the lower court:

(a) any parts of the record relied upon in the brief, and in a criminal case, a copy of the complaint or indictment;

(b) any document, or portion thereof, filed in the case relating to an issue which is to be argued on appeal;

(c) any findings or memorandum of decision or order by the lower court pertinent to an issue on appeal, including a typed version of any pertinent handwritten or oral endorsement, notation, findings, or order made by the lower court;

(d) the judgment, decree, order, or adjudication in question; and

(e) the notice(s) of appeal.

(B) Except where they have independent relevance, memoranda of law in the lower court should not be included in the appendix.

(C) The first volume of a multi-volume appendix shall include a complete table of contents referencing all volumes of the appendix, and each individual volume shall include a table of contents for that volume.

(D) The court may decline to permit the parties to refer to portions of the record omitted from the appendix, but the fact that parts of the record are not included in the appendix shall not prevent the court from relying on such parts.

(E) When an appendix contains materials from more than 1 lower court case, the table of contents shall clearly indicate, by reference to the lower court docket number, the case in which each paper was filed and by whom it was filed.

(F) Any reproduction of an exhibit in an appendix shall be of high quality to ensure a legible and accurate representation of the exhibit, including color if color is relevant. A color photograph marked or admitted as an exhibit in the lower court and included in the appendix must be reproduced in color. Lower court color-coded forms need not be reproduced in color.

(2) Additional Requirements in a Criminal Case.

(A) The appellee in a criminal case must include any part of the record relied on by the appellee not otherwise included in the appellant's appendix or contained in the transcript.

(B) An appendix may contain relevant excerpts of the transcript, but should not duplicate the entire transcript transmitted from the lower court to the appellate court.

(b) Determination of Contents of Appendix in Civil Cases; Cost of Producing; Supplemental Appendix.

(1) The parties are encouraged to agree as to the contents of the appendix. In the absence of agreement, the appellant shall, not later than 14 days after receiving from the clerk of the lower court the notice of assembly of the record, serve on the appellee a designation of the parts of the record which the appellant intends to include in the appendix and a statement of the issues which the appellant intends to present for review. If the appellee deems it necessary to direct the particular attention of the court to parts of the record not designated by the appellant, the appellee shall, within 14 days after receipt of the designation, serve upon the appellant a designation of those parts. The parties shall not engage in unnecessary designation and may refer to parts of the record not included in the appendix if permitted by the appellate court or a si ngle justice pursuant to the provision of Rule 18(a)(1)(D). However, this does not affect the responsibility of the parties to include materials necessary to their appeal, including exhibits, in the appendix.

(2) Where a party designates as part of the record any matter that has been impounded or has been made confidential by statute, rule, or order, the designation shall so state.

(3) Unless the parties otherwise agree, the cost of producing the appendix shall initially be paid by the appellant, but if the appellant considers that parts of the record designated by the appellee for inclusion are unnecessary for the determination of the issues presented the appellant may so advise the appellee and the appellee shall advance the cost of including such parts. In the event of a dispute as to the parts to be included or the cost advance required to include them, the matter shall be settled by the lower court on motion and notice. The cost of producing the appendix shall be taxed as costs in the case, but if either party shall cause matters to be included in the appendix unnecessarily the court may impose the cost of producing such parts on the party.

(4) Depending on the issues raised on appeal and the applicable standards of review, it may be necessary for the party filing the appendix to reproduce the entire transcript of the relevant lower court proceedings. Failure to reproduce the entire transcript may result in waiver of the issue. If the party does not reproduce a transcript of the entire proceedings, the party shall, preceding each portion of transcript reproduced, insert a concise statement identifying:

(A) the witness whose testimony is being reproduced;

(B) the party originally calling the witness;

(C) the party questioning the witness;

(D) the classification of the witness's examination (direct, cross, or other); and

(E) the transcript volume and page number from which the reproduced testimony is derived.

(5) Supplemental Appendix in a Civil Case. Except with leave of the appellate court or a single justice granted on motion, an appellee or cross-appellee in a civil case shall not file a supplemental appendix. Where such leave is granted, the appendix shall

(A) be filed and served with the brief pursuant to Rule 18(f) and 19, unless otherwise ordered;

(B) include only materials that are part of the record;

(C) not generally include materials already in the appellant's appendix, unless necessary for context; and

(D) be in the form prescribed by Rules 18(a)(1) and 20(a)(5) and (a)(6).

(c) Reproduction of Transcripts in Civil Cases. In a civil case, transcripts or portions thereof shall be reproduced for inclusion in the appendix consistent with Rule 18(b)(4).

(d) Reproduction of Impounded Materials. If the entire case has been impounded, the cover of the appendix shall clearly indicate that the appendix is impounded. If the entire case has not been impounded, a separate appendix volume shall be filed containing the impounded material and a copy of any lower court order(s) impounding the material, and the cover thereof shall clearly indicate that it contains impounded material.

(e) Reproduction of electronic audio or audiovisual exhibit. At the time of filing an appendix containing a reproduction of an electronic audio or audio-visual exhibit that was part of the lower court record, the filing party shall file a written notice with the clerk, with a copy of the notice sent to all parties, so indicating the inclusion of such reproduction, and specifying the form in which it is reproduced.

(f) Filing and Service. Any appendix, including exhibits and transcripts or portions thereof in a civil case, shall be filed and served with the brief in accordance with Rule 19.

(g) Amendment of Appendix. On motion for good cause, the court may grant leave for a party to file an amended appendix volume. The motion shall describe the nature and reason for the amendment. The party shall file with the motion the amended appendix volume marked as such on the front page or cover. Except as the court otherwise orders, the filing of an amended appendix volume has no effect on any filing deadlines.

Rule 19. Filing and Serving of Briefs, Appendices, and Certain Motions

(a) Time for Serving and Filing Briefs and Appendices in All

Cases Except Cross Appeals. Except as provided in Rule 19(c) (first degree murder appeals), Rule 11(g)(4) (direct appellate review), and Rule 27.1(f) (further appellate review), the following briefs and appendices shall be due as stated below:

(1) Appellant Brief and Appendix. The appellant shall serve and file a brief and appendix within 40 days after the date on which the appeal is docketed in the appellate court.

(2) Appellee Brief. The appellee shall serve and file a brief within 30 days after service of the brief of the appellant (or, in the case of multiple appellants, service of the last appellant brief).

(3) Reply Brief. Except by leave of court, any reply brief must be served and filed by the earlier of

(A) 14 days after service of the brief of the appellee (or, in the case of multiple appellees, service of the last appellee brief), or

(B) 7 days before argument.

(b) Time for Serving and Filing Briefs and Appendices in Cases Involving Cross Appeals. Except as provided in Rule 19(c) (first degree murder appeals), Rule 11(g) (direct appellate review), and Rule 27.1(f) (further appellate review), the following briefs and appendices shall be due when stated:

(1) Appellant's Principal Brief and Appendix. The appellant/cross-appellee shall serve and file a brief and appendix within 40 days after the date on which the appeal is docketed in the appellate court.

(2) Appellee's Principal and Response Brief and Appendix. The appellee/cross-appellant shall serve and file a brief and appendix within 30 days after service of the brief and appendix of the appellant (or, in the case of multiple appellants, service of the last appellant brief).

(3) Appellant's Response and Reply Brief. The appellant/cross-appellee reply brief must be served and filed within 30 days after service of the brief of the appellee/crossappellant.

(4) Appellee's Reply Brief. Except by leave of court, any reply brief must be served and filed by the appellee/cross-appellant by the earlier of (A) 14 days after service of the brief of the appellant/cross-appellee (or, in the case of multiple appellant/cross-appellees, service of the last appellant/cross-appellee brief), or (B) 7 days before argument.

(c) Time for Serving and Filing Briefs, Appendices, and Motions for New Trial in First Degree Murder Appeals.

(1) In the case of a direct appeal by an appellant who has been convicted of first degree murder, the appellant shall within 120 days after the date on which the appeal is docketed in the Supreme Judicial Court: (A) serve and file the appellant's brief and appendix; (B) serve and file a motion for a new trial; or (C) for good cause shown, seek a further enlargement of time for filing a brief and appendix or a motion for a new trial. The Commonwealth shall serve and file its brief within 90 days after service of the brief of the appellant. The appellant may serve and file a reply brief within the 30 days after service of the brief of the Commonwealth.

(2) If during the pendency of the direct appeal a motion for a new trial is remanded to the Superior Court, the direct appeal of the conviction will ordinarily be stayed until the motion is decided. The matter shall be heard and determined expeditiously in the Superior Court. The appellant shall file with the Clerk of the Supreme Judicial Court for the Commonwealth status reports as directed by the Court. An appeal by the defendant from the denial of a motion for a new trial shall be consolidated with the direct appeal.An appeal by the Commonwealth or by the defendant from the determination of a motion for a new trial shall have the same docket number as the direct appeal. The Clerk of the Supreme Judicial Court for the Commonwealth shall establish a briefing schedule.

(d) Number of Copies to Be Filed and Served.

(1) Briefs and Appendices.

(A) Appeals Court. Except as provided in the Appeals Court Standing Order Concerning Electronic Filing, on appeal to the Appeals Court, 4 copies of each brief and appendix shall be filed with the clerk, unless the court by order in a particular case shall direct a different number, and 2 copies shall be served on counsel for each party separately represented, 2 copies of each shall be served on counsel for all jointly represented parties, and 2 copies of each shall be served on each self-represented party to the appeal, unless the parties agree in writing or the court shall by rule or by order direct the filing or service of a different number.

(B) Supreme Judicial Court.

(i) On appeal to the Supreme Judicial Court, 7 copies of each brief and appendix shall be filed with the clerk, unless the court by order in a particular case shall direct a different number, and 2 copies shall be served on counsel for each party separately represented, 2 copies of each shall be served on counsel for all jointly represented parties, and 2 copies of each shall be served on each self-represented party to the appeal, unless theparties agree in writing or the court shall by rule or by order direct the filing or service of a different number.

(ii) Appeals Transferred to the Supreme Judicial Court from the Appeals Court. In any appeal transferred to the full Supreme Judicial Court, in which briefs and appendices have already been filed in the Appeals Court, 7 copies of each brief and appendix shall be promptly filed with the clerk of the Supreme Judicial Court, unless the court by order in a particular case shall direct a different number.

(2) Exhibits and Transcripts in Civil Cases. Exhibits and transcripts or portions thereof in civil cases, designated for inclusion in the appendix, may be contained in separate volumes, suitably indexed.

(A) Appeals Court. Except as provided in the Appeals Court Standing Order Concerning Electronic Filing, on appeal to the Appeals Court, 2 copies of the exhibit volume or volumes, and 1 copy of the transcript volume or volumes shall be filed with the brief and appendix and 1 copy of each shall be served on counsel for each party separately represented, 1 copy of each shall be served on counsel for all jointly represented parties, and 1 copy of each shall be served on each selfrepresented party to the appeal, unless the parties agree in writing or the court shall by rule or order direct the filing or service of a different number.

(B) Supreme Judicial Court.

(i) On appeal to the Supreme Judicial Court, and on further appellate review, 2 copies of the exhibit volume or volumes and 2 copies of the transcript volume or volumes shall be filed with the brief and appendix and 1 copy of each shall be served on counsel for each party separately represented, 1 copy of each shall be served on counsel for all jointly represented parties, and 1 copy of each shall be served on each selfrepresented party to the appeal, unless the parties agree in writing or the court shall by rule or by order direct the filing or service of a different number.

(ii) Appeals Transferred to the Supreme Judicial Court from the Appeals Court. In any appeal transferred to the full Supreme Judicial Court, in which copies of the exhibits and transcripts have already been filed in the

Appeals Court pursuant to this rule, 2 copies of the transcript volume or volumes shall be promptly filed with the clerk of the Supreme Judicial Court, unless the court by order in a particular case shall direct a different number.

(e) Consequence of Failure to File Briefs and Appendices. If an appellant fails to file a brief and appendix, other than a reply brief, within the time provided by this rule, or within the time as extended, the appellate court may, upon motion or sua sponte, dismiss the appeal. Any appellee who elects not to file a principal brief shall timely notify the appellate court and all parties that no brief will be filed. If an appellee fails to file a brief within the time provided by this rule, or within the time as extended, the appellate court may, upon motion or sua sponte, deem the case ready for consideration by the appellate court. An appellee who fails to file a timely brief will not be heard at oral argument except by permission of the appellate court.

Rule 20. Form and Length of Briefs, Appendices, and Other Documents

(a) Form and Length of Briefs, Appendices, and Applications for and Responses to Direct and Further Appellate Review.

(1) Form. Except on order of the appellate court or a single justice, or if filed on behalf of a party allowed to proceed as an indigent party, all briefs, appendices, and applications for and responses to direct and further appellate review shall be produced by any duplicating or copying process which produces a clear black image on white paper.

However produced, the page shall be 8.5 inches in width and 11 inches in height. Pages shall be firmly bound at the left, and a cover or front page shall be used.

(2) Length of Briefs in All Cases Other than Cross Appeals. The following rules shall govern the length of briefs in all cases other than cross appeals:

(A) A principal brief shall either be produced in a monospaced font and not contain more than 50 pages, or be produced in a proportionally spaced font and not contain more than 11,000 words.

(B) A reply brief shall either be produced in a monospaced font and not contain more than 20 pages, or be produced in a proportionally spaced font and not contain more than 4,500 words.

(C) An amicus curiae brief shall either be produced in a monospaced font and not contain more than 35 pages, or be produced in a proportionally spaced font and not contain more than 7,500 words.

(D) In all briefs, only those parts required by Rule 16(a)(5)-(11), including headings, footnotes, and quotations, count towards the length limits.

(E) A motion to exceed these length limits shall specify the relevant issue or issues and why such issues merit additional pages or words, and will not be granted except for extraordinary reasons.

(F) The certification required pursuant to Rule 16(k) shall specifically state how compliance with the length limits of this rule was ascertained, as specified therein.

(3) Length of Briefs in Cases Involving Cross Appeals. The following rules shall govern the length of briefs in cases involving cross appeals:

(A) An appellant's principal brief shall either be produced in a monospaced font and not contain more than 50 pages, or be produced in a proportionally spaced font and not contain more than 11,000 words.

(B) An appellee's principal and response brief shall either be produced in a monospaced font and not contain more than 60 pages, or be produced in a proportionally spaced font and not contain more than 13,000 words.

(C) An appellant's response and reply brief shall either be produced in a monospaced font and not contain more than 50 pages, or be produced in a proportionally spaced font and not contain more than 11,000 words.

(D) An appellee's reply brief shall either be produced in a monospaced font and not contain more than 20 pages, or be produced in a proportionally spaced font and not contain more than 4,500 words.

(E) An amicus curiae brief shall either be produced in a monospaced font and not contain more than 35 pages, or be produced in a proportionally spaced font and not contain more than 7,500 words.

(F) In all briefs, only those parts required by Rule 16(a)(5)–(11), including headings, footnotes, and quotations, count towards the length limits.

(G) A motion to exceed these length limits shall specify the relevant issue or issues and why such issues merit additional pages or words, and will not be granted except for extraordinary reasons.

(H) The certification required pursuant to Rule 16(k) shall specifically state how compliance with the length limits of this rule was ascertained, as specified therein.

(4) Format and Pagination of Text. The following rules shall govern the format of text on the pages of all briefs and applications for and responses to direct or further appellate review:

(A) If a monospaced font is used, the top and bottom margins shall be at least 1 inch. The left and right margins shall be at least 1.5 inches. If a proportionally spaced font is used, the top, bottom, left, and right margins shall be at least 1 inch. Page numbers shall appear in the margin with the cover paginated as page 1 pursuant to Rule 20(a)(6)(B)(vii) and pages thereafter numbered consecutively through the last page, including any addendum.

(B) The typeface of all text, including footnotes, shall be either (i) a monospaced font (such as Courier New) of 12 point or larger size and not exceeding 10.5 characters per inch; or (ii) a proportionally spaced font (such as Times New Roman) of 14 point or larger size.

(C) Text shall be double-spaced, except that argument headings, footnotes, and indented quotations may be single-spaced. For purposes of this rule, single spacing means not more than 6 lines of text per vertical inch; double spacing means not more than 3 lines of text per vertical inch and not more than 27 doublespaced lines on a page.

(D) The text may appear on both sides of the page.

(5) Format, Pagination, and Length of Appendix. The following rules shall govern the format of appendices:

(A) The cover of each volume of the appendix shall be designated by a Roman numeral and paginated as page 1, and pages thereafter numbered consecutively through the volume's last page. The cover shall also contain the information identified in Rule 20(a)(6)(B).

(B) Each volume of the appendix shall be separately paginated, beginning at page 1.

(C) No single volume of an appendix, transcript or exhibit shall be more than 1.5" thick.

(D) The text of appendices filed on paper may appear on both sides of the page.

(6) Color and Contents of Cover. The following rules shall govern the color and contents of the cover of all briefs, appendices, and applications for or responses to direct or further appellate review:

(A) Color. The cover of the brief of the appellant shall be blue; that of the appellee, red; that of a party intervening in the appeal, yellow; that of an amicus curiae, green; that of any reply brief, gray. The cover of the appendix shall be white. The cover or front page of an application for or response to direct orfurther appellate review shall be white. A color cover is not required for any electronically filed brief.

(B) Contents. The front covers of the briefs and appendices, in addition to the requirements for covers of appendices in Rule 20(a)(5), and of applications for or responses to direct or further appellate review shall contain: (i) the name of the court and the number of the case; (ii) the title of the case (see Rule 10(a)); (iii) the nature of the proceeding in the appellate court (e.g., Appeal; Application for Review) and the name of the lower court; (iv) the title of the document (e.g., Brief for Appellant, Appendix); (v) the name(s), Board of Bar Overseers (BBO) number(s), if any, mailing and electronic addresses, and telephone number(s) of the person(s) filing the document, and, if any individual counsel is affiliated with a firm or office, the office name; and (vi) where it is necessary to include impounded material in a brief, thenotification required by Rule 16(m). (vii) The cover shall be paginated as page 1.

(7) Substantial Compliance Required. Briefs, appendices, or applications for or responses to direct or further appellate review not in substantial compliance with these rules shall not be docketed unless the appellate court or a single justice shall otherwise order.

(b) Form of Other Documents.

(1) Motions for Reconsideration or Modification. Motions for reconsideration or modification shall be produced in a manner prescribed by Rule 27(b).

(2) Motions and Other Documents.

(A) A motion or other document addressed to an appellate court shall contain a caption setting forth the name of the court, the title of the case, the docket number, and a brief descriptive title indicating the purpose of the document; the caption shall appear on the first page. Lines of text shall be double-spaced and shall be in 12 point or larger font, with side and top margins no less than 1 inch, and shall be no longer than reasonably necessary. Consecutive pages shall be stapled at the upper left margin.

(B) Such motion or document shall contain, at the end thereof (i) the printed and signed name(s), Board of Bar Overseers (BBO) number(s), if any, mailing and electronic addresses, and telephone number(s) of the person(s) filing the document, and, if any individual counsel is affiliated with a firm or office, the office name, and (ii) the date of signing.

Rule 21. Protection of Personal Identifying Information

Publicly accessible documents filed with the court shall conform to Supreme Judicial Court Rule 1:24, Protection of Personal Identifying Information in Publicly Accessible Court Documents.

Rule 22. Oral Argument

(a) Notice of Argument; Postponement. The clerk shall advise all parties of the time and place at which oral argument will be heard. A request for postponement of the argument must be made by motion filed reasonably in advance of the date fixed for hearing.

(b) Time Allowed for Argument. Unless otherwise enlarged or limited by the appellate court, each side will be allowed 15 minutes for argument, except in a criminal case in which the defendant is appealing from a conviction of murder in the first degree, in which case each side will be allowed 20 minutes for argument. Reasonably in advance of the date fixed for oral argument, a party may move for additional time for good cause shown. The appellate court may terminate the argument whenever in its judgment further argument is unnecessary.

(c) Order and Content of Argument.

(1) Oral Argument. The appellant will argue first. Nothing argued in the brief shall be deemed to be waived by a failure to argue orally.

(2) Post-Argument Filings. After the oral argument of a case has been concluded or the case has been submitted on the documents without oral argument, no brief, memorandum, or letter relating to the case, except a citation of supplemental authorities letter filed pursuant to Rule 16(l), shall be submitted to the court, except to correct a factual misstatement during oral argument, or when such a writing was expressly allowed or requested by the court during the argument, or upon allowance of a motion to submit such a writing. Any such writing allowed during oral argument shall state that the court allowed the submission. A submission containing argument on the merits and not otherwise in compliance with this rule may be struck by the court.

(d) Cross and Separate Appeals. A cross or separate appeal shall be argued with the initial appeal at a single argument, unless the appellate court otherwise directs. If separate appellants support the same argument, care shall be taken to avoid duplication of argument.

(e) Non-appearance of Parties. Parties are expected to appear for oral argument unless prior arrangements have been made with the court. If the appellee fails to appear to present argument, the appellate court will hear argument on behalf of the appellant, if present. If the appellant fails to appear, the court may hear argument on behalf of the appellee, if present. If neither party appears, the case will be decided on the briefs unless the appellate court shall otherwise order.

(f) Submission on Briefs. By agreement of the parties, a case may at any time be submitted for decision on the briefs, but the appellate court may direct that the case be argued. At any time, any party may, by written notice filed and served, waive the party's right to oral argument. No criminal case in which the defendant was convicted of murder in the first degree may be submitted for decision on the briefs without oral argument unless the appellate court or a justice thereof shall have approved the submission prior to the week the case has been scheduled for argument.

(g) Use of Physical Exhibits at Argument; Removal. If physical exhibits other than documents are to be used at the argument, the party shall arrange to have them placed in the court room before the court convenes on the date of the argument. After the argument, the exhibits shall be left with the clerk unless the court otherwise directs. If exhibits are not reclaimed by the party within a reasonable time after notice is given by the clerk, they shall be destroyed or otherwise disposed of as the clerk shall think best.

Rule 23. Notice of Decision; Issuance of Rescript; Stay of Rescript

(a) The clerk of the appellate court shall send to all parties copies of or a link to the rescript and the decision, if one was written, on the day the decision is released.

(b) The rescript and the decision of the appellate court shall issue to the lower court 28 days after the date of the decision unless the time is shortened or enlarged by order, except as provided by Rule 23(c).

(c) The issuance of the rescript will automatically be stayed, unless otherwise ordered by the appellate court, by the timely filing of: (1) a motion for reconsideration or modification pursuant to Rule 27; or (2) an application for further appellate review pursuant to Rule 27.1. The rescript shall issue forthwith after both the disposition of any motions for reconsideration or modification and the denial of any applications for further appellate review, unless the appellate court or a single justice orders otherwise. If an application for further appellate review is granted, the rescript of the Appeals Court shall not issue to the lower court.

Rule 24. Justices' Participation

(a) Other Justices May Participate Without Reargument. Whenever the justices before whom a case has been heard so desire, others of the justices may be called in to take part in the decision, upon a review of the record and briefs, and the recording of any oral argument, without reargument.

(b) Replacement of Justices. If a justice who has participated in a case becomes unable to participate further, then the Chief Justice of the appellate court may substitute another justice.

(c) Justice May Review Own Ruling in Certain Cases. No justice shall sit on the hearing of any proceeding in the nature of a review of any judgment, decree, order, or ruling made by that justice; provided, however, that this shall not apply where it is necessary to secure a quorum or where the other justices of the court shall be equally divided in opinion.

Rule 25. Damages for Frivolous Appeal in Civil Cases

If an appellate court determines that an appeal in a civil case is frivolous, it may award just damages and single or double costs to the appellee, and such interest on the amount of the judgment as may be allowed by law. The appellate court shall calculate the amount of any award after a separately filed motion or notice from the court and reasonable opportunity to respond.

Rule 26. Costs in Civil Cases

This rule applies only to civil cases.

(a) To Whom Allowed. Except as otherwise provided by law or ordered by the court, (1) if an appeal is dismissed, costs shall be taxed against the appellant unless otherwise agreed to by the parties; (2) if a judgment is affirmed, costs shall be taxed against the appellant; (3) if a judgment is reversed, costs shall be taxed against the appellee; (4) if a judgment is affirmed in part, reversed in part, modified, or vacated, costs are taxed only as ordered by the appellate court. Costs shall not be taxed against a party determined indigent in the same proceeding.

(b) Costs For and Against the Commonwealth. In cases involving the Commonwealth or an agency or officer thereof, if an award of costs against the Commonwealth is authorized by law, costs shall be awarded in accordance with the provisions of Rule 26(a); otherwise, costs shall not be awarded for or against the Commonwealth.

(c) Costs of Briefs and Appendices. The cost of printing or otherwise producing necessary copies of briefs and appendices shall be taxable in the lower court at rates not higher than those generally charged for such work in the Commonwealth. A party who desires such costs to be taxed shall state them in an itemized and verified bill of costs which shall be filed with the clerk of the lower court, with proof of service, within 14 days after the entry of judgment.

(d) Clerk to Insert Costs in Lower Court Judgment; Costs Taxable. The clerk of the lower court shall prepare and certify an itemized statement of costs on appeal for insertion in the lower court judgment. The following costs on appeal are taxable in the lower court for the benefit of the party entitled to costs under this rule:

(1) copies under Rule 26(c);

(2) costs incurred in the preparation and transmission of the record;

(3) the reporter's transcript, if necessary to determine the appeal;

(4) the premiums paid for any bond to preserve rights pending appeal;

(5) the fee for docketing the appeal under Rule 10(a)(1); and

(6) the cost of any convenience fees and other administrative fees levied for the privilege of paying fees or costs by credit card or other means, including, but not limited to, fees for electronic filing of documents or pleadings with the court.

Rule 27. Motion for Reconsideration or Modification of Decision

(a) Time for Filing; Content; Action by Court if Granted. Within 14 days after the date of the decision of the appellate court, any party to an appeal may file a motion for reconsideration or modification of decision unless the time is shortened or enlarged by order. It shall state with particularity the points of law or fact which it is contended the court has overlooked or misapprehended and shall contain such argument in support of the motion as the movant desires to present. Oral argument in support of the motion will not be permitted, except by order of the appellate court which decided the appeal. The motion shall be decided by the quorum or panel of the appellate court which decided the appeal.

(b) Form of Motion; Length. Except by permission of the appellate court, a motion shall not exceed either 10 pages of text in monospaced font or 2,000 words in proportional font, as defined in Rule 20(a)(4)(B), and shall contain a certification of such compliance, including a statement of how compliance with the foregoing length limit was ascertained, as specified in Rule 16(k).

(c) Response. No response to a motion for reconsideration or modification will be docketed unless requested by the appellate court, but reconsideration will ordinarily not be granted in the absence of such a request. Any response filed pursuant to this provision shall comply with the form and length requirements in Rule 27(b).

(d) Filing and Service. The motion, and any requested response, shall be filed in the office of the clerk of the appellate court that released the decision. In the Supreme Judicial Court, a paper original and 7 copies of the motion shall be filed. In the Appeals Court, the motion shall be filed in electronic form and no paper original or copies are required. Service of the motion, and any requested response, shall comply with Rule 13.

(e) Ruling on Motion. Upon consideration of a motion and any response, the appellate court may make a final disposition of the case without reargument or may restore it to the calendar for reargument or resubmission or may make such other orders as are deemed appropriate under the circumstances of the particular case. Action upon a motion is in the discretion of such appellate court, which may award costs, including a reasonable attorney's fee, to the prevailing party.

(f) Notice to Supreme Judicial Court. A party seeking further appellate review shall promptly notify the Supreme Judicial Court of any action taken on the motion.

Rule 27.1. Further Appellate Review

(a) Application; When Filed; Grounds. Within 21 days after the date of the decision of the Appeals Court, any party to the appeal may file an application for further appellate review of the case by the Supreme Judicial Court. Such application shall be founded upon substantial reasons affecting the public interest or the interests of justice. Oral argument in support of an application shall not be permitted except by order of the court.

(b) Contents of Application; Form. The application for further appellate review shall contain, in the following order: (1) a request for leave to obtain further appellate review; (2) a statement of prior proceedings in the case (including whether any party is seeking a reconsideration or modification in the Appeals Court); (3) a short statement of facts relevant to the appeal (but facts correctly stated in the decision of the Appeals Court shall not be restated); (4) a statement of the points with respect to which further appellate review of the decision of the Appeals Court is sought; and (5) a brief statement (consisting of not more than either 10 pages of text in monospaced font or 2,000 words in proportional font as defined in Rule 20(a)(4)(B)), including appropriate authorities, indicating why further appellate review is appropriate. A copy of the rescript and decision of the Appeals Court shall be appended to the application. In addition, if the Appeals Court entered a memorandum and order under Appeals Court Rule 1:28 which refers to another document, such as a brief or judge's findings and rulings, a copy of that document, or, if appropriate, the pertinent pages of that document, shall be appended to the application. The application shall comply with the requirements of Rule 20(a), and shall contain a certification of such compliance, including a statement of how compliance with the foregoing length limit was ascertained, as specified in Rule 16(k).

(c) Response; Form. Within 14 days after the filing of the application, any other party to the appeal may, but need not, file and serve a response thereto (consisting of not more than either 10 pages of text in monospaced font or 2,000 words of text in proportional font, as defined in Rule 20(a)(4)(B)) setting forth reasons why the application should or should not be granted. The response shall not restate matters described in Rule 27.1(b)(2) and (3) unless the opposing party is dissatisfied with the statement thereof contained in the application. A response shall comply with the requirements of Rule 20(a), and shall contain a certification of such compliance, including a statement of how compliance with the foregoing length limit was ascertained, as specified in Rule 16(k). A response may be filed in a different form as permitted by the court.

(d) Filing; Service. One copy of the application and of each response shall be filed in the office of the clerk of the full Supreme Judicial Court. No copy of the application or any response need be filed in the Appeals Court. Filing and service of the application and of any response shall comply with Rule 13.

(e) Vote for Further Appellate Review; Certification. If any 3 justices of the Supreme Judicial Court shall vote for further appellate review for substantial reasons affecting the public interest or the interests of justice, or if a majority of the justices of the Appeals Court or a majority of the justices of the Appeals Court deciding the case shall certify that the public interest or the interests of justice make desirable a further appellate review, an order allowing the application or the certificate, as the case may be, shall be transmitted to the clerk of the Appeals Court with notice to the lower court. The clerk of the Appeals Court shall forthwith transmit to the clerk of the full Supreme Judicial Court all documents filed in the case.

(f) Briefs. Any party may apply to the Supreme Judicial Court within 14 days after the date on which the appeal is docketed in the full Supreme Judicial Court for permission to file a new brief. If the application is granted, the new brief must be filed in accordance with the briefing schedule established by the clerk of the Supreme Judicial Court, and the court may impose terms as to the length and filing of such brief and any response thereto. If a new brief is filed, it will be considered in lieu of the Appeals Court brief. If permission to file a new brief is denied or not sought, cases in which further appellate review has been granted shall be argued on the briefs filed in the Appeals Court.

(g) Equally Divided Vote on Further Appellate Review. If, following allowance of an application for further appellate review, the justices of the Supreme Judicial Court are equally divided in opinion, unless a majority of the participating justices decides otherwise, the court shall issue an order noting such equal division, the effect of which shall be the same as if the court had denied the application for further appellate review.

Rule 28. Procedure in Lower Court Following Rescript

(a) Civil Cases. In a civil case, when the rescript from the appellate court sets forth the text of the judgment to be entered, the clerk of the lower court shall, upon receipt of the rescript, prepare, sign, and enter the judgment which has been ordered. If the rescript orders settlement of the form of the judgment in the lower court, the clerk of the lower court shall sign and enter the judgment after settlement. Notation of a judgment in the lower court docket constitutes entry of the judgment.

(b) Criminal Cases. If the rescript has the effect of entitling the defendant to immediate release from custody, counsel for the defendant, the Commonwealth, and the clerk of the lower court shall immediately take any action necessary to ensure that the defendant is released from custody forthwith. In all other criminal cases, unless the rescript affirms the lower court, the clerk of the lower court shall, upon receipt of the rescript, schedule a hearing forthwith to be held no later than 30 days from the clerk's entry of the rescript.

Rule 29. Voluntary Dismissal of Appeal or Other Proceeding

(a) Voluntary Dismissal in the Lower Court. Before an appeal has been docketed in the appellate court, the lower court may dismiss the appeal on the filing of a stipulation signed by all the parties or on the appellant's motion with notice to all parties.

(b) Voluntary Dismissal in the Appellate Court.

(1) Civil Cases. If the parties to a civil appeal or other civil proceeding shall sign and file with the clerk of the appellate court a stipulation or motion that the proceeding be dismissed with prejudice, specifying the terms as to payment of costs and attorney's fees, and shall pay whatever fees are due, the clerk shall enter the case as dismissed. An appeal may be dismissed on motion of the appellant on such terms as may be agreed upon by the parties or fixed by the court.

(2) Criminal Cases. A criminal appeal or other criminal proceeding may be dismissed by the appellate court on motion of the appellant, and the clerk shall enter the case as dismissed. If the appellant is the defendant, the motion shall include an affidavit by the defendant, or an attestation by counsel, that the defendant assents to the court's dismissal of the appeal with prejudice. If the motion states that the appeal is moot, an affidavit by the defendant is not required.

(c) Settlement; Obligation of Appellant. In the event a case is settled or otherwise disposed of while an appeal is pending, it shall be the duty of the appellant to notify the clerk of the appellate court forthwith.

(d) Notice to Lower Court. The clerk of the appellate court shall promptly notify the clerk of the lower court whenever an appeal is dismissed pursuant to this rule.

Rule 30. Substitution of Parties in Civil Cases

This rule applies only to civil cases.

(a) Death of a Party. If a party dies after a notice of appeal is filed in the lower court or while a proceeding is pending in the appellate court, the personal representative of the deceased party may be substituted as a party on motion filed by the representative or by any party with the clerk of the appropriate court. The motion of a party shall be served upon the representative in accordance with the provisions of Rule 13. If the deceased party has no representative, any party may suggest the death on the record and proceedings shall then be had as the appellate court or a single justice may direct. If a party against whom an appeal may be taken dies after entry of a judgment or order in the lower court but before a notice of appeal is filed, an appellant may proceed as if death had not occurred. After the appeal is docketed, substitution shall be effected in the appellate court in accordance with this subdivision. If a party entitled to appeal shall die before filing a notice of appeal, the notice of appeal may be filed by the party's personal representative, or, if the party has no personal representative, by the party's attorney of record within the time prescribed by these rules. After the appeal is docketed, substitution shall be effected in the appellate court in accordance with this subdivision.

(b) Substitution for Other Causes. If substitution of a party in the appellate court is necessary for any reason other than death, substitution shall be effected in accordance with the procedure prescribed in Rule 30(a).

(c) Public Officers; Death or Separation from Office.

(1) When a public officer is a party to an appeal or other proceeding in an appellate court in the public officer's official capacity and during its pendency dies, resigns, or otherwise ceases to hold office, the action does not abate and the public officer's successor is automatically substituted as a party. Proceedings following the substitution shall be in the name of the substituted party, but any misnomer not affecting the substantial rights of the parties shall be disregarded. An order of substitution may be entered at any time, but the omission to enter such an order shall not affect the substitution.

(2) When a public officer is a party to an appeal or other proceeding in the public officer's official capacity, the public officer may be described as a party by official title rather than by name; but the court may require the public officer's name to be added.

Rule 31. Duties of Clerks

(a) General Provisions. The Supreme Judicial Court and the Appeals Court shall be deemed always open for the purpose of filing any proper document, of issuing and returning process, and of making motions and orders. The office of the clerk with a clerk in attendance shall be open during regular court business hours on all weekdays except State and Federal holidays recognized by the Commonwealth.

(b) The Docket; Calendar; Other Records Required.

(1) The clerk shall keep an electronic docket, in such form and style as may be prescribed by the appellate court, and shall enter therein each case. Cases shall be assigned consecutive docket numbers. All filings, orders, decisions, and rescripts shall be entered chronologically on the docket. Entries shall show the nature of each filing, order, decision, or rescript.

(2) The clerk shall prepare, under the direction of the appellate court, a calendar of cases awaiting argument. In placing cases on the calendar for argument, the clerk shall give preference to appeals in child welfare and criminal cases, and to appeals and other proceedings entitled to preference by law.

(3) The clerk shall keep such other records as may be required from time to time by law or by the appellate court.

(c) Notice of Orders, Decisions, or Rescripts. Upon the entry of an order, decision, or rescript, including an order on an application for direct or further appellate review, the clerk of the appellate court shall send a notice of entry to each party, and include a copy of or a link to any decision and rescript. The clerk shall send such notice to the electronic business address of an attorney that is registered with the Board of Bar Overseers, and may send paper notice by conventional mail. The clerk shall send such notice to the mailing or electronic address of a selfrepresented party, depending upon such party's address preference as registered with the clerk.

(d) Custody of Records and Documents. The clerk shall have custody of the records and documents of the appellate court. The clerk shall not permit any original record or document to be taken from the clerk's custody except as authorized by the orders or instructions of the court or a single justice. Original documents transmitted as the record on appeal or review shall be returned to the lower court.

Massachusetts Juvenile Court

Juvenile Court Rules for the Care and Protection of Children

[Amended effective Nov. 5, 2018.]

Rule 1. Scope of Rules

These rules apply to all actions in the Juvenile Court Department for the care and protection of children, including actions for guardianship of minors, child support, parentage, name change and actions seeking to dispense with parental consent to adoption, custody, guardianship or any other disposition of the child pursuant to G.L. c. 119 and c. 210.

Note

Throughout these rules "paternity" has been replaced by the gender-neutral term "parentage." *See Partenan v. Gallagher*, 475 Mass. 632 (2016).

See G.L. c. 119, § 24 (care and protection), c. 190B, §§ 1-401 and 5-101 (guardianship of minors), c. 209C, § 3(c) (parentage and support), c. 119, § 28 (temporary support), and c. 210, § 1 (authority of the Juvenile Court to hear cases pursuant to c. 210 with respect to pending proceedings in the Juvenile Court). Proceedings that seek equitable relief are governed by the Massachusetts Rules of Civil Procedure, including proceedings pursuant to G.L. c. 210, § 6D (enforcement of post-adoption agreements). *See* G.L. c. 218, § 59 and Mass. R. Civ. P., Rule 1. Permanency Hearings are governed by the Massachusetts Trial Court Rule VI Uniform Rules for Permanency Hearings.

Rule 2. Definition of Terms

For these rules the terms below shall have the following definitions:

"Child" means the person who is the subject of the petition or complaint.

"Department" means the Department of Children and Families or its successor.

"Order or Decree Dispensing with Consent to Adoption" means an order or decree dispensing with the need for consent to adoption, guardianship or any other disposition of the child, commonly referred to as "termination of parental rights."

"Precept" means an order of the court to take and bring the child who is the subject of the care and protection petition before the court.

Rule 3. Precepts

A. Procedure. The court may order a precept sua sponte or upon the request of the petitioner or the Department. The precept shall be served by a court officer, constable, deputy sheriff, sheriff, police officer, or other person designated by the court and shall be on a form approved by the Chief Justice of the Juvenile Court.

B. Service. The precept shall be served forthwith. The child shall be brought to the court within court hours and identified.

Nothing in this rule limits the authority or responsibility of the Department regarding the care and custody of children as set forth in statutes, case law and Department regulations.

C. Return of Service. The officer or other person making service in accordance with this rule shall make a return of service on the precept and file it promptly with the court.

Note

If the precept is served and the child cannot be brought before the court the same day, the Department shall bring the child to the court for identification as soon thereafter as practicable. If available and with prior arrangement, the child may be identified by way of videoconference. *See* Executive Office Transmittal 14-4 Trial Court Videoconferencing Policy. The child should be identified by a judge from the court that issued the precept. However, if necessary and with prior arrangement, the child may be identified by a judge from a different Juvenile Court. *See* Order of Assignment dated February 12, 2014 authorizing justices appointed to a particular division of the Juvenile Court Department and circuit justices appointed to the Juvenile Court Department to sit and act as justices in all divisions of the Juvenile Court Department.

Rule 4. Appointment of Counsel

Counsel shall be appointed in accordance with the provisions of G.L. c. 119, § 29 and c. 211D, the Massachusetts Rules of the Supreme Judicial Court, Rule 3:10, and applicable case law.

Note

See Dept. of Pub. Welfare v. J.K.B., 379 Mass. 1 (1979) (indigent parent entitled to court- appointed counsel in termination of parental rights proceedings pursuant to G.L. c. 210, § 3), *Guardianship of V.V.*, 470 Mass. 590 (2015) (indigent parent entitled to court-appointed counsel on a guardianship petition pursuant to G.L. c. 190B) and *L.B. v. Chief Justice of the Probate and Family Court Dept.*, 474 Mass. 231 (2016) (indigent parent entitled to court-appointed counsel in petitions to remove guardian and/or seek visits with the child under the guardianship provided the parent presents a meritorious claim for removal and/or modification of visitation).

Rule 5. Process

A. Summons to Parent/Guardian; Service of Process by Publication

1. Care and Protection Cases

After the filing of the care and protection petition, the petitioner shall cause a summons or order of notice and a copy of the petition to be served by a court officer, constable, deputy sheriff, sheriff, police officer, or other person approved by the court on each of the parents of the child, the legal guardian, if any, the legal custodian, if any, and the Department, if the legal custodian. The summons or order of notice shall be on a form approved by the Chief Justice of the Juvenile Court and shall be served on each of the above in the following manner:

(a) If the place of residence or whereabouts of the persons above is known, service shall be accomplished by delivery in hand. Service shall be accomplished on the Department by delivering the summons or order of notice to the appropriate Office of the Regional Counsel.

(b) Personal service may be accomplished the first time the matter comes before the judge or at the temporary custody hearing on persons above, if present, and upon a representative of the Department.

(c) If the Department is not the legal custodian, the petitioner shall provide notice to the Department of the filing of the petition by certified or registered mail, return receipt requested, to the appropriate Office of Regional Counsel, attention to the Regional Counsel.

(d) If the place of residence or whereabouts of persons above, except the parent(s), is known but the petitioner has been unable to accomplish in-hand service despite diligent efforts to do so, on the petitioner's written motion for alternate manner of service setting forth the diligent efforts made to accomplish in-hand service, the court may order that service be accomplished by certified or registered mail, return receipt requested, to the last known place of residence, the mailing to be at least twenty-one days before the date of the pretrial conference, unless the court otherwise orders.

(e) If the place of residence or whereabouts of a parent is known but the petitioner has been unable to accomplish in-hand service despite diligent efforts to do so, or the place of residence or whereabouts of a parent cannot be found after diligent efforts, on the petitioner's written motion for alternate manner of service setting forth the diligent efforts made to accomplish in-hand service or ascertain the place of residence or whereabouts, the court may order that service be accomplished on that parent, either within or outside of the Commonwealth, by:

(i) certified or registered mail, return receipt requested, to the last known place of residence of the parent, the mailing to be at least twenty-one days before the date of the pretrial conference, unless the court otherwise orders, and

(ii) publication in accordance with subsection (g), below.

(f) If the identity of a parent is not known, service shall be accomplished on that parent by publication in accordance with subsection (g), below.

(g) Whenever service by publication is required in a care and protection case, the court shall, upon motion of the petitioner, other party, or sua sponte, issue an Order for Service by Publication. The petitioner shall cause notice to be published in accordance with the order in the newspaper or newspapers designated by the court once in each of three successive weeks, the final publication to appear no later than the pretrial conference date unless the court otherwise orders. Whenever the court orders service by publication the court shall also require the petitioner to file a Military Affidavit on a form approved by the Chief Justice of the Juvenile Court as to the parent to be served by publication.

(h) If, after the petitioner has perfected service of process in accordance with this rule, no parent has appeared or can be found, and the legal guardian, if any, has not appeared and the legal custodian, if any, has not appeared, a summons shall be issued to the person with whom such child last resided, if known.

2. Guardianship of a Minor Cases

Except as provided for in subsection (i), after the filing of a guardianship petition, the petitioner shall cause notice and a copy of the petition to be served by a court officer, constable, deputy sheriff, sheriff, police officer, or other person approved by the court on the person(s) set forth in G.L. c. 190B, § 5-206. The notice shall be on a form approved by the Chief Justice of the Juvenile Court and shall be served with a copy of the petition in the following manner:

(a) If the place of residence or whereabouts of persons entitled to notice pursuant to G.L. 190B, § 5-206 is known, service shall be accomplished by delivery in hand on the:

(i) parent(s);

(ii) child if age fourteen or older and not the petitioner;

(iii) person given care or custody of the child by court order and with whom the child has resided within sixty days prior to the filing of the petition, excluding foster parent(s);

(iv) current guardian or conservator for the child; and

(v) the Department, if the legal custodian. In-hand service shall be accomplished on the Department by delivering the notice to the appropriate Office of the Regional Counsel.

(b) Personal service may be accomplished on person(s) entitled to in-hand service pursuant to paragraph (a), if present, and upon a representative of the Department, if the legal custodian, when the matter comes before the judge.

(c) Service shall be accomplished on all others entitled to notice pursuant to G.L. c. 190B, § 5-206 by certified or registered mail, return receipt requested, to the last known place of residence or whereabouts, if known. Service shall be accomplished on the Department, if not the legal custodian, by certified or registered mail, return receipt requested, to the appropriate Office of Regional Counsel, attention to the Regional Counsel.

(d) If the place of residence or whereabouts of a person, except the parents, entitled to in-hand service pursuant to paragraph (a) is known but the petitioner has been unable to accomplish in-hand service despite diligent efforts to do so, on the petitioner's written motion for alternate manner of service setting forth the diligent efforts made to accomplish in-hand service, the court may order that service be accomplished by certified or registered mail, return receipt requested, to the last known place of residence, the mailing to be at least fourteen days before the petition for guardianship is heard, unless the court otherwise orders.

(e) If the place of residence or whereabouts of a parent is known but the petitioner has been unable to accomplish in-hand service despite diligent efforts to do so or the place of residence or whereabouts of a parent cannot be found after diligent efforts, on the petitioner's written motion for alternate manner of service setting forth the diligent efforts made to accomplish in-hand service or ascertain the place of residence or whereabouts, the court may order that service be accomplished on that parent, either within or outside of the Commonwealth, by:

(i) certified or registered mail, return receipt requested, to the last known place of residence of the parent, the mailing to be at least fourteen days before the petition for guardianship is heard, unless the court otherwise orders, and

(ii) publication in accordance with subsection (g), below.

(f) If the identity of a parent is not known, service shall be accomplished on that parent by publication in accordance with subsection (g), below.

(g) Whenever service by publication is required in a guardianship case the court shall, upon motion of the petitioner, other party, or sua sponte, issue an Order for Service by Publication. The petitioner shall cause notice to be published in accordance with the order at least once in the newspaper or newspapers designated by the court, the publication to appear at least seven days before the petition for guardianship is heard, unless the court otherwise orders. Whenever the court orders service by publication the court shall also require the petitioner to file a Military Affidavit on a form approved by the Chief Justice of the Juvenile Court, as to the parent to be served by publication.

(h) If the minor is entitled to any benefit, estate, or income paid or payable through the United States Veterans Administration or its successor, service shall be made on the Veterans Administration or its successor by certified or registered mail, return receipt requested, unless the court otherwise orders.

(i) No notice need be given in the following circumstances: (1) to a person entitled to notice under this rule who has assented in writing to the allowance of the petition if the assent is filed in court; (2) to a parent who executes an adoption surrender in conformance with G.L. c. 210, § 2; or (3) if the court has terminated parental rights pursuant to G.L. c. 119, § 26 or c. 210, § 3.

(j) A motion for the appointment of a temporary guardian may not be filed unless a guardianship petition has been filed. If service of the notice of the guardianship petition has not been made in accordance with this rule, a copy of the motion for the appointment of temporary guardian and written notice of its hearing shall be served with the notice of the guardianship petition, unless the court otherwise orders.

3. Parentage and Child Support Cases

After the filing of a complaint for parentage or an order of child support, or both, the plaintiff shall cause notice and a copy of the complaint to be served by a court officer, constable, deputy sheriff, sheriff, police officer, or other person approved by the court on each of the parents of the child unless a parent has assented to the filing of the complaint, on the child, if the child is age fourteen years or older, on the Department, if the legal custodian, and on the person entitled to notice pursuant to G.L. c. 209C, § 6. The notice shall be on a form approved by the Chief Justice of the Juvenile Court and shall be served with a copy of the complaint in the following manner:

(a) If the place of residence or whereabouts of a parent is known, service shall be accomplished on that parent by delivery in hand to the parent. If the child is age fourteen years or older, service shall be made in the same manner on the child. Service shall be accomplished on the Department by delivering the notice to the appropriate Office of the Regional Counsel, attention to the Regional Counsel.

(b) Personal service may be accomplished on the parent or child who is age fourteen years or older, if present, and on a representative of the Department, if the legal custodian, when the matter comes before the judge.

(c) If the Department is not the legal custodian of the child, the plaintiff shall provide notice to the Department of the filing of the complaint by certified or registered mail, return receipt requested, to the appropriate Office of Regional Counsel, attention to the Regional Counsel.

(d) If the place of residence or whereabouts of a parent is known but the plaintiff has been unable to accomplish in-hand service despite diligent efforts to do so or the place of residence or whereabouts of a parent cannot be found after diligent efforts, on the plaintiff's written motion for alternate manner of service setting forth the diligent efforts made to accomplish in-hand service or ascertain the place of residence or whereabouts, the court may order that service be accomplished on that parent, either within or outside of the Commonwealth, by:

(i) certified or registered mail, return receipt requested, to the last known place of residence of the parent, the mailing to be at least fourteen days before the complaint for parentage or support is heard, unless the court otherwise orders, and

(ii) publication in accordance with subsection (e), below.

(e) Whenever service by publication is required in a parentage or child support case the court shall, upon motion of the plaintiff, other party, or sua sponte, issue an Order for Service by Publication. The plaintiff shall cause notice to be published in accordance with the order at least once in the newspaper or newspapers designated by the court, the publication to appear at least seven days before the complaint for parentage or support is heard, unless the court otherwise orders. Whenever the court orders service by publication the court shall also require the plaintiff to file a Military Affidavit on a form approved by the Chief Justice of the Juvenile Court as to the person to be served by publication.

4. Change of Name Cases

Except as provided in subsection (e), after the filing of a change of name petition, the petitioner shall serve notice on each of the parents of the child and upon the Department if the legal custodian or if there is a care and protection case pending, in accordance with an order of notice. An order of notice shall be on a form approved by the Chief Justice of the Juvenile Court and shall be served with a copy of the petition in the following manner:

(a) Service shall be accomplished by certified or registered mail, return receipt requested, on the parent to the last known place of residence of the parent and on the Department to the appropriate Office of the Regional Counsel, attention to the Regional Counsel, the mailing to be at least fourteen days before the petition for change of name is heard, unless the court otherwise orders.

(b) Service may be accomplished by a court officer on the parent, if present, and on a representative of the Department when the matter comes before the judge.

(c) If the place of residence or whereabouts of a parent is known but the petitioner has been unable to accomplish service by certified or registered mail despite diligent efforts to do so or if the place of residence or whereabouts of a parent cannot be found after

2

diligent efforts, on the petitioner's written motion for alternate manner of service setting forth the diligent efforts made to accomplish service or ascertain the place of residence or whereabouts, the court may order that service be accomplished on that parent, either within or outside of the Commonwealth, by publication in accordance with subsection (d), below.

(d) Whenever service by publication is required in a change of name case the court shall, upon motion of the petitioner, or sua sponte, issue an Order for Service by Publication. The petitioner shall cause notice to be published in accordance with the order at least once in the newspaper or newspapers designated by the court, the publication to appear at least seven days before the petition is heard, unless the court otherwise orders. Whenever the court orders service by publication the court shall also require the petitioner to file a Military Affidavit on a form approved by the Chief Justice of the Juvenile Court, as to the parent to be served by publication.

(e) No notice need be given in the following circumstances: (1) to a person entitled to notice under this rule who has assented in writing to the allowance of the petition if the assent is filed in court; (2) to a parent who executes an adoption surrender in conformance with G.L. c. 210, § 2; or (3) if the court has terminated parental rights pursuant to G.L. c. 210, § 3.

B. Filing Proof of Publication. Following publication in accordance with the order, counsel for the petitioner or plaintiff shall promptly complete and file in the Clerk's office an Affidavit of Notice of Publication on a form approved by the Chief Justice of the Juvenile Court and shall file a completed Military Affidavit as to the person served by publication.

C. Joint Publication. In a case involving two or more children who have the same parents, the petitioner or plaintiff may accomplish service by joint publication. In all other cases, there shall be a separate publication for each child who is a subject of a case.

D. Filing of Return of Service. The officer or other person making service in accordance with this rule shall make a return of service on a copy of the summons or order of notice that the petitioner or plaintiff shall promptly file with the court.

Note

See Trial Court Rules, Rule IV Uniform Rule Requiring Disclosure of Pending and Concluded Care or Custody Matters and Rule X Uniform Rule Requiring Disclosure of Present or Past Receipt of Public Assistance Benefits by Minor Children. Current Juvenile Court forms are available online on the Juvenile Court website.

Subsection A. Service on the Department. When providing service in hand or by certified or registered mail on the Department, the address to be used is that of the Office of the Regional Counsel for the region in which the case is filed.

Subsection A.3. See G.L. c. 209C, § 6, relative to persons who must be joined as a party and the manner of notice required.

Subsection A. 4. Petitions for change of name pursuant to G.L. c. 210, § 12 are for name changes other than those that occur in the context of adoption cases or, in some instances, parentage cases. After the petition for change of name is allowed, the clerk may, upon request, issue a Certificate of Name Change. Allowance of the petition for change of name will not result in an amendment of the birth certificate. The birth name remains the same. The new name is considered an alias or an "also known as" ("aka"). See G.L. c. 210, §§ 12 -14.

Rule 6. Filing of Birth Certificates

A. Care and Protection Cases. The petitioner shall file, within sixty days of commencement of the action, a certified copy of the birth certificate issued after the date of the filing of the petition, of each child named in the petition. In rare circumstances and for good cause shown, the judge may extend the time or waive the filing of the birth certificate. The petitioner may request an order from the court to produce a birth certificate pursuant to G.L. c. 46, § 2A if the petitioner does not have custody of the child.

B. Guardianship, Parentage and Change of Name Cases. The petitioner or plaintiff shall file along with the petition or complaint, a certified copy of the birth certificate for each child named in the petition or complaint. For good cause shown, the judge may extend the time or waive the filing of the birth certificate. The certified birth certificate shall have been issued within sixty days of filing the petition or complaint. The petitioner or plaintiff may request an order from the court to produce a birth certificate pursuant to G.L. c. 46, § 2A if the petitioner or plaintiff does not have custody of the child. If there is a certified copy of the child's birth certificate on file in the care and protection case, the clerk may copy and file it in the guardianship, parentage or change of name case provided that it was filed in the care and protection case within sixty days of the filing of the guardianship petition, parentage complaint or change of name petition.

Note

A. The importance of having a recent certified copy of the child's birth certificate to determine parentage in order to provide parents with notice and the opportunity to be heard cannot be overstated. "Good cause" should be construed narrowly and constitute more than mere inconvenience; however, there may be circumstances in which a certified copy of the birth certificate cannot be obtained or obtaining it would cause unreasonable delay in the disposition of the case. In such circumstances, including but not limited to instances in which a foreign birth certificate cannot be obtained, a judge may waive the filing of a certified copy of a birth certificate. In the event a foreign birth certificate is obtained, the burden is on the petitioner to provide an English translation of a foreign birth certificate.

B. There may be circumstances in which the certified copy of the birth certificate in the care and protection case does not satisfy the requirements of this rule and cannot be used when filing a guardianship, change of name petition, or a parentage complaint. In those instances, if the petitioner or the plaintiff does not have custody of the child and cannot otherwise obtain a certified copy of the birth certificate, he/she may file a motion in the underlying care and protection case for a court order to produce the birth certificate for filing with the petition or complaint. The person seeking such an order may be permitted to appear in the care and protection case for the sole purpose of filing such a motion. An appearance for this limited purpose does not make the person a party to the care and protection case.

Rule 7. Service and Form of Papers

A. Form of Motion. Every motion or other document filed with the court, other than documents offered in evidence, shall be on 8 ½" x 11" paper, or in an electronic or digital manner approved by the court, and shall have a heading which includes the name, division and county of the court, the docket number, the title of the action and a designation of the nature of the motion or document. Every such motion or document shall set forth the name, address, telephone number and email address of the attorney or pro se party filing it, the Board of Bar Overseers registration number of the attorney, and the date on which the motion or other document was filed with the court.

B. Requirement of Affidavit. Unless a motion, other than a motion to dismiss as provided in paragraph C, is made during a hearing or trial, any request for a court order shall be made by written motion accompanied by an affidavit signed by the person with personal knowledge of the factual basis of the motion, and shall state with particularity the grounds therefor, and shall set forth the relief or order sought, provided however, that the following types of motions are not required to be accompanied by an affidavit: motions in limine, motions to strike, motions for discovery, motions for appointment of appellate counsel, motions to correct a name on the petition and motions for continuance or change of court date. Whenever a motion is supported by an affidavit or memorandum, the affidavit or memorandum shall be served with the motion.

C. Motions to Dismiss. All motions to dismiss shall be in writing accompanied by an affidavit signed by the person with personal knowledge of the factual basis of the motion and shall state with particularity the grounds therefor.

D. Notice. All motions other than those which do not require a hearing shall be scheduled by the court in accordance with procedures established by the court division. A written motion, other than one that may be heard ex parte, and notice of the hearing of the motion, shall be served pursuant to paragraph E of this rule, no later than seven days prior to the hearing. When service is made by mail, the motion and notice of the hearing shall be served no later than ten days prior to the hearing. An application for ex parte relief from the seven day notice requirement shall be made by motion for a short order of notice and supported by affidavit setting forth the nature of the emergency.

E. Manner of Service. Every motion, except an ex parte motion, or document filed in court shall be served by the attorney or party filing it by mailing or delivering a copy or electronically in accordance with court procedure, to each attorney of record, and each party appearing pro se.

Rule 8. Appearances

All counsel, including court-appointed counsel, shall file a notice of appearance in the Clerk's Office by hand delivery or mail that shall include the name of the attorney, address, telephone number, email address and Board of Bar Overseers registration number. A copy of the appearance shall be served on all parties.

Note

This rule applies to all private and court-appointed counsel and to attorneys employed by state agencies, including but not limited to, the Department and the Committee for Public Counsel Services.

Rule 9. Temporary Custody Hearing and Waiver

The temporary custody hearing pursuant to G.L. c. 119, § 24 or § 25 may be waived by a parent, guardian, custodian or child. The waiver of the parent, guardian or custodian shall be in writing signed by the parent, guardian or custodian and, unless such person is self-represented, accompanied by a certification by his/her attorney. The certification shall include a statement that the attorney has discussed the waiver with his/her client and advised the client that he/she is giving up the right to object and present evidence at the hearing in opposition to the court's orders, including orders regarding his/her child's custody, and the right to appeal the court's orders. The waiver and the certification shall be on a form approved by the Chief Justice of the

Juvenile Court. The court shall conduct a colloquy with the parent, guardian or custodian and determine whether the waiver was intelligently and voluntarily made. The attorney for the child may waive the temporary custody hearing by signing a waiver and certification form on behalf of his/her client.

Note

This temporary custody hearing may be held pursuant to one of two mutually exclusive statutory provisions, G.L. c. 119, § 24 (so-called "72 hour" hearing) or § 25 (non-emergency temporary custody hearing). At the temporary custody hearing, the judge must determine whether custody should be removed from the child's parent, guardian or custodian, or whether the initial temporary custody order should be continued, depending on the circumstances. The judge must consider any nomination by the child or the parents of a relative or other individual to become the temporary legal custodian pending the hearing on the merits. *See Care and Protection of Manuel*, 428 Mass. 527 (1998). The judge must also make the written certification and determinations required by G.L. c. 119, § 29C (contrary to the welfare certification and reasonable efforts determination). *See Care and Protection of Walt*, 478 Mass. 212 (2017).

This rule addresses waiver of a parent, guardian, custodian or child of either a § 24 or § 25 temporary custody hearing. By waiving the temporary custody hearing, the parent, guardian, custodian or child is relinquishing his/her right to be heard, to object to the court's orders and to appeal the orders. A parent, guardian, custodian or child may waive the hearing by formal action as provided in this rule or may forfeit the hearing by failure to appear or participate after having received notice of such hearing. Waiver or forfeiture of the hearing is distinguished from the circumstance in which a parent, guardian, custodian or child agrees to a temporary transfer of custody but seeks to nominate a relative or other individual to be appointed the child's temporary custodian pending the hearing on the merits or be heard on the issue of reasonable efforts. Although that party may have acknowledged or stipulated that there is sufficient evidence to support a temporary transfer of custody, he/she has not waived the opportunity to be heard on the issue of a third party temporary custody order or the issue of reasonable efforts. There may be situations in which a parent, guardian, custodian or child requests a reasonable amount of time beyond the scheduled 72 hour hearing to nominate another individual or family member, or more time is necessary to complete a home study of the proposed nominee. In those cases, after the hearing has commenced, the judge may continue the temporary custody hearing to another date for this purpose.

A temporary custody hearing held pursuant to either G.L. c. 119, § 24 or § 25 is not a so called "placement hearing". Placement decisions are within the discretionary powers of the legal custodian as one of the usual incidents of custody. *See* G.L. c. 119, § 21. Decisions related to the normal incidents of custody generally are committed to the Department or third party legal custodian and are reviewable only under § 21 for abuse of discretion or error of law. The court does not have authority to subject the Department to conditions regarding placement. *See Care and Protection of Isaac*, 419 Mass. 602 (1995), *Care and Protection of Jeremy*, 419 Mass. 616 (1995) but *see Care and Protection of Walt*, 478 Mass. 212. In contrast, if the court grants custody to a third party, it may subject the grant of custody to conditions, including conditions that restrict the third party custodian from changing the child's placement.

Rule 10. Written Reports by the Department

The Department shall file a written report with the court each time the case is before a judge for hearing or report. The report shall be filed in the Clerk's Office at least two days in advance of the scheduled court date and shall contain relevant information regarding the child, the parents, caregivers, the services being offered and provided and the progress towards the permanency goal. The failure of the Department to provide the report in advance of the scheduled court date shall not preclude the judge from proceeding with the hearing.

Rule 11. Investigator's Report in Care and Protection Cases

In a care and protection case, including a case in which the need for parental consent to adoption is an issue, the report of the court-appointed investigator required by G.L. c. 119, §§ 21A and 24 shall be filed in the Clerk's Office within sixty days after the appointment of the investigator, unless the court otherwise orders. A request for extension of time to file the court investigator's report shall be made by motion on a form approved by the Chief Justice of Juvenile Court, signed by the court investigator and approved by a justice of the Juvenile Court. Any motion for extension of time shall be filed no later than fourteen days prior to the date the report is due, provided however, that the court may permit the filing of a motion for an extension of time at some other time in the interests of justice. If the court approves a motion for extension of time, the court investigator shall provide a copy of the approved motion to all counsel of record and to any party who is not represented by counsel.

Note

Counsel of record may obtain from the Clerk's Office a copy of the court investigator's report without filing a motion to do so. Standing Order 1-84 applies to all court-appointed investigator reports.

Rule 12. Assignment of Care and Protection Cases

At the conclusion of the temporary custody hearing in a care and protection case, if not before, a judge shall be assigned to that case in accordance with procedures established by the Chief Justice of the Juvenile Court. Nothing in this rule shall preclude changing the assignment of a case to, or matters being heard by, a different judge for good cause.

Rule 13. Discovery

A. Department or Licensed Placement Agency. In any care and protection case in which the Department or a licensed placement agency is or becomes a party, the Department or the licensed placement agency shall produce for each party a copy of its entire social services file, including reports made pursuant to G.L. c. 119, § 51A and § 51B, within sixty days from the date the case is commenced, or within sixty days from the date the Department or the licensed placement agency becomes a party, whichever is later. No party receiving material produced pursuant to this rule shall further duplicate or divulge the material to any person not a party to the case unless by order of court, except that counsel for a party may disclose the material to an expert retained by counsel. The expert shall not further duplicate or divulge the material and shall return the material to the counsel that retained him/her.

When producing a copy of its social services file in compliance with this rule, the Department or the licensed placement agency may withhold privileged material and work product of its attorney, and may withhold the names, and other reasonable, identifying data, of past or present foster parents of a child who is a subject of the case or of an adoptive parent or prospective adoptive parent of a child who is a subject of the case or of the reporter on reports made pursuant to G.L. c. 119, § 51A, subject to orders for further production.

The attorney for the Department or the licensed placement agency shall produce with the copy of the file a list of the materials and information withheld. The attorney for the Department or the licensed placement agency shall have an ongoing duty to produce for each other party on a timely basis any additions to the social services file made after initial production required in this subsection.

B. Other Discovery. Other discovery may be had only by court order on such terms as the court prescribes. A court order shall be requested by motion in accordance with Rule 7.

Note

Section A. *See* Juvenile Court Standing Order 1-84, Juvenile Court Case Records and Reports.

Rule 14. Status Hearing

There shall be a status hearing within ninety days after the commencement of a care and protection case, provided however, that it shall be scheduled to occur after the court investigator's report has been filed. All parties are required to be present with counsel at the status hearing, except that counsel for the child may appear without his/her client. Failure of one or more parties to appear shall not preclude the court from proceeding with the status hearing.

A. Summons to the Court Investigator. The court may issue, or one or more of the parties may request, a summons to the court investigator to attend the status hearing. When so summoned, the court investigator shall attend the status hearing to respond to any questions regarding the process of the investigation or the report filed in accordance with Rule 11 and G.L. c. 119, §§ 21A and 24. Failure of the court investigator to be present without good cause or the report to be available shall not preclude the court from proceeding with the status hearing.

B. Issues to be Addressed. Unless previously addressed and resolved, at the status hearing the court shall address but is not limited to addressing: the process of the court investigation or the report; service of process in accordance with Rule 5; discovery motions; child identification; the Indian Child Welfare Act; any special evidentiary issues; the Department's plan to achieve permanence; any issues regarding services being offered or delivered to the family pending trial; the scheduling of a pretrial conference; and compliance with the standing order regarding time standards. Nothing in this rule shall preclude the court from hearing motions, including discovery motions, at other times in the interests of justice.

C. Court Investigator's Report. The court shall attach the court investigator's report to the petition at the status hearing, or at the next court date after the filing of the report. The report shall then become a part of the record in accordance with G.L. c. 119, § 24.

D. Orders. At the conclusion of the status hearing, the court shall issue any necessary and appropriate orders to resolve the matters before the court.

Note

The purpose of the status hearing is to address any matters that may impact the timely resolution of the case and permanency for the child.

This rule differs from the prior rule in that it provides a uniform procedure to secure the presence of the court investigator and addresses how the court investigator's report becomes part of the record and evidence in the case.

When summoned to attend the status hearing by the Clerk's Office, the court investigator is present to answer any questions from the parties, their attorneys or the court regarding the process of the investigation and to identify sources of information. It is not the purpose of the attendance of the court investigator at the status hearing to address the factual content of the investigator's report, or assess the credibility of the investigator or the reliability of the information in the report. When the court investigator is summoned to attend the status hearing, the court should make every effort to conduct the hearing as early as possible on the scheduled date in order to avoid and/or reduce the wait time for the court investigator.

This rule makes it clear that the court investigator's report automatically becomes part of the record in accordance with G.L. c. 119, § 24. The court investigator's report becomes part of the record and evidence not by its physical "attachment" to the petition but by operation of law. General Laws c. 119, § 24, requires that "the court shall appoint a person qualified under section 21A to investigate the conditions affecting the child and to make a report under oath to the court, which shall be attached to the petition *and be a part of the record*." (emphasis added). Accordingly, the Appeals Court has held that there is "no question that § 24 anticipates use of the report by the trial judge." *In re Zita*, 455 Mass. 272, 281 (2009) (citing *Custody of Two Minors*, 19 Mass. App. Ct. 552, 559 (1985)). *See also Custody of Michel*, 28 Mass. App. Ct. 260, 267 (1990). ("Primary reliance concerning the family picture will be on the § 24 report. Such is the import of the statutory language . . .")

Because the investigator's report is part of the record of the case, there can be no objection in general to the receipt or use of the investigator's report in arriving at decisions in care and protection cases. *Custody of Michel*, 28 Mass. App. Ct. at 265. The report may contain hearsay statements from a wide variety of sources and the cases do not distinguish between levels of hearsay. *Id.* at 266. Parties have a fair opportunity to rebut allegations in the report by cross examining the court investigator and his/her sources or by other means at trial, so it is vital that all sources of statements and information in the report be clearly identified. Specific objections may be made by motions in limine. *Custody of Tracy*, 31 Mass. App. Ct., 481 (1991) and *Custody of Michel. See also* Mass. G. Evid. § 1115(c)(1) and (e)(6) regarding court investigator reports in general.

Rule 15. Pretrial Conference in Care and Protection Cases

A pretrial conference shall be scheduled to occur no later than thirty days before the trial on the merits, except for good cause shown provided however, that it shall be scheduled to occur after the date upon which the court investigator's report is due. All parties are required to be present with counsel at the pretrial conference, except that counsel for the child may appear without his/her client. Failure of one or more parties to appear shall not preclude the court from proceeding with the pretrial conference.

A. Witness and Exhibit Lists. The parties shall file written witness and exhibit lists with the court at the pretrial conference. As a matter of discretion in a particular case, the trial judge may order the parties to submit a written joint or individual pretrial memorandum that covers any or all of the issues set forth below in subsection B of this rule. Parties shall be bound by the witness and exhibit lists filed separately or set forth in a pretrial memorandum, except by court order for good cause shown.

B. Issues to be Addressed. At the pretrial conference, the court shall address the matters set forth below:

1. Whether parents have been served by the petitioner and the date(s) of service
2. Whether discovery has been completed; and if discovery has not been completed, a list of discovery items not yet provided and the compliance date
3. Relief sought, including whether or not there will be a request for a decree dispensing with the need for parental consent to the adoption, custody, guardianship or other disposition of the child named in the petition
4. Identification of the specific contested issues to be litigated at trial
5. A stipulation of all uncontested facts and issues
6. A list of proposed exhibits to be introduced at trial

7. A list of proposed witnesses which shall include the names of any expert witnesses, a delineation of the issues to which the expert is expected to testify, and a copy of his or her curriculum vitae

8. Issues regarding the admissibility of evidence at trial

9. Scheduling a date for the submission of motions in limine, if any, and scheduling a hearing thereon, if necessary

10. Any unaddressed motions

11. Whether a writ of habeas corpus will be required to ensure attendance of a party or witness, or whether a witness needs to participate telephonically or by other means

12. Whether an interpreter is required

13. Whether a child witness needs an accommodation to testify

14. Whether, if the Indian Child Welfare Act (ICWA) applies, the tribe has been notified and has responded and whether other legal requirements under ICWA have been satisfied

15. An estimate of trial time

16. Any other matters that may aid in the disposition of the action

The court shall address, where applicable:

17. Whether the possibility of settlement has been discussed

18. Whether counsel for the parties have discussed mediation with their client(s) pursuant to Rule 5 of Rule 1:18 of the Supreme Judicial Court

19. The Department's plan to provide timely notice of the trial to the foster parent, pre-adoptive parent or relative providing care.

C. Scheduling the Hearing on the Merits. At the pretrial conference, unless previously scheduled, the court shall schedule a hearing on the merits to be heard within twelve months of the filing of the petition unless a later date is necessary in the interests of justice.

Note

This rule differs from the prior 2007 rule in that it retains the pretrial conference and written witness and exhibit lists but removes the requirement of a written pretrial conference memorandum unless ordered by the trial judge. Pretrial memoranda that contain mere boilerplate paragraphs relative to the issues to be addressed or a list of all possible witnesses are of no value to the court.

In some divisions, proposed exhibits are marked for identification at various stages of the proceedings. In those divisions, when listing exhibits marked for evidence under Rule 15 B. 6, counsel should use the same numbers used by the court to mark the exhibits for identification.

If a date has not been set for the submission of, or to hear, motions in limine, the trial judge should schedule said date(s) at the pretrial conference.

Rule 16. Notice to Foster Parent, Pre-adoptive Parent, or Relative Providing Care for a Child

The Department shall file a certification with the court that the Department has provided notice and informed the foster parent, pre-adoptive parent or relative providing care for a child, who is the subject of a care and protection petition, of his/her right to attend and be heard at a hearing held pursuant to G.L. c. 119, §§ 26 and 29B. The certification shall be on a form approved by the Chief Justice of the Juvenile Court. In the event the foster parent, pre-adoptive parent or relative chooses to exercise his/her right to be heard, he/she shall testify in court under oath. Failure by the Department to provide timely notice does not preclude the judge from proceeding with the hearing.

Note

General Laws c. 119, § 29D requires the Department to provide notice and inform the foster parent, pre-adoptive parent or relative providing care of a child who is the subject of a care and protection petition of the right to attend and be heard at hearings pursuant to G.L. c. 119, §§ 26 and 29B. This includes hearings on the merits, (including the termination or so called "best interests" hearing) review and redetermination hearings, and permanency hearings. The statute expressly provides that the foster parent, pre-adoptive parent or relative does not become a party to the case by exercising his/her right to attend and be heard. Although the rule provides that the hearing may proceed in the absence of timely notice by the Department, the court may provide an opportunity for the foster parent, pre-adoptive parent or relative to be heard on another date. The rule does not require the foster parent, pre-adoptive parent or relative to inform the court in advance of the hearing of his/her intention to attend and be heard but he/she may do so. *See Adoption of Sherry*, 435 Mass. 331 (2001) (usual rules of evidence apply; testimony of foster parent must be under oath and subject to cross examination; unsworn written statement is inadmissible.)

Rule 17. Sanctions and Contempt

A. Sanctions. If a party, or an attorney, or both, engages in conduct that either delays the progress of litigation, wastes judicial resources or causes an unnecessary increase in expenses on a party, or otherwise impedes the full and effective administration of justice, without sufficient justification as determined by the court, the court may order the party, or the attorney, or both to pay reasonable costs and expenses. The court shall provide notice and a hearing before final imposition of costs or expenses. The court shall articulate, in writing, the reasons for the imposed sanctions.

B. Contempt. Enforcement of compliance with court orders may be sought by means of civil contempt, which shall proceed in accordance with the provisions of Mass. R. Civ. P. 65.3 (b) - (h). Proceedings for summary contempt shall be held in accordance with the provisions of Mass. R. Crim. P. 43. Prosecutions for criminal contempt shall proceed in accordance with the provisions of Mass. R. Crim. P. 44.

Rule 18. Subpoenas

Subpoenas shall be served and enforced as provided by Mass. R. Civ. P. 45 and may be issued by the Clerk's Office or as otherwise provided in Mass. R. Civ. P. 45.

Rule 19. Trial Judge's Order, Findings of Fact and Conclusions of Law and Notification by Clerk of Issuance of Findings of Fact and Conclusions of Law

A. Entry of Adjudication, Order of Commitment, Order Dispensing with the Need for Consent to Adoption, Allowance or Denial of Guardianship Petition. Upon adjudication, order of commitment, or order dispensing with the right of the parents to receive notice of or consent to the adoption, custody, or guardianship or any other disposition of the child or an allowance or denial of a guardianship petition, the clerk shall forthwith enter that adjudication, order, allowance or denial on the court's docket. If the court issues a permanent mittimus or grants permanent custody of a child to the Department, the court shall schedule the case for review which shall be no later than six months from the date of the mittimus or custody order and every six months thereafter until permanency has been achieved for the child.

B. Notice. Immediately following the clerk's entry of the above adjudication, order, allowance or denial on the docket, the clerk shall notify all attorneys of record and parties who are self-represented by mail or electronically, of the entry of that adjudication, order, allowance or denial. The clerk shall note on the docket, or otherwise record electronically, the names of the persons to whom the notice was sent, with the date notified. This notice shall include: 1) a copy of the adjudication, order, allowance or denial; 2) the date of the clerk's entry; and 3) notice that each party has thirty (30) days from the date of entry within which to file a claim of appeal.

C. Order or Decree Dispensing with Consent to Adoption. In all cases in which the court issues an order dispensing with the right of the parents to receive notice of or consent to the adoption, custody, or guardianship or any other disposition of the child, the court shall enter the order or decree on a document separate from any findings of fact and conclusions of law.

D. Trial Judge's Findings of Fact and Conclusions of Law. The trial judge, upon making an adjudication or issuing an order of commitment or an order dispensing with the right of the parents to receive notice of or consent to the adoption, custody, or guardianship or any other disposition of the child, shall file with the clerk, consistent with time standards promulgated by the Chief Justice of the Juvenile Court, findings of fact and conclusions of law to support the order and/or adjudication.

E. Notification to All Parties by Clerk. Immediately upon the filing of the findings of fact and conclusions of law, the clerk shall mail or transmit a copy to each attorney of record and party who is self-represented.

2

Note

After an adjudication, the judge may make any appropriate dispositional order including conditions and limitations relative to the care and custody of the child. The dispositional order may include, but is not limited to, reunification with the parent, guardian, or other custodian found by the court to be qualified to care for the child; custody to any agency or private organization licensed or otherwise authorized to provide care for the child; or custody to the Department. G.L. c. 119, § 26(b).

Although issuance of a permanent mittimus or grant of permanent custody to the Department is a permissible post-adjudication order under § 26(b), these alternatives are not considered to be permanent plans for children under Rule 9(a)(1) of Trial Court Rule VI Uniform Rules for Permanency Hearings. Accordingly, this rule requires the court to schedule a review of these cases no later than six months after the date of the issuance of a permanent mittimus or order of permanent custody to the Department and every six months thereafter until the child is returned to his/her parents, is adopted, is placed with a third party custodian, a permanent guardian is appointed, or the child ages out of the system.

While an alternative planned permanent living arrangement ("APPLA") is considered to be a possible permanency plan for a child sixteen years of age or over under Rule 9(a)(1) of the Uniform Rules for Permanency Hearings, it does not achieve legal permanency for the child. Therefore, if APPLA is approved by the court as the permanency plan, the court must schedule a review of the case every six months thereafter until the child is returned to his/her parents, is adopted, is placed with a third party custodian, a permanent guardian is appointed, or the child ages out of the system. The review required in section A of this rule is different from the right of review and redetermination under G.L. c. 119, § 26(c); rather it is established by this rule to permit the court to assess progress toward permanency in keeping with the best practices for achieving legal permanency for children.

Rule 20. Appeal

A. Claim of Appeal. An appeal, as permitted by G.L. c. 119, § 27, shall be governed by the Massachusetts Rules of Appellate Procedure. The claim of appeal shall be on a form approved by the Chief Justice of the Juvenile Court and shall be taken to constitute the "notice of appeal" for the purposes of complying with the Massachusetts Rules of Appellate Procedure. The claim of appeal and any request for a transcript, if required, shall be signed by the appealing party or parties unless the appellant is the child; a claim of appeal that is not so signed by the party or parties shall not be accepted for filing by the clerk.

B. Record on Appeal. In addition to the requirements of the Rules of Appellate Procedure, the record on appeal as assembled shall include a copy of the trial judge's findings of fact and conclusions of law.

Standing Orders of the Juvenile Court

Standing Order 1-82. Court Hours

[Adopted Feb. 3, 1982.]

The hours during which the Divisions of the Juvenile Court Department shall be open for business to the general public shall be 8:30 a.m. to 4:30 p.m., Monday through Friday.

Standing Order 1-84. Juvenile Court Case Records and Reports

[Applicable to all divisions. Adopted May 8, 1984.]

All juvenile court case records and reports are confidential and are the property of the court.

Reports loaned to or copied for attorneys of record, or such other persons as the court may permit, shall be returned to the court after their use or at the conclusion of the litigation, whichever occurs first.

Said reports shall not be further copied or released without permission of the court.

Standing Order 2-09. Sound Recording of Court Proceedings

[Adopted effective Nov. 1, 2009.]

A. Definitions.

1. *Sound Recording*: a recording, such as but not limited to a cassette tape or compact disc, used to store recorded sound.

B. Official Recordings.

1. *When required.* In all divisions of the Juvenile Court Department all courtroom proceedings shall be recorded electronically, subject to the availability and functioning of appropriate recording devices, except that the following may but need not be recorded: (a) the call of the list and similar matters of an administrative nature; and (b) proceedings conducted by a magistrate other than a judge. Said recording shall take place whether or not a court stenographer is present in the courtroom.

2. *Logging*. During every proceeding which is required to be recorded, the clerk shall: (a) announce clearly the name of the case and its docket number at the beginning of the proceeding; and (b) log, whenever practicable, the sound recording number and the index numbers or dates representing the beginning and end points of the proceeding.

3. *Counsel's Responsibility*. Counsel shall be responsible for assisting in the creation of an audible record by properly using the microphones provided. Counsel shall speak with sufficient clarity and in sufficient proximity to the microphones to ensure an audible record, and shall be responsible for requesting the judge, when necessary, to instruct other counsel, witnesses or others as to the proper use of the microphones in order to ensure an audible record.

4. *Preservation of Recordings*. The clerk-magistrate shall preserve for at least three years the original recording of any trial, evidentiary hearing, guilty plea or admission to sufficient facts that was presided over by the judge.

5. *Access to Copies of Sound Records.*

(a) *Open proceedings.* Any person whether or not a party, shall be permitted to obtain a sound recording copy of an original recording, or any portion thereof, of any proceeding which was open to the public, unless the record of such proceeding has been sealed or impounded.

(b) *Closed proceedings.* The original recording of a proceeding which was not open to the public, or of a proceeding whose record has been sealed or impounded, shall be deemed to be impounded and a sound recording copy of the original recording, or any portion thereof, shall be made available only in accordance with the following provisions:

(i) *Sound recording copies of closed proceedings for purposes of appeal.* Counsel for any party, or any party who has entered an appearance pro se, shall be permitted to obtain a sound recording copy of such a proceeding upon certifying that such sound recording copy will be used solely for an appeal, or to determine whether to claim an appeal, in the same matter. Unless the judge who presided over the proceeding has ordered otherwise, the clerk-magistrate shall provide such sound recording copy upon such certification without requiring a judge's approval of the request.

(ii) *Sound recording copies of closed proceedings for other purposes.* A sound recording copy of such a proceeding may be made available to other persons or for other purposes only with the approval of the judge who presided over the proceeding or, if that judge is unavailable for an extended period or the proceeding was conducted by a magistrate other than a judge, any judge of the court. Any such request shall be accompanied by an affidavit, setting forth the reason for the request and the specific use to be made of the sound recording copy, and shall be served on all parties to the proceeding. Any other party or interested person may file a statement in support of or in opposition to such a request. A judge may determine such a request with or without hearing wherever he or she is then sitting. A judge may permit access subject to appropriate restrictions upon the use and dissemination of the sound recording copy of such proceeding.

(c) *Ordering sound recording copies.* A request for a sound recording copy shall be filed with the clerk-magistrate on a form prescribed by the Chief Justice of the Juvenile Court. In order that multiple sound recording copies may be made simultaneously whenever possible, any person making such a request regarding a proceeding that is presently pending on appeal shall certify that he has notified all other parties of his request.

The cost of a sound recording copy shall be as established by the Chief Administrative Justice of the Trial Court pursuant to G.L. c. 262, s. 4B. The clerk-magistrate shall require prepayment of all or some portion of such cost. There shall be no cost for a sound recording copy produced for the use of the court, the Attorney General's office, a district attorney's office, any other agency of the Commonwealth, a police prosecutor, or a party represented by an attorney provided by the Committee for Public Counsel Services. General Laws c. 261, ss. 27A–27G shall apply to any request on behalf of an indigent party who is not represented by an attorney provided by the Committee for Public Counsel Services, and in such case the cost of a sound recording copy shall be deemed an "extra cost" as defined in s. 27A.

6. *Impermissible Uses.* No sound recording copy shall be used for a commercial purpose, for public or private entertainment or amusement, or for any other purpose detrimental to the administration of justice. No sound recording copy shall be duplicated or tampered with. No sound recording copy shall be erased, nor its labels removed or defaced, while the matter is pending in any court, or is subject to direct appellate review. Any sound recording copy which is thereafter erased shall be erased in its entirety.

Any further dissemination of the sound recording copy of a closed proceeding, or its contents, is permissible only: (a) for the purposes for which access was permitted; (b) subject to all provisions of law and court rules governing the records of such closed proceedings; and (c) subject to any additional restrictions with regard to its use which have been prescribed by the judge permitting access.

Any person requesting a sound recording copy shall take all reasonable precautions to assure compliance with the requirements of this rule, including notifying anyone permitted to use the sound recording copy of such requirements. Any person violating any such requirements shall be subject to appropriate sanctions, including contempt proceedings.

C. Unofficial Recordings.

1. *Covert Recording Forbidden.* No person shall make any electronic recording in any courtroom, hearing room, office, chambers or lobby of a judge or magistrate without prior authorization from the judge or magistrate then having immediate supervision over such place.

2. *Recording by the News Media.* The recording by the news media of a proceeding open to the public is governed by the provisions of the Supreme Judicial Court Rule 1:19.

Standing Order 1-10. Scheduling Care and Protection and Termination of Parental Rights Trials

[Adopted effective Sept. 1, 2010.]

1. **Purpose.** The purpose of this Standing Order is to establish procedures and standards and promote uniformity to ensure that care and protection and termination of parental rights trials are completed within a reasonable time after commencement of trial.

2. **Applicability.** This Standing Order is applicable to all Divisions of the Juvenile Court and to all care and protection and termination of parental rights trials.

3. **Definitions.** *Commencement of Trial*—the date when testimonial evidence is presented by witnesses called to testify before the court; the date that a document is submitted to the court, accepted and admitted into evidence as an exhibit. *Close of Evidence*—the date when all parties have completed the submission of all evidence.

4. **Length of Trial.** All care and protection and termination parental rights trials will conclude no later than thirty (30) calendar days after commencement of trial. Trial dates should be scheduled for consecutive days, wherever possible. Potential exhibits should be "marked for identification" prior to trial whenever possible.

5. **Cases Under Advisement.** An adjudication that a child is, or is not, in need of care and protection, or an order terminating, or a decision not to terminate, parental rights shall be made no later than thirty (30) days after the close of evidence.

6. **Emergency Extension for Trial or Cases Under Advisement.** In extraordinary circumstances, the justice presiding over the trial may request approval from the Chief Justice to extend the time for trial, or extend the time for adjudication, order or decision, for an additional fifteen (15) calendar days. Such request should be submitted in writing, should identify the extraordinary circumstances that necessitated the request and should be submitted no later than ten (10) calendar days prior to the expiration of the thirty (30) day period, except when the request for additional time is due to unforseen circumstances which occur subsequent to the ten (10) calendar day period.

[*Note: there is no paragraph 7.*]

8. **Dedicated Trial Sessions.** Dedicated trial sessions for care and protection and termination of parental rights cases are encouraged where there are available judicial resources, sufficient attorneys to represent the parties and where multiple demands upon court time do not make such sessions impractical or inefficient.

9. **Effective Date.** This Standing Order and the procedures and standards contained herein shall apply to all care and protection and termination of parental rights trials commenced on or after September 1, 2010.

Standing Order 1-15. Provision of Respondents' Non-Clinical Identifying Information in Commitment Proceedings Under G.L. c. 123, §§ 7, 8, and 12(e), or G.L. c. 123, § 35

[Adopted effective June 1, 2015.]

1. The purpose of this Order is to provide for the collection of non-clinical identifying information in commitment proceedings in the Juvenile Court Department necessary to comply with the courts' reporting requirements pursuant to Chapter 284, Acts of 2014, An Act Relative to the Reduction of Gun Violence.[1]

IT IS THEREFORE ORDERED:

An applicant seeking a court order to commit a respondent to a mental health facility pursuant to G.L. c. 123, § 12(e), a petitioner seeking a court order to commit or retain a respondent for inpatient care pursuant to G.L. c. 123, §§ 7 and 8, and a petitioner seeking a court order to commit a respondent for treatment for alcoholism and/or substance abuse pursuant to G.L. c. 123, § 35, shall provide the respondent's date of birth and social security number, if available, to the court.

[1] Although commitment matters are also brought under G.L. c. 123, §§ 15(b), 16(b) or (c), or 18 that arise out of criminal proceedings, the respondent's or defendant's date of birth and social security number is obtained and provided to the court through the Defendant Identification Information System in those cases.

Standing Order 2-15. Relief from Notification Requirements of Rule 13(b) of the Trial Court Rule VIII, Uniform Rules of Impoundment Procedure

[Adopted effective Oct. 1, 2015.]

Any party or interested nonparty filing materials in a Juvenile

2

Court case that is impounded by statute, caselaw, court rule or standing order, is not required to file a notice identifying the case and/or the material as 'impounded' as required by Rule 13(b) of the Uniform Rules of Impoundment Procedure. In the Juvenile Court, any cases or case records that are confidential or not available for public inspection are considered to be impounded by statute, caselaw, court rule or standing order. These cases include but are not limited to care and protection and delinquency cases. Rule 13(b) of the Uniform Rules of Impoundment Procedure applies only to Juvenile Court cases and case records that are open to the public and to public inspection, such as Youthful Offender and adult criminal cases.

Standing Order 1-17. Violation of Probation Proceedings

[Adopted effective Sept. 25, 2017.]

I. SCOPE AND PURPOSE

This standing order prescribes procedures in the Juvenile Court to be followed upon the allegation of a violation of an order of probation issued in a delinquency, youthful offender or criminal case after a finding of delinquency, youthful offender, or guilty, or after a continuance without a finding. This standing order does not apply to an alleged violation of pretrial probation, as the latter term is defined herein.

The purpose of this standing order is to ensure that judicial proceedings undertaken upon the allegation of a violation of probation are conducted in a manner consistent with the Commonwealth's policy regarding children as set forth in G. L. c. 119 and in full compliance with all applicable law, promptly and with an appropriate degree of procedural uniformity. This standing order supersedes Standing Order 1-07 Violation of Probation Proceedings.

COMMENTARY

The first purpose of the violation hearing is to adjudicate the factual question of whether a probationer has violated his or her probation order. The second purpose is to revoke probation or order any other disposition. The issue of violation is essentially a factual matter whereas the dispositional decision of whether to revoke probation is essentially a matter of discretion.

Throughout this standing order the person who is the subject of probation violation proceedings is usually referred to as the "probationer" rather than the "defendant." With respect to the probation proceedings, such a person is not a defendant; he or she has either been adjudicated or convicted, after trial or based on a plea of delinquent, youthful offender or guilty, or has formally submitted an admission to the facts of a criminal charge. Use of the term "probationer" is intended to underscore the legal status of the person charged with a probation violation, which is fundamentally distinct from the status of a person who is a defendant on a delinquency, youthful offender or criminal case, particularly in terms of procedural rights.

II. DEFINITION OF TERMS

In construing this standing order, the following terms shall have the following definitions:

"Continuance without a finding" is the order of a court, following a formal submission and acceptance of a plea of guilty or an admission to sufficient facts in a youthful offender case or criminal case; or, in a delinquency case, following a formal submission and acceptance of a plea of delinquency or an admission to sufficient facts or after a trial in which the allegations are proven beyond a reasonable doubt, whereby the case is continued to a date certain without the formal entry of a delinquency, youthful offender, or guilty finding. A continuance without a finding may include conditions imposed in an order of probation (1) the violation of which may result in the revocation of the continuance, entry of a finding of guilty, youthful offender or delinquency and imposition of sentence or commitment to the Department of Youth Services and (2) compliance with which will result in dismissal of the case.

"Defendant" is a juvenile adjudged delinquent or youthful offender or an adult convicted of a crime.

"District Attorney" is the criminal prosecuting authority and includes the Attorney General if the delinquency, youthful offender, or criminal case in which probation was ordered was prosecuted by the Office of the Attorney General.

"General conditions of probation" are the conditions of probation that are imposed as a matter of course in every order of probation, as set forth in the official form promulgated by the Chief Justice of the Juvenile Court for such orders.

"Probation order" is the formal, written court order whereby a defendant is placed on probation and which expressly sets forth the conditions of probation. A probation order is not a contract.

"Pretrial probation" is the probationary status of a defendant pursuant to a probation order issued prior to a trial or prior to the formal submission and acceptance of a plea of delinquent, youthful offender or guilty, or prior to an admission to sufficient facts, as provided in G.L. c. 276, § 87.

"Revocation of probation" is the revocation by a judge of an order of probation as a consequence of a determination that a condition of that probation order has been violated.

"Special conditions of probation" are any condition of probation other than one of the general conditions of probation.

"Surrender" is the procedure by which a probation officer requires a probationer to appear before the court for a judicial hearing regarding an allegation of a probation violation.

III. COMMENCEMENT OF VIOLATION PROCEEDINGS: CHARGED CRIMINAL CONDUCT

(a) General. This standing order prescribes the procedures to be undertaken upon the issuance of a delinquency or criminal complaint or youthful offender indictment against a probationer.

(b) Where Probation Order and Delinquency or Criminal Complaint or Youthful Offender Indictment Involve Same Court Division.

(i) Issuance and Service of Notice of Violation; Termination of Proceedings; Withdrawal of Notice of Violation. When a delinquency or criminal complaint is issued by a court division or a youthful offender indictment is returned by a grand jury and remitted to a court division of the Juvenile Court against a defendant who is the subject of a probation order previously issued by that same court division, the Probation Department shall commence violation proceedings against that probationer. Such proceedings shall be commenced by the issuance by the Probation Department of a Notice of Probation Violation/Hearing at or before the arraignment on the delinquency or criminal complaint or youthful offender indictment, or as soon thereafter as possible. The Notice shall be served on the probationer in hand following the assignment of a date and time for a probation violation hearing as provided in Section III(b)(ii) and such service shall be entered in the case docket, provided that if such in-hand service is not possible, the Notice shall be served on the probationer by first-class mail, unless the court orders otherwise. Service of the Notice by first-class mail shall be entered in the case docket. Out of court service other than by mail shall require a written return of service. The Probation Department shall provide a copy of each Notice of Probation Violation/Hearing to the District Attorney forthwith upon its issuance.

At any time during violation proceedings, the court, upon review of the Notice and as a matter of its discretion, may order termination of the proceedings. A Notice of Probation Violation may be withdrawn only with the permission of the court and such withdrawal and permission shall be entered in the case docket.

(ii) Contents of Notice of Violation. The Notice of Probation Violation/Hearing shall set forth the criminal conduct alleged to have been committed by the probationer as indicated in the delinquency or criminal complaint or youthful offender indictment, and shall set forth any other specific conditions of the probation order that the Probation Department alleges have been violated with a description of each such alleged violation. The Notice shall also state the date, time, and place of the probation violation hearing.

(iii) Scheduling of Hearing. The probation violation hearing shall be scheduled to commence on the date of the pretrial hearing for the new delinquency or criminal complaint or youthful offender indictment, unless the court expressly orders an earlier hearing. The hearing shall be scheduled for a date certain no less than seven days after service on the probationer of the Notice of Violation/Hearing unless the probationer waives said seven day notice period. The hearing date shall not be later than fifteen days after service of the Notice of Violation/Hearing without the probationer's consent if he or she is held pursuant to Section V of this standing order. In any case, the hearing shall not be later than thirty days after service of the Notice of Violation/Hearing, except in extraordinary circumstances. In scheduling the pretrial hearing on the new delinquency or criminal complaint or youthful offender indictment together with the probation violation hearing, the court shall give primary consideration to the need for promptness in conducting the probation violation hearing.

(c) Where Probation Order and Delinquency or Criminal Complaint or Youthful Offender Indictment Involve Different Divisions.

(i) Issuance and Service of Notice of Violation. When a delinquency or criminal complaint is issued by a court division of the Juvenile Court or a youthful offender indictment is returned by a grand jury (hereinafter the "criminal court") against a defendant who is the subject of a probation order issued by a different court division of the Juvenile Court Department (hereinafter the "probation court"), the Probation Department in the criminal court shall issue a Notice of Probation Violation/Hearing to the probationer at or before arraignment on the new delinquency or criminal complaint or youthful offender indictment, or as soon thereafter as possible. The Notice, as provided in paragraph (c)(ii) below, shall be served on the probationer in hand and such service shall be entered in the case docket. Nothing in this section shall preclude the later issuance and service on the probationer of a Notice of Probation Violation/Hearing by the Probation Department of the probation court.

(ii) Contents of Notice of Violation. The Notice of Probation Violation/Hearing shall set forth the name of the probation court and criminal conduct alleged to have been committed by the probationer as indicated in the delinquency or criminal complaint or youthful offender indictment and shall order the probationer to appear at a specific date and time at the probation court for the express purpose of appointment of counsel, if necessary, and scheduling of a probation violation hearing.

(iii) Transmission of Notice of Violation and Other Documents to Probation Court. Prior to the service of the Notice of Violation/Hearing on the probationer, the Probation Department at the criminal court shall send to the probation officer on duty in the probation court or, if there is no probation officer on duty, to the Chief Probation Officer at the probation court, by electronic transmission, copies of the following documents: the notice of violation; the delinquency or criminal complaint or youthful offender indictment and related police report on the new criminal charge that constitutes the alleged probation violation; and a request for the following information: whether the probation court recommends that the probationer be transported in custody, and, if not, the date and time for the non-custodial appearance of the probationer at the probation court.

(iv) Response by the Probation Court. At the probation court, the probation officer on duty, the Chief Probation Officer, an Assistant Chief Probation Officer, or a probation officer designated by either shall respond by electronic transmission to the request for information no later than one hour from receipt thereof. The response shall include a recommendation on whether the probationer should be transported to the probation court in custody, and, if not, the date and time for the probationer's non-custodial appearance at the probation court.

(v) The Decision to Transport. A judge at the criminal court shall decide whether the probationer is to be transported in custody to the probation court. The judge shall provide the probationer an opportunity to be heard and, unless exceptional circumstances require otherwise, shall wait at least one hour for receipt of the recommendation from the probation court before making such decision. If the criminal court orders custodial transport, it shall issue a probation transportation order on behalf of the probation court, and the probation court shall be so notified. The probationer promptly shall be transported in accordance with the probation transportation order, provided that, if the probationer is held in custody in the criminal proceeding, the probation transportation order shall be lodged with custodial authority to ensure that the probationer will be detained and transported to the probation court. The Probation Department at the criminal court shall so notify the Probation Department at the probation court.

If the criminal court decides not to order custodial transport, it shall enter the probation court appearance date and other required information on the notice of violation and serve it on the probationer in accordance with Section III (c)(i). For good cause, the criminal court may hold the probationer in custody pending its decision regarding custodial transport. Nothing in this rule shall preclude the issuance of an arrest warrant for a violation of probation by the probation court to secure the appearance of a probationer for a probation violation proceeding.

(vi) Probationer's Appearance at the Probation Court; Service of a New Notice. Upon appearance of the probationer at the probation court, the court shall appoint counsel, if necessary, and shall schedule a probation violation hearing for a date certain, the date to be no less than seven days later unless the probationer waives said seven-day period. The hearing date shall not be later than fifteen days after said appearance without the probationer's consent if he or she is held pursuant to Section V of this standing order, or in any case no later than thirty days after said appearance, except in extraordinary circumstances. If the Probation Department at the probation court alleges additional violations, it shall prepare and serve on the probationer a new Notice of Probation Violation/Hearing which shall set forth all alleged violations. The Notice shall also include the date, time and place of the violation hearing and shall be served on the probationer in hand while he or she is before the court, or as soon thereafter as possible. Such service shall be entered in the case docket. The Probation Department shall provide a copy of the new Notice to the District Attorney at the time of, or before such service on the probationer.

At any time during the proceeding, the probation court, upon review of the Notice and as a matter of its discretion, may order termination of the proceedings The Notice may be withdrawn only with the permission of the court and such withdrawal and permission shall be set forth on the record and entered in the case docket.

(vii) Procedure When a Defendant is a Probationer in More than One Other Court Division within the Juvenile Court. When a defendant appearing in a court division on a new delinquency, youthful offender, or criminal charge is on probation at more than one other court division within the Juvenile Court, the criminal court shall select one of the latter divisions to be the probation court and shall issue a Notice of Violation/Hearing for that division. The criminal court shall interact as provided in this section with the selected probation court. The other probation court or courts each shall be responsible for the issuance and service on the probationer of a Notice of Violation/Hearing based on the new criminal conduct, and for securing the presence of the probationer for a violation hearing by means of such Notice or by means of an arrest warrant for a violation of probation or other process.

(d) When Probation Order and New Criminal Charge Involve Different Court Departments. When a criminal complaint is issued by a court or an indictment is returned against a defendant who is the subject of a probation order issued by a court in a different court department, the criminal and probation court personnel shall proceed in accordance with Trial Court Standing Order 2-16, Uniform Interdepartmental Procedures for Probation Violation Proceedings.

2

COMMENTARY

This section involves cases in which an alleged probation violation consists of new criminal conduct charged against the probationer. Such cases can arise in two contexts: where the probationer is on probation at the same court division that issued the new charges (the "same court" situation), and where the new charges were issued by a court division or department other than the one where the probationer is on probation (the "different court" situation).

For both situations, this section contains a provision by which a Notice of Probation Violation/Hearing may be "withdrawn." Such withdrawals have been a method by which probation violation proceedings may be terminated. There has been no requirement for court approval or permission. The provision imposes two new requirements: (1) that such withdrawals must receive the permission of the court, and (2) that such permission and the fact of the withdrawal must be entered on the case docket. By requiring judicial permission and entry on the record, the provision reflects the importance of a process by which a probation violation proceeding that has been formally commenced may be terminated without adjudication.

New subsections (c)(iii)–(v) have been added to provide a detailed process by which, in the "different court" situation, the "criminal court" must interact with the "probation court." The purpose of this interaction is to effect the transfer of the probation proceeding and, in some instances, the custodial transfer of the probationer, to the probation court.

Under the former procedure, the decision to transport a probationer was made at the probation court, a warrant issued there and was sent to the criminal court. This meant that a probation officer had to seek the issuance of a warrant by a judge of that court, a judge who was otherwise unaware of the matter and was usually engaged in that court's daily business. This would often delay the process, particularly in those cases where the judge at the probation court required a more detailed description of the underlying allegations before issuing the warrant.

This standing order has been changed because the judge in the criminal court will be addressing an issue in a case that is before the court at that time, will be immediately aware of the criminal case which constitutes the alleged probation violation, and will have all relevant information regarding the probationer's criminal record and pending probation status.

Section (c)(vii) has been added to address a circumstance not previously addressed, namely, where the defendant before the criminal court is currently on probation in more than one other court division within the Juvenile Court. It provides that in such cases the judge at the criminal court must decide the probation court with which the criminal court will interact. This decision will determine which of the probation courts will be "first in line" to address the probationer's alleged violation based on new charged criminal conduct. The standing order provides that the other courts at which the individual is on probation are responsible for charging the new criminal conduct as an alleged violation, and initiating a violation proceeding by issuing a Notice of Violation/Hearing and mailing it to the probationer or obtaining the appearance of the probationer by means of an arrest warrant for a violation of probation or other process such as a writ of habeas corpus.

IV. COMMENCEMENT OF VIOLATION PROCEEDINGS: VIOLATIONS OTHER THAN NEW CHARGED CRIMINAL CONDUCT

(a) General. This section prescribes the procedures to be undertaken regarding alleged violations of probation that do not involve or include criminal conduct charged in a new delinquency or criminal complaint or youthful offender indictment.

(b) Issuance and Service of Notice; Termination of Proceedings, Withdrawal of Notice. When a probation officer of a court division that has issued a probation order determines that a probationer has violated any condition of that order other than alleged criminal conduct as charged in a new delinquency or criminal complaint or youthful offender indictment, that probation officer shall decide whether to commence probation violation proceedings. Such decision shall be made in accordance with the rules and regulations of the Office of the Commissioner of Probation, provided, however, that probation violation proceedings shall be commenced (1) upon the issuance of a criminal complaint or indictment, (2) when the judge issuing the probation order orders that such proceedings are to be commenced upon an alleged violation of one or more conditions of probation, or (3) when the commencement of such proceedings is required by statutory mandate. In any case, a judge of the court division may order the commencement of violation proceedings.

Violation proceedings shall be commenced by the issuance by the Probation Department of a Notice of Probation Violation/Hearing which shall be served on the probationer in hand or by first-class mail, unless the court orders otherwise. Service of the Notice in hand or by first-class mail shall be entered in the case docket. Out-of-court service other than by first-class mail shall require a written return of service. The Probation Department shall provide a copy of each Notice of Probation Violation/Hearing to the District Attorney forthwith upon its issuance.

If deemed appropriate, because of the seriousness of the alleged violation or for other good reason, the court may issue an arrest warrant for a violation of probation. The clerk shall forthwith enter such warrant in the Warrant Management System. Upon the probationer's first appearance before the court, the probationer shall be served in hand with the Notice of Violation/Hearing.

At any time during the proceedings, the court, upon review of the Notice and as a matter of its discretion, may order termination of the proceedings. The Notice may be withdrawn only with the permission of the court and such withdrawal and permission shall be set forth on the record and entered in the case docket.

(c) Contents of Notice. The Notice of Probation Violation/Hearing shall set forth the conditions of the probation order that the Probation Department alleges have been violated and shall order the probationer to appear at a specific date and time for the express purpose of the appointment of counsel, if necessary, and the scheduling of a probation violation hearing.

(d) Scheduling of Hearing. Upon appearance of the probationer in accordance with the Notice required by paragraph (c) above, the court shall appoint counsel, if necessary, and schedule a probation violation hearing for a date certain, said date to be no less than seven days later unless the probationer waives said seven-day notice period. The hearing date shall not be later than fifteen days after said appearance without the probationer's consent if he or she is held pursuant to Section V of this standing order, or in any case no later than thirty days after said appearance, except in extraordinary circumstances.

V. PROBATION DETENTION HEARINGS

(a) Purpose. A probation detention hearing may be conducted to determine whether a probationer shall be held in custody pending the conduct of a probation violation hearing. The issues to be decided at a probation detention hearing are whether probable cause exists to believe that the probationer has violated a condition of the probation order, and, if so, whether the probationer should be held in custody.

(b) Notice of Hearing. The probationer shall be given a written notice of probation detention hearing indicating the purpose of the hearing and referring to the probation violations alleged in the Notice of Violation/Hearing which is required to be served on the probationer under this standing order. The probation detention proceeding shall be commenced by the service of such notice on the probationer. The court may, for good cause, order that the probationer be taken into custody pending the completion of the proceeding. The notice of probation detention hearing shall be served in hand when the probationer is before the court having been arrested on a new delinquency or criminal complaint or youthful offender indictment, having been arrested for a probation violation, or for any other reason. The notice of probation detention hearing shall be prepared and served by the Probation Department at the discretion of a probation officer or as directed by the court.

(c) Conduct of Hearing. Probation detention hearings shall be conducted by a judge or, if a judge is not available, by a clerk-magistrate. When a clerk-magistrate conducts a probation detention hearing, a resulting custody order shall not extend beyond the date on which a judge will next be available at the court. On such date, the probationer shall be brought before the court and any further custody order will require the conduct of a detention hearing by a judge.

Probation detention hearings shall be conducted in a courtroom on the record. The probationer shall be entitled to counsel. Following service of notice as provided in paragraph (b) above, the appointment of counsel, the appearance of private counsel or the knowing and voluntary waiver of the right to counsel in accordance with G.L. c. 119, § 55A, the probationer shall be allowed a reasonable time to prepare for the hearing. At the hearing, the probation officer shall be required to present evidence to support a finding of probable cause. The District Attorney may assist in the presentation of such evidence. The probationer shall be entitled to be heard in opposition. Testimony, including the testimony of the probation officer, shall be taken under oath. The court shall admit such evidence as it deems relevant and appropriate. The scope of the inquiry shall be limited to the issue of whether there is probable cause to believe that the alleged violation of probation has occurred.

If probable cause is found, the court may order the probationer to be held in custody pending the conduct and completion of the violation hearing. The court's decision whether to order such custody, shall include, but not necessarily be limited to consideration of the following:

i. the probationer's criminal or juvenile record;

ii. the nature of the offense for which the probationer is on probation;

iii. the nature of the offense or offenses with which the probationer is newly charged, if any;

iv. the nature of any other pending alleged probation violations;

v. the likelihood of probationer's appearance at the probation violation hearing if not held in custody; and

vi. the likelihood of incarceration or commitment if a violation is found following the probation violation hearing.

If probable cause is found and the court does not order the probationer held in custody, the court may order the probationer released upon such terms it deems necessary and appropriate to insure the safety of an individual or the community. In the case of a juvenile, the court may impose terms of release that balance the issues of public safety and the best interests of the juvenile. These terms may include, but are not limited to, an earlier curfew, restrictions on the juvenile's activities, or terms that permit a juvenile to attend school and/or receive services available only in the community. Terms of release shall be set forth in writing and served in hand on the probationer. Terms of release imposed under this section are not conditions of probation. A violation of a term of release shall not itself be the basis for a finding of a violation of probation, although the judge may consider such violation of a term of release in determining a proper disposition under section VIII(d) and IX(b).

If no probable cause is found, the court may terminate the proceedings or schedule a probation violation hearing serving the probationer with notice thereof, but the probationer may not be held in custody nor shall an order with terms of release be issued pending the hearing based on the alleged probation violation.

(d) Bail. Bail and other conditions of pretrial release pursuant to G.L. c. 276, §§ 58 and 58A do not apply to a probation detention hearing. However, the court shall proceed to determine the issues of bail and pretrial detention ("dangerousness") on any new delinquency or criminal complaint or youthful offender indictment, as provided by law.

COMMENTARY

This section differs from its antecedent, in its replacement throughout of the terms "preliminary probation hearing" and "final [or 'full'] probation hearing" with the terms "probation detention hearing" and "probation violation hearing," respectively. The purpose of these changes is to use terms that more accurately describe and clearly differentiate these proceedings.

Paragraph (b) contains a new sentence indicating that a probation detention proceeding is commenced when the notice thereof is served on the probationer. Another new sentence indicates that the court has the authority to hold the probationer in custody pending the completion of the proceedings for good cause.

Paragraph (b) contains a new, final sentence indicating that a probation detention hearing may be conducted at the direction of the court as well at the initiative of the Probation Department.

When probable cause is found and the court does not order the probationer held in custody, Section V authorizes the court to impose terms of release. Authorizing the court to impose terms of release is consistent with the Juvenile Court's mission to further the best interests of children who appear before the court by offering a course of rehabilitation rather than punishment, consistent with the provisions of G.L. c. 119. See also *Jake J. v. Commonwealth*, 433 Mass. 70, 75 (2000). If a probationer fails to comply with the order of terms of release, the probationer may be subject to arrest and brought before the court for a review of custody status.

When the court does not find probable cause, the court must exercise its discretion whether to terminate proceedings or to schedule a probation violation hearing nonetheless. Because of the need for dispatch in conducting a detention hearing, the absence of evidence, witnesses, or assistance from the District Attorney may result in the probation officer's being unable to establish probable cause for the purpose of detention but still having a reasonable prospect of proving the probation violation at a full hearing. The court will decide whether further proceedings are in the interests of justice, but in no event may the probationer be held or subject to terms of release on the probation matter pending a probation violation hearing.

Paragraph (d) makes clear that bail and other terms of pretrial release have no application to a probationer's custody pending the conduct and completion of a violation hearing. Bail and other conditions of pretrial release, including pretrial detention based on "dangerousness" under G.L. c. 276, § 58 and 58A, relate solely to a newly alleged crime. If the court finds probable cause for a probation violation, it may order the defendant into custody pending the violation hearing. If the court does not find probable cause, the probationer cannot be held in custody on the alleged violation. Even if the probationer is held on the probation allegation, if he or she is also before the court on a new delinquency, youthful offender or criminal charge, the court must address the terms of pretrial release on the new charge(s). This issue is unrelated to custody on the probation charge. The prosecutor may want to be heard on the issue of bail or dangerousness because if the probation matter is promptly resolved, the defendant may be released from custody on the probation matter well before the new delinquency, youthful offender or criminal case is concluded.

Conversely, the issue of probation custody should be addressed regardless of whether or not the prosecutor plans to ask for high bail or pretrial detention based on dangerousness on the new charge(s).

VI. CONDUCT OF HEARINGS

(a) In General. Probation violation hearings shall be conducted by a judge, on the record. All testimony, including that of a probation officer, shall be taken under oath. The presentation of the case against the probationer shall be the responsibility of the probation officer assigned by the Chief Probation Officer of the court. The probationer shall be entitled to the assistance of counsel, including the appointment of counsel for probationers determined by the court to be indigent. A waiver by the probationer of the right to counsel shall be accepted by the court only if the court determines that such waiver is being made knowingly and voluntarily and in accordance with G.L. c. 119, § 55A.

(b) Requirement of Two Step Procedure. Probation violation hearings shall proceed in two distinct steps, the first to adjudicate the factual issue of whether the alleged violation or violations occurred, the second to determine the disposition of the matter, if a violation of probation is found to have occurred.

(c) Adjudication of Alleged Violation. Probation violation hearings shall commence with testimony by the probation officer describing the violation or violations alleged in the Notice of Violation/Hearing, and shall proceed with a presentation of the evidence supporting the allegations. The probationer shall be permitted to present evidence relevant to the issue of the alleged violation. Each party shall be permitted to cross-examine witnesses produced by the opposing party. Hearsay evidence shall be admitted by the court in accordance with section VII of this standing order, provided that the court shall enforce any statutory privileges unless waived and any legally required disqualifications. The probation officer shall have the burden of proving the alleged violations with or without the participation of the District Attorney as provided below. The standard of proof at such hearings shall be the preponderance of the evidence. After the presentation of evidence, both parties or their counsel shall be permitted to make a closing statement.

(d) Dispositional Decision. If the court finds that the probationer has violated one or more conditions of probation as alleged, the probation officer shall recommend to the court a disposition consistent with the dispositional options set forth in sections VIII(d) and IX(b), and may present argument and evidence in support of that recommendation. The probationer shall be permitted to present argument and evidence relevant to disposition and to propose a disposition.

(e) Continuances. Probation violation hearings shall be continued only by a judge and only for good cause shown. No continuance shall be ordered other than to a date certain and for a specific purpose, and as provided in section VIII(a). The pendency of a delinquency or criminal complaint or youthful offender indictment which also constitutes an alleged violation of probation shall not be grounds for a continuance of the probation violation hearing unless a judge determines the interests of justice require it. The reason of any continuance shall be stated by the judge and entered in the case docket.

(f) Participation of the District Attorney.

(i) In General. The District Attorney may participate in probation violation hearings as provided in G.L. c. 279, § 3, and such participation shall be permitted in any such proceeding regardless of whether the delinquency or criminal or youthful offender case in which the probation order was issued involved a felony charge.

(ii) Coordination with the Probation Department. If the District Attorney intends to appear at a probation violation hearing, he or she shall confer prior to the hearing with the probation officer responsible for presenting the matter to the court, for the purpose of coordinating the District Attorney's involvement in the hearing with the planned presentation of the probation officer.

(iii) Presentation of Evidence. The District Attorney may present and examine witnesses at the hearing and may examine witnesses presented by the probation officer, and may cross- examine witnesses presented by the probationer. The probationer may cross-examine witnesses presented by the District Attorney. The District Attorney shall be responsible for the attendance of every witness he or she wishes to present, and for the summoning of such witnesses.

(iv) Finding and Disposition. After the presentation of evidence, the District Attorney may be heard on the strength of that evidence in supporting a finding of violation. If the court finds that the probationer has violated one or more of the conditions of probation as alleged in the Notice of Violation/Hearing, the District Attorney may be heard regarding the court's disposition of the matter. The District Attorney may present a recommendation on disposition orally or in writing.

(g) Admission to Violation and Waiver of Right to Hearing. The court may accept an admission to an alleged probation violation and a waiver of the right to a violation hearing only upon a determination that the admission and waiver have been made knowingly and voluntarily.

Such an admission and waiver shall not be accepted by the court subject to any condition regarding the disposition of such violation or the disposition of any other probation violation or any pending delinquency or criminal complaint or youthful offender indictment. A probationer shall not be entitled to withdraw an admission as of right after it has been accepted by the court.

(h) Ensuring Probationer's Presence in Courtroom. For good cause, the court may order that the probationer be taken into custody pending the commencement and completion of the violation hearing.

COMMENTARY

District Attorney Participation

Section (f) addresses participation by the District Attorney. Sections III and IV of this standing order require the probation officer to provide a copy of every Notice of Probation Violation and Hearing to the District Attorney. Section (f) is intended to clarify the involvement of the District Attorney in those cases where he or she decides to participate, consistent with the statutory provisions of G.L. c. 279, § 3.

It should be noted that as a constitutional matter, probation functions are within the judicial branch, and the office of the District Attorney is considered within the executive branch. *Commonwealth v. Tate*, 34 Mass.App.Ct. 446 (1993). Under the Massachusetts Constitution, Pt. 1 Art. 30, the branches must maintain a separation of governmental powers. That separateness does not, however, lead to the conclusion that a district attorney's office may not assist the probation service in presenting evidence in support of a position that the probation service had decided upon. Probation officers are only aided, not interfered with, when district attorneys, upon invitation, conduct examination of witnesses and present evidence. *Commonwealth v. Tate* at 448 and cases cited.

Thus the right of District Attorneys to present evidence and witnesses, and to examine and cross-examine witnesses at these proceedings would appear to be constitutionally acceptable as long as it does not fundamentally interfere with probation.

VII. HEARSAY EVIDENCE

(a) Admissibility of Hearsay Evidence. Hearsay evidence shall be admissible at probation violation hearings.

(b) Legal Sufficiency of Hearsay Evidence. The court may rely on hearsay as evidence of a probation violation only if the court finds in writing that the hearsay is substantially reliable. In determining if hearsay is substantially reliable, the court may consider, among any other relevant factors, whether that evidence

(1) is based on personal knowledge and/or direct observation, rather than on other hearsay;

(2) involves observations recorded close in time to the events in question;

(3) is factually detailed, rather than generalized and conclusory;

(4) is internally consistent;

(5) is corroborated by any evidence provided by the probationer;

(6) was provided by a disinterested witness; or

(7) was provided under circumstances that support the veracity of the source (e.g., was provided under the pains and penalties of perjury or subject to criminal penalties for providing false information).

VIII. FINDING AND DISPOSITION

(a) Requirement of Finding. Upon the completion of the presentation of evidence and closing arguments on the issue of whether the probationer has violated one or more conditions of a probation order, as alleged, the court shall make a determination of that issue. The court shall decide the matter promptly and shall not continue the proceeding generally.

(b) Finding of No Violation. If the court determines that the probation officer has failed to prove by a preponderance of the evidence that the probationer committed a violation alleged in the Notice of Probation Violation/Hearing, the court shall expressly so find and said finding shall be entered in the case docket.

(c) Finding of Violation; Written Findings of Fact. If the court determines that the Probation Department has proved by a preponderance of the evidence that the probationer has violated a condition of probation as alleged in the Notice of Probation Violation/Hearing, or if the probationer waives the hearing and admits such violation and the court accepts such admission in accordance with section VI(g), the court shall expressly so find, and said finding shall be entered in the case docket. In a contested proceeding, the court shall make written findings of fact to support the finding of violation, stating the evidence upon which the court relied. A finding of violation based on an admission may be recorded as such.

(d) Disposition After Finding of Violation. After the court has entered a finding that a violation of probation has occurred, the court may order any of the following dispositions set forth below, as it deems appropriate. These dispositional alternatives shall be the exclusive options available to the court. The court shall proceed to determine disposition promptly following the entry of a finding of violation. General continuances are prohibited. In determining its disposition, the court shall give such weight as it may deem appropriate to the recommendation of the Probation Department, the probationer, and the District Attorney, if any, and to such factors as public safety; the seriousness of any offense of which the probationer was placed on probation; the nature of the probation violation; the occurrence of any previous violations and the impact of the underlying offense on any person or community, as well as any mitigating factors.

(i) Continuance of Probation. The court may decline to modify or revoke probation and, instead, issue to the probationer such admonition or instruction as it may deem appropriate.

(ii) Termination. The court terminate the probation order.

(iii) Modification. The court may modify the conditions of probation. Such modification may include the addition of reasonable conditions and the extension of the duration of the probation order.

(iv) Revocation. The court may order that the order of probation be revoked. If the court orders revocation, it shall state the reasons therefor in writing.

(e) Execution of Suspended Sentence or Commitment; Stay of Execution. Upon revocation of a probation order, any sentence or commitment that was imposed for the offense involved, the execution of which was suspended, shall be ordered executed forthwith; provided, however, that such execution may be stayed (1) pending appeal in accordance with Mass.R.Crim.P. 31, or (2) at the court's discretion, and upon the probationer's motion, to provide a brief period of time for the probationer to attend to personal matters prior to commencement of a sentence of incarceration or commitment to the Department of Youth Services. The execution of such sentence or commitment shall not be otherwise stayed.

(f) Imposition of Sentence or Commitment Where No Sentence or Commitment Previously Imposed. Upon revocation of probation in a case where no sentence or commitment was imposed following conviction or adjudication, the court shall impose a sentence, commitment, or other disposition as provided by law.

IX. VIOLATION OF CONDITIONS OF A CONTINUANCE WITHOUT A FINDING

(a) Notice, Conduct of Hearing, Adjudication. The procedures set forth in this standing order regarding notice for, and the conduct and adjudication of, probation violation hearings shall also apply where the Probation Department alleges a violation of one or more conditions of probation imposed together with a continuance without a finding.

(b) Disposition. The dispositional options available to the court following a determination that one or more conditions of probation imposed together with a continuance without a finding have been violated shall be as follows:

(i) Termination of Probation. The court may terminate the order of probation and the continuance without a finding and enter a dismissal on the underlying criminal case.

(ii) Continuation of the Continuance Without a Finding With No Probation Modification. The court may continue the continuance without a finding and issue to the probationer such admonition or instruction as it may deem appropriate.

(iii) Continuance of the Continuance Without a Finding With Modification of Probation. The court may continue the continuance without a finding and modify the conditions of probation including the duration of the continuance.

(iv) Termination of the Continuance Without a Finding and No Revocation of Probation. The court may terminate the continuance without a finding without revoking probation and, if a finding of sufficient facts was entered at the time the continuance without a finding was ordered, shall proceed to enter a guilty, delinquency or youthful offender finding. The order of probation, with or without modifications, may thereupon constitute the disposition on the finding if the probationer consents.

(v) Termination of the Continuance Without a Finding and Revocation of Probation. The court may terminate the continuance without a finding and revoke the order of probation. If the court orders revocation, it shall state the evidence relied upon in writing, and, if a finding of sufficient facts was entered at the time the continuance without a finding was ordered, the court shall enter a guilty, delinquency or youthful offender finding and impose a sentence, commitment or other disposition as provided by law.

Standing Order 1-18. Notification Requirements and Counsel Appointment Procedures for Permanency Hearings Held Pursuant to G.L. c. 119, § 29B and Trial Court Rule VI, Uniform Permanency Hearings

[Adopted effective Mar. 1, 2018.]

1. Purpose. The purpose of this Standing Order is to establish procedures for notification to parties and attorneys and for appointment of counsel for permanency hearings held pursuant to G.L. c. 119, § 29B and Trial Court Rule VI.

2. Applicability. This Standing Order is applicable to all Divisions of the Juvenile Court and to all matters where a permanency hearing is required pursuant to G.L. c. 119, § 29B.

3. Scheduled Hearing List. (a). No less than ninety (90) days prior to the required scheduled hearing date in accordance with G.L. c. 119, § 29B and Rule 3 of Trial Court Rule VI, the clerk's office of the court wherein the hearing is to be convened shall send a list of cases scheduled for permanency hearings to the Department of Children and Families ('Department').

(b). The Department shall, within thirty (30) days of receipt of the list, advise the court in writing of the name of any child or young adult on the list who is no longer in the care or custody of the Department and therefore no longer requires a permanency hearing. In addition, the Department shall advise the court in writing whether the parents' rights to consent or receive notice of any petition for adoption, custody, guardianship or other disposition have been dispensed with pursuant to G.L. c. 119, § 26 or G.L. c. 210, § 3, whether the parents have signed voluntary surrenders under G.L. c. 119, § 23(a) or G.L. c. 210, § 2 or whether the young adult or the Department terminated the agreement to continue responsibility for the young adult under G.L. c. 119, § 23(f).

4. Notice. No less than forty-five (45) days prior to the hearing date, the clerk's office shall send notice of the hearing to the Department, to the petitioner, if different from the Department, to the child or young adult's attorney, and unless the parents' rights to consent or receive notice of any petition for adoption, custody, guardianship or other disposition of the child have been dispensed with, or the parents have signed voluntary surrenders or the subject of the hearing is a young adult, to the parents, by mailing to their last known addresses, or if the parents are represented by counsel, to their attorney(s) of record. Such notice shall inform the parties of the date, time, and location of the hearing, of their right to counsel pursuant to G.L. c. 119, § 29, and of the right to file objections pursuant to Rule 6. If a case is scheduled for permanency hearing and the child or young adult is no longer in the care or custody of the Department, the Department shall notify the court and all parties, or if the parties are represented by counsel, the attorneys of record, and the court will take the case off the hearing list. The time for notice provided in this paragraph shall not apply if the court has determined that reasonable efforts to reunify the family are not required pursuant to G.L. c. 119, § 29C.

5. Appointment of Counsel. (a). All parties have the right to counsel. If a party was represented by counsel at the trial, that counsel shall continue to represent the party until the court permits him/her to withdraw his/her appearance or until an appearance is filed by successor counsel. If trial counsel wishes to withdraw his/her appearance, and if the party has been determined to be indigent, a motion for withdrawal requesting appointment of successor counsel shall be filed. Any motion under this paragraph shall be scheduled for hearing no later than seven (7) days after filing. Counsel wishing to withdraw shall ensure that the motion to withdraw and appoint successor counsel is scheduled for hearing no less than thirty (30) days prior to the date of the scheduled permanency hearing. A permanency hearing shall not be taken off a court calendar to accommodate a motion to withdraw.

(b). If the attorney of record is no longer available to represent the child or young adult, the court shall remove the attorney and appoint successor counsel. The clerk's office shall send notice of the permanency hearing as set forth in section 4 of this Standing Order to the newly appointed counsel.

(c). If the attorney of record is no longer available to represent a parent and if the parent is indigent and their rights have not been dispensed with or the parent has not signed a voluntary surrender, the court shall remove the attorney and appoint successor counsel. The clerk's office shall send notice of the permanency hearing as set forth in section 4 of this Standing Order to the newly appointed counsel.

6. Effective Date. This Standing Order is effective on March 1, 2018.

_____

Amy L. Nechtem
Chief Justice of the Juvenile Court
Date: _____

Standing Order 2-18. Time Standards

[Adopted effective Nov. 5, 2018.]

The Juvenile Court Department has jurisdiction over a variety of criminal and civil case types including delinquency and youthful offender proceedings, child requiring assistance proceedings (CRA) and care and protection/termination of parental rights proceedings. The vast majority of cases addressed by the Juvenile Court fall within the parameters of these four case types. The Juvenile Court has jurisdiction, by statute, of matters ancillary to these four case types including guardianship petitions, parentage complaints, change of name petitions and adoption petitions.

The work of the Juvenile Court often reflects shifting community expectations and social science theory regarding children. Those shifts in expectations often unpredictably alter Juvenile Court caseloads.

The purpose of the time standards is to provide guidelines for application in the great majority of cases; it being understood that, as a matter of discretion in specific situations, a judge may extend time periods and vary requirements in the interest of justice. The time standards set forth below for the trial, settlement or other disposition of cases are applicable to cases filed in any division of the Juvenile Court Department on or after November 5, 2018. The benchmarks are not part of the time standards but are provided to offer guidance in achieving compliance with the standards.

I. DELINQUENCY AND YOUTHFUL OFFENDER PROCEEDINGS (G.L. c. 119, §§ 52–74, MA Rules of Criminal Procedure)

A. Filing of complaint or indictment to adjudication/disposition (bench trial): Six months (180 days).

Indictment of a juvenile as a Youthful Offender proceeds only at the option of the District Attorney for whom there are no time requirements for the exercise of that option.

B. Filing of complaint or indictment to adjudication/disposition Gury trial): Eight months (240 days).

Benchmarks:

1. Arraignment: within fifteen (15) days from the issuance of the complaint, unless the juvenile has been referred to diversion.

2. Pre-trial Conference: within thirty (30) days from the arraignment.

The prosecuting attorney and defense counsel shall confer prior to the scheduled pretrial hearing in order to conference the case and to prepare a written pretrial conference report. In addition to those matters set forth in the Rules of Criminal Procedure, counsel shall also discuss whether the case can be disposed of by means of a plea and, if so, shall propose a date for a change of plea within the conference report. Special circumstances should be identified, including but not limited to: unavailability of victim or essential witness; information relating to the victim's capacity to testify at trial within the time frame established by the standards; existence of multiple defendants; anticipated delays occasioned by necessary forensic or scientific testing (e.g. DNA testing, drug analysis, etc.); delays due to issues related to the juvenile's competency, or the necessity for extended pretrial hearings such as those relating to the pretrial inspection of third party records or similar proceedings but not including motions to dismiss or motions to suppress statements, evidence, search warrants, or identifications.

II. CHILD REQUIRING ASSISTANCE PROCEEDINGS (G.L. c. 119, §§ 39E–I)

A Filing of application to preliminary hearing: Fifteen (15) days.

B. Acceptance of application to determination/disposition: Six (6) months.

Numerous reasons may delay the final disposition of cases, such as an outstanding warrant, the unavailability or inappropriateness of a home to which the child can return, and frequently, serious mental health issues which defy easy and quick resolution. In addition, the preliminary hearing may result in a referral to informal assistance which is not to exceed ninety (90) days and which may, with the agreement in writing of the parents and child, last an additional ninety (90) days for a total of one hundred and eighty (180) days.

III. CARE AND PROTECTION/TERMINATION OF PARENTAL RIGHTS PROCEEDINGS (G.L. c. 119, §§ 24–29D, G.L. c. 210, § 3 and Juvenile Court Rules on Care and Protection Cases, Standing Order 1-10, Scheduling Care and Protection and Termination of Parental Rights Trials)

A Filing of petition to final order of adjudication and permanent disposition: Fifteen (15) months, which may be extended once for a period not to exceed 3 months.

Benchmarks:

1. Temporary custody hearing: within seventy-two (72) hours of ex parte transfer of custody except by agreement of parties for good cause shown.

2. Filing of court investigator report: within sixty (60) days after the appointment of the investigator unless the court otherwise orders.

3. Status Hearing: within ninety (90) days after filing of the petition.

4. Pre-trial Conference: no later than thirty (30) days before trial.

5. Permanency hearings for children in the custody of the Department of Children and Families: twelve (12) months from the transfer of custody and annually thereafter.

B. Trial: Twelve (12) to fifteen (15) months after filing of the petition.

C. Decision and Written Findings: within ninety (90) days from the close of evidence. See Standing Order 1-10, requiring that an adjudication, termination of parental rights or decision not to terminate parental rights shall be made no later than thirty (30) days after the close of evidence.

D. Permanency Review: Following the entry of an order granting permanent custody of the child to the Department of Children and Families, the court shall hold a permanency review every six (6) months until legal permanency is achieved for the child. Legal permanency is achieved upon the closure of the case to reunification, adoption, guardianship or third party custody.

E. Legal Permanency: within 24 months after filing of the petition.

Amy L. Nechtem
Chief Justice
Dated: 10/5/18
Effective November 5, 2018

Selected Juvenile Court Uniform Practices and Procedures

Uniform Practice 01-10. Procedures for the Use of Juvenile Court Videoconferencing Equipment

1. **Purpose.** The purpose of this uniform practice is to establish procedures for the use of Juvenile Court videoconferencing equipment.

2. **Definitions.** "Videoconferencing", using a set of interactive telecommunication technologies, which allow two or more locations to interact via video and audio transmission simultaneously. "Remote Site", location from which a party or witness is appearing via videoconferencing.

3. **Use of Juvenile Court Videoconferencing Equipment in Juvenile Court.** Upon the written motion of any party to a proceeding in Juvenile Court, a Juvenile Court judge may allow the use of videoconferencing at any stage of the proceeding, subject to the procedures set forth in this Interim Uniform Practice. Any party seeking to use videoconferencing at a court event shall file a written motion with the court thirty (30) calendar days prior to the scheduled date of the court event at which the party is seeking to use videoconferencing. The moving party shall serve all other parties with a copy of any motion filed under this procedure. Any party may file a written objection to the motion within seven (7) calendar days after the filing of the motion and such party shall serve all other parties with a copy of said objection. A Juvenile Court judge in the exercise of discretion may waive the time period for filing said motion and any objection thereto for good cause.

A Juvenile Court judge may at any time during a proceeding recommend the use of videoconferencing to the parties to further judicial efficiency. In a criminal trial, if the prosecution files a motion for the use of videoconferencing for the appearance of a defendant or a witness and the defendant has not assented to the motion, the court shall deny the prosecution's motion as to the defendant, and deny the prosecution's motion as to the witness, unless the prosecution shows that the appearance of the witness in the courtroom creates a security or health risk to the defendant, witness or participants in the proceeding which cannot be addressed by the application of reasonable procedures which alleviate the security or health risk.

4. **Affidavits.** The moving party shall file an affidavit in support of the motion and any party may file an affidavit in support of any objection to the motion. The judge may rule on a motion filed pursuant to this Interim Uniform Practice on the basis of facts alleged in the affidavits without further hearing.

5. **Criteria Considered by the Judge When Ruling on the Motion.** In determining whether a motion seeking the use of videoconferencing in a proceeding shall be allowed, a Juvenile Court judge shall consider the following, if applicable: (1) whether the party filing the motion is unable, after a diligent effort, to procure the physical presence of a party or witness in the courtroom, (2) whether full and effective cross-examination can occur, especially when the cross-examination may involve documents or other exhibits, (3) whether there is sufficient control of the proceedings at the remote site so as to effectively extend the courtroom to the remote site, (4) whether transporting the person proposed to appear by videoconferencing to the courtroom presents a significant security or health risk, (5) whether security would be required and available at the remote site to commit to videoconferencing on the date(s) and time requested in the motion, (6) the cost of producing a witness in person in relation to the importance of the offered testimony, (7) the convenience of the parties and the proposed witness, and (8) any other factors that the court may determine to be relevant. Any order issued pursuant to this procedure is subject to (a) the ability to compatibly utilize the videoconferencing equipment between the court and the remote site, (b) the operational needs of the remote site, and (c) the cost to the court to utilize said equipment.

6. **Coordination with the Remote Site When the Remote Site is a Juvenile Court Location.** Prior to filing said written motion, the moving party shall contact the Office of the Clerk-Magistrate for the Juvenile Court where the motion is to be filed and obtain, complete and submit a "Videoconferencing Availability Form" which will be forwarded to the videoconferencing liaison at that site. The form will request the videoconferencing liaison to provide the following information: (1) whether the videoconferencing equipment will be available at the court where the motion is to be filed and at the remote site on the date(s) and time to be requested in the motion, (2) whether there is a room or courtroom at the court where the motion is to be filed and at the remote site which is compatible and available to utilize the equipment on the requested date(s) and time, and (3) whether the videoconferencing liaison, or other designated contact person, at the court where the motion is to be filed and at the remote site will be available on the requested date(s) and time to ensure that the equipment is operational and that it is being properly utilized. The videoconferencing liaison for the court where the motion is to be filed shall contact the videoconferencing liaison for the remote site to obtain the requested information. If the videoconferencing equipment, room or courtroom and contact person are available in both locations, the videoconferencing liaisons at both locations will note in their records that a request to use the equipment is pending. The videoconferencing liaison for the court where the motion is to be filed shall return the completed "Videoconferencing Availability Form" marked either "Available" or "Not Available" to the Office of the Clerk-Magistrate who shall contact and provide the same to the moving party. A copy of the completed "Videoconferencing Availability Form" shall be included as an attachment to the motion. The videoconferencing liaison shall keep a copy of the "Videoconferencing Availability Form" in their records.

7. **Coordination with the Remote Site When the Remote Site is Not a Juvenile Court Location.** Prior to filing said written motion, the moving party shall contact the Office of the Clerk-Magistrate for the Juvenile Court where the motion is to be filed and obtain complete and submit a "Videoconferencing Availability Form" which will be forwarded to the videoconferencing liaison.

2

The form will request the videoconferencing liaison to provide the following information: (1) whether the videoconferencing equipment will be available at the court where the motion is to be filed on the date(s) and time to be requested in the motion, (2) whether there is a room or courtroom at the court where the motion is to be filed which is compatible and available to utilize the equipment on the requested date(s) and time, and (3) whether the videoconferencing liaison, or other designated contact person, at the court where the motion is to be filed will be available on the requested date(s) and time to ensure that the equipment is operational and that it is being properly utilized. If the videoconferencing equipment, room or courtroom and contact person is available in the Juvenile Court where the motion is to be filed, the videoconferencing liaison will note in their records that a request to use the equipment is pending. The videoconferencing liaison for the court where the motion is to be filed shall return the completed "Videoconferencing Availability Form" to the Office of the Clerk-Magistrate who shall contact and provide the same to the moving party. A copy of the completed "Videoconferencing Availability Form" shall be included as an attachment to the motion. The videoconferencing liaison shall keep a copy of the "Videoconferencing Availability Form" in their records.

The moving party shall also contact the individual who is responsible for the videoconferencing equipment at the remote site which is not a Juvenile Court location to determine the following information: (1) whether the videoconferencing equipment at the remote site is compatible with the videoconferencing equipment utilized by the Juvenile Court, (2) whether said equipment will be available at the remote site on the date(s) and time requested in the motion, (3) whether there is a room at the remote site which is compatible and available to utilize the equipment on the requested date(s) and time, and (4) whether a designated contact person at the remote site will be available on the requested date(s) and time to ensure that the equipment is operational and that it is being properly utilized. Said information shall be included and affirmatively stated in the affidavit attached to the motion along with the name and contact information of the individual at the remote site who will be responsible for ensuring that the equipment is available and operational on the requested date(s) and time.

8. **Communications between Courtroom and Remote Site.** When a party or witness appears via videoconference in a proceeding, the court shall confirm that all participants are able to hear, see and communicate with each other as well as view any physical evidence or exhibits to be presented prior to the start of the proceeding. Copies of documents may be transmitted at the direction of the court between the courtroom and the remote site.

9. **Videoconferencing Liaison; Scheduling the Use of Videoconferencing Equipment in Courtroom Proceedings.** Each court location with videoconferencing equipment shall designate a person to act as a videoconferencing liaison. The videoconferencing liaison shall be responsible for (1) scheduling the use of videoconferencing equipment, (2) contacting the videoconferencing liaison for remote sites in other Juvenile Courts to obtain information, (3) completion of "Videoconferencing Availability Forms," (4) maintaining records of pending requests, (5) compiling the monthly report, (6) ensuring that the equipment is operational and being properly utilized on those dates and time scheduled for use, and (7) providing technical guidance for the use of the videoconferencing equipment. The videoconferencing liaison shall schedule the use of videoconferencing equipment in a Juvenile Court proceeding only upon the filing of a motion approved by the court allowing for the use of videoconferencing pursuant to section 3 of this Interim Uniform Practice. Scheduling shall normally occur in the order in which requests are submitted to the videoconferencing liaison. Priority shall be given to emergency hearings and hearings which must occur within a limited specified period of time, such as temporary custody hearings. The Office of the Clerk-Magistrate shall notify the videoconferencing liaison when a motion has been allowed or denied by a judge and the videoconferencing liaison shall note the court action in their records.

10. **Use of Videoconferencing Equipment for Juvenile Court Meetings or Trainings.** Juvenile Court personnel may use videoconferencing equipment for meetings or trainings. Requests for the use of videoconferencing equipment for meetings or trainings must be submitted to the videoconferencing liaison with a copy to the First Justice of the respective division(s) no later than ten (10) calendar days prior to the date of the scheduled meeting or training. Such requests shall be submitted in writing or by email and describe or identify the date and time, the purpose and the location of the meeting or training. Prior to filing such request, the requesting party shall contact the videoconferencing liaison for the Juvenile Court where the meeting or training is to be held, to determine (1) whether the videoconferencing equipment will be available at the court(s) where the meeting or training is to be held on the date(s) and time to be requested, (2) whether there is a room at the court(s) where the meeting or training is to be held which is compatible and available to utilize the equipment on the requested date(s) and time, and (3) whether the videoconferencing liaison, or other designated contact person, at the court(s) where the meeting or training is to be held will be available on the requested date(s) and time to ensure that the equipment is operational and that it is being properly utilized. Priority will be given to requests for the use of videoconferencing in a Juvenile Court emergency court proceeding even if a request for use of equipment for a meeting or training from another source is received prior to a request for use of the equipment in a Juvenile Court emergency court proceeding, however, every effort should be made to accommodate prior scheduled meetings or trainings.

11. **Use of Videoconferencing Equipment by Other Trial Court Departments.** Other Trial Court departments may submit a request to use Juvenile Court videoconferencing equipment. The requesting Trial Court department shall be responsible for safely transporting the equipment to an available area within the court facility where the equipment is located which has the ability to compatibly utilize the equipment. Said department shall be responsible for the security, operation and the timely return of the videoconferencing equipment to the Juvenile Court. Said requests shall be made in writing to the First Justice of the respective Juvenile Court division where the equipment is located no later than twenty-one (21) calendar days prior to the date of the proposed use of the equipment. Said requests should describe or identify (1) the date and time, (2) the purpose and proposed length of use, (3) the proposed location where the equipment will be used, and (4) the qualified person from the requesting department who will be responsible for the security, operation and timely return of the equipment. The qualified person from the requesting department must be properly trained to operate, maintain, transport and protect the videoconferencing equipment. The First Justice shall consult with the videoconferencing liaison and shall inform the requesting Trial Court department whether said equipment will be available on the requested date and time. Priority shall be given to requests from the Juvenile Court for the use of videoconferencing in Juvenile Court court proceedings, meetings and trainings. Any request from other Trial Court departments is subject to the ability to compatibly utilize the videoconferencing equipment between the court and the remote site, the operational needs of the remote site and the cost to the court to utilize said equipment.

12. **Report.** The First Justice for each Juvenile Court division shall maintain a monthly report of the usage of videoconferencing equipment by the Juvenile Court and by other Trial Court departments. Said report shall be compiled by the videoconferencing liaison. A copy of the report shall be forwarded by the First Justice

to the Chief Justice of the Juvenile Court on the second Wednesday of each month.

13. **Conflicts Regarding Scheduling the Use of Videoconferencing Equipment.** Any conflicts within the Juvenile Court department regarding the scheduling of videoconferencing equipment for Juvenile Court court proceedings, meetings or trainings, or for use of videoconferencing equipment by other Trial Court departments which cannot be resolved by the First Justice(s) of the respective Juvenile Court division(s) will be resolved by the Chief Justice of the Juvenile Court.

Uniform Practice 01-11. Scheduling Permanency Hearings for Young Adults and Children Who Choose to Remain in the Care of the Department of Children and Families Upon or After Turning 18 Years Old

I. INTRODUCTION

This uniform practice sets forth the practice and procedure for scheduling permanency hearings for young adults and children who choose to remain in the care of the Department of Children and Families (DCF) upon or after turning 18 years old. For the purposes of this uniform practice: **'Care'** is a written agreement between the young adult and DCF to continue to provide services and support to the young adult in preparing for their future outside of DCF; **'Young Adult'** is a person between the ages of 18 and 22; **'Child'** is a person who has not yet attained the age of 18.

This uniform practice addresses the following three groups of young adults and children:

- **GROUP ONE:** young adults, who turned 18 on or before January 3, 2011, are not yet 22, and are in the care of DCF on January 3, 2011.
- **GROUP TWO:** children, in the care and custody of DCF, who turn 18 after January 3, 2011.
- **GROUP THREE:** children, in the care and custody of DCF, who turn 18 after January 3, 2011, who subsequently leave the care of DCF but return to the care of DCF at a later date, prior to turning 22. An example of this group is a child, in the care and custody of DCF, who, upon turning 18, decides to not remain in the care of DCF, but then returns to the care of DCF prior to turning 22. Another example of this group is a child, in the care and custody of DCF, who upon turning 18, decides to remain in the care of DCF, but then decides to leave DCF, only to return to the care of DCF, prior to turning 22.

II. GROUP ONE: YOUNG ADULTS WHO TURNED 18 ON OR BEFORE JANUARY 3, 2011, ARE NOT YET 22, AND ARE IN THE CARE OF DCF ON JANUARY 3, 2011

A. Identifying the Young Adult

DCF will identify every young adult currently in its care. The names of these young adults will be provided to the court that entered the final custody order in either a care and protection or CHINS case.

B. Motion to Schedule a Permanency Hearing for a Young Adult

DCF will file a **Motion to Schedule a Permanency Hearing for a Young Adult (JV-F)** for each young adult on the list provided to the court. The **Motion** includes a request that if the underlying case was dismissed by the court in order to dispose of the case or the young adult was dismissed from a care and protection case that is currently active due to other children on the case, that the dismissal be vacated in order for the new permanency hearings to be entered on the same docket.

- The court will docket the **Motion** under the original docket number of the care and protection or CHINS case.
- The court shall schedule the **Motion** for a hearing to be held ex parte.
- More than one **Motion** may be scheduled for the same date and time.
- **All permanency hearings for Group One must be scheduled by April 1, 2011.**

Session Code:	MO
MOTF:	Motion for [C][C] filed. Motion *for scheduling a permanency hearing for a young adult* filed.

C. Hearing on the Motion

A legal representative of DCF shall be present at the hearing on the **Motion**. Once the **Motion** is allowed, the permanency hearing shall be scheduled. The permanency hearing shall be held within 180 days of January 3, 2011. **Therefore all permanency hearings for young adults in Group One shall be <u>held</u> on or before July 1, 2011.** Please use the new session code PY when scheduling a permanency hearing for a young adult.

MOTA:	Motion for [C][C] allowed. Motion *for scheduling a permanency hearing for a young adult* allowed.
Session Code:	PY

1. If Case/Child was Dismissed

Included in the **Motion to Schedule a Permanency Hearing for a Young Adult** is a request that if the underlying case was dismissed by the court in order to dispose of the case or the young adult was dismissed from a care and protection case that is currently active due to other children on the case, that the **dismissal be vacated** in order for the new permanency hearings to be entered on the same docket. If the case was dismissed, the judge must vacate the dismissal. After entering **MOTA**, please enter the following new major action code to vacate the dismissal:

DISV	Dismissal vacated for the limited purpose of holding a permanency hearing as required by G.L. c. 119, sec. 29B.

2. If Case/Child was not Dismissed

If the underlying case was disposed of using the major action code **CPNJ** (Child attained age 18 and is no longer subject to the court's jurisdiction), that major action code is not considered a dismissal and therefore only the filing of the motion and its allowance is required on the docket in order to schedule the new permanency hearings. Therefore if **CPNJ** was used to dispose of the underlying case, you only need to enter the major action code **MOTA**.

D. Appointment of Counsel for the Young Adult

The young adult is entitled to counsel. Whenever practicable, counsel who previously represented the young adult on the care and protection or CHINS, shall be appointed. The Clerk's Office shall determine the name of the last appointed counsel for the young adult on the underlying case. The Clerk's Office shall contact the attorney to determine whether he/she would like to represent the young adult for the permanency hearings. If the attorney agrees to represent the young adult that attorney shall be appointed. If the attorney declines to represent the young adult, then an attorney shall be appointed following the normal appointment procedures.

E. Permanency Hearing

The judge who entered the final custody order in the underlying case shall be the judge presiding over the permanency hearing, to the extent that it is practicable. DCF will notify the young adult of the opportunity to attend the hearing. The young adult should be present at the hearing unless he/she chooses otherwise. If the young adult is not present, the hearing may still go forward. The court must determine whether DCF had made reasonable efforts to achieve the permanent plan and that the plan is an appropriate transition plan for a young adult. Once the plan is approved, the court shall schedule the next permanency hearing to be held within a year. The court shall schedule the hearings on an annual basis, until the young adult turns 22 or leaves the care of DCF, whichever occurs first. The court may, in its discretion, schedule a permanency hearing on a more frequent basis than once a year. Please use the new session code **PY** for scheduling these hearings.

F. Disposing of the Case Once Young Adult Turns 22

If the young adult remains in the care of DCF until he/she turns 22, after the final permanency hearing, please enter the following new major action code to dispose of the case:

CP22	Young adult attained age 22 and is no longer subject to the court's jurisdiction.

III. GROUP TWO: CHILDREN IN THE CARE AND CUSTODY OF DCF WHO TURN 18 AFTER JANUARY 3, 2011

A. Permanency Hearing Held on the Child's 18th Birthday or Just Prior to the Child's 18th Birthday

This section refers to the permanency hearing held on the child's 18th birthday or just prior to the child's 18th birthday. Prior to this hearing, DCF will notify the child of the opportunity to attend the hearing. The child should be present at the hearing unless he/she chooses otherwise. If the child is not present, the hearing may still go forward.

At this hearing, DCF shall notify the court of whether the child is requesting to remain in the care of DCF following his/her 18th birthday. DCF shall indicate this in the written permanency plan for the child.

Regardless of whether DCF indicates that the child will remain in the care of DCF after his/her 18th birthday, the court shall schedule another permanency hearing to be held 6 months from the date of this hearing. Please use the following new session code **PY** to schedule the next permanency hearing.

B. Permanency Hearing Held After the Child Turns 18

This section refers to the hearing scheduled to be held 6 months after the child's 18th birthday. Prior to this hearing, DCF will notify the young adult of the opportunity to attend the hearing. The young adult should be present at the hearing unless he/she chooses otherwise. If the young adult is not present, the hearing may still go forward.

At this hearing, DCF shall notify the court of whether the young adult remains in the care of DCF following his/her 18th birthday. DCF shall indicate this in the written permanency plan for the young adult.

1. Child Remains in DCF Care after 18th Birthday

If the child remains in DCF care after his/her 18th birthday, then a permanency hearing shall be held for him/her on an annual basis until he/she turns 22 or leaves the care of DCF, whichever occurs first. Please use the new session code PY when scheduling these hearings. The court may, in its discretion, schedule a permanency hearing on a more frequent basis than once a year.

2. Child No Longer Remains in DCF after 18th Birthday

If DCF notifies the court that the child, upon turning 18, chose not to remain in the care of DCF, then no more permanency hearings shall be scheduled. The court may enter the following major action code in order to dispose of the case:

PNX:	Permanency hearing notice filed by DCF that child/young adult is no longer in the care or custody of DCF.

IV. GROUP THREE: CHILDREN, IN THE CARE AND CUSTODY OF DCF, WHO TURN 18 AFTER JANUARY 3, 2011, WHO SUBSEQUENTLY LEAVE THE CARE OF DCF BUT RETURN TO THE CARE OF DCF AT A LATER DATE, PRIOR TO TURNING 22

The amendments to G.L. c. 119, as appearing in Chapter 359 of the Acts of 2010, permits a child in the care and custody of DCF who turns 18 after January 3, 2011, and who subsequently leaves the care of DCF, to return to the care of DCF, prior to turning 22. This section addresses the procedure for those young adults which is similar to the procedure for **GROUP ONE.**

A. Motion to Schedule a Permanency Hearing for a Young Adult

DCF will file a **Motion to Schedule a Permanency Hearing for a Young Adult (JV-F)** for each young adult who returns to the care of DCF. The Motion includes a request that if the underlying case was dismissed by the court in order to dispose of the case or the young adult was dismissed from a care and protection case that is currently active due to other children on the case, that the dismissal be vacated in order for the new permanency hearings to be entered on the same docket. Along with the **Motion**, DCF shall file an affidavit that includes the date on which the young adult returned to the care of DCF.

- The court will docket the Motion under the original docket number of the care and protection or CHINS case.
- The court shall schedule the Motion for a hearing to be held ex parte.

Session Code:	MO
MOTF:	Motion for [C][C] filed. Motion *for scheduling a permanency hearing for a young adult* filed.

B. Hearing on the Motion

A legal representative of DCF shall be present at the hearing on the Motion. Please use the new session code PY when scheduling a permanency hearing for a young adult.

MOTA:	Motion for [C][C] allowed. Motion *for scheduling a permanency hearing for a young adult* allowed.
Session Code:	PY

1. If Case/Child was Dismissed

Included in the **Motion to Schedule a Permanency Hearing for a Young Adult** is a request that if the underlying case was dismissed by the court in order to dispose of the case or the young adult was dismissed from a care and protection case that is currently active due to other children on the case, that the **dismissal be vacated** in order for the new permanency hearings to be entered on the same docket. If the case was dismissed, the judge must vacate the dismissal. After entering **MOTA**, please enter the following new major action code to vacate the dismissal:

DISV	Dismissal vacated for the limited purpose of holding a permanency hearing as required by G.L. c. 119, sec. 29B.

2. If Case/Child was not Dismissed

If the underlying case was disposed of using the major action codes **CPNJ** or **PNX**, those major action codes are not considered dismissals and therefore only the filing of the **Motion** and its allowance is required on the docket in order to schedule the new permanency hearings. Therefore if **CPNJ** or **PNX** was used to dispose of the underlying case, you only need to enter the major action code **MOTA.**

C. Appointment of Counsel for the Young Adult

The young adult is entitled to counsel. Whenever practicable, counsel who previously represented the young adult on the care and protection or CHINS, shall be appointed. The Clerk's Office shall determine the name of the last appointed counsel for the young adult on the underlying case. The Clerk's Office shall contact the attorney to determine whether he/she would like to represent the young adult for the permanency hearings. If the attorney agrees to represent the young adult that attorney shall be appointed.

If the attorney declines to represent the young adult, then an attorney shall be appointed following the normal appointment procedures.

D. Permanency Hearing

The judge who entered the final custody order in the underlying case shall be the judge presiding over the permanency hearing, to the extent that it is practicable. DCF will notify the young adult of the opportunity to attend the hearing. The young adult should be present at the hearing unless he/she chooses otherwise. If the young adult is not present, the hearing may still go forward. The court must determine whether DCF had made reasonable efforts to achieve the permanent plan and that the plan is an appropriate transition plan for a young adult. Once the plan is approved, the court shall schedule the next permanency hearing to be held within a year. The court shall schedule the hearings on an annual basis, until the young adult turns 22 or leaves the care of DCF, whichever occurs first. The court may, in its discretion, schedule a permanency hearing on a more frequent basis than once a year. Please use the new session code **PY** for scheduling these hearings.

E. Disposing of the Case Once Young Adult Turns 22

If the young adult remains in the care of DCF until he/she turns 22, after the final permanency hearing, please enter the following new major action code to dispose of the case:

CP22	Young adult attained age 22 and is no longer subject to the court's jurisdiction.

Uniform Practice 01-12. Uniform Practice and Procedure Regarding the Appointment of Court Investigators

[Effective July 1, 2012; revised Feb. 20, 2013.]

I. INTRODUCTION

This uniform practice and procedure sets forth the application process and qualifications for appointment of court investigators in the Juvenile Court. This practice is effective on July 1, 2012.

II. COURT INVESTIGATOR QUALIFICATIONS

A. Qualifications for Appointment

1. Applicant shall be a licensed social worker with 3 years experience in child welfare protective cases, or a person with a Masters degree or higher in counseling psychology or clinical psychology with at least 1 year experience in child welfare protective cases, or a person with an undergraduate degree and knowledge of child welfare protective cases with demonstrable competence and at least 3 years experience in conducting investigations, or an attorney or retired judge with at least 3 years experience in child welfare protective cases.

2. Applicant shall have a business or residential address in the county where they are an applicant for appointment or in a county contiguous to the county of their business location or residence. If the applicant wishes to have his/her residential address remain confidential, he/she may use a post office box for mailing purposes.

B. Continuing Legal Education Requirements for Court Investigators

Any person qualified by the Administrative Office of the Juvenile Court (AOJC) to be appointed as a court investigator shall participate in six hours of continuing legal education per year. The AOJC shall approve all continuing legal education programs. The AOJC reserves the right to identify certain programs as mandatory. Any person eligible for appointment as a court investigator is responsible for providing certification of completed legal education hours to the AOJC no later than June 30 of each year. Failure to provide certification will result in the person being ineligible to receive further appointments.

III. GUIDELINES

Every court investigator shall comply with the Juvenile Court Guidelines on Court Investigator Reports promulgated by the AOJC.

IV. APPLICATION PROCESS

A. Application Submissions

Anyone seeking to be eligible for appointment as a court investigator shall submit the following to the AOJC:

1. A letter of interest addressing their qualifications

2. Application for Appointment, on a form approved by the Chief Justice of the Juvenile Court, noting counties in which they seek to accept appointments

3. Current resume, listing relevant educational training or classes attended or taught

4. Three references from persons who can speak to the applicant's qualifications

5. Consent to Criminal Record Check

B. Applicants Who Received Previous Appointments

The First Justices of all divisions in which the applicant previously accepted appointments as a court investigator will be consulted during the application process regarding the past performance and quality of written reports. An applicant who has met the qualifications for appointment but has submitted unsatisfactory reports in the past may be placed on a probationary status by the First Justice in accordance with section IV(D) of this Uniform Practice and Procedure.

C. Length of Appointment

Applicants who are qualified by the AOJC to serve as a court investigator shall be eligible to receive appointments in a county for a five year period, commencing on the date on which he/she receives approval by the AOJC. At the end of the five year period, anyone wishing to continue to receive appointments as a court investigator shall re-apply under the same application process.

D. Probationary Period

All court investigators are subject to being placed on probation during their five year appointment for failure to comply with the Juvenile Court Guidelines for Court Investigator Reports. Upon submission of an investigatory report, determined unsatisfactory by one or more judges in a division, the court investigator may be placed on probation by the First Justice. The First Justice shall identify the deficiencies in the report to the court investigator. A court investigator who is placed on probation will be so notified by the First Justice and shall be required to participate in remedial training as determined by the First Justice and the AOJC. The First Justice shall notify the AOJC when a person is placed on probation. If placed on probation, the court investigator shall submit all reports completed during the probationary period to the First Justice for review. The First Justice shall notify AOJC when the person has successfully completed the probationary period.

Pursuant to Supreme Judicial Court Rule 1.07, failure to correct deficiencies in the reports or continued noncompliance with Juvenile Court Guidelines may result in the First Justice reporting the investigator to the AOJC, requesting removal from the list of court investigators qualified for appointment. Nothing within this Uniform Practice and Procedure precludes a First Justice from requesting removal of an investigator from the list without placing the investigator on probation.

V. REVIEW AND APPROVAL OF APPLICATIONS

Applications submitted in accordance with this procedure will be reviewed within 60 days.[1] Each application shall be reviewed and a determination made as to whether the person qualifies for inclusion on the list. Each person shall be notified of the results of the review.

[1] This provision is effective October 1, 2012.

Uniform Practice 01-15. Uniform Practice and Procedure Regarding the Appointment of Guardians Ad Litem

[Effective July 6, 2015.]

I. Introduction

This Uniform Practice and Procedure sets forth the categories,

2

descriptions, qualifications and application process for the appointment of guardians ad litem in the Juvenile Court Department. This Uniform Practice and Procedure is effective on July 6, 2015.

II. Categories and Descriptions

A. *Guardian Ad Litem/Extraordinary Medical Treatment.* A guardian ad litem in this category is appointed to make recommendations regarding the authorization of extraordinary medical treatment. Extraordinary medical treatment includes administration of medical treatment and/or procedures not considered routine, refusal of medical treatment and/or procedures on religious or other grounds, administration of antipsychotic medication, and forgoing or discontinuing life sustaining medical treatment pursuant to G.L. c. 119, § 38A.

B. *Guardian Ad Litem/Treatment Monitor.* A guardian ad litem in this category is appointed after the judge has approved an extraordinary medical treatment plan ("plan") to monitor compliance with the plan and the effects of treatment.

C. *Guardian Ad Litem/Education Surrogate.* A guardian ad litem in this category is appointed to stand in the place of the parent(s) to make all special education decisions on behalf of the child including, but not limited to, assessment of the Individualized Educational Plan ("IEP"), participation in all Team meetings, acceptance or rejection of the proposed IEP (in whole or in part), and filing complaints with the Department of Elementary and Secondary Education when necessary in accordance with the Individuals with Disabilities Education Act (IDEA 2004), Federal Regulation 34 CFR 300 and Massachusetts Regulation 603 CMR 28. A guardian ad litem in this category must satisfy the criteria set forth in Federal Regulation 34 CFR 300.519, to act as Special Education Surrogate Parent.

A guardian ad litem appointment under this section does not include the authority to litigate educational issues in federal or state courts.

Note: These appointments are limited to Care and Protection cases in which custody of the child has been transferred to the Department of Children and Families.

D. *Guardian Ad Litem/Legal Rights.* A guardian ad litem in this category is appointed to enforce and defend the child's legal rights and does not include appointment as the child's attorney. The scope of the appointment may include the authority to:

1. Legal Rights/Privilege. Assert or waive a statutory privilege (e.g., psychotherapist-patient privilege pursuant to G.L. c. 233, § 20B, social worker-client privilege pursuant to G.L. c. 112, §§ 135A & B, etc.);

2. Legal Rights/Claims. Protect the child's legal claims including, but not limited to, the authority to consult with counsel or other experienced professionals in the field(s) to determine whether or not the child may have a tort, estate or other claim and if there is a reasonable basis to retain counsel, to retain counsel to initiate litigation on the child's behalf, where appropriate, and to approve settlements arising out of any claims and/or litigation on the child's behalf unless otherwise ordered by the judge. This appointment includes petitioning the appropriate court for the appointment of a conservator to manage the child's assets. A GAL in this category is not authorized to litigate any matters or file an appearance as an attorney for the child in any proceeding. A GAL in this category may not obligate the Commonwealth financially or in any other manner. A GAL in this category is not entitled to receive any funds or compensation from the resolution of any such claims(s) or litigation;

3. Legal Rights/Advisor. Advise the child on matters arising in delinquency and youthful offender cases (e.g., waiver of right to a jury trial, tender of plea), in the absence of a parent or interested adult, to the same extent and in the same manner as the parent(s) or interested adult whose responsibility it is to consult and advise the child. Therefore, the appointment does not extend to the actual assertion or waiver of the child's constitutional rights. The child asserts or waives his or her rights after consultation with the GAL.

E. *Guardian Ad Litem/Evaluator.* A guardian ad litem in this category is appointed to report on a narrowly defined issue where the judge deems an updated court investigation is not appropriate and where the appointment does not fall into one of the other categories of GAL appointments.

F. *Guardian Ad Litem/Diminished Capacity.* A guardian ad litem in this category is appointed, at the request of the attorney for an adult party, in civil matters to direct the attorney in the representation of the adult party after the judge has determined that the adult is unable to assist his/her attorney in the preparation and/or presentation of the case. This appointment does not extend to the actual assertion or waiver of the adult's constitutional rights (See Massachusetts Rules of Professional Responsibility S.J.C. Rule 3:07, Rule 1.14).

III. Qualifications for Guardian Ad Litem Categories

A. *Extraordinary Medical Treatment.* An attorney who is a member in good standing of the Massachusetts Bar with five (5) years experience in child welfare protective cases or five (5) years experience representing adults in extraordinary medical care matters.

B. *Treatment Monitor.* An attorney who is a member in good standing of the Massachusetts Bar with three (3) years experience in child welfare protective cases or with three (3) years experience representing adults in extraordinary medical care matters.

C. *Education Surrogate.* An individual who is not employed by an agency involved in the care or education of his/her assigned student, who does not have personal or professional interests that conflict with the assigned student's interest and who has or is willing to obtain adequate knowledge in special education and IEP process or a member in good standing of the Massachusetts Bar with three (3) years experience representing the interests of children in educational matters.

D. *Legal Rights/Privilege and Legal Rights/Claims.* An attorney who is a member in good standing of the Massachusetts Bar with three (3) years experience in child welfare protective cases.

E. *Legal Rights/Advisor.* An attorney who is a member in good standing of the Massachusetts Bar with three (3) years experience in child welfare protective cases or with three (3) years experience in delinquency and/or youthful offender cases.

F. *Evaluator.* An individual with a Masters degree or higher degree who holds a Massachusetts license in social work, counseling psychology or clinical psychology or a registered nurse with at least three (3) years experience in child welfare protective cases, or an attorney who is a member in good standing of the Massachusetts Bar with at least five (5) years experience in child welfare protective cases.

G. *Diminished Capacity.* An individual with a Masters degree or higher degree who holds a Massachusetts license in social work, counseling psychology or clinical psychology.

IV. Continuing Educational Requirements for All Guardian Ad Litem Categories

Any person qualified by the Administrative Office of the Juvenile Court ("AOJC") to be appointed as a guardian ad litem, regardless of category, shall participate in six hours of continuing legal education per year. The AOJC shall approve all continuing legal education programs and reserves the right to identify certain programs as mandatory. Any person eligible for appointment as a guardian ad litem is responsible for providing certification of completed legal education hours to the AOJC no later than June 30 of each year. Failure to provide certification will result in the person being ineligible to receive further appointments.

V. Guidelines

Every guardian ad litem shall comply with the Juvenile Court Guidelines for Guardians Ad Litem promulgated by the AOJC.

VI. Application Process

A. *Application Submissions.* Anyone seeking to be eligible for appointment as a guardian ad litem shall submit the following to the AOJC:

1. A letter of interest addressing his/her qualifications

2. Application for Appointment on a form approved by the Chief Justice of the Juvenile Court, noting categories and county divisions in which he/she seeks to accept appointments [Note: "County Division" includes all court locations within the County Division]

3. Current resume, including relevant educational training or classes attended or taught

4. Three references from persons who can speak to the applicant's qualifications

5. Notarized Consent to Criminal Offender Record Information Check

B. *Applicants Who Received Previous Appointments.* The First Justices of all divisions in which the applicant previously accepted appointments as a guardian ad litem will be consulted during the application process regarding the past performance and quality of written reports. An applicant who has met the qualifications for appointment but whose work has been unsatisfactory or has submitted unsatisfactory reports in the past may be placed on a probationary status by the First Justice in accordance with section VI(D) of this Uniform Practice and Procedure.

C. *Length of Eligibility for Appointment.* Applicants who are qualified by the AOJC to serve as a guardian ad litem shall be eligible to receive appointments in a division for a five-year period, commencing on the date on which he/she receives approval by the AOJC. At the end of the five-year period, anyone wishing to continue to receive appointments as a guardian ad litem shall reapply under the same application process.

D. *Probationary Period.* All guardians ad litem are subject to being placed on probation during their five-year period of eligibility for failure to comply with the Juvenile Court Guidelines for Guardians Ad Litem. If the quality of the work performance or written report is determined unsatisfactory by one or more judges in a division, the First Justice may place the guardian ad litem on probation. The First Justice shall identify the deficiencies in the work and/or report to the guardian ad litem. A guardian ad litem who is placed on probation will be so notified by the First Justice and shall be required to participate in remedial training as determined by the First Justice and the AOJC. The First Justice shall notify the AOJC when a person is placed on probation and establish a method to monitor progress based on the deficiencies identified and the remedial training required. The First Justice shall notify the AOJC when the person has successfully completed the probationary period.

Pursuant to Supreme Judicial Court Rule 1.07, failure to correct deficiencies in work performance or written reports or continued noncompliance with Juvenile Court Guidelines may result in the First Justice reporting the guardian ad litem to the AOJC, requesting removal from the list of guardians ad litem eligible for appointment. Nothing within this Uniform Practice and Procedure precludes a First Justice from requesting removal of a guardian ad litem from the list without placing the guardian ad litem on probation.

VII. Review and Approval of Applications

Applications submitted in accordance with this Uniform Practice and Procedure will be reviewed within 60 days by the AOJC. Each application shall be reviewed and a determination made as to whether the person qualifies for inclusion on the list(s). Each person shall be notified of the results of the review.

2

COUNTY[IES] DIVISION	TRIAL COURT OF MASSACHUSETTS JUVENILE COURT DEPARTMENT	DOCKET NO.

MOTION TO SCHEDULE A PERMANENCY HEARING FOR A YOUNG ADULT

1. The Department of Children and Families respectfully requests the Juvenile Court to schedule a permanency hearing in accordance with G.L. c. 119, s. 29B for the following young adult who remains in the agency's care:

____________________ (Young Adult's Name) ____________________ (Date of Birth)

2. The Department of Children and Families further requests that if the young adult's case has been dismissed, the court vacate the dismissal for the limited purpose of holding permanency hearings as required by G.L. c. 119, s. 29B.

3. The young adult has signed an agreement to remain in the care of the Department of Children and Families beyond his/her eighteenth birthday.

4. The young adult entered the Department of Children and Families' custody prior to his/her eighteenth birthday as the result of a

☐ Care and Protection
☐ Children in Need of Services

Department of Children and Families

____________________ (Area Office)

Signed under the pains and penalties of perjury.

____________________ (Regional/Assistant Regional Counsel)

____________________ (Telephone No.)

____________________ (BBO No.)

____________________ (Date)

FOR COURT USE ONLY

ORDER

Motion to schedule a permanency hearing and to vacate the dismissal, if necessary, for the limited purpose of holding a permanency hearing as required by G.L. c. 119, s. 29B.

☐ **ALLOWED**

☐ **DENIED** ____________________

____________________ (Date) ____________________ (Justice)

JV-59 (12/10/2010)

Procedures Governing Intra-Departmental Transfers and Assignments

[Adopted effective Apr. 1, 2004.]

These procedures govern the method for requesting intra-departmental transfers or judicial assignments.

Pursuant to G.L. c. 211B, § 10(ii), the Chief Justice of the Juvenile Court is authorized to assign or to transfer a judge appointed to any Juvenile Court Division to sit in any other Juvenile Court Division for such period or periods of time as will best promote the speedy dispatch of judicial business. Further, pursuant to c. 211B, § 10(iv), the Chief Justice is authorized to transfer cases and matters from a court to any other court within his department, to consolidate cases, and to make such periodic adjustments in the scheduling and locations of court sessions as are deemed necessary for the proper administration of justice.

For purposes of these procedures, the term "party" shall mean the attorney of record for a party, if represented by counsel, or, if a party is not represented by counsel, the party acting pro se.

1. Purpose. If two or more actions are pending in different divisions of the Juvenile Court, and if a judge or party determines that the separate actions are related actions involving substantially the same or similar issues and parties, the judge or party may request that the Chief Justice make an appropriate intra-departmental assignment or transfer so that one judge may hear all related matters; or, if a case is pending in a division of the Juvenile Court Department and if a judge or party determines that the matter should be transferred to another division of the Juvenile Court Department, the judge or party may request that the chief justice make an appropriate intra-departmental transfer so that the case may be heard in another division in the interests of justice. Such assignments or transfers shall be made to accomplish one or more of the following purposes:

- to promote speedy disposition of cases, reduce duplication of hearings and promote judicial economy when each pending action will require a hearing or trial;
- to afford complete and permanent relief which might not be obtained unless the actions are consolidated for hearing and heard by one judge;
- to effectuate a proposed settlement of one case through the filing of a subsequent action in another juvenile court division; or
- where there is some other reason, consistent with the speedy and efficient dispatch of judicial business, why the cases should be assigned to and heard by a judge in another division.

2. Content and Timing of Request made by Parties: If a request for an intradepartmental judicial assignment or transfer is made by one or more parties, the request shall be made in a letter to the Chief Justice, with copies to the First Justice(s) of the Divisions in which the action(s) is/are pending and any specially assigned justice, and to the Clerk-Magistrates of each Division. A party making a request pursuant to these procedures shall at the same time send a copy of such request to all parties in the related cases.

Letters requesting intra-departmental judicial assignment: Should identify by title, name of court division, and docket number each of the related cases; list all parties and counsel of record, with addresses; describe the nature of the cases; and include a specific, individualized statement of reasons why the separate actions are deemed related and an intra-departmental assignment or transfer would be appropriate, with particular attention to the latter in situations in which at least one of the related cases will not require a hearing or trial.

Letters requesting a transfer of a case from one division to another division of the Juvenile Court Department: Should identify by title, name of court division, and docket number of the case and include a specific statement of the reasons why a transfer of the case would be appropriate. Every request must be accompanied by a copy of the current docket entries in the related case(s), with the most recent court activity listed thereon. Requests which are submitted without current docket sheets need not be considered.

Objections: Any party opposing the request will have seven days from receipt of the request to submit to the Chief Justice with copies to the First Justice(s) of the respective Division(s), any specially assigned justice, and the Clerk-Magistrate(s) of the respective Division(s), a letter in opposition with a statement of the reasons therefor.

Except for good cause shown and described in the request, a request for an intradepartmental judicial assignment or transfer will not be considered if made within 60 days prior to an established trial date. Cases shall not be removed from a trial list solely because a request for an intra-departmental judicial assignment or transfer is pending.

3. Applicable Considerations. Factors to be considered in determining whether actions are related include the following:

- whether the actions involve the same parties (including children) and the same attorneys;
- whether, in child welfare cases in which all parties are not identical, the person who is not a party to one of the cases sought to be consolidated is a parent, foster parent, guardian, relative or caretaker who seeks custody, visitation, or related orders regarding the child;
- whether the actions involve common, or substantially the same or similar, questions of law and fact;
- whether the witnesses and the evidence to be presented in the separate actions will be the same or similar; and
- whether the requested forms of relief are similar or related.

Factors to be considered in determining whether allowance of the request would tend to promote the speedy dispatch of court business and to reduce delay and duplication include the following:

- whether the actions are in similar stages of readiness;
- whether either action has an established trial date;
- whether the request was made to take advantage of an existing trial date in one case for use in the other case(s);
- whether allowance of the request might require that an established trial date for one of the cases be rescheduled to afford additional time for preparation or for trial of the other, unscheduled case(s); and
- whether, notwithstanding the provisions of these procedures, a party already has caused a case to be removed from a trial list by informing the court that a request for an intradepartmental judicial assignment or transfer was or will be made.

Additional factors to be considered may include the following:

- whether, if the request is allowed, there will be a continuing or long-term need for a judge of one court Division to exercise the powers normally vested within another court Division or whether the assignment or transfer only will be needed for one hearing;
- especially in cases involving child welfare, whether, due to special assignment to, or continuing familiarity with, one of the cases, it would be appropriate for the same judge to hear the related matter(s) to promote case continuity or permanency planning;
- whether the request should have been made earlier in order to reduce resulting delay; and
- any other special considerations that are not apparent from the docket entries or other portions of the written request.

4. Action by Chief Justice. The Chief Justice will review the request and consult with the First Justice(s) and any specially assigned Justice, and, if the interests of the Juvenile Court and of the parties would be served thereby, may make an appropriate order of assignment or transfer which would allow one judge to hear the related actions. When possible, the order of assignment or transfer or disallowance of the request shall be made by the Chief Justice within 45 days of receipt of a complete request. In cases with an established trial date, the decision on the request shall be made prior to the trial date. The Chief Justice will notify the First Justices, any justice assigned to the case(s), the Clerk-Magistrates and all parties of his decision on each request. Notwithstanding the provisions of this paragraph, in no event shall the pendency of a request be the sole cause for a case to be removed from a trial list.

6. Presumption in Certain Cases. There shall be a presumption in favor of allowance of the request if the parties to all the actions sought to be heard together are identical, if each case will require a hearing or trial, and if the issues are substantially related. This presumption shall not apply with respect to the consolidation of hearings or reviews conducted pursuant to c. 119, § 29B with post-decree reviews of c. 210, § 3 matters.

7. Authority of Chief Justice in Absence of a Request. The Chief Justice may make such assignments or transfers in the absence of a request by a judge or party.

Guidelines for Court Investigation Reports

[Dated Jan. 25, 2002; reissued Nov. 1, 2013.]

I. ROLE OF THE COURT INVESTIGATOR

A court investigator holds a position of public confidence and trust and, as such, court investigators shall conduct themselves in a professional manner and refrain from any conduct, which may result in a breach of such trust and confidence. In a care and protection proceeding, a judge must have as much relevant information available as possible. One important source of information is the report of the court investigator, because it provides the court with useful information that otherwise may not be presented by any of the parties in the proceedings. *See Custody of Tracy*, 31 Mass. App. Ct. 481, 485, 579 N.E.2d 1362 (1991). Due to the importance of this report, a court investigator shall have the ability to develop the investigative information in a written report that displays excellent communications skills, solid analytical ability, and the aptitude to exercise sound independent judgment. Armed with this information, a judge is better able to undertake the challenging task of deciding the outcome of a care and protection case.

II. COURT INVESTIGATION REPORT: PURPOSE AND USE

By statute, the investigator is required to "investigate the conditions affecting the child and make a report to the court under oath." G.L. c. 119, § 24. The investigation report should contain all the facts obtained as a result of the investigation. *See* G.L. c. 119, § 21A. Additionally, the report should be limited to factual information collected from identified sources. *See Custody of Tracy*, 31 Mass. App. Ct. at 484. Investigators should avoid reproducing clinical reports in their entirety. The better practice is to extract pertinent quotes and present the facts.

Furthermore, Chapter 119, § 21A provides an exception to the hearsay rule for court investigator reports. Therefore, although a court investigation report may contain hearsay, it is admissible evidence. *See Section V. Hearsay*. The investigator, however, must clearly indicate the source of any information contained therein. *See Duro v. Duro*, 392 Mass. 574, 579-580, 467 N.E.2d 165, 169-170 (1984); *Custody of Two Minors*, 19 Mass. App. Ct. 552, 559, 476 N.E.2d 165, 169-170 (1985).

Once submitted to the court, the investigation report is available for inspection by all counsel and subject to motions in limine.

Because of the importance of the court investigation report, these guidelines were created to assist the court investigator with his/her statutory task. The guidelines will:

- address basic elements that all court investigators' reports should contain;
- suggest sources the investigator should use to obtain the facts to be included in the report;
- discuss the use of hearsay in the report;
- discuss the propriety of addenda to the report;
- comment on how to best organize the contents of the report; and
- address the "Summary" and/or "Recommendation" sections.

III. BASIC ELEMENTS

The following list provides general guidelines for the overall format of the court investigation report.

A. The report shall be thorough, professional, and contain accurate information.

1. The report should provide current information and relevant history rather than merely relying upon or incorporating prior existing reports.

2. The report should reflect a balanced picture of the family, listing all positive and negative information relevant to the case.

3. The report should utilize multiple sources. The importance of contacting all known collaterals cannot be overemphasized.

4. The information contained in the report should be as factual as possible. Primary source information is preferable to secondary source information. Opinions and conclusions of the investigator should be limited to the summary and recommendation sections of the report.

Example: If the Department of Children and Families (DCF) social worker informs the court investigator that a physician provided information to the worker, the court investigator not only should include the DCF worker's statement, but should also contact the physician to verify the information from its primary source.

5. The report should have a professional appearance. It should not contain spelling or grammatical errors and the report should be paginated.

6. The report should explain and discuss medical, psychiatric, and social conditions in language understandable to the average layperson.

7. The report should state the child(ren)'s needs in detail.

B. The report should not be biased.

1. The family should not be described in derogatory or judgmental terms.

2. All family members should be approached with respect and openness, so that the investigator may hear their versions of the events and circumstances regardless of the allegations.

3. Avoid incorporating statements from sources that contain negative data in judgmental terms:

Example: "Father is a well known drunk." Ask the source to be more specific and provide factual information about the statement:

Example: "I saw father yesterday on the street; he was unable to stand and was slurring his words."

4. Exclude *biases* of any of the parties toward DCF as a whole, any specific area office or social worker. The purpose of the investigation is to provide the court with information pertaining to the specific child(ren) and family before the court. Positive and negative interactions between any of the parties and DCF may be included if relevant as well as any of the facts regarding actions or inactions of DCF.

5. Seek out sources who may have differing viewpoints.

6. Consult any sources offered by the parents.

7. When writing the report, give a balanced presentation that includes parent(s)' strengths and weaknesses, and any relevant information that is factual, but which may not support your conclusions.

C. Reported information should be descriptive not evaluative.

1. *Example of improper evaluative statement:* "The apartment was filthy."

2. *Example of proper descriptive statement:* "The kitchen sink was filled with dishes covered with dried food and there were dozens of flies and roaches in the apartment."

3. If a source's comment is evaluative rather than descriptive, attempt to clarify the statement or have the source be more specific. Remember that investigation reports (in contrast to guardian ad litem reports) are factual and not evaluative in nature. Nevertheless, an investigator may wish to include statements of opinion.

D. Sources should be easily identifiable.

The report should clearly show the following for each factual allegation: who the informant is or the type of record reviewed, what the source's position is, what his relationship is to the family, when the information was obtained or person interviewed, how the information was obtained, and why the source is important.

1. *Example of improper attribution:* "Hospital staff said that . . ."

2. *Example of proper attribution:* "Nurse Ruth Smith, the child's nurse at Children's Hospital on June 6, 2011, said that . . ."

E. Parents should be interviewed, and a home visit performed.

1. The court investigator shall contact the parents' attorneys, informing them of the date and time the investigator would like to meet with parents; the investigator should give the attorney a reasonable opportunity to be present, but not let the attorney's schedule control the investigation. The investigator shall notify the attorney that if the attorney does not respond to the court investigator within three days of contact, the investigator shall initiate contact with the parent. An attorney may not prevent the investigator from performing his or her job, but may advise a client not to meet with the investigator or not to answer a particular question. If a parent's attorney informs the investigator that the investigator may not meet with the attorney's client, the investigator shall not meet with the parent and shall include the details of such restrictions in the report.

2. Unannounced visits should be avoided unless the condition or occupants of the home is an issue.

3. Prior to meeting with parents, the court investigator should obtain basic background information including why the petition was filed (e.g. read the affidavit, 51A and B reports, police reports, prior court investigation reports, etc.).

4. A court investigator who must interview a parent who has difficulty communicating and understanding English, or a parent, who is deaf, must obtain the services of a court-approved interpreter for the interview. A court investigator may arrange for the assistance of a court interpreter by faxing a completed Court Investigator Request form to the Office of Court Interpreter Services (O.C.I.S.) at 617-367-9293. *See Appendix C.* Due to the needs of the court for interpreter services, it is important that you schedule your interview with the party for 3:00 p.m. or after. It is not necessary to file a motion for funds or for the services of a court investigator. The interpreter will bill the Office of Court Interpreter Services directly for payment upon completion of the assignment. If you later determine that you do not need the services of an interpreter, contact the Office of Interpreter Services by telephone (800-572-5027 x343) or (617-742-8383) or by email at Interpreter.requests@jud.state.ma.us to cancel the service. Thereafter fax the O.C.I.S. Service Request Cancellation form to (617-367-9293). *See Appendix D.*

F. Children who are the subject of the petition shall be interviewed (if age appropriate), and a home visit performed.

The court investigator shall contact the children's attorney(s), informing the attorney(s) of the date and time the investigator would like to meet and interview the children and a home visit performed. The investigator should give the attorney a reasonable opportunity to be present, but not let the attorney's schedule control the investigation. An attorney may not prevent the court investigator from meeting with the children who are the subject of the petition.

G. A Lamb-type warning should be given before interviewing a party.

1. The court investigator must explain to the party the role of the investigator, the purpose of the interview, as well as how the information gathered is going to be used, including the fact that information the party gives to the investigator is not confidential. There cannot be any "off the record" discussion prior to interviewing a party. *See Commonwealth v. Lamb*, 1 Mass. App. Ct. 530 (1973). A similar disclosure should be made to a mature child, modified to reflect the child's age and understanding.

2. To verify that the party understands the warning, a court investigator should ask the parent to summarize the warning for the investigator.

3. The investigator should indicate in the report that the *Lamb*-type warning was given and whether the party understood.

4. The court investigator should instruct the party to be truthful, that an attorney may be present if desired, and that the party does not have to answer a question if he or she does not want to, but that the investigator may include any refusal to answer questions in the report.

H. The report should be filed in a timely manner.

In accordance with Rule 7 of the Juvenile Court Rules for the Care and Protection of Children, the report of the court investigator shall be filed in the Clerk Magistrate's Office within sixty days after the appointment of the investigator, unless the court orders otherwise. A motion for extension of time for the filing of the court investigation report shall be in writing, signed by the court investigator and approved by a justice of the juvenile court. The court investigator shall file a motion for extension of time no later than fourteen days prior to the date the report is due, provided however, that the court may permit the filing of a motion for an extension at some other time in the interests of justice. If the court approves a motion for an extension, the court investigator shall provide a copy of any such approved motion to all counsel of record and to any party who is not represented by counsel. *See Appendix B. Juvenile Court Form: Motion for Additional Hours or Extension of Time to File Report.*

I. Other key information should be included in the report.

1. Efforts made to locate an absent parent.

2. Information about minor children who are not included on the petition.

a) If such children are in the custody of the parents, the investigator should see them and interview them. If they are not, a statement should be included indicating where they are placed, with whom, and why they are not in the parents' custody. If the child(ren) is/are in the custody of DCF, the names and addresses of their foster parents should be omitted from the report.

b) If the court investigator becomes aware of information that raises concerns about the safety of the child, the court investigator shall bring the information to the court's attention and include it in the court investigation report.

3. Information regarding previous care and protection proceedings on the same child(ren).

4. Extended family members and those who have provided care for the child should be contacted for background history. The court investigator may ask the parent(s) about extended family members through the use of open-ended questions. After obtaining information regarding family members, the court investigator should, as a courtesy, disclose to the parent(s) that he/she would be contacting the family members and those who have provided care for the child. The court investigator may ask the parent(s) whether there is any information that he/she would like to disclose regarding any family members (e.g. any potential biases).

5. Court Activity Record Information (CARI) data regarding the parents, subject children, adult children residing in the home, and other adults living in the home should be reported.

6. Report any discrepancies or omissions noticed during the investigation and report information subsequently obtained to resolve those discrepancies.

a) *Examples:* Service plan is out of date; the parent may not have seen the service plan; service plan is missing information; social worker may or may not have seen the child or family for some time—*verify* this with DCF social worker; note any explanations.

J. Facts should be separated from the conclusions and other personal views of the investigator.

1. Only facts and opinions of experts and professionals should be contained in the body of the investigation.

2. Expert witness or professional opinion information should be included in separate paragraphs within the body of the investigation so that such information and the identity of the person who provided it are easily identified.

3. The investigator's opinions should be confined to the summary and recommendations sections of the report. However, the report should never include conclusory statements as to whether DCF (or other petitioner) has met its burden.

K. Be cognizant of any domestic violence risk to a parent or child.

Certain information in the report could pose risks or dangers to parents or children involved in a case, especially if there is evidence of domestic violence. It is important to bring that information to the attention of the court. In those instances where the investigator believes that including the information in the report likely would be dangerous, the investigator may request a hearing before the court to bring the matter to the attention of the judge and attorneys in the case.

IV. SOURCES OF INFORMATION

The following are suggestions of possible sources from which a court investigator can obtain factual information. *This list is not exhaustive*. It is important to keep in mind that each case is unique and may require contacting sources beyond those commonly contacted by an investigator.

A. Privileged and/or Confidential Information

The court investigator's appointment form issued by the court orders access to both statutorily privileged or other restrictive information. However some privileged record holders may require a release of the information by the holder of the privilege or a specific order issued by the court prior to releasing such information. The court investigator may ask the holder of the privilege to sign a release or may file a motion to the court with notice to the attorneys and pro se litigants requesting access to the records.

B. Petitioner and Petitioner's Records

1. Reason for filing care and protection petition

2. History and involvement with family

3. Review entire case file, both that which is computer-generated and that which is in the on-going social worker's binder, 51A/51B investigations, service plans, case reviews, voluntary agreements or contracts, and day-to-day dictation of the social worker.

4. Current situation and relationship with parent(s)

C. Biological parent(s)

1. Interview each parent separately from one another.

2. Conduct home visit with parent(s), especially if parent(s) wish to have physical custody of children.

3. Inquire as to parent's understanding of why care and protection was filed; obtain parent's response(s) to the allegations.

4. Inquire as to parent's understanding of each child's personality and needs, what parent wishes for the child and how parent would like to see child's situation be different.

5. Inquire as to the background and history of each parent as an individual, as a couple, as parents.

6. Inquire as whether either parent is of Native American ancestry or eligible for membership in an Indian Tribe. If yes, ask the name of the tribe or tribes and the parent's connection with the tribe. For example, *did the parent live on the reservation*?

7. Inquire whether paternity has been established, if the child was born out of wedlock and/or the father's name is not listed on the child's birth certificate.

8. Inquire as to what parent would like the court to know.

D. Child(ren) on the Petition

1. Focus on age, developmental level, and mental health concerns.

2. Inquire as to his/her understanding of why the family is involved with the court; why he/she is in placement; where he/she want to reside and with whom in the short and long-term.

3. Use open-ended questions when interviewing the child.

Example: What would you like the judge to know about you?

Not: "Do you want to live with your mother or your aunt?"

4. Review current functioning: school performance, peer relationships, interests, wishes, and ambitions.

E. Information from other sources

1. All key collaterals should be included: hospitals, physicians, dentists, mental health, substance abuse, domestic violence and other treatment providers, parent aides, teachers, day care, early intervention, special education evaluations, home assessments, health records, police, relatives, neighbors.

2. Any privilege issues regarding obtaining information from mental health or substance abuse treatment providers should be brought to the attention of the parties and the court so that special orders may be issued if warranted.

3. Reasons should be given for omissions.

Example: "Father's whereabouts are unknown."

4. Balance of sources should be sought: sources suggested by family, as well as sources suggested by service providers and petitioner.

5. Probation officer assigned to the care and protection case.

F. Documentary Sources

1. Court Activity Record Information (CARI) check

The court upon the filing of a petition should automatically order the parents' CARIs. The court may order CARIs for other individuals relevant to the petition. The court investigator may review the CARIs in the Clerk Magistrate's or Probation Office, depending on local practice. A copy of the CARI should not be attached to the court investigation report.

2. Probate and Family Court records; other court records

V. HEARSAY

Hearsay, including totem-pole hearsay and hearsay from a child, is allowed in the court investigation report both in care and protection proceedings and in proceedings dispensing with consent to adoption, guardianship, or other custody proceedings.

For hearsay contained in an investigation report to withstand a motion to strike, the parties must be afforded an opportunity to refute the court investigator and the investigator's sources through cross examination and other means. Therefore, all out-of-court statements in the report must be attributed to a specific source by the investigator in the report. Whether a hearsay statement in an investigation report will be allowed to stand or will be stricken is for the court to decide. The obligation of the investigator is to include any such statement, if relevant, in the report.

Hearsay is an out-of-court statement made by a person that is offered by another to prove the truth of the matter asserted. For example, anything that is reported to the court investigator by someone, which is then in turn incorporated by the court investigator in his/her report is hearsay. Pursuant to G.L. c. 119, § 24, a court investigation report is admissible as evidence in a care and protection proceeding and cases involving the dispensing of parental consent to adoption, guardianship, or other custody proceeding, despite the fact that it includes hearsay. *Custody of Jennifer*, 25

Mass. App. Ct. 241, 245, 517 N.E.2d 187 (1988); *Custody of Michel*, 28 Mass. App. Ct. 260, 265, 549 N.E.2d 440 (1990); *see also Adoption of Astrid*, 45 Mass. App. Ct. 538, 546, 700 N.E.2d 275, *further rev. den'd*, 428 Mass. 1109, 707 N.E.2d 367 (1998) (no error in admitting court investigation report in a proceeding to dispense with consent to adoption, including opinions, recommendations, and conclusions, where investigator' testified, her sources were identified and the parents had an opportunity to rebut any adverse or erroneous material). The hearsay exception for court investigator reports exists "because of the importance of providing needed information to the court." *Custody of Tracy*, 31 Mass. App. Ct. 481, 484, 579 N.E.2d 1362 (1991). It also recognizes the difficulty and time constraints inherent in collecting adequate confidential information to be presented at the adjudicatory hearing. *Id.* Furthermore, it permits the judge to "steer as wide a course as possible" through all of the information presented regarding the fitness of parents. *Id.* at 485.

"Totem-pole" hearsay is different from regular hearsay. "Totem-pole" hearsay is an out-of-court statement made by a declarant to another individual who then reports it to a third person who offers it in court for the truth of the matter asserted. One example of totem-pole hearsay would be a neighbor reporting to the court investigator that she overheard the child, who is the subject of the care and protection proceeding, say that her bruises came from a beating by her parent. Under the law, however, no distinction between levels of hearsay is made as regards to their inclusion in a court investigation report. Therefore, investigators should report totem-pole hearsay so long as there is an identified source capable of being cross-examined as to each level of the hearsay. *Custody of Michel*, 28 Mass. App. Ct. at 266. It is reasonable to assume that as a part of the investigation, an investigator will talk to neighbors, teachers, social workers, mental health workers, relatives and friends, who will describe what they heard from third persons. *Id.* Each such third person, as well as the person interviewed, must be clearly identified, by name, as the source of the information provided.

The investigation report "should be limited to factual information collected from identified sources in order to permit a fair cross-examination of the investigator as to all contributions to his/her report." *See Custody of Tracy*, 31 Mass. App. Ct. at 487.

This provides the parties with an opportunity to adequately challenge any material in the investigation report with evidence of his/her own or to call any contributor to the report. *Care and Protection of Leo*, 38 Mass. App. Ct. at 243. Although the inclusion of hearsay in a court investigation report is expected and permitted, it is recommended that with totem-pole hearsay, the investigator seek to confirm any such totem-pole information from the primary source of the information.

VI. ATTACHING DOCUMENTS TO THE REPORT

A court investigator report should stand on its own merit with no attachments. To ensure that important information from letters, reports, evaluations and the like, is read and considered by the trial judge, any such important information should be included in the body of the report and properly attributed, not added as an attachment to the investigation report.

VII. ORGANIZATION OF REPORT

A. Overview

1. Make use of bold type and underlining and or headings to identify sources

2. Provide specific dates or time frames if possible

a) Avoid use of "on 1 or 2 occasions"

b) Avoid use of "in the past"

3. Identify sources of statements

4. Define all medical/psychiatric terms using a medical dictionary or a current edition of the Diagnostic and Statistical Manual of Mental Disorders.

5. 51A and 51B information (subject, alleged perpetrator, when filed, allegations, outcome of investigation, recommendations)

6. Service plan tasks and details of compliance/noncompliance with each task

7. Court and criminal records

B. Outline of the Report

The following is a suggested outline for a court investigation report. It is the intention of this outline to help the investigator make the information easily accessible to the reader. The purpose of the outline is to provide the court investigator with the type and quantity of information to be contained in the report. The data should be presented in the order that makes the most sense logically in that particular case. In the report, the investigator should refrain from using evaluative terms. Rather, the investigator should state the facts with respect to each category. The outline is not exhaustive as the facts of each case are unique and may require the review of additional factors or sections. Further, this outline may identify issues that are not of concern in the particular case being investigated. If an issue is not germane to the particular case, it should not be included in the report.

1. Case Caption

a. Case Name

b. Docket Number

c. County

d. Division

2. Parties

a. Names and dates of birth of the parties including the children

3. Summary of Allegations

4. Parents

a) Names—including stepparents, any putative fathers

b) Addresses—present or last known if applicable

c) Age and date of birth

d) Marital status including history of present and past marriages; dates of divorce

e) Relationship with spouse/partner

f) Education history

g) Employment history

h) Source of any income or financial assistance

i) Religion, if known

j) Cultural considerations including ICWA issues

k) Physical status—ailments; addictions; substance abuse

l) Psychological status—mental health (including diagnosis, treatment, medication history)

m) Impulse control & response to stress

n) Relationship with extended family

o) Relationships with supports

p) Relationship with individual children (note any paternity issues)

q) Prior history, if any, with any state or private social service agency, court, police including, but not limited to:

i) Chronological history of G.L. c. 119, § 51As—when, where, by whom, allegation, whether substantiated/unsubstantiated, recommendation

ii) Chronological history of any G.L. c. 209A actions, temporary restraining orders, violations of 209A orders

iii) Court proceedings, including prior C&P/TPR cases and outcomes

iv) Criminal record

r) Parent's view of C&P allegation(s)

s) Parent's view of child(ren)'s character and needs

5. Each child on the petition

a) Background

i. Name

ii. Age and date of birth

iii. Mother

iv. Father (note any paternity issues)

2

v. Address
vi. School and grade
a. Attendance
b. Appearance
c. Behavior
e. Grades
f. Relationships in school
g. Early intervention, special education and other evaluations
h. IQ
i. Other
vii. Special needs in school and in the home and community
viii. Medical needs
ix. Psychological needs
x. Prescribed medication
xi. Other court proceedings
xii. Other
b) Foster care
i. Duration
ii. Behavior
iii. Attitude
iv. Verbal and behavioral reaction before and after visitation
v. Relationship with foster parent(s) and other adults in the foster home
vi. Relationship with & behavior toward any other children in the foster home, if applicable
vii. Level of communication with biological parent
viii. Other
c) Nature of alleged parental abuse / neglect
i. Sexual abuse
ii. Physical abuse and/or neglect
iii. Emotional abuse and/or neglect
iv. Educational neglect
v. Lack of supervision; placing child in high-risk situations
vi. Other
d) Effect of abusive or neglectful treatment on child.
i. Educational status, including any special needs
ii. Social / Emotional/Psychological/Behavioral status
iii. Physical health
e) Relationship with parent(s) or extended family members
i. Visitation or other contact with parents
ii. Visitation or other contact with extended family members
f) Relationship with siblings
i. Nature of relationship
a. Time spent living together
b. If not in same placement, type and extent of visitation if applicable; note any court action regarding sibling visitation
ii. Siblings expressed desire to live together
iii. Child's preference for placement
iv. Other
g) Child(ren)'s view of the situation (if age appropriate)
i. Child(ren)'s view of family, self and predicament
ii. Child(ren)'s feelings about:
a. Placement
b. Parents
b. Extended family, if appropriate
b. Reunification
iii. Other

6. Other caretakers, if applicable

a) Name (if necessary. To protect substitute caretakers not known to parents, use first initial of last name only.)
b) Address (if necessary. To protect substitute caretakers not known to parents, street addresses may be excluded.)
c) Date of birth
d) Time spent living with child(ren) in present care and protection case.
e) Marital status including history or present and past marriages; dates of divorce
f) Relationship with spouse/partner
g) Last grade of education
h) Employment history
i) Source of any income or financial assistance
j) Religion, if known, and religious considerations, if any
k) Cultural considerations
l) Physical status—ailments; addictions; substance abuse
n) Psychological status—mental health
m) Impulse control & response to stress
o) Relationship with extended family
p) Relationships with supports
q) Relationship with individual children
r) Prior history, if any, with any state or private social service agency, court, police including, but not limited to:
i. Chronological history of G.L. c. 119, § 51As—when, where, by whom, allegation, whether substantiated/unsubstantiated, recommendation
ii. Chronological history of any G.L. c. 209A actions, temporary restraining orders, violations of 209A orders
iii. Court proceedings
iv. Criminal record
s) Caretaker'(s) view of allegation(s) in the care and protection petition
t) Caretaker'(s) view of child(ren)'s character and needs
u) Caretaker's ability to advocate for and participate in any services provided to children in their care

7. Children of the respondent mother and father not included in the petition.

a) Background
i. Name
ii. Age and date of birth
iii. Mother
iv. Father (note any paternity issues)
v. Address
b) School and grade
i. Attendance
ii. Appearance
iii. Behavior
iv. Grades
v. Relationships in school
vi. Special education evaluation
vii. IQ
viii. Other
c) Special needs
d) Medical needs
e) Psychological needs
f) Prescribed medication
g) Other court proceedings
h) With whom are child(ren) living. If not with parent, why not?
i) Explain why child(ren) are not included on the petition.

8. Extended Family

a) Maternal/paternal grandparent(s), if living
i. Names
ii. Addresses
iii. Information or knowledge about the allegations in the petition, and care of children
iv. Interest in helping family, including financially
v. Willingness and capacity to take children
b) Maternal/paternal aunts and uncles
i. Review factors (a)–(e) above for grandparents
c) Adult siblings
i. Review factors (a)–(e) above for grandparents

9. Parenting

a) Children's nutrition

b) Children's clothing
c) Family Housing (describe setting)
d) Education of children
i. Parental involvement and interest in school/daycare
ii. Parent(s)' explanation for any school related problems
iii. Describe level of parental understanding and support for child's educational needs
e. Medical/Physical/Psychological Welfare of Children
i. Medical care
ii. Emotional status
iii. Physical care
f) Cultural considerations, if applicable
g) Religious considerations, if applicable
h) Visitation and communication with child
i. Attendance at visits, if problems, describe in detail [including date(s)]
ii. Interaction with child(ren)—describe in detail (including date(s)
a. Affection/attention
b. Ability to set appropriate limits
c. Ability to communicate with children
d. Ability to appropriately stimulate child(ren)
e. Other
i) If investigator observed visit(s) between parent:
i. When, where, arranged by whom
ii. Parent and child present
iii. Describe visit especially parent/child interactions in detail

10. Parental Involvement with DCF

a) Cooperation
b) Position regarding service plan
c) Motivation to make use of services
d) Capacity to utilize support services
e) Previous experiences with other children
f) Parent(s)' willingness and ability to modify behavior that led to filing of care and protection petition
g) Cooperation with court ordered evaluation

11. Maternal/Paternal Compliance with Recommended Treatment Programs and Evaluation

1. Psychotherapy
2. Drug/Alcohol Evaluation/Counseling
3. Domestic Violence Counseling/Batterer's Program
4. Homemaker/Home Health Aide (if applicable)
5. Parenting Programs
6. Court Clinic evaluation, parenting evaluation, substance abuse evaluation, etc.

IX. SUMMARY SECTION

After the body of the report, the investigator may include a section that summarizes key facts. No facts that do not appear in the body of the investigation report should be added to the summary section. This section allows the court investigator to state the implications of all the data collected with regard to the petitioner's allegations and the possible case disposition. It is an opportunity to underline strengths and weaknesses of the family that may not be readily apparent. Furthermore, this section can speak to the willingness and ability of the parents to work on the issues that originally brought them to the attention of the court. The summary section should not, however, be an opportunity for the court investigator to discuss whether the investigator liked or disliked the family or agreed or disagreed with the family lifestyle.

X. COURT INVESTIGATOR'S OATH

Court investigators should conclude their reports with an oath swearing under pains and penalties of perjury that the statements are accurately quoted, that the observations are accurately presented, that the facts written are true to the best of the investigator's knowledge and that the opinions expressed within the report are rendered through the exercise of their best professional judgment. See Appendix A: Court Investigator's Oath.

XI. RECOMMENDATIONS

Although the court investigator's central function is to bring facts to the attention of the court, in some cases, the recommendations of the court investigator also are permitted. *See Adoption of Astrid*, 45 Mass. App. Ct. 538, 546 (1998) (no error in admitting an investigation report, including opinions, recommendations, and conclusions, where the investigator testified, her sources were identified and the parents had the opportunity to rebut any adverse or erroneous material).

The recommendation section should be consistent with factual data presented in the body of the report. The ultimate legal question of fitness/unfitness and/or best interests is for the court to decide. Therefore, the court investigator should refrain from recommending that the child be adjudicated "in need of care and protection," or that parents be found "unfit."

The recommendation section may serve a useful purpose to the court. It may contain recommendations for services that may be helpful to the child(ren) and family. In addition, the court investigator, in a recommendation section can make the court aware of alternatives which DCF, because of policy, regulations, or otherwise, did not present. It is important for the court investigator to have considered what his/her recommendations are, if any, because the investigator may be called upon to testify as an expert witness. *See* G.L. c. 119, § 21.

XII. UPDATES

The investigator may be called upon to "update" his/her investigation and file an addendum to the original report. This may occur, for example, when circumstances change, when a missing parent is located, or when the parent has petitioned for his/her review and redetermination right pursuant to G.L. c. 119, § 26. When an update is requested, except when an update is ordered because a missing parent has been located, the investigator should focus on all circumstances and facts since the date of the previous report. In some cases, the investigator may be ordered to provide an update with a focus around a specific person and/or issue.

Appendix A

COURT INVESTIGATOR'S OATH
Commonwealth of Massachusetts

_____, ss

I hereby swear and affirm under the pains and penalties of perjury that the statements contained in this report are accurately quoted, that the observations are accurately presented, that the facts written are true to the best of my knowledge and that the opinions expressed within the report are rendered through the exercise of my best professional judgment.

_____ _____
Court Investigator Date
Juvenile Court

Appendix B

2

COURT INVESTIGATOR MOTION FOR ADDITIONAL HOURS/EXTENSION	DOCKET NO(S).	TRIAL COURT OF MASSACHUSETTS JUVENILE COURT DEPARTMENT
CASE NAME	APPOINTMENT DATE: NEXT COURT DATE:	DIVISION

MOTION TO REQUEST ADDITIONAL HOURS OR EXTENSION OF TIME TO FILE REPORT

I ______________________________ request the court for:
(NAME)

☐ Additional hours.
No. of previously approved requests for additional hours: ______________

☐ Extension of time to file my report.
No. of previously approved requests for extension of time: ______________

REASON(S) FOR REQUEST

(Must be completed)

Note: If additional space is needed, please fill out and attach a separate sheet.

______________________ Date

______________________ Court Investigator

TO BE COMPLETED BY COURT

Motion is hereby allowed ☐

__________ Hours
(not to exceed 10 hours)

__________ Due Date

Motion is hereby denied ☐

DATE	JUSTICE

JV-127 09/25/2013

Appendix C

COURT INVESTIGATOR

Interpreter Request Form

(Please type or print clearly)

Investigator Name: __________
Investigator Phone Number: __________
Case Name: __________
Party in Need of Interpreter: __________
Court of Jurisdiction: __________
Docket Number: __________
Case Type/Matter: __________
Date of Interview: __________
Time of Interview: __________
Duration: __________
Address/Location of Interview: __________
Language Requested: __________
Notes: __________

[ ] If you need an interpreter's assistance to establish a meeting time, please check this box. An OCIS staff member will call you to make arrangements.

July 2010

Appendix D

O.C.I.S. SERVICE REQUEST CANCELLATION PRINT OR TYPE CLEARLY		
Date of Service	**Language**	**COURT**
Case Name	Docket #	
Cancelled by:		
Telephone:		
Email:		
Comments:		
OCIS FAX LINE: 617-367-9293		
Reminder: This is a Cancellation Notice. A rescheduled matter becomes a **New Service Request**. Please fill out a new request form.		
DO NOT WRITE IN THIS SPACE Received at OCIS on: (Please Stamp)		
OCIS/2000		

Guidelines for Guardians Ad Litem

Juvenile Court Department

Effective July 6, 2015.

I. INTRODUCTION

The *Guidelines for Guardians Ad Litem* set forth the role and the duties and responsibilities for each category of appointment. These *Guidelines for Guardians Ad Litem* are effective July 6, 2015.

II. ROLE OF THE GUARDIAN AD LITEM

A guardian ad litem ("GAL") holds a position of public confidence and trust and, as such, guardians ad litem ("GALs") shall conduct themselves in a professional manner and refrain from any conduct that may result in a breach of public trust and confidence. GALs must know and understand the scope of appointment, know the due date of any report that may be required, and know the number of hours that are approved. Additional duties and responsibilities vary depending on the category of appointment.

III. DUTIES AND RESPONSIBILITIES BY CATEGORY OF APPOINTMENT

A. GAL EXTRAORDINARY MEDICAL TREATMENT

Description

A GAL in this category is appointed to make recommendations regarding the authorization of extraordinary medical treatment. Extraordinary medical treatment includes administration of medical treatment and/or procedures not considered routine, refusal of medical treatment and/or procedures on religious or other grounds, administration of antipsychotic medication, and forgoing or discontinuing life sustaining medical treatment pursuant to G.L. c. 119, § 38A.

Duties and Responsibilities

GAL Extraordinary Medical Treatment must:

1. Review medical records
2. Interview medical personnel
3. Review affidavit of licensed medical personnel, if any
4. Meet with child
5. Interview legal parent(s) and/or caretakers(s)
6. File a report with the court that identifies sources of information includes a recommendation to the court regarding the petitioner's request to authorize, forego or withdraw treatment, an analysis of the below factors

Report must provide background information regarding the child and address the following factors of substituted judgment/best interests determination:

1. Child's expressed preferences, if any
2. Child's religious beliefs (strength of child's religious convictions to the extent that they may contribute to refusal of treatment)
3. Impact on the child's family of ordering or foregoing treatment
4. Probability of adverse side effects of treatment, including severity
5. Prognosis without treatment
6. Prognosis with treatment
7. Present and future competency of the child
8. Any other relevant factors

B. GAL TREATMENT MONITOR

Description

A GAL in this category is appointed after the judge has issued a Substituted Judgment Order ("SJO") and approved a Treatment Plan ("plan") to monitor compliance with the plan and the effects of treatment.

Duties and Responsibilities

GAL Treatment Monitor must:

1. Review treatment order
2. Review medical records and speak with treating medical personnel
3. Meet with child
4. Interview caretaker(s)
5. Interview DCF staff
6. Interview teacher(s), if any
7. Consult with child's counsel
8. File a report with the court that includes a recommendation of whether or not the judge should schedule a Substituted Judgment Hearing to review the SJO

Report must address the following:

1. Treating medical personnel/caretaker's compliance with the plan
2. Child's general condition and tolerance of treatment, including any side effects [behavioral, medical and psychiatric/psychological]
3. Effectiveness of treatment on presenting medical/psychiatric issue

4. Child's expressed preferences, if any, for continuance with the plan

5. Changed circumstances, if any, which may require a modification of the SJO or plan [Note: any modification of a SJO or plan requires a Substituted Judgment Hearing]

C. GAL EDUCATION SURROGATE

Description

A GAL in this category is appointed to stand in the place of the parent(s) to make all special education decisions on behalf of the child, including but not limited to assessment of the Individualized Educational Plan ("IEP"), participation in all Team meetings, acceptance or rejection of the proposed IEP (in whole or in part), and filing complaints with Department of Elementary and Secondary Education when necessary in accordance with the Individuals with Disabilities Education Act (IDEA 2004), Federal Regulation 34 CFR 300 and Massachusetts Regulation 603 CMR 28. A GAL in this category must satisfy the criteria set forth in Federal Regulation 34 CFR 300.519, to act as Special Education Surrogate Parent.

A GAL appointment under this section does **not** include the authority to litigate educational issues in federal or state courts.

Note: These appointments are limited to Care and Protection cases in which custody of the child has been transferred to the Department of Children and Families.

Duties and Responsibilities

GAL Education Surrogate must:

1. Review educational records
2. Review and determine status of the IEP, if any
3. Interview child
4. Interview caretaker(s)
5. Interview teacher(s)
6. Interview collaterals
7. Attend Team and other education meetings
8. Stand in the place of parent(s) in all matters relating to the identification, evaluation, education program and educational placement of the child and the provision of a free and appropriate public education to the child
9. File a report with the Court

Report must address the following:

1. Status of current IEP, if any
2. Barriers, if any, to the implementation of the IEP
3. Recapitulation of relevant actions and outcomes, including meetings, that occurred since the appointment or most recent court review
4. Effectiveness of the current IEP
5. Recommendations or prospective actions, if any, to improve and/or modify the IEP

D. GAL LEGAL RIGHTS

Description

A GAL in this category is appointed to enforce and defend the child's legal rights and does not include appointment as the child's attorney. The scope of the appointment may include the authority to:

1. *Legal Rights/Privilege.* Assert or waive a statutory privilege (e.g., psychotherapist-patient privilege pursuant to G.L. c. 233, § 20B, social worker-client privilege pursuant to G.L. c. 112, §§ 135A & B, etc.);

2. *Legal Rights/Claims.* Protect the child's legal claims including, but not limited to, the authority to consult with counsel or other experienced professionals in the field(s) to determine whether or not the child may have a tort, estate or other claim and there is a reasonable basis to retain counsel, to retain counsel to initiate litigation on the child's behalf, where appropriate, and to approve settlements arising out of any claims and/or litigation on the child's behalf unless otherwise ordered by the judge. This appointment includes petitioning the appropriate court for the appointment of a conservator to manage the child's assets. A GAL in this category is **not** authorized to litigate any matters or file an appearance as an attorney for the child in any proceeding. A GAL in this category may not obligate the Commonwealth financially or in any other manner. A GAL in this category is not entitled to receive any funds or compensation from the resolution of any such claims(s) or litigation;

3. *Legal Rights/Advisor.* Advise the child on matters arising in delinquency and youthful offender cases (e.g., waiver of right to a jury trial, tender of plea), in the absence of a parent or interested adult, to the same extent and in the same manner as the parent(s) or interested adult whose responsibility it is to consult with and advise the child. Therefore, the appointment does **not** extend to the actual assertion or waiver of the child's constitutional rights. The child asserts or waives his or her rights after consultation with the GAL.

Duties and Responsibilities

GAL Legal Rights/Privilege must take the following steps:

1. Determine whether a recognized privilege exists
2. Determine if the information sought is available from another source
3. Review medical records and/or speak with treatment professionals
4. Speak with child's attorney
5. Speak with child
6. Speak with the caseworker from the Department of Children and Families, if appropriate
7. Speak with the child's legal parent(s) or guardian(s), if appropriate
8. Determine if it is more important to the child's best interests that the information be communicated rather than that the relationship between the child and psychotherapist/social worker be protected
9. File a report with the court, unless otherwise ordered by the judge

Report must include:

1. List of persons consulted
2. Considerations/basis for decision to assert or waive the privilege

GAL Legal Rights/Claims, as directed by the judge, and where appropriate, must:

1. Explore potential legal claims on behalf of the child, including entitlement to benefits
2. Consult with child's attorney
3. Speak with child
4. Consult with relevant experienced professionals
5. Consult with a minimum of three (3) attorneys relative to potential litigation
6. Retain the services of counsel, after consultation listed above, to litigate claims on behalf of the child
7. Initiate litigation by directing counsel to file claim(s) on behalf of the child
8. Approve settlements on behalf of the child, unless otherwise ordered by the judge
9. File a report with the court

Report must include:

1. List of person(s) consulted, including attorneys, and the information he/she/they provided
2. Events, if any, that occurred since the date of the appointment or last court hearing, including any administrative or other meetings
3. Action(s) taken and their outcome(s)
4. Proposed action(s), the purpose(s)/reason(s), and the anticipated outcome(s)

GAL Legal Rights/Advisor must:

1. Consult with the child's attorney
2. Speak with the child
3. Consult/speak with others, if appropriate, who may have relevant information

2

E. GAL EVALUATOR

Description

A GAL in this category is appointed to report on a narrowly defined issue where the judge deems an updated court investigation is not appropriate and where the appointment does not fall into one of the other categories of GAL appointments.

Duties and Responsibilities

GAL Evaluator must:

1. Investigate, evaluate and make a recommendation to the court on the narrowly defined issue set forth in the court's order

2. File a report with the court in accordance with the court's order

Report must address the following and include a recommendation on the narrowly defined issue set forth in the court's order:

1. Description of narrowly defined issue contained in court's order

2. Summary of work done to accomplish the objective of the court's order, such as interviews, consultations, record review, and actions

3. List of person(s) consulted and/or interviewed and the information he/she/they provided

F. GAL DIMINISHED CAPACITY

Description

A GAL in this category is appointed, at the request of the attorney for an adult party, in civil matters to direct the attorney in the representation of the adult party after the judge has determined that the adult is unable to assist his/her attorney in the preparation and/or presentation of the case. This appointment does not extend to the actual assertion or waiver of the adult's constitutional rights (Massachusetts Rules of Professional Responsibility S.J.C. Rule 3:07, Rule 1.14).

Duties and Responsibilities

GAL Diminished Capacity must:

1. Speak with the adult

2. Consult with the adult's attorney

3. Consult/speak with others, if appropriate, who may have relevant information

IV. FILING THE REPORT

If the appointment requires the production of a written report, then the GAL shall file the original report, along with copies for each party, in the Clerk Magistrate's office.

V. REQUEST FOR ADDITIONAL HOURS OR EXTENSION OF TIME TO FILE THE REPORT

A. REQUEST FOR ADDITIONAL HOURS

Additional hours may be requested when necessary to complete the objectives of the appointment. A request for additional hours shall be made by typed motion, on a form approved by the Chief Justice of the Juvenile Court, which sets forth the specific reasons for the request. Requests for additional hours shall be limited to increments not to exceed 10 hours. GALs must receive written authorization for additional hours by a justice of the appointing Juvenile Court division prior to the provision of services. Requests for additional hours made after services have been provided shall not be approved by the Court.

B. REQUEST FOR EXTENSION OF TIME TO FILE REPORT

A request for an extension of time to file the GAL's report shall be made by typed motion, on a form approved by the Chief Justice of the Juvenile Court, which sets forth the specific reasons for the request. GALs must receive prior written authorization by a justice of the appointing Juvenile Court division for such request. A request for an extension of time shall be filed no later than fourteen days prior to the date the report is due. The Court may, however, permit the filing of a request for an extension at some other time in the interests of justice.

VI. PAYMENT FOR SERVICES

GALs shall submit requests for payment of services rendered in accordance with procedures and forms established and approved by the Chief Justice of the Juvenile Court.

Information on Juvenile Court Department Forms

Juvenile Court Department forms are available in electronic format on the Massachusetts court system website at https://www.mass.gov/lists/juvenile-court-forms.

Massachusetts Probate and Family Court

Selected Supplemental Rules of the Probate and Family Court

[These rules combine the Rules of the Probate Court and the Supplemental Rules of the Probate Court, effective Jan. 2. 2012.]

Selected Standing Orders of the Probate and Family Court

Selected Supplement Rules of the Probate and Family Court

Rule 1. Effect of Rules

The provisions of these rules shall apply to all proceedings in the Probate and Family Court unless a contrary intent appears.

Whenever a Supplemental Rule of the Probate and Family Court refers to a rule in the Massachusetts Rules of Civil Procedure, or to a rule in the Massachusetts Rules of Domestic Relations Procedure, it shall mean the rule in the Massachusetts Rules of Civil Procedure or in the Massachusetts Rules of Domestic Relations Procedure as it may be amended from time to time.

Rule 2. Appearances

In all cases not governed by the Mass.R.Dom.Rel.P., appearances and pleadings shall be governed by Mass.R. Civ.P. 11.

If the person appearing is an attorney-at-law, the written appearance shall also include the person's Board of Bar Overseers number.

Except for joint petitions for divorce, petitions for grandparent visitation and joint petitions for modification of child support, no appearance in a case commenced by petition shall be filed after 10:00 a.m. on the return day except by leave of court or in substitution or addition of attorneys.

An appearance may specify that it is not an objection to the petition, and such an appearance may be filed after 10:00 a.m. on the return day without leave of court.

Rule 3. Giving Service of Notice

In all cases not governed by the Mass.R.Dom.Rel.P., service and filing of pleadings and other papers shall be governed by Mass.R.Civ.P. 5. Wherever the word "complaint" appears in said rule, it shall also mean, where applicable, "petition."

When notice of a petition has been given by service of a citation, notice of any pleading asserting new or additional claims for relief not asserted in the original petition shall be given by service of a new citation.

Rule 4.

[Repealed effective Jan. 2, 2012.]

Rule 5. Guardians ad Litem

In addition to making appointments of guardians ad litem in cases required by statute, whenever it shall appear that a minor, intellectually disabled person, a person under disability, an incapacitated person, a person to be protected or a person not ascertained or not in being is interested in any matter pending, a guardian ad litem for said person may be appointed by the court at its discretion. No Judge of Probate and Family Court shall be appointed a guardian ad litem.

Rule 6. Citations: Return Days; Service; Publication

A. Return Days. All citations shall be made returnable not later than three months after the date of such citation except as otherwise provided by statute. Every day when a court session is scheduled in the city or town where the registry is located shall be a return day for probate citations. A return day is not a hearing date, but a date by which an interested person must file his or her appearance to contest a probate proceeding.

B. Extension of the Return Day. There shall be only one return day outstanding, and no return day shall be changed or extended before the return day unless it is certified in writing by the party or his or her attorney that no service has been made on the original citation. Notwithstanding the foregoing, if counsel is appointed to represent an alleged incapacitated person, incapacitated person, person to be protected, protected person, minor or ward at any point prior to the entry of a decree on the petition, the court may provide a separate date by which said counsel may file an appearance and objection.

C. Service within the Commonwealth. Except where otherwise required by statute or ordered by the court, service of a citation within the Commonwealth shall be given by delivering in hand or by mailing by certified, registered or ordinary first class mail at least fourteen (14) days before the return day.

D. Service outside the Commonwealth. Except where otherwise required by statute or ordered by the court, if it shall appear from the petition that there is anyone interested who is outside the Commonwealth in any part of the United States, its Commonwealths or territories, service of the citation shall be given by delivering in hand or by mailing by certified, registered or ordinary first class mail at least fourteen (14) days before the return day; if in other parts, one (1) month.

E. Service. When Whereabouts Unknown. Except where otherwise required by statute or ordered by the court, if it shall appear from the petition that there is anyone interested who is of parts unknown, service of the citation shall be given by delivery or mailing to the last known address at least one (1) month before the return day.

F. Service by Publication. Except where otherwise required by statu[t]e or ordered by the court, and in addition to the service requirements above, publication shall be required if any interested person's whereabouts, address or identity is unknown. Publication shall also be required in all formal testacy and appointment proceedings. A copy of the citation shall be published once in a newspaper designated by the register of probate having general circulation in the county where the proceeding is pending at least seven (7) days before the return date.

Rule 7. Amendments

In all cases not governed by the Mass.R.Dom.Rel.P., amended and supplemental pleadings shall be governed by Mass.R. Civ.P. 15. In all cases commenced by petition, except for joint petitions for divorce, petitions for grandparent visitation and joint petitions for modification of child support, a "responsive pleading" shall include an appearance filed before 10:00 a.m. on the return day.

Rule 7A. Time

In cases not governed by the Mass.R.Dom.Rel.P., the time for acts to be performed shall be governed by Mass.R.Civ.P. 6.

Rule 8. Further Notice

If a notice, given in accordance with the forms approved as provided by General Laws Chapter 215, Section 30, General Laws

Chapter 217, Section 8, or otherwise provided by these rules, is held by the judge to be insufficient, the judge may order such further notice as the case requires.

Rules 9–12.

[Repealed effective Jan. 2, 2012.]

Rule 13. Examination of Witnesses

In cases not governed by the Mass.R.Dom.Rel.P., the examination of witnesses shall be governed by Mass.R. Civ.P. 43(g).

Rule 14. Writ of Protection

A writ of protection shall issue only upon the application of the person for whom such writ is to be issued, or some person in his behalf, and upon order of the court, and then only if it is made to appear to the court, by affidavit and any other evidence that the court may require, (1) that the application is made in good faith and for the purpose of enabling such person to attend this court as a party or witness in some specified proceeding pending, (2) if such person is a party, that such proceeding has not been brought collusively to enable him to obtain a writ of protection, and (3) if such person is a witness, that he has not been required to attend as a witness by his own request or procurement, to enable him to obtain a writ of protection.

Rule 15. Interlocutory Hearings

The court may hear motions and other interlocutory matters in chambers or in open court at such times, and upon such notice as may be otherwise required by law provided the proceedings are recorded as required by Rule 201.

Rule 17. Foreign Law

In cases not governed by the Mass.R.Dom.Rel.P., the determination of foreign law shall be governed by Mass.R. Civ.P. 44.1. In addition, it shall be the duty of counsel to call to the attention of the court such authorities or other material relating to the question as they wish the court to consider.

Rule 18. Appointment of Stenographers

Request for the appointment of a stenographer to take the testimony at a trial for the purpose of reporting the testimony on appeal to the Appeals Court or the Supreme Judicial Court shall be given to the Register in writing not later than forty-eight hours before trial. If trial is cancelled at the request of either party, cost of the stenographer may be assessed by the presiding judge unless twenty-four hours notice in writing is given to the register to cancel the request for the stenographer.

Rule 19. Report of Evidence

Upon an appeal, where the court under General Laws Chapter 215, Section 18, has appointed a stenographer to take the evidence to be reported to the Appeals Court or the Supreme Judicial Court, the appellant, unless he files with the appeal a disclaimer of any right to rely upon the transcript of the evidence, shall, within sixty days of the date of the appeal file with the register for the use of the court and for use in the preparation of the record on appeal one certified transcript of the stenographic notes taken by the stenographer. The court, at any time, may extend the time for filing the transcript. The transcript shall be subject to the right of the court, before copies thereof are prepared for the use of the Appeals Court or the Supreme Judicial Court, to direct that the transcript be submitted to it for such correction as it may direct after hearing.

When decree or judgment after rescript has been entered or after dismissal of appeal, the register shall notify the persons supplying the transcript to call for the same within ten days, and, if not so called for, the transcript may be destroyed.

Rule 26. Exhibits

Exhibits which are placed in the custody of the register shall be retained by him for one year after the trial or hearing at which they were used, unless sooner delivered to the parties or counsel to whom they respectively belong or by whom they were respectively presented or introduced. If in doubt as to the party or counsel entitled to delivery, the register may require an agreement of parties or counsel or order of the court, before delivery. The register may destroy or discard such exhibits, but not earlier than thirty days after notice by him to the party presenting or introducing such exhibits, requesting him to remove them, nor earlier than one year after such trial or hearing.

Rule 27A. Depositions and Discovery

In all cases not governed by the Mass.R.Dom.Rel.P., depositions and discovery shall be governed by Rules 26 through 37 of the Mass.R.Civ.P.

Rule 27B. Summary Judgment

In all cases not governed by the Mass.R.Dom.Rel.P., summary judgment may be granted in accordance with the provisions of Rule 56 of the Mass.R.Civ.P.

Rule 27C. Summary Judgment Procedure

(a) Form of Motions for Summary Judgment and Oppositions Thereto.

(1) Motions. A moving party shall serve with the motion for summary judgment a separate memorandum stating the reasons, including supporting authorities, why the motion should be granted. Affidavits and other documents setting forth or offering evidence of facts on which the motion is based shall be served with the motion.

(2) Oppositions to Motions. A party opposing a motion for summary judgment may serve a memorandum in opposition. The memorandum in opposition may include a statement of reasons, with supporting authorities, why the motion should not be allowed and may include a request for a hearing. Affidavits and other documents setting forth or offering evidence of facts on which the opposition is based shall be served with the memorandum in opposition.

(3) Reply and Sur-reply Memoranda. A reply memorandum may be filed only with leave of court. Such leave must be sought within 5 days of service of a memorandum in opposition. A reply memorandum shall be limited to addressing matters raised in the opposition that were not and could not reasonably have been addressed in the moving party's initial memorandum. In view of the limitations upon a reply memorandum, a sur-reply is strongly disfavored and may not be filed without leave of court sought within 5 days of service of the reply. To request leave of court, a party shall file and serve a motion setting forth the grounds to support the request and shall have the motion scheduled for hearing. If the motion is allowed granting leave, the requesting party shall serve notice of the grant of leave with its reply memorandum or sur-reply.

(4) Facts Verified by Affidavit. The court need not consider any motion for summary judgment or opposition thereto unless the facts are verified by affidavit, are apparent upon the record, or are agreed to in writing, signed by interested parties or their counsel.

(5) Format and Length. All motions, memoranda of law and other papers, except for exhibits, filed pursuant to this rule shall be filed on 8-1/2" by 11" paper and, except for exhibits, shall be typed in no less than 12-point type and double-spaced, provided that the title of the case, footnotes and quotations may be single spaced. The title of each document shall appear on the first page thereof. Unless leave of court has been obtained in advance by motion with notice, all memoranda of law and the oppositions thereto shall not exceed 20 pages, and any reply memoranda shall not exceed 10 pages. Any document package permitted by paragraph b(2) of this rule shall not be included in the page limit. To request leave of court, a party shall file and serve a motion stating the number of pages the party desires, and why the party's objective cannot be achieved within the applicable page limit. The party shall have the

motion scheduled for hearing. Any leave of court obtained by a moving party shall apply to all opposing parties. The moving party shall serve notice of the grant of leave of court with the moving party's memorandum.

(6) Email Addresses. Each party or attorney filing a motion for summary judgment or opposition papers shall include his or her email address on the papers, unless he or she does not have an email address.

(b) Procedure for Serving and Filing Motions for Summary Judgment.

(1) General. All motions for summary judgment and oppositions shall be served on all parties and filed with the register in accordance with the procedure set forth in this paragraph (b). Compliance with this paragraph is compliance with the "reasonable time" provisions of the first sentence of Mass. R. Civ. P. 5(d)(1) or Mass. R. Dom. Rel. P. 5(d)(1).

(2) Service and Filing of Motions for Summary Judgment and Oppositions. The moving party shall serve a copy of the motion and the other documents specified by this rule on every other party. Every opposing party shall serve on the moving party an original and a copy, and on every other party a copy, of the opposition and the other documents specified by this rule. The opposition to a motion shall be served within (A) 21 days after service of a motion for summary judgment or (B) such additional time as is allowed by statute or order of the court. Upon receipt of the opposition and associated documents, if any, the moving party shall attach the original of the opposition and associated documents to the original motion and associated documents and within 10 days shall file with the register the combined documents ("the document package"), unless within the same 10-day period the moving party notifies all counsel that the motion has been withdrawn. If leave to file a reply memorandum is allowed, the reply shall be served and filed within 10 days of the allowance, unless the court orders otherwise. If leave to file a reply has been allowed, or, if a motion to strike has been served in response to the opposition to a motion or a cross-motion, the period for filing the document package is extended to the time granted for serving the reply or the opposition to the motion to strike. If the party opposing a summary judgment motion serves an additional statement of material facts under paragraph (b)(5)(iv), the moving party shall have 21 days to file the document package or to notify all counsel that the motion has been withdrawn. If the moving party does not receive an opposition within 3 business days after expiration of the time permitted for service of an opposition, then the moving party shall file with the register the motion and other documents initially served on the other parties with an affidavit reciting compliance with this rule and receipt of no opposition in timely fashion, unless the moving party has notified all parties that the motion has been withdrawn. The moving party shall give prompt notice of the filing of the document package to all other parties by serving thereon a copy of a certificate of notice of filing on a separate document. A separate document accompanying the filing shall list the title of each document in the document package.

(3) Cross-Motions. A cross-motion for summary judgment, accompanied by the other documents specified in paragraph (a)(1) of this rule, shall be served on the moving party with the opposition to the original motion. A party opposing a cross-motion may serve a memorandum in opposition within (A) 21 days after service of a cross-motion for summary judgment or (B) such additional time as is allowed by statute or order of the court.

(4) Motions to Strike.

(i) A motion to strike brought in response to a motion for summary judgment shall be served along with the opposition to the original motion. An opposition to the motion to strike shall be served within 10 days of service of the motion to strike. The motion to strike and the opposition thereto shall be filed with the document package relating to the original motion in the manner specified in Paragraph (b)(2) of this rule.

(ii) A motion to strike brought in response to the opposition to the original motion shall be served within 10 days of service of the opposition. An opposition to the motion to strike shall be served within 10 days of service of the motion to strike. The motion to strike and the opposition thereto shall be filed with the document package relating to the original motion in the manner specified in paragraph (b)(2) of this rule. Compliance with the times for service contained herein shall extend the time for filing prescribed in paragraph (b)(2) of this rule.

(iii) A motion to strike brought in response to a cross-motion shall be served along with the opposition to the cross-motion. An opposition to the motion to strike shall be served within 10 days of service of the motion to strike. The motion to strike and the opposition thereto shall be filed with the document package relating to the original motion and the cross-motion in the manner specified in paragraph (b)(2) of this rule. Compliance with the times for service contained herein shall extend the time for filing prescribed in paragraph (b)(2) of this rule.

(5) Statement of Material Facts and Response.

(i) A motion for summary judgment shall be accompanied by a statement of the material facts as to which the moving party contends there is no genuine issue to be tried, set forth in consecutively numbered paragraphs, with page or paragraph references to supporting pleadings, depositions, answers to interrogatories, responses to requests for admission, affidavits, or other evidentiary documents. Failure to include the foregoing statement shall constitute grounds for denial of the motion. In addition to the service specified in Paragraph (b)(2) of this rule, the statement of material facts shall be contemporaneously sent in electronic form by email to all parties against whom summary judgment is sought in order to facilitate the requirements of the following paragraph. The statement of material facts in electronic form shall be sent as an attachment to an email and shall be in Rich Text Format (RTF) unless the parties agree to use another word processing format. The requirement to email the statement of material facts to the opposing party does not alter the date or method of service, which continues to be governed by Mass. R. Civ. P. 5(b) or Mass. R. Dom. Rel. P. 5(b). The requirement for transmission by email of the statement of material facts in electronic form shall be excused if (A) the moving or any opposing party is appearing *pro se*, (B) the attorney for the moving party certifies in an affidavit that he or she does not have access to email, or (C) the attorney for the moving party certifies in an affidavit that an opposing party's attorney has no email address or has not disclosed his or her email address.

(ii) An opposition to a motion for summary judgment shall include a response to the moving party's statement of facts as to which the moving party claims there is no genuine issue to be tried. To permit the court to have in hand a single document containing the parties' positions as to material facts in easily comprehensible form, in preparing this response the opposing party shall reprint the moving party's statement of material facts and shall set forth a response to each directly below the appropriate numbered paragraph. Where the obligation to send the statement of material facts in electronic form has been excused, the response to the statement of material facts may be in a separate document. For purposes of summary judgment, the moving party's statement of a material fact shall be deemed to have been admitted unless controverted as set forth in this paragraph.

(iii) Neither the statement of material facts as to which there is no genuine issue to be tried nor the response thereto shall be subject to the 20-page limitation in paragraph (a)(5) of this rule.

(iv) An opposing party, with the response to the moving party's statement of facts, may assert an additional statement of material facts with respect to the claims on which the moving party seeks summary judgment, each to be supported with page or paragraph references to supporting pleadings, depositions, answers to interrogatories, responses to requests for admission, affidavits, or other evidentiary documents. Such an additional statement shall be a continuation of the opposing party's response described in paragraph (b)(5)(ii), with an appropriate heading, and shall not be a separate document. In addition to the service specified in paragraph (b)(2) of this rule, where the party opposing summary judgment includes such an additional statement in its response, the response, including the additional statement, also shall be sent in electronic form by email to the moving party, unless excused as provided in paragraph (b)(5)(I). The moving party shall respond to the opposing party's additional statement of material facts within the time prescribed by paragraph (b)(2)(A), resulting in a single document for the court's consideration, unless the obligation to send the additional statement of material facts in electronic form has been excused. For purposes of summary judgment, the opposing party's additional statement of a material fact shall be deemed to have been admitted unless controverted as set forth in this paragraph.

(v) Cross-motions for summary judgment and oppositions thereto shall comply with the requirements of paragraph (b)(5), with the result that there shall be a single consolidated document containing the respective statements of material facts and responses thereto, unless excused as provided in paragraph (b)(5)(I).

(vi) All exhibits referred to in a motion, a cross-motion, or opposition thereto shall be filed as a joint appendix, which shall include an index of the exhibits. The initial moving party, with the cooperation of each opposing party, shall be responsible for assembling the joint appendix and the index. Unless all the pages of the joint appendix are consecutively numbered, each exhibit shall be separated by an off-set tab divider. Where such dividers are used, the exhibits in the joint appendix shall be numbered consecutively. The moving party shall serve a copy of its exhibits to each opposing party with the motion. If a party opposing the initial motion designates additional exhibits, the additional exhibits shall begin with the next consecutive designation following the last designation by the initial moving party. Where an opposing party relies upon any evidence contained in the exhibits supporting the motion for summary judgment, the opposing party in its memorandum shall cite to that evidence using the form of designation of the moving party.

Where the opposing party relies upon evidence not contained in such exhibits, the opposing party shall treat such additional evidence as new exhibits. Such new exhibits, as well as an index of the new exhibits, shall be served with the opposition. The initial moving party shall certify that the joint appendix includes all exhibits served upon the initial moving party with the opposition to the summary judgment motion. If the initial moving party does not receive with the opposition an exhibit designated by the opposing party, then the moving party shall file with the register the joint appendix of exhibits without that designated exhibit, with the certification required by this rule. The burden will then rest with the opposing party to move to file any designated exhibit not timely submitted.

(vii) The initial moving party, upon filing a motion for summary judgment, shall serve upon the opposing parties, in paper and electronic form, unless electronic form is excused, the consolidated statement of material facts and responses filed with the register, unless the response is filed as a separate document in accordance with this rule. The moving party shall also serve upon the opposing parties the joint appendix of exhibits, including the index of the exhibits, filed with the register, unless the parties otherwise agree. If the joint appendix of exhibits, including the index, is in electronic form, an electronic copy shall also be sent, unless the parties otherwise agree.

(6) Sanctions for Noncompliance. The court need not consider any motion for summary judgment or opposition that fails to comply with the requirements of this rule.

(7) Applicability. This rule applies to all actions in the Probate and Family Court in which motions for summary judgment are permitted.

(8) Hearing. It is the responsibility of the moving party to obtain a hearing date for the motion for summary judgment and any cross motions.

2

Rule 28. Signatures to Pleadings

In all cases not governed by the Mass.R.Dom.Rel.P., any matter that is not required to be signed under oath or under penalties of perjury by the petitioner or an interested party may be signed by counsel of record, and Mass.R. Civ.P. 11(a) shall apply to such signings.

Returns of service and military affidavits may be signed by counsel of record, and Mass.R.Civ.P. 11(a) shall apply to such signings.

Rule 29

In all cases not governed by the Mass.R.Dom.Rel.P., time for service and giving of notice shall be governed by Mass.R.Civ.P. 5 and 6. Wherever the word "complaint" appears in said rule, it shall also mean, where applicable, 'petition."

Rule 29B. Temporary Conservatorships and Guardianships

Written notice of a hearing on a petition for a temporary conservatorship or guardianship shall be given at least seven (7) days in advance of said hearing, as follows:

(1) Temporary Guardianship of a Minor.

a. To the minor, if he is fourteen or more years of age; and

b. To all persons named in said petition.

(2) Temporary Guardianship of an Incapacitated Person and Temporary Conservatorship.

a. To the person alleged to be incapacitated or the person to be protected and his or her spouse and children, or, if none, parents, brothers and sisters, or, if none, heirs apparent or presumptive;

b. To any person who is serving as guardian, conservator, or who has the care or custody of the person or with whom the person has resided during the sixty (60) days (exclusive of any period of hospitalization or institutionalization) preceding the filing of the petition;

c. In case no other person is notified under paragraph (a), to at least one of the nearest adult relatives, if any can be found;

d. To all other persons named in the petition;

e. If the person is alleged to be intellectually disabled, to the Department of Developmental Services;

f. To the United States Veterans Administration or its successor, if the person is entitled to any benefit, estate or income paid or payable by or through said Administration or its successor; and

g. To any other person as directed by the court.

Notice shall be given to the respondent in hand and to all other interested persons by delivery or mail.

No extension of a temporary appointment of a conservator will be allowed unless an inventory and bond of the temporary fiduciary has been filed.

Rule 29C. Uniform Forms

The Chief Justice of the Probate and Family Court shall prescribe and promulgate uniform probate and domestic relations forms, and shall designate the specifications under which such forms may be printed or computer generated.

Rule 30. Dismissal of Abandoned Appeals

If the appellant has failed to (i) file the transcript of the proceedings or the designated portions thereof or the statement of certification within the time required by Rule 8(b)(3) and Rule 9(c) of the Massachusetts Rules of Appellate Procedure (unless such time shall previously have been enlarged as permitted by Rule 10(c)); (ii) docket the appeal within the time required by Rule 10(a)(1) of the Massachusetts Rules of Appellate Procedure (unless such time shall previously have been enlarged or the late docketing allowed as permitted by Rule 10(a)(3)); or (iii) failed to file the transcript of the proceedings or the designated portion thereof within six (6) months of filing the statement of certification, the register shall send written notice by first class mail that the appeal will be dismissed for lack of prosecution to the attorney of record for each party, or to the party at his last known address if he is not represented by an attorney. A copy of this rule shall accompany said written notice. The sending of every notice required by this rule shall be noted on the docket.

Fourteen (14) days after the date of such notice, the register shall forthwith dismiss such appeal for lack of prosecution and shall note said dismissal on the docket, unless the register receives a) a motion to enlarge to a date certain set forth therein the time for complying with this rule and the requirements of said Rule 8(b)(3) and Rule 9(c) and/or Rule 10(a)(1) or (3) which has been marked for hearing and b) an affidavit of the movant which shall set forth all the facts which such movant wishes to have considered by the court which will act on such motion in accordance with the provisions of this rule and Rule 10(c).

Rule 31. Pre-Trial Procedure

In all cases not governed by the Mass.R.Dom.Rel.P., pre-trial procedure shall be governed by Mass.R.Civ.P. 16.

Rule 40. Assignment of Cases for Trial: Continuances

In all cases not governed by the Mass.R.Dom.Rel.P., assignment of cases for trial and granting of continuances shall be governed by Mass.R.Civ.P. 40.

Rule 43. Evidence

In all cases not governed by the Mass.R.Dom.Rel.P., taking of evidence shall be governed by Mass.R.Civ.P. 43. A judge may, in the judge's discretion, take evidence at a place other than a courthouse.

Rule 44. Proof of Official Records

In all cases not governed by the Mass.R.Dom.Rel.P., proof of official records shall be governed by Mass.R. Civ.P. 44.

Rule 45. Subpoena

In all cases not governed by the Mass.R.Dom.Rel.P., subpoenas shall be governed by Mass.R.Civ.P. 45.

Rule 46. Exceptions Unnecessary

In all cases not governed by the Mass.R.Dom.Rel.P., exceptions shall be unnecessary as provided in Mass.R.Civ.P. 46.

Rule 52. Findings by the Court

In all cases not governed by the Mass.R.Civ.P.

(a) Effect. Except in actions to which G.L. c. 208, § 34, applies, the court shall upon written motion made prior to final argument, providing either party or the court has requested appointment of a stenographer pursuant to Rule 18 or the trial was recorded electronically, find the facts specially and state separately its conclusions of law thereon. Where the court enters judgment pursuant to G.L. c. 208, § 34 it shall issue findings of fact and conclusions of law thereon within sixty (60) days of the filing of a notice of appeal. Requests for findings are not necessary for purposes of review. Findings of fact shall not be set aside unless clearly erroneous, and due regard shall be given to the opportunity of the Trial Court to judge the credibility of the witnesses. The findings of a master, to the extent that the court adopts them, shall be considered as the findings of the court. If an opinion or memorandum of decision is filed, it will be sufficient if the findings of fact and conclusions of law appear therein. Findings of fact and conclusions of law are unnecessary on decisions of motions except as provided in Mass.R.Civ.P. 41(b)(2).

(b) Amendment. Upon motion of a party made not later than 10 days after entry of its findings the court may amend its findings or make additional findings and may amend the judgment accordingly. The motion may be made with a motion for a new trial. When findings of fact are made in actions tried by the court without a jury, the question of the sufficiency of the evidence to support the findings may thereafter be raised whether or not the party raising the question has made in the trial court an objection to such findings or has made a motion to amend them or a motion for judgment.

(c) Transcript of Proceedings Upon Request for Special Findings. Upon a written motion under paragraph (a) of this rule, the party making such request shall order from the stenographer and file with the court the original of a transcript of such parts of the proceedings not already on file as the court may determine material to any facts essential to a determination of the case. At the time of ordering, a party shall make satisfactory arrangements with the stenographer for payment of the cost of the transcript.

Rule 59. New Trials: Amendment of Judgments

In all cases not governed by the Mass.R.Dom.Rel.P., new trials and amendment of judgments shall be governed by Mass.R. Civ.P. 59.

Rule 60. Relief from Judgment or Order

In all cases not governed by the Mass.R.Dom.Rel.P., motions for relief from judgment or order shall be governed by Mass.R. Civ.P. 60.

Rule 61. Harmless Error

In all cases not governed by the Mass.R.Dom.Rel.P., harmless error shall be governed by Mass.R.Civ.P. 61.

Rule 101.

[Repealed effective Jan. 2, 2012. See Rules 15 & 29.]

Rule 102.

[Repealed effective Jan. 2, 2012. See Rule 8.]

Rule 103.

[Repealed effective Jan. 2, 2012. See Rule 14.]

Rule 201. Recording of Court Proceedings

(1) In all Probate and Family Court divisions, all proceedings shall be held in a courtroom and recorded electronically, subject to the availability and functioning of appropriate recording devices. Said recording shall take place whether or not a court stenographer is present in the courtroom. Uncontested adoption hearings may be held in the lobby and need not be recorded. Proceedings, if recorded, may be held in a hospital or other location when a litigant is, for health reasons, unable to come to the courthouse or in other exigent circumstances.

(2) A copy of the original recording, or any portion thereof, may be requested by counsel or by litigants or by an agency party to the proceedings within one year of the date the proceedings are recorded, provided that failure to request said copy seasonably shall not be grounds for the delay of subsequent proceedings. Upon motion for good cause shown, the court may extend the time period within which a copy may be requested. The copy shall consist of a cassette or disk copy of the original recording, or such portion thereof as is requested, which copy shall be produced pursuant to such process and procedure as is prescribed by the Chief Justice for Administration and Management of the Trial Court and the Chief Justice of the Probate and Family Court, and which shall be playable on standard cassette or disk devices designed for home or office use. Said request for a cassette or disk copy of an original court proceeding shall be filed with the Register of the Probate and

Family Court in the division in which the case was heard. Such request shall be on a form prescribed by the Chief Justice of the Probate and Family Court. Any person making such a request shall, in advance, notify all parties of the intention to make said request, to the end that multiple requests shall be made simultaneously wherever possible. The cost of said cassette or disk copy, which shall be prepaid, shall be determined by the Chief Administrative Justice pursuant to G.L. c. 262, § 4B, plus postage, except that there shall be no cost for a cassette or disk copy produced for the use of the court. Sections 27A through 27G of Chapter 261 of the General Laws shall be deemed applicable to a request by or on behalf of an allegedly indigent party and the cost of a cassette or disk copy shall be deemed an "extra cost" as defined in said section 27A.

(3) A cassette or disk copy shall, upon request as aforesaid, be made available to any party to a proceeding so recorded or to his counsel of record. A cassette or disk copy may be made available to any other interested person or interested agency in the discretion of the judge who presided over the proceedings. After the submission by said person or agency of a request in writing setting forth the basis of the request and the specific use to be made of the cassette or disk copy, said request is to be acted upon promptly, and any denial thereof or undue delay in obtaining a copy may be referred to the Chief Justice of the Probate and Family Court.

(4) A cassette or disk shall not be erased or tampered with nor its labels removed or defaced as long as the matter recorded is pending in any court or is subject to or the subject of appellate review. A cassette or disk which is thereafter erased shall be erased in its entirety. No cassette or disk shall be erased until a period of three years has expired from the date of the original recording. Duplication of a cassette or disk is expressly prohibited except where specifically authorized by the presiding justice of a Probate and Family Court, the Chief Justice of the Probate and Family Court, or the Chief Justice for Administration and Management of the Trial Court, as the case may be.

(5) A copy of a cassette or disk or a copy of any portion of the material contained in a cassette or disk shall not be used for a commercial purpose, for the purpose of public or private entertainment or amusement or for any other purpose detrimental to the administration of justice. A cassette or disk copy of an original recording of a proceeding from which the public was excluded shall be deemed confidential and subject to such additional restrictions with regard to its use as may be prescribed by the judge who presided over the session so recorded.

(6) All persons receiving a cassette or disk copy shall comply with the provisions of sections (4), (5) and (6) of this rule and shall be subject to the imposition of appropriate sanctions for non-compliance, including contempt proceedings. It shall be the responsibility of a person requesting a copy of a cassette or disk from the register of probate to take all necessary and reasonable precautions to prevent any incident of non-compliance with said sections, including but not necessarily limited to notifying persons who are permitted to use said copy of the provisions of said sections.

Rule 202.

[Repealed effective Jan. 2, 2012. See Rule 18.]

Rule 203.

[Repealed effective Jan. 2, 2012. See Rule 26.]

Rule 204.

[Repealed effective Jan. 2, 2012. See Rule 29C.]

Rule 402. Assignment of Counsel

If any party appears in court in a matter in which the laws of the Commonwealth or the rules of the Supreme Judicial Court establish a right to be represented by counsel, the judge shall follow the procedures established in G.L. c. 211D and in Supreme Judicial Court Rules 1:07 and 3:10.

Rule 406. Allowance for Fees, Costs, and Expenses

An application by a party for an allowance from the other party to prosecute or defend a complaint shall contain a statement that the party intends in good faith to defend or prosecute such complaint, and shall be accompanied by a certificate of the party's attorney that the attorney believes such statement to be true. The judge shall review the financial statements of the parties and other relevant evidence, including affidavits, and shall order an allowance, if appropriate, for counsel fees and necessary expenses. If such allowance is granted, it shall be paid as the court may direct.

2

Rule 410. Mandatory Self-Disclosure

(a) Initial Disclosures.

(1) Except as otherwise agreed by the parties or ordered by the court, each party to a divorce action, each party to a complaint for separate support, and each parent who is a party to an action under Chapter 209C that includes a claim for child support where paternity has already been adjudicated or where the parents have completed a notarized voluntary acknowledgment of paternity shall deliver to the other party or parties within 45 days from the date of service of the summons the following documents:

(a) The parties' federal and state income tax returns and schedules for the past three (3) years and any non- public, limited partnership and privately held corporate returns for any entity in which either party has an interest together with all supporting documentation for tax returns, including but not limited to W-2's, 1099's 1098's, K-1, Schedule C and Schedule E.

(b) The four (4) most recent pay stubs from each employer for whom the party worked.

(c) Documentation regarding the cost and nature of available health insurance coverage.

(2) Except as otherwise agreed by the parties or ordered by the court, each party to a divorce action and each party to a complaint for separate support shall also deliver to the other party within 45 days from the date of service of the summons the following documents:

(a) Statements for the past three (3) years for all bank accounts held in the name of either party individually or jointly, or in the name of another person for the benefit of either party, or held by either party for the benefit of the parties' minor child(ren).

(b) Statements for the past three (3) years for any securities, stocks, bonds, notes or obligations, certificates of deposit owned or held by either party or held by either party for the benefit of the parties' minor child(ren), 401K statements, IRA statements, and pension plan statements for all accounts listed on the 401 financial statement.

(c) Copies of any loan or mortgage applications made, prepared or submitted by either party within the last three (3) years prior to the filing of the complaint.

(d) Copies of any financial statement and/or statement of assets and liabilities prepared by either party within the last three (3) years prior to the filing of the complaint.

(b) Additional Disclosures.

(1) Except as otherwise agreed by the parties or ordered by the court, each party to an action under Chapter 209C that includes a claim for child support where paternity has already been adjudicated or where the parents have completed a notarized voluntary acknowledgment of paternity may serve on a parent who is a party to the action a separate written request entitled "Request for Additional Rule 410 Documents," and the parent served shall, within 45 days from the date of service of the request, deliver to the other party or parties the documents set out in (a)(2)(a)–(d) above.

(2) When a request for child support is first added to an action under Chapter 209C by counterclaim or by amendment of the complaint, a party may serve on a parent who is a party to the action a separate written request entitled "Request for Rule 410 Documents,"

and the parent served shall, within 45 days from the date of service of the request, deliver to the other; party or parties the documents set out in (a)(1)(a)–(c) above.

(3) The parties shall supplement all disclosures as material changes occur during the progress of the case. No party required to deliver documents under this rule shall be permitted to file any discovery motions prior to making the initial disclosure as described herein, and no party to a divorce or separate support action shall be permitted to file any discovery motions prior to making both the initial and the additional disclosures as described herein.

(c) Unavailability of Documents. In the event that any party required to deliver documents under this rule does not have any of the documents required pursuant to this rule or has not been able to obtain them in a timely fashion, he or she shall state in writing, under the penalties of perjury, the specific documents which are not available, the reasons the documents are not available, and what efforts have been made to obtain the documents. As more information becomes available there is a continuing duty to supplement.

Rule 412. Uncontested Actions to Modify a Judgment or Order

[Amended effective Aug. 1, 2013.]

In order to facilitate uncontested actions to modify a judgment or order, including, but not limited to, actions to modify child support consistent with the Child Support Guidelines, the following uniform procedure is to be followed:

(a) The parties shall file with the court a joint petition to modify a judgment or a joint motion to modify an order, on a form approved by the Probate and Family Court. The petition or motion shall be accompanied by a copy of the judgment or order to be modified and:

(1) an agreement setting forth the agreed upon modification(s), which must be notarized if modifying a judgment. If a child's primary residence or custody is being modified, the agreement must specifically state whether any terms in a prior judgment or order related to child support, health, dental, vision or life insurance coverage are also modified, or if they remain in effect. If child support is being modified and the parties deviate from the guidelines amount, the agreement must include specific facts that justify departure from the guidelines, and if the parties agreement terminates child support upon the age of 18, the agreement must acknowledge that G.L. c. 208, § 28 or G.L. c. 209C, § 9 is not applicable;

(2) complete and accurate financial statements signed by each party and counsel, if any, pursuant to Supplemental Probate and Family Court Rule 401, with supporting documentation (attach W-2 and 1099 forms for prior year), if financial issues are being modified;

(3) a complete and accurate Child Support Guidelines Worksheet, if child support or medical, dental or vision insurance is being modified;

(4) a written assent from the Department of Revenue Child Support Enforcement Division as the IV-D agency when a party, and/or a dependent child, is a current recipient of public assistance or owes a past-due child support debt assigned to the Commonwealth, and any term relating to child support or medical insurance is being modified;

(5) a proposed Child Support Findings form, if child support is being modified and the parties deviate from the guidelines amount;

(6) an Affidavit Disclosing Care or Custody Proceeding form by each party, pursuant to Trial Court Rule IV, if the care, custody or visitation of a child is being modified;

(7) any other assent or document required by statute or court rule; and

(8) a proposed judgment or order on a form approved by the Probate and Family Court.

(b) Formal notice or service shall not be required.

(c) Neither party shall mark the joint petition or joint motion for hearing. In the event that the court believes that a hearing is necessary or helpful to a disposition of the matter, the court will set the time and date of the hearing and will notify the parties within twenty-one (21) days of the filing of the petition or motion. If the pleadings are deficient or incomplete, an in-person hearing will be required.

(d) A joint petition or joint motion that is not scheduled for a hearing will be decided on the papers filed in accordance with this rule within thirty (30) days of such filing.

(e) A judgment or order entered on a joint petition or joint motion involving child support will be entered in the State Case Registry pursuant to G.L. c. 119A § 4.

(f) This rule cannot be applied to actions governed by G.L. c. 209A.

Selected Standing Orders of the Probate and Family Court

Standing Order 2-97. Service

[Effective Nov. 1, 1997.]

Service by facsimile or other electronic or telephonic transmittal is not service within the meaning of Mass. R. Dom. Rel. P. 5 unless expressly permitted by a specific rule for a specific purpose, by order of the court for cause shown, or pursuant to a written stipulation of the parties allowing for service by facsimile.

Standing Order 2-98. Tracking of Appointments of Guardians ad Litem and Probation Officers to Conduct Investigations in Domestic Relations and Child Welfare Matters

[Effective Oct. 1, 1998.]

It is ordered that the Probation Department of each Division shall track all appointments of Guardians Ad Litem and Probation Officers to conduct investigations in Domestic Relations* and Child Welfare** matters.

** Domestic Relations refers to: Divorce G.L. c. 208; Paternity G.L. c. 209C; Separate Support G.L. c. 209; and Abuse Prevention G.L. c. 209A.*

*** Child Welfare refers to: Termination of Parental Rights G.L. c. 210, § 3; Care and Protection G.L. c. 119, § 23C; and Guardianship of Minor G.L. c. 201, § 5.*

The following procedure will be followed:

1. When a Judge appoints a Guardian Ad Litem (G.A.L.) or a Probation Officer (P.O.) to conduct an investigation in Domestic Relations or Child Welfare matters, the person preparing the appointment form will provide the Probation Department with a copy of the completed form.

2. Upon receipt of the copy of the appointment form the Probation Department will prepare a tracking system which will record, at a minimum, the following:

a. Docket number;
b. Name of the case;
c. Date of appointment;
d. Name of the Judge making the appointment;
e. Whether the appointing judge wants to be notified when the Report is filed;
f. Name(s) of Attorney(s) of record;
g. Name of G.A.L. or P.O.;
h. Due date of the Report;
i. Extension date, if any, granted by the judge;
j. Date Report is received;
k. Date Parties are notified of receipt of Report;
l. Pre-trial date; and
m. Trial date.

3. The G.A.L. will file his/her report with the Probation Department on or before the due date. In situations where the G.A.L. has not filed his/her report in a timely fashion, the Probation Department will contact the G.A.L., either by telephone or in writing, to notify him/her of the need to file the Report and determine if an extension is necessary. If the G.A.L. fails to respond or fails to

meet the agreed upon due date, the Probation Department shall notify the Judge who made the appointment of this fact and seek further instruction. It is expected that the Probation Department has in place a mechanism to ensure the timeliness of Reports on investigations performed by its Probation Officers in accordance with the Standards of the Office of the Commissioner of Probation.

4. Once the Report is filed, the Probation Department will notify in writing the attorney(s) of record, if any, or the litigant(s) if pro se that the Report has been filed and is available for inspection; how to inspect the Report; and that it is required that counsel or a party, within thirty (30) days from the date of the notice, request the hearing of the matter as an uncontested matter or the scheduling of a pre-trial conference. In its notice the Probation Department shall give a brief description of the process for requesting an uncontested hearing or pre-trial conference. For pro se litigants, a Trial Request Form shall be sent with the notice.

5. Once the Probation officer has recorded the receipt of the G.A.L. Report, the Report shall be filed and stored in accordance with the directions of the First Justice.

6. After thirty (30) days from the date of notice to counsel or the parties the Probation Department will contact the Trial Department to establish whether a Trial Request Form has been received requesting an uncontested hearing or a pre-trial conference. If no request has been received, the Trial Assignment Clerk shall schedule a pre-trial conference.

7. On the first day of each month, the Probation Department will supply each judge with a status report on his/her outstanding G.A.L. and/or Probation Officer investigations and a report to the First Justice as to the status of all Guardian Ad Litem and Probation officer investigations in the Division.

The court shall provide a copy of this protocol to the Guardian Ad Litem with each appointment.

Standing Order 2-99. Procedure for Submission and Disposition of Certain Post-Hearing Motions

[Effective Oct. 1, 1999; amended effective July 2, 2012.]

Pursuant to Rule 78 of the Rules of Civil Procedure and Domestic Relations Procedure, the provisions of this Standing Order shall apply to the following post-hearing motions:

i) to Amend Findings of Fact (Rule 52)
ii) to Amend Conclusions of Law (Rule 52)
iii) for New Trial (Rule 59)
iv) to Amend Judgments (Rule 59(e))
v) for Relief from Judgment and Order (Rule 60)

The purpose of this Standing Order is to set out the procedures by which relief pursuant to subparagraphs i) through v) above, is sought. This Standing Order does not create any substantive right to relief, other than as set forth above.

Motions for post-hearing relief should be titled to reference the rule the moving party asserts is applicable to the relief requested. Even if the rule is not specifically identified, the motion shall be disposed of by the Court in accordance with the factors and time limitations set out in the applicable Rule specified in subparagraphs i) through v) above, since no other relief is available. The provisions of this Standing Order shall not apply to the following:

i) Objections to a Judgment of Divorce Nisi- pursuant to Rule 58(c) of the Rules of Domestic Relations Procedure

ii) Motions to Stay Proceedings to Enforce a Judgment (Rule 62)

(a) Submission of the Motion and Opposition Thereto.

(1) Submission of Motion. The moving party shall serve with the motion a copy of the order or judgment at issue and a concise statement of facts and law in support of why the motion should be granted. The statement shall be no longer than five (5) pages and shall be signed under the penalties of perjury. All documents required to be served with the motion shall be filed with the court on the date of service or within five (5) days after service. Compliance with this paragraph is compliance with the "reasonable time" provisions of Mass.R. Civ.P. 5(d)(1) and Mass.R. Dom. Rel.P. 5(d)(1).

(2) Submission of Statement in Opposition or Support of the Motion. Except by leave of court, upon motion, within ten (10) days after service of the motion, the non-moving party(ies) opposing or supporting the motion may file and serve a concise statement of facts and law in opposition to or in support of the motion. Said statement shall be no longer than five (5) pages, should explain why the motion should or should not be allowed, and shall be signed under the penalties of perjury.

(3) Additional Papers. With the exception of the certificate of service or, when applicable, the motion to extend the time for filing the statement in opposition or support of the motion provided for under paragraph (a)(2) of this rule, papers not served with the motion or statement in opposition or support may be filed only with leave of court.

(4) Form of the Motion. The moving party shall indicate in the title of the motion the name of the Justice who decided the original order or judgment and identify the applicable rule.

(5) Filing the Motion and Statement in Opposition or Support by Mail. If the motion and/or the statement in opposition or support is filed by mail, the bottom left-hand comer of the envelope should clearly indicate "Post-Hearing Motion".

(b) Hearing on Motion.

(1) Marking. No party shall mark the motion for hearing. No later than twenty (20) days from the date the motion is filed, the motion, supporting papers and any statement(s) of opposition or support shall be transmitted to the justice who decided the original order or judgment, unless the court has extended the time for filing the statement in opposition or support of the motion. In such case, the motion and supporting papers shall be transmitted to the justice who decided the original order or judgment within five (5) days from the date the certificate of service is filed with the court on the statement in opposition or support of the motion. In the event the court believes that a hearing is necessary or helpful to the disposition of the motion, the court will set the time and date for the hearing and will notify the parties of that date and time.

(2) Request for Hearing. If a party wishes to request a hearing on the motion, said request shall be filed and served with the motion or the statement in opposition or support of the motion. A request for a hearing shall set forth any statute, rule of court or case law which, in the opinion of the submitting party, mandates a hearing on the motion. After reviewing the motion, the statement in opposition or support of the motion, and the request for hearing, the court will determine whether a hearing should be held and, if a hearing is to be held, will notify the parties of that date and time. Failure to request a hearing shall be deemed a waiver of any right to a hearing afforded by statute, court rule or case law.

(c) Disposition of Motion.

Motions which are not set down for hearing shall be decided on the written submissions filed in accordance with this order.

(d) Sanction for Noncompliance.

Failure to comply with any and all of the provisions of this order may result in the Court's refusal to entertain the motion and/or the imposition of sanctions and/or costs against a party or his/her counsel.

Standing Order 1-05. Standards for Category F Guardian ad Litem/Investigators

[Effective Jan. 24, 2005.]

1. The Standards for Category F, Guardians ad Litem/Investigators in actions involving: Domestic Relations or Custody/Visitation/Adoption G.L. c. 215, § 56A; c. 208, § 16, (hereinafter "Standards") are effective January 24, 2005.

2. The purpose of these Standards is to:

- provide accountability related to guardian ad litem/ investigations;
- improve custody, visitation, and other outcomes for children;
- promote uniformity and consistency in guardian ad litem/ investigations; and
- promote respect for the rights of parties and their children, including their safety.

3. It is ordered that all guardians ad litem/investigators appointed pursuant to G.L. c. 215, § 56A, c. 208, § 16 utilize the Standards in conducting these investigations. Guardians ad litem/ investigators who are certified by the Probate and Family Court Administrative Office to receive appointments under Supreme Judicial Court Rule 1:07, and those persons not on the list who are appointed in accordance with Section (4) of Rule 1:07, are governed by this Order and shall conduct their investigations in accordance with the Standards.

Standards for Category F Guardian ad Litem Investigators

[Effective Jan. 24, 2005.]

INTRODUCTION

A Category F Guardian ad Litem investigator (GAL) is appointed by the Probate and Family Court to investigate facts in cases involving the care and custody of minor children and other matters that implicate the interests or rights of children. G.L. c. 215, § 56A; G.L. c. 208, § 16. A GAL is often appointed in cases that raise questions about:

- a child's best interests as related to custody and visitation;
- advantages or disadvantages of removing a child from the Commonwealth;
- changes in circumstances that might warrant modification of a judgment;
- existence of a de facto parent-child relationship;
- parental fitness as related to termination of parental rights or guardianship;
- paternity of a minor child; or
- other matters implicating the rights and interests of a minor child.

The purpose of these standards is to:

- provide accountability related to GAL investigations;
- improve custody, visitation, and other outcomes for children;
- promote uniformity and consistency in GAL investigations; and
- promote respect for the rights of parties and their children, including their safety.

These standards apply to all Category F guardian ad litem investigators.

1. THE ROLE OF THE GAL INVESTIGATOR

The GAL performs duties that are within the scope of the court order of appointment.

1.1 The GAL Shall Gather and Report Factual Data to the Court.

The role of the Category F GAL investigator is to gather and report factual information that will assist the court in making custody, visitation, or other decisions related to the welfare of a child. Unless the appointing judge specifies otherwise, the GAL investigator's role is limited to gathering and reporting information to the court. The GAL may include recommendations in the report if the order of the court authorizes inclusion of such recommendations.

COMMENTARY

The court, not the GAL, decides legal issues and ultimately makes credibility determinations and factual findings when facts are in dispute. The GAL reports on facts and avoids providing legal conclusions or legal analysis.

Inappropriate analysis: "This case presents a legal question of first impression as to whether the mother is entitled to relief from judgment. The national trend is to deny relief in this situation and in a recent case, the SJC hinted that it also would reject a claim based on weak facts such as those in this case."

A. The GAL Investigator is Not a Clinical Evaluator and Shall Not Perform Clinical Assessments or other Clinical Functions.

The GAL should provide descriptive information without clinical interpretations, even if the GAL is a mental health professional.

Example of a descriptive statement: "Mr. Jones said that he has felt very sad since his separation with his wife; he said he has trouble sleeping, has no appetite, and has missed numerous days of work because he is too depressed to get up."

Example of improper clinical interpretation: "Mr. Jones appears to be clinically depressed."

B. The GAL Shall Investigate Only those Areas Specified by the Court.

If the GAL sees a need to broaden the scope of the investigation, the GAL shall seek authority from the court before broadening the investigation. For example, a GAL appointed to investigate the issue of visitation discovers that the major conflict between the parties involves a parent's plan to remove the child out of state. The GAL must file a motion with the court before expanding the investigation to encompass fact gathering relating to the removal issue. Copies of any and all motions filed by a GAL must be sent to counsel of record and any pro se parties.

COMMENTARY

This standard does not preclude a GAL from investigating factual issues that were not identified at the time of the appointment if they are relevant to the legal issues identified in the appointment.

1.2 The GAL's Role Requires Participation in the Trial and Discovery.

After conducting the investigation and writing a report, the GAL shall be available for trial and for possible deposition. If the parties do not reach an agreement about their case, the GAL may be subpoenaed by a party or the court may request that the GAL be present for trial.

COMMENTARY

Absent a protective order of the court, the GAL shall appear for deposition as required under the applicable rules and statutes as part of his or her responsibilities as the GAL.

1.3 The GAL Shall Serve as an Impartial Investigator and Reporter.

The GAL is an impartial investigator and reporter in all cases.

A. The GAL Shall Decline or Withdraw from the Appointment if a Conflict of Interest Exists, or the GAL has Information or Personal Relationships that Will Bias the Process or Outcome of the Investigation.

If the GAL has any prior or existing direct or indirect relationships with parties, their families, their attorneys, material witnesses, or someone else connected with the family, the GAL must consider whether the GAL's impartiality is compromised as a result of these relationships. The GAL shall decline the appointment if:

- The GAL or the GAL's law firm previously advised or acted as counsel for a party, child, or other person closely aligned to a party, including but not limited to a party's spouse, non-marital partner, or a material witness;
- The GAL has or had a dating or intimate relationship with any counsel of record, or a close personal relationship with any counsel of record that will impact the GAL's ability to be unbiased;
- The GAL provided counseling or other services to a party or members of the family, or a material witness;
- The GAL was married to or had a personal relationship with a party, a member of the party's family, a material witness, or another person closely aligned to a party;
- The GAL has or had pecuniary interests or financial involvement with a party, the party's spouse or non-marital partner, a material witness, counsel for a party or other person closely aligned to a party;

- The GAL' s concerns about reprisal or adverse personal consequences if the report is unfavorable to a party will impede the GAL's candor or ability to be impartial and render an unbiased report;
- The GAL is aware of other circumstances that will impede the GAL's candor or ability to be impartial and render an unbiased report.

COMMENTARY

If a GAL is aware of circumstances that indicate that the GAL may have a conflict of interest or other circumstances that may make it inappropriate for the GAL to serve as the investigator, the GAL shall disclose the information to counsel of record and any pro se parties. The GAL also shall immediately file a motion for instructions from the appointing judge as appropriate with notice to counsel and any pro se parties.

B. The GAL Engages in Nondiscriminatory Practices.

The GAL shall not engage in conduct manifesting bias or prejudice based on race, gender, religion, ethnicity, disability, age, socioeconomic status, marital status or sexual orientation against a party, witness, counsel, or other persons involved in the case.

COMMENTARY

The GAL must be aware of how societal and personal biases may interfere with an objective investigation and recommendations. The GAL recognizes and strives to overcome any such biases. If the GAL is not able to do so, he or she must promptly decline or withdraw from the appointment. If the GAL considers factors related to race, gender, religion, ethnicity, disability, age, sexual orientation, marital status or socioeconomic status concerning a party in the investigation or report, the GAL must explain the relevance of these factors to the issues before the court.

C. The GAL Investigator Shall Not Act as an Attorney or Legal Advocate for the Child.

The GAL is an objective and even-handed reporter. The GAL shall not give legal advice or act as advocate or attorney for the child. In some cases, the child's wishes may be contrary to the child's best interests.

COMMENTARY

A GAL is not a party to the case. A GAL is a witness to the case. A GAL shall not engage in direct or cross examinations of witnesses or conduct depositions. The GAL shall not file motions except as related to performance of the GAL's responsibilities and as provided in these standards.

D. The GAL Does Not Represent Parties or Give Them Legal Advice.

The GAL refrains from giving legal advice to parties, including but not limited to advice about how the law applies to the facts of their case, how to obtain or modify court orders, or how to draft legal documents. The GAL refers parties to their attorneys for legal advice. If a party is pro se, the GAL suggests that the party seek legal advice from an attorney.

COMMENTARY

Many courts have "Lawyer of the Day" programs for indigent parties and many bar associations have lawyer-referral panels. Nonprofit "legal aid" (a/k/a "legal services") programs may be able to provide free legal advice and representation to low income or indigent parties.

The GAL shall refrain from giving a party legal advice that he or she should drop a restraining order so that the parties may meet together with the GAL or engage in mediation pertaining to the restraining order. *See* G.L. c. 209A, § 3.

1.4 The GAL Avoids Dual or Multiple Roles.

The GAL shall not provide legal, mental health, mediation or other professional services to any party or the child during the investigation or pendency of the case.

COMMENTARY

To provide such services during the investigation or pendency of the case is inconsistent with the GAL's role as an impartial investigator and reporter. The GAL, however, may provide information to the parties, the court, and counsel about community resources available to the parties, such as but not limited to substance abuse treatment programs or other professional services that may be helpful to the parties and their children.

1.5 The GAL Adheres to Applicable Ethical and Professional Standards.

The GAL shall adhere to the ethical guidelines and standards for his or her profession to the extent that these guidelines apply. An attorney must remain in good standing as a member of the bar and adhere to the Rules of Professional Conduct that apply to lawyers. *See* Mass. R. S. Ct. Rule 3:07. Likewise, mental health professionals must adhere to ethical and professional standards that govern their respective professions.

COMMENTARY

There is no attorney-client confidentiality when an attorney serves as a GAL investigator because the investigator does not represent any party. If an attorney or mental health professional serving as a GAL is unable to perform his or her investigatory responsibilities because of a conflict with applicable professional standards, the GAL shall promptly file a motion to withdraw as the GAL with notice to counsel and any pro se parties.

2

2. COMPENSATION

GAL investigator's fees paid by the Commonwealth are set by the Administrative Office of the Trial Court. If the court order lacks clarity about who will pay for GAL services, the GAL shall file a motion for clarification by the appointing judge with notice to counsel and any pro se party. If the order specifies that compensation will be paid by the Commonwealth, the GAL is prohibited from charging additional fees to the parties. The GAL files the report in a timely fashion whether or not compensation has been paid.

COMMENTARY

At present, Category F Guardian ad litem investigators paid by the Commonwealth are compensated in accordance with Memo No. 14 (February 28, 1997, Fiscal Year 1997) issued by the Administrative Office of the Trial Court. The GAL also may file a motion with notice to counsel and any pro se party for an extension of hours beyond the number of hours set forth in the order of appointment for approval by the judge who appointed the GAL.

3. UPON RECEIVING THE APPOINTMENT

The GAL carefully reviews the order of appointment to determine the scope of the investigation and the duties to be performed.

3.1 The GAL Clarifies the Scope of the Appointment and Duties as Necessary.

If the GAL is uncertain about the areas to be investigated or the GAL's responsibilities, the GAL shall file a motion for clarification for hearing before the appointing judge with notice to counsel and pro se parties.

COMMENTARY

A Category F investigative appointment should indicate that the GAL shall "investigate" certain issues, rather than "evaluate" the issues. If the order includes both mandates, the GAL should file a motion for clarification for hearing before the appointing judge with notice to counsel and any pro se party.

3.2 The GAL Determines Whether he or she has the Requisite Expertise and Competence in the Areas to be Investigated.

If the GAL lacks the necessary experience, expertise or competence to conduct an investigation of the issues, the GAL shall decline the appointment.

3.3 The GAL Determines Whether the GAL's Personal and Professional Schedule Permit a Timely Report.

The GAL reviews the areas to be investigated and the tasks to be performed. If the GAL will not be able to complete a report by the designated deadline, the GAL shall promptly decline the appointment.

COMMENTARY

If the GAL determines after commencement of the investigation that additional time will be needed to complete the investigation, the GAL may file a motion to extend the deadline with notice to counsel and any pro se party. The motion shall include a new proposed due date for the report so that the judge may determine whether the deadline should be extended or the appointment should be vacated.

3.4 The GAL Promptly Accepts or Rejects any Appointment.

The GAL shall promptly accept or reject the appointment no later than twenty days after the GAL receives it, or earlier if requested by the court. The GAL accepts or rejects the appointment by returning the completed form to the court.

4. THROUGHOUT THE CASE

4.1 The GAL Maintains an Attitude of Respect.

The GAL shall approach all family members and parties with an attitude of respect and openness to hear their account of the relevant facts regardless of any allegations that have been made. The GAL shall be patient, courteous, and dignified in his or her interactions with litigants, witnesses, attorneys, and others with whom the GAL deals in this official capacity.

COMMENTARY

The GAL may limit the number of telephone calls and contacts made by a party or attorney as is reasonable given the particular circumstances. The GAL may seek assistance from the court on issues related to the GAL's safety or to address inappropriate conduct by a party related to the investigation. In such instances, a motion must be filed with the court with a copy sent to counsel of record and any pro se parties.

4.2 The GAL is Diligent and Adheres to Time Deadlines.

The GAL shall adhere to all time frames set forth in the order of appointment as applicable.

COMMENTARY

If the report is not filed on time, the Probation Office notifies the judge and seeks further instruction from the court. Probate and Family Court Standing Order 2-98. If the GAL needs more time to complete the report, the GAL shall file a motion with notice to counsel and pro se parties to extend the deadline prior to the date when it is due. The motion shall indicate the proposed due date for the report. The GAL shall complete the report even if a party declines to participate or an attorney indicates that the case may settle.

4.3 The GAL Maintains Safety.

The GAL shall make every reasonable effort to ensure the safety of all parties and their children. To implement this requirement, the GAL shall:

A. Arrange joint parent-child interviews, home visits, or observations of a party with the children only when such processes are safe.

B. Arrange interview schedules so that parties do not come into contact during the interview process when domestic violence is alleged or identified as a possible issue.

C. Inquires about and refrains from disclosing, directly or indirectly, residential, telephone, work, or other location information that a party has kept confidential for safety reasons.

D. Refrain from recommending visitation or other arrangements that bring the parties into contact when an abuse prevention order is in effect, or when the investigator has reasonable cause to believe that such contact may be dangerous or harmful for either party or the child.

E. Warn the party, the party's attorney and contact police as appropriate if the GAL believes that a party or child is in danger of imminent physical harm from the other party in the case.

COMMENTARY

To ensure the safety of the parties and their children, the GAL should screen for previously undisclosed safety issues in separate interviews with the parties early in the investigation. Depending on the circumstances, the other party, the child, the GAL, or others may be at risk if there are issues of mental illness, domestic violence, child abuse, or substance abuse. The GAL should attempt to gather and communicate information in ways that avoid harm to parties, the child or children, or others involved in the case. The GAL shall consider the safety of the parties and other family members when he or she makes recommendations and determines how the information he or she has collected will be reported to the court.

4.3.1 The GAL Files Mandatory "51A" Reports When Required and as Appropriate.

In cases of suspected child maltreatment, many mental health professionals are required to file a "51A" report. G.L. c. 119, § 51A. However, a lawyer or mental health professional, who is not a mandated reporter, may still report suspected abuse or neglect as necessary if a child is at risk. If the GAL has reasonable cause to believe a child is in imminent danger, the GAL should report this information to the police department and should also report the information to the Court through an emergency motion for instructions with the required notice to counsel and pro se parties.

4.4 The GAL Shall Use a Process for Communication and Collection of Information that is Conducive to Disclosure of Information and Fair to the Parties.

The GAL shall provide each party with a separate interview so that each party may speak with candor. The GAL encourages parties and their attorneys to provide additional relevant information and documents. The process for communications must be even-handed and provide each party with the opportunity to present relevant information and respond to relevant allegations by the opposing party. The GAL also affords a pro se party the same procedural protections that the GAL affords a party with an attorney.

4.4.1 The GAL Shall Conduct All Oral and Written Communications with Attorneys and Pro Se Parties in a Manner that Avoids the Question of Bias.

The GAL shall send counsel of record and pro se parties copies of any motions and other documents filed by the GAL in court, except for the GAL report. If the GAL sends a substantive written communication to one counsel or a pro se party, the GAL shall send a copy of the communication to the opposing counsel or pro se party.

COMMENTARY

A GAL's written communications to one party or attorney about administrative or scheduling matters, such as arranging a time for an interview or signing releases, are not substantive matters. While it is not required by any statute or rule, attorneys may agree to send copies of all written correspondence addressed to the guardian ad litem to the opposing counsel.

4.4.2 The GAL Arranges for a Qualified Interpreter if a Party or Child is Unable to Understand or Use the English language.

The need for an interpreter goes beyond the courtroom if a party is not completely fluent or comfortable in using the English language. The party, child or child's guardian should be interviewed to determine the communication system to be used and the party's or child's comfort with it. In the case of a deaf or hard-of-hearing person, this communication system could be oral, cued-speech, finger spelling, sign language, or a combination of all of them. People may prefer to use their native language. Using a child as an interpreter is not appropriate, and using relatives or friends may have a chilling effect on what is disclosed. If the child or a party has limited or no English language skills and the GAL does not speak the language, every effort should be made to ensure that only qualified interpreters are used. Any authorizations for release of information and other forms should be translated for such parties. Likewise, a party or child may have a need for a sign language interpreter.

COMMENTARY

If a party does not supply a qualified interpreter, the GAL may file a motion in court for appointment of a qualified interpreter that includes a request that the Commonwealth pay for the interpreter's services if a party is indigent, or that a party or parties who are not indigent pay for the interpreter. Counsel and pro se parties shall be given notice of the motion. If the GAL desires payment from or reimbursement from the Commonwealth for the cost of using an interpreter, the GAL must receive approval from the court before incurring the expense. Bias or incompetence of an interpreter can lead to omitted and inaccurate communications with the GAL. The interpreter should not have a conflict of interest or a relationship with a party or other person that will bias the interpretation. The Supreme Judicial Court has promulgated standards for court interpreter services and qualifications which are available on the internet at: http://www.state.ma.us/courts/formsandguidelines/index.html.

Certain cases may require that the GAL possess or utilize cross-cultural competence and expertise. For example, if the parents dispute whether a certain religious ritual was integral to a certain faith and whether the ritual should be performed on the child. The role of the interpreter, however, is to facilitate communication rather than serve as a substitute for an expert on a particular culture.

4.5 The GAL Answers Appropriate Questions about the GAL's Credentials or Role.

The GAL answers appropriate questions about the GAL's education, training, experience, practice areas, professional affiliations, and the process of the GAL investigation.

COMMENTARY

If requested by counsel or a pro se party, the GAL shall provide a copy of his or her curriculum vitae to said counsel or party. However, questions pertaining to the GAL's personal life need not be answered.

4.6 The GAL Maintains Confidentiality.

The information gathered by the GAL for the court is confidential. The GAL shall not disclose confidential and personally identifiable information about the parties, their children, or the services rendered by the GAL to a person who is not a party or counsel in the case, except as necessary to gather information to complete the investigation and report, or to perform responsibilities related to the order of appointment. This prohibition is permanent and applies to the GAL's writings, lectures, or other media communications.

COMMENTARY

If a GAL has questions regarding release of information pertaining to the parties, child, or the investigation and report, the GAL may file a motion for instructions with the court with notice to counsel and any pro se party.

4.6.1 The GAL Obtains Appropriate Release Forms or Court Orders before Obtaining Privileged and Confidential Information about the Parties and their Children.

Many of the most common and relevant records that are subject to statutory privileges or other restrictions can be obtained with an appropriate authorization for release of the information or a court order.

- Department of Social Services (DSS) records. A party's release form or court order is needed to access records. The GAL can obtain the DSS file with a release from a party but privileged information must be redacted. 10 C.M.R. § 12.09(l)–(3).
- Medical, health and hospital records. A party's release form or court order is needed to access records. G.L. c. 111 § 70, § 70E(b); The Health Insurance Portability and Accountability Act of 1996, Pub. L. 104-19 1 (HIPAA).
- Psychotherapist records. A party's release form or court order is needed to access records pertaining to an adult from a psychotherapist whose communications are privileged. G.L. c. 112, § 8GB; *Commonwealth v. Bernard*, 424 Mass. 32, 673 N.E.2d 1220 (1996). G.L. c. 233, § 20B.
- Social Worker records. A party's release form or court order is needed to access records. G.L. c. 112, §§ 135A, 135B.
- Alcohol and drug abuse programs records. A party's release form and/or court order may be needed to access records. 42 U.S.C. §§ 1 175, 290 dd-3.
- School records. If a party has shared or sole legal custody, he or she may authorize release of records, except for a parent or party whose access is restricted by a Chapter 209A or other court order. G.L. c. 71, § 34H; G.L. c. 208, § 31.
- Criminal Offender Record Information (CORI and CARI). The GAL can most easily review these records with a court order through the Probation Department, or request the records through the Criminal History Systems Board.
- Prior GAL reports, Probation Office or Court Clinic reports involving the parties. The GAL must file a motion with the court with notice to the parties to access these records.
- Domestic Violence or Sexual Assault Victim-Counselor records. Confidential communications cannot be disclosed in civil actions by court order and are not discoverable without the victim's prior consent. G.L. c. 233, §§ 20J, 20K.
- Victim program locations. Locations of battered women's shelters, domestic violence, and rape crisis programs may not be disclosed by court order, or otherwise to the GAL. G.L. c. 233, §§ 20J, 20K.
- Mediator Records. Communications made during mediation with a mediator are privileged and the court cannot order disclosure. G.L. c. 233, § 23C.
- Alternative dispute resolution information. The Probation Department of the Probate and Family Court may release the information to the GAL if the court orders release of the information or the parties consent to the release of information.

2

The Health Insurance Portability and Accountability Act of 1996, Pub. L. 104-19 1 (HIPAA) requires that health providers may only release personal health information if the release signed by a party complies with the provisions of the federal law. Even if no statutory privilege applies to the information sought by the GAL, the provider or keeper of other records (e.g. unlicensed support group leaders, batterer intervention programs) may also request a written release from their client. In some instances, the order for appointment of the GAL will provide that the GAL is permitted to access certain records and information; this obviates the need for a party's authorization for release of the information.

COMMENTARY

Some third parties or providers may be unaware of protections that apply to records or confidential information relating to the parties or the children. The GAL, however, shall only review the information after appropriate releases or court orders for access to the information have been provided to the holder of the information. If a privilege is not properly waived, a judge may allow a motion to strike reference to the information from the GAL report.

4.6.2 The GAL Recognizes that Children's Rights to Confidentiality are Different than Other Parties' Rights to Confidentiality.

The GAL shall obtain authorizations for release of information pertaining to children from the children's parents or legal guardians. A parent, however, cannot waive a child's psychotherapy or social worker privilege. If the counseling information is needed but protected by a privilege, the GAL or counsel must return to the appointing judge and present a motion for appointment of another guardian ad litem to investigate whether waiver of the child's psychotherapy privilege is in the child's best interest. *Adoption of Diane*, 400 Mass. 196, 201 (1987); G.L. c. 233, § 20B. The motion should indicate the scope of the information sought and the GAL's reason for seeking the information. Counsel and pro se parties must have notice of the motion. If the court later waives the privilege, the GAL may access the information.

COMMENTARY

A parent or parents with legal custody of the child, or a party granted legal guardianship of the child, may authorize access to most other records of the child. If a parent or parents refuse to authorize release of information that is important to the investigation, the GAL may file a motion for access to the information with notice to counsel and pro se parties.

5. COMMENCEMENT OF THE INVESTIGATION

After the GAL accepts the appointment, he or she promptly schedules initial investigatory contacts with each of the parties and their attorneys if they are represented.

COMMENTARY

If a party has an attorney, the GAL should first make contact with the attorney. The GAL may find it helpful to send a letter of introduction to counsel and pro se parties outlining the investigative process. The GAL should use additional means of communication, however, if a party's primary language is not English, or there are literacy or other barriers impacting written communication. The GAL can determine more easily if a party understands what is communicated in a face-to-face interview.

5.1 The GAL Provides an Explanation of the GAL's Role and a Lamb-type Warning at the Commencement of the Investigation.

The GAL must explain the GAL's role and the purpose of the investigation to the parties. The GAL shall inform the parties how the information gathered by the GAL will be used. The GAL must provide a "Lamb warning" that explains there are no "off the record" discussions and any information collected by the GAL may appear in the GAL report, be disclosed in court or to the other party, *Commonwealth v. Lamb*, 1 Mass. App. Ct. 530 (1973), or otherwise disclosed as required or permitted by law. As appropriate based on the child's level of maturity, the GAL should provide a similar explanation of the investigative process and a Lamb warning to a child, but modified to reflect the child's age and level of understanding. If the GAL interviews other witnesses, they also must receive a Lamb warning.

COMMENTARY

To ensure a person understands the Lamb warning, the GAL should ask the person to summarize it for the GAL. The parties or witnesses should be informed that while they are encouraged to provide information, they may decline to answer a question and have an attorney present during any interview. Increasingly, parties represent themselves in court. Therefore, the GAL should avoid use of professional jargon or legalese that a party may not understand. The GAL should strive to explain things in simple language and terms as appropriate so that a party with a limited educational background or language ability can better understand what the GAL is communicating.

5.2 The GAL Inquires if the Parties have Relevant Safety Concerns.

The GAL shall inquire at the outset of the investigation about any safety risks related to the investigation for either party, the child, or others because of any party's mental illness, substance abuse, domestic violence, child abuse, or history of violence against others. The GAL should attempt to conduct the investigation in such a manner as appropriate to avoid likely harm to the child, a party, the GAL, or others.

5.3 The GAL Explains the Limits on Confidentiality and Complies with Legal and Ethical Standards Governing Disclosure of Privileged Communications.

The GAL shall obtain information or review records after appropriate authorizations for release of information are executed or the court orders release of the information. The GAL shall respect the parties' and their children's right to confidentiality. Before obtaining an authorization for release of records or other information from a party, the GAL should inform the party how the information will be used. The GAL should also disclose that any information obtained by the GAL could appear in the GAL report, be disclosed to the other party, put into evidence during court proceedings or depositions, or disclosed to others as necessary to complete the investigation, discovery, or trial of the case. The authorization for release of information form given to a party by the GAL shall include but is not limited to who the information is sought from and the duration of the authorization of the release. A party should also be informed that he or she has a right to seek legal advice before signing a release and may decline to sign an authorization for release of information. A party may direct that all release forms be sent directly to counsel of record. If a party consents to release of information, the GAL should use forms for release of information that comply with applicable laws and that are acceptable to providers. The Health Insurance Portability and Accountability Act of 1996, Pub. L. 104-19 1 (HIPAA) requires that health providers may only release personal health information if the release form complies with the provisions of the federal law.

COMMENTARY

The GAL should not seek confidential information unless it is necessary. If a party objects to release of certain information, the GAL may file a motion to obtain this information. G.L. c. 233, § 20B; G.L. c. 112, § 135B; *Commonwealth v. Bernard*, 424 Mass. 32 (1996). A parent cannot consent to release of a child's psychotherapy information. See Section 4.9.2.

6. INVESTIGATION SOURCES AND METHODS

The GAL shall conduct the investigation in a fair and balanced manner. The GAL should obtain similar types of information about each party. If the case involves more than one child, each child's best interests must be addressed unless the court orders otherwise. If the GAL is unable to report on all of the children, the GAL shall indicate why in the report.

COMMENTARY

Depending on the circumstances, the GAL may need to spend more time investigating facts that relate only to one party, especially if such facts are disputed, difficult to investigate, or new information arises about that parent. The GAL may have satisfactory information about one parent, but incomplete data about the other parent. For example, further investigation of alleged drug use might be needed if a party's drug testing results are unreliable because the facility did not monitor how samples from the party were collected, or new sources indicate that the party has used drugs since the time of the last testing.

6.1 The GAL Spends Sufficient Time Interviewing Parties and Investigating their Concerns as Necessary to Gather Relevant Information.

The GAL conducts an initial interview with each party and additional interviews with each party and other witnesses as necessary to gather relevant information. In addition, the GAL may gather information by telephone, email, and or other means.

COMMENTARY

A party is permitted to have counsel present during an interview, but the GAL controls the interview and conducts the questioning. If counsel directs a party to refuse to answer a question or plead the Fifth Amendment against self-incrimination, the GAL moves on to other questions, noting the objection. Such objections do not prohibit the GAL from using other sources to obtain the information. If the GAL does not meet with any party, the GAL explains why in the report.

6.2 The GAL Asks Each Party about Relevant Witnesses and Documents and Investigates these Sources of Information as Appropriate.

As a starting point, the GAL invites counsel and parties to provide relevant information, including a fact summary, procedural history, relevant documents, and a list of witnesses and professionals who can provide relevant information. In deciding what records to review or witnesses to interview, the GAL considers the likelihood that relevant information will be obtained, with reasonable convenience, efficiency, cost, and physical safety of a party, child or informant. The order of appointment also may direct the GAL to contact certain witnesses or sources.

COMMENTARY

In determining what witnesses to interview, the GAL may also consider: the number of witnesses suggested, whether the witness directly witnessed important events or the aftermath of important events, the potential bias of the witness, the importance of the interview to a party, and other relevant considerations. At the beginning of each collateral witness or party interview, it is important that the GAL explain the GAL's role and the limits of confidentiality. The GAL shall access information after appropriate release forms are provided to professionals. In addition to oral communications, the GAL may provide written questions and accept additional written responses from witnesses or collateral sources.

6.3 The GAL Accesses Original Sources When Possible.

To increase the reliability of reported information, the GAL investigates original sources of information.

For example: John Jones says that Jane Doe saw the parties' son drinking beer at a soccer game. The GAL speaks with Jane Doe to ascertain what she observed.

For example: a police report indicates that the child told his soccer coach that the child's parent supplied the beer. The GAL speaks with the coach and the child.

6.4 The GAL Uses Multiple Fact Sources When Possible.

If certain events or facts are disputed, the GAL should investigate more than one source of information relating to the events or allegations when possible. The parties should be encouraged to provide names of witnesses who were present, written reports, or other relevant evidence related to the event or allegation.

COMMENTARY

For example, the husband disputes the wife's claim that the husband told her that he was treated at Cambridge Hospital after he attempted suicide by taking an overdose of sleeping pills and cocaine. The GAL contacts the hospital and interviews any other witnesses with direct knowledge about the disputed event or his statements about it. Hospital records in the case lead to other relevant sources of information such as "911" call records, a police report, and an ambulance report, including a copy of a suicide note found in the ambulance. The GAL reports all the relevant facts collected about the disputed allegation.

6.5 The GAL Conducts a Home Visit When Appropriate.

Ordinarily, home visits can yield valuable information, but on occasion a home visit is not indicated. Factors to consider in deciding whether to conduct home visits include: whether issues or problems with either home are alleged, cost and time involved, location, and the likelihood of obtaining relevant information not accessible in other ways. If no home visit is conducted, the GAL shall explain why that decision was made in the report.

COMMENTARY

If home visits are conducted, care must be exercised so that inequality in housing conditions or perceived wealth do not lead to bias. A person, who is a fit parent and caretaker for the child, also may experience transitional or temporary housing difficulties as a result of separation from the other party, nonpayment of support, inadequate financial support, or relocation related to domestic violence or loss of income.

6.6 The GAL Meets with the Children.

The GAL meets with the children as part of the investigation. Children can offer useful information and should be offered the opportunity to provide information about themselves and their family. The conditions under which children are interviewed must be carefully considered, including what conditions will put the child most at ease and yield the most useful information. The GAL shall explain the reasons for not meeting with any of the children in the GAL report.

COMMENTARY

Some children may be much less candid in the interview if a parent or the parents are present during the child's interview, or are visible or able to hear the interview.

6.7. The GAL Observes Children with Each Parent When Appropriate.

The GAL should observe the child with each parent when appropriate. This often provides valuable information about the parent-child relationship.

COMMENTARY

The GAL has a duty to avoid further harm to children when possible. If concerns are raised that a child will be traumatized or at risk by contact with a parent (e.g., due to severe neglect or abuse, exposure to domestic violence, traumatic or unpredictable absence, or other inappropriate behavior) a parent-child observation may not be indicated. The GAL explains the reasons for not observing children with each parent in the report.

6.8 The GAL Considers the Need for any Further Information Necessary to Complete the GAL investigation and Provide a Comprehensive Report.

The GAL shall collect and review documents as well as conduct additional interviews of the parties, each of the children and other witnesses until the necessary information is fully gathered.

7. SCOPE AND CONTENT OF THE INVESTIGATION

A comprehensive history creates a context for understanding the current issues in dispute. The nature and extent of the family history obtained, through both interviews as well review of documents depends on the particular family's circumstances and the directives contained in the order of appointment. However, it is commonplace to obtain the:

A. History of legal proceedings and prior investigations.

- The nature of the case, including the parties and children involved, relevant procedural history, current orders, and the relief sought by each party;
- History of other cases involving the parties, including prior cases pertaining to parties or the children including, but not limited to Probate and Family Court, Juvenile Court, criminal, abuse prevention, or other relevant cases;
- Prior custody related investigations and evaluations, including GAL, Court Clinic, Probation, Department of Social Services, or other evaluations or assessments;

B. Facts designated by court order and the applicable law.

- The issues that the court specifies for investigation in the order of appointment;
- Facts relevant to the legal standard that applies to the case for:
  1. modification of custody or visitation;
  2. termination of parental rights;
  3. guardianship of a minor;
  4. removal of the child from the Commonwealth;
  5. custody or visitation by a parent.

C. Relevant concerns raised in the case by each parent, including facts related to how each parent's proposed outcome serves or conflicts with the child's best interests.

D. Parenting history.

- With whom have the children lived and for how long;
- What parenting tasks have each parent performed, when, for how long;
- The competence with which each parent carried out parenting tasks;
- History of parents' past joint decision-making regarding children;
- Parent's present ability to communicate or make joint decisions;
- Whether a third party or either party is or was a primary caretaker;
- History and impact of a parent's substance abuse, mental illness, or domestic violence on the children and the parent's parenting ability;
- History of physical, sexual or emotional abuse of the children;
- History of past restraining orders and violence against others;
- Each parent's past and present parenting skills and deficits;
- The strength and quality of the parent-child relationships, emotional closeness, attachment, and perceptions of each other;
- Each parent's or potential caretaker's knowledge of the children, knowledge of parenting techniques, disciplinary practices, ability to distinguish his or her own needs from the needs of the children, and to understand and respond to the children's needs;
- The ability of the parent to promote and support appropriate social, emotional, and educational development in the children, and to provide a stable home environment for the children;
- Each parent's or potential caretaker's ability to support the children's relationship with the other parent as appropriate;
- Each party's ability to communicate and cooperate with the other parent regarding the children as appropriate, including the impact of substance abuse, mental illness or domestic violence on that ability.

E. The family history.

- History of parents' relationship, including if and for how long the parties lived together as a family;
- Parties' accounts of how difficulties began, how they were disclosed, or if they persist;
- Prior Department of Social Services involvement with family members;
- Children's present and past school functioning;
- Criminal history of both parties (CORI (Criminal Offender Record Information) or CARI (Court Activity Record Information) ;
- Sexual offense history (Sexual Offender Registry Information, or SORI);
- Substance abuse and substance use history of family members;
- Mental health treatment and history of family members;
- Relevant medical history or problems of family members;

2

- Presence of new relationships, partners or their children;
- Relationships with significant caretakers, grandparents, relatives, child care providers;
- Each parent's relationship with family of origin and partner's family;
- Education and employment history of parents;
- If relevant, ethnic, cultural, lifestyle, and religious factors.

2

F. Developmental status and parenting needs of the children.

- Each child's developmental history, functioning in school, peer relationships, medical and mental health history, activities, schedules ;
- Special needs of each child: medical, learning or developmental problems;
- Assessment of each child's adjustment to school, friends, community, and extended families;
- Child's temperament and response to transitions;
- Impact of change on child's routines, attachments, familiar environs;
- Child's exposure to, understanding of or concerns about a parent's needs, wishes, concerns, safety, or problems;
- Quality of relationship between siblings;
- Particular challenges for either parent or the child with each other.

8. REPORT WRITING

The report should address and relate to the areas of investigation designated by the order of appointment. The report should provide accurate, detailed and balanced information about the parties and their children.

8.1 The Report Should Appear Professional in Appearance, Format and Writing Style.

The report should be typed, well-written and neat in appearance. Pages must be numbered. The GAL shall attempt to avoid spelling, grammar or typographical errors in the report. The GAL should write the report in a way that is concise in words, yet able to encompass all the relevant facts and provide detailed information. The language used in the report should be understandable to the average layperson and avoid jargon that may be confusing. The GAL should prepare a report that is well-organized. Use of headings, bold type, or underlining to separate sections or topics in the report may make a report easier to comprehend. The report shall be dated and signed by the GAL with the GAL's name typed below the signature. The report shall include the GAL's mailing or office address and telephone number.

8.2 The Report Should be Accurate, Objective and Unbiased.

When writing the report, the GAL provides a balanced view of the parties that includes all of their relevant strengths and weaknesses. The information contained in the report should be accurate. It also should be as factual and detailed as possible. The GAL report should:

A. Use descriptive statements rather than evaluative statements.

Evaluative statement: "Michael is a cruel and aggressive boy."

Descriptive statements: "In his interview, Michael said he punches his younger brother, Joseph, almost every day. Michael's father reports that he had to interfere three times last week when Michael hit the family dog with a hockey stick."

B. Provide ample details, but avoid inflammatory characterizations if possible.

Derogatory statement: "Mr. Jones is well-known to the courts as a drunk." Descriptive statement: "Mr. Jones was convicted in Somerville District Court of driving under the influence of alcohol in 1986, 1996, 2001, and in July, 2003."

C. Provide past and present relevant facts relating to both parties and the children.

1. Include all relevant facts that address the court's directives.
2. Include all relevant facts collected from all sources, including facts that are consistent and inconsistent with other reported facts.
3. Provide balanced and similar information about both parties;
4. Provide relevant and detailed information about all of the children.
5. Include facts that do not support the GAL's recommendations or conclusions.
6. Disclose what important information may be missing and why it missing.

D. Include specific information and provide dates and pinpoint time frames if at all possible.

Avoid use of vague phrases or time frames such as "in the past" or "occasionally" or "sometimes" if a more precise time frame is available. The GAL should provide detailed information.

Vague: "John says he used heroin in the past." Specific: "John says he used heroin in May, 1996 and June, 1998."

Vague: "Mary states that John occasionally uses drugs."

Specific: "Mary states that she saw John use cocaine twice in August, 1998."

Vague: "The child has health problems."

Specific: "The child has diabetes."

8.3 The GAL Identifies the Sources of Information.

Sources should be easily identified in the report. The GAL must list every person interviewed and the records reviewed with any relevant information about the informant or source.

- Date and Name of each person interviewed (e.g. Dr. Tom Jones on 9/5/03),
- Position, profession, place of employment (psychiatrist, General Hospital);
- Description of record reviewed (Dr. Jones' records regarding mother);
- Date the record was made and period it encompasses (July, 2002 to July, 2003);
- How information was obtained (e.g. in person, telephone call, written request);
- Date records were reviewed or obtained by the GAL (9/5/03);
- Informant or record author's relationship to the parties, child or family

(Dr. Jones is mother's psychiatrist, but also saw her and the husband for marriage counseling in May, 2001).

If a source is not clearly identified, a party can move to strike the statement from the report.

Example of improper attribution: "Hospital staff said that Drew Smith was hospitalized there for three months last year." (Names of the staff and hospital are missing).

Use of hearsay statements is permitted in the report, but the GAL should always attempt to contact and also quote the original source in the report if possible.

8.4 If a Party Fails or Refuses to Participate, the GAL Includes the Information that the GAL has Obtained in the Report.

The GAL encourages parties to participate in the investigation. If a party does not participate, the GAL is still permitted to file a report and to disclose whatever information has been collected about that party from other sources. The report should disclose that such a party has not participated or declined to provide information.

COMMENTARY

The GAL shall refrain from drawing conclusions about a party without a factual basis.

8.5 Facts Shall be Separated in the Report from Recommendations or Conclusions.

Only facts should be contained in the body of the investigation. The investigator's inferences, conclusions or recommendations based on the facts shall be confined to separate summary or recommendations sections of the report. Such material is then easier to redact if it is later excluded from evidence at trial and stricken from the report.

COMMENTARY

The GAL's conclusions or recommendations should be consistent with the information that is collected; the GAL shall set forth the connection between the facts and the conclusions or recommendations. The trial judge is the ultimate fact finder. Thus, the GAL's conclusions as to whether a party has met his or her burden of proof should be avoided.

8.6 The GAL Files a Timely Report and Informs Counsel and Pro Se Parties.

The GAL should inform counsel and pro se parties when the report is filed at the court so that the parties can read the report. The GAL should inform parties requesting a copy of the report that the report is property of the court; it cannot be given out or shown to anyone, except the parties or their counsel. A court order may be required for any distribution of the report, even to parties or their counsel. The GAL shall not distribute copies of the report to the parties, counsel of record or anyone else unless the court orders that the GAL may release copies to such individuals.

COMMENTARY

If information or recommendations in the GAL report have the potential of exposing a party or the child to danger, the GAL should consider advising the endangered parent or party about the date that he or she expects to file the report in court.

8.7 The GAL Shall Retain Any Materials Gathered or Created During the Investigation

The GAL shall retain any notes, records, documents, taped recordings, videos, or other material gathered or created during the investigation so that these materials are available for trial, discovery, appeal and remand of the case.

COMMENTARY

Notes or other materials created or obtained by a GAL may be sought by a party through discovery. The GAL's notes, written observations, or other materials created during interviews or telephone conversations should be descriptive, factual, and respectful in tone. Note taking should be objective and include quotations of witnesses and parties when possible.

Standing Order 1-06. Case Management and Time Standards for Cases Filed in the Probate and Family Court Department

[Effective Apr. 3, 2006. Replaced Standing Order 1-04.]

PREAMBLE

The fair and efficient administration of justice requires that all cases and actions before the Probate and Family Court receive timely attention and action from the court. This requires that the judicial system dispose of cases as expeditiously as is consistent with care, fairness and cases before the court. These time standards are intended to provide the Probate and Family sound decisions. It is the responsibility of the court to manage the process and disposition of the Court with recognized goals for the timely disposition of cases.

These time standards represent aspirational goals to measure the movement of cases in the Probate and Family Court. Each case is unique and the Judges must, consistent with the rules of court and statutes, exercise sound judgment in such a manner as to provide the parties with a fair opportunity to be heard and to allow the court to achieve a reasoned disposition. Those individuals who appear before our courts have distinct needs that must be addressed on an individual basis, case by case.

These time standards preserve discretion for judges to schedule individual cases according to the particular needs of the individuals involved. These time standards recognize that there are many factors that determine the flow of cases in the Probate and Family Court which are not within the control of the court. These standards also recognize that the cases heard in the Probate and Family Court require consideration of the individual needs of the families who come before the court.

Accordingly:

1. GENERAL PROVISIONS

This Standing Order applies to all actions filed in the Probate and Family Court.

This Standing Order applies to all Divisions of the Probate and Family Court.

The timing for the completion of the case, from filing to trial, settlement, or dismissal, shall be calculated from the date of filing the petition or complaint.

At time of filing, all cases shall be assigned to a caseflow track according to the type of case. Most cases shall be assigned to one of the following tracks; 3–6 months to trial, 8 months to trial, or 14 months to trial.

2. TRACK ASSIGNMENT AND CASE MANAGEMENT

a. Track Assignment

At filing each case is assigned to a track.

The Plaintiff/Petitioner shall be provided with a Track Assignment Notice except as set forth below. The Plaintiff/Petitioner shall serve the Track Assignment Notice upon the Defendant/Respondent along with the summons or notice (citation). No service of the Track Assignment Notice will be required in cases where service is by publication.

No Track Assignment Notice shall be issued for cases in the 3–6 month track: Probate of Will, Administration, Accounts, Real Estate Sales, and Change of Name. No Track Assignment Notice shall be issued for cases described in sections 10 through 17 of this Standing Order. No Track Assignment Notice shall be issued at the time of filing for any case filed by the Department of Revenue, Child Support Enforcement Division.

The goals for completion of all cases filed in the Probate and Family Court are outlined in the chart in section 7(a) and in sections 10 through 17 of this Standing Order. A Judge, at any time, may change the track designation for a case and issue a new Track Assignment Notice.

b. Next Event Scheduling

At the conclusion of every court event, until a judgment has issued or the complaint has been dismissed, or until a permanent decree has issued or the petition has been dismissed, the Court shall schedule the next court event for the case.

Once a motion hearing, conference, or any other court event has been scheduled and placed on a court list, whether at the request of a party, a party's lawyer, the Register, or the Court, it can be removed from the list or continued only if a next court event is scheduled.

c. Case Management Conferences: Generally

Case Management Conferences will be scheduled by the court for the case types set forth in sections 2(d),(e), and (f) below, when a return of service, answer, objection, or counterclaim is filed and there is no future court event scheduled for the case.

In scheduling a case management conference, the Register shall issue a Case Management Conference Notice and Order in the format specified by the Chief Justice of the Probate and Family Court.

The purpose of the Case Management Conference is to establish the Court's control of the progress of the case, to provide early intervention by the Court, to offer Alternative Dispute Resolution processes, to establish discovery limitations and deadlines, to discuss settlement progress and opportunities for settlement, and to assign a date for the pre-trial conference, if needed.

d. Case Management Conference: Equity, Petition to Partition, and Domestic Relations, including Paternity (except Joint Petitions for Divorce, Joint Petitions for Modification and Complaint for Divorce filed under G.L. c. 208, § 1B).

Upon the filing of the return of service, answer, objection, or counterclaim, the Register shall review the case to determine if a future court event has been scheduled in the case. If no future court event has been scheduled, the Register shall schedule a Case Management Conference on the next available date, but no sooner than thirty (30) days from the filing of the return of service, answer, objection, or counterclaim. The Register shall send the Case Management Conference Notice and Order to all parties.

e. Case Management Conference: 1B Divorce, Guardianship and Conservatorship

All G.L. c. 208, § 1B Divorce Cases

The Register shall review the case one hundred twenty (120) days after the case is filed. If no return of service has been filed, and no answer, appearance, motion, or other paper has been filed by a defendant, the Register shall mail to the plaintiff a written notice of dismissal in accordance with section 3 of this Standing Order. If the return of service or an answer, objection, or counterclaim has been filed, but no future court event has been scheduled, a Case Management Conference shall be scheduled on the next available date, but no sooner than thirty (30) days from the filing of the return of service. The Register shall send the Case Management Conference Notice and Order to all parties.

Guardianship and Conservatorship Cases

The Register shall review the case one hundred twenty (120) days after the case is filed. If no future court event has been scheduled, the Register shall schedule a Case Management Conference on the next available date. The Register shall send the Case Management Conference Notice and Order to all parties. All temporary guardianships shall include an expiration date and a further hearing date. All guardianships with approval and authorization of an antipsychotic medication treatment plan shall include an expiration date and a review date, which may be the same date. All guardianships with authority to approve other extraordinary medical treatment shall include an expiration date for the authority.

f. Case Management Conference for Certain Probate Matters

A Track Assignment Notice shall not be issued at the time of filing for the cases assigned to the 3–6 Month Track: Probate of Will, Administration, Accounts, Real Estate Sales, and Change of Name. If a timely appearance in opposition or objection is filed in a case initially assigned to the 3-6 Month Track, the Register shall reassign the case to the 8 Month Track and issue to all parties a Track Assignment Notice. The Register shall also issue a Pre-Trial Notice and Order in the form specified by the Chief Justice of the Probate and Family Court with an established date for a Pre-Trial Conference unless another future court event has been scheduled. The date for the Pre-Trial Conference shall be after the return date, but no more than forty-five (45) days after the return date.

g. Case Management Conference conducted at Motion Hearing

If a motion, or other hearing, is scheduled and held prior to the date of the Case Management Conference, the Judge may conduct a Case Management Conference in connection with the motion hearing, even if there has been no notice of a Case Management Conference for that day, and may cancel any previously scheduled Case Management Conference, making sure to schedule a next event in the order on the motion or the order after Case Management Conference.

Motions shall not be heard at a scheduled Case Management Conference without prior approval of the Court. As a general rule, the discovery schedule and deadline and a Pre-Trial Conference date should be assigned the first time the case is before a Judge with both parties or counsel present.

h. Joint Stipulation on Case Management Conference

Counsel and pro se parties may, at any time after a complaint is filed, file a Joint Stipulation signed by counsel for each represented party and by each pro se party which, at a minimum, requests a pre-trial conference date and agrees to a specific date to be the discovery deadline for that case. The discovery deadline date shall be not more than 180 days after the date of filing of the complaint.

Counsel and pro se parties may, after receiving notice that a Case Management Conference has been scheduled, file, on or before the date of the Case Management Conference, a Joint Stipulation signed by counsel for each represented party and by each pro se party which, at a minimum, requests a pre-trial conference date and agrees to a specific date to be the discovery deadline for that case. The discovery deadline date shall be not more than 120 days after the date of filing of the Joint Stipulation. If the Joint Stipulation is filed prior to the time scheduled for the Case Management Conference, no one need appear for the Case Management Conference.

Upon the filing of such a Joint Stipulation, the Register shall schedule a pre-trial conference for the next available date not sooner than 14 days after the discovery deadline and issue a Pre-Trial Notice and Order in the form specified by the Chief Justice of the Probate and Family Court. The scheduled pre-trial conference is a "future court event" so that a Case Management Conference will not be automatically scheduled upon the 120 day review or upon the filing of a return of service, answer, objection or counterclaim.

i. Joint Requests to Continue Case Management Conference

Parties engaged in alternative dispute resolution may request an extension of a scheduled Case Management Conference date by filing a joint or assented to motion which attests that the parties are engaged in alternative dispute resolution and includes:

- the name of the alternative dispute resolution provider;
- the dates and number of sessions held and;
- the dates and number of future sessions scheduled.

All other joint requests to continue shall be by written motion stating detailed and specific reasons for the request. All motions shall include proposed dates for the rescheduling of the Case Management Conference. Joint or assented to motions shall be considered without an in person hearing, unless otherwise ordered by the Court. If the motion is allowed, the court shall reschedule the Case Management Conference and send notice to all parties.

j. Citations in Probate, Guardianship, Child Welfare, and Adoption Petitions

Unless all required assents are filed with a probate petition, including guardianship petitions, custody petitions under G.L. c. 119, and adoption petitions, the Register shall issue a citation no later than three (3) court days after the date of filing.

k. General Provisions

Nothing in this Standing Order precludes the marking of an earlier hearing date for a motion or other case event when appropriate. The Court may schedule conferences, including Case Management, Pre-Trial and Status Conferences, as well as Trials, in its discretion.

Any party to any matter filed in the Probate and Family Court may request a Case Management Conference or Pre-Trial Conference after service of the complaint or petition, with notice to the other side of such request.

When a Case Management Conference is held, the conference will include discussion of all actions pending between the named parties. Other pending actions shall be scheduled for a future court event or shall be dismissed.

3. DISMISSAL FOR LACK OF SERVICE

The Register shall review all Domestic Relations and Equity cases 120 days after filing of the complaint to determine whether a return of service has been filed. If a return of service has not been filed, and no future court event has been scheduled, the Register shall issue a notice in a format specified by the Chief Justice of the Probate and Family Court. The notice shall inform the plaintiff that, because no return of service has been filed to show that service was made within 90 days of filing as required by Mass. R. Civ. P./Mass. R. Dom. Rel. P. 4 (j), the case will be dismissed 21 days after the date of the notice unless the plaintiff files the return of service showing that service was made within ninety (90) days after the filing of the complaint or unless within those twenty-one (21)days, the plaintiff files and has scheduled a motion for extension of time which shows good cause why service was not made within ninety (90) days after the filing of the complaint.

4. CONDUCT OF CASE MANAGEMENT CONFERENCE

a. Counsel and/or Parties Encouraged to Confer.

Prior to the Case Management Conference, counsel and/or parties are encouraged to confer for the purpose of agreeing on a proposed schedule of deadlines and dates through trial.

If a domestic violence restraining order (G.L. c. 209A) or a domestic violence protective order (G.L. c. 208) has been issued for one party against the other, then the parties are not expected to confer. The Case Management Conference shall still be held.

b. At a Case Management Conference the Court may:

(1) explore the possibility of settlement including but not limited to exploring the use of Alternate Dispute Resolution (ADR) processes;

(2) identify or formulate (or order attorneys or parties to formulate) the principal issues and disputes;

(3) prepare (or order attorneys or parties to prepare) a discovery schedule including discovery parameters and deadlines;

(4) establish deadlines for filing motions, including but not limited to motions for summary judgment and a time frame for their disposition;

(5) explore any other matters that the court determines appropriate for the fair and efficient management of the litigation;

(6) hear the case on an uncontested basis if settlement has been achieved, or if no appearance or answer is filed after service and return of service and there is no opposition; or

(7) dismiss the case if no parties are present for the Case Management Conference or if the plaintiff or petitioner is not present.

c. Next Event Scheduling

At the Case Management Conference, the next court date shall be assigned unless a judgment or permanent decree is issued or the case is dismissed.

d. Requirement to Appear

Counsel and parties, or parties alone if not represented by counsel, shall be required to appear at the Case Management Conference, except as provided in section 2(h) above. The Court, in its discretion, may waive the requirement for the appearance of the parties if they are represented by counsel. The Court may conduct Case Management Conferences by telephone, in its discretion.

e. Sanctions for Failure to Appear.

The court may impose sanctions for failure to attend the Case Management Conference without good cause, including dismissal, or may hear the case as if it were uncontested.

5. ALTERNATE DISPUTE RESOLUTION SERVICES

When appropriate, cases may be referred to:

a. Probation Officers for dispute intervention services in contested matters at any court event; or

b. Other approved providers of court connected dispute resolution services as defined in S.J.C. Rule 1:18, Uniform Rules on Dispute Resolution.

6. CHANGES TO TRACK ASSIGNMENT AND RESCHEDULING OF SCHEDULED EVENTS

a. A party may file and serve a motion requesting a change in track assignment or rescheduling of scheduled events. Changes in track assignment or rescheduling of scheduled events shall be allowed only at the discretion of the Judge. A Probation Officer, in connection with an investigation, may file and serve on all parties a motion requesting a change in track assignment or rescheduling of scheduled events.

b. Motions to continue a trial may be allowed, only for good cause shown, with notice and hearing, in accordance with Mass. R. Dom. Rel. P. 40(b) and Mass. R. Civ. P. 40(b).

c. All requests for rescheduling shall include proposed future dates. No action shall be "continued generally." Any rescheduling shall be to a date and event certain.

d. In cases involving allegations or a history of domestic violence, or a prior or current abuse prevention order, the Judge shall take into account the safety of alleged victims and victims and the reduction of conflict when considering any requests for changes in track assignment or rescheduling of scheduled events.

7. ASSIGNMENT TO TRACKS:

a. At filing, all Probate, Equity, Domestic Relations (including Paternity) cases (except Joint Petitions for Divorce, Joint Petitions for Modification of Child Support, and Complaints for Contempt, which shall be heard as outlined in sections 10 through 12) shall be assigned to a track according to the chart below:

3–6 Month Track[1]

Probate of Wills and Administration of Estates
Accounts
All Other "Probate" except Guardianships and Conservatorships
Real Estate Sales
Change of Name

[1] As described in section 2(f) above, if a case assigned to this track becomes contested due to the filing of an appearance and, if required, objections, the Register shall change the track designation to an 8 month track.

8 Month Track

Complaint to Establish Paternity
Complaint for Custody, Visitation, and Support (Paternity)
Complaint for Modification (except Joint Petition for Modification of Child Support)
Probate-Guardianships
Conservatorships
Complaint for Separate Support
Other Paternity Case Types

14 Month Track

Complaint for Divorce
Complaints in Equity
Petitions to Partition
Other "Divorce" Case Types (except Joint Petition for Divorce)

b. G.L. c. 209A Complaints and G.L. c. 19A Petitions for Protection from Abuse, cases concerning the custody of children under G.L. c. 119, § 23A, G.L. c. 119, § 23C, and G.L. c. 210, § 3, and Adoptions shall be heard as outlined below in sections 13 through 17.

c. Assignment to a track indicates the maximum amount of time in which a case should be tried, settled, or dismissed. Most cases should be tried, settled, or dismissed before the maximum time period of the track.

d. There may be extraordinary cases which cannot be disposed of within the time frames set forth in their track designations.

e. The Register shall issue a Track Assignment Notice for each case in the 8 month and 14 month tracks, except as outlined in section 2 (a) of this Standing Order, in a format specified by the Chief Justice of the Probate and Family Court. The Track Assignment Notice shall reflect the time requirements for each track.

8. CONDUCT OF PRE-TRIAL CONFERENCES

a. The Pre-Trial Conference shall be conducted in accordance with Rule 16 of the Massachusetts Rules of Domestic Relations Procedure or the Massachusetts Rules of Civil Procedure.

b. In scheduling a Pre-Trial Conference the court shall issue a Pre-Trial Notice and Order in a format specified by the Chief Justice of the Probate and Family Court.

c. If a case is not resolved at the Pre-Trial Conference, an Order After Pre-Trial Conference shall be issued which shall include provisions specified by the Chief Justice of the Probate and Family Court, and may also include additional provisions at the discretion of the Judge conducting the Pre-Trial Conference.

9. SEQUENTIAL TRIAL DAYS

When trial dates are originally assigned, they shall be scheduled on days as close to sequential trial days as the calendar of the trial Judge permits. When trials are not completed in the number of days originally scheduled, the Court shall schedule the remaining trial days as soon as possible using the earliest available trial days, with the goal of minimizing intervals between trial days.

10. TRACK FOR COMPLAINTS FOR CONTEMPT

At time of filing, a summons shall issue with the date for the contempt hearing. The hearing date shall be set for no later than twenty-eight (28) days from the date of filing.

11. JOINT PETITIONS FOR DIVORCE UNDER G.L. c. 208, § 1A

All Joint Petitions for Divorce shall be scheduled for hearing within thirty (30) days of filing of all required documents.[2]

[2] If a case is ready for hearing at time of filing, a hearing shall be scheduled within 30 days. If a case is uncontested at time of filing, but incomplete, the case shall be scheduled for hearing within thirty (30) days of the date of filing all required documents.

12. JOINT PETITION FOR MODIFICATION OF CHILD SUPPORT

Pursuant to Probate and Family Court Supplemental Rule 412 and Protocol, these cases shall be decided on the pleadings without hearing, within fourteen (14) days of filing, unless otherwise ordered by the Court. If a hearing is ordered by the Court, the Court shall set the time and date for the hearing and shall notify the parties within fourteen (14) days of the filing of the joint petition.

13. G.L. c. 209A COMPLAINT FOR PROTEC-TION FROM ABUSE

All proceedings pursuant to G.L. c. 209A shall be processed in accordance with the existing statutory time requirements and each order shall specifically state the next hearing date and expiration date of the order, unless the order is permanent. If the order is permanent, it shall so specify.

14. COMPLAINTS FOR PROTECTION FROM ELDER AND DISABLED ABUSE, G.L. c. 19A, § 20, G.L. c. 19C, § 7

An initial hearing shall be held within fourteen (14) days of the filing of a petition. Emergency hearings may be held with at least twenty-four (24) hours notice to the elderly or disabled person. The court may dispense with notice upon finding that immediate and foreseeable physical harm to the individual or others will result from the twenty-four (24) hour delay and that reasonable attempts have been made to give notice.

15. TRACK FOR PETITIONS FILED PURSUANT TO G.L. c. 210, § 3 AND PETITIONS FILED PURSUANT TO G.L. c. 119, § 23C

a. If the Petition is uncontested, due to the assent of all parties or completion of proper notice, with appearance in opposition filed, the Register shall, within fourteen (14) days of the return date, notify the petitioners that the case is uncontested, and schedule an uncontested hearing within 30 days of the return date. For cases filed under G.L. c. 210, § 3, an adoption plan shall be filed, in accordance with Uniform Probate Court Practice X prior to the hearing date.

b. If, by virtue of an appearance the case is contested, the Register shall issue a Track Assignment and Scheduling Notice for a Case Management Conference to be held not more than thirty (30) days after the return date.

c. At the Case Management Conference, referral to Permanency Mediation shall be considered and a Pre-Trial Conference shall be scheduled for a date within seventy-five (75) days of the Case Management Conference. At the Pre-Trial Conference, a trial date shall be set for no later than one hundred twenty (120) days from the date of the Pre-Trial Conference.

d. If a sua sponte or ex parte custody order under G.L. c. 119, § 23C is issued, the Court shall schedule a hearing within 72 hours of the sua sponte or ex parte custody order, unless a prior evidentiary hearing has been held. Notice shall be given to all parties and counsel.

16. TRACK FOR ADOPTION PETITIONS

a. If a Petition is filed as uncontested, due to the filing of necessary surrenders or termination decrees, and notice is not required, a hearing shall be scheduled within thirty (30) days of the filing of the Petition.[3]

[3] If a case is ready for hearing at time of filing, a hearing shall 3 be scheduled within 30 days. If a case is uncontested at time of filing, but incomplete, the case shall be scheduled for hearing within thirty (30) days of the date of filing all required documents.

b. If a timely appearance is filed, a Case Management Conference shall be scheduled for not more than thirty (30) days after the return date.

c. At the Case Management Conference, a Pre-Trial Conference shall be scheduled for a date within seventy-five (75) days of the Case Management Conference. At the Pre-Trial Conference, a trial date shall be set for no later than one hundred twenty (120) days from the date of the Pre-Trial Conference.

17. PETITIONS FILED PURSUANT TO G.L. c. 119, § 23(A), VOLUNTARY PLACEMENT WITH DEPART MENT OF SOCIAL SERVICES

At time of filing, all petitions filed pursuant to G.L. c. 119, § 23(A) shall be scheduled for hearing within thirty (30) days.

18. ISSUANCE OF TEMPORARY ORDERS

Temporary orders shall be issued as expeditiously as possible, but in no event more than fourteen (14) days from the conclusion of the hearing, or the receipt by the court of all written submissions. On motions for summary judgment, orders shall be issued within thirty (30) days of the conclusion of the hearing, or the receipt by the court of all written submissions.

19. ISSUANCE OF JUDGMENT OR DECREE

Except as otherwise indicated in this Standing Order, or with notice to the Chief Justice of the Probate and Family Court, and counsel or parties, the judgment or decree shall be issued as follows:

Trial Time	Entry of Judgment or Decree
One day or less	Within 30 days of the conclusion of the trial
Two days	Within 60 days of the conclusion of the trial
Three to Seven days	Within 90 days of the conclusion of the trial
Exceeds Seven days	Within 120 days of the conclusion of the trial

Standing Order 1-08. Standards for Guardians ad Litem/ Evaluators

[Effective Jan. 14, 2008.]

1. The Standards for Category E, Guardians ad Litem/ Evaluators in actions involving:

Domestic Relations or Custody/Visitation/Adoption G.L. c. 215, § 56A; c. 208, § 16, (hereinafter "Standards") are effective January 14, 2008.

2. The purpose of these Standards is to:

- provide accountability related to guardian ad litem/evaluations;
- improve custody, visitation, and other outcomes for children;
- promote uniformity and consistency in guardian ad litem/ evaluations; and
- promote respect for the rights of parties and their children, including their safety.

3. It is ordered that all guardians ad litem/evaluators appointed pursuant to G.L. c. 215, § 56A, c. 208, § 16 utilize the Standards in conducting these evaluations. Guardians ad litem/evaluators who are certified by the Probate and Family Court Administrative Office to

receive appointments under Supreme Judicial Court Rule 1:07, and those persons not on the list who are appointed in accordance with Section (4) of Rule 1:07, are governed by this Order and shall conduct their evaluations in accordance with the Standards.

Standing Order 2-08. Impoundment of Guardian ad Litem Reports

[Effective Mar. 10, 2008.]

Unless otherwise ordered by the court, all guardian ad litem reports except those filed in cases involving accounts, licenses to sell and estate plans are impounded. As used herein, "impounded" shall mean the act of keeping the guardian ad litem report separate and unavailable for public inspection. The reports shall be kept in the Registry of Probate unless otherwise determined by the First Justice. The following procedure will be followed:

1. Upon filing with the court, guardian ad litem reports shall be kept separate from the case file and unavailable for public inspection. Access to inspect the impounded reports shall be limited to the court, the attorney(s) of record, if any, and the party(ies), unless otherwise ordered by the court. Where appropriate, the court may instruct the guardian ad litem to send a copy of a report to the attorney(s) of record or the parties.

2. Unless otherwise ordered by the court, the attorney(s) of record, if both parties are represented by counsel, shall be entitled to receive a copy of a report. If a party wishes to obtain a copy of the report, the party or their attorney must file a Motion with the Court. If a party is unrepresented by counsel and wishes to obtain a copy of the report, they must file a Motion with the Court. The attorney(s) of record or the party(ies) who are authorized to have a copy of the guardian ad litem report:

a. Shall make no further copies of the report for use outside of counsel's office except as provided below;

b. Shall not show the report to any person except, to his or her client or, to an expert engaged or consulted regarding the case;

c. Shall, in the case of an attorney, return the copy of the report to the court upon withdrawal or conclusion of the case, and in the case of a party, return the copy of the report to the court at the conclusion of the case,

d. Shall comply with such conditions as the Trial Judge may impose.

e. May provide a copy to an expert engaged or consulted on the case, provided the expert certifies in writing that he or she will be bound by this Standing Order, and;

f. Shall not provide a copy to his or her client except upon the allowance of a motion.

3. In accordance with Trial Court Rule IX, Rule 2, Uniform Rules on Subpoenas to Court Officials, the Register shall not provide a copy of an impounded guardian ad litem report to a person who is not a party to the case.

4. Relief from impoundment may be sought by Motion supported by affidavit, and may be granted after notice by the court only upon written findings.

5. Service of the Motion for Relief from Impoundment and affidavit shall be made on all parties in accordance with Rule 5 of the Massachusetts Rules of Domestic Relations Procedure. The time periods for hearing shall be as set forth in Rule 6 of the Massachusetts Rules of Domestic Relations Procedure.

6. The attorney(s) of record, if any, or the party(ies) if unrepresented by counsel, shall receive a copy of this Standing Order when they are notified in writing by the Court in accordance with Standing Order 2-98 that a report has been filed and is available for inspection.

Standing Order 3-08. Impoundment of Qualified Domestic Relations Orders, Domestic Relations Orders and Orders Commonly Known as *Mangiacotti* Orders

[Effective Mar. 10, 2008.]

Unless otherwise ordered by the court, all qualified domestic relations orders, domestic relations orders and orders issued pursuant to *Contributory Retirement Board of Arlington v. Mangiacotti*, 406 Mass. 184, (1989) are impounded. As used herein, "impounded" shall mean the act of keeping the orders separate and unavailable for public inspection. The following procedure will be followed:

1. Upon filing with the court, the orders shall be kept separate from the case file and unavailable for public inspection. Access to inspect the impounded orders is limited to the court, the attorney(s) of record, if any, and the party(ies), unless otherwise ordered by the court.

2. In accordance with Trial Court Rule IX, Rule 2, Uniform Rules on Subpoenas to Court Officials, the Register shall not provide a copy of the impounded orders to a person who is not a party to the case.

3. Relief from impoundment may be sought by Motion supported by affidavit, and may be granted after notice by the court only upon written findings.

4. Service of the Motion for Relief from Impoundment and affidavit shall be made on all parties in accordance with Rule 5 of the Massachusetts Rules of Domestic Relations Procedure. The time periods for hearing shall be as set forth in Rule 6 of the Massachusetts Rules of Domestic Relations Procedure.

Standing Order 1-09. Impoundment of Personal Medical Information

[Effective July 1, 2009.]

IT IS HEREBY ORDERED THAT:

1. Whenever a Medical Certificate or Clinical Team Report is required to be filed under Article V of G.L. c. 190B, it must be in possession of the Court or accompany the petition or motion. The Medical Certificate must be dated and an examination must have taken place within 30 days of the filing of the petition or motion or, in the case of a person alleged to be mentally retarded, the Clinical Team Report must be dated and an examination must have taken place within 180 days of the filing of the petition or motion.

2. The Court may waive or postpone the requirement of filing of a Medical Certificate or Clinical Team Report. Such a statement of impossibility shall be supported by an affidavit or affidavits meeting the requirements set forth in Massachusetts Rules of Civil Procedure 4.1(h).

3. All Medical Certificates, Clinical Team Reports, treatment plans and medical affidavits shall be impounded and kept separate from other papers in the case and shall not be available for public inspection. These documents shall be available for inspection to authorized Court personnel, the Respondent, the attorneys who have filed an appearance in the case, all persons named in the petition who make a written request, and any Guardian ad litem appointed in the case. They may not be copied without further order of the Court, but Registry staff may scan them into an impounded computer file.

4. Authorized Court personnel, parties, attorneys, and Guardians ad litem with access to a Medical Certificate, Clinical Team Report, treatment plan or medical affidavit are prohibited from using or disclosing the information on the form for any purpose other than the Guardianship or Conservatorship case for which it was filed.

Standing Order 2-09. Application of G.L. c. 190B, Article V to Guardianship and/or Conservatorship Cases Pending on July 1, 2009 or with a Decree Issued Thereto

[Effective July 1, 2009.]

On July 1, 2009, certain provisions of the Massachusetts Uniform Probate Code, G.L. c. 190B ("the Code"), become effective. The provisions are primarily contained in Article V of the Code, Protection of Persons under Disability and Their Property. The

2

Code significantly reforms the practice of Guardianship and Conservatorship law.

The Probate and family Court interprets the Massachusetts Uniform Probate Code to apply to any Guardianship and Conservatorship case:

(a) pending on July 1, 2009 without a permanent decree having entered;

(b) where a permanent decree has previously entered and the Guardianship or conservatorship has not terminated; or

(c) commenced on or after July 1, 2009.

Accordingly:

1. PENDING CASES WITH NO PERMANENT DECREE

Any Petition for Guardianship of the person and/or estate or Conservatorship filed prior to and pending as of July 1, 2009 generally does not need to be amended. If the petitioner seeks authority to admit the alleged incapacitated person to a nursing facility and such authorization was not explicitly requested on the petition, the petition must be amended to include a request for such authorization and a new citation must issue.

Any citation issued before July 1, 2009 shall be accepted by the Court after July 1, 2009 as sufficient even if the return date is after July 1, 2009. Any citation issued after July 1, 2009 must be served in accordance with the notice requirements of the applicable MUPC sections.

Any petition for Guardianship of the person and/or estate or Conservatorship filed prior to and pending as of July 1, 2009 must be accompanied by the new Medical Certificate or Clinical Team Report form.

Any petition requesting the appointment of a Guardian of the estate pending as of July 1, 2009 shall be treated as a Petition for the Appointment of a Conservator. At the time of allowance, an Order and Decree of Appointment of Conservator shall be issued (in addition to an Order and Decree of Appointment of Guardian if appointment of a Guardian was requested) and docketed in a Conservator file. The Conservator case file shall include a copy of the Petition for Guardianship docket sheet up to the time of appointment. There shall be no fee charged when a new Conservator case initiation is required. Thereafter, the Conservator shall file any and all required Financial Plan, Inventory and Accounts with the Conservator file.

2. CASES WHERE A GUARDIAN OF THE PERSON AND/OR ESTATE OR A CONSERVATOR WAS APPOINTED PRIOR TO JULY 1, 2009

a. Issuance of Letters of Appointment.

When any party seeks a certified copy of the Decree appointing the Guardian of the person, a Letter of Appointment of Guardian shall be issued in accordance with the prior Decree and the Code.

When any party seeks a certified copy of the Decree appointing the Guardian of the estate or the Conservator, a Letter of Appointment of Conservator shall be issued indicating all powers vested in the Conservator in accordance with the prior Decree and the Code and a new Conservator filed opened.

The Letter of Conservatorship shall be placed in the new case file. The new case file shall include a copy of the Petition for Guardianship docket sheet up to the time of the issuance of the Letter of Conservatorship. There shall be no fee charged if a new Conservator case initiation is required.

b. Reporting Requirements

Guardians of Incapacitated Persons are required to file a Care Plan/Report within 60 days following their appointment. All Guardians of Incapacitated Persons and Guardians of Wards, regardless of the date of appointment, must file a Report annually thereafter. G.L. c. 190B, § 5-309(b). Whenever any Guardian of the person is before the Court, the Court shall insure the timely filing and review of any and all Care Plans/Reports. If Care Plans/Reports have not been filed, the Court shall order the filing of a Care Plan/Report.

A Conservator may be required to file a Conservator Financial Plan for managing, expending and distributing the assets of the estate. G.L. c. 190B, § 5-416(c). Whenever any Guardian of the estate or Conservator is before the Court, the Court may order the filing of a Conservator Financial Plan.

c. Accounting Requirements

Any Guardian of the estate or Conservator is subject to the accounting requirements of G.L. c. 190B, § 5-418 of the Code. Whenever any Guardian of the estate or Conservator is before the Court, the Court shall insure the timely filing and review of any and all required Inventory and Accounts.

d. Nursing Facility Admissions

Any nursing facility admission made by a Guardian before July 1, 2009 shall continue to be considered a valid admission after July 1, 2009 without the need for further Court authorization. If the incapacitated person is temporarily hospitalized, the Guardian may readmit the incapacitated person to the nursing facility the incapacitated person was in immediately before being hospitalized, without further authorization, notwithstanding the fact that this admission may be considered a new admission due to the length of hospitalization and/or loss of the prior bed. However, if the incapacitated person is being admitted to a nursing facility other than one the incapacitated person was in immediately before being hospitalized or, if it is a first-time admission after July 1, 2009, Court authorization for admission must be sought by the filing of a General Petition.

e. Previous Authority to Admit/Commit

Beginning July 1, 2009, the Probate and Family Court no longer has the authority to authorize a Guardian to admit or commit an incapacitated person to a mental health facility or a mental retardation facility as defined in the regulations of the department of mental health. G.L. c. 190B, § 5-309(f). In addition, beginning July 1, 2009, the Probate and Family Court will no longer have the authority to review or extend an admit/commit order previously authorized by the Court. An initial commitment order is generally valid for six months, and subsequent commitment orders are valid for one year. G.L. c. 123, § 8(d). *Guardianship of Weedon*, 409 Mass. 196 (1991).

If the authority to admit/commit is in an existing decree allowed before July 1, 2009, but the incapacitated person is not admitted/committed before July 1, 2009, this authority shall be considered to have expired on July 1, 2009 and the authority to admit/commit may not be relied upon after July 1, 2009. A new order must be sought through the appropriate District Court proceeding. If the authority to admit/commit is in an existing decree allowed before July 1, 2009, and the incapacitated person is admitted/committed before July 1, 2009, this authority shall continue to be valid, but will expire six months after the date of admission/commitment.

If the authority to admit/commit issued before July 1, 2009 has expired, it cannot be relied upon nor can the Probate and Family Court review or extend the prior authorization. Any such order must now be sought through the appropriate District Court proceeding.

3. STANDBY OR EMERGENCY GUARDIANSHIP PROXY

The current provisions of G.L. c. 201, § 2(A)–(H) regarding Standby or Emergency Guardianship Proxies will be repealed as of July 1, 2009. Under G.L. c. 190B, § 5-202(a) and (b), a parent or a current Guardian may appoint a Guardian for any minor child in a writing that must be attested to by at least two witnesses. This requirement is similar to the requirements of G.L. c. 201, § 2B, which provides that the standby Guardianship proxy must be in writing, designate an adult and be "witnessed by two or more persons, at least eighteen years of age, neither of whom is to be designated as the proxy." Therefore, the Court shall deem designations executed in accordance with G.L. c. 201, § 2B valid parental or Guardian appointments under G.L. c. 190B, § 5-202 regardless of the date of execution.

Standing Order 3-09. Notice in Guardianship of Incapacitated Persons and Conservatorship Matters

[Effective July 1, 2009.]

In all Guardianship of incapacitated person and Conservatorship matters, notice pursuant to G.L. c. 190B, § 1-401(c) will be presumed insufficient unless:

(1) Proof of mailing is provided for all notice given by first class mail; and

(2) Proof of publication is provided for all cases where there are interested persons whose address or identity is not known or cannot be ascertained with reasonable diligence.

This Standing Order does not preclude the Court from requiring additional proof of notice as the case requires.

Standing Order 4-09. Notice in Guardianship of Minors Matters

[Effective July 1, 2009; amended effective Feb. 8, 2010.]

Pursuant to G.L. c. 190B, § 1-401(b) of the Massachusetts Uniform Probate Code, to promote the well-being of the children of the Commonwealth who are the subjects of Guardianship proceedings, the Probate and Family Court establishes the following order for notice to parties in all Petitions for Appointment of Guardian of a Minor proceedings.

Petition for Appointment of Guardian of a Minor

Notice to Interested Parties

Definitions:

Interested Parties under G.L. c. 190B, § 5-206:

(1) The minor, if the minor is 14 or more years of age and is not the petitioner;

(2) Any person who has been awarded care or custody of the minor by a Court of competent jurisdiction, who is alleged to have had the principal care or custody of the minor, or with whom the minor has resided during the 60 days preceding the filing of the petition, excluding foster parents. If the Department of Children and Families has custody of the minor, it must be served;

(3) Any living parent of the minor, excluding a parent whose parental rights have been terminated or a parent who has signed a voluntary surrender or, if none, brothers and sisters 18 years or older or, if none, heirs apparent or presumptive;

(4) The spouse if the minor is married;

(5) Any person nominated as Guardian by the minor if the minor has attained 14 years of age;

(6) Any parental or Guardian appointee whose appointment has not been prevented or terminated under G.L. c. 190B, § 5-203.

(7) Any Guardian or Conservator currently acting for the minor in this Commonwealth or elsewhere; and

(8)The United States Veterans Administration or its successor if the minor is entitled to any benefit, estate or income paid or payable by or through said administration or its successors.

Order:

Upon the filing of the Petition for Appointment of Guardian of a Minor, the Court shall establish a date for hearing on the Petition and enter this date on the "Order and Notice." For Petitions that also include a request for the appointment of a temporary Guardian (either with notice or ex parte), the date for hearing on the Petition shall be on or before the expiration of the temporary Guardianship. For all other Petitions, the date for hearing on the Petition shall be at least twenty-one (21) days after the filing of the Petition, but no more than forty-five (45) days after the filing of the petition.

Except as provided for in subsection "c" of this order, following the filing of Petition, the petitioner shall case an "Order and Notice" and a copy of the Petition to be served by a constable, deputy sheriff, sheriff or other persons approved by the Court and shall be served with a copy of the Petition in the following manner:

(a) If the place of residence or whereabouts of an interested parts is known, service shall be accomplished on the interested party by:

(i) Delivery in hand to the party at least fourteen days before the date of hearing for the Petition. If the minor is above the age of fourteen years and has not nominated the Guardian proposed in the petition in conformance with the requirements of G.L. c. 190B, § 5-207, then service shall be made in the same manner on the minor; or

(ii) Written and duly notarized endorsement of the party's acceptance of service on the Order and Notice of hearing, whether within or without the Commonwealth.

(b) If the place of residence or whereabouts of an interested party is known, but the petitioner has been unable to accomplish service by delivery despite efforts to do so, the Petitioner may accomplish service on that interested party, either within or without the Commonwealth, by leaving a copy of the Petitioner and Order and Notice at his or her last and usual place of residence, and by mailing by first-class mail copies to the interested party at least fourteen (14) days before the date of the hearing for the Petition, or by some other method as ordered by Court.

(c) If the place of residence or whereabouts of an interested party is not known or cannot be ascertained with reasonable diligence, the Court shall order that service be accomplished on that interested party, either within or without the Commonwealth, by mailing by first-class mail to the interested party at his or her last known address, at least fourteen (14) days before the date of the hearing for the Petition, or by some other method as ordered by the Court. In addition, the Court shall issue an Order for Service by Publication, and the petitioner shall cause notice to be published at least one time in the newspaper or newspapers designated by the Register of Probate having general circulation in the county where the proceeding is pending, the publication to appear at least seven days before the date of the hearing for the Petition, unless otherwise directed by the Court.

(d) If the identity of an interested party is not known, service shall be accomplished on that interested party by publication as follows: the Court shall issue an Order for Service by Publication, and the petitioner shall cause notice to be published at least one time in the newspaper or newspapers designated by the Register of Probate having general circulation in the county where the proceeding is pending, the publication to appear at least seven days before the date of the hearing for the Petitioner, unless otherwise ordered by the Court.

(e) If the minor is entitled to any benefit, estate, or income paid or payable through the United States Veterans Administration or its successor, service shall be made on the Veterans Administration by regular first-class mail at least seven days before the date of the hearing for the Petition.

(f) If the minor is in the custody of the Department of Children and Families, service shall be made on the Department of Children and Families by regular first-class mail at least seven days before the date of the hearing for the Petition.

(g) No notice need be given in the following circumstances:

(1) to a person entitled to notice under this rule who has consented in writing to the allowance of the Petition, if the consent is filed in Court;

(2) to a parent who signed a voluntary surrender in conformance with G.L. c. 210, § 2, or

(3) if the Court has terminated parental rights pursuant to G.L. c. 210, § 3.

(h) The officer or other person making service in accordance with this rule shall make a return of service on a copy of the Order and Notice, which the petitioner shall promptly file with the Court. The return of service shall indicate the method of service. If service is made by leaving at the last and usual address and first class mail, the officer or other person making service shall describe the efforts made to complete in-hand service.

2

APPLICABILITY OF ORDER TO OTHER PROCEEDINGS

This order for notice shall apply to all petitions relating to the Guardianship of a Minor, Petitions for Removal of Guardian of a Minor, Petitions for Visitation, and Petitions for Support.

Standing Order 5-09. Medical Certificates in Conservatorship of Minor Matters

[Effective July 1, 2009.]

No Medical Certificate or Clinical Team Report shall be required in proceedings for Conservatorship of a minor filed pursuant to G.L. c. 190B, § 5-401(b) unless ordered by the Court.

Standing Order 1-10. Special Procedures for Cases Involving Children

[Effective May 5, 2010.]

Preamble

The Hampshire Division of the Probate and Family Court is committed to a child-focused procedural model for all cases involving children and has developed a pilot project for this purpose.

This Standing Order applies to all cases involving children filed in the Hampshire Division and will be liberally construed and applied to establish, endure and support child-focused parenting and care giving, professional conduct and court procedures by and for families served by this Court.

The purposes of the child-focused model are as follows:

- to provide early opportunities for parents and care givers to learn the effects of hostile litigation on children;
- to provide early opportunities for non-adversarial planning of all unresolved issues;
- to establish a problem-solving environment in which each parent, care giver and attorney is expected to be a problem solver; and
- to establish an atmosphere in which parents and care givers are encouraged to experiment responsibly with multiple child care models as they observe children's adjustment to parenting in two households.

A. Application of the Rule

This Standing Order applies:

1. to all cases involving children filed in the Hampshire Division, including Divorce, Separate Support, Paternity, Support/Custody/Visitation, Modification, Contempt, Guardianship and Termination of Parental Rights; and

2. to all attorneys, parents and care givers involved in each such case. A "care giver" is a party to a case who is either a guardian, potential guardian, grandparent seeking visitation, de facto parent or person seeking de facto parent status.

B. Domestic Violence and Application of the Rule

Parents, care givers and attorneys will not be expected to adhere to the requirements of Paragraph E of this Standing Order if there is an abuse prevention order in effect.

C. Introductory Letter

1. After the commencement of an action, the Court will send an Introductory Letter to each parent, care giver or to the attorney representing each parent or care giver.

2. The attorney, upon receipt of the Introductory Letter, shall provide the original letter to his or her client.

D. Duties of Attorneys, Parents, Care Givers and the Court

1. Problem solving

Attorneys, parents and care givers shall make all efforts to solve problems before seeking the decision making intervention of the Court and shall seek that intervention only as needed.

2. Conduct

Parents, care givers, attorneys and the Court shall consistently observe the following conduct:

a. consistent, focused attention on each child's needs including maintaining an awareness that children suffer when their parents or care givers fight about them;

b. consistent, focused attention on each parent or care giver's needs, including maintaining an awareness

i. that children will be well served if each parent or care giver's ability to provide safe, health and responsible parenting time with the children is supported by each parent or care giver;

ii. that children will be well served if there is reasonable financial security in each household; and

iii. that children will be well served if parents or care givers are able to resolve conflicts in a constructive matter.

3. Resources

a. Attorneys shall inform their clients about resources available for counseling, mediation, conciliation or other assistance to help parents, care givers and children improve their relationships and functioning, and to adjust to the realities of parenting or care giving in two households.

b. The Court shall maintain and make available to the public information about the following court-related resources, which parents are encouraged (and may be ordered) to use:

i. Parenting websites

www.uptoparents.org

www.proudtoparent.org

ii. Mediation/Conciliation

Hampshire Introductory Mediation Program

Hampshire Conciliation Program

iii. Referrals to bar association lawyer referral services and the Massachusetts Justice project.

4. Planning

Parents, care givers, attorneys and the Court shall engage in consistent and, if necessary, repeated attempts to improve the circumstances of the children by cooperative planning on each relevant issue at each stage of the court process.

5. Administrative Efficiency

The Court shall establish an administrative process to accept full written agreements for temporary orders without the necessity of a hearing.

E. Introductory Meeting

1. General Requirement

All parties and attorneys shall schedule and participate in an Introductory Meeting at a time and place to be agreed upon by the attendees which shall take place as set forth below and, except in an emergency, no less than two days prior to a motion hearing.

The Introductory Meeting shall take place no later than forty-five days after the filing of an Answer or other relevant responsive pleading.

2. Content and Process of the Introductory Meeting shall:

a. explore whether the parents or care givers need assistances gaining access to resources that could help them resolve the open issues or improve relevant relationships or functioning, and adjust to the realities of parent or care giving in two households;

b. confirm, if applicable, whether the parents or care givers have completed their website work, and if so, discuss the Agreed Commitments reached;

c. work on a parenting or care giving plan;

d. identify

i. issues that require immediate resolution;

ii. issues that require additional planning prior to resolution;

iii. tasks to be performed as to each issue;

iv. person(s) responsible for completing each task; and

v. the completion date for each task.

e. attempt to resolve all issues that require resolution by the parties;

f. confirm that each parent has complied with the parent education program required of them; and

g. write, for presentation in court, any agreements or partial agreements achieved by the parties in the Introductory Meeting.

3. Facilitation Services

The family services resources of the Probation Department of the Court are available to assist in (a) facilitating the Introductory Meeting or any follow-up meeting, (b) suggesting resources available to the parents and care givers, and (c) writing any agreements or partial agreements reached in any meeting. In order to make use of these resources, the parents or care givers or counsel shall, in sufficient time to be in compliance with the scheduling requirements of this Standing Order, make an appointment with the Probation Department for assistance on a day before the date on which a motion or Case Management Conference is scheduled to be heard.

4. Non-Compliance

If parents or care givers and/or attorneys representing each parent or care giver fail to comply with the requirements of the Introductory Meeting, they shall be prepared to report to the Court the reasons therefore. In the event of an unexcused non-compliance, the Court has the discretion to refuse to hear the motion, alter the Case Management Order and issue sanctions, including but not limited to attorney's fees.

5. Follow Up Meetings

A follow-up meeting shall be held upon the request of any attorney or self-represented parent or care giver at any time, and at least two days prior to any hearing on each subsequently filed motion. Such a follow-up meeting may be held in person or by conference call, and shall, as applicable, address the same issues addressed in the Introductory Meeting.

6. Summary of Cooperative Efforts

Parents, care givers and attorneys, in compliance with Pre-Trial Notice and Order, shall present at the Pre-Trial Conference a summary of the steps they have taken under this Standing Order toward the cooperative resolution of the unresolved issues.

F. Training

The Court, in collaboration with the Hampshire County Bar Association, shall offer training to attorneys on such topics as:

- representing children, parents and care givers in the context of this Standing Order;
- special skills needed to represent children, parents and care givers in the context of this Standing Order;
- processes developed in this Court and other Courts to carry out the purpose of the Standing Order; and
- ethical considerations in representing children, parents and care givers.

Standing Order 2-10. Medical Certificate Affidavit

[Effective Nov. 16, 2010.]

A court-promulgated Medical Certificate Affidavit Form (Medical Certificate Affidavit) may be used prior to a determination of incapacity or disability, or, in limited circumstances at a hearing for a final determination of incapacity or disability for a person who has been and continues to be medically stable as indicated on the most recently filed Medical Certificate Form (Medical Certificate), particularly Part I, A, B & C. A Medical Certificate Affidavit may be used at the time of a final determination of incapacity or disability in the limited circumstances where counsel for the Incapacitated or Protected Person has been appointed and does not object to its use. A Medical Certificate Affidavit shall be completed by a registered physician, a licensed psychologist, a certified psychiatric nurse clinical specialist or a nurse practitioner and must be dated and the examination must have taken place within thirty (30) days prior to the entry of each decree, temporary or permanent. This Standing Order does not preclude the Court from requiring additional medical information, including a Medical Certificate, as the case requires.

Standing Order 1-11. Probate and Family Court's Use of Information Contained in the Court Activity Record Information (CARI) Report

[Effective June 1, 2011.]

1. The Probation Department shall obtain Court Activity Record Information (CARI) and Warrant Management system information (WMS) for all parties referred by a judge of the Probate and Family Court for probation services. Such services include, but are not limited to, dispute intervention, short-term investigation, full investigation, supervision and case intervention.

2. CARI includes Criminal Offender Record Information (CORI), juvenile records and civil restraining order information.

3. The Court has an obligation to obtain CARI in all cases pertaining to abuse prevention orders pursuant to Chapter 209A and domestic relations protective orders pursuant to Chapters 208, 209 or 209C. Nothing in this Standing Order is intended to restrict access that the Court would otherwise have to CORI/CARI records.

4. Prior to the delivery of any probation services, the Probation Department shall disclose to a party who is the subject of a CARI record, and his or her counsel, that the party's CARI record has been reviewed by the Probation Department.

5. In a dispute intervention where all parties and their counsel, if any, are present, the Probation Department shall advise all of the parties, and their counsel, whether CARI information of any party has been considered. If safety concerns are raised by either party, the CARI information shall be discussed separately.

6. The Probation Department shall inform each party who is the subject of a CARI record, and his or her counsel, of the information in his or her CARI record that has been considered by the Probation Department in the context of completing the referred service. The Probation Department shall provide the party and his or her counsel the opportunity to review the CARI record.

7. A party may consent to the disclosure to the other party of the information contained in his or her CARI record in order to complete the referred services. Absent such consent, a party seeking disclosure of CARI information may request an order from the judge for disclosure of the CARI information. Subject to the judge's discretion, including the entry of appropriate protective orders, CARI information may be disclosed pursuant to a court order to adverse counsel and/or the adverse litigant, in order to complete the referred services, including, but not limited to, dispute interventions and court hearings.

8. The Probation Department is authorized to provide the CARI record to the judge. If the judge reviews the CARI record, the judge shall explain on the record or by written findings the information relied upon and any inferences or conclusions made as a result of the review of the CARI information.

9. The judge shall afford a party a reasonable and meaningful opportunity to rebut any adverse information that might appear in the party's CARI record, and to otherwise respond to the CARI record. Upon request, additional time to rebut such adverse information may be allowed in the judge's discretion. The Court shall enter an order if necessary to protect the interests of a party or the child or children involved prior to the continued hearing.

10. Upon receipt of information that an outstanding warrant exists for either party, a member of the Probation Department shall notify the judge.

11. No CARI/WMS information shall be stored in the court case file. All CARI/WMS information shall be shredded unless a party or the judge requests that it be returned to the Probation Department and kept in the Probation file.

12. No dissemination or use of any CARI information obtained under this order may be used outside the context and purpose for which it was sought without further order of the court unless otherwise permitted by law.

Standing Order 2-11. Probate and Family Court's Use of Information Obtained by the Department of Children and Families

2

[Effective June 1, 2011.]

1. Whenever the Probate and Family Court determines that it requires information from the Department of Children and Families (DCF) in order to make a determination relating to the care and custody of a child, the Court shall either obtain the written, informed consent of the party(ies), after identifying the documents requested on the form entitled "Consent and/or Order for Production of Department of Children and Families Documents", and/or issue an order identifying the documents to be produced. Such orders may, in the judge's sound discretion, be made under G.L. c. 119, §§ 51E and 51F, or any other applicable provision of law. Any written, informed consent and/or order shall be docketed. Parties may request a hearing on the issue of the need for DCF documents.

2. Circumstances where documents may be requested include, but are not limited to, where (a) a party's "Affidavit Disclosing Care or Custody Proceedings (Trial Court Uniform Rule IV)" or other filing reveals a pending child welfare case; (b) a Probation or guardian ad litem report reveals a party's past or pending child welfare case, past or present DCF involvement, or history of child abuse or neglect; (c) witness testimony reveals a party's past or pending child welfare case, past or present DCF involvement, or history of child abuse or neglect; or (d) a party discloses his or her own, or alleges another party's, past or pending child welfare case, past or present DCF involvement, or history of child abuse or neglect.

3. The Court shall provide DCF with a copy of the written, informed consent or order, which identifies the requested documents.

4. The parties and counsel shall be given the opportunity to review all documents obtained from DCF prior to the hearing, and be provided with an adequate and meaningful opportunity to respond. Upon the request of counsel or a party for additional time to rebut or respond to the DCF documents, the matter may be continued for up to 7 days for hearing. Leave to continue shall be freely granted. The Court shall enter an order if necessary to protect the interests of the child or children prior to the continued hearing. At the hearing, the DCF documents shall be available to the Court and to the parties and shall be admissible in accordance with applicable rules of evidence.

5. Upon its own initiative, or upon the request of any party, or upon the request of DCF, the Court may issue an order allowing a representative of DCF to present oral testimony at a hearing or trial by electronic means. The phrase "electronic means" shall include communication by telephone, video teleconference, or the Internet. Testimony presented by electronic means shall be admissible in accordance with the applicable rules of evidence.

6. The Court shall afford a party the opportunity to object to and rebut information about the party that appears in the DCF documents and otherwise to respond to the DCF documents or information presented in person by DCF.

7. Parties and counsel shall have the right to view the DCF documents as often as they wish, upon reasonable request. Handwritten notes may be taken, however, no electronic reproductions shall be allowed. This restriction includes, but is not limited to, scanning and photography, by mobile device or otherwise.

8. Unless otherwise ordered by the court, the attorney(s) of record, if both parties are represented by counsel, shall be entitled to copies of the DCF documents. In the event only one party, or neither party, is represented by counsel and a party wishes to obtain a copy of the DCF documents, the party or his/her attorney must file a motion with the Court. Service of the motion and the time periods for hearing shall be in accordance with the Massachusetts Rules of Domestic Relations Procedure, or the Massachusetts Rules of Civil Procedure, as applicable.

9. In order to protect the privacy of the parties and the children involved, all documents received from DCF will be segregated by the Court and will be made available to parties, counsel and any other individual who would otherwise be authorized to have access to such information, who shall treat such information as confidential. Any individual who views DCF documents, including counsel, is prohibited from disclosing an impounded address or using information in the DCF documents except as allowed by order of the Court. Any DCF documents produced pursuant to the procedures set forth in this Standing Order will be maintained in the Probation Department of each division of the Probate and Family Court. In the event DCF records are subpoenaed for trial or evidentiary hearing, the records shall be kept in the Registry of Probate, in the customary manner.

10. This Standing Order shall be construed to authorize a judge to issue such other or additional orders or rulings as are necessary and appropriate under the circumstances and consistent with due process.

11. Once the Court has placed a child with DCF pursuant to G.L. c. 119, § 23(a)(3), the provisions of this Standing Order no longer apply and the protections and procedures of Chapter 119 apply.

Standing Order 4-11. Administrative Process for Uncontested *Rogers* Reviews and Extensions

[Effective July 1, 2011.]

In order to provide for the orderly and efficient administration of uncontested *Rogers* review cases and extensions, and for the convenience of Incapacitated Persons (hereinafter "IP") and other interested parties, all requests for review and/or extension of court orders authorizing the use of antipsychotic medications may be submitted to the Court for administrative allowance without a hearing where the requests are uncontested.

Unless otherwise ordered by the Court and subject to the terms and conditions stated below, uncontested requests for reviews and extensions of *Rogers* Orders shall be considered by Judicial Case Managers, Assistant Judicial Case Managers, or other designees of the First Justice of each Probate and Family Court Division (hereinafter collectively referred to as "judicial designees"). See *Rogers v. Commissioner of the Department of Mental Health*, 390 Mass. 489 (1983).

Initial petitions for guardianship seeking authority to administer antipsychotic medication to an IP shall be heard by a judge. Initial petitions and all annual reviews for wards (minors) shall also be heard by a judge.

The Administrative Process for Uncontested *Rogers* Reviews and Extensions shall be as follows:

1. An uncontested Motion to Extend and/or Amend an existing Treatment Order for a period not to exceed twelve (12) months may be allowed without a judicial hearing provided the following court-approved pleadings and documents have been filed, and are in proper order. The documents listed below shall constitute a completed package.

a. Motion to Extend and/or Amend Treatment Plan.

b. Motion to Waive Appearance of the IP brought by counsel for the IP.

c. Clinician's Affidavit and Treatment Plan completed by the IP's treating physician, certified psychiatric nurse clinical specialist, or other person(s) so authorized by law. The Clinician's Affidavit shall include any proposed changes in medication or dosage, the reasons therefore, and any possible side effects. No more than four (4) alternative and different class antipsychotic medications shall be permitted absent judicial approval. The affidavit must indicate that the examination of the IP was completed within sixty (60) days of the filing of the pleadings for administrative review.

d. *Rogers* Monitor's Report in accordance with the terms of the Appointment of *Rogers* Monitor. The *Rogers* Monitor is to meet with the IP a reasonable time prior to the review date. The *Rogers* Monitor is to provide a copy of the report to Petitioner and/or counsel, and to the IP's counsel, at least thirty (30) days prior to the review date.

e. Representations of Respondent's (IP's) Counsel indicating that counsel has met with the Respondent, reviewed the Clinician's Affidavit and the Monitor's Report, and that Respondent does not object to the proposed Order and Treatment Plan. Respondent's counsel shall list the date(s) s/he has seen the IP within the last 12 months. The lack of objection by Respondent's counsel to a proposed Treatment Plan shall not constitute a waiver or partial waiver of the attorney-client privilege.

f. A proposed Review Order which shall include the new treatment plan.

g. A Motion for Fees pursuant to *Rudow v. Commissioner of the Division of Medical Assistance*, 429 Mass. 218 (1999) may be presented for services, provided there is an Affidavit supporting the fees, and provided the Motion is assented to by Counsel for the IP.

2. Proposed changes to medication or dosage that offer increased treatment options for the IP, and that are assented to by the IP's counsel, may be considered by the judicial designee at the time of the extension of the Order without a judicial hearing.

3. If no changes to the original Treatment Plan are proposed other than those permitted in this standing order, and there is no contest, the treatment plan may be allowed as amended, or the previous treatment plan may be extended administratively, for up to twelve (12) months. The review date shall be the same as the expiration date of the Order. The newly approved Treatment Plan will expire twelve (12) months from the date of allowance, unless extended before then.

4. Upon completion of the review by the judicial designee, the filings will be submitted to the judge with a recommendation for allowance, or a recommendation that the matter be scheduled for a hearing before a judge.

5. If a completed uncontested package is filed within sixty (60) days of the expiration of a Treatment Plan Order, the matter may be considered for administrative allowance.

6. Any requests for renewal, extension, or amendment of a Treatment Plan Order filed more than sixty (60) days after the review date set in the most recent Order may be initiated by a Motion to Reinstate Rogers Authority, and must be presented to a judge.

7. Any interested party may seek judicial review at any time should circumstances warrant a hearing.

8. When deemed appropriate to do so, Orders may be entered nunc pro tunc; however, nunc pro tunc Orders shall only be issued at the discretion of a judge.

Standing Order 1-15. Application of Rule 13(b) of the Uniform Rules of Impoundment Procedure to the Probate and Family Court

[Effective Oct. 1, 2015.]

Rule 13(b) of the Uniform Rules of Impoundment Procedure provides as follows:

> Notice to the Clerk. The filer of a document containing impounded information shall simultaneously file a notice that shall (i) notify the clerk that impounded information is included within the document being filed; (ii) identify the specific legal authority requiring impoundment of the identified information; and (iii) identify the precise location of the impounded information within the document being filed. The clerk shall docket the notice and designate the referenced document as impounded. The cover page of the document containing the impounded information shall identify that it is impounded.

As written, the filer of a document shall file the notice even if the information or document is impounded by statute, court rule, standing order, or case law.

In the Probate and Family Court, the filer of the documents listed below is exempt from filing the Rule 13(b) notice:

a. affidavit of indigency—by order of the SJC;

b. financial statement—Supplemental Probate and Family Court Rule 401(d);

c. qualified domestic relations order, domestic relations order, and Mangiacotti order—Probate and Family Court Standing Order 3-08;

d. guardian ad litem report—Probate and Family Court Standing Order 2-08;

e. medical certificate, clinical team report, treatment plan and medical affidavit—Probate and Family Court Standing Order 1-09 and G.L. c. 190B;

f. all filings in an adoption case—G.L. c. 210, § 5C;

g. all filings in a child welfare case—G.L. c. 119 and

h. all filings in a paternity case after there has been a judgment of non-paternity—G.L. c. 209C, § 13.

The exemption applies only when the documents are filed in the Probate and Family Court. If any of the documents listed above are filed in connection to a case in another court department, the Rule 13(b) notice is required, unless that court department has a standing order exempting the filer.

Standing Order 3-16. Remote Access to Electronic Court Records for Probate and Family Records

[Effective Nov. 1, 2016.]

Rule 5(a)(iii) of the Trial Court Rule XIV, Uniform Rules on Public Access to Court Records, provides that each Department of the Trial Court, subject to the approval of the Chief Justice of the Trial Court after notification to the SJC, may exempt certain civil case types or categories of information from remote access.

Probate and Family Court Estate Administration electronic case information is currently available remotely. Effective November 1, 2016 electronic case information for Equity cases will be available remotely, with the exception of Paternity cases filed in equity pursuant to G.L. c. 215, § 6.

The following exemptions have been approved for these case types and types of information of the Probate and Family Court:

For all Divorce, Paternity, Guardianship, Conservatorship, Trust, Separate Support, Modification, Contempt, and Change of Name case types not restricted or impounded by other standing orders, rules or orders of the court, the following information shall be available through remote public access:

- Case Name
- Party Names
- Attorney Information
- Event Dates
- Subsequent Actions
- Case Disposition

For all Divorce, Paternity, Guardianship, Conservatorship, Trust, Separate Support, Modification, Contempt, and Change of Name case types not restricted or impounded by other standing orders, rules or orders of the court, the following information shall NOT be available through remote public access:

- Addresses for parties, whether represented by counsel or not
- Docket entries

2

Probate and Family Court Uniform Practice X

Plan of Adoption Required in Petitions to Establish Consent

[Amended effective Jan. 28, 1980; July 1, 1989.]

In an uncontested adoption, filed pursuant to Chapter 210, Section 3, requiring the submission of a plan, the Department of Social Services or other agency shall submit to the Court at the time of allowance a written report. The report shall consist of:

1. a. The name, date of birth and age of the child who is the subject of the proceeding.

b. The name(s), current address(es), and age(s) of the biological/legal parents, to the extent the information is available.

c. History of legal actions including the present action; Date of petition, Return date, how notice was accomplished, if a valid surrender was filed and by whom, that the petition was uncontested.

d. Brief background on the fitness, availability, capacity and readiness of parents to assume parental responsibility for the child; Acts of neglect, emotional/physical/sexual abuse, psychiatric/psychological evaluations, interactions and attachments between parents and child, and the timetable, if any, when parent(s) will be able to assume the care and custody of the child and the effect of this change on the minor.

e. The needs of the child.

2. The agency's plan for the child upon the release of the required parental consent. A plan that elaborates in detail what steps the agency plans to employ to find a suitable adoptive parent may be deemed sufficient without further specificity.

Probate and Family Court Scheduling Practices and Procedures

[Effective Apr. 15, 2010.]

Purpose:

To promote predictability and uniformity of practice to the mechanisms, practices and procedures utilized for the scheduling of all types of hearings in the Probate and Family Courts throughout the Commonwealth.

Applicability:

These practices and procedures apply to all divisions of the Probate and Family Court and are applicable in all cases, regardless of whether or not litigants are represented by counsel or self-represented.

Case Management

Pursuant to Standing Order 1-06, the Time Standards of the Probate and Family Court, all Domestic Relations and Equity cases shall be reviewed 120 days after the filing of the complaint to determine if service of process has been made. If no service has been made a notice shall be sent informing the Plaintiff that the case will be dismissed 21 days after the date of the notice unless the Plaintiff files with the court the return of service, or schedules a motion for an extension of time to complete service.

If service has been accomplished and returned to the Court within the requisite period of time, pursuant to Standing Order 1-06, section e., a case management conference will be scheduled by the court to be held on a date certain (approximately six weeks after the date upon which the return of service is due) and specified in the notice.

(N.B. A scheduled case management conference may be canceled if the case is before the Court prior to the date scheduled for the case management conference. Also, a joint stipulation may be filed by all parties in lieu of appearing at a case management conference. This process is detailed in Standing Order 1-06. The joint stipulation must, upon receipt by the Court, be incorporated by a Judge into a formal order).

Mandatory Next Event Scheduling

Pursuant to Standing Order 1-06, section 2.b., whenever a case is, for whatever reason, in Court, if the proceeding before the Court does not result in the matter being brought to final judgment, a next event date will be issued, preferably after consultation with counsel and/or the parties. The assigned date must be made before the parties leave the courthouse. There are to be no exceptions to the issuance of a next event date, unless the case already has a scheduled next event. In cases where the parties have reached any out of Court agreement and have a complete stipulation which the parties intend to have the Court incorporate into an order, the case may *not* be released until: the case has been given a next event date *in* the courtroom; the next event date is in the stipulation; or, a future event date had previously been scheduled. Cases referred to the Probation Department for Dispute Intervention which result in a stipulation that does not require further court appearance by the parties or their attorneys on that day, *shall* include a next event date, if the case is not going to judgment or decree. If the stipulation does not include a next event date, the case *must* return to the courtroom to receive a next event date.

Scheduling of Motions

Any party may mark a motion for hearing, with proper service upon the opposing party, for any date upon which the Judge to whom a case is assigned, is sitting and generally hears motions, except as follows. In the First Justice's discretion, with the approval of the Chief Justice of the Probate and Family Court, marking to a particular motion session, in a particular division, may be limited, as justice requires. Any limitation on motion sessions approved by the Chief Justice shall be posted in the division (Registry of Probate and courtrooms) and on the web site of the Probate and Family Court. In the First Justice's discretion an individual Judge may from time to time as circumstances may warrant, limit the number of matters which may be scheduled on a particular day.[1]

[1] The Probate and Family Court is committed to providing timely access to our Court for all parties in all cases. There are however instances where the number of motions per day must be limited, in order to insure the allocation of sufficient time to adequately hear each case. Parties are encouraged to consolidate the number of appearances in their case on issues requiring temporary relief.

There shall be no restrictions on the number or timing of motions which may be filed except as set forth above regardless of the nature of the underlying complaint, except that all motions (and complaints for contempt) shall be scheduled to be heard at the commencement of the Court's day unless otherwise allowed by the Court, or advance permission has been obtained from the Court to have a motion (or a contempt) heard at another time during the day. In the Court's discretion, motions that are expected to require greater than 20 minutes of time before the Court shall be specifically assigned by the Judge. The Court must be provided with the motion, and notice of the date and time of the motion, at the same time that the opposing party is given notice thereof. Advanced permission to schedule a motion need not be obtained from the Court, except as set forth above.

Exceptions to number and timing of motion scheduling.

a. Dispositive Motions (i.e., Motion for Summary Judgment) shall be scheduled by the Judge assigned to the case. Motions for Summary Judgment and responses must be filed with the Court in accordance with Mass. R. Civ. P. 56 and Probate Court Rule 27C in advance of the hearing.

b. All ex-parte motions shall be reviewed, as directed by the Court, prior to presentment to a Judge. Any *ex parte* motion must be supported by an affidavit setting forth the nature of the emergency and shall be submitted in person. After review, such requests shall be heard by the Court at an appropriate time during the course of a judge's session.

c. Motions for permission to file a complaint or pleading must be presented in person to the Court;

d. Requests for a short order of notice must be presented to the Court in person, unless otherwise allowed by the Court.

Scheduling of Status and Pre-trial Conferences

If any action has not been before the Court, or for whatever reason does not have a next event date scheduled, either party may request that the case be assigned for a status conference or a pre-trial conference. In such event, the Court, and not a party, shall select the date (although a party may request a particular date or dates).

When multiple pre-trial conferences are to be heard on the same day, the Court should stagger the scheduling of pre-trial conferences throughout the day, for example, at 9:00 a.m., 10:30 a.m., 12:00 p.m., and 2:00 p.m. Pre-trial conferences shall be heard on the record in open session before the judge to whom the case is assigned. A pre-trial conference may be referred to a Judicial Case Manager, Assistant Judicial Case Manager, or Probation Officer in the discretion of the judge, with approval of the parties or their counsel.

Continuances

Motions, case management conferences, contempts, reviews and status conferences may, for good cause shown, be continued at the joint request (in writing) of the parties to a date certain if the case does not already have a next event date. Any such agreement to continue a matter may be either presented in person or faxed to the Court (e-mailing not permitted) prior to the date upon which the matter is scheduled to be heard. The request for a continuance will be reviewed by the Court for consideration. The Court reserves the right to deny any such request or to require the parties (either or both) to appear before the Court (either in person or by tele-conference) to present any such motion. It shall be the responsibility of the parties to check with the Court, prior to the day of the hearing, to assure that the request for a continuance was granted as the case may be subject to dismissal, (if the case does not already have a next event scheduled), or a party subject to sanctions, for failure to appear should the request for a continuance not have been granted.

Pre-trial conferences may, for good cause shown, be continued *once, by joint request, to a date certain, unless the Court orders that there will be no continuances when the Pre-trial conference is assigned.*[2] Any such agreement to continue a pre-trial conference may be either presented in person or faxed to the Court (e-mailing not permitted) prior to the date upon which the matter is scheduled to be heard. The Court reserves the right to deny any such request or to require the parties (either or both) to appear before the Court (either in person or by tele-conference) and present any such motion. It shall be the responsibility of the parties to check with the Court, prior to the day of the hearing, to assure that the request for a continuance was granted as the case may be subject to dismissal, or a party subject to sanctions, for failure to appear should the request for a continuance not have been granted. Any further requests to continue a pretrial conference, whether by agreement or not, must be presented to the court for hearing.

[2] If needed, requests for extension of discovery deadlines should be included with motions to continue.

Any motion, even a joint motion, to continue a **trial date** *must* be presented in person (teleconference, if authorized by the Court, would constitute a personal appearance), and should be presented to the Court at least 30 days prior to the trial date, (except in emergency circumstances) with proper notice to the opposing party. In accordance with Mass. R. Dom. Rel. P. 40(b) and Mass. R. Civ. P. 40(b), a motion to continue a trial may be allowed only for good cause shown.

Scheduling of Hearings on Uncontested Matters

The Court will hear any agreement or uncontested pleading which results in any complaint going to final judgment within thirty days of the filing of the pleadings or request for uncontested final hearing. Individual Divisions may adopt a policy to hear uncontested matters resulting in final judgment on a walkin or expedited basis, but at a minimum, must establish procedures to hear such uncontested matters *within thirty days of filing* or request for hearing. Prior to the hearing, the case must have been filed in the Registry to assure that all required paperwork is in the file and then reviewed by a member of the Court staff for technical sufficiency. Requests may be made to hear uncontested matters resulting in final judgment in satellite sessions. Uncontested hearings for final judgment shall be heard by the judge to whom the case is generally assigned, with the exception of satellite sessions or if the case cannot be heard by the assigned judge within thirty days of filing or request.

Contested Discovery Motions

The parties may, by agreement, or at the direction of the Court be required to submit any such motion, without hearing, to the Court for determination on the pleadings and accompanying memoranda. After initial review by the Judge who would be hearing the motion, on the day of hearing, but prior to any appearance before the Court, the Judge may, in his or her discretion, refer all contested discovery motions to the Judicial Case Manager or to an Assistant Judicial Case Manager for review and recommendations. Cases not resolved through this referral shall be heard by the Judge. For Domestic Relations and Equity cases, prior to any such hearing or submission, the parties must have complied with the requirements of Mass. R. Dom. Rel. P. 26(f) and submitted an affidavit affirming such compliance.

Scheduling of Tele-Conferences

The use of tele-conferences is encouraged in the following types of events:

- motions, in which participation of the litigants is not required;
- discovery motions;
- case management conferences;
- status conferences; and,
- any other matter at the direction of, and in the discretion of, the Court.

Any party seeking the participation at any proceeding of an attorney, litigant or witness via tele-conference must request permission for such participation by motion, with proper notice to the opposing party or parties, to be heard, or ruled upon, at least seven days prior to the scheduled event, by the Court. These motions will be handled administratively. If the Court approves the request, the Court will notify the requesting party of the time of the hearing and the telephone number to call.

Implementation and Effect

The provisions set forth in these Practices and Procedures shall supersede any local rules, practices, or promulgated procedures where there is a conflict.

Modifications to Probate and Family Court Scheduling Practices and Procedures, Barnstable, Bristol, and Middlesex Divisions of the Probate and Family Court

At the request of certain First Justices, the Chief Justice of the Probate and Family Court, Paula M. Carey has determined that the following Divisions of the Probate and Family Court will be permitted to modify their motion practice as set forth in the Scheduling Practices and Procedures promulgated and effective April 15, 2010.

1. Bristol Division of the Probate and Family Court (New Bedford)—Scheduled motions in New Bedford shall be limited to 55 per motion session. Attorneys and parties shall be permitted to mail in or hand deliver their motion and choose their own dates, on a motion day of the assigned case Judge, rather than the Court choosing a motion date. If the date fills, the parties or counsel will be notified and they will be required to choose another date for their hearing. This exemption was granted to ensure that no fire code is violated in New Bedford.

2. Barnstable Division of the Probate and Family Court—Motions may be scheduled on Monday, Thursday, and Friday mornings beginning May 3, 2010. Motions may be scheduled on

Wednesdays only if the parties have a scheduled pre-trial conference that day. There will be no limit to the number of motions scheduled on a particular day, except in the event of vacation or other anomaly circumstance. Attorneys and parties may send motions in to the Court, with proper notice, without having to call the Court in advance.

3. Middlesex Division of the Probate and Family Court—Scheduled motions in the Middlesex Division shall be limited to 55 per motion session. Attorneys and parties shall be permitted to mail in or hand deliver their motion and choose their own dates, on a motion day of the assigned case Judge, rather than the Court choosing a motion date. If the date fills, the parties or counsel will be notified and they will be required to choose another date for their hearing. This exemption was granted in light of the significant shortage of Probation Officers in Middlesex County, the fact that four days a week two motion sessions are running, and at times three court locations operate on one day.

Memorandum Re Permanency Hearings for Young Adults in Child Welfare Cases

MEMORANDUM

To: Judges of the Probate and Family Court; Registers of Probate; Chief Probation Officers

From: Hon. Paula M. Carey, Chief Justice

Date: March 21, 2011

Re: Permanency Hearings For Young Adults in Child Welfare Cases in Probate and Family Court

cc: Judicial Case Managers, Assistant Judicial Case Managers

On October 15, 2010, Governor Patrick signed into law changes to c.119 of the Massachusetts General Laws which require DCF to continue to provide educational and rehabilitative services to young adults in its care and custody, and to support those young people in preparing for their future outside the care of DCF under conditions agreed upon by both DCF and the young adult. A young adult is defined as a person between the ages of 18 and 22. In addition, permanency hearings for these young adults are required by the amendments to c.119 included in the outside sections of Chapter 359 of the Acts of 2010 (Supplemental Budget FY 10, October 15, 2010).

The chart below outlines procedures for scheduling these permanency hearings. The young adults impacted fall into three groups; those over 18 currently in DCF care, (third column in chart), those in DCF care who turned 18 after January 3, 2011, (first column in chart) and those who leave DCF care and return after they are 18, (second column in chart). There are slight differences in the procedures for each group. These are detailed below. For young adults who turned 18 prior to January 3, 2011, the permanency hearings must be held by approximately June 3, 2011. DCF will contact each court with a list of cases that require the permanency hearings before June.

Please feel free to contact Ilene Mitchell in the Administrative Office with any questions or comments.

Steps for Scheduling and Conducting Permanency Hearings	**Children in Care of DCF Who Turn 18 while in DCF Care**	**Children in Care of DCF Who Turn 18 and Leave and Then Return**	**Young Adults Age 18-22 in DCF Care**
If child's Date of Birth is:	**18 after 1/3/2011**	**18 after 1/3/2011**	**18 on or before 1/3/2011**
1. Identifying Young Adult and setting hearing date	Will be identified at last permanency hearing before turning 18 at which child, if chooses, shall be present and next permanency hearing set for 6 months from previous hearing.	DCF will file affidavit with young adult returned to care of DCF, file permanency plan, ask court to vacate dismissal, if necessary, and request hearing within 30 days of filing.	DCF will identify and give list of names to the court that entered final custody order and request hearing.
2. Register/ Court responsibilities	No less than 60 days prior to hearing, Court shall send notice of hearing to DCF, child's attorney, to parents or their attorneys unless parental rights terminated.	Docket pleadings filed by DCF under original case file number and schedule in court where previously heard for hearing within 30 days of filing to consider permanency plan. DCF shall give notice to all parties or counsel of record.	Docket pleadings filed by DCF under original case file number and schedule for hearing to consider permanency plan. To be heard with siblings on case if still active. Notify DCF of hearing dates. DCF shall give notice to all parties or counsel of record.
3. Filing of Permanency Plan	30 days prior to hearing DCF shall file plan with Court with copies to all parties or counsel.	With request for hearing, Permanency Plan filed by DCF.	30 days prior to hearing DCF shall file plan with Court with copies to all parties or counsel.
4. Appointment of Counsel	Parties entitled to counsel. Counsel of record shall continue to represent child at permanency hearings.	Parties entitled to counsel. Court shall determine and contact last counsel for young adult, and reappoint unless that attorney declines, then follow normal procedure to appoint new counsel.	
5 Notification of Hearing	DCF shall notify young adult prior to hearing of opportunity to attend, either verbally or in writing. Child's attorney will notify young adult.		
6. At the Permanency Hearing	Court will review plan and make reasonable efforts finding	If underlying case was dismissed, DCF attorney asks Court to vacate dismissal, review plan and make reasonable efforts finding.	
7. Child/young adult in Court	Court shall consult with the young adult re: Permanency Plan. Young adult may choose to attend court or not.		
8. Court inquires re: Permanency Hearing Report	Has young adult helped develop plan? If placed out of state, is placement there in the best interest of young adult? Is placement appropriate? Does plan include specific options on housing, health insurance, education, local opportunities for mentors and continuing support services, and work force supports and employment services? Is plan as detailed as the young adult may elect? Can young adult identify significant adult relationships or lifelong connections? Does young adult have information about how to obtain and have in place a power of attorney or health care proxy in case young adult becomes unable to make health care decisions?		

Steps for Scheduling and Conducting Permanency Hearings	Children in Care of DCF Who Turn 18 while in DCF Care	Children in Care of DCF Who Turn 18 and Leave and Then Return	Young Adults Age 18-22 in DCF Care
If child's Date of Birth is:	**18 after 1/3/2011**	**18 after 1/3/2011**	**18 on or before 1/3/2011**
9. Court must make a Reasonable Efforts Finding	Has DCF made reasonable efforts to achieve the permanent plan?		
10. Schedule Next Hearing	At least within 12 months and annually thereafter while in care.		
11. If Young Adult leaves care after age 18	If DCF notifies Court that young adult is no longer in care, then no more permanency hearings scheduled.		
12. When young adult turns 22	No further action required by Court.		

Amendments to G.L. c. 119, § 29B in Chapter 359 of the Acts of 2010 (new language is [italicized]):

SECTION 18. *Section 21 of chapter 119* of the General Laws, as appearing in the 2008 Official Edition, is hereby amended by adding the following definition:—*"Young adult", a person between the ages of 18 and 22.*

SECTION 19. *Section 23 of said chapter 119* is hereby amended by *striking out subsection (f), as so appearing, and inserting in place thereof the following subsection:—*

(f) The department shall offer to continue its responsibility to any young adult who is under the custody, care, or responsibility of the department including, but not limited to, those persons who meet any of the criteria set forth in 42 USC § 675(8)(B)(iv): (i) for the purposes of specific educational or rehabilitative programs, or (ii) to promote and support that person in fully developing and fulfilling that person's potential to be a participating citizen of the commonwealth under conditions agreed upon by both the department and that person. *The department's continued responsibility for such persons is contingent upon the express written consent of the person or their guardian unless: (i) before reaching the age of 18, the person had an intellectual disability and was declared mentally incompetent under clause (3) of subsection (a) while under the responsibility of the department; or (ii) the person is under the responsibility of the department pursuant to section 5-305 of chapter 190B.* The purposes and conditions of such responsibility may be reviewed and revised or terminated by either the person or the department; *provided, however, that within 90 days before the termination of such responsibility, the department shall provide the person with assistance and support in developing a transition plan which fulfills the requirements of 42 USC § 675(5)(H).* If after termination the person requests that the department renew its responsibility therefor, the department shall make every reasonable attempt to provide a program of support which is acceptable to the person and which permits the department to renew its responsibility; *provided, however, that the department may require the person to meet 1 of the criteria set forth in 42 USC § 675(8)(B)(iv).* If the department renews its responsibility, all other provisions of this subsection shall apply. The department shall report annually to the child advocate, the senate and house chairs of the joint committee on children, families and persons with disabilities and the chairs of the senate and house committees on ways and means on the number of persons it serves and declines to serve under this subsection.

SECTION 20. *Section 29 of said chapter 119,* as so appearing, is hereby amended by *striking out the first 2 paragraphs and inserting in place thereof the following 2 paragraphs:—*

The following persons shall have and shall be informed of the right to counsel, and the court shall appoint counsel for all such persons if the person is not able to retain counsel: (i) an adult who is under the responsibility of the department under clause (1) of subsection (a) of section 23; (ii) a child who is before the court under clauses (1) and (3) of said subsection (a) of said section 23, sections 24 to 27, inclusive, or section 29B; (iii) a child in a custody proceeding where the department or a licensed placement agency is a party; and (iv) any young adult to whom subsection (f) of section 23 applies. Whenever the department or a licensed child placement agency is a party to child custody proceedings, the parent, guardian or custodian *of the child, or a parent or guardian of an adult who is the responsibility of the department under clause (3) of subsection (a) of section 23: (i)* shall have and be informed of the right to counsel at all such hearings, including proceedings under *sections 5-201, 5-204 or 5-206 of chapter 190B,* and that the court shall appoint counsel if the *parent, guardian or custodian* is financially unable to retain counsel; and (ii) shall have and be informed of the right to a service plan or case plan *for the child and the child's family, or an adult who is the responsibility of the department under clause (3) of subsection (a) of section 23,* which complies with applicable state and federal laws and regulations for these plans. *Any young adult to whom subsection (f) of section 23 applies is also entitled to such service plan or case plan.* The probate and family court and the juvenile court departments of the trial court shall establish procedures for: (i) notifying the parent, guardian or custodian of these rights; and (ii) appointing counsel for an indigent parent, guardian or custodian within 14 days of a licensed child placement agency filing or appearing as a party in any such action. The department or agency shall provide a copy of the service or case plan to the parent, guardian or custodian of the child or of an adult who *is the responsibility of the department under clause (3) of subsection (a) of section 23, or to an adult who is the responsibility of the department under clause (3) of subsection (a) of section 23 or section 5-305 of chapter 190B, or any young adult to whom subsection (f) of section 23 applies* and to the attorneys for all parties appearing in the proceeding within 45 days of the department or agency filing an appearance in such proceeding. Thereafter, any party may have the original or changed plan introduced as evidence, and with the consent of all parties the plan shall be filed with the court. Notwithstanding this section, the court may make such temporary orders as may be necessary to protect the adult *who is under the responsibility of the department under clause (3) of subsection (a) of section 23 or the child and society.*

SECTION 21. Said *chapter 119 is hereby further amended by striking out section 29B, as so appearing, and inserting in place thereof the following section:—*

Section 29B. *(a)* Except as provided in subsection (d), within 12 months of the original commitment, grant of custody or transfer of responsibility of a child to the department by a court of competent jurisdiction and not less than every 12 months thereafter while the child remains in the care of the department, the committing court shall conduct a permanency hearing, in accordance with rules established by the chief justice for administration and management, to determine and periodically review thereafter the permanency plan for the child. The plan shall address whether and, if applicable, when: (i) the child will be returned to the parent; (ii) the child will be placed for adoption and the steps the department will take to free the child for adoption; (iii) the child will be referred for legal guardianship; (iv) the child will be placed in permanent care with relatives; or (v) the child will be placed in another permanent planned living arrangement. The department shall file a permanency plan prior to a permanency hearing that shall address the above placement alternatives. *The court shall consult with the child in an age-appropriate manner about the permanency plan developed for the child.*

(b) The committing court shall continue to hold annual permanency hearings as described in subsection (a) for young adults to whom subsection (f) of section 23 applies. The young adult shall be entitled to counsel under section 29.

(c) If a child *or a young adult* is not to be returned to the child or young adult's parents, the permanency plan shall consider in-state and out-of-state placement options. In the case of a child placed in foster care outside the state in which the home of the parents of the child is located or a *young adult in* an out-of-state placement, the permanency plan shall also address whether the out-of-state placement continues to be appropriate and in the best interests of the child *or young adult.* In the case of a child who has attained age 16 *or any young adult,* the permanency plan shall also address the services needed to assist the child *or young adult* in making the transition from foster care to independent living; provided, *however,* that the court shall consult with the child *or young adult* in an age-appropriate manner about the permanency plan. *If a person in the custody of or under the responsibility of the department has attained the age of 17 years and 9 months, the permanency plan shall also address the status of and the topics of the transition plan required under 42 USC § 675(5)(H); provided, however, that the court shall retain jurisdiction until it finds, after a hearing at which the person is present unless the person chooses otherwise, that a satisfactory transition plan has been provided for the person.*

(d) In conducting a permanency hearing, the court may make any appropriate order as may be in the child or the young adult's best interests including, but not limited to, orders with respect to care or custody. At the same time, the court shall consider the provisions of section 29C, and shall make the written certification and determinations required by said section 29C. The health and safety of the child or young adult shall be of paramount, but not exclusive, concern.

The permanency hearing *for a child or young adult* shall be held within 30 days of a hearing at which a court determines that reasonable efforts to preserve and reunify families are not required pursuant to section 29C. The court may, however, make such determination at the time of the permanency hearing. If continuation of reasonable efforts to return a child *or young adult safely to the child or young adult's* parent or guardian are found to be inconsistent with the permanency plan for the child *or young adult or* if reasonable efforts are not required pursuant to section 29C, *or in the case of any young adult to whom subsection (f) of section 23 applies,* the department shall make reasonable efforts to place the child *or young adult* in a timely manner in accordance with the permanency plan including, if appropriate, through an interstate placement, and to complete whatever steps are necessary to finalize the permanent placement of the child *or young adult.* In subsequent permanency hearings held on behalf of the child *or young adult,* the court shall determine whether the department has made such efforts in accordance with section 29C.

(e) A child, parent *of a child,* guardian, *young adult,* or the department may appeal to the appeals court from the determination or order of the trial court. The claim of appeal shall be filed in the office of the clerk or register of the trial court within 30 days following the court's determination or order. Thereafter, the appeal shall be governed by the Massachusetts Rules of Appellate Procedure. The scope of appellate review shall be limited to abuse of judicial discretion.

SECTION 22. *Section 29C* of said chapter 119, as so appearing, is hereby amended by inserting after the first paragraph the following paragraph:—

If a young adult continues under the responsibility of the department pursuant to subsection (f) of section 23, the committing court shall continue to annually determine whether the department or the department's agent has made reasonable efforts to achieve the permanent plan approved by the court under section 29B.

P.L. 111-148 "The Patient Protection and Affordable Care Act" of Congress

SEC. 2955. INCLUSION OF INFORMATION ABOUT THE IMPORTANCE OF HAVING A HEALTH CARE POWER OF ATTORNEY IN TRANSITION PLANNING FOR CHILDREN AGING OUT OF FOSTER CARE AND INDEPENDENT LIVING PROGRAMS. (a) Transition Planning.—Section 475(5)(H) of the Social Security Act (42 U.S.C. 675(5)(H)) is amended by inserting "includes information about the importance of designating another individual to make health care treatment decisions on behalf of the child if the child becomes unable to participate in such decisions and the child does not have, or does not want, a relative who would otherwise be authorized under State law to make such decisions, and provides the child with the option to execute a health care power of attorney, health care proxy, or other similar document recognized under State law," after "employment services,". (b) Independent Living Education.—Section 477(b)(3) of such Act (42 U.S.C. 677(b)(3)) is amended by adding at the end the following: "(K) <<NOTE: Certification.>> A certification by the chief executive officer of the State that the State will ensure that an adolescent participating in the program under this section are provided with education about the importance of designating another individual to make health care treatment decisions on behalf of the adolescent if the adolescent becomes unable to participate in such decisions and the adolescent does not have, or does not want, a relative who would otherwise be authorized under State law to make such decisions, whether a health care power of attorney, health care proxy, or other similar document is recognized under State law, and how to execute such a document if the adolescent wants to do so.". ©) Health Oversight and Coordination Plan.—Section 422(b)(15)(A) of such Act (42 U.S.C. 622(b)(15)(A)) is amended—(1) in clause (v), by striking "and" at the end; and (2) by adding at the end the following: "(vii) steps to ensure that the components of the transition plan development process required under [[Page 124 STAT. 353]] section 475(5)(H) that relate to the health care needs of children aging out of foster care, including the requirements to include options for health insurance, information about a health care power of attorney, health care proxy, or other similar document recognized under State law, and to provide the child with the option to execute such a document, are met; and". (d) <<NOTE: 42 USC 622 note.>> Effective Date.—The amendments made by this section take effect on October 1, 2010.

* * * * *

Relevant Federal Regulations

42 USC § 675(8)(B)(iv) (referred to above in amendment to G.L. c. 119, § 23(f)):

(iv) [young adult] who is—

(I) completing secondary education or a program leading to an equivalent credential;

(II) enrolled in an institution which provides post-secondary or vocational education;

(III) participating in a program or activity designed to promote, or remove barriers to, employment;

(IV) employed for at least 80 hours per month; or

(V) incapable of doing any of the activities described in subclauses (I) through (IV) due to a medical condition, which incapability is supported by regularly updated information in the case plan of the child.

42 USC § 675(5)(H): (referred to above in amendment to G.L. c. 119, §§ 23(f), 29B(c):

H) during the 90-day period immediately prior to the date on which the child will attain 18 years of age, or such greater age as the State may elect under paragraph (8)(B)(iii), whether during that period foster care maintenance payments are being made on the child's behalf or the child is receiving benefits or services under section 677 of this title, a caseworker on the staff of the State agency, and, as appropriate, other representatives of the child provide the child with assistance and support in developing a transition plan that is personalized at the direction of the child, includes specific options on housing, health insurance, education, local opportunities for mentors and continuing support services, and work force supports and employment services, and is as detailed as the child may elect.

Standards for Category E
Guardians ad Litem/Evaluators

Table of Contents

Introduction

A Category E Guardian ad Litem/Evaluator (GAL) is appointed by the Probate and Family Court to investigate and evaluate facts in cases involving the care and custody of minor children and other matters that implicate the interests or rights of children. G.L. c. 215, § 56A; G.L. c. 208, § 16. A GAL is often appointed in cases that raise questions about:

- a child's best interests as related to custody and visitation;
- advantages or disadvantages of removing a child from the Commonwealth;
- changes in circumstances that might warrant modification of a judgment;
- existence of a de facto parent-child relationship;
- parental fitness as related to termination of parental rights or guardianship;
- paternity of a minor child; or
- other matters implicating the rights and interests of a minor child.

The purpose of these standards is to:

- provide accountability related to GAL evaluations;
- improve custody, visitation, and other outcomes for children;
- promote uniformity and consistency in GAL evaluations; and
- promote respect for the rights of parties and their children, including their safety.

These standards apply to all Category E Guardians ad Litem/Evaluators.

1. THE ROLE OF THE GAL EVALUATOR

The GAL performs duties that are within the scope of the court order of appointment.

1.1 The GAL Shall Gather and Report Factual Data to the Court, and, when Competent to do so, Offer Clinical Opinions

The role of the Category E GAL evaluator is to gather and report factual information, use clinical knowledge to interpret that data, and formulate clinical opinions to assist the court in making custody, visitation, or other decisions related to the welfare of a child. Unless the appointing judge specifies otherwise, the GAL's role it limited to gathering and evaluating information and reporting it to the court. The GAL may include recommendations in the report if the order of the court authorizes inclusion of such recommendations. The GAL shall not offer clinical assessment or conclusions unless the GAL has the requisite expertise to offer such opinions.

COMMENTARY

The court, not the GAL, decides legal issues and ultimately makes credibility determinations and factual findings when facts are in dispute. The GAL reports on facts and avoids providing legal conclusions or legal analysis.

A. The GAL Shall Investigate and Evaluate Only those Areas Specified by the Court.

If the GAL sees a need to broaden the scope of the evaluation, the GAL shall seek authority from the court before broadening the evaluation. Copies of any and all motions filed by a GAL must be sent to counsel of record and any pro se parties.

COMMENTARY

This standard does not preclude a GAL from investigating and evaluating factual issues that were not identified at the time of the appointment if they are relevant to the legal issues identified in the appointment.

1.2 The GAL's Role Requires Participation in the Trial and Discovery.

After conducting the evaluation and writing a report, the GAL shall be available for trial and for possible deposition. If the parties do not reach an agreement about their case, the GAL may be subpoenaed by a party or the court may request that the GAL be present for trial.

COMMENTARY

Absent a protective order of the court, the GAL shall appear for deposition as required under the applicable rules and statutes as part of his or her responsibilities as the GAL.

1.3 The GAL Serves as an Impartial Investigator, Evaluator and Reporter.

The GAL is an impartial investigator, evaluator and reporter in all cases.

A. The GAL Shall Decline or Withdraw from the Appointment if a Conflict of Interest Exists, or the GAL has Information or Personal Relationships that Will Bias the Process or Outcome of the Evaluation.

If the GAL has any prior or existing direct or indirect relationships with parties, their families, material witnesses, or someone else connected with the family, the GAL must consider whether the GAL's impartiality is compromised as a result of these relationships. The GAL shall decline the appointment if:

- The GAL has or had a dating or intimate relationship with any counsel of record, or a close personal relationship with any counsel of record that will impact the GAL's ability to be unbiased;
- The GAL provided counseling or other services to a party or members of the family, or a material witness;
- The GAL, by virtue of a professional relationship with a colleague (e.g. members of the same practice, members of a peer review/case review/professional development group, supervisory/consulting relationship), has or has had access to information about the parties, children, material witnesses, that would otherwise not be available to the GAL in the normal course of the evaluation;
- The GAL was married to or had a personal relationship with a party, a member of the party's family, a material witness, or another person closely aligned to a party;
- The GAL has or had pecuniary interests or financial involvement with a party, the party's spouse or nonmarital partner, a material witness, counsel for a party or other person closely aligned to a party;
- The GAL's concerns about reprisal or adverse personal consequences if the report is unfavorable to a party will impede the GAL's candor or ability to be impartial and render an unbiased report;
- The GAL is aware of other circumstances that will impede the GAL's candor or ability to be impartial and render an unbiased report.

COMMENTARY

If a GAL is aware of circumstances that indicate that the GAL may have a conflict of interest or other circumstances that may make it inappropriate for the GAL to serve as the evaluator, the GAL shall disclose the information to counsel of record and any pro se parties. The GAL also shall immediately file a motion for instructions from the appointing judge as appropriate with notice to counsel and any pro se parties.

B. The GAL Engages in Nondiscriminatory Practices

The GAL shall not engage in conduct manifesting bias or prejudice based on race, gender, religion, ethnicity, disability, age, socioeconomic status, marital status or sexual orientation against a party, witness, counsel, or other persons involved in the case.

COMMENTARY
The GAL must be aware of how societal and personal biases may interfere with an objective evaluation and recommendations. The GAL recognizes and strives to overcome any such biases. If the GAL is not able to do so, he or she must promptly decline or withdraw from the appointment. If the GAL considers factors related to race, gender, religion, ethnicity, disability, age, sexual orientation, marital status or socioeconomic status concerning a party in the evaluation or report, the GAL must explain the relevance of these factors to the issues before the court.

C. The GAL Evaluator Shall Not Act as an Attorney or Legal Advocate for the Child.

The GAL is an objective and evenhanded reporter. The GAL shall not give legal advice or act as advocate or attorney for the child. In some cases, the child's wishes may be contrary to the child's best interests.

COMMENTARY
A GAL is not a party to the case. A GAL is a witness to the case. The GAL shall not file motions except as related to performance of the GAL's responsibilities and as provided in these standards.

D. The GAL Does Not Give Legal Advice or Act as Either Party's Legal Advocate.

The GAL refrains from giving legal advice to parties including but not limited to advice about how the law applies to the facts of their case, how to obtain or modify court orders, or how to draft legal documents. The GAL refers parties to their attorneys for legal advice. If a party is pro se, the GAL suggests that the party seek legal advice from an attorney.

COMMENTARY
Many courts have "Lawyer of the Day" programs for indigent parties as well as family law facilitators and many bar associations have lawyer-referral panels. Nonprofit "legal aid" (a/k/a "legal services") programs may be able to provide free legal advice and representation to low income or indigent parties.

The GAL shall refrain from giving a party legal advice that he or she should drop a restraining order so that the parties may meet together with the GAL or engage in mediation pertaining to the restraining order. *See* G.L. c. 209A, § 3.

1.4 The GAL Avoids Dual or Multiple Roles.

The GAL shall not provide legal, mental health, parent coordination, mediation or other professional services to any party or the child during the evaluation or pendency of the case.

COMMENTARY
To provide such services during the Evaluation or pendency of the case is inconsistent with the GAL's role as an impartial evaluator and reporter. The GAL, however, may provide information to the parties, the court, and counsel about community resources available to the parties, such as but not limited to substance abuse treatment programs or other professional services that may be helpful to the parties and their children.

1.5 The GAL Adheres to Applicable Ethical and Professional Standards.

The GAL shall adhere to the ethical guidelines and standards for his or her profession to the extent that these guidelines apply.

COMMENTARY
If the mental health professional serving as a GAL is unable to perform his or her evaluative responsibilities because of a conflict with applicable professional standards, the GAL shall file a motion to withdraw as the GAL with notice to counsel and any pro se parties.

2. COMPENSATION

GAL evaluator's fees paid by the Commonwealth are set by the Administrative Office of the Trial Court. If the court order lacks clarity about who will pay for GAL services, the GAL shall file a motion for clarification by the appointing judge with notice to counsel and any pro se party. If the order specifies that compensation will be paid by the Commonwealth, the GAL is prohibited from charging additional fees to the parties. The GAL files the report in a timely fashion whether or not compensation has been paid.

COMMENTARY
At present, Category E Guardians ad Litem/Evaluators paid by the Commonwealth are compensated in accordance with Memo No. 14 (February 28, 1997, Fiscal Year 1997) issued by the Administrative Office of the Trial Court. The GAL also may file a motion with notice to counsel and any pro se party for an extension of hours beyond the number of hours set forth in the order of appointment for approval by the judge who appointed the GAL.

3. UPON RECEIVING THE APPOINTMENT

The GAL carefully reviews the order of appointment to determine the scope of the evaluation and the duties to be performed.

3.1 The GAL Clarifies the Scope of the Appointment and Duties as Necessary.

If the GAL is uncertain about the areas to be evaluated, or the GAL's responsibilities, the GAL shall file a motion for clarification for hearing before the appointing judge with notice to counsel and pro se parties.

3.2. The GAL Determines Whether he or she has the Requisite Expertise and Competence in the Areas to be Evaluated.

If the GAL lacks the necessary experience, expertise or competence to conduct an evaluation of the issues, the GAL shall decline the appointment.

3.3 The GAL Determines Whether the GAL's Personal and Professional Schedule Permit a Timely Report.

The GAL reviews the areas to be evaluated and the tasks to be performed. If the GAL will not be able to complete a report by the designated deadline, the GAL shall decline the appointment.

COMMENTARY
If the GAL determines after commencement of the evaluation that additional time will be needed to complete the evaluation, the GAL may file a motion to extend the deadline with notice to counsel and any pro se party. The motion shall include the reasons for the proposed extension and a new proposed due date for the report so that the judge may determine whether the deadline should be extended or the appointment should be vacated.

3.4 The GAL Promptly Accepts or Rejects any Appointment.

The GAL shall promptly accept or reject the appointment no later than twenty days after the GAL receives it, or earlier if requested by the court. The GAL accepts or rejects the appointment by returning the completed form to the court.

4. THROUGHOUT THE CASE

4.1 The GAL Maintains an Attitude of Respect.

The GAL shall approach all family members and parties with an attitude of respect and openness to hear their account of the relevant facts regardless of any allegations that have been made. The GAL shall be patient, courteous, and dignified in his or her interactions with litigants, witnesses, attorneys, and others with whom the GAL deals in this official capacity.

COMMENTARY
The GAL may limit the number of telephone calls and contacts made by a party or attorney as is reasonable given the particular circumstances. The GAL may seek assistance from the court on issues related to the GAL's safety or to address inappropriate conduct by a party related to the evaluation. In such instances, a motion must be filed with the court with a copy sent to counsel of record and any pro se parties.

4.2 The GAL is Diligent and Adheres to Time Deadlines.

The GAL shall adhere to all time frames set forth in the order of appointment as applicable.

COMMENTARY
If the report is not filed on time, the Probation Office notifies the judge and seeks further instruction from the court in accordance with Probate and Family Court Standing Order 298. If the GAL needs more time to complete the report, the GAL shall file a motion with notice to counsel and pro se parties to extend the deadline prior to the date when it is due. The motion shall indicate the proposed due date for the report. The GAL shall complete the report even if a party declines to participate or an attorney indicates that the case may settle. A party or GAL may file a motion to terminate the GAL appointment with notice to the parties or GAL as applicable if a case settles and the GAL's services are no longer necessary.

4.3 The GAL Maintains Safety.

The GAL shall make every reasonable effort to ensure the

2

safety of all parties and their children. To implement this requirement, the GAL shall:

A. Arrange joint parent and child interviews, home visits, or observations of a party with the children

B. Avoid interview strategies which put the child(ren) at risk of physical or psychological harm from one or both parents after the interview.

C. Arrange interview schedules so that parties do not come into contact during the interview process when domestic violence is alleged or identified as a possible issue.

D. Inquire about and refrains from disclosing, directly or indirectly, residential, telephone, work, or other location information that a party has kept confidential for safety reasons.

E. Refrain from recommending visitation or other arrangements that bring the parties into contact when an abuse prevention order is in effect, or when the evaluator has reasonable cause to believe that such contact may be dangerous or harmful for either party or the child.

F. Warn the party, the party's attorney and contact police as appropriate if the GAL believes that a party or child is in danger of imminent physical harm from the other party in the case.

COMMENTARY

To ensure the safety of the parties and their children, the GAL should screen for previously undisclosed safety issues in separate interviews with the parties early in the evaluation. Depending on the circumstances, the other party, the child, the GAL, or others may be at risk if there are issues of mental illness, domestic violence, child abuse, or substance abuse. The GAL should attempt to gather and communicate information in ways that avoid harm to parties, the child or children, or others involved in the case. The GAL shall consider the safety of the parties and other family members when he or she makes recommendations and determines how the information he or she has collected will be reported to the court.

4.3.1 The GAL Files Mandatory "51A" Reports When Required.

In cases of suspected child maltreatment, many mental health professionals are required to file a "51A" report. G.L. c. 119, § 51A. However, a mental health professional who is not a mandated reporter may still report suspected abuse or neglect as necessary if a child is at risk. If the GAL has reasonable cause to believe a child is in imminent danger, the GAL should also report the information to the police department and should also report the information to the Court through an emergency motion for instructions with the required notice to counsel and pro se parties.

COMMENTARY

If a GAL files a 51A report, the GAL should assess whether he or she can remain neutral and complete his or her duties free of bias.

4.4 The GAL Shall Use a Process for Communication and Collection of Information that is Conducive to Disclosure of Information and Fair to the Parties.

The GAL provides each party with a separate interview so that each party may speak with candor. The GAL encourages parties and their attorneys to provide additional relevant information and documents. The process for communications must be even-handed and provide each party with the opportunity to present relevant information and respond to relevant allegations by the opposing party. The GAL also affords a pro se party the same procedural protections that the GAL affords a party with an attorney.

4.4.1 The GAL Shall Conduct All Oral and Written Communications with Attorneys and Pro Se Parties in a Manner that Avoids the Question of Bias.

The GAL shall send counsel of record and pro se parties copies of any motions and other documents filed by the GAL in court, except for the GAL report. If the GAL sends a substantive written communication to one counsel or a pro se party, the GAL shall send a copy of the communication to the opposing counsel or pro se party.

COMMENTARY

A GAL's written communications to one party or attorney about administrative or scheduling matters, such as arranging a time for an interview or signing releases, are not substantive matters. While it is not required by any statute or rule, attorneys may agree to send copies of all written correspondence addressed to the guardian ad litem to the opposing counsel.

4.4.2 The GAL Arranges for a Qualified Interpreter if a Party or Child is Not Fluent in the English language or a Sign Language Interpreter is Needed.

The need for an interpreter goes beyond the courtroom if a party is not completely fluent or comfortable in using the English language or needs an American Sign Language interpreter. Using a child as the interpreter is not appropriate, and using relatives or friends may have a chilling effect on what is disclosed. If the child or a party has limited or no English language skills and the GAL does not speak the language, a qualified interpreter should be used. Any authorizations for release of information and other forms should be translated for such parties. Likewise, a party or child may have a need for a sign language interpreter.

COMMENTARY

If a party does not supply a qualified interpreter, the GAL may file a motion in court for appointment of a qualified interpreter that includes a request that the Commonwealth pay for the interpreter's services if a party is indigent, or that a party or parties who are not indigent pay for the interpreter. Counsel and pro se parties shall be given notice of the motion. If the GAL desires payment from or reimbursement from the Commonwealth for the cost of using an interpreter, the GAL must receive approval from the court before incurring the expense. Bias or incompetence of an interpreter can lead to omitted and inaccurate communications with the GAL. The interpreter should not have a conflict of interest or a relationship with a party or other person that will bias the interpretation. The Supreme Judicial Court has promulgated standards for court interpreter services and qualifications which are available on the internet at: http://www.state.ma.us/courts/formsandguidelines/index.html.

Certain cases may require that the GAL possess or utilize cross-cultural competence and expertise. For example, if the parents dispute whether a certain religious ritual was integral to a certain faith and whether the ritual should be performed on the child. The role of the interpreter, however, is to facilitate communication rather than serve as a substitute for an expert on a particular culture.

4.5 The GAL Answers Appropriate Questions about the GAL's Credentials or Role.

The GAL answers appropriate questions about the GAL's education, training, experience, practice areas, professional affiliations, and the process of the GAL evaluation.

COMMENTARY

If requested by counsel or a pro se party, the GAL shall provide a copy of his or her curriculum vitae to said counsel or party. However, questions pertaining to the GAL's personal life need not be answered.

4.6 The GAL Maintains Confidentiality.

The information gathered by the GAL for the court is confidential. The GAL shall not disclose confidential and personally identifiable information about the parties, their children, or the services rendered by the GAL to a person who is not a party or counsel in the case, except as necessary to gather information to complete the evaluation and report, or to perform responsibilities related to the order of appointment. This prohibition is permanent and applies to the GAL's writings, lectures, or other media communications.

COMMENTARY

If a GAL has questions regarding release of information pertaining to the parties, child, or the evaluation and report, the GAL may file a motion for instructions with the court with notice to counsel and any pro se party.

4.6.1 The GAL Obtains Appropriate Release Forms or Court Orders before Obtaining Privileged and Confidential Information about the Parties and their Children.

Many of the most common and relevant records that are subject to statutory privileges or other restrictions can be obtained with an appropriate authorization for release of the information or a court order.

- Department of Social Services (DSS) records. A party's release form or court order is needed to access records. The GAL can obtain the DSS file with a release from a party but privileged information must be redacted. 10 C.M.R. § 12.09(l)(3).
- Medical, health and hospital records. A party's release form or court order is needed to access records. G.L. c. 111, § 70, § 70E(b); The Health Insurance Portability and Accountability Act of 1996, Pub. L. 10419 1 (HIPAA).
- Psychotherapist records. A party's release form or court order is needed to access records pertaining to an adult from a psychotherapist whose communications are privileged. G.L. c. 112, § 8GB; *Commonwealth v. Bernard*, 424 Mass. 32, 673 N.E.2d 1220 (1996). G.L. c. 233, § 20B.
- Social Worker records. A party's release form or court order is needed to access records. G.L. c. 112, §§ 135A, 135B.
- Alcohol and drug abuse programs records. A party's release form and/or court order may be needed to access records. 42 U.S.C. §§ 1-175, 290 dd-3.
- School records. If a party has shared or sole legal custody, he or she may authorize release of records, except for a parent or party whose access is restricted by a Chapter 209A or other court order. G.L. c. 71, § 34H; G.L. c. 208, § 31.
- Criminal Offender Record Information (CORI and CARI). The GAL can most easily review these records with a court order through the Probation Department, or request the records through the Criminal History Systems Board.
- Prior GAL reports, Probation Office or Court Clinic reports involving the parties. The GAL must file a motion with the court with notice to the parties to access these records.
- Domestic Violence or Sexual Assault Victim Counselor records. Confidential communications cannot be disclosed in civil actions by court order and are not discoverable without the victim's prior consent. G.L. c. 233, §§ 20J, 20K.
- Victim program locations. Locations of battered women's shelters, domestic violence, and rape crisis programs may not be disclosed by court order, or otherwise to the GAL. G.L. c. 233, §§ 20J, 20K.
- Mediator Records. Communications made during mediation with a mediator are privileged and the court cannot order disclosure. G.L. c. 233, § 23C.
- Alternative dispute intervention information. The Probation Department of the Probate and Family Court may release the information to the GAL if the court orders release of the information or the parties consent to the release of information.

The Health Insurance Portability and Accountability Act of 1996, Pub. L. 10419 1 (HIPAA) requires that health providers may only release personal health information if the release signed by a party complies with the provisions of the federal law. Even if no statutory privilege applies to the information sought by the GAL, the provider or keeper of other records (e.g. unlicensed support group leaders, batterer intervention programs) may also request a written release from their client. In some instances, the order for appointment of the GAL will provide that the GAL is permitted to access certain records and information; this obviates the need for a party's authorization for release of the information.

COMMENTARY

Some third parties or providers may be unaware of protections that apply to records or confidential information relating to the parties or the children. The GAL, however, shall review the information only after appropriate releases or court orders for access to the information have been provided to the holder of the information. If a privilege is not properly waived, a judge may allow a motion to strike reference to the information from the GAL report.

4.6.2 The GAL Recognizes that Children's Rights to Confidentiality are Different than Other Parties' Rights to Confidentiality.

The GAL shall obtain authorizations for release of information pertaining to children from the children's parents or legal guardians. A parent, however, cannot waive a child's psychotherapy or social worker privilege. If the counseling information is needed but protected by a privilege, the GAL or counsel must return to the appointing judge and present a motion for appointment of another guardian ad litem to evaluate whether waiver of the child's psychotherapy privilege is in the child's best interest. *Adoption of Diane*, 400 Mass. 196, 201 (1987); G.L. c. 233, § 20B. The motion should indicate the scope of the information sought and the GAL's reason for seeking the information. Counsel and pro se parties must have notice of the motion. If the privilege is waived, the GAL may access the information.

COMMENTARY

A parent or parents with legal custody of the child, or a party granted legal guardianship of the child, may authorize access to most other records of the child. If a parent or parents refuse to authorize release of information that is important to the evaluation, the GAL may file a motion for access to the information with notice to counsel and pro se parties.

5. COMMENCEMENT OF THE EVALUATION

After the GAL accepts the appointment, he or she promptly schedules initial contacts with each of the parties and their attorneys if they are represented.

COMMENTARY

If a party has an attorney, the GAL should first make contact with the attorney. The GAL may find it helpful to send a letter of introduction to counsel and pro se parties outlining the evaluation process. The GAL should use additional means of communication, however, if a party's primary language is not English, or there are literacy or other barriers impacting written communication. The GAL can determine more easily if a party understands what is communicated in a face-to-face interview.

5.1 The GAL Provides an Explanation of the GAL's Role and a Lamb-type Warning at the Commencement of the Evaluation.

The GAL must explain the GAL's role and the purpose of the evaluation to the parties. The GAL shall inform the parties how the information gathered by the GAL will be used. The GAL must provide a "Lamb warning" that explains there are no "off the record" discussions and any information collected by the GAL may appear in the GAL report, be disclosed in court or to the other party, *Commonwealth v. Lamb*, 1 Mass. App. Ct. 530 (1973), or otherwise disclosed as required or permitted by law. As appropriate based on the child's level of maturity, the GAL should provide a similar explanation of the evaluative process and a Lamb warning to a child, but modified to reflect the child's age and level of understanding. If the GAL interviews other witnesses, they also must receive a Lamb warning.

COMMENTARY

To ensure a person understands the Lamb warning, the GAL should ask the person to summarize it for the GAL. The parties or witnesses should be informed that while they are encouraged to provide information, they may decline to answer a question and have an attorney present during any interview. Increasingly, parties represent themselves in court. The GAL should avoid use of professional jargon or legalese that a party may not understand. The GAL should strive to explain things in simple language and terms as appropriate so that a party with a limited educational background or language ability can better understand what the GAL is communicating.

5.2 The GAL Inquires if the Parties have Relevant Safety Concerns.

The GAL shall inquire at the outset of the evaluation about any safety risks related to the evaluation for either party, the child, or others because of any party's mental illness, substance abuse, domestic violence, child abuse, or history of violence against others. The GAL should attempt to conduct the investigation and evaluation in such a manner as appropriate to avoid likely harm to the child, a party, the GAL, or others.

2

5.3 The GAL Explains the Limits on Confidentiality and Complies with Legal and Ethical Standards Governing Disclosure of Privileged Communications.

The GAL shall obtain information or review records after appropriate authorizations for release of information are executed or the court orders release of the information. The GAL shall respect the parties' and their children's right to confidentiality. Before obtaining an authorization for release of records or other information from a party, the GAL should inform the party how the information will be used. The GAL should also disclose that any information obtained by the GAL could appear in the GAL report, be disclosed to the other party, put into evidence during court proceedings or depositions, or disclosed to others as necessary to complete the evaluation, discovery, or trial of the case. The authorization for release of information form given to a party by the GAL should include who the information is sought from and the duration of the authorization of the release. A party should also be informed that he or she has a right to seek legal advice before signing a release and may decline to sign an authorization for release of information. A party may direct that all release forms be sent directly to counsel of record.

If a party consents to release of information, the GAL should use forms for release of information that comply with applicable laws and that are acceptable to providers. The Health Insurance Portability and Accountability Act of 1996, Pub. L. 10419 1 (HIPAA) requires that health providers may only release personal health information if the release form complies with the provisions of the federal law.

COMMENTARY

The GAL should not seek confidential information unless it is necessary. If a party objects to release of certain information, the GAL may file a motion to obtain this information. G.L. c. 233, § 20B; G.L. c. 112, § 135B; *Commonwealth v. Bernard*, 424 Mass. 32 (1996). A parent cannot consent to release of a child's psychotherapy information. *See* Section 4.6.2.

6. EVALUATION SOURCES AND METHODS

The GAL shall conduct the evaluation in a fair and balanced manner. The GAL should obtain similar types of information about each party. If the case involves more than one child, each child's best interests must be addressed unless the court orders otherwise. If the GAL is unable to report on all of the children, the GAL shall indicate why in the report.

COMMENTARY

Depending on the circumstances, the GAL may need to spend more time investigating facts or evaluating issues that relate only to one party, especially if such facts are disputed, difficult to investigate, or new information arises about that parent. The GAL may have satisfactory information about one parent, but incomplete data about the other parent. For example, further investigation of alleged drug use might be needed if a party's drug testing results are unreliable because the facility did not monitor how samples from the party were collected, or new sources indicate that the party has used drugs since the time of the last testing.

6.1 The GAL Shall be Familiar with Applicable Legal Standards and Procedures

The GAL shall be familiar with the law and the legal standards applicable to the questions the GAL has been appointed to evaluate.

COMMENTARY

A GAL who is not an attorney, shall nonetheless have a sufficient understanding of the law to provide the judge with the facts that the judge will need to apply the applicable legal standard.

6.2 The GAL Spends Sufficient Time Interviewing Parties and Investigating their Concerns as Necessary to Gather Relevant Information.

The GAL conducts an initial interview with each party and additional interviews with each party and other witnesses as necessary to gather relevant information. In addition, the GAL may gather information by telephone, email, and or other means.

COMMENTARY

A party is permitted to have counsel present during an interview, but the GAL controls the interview and conducts the questioning. If counsel directs a party to refuse to answer a question or plead the Fifth Amendment against self-incrimination, the GAL moves on to other questions, noting the objection. Such objections do not prohibit the GAL from using other sources to obtain the information. If the GAL does not meet with any party, the GAL explains why in the report.

6.3 The GAL Asks Each Party about Relevant Witnesses and Documents and Investigates these Sources of Information as Appropriate.

As a starting point, the GAL invites counsel and parties to provide relevant information, including a fact summary, procedural history, relevant documents, and a list of witnesses and professionals who can provide relevant information. In deciding what records to review or witnesses to interview, the GAL considers the likelihood that relevant information will be obtained, with reasonable convenience, efficiency, cost, and physical safety of a party, child or informant.

The order of appointment also may direct the GAL to contact certain witnesses or sources.

COMMENTARY

In determining what witnesses to interview, the GAL may also consider: the number of witnesses suggested, whether the witness directly witnessed important events or the aftermath of important events, the potential bias of the witness, the importance of the interview to a party, and other relevant considerations. At the beginning of each collateral witness or party interview, it is important that the GAL explain the GAL's role and the limits of confidentiality. The GAL shall access information after appropriate release forms are provided to professionals. In addition to oral communications, the GAL may provide written questions and accept additional written responses from witnesses or collateral sources. If a GAL declines to interview some or all of suggested witnesses, the GAL shall provide an explanation why the witnesses were not interviewed.

6.4 The GAL Shall Use Methods Designed to Assess the Accuracy of Information Gathered

The GAL uses interview and fact gathering techniques designed to test the factual accuracy and reliability (i.e. objective truth) of the information gathered. The GAL compares sources of information, looks for consistencies and inconsistencies in reports, and appraises the value of the information gathered.

6.4.1 The GAL Uses Multiple Fact Sources When Possible.

If certain events or facts are disputed, the GAL should investigate more than one source of information relating to the events or allegations when possible. The parties should be encouraged to provide names of witnesses who were present, written reports, or other relevant evidence related to the event or allegation.

COMMENTARY

For example, the husband disputes the wife's claim that the husband told her that he was treated at Cambridge Hospital after he attempted suicide by taking an overdose of sleeping pills and cocaine. The GAL contacts the hospital and interviews any other witnesses with direct knowledge about the disputed event or his statements about it. Hospital records in the case lead to other relevant sources of information such as "911" call records, a police report, and an ambulance report, including a copy of a suicide note found in the ambulance. The GAL reports all the relevant facts collected about the disputed allegation.

6.4.2 The GAL Accesses Original Sources When Possible.

To increase the reliability of reported information, the GAL investigates original sources of information.

For example: John Jones says that Jane Doe saw the parties' son drinking beer at a soccer game. The GAL speaks with Jane Doe to ascertain what she observed.

For example: a police report indicates that the child told his soccer coach that the child's parent supplied the beer. The GAL speaks with the coach and the child.

6.5 The GAL Conducts a Home Visit When Appropriate.

Ordinarily, home visits can yield valuable information, but on occasion a home visit is not indicated. Factors to consider in deciding whether to conduct home visits include: whether issues or problems with either home are alleged, cost and time involved, location, and the likelihood of obtaining relevant information not accessible in other ways. If no home visit is conducted, the GAL shall explain why that decision was made in the report.

COMMENTARY

If home visits are conducted, care must be exercised so that inequality in housing conditions or perceived wealth do not lead to bias. A person, who is a fit parent and caretaker for the child, also may experience transitional or temporary housing difficulties as a result of separation from the other party, nonpayment of support, inadequate financial support, or relocation related to domestic violence or loss of income.

6.6 The GAL Meets with the Children and Interviews them in a Developmentally Appropriate Manner

The GAL meets with the children as part of the investigation. Children can offer useful information and should be offered the opportunity to provide information about themselves and their family. The GAL uses developmentally appropriate techniques to observe, interview and evaluate each child in the family. The conditions under which children are interviewed must be carefully considered, including what conditions will put the child most at ease and yield the most useful information. The GAL shall explain the reasons for not meeting with any of the children in the GAL report.

COMMENTARY

Some children may be much less candid in the interview if a parent or the parents are present during the child's interview, or are visible or able to hear the interview.

6.7 The GAL Observes Children with Each Parent When Appropriate.

The GAL should observe the child with each parent when appropriate. This often provides valuable information about the parent-child relationship.

COMMENTARY

The GAL has a duty to avoid further harm to children when possible. If concerns are raised that a child will be traumatized or at risk by contact with a parent (e.g. due to severe neglect or abuse, exposure to domestic violence, traumatic or unpredictable absence, or other inappropriate behavior) a parent-child observation may not be indicated. The GAL explains the reasons for not observing children with each parent in the report.

6.8 The GAL Considers the Need for any Further Information Necessary to Complete the GAL Evaluation and Provide a Comprehensive Report.

The GAL shall collect and review documents as well as conduct additional interviews of the parties, each of the children and other witnesses until the necessary information is fully gathered.

The GAL may consider the usefulness of specialized evaluation tools such as behavioral information surveys; psychological and neuropsychological testing of mental health, adaptive functioning and/or medication needs; evaluations of substance abuse, sexual offending behavior, domestic violence, educational/learning needs; or clinical determinations of child sexual abuse.

7. USE OF SPECIALIZED CLINICAL METHODS IN THE FORENSIC CONTEXT

Specialized methods include primarily psychological testing and sexual abuse evaluations. Other specialized methods such as educational or medical evaluations are subject to the same general requirements as those set forth here.

7.1 The GAL Shall use Specialized Methods Only when Doing so is Likely to Produce Necessary, Relevant and Useful Information to Evaluate the Forensic Questions in the Case.

The GAL must evaluate the merits of using a specialized method and consider the costs (e.g. financial and time) to the parties or to the Court. If the GAL chooses to use a specialized method, the GAL explains the reasons to the parties and counsel, and documents those reasons in the report.

Psychological Testing

Psychological testing is not required in most cases. The GAL shall obtain an order of the court before performing psychological testing unless previously authorized to do so by the court. In each case the GAL must balance likelihood of obtaining relevant and reliable information against the financial costs, the time involved and the potential invasiveness of the testing. Testing may be necessary when the psychological health or functioning of a party or child is directly relevant to the issues the GAL has been appointed to evaluate, or when psychological limitations of the parties make it difficult to obtain relevant information without psychological testing. When considering psychological testing, the GAL should first determine whether the information sought by the testing could be obtained in other ways.

When selecting a particular psychological test, the GAL ensures and is prepared to explain how any chosen test measures factors relevant to the issues before the court. The GAL shall consider and be prepared to articulate for the Court the reliability and validity of any chosen test. (See *Daubert v. Merrell Dow Pharmaceuticals, Inc.* 509 U.S. 579 (1993) and *Commonwealth v. Lanigan*, 413 Mass. 154 (1994). Elements of reliability and validity include: commercial availability of the test or measure including a comprehensive test manual; relevant measures of reliability for the test or measure; relevant measures of validity for the test or measure; appropriateness of use with the examinee (e.g. relevance of race, ethnicity, primary language, reading level); peer reviews of the test or measure; relevant error rates of the test or measure or of components (e.g. index or scale) of the test or measure; method of scoring and interpreting including the published system (e.g. Rorschach Comprehensive System); appropriateness of use in the context for which it is being used.

Sexual Abuse Evaluations

In determining the appropriateness of conducting a sexual abuse evaluation, the GAL shall first consider the nature and extent of the alleged sexual abuse, the context in which the sexual abuse allegations were raised (e.g. custody conflict) and the relationship of potential findings from the sexual abuse evaluation to the questions that the GAL has been appointed to evaluate.

As with psychological testing, the GAL takes reasonable steps to ensure the relevance, reliability, and validity of the sexual abuse evaluation procedure the GAL uses. The GAL shall consider and be prepared to articulate for the Court the reliability and validity of the sexual abuse evaluation procedure.

7.2 The GAL shall Only use those Specialized Methods that the GAL is Competent to use in the Forensic Context.

The GAL adheres to relevant standards of ethics and conduct including those which govern psychological testing and other specialized methods, and does not practice outside his or her areas of competence. The GAL shall also be competent to use these specialized methods in a forensic context.

COMMENTARY

The GAL or designee does not succumb to pressure by legal actors to overstate or inaccurately represent tests, test interpretations, or the results of sexual abuse evaluations or other specialized methods.

Psychological Testing

The GAL must be qualified to administer and interpret each test instrument used, or ensure that his or her designee is qualified to perform these functions. In addition, the GAL or designee must be familiar with applicable testing standards such as the current American Psychological Association's Standards for Educational and Psychological Testing. The GAL must also be knowledgeable about psychological testing in the forensic context, and must be able to link the data, hypotheses and interpretations generated by testing to the forensic questions the GAL has been appointed to evaluate, and must be able to articulate to the Court the limitations of the each test used and its role in the comprehensive GAL evaluation.

Sexual Abuse Evaluations

The GAL or designee must be qualified to perform sexual

2

abuse evaluations. Qualifications include: training in child and adolescent psychology; supervised training and practice in conducting sexual abuse evaluations in the forensic context, knowledge of the literature of sexual abuse as it pertains to the family court context and knowledge of the relevant practice guidelines and standards (an example of one well known set of standards is the American Professional Society on the Abuse of Children [APSAC] Standards). In addition, the GAL must be able to link the evaluation data, hypotheses and interpretations generated by the sexual abuse evaluation to the forensic questions before the evaluator, and to articulate to the Court the limitations of the sexual abuse evaluation and its role in the comprehensive GAL evaluation.

7.2.1 If the GAL is not Competent to Perform Psychological Testing or a Sexual Abuse Evaluation, the GAL shall make a Referral to, or Obtain a Consultation with, an Appropriate Clinical Evaluator (henceforth, the "Designee.").

The GAL seeks a Court order to have an additional professional conduct the specialized evaluation. The GAL takes reasonable steps to ensure the designee is competent to perform psychological testing or a sexual abuse evaluation.

Before making a referral to a designee for psychological testing or a sexual abuse evaluation, a GAL should consider obtaining a consultation from an appropriate professional. The purpose of this consultation is to determine whether or not psychological testing or a sexual abuse evaluation would provide useful information to the Court.

The GAL shall inform the designee that the designee is subject to the requirements of these standards where applicable.

7.2.2 If the GAL is Competent to Perform Psychological Testing or a Sexual Abuse Evaluation, the GAL shall Consider Whether it is Nevertheless Useful or Necessary to have Another Professional Conduct the Testing or Sexual Abuse Evaluation.

If the Court has not already clarified whether the GAL or another professional should conduct the testing or sexual abuse evaluation, factors for the GAL to consider in making that determination include: the clinical appropriateness of having the GAL conduct the evaluation. (e.g. an eight year old female alleged sexual abuse victim might feel frightened or uncomfortable with a male evaluator.); the need for consultation from another professional, whether performing the overall GAL evaluation biases, or appears to bias, the GAL's interpretation of testing/sexual abuse evaluation data.

7.3 The GAL Shall Only Interpret the Results of Psychological Testing and Sexual Abuse evaluations in the Context of Multiple Sources of Data.

The GAL should not use psychological testing data as the sole source of information from which to draw conclusions about a party or child. The GAL should consider psychological tests as a means of supporting, disconfirming or generating hypotheses that are to be further investigated and confirmed or disconfirmed through clinical interviews, collateral interviews, document reviews, observations and other available data. If test data conflicts with other sources of data, the GAL is obliged to explain how the GAL understands the discrepancies.

It is particularly important that the GAL be knowledgeable about the ways in which specialty issues (such as Domestic Violence, Child Abuse and Substance Abuse) may contribute to the interpretation of test data.

The results of a sexual abuse evaluation are not, by themselves, determinative of parenting capacity. The sexual abuse evaluation data must be reviewed in the context of the broader forensic question that the GAL has been appointed to evaluate.

7.4 The GAL Avoids Offering Psychiatric Diagnoses, Except when Special Circumstances Require the GAL to do so.

The role of the GAL in most Probate and Family Court matters does not require or warrant the formulation of psychiatric diagnoses. The GAL does gather information relevant to the psychological functioning and mental health histories (both directly and through collateral sources) of both parties and the child(ren). The GAL recognizes that a diagnostic label is not determinative of parenting capacity. Rather than making diagnoses, the GAL describes the impact of clinical symptoms or known diagnoses on the functional abilities of a parent or child and the relationship between the parent and child.

COMMENTARY

In the unusual circumstance where formulating a new diagnosis might be appropriate, the GAL considers the potential risks and benefits of making the diagnosis, and the relevance of such a diagnosis to the referral question. The GAL assures that s/he has all the information necessary to make such a diagnosis and is competent to do so. The GAL is particularly sensitive to the potentially pejorative and prejudicial aspects of a diagnosis in the legal context. The GAL provides the rationale for making the diagnosis in the report.

8.0 SPECIALTY EVALUATION TOPICS

In the context of disputed Probate and Family Court matters, some allegations require specialized investigation and evaluation. Examples of such specialty topics which frequently arise in Category E GAL evaluations include: substance abuse, domestic violence, mental illness, and child abuse. Specialty evaluation topics demand both process and content considerations.

8.1 The GAL Asks the Parties about Key Issues which Might Warrant Specialized Attention.

As part of the comprehensive evaluation, the GAL gathers a background history of each party designed to screen for specialty concerns (see 9.1E). The GAL is also attentive to allegations raised by all parties. The GAL should phrase questions about the specialized topics in non-judgmental language, and ask them in multiple ways. This affords the parties the greatest opportunity to answer openly and accurately.

8.2 The GAL Considers Whether the GAL is Competent to Evaluate Questions that Require Specialized Expertise.

The GAL assesses his or her competence to address the specialty issues that are present in the case. The GAL makes this assessment at the outset of the case, and throughout the case.

If the GAL is not competent to evaluate the specialized questions, the GAL considers:

- Referring the specialized assessment component of the comprehensive GAL evaluation to a competent mental health professional with specialized expertise,
- Seeking consultation and/or supervision from a professional with specialized expertise,
- Withdrawing from the case because the specialized issue warrants that a person with specialized expertise conduct the comprehensive GAL evaluation.

COMMENTARY

The GAL also considers the level of attention required to appropriately address the concerns or allegations. In making decisions about whether to refer or seek consultation with a person with specialized expertise, the GAL takes reasonable steps to ensure that the professional to whom the referral is made is competent as per standard 8.2 and does not have a conflict of interest or role conflict as per 1.3 A or 1.4. Finally, the GAL considers the issues of cost, inefficiency, and delay in assigning such assessments to other professionals.

8.3 The GAL Shall be Competent to Evaluate Specialized Topics Within a Forensic Context.

- The GAL or designee must have the education or training, knowledge and experience necessary to evaluate a specialty topic within the forensic context.
- The GAL or designee must be knowledgeable about any relevant laws, legal standards or rules particular to specialty topics.
- The GAL or designee must be aware of any relevant standards of practice relevant to the evaluation of specialty topics. These include the Massachusetts Standards on Substance Abuse by the Justices of the Supreme Judicial

Court in collaboration with the Massachusetts Trial Court (1998) at: http://www.mass.gov/courts/formsandguidelines/substancev.html, and the Standards on Judicial Practice, Abuse Prevention Guidelines by the Administrative Office of the Trial Court (2000) at: http://www.mass.gov/courts/formsandguidelines/domestic/dvtoc.html

- The GAL or designee must be knowledgeable about ways that specialty topics might present in the forensic context.
- The GAL must be able to access and interpret collateral sources relevant to each specialty topic.
- The GAL or designee must maintain a current knowledge of the literature and critical issues in specialty topics in the forensic context.

8.4 The GAL Incorporates the GAL's Conclusions from the Specialty Areas with all other Data Gathered in the Evaluation to Complete a Functional Assessment of Parenting as it Relates to the Forensic Questions to be Addressed.

A. **Substance abuse and Mental Illness**—Conclusions about a party related to his/her substance abuse, mental illness, are not dispositive on the question of parenting capacity. The applicable case law states that a determination that one party has or had an active substance abuse problem or mental illness does not constitute unfitness, in and of itself. (See, for example, *Adoption of Katharine*, 674 N.E. 2d 256 (Mass. App. Ct. (1997)).

B. **Domestic violence**—Conclusions that a party has been a victim of domestic violence are not dispositive of parenting capacity. Conclusions that a party has been the perpetrator of domestic violence are considered direct indicia of parenting capacity, but do not predetermine the answer to the forensic question (e.g. the specifics of a custody/visitation plan). Some conclusions by the GAL about domestic violence may lead to findings by the Court which trigger the requirements of the custodial presumption in favor of custody to the non-perpetrating parent. (G.L. c. 208, § 31a)

C. **Child Abuse**—Conclusions that a party has perpetrated abuse against a child are direct indicia of parenting capacity. As above, however, such conclusions do not dictate the answer to the forensic question to be addressed.

COMMENTARY

The GAL recognizes that an adequate assessment of any of these specialized topics involves consideration of co-existing issues that may complicate the resolution of the problem, or mitigate the importance of the problem. For example, resolving a substance dependence problem does not necessarily resolve the other mental health problems, nor does it automatically improve parenting. On the other side, a mentally ill parent may have a support and resource network which allows adequate caretaking of the children even when flagrantly ill or incapacitated.

8.5 In Cases Involving but not Limited to Domestic Violence, Substance Abuse, Child Abuse and Mental Illness, the GAL Should Identify the Types of Supportive Services Believed Necessary to Successfully Implement a Custody and Access Plan

Examples. Such resources may include: substance abuse assessment and treatment, mental health evaluation and treatment, sexual abuse or certified batterers' treatment; supervised visitation; counseling; parenting education; educational assessment for the child(ren); medication assessment; recreational or social services; housing or public benefits advocacy; regular payment of court ordered child support; DSS provided in-home services.

COMMENTARY

Standard VII of the Massachusetts Substance Abuse Standards promulgated by the Supreme Judicial Court and the Trial Court requires prompt screening to alert the court to the possible need for an immediate substance abuse assessment or treatment program. The Substance Abuse Standards depend to some extent on resources that are not yet fully available to the Court. This may limit the GAL's ability to perform the tasks set out in the standards. It is nonetheless important that the GAL be aware of the standards and consider which elements the GAL has the resources to perform.

8.6 In Cases Where it is Appropriate that a Party's Access to Children Proceeds in Stages, the GAL may Suggest a Process for Monitoring Such Access.

In some cases involving domestic violence, child abuse, substance abuse or mental illness, it may be appropriate that access to the child on the part of the "visiting" party proceed in stages. When appropriate, the GAL may suggest, a process for monitoring a plan built on access increasing in stages.

2

COMMENTARY

The Massachusetts Substance Abuse Standards require a monitoring plan in cases where a party's substance abuse problem is a factor in behavior related to the case. Specifically, Standard XII requires that the Court monitor compliance and Standard XIII requires the Court to implement strategies to prevent relapse. (But see commentary to 8.5 above).

Planning for shifts in access requires many considerations including the recognition that predicting behavior over lengthy time frames has serious potential for inaccuracy. The following is a non-inclusive list of considerations: Whether a parent can comply with the recommendations; How likely is it that compliance with recommended interventions will translate into changes related to parenting?; How important it is that the child have access to the parent even if the parent is non-compliant?; What conditions need to be required of the parent without the problem (e.g. substance abuse, mental illness, etc.) in order for a child to better benefit from contact with the parent with the problem?

9. SCOPE AND CONTENT OF THE EVALUATION

A comprehensive history creates a context for understanding the current issues in dispute. The nature and extent of the family history obtained, through both interviews as well as review of documents depends on the particular family's circumstances and the directives contained in the order of appointment. However, it is commonplace to obtain the following information unless it is not relevant:

A. History of legal proceedings and prior investigations and evaluations.

- The nature of the case, including the parties and children involved, relevant procedural history, current orders, and the relief sought by each party;
- History of other cases involving the parties, including prior cases pertaining to parties or the children including, but not limited to Probate and Family Court, Juvenile Court, criminal, abuse prevention, or other relevant cases;
- Prior custody related investigations and evaluations, including GAL, Court Clinic, Probation, Department of Social Services, or other evaluations or assessments;

B. Facts designated by court order and the applicable law.

- The issues that the court specifies for investigation and evaluation in the order of appointment;
- Facts relevant to the legal standard that applies to the case for:
  - modification of custody or visitation;
  - termination of parental rights;
  - guardianship of a minor;
  - removal of the child from the Commonwealth;
  - custody or visitation by a parent.

C. Relevant concerns raised in the case by each parent, including facts related to how each parent's proposed outcome serves or conflicts with the child's best interests.

D. Parenting history.

- With whom have the children lived and for how long;
- What parenting tasks have each parent performed, when, for how long;
- Each parent's past and present parenting capacities including both skills and deficits;
- The competence with which each parent carried out parenting tasks;
- History of parents' past joint decision-making regarding children;

- Parent's present ability to communicate or make joint decisions;
- Whether a third party or either party is or was a primary caretaker;
- History and impact of a parent's substance abuse, mental illness, or domestic violence on the children and the parent's parenting ability;
- History of physical, sexual or emotional abuse of the children;
- History of past restraining orders and violence against others;
- Each parent's past and present parenting skills and deficits;
- The strength and quality of the parent-child relationships, emotional closeness, attachment, and perceptions of each other;
- Each parent's or potential caretaker's knowledge of the children, knowledge of parenting techniques, disciplinary practices, ability to distinguish his or her own needs from the needs of the children, and to understand and respond to the children's needs;
- The ability of the parent to promote and support appropriate social, emotional, and educational development in the children, and to provide a stable home environment for the children;
- Each parent's or potential caretaker's ability to support the children's relationship with the other parent as appropriate;
- Each party's ability to communicate and cooperate with the other parent regarding the children as appropriate, including the impact of substance abuse, mental illness or domestic violence on that ability;
- Each parent's ability to recognize his or her own and the other parents strengths and weaknesses as parent.

E. The family history.

- History of parents' relationship, including if and for how long the parties lived together as a family;
- Parties' accounts of how difficulties began, were disclosed, or persist;
- Prior Department of Social Services involvement with family members;
- Children's present and past school functioning;
- Criminal history of both parties (CORI (Criminal Offender Record Information) or CARI (Court Activity Record Information);
- Sexual offense history (Sexual Offender Registry Information, or SORI);
- Substance abuse and substance use history of family members;
- Mental health treatment and history of family members;
- Relevant medical history or problems of family members;
- Presence of new relationships, partners or their children;
- Relationships with significant caretakers, grandparents, relatives, child care providers;
- Each parent's family history and current relationship with family of origin and partner's family;
- Education and employment history of parents;
- If relevant, ethnic, cultural, lifestyle, and religious factors.

F. Developmental status and parenting needs of the children.

- The child's preferences for custody and access.
- Each child's developmental history, functioning in school, peer relationships, medical and mental health history, activities, schedules;
- Special needs of each child: medical, learning or developmental problems;
- Assessment of each child's adjustment to school, friends, community, and extended families;
- Child's temperament and response to transitions;
- Impact of change on child's routines, attachments, familiar environs;
- Impact of the divorce or separation on the child, if any.
- Child's exposure to, understanding of or concerns about a parent's needs, wishes, concerns, safety, or problems;
- Quality of relationship between siblings;
- Particular challenges for either parent or the child with each other.

10. REPORT WRITING AND ANALYSIS

The report should address and relate to the areas of investigation and evaluation designated by the order of appointment. The report should provide accurate, detailed and balanced information about the parties and their children.

10.1 The Report Should Appear Professional in Appearance, Format and Writing Style.

The report should be typed, well-written and neat in appearance. Pages must be numbered. The GAL shall attempt to avoid spelling, grammar or typographical errors in the report. The GAL should write the report in a way that is concise in words, yet able to encompass all the relevant facts and provide detailed information. The language used in the report should be understandable to the average layperson and avoid jargon that may be confusing. The GAL should prepare a report that is well-organized. Use of headings, bold type, or underlining to separate different sections or topics in the report may make a report easier to comprehend. The report shall be dated and signed by the GAL with the GAL's name typed below the signature. The report shall include the GAL's mailing or office address and telephone number.

10.2 The Report Should be Accurate, Objective and Unbiased.

When writing the report, the GAL provides a balanced view of the parties that includes all of their relevant strengths and weaknesses. The information contained in the report should be accurate. It also should be as factual and detailed as possible. The GAL report should:

A. Use descriptive statements and provide ample details, but avoid inflammatory characterizations if possible.

Inflammatory characterization: "Mr. Jones is well-known to the courts as a drunk."

Descriptive statement: "Mr. Jones was convicted in Somerville District Court of driving under the influence of alcohol in 1986, 1996, 2001, and in July, 2003."

B. Provide past and present relevant facts relating to both parties and the children.

1. Include all relevant facts that address the court's directives.
2. Include all relevant facts collected from all sources, including facts that are consistent and inconsistent with other reported facts.
3. Provide balanced and similar information about both parties;
4. Provide relevant and detailed information about all of the children.
5. Include facts that do not support the GAL's recommendations or conclusions.
6. Disclose what important information may be missing and why it is missing.

C. Include specific information and provide dates and pinpoint time frames if at all possible.

Avoid use of vague phrases or time frames such as "in the past" or "occasionally" or "sometimes" if a more precise time frame is available. The GAL should provide detailed information.

Vague: "John says he used heroin in the past."

Specific: "John says he used heroin in May, 1996 and June, 1998."

Vague: "Mary states that John occasionally uses drugs."

Specific: "Mary states that she saw John use cocaine twice in August, 1998."

Vague: "The child has health problems."

Specific: "The child has diabetes."

10.3 The GAL Identifies the Sources of Information.

Sources should be easily identified in the report. The GAL must list every person interviewed and the records reviewed with any relevant information about the informant or source.

- Date and Name of each person interviewed (e.g. Dr. Tom Jones on 9/5/03),
- Position, profession, place of employment (psychiatrist, General Hospital);
- Description of record reviewed (Dr. Jones' records regarding mother);
- Date the record was made and period it encompasses (July, 2002 to July, 2003);
- How information was obtained (e.g. in person, telephone call, written request);
- Date records were reviewed or obtained by the GAL (9/5/03);
- Informant or record author's relationship to the parties, child or family (Dr. Jones is mother's psychiatrist, but also saw her and the husband for marriage counseling in May, 2001).

If a source is not clearly identified, a party can move to strike the statement from the report.

Example of improper attribution: "Hospital staff said that Drew Smith was hospitalized there for three months last year." (Names of the staff and hospital are missing).

Use of hearsay statements is permitted in the report, but the GAL should always attempt to contact and also quote the original source in the report if possible.

10.4 If a Party Fails or Refuses to Participate, the GAL Includes the Information that the GAL has Obtained in the Report.

The GAL encourages parties to participate in the evaluation. If a party does not participate, the GAL is still permitted to file a report and to disclose whatever information has been collected about that party from other sources. The report should disclose that such a party has not participated or declined to provide information.

COMMENTARY

The GAL shall refrain from drawing conclusions about a party without a factual basis.

10.5 Facts Shall be Separated in the Report from Recommendations or Conclusions.

The investigative and evaluative information shall be separated from the GAL's conclusions and recommendations. The report shall include a section on the facts of the case in the body of the evaluation.

10.6 The GAL's Conclusions or Recommendations Shall Follow Clearly from the Data Gathered and the Analysis of that Data

The GAL shall set forth the connection between the facts, the analysis of the facts, and the GAL's conclusions and recommendations. The GAL shall explain the basis for any opinions or conclusions drawn.

COMMENTARY

This includes stating in the report: alternative explanations the GAL considered, how conflicting data was reconciled, and the clinical or theoretical framework, if any, which informed the GAL's opinions.

10.7 The GAL shall Identify any Limits of the Completed GAL Evaluation

The GAL shall list any important sources of information that were not obtained and why. The GAL shall articulate any limits to the usefulness of the report's final conclusions. The GAL shall not draw any conclusions for which s/he does not have the adequate supporting data.

Example: The GAL discovers that a party's medical records from a particular hospital have been lost. The records were alleged to be evidence of mother's injuries due to domestic violence. The GAL documents the attempts to acquire these records, and that without them mother's allegations of physical injury cannot be confirmed.

10.8 The GAL Files a Timely Report and Informs Counsel and Pro Se Parties.

The GAL should inform counsel and pro se parties when the report is filed at the court so that the parties can read the report. The GAL should inform parties requesting a copy of the report that the report is property of the court; it cannot be given out or shown to anyone, except the parties or their counsel. A court order is required for any distribution of the report, even to parties or their counsel. The GAL shall not distribute copies of the report to the parties, counsel of record or anyone else unless the court orders that the GAL may release copies to such individuals.

COMMENTARY

If information or recommendations in the GAL report have the potential of exposing a party or the child to danger, the GAL should consider advising the endangered parent or party about the date that he or she expects to file the report in court.

11. THE GAL SHALL RETAIN ANY MATERIALS GATHERED OR CREATED DURING THE EVALUATION

The GAL shall retain any notes, records, documents, taped recordings, videos, or other material gathered or created during the evaluation so that these materials are available for trial, discovery, appeal and remand of the case.

COMMENTARY

Notes or other materials created or obtained by a GAL may be sought by a party through discovery. The GAL's notes, written observations, or other materials created during interviews or telephone conversations should be descriptive, factual, and respectful in tone. Note taking should be objective and include quotations of witnesses and parties when possible.

Massachusetts Trial Court

Rule IV—Uniform Rule Requiring Disclosure of Pending and Concluded Care or Custody Matters

[Amended effective July 1, 1984, Sept. 1, 1993, Aug. 1, 1995, July 1, 2009.

Applicable to Boston Municipal, District, Juvenile, Probate and Family and Superior Court Departments.]

Upon the filing or issuance of any petition or complaint involving the care, custody, visitation, or change of name of a child, pursuant to G.L. c. 119 (except delinquency actions under G.L. c. 119), G.L. c. 190B, G.L. c. 207, G.L. c. 208, G.L. c. 209, G.L. c. 209A, G.L. c. 209C, G.L. c. 210, or any other provision of law concerning the care or custody of a child, the plaintiff shall file an affidavit. Such affidavit shall contain relevant information concerning such child including, but not limited to, a list of all other known proceedings involving the care or custody of said child which are pending or have been concluded in any court in the Commonwealth of Massachusetts or in any court in any other state or foreign country. All other parties appearing in the action shall likewise file such affidavit. No pleading shall be accepted for filing without such affidavit unless the plaintiff or other party has already filed an affidavit, or unless the court, on written motion for good cause shown, extends the time for filing such affidavit. No such extension shall exceed 30 days. A copy of the affidavit shall be furnished by the plaintiff or other party filing it to all other parties to the action. Upon the discovery of new information subsequent to the filing of such affidavit, the plaintiff or other party shall file a revised affidavit.

The plaintiff shall attach to the affidavit certified copies of each pleading and of any determination entered in any care or custody proceeding which the plaintiff knows of, or has participated in, involving the child in any court in any state other than the Commonwealth of Massachusetts or in any foreign country, unless the court, on written motion for good cause shown, extends the time for filing such pleadings and determinations. No such extension shall exceed 30 days, unless the court, on written motion for good cause shown, finds an extension in excess of 30 days is warranted. All other parties shall attach to the affidavit certified copies of each pleading and of any determination entered in any care or custody proceeding as required above, unless previously filed by the plaintiff or unless the plaintiff has been granted an extension for filing such pleadings and determinations.

The court, upon written motion of any party, or upon its own motion, may order the impoundment of an affidavit which discloses the adoption of a child. Impounded affidavits shall not be available for public inspection, but shall be available to the court and its employees, attorneys whose appearances are entered in a case, the parties, the Department of Social Services or its licensed adoption agencies, and such other persons whom the court, upon written motion, may permit.

The affidavit shall be on a form prescribed by the Chief Administrative Justice of the Trial Court, which upon its filing, shall be deemed in compliance with the provisions of G.L. c. 209B, the Massachusetts Child Custody Jurisdiction Act.

Rule VI—Uniform Rules for Permanency Hearings

[Effective July 1, 1985; amended effective Sept. 5, 2000; Mar. 1, 2018.]

Rule 1. Purpose

The Uniform Rules for Permanency Hearings provide a consistent procedure for hearings conducted pursuant to G.L. c. 119, § 29B. This procedure is intended to encourage meaningful participation by the parties. Permanency hearings provide the child or young adult an important opportunity to have individual needs addressed by the court to ensure that the child or young adult is receiving the necessary supports to timely reach a permanent, safe, and healthy home and a successful adulthood.

Rule 2. Scope of Rules and Definitions

(a) Scope

These rules govern the procedure for hearings conducted pursuant to G.L. c. 119, § 29B in the Juvenile, District, and Probate and Family Court Departments. Procedures not addressed by these rules shall be governed by the rules of procedure applicable to the court in which the matter is heard.

(b) Definitions

The following definitions apply in this Rule:

(1) "APPLA"—another permanent planned living arrangement or an alternative planned permanent living arrangement in which the Department maintains care and custody or responsibility of a child age 16 or older or of a young adult and arranges a stable living situation for that child or young adult when it continues not to be in the best interest of the child or young adult to pursue another permanency option.

(2) "Child"—a person under the age of eighteen.

(3) "Clerk's Office"—the office of the Clerk-Magistrate or Register of Probate of the court where the permanency hearing is scheduled.

(4) "Department"—the Department of Children and Families, or its successor agency.

(5) "Indian Child"—an unmarried child who either is a member of a federally recognized Indian tribe or is eligible for membership in a federally recognized Indian tribe and a biological child of a member pursuant to the Indian Child Welfare Act, 25 U.S.C. § 1903.

(6) "Kin"—any person to whom a child and/or the child's parent(s) and family members ascribe a "family" relationship. Such individual may be related by blood, marriage or adoption or a person to whom the child and/or parent(s) ascribe the role of family based on cultural and affectional ties or individual family values.

(7) "Parent"—a child's biological, adoptive, or legal mother or father.

(8) "Party"—a person who is a party in the underlying case, except the parent of a young adult or a parent whose parental rights have been terminated under G.L. c. 119, § 26 or G.L. c. 210, § 3 or who has signed a voluntary surrender under G.L. c. 119, § 23(a)(2) or G.L. c. 210, § 2.

(9) "Permanency Hearing"—a hearing conducted pursuant to G.L. c. 119, § 29B and as described in these Rules.

(10) "Permanency Plan"—a plan for the child as determined by the court pursuant to G.L. c. 119, § 29B and Rule 9, that addresses whether, and if applicable when, the child or young adult will be: (i) returned to the parent; (ii) placed for adoption and the steps the Department will take to free the child for adoption; (iii) referred for legal guardianship; (iv) placed in permanent care with kin; or (v) placed in APPLA.

(11) "Permanency Report"—a written document prepared by the Department and reviewed by the court at the permanency hearing regarding a child in the care or custody or under the responsibility of the Department or a young adult, which sets forth the Department's proposed permanency plan and the efforts it has made and will make to implement the permanency plan in a timely manner as detailed in Rule 4.

(12) "Transition Plan"—a plan which includes the components listed in Rule 4(c), approved by the court pursuant to G.L. c. 119, § 29B(c) for a child who is age 17 years and 9 months or older or for a young adult who will be leaving care within the next 90 days.

(13) "Young Adult"—a person between the ages of 18 and 22 under the responsibility of the Department pursuant to G.L. c. 119, § 23(f).

COMMENTARY

Rule 2(b)(l) APPLA. Federal law uses the term another planned permanent living arrangement. 42 U.S.C. § 675a. State law uses the term another permanent planned living arrangement. G.L. c. 119, § 29(a)(v). The Department of Children and Families (DCF) uses the term alternative planned permanent living arrangement. DCF Permanency Planning Policy #2013-01 (July 1, 2013) at 22, 51. For purposes of this Rule, the terms are interchangeable and expressed as APPLA.

Rule 2(b)(12) Transition Plan. Federal law also describes the components of a transition plan. See 42 U.S.C. § 675(5)(H).

Rule 3. Notice—Scheduling the Permanency Hearing

(a) Scheduling

The committing court shall schedule the first permanency hearing at the original commitment, grant of care or custody, or transfer of responsibility of a child or young adult to the Department by order of a court of competent jurisdiction, and at each permanency hearing, the court shall schedule the next permanency hearing. Except, however, if the underlying case is a child requiring assistance petition, the court shall schedule a permanency hearing at the first dispositional review hearing. Nothing in this rule shall be read to prevent the parties from requesting, or the court from scheduling, a permanency hearing more frequently than required.

(1) The court shall conduct the first permanency hearing within twelve (12) months of the date the child or young adult first entered the care, custody, or responsibility of the Department. Subsequent permanency hearings shall be held no less frequently than every twelve (12) months thereafter, while the child or young adult remains in the care or custody or under the responsibility of the Department.

(2) If the court has determined that reasonable efforts to preserve and reunify the family are not required pursuant to G.L. c. 119, § 29C, a permanency hearing shall be held within thirty (30) days of the court's determination that no reasonable efforts are required.

(b) Announcement

The court shall announce the date on which the permanency report is due and the date of the permanency hearing in open court at each court event until the permanency hearing is held. Failure of the court to announce the date of the permanency hearing shall not preclude the court from proceeding with the permanency hearing.

(c) Hearing on the permanency report and the transition plan

Upon the request of any party, the court shall schedule and/or hold a hearing on the Department's permanency report, particularly the proposed transition plan, for a child in the care and custody or under the responsibility of the Department who has attained the age of 17 years 9 months or for a young adult who plans to leave the responsibility of the Department in the next 90 days.

COMMENTARY

Rule 3(a). In order to encourage the participation of a child or a young adult in his or her permanency hearing, the parties may request and the court shall make every effort to schedule a hearing day and time that accommodates the schedule of the child or young adult and that is within the prescribed timeframes.

Rule 3(a)(1). For a child or young adult who has experienced interruptions in care or custody, responsibility, or placement with the Department, a permanency hearing may still be required. See 45 C.F.R. § 1356.21(e) (describing a trial home visit). For example, if a child in the care or custody or under the responsibility of the Department or a young adult has been placed at home for less than six months, a permanency hearing is still required for that child or young adult. U.S. Department of Health and Human Services Administration for Children and Families, Children's Bureau, Child Welfare Policy Manual Tit. IV-E 8.3C.5, available at https://www.acf.hhs.gov/cwpm/programs/cb/laws_policies/laws/cwpm/policy (last accessed May 24, 2016).

Rule 4. Permanency Reports

(a) Permanency reports for all children and young adults

Permanency reports for all children and young adults shall be in writing and shall include the following:

(1) identifying information about the child or young adult and biological family including siblings as well as the Department's efforts to identify whether the child is an Indian Child and the result of those efforts;

(2) a brief history of the legal and clinical case, including placement history;

(3) the efforts the Department has made to engage and include the family in the development of the permanency plan, including the child, as appropriate, or young adult.

(4) the proposed permanent plan for the child or young adult, including:

i. when the plan will be accomplished,

ii. what steps the Department has taken and will take to implement the permanency plan for the child or young adult, and

iii. if the plan is APPLA, the compelling reason for proposing that plan, and why it continues to not be in the best interests of the child to return home; be placed for adoption; be placed with a legal guardian; or be placed with fit and willing kin.

(5) services and other assistance provided, currently and in the past, to safely reunify the child with his or her parent or guardian, or, if the court has previously determined a plan other than reunification, to further that permanency plan, and the engagement of all parties with those services. The report shall include any services and needed assistance provided to accommodate a parent, child, or young adult's disability, and how the services and assistance provided are specifically tailored to meet the parent, child, or young adult's cultural background and language needs;

(6) information about the current placement including: how it meets the child's or young adult's current needs and furthers the permanency plan; if the child is not placed in family foster care, the reasons the Department determined the child is in need of special care, treatment or education, and if the child is placed in foster care outside the state in which the child's parents' home is located, why the out-of-state placement continues to be appropriate and in the child's best interests;

(7) medical information about the child or young adult, including ongoing treatment and medications being provided to the child or young adult, and, if the child or young adult is medically needy, a description of his or her individualized health care plan;

(8) the plan for visits and/or contact with parents and among siblings;

(9) results of any internal reviews by the foster care review unit;

(10) a description of the child's or the young adult's educational history, needs, and current status, including efforts made to maintain school stability;

(11) information about the regular, ongoing opportunities the child or young adult has had to engage in age and developmentally appropriate activities; and

(12) if the proposed permanency plan for the child or young adult is APPLA:

i. the intensive, ongoing, and, as of the date of the report, unsuccessful efforts made by the Department to return the child or young adult home or secure a placement for the child or young adult with kin, a legal guardian, or an adoptive parent, including efforts that utilize search technology to find biological family members, and

ii. what steps the Department has taken to ensure that the foster care provider of the child or young adult is following the reasonable and prudent parent standard.

(b) Permanency reports for children age 14 or older and young adults

For a child age 14 or older or a young adult, the permanency report shall include the information required under Rule 4(a) as well as information about any additional or specialized services provided to the child or young adult to assist with the transition to successful adulthood. Such services include those designed to help the child or young adult:

(1) build relationships with other caring adults, particularly with life-long connections;

(2) make an education plan;

2

(3) find vocational, employment, and career counseling and placement;

(4) secure stable housing;

(5) develop expertise in daily living skills;

(6) maintain physical and mental health care and health insurance;

(7) learn how to access community resources and public benefits and services;

(8) connect with other state agencies; and

(9) develop financial skills including receiving, understanding, and correcting, if applicable, his/her consumer credit report.

(c) Permanency reports for children who are age 17 years and 9 months or older and for young adults

For a child in the care or custody or under the responsibility of the Department who is age 17 years and 9 months or older or for a young adult, the permanency report shall include the information required under Rule 4(a) and Rule 4(b) as well as a proposed transition plan. Proposed transition plans shall be personalized at the direction of the child or young adult, be as detailed as the child or young adult shall elect, and include specific options on:

(1) stable housing;

(2) health insurance;

(3) physical and mental health care including the designation of a health care proxy;

(4) educational services;

(5) long-term connections with mentors and caring adults;

(6) continuing support services including state agencies;

(7) workforce supports and employment services; and

(8) maintaining contact with siblings still in DCF custody or care.

COMMENTARY

Rule (4)(a)(3). Permanency plan options include: reunification, adoption, guardianship, permanent care with kin, and APPLA. See 42 U.S.C. § 675(5)(C)(i); G.L. c. 119, § 29(a)(v); DCF Permanency Planning Policy #2013-01 (July 1, 2013) at 22, 29-51.

Rule 4(a)(5) Information about the placement may include: (i) the type and level of placement; (ii) whether the child is placed with kin and, if not, the reasons why not; (iii) whether the child is placed with siblings and, if not, the reasons why the department determined placement with siblings is not in the child's best interests; (iv) if the child is not placed in family foster care, the reasons why the child requires a more restrictive setting; (v) if an Indian child is placed in a non-preferred placement as described in Rule 9(c)(3), why the department determined there was "good cause" to not follow the placement preferences required by 25 U.S.C. § 1915(b).

Rule 4(a)(11)(ii). See 42 U.S.C. § 675(10)(A) (definition of the reasonable and prudent parent standard). The reasonable and prudent parent standard means the standard a caregiver shall use to ensure that children are participating in age and developmentally appropriate extracurricular, enrichment, cultural, and social activities.

Rule 4(b). For a child who is age 14 or older or for a young adult, the Department may already have developed a Youth Readiness Assessment Tool, which identifies and prioritizes the skill development needed to prepare the child or young adult for the transition to adulthood.

Rule 4(b)(5). Examples of daily living skills include driving, navigating public transportation, maintaining healthy relationships, opening a bank account, and budgeting. The child or young adult may need, and the Department is required to provide, certain personal documents in order to develop these skills, such as a birth certificate, social security card, other identification, a credit report (annually), and a document that describes the right of the child or young adult to education, health care, visitation, and court participation.

Rule 5. Notice

The Department shall provide notice of the scheduled permanency hearing date to the foster parent, pre-adoptive parent or relative providing care for the child who is the subject of the petition pursuant to G.L. c. 119, § 29D. The Department shall provide notice of the scheduled permanency hearing date to the Department of Youth Services if the child or young adult is committed to the care or custody of the Department of Youth Services. Failure of the Department to comply with this section shall not preclude the court from proceeding with the permanency hearing.

Rule 6. Submission of Report and Response or Objections

(a) Filing of the permanency report

For a child in the care or custody or under the responsibility of the Department or for a young adult, no less than thirty (30) days prior to the scheduled permanency hearing date the Department shall file the permanency report with the clerk's office and shall send copies to all parties or, if the parties are represented by counsel, to the counsel of record.

(b) Filing of the permanency report for an expedited permanency hearing

If the court has determined that reasonable efforts to reunify the family are not required pursuant to G.L. c. 119, § 29C, the Department shall file the permanency report and send copies as provided above within ten (10) days of entry of the "no reasonable efforts required" order.

(c) Filing of response or objection to the permanency report

Any party may file a response or objection to the permanency report no less than ten (10) days prior to the scheduled permanency hearing date.

Rule 7. Counsel

(a) Right to counsel

All parties have the right to be represented by counsel at the permanency hearing.

(b) Attendance of counsel

All counsel of record shall attend the permanency hearing. Failure of counsel to attend, without good cause, shall not require that the hearing be postponed unless the interests of justice so require.

Rule 8. The Permanency Hearing

(a) Purpose of the permanency hearing

The purpose of the Permanency Hearing shall be to:

(1) determine the permanency plan for the child or young adult and when the plan will be implemented;

(2) aid in the timely implementation of such plan; and

(3) determine whether the Department has made reasonable efforts to safely reunify the child or young adult with his or her parent or guardian, or if the court has previously determined under Rule 9(c) a plan other than reunification, to implement the previously determined plan.

(b) Parties and non-parties

(1) Any child or young adult who is a party has a right to attend the permanency hearing. There shall be a presumption that the child who is age 14 or older or the young adult will attend the permanency hearing. If the child age 14 or older or the young adult is not present at the hearing, the court will inquire of counsel for the child or young adult as to the reason his or her client is not present.

(2) Pursuant to G.L. c. 119, § 29D, foster parents, pre-adoptive parents or relatives providing care for the child have the right to attend the permanency hearing and be heard. Nothing in this provision shall be construed to provide that such foster parent, pre-adoptive parent or relative shall be made a party to the proceeding by exercising his/her right to attend and be heard.

(3) Failure of one or more parties or non-parties to appear shall not preclude the court from proceeding with the permanency hearing.

(c) The hearing

(1) The permanency hearing, including the hearing as described in Rule 3(c), shall be conducted in the same manner as any other hearing unless otherwise stated in these Rules. At the hearing, the judge will review the permanency report, any objections and responses, and make the determinations required by these Rules.

(2) The author of the Department's permanency report shall be available for cross-examination by each of the parties.

(3) The judge who entered the adjudication, or if there has not been an adjudication, who entered the original order of commitment, grant of custody, or transfer of responsibility of a child or young adult to the Department shall conduct the hearing unless impractical or would cause undue delay.

(4) The court shall consult with the child or young adult in an age-appropriate manner about the permanency report and the permanency plan. Counsel for the child or young adult shall be prepared to provide the court with the child's position regarding the permanency report and the permanency plan.

(5) The permanency hearing, including the hearing as described in Rule 3(c), may be held simultaneously with a trial, review and redetermination, other hearing, or other proceeding in the matter, but no later than the scheduling requirements contained in Rule 3(a)(1).

Rule 9. Orders

(a) Permanency plan

The court shall determine the permanency plan for the child or young adult going forward and when that plan will be implemented.

(1) Permanency plan options include: reunification, adoption, guardianship, permanent care with kin, and APPLA.

(2) In determining the permanency plan, the health and safety of the child or young adult shall be of paramount, but not exclusive, concern.

(3) If the child is an Indian child, the court shall determine and document in writing whether the placement preferences required by 25 U.S.C. § 1915 have been applied in any foster care, pre-adoptive, or adoptive placement, unless it determines that good cause exists to not apply those placement preferences.

(4) If the court determines the permanency plan for a child or young adult to be APPLA, the court shall make findings regarding why APPLA is the best permanency plan for the child or young adult and the compelling reasons why it continues to not be in the best interests of the child or young adult to return home, be placed for adoption, be placed with a legal guardian, or be placed with a fit and willing relative.

(b) Reasonable efforts pursuant to G.L. c. 119, §§ 29B, 29C

The court shall determine whether the Department has made reasonable efforts to safely reunify the child or young adult with his or her parent or guardian, or, if the court has previously determined under Rule 9(c) a permanency plan other than reunification, to implement the previously determined permanency plan. The court is not required to make a reasonable efforts determination at an expedited permanency hearing as described in Rule 3(a)(2). A determination by the court that the Department has not made reasonable efforts does not preclude the court from entering any appropriate order as may be in the child or young adult's best interests.

(c) Services needed for children age 14 or older or young adults

For a child age 14 or older and for a young adult, the court shall determine whether the services the child or young adult needs are in place to assist him or her to make a transition from foster care to a successful adulthood.

(d) Satisfactory transition plan

After a hearing conducted pursuant to Rule 3(c), the court shall determine whether the proposed transition plan is satisfactory and shall retain jurisdiction of the matter until it finds that a satisfactory transition plan has been provided for the child or young adult.

(e) Orders in the best interest of the child or young adult

At a permanency hearing, including at a hearing conducted pursuant to Rule 3(c), the court may make any appropriate order in the child's or young adult's best interest, including but not limited to orders with respect to the child's or young adult's care or custody or that will aid in the implementation of the permanency plan.

(f) Findings

The court need not enter findings absent an appeal from its order with the exception of those findings required by law or this Rule.

COMMENTARY

Rule 9(a)(3). "Good cause" is defined pursuant to 25 C.F.R. § 23.132 (effective December 12, 2016). There are two sets of placement preferences. In adoptive placements, where the Indian child's tribe has not established a different order of preference, placement preferences for the child must descend as follows: 1) a member of the Indian child's extended family; 2) other members of the Indian child's Tribe; or 3) other Indian families. 25 C.F.R. § 23.130(a). If the Indian child's Tribe has established by resolution a different order of preference than that specified in ICWA, the Tribe's placement preferences apply. 25 C.F.R. § 23.130(b). The court must, where appropriate, also consider the placement preference of the Indian child or Indian child's parent. 25 C.F.R. § 23.130(c)(effective December 12, 2016). In any foster care or pre-adoptive placement, including changes in foster-care or pre-adoptive placement, the child must be placed in the least restrictive setting that most approximates a family, taking into consideration sibling attachment; that allows the Indian child's special needs (if any) to be met; and is in reasonable proximity to the Indian child's home, extended family, or siblings. In any foster care or pre-adoptive placement, including changes in foster care or pre-adoptive placement, where the Indian child's Tribe has not specified a different order, placement preferences for the child must descend as follows: 1) a member of the Indian child's extended family; 2) a foster home licensed, approved or specified by the Tribe; 3) an Indian foster home licensed or approved by an authorized, non-Indian licensing authority; and 4) an Indian institution. The court must, where appropriate, also consider the preference of the Indian child or the Indian child's parent. See Indian Child Welfare Act 25 U.S.C. §1915; 25 C.F.R. §§ 23.130-134 (effective December 12, 2016).

Rule 9(e). See G.L. c. 119, § 29B(c) ("the court shall retain jurisdiction until it finds, after a hearing at which the person is present unless the person chooses otherwise, that a satisfactory transition plan has been provided for the person").

Rule 10. Appeals

(a) Timing

Any party may appeal the court's determination(s) and/or order(s) to the Appeals Court by filing a notice of appeal in the clerk's office no later than thirty (30) days following the entry of such determination(s) and/or order(s) on the court's docket.

(b) Notice to the judge

The clerk's office shall inform the judge within five (5) days from the filing of the notice of appeal that the determination(s) and/or order(s) have been appealed.

(c) Findings

The judge shall file written findings within sixty (60) days from the filing of the notice of appeal.

Rule VIII—Uniform Rules on Impoundment Procedure

[Effective Sept. 1, 1986; amended effective Oct. 1, 2015.]

Rule 1. Applicability and Definitions

(a). Applicability. The Uniform Rules on Impoundment Procedure (URIP) govern impoundment of otherwise public case records that are filed in civil and criminal proceedings in each Department of the Trial Court. Case records are presumed to be open to the public, unless they are impounded or sealed as a matter of law, or impounded by a court order. These rules are inapplicable to case records that are required to be impounded by statute, court rule, standing order, or case law, except as otherwise provided in Rules 9, 11, and 13. These rules shall not be construed to deprive a person of any rights or remedies regarding impoundment that are otherwise available under law.

(b). Definitions. As used herein:

(1). "Case" shall include any matter that has been entered in any Department of the Trial Court. Each case shall always have a case caption and an assigned case number visible on the court's docket and index, even if a pseudonym must be used for a party whose identity is impounded.

(2). "Case Caption" shall mean the official title of the case. For example, Commonwealth v. Smith, Jones v. Jones, or Impounded Plaintiff v. Jones.

(3). "Case record" shall mean all or any portion of court papers, documents, exhibits, orders, and other records, including an audio recording or official transcript of a proceeding, that are made, entered, or filed and maintained by the clerk in connection with a transaction of court business.

(4). "Case law" shall mean appellate decisions that are binding precedent for a Massachusetts court.

(5). "Clerk" shall mean Clerk, Clerk-Magistrate, Register of Probate, Recorder of the Land Court, their assistants, and designated court personnel.

(6). "Court" shall mean a judge or justice.

(7). "Docket" shall mean the paper or electronic list of case information maintained by the clerk that contains the case caption, case number, and a chronological entry identifying the date and title of each paper, document, exhibit, order, or judgment filed in a case, and the scheduling and occurrence of events in the case.

(8). "Final Disposition" shall mean, in a civil or criminal proceeding, when (i) a final judgment, sentence, decree, or order of dismissal has entered as to all claims, counts, and parties, (ii) any timely post-judgment motions have been disposed, and (iii) any appeal has been concluded and the rescript entered.

(9). "Impoundment" shall mean the act of keeping some or all of the case record separate and unavailable for public inspection. Impounded records are not accessible to anyone other than the court, clerk, authorized court personnel, attorneys of record, and the parties to the case, unless otherwise ordered. Any order of impoundment shall not restrict the clerk, as keeper of the records, from accessing information sufficient to file the impounded documents and carry out the clerk's duties required under URIP Rule 9. "Impounded" information includes material that a statute, court rule, standing order, case law, or court order designates must be withheld as "impounded," "withheld from public inspection," "not available for public inspection," "segregated," or "confidential," though these terms are not exhaustive. "Sealed" records are distinct from "impounded" records, in that sealed records are available to the court only, unless otherwise ordered.

(10). "Index" or "indices" shall mean the clerk's list of cases, whether maintained alphabetically or chronologically.

(11). "Interested nonparty" shall mean a person who is not or was not a party to the underlying matter in which an impoundment issue has arisen, but who nevertheless expresses to the court (through a motion, an appearance limited to impoundment, filing, or otherwise) an interest in the impoundment proceeding, or who has been named by the court as a person who shall receive notice.

(12). "Party" shall mean a person who is a litigant in the civil or criminal matter in which the impoundment proceeding has arisen.

(13). "Person" shall mean any natural person or any business, legal, or government entity.

(14). "Public record" or "public case record" shall mean a record that is accessible to any and all persons.

(c). Impoundment and Discovery.

(1) Where impoundment is sought in connection with discovery, these rules shall be applied in a manner consistent with any applicable provisions of Rule 26(c) of the Massachusetts Rules of Civil Procedure, Rule 26(c) of the Massachusetts Rules of Domestic Relations Procedure, or Rule 14(a)(6) of the Massachusetts Rules of Criminal Procedure.

(2) In civil and criminal proceedings, material received by the clerk directly from a third person or nonparty in response to a subpoena, summons, or court order for discovery purposes is not available for public inspection until either a party files the material as an attachment to a pleading or motion, introduces the material as evidence, or the court so orders. The clerk shall make a notation on the docket indicating that impounded materials were filed in response to court order or discovery request.

Rule 2. Motion for Impoundment

(a). Content of Motion.

(1). Motion. Any party or interested nonparty may file a written motion for impoundment of a portion or all of the case record in any judicial proceeding. The motion shall describe with particularity (i) the material sought to be impounded, (ii) the duration for which impoundment is sought, (iii) the reasons impoundment is necessary, and (iv) the reasons other alternatives to impoundment will not afford adequate protection. The movant shall include proposed findings and a proposed order, conforming to URIP Rule 8, with the motion.

(2). Affidavit. A motion for impoundment shall be accompanied by an affidavit in support thereof. Unless otherwise provided herein, the rules governing motions and affidavits in civil or criminal proceedings generally shall apply to requests for impoundment.

(3). Public Nature of Motion and Affidavit. The clerk shall enter the motion and affidavit on the case docket. Unless the court impounds the motion and affidavit by separate order, they remain publicly available documents.

(b). Submission of the Material Sought to Be Impounded.

(1). Material Outside of the Case Record. A motion for impoundment must be filed and ruled upon prior to submission of the actual material sought to be impounded. The clerk shall not accept any document that the movant seeks to be impounded until the court has ruled on the motion or ordered otherwise.

(2). Materials for in camera Review. If the court orders the movant to file the materials sought to be impounded for the court's in camera review, the movant shall first place them in an envelope bearing the case caption and a prominent notation that the documents within are "PROVISIONALLY IMPOUNDED PENDING COURT ORDERED IN CAMERA REVIEW." The clerk shall withhold the submission from public inspection until there is a ruling on the motion. If the court allows the motion, the allowance shall be noted on the envelope and the materials shall be impounded for the duration of the order. If the court denies the motion, within fourteen days, the movant must retrieve the materials from the clerk or notify the clerk that the materials should be filed in their entirety. Should the same materials be filed, they will be placed in the public case record. The clerk will destroy any materials that have not been retrieved or filed by the fifteenth day.

(3). Materials Previously Filed in the Case Record. A motion may be made for impoundment of information that is currently contained in the case record. Upon receipt of such a motion, the clerk shall remove the subject material from the case record and withhold it from public dissemination pending the court's ruling on the motion. A hearing on the motion shall be held within three days unless otherwise agreed by the parties or ordered by the court.

Rule 3. Ex Parte Impoundment

(a). Motion and How Allowed. An ex parte order of impoundment may be issued by the court without prior notice only upon either the filing of a written motion supported by affidavit in the manner provided in URIP Rule 2, or by the court sua sponte, and only upon a showing that immediate and irreparable injury may result before a party or interested nonparty can be heard in opposition. The court may conduct an ex parte hearing prior to issuing an order.

(b). Limited Duration of Ex Parte Impoundment Order. An ex parte order of impoundment shall include the date of issuance and the clerk shall record the filing of the order on the docket and store the order with the underlying materials. An ex parte order of impoundment shall expire ten days from the date of issuance unless otherwise ordered by the court for good cause shown.

(c). Notice. After the court has ruled on the ex parte motion for impoundment, the movant, unless the ruling was sua sponte by the court, shall serve a copy of the motion, supporting affidavit, and any other related documents, on the parties and any interested nonparty. The court shall provide notice of the ex parte order or the sua sponte order and the scheduling of any subsequent hearing. The court has discretion to order that certain notice requirements be withheld for good cause shown.

(d). Motion to Modify or Terminate Ex Parte Impoundment Order. Any party or interested nonparty aggrieved by an ex parte order may file a written motion to vacate or modify the ex parte order. The motion may request a hearing not fewer than two days from the date of filing. Any motion to modify or terminate an ex parte order shall be accompanied by a certificate of service that notice has been provided to all parties, any interested nonparty, and any other person named by the court.

(e). Search Warrants.

(1). Ex Parte Motion for Impoundment, Order, and Notice. An ex parte motion to impound materials related to the issuance and/or execution of a search warrant may be filed and allowed in conformance with Rule 3(a). The court may enter, contemporaneously with or subsequent to the issuance of a search warrant, an ex parte order that the search warrant application and any related materials be impounded upon their return to the court. An ex parte order of impoundment shall expire ten days from the date of issuance unless otherwise ordered by the court for good cause shown. The clerk shall record the filing of any order on the docket or, if a docket for search warrants is not maintained, on the clerk's application folder. The court has discretion to order that the notice requirements of Rule 3(c) be withheld for good cause shown.

(2). Motion to Modify or Terminate an Ex Parte Order Related to a Search Warrant. After an order to impound a search warrant or related materials has issued, any motion for relief from the impoundment order shall be filed in the court or division where the search warrant was returned. A judge in the court or division where the search warrant was returned may request the transfer of a hearing on a motion to impound a search warrant or motion for relief of an impoundment to a different court department or division (i) if the impoundment order was ordered by a judge of a different court department or division or (ii) if a criminal case relating to the search warrant is pending in a different court department or division.

Rule 4. Service

(a). Service. Except as otherwise provided by these rules, a movant shall serve any motion or opposition related to impoundment, or motion to modify or terminate impoundment, and any supporting materials on all parties, interested nonparties, and any other person named by the court, by mailing or delivering a copy to counsel for any represented person and to any self-represented person. Service on a represented person shall be made on the person's attorney unless service on the represented person is ordered by the court. Service shall be made in the manner provided by Rule 5 of the Massachusetts Rules of Civil Procedure or by any alternative means ordered by the court. In the event an order of impoundment is sought at the time of, or prior to, service of the original complaint, service shall be made in accordance with Rule 4 of the Massachusetts Rules of Civil Procedure. The time periods for hearing shall be as set forth in Rule 6 of the Massachusetts Rules of Civil Procedure.

(b). Service on Parties Prior to, or Simultaneously with, Service of Complaint in Civil Proceedings. When an order of impoundment is sought at the time of, or prior to, service of the original complaint in a civil proceeding, service shall be made in the manner provided by Rule 4 of the Massachusetts Rules of Civil Procedure.

(c). Service on Interested Nonparty. The court may, prior to hearing, order notice to be given to any interested nonparty. Notice to such interested nonparty shall be given in such manner as the court may direct. If a person who receives notice under this subsection seeks to participate in the impoundment proceedings, the person must comply with URIP Rule 6.

(d). Service on the Office of the Attorney General by Interested Nonparty in Criminal Cases. The movant shall serve notice on the Office of the Attorney General, in addition to the parties to the case, of any motion filed in any court by an interested nonparty to obtain access to impounded documents in a criminal case. The Office of the Attorney General shall have an opportunity to be heard on the motion. The movant shall also notify the court of that office's right to be heard on the motion.

(e). Affidavit of Service. Service shall be proved by an affidavit containing a particular statement thereof, including the names and addresses of all parties, their counsel, and all interested nonparties who have been given notice, and the method and date of service. The affidavit shall be served and filed with the motion.

(f). Timing. The motion for impoundment and supporting materials shall be served before or at the same time as such documents are mailed or delivered to the court.

Rule 5. Opposition

Any party or interested nonparty may serve and file an opposing affidavit not later than one day before any hearing, if scheduled, unless otherwise ordered. Service of any opposing affidavit shall be made in accordance with the procedures provided in URIP Rule 4 unless otherwise ordered.

Rule 6. Involvement of Interested Nonparties

(a). Motion and Appearance in Pending Civil or Criminal Cases. An interested nonparty who seeks, pursuant to URIP Rules 2, 3, 5, or 10, to request, oppose, modify, or terminate an order of impoundment pertaining to the case record of a pending civil or criminal case shall file a motion for such relief with the court and shall serve the motion in accordance with URIP Rule 4 and subsection (c) of this rule. Such a motion shall (i) specify the relief requested, (ii) specify the grounds therefor, (iii) be accompanied by an affidavit setting forth the nature of the movant's interest in the matter of impoundment and any facts on which the motion relies, and (iv) be accompanied by a notice of appearance for the limited purpose of participating in the impoundment proceeding, but without making the person a party to the case for other purposes. Proceedings on the motion shall be in accordance with the procedures described in URIP Rules 2, 3, 5, or 10, as applicable.

(b). Cases in Which a Final Disposition Has Entered. An interested nonparty who seeks, pursuant to URIP Rules 2, 3, 5, or 10, to request, oppose, modify, or terminate an order of impoundment pertaining to the case record of a prior civil or criminal case in which a final disposition has been entered shall file a separate civil action in the court where the prior action commenced, specifying the relief sought. The civil action shall name, as defendants, the clerk of court in his or her official capacity and (1) if the prior case was a civil case, all parties to the prior case, or (2) if the prior case was a criminal case, the defendant(s) in the prior case, the Office of the Attorney General, and the Office of the District Attorney of the county where the case commenced.

(c). Service on the Office of the Attorney General by Interested Nonparty in Criminal Cases. The interested nonparty movant shall serve notice on the Office of the Attorney General, in addition to the parties to the case, of any motion filed in any court to obtain access to impounded documents in a criminal case in accordance with the provisions of URIP Rule 4(d).

Rule 7. Hearing

(a). Hearing Required. The court may enter an order of impoundment for good cause shown and in accordance with applicable law only after a hearing, except as provided in URIP Rule 2(b)(3), URIP Rule 3(a), or URIP Rule 7(e). During the hearing, those present shall preserve the confidentiality of the material that is at issue. A record of the proceedings, including the record of any in camera hearing, shall be preserved stenographically or by a recording device.

(b). Good Cause. In determining good cause, the court shall consider all relevant factors, including, but not limited to, (i) the nature of the parties and the controversy, (ii) the type of information and the privacy interests involved, (iii) the extent of community interest, (iv) constitutional rights, and (v) the reason(s) for the request. Agreement of all parties, interested nonparties, or other persons in favor of impoundment shall not, in itself, be sufficient to constitute good cause.

(c). Interested Nonparties. The court may, in its discretion, permit an interested nonparty who files a notice of appearance limited to participation in the impoundment proceeding to be heard at any impoundment hearing.

(d). In Camera Hearing. Where a public hearing may risk disclosure of the information sought to be impounded, the court may, upon a written finding of good cause, conduct in camera only that portion of the hearing that would risk disclosure. The record of any in camera hearing shall be impounded until a court orders otherwise.

(e). Trade Secret Exception. The court may, upon a written finding of good cause under URIP Rule 7(b), allow a motion for impoundment without a hearing when (1) the reason for the impoundment is to protect trade secrets or other confidential research, development, or business information, (2) the motion is by agreement or the motion is unopposed, (3) no party or other person has requested a hearing, and (4) the information does not involve an alleged or potential public hazard or risk to public safety.

Rule 8. Order of Impoundment

(a). Good Cause. An order of impoundment, whether ex parte or after notice, may be entered only upon a written finding of good cause.

(b). Specificity. An order of impoundment shall state specifically what material is to be impounded, and, where appropriate, may specify how impoundment is to be implemented. An order of impoundment shall include the date of issuance and shall specify the duration of the order with a date certain for expiration of the order. In its order, the court may allow persons other than those described in Rule 9 of these rules to have access to impounded material, and may order that appropriate redactions or notations be made in the docket and indices kept by the clerk.

(c). Narrow Tailoring. The court shall tailor the scope of the impoundment order so that it does not exceed the need for impoundment. The court may order that the movant or the filer of any material submit a redacted copy of the impounded document to the clerk for public inspection.

(d). Public Inspection. The order shall be entered on the docket, kept in the public file, and made available for public inspection. The order shall provide sufficient information for the public to identify the case caption, the case number, and to ascertain the grounds, duration, and scope of the impoundment. All information stating or disclosing the impounded material shall be omitted or redacted from the order prior to public inspection. A copy of the order shall be affixed to the envelope or other receptacle containing the court's copy of the impounded materials.

Rule 9. Clerk's Duties

Upon entry of an order of impoundment, or pursuant to an impoundment designation set forth in a statute, court rule, standing order, or case law, the clerk shall make a notation in the docket indicating what material has been impounded and the duration of its impoundment status. All impounded material shall be clearly marked, and kept separate and unavailable for public inspection. The impounded material shall be available to the court, the clerk and designated court personnel, the attorneys of record, the parties to the case, and other persons designated by the court, unless otherwise ordered by the court. Upon expiration or other termination of the order of impoundment, the material shall be returned to the public case record, unless other arrangements have been ordered, and the docket marked accordingly.

Rule 10. Modification or Termination of Order of Impoundment

A party or interested nonparty may, by motion supported by affidavit, seek to modify or terminate an order of impoundment. The motion shall be served in accordance with URIP Rule 4 and 6(c).

No order of impoundment may be modified or terminated, except upon an order of the court and upon written findings in support thereof.

Rule 11. Material Impounded by Statute, Court Rule, Standing Order, or Case Law

Any party or interested nonparty may file a motion supported by affidavit for relief from impoundment or for release of material required to be impounded pursuant to a statute, court rule, standing order, or case law, except where a different procedure is otherwise provided. The procedures set forth in these rules shall govern requests for relief from impoundment to the extent practicable.

Relief from impoundment shall be granted by the court only upon written findings.

Rule 12. Appellate Review

[Added effective Jan. 1, 1988.]

(a). Review of Orders Entered in Ongoing Proceedings. A party or interested nonparty aggrieved by an order impounding or refusing to impound material, or vacating, modifying, or refusing to modify a prior order of impoundment in an ongoing proceeding, may enter in the Appeals Court, within thirty days of the entry of such order, a petition for review by the single justice. The single justice's review shall proceed in accordance with the law and procedures governing petitions to the single justice.

(b). Review of Orders Entered in Proceedings Which Have Concluded. Upon the entry of judgment, including in an action commenced pursuant to URIP Rule 6(b), or other final disposition of the proceeding, any appeal of an impoundment order proceeds pursuant to the Massachusetts Rules of Appellate Procedure.

(c). Notice to the Clerk. In any matter entered or pending in an appellate court, the filer of any document shall provide written notice to the clerk of the appellate court of any document that contains impounded information. Such notification shall accompany the document and specify those papers, documents, or exhibits, or portions thereof, that are impounded and shall include a copy of the order of impoundment, if any, or a reference to other authority for the impoundment. Unless otherwise ordered, material impounded in the Trial Court shall remain impounded in the appellate court.

Rule X—Uniform Rule Requiring Disclosure of Present or Past Receipt of Public Assistance Benefits by Minor Children

[Adopted effective Feb. 1, 1993; amended effective Dec. 27, 1995, July 1, 2009.]

Upon the filing or issuance of any petition or complaint pursuant to G.L. c. 190B, G.L. c. 208, G.L. c. 209, G.L. c. 209A, G.L. c. 209C or G.L. c. 209D or any other provision of law concerning the support and maintenance of a minor child, the plaintiff in the action, should any minor child who is named in the petition or complaint be either a past or present recipient of public assistance through Aid to Families with Dependent Children, General Assistance, Medicaid, or Foster Care or any other program established pursuant to G.L. c. 117A, G.L. c. 118, or G.L. c. 118E, shall notify the Child Support Enforcement Division of the Department of Revenue of the pendency of the petition or complaint within three (3) days of its filing. The moving party must thereafter serve notice on the Child Support Enforcement Division of each hearing or trial date with respect to any such petition or complaint.

Notice in compliance with this rule shall be served upon the Department of Revenue at the office of the Child Support Enforcement Division for the county in which the petition or complaint is pending.

Said notice shall identify the division and department of the Trial Court in which the action has been filed, the title and docket number of the action, the name of the parents of any such child, the Social Security number of each parent and the name or names of any such child or children.

Rule XII—Requests for Interdepartmental Judicial Assignments

[Adopted effective Dec. 2, 1996; amended effective July 1, 2005.]

This Rule governs the method for requesting interdepartmental judicial assignments. Pursuant to G.L. c. 211B, section 9, the Chief Justice for Administration and Management of the Trial Court (hereafter, "CJAM") is authorized to assign a judge appointed to any Department of the Trial Court to sit in any other Department of the Trial Court for such period or periods of time as will best promote the speedy dispatch of judicial business.

The assignments may authorize a judge to sit simultaneously as a judge of several Departments for the purpose of reducing delay and duplication in actions pending in the Trial Court.

As used herein, the term "party" shall mean the attorney of record for a party, if represented by counsel, or, if a party is not represented by counsel, the party acting pro se.

1. Interdepartmental Assignment and Consolidation of Cases—Purpose and Procedure. If two or more actions are pending in different departments of the Trial Court, and if a judge, Clerk-Magistrate, register, or party determines that the separate actions are related actions involving substantially the same or similar issues and parties, the judge, Clerk-Magistrate, register, or party may request that the Chief Justice for Administration and Management make an appropriate interdepartmental assignment so that one judge may hear all related matters. The requests should be directed to the CJAM, with copies to the Chief Justice of each Department in which the related actions are pending.

Such assignments shall be made to accomplish one or more of the following purposes:

- to promote speedy disposition of cases, reduce duplication of hearings and promote judicial economy when each pending action will require a hearing or trial;
- to afford complete and permanent relief which might not be obtained unless the actions are consolidated for hearing and heard by one judge;
- to effectuate a proposed settlement of one case through the filing of a subsequent action in another court department; or
- where there is some other reason, consistent with the speedy and efficient dispatch of judicial business, why the cases should be assigned to and heard by one judge.

2. Content and Timing of Request. If a request for an interdepartmental assignment is made by one or more parties, the request shall be made in a letter to the CJAM and the Chief Justices of the Departments in which the actions are pending. The letter should identify by title, name of court division, and docket number each of the related cases; list all parties and counsel of record, with addresses; describe the nature of the cases; and include a specific, individualized statement of reasons why the separate actions are deemed related and an interdepartmental assignment would be appropriate, with particular attention to the latter in situations in which at least one of the related cases will not require a hearing or trial. Every request must be accompanied by a copy of the current docket entries in the related cases, with the most recent court activity listed thereon. Requests which are submitted without current docket sheets need not be considered.

A party making a request pursuant to this Rule shall at the same time send a copy of such request to all parties in the related cases, and to any judge who has been specially assigned to any of the cases, and, as to any case to which no judge has been specially assigned, to the first justice of the court in which that case is pending. Any party opposing the request will have seven days from receipt of the request to submit to the CJAM and Chief Justices of the respective Departments a letter in opposition with a statement of the reasons therefor.

Except for good cause shown and described in the request, a request for an interdepartmental judicial assignment will not be considered if made within 60 days prior to an established trial date. Cases shall not be removed from a trial list solely because a request for an interdepartmental judicial assignment is pending.

3. Applicable Considerations. Factors to be considered in determining whether actions are related include the following:

- whether the actions involve the same parties (including children) and the same attorneys;
- whether in child welfare cases in which all parties are not identical, the person who is not a party to one of the cases sought to be consolidated is a parent, foster parent, guardian, relative or caretaker who seeks custody, visitation, or related orders regarding the child;
- whether the actions involve common, or substantially the same or similar, questions of law and fact;
- whether the witnesses and the evidence to be presented in the separate actions will be the same or similar; and
- whether the requested forms of relief are similar or related.

Factors to be considered in determining whether allowance of the request would tend to promote the speedy dispatch of court business and to reduce delay and duplication include the following:

- whether the actions are in similar stages of readiness;
- whether either action has an established trial date;
- whether the request was made to take advantage of an existing trial date in one case for use in the other case(s);
- whether allowance of the request might require that an established trial date for one of the cases be rescheduled to afford additional time for preparation or for trial of the other, unscheduled case(s); and
- whether, notwithstanding the provisions of this Rule, a party already has caused a case to be removed from a trial list by informing the court that a request for an interdepartmental judicial assignment was or will be made.

Additional factors to be considered may include the following:

- whether, if the request is allowed, there will be a continuing or long-term need for a judge of one court Department to exercise the powers normally vested within another court Department, or whether the assignment only will be needed for one hearing;
- especially in cases involving child welfare, whether, due to special assignment to, or continuing familiarity with, one of the cases, it would be appropriate for the same judge to hear the related matter(s) to promote case continuity or permanency planning;
- whether the request should have been made earlier in order to reduce resulting delay; and
- any other special considerations that are not apparent from the docket entries or other portions of the written request.

4. Action by Chief Justices. Upon receipt of a complete request, the Chief Justices will review the request and any letters in opposition to determine whether the cases are related and whether the efficient administration of judicial business would be served by having the several actions heard by one judge. The Chief Justices will then forward their recommendations to the CJAM. When possible, the recommendations shall be forwarded to the CJAM within 30 days of receipt of a complete request.

5. Action by CJAM. The CJAM will review the request and the recommendations of the Chief Justices, and, if the interests of the Trial Court and of the parties would be served thereby, may make an appropriate order of assignment which would allow one judge to hear the related actions. When possible, the order of assignment or disallowance of the request shall be made by the CJAM within 45 days of receipt of a complete request. In cases with an established trial date, the decision on the request shall be made prior to the trial date. The CJAM will notify the Chief Justices and all parties of his decision on each request. Notwithstanding the provisions of this paragraph, in no event shall the pendency of a request be the sole cause for a case to be removed from a trial list.

2

6. Presumption in Certain Cases. There shall be a presumption in favor of allowance of the request if the parties to all the actions sought to be consolidated are identical, if each case will require a hearing or trial, and if the issues are substantially related. This presumption shall not apply with respect to the consolidation of hearings or reviews conducted pursuant to G.L. c. 119, § 29B with post-decree reviews of G.L. c. 210, § 3 matters.

7. Authority of CJAM in Absence of a Request. The CJAM may make such assignments in the absence of a request by a judge, Clerk-Magistrate, register, or party.

8. Requests to Have Related Actions Heard by Single Justice. This rule shall not apply to a request by a party for the interdepartmental judicial assignment of a justice of the Superior Court Department to hear related actions pending in the Superior Court Department, the District Court Department and/or the Boston Municipal Court Department nor shall it apply to a joint request by all the principal parties for an interdepartmental assignment of a justice of the District Court Department or the Boston Municipal Court Department to hear related actions pending in the Superior Court Department, the District Court Department and/or the Boston Municipal Court Department. A party or parties seeking to have such related actions heard by a single justice shall file a motion to transfer in the Superior Court Department pursuant to G.L. c. 223, Sec. 2B and then a motion to consolidate pursuant to Mass. R. Civ. P. 42(a) in the court to which the transfer is made.

Rule XIII—Uniform Trial Court Rules for Civil Commitment Proceedings for Alcohol and Substance Use Disorders, G.L. c. 123, § 35

[Effective July 1, 2015. Amended effective Sept. 6, 2016.]

Rule 1. Commencement of Proceedings

(a) Proceedings under the provisions of G.L. c. 123, § 35 in the District Court, Boston Municipal Court, and Juvenile Court Departments shall be commenced by the filing of a written petition, signed under the penalties of perjury, by a police officer, physician, spouse, blood relative, guardian, or court official seeking the issuance of an order of commitment of a person (hereinafter the "respondent") who the petitioner has reason to believe is an individual with an alcohol or substance use disorder, as those terms are defined in G.L. c. 123, § 35. Such a petitioner, including a court official, may petition on behalf of the respondent.

(b) Proceedings may be commenced in any Division of any of the three Departments without regard to the age, residence, or location of the respondent, but the age, residence, or location of the respondent may determine to which Division or Department any warrant or summons will be returnable pursuant to Rule 3.

(c) Following commencement, a petition may not be withdrawn without leave of court.

Rule 2. Review of Petition

Upon the filing of a petition and any sworn statements the court may request from the petitioner at the time of such filing, the case shall be brought expeditiously before a judge who shall review the petition on the record in court. If the judge determines that either (1) the petitioner is statutorily unqualified to file a petition under the provisions of G.L. c. 123, § 35; or (2) the petitioner's allegation that the respondent is an individual with an alcohol or substance use disorder has no reasonable basis, the judge shall dismiss the case. Otherwise, if the respondent is present, the court shall immediately proceed in accordance with Rules 4 and 5. If the respondent is not present, the court shall immediately proceed in accordance with Rule 3.

Rule 3. Issuance of Warrant or Summons; Execution of Warrant

(a) If the judge determines that there are reasonable grounds to believe that the respondent will not appear at the hearing and that any further delay in the proceeding would present an immediate danger to the physical well-being of the respondent, the court may issue a warrant for the apprehension and appearance of the respondent.

(b) If the court does not issue a warrant pursuant to Rule 3(a), the court shall cause a summons and a copy of the petition to be served on the respondent in the manner provided in G.L. c. 276, § 25. Following such service, if the respondent fails to appear at the time summoned, the court may issue a warrant for the apprehension and appearance of the respondent. The issuance of such a warrant shall not require a determination of immediate danger to the physical well-being of the respondent.

(c) The judge shall determine how long the warrant shall be effective, but shall not make any warrant effective for more than five business days. A warrant issued under this rule shall provide that it may be executed only when the respondent may be presented immediately after apprehension before a judge pursuant to Rule 4 or Rule 10.

(d) If the judge determines that the case should be heard in another Division or Department, because of the respondent's age or location or for other good reason, the judge may, in the exercise of discretion, make the warrant or summons returnable to an appropriate court in another Division or Department. The clerk shall notify the return court of the warrant or summons and transmit the papers listed in Rule 10(a) to the return court.

Rule 4. Appointment of Counsel

Unless the respondent is represented by counsel, the court shall appoint counsel pursuant to Supreme Judicial Court Rule 3:10(1)(f)(iii) before or upon the respondent's appearance before the court.

Rule 5. Order for Examination

The judge shall order an examination of the respondent to be conducted by a qualified physician, a qualified psychologist, or a qualified social worker.

Rule 6. Conduct of the Hearing; Standard of Proof

(a) After the completion of the examination ordered under Rule 5, the judge shall hold a hearing expeditiously to determine whether there is clear and convincing evidence that (1) the respondent is an individual with an alcohol or substance use disorder, as defined in G.L. c. 123, § 35; and (2) there is a likelihood of serious harm, as defined in G.L. c. 123, § 1, as a result of the respondent's alcohol or substance use disorder, to the respondent, the petitioner, or any other person.

(b) The judge may inquire of the petitioner and may accept testimony or other evidence from the petitioner or any other person, including a court official.

(c) The respondent shall have the right to cross-examine witnesses, present independent expert evidence, call witnesses, and submit documents or other evidence.

(d) All testimony shall be taken under oath and shall be recorded or transcribed.

Rule 7. Evidence

(a) The rules of evidence shall not apply in proceedings under G.L. c. 123, § 35, except that privileges and statutory disqualifications shall apply. Hearsay evidence shall be admissible, but may be relied upon only if the judge finds that it is substantially reliable.

(b) The judge shall not draw any adverse inference from a respondent's refusal to testify or to speak during the examination ordered pursuant to Rule 5 or at any other time during the proceedings. This shall not prohibit the clinician from offering an opinion despite such refusal and reporting such refusal to the court.

(c) The court shall base its findings on credible and competent evidence, including medical testimony and such other evidence as maybe admitted.

Rule 8. Findings and Issuance of Commitment Order

(a) If the judge makes the findings required by Rule 6(a), the court may then issue an order of commitment consistent with the terms and requirements set forth in G.L. c. 123, § 35, which shall be for a period not to exceed 90 days. The order shall specify whether the commitment is based on a finding of alcohol use disorder, substance use disorder, or both. The commitment shall be to a facility designated by the department of public health. The order shall specify that the receiving facility, or any facility to which the respondent is transferred, is responsible for providing and maintaining custody of the respondent until expiration or termination of the order, as provided by law.

(b) The judge shall include a provision in the order requiring the facility, or any facility to which the respondent is transferred, to provide the clerk of the committing court with notice, in the manner directed by the court, of the release, the transfer, or of any escape by the respondent.

(c) The commitment shall be made to a facility approved by the department of public health for the care and treatment of individuals with an alcohol or substance use disorder. If (i) the judge finds that the only appropriate setting for the treatment of the respondent is a secure facility or (ii) the department of public health informs the court that there are no suitable facilities available for treatment licensed or approved by the department of public health or the department of mental health, the judge may commit the respondent to the Massachusetts correctional institution at Bridgewater, for an adult male respondent, or to a secure facility for women approved by the department of public health or the department of mental health, for an adult female respondent.

(d) Upon issuance of a commitment order, the court shall notify the respondent that the respondent is prohibited from being issued a firearm identification card pursuant to G.L. c. 140, § 129B , or a license to carry pursuant to G.L. c. 140, §§ 131 and 131F, unless a petition for relief pursuant to G.L. c. 123, § 35 is subsequently granted.

Rule 9. Security of Respondent

The court shall take such action and issue such orders as maybe necessary to secure the presence of the respondent after the respondent's arrival at the court, prior to or during the hearing, and while awaiting transport following the issuance of a commitment order, as the circumstances may require

Rule 10. Proceedings When a Respondent Appears Before a Court Other than the Court that Issued the Warrant or Summons

(a) When (1) a warrant or summons is issued pursuant to Rule 3(d) or (2) a warrant is executed where it is impractical to transport the respondent to the return court, the respondent may be brought before a court having jurisdiction of cases under G.L. c. 123, § 35 (hereinafter the "new court"). The new court shall immediately contact the issuing court and obtain copies of (1) the docket in the case; (2) the petition; and (3) any other documents in the case file.

(b) The new court shall open a new case file for the matter and make reasonable efforts to notify the petitioner of the location of the new court. The new court, in its discretion, may wait a reasonable time for the petitioner to arrive.

(c) The new court shall proceed to adjudicate the case in accordance with Rules 4 through 9. The new court shall promptly inform the issuing court of its disposition-by transmitting to the issuing court a copy of its docket entries.

Rule 11. Appeal

(a) Any person aggrieved by a decision of the District Court Department or the Boston Municipal Court Department may appeal to the Appellate Division of such Department within seven days. Upon request, the Appellate Division shall expedite consideration of any appeal.

(b) Any person aggrieved by a decision of the Juvenile Court Department may appeal to the Appeals Court within seven days. Upon request, the Appeals Court shall expedite consideration of any appeal.

(c) The clerk shall serve notice of the filing of the appeal to any adverse party and to the facility to which a respondent was committed, if any.

Trial Court Guidelines for Pretrial Conditions of Release

[Effective Nov. 1, 2016.]

Preamble

The Executive Office of the Trial Court is pleased to provide you with the Pretrial Conditions of Release Guidelines developed by the Probation Pretrial Services Task Force. The Guidelines, which can be found at the link below are intended to assist judges, clerk magistrates, assistant clerk magistrates and others authorized to set bail when determining whether to set pretrial conditions of release, and if released, which conditions to impose.

Presently there are approximately 11,000 defendants on pretrial conditions of release across court departments. The goal of these Guidelines is to promote consistency in procedures relating to the setting of pretrial conditions of release on criminal defendants. These Guidelines are **not** intended to interfere with the discretion of those setting conditions of release.

The Guidelines were prepared with the assistance of the members of the Trial Court Pretrial Services Committee, whose members include: Hon. Paul C. Dawley, Co-chair, Commissioner Edward J. Dolan, Co-Chair, Hon. Kenneth Fishman, Hon. Andrew Mandell, Hon. Lawrence Moniz, Hon. Richard Savignano, Hon. Raymond Veary, Anthony Beneditti, Esq., Sheriff Frank Cousins, Sheriff Peter Koutoujian, Tara McGuire, Esq., Clerk Magistrate Keith McDonough, District Attorney Michael O'Keefe, Dr. Debra Pinals, and Chief Probation Officer Vincent Piro, Jr. In addition, the Committee received numerous comments reviewing the proposed Guidelines from court staff and others, including representatives from the Committee for Public Counsel Services and the Massachusetts District Attorney's Association.

Pretrial Conditions of Release Definition

Although the legal presumption for all criminal charges excluding capital cases is that an individual will be released on personal recognizance, pretrial conditions of release are conditions that may be ordered in addition to, or in lieu of, cash bail under any of the following bail statutes: G.L. c. 276, § 42A, § 57, § 58, § 58A, § 58B, or § 87.[i] Pretrial conditions of release may be ordered by any person authorized to take bail prior to arraignment or at arraignment, or by a judge at or after arraignment. Unless otherwise ordered or modified, pretrial conditions of release remain in effect until the case pursuant to which they are ordered is disposed.

Conditions ordered pursuant to G.L. c. 276, § 87 as a conditional disposition ("pre-trial probation"), anticipating dismissal of the criminal charges upon compliance with the conditions for a set period of time, are *not* considered pretrial conditions of release.

The Purposes of Pretrial Conditions of Release

1. To ensure the defendant's return to court while the criminal charges are pending.

2. To restrict or compel the defendant's conduct in a manner authorized by the bail statute under which release is ordered.

3. To protect alleged victims, other individuals, and the community through the imposition of appropriate pretrial conditions and / or supervision.

4. To prevent, as appropriate, any negative collateral consequences of pretrial incarceration.

Considerations in Setting Pretrial Conditions of Release

1. Pretrial conditions of release should be imposed only when personal recognizance without conditions is determined to be insufficient to ensure the defendant's return to court, or pretrial conditions of release satisfy a purpose set forth in one of the bail statutes.[ii]

2. Ordering pretrial conditions of release is entirely within the court's discretion.

3. The court should impose only pretrial conditions of release that, if violated, the court reasonably would expect to enforce.

4. The pretrial conditions of release should be tailored to address the particular characteristics of the defendant and the charged offense(s).[iii]

5. The number and type of pretrial conditions and / or supervision should correlate with the risks a defendant poses to default and / or to commit criminal offenses or otherwise endanger others.

6. The imposition of pretrial conditions of release does not detract from the defendant's presumption of innocence.

7. Pretrial conditions of release are not subject to supervision fees under G.L. c. 276, § 87A.[iv]

8. Probation shall supervise the pretrial conditions of release as necessary to implement the orders of the court.

9. The court may require the probation department to be heard at the time the court considers the imposition of pretrial conditions of release.[v]

Violations of Pretrial Conditions of Release

Alleged violations of pretrial conditions of release are subject to arrest by the police if the violation is the allegation of a new criminal act for which the police have a right of arrest, by a probation officer on a warrant for temporary custody pursuant to G.L. c. 279, § 3, ¶ 3,[vi] or by any officer upon the issuance of a warrant either by the court or by a probation officer pursuant to G.L. c. 279, § 3, ¶ 3. Notice of a hearing for a violation may also be given to a defendant by letter or summons.

Alleged violations of pretrial conditions of release may be brought before the court by the prosecution in a motion to revoke or modify bail or pretrial conditions of release. In addition, a probation officer may arrange for the appearance of the defendant before the court pursuant to G.L. c. 279, § 3, ¶¶ 1, 3 for an alleged violation of pretrial conditions of release. When the court is notified or becomes aware of an alleged violation of pretrial conditions of release, the court shall conduct a hearing pursuant to G.L. c. 276, § 58, ¶ 6[vii] or G.L. c. 276, § 58B.

Violations of pretrial conditions of release based on a new criminal charge are subject to bail revocation in the Superior Court pursuant to G.L. c. 276, § 57, and in the District Court pursuant to G.L. c. 276, § 58, ¶ 6 for up to 60 days, or pursuant to G.L. c. 276, § 58B for up to 90 days. Violations of pretrial conditions of release that are not based on a new criminal charge are subject to bail revocation pursuant to G.L. c. 276, § 58B for up to 90 days. Bail revocation and incarceration are not the only alternatives in the case when a violation of pretrial conditions of release has been found. Following a hearing on an alleged violation, upon a finding of violation, the court may release the defendant on the same conditions, alter or add pretrial conditions of release,[viii] set a cash bail,[ix] or revoke the defendant's bail and detain the defendant for up to 90 days.

END NOTES

[i] The legislature has provided in six separate statutes the specific circumstances under which pretrial release may be made subject to certain conditions.

G.L. c. 276, § 42A: "the court may, in lieu of or in addition to any terms of personal recognizance, and after a hearing and finding, impose such terms as will insure the safety of the person allegedly suffering the physical abuse or threat thereof, and will prevent its recurrence. Such terms and conditions shall include reasonable restrictions on travel, association or place of abode of the defendant as will prevent such person from contact with the person abused."

G.L. c. 276, § 58, ¶ 1: "the defendant may be ordered to abide by specified restrictions on personal associations or conduct including, but not limited to, avoiding all contact with an alleged victim of the crime and any potential witness or witnesses who may testify concerning the offense, as a condition of release."

Pursuant to **An Act Relative to Domestic Violence**, G.L. c. 276, §§ 42A, 57, and 58 state, "Any person authorized to take bail for such [domestic abuse] violation may impose conditions on a person's release in order to ensure the appearance of the person before the court and the safety of the alleged victim, any other individual or the community."

Conditional release, pursuant to **G.L. c. 276, § 58A**, may be ordered, on a motion by the prosecutor, for certain categories of defendants who have been charged with felonies that have as an element of the crime "the use, attempted use, or threatened use of physical force against the person of another, or any other felony that by its nature involves a substantial risk that physical force against the person of another may result" or with certain specified charges. *See Commonwealth v. Dodge*, 42 Mass 860, 864 n.7 (1999).

G.L. c. 276, § 58B, ¶ 2: "if the judicial officer finds that there are conditions of release that will assure that the person will not pose a danger to the safety of any other person or the community, and that the person will abide by such conditions, the judicial officer shall treat the person in accordance with the provisions of this section and may amend the conditions of release accordingly."

G.L. c. 276, § 87: "The superior court, any district court and any juvenile court may place on probation in the care of its probation officer any person before it charged with an offense or a crime for such time and upon such conditions as it deems proper, with the defendant's consent, before trial and before a plea of guilty." Conditions ordered pursuant to G.L. c. 276, § 87 as a conditional disposition ("pre-trial probation"), anticipating dismissal of the criminal charges upon compliance with the conditions for a set period of time, are not considered pretrial conditions of release.

[ii] The preferred disposition under the bail statute (G.L. c. 276, § 58) is release on personal recognizance. *Commonwealth v. Dodge*, 428 Mass. 860, 865 (1999), citing *Mendonza v. Commonwealth*, 423 Mass. 771, 774 (1996). See *Commonwealth v. Perito*, 417 Mass. 674, 678 (1994); *Delaney v. Commonwealth*, 415 Mass. 490, 495 (1993) ("Our Legislature intended § 58 to protect the rights of the defendant by establishing a presumption that he or she will be admitted to bail on personal recognizance without surety and by delineating carefully the circumstances under which bail may be denied").

[iii] "The goals of probation 'are best served if the conditions of probation are tailored to address the particular characteristics of the defendant and the crime.'" *Commonwealth v. Gomes*, 73 Mass. App. Ct. 857, 859 (2009), citing *Commonwealth v. Pike*, 428 Mass. 393, 403 (1998). Although a probationary condition is not necessarily invalid simply because it affects constitutional rights, the condition must be reasonably related to legitimate probationary goals in order to withstand constitutional scrutiny. *Id.*, citing *Commonwealth v. Lapointe*, 435 Mass. 455, 459 (2001); *Commonwealth v. Power*, 420 Mass. 410, 416-417 (1995), *cert. denied*, 516 U.S. 1042 (1996) ("As long as the condition meets the 'reasonably related' test, it is not per se unconstitutional even if it restricts a probationer's fundamental rights"). "Ordering a defendant to submit to random drug or alcohol testing as a condition of probation, therefore, is not permissible unless it is reasonably related to one or more of the goals of probation: punishment, deterrence, retribution, protection of the public, or rehabilitation." *Gomes*, 73 Mass. App. Ct. at 859. "This is a fact-intensive inquiry, dependent on the circumstances and characteristics of the particular defendant and his offenses." *Id.*

[iv] G.L. c. 276, § 87A dictates that "[t]he court shall assess upon every person placed on supervised probation, including all persons placed on probation for offenses under c. 90 § 24, a monthly probation supervision fee, hereinafter referred to as 'probation fee', in the amount of $60 per month. Said person shall pay said probation fee once each month during such time as said person remains on supervised probation. Said person shall pay said probation fee once each month during such time as said person remains on supervised probation. The court shall assess upon every person placed on administrative supervised probation a monthly administrative probation supervision fee, hereinafter referred to

as 'administrative probation', in the amount of $45 per month. Said person shall pay said administrative probation fee once each month during such time as said person remains on administrative supervised probation."

[v] This guideline applies the probation clause of District & Municipal Courts Rules of Criminal Procedure 4(c) to the pretrial context. Dist./Mun. R. Crim. P. 4(c): "if the proposed dispositional terms involve any probationary terms or conditions, the parties shall consult with the probation department, so as to enable the probation department to be heard as may be required by the court at the time the court considers the tendered plea or admission."

[vi] Pursuant to G.L. c. 279, § 3, ¶ 3, "if a probation officer has probable cause to believe that a person placed under probation supervision or in the custody or care of a probation officer pursuant to sections 42A, 58A or 87 of chapter 276 or any other statute that allows the court to set conditions of release, has violated the conditions set by the court, the probation officer may arrest the probationer or may issue a warrant for the temporary custody of the probationer for a period not to exceed 72 hours or until the next sitting of the court, during which period the probation officer shall arrange for the appearance of the probationer before the court pursuant to [G.L. c. 279, § 3, ¶ 1]."

[vii] G.L. c. 276, § 58, ¶ 6 provides in part that "[t]he hearing shall be held upon the person's first appearance before the court before which the person is charged with committing an offense while on release pending adjudication of a prior charge, unless that person, or the attorney for the commonwealth, seeks and the court allows, a continuance because a witness or document is not immediately available." Said person has the right to be represented by counsel at the hearing. If the court "finds probable cause to believe that the person committed a crime during said period of release, the court shall then determine, in the exercise of its discretion, whether the release of said person will seriously endanger any person of the community."

[viii] Pursuant to G.L. c. 276, § 58B, ¶ 2, if there is probable cause to believe that, while on release, the defendant committed a federal or state crime or clear and convincing evidence that the defendant violated any other condition of release, but "the judicial officer finds that there are conditions of release that will assure that the person will not pose a danger to the safety of any other person or the community, and that the person will abide by such conditions, the judicial officer shall treat the person in accordance with the provisions of this section and may amend the conditions of release accordingly."

[ix] Pursuant to G.L. c. 276, § 58, ¶ 9, "if any court, in its discretion, finds that changed circumstances or other factors not previously known or considered, make the order of bail or recognizance ineffective to reasonably assure the appearance of said defendant before the court, the court may make a further order of bail, either by increasing the amount of the recognizance or requiring sufficient surety or both, which order will not revoke the order of bail or recognizance previously in force and effect. The court may also review such changed circumstances or other factors not previously known or considered in accordance with [G.L. c. 276, § 58, ¶ 6]."

Amended Standards for Care and Protection Cases for Probation Officers of the Juvenile Court Department

Statement of Purpose

The purpose of these Standards is to monitor and enforce the orders of the Court to insure safety and well being of the children, to provide information to the Court and to assist in timely permanency planning.

Scope

These Probation Standards shall govern the procedures and duties to be followed by Probation Officers in the Juvenile Court Department when they are assigned to supervise cases arising pursuant to MGL c. 119, section 24, i.e. "Care and Protection cases," and Guardianship cases arising pursuant to c. 190B unless otherwise directed by a justice. These standards shall continue to apply to children involved in such proceedings in the Juvenile Court Department until the case is dismissed or closed; the child attains the age of majority; or the child is adopted.

Statement of Roles

The *Chief Probation Officer*, as the Department Head, exercises executive control and supervision of the Probation office. She/he is responsible for implementing, monitoring. and maintaining the Care and Protection established by the Office of the Commissioner of Probation.

The *First Assistant Chief Probation Officer*, under the direction of the Chief Probation Officer, exercises direct control and supervision over the Probation office. She/he is responsible for the supervision of the Assistant Chief Probation Officers to insure the Care and Protection Standards are implemented.

The *Assistant Chief Probation Officer*, as supervisor, under the direction of the Chief Probation Officer and where applicable, the First Assistant Chief Probation Officer, is responsible for the supervision of Probation Officers in their duties as they pertain to the Care and Protection Standards.

The *Probation Officer*, under the direction of the Chief Probation Officer or her/his designate, performs duties and responsibilities as promulgated in the Care and Protection Standards.

Care and Protection Standards

Standard 1:00. Case Assignment

1:01 Case assignments shall occur upon receipt of an affidavit. The assignments of levels of supervision shall be made within 48 hours after the custody determination is made pursuant to the 72 hour hearing. Prior to the completion of the 72 hours, the role of probation shall be determined by a judge or the Chief Probation Officer.

The Chief Probation Officer shall be responsible for establishing local written policies and procedures to ensure that Care and Protection cases under Probation Officer supervision are assigned in a timely and efficient manner.

1:02 The First Assistant Chief Probation Officer under the direction of the Chief Probation Officer, shall be responsible for supervising Assistant Chief Probation Officers in their assignment, tracking and supervision of Probation Officers in Care and Protection cases.

1:03 The Assistant Chief Probation Officer, under the direction of the Chief Probation Officer and the First Assistant Chief Probation Officer (where applicable), shall be responsible for initial assignment of Care and Protection cases upon notice from the Clerk Magistrate's Office of the filing of the Care and Protection petition.

1:04 In each division there shall be a master assignment system and a case tracking system. It shall be the responsibilities of the Chief Probation Officer, as department head, to ensure that these systems are implemented and maintained accurately and in a timely fashion.

1:05 The Assistant Chief Probation Officer shall be responsible for developing and monitoring a case tracking system for all cases assigned to each Probation Officer under his/her supervision.

1:06 Under the Direction of the Chief Probation Officer and the First Assistant Chief Probation Officer, where applicable, the Assistant Chief Probation Officer shall be responsible for any other assignments and tracking of Care and Protection case responsibly, including but not limited to Intra-state Courtesy Placements and Home Studies pursuant to c. 119, section 26(2)(i), where applicable.

COMMENTARY

As Department Head, the Chief Probation Officer manages case flow control within the office. The intent of the master assignment and case tracking systems is to provide management instruments for the CPO or his/her designee to insure the following:

- The time assignment of all Care and Protection cases;

- The development of a management information system to provide date as to the amount of time expended on each essential function of the duties of the Probation Officer;
- Maintenance of a reliable database and submission of monthly statistics as required;
- Tracking all due dates for the review of cases assigned to Probation Officers.

Standard 2:00. Case Management

2:01 The Probation Officer shall complete an Intake form which shall include information as to each child who is subject to the petition, and as to each parent(s)/guardian(s) and any other person residing in the household.

2:02 Indigency information shall be obtained on parent(s)/guardian(s) on the required Form(s).

2:03 The Probation Officer shall complete an Indigency Report as to each parent or guardian of each child named in the petition who claims indigency pursuant to Rule 3:10 of the Supreme Judicial Court.

2:04 The Probation Officer shall conduct an inquiry in the CARI system as to each parent (or guardian) who is before the court and as to any other person residing in the home as part of the intake process. The Probation Officer shall bring to the attention of the court any information obtained as a result of said inquiring

2:05 The Probation Officer shall conduct a CARI inquiry as to any person who is being considered by the Court as a possible placement for a child. The Probation Officer shall bring to the Court's attention any information obtained as a result of said inquiry.

2:06 The probation officer shall also conduct a CARI inquiry: as to any person 1) who may commence residing in the home; 2) whenever there are allegation of criminal conduct mad against any person residing in the home; 3) at every subsequent court appearance; and when so directed by the Court.

2:07 Absent an express court order the Probation Officer shall not provide any printed CARI records to any party.

2:08 The Probation Officer shall maintain a Probation case folder of the chronological record, to include a record of court hearings, home studies, home visits, placement visits, collateral contacts and all other Probation activities. Court orders shall be entered in the Probation chronological notes and/or copies of such written orders shall be incorporated into the Probation case folder.

2:09 The Probation Officer shall verify compliance of court orders and shall report to the Court as necessary.

2:10 The Probation Officer shall maintain contact with the parent(s)/guardians(s), the Department of Children and Families, and/or other sources, regarding the placement, safety and welfare of the child(ren). All contacts are to be recorded in the chronological notes. The level and frequency of contact shall be determined by the classification of the case, as required by Standard 4.00 of these Standards pertaining to Case Supervision.

COMMENTARY

With respect to Standard 2:01, the Care and Protection intake forms shall be commenced within seventy-two (72) hours, provided, however, the intake form must be completed no later than 30 calendar days from the initial filing. The Standard makes clear that the Probation Officer shall complete an indigency form as to each parent or guardian of each child pursuant to the Rules of the Supreme Judicial Court pertaining to claims of indigency in regards to the appointment of counsel.

With respect to Standard 2:03, the Probation Officer shall conduct a CARI inquiry at the time of filing the petition, on each parent(s)/guardian(s), caregiver and occupant in the primary home. A CARI inquiry should be conducted on a proposed caregiver and on each resident of the proposed home. Thereafter, subsequent CARI checks may be conducted as determined necessary and appropriate by the Probation Officer. The purpose of conducting these CARI inquiries is to inform the Judge about an concerns regarding any persons residing in the home in which the child is residing or in which the child may be placed. When doing a home study on a proposed placement, a CARI inquiry should be conducted on each person residing in the home and/or having care-giving responsibilities.

With respect to Standard 2;08, chronological notes documenting court actions, collateral contacts and all other Probation activities can reference supporting documents/verifications in the folder which reflect compliance to Standards.

With respect to Standard 2:10, the Probation Officer will maintain collateral contact with sources who provide credible information regarding the current safety and well-being of the child(ren). Sources may include the Court Appointed Special Advocate (CASA), foster parent/caretaker, teacher/school adjustment counsel, therapist, attorney, social worker, etc. Probation Officers are expected to maintain contact with a variety of sources throughout the duration of the case. The Probation Officer shall maintain and record contact information for all sources who provide information about the child. The contact and corresponding chronological entry shall include the following:

- Date of contact
- Source of information
- Source's relationship to child(ren) (attorney, therapist, etc)
- Current address of child(ren)
- Most recent date the source had direct contact with the child(ren)

A chronological entry stating that no collateral sources could be reached shall prompt an immediate Placement Visit to the last known residence by the Probation Officer with all information documented as to comply with the Standards.

Standard 3:00. Home Studies/Investigations, Placement Visits (Including Courtesy)

3:01 The Probation Officer shall conduct home studies/investigations and placement visits for every subject child in every Care and Protection case, as defined in accordance with these standards.

3:02 The Probation Officer shall make an initial placement visit to the current residence of each subject child and make subsequent visits during the duration of the case in accordance with case supervision Standard 4:00 unless an alternative schedule of visits is ordered by the court.

3:03 The Probation Officer also shall conduct a Home Study/Investigation whenever ordered to do so by the Court.

3:04 At the request of another Probation Department, a Probation Officer shall conduct a courtesy placement visit and return the report no later than 30 calendar days after receipt of the original request. (A)CPO's from each division shall ensure that the assignment and time standards for courtesy placement visits are met from both the sending and receiving court.

3:05 Courtesy home study/investigation shall be conducted by a Probation Officer at the request of another Probation Department. The home study/investigation report shall be returned to the requesting court no later than 45 calendar days unless otherwise ordered from the court. (A)CPO's from each division shall ensure that the assignment and time standards for courtesy home study/investigations are met from both the sending and receiving court.

COMMENTARY

With respect to Standard 3:01, the purpose of this home study is to provide basic information to the Court regarding the proposed placement of a short-term uncontested, third-party or kinship placement.

With respect to Standard 3:03, the purpose of the home investigation is to provide more extensive information to the Court.

With respect to Standard 3:00 and all sub-sections thereof, for every placement visit, home study, home investigation or courtesy placement visit, the probation officer will complete the approved, corresponding report forms, which shall contain all of the information identified as necessary and appropriate. A written explanation will be included if necessary information was not obtained.

With respect to Standards 3:04 and 3:05, the term "courtesy" identifies those instances when Probation Officers have been asked to conduct placement visits, home studies and or home investigations within their jurisdiction for another Court. Every request for a courtesy visit, home study or home investigation shall be honored and conducted within required time lines, unless the CPO's from both the sending and receiving Courts have determined that it would not be feasible.

Standard 4:00. Case Supervision

4:01 Case supervision shall be categorized Level I, Level II, Level III and Level IV as defined in the following Standards. Supervision Level I, Level II, Level III, or Level IV is defined by each child's current living situation and the length of the custody order. The initial Level for Supervision determination will be made using existing information from the petition, affidavit and address from DCF and will be documented in the chronological record. This initial determination shall be made for each child in the petition, pursuant to the provisions of Section 1:01 and this Section, to make sure that the placement visit will be made within the required time standard.

The assigned PO shall write and submit the initial Supervision Plan, based upon the preliminary hearing information and the initial determination. Such supervision plans will include the supervision level of each child, the residence of each child and the date of placement at such residence(s), the social worker's name, telephone number and email address, and the time and place of the next placement visit. All supervision plans must be submitted for approval by the (A)CPO within 21 calendar days. The (A)CPO will have up to five calendar days to review the proposed plan. In cases where there is more than one child named in the Care and Protection petition and the children are on different supervision levels, the Probation Officer will supervise each child at his/her specific level in accordance with the established guidelines and the level will be entered in the supervision plan. Whenever a child's placement changes or whenever the court orders a change in placement or the PO discovers new information, the PO shall redetermine the appropriate level of supervision, conduct a new placement visit report and submit the required documentation to his/her (A)CPO, in the time frame determined by the level.

4:02 Level 1: Child(ren) named in a Care and Protection petition who are placed in the custody of a parent or third party for less than year, not in the custody of the Department of Children and Families (DCF) shall be classified as Level I. The Probation Officer shall conduct an initial home visit for every subject child, with the child present, within twenty-one (21) calendar days of the case assignment. A Home visit with the child present shall occur at least one time at the placement and every 30 calendar days thereafter. In the event there is a change in placement, the Probation Officer shall conduct a home visit within twenty-one (21) calendar days.

4:03 Level II: Child(ren) named in a Care and Protection petition who are in the custody of DCF shall classified as Level II. These children may be placed with a parent/guardian, regular or contracted foster home, licensed group care facility, or other setting. The Probation Officer shall maintain contact with DCF personnel, the child's custodian/caretaker or any other significant care or service provider, at least once every ninety (90) calendar days regarding the health and welfare of the child, status of the case, and placement of the child. This contact shall include face-to-face, telephone or email contact, or the receipt of a written report. The Probation Officer shall verify the information received with another source within the 90 calendar day period.

4:04 At Level II, the Probation Officer shall conduct a home visit for every subject child, with the child present, within forty-five (45) calendar days of the case assignment except for a child who is placed in a DCF approved child specific licensed group home.

4:05 Level III: Children named in a Care and Protection petition who are hospitalized or placed in any long-term placement pending guardianship or adoption, with or without a plan for adoption shall be classified as Level III. Open Care and Protection cases where the child runs away and a warrant or precept has issued shall be classified as Level III. Upon arrest or appearance in court, the classification of the case shall be redetermined. There is no mandatory placement visit requirement for Level III, however, if the child is discharged from the hospital setting or long-term placement, a re-determination of the level of supervision shall be conducted with 30 calendar days, which shall include a Home/placement visit report. The Probation Officer shall review the placement, record such review in writing and submit the Assistant Chief Probation Officer for approval no less than every six (6) months, or any time there is a change in the child's placement.

4:06 Level IV: Children named in a Care and Protection Petition for whom an order of permanent guardianship, permanent custody with parental rights terminated, young adults (ages 18-22) or for whom an order of long term third party custody of a year or more has entered, children placed out of state by court order, or cases open for collection of monies only shall be classified as Level IV. In the event there is a disruption in the guardianship, the Probation Officer shall redetermine and establish the level of supervision and supervise according to the care and protection standards.

4:07 Whenever the court orders a change in custody of the child(ren), the Probation Officer shall determine whether a different level of supervision applies, and shall note the level of supervision in the new supervision plan, submitted within the same time Standards as directed in Standard 4:01.

4:08 After the initial supervision plan has been approved, Level I cases shall be submitted for review every four (4) months thereafter. Level II and Level II cases shall be submitted for review every six (6) months thereafter. For each review, the Probation Officer shall note the placement address and custody status of each child named in the petition and the corresponding level of supervision. For Level IV cases, once a determination is made that the case is a Level IV, there are no mandatory requirements for the Probation Officer or the Assistant Chief Probation Officer however, should the case go back before the judge, a new level determination may be required.

4:9 The Assistant Chief Probation Officer (ACPO) shall record in writing on the chronological notes his/her approval of the initial plan/case review, including the ACPO's initials and the date of the review. If the (A)CPO is not in agreement with the management of the case, the ACPO shall take action to resolve the differences and shall note the necessary changes, incomplete actions, or what further information or action is required, in the chronological record.

COMMENTARY

With respect to Standards 4:01 and 4:07 the initial supervision plan and all subsequent reviews, shall minimally include custody status, placement address of each child, special court orders, level of supervision, placement visit date or scheduled date. The supervision plan determination shall be based on the care and custody, safety and well being of each subject child. With respect to Standard 4:01, circumstances or changes of the child's placement will dictate whether a new level of supervision or new supervision plan is necessary. Short term third party custody shall be supervised as Level I.

With respect to Standard 4:03, the purpose of Probation Officers supervising Care and Protection cases is to enhance the safety and well-being of the child(ren); the Probation Officer shall maintain collateral contacts with sources that provide credible and current information regarding the safety and well-being of each subject child. Credible and current sources may include but are not limited to: foster parent/caretaker, teacher/school adjustment counsel, therapist, attorney, Court Appointed Special Advocate or social worker, etc.

The Probation Officer is expected to contact different sources over the period of supervision. Each contact, and corresponding chronological entry, shall contain the date of the contact, the source of information, the source's relationship to the child(ren), the current address of each child and the date when the source last had contact.

If no collateral sources could be reached within the required time interval, this shall prompt the Probation Officer to conduct an immediate placement visit to ensure the safety and well-being of the child(ren). The Probation Officer shall then document all information in the case file chronological record.

Due to the fact that hearings (not continuances) provide the Court with updated information as to the status, the substantive court hearings can take the place of a collateral contact but cannot be used for consecutive contacts.

With respect to Standard 4:05, the term "hospitalization" shall also include acute/long term placement for psychiatric stabilization, evaluation, and assessment.

Long term third party custody shall be defined as a year or more and shall be supervised at Level IV.

Home visits should be made during normal work hours. It is understood that some visits may have to be made outside the normal work hours with the approval of the Chief Probation Officer.

2

2

Standard 5:00. Advancing Care & Protection Cases

5:01 The Probation Officer shall advance the case before the court in the event that one or more parties fail to comply with a specific court order. If the non-compliances results in risk to the health or well-being of the child(ren), the Probation Officer shall advance the case immediately with notification to all parties and in accordance with court practices. If the non-compliances does not jeopardize the health or well-being of the child(ren), the Probation Officer shall document the failure to comply in the Probation chronological notes and bring such failure to the attention of the court at the next scheduled date, unless the Court and/or (A)CPO directs otherwise.

5:02 The Probation Officer shall advance the case before the court in the event s/he discovers facts or circumstances that may be detrimental to the health and welfare of the child(ren). These facts or circumstances may or may not be based on non-compliance with court orders. The Probation Officer shall bring the case forward immediately with notification to all parties and in accordance with court practices.

5:03 When a Probation Officer determines that a case may require advancement, the Probation Officer shall consult with the (A)CPO. This consultation may be written or verbal, and shall be documented in writing in the Probation chronological notes.

5:04 Cases that require advancement include the cases described in Standard 5:01 and 5:02 and also shall include cases in which a collateral contact cannot be made and the Probation Officer has not be able to complete a placement visit.

5:05 A Care and Protection Case Advancement Report shall be completed and submitted to the (A)CPO for review and approval prior to submission to the court.

COMMENTARY

The fundamental role of Probation Officers is to monitor and enforce court orders to ensure the safety and well being of the children and to provide information to the Court. Advancing cases is consistent with that role and the purpose of these standards.

With respect to Standard 5:00 in its entirety, Probation Officers, with the approval of the (A)CPO, have the responsibility to make certain that cases are brought back into court for judicial intervention if there are significant changes in circumstances that may affect the child and the Probation Officer determines it is in the best of the child(ren).

Standards for Children in Need of Services (CHINS) for Probation Officers of the District Court Department and the Juvenile Court Department

NOTE These standards were drafted before Children in Need of Services (CHINS) was replaced by Children Requiring Assistance (CRA), updated standards were in progress by the court but not available to MCLE by this book's publication date.

Statement of Purpose

The purpose of these standards is to promote law abiding, productive behavior, by coordinating appropriate services and providing supervision to children involved in Children In Need Of Services proceedings.

Statement of Roles

The CHIEF PROBATION OFFICER* is responsible for implementing, monitoring and maintaining the standards, forms, and procedures governing the CHINS Standards established by the Commissioner of Probation.

** The responsibilities set forth in these standards as applicable to the Chief Probation Officer shall, in the instance of a one person office, be applicable to the Probation Officer-in-Charge.*

The ASSISTANT CHIEF PROBATION OFFICER** under the direction of the Chief Probation Officer, is responsible for training and supervising the probation officers in the implementation of the CHINS Standards.

***The First Assistant Chief Probation Officer is responsible for performing those functions with respect to the standards which are delegated to him/her by the Chief Probation Officer.*

The PROBATION OFFICER is responsible for carrying out the CHINS Standards.

Standard 1:00. Screening/Intake

1:01 The Chief Probation Officer shall be responsible for establishing written procedures to ensure that each person seeking CHINS assistance or information from the probation office, or who is referred to the probation office for CHINS screening or services, receives immediate attention and is provided with appropriate assistance.

1:02 The Chief Probation Officer shall be responsible for establishing written procedures to ensure that a probation officer completes Part I Sections A–E of the CHINS Preliminary Inquiry Report (CHINS-R-1) for each individual referred to the probation office for assistance.

1:03 The probation officer, prior to collecting the initial intake information, shall provide the individual(s) seeking assistance with an explanation of the CHINS process, including the options which are available (M.G.L. c. 119 § 39E–39J).

1:04 The probation officer, after completing the screening process, shall refer the applicant to the clerk/magistrate for assistance, if he/she believes that the best interest of the child would be served by a more formal process.

COMMENTARY

The intent of Standard 1:01, is to establish a procedure by which the probation officer can, at the earliest possible moment, evaluate the need for service and respond appropriately.

The intent of Standard 1:02, is to ensure that basic background information is collected on each individual referred to the probation office for services. This includes individuals who request assistance directly from a probation officer, as well as those referred directly from the clerk/magistrate prior to the issuance of an application.

The intent of Standard 1:03, is to provide the individual(s) seeking assistance with guidance and direction concerning the CHINS process, keeping in mind that the goal should be to determine what is in the best interests of the child.

Standard 2:00. Preliminary Inquiry

2:01 Prior to a hearing concerning the issuance of a petition, or subsequent to a petition being issued when a child is before the court on an arrest, the probation officer shall complete the CHINS Preliminary Inquiry Report, including a written recommendation as to whether the interests of the child can be best served by informal assistance without issuance of a petition, informal assistance without a trial on the merits, or by issuing a petition and proceeding with a trial on the merits.

2:02 The probation officer completing the preliminary inquiry shall review all pertinent identifying and investigative information prior to making a recommendation to the court.

2:03 The probation officer completing the report shall make every attempt to verify the information obtained during the preliminary inquiry, in order to provide the court with accurate information regarding the CHINS action.

2:04 Prior to making a recommendation to the court, the probation officer, in those instances where informal assistance is being recommended, shall discuss the recommendation with the parties in an effort to reach a consensus regarding the specific terms of the agreement. If the effort is successful, the terms of the agreement shall be presented to the court for its consideration.

COMMENTARY

With respect to Standard 2:01, it is the practice in some courts to refer the applicant to the probation office for screening after the clerk/magistrate has verbally granted the application, but prior to signing the application, when the applicant has not been previously screened by a probation officer. In those instances the probation officer should complete sections Part I, A–E of the CHINS Preliminary Inquiry Report prior to completing the remaining sections of the report.

With respect to Standard 2:03, the information obtained during the preliminary inquiry may be verified through home/school visits, medical/psychological reports, telephone calls to appropriate agencies/individuals and other collateral contacts. The probation officer should mark the appropriate response (yes—no) under "Information Verified" on the Preliminary Inquiry Report, indicating whether the information in each particular section was verified through reliable sources.

With respect to Standard 2:04, the probation officer should be aware that any agreement is voluntary, and therefore it is in the best interest of everyone involved to attempt to reach a consensus which will allow for an amicable solution to the problem.

Any agreement between the parties should be reduced to writing, and if approved by the court, all parties should receive a copy of the agreement.

Standard 3:00. Terms of Agreement/Conditions of Order

3:01 The Chief Probation Officer shall be responsible for establishing written procedures designed to ensure that each child referred by the court for probation officer assistance receives, forthwith, a written copy of the terms of the agreement/conditions of the order signed by the child, the parents)/guardian(s), and the probation officer, a copy of which shall be retained in the case folder.

3:02 The probation officer shall, at the time of the signing of the terms of the agreement/conditions of the order, ensure that the child and his parent(s)/guardian(s) understand the obligations and requirements for each party to the agreement/ order.

3:03 The probation officer shall inform the parties to any agreement/order that he/she will monitor compliance with the terms of the agreement/conditions of the order. The probation officer shall explain the likely action and possible consequences of non-compl iance with any of the terms or conditions.

COMMENTARY

With regard to Standard 3:01, in those instance (provided for in M.G.L. c. 119. § 39E) where the court finds that the interests of the child would be best served by informal assistance without a trial on the merits, the probation officer should utilize the CHINS AGREEMENT. This includes those situations where a petition issued because of an arrest, and the court referred the child to the probation officer for assistance without a trial on the merits.

The CHINS AGREEMENT contains a voluntary set of terms agreed to by the parties with the assistance of the probation officer, though the parties are required to participate in good faith with probation officer referrals and conferences.

The CHINS ORDER should be utilized in those instances where the court has adjudicated the child to be in need of services after a trial on the merits (M.G.L. c. 119 § 39G). It is a set of conditions which reflect and specify the court's orders.

In addition, anytime the court alters the terms of the agreement/conditions of the order, the probation officer shall be responsible for ensuring that a new written agreement/order is executed by the parties.

With respect to Standard 3:03, the probation officer has the authority and responsibility to refer the child to any appropriate public or private organization for assistance and conduct conferences with the child and the family/guardian for the Purpose of avoiding judicial trial on the merits. If the child or the parents/guardian fail to participate in good faith and fail to comply with the terms of agreement/conditions of order, the probation officer shall take appropriate action (see Section 7:00, Case Review/Court Action).

Standard 4:00. Case Assignment

4:01 The Chief Probation Officer shall be responsible for establishing written procedures to ensure, when a child is referred by the court for probation officer assistance, or otherwise, when the court places a child under probation officer supervision, that the case is assigned to a probation officer no later than the next working day following action by the court.

COMMENTARY

Standard 4:01 requires each Chief Probation Officer to establish a timely and efficient procedure for assigning children to probation officers for services. The intent of the standard is to establish a system which will ensure that the child begins receiving services immediately upon being referred to probation by the court. The current practice in some courts is to assign a probation officer at date of application. If this is not the case, a system must be established by the CPO, which will ensure that a probation officer is assigned at the time of the agreement/order by the court. It is imperative that a probation officer be assigned to establish a supervision plan, to make appropriate referrals to public or private organizations or individuals, and to ensure that the terms of agreement/conditions of order are enforced.

2

Standard 5:00. Case Planning

5:01 For each child referred by the court for assistance, or when the court p1aces a child under probation officer supervision, the probation officer shall commence appropriate contact with the child forthwith.

5:02 The probation officer shall review and assess all available investigative and evaluative material, and shall develop a written supervision plan which shall be recorded on the chronological supervision sheet, in the following instances: where the court has referred a child to the probation officer for assistance; or where the court intends the probation officer to monitor and/or implement the conditions and limitations prescribed by the court.

5:03 The written supervision plan shall address any informal agreement(s) made between the child and the other parties, on the basis of which the court has agreed to continue the case. In addition, the plan shall include any orders of the court, and shall include the steps to be taken by the child, the parents/guardian, other persons or agencies and the probation officer to resolve the issues which resulted in the CHINS action.

5:04 The written supervision plan shall be completed by the probation officer within 15 calendar days from the date of the agreement/order and shall be reviewed and approved by the (A)CPO within 30 calendar days from the date of the agreement/order.

5:05 The (A)CPO approval of the written supervision plan shall be evidenced by the (A)CPO's initials and date of approval adjacent to the supervision plan and recorded on the chronological supervision sheet.

5:06 If the (A)CPO is not in agreement with the initial supervision plan, the (A)CPO shall confer with the probation officer to resolve any differences. When necessary, the probation officer shall immediately revise the supervision plan and record the revised plan on the chronological supervision sheet.

COMMENTARY

With respect to Standard 5:02, it is expected that the probation officer will review the CHINS PRELIMINARY INQUIRY REPORT as well as any relevant reports from schools/social service, or other appropriate agencies prior to developing a plan of action for the child.

With respect to Standard 5:03, it is intended that the probation officer will develop a supervision plan that is consistent with any voluntary agreements that are made between the child, his parents, or other parties to the CHINS action, on the basis of which the court has agreed to continue the case, and with any orders or suggestions made by the court which are intended to provide a solution to the problem.

With respect to Standard 5:05 the (A)CPO when reviewing the initial supervision plan, should also review all entries made on the chronological supervision sheet subsequent to the recording of the plan to determine if they are consistent with the objectives of the plan.

Standard 6:00. Supervision Plan Implementation

6:01 The probation officer shall implement and monitor the supervision plan, including any informal agreements or orders of the court.

6:02 The date, type of contact and a summary of each activity which relates to the CHINS case shall be recorded on the chronological supervision sheet.

6:03 The probation officer shall have contact with the child, the child's parents/guardian or other appropriate individuals/

agencies at least once every thirty (30) calendar days to ensure compliance with all terms of the agreement/orders of the court.

6:04 When circumstances occur which substantially change the nature of the supervision, the probation officer, with the approval of the (A)CPO, shall revise the supervision plan in a manner consistent with the terms of agreement/conditions of order and with any other conditions and limitations prescribed by the court.

6:05 The probation officer and the (A)CPO shall meet to discuss a case at the request of either individual. A notation as to the outcome of that meeting shall be recorded on the chronological supervision sheet.

COMMENTARY

With regard to Standard 6:01, in order to implement a supervision plan which will provide the child and his family with an opportunity to resolve their difficulties, the probation officer should act as a resource broker with appropriate individuals/agencies to ensure that psychiatric, psychological, educational, occupational, medical, dental and/or social services are provided.

With respect to Standard 6:02, all entries made on the chronological supervision sheet should be brief, succinct and primarily focused on the implementation of the supervision plan, including all terms of agreement/conditions of order. The probation officer, during the supervision period, should review the case folder, as necessary, to ensure familiarity with the child's current status, as well as to help ensure compliance with the terms of agreement/conditions of order, and the full implementation of the supervision plan.

With respect to Standard 6:03, the probation officer contacts with the child, parents/guardian or other appropriate individuals/agencies could include face to face, telephone or letter contacts, or written status reports. The intent is to ensure that the probation officer monitors the case and verifies the information received regarding the status of the child, in accordance with the supervision plan.

Upon the court's adjudicating a child to be a Child In Need of Services (CHINS) and committing the child to the Department of Social Services (DSS), the probation officer's responsibility terminates as it relates to the supervision contact level. However, the probation officer may, at the court's direction, continue to monitor compliance with the order, including any conditions and limitations prescribed by the court.

With respect to Standard 6:04, whenever circumstances occur which might affect the supervision plan, the probation officer should reassess the plan and, if necessary, record a revised plan on the chronological supervision sheet.

Standard 7:00. Case Review/Court Action

7:01 The (A)CPO, shall review each case at least every ninety (90) days from the date of the initial agreement/order, to determine if contact levels are being maintained, and to ensure compliance with agreements/orders.

7:02 Whenever the (A)CPO reviews a case, he/she shall indicate his/her approval of the supervision, by placing his/her initials and the date next to the last entry on the chronological supervision sheet.

7:03 Whenever the probation officer believes that a child or the child's parents have failed to comply with the terms of agreement/conditions of the order, or when other persons or agencies have failed to comply with any other conditions or limitations prescribed by the court, shall bring the case to the attention of the (A)CPO for review. If after such consideration, further action is determined to be appropriate, the probation officer shall inform the parties in writing of his/her intent to bring the matter before the court for review, as well as the basis for a such review. A copy of the notification shall be filed with the clerk/magistrate.

COMMENTARY

Standards 7:01, requires that the (A)CPO review each case every ninety days as long as the agreement/order remains in effect. In addition to approving the initial supervision plan within the first 30 days of the agreement/order, the (A)CPO must review the case within 90 days of the initial agreement/order, and every 90 days subsequent to that date, for compliance with the agreement/order, as well as for compliance with the contact levels.

Standard 7:03, provides a mechanism to respond appropriately to instances of non-compliance with terms of the agreement/conditions of the order, or with any other conditions or limitations prescribed by the court. The notice of VIOLATION OF CHINS AGREEMENT/ORDER should be utilized, and a copy should be retained in the case folder.

Standard 8:00. Extension/Termination

8:01 The probation officer, not less than two weeks prior to the expiration of the initial application for services, and prior to the expiration of any other time intervals imposed by the court for services/care, shall meet with the (A)CPO to review the case and to determine what recommendations shall be made to the court regarding the child.

8:02 After consultation with the (A)CPO, the probation officer shall enter his/her written recommendation on the chronological supervision sheet along with the rationale for this recommendation.

8:03 The probation officer, in those instances when the recommendation to the court is to extend the period of court involvement beyond the expiration date of the initial agreement/order, shall notify all parties, in writing, of his/her intent.

8:04 The probation officer, in those instances when the agreement/order has been extended beyond the initial period by the court, shall complete a new terms of agreement/conditions of order form, develop a new supervision plan and record the plan on the chronological supervision sheet.

8:05 Where court policy permits, the probation officer, with the approval of the (A)CPO, shall have the discretion to recommend to the court early termination of probation officer assistance/supervision.

COMMENTARY

With respect to Standard 8:02, the probation officer should be prepared to provide the court with a detailed explanation as to the reason(s) for recommending a continuation of probation officer assistance. The M.G.L. c. 119 § 39E indicates that unless the parents and child voluntarily agree, in writing, to a continuation (for an additional period not to exceed six months), then the petition shall be dismissed, or if not already issued, a petition shall be issued and a date set for a trial on the merits. The court may rely heavily on the information provided by the probation officer when determining what course of action to take to ensure that the best interests of the child is considered. M.G.L. c. 119, § 39G requires a finding by the court that the purposes of an order of disposition have not been met, and that an extension of such order of disposition would be reasonably likely to further those purposes.

With respect to Standard 8:03, the parties to the application for the petition may include the school, the police, an attorney(s), DSS or other persons or agencies charged by the court with the care of the child, in addition to the parents.

With respect to Standard 8:04, where the terms of agreement/conditions of order do not change, and where no changes in the supervision plan are necessary, the probation officer may record "no changes in the supervision plan" on the chronological supervision sheet.

With respect to Standard 8:05, a probation officer should exercise his/her judgment and recommend to the court early termination when intervention is no longer necessary and the child is no longer in need of services. In addition, the probation officer shall bring to the attention of the (A)CPO any cases where a child has attained the age of eighteen and is under probation officer assistance/care as a stubborn child or runaway. Similarly, the probation officer shall give such notification on truancy and school offender cases when the child has attained the age of sixteen.

Additional Materials

Note: The following materials are available in the eBook version of this Sourcebook. See the Electronic Download page at the front of this book for instructions on downloading a copy of the eBook.

Supreme Judicial Court Rule 1:18—Uniform Rules on Dispute Resolution
Juvenile Court Dispositional and Sentencing Best Practices for Delinquent and Youthful Offender Matters, Apr. 2016
Summary of Ronald P. Corbett, Jr., "The Burdens of Leniency: The changing Face of Probation," *Minnesota Law Review*, Vol. 99, Issue 5.
Supreme Judicial Court Committee on Voir Dire Final Report to the Justices, July 12, 2016
Juvenile Court Form JV-170—Written Agreement Between the Parties Pursuant to a Conditional Tender of Plea—Mass. R. Crim. P. 12(b)(6)

PART 3

Care and Protection: An Evidentiary View

Abandonment

1. General Laws c. 210, § 3 defines "abandoned" as "left without any provision for support and without any person responsible to maintain care, custody and control because the whereabouts of the person responsible therefor is unknown and reasonable efforts to locate such person have been unsuccessful." "While we agree that the statutory meaning of the word 'abandoned' in this context does not entirely apply to the situation here, the judge's use of the word is not unwarranted on the particular facts of this case. The parents have done little to express interest in their child." *Adoption of Astrid*, 45 Mass. App. Ct. 538, 544 (1998).

2. "Benevolent abandonment is abandonment nonetheless." *Adoption of Fran*, 54 Mass. App. Ct. 455, 463 (2002).

3. On the facts of this case, comparing deportation to incarceration, the Appeals Court held that deportation was not sufficient to warrant the trial judge's finding of abandonment, *Adoption of Posey*, 94 Mass. App. Ct. 748, 753 n.11 (2019).

Abuse of Discretion

"Abuse of discretion here means the failure to avoid idiosyncratic choice brought on by arbitrary determination, capricious disposition, or whimsical thinking." *Adoption of Iris*, 427 Mass. 582, 588 (1998).

Abuse of Discretion (Judicial)

The Supreme Judicial Court has adopted a new standard of review for judicial abuse of discretion. *L.L. v. Commonwealth*, 470 Mass. 169, 185 n.27 (2014) ("When an appellate court concludes that a judge abused his or her discretion, the court is not, in fact, finding that the judge was not conscientious or, for that matter, not intelligent or honest. Borrowing from other courts, we think it more accurate to say that a judge's discretionary decision constitutes an abuse of discretion where we conclude the judge made 'a clear error of judgment in weighing' the factors relevant to the decision, such that the decision falls outside the range of reasonable alternatives.") (citations omitted).

Access to Children in DCF [Formerly DSS] Custody

Although "[w]itnesses belong to neither the Commonwealth nor to the defense," the Department of Social Services has the same right as a biological parent to consent to or decline an interview of a child in its care by defense counsel or anyone acting on the defendant's behalf (except when responding to lawful process); and, when consent is granted, "to impose reasonable conditions on the conduct of the interview." *Commonwealth v. Adkinson*, 442 Mass. 410, 416–18 (2004).

Access to Information Relating to Children in DCF Custody

"Thus, whatever confidentiality the statute [G.L. c. 119, § 51F] may provide to children within the department's purview, that protection cannot be said to be 'closely associated' with a constitutional right." *Commonwealth v. Demetrius D.*, 94 Mass. App. Ct. 12, 18 (2018) (police department contacted DCF to obtain address of juvenile in foster care who was a suspect in a criminal investigation).

Action Plans (Formerly Called Service Plans)

Compliance. "The judge was not obliged to believe that the parenting skills of the mother or the father had improved simply because of their recent cooperation with the department, or that their good intentions eliminated risk of future abuse." *Adoption of Lorna*, 46 Mass. App. Ct. 134, 143 (1999). *See also Care & Protection of Quinn*, 54 Mass. App. Ct. 117, 126–27 (2002).

Mass. G. Evid. § 1115(b)(2)(C) (2019).

Adoption Plan

3

1. "General Laws c. 210, § 3(c), requires a trial judge to consider the plan proposed by the department or other agency initiating the petition. Judges also consider parental nominations of caretakers in an extended family, just as they do in other types of child custody cases. . . . [A] plan proposed by a parent is not entitled to any artificial weight in determining the best interests of the child." *Adoption of Hugo*, 428 Mass. 219, 226 (1998). The fact "that the judge [is] obliged to consider which of the two competing plans would be in the child's best interests does not determine who is entitled to assert a claim that he performed that task incorrectly." *Adoption of Malik*, 84 Mass. App. Ct. 436, 439 (2013) (dismissing mother's appeal).

2. "Once the judge concluded that parental unfitness was established, he correctly determined that the central question was whether it was in Hugo's best interests to remain with his foster mother or to be transferred to the care and custody of his aunt. G.L. c. 210, § 3(c). The best interests of a child is a question that presents the trial judge with a classic example of a discretionary decision. We recognize that in this field it is neither possible nor desirable to make decisions with precision, and that much must be left to the trial judge's experience and judgment. It is for this reason . . . that our attitude toward a trial judge's decision in a custody appeal is one of substantial deference. Particularly where, as here, close scrutiny of lay and expert witnesses was central to the judge's decision, our task is not to decide whether we, presented with the same facts, would have made the same decision, but to determine whether the trial judge abused his discretion or committed clear error of law." *Adoption of Hugo*, 428 Mass. 219, 225 (1998); *see Adoption of Nanette*, 81 Mass. App. Ct. 1134 (2012) (Rule 1:28 decision) (applying same standard of review).

3. "It is not essential, albeit beneficial to that consideration, that the proposed plan be fully developed. Nor need the plan identify the prospective adoptive parents. The adoption plan must, however, have content and substance enough to permit the court meaningfully to evaluate and consider what DSS proposes to do for the child by way of adoption. In keeping with the obligation to demonstrate that close attention has been given the evidence, the judge considering an adoption plan must make specific findings reflecting careful evaluation of the suitability of the DSS proposal." *Adoption of Lars*, 46 Mass. App. Ct. 30, 31 (1999); *see Adoption of Richard*, 77 Mass. App. Ct. 1103 (2010) (Rule 1:28 decision).

4. A judge must "consider the plan proposed by the department or other agency initiating the petition." G.L. c. 210, § 3(c). It is not essential that the proposed plan be "fully developed," *Adoption of Paula*, 420 Mass. 716, 722–23 n.7 (1995), or that it identify the prospective parents. *Care & Protection of Three Minors*, 392 Mass. 704, 717 (1984). "The adoption plan must, however, have content and substance enough to permit the court meaningfully to evaluate and consider . . . what [the department] proposes to do for the [children] by way of adoption." *Adoption of Stuart*, 39 Mass. App. Ct. 380, 393 (1995). The judge, in considering the adoption plan, must make specific findings reflecting careful evaluation of the suitability of the DSS proposal. *See Adoption of Gabrielle*, 39 Mass. App. Ct. 484, 488 (1995).

5. "The adoption plan need not be fully developed to support a termination order; it need only provide sufficient information about the prospective adoptive placement 'so that the judge may properly evaluate the suitability of the department's proposal.' *Adoption of Vito*, 431 Mass. 550, 568 n.28 (2000), quoting *Care and Protection of Three Minors*, 392 Mass. 704, 714 (1984). See *Adoption of Paula*, 420 Mass. 716, 722–723 n.7 (1995)." *Adoption of Willow*, 433 Mass. 636, 652–53 (2001); *see also Adoption of Mariano*, 77 Mass. App. Ct. 656, 663 (2010).

6. "Although the better practice would have been for the judge to make explicit findings of fact from which we could determine her assessment of the cousin's [father's proposed placement] credibility at trial and her suitability as Ilian's caregiver, we think it is implicit in the findings that the judge did make that she considered placement with the cousin and concluded such placement was not in Ilian's best interests. In these circumstances, where the child was thriving in a stable environment with the preadoptive foster parents, and the economic and emotional stability of a placement with the cousin was uncertain, the judge acted well within her discretion in concluding that Ilian's best interests were served by DCF's plan that Ilian be adopted by his preadoptive foster parents." *Adoption of Ilian*, 91 Mass. App. Ct. 727, 732 (2017) (Father contended that judge failed to conduct an "even-handed assessment" of his plan and DCF's plan. Court concluded, "judge adequately considered the father's alternative plan and properly concluded such plan was not in Ilian's best interests. 91 Mass. App. Ct. at 728.).

7. Mass. G. Evid. § 1115(f)(1) (2019).

8. In order for an adoption plan to be adequate, the plan must "convey enough information for the judge to assess the various options that the department [is] actively considering. . . . In the present case, the adoption plan submitted by the department outlined the goal for Varik's adoption but failed to specify the type of adoptive parents and the characteristics of the home environment best suited to meet his specific needs. Although the plan contained some details of Varik's medical history, placement history, and ongoing behavioral issues, this was not a substitute for information describing the kind of home environment and adoptive family makeup that ideally would best meet Varick's particular needs." *Adoption of Varik*, 95 Mass. App. Ct. 762, 771 (2019) (In remanding the case, the court recognized that circumstances may change after an adequate plan is approved creating a situation where the department and judge may exercise discretion. "We do not hold nor are we suggesting that an adequate plan once approved by the judge is binding on the department, because circumstances may change and the best interests of Varik may require adjustments in the adoption plan. . . ." *Id.* at 772 n.13.).

Adverse Inference/Negative Inference

1. "Where, as here, the production of documentation to support Fong's claimed expenditures was a matter entirely within his control, his making these important records unavailable for examination could properly be treated by the court as conduct in the nature of an admission. Accordingly, the judge was entitled not only to regard Fong as an evasive witness, but to draw inferences adverse to him from the uncertainties surrounding his financial affairs." *Crowe v. Fong*, 45 Mass. App. Ct. 673, 679 (1998).

2. While a parent may assert his or her privilege against self-incrimination if called to testify in a care and protection proceeding, the court may draw a negative inference from the failure to testify; the court need not limit the scope of prospective cross-examination of the parent in order to permit his or her testimony on matters unrelated to the criminal case against him or her; and the court need not continue the care and protection proceeding until the pending criminal case has been disposed of, as long as the court has balanced the possible prejudice to the other litigants against the potential harm to the party claiming the privilege. *Care & Protection of Quinn*, 54 Mass. App. Ct. 117, 120–25 (2002).

3. Mass. G. Evid. § 1115 (e)(3) (2019).

4. "[A]n adverse inference may be drawn against a parent who, despite having received notice, is absent from a child custody or termination proceeding, even though such an inference would be impermissible in a criminal matter absent affirmative evidence showing consciousness of guilt. [footnote omitted] Where a parent has notice of a proceeding to determine his parental rights and the parent does not attend or provide an explanation for not attending, the absence may suggest that the parent has abandoned his rights in the child or cannot meet the child's best interests." *Adoption of Talik*, 92 Mass. App. Ct. 367, 371–73 (2017) (judge did not err in drawing a negative inference from mother's failure to attend trial).

5. "The judge was permitted to draw a negative inference from the mother's unexplained refusal to cooperate with the department; the judge was not obligated to credit her testimony that there was nothing amiss in the home." *Care and Protection of Vieri*, 92 Mass. App. Ct. 402, 406 (2017) (mother refused to provide access to her home to workers, among other conduct).

Allegations

"It is a bedrock principle that parental rights may not be terminated on the basis of an unproven allegation. . . . For this reason, it is essential that trial judges who recite allegations explain their significance to the disposition of the case." *Adoption of Eden*, 88 Mass. App. Ct. 293, 296 (2015) (allegations of sexual abuse by father).

Amendment of Petition

"[C]onsolidation of a care and protection petition with a termination proceeding is expressly authorized, and may provide a mechanism for avoiding delay in the litigation of custody and adoption disputes." *Adoption of Astrid*, 45 Mass. App. Ct. 538, 548 (1998) (citing *Care & Protection of Martha*, 407 Mass. 319, 328–29 (1990)).

Americans with Disabilities Act (ADA)

1. Because proceedings to terminate parental rights "do not constitute services, programs, or activities" for the purposes of 42 U.S.C. § 12132, "the ADA may not be raised as a defense to these proceedings." Rather, because the parents' rights are secondary to the child's best interests, the proper focus of termination proceedings is the welfare of the child. The ADA does require DSS to accommodate the parents' special needs in its provisions of services prior to the termination proceeding, but the onus is on the parent to make any ADA claims in a timely manner so that reasonable accommodations may be made. *Adoption of Gregory*, 434 Mass. 117, 120–21 (2001); *see also Adoption of Ilona*, 76 Mass. App. Ct. 481, 486 (2010), *aff'd*, 459 Mass. 53 (2011).

2. "Courts do not determine whether an agency's allocation of resources or provision of services is efficient or in proportion to the obvious and pressing need of the disabled within the Commonwealth. On this record, the plaintiffs have not shown that the practices and policies of the DMH [Department of Mental Health] discriminate against these individuals with disabilities in violation of the provisions or regulations of the Americans with Disabilities Act or the Federal Rehabilitation Act." *Williams v. Sec'y of Exec. Office of Human Servs.*, 414 Mass. 551, 560–61 (1993).

"The plaintiffs point to programs outside the Commonwealth as models for the methods by which the DMH could provide services to the individuals with dual diagnoses; however, the ADA does not require the DMH to change the structure of its services or funding to conform to other programs that the plaintiffs claim are more efficient." *Williams v. Sec'y of Exec. Office of Human Servs.*, 414 Mass. at 561.

Appeal Time Period

1. An appeal from an order or adjudication under the provisions of G.L. c. 119, § 26 must be made within 30 days. G.L. c. 119, § 27.

2. Chapter 210 cases are governed by the Rules of Appellate Procedure (30 days). *See also Adoption of Donald*, 44 Mass. App. Ct. 857, 859–60 (1998) ("We are of opinion that once the judge dispensed with parental consent to adoption in the care and protection proceeding, the appeal period was governed by Mass. R. App. Proc. 4(a) [30 days] and not G.L. c. 119, § 27 [10 days].").

3. Practice Note: Counsel is wise to appeal any adverse Chapter 119 or Chapter 210 ruling within 30 days.

4. "A party aggrieved by an interlocutory order of a trial court justice in . . . the juvenile court department . . . may file, within thirty days of the entry of such order, a petition in the appropriate appellate court seeking relief from such order." G.L. c. 231, § 118.

Appellate Standard

1. "[W]e require that a judge make specific and detailed findings demonstrating that close attention has been given to the evidence. Subsidiary findings, in turn, must be proved by a fair preponderance of the evidence. When a judge complies with these mandates, we do not disturb his findings unless they are clearly erroneous. . . . [The appellate court's] task is not to decide whether [it], presented with the same facts, would have made the same decision, but to determine whether the trial judge abused his discretion or committed a clear error of law." *Adoption of Hugo*, 428 Mass. 219, 224–25 (1998).

2. "Appellate review in custody appeals is not done to assess the evidence de novo, but rather to determine whether the judge's findings were clearly erroneous and whether they proved parental unfitness by clear and convincing evidence." *Custody of Eleanor*, 414 Mass. 795, 802 (1993).

Bonding

1. "The . . . issue raised by the mother on appeal is whether the . . . judge improperly relied upon the deterioration of the mother-son relationship caused by the child's placement in a foster home, where visitation with the mother was supervised and limited to a single one-hour weekly session. The mother's argument is without merit. In *Petitions of Dep't of Social Servs. to Dispense With Consent to Adoption*, 399 Mass. 279, 289–290 (1987), we indicated that a lengthy separation between parent and child, the growth of emotional ties between the child and a different custodian, and the effect of a forced return of the child to the biological parent are all factors that should be weighed by the judge, with no one factor being determinative." *Adoption of Frederick*, 405 Mass. 1, 7 (1989).

2. "Although the bonding of a child with foster or adoptive parents is not a dispositive consideration, it is a factor that has weight in the ultimate balance." *Adoption of Nicole*, 40 Mass. App. Ct. 259, 262–63 (1996).

3. In Massachusetts case law applying G.L. c. 210, § 3, the bond of a child with foster parents is not dispositive, but is a factor that has weight in the ultimate balance. To the extent that the factor becomes decisive, findings that address directly the nature of the harm that a child is likely to suffer, among other considerations, are required. Expert testimony may be necessary, although it is not a requirement in all cases. "[W]hen bonding and the potential effects of severance are the issues, it is the effect on the child, not the disappointment or loss of the foster parent, to which attention must be paid." *Adoption of Daniel*, 58 Mass. App. Ct. 195, 202–03 & n.10 (2003).

4. Mass. G. Evid. § 1115(f)(2) (2019).

Burden of Proof

"[T]he burden of proving current parental unfitness remains squarely upon the petitioner." *Care & Protection of Ian*, 46 Mass. App. Ct. 615, 616 (1999).

CASA (Court-Appointed Special Advocate)

1. Reports made by a CASA may be admitted into evidence. "Once appointed, the CASA becomes an officer of the court . . . and could be considered the functional equivalent of a guardian ad litem." *Adoption of Georgia*, 433 Mass. 62, 68 (2000) (quoting R. L. Ireland, *Juvenile Law* § 124, at 536 (1993)). "[Their reports] are analogous to investigator's reports pursuant to G.L. c. 119, § 24, which we have held admissible even when multiple level hearsay (and clinical evaluations) have been contained therein. All that is required is that the guardian ad litem be available to testify at trial and that the source of the material be sufficiently identified so that the affected party has an opportunity to rebut any adverse or erroneous material contained therein." *Adoption of Georgia*, 433 Mass. 62, 68–69 (2000).

2. Mass. G. Evid. § 1115(c)(3) (2019).

Case Caption

"[T]he label attached to a pleading or motion is far less important than its substance." *Lambley v. Kameny*, 43 Mass. App. Ct. 277, 280 (1997).

Chapter 210, § 3 Factors

Chapter 210, § 3(c) Factors. Factors to consider in assessing fitness:

i. Abandonment;
ii. Abuse or neglect
  a. Services not utilized; or
  b. Services of no avail;
iii. Custody of child with DCF for 6 months or longer with no parental "significant and meaningful contact" with the child;
iv. Child, 4 years or older, cannot be returned to the parents after 15 months, 12 of which the child was in DCF custody;
v. Child, under 4, cannot be returned to the parents after 12 months, 6 of which the child was in DCF custody;
vi. Parent has not and will not be able to provide appropriate care;
vii. Child's bond with substitute caretaker;
viii. Lack of effort to remedy conditions;
ix. Physically, emotionally or sexually abusive severe or repetitive conduct or neglectful nature toward child or another child in household;
x. Willful failure to visit;
xi. Willful failure to support;
xii. Continuing condition, i.e., alcoholism, drug addiction, mental deficiency/illness resulting in "minimally acceptable care";
xiii. Felony conviction resulting in a lengthy, unstable home environment; or
xiv. Prior pattern of neglect or misconduct; or felony assault resulting in serious bodily injury and the likelihood of future harm.

"[T]he following circumstances shall constitute grounds for dispensing with the need for consent to adoption, custody, guardianship or other disposition. . . ."

i. Abandonment;
ii. Parent convicted of murder or voluntary manslaughter of another child of the parent or in aiding, abetting, etc. in murder or involuntary manslaughter or assault resulting in serious bodily injury to child or another child of the parent.

Child's Wishes

1. "Although the boy was described in testimony as 'a really bright student,' we note that the preference of an eleven year old is not given decisive weight, although it is a factor to be considered." *Custody of Vaughn*, 422 Mass. 590, 599 n.11 (1996).

2. "In situations involving younger children who are not yet sufficiently mature to comprehend where their welfare lies, the courts are empowered, indeed obligated, to substitute their judgment for that of the child. However, it has long been the law of Massachusetts that the preferences of children of sufficient maturity may be considered. Where a child has been placed in someone's care by agreement of the parents, the wishes of the child to remain

in that person's care have been given weight." *Custody of a Minor*, 383 Mass. 595, 602 (1981).

3. "There is no question that the children are entitled to counsel, that their autonomy and rights to be heard on issues affecting their interest should be respected, and that their positions, based on mature expression, are entitled to weight in custody proceedings (although not determinative). *See Custody of a Minor*, 383 Mass. 595, 602 (1981); *Adoption of Arthur*, 34 Mass. App. Ct. 914, 915 (1993). Nonetheless, we have noted that, 'even where it is undisputed that a child and her attorney disagree, the law is unclear as to whether the attorney is always bound by her minor client's decision when the attorney feels that the child's decision is not in her own best interests.' *Adoption of Erica*, 426 Mass. 55, 63–64 n.9 (1997). In that decision, we felt 'particularly hesitant to conclude that a difference of opinion between what a young child . . . expresses as her wish and the position of her attorney necessarily suggests a conflict of interest.' *Id.* We also pointed out that 'the notion that an attorney might zealously advocate for a result opposed by the client clearly sets the representation of children apart from the normal context in which attorneys operate.' *Id.*" *Care & Protection of Georgette*, 439 Mass. 28, 36, *aff'd*, 439 Mass. 28 (2003).

4. "The judge noted Garret's wish to remain in the custody of the mother, but ultimately decided that placing him in the custody of his maternal grandmother, with whom he had previously lived for an extended period of time, was in his best interests. The record makes clear that Garret's wishes were properly considered in determining which placement would best serve his interests, and the judge was not required to make a custody determination in accordance with his views on the matter." *Adoption of Garret*, 92 Mass. App. Ct. 664, 676 (2018) (citation omitted).

Clear and Convincing Proof

1. "Clear and convincing proof involves a degree of belief greater than the usually imposed burden of proof by a preponderance of the evidence, but less than the burden of proof beyond a reasonable doubt imposed in criminal cases." *Custody of Eleanor*, 414 Mass. 795, 800 (1993).

2. "[B]ecause circumstantial evidence is sufficient to establish guilt beyond a reasonable doubt, even for the conviction of the highest crimes, such evidence is sufficient in child custody cases. Nor is it necessary to the reasonable doubt standard—nor, by implication, to the clear and convincing one—for the Commonwealth to show that no one else could have committed the crime charged. If conflicting inferences are both reasonable and possible, it is for the trier of fact to determine which is true." *Adoption of Keefe*, 49 Mass. App. Ct. 818, 825 (2000).

3. "The burden of persuasion . . . in those cases requiring a showing of clear and convincing proof is sustained if evidence induces in the mind of the trier a reasonable belief that the facts asserted are highly probably true, that the probability that they are true or exist is substantially greater than the probability that they are false or do not exist." *In the Matter of G.P.*, 473 Mass. 112, 120 n.13 (2015) (citations omitted).

Clearly Erroneous

"A finding is clearly erroneous when there is no evidence to support it, or when, although there is evidence to support it, the reviewing court on the entire evidence is left with the definite and firm conviction that a mistake has been committed. . . . [However, we] do not sit as a trial court to review de novo the evidence presented by the parties." *Guardianship of Clyde*, 44 Mass. App. Ct. 767, 774–75 (1998).

Commitment Proceedings for Alcohol and Substance Use Disorders

Trial Court Rule XIII: Uniform Trial Court Rules for Civil Commitment Proceedings for Alcohol and Substance Use Disorders. Discussed in *In the Matter of G.P.*, 473 Mass. 112 (2015).

Competency

Competency to stand trial. "Competency to stand trial requires that the defendant have the capacity to understand the nature and object of the proceedings against him, to consult with counsel, and to assist in preparing his defense. *Commonwealth v. Crowley*, 393 Mass. 393, 398 (1984), [abrogated by *Medina v. California*, 505 U.S. 437 (1992),] quoting *Dusky v. United States*, 362 U.S. 402 (1975). The burden of proof is on the Commonwealth to show that the defendant is competent. *Crowley, supra* at 400. . . . A competency hearing must be held 'where there exists doubt as to whether the defendant satisfied the [*Dusky*] test.' *Crowley, supra* at 398, quoting *Commonwealth v. Vailes*, 360 Mass. 522, 524 (1971)." *Commonwealth v. L'Abbe*, 421 Mass. 262, 266 (1995).

"The judge's determination that the defendant was competent to stand trial was within her discretion. *See Commonwealth v. DeMinico*, 408 Mass. 230, 234–235 (1990) (defendant competent to stand trial despite testimony during trial that defendant experiencing psychotic episode); *Commonwealth v. Kostka*, 370 Mass. 516, 522 (1976) (defendant competent despite some psychiatric testimony to contrary)." *Commonwealth v. L'Abbe*, 421 Mass. 262, 266–67 (1995). A defendant's demeanor at trial and response to questioning by the judge are relevant to a decision on the merits of the competency issue. *Commonwealth v. L'Abbe*, 421 Mass. 262, 266–67 (1995). *See also Commonwealth v. Lyons*, 426 Mass. 466, 468–69 (1998) ("Competency to stand trial requires that the defendant have (1) sufficient present ability to consult with his lawyer with a reasonable degree of rational understanding and . . . (2) a rational as well as factual understanding of the proceedings against him. The Commonwealth has the burden to prove by a preponderance of the evidence that the defendant was competent. When reviewing the judge's finding of competency, we give substantial deference to his findings of fact.").

If the defendant has not raised the issue of competency to stand trial, the trial judge has an obligation to raise the issue on the judge's own motion if developments in the trial raise "a substantial question of possible doubt" about the defendant's competence. *Rhay v. White*, 385 F.2d 883, 886 (9th Cir. 1967); *Commonwealth v. Simpson*, 44 Mass. App. Ct. 154, 162 (1998), *rev'd*, 428 Mass. 646 (1999).

Competency to testify. "[T]here is a two-pronged test for competency. The witness must (1) have the general ability or capacity to observe, remember and give expression to that which she has seen, heard, or experienced; and (2) have understanding sufficient to comprehend the difference between truth and falsehood, the wickedness of the latter and the obligation and duty to tell the truth, and, in a general way, belief that failure to perform the obligation will result in punishment. A trial judge has broad discretion to determine whether a competency hearing is required, and whether a witness is competent to testify. Whether the test is met is peculiarly for the trial judge, and his determination will be rarely faulted on appellate review." *Commonwealth v. Allen*, 40 Mass. App. Ct. 458, 461 (1996); *see Commonwealth v. Thibeault*, 77 Mass. App. Ct. 419, 423–31, *review denied*, 458 Mass. 1107 (2010).

Condition of Child

"It was not error for the judge to consider evidence of the child's condition in 1981, while he lived with the mother, and contrast it with the development of the child since he had been removed from the mother's custody. The evidence supported the judge's conclusion that the best interests of the child necessitated his living with a parent or parents who were able to contribute to his continued positive development." *Petition of Catholic Charitable Bureau to Dispense with Consent to Adoption*, 395 Mass. 180, 187 (1985).

Contempt

Where parents, ordered to present their child for identification pursuant to G.L. c. 119, § 24, fail to do so, the order may be enforced by means of contempt. *In re Care & Protection Summons*, 437 Mass. 224, 237 (2002).

Counsel

"[B]efore a constitutional right to counsel, or a statutory right to counsel under G.L. c. 119, § 29, attaches, a parent must first come forward and appear, or in some way indicate a desire to be heard or to contest the petition, and must demonstrate his or her indigence." *Adoption of Holly*, 432 Mass. 680, 687–88 (2000).

"Indigent parents in termination and adoption proceedings are entitled to counsel because [t]he interest of parents in their relationship with their children has been deemed fundamental, and is constitutionally protected. Before the State deprive[s] a legitimate parent of all that parenthood implies, the requirements of due process must be met." *Adoption of Meaghan*, 461 Mass. 1006, 1007 (2012).

"The decision whether to terminate is of enormous consequence to the child. The child cannot have a meaningful opportunity to be heard in a contested proceeding without the assistance of counsel, regardless whether the case is initiated by the department or other agency or by a private party." *Adoption of Meaghan*, 461 Mass. 1006, 1007 (2012).

The right to counsel established in *Adoption of Meaghan* has retroactive applicability to adoption cases not final as of the date of the decision (January 30, 2012). *Adoption of Gabe*, 84 Mass. App. Ct. 286 (2013).

Indigent parents' right to counsel was extended to contested guardianship cases in *Guardianship of V.V.*, 470 Mass. 590 (2015).

"[T]he equitable powers of the Probate and Family Court allow a judge of that court to grant a motion requesting the appointment of counsel for an indigent guardian who is the subject of a removal proceeding, G.L. c. 190B, § 5-212, where the judge, based on the exercise of his or her sound discretion, concludes that doing so would materially assist in determining the best interest of the child and parental fitness." *Guardianship of K.N.*, 476 Mass. 762, 766 (2017) (court found that a guardian who is a de facto parent does not have a liberty interest which would warrant appointment of counsel but found that the Probate and Family Court equitable powers authorize a judge to allow a motion for appointment of counsel for a guardian in a removal proceeding in certain circumstances).

Court Investigator's Report

1. **Recommendations.** "There was no reversible error in the admission of the investigator's report, even including her recommendations, because she testified and the report identified, for the most part, her sources. The parents, therefore, had the opportunity to rebut any adverse or erroneous material." *Adoption of Astrid*, 45 Mass. App. Ct. 538, 546 (1998).

2. **Hearsay.** "[A]lthough the mother criticizes the 'hearsay' statement contained in the investigator's report that Keefe had a positive laxative screen, facts contained in such reports are admissible by statute where opposing parties have an opportunity to refute the report through cross-examination." *Adoption of Keefe*, 49 Mass. App. Ct. 818, 826 (2000).

G.L. c. 119, § 24; Mass. G. Evid. § 1115(c)(1) (2019).

Credibility

"It is within the judge's discretion to evaluate the credibility of witnesses and to make his findings of fact accordingly. He was not obligated to believe the mother's testimony or that of any other witness. [T]he judge who has heard the testimony and seen the witnesses face to face has a better opportunity for determining the credibility of their conflicting statements than can possibly arise from reading a record. The credibility of witnesses, particularly, is a preserve of the trial judge upon which an appellate court treads with great reluctance." *Custody of Eleanor*, 414 Mass. 795, 800 (1993).

Criminal Records

1. "Probation records are records of the court system, *Police Commr. of Boston v. Municipal Court of the Dorchester Dist.*, 374 Mass. 640, 648 (1978), and are by statute (G.L. c. 276, § 100) available for use by the courts of the Commonwealth. *Id.* at 650. There was no reason to qualify them as business records, because they were admissible as official written records. *Furtado v. Furtado*, 380 Mass. 137, 149 (1980). *See Adoption of George*, 27 Mass. App. Ct. 265, 271–72 (1989). Their contents recorded primary facts rather than judgmental observations. [*Adoption of George*, 27 Mass. App. Ct.] at 272–74." *Adoption of Irwin*, 28 Mass. App. Ct. 41, 43 (1989).

2. Mass. G. Evid. § 1115(b)(1) (2019).

3

De Facto Parent

1. "A de facto parent is one who has no biological relation to the child, but has participated in the child's life as a member of the child's family. The de facto parent resides with the child and, with the consent and encouragement of the legal parent, performs a share of caretaking functions at least as great as the legal parent. The de facto parent shapes the child's daily routine, addresses his developmental needs, disciplines the child, provides for his education and medical care, and serves as a moral guide [for reasons primarily other than financial compensation]." *E.N.O. v. L.M.M.*, 429 Mass. 824, 829 (1999).

2. The Appeals Court cites three Supreme Judicial Court decisions to a requirement that a person must live with a child and perform care taking functions for two years before being deemed as a de facto parent. "The court's repeated references to the two-year requirement indicate that the length of time a person seeking de facto parent status has lived with the child is relevant to the court's determination, but is not the sole factor. . . . As she is not his de facto parent, the mother is not entitled to court-ordered visitation with Garret." *Adoption of Garret*, 92 Mass. App. Ct. 664, 678–79 (2018) (Appeals Court refused to recognize stepmother as de facto parent for purposes of considering visitation) (citations omitted).

Delay in Proceedings

"[T]he best interests of Bianca strongly militate against reopening the trial record. Stability is important for every child, and it is particularly necessary for Bianca. Bianca's healthy development depends upon finality in this matter. In circumstances such as these, a parent's postdecree improvements cannot be permitted to continually upend an unfitness determination. It is therefore not appropriate to prolong these proceedings to expand the record." *Adoption of Bianca*, 91 Mass. App. Ct. 428, 431 (2017) (two years and four months passed between the beginning of the termination trial and assembly of the record for appeal; mother argued that the delay made stale the facts on which the judge relied; mother failed to demonstrate material prejudice due to the delay).

Domestic Violence

1. "We endorse the Appeal Court's commitment to the propositions that physical force within the family is both intolerable and too readily tolerated, and that a child who has been either the victim or the spectator of such abuse suffers a distinctly grievous kind of harm." *Custody of Vaughn*, 422 Mass. 590, 595 (1996); *see Loebel v. Loebel*, 77 Mass. App. Ct. 740, 748, *review denied*, 458 Mass. 1109 (2010).

2. "The Gender Bias Study concludes that our courts have too often failed to appreciate the fundamental wrong and the depth of the injury inflicted by family violence." *Custody of Vaughn*, 422 Mass. 590, 596 (1996).

3. "Where the victim of violence is a family member, the violence is not less but more of a threat to the victim's basic sense of security." *In re Grella*, 438 Mass. 47, 52 (2002).

4. A judge's determination of whether a particular permanency plan is in a child's best interests cannot stand where the judge

fails to make specific and detailed findings regarding domestic violence in the proposed home and its effects on the child. *Adoption of Imelda*, 72 Mass. App. Ct. 354, 364 (2008).

5. "The judge should have made specific findings on domestic violence in the paternal grandmother's home and its effects on Imelda. Such findings are needed to show that a full and fair hearing took place and that the judge's findings were an 'even-handed assessment of the evidence' addressing the '[t]roublesome facts' of the proposed placement." *Adoption of Imelda*, 72 Mass. App. Ct. 354, 365 (2008).

Double Jeopardy

3

"We have previously rejected the claim that double jeopardy applies to care and protection proceedings under G.L. c. 119. Custody proceedings are not criminal in nature and, accordingly, the full panoply of constitutional rights afforded criminal defendants does not apply in these cases." *Adoption of Iris*, 427 Mass. 582, 586 (1998).

Drug and Alcohol Treatment Records

1. "Because the interests of the children in being free from abuse and neglect substantially outweigh any unlikely injury to the mother from this limited disclosure of confidential information, we conclude that the judge had good cause to order the program manager to disclose by affidavit the reasons for the mother's discharge from her treatment program, in accordance with 42 U.S.C. § 290dd-2." *Adoption of Lisette*, 93 Mass. App. Ct. 284, 292 (2018) (citing *Adoption of Virgil*, 93 Mass. App. Ct. 298, 305 (2018)).

2. Mass. G. Evid. § 1115(b)(3) (2019).

Drugs

1. "What the evidence does not support is that the parents' cocaine habit has to date caused them to provide less than minimally acceptable care of Katherine. In the absence of a history of unacceptable care or testimony from an expert that child abuse and neglect is the inevitable end result of a cocaine habit, the prediction that such will occur is impermissible speculation." *Adoption of Katharine*, 42 Mass. App. Ct. 25, 31 (1997).

2. "[T]he Legislature has recognized that prenatal exposure to a controlled substance is probative of neglect by the mother. See G.L. c. 119, Section 51A (presence of drug addiction in newborn constitutes abuse)." *Commonwealth v. Pelligrini*, 414 Mass. 402, 409 (1993).

DCF Records

1. "DSS records [are] admissible as records of [a] public agency under official records exception to the hearsay rule." *Adoption of Astrid*, 45 Mass. App. Ct. 538, 546 (1998) (citing *Adoption of George*, 27 Mass. App. Ct. 265, 271–72 (1989)).

2. Mass. G. Evid. § 1115(b)(2) (2019).

Expert Testimony

1. "The admission of expert testimony is largely within the discretion of the trial judge and will be reversed only where it constitutes an abuse of discretion or error of law. . . . The crucial issue, in determining whether a witness is qualified to give an expert opinion, is whether the witness has sufficient education, training, experience and familiarity with the subject matter of the testimony. . . . There is no requirement that testimony on a question of discrete knowledge come from an expert qualified in a subspecialty rather than from an expert more generally qualified." *Adoption of Hugo*, 428 Mass. 219, 232–33 (1998), *cert. denied sub nom. Hugo P. v. George P.*, 526 U.S. 1034 (1999).

2. Mass. G. Evid. § 1115(e)(7) (2019).

3. Mass. G. Evid. §§ 702, 703, 704, 705, 706 (2019).

51A and 51B Reports

1. "The utility of the § 51A and § 51B reports is to set the stage [as to how and why the proceedings were initiated]. . . . It may be added that the § 51B report is a required government report and may be considered for statements of fact, e.g., that there was screaming or beating or no food or clean diapers in the house, although not for purposes of diagnosis, prognosis, and evaluation." *Custody of Michel*, 28 Mass. App. Ct. 260, 267 (1990).

2. G.L. c. 119, § 51A; Mass. G. Evid. § 1115(b)(2)(A) (2019).

3. G.L. c. 119, § 51B; Mass. G. Evid. § 1115(b)(2)(B) (2019).

Findings

1. "The judge's findings in a custody proceeding must be specific and detailed so as to demonstrate that close attention has been given the evidence and such findings must prove current parental unfitness clearly and convincingly. The requisite proof must be strong and positive; it must be full, clear and decisive." *Care & Protection of Ian*, 46 Mass. App. Ct. 615, 616 (1999).

2. "A finding is clearly erroneous when there is no evidence to support it, or when, although there is evidence to support it, the reviewing court on the entire evidence is left with the definite and firm conviction that a mistake has been committed." *Custody of Eleanor*, 414 Mass. 795, 799 (1993).

Fitness

1. "The term 'fitness' represents more than a test by which the limits of acceptable parental conduct are measured. The term is a standard by which we measure the circumstances within the family as they affect the child's welfare. Therefore, if returning custody to the natural parents would be seriously detrimental to the welfare of the child, then the parents could be considered to be unfit." *Guardianship of Clyde*, 44 Mass. App. Ct. 767, 773 (1998).

2. "Parental unfitness, as developed in the case law, means more than ineptitude, handicap, character flaw, conviction of a crime, unusual life style, or inability to do as good a job as the child's foster parent. Rather, the idea of 'parental unfitness' means 'grievous shortcomings or handicaps' that put the child's welfare 'much at hazard.' Endangerment of the child from abuse, neglect, or other activity harmful to the children must be in the picture. At the core of the inquiry is the question of what is in the best interests of the child, although the answer to that question in any given case is bound up with the determination of unfitness. The child's best interests may bear on how much parental deficiency is tolerable, or, conversely, the degree of parental deficiency may determine the child's best interests." *Adoption of Katharine*, 42 Mass. App. Ct. 25, 28 (1997); *see Adoption of Zoltan*, 71 Mass. App. Ct. 185, 187–90 (2008). *See also Care & Protection of Laurent*, 87 Mass. App. Ct. 1 (2015) (mother had cognitive disabilities).

3. "Where the child was surviving in deplorable conditions, with a mother who obstinately and defiantly refused to allow DCF access to the home, the judge's conclusion that the child was 'at near certain risk of future harm' was supported by clear and convincing evidence." *Care & Protection of Vick*, 89 Mass. App. Ct. 704, 709 (2016). "Regardless, the mother's inability to provide for the child's overall welfare and best interests was the central determination of her unfitness." *Care & Protection of Vick*, 89 Mass. App. Ct. at 709.

Foster Parents' Rights

While G.L. c. 119, § 29D gives foster parents the right to attend care and protection proceedings and to be heard, they do not have the right to submit information for judges' consideration "unconstrained by the usual evidentiary rules (i.e., relevance, personal knowledge, oath or affirmation, and cross-examination)." *Adoption of Sherry*, 435 Mass. 331, 338 (2001).

Future Fitness

1. "In determining whether that extreme step [terminating the parent-child relationship] should be taken, consideration of the future is a necessity. For instance, the judge should explore whether there is a reasonable likelihood that the parent's unfitness at the

time of trial may be only temporary. Consideration of future fitness, however, should never be made at the expense of the child, whose interest is paramount." *Adoption of Inez*, 428 Mass. 717, 723 (1999) (quoting and citing *Adoption of Carlos*, 413 Mass. 339, 350 (1992)).

2. "Minor parents should not retain parental rights until their maturation is sufficiently complete while adult parents are given no opportunity to 'mature.' Most importantly, to permit a minor parent time to mature before freeing a child for adoption could harm the child." *Adoption of Inez*, 428 Mass. 717, 724 (1999).

Grandparent Visitation

1. In light of *Blixt v. Blixt*, 437 Mass. 649 (2002), trial judge "must allow a parent's motion to dismiss a grandparent's petition for visitation if the petition does not sufficiently allege why visitation is necessary to protect the child from significant harm." *Martinez v. Martinez-Cintron*, 93 Mass. App. Ct. 202–04 (2018) (Appeals Court reversed trial court's denial of mother's Mass. R. Civ. P. 12(b)(6) motion to dismiss grandparent's petition for visitation).

2. G.L. c. 119, §§ 26B, 39D.

Guardianship

1. "In the context of a guardianship proceeding, evidence that is at least clear and convincing is constitutionally required for a finding of parental unfitness." *Guardianship of Clyde*, 44 Mass. App. Ct. 767, 773 (1998).

2. Where a father files a petition seeking to vacate a guardianship and to take custody of his child, "the comparison of the life the father can offer his child with the 'better life' the guardians can provide is inappropriate, for it does not clearly recognize the father's presumptive right to raise his child." *Guardianship of Yushiko*, 50 Mass. App. Ct. 157, 160 (2000).

3. The Appeals Court affirmed a Probate and Family Court judge's decision to find the biological father unfit and allow the child to remain with the husband of the deceased mother. Citing *Guardianship of Estelle*, 70 Mass. App. Ct. 575 (2007) as holding that a "trial judge must determine whether 'the father is fit to parent this child in these circumstances at this time,'" the court found that the removal of the child from the husband would be harmful to the child and not be in the child's best interests. *C.P. v. R.S.*, 81 Mass. App. Ct. 223, 226–28 (2012).

Petition to remove guardian. A petitioner has the initial burden of producing some credible evidence of changed circumstances that the minor may not be in need of a guardian. Once the petitioner satisfies the initial burden of production, the guardian bears the burden of proving by clear and convincing evidence that the guardian remains unfit and that continuation of the guardianship is in the minor's best interest. "On remand, after hearing such additional evidence as the judge deems appropriate, and applying the standards we have articulated, the judge shall determine, with detail and specificity, first, whether the mother has presented some credible evidence showing some change in circumstances from the initial appointment of the guardian, and second, whether the guardian has established, by clear and convincing evidence, that the mother remains currently unfit and that Kelvin's best interest would be served by continuation of the guardianship." *Guardianship of Kelvin*, 94 Mass. App. Ct. 448,456 (2018) (Court cites G.L. c. 119 and review and redetermination cases for guidance as to its determination of burdens of production and proof and concludes that "[a]lthough these two types of proceeding are not identical (citation omitted) the parent's same liberty interests are at stake and, thus, our determination as to who shoulders the burden of proof in a proceeding on a petition to remove a guardian is guided by the well-established principles governing a care and protection proceeding under G.L. c. 119, § 26(c) [the review and redetermination section].

Hearsay

1. "That a child's hearsay statements [containing disclosures of sexual abuse] appear in an admissible report[8] does not render the statements admissible for their truth." *Adoption of Tina*, 45 Mass. App. Ct. 727, 732 & n.8 (1998). Provisions of G.L. c. 233, §§ 82 or 83 apply.

2. "Hearsay contained in an investigator's report is admissible for its truth when there is an opportunity 'to refute the investigator and the investigator's sources through cross-examination and other means.' 'Other means' with respect to a statement as to sexual abuse by a child under the age of ten refers to the determination required under G.L. c. 233, § 82 or § 83, that such evidence be reliable." *Adoption of Tina*, 45 Mass. App. Ct. 727, 732 (1998) (quoting *Care & Protection of Rebecca*, 419 Mass. 67, 83 (1994) (quoting *Adoption of Carla*, 416 Mass. 510, 514 (1993))).

3. "Unlike [G.L. c. 233,] § 82, which is applicable to a proceeding to dispense with consent to adoption, § 83, which relates to admissibility of hearsay in a care and protection proceeding, does not require a finding that the child be unavailable." *Adoption of Tina*, 45 Mass. App. Ct. 727, 733 n.10 (1998).

4. "Hearsay is an out-of-court statement offered to prove the truth of the matter asserted in the statement. *See* Mass. G. Evid. § 801(c)(2) (2017). If a statement is offered for any purpose other than for its truth, it is not hearsay. *See* P.C. Giannelli, *Understanding Evidence* 446 (4th ed. 2013)." *Commonwealth v. Keown*, 478 Mass. 232, 245 (2017) (discussion of hearsay in context of assessing murder victim's state of mind).

5. **911 calls.** Certain contents of a 911 call to the police may be admissible if it is an exception to the hearsay rule, i.e., an excited utterance. "[W]e are satisfied that the judge did not abuse his discretion in concluding that when the defendant's wife made the 911 call, she was under the influence of the criminal assault that she was reporting had just occurred and what she related to the dispatcher during the admitted portion of the call was not the product of reflective thought." *Commonwealth v. Wilson*, 94 Mass. App. Ct. 416, 423 (2018) (911 call was six minutes long but trial judge allowed only the first part of the call, until the caller was placed on hold, to be admitted.) Mass. G. Evid. Art VIII (2019), see Introductory Note.

Multiple Level Hearsay.

6. "Guardian ad litem reports may properly contain hearsay information. *Jones v. Jones*, 349 Mass. 259, 264 (1965). They are analogous to investigator's reports pursuant to G.L. c. 119, § 24, which we have held admissible even when multiple level hearsay (and clinical evaluations) have been contained therein. *Custody of Michel*, 28 Mass. App. Ct. 260, 265–267 (1990). *Custody of Tracy*, 31 Mass. App. Ct. 481, 483–487 (1991). All that is required is that the guardian ad litem be available to testify at trial and that the source of the material be sufficiently identified so that the affected party has an opportunity to rebut any adverse or erroneous material contained therein. *Gilmore v. Gilmore*, 369 Mass. 598, 604–605 (1976). *Adoption of Carla*, 416 Mass. 510, 514 (1993). *Custody of Michel*, 28 Mass. App. Ct. at 266. *See Custody of Tracy*, 31 Mass. App. Ct. at 484–87." *Adoption of Sean*, 36 Mass. App. Ct. 261, 263–64 (1994); *see Adoption of Georgia*, 433 Mass. 62, 68–69 (2000).

7. Dictation notes of a deceased social worker were admitted as official records, and properly redacted and "the document admitted was a record of primary fact." *Adoption of Luc*, 94 Mass. App. Ct. 565, 468 (2018) (direct testimony of deceased social worker was properly struck from record but primary facts in his dictation were admissible.) (Further Appellate Review was granted and the case was argued before the Supreme Judicial Court this court year. The court has affirmed trial court judge's termination of mother's parental rights, and a published decision will follow.)

Hospital Records

1. While the certification of the hospital records, *see* G.L. c. 233, § 79, could have been "more artfully" drawn, the court found no error in their admission. "In the circumstances an acknowledgment that the statement was her free act and deed implies an assertion that she is not making a careless or false presentation. The contemporaneous signing by the notary assures that the statement was solemnized." *Custody of Two Minors*, 19 Mass. App. Ct. 552, 560–61 (1985).

2. Mass. G. Evid. § 803(3)(B) (2019).

Immunity Agreement

3

"The mother [under a grant of immunity] gave a statement to authorities in her home State in which she provided an account of the first baby's death." That statement was properly admitted in this case at the termination trial. *Adoption of Astrid*, 45 Mass. App. Ct. 538, 541 (1998).

Impounded Records of Juvenile Court Proceedings

All records of care and protection cases, "except those related to court orders to not resuscitate or to withdraw life-sustaining medical treatment for children in the custody of the department [of children and families] under a care and protection order," are impounded by statute, G.L. c. 119, § 38, and court rule, Juvenile Court Standing Order 1–84. In order to provide access to impounded records in care and protection cases, the Supreme Judicial Court decided that a party seeking access should follow the Uniform Rules on Impoundment Procedure, that the juvenile court judge should consider whether good cause exists under Rule 7, that the proponent of the motion to release the records from impoundment bears the burden of establishing good cause for their release, that by her testifying at the care and protection trial the mother's privilege against self-incrimination was not waived with regard to her criminal trial, and that by admitting psychiatric evidence at the care and protection trial the mother's waiver of her patient-psychotherapist privilege was not waived with regard to her criminal trial, as well. *Care & Protection of M.C.*, 479 Mass. 246 (2018) (mother and father of a child named in a care and protection petition were charged criminally and the father and the Commonwealth sought access to the records of the care and protection case to assist in their preparation for the criminal prosecution).

After remand of *Care & Protection of M.C.*, 479 Mass 246 (2018), the trial court judge issued new orders which were appealed. The case was argued before the Supreme Judicial Court last court year. A decision will be published soon.

In-Camera Examination of Child

"Although it would have been preferable for the judge to have made an explicit finding of trauma to the eldest child prior to allowing her to testify in camera, in view of the indication of trauma, . . . the judge did not abuse her discretion in holding an in camera hearing." *Adoption of Tina*, 45 Mass. App. Ct. 727, 734 (1998).

Incarceration

"Section 3(c)(xiii) of c. 210 . . . provides that when assessing the fitness of a parent, the judge shall consider 'the conviction of a parent . . . of a felony offense that the court finds is of such a nature that the child will be deprived of a stable home for a period of years; provided, however, that incarceration in and of itself shall not be grounds for termination of parental rights.'" *Adoption of Nicole*, 40 Mass. App. Ct. 259, 260–61 (1996) (quoting G.L. c. 210, § 3(c)(xiii)).

Indian Child Welfare Act (ICWA)

1. The ICWA, 25 U.S.C. § 1901 et seq., created a dual jurisdictional framework with respect to child custody cases involving Native American children, which balances tribal and state court authority. If a child is domiciled on a reservation, the tribe has exclusive jurisdiction. If a child is not domiciled on a reservation, state and trial courts have concurrent jurisdiction, and the state is required to notify the tribe if it has reason to believe that the proceedings involve an Indian child. Jurisdiction will remain in the state court if the tribe or either parent declines tribal jurisdiction, but the state court may also decline to transfer the proceedings to tribal court if it finds "good cause" not to do so. "When termination is warranted, the ICWA requires preference 'be given, the absence of good cause to the contrary, to a placement with (1) a member of the child's extended family; (2) other members of the Indian child's tribe; or (3) other Indian families.'" *See Adoption of Arnold*, 50 Mass. App. Ct. 743, 748 (2001) (quoting 25 U.S.C. § 1915(a)).

2. *See Adoptive Couple v. Baby Girl*, 133 S. Ct. 2552 (2013) (recent analysis of ICWA).

3. "We permitted the department to file a supplemental record appendix in which the department submitted letters from the three federally recognized Cherokee tries . . . all to the effect that Uday does not qualify as an "Indian child" under 25 U.S.C. § 1903(4) (2012). . . . These responsive letters demonstrate that the department in fact did comply with the ICWA notice provision. . . . Thus, in the future, documentation of compliance with ICWA is to be included in the trial court record." *Adoption of Uday*, 91 Mass. App. Ct. 51, 52–53 (2017) (father's claim of department's failure to comply with the notification requirement of ICWA rejected by Appeals Court).

Injury to Child

1. DSS must establish that the cause of the injury was due to abuse and not accident. *Adoption of Lorna*, 46 Mass. App. Ct. 134, 139 (1999).

2. "[T]he judge's findings of abuse were not limited to whether either parent was the perpetrator of the abuse. While at least one had to have abused Abby, both were deemed unfit for their inability to protect the children from future abuse." *Adoption of Lorna*, 46 Mass. App. Ct. 134, 140 (1999).

3. "The mother's refusal to accept responsibility for failing to recognize and avoid circumstances having high potential to jeopardize the safety and well-being of her children is the denial of responsibility about which the judge spoke." *Adoption of Lorna*, 46 Mass. App. Ct. 134, 140–41 (1999).

4. "Even if [the father] did not inflict any of Abby's injuries, he never recognized that she had been injured seriously." *Adoption of Lorna*, 46 Mass. App. Ct. 134, 141 (1999).

5. "It was not necessary to sort out the identity of the actual abuser for each incident of abuse. Both lacked the ability to protect the children: one, unable to protect them from his (or her) own abuse; and the other, unable to protect them from the abuser. [The judge] found both parents unfit because both remain unable to recognize abuse and confront it preventively. The case against each parent rested on independent footing, and there was no burden shifting." *Adoption of Lorna*, 46 Mass. App. Ct. 134, 141 (1999).

Interstate Compact

"The regulations governing the placement of children across State lines, which were promulgated in accordance with the Interstate Compact, specifically address the situation where a State agency places a child with a parent in another State. Section 7.507(4) of the Code of Massachusetts Regulations provides that '[w]henever a state agency has custody of a child or care of a child pursuant to a voluntary placement agreement, and such agency places a child with his/her parent(s) in another state, this constitutes a placement under the Interstate Compact.' 110 C.M.R. § 7.507(4) (1993). DSS had been granted temporary custody of Warren, and his mother had voluntarily surrendered him to the care and custody of DSS for the purpose of adoption. The placement of Warren with his father in New York by DSS would constitute a placement under the Interstate Compact, thereby rendering the provisions of the Interstate Compact applicable to the present case." *Adoption of Warren*, 44 Mass. App. Ct. 620, 623–24 (1998).

"The Interstate Compact also is applicable to the present case pursuant to Section 7.503(8) of the Code of Massachusetts Regulations which provides that '[t]he Interstate Compact shall apply to any stay across state borders whenever the sending agency requests a homestudy or supervision of a child by the receiving state.' 110 C.M.R. § 7.503(8) (1993). . . . Since DSS, as the sending agency, requested a home study by the State of New York, as the receiving State, in order to determine whether Warren could stay with his father, the provisions of the Interstate Compact apply." *Adoption of Warren*, 44 Mass. App. Ct. 620, 624 (1998).

Jurisdiction

1. Federal immigration law specifically recognizes the jurisdiction of state juvenile courts over determinations regarding the custody and best interests of children who have been abused or neglected, regardless of their immigration status. *Adoption of Peggy*, 436 Mass. 690, 699 (2002).

2. Where a child is subject to outstanding orders in an ongoing child protection case in a foreign state, Massachusetts courts should not exercise jurisdiction on a care and protection petition here, except in an emergency to protect the child from mistreatment or abuse, or if the child has been abandoned in Massachusetts. Exercise of jurisdiction should be "limited to issuing temporary orders designed to effectuate [the foreign state's] exercise of jurisdiction yet keep the child safe." *Adoption of Yvette*, 71 Mass. App. Ct. 327, 341, *further appellate review denied*, 451 Mass. 1103 (2008).

3. G.L. c. 209B, the Massachusetts Child Custody Jurisdiction Act (MCCJA). "The MCCJA 'encourage[s] communication, cooperation, and mutual assistance between courts and seek[s] to avoid jurisdictional competition and conflict.'" *Adoption of Anisha*, 89 Mass. App. Ct. 822, 827–28 (2016) (citing *Redding v. Redding*, 398 Mass. 102, 105 (1986)).

The MCCJA is the starting point in any evaluation of multistate jurisdictional conflicts. The "purpose of MCCJA, as well as other States' acts governing custody determinations, is to 'encourage cooperation and avoidance of jurisdictional conflict between courts of different States in order to protect a child's welfare when litigating custody matters.'" *Adoption of Anisha*, 89 Mass. App. Ct. at 828 (quoting *Custody of Victoria*, 473 Mass. 64, 68 (2015)).

The Juvenile Court judge was correct to assert jurisdiction over a subject child who was taken from the Commonwealth after a care and protection petition was filed. *Adoption of Anisha*, 89 Mass. App. Ct. 822 (2016).

Life Style

"A judge's custody decision must not be based on inappropriate factors, such as disapproval of a parent's life-style . . . ." *Adoption of Hugo*, 428 Mass. 219, 226–27 (1998), *cert. denied sub nom. Hugo P. v. George P.*, 526 U.S. 1034 (1999).

Massachusetts Guide to Evidence

The *Massachusetts Guide to Evidence* includes a section dedicated to child welfare cases: Section 1115, Evidentiary Issues in Care and Protection and Termination of Parental Rights Cases.

Material Advantage

"A judge's custody decision must not be based on inappropriate factors, such as . . . a comparison of the material opportunities a foster parent may offer with those offered by a natural parent." *Adoption of Hugo*, 428 Mass. 219, 226–27 (1998), *cert. denied sub nom. Hugo P. v. George P.*, 526 U.S. 1034 (1999).

Mental Impairment/Illness

"When assessing parental fitness, it is not enough to state that a parent is mentally impaired, rather there must be a showing that the condition affects the parent's ability to care for the child." *Adoption of Quentin*, 424 Mass. 882, 888 (1997).

G.L. c. 233, § 20B (psychotherapist-client privilege) "protects from compelled disclosure conversations and other communicative conduct ('correspondence, actions and occurrences') which relate to diagnosis or treatment, but not the diagnosis itself." *Adoption of Saul*, 60 Mass. App. Ct. 546, 551 (2004) (quoting G.L. c. 233, § 20B).

"A parent may be found unfit because of mental deficiencies, but only when it is shown that such "deficiencies impaired her ability to protect and care for the children." (Citation omitted). "Where a parent, as here, has cognitive or other limitations that affect the receipt of services, [DCF's] duty to make reasonable efforts to preserve the natural family includes a requirement that [DCF] provide services that accommodate the special needs of a parent." (Citation omitted)."

3

"Having stated these background principles of law, we now turn to examining the ground on which the judge relied, the mother's inability to address the children's special needs. . . . First, the judge's finding that both children have serious special needs (not the least of which relate to the sexualized behavior they both have exhibited) is unassailable. Second, it is indisputable that the mother lacks the capacity to address those special needs on her own, whether due to her cognitive limitations, depression, or weight-related immobility. Thus, the concerns that animated the termination decrees are both serious and well substantiated."

"At the same time, while it is undisputed that the mother could not address the children's special needs on her own, it is also undisputed that their special needs could not be managed by other individuals either. . . . In addition, the judge's analysis does not take into account the availability of support resources to help the mother manage her life, including her role as a parent. [footnote omitted] The judge did not speak directly to the nuanced question that the mother's situation posed: whether, with available assistance, the mother would be able to leverage the outside support that both children plainly need." *Adoption of Chad*, 94 Mass. App. Ct. 828, 838-840 (2019) (decrees terminating the mother's parental rights vacated, insufficient evidence of relationship between mother's mental disability and her ability to serve the children's best interests).

Minor Parents

"Minor parents should not retain parental rights until their maturation is sufficiently complete while adult parents are given no opportunity to 'mature.' Most importantly, to permit a minor parent time to mature before freeing a child for adoption could harm the child." *Adoption of Inez*, 428 Mass. 717, 724 (1999).

Munchausen Syndrome by Proxy/Factitious Disorder by Proxy (FDP)

1. "Munchausen Syndrome by Proxy is a medical diagnosis . . . which was first described by a British pediatrician, Roy Meadow, who published two case studies of mothers who faked or caused illnesses in their children to gain attention and sympathy for themselves." *Adoption of Keefe*, 49 Mass. App. Ct. 818, 819 n.2 (2000); *see Adoption of Willamina*, 71 Mass. App. Ct. 230, 230, *review denied*, 451 Mass. 1103 (2008).

2. "Like battered child syndrome, a diagnosis of [Munchausen Syndrome by Proxy] is dependent on inferences, not a matter of common knowledge, but within the area of expertise of physicians whose familiarity with numerous instances of genuine illnesses qualifies them to express with reasonable probability that a particular illness or group of illnesses is not genuine but is instead the result of induction or fabrication of symptoms." *Adoption of Keefe*, 49 Mass. App. Ct. 818, 823–24 (2000).

3. Profile evidence is not admissible. *Adoption of Keefe*, 49 Mass. App. Ct. 818, 824 (2000).

4. "Factitious disorder by proxy is also known as Munchausen syndrome by proxy. Stedman's Medical Dictionary 1906 (28th ed. 2006). The definition of Munchausen syndrome by proxy has not changed since *Adoption of Keefe*, 49 Mass. App. Ct. 818, 819 n.2 (2000), where we cited to the 26 edition of Stedman's Dictionary. A person with FDP fabricates or exaggerates illnesses or physical ailments suffered by another person, typically the child of the person with FDP. In extreme cases, a parent with FDP may induce physical injury to the child, to support the assertion that the child is in need of medical treatment." *Adoption of Willamina*, 71 Mass. App. Ct. 230, 231 n.3 (2008).

3

5. A child suffered "horrible injuries . . . inflicted in her own home," the investigation of which led to the conviction of her mother's boyfriend of a number of charges involving battery and substantial bodily injury. *Commonwealth v. Strickland*, 87 Mas. App. Ct. 46, 47 (2015) (defendant claimed that victim's mother suffered from Munchausen Syndrome by Proxy; convictions and order denying defendant's motion for a new trial affirmed). *See Care & Protection of Sharlene*, 445 Mass. 756 (2006).

New Trial

The decision to grant a new trial rests in the discretion of the trial judge, and an appellate court will not vacate such an order unless the judge has abused that discretion. *Adoption of Iris*, 427 Mass. 582, 588 (1998).

Newly Discovered Evidence

"In the circumstances of this case, where the parent had played a marginal role in the child's upbringing since birth, we hold that the judge's earlier finding regarding lack of proof of unfitness did not preclude her subsequent finding of unfitness, based on new or newly discovered evidence." *Adoption of Karla*, 46 Mass. App. Ct. 64, 70 (1998).

Notice

1. "The department should have set forth in its motion seeking service by publication what 'diligent efforts' had been made to locate [the father]. This oversight, however, did not deprive [the father] of his constitutional right to notice because the department had in fact made 'diligent efforts' to locate [him]; additional efforts would have been futile; and [the father] was afforded constructive notice, by publication, reasonably calculated, under all the circumstances, to apprise him of pendency of the action and afford him an opportunity to present his objections." *Adoption of Holly*, 432 Mass. 680, 686 (2000).

2. "State action terminating a parent-child relationship must comport with due process, including notice and an opportunity to be heard at a meaningful time and in a meaningful manner." *Adoption of Zev*, 73 Mass. App. Ct. 905, 905 (2009).

3. "Indeed, the adoption statute does not require that notice of an adoption of a marital child be given to a putative father whose parental rights have not been determined." *Adoption of a Minor*, 471 Mass. 373, 379 (2015) (child was conceived through in-vitro fertilization; Supreme Judicial Court determined that notice of a petition for adoption is not required to be provided to a known sperm donor; sperm donor was the brother of one of the married same-sex parents).

Oath

"[The judge did not] abuse her discretion in not requiring an oath, where she determined that the child knew the importance of telling the truth." *Adoption of Tina*, 45 Mass. App. Ct. 727, 734 (1998).

Open Adoption Agreement Enforcement

When a party has filed an equity complaint seeking enforcement of the conditions of an open adoption agreement where the adoptive parents have terminated the agreement alleging a breach by the biological parents, in order to modify the terms of the agreement, a judge must find "a material and substantial change in circumstances." *S.M. v. M.P.*, 91 Mass. App. Ct. 775, 779–80 (2017). Then, "[t]he judge must follow the requirements of the relevant statutes, applicable provisions of the agreement, and our common law as related to contract interpretation and enforcement. Finally, the judge should consider whatever evidence is probative, and necessary, to determine whether the adoptive parents acted honestly and in good faith in terminating the agreement. Pending final disposition, the judge may make such temporary orders for continued visitation as she may deem appropriate. *S.M. v. M.P.*, 91 Mass. App. Ct. at 786. G.L. c. 210, §§ 6C–6E.

Out-of-State Records

"As a general matter, however, we remind counsel that parties submitting records such as those at issue here, particularly when the records are from out of State, should adhere to the rules of evidence as to authentication and certification, or risk having the evidence excluded." *Adoption of Astrid*, 45 Mass. App. Ct. 538, 547 (1998).

Parent-Child Disqualification

G.L. c. 233, § 20. Fourth. A parent shall not testify against the parent's minor child and a minor child shall not testify against the child's parent in a proceeding before an inquest, grand jury, trial of an indictment or complaint or any other criminal, delinquency or youthful offender proceeding in which the victim in the proceeding is not a family member and does not reside in the family household; provided, however, that for the purposes of this clause, "parent" shall mean the biological or adoptive parent, stepparent, legal guardian or other person who has the right to act in loco parentis for the child; provided further, that in a case in which the victim is a family member and resides in the family household, the parent shall not testify as to any communication with the minor that was for the purpose of seeking advice regarding the child's legal rights

Mass. G. Evid. §§ 504(c)(1) and (2). See Note to § (c)(2), "[t]he statutory disqualification does not prohibit the child from testifying in a civil case, including but not limited to a divorce or custody case."

Parent's Privilege Against Self-Incrimination

1. "Due to the separate concerns of a trial on the termination of parental rights and a criminal trial, we conclude that the waiver of the privilege against self-incrimination at a trial of parental rights does not result in a waiver of that privilege in a subsequent criminal trial. In any future criminal proceeding, with entirely different stakes and rights at issue, [a parent] may reassert the privilege against self-incrimination." *Care & Protection of M.C.*, 479 Mass. 246, 261–62 (2018) (mother and father of a child named in a care and protection petition were charged criminally, mother testified at the care and protection trial, Commonwealth argued that mother's testimony would be admissible at criminal trial; Supreme Judicial Court found otherwise).

2. Mass. G. Evid. §§ 511(b), 1115(e)(3) (2019).

Parentage

A person may establish himself or herself as a child's presumptive parent in the absence of a biological relationship with the child. *Partanen v. Gallagher*, 475 Mass. 632 (2016).

Parental Discipline and the Parental Privilege Defense

In *Adoption of Varik*, 95 Mass. App. Ct. 762 (2019), the Appeals Court provides an analysis of the right of a parent to use force to discipline his or her child, a child's right to be safe from abuse and neglect, and the use of the parental discipline privilege when parents have been charged in a criminal prosecutions for their actions. The court compares the holdings in *Custody of Vaughn*, 422 Mass. 590 (1996) and *Commonwealth v. Dorvil*, 472 Mass. 1 (2015), and further includes "cases involving parental conduct that was determined to be criminal notwithstanding an assertion of the parental privilege to discipline a child, see *Commonwealth v. Rosa*, 94 Mass. App. Ct. 458, 464 (2018); *Commonwealth v. Dobson*, 92 Mass. App. Ct. 355, 357-358 (2017); *Commonwealth v. Lark*, 89 Mass. App. Ct. 905, 906 (2016)." *Id.* at 767 n.8.

See Criminal Model Jury Instructions for Use in the District Court (2009 & Supps.), § 9.250.

Parents' Rights

1. "The resolution of any custody dispute involving a natural parent necessarily begins with the premise that parents have a natural right to the custody of their children. . . . The right of parents to be free from State intrusion in childrearing matters, however, is not absolute." *Guardianship of Clyde*, 44 Mass. App. Ct. 767, 772 (1998).

2. "Parents have a constitutionally protected interest in maintaining a relationship with their children. Before that relationship is severed, due process requires that there be notice and an opportunity to be heard at a meaningful time and in a meaningful manner." *Adoption of Simone*, 427 Mass. 34, 39 (1998); *see Brantley v. Hampden Div. of Prob. & Fam. Court Dep't*, 457 Mass. 172, 187 (2010).

3. Parents have the right to a meaningful opportunity to rebut evidence presented at trial, which may include presence at trial, through video or telephonic conferencing, or through documentary submissions, deposition testimony or other reasonable means. The responsibility for devising a mechanism for meaningful participation, *once requested*, rests with the trial judge. *Adoption of Whitney*, 53 Mass. App. Ct. 832, 836 (2002); *see Brantley v. Hampden Div. of Prob. & Fam. Court Dep't*, 457 Mass. 172, 185 (2010); *Adoption of Parker*, 77 Mass. App. Ct. 619, 622–23, *review denied*, 458 Mass. 1106 (2010).

Past Conduct

1. "When a parent's living situation has changed, judge nonetheless properly may rely on evidence of past parental abuse or neglect in deciding parental unfitness to the extent that this evidence has relevance to current parental fitness." *Adoption of Paula*, 420 Mass. 716, 729 (1995); *see Care & Protection of Zita*, 455 Mass. 272, 282 (2009).

2. "[Judges] may consider past conduct to predict future ability and performance. It is one thing, however, to make a prognosis of damage to a child because of a previous pattern of abuse or neglect and quite another to predict catastrophe when the care of the child to date has been, on the whole, satisfactory and, certainly, free of abuse or neglect." *Adoption of Katharine*, 42 Mass. App. Ct. 25, 32–33 (1997).

3. "Fairly construed, the record reveals a family that was profoundly affected by drug abuse and domestic violence, the effects of which left the three children with an intense need for care, attention, and therapy. During the approximately two years between the time of the department's initial intervention and the time of trial, the parents had made progress in dealing with their difficulties. The mother's progress was aided by assistance the department provided and the father's was aided largely by the assistance he received while incarcerated. Although that progress, and its impact on the likelihood of future fitness, require recognition, *see Adoption of Paula*, 420 Mass. 716, 731 (1995), that progress does not preclude consideration of past behavior as a means of predicting the likely future. *Id.* at 729. *Cf. Adoption of Rhona*, [57 Mass. App. Ct.] 479, 485 (2003). Overall, the essential question remains whether the parents, or either of them, were fit at the time of trial 'to assume the duties and responsibilities required of a parent,' *Adoption of Mary*, 414 Mass. 705, 710 (1993), taking into account their potential for future growth and improvement. *See, e.g., Adoption of Carlos*, 413 Mass. 339, 350 (1992). Beyond that, the assessment of parental fitness must focus on the children actually involved in the proceedings, with their specific needs, interests and requirements, and not on some hypothetical child or children. *See Adoption of Frederick*, 405 Mass. 1, 7-8 (1989); *Adoption of Vito*, 431 Mass. 550, 566 (2000). In the end, the children's best interests are of paramount importance. *Adoption of Willow*, 433 Mass. 636, 644-645 (2001)." *Care & Protection of Olga*, 57 Mass. App. Ct. 821, 830 (2003).

Paternity Testing

"Paternity, by the express terms of G.L. c. 209C, § 7, must be established by clear and convincing evidence, and the proceedings are civil in nature. A mother's testimony that, at the relevant times, she had sexual intercourse exclusively with her child's putative father may support a finding of paternity. It is the function of the trial court judge to determine the weight and credibility of witness testimony and the judge's findings of fact will not be set aside unless they are clearly erroneous." *A.B. v. C.D.*, 44 Mass. App. Ct. 331, 334 (1998).

"When there is evidence of sexual intercourse between a child's mother and a putative father, G.L. c. 209C, § 17, provides that "[u]nless a party objects in writing to the [blood or genetic marker] test results upon notice of the hearing date or within thirty days prior to the hearing, whichever is shorter, the report of results of blood grouping or genetic marker tests, including a statistical probability of the putative father's paternity based upon such tests, shall be admissible in evidence without the need for laying a foundation or other proof of authenticity or accuracy. . . . General Laws c. 209C, § 17, further provides that "[i]f such report indicates a statistical probability of paternity of ninety-seven percent or greater, there shall be a rebuttable presumption that the putative father is the father of such child." *A.B. v. C.D.*, 44 Mass. App. Ct. 331, 334–35 (1998).

"In making a determination about paternity, G.L. c. 209C, § 16(e) . . . also states that 'the court may view the mother, the child, and the putative father to note any resemblance among the parties notwithstanding the absence of expert testimony.' It is not error for the trial judge, in making his decision, to rely on the physical resemblance between the child and the defendant." *A.B. v. C.D.*, 44 Mass. App. Ct. 331, 335 (1998).

Physical Abuse

1. "The department's regulations, promulgated pursuant to authority expressly granted by the Legislature, see G.L. c. 119, § 51B(8), clearly draw a line between permissible physical discipline and prohibited abuse, specifying the types of physical injuries which may not be inflicted on children and, consistent with the statute, defining abuse as nonaccidental conduct that actually inflicts these injuries or creates the substantial risk that they will result. See 110 Code Mass. Regs. § 2.00." *Cobble v. Comm'r of DSS*, 430 Mass. 385, 395 (1999).

2. Where the evidence did not establish whether it was the mother or father who abused the child, "the department could prevail against the mother only if it could show that, even if she did not abuse [the child], she nonetheless was unfit because she was unable to protect him from future harm." *Adoption of Larry*, 434 Mass. 456, 470 (2001).

3. A parent or guardian may not be subjected to criminal liability for subjecting a child under his or her care or supervision to corporal punishment if: (1) the force is reasonable, (2) the force is reasonably related to the purpose of safeguarding or promoting the welfare of the minor, including the prevention or punishment of the minor's misconduct, and (3) the force used neither causes, nor creates substantial risk of causing physical harm (beyond fleeting pain or minor transient marks), gross degradation, or severe mental stress. *Commonwealth v. Dorvil*, 472 Mass. 1 (2015) (establishing the contours of a parental privilege affirmative defense in criminal cases). While *Dorvil* is a criminal case, the case may provide guid-

ance in the context of care and protection cases. *Commonwealth v. Packer*, 88 Mass. App. Ct. 585 (2016) (stepmother [stepparent] is entitled to a parental discipline instruction if the facts support she served an in loco parentis role). *See also* District Court Criminal Model Jury Instruction 9.250 (issued June 2016).

4. DCF may rightly deny an application to become foster and preadoptive parents because of the applicants' use of corporal punishment in their home. *Magazu v. Dep't of Children & Families*, 473 Mass. 430 (2016) (upholding DCF regulation and stating that while "the department's decision imposes a substantial burden on the [applicants'] sincerely held religious beliefs, this burden is outweighed by the department's compelling interest in protecting the physical and emotional well-being of foster children").

5. "There was no indication that the discipline was used for the child's safety—for example, to keep him from going into the street or touching something hot. On this evidence, the judge rationally could have found that it was unreasonable for the mother to strike her five year old child in the face with a leather belt for unspecified misbehavior in his kindergarten classroom." *Commonwealth v. Dobson*, 92 Mass. App. Ct. 355, 358 (2017) (footnote omitted) (analysis of whether force was reasonable where mother claimed parental privilege discipline).

6. "Although little evidence was presented at trial as to the physical abuse of any child in the home apart from Elizabeth, we agree with the judge's conclusions that the exposure of the other children in the care of the mother to the abuse of Elizabeth, in addition to the mother's role in the physical abuse of Elizabeth, her refusal to acknowledge and take responsibility for such abuse, and her continued commitment to the father, rendered the mother unfit to parent the children who were not directly subjected to physical abuse." *Adoption of Garret*, 92 Mass. App. Ct. 664, 674 (2018).

Placement Decisions

"Placement decisions, as opposed to custody decisions, fall within the discretionary powers of the legal guardian as one of the usual incidents of custody. See G.L. c. 119, § 23. While the judge certainly may offer guidance to the [custodian] concerning a child's residence, the ultimate decision regarding placement is the custodian's. That decision is reviewable under § 21 for abuse of discretion or error of law only." *Care & Protection of Manuel*, 428 Mass. 527, 534 (1998).

Plan

1. A finding of unfitness may be buttressed if a parent fails to "formulate any realistic plan by which [the parent] could care for her [or his] children already in the department's custody." *Custody of a Minor (No. 1)*, 377 Mass. 876, 883 (1979).

2. "Although it would have been better practice for the department to explain why the goal was changed from adoption to guardianship, this is not fatal. The controlling consideration is the welfare of the child. (Citation omitted)." *Adoption of Xarina*, 93 Mass. App. Ct. 800, 805 (2018).

Police Reports

1. "Admission of the police report as a business record was proper. . . . The report was a record of the officers' first-hand observations of conditions in the marital home in October, 1988, when police executed a search warrant on the premises." *Adoption of Paula*, 420 Mass. 716, 727 (1995).

2. Mass. G. Evid. § 1115(b)(5) (2019).

Postadoption Visitation

1. "The decision as to whether to allow [it] is more a question of what is in the interests of the child, rather than one of the rights of the parent. *Adoption of Abigail*, 23 Mass. App. Ct. 191, 199–200 (1986)." *Adoption of Warren*, 44 Mass. App. Ct. 620, 626 n.5 (1998).

2. "Here, where the children had not yet been placed in a prospective adoptive home as of the time of trial, visitation has not been judicially thrust upon identified adoptive parents. When such prospective parents have been chosen, they will, by their willingness to adopt, have implicitly, if not expressly, consented to the visits ordered by the judge. We distinguish and intimate no opinion as to a visitation order in a G.L. c. 210, § 3, proceeding entered after a child has been placed with a prospective adoptive family." *Adoption of Lars*, 46 Mass. App. Ct. 30, 36 (1998); *see Adoption of Rico*, 72 Mass. App. Ct. 219–20 (2008), *aff'd on other grounds*, 453 Mass. 749, 754–58 (2009); *see also Adoption of Jacques*, 82 Mass. App. Ct. 601, 610 (2012) (affirming trial judge's decision not to order postadoption visitation where adoptive parents were not yet identified because it might "reduce the pool of potential adoptive parents and hamper the department's efforts to recruit an adoptive home for [the child], and would also affect the rights of any adoptive parents once they are identified").

3. "The decision regarding visitation by the father will be made by the adoptive parents. This is consistent with our prior decisions in such matters, to the effect that the trial judge may, in his discretion, leave postadoption visitation in the hands of the adoptive parents. *See Adoption of Mary*, 414 Mass. 705 (1993); *Adoption of Gwendolyn*, 29 Mass. App. Ct. 130, 138–39 (1990)." *Adoption of Wesley*, 48 Mass. App. Ct. 1114 (2000). *See also Adoption of Ilona*, 459 Mass. 53 (2011) (clarifying that a judge has discretion to leave the visitation decision up to the adoptive parents and is not *required* to order visitation when he or she concludes it is presently in the child's best interest).

4. "[W]e hold that a judge may order limited post-adoption contact, including visitation, between a child and a biological parent where such contact is currently in the best interests of the child." *Adoption of Vito*, 431 Mass. 550, 553 (2000); *Adoption of Rico*, 72 Mass. App. Ct. 219–20 (2008), *aff'd on other grounds*, 453 Mass. 749, 754–58 (2009).

a. "Generalities about what may be in the best interests of some children, without more, cannot be the basis of judicial orders concerning postadoption contact of a particular child; the best interests of the child standard is one grounded in the particular needs and circumstances of the individual child in question." *Adoption of Vito*, 431 Mass. 550, 566 (2000); *Adoption of Rico*, 72 Mass. App. Ct. 219–20 (2008), *aff'd on other grounds*, 453 Mass. 749, 754–58 (2009).

b. "[A] judicial order for postadoption contact may be warranted where the evidence readily points to significant, existing bonds between the child and a biological parent, such that a court order abruptly disrupting that relationship would run counter to the child's best interests." *Adoption of Vito*, 431 Mass. 550, 563 (2000); *Adoption of Rico*, 72 Mass. App. Ct. 219–20 (2008), *aff'd on other grounds*, 453 Mass. 749, 754–58 (2009); *Adoption of Greta*, 431 Mass. 577, 588 (2000).

5. "The United States Supreme Court has never concluded that there exists a fundamental liberty interest in the sibling relationship. When addressing the sibling relationship, the Supreme Judicial Court has rejected the argument that the sibling relationship is entitled to any heightened protection, *Adoption of Hugo*, 428 Mass. 219, 230-231 (1998), and has concluded that while it is "preferable that siblings be raised together . . . the weight to be accorded sibling relations in the application of the best interests standard . . . 'will vary with the circumstances.'" *Adoption of Willow*, 433 Mass. 636, 651 (2001), quoting from *Adoption of Hugo*, *supra* at 231.

Furthermore, visitation orders concerning other relationships have been evaluated by the best interests standard. *See Youmans v. Ramos*, 429 Mass. 774, 785 (1999) (court may order visitation between child and de facto parent when it is in best interests of child); *Adoption of Vito*, 431 Mass. at 563-567 (postadoption visitation with biological mother); *Blixt v. Blixt*, 437 Mass. 649, 657-60 (2002), *cert. denied*, 123 S. Ct. 1259 (2003) (grandparents where parents are unmarried); *R.J.A. v. K.A.V.*, 34 Mass. App. Ct. 369, 373 (1993) (best interest of child standard should be predominant factor in determining what rights, if any, putative father had). It would make little sense to accord the sibling relationship greater protections than are provided other family relationships." *Adoption of Pierce*, 58 Mass. App. Ct. 342, 347 (2003).

6. Where a trial judge found significant attachment between a parent and child, and the judge (1) concluded that continued contact was in the child's best interests; (2) did not enter an order requiring such visits; and (3) left the extent and frequency of contact to the informed decision-making of the preadoptive parents, there was no error because the trial judge had an evidentiary basis for concluding that the preadoptive mother would support and permit such contact unless it became harmful to the child. *Adoption of Ilona*, 459 Mass. 53, 64–66 (2011), reversing *Adoption of Ilona*, 76 Mass. App. Ct. 481, 488 (2010).

7. "In the ordinary case, the adoptive parents must be relied upon to ensure that the child is exposed to her ethnic and religious heritage, and to make certain, where appropriate and permitted, that there is continued contact with the child's biological extended family." *Adoption of Odetta*, 87 Mass. App. Ct. 576 (2015). However, in *Odetta*, the court upheld a narrowly tailored order for visitation with the child's paternal uncle as in the child's best interest, where there was animosity between the child's maternal and paternal families due to the fact that the child's father was convicted of killing her mother and visitation with her paternal uncle would provide her with exposure to the religion of the paternal side of her family.

Prima Facie Evidence

1. "Prima facie evidence is evidence that, until its effect is overcome by other evidence, compels the conclusion that the evidence is true. When evidence is introduced that contradicts the prima facie evidence, however, the prima facie evidence loses its artificial force and a factual issue arises. In these circumstances, the prima facie evidence is no more significant than any other evidence, but must be weighed equally with all other evidence to determine whether a particular fact has been proved. Furthermore, the burden of persuasion always remains on the party who must prove the point, even though the party is aided by prima facie evidence." *Burns v. Commonwealth*, 430 Mass. 444, 450–51 (1999).

2. Mass. G. Evid. § 301(c) (2019).

Primary Caregiver

1a. Where "[t]he mother argues that the judge failed to give 'proper weight' to her role as primary caretaker of the child as required by G.L. c. 209C, § 10(a), as amended through St. 1998, c. 179, § 6, . . . we decline the mother's request . . . that we create, presumably through interpretation of § 10(a), a *presumption* that custody should be awarded to the primary caretaking parent. Indeed, we have stated, in the context of c. 209C, that a parent's role as a primary caregiver 'should not be afforded substantial weight without a determination as to the quality of that care.' *R. H. v. B. F.*, 39 Mass. App. Ct. 29, 42 (1995), *S.C. sub nom. Custody of Vaughan*, 422 Mass. 590 (1996). . . . *See also Adoption of Hugo*, 428 Mass. 219, 231–232 n.21 (1998), *cert. denied sub nom. Hugo P. v. George P.*, 526 U.S. 1034 (1999) (in considering widest range of permissible evidence in child custody cases, court should not give presumptive consideration to one factor or another when legislature has not recognized a presumption as such); *Opinion of the Justices*, 427 Mass. 1201 (1998) (discussing the constitutional ramifications of creating a presumption in child custody matters); Kindregan & Inker, Family Law and Practice §§ 47.12 & 47.12.1 (2d ed. 1996 & Supp. 2000)." *Custody of Zia*, 50 Mass. App. Ct. 237, 241–43 (2001). Neither does G.L. c. 209C, § 10(a) establish a "preference" for retaining custody with the primary caretaker. *See Custody of Zia*, 50 Mass. App. Ct. 237, 243–44 (2000).

b. "'[C]ustody orders and judgments [including those under G.L. c. 209C] are made on the basis of a determination of the best interests of the child. . . [,]' *R. H. v. B. F.*, 39 Mass. App. Ct. at 39[; s]ee *Bak v. Bak*, 24 Mass. App. Ct. 608, 616 (1987); *Carr v. Carr*, 44 Mass. App. Ct. at 925; *Freedman v. Freedman*, 49 Mass. App. Ct. 519, 522 (2000), and a judge may consider any factors found pertinent to those interests in the circumstances of the dispute. See *R. H. v. B. F.*, 39 Mass. App. Ct. at 40; *Rosenberg v. Merida*, 428 Mass. 182, 191; *Ardizoni v. Raymond*, 40 Mass. App. Ct. 734, 738 (1996); *Freedman v. Freedman, supra*. 'It is the duty of the judge to consider the welfare of the child[ren] in reference not merely to the present, but also to the probable future. . . .' *Rolde v. Rolde*, 12 Mass. App. Ct. 398 at 403, quoting from *Jenkins v. Jenkins*, 304 Mass. 248, 250 (1939). 'The decision of which parent will promote a child's best interests "is a subject peculiarly within the discretion of the judge."' *Ardizoni v. Raymond, supra* at 738, quoting from *Bak v. Bak, supra*." *Custody of Zia*, 50 Mass. App. Ct. 237, 243 (2000).

3

2. General Laws c. 209C, § 10(a) "gives direction to the judge's consideration of a child's 'best interests' by 'evincing a general intent on the part of the Legislature to maintain the bonds between the child and her caregiver.' It cautions against rearranging a child's living arrangements in an attempt to achieve some optimum from all the available permutations and combinations of custody and visitation, when it is generally wiser and safer not to meddle in arrangements that are already serving the child's needs. If the parenting arrangement in which a child has lived is satisfactory and is reasonably capable of preservation, it is ordinarily in the child's best interests to maintain that arrangement, and contrary to the child's best interests to disrupt it. Stability is itself of enormous benefit to a child, and any unnecessary tampering with the status quo simply increases the risk of harm to the child." *Custody of Kali*, 439 Mass. 834, 843 (2003) (quoting *Custody of Zia*, 50 Mass. App. Ct. at 244); *see Smith v. McDonald*, 458 Mass. 540 (2010); *Charara v. Yatim*, 78 Mass. App. Ct. 325, 334–36 (2010).

Prior Findings

1. "The findings from the care and protection proceeding may be introduced in evidence at the trial on a petition to dispense with consent to adoption to the extent they are both relevant and material." *Adoption of Simone*, 427 Mass. 34, 43 (1998) (quoting *Adoption of Frederick*, 405 Mass. 1, 12 (1989), and citing with approval *Adoption of Paula*, 420 Mass. 716, 721 (1995)).

"We went on to note, however: 'We think . . . that the better practice would be for a judge to decline to admit as evidence in an adoption proceeding findings from an underlying care and protection proceeding that are on appeal." *Adoption of Simone*, 427 Mass. 34, 43 (1998) (quoting with approval *Adoption of Paula*, 420 Mass. 716, 722 (1995)).

"While expressing a preference for fresh findings in the second proceeding, we were clearly mindful that the earlier findings might, in appropriate cases, be relevant and reliable." *Adoption of Simone*, 427 Mass. 34, 44 (1998). *Cf. Adoption of Tina*, 45 Mass. App. Ct. 727, 731 (1998) ("Findings from a care and protection case are to be treated with caution before admission in an adoption proceeding. The better practice may be to exclude such findings, especially where they relate to children other than the child before the court."). In *Tina*, it was error for the judge to preclude evidence to contradict earlier findings.

2. Mass. G. Evid. § 1115(f)(3) (2019).

Reasonable Efforts

"[1] [A] judge must make a reasonable efforts determination when issuing an order transferring custody of the child to the department [DCF] for up to seventy-two hours at the emergency hearing, and must revisit that determination at the temporary custody hearing that must follow, commonly known as the "seventy-two hour hearing" if the judge continues the department's temporary custody of the child . . . [2] § 29C provides that reasonable efforts by the department prior to removal of a child from the home are not required if the judge finds that one of four exceptions applies. We hold that, where none of the four exceptions in § 29C applies exigent circumstances do not excuse the department from making reasonable efforts, but we recognize that a judge must determine what is reasonable in light of the particular circumstances in each case, that the health and safety of the child must be the paramount concern, and that no child should remain in the custody of his or her parents if immediate removal is necessary to protect the child from serious abuse or neglect . . . [3] where a judge or single justice finds that the department failed to make reasonable efforts before removing a child from his or her home, the judge or single justice has the equitable authority to order the department to take reasonable remedial steps to diminish the adverse consequences of the department's failure to do so." *Care & Protection of Walt*, 478 Mass. 212, 213–14 (2017) (where department has duty to make reasonable efforts to prevent or eliminate the need for removal from the home prior to removal and fails to do so, a judge has equitable authority to issue orders to remedy adverse consequences resulting from removal).

G.L. c. 119, §§ 24, 25, 26, 29C.

Reunification/Services

DCF is not required to provide services geared toward reunification once the goal is changed to adoption. *See Adoption of Nicole*, 40 Mass. App. Ct. 259, 263 (1996).

Review and Redetermination

1. "General Laws c. 119, § 26, governs review and redetermination hearings. . . . This provision is primarily the means by which a parent or other interested party, including the department, may bring to a judge's attention a change in the situation of a child, or of a child's parent, which might warrant reconsideration or modification of the original order adjudicating the child in need of care and protection." *Adoption of Helen*, 429 Mass. 856, 861 (1999); *see Care & Protection of Thomasina*, 75 Mass. App. Ct. 563, 569–70, *review denied*, 455 Mass. 1107 (2009); *cf. Care & Protection of Joselita*, 77 Mass. App. Ct. 28, 31–33, *review denied*, 458 Mass. 1101 (2010).

2. This statute applies to C&P cases, not termination cases. *Adoption of Helen*, 429 Mass. 856, 861–62 (1999); *see Care & Protection of Thomasina*, 75 Mass. App. Ct. 563, 569–70, *review denied*, 455 Mass. 1107 (2009); *cf. Care & Protection of Joselita*, 77 Mass. App. Ct. 28, 31–33, *review denied*, 458 Mass. 1101 (2010).

3. As per the statute, such review is not more than once every six months. *Adoption of Helen*, 429 Mass. 856, 861 (1999); *see Care & Protection of Thomasina*, 75 Mass. App. Ct. 563, 569–70, *review denied*, 455 Mass. 1107 (2009); *cf. Care & Protection of Joselita*, 77 Mass. App. Ct. 28, 31–33, *review denied*, 458 Mass. 1101 (2010).

4. "[T]he moving party [on a petition for review and determination] bears an initial burden to produce some credible evidence that circumstances have changed since the initial determination such that the child[ren] may no longer be in need of care and protection. Once such a showing is made, the department [has the burden of proving by clear and convincing evidence] . . . that the parent is still unfit and [that] the child[ren]'s best interests are served by remaining removed from parental custody." *Care & Protection of Erin*, 443 Mass. 567, 568 (2005); *see Care & Protection of Thomasina*, 75 Mass. App. Ct. 563, 575, *review denied*, 455 Mass. 1107 (2009); *Adoption of Melvin*, 71 Mass. App. Ct. 706, 713, *review denied*, 451 Mass. 1108 (2008).

5. G.L. c. 119, § 26(c).

Rule 1:28 Decisions

"We have never suggested that summary decisions of this court issued pursuant to rule 1:28 . . . may be relied upon or cited as authority in other cases." *Horner v. Boston Edison Co.*, 45 Mass. App. Ct. 139, 140 (1998). *But see* Mass. App. Ct. R. 1:28, as amended effective Jan. 1, 2009 (parties may cite to Rule 1:28 decisions except that "[n]o such order issued before February 28, 2008, may be cited").

School Records

1. Mass. G. Evid. § 1115(b)(4) (2019).

2. "[T]he school had a statutory duty, pursuant to the Federal Individuals with Disabilities Education Act, 20 U.S.C. §§ 1400 et seq. (2012) (IDEA), to disclose information relating to the IEP to the prosecutor in order for the Commonwealth to make a reasoned, informed decision whether to move forward with the prosecution." *Commonwealth v. Geordi G.*, 94 Mass. App. Ct. 82, 88 (2018) (Appeals Court vacated dismissal of school-related assault and battery charges for lack of probable cause and took "this opportunity to remind school officials of their obligation, when seeking a delinquency complaint against a student with an individualized education program (IEP), to make the prosecutor aware of the juvenile's special needs in a timely manner," *Commonwealth v. Geordi G.*, 94 Mass. App. Ct. at 83.).

Schooling

1. "We conclude that the parents' refusal to provide the [school] committee with the bare essentials of their educational plan and to allow for any evaluation of their children's educational attainments transgresses the mandate of *Care & Protection of Charles*, 399 Mass. 324, 337–40 (1987) and affirm the decision . . . that the children are in need of care and protection and committing them temporarily to [DSS]." *Care & Protection of Ivan*, 48 Mass. App. Ct. 87, 87–88 (1999).

2. Where a child on whose behalf the Department of Social Services filed a care and protection petition was no longer required to attend school by reason of G.L. c. 76, § 1, a judge of the Juvenile Court erred in depriving her of her relationship with her mother solely on the ground that it might be better for her to continue her education beyond the age of sixteen. "The legislative standard of G.L. c. 76, § 1, establishing the maximum age during which children are required to attend school, accommodates the governmental interest in the compulsory education of citizens . . . we consider that standard to be the appropriate guide implicit in G.L. c. 119, § 24, for determining what constitutes 'necessary and proper . . . educational care and discipline.' Since Emily is no longer required to attend school by reason of G.L. c. 76, § 1, the State may not deprive her of her relationship with her mother solely on the ground that it might be better for her to continue her education beyond the age of sixteen; her mother, as well, may not be deprived of Emily's custody solely because in her mother's house, Emily may decide not to continue to attend school." *Care & Protection of Emily*, 58 Mass. App. Ct. 190, 193 (2003).

Service Plan

See **Action Plans**.

Sexual Abuse

1. The legislature, in 1990, enacted three separate statutes regarding the testimony of children in sexual abuse cases. General Laws c. 233, § 81 deals with criminal proceedings; G.L. c. 233, § 82 deals with any civil proceeding except G.L. c. 119, §§ 23(C) and 24; and G.L. c. 233, § 83 deals with G.L. c. 119, §§ 23(C) and 24 actions (care and protection).

2. "*Adoption of Quentin*, 424 Mass. 882, 893 (1997), [a G.L. c. 210, § 3 termination case], suggested that the following procedures be incorporated into G.L. c. 233, § 82 proceedings:

(1) DSS must give prior notice to the parents that it will seek to use such statements;

(2) DSS must show by more than a mere preponderance of evidence a compelling need for use of such a procedure;

(3) Any separate hearing regarding the reliability of a child witness's out-of-court statement must be on the record and a judge's basis for determining reliability must be supported by specific findings; and

(4) There should be independently admitted evidence that corroborates the out-of-court statement." *Adoption of Tina*, 45 Mass. App. Ct. 727, 733–34 (1998).

3a. "The Legislature obviously intended to authorize the introduction of out-of-court statements by a child under the age of ten concerning sexual abuse in care and protection proceedings without regard to the availability of the child, where the remaining statutory prerequisites for admissibility are met." *Care & Protection of Rebecca*, 419 Mass. 67, 77 (1994) (As *Rebecca* was a C&P case, G.L. c. 233, § 83, not G.L. c. 233, § 82, was applicable.); *see Adoption of Daisy*, 77 Mass. App. Ct. 768, 777–78 (2010).

3b. "[T]he phrase, 'out-of-court statements of a child under the age of ten,' in G.L. c. 233, § 82, refers to hearsay statements made by a child when the child was under the age of ten, not to hearsay statements made by a child who is under the age of ten at the time the statement is offered at trial." *Adoption of Daisy*, 460 Mass. 72, 78 (2011).

4. "[G.L. c. 233, §§ 81 and 82] explicitly require the proponent of an out-of-court statement made by a child under the age of ten to 'demonstrate a diligent and good faith effort to produce the child' and 'specific findings on the record' demonstrating unavailability. The circumstances in which a declarant may be found unavailable are carefully delineated. This unavailability requirement is conspicuously absent from § 83." *Care & Protection of Rebecca*, 419 Mass. 67, 76–77 (1994); *see Adoption of Daisy*, 77 Mass. App. Ct. 768, 777–78 (2010).

5. "[T]he judge found that the mother placed her own needs to continue involvement with [Bob] before the needs of her children, that the mother was very slow to acknowledge and deal with the impact of the sexual abuse and the mother has a history of having failed to protect these two minor children from abuse and neglect and in fact has contributed to some of what they have suffered. . . . Because of the evidence of Bob's abuse, the mother's continuing relationship with Bob, and the children's improvement since living with the grandparents, the judge's findings and disposition of these cases were not clearly erroneous." *Adoption of Kimberly*, 414 Mass. 526, 530–31 (1993).

6. DSS regulations do not limit "sexual contact" to physical touching. Purely verbal sexual contact may support a conclusion by DSS that a § 51B report should be supported. *See John D. v. Dep't of Social Servs.*, 51 Mass. App. Ct. 125, 128–32 (2001).

Shaken Baby Syndrome (Abusive Head Trauma)

Two criminal cases have addressed the diagnosis of shaken baby syndrome. *See Commonwealth v. Millien*, 474 Mass. 417 (2016); *Commonwealth v. Epps*, 474 Mass. 743 (2016).

In the first case, the defendant's convictions were vacated and the case was remanded for a new trial due to ineffective assistance of counsel in that the defense counsel's failure to introduce expert testimony concerning the controversy in the medical community around shaken baby syndrome deprived the defendant of a defense "by not providing the jury with the other side of this debate." *Commonwealth v. Millien*, 474 Mass. at 418. The case provides an analysis of the controversy in the medical community concerning the diagnosis of shaken baby syndrome. *Commonwealth v. Millien*, 474 Mass. at 418. "In 2009, the American Academy of Pediatrics (AAP) in a policy statement recommended that pediatricians 'use the term "abusive head trauma" rather than a term that implies a single injury mechanism, such as shaken baby syndrome, in their diagnosis and medical communications.'" *Commonwealth v. Millien*, 474 Mass. at 423 n.7 (citation omitted).

In the second case, the defendant's conviction was vacated and the case remanded for a new trial. "[T]he absence of expert testimony that the child's injuries might have been caused by her accidental fall deprived the defendant of an available, substantial ground of defense . . ." *Commonwealth v. Epps*, 474 Mass. at 744.

Sibling Visitation

1. *See* G.L. c. 119, § 26B(b) relative to the right to sibling visitation.

2. "Whether a court has jurisdiction in particular cases brought under G.L. c. 119, § 26B(b), will . . . turn on whether, by virtue of State intervention, siblings were placed in different homes and thereby separated from one another, and not on whether, at the time a child petitions for visitation, siblings are in particular types of custodial arrangements." *Care & Protection of Jamison*, 467 Mass. 269, 279 (2014).

3. "The plain language of the statute [G.L. c. 119, § 26B(b)] states that posttermination sibling visitation may be managed by either the court or DCF. Here, evidence was presented that sibling visitation was being provided by DCF, and the judge was thus under no obligation to order visitation pursuant to G.L. c. 119, § 26B(b)." *Adoption of Garret*, 92 Mass. App. Ct. 664, 680–81 (2018) (trial court did not err in declining to make sibling visitation order, statute allows DCF to provide and manage sibling visits).

Siblings

"The courts of this Commonwealth have recognized the importance of siblings' being raised together. But we have been careful to observe that a sibling relationship is but one factor, albeit an important one, that a judge should consider in custody cases." *Adoption of Hugo*, 428 Mass. 219, 230 (1998), *cert. denied sub nom. Hugo P. v. George P.*, 526 U.S. 1034 (1999). See G.L. c. 119, § 26B(b) relative to the right to sibling visitation in cases where the siblings are separated by adoption or long or short-term placements in state care. *Care & Protection of Jamison*, 467 Mass. 269 (2014).

Sobriety

Where a parent's lengthy addiction was unmarked by serious or significant periods of sobriety, "more than a few months of sobriety in prison, unaccompanied by proof of effective drug treatment while there, was required to establish convincingly that, on release, the [parent] would be able to maintain sobriety sufficiently to become a fit parent." *Adoption of Serge*, 52 Mass. App. Ct. 1, 7 (2001).

Special Immigrant Juvenile (SIJ) Status

1. "In Massachusetts, the Juvenile Court and the Probate and Family Court have jurisdiction to make judicial determinations about the care and custody of juveniles despite only one court being designated as a juvenile court. Therefore, in Massachusetts, an immigrant may petition for special findings in either the Juvenile Court or the Probate and Family Court. Because of the distinct expertise State courts possess in the area of child welfare and abuse, Congress has entrusted them with the responsibility to perform a best interest analysis and to make factual determinations about child welfare for purposes of SIJ eligibility." *Recinos v. Escobar*, 473 Mass. 734, 738 (2016) (citation omitted) (twenty-year-old unmarried immigrant filed a complaint in equity in the Probate and Family Court applying for SIJ status). "Before an immigrant child can apply for SIJ status, she must receive the following predicate findings from a 'juvenile court': (1) she is dependent on the juvenile court; (2) her reunification with one or both parents is not viable due to abuse, neglect, or abandonment; and (3) it is not in her best interests to return to her country of origin." *Recinos v. Escobar*, 473 Mass. at 735 (citing 8 U.S.C. § 1101(a)(27)(J)(i)).

2. "Acting within the limits of the fact-finding role, the judge must make the special findings even if he or she suspects that the immigrant child seeks SIJ status for a reason other than relief from neglect, abuse, or abandonment. The immigrant child's motivation for seeking the special findings, if relevant to the child's entitlement to SIJ status, ultimately will be considered by USCIS [United States Citizenship and Immigration Services] in its review of the application. The immigrant child's motivation is irrelevant to the judge's special findings." *Guardianship of Guadalupe Penate. Department of Revenue v. Lopez*, 477 Mass. 268, 275 (2017) (a judge may not decline to make special findings based on an assessment of the merits of an applicant's application for SIJ status or the applicant's motivation for seeking SIJ status).

3 3. "A judge may not decline to make special findings based on his or her assessment of the likelihood that the SIJ application ultimately will be successful before the Federal authorities, or on any consideration of the juvenile's motivation for seeking SIJ status (citation omitted). . . . A judge simply may not decline to make findings; he or she must make the findings—whether favorable or not—concerning those criteria." *Hernandez-Lemus v. Arias-Diaz*, 480 Mass. 1002, 1003 (2018) (trial court judgment to decline to enter special findings vacated).

Stability

Stability in the life of a child, especially a young child, is important. *Adoption of Hugo*, 428 Mass. 219, 228–29 (1998), *cert. denied sub nom. Hugo P. v. George P.*, 526 U.S. 1034 (1999).

Staleness

"Stale information cannot be the basis of current unfitness but prior parental conduct is relevant in assessing capacity and ability to care for the child." *Care & Protection of Ian*, 46 Mass. App. Ct. 615, 618 (1999). *See also Adoption of Querida*, 94 Mass. App. Ct. 771, 779 (2019) (mother's history with DCF properly considered "for its predictive value on the risk of future abuse or neglect").

Standard (Dispense with Parental Consent)

"The critical consideration in deciding whether to dispense with the need for parental consent to adoption is whether the natural parents are currently fit to further the welfare and best interests of their children. *Petitions of the Dept. of Social Servs. to Dispense with Consent to Adoption*, 389 Mass. 793, 799 (1983). See G.L. c. 210, § 3. '[I]n deciding whether natural parents may be deprived of the custody of their minor children, both the fitness of the parents and the needs of the particular children must be examined.' *Petitions of the Dept. of Social Servs. to Dispense with Consent to Adoption, supra* at 800. Natural parents may not be deprived of the custody of their minor children absent a showing that they 'have grievous shortcomings or handicaps that would put the child's welfare in the family milieu much at hazard' or that 'some factor such as lengthy separation and a corresponding growth in the ties between the child and the prospective adoptive parents indicated that the child would be hurt by being returned to the natural parents.' *Petition of the New England Home for Little Wanderers to Dispense with Consent to Adoption*, 367 Mass. 631, 639, 646 (1975)." *Adoption of Warren*, 44 Mass. App. Ct. 620, 625 (1998).

"'The specialized needs of a particular child when combined with the deficiencies of a parent's character, temperament, capacity, or conduct may clearly establish parental unfitness.' *Petitions of the Dept. of Social Servs. to Dispense with Consent to Adoption*, 18 Mass. App. Ct. 120, 125 (1984). Because parental fitness must be evaluated in the context of a particular child's needs, parents might be fit to bring up one child and not fit to bring up another in light of the fact that the needs of one child may be different from those of another. *Petition of Catholic Charitable Bureau of the Archdiocese of Boston, Inc., to Dispense with Consent to Adoption*, 18 Mass. App. Ct. 656, 661 (1984). While raising siblings together is important, it is not dispositive of custody matters. *Ibid.*" *Adoption of Warren*, 44 Mass. App. Ct. 620, 625–26 (1998).

Standard of Proof

"[I]n care and custody proceedings, subsidiary evidentiary findings need only be proved by a fair preponderance of the evidence. Taken together, these facts must then prove parental unfitness, since it is the 'critical inquiry,' by clear and convincing evidence." *Care & Protection of Laura*, 414 Mass. 788, 793 (1993).

Standing

"[T]he parents retained standing here because the remand proceeding was part of the same proceeding to which the parents were already a party." *Adoption of Zak*, 90 Mass. App. Ct. 840, 844 (2017) (parents have standing to participate in remand hearing concerning visitation order). "[T]he fact that the termination was final did not divest the parties of standing to participate in a hearing that was a continuation of the very proceeding in which they had participated." *Adoption of Zak*, 90 Mass. App. Ct. at 844.

"Until parental rights have been terminated by entry of a decree, parents have the right to participate in proceedings to determine issues such as placement and visitation arrangements concerning their children." *Adoption of Douglas*, 473 Mass. 1024, 1025 (2016) (parents stipulated to unfitness and termination of parental rights, but the right to appeal decisions concerning the proposed adoption plan and visitation were reserved).

Stay

1. "Relying on the general rule that a stay serves 'to preserve the rights of the parties during the pendency of an appeal,' the mother next argues that a stay of the decree dispensing with consent, issued by a single justice of the Appeals Court, preserves her rights to visitation and a review and redetermination hearing pending appeal." The Supreme Judicial Court rejected the argument. "The stay simply prevents the department from asking the court to allow the adoption of the child pending appeal." *Adoption of Helen*, 429 Mass. 856, 864–65 (1999).

2. When seeking a stay a parent "should include sufficient evidentiary material and argument to allow the single justice to make an informed threshold assessment whether the new trial motion has a sufficiently strong likelihood of success on the merits to justify the resulting delay in completion of appellate review." *Adoption of Ulrich*, 94 Mass. App. Ct. 668, 675 (2017).

Sufficiency of Petition

1. G.L. c. 119, § 24.

2. A care and protection petition is legally sufficient if it alleges facts, based on personal information and belief, that, if true, fall within one of the four enumerated concerns contained in the first sentence of G.L. c. 119, § 24. *Care & Protection of Lillian*, 445 Mass. 333, 334 (2005).

Temporary Custody Hearing

1. G.L. c. 119, §§ 24, 25.

2. "The relevant provisions of § 24, pertaining to so-called seventy-two hour hearings, and § 25, pertaining to nonemergency preliminary hearings, provide alternative, mutually exclusive means of conducting a temporary custody hearing pending the final adjudicatory hearing that takes place under § 26. If . . . custody of the child has been transferred to the department by an emergency order of the court, the child and his parents or custodians are entitled to a temporary custody hearing under § 24 within seventy-two hours of issuance of that emergency order. If, on the other hand, there has been no emergency custody order or emergency removal of the child, then the temporary custody hearing would be held pursuant to § 25." *Care & Protection of Manuel*, 428 Mass. 527, 532–33 (1998).

"In key respects, a temporary custody hearing held under § 25 is identical to one held under § 24. The parties, including the child named in the petition, have the right to be heard regarding, for example, their possible nominations of temporary custodians for the child and whether (or what) temporary custody orders should be issued—particularly where such orders often remain in effect for a year or more until final adjudication of the petition. Furthermore, both sections give the judge essentially the same range of options of awarding temporary care or custody of the child to the department, or to another licensed child care agency, or to an individual nominated by the child or parents and approved by the court as provided in § 26(2)(i). Because the interests affected . . . are the same, we believe that the same 'fair preponderance of the evidence' standard that governs temporary custody orders under § 24, should also govern orders under § 25." *Care & Protection of Manuel*, 428 Mass. 527, 533–34 (1998) (quoting *Care & Protection of Robert*, 408 Mass. 52, 68 (1990)).

3. When a probate court removes a child from parents' custody under G.L. c. 119, § 23(c), due process requires the same protection of a seventy-two–hour hearing as is provided in G.L. c. 119, § 24. *Custody of Lori*, 444 Mass. 316, 319–21 (2005).

4. A judge at a seventy-two–hour hearing may not rely on the contents of "an unsworn petition filed by a social worker that commenced [the child's] care and protection proceedings." *Care & Protection of Zita*, 455 Mass. 272, 281 (2009).

Termination of Parental Rights

1. "To determine whether to dispense with parental consent to adoption, the judge must evaluate whether the parent can assume the duties and responsibilities required of a parent and whether dispensing with consent will be in the best interests of the child. Before a judge may remove custody from a parent and reward it to the department, the judge must find, by clear and convincing evidence, that the natural parent is unfit to further the welfare and best interests of the child. Subsidiary findings must be proven by a fair preponderance of the evidence. We will not disturb these findings absent a showing that they are clearly erroneous." *Adoption of Helen*, 429 Mass. 856, 859 (1999).

"The judge made fifty-nine findings that demonstrate a history of substance abuse, a pattern of late and missed appointments, failure to communicate her whereabouts to the department, and a minimal amount of communication with the child over a significant period of time." *Adoption of Helen*, 429 Mass. 856, 859–60 (1999).

2. "Termination denies the natural parents physical custody, as well as the rights ever to visit, communicate with, or regain custody of the child." *Adoption of Helen*, 429 Mass. 856, 864 (1999) (quoting *Petition of Catholic Charitable Bureau of the Archdiocese of Boston, Inc., to Dispense with Consent to Adoption*, 392 Mass. 738, 741 (1984) (quoting *Santosky v. Kramer*, 455 U.S. 745, 749, 753 (1982))).

3. There was no error in the determination of a trial judge to terminate parental rights as to the biological mother, but not as to the biological father, of the subject children. "We do not agree . . . that the legislative scheme authorizes only an order terminating the parental rights of both parents." *Adoption of Willow*, 433 Mass. 636, 645 (2001).

Testimony Offered by Electronic Means

"[T]he denial of the wife's request to testify by electronic means was an abuse of discretion." *Bonaparte v. Devoti*, 93 Mass. App. Ct. 603, 608 (2018) (mother's presence at hearing was precluded by immigration status and she requested to participate in the hearing by telephonic or audiovisual means).

Unavailability

In G.L. c. 233, § 82(b), a child is unavailable under the following circumstances: (1) death or existing physical or mental illness or infirmity; (2) privilege; (3) lack of memory; (4) child is absent and attendance cannot be procured; (5) testimony would cause severe psychological or emotional trauma; or (6) incompetency. *See also Care & Protection of Rebecca*, 419 Mass. 67, 84 (1994).

The Supreme Judicial Court took the "opportunity to adopt as a matter of common law Proposed Mass. R. Evid. 804(a)(3) (1980), which would allow a declarant, in a civil case, to be deemed unavailable if he or she testifies to a lack of memory about the subject matter in question." *Hedberg v. Wakamatsu*, 482 Mass. 613, 614 (2019) (in a medical malpractice case the Supreme Judicial Court found that out of court statements made by a medical student should have been admitted as statements against interest by an unavailable party when the student testified that he did not remember the patient's surgery or postsurgery care other than a vague memory of a conversation concerning a consult).

3

Unsupported 51A Report

"The mother cites no authority for the proposition that evidence regarding an incident which was the subject of an *unsupported* 51A report may not be offered as evidence of current parental unfitness. The department did not conclude in 1992 that the mother did not cause Lorna's injuries. It determined that the 51A report was unsupported because of the absence of other signs of abuse. . . . [Additionally], the use of such evidence was not precluded by principles of collateral estoppel." *Adoption of Lorna*, 46 Mass. App. Ct. 134, 141 (1999).

Visitation Rights

1. "Before visitation rights may be terminated, the trial judge must make specific findings demonstrating that parental visits will harm the child. The same standard of clear and convincing evidence controls the decision to terminate a parent's visitation rights as it does the decisions concerning parental unfitness in both care and protection and adoption proceedings." *Care & Protection of Ian*, 46 Mass. App. Ct. 615, 620 (1999) (citations and quotation marks omitted); *see also Care & Protection of Thomasina*, 75 Mass. App. Ct. 563, 576–77, *review denied*, 455 Mass. 1107 (2009).

2. A judge may order visitation between the child and a guardian with whom she had lived for many years, and who long filled the role of the only parent for the child. *Youmans v. Ramos*, 429 Mass. 774 (1999).

3. Visitation between child and de facto parent was permissible as it was in the best interests of the child. *E.N.O. v. L.M.M.*, 429 Mass. 824, 829–31 (1999).

4. "While posttermination visitation may be allowed, the proper focus is on the best interests of the child. Here, the judge properly dispensed with the mother's right to consent to adoption after determining that she was an unfit parent. The judge then declined to permit further visitation. There was no error." *Adoption of Helen*, 429 Mass. 856, 863 (1999).

5. "[T]he question of visitation is separate and distinct from the question whether the child's best interests require termination of parental rights. There may be a variety of reasons why a child's postadoption best interests may include contact with a biological parent, including, as here, the parent's service as a resource for the child's developmental needs. That is a matter of the best interests of the child, however, and not an enforceable right of the biological parent." *Adoption of Vito*, 47 Mass. App. Ct. 349, 354 (1999).

6. Where it is in the best interests of the child, a judge may order postadoption visitation with a relative who is not a parent, de facto parent, sibling, or grandparent. *Adoption of Odetta*, 87 Mass. App. Ct. 576 (2015).

Waiver

"[T]he intent to give up a known right is necessary for waiver. Even in the case of a waiver of nonconstitutional, civil procedural rights, some present act or omission, or a prior agreement to waive, is required. It would be inconsistent with these principles to say that a waiver made in 1996, induced by the then-existing circumstances, would be effective in 1997 to bar a new [temporary custody] hearing precipitated by a change in those very circumstances." *Care & Protection of Manuel*, 428 Mass. 527, 536 (1998).

"Waiver by conduct may occur where a parent engages in misconduct after having been warned by the judge that such behavior will result in the loss of the right to counsel." *Adoption of Raissa*, 93 Mass. App. Ct. 447, 452 (2018) (citing *Commonwealth v. Gibson*, 474 Mass. 726, 741 (2016)).

Additional Materials

Note: The following materials are available in the eBook version of this Sourcebook. See the Electronic Download page at the front of this book for instructions on downloading a copy of the eBook.

Mental Health Reference Materials, by Virginia Merritt, M.D.
Brief Reference Table to Psychiatric Medications Used in Children, by Virginia Merritt, M.D.
Psychoactive Medication for Children and Adolescents: Orientation for Parents, Guardians, and Others, by Massachusetts Department of Mental Health
Psychoactive Medication for Children and Adolescents: Orientation for Parents, Guardians, and Others, by Massachusetts Department of Mental Health.

PART 4

Children Requiring Assistance: General Principles and Practices

NOTE Children in Need of Services (CHINS) was replaced by Children Requiring Assistance (CRA) pursuant to 2012 Mass. Acts c. 240, effective Nov. 5, 2012. See G.L. c. 119, §§ 39E–39L in Part 1 of this book for the entirety of the CRA statute. Some case law cited in this section was decided under CHINS, but remains relevant. Supplementary reference materials on CRA are included in this part's additional materials: Quick Reference Guide on CRA (prepared by the Children's Law Center of Massachusetts); CRA: Filing to Preliminary Hearing (chart prepared by the Juvenile Court Administrative Office); and CRA: Fact-Finding Hearing to Disposition (chart prepared by the Juvenile Court Administrative Office). For resources on mental health and clinical issues, please see the additional materials in Part 3 of this book.

Appeal

"A child, parent, legal guardian or custodian may appeal from any order or determination, whether final or not final, made under [G.L. c. 119, §§ 39E through 39H]." G.L. c. 119, § 39I.

Contempt

"Although we conclude that the Juvenile Court does not have the power of contempt for violation of conditions of custody because the plain language of G.L. c. 119, § 39G, as well as our case law, precludes Juvenile Court judges from issuing direct orders in CHINS cases, thereby prohibiting that court from charging a child with criminal contempt, we urge the Legislature to address and resolve this well-known and long-standing problem." *Commonwealth v. Florence F.*, 429 Mass. 523, 523 (1999).

Definitions

A child requiring assistance is "a child between the ages of 6 and 18 who: (i) repeatedly runs away from the home of the child's parent, legal guardian or custodian; (ii) repeatedly fails to obey the lawful and reasonable commands of the child's parent, legal guardian or custodian, thereby interfering with their ability to adequately care for and protect the child; (iii) repeatedly fails to obey the lawful and reasonable regulations of the child's school; (iv) is habitually truant; or (v) is a sexually exploited child." G.L. c. 119, § 21.

"Habitually truant" means "a school-aged child, not excused from attendance under the lawful and reasonable regulations of such child's school, who willfully fails to attend school for more than 8 school days in a quarter." G.L. c. 119, § 21. A "child 'willfully fails to attend school' when he or she acts purposefully, such that his or her behavior arises from reasons portending delinquent behavior." *Millis Pub. Sch. v. MP*, 478 Mass. 767, 783 (2018).

Dispositional Options

General Laws c. 119, § 39G provides for three alternatives for disposition. The court may:

(a) "subject to any conditions and limitations the court may prescribe, . . . permit the child to remain with his parents, legal guardian or custodian";

(b) "subject to such conditions and limitations as the court may prescribe, . . . place the child in the care of . . . a relative, probation officer or other adult individual . . . a private charitable or childcare agency . . . or . . . a private organization";

(c) "subject to the provisions of sections 32 and 33 and with such conditions and limitations as the court may recommend, place the child in the custody of the department of children and families."

A child who is the subject of a CRA petition "may not be confined in shackles or similar restraints or . . . placed in a locked facility or any facility designated or operated for juveniles who are alleged to be delinquent or who have been adjudicated delinquent." G.L. c. 119, § 39G.

a. A judge did not have the authority, under G.L. c. 119, §§ 39G and 39J, to order that the juvenile be enrolled in a specifically named, specialized private school and that the county pay for those educational expenses. *Oscar F. v. County of Worcester*, 412 Mass. 38, 40–42 (1992).

b. A Juvenile Court judge did not have the authority, under G.L. c. 119, § 39G to declare unconstitutional a Worcester school committee policy which called for the expulsion of any high school student who brought a weapon onto school premises. *Sch. Comm. of Worcester v. Worcester Div. of the Juvenile Court Dep't*, 410 Mass. 831, 832, 836–38 (1991).

c. "We held in [*In re Vincent*, 408 Mass. 527 (1990)] that § 39G authorized the judge to make an order determining the custody of the juvenile, and to make the custody subject to various conditions, but that § 39G does not authorize a judge to order a juvenile directly to attend school." *Sch. Comm. of Worcester v. Worcester Div. of the Juvenile Court Dep't*, 410 Mass. 831, 836 (1991).

d. If a child is in the custody of DSS, the court does not have the authority to order DSS to place that child in a specific program. *Care & Protection of Jeremy*, 419 Mass. 616, 621–23 (1995); *Care & Protection of Isaac*, 419 Mass. 602, 604 (1995).

Length of Disposition

The initial duration of any court-ordered CRA disposition may not exceed 120 days. G.L. c. 119, § 39G. After a hearing, the court that entered the initial dispositional order may "extend its duration for up to 3 additional periods, each such period not to exceed 90 days if the court finds that the purposes of the order have not been accomplished and that such extension would be reasonably likely to further those purposes." G.L. c. 119, § 39G. No dispositional order may continue "after the eighteenth birthday of a child named in an application for assistance authorized to be filed by a parent, a legal guardian or custodian or a police officer or after the sixteenth birthday of a child named in a petition authorized to be filed by a school district." G.L. c. 119, § 39G.

The standard for a judicial finding that the purposes of a dispositional order have not been accomplished, and that an extension for a period not to exceed six months would further those purposes, is a preponderance of the evidence. No "redetermination" or "readjudication" is required for such a dispositional extension. *In re Angela*, 445 Mass. 55, 55, 61–62 (2005).

Dismissal

The petitioner or any party may file a motion to dismiss at any time prior to a dispositional hearing, which motion may be allowed by the court if dismissal is in the best interests of the child or if all parties agree to the dismissal. G.L. c. 119, § 39G.

Expungement

When a CRA petition is dismissed prior to a factfinding hearing under Section 39G, the court shall order the expungement of any and all records pertaining to the case. G.L. c. 119, § 39E.

Parent's Right to Counsel

A parent has a "right to counsel at any hearing or proceeding regarding custody" of his or her child. G.L. c. 119, § 39F.

Process and Procedure

See G.L. c. 119, §§ 39E–39G.

Recusal

"The judge who conducted the hearing on the acceptance of the application for assistance shall not preside at any subsequent hearing." G.L. c. 119, § 39E. (Note: For practical considerations, these rights are often waived.)

Standard of Proof

The standard of proof is proof beyond a reasonable doubt. G.L. c. 119, § 39G.

Additional Materials

Note: The following materials are available in the eBook version of this Sourcebook. See the Electronic Download page at the front of this book for instructions on downloading a copy of the eBook.

Children's Law Center Quick Reference Guide on CRA
CRA: Filing to Preliminary Hearing (Chart)
CRA: Fact Finding Hearing to Disposition (Chart)

PART 5

Department of Children and Families Regulations

NOTE
The Department of Children and Families was in the process of rewriting its regulations as this book went to press. For the latest updates, practitioners are advised to consult the DCF website at http://www.mass.gov/orgs/massachusetts-department-of-children-families.

110 CMR 1.00. Principles and Responsibilities of the Department of Children and Families

110 CMR 1.01. Statement of Philosophy

The policy of the Commonwealth of Massachusetts and therefore of the Department of Children and Families (Department) is to strengthen and encourage family life so that every family can care for and protect its children. To that end, the Department will make every reasonable effort to encourage and assist families to use all available resources to maintain the family unit intact. However: for so long as a family cannot or does not provide the necessary amount of care and protection for its children, the Department will intervene to protect the right of children to sound health and normal physical and mental development. These dual obligations—to protect children and yet simultaneously to respect the right of families to be free from unwarranted state intervention—present an inherently difficult balance to strike. Yet, this is precisely the Department's mandate. The effort to balance these two basic obligations, above all others, shall govern the Department's activities.

110 CMR 1.02. Principles of Service

In delivering services to children and families the Department shall:

(1) seek to ensure the safety of children;

(2) recognize that, consistent with the need to ensure the safety of children, the family is the best source of child rearing, and so require that state intervention into a family unit be used only when it is clearly needed to protect a child;

(3) reflect the understanding that every child needs stability and permanency;

(4) recognize that substitute care is a temporary solution, and require the Department and the parent(s) to direct their efforts toward reunification of child(ren) and parent(s). As soon as it is determined that reunification is not feasible, the Department shall take swift action to implement another permanent plan, such as adoption or guardianship.

The Department recognizes that it operates not in isolation but in partnership with families. The Department seeks to assist parents in meeting their parental responsibilities, among which are:

(5) to maintain meaningful contact with the child(ren);

(6) to seek and utilize appropriate services to assist family reunification;

(7) to make good faith efforts to participate with the Department in developing and implementing a service plan;

(8) to maintain contact with the Department, especially concerning any change of address;

(9) to pay reasonable sums toward the support of the child(ren) within the limits of their ability to pay.

110 CMR 1.03. Goals for Children in Substitute Care

When parents are unable to care for their children in their own homes the Department is obligated to provide substitute care. These children come to the Department either through a court order or through a parent's voluntary request for substitute care. In either case the Department's goal is to alleviate or mitigate the causes necessitating placement; or in those circumstances where a child is unable to return home, to provide the child with a permanent new home in a timely fashion.

5

110 CMR 1.04. Courteous and Prompt Service

Each individual served by the Department shall receive courteous treatment at all times, and each such individual's personal dignity shall be respected. Services shall be provided as promptly as possible.

110 CMR 1.05. Fair, Just, and Equitable Provision of Services

The Department's services shall be provided on a fair, just, and equitable basis.

110 CMR 1.06. Special Provisions Relating to Linguistic and Cultural Minorities

The Department recognizes the special concerns of linguistic and cultural minorities in the Commonwealth. The Department shall be responsive to issues of ethnic and cultural diversity by utilizing social workers who are attuned to ethnic and cultural values and traditions. The Department shall ensure that both the services it provides directly and those it provides through providers or contracts are culturally sensitive to the various minority groups in the client population. In addition, the Department shall make all reasonable efforts to ensure that communications with every client, whether written or oral, are made in a language, or in a manner, that the client can understand. This requirement shall be satisfied as follows:

(1) The Department shall ensure that its social work activities are conducted by a social worker fluent in a language understood by the client. If such a person is unavailable, then the Department shall utilize an interpreter who can effectively communicate with the client.

(2) Deaf persons for whom American Sign Language is the primary language are rightly considered as a special linguistic minority population, and the Department shall utilize qualified oral or Sign Language interpreters who can effectively communicate with a deaf client.

(3) The Department shall ensure that any written communications from the Department to a client are in a language or a manner of communication that is understood by the client.

(4) Whenever a client is unable to read in any language, communications shall be made orally.

110 CMR 1.07. Special Provisions Relating to Native Americans

(1) The Department recognizes the special concerns of Native Americans in the Commonwealth. Accordingly, decisions affect-

ing Native Americans shall respect the unique values of Indian culture, whether or not the Indian child or family in question is a member of an Indian tribe as defined in 25 U.S.C. § 1903(8).

(2) The Department shall adhere to the provisions of the Indian Child Welfare Act (25 U.S.C. § 1901 et seq.). Where procedures or rights under Massachusetts law or regulation afford more protection than U.S.C. § 1901 et seq., then the former procedures or rights shall apply.

110 CMR 1.08. Special Provisions Relating to Handicapping Conditions

The Department recognizes the special needs of handicapped clients. The Department shall make reasonable accommodations to ensure that its services, facilities, communications, and meetings are accessible to all handicapped persons. The Department shall make reasonable accommodations to clients who have impaired sensory (i.e. visual, auditory) skills, including but not limited to sign language, Braille, large print type, and TTD (telephonic telecommunication device). The Department shall be responsive to issues of handicapping conditions by utilizing social workers who are attuned to the special needs of handicapped persons.

110 CMR 1.09. Special Provisions Relating to Nondiscrimination

(1) No applicant for or recipient of Department services shall, on the ground of race, creed, color, religion, age, ancestry, marital status, sex, sexual orientation, language, disability, veteran status, or national origin, be excluded from participation in, be denied the benefits of, or otherwise be subjected to discrimination in connection with, any service, program, or activity administered or provided by the Department.

(2) 110 CMR 1.00 does not prohibit the Department from recruiting foster parents or adoptive parents from groups of persons of specific race, creed, color, religion, age, ancestry, marital status, sex, language, or national origin to permit the pool of available foster and pre-adoptive families to reflect the ethnic and racial diversity of the children needing placement in substitute care.

(3) The Department shall not deny to any person the opportunity to become an adoptive or foster parent, on the basis of the race, creed, color, religion, age, ancestry, marital status, sex, sexual orientation, language, disability, veteran status or national origin of the person, or of the child, involved; or delay or deny the placement of a child for adoption or into foster care, on the basis of the race, color or national origin of the adoptive or foster parent, or the child, involved.

110 CMR 1.10. Special Provisions Relating to Incarcerated Parents

The Department recognizes the special efforts required to prevent permanent or irremediable separation of children from their incarcerated parents. Therefore, the Department shall make all reasonable efforts to work in cooperation with incarcerated parents to promote a healthy relationship with their children, and to avoid permanent separation. The Department's efforts shall include regular visitation at the correctional facility, as well as the holding of case conferences and other consultations at the correctional facility.

110 CMR 1.11. Special Provisions Relating to Homeless Families

In accordance with the Department's established policy of maintaining the integrity of families, the Department shall make all reasonable efforts to serve homeless families. Ensuring that families remain together whenever possible is a primary goal in serving the homeless. The Department's efforts on behalf of a homeless family shall include efforts to provide access to facilities which allow a family to feed, bathe, and care for their children, and which provide meals and a safe place to sleep for the adults and children. The Department confirms its commitment to provide comprehensive information and referral services for homeless families at the local area office level. Since many factors can cause or contribute to homelessness (including unemployment, substance abuse, domestic violence, inadequate income, inadequate shelter, and natural disasters) the Department also confirms its commitment to a multi-disciplinary and possibly multi-department approach to service delivery to a homeless family. Lastly, the Department affirms its policy that poverty or homelessness are not per se indicative of child abuse or neglect; and that children should never be removed from their parents and placed into substitute care on the sole basis of homelessness of a family.

110 CMR 1.12. Special Provisions Relating to Refugees/ Unaccompanied Refugee Minors

(1) The Department provides a range of social services to refugee families, in conjunction with the services of other departments (e.g. Transitional Assistance, Mental Health, etc.) and in cooperation with the Governor's Advisory Council for Refugees and Immigrants (GACRI) and the Massachusetts Office for Refugees and Immigrants (MORI). The Department offers refugees the full range of services described in 110 CMR. For services available to refugees beyond the social services offered by the Department (e.g. food stamps, SSI, ESL training, etc.) more information is available by contacting MORI directly, at 727-7888.

(2) The Department shall periodically offer training to its social work staff on the cultural and ethnic issues of those refugee populations which are statistically significant in Massachusetts.

(3) The Department operates an Unaccompanied Refugee Minors Program, which provides foster care and case management services to Indochinese (Vietnamese, Cambodian and Laotian) refugee children who arrive in Massachusetts unaccompanied by a parent or immediate relative. In every case the parents of such children are either deceased or of parts unknown. The intent of this program is to reunite such children with a member or members of their family. Services are provided to these minors by providers under contract with the Department. These providers are required to have a demonstrated ability to respond to the cultural and linguistic needs of the refugees they serve. The Unaccompanied Refugee Minors program is fully funded by the federal government through the Office of Refugee Resettlement. At present, a federal regulation requires that such children not be freed for adoption by the states. A proposed amendment to the federal regulation, to allow states to free such children for adoption, awaits enactment. The Department will adhere to the federal regulation in question.

110 CMR 1.13. Use of Commentaries

Commentaries are used throughout 110 CMR to clarify certain issues, concepts, or problems; as well as to give concrete examples of typical situations. The commentaries are intended to be illustrative, but they are *examples only*, and should not be read more broadly than the specific facts presented, nor to apply to fact situations different than those specifically described.

110 CMR 1.14. Future Changes

As 110 CMR go to press, several legislative, fiscal, or programmatic changes, which may be implemented over the next several months, are pending. As such changes are in fact implemented, 110 CMR will be revised, and substitute pages will be issued. In addition, several lists contained within 110 CMR (for example, list of antipsychotic drugs) will be revised as needed so that they continue to be up to date.

110 CMR 1.15. Severability

If any regulation or section, sub-section, sentence, clause, phrase or portion thereof is found to be invalid by a court of competent jurisdiction for any reason, said portion shall be deemed a separate, distinct, and independent provision, and the validity of the other regulations shall not be affected.

Regulatory Authority—110 CMR 1.00: M.G.L. c. 18B, § 7(i).

5

110 CMR 2.00. Glossary

Whenever used throughout 110 CMR, the following words shall have the following meanings, unless the context plainly requires otherwise.

Abuse means the non-accidental commission of any act by a caretaker upon a child under age 18 which causes, or creates a substantial risk of physical or emotional injury, or constitutes a sexual offense under the laws of the Commonwealth or any sexual contact between a caretaker and a child under the care of that individual. Abuse is not dependent upon location (*i.e.*, abuse can occur while the child is in an out-of-home or in-home setting.)

Antipsychotic Drugs shall mean drugs which are considered neuroleptics, in that they are used to treat certain psychotic symptoms. Such antipsychotic drugs shall include, but shall not be limited to:

Generic Name	Trade Name
1 Acetophenazine	Tindal
2 Amoxapine	Asendin
3 Butaperazine	Repoise
4 Carphenazine	Proketazine
5 Chlorpromazine	Thorazine
6 Chlorprothizene	Taractan
7 Fluphenazine	Prolixin, Permitil
8 Haloperidol	Haldol
9 Loxapine	Loxitane
10 Mesoridazine	Serentil
11 Molindone	Moban
12 Perphenazine	Trilafon, Etrafon, Triavil
13 Pimozide	Orap
14 Piperacetezine	Quide
15 Prochlorperazine	Compazine
16 Promazine	Sparine
17 Reserpine	—
18 Thioridazine	Mellaril
19 Thiothixene	Navane
20 Trifluoperazine	Stelazine
21 Trifluoperazine	Vesprin

Antipsychotic drugs include the above-listed drugs by whatever official name, common or usual name, chemical name, or brand name they may be designated. All isomers, esters, ethers, and salts of; and any combination of; drugs listed above are deemed to be antipsychotic drugs.

Area means one of the 29 geographic areas of the Department of Children and Families.

Area Director means the director of one of the Areas of the Department of Children and Families.

Caretaker means a child's:

(a) parent

(b) stepparent

(c) guardian

(d) any household member entrusted with the responsibility for a child's health or welfare

(e) any other person entrusted with the responsibility for a child's health or welfare whether in the child's home, a relative's home, a school setting, a day care setting (including babysitting), a foster home, a group care facility, or any other comparable setting. As such "caretaker" includes (but is not limited to) school teachers, babysitters, school bus drivers, camp counselors, *etc.* The "caretaker" definition is meant to be construed broadly and inclusively to encompass any person who is, at the time in question, entrusted with a degree of responsibility for the child. This specifically includes a caretaker who is him/herself a child (*i.e.* a babysitter under 18 years of age).

Central Registry means a subset of the Department's computerized system. Every area and regional office of the Department, as well as the Central Office of the Department, shall have access to the computerized system, via terminals and printers which shall be located in each such office. The computerized system shall have security procedures which protect the data contained therein against unauthorized users or access. The Department's Central Registry shall consist exclusively of data located within the designated subset of the Department's computerized system. No files, papers, index card systems, or any other form of document shall constitute a part of the Department's Central Registry.

Child means a person who has not reached his/her 18th birthday, but does not include unborn children.

Child in the Care of the Department means a child receiving services from the Department pursuant to a Voluntary Placement Agreement.

Child in the Custody of the Department means a child placed in the Department's custody through court order, including an order under a Child in Need of Services (CHINS) petition, or through adoption surrender.

Closed Referral means that a client may be referred to a provider only by the Department, *i.e.*, the provider may only be reimbursed by the Department for delivering the service(s) if the client was so referred. *Compare*, "Open Referral".

Commissioner means the Commissioner of the Department of Children and Families.

5

Contract means any agreement between the Department and a provider, and shall specifically include Purchase of Service Agreements, Master Agreements, *etc.*

Day means calendar day, unless noted to the contrary (*i.e.* "working day").

Department means the Department of Children and Families.

Designee means any Department employee designated by means of a written memorandum, bearing the written approval of the Commissioner or Deputy Commissioner, and filed with the General Counsel of the Department.

Diseases Dangerous to the Public Health is defined under 105 CMR 300.100 and 105 CMR 310.020 and includes the following:

(a) Actinomycosis

(b) AIDS (Acquired Immune Deficiency Syndrome)

(c) Animal Bite

(d) Anthrax

(e) Brucellosis (Undulant Fever)

(f) Chickenpox (Varicella)

(g) Cholera

(h) Diarrhea of the Newborn

(i) Diphtheria

(j) Dysentery, Amebic

(k) Dysentery, Bacillary (Shigellosis)

(l) Encephalitis (specify if known)

(m) Food Poisoning by:

1. Botulism

2. Mushrooms and other poisonous vegetable and animal products

3. Mineral or organic poisons such as arsenic, lead, etc.

4. Staphylococcal

(n) German Measles (Rubella)

(o) Glanders

(p) Hepatitis, Viral (includes Infectious and Serum Hepatitis)

(q) Impetigo of the Newborn

(r) Leprosy

(s) Leptospirosis (including Weil's Disease)

(t) Lymphocytic Choriomeningitis

(u) Malaria

(v) Measles (Rubeola)

(w) Meningitis (B. Influenzal, meningococcal, pneumococcal, streptococcal and other forms)

(x) Mumps

(y) Ophthalmia Neonatorum

(z) Plague

(aa) Poliomyelitis

(bb) Psittacosis

(cc) Rabies—Human

(dd) Rickettsialpox

(ee) Rocky Mountain Spotted Fever

(ff) Salmonellosis (except Typhi and Paratyphi)

(gg) Salmonellosis: Typhi and Paratyphi (Typhoid and Paratyphoid Fevers)

(hh) Smallpox (Variola)

(ii) Smallpox Vaccination Reactions—Generalized Vaccinia, Eczema Vaccinatum

(jj) Streptococcal Infections (including Erysipelas Scarlet Fever, Streptococcal Sore Throat, *etc.*)

(kk) Tetanus

(ll) Trachoma

(mm) Trichinosis

(nn) Tuberculosis

(oo) Tularemia

5

(pp) Typhus Fever (including Brills' Disease)

(qq) Whooping Cough (pertussis)

(rr) Yellow Fever

Electroconvulsive Treatment or **ECT** means a process that passes a controlled electric current into the brain to induce a seizure.

Emergency means a situation where the failure to take immediate action would place a family and/or child at substantial risk of serious and imminent family disruption, or death, or serious emotional or physical injury.

Extraordinary Medical Treatment shall include No-code orders, sterilization, electroconvulsive treatment, antipsychotic medication, withholding or providing life-prolonging treatment (as defined in this Glossary), and any other treatment determined to be extraordinary by using the following analysis:

Recognizing that it is impossible to itemize every extraordinary medical treatment, the Department shall utilize the following factors to determine whether a medical treatment is extraordinary:

(a) Complexity, risk and novelty of the proposed treatment: The more complex the treatment, the greater the risk of death or serious complications, the more experimental the procedure, then the greater the need to determine that the treatment is extraordinary, and to obtain parental consent or to seek judicial approval prior to authorizing treatment. *See, In the Matter of Guardianship of Richard Roe III*, 421 N.E.2d 40, 53 (1981). *In the Matter of Spring*, 405 N.E.2d 115 (1980). *In the Matter of Moe*, 432 N.E.2d 712 (1982).

(b) Possible side effects: The more serious and permanent the side effect, the greater the need to determine that the treatment is extraordinary, and to obtain parental consent or to seek judicial approval prior to authorizing treatment. *See, Superintendent of Belchertown State School v. Saikewicz*, 370 N.E.2d 417 (1977). *Rogers v. Commissioner of DWH*, 390 Mass. 489, 501-502 (1983). *In the Matter of Guardianship of Richard Roe III*, 421 N.E.2d 40 (1981). *Custody of a Minor*, 385 Mass. 697, 434 N.E.2d 601 (1982).

(c) Intrusiveness of proposed treatment: The more intrusive the treatment, the greater the need to determine that the treatment is extraordinary, and to obtain parental consent or prior judicial approval. *See, In the Matter of Hier*, 18 Mass. Appeals Court 200 (1984). *Superintendent of Belchertown State School v. Saikewicz, supra. In The Matter of Moe, supra. In The Matter of Spring, supra.*

(d) Prognosis with and without treatment: The less clear the benefit from the proposed treatment, the greater the need for parental consent or prior judicial approval. *See, Superintendent of Belchertown State School v. Saikewicz, supra*; *Custody of a Minor*, 385 Mass. 697, 434 N.E.2d 601 (1982); *In The Matter of Spring, supra.*

(e) Clarity of professional opinion: The more divided the medical opinion, the greater the need for parental consent or prior judicial approval. *See, In The Matter of Spring, supra.*

(f) Presence or absence of an emergency: In a medical emergency a physician can act without anyone's consent. *See*, M.G.L. c. 112, § 12F.

(g) Prior judicial involvement: if a court has been involved in past medical decisions, this argues for judicial involvement in any future medical treatment decision, but this is not conclusive. *See, In The Matter of Guardianship of Richard Roe III, supra* at 56.

(h) Conflicting Interests: Where the interests of the decision maker conflict with the interests of the child, the greater the need for obtaining parental consent or prior judicial approval. *In the Matter of Guardianship of Richard Roe III*, 421 N.E.2d 40 (1981).

Family Planning Services means medical, educational and social services, excluding abortion and sterilization, which enable individuals voluntarily to limit family size or plan spacing of children. Family planning services include the below-listed services. *See*, 106 CMR 269.030(A)(B) and 106 CMR 421.412.

(a) Information and referral (including outreach & follow-up)

(b) Individual and group counseling

(c) A physical examination:

1. for a female, includes thyroid, breast, heart, abdominal, speculum, pelvic, and rectal examinations, and measurements of height, weight and blood pressure;

2. for a male, includes thyroid, heart, genital, abdominal, and rectal examinations, and measurements of height, weight and blood pressure. *See*, 106 CMR 421.412(2).

(d) A pap smear for females. *See*, 106 CMR 421.412(3).

(e) Any laboratory test indicated by the child's history or examination. *See*, 106 CMR 421.412(4).

(f) A medically approved method of contraception. *See*, 106 CMR 421.427(5).

(g) Medical examinations, consultations, laboratory tests and contraceptive services rendered by a licensed physician

(h) Medical treatment for related conditions, such as venereal diseases or vaginal infections

(i) Prescriptions and medical items related to family planning services including drugs, supplies and devices

(j) Clinical follow-up

Foster Parent Applicant means a person who has applied to be a foster parent and meets the initial eligibility criteria set forth at 110 CMR 7.100.

Foster Parent means a person approved by the Department to be a foster parent in accordance with 110 CMR 7.100 *et seq.*

Guardian means the individual, organization or agency which has been appointed guardian of the person by a Court of the Commonwealth, in accordance with M.G.L. c. 201, or a court of competent jurisdiction in another state.

Guardian Ad Litem means the person appointed by a court to serve as an independent investigator for the court, not as an advocate for the ward, in a particular legal proceeding, without control over either the individual's person or property.

Handicapped Person means any person who:

(a) has a physical or mental impairment which substantially limits one or more of such person's major life activities,

(b) has a record of such an impairment, or

(c) is regarded as having such an impairment.

Incompetent means determination made by a court, in accordance with M.G.L. c. 201, that an individual does not have the legal power to direct his personal or financial affairs.

Institutional Abuse or Neglect means abuse or neglect which occurs in any facility for children, including but not limited to group homes, residential or public or private schools, hospitals, detention and treatment facilities, family foster care homes, group day care centers, and family day care homes.

Life-prolonging Treatment, as distinguished from live-saving treatment, means intrusive medical treatment where there is no prospect of recovery. *In the Matter of Earle A. Spring*, 380 Mass. 629, 405 N.E.2d 115, 120 (1980). Recovery does not mean the ability to remain alive but rather life without intolerable suffering. *Saikewicz*, 373 Mass. 728, 370 N.E.2d 417 (1977).

Mandated Reporters are defined at M.G.L. c. 119, § 51A and include: any physician; medical intern; hospital personnel engaged in the examination, care or treatment of persons; medical examiner; psychologist; emergency medical technician; dentist; nurse; chiropractor; podiatrist; osteopath; public or private school teacher; educational administrator; guidance or family counselor, day care worker or any person paid to care for or work with a child in any public or private facility, or home or program funded by the Commonwealth or licensed pursuant to the provisions of M.G.L. c. 28A, which provides day care or residential services to children or which provides the services of child care resource and referral agencies, voucher management agencies, family day care systems and child care food programs; probation officer, clerk/magistrate of the district courts; parole officer, social worker; foster parent; firefighter; or police officer, office for children licensor, school attendance officer, allied mental health and human services professional as licensed pursuant to the provisions of M.G.L. c. 112, § 165, drug and alcoholism counselor, psychiatrist, and clinical social worker.

Mature Child means a child who is able to understand the circumstances and implications of the situation in which he/she is involved and is able to participate in the decision-making process without excessive anxiety or fear. A child who is 14 years of age or older is presumed to be a mature child. Other relevant sources of law concerning a "mature child" include:

(a) M.G.L. c. 119, § 21 (CHINS);
(b) M.G.L. c. 210, § 2 (adoptions);
(c) M.G.L. c. 112, § 12F (certain medical treatment);
(d) M.G.L. c. 4, § 7 (general age of majority).

Medical Emergency means any immediately life threatening condition and shall include, but is not limited, to the following conditions.

(a) severe, profuse bleeding
(b) choking, blocked airway
(c) unconsciousness
(d) cardiac arrest
(e) cardio-vascular accident
(f) any fracture
(g) extensive burns
(h) severe cuts
(i) other similar severe injury
(j) other sudden signs of serious physical illness
(k) any condition where delay in treatment will endanger the life, limb or mental well being of the patient. *See*, M.G.L. c. 112, § 12F.

Possibility that a disease may deteriorate to an irreversible condition at an uncertain but relatively distant date is not an emergency. *See*, 104 CMR 2.11(3) and *In the Matter of Guardianship of Richard Roe, III*, 421 N.E.2d 40, 55; 383 Mass. 415 (1981).

In determining whether a medical emergency exists the relevant time period to be examined begins when the claimed emergency arises, and ends when the individual who seeks to act in the emergency could, with reasonable diligence, obtain parental consent or judicial review, as applicable. *See, Roe* at 55.

Mental Health Facility means a public or private facility for the in-patient care or treatment or diagnosis or evaluation of mentally ill or mentally retarded persons, except for the Bridgewater State Hospital. *See* M.G.L. c. 123, § 1. Community residential care facilities for children (as defined at 110 CMR 7.120) are not mental health facilities for purposes of 110 CMR.

Neglect means failure *by a caretaker*, either deliberately or through negligence or inability, to take those actions necessary to provide a child with minimally adequate food, clothing, shelter, medical care, supervision, emotional stability and growth, or other essential care; provided, however, that such inability is not due solely to inadequate economic resources or solely to the existence of a handicapping condition. This definition is *not* dependent upon location (*i.e.*, neglect can occur while the child is in an out-of-home or in-home setting.)

No Code order means a medical order regarding a terminally ill patient directing a hospital and its staff not to use heroic medical efforts in the event of cardiac or respiratory failure. Heroic medical efforts include invasive and traumatic life-saving techniques such as intracardial medication, intracardial massage and electric shock treatment. No code orders include "do not resuscitate" orders or orders stated in different language attempting to accomplish substantially the same result as a "no code" order. *See, Custody of a Minor*, 385 Mass. 697, 434 N.E.2d 601 (1982).

Non-mandated Reporters are all persons who are not mandated reporters.

Open Referral means that a client may be referred to a provider in any fashion (including client self-referral) and that the provider may thereafter be reimbursed by the Department for delivering the service(s), regardless of how the client was referred to the provider. *Compare*, "Closed Referral".

5

Outreach means those Department activities conducted in the community to make the community aware of the philosophy of the Department, the variety of social services offered by the Department, the ways to obtain Department services, and the Department's desire to work in conjunction with other community resources and agencies to meet clients' needs. Outreach activity provides a way for the Department to identify existing resources, duplications and gaps in services, and unmet service needs in the community.

Partner means a non-Department entity that is providing cash contributions to a provider, which, when joined with Department funds, result in funding the total cost of one or more services which are provided by a provider.

Preadoptive Parent means a person approved by the Department to be an adoptive parent in accordance with 110 CMR 7.200 *et seq.*

Pre-adoptive Parent Applicant means a person who has applied to be an adoptive parent and meets the eligibility criteria established by 110 CMR 7.100 and 7.200.

Pre-adoptive Placement means the provision of substitute care by pre-adoptive parents, pending their adoption of the child placed in substitute care with them.

Provider means any party agreeing by contract with the Department to provide one or more services, or agreeing by a Purchase of Service Agreement to serve Department clients. Some providers provide a comprehensive array of activities and services (investigation, case management, legal services, *etc.*) which parallel those of the Department. Other providers merely provide a single service (day care, counseling, *etc.*)

Region means one of the six geographic regions of the Department of Children and Families.

Regional Director means the director of one of the Regions of the Department of Children and Families.

Routine Medical Care shall include but is not limited to the following:

(a) Allergy Shots.
(b) Blood Pressure Test. *See*, 106 CMR 421.445(J).
(c) Comprehensive Physical Examination—documenting the finding of an unclothed physical examination including a complete system review pertinent to the age of the child, fundoscopic exam-

ination of the eyes for children over five years of age, and observation of the teeth and gums for children three years of age or older. *See*, 106 CMR 421.445(D).

(d) Dental Care.

(e) Developmental Assessment—the child's current levels of functioning in the below-listed areas, as appropriate to the child's age. *See*, 106 CMR 421.445(F).

1. gross motor development, including strength, balance, and locomotion

2. fine motor development, including eye-hand coordination

3. language development, including expression, comprehensive and articulation

4. self-help and self-care skills

5. social interaction and emotional development

6. cognitive skills, including problem-solving and reasoning abilities

(f) Diseases Dangerous to the Public Health Treatment of. *See*, M.G.L. c. 112, § 12F and 105 CMR 300.100.

(g) Drug Dependency Treatment. *See*, M.G.L. c. 112, § 12E.

(h) Family Planning Services. *See*, 106 CMR 421.401 *et seq.*

(i) Fractures, Treatment of

(f) Hearing Test. *See*, 106 CMR 421.445(K).

(k) Immunization—against diphtheria, pertussis, tetanus, measles, poliomyelitis, mumps, rubella and such other communicable diseases as may be specified by the Department of Public Health. *See*, M.G.L. c. 76, § 15 and 105 CMR 220.100.

(l) Laboratory Tests and Special Medical Studies—when determined by the examining physician to be necessary.

(m) Lead Poisoning Test. *See*, 106 CMR 421.445(P).

(n) Nutritional Status Assessment—the evaluation of the child's nutritional health in light of dietary practice and the entire health assessment (that is, history, physical examination, height and weight measurements, and the laboratory tests) and documentation of any nutritional disturbance or dysfunction. *See*, 106 CMR 421.445(G).

(o) Pelvic Examination. *See*, 106 CMR 421.445(0).

(p) Pregnancy Treatment—except abortion or sterilization. *See*, M.G.L. c. 112, § 12F.

(q) Preventive Health Services.

(r) Psychiatric Assessment. Evaluation or Treatment on outpatient basis, or up to 90 days on in-patient basis.

(s) Treatment—commonly prescribed for a specific physical illness, which treatment does not pose risks of permanent serious side effects or risk of death, *See, Custody of a Minor*, 375 Mass. 733, 379 N.E.2d 1053, 1064 (1978) or is determined not to be extraordinary medical treatment by using the analysis outlined in 110 CMR.

(t) Tubercular Skin Test or Chest X-ray.

(u) Venereal Disease Treatment. *See*, M.G.L. c. 112, § 12F; 105 CMR 300.140.

(v) Vision Test. *See*, 106 CMR 421.445(L).

Emotional Injury means an impairment to or disorder of the intellectual or psychological capacity of a child as evidenced by observable and substantial reduction in the child's ability to function within a normal range of performance and behavior.

Physical Injury means

(a) death; or

(b) fracture of a bone, a subdural hematoma, burns, impairment of any organ, and any other such nontrivial injury; or

(c) soft tissue swelling or skin bruising depending upon such factors as the child's age, circumstances under which the injury occurred, and the number and location of bruises; or

(d) addiction to drug at birth; or

(e) failure to thrive.

Sterilization means any medical procedure, treatment, or operation intended to render an individual permanently incapable of reproducing. *See, Matter of Moe*, 385 Mass. 555, 432 N.E.2d 712, 716 [n.]3 (1982); 106 CMR 485.002.

Substitute Care means the provision of planned, temporary 24 hour a day care when the parent or principal caretaker is unable or unavailable to provide care on a daily basis. Substitute care encompasses the provision of foster care, community residential care, and supervised independent living. The Department shall protect and promote the basic principle that every child has a right to permanent family by providing substitute care which is time-limited, community-based and in the least restrictive setting possible.

Substitute Judgment means a decision regarding proposed health care made for an individual incapable of consenting to his/her own health care, which would be made by the incapable individual if s/he were capable, taking into account his/her actual interests and preferences and also his/her present and future incapability. *See, Rogers v. Commissioner of Dept. of Mental Health*, 390 Mass. 489 (1983).

Support means to find after an investigation that there is reasonable cause to believe a report that a child has suffered abuse or neglect inflicted *by a caretaker*. Support shall mean the same as the earlier phrase Substantiate.

Unsupport means to find after an investigation a lack of reasonable cause to believe a report that a child has suffered abuse or neglect inflicted *by a caretaker*. Unsupport shall mean the same as the earlier phrase Unsubstantiate.

Venereal Diseases is defined in accordance with 105 CMR 300.100, 105 CMR 300.140 and 105 CMR 340.100 and includes.

(a) Chancroid

(b) Gonorrhea

(c) Granuloma Inguinale

(d) Lymphogranuloma Venereum

(e) Syphilis

Volunteer means any person who gives his/her services to the Department without any express or implied promise of remuneration.

Ward means a person who has been adjudicated incompetent and for whom a guardian has been appointed by a Probate Court in accordance with M.G.L. c. 201.

Regulatory Authority—110 CMR 2.00: M.G.L. c. 18B.

110 CMR 3.00. Information and Referral Services

110 CMR 3.01. Introduction

Information and referral services are services provided, upon request, to refer individuals with unmet social service needs to the most appropriate resource. Information and referral services include but are not limited to: evaluation of requests for social services; provision of information about the spectrum of service resources including Department services; referral of the person to one or more appropriate agency(s); and outreach services.

110 CMR 3.02. How to Request Information and Referral Services

Requests for information and referral services may be made in person, by telephone (telephone access shall be assured to deaf and hearing impaired persons through the Department's use of TTD (telephonic telecommunications device) equipment), in writing, or via the mail. A client may request information and referral services directly from the Department, or the client may be referred to the

Department by an agency or community professional. A Department employee shall collect the following information on every request or referral for information and referral services:

(1) date of request/referral;

(2) type of request;

(3) Department action taken;

(4) such other information as may be required.

110 CMR 3.03. Eligibility for Information and Referral Services

The Department shall provide information and referral services to all persons requesting such services. No other indication of need is required nor are there any eligibility requirements to be met prior to the delivery of this service.

110 CMR 3.04. Case Record

If as a result of information and referral services, the client wishes to apply for other services, then the Department shall establish a case record.

110 CMR 3.05. How Services Provided

Information and referral services are provided either directly by the social work staff of the Department or the Department may purchase comprehensive information and referral services, to supplement the Department's information and referral system.

Regulatory Authority—110 CMR 3.00: M.G.L. c. 18B, § 2(A)(15).

110 CMR 4.00. Intake

Selected Sections

110 CMR 4.01. Requests for Services

(1) 110 CMR 4.01 through 4.15 do not apply to single service cases. For single service cases, see 110 CMR 4.70 et seq.

(2) Any person located within the Commonwealth may request social services from the Department. Persons requesting social services must complete a written application form. Persons needing assistance in completing the written application form shall be furnished with assistance by the Department.

COMMENTARY

The Department frequently receives requests for services from persons who, while physically located within the Commonwealth, might be classified as "transients" or "temporary residents". Examples include families who have stopped in Massachusetts while moving from Florida to Maine and who are living with relatives, families who are temporarily residing at the Ronald McDonald House while their child receives specialized care at Children's Hospital, etc. The Department will not exclude such families from eligibility for Department services on the basis of these residency characterizations. Instead, the Department will accept applications from any person who has a bona fide physical location within Massachusetts, and the Department will thereafter proceed to review and assess the application in accordance with 110 CMR.

110 CMR 4.02. Review of Application

(1) When the Department receives a written application for social services, it shall first review the application to determine:

(a) the nature of the social service(s) requested,

(b) whether the service(s) requested lie within the mandate of the Department, and

(c) whether services are needed on an emergency basis.

110 CMR 4.03. Response Time for Application

(1) If after review it is determined that the social service(s) requested lie within the mandate of the Department, and that the services are not needed on an emergency basis, then the Department (or provider) shall next conduct an assessment. See 110 CMR 5.00. The assessment shall be completed within 45 working days after receipt of the application by the Department. Thereafter, if the applicant is found eligible, the Department shall proceed in accordance with 110 CMR 6.00: Service Plans and Case Reviews.

(2) If after review it is determined that the social service(s) requested lie within the mandate of the Department, and that the services are needed on an emergency basis, the Department shall

make a preliminary determination of the applicant's eligibility to receive social services. If the applicant is found eligible, the Department shall provide or authorize services within seven days from the date of receipt of the application; provided, however, that such determination of eligibility and provision or authorization of services will be made earlier if necessary to avoid serious and imminent risk to the health or safety of the applicant or a member of the applicant's family.

110 CMR 4.04. Eligibility to Receive Social Services

As part of the assessment or evaluation process (as well as during each case review—see 110 CMR 6.00), the Department shall determine an applicant's eligibility to receive social services. The Department shall make this determination on the basis of whether the applicant is in need of the social service(s) requested, in that the service, if provided, will assist the applicant to reach at least one of the departmental goals enumerated in M.G.L. c. 18B.

110 CMR 4.05. Decision to Provide Social Services to Eligible Applicants

(1) The decision to provide voluntarily requested social services to eligible applicants shall take into consideration:

(a) the availability of the service(s); and

(b) the client's willingness to pay all or a portion of the cost of the service(s), according to a sliding fee scale established by the Department, unless the service(s) in question is/are not subject to sliding fee.

(2) If no Department (or provider) service resources are currently available, the eligible applicant shall be placed on a waiting list.

(3) If an eligible applicant has an assessed ability to pay the entire cost of the social service, the applicant shall be provided information and referral services only, unless the service in question is exempted from the sliding fee requirement.

COMMENTARY

M.G.L. c. 18B, § 4 states that "subject to appropriation, services of the Department shall not be denied to any person on the basis of such person's financial assets or income." Thus, the availability of the Department's services is always subject to sufficient appropriation of funds to the Department by the Legislature, in order to meet the amount of demand. Beyond that limitation, the availability of the Department's services is secondarily limited by a client's ability and willingness to pay a portion of the cost of those services—for the Department is statutorily required to "establish a schedule of fees" in proportion to the client's ability to pay for the services. See, M.G.L. c. 18B, § 4.

On the basis of these statutory provisions, the Department has developed 110 CMR 4.00, which draw the distinction between universal eligibility to receive social services, and the consideration of assets and income in the Department's decision to provide social services subject to a sliding fee requirement. Thus, while no applicant will be ineligible for services on the basis of assets or income per se, the Department may take assets or income into consideration in a subsequent decision to offer services subject to a sliding fee agreement.

110 CMR 4.06. Notification of Eligibility

If the Department determines that an applicant is ineligible, then the Department shall give notice to said applicant. The notice shall be in writing and shall conform to the requirements set forth in 110 CMR 8.00.

110 CMR 4.07. Redetermination of Eligibility

(1) The Department shall redetermine each recipient's eligibility for services at the following times in connection with the case review process:

(a) At least every six months; or

(b) More often than every six months, when required on the basis of reliable information obtained by the Department or provider about actual or anticipated changes in an individual's circumstances and ability to pay for the service(s).

(2) Upon each redetermination of eligibility the Department (or provider) shall give notice to the recipient of the results of said redetermination. Whenever the recipient is found ineligible for services or whenever services are being reduced or terminated, the notice shall be in writing, and shall conform to the requirements set forth in 110 CMR 8.00.

110 CMR 4.08. Sliding Fee for Services

All Department services may be subject to a sliding fee as established by the Department, except for the following services:

(1) Information and referral services.

(2) Family planning services to persons under 18 years of age.

110 CMR 4.08A. Fees for Voluntary Substitute Care Services

(1) The Department will assess a fee when it determines that a child will be entering out-of-home care on a voluntary basis. The fee will include a portion based on the family's income and a portion based on an amount equal to 75% of the child's Supplemental Security Income (SSI) benefit, 75% of the child's Title II benefits, and/or an amount equal to 75% of the child's adoption or guardianship subsidy, if the child receives SSI benefits, Title II benefits, or an adoption or guardianship subsidy. Guardians will not be subject to the income based portion of the fee. The fee for services will never exceed the actual cost of services.

No fee will be charged to any family whose income is at or below 150% of the federal poverty level as revised annually and published by the United States Department of Health and Human Services in the Federal Register. When determining whether a family's income falls at or below 150% of the federal poverty level the federal poverty levels for each size family will be used.

The fee for substitute care services will be calculated as follows:

(a) The Department will determine the family's gross income. Supplemental Security Income (SSI), Title II benefits, and adoption or guardianship subsidy for a child will not be included in calculating gross income.

(b) If the family's gross income is at or below 150% of the federal poverty level for that size family unit, none of the fees listed in 110 CMR 4.08A will be charged.

(c) If the family's income is above 150% of the federal poverty level, the family will be charged as a portion of the fee, a specified amount based upon their income as set forth in a sliding fee scale established by the Department. Guardians will not be subject to the income based portion of the fee.

(d) If the family's income is above 150% of the federal poverty level and the child in placement receives SSI benefits, Title II benefits, or an adoption or guardianship subsidy, and the parent(s) is the representative payee of such benefits, the fee will also include an amount equal to 75% of the child's SSI benefit, 75% of the child's Title II benefits, and/or 75% of the child's adoption or guardianship subsidy. An amount equal to the remaining 25% will be retained by the parent or representative payee.

(2) The fee is computed on a daily rate and is due monthly.

(3) The Department will provide written notice to the family of the procedures for requesting a full or partial waiver to the fee at the time that the fee is first imposed.

(4) The Commissioner, or designee, may authorize a full or partial waiver of the fee if the family establishes:

(a) that the imposition of the fee would create an extreme financial hardship and/or;

(b) that the actual and reasonable monthly expenses directly attributable to the child in placement exceed 25% of the child's monthly SSI benefit. A waiver under 110 CMR 4.08A(4)(b) shall be in the amount by which the directly attributable reasonable expenses exceed the 25% figure.

COMMENTARY

This commentary is to provide examples where the actual and reasonable expenses directly attributable to the child in placement exceed 25% of the child's SSI benefit.

Family A is composed of two parents and two children, a son and a daughter. The daughter is in residential care but returns to the family home on weekends and vacations. The family is able to demonstrate

5

through bills, receipts, etc., that the actual expenses of the clothing, food and recreational activities for their daughter is $200.00 per month and that those expenses are reasonable. The daughter's SSI benefit is $350.00 per month. The family may receive a partial waiver of the fee by $112.50, the difference between $87.50 (an amount equal to 25% of the child's SSI benefit) and the actual cost of the child's care and expenses.

Family B is composed of a mother and her son. The son is placed in a residential program and spends weekends and vacations with his mother. When the son visits his mother a nurse is required to assist in the child's care. The nurse costs $75.00 per weekend for a total cost of $300.00 per month. The son receives $400.00 per month in SSI benefits. Under the Department's regulations, the mother would have paid $300.00 to DSS and would have retained an amount equal to $100.00 for the child's expenses. Upon request, the mother would receive a partial waiver of her fee by $200.00 as well as an amount equal to any other documented expenses which are reasonable and directly attributable to the child, such as those set forth in Family A.

Family C is composed of a father and a thirteen year old daughter. The daughter receives $375.00 in SSI benefits per month. The father uses a portion of that money to pay for a two bedroom apartment for his daughter and himself. The daughter is placed in a residential program through the Department. The father must maintain a two bedroom apartment for those times when his daughter visits on weekends and holidays. The father is able to demonstrate that the rental difference between a one bedroom and a two bedroom apartment is $150.00. Under the Department's regulations the father is requested to pay a fee of $371.25. The fee is composed of $90.00 based on the family gross income and $281.25, an amount equal to 75% of the child's SSI benefit. Upon request, the father may receive a partial waiver in the amount of $56.25, which is the difference between (1) $93.75, an amount equal to 25% of the child's SSI benefit, and (2) $150.00, the rental difference between a one bedroom and a two bedroom apartment.

(5) Any family may initiate a request for a full or partial waiver of the fee by filing a written request with the appropriate regional director and by providing appropriate documentation establishing that the fee would create an extreme financial hardship and/or that the actual and reasonable monthly expenses directly attributable to the child in placement exceed 25% of the child's monthly SSI benefit.

The Department's response to a request for a full or partial waiver shall be in writing. If the Department denies the request for a waiver in full or in part, the response shall include notice to the family of their right to request a fair hearing and the procedures for requesting such a hearing.

(6) If a family fails to pay the assessed fee, the family shall receive a warning letter. If a family receives a warning letter for three consecutive months, the family may receive a notice of termination and the Department may refer the case for debt collection.

(7) The family may request a fair hearing if:

(a) The family requested a full or partial waiver to the fee for substitute care services and the family disagrees with the denial of a waiver or the amount of the partial waiver;

(b) The family wants to dispute the computation of the fee or the termination of the service due to non-payment; or

(c) The family maintains that the Department erroneously has determined that family's gross income exceeds 150% of the federal poverty level for that size family unit.

If the family requests a fair hearing, services shall not be terminated until a fair hearing is held as long as the family continues to pay all assessed fees. If the issue for the fair hearing is the denial of a request for a waiver or the amount of a partial waiver of a fee for substitute care services under 110 CMR 4.08A(7)(a) then only the undisputed portion of the fee must be paid pending the fair hearing. If the issue for the fair hearing is whether the family's income falls at or below 150% of the federal poverty level under 110 CMR 4.08(7)(b) no fee is required pending the outcome of the fair hearing. However, if the denial of the full or partial waiver or the determination that the family's income is above 150% of the federal poverty level is upheld at the fair hearing, the total fee will be applied retroactively to the date the sliding fee agreement was signed, and the family will be responsible for paying past due amounts.

COMMENTARY

This commentary is to provide an example of a situation where a family would pay the undisputed portion of a fee pending a fair hearing on a denial of a partial waiver to the fee.

Example. Family A is assessed a fee of $250.00 for their child's placement. The family requests and is denied a partial waiver of the fee in the amount of $50.00. During the pendency of the fair hearing the family would be required to pay a $200.00 fee, which is the undisputed portion of the total assessed fee. If the denial of the partial waiver of the fee is upheld by the fair hearing, and it had been three months since the original fee was assessed, Family A would owe the Department $150.00 for the past due amount of the fee.

110 CMR 4.08B. Fees for Nonvoluntary Substitute Care Services

(1) The Department will assess a fee when nonvoluntary substitute care services are provided to a child. The fee will include a portion based on the family's income and a portion based on an amount equal to 75% of the child's Supplemental Security Income (SSI) benefit, 75% of the child's Title II benefits, and/or 75% of the child's adoption or guardianship subsidy, if the child receives SSI benefits, Title II benefits, an adoption subsidy or a guardianship subsidy. Guardians will not be subject to the income portion of the sliding fee. The fee for services will never exceed the actual cost of services.

No fee will be charged to any family whose income is at or below 150% of the federal poverty level as revised annually and published by the United States Department of Health and Human Services in the Federal Register. When determining whether a family's income falls at or below 150% of the federal poverty level, the federal poverty levels for each size family will be used.

5

The fee for nonvoluntary substitute care services will be calculated as follows:

(a) The Department will determine the family's gross income. Supplemental Security Income (SSI), Title II benefits, an adoption subsidy, or a guardianship subsidy for a child will not be included in calculating gross income.

(b) If the family's gross income is at or below 150% of the federal poverty level for that size family unit, none of the fees listed in 110 CMR 4.08B will be charged.

(c) If the family's income is above 150% of the federal poverty level, the family will be charged as a portion of the fee, a specified amount based upon their income as set forth in a sliding fee scale established by the Department. Guardians will not be subject to the income portion of the sliding fee.

(d) If the family's income is above 150% of the federal poverty level, and the child in placement receives SSI benefits, Title II benefits, an adoption subsidy, or a guardianship subsidy and the parent is the representative payee of such benefits, the fee will also include an amount equal to 75% of the child's SSI benefit, 75% of the child's Title II benefits, and/or 75% of the child's adoption or guardianship subsidy. An amount equal to the remaining 25% will be retained by the parent or representative payee.

(2) If a family fails to pay the assessed fee for nonvoluntary substitute care, the family shall receive a warning letter. If a family receives a warning letter for three consecutive months, the family may receive a notice of termination and the Department may refer the case for debt collection.

(3) The provisions of 110 CMR 4.08A(2) through 4.08A(5) and 4.08A(7) apply equally to 110 CMR 4.08B.

110 CMR 4.08C. Fees for All Services Other than Substitute Care

(1) For all Department services subject to a sliding fee, other than substitute care services, the Department may assess a fee based solely on the family's income. Guardians will not be subject to this fee. The fee for services will never exceed the actual cost of services.

No fee will be charged to any family whose income is at or below 150% of the federal poverty level as revised annually and published by the United States Department of Health and Human

Services in the Federal Register. When determining whether a family's income falls at or below the federal poverty level, the federal poverty levels for each size family will be used.

The fee for all services other than substitute care will be calculated as follows:

(a) The Department will determine the family's gross income. Supplemental Security Income (SSI), Title II benefits, an adoption subsidy, or a guardianship subsidy for a child will not be included in calculating gross income.

(b) If the family's gross income is at or below 150% of the federal poverty level for that size family unit, none of the fees listed in 110 CMR 4.08C will be charged.

(c) If the family's income is above 150% of the federal poverty level, the family will be charged as the fee, a specified amount based upon their income as set forth in a sliding fee scale established by the Department.

(2) If a family fails to pay the assessed fee, the family shall receive a warning letter. If a family receives a warning letter for three consecutive months, the family may receive a notice of termination and the Department may refer the case for debt collection.

(3) The provisions of 110 CMR 4.08A(2) through 4.08A(5) and 4.08A(7) apply equally to 110 CMR 4.08C.

5

110 CMR 4.09. Parents of Children Who Are in Substitute Care and Are Entitled to S.S.I./Soc. Sec./VA/Other Benefits

(1) The Department will require parents of children entitled to S.S.I./Soc. Sec./VA/Other Benefits to participate in the financial support of their children while in Department-funded substitute care. When children are placed in substitute care pursuant to either a Voluntary Placement Agreement or court-ordered custody, either:

(a) The parents will continue to serve as Representative Payee on behalf of their entitled children and pay the Department an amount equal to 75% of the monthly benefits towards, but not exceeding, the actual cost of each child's care provided by the Department. However, if the family's gross income as defined in 110 CMR 4.08A is at or below 150% of the federal poverty level, no payment will be requested; or

(b) The Department will apply for benefits and/or to be designated as Representative Payee on behalf of the entitled children. As Representative Payee, the Department will set aside in a Personal Needs Account (PNA) 10% of the benefits up to but not to exceed the amount of $2,000, to be used only for the entitled child's personal needs. The remaining 90% of the benefits (100% of the benefits whenever the PNA reaches $2,000) will be used to reimburse the Department for the cost of the entitled child's care. The Department periodically establishes a uniform "personal needs allowance" for children who receive third party benefits.

(2) The entitled child shall be allowed, subject to approval by the Representative Payee, to spend from his/her PNA for personal needs. Whenever money is spent from the PNA, the PNA will be refunded with 10% of the entitled child's future benefits until the PNA reaches an amount of $2,000.

The Department will use a standard form of Voluntary Placement Agreement which will contain an express agreement between the Department and the parents that the parents will comply with requirement 110 CMR 4.09(a) or (b).

It should be noted, in contrast, that in cases of adoption or guardianship, the adoptive parent/legal guardian retains the child's entire S.S.I./Soc. Sec./or other payment, which is then supplemented by the Department, up to the full amount of the child's adoption or guardianship subsidy.

110 CMR 4.10. Voluntary Placement Agreements—Execution

Upon the request of one or both parent(s) or parent substitute(s) and when supported by an assessment of the needs of the child which has been conducted by the Department, the Department may agree to provide substitute care for a child. Every voluntary placement into substitute care shall be accomplished by completion of the Department's standard form of Voluntary Placement Agreement, between the parent(s) or parent substitute and the Department.

110 CMR 4.11. Voluntary Placement Agreements—Form

The Department shall utilize a standard form of Voluntary Placement Agreement, as established by the Department. This Voluntary Placement Agreement shall automatically expire after six months, and must be re-executed if the voluntary placement is to be continued. All Voluntary Placement Agreements shall be approved by, and then signed by, a departmental Area Director or Assistant Area Director or his/her designee. The Voluntary Placement Agreement is intended to be a flexible document adaptable to the individual needs and circumstances of the client or family—thus the standard form may be modified as appropriate, so long as any such modifications are in writing and are approved by both the client and the Department.

110 CMR 4.12. Voluntary Placement Agreements—Termination

(1) Any Voluntary Placement Agreement may be terminated by one or both parent(s) who have legal custody of the child giving written notice to the Department, regardless of which parent has signed the Voluntary Placement Agreement (i.e., if mother signs the Voluntary Placement Agreement, father may terminate it so long as he has some form of legal custody of the child).

(2) In any case where a parent gives notice to the Department terminating a Voluntary Placement Agreement (including but not limited to cases where one parent has signed the agreement and the other parent gives notice to terminate it) the Department shall honor the Agreement for a period of 72 hours thereafter. If, during said 72 hour period, the Department determines that the child would be at risk of abuse or neglect if returned home, the Department may institute court proceedings to obtain custody of the child.

(3) If any child(ren), who was placed in substitute care as a result of a voluntary placement agreement, is returned home to live with her/his parent(s), the voluntary placement agreement shall automatically terminate. If the parent wishes to voluntarily place the child back into substitute care, a new voluntary placement agreement must be executed pursuant to 110 CMR 4.10. 110 CMR 4.12(3) does not apply if the child(ren) is visiting her/his parents.

110 CMR 4.13. Voluntary Placement Agreements—Mature Child

The Department may accept a Voluntary Placement Agreement from a mature child, without signature of any parent(s). However, such Voluntary Placement Agreements (signed only by the mature child) will only be accepted and honored by the Department for a period of 72 hours thereafter. During that 72 hour period, the Department shall notify the parent(s) of the child, verbally or in writing, that the child has signed a Voluntary Placement Agreement with the Department and is in substitute care. During that 72 hour period, parent(s) shall not have the right to revoke or terminate the Voluntary Placement Agreement, nor shall they have the right to know the whereabouts of the child, unless the child specifically agrees and unless the Department determines that to so inform the parent(s) would not be contrary to the child's best interests. At the conclusion of the 72 hour period, the Department shall either return the child to his/her parent(s), or shall institute court proceedings to obtain custody of the child, or shall obtain a Voluntary Placement Agreement signed by the mature child's parent(s).

110 CMR 4.14. Voluntary Placement Agreements—Miscellaneous

In addition to the rights and duties enumerated in the standard form Voluntary Placement Agreement, the Department shall also exercise the following rights:

(1) Interviews of Children. The Department may receive requests from various sources to allow third parties to interview

child(ren). Examples include: media, police officers, district attorneys, other social work professionals (however 110 CMR 4.14 does not apply to interviews of children conducted by social workers employed by the Department), etc.

(a) From a Police Officer or a Representative of the District Attorney's Office. the parent(s) retain the right to determine if their child will be available for an interview unless the child is a mature minor and consents on his/her own. If a child is a possible or known defendant in a criminal action, the Department, Department foster/pre-adoptive parents or other Department providers caring for children in the Department's care cannot consent to having the child interviewed irrespective of whether or not the child is considered by the Department to be mature. In this situation, the Department may go to court and request the appointment of a Guardian Ad Litem with authority to determine whether the child should/will consent to participate in any kind of police interrogation.

(b) All Other Requests. The Department, upon receipt of such requests, will make all reasonable efforts to consult with the parent(s) by telephone. If contact with the parent(s) is made, the Department will honor the parent(s) wishes. If the Department is unable to contact the parent(s), the Department shall not consent to such interviews, unless there are special circumstances under which the interview would further the best interests of the child, in which case the Department may consent.

(2) School Permissions. If the child is enrolled in any public school, private school, group care facility, day care facility, residential placement, or other such facility, the facility may request or require a variety of consent forms to be signed. Examples include: sports participation forms, field trip forms, driving forms, etc. The Department (including departmental foster parents) will exercise its clinical judgment to determine whether or not it is in the child's best interests to have the form signed, and the Department (including departmental foster parents) will consent or deny on that basis.

(3) Permits, Licenses. The child may wish to obtain various permits or licenses. Examples include: hunting and fishing permits, driver's licenses, motorcycle licenses, etc. Such permit(s) or license(s) may require parental consent or signature. If this occurs, the Department will make all reasonable efforts to consult with the parent(s) by telephone. If contact with the parent(s) is made, the Department will honor the parent's wishes. If the Department is unable to contact the parent(s), the Department will exercise its clinical judgment to determine whether or not it is in the child's best interests to obtain such permit or license, and the Department will consent or deny on that basis.

(4) Permission to Marry. The Department (including departmental foster parents) will not consent to the marriage of any minor child in its care pursuant to a Voluntary Placement Agreement.

(5) Enlistments to Military. Upon receipt of a request from a child to enlist into military services, the Department will make all reasonable efforts to contact the parent(s). If contact with the parent(s) is made, the Department will honor the parent(s) wishes. If the Department is unable to contact the parent(s), the Department will exercise its clinical judgment to determine whether or not it is in the child's best interests to enlist, and the Department will consent or deny on that basis.

(6) For all Issues Relative to Medical Authorizations. See 110 CMR 11.00.

(7) Religion. The Department (including departmental foster parents) will not procure or authorize any baptism or other religious ceremony for any minor child in its care pursuant to a Voluntary Placement Agreement.

110 CMR 4.15. Surrenders for Adoption

(1) The Department's social services are available to any birth parent(s) who voluntarily surrender their child(ren), to assist the parent(s) with the loss of their child(ren). Such services may include, but need not be limited to:

(a) counseling on separation and loss;

(b) involvement in a surrendering parent support group.

(2) The Department shall observe the following procedures prior to taking a voluntary Surrender from a birth parent:

(a) Explore alternatives to voluntary surrender with the parent(s), including casework services to assist parent(s) and child(ren) to remain together.

(b) If casework services are accepted, provide the services set forth in the service plan.

(c) If services are declined, the social worker shall record in writing in the case record the offer and declination of services.

(d) Before accepting a surrender, the social worker shall collect and record in the case record psycho-social and medical information about the child and the child's biological family.

(e) When one of the birth parent(s) is not present, the social worker shall obtain information relevant to assisting in locating the parent, so that placement or surrender can be explored.

(3) All surrenders shall be taken in conformity with M.G.L. c. 210, § 2. In addition:

(a) Parent(s) seeking to surrender their child(ren) shall be encouraged to bring two witnesses of their own choice in order to execute the surrender(s).

(b) In the event parent(s) decline to bring two witnesses of their own choice, one or more department employees shall act as witness on the parents' behalf.

(c) The Department will accept a voluntary surrender from any parent, including any parent who is a mature child, in conformity with 110 CMR 4.01 through 4.15. When a parent who is a mature child seeks to voluntarily surrender a minor child, the Department shall first explore with the mature child parent alternative family resources, including adoption by an extended family member.

(d) Parents of Indian (Native American) heritage shall be informed of their rights pursuant to the Indian Child Welfare Act.

110 CMR 4.16 to 4.19. Reserved

110 CMR 4.20. Receipt of Reports of Alleged Abuse or Neglect—Reporting Process

(1) During Business Hours on Business Days. To report known or suspected abuse or neglect of children, telephone calls by mandated and non-mandated reporters should be directed to the Department. The caller should select the area or regional office which covers the residence of the parent(s) or caretaker(s) of the child(ren) in question. When the residence of the child's parent(s) or caretaker(s) is unknown or outside the Commonwealth, or if the child is located in a hospital, the report should be made to the area or regional office closest to the caller, but shall be accepted by the Department if made to any area or regional office of the Department. Each area and regional office of the Department shall have one or more employees designated to receive "51A" reports.

(2) During Evenings, Weekends, and Holidays. To report known or suspected abuse or neglect of children, telephone calls by mandated and non-mandated reporters should be directed to the statewide Child-At-Risk-Hotline (1-800-792-5200).

(3) Reports Not Constituting Child Abuse or Child Neglect. The Department sometimes receives reports of subject matter or events which clearly do not fall within the Department's mandate (i.e. abuse or neglect of children). Examples include: reports of abuse of young adults (over 18 years of age); reports of elder abuse; reports that a certain teenager is not being allowed to date or is not being given money for the high school prom; reports that a certain department store mail order catalogue contains pornographic pictures of children. If an individual attempts to report a matter which is not child abuse or neglect to the Department or to the Child-At-Risk-Hotline, the reporter shall be advised that the

report is not appropriate. The Department shall treat such call not as a report of abuse or neglect, but rather as a request for information and referral services. See, 110 CMR 3.00. The Department shall also treat incomplete reports as requests for information and referral services. Example: Caller reports seeing an unknown child struck by an unknown adult; but has neither name nor address nor other identifying information for either the child or the adult.

(4) Transcription of Information. For any calls received which report child abuse or child neglect, the Department or Hotline employee shall transcribe the information into a computerized data base maintained by the Department. The information entered into the database will be printable onto a "51A" standard report form, as established by the Department.

(5) Identity of Reporter/Anonymous Reports. The caller must give his/her name and address if s/he is a mandated reporter. The Department will accept anonymous reports from non-mandated reporters if the caller refuses to identify him/herself. However, if the reporter gives identifying information the name will in fact be recorded for later use by the investigator. Mandated reporters shall be informed that they are required by law to submit a written report to the Department within 48 hours after making the oral report. (See, M.G.L. c. 119, § 51A).

5

110 CMR 4.21. Screening of Reports of Alleged Abuse or Neglect

Upon receipt of any oral or written "51A" report (whichever is received first), the Department shall immediately screen such report. The purpose of screening is to identify children at risk of abuse or neglect from a caretaker, and to distinguish the need for an emergency or non-emergency response. The screener may also provide the caller with information about other authorities (police, District Attorney, licensing agency, etc.) who should be called. Three examples of "screen out" situations are: (a) report where the identified alleged perpetrator is not a caretaker (but the Department shall not screen out reports on the sole basis that no alleged perpetrator is identified or that the perpetrator is unknown); (b) report where the incident or condition reported by the caller is so old that it should be screened out because of its outdated character; (c) demonstrably unreliable or counterproductive multiple reports.

Reports involving Department employees, household or family members of Department employees, foster parents, pre-adoptive parents or area board members shall be screened in accordance with 110 CMR 4.28.

COMMENTARY

This Commentary further explains the three screening decisions set forth in 110 CMR 4.21(a) through (c):

(1) The "caretaker" distinction is an important one, for the Department's primary duty is to protect children from abuse or neglect *inflicted by their parents or parent substitutes*. See, M.G.L. c. 119, § 1, paragraph 2: "The purpose of this chapter is to insure that the children of the Commonwealth are protected against the harmful effects resulting from the absence, inability, inadequacy or destructive behavior *of parents or parent substitutes*" (emphasis added). See also, 42 U.S.C. § 5102: "'[Child abuse and neglect' means the physical or mental injury, sexual abuse or exploitation, negligent treatment, or maltreatment of a child under the age of eighteen . . . *by a person who is responsible for the child's welfare*" (emphasis added).

For example, the rape of a small girl by a stranger in a vacant lot, while certainly an incident of "child abuse" in the broad sense, is not the type of child abuse which the Department's investigation process was created to address. The criminal justice system remains primarily responsible for the investigation of such acts.

Thus, if the Department receives a report where the alleged perpetrator is identified and is clearly a non-caretaker, the Department shall screen out such a report. However, Department employees shall refer the case to the District Attorney if the allegations contained in the report fall into one of the categories under M.G.L. c. 119, § 51B(k). The Department shall also provide the caller with the name, address, and telephone number of the local police and/or appropriate District Attorney. The Department can also offer voluntary services to the child-victim and his/her family, as appropriate. (See, 110 CMR 4.50 through 4.54 for mandatory referral to the District Attorney).

(2) The Department sometimes receives reports of incidents which the caller identifies as very outdated (for example, a caller who reports an incident of a parent seen striking a child five years ago). The Department shall "screen out" reports for age where the reporter has no reasonably current information to convey, and where there is no reason to suspect that the child is still at risk of ongoing abuse. When a social worker determines that a call should be screened out, the screening information and recommendation to screen out shall be forwarded to the Area Director, or his/her designee, who shall make the final decision.

(3) In extreme cases, reports may also be screened out for a demonstrated history of unreliability (i.e., a series of similar reports from the same reporter, which have on several occasions been investigated and found to be without merit.) The Department shall "screen out" reports for unreliability in cases where the repetitive and meritless nature of the reports is well established. When a social worker determines that a call should be screened out, the screening information and recommendation to screen out shall be forwarded to the Area Director, or his/her designee, who shall make the final decision.

Reliable but repetitive reports may be "screened out" by the Department:

Multiple 51A's on the same incident:

It is not unusual for professionals and nonprofessionals to learn of an abusive incident over a broad range of time. Once learning of the incident, they quite appropriately file a 51A report.

Example: Child is brought to Hospital A by parents. Hospital A believes injuries were the result of abuse, and files a 51A. However, Hospital A is a small community hospital, and a large well-known hospital with more pediatric expertise is not far away. Hospital A refers or transfers the child to Hospital B the next morning, for further examination and testing. Hospital B, upon examining the child, also files a 51A.

Example: Mrs. H.'s daughter Tina was severely sexually abused while in the care of a babysitter. The doctor and police involved in the incident file their 51A reports. The Department investigates and supports the report. Nine days later, Tina begins to tell her story to her new therapist who is mandated to report. Six months later, a relative learns of the incident and calls to report sexual abuse. A year later, Mrs. H. changes therapists . . . etc.

Duplicate investigations are unnecessarily intrusive to a family and do not permit effective use of the Department's staff resources. In situations such as this, the screening decision shall be made by the Area Director, or his/her designee.

110 CMR 4.22. Screening—Collateral Contacts

In addition to consultation with the reporter, screening will include checking of Department files and the Department's Central Registry. Screening may also include collateral contacts with third parties. Any such collateral contacts made shall be documented in writing on the 51A form.

110 CMR 4.23. Screening—Entry Into Central Registry

Each 51A report (whether or not "screened out") shall thereafter be entered into the Department's Central Registry.

110 CMR 4.24. Screening—Notification to Mandated Reporters

The Department shall notify mandated reporters in the event that it decides to screen out a 51A report filed by said mandated reporter. Said notification of the Department's screen out decision shall be accomplished by means of a standard form letter established by the Department.

110 CMR 4.24A. Screening—Identification of Family Members

Prior to the initiation of an investigation, the screener shall identify all family members that are known to the screener. For the purpose of screening and investigation, family is defined as all family members and other individuals residing in the home, children in DCF placements, children residing out of the home, and any parent/parent substitute living out of the home.

110 CMR 4.25. Screening—Emergency and Non-Emergency Responses

(1) If the screener determines:

(a) that the report constitutes an event or subject matter within the Department's mandate; and

(b) that the reported condition poses a threat of immediate danger to the life, health, or physical safety of the child, then the screener shall designate the report an "emergency report" and cause the matter to be assigned for an immediate investigation as provided hereafter in 110 CMR.

(2) If the screener determines:

(a) that the report constitutes an event or subject matter within the Department's mandate; and

(b) that the reported condition does not pose a threat of immediate danger to the life, health or physical safety of the child, then the screener shall designate the report a "non-emergency report" and cause the matter to be assigned for an investigation as provided hereafter in 110 CMR 4.27.

110 CMR 4.26. Investigation of Emergency Reports

(1) Once a report is designated an "emergency report", the Department shall immediately initiate an emergency response. The first priority of an emergency response is to view the child(ren) in question, and to determine the condition of any other children residing in the same household. The children are visited a minimum of one time within 24 hours after receipt of the report. This meeting should occur in the home; however, in certain situations the social worker and supervisor may decide that another location is more appropriate (e.g., the child is hospitalized, the injury/incident occurred outside the home, the child would be placed at greater risk if interviewed in the home).

Parents and other individuals living in the home are visited a minimum of one time, within 24 hours after the receipt of the report. The investigator and supervisor determine which family members will be contacted based on their determination of which individuals would be expected to provide significant information regarding the current allegations.

(2) If an emergency report is received by the Child-At-Risk Hotline during evenings, weekends or holidays, the Child-At-Risk Hotline staff may request the assistance of local law enforcement personnel if on-call investigation personnel cannot immediately respond. This will occur in circumstances where there is an apparent immediate threat to the safety of the child and where due to geographic distances the on-call social worker cannot respond as quickly as the situation demands. In these circumstances, the Hotline will contact the local police department and ask the police to verify the allegations (e.g., abandonment, intoxicated caretaker, violent domestic dispute) and if necessary to provide temporary protection for the child until the Department's on-call personnel can reach the child's location.

(3) If an individual or family prevents an investigator from viewing a child who is the subject of the report or from determining the name, age or condition of other children in the same household that the investigator has determined should be viewed, the investigator shall, if the investigator has reason to believe that the child is in immediate danger of serious physical harm resulting from abuse or neglect, seek the aid of the local police in entering the home or otherwise viewing the child. The investigator shall, if practicable, obtain the approval of his/her supervisor, and may in addition choose to consult with a member of the legal staff to determine what legal action may be warranted. In the alternative, the investigator may use the 24-hour Judicial Hotline to obtain judicial assistance, with the approval of his/her supervisor. If the investigator remains unable to view the child, the investigator's supervisor will make the investigation decision based on his/her evaluation of the nature and contents of the 51A report and any collateral information.

(4) Once the child(ren) have been viewed and their condition determined, the Department must make an initial determination of the child(ren)'s safety and a determination of whether to seek custody of the child(ren) within 24 hours of receipt of the report and may:

(a) determine that the child's condition presents an emergency, in which case the investigation of the emergency report shall be completed as soon as possible and in no event later than five working days from the time the report is received. The investigation shall be conducted in the same manner as investigations of non-emergency reports (set forth in 110 CMR 4.27).

(b) determine that the child's condition does not present an emergency, in which case the investigation of the emergency report shall be conducted in the same manner and in the same timeframe as investigation of non-emergency reports (set forth in 110 CMR 4.27).

110 CMR 4.27. Investigation of Non-Emergency Reports

(1) The investigation shall include a viewing of the child who is the subject of the report and a visit to the home of the child who is the subject of the report both of which shall occur within three working days after the screening decision. (See 110 CMR 4.27(3) for procedures when an individual or family refuses to permit a viewing of the child.) The investigator may waive the visit to the home of the child in appropriate circumstances (for example, if the abuse alleged occurred outside the child's home in a day care facility and if the child is viewed at the day care facility). The investigation shall include a determination of the name, age, and condition of other children in the same household. The Department will ensure that the investigation includes the linguistic capacity and cultural knowledge needed to perform a fair and comprehensive investigation of the reported child and family.

5

(2) The investigation shall include consulting with the reporter, checking Department files and the Central Registry, arranging medical examination(s) where appropriate, and making any collateral contacts necessary to obtain reliable information which would corroborate or disprove the reported incident and the child's condition. In the course of making such collateral contacts, Department social workers may disclose sufficient information about the child(ren) and the family as is reasonably necessary to investigate the allegations made in the 51A report. However, the parent(s) or caretaker(s) of the reported child, the reported child him/herself, and the reporter, are to be considered the primary sources of information. Parents and other individuals living in the home are visited a minimum of one time, the initial visit occurs in the home within three working days after the screening decision. Any parent or parent substitute living out of the home, who can be located, is contacted a minimum of one time. The nature of the contact is determined by the investigator and supervisor.

(3) If an individual or family prevents an investigator from viewing a child who is the subject of the report or from determining the name, age or condition of other children in the same household that the investigator has determined should be viewed, the investigator shall, if the investigator does not have reason to believe that the child is in immediate danger of serious physical harm resulting from abuse or neglect, immediately inform his/her supervisor. The supervisor shall confer with a member of the legal staff to determine what legal action may be warranted. The Department may choose to waive a home visit if it is able to view the child in some other location. If the investigator remains unable to view the child, the investigator's supervisor will make the support/unsupport decision based on his/her evaluation of the nature and contents of the 51A report and any collateral information.

(4) The manner in which the investigator views the child who is the subject of a 51A report shall take into account and shall respect the child's age, sex, and other circumstances, particularly with respect to removal of the child's clothing.

(5) At the time of the first contact with parent(s) or caretaker(s), the investigator shall deliver to said individual a statement of rights which shall include written notice that a 51A report has been made, the nature and possible effects of the investigation, and that information given could and might be used in subsequent court hearings. Such notice shall be in a form prescribed by the Department.

(6) Based on the investigation, the investigator shall determine:

(a) the existence, nature, extent and cause or causes of the alleged abuse or neglect;

(b) the identity of the person or persons alleged to be responsible therefor, if possible;

(c) the name, age and condition of all other children in the same household; and

(d) all other pertinent facts or matters which in the opinion of the investigator are necessary to support or unsupport the allegation which was reported to the Department.

110 CMR 4.28. Screening and Investigation of Reports Involving Department Employees, Department Employee's Household or Family Members, Foster Parents, Pre-Adoptive Parents or Area Board Members

Whenever the Department receives a 51A report involving a Department employee, or a member of a Department employee's immediate household, the report shall immediately be referred to the Commissioner or designee. The Commissioner or designee will assign the report to the Central Office Special Investigations Unit or to an independent contracted agency for screening and/or investigation.

Whenever the Department receives a 51A report involving a Department employee's non-household family member, Department foster parent, pre-adoptive parent, or area board member, the report shall be screened by the area where the home is located and if the report is screened in, the matter shall thereafter be referred to the Central Office Special Investigation Unit, or to another Area or Regional Office of the Department (not the Area or Regional Office which has primary responsibility for the family member, foster home, pre-adoptive parent, or area board member) or to an independent, contracted agency (provider) for investigation. The Central Office Special Investigations Unit shall also investigate any other 51A report at the request of the Commissioner.

5

110 CMR 4.29. Emergency Removal

(1) Emergency removal pursuant to M.G.L. c. 119, § 51A is an extreme measure requiring dire circumstances. Before arriving at a decision to effect an emergency removal, the Department shall consider the harm to the child that such removal inevitably entails.

(2) A child may be immediately taken into custody by the social worker if, after viewing the child, the social worker finds reasonable cause to believe:

(a) that a condition of serious abuse or neglect (including abandonment) exists, and

(b) that, as a result of that condition, removal of the child is necessary in order to avoid the risk of death or serious physical injury of the child, and

(c) that the nature of the emergency is such that there is inadequate time to seek a court order for removal.

(3) If an emergency removal occurs, the removing social worker shall on the next working day make a written report which shall state the reason(s) for such removal, shall be reviewed by the Supervisor, and shall thereafter be filed in court together with a petition pursuant to M.G.L. c. 119, § 24.

110 CMR 4.30. Assignment of Second or Subsequent Reports for Investigation

In the event that a second or subsequent report is received and screened in on an open case or any case which has been closed during the previous twelve months, the Department shall not assign such report for investigation to any social worker who has had any previous responsibility for the case, unless a second report is received and screened in during the investigation of the initial report (in which case the same social worker may be assigned to investigate both reports) or unless there is no social worker meeting the foregoing description among the staff of the office in question.

110 CMR 4.31. Time Frames for Completion of Investigation

(1) The investigation of all "emergency reports" shall commence within two hours of initial contact and shall be completed within five working days after receipt of the report by the Department. The results of the investigation shall be in writing, transcribed onto a "51B" standard investigation form, as established by the Department.

(2) The investigation of all "non-emergency reports" shall commence within two working days of initial contact and shall be completed within 15 working days following the receipt of the report by the Department. The results of the investigation shall be in writing, transcribed onto a "51B" standard investigation form, as established by the Department.

110 CMR 4.32. Decision to Support/Unsupport a Report

(1) After completion of its 51B investigation, the Department shall make a determination as to whether the allegations in the report received are "supported" or "unsupported".

(2) To "support" a report means that the Department has reasonable cause to believe that an incident (reported or discovered during the investigation) of abuse or neglect by a caretaker did occur. To "support" a report does not mean that the Department has made any finding with regard to the perpetrator(s) of the reported incident of abuse or neglect. It simply means that there is reasonable cause to believe that some caretaker did inflict abuse or neglect upon the child in question. "Reasonable Cause to believe" means a collection of facts, knowledge or observations which tend to support or are consistent with the allegations, and when viewed in light of the surrounding circumstances and credibility of persons providing information, would lead one to conclude that a child has been abused or neglected.

Factors to consider include, but are not limited to, the following: direct disclosure by the child(ren) or caretaker; physical evidence of injury or harm; observable behavioral indicators; corroboration by collaterals (e.g., professionals, credible family members); and the social worker and supervisor's clinical base of knowledge.

(3) Each determination by the Department that the allegations of a 51A report are "unsupported" shall be communicated to the parent(s) or parent substitute(s), or, in the case of divorced parents, to both parents if both have some form of court-ordered custody, and if not, then only to the parent with court-ordered custody, within 48 hours after the determination that the allegations are unsupported, in a form letter established for use by the Department. All collaterals who were contacted by the investigator, shall be notified in writing of the decision to unsupport the report, unless the target of the investigation requests that such notification not occur. If the 51A report in question was filed by a mandated reporter, the mandated reporter is notified of the decision on a form established by the Department. If the 51A report in question contained an allegation of institutional abuse or neglect which occurred at a facility owned, operated, or funded, in whole or in part, by any department or office listed in 110 CMR 4.43, or at a facility operated by a person or entity subject to licensure or approval by any department or office listed in 110 CMR 4.43, then the director or owner of such facility shall also be sent a copy of said letter.

(4) Each determination by the Department that the allegations of a 51A report are "supported" shall be communicated to the parent(s) or parent substitute(s), or, in the case of divorced parents, to both parents if both have some form of court-ordered custody, and if not, then only to the parent with court-ordered custody, within 48 hours after the determination that the allegations are supported, in a form letter established for use by the Department. If the 51A report in question was filed by a mandated reporter, a copy of the letter shall also be provided to the mandated reporter is notified on a form established by the Department. In addition, upon request by any mandated reporter of a supported 51A report, the Department

shall inform the mandated reporter of the social service(s), if any, that the Department intends to provide to the child and/or the child's family. If the 51A report in question contained an allegation of institutional abuse or neglect which occurred at a facility owned, operated, or funded, in whole or in part, by any department or office listed in 110 CMR 4.43, or at a facility operated by a person or entity subject to licensure or approval by any department or office listed in 110 CMR 4.43, then the director or owner of such facility shall also be sent a copy of said letter.

110 CMR 4.33. Perpetrator/Caretaker

(1) Perpetrator: For any investigated and supported report of abuse or neglect, the Department shall record the identity(ies) of alleged perpetrator(s) when:

The incident of child abuse or neglect has been supported and referred to the District Attorney pursuant to M.G.L. c. 119, § 51B(k) and there is substantial evidence indicating that the alleged perpetrator was responsible for the abuse or neglect. See 110 CMR 4.37.

(2) Perpetrator: For any investigated and unsupported report of abuse or neglect, the Department's Central Registry shall automatically record perpetrator "not applicable".

(3) Perpetrator: Whenever the Department "supports" a 51A report and whenever the name(s) of alleged perpetrator(s) are recorded as such on the Registry of Alleged Perpetrators, the Department shall 20 working days after the referral is made to the District Attorney notify each alleged perpetrator that his/her name will be maintained on the Registry of Alleged Perpetrators. The Department shall utilize a form letter established for use by the Department. The form letter shall include notification to the alleged perpetrator(s) of the right to a fair hearing to appeal said listing. If the alleged perpetrator is a child under age 18, the letter shall be directed to the child, with a copy to the child's parent(s) and/or guardian. (See, 110 CMR 10.06(9)(c) for a stay of fair hearing proceeding at request of the District Attorney.)

(4) Caretaker: Where the Department has no reasonable cause to believe that a caretaker was the perpetrator of abuse or neglect, the Department will "unsupport" the report. (Note, however, that the Department may voluntarily refer or be required to refer the matter to appropriate law-enforcement agencies. See 110 CMR 4.50 et seq. Note also that the Department may offer voluntary services as appropriate.)

COMMENTARY

The meaning of a "supported" or "unsupported" report is often misunderstood, primarily because the Department sometimes unsupports a report where a child has clearly suffered an injury. While at first blush this can appear contradictory, it is in fact most often the result of the application of the important distinction between caretakers and non-caretakers.

The "caretaker" distinction is an important one, for the Department's primary duty is to protect children from *abuse or neglect inflicted by their parents or parent substitutes*. See, M.G.L. c. 119, § 1, paragraph 2: "The purpose of this chapter is to insure that the children of the Commonwealth are protected against the harmful effects resulting from the absence, inability, inadequacy or destructive behavior of parents or parent substitutes." (emphasis added).

The following examples may serve to clarify.

Example A: The Department receives a report of a small boy with burns around his lips and nose. It is screened in. It is investigated. The investigator determines that the injury occurred when the small boy pulled a heat lamp from his parents' bathroom onto his face. There is no evidence that the accident occurred as a result of either parents' neglect. The report is unsupported, as no incident of abuse or neglect is determined to have occurred. Note that if the facts were slightly different (for example, if the Department determined that the injury occurred because the small boy had been left alone at home all day) then the Department could have supported the report as neglect.

Example B: Teenaged girl reports that father has been sexually molesting her. In these circumstances, the Department will list the father as the alleged perpetrator. Since he is a caretaker, the Department will support the report, if the Department determines it has reasonable cause to believe the reported incident(s). The Department will also refer the matter to the District Attorney (See, 110 CMR 4.50 et seq.) and offer services as appropriate.

Example C: A school nurse reports that a sixteen year old female high school student has been sexually molested. After investigation, the Department determines that the perpetrator is the girl's sixteen year old boyfriend. Since he is not a caretaker, the Department will unsupport the report. Note that the Department may refer the case to the District Attorney (See, 110 CMR 4.50 et seq.) and offer voluntary services as appropriate.

Example D: Infant is brought to pediatrician by mother with numerous fresh facial bruises. Pediatrician characterizes them as non-accidentally inflicted. Mother claims infant was in bruised condition when returned by her ex-husband (infant's father) from weekend visitation. Father claims infant was unblemished when returned to mother by him. Both mother and father state no other caretakers had child recently. In this circumstance, mother and father are both listed as alleged perpetrators on the Department's records, and the Department will support the report. Once again, the Department's supported decision in no way reflects a determination by the Department of the identity of the perpetrator. Note that the Department will offer voluntary services as appropriate.

Example E: 12-year old boy is taken to hospital emergency room with broken ribs. Parent(s) cannot be located. Boy tells doctor he was attacked by gang of neighborhood youths he does not know, and robbed. Hospital files 51A report, and report is screened in to investigate possible neglect. Parents are thereafter located and it is determined they were not neglectful with regard to the boy's injury. The Department will unsupport the report, because even though the young boy suffered a clear incident of physical injury, the abuse was not caused by caretaker(s), and there was no neglect by his caretakers. Note that the Department will offer voluntary services as appropriate.

Example F: The Department receives a report of a young teenager currently in foster care who has had several front teeth knocked out. It is screened in. It is investigated. The investigator determines that the young teenager has at various times given divergent explanations for his injury: sometimes he says his biological father punched him, sometimes he says his grandfather punched him. Both father and grandfather deny punching him. There are no witnesses to the event. There is no suggestion that the injury was accidental and a dental examination confirms this. The report is supported. Both father and grandfather are listed as alleged perpetrators. The Department's supported decision means the Department has determined it has reasonable cause to believe an incident of abuse by a caretaker occurred to the young teenager. The supported decision in no way reflects a determination by the Department of the identity of the perpetrator.

110 CMR 4.34. Department's Custodial Powers—Miscellaneous

If the Department seeks and obtains court-ordered custody of a child, in addition to the rights and duties enumerated in M.G.L. c. 119, § 21 pertaining to the definition of "custody", the Department shall also exercise the following rights with respect to any child in the court-ordered custody of the Department:

(1) Interviews of Children. The Department may receive requests from various sources to allow third parties to interview child(ren). Examples include: media, police officers, district attorneys, other social work professionals (however 110 CMR 4.34 does not apply to interviews of children conducted by social workers employed by the Department), etc.

(a) From a Police Officer or a Representative of the District Attorney's Office: the Department will exercise its clinical judgment to determine whether or not it is in the child's best interest to be interviewed, and the Department will consent or deny on that basis. If a child is a possible or known defendant in a criminal action, the Department, Department foster/pre-adoptive parents or other Department providers caring for children in the Department's custody cannot consent to having the child interviewed irrespective of whether or not the child is considered by the Department to be mature. In this situation, the Department may go to court and request the appointment of a Guardian Ad Litem with authority to determine whether the child should/will consent to participate in any kind of police interrogation.

(b) All Other Requests: The Department, upon receipt of such requests, will make all reasonable efforts to consult with the parent(s) by telephone. If contact with the parent(s) is made, the Department will honor the parent(s)' wishes, unless the Department believes that the parents' wishes are contrary to the best interests of

5

the child. If the Department is unable to contact the parent(s), the Department shall not consent to such interviews, unless there are special circumstances under which the interview would further the best interests of the child, in which case the Department may consent.

(2) School Permissions. If the child is enrolled in any public school, private school, group care facility, day care facility, residential placement, or other such facility, the facility may request or require a variety of consent forms to be signed. Examples include: sports participation forms, field trip forms, driving forms, etc. The Department (including departmental foster parents) will exercise its clinical judgment to determine whether or not it is in the child's best interests to have the form signed, and the Department (including departmental foster parents) will consent or deny on that basis.

(3) Permits, Licenses. From time to time the child may wish to obtain various permits or licenses. Examples include: hunting and fishing permits, driver's licenses, motorcycle licenses, etc. Such permit(s) or license(s) may require parental consent or signature. The Department will exercise its clinical judgment to determine whether or not it is in the child's best interests to obtain such permit or license, and the Department will consent or deny on that basis.

(4) For all Issues Relative to Medical Authorizations: See 110 CMR 11.00 et seq.

(5) Religion: The Department (including departmental foster parents) will not procure or authorize any baptism or other religious ceremony for any minor child in its custody.

110 CMR 4.35. Access to the Central Registry

(1) Department staff may have access to the Central Registry for the purpose of:

(a) screening applicants for employment, including volunteers and student interns, by the Department, or one of its contracted providers, in a position with direct contact with clients or children;

(b) screening applicants to become foster or adoptive parents;

(c) screening a report filed under M.G.L. c. 119, § 51A;

(d) conducting an investigation under M.G.L. c. 119, § 51B;

(e) assisting in providing appropriate services to any child in the care or custody of the Department; or

(f) assisting in providing appropriate services to any family having an open case with the Department

(2) State child welfare agencies of another state may, upon request, receive information from the Central Registry for the purpose of:

(a) determining whether to approve a prospective foster or adoptive parent; or

(b) to carry out the agencies responsibilities under the law to protect children from abuse and neglect.

(3) The Department may enter into agreements with other state agencies to permit access to the Central Registry for the purpose of screening applicants for employment, volunteers, interns, foster or adoptive parents or other entities licensed by the agency who may have unsupervised contact with children.

(4) No other individual, group, agency or department, including law enforcement, child welfare or educational agencies, may have access to the Central Registry without the written approval of the Commissioner, an order of a court of competent jurisdiction, or as authorized by M.G.L. c. 119, § 51F.

(5) Upon request, the Child Advocate shall have access to information contained in the Central Registry in order to fulfill the responsibilities of the Office of the Child Advocate.

110 CMR 4.36. Registry of Alleged Perpetrators

The Department shall pursuant to M.G.L. c. 18B, § 7(b) create and maintain a Registry of Alleged Perpetrators as a component of the Central Registry maintained pursuant to M.G.L. c. 119, § 51F. The Registry of Alleged Perpetrators shall be indexed by the name of the alleged perpetrator. The Registry of Alleged Perpetrators shall contain the following information on the alleged perpetrator: (1) Name, (2) Date of birth, (3) Social Security Number, (4) Sex, (5) Address, (6) Date of Listing, (7) Allegation, (8) Cross reference to victim, (9) Relationship to victim.

110 CMR 4.37. Listing of Alleged Perpetrators

The name of the alleged perpetrator shall be added to the Registry of Alleged Perpetrators if: (a) the allegation of child abuse or neglect has been supported and referred to the District Attorney pursuant to M.G.L. c. 119, § 51B(k) and (b) there is substantial evidence indicating that the alleged perpetrator was responsible for the abuse or neglect. Pursuant to M.G.L. c. 30A, § 1(6) substantial evidence is defined as "such evidence as a reasonable mind might accept as adequate to support a conclusion."

The name of the alleged perpetrator shall remain on the Registry of Alleged Perpetrators for 75 years or until the decision to list the name of the alleged perpetrator is reversed pursuant to 110 CMR 10.00 et seq., or by a court of competent jurisdiction.

110 CMR 4.38. Access to the Registry of Alleged Perpetrators

(1) Department staff may have access to the Registry of Alleged Perpetrators for the purpose of:

(a) screening applicants for employment, including volunteers and student interns, by the Department, or one of its contracted providers, in a position with direct contact with clients or children;

(b) screening applicants to become foster parents or adoptive parents;

(c) screening a report filed under M.G.L. c. 119, § 51A;

(d) conducting an investigation under M.G.L. c. 119, § 51B;

(e) assisting in providing appropriate services to any family having an open case with the Department[.]

(2) State child welfare agencies of another state may, upon request, receive information from the Registry of Alleged Perpetrators for the purpose of:

(a) determining whether to approve a prospective foster or adoptive parent; or

(b) to carry out the agencies responsibilities under the protect children from abuse and neglect.

(3) Any data subject or duly authorized representative may obtain official confirmation or denial of the fact that the data subject's name appears on the Registry of Alleged Perpetrators and a copy of the information maintained on the Registry of Alleged Perpetrators by making a specific written request to the Fair Hearing Unit, pursuant to this provision, accompanied by sufficient proof of identity. The data subject may direct that the information be provided to another individual, or agency. Pursuant to the Fair Information Practices Act (FIPA) M.G.L. c. 66A, § 2(j), a data subject or duly authorized representative may contest the accuracy of the data maintained in the Registry of Alleged Perpetrators.

(4) No other individual, group, agency or department, including law enforcement, child welfare or educational agencies, may have access to the Registry of Alleged Perpetrators without the written approval of the Commissioner, or an order of a court of competent jurisdiction or as authorized by M.G.L. c. 119, § 51E. A state agency may have access to the Registry of Alleged Perpetrators for purposes of conducting an investigation of an allegation of child abuse or neglect pursuant to a duly promulgated regulation.

(5) The Department may enter into agreements with other state agencies to permit access to the Registry of Alleged Perpetrators for the purpose of screening applicants for employment, volunteers, interns, foster or adoptive parents or other entities licensed by the agency who may have unsupervised contact with children.

(6) Upon request, the Child Advocate shall have access to information contained in the Registry of Alleged Perpetrators in order to fulfill the responsibilities of the office of the Child Advocate.

(5) Upon a written request to the Fair Hearing Unit, the Department may release aggregate data for research purposes. All identifying information will be removed.

110 CMR 4.39. Reserved

110 CMR 4.40. To Whom Reported

All reports of abuse or neglect of children in an institutional setting shall be made to the Department pursuant to the provisions of M.G.L. c. 119, §§ 51A through F.

110 CMR 4.41. How Handled

All reports of abuse or neglect of children in an institutional setting shall be handled by the Department in the same manner as all other reports (see, 110 CMR 4.20 et seq.) except that the Department's investigator shall also visit the institution in question in connection with the investigation.

110 CMR 4.42. Reserved

110 CMR 4.43. Telephone Notice

The Department may, in appropriate circumstances, notify the Department of Early Education and Care (EEC), Department of Elementary and Secondary Education (DESE), Department of Mental Health (DMH), Department of Developmental Services (DDS), Department of Public Health (DPH), or Department of Youth Services (DYS) by telephone in an instance where the Department has received and screened in a report alleging that abuse or neglect of a child has occurred at a facility owned, operated, or funded, in whole or in part, by any of said departments or office, or at a facility operated by a person or entity subject to licensure or approval by any of said departments or office. Said telephone notice may be given in appropriate cases where coordination between agencies during the investigation would minimize interviews of and trauma to any child-victim, or would otherwise be beneficial.

110 CMR 4.44. Accompaniment of Department Investigator

During the Department's investigation process, the Department's investigator may be accompanied by an employee of EEC, DMH, DDS, DPH, or DYS, if said department or office is responsible for the institution in question, and if the Department and said department or office have previously entered into an Interagency Agreement which details procedures for such joint activities including but not limited to procedures to minimize the number of interviews of and trauma to any child-victim.

110 CMR 4.45. Information Sharing

(1) After completion of its investigation, the Department shall notify EEC, DESE, DMH, DDS, DPH, or DYS in writing by transmitting to the commissioner or director of that department a copy of the report received by the Department under M.G.L. c. 119, § 51A and a copy of the report prepared by the Department under M.G.L. c. 119, § 51B, if (a) the Department has supported said report, and (b) the Department has reason to believe that abuse or neglect may have occurred at a facility approved, owned, operated, or funded, in whole or in part, by any of said departments. In the event that EEC shares with one or more other state department(s) (DMH, DDS, DPH, or DYS) responsibility for licensing, funding or approving a facility as set forth 110 CMR 4.45(a) and (b), the Department shall always notify EEC and may at the Regional Director's discretion also notify DMH, DPH, DYS, or DDS.

(2) In any investigation in which the Department has notified EEC, DMH, DMR, DPH, DYS or DESE in accordance with the previous paragraph, the Department shall also notify the OCA in writing by transmitting a copy of the 51A report and 51B investigation report to the Office of the Child Advocate.

(3) If as a result of any 51A report or 51B investigation, the Department discovers information or circumstances which might indicate poor quality of care provided to children, or licensing violations, in any facility operated by a person or entity subject to licensure or approval by EEC, DESE, DMH, DDS, DPH, or DYS; that information shall be recorded by the Department's investigator on the 51B form, and (a) the information regarding poor quality of care or possible licensing violation shall be immediately communicated to the department in question; and (b) if supported, the 51B form shall be sent to the department in question.

110 CMR 4.46. Testimony by Department Employees

Department employees shall be made available to testify at administrative hearings held by EEC, DESE, DMH, DDS, DPH, or DYS in connection with matters reported by the Department to any of said departments or office pursuant to 110 CMR 4.00.

110 CMR 4.47. Follow-Up Actions

After the Department has provided a copy of the 51A/51B report to any department pursuant to 110 CMR 4.00, the department or office in question will be responsible for any further action to insure that adequate steps have been or will be taken to prevent reoccurrence of incidents of abuse and/or neglect of children in the institution in question. The Department will maintain the responsibility for monitoring the quality of services for any children who are in the care or custody of the Department and who are placed by the Department at the institution in question.

110 CMR 4.48. Information Requests from Day Care Facilities, Schools, and Other Child Care Facilities

Each determination by the Department to "support" or "unsupport" a report of abuse or neglect in an institutional setting shall be communicated to the director or owner of the institution in question, in a form letter established for use by the Department. See, 110 CMR 4.32.

If a request for copies of a 51A/51B report, pursuant to M.G.L. c. 119, § 51E, is made to the Department by any owner or operator or director of a day care facility, or any superintendent or director of a public or private school, or any director of any other child care facility (such as group care facilities, etc.) said owner or operator or director of a day care facility or superintendent or director of a public or private school or director of any other child care facility may, subject to the approval of the Commissioner or his/her designee, receive a copy of the 51A/51B report regardless of whether the report has been "supported" or "unsupported", if said report contains an allegation that an incident of abuse or neglect occurred on the premises of the day care facility, school, or other child care facility. However, before copies of the reports are released, the name of the reporter shall be redacted. See, 110 CMR 12.08.

110 CMR 4.50. Introduction

M.G.L. c. 119, §§ 51B(k) requires that the Department notify and provide information to the appropriate District Attorney and local law enforcement concerning certain enumerated conditions caused by child abuse or neglect. The Department is permitted to notify the District Attorney of other matters involving possible criminal conduct.

110 CMR 4.51. Mandatory Reporting to the District Attorney

(1) The Department shall immediately notify the district attorney and local law enforcement when early evidence, either during the receipt of the 51A report or during the investigation conducted under 51B indicates that there is reasonable cause to believe that one of the conditions listed in 110 CMR 4.51(2) resulted from abuse or neglect. Notification may include transmitting a copy of the 51A report.

(2) If, after an investigation pursuant to M.G.L. c. 119, § 51B, the Department supports a 51A report, the Area Director shall, no later than five working days after the supported decision is made, mail or deliver a copy of the completed 51A report and a copy of the completed 51B investigation to the District Attorney and the local law enforcement authorities for the county in which the offense occurred, if:

(a) a child has died;

(b) a child has been sexually assaulted;

(c) a child has suffered brain damage, loss or substantial impairment of a bodily function or organ, or substantial disfigurement;

(d) a child has been sexually exploited;

(e) a child has suffered serious physical abuse or injury that includes, but is not limited to:

1. a fracture of any bone, severe burn, impairment of any organ, or any other serious injury;

2. an injury requiring the child to be placed on life-support systems;

3. any other disclosure of physical abuse involving physical evidence which may be destroyed;

4. any current disclosure by the child of sexual assault; or

5. the presence of physical evidence of sexual assault.

(3) If a report is either screened out, or unsupported, on the basis that the alleged perpetrator did not meet the definition of caretaker, but the allegations fall within one of the categories under M.G.L. c. 119, § 51B(k), as listed in 110 CMR 4.51(2), the Area Director shall, no later than five working days after the screen out, or unsupport, decision, mail or deliver a copy of the completed 51A report and the completed 51B report, if applicable, to the District Attorney, and the local law enforcement authorities for the county where the child resides and for the county in which the offense occurred.

5

110 CMR 4.52. Discretionary Reporting to the District Attorney

The Department may refer other matters involving possible criminal conduct (including but not limited to cases of abuse or neglect resulting in conditions other than those listed in 110 CMR 4.51(2) to the District Attorney for investigation, regardless of whether the 51A report is supported or unsupported by the Department. Decisions as to which matters to refer to a District Attorney as a discretionary report shall be made by the Area Director. Such referral shall be accomplished by mailing or delivering to the District Attorney for the county in which the child resides a copy of the completed 51A report and the completed 51B investigation.

110 CMR 4.53. Procedures

(1) After a mandatory or discretionary referral has been made to a District Attorney, a social worker or other Department employee may discuss with the District Attorney any information obtained by the social worker in connection with the 51A report or 51B investigation. Further documents (other than the completed 51A report and 51B investigation already furnished to the District Attorney) from the Department's files shall be released to the District Attorney upon request, if the Commissioner or his/her designee determines that such documents are directly relevant to the investigation or prosecution of the matter referred to the District Attorney, and that release would not be contrary to the best interests of the child(ren) in question.

(2) After a mandatory or discretionary referral to a District Attorney, the Area Director shall advise the family that their case has been referred to the District Attorney, unless within six working days after the Area Director notifies the District Attorney, the District Attorney, in writing, requests that such notification not occur.

(3) Any documents provided to a District Attorney in accordance with 110 CMR 4.00, which are thereafter subpoenaed from the District Attorney or otherwise requested from the District Attorney by any party to any pending criminal matter, shall be released or not released by the District Attorney solely in accordance with the applicable rules or procedures governing the District Attorney, and no notice to or consent from the Department shall be required.

(4) Any documents from Department files which are subpoenaed directly from the Department by any party to a criminal matter to which the Department is not a party, is governed by the procedures set out in *Commonwealth v. Dwyer*, 448 Mass. 122 (2006). M.G.L. c. 119, §§ 51E through 51F and M.G.L. c. 66A and M.G.L. c. 112, § 135 through 135B apply to Department records and a specific order is required to produce Department records in a criminal matter.

110 CMR 4.54. Multi-disciplinary Service Team

(1) Following each referral made to a District Attorney pursuant to 110 CMR 4.00, the Regional Director shall, in cooperation with the District Attorney and the Area Director, select the members of a multi-disciplinary team which will be assigned to review the service plan, unless the Regional Director and the District Attorney mutually agree to waive the multi-disciplinary team procedure. The multi-disciplinary service team shall consist of the social worker responsible for servicing the family, a representative of the District Attorney, and at least one other member who is not employed by either the Department or the District Attorney. This other member shall be appointed by the Regional Director and shall have experience and training in the field of child welfare and criminal justice.

(2) Members of the multi-disciplinary service team shall have full access to the service plan and any information from the family's social service file which is directly related to the implementation of the plan. The data shared with the members of the multi-disciplinary team shall be confidential and shall be utilized by the members solely to carry out the responsibilities of the team.

(3) Within 30 working days of the selection of the service team, the service team shall meet:

(a) to discuss the current status of the child and family and any intervention initiated;

(b) to discuss any existing service plan for the family;

(c) to make recommendations as to the advisability of prosecuting any members of the family; and

(d) to discuss the possible effects of prosecution on the child and attempt to minimize the possibility of multiple interviews of the child.

(4) Within 55 working days of the referral of any case to the District Attorney, the Regional Director will forward a copy of the Department's service plan for the child and family to the District Attorney.

(5) If the multi-disciplinary service team finds that the service(s) identified in the service plan is/are not being provided due to unavailability, the team shall refer the case to the Commissioner.

(6) The multi-disciplinary service team may notify the District Attorney when a family has failed to participate or cooperate in the service plan.

(7) The Regional Director, in consultation with the District Attorney, shall determine when the multi-disciplinary team's involvement with a case is no longer warranted, and the Regional Director may thereafter authorize the dissolution of the team.

110 CMR 4.60. Scope of 110 CMR 4.60 through 4.67

110 CMR 4.60 Through 4.67 set forth the Department's responsibilities to children and their families under the Children In Need of Services (CHINS) statute found at M.G.L. c. 119, §§ 39E through 39J.

110 CMR 4.61. General Provisions

After an application for a CHINS petition is filed with any court, the child may come to the attention of the Department in four different ways: [1] court referral, [2] court-ordered pre-trial detention, [3] court-prescribed services, and [4] court-ordered commitment of the child to the custody of the Department.

110 CMR 4.62. Court Referral

(1) A probation officer of a court in which a CHINS petition has been filed may refer the child or his/her family to the Department for provision of social services by instructing the child or his/her family to contact the Department and apply for services.

(2) If the child, or the child and his/her parents, apply for services, the application shall be treated in the same manner as a voluntary application for services.

(3) A referred child who reasonably appears to be mentally ill and in danger of serious harm if not hospitalized should be the subject of an application for a commitment hearing before a district court under M.G.L. c. 123, § 12. No Department employee shall make such an application. The referring probation officer shall be informed immediately by the Department that in the Department's opinion the referred child is mentally ill and that without hospitalization serious harm is likely.

(4) If any child is referred to the Department for services under circumstances which indicate that the child may be in need of care and protection, a case conference shall be held to determine if legal action is warranted, and thereafter the Department may initiate court proceedings under M.G.L. c. 119.

110 CMR 4.63. Court-Ordered Pre-Trial Detention

(1) If a court finds that a child alleged to be in need of services is not likely to appear at the trial of the CHINS petition, the court may set bail or other terms and conditions for the child's release, or may order the Department to secure the child in lieu of bail and to hold the child in pre-trial detention.

(2) Detention is a period of custodial deprivation of liberty between the issuance of a CHINS petition and the trial on the merits. The only legally permissible purpose of detention is to secure the presence of the child at trial.

(3) Court-ordered detained children shall be placed by the Department in a setting which, consistent with humane practice and the requirements of law, reasonably appears to be able to ensure the child's availability on the trial date. Such children shall be placed in the least restrictive setting possible, including placement in the child's own home.

110 CMR 4.64. Court-Prescribed Services (No Custody to Department)

(1) Following a trial on a CHINS petition, if the court finds that the allegations have been proved beyond a reasonable doubt, it may adjudicate the child in need of services.

(2) Once the child has been adjudicated, the court may order provision of specified services (without committing the child to the custody of the Department).

(3) The Department may provide such court-prescribed services if the services are available, and the Department determines in its clinical judgment that the services are appropriate for the child and her/his family, and to the extent the Department is reasonably able to comply.

(4) A child receiving court-prescribed services (but not in the court-ordered custody of the Department) who reasonably appears to be mentally ill and in danger of serious harm if not hospitalized should be the subject of an application for a commitment hearing before a district court under M.G.L. c. 123, § 12. No Department employee shall make such an application. A probation officer or other employee of the Court which ordered the provision of services shall be informed immediately by the Department that in the Department's opinion the child is mentally ill and that without hospitalization serious harm is likely.

(5) If the court orders the Department to provide particular services or treatment, the Department shall carefully review the order. The Department may only be ordered to provide those services that it is legally required to provide. (*Charrier v. Charrier*, 416 Mass. 105 (1993)) Until such time as a court's order is vacated, changed or dismissed, the court's order shall nevertheless be complied with, if the services are available and to the extent the Department is reasonably able to comply-but at the same time the Department's legal counsel shall be contacted, so that an appeal may be considered.

110 CMR 4.65. Court-Ordered Commitment (Custody to Department)

(1) After a trial on a CHINS petition, a child may be adjudicated to be in need of services. The court may then commit the child to the custody of the Department for a period of up to six months.

(2) Following such a commitment order, the child shall be considered to be in the temporary custody of the Department.

(3) A child committed to the temporary custody of the Department shall be placed in the home of his/her parents unless substitute care would better serve the child's interests.

(4) Children may only be committed to the custody of the Department by a court after a CHINS adjudication has been entered.

(5) A CHINS child committed to the custody of the Department who reasonably appears to be mentally ill and in danger of serious harm if not hospitalized should be the subject of an application for a commitment hearing before a district court under M.G.L. c. 123, § 12. Department social workers, after consultation with a member of the Department's legal staff, shall be responsible for making such applications.

(6) If the court orders the Department to provide particular services, treatment or placement, the Department shall carefully review the order. The Department may only be ordered to provide those services that it is required by law to provide. *Charrier v. Charrier*, 416 Mass. 105 (1993). In addition, a court in a CHINS matter may recommend out-of-home placement of a child. If such placement is recommended the Department may not refuse the out-of-home placement, but the Department shall direct the type and length of the out-of-home placement. The Department shall also give consideration to a request of the child that s/he be placed outside the home of a parent or guardian when there is a history of abuse and neglect in the home of the parent or guardian. Until such time as the order is vacated, changed or dismissed the court's order shall nevertheless be complied with, to the extent the services are available and to the extent the Department is reasonably able to comply-but at the same time the Department's legal counsel shall be contacted, so that an appeal may be considered.

(7) After any order committing a child to the custody of the Department after a CHINS adjudication, the Department shall complete a service plan in accordance with 110 CMR 6.00.

(8) When preparing the service plan, the Department's social worker shall involve other interested persons such as relatives, friends, or community agencies who may be willing to provide helpful services.

(9) Where a child's service plan will affect the child's educational placement, the Department social worker shall consult with the child's school system in the development of such plan. This consultation shall occur prior to placement except in emergencies. Whenever the Department social worker has reason to believe that a child is in need of special education, the Department social worker shall initiate a request for an evaluation of the child under procedures set forth in 110 CMR 7.400.

110 CMR 4.67. Department Employees at CHINS Court Proceedings

Members of the Department's social work staff may attend all CHINS court proceedings if informally requested to do so by a Court, or if formally subpoenaed. Members of the Department's legal staff shall attend pre-adjudication CHINS court proceedings, in those cases where a request is made by an Area or Regional Director.

COMMENTARY

Traditionally, Department attorneys have not appeared at any pre-adjudication CHINS court proceedings because technically the Department is not a party to such actions. However, recognizing that some pre-adjudication CHINS matters present difficult or complex legal problems for the social work staff, the Department will make members of the legal staff available on an as-needed basis.

5

110 CMR 4.70. Eligibility for Single Service Cases

A family receives a single service when the family is assessed to need only one service purchased in whole or in part by the Department. A single service is provided when, in the judgment of the Department, the service is needed to maintain or support the family, and comprehensive case management is not needed.

Limitation upon hours of service and duration of service are set forth in each service-specific chapter of 110 CMR.

Any person located within the Commonwealth may request social services from the Department. Persons requesting social services must complete a written application form. Persons needing assistance in completing the written application form shall be furnished with assistance by the Department.

COMMENTARY

The Department frequently receives requests for services from persons who, while physically located within the Commonwealth, might be classified as "transients" or "temporary residents". Examples include families who have stopped in Massachusetts while moving from Florida to Maine and who are living with relatives, families who are temporarily residing at the Ronald McDonald House while their child receives specialized care at Children's Hospital, etc. The Department will not exclude such families from eligibility for Department services on the basis of these residency characterizations. Instead, the Department will accept applications from any person who has a bona fide physical location within Massachusetts, and the Department will thereafter proceed to review and assess the application in accordance with 110 CMR 4.70 through 4.76.

110 CMR 4.71. Case Management

Requests for a single service, and case management of single service cases, shall be in accordance with the applicable chapters of 110 CMR 4.00, including: 110 CMR 4.00: Intake; 110 CMR 5.00: Assessment; 110 CMR 6.00: Service Plans and Case Reviews; and 110 CMR 7.000: Services.

In particular, the need for single service provision shall be reviewed every six months, in conjunction with review of the service plan.

110 CMR 4.72. Application Information Required

Any client seeking a single service shall be required to provide sufficient information to allow the Department to assess the applicant's need and eligibility for a single service. In addition, an individual applying for a single service may be required to provide such authorization(s) for collateral contacts as are necessary for the Department to verify or assess the individual's need for a single service.

110 CMR 4.73. Limited Assessment for Single Service Cases

Single service cases shall require a limited assessment only. See, 110 CMR 5.00 (Assessment). The limited assessment shall determine the applicant's need for the single service and whether the service is appropriate.

110 CMR 4.74. Delivery of Service

After completion of the limited assessment, if the applicant is determined to need the single service and if the single service is determined to be appropriate, the Department shall provide the single service, or authorize provision of the single service, within ten (10) working days of completion of the limited assessment. If no Department (or provider) service resources are currently available, the applicant shall be placed on a waiting list.

110 CMR 4.75. Sliding Fee

All single services may be subject to a sliding fee.

110 CMR 4.76. Denial, Reduction, or Termination of Services

Any client aggrieved by the denial, reduction, or termination of a single service may request a fair hearing on the matter pursuant to 110 CMR 10.00 et seq.

All Department clients who receive a single service (such as chore, homemaker, respite, etc.) shall, upon attaining the age of sixty (60), be transferred to the Department of Elder Affairs. The transfer of a client's case, at age 60, to the Department of Elder Affairs is not appealable.

Regulatory Authority—110 CMR 4.01: M.G.L. c. 18B, § 7(i); M.G.L. c. 18B, § 4; M.G.L. c. 119, § 23(A); M.G.L. c. 210, § 2; 4.20: M.G.L. c. 119, §§ 51A, 51B; 4.40: M.G.L. c. 119, §§ 51A through F; M.G.L. c. 66A; 4.50: M.G.L. c. 119, §§ 51A, B, and D; 4.60: M.G.L. c. 119, §§ 39E through 39J; 4.70: M.G.L. c. 18B.

110 CMR 5.00. Assessment

Section

110 CMR 5.01. Introduction

(1) Assessment is the process of gathering and evaluating information regarding a family or individual's situation, in order to determine:

(a) whether services are necessary,

(b) which services would be appropriate, and

(c) who could best provide the needed services.

(d) the desired outcome(s)/behavioral changes to be achieved.

(2) After the assessment process, a written "Assessment" document shall be prepared by the social worker, in accordance with a standard format established by the Department. The assessment document shall include relevant information regarding the family's composition, the home environment, the family's financial situation, the family's functioning, and an evaluation of the family's general situation. The social worker shall inform the client of the assessment outcome.

(3) Assessment shall include:

(a) face-to-face contact with the client; and

(b) collateral contacts with such persons as the social worker deems necessary, including but not limited to extended family, previous or current service providers, and any other information resources identified by the client.

(4) During the course of the assessment process, the social worker shall establish an initial relationship with the client and shall respond to the client's immediate needs, including authorizing any immediately necessary services for the client and providing any necessary casework services.

110 CMR 5.02. When Required

An assessment of a family's or individual's needs for services must be completed for each new case. For cases which were previously assessed, closed, and are re-opened, a new assessment is not required. However, an update of the assessment, in particular a current evaluation of family functioning, must be completed.

110 CMR 5.03. When Completed

A *full* assessment must be completed within 45 working days after the initial contact event/case opening (i.e., the date of a supported investigation, Voluntary Application, or a referral from a court) and includes evaluations of risk to children based on factors identified in the Department's Risk Factor Matrix.

110 CMR 5.04. How Conducted

(1) Upon assignment, the social worker reviews the material included in the case record. If the material indicates that a previous case record exists, the social worker accesses and reviews the previous record(s).

(2) The social worker, together with the client, identifies family members who will be included in the assessment. The assessment process includes the active involvement of all family members. For the purpose of assessment, family is defined as: all family members and other individuals residing in the home, children in Department placement, children residing out of the home, and any parent/parent substitute living out of the home.

(3) The assessment involves collateral contacts with extended family, service providers, and other resources identified by the social worker and family. If the family is willing to sign the required releases permitting the Department to contact these collateral sources, the social worker proceeds to contact these collaterals. If the family is not willing to sign releases, the social worker documents this in the dictation and proceeds with the assessment without the benefit of collateral contacts.

(4) During the course of the assessment, the social worker shall have a minimum of three face-to-face contacts with parents and other individuals who reside in the home, the first of which occurs within five working days after the assignment of the case to the social worker responsible for completing the assessment. Two of the three face-to-face contacts take place in the home. If an out-of-home parent/parent substitute can be located, s/he is visited a minimum of one time, at a mutually agreeable location, during the assessment. All children are visited a minimum of two times during the assessment. The first face-to-face contact occurs in the child's current residence within five working days after the assignment of the case to the social worker responsible for completing the assessment.

(5) If the social worker is not able to meet with the individuals in the family, cannot conduct the expected number of visits, and/or it is not possible or appropriate to conduct a visit in the expected location set forth in 110 CMR 5.04(4), the social worker discusses this with his/her supervisor prior to the completion of the assessment. The reason(s) why the visits were not conducted, and/or occurred at a different location, and the outcome of the discussion with the supervisor are documented in the case record.

(6) In cases which were opened as a result of a supported investigation, under M.G.L. c. 119, § 51B, the social worker informs the family that they may submit information to her/him regarding the investigation decision which will be reviewed at the completion of the assessment.

(7) As part of the assessment, the social worker should request a check of the Registry of Alleged Perpetrators for all household members. For protective cases only, the social worker, in consultation with his/her supervisor, should determine if there is a need to conduct a Criminal Offender Record Information (CORI) check on a household member. When such a determination is made, the social worker should submit a request in accordance with the Department's Policy and Procedures for Accessing Name Search, Central Registry, Registry of Alleged Perpetrators, and CORI Checks policy, (Department Policy #86-014(R).

(8) If an assessment is being completed as the result of a supported investigation under M.G.L. c. 119, § 51B, and the family refuses, despite reasonable casework efforts, to participate in the assessment process, the social worker and supervisor consult with the Area Director, or designee, to determine risk to the child(ren) and, in consultation with a Department attorney, to determine if there are reasons to pursue legal action.

(9) Documentation. Information gathered during the assessment process is documented, by the social worker, in consultation with the supervisor, utilizing a form or an electronic method established by the Department's Assessment policy, Department Policy # 85-011. The assessment is based on an evaluation of information learned from the interviews with all family members and collateral contacts and the use of the Department's Risk Factor Matrix.

(10) Outcome. Following completion of the assessment, the social worker and supervisor determine if the case will remain open or be closed.

For cases remaining open the social worker and supervisor determine who in the family will be receiving services and be included in the service plan. The social worker verbally informs the family of the outcome of the assessment and also provides the family with written notification.

For cases that will be closed after the assessment, the social worker verbally informs the family of the outcome of the assessment and proceeds in accordance 110 CMR 9.00 et seq. and the Department's Case Closing Policy (Department Policy #86-007(R)).

110 CMR 5.05. Administrative Review

(1) Supported decisions in new cases, made by the Department on or after December 1, 1988, will be automatically reviewed following the Department's assessment, by Administrative Review.

5

(2) Each Administrative Review will consider all information gathered during assessment, as well as the original information gathered during investigation which formed the basis of the "supported" decision. The purpose of each Administrative Review is to determine whether the "supported" decision should be changed to "unsupported", because:

(a) based on information available during the investigation, the decision at the time it was made was not in accordance with 110 CMR or policies, or was not reasonable; or

(b) based upon new information not available during the investigation, the decision is not in accordance with 110 CMR or policies, or is not reasonable.

(3) In any case where the Department changes, via the above Administrative Review process, a decision from "supported" to "unsupported".

(a) The Department's Central Registry shall reflect said change, and shall be expunged according to the timetable as if the original decision had been "unsupported";

(b) Any alleged perpetrator listing on the Central Registry will be automatically eliminated;

(c) The parents, the mandated reporter who filed the report, if applicable, and any individual identified on the Registry of Alleged Perpetrators as a result of the supported investigation, shall be notified that the supported decision has been unsupported and that any perpetrator listing that resulted from the support decision has been eliminated; and

(d) The M.G.L. c. 119, §§ 51A and 51B reports and related case record materials shall be filed with other closed record files.

(4) An individual may waive his/her right to the Department's assessment and Administrative Review (for example, where the Department proposes and the individual agrees, to support the allegation(s) after investigation but to close the case thereafter).

Regulatory Authority—110 CMR 5.00: M.G.L. c. 18B.

110 CMR 6.00. Service Plans and Case Reviews

(Effective until Sept. 6, 2019. For the version of the regulations effective on Sept. 6, 2019, see below.)

Section

110 CMR 6.01. Service Plan—Description and Purpose

(1) A service plan is a written document which describes in detail the behavioral changes needed, the tasks to be undertaken and the services to be provided to either:

(a) strengthen a family unit; or

(b) reunify a family unit for a child who has been removed from his/her home; or

(c) provide an alternative permanent home for a child who has been removed from his or her home;

(2) The service plan shall provide a basis for assessing the progress of family members in meeting the goal of the service plan.

110 CMR 6.02. Service Plan—Requirement

Every family receiving services from the Department shall have a service plan. The service plan should include both parents, including the non-resident parent when possible. If either parent is not included in the service plan an explanation should be included in the case record.

110 CMR 6.03. Service Plan—Elements (Generally)

Each service plan shall contain the following elements:

(1) A statement indicating whether the goal of the service plan is to:

(a) strengthen the family unit; or

(b) reunify the family unit; or

(c) provide an alternative permanent home for a child who has been removed from his or her home;

(2) A statement of the strengths of the family, the areas needing improvement and behavioral change(s) family members need to make to achieve the goal of the service plan and close the case.

(3) A statement of each task the family member must complete to achieve the goal of the service plan and the time by which or the frequency at which the task is to be completed.

(4) A statement of the task(s) the Department and other parties must complete and the time by which or the frequency at which the task is to be completed.

(5) A listing of the services to be provided to family members and the time by which or the frequency at which the service is to be provided.

110 CMR 6.04. Service Plan—Elements (Children in Substitute Care)

A service plan for a family with a child in substitute care shall contain the elements listed above and each of the following additional elements about the child:

(1) The type of placement (foster care, intensive foster care, congregate care, etc.).

(2) The history of any previous placements.

(3) The reason for the child's current placement.

(4) Efforts made by the Department and the family to prevent the need for placement.

(5) The visiting schedule between the family and the child, or, if no visits are to be scheduled, the reason why visits are not in the best interest of the child.

(6) The identification of the permanent plan for the child. The permanent plan may be either:

(a) Permanency through stabilization;

(b) Permanency through reunification;

(c) Permanency through adoption;

(d) Permanency through guardianship;

(e) Permanency through living with Kin; or

(f) Alternative Permanency Planned Living Arrangement.

(7) The projected date by which the child may return home or be placed in another permanent living situation.

(8) A description of the child's specific health, dental and educational needs while in placement.

110 CMR 6.05. Service Plan—Time for Completion; Case Opening

(1) A service plan shall be completed within the following time periods:

(a) for all cases within ten working days after a comprehensive assessment is completed, but in no event later than 55 working days after the opening of the case.

(b) for a placement made on an emergency basis to ensure the immediate safety of a child, where there is no service plan, a service plan shall be completed within 30 working days after the placement.

(2) Except in an emergency, every family shall have a service plan prior to placing a child in substitute care.

(3) For purposes of developing a service plan the opening of the case occurs upon one of the following:

(a) the decision to support a 51A report after an investigation; or

(b) the decision to open a case for services after an initial assessment; or

(c) the receipt of an application for voluntary services; or

(d) a court order giving custody to the Department.

110 CMR 6.06. Service Plan—Agreement by Family

(1) A service plan shall be, to the maximum extent possible, jointly developed by the Department and the family receiving services from the Department. If the parties are in agreement about the service plan it shall be signed by all parties and a copy shall be provided to the family.

(2) If the parties are not in agreement about the service plan the Department shall prepare the service plan and a copy shall be provided to the family. The Department shall also inform the family that the family may seek a review of the service plan by using the Department's grievance procedure.

(3) If the parties are in agreement about some but not all of the service plan, the family member has the option of noting and initialing the sections he/she does agree with, or adding services he/she would like the Department to offer, and signing the service plan with reservations.

110 CMR 6.07. Service Plan—Review of Existing Plan

A service plan shall at a minimum be reviewed during each case review or every six months.

110 CMR 6.08. Service Plan—Writing a New Plan

A new service plan must be written when there has been a change in the goal of the plan. An existing service plan may be updated and renewed if the goal of the plan is unchanged. However, no service plan may be renewed a second time.

110 CMR 6.09. Case Review—Types of Case Reviews

There are two types of case reviews:

(1) Foster Care Review. A Foster Care Review (FCR) is a review, conducted by a panel under the auspices of the Department's independent Foster Care Review Unit (FCRU) established under M.G.L. c. 18B, § 6A, of the service plan and status of any family with a child

(a) who is either:

(1) committed by a court to the custody of the Department or an agent of the Department; or

(2) in the custody of the Department via an adoption surrender, executed in conformance with M.G.L. c. 210, § 2; or

(3) in the voluntary care of the Department pursuant to a Voluntary Placement Agreement; and

(b) who is not living at home six months from the time such child came into the care or custody of the Department or the custody of an agent of the Department.

(2) Permanency Hearing. A Permanency Hearing is a re-view conducted in the court which granted custody of a child to the

Department. The review is conducted under the provisions of G.L. c. 119, § 29B.

110 CMR 6.10. Case Review—Foster Care Review (FCR)

(1) Requirement. The Department shall conduct a FCR within six months after a child is placed and every six months thereafter for a child who remains out of the home.

(2) Content. A FCR shall include consideration of the following issues:

(a) the necessity and appropriateness of the services to the family; and

(b) a review of the purpose of the service plan; and

(c) a review of the past six months' activities, including:

(1) the Department's fulfillment of the tasks identified in the service plan;

(2) the parent's fulfillment of the tasks identified in the service plan, including the visitation schedule;

(3) the provider's fulfillment of the tasks identified in the service plan;

(4) where appropriate, the child's fulfillment of the tasks identified in the service plan; and

(5) progress made toward resolving the problems identified in the assessment or previous case review; and

(d) a review of the safety of the child and the necessity and appropriateness of the child's continued placement; and

(e) a review of the extent of progress made toward alleviating or mitigating the causes necessitating the child's placement; and

(f) a review of the goal and the projected date by which the child will achieve permanency either through

1. stabilization with his or her parents or guardian;

2. reunification and safely maintaining with his or her parents or guardian;

3. adoption;

4. guardianship by a person other than the Department or its agent;

5. permanently living with Kin; or

6. another permanent planned living arrangement; and

(g) a review of the proposed direction of service planning for the next six months, including:

1. the steps necessary to achieve permanency for the child; and

2. the visitation schedule for the parents and the means by which the schedule will be implemented; and

(h) a review of the child's medical and dental checkups, consistent with the well-child schedule.

(3) Structure and Format. A FCR shall be conducted a three member panel consisting of:

(a) a member of the FCRU, who shall convene and chair the panel; and

(b) a person who may or may not be a Department em-ployee, provided that such person may not be social worker or the supervisor of the case under review; and

(c) a volunteer, provided

1. the volunteer shall represent to the maximum extent feasible the various socio-economic, racial and ethnic groups served by the panel; and

2. the volunteer has, prior to participation, attended FCRU orientation and follow up training sessions; and

3. the volunteer is not an employee of the Department (but may be a Department foster parent); and

4. the volunteer is not an employee of, board member of, or volunteer associated with, an agency contracted to provide services to the child or family whose case is under review; and

5. the volunteer does not know and is not known by the family; and

6. the volunteer has signed an agreement to be a foster care review panel volunteer with the Department and acknowledged the circumstances which could lead to termination or non-renewal of the agreement.

(d) The format of the case review may vary depending on the family's needs and circumstances, and the number of participants in the case review. However, the following guidelines shall apply to each FCR review:

1. The review shall be a structured discussion; and

2. All participants shall be encouraged to participate and afforded the opportunity to express their views.

(4) Participants. A FCR shall at a minimum invite the following people, who shall be notified in writing to attend the case review prior to its scheduled date:

(a) parents of the child in placement, unless parental rights have been terminated or surrendered, under M.G.L. c. 210 §§ 2 or 3, or under M.G.L. c. 119, § 26, or unless a parent has a documented history of violent or assaultive behavior that is not mitigated by treatment and changes in behavior by the parent (in which case approval to exclude the parent from in-person participation in the case review shall be obtained from the FCRU member, and the parent shall be notified by the social worker of the reasons for such exclusion and shall be advised of alternative methods of providing input into the review.) The parents may invite other persons to provide support. While this may include an attorney, an attorney is not required.

(b) a putative or unwed father, unless his parental rights have been surrendered or terminated, if:

1. he is named on any legal papers (i.e. petitions, birth certificate, or other judicial decree); or

2. he has formally acknowledged paternity; or

3. he has been named as the father by the mother.

(c) the child, if 14 years of age or older, unless the child is a danger to him/herself or other participants or exhibits behavior that would make it impossible for the review to be conducted.

(d) the social worker assigned to the family and the children.

(e) the supervisor of the social worker assigned to the family and the children, provided such supervisor may but is not required to attend.

(f) foster parents.

(g) substitute care provider, if a child is receiving substitute care services from an agency under contract with the Department.

(h) the child's attorney or Guardian Ad Litem, if any.

(i) staff of other public or private agencies and other individuals important to the child or family.

Any of the above persons who are invited, but unable to attend the case review shall be permitted to submit written comments in lieu of attendance.

(5) Responsibilities of Social Workers. As part of a FCR a social worker shall:

(a) verify periodic lists furnished him/her of all families in his/her caseload who are to be scheduled for case review; and

(b) notify the FCRU of the names and current addresses of the individuals who are to be invited; and

(c) notify the FCRU if the family's primary language is other than English and advise the FCRU of resources available for an interpreter; and

(d) ensure that a current service plan is available for the case review; and

(e) discuss the pending case review with parents, foster parents, and the child prior to the review, to insure that all parties understand its format and purpose; and

(f) discuss any change in the service plan with the client, parents, supervisor, foster parents and providers prior to the case review, if such a change will be proposed at the case review; and

(g) notify FCRU staff of any casework issues which may require particularly sensitive handling during the review, or of any recent significant events which have occurred which might affect the case review; and

(h) attend the case review and provide clarification and information about the service plan; and

(i) notify his/her supervisor if he/she disagrees with the determinations of the case review panel; and

(j) write the service plan for the next six month period in a manner consistent with the determinations of the case review panel, unless such determinations are appealed.

(6) Responsibilities of Supervisors. For a FCR, a su-pervisor shall:

(a) in instances in which the social worker cannot attend the case review due to an emergency or illness, either attend the case review or provide for alternative staff representation; and

(b) ensure that the determinations of the case review panel are implemented unless:

1. there is an appeal and reversal of those determinations by the Regional Director, as set forth below; or

2. changes in case circumstances necessitate changes in the service plan, provided that the Area Director approves such changes.

(c) notify the Area Director if the determinations of the case review panel will be appealed.

(7) Responsibilities of Area Directors. The Area Director or his/her designee shall:

5

(a) in instances in which the social worker cannot attend the case review due to an emergency, illness, or scheduled vacation, provide for alternative staff representation; and

(b) ensure that all clients have up to date service plans; and

(c) review the monthly preliminary list of families due for review and make such adjustments as are necessary to case review scheduling; and

(d) ensure that the determinations of the case review panel are implemented unless:

1. there is a reversal of those determinations pursuant to 110 CMR of the Department; or

2. changes in case circumstances necessitate changes in the service plan, provided that the Area Director approves such changes.

(8) Responsibilities of FCRU Staff. FCRU staff shall:

(a) schedule the date, time and place of the review and select the volunteer panel member; and

(b) invite all necessary parties to attend the review; and

(c) review the family's case record, including any prior service plan; and

(d) if necessary, seek out additional information from appropriate staff which will facilitate an effective review; and

(e) chair the case review; and

(f) prepare a written summary of the case review panel's determinations and recommendations.

(9) Responsibilities of Panel Members. Case review panel members shall:

(a) have equal authority during the case review; and

(b) prepare for the case review according to procedures established by the FCRU; and

(c) maintain the confidentiality of all client related information; and

(d) attend the case review as scheduled; and

(e) actively participate in the case review, in an objective and unbiased manner; and

(f) notify the FCRU if they have personal knowledge of the client or family whose case is to be reviewed.

(10) Determinations Made by the Panel. The panel mem-bers shall discuss and determine:

(a) the necessity and appropriateness of the child's continued placement in substitute care; and

(b) the extent of the parties' compliance with the written service plan and the actions which must be undertaken within specified time limits by all parties to achieve identified service goals; and

(c) the extent of progress which has been made toward alleviating or mitigating the causes necessitating the child's placement in substitute care; and

(d) the goal and the projected date by which the child may achieve permanency either through

1. stabilization with his or her parents or guardian;

2. reunification and safely maintaining with his or her parents or guardian;

3. adoption;

4. guardianship by a person other than the Department or its agent;

5. permanently living with Kin; or

6. another permanent planned living arrangement; and

(e) The FCRU panel member shall record the panel's determinations and recommendations on a form prescribed by the Department. Copies of the form shall be mailed by the FCRU to the:

1. Area Director;

2. social worker;

3. parents;

4. child age 14 or older;

5. substitute care provider;

6. child's attorney and/or GAL, if applicable.

The social worker shall put a copy of the form into the family's case record.

(11) Panel Disagreement with Service Plan. If the determinations of the panel conflict with the service plan as written, the determination of the panel shall be binding upon the Department and shall be incorporated into a revised or new service plan unless the panel's determinations are successfully appealed as set in 110 CMR 6.12(12).

(12) Appeal of FCR Determination.

(a) Parents, foster parents, the child's attorney, and children over the age of 14 may appeal the Foster Care Review determina-tion to change the service plan goal by requesting a Fair Hearing within 30 days after receiving the Foster Care Review Report. All other FCR determinations may be appealed through the grievance process.

(b) If the department social worker or supervisor disagree with any of the FCR determinations, the area staff and FCR staff will attempt to resolve the disagreement in accordance with the Foster Care Review Policy.

(13) Goal Change. Whenever the Foster Care Review panel determines, under 110 CMR 6.10(10)(d), that the goal for the child should be changed, the department must schedule the case for a permanency planning conference. The goal does not change until a permanency planning conference is held. If the permanency planning conference goal determination differs with the foster care review goal determination, the case will be referred to the Regional Director who will determine the goal.

110 CMR 6.11. Permanency Hearing

A Permanency Hearing is a review conducted by a court of competent jurisdiction under M.G.L. c. 119, § 29B, of a child under the age of 18 in substitute care. The Department shall participate in a permanency hearing to determine a child's permanency plan within 12 months of an initial order of commitment, or grant of custody to the Department, and every 12 months thereafter as long as the child remains in substitute care. If a child has entered substitute care through a voluntary placement agreement as set forth in 110 CMR 4.10 through 4.14, the per-manency hearing will be held within 12 months of the child en-tering placement or within 60 days of the Department obtaining court custody, whichever is later. For children who remain in the Department's custody after they are placed home, a permanency hearing will be conducted if at the time the review is scheduled the child has been home for less then 6 months.

The process utilized for a permanency hearing shall be in accordance with Trial Court Rule VI Uniform Rules for Permanency Hearings. The Department shall file with the court which committed the child to the Department's custody a permanency plan report 30 days prior to the permanency hearing date, and shall send a copy of the plan to the attorneys of record, or to a party who is unrepresented. If a parent has signed an adoption surrender, or if a parent's parental rights have been terminated by a court of law, the parent or counsel will not be sent a copy of the permanency plan.

The Department shall notify the child's current foster/pre-adoptive parent of the date of the permanency hearing. The current foster/pre-adoptive parent has the right to be heard at the permanency hearing.

At the permanency hearing the court shall determine the permanent plan for the child. In making such determination the court shall consult with the child, in an age-appropriate manner, the proposed permanency plan for the child. Such consultation may be through a report by the Department Social Worker, the Child's attorney or a guardian ad litem whose has discussed with the child the proposed permanent plan. A child age 16 and over may attend the permanency hearing review. The Department shall use reasonable efforts to achieve the permanency plan determined by the court. The Department may concurrently use reasonable efforts to achieve an alternative permanent plan if the permanent plan determined by the court is reunification with the family and the goal established through the Department's permanency planning conference is other than reunification.

Regulatory Authority—110 CMR 6.00: M.G.L. c. 18B, § 6A; M.G.L. c. 119, § 29B.

110 CMR 6.00. Case Reviews

(Effective Sept. 6, 2019.)

Section

110 CMR 6.01. Foster Care Review and Permanency Hearing—Generally

(1) Foster Care Review. A Foster Care Review (FCR) is a review, conducted by a panel under the auspices of the Department's independent Foster Care Review Unit (FCRU) established under M.G.L. c. 18B, § 6A, of the action plan and progress toward permanency and the safety and well-being of a child or young adult.

(a) who is either:

1. committed by a court to the custody of the Department or an agent of the Department;

2. in the custody of the Department via an adoption surrender, executed in conformance with M.G.L. c. 210, § 2;

3. in the voluntary care of the Department pursuant to a Voluntary Placement Agreement or a petition under M.G.L. c. 119, § 23(a)(1); and

(b) who is not living at home at the time the foster care review is scheduled to occur.

(2) Permanency Hearing. A Permanency Hearing is a review conducted by the court which granted custody of a child to the Department. The review is conducted under the provisions of M.G.L. c. 119, § 29B and includes reviews for any child or young adult up to 22 years of age.

(3) Definitions.

(a) Age or Developmentally Appropriate Activities:

1. activities or items that are generally accepted as suitable for children, youth and young adults of the same chronological age or level of maturity or that are determined to be developmentally-appropriate based on the development of cognitive, emotional, physical, and behavioral capacities that are typical for an age or age group; and

2. in the case of a specific child, youth or young adult, activities or items that are suitable based on the developmental stages attained by the child, youth or young adult with respect to their cognitive, emotional, physical, and behavioral capacities.

(b) Reasonable and Prudent Parent Standard. The standard characterized by careful and sensible parental decisions that maintain the health, safety, and best interests of a child, youth or young adult while at the same time encouraging the emotional and developmental growth of the child, youth or young adult. The caregiver shall employ this standard when determining whether to allow a child, youth or young adult in foster care to participate in extracurricular, enrichment, cultural, and social activities.

110 CMR 6.02. Foster Care Review (FCR)

(1) Requirement. The Department shall conduct a FCR within six months after a child or young adult is placed out of the home and every six months thereafter as long as the child or young adult remains out of the home.

(2) Content. A FCR shall include consideration of the following:

(a) a review of the family assessment and action plan and any updates since the last foster care review, including the reason for the Department's continued involvement with the family; and

(b) a review of the tasks, services and supports within the action plan since the last foster care review, including:

1. the Department's actions and efforts to address the reason for the Department's involvement and to achieve safety, permanency and well-being for the child/young adult, including contact with parent(s) and children and placement resource;

2. each parent's actions and efforts toward participation in the tasks, services and supports identified in the action plan, including participation in scheduled visits, intended to reduce or alleviate the danger to, or need for placement of, the child(ren) or young adult and whether desired outcomes were achieved;

3. where appropriate, the child/young adult's actions and efforts toward participation in the tasks, services and supports identified in the action plan and the extent to which the outcomes of safety, permanency and well-being were achieved;

4. progress made toward resolving the issues identified in the family assessment and action plan, updates to the family assessment and action plan or the previous FCR;

5. the placement provider's actions and efforts toward the fulfillment of the expectations necessary to meet the needs of the child, including providing regular opportunities to engage in age or developmentally appropriate activities; and

6. the Department's actions and efforts to ensure the child's placement is following the reasonable and prudent parent standard;

(c) a review of the safety of the child or young adult, including children living at home, and the necessity and appropriateness of the child or young adult's continued placement;

(d) a review of the extent of progress made toward alleviating or mitigating the causes necessitating the child/young adult's placement and achieving desired outcomes;

(e) a review of the Department's permanency plan for the child or young adult and the projected date by which the child or young adult will achieve permanency either through:

1. stabilization with their parents or guardian;

2. reunification and safely maintaining with their parents or guardian;

3. adoption;

5

4. guardianship by a person other than the Department or its agent;

5. permanently living with Kin; or

6. another planned permanent living arrangement for a child 16 years of age or older; and

(f) a review of the proposed action planning for the next six months, including:

1. the steps necessary to achieve permanency for the child or young adult; and

2. the visitation schedule for the parents, siblings and grandparents if applicable and the means by which the schedule will be implemented.

(g) a review of the child or young adult's medical and dental checkups, consistent with the well-child schedule;

(h) a review of the child or young adult's educational needs and the stability of the educational setting;

(i) a review of the child or young adult's regular opportunities to engage in age or developmentally appropriate activities;

(j) a review of the services and supports for the child or young adult 14 years of age or older that will assist them in transitioning from foster care to a successful adulthood; and

(k) for any child who have reached the age of 17 years and six months, a review of a child's request to receive young adult services through the Department beyond 18 years of age.

(3) Structure and Format. A FCR should be conducted by a three member panel consisting of:

(a) a member of the FCRU, who shall convene and chair the panel;

(b) a person who may or may not be a Department employee, provided that such person may not be the social worker, supervisor or manager assigned to the case under review;

(c) a volunteer, provided:

1. the volunteer shall be recruited to represent to the maximum extent feasible the various socio-economic, racial and ethnic groups of the community served by the Department;

2. the volunteer has, prior to participation, attended FCRU orientation and follow up training sessions;

3. the volunteer is not an employee of the Department (but may be a Department foster parent);

4. the volunteer is not an employee of, board member of, or volunteer associated with, an agency contracted to provide services to the child or family whose case is under review;

5. the volunteer does not know and is not known by the family; and

6. the volunteer has signed an agreement to be a foster care review panel volunteer with the Department and acknowledged the circumstances which could lead to termination or non-renewal of the agreement.

(d) The format of the FCR may vary depending on the family's needs and circumstances, and the number of participants in the FCR. However, the following guidelines shall apply to each FCR:

1. The review shall be a structured discussion; and

2. All participants shall be encouraged to participate and afforded the opportunity to express their views.

(4) Participants. A FCR shall at a minimum invite the following people, who shall be notified in writing to attend the FCR prior to its scheduled date:

(a) parent(s), or guardian if applicable, of the child(ren) being reviewed, unless parental rights have been terminated or surrendered, under M.G.L. c. 210, §§ 2 or 3, or under M.G.L. c. 119, § 26, or the review only concerns a young adult, or unless a parent has a documented history of violent or assaultive behavior that is not mitigated by treatment which results in behavioral changes by the parent. In such case approval to exclude the parent from in-person participation in the FCR shall be obtained from the Area Director/designee in consultation with the FCRU manager, and the parent shall be notified by the Area Director/designee of the reasons for such exclusion and shall be advised of alternative methods of providing input into the review. The parents may invite other persons to provide support. While this may include an attorney, an attorney is not required.

(b) a putative or unwed father, unless his parental rights have been surrendered or terminated, if:

1. he is named on any legal papers (i.e. petitions, birth certificate, or other judicial decree);

2. he has formally acknowledged paternity;

3. he has been named as the father by the mother; or

4. he has been determined to be the father by genetic marker testing.

(c) the child or young adult, if 14 years of age or older, as well as any individual invited by the child or young adult to provide support, unless the child or young adult is a danger to themselves or other participants or exhibits behavior that would make it impossible for the review to be conducted;

(d) the social worker(s) assigned to the family and the children or young adult, including an adolescent outreach worker;

(e) the supervisor(s) of the social worker(s) assigned to the family and the children or young adult, provided such supervisor(s) may but is not required to attend;

(f) the family resource worker assigned to the foster home of the child(ren)'s placement

(g) foster parents;

(h) placement provider, if a child or young adult is receiving congregate care services from an agency under contract with the Department;

(i) the child's attorney or guardian ad litem, if any;

(j) the parent's attorney, unless their clients rights have been terminated;

(k) the Department Attorney;

(l) staff of other public or private agencies and other individuals important to the child/young adult or family; and

(m) the Guardian for an Incapacitated young adult.

Participants will be notified of the date and time for the FCR 30 calendar days prior to the scheduled FCR. Any of the above persons who are invited, but unable to attend the FCR shall be permitted to submit written comments to the Foster Care Review Unit in lieu of attendance.

(5) Responsibilities of Social Workers. As part of the FCR process, a social worker shall, and their supervisor shall ensure the social worker:

(a) verify periodic lists furnished to them of all families in their caseload who are to be scheduled for a FCR;

(b) inform the FCRU of the names of the individuals who are to be invited to the review, including those individuals the family or child or young adult 14 years or age or older wishes to invite and ensure the current addresses of the participants listed in 110 CMR 6.02(4) and other invitees are reflected in the electronic case record;

(c) arrange for a child or young adult 14 years of age or older to be transported to the FCR if the child or young adult wishes to attend;

(d) inform the FCRU if the family's primary language is other than English;

(e) ensure that a current family assessment and action plan is available for the FCR including updating the electronic and physical record as needed;

(f) ensure a copy of any action plan(s) that will be reviewed at the FCR are provided to the parents, as well as any child or young adult 14 years of age or older prior to the FCR;

(g) discuss the pending FCR with parents, foster parents, and the child or young adult prior to the review, to ensure all parties understand its format and purpose;

(h) discuss any change in the action plan with the, parents, child(ren) or young adult 14 years of age or older, supervisor, foster parents and providers prior to the FCR, if such a change will be proposed at the FCR;

(i) notify FCRU staff of any casework issues, including any concerns about participants safety, which may require particularly sensitive handling during the review, or of any recent significant events which might affect the FCR;

(j) discuss with their supervisor the action plan, family progress and proposed permanency plan in supervision prior to the FCR;

(k) attend the FCR and provide clarification and information about the action plan and other information about the family as needed; and

(l) revise the family assessment and action plan with the family and child(ren) or young adult 14 years of age or older, if needed, for the next six-month period in a manner consistent with the determinations.

(6) Responsibilities of Area Directors. The Area Director or designee shall:

(a) provide for alternative staff representation in instances in which the social worker cannot attend the FCR due to an emergency, illness, or scheduled vacation;

(b) ensure that all families have up to date family assessments and action plans;

(c) ensure a copy of any action plan(s) that will be reviewed at the FCR has been provided to the parents, child(ren) or young adult 14 years of age or older prior to the FCR;

(d) review the monthly preliminary list of families due for review and notify the FCRU if adjustments are necessary to FCR scheduling;

(e) provide a person to participate as a member of the foster care review panel, provided that such person may not be the social worker, supervisor or manager assigned to the case under review;

(f) arrange for an interpreter if one is needed for the review;

(g) ensure there is a room available in the Area Office for the FCRs scheduled each month; and

(h) ensure the determinations of the FCR panel are implemented.

(7) Responsibilities of FCRU Staff. FCRU staff shall:

(a) schedule the date, time and place of the review and select the volunteer panel member;

(b) invite all necessary parties to attend the review;

(c) review the family's case record, or the record for the young adult as applicable, including the family assessment any prior service or action plan;

(d) if necessary, seek out additional information from appropriate staff which will facilitate an effective review;

(e) chair the FCR;

(f) ensure that all participants have the opportunity to have their views heard;

(g) facilitate an alternative method of participation when needed for any participant listed under 110 CMR 6.02(4) who cannot attend in person; and

(h) prepare a written summary of the FCR panel's determinations and recommendations, including minority opinions and objections, in a format established by the Department.

(8) Responsibilities of Panel Members. FCR panel members shall:

(a) have equal authority during the FCR;

(b) prepare for the FCR according to procedures established by the FCRU;

(c) maintain the confidentiality of all client related information;

(d) attend the FCR as scheduled;

(e) actively participate in the FCR, in an objective and unbiased manner; and

(f) notify the FCRU if they have personal knowledge of the client or family whose case is to be reviewed.

(9) Determinations Made by the Panel. The panel members shall discuss and determine:

(a) whether there are any concerns for the child(ren)'s safety identified during the FCR process;

(b) whether the child's or young adult's placement in substitute care is necessary as of the FCR;

(c) whether the child's current placement is appropriate;

(d) the extent of each parties' participation and progress as follows:

1. The parent(s) participation in the action plan and whether they have demonstrated observable changes that reduce or alleviate danger to their child(ren) or the need for the child(ren)'s placement or to achieve other outcomes necessary to improve their capacity to keep their child(ren) safe and provide for the child(ren)'s well-being;

2. The child(ren) or young adult's participation in the action plan and whether they have demonstrated progress in achieving the outcomes to improve their safety and well-being;

3. The Department's actions and efforts to address the needs of the family; and

4. The placement provider's fulfillment of the placement expectations to meet the child(ren) or young adult's needs.

(e) the extent of progress which has been made by all parties to achieve the Department's identified permanency plan(s) in the action plan;

(f) whether the Department has taken steps to:

1. ensure the child(ren)'s or young adult's placement resource is following the reasonable and prudent parent standard; and

2. ascertain whether the child(ren) or young adult has regular, ongoing opportunities to engage in age or developmentally appropriate activities, including consulting with the child or young adult in an age appropriate manner about the child(ren)'s or young adult's opportunities to participate in the activities;

(g) the Department's permanency plan for the child(ren) or young adult and the projected date by which the child(ren) or young adult may achieve permanency either through:

1. stabilization with their parents or guardian;

2. reunification and safely remaining with their parents or guardian;

3. adoption;

4. guardianship by a person other than the Department or its agent;

5. permanently living with Kin; or

6. another planned permanent living arrangement for a child 16 years of age or older.

(10) In addition, the panel may make and record nonbinding recommendations designed to further the child's progress towards permanency.

(11) At the FCR that occurs within six months of a child's 18th birthday, the FCR panel, the child and the Department review a child's request to receive young adult services with the Department after 18 years of age.

(a) If all parties agree to the child receiving young adult services and the child meets the criteria for young adult services under 110 CMR 23.00: Services for Young Adults, the child will continue to receive services through the Department.

(b) If the Department and child agree that the child is not interested in receiving young adult services at 18 years of age, the Department works with the child on transition planning for a discharge at 18 years of age.

(c) If the child is requesting young adult services beyond 18 years of age and either the Department or the FCR Panel disagrees, the child's request is sent to a Young Adult Review Panel at the Area Office responsible for the child's case for a final decision.

(12) The FCRU panel member shall record the panel's determinations and recommendations, including minority opinions and objections, and a summary of the review in the electronic case record in a format prescribed by the Department. The FRCU will notify applicable agency staff when the report is completed and will provide copies of the report to the:

(a) parents, unless their parental rights were terminated;

(b) child or young adult 14 years of age or older;

(c) placement provider;

(d) child's or young adult's attorney and/or GAL, if applicable; and

(e) parent's attorneys, unless their client's parental rights were terminated.

(13) Panel Disagreement with Action Plan. If the determinations of the panel conflict with the action plan as written, the determination of the panel, shall be binding upon the Department and shall be incorporated into a revised action plan, unless the panel's determinations are successfully appealed as set forth in 110 CMR 6.02(14).

(14) Appeal of FCR Determination.

(a) Parents, foster parents, the child's or young adult's attorney, as well as any child or young adult 14 years of age or older may appeal the FCR determination to change the permanency plan for the child or young adult by requesting a Fair Hearing within 30 days after receiving the FCR Report. All other FCR determinations may be appealed through the grievance process.

5

(b) If the departent social worker or supervisor disagree with any of the FCR determinations, the area staff and FCR staff will attempt to resolve the disagreement in accordance with the Foster Care Review Policy.

(15) Permanency Plan Change. Whenever the FCR panel determines, under 110 CMR 6.02(9)(g), that the permanency plan for the child or young adult should be changed, the department must schedule the case for a permanency planning conference. The permanency plan does not change until a permanency planning conference is held. If the permanency planning conference determination differs with the FCR permanency plan determination, the case will be referred to the Regional Director who will determine the permanency plan.

110 CMR 6.03. Permanency Hearing

A Permanency Hearing is a review conducted by a court of competent jurisdiction under M.G.L. c. 119, § 29B, of a child or young adult younger than 22 years old in substitute care. The Department shall participate in a permanency hearing to determine a child's or young adult's permanency plan within 12 months of an initial order of commitment, or grant of custody to the Department, and every 12 months thereafter as long as the child or young adult remains in substitute care. If a child or young adult has entered substitute care through a voluntary placement agreement as set forth in 110 CMR 4.10 through 4.14, the permanency hearing will be held within 12 months of the child or young adult entering placement or within 60 days of the Department obtaining court custody, whichever is later. For children who remain in the Department's custody after they are placed home, a permanency hearing will be conducted if at the time the review is scheduled the child has been home for less than six months.

The process utilized for a permanency hearing shall be in accordance with Trial Court Rule VI Uniform Rules for Permanency Hearings. The Department shall file with the court which committed the child to the Department's custody a permanency report prior to the permanency hearing date, and shall send a copy of the report to the attorneys of record, or to a party who is unrepresented. The outcome of the Department's FCR and Permanency Planning Conference is included in the permanency report. If a parent has signed an adoption surrender, or if a parent's parental rights have been terminated by a court of law, the parent or his or her counsel will not be sent a copy of the permanency report.

The Department shall notify the child's current foster/pre-adoptive parent of the date of the permanency hearing. The current foster/pre-adoptive parent has the right to be heard at the permanency hearing.

At the permanency hearing the court shall determine the permanent plan for the child. In making such determination the court shall consult with the child, in an age-appropriate manner, about the proposed permanency plan for the child. Such consultation may be through a report by the Department social worker, the child's attorney or a guardian ad litem whose has discussed with the child the proposed permanent plan. A child 14 years of age or older may attend the permanency hearing review. The Department shall use reasonable efforts to achieve the permanency plan determined by the court. The Department may concurrently use reasonable efforts to achieve an alternative permanent plan if the permanent plan determined by the court is reunification with the family and the permanency plan established through the Department's permanency planning conference is other than reunification.

Regulatory Authority—110 CMR 6.00: M.G.L. c. 18B, §§ 6A,7; c. 119, §§ 37 and 29B.

110 CMR 7.00. Services

Selected Sections

110 CMR 7.001. Introduction to Purchase of Services

The Department provides services in two basic ways: through its own direct service staff and from a wide variety of private social service providers. The Department purchases a wide array of social services. Most of these services are purchased only for the referral of Department clients, but several are open to any eligible citizen of the Commonwealth without direct Departmental contact.

110 CMR 7.002. Providers—Procedures for the Purchase of Services

(1) The purchase of services by the Department is governed by the Regulations of the Executive Office of Administration and Finance at 801 CMR 25.00: Procurement Procedures Governing the Purchase of Social and Rehabilitative Services and 801 CMR 4.00 Service Contract Regulations and any administrative bulletin(s) issued in connection thereto.

(2) All written contracts between the Department and any provider shall include and incorporate the General Conditions, as required by the Executive Office of Human Services, for the fiscal year in which the services are to be provided.

(3) All written contracts between the Department and any provider shall obligate the provider to comply with all of 110 CMR, service delivery standards, and policies. This requirement shall expressly include, but is not limited to, observance by the provider of the requirements for special provisions relating to linguistic and cultural minorities (see 110 CMR 1.06), for Native Americans (see 110 CMR 1.07), handicapped clients (see 110 CMR 1.08), and nondiscrimination (see 110 CMR 1.09). Failure to conform to such obligations shall be grounds for terminating any provider's contract.

(4) All purchases of services by the Department are subject to the proposal review of the Department's area boards as mandated by M.G.L. c. 18B, § 15, and of the local councils for children recognized by the Office for Children, as mandated by M.G.L. c. 28A, § 7.

110 CMR 7.003. Providers—Delivery of Services

(1) Every provider shall deliver services in conformance with the provisions of the contract.

(2) Every provider shall utilize the eligibility criteria as set forth in the contract or the Department's regulations in determining

whether an applicant is eligible for the services enumerated in the provider's contract with the Department.

(3) No provider shall require a recipient of services to sign any agreement which purports to limit the provider's liability with respect to the provision of those services.

(4) The Department, in conformance with the provisions of the contract, may conduct periodic monitoring activities of the provider's programmatic and fiscal performance and status.

110 CMR 7.004. Providers—Contract Termination

Termination of any contract between the Department and a provider shall be in conformance with the terms of the contract.

110 CMR 7.005. Public Private Partnership Program ("PPPP")

The Public Private Partnership Program (PPPP) is the program established annually by the Legislature in the budget appropriation of the Department, whereby the Department is authorized to purchase services from providers jointly with entities known as "partners".

110 CMR 7.006. PPPP—Eligible Partners

(1) The following entities are eligible to participate as partners:

(a) Political subdivisions of the Commonwealth (including but not limited to, cities, towns, counties, boards, commissions, school districts, and housing authorities).

5

(b) Not-for-profit organizations whose purposes are among those listed in Sections 501(c)(3), 501(c)(4), and 502(c)(6) of the Internal Revenue Code, and who are incorporated under state law as not-for-profit corporations (including but not limited to corporations, foundations, trusts and federated fund-raising organizations).

(c) For-profit organizations (including but not limited to corporations, partnerships, trusts, and sole proprietorships).

(d) Providers already participating in the Public Private Partnership Program (PPPP) or potential providers submitting proposals for funding under this program.

(2) The following entities are ineligible to participate as partners:

(a) Other state agencies, or departments, or branches of state government or federal agencies or branches of federal government. However, these parties may make financial contributions to eligible partners.

(b) Individuals. However, individuals may make financial contributions to eligible partners.

110 CMR 7.007. PPPP—Administration

(1) The Commissioner shall appoint an advisory committee which may make recommendations on issues such as the services to be eligible for funding under this program, the priorities for services to be provided, the target populations to be served through the program, and composition of the partner share.

(2) The Department retains final authority to determine priorities and eligible services.

110 CMR 7.008. PPPP—Procurement Procedures

(1) All procurements under the PPPP shall be subject to the requirements set forth in 110 CMR 7.001 through 7.009.

(2) Potential providers seeking to procure a contract with the Department funded through this program shall obtain and complete an "Expression of Intent to Participate" form from a potential partner, unless the potential provider has already obtained a Partner Commitment as described in 110 CMR 7.008(3).

(3) The Expression of Intent to Participate form shall be in writing and shall include, at a minimum:

(a) the total proposed amount to be contributed by the partner;

(b) the period (date from and date to) for which the services will be provided;

(c) the signature of an officer of the partner organization authorized to express such intent; and

(d) the date of the written statement and date of expiration of the intent to participate, if any.

(4) An eligible partner may designate the following in its Expression of Intent to Participate:

(a) the service to be provided under a proposed Purchase Agreement; and

(b) the geographic area(s) where the services will be delivered.

110 CMR 7.009. PPPP—The Partner Commitment

(1) Once a provider has been selected by the Department, the provider shall be responsible for submitting, or causing the partner to submit, to the Department, a written commitment from the partner to provide the partner's share.

(2) The Partner Commitment may be in the form of a contract, note, letter or other document and shall contain, at a minimum:

(a) the dollar amount to be contributed by the partner;

(b) the period (date from and date to) for which the services will be provided;

(c) a schedule of installments and amount of each installment;

(d) the name and address of the provider intended to be the recipient of the funds;

(e) the full name and business address of the partner and the name and title of the person signing the commitment; and

(f) the signature of an officer of the partner confirming the Commitment.

(3) The Department retains the authority to request further information and documents from the partner in addition to those set forth in 110 CMR 7.009(2).

(4) An executed Partner Commitment shall be attached to but not incorporated into the Purchase Agreement and such execution and attachment shall be a condition precedent to a binding Purchase Agreement.

(5) The partner may participate in the program monitoring and auditing of the provider pursuant to the provisions of the Executive Office of Human Services General Conditions and the contract.

110 CMR 7.010. Services of Other Agencies

(1) When appropriate or necessary, the Department may make referrals to, or provide services in conjunction with, local education agencies (LEAs), the Department of Elementary and Secondary Education, the Department of Early Education and Care, and/or other agencies within the Executive Office of Human Services such as: the Department of Mental Health, Department of Public Welfare, Department of Youth Services, Department of Public Health, Commission for the Blind, Massachusetts Rehabilitation Commission.

(2) Referrals to other agencies will be made if a service requested or needed by an individual or family is not provided by the Department, or if the service requested or needed is within the mandate of another agency or Department of the Commonwealth.

110 CMR 7.011. Interagency Children's Services Team

(1) Whenever a dispute arises between or among the Department and another agency or department as to which agency or department is responsible for the appropriate provision of services, the matter shall be referred to the Office for Children (OFC) for resolution by the interagency children's services team, pursuant to M.G.L. c. 28A, § 6A, for resolution.

(2) In any case where such a dispute has arisen between or among agencies or departments, the Department shall inform any client seeking services from the Department of the procedures for referring the case to the interagency children's service team.

(3) Referral of a case to the interagency children's service team shall not preclude the Department from providing immediate placement, or services, to the child in question, when the child is determined by the Department to be at risk of suffering abuse or neglect.

(4) Referral of a case to the interagency children's service team shall not preclude any client from exercising any other rights s/he may have to either a fair hearing or a grievance consistent with 110 CMR 10.00.

110 CMR 7.012. Interagency Agreements

At the direction of the Commissioner, the Department may enter into written agreements with other departments or agencies, concerning matters of mutual interest. Such agreements shall be signed by the Commissioner on behalf of the Department.

110 CMR 7.020. Introduction to Homemaker Services

Homemakers provide support, assistance and training to families in the activities of daily functioning. Homemakers provide a monitoring and teaching function within a family. Homemakers help care for children, act as a role model for parents, assist in family budgeting, etc.

110 CMR 7.021. Eligibility

In order to be eligible for homemaker services paid for in whole or in part by the Department, there must be an assessed need for homemaker services. The Department will assess a need for homemaker services when:

(1) Emergency Services: During a period of temporary crisis or injury to the parent or primary caretaker, if a caretaker is needed to maintain children in their own home, homemaker services may be authorized.

(2) Ongoing Services: If in the judgment of the Department homemaker services are necessary to assist the parent in meeting the goals of the service plan, homemaker services may be authorized. Such needs may include:

(a) assisting the parents in home management skills;

(b) assisting and teaching the parents when the special needs of the child(ren) in the home so require, in order to meet the child's needs; or

(c) assisting the family in ensuring that abuse and neglect are not occurring in the home.

110 CMR 7.022. Limitation

(1) Emergency Services: Emergency homemaker services may be authorized for a maximum of 24 hours per day, for a maximum of 30 consecutive days.

(2) Ongoing Services: Ongoing homemaker services may be provided for a maximum of six months at a maximum rate of ten hours per week. Homemaker services will be reviewed during each case review, and a six month extension may be authorized. If homemaker services are to be provided for a period longer than one year, or for a maximum rate of more than ten hours per week, such services must be authorized in writing by the Area Director or his/her designee. If homemaker services are to be provided for a period longer than two years, or for a maximum rate of more than 30 hours per week, such services must be authorized in writing by the Regional Director.

110 CMR 7.023. Application Information Required

Any client seeking homemaker services shall be required to provide sufficient information to allow the Department to assess the applicant's need and eligibility for homemaker services. In addition, an individual applying for homemaker services may be required to provide such authorization(s) for collateral contacts as are necessary for the Department to verify or assess the individual's need for homemaker services.

110 CMR 7.024. Sliding Fee

Homemaker services which are, in the judgment of the Department, provided on a protective basis, shall not be subject to any sliding fee requirement. All other homemaker services provided by the Department may be subject to a sliding fee requirement.

110 CMR 7.025. Denial, Reduction, or Termination of Services

Any client aggrieved by the denial, reduction, or termination of homemaker services may request a fair hearing on the matter pursuant to 110 CMR 10.00 et seq. However, the transfer of a client's case, at age 60, to the Department of Elder Affairs is not appealable.

110 CMR 7.030. Introduction to Family Support Services

Family support services is a spectrum of services that supports maintenance of the family unit, and enables adults or children to meet the goals of a service plan. Family support services include active home management (e.g. chore services) and the purchase of items or services that provide social and developmental opportunities for a family or for individual family members.

110 CMR 7.031. Eligibility

(1) Family support services are used to strengthen the family unit, and eliminate the need for placement of children into substitute care.

(2) Family support services may be approved for families who are receiving other Department services, and when, in the judgment of the Department, the family support services will strengthen the family unit and thereby eliminate the need for placement of children into substitute care.

5

110 CMR 7.032. Limitation

(1) Specific family support services to be provided, or items to be purchased, and the reasons therefor, shall be stated in the service plan.

(2) Family support services of active home management (e.g. chore services) may be provided for a maximum of six months at a maximum rate of ten hours per week. Family support services will be reviewed during each case review, and a six month extension may be authorized. If family support services are to be provided for a period longer than one year, or for a maximum rate of more than ten hours per week, such services must be authorized in writing by the Area Director or his/her designee. If family support services are to be provided for a period longer than two years, or for a maximum rate of more than 30 hours per week, such services must be authorized in writing by the Regional Director.

(3) All Department clients who receive chore services as a single service (see 110 CMR 4.70) shall, upon attaining the age of 60, be transferred to the Department of Elder Affairs.

(4) Any items to be purchased must be authorized in writing by the Area Director or his/her designee.

110 CMR 7.033. Application Information Required

Any client seeking family support services shall be required to provide sufficient information to allow the Department to assess the applicant's need and eligibility for family support services. In addition, an individual applying for family support services may be required to provide such authorization(s) for collateral contacts as are necessary for the Department to verify or assess the individual's need for family support services.

110 CMR 7.034. Sliding Fee

Family support services which are, in the judgment of the Department, provided on a protective basis, shall not be subject to any sliding fee requirement. All other family support services provided by the Department may be subject to a sliding fee requirement.

110 CMR 7.035. Denial, Reduction, or Termination of Services

Any client aggrieved by the denial, reduction, or termination of family support services may request a fair hearing on the matter pursuant to 110 CMR 10.00 et seq. However, the transfer of a client's case, at age 60, to the Department of Elder Affairs is not appealable.

110 CMR 7.040. Introduction to Babysitting Services

Babysitting services provide direct care, protection and supervision to children during some portion of a day. Babysitting services are provided to parents (including foster parents) on either an occasional, short-term basis or, under certain circumstances, on a regular, ongoing basis. Babysitting services shall not be authorized on an overnight basis. Babysitting services may be authorized on a night shift basis, but shall not be authorized on an overnight basis.

110 CMR 7.041. Eligibility

In order to be eligible for babysitting services paid for in whole or in part by the Department, there must be an assessed need for babysitting services. The Department may assess a need for babysitting services:

(1) *Occasional, Short-Term Babysitting Services.*

(a) Non-Emergency. When the client needs babysitting services to participate in other services contained in the client's service plan.

(b) Emergency. When the client needs babysitting services to correct a temporary emergency situation or during a period of injury of the parent and primary caregiver.

(2) *Regular Ongoing Babysitting Services.* The Department may provide regular ongoing babysitting services when:

5

(a) in the judgment of the Department, the provision of babysitting services will aid in protecting a child who is the subject of a supported 51A report from further abuse and/or neglect; or

(b) in the judgment of the Department, the provision of babysitting services will aid in preventing the occurrence of abuse and/or neglect, in preventing the placement of children in substitute care, and/or in reuniting families as children return home from substitute care; or

(c) in the judgment of the Department, the need for babysitting services is caused by a physical, mental or emotional disability of the child; or

(d) in the judgment of the Department, day care services (through the Department or otherwise) are unavailable or inappropriate.

110 CMR 7.042. Limitation

(1) Emergency: Emergency babysitting services may be authorized for a maximum of ten hours per day for a maximum period of 30 days.

(2) Non-emergency: Non emergency babysitting services may be authorized for a maximum of ten hours per week for a maximum period of six months. Babysitting services will be reviewed during each case review, and six month extensions may be authorized as often as is, in the judgment of the Department, necessary.

110 CMR 7.043. Application Information Required

Any client seeking babysitting services shall be required to provide sufficient information to allow the Department to assess the applicant's need and eligibility for babysitting services. In addition, an individual applying for babysitting services may be required to provide such authorization(s) for collateral contacts as are necessary for the Department to verify or assess the individual's need for babysitting services.

110 CMR 7.044. Sliding Fee

Babysitting services which are, in the judgment of the Department provided on a protective basis, shall not be subject to any sliding fee requirement. All other babysitting services provided by the Department may be subject to a sliding fee requirement.

110 CMR 7.045. Babysitting Providers

(1) Providers utilized by the Department to provide out-of-home babysitting services shall comply with OFC regulations for licensure. Babysitters providing services in the child(ren)'s home need not be registered, licensed, or approved by the Office for Child Care Services (OCCS); however, such babysitters must meet the standards of the Department, as established from time to time.

(2) Babysitters shall not provide services for more than six children at a time, including the babysitter's own children (if any). No more than two children under two years of age shall receive babysitting services at the same time from the same babysitter unless the babysitter is aided by an approved assistant.

(3) In-home babysitters shall be at least 16 years of age.

(4) If, in the judgment of the Department, a relative or other alternative individual becomes available as a babysitter, babysitting services shall be terminated.

(5) No approval for payment shall be given to relatives or other adults living in the home of the family requesting babysitting services. No parent shall be approved for babysitting services to his or her child or children even if the parent is not living in the home of the child or children. Other relatives approved to provide babysitting who are living outside the home where care is to be provided must comply with 110 CMR 7.045(1) through (3).

110 CMR 7.046. Denial, Reduction, or Termination of Services

Any client aggrieved by the denial, reduction, or termination of babysitting services may request a fair hearing on the matter pursuant to the provisions of 110 CMR 10.00 et seq.

110 CMR 7.050. Respite Care for Families with Developmentally Disabled Members

Families with developmentally disabled children may be eligible to receive respite services from the Department of Mental Retardation, under the auspices of an Interagency Agreement between the Department and DMR. (This Interagency Agreement, as of July 1, 1988, transferred the responsibility for providing those respite care services for developmentally disabled persons that were previously defined in 110 CMR 7.00, (specifically 7.50 through 7.57), to the Department of Mental Retardation.)

110 CMR 7.051. Other Respite Care

The Department may develop and make available other forms of respite care for other populations of families and/or children served by the Department.

110 CMR 7.060. Introduction to Parent Aide Services

Parent Aide services provide a consistent relationship between a trained and supervised individual and a parent or primary caretaker whose family is at risk of or is currently experiencing problems with child abuse or neglect. Parent Aide services provide support and encouragement; build self-esteem; assist in ability to mobilize personal resources; enhance parenting skills; and reduce isolation. The objectives of Parent Aide services are to assist in the prevention of child abuse and neglect and its recurrence; improve self-esteem and promote the emotional growth and independent functioning of the parent or primary caretaker; strengthen parent-child relationships and enhance parenting skills; promote the effective and appropriate use of community resources; enable the parent or primary caretaker to develop appropriate relationships with others; enable the parent or primary caretaker to cope with normal periods of stress and adjust to changes associated with developmental stages of growth; reduce or eliminate stress leading to the abuse or neglect of children; support efforts to prevent placement of children or to assist in the acceptance of placement when necessary; prepare a parent or primary caretaker for eventual reunification when substitute care has been used and assist when reunification occurs; and reduce isolation resulting from cultural and linguistic barriers.

110 CMR 7.061. Target Population

The Department may offer or authorize Parent Aide services when, in the judgment of the Department, the individual(s) in question are members of the target population. The target population for Parent Aide services shall consist of parents, expectant parents, or primary caretakers whose families are at risk of or are currently experiencing problems with child abuse or neglect, which may include situations of:

(1) Physical abuse/neglect
(2) Emotional abuse/neglect
(3) Inexperience in parenting
(4) Inadequate support systems
(5) Isolation resulting from cultural or linguistic barriers
(6) Marital difficulties
(7) Family dysfunction resulting from a variety of situational or social factors
(8) Risk due to physical, developmental and/or emotional disability
(9) Sexual Abuse
(10) Substance Abuse

110 CMR 7.062. Purchased Parent Aide Services

The Department purchases parent aide services directly or through providers, who in turn may utilize volunteer or paid employees. In either case, parent aides must meet the following criteria:

(1) Training. Prior to matching a Parent Aide with a client, the Parent Aide shall receive from the provider or volunteer organization a minimum of 12 hours of initial training, which shall include the following topics:

(a) Overview of child abuse and neglect including the protective service delivery system and M.G.L. c. 119.

(b) Community resources.

(c) Basic Parent Aide skills including: communicating, listening, problem solving, relationship building, values clarification, identifying and understanding parental stress factors and preparing for an initial home visit.

(d) Roles and responsibilities of the Parent Aide in relation to the clients, his/her agency, and the Department.

(e) The purpose of supervision.

(f) Crisis intervention procedures.

(g) Confidentiality and ethics.

(2) Supervision. The Parent Aide shall receive supervision at regular intervals, which shall include:

(a) The integration of training with practice.

(b) The support of the Parent Aide in carrying out his/her roles and responsibilities.

(c) The assessment of client needs and the establishment of goals and plans for service provision in the context of the developmental stages of the case (i.e. engagement, ongoing, termination).

(d) The monitoring and assessment of the Parent Aide's performance.

(3) Confidentiality. The Parent Aide must demonstrate that the client's right to privacy, autonomy and self-determination shall be safe-guarded, and that no information obtained during Parent Aide visits will be divulged without the client's prior notification and consent, except as may be required by law.

(4) Recognition of Cultural and/or Linguistic Differences. Whenever possible the Parent Aide should be of the same racial, ethnic or linguistic background as the client to be served; or at a minimum must demonstrate the ability to recognize and respect the diverse racial, ethnic and linguistic minority groups within the target populations.

110 CMR 7.063. Limitation

Parent Aide services will be provided to a family for a maximum period of 12 months. This limitation may be extended for a maximum total of 18 months, but only with the written approval of the Area Director.

110 CMR 7.064. Denial, Reduction, or Termination of Services

Any client aggrieved by the denial, reduction, or termination of Parent Aide services may request a fair hearing on the matter pursuant to 110 CMR 10.00 et seq.

110 CMR 7.070. Introduction to Supportive Child Care Services

Supportive child care is a program of transportation and supportive social services providing direct child care to children who have open cases with the Department.

110 CMR 7.071. Supportive Child Care

Supportive child care is offered to protect a child who has an open case with the Department. Supportive child care subsidies are administered by the Department of Early Education and Care (EEC) in accordance with 102 CMR 10.00: *Subsidized Child Care* and policies. The Department or its designee, a contracted partnership agency, will determine appropriateness and authorize all referrals for supportive child care.

110 CMR 7.072. Eligibility—Need

In order to be authorized for child care services by the Department, there must be an assessed need for child care services. The Department will assess a need for child care services when, in the judgment of the Department, the provision of child care will aid in protecting a child who has an open case with the Department.

110 CMR 7.073. Intake for Supportive Child Care Services

When child care is requested, the Department social worker and supervisor shall assess whether supportive child care is required as part of the family's service plan. Utilization and continuation of child care services shall be reviewed as needed, but not less than every six months, to determine the appropriateness of continuing supportive child care. Area director approval is required for continuation of supportive child care services beyond 12 months.

110 CMR 7.074. Sliding Fee

(1) A family with a documented need for protection from abuse or neglect must meet income requirements unless waived on a case by case basis by the Department.

(2) Families of children who are approved by the Department to receive supportive child care services may be required to contribute to the cost of the child care services they receive in accordance with a sliding fee established by the EEC.

110 CMR 7.075. Denial, Reduction or Termination of Services

Any client aggrieved by the denial, reduction, or termination of supportive child care services may request a fair hearing from the Department on the matter pursuant to the provisions of 110 CMR 10.00 *et seq.*

110 CMR 7.076. Exceptions to Sliding Fee

Families of children with a need as documented by the Department for protection from abuse and/or neglect, may have fees assessed or waived on a case by case basis. Teen parents enrolled in services for teen parents and their children may have fees waived for the first year at the discretion of the provider, and subsequent years, if they have no income. In lieu of fees, a work contribution must be documented. Children placed in foster care and children living with relatives not legally responsible for them are exempt from the sliding fee requirements of 110 CMR 7.070 through 7.076.

110 CMR 7.077. Redetermination

The Department shall redetermine the fee status of each family receiving child care services at least once every six months. In addition, the Department may redetermine the fee status at any time it learns of a change in family size or income which may dictate a new fee. The Department may require a family to submit appropriate income verification to support the income reported, and to report any change in income or circumstances.

110 CMR 7.078. Delinquent Payments—Termination of Basic Child Care Services

(1) All child care fees must be paid no later than the last business day of the week prior to the week being paid for.

(2) A fee is delinquent if it is not received by the Department or provider agency by the end of the day on which it is due.

(3) Clients who fail to pay a weekly fee on time will be sent a notice that their services will be terminated unless the delinquent fee is paid. Payment must be made by the 14th calendar day after the notice is issued or the services will be terminated the following service day. Families who are habitually late and therefore receive five such notices in a fiscal year will be terminated on the fifth notice even though they pay their late fee.

However, a client may appeal any termination notice via the fair hearing process. In order to have services continue pending the outcome of the fair hearing, the client must pay any delinquent fees by the date stated and must continue to pay all current fees as they become due. If this is not done, the fair hearing may still be held but services will be terminated and will only be reinstated if the decision is favorable to the client.

110 CMR 7.079. Denial, Reduction or Termination of Services

Any client aggrieved by the denial, reduction, or termination of child care services may request a fair hearing on the matter pursuant to the provisions of 110 CMR 10.00 *et seq.*

110 CMR 7.080. Introduction to Counseling and Case Management Services

Counseling and case management services are services provided by a trained individual of support, intervention and/or treatment services, through a range of methods, to an individual or family, on an individual, family, or group basis.

110 CMR 7.081. Eligibility

Counseling and case management services are provided both directly by the Department's direct service staff and by purchase of services. Purchased counseling and case management services are available on both an open referral and closed referral basis. Closed referral case management services are required to conform to the Department's policies, practices, procedures, and regulations, as reflected in the provider's contract. Counseling services are provided to meet a wide variety of needs, including:

(1) to prevent placement of children in substitute care;

(2) to reduce or eliminate stress leading to abuse or neglect of children or adults;

(3) to assist victims of abuse, neglect, sexual abuse, and domestic violence to cope with and respond to these experiences;

(4) to prepare families for eventual reunion when substitute care has been used and to assist families when reunions occur;

(5) to assist families or individuals to achieve a higher level of independent functioning;

(6) to assist families or individuals to cope with normal periods of stress and adjusting to changes caused by the developmental stages of growth;

(7) to assist parents and foster parents to strengthen their parenting skills;

(8) to assist families, foster families or individuals to cope with crisis and develop ways to resolve the crisis;

(9) to prepare children in the Department's care and all members of permanent alternative families for their new living experience;

(10) to assist individuals and their families and foster families in coping with developmental disabilities;

(11) to prepare children and adolescents, as well as their families and foster families, for substitute care placement;

(12) to assist children and adolescents in substitute care, and their families and foster families, to attain agreed upon service goals;

(13) to prevent families and individuals from becoming homeless, and to assist the homeless and those living in inadequate or substandard housing to locate and retain appropriate housing; and

(14) to assist recently immigrated and refugee families and individuals in adjusting to living in a new culture.

110 CMR 7.082. Application Information Required

Any individual applying for counseling services directly to the Department shall be required to provide sufficient information to allow the Department to assess the applicant's need and eligibility for counseling. In addition, an individual applying for counseling services may be required to provide such authorization(s) for collateral contacts as are necessary for the Department to verify or assess the individual's need for counseling.

110 CMR 7.083. Sliding Fee

Case management services are not subject to any sliding fee requirement. Counseling services which are, in the judgment of the Department, provided on a protective basis, shall not be subject to any sliding fee requirement. All other counseling services provided by the Department may be subject to a sliding fee requirement.

110 CMR 7.084. Denial, Reduction, or Termination of Services

Any client aggrieved by the denial, reduction, or termination of counseling services may request a fair hearing on the matter pursuant to the provisions of 110 CMR 10.00 et seq.

110 CMR 7.090. Introduction to Emergency Shelter Services

Emergency Shelter is a service which provides short-term residential placement for women, children, families, and adolescents who are in crisis because they have suffered or are at substantial risk of suffering serious physical or emotional injury as a result of abuse, neglect or abandonment; or who are, due to financial constraints, unable to obtain housing.

Services to Women in Transition is a program of services which offers safety, protection, and support to women (with or without children) who have been threatened with or have experienced harassment, intimidation, or assault by someone within their household.

110 CMR 7.091. Scope of Services

(1) Emergency shelter for adolescents shall be provided by agencies or individuals under contract to the Department and licensed by EEC, and shall be available on a 24-hour-a-day, seven-day-a-week basis. These shelters may be either self-contained facilities or foster homes designated as emergency shelters.

(2) Emergency shelter for homeless women with children shall be provided at the Department's New Chardon Street Shelter in Boston or by referral to other appropriate facilities or agencies on a 24-hour-a-day, seven-day-a-week basis.

(3) Services to women in transition shall be provided by agencies or individuals under contract to the Department. Shelters shall be located in facilities that provide a safe, temporary residence in an anonymous location and shall be accessible on a 24-hour-a-day, seven-day-a-week basis.

110 CMR 7.092. Application for Emergency Shelter Services

Clients may apply for emergency shelter services in the following manner:

(1) by applying directly to the Department;

(2) by applying directly to an emergency shelter service provider under contract with the Department; or

(3) by applying to another agency, which may refer the client to the Department or to an emergency shelter service provider under contract with the Department.

110 CMR 7.093. Approval of Application for Emergency Shelter Services

Emergency shelter service may be provided if one or more of the following conditions exist at the time of application:

(1) children have suffered or are in immediate danger of suffering physical or emotional injury as a result of abuse or neglect.

(2) children have been abandoned and are in need of temporary placement pending completion of an assessment and a search for parents and family.

(3) children are placed into the Department's custody by a court pending a hearing on a CHINS petition.

(4) children have had difficulty with previous placements and need a short-term placement pending resolution of the immediate crisis and development of a new service plan.

(5) children have run away from home.

(6) women have been threatened with or have experienced harassment, intimidation or abuse by a member of their household.

(7) families with children are homeless.

110 CMR 7.094. Sliding Fee

(1) Emergency shelter services, if approved by the Department, are available without regard to income, and are not subject to a sliding fee.

(2) Shelter services to families temporarily placed at the New Chardon Street Home shall be subject to a sliding fee for services, as determined by the Department.

(3) Services to women in transition are available without regard to income, and are not subject to a sliding fee.

110 CMR 7.095. Limits on Use of Emergency Shelter Services

(1) Emergency shelter for an individual child shall be provided for a maximum period of 30 days in a six month period. Those 30 days may be consecutive or may accumulate. In the event of a court order for out-of-home placement of a child, emergency shelter for an individual child shall be utilized for a maximum period of 45 days in a six-month period.

(2) Emergency shelter to women in transition shall be provided for a maximum period of six consecutive weeks.

(3) Emergency shelter facilities may provide placement for children without parental consent for up to 72 hours, during which time either the parents' consent must be obtained or a court order allowing continued placement must be obtained. If the client is a mature child, he/she may be required to sign a Voluntary Placement Agreement with the Department in order for the Department to provide placement for 72 hours without parental consent or court order.

110 CMR 7.100. Eligibility and Recruitment of Foster/ Pre-Adoptive Parent Applicants

(1) Whenever the Department needs foster parents or adoptive parents, it shall recruit individuals who meet the standards set forth at 110 CMR 7.100 through 7.105. The Department may, in appropriate circumstances, use resources outside the Department to assist in such recruitment, including, but not limited to: private foster care and adoption agencies, foster parent associations, media-assisted recruitment, recruitment by culture based and faith based organizations.

(2) Whenever an individual contacts the Department for the purpose of applying to be a foster or pre-adoptive parent, the Department shall conduct an initial screening process to determine if the individual and any household member meets the Department's initial eligibility criteria as set forth at 110 CMR 7.100(3) and (4).

(3) An individual will be eligible to apply to be a foster or pre-adoptive parent if she/he, or a member of their/her/his household,

(a) does not have a criminal record which, in the judgment of the Department bears adversely upon the individual's ability to assume and carry out the responsibilities of a foster or pre-adoptive parent, as established by Department Policy on background record check and 110 CMR 18.00 et seq.; and

(b) has not had an open case with the Department during the 12 months immediately preceding the initial screening process except:

1. The individual/household member has an open case to receive services following an adoption legalization;

2. The individual/household member has an open case to receive services on behalf of a child for whom they are a guardian;

3. The individual is a prospective Kinship placement and the household member with the open case is the teen parent of a child to be placed, the teen parent is not alleged to be responsible for the physical or sexual abuse of any child in a supported child abuse/ neglect investigation under M.G.L. c. 119, § 51B, and it is considered to be in the child's best interest for the teen parent to be a member of the kinship household;

4. Where the household member with an open case is a biological parent, but not an applicant, who is unable to parent their child due to a disability and the foster parent is approved by the commissioner after a recommendation by a central office clinical review team.

5. Any circumstance other than those listed above when approved by the Assistant Commissioner over foster care and adoption, upon the recommendation of a Regional clinical review team; and

(c) is not identified by the Department as alleged to be responsible for abuse or neglect of a child in a screened out report of child abuse/neglect under M.G.L. c. 119, § 51A or supported 51B investigation which was referred to the District Attorney pursuant to M.G.L. c. 119, § 51B(k), unless approved by the Regional Director, upon the recommendation of a Regional clinical review team; and

(d) does not have a history of involvement with the Department, including but not limited to, being the victim or the perpetrator of child abuse or neglect, which in the judgment of the Department would bear adversely on the person's ability to assume and carry out the responsibilities of a foster or pre-adoptive parent; and

(e) is a resident of the Commonwealth. If the individual is a resident of another state, they will be referred to the child welfare agency in the state where they reside. This does not preclude the Department from utilizing, or paying foster care payments to, foster/pre-adoptive homes outside of the Commonwealth if that home has been approved by the resident state.

In making the determination under 110 CMR 7.100(4)(b), (c) and (d), the Department will check its Central Registry and its computerized data system to determine if there is current, or has been previous, involvement with the Department and the nature of that involvement.

For any applicant who has lived outside the Commonwealth in the five years prior to applying to become a foster/pre-adoptive parent, the Department will check the central registry of child abuse and neglect in each state or other jurisdiction the applicant lived in.

(4) An individual will not be eligible to apply to be a foster or pre-adoptive parent if:

(a) the individual's home, which will be used to provide foster or pre-adoptive care, does not meet the physical standards as set forth at 110 CMR 7.105 or does not currently have space sufficient to accommodate one additional household member,

(b) the individual's schedule would not require that a foster child of pre-school age spend in excess of 50 hours per week in child care, or that a foster child in the first grade or beyond spend more than 25 hours in child care each week,

(c) the individual has a stable source of income sufficient to support his/her current household members,

(d) the individual has a stable housing history,

(e) the individual possesses the basic ability to read and to write in English or in his/her primary language, or unless another household member who is requesting consideration as a foster/pre-adoptive parent can meet this criteria.

(f) the individual has a working telephone in his/her home for both incoming and outgoing calls,

(g) the individual has reached his/her 18th birthday,

(h) the individual is not the parent of the child for whom she/he seeks to provide foster or adoptive care, and

(i) is a citizen of the United States or been granted legal permanent resident status, asylum, refugee or other indefinite legal status by the U.S. Immigration officials.

(j) the premises of the individual's home are free of any animal that would pose a danger to a foster/pre-adoptive child.

This initial eligibility process will include at least one visit to the foster/pre-adoptive home, an interview with at least one of the potential foster/pre-adoptive parents and an assessment of the physical requirements for foster/pre-adoptive homes set forth at 110 CMR 7.105. The Department will provide the potential foster/pre-adoptive parent with the Department's Family Resource Application.

(5) If the Department determines that an individual is ineligible to apply to be a foster or adoptive parent it shall notify the individual in writing and shall include the reason(s) for the ineligibility.

(6) If as a result of the Department's initial screening process an individual is determined to be ineligible to apply to be a foster or adoptive parent, that determination shall be final and the individual shall not have a right to have that decision reviewed through the Department's fair hearing process.

However, if the sole basis for ineligibility is based on the individual's, or a household member's, criminal record, the individual has the right to submit information demonstrating the inaccuracy of, or the lack of relevance of, the criminal record.

(7) If as a result of the Department's initial screening process an individual decides to withdraw from consideration as a foster/pre-adoptive parent, the Department will confirm the individual's decision in writing and document the decision in the foster/pre-adoptive parent file.

110 CMR 7.101. Out-of-Home Placements

(1) All out-of-home placement decisions shall be made in the best interests of the child, based upon safety, well-being and permanency of the child and the child's individual needs. Placement decisions should be made in a manner conducive to permanency planning and the safe and timely return of children to their homes or their placement into a new permanent setting. The following factors shall be taken into consideration:

(a) the least restrictive setting for the child;

(b) close proximity to the home of the child's family and/or the child's school;

(c) ability for frequent visits between child and his/her family;

(d) the child's individual needs including those related to his/her physical, mental, and emotional well-being and the capacity of the prospective foster or pre-adoptive parents to meet those needs;

(e) a placement that can serve as the placement for any of the child's siblings in the Department's care or custody; and

(f) a mature child's choice of residence.

(2) The Department shall consider, consistent with the best interests of the child, the following placement resources in the following order:

(a) placement with a kinship family;

(b) placement with a child-specific family;

(c) placement in a family foster care home where the child was previously placed;

(d) placement in family foster care;

(e) placement in a shelter/short term program or group home;

(f) placement in community residential care.

Every reasonable effort should be made to place a child in accordance with 110 CMR 7.101(1) and (2).

(3) Whenever the Department places a child in foster care, the Department shall seek from the child's parents the names of relatives or other kin who may be available to become a foster placement for the child(ren). The Department shall also begin a search for other relatives of the child or for other adult persons who have played a significant positive role in the child's life in order to determine whether the child may appropriately be placed with a relative or person if, in the judgment of the department, that placement would be in the best interests of the child.

(4) The Department shall place a child with the child's full or half sibling(s) unless doing so would be contrary to the safety or well-being of the child or sibling(s), or otherwise not in the child's best interest. If siblings are not placed together, reasonable efforts will be made to provide for visitation with siblings, unless such visitation would be harmful to the child or sibling.

(5) Within 30 days after the child is removed from the custody of the parent(s), the Department shall provide notice to the kin and other adults identified under 110 CMR 7.101(3), unless the kin or other adult could not be approved as a foster parent due to known family or domestic violence. The notice shall include the following information:

(a) The Child has been removed from the custody of the parents;

(b) The process for applying to become the child(ren)'s foster parent and the standards for becoming a foster parent;

(c) The child is placed with kin, if applicable;

(d) The availability of DCF foster care payments and Mass Health medical insurance for the child;

(e) The Departments process for considering kin placements when more than one kin applies at the same time;

(6) When considering a kinship or child-specific placement, the Department shall require that the relative or extended family member or individual chosen by parent(s) meet the Department's requirements as set forth at 110 CMR 7.104 and 7.105.

(7) If more than one kinship or child-specific family is available and willing to be considered as a placement for the same child at the same time the Department reserves the right to prioritize which family(s) will be studied and in which order in accordance with factors set forth in the Department's family resource policy.

(8) If placement is not made in a kinship home, the child's service plan shall indicate in writing:

(a) which kinship placements were given consideration; and

(b) the reason(s) why said persons were not utilized by the Department.

(9) The Department will promote early permanency decisions and outcomes for children in substitute care. The Department will seek to have no more than 1/3 of all children (under the age of 18) who have been in foster care for over 24 months that remain in foster care at any given time during the fiscal year.

110 CMR 7.102. Applicability of 110 CMR 7.100 through 7.303

(1) 110 CMR 7.100 through 7.199 apply to foster and pre-adoptive homes, foster and pre-adoptive parents, and foster and pre-adoptive parent applicants; as well as children placed in community residential care.

(2) 110 CMR 7.200 contains special provisions relating to pre-adoptive placements.

(3) 110 CMR 7.300 applies to persons who wish to become legal guardians of children in the Department's care or custody.

(a) When used in 110 CMR 7.100 through 7.303, the term custody shall mean child in either the care or custody of the Department unless other specified.

(b) When used in 110 CMR 7.100 through 7.303, the term days shall mean calendar days unless otherwise specified.

110 CMR 7.103. Application to Become a Foster Parent/ Pre-Adoptive Parent

Whenever an individual who has contacted the Department for the purpose of applying to be an unrestricted, kinship or child-specific foster or pre-adoptive parent has been deemed eligible under 110 CMR 7.100 the following procedures shall be observed:

(1) The Department shall open a file for the foster/pre-adoptive parent applicant, if not previously opened, with either the Department or a Department contracted provider of foster care.

(2) The Department shall provide the foster/pre-adoptive parent applicant with the following materials: an application form if not previously provided during the initial screening process, and information regarding the evaluation process and the standards for licensing foster/pre-adoptive applicants, in addition to the information required by 102 CMR 5.10(1).

(3) Application forms shall require at least the following information and consent:

(a) the name, date of birth, social security number, address, out of state addresses in the five years prior to the application date, telephone number, sex, sexual preference/ orientation, ethnicity, and occupation of the applicant;

(b) the name, date of birth, social security number, sex and relationship to the applicant of all household members;

(c) the current physical, mental and emotional condition of the applicant and all household members;

(d) the name, address and telephone number of the applicant's employer and the employer of the head of the household, if the applicant is not the head of the household;

(e) the name, address and telephone number of the last physician who has examined or treated the applicant;

(f) the name(s), address(es) and telephone number(s) of any physician(s), psychologist(s) or other professional(s) who have treated the applicant or other household member within the last year for any serious or chronic illness, drug abuse, or alcohol abuse;

(g) any crimes of the applicant or other household member who have been charged with or convicted of;

(h) any current or previous applications to become a foster or pre-adoptive parent submitted by the applicant or other household member, and the results thereof;

(i) whether the applicant or any other household member has ever been identified as allegedly responsible for an incident of child abuse or neglect in a 51B investigation supported by the Department or other child protective agency;

(j) the names and addresses of at least two personal references;

(k) languages spoken in the household, and the language predominantly used in the household;

(l) whether the applicant is seeking placement of a specific child in the home, and, if so, the name, date of birth, address, sex and relationship to the applicant and other household members' relationship to the child;

(m) the consent of the applicant, and other household members if appropriate, for the Department to make collateral contacts with any individuals named in response to requests for information under 110 CMR 7.103(3)(d), (e), (f), (g) and (j) and any other individuals seen by the Department as useful to the evaluation of the application, and

(n) an agreement to allow the Department to conduct an examination of the applicant's status with the criminal offender information system as defined by M.G.L. c. 6, §§ 167 through 172.

(4) The Department shall record in the foster parent/pre-adoptive applicant file opened pursuant to 110 CMR 7.103(1) the date when the foster/pre-adoptive parent applicant contacted the Department for the purpose of applying to become a foster/pre-adoptive parent, and the date when application materials were given or mailed to the foster/pre-adoptive parent applicant.

(5) If the Department does not receive a completed application form from the foster/pre-adoptive applicant within 30 days after giving or mailing the application materials to the applicant, the Department shall attempt to contact the applicant to determine whether the applicant still wishes to become a foster/pre-adoptive parent. If, after the Department has contacted the foster/pre-adoptive parent applicant, the Department does not receive the completed application form within another 30 days, or the Department determines that the applicant no longer wishes to become a foster/pre-adoptive parent, the Department shall note that fact in the foster/pre-adoptive parent applicant file and close the file. If the Department was unable to contact the foster/pre-adoptive parent applicant, the Department will send written notice of the foster/pre-adoptive parent applicant that their file will be closed if the Department does not receive a completed application form within 30 days after mailing the notice to the applicant if the Department does not receive a completed application after the 30th day passes the Department shall note that fact in the foster/pre-adoptive parent applicant file and close the file.

In either case, if the individual later determines that she/he desires to be a foster/pre-adoptive parent, she/he shall recommence the process in accordance with 110 CMR 7.100.

(6) After the Department receives the completed foster/pre-adoptive application, the Department shall, arrange for the foster/pre-adoptive applicant to attend the Department's approved foster/pre-adoptive pre-service orientation, education and support training program for the type of foster care they seek to provide. The training program will include, but not be limited to, the information required by 102 CMR 5.10(2). The training is designed to ensure that the foster/pre-adoptive family will provide adequate foster care (including health care), abide by the foster/pre-adoptive parent agreement, and comply with applicable state and federal laws and regulations. The foster/pre-adoptive applicant's participation will be recorded in the foster/pre-adoptive parent applicant's record.

110 CMR 7.104. Standards for Licensure as Foster/ Pre-Adoptive Parent

In order to be licensed as a foster/ adoptive parent, a foster/pre-adoptive parent applicant must meet the following requirements:

(1) A foster/pre-adoptive parent applicant must demonstrate, to the satisfaction of the Department the ability:

(a) to assure that a child placed in his or her care will experience a safe, supportive, nurturing and stable family environment which is free from abuse or neglect;

(b) to assure that a child placed in his or her care will be provided with adequate food, clothing, shelter, supervision and other essential care at all times;

(c) to assure that a child placed in his or her care will be provided with routine and emergency medical and dental care;

(d) to promote the physical, mental, and emotional well-being of a child placed in his or her care; including supporting and respecting a child's sexual orientation or gender identity;

(e) to respect and make efforts to support the integrity of a child's racial, ethnic, linguistic, cultural and religious background;

(f) to manage the stressful situations which are frequently associated with the placement of a child in substitute care, such as the temporary nature of such placement, the integration of a child in crisis into the foster/adoptive family, and the potential return of the child to his/her family;

(g) to respect and be bound by the same standards of confidentiality as the Department and its employees;

(h) to accept and support the child's relationship with his/her parents, siblings and other family members and with the Department;

(i) to assist a child in handling his/her situations such as removal from the home of their parent(s), placement in a new home environment, placement in a new school (when applicable), visits with parents and siblings, and possible return to the home of the parent(s) or placement in other substitute care;

(j) to assure that a child placed in his /her care will be expected to attend school regularly and will have the opportunity to participate in an educational program and in extracurricular activities that meet the child's educational and social needs;

(k) to work with the Department and the foster child's parents in implementing the child's service plan in order to meet development goals and outcomes;

(l) in collaboration with the Department, to develop and participate in an annual plan for trainings, education and support that will assist the foster/pre-adoptive parent in meeting the needs of the child(ren) to be placed in his/her care;

(m) to draw upon community and professional resources as needed;

(n) to transport children safely, within the standards set by state law;

(o) to deal with difficult issues in the child's background, and be able to talk with the child comfortably and constructively about his/her birth parents and family;

(p) to have reasonable expectations of a child's behavior and potential growth; and

(q) to assume and carry out all other responsibilities of a foster/pre-adoptive parent as detailed in the standard written agreement between the Department and foster/pre-adoptive parents.

(2) A foster/pre-adoptive parent applicant or any member of her/his household must be free of any physical, mental or emotional illness or handicap which, in the judgment of the Department, would impair his or her ability to assume and carry out the responsibilities of a foster/pre-adoptive parent. However, no illness or handicap in and of itself shall disqualify an individual from becoming a foster/pre-adoptive parent.

(3) A foster/pre-adoptive parent applicant or any member of his/her household must have a record which is free of criminal conduct which, in the judgment of the Department, bears upon his/her ability to assume and carry out the responsibilities of a foster/pre-adoptive parent, as established by Department Policy on background checks and 110 CMR 18.00 *et seq.*

(4) A foster/pre-adoptive parent applicant shall maintain a household that has sufficient income and appropriate fiscal management to maintain stability and security without foster or adoptive parent reimbursement or subsidies provided under 110 CMR 7.130 and 110 CMR 7.209. Foster/adoptive reimbursement and subsidy shall be used to meet the individual needs of the child.

(5) A foster/pre-adoptive parent applicant must live in a home which meets the requirements for foster/pre-adoptive homes set forth in 110 CMR 7.105.

(6) A foster/pre-adoptive applicant must be a citizen of the United States or been granted legal permanent resident status, asylum, refugee or other indefinite legal status by U.S. Immigration officials, unless a waiver is granted under 110 CMR 7.105A.

(7) A foster/pre-adoptive applicant must meet the initial eligibility criteria set forth at 110 CMR 7.100.

110 CMR 7.105. Standards for Licensure of Foster/ Pre-Adoptive Homes

In order to be licensed as a foster/pre-adoptive parent, a foster/pre-adoptive parent applicant must live in a home which meets the requirements of 102 CMR 5.10(4) and the following requirements:

(1) The home must be clean; safe; free of obvious fire and other hazards; and of sufficient size to accommodate comfortably and appropriately all members of the household and the approved number of foster/pre-adoptive children.

(2) The home must have safe and adequate lighting, ventilation, hot and cold water supply, plumbing, electricity, and heat.

(3) The home must be furnished with a refrigerator and cooking stove in safe, working condition.

(4) No foster child over one year of age shall share a bedroom with an adult, except if the foster children had been sharing a bedroom in the foster home prior to their 18th birthday and one of the children turns 18 years of age.

(5) The home must have sufficient furniture to allow each child to sleep in a separate bed and to have adequate storage space for his or her personal belongings.

(6) No foster child over four years of age, except for siblings up to age eight, shall share a bedroom with a child of the opposite sex.

(7) The home must have bedrooms which provide at least 50 square feet per child, except the Department may waive this requirement for kinship homes if the bedrooms provide at least 35 square feet per child, and shall accommodate no more than four children per bedroom.

(8) No bedroom to be used by foster children shall be located above the second floor unless any such floor has two safe means of egress.

(9) No bedroom to be used by foster children shall be located below the first floor unless it contains a ground level, standard door exit and at least one operable window.

(10) Each floor of the home, including the basement, shall be equipped with smoke detectors in working order.

(11) If the home uses well water, it shall be tested and determined safe, and a report of the test shall be furnished to the Department.

(12) No more than four foster children shall reside in the foster/per-adoptive home at any one time, and at no time shall the total number of children residing in the foster/pre-adoptive home exceed six. Of the total of six children being cared for in the foster/pre-adoptive home, up to two children may be age 24 months or younger; however, only one child may be age one month or younger, provided, however:

(a) The Regional Director whose area office oversees the foster/pre-adoptive home may authorize additional children to be placed in a foster/pre-adoptive home under the following circumstances, as long as the total number of foster children in the foster home does not exceed six and the total number of children in the home does not exceed eight:

1. in the event of a multiple birth to allow siblings under the age of one month to be placed together; or

2. for an emergency short-term placement in a Hotline, respite, or family child care home; or

3. to place siblings together; or

4. for the replacement of a foster/pre-adoptive child in a foster/pre-adoptive home where she or he previously resided; or

5. to place siblings together where one sibling is already residing in the foster/pre-adoptive home; or

6. to place siblings together where one or more of the siblings has a previously established relationship with the foster/pre-adoptive home.

A capacity waiver for reasons 110 CMR 7.105(12)(a)1., 2., or 3. is not permitted unless there are no more than three foster children in the home and no more than five children in the home at the time the waiver is granted.

(b) The Commissioner/designee may authorize the placement of additional children in a foster/pre-adoptive home over the 4/6 limits outlined above for any reason other than the reasons listed in 110 CMR 7.104(12)(a) when the placement of a child(ren) is in the best interest of the child(ren) and the Commissioner/designee has received a recommendation of a Department clinical review team and consulted with professionals or others involved with the child(ren).

The Department may limit the number of children placed in a foster/pre-adoptive home during the first six months a home is licensed.

For the purpose of 110 CMR 7.000, the Department includes in the four/six limits any youth over the age of 18 who is in the Department's care or custody unless the youth receives care and maintenance payments directly.

COMMENTARY

The Department establishes capacity limits regarding the maximum number of foster/preadoptive children a family can accept for a number of reasons. By limiting the number of children placed with a foster/pre-adoptive family, the Department seeks to ensure that the family is able to meet each placed child's needs as well as those of other household members. The Department is particularly concerned that the family is able to meet these needs on the sustained, intensive level required when caring for children who have been abused or neglected, while carrying out their other responsibilities in this important partnership role.

(13) Any home which is used for family childcare must be in compliance with the requirements of the EEC, as set forth in 102 CMR 8.07 through 8.09.

(14) The home may not have any household member, frequent visitor or alternative caretaker, who would, in the judgment of the Department, pose a threat of abuse or neglect to foster children placed in the home, or who would impede or prevent the provision of adequate foster care in the foster home.

(15) The home must be equipped with a telephone in working order for both incoming and outgoing calls.

(16) Any firearm located in the home shall be licensed and registered in accordance with state law and shall be trigger-locked or fully inoperable, and stored without ammunition in a locked area. Ammunition shall be stored in a separate locked area.

(17) Any pet/animal maintained on the premises of the foster/pre-adoptive home must have up to date vaccinations, rabies shots, and be licensed in accordance with the municipality in which the pet/animal is maintained.

(18) No foster child under the age of 12 will be placed in a home where a Rottweiler, Pit Bull or German Shepard dog, or a mixture of the these three breeds, is maintained on the premises of a foster/pre-adoptive home, unless the Department after review determines that such a placement is in the best interest of the child(ren), except for a dog which is being used as a service animal for a household member whose disability has been verified.

In reviewing a request for the placement of a child under the age of 12 in a foster/pre-adoptive home that maintains a Rottweiler, Pit Bull, or German Shepherd, or a mixture of these three breeds, on the premises the Department shall contact the animal control officer in any town where the animal has been maintained and the Department may consider, but is not limited to, the following factors:

(a) Any prior relationship between the child and the dog;

(b) The age, sex and size of the child;

(c) The age, sex and size of the dog;

(d) Whether the dog has been neutered;

(e) Any prior incidents of dangerous behavior/incidents by the dog;

(f) Behavioral aspects of the child(ren);

(g) Number of dogs on the premises; and

(h) Whether the dog is penned or caged at anytime, and if so, under what circumstance and for what purpose.

The Department reserves the right to request that a foster/pre-adoptive parent applicant or foster/pre-adoptive parent obtain and provide a copy of a behavior/temperament assessment and/or provide veterinary records on any animal maintained on the premises used as a foster/pre-adoptive home. The cost of the behavior/temperament assessment will be borne by the foster/pre-adoptive parent or applicant.

110 CMR 7.105A. Waiver of Standards for Approval of Foster/Pre-Adoptive Parents or Home

The requirement set forth in 110 CMR 7.104(6) may be waived for an applicant for a child specific or kinship home as set forth in 110 CMR 7.108, provided the applicant otherwise meets the eligibility criteria set forth for child specific and kinship applicants and a determination is made that it would be in the child's best interest to be placed in the applicant's home.

In determining whether a waiver is in the child's best interest, the decision maker(s) shall consider the nature and length of the applicant's relationship with the child(ren), the applicant's ability to support and maintain the child's connection to family, community and culture and the child's anticipated length of stay in placement.

The decision whether to waive the requirement shall be made by a Regional Clinical Review Team (RCRT), or in an emergency placement situation, by the Regional Director who shall then arrange for a final decision by the RCRT after the comprehensive assessment under 110 CMR 7.107. Waiver decisions made in connection with an emergency placement may be changed as a result of information obtained or reassessed during the comprehensive assessment under 110 CMR 7.107. There shall be no appeal from a decision not to waive the requirement for an emergency placement.

110 CMR 7.106A. Non-Department State Employees as Foster/Pre-Adoptive Parents

Any state employee, including a special state employee, full or part time who is licensed as a foster/pre-adoptive parent, must file with the State Ethics Commission a disclosure of financial interest on a form prescribed by the Ethics Commission. The disclosure of financial interest form must be filed with the Ethics Commission prior to the placement of a child in the foster/pre-adoptive home.

110 CMR 7.106B. Department Employees as Foster/Pre-Adoptive Parents

(1) Encouraging individuals to become foster or adoptive families is a critical Department priority. The Department shall therefore support its own employees who wish to become foster or pre-adoptive parents by providing opportunities for them to do so.

(2) Upon written request to and written approval by the Deputy Commissioner for Field Operations, a Department employee may be referred to a private agency for foster/pre-adoptive parent purposes through an existing Department contract, to obtain a foster/pre-adoptive parent home study and/or monitor the home if approved. The Deputy Commissioner may also choose to refer the Department employee to a Department area office or regional office where the employee does not currently work, nor has previously worked, to obtain a foster/pre-adoptive parent home study and/or to monitor the home if approved.

(3) Prior to the placement of a child in Department care or custody in a Department employee's home, including a Department special state employee, the Department employee must file with the State Ethics Commission a disclosure of financial interest on a form prescribed by the Ethics Commission.

(4) Prior to the initiation of contact for the purposes of placement, or prior to the placement of a child in the care or custody of the Department with a Department employee, or a Department special state employee, a committee consisting of the Deputy Commissioner for Field Operations, the General Counsel and the Assistant Commissioner for Foster Care, Adoption and Adolescent Services, must grant written approval of the placement.

(5) (a) A child in the care or custody of the Department and whose case is managed by the Department may be placed in a Department employee's home (approved and supervised by a private agency or by a Department area office or regional office where the employee does not currently work, nor has previously worked) unless the child is from the employee's own area if the

5

employee works in an area office or the employee's region if the employee works in a regional office. For the purpose of this regulation, Department legal staff is deemed regional employees. For employees in the Department's Central Office, placements will be limited based on the employee's area of responsibility and oversight.

(b) The Department may permit a placement that would not be permitted under 110 CMR 7.106B(5)(a) under the following circumstances:

1. A voluntary or involuntary termination of parental rights has issued, there are no available kin willing and able to care for the child and it is in the child's best interest to be placed with the Department employee;

2. The Department employee is a kin of the child to be placed and it is in the child's best interest to be placed with the Department employee;

3. The child's parent or the child has identified the Department employee as a potential placement, the child's parents do not object to the placement, and it is in the child's best interest to be placed with the Department employee.

(c) In any case in which an exception is granted under 110 CMR 7.106B(5)(b), the parent's and child's Department clinical and adoption case will be transferred to another Department area office or to a contracted agency.

5

COMMENTARY

If a department employee is a kin of the child, a placement may occur on an emergency basis in accordance with 110 CMR 7.108(1) as long as 110 CMR 7.106B (3) and (4) are complied with prior to placement.

(6) Any Department employee wishing to be approved as a pre-adoptive parent for a child not in the Department's care or custody may make application to any private, licensed placement agency, regardless of whether that agency has a contract with the Department, in accordance with the procedures and fee schedule of that agency.

110 CMR 7.106C. Department Employees as Mentor, Visiting Resource or Other Significant Adult to Child in Department Care or Custody

The Department is committed to developing opportunities that will provide youth in its care or custody with positive, sustainable adult connections. In some cases, this adult connection may be a Department employee. A Department employee, or Department special state employee, who seeks to continue or establish a relationship with a child in Department care or custody outside of the employee's duties must obtain prior written permission of the Deputy Commissioner for Field Operations, Assistant Commissioner for Foster Care, Adoption and Adolescent Services and the General Counsel in accordance with the Department family resource policy.

110 CMR 7.106D. Employees of Department Contracted Agencies as Foster/Pre-Adoptive Parents

Any employee of an agency on contract with the Department, who is providing services under the Department contract who wishes to become a foster/pre-adoptive parent, mentor, or visiting resource for a child in Department care or custody, must inform, and obtain the permission of, the Department prior to initiating a license study process and the placement of a foster/pre-adoptive child by writing to the Deputy Commissioner for Field Operations. The Deputy Commissioner will consult with the General Counsel and the Assistant Commissioner for Foster Care, Adoption and Adolescent Services to ascertain that there are no ethical or other conflicts with the proposed home-study or placement, in accordance with the Department's Family Resource Policy.

110 CMR 7.106E. Department Contracted Foster/Adoptive Parents

The Department may utilize foster or adoptive care agencies licensed under the laws of the Commonwealth to provide foster/pre-adoptive services to children in Department care or custody. When it does so, the contracted foster/pre-adoptive homes must comply with the standards set forth at 110 CMR 7.100(3) and (4), 7.103 and 7.104. The Department reserves the right, through its procurement and contracting process, to further define standards that the contracted foster/pre-adoptive homes must meet, such as further limiting the number of children that may be placed in a foster/pre-adoptive home, or requiring additional skills of the foster/pre-adoptive parents,

110 CMR 7.107. Assessment and Licensing of Foster/Pre-Adoptive Parent Applicants

(1) All applicants seeking licensure as an unrestricted foster/pre-adoptive parent are required to complete the Department's foster/pre-adoptive parent pre-service training program. Within 30 working days after the applicant's completing the training, the Department shall complete a comprehensive assessment of the foster/pre-adoptive applicant, unless the foster/pre-adoptive applicant requests, and the Department approves, an extension of time to complete the assessment.

(2) The comprehensive assessment will be performed by the Department in accordance with 102 CMR 5.10(5) and shall include at least the following:

(a) an interview with each household member as appropriate to her/his age and verbal capacity including an individual interview with each applicant;

(b) Home visit(s); and

(c) Contact(s) with personal references supplied by the applicant and other individuals seen by the Department as useful to the assessment; and

(d) Contact(s) with a licensed physician who has conducted a current medical examination of the applicant and each household member; and

(e) contact with the employer for each employed applicant; and

(f) contact with the school for the school age children living in the home and younger children who participate in pre-school or a child care program; and

(g) a check of the Department's Central Registry and the Department's computerized data system; and

(h) for any applicant who has lived out of state within the five years prior to application, a check of the Central Registry of child abuse and neglect of each state in which the applicant lived in the prior five years; and

(i) a check of the state criminal offender record information as defined pursuant to M.G.L. c. 6, §§ 167 and 172; and

(j) a fingerprint-based check of the national crime information databases for each foster/pre-adoptive parent during the initial license study. This requirement will begin October 1, 2008 for new applicants only; and

(k) A specific assessment of the applicant's ability to meet the special needs of children the Department will be placing; and

(l) Successful completion of the Department's training program, unless waived; and

(m) confirmation that the applicant(s) and the home meet the standards established by 110 CMR 7.104 and 7.105.

(3) The Department shall enter all information obtained as a result of its comprehensive assessment [except for any information obtained as a result of any check required by 110 CMR 7.107(2)] in the foster parent file, which may be a combination of an electronic file and a hardcopy file.

Any information obtained as a result of any check required by 110 CMR 7.107(2)(i) and (j) shall be stored separately in a locked file cabinet, as required by the Criminal History Systems Board.

(4) If at any time during the application or comprehensive assessment process the Department obtains information, which if known at the time of the initial eligibility screening process,

would, for any of the reasons set forth in 110 CMR 7.100(3) and (4), have excluded the individual from applying to become a foster/pre-adoptive parent, as set forth at 110 CMR 7.100, the Department shall discontinue the comprehensive assessment process and notify the individual that she/he is ineligible to apply to be a foster/pre-adoptive parent. This may include events which occur after the initial eligibility screening process, such as a report of child abuse/neglect is supported after an investigation under M.G.L. c. 119, § 51B or the individual is charged with a crime which poses a risk to a child's safety. This determination shall be final and the individual shall not have a right to appeal this decision through the Department's fair hearing process.

(5) Within ten working days after completing the comprehensive assessment, the Department shall reach one of the following decisions:

(a) The foster/pre-adoptive parent applicant shall be licensed.

(b) The foster/pre-adoptive parent applicant shall not be licensed.

(6) Within ten working days after reaching a decision to license or not to license a foster/pre-adoptive parent applicant as a foster/pre-adoptive parent, the Department shall give written notice of its decision to the foster/pre-adoptive parent applicant. The written notice shall include:

(a) if the decision reached is to license the age, sex or other characteristics of the children who may be placed in the foster/pre-adoptive home; or

(b) if the decision reached is not to license the reason(s) for the decision, notice of the foster/pre-adoptive parent applicant's right to appeal the decision, and the procedure for taking such an appeal.

A copy of the written notice shall be entered in the foster/pre-adoptive parent file. Upon written request, the foster/pre-adoptive applicant is entitled to receive a copy of the completed assessment.

(7) Either together with or subsequent to the notice of the decision to license, the Department shall issue a foster/pre-adoptive license.

(8) The duration of a foster/pre-adoptive license shall be two years but, in any event, shall be subject to the provisions of 110 CMR 7.107 (9), 110 CMR 7.113, 7.113A, 7.113B, 7.113C, and 7.116. In any case in which the Department is delayed in completing its re-assessment of the foster/pre-adoptive license, the foster/pre-adoptive license shall continue in effect until such time as the Department completes its re-assessment process and sends notice of its decision to the foster/pre-adoptive parent(s). If a foster/pre-adoptive home files for a fair hearing to challenge the Department's decision to terminate their license, the license shall remain in effect until the fair hearing decision is issued.

(9) A license applies only to the home in which the foster/pre-adoptive parent(s) resides at the time of the comprehensive assessment. Except in the case of an emergency, a foster/pre-adoptive parent(s) must notify the Department of any planned change of residence at least 60 days in advance. If a change of residence is necessitated by an emergency, the foster/pre-adoptive parent(s) must notify the Department within 24 hours after the change. If a foster/pre-adoptive parent(s) changes his/her residence without providing the required notice to the Department, or if the foster/pre-adoptive parent(s)' new home does not meet all of the standards set forth in 110 CMR 7.105, the license shall be revoked. In the latter circumstance, there shall be no right to appeal from the revocation of the license.

110 CMR 7.108. Kinship or Child-Specific Placements

Kinship or child-specific placements may occur when a specific child is to be placed into a specific home and that home is not available for other foster children.

(1) Emergency Placements. If the Department determines that an emergency kinship or child-specific placement is necessary for a child(ren), the Department will first conduct an initial eligibility screening of the individual seeking to become the child(ren)'s foster parent, all household members and the home which shall include the following:

(a) background checks (CORI and Department history) on all household members 14 years and older, and on those younger about whom concerns exist;

(b) a home visit;

(c) a determination that the home meets the physical standards set forth at 110 CMR 7.105;

(d) an initial interview is completed on all household members present, as appropriate to age and verbal capacity, including an individual interview with at least one potential foster/pre-adoptive parent and that person has committed to completing the full assessment and approval process;

(e) completion of the Family Resource Application;

(f) if a Department employee, the placement has been approved in accordance with 110 CMR 7.106B(4)

If the proposed placement meets the requirements in 110 CMR 7.108, the Department may place the child(ren). If the proposed placement does not meet the requirements in 110 CMR 7.108, the placement shall be deemed ineligible for an emergency placement, and the Department shall not place the child(ren). A determination of ineligibility under 110 CMR 7.108(1) is final, and is not subject to appeal.

Nothing in 110 CMR 7.108 precludes the kinship/child specific home from being considered as a non-emergency placement as set forth in 110 CMR 7.108(2).

If an emergency kinship or child-specific placement is made, the individual who has been deemed eligible to apply to become the approved family for the child(ren) shall submit to the Department a completed foster/pre-adoptive application. The Department shall complete a comprehensive assessment of the foster/pre-adoptive application within 40 working days after placement.

If the comprehensive assessment reveals compliance with the standards set forth at 110 CMR 7.100, 7.104 and 7.105, the placement shall be approved, solely for the child(ren) for whom an emergency placement had been made. If the assessment reveals that the requisite standards are not met, the placement shall not be approved, and the child(ren) for whom an emergency placement had been made shall be removed forthwith. The kinship or child-specific placement resource shall be notified in writing, of the outcome of the comprehensive assessment, within ten working days after completion of the comprehensive assessment. There is no right of appeal from the removal of a child(ren) from an unapproved home, but the denial of a foster/pre-adoptive application may be appealed via the Department's fair hearing process, set forth at 110 CMR 10.00 et seq.

(2) Non-emergency Placements. Where the Department is not considering the kinship or child-specific home for an emergency placement, the Department shall conduct an initial eligibility screening of the proposed caregivers in accordance with 110 CMR 7.100(3) and (4). If as a result of the initial eligibility screening the proposed caregivers are determined to be ineligible, that determination shall be final, and there shall be no right of appeal. See 110 CMR 7.100(6). If the proposed caregivers are determined to be eligible, they shall submit a completed foster/pre-adoptive application to the Department, and the Department shall complete a foster/pre-adoptive assessment within 40 working days after receiving the completed application.

If the assessment reveals compliance with the standards set forth at 110 CMR 7.100, 7.104 and 7.105, the applicant shall be licensed as a kinship or child-specific placement for the child(ren) named in the foster/pre-adoptive application, and the child(ren) may be placed in the home. The kinship or child-specific placement parent(s) shall be notified in writing, of the outcome of the comprehensive assessment, within ten working days after completion of the comprehensive assessment. Applicants may appeal the denial of a foster/pre-adoptive application via the Department's fair hearing process, set forth at 110 CMR 10.00 et seq.

(3) Miscellaneous Provisions.

(a) Kinship or child-specific parent(s) shall be paid at the Department's regular foster care rates for the care of the children placed pursuant to 110 CMR 7.108.

(b) A foster/pre-adoptive applicant licensed pursuant to 110 CMR 7.108 may not be used as a placement for any child(ren) not named in the foster/pre-adoptive application, unless the comprehensive assessment and training program, as set forth in 110 CMR 7.107(2), is completed, and the applicant is thereafter licensed as an unrestricted foster/pre-adoptive parent in accordance with 110 CMR 7.107.

(c) All new kinship or child-specific foster/pre-adoptive parent(s) will be notified of the approval and payment requirements of 110 CMR 7.100 et seq. either before or at the time they submit a completed foster/pre-adoptive application to the Department.

(d) When the child(ren) for whom the kinship or other child specific family was licensed leaves the placement, the kinship or other child specific family shall cease to be licensed. In these circumstances, there shall be no right to appeal the fact that the family is no longer licensed. However, depending upon the reason for the child(ren)'s departure from the placement and as more fully set forth in 110 CMR 7.116, there may be a right to appeal the fact of the child(ren)'s departure from the placement.

5

COMMENTARY

An emergency kinship or child specific placement may be made on the basis of an initial eligibility screening, but the Department must license the placement as a kinship or child-specific family within 40 working days after the emergency placement. Because the Department is prohibited by law from keeping a child(ren) in an unapproved placement (See M.G.L. c. 15D), the child(ren) must be removed upon a determination that the applicant/home will not be licensed and, in these circumstances, there is no right of appeal from the removal of the child(ren). Similarly, because a kinship or child specific family is approved solely for a specific child(ren), the departure of that child(ren) from the placement automatically terminates the license of the family, and there is no right of appeal from the loss of license.

110 CMR 7.109. TAFDC Grantee Relative vs. Department Foster Care Payments

If a home is approved or licensed as a foster/pre-adoptive home by the Department, and if the family is or could be receiving TAFDC Grantee Relative payments from the Department of Transitional Assistance, the family must choose to receive either TAFDC Grantee Relative payments or foster care payments. The family may not receive payments from both programs simultaneously.

110 CMR 7.111. Written Agreement Between Department and Foster/Pre-Adoptive Parents

Once a foster/pre-adoptive parent applicant has been licensed by the Department as a foster/pre-adoptive parent and has completed pre-service foster/pre-adoptive parent training, the Department and the foster/pre-adoptive parent shall enter into a written agreement. The written agreement shall be signed by each foster/pre-adoptive parent and the Department's authorized agent, shall be renewed annually, and shall include at least the following terms:

(1) a statement of the responsibilities of the foster/pre-adoptive parent, including a recognition that foster care is a temporary arrangement which envisions the eventual reunification of the child with his/her birth family and the obligation of the foster/pre-adoptive parent to support that reunification;

(2) a statement of the Department's responsibilities to the foster/pre-adoptive parents;

(3) a prohibition against the use of any form of corporal punishment by foster/pre-adoptive parents upon any foster child(ren);

(4) a statement of any limitations on the identity or individual characteristics of children who may be placed in the foster/pre-adoptive home;

(5) any other terms required by the EEC under its regulations at 102 CMR 5.10(7)(a); and

(6) a statement that the foster/pre-adoptive parent is bound by the same standards of confidentiality as the Department and its employees.

110 CMR 7.112. Department Obligations to Foster/Pre-Adoptive Parents

(1) Pre-placement. Before a child is placed in a foster/pre-adoptive home, the Department shall provide the prospective foster/pre-adoptive parent with sufficient information about the child to enable the foster/pre-adoptive parent to determine whether to accept placement of the child. The foster/pre-adoptive parent will receive information about the service plan for the child, behavior management guidelines and techniques, the child's medical needs, the child's educational needs, the current health and education information and/or records available, legal status and any other special conditions or requirements.

(2) Post-placement. During the period of a specified child's placement in a foster/pre-adoptive home, the Department shall:

(a) provide the foster/pre-adoptive parent with sufficient information about the foster child on a continuous basis to enable the foster/pre-adoptive parent to provide adequate foster/adoptive care to that child and to meet the individual needs of that child;

(b) assign a social worker who will be responsible for providing direct service to the foster child and support to the foster/pre-adoptive family;

(c) provide the foster/pre-adoptive parent with a copy of the Department's service plan for the foster child, and solicit the foster/pre-adoptive parent's involvement in the implementation and review of the service plan;

(d) provide the foster/pre-adoptive parent with a Medical Passport for the foster child and if not contained in the medical passport, a document(s) that contain the following information: the name and address of the child's medical provider(s), the child's immunization record, the child's known medical problems, the child's medications and any other relevant health information needed to care for the child;

(e) provide the foster/pre-adoptive parent with either a copy of that portion of the child's educational records that include the child's current educational provider, the child's grade level performance, the child's current school record, and any other relevant education information needed to care for the child, or a document(s) that contain such information;

(f) notify the foster/pre-adoptive parent of all court hearings and case reviews involving the foster child, as far in advance of each hearing as possible;

(g) notify the foster/pre-adoptive parent if the Department decides to pursue legal guardianship or adoption for a child placed in the foster/pre-adoptive home, and afford the foster/pre-adoptive parent adequate opportunity to apply to become the legal guardian or adoptive parent for that child;

(h) provide the foster/pre-adoptive parent with any subsidy or benefits to which they are entitled under the Department's regulations, standards or policies; and

(i) provide the foster/pre-adoptive parent with notice of a review or hearing held pursuant to M.G.L. c. 119, §§ 26 and 29B and c. 210, § 3. The notice shall include notice of the time and place of the hearing and notice of the foster/pre-adoptive parent's right to be heard at the proceeding.

110 CMR 7.113. Reassessment and License Renewal of Foster/Pre-Adoptive Parents and Foster/Pre-Adoptive Homes

(1) The Department shall annually re-assess foster/pre-

adoptive parents and foster/pre-adoptive homes whether unrestricted, kinship or other child-specific, in accordance with the procedure set forth in 110 CMR 7.113(1)(a). Every two years a license renewal will be conducted in place of the annual reassessment.

(a) The Department shall send re-assessment materials to the foster/pre-adoptive parent 45 working days prior to the re-assessment due date:

(b) The Department will thereafter:

1. interview the foster/pre-adoptive parents and other household members in the foster/pre-adoptive home;

2. obtain information from any Department social worker who has had a child in his/her caseload placed in the home in the previous year, and include information from any foster child then placed in the home, and thereafter enter a written summary of the interview results in the foster/pre-adoptive parent file;

3. review the foster/pre-adoptive parent file to examine written correspondence between the Department and the foster/pre-adoptive parent during the preceding year to review the Child Placement Agreements for children in the home in the year preceding the re-assessment, to determine the foster/pre-adoptive parent's compliance with training requirements established by the Department; and determine the nature and extent of the foster/pre-adoptive parent's involvement in the implementation and review of the service plan for children placed in the home during the preceding year;

4. prepare a written evaluation of the foster/pre-adoptive parent(s) which may include a general description of the foster/pre-adoptive parent's performance in providing foster/pre-adoptive care; identification of the foster/pre-adoptive parent's particular strengths and weaknesses in providing foster/pre-adoptive care; and recommendations for eliminating weaknesses and capitalizing on strengths identified;

5. request criminal record and Central Registry checks and other background checks as required by Department Background Record Check Policy and 110 CMR 18.00 *et seq.* for all household members, other than foster children;

6. contact references seem by Department staff as useful to the re-evaluation;

7. review and update of the foster/pre-adoptive parent professional development plan;

8. review of the physical standards for foster/pre-adoptive homes, as set forth in 110 CMR 7.105 and Department Family Resource Policy, to ensure the home continues to meet these standards;

9. notify the foster/pre-adoptive parent, at least 15 working days prior to the re-assessment due date, of any issues that need resolution to continue the foster/pre-adoptive parent license;

10. develop with the foster/pre-adoptive parent a plan to meet the identified outstanding issues needing resolution and a time frame for completion.

(c) Within ten working days after completing the re-assessment, the Department shall reach one of the following decisions shall notify the foster/pre-adoptive parents and shall enter a copy of the notification in the foster/pre-adoptive parent file:

1. The foster/pre-adoptive parent and foster/pre-adoptive home license is continued on the same terms, and with the same conditions, as existed prior to the re-assessment. For kinship or child-specific placement this means the child currently in the home remains.

2. The foster/pre-adoptive parent and foster/pre-adoptive home license is continued on terms, and with conditions, different from those which existed prior to the re-assessment, which new and different terms and conditions shall be set forth in writing. For kinship or child-specific placements this may mean that the home was licensed for a different or additional specific child.

3. The foster/pre-adoptive parent and/or the foster/pre-adoptive home license will not continue unless specific changes in circumstances or conditions are effected within a specified time period, not to exceed 14 days, and that if such changes are not effected within the time allotted, the child or children currently placed in the foster/pre-adoptive home will be removed from the placement and the placement will cease to be approved.

4. For an unrestricted foster/pre-adoptive parent the license continues but the home's status is changed to a child-specific home.

5. The foster/pre-adoptive parent and/or the foster/pre-adoptive home are not reapproved, and all foster children residing in the home shall be removed.

(d) In any case in which the Department is delayed in completing the annual re-assessment, the unrestricted foster/pre-adoptive parent(s) and home shall continue to be licensed, until the Department completes the re-assessment and sends notice of its decision to the foster/pre-adoptive parent(s).

If the foster/pre-adoptive parent(s) appeal the revocation of their license via the fair hearing process, the license shall remain in effect until the fair hearing decision is issued.

(e) The foster/pre-adoptive parents shall receive a copy of the written evaluation upon request.

(2) The Department may, six months after a foster/pre-adoptive home is first licensed, conduct a review of the foster/pre-adoptive home whether unrestricted, kinship or child-specific. The review held under 110 CMR 7.113(2) may include, but not be limited to, the procedures set forth in 110 CMR 7.113(1). At the conclusion of the review the Department shall reach one of the decisions set forth in 110 CMR 7.113(1)(d). The Department shall send written notice to the foster/pre-adoptive parent of the outcome of the review.

5

(3) The Department shall conduct a license renewal study of all foster/pre-adoptive parent(s) and foster/pre-adoptive homes every two years, prior to the expiration date of the existing license, provided, however, that an existing license shall continue in full force and effect until the Department reaches decision as a result of the license renewal study and notifies the foster/pre-adoptive parent(s), in writing, of that decision. The license renewal study shall substitute for the annual re-assessment during the year that the license renewal study is conducted.

License renewal studies shall be conducted in accordance with the procedures set forth in 110 C.M.R. 7.113(1)(a) and (b) and Department Family Resource Policy #2006-01 as well as the following:

(a) obtain and review a school reference for each school age child living in the foster/pre-adoptive home and for any child participating in pre-school or a child care program;

(b) when necessary, obtain and review an employer reference for each foster/pre-adoptive parent and head of household whose employment status has changed since the last annual reassessment;

(c) when necessary, obtain and review a medical reference for each household member.

Within ten working days after completing a license renewal study, the Department shall reach one of the decisions set forth in 110 CMR 7.113(1)(c), and shall notify the foster/pre-adoptive parent(s) of the decision in writing and shall enter a copy of the notification in the foster/pre-adoptive parent(s) file.

(4) Whenever the Department has revoked or not renewed a license for a licensed foster/pre-adoptive parent(s), as a result of an annual or limited re-assessment, the Department shall remove all children from the foster/pre-adoptive home, unless the Department determines that it is in the child(ren)'s best interest to remain in the foster/pre-adoptive home. If the Department determines that it is in the child(ren)'s best interest to remain in the foster/pre-adoptive home, the home shall become a child specific home and subject to the same terms and conditions as any home approved under 110 CMR 7.108.

(5) The rights of foster/pre-adoptive parent(s) to appeal Department decisions under 110 CMR 7.113 or 7.113A are set forth in 110 CMR 10.06.

110 CMR 7.113A. Limited Reassessments

In addition to the annual reassessment or license study, the Department may perform a limited re-assessment of the foster/pre-adoptive parent and/or foster/pre-adoptive home at other times.

(1) The Department shall conduct a limited reassessment whenever the Department:

(a) investigates and supports a report of abuse or neglect under G.L. c. 119, § 51B and the foster/pre-adoptive parent or other household member is identified as responsible for abuse or neglect; or

(b) learns that a foster/pre-adoptive parent has moved to a new residence; or

(c) learns that corporal punishment has been used on a foster/pre-adoptive child placed in the home; or

(d) removes a foster/pre-adoptive child from the foster/pre-adoptive home on an emergency basis.

(2) The Department may conduct a limited reassessment whenever the Department;

(a) removes a foster child from a foster/pre-adoptive home on a non-emergency basis, whether the foster/pre-adoptive home is an unrestricted licensed home or a kinship or child-specific home; or

5

(b) learns of any circumstance which could affect the foster/pre-adoptive parent's provision of, or ability to provide, adequate foster care; or

(c) learns of any circumstance which would cause the Department to impose or remove any restrictions or limitations on the identity or characteristics of children to be placed or already placed in the foster/pre-adoptive home; or

(d) learns of any circumstance which would cause the Department to increase or decrease the maximum number of children who may be placed in the foster/pre-adoptive home;

(e) learns of additional household members or pets/animals;

(f) screens out or unsupports a report of child abuse or neglect on the foster/pre-adoptive family or supports a report of child abuse or neglect on a child residing in the home where the individual responsible for the abuse or neglect is not a household member; or

(g) learns of any possible violations of Department foster/pre-adoptive parent of home standards or of the Foster/Pre-Adoptive Parent Agreement.

(3) In conducting the limited reassessment the Department will follow the following procedure:

(a) The Department shall give written notice to the foster/pre-adoptive parent as soon as possible. Such written notice shall include at least the following information:

1. the fact that the Department intends to perform a limited re-assessment of the foster/pre-adoptive parent, the foster/pre-adoptive home, or both;

2. the reason(s) for performing the limited re-assessment; and

3. the steps which the Department intends to take in order to complete the limited re-assessment.

A copy of the written notice shall be entered in the foster/pre-adoptive parent file.

(b) Within 30 days after the written notice has been given, the Department shall perform and complete the limited re-assessment of the foster/pre-adoptive parent and/or foster/pre-adoptive home. The limited re-assessment may consist of one or more of the steps described under 110 CMR 7.113(1) and in the Department's Family Resource Policy.

(c) The Department shall prepare a written report of findings and conclusions made as a result of the completed limited re-assessment. A copy shall be entered in the foster/pre-adoptive parent file. The foster/pre-adoptive parent may receive a copy upon request.

(d) At the conclusion of the limited re-assessment, the Department shall reach one of the decisions in 110 CMR 7.113(4)(c).

(e) The Department may combine an annual reassessment or Licensed renewal study with a limited reassessment if the annual reassessment or license renewal study is due within three months of the commencement of the limited reassessment. If the reassessments are combined, all steps in the annual reassessment or license renewal study will be conducted.

110 CMR 7.113B. License Revocation

(1) Except as provided otherwise in 110 CMR 7.100 *et seq.*, whenever the Department reaches a decision to revoke a license, it shall give written notice to the foster/pre-adoptive parent. The written notice shall include at least the following information:

(a) notice that the Department will no longer place any foster children in the home;

(b) notice that agreement(s) between the Department and the foster/pre-adoptive home is terminated and that the license should be returned to the Department;

(c) the reason(s) for the license revocation; and

(d) if applicable, notice of the foster/pre-adoptive parent's right to appeal and the procedures for taking such appeal.

A copy of the written notice shall be entered in the foster/pre-adoptive parent file.

(2) If the decision to revoke the license is concurrent with a decision to remove one or more children from the foster/pre-adoptive home, the written notice required under 110 CMR 7.00 may be modified as necessary and combined with the written notice of the decision to remove the foster children from the foster/pre-adoptive home as required under 110 CMR 7.116.

110 CMR 7.113C. Closing a Foster/Pre-Adoptive Home

Foster/pre-adoptive homes may be closed either at the request of the foster/pre-adoptive parent or as a result of a decision by the Department. The basis and process for decisions by the Department are set forth above in 110 CMR 7.113 through 7.113B. Whenever a foster/pre-adoptive parent requests that their foster/pre-adoptive home be closed they shall do so in writing. Prior to closing the home, the Department will meet with the foster/pre-adoptive parent to discuss the reasons for closing the home, plans to remove any foster child(ren) placed in the home and to establish dates for the removal of the foster child(ren) and the closure of the home. The Department will confirm in writing the decisions agreed upon at that meeting, the reasons for those decisions, and provide a copy to the foster/pre-adoptive parent.

110 CMR 7.113D. Reopening of Former Foster/Pre-Adoptive Home

If a foster/pre-adoptive family seeks to resume the provision of foster/pre-adoptive care within six months after their home was closed at their request, the Department shall conduct an annual reassessment or license renewal study, which ever would have been due had they remained open with the Department. After the six months, the Department shall conduct a new licensed study and they shall be treated as a new applicant.

110 CMR 7.114. Temporary Placement of Foster Children in Care of Persons Other Than Foster/Pre-Adoptive Parents

(1) 110 CMR 7.114 applies to situations where a foster child who has been placed in a foster/pre-adoptive home is, or will be, placed temporarily in the care of someone other than the foster/pre-adoptive parent. (Examples of such situations are: day, overnight or weekend visits with parents or relatives; work-related day care; and extended trips or appointments for the child unaccompanied by the foster/pre-adoptive parent.) 110 CMR 7.114 does not apply to overnight visits with friends, use of babysitters, etc.

(2) The Department shall have the sole and exclusive power to determine whether a foster child may be placed temporarily in

the care of someone other than the foster/pre-adoptive parent. Whenever a foster/pre-adoptive parent wishes to place a temporarily in the care of another person, the foster/pre-adoptive parent shall make a request for such placement to the Department in advance of such placement.

(3) After a foster/pre-adoptive parent has made such a request to the Department, if the Department determines that it is not necessary or desirable for the foster child to be placed temporarily in the care requested by the foster/pre-adoptive parent, the Department shall give written notice to the foster/pre-adoptive parent that the foster/pre-adoptive parent's request has been denied.

110 CMR 7.115. Runaway Foster Children

(1) Whenever a foster/pre-adoptive parent knows, or reasonably believes, that a foster child intends to run away from the foster/pre-adoptive home, the foster/pre-adoptive parent shall immediately notify the Department (or the Child-At-Risk Hotline if after hours) of that fact.

(2) When the Department knows that a child who will be placed in a foster/pre-adoptive home has run away from his/her parent's home or from any previous placements in substitute care, the Department shall notify the prospective foster/pre-adoptive parent of that fact. In either case, the Department shall also inform the foster/pre-adoptive parent or prospective foster/pre-adoptive parent of measures which the foster/pre-adoptive parent or prospective foster/pre-adoptive parent may take to prevent the child from running away from the foster/pre-adoptive home, and of the procedures which the foster/pre-adoptive parent or prospective foster/pre-adoptive parent should follow if the child does run away from the foster/pre-adoptive home.

(3) Whenever a foster/pre-adoptive parent learns that a foster child has run away or is missing from the foster/pre-adoptive home, the foster/pre-adoptive parent shall immediately notify the Department, and then the local police. Such notice shall include at least the following information:

(a) the name and age of the child who ran away;

(b) the time when the child was last seen;

(c) the location where the child was last seen;

(d) a physical description of the child when last seen, including a description of the clothing worn by the child at that time; and

(e) any known or suspected locations where the child might be found, and any known or suspected individuals who might know the whereabouts of the child.

(4) Whenever the Department learns that a foster child has run away or is missing from the foster/pre-adoptive home, or from any temporary substitute care placement, the Department shall immediately do the following:

(a) notify the local police department or other appropriate law enforcement agencies that the child has run away or is missing, (or ensure that the foster/pre-adoptive parent(s) have done so) and provide such agencies with all known information which would assist them in locating the child, and the name and telephone number of the Department employee who should be notified if the child is located;

(b) notify the child's parent(s), (unless the parents have surrendered the child for adoption or a court of competent jurisdiction has entered a decree dispensing with the need for parental consent to the child's adoption), and notify the foster/pre-adoptive parent(s) that the child has run away or is missing, and provide them with the name and telephone number of the Department employee who should be notified if the child is located;

(c) if the child was committed to the Department by court order, notify the juvenile probation office of the court which issued the order; and

(d) contact any individuals who might know the whereabouts of the child, attempt to obtain any information such individuals have concerning the whereabouts of the child, and provide such individuals with the name and telephone number of the Department employee who should be notified if the child is located.

(5) Whenever the Department receives information concerning the possible or suspected current whereabouts of a child who has run away or is missing from a foster/pre-adoptive home, or from any temporary substitute care placement, the Department shall immediately notify the appropriate law enforcement agencies and provide such information to them. If possible, the assigned Department social worker shall also attempt to locate the child by going to the suspected location of the child.

(6) When a child who has run away or is missing from a foster/pre-adoptive home, or from any temporary substitute care placement, is located by the foster/pre-adoptive parent, or returns to the foster/pre-adoptive home, the foster/pre-adoptive parent shall immediately give notice to the Department.

Such notice shall include at least the following information:

(a) the fact that the child has been located or has returned to the foster/pre-adoptive home;

(b) the current location of the child;

(c) the current physical and emotional condition of the child, and whether it appears likely that the child requires medical, psychiatric or other treatment; and

(d) whether it appears likely that the child will attempt to run away from his or her current location.

(7) When a child who has run away from a foster/pre-adoptive home, or from any temporary substitute care placement, is located by the Department, the Department shall do the following:

(a) assure that the child receives any required medical, psychiatric or other treatment as soon as needed;

(b) notify the appropriate law enforcement agencies, the child's parent(s) (unless the parent(s) have surrendered the child for adoption or a court of competent jurisdiction has entered a decree dispensing with the need for parental consent to the child's adoption), and foster/pre-adoptive parent(s), and, if appropriate, the juvenile probation office of the court which committed the child to the Department, that the child has been located;

(c) interview the child as soon as possible to determine what changes, if any, should be made in the circumstances or conditions of the child's care or placement; and

(d) if the child has not returned to the foster/pre-adoptive home, notify the foster/pre-adoptive parent(s) whether the child will be placed back in that foster/pre-adoptive home, and

1. if so, the date and time when the child will return to the foster/pre-adoptive home; or

2. if not, the reason for the child not being placed back in that foster/pre-adoptive home.

(8) For purposes of appeal under 110 CMR 10.00 et seq., a decision made by the Department not to return a runaway to the foster/pre-adoptive home where the child had been placed at the time he or she ran away shall be treated as a decision to remove the child from the foster/pre-adoptive home.

110 CMR 7.116. Removal of Foster Children from Foster/Pre-Adoptive Homes

(1) Whenever the Department receives a request from a foster/pre-adoptive parent to remove a foster child from the foster/pre-adoptive home, the Department shall do the following:

(a) interview the foster/pre-adoptive parent to determine the reason(s) for the request;

(b) interview the foster/pre-adoptive parent, the foster child, other household members, and/or any other individual deemed necessary for the purpose of determining whether the situation giving rise to the request might be resolved without removing the child;

(c) if the situation giving rise to the request appears to be resolvable, provide, or offer to provide, services or assistance available

5

from the Department to facilitate resolution of the situation without removing the child;

(d) if the situation giving rise to the request is not resolved, or if the foster/pre-adoptive parent still wishes the child removed from the foster/pre-adoptive home after attempts to resolve the situation have been made, the Department shall make arrangements for moving the child to another placement and notify the foster/pre-adoptive parent and the foster child of the actual or estimated date when the child will be removed from the foster/pre-adoptive home;

(e) as appropriate, notify the child's parents, (unless they have surrendered the child for adoption or a court of competent jurisdiction has issued a decree dispensing with the need for parental consent to the child's adoption); school officials, juvenile probation officers, and/or other individuals interested in the child's whereabouts, of the change in the child's placement; and

(f) prepare a written report concerning the request for removal of the foster child from the foster/pre-adoptive home and the reason(s) therefor, and enter the written report in the foster/pre-adoptive parent file. No right of appeal shall exist when the child is being removed from the foster/pre-adoptive home at the request of the foster/pre-adoptive parent(s).

(2) Whenever the Department determines that a foster child should be removed from a foster/pre-adoptive home for the purpose of achieving a more suitable placement for permanency, safety or well-being, and not because of a request made by the foster/pre-adoptive parent(s) for removal of the foster child nor because of the occurrence or threat of abuse or neglect of the child in the foster/pre-adoptive home, the Department shall do the following:

(a) give written notice to the foster/pre-adoptive parent(s) as soon as the determination is made but absent an emergency at least 14 days prior to the intended removal of the foster child(ren). The written notice shall include at least the following:

1. the fact that the Department intends to remove the foster child from the foster/pre-adoptive home;

2. the reason(s) for the intended removal;

3. the actual or estimated date when the foster child will be removed from the foster/pre-adoptive home;

4. if the reason for the intended removal is to place the child with a prospective guardian or adoptive parent, notice that the foster/pre-adoptive parent(s) may apply to become the child's guardian(s) or adoptive parent(s) and the procedure for so applying; and

5. notice of the foster/pre-adoptive parent's right to appeal the decision to remove the foster child from the foster/pre-adoptive home, under the fair hearing or grievance procedure, provided however that no right of appeal exists if the child is to be removed in order to be placed:

a. with his or her parent(s);

b. in an independent living situation;

c. in a different foster home after the foster home was not licensed or whose license was revoked following a license study, reassessment study, license renewal study or a limited reassessment study.

d. In a department foster home from an intensive foster care home, where the child is no longer in need of intensive foster care, unless the intensive foster care foster parent is seeking to become a pre-adoptive or guardian placement and has not been denied by the Department.

e. in one of the following placements, if the current placement is not such a placement, unless the foster parent(s) has applied to be a pre-adoptive or guardian placement for the child and has not been rejected by the Department as a pre-adoptive or guardian placement for the child, or there is a fair hearing pending challenging the denial of the current foster parent as the child's pre-adoptive or guardian placement:

i. in a pre-adoptive home;

ii. with a legal guardian;

iii. in a home where one or more of the child's siblings is residing; or

iv. in a kinship home of the foster child if the current foster parent is not a kinship home of the foster child.

6. Notice that if the foster/pre-adoptive parent(s) intend to file for a fair hearing from the decision to remove the child, they must do so within ten days of receipt of the notice in order to prevent the removal of the child(ren) pending the fair hearing.

A copy of the written notice shall be entered in the foster/pre-adoptive parent file.

(b) make arrangements for moving the child to the new placement;

(c) if the foster/pre-adoptive parent files an allowable fair hearing claim of appeal of the removal decision within ten working days after receiving the written notice, the foster child shall not be removed until ten working days following the issuance of a decision of the hearing officer adverse to the foster/pre-adoptive parent's claim, or until the child is removed for non-appealable reasons, or until the child is removed in accordance with the provisions of 110 CMR 7.116(1) or (3), or until it is determined by an Area or Regional Director that the foster child's physical, mental, or emotional well-being would be endangered by leaving the child in the foster/pre-adoptive home, whichever occurs first;

(d) if the foster child is removed from the foster/pre-adoptive home, the Department shall notify, as appropriate, the child's parents, (unless they have surrendered the child for adoption or a court of competent jurisdiction has issued a decree dispensing with the need for parental consent to adoption), school officials, juvenile probation officers, and/or other individuals interested in the child's whereabouts, of the change in the child's placement.

(3) Whenever the Department has received, investigated, and supported a report of abuse or neglect of any foster child and the foster/pre-adoptive parent is named as the person believed to be responsible for the abuse or neglect of the child, the following procedures shall be observed:

(a) the foster/pre-adoptive home shall be closed to any future placements of children.

(b) The license shall be changed and, pending a determination under 110 CMR 7.116(3)(b) or (c), the placement will be deemed a child specific placement for any children who remain in the foster/pre-adoptive home.

(c) As to any foster child(ren) already in the foster/pre-adoptive home, if the Department determines that the foster child's physical, mental or emotional well-being would be endangered by leaving the child in the foster/pre-adoptive home, it shall immediately remove the foster child from the foster/pre-adoptive home and arrange an alternative placement. The foster/pre-adoptive parent shall be given verbal notice as soon as possible after the child is removed, and written notice within five days after the removal. The written notice shall include at least the following information:

1. the reason(s) for the removal;

2. notice of the foster/pre-adoptive parent's right to appeal the removal decision, and the procedures for taking such an appeal;

3. notice that the Department intends to perform a limited re-assessment of the foster/pre-adoptive parent(s) and the foster/pre-adoptive home.

A copy of the written notice shall be entered in the foster/pre-adoptive parent file. The Department shall then conduct a limited re-assessment of the foster/pre-adoptive parent(s) and foster/pre-adoptive home in accordance with the provisions of 110 CMR 7.113(1).

(d) If the Department determines that the foster child's physical, mental or emotional well-being would not be endangered by leaving the child in the foster/pre-adoptive home, it shall not remove the foster child, and shall proceed to perform a limited re-assessment of the foster/pre-adoptive parent(s) and the foster/pre-adoptive home. If the limited re-assessment is satisfactory, the placement shall become a child-specific placement as to the foster child remaining in the home.

(e) The limited re-assessment performed for purposes of 110 CMR 7.116(3) shall be conducted for the purpose of determining:

1. whether the removal of the foster child should be sustained if the foster child has already been removed; and

2. whether any other foster children in the foster/pre-adoptive home should be removed.

(f) If the limited re-assessment results in a decision to remove one or more foster children from the foster/pre-adoptive home, the Department shall make arrangements for removing any of those children still remaining in the foster/pre-adoptive home and moving them to new placements. If the limited re-evaluation does not result in a decision to remove one or more foster children from the foster/pre-adoptive home, the reason(s) for said determination shall be recorded in writing in the case file and approved in writing by the Hosting Area Director.

(g) Whenever a foster child is removed under 110 CMR 7.116, the Department shall notify, as appropriate, the child's parents (unless they have surrendered the child for adoption or a court of competent jurisdiction has issued a decree dispensing with the need for parental consent to adoption), school officials, juvenile probation officers, and/or other individuals interested in the child's whereabouts of the change in the child's placement.

(4) Whenever the Department has received, investigated, and supported a report of abuse or neglect of any child and a member of the foster/pre-adoptive household, other than the foster/pre-adoptive parent(s), is named as the person believed to be responsible for the abuse or neglect, the Department shall conduct a limited reassessment in accordance with 110 CMR 7.116(3).

As part of the limited reassessment the Department will determine whether the home will remain open to future placements, whether the home should be restricted to a child-specific home for any children remaining in the home and whether it is in the best interest of the children placed in the home to remain in that home.

(5) Whenever the Department has revoked or not renewed a license for a licensed foster/pre-adoptive parent(s) and foster/pre-adoptive home, as a result of an annual or limited re-assessment, the Department shall remove all children from the foster/pre-adoptive home, unless the Department determines that it is in the child(ren)'s best interest to remain in the foster/pre-adoptive home. If the Department determines that it is in the child(ren)'s best interest to remain in the foster/pre-adoptive home, the home shall become a child specific home and subject to the same terms and conditions as any home approved under 110 CMR 7.108.

When a foster child is removed under this provision, the Department will provide the foster/pre-adoptive parent(s) 14 days notice in advance of the decision to remove the foster child, unless the Area Director has determined that the child's physical, mental or emotional well-being would be endangered by remaining in the foster/pre-adoptive home, in which case the Department will provide less then 14 days notice.

(6) The removal of foster children from a foster/pre-adoptive home following an annual or limited reassessment is governed by 110 CMR 7.113(1)(c).

(7) The rights of foster/pre-adoptive parent(s) to appeal Department decisions issued under 110 CMR 7.116 are set forth in 110 CMR 10.06.

110 CMR 7.118. Foster/Pre-Adoptive Parent Appeals

The appeal process for foster/pre-adoptive parents is the Department's fair hearing and grievance process as set forth at 110 CMR 10.00 et seq.

110 CMR 7.119. Access to Foster/Pre-Adoptive Parent File

Foster/pre-adoptive parents have the right to review and obtain a copy of any and all documents contained in their foster/pre-adoptive parent file, subject to the provisions of 110 CMR 12.00 et seq. governing confidentiality and other applicable state and federal laws concerning confidentiality. Foster/pre-adoptive parents should address a request to view their file to the Hosting Area Director.

110 CMR 7.120. Community Residential Care

(1) Community residential care is a form of substitute care which provides planned, temporary care in a licensed or approved residential facility on a 24 hour basis.

(2) Community residential care shall be goal-directed, time limited, community-based, and in the least restrictive setting possible. Community residential care may be the placement of primary choice when a child's behavioral, emotional, or physical needs cannot be met in a less restrictive setting, i.e. in their own home, or in a foster/pre-adoptive home setting.

(3) A community residential placement is an interim placement for a child with the long term goal(s) of either the child's return home, movement of the child to a less restrictive setting, or transitioning the child to another permanent placement, i.e. adoptive home, guardianship, or an independent living situation.

(4) When the Department determines, in its clinical judgment, that a child's best interests would be served by placement into a community residential care facility, the Department shall select from the facilities available, which have a valid Department Community Residential Care Purchase Agreement, the one which best meets the child's needs, and place the child in the selected residential care facility. The Department may utilize the following kinds of facilities:

(a) a facility licensed or approved by EEC;

(b) a facility not subject to the jurisdiction of EEC, which is approved as a special education school by the Department of Elementary and Secondary Education (ESE);

(c) a facility not included in 110 CMR 7.120(4)(a) or (b) if otherwise approved by the Department; or

(d) a facility located outside of Massachusetts if the procedures of the Interstate Compact are utilized, and if the facility is licensed or approved by the applicable licensing/regulatory agency of that state.

(5) The Department recognizes that certain children may occasionally require some degree of seclusion or restraint in order to enable staff to effectively implement the child's treatment plan and provide for his/her safety. Issues of seclusion and physical restraint, to the extent they are regulated by EEC or DMH or ESE, shall be governed by EEC's or DMH's or ESE's regulations and requirements. (*See* 102 CMR and 104 CMR and 603 CMR). In addition to and to the extent not inconsistent with EEC's and DMH's and ESE's regulations and requirements, the Department will permit providers of residential or group care to use the least restrictive effective amount of restraint or seclusion which enables staff to effectively implement the child's treatment plan and provide for his/her safety. Examples of permissible restraint or seclusion include:

(a) physical restraint of child's arms and legs by staff members holding the child;

(b) use of a "seclusion" or "cool off" or "time out" room, if the child is, at all times therein, accompanied by or in view of a staff member;

(c) use of high staff: children ratio to create a "staff secure" environment.

Use of greater amounts or types of restraint or seclusion by any provider, or use of any cruel or unusual punishment by any provider, is prohibited by the Department. Examples of such impermissible restraint or seclusion or punishment include:

(d) use of "seclusion" room for excessive periods of time or without constant surveillance by a staff member;

(e) food deprivation;

(f) physical exercises when used solely as a means of punishment;

(g) use of any type of drug for the purpose of restraining behavior, unless the administration of such drug is on an emergency basis, has been court-approved, or is administered with parental consent; and

(h) use of any facility (except a mental health facility) which is wholly locked or barred at all times.

Nothing in 110 CMR 7.000 shall affect or preclude the Department's use of mental health and mental retardation facilities, which are subject to the provisions of M.G.L. c. 123, and which may employ locked and/or barred facilities, and drug therapy, for placement of children who have been adjudicated mentally ill or incompetent and committed to such a facility by court order.

(6) The Department shall conduct periodic evaluations of all community residential care providers under contract with the Department. Such evaluation shall be conducted jointly with the Department or ESE for all 766-approved providers. The Department's evaluation shall include a site visit to the provider. The Department shall maintain records of the evaluations it conducts. A copy of the written evaluation shall be provided to the director of each facility evaluated, and said director shall be afforded the opportunity to attach his/her comments concerning the evaluation.

110 CMR 7.121. Periodic Health Care—Generally

The Department's philosophy regarding health care reflects the principles and standards of Project Good Health. The Project Good Health (PGH) program is a federally-funded, Medicaid-reimbursable program aimed at ensuring that children receive quality, comprehensive health services on a periodic and continual basis. The Department is committed to preventative health care and to the early diagnosis and treatment of children's illnesses. In order to help promote good health maintenance and to minimize the incidence of chronic and disabling diseases among the high risk population it serves, the Department has established 110 CMR 7.121 through 7.127.

For its substitute care population, the Department assumes responsibility for assuring that the children receive medical examinations at the time of placement if needed, routine medical and dental examinations within age-specific time-frames (i.e., within the Department's periodicity schedule [FN*]), any required follow-up, and routine and emergency mental health care.

* The periodicity schedule for health care examinations which the Department shall adhere to is as follows:

Routine medical examinations at the following times:
two-six weeks of age
eight-ten weeks of age
four months of age
six months of age
nine months of age
one year of age
15 months of age
20 months of age
two years of age
30 months of age
three years of age
After age three, annually
Routine dental examinations at the following times:
Starting at age three, routine dental examinations annually.

110 CMR 7.122. Periodic Health Care-Training

Health care training for social work staff and substitute care providers shall be provided by the Department on an ongoing and periodic basis.

110 CMR 7.123. Periodic Health Care—Project Good Health

The Department's health care periodicity schedule is identical to that of PGH, and the Department will adhere to the PGH periodicity. The Department will attempt to utilize PGH providers for medical service delivery, and the Department will work with the Department of Public Welfare to promote participation in the PGH program. When utilization of a PGH provider is not feasible, the Department will promote the utilization of other medical providers who adhere to PGH standards of care.

110 CMR 7.124. Periodic Health Care—Medical Passport

The Department shall implement a program of utilization of a "medical passport" for all children in substitute care. The medical passport shall record pertinent and available medical/dental/mental health and developmental data about the child. Department social workers and medical providers shall each complete relevant portions of the passport. The passport shall be held by the substitute care provider and shall remain with the child for the duration of his/her placement. If a child moves to a new substitute care placement or returns home, the medical passport moves with the child.

110 CMR 7.125. Periodic Health Care—Emergency Treatment at Time of Placement

At the time of placement, children will be provided with emergency medical/dental/mental health care if needed. If such care is necessary the social worker shall arrange for the provision of emergency care with an appropriate health care provider. If appropriate and if time permits, the social worker may delegate all or part of the responsibility for the procurement of emergency medical/dental/mental health treatment to the substitute care provider (i.e., foster/pre-adoptive parents, group care facility, etc.). If the child does not have a medicaid card at the time of placement and requires emergency treatment, the social worker shall obtain a temporary Medicaid card to ensure the provision of needed treatment. Following the provision of emergency medical/dental/mental health treatment at time of placement, a record of such treatment shall be entered into the child's case record. When a "Medical Passport" is completed for this child, the social worker, in completing the relevant portions, shall make reference to the emergency treatment provided at placement.

110 CMR 7.126. Periodic Health Care—Routine Treatment After Placement

At time of placement, the Department will determine if a child is in need of routine medical and/or dental examinations by determining the date of the child's most recent routine medical and dental examinations and will assume responsibility for ensuring that such examinations are arranged if such examinations have not occurred within the required periodicity schedule. At time of placement the social worker shall complete an application for Medicaid and shall obtain a temporary Medicaid card if necessary. As soon as practicable after placement, the social worker shall provide the child with a "Medical Passport". If routine medical and dental examinations have occurred within the required periodicity schedule prior to placement, the social worker shall obtain records of these examinations for the medical passport.

If, prior to placement, medical and dental examinations have not occurred within the required periodicity schedule, the social worker shall insure that a medical examination is scheduled within two weeks of substitute care placement and that a dental examination is scheduled as soon as possible. The social worker may delegate all or part of the process of health care procurement to the substitute care providers and/or biological parents, but only if the social worker has clearly delineated those responsibilities to be assumed to the substitute care providers and/or biological parents.

110 CMR 7.127. Periodic Health Care—Responsibilities of Substitute Care Providers

It is the policy of the Department that substitute care providers, at the request of the social worker, will assume responsibility for the provision of health care services. Substitute care providers will:

(1) Arrange for emergency treatment when necessary.

(2) Schedule appointments for routine health care and any needed follow-up and will insure that these appointments are kept.

(3) Hold the child's medical passport and request written documentation from medical providers for inclusion in the passport.

(4) Provide non-specialized care (e.g., administration of oral medication) as required.

(5) Arrange for or coordinate the provision of specialized care (e.g., physiotherapy) as required.

(6) Advise the responsible social worker of changes in the child's health status.

(7) Access available nutrition programs for eligible children in placement.

110 CMR 7.128. Visitation

The Department will plan and promote regular and frequent visitation between children in substitute care and their parents, and/or siblings consistent with the terms of the service plan. For children who are the subject of a Voluntary Placement Agreement, parents may use the Department's grievance procedure (110 CMR 10.37 through 10.39) to address complaints concerning visitation matters. For all children in the court-ordered custody of the Department, if the Department seeks to terminate visitation between the child and the parents, it will not do so unless the matter is brought before a judge, and the judge makes specific findings demonstrating that parental visits will harm the child or the public welfare, unless a parent(s)'s right to notice of and consent to a child's adoption has been voluntarily or involuntarily dispensed with, whether or not the judgment dispensing with that right is on appeal. *See, Custody of a Minor (No. 2)*, 392 Mass. 719, 725-726 (1984).

For all children in the custody of the Department, where a parent(s)'s right to notice of and consent to a child's adoption has been voluntarily or involuntarily dispensed with, or where the judgment to dispense with a parent's right to consent to the child's adoption is on appeal, the Department may continue parental visitation if, in the judgment of the Department, it is in the best interest of the child(ren). See, *Adoption of Gwendolyn*, 29 Mass. App. Ct. 130, 134 n.3 (1990).

110 CMR 7.129. Legal Representation for Injured Children in Substitute Care

(1) Neither Department social work nor legal staff shall represent any child, injured because of someone's negligence or intentional actions, in personal injury cases; shall not negotiate settlement of any personal injury claim with an insurer; shall not commence suit on behalf of such child; and shall not refer such child's case to any private attorney.

(2) The Department's legal staff will make reasonable efforts to insure that children who are in substitute care receive legal assistance when they have been injured because of someone's negligence or intentional actions. Department social work staff shall report cases of serious injury of children in substitute care to the Department's General Counsel.

(3) The Department's legal staff shall check with the child(ren)'s parents, if appropriate, to determine whether the parent(s) will bring suit on behalf of the child(ren). If the parent(s) will not or do not, the Department's legal staff shall, if appropriate, seek the appointment of a Guardian Ad Litem to investigate the matter and thereafter determine whether to retain an attorney to represent the injured child on a contingent fee basis.

110 CMR 7.130. Reimbursement/Stipend to Foster/Pre-Adoptive Parents

(1) Reimbursement for Foster Care Services. Department foster/pre-adoptive parents shall receive reimbursement for providing foster care at rates the Department establishes. The Department shall reimburse all foster/pre-adoptive parents a basic minimum rate for each child in their home based on the age of the child. In addition, the Department may reimburse foster/pre-adoptive parents using a tiered system based on:

(a) the special medical, psychological and/or social needs of the child(ren) and the additional expectations on a foster/pre-adoptive family who have such child(ren) placed with them, and

(b) specialized training and certification requirements as the Department determines are needed to meet the child's special behavioral, cognitive, emotional, physical and medical needs.

(2) Quarterly Clothing Allowance. Department foster parents may receive a quarterly clothing allowance for foster children in their care at rates the Department establishes.

(3) Foster/Pre-Adoptive Parent Extraordinary Out-of-pocket Expenses: The Department shall administer a program of reimbursement to foster/pre-adoptive parents for extraordinary out of pocket expenses incurred by foster/pre-adoptive parents as a result of providing foster/pre-adoptive care, except those reimbursed by MassHealth if such expenses are:

5

(a) necessary to enable foster/pre-adoptive parents to provide appropriate foster/pre-adoptive care services (for example, specialized medical or educational training to enable foster/pre-adoptive parents to care for special needs children; or specialized handicap accommodations for handicapped foster children; or transportation and child care stipend to enable foster/pre-adoptive parents to attend skill specific training; or to purchase specialized medical or other equipment such as intercoms, bars and handles, specialized toys, mattresses, etc. meeting the special needs of the foster child; or for participation in special activities necessary for provision of foster care to a special needs foster child, etc); and

(b) agreed upon in writing in advance of the expenditure.

(4) Other: Department foster/pre-adoptive parents may from time to time receive other payments, such as a birthday supplement or holiday supplement for the child or a retainer for on-call home status, etc.

(5) Written Notice: Foster/pre-adoptive parents shall receive written notice of the availability of these reimbursements/stipends as a part of the Department's mandatory pre-service foster/pre-adoptive parent training.

110 CMR 7.131. Department Certification

In administering federal grants under Titles IV-E and IV-B, which monies aid the Department in providing effective service delivery, the Department will comply with the following Federal Regulations:

1. 45 CFR Part 16—Department Grant Appeals Process
2. 45 CFR Part 30—Federal Claims Collection
3. 45 CFR Part 74—Administration of Grants (except for §§ 74.23 and 74.52)
4. 45 CFR Part 76—Government Debarment and Suspension
5. 45 CFR Part 80—Nondiscrimination
6. 45 CFR Part 81—Hearings under Part 80
7. 45 CFR Part 84—Nondiscrimination on basis of handicap
8. 45 CFR Part 91—Nondiscrimination on basis of age
9. 45 CFR Part 93—New restrictions on lobbying
10. 45 CFR Part 95—General Administration-Grant Programs (Public Assistance and Medical Assistance)
11. 45 CFR Part 97—Consolidation of grants to insular areas
12. 45 CFR Part 95, Section 95.517 (supersedes section 205.150)—Cost Allocation Plans

13. 45 CFR Part 201, Section 201.5—Grants (except that ACYF shall supply appropriate forms and instructions)

14. 45 CFR Part 201, Section 201.6—Withholding/Reduction of FFP

15. 45 CFR Part 201, Section 201.7—Judicial Review

16. 45 CFR Part 201, Section 201.15—Deferral

17. 45 CFR Part 201, Section 201.66—Repayment of Federal Funds in Installments

18. 45 CFR Part 204, Section 204.1—Submittal of State Plans for Governor's Review

19. 45 CFR Part 205, Section 205.5—Plan Amendments

20. 45 CFR Part 205, Section 205.10—Hearings

21. 45 CFR Part 205, Section 205.50—Safeguarding Information

22. 45 CFR Part 205, Section 205.100—Single State Agency

23. 45 CFR Part 205, Section 205.101—Organization for Administration

110 CMR 7.200. Special Provisions Regarding Pre-Adoptive Placements

COMMENTARY

It is the primary responsibility of the Department to find families for children, rather than to find children for families.

5

(1) Foster Parent(s) as Pre-adoptive Placements. Any foster parent(s) may seek to become the pre-adoptive placement for a child for whom the Department's long-term goal is adoption. A foster parent(s) may be approved as the pre-adoptive placement for a particular child if the Department determines, after assessment, that adoption by the foster parent(s) will further the best interests of that child.

(2) Priority. Although all foster pre-adoptive parent(s) who seek to become a pre-adoptive placement will be considered and assessed, priority will be given to those who are interested in the kinds of children currently waiting for and in need of homes. This includes, but is not limited to, the following types of children: school age, special needs, legal risk, siblings, Black, Hispanic, and mixed racial. Special needs includes a wide variety of emotional problems, behavioral disorders, learning disabilities, and other handicapping medical conditions. Applicants interested only in healthy infants will be considered as the need for such homes presents itself.

(3) Department Obligations. Whenever a child is placed with a family who has been approved as a pre-adoptive placement and the child is not yet free for adoption (i.e., the parents have not surrendered the child for adoption, and no court of competent jurisdiction has issued a decree dispensing with the need for the biological parent's consent to adoption, or such a decree has been issued but has been appealed and/or stayed, or), the pre-adoptive family:

(a) shall be informed, plainly and clearly, that the child placed with them is not yet and may not become free for adoption;

(b) shall be required to acknowledge their understanding and voluntary assumption of the "legal risk" nature of the placement;

(c) shall periodically be updated by the assigned social worker or adoption worker about the legal status of the child in their care;

(d) shall be informed they are not parties to and should not expect to become parties to any proceeding brought by the Department pursuant to M.G.L. c. 210, § 3 or M.G.L. c. 119, § 26(4), or to receive legal advice from Department legal staff in connection with any such proceeding.

(4) Re-evaluation of Pre-adoptive Placements. All pre-adoptive parent(s) who have a child in pre-adoptive placement shall have a full or abbreviated re-evaluation, as appropriate:

(a) whenever the Department learns of factors affecting the suitability of the placement; and

(b) within 30 days prior to an adoption if the adoption occurs more than one year after approval of the pre-adoptive placement; and

(c) Annually in accordance with 110 CMR 7.113

The re-evaluation shall be in writing and a copy shall be given to the pre-adoptive parents.

(5) Withdrawal of Adoption Sponsorship. At any time after deciding to sponsor an adoption, and before the adoption occurs, the Department may, for good cause, withdraw its sponsorship of an adoption and its approval of a pre-adoptive placement.

(6) Obligations of the Department to Pre-adoptive Parents.

(a) The Department shall assign an adoption worker who will be responsible for providing direct service to the pre-adoptive family.

(b) The Department shall provide the pre-adoptive parent with all relevant information about a child to enable the pre-adoptive parent to knowledgeably determine whether to accept the child for adoption. *See* Department Policy #91-001.

(c) The Department shall notify pre-adoptive parents of all court hearings regarding a child placed in their home. *See* 110 CMR 7.112(2)(h).

(d) Pending an adoption, the Department may offer to pay pre-adoptive parents at established rates equal to the rate for foster care. *See* 110 CMR 7.130.

110 CMR 7.209. Adoption Subsidy

(1) Definition of Adoption Subsidy. The Department operates two adoption subsidy programs to support the adoption of children with special needs: a federally supported program governed by the provisions of Title IV-E of the Social Security Act, 42 U.S.C. § 673, (hereinafter "Title IV-E adoption subsidy"), and a state funded program created pursuant to M.G.L. c. 18B, § 21, (hereinafter state adoption subsidy"). In both programs, adoption subsidy consists of financial assistance and/or medical assistance through the State's Division of Medical Assistance and is provided on behalf of a child with special needs after the child has been adopted. Financial assistance is intended to aid in the support of the child with special needs and is paid directly to the adoptive parent(s). Medical assistance is intended to supplement family health insurance for the child with special needs and is paid directly to the vendor according to the current Division of Medical Assistance fee schedule. Financial assistance provided through adoption subsidy may not exceed the amount that would have been authorized during the period had the child been in family foster care.

(2) Definition of Child with Special Needs. A child is a "child with special needs" if the Department determines that the child meets the following three criteria.

(a) The child cannot or should not be returned to the home of his parents. Evidence that the child is legally free for adoption meets this criterion.

(b) At least one of the following circumstances applies:

1. The child has one or more special needs as a result of a mental, emotional or physical impairment, behavioral disorder, or medical condition that has been diagnosed by a licensed professional who is qualified to make the diagnosis.

2. The child is difficult to place for one or more of the following reasons:

a. The child is a member of a sibling group of two to be adopted together and one of the children is eight years of age or older;

b. The child is a member of a sibling group of three or more to be adopted together; or

c. The child is a member of an ethnic or cultural minority for whom reasonable, but unsuccessful, efforts to place the child in an adoptive home were made and documented.

3. The child's birth and/or family history places the child at risk of having special needs but, due to the child's age, a reliable diagnosis cannot be made.

(c) Reasonable efforts have been made to place the child for adoption in the most appropriate home without providing adoption subsidy. The requirement to make such efforts may be waived for any child whose best interests would not be served by a new placement because the child has developed significant emotional or psychological ties with the preadoptive parent(s) while in the care of such parent(s), and the pre-adoptive parent(s) cannot adopt the child without adoption subsidy.

(3) Eligibility Criteria—Title IV-E Adoption Subsidy. In order to be eligible for Title IV-E adoption subsidy, a child must meet the following criteria.

(a) The child is a child with special needs as defined in 110 CMR 7.209(2).

(b) The child is in substitute care and in the custody of the Department, or the child is in the custody of a licensed nonprofit placement agency, as defined in M.G.L. c. 28A, § 9, which has placed the child for adoption.

(c) Adoption is the plan for the child.

(d) The child resides in the pre-adoptive home.

(e) The child is a U.S. citizen or a qualified alien within the meaning of the Personal Responsibility and Work Opportunity Reconciliation Act of 1996.

(f) If the child is in substitute care and in the custody of the Department, one of the following is established:

1. The child has been eligible for Title IV-E foster care payments; or

2. The costs of the child's foster care have been covered by Title IV-E foster care payments made on behalf of his/her minor parent; or

3. The child is S.S.I. eligible.

(g) If the child has been placed for adoption in a pre-adoptive home by a licensed non-profit placement agency, as defined in M.G.L. c. 28A, § 9, one of the following is established:

1. The child is S.S.I. eligible; or

2. The child meets the following criteria.

a. At the time the adoption proceedings were initiated, the child met or would have met the AFDC requirements as they existed in July 16, 1996 but for the child's removal from his/her home, either as a result of an adoption surrender or voluntary placement agreement, or a judicial determination to the effect that continuation in the home would be contrary to the child's welfare.

b. A court document(s) establishes that the child's removal from the home was the result of a judicial determination to the effect that continuation in the home would be contrary to the child's welfare. Provided however, if the child's removal from his/her home was the result of an adoption surrender or voluntary placement agreement, a court document(s) establishes that there was a judicial determination within 180 days of the initial placement with the agency to the effect that such placement is in the child's best interests.

(4) Eligibility Criteria—State Adoption Subsidy. In order to be eligible for state adoption subsidy, the child must meet the following criteria.

(a) The child is a child with special needs as defined in 110 CMR 7.209(2).

(b) The child is in substitute care and in the custody of the Department.

(c) Adoption is the plan for the child.

(d) The child resides in the pre-adoptive home.

(5) Application for Adoption Subsidy.

(a) Children with Special Needs in the Custody of the Department. When a child has been legally freed for adoption and placed in a pre-adoptive home, after informing the child's preadoptive parents about the adoption subsidy program, the Department social worker shall refer the child to the Subsidy Unit and provide information relevant to a determination of eligibility. The Subsidy Unit shall determine the child's eligibility for Title IV-E or state adoption subsidy, as applicable.

(b) Children with Special Needs in the Custody of a Licensed Nonprofit Placement Agency, as Defined in M.G.L. c. 28A, § 9. The pre-adoptive parent(s) or the placement agency may request an application for adoption subsidy by contacting the Department's Subsidy Unit. The application must be completed with the information necessary for an eligibility determination pursuant to 110 CMR 7.209(3) and returned to the Subsidy Unit. The Subsidy Unit will determine the child's eligibility for Title IV-E adoption subsidy.

(c) Adopted Children with Special Needs in the Custody of their Parents. The parent(s) of an (adopted child with special needs may assert the right to an adoption subsidy in extenuating circumstances as set forth in 110 CMR 7.209(11) and (12). Where such circumstances are alleged, the adoptive parent(s) must write to the Department's Fair Hearing Unit to request a fair hearing and send a copy of the request to the Department's Subsidy Unit. The request for a fair hearing must include the following information: name, address and telephone number of the adoptive parent(s) and child; a brief statement of the reason(s) why the adoptive parent(s) believe that extenuating circumstances exist for entering into an adoption subsidy agreement after the adoption has been finalized; and whether the adoptive parent(s) adopted through the Department or licensed nonprofit placement agency as defined in M.G.L. c. 28A, § 9. A hearing officer shall decide whether extenuating circumstances exist and, if so, whether the child meets the eligibility criteria for adoption subsidy. The Department is under no obligation to provide adoption subsidy after a child has been adopted unless there are extenuating circumstances as set forth herein and the child meets the eligibility criteria for Title IV-E or state adoption subsidy.

5

(6) *Adoption Subsidy Agreement.* If the Department determines that the child is eligible for a Title IV-E adoption subsidy, the type of assistance and, as applicable, the amount of assistance, will be determined through discussion and negotiation with the pre-adoptive parent(s), taking into consideration the circumstances of the pre-adoptive parent(s) and the needs of the child being adopted. If the Department determines that the child is not eligible for a Title IV-E adoption subsidy but is eligible for a state adoption subsidy, the Department will inform the preadoptive parent(s) of the determination, the type of assistance and, as applicable, the amount of assistance to be provided, taking into consideration the circumstances of the pre-adoptive parent(s) and the needs of the child being adopted, and of the right to challenge the denial of the child's Title IV-E eligibility in a fair hearing. Except as provided in 110 CMR 7.209(7), in both subsidy programs, the Department will provide the pre-adoptive parent(s) with an adoption subsidy agreement describing the subsidy program for which the child is eligible, the type of assistance and, if applicable, amount of assistance, and the circumstances under which the adoption subsidy may be terminated. The Department will inform the pre-adoptive parent(s) in writing that the adoption subsidy agreement must be signed and returned to the Department prior to finalization of the child's adoption and before the subsidy may be initiated.

(7) Deferred Subsidy Agreement.

(a) Initial Determination. If the Department determines that a child meets the eligibility criteria set forth in 110 CMR 7.209(3) or (4) and is at risk in the future of having special needs as set forth in 110 CMR 7.209(2)(b)3., the Department will provide a deferred subsidy agreement. In such cases, the Department will inform the pre-adoptive parent(s) that financial and/or medical assistance may be provided at a future date if the parent requests a redetermination of the decision to provide a deferred subsidy as set forth in 110 CMR 7.209(7)(b), but that no such request will be considered for at least one year from the date of the initial deferred subsidy agreement. The Department will also inform the preadoptive parent(s) in writing that the deferred subsidy agreement must be signed and returned prior to finalization of the child's adoption to preserve the child's eligibility and of the right to a fair hearing to challenge the Department's decision as provided in 110 CMR 10.06(5)(d). A deferred subsidy agreement shall terminate on the child's 18th birthday.

(b) Re-determination. If an adoptive parent of a child who is the subject of a deferred subsidy agreement submits a request for re-determination to the Subsidy Unit along with documentation from a qualified professional diagnosing the child's special needs, the Department shall determine, whether the child meets the criteria sets forth in 110 CMR 7.209(2)(b)1., and, if so, whether there is reasonable cause to believe that the child's mental, emotional or physical impairment, behavioral disorder or medical condition is related to the child's birth or family history prior to adoption. If the Department concludes that the child meets said requirements, the Department will enter into a Title IV-E or state adoption subsidy agreement, as applicable, as set forth in 110 CMR 7.209(6). If said requirements are not met, the Department will notify the adoptive parent in writing of the results of the redetermination, including the rationale for its decision, and of the right to challenge the Department's decision to deny an adoption subsidy agreement.

(8) *Arrangements Prior to Finalization of Adoption: Initiation of Benefits*. Except as provided in 110 CMR 7.209(11) and 7.209(12), only adoptive parents who have completed an adoption subsidy agreement with the Department prior to finalization of the adoption of their child with special needs shall be entitled to receive an adoption subsidy. Adoption subsidy benefits shall begin no earlier than the finalization of the adoption unless the Department determines that an earlier start date is in the best interest of the child.

5

(9) *Re-evaluation Requirement*. Adoption subsidy agreements are re-evaluated periodically at the discretion of the Department, or in the case of Title IV-E adoption subsidies, as agreed to by the Department and the adoptive parent(s). At the time of the re-evaluation, the amount of the subsidy may be adjusted based on a change in the circumstances of the adoptive family and/or the child's special needs, or the subsidy may be terminated for the reasons set forth in 110 CMR 7.209(13). A Title IV-E adoption subsidy may be adjusted only after negotiation with, and agreement by, the adoptive parent except the Department may terminate the subsidy after providing written notice of the decision and the right to a fair hearing. In the case of a state adoption subsidy, the Department will notify the adoptive parent(s) in writing of the Department's decision upon re-evaluation and the reasons for it, and of the right to a fair hearing to challenge a decision to reduce or terminate the adoption subsidy.

(10) *Denial*. If a request for an adoption subsidy is denied, the Department shall notify the pre-adoptive parent(s) in writing of the denial. A statement of reasons shall be included along with notice of the right to request a fair hearing to appeal the decision. Requests for adoption subsidy after finalization of the adoption shall be governed by the provisions set forth in 110 CMR 7.209(11) and (12), as applicable.

(11) *Extenuating Circumstances—Title IV-E Adoption Subsidy*.

(a) If, after the adoption of a child with special needs as defined herein, an adoptive parent believes that he/she has been wrongly denied access to a Title IV-E adoption subsidy, the adoptive parent(s) has the right to request a fair hearing to establish that:

1. extenuating circumstances exist for entering into an adoption subsidy agreement after the adoption has been finalized; and

2. the child meets the criteria for Title IV-E adoption subsidy. The adoptive parent(s) shall have the burden of proof on both issues. Extenuating circumstances shall be limited to the following:

a. relevant facts regarding the child's special needs, birth history or family history, which would have established that the child is a child with special needs as defined in 110 CMR 7.209(2), were known to the Department but not presented to the adoptive parent(s) prior to the finalization of the adoption;

b. the Department previously denied a Title IV-E adoption subsidy based on a means test of the adoptive family;

c. the Department made an erroneous determination that the child was ineligible for a Title IV-E adoption subsidy;

d. the Department or its contracted agency failed to advise the adoptive parent(s) of the availability of an adoption subsidy before the child's adoption; or

e. the adoptive parent(s) adopted a child with special needs in Massachusetts through a licensed nonprofit placement agency, as defined in M.G.L. c. 28A, § 9, prior to April 14, 2000, and said agency failed to advise the adoptive parent(s) of the availability of an adoption subsidy or advised the adoptive parent(s) that such subsidies were not available.

(b) If a hearing officer determines that extenuating circumstances exist and the child meets the eligibility criteria for Title IV-E adoption subsidy, the hearing officer may direct the Department to provide Title IV-E adoption subsidy from a date beginning no earlier than the date the adoptive parent notified the Department in writing that an adoption subsidy was wrongly denied or withheld. The type of assistance and, if applicable, the amount of assistance, shall be determined in accordance with 110 CMR 7.209(6) as applicable to Title IV-E adoption subsidies.

(12) *Extenuating Circumstances—State Adoption Subsidy*.

(a) If, after the adoption of a child with special needs as defined herein, the adoptive parent(s) believes that he/she has been wrongly denied access to a state adoption subsidy, the adoptive parent(s) has a right to request a fair hearing to establish that:

1. extenuating circumstances exist for entering into an adoption assistance agreement after the adoption has been finalized; and

2. the child is eligible for a state adoption subsidy. The adoptive parent(s) shall have the burden of proof on both issues. Extenuating circumstances shall be limited to the following:

a. relevant facts regarding the child's special needs, birth history or family history, which would have established that the child is a child with special needs as defined in 110 CMR 7.209(2), were known to the Department but not presented to the adoptive parent(s) prior to the finalization of the adoption; or

b. the Department failed to advise the adoptive parent(s) of the availability of an adoption subsidy before the child's adoption.

(b) If a hearing officer determines that extenuating circumstances exist and that the child meets the eligibility criteria for state adoption subsidy, the hearing officer may direct the Department to provide adoption subsidy from a date beginning no earlier than the date the adoptive parent notified the Department in writing that an adoption subsidy was wrongly denied or withheld. The Department shall determine the type of assistance and, if applicable, the amount of financial assistance in accordance with 110 CMR 7.209(6) as applicable to state adoption subsidies.

(13) *Termination of Adoption Subsidy*. The Department will terminate an adoption subsidy when any of the following occurs and provide written notice to the adoptive parent(s) of the termination and of the right to a fair hearing to challenge the action:

(a) the child with special needs turns 18 years of age. In exceptional circumstances, the Department in its discretion may continue a Title IV-E adoption subsidy until the child turns 21 or a state adoption subsidy until the child turns 22 years of age;

(b) the child's mental, emotional or physical impairment, behavioral disorder or medical condition is corrected or cured provided this condition of termination is contained in the initial adoption subsidy agreement and was accepted by the parent(s);

(c) the adoptive parent(s) are no longer legally responsible for the support of such child; or

(d) the child is no longer receiving assistance from the adoptive parent(s).

(14) *Responsibilities of Adoptive Parents.* Adoptive parent(s) receiving an adoption subsidy shall inform the Department of any change of address and of circumstances which would make the child ineligible for adoption subsidy, and shall cooperate with the Department in providing requested information at the time the adoption subsidy is re-evaluated. If the adoptive parent(s) fails to carry out these responsibilities, the Department may suspend, reduce or terminate the adoption subsidy and take appropriate action to recoup financial assistance incorrectly paid. The Department shall provide written notice of said action and of the right to a fair hearing to challenge the Department's action. If the adoptive parent(s) request a hearing in a timely manner, the adoption subsidy shall continue pending the results of the hearing.

(15) *Continuing Eligibility for Adoption Subsidy.* If a child with special needs who has been determined eligible by the Department for adoption subsidy and has been adopted, then reenters substitute care and becomes available for adoption again because the rights of the adoptive parents were terminated, voluntarily or involuntarily, or because the child's adoptive parents have died, the child shall be eligible for an adoption subsidy in the event of a subsequent adoption.

110 CMR 7.209A. Nonrecurring Adoption Expenses

If requested, the Department shall make a one time payment to the pre-adoptive parent(s) of a child with special needs, as defined in 110 CMR 7.209(2), to reimburse the family for expenses directly related to said child's adoption, provided the child is adopted through a placement made by the Department or its contracted agency, or a licensed nonprofit placement agency as defined in M.G.L. c. 28A, § 9. In all cases, requests for nonrecurring adoption expenses must be made and agreements for same completed, before the child's adoption is finalized. Payment shall be made after the finalization of the adoption. Nonrecurring adoption expenses include reasonable and necessary adoption fees, court costs, attorneys fees and other costs directly related to the adoption and which are not incurred in violation of law, but shall not include out-of-pocket expenses for which the family may be, or has been, reimbursed by other sources. The Department shall periodically determine the maximum amount to be paid for nonrecurring adoption expenses.

110 CMR 7.210. Post Adoptive Services

Any family who has adopted a child shall be eligible for any service offered by the Department under the same terms and conditions as any other family or individual.

COMMENTARY

Within the last decade the social work profession has come to realize and acknowledge that many of an adoptees' problems occur after legalization. In the traditional adoption, support services ceased on the day of legalization, but we now know that post-legalization services may be important for adoptive families. The Department recognizes that the provision of appropriate and timely services after the adoption legalization may make the difference between a secure permanent placement or a painful adoption disruption. The Department recognizes the difficulty of integrating a new family member into an existing family system. No one should expect the placement to be problem-free. The Department fully recognizes that for those families seeking post-legalization services, this does not in any way indicate failure on their part. In order to better service families who have adopted children a variety of services are available: routine services by a caseworker trained in the field of adoption; the option of being in a parent support group; community services such as school counseling, individual or family psychological counseling or therapy; respite care; etc.

110 CMR 7.211. Adoption Records

(1) No records or information of any kind about an adoption which has occurred may be released by any Department employee or any Department agent to any inquiring party outside the Department unless that inquiring party has:

(a) obtained a written order from a Probate Court (see M.G.L. c. 210, § 5D.)

(b) Received approval from a placement agency for release of non-identifying information under M.G.L. c. 210, § 5D; or

(c) Obtained a written order from a probate court for all other adoption records which are not subject to release under M.G.L. c. 210, § 5D. See M.G.L. c. 210, § 5C and 5D(e).

(2) Whenever an inquiring party contacts any Department employee or any Department agent concerning records or information about an adoption that has occurred, the inquiring party shall be informed that:

(a) M.G.L. c. 210, § 5D governs the release of certain non-identifying information to adopted persons, biological parents and adoptive parents; and

(b) The Department will give to the inquiring party a form request for release of adoption records, as established by the Department, and inform the inquiring party as to the types of records which shall be released upon submission of the request form; and

(c) The Department will give to the inquiring party an information sheet, as established by the Department, which shall inform the inquiring party of the name of the applicable Probate Court, and the procedures by which the inquiring party may seek an order from that court for release of adoption records which are not subject to release by the Department pursuant to M.G.L. c. 210, § 5D.

(3) Upon presentation to the Department of a written Probate Court order the Department shall release such information as is provided for in the court's order, in the manner directed by the court.

110 CMR 7.212. Fair Hearings and Grievances on Adoption-Related Matters

(1) Adoption-related matters that may be appealed via the Fair Hearing process are set forth at 110 CMR 10.06(5).

(2) All other adoption-related matters will be reviewed under the Department's grievance process established by 110 CMR 10.37 through 10.39.

110 CMR 7.214. Claims of Paternal Responsibility

The Department shall maintain a system for the filing of claims of paternal responsibility in accordance with M.G.L. c. 210, §§ 3 and 4A. No petition for adoption shall be filed by any Department employee without having searched said records to determine whether a claim of paternal responsibility has been filed, in a case where a child has been born out of wedlock.

110 CMR 7.215. Open Adoption

(1) Availability. In appropriate circumstances the Department may propose, as part of its adoption plan, that some limited contact between a child and his/her biological parents or grandparents or other extended family members occur after the child has been adopted. An open adoption will not be recommended for any child under 12 years of age, except in special circumstances, and only with the approval of the Area or Regional Director.

(2) *Criteria.* An open adoption may be recommended by the Department to the Court hearing an adoption petition only under the following conditions:

(a) severance of a relationship between a child and his/her parents or other extended family members will prove harmful to the child; and

(b) both the adoptive parents and the biological parents consent; and

(c) the child, if over 12 years of age, consents; and

(d) the Department believes an open adoption is in the best interests of the child.

(3) *Review.* The decision of the Department to recommend or not recommend an open adoption plan for a child is not a decision subject to review via the fair hearing process.

COMMENTARY

Parents, both biological and adoptive, should be aware that the terms and conditions of an open adoption agreement, after the adoption has taken place, are not under the control of the Department, and any subsequent disagreements must be resolved by the parties themselves. It takes maturity and commitment by both parties to carry out an open adoption successfully. Thus, open adoption needs to be a mutually consensual plan. Likewise, because social workers and lawyers must be careful that open adoption is not used as a vehicle in coercing an adoption surrender, nor as a quick solution to a problem case, and because open adoption must always be in the child's best interests, in every case where open adoption is proposed by the Department, the court where the legalization is to occur will be apprised of the terms of the proposed open adoption agreement.

110 CMR 7.300. Policy on Guardianship

The Department is committed to establishing permanent placements for all children in its care and custody. Pursuant to this commitment, the Department may sponsor a guardianship for selected children. The children selected will be those who are not likely to return to their parents and who, for whatever reason, are not candidates for adoption.

110 CMR 7.301. Selecting Children to Be Considered for Department Sponsored Guardianship

5

The Department shall consider sponsoring a guardianship for a child in its care or custody if the child meets all the following criteria:

(1) The child will not be able to return to his/her biological parents. This determination is made by the Department based upon the history of the case and the clinical judgment of Department social work staff.

(2) In the judgment of the Department, there is no reasonable likelihood that the child will be adopted. This determination may be made by the Department when, for example, the child is unwilling to be adopted, or when in the clinical judgment of the Department social work staff adoption would not be in the child's best interests.

(3) The child has resided with the potential guardians for at least one year. This requirement may be waived if waiver is determined by the Department to be in the best interests of the child.

(4) The child is at least 12 years of age. This requirement may be waived if waiver is determined by the Department to be in the best interests of the child (for example, to keep sibling groups together).

110 CMR 7.302. Implementation of Guardianship

The Department shall proceed to implement the guardianships it sponsors as follows:

(1) The Department determines that the child meets the criteria set forth in 110 CMR 7.301(1) through (3).

(2) The child's assigned social worker meets with the child and potential guardian. The guardianship plan is presented to them at this time for their consideration and approval.

(3) If guardianship is acceptable to the child and potential guardian, the social worker will make reasonable and diligent efforts to contact the child's parents. If the parents are contacted, they will be informed of the proposed guardianship proceeding, of their right to contest the guardianship proceeding, and of their right, if indigent, to court-appointed counsel. The parents' consent will then be sought.

(4) An employee of the legal staff of the Department will prepare the appropriate court papers. If the parents of the child have consented, their consent shall be noted upon the court papers by obtaining their signature. If the parents of the child have not consented to the guardianship in writing, they will be given notice as required by law.

(5) An employee of the legal staff of the Department will initiate and prosecute all court proceedings necessary to finalize the guardianship. The guardianship plan will be presented to the court for review as part of the proceeding, and said plan shall address the appropriateness of the proposed placement and the suitability of the proposed guardians.

110 CMR 7.303. Guardianship Subsidy

As used in 110 CMR 7.303, the term guardianship, means guardianship of a minor.

(1) *Definition of Guardianship Subsidy*. The Department operates two guardianship subsidy programs to support the permanency of children who are in the Department's care or custody: a federally supported program governed by the provisions of Title IV-E of the Social Security Act, 42 U.S.C. § 673, (Title IV-E guardianship subsidy), and a state funded program created pursuant to M.G.L. c. 18B, §§ 2 and 3, (state guardianship subsidy). In both programs, the guardian will receive financial assistance which is intended to aid in the support of the child and is paid directly to the guardians of the child, and the child will receive medical assistance through the MassHealth program which is intended to provide the child with health insurance and is paid directly to the vendor according to the current MassHealth fee schedule. Financial assistance provided through guardianship subsidy may not exceed the amount that would have been authorized during the period had the child been in family foster care.

(2) *Eligibility Criteria—Title IV-E Guardianship Subsidy*. In order to be eligible for Title IV-E guardianship subsidy, the following criteria must be met:

(a) The child is in substitute care and in the care or custody of the Department.

(b) The child was removed from his or her home pursuant to a voluntary placement agreement or as a result of a judicial determination that continuation in the home would be contrary to the welfare of the child.

(c) Guardianship is the permanent plan for the child.

(d) The proposed guardian(s) is a kinship/relative foster home licensed by the Department or an agency under contract with the Department which licensure includes:

1. a fingerprint-based criminal records check of the national crime information databases; and

2. a child abuse and neglect check of the proposed guardian(s) and other adults living in the home of the proposed guardian(s) for Massachusetts and any state the proposed guardian(s) or other adults living in the home have lived within the five years prior to the license study.

(e) The proposed guardian(s) has not been convicted of:

1. a felony for child abuse or neglect, spousal abuse, a crime against a child or a crime involving violence, such as rape, sexual assault or homicide, but not including simple assault and battery; or

2. a felony for physical assault, battery or a drug or alcohol related offense committed in the five years prior to being licensed.

(f) The child has been residing in the home of the proposed guardian(s) for at least six consecutive months prior to the guardianship.

(g) The child has been eligible for Title IV-E foster care payments during at least six consecutive months he or she has resided with the proposed guardians prior to the guardianship.

(h) The Department has determined:

1. Returning home or adoption are not appropriate permanency options for the child;

2. The child demonstrates a strong attachment to the prospective kinship/relative guardian(s);

3. The kinship/relative prospective guardian(s) has a strong commitment to caring permanently for the child; and

4. If the child is 14 years of age or older, the child consents to the kinship/relative guardianship arrangement.

(i) The guardian(s) and the Department have entered into a guardianship subsidy agreement, signed by both the guardian(s) and Department prior to the guardianship being granted.

(3) *Eligibility Criteria—Title IV-E Guardianship Subsidy for Sibling of Title IV-E Child.* A child is eligible for a Title IV-E guardianship subsidy if:

(a) the child is the sibling of a child who:

1. has been deemed eligible for a guardianship subsidy under 110 CMR 7.303(2); or

2. is receiving a Title IV-E guardianship subsidy; and

(b) the child is placed with the same kinship/relative guardian(s); and

(c) the kinship/relative guardian(s) agree that the placement is appropriate.

The guardianships need not occur at the same time for the sibling to be Title IV-E eligible.

COMMENTARY

As long as the children are placed in the same kinship guardianship arrangement and one of the siblings is Title IV-E eligible for a guardianship subsidy, the other sibling(s) will be Title IV-E eligible, even if the sibling who is Title IV-E eligible has their guardianship finalized after the non-Title IV-E eligible sibling. The Non-Title IV-E sibling becomes eligible once the Title IV-E eligible sibling's guardianship is finalized and the guardianship agreement is modified.

(4) *Eligibility Criteria—State Guardianship Subsidy.* In order to be eligible for state guardianship subsidy, the following criteria must be met:

(a) The child is in substitute care and in the care or custody of the Department.

(b) Guardianship is the permanent plan for the child.

(c) The child has resided in the home of the proposed guardian(s) for at least six months, unless a shorter time has been approved by the Director of Areas.

(d) The proposed guardian(s) is licensed as a foster home by the Department or an agency under contract with the Department.

(e) If the child is age 14 or older, he or she consents to the guardianship.

(f) The guardian(s) and the Department have entered into a guardianship subsidy agreement, signed by both the guardian(s) and the Department prior to the guardianship being granted.

(5) *Application for Guardianship Subsidy.*

(a) Children in the Custody of the Department. Prior to completing the guardianship petition, the Department will inform the proposed guardian(s) about the guardianship subsidy program. Prior to the guardianship petition being filed in court, the Department social worker shall refer the child to the Subsidy Unit and provide information relevant to a determination of eligibility. The Subsidy Unit shall determine the child's eligibility for Title IV-E or state guardianship subsidy, as applicable.

(b) Children in the Custody of Guardian(s). The guardian(s) of a child whose guardianship was sponsored by the Department may assert the right to a state guardianship subsidy in extenuating circumstances as set forth in 110 CMR 7.303(11) and (12). Where such circumstances are alleged, the guardian(s) must write to the Department's Subsidy Unit. The request must include the following information: name, address and telephone number of the guardian(s) and child; a brief statement of the reason(s) why the guardian(s) believe that extenuating circumstances exist for entering into a guardianship subsidy agreement after the guardianship has been finalized; and the court and date when the Department sponsored guardianship was granted. A subsidy administrator/designee shall decide whether extenuating circumstances exist and, if so, whether the child meets the eligibility criteria for a state guardianship subsidy. The Department is under no obligation to provide guardianship subsidy after a guardianship petition is granted unless there are extenuating circumstances as set forth in 110 CMR 7.303(11) and the child meets the eligibility criteria for a state guardianship subsidy. If the subsidy is denied, the guardian(s) will be provided notice of their right to appeal the denial through the Department's Fair Hearing process.

(6) *Guardianship Subsidy Agreement.* If the Department determines that the child is eligible for a Title IV-E guardianship subsidy, the type of assistance and, as applicable, the amount of assistance, will be determined through discussion and negotiation with the guardian(s), taking into consideration the circumstances of the guardian(s) and the needs of the child who is the subject of the guardianship. If the Department determines that the child is not eligible for a Title IV-E guardianship subsidy but is eligible for a state guardianship subsidy, the Department will inform the guardian(s) of the determination, the type of assistance and, as applicable, the amount of assistance to be provided, taking into consideration the circumstances of the guardian(s) and the needs of the child, and of the right of the guardian(s) to challenge the denial of the child's Title IV-E eligibility in a fair hearing.

In both subsidy programs, the Department will provide the guardian(s) with a guardianship subsidy agreement describing the subsidy program for which the child is eligible, the type of assistance and, if applicable, amount of assistance, and the circumstances under which the guardianship subsidy may be increased, decreased or terminated, the verification requirements, the additional services and assistance which the child or guardian may be eligible for and the process for applying and the circumstances under which the Department will pay for nonrecurring expenses associated with obtaining the guardianship. If the child is eligible for a Title IV-E guardianship subsidy the agreement will remain in effect regardless of the state residence of the kin guardian. The Department will inform the guardian(s) in writing that the guardianship subsidy agreement must be signed and returned to the Department prior to finalization of the child's guardianship and before the subsidy may be initiated.

(7) *Arrangements Prior to Finalization of Guardianship; Initiation of Benefits.* Except as provided in 110 CMR 7.303(11), only guardian(s) who have completed a guardianship subsidy agreement with the Department prior to finalization of the guardianship of the child are entitled to receive a guardianship subsidy. Guardianship subsidy benefits shall begin no earlier than the finalization of the guardianship unless the Department determines that an earlier state date is in the best interest of the child.

(8) *Verification Requirement.*

(a) Guardianship subsidy agreements are verified periodically at the discretion of the Department. At the time of the verification, the amount of the subsidy may be adjusted based on a change in the circumstances of the guardianship family and/or the child's needs, or the subsidy may be terminated for the reasons set forth in 110 CMR 7.303 (12). A Title IV-E guardianship subsidy may be adjusted only after negotiation with, and agreement by, the guardian(s) except the Department may terminate the subsidy after providing written notice of the decision and the right to a fair hearing for the reasons set forth in 110 CMR 7.303(12). If the Department modifies the subsidy, the Department will notify that guardian(s) in writing of the Department's decision, the reasons for it, and of the right of the guardian(s) to a fair hearing to challenge a decision to reduce or terminate the guardianship subsidy.

(b) The periodic verification process will include verification that the child is still living with the guardian(s), the guardian(s) continue to be legally responsible for the child, whether the guardian(s) has received third-party payments on behalf of the child, whether the guardian(s) has moved and whether the child remains in school, if of school age. For youth whose subsidy is extended beyond age 18, the verification process will include specific documentation that the youth continues to meet the criteria for an extended subsidy set forth in 110 CMR 7.303(13).

(c) The Department may periodically check the names and other identifying information of recipients of guardianship subsidy with the Title IV-A (the Department of Transitional Assistance) and the Title IV-D (the Department of Revenue/Child Support

Enforcement) agencies to assist the Commonwealth with federal reimbursement and to prevent fraud in Commonwealth programs.

(9) *Denial*. If a request for a guardianship subsidy is denied, the Department shall notify the proposed guardian(s) in writing of the denial. A statement of reasons shall be included along with notice of the right to request a fair hearing to appeal the decision. Requests for guardianship subsidy after finalization of the guardianship shall be governed by the provisions set forth in 110 CMR 7.303(11), as applicable.

(10) *Responsibility of Guardian(s)*. Guardian(s) receiving an adoption subsidy shall inform the Department of any change of address and of circumstances which would make the child ineligible for a guardianship subsidy, and shall cooperate with the Department in providing requested information at the time the guardianship subsidy is verified. If the guardian(s) fails to carry out these responsibilities, the Department may suspend, reduce or terminate the guardianship subsidy and take appropriate action to recoup financial assistance incorrectly paid. The Department shall provide written notice of said action and of the right of the guardian(s) to request a fair hearing to challenge the Department's action. If the guardian(s) requests a hearing in a timely manner, the guardianship subsidy shall continue pending the results of the hearing.

(11) *Extenuating Circumstances—State Guardianship Subsidy.*

(a) If, after the finalization of a guardianship of a child who had been in the Department care or custody, the guardian(s) believes that he or she has been wrongly denied access to a state guardianship subsidy, the guardian(s) has a right to submit an application, and supporting documentation, for a state funded guardianship subsidy to establish that:

1. extenuating circumstances exist for entering into a state funded guardianship assistance agreement after the guardianship has been finalized. Extenuating circumstances shall be limited to the following:

a. the Department failed to submit or process an application for guardianship subsidy prior to the guardianship legalization;

b. the Department failed to advise the guardian(s) of the availability of a guardianship subsidy before the child's guardianship is finalized;

c. The Department failed to advise the guardian(s) of the requirement that the guardianship subsidy agreement must be signed and entered into prior to the allowance of the guardianship petition; or

d. The Department was in the process of finalizing the guardianship subsidy application and a Court finalized the guardianship before the guardianship agreement could be signed by both parties; and

2. the child is eligible for a state guardianship subsidy.

(b) If the Department's subsidy administrator/designee determines that extenuating circumstances exist and that the child meets the eligibility criteria for state funded guardianship subsidy, the Department will provide guardianship subsidy from a date beginning no earlier than the date the guardian(s) notified the Department in writing that a guardianship subsidy was wrongly denied or withheld. The Department shall determine the type of assistance and, if applicable, the amount of financial assistance in accordance with 110 CMR 7.303(5) and (6) as applicable to state guardianship subsidies.

(c) If a request for a guardianship subsidy is denied, the Department shall notify the proposed guardian(s) in writing of the denial. A statement of reasons shall be included along with notice of the right to request a fair hearing to appeal the decision.

(12) *Termination of Guardianship Subsidy*. The Department will terminate a guardianship subsidy when any of the following occurs and provide written notice to the guardian(s) of the termination and of the right to a fair hearing to challenge the action;

(a) the child turns 18 years of age, unless prior to age of 18 the guardian requests an extension of the guardianship subsidy and the child meets the criteria for an extension set forth at 110 CMR 7.303(13).

(b) the guardian(s) are no longer legally responsible for the child;

(c) the child is no longer receiving assistance from the guardian(s); or

(d) the child or guardian has died; or

(e) the youth over 18 years of age no longer meets the criteria for an extension of the guardianship subsidy; or

(f) the youth over 18 years of age has reached the age of 21 for an extended federally supported guardianship subsidy or has reached the age of 22 for a state funded guardianship subsidy.

(13) *Extension of Guardianship Subsidy Over Age 18*. For the purpose of 110 CMR 7.303(13), young adult shall mean a person between the ages of 18 and 23.

(a) State Funded: If requested by the guardian(s), the Department may extend a guardianship subsidy up to the age of 22 for a young adult who is enrolled in a school, vocational program or a college program.

(b) Federally Supported: If requested by the guardians, the Department may extend a federally supported guardianship subsidy to a young adult who reaches the age of 18 up to age 21 if one of the following criteria are met:

1. the young adult has a mental or physical handicap which warrants the continuation of assistance; or

2. the state has adopted the expanded definition of child pursuant to 42 USC 465(8)(B) and the guardianship subsidy was entered into after the child turned age 16, and the young adult will be:

a. completing a secondary school or the equivalent; or

b. enrolled in post-secondary or vocational school; or

c. participating in a program or activity that promotes or removes barriers to employment; or

d. employed 80 hours a month; or

e. incapable of any in 110 CMR 7.303(13)(b)2.a. through d. due to a documented medical condition.

(c) Documentation: The Department will require documentation from the guardian to support a request for an extension of a guardianship subsidy over age 18 and may periodically require the guardian to provide documentation that the youth over 18 continues to meet the criteria for an extended guardianship subsidy.

1. For an extension based on a mental or physical handicap, or based on the young adult being incapable of doing any of the activities outlined in 110 CMR 303(13)(2)(b)1.a. through d., the Department will require documentation of the young adult's mental or physical handicap or condition by a licensed professional qualified to make the diagnosis.

2. For an extension based on the criteria set forth in 110 CMR 7.303(13)(2)(b)a. through d., the Department will require documentation from the school, program or employer verifying the young adult's enrollment, participation or employment including the amount of time the young adult is involved.

(14) *Successor Guardian.*

(a) When a guardian dies, or is no longer capable of caring for the child who is the subject of a guardianship subsidy, and a successor guardian is appointed by a court of competent jurisdiction, the Department may authorize the guardianship subsidy to be transferred to the successor guardian who resides within the state of Massachusetts. The guardianship subsidy provided to a successor guardian will be a state guardianship subsidy, not a Title IV-E subsidy. Prior to the subsidy being transferred the Department will:

1. Conduct a background check of the successor guardian, which includes both a check of the Criminal Offender Record Information system and the Department's statewide automated child welfare information system to determine whether the successor guardian might impair their ability to assume and carry out the responsibilities of being the child's guardian.

2. Conduct a home visit of the successor guardian and complete a physical standards review of the home.

(b) The determination of whether to transfer the subsidy to a successor guardian is solely with the discretion of the Department is subject to appropriation and it not the subject for a fair hearing.

110 CMR 7.303A. Fair Hearing and Grievances on Guardianship Subsidy Related Matters

(1) Guardianship subsidy related matters that may be appealed via the Fair Hearing process are set forth at 110 CMR 10.06(6).

(2) All other guardianship subsidy related matters will be reviewed under the Department's grievance process established by 110 CMR 10.37 through 10.39.

110 CMR 7.304. Nonrecurring Guardianship Expenses

The Department shall make a one time payment to the proposed kinship/relative guardian(s) of a child in the Department's care or custody, to reimburse the family for expenses directly related to said child's guardianship, provided the child's guardianship is through a placement made by the Department, or an agency under contract with the Department. Payment shall be made after the finalization of the guardianship by submitting a request for nonrecurring guardianship expenses with receipts to the guardianship subsidy unit Nonrecurring guardianship expenses include reasonable and necessary guardianship fees, court costs, attorneys fees, travel costs and other costs directly related to the guardianship and which are not incurred in violation of law, but shall not include out-of-pocket expenses for which the family may be, or has been, reimbursed by other sources. The Department will pay up to $2,000 of Title IV-E guardianship expenses and $400 of state sponsored guardianship expenses.

110 CMR 7.400. Provision of Education Services to Children in Department Care or Custody

All handicapped children in the Department's care or custody are entitled to a free appropriate education. Whenever special education is necessary for children in its care or custody, the Department will pursue special education services, through the local public schools.

110 CMR 7.401. Special Education Definitions

As used 110 CMR 7.400 through 7.499 only the following terms shall have the following meanings:

(1) *Child*. Any person aged three through 21 years of age who has not obtained a high school diploma or its equivalent.

(2) *Child in Need of Special Education*. Any child aged three through 21 years of age who, because of temporary or permanent adjustment difficulties or attributes arising from intellectual, sensory, emotional or physical factors, cerebral dysfunctions, perceptual factors, or other specific learning impairments, or any combination thereof, is unable to progress effectively in a regular educational program.

(3) *Educational Advocate*. A person assigned by the Department of Education (DOE) to act in educational matters on behalf of a child.

(4) *Grandfathered Children*. All children placed and funded in institutions by the Department of Public Welfare (DPW) prior to September 1, 1974 (effective date of M.G.L. c. 71B) are considered "grandfathered" and will continue to be funded in those institutions by the Department for so long as they remain in the Department's care or custody. In addition, all formal or informal agreements made before May 1, 1976 (effective date of the Interagency Agreement on the Clarification of Responsibility for Children in the Custody of Human Services Agencies) between a local educational agency (LEA) and DPW regarding placement and funding of children in special education programs shall continue in effect for so long as the child continues in the special education program and remains in the Department's care or custody.

(5) *Individualized Education Plan (IEP)*. A written statement of special educational needs and services, developed for a child in need of special education at a meeting of at least:

(a) a representative of the local public school district who shall be qualified to provide, or supervise provision of, specifically designed instruction to meet the unique needs of the child,

(b) the teacher,

(c) the parents, guardian, custodian, or educational advocate of the child, and

(d) whenever appropriate, the child.

(6) *Local Educational Agency (LEA)*. The local public school district which is responsible for providing educational services to the child in need of special education.

(7) *Prototype*. Numerical scale developed by the Department of Education (DOE) which reflects the amount of time that a child in need of special education is separated from children not receiving special education services. Prototypes include:

502.1 Regular education with modifications

502.2 Regular education with less than 25% time spent outside the regular education classroom.

502.3 Regular education with less than 60% time spent outside the regular education classroom.

502.4 More than 60% time spent outside the regular education classroom.

502.5 Private school day program.

502.6 Private school residential program.

502.7 Home or hospital instruction.

502.8 Preschool special education program.

502.9 Diagnostic program.

502.11 Program for children aged 16 through 21.

110 CMR 7.402. Advocacy on Behalf of Children with Special Needs in Department Care or Custody

(1) *Children in the Custody of the Department*. The child's educational advocate in the special education process shall be:

(a) An educational advocate appointed by an authorized educational advocacy program established by the Department of Education pursuant to 20 U.S.C. § 1401; or, if no educational advocate is available;

(b) A foster parent if the Department has delegated this authority to the foster parent via written agreement; or if there are compelling reasons why no such delegation can be made;

(c) A Department social worker.

Special education advocacy shall in any event be done in conjunction with the child's natural or foster parent(s) whenever possible; however, in the event of a disagreement between the Department and the natural parent(s) concerning an educational program, Department rights supersede parental rights for children in the custody of the Department.

(2) *Children in the Care of the Department*. For children in the care of the Department, the Department shall not exercise special education parental rights unless there is specific language in the Voluntary Placement Agreement delegating special education parental rights to the Department.

The Department shall only request delegation of special education parental rights for children placed in Department care voluntarily when supported by an assessment which determines that exercise of those parental rights is essential to the provision of social services to the family.

The Department will not enter into voluntary placement agreements with the child's parent(s) solely for the purpose of sharing the costs of any residential school placement with an LEA.

(3) *Signature Authority on Cost Shared IEP's and Cost Sharing Agreements*. Education plans (IEPs) raising cost sharing issues and cost sharing agreements will be binding upon the Department only if signed by a Department Area Director or his/her designee.

110 CMR 7.403. Referral for Special Education Assessment and Services

(1) *Generally*. Whenever it appears to a Department social worker that a child is in need of special education services, the worker shall refer the child, in writing, to the child's LEA for assessment and services.

(2) *Referral Upon Change in Placement*. Whenever educational responsibility for a child in Department care or custody shifts from one LEA to another because of a shift in the child's custody or placement, the Department social worker shall notify both the old LEA and the new LEA, in writing, of the change as soon as the Department becomes aware that a shift in educational responsibility is likely or has occurred.

(3) *Referral Upon Placement in a Residential School Facility*. Except in emergencies, all children referred for placement in a residential care facility shall be referred for special education assessment and services prior to the child's entry into the residential facility. Where, in an emergency, a child must be placed in a residential facility prior to being referred for special education assessment, a special education referral shall be made within one week following placement.

110 CMR 7.404. Cost Sharing

5

(1) *Public School Special Education Placements*. The Department will not fully fund, nor cost share, public school special education placements. However, where the Department places a child in a residential educational facility because no adequate community-based residential program exists for the child, but the LEA has an adequate community-based educational program for the child, the Department shall bear the full cost of both the educational and care/support components of the residential placement. This regulation in no way limits the right of the Department to test the adequacy of the proposed community-based educational program through the due process hearing procedure of the special education statutes and regulations, or to arrange for the provision of the proposed community-based educational program near the child's residential facility.

(2) *Private Residential School Special Education Placements*. If a child's IEP specifies that a private day school program (prototype 502.5) is necessary to meet the child's special education needs and the Department determines that the child should be placed in community residential care for non-educational reasons, then the Department shall share the cost of the placement with the local educational agency.

Where a child with a 502.5 prototype is placed in a residential school facility, the Department and the LEA will share the cost of the placement equally, if the facility has no Day Rate established by the Massachusetts Rate Setting Commission. Where the Rate Setting Commission has established both Day and Residential Rates for the facility, the LEA shall pay the Day Rate and the Department will pay the difference between the Day Rate and the full Residential Rate. The Department will not enter into a cost sharing agreement at a rate other than that established by the Massachusetts Rate Setting Commission or at a percentage that differs from 50%/50% for placements where no Day Rate is established, unless more than two agencies are involved in sharing the placement cost.

(3) *Other specific Education Placements*. If a child's prototype is 502.6, 502.7, 502.8, 502.9, or 502.11, M.G.L. c. 71B requires the responsible LEA to fully fund the placement. Therefore, the Department will not pay for or cost share 502.6–502.11 placements. In addition, the Department will not provide substitute care to any child in need of special education whose individualized education plan (IEP) specifies that a residential school program is necessary to meet the educational goals and objectives of the IEP (i.e., the IEP bears a 502.6 prototype).

110 CMR 7.500. Introduction to Interstate Placement Services

110 CMR 7.500 through 7.523 set forth the responsibilities of all persons and agencies involved in the placement of children across state lines and across national borders, consistent with Massachusetts law, including M.G.L. c. 119, Appendix §§ 2-1 et seq. (the Interstate Compact on the Placement of Children, hereinafter called "the Compact"); M.G.L. c. 119, § 36; M.G.L. c. 18B; M.G.L. c. 28A; and M.G.L. c. 210.

110 CMR 7.501. Interstate Placement Definitions

As used in 110 CMR 7.500 through 7.523 only the following terms shall have the following meanings:

Appropriate Authorities as used in M.G.L. c. 119, Appendix §§ 2-1 Article I(b) and Article V(a), and "appropriate public authority" as used in Article III, mean the Compact Administrator for Massachusetts when the child is to be placed in Massachusetts.

Appropriate Officer or Agency as used in M.G.L. c. 119, Appendix, §§ 2-1 Article III(c) and §§ 2 through 6, means the Compact Administrator for Massachusetts when the child is to be placed from Massachusetts to another state.

Hospital means an institution for the acutely ill which discharges its patients when they are no longer acutely ill, which does not provide or hold itself out as providing child care in substitution for parental care or foster care, and in which a child is placed for the primary purpose of treating an acute medical problem. Outpatient care does not fall within this definition.

Institution means a residential setting where children are cared for on a 24-hour-a-day basis.

Institution Caring for the Mentally Ill or Mentally Defective means an institution which provides medical care and treatment, psychiatric care and treatment, corrective, and therapeutic or rehabilitative treatment, for mentally ill or mentally defective or retarded persons. Such an institution is not altered in its character as an institution for the mentally ill or mentally defective merely because it provides child care services to these patients as part of a comprehensive regime of treatment. Outpatient care does not fall within 110 CMR 7.501: Institution Caring for the Mentally Ill or Mentally Defective.

Institution Primarily Educational in Character means an institution which operates one or more programs that can be offered in satisfaction of compulsory school attendance laws, in which the primary purpose of accepting children is to meet their educational needs, and which: (a) does not accept responsibility for children during the entire year; and (b) does not provide or hold itself out as providing child care constituting foster care or similar nurture sufficient to substitute for parental supervision and control; and (c) does not provide any other services to children, except for those customarily regarded as extracurricular or cocurricular school activities, pupil support services, and those services necessary to make it possible for the children to be maintained on a residential basis in the aforementioned school program or programs.

Placement means the arrangement for the care of a child in a family or boarding home or in a child-caring agency or institution but does not include any institution caring for the mentally ill, mentally defective or epileptic or any institution primarily educational in character, or any hospital or other medical facility.

Proper Authorities as used in M.G.L. c. 119, Appendix § 2-1 Article I(c) means the Compact Administrator for Massachusetts when the child is to be placed from Massachusetts to another state.

Receiving Agency means any state; an officer or employee of any state, or an officer or employee of any political subdivision of any state; a court of any state; any person, corporation, association, charitable agency or other entity which receives any child from another state.

Receiving State means the state to which a child is sent, brought or caused to be sent or brought, whether by public authorities or private persons or agencies, and whether for placement with state or local public authorities or for placement with private agencies or persons.

Sending Agency means any state; an officer or employee of any state, or an officer or employee of any political subdivision of any state; a court of any state; any person, corporation, association, charitable agency or other entity which sends, brings or causes to be sent or to be brought any child to another state.

Sending State means the state in which the sending agency is located or resides, or the state from which the sending agency sends the child.

Visit means a stay of less than 30 days to provide the child with a social or cultural experience of short duration, such as a stay in a camp or with a friend or relative who has not assumed legal responsibility for providing child care services. A stay of more than 30 days shall be considered a visit if it begins and ends within the period of a child's vacation from school. A visit may not extend beyond 30 days (or the duration of the school vacation period). A stay without an express or implied termination date is a placement and not a visit.

110 CMR 7.502. Interstate Compact Administrator for Massachusetts

The Department shall conduct all interstate placement activities through the Office of the Deputy Commissioner, Department of Social Services. The "Compact Administrator" for Massachusetts is the Deputy Commissioner of the Department of Social Services, or his/her designee.

110 CMR 7.503. Applicability of the Interstate Compact and M.G.L. c. 119, § 36

(1) The Interstate Compact shall apply whenever a sending agency from a state which is a party to the Compact sends, brings, or causes to be sent or to be brought into any other state which is a party to the Compact, any child for placement in foster care or residential or group care, or for placement in a relative's home [other than those persons named in 110 CMR 7.503(3)] or for placement preliminary to a possible adoption.

(2) Placements made to the Commonwealth by sending agencies from non-member states and foreign countries, or made by the Commonwealth to non-member states and foreign countries, are not subject to the Compact but such placements made to the Commonwealth are subject to the provisions of M.G.L. c. 119, § 36 unless the placement is between persons both of whom are persons listed in 110 CMR 7.503(3).

(3) Neither the Interstate Compact procedures nor the provisions of M.G.L. c. 119, § 36 shall apply when the sending agency is the child's parent, step-parent, grandparent, adult brother or adult sister, adult uncle or adult aunt, or non-agency guardian and the receiving agency is likewise any such relative of the child or a non-agency guardian.

(4) The Interstate Compact shall apply to court orders unless they relate to cases exempted by Article VIII of the Compact.

(5) The Interstate Compact shall not apply to placements which occurred prior to the date of enactment of the Compact by either the state of the sending agency or the state of the receiving agency; however, the provisions of M.G.L. c. 119, § 36 shall apply if otherwise applicable.

(6) Neither the Interstate Compact nor the provisions of M.G.L. c. 119, § 36 shall apply to any placement with an institution primarily educational in character, any institution caring for the mentally ill or mentally defective or epileptic, or any hospital or other medical facility.

(7) Neither the Interstate Compact nor M.G.L. c. 119, § 36 shall apply to a visit.

(8) The Interstate Compact shall apply to any stay across state borders whenever the sending agency requests a homestudy or supervision of a child by the receiving state.

(9) The provisions of M.G.L. c. 119, § 36 shall not apply to a sending agency which is a public agency in another state that is a party to the Interstate Compact.

(10) Adoptions by residents of Massachusetts who finalize the adoption of out-of-state or out-of-country children in another state or country are not governed by either the Interstate Compact or by M.G.L. c. 119, § 36. This exception applies only to cases where the adoption of the child is completed before the child enters the Commonwealth for the first time.

(11) Both the Interstate Compact and M.G.L. c. 119, § 36 apply, if otherwise applicable, to adoption by residents of Massachusetts who send, bring or cause to be sent or to be brought a child into the Commonwealth pending the finalization of the adoption in another state or country.

(12) The Interstate Compact shall not apply when a placement is made pursuant to any other interstate compact to which both the sending state and the receiving state are parties or pursuant to any other agreement between the states which has the force of law.

110 CMR 7.504. Placement of Out-of-State Children in Educational Institutions

(1) Programs conducted by public or private agencies in which children are placed in family homes incident to their attendance at educational institutions in other states are foster care placements within the meaning of the Interstate Compact, because the home rather than the educational institution provides child care and supervision during the time when the child is not in attendance at the school program.

(2) To facilitate the conduct of such a program, the agency administering it may investigate and prepare reports on the Massachusetts homes in question in advance, and may offer such reports to the Compact Administrator of the Commonwealth as part of the information required in connection with an intended placement, provided that any such report must be current to within six months of the date of its submission.

(3) Any home in which a child is placed or proposed to be placed pursuant to 110 CMR 7.000 shall obtain and maintain such license or approval as a child care or foster home as the laws and regulations of the Commonwealth require. The license or approval must be in full force and effect at the time the sending agency gives notice of the intended placement and at all times during the continuance of the placement. Failure to meet this condition shall be sufficient ground for the Compact Administrator to deny or terminate the placement.

(4) The operator of a program to which 110 CMR 7.504 applies shall:

(a) notify the Compact Administrator of the Commonwealth promptly in writing if the child is returned to his parent's or guardian's home or is sent to another home during the school year.

(b) notify the Compact Administrator of the Commonwealth promptly in writing upon the child's return to his parent's or guardian's home at the end of the school year.

(5) If a child in a program to which 110 CMR 7.000 applies is placed from one home to another the action shall be considered a new placement and shall require the same notifications, furnishing of information and documentation, and receipt of a notice pursuant to Article III(b) of the Compact as an initial placement.

(6) The special procedures of 110 CMR 7.000 shall be available only for programs in which the parents or guardians retain full custodial rights to control (by the giving or withholding of consent or otherwise) the place of abode and participation in the program of the child. Further, this regulation applies only to programs one purpose of which is to afford children educational opportunities but in which residential schools or other residential institutions are not utilized to provide the educational component of the program.

110 CMR 7.505. Placement of Out-of-State Children in Medical Institutions

(1) Placement of a child in a medical institution of whatever kind in another state is a placement within the meaning of the Interstate Compact unless the room, board, care and supervision provided at the medical facility are merely incident to medical or psychiatric treatment which the child is receiving, and are to be terminated when the child's medical or psychiatric treatment ends.

(2) Placement in a home for unwed pregnant mothers is a placement within the meaning of the Interstate Compact if the purpose of the facility is to meet the expectant mother's social and emotional needs as well as to provide room and board during pregnancy. Only if the home's services are primarily medical and are confined to the period of the actual delivery and customary post-delivery stay is the placement outside the Compact.

110 CMR 7.506. Placement of Out-of-State Children in Residential Institutions

(1) Placement of a child in a residential institution is a placement within the meaning of the Interstate Compact if the institution provides child care or other services which, if provided by a family or individual other than the child's parents, would constitute foster care, with or without payment.

5

(2) Where children attend school or other educational programs, but are not housed or cared for on a 24-hour basis by the school or educational program and where a placement within the meaning of the Compact occurs, the placement shall be deemed to be with the person, family, agency or institution which provides the 24-hour a day housing and care during the period of school or other educational attendance.

(3) The type of license, if any, held by an institution may be used as evidence of its character, but whether an institution is either generally exempt from the need to comply with the Interstate Compact procedures or exempt in a particular instance shall be determined by the services the institution actually provides or offers to provide.

110 CMR 7.507. Placement with Parent(s)

(1) No placement under the Interstate Compact occurs nor do the provisions of M.G.L. c. 119, § 36 apply when a court in one state, in connection with the granting of a divorce, awards any form of custody to a parent residing in another state.

(2) If a court enters an order which alters custodial rights which had been previously adjudicated in a divorce, separation or other legal proceeding, and such order places a child with a previously non-custodial parent in a state other than the one in which the child currently resides, there is a placement within the meaning of the Compact.

(3) No placement under the Interstate Compact occurs nor do the provisions of M.G.L. c. 119, § 36 apply when divorced parents agree to a placement of their child with a relative listed in 110 CMR 7.503(3), or when one divorced parent places his/her child with the other non-custodial divorced parent across state lines.

(4) Whenever a state agency has custody of a child or care of a child pursuant to a voluntary placement agreement, and such agency places a child with his/her parent(s) in another state, this constitutes a placement under the Interstate Compact.

(5) Whenever a court in a divorce proceeding awards custody of a child to any third party including a relative listed in 110 CMR 7.503(3) against the wishes of the parents, this constitutes a placement under the Interstate Compact.

110 CMR 7.508. Independent Adoptions

(1) "Independent adoption" is any placement of a child for adoption in the Commonwealth made or facilitated by anyone other than the Department or by anyone other than an adoption or placement agency licensed or approved by the Department of Early Education and Care; any placement of a child from the Commonwealth for adoption in another state made or facilitated by anyone other than a placement agency licensed by the receiving state and anyone other than the Department or an adoption or placement agency licensed or approved by the Department of Early Education and Care.

(2) Independent adoptions are illegal in the Commonwealth. See, M.G.L. c. 28A, § 11(c). Independent adoptions, for purposes of 110 CMR 7.508, shall include both children placed in the Commonwealth and children placed from the Commonwealth, for purposes of adoption.

110 CMR 7.509. Identified Adoptions

(1) An "identified adoption" means an adoption where the parent executes a written surrender of his/her child directly to a particular person or agency.

(2) Identified adoptions of children brought into the Commonwealth are permitted provided that the placement is made by the Department or by an adoption or placement agency licensed or approved by the Office for Children, and is approved by the Compact Administrator for the Commonwealth.

(3) Identified adoptions of Massachusetts children in another state are permitted provided that a home study is prepared in accordance with the laws of the receiving state and is submitted for approval to the Compact Administrator for the Commonwealth, prior to the placement.

(4) Any adoption or placement agency licensed or approved by the Office for Child Care Services (including the Department of Children and Families) which agrees to accept a child from another state and to place that child in a particular identified home in the Commonwealth can thereafter refuse to place the child in that particular home based on the results of a completed home study.

(5) The Interstate Compact shall apply to all identified adoptions of children born to mothers who are out-of-state residents, regardless of whether the surrender was executed in the sending state or in Massachusetts, unless the child is surrendered directly to one of the exempt relatives or guardian as enumerated in 110 CMR 7.503(3).

110 CMR 7.510. Guardians

(1) The Interstate Compact procedures shall not apply to a non-agency guardian sending or bringing a child into a receiving state and leaving the child with a non-agency guardian or any of the exempt relatives enumerated in 110 CMR 7.503(3) in the receiving state.

(2) The Interstate Compact and the provisions of M.G.L. c. 119, § 36 shall apply whenever a resident of the Commonwealth is appointed guardian of a child by a court of another state for the purpose of securing an adoption in the Commonwealth.

110 CMR 7.511. Foreign Children

(1) The Interstate Compact procedures do not apply to intercountry placement of children. M.G.L. c. 119, § 36 governs the placement of foreign-born children into the Commonwealth for the purpose of adoption.

(2) The Interstate Compact procedures shall apply to the interstate placement of foreign-born children, whether or not the child was ever physically in the sending state, so long as such sending state caused the child to be sent or brought into another state.

110 CMR 7.512. Moves Across State Borders

(1) Move by child. An intra-state placement not subject to the Compact becomes an interstate placement subject thereto when the child moves to another state.

Example: The Department has custody or care of a child and places the child with a foster family in Massachusetts. If the foster family and child thereafter move to Vermont, the Interstate Compact procedures must be followed.

(2) Move by parents. An intra-state placement not subject to the Compact does not become subject to the Compact when the parent(s) move to another state but the child remains in the state where the original placement occurred.

Example: The Department has custody or care of a child and places the child with a foster family in Massachusetts. If the parents who placed the child with the Department thereafter move to Vermont, but the child remains in Massachusetts, the Interstate Compact is not involved.

110 CMR 7.513. Runaway Children

Whenever a child is a runaway and crosses state borders, the provisions of M.G.L. c. 119, App. §§ 1–7 shall govern the return or retention of the child.

110 CMR 7.514. Procedural Requirements When Sending Agency Is Within the Commonwealth

(1) Any sending agency which intends to send, bring, or place a Massachusetts child into another state shall give advance written notice of its intention to the Compact Administrator of the Commonwealth and of the receiving state.

(2) The sending agency shall thereafter furnish the Compact Administrator of the Commonwealth and of the receiving state with all information requested by each Compact Administrator, provided that such information will consist of at least the following;

(a) The name, date and place of birth of the child.

(b) The identity and address(es) of the parent(s) and legal guardian(s).

(c) The name and address of the person, agency or institution to or with which the sending agency proposes to send, bring or place the child.

(d) A full statement of the reasons for such proposed action.

(e) Social assessment of the child and family (Form ICPC-101).

(f) Copy of all court documents relating to custody or adoption of the child, if applicable.

(g) A full statement of what the receiving state is being asked to do regarding the child.

(h) Copy of Request to Place Child (Form 100A), if applicable.

(i) Copy of Report on Placement Status Change of Child (Form ICPC-100B) for all retroactive applications, if applicable.

(j) Evidence that surrenders by parent(s) and/or termination of parental rights were accomplished fully in accordance with the laws of Massachusetts, or evidence that the process of terminating such rights has been commenced in accordance with the laws of Massachusetts.

(k) A home study of the proposed placement site conducted by a placement agency licensed or approved by the receiving state.

(l) In the case of placement for purposes of adoption, a description of each expense incurred or to be incurred by the adoptive parents, the amount of each such expense, the name and address of the payee, and the date of payment.

(m) In the case of placement for purposes of adoption, medical background information on the child (if born) and on the natural parents.

(n) Evidence of authority of sending agency to place child which may consist of any of the following as appropriate.

1. Court order;

2. Executed Voluntary Placement Agreement;

3. A notarized statement by a parent or legal guardian acting as a sending agency;

4. Executed surrender form executed in accordance with the requirements of M.G.L. c. 210.

(o) Whenever a private child welfare agency is the sending agency, a copy of its current license.

(p) If a child is of Indian heritage, verification that the placement is in compliance with the Indian Child Welfare Act.

(q) A pre-placement visitation plan which is consistent with good social work practice.

(3) The Compact Administrator of the sending state shall send copies of the information outlined above to the Compact Administrator in the receiving state.

110 CMR 7.515. Financial Responsibility for the Child

(1) A sending agency in the Commonwealth shall continue to have financial responsibility for support and maintenance of any Massachusetts child placed out-of-state, during the period of the out-of-state placement (including any subsidized adoption which occurs out-of-state).

(2) An out-of-state sending agency shall continue to have financial responsibility for support and maintenance of any child placed in the Commonwealth during the period of the placement (including any subsidized adoption which occurs in the Commonwealth).

(3) A sending agency in the Commonwealth may contract with any third party to shift financial responsibility for an out-of-state placement to such third party, provided that in the event of default by the third party financial responsibility for the child as between the receiving state and sending agency remains with the sending agency in the Commonwealth.

(4) A sending agency in the Commonwealth shall not condition a placement with a receiving state upon the latter's assumption of financial responsibility for the child.

(5) The laws of the receiving state shall govern whether a particular cost is a cost of placement which shall be borne by the sending agency, provided that the rate at which foster care payments shall be paid shall be the rate established by the Commonwealth, regardless of whether it is the sending or receiving state.

(6) Nothing in 110 CMR 7.00 shall prevent the sending agency from pursuing its right to reimbursement from parties responsible for the support of the child.

(7) Whenever parent(s) terminate their parental rights and surrender the child to a person or agency in the Commonwealth, such parents by virtue of such surrender shall not retain any jurisdiction over the child but jurisdiction and financial responsibility for the child shall be vested in a state child welfare agency or other financially responsible entity which must be named as the sending agency. Financial responsibility shall include the support and maintenance of the child during the pre-adoption period of the child's placement in the Commonwealth.

110 CMR 7.516. Procedural Requirements When the Commonwealth Is the Receiving State

(1) Whenever the Interstate Compact procedures or the provisions of M.G.L. c. 119, § 36 are applicable, all placements of children across state borders into the Commonwealth shall require the advance approval, in writing, of the Compact Administrator of the Commonwealth.

(2) The Compact Administrator of the Commonwealth shall approve the placement so long as the proposed placement conforms to the laws of the Commonwealth, and does not appear to be contrary to the interests of the child. The placement need not be the best possible placement to be approved, so long as it is reasonable and satisfactory considering all the relevant circumstances.

(3) The Compact Administrator shall not approve a placement of a child into the Commonwealth whenever the provisions of the Interstate Compact or the provisions of M.G.L. c. 119, § 36 are applicable, unless the following are submitted in advance to the Compact Administrator, except that 110 CMR 7.516(a) and (b) shall not be required from a public sending agency in a state which is a party to the Interstate Compact:

(a) An individual or blanket bond running to the Commonwealth in such penal sum and with such surety or sureties as the Department may approve.

5

(b) A written application containing such information relative to such child as the Department may require and which includes the statement:

1. that all statements contained in such an application are true;

2. that any such child becoming a public charge during his minority shall be removed from the state by the sending agency not later than 30 days after notice from the Department;

3. that such child shall be removed from the state by the sending agency immediately upon his release from any penal or reformatory institution or training school to which he has been committed, within three years of his arrival within the state, for juvenile delinquency or crime;

4. that such child shall be placed or boarded by the sending agency under such agreement as will secure to him a proper home and surroundings, and as will render his custodian responsible for his proper care, education and training, under adequate supervision and subject to annual visitation by an agent; and

5. that such reports relative to the child shall be made to the Department as it may require.

(c) The name, date and place of birth of the child.

(d) The identity and address(es) of the parent(s) and legal guardian(s).

5

(e) The name and address of the person, agency or institution to or with which the sending agency proposes to send, bring or place the child.

(f) A full statement of the reasons for such proposed action.

(g) Social assessment of the child and family (Form ICPC-101).

(h) An opinion letter from a member of the Bar of the sending state that surrenders by parent(s) and/or termination of parental rights were accomplished fully in accordance with the laws of the sending state, or evidence that the process for terminating such rights has been commenced in accordance with the laws of the sending state.

(i) Copy of all court documents relating to custody or adoption of the child, if applicable.

(j) A full statement of what the Commonwealth is being asked to do regarding the child.

(k) Copy of Request to Place Child (Form ICPC 100A), if applicable.

(l) Copy of Report on Placement Status Change of Child (Form ICPC 100B), for all retroactive applications.

(m) A home study of the proposed placement site in the Commonwealth conducted by a placement agency licensed or approved by the Office for Children.

(n) If a child is of Indian heritage, verification that the placement is in compliance with the Indian Child Welfare Act.

(o) In any case where parent(s) have terminated their parental rights and have surrendered their child to a person or agency in the Commonwealth, a statement naming as the sending agency, a state child welfare agency or other financially responsible entity, signed and acknowledged by said financially responsible entity as to its financial obligation.

(p) In the case of placement for purposes of adoption, a description of each expense incurred or to be incurred by the adoptive parents, the amount of each such expense, the name and address of the payee and the date of payment.

(q) In the case of placement for purposes of adoption, medical background information on the child (if born) and on the natural parents.

(r) Evidence of authority of sending agency to place child which may consist of any of the following as appropriate:

1. Court order;

2. Executed Voluntary Placement Agreement;

3. A notarized statement by a parent or legal guardian acting as a sending agency;

4. Executed surrender form executed in accordance with the requirements of the sending state.

(s) Whenever a private child welfare agency is the sending agency, a copy of its current license.

(t) A pre-placement visitation plan which is consistent with good social work practice.

(4) The receiving agency shall arrange for the actual placement of the child and shall supervise the placement if requested to do so by the sending agency.

The receiving agency may make recommendations regarding the placement, but the sending agency shall make all the decisions, provided that whenever the receiving agency requests the removal of the child out of the Commonwealth, the sending agency shall remove such child.

(5) The receiving agency shall conduct a home study of the family with whom placement is to be made. Within 30 days of receiving a request for the conduct of such home study, the receiving agency shall prepare such home study and shall make a recommendation on the suitability of the placement to the Compact Administrator of the Commonwealth.

(6) Notwithstanding any provisions to the contrary, whenever a child is placed into the Commonwealth under the provisions of the Interstate Compact or M.G.L. c. 119, § 36, and such child is emotionally, physically or mentally handicapped so that the need for such placement will reasonably be expected to continue past the child's 18th birthday, the Commonwealth, as the receiving state, shall condition the acceptance of the child into the Commonwealth on the execution of an agreement with the sending agency that the financial responsibility for such individual shall continue with the sending agency so long as the individual remains in the Commonwealth and requires financial assistance, provided, however, that the sending agency shall no longer be financially responsible if the individual is adopted or is discharged from the placement with the concurrence of the Compact Administrator for the Commonwealth.

110 CMR 7.517. Jurisdiction under the Interstate Compact

(1) The sending agency shall have jurisdiction over the child sufficient to determine all matters relative to the custody, supervision, care, treatment and disposition of the child in the same manner as if the child had remained in the sending agency's state, until the child is adopted, reaches majority age, becomes self-supporting or is discharged from the placement in question with the concurrence of the appropriate authority in the receiving state.

(2) The child's legal residence shall be in the state of the sending agency until one of the events stated in the 110 CMR 7.517(1) occurs.

(3) The sending agency shall have jurisdiction sufficient to effect or cause the return of the child or his/her transfer to another location.

(4) The sending agency shall have the power to secure periodic reports from the receiving state concerning the course of the placement.

(5) Whenever parent(s) terminate their parental rights and surrender their child to a person or agency in the Commonwealth, such parents by virtue of such surrender shall not retain any jurisdiction over the child but jurisdiction and financial responsibility over the child shall be vested in a state child welfare agency or other financially responsible entity which must be named as the sending agency.

(6) The receiving state shall be responsible for providing supervision of the placement, if so requested by the sending agency.

(7) The receiving state shall have jurisdiction over the child sufficient to deal with an act of delinquency or crime committed in the receiving state.

(8) The receiving state shall have jurisdiction over the child sufficient to deal with protecting the child from abuse or neglect committed in the receiving state.

(9) Both the sending state and the receiving state shall have jurisdiction sufficient to punish or subject to penalty anyone violating the terms of the Interstate Compact.

110 CMR 7.518. Law Governing

(1) Whenever a child is placed across state borders, the sending agency shall comply with the applicable laws of the receiving state governing the placement of children therein.

(2) After the child has been placed across state borders the laws of the receiving state shall govern all matters relating to the child, other than all matters in relation to the custody, supervision, care, treatment and disposition of the child which shall be governed by the laws of state of the sending agency retaining jurisdiction over the child.

(3) The laws of the receiving state shall apply at a minimum:

(a) to a care and protection proceeding brought against the placement in the receiving state;

(b) to a determination of whether medical, educational, support or other payments shall be made on behalf of the child;

(c) to a determination of the legality of the placement in the receiving state;

(d) to a determination of the age of majority.

(4) In the event that the laws of the sending state and receiving state are in conflict regarding the placement of the child, the laws of the receiving state shall govern.

(5) Whenever a sending state or a receiving state exercise jurisdiction to punish or subject to penalty anyone for violation of the Interstate Compact, the laws of the state exercising jurisdiction shall apply.

110 CMR 7.519. Enforcement

(1) Whenever the Compact is applicable anyone sending, bringing or causing to be sent or brought into any receiving state a child in violation of the terms of the Compact shall also be deemed to be in violation of the laws respecting the placement of children of the receiving state and of the state in which the sending agency is located or from which it sends or brings the child. The term anyone in the preceding sentence shall include a court of competent jurisdiction.

(2) A violation of the terms of the Interstate Compact shall also be a violation of M.G.L. c. 119, § 36; M.G.L. c. 15D, §§ 6(c), 6(e), and 15(a) and M.G.L. c. 210, as applicable, together with such other statutes and regulations of the Commonwealth as are applicable to the placement of children.

(3) The Department may, in its discretion, refer matters involving violation of the terms of the Interstate Compact or any of the above-listed statutes to any appropriate investigatory or prosecutorial agency or board in the sending state or the receiving state, including but not limited to the Office of the Attorney General, Office of the District Attorney, Executive Office of Health and Human Services, Department of Early Education and Care, Board of Bar Overseers.

110 CMR 7.520. Effect of Violation on Placements

(1) Failure by any receiving agency or sending agency, including a court, to utilize Interstate Compact procedures whenever the Compact applies renders the placement illegal.

(2) Such illegal placement shall not permit the sending agency to avoid the financial responsibility for the placement or other requirements of the Compact which would rest with the sending agency had the Compact not been violated.

(3) Whenever a placement is illegal because the Compact, which was applicable, was either not used or its provisions were violated, such placement shall be brought into compliance with the Compact or the placement shall be terminated.

(4) Whenever the provisions of M.G.L. c. 15D, §§ 6(c) or 6(e) have been violated the Department of Early Education and Care may petition the Superior Court to enjoin any such violation or to take such other action as equity and justice may require. *See* M.G.L. c. 28A, § 16.

110 CMR 7.521. Termination of Placements

(1) A placement made pursuant to the Interstate Compact or the provisions of M.G.L. c. 119, § 36 shall terminate only when the child is adopted, reaches majority under the laws of the receiving state, becomes self-supporting, or is discharged from the placement in question with the concurrence of the Compact Administrator in the receiving state.

(2) If the placement is in violation of the Interstate Compact or M.G.L. c. 119, § 36, the sending agency may not unilaterally terminate its responsibilities as to such placement.

(3) If the placement is in violation of the Interstate Compact or M.G.L. c. 119, § 36, such placement may be terminated only upon the conditions set forth at 110 CMR 7.521(1).

110 CMR 7.522. Confidentiality

(1) A receiving agency of the Commonwealth which has been requested to perform a home study by a sending agency shall release the information contained in the home study to the sending agency upon the same conditions as would apply if the sending agency were a Massachusetts agency with jurisdiction over the child to be placed.

(2) The laws of the Commonwealth regarding confidentiality shall govern the release of information by the sending agency and the Compact Administrator.

(3) *See* Confidentiality, generally at 110 CMR 12.00 et seq.

110 CMR 7.523. Administrative Review

Any person aggrieved by any action or inaction of the Department involving the placement of children across state lines shall have the right to a fair hearing on the matter pursuant to 110 CMR 10.00 et seq.

Regulatory Authority—110 CMR 7.000: M.G.L. c. 18B, §§ 3(B), 15; M.G.L. c. 28A, § 7; M.G.L. c. 119, §§ 51B(7) and 51B(8); 7.010: M.G.L. c. 18B, § 7; M.G.L. c. 28A, § 6A; 7.020: M.G.L. c. 18B, § 2(A)(6); M.G.L. c. 119, § 51B(7); 7.030: M.G.L. c. 18B, § 2(A)(13); M.G.L. c. 119, § 51B(7); 7.040: M.G.L. c. 18B, §§ 2, 3, 4, 7; M.G.L. c. 119, § 51B(7); 7.050: M.G.L. c. 18B, §§ 2(A)(8) and 2(A)(13); 7.060: M.G.L. c. 18B, § 2(A)(10); M.G.L. c. 119, § 51B(7); 7.070: M.G.L. c. 18B, § 2(A)(7); M.G.L. c. 119, § 51B(7); 7.080: M.G.L. c. 18B, § 2(A)(1); 7.090: M.G.L. c. 18B, §§ 2(a)(14) and 2(A)(16); M.G.L. c. 119, § 51B(7); M.G.L. c. 119, § 23G; 7.100: M.G.L. c. 18B,§ 2; M.G.L. c. 119, Appendix; M.G.L. c. 119, §§ 39E through J; M.G.L. c. 119, §§ 51A through F.; 7.200: M.G.L. c. 18B, § 2(A)(5); M.G.L. c. 18B, § 21; M.G.L. c. 210; 7.300: M.G.L. c. 119, § 23; M.G.L. c. 18B, § 2(A)(3); 7.400; M.G.L. c. 71B; 7.500; M.G.L. c. 119, Appendix ("The Interstate Compact"); M.G.L. c. 119, § 36; M.G.L. c. 28A, § 11(c).

110 CMR 8.00. Service Denial, Reduction, or Termination

Section

110 CMR 8.01. Notice of Action

(1) The Department or provider shall give written notice to a client if the Department intends to deny, reduce, or terminate services, or increase the cost thereof. The written notice shall contain:

(a) a statement of what action the Department intends to take;

(b) the reasons for the action;

(c) the date on which the action shall become effective;

(d) the address and telephone number of the Department office making the decision;

5

(e) an explanation of the applicant's or recipient's right to request a fair hearing;

(f) the process used to request a fair hearing; and

(g) an explanation of the circumstances, if any, under which services will be continued pending the fair hearing.

(2) The Department or provider shall mail or hand-deliver the written notice set forth in 110 CMR 8.01(1) to the applicant or recipient at least 15 days prior to the date of the intended action or 30 calendar days if the intended action relates to young adult services except as set forth in 110 CMR 8.01(3).

(3) The Department or provider shall mail or hand deliver the written notice set forth in 110 CMR 8.01(1) without advance notice but no later than the date of action when:

(a) the Department or provider has factual information confirming the death of the recipient of services;

(b) the Department or provider has received a clear, written statement from the recipient that he or she no longer wishes services;

(c) the recipient gives to the Department information which requires termination or reduction of services, and the recipient has indicated, in writing, that he or she understands that this must be the consequence of supplying such information;

(d) the recipient has been accepted as a recipient of services in a new jurisdiction; or

(e) a service was granted for a specific period and the recipient had been informed in writing at the time of initiation that the service would terminate at the end of the specified period; or

(f) the department is unable to locate the applicant or recipient after using diligent efforts.

110 CMR 8.02. Service Continuation for 18 through 22 Years of Age

The Department is committed to assisting older adolescents and young adults in their transition to independence and self sufficiency.

Regulatory Authority—110 CMR 8.00: M.G.L. c. 18B, §§ 3, 7, and c. 119, § 37.

110 CMR 9.00. Case Closure

5

Section

110 CMR 9.01. Introduction

Case closing is the set of activities which leads to the termination of Department services to an individual or a family.

110 CMR 9.02. Required Closings

Case closing shall include, but is not limited to, the following events.

(1) A case must be closed when a case opened with a 51A report subsequently is not supported and the family does not wish to make a voluntary application for services.

(2) A case must be closed when the child(ren) have been adopted or placed with a legal guardian and the adoptive/guardian family no longer needs Department services. Adoption or guardianship subsidy can continue to be provided, regardless of case closure.

(3) A case must be closed when the social worker and client jointly agree that Department services are no longer necessary.

(4) A case must be closed when a voluntary applicant for Department services withdraws the application or refuses to participate in assessment, service planning or case review.

(5) A case must be closed when, after reasonable social work efforts and offers of service, a family which is the subject of a supported 51A report refuses further Departmental services and there are no grounds for either legal action or a new 51A report.

(6) A case must be closed when a CHINS petition is dismissed and no family members are requesting or receiving Departmental services.

110 CMR 9.03. Procedures

(1) The Social Worker And His/Her Supervisor Make The Case Closing Decision. Case closing is a clinical decision between a social worker and his/her supervisor, which decision is thereafter discussed with the client family. Case closing takes into consideration the stated goals of the case, the individual's or family's participation in services, the reduction of risk to the child, legal issues, and the Department's responsibility to provide services. When a family which is the subject of a supported 51A report refuses further Department services, and if the social worker and/or supervisor wish to seek court-ordered custody of the children in question, then a consultation with a Department attorney shall be conducted to determine if there are grounds for legal action. The social worker documents in writing in the case record the outcome of this consultation. If legal action is not warranted and despite reasonable casework efforts, the family persists in refusing Department services, the social worker documents this in the case record and proceeds to close the case, by following the procedures set forth in 110 CMR 9.00.

(2) A Plan Is Developed For Case Closure. The social worker and his/her supervisor determine what activities are necessary to prepare the case for closing, and complete these activities.

(3) Area Director Reviews Case Closing. There shall be a review of every case closing decision by either the Area Director or his/her designee. If the Area Director or designee approves, s/he shall sign a case closing form to approve the closing.

(4) The Social Worker Notifies The Family In Writing Of The Decision To Close The Case. The social worker shall notify the family in writing that the case is to be closed. An outline of the fair hearing/grievance procedures shall be attached to the letter.

110 CMR 9.04. Closing a Supported Case

The Department may close a case with a supported 51A at any time after completion of its investigation.

COMMENTARY

It is generally but erroneously assumed that the decision to support a 51A report after investigation automatically means that the case should be left open. However, there are some types of circumstances where "support and close" would be the decision of choice:

(1) Supporting an allegation of child abuse or neglect does not necessarily mean that a child is at ongoing risk. Example: abuse that is found to have occurred by a babysitter. The child was definitely injured, by a caretaker.

However, the family is in no way responsible for the injury, or for choosing an inappropriate caretaker. Also, the family is appropriate in preventing any further contact between the child and babysitter. The incident must be supported, (as well as perhaps reported to the District Attorney—see 110 CMR 4.50), but the Department does not need to conduct an assessment, nor to keep the case open, if there is no ongoing risk to the child. Of course, the Department's services would be offered to the child and family.

(2) The second set of circumstances has to do with families that have disappeared. Example: Boston City Hospital examines a child and discovers welt marks on his back. The parents are interviewed, admit that they struck their child, and are informed that a 51A report will be filed. When the Department investigator goes out, s/he discovers that the address given does not exist. The investigator spends the rest of ten days attempting to locate the family through all other means, but is unsuccessful. There is reasonable cause to believe that the incident of abuse did occur, so the 51A must be supported. However, the Department can provide no services because the family cannot be located. Therefore, the Department does not keep the case open.

110 CMR 9.05. Court Approval Requirement for Closing Certain Cases

When a decision is made to close any case in which the Department has court ordered custody of child(ren), the Department will not close the case until the Department seeks from the court a return of full custody to the parents, and dismissal of the case.

COMMENTARY

By statute (M.G.L. c. 119, § 26) the Department does have the option to close cases by "administrative decision" without court action. However, in the interest of consistent casework and in order to afford Department social workers maximum support in making such decisions, the Department will seek the court's approval of the decision to close the case. In these instances, a member of the Department's legal staff will file a Motion to Dismiss the court case. If the court approves the Department's motion, the Department will proceed to close the case. If the court declines to make any ruling on the Department's motion in light of the Department's administrative prerogative contained in M.G.L. c. 119, § 26, the Department will proceed to close the case. If the court denies the Department's motion, the Department will not proceed to close the case.

Regulatory Authority—110 CMR 9.00: M.G.L. c. 119, § 26; M.G.L. c. 119, §§ 51A through D.

110 CMR 10.00. Fair Hearing and Grievances

[Amended Jan. 31, 2014.]

Selected Sections

110 CMR 10.01. Policy

The Department strives to provide services to clients equitably and fairly. Toward that end, clients shall have the opportunity to appeal certain matters via a Fair Hearing Process, and to present other matters to the department via a Grievance Process. The Fair Hearing Process is designed to enable a client who is dissatisfied with certain actions or inactions by the Department or a provider under contract with the Department, to present his or her position in an informal hearing and to receive a just and fair decision from an impartial hearing officer based on the facts and applicable policies, regulations, statutes and/or case law. The provisions of 801 CMR 1.01: Formal Rules through 1.03: Miscellaneous Provisions Applicable to All Adjudicatory Proceedings shall not apply to the Department's Fair Hearings. The Grievance Process is likewise designed to offer an informal dispute resolution process for clients.

110 CMR 10.02. Definitions

As used in 110 CMR 10.00, unless the context otherwise requires, the following terms shall have the following meanings:

Adolescent. An individual between 14 and 18 years of age.

Aggrieved Party. Any individual who challenges a decision of the Department pursuant to 110 CMR 10.36 through 10.38.

Alleged Perpetrator. An individual who the Department has identified, by substantial evidence, as responsible for the abuse or neglect of a child, referred the person's name to the District Attorney's office under MGL c. 119, § 51B(k), and listed the person on the Department's Registry of Alleged Perpetrators.

Appellant. Any individual who challenges a decision of the Department pursuant to 110 CMR 10.03 through 10.36.

Authorized Representative. Any person, such as a lawyer, advocate, relative or friend, who is authorized in writing by any party to represent that party.

Client. An applicant for or recipient of Department services. Foster parents, pre-adoptive parents or adoptive parents in their status as such shall be considered clients for purposes of 110 CMR 10.00.

Clinical Review Team. A team of not less than five individuals, each of whom must have extensive social work experience, convened by a Regional Director for the purpose of reviewing a decision referred to the team pursuant to 110 CMR 10.08.

Director of Areas. The term Director of Areas when used in 110 CMR 10.00 means the director of the Department's Area Office and shall include the director of any provider.

Fair Hearing Office. The centralized hearing office for Fair Hearings statewide, located at the Central Office of the Department, and within the Office of the General Counsel.

OCA. The Office of the Child Advocate pursuant to M.G.L. c. 18C.

Provider. An organization with a contract with the Department to provide services for Department Clients.

Young Adult. An individual between 18 and 22 years of age.

110 CMR 10.03. Hearings Officers

The Department shall employ one or more impartial hearings officers, whose sole duty shall be to conduct Fair Hearings statewide. No officer shall hear, or involve themselves in any way, in any matter in which they have, or have had, any direct or indirect interest, personal involvement or bias. Said officer shall attest to this impartiality in his or/her written decision.

In the event that the assigned Fair Hearing Officer is unable to hear the matter due to a lack of impartiality, the officer shall notify the Director of Fair Hearings or designee, in writing, that the officer must recuse himself or herself from the matter. The Director of Fair Hearings or designee shall appoint another officer to hear the case.

The Hearing Office, as defined in 110 CMR 10.02, shall be under the direction of the Department's Director of Fair Hearings. Fair Hearing Officers employed by the Department shall have, at a minimum, two years of direct service experience as well as legal training and/or experience.

In addition, each Fair Hearing Officer shall receive the following hours of in-service training: 40 hours of pre-service training before she/he is eligible to conduct Fair Hearings, and, on an

5

annual basis, shall receive 25 hours of training in the following areas, including but not limited to: legal/administrative, trauma/abuse, health, poverty, and conflict resolution, and conflict of interest. However, the failure to comply with 110 CMR 10.03 shall not prevent an individual from serving as a Hearing Officer.

110 CMR 10.03A. Reports

The General Counsel's Office shall report, on an annual basis, the activities of the office, including but not limited to, the number of fair hearing requests, the number of hearings held, the number of decisions issued and the number of open Fair Hearing cases.

110 CMR 10.04. Providers

110 CMR 10.00 shall apply to clients who obtain or apply for services from the Department or from any Department provider. Providers may not avail themselves of the Fair Hearing or Grievance processes.

110 CMR 10.05. Standards for Review

A Fair Hearing shall address whether, based upon the evidence and the hearing record as a whole:

(a) the Department's or Provider's decision or procedural action violated applicable statutory or regulatory requirements, including but not limited to 110 CMR, or the Department's or Provider's policies or procedures, and resulted in substantial prejudice to the Appellant; or

(b) if there is no applicable statute, policy, regulation or procedure, the Department or Provider failed to act with a reasonable basis or in a reasonable manner which resulted in substantial prejudice to the Appellant; or

(c) for a decision to support a report of abuse or neglect, whether based on the record as a whole, and giving due weight to the clinical judgments of the Department social workers, there is reasonable cause to believe that a child has been abused or neglected; or

(d) for a decision to list a person on the registry of alleged perpetrators, whether based on the record as a whole, there is substantial evidence that the person is responsible for the abuse or neglect.

110 CMR 10.06. Allowable Grounds for Appeal

The following matters are the exclusive grounds that may be appealed via the Fair Hearing process pursuant to 110 CMR 10.00:

(1) *Applicant's Grounds for Appeal.* An applicant for services has the right to appeal:

(a) the failure of the Department to follow 110 CMR, which resulted in substantial prejudice to the applicant;

(b) the computation of a fee for services in excess of the minimum fee set by the Department if the applicant is claiming that the fee was incorrectly calculated;

(c) the imposition of the minimum fee set by the Department if the applicant can show cause that she or he is exempt from that fee;

(d) any action or inaction of the Department involving the placement of children across state lines, pursuant to the provisions of 110 CMR 7.500: Introduction to Interstate Placement Services.

(2) *Biological Parents' Grounds for Appeal.* In addition to any other matters which are appealable pursuant to 110 CMR 10.06(1) and (3), biological parents may appeal when a goal determination made at a Foster Care Review changes pursuant to 110 CMR 6.12(10): Appeal of FCR Determination.

(3) *Recipients' Grounds of Appeal.* A recipient of services from the Department has the right to appeal the following actions by the Department or Provider:

(a) the suspension, reduction or termination of a service; however, there shall be no right to a Fair Hearing if:

1. the termination of a service is due to a judicial determination that the recipient's parental rights were terminated;

2. the termination of a service is due to a judicial determination that all of the recipient's minor children are under a permanent custody order to another individual pursuant to M.G.L. c. 119 § 26, and/or are under a guardianship to another pursuant to M.G.L. c. 190B;

3. the service being terminated is to a parent(s) whose child has turned 18; or

4. the service being terminated is to an individual over the age of 22 years of age.

(b) the calculation or recalculation of a fee if the recipient can show cause that the fee was calculated incorrectly;

(c) the imposition of the minimum fee if the recipient can show cause that she/he is exempt from that fee;

(d) the failure of the Department to follow 110 CMR, which resulted in substantial prejudice to the recipient.

(4) Foster Parents' Grounds of Appeal. A foster parent has a right to appeal the following actions by the Department although a right to appeal does not confer or create a liberty or property interest to a foster parent:

(a) the removal of a foster child from the foster home, except that no right of appeal exists if the child is to be removed in order to be placed:

1. with her/his biological or adoptive parent(s);

2. in one of the following placements, if the current placement is not such a placement, unless the foster parent(s) has applied to be a pre-adoptive or guardian placement for the child and has not been rejected by the Department as a pre-adoptive or guardian placement for the child, or there is a Fair Hearing appeal pending challenging the denial of the current foster parent as the child's pre-adoptive or guardian placement;

a. in a pre-adoptive home;

b. with a prospective guardian;

c. in a home where one or more of the child's siblings is residing; or

d. in a kinship home of the foster child if the current foster parent is not a kinship home of the foster child.

3. in an independent living situation;

4. in a different foster home because the child specific or kinship home was not approved as a foster/pre-adoptive home for the specific child, or was not reapproved after a reassessment under 110 CMR 7.113: Reassessment of Foster/Pre-adoptive Parents and Foster/Pre-adoptive Homes;

5. in a different foster home because the foster parent's license is either terminated or is not renewed after a reassessment under 110 CMR 7.113: Reassessment of Foster/Pre-adoptive Parents and Foster/Pre-adoptive Homes;

6. in a Department foster home, if that child is being moved from an intensive foster care home, and the child is no longer in need of intensive foster care, unless the intensive foster parent is seeking to become a pre-adoptive or prospective guardian placement and has not been denied by the Department.

(b) closure of the foster home, termination of a license as a foster parent/home or denial of a renewal of a foster parent/home license;

(c) denial of the foster parent as a legal guardian or adoptive parent for a child who has been in his or her foster home for at least six months;

(d) the failure of the Department to follow 110 CMR, which resulted in substantial prejudice to the foster parent.

(e) a Foster Care Review determination to change the service plan goal pursuant to 110 CMR 6.12(12): Appeal of FCR Determination to change a goal.

(5) *Pre-adoptive and Adoptive Parents' Grounds of Appeal.* A pre-adoptive and adoptive parent has the right to appeal the following decisions by the Department:

(a) denial of an application to become a Pre-adoptive placement;

(b) withdrawal of Department sponsorship of a Pre-adoptive placement;

(c) removal of a child from a Pre-adoptive placement, except that no right of appeal exists if the child was or will be placed with his or her parents, in an independent living situation, or if the pre-adoptive parent is either not reapproved for a child specific or kinship home, or his or her license is either terminated or not renewed for an unrestricted adoptive home after an evaluation under 110 CMR 7.113: Reassessment of Foster/Pre-adoptive Parents and Foster/Pre-adoptive Homes;

(d) decisions related to the adoption subsidy program, including:

1. the denial, reduction, suspension or termination of an adoption subsidy, except that there shall be no right to challenge a decision to terminate a subsidy if the child is 21 years of age and has been receiving a Title IV-E subsidy, or the child is 22 years of age and has been receiving a state adoption subsidy;

2. the decision to provide a deferred subsidy or to continue a deferred subsidy after a request for re-determination;

3. the existence of extenuating circumstances for an adoption subsidy after finalization of the adoption of a child with special needs;

(e) closure of a foster home which is also a Pre-adoptive placement;

(f) the failure of the Department to follow 110 CMR, which resulted in substantial prejudice to the Appellant.

(g) the delay or denial of the placement of a child for adoption when an approved family is available out of state.

(6) *Prospective Guardians' or Guardians' Grounds for Appeal.* A Prospective Guardian or Guardian has the right to appeal the following actions by the Department:

(a) denial of an application to become a guardian for a child in Department care or custody;

(b) withdrawal of the sponsorship of a guardianship;

(c) removal of a child from a prospective guardianship placement, except that no right of appeal exists if the child was or will be placed with her/his parents, in an independent living situation, or if the Prospective Guardian or Guardian is either not reapproved as a child specific or kinship home, or his or her license is either terminated or not renewed for an unrestricted adoptive home, after an evaluation under 110 CMR 7.113: Reassessment of Foster/Pre-adoptive Parents and Foster/Pre-adoptive Homes;

(d) decisions related to the guardianship subsidy program, including the:

1. denial, reduction, suspension or termination of a guardianship subsidy, except that there shall be no right to challenge a decision to terminate a subsidy if the child has turned 18 unless a request for an extension has been granted under 110 CMR 7.303(13): Extension of Guardianship Subsidy Over Age 18;

2. denial of a state funded guardianship which was requested on the ground that extenuating circumstances exist for a guardianship subsidy after finalization of the guardianship;

3. denial of a request for an extension of a guardianship subsidy under 110 CMR 7.303(13): Extension of Guardianship Subsidy Over Age 18 for a Young Adult unless the Young Adult has turned 22.

(e) a decision to close a foster home which is also a proposed guardianship placement;

(f) the failure of the Department to follow 110 CMR which resulted in substantial prejudice to the Appellant.

(7) *Foster and Pre-adoptive Parent Applicants' Grounds for Appeal.* Foster and Pre-adoptive parent applicants have the right to appeal the Department's decision to deny an application to become a Foster parent or Pre-adoptive parent, except that no right of appeal exists if the decision is based on the applicant's failure to effect specified changes within the allotted time after receiving notice from the Department.

(8) *Adolescents' Grounds for Appeal.* In addition to any other matters which are appealable pursuant to 110 CMR 10.06(1) and (3), an Adolescent has the right to appeal.

(a) a Foster Care Review determination to change the service plan goal pursuant to 110 CMR 6.12(12): Appeal of FCR Determination;

(b) the denial of a request to receive services, including placement services, from the Department over the age of 18.

(9) *Children's Grounds for Appeal.* In addition to any other matters which are appealable pursuant to 110 CMR 10.06(1) and (3), a child under 14 years of age has the right to appeal, through an attorney or authorized representative, a Foster Care Review determination to change the service plan goal made pursuant to 110 CMR 6.12(12): Appeal of FCR Determination.

(10) *Young Adults' Grounds for Appeal.* In addition to any other matters which are appealable pursuant to 110 CMR 10.06(1) and (3), a Young Adult may appeal:

(a) the denial of a request to continue to receive services, including placement services, from the Department over the age of 18;

(b) the denial of a request to return to the Department's care and receive services if the Young Adult was in the care or custody of the Department at the age of 18 and is not yet 22;

(c) the termination of services, except that no right of appeal exists if the Young Adult has reached the age of 22.

(11) *Supported Decision Appeal.* Whenever the Department has supported a report of abuse or neglect of a child, any parent of the subject child, any caregiver who has been identified in the Department's Central Registry as the person believed to be responsible for the abuse or neglect, any caregiver of the subject child and any Adolescent, who is the subject child has the right to appeal the Department's decision to support the report,

(a) Following the Department's decision to support a report of abuse or neglect, the Department shall notify the parties involved that they have the right to appeal the support decision via the Fair Hearing Process.

(b) In situations involving a support decision on a case not currently opened but opened after the support decision, the Fair Hearing will be conducted after an assessment has been completed or after the assessment period, whichever is earlier.

(12) *Alleged Perpetrators' Grounds for Appeal.*

(a) An individual who is listed on the Department's Registry of Alleged Perpetrators may appeal such listing.

1. based on information available during the initial investigation and/or any new information not available during the investigation, the Department's decision was not in accordance with 110 CMR 4.33 Perpetrator/Caretaker; or

2. the Department's procedural actions were not in conformity with the Department's policies and/or regulations, and/or any applicable statute or case law, and resulted in substantial prejudice to the Appellant.

(b) In reviewing a decision to list a person on the Registry of Alleged Perpetrators, the Area Office and the Fair Hearing Officer shall review any related support decision. The Area Office shall notify the Fair Hearing Office of any support decisions and other determinations arising from the same incident that have been challenged by the Appellant. If the Director of Areas of the office which made the initial decisions reverses the underlying support decision, the determination to list a person(s) on the Registry of Alleged Perpetrators shall be changed to reflect that there is no longer reasonable cause to believe that the person is responsible for the abuse or neglect and the name shall be removed from the Registry of Alleged Perpetrators. *See* 110 CMR 4.32: Decision to

5

Support/Unsupport a Report for procedures to follow if the Department finds that a 51A report is unsupported.

110 CMR 10.07. Disallowed Grounds for Appeal

No matter except those listed in 110 CMR 10.06 may be the subject of a Fair Hearing. Without limiting the generality of the foregoing, the following are specifically among the matters for which there is no right to a Fair Hearing.

(1) When the only reason for the Department's failure to grant a request for services or increased services, or for the Department's reduction or termination of services, is the unavailability of funds, or the unavailability of a particular service, there is no right to a Fair Hearing if:

(a) services are authorized on a first come-first serve basis unless the Appellant submits an offer of proof that other individuals received the services before them although their application was received later than that of the Appellant. The Appellant may submit such offer of proof with the request for the Fair Hearing or upon request of the Hearing Office; or

(b) the reduction or termination is applied uniformly to all recipients of the particular service in that area office, unless the Appellant submits an offer of proof that such reduction or termination was not applied uniformly to all recipients of the particular service in that area office. The Appellant may submit such offer of proof with the request for the Fair Hearing or upon request by the Hearing Office.

5

(2) A decision by the Department that a particular person, or that person's home, is not eligible to apply to become a foster/pre-adoptive parent for the Department, in accordance with 110 CMR 7.100: Eligibility and Recruitment of Foster Parent and Pre-adoptive Parent Applicants.

(3) A decision by the Department not to continue its comprehensive assessment for a foster/pre-adoptive parent when the Department has obtained new information, which if known at the time of the initial eligibility screening process, would have excluded the individual from applying to become a foster/pre-adoptive parent, as set forth at 110 CMR 7.100: Eligibility and Recruitment of Foster Parent and Pre-adoptive Parent Applicants.

(4) A decision to remove a child from a foster/pre-adoptive home when

(a) a child specific or kinship family is not approved, or when a child specific or kinship family is not reapproved following a limited or annual reassessment in accordance with 110 CMR 7.113: Reassessment of Foster/Pre-adoptive Parents and Foster/Pre-adoptive Homes; or

(b) a licensed foster/pre-adoptive parent whose license is revoked, or is not renewed following a limited or annual reassessment, or license renewal study, in accordance with 110 CMR 7.113: Reassessment of Foster/Pre-adoptive Parents and Foster/Pre-adoptive Homes.

110 CMR 10.08. Fair Hearing Processes

(1) *Appellant's Initiation of a Fair Hearing*

(a) to initiate an appeal, the Appellant shall file a written request for a Fair Hearing with the Hearing Office of the Department within 30 calendar days from the decision complained of or, if notice of such decision is required under the Department regulations, policy or procedures, then 30 calendar days from receipt of such written notice.

(b) the Appellant is encouraged to use the form provided by the Department's Hearing Office to request a Fair Hearing, but a request which contains the following information is sufficient: the name, address, and telephone number of the Appellant, the date the alleged action occurred, the name and address of the office which made the decision being appealed, and a request for review of the decision. The Appellant must provide a copy of the request to the Director of Areas of the office where the challenged decision was made.

(2) *The Director of Areas Response*. The Director of Areas or the designee of the office where the challenged decision was made,

(a) shall have 15 business days from receipt of a request for a Fair Hearing, or from the completion of an assessment following an initial support decision, whichever is later, to review the request for a Fair Hearing and the decision upon which it is based;

(b) may, at his or her sole discretion, hold a meeting with the Appellant prior to the Fair Hearing in order to resolve disputes and to clarify issues, with the goal of reaching an agreement which would dispose of the need for, or limit the issues to be resolved at the Fair Hearing;

(c) shall have the authority to reverse the underlying decision that is the basis for the Fair Hearing request, thereby nullifying the need for a Fair Hearing.

(3) *Referral to the Clinical Review Team.*

(a) the Director of Areas or designee may refer the decision to the Clinical Review Team within the 15 day Review Period if he declines to reverse the decision pursuant to 110 CMR 10.08(2)(c); and

1. the decision involves: the removal of a child from a Foster home or Pre-adoptive home; a mandatory referral to the District Attorney, or a change to Foster Care Review goal determination, or

2. any other type of decision that the Director determines should be referred to the Clinical Review Team.

(b) the referral should be made during the 15 day review period, prior to the scheduled date of the Fair Hearing and after the completion of an assessment following an initial support decision.

(c) the Director of Areas or designee shall be a member of the Clinical Review Team.

(d) in considering a determination to list a person on the Registry of Alleged Perpetrators the Clinical Review Team will consider the underlying support decision.

(e) the Clinical Review Team shall, within ten calendar days, issue written findings.

1. the Clinical Review Team shall have authority to support the decision, reverse the decision, or remand the action to the area office for the purposes of gathering further information,

2. if the Clinical Review Team recommends that a decision be reversed over the objection of the Director of Areas, the matter will be resolved by the Deputy Commissioner of Field Operations within 15 business days.

3. the written report of the Clinical Review team may be admitted as evidence in the Fair Hearing.

(f) the Director of Areas or designee shall notify the Fair Hearing Office of the determination to support the challenged decision, to reverse the decision or to remand to the area office for additional information. If the determination is to reverse or remand the decision, the Director of Areas or designee shall notify the Appellant of the determination.

(g) the Director of Areas or designee, a member of the Clinical Review Team or a Regional Director shall not review any matter in which he or she has or has had any direct or indirect personal interest, involvement, or bias. In the event that the Director of Areas or designee is unable to review the matter due to the reasons stated above, the Regional Director shall review the matter. In the event that the Regional Director is unable to review the matter due to the reasons stated above, the Deputy Commissioner for Field Operations shall review the matter.

(4) The Director of Areas of the office which made the initial decision may review the decision and reverse it even if the decision has not been challenged by the client. If the reversal involves a support decision, any determination to list a specific person(s) on the Registry of Alleged Perpetrator that arises from the same incident shall also be reversed and the Department's records shall be

adjusted to remove the person's name from the Registry of Alleged Perpetrators. All decisions which are reversed as a result of actions taken by a Director of Areas or designee or by the Clinical Review Team pursuant to 110 CMR 10.08(2) or (3) shall be documented by the Area Office which vacated the underlying decision.

110 CMR 10.09. Continuation of Service or Placement Pending Appeal

(1) The filing of a request for a Fair Hearing shall not stay or otherwise affect the implementation of the challenged decision, except as provided in 110 CMR 10.09.

(2) The filing of a request for a Fair Hearing regarding a decision to deny services or to reduce the quantity of services shall stay the effect of the challenged decision until after the final decision of the agency is made pursuant to 110 CMR 10.00, provided further that the Appellant continues to pay the pre-established fee, if any for the services in question.

(3) The filing of a request for a Fair Hearing regarding a decision to remove a child from a foster or pre-adoptive placement shall stay the effect of the challenged decision until after the final decision of the agency is made pursuant to 110 CMR 10.00. A decision to remove a child from a foster or pre-adoptive placement on an immediate basis because the Director of Areas or Regional Director has determined that the child's physical, mental, or emotional well-being would be endangered by leaving the child in the foster home, as provided by 110 CMR 7.116: Removal of Children from Foster/Pre-adoptive Homes, shall not be stayed by the filing of a request for a Fair Hearing regarding that decision.

(4) The filing of a request for a Fair Hearing regarding a decision to close a recipient's Department case shall stay the closure until after the final decision of the agency is made pursuant to 110 CMR.

(5) The filing of a request for a Fair Hearing regarding a decision to suspend, reduce or terminate an adoption or guardianship subsidy shall stay the suspension, reduction or termination of the adoption or guardianship subsidy until the final decision of the agency is made pursuant to 110 CMR, unless the reason for the termination of the subsidy is because the child reached 18 years of age and no request for an extension of subsidy had been received by the Department before the 18th birthday, or the Young Adult reached 21 years of age and qualifies for a Title IV-E subsidy or 22 years of age and qualifies for a state subsidy.

110 CMR 10.10. Scheduling

(1) *Time Requirements for Hearing*. The hearing shall be scheduled to be held within 65 business days from receipt of a request for a Fair Hearing.

(2) *Notification*. Within 20 business days of receipt of a request for a Fair Hearing, the Hearing Office shall send notification of the scheduled hearing date to the Appellant and to the appropriate area office of the Department.

(3) *Expedited Hearings*. The Director of Fair Hearings or designee may, upon request, schedule a hearing in an expedited manner. Examples of appropriate reasons to expedite a hearing include: loss of licensure, employment-related issues or other good cause shown. In addition, the Department will expedite Fair Hearing requests that involve the removal of a child from a Foster/Pre-adoptive home or kinship home, the reduction or termination of services, denial of subsidy or the closure of a Department case. The Department shall use its best efforts to schedule expedited hearings within 45 business days of such request.

(4) *Content of Notice of Scheduled Hearing*. The notice of scheduled hearing shall inform the aggrieved patty:

(a) of the date, time and location of the hearing,

(b) that the Appellant may examine and request copies of those portions of her/his file which she/he is legally entitled to subject to any confidentiality requirements;

(c) that the Appellant may bring witnesses and an Authorized Representative;

(d) that in accordance with 110 CMR 10.13 the Department may issue subpoenas for witnesses upon request made at least 15 calendar days in advance of the scheduled hearing;

(e) that a translator or interpreter and reasonable accommodations for handicapped persons will be provided if necessary.

(f) that the Appellant may request a rescheduling of the Fair Hearing for good cause and that if such continuance is granted, the Department will schedule the hearing within the next 45 business days, unless the Appellant requests more time and such is granted.

(5) *Stay of Fair Hearing for Support Decision and/or Alleged Perpetrators*. If the Department receives a written request from any District Attorney's Office stating that there is an open criminal investigation pending or formal criminal charges have been instituted (i.e., indictment or complaint returned or issued), the Department shall stay its review by Fair Hearing of the related agency decisions for six months and notify the parties.

110 CMR 10.11. Representation

(1) An Appellant may appear on his or her own behalf and represent himself or herself, or may, if he or she chooses, be accompanied, represented, and advised by any Authorized Representative. Any child may be represented by an authorized representative which may include an attorney assigned to represent the child.

(2) The authorized representative shall, prior to the scheduled hearing date, submit an appearance to the hearing office containing his or her name, address, telephone number, signature, and the date. The appearance may be on the Request for a Fair Hearing form.

(3) The authorized representative may exercise all of the rights and powers of the aggrieved party.

(4) The Department or Provider may appear through a representative and be represented by a departmental attorney. In those circumstances where the Department is represented by a departmental attorney, in order to avoid the appearance of a conflict of interest, that attorney shall not consult with or seek supervision from anyone supervising the Hearing Office or any Hearing Officer assigned to hear the matter.

110 CMR 10.12. Non-English Speaking Parties

(1) *Notice*. All notices regarding appellate rights shall contain a provision printed in languages to be determined by the Department that the document is important and should be translated immediately.

(2) *Interpreters*. If the Appellant cannot fluently speak or read English, he or she may bring an interpreter or she or he may request at the time a Fair Hearing is sought that the Department pro vide an interpreter.

110 CMR 10.13. Fair Hearings—Subpoenas

(1) *Department or Provider Employees*.

(a) The Appellant shall be able to require the attendance of any Department or Provider employee(s) who can provide information relevant to the decision that the Appellant is appealing by submitting a written request to the Hearing Officer at least 15 calendar days before the hearing.

(b) If the requested employee is not available to testify, written notification must be provided to the Appellant at least five calendar days before the hearing, indicating the identity of another employee with direct knowledge of the challenged decision who will be present to testify at the hearing.

(c) If the employee is not available and notice is given to the Appellant, the Appellant may request a continuance until such time as the employee is available; however, if the Appellant requests such continuance the time requirement for scheduling as set for in 110 CMR 10.10 shall not apply.

(2) *Other Persons*

(a) Child victims shall not be required to testify at a Fair Hearing, unless a compelling reason can be shown as to why the child's testimony is essential. In no event will a child be required to testify if the testifying will harm the child. Evidence demonstrating the harm shall be produced to the Fair Hearing Officer.

(b) Any party to a hearing shall have the right to subpoena witnesses and/or the production of documents pursuant to M.G.L. c. 30A, § 12(3). The party may have the subpoena issued in any way permitted by law or may request the Hearing Office to issue a subpoena. Any request that the Hearing Officer issue a subpoena must be made at least 15 calendar days prior to the scheduled hearing and must include the person's correct name and address. Upon the request of such subpoena, the Hearing Officer, the Director of Fair Hearings or designee may issue an Order to Quash such subpoena if it is determined that the subpoena is being used to intimidate, harass, is contrary to 110 CMR 10.13(2)(a), is overly burdensome or oppressive or lacks a reasonable period of notice. If such order issues, the Appellant may request the Hearing Officer, the Director of Fair Hearings or designee to reconsider, provided said party submits additional information setting forth such facts as to why the subpoena should issue.

(c) In the event that a subpoena has been issued, any party or the person subpoenaed may file a written request with the hearing office to vacate or modify the subpoena pursuant to M.G.L c. 30A, § 12(4). The Hearing Officer, Director of Fair Hearings or designee shall give notice of a request to vacate or modify the subpoena to all parties either orally or in writing. The notice shall recite the contents of the request or summarize the request. If time does not permit a party to respond to the request to vacate or to modify the subpoena, the hearing on the merits shall be postponed long enough to permit the party to do so. No hearing on the request shall be required. Grounds to vacate or modify a subpoena shall include, but not be limited to, requests that are overly burdensome, seek privileged information, are irrelevant to the action, are unreasonable or impose insufficient time for the party to comply.

(d) Pursuant to M.G.L c. 30A, § 12(5), if any person fails to comply with a properly issued subpoena, which has not been vacated or modified by the Hearing Office, the party requesting the issuance of the subpoena may petition any justice of the superior court for an order requiring compliance with the terms of the subpoena.

110 CMR 10.14. Discovery

(1) The Appellant and/or his or her authorized representative may examine and/or request copies of the Appellant's file to which they are legally entitled, subject to the confidentiality requirements which govern the Department at 110 CMR 12.00: Records, by submitting a written request to the area office or provider at least 30 calendar days prior to the time the Appellant wishes to see the material.

(2) An Appellant shall be entitled to obtain a copy of the "51A and 51B" reports if any, which form the basis of the appeal. To request such documents, the Appellant shall make a written request to the Director of Areas, at least 30 calendar days in advance of the scheduled hearing date. The Area Office shall ensure that the record is available to the Appellant within 30 days from receipt of the request or ten calendar days prior to the hearing, whichever is earlier. In releasing copies of these reports the name of (and any other reasonably identifying data concerning) the reporter shall be redacted. Other information may be redacted if it is privileged (e.g. attorney-client communication) or if the release of the information would be contrary to the best interest of the child.

(3) Upon request, copies of papers contained in the Appellant's file shall be provided to the Appellant at a rate of $.10 per page. However, the Department shall waive the fee for 20 or fewer pages.

(4) Requests for any other form of discovery must be made in writing and may be made any time after a request for a Fair Hearing has been filed and up to 30 calendar days before the scheduled hearing date. Such requests should include not only the type of discovery requested but the reasons for the necessity of such discovery. The Hearing Officer, the Director of Fair Hearings or designee shall rule upon such requests, and shall give each party written notice of this ruling.

(5) It is the Department's specific intention that Fair Hearings not be abused as an opportunity for criminal or civil discovery. The Department's Fair Hearing Officers may, in his or her discretion, limit the Fair Hearing in order to ensure that the Fair Hearing is not so used.

110 CMR 10.15. Motions During Hearing

The Appellant, the Department, or the provider may file written motions prior to or during the hearing. The Hearing Officer, the Director of Fair Hearings or designee shall rule on all such motions.

110 CMR 10.16. Consolidated Hearings

If requests for Fair Hearings involve the same issues of fact or law, the hearings may be consolidated upon motion by any party or on motion of the Hearing Officer, if all parties to the matters to be consolidated agree to the consolidation. Such consent to consolidation shall constitute a waiver of any claim of confidentiality for the sole purposes of the hearing.

110 CMR 10.16A. Dismissal for Failure to Go Forward

If the Appellant fails to file documents, respond to notices, appear at the scheduled hearing or otherwise indicates an intention not to pursue the request for a Fair Hearing or a Fair Hearing, the Hearing Officer, the Director of Fair Hearings or designee may dismiss the matter with or without prejudice.

110 CMR 10.17. Rescheduling

The Hearing Officer, the Director of Fair Hearings or designee may reschedule a hearing for good and sufficient cause. The Hearing Officer, the Director of Fair Hearings or designee shall consider how much advance notice of non-attendance was given and the reason for the request. Should any party be granted such request, the Department shall schedule the hearing within 45 business days, unless the Appellant requests additional time and such time is granted, and the time requirement for scheduling as set forth in 110 CMR 10.10(1) shall be extended by the number of continuance days granted.

110 CMR 10.18. Submission Without a Hearing

The Appellant may elect in writing to waive a hearing and to have a decision issued based upon written documentation and written argument. The Director of the Fair Hearing Office or designee shall have the authority to grant or deny such a request. If the request to waive the hearing is granted the Appellant may submit documents or other material without appearing.

110 CMR 10.19. Conduct of Hearings

Hearings shall be as informal as possible, but the Hearing Officer shall ensure that the hearing is orderly.

110 CMR 10.20. Hearing Officer's Duties and Powers

The Hearing Officer shall have the duty to conduct a Fair Hearing so as to ensure that the rights of all parties are protected, and to render an impartial decision based upon the issues and evidence presented at the hearing and in accordance with the law. He or she shall have the following specific duties:

(1) place witnesses under oath or affirmation and to sequester witnesses;

(2) assist all the witnesses in making a full and free statement of the facts in order to bring out all the information necessary to decide the issues involved;

(3) ensure that all parties have a full opportunity to present their claims;

(4) receive, rule on, exclude, or limit evidence (which shall include the right to request that any party produce additional evidence such as witnesses, documents, etc.-but shall not include the right to require any party to do so);

(5) permit introduction into the record of any regulations, statutes, memoranda, or other materials offered by any party which the Hearing Officer believes relevant;

(6) define the issues;

(7) regulate the presentation of the evidence and the participation of the parties to ensure an adequate and comprehensible record of the proceedings;

(8) issue subpoenas upon request of a party;

(9) examine witnesses;

(10) reconvene the hearing prior to the decision upon ten calendar days written notice of the parties, if necessary.

110 CMR 10.21. Evidence

(1) *General*. The Hearing Officer need not strictly follow the rules of evidence. The Massachusetts Rules of Evidence do not apply but the Hearing Officer shall observe any privilege conferred by statute such as social worker-client, doctor-patient and attorney-client privileges. Only evidence which is relevant and material may be admitted and may form the basis of the decision. Unduly repetitious or irrelevant evidence may be excluded.

(2) *Oral Testimony*. Oral testimony shall be given under oath or affirmation; however, changes may be made in the oath if requested on the grounds of religious principles. All testimony shall be subject to the pains and penalties of perjury. Witnesses shall be available for examination and cross-examination.

(3) *Regulations*. Statutes and regulations of a state or federal agency shall be admitted into evidence upon the submission of a copy.

(4) *Other Documents or Written Material*. All documents and written material admitted into evidence shall be authenticated to the satisfaction of the Hearing Officer. Written material from the Appellant's Department file shall be admitted without further authentication.

(5) *Stipulations*. The parties may stipulate to facts or to testimony that a witness would have given.

(6) *Fair Hearings of Support decision and Alleged Perpetrator Listing*. In any case in which an appellant is challenging a Department decision to support a report of abuse or neglect or to list a person's name on the Registry of Alleged Perpetrators, a copy of the report and investigation required by M.G.L. c. 119 § 51A and B shall be admitted into evidence. When reviewing a support decision or an Alleged Perpetrator listing, the hearing officer may consider information available during the investigation and new information subsequently discovered or provided that would either support or detract from the Departments decision.

110 CMR 10.22. Order of Presentation

The Department or Provider will proceed first to produce evidence upon which its decision was based and to show that its decision was in conformity with the applicable regulation, policy, statute or case law. The Hearing Officer shall determine the order of presentation for all other parts of the hearing. After each witness is presented, the opposing party shall have the opportunity for cross-examination of that witness.

110 CMR 10.23. Burden of Proof

To prevail, the Appellant must show based upon all of the evidence presented at the hearing, by a preponderance of the evidence that:

(a) the Department's or Provider's decision was not in conformity with the Department's policies and/or regulations and/or statutes and/or case law and resulted in substantial prejudice to the Appellant,

(b) the Department's or Provider's procedural actions were not in conformity with the Department's policies, and/or regulations, and resulted in substantial prejudice to the Appellant; or

(c) if there is no applicable policy, regulation, or procedure, that the Department or Provider acted without a reasonable basis or in an unreasonable manner which resulted in substantial prejudice to the Appellant; or

(d) if the challenged decision is a supported report of abuse or neglect, that the Department has not demonstrated there is reasonable cause to believe that a child was abused or neglected; or

(e) if the challenged decision is a listing on the alleged perpetrators list, that there is not substantial evidence indicating the person is responsible for the abuse or neglect of a child.

110 CMR 10.24. Memoranda

The Hearing Officer may order or permit that memoranda be filed at any time prior to issuance of the decision. The record shall remain open until the expiration of the date on which memoranda are due.

110 CMR 10.25. The Record

The record shall consist of the documents, other exhibits, and testimony accepted into evidence, as well as all pleadings, notices and decisions.

110 CMR 10.26. Recordings of Hearing

All Fair Hearings shall be recorded. The choice of means shall be at the election of the Department, and at the expense of the Department, and shall be arranged by the Department. Such recordings shall be available to the parties upon request. The Hearing Officer may permit any party to make his/her own recording, but any such recording shall be unofficial and shall not constitute the record nor become part of the record.

110 CMR 10.27. Copies of Recording

If an Appellant desires a transcript it shall be prepared at the expense of the Appellant in accordance with M.G.L. c. 30A, § 11(6). Upon request, a copy of the recordation will be provided to the Appellant.

110 CMR 10.28. Special Requests

(1) An Appellant may withdraw a request for a Fair Hearing at any time by filing a written withdrawal signed by the Appellant.

(2) The Hearing Officer may shorten the notice period of scheduling a hearing, for good cause or for emergency purposes.

110 CMR 10.29. Decision

(1) The Hearing Officer shall render a written decision within 60 business days after the close of the record unless notice is provided to the Appellant that a longer period of time is needed to reach a decision and the time for issuance of such decision shall be extended for an additional 30 business days.

(a) the Hearing Officer may not extend such time for hearings deemed to be expedited hearings and must issue such decisions within 60 business days after the close of the record.

(2) The Hearing Officer may affirm the challenged decision, reverse the challenged decision or remand the decision to the Area Office or Provider to obtain additional information or to take further action. In making a determination on these questions, the Fair Hearing Officer shall give due weight to the clinical decision made by a Department social worker.

(3) If the Hearing Officer recommends to reverse the decision of the Area Office or provider, the Hearing Officer shall submit to the Commissioner or designee the Hearing Officer's written decision within the timeframe as set forth above. Simultaneously the Hearing Officer shall send to the Appellant notification that the Hearing Officer has submitted his/her decision to the Commissioner or designee recommending a reversal of the Area Office's

decision. Such notice shall inform the Appellant that if the Commissioner or designee does not issue a decision within 21 business days, the recommendation of the Hearing Officer shall become the final decision of the Department. The Commissioner or designee may accept the Hearing Officer's recommendation or may overturn the Hearings Officer's decision. If the Commissioner or designee determines that he or she will overturn the Hearing Officer's decision to reverse the decision of the Department, the Commissioner or designee shall write the reasons why he or she does not agree with the decision of the Hearing Officer and why he or she holds that the analysis of the findings by the Hearing Officers is not accepted and shall append to the Hearings Officer's findings and recommendation to such decision. The Commissioner or designee may not make additional findings of fact to the Hearing Officer's findings, which shall be binding on the Commissioner. The decision to overturn the Hearing Officer shall be solely based upon an analysis of the Hearing Officer's findings and the Department's regulations, policy, procedures and the applicable statutes and case law. The decision to either accept or overturn the Hearing Officer's decision must be issued within 21 business days of the Hearing Officer's submitted decision and shall be the final decision of the agency. If the Commissioner or designee fails to issue any written order within 21 business days from the submitted decision, then the Hearing Officer's decision shall issue without such Commissioner's review and shall be the final decision of the agency. The Hearing Officer shall promptly forward a copy of the decision by mail to each of the parties.

(4) For the purpose of 110 CMR 10.29(3) the Commissioner's designee shall not be the General Counsel.

(5) In the event a hearing office becomes unavailable before completing the written decision, the Director of Fair Hearings or designee shall appoint a successor to assume the case and render the fair hearing decision. If the presentation of the evidence has been completed and the record is closed, the successor shall decide the case on the basis of the record, including reviewing all exhibits and the recording of the hearing. Otherwise, the successor may either proceed with evidence or require presentation of evidence again from the beginning.

110 CMR 10.30. Form of Decision

The decision will be in written form and in a manner consistent with M.G.L. c. 30A and may include: a summary of the issues considered; clear and concise findings of fact including credibility determinations; the reasons for the decision reached on each issue; the statute, case law, policy, practice and/or regulation, if any, on which the decision is based; and an order for relief if appropriate. The decision shall be signed and dated by the Hearing Officer and the Director of Fair Hearing or designee. All decisions shall notify the Appellant that the Fair Hearing decision, or where applicable, the decision of the Commissioner or designee, is the final decision of the agency and that the Appellant has the right to seek review under M.G.L. c. 30A.

110 CMR 10.31. Ex Parte Communications

The Hearing Officer shall not consider any evidence, whether written or oral, regarding any matter at issue in a Fair Hearing, unless such submission is part of the record or made in the presence of all parties. No person, other than the Director of Fair Hearings or designee, shall communicate directly or indirectly with the Hearing Officer about a pending matter from the time the hearing is requested until such time as a final agency decision is rendered unless such communication is in the presence of all the parties or submitted in writing with copies to all parties, except that the Commissioner or designee may discuss with the Hearing Officer or the Director of Fair Hearings or designee any decision she/he is reviewing.

110 CMR 10.32. Special Provisions for Fee-Paying Clients

When a fee-paying Appellant requests a Fair Hearing, the Hearing Officer shall include in the decision an order relative to the recoupment of fees as set forth below:

(1) If the Appellant's challenge to the fee is successful, any extra fees paid shall be refunded within 14 days of the decision.

(2) If the Appellant's challenge to the fee is unsuccessful, the aggrieved party shall be notified that he or she must pay any fees owed within 14 days of the decision, and that failure to pay such fees shall result in a termination of service without further hearing. 110 CMR 10.32 in no way negates the Appellant's obligation to continue to pay any pre-established fees pending the outcome of the hearing.

110 CMR 10.33. Confidentiality

The confidentiality requirements of 110 CMR 12.00: Records apply to the Fair Hearing process including the hearing, record, and decision(s). If the subject of the Fair Hearing involves a report and investigation of abuse or neglect that was sent to a licensing agency, the Department of Elementary and Secondary Education (ESE) and/or the OCA under M.G.L. c. 119, § 51B(1), the Department shall forward a copy of any Fair Hearing decision that reverses the 51B decision or reverses the listing of a person's name on the registry of alleged perpetrator's to such agency, ESE and/or the OCA. If such agency, ESE or the OCA requests a copy of any other Fair Hearing decision that involves a report previously sent to the agency, ESE or the OCA the Department may release the Fair Hearing decision to the agency, ESE or the OCA. If the subject of the Fair Hearing involves a report and investigation of abuse or neglect that was sent to a District Attorney's Office pursuant to M.G.L. c. 119, § 51B, then upon request, the Director of the Fair Hearing Unit or designee may inform such District Attorney of the outcome of the Fair Hearing and may provide the District Attorney with a copy of the written decision.

110 CMR 10.34. Time

(1) All papers which must be submitted to the hearing office will be considered to be filed as follows:

(a) Papers hand delivered during business hours shall be considered filed that day;

(b) Papers hand delivered after business hours or on weekends or holidays shall be considered filed the next business day;

(c) Papers which are mailed shall be considered filed on the date postmarked.

(2) Any written notices or other papers mailed by the Department Hearing Office shall be considered to be received five days after mailing.

(3) Time periods shall be computed starting with the day after the act which initiates the time period. If the final day falls on a non-business day, the deadline is extended to the next business day.

(4) Any time limit in 110 CMR 10.00 may be extended if there is good cause for doing so and the extension is not inconsistent with state or federal law or regulation. Requests for extension of time must be in writing and must be filed before the deadline expires. Filing a request shall automatically extend the deadline until the Hearing Office rules on the request.

110 CMR 10.36. Fair Hearing Data Base

The Department shall maintain a database that shall include, among other data, information on requests and outcomes of fair hearings, including for each request, the number of days between the request and the hearing, the number of days between the hearing and the decision and the actual outcome of the hearing. This information shall be available for inspection and copying by the public during normal business hours of the Department.

110 CMR 10.37. Grievance Process

The grievance process is intended to supplement the Fair Hearing procedure. The grievance procedure, like the Fair Hearing procedure, is designed to offer an informal dispute resolution process. Any matter, except as excluded in 110 CMR 10.37, may be the subject of a grievance.

110 CMR 10.38. Grievances—Allowable Subjects

The grievance process is not available to complain of conduct which can be the subject of a Fair Hearing. If an Aggrieved Party files a grievance involving such conduct, the grievance shall be treated as a request for a Fair Hearing. The grievance process is otherwise available for all Aggrieved Party complaints.

110 CMR 10.39. Grievances—Procedures

(1) To initiate the grievance procedure, the Aggrieved Party must file a written complaint with the Area Office, Regional Office or Foster Care Review Unit whose decision is complained of or which employs the employee whose conduct is complained of, within 30 days of the action or inaction complained of. The Director of Areas, Regional Director or Director of Foster Care Review shall assign the complaint to a Regional Clinical Director, Area Clinical Manager, Area Program Manager or to the Assistant Director of Foster Care Review as the case may be.

(2) The Regional Clinical Director, Area Clinical Manger, Area Program Manager or Assistant Director of Foster Care Review shall review the decision or conduct complained of by the aggrieved party within 21 calendar days of receipt of the complaint. The review shall include any facts and/or arguments submitted by the aggrieved party in written form. The Regional Clinical Director, Area Clinical Manager, Area Program Manager or Assistant Director of Foster Care Review may, upon the approval of the Regional Director, Director of Areas or the Director of Foster Care Review, meet with the Aggrieved Party and/or with other Department or Provider agency staff in order to resolve the dispute.

(3) Upon completion of the review, the Regional Clinical Director, Area Clinical Manager, Area Program Manager or Assistant Director of Foster Care Review shall send written notice of his or her decision to the Aggrieved Party and to the employee(s) in question. The notice shall recite the grounds of the complaint, the facts of the case, and any action taken by the Department or Provider.

(4) The decision of the Regional Clinical Director, Area Clinical Manger, Area Program Manager or Assistant Director of Foster Care Review shall be final. If the Aggrieved Party is still dissatisfied, she or he has recourse to such further rights or remedies as are available by law.

Regulatory Authority—110 CMR 10.00: M.G.L. c. 18B, §§ 3, 4 and 7; c. 30A.

5

110 CMR 11.00. Medical Authorizations

Section

110 CMR 11.01. Introduction

To determine who can consent to medical care, the first determination is whether an emergency exists as defined in 110 CMR 11.03 and 11.14. If it is an emergency, no one's consent is required. If there is no emergency, the question is whether the treatment is routine as defined in 110 CMR 11.04 or extraordinary as identified in 110 CMR 11.11, 11.12, 11.13, 11.14 and 11.15. If the particular treatment is not identified specifically in 110 CMR 11.00, it is necessary to weigh the factors outlined in 110 CMR 11.17 to determine whether the contemplated treatment is extraordinary. If it is not extraordinary, it is routine. There is no other possibility.

If the treatment is routine, the Department may consent. In the case of treatment for drug dependency, pregnancy (except abortion and sterilization), family planning, and treatment for a venereal disease or a disease dangerous to the public health, the consent of the minor is sufficient. If the treatment is extraordinary the Department may never consent, but must obtain parental consent for children in the care of the Department and prior judicial approval for wards and children in the custody of the Department. The terms "emergency"," routine", and "extraordinary" medical treatment are extensively defined in 110 CMR 11.00 and only those definitions apply. Neither common parlance nor medical terminology may be used in their place.

110 CMR 11.02. Medical Authorization Definitions

In the Custody of the Department: means a child placed in the Department's custody through court order or through adoption surrender. For purposes of 110 CMR 11.00 only, this phrase shall also include the period occasioned by an emergency removal pursuant to M.G.L. c. 119, § 51B between removal and appearance in Court on the next available court date.

In the Care of the Department: means a child receiving services from the Department pursuant to a Voluntary Placement Agreement. For purposes of 110 CMR 11.00 only, this phrase shall also include the involvement of the Department after the issuance of a mittimus which commits a CHINS child to the custody of the Department, pursuant to a CHINS proceeding. Although the Department has custody of CHINS children and therefore has the power to determine the child's medical care, for purposes of these medical authorization regulations, the Department shall be deemed to have delegated back to the parents the power to determine the CHINS child's extraordinary medical care.

110 CMR 11.03. Emergency Medical Care

(1) "Medical emergency" means any immediately life threatening condition and shall include but is not limited to the below-listed conditions.

(a) severe, profuse bleeding
(b) choking, blocked airway
(c) unconsciousness
(d) cardiac arrest
(e) cardio-vascular accident
(f) any fracture
(g) extensive burns
(h) severe cuts
(i) other similar severe injury
(j) other sudden signs of serious physical illness
(k) any condition where delay in treatment will endanger the life, limb or mental well being of the patient. See, M.G.L. c. 112, § 12F.

(2) Possibility that a disease may deteriorate to an irreversible condition at an uncertain but relatively distant date is not an emergency. See, *In the Matter of Guardianship of Richard Roe, III*, 421 N.E.2d 40, 55; 383 Mass. 415 (1981). In determining whether a medical emergency exists the relevant time period to be examined begins when the claimed emergency arises, and ends when the individual who seeks to act in the emergency could, with reasonable diligence, obtain parental consent or judicial review, as applicable.

(3) Consent. When there is a medical emergency, no one's consent is required in order to allow a child to receive necessary medical care. See, M.G.L. c. 112, § 12F.

110 CMR 11.04. Routine Medical Care

(1) "Routine medical care" shall include but is not limited to the following:

(a) Allergy Shots.

(b) Blood Pressure Test. See, 106 CMR 421.445(J).

(c) Comprehensive Physical Examination—documenting the finding of an unclothed physical examination including a complete system review pertinent to the age of the child, fundoscopic examination of the eyes for children over five years of age, and observation of the teeth and gums for children three years of age or older. See, 106 CMR 421.445(D).

5

(d) Dental care.

(e) Developmental Assessment—the child's current levels of functioning in the below-listed areas, as appropriate to the child's age. See, 106 CMR 421.445(F).

1. gross motor development, including strength, balance, and locomotion

2. fine motor development, including eye-hand coordination

3. language development, including expression, comprehensive and articulation

4. self-help and self-care skills

5. social interaction and emotional development

6. cognitive skills, including problem-solving and reasoning abilities.

(f) Diseases dangerous to the public health, treatment of. See, M.G.L. c. 112, § 12F and 105 CMR 300.100.

(g) Drug dependency treatment. See, M.G.L. c. 112, § 12E.

(h) Family planning services. See, 106 CMR 421.401 et seq.

(i) Fractures, treatment of

(j) Hearing Test. See, 106 CMR 421.445(K).

(k) Immunization—against diphtheria, pertussis, tetanus, measles, poliomyelitis, mumps, rubella and such other communicable diseases as may be specified from time to time by the Department of Public Health. See, M.G.L. c. 76, § 15 and 105 CMR 220.100.

(l) Laboratory tests and special medical studies -when determined by the examining physician to be necessary.

(m) Lead Poisoning Test. See, 106 CMR 421.445(P).

(n) Nutritional Status Assessment—the evaluation of the child's nutritional health in light of dietary practice and the entire health assessment (that is, history, physical examination, height and weight measurements, and the laboratory tests) and documentation of any nutritional disturbance or dysfunction. See, 106 CMR 421.445(G).

(o) Pelvic Examination. See, 106 CMR 421.445(O).

(p) Pregnancy Treatment—except abortion or sterilization. See, M.G.L. c. 112, § 12F.

(q) Preventive health services.

(r) Psychiatric assessment, evaluation, or treatment on outpatient basis or up to ninety (90) days on in-patient basis.

(s) Treatment—commonly prescribed for a specific physical illness, which treatment does not pose risks of permanent serious side effects or risk of death, See, *Custody of a Minor*, 375 Mass. 733, 379 N.E.2d 1053, 1064 (1978) or is determined not to be extraordinary medical treatment by using the analysis outlined in 110 CMR 11.00.

(t) Tubercular skin test or chest x-ray.

(u) Venereal Disease Treatment. See, M.G.L. c. 112, § 12F; 105 CMR 300.140.

(v) Vision Test. See, 106 CMR 421.445(L).

(2) Consent. The Department may consent to routine medical care for a child in the care of the Department or a child in the custody of the Department or a child who is a ward of the Department.

(3) Parent's Religious Beliefs Regarding Routine Medical Treatment. If parents refuse to sign a standard Voluntary Placement Agreement because they refuse to delegate to the Department the power to consent to routine medical treatment for their child on the basis that such routine medical treatment conflicts with the parents' sincere religious beliefs, the Department shall elect one of the following actions:

(a) Amend the standard Voluntary Placement Agreement by adding the following paragraph:

"Whereas the undersigned parents hold sincere religious beliefs opposed to all medical treatment, the Department shall have the right to approve only medical, psychological and dental care, testing or studies for the child relative to: (i) drug dependency; (ii) diseases dangerous to the public health; (iii) venereal diseases; (iv) emergency medical treatment; and (v) routine physical examination and laboratory test."

(b) Determine whether the parents' refusal to delegate to the Department the power to consent to the medical treatment constitutes medical neglect, and if so, institute appropriate court action on that basis.

110 CMR 11.05. Family Planning Services

(1) "Family Planning Services" means medical, educational and social services, excluding abortion and sterilization, which enable individuals voluntarily to limit family size or plan spacing of children. Family planning services include the below-listed services. See, 106 CMR 269.030(A)(B) and 106 CMR 421.412.

(a) Information and referral (including outreach & follow-up)

(b) Individual and group counseling

(c) A physical examination

1. for a female, includes thyroid, breast, heart, abdominal, speculum, pelvic, and rectal examinations, and measurements of height, weight and blood pressure;

2. for a male, includes thyroid, heart, genital, abdominal, and rectal examinations, and measurements of height, weight and blood pressure. See, 106 CMR 421.412(2).

(d) A pap smear for females. See, 106 CMR 421.412(3).

(e) Any laboratory test indicated by the child's history or examination. See, 106 CMR 421.412(4).

(f) A medically approved method of contraception. See, 106 CMR 421.427(5).

(g) Medical examinations, consultations, laboratory tests and contraceptive services rendered by a licensed physician

(h) Medical treatment for related conditions, such as venereal diseases or vaginal infections

(i) Prescriptions and medical items related to family planning services including drugs, supplies and devices

(j) Clinical follow-up

(2) Provision of Information.

(a) Department staff shall inform a child in the care or custody of the Department, or a child who is a ward of the Department, about family planning services available to sexually active minors if such child requests this information or if in the judgment of Department staff such child has need for this information. See, 106 CMR 421.401 et seq.

(b) Department staff shall not coerce any child in any way to receive family planning services or to employ any particular method of family planning. A child's use of family planning services must be completely voluntary. See, 106 CMR 421.427(B).

(3) Consent by Child. Any child who requests family planning services, whether such child is in the care or custody of the Department, or is a ward of the Department, may consent to his/her own medical and laboratory family planning services. The consent of the Department is not necessary in such cases. (See, 106 CMR 421.427(A) which provides that "services must be made available to all recipients who request services, without regard to . . . age . . .".)

(4) Consent by Department or Parent. If the child consents to family planning services but the medical provider insists on parental or Department consent, the Department may consent. If the child is not able to consent, the Department may consent.

110 CMR 11.06. Pregnancy

(1) Consent By Child. A child who is pregnant or believes herself to be pregnant may give consent to her own medical and dental care (except abortion or sterilization). The consent of the Department is not necessary to authorize medical or dental care for any such child in the care or custody of the Department, or any such ward of the Department. See, M.G.L. c. 112, § 12F.

(2) Consent By Department or Parent. If a medical provider refuses to treat a child who is pregnant or believes herself to be pregnant without parental or Department consent, or if such child refuses to consent or is not able to consent to medical or dental care, the Department may consent (except to abortion or sterilization).

110 CMR 11.07. Abortion

(1) Consent By Child in Care of Department.

(a) If a minor in the care of the Department is pregnant both the minor and both of her parents must consent to an abortion, or she must obtain prior judicial approval pursuant to M.G.L. c. 112, § 12S.

(b) If one of the pregnant minor's parents has died or is unavailable to give consent within a reasonable time, consent of the remaining parent shall be sufficient. See, M.G.L. c. 112, § 12S.

(c) If both parents have died or are otherwise unavailable to the physician within a reasonable time, and in a reasonable manner, consent of the minor's guardian or guardians shall be sufficient. See, M.G.L. c. 112, § 12S.

(d) If the pregnant minor's parents are divorced, consent of the parent having custody shall be sufficient. See, M.G.L. c. 112, § 12S.

(e) If one or both of the pregnant minor's parents or guardians refuse to consent to the performance of an abortion or if she elects not to seek the consent of one or both of her parents or guardians, the minor must seek authorization for an abortion from a judge of the Superior Court, pursuant to M.G.L. c. 112, § 12S.

(2) Consent By Child in Custody of Department.

(a) If a minor, in the custody of the Department, is pregnant and wants to have an abortion, Department staff shall not consent to the abortion. Such a minor must obtain prior judicial approval pursuant to M.G.L. c. 112, § 12S.

(b) If the minor requests assistance from the Department in seeking court authorization for an abortion, or if in the judgment of the Department's social work staff such minor has need for this information, the Department social work and legal staff shall provide her with the necessary information on how to go to court to file a petition or motion under the provisions of M.G.L. c. 112, § 12S. However, Department attorneys shall not represent pregnant minors in their petition or motion pursuant to M.G.L. c. 112, § 12S.

(3) Consent By Department As Guardian. If a minor is pregnant and wants an abortion, and both her parents have died or are otherwise unavailable to the physician within a reasonable time and in a reasonable manner, and if the Department has been appointed guardian of the minor by a Probate Court, the Department shall follow the requirements and procedures of M.G.L. c. 112, § 12S.

110 CMR 11.08. Drug Dependency

(1) Consent. A child 12 years of age or older who is found to be drug dependent by two or more physicians may give his/her consent to the furnishing of hospital and medical care related to the diagnosis or treatment of such drug dependency. The consent of the Department is not necessary to authorize hospital or medical care related to drug dependency of any child over 12 years of age in the Department's care or custody, or any child for whom the Department has been appointed guardian. See, M.G.L. c. 112, § 12E.

(2) Consent By Department or Parent. If a medical provider refuses to treat a child without parental or Department consent, or if a child refuses to consent or is not able to consent to medical or hospital care related to the diagnosis or treatment of drug dependency, the Department may consent; provided that the Department shall not consent to the administration of antipsychotic medication or shock therapy or any other extraordinary medical treatment for diagnosis or treatment of drug dependency.

110 CMR 11.09. Diseases Dangerous to the Public Health

(1) "Diseases dangerous to the public health" means the following. See, 105 CMR 300.100; 105 CMR 310.020.

(a) Actinomycosis
(b) AIDS (Acquired Immune Deficiency Syndrome)
(c) Animal Bite
(d) Anthrax
(e) Brucellosis (Undulant Fever)
(f) Chickenpox (Varicella)
(g) Cholera
(h) Diarrhea of the Newborn
(i) Diphtheria
(j) Dysentery, Amebic
(k) Dysentery, Bacillary (Shigellosis)
(l) Encephalitis (specify if known)
(m) Food Poisoning by:
1. Botulism
2. Mushrooms and other poisonous vegetable and animal products
3. Mineral or organic poisons such as arsenic, lead, etc.
4. Staphylococcal
(n) German Measles (Rubella)
(o) Glanders
(p) Hepatitis, Viral (includes Infectious and Serum Hepatitis)
(q) Impetigo of the Newborn
(r) Leprosy
(s) Leptospirosis (including Weil's Disease)
(t) Lymphocytic Choriomeningitis
(u) Malaria
(v) Measles (Rubeola)
(w) Meningitis (B. Influenzal, meningococcal, pneumococcal, streptococcal forms)
(x) Mumps
(y) Ophthalmia Neonatorum
(z) Plague
(aa) Poliomyelitis
(bb) Psittacosis
(cc) Rabies—Human
(dd) Rickettsialpox
(ee) Rocky Mountain Spotted Fever
(ff) Salmonellosis (except Typhi and Paratyphi)
(gg) Salmonellosis: Typhi and Paratyphi (Typhoid and Paratyphoid Fevers)
(hh) Smallpox (Variola)
(ii) Smallpox Vaccination Reactions—Generalized Vaccinia, Eczema Vaccinatum
(jj) Streptococcal Infections (including Erysipelas Scarlet Fever, Streptococcal Sore Throat, etc.)

5

(kk) Tetanus
(ll) Trachoma
(mm) Trichinosis
(nn) Tuberculosis
(oo) Tularemia
(pp) Typhus Fever (including Brills' Disease)
(qq) Whooping Cough (pertussis)
(rr) Yellow Fever

(2) Consent by Child. If any ward or child in the care or custody of the Department reasonably believes herself or himself to be suffering from or to have come in contact with any disease dangerous to the public health, such child may consent to his or her own medical care or dental care related to the diagnosis or treatment of such disease. The consent of the Department is not necessary to authorize medical or dental care related to the diagnosis or treatment of diseases dangerous to the public health for any ward or child in the Department's care or custody. See, M.G.L. c. 112, § 12F.

(3) Consent by Department or Parent. If a medical provider refuses to treat the child without parental or Department consent, or if a child refuses to consent or is not able to consent to medical or dental care related to the diagnosis or treatment of a disease dangerous to the public health, the Department may consent.

(4) AIDS. The Department shall establish and consult with an AIDS Advisory Board, comprised of Department personnel, Department of Public Health personnel, a physician consultant, a legal consultant, a foster parent representative, in making AIDS-related decisions.

5

COMMENTARY

Children with AIDS are to be treated as any other children with serious diseases. However, the Department strongly emphasizes the importance of confidentiality for these children and families. Additionally, the Department supports, as policy, the "case by case" review of these infants and children, due to the constantly emerging knowledge about HIV infection from the medical and scientific communities.

To achieve this goal, the Department has established a Central AIDS Review Board comprised of experts in the field of AIDS and representatives of DSS who will review cases involving testing, placement and other AIDS issues of any child in the care or custody of the Department. The Board will evaluate the information and make recommendations to the Deputy Commissioner, who will make final decisions involving testing and placement of these children.

110 CMR 11.10. Venereal Disease

(1) "Venereal diseases" means the following. See, 105 CMR 300.100; 105 CMR 300.140; 105 CMR 340.100.
(a) Chancroid
(b) Gonorrhea
(c) Granuloma Inguinale
(d) Lymphogranulom Venereum
(e) Syphilis

(2) Consent by Child. If any ward of the Department or child in the care or custody of the Department reasonably believes himself or herself to be suffering from or to have come in contact with any venereal disease, such child may consent to his or her own medical care or dental care related to the diagnosis or treatment of such venereal disease. The consent of the Department is not necessary to authorize medical or dental care related to the diagnosis or treatment of venereal disease for any ward or child in the Department's care or custody. See, M.G.L. c. 112, § 12F.

(3) Consent by Department or Parent. If a medical provider refuses to treat the child without parental or Department consent, or if a child refuses to consent or is not able to consent to medical or dental care related to the diagnosis or treatment of venereal diseases, the Department may consent.

110 CMR 11.11. Sterilization

No Consent By Department. Department staff shall not consent to the sterilization of any ward or child in its care or in its custody. Prior judicial approval is necessary under all circumstances for the performance of a sterilization upon any child who is a ward of the Department, or who is in the care or custody of the Department. See, *Matter of Moe*, 385 Mass. 555, 559, 432 N.E.2d 712 (1982); M.G.L. c. 112, § 12W.

110 CMR 11.12. No Code Orders

(1) "No code" order means a medical order regarding a terminally ill patient directing a hospital and its staff not to use heroic medical efforts in the event of cardiac or respiratory failure. Heroic medical efforts include invasive and traumatic life-saving techniques such as intracardial medication, intracardial massage and electric shock treatment. No code orders include "do not resuscitate" orders or orders stated in different language attempting to accomplish substantially the same result as a "no code" order. See, *Custody of a Minor*, 385 Mass. 697, 434 N.E.2d 601 (1982).

(2) No Consent By Department. Department staff shall not consent to the entry of a "no code" order for any ward or child in its care or custody. See, *Custody of a Minor*, 434 N.E.2d 601 (1982).

(3) Consent By Parents.

(a) With respect to a child who is in the care of the Department, the right to consent or to refuse to consent to the entry of a "no code" order shall remain with the child's parents, unless otherwise limited by court order. If the Department has reason to believe that the parents are guilty of medical neglect by their consent to a "no code" order, the Department shall seek custody through a court proceeding which alleges medical neglect.

(b) With respect to a child who is a ward of the Department or is in Department custody, when a medical provider seeks the Department's consent to the entry of a "no code" order, the Department shall not consent unless it seeks and receives prior judicial approval for the entry of a "no code" order, even if the child's biological parents have consented to the entry of such order. See, *Custody of a Minor*, 434 N.E.2d 601, 608 (1982). When seeking prior judicial approval, the Department shall file a Motion for Appointment of a Guardian ad Litem to investigate whether such order should enter.

110 CMR 11.13. Life-Prolonging Medical Treatment

(1) "Life-prolonging medical treatment", as distinguished from life-saving treatment, means intrusive medical treatment where there is no prospect of recovery. *In the Matter of Earle A. Spring*, 380 Mass. 629, 405 N.E.2d 115, 120 (1980). Recovery does not mean the ability to remain alive but rather life without intolerable suffering. *Saikewicz*, 373 Mass. 728, 370 N.E.2d 417 (1977).

(2) No Consent By Department. Department staff shall not consent to the giving or withholding of life-prolonging medical treatment for any child who is a ward of the Department or for any child in its care or custody. See, *Spring*, supra; *Superintendent of Belchertown State School v. Saikewicz*, supra.

(3) Consent By Parents or Court.

(a) With respect to a child who is in the care of the Department, the right to consent or to refuse to consent to the giving or withholding of life-prolonging medical treatment shall remain with the child's parents unless otherwise limited by statute or court order. If the Department has reason to believe that the parents are guilty of medical neglect by their consent to giving or withholding of life-prolonging medical treatment, the Department shall seek custody through a court proceeding which alleges medical neglect.

(b) With respect to a child who is a ward of the Department or is in the Department's custody, when a medical provider seeks the Department's consent to an order giving or withholding life-prolonging medical treatment, the Department shall seek prior judicial approval for the giving or withholding of life-prolonging medical treatment, even if the child's biological parents have consented to the entry of such order. When seeking prior judicial approval, the Department shall file a Motion for Appointment of a

Guardian ad Litem to investigate whether such order should enter for a ward of the Department or child in the Department's custody.

110 CMR 11.14. Antipsychotic Drugs

(1) "Antipsychotic drugs" shall mean drugs which are used in treating psychosis. Antipsychotic drugs include the below-listed drugs by whatever official name, common or usual name, chemical name, or brand name they may be designated. All isomers, esters, ethers, salts of, or any combination of, drugs listed below are deemed to be antipsychotic drugs. Such antipsychotic drugs shall include, but shall not be limited to:

Generic Name	Trade Name
1 Acetophenazine	Tindal
2 Butaperazine	Repoise
3 Carphenazine	Proketazine
4 Chlorpromazine	Thorazine
5 Chlorprothizene	Taractan
6 Fluphenazine	Prolixin
7 Haloperidol	Haldol
8 Loxapine	Loxitane
9 Mesoridazine	Serentil
10 Molindone	Moban
11 Perphenazine	Trilafon
12 Piperacetezine	Quide
13 Prochlorperazine	Compazine
14 Promazine	Sparine
15 Thioridazine	Mellaril
16 Thiothixene	Navane
17 Trifluoperazine	Stelazine
18 Triflupromazine	Vesprin

(2) No Consent By Department. The Department shall not consent to the administration of antipsychotic medication for any individual, but shall in all cases seek parental consent for children in Department care, or prior judicial approval for children in Department custody and wards of the Department.

(3) Consent by Parents for Children in Department Care.

(a) When any individual, organization, facility or medical provider seeks to medicate with antipsychotic drugs a child, who is in the care of the Department, Department staff shall not consent to such medication nor shall the Department seek prior judicial approval for administration of such medication. The decision of whether to consent to such medication shall remain with the parents.

(b) If the Department has reason to believe that the parents are guilty of medical neglect by their consent to medicate with antipsychotic drugs or by their refusal to consent to medicate with antipsychotic drugs, the Department shall seek custody of the child through a court proceeding which alleges medical neglect.

(c) The 110 CMR 11.14(3)(a) and (b) apply whether or not the child consents to the administration of antipsychotic medication.

(4) Judicial Approval for Wards and Children in Department Custody.

(a) When any individual, organization, facility, or medical provider seeks the Department's consent to medicate with antipsychotic drugs a child, who is a ward of the Department or who is in Department custody, the Department shall seek prior judicial approval for administration of such drugs even if the child's biological parents have consented to the medication. See, *Rogers v. Commissioner of the Department of Mental Health*, 390 Mass. 489 (1983); M.G.L. c. 210, § 6.

(b) Where antipsychotic medications have been previously prescribed for a child who is a ward of the Department or who is in the custody of the Department, and that child is currently being treated with antipsychotic drugs without judicial authorization, the Department shall initiate the process for judicial review and application of substituted judgment. Pending judicial review the Department shall not discontinue the prescribed treatment with antipsychotic drugs, because interruption or discontinuance of the treatment might cause severe medical complications and might violate the individual's legal right to treatment.

(c) Neither a ward of the Department who has attained age 16 nor a child in the custody of the Department who has attained age 16 and who has voluntarily admitted him/herself to a mental health facility, shall have the power to consent to the administration of anti-psychotic drugs. The Department shall seek prior judicial approval for medicating such a child with antipsychotic drugs, even if such child consents to its administration. See, M.G.L. c. 201, § 6.

(5) Guardianship for Individuals Over Age 18.

(a) The Department shall not consent to the administration of antipsychotic drugs to an individual over 18 years of age who is in the care or custody of the Department.

(b) Any individual over the age of 18 who is in the care or custody of the Department, and who is competent to make medical decisions, may consent to the administration of his/her antipsychotic medication.

(c) If the Department believes that an individual over the age of 18 in the care or custody of the Department is not competent to make medical decisions, and failing action by the individual's parents, the Department of Mental Health, or other third person, the Department will file incompetency proceedings under M.G.L. c. 201. If the individual is adjudicated competent, then only such individual may consent to the administration of antipsychotic drugs. If the individual is adjudicated incompetent then the judge will apply a substituted judgment standard to determine whether antipsychotic drugs ought to be administered, and will issue appropriate orders.

(6) Emergency Treatment with Antipsychotic Drugs.

(a) Antipsychotic drugs may be administered for treatment purposes without parental consent or prior judicial approval only in an emergency (even though no threat of violence exists) and only if there is no less intrusive alternative to antipsychotic drugs.

(b) An emergency for purposes of administering antipsychotic drugs for treatment purposes is an unforeseen combination of circumstances or the resulting state that calls for immediate action. See Roe at 42. It includes a situation where doctors, in their professional judgment, determine that the medication is necessary to prevent the immediate, substantial, and irreversible deterioration of a serious mental illness. See Rogers at 511. The possibility that a mental condition might deteriorate into a chronic, irreversible condition at an uncertain but relatively distant date is not an emergency. Roe at 55.

(c) In situations that fall within the purview of 110 CMR 11.00, no consent by the Department or parents is necessary (since the medical provider may make such determination) and therefore the Department shall not give consent nor seek parental consent.

(d) If a child is medicated with antipsychotic drugs in an emergency situation and the doctors determine that the antipsychotic drugs should continue, then the Department shall follow the procedures for obtaining consent as though no emergency existed. See, Rogers at 512.

(7) Use of Antipsychotic Drugs for Restraint.

(a) Antipsychotic drugs shall not be administered as a restraint of any ward or child in the care or custody of the Department when such restraint is for disciplinary reasons or for administrative convenience.

(b) Antipsychotic drugs may be used for restraint only in cases of emergency, and only if there is no less intrusive alternative to antipsychotic drugs. An emergency for purposes of administering antipsychotic drugs for restraint is the occurrence of, or serious threat of, extreme violence, personal injury, or attempted suicide. Such emergency cases shall only include situations where there is the occurrence or a substantial risk of serious self-destructive behavior, or the occurrence or a substantial risk of serious physical assault. A substantial risk includes only the serious, imminent threat of bodily harm, where there is present ability to effect such harm. Predictable crises are not within the definition of emergency. Antipsychotic drugs may be administered for restraint only in accordance with the procedures set forth in the Regulations of the Department of Mental Health.

110 CMR 11.15. Electroconvulsive Treatment or ECT ("Shock Treatment")

(1) Consent by Child If Age 16 or Older. No person other than the child may consent to ECT if the child is 16 years of age or older and:

(a) is not a patient at a mental health facility; or

(b) is on voluntary admission status or conditional voluntary admission status to a mental health facility.

(2) Consent by Parents for Children in Department Care.

(a) When any individual, organization, facility or medical provider seeks to administer ECT to a child under 16 years who is in the care of the Department, the Department shall not consent to such treatment nor shall the Department seek prior judicial approval for administration of such treatment. The decision of whether to consent to ECT shall remain with the parents.

5

(b) If the Department has reason to believe that the parents are guilty of medical neglect by their consent to ECT or by their refusal to consent to ECT, the Department shall seek custody of the child through a court proceeding which alleges medical neglect.

(c) The 110 CMR 11.15(2)(a) and (b) apply to any child under 16 years of age whether or not the child consents to the administration of ECT.

(3) Judicial Approval for Children in Department Custody.

(a) When any individual, organization, facility or medical provider seeks the Department's consent to administer ECT to a child who is in Department custody, or to a ward of the Department, the Department shall seek prior judicial approval for administration of such treatment, even if the child's biological parents have consented to the ECT.

(b) Where ECT has been previously prescribed for a child in the custody of the Department, and that child is currently being treated with ECT without judicial authorization, the Department shall immediately initiate the process for judicial review and application of substituted judgment. Pending judicial review the Department shall not attempt to discontinue the prescribed treatment with ECT, because interruption or discontinuance of the treatment might cause severe medical complications and might violate the child's legal right to treatment.

110 CMR 11.16. Commitment to a Mental Health Facility

(1) Definition.

Mental health facility means a public or private facility for the inpatient care or treatment or diagnosis or evaluation of mentally ill or mentally retarded persons, except for the Bridgewater State Hospital. See M.G.L. c. 123, § 1. Community residential care facilities for children (as defined at 110 CMR 7.120) are not mental health facilities for purposes of 110 CMR 11.00.

(2) Consent By Child If Age 16 Or Older. Any child who has attained the age of 16 may apply for voluntary admission to a mental health facility. In the case of such an application by the child, no additional consent either from the Department or from parents is necessary. See M.G.L. c. 123, § 10(a).

(3) Consent By Parent. A parent may consent to the admission of his/her child to a mental health facility when:

(a) the child is in the care of the Department and is under 16 years of age; or

(b) the child is in the care of the Department and is between 16 and 18 years of age and does not consent to admission to a mental health facility.

(4) Consent By Department Area or Regional Director. The Department (by an Area or Regional Director only) may consent to the admission of a person:

(a) (custody:) in the custody of the Department

(b) (care:) in the care of the Department if that person's parent(s) is unavailable for consultation or if that person's parent(s) after consultation consent or authorize the Department to consent; but the Department may not consent to the admission of a person in the care of the Department if that person's parent(s) after consultation refuse to consent or refuse to authorize the Department to consent

(c) (ward:) who is a ward of the Department only if the Department as guardian has the specific power to consent to the admission of the ward to a mental health facility for an initial period of time not to exceed a maximum of 90 days.

(5) Judicial Review After 90 Days. In any case where the Department has consented to the admission of a person to a mental health facility, the Department shall seek judicial review before it consents to an extension of the admission of such person to a mental health facility beyond a period of 90 days.

(6) Antipsychotic Drugs. The determination of who may consent to the administration of antipsychotic drugs to a child shall be made according to 110 CMR 11.14.

110 CMR 11.17. Other Extraordinary Medical Treatment

(1) Recognizing that it is impossible to itemize every extraordinary medical treatment, the Department shall utilize the following factors to determine whether a medical treatment is extraordinary:

(a) Complexity, risk and novelty of the proposed treatment: The more complex the treatment, the greater the risk of death or serious complications, the more experimental the procedure, then the greater the need to determine that the treatment is extraordinary, and to obtain parental consent or to seek judicial approval prior to authorizing treatment. *See, In the Matter of Guardianship of Richard Roe III*, 421 N.E.2d 40, 53 (1981). *In the Matter of Spring*, 405 N.E.2d 115 (1980). *In the Matter of Moe*, 432 N.E.2d 712 (1982).

(b) Possible side effects: The more serious and permanent the side effect, the greater the need to determine that the treatment is extraordinary, and to obtain parental consent or to seek judicial approval prior to authorizing treatment. *See, Superintendent of Belchertown State School v. Saikewicz*, 370 N.E.2d 417 (1977). *Rogers v. Commissioner of DMH*, 390 Mass. 489, 501-502 (1983). *In the Matter of Guardianship of Richard Roe III*, 421 N.E.2d 40 (1981). *Custody of a Minor*, 385 Mass. 697, 434 N.E.2d 601 (1982).

(c) Intrusiveness of proposed treatment: The more intrusive the treatment the greater the need to determine that the treatment is extraordinary, and to obtain parental consent or prior judicial approval. *See, In the Matter of Hier*, 18 Mass. App. Ct. 200, 464 N.E.2d 959, (1984). *Superintendent of Belchertown State School v. Saikewicz*, supra. *In The Matter of Moe*, supra. *In The Matter of Spring*, supra.

(d) Prognosis with and without treatment: The less clear the benefit from the proposed treatment the greater the need for parental consent or prior judicial approval. *See, Superintendent of Belchertown State School v. Saikewicz*, supra; *Custody of a Minor*, 385 Mass. 697, 434 N.E.2d 601 1982); *In The Matter of Spring*, supra.

(e) Clarity of professional opinion: The more divided the medical opinion, the greater the need for parental consent or prior judicial approval. *See, In The Matter of Spring*, supra.

(f) Presence or absence of an emergency: In a medical emergency a physician can act without anyone's consent. See, M.G.L. c. 112, § 12F.

(g) Prior judicial involvement: if a court has been involved in past medical decisions, this argues for judicial involvement in any future medical treatment decision, but this is not conclusive. *See, In The Matter of Guardianship of Richard Roe III*, supra at 56.

(h) Conflicting Interests: Where the interests of the decision maker conflict with the interests of the child, there is greater need for obtaining parental consent or prior judicial approval. *In the Matter of Guardianship of Richard Roe III*, 421 N.E.2d 40 (1981).

(2) No Consent By Department. The Department shall not give its consent to extraordinary medical treatment for any child in the care or custody of the Department. For all such children, the Department shall seek prior judicial approval for any extraordinary medical treatment (unless parental consent is obtained for children in the care of the Department, as set forth at 110 CMR 11.17(3)).

(3) Consent By Parent. With respect to a child in the care of the Department, the right to consent to extraordinary medical treatment shall remain with the parent(s), except to the extent such right has been specifically limited by the legislature or by the findings of a court or by written agreement between the parents and the Department.

(4) Guardianship. The Department shall not give its consent to extraordinary medical treatment for its ward, except where it is specifically empowered to do so by statute, regulation or case law. In all other cases the Department shall seek prior judicial approval for extraordinary medical treatment.

110 CMR 11.18. Legal Proceedings

(1) Whenever the Department may not consent to a medical procedure, but must seek prior judicial approval for such procedure, the Department shall seek the appointment of a guardian ad litem to investigate whether such procedure should be administered, and thereafter report back to the court.

(2) At any subsequent hearing when the court is considering the question of whether such treatment ought to be administered, the Department shall not request that the court authorize the Department to consent to such treatment; but rather the Department shall request that the court, using a substituted judgment standard, make the decision whether to authorize such treatment.

110 CMR 11.19. Autopsy

For children in the care of the Department at the time of their death, the right to consent or refuse to consent to an autopsy belongs to the parent(s). The Department shall not consent to an autopsy for children who die while in the care of the Department, unless the Department, after diligent efforts, is unable to contact the parent(s) to seek their consent, in which case the Department may then consent.

For wards or children in the custody of the Department at the time of their death, the Department may request and may consent to an autopsy.

110 CMR 11.20. Burial

Burial of wards or children in the care or custody of the Department at the time of their death shall be accomplished by consulting with the parents, in the first instance. If the parents refuse to make burial arrangements or cannot be contacted, the Department shall make and pay for appropriate burial arrangements, consistent with the provisions of M.G.L. c. 119, § 23(H).

110 CMR 11.21. Organ Donation

For children in the care of the Department at the time of their death, the right to consent or refuse to consent to a request for organ donation after the child's death belongs to the parent(s). The Department shall not consent to organ donation by children who die in the care of the Department.

For wards or children in the custody of the Department at the time of their death, the Department shall determine on a case-by-case basis whether to consent to a request for organ donation.

110 CMR 11.22. Confidentiality of Medical Records and Information

(1) Except for cases in litigation (in which case 110 CMR 12.09 shall govern), with respect to the medical records of a child in the care or custody of the Department or a child who is a ward of the Department:

(a) The Department shall not distribute or release medical documents or information contained anywhere in a child's record or case file to any unauthorized person (as defined at 110 CMR 11.22(3)) without the written consent of one of the child's parents or without an order of a court of competent jurisdiction.

(b) The child's parent(s) or attorney or guardian or guardian ad litem shall have access to all medical documents or information contained anywhere in a child's record or case file; unless the person who contributed such information has requested in writing to the Department that the information not be disclosed (for which purpose the mere stamp "Confidential" shall not be sufficient), or unless otherwise provided by statute. The child's parent(s) may also request medical documents regarding their child directly from the hospital or medical provider pursuant to the provisions of the "Patient's Bill of Rights" at M.G.L. c. 111, § 70E.

(2) With respect to the medical records of a child surrendered for adoption to the Department or in the custody of the Department after an adjudication under M.G.L. c. 210, § 3:

(a) The Department shall not distribute or release information in a child's medical record to any unauthorized person without court order.

(b) Unauthorized person for purposes of 110 CMR 11.22(2) shall include the parents of the child.

(3) Unauthorized person for purposes of 110 CMR 11.22(1) and (2) shall include everyone except: the child's physician or any other medical provider, the child's foster parents, the appropriate authorities at a residential facility in which the child is or is intended to be living, the appropriate authorities at any school the child is attending, the child's substitute care provider, the subject child if over 14 years of age, or any other person who the Department determines requires such information to render medical or other professional assistance to the subject child.

(4) When any ward or child in the care or custody of the Department requests that the Department not notify his or her parents of intended medical treatment, the Department shall determine on a case-by-case basis whether to consent to the child's request, but shall comply with the provisions of M.G.L. c. 112, § 12F.

110 CMR 11.23. Children as Research Subjects

Parents shall retain the right to consent to participation by their child in any medical or psychological research. If the parents consent, the Department shall also consent. If the parents refuse to consent, the child shall not participate. Medical research includes physical examinations, laboratory tests of any kind, and psychological examinations and tests. For children in the custody of the Department pursuant to a surrender for adoption, termination of parental rights, or where parents cannot be located, the Department shall seek prior judicial approval.

110 CMR 11.24. Consent Standard

In all cases where the Department has the right to consent to medical care for a ward or a child in its care or in its custody, the Department shall consider exclusively what will serve the child's best interests.

Regulatory Authority—110 CMR 11.00: M.G.L. c. 112, § 12; M.G.L. c. 201; M.G.L. c. 123, § 10; M.G.L. c. 119, § 23(H).

5

110 CMR 12.00. Records

Section

110 CMR 12.01. Purpose

110 CMR 12.00 defines how the Department shall fulfill the statutory mandate of M.G.L. c. 119, § 51F to "maintain a Central Registry." 110 CMR 12.00 also specifies the information kept in the Registry and enumerates the rules for access to information kept in the Registry. Lastly, 110 CMR 12.00 sets forth rules for access to other Department files or information.

5

110 CMR 12.02. Confidentiality of Department Records

Access to the Department's records is governed by several sources of law:

(1) M.G.L. c. 119, §§ 51E and F

(2) M.G.L. c. 66A ("FIPA")

(3) M.G.L. c. 4, § 7 clause 26 and M.G.L. c. 30, § 42 and M.G.L. c. 66 ("Public Records Law")

(4) M.G.L. c. 210, § 5C and 5D (adoption records)

(5) (see also M.G.L. c. 112, § 135 for limitation upon oral testimony by certain Department employees).

110 CMR 12.00 which follow define how the Department will act to safeguard the confidentiality of client records.

110 CMR 12.03. Central Registry—Contents

The Central Registry shall contain, but need not be limited to, all identifying data that is known ("identifying data" shall mean name, date of birth, sex, ethnicity, and address) for each child who is the subject of a report pursuant to M.G.L. c. 119, § 51A.

110 CMR 12.04. Central Registry—Expungement

Expungement, as mandated by M.G.L. c. 119, § 51F, shall be a computerized process whereby, with respect to a particular reported incident, the name and all other identifying characteristics relating to any child which is contained in the Central Registry, or to his parents or guardian, is permanently removed from the Central Registry.

110 CMR 12.05. Department Records—Expungement

Expungement, as mandated by M.G.L. c. 119, § 51E, shall be either: [1] a manual redaction process whereby, with respect to a particular reported incident, the name and all other identifying characteristics relating to any child or to his parents or guardian, is permanently removed or redacted from the Department's 51A standard report form, and the Department's 51B standard investigation form; or [2] the shredding of the 51A and 51B forms. The Department may elect either of the above expungement options.

110 CMR 12.06. Release of Information—Providers

(1) The Department may release to any Department provider or other individual or entity acting at the Department's request, any records, documents, or information which in the judgment of the Department is necessary for service delivery to children in the care or custody of the Department.

COMMENTARY

In order to adequately serve the children in its care and custody, the Department must necessarily release a variety of personal information about a child (as well as the child's family and other third parties) to a variety of providers or other individuals who serve the child, such as the child's doctor, dentist, psychiatrist, hospital, school, foster parents, day care center, private placement or adoption agency, camp, etc. Providers (e.g. day care centers, camps, etc.) under contract with the Department may receive and hold information from the Department, subject to the same restrictions upon release as apply to the Department. Other individuals or entities (e.g. doctors, hospitals, schools, etc.) may be given so much information as is, in the Department's judgment, necessary for them to provide needed services.

(2) Only employees of the Department may release information from Department files. Only the Commissioner or his/her designee may release information from the Department's Central Registry. Agencies or providers under contract with the Department holding Department records must consult the Department before releasing any information or documents from the Department's files.

110 CMR 12.07. Release of Information—Subpoena or other Legal Process

Whenever any Department records, documents or information are sought by compulsory legal process (subpoena, etc.) in any civil proceeding (for criminal proceedings, see 110 CMR 4.53) the Department shall not release such records until the Department has made reasonable efforts to notify each data subject identified in the records, so that s/he has reasonable time to seek to have the process quashed, in accordance with M.G.L. c. 66A, § 2(k). The Department's efforts to notify the data subject(s) may be written or oral, including notice by telephone. If the Department is unable to contact a data subject, the Department shall document in the case record the efforts made to contact the data subject, and thereafter the Department shall release the records sought.

In the alternative (and especially for voluminous records or files) the Department may elect to bring the entire file (unredacted, and without prior notification to any third parties named therein) before a judge in camera, and seek an order from said judge as to which records must be released by the Department. Then, before releasing such records as ordered by the judge, the Department shall attempt to notify third parties, as set forth in 110 CMR 12.07.

110 CMR 12.08. Release of 51A and 51B Forms

(1) The Department's release of 51A reports and 51B investigations is governed by M.G.L. c. 119, § 51E. Copies of 51A reports and 51B investigations shall be made available only if one of the following is obtained:

(a) The written consent of the child's parent(s) ("parent" shall mean the child's mother, or the child's father as "father" is defined by M.G.L. c. 209C, § 6) or guardian(s) or counsel. Regardless of whether parental or guardian consent is obtained, the Commissioner or his/her designee shall have the discretionary authority to grant or deny the request in order to promote and protect the best interests of the child.

(b) The written approval of the Commissioner or his/her designee.

(c) An order of a court of competent jurisdiction. A "court of competent jurisdiction" may include an out-of-state (non-Massachusetts) court, or a military court, so long as that court has some form of jurisdiction over the subject matter or the party(s).

All requests for 51A reports/51B investigations should be in writing or by telephone, and should be directed to the Regional Director, as the Commissioner's designee. Letter requests (but not telephone requests) will be accepted if made by an attorney on behalf of his/her client, as long as the attorney's request letter specifically states that the attorney is authorized to act on behalf of the client and is accompanied by a release or authorization signed by the client. Upon receipt of a request for the release of 51A/51B reports, the Regional Director or his/her designee contacts the Area Office which is currently responsible for the particular case. The Regional Director, or his/her designee, requests from the Area Director of his/her designee, a copy of the 51A report and 51B investigation, together with a recommendation from the Area Director or his/her designee as to whether granting the request of the requesting party would be contrary to the child's best interests. The Area Director sends a copy of the 51A report and 51B investigation, together with his/her recommendation, to the Regional Director. Upon receipt of the 51A report, 51B investigation, and recommendation from the Area Director or his/her designee, the Regional Director or his/her designee decides whether to release all or portions of the information based upon an analysis of whether such release to the requesting party would be contrary to the child's best interests. Upon a decision to grant all or part of the request, the material will be made available to the requesting party from the Regional Office within 30 calendar days of the initial request (or 45 calendar days if the requested material is voluminous). As to all persons other than an attorney who has complied with the above requirements of 110 CMR 12.00, if the requesting party:

(d) wishes to personally appear to obtain his/her copies from the Regional Office, some positive form of identification (photo drivers license, birth certificate, etc.) will be required; or

(e) wishes to have the material mailed some positive form of identification (photocopy of photo drivers license, photocopy of birth certificate) must be furnished in advance.

(2) A request may be granted by the Regional Director as the Commissioner's designee, but only when, in the opinion of the Regional Director, granting the request would not be contrary to the best interests of the child. The Regional Director shall send written notice of any denial to the requesting party stating the reasons for denying the request. No fair hearing or grievance shall be available concerning such a denial by the Regional Director, but an aggrieved party may exercise any other rights or remedies available at law.

(3) A request may be allowed in part and denied in part by the Regional Director as the Commissioner's designee, but in such cases the Regional Director shall so inform the requesting party and shall inform said party of the type of information withheld. Information which may be withheld, where appropriate, includes such material as attorney-client communications, other privileged material, portions which would be contrary to the best interests of the child if released, etc. No fair hearing or grievance shall be available concerning such a denial by the Regional Director, but an aggrieved party may exercise any other rights or remedies available at law.

(4) A non-custodial parent (i.e., divorced, adjudicated unfit, etc.) shall have the same right of access to said 51A and 51B reports as does the custodial parent, and is equally subject to the limitations of 110 CMR 12.08(2) and

(3). For purposes of 110 CMR 12.08, the request of one parent or guardian (not both parents nor both guardians) shall be sufficient to cause the Department to release to that individual a copy of the 51A report and 51B investigation, subject to the other limitations of 110 CMR 12.08.

(5) Whenever the Department releases any copy of a 51A report or 51B investigation, the name of (and any other reasonably identifying data concerning) the reporter shall be redacted. Other information may be redacted as set forth in 110 CMR 12.08(3) (i.e. attorney-client communications, privileged material, material contrary to the best interests of the child, etc.). However, this provision shall not apply to release of a 51A report or 51B investigation to a District Attorney, which shall not be redacted.

(6) See also 110 CMR 10.14, Regarding release of 51A/51B reports to alleged perpetrators for purposes of fair hearing.

110 CMR 12.09. Release of Information—Litigation

(1) In all court proceedings (including but not limited to care and protection actions, termination of parental rights actions, etc.) in which the Department or a provider under contract with the Department is a party, a copy of the entire social services file, including the pertinent 51A reports and 51B investigations, shall be made available, upon written request, to any of the following individuals:

(a) A court investigator appointed pursuant to M.G.L. c. 119, § 24

(b) A court-appointed guardian ad litem

(c) An officer of the court assigned by the judge to the case

(d) An attorney for the child, parent or legal guardian, if that attorney has been appointed or retained for the particular proceeding

(2) The written request must contain a statement from the requesting party that any material disclosed shall not be further duplicated nor divulged to any person not a party to the particular proceeding, unless by order of court. Fees for copying records shall be charged in accordance with the Department's fee schedule.

(3) Before releasing said file(s), a member of the Department's legal staff shall review the file(s), and remove any records of attorney-social worker conversations which may be considered attorney work product and/or privileged.

(4) Whenever the Department releases any copy of a 51A report or 51B investigation, the name of (and any other reasonably identifying data concerning) the reporter shall be redacted.

(5) Whenever the Department has reason to believe that disclosure to any individual named in 110 CMR 12.09(1)(a) through (d) of all or a portion of the social service file would be contrary to the child's best interest, the Department shall deny access and shall bring to the court's attention the reason(s) for denying access.

110 CMR 12.10. Release of Information—Non-Litigation

(1) Unless specifically governed by another provision in 110 CMR 12.10, all records held by the Department about a person are available to that person, with all third-party identifiers redacted, except for identifiers of third parties who are employees or providers of the Department, which shall not be redacted.

(2) Parent(s) may have access to their minor child's records until the child reaches 18. After a child reaches 18, parent(s) do not have access to their child's records without the child's consent.

(3) In order to obtain records, an individual must file a written request directed to the Area or Regional Director where the records are located. (In the event of uncertainty, such a written request may be directed to either). Fees for copying records shall be charged in accordance with the Department's fee schedule.

(4) Before releasing said record(s), a member of the Department's legal staff shall review the record(s), and remove any records of attorney-social worker conversations which may be considered attorney work product and/or privileged.

(5) Whenever the Department has reason to believe that disclosure to any requesting individual of all or a portion of the Department's records would be contrary to a child's best interests, the Department shall deny access and shall furnish to the requesting individual a written explanation of the reason(s) for denying access.

(6) Whenever the Department releases any copy of a 51A report or 51B investigation, the name of (and any other reasonably identifying data concerning) the reporter shall be redacted.

110 CMR 12.11. Release of Information—Consent of Data Subject

Whenever information may be released if the data subject "consents", the Department may obtain such consent in writing or orally, including by telephone; however, the Department shall make reasonable efforts to verify the data subject's identity; and shall, if no written consent is given, file a record of any oral approval in the case record.

110 CMR 12.12. Release of Information—Adoption Records

Release of any records, documents, or information from an adoption file is governed by 110 CMR 7.211.

110 CMR 12.13. Release of Information—Medical Records

Release of any medical records, documents or information ("medical" shall include psychiatric and dental) from any Department file is governed by 110 CMR 11.22.

110 CMR 12.14. Release of Information—Bureau of Special Investigations

Any authorized agent or representative of the Bureau of Special Investigations may have access to any documents, records, or files of the Department. See, M.G.L. c. 7, § 30(R) and (T).

110 CMR 12.15. Release of Information—Department of Youth Services

Any authorized agent of the Department of Youth Services (DYS) may have access to any documents, records, or files of the Department regarding a child who is at the time of the request for access, in the custody of DYS. See, M.G.L. c. 119, § 69A.

110 CMR 12.16. Correction of Information by Client

A Department client shall have the right to furnish to the Department, for inclusion in his/her record, a written statement of his/her version of any fact(s), in order to correct, supplement, or clarify any matter contained in the Department's file with which the client disagrees or is dissatisfied.

110 CMR 12.17. Release of Information—Other State Agencies

The Department may provide personal data, as that term is defined by M.G.L. c. 66A, § 1, to other state agencies for the sole purpose of enabling the receiving state agency to apply for and to receive federal funds, provided that the receiving state agency uses the personal data for that purpose and none other.

Regulatory Authority—110 CMR 12.00: M.G.L. c. 119, §§ 51E through F; c. 7, § 30(R), (T); c. 66A; c. 112, § 135; c. 4, § 7; c. 210, § 5C.

110 CMR 13.00. Case Investigation Unit

5

Section

110 CMR 13.01. Introduction

(1) The Department shall have a Case Investigation Unit (hereinafter "C.I.U") within the Central Office of the Department. The C.I.U. shall conduct internal reviews of all Department and contracted casework provider agency cases involving the death of any child who was:

(a) a member of a family with an open case; or

(b) a member of a family being investigated as a result of a M.G.L. c. 119, § 51A report received prior to the child's death; or

(c) a member of a family who had an open case within the six months preceding the child's death; or

(d) a member of a family who had a supported 51A report, but a case was not open for services, within the six months proceeding the child's death.

The CIU shall also conduct case investigations on any case which does not fall within the criteria above, if requested to do so by the Commissioner.

(2) The purpose of each C.I.U. investigation shall be to determine:

(a) the circumstances surrounding the child's death;

(b) if the child's death has any implications for the Department's policy, regulations, training and/or contracted service resources; and

(c) if case management activities and other services provided to the deceased child and her/his family were adequate, appropriate, and complied with Department policy and regulations.

110 CMR 13.02. Procedures

(1) Upon learning of the death of a child the social worker shall:

(a) immediately notify her/his supervisor, Area Program Man[a]ger and Area Director of the death of the child and the circumstances surrounding the death;

(b) collect as much information as possible about the cause of death and circumstances surrounding the death; and

(c) collect as much information as possible to assess the risk and safety issues for the surviving siblings and/or other children in the setting.

(2) Upon learning of the death of a child the Area Director, or the Director of a contracted casework provider agency, shall:

(a) immediately provide verbal notification to the Regional Director and the CIU Director, or designee, of the child's death and provide as much information as is available regarding the circumstances surrounding the death and other children in the setting, and

(b) if the child was residing in an out-of-home setting at the time of her/his death, immediately notify the Director(s) of any other Department Area Office(s), or Director of a contracted provider agency, who has a child in the setting; and

(c) within one working day convene a meeting to coordinate the Department's activities and response to the death; and

(d) ensure that a copy of the Department case record is provided to the Case Investigator at the time of the investigation interview.

(3) Upon learning of the death of a child the Care Investigation Unit shall:

(a) immediately notify other central office staff as set forth in the Department's Responding to a Child Fatality Policy (Department Policy #10-002(R)); and

(b) notify the Early Education and Care (EEC) if at the time of her/his death the child was residing in a placement subject to EEC licensure (i.e., foster home, pre-adoptive home, group home, shelter, residential facility), or was with a licensed day care provider; and

(c) on the day the CIU is notified of the child's death, assign a case investigator who shall immediately contact the Area Director, or designee, and schedule an investigation interview to be conducted within two working days after receiving notification of the child's death; and

(d) the assigned case investigator shall proceed to conduct the investigation following the procedures set forth in the Department Responding to Child Fatality Policy (Department Policy #90-002(R)).

These procedures include but are not limited to:

1. interviewing Department staff involved with the child, the child's family, and/or the child's placement;

2. non-Department staff, if appropriate;

3. forward a copy of the case record to an identified member of the Department Professional Advisory Committee (PAC) who reviews the case record in conjunction with the case investigator;

4. requesting, in writing, a copy of the child's autopsy report from the Medical Examiner's office.

(4) After the C.I.U. investigation is completed, a written report shall be prepared and submitted for comments and approval to the Deputy Commissioner for Field Operations, the designated Professional Advisory Committee member, the General Counsel and the Commissioner. The report may contain or address recommendations and/or comments covering a range of issues including: commendable or deficient casework practices demonstrated in the

case, compliance with existing regulations and procedures, the need for new or revised policies or procedures, operational and administrative issues, etc. When approved by the Commissioner, the C.I.U. report shall be delivered to the Deputy Commissioner for Field Operations and to the involved Regional and Area Director. The report shall include a narrative of the facts of the case based upon the information gathered by the C.I.U. The C.I.U. may issue a preliminary report, followed by a final report if requested to do so by the Commissioner. A final written report shall be delivered to the Commissioner within 30 calendar days after the CIU received notification of the death, unless the child died of natural causes, If the child died of natural causes the final written report shall be delivered to the Commissioner within 60 calendar days after the CIU received notification of the child's death.

(5) The Area Director and/or any Department staff interviewed during the CIU process may request an exit interview with the case investigator. Requests for an exit interview must be made, within 30 days after receipt of the CIU report, through the Area Director and are directed to the Deputy Commissioner or the Director of CIU.

The exit interview must include the Area Director, or designated manager, and may include the social worker, supervisor, Regional Director, or designee, or other DSS staff interviewed during the CIU process.

110 CMR 13.03. Participation of Department Employees

(1) Department employees, if they so request, are entitled to union representation during the C.I.U. investigatory process. The union representative attends at the staff members requests but does not participate in any discussions pertaining to the case materials during the interview.

(2) All Department staff involved with service provisions to the child and her/his family shall have the opportunity to review the final report of the C.I.U. and to provide a written response to the report.

Any written response from any involved staff is submitted, through the Area Director, within 30 working day after the Area Office receives the report or the exit interview, which ever is later.

(3) Notes from the exit interview and the Area Office's written response to the C.I.U. report shall be included in the C.I.U. file.

110 CMR 13.04. Public Access to C.I.U. Report

The Department's CIU report shall remain confidential, and shall not be released to any person or entity outside the Department, except:

(1) that portion of the CIU report which contains conclusions or recommendations may be released, in whole or in part, with all identifying data removed, if a written request is directed to the Commissioner and if the Commissioner determines that release of this portion, so redacted, would not be contrary to the best interests of the Department's client(s) or other involved parties, or effective law enforcement. In those limited number of cases where publicity accorded the events under investigation is so extensive that mere removal of identifying data would be insufficient to protect existing privacy interests, the report shall remain confidential; and

(2) members of the Department's Professional Advisory Committee may review C.I.U. reports in connection with their advisory function.

Regulatory Authority—110 CMR 13.00: M.G.L. c. 18B, § 7.

110 CMR 14.00. Volunteers

(May 3, 2019.)

110 CMR 14.01. Use of Volunteers

The Department's enabling legislation authorizes collaboration with volunteer agencies or organizations to assure efficient and high quality social and educational services for persons who are unable for social or economic reasons to provide such services for themselves (see, M.G.L. c. 18B, § 3). In addition, volunteers are needed to serve as independent third party representatives on the Department's foster care review panels (see M.G.L. c. 18B, § 6A) and multidisciplinary service teams (see M.G.L. c. 119, § 51D). As such, volunteers provide a valuable resource to the Department as it strives to maximize its delivery of a comprehensive social service program. Furthermore, volunteers may be utilized by area, regional or central offices in duties the office determines may best assist the agency in its mission.

110 CMR 14.02. Selection of Volunteers

(1) The manner utilized to recruit volunteers shall be designed to encourage participation from all cities and towns within the area or region, from all racial and ethnic groups, and from all economic levels.

(2) Volunteer applicants shall be asked to complete an application which lists educational and employment background, to provide at least two references, and to authorize a check of the Department's Central Registry, the Criminal Offender Record Information (CORI) and Sex Offender Registry Information (SORI) systems.

(3) Volunteer applicants shall be notified in writing whether they have been accepted as a volunteer with the Department.

(4) All volunteers serve at the will of the Department and may be terminated at any time for any reason.

110 CMR 14.03. Volunteer Requirements

(1) Before beginning work for the Department, all volunteers shall receive training. The training shall include information on the mandates and operations of the Department, with a particular emphasis on the laws and regulations governing client confidentiality.

(2) Every volunteer shall sign an Agreement agreeing to comply with 110 CMR and the applicable laws regarding client confidentiality.

(3) Volunteers shall be supervised in the performance of their duties by Department employees.

(4) Volunteers shall comply with any guidelines which may be issued by the Commissioner.

(5) Failure to comply with the Department's applicable laws, regulations or guidelines shall result in the volunteer's removal, by written notice to the volunteer from the Department.

Regulatory Authority—110 CMR 14.00: M.G.L. c. 18B, §§ 3(B)(5), 6A, 7(i); c. 119, §§ 37, 51B(j), 51D.

110 CMR 15.00. Area Boards and Statewide Advisory Council

110 CMR 15.01. Introduction

Under M.G.L. c. 18B, § 13, the Department is mandated to operate with the advice of 40 area boards which consist of a representative cross-section of the community. Area boards provide citizens with an opportunity to plan, develop, and implement the social services provided in their community.

Under M.G.L. c. 18B, § 16, the Department is mandated to operate with the advice of one (1) statewide advisory council. The statewide advisory council is composed of representatives from the area boards as well as members appointed by the Commissioner. The statewide advisory council provides citizens with an opportunity to advise the Commissioner in matters of statewide interest.

110 CMR 15.00 govern the operation, duties, and responsibilities of social service area boards and the statewide advisory council.

110 CMR 15.02. Area Board Membership

(1) Each area board shall have 21 members. No employee of the Department may be a member of an area board. No more than seven members of an area board may be employees of the Commonwealth or any of its political subdivisions (county employees, city employees, etc).

5

(2) Area boards shall consist of the following representatives:

(a) Four area consumers;

(b) Three area providers;

(c) One member of the mental health area board;

(d) One member knowledgeable in the field of mental retardation;

(e) Two members of the councils for children;

(f) Two members of the financial or business profession with special fiscal or budgetary skills;

(g) Two members of the community service area boards.

If after diligent efforts, it proves to be impossible to obtain individuals as listed above, then other individuals who are knowledgeable about the required subject matter may be temporarily appointed.

Every effort will be made to ensure that Area Boards reflect the demographic composition in their communities, and to ensure that all minority groups (blacks, hispanics, handicapped, etc.) are represented.

(3) In order to provide geographical representation in the membership of area boards, each area board shall include at least one member from each city, and if practicable each town, in the area.

(4) At least two members of the area board must be, at the time of their appointment, members of the financial or business professions and have competence in fiscal or budgetary matters.

110 CMR 15.03. Appointment to Area Board; Term of Office

(1) Area board members shall be appointed by the Commissioner. The term of appointment shall be three years. Members shall serve no more than two full consecutive terms of three years each.

(2) Area board members may be removed at any time by the Commissioner, according to the provisions of 110 CMR 15.00.

(3) The Commissioner may appoint an individual to serve during the remainder of the term of any board member whose seat becomes vacant for any reason.

(4) The area board shall provide, for the Commissioner's consideration, one or more names of candidates for each expiring term or vacancy.

(5) Area board members shall be sworn to the faithful performance of their duties, pursuant to the provisions of M.G.L. c. 30, § 11 and M.G.L. c. 222, § 3, by taking the oath prescribed by the Constitution of the Commonwealth.

(6) The area board shall notify the Commissioner in the event that it ceases to meet the qualifications of membership enumerated in 110 CMR 15.00. The Commissioner may authorize a period of time during which said requirements may be suspended, while requiring that efforts be made to meet said qualifications.

110 CMR 15.04. Rules

With the prior written approval of the Commissioner, each area board may adopt such rules as it may decide are necessary or helpful for the conduct of its business. Proposed rules shall be reduced to writing and adopted by a majority of the area board members present and voting. Within three days of the board's adoption of such rules, a copy shall be forwarded to the Commissioner who shall have 30 days to approve or disapprove, and to notify the board of approval or disapproval in writing.

110 CMR 15.05. Officers

(1) Each area board shall annually elect one member as president and such other officers as may be required. The election of officers shall occur no later than the second regularly scheduled meeting of a calendar year. The election shall be by secret ballot. Prior to the annual election of officers, the board shall insure that the members of the board are apprised of the qualifications of the candidates for president and any other officers to be elected.

(2) No person may serve more than two consecutive full terms of one year each as president. Upon election the president shall preside over each meeting, unless the board provides otherwise in its rules. The president shall have the sole and exclusive power to appoint members of the board to committees.

110 CMR 15.06. Committees

(1) The area board may establish such standing committees, special committees, or sub-committees as it deems necessary to conduct the business of the board.

(2) Each area board shall establish one committee which shall conduct the annual needs assessment for social services, as set forth in 110 CMR 15.00.

(3) In order to broaden citizen participation on area boards, the president may appoint persons who are not board members to committees. Non-board members may be appointed to any committee except an executive committee, if they have expressed a willingness to serve and if they have a particular expertise or perspective which would contribute to the committee's work.

110 CMR 15.07. Meetings and Proceedings of the Area Board

(1) Each area board shall hold meetings as often as the President shall require, but must meet at least four times in each calendar year.

(2) Area board meetings shall be held in conformance with the Open Meeting Law, M.G.L. c. 30A §§ 11A and 11A½. Notice of area board meetings shall be filed with the Secretary of the Commonwealth and the Secretary of Administration and Finance at least two calendar days prior to the scheduled meeting.

(3) Notice of regularly scheduled meetings must be given to all board members and to the Area Director in writing at least ten days in advance of the meeting.

(4) A special meeting of the board may be called by the president, by the Area Director, or by at least ten members of the board, by written notice to all members and to the area director. Any such notice of a special meeting shall be issued at least three days in advance of the meeting and shall contain the names of the person or persons calling the meeting and the proposed agenda.

(5) The Area Director shall provide staff support to the Area Board, shall work with the Board to achieve its purposes, and shall work with the Board's President regarding the Board's agenda.

110 CMR 15.08. Quorums; Voting

(1) Any proposed business requiring a vote shall be considered carried and adopted if it is supported by the vote of a majority of those members present.

(2) No proposed business requiring a vote shall be acted upon or voted upon unless at least seven members of the board are present.

110 CMR 15.09. Area Director Selection

(1) The Department shall recruit qualified applicants whenever there is a vacancy in the position of Area Director. The Department shall submit the name(s) of the final candidate(s) to the area board. The area board shall have the opportunity to interview the final candidate(s). The Commissioner, with the advice of the area board, shall appoint the Area Director.

(2) The Commissioner may designate any person to act as temporary Area Director in any case in which the office is vacant, until such time as a replacement selection is made.

110 CMR 15.10. Annual Needs Assessment

(1) Each area board shall participate in the needs assessment for social services in its area. The needs assessment shall be conducted annually.

(2) The purpose of the needs assessment process is to identify social services needed by area residents, which are either not being offered by the Department, or are not offered in sufficient quantity or quality. The needs assessment shall be conducted and reduced to writing following uniform guidelines developed by the Department.

110 CMR 15.11. Area Plans

(1) Annually, the Area Director shall furnish to each area board member a copy of the draft annual area plan and a proposed budget for the following fiscal year. The draft area plan shall describe the resources which will be utilized to provide social services in the area, and each category of planned social services. The proposed budget shall specify the amount of funds which are to be allocated for each category of planned social services contained in the area plan.

(2) The area board shall review the draft area plan and budget and shall submit its recommendations in writing to the Area Director. Any sections which the board disapproves shall be accompanied with a proposed, revised section. The Area Director shall meet with the board to attempt to resolve any differences between the draft area plan and the board's recommendations. However, the decision of the Area Director shall be final.

(3) The board shall certify to the Area Director, the Regional Director and the Commissioner whether it has or has not approved the annual area plan.

110 CMR 15.12. Regional Review

(1) The Regional Director shall call an annual meeting of all of the area boards in the region. The Regional Director shall preside at such meeting.

(2) The purpose of the regional meeting is to consider the needs assessment and the proposed area plans from a regional perspective. The meeting shall attempt to balance competing needs for resources and shall also designate area responsibility for new program development.

110 CMR 15.13. Receipt of Funds and Incorporation

(1) Subject to the prior written approval of the Commissioner, area boards may receive or solicit funds. The Commissioner shall issue guidelines which shall govern the solicitation, receipt, and expenditure of any funds by area boards.

(2) No area board may incorporate itself, nor may any group of area board members incorporate, for a purpose relating in any way to the delivery of social services.

110 CMR 15.14. Review of Proposals

(1) Each area board (or sub-committee established for that purpose) shall review, and make recommendations concerning, proposals submitted to the Department for the provision of social services within the area.

(2) The Area Director shall determine annually the manner in which proposal review shall be accomplished by the area board.

(3) The board shall make one of the following written recommendations following its review of each proposal:

(a) "Recommended". The board may include detailed comments which describe how the proposal could be further strengthened.

(b) "Not recommended". The board shall include a detailed statement indicating the reasons for this determination.

110 CMR 15.15. Review of Contracts

No more frequently than twice per calendar year, the Board may request from and receive from the Area Director a list of all contracts for programs or services which have been entered into which are a part of the area program of social services. The board may in addition request and receive a copy of the actual contract(s). Following its review, the area board may make written recommendations to the Area Director.

110 CMR 15.16. Statewide Advisory Council

(1) There shall be a statewide advisory council which shall advise the Commissioner in matters of statewide interest relating to the delivery of social services.

(2) The council shall have 45 members elected or appointed in the following manner:

(a) Each area board shall elect one of its members to serve for a term of one year; and may elect an alternate delegate to serve and vote in the absence of the elected delegate.

(b) The Commissioner shall appoint five members to serve on the council. Each appointed member shall serve for a term of one year.

(3) No member shall serve more than three consecutive terms.

(4) The council shall hold meetings as often as its business requires but must meet at least once in each calendar year.

(5) The council shall adopt such rules as are necessary for the conduct of its business. The rules shall be subject to the approval of the Commissioner.

110 CMR 15.17. Conflict of Interest

(1) Area board and statewide advisory council members shall comply with all provisions of the state conflict of interest law as mandated under M.G.L. c. 268A.

(2) If any matter comes before the board in which any board member or statewide advisory council member (or any member of his or her immediate family) has a financial interest, that member shall immediately inform both the Commissioner and the State Ethics Commission, in writing, of his/her financial interest in the matter. Furthermore, that area board or statewide advisory council member shall not participate in any proceedings or votes of the board which concern the matter in which the member (or any member of his or her immediate family) has a financial interest.

(3) No area board or statewide advisory council member shall directly or indirectly advocate to any other member a position which would benefit his or her financial interest or that of any member of his or her immediate family.

(4) No member of the statewide advisory council or any area board shall:

(a) improperly disclose confidential information acquired in the course of official duties nor use such information to further personal interests;

5

(b) use or attempt to use his or her official position to secure unwarranted privileges or exemptions or give the appearance of any such action;

(c) by his or her conduct give reasonable basis for the impression that any person can improperly influence him or her; or

(d) pursue a course of conduct which will raise suspicion among the public that he or she is likely to be engaged in acts that are in violation of the trust of the office of a board or council member.

(5) Members of any area board or the statewide advisory council shall request an advisory ruling from the State Ethics Commission whenever the Department informs such member in writing that in the judgment of the Department a potential conflict exists.

(6) Any violation of the provisions of 110 CMR 15.17 may result in the removal of the member from the area board or statewide advisory council by the Commissioner.

Regulatory Authority—110 CMR 15.00: M.G.L. c. 18B, §§ 7(i), 13, 14, 15, and 16; M.G.L. c. 30A, §§ 11A and 11A 1/2; M.G.L. c. 268A.

110 CMR 16.00. Requests for Research

Section

110 CMR 16.01. Introduction

110 CMR 16.02 shall be the criteria for approval or denial of research requests when the Department receives requests for access to Department data by independent researchers. 110 CMR 16.00 shall apply to projects originating outside of the Department, to research requested and contracted for by the Department or to routine requests from outside individuals or organizations for aggregate data.

5

110 CMR 16.02. Criteria for Approval of Research Requests

(1) The expected end-product(s) of the research will benefit the Department in one or more of the following ways:

(a) it will provide significant information that is not otherwise available and will be of use in improving case practice or service delivery, or in developing new or improving current service delivery; and/or

(b) it will result in provision of useful training for the Department by the research team or their associates, that is otherwise unavailable for Department staff, foster parents and/or providers; and/or

(c) it can be used to improve management of service delivery by:

1. increasing knowledge of family needs, service costs, effectiveness and/or benefits; and/or

2. it will aid the development of new mechanisms for service, personnel, systems or fiscal administration.

(2) The person or persons conducting the research will be professionally qualified to carry it out. Evidence of such qualifications must include one or more of the following:

(a) a degree that requires demonstration of research competency from an accredited university, e.g., Ph.D. or Ed.D.;

(b) publication(s) of prior research;

(c) a faculty or research unit or educational department appointment or student status requiring research activity at an accredited college, university or hospital, or an appointment requiring research competency at a social service organization.

(3) The external research project will be time limited from initiation to completion of end-product(s) preferably lasting no more than six–nine months, unless the benefits to the Department are such that a longer period is warranted.

(4) Proposed research projects requiring data collection from case records or other confidential materials, although not totally prohibited, shall be approved only under circumstances warranting the increased Department supervision and staff involvement necessary in such cases. This increased Department supervision and staff involvement is necessary because researchers who are not Department employees may not have access to families' records (whether stored in written or electronic form) due to confidentiality constraints. As a result, research requiring confidential information must involve Department staff in order to protect the confidentiality of such records. While the Department supports the concept of social research, and recognizes the value of the Department's data base to researchers, the Department must nevertheless set priorities for use of its limited staff resources. The Department requires, therefore, that the investment of Department staff time and other resources be commensurate with the results to be derived from the research. As a result, projects by independent researchers that require use of confidential materials will be limited to those expected to be of benefit to the Department equal to or greater than the resulting drain upon Department resources. Unless written consent is obtained from the parent(s) and/or a child over the age of 18, Department information will be released to researchers only in forms that do not allow identification of Department family members, i.e., either as aggregated data or as case data that has been redacted in order to remove any information that could be used to identify the family members, and any other persons mentioned in the case record, or Department staff.

(5) Researchers must agree to: a) provide a copy of the final draft research study; report or product to the Department for review; and b) acknowledge the Department support in any article published as a result of the approved research proposal; and c) provide the Department with a copy of any reports or publications produced as a result of the approved research proposal.

(6) Data sources (including redacted case records) that are required for research projects may be made available as copies of materials already collected or prepared, and charges will be made to the researcher to cover costs of provision (e.g., copying costs). When responding to the date request requires extensive programming or comparable use of Department staff time or resources, the Department will estimate the costs to the researcher in advance.

(7) Consent for participation of children in Department care or custody in research studies is governed by 110 CMR 11.23.

110 CMR 16.03. Department Research Review Committee

The Department will establish a research review committee which will consist of three to five standing members appointed by the Commissioner to provide clinical, legal, operational, research and information system expertise. The Commissioner will designate one member as the chair.

The purpose of the research review committee is to review requests for access to Department data by researchers. The committee will convene as necessary to consider all conforming research proposals. Proposals will be evaluated according to the criteria for approval set forth in 110 CMR 16.02.

110 CMR 16.04. Procedures for Processing Research Proposals

(1) A researcher must contact the Department's Research Review Committee Chair to initiate a research proposal, who will provide the researcher with a copy of the Department research policy.

(2) Research proposals are initially reviewed by the Department for conformity with the following required components:

(a) A research proposal including at least the following:

1. objective(s) of research;

2. preliminary description of research methodology;
3. type(s) of data needed;
4. expected data source(s);
5. expected end-products of the research;
6. estimate of completion times for entire project and principal stages;

(b) letters of approval from the Department Area Director and/or Regional Director, when the research is anticipated to have an impact on staff or families in a participating Area and/or Regional Office;

(c) letters of support from other involved Department offices or units, agencies, residential facilities, institutions, or organizations, as available;

(d) resume(s) of principal researcher(s);

(e) description of any relevant institutional or organizational involvement;

(f) copies of University and/or Hospital Human Subjects Committee or Internal Review Board approval of project, if relevant;

(g) copy of informed consent form that meets Department approval;

(h) source(s) of funding for project;

(i) description of benefits expected to accrue to the Department's families, or staff, or to the management of service delivery;

(j) evidence that Department consent and confidentiality requirements will be maintained; and

(k) an estimate of staff time and/or other Department resources needed for the project.

110 CMR 16.05. Notification of Approval/Disapproval

The Committee shall determine whether to approve or disapprove a research request, and shall thereupon notify the requesting researcher(s) as soon as possible in writing. If a request is approved, further arrangements regarding collection and/or provision of data will be made between the researcher and the Department.

Regulatory Authority—110 CMR 16.00: M.G.L. c. 18B, §§ 2, 3, 7.

110 CMR 17.00. Reserved

110 CMR 18.00. Criminal Offender Record Checks

5

NOTE Effective July 15, 2014, G.L. c. 119, § 26A was amended to provide new resources for DCF review of criminal records of prospective foster parents. Section 26A will control over inconsistent provisions in 110 CMR 18.00 et seq.

Section

110 CMR 18.01. Purpose

The purpose of 110 CMR 18.00 et seq. is to establish standardized procedures for the Department and Department funded or operated programs regarding the review of criminal records of candidates for employment or regular volunteer or training positions, as well as for foster and pre-adoptive parents. The Criminal History Systems Board (CHSB) has authorized Executive Office of Health and Human Services (EOHHS) agencies and their vendor agencies to receive criminal record information regarding present or prospective employees in any program funded or operated by such agencies. The CHSB has also authorized the Department to receive criminal record information regarding present or prospective foster and adoptive parents and their household members.

110 CMR 18.02. Policy

In order to ensure that employees or other persons regularly providing client or support services, including foster/pre-adoptive parents, in any program or facility of the Department or in vendor agency programs funded by the Department are appropriate for serving in their positions with potential for unsupervised contact, a Criminal Offender Record Information (CORI) check shall be performed on candidates for positions in such programs or facilities, as provided in 110 CMR 18.00. It is the policy of EOHHS and the Department that convictions of certain crimes pose an unacceptable risk to the vulnerable populations served by the Department and its vendor agencies. 110 CMR 18.00 sets forth minimum standards.

110 CMR 18.03. Scope

110 CMR 18.00 applies to:

(a) applicants for positions, including employment, trainee, volunteer or intern, which entail potential unsupervised client contact in the Department and/or Department funded vendor agency programs that provide people with Department services;

(b) persons seeking to apply to become foster/pre-adoptive parents, foster/pre-adoptive parent applicants and foster/pre-adoptive parents for Department and any vendor agency providing foster or adoptive services for the Department;

(c) candidates for positions in the Department, including employment, trainee, volunteer or intern, which do not entail the potential for unsupervised client contact; and

(d) At the discretion of the Department vendor agency programs, the scope of 110 CMR 18.00 may be expanded to include volunteers, interns, students or other persons regularly offering support to any program or facility in either a paid or unpaid capacity whose services do not entail the potential for unsupervised client contact.

110 CMR 18.04. Definitions

Applicant: Any person seeking employment or a position as a regular volunteer or trainee to provide services for or on behalf of the Department or its vendor agency programs, where such employment or position involves potential unsupervised contact with program clients. Employment includes but is not limited to placement in: state positions; federal positions; positions funded by grants, bonds or other capital outlay, and, vendor agency positions.

Candidate: Any person receiving a conditional offer for employment or a position as a regular volunteer or trainee or intern, subject to consideration of any criminal record, to provide services for or on behalf of the Department or its vendor agency programs, where such employment or position involves potential unsupervised contact with program clients. Employment includes but is not limited to placement in: state positions; federal positions; positions funded by grants, bonds or other capital outlay; and vendor agency positions.

Community Service Worker: Any individual who, as a condition of probation, is applying for a position.

CORI Cleared Employee: Any candidate hired as an employee after successfully satisfying the requirements of 110 CMR 18.00.

CORI Coordinator: The person designated by the hiring authority to send requests and receive responses from the CHSB EOHHS CORI Unit.

CORI Investigation: The process of requesting, receiving and evaluating CORI related to candidates for a position with the Department or a vendor agency program.

Criminal History Systems Board (CHSB) EOHHS CORI Unit: The EOHHS sponsored unit within the Criminal History Systems Board which processes requests for CORI information from EOHHS agencies and offers technical assistance with any question arising from the results of a search.

Criminal Justice Official: Either the candidate's probation officer, parole officer or correctional facility superintendent (or designee), depending upon the person having the most recent responsibility for supervision of the candidate. In cases where the candidate was last supervised in a correctional facility, the candidate may advise the hiring authority of any employee of the correctional facility who may have specific information about the candidate that would assist the superintendent or designee in his/her assessment process.

Criminal Offender Record information (CORI): Information regulated by the Criminal History Systems Board and maintained by the Board of Probation regarding the criminal histories of persons within the Massachusetts Court system.

5

Discretionary Disqualification: A candidate shall be ineligible for a position that entails potential unsupervised contact with persons receiving services at a Department funded or operated program if he or she has been convicted of any crime, or has pending any charge for any crime in 110 CMR 18.16: Table B or Table C, unless the hiring authority has complied with the provisions of 110 CMR 18.11.

Department Background Record Check (BRC): The Department Central Office unit which conducts all CORI investigations for the Department.

Department Funded or Operated Program: Any program operated by the Department or contracted and funded by the Department with a vendor agency that provides services for or on behalf of Department clients.

Foster/Pre-adoptive Parent: For the purpose of 110 CMR 18.00 et seq. Foster/pre-adoptive parent shall refer to persons seeking to apply to become foster/pre-adoptive parents, foster/pre-adoptive parent applicants and current foster/pre-adoptive parents.

Hiring Authority: The person legally authorized or designated to make hiring decisions within the affected agency, department, office, program, or facility. For the purpose of foster/pre-adoptive parents, the hiring authority shall be the management level of the agency authorized to make approval/licensing decisions in accordance with Department policy.

Household Member: Any individual, regardless of age, who resides or spends substantial time in the home. This may include, but is not limited to, a non-custodial parent who visits the home; relatives, paramours, and/or other individuals who spend overnights in the home; an individual who routinely baby-sits in the home and/or otherwise assumes some degree of caretaking responsibility, in the home, for any child in that home.

Kinship Placement: The placement of a child, who is in Department care or custody, with a person(s) related either by blood, marriage or adoption (i.e. adult sibling, grandparent, aunt, uncle, first cousin) or a significant other adult to whom a child and the child's parent(s) ascribe the role of family based on cultural and affectional ties or individual family values.

Lifetime Presumptive A category of offenses, compiled as 110 CMR 18.16: Table A, for which conviction of any such offense results in a presumption of disqualification for employment or other service which entails potential unsupervised contact with persons receiving services in Department or any Department funded or operated program, due to the presumed unacceptable risk posed by the nature of the crime to person receiving services. A lifetime presumptive disqualification shall become a discretionary disqualification:

(a) if the candidate's criminal justice official concludes in writing that the candidate, within the position sought, does not pose an unacceptable risk of harm to the person served by the program, or

(b) if the criminal justice official has been determined by the hiring authority to be unavailable or has indicated to the hiring authority that she has insufficient information to render an assessment, then the hiring authority shall, at the candidate's request, seek an assessment of the candidate's risk of harm from a qualified mental health professional and the qualified mental health professional concludes in writing that the candidate, within the position sought, does not pose an unacceptable risk of harm to the persons served by the program.

(c) For foster/pre-adoptive parents one of the provisions of 110 CMR 18.10(1) apply.

No Record: The conclusion from a CORI search that convictions or pending charges relating to the candidate have not been found. A finding of "no record" does not necessarily mean, however, that criminal information is not present in the CORI database.

Pending: A criminal offense shall be considered pending if the CORI report indicates that the offense remains open and without final resolution, including that the case has been continued without a finding.

Position: Employment, service by a regular volunteer, trainee, or intern.

Potential Unsupervised Contact: Potential for contact with a person who is receiving or applying for services in Department or Department vendor agency program when no other CORI cleared employee is present. A person having only the potential for incidental unsupervised contact with clients in commonly used areas such as elevators, hallways and waiting rooms shall not be considered to have the potential for unsupervised contact for purposes of 110 CMR 18.00. These excluded areas do not include bathrooms and other isolated areas (not commonly utilized or separated by sight and sound from other staff) that are accessible to clients.

Qualified Mental Health Professional: A psychiatrist, licensed to practice medicine under M.G.L. c. 112, § 2, a psychologist, licensed under M.G.L. c. 112, §§ 118 through 121, or a licensed independent clinical social worker licensed under M.G.L. c. 112, §§ 130 through 132; provided that the psychiatrist, psychologist, or licensed independent clinical social worker (LICSW) has at least 1,000 hours of experience over a minimum or two years involving assessment, treatment, and consultation concerning individuals with behavior that presents a risk of harm to others in the community, in the workplace, in treatment settings, or in correctional facilities; provided further that the psychiatrist, psychologist, or licensed independent clinical social worker has not provided treatment to the candidate.

Trainee: Any person enrolled in an academic program or participating in a pre or post-doctoral training program that is affiliated with an accredited educational institution or hospital, who receives a placement within the Department or a vendor agency program.

Vendor Agency Program: The provision of client services by any individual, corporation, partnership, organization, trust, association or other entity through funding by the Department.

Volunteer: Any person who works in an unpaid capacity on a regular basis for the Department or a vendor agency program. For the purposes of 110 CMR 18.04: Volunteer, means a current client of services at a facility or program who provides unpaid services at that facility or program shall not be considered a volunteer at that facility or program.

Work Release Program: A program of unpaid work performed by any individual who is under the custody of the state or county correctional system.

110 CMR 18.05. Applicant Disclosure of Criminal Record Information

All applicants for a position in the Department or a vendor agency program shall complete an application form that contains a section requiring the applicant to disclose whether or not he/she has a criminal record and what crimes, if any, he or she has been convicted of, consistent with the requirements of M.G.L. c. 151B, § 4, para 9. The application shall not require an applicant to disclose:

(a) an arrest, detention, or disposition regarding any violation of law in which no conviction resulted; or

(b) a first conviction for any of the following misdemeanors: drunkenness, simple assault, speeding, minor traffic violations, affray, or disturbance of the peace; or

(c) any conviction of a misdemeanor where the date of such conviction or the completion of any period of incarceration resulting therefrom, whichever date is later, occurred five or more years prior to the date of such application for employment or such request for information, unless such person has been convicted of any offense within five years immediately preceding the date of such application for employment or such request for information. No application for employment shall be considered complete unless the applicant completes this section.

Prospective foster/pre-adoptive parents or foster/pre-adoptive parent applicants for Department or a vendor agency program will be required to disclose whether or not he/she has a criminal record, including the crimes charged and the disposition of the charge.

110 CMR 18.06. Community Service and Work Release Workers

Any Department or vendor agency program that participates in either a criminal justice related community service program or a work release program shall require all individuals who participate and would have potential unsupervised contact with clients to disclose his/her criminal record in conformance with 110 CMR 18.05 on a form signed by the candidate's criminal justice official. In addition, as a condition of participation, the candidate's criminal justice official must conclude in writing that the individual will not pose an unacceptable risk to program clients or the community service program or work release program will take responsibility for providing supervision for the individual at all times.

110 CMR 18.07. Hiring Authority Responsibilities

(1) The hiring authority shall ensure that each applicant provides consent to a CORI investigation as part of his/her application and to the periodic conduct of further CORI investigations during the course of employment with Department or vendor agency program. The hiring authority shall also inform the applicant that his or her CORI may be utilized by the criminal justice official or qualified mental health professional conducting themselves in conformance with 110 CMR 18.06, 18.10, 18.11; and Department personnel responsible for carrying out the provisions of 110 CMR 18.08, 18.09, 18.10, 18.11, and 18.13. Such consent and notification shall be included in the hiring authority's employment application form.

(2) The hiring authority shall require, as a condition of an offer of a position, the satisfactory completion of the CORI investigation. The hiring authority shall confirm an offer of a position only after the hiring authority receives written confirmation that the criminal record investigation has resulted in a finding of "no record" or until the hiring authority has complied with the requirements of 110 CMR 18.08, 18.09, 18.10 and 18.11.

(3) The hiring authority shall review positive findings from the CORI.

(4) The hiring authority shall not permit any candidate to commence employment or other service until after the candidate is cleared as a result of the CORI investigation, in accordance with 110 CMR 18.00.

(5) For all foster/pre-adoptive parents, the hiring authority shall conduct a CORI investigation on the foster/pre-adoptive parents as well as any household member age 14 years or older. The hiring authority may conduct a CORI investigation on any household member under the age of 14 about whom the hiring authority has concerns that the person may pose a risk to a child placed in the home.

110 CMR 18.08. CORI Investigations

(1) Department Employees, Volunteers, Interns, Trainees.

(a) All applicants shall complete the appropriate CORI request form.

(b) After the hiring authority makes a conditional offer of a position to an individual, subject to consideration of any criminal record, the completed CORI request form or electronic equivalent shall be forwarded to the Department Central Office Background Record Check (BRC) Unit, in accordance with Department policy.

(c) All CORI investigations that result in a finding of "no record" shall be transmitted back to the hiring authority and shall provide sufficient evidence of suitability for hire for 60 business days. A "no record" finding may be valid for consideration for other positions during this 60 day period.

(d) All CORI investigations that show findings of criminal records shall be sent immediately to the hiring authority for review consistent with 110 CMR 18.00.

(2) Department Foster/Pre-adoptive Parents.

(a) Whenever an individual contacts the Department for the purpose of applying to be a foster or pre-adoptive parent, the Department shall conduct a CORI investigation as part of the Department initial screening process on the individual(s) applying and household members age 14 years and older.

(b) The Department shall conduct a CORI investigation of any household member age 14 or older during the initial home-study/evaluation of the foster/pre-adoptive home and during the annual reassessment of the foster/pre-adoptive home.

(c) The Department BRC Unit shall conduct the CORI investigations for the Department in accordance with policies and procedures established by the Department.

(d) The results of the CORI investigation shall be transmitted back to the Department employee requesting the CORI investigation. If the CORI investigation shows findings of a criminal record, the Department shall proceed consistent with 110 CMR 18.00, M.G.L. c. 119, § 26A, M.G.L. c. 210, § 3B and Department policy and procedures for background record checks.

(3) Department Vendors not Licensed by the Office for Child Care Services.

(a) All applicants shall complete the appropriate CORI request form.

(b) After the hiring authority makes a conditional offer of a position to an individual, subject to consideration of any criminal record, the completed CORI request form or electronic equivalent shall be forwarded to the CHSB EOHHS CORI Unit, in accordance with the policies of the CHSB.

(c) All CORI investigations that result in a finding of "no record" shall be transmitted back to the hiring authority and shall provide sufficient evidence of suitability for hire for 60 business days. A "no record" finding may be valid for consideration for other positions during this 60 day period.

(d) All CORI investigations that show findings of criminal records shall be sent immediately to the hiring authority for review consistent with 110 CMR 18.00.

(4) Department Vendors Licensed by the Department of Early Education and Care. Department Vendors Licensed by the (EEC) shall conduct CORI investigations in accordance with the EEC regulations found at 102 CMR.

(5) Foster/Pre-adoptive Parents Approved and/or Licensed by a Department Contracted Provider Agency.

(a) Before a child in Department care or custody can be placed in a foster/pre-adoptive home of a Department vendor agency, a CORI investigation must have been conducted on the foster/pre-adoptive parent(s) and any household member age 14 or older.

(b) The CORI investigation may be conducted by the Department BRC Unit in accordance with policy and procedures established by the Department.

(c) If the Department conducts the CORI investigation, the results shall be transmitted back to the Department unit having responsibility for overseeing the contracted provider agency.

(d) The Department unit having responsibility for overseeing the contracted provider agency shall contact the provider agency to discuss the CORI Investigation results and determine, if needed, whether to proceed in accordance with 110 CMR 18.10 and 110 CMR 18.11, 119, § 26A, M.G.L. c. 210, § 3B and Department policy and procedures for background record checks.

110 CMR 18.09. Findings from CORI Investigations

(1) If the CORI investigation reveals a finding of "no record," such finding shall be documented in the candidate's file.

(2) If the CORI investigation reveals a "lifetime presumptive disqualification" on the candidate's record, as specified in 110 CMR 18.10(1), the candidate shall be informed by the hiring authority that he or she is ineligible for any position in a Department or a vendor agency program where there is potential unsupervised contact with persons applying for or receiving services, unless there is compliance with the provisions of 110 CMR 18.10 and 18.11. If the CORI investigation reveals a "lifetime presumptive disqualification" on the foster/pre-adoptive parent's record, as specified in 110 CMR 18.10(1), the foster/pre-adoptive parents shall be informed by the Department or vendor agency program that he or she is ineligible to be a foster/pre-adoptive parent unless there is compliance with the provisions of 110 CMR 18.10 and 18.11.

(3) If the CORI investigation reveals a "discretionary disqualification" on the candidate's record, as specified in 110 CMR 18.10(2), the candidate shall be informed by the hiring authority that he or she is ineligible for any position in a Department or vendor agency program where there is potential unsupervised contact with persons applying for or receiving services, unless there is compliance with the provisions of 110 CMR 18.10 and 18.11. If the CORI investigation reveals a "discretionary disqualification" on the foster/pre-adoptive parent's record, as specified in 110 CMR 18.10(3), the foster/pre-adoptive parents shall be informed by the Department or vendor agency program that he or she is ineligible to be a foster/pre-adoptive parent unless there is compliance with the provisions of 110 CMR 18.10 and 18.11.

(4) If the CORI investigation reveals that the candidate has an outstanding warrant for any offense, the candidate shall be informed by the hiring authority that he or she is ineligible for any position in the Department or a Department funded or operated program where there is potential unsupervised contact with persons applying for or receiving services, unless the warrant is removed.

110 CMR 18.10. Disqualification

(1) Lifetime Presumptive Disqualification. A candidate shall be ineligible for a position in a Department or a Department funded or operated program which entails potential unsupervised contact with persons receiving services if he or she has been convicted of, has any pending charges, involving crimes listed in 110 CMR 18.16: *Table A* unless:

(a) the candidate's criminal justice official

(1) concludes in writing that the candidate, within the position sought in Department or in a Department vendor agency program, does not pose an unacceptable risk of harm to the persons served by the program, or

(2) has been determined by the hiring authority to be unavailable or has indicated to the hiring authority that he/she has insufficient information to render an assessment, then the hiring authority shall, at the candidate's request, seek an assessment (the cost of which shall be borne by the hiring authority) of the candidate's risk of harm from a qualified mental health professional and the qualified mental health professional concludes in writing that the candidate, within the position sought in Department or a Department funded or operated program, does not pose an unacceptable risk of harm to the persons served by the program; and

(b) the hiring authority has complied with the provision of section 110 CMR 18.11.

(c) In the case of an individual seeking to serve as a foster/pre-adoptive kinship placement for a child in the care or custody of Department, the Department shall not be precluded from placing the child(ren) in a kinship foster/pre-adoptive home where the Commissioner, Deputy Commissioner for Field Operations and General Counsel have conducted a review pursuant to 110 CMR 18.11(9) and determined the placement is in the best interest of the child.

(2) Discretionary Disqualification. A candidate shall be ineligible for any position in Department or a Department funded or operated program which entails potential unsupervised contact with persons receiving services if he/she has been convicted of, has any pending charges, involving any of the crimes listed in 110 CMR 18.16: *Table B or Table C*, unless the hiring authority has complied with the provisions of 110 CMR 18.11.

(3) Provisions Pertaining to Foster/Pre-Adoptive Parents.

(a) In the case of a foster/pre-adoptive parent, 110 CMR 18.10(1)(2) shall apply as if the foster/adoptive parent was a candidate for a position.

(b) When determining eligibility, approval or licensing of a foster/pre-adoptive parent the Department shall conduct a review of any misdemeanor offense in accordance with 110 CMR 18.11(10) in order to assist the Department in accurately evaluating whether the mere existence of the offense has a substantial effect on the foster/pre-adoptive parent's current or future ability to assume and carry out the responsibilities of a foster/pre-adoptive parent in such a manner that the rights of the child to sound health and normal physical, mental, spiritual and moral development are insured.

110 CMR 18.11. Provisions for Review of a Candidate in Any Discretionary Category

(1) Each candidate for whom the CORI investigation reveals a "lifetime presumptive disqualification", who has otherwise met the requirements for further consideration set forth in 110 CMR 18.10, or a "discretionary disqualification" shall, unless the hiring authority has decided to withdraw the conditional offer of a position, receive additional review by the hiring authority to determine if the candidate poses an unacceptable risk of harm to the persons served by the program within the position sought. In reviewing the candidate's appropriateness for employment given the concern for client safety, due weight shall be given to the following factors:

(a) Time since the conviction;

(b) Age of the candidate at the time of the offense;

(c) Seriousness and specific circumstances of the offense;

(d) The nature of the work to be performed;

(e) The number of offenses;

(f) Any relevant evidence of rehabilitation or lack thereof;

(g) Any other relevant information, including information submitted by the candidate or requested by the hiring authority.

Information considered pursuant to 110 CMR 18.11(1)(g) may include documentation from the candidate's criminal justice official, if not already supplied pursuant to 110 CMR 18.10(1), or treating professional or other knowledgeable source, such as, the police, courts, or prosecuting attorneys.

(2) Following the review, the hiring authority shall determine whether:

(a) To hire the candidate based upon a determination that the candidate does not pose a danger to the program's clients; or

(b) To not hire the candidate;

Nothing in 110 C.M.R. 18.11(1) shall be construed as preventing the hiring authority from deciding not to hire the candidate for any other reason.

(3) If a decision is made to hire the candidate, the hiring authority shall make a written determination of such decision, documenting the considerations outlined in 110 CMR 18.11(1)(a) through (g), and the rationale for the conclusion that the candidate does not pose a danger to the program's clients within the position sought.

(4) The hiring authority shall submit such written determination to the Department immediately upon a decision to hire the individual.

(a) If the candidate has been convicted of or has a pending charge for any of the crimes listed in 110 CMR 18.16: *Tables A* and *B*, the hiring authority shall not proceed to hire the individual for five business days during which time the Commissioner may, after review of the determination, disapprove the hire.

(b) If the candidate has been convicted of or has a pending charge for any of the crimes listed in 110 CMR 18.16: *Table C*, the hiring authority may proceed to hire the individual, unless the provisions of 110 CMR 18.11(6) apply.

(5) The Department shall conduct an annual review of such written determinations for candidates with crimes listed in 110 CMR 18.16: *Table C* to ensure compliance with the requirements of 110 CMR 18.09, 18.10, and 18.11.

(6) Based on the annual review pursuant to 110 CMR 18.11(5) or other relevant information obtained by the Department that raises concerns about the hiring authority's compliance with these requirements, the Department may require the hiring authority to submit such written determinations prior to hiring the individual. The Commissioner shall have five business days following receipt of the determination to disapprove the hire. The Department may require the hiring authority to follow such prior review process for as long a period as it determines is necessary to ensure that the hiring authority is complying with the requirements of 110 CMR 18.09, 18.10, and 18.11.

(7) In the case of a foster/pre-adoptive parent, 110 CMR 18.11(1)(2)(3) shall apply as if the foster/adoptive parent was a candidate for a position.

(8) In the case of a foster/pre-adoptive parent who is being considered or has been approved and/or licensed by the Department, the Department shall proceed in accordance with its policy in meeting the requirements of 110 CMR 18.11(4), (5) and (6).

In the case of a foster/pre-adoptive parent who is being considered or has been approved and/or licensed by the Department vendor agency program and will be used as a placement for a child in the Department's care or custody, the Department vendor agency must proceed in accordance with the Department policy and procedures on background record checks in meeting the requirements of 110 C.M.R. 18.11(4), (5) and (6).

(9) In reviewing a request for an individual to serve as a kinship foster/pre-adoptive parent pursuant to 110 CMR 18.10(1) the Commissioner, Deputy Commissioner for Field Operations and General Counsel must find :

(a) That the prospective foster/pre-adoptive parent, or any household member, does not present a risk of harm to the child based on the existence of a criminal conviction;

(b) That the conviction did not involve a crime against or involving a child;

(c) That the foster/pre-adoptive parent has a pre-existing relationship and bond with the child;

(d) That the foster/pre-adoptive parent agrees to submit to an assessment by a qualified mental health professional within 30 days of placement; and

(e) That the Department has reviewed the enumerated factors set forth in 110 CMR 18.11(1) in determining that it is in the best interests of the child to be placed with the kinship foster/pre-adoptive parent notwithstanding the existence of a criminal conviction that would otherwise disqualify them.

(10) In reviewing a misdemeanor crime for any foster/pre-adoptive parent the Department shall consider at a minimum the following:

(a) the time that has elapsed between the date of the offense and the date of the screening, assessment or reassessment;

(b) The seriousness and specific circumstances of the offense;

(c) The number and nature of other offenses;

(d) The age of the offender at the time at the time of the offense;

(e) The findings and recommendations of the family resource worker assigned by the Department to discuss the facts surrounding the misdemeanor with the foster/pre-adoptive parent;

(f) The recommendations given to the family resource worker by personal or employment references chosen by the foster/pre-adoptive parent or received otherwise;

(g) The current and future needs of the child to be placed and the probable effect that the misdemeanor would have on the foster/pre-adoptive parent's ability to fulfill those needs;

(h) Any reports or recommendations received by the Department from the foster/pre-adoptive parent's parole or probation officer should one have been assigned;

(i) A copy of the police report pertaining to the offense in question if obtainable within a reasonable period of time or discussions with a police officer familiar with the facts surrounding the offense; and

(j) Unless inappropriate, discussions with the child to be placed regarding his/her current and past relationship with the foster/pre-adoptive parent.

Nothing in 110 CMR 18.11(7), (8), or (9) shall be construed as preventing the Department or a vendor agency program from deciding not to approve or license a foster/pre-adoptive home for any other reason.

110 CMR 18.12. Dissemination

CORI records may be disseminated only to individuals certified by the CHSB to receive such information, such as designated representatives of the hiring authority or the CORI Coordinator. The hiring authority shall maintain a listing of persons so certified. Willful dissemination of Criminal Offender Record Information to unauthorized individuals is punishable by a jail sentence of up to one year and/or a fine of $5,000 in addition to civil penalties, pursuant to M.G.L. c. 6, § 178.

110 CMR 18.13. Incidents

Any hiring authority receiving an allegation that an employee with a positive CORI history has harmed a client in a Department or vendor agency program shall immediately report the allegation to the person designated by the Department for such purposes. Upon request, the hiring authority shall provide the Department with documentation of the basis for the hiring decision.

110 CMR 18.14. Severability

If any provisions of 110 CMR 18.01 through 18.14, inclusive, or the applications of such provisions to any person or circumstance are held invalid, the other provisions of said 110 CMR 18.01 through 18.14, inclusive, or the application of such provisions to any person or circumstance other than that as to which it is held invalid, shall not be affected thereby.

110 CMR 18.15. Application

To the extent 110 CMR 18.00 conflicts with existing Department regulation or policy, 110 CMR 18.00 shall control. 110 CMR 18.00 shall apply to persons who apply to the Department on or after October 12, 2001.

110 CMR 18.16. Tables of Offenses

All of the offenses included in 110 CMR 18.16: Tables A, B, and C, are to be construed as including all violations of Massachusetts law or like violation of the law of another state, the United States, or a military, territorial or Native American tribal authority. The Hiring Authority shall contact the CHSB EOHHS CORI Unit whenever a CORI investigation reveals an offense that is not included in 110 CMR 18.16: Tables A, B, and C and it appears similar in seriousness to included offenses. The CHSB EOHHS CORI Unit, in consultation with the EOHHS General Counsel, shall determine, taking into account the purposes of 110 CMR 18.00, if the offense is similar to one of the included offenses. If it is determined to be similar, then it shall be considered to be included in the same table as the included offenses. If it is determined to be not similar, then it shall be considered for inclusion into the appropriate table through the regulatory process. Nothing herein shall preclude the hiring authority from considering any criminal conviction not included in 110 CMR 18.16: Tables A, B, and C.

TABLE A	MGL
A&B, Dangerous Weapon, Vict 60+	c. 265, § 15A(a)
A&B Child W/ Injury	c. 265, § 13J
A&B On Retarded Person	c. 265, § 13F
Administering Drugs/Sex	c. 272, § 3
Armed Assault W/Intent To Murder Or Rob	c. 265, § 18(b)
Armed Assault W/Intent To Murder Or Rob, Vict 60	c. 265, § 18(a)
Armed Assault, Dwelling, W/Felony Intent	c. 265, § 18A
Armed Carjacking	c. 265, § 21A
Armed Robbery	c. 265, § 17
Assault W/Intent To Murder Or Maim	c. 265, § 15
Assault W/Intent To Rape	c. 265, § 24
Assault W/Intent To Rape Child	c. 265, § 24B
Attempt Escape Or Escape By Prisoner Or Sex/Dang	c. 268, § 16
Attempt To Murder	c. 265, § 16
Burning Dwelling House	c. 266, § 1
Distribute Controlled Substan, Minor	c. 94C, § 32F
Exhibit Posing Child	c. 272, § 29A
Extortion	c. 265, § 25
Home Invasion	c. 265, § 18C
Incest	c. 272, § 17
Indecent A&B, Child 14 Or Over	c. 265, § 13H
Indecent A&B, Child Under 14	c. 265, § 13B
Indecent A&B, Retarded Person	c. 265, § 13F
Induce Minor To Prostitution	c. 272, § 4A
Intimidation Of Witness	c. 268, § 13B
Kidnapping	c. 265, § 26
Malicious Explosion	c. 266, §101
Manslaughter, Negligence (Minor/Child)	c. 265, § 13
Manslaughter	c. 265, § 13
Mayhem	c. 265, § 14
Murder	c. 265, § 1
Perjury	c. 268, § 1
Rape	c. 265, § 22(b)
Rape Aggravated	c. 265, § 22(a)
Rape, Statutory	c. 265, § 23
Trafficking In Cocaine	c. 94C, § 32E(b)(4)
Trafficking In Heroin	c. 94C, § 32E(c)(4)
Trafficking In Marijuana	c. 94C, § 32E(a)(4)
Unnatural Acts W/Child Under 16	c. 272, § 35A
Conspiracy To Commit Any Of Above Offenses	
Accessory Before Any Crime In This Category	
Attempts To Commit Any Crime In This Category	

TABLE B	MGL
A& B Dangerous Weapon	c. 265, § 15A
A&B Intimidation, Race/Color/Religion	c. 265, § 39(a)
Accessory After Fact (Variable)	c. 274, § 4
Accessory Before Fact	c. 274, § 2
Aid Escape From Custody	c. 268, § 17
Assault By Dangerous Weapon	c. 265, § 15B(b)
Assault By Dangerous Weapon, Victim 60 And Older	c. 265, § 15B(a)
Attempt To Burn Dwelling House	c. 266, § 5A
Attempted Extortion	c. 265, § 25
Bomb Scare	c. 269, § 14
B&E Day, Intent Comm Felony	c. 266, § 18
B&E Day, Intend Comm Felony, Fear	c. 266, § 17
B&E Night, Bldg/Ship/M/V, Intend Comm Felony	c. 266, § 16
B&E Truck, Intend Comm Felony	c. 266, § 20A
Bribery Of A Police Officer	c. 268, § 2
Burglary, Armed	c. 266, § 14
Burglary, Unarmed	c. 266, § 15
Burning Building	c. 266, § 2
Burning M/V Or Personal Property	c. 266, § 5
Burning To Defraud Insurance Co.	c. 266, § 10
Carrying Dangerous Weapon, Committing Felony	c. 269, § 10(b)
Carrying Dangerous Weapon, Sub Offense	c. 269, § 10(d)
Carrying Loaded Rifle/Shotgun, Public Way	c. 269, § 12D
Civil Rights Violation, Bodily Injury	c. 265, § 37
Compounding Felony	c. 268, § 36
Contribute Delinquency Child	c. 119, § 63
Deliver Articles To Inmate	c. 268, § 31
Deliver Drugs To Prisoner	c. 268, § 28
Deriving Support From Prostitute	c. 272, § 7
Distributing Obscene Pictures	c. 272, § 28
Drug Paraphernalia	c. 94C, § 32I(a)
Enter W/O Brk, Bldg/Shp/M/V, Int Fel. Fear	c. 266, § 17
Enter W/O Brk, Night, Dwell, Intend Comm Felony	c. 266, § 18
Entice Female, Sex, Intercourse	c. 272, § 2
Escape, Furlough	c. 268, § 16
Escape By Prisoner	c. 268, § 16
False Information For Gun Permit	c. 140, § 129
Forgery, Alter Prescription	c. 94C, § 33(b)
Fugitive From Justice	c. 276, § 20A
Induce Prostitution	c. 272, § 6
Induce Sex, Minor	c. 272, § 4
Involuntary Manslaughter	c. 265, § 13
Kidnapping Minor By Relative	c. 265, § 26A
Kidnapping Minor By Relative, Endanger Safety	c. 265, § 26A
Larceny, Bank Employee Or Officer	c. 266, § 52
Larceny, Controlled Substance, From Authorized Person	c. 94C, § 37
Larceny Firearm	c. 266, § 30
Larceny, Person	c. 266, § 25
Larceny, Person 65+	c. 266, § 25
Manufacture/Distribute Class A Substance	c. 94C, § 32

TABLE B	MGL
Manufacture/Distribute Class B Substance	c. 94C ,§ 32A
Manufacture/Distribute Class C Substance	c. 94C, § 32B
Manufacture/Distribute Class D Substance	c. 94C, § 32C
Manufacture/Distribute/Dispense Class B Substance	c. 94C, § 32A
Mfg/Dist/Dispense Cl A W/In 1000ft School	c. 94C, § 32J
Mfg/Dist/Dispense Cl B W/In 1000ft School	c. 94C, § 32J
M/V Homicide, Negligent Operation	c. 90, § 24G(b)
M/V Homicide, Reckless Operation	c. 90, § 24G(b)
M/V Homicide, Under Influence Drugs, Negligent Or Reckless	c. 90, § 24G(a)
M/V Homicide, Under Influence Liquor	c. 90, § 24G(b)
M/V Homicide, Under Influence Liquor, Negligent Or Reckless	c. 90, § 24G(b)
Operate M/V Under Influence, Serious Injury	c. 90, § 24(1)(a)(1)
Operate M/V Under Influence, Drugs, 3rd Offense	c. 90, § 24(1)(a)(1)
Operate M/V Under Influence, Liquor, 3rd Offense	c. 90, § 24
Possess Burglarious Tools	c. 266, § 49
Poss Cl A Sub W/Int To Dist W/Int 1000ft School	c. 94C, § 32J
Poss Cl B Sub W/Int To Dist W/Int 1000ft School	c. 94C, § 32J
Poss Cl B Sub W/Int To Dist/Mfg/Cult W/Int 1000ft School	c. 94C, § 32J
Possess Class A Substance	c. 94C, § 34
Possess Class A Substance, Intent To Distribute	c. 94C, § 32(a)
Possess Class B Substance	c. 94C, § 34
Possess Class B Substance, Intent To Distribute	c. 94C, § 32A(a)
Possess Class B Substance, W/Intent Dist/Mfg	c. 94C, § 32A
Possess Class C Substance, Intent To Distribute	c. 94C, § 32B(a)
Possess Class C Substance, Sub Offense	c. 94C, § 34
Possess Class D Substance, Sub Offense	c. 94C, § 34
Possess Class D Substance, Intent To Distribute	c. 94C, § 32C(a)
Poss Class D Sub W/Int To Dist W/Int 1000ft School	c. 94C, § 32J
Possess Class E Substance, Intent To Distribute	c. 94C, § 32D
Possess Controlled Sub W/Intent Distrib, Sub Off	c. 94C, § 32(b)
Possess Firearm W/O License	c. 269, § 10(h)
Possess Firearm, Serial/Id Num Oblit	c. 269, § 11C
Possess Firearm, Serial/Id Num Oblit, Comm Felony	c. 269, § 11B
Possess Infernal Machine	c. 266, § 102A
Possess Machine Gun W/O License	c. 269, § 10(c)
Possess Machine Gun Or Sawed Off Shot Gun, Sub Offense	c. 269, § 10(d)
Possess M/V Master Key	c. 266, § 49
Possess Matter Harmful Minor	c. 272, § 28
Possess Shotgun, Barrel Und 18 "Sawed Off"	c. 269, § 10C
Possess Shotgun, Barrel Und 18 "Sawed Off, Sub Off	c. 269, § 10D
Receive/Buy Stolen M/V	c. 266, § 28(a)
Sell Ammuniton W/O License	c. 140, § 122B
Sell Obscene Literature, Under 18	c. 272, § 28
Sell Firearm W/O License	c. 140, § 128
Throw Explosives	c. 266, § 102
Trafficking In Cocaine W/ In 1000ft School	c. 94C, § 32J
Trafficking In Heroin W/ In 1000ft School	c. 94C, § 32J
Trafficking In Marij W/ In 1000ft School	c. 94C, § 32J
Unarmed Assault, Intent To Rob	c. 265, § 20
Unarmed Robbery	c. 265, § 19(b)
Unarmed Robbery, Victim 60	c. 265, § 19(a)
Unlawful Possession, Bomb	c. 148, § 35
Unlawful Possession, Firearm, Commission Felony	c. 265, § 18B
Unlawfully Place Explosives	c. 266, § 102
Unnatural Acts	c. 272, § 35
Utter False Prescription	c. 94C, § 33

TABLE B	MGL
Vandalize Church/Synagogue/Cemetery	c. 266, § 127A
Vandalize School/Church/Educational Bldg	c. 266, § 98
Violate Domestic Protective Order	c. 208, § 34C
Violate Stalking Law	c. 265, § 43(a)
Violation Of Protective Order (209a)	c. 209A, § 7
Conspiracy To Commit Any Of Above Offenses	
Attempts To Commit Any Crime In This Category	
Accessory Before Any Crime In This Category	

TABLE C	MGL
A&B	c. 265, § 13A
A&B On Public Servant	c. 265, § 13D
A&B On Police Officer	c. 265, § 13D
A&B Or Assault On Correctional Officer	c. 127, § 38B
Abandon W/O Support Of Spouse, Or Minor Child	c. 273, § 1(1)
Abandon M/V	c. 90, § 22B
Accosting	c. 272, § 53
Adulteration Alcoholic Beverage	c. 138, § 16
Affray	c. 272, § 53
Alien In Possess Of Firearm	c. 140, § 131H
Annoying Phone Calls	c. 269, § 14A
Assault	c. 265, § 13A
Attempt To Injure Depository Of Valuables	c. 266, § 16
B&E, Intend To Comm Misdemeanor	c. 266, § 16A
B&E Railroad Car	c. 266, § 19
B&E Recognizance Violation	c. 276, § 82A
Being Present Where Heroin Kept	c. 94C, § 35
Civil Rights Violation, No Bodily Injury	c. 265, § 37
Credit Card, Larceny Of	c. 266, § 37B
Cruelty To Animals	c. 272, § 77
Discharging Firearm, 500ft	c. 269, § 12E
Discharging Weapon Near Highway/Dwell, Hun	c. 131, § 58
Dispense Controlled Substance, Not Registered	c. 94C, § 25
Distribute Controlled, Substan W/O Prescription	c. 94C, § 25(1)
Engaging In Sex, Prostitution, "John"	c. 272, § 53A
Enter W/O Brk, Truck, Intend Comm Felony	c. 266, § 20A
Fail To Keep Records On Controlled Substance	c. 94C, § 15
Gaming, Implements Found Present, Manager	c. 271, § 17
Gaming, Implements Found Present, Owner	c. 271, § 17
House Of Ill Fame	c. 272, § 24
Illegal Possess Class C Substance	c. 94C, § 34
Illegal Possess Class D Substance	c. 94C, § 34
Illegal Possess Class E Substance	c. 94C, § 34
Indecent Exposure	c. 272, § 53
Larceny By Check	c. 266, § 37
Larceny More	c. 266, § 30
Larceny In Bldg, Ship, Vessel, Or Rr Car	c. 266, § 20
Larceny In Truck/Trailer	c. 266, § 20B
Larceny, M/V Or Trailer	c. 266, § 28
Leave Comm W/O Support Minor Child Out Of Wdlock	c. 273, § 15
Leave Comm W/O Support Of Spouse & Minor Child	c. 273, § 1
Leave Scene After Personal Injury, M/V	c. 90, § 24(2)(a½)(1)
Lewd & Lascivious Speech & Behavior	c. 272, § 53
Malicious Destruc, Pers/Real Prop, Over $250	c. 266, § 127
Manufacture/Distribute Class E Substance	c. 94C, § 32D(a)
Non-Support Of Minor Child Out Of Wedlock	c. 273, § 15
Non-Support Of Minor Child(Ren)	c. 273, § 1
Obscene Telephone Calls	c. 269, § 14A
Obstruct Justice	c. 268, § 34

TABLE C	MGL
Open & Gross Lewdness	c. 272, § 16
Operate M/V After License Revoked For Drunk Driving	c. 90, § 23
Operate M/V Under Influence, Drugs	c. 90, § 24(1)(a)(1)
Operate M/V Under Influence, Liquor	c. 90, § 24
Possess Altered Fid Card	c. 140, § 131I
Possess Counterfeit Subs W/Intent Distribute	c. 94C, § 32G
Possess Dangerous Weapon Unlawfully	c. 269, § 10(b)
Possess Hypodermic Syringe Or Needle	c. 94C, § 27
Possess Obscene "Pornographic" Material	c. 272, § 29
Procure Liquor For Minor	c. 138, § 34
Prostitution	c. 272, § 53A
Receive Stolen Property, Over 250	c. 266, § 60
Riot	c. 269, § 1
Sell/Deliver Alcoholic Beverages Person Under 21	c. 138, § 34
Soliciting Prostitute	c. 272, § 8
Shoplifting, 3rd Or Sub Offense	c. 266, § 30A
Sodomy	c. 272, § 34
Taking M/V W/O Authority, Steal Parts	c. 266, § 28
Telecommunications Fraud	c. 166, § 42A
Unauthorized Use, Credit Card, Over $250	c. 266, § 37C
Unlawful Possession, Shotgun	c. 140, § 129C
Unlawfully Obtain Controlled Substance	c. 94C, § 33
Use M/V, Commission Of Felony	c. 90, § 24(2)(a)
Utter Forged Instrument	c. 267, § 5
Violate Support Order	c. 273, §1
Violate Support Order, Minor Child Out Of Wdlock	c. 273, § 15
Wanton Destruction, Pers/Real Property	c. 272, § 73
Willfully & Maliciously Burn M/V	c. 266, § 127
Willfully & Maliciously Kill Beast	c. 266, § 127
Conspiracy To Commit Any Of Above Offenses	
Attempts To Commit Any Crime In This Category	
Accessory Before Any Crime In This Category	

Regulatory Authority 110 CMR 18.00: M.G.L. c. 18B, § 7(i) and M.G.L. c. 30A.

110 CMR 23.00. Services for Young Adults

5

(Sept. 6, 2019.)

Section

110 CMR 23.01. Introduction to Services for Young Adults

The Department is committed to assisting older adolescents and young adults in their transition to independence and self-sufficiency. Services for young adults assist individuals transitioning from foster care to young adulthood. These services are provided under conditions agreed upon by both the Department and the young adult, and based upon the availability of resources. The Department will collaborate with the young adult to develop a plan for services that are individualized in accordance with a shared understanding of the young adult's needs. The Department will make reasonable efforts to provide an array of supports typically needed by young adults.

110 CMR 23.02. Duration of Services

(1) The Department only provides services to young adults up to 22 years of age. The Department may continue services to young adults until 23 years of age if the individual demonstrates that without the provided services the individual will not complete an Associate's or higher degree program.

(2) To the extent that another state agency, including but not limited to, the Department of Mental Health (DMH) or the Department of Developmental Services (DDS), is primarily responsible for such person, the Department may terminate services prior to the young adult's 22nd birthday.

110 CMR 23.03. Eligibility

For a young adult to receive services from the Department beyond 18 years of age, the young adult must meet one of the age criteria listed in 110 CMR 23.03(1), and one of the criteria for either state-supported services listed below in 110 CMR 23.03(2)(a), or Title IV-E supported services listed in 110 CMR 23.03(2)(b).

(1) Age Criteria.

(a) For a young adult to receive state-supported services beyond 18 years of age, the young adult must be:

1. in the care or custody of the Department at 18 years of age and continue under the responsibility of the Department after 18 years of age pursuant to a voluntary placement agreement with the Department;

2. in the care or custody of the Department at 18 years of age or continued under the Department's responsibility after18 years of age, and after termination at 18 years of age or older, later seeks Department services prior to 22 years of age; or

3. a consumer in an open case with the Department at 18 years of age or older.

(b) For a young adult to receive Title IV-E supported services beyond 18 years of age, the young adult must be:

1. the care or custody of the Department at 18 years of age and continues under the responsibility of the Department after 18 years of age; or

2. the care or custody of the Department at 18 years of age or continued under the Department's responsibility after 18 years of age, and after termination at 18 years of age or older, later seeks Department services prior to 21 years of age.

(2) Participation.

(a) A young adult is eligible for state-supported services when the young adult is:

1. enrolled in secondary education or a program leading to a GED;

2. enrolled in a post-secondary or vocational education program or trade school;

3. participating in a program or activity designed to promote, or remove barriers to employment;

4. employed for at least 80 hours per month;

5. incapable of doing any of the education or employment activities listed in 110 CMR 23.03(2)(a)1. through 4. due to a medical condition;

6. participating in another program or plan which promotes specific educational or rehabilitative programs; or

7. participating in another program which promotes and supports the youth in fully developing and fulfilling the youth's potential to be a participating citizen of the commonwealth.

(b) A young adult is eligible for Title IV-E-supported services when the young adult is:

1. completing secondary education or a program leading to a GED;

2. enrolled in a post-secondary or vocational education program or trade school;

3. participating in a program or activity designed to promote, or remove barriers to employment;

4. employed for at least 80 hours per month; or

5. incapable of doing any of the above education or employment activities listed in 110 CMR 23.03(2)(b)1. through 4. due to a medical condition.

In addition to the criteria in 110 CMR 23.03(2)(b)1. through 5., for a young adult to be eligible for Title IV-E supported services the eligibility criteria set forth in 42 USC § 672 must be met.

110 CMR 23.04. Verification/Documentation

The young adult will be required to provide periodic documentation that they meet one of the criteria listed in 110 CMR 23.03. The Department will utilize the documentation, and other sources, to verify a young adult's Title IV-E eligibility a minimum of twice per year.

110 CMR 23.05. Substitute Care Services

(1) Young adults who remain in placement with the Department are to live in either a:

(a) Department licensed foster home;

(b) Department contracted placement such as a foster home, IFC home, congregate care facility, teen living program, independent living program;

(c) another supervised independent living setting, such as a dorm, an apartment, a friend or relative's home;

(d) another setting where the young adult is living and/or renting space; or

(e) upon approval of the Area Director and the Assistant Commissioner over Adolescent Services, another living environment.

(2) The Department may make care and maintenance payments directly to the contracted placement or may make young adult support payments directly to the young adult. The Department's continued responsibility for such persons is contingent upon the express written consent of the person or their guardian unless:

(a) before reaching 18 years of age, the person had an intellectual disability and was declared mentally incompetent under M.G.L. c. 119, § 23(a)(3) while under the responsibility of the Department; or

(b) the person is under the responsibility of the Department pursuant to M.G.L. c. 190B, § 5-305.

110 CMR 23.06. Young Adult Support Payments

(1) The Department may make young adult support payments when the young adult:

(a) demonstrates responsibility and compliance with the agreements made with the Department as set forth in the voluntary placement agreement and the action plan and in monthly meetings with their Department social worker;

(b) is living in a supervised independent living setting;

(c) agrees to monthly visits by the Department Social Worker, or for young adults living out of state with a social worker from the state in which they are living; and

(d) agrees to use the young adult support payments for housing, food and other living expenses.

(2) The Department will establish guidelines to determine the amount of the young adult support payment. Payments may be suspended or terminated if the Department determines there are significant changes in the young adult's circumstances or the young adult's ability to manage the payments. Before young adult support payments are suspended or terminated, the young adult shall be provided an opportunity to submit information to the Area Director in support of his or her request to continue payments through the Department's grievance process.

(3) The Area Director must approve the initiation, suspension or termination of young adult support payments. In rare circumstances, a youth between 17 and 18 years of age may be approved by the Area Director to receive young adult support payments.

(4) The Department shall notify a young adult in writing 30 days prior to termination of young adult support payments unless the Area Director determines that immediate termination is needed due to fraud or misuse of funds.

110 CMR 23.07. Discharge Support Services

The Department may provide discharge financial support to young adults who are transitioning to living independently as adults. Discharge support payments may include payments toward first and last months rent, security deposit, essential household items, or other related needs. These services are subject to the limitation of funding received from the federal government.

(1) Eligibility. A young adult is eligible for discharge financial support if the young adult is:

(a) under the care and responsibility of the Department;

(b) between 18 and 21 years of age;

(c) within three months prior to discharge from a Department placement or is planning to live independently as an adult;

(d) making progress toward development of life skills as specified in the young adult's action plan;

(e) willing to participate in the discharge planning process; and

(f) able to afford the ongoing cost of the apartment or other living arrangement after the discharge support payments have been provided.

(2) Application. In order to receive discharge financial support, the Department's social worker assigned to the young adult's case must apply prior to the young adult's anticipated discharge from placement, for discharge support funding from the Department's Adolescent Support Services Unit.

(3) Decision. The Department's Adolescent Support Services Unit will notify the young adult's social worker of the outcome of the application and the process for payments. The young adult's social worker will notify the young adult of the outcome.

110 CMR 23.08. Denial, Reduction, or Termination of Services

(1) Young adult support services may continue until 22 years of age as long as the young adult continues to meet one of the criteria listed in 110 CMR 23.03, regularly meets with their Department Social Worker, and cooperates with other reasonable requests made by the Department. The young adult's continued participation in such Department services must be under conditions agreed upon by both the Department and the young adult.

(2) The Department will work with the young adult to develop a transition plan beginning 90 days prior to the end of services to the young adult or 90 days prior to discharge from placement, whichever is earlier. The transition plan must be personalized at the direction of the young adult, be as detailed as they choose and include specific options regarding housing, health insurance, education, local opportunities for a mentor or continuing support services, work force supports and employment services, and information about the importance of a health care proxy. The Department will provide the young adult with the documents/information required by 42 USC § 675(5)(I).

(3) The Department may deny, reduce or terminate any or all of services to the young adult if the young adult does not meet one of the criteria in 110 CMR 23.03, does not meet regularly with the Department social worker, or otherwise does not cooperate with the Department's requests as outlined in the action plan. If the Department decides to deny, reduce or terminate young adult support services, it must do so in writing at least 30 days prior to the agency action and must state the reasons for the denial, reduction or termination. In a situation where the agency is terminating all services the Department must complete the transition planning with the young adult as required above. The process to deny, reduce

or terminate young adult support services is governed by 110 CMR 8.00: *Service Denial, Reduction, or Termination.*

(4) Any young adult aggrieved by the denial, reduction, or termination of young adult support services, excepting young adult support payments, may request a fair hearing on the matter up to 22 years of age, pursuant to 110 CMR 10.00: *Fair Hearings and Grievances*. If the request for a fair hearing is made within 30 days of notice of the denial, reduction or termination of young adult support services, the services shall continue pending the outcome of the fair hearing. Any young adult aggrieved by the denial, reduction or termination of young adult support payments shall receive 30 days written notice from the Department, unless the Area Director determines that immediate termination is needed due to fraud or misuse of funds, and may request a grievance and have an opportunity to present information/documentation to the Area Director in support of their request to have Young Adult Support payments or to not have payments suspended or terminated.

Regulatory Authority—110 CMR 23.00: M.G.L. c. 18B, §§ 3 and 7; M.G.L. c. 30A; M.G.L. c. 119, § 37.

Additional Materials: Department of Children and Families Policies

Note: The following materials are available in the eBook version of this Sourcebook. See the Electronic Download page at the front of this book for instructions on downloading a copy of the eBook. To go directly to any policy, use the eBook's "bookmarks" feature to select the policy number in the expandable bookmarks list in the eBook's left-hand column.

Some DCF policies are available on the department's website at https://www.mass.gov/lists/review-dcf-policies.

1984-002 (r2008)—Policy for 51A Reports Involving Department Employees, Relatives/Household Members of Department Employees, Department Foster/Pre-Adoptive Parents, or Department Area Board Members

1984-004 (r2008)—Clothing Grant

1984-005 (r1989)—Guardianship

1984-007 (r2018)—SSI and RSDI Child Benefits Policy

1984-010 (r2008)—Emergency Judges After Court Hours Policy

1984-012 (r2008)—Policy for Closing Court-Involved Cases

1985-001 (r2015)—Case Transfer

1985-003 (r2008)—Health Care Services for Children in Placement

1985-005 (r2008)—51A Investigations in Certain Institutional Settings

1985-007 (r2013)—Adoption Subsidy Policy

1985-012 (r2017)—Policy for Referrals to the District Attorney and Local Law Enforcement Authority

1985-013 (r2008)—Conflict of Interest

1986-002 (r2008)—Appeal of Court Orders or Decisions

1986-003 (r2008)—Information and Referral

1986-004 (r1989)—Case Assignment

1986-005 (r2008)—Voluntary Intake

1986-006 (r1989)—Intake Policy and Procedures for CHINS Children Committed or Ordered into Detention at the Time of Referral

1986-007 (r2017)—Case Closing

1986-008 (r1994)—Policy for the Periodic Review of Cases—Progress/ Supervisory Review

1986-009 (r2019)—Foster Care Review Policy

1986-010 (r2008)—Reports Alleging Medical Neglect of Infants with Life-Threatening Conditions

1986-011 (r2008)—Ongoing Casework and Documentation Policy

1986-012 (r1989)—Transitional Planning for Special Education Students Turning 22 or Graduating High School

1986-014 (r2018)—Background Records Check Policy

1986-015 (r2016)—Protective Intake Policy

1987-003 (r2008)—Policy and Procedure for Release of Adoption Records and Information

1987-007A (r1989)—Procedures for Assessing "Psych. Under 21 Medicaid" and DMH Hospital Beds for Children up to the Age of 21 in the Care or Custody of the Department of Social Services

1988-001 (r2008)—Indian Child Welfare Act

1988-002—DSS Children Committed to DYS

1989-002 (r2008)—Supplemental Reimbursement Policy

1989-003 (r2008)—Decision-Making for Children in Department Care or Custody Who Have AIDS, are HIV+, or Are at Risk of HIV Infection

1989-004 (r1990)—Obtaining Medicaid

1990-002 (r1995)—Responding to a Child Fatality

1990-003 (r2008)—Voluntary Adoption Surrender

1990-004 (r1996)—Placement Prevention and Placement Policy

1990-006 (r2008)—Sliding Fee Policy

1991-001 (r1992)—Adoption Information Disclosure Policy

1991-002 & 1991-004—Policy for Reimbursement of Non-Recurring Expenses for Families Adopting Special Needs Children; PAYA Program

1991-003 (r1991)—MAPP (Massachusetts Approach to Partnerships in Parenting)

1991-005 (r2008)—Policy for Approval of Research Proposals and Survey Participation Requests

1991-006—Subsidized Day Care Services

1992-001 (r2008)—Adolescent Sexual Offender Policy

1994-001 (r2008)—Fair Hearing Office and Grievance Policy

1997-001—Community Residential Care Policy for Diagnostic Assessment, Group Home, Independent Living, 766-Approved Private School, and Commonworks Programs

1997-002 (r2014)—Education Policy for Children Birth Through 22

2005-01 (r2008) Summary of Workplace Violence Prevention Policy

2005-01 (r2008)—Department Workplace Violence Prevention Policy

2006-01 (r2008)—Family Resource Policy

2007-01 (r2008)—Forgoing or Discontinuing Life-Sustaining Medical Treatment

2008-01—Foster/Pre-Adoptive Parent Damage and Theft Reporting and Compensation

2010-01—Medical Examinations for Children Entering DCF Placement or Custody

2011-01—Early Intervention Referral Policy

2011-01—Referral Letter for Early Intervention

2011-02—Guardianship Subsidy Policy

2013-01—Permanency Planning Policy

2016-001—Rental Car Policy

2016-01—Supervision Policy

2016-02 (r2019)—Children Who Are Missing or Absent

2017-001—Travel Reimbursement Documentation, Submission, and Approval Policy

2017-01—Family Assessment and Action Planning Policy

PART 6

Selected Massachusetts Department of Elementary and Secondary Education Regulations

603 CMR 28.00. Special Education

[Amended effective July 1, 2018.]

Section

603 CMR 28.01. Authority, Scope and Purpose

(1) 603 CMR 28.00 is promulgated pursuant to the authority of the Board of Elementary and Secondary Education under M.G.L. c. 69, § 1B and c. 71B.

(2) 603 CMR 28.00 governs the provision by Massachusetts public schools of special education and related services to eligible students and the approval of public or private day and residential schools seeking to provide special education services to publicly funded eligible students. The requirements set forth in 603 CMR 28.00 are in addition to, or in some instances clarify or further elaborate, the special education rights and responsibilities set forth in state statute (M.G.L. c. 71B), federal statute (20 U.S.C. § 1400 et seq. as amended) and federal regulations (34 C.F.R. § 300 et seq. as amended).

(3) The purpose of 603 CMR 28.00 is to ensure that eligible Massachusetts students receive special education services designed to develop the student's individual educational potential in the least restrictive environment in accordance with applicable state and federal laws.

603 CMR 28.02. Definitions

(1) *Approved private special education school or approved program* shall mean a private day or residential school, within or outside Massachusetts, that has applied to, and received approval from, the Department according to the requirements specified in 603 CMR 28.09.

(2) *Approved public special education school* shall mean a program operated by a public school or an educational collaborative providing full day or residential special education services to eligible students in a facility serving primarily students with disabilities. Such program shall be approved when it has applied to, and received approval from, the Department according to the requirements specified in 603 CMR 28.09.

(3) *Certified special educator* shall mean a person with a teaching certificate or license in an area of special education or a related service provider with appropriate certification or license in his or her professional area. Licensure shall meet the requirements of the Massachusetts Regulations for *Educator Licensure and Preparation Program Approval* at 603 CMR 7.00 and the requirements for renewal of license at 603 CMR 44.00: *Recertification*, as necessary. A certified or licensed special educator may provide, design, or supervise special education services.

(4) *Consent* shall mean agreement by a parent who has been fully informed of all information relevant to the activity for which consent is sought, in his/her native language or other mode of communication, understands and agrees in writing to the carrying out of the activity, and understands that the granting of consent is voluntary and may be revoked at any time. The consent describes the activity and lists the records (if any) that will be released and to whom.

(5) *Day* shall mean calendar day unless the regulation specifies *school day*, which shall mean any day, including a partial day, that students are in attendance at school for instructional purposes.

(6) *Department* shall mean the Massachusetts Department of Elementary and Secondary Education.

(7) *Disability* shall mean one or more of the following impairments:

(a) *Autism*. A developmental disability significantly affecting verbal and nonverbal communication and social interaction. The term shall have the meaning given it in federal law at 34 CFR § 300.8(c)(1).

(b) *Developmental Delay*. The learning capacity of a young child (3–9 years old) is significantly limited, impaired, or delayed and is exhibited by difficulties in one or more of the following areas: receptive and/or expressive language; cognitive abilities; physical functioning; social, emotional, or adaptive functioning; and/or self-help skills.

(c) *Intellectual Impairment*. The permanent capacity for performing cognitive tasks, functions, or problem solving is significantly limited or impaired and is exhibited by more than one of the following: a slower rate of learning; disorganized patterns of learning; difficulty with adaptive behavior; and/or difficulty understanding abstract concepts. Such term shall include students with mental retardation.

(d) *Sensory Impairment*. The term shall include the following:

1. *Hearing Impairment or Deaf*. The capacity to hear, with amplification, is limited, impaired, or absent and results in one or more of the following: reduced performance in hearing acuity tasks; difficulty with oral communication; and/or difficulty in understanding auditorally-presented information in the education environment. The term includes students who are deaf and students who are hard-of-hearing.

2. *Vision Impairment or Blind*. The capacity to see, after correction, is limited, impaired, or absent and results in one or more of the following: reduced performance in visual acuity tasks; difficulty with written communication; and/or difficulty with understanding information presented visually in the education environment. The term includes students who are blind and students with limited vision.

3. *Deafblind*. Concomitant hearing and visual impairments, the combination of which causes severe communication and other developmental and educational needs.

(e) *Neurological Impairment*. The capacity of the nervous system is limited or impaired with difficulties exhibited in one or more of the following areas: the use of memory, the control and use of cognitive functioning, sensory and motor skills, speech, language, organizational skills, information processing, affect, social skills, or basic life functions. The term includes students who have received a traumatic brain injury.

(f) *Emotional Impairment*. As defined under federal law at 34 CFR § 300.8(c)(4), the student exhibits one or more of the following characteristics over a long period of time and to a marked degree that adversely affects educational performance: an inability to learn that cannot be explained by intellectual, sensory, or health factors; an inability to build or maintain satisfactory interpersonal relationships with peers and teachers; inappropriate types of behavior or feelings under normal circumstances; a general pervasive mood of unhappiness or depression; or a tendency to develop physical symptoms or fears associated with personal or school problems. The determination of disability shall not be made solely because the student's behavior violates the school's discipline code, because the student is involved with a state court or social service agency, or because the student is socially maladjusted, unless the Team determines that the student has a serious emotional disturbance.

(g) *Communication Impairment.* The capacity to use expressive and/or receptive language is significantly limited, impaired, or delayed and is exhibited by difficulties in one or more of the following areas: speech, such as articulation and/or voice; conveying, understanding, or using spoken, written, or symbolic language. The term may include a student with impaired articulation, stuttering, language impairment, or voice impairment if such impairment adversely affects the student's educational performance.

(h) *Physical Impairment.* The physical capacity to move, coordinate actions, or perform physical activities is significantly limited, impaired, or delayed and is exhibited by difficulties in one or more of the following areas: physical and motor tasks; independent movement; performing basic life functions. The term shall include severe orthopedic impairments or impairments caused by congenital anomaly, cerebral palsy, amputations, and fractures, if such impairment adversely affects a student's educational performance.

6

(i) *Health Impairment.* A chronic or acute health problem such that the physiological capacity to function is significantly limited or impaired and results in one or more of the following: limited strength, vitality, or alertness including a heightened alertness to environmental stimuli resulting in limited alertness with respect to the educational environment. The term shall include health impairments due to asthma, attention deficit disorder or attention deficit with hyperactivity disorder, diabetes, epilepsy, a heart condition, hemophilia, lead poisoning, leukemia, nephritis, rheumatic fever, and sickle cell anemia, if such health impairment adversely affects a student's educational performance.

(j) *Specific Learning Disability.* The term means a disorder in one or more of the basic psychological processes involved in understanding or in using language, spoken or written, that may manifest itself in an imperfect ability to listen, think speak, read, write, spell, or to do mathematical calculations. Use of the term shall meet all federal requirements given in federal law at 34 CFR §§ 300.8(c)(10) and 300.309.

(8) *District or school district* shall mean a Massachusetts municipal school department or regional school district, acting through its school committee or superintendent of schools; a county agricultural school, acting through its board of trustees or superintendent/director; and any other Massachusetts public school established by statute, certificate, or charter, acting through its governing board or director. School districts have programmatic and financial responsibility in accordance with the procedures of 603 CMR 28.10.

(9) *Eligible student* shall mean a person aged three through 21 who has not attained a high school diploma or its equivalent, who has been determined by a Team to have a disability(ies), and as a consequence is unable to progress effectively in the general education program without specially designed instruction or is unable to access the general curriculum without a related service. An eligible student shall have the right to receive special education and any related services that are necessary for the student to benefit from special education or that are necessary for the student to access the general curriculum. In determining eligibility, the school district must thoroughly evaluate and provide a narrative description of the student's educational and developmental potential.

(10) *In-district program* shall mean a special education program operated in a public school building or other facility that provides educational services to students of comparable age, with and without disabilities.

(a) For young children ages three to five years, the term shall include programs provided by the public school in the eligible child's home if such setting has been identified by the Team as the natural or least restrictive setting to deliver the services on the child's IEP.

(b) For students of ages three through 21, the term shall include programs provided by the district in a home or hospital setting if such setting is required by the student's physician and the student would otherwise have been served in an in-district program.

(c) For students aged 14 years or older, when the Team has determined that a vocational program is appropriate, work settings shall be considered in-district programs if such programs offer ongoing opportunities for students to interact with community members and/or other workers without disabilities engaging in similar activities.

(d) A program operated solely by an individual, not for profit corporation or agency, or proprietary corporation shall not be considered an in-district program unless it is located within a public school building.

(11) *Individualized Education Program (IEP)* shall mean a written statement, developed and approved in accordance with federal special education law in a form established by the Department that identifies a student's special education needs and describes the services a school district shall provide to meet those needs.

(12) *Least restrictive environment (LRE)* shall mean the educational placement that assures that, to the maximum extent appropriate, students with disabilities, including students in public or private institutions or other care facilities, are educated with students who are not disabled, and that special classes, separate schooling, or other removal of students with disabilities from the general education environment occurs only when the nature or severity of the student's disability is such that education in regular classes with the use of supplementary aids and services cannot be achieved satisfactorily.

(13) *Notice* shall mean the notice and content required in accordance with the federal special education law whenever the school district proposes or refuses to initiate or change the identification, evaluation, or educational placement or the provision of special education services to the student.

(14) *Out-of-district program* shall mean a special education program located in a building or facility outside of the general education environment that provides educational services primarily to students with disabilities and shall include all programs approved under 603 CMR 28.09. Such program may be operated by a private organization or individual, a public school district, or a collaborative.

(15) *Parent* shall mean father or mother. For purposes of special educational decision-making, parent shall mean father, mother, legal guardian, person acting as a parent of the child, foster parent, or an educational surrogate parent appointed in accordance with federal law. Legal authority of the parent shall transfer to the student when the student reaches 18 years of age.

(16) *Program school* shall mean the school in which the student is enrolled according to the provisions of M.G.L. c. 71, § 89 (charter schools); M.G.L. c. 71, § 94 (Commonwealth of Massachusetts virtual schools); M.G.L. c. 74 (vocational schools); M.G.L. c. 76, § 12A (Metco) or M.G.L. c. 76, § 12B (school choice), and shall not include schools approved under 603 CMR 28.09 or institutional school programs as described in 603 CMR 28.06(9).

(17) *Progress effectively in the general education program* shall mean to make documented growth in the acquisition of knowledge and skills, including social/emotional development,

within the general education program, with or without accommodations, according to chronological age and developmental expectations, the individual educational potential of the student, and the learning standards set forth in the Massachusetts Curriculum Frameworks and the curriculum of the district. The general education program includes preschool and early childhood programs offered by the district, academic and non-academic offerings of the district, and vocational programs and activities.

(18) *Related services* shall have the meaning set forth in federal special education law at 34 CFR § 300.34. Individuals providing interpreting services for students who are deaf or hard of hearing shall be registered with the Massachusetts Commission for the Deaf and Hard of Hearing.

(19) *State agency* shall mean a Massachusetts state agency.

(20) *Special education* shall mean specially designed instruction to meet the unique needs of the eligible student or related services necessary to access the general curriculum and shall include the programs and services set forth in state and federal special education law.

(21) *Team* shall mean a group of persons, meeting participant requirements of federal special education law as provided at 34 CFR §§ 300.321 and 300.116(a)(1), who, together, discuss evaluation results, determine eligibility, develop or modify an IEP, or determine placement.

603 CMR 28.03. School District Administration and Personnel

(1) *General Responsibilities of the School District.*

(a) *General.* Each school district shall provide or arrange for the provision of special education and related services for eligible students in accordance with the provisions of state and federal law and regulation.

1. The school district shall provide training to all school district staff, including general and special educators, administrators, and paraprofessionals, on the requirements of special education.

2. The school district shall provide such staff training in analyzing and accommodating diverse learning needs of all students in the general education classroom.

3. The school district shall provide such staff training in methods of collaboration among teachers, paraprofessionals, and teacher assistants to accommodate diverse learning needs.

4. The district shall conduct, in cooperation with the parent advisory council, at least one workshop annually within the school district on the rights of students and their parents and guardians under state and federal special education laws.

(b) *Facilities.* The school district shall provide facilities and classrooms for eligible students to maximize the inclusion of such students into the life of the school. Facilities and classrooms serving only students with disabilities shall be at least equal in all physical respects to the average standards of general education facilities and classrooms. Resource rooms and separate classrooms for students with disabilities shall be given the same priority as general education programs for access to and use of instructional and other space in public schools in order to minimize the separation or stigmatization of eligible students.

1. All eligible students shall have access to school facilities including, but not limited to, those areas necessary to implement the student's IEP.

2. School districts shall provide whatever equipment and make whatever physical adaptations are necessary to comply with this provision, including acoustical and lighting treatments to remove physical communication barriers for students who are deaf or hard of hearing.

3. The Department may make unannounced inspections of facilities.

4. The following examples illustrate aspects of this requirement and shall not be construed as limiting or defining its scope:

(i) Placing a classroom serving only older students with disabilities in a part of the school building in which all the classrooms are occupied by elementary school students would violate the requirements of 603 CMR 28.03(1)(b).

(ii) Placing a sign saying "special class" on the front of a substantially separate classroom would violate the requirements of 603 CMR 28.03(1)(b).

(iii) Placing all special education facilities together in one part of a school building would violate the requirements of 603 CMR 28.03(1)(b).

(iv) Moving classrooms of students with disabilities to locations apart from the general education program because of financial or construction considerations violates the requirements of 603 CMR 28.03(1)(b).

(c) *Change of residence.*

1. When an eligible student or student's family changes residence from one Massachusetts school district to another, the last IEP written by the former school district and accepted by the parent shall be provided in a comparable setting without delay until a new IEP is developed and accepted.

2. If a student found eligible in another state moves to Massachusetts, the new Massachusetts district of residence shall provide the student with a free appropriate public education, including special education services comparable to those in the IEP from the former state, in consultation with the parents, until the Massachusetts district determines if it will accept the finding of eligibility and/or the current IEP developed for the student in the former state of residence. If the Massachusetts district determines that the finding of eligibility and the IEP developed for the student continues to accurately represent the needs of the student, then the Massachusetts district shall continue to implement the IEP. If the Massachusetts district determines that a new evaluation is necessary to determine continued eligibility or services, or a parent or another person concerned with the child's development requests an evaluation, the district shall immediately provide written notice to the parents as required under 603 CMR 28.04(1).

(d) *Preschool Screening.* Each school district shall conduct screening for three and four year olds and for all children who are of age to enter kindergarten. Such screening shall be designed to review a child's development and to assist in identification of those children who should be referred for an evaluation to determine eligibility for special education services.

1. The school district shall submit information to the Department describing the screening program and its elements as part of the local special education plan, when so requested.

2. Participation in the screening program for three and four year olds shall be optional on the part of the parents.

(e) *Private Schools at Private Expense.* Nothing in 603 CMR 28.00 shall be construed to limit the rights of parents to have their children educated at private schools, completely at private expense. To the extent that public school districts provide and pay for special education services for eligible students enrolled in private schools at private expense, the following requirements shall apply:

1. Each school district shall provide special education designed to meet the needs of eligible students who are attending private schools at private expense and whose parents reside in the jurisdiction of the school district. The school district shall provide to such students genuine opportunities to participate in the public school special education program consistent with state constitutional limitations.

2. The school district shall provide or arrange for the provision of evaluation services and an IEP for any eligible private school student whose parent resides in the jurisdiction of the school district. The evaluation may take place in the public school, the private school, or an appropriate contracted facility, provided that the school district shall ensure that a representative of the student's

private school is invited to participate as a member of the Team pursuant to 603 CMR 28.05.

3. The school district shall provide or arrange for the provision of the special education described by the student's IEP provided that school districts shall ensure that special education services funded with state or local funds are provided in a public school facility or other public or neutral site. When services are provided using only federal funds, services may be provided on private school grounds.

4. Special education provided by the school district to a private school student shall be comparable in quality, scope, and opportunity for participation to that provided to public school students with needs of equal importance. Programs in which both public and private school students participate may not include classes that are separated on the basis of school enrollment or the religious affiliation of the students.

(2) *Administrator of Special Education.* Each school district shall appoint a person to be its Administrator of Special Education. The Administrator shall supervise all special education for the school district and shall ensure compliance with all federal and state special education laws. As appropriate, and in accordance with the requirements of M.G.L. c. 71B, § 3A, the Administrator may designate other school district personnel to carry out some of the duties of the Administrator.

(3) *Responsibilities of the School Principal.*

(a) *Instructional support.* The principal shall implement the plan developed and adopted by the district to ensure that efforts have been made or will be made to meet the needs of diverse learners in the general education program. As part of his/her responsibilities, the principal shall promote instructional practices responsive to student needs and shall ensure that adequate instructional support is available for students and teachers. Instructional support shall include remedial instruction for students, consultative services for teachers, availability of reading instruction at the elementary level, appropriate services for linguistic minority students, and other services consistent with effective educational practices and the requirements of M.G.L. c. 71B, § 2. The principal may consult with the Administrator of Special Education regarding accommodations and interventions for students. Such efforts and their results shall be documented and placed in the student record. Additionally, if an individual student is referred for an evaluation to determine eligibility for special education, the principal shall ensure that documentation on the use of instructional support services for the student is provided as part of the evaluation information reviewed by the Team when determining eligibility.

(b) *Coordination with special education.* The principal with the assistance of the Administrator of Special Education shall coordinate the delivery and supervision of special education services within each school building.

(c) *Educational services in home or hospital.* Upon receipt of a physician's written order verifying that any student enrolled in a public school or placed by the public school in a private setting must remain at home or in a hospital on a day or overnight basis, or any combination of both, for medical reasons and for a period of not less than fourteen school days in any school year, the principal shall arrange for provision of educational services in the home or hospital. Such services shall be provided with sufficient frequency to allow the student to continue his or her educational program, as long as such services do not interfere with the medical needs of the student. The principal shall coordinate such services with the Administrator of Special Education for eligible students. Such educational services shall not be considered special education unless the student has been determined eligible for such services, and the services include services on the student's IEP.

(4) *Standard Procedures and Forms.* The Department may prepare standard forms to assist school districts in meeting state and federal special education requirements.

(a) The school district shall use forms that, at a minimum, contain the elements of those forms issued by the Department.

(b) School districts shall maintain required data on eligible students receiving special education services, shall ensure that such data remains current and accurate, and, on request, shall report such data in the form required by the Department and in accordance with 603 CMR 10.00 and the guidelines for reporting student and financial data.

(5) *Waivers.* A school district, collaborative, or approved special education school program may submit in writing a proposal for approval by the Department for the satisfaction of any requirement in 603 CMR 28.00 in a manner different from that specified in 603 CMR 28.00. The Department may approve such proposal if it shows substantial promise of contributing to improvements in the methods for meeting the goals of 603 CMR 28.00 and if such proposal does not conflict with any provision of law. No such proposal shall be implemented until approved by the Department.

(6) *Enforcement: Withholding of Funds.* The Department may withhold funds for special education from cities, towns, school districts, or private schools or agencies that do not comply with regulations or statutes related to special education or do not carry out plans for such compliance within a reasonable period of time; provided, however, that nothing in 603 CMR 28.03(6) shall be construed to prevent the Department from withholding state and federal funds to the extent it deems necessary consistent with state and federal law, or from taking such other enforcement action as may be authorized by law.

603 CMR 28.04. Referral and Evaluation

(1) *Referral for Initial Evaluation.* A student may be referred for an evaluation by a parent or any person in a caregiving or professional position concerned with the student's development.

(a) When a student is referred for an evaluation to determine eligibility for special education, the school district shall send written notice to the student's parent(s) within five school days of receipt of the referral.

(b) The notice required by 603 CMR 28.04(1)(a) shall meet all of the content requirements set forth in M.G.L. c. 71B, § 3, and in federal law and shall seek the consent of a parent for the evaluation to occur, and provide the parents with the opportunity to express any concerns or provide information on the student's skills or abilities.

(c) School districts shall provide the student's parents with an opportunity to consult with the Special Education Administrator or his/her designee to discuss the reasons for the referral, the content of the proposed evaluation, and the evaluators used.

(d) Upon referral, school districts shall evaluate children who are two and a half years of age and who may be receiving services through an early intervention program. An initial evaluation shall be conducted in order to ensure that if such child is found eligible, special education services begin promptly at age three.

(2) *Initial Evaluation.* Upon consent of a parent, the school district shall provide or arrange for the evaluation of the student by a multidisciplinary team within 30 school days. The assessments used shall be adapted to the age of the student and all testing shall meet the evaluation requirements set out in state and federal law. The school district shall ensure that appropriately credentialed and trained specialists administer all assessments.

(a) *Required assessments.*

1. An assessment in all areas related to the suspected disability.

2. An educational assessment by a representative of the school district, including

(i) a history of the student's educational progress in the general curriculum. Such assessment shall include information provided by a teacher(s) with current knowledge regarding the student's specific abilities in relation to learning standards of the

Massachusetts Curriculum Frameworks and the district curriculum; and

(ii) an assessment of the student's attention skills, participation behaviors, communication skills, memory, and social relations with groups, peers, and adults.

(iii) The school district shall also thoroughly evaluate and provide a narrative description of the student's educational and developmental potential.

(iv) When a child is being assessed to determine eligibility for services at age three, an observation of the child's interactions in the child's natural environment or early intervention program is strongly encouraged.

(v) For children who are receiving early intervention services, school districts are encouraged to use current and appropriate assessments from early intervention teams, whenever possible, to avoid duplicate testing.

(b) *Optional assessments*. The Administrator of Special Education may recommend or a parent may request one or more of the following:

1. A comprehensive health assessment by a physician that identifies medical problems or constraints that may affect the student's education. The school nurse may add additional relevant health information from the student's school health records.

2. A psychological assessment by a licensed school psychologist, licensed psychologist, or licensed educational psychologist, including an individual psychological examination.

3. A home assessment that may be conducted by a nurse, psychologist, social worker, guidance or adjustment counselor, or teacher and includes information on pertinent family history and home situation and may include a home visit, with the agreement of a parent.

(c) *Reports of assessment results*. Each person conducting an assessment shall summarize in writing the procedures employed, the results, and the diagnostic impression, and shall define in detail and in educationally relevant and common terms, the student's needs, offering explicit means of meeting them. The assessor may recommend appropriate types of placements, but shall not recommend specific classrooms or schools. Summaries of assessments shall be completed prior to discussion by the Team and, upon request, shall be made available to the parents at least two days in advance of the Team discussion at the meeting occurring pursuant to 603 CMR 28.05(1).

(3) *Annual reviews and three-year reevaluations*. The school district shall review the IEPs and the progress of each eligible student at least annually. Additionally, every three years, or sooner if necessary, the school district shall, with parental consent, conduct a full three-year reevaluation consistent with the requirements of federal law.

(4) *Unscheduled evaluations for medical reasons*. If, in the opinion of the student's physician, an eligible student is likely to remain at home, in a hospital, or in a pediatric nursing home for medical reasons and for more than 60 school days in any school year, the Administrator of Special Education shall, without undue delay, convene a Team to consider evaluation needs and, if appropriate, to amend the existing IEP or develop a new IEP suited to the student's unique circumstances.

(5) *Independent education evaluations*. Upon receipt of evaluation results, if a parent disagrees with an initial evaluation or reevaluation completed by the school district, then the parent may request an independent education evaluation.

(a) All independent education evaluations shall be conducted by qualified persons who are registered, certified, licensed or otherwise approved and who abide by the rates set by the state agency responsible for setting such rates. Unique circumstances of the student may justify an individual assessment rate that is higher than that normally allowed.

(b) The parent may obtain an independent education evaluation at private expense at any time.

(c) *Public Funding of Independent Education Evaluations*. When the parent requests public funding for an independent education evaluation, the district shall abide by the following provisions for a sliding fee scale:

1. If the student is eligible for free or reduced cost lunch or is in the custody of a state agency with an Educational Surrogate Parent appointed in accordance with federal law, then the school district shall provide, at full public expense, an independent education evaluation that is equivalent to the types of assessments done by the school district. No additional documentation of family financial status is required from the parent.

2. If the family financial status is not known, the district shall offer the parent information about the sliding fee scale and the opportunity to provide family income information to determine if the family may be eligible for public funding of all or part of the costs of an independent education evaluation. Provision of financial information by the family is completely voluntary on the part of the family. The lack of financial information provided by the family will disqualify the family from such additional public funding of all or part of the costs of an independent education evaluation under 603 CMR 28.04(5)(c) but shall not limit the rights of parents to request public funding under 603 CMR 28.04(5)(d).

3. If the family agrees to provide financial information, such information shall include anticipated annual income of the family, including all sources of income and verifying documents. Financial information shall be reviewed by the district, shall be kept confidential during review by the district, shall not be copied or maintained in any form at the district except to note that information was provided and reviewed and met or did not meet sliding fee scale standards. Financial documents shall be promptly returned to the parent upon the district's determination of financial income status.

4. The district shall consider family size and family income information in relation to Federal Poverty Guidelines and shall contribute public funds to the costs of the independent education evaluation according to the following standards:

(i) If the family income is equal to or less than 400% of the federal poverty guidelines, the district shall pay 100% of the costs of an independent education evaluation.

(ii) If the family income is between 400% and 500% of the federal poverty guidelines, the district shall pay 75% of the costs of an independent education evaluation.

(iii) If the family income is between 500% and 600% of the federal poverty guidelines, the district shall pay 50% of the costs of an independent education evaluation.

(iv) If the family income is over 600% of the federal poverty guidelines, the district shall have no obligation to cost-share with the parent.

5. When the parent seeks and receives public funding for an independent education evaluation under these provisions, the parent may request independent assessments in one, more than one, or all of the areas assessed by the school district.

6. The right to this publicly funded independent education evaluation under 603 CMR 28.04(5)(c) continues for 16 months from the date of the evaluation with which the parent disagrees.

(d) If the parent is requesting an independent education evaluation in an area not assessed by the school district, the student does not meet income eligibility standards, or the family chooses not to provide financial documentation to the district establishing family income level, the school district shall respond in accordance with the requirements of federal law. Within five school days, the district shall either agree to pay for the independent education evaluation or proceed to the Bureau of Special Education Appeals to show that its evaluation was comprehensive and appropriate. If the Bureau of Special Education Appeals finds that the school district's evaluation was comprehensive and appropriate, then the school district shall not be obligated to pay for the independent education evaluation requested by the parent.

(e) Whenever possible, the independent education evaluation shall be completed and a written report sent no later than 30 days after the date the parent requests the independent education evaluation. If publicly funded, the report shall be sent to the parents and to the school district. The independent evaluator shall be requested to provide a report that summarizes, in writing, procedures, assessments, results, and diagnostic impressions as well as educationally relevant recommendations for meeting identified needs of the student. The independent evaluator may recommend appropriate types of placements but shall not recommend specific classrooms or schools.

(f) Within ten school days from the time the school district receives the report of the independent education evaluation, the Team shall reconvene and consider the independent education evaluation and whether a new or amended IEP is appropriate.

603 CMR 28.05. The Team Process and Development of the IEP

(1) *Convening the Team.* Within 45 school working days after receipt of a parent's written consent to an initial evaluation or reevaluation, the school district shall: provide an evaluation; convene a Team meeting to review the evaluation data, determine whether the student requires special education and, if required, develop an IEP in accordance with state and federal laws; and provide the parents with two copies of the proposed IEP and proposed placement, except that the proposal of placement may be delayed according to the provisions of 603 CMR 28.06(2)(e); or, if the Team determines that the student is not eligible for special education, the school district shall send a written explanation of the finding that the student is not eligible. The evaluation assessments shall be completed within 30 school working days after receipt of parental consent for evaluation. Summaries of such assessments shall be completed so as to ensure their availability to parents at least two days prior to the Team meeting. If consent is received within 30 to 45 school working days before the end of the school year, the school district shall ensure that a Team meeting is scheduled so as to allow for the provision of a proposed IEP or written notice of the finding that the student is not eligible no later than 14 days after the end of the school year.

6

(2) *Determinations of the Team.*

(a) *Eligibility Determination.* The Team shall examine the evaluative data, including information provided by the parent, and make one of the following determinations:

1. The student is eligible. If the student has one or more of the disabilities defined at 603 CMR 28.02(7) and if, as a result of the disability(ies), the student is unable to progress effectively in the general education program without the provision of specially designed instruction, or is unable to access the general curriculum without the provision of one or more related services, the Team shall determine that the student is eligible.

(i) Consistent with state and federal special education law, the Team shall establish whether a student has a disability(ies) as defined in 603 CMR 28.02(7), determine the type(s) of disability(ies) and shall ensure that the student's inability to progress is a result of the disability(ies) and not a result of an inability to meet the school discipline code, limited English proficiency, social maladjustment, or lack of instruction in reading or math.

(ii) Once eligibility has been determined, the type of disability of the student shall not be used to provide a basis for labeling or stigmatizing the student. Additionally, the type of disability shall not define the needs of the student and shall in no way limit the services, programs, or inclusion opportunities provided to the student.

(iii) If the Team determines that the student is an eligible student, the Team shall develop an individualized education program (IEP).

2. The student is not eligible. If the Team determines that the student is not eligible, the Team chairperson shall record the reason for such finding, list the meeting participants, and provide written notice to the parent of their rights in accordance with federal requirements within ten days of the Team meeting.

(b) *Evaluation Information is Inconclusive.* If the Team finds the evaluation information insufficient to develop an IEP, the Team, with parental consent, may agree to an extended evaluation period.

1. The extended evaluation period shall not be used to deny programs or services determined to be necessary by the Team. If, prior to the extended evaluation, the Team determines that sufficient information is available to identify some necessary objectives and services, the Team shall write a partial IEP that, if accepted by the parent, shall be immediately implemented by the district while the extended evaluation is occurring.

2. The extended evaluation period shall not be used to allow additional time to complete the required assessments under 603 CMR 28.04(2)(a).

3. If the parent consents to an extended evaluation, the Team shall document its findings and determine what evaluation time period is necessary and the types of information needed to develop an IEP, if appropriate. The Team may decide to meet at intervals during the extended evaluation, but in all cases shall reconvene promptly to develop or complete an IEP when the evaluation is complete.

4. The extended evaluation may extend longer than one week, but shall not exceed eight school weeks.

5. The extended evaluation shall not be considered a placement.

(3) *Developing the IEP.* Upon determining that the student is eligible for special education, the Team shall develop an IEP using the evaluation data to guide development of goals and objectives for the student.

(a) Parent disagrees with evaluation and seeks an independent education evaluation. If a parent disagrees with the evaluation results, the Team may, with the agreement of the parent, delay writing some or all of the IEP until an independent education evaluation can be completed.

(b) If the Team writes a partial IEP, a parent may consent to the proposed partial program prior to completion of the full IEP. In such case, the partial program shall be implemented immediately.

(c) The IEP shall be completed using the standard IEP format provided by the Department. If the Team members are unable to agree on the IEP, the Team chairperson shall state the elements of the IEP proposed by the school district.

(4) *Contents of the IEP.* Upon determining that the student requires special education and based upon the evaluative data, the Team shall write an IEP for the student and decide the student's placement. The IEP shall describe the special education and related services that the student requires and shall include all elements required under federal and state law.

(a) The IEP shall include specially designed instruction to meet the needs of the individual student and related services that are necessary to allow the student to benefit from the specially designed instruction, or may consist solely of related services that are necessary to allow the student to access the general curriculum, consistent with federal and state requirements.

(b) The Team shall carefully consider the general curriculum, the learning standards of the Massachusetts Curriculum Frameworks, the curriculum of the district, and shall include specially designed instruction or related services in the IEP designed to enable the student to progress effectively in the content areas of the general curriculum.

(c) For any student approaching graduation or the age of twenty-two, the Team shall determine whether the student is likely to require continuing services from adult human service agencies. In such circumstances, the Administrator of Special Education shall make a referral to the Bureau of Transitional Planning in the

Executive Office of Health and Human Services in accordance with the requirements of M.G.L. c. 71B, § 12A through C (known as Chapter 688).

(d) The daily duration of the student's program shall be equal to that of the regular school day, unless the Team states that a different duration is necessary to provide a free appropriate public education to the student. In such case, the Team shall specify the daily duration of the program, and the Team shall state on the IEP the reason for such different duration.

1. An extended year program may be identified if the student has demonstrated or is likely to demonstrate substantial regression in his or her learning skills and/or substantial difficulty in relearning such skills if an extended program is not provided.

2. If residential services are required, the IEP must clearly specify the reasons for such determination and how such services will be coordinated with the day education services provided to the student. Additionally, the goals and services on the student's IEP must reflect the comprehensive nature of the educational program required.

3. If a longer program is required, the student's IEP must specify why a longer program is necessary.

4. Camping or recreation programs provided solely for recreational purposes and with no corresponding IEP goals or specially designed instruction shall not be considered extended year programs.

(5) *Transportation.* The Team shall determine whether the student requires transportation because of his or her disability in order to benefit from special education.

(a) *Regular Transportation.* If the student does not require transportation as a result of his or her disability, then transportation shall be provided in the same manner as it would be provided for a student without disabilities. In such case, the IEP shall note that the student receives regular transportation, and if the school district provides transportation to similarly situated students without disabilities, the eligible student shall also receive transportation.

1. If regular transportation is noted on the student's IEP and the student is placed by the school district in a program located at a school other than the school the student would have attended if not eligible for special education, the student is entitled to receive transportation services to such program.

2. If regular transportation is noted on the student's IEP and the student is enrolled by his or her parents in a private school and receiving services under 603 CMR 28.03(1)(e), such student is not entitled to transportation services unless the school district provides transportation to students without disabilities attending such private school.

(b) *Special Transportation.* If the Team determines that the student's disability requires transportation or specialized transportation arrangements in order to benefit from special education, the Team shall note on the student's IEP that the student requires special transportation. In such circumstances, transportation is a related service.

1. The Team shall determine necessary modifications, special equipment, assistance, need for qualified attendants on vehicles, and any particular precautions required by the student and shall document such determinations in the student's IEP. If specialized arrangements can be provided on regular transportation vehicles, the school district shall make such arrangements.

(i) The district shall arrange to have eligible students who use wheelchairs transported in vehicles that do not require such students to be removed from their wheelchairs in order to enter or leave the vehicles; provided, however, that this requirement shall not be applicable where a Team or the student's physician recommends that the student regularly transfer in and out of conventional vehicles to or from a wheelchair for therapeutic or for independence training reasons.

(ii) The Team shall specify whether the student requires assistance in or out of the home, on or off of the vehicle, and in or out of the school. If such assistance is specified, the district shall ensure that it is provided.

(iii) The Team shall specify if the student has a particular need or problem that may cause difficulties during transportation, such as seizures, a tendency for motion sickness, behavioral concerns, or communication disabilities.

2. If special transportation is noted on the student's IEP, the student is entitled to receive transportation services to any program provided by the public school and in which the student participates.

3. If special transportation is noted on the student's IEP and the student is enrolled by his or her parents in a private school and receiving services under 603 CMR 28.03(1)(e), the school district's obligation to provide transportation shall be limited to transportation services within the geographic boundaries of the school district.

(c) In no event shall a school district allow transportation considerations to influence, modify, or determine the educational program required by any student in need of special education.

(6) *Determination of Placement.* At the Team meeting, after the IEP has been fully developed, the Team shall determine the appropriate placement to deliver the services on the student's IEP. Unless the student's IEP requires some other arrangement, the student shall be educated in the school that he or she would attend if the student did not require special education.

(a) Identification by the Team of placement shall proceed in accordance with the options delineated in 603 CMR 28.06.

(b) Lack of an identified placement shall not delay the proposal of the IEP to the parent following the Team meeting.

(7) *Parent Response to Proposed IEP and Proposed Placement.* Immediately following the development of the IEP, and within 45 school working days after receipt of the parent's written consent to an initial evaluation or reevaluation, the district shall provide the parents with two copies of the proposed IEP and proposed placement along with the required notice, except that the proposal of placement may be delayed according to the provisions of 603 CMR 28.06(2)(e) in a limited number of cases.

(a) No later than 30 days after receipt of the proposed IEP and proposed placement, the parents shall:

1. Accept or reject the IEP in whole or in part; request a meeting to discuss the rejected portions of the IEP or the overall adequacy of the IEP; or if mutually agreed upon, accept an amended proposal; and

2. accept or reject the proposed placement.

(b) Upon parental response to the proposed IEP and proposed placement, the school district shall implement all accepted elements of the IEP without delay.

603 CMR 28.06. Placement and Service Options

(1) *Reporting.* The Department shall determine specific protocols for school districts to report level of services and placements made for eligible students. School districts shall use such protocols for the purposes of reporting information only. No reporting protocol shall be used as the basis for specifying services, delaying, or otherwise limiting services or programs for eligible students.

(2) *Determining placement.* At the Team meeting, after the IEP has been developed, the Team shall consider the identified needs of the student, the types of services required, and whether such services may be provided in a general education classroom with supplementary aids and/or services or in a separate classroom or school. The Team shall consider all aspects of the student's proposed special education program as specified in the student's IEP and determine the appropriate placement to provide the services. The Team shall determine if the student shall be served in an in-district placement or an out-of-district placement and shall determine the specific placement according to the following requirements:

(a) The decision regarding placement shall be based on the IEP, including the types of related services that are to be provided to the student, the type of settings in which those services are to be provided, the types of service providers, and the location at which the services are to be provided.

(b) The placement selected by the Team shall be the least restrictive environment consistent with the needs of the student. In selecting the least restrictive environment, consideration must be given to any potential harmful effect on the student or on the quality of services that the student needs.

(c) *Least restrictive environment (LRE).* The school district shall ensure that, to the maximum extent appropriate, students with disabilities are educated with students who do not have disabilities, and that special classes, separate schooling, or other removal of students with special needs from the general education program occurs only if the nature or severity of the disability is such that education in general education classes with the use of supplementary aids and services cannot be achieved satisfactorily.

(d) *In-district placement.* The placement decision made by the Team shall indicate the specific program setting in which services will be provided. The Team shall first consider in-district settings such as a general education classroom, a resource setting, a separate classroom, a work setting, a vocational school program, and/or another type of setting identified by the Team as appropriate and able to provide the services on the IEP in a natural or less restrictive environment. If an in-district setting is able to deliver the services on the IEP, the Team shall identify such placement and include such determination with the proposed IEP.

1. The school district shall determine specific instructional personnel and shall work jointly with the Team to arrange the specific classroom or school, in order to implement the placement decision and to assure that services begin promptly when parental consent to the IEP and placement has been received.

2. The school district shall not delay implementation of the IEP due to lack of classroom space or personnel, shall provide as many of the services on the accepted IEP as possible and shall immediately inform the parent in writing of any delayed services, reasons for delay, actions that the school district is taking to address the lack of space or personnel and shall offer alternative methods to meet the goals on the accepted IEP. Upon agreement of a parent, the school district shall implement alternative methods immediately until the lack of space or personnel issues are resolved.

(e) *Placement meeting.* Upon developing the IEP, if the needs of the student and the services identified by the Team are complex, and the Team is considering an initial placement out-of-district or a different setting for a student who has been served in an out-of-district program, the school district may schedule a separate Team meeting to determine placement. The placement meeting shall meet the participant requirements of federal special education law as outlined at 34 CFR § 300.116(a)(1) and shall be held within ten school days following the meeting at which the Team developed the IEP. At the request of the parent, the placement meeting may be held at a later date.

1. Any other school district that may be financially or programmatically responsible for the student shall be invited to participate in the placement meeting and shall receive notice of such meeting at least five school days prior to the meeting. The Department or other state agency involved with the student may designate a representative to participate in the placement meeting.

2. Prior to the placement meeting, the school district and parent shall investigate in-district and out-of-district placement options in light of the student's needs and identified services required.

3. At the placement meeting, the district and the parent shall report on the investigation of in-district and out-of-district options. If an in-district program can provide the services on the IEP, such program shall be identified at the placement meeting and provided by the district; if not, the placement Team shall identify an out-of-district placement.

(f) *Out-of-district placement.* If an out-of-district placement is designated by the Team, the Team shall state the basis for its conclusion that education of the student in a less restrictive environment with the use of supplementary aids and services could not be achieved satisfactorily.

1. Students in out-of-district placements shall be entitled to the full protections of state and federal special education law and regulation. Out-of-district options include, but are not limited to, special education schools approved under 603 CMR 28.09.

2. When an out-of-district placement is identified by the Team, the determination shall ensure that the student's placement is as close as possible to the student's home. The Team shall not recommend a day or residential school program outside of the city, town, or school district in which the student resides unless there is no suitable program within the city, town, or school district. The school district shall implement the placement decision of the Team and shall include consulting with personnel of the school contemplated to provide the program for the student to determine that the school is able to provide the services on the student's IEP. The Team shall not recommend a specific program unless it is assured that the adequacy of said program has been evaluated and the program can provide the services required by the student's IEP. Team identification of specific schools, however, shall not supercede LRE considerations, IEP considerations, or requirements to give preference to approved programs as provided in 603 CMR 28.06(3)(d).

(3) *General requirements for out-of-district placements.* For the duration of any student's placement in an out-of-district setting in Massachusetts, the Administrator of Special Education shall make a good faith effort to ensure that the student's IEP is being appropriately implemented and that service delivery in the out-of-district setting is aimed at assisting the student to meet the goals identified on the student's IEP.

(a) *Program oversight:* The Department shall determine that programs approved under 603 CMR 28.09 have appropriate policies, procedures, and appropriately credentialled staff as may be necessary to provide special education services to publicly funded students. The Department shall investigate and resolve concerns raised through the Problem Resolution System of the Department. The approval activities and oversight of the Department for the approved programs does not relieve school districts of their responsibility to monitor the programs of individual students enrolled in the approved programs by the school districts. The approval activities and oversight of the Department for the approved programs does not make the Department a guarantor or insurer for services or programs provided to individual students.

(b) *Individual student program oversight:* The school district is required to monitor the provision of services to and the programs of individual students placed out-of-district. Documentation of monitoring plans and all actual monitoring shall be placed in the files of every eligible student who has been placed out-of-district. To the extent that this monitoring requires site visits, such site visits shall be documented and placed in the students' files for review. The duty to monitor out-of-district placements cannot be delegated to parents or their agents, to the Department, or to the out-of-district placement. The school district may, however, contract directly with a person to conduct such monitoring.

(c) *Student right to full procedural protections:* School districts that place eligible students in out-of-district programs retain full responsibility for ensuring that the student is receiving all special education and related services in the student's IEP, as well as all procedural protections of law and regulation, including but not limited to those specified in 603 CMR 28.09. Any Team meetings conducted during the time that a student is enrolled in the out-of-district program shall be initiated by the school district in coordination with the out-of-district placement.

(d) *Preference to approved programs:* The school district shall, in all circumstances, first seek to place a student in a program approved by the Department pursuant to the requirements of 603 CMR 28.09. Preference shall also be given to approved programs located within the Commonwealth of Massachusetts if the choice of such program is consistent with the needs of the student and choice of such program complies with LRE requirements. No student in an out-of-state placement as of June 1, 2000 shall be required to transfer to a facility in Massachusetts unless such transfer is consistent with the student's IEP and the LRE requirements of the law. When an approved program is available to provide the services on the IEP, the district shall make such placement in the approved program in preference to any program not approved by the Department.

(e) *Use of unapproved programs:* If the Team is unable to identify an appropriate placement in an approved school, the Administrator of Special Education may request assistance from the Department. Such request shall be in writing and shall contain copies of all assessments from the evaluation or reevaluation. the complete referral package that had been sent to approved schools, a listing of all approved schools that had been considered, and the decision given by such schools to refuse admission. A school district that places a student in a program that has not been approved by the Department according to the requirements under 603 CMR 28.09 must ensure that such programs and services are provided in appropriate settings by appropriately credentialed staff able to deliver the services on the student's IEP. Students placed by the school district in such programs shall be entitled to the full protections of state and federal special education law and regulation, including but not limited to those protections specified in 603 CMR 28.09 and in 603 CMR 18.00. The following documentation is required and may be reviewed by the Department of Elementary and Secondary Education at any time:

1. *Search:* The Administrator of Special Education shall document the search for and unavailability of a program approved by the Department under 603 CMR 28.09. The Administrator shall place such documentation in the student record.

2. *Evaluation of facility:* The Administrator of Special Education or his/her designee shall thoroughly evaluate the appropriateness of any unapproved facility prior to placement of the student in such program. Such evaluation shall determine whether the unapproved facility can appropriately implement the student's IEP in a safe and educationally appropriate environment. Such evaluation shall additionally determine whether the unapproved facility can and will provide the student with all the rights that are accorded to the student under state and federal special education law. Such evaluation shall be documented in detail and placed in the student record for review. To the extent that this evaluation requires a site visit, such site visits shall be documented and placed in the student record for review. The duty to evaluate the appropriateness of any unapproved facility cannot be delegated to the parents or their agents or the proposed unapproved facility. The school district may, however, contract directly with a person to conduct such evaluation activities.

3. *School district approval to operate a private school in Massachusetts:* If services in an unapproved program are provided in a school setting, the Administrator of Special Education must ensure that such school has received approval from the local school committee under M.G.L. c. 76, § 1 and that a copy of such approval is retained in the student record.

4. *Notification to the department:* Prior to placement, the Administrator shall notify the Department of the intent to place the student and the name and location of the proposed placement.

(i) Pursuant to the requirements for Compliance, Reporting and Auditing for Human and Social Services at 808 CMR 1.00, the Administrator shall obtain pricing forms required to set program prices for programs receiving publicly funded students. Such pricing forms shall be completed by the proposed placement and shall document that the price proposed for the student's tuition is the lowest price charged for similar services to any student in that program.

(ii) The Administrator shall forward the notice of proposed placement and completed pricing forms to the Department along with the information on the proposed terms of the contract that will govern such placement. The Department shall notify the district within ten days if there are any objections to such placement, and if none, shall forward the pricing forms to the state agency responsible for setting program prices. Such agency shall, according to its procedures, set an approved price for publicly funded students and shall forward such information to the school district making the placement.

(iii) The Department reserves the right to request any additional documentation or information regarding student placements in educational settings not approved under 603 CMR 28.09, including but not limited to documentation of a monitoring plan pursuant to 603 CMR 28.06(3)(b) and a plan detailing the time and resources necessary to establish or locate a program able to meet the student's needs in the city, town or school district where the student resides or in an approved program.

5. *Out-of-state:* If such services are provided in a placement outside of Massachusetts, and such school has not received approval by the Department under 603 CMR 28.09, the Administrator of Special Education must ensure that such school has received approval from the host state. No placements of Massachusetts students may be made in out-of-state programs without approval of the program by the host state or, if the host state does not have an approval process, then the program must provide documentation of reputable accreditation. The requirements of 603 CMR 28.06(3)(b through e), apply to all such placements.

6. *Department review:* The Department shall periodically, and at its discretion, review all required documentation and if such documentation is not available or is not appropriate, the Department may take action pursuant to 603 CMR 28.03(7). Such a review, however, does not make the Department a guarantor or insurer for services or programs provided to individual students.

(f) *Written contracts:* School districts shall enter into written contracts with all out-of-district placements. Each such contract shall include, but not be limited to, the following terms:

1. The out-of-district placement shall comply with all elements of the IEP for the student and shall provide, in writing, to the Administrator of Special Education detailed documentation of such compliance through completion of required student progress reports.

2. The out-of-district placement shall allow the placing school district to monitor and evaluate the education of the student and shall make available, upon request, any records pertaining to the student to authorized school personnel from the school district and the Department in accordance with 603 CMR 23.00: *Student Records*.

3. The out-of-district placement shall allow the placing school district and/or the Department to conduct announced and unannounced site visits and to review all documents relating to the provision of special education services to Massachusetts students at public expense. Access to documents for the placing school district shall include general documents available to the public, documents specifically related to the student placed by such district, and other documents only to the extent they are necessary to verify and evaluate education services provided at public expense.

4. The out-of-district placement shall afford publicly-funded students all the substantive and procedural rights held by eligible students, including but not limited to those specified in 603 CMR 28.09, and shall comply with all other applicable requirements of 603 CMR 28.00 and applicable policy statements and directives issued by the Department.

5. No school district shall contract with any out-of-district placement that discriminates on the grounds of race, color, religion,

sexual orientation, or national origin, or that discriminates against qualified persons with disabilities.

(4) *Programs for older students.* The school district shall ensure that options are available for older students, particularly those eligible students of ages 18 through 21 years. Such options shall include continuing education; developing skills to access community services; developing independent living skills; developing skills for self-management of medical needs; and developing skills necessary for seeking, obtaining, and maintaining jobs. Such programs may have an educational and/or vocational focus and shall be considered in-district programs if the program is operated by the public school and offers the student ongoing opportunities to interact with students or young adults without disabilities. Participation in such options for students younger than age 18 shall not relieve the school district of its obligation to ensure that students have access to instruction in the general curriculum.

(5) *Access to district programs.* All students receiving special education, regardless of placement, shall have an equal opportunity to participate in and, if appropriate, receive credit for the vocational, supportive, or remedial services that may be available as part of the general education program as well as the non-academic and extracurricular programs of the school.

(6) *Instructional grouping requirements.* When eligible students aged five and older receive special education services for some or all of the school day outside of the general education environment, the school district shall make every effort to maintain the student's access to the general curriculum and participation in the life of the school. The school district shall devote resources to develop the school district's capacity for serving such eligible students in less restrictive alternatives.

6

(a) Programs serving young children shall meet instructional grouping requirements of 603 CMR 28.06(7).

(b) The size and composition of instructional groupings for eligible students receiving services outside the general education classroom shall be compatible with the methods and goals stated in each student's IEP.

(c) Instructional grouping size requirements are maximum sizes and school districts are expected to exercise judgment in determining appropriate group size and supports for smaller instructional groups serving students with complex special needs. When eligible students are assigned to instructional groupings outside of the general education classroom for 60% or less of the students' school schedule, group size shall not exceed eight students with a certified special educator, 12 students if the certified special educator is assisted by one aide, and 16 students if the certified special educator is assisted by two aides.

(d) Eligible students served in settings that are substantially separate, serving solely students with disabilities for more than 60% of the students' school schedule, shall have instructional groupings that do not exceed eight students to one certified special educator or 12 students to a certified special educator and an aide.

(e) After the school year has begun, if instructional groups have reached maximum size as delineated in 603 CMR 28.06(6)(c) and (d), the Administrator of Special Education and the certified special educator(s) providing services in an instructional group may decide to increase the size of an instructional grouping by no more than two additional students if the additional students have compatible instructional needs and then can receive services in their neighborhood school. In such cases, the Administrator must provide written notification to the Department and the parents of all group members of the decision to increase the instructional group size and the reasons for such decision. Such increased instructional group sizes shall be in effect only for the year in which they are initiated. The district shall take all steps necessary to reduce the instructional groups to the sizes outlined in 603 CMR 28.06(6)(c) and (d) for subsequent years.

(f) The ages of the youngest and oldest student in any instructional grouping shall not differ by more than 48 months. A written request for approval of a wider age range may be made to the Department, which may approve such request.

(g) Instructional group sizes in all programs approved under 603 CMR 28.09 shall be limited to those outlined in 603 CMR 28.06(6)(d), and no such instructional groups shall have an age range greater than 48 months.

(7) *Programs for young children.* The school district shall ensure programs are available for eligible children three and four years of age. Such programs shall be developmentally appropriate and specially designed for children ages three and four years.

(a) The requirements of 603 CMR 28.00 shall apply to the extent that they can be adapted to reflect the fact that such children may not be receiving services in the public school.

(b) School districts are encouraged to accept referrals from the Department of Public Health, other agencies, and individuals for young children when or before the child turns two-and-one-half years old in order to ensure continuity of services and to ensure the development and implementation of an IEP for eligible children by the date of the child's third birthday in accordance with federal requirements.

(c) The school district may elect, consistent with federal requirements as outlined at 34 CFR § 300.323(b), to use the format and services of the Individualized Family Service Plan (IFSP), if appropriate, for an additional year as a means of transitioning eligible children to public school services.

(d) The Team may allow a child to remain in a program designed for three and four year old children for the duration of the school year in which the child turns five years old (including the summer following the date of the child's fifth birthday).

(e) *Type of Setting—Inclusionary.* Inclusionary programs for young children shall be located in a setting that includes children with and without disabilities and shall meet the following standards:

1. Services in such programs may be provided in the home, the public school, Head Start, or a licensed childcare setting.

2. For public school programs that integrate children with and without disabilities, the class size shall not exceed 20 with one teacher and one aide and no more than five students with disabilities. If the number of students with disabilities is six or seven then the class size may not exceed 15 students with one teacher and one aide.

(f) *Type of Setting—Substantially Separate.* Substantially separate programs for young children shall be those programs for three and four year olds that are located in a public school classroom or facility that serves primarily or solely children with disabilities. Substantially separate programs shall adhere to the following standards:

1. Substantially separate programs shall be programs in which more than 50% of the children have disabilities.

2. Substantially separate programs operated by public schools shall limit class sizes to nine students with one teacher and one aide.

(8) *Transportation Services.* The term transportation providers shall include the driver of the vehicle and any attendants or aides identified by the Team. The school district shall provide a qualified attendant on each vehicle that transports one or more students in need of special education, when such attendant is recommended by the Team in accordance with 603 CMR 28.05(5)(b).

(a) The district shall not permit any eligible student to be transported in a manner that requires the student to remain in the vehicle for more than one hour each way except with the approval of the Team. The Team shall document such determination on the IEP.

(b) The school district shall give transportation providers clear, written information on the nature of any need or problem that may cause difficulties for a student receiving special transportation along with information on appropriate emergency measures that may be necessary.

(c) The district shall provide an in-service training program for transportation providers. Such training program shall acquaint transportation providers with the needs of the students they are transporting and shall be designed to enable the transportation providers to meet those needs. All transportation providers shall be required to complete such in-service training prior to providing transportation services to eligible students.

(d) The district shall make sufficient inspections of equipment and unannounced spot checks throughout the year to ensure compliance with these requirements, and with all applicable state and federal safety and equipment laws, including M.G.L. c. 90.

(9) *Educational Services in Institutional Settings.* The Department shall provide certain special education services to eligible students in certain facilities operated by or under contract with the Department of Mental Health, the Department of Youth Services, County Houses of Corrections, or the Department of Public Health. The Department shall retain the discretion to determine based upon resources, the type and amount of special education and related services that it provides in such facilities.

(a) Decisions about admission to and discharge from institutional facilities are within the authority of institution administrators, not the school district. However, school districts are not relieved of their obligations to students in such settings. School districts are responsible for students in institutional settings in accordance with 603 CMR 28.10. Such students have the same rights for referral, evaluation, and the provision of special education in accordance with state and federal law as students in public schools.

(b) Non-educational services such as residential, medical and clinical services shall be provided by the state agency that controls the facility. The provision of such services shall be governed by the state agency in accordance with applicable laws, interagency agreements, or agency policies.

(c) Where a student's IEP requires a type or amount of service that the facility does not provide, it shall remain the responsibility of the school district where the father, mother or legal guardian resides, except as provided in 603 CMR 28.10(3)(c)1 and 2, to implement the student's IEP by arranging and paying for the provision of such services.

(d) The responsible school district coordinate with the Department and ensure that the student receives an evaluation, an annual review, and special education services as identified by the Team at a Team meeting convened by the responsible school district. The Department shall participate in Team meetings for any student receiving special education services in an institutional setting. To the extent that special education services are provided by the Department in such facilities, the Department will make every effort to provide services consistent with the student's IEP and available resources.

603 CMR 28.07. Parent Involvement

(1) *Parental consent.* In accordance with state and federal law, each school district shall obtain informed parental consent as follows:

(a) The school district shall obtain written parental consent before conducting an initial evaluation or making an initial placement of a student in a special education program under 603 CMR 28.00. Written parental consent shall be obtained before conducting a reevaluation and before placing a student in a special education placement subsequent to the initial placement in special education.

1. The school district shall obtain consent before initiating extended evaluation services as described in 603 CMR 28.05(2)(b).

2. A parent may revoke consent at any time. Except for initial evaluation and initial placement, and as prescribed by 603 CMR 28.00, consent may not be required as a condition of any benefit to the student.

3. Parents have the right to observe any program(s) proposed for their child if the child is identified as eligible for special education services.

4. A parent may discontinue special education and related services provided to his or her child by notifying the school district in writing that the parent revokes consent to the continued provision of all special education and related services to the child. The school district shall respond promptly by sending notice to the parent of the district's intention to discontinue all special education and related services to the student 10 school days from the date of the district's notice based on the parent's revocation of consent. The school district may not challenge the parent's decision through the dispute resolution processes provided under 603 CMR 28.08. Nothing in this regulation shall prevent a school district and a parent from meeting to discuss discontinuation of all special education and related services provided the parent's participation is voluntary.

(b) If, subsequent to initial evaluation and initial placement and after following the procedures required by 603 CMR 28.00, the school district is unable to obtain parental consent to a reevaluation or to placement in a special education program subsequent to the initial placement, or the parent revokes consent to such reevaluation or placement, the school district shall consider with the parent whether such action will result in the denial of a free appropriate public education to the student. If, after consideration, the school district determines that the parent's failure or refusal to consent will result in a denial of a free appropriate public education to the student, it shall seek resolution of the dispute through the procedures provided in 603 CMR 28.08. Participation by the parent in such consideration shall be voluntary and the failure or refusal of the parent to participate shall not preclude the school district from taking appropriate action pursuant to 603 CMR 28.08 to resolve the dispute. This provision shall not apply if the parent has revoked consent to all special education and related services as provided in 603 CMR 28.07(1)(a)(4).

(c) When the participation or consent of the parent is required and the parent fails or refuses to participate, the school district shall make and document multiple efforts to contact the parent. Such efforts may include letters, written notices sent by certified mail, electronic mail (e-mail), telephone call, or, if appropriate, TTY communications to the home, and home visits at such time as the parent is likely to be home. Efforts may include seeking assistance from a community service agency to secure parental participation. The school district shall ensure that its efforts to involve the parent and gain parental consent meet a reasonable measure standard as articulated in federal law at 34 CFR §§ 300.300(c)(2) and 300.322(d). If the above efforts are attempted and documented and the district is unable to secure parental consent to a reevaluation or placement subsequent to the initial placement in a special education program, the school district shall proceed in accordance with 603 CMR 28.07(1)(b). This provision shall not apply if the parent has revoked consent to all special education and related services as provided in 603 CMR 28.07(1)(a)(4).

(2) *Parent right to waive assessments.* Any individual assessment may be waived with the approval of the parents if an equivalent assessment has been recently completed and if the person conducting the school assessment determines that the assessment results are still accurate.

(a) All efforts shall be made to avoid duplicative or unnecessary testing.

(b) In accordance with federal requirements, if recommended by the school district, parents may agree to waive some or all assessments when the three-year reevaluation is required.

(3) *Reports to parents.* Written progress reports for eligible students shall be submitted to parents at least as often as report cards or progress reports for students without disabilities.

(4) *Parent advisory participation.* Each school district shall create a districtwide parent advisory council offering membership

6

to all parents of eligible students and other interested parties. The parent advisory council duties shall include but not be limited to: advising the district on matters that pertain to the education and safety of students with disabilities; meeting regularly with school officials to participate in the planning, development, and evaluation of the school district's special education programs. The parent advisory council shall establish by-laws regarding officers and operational procedures, and, in the course of its duties, the parent advisory council shall receive assistance from the district without charge, upon reasonable notice, and subject to the availability of staff and resources.

(5) *Student participation and consent at the age of majority.* When the student reaches 18 years of age, he or she shall have the right to make all decisions in relation to special education programs and services. The school district shall have the obligation to obtain consent from the student to continue the student's special education program. The parents will continue to receive written notices and information but will no longer have decision-making authority, except as provided in 603 CMR 28.07(5)(a) through (c).

(a) If a parent has sought and received guardianship from a court of competent jurisdiction, then the parent retains full decision-making authority. The parent shall not have authority to override any decision or lack of decision made by the student who has reached the age of majority unless the parent has sought or received guardianship or other legal authority from a court of competent jurisdiction.

(b) The student, upon reaching 18 years of age and in the absence of any court actions to the contrary, may choose to share decision-making with his or her parent (or other willing adult), including allowing the parent to co-sign the IEP. Such choice shall be made in the presence of the Team and shall be documented in written form. The student's choice shall prevail at any time that a disagreement occurs between the adult student and the parent or other adult with whom the student has shared decision-making.

6

(c) The student, upon reaching 18 years of age and in the absence of any court actions to the contrary, may choose to delegate continued decision-making to his or her parent, or other willing adult. Such choice shall be made in the presence of at least one representative of the school district and one other witness and shall be documented in written form and maintained in the student record.

(6) *When a parent provides transportation.* If a parent provides transportation to an eligible student requiring special transportation consistent with the requirements of 603 CMR 28.05(5)(b), the school district shall reimburse such parent the prevailing rate per mile for state employees. Reimbursement shall be for no more than the round-trip distance between the home and the school for school attendance and school-sponsored extracurricular activities. Mileage shall be determined based on a direct route between the student's home and school. No parent shall be obligated to provide such transportation.

(7) *Educational surrogate parent—district responsibility.* When a student is without parental representation and requires an educational surrogate parent to be appointed in accordance with federal law and regulations, the Department may request assistance from the district responsible for services to the student in identifying a person willing to serve as an educational surrogate parent.

(a) Upon assignment by the Department, such educational surrogate parent shall have all the rights and responsibilities of a parent in making decisions regarding eligibility and services for special education for the assigned student. The Department shall provide notice of appointment to the school district and any state agency with custody of the student.

(b) A person identified by the district and willing to serve as an educational surrogate parent shall have no conflict of interest and shall not be in the employ of the school district or any state or local agencies involved with the care of the student.

(c) A person identified by the district, appointed by the Department, and serving as an educational surrogate parent shall not receive financial remuneration from the district except that the school district shall reimburse the person for reasonable expenses related to the exercise of his or her responsibilities as an educational surrogate parent for a student enrolled in the district.

(8) *Communications with parents and students.* Each district shall ensure that all communications and meetings with parents and students pursuant to 603 CMR 28.00 meet the following standards:

(a) Communications shall be in simple and commonly understood words.

(b) Communications shall be in both English and the primary language of the home, if such primary language is other than English. Any interpreter used to implement this provision shall be fluent in the primary language of the home.

(c) Where the parents or the student are unable to read in any language or are blind or deaf, communications shall be made orally in English or with the use of a foreign language interpreter, in Braille, in sign language, via TDD, or in writing, whichever is appropriate.

603 CMR 28.08. Continuum of Options for Dispute Resolution

(1) *Local School District Procedures.* School districts are encouraged to develop local problem resolution procedures that allow parents to present a concern to a district representative and receive a response related to the concern. Local procedures shall not be used to delay or deny a parent's right to access other dispute resolution mechanisms.

(2) *Department Procedures.* The Department maintains a Problem Resolution System that provides for the investigation of complaints and the enforcement of compliance with 603 CMR 28.00, as well as with other statutes and regulations relating to the provision of publicly funded education. The Department can make findings on procedural issues and issues related to implementation of requirements. Any party wishing to file a complaint may do so through the Department. Use of the Department Problem Resolution procedures shall not prevent a party from requesting alternative administrative remedies of mediation or hearing on any matter, at any time. Copies of the Problem Resolution System Guidelines and Procedures are available from the Department upon request. Findings and orders issued by the Department on complaints and the Department's processing of a complaint are not reviewable by the Bureau of Special Education Appeals. Additionally, the pendency of a complaint before the Department does not make the Department a necessary party to actions on related issues pending before the Bureau of Special Education Appeals.

(3) *Bureau of Special Education Appeals: Jurisdiction.* In order to provide for the resolution of differences of opinion among school districts, private schools, parents, and state agencies, the Bureau of Special Education Appeals, pursuant to G.L. c. 71B, § 2A, shall conduct mediations and hearings to resolve such disputes. The jurisdiction of the Bureau of Special Education Appeals over state agencies, however, shall be exercised consistent with 34 CFR § 300.154(a). The hearing officer may determine, in accordance with the rules, regulations and policies of the respective agencies, that services shall be provided by the Department of Children and Families*, the Department of Developmental Disabilities*, the Department of Mental Health, the Department of Public Health, or any other state agency or program, in addition to the IEP services to be provided by the school district. Mediations and hearings shall be conducted by impartial mediators and hearing officers who do not have personal or professional interests that would conflict with their objectivity in the hearing or mediation and who are employed to conduct those proceedings.

(a) A parent or a school district, except as provided in 603 CMR 28.08(3)(c) and (d), may request mediation and/or a hearing at any time on any matter concerning the eligibility, evaluation, placement, IEP, provision of special education in accordance with 603 CMR 53.00of the free appropriate public education guaranteed by Section 504 of the Rehabilitation Act of 1973, as set forth in 34 CFR §§ 104.31–104.39.

(b) No later than five days after receipt of a request for hearing or notice that an IEP, or proposed placement, or finding of no eligibility for special education has been rejected by the parent, the school district shall send a copy of such request or notice to the Bureau of Special Education Appeals. The Bureau of Special Education Appeals shall then give notice in writing to the parties of the rights of the parents and school district to request mediation and a hearing.

(c) A school district may not request a hearing on a parent's failure or refusal to consent to initial evaluation or initial placement of a student in a special education program, or on a parent's decision to revoke consent to the continued provision of all special education and related services to his or her child under 603 CMR 28.07(1)(a)(4).

(d) A school district may request a hearing to appeal the Department's assignment of school district responsibility under 603 CMR 28.10 according to the procedures in 603 CMR 28.10(9).

(4) *Mediation*. A voluntary dispute resolution procedure, called mediation, shall be provided by mediators employed by the Bureau of Special Education Appeals and may be used by parents and school districts to seek resolution of their dispute. Mediations shall be provided at no cost to the parties. No parent shall be required to participate in mediation.

(a) Within 30 days of receipt of a request for mediation, the mediator shall schedule a mediation session at a time and place convenient to the parties. The mediation shall include the parents, any representative of the parents' choosing, and a representative(s) of the school district, with one representative who is authorized to resolve the dispute on behalf of the school district. When the parties reach agreement, it shall be set forth in written form. Concurrent with a request for mediation or if no agreement is reached, the parents or school district may request a hearing.

(b) All discussions that occur during mediation are confidential and may not be used as, evidence in a hearing. Parents and school districts may request a hearing without participating in mediation.

(5) *Hearings*. Five (5) days after receipt of a written request for hearing, the Bureau of Special Education Appeals shall notify the parties in writing of the name of the assigned hearing officer and, as appropriate, shall provide either a date for the hearing or a statement of federally required procedures to be followed before a hearing date can be assigned.

(a) The Bureau of Special Education Appeals shall issue Rules that state the parties' rights and obligations as to the hearing process, which shall be consistent with all state and federal laws. Such Rules shall be available to the public on request.

(b) Except as provided otherwise under federal law or in the administrative rules adopted by the Bureau of Special Education Appeals, hearings shall be conducted consistent with the formal Rules of Administrative Procedures contained in 801 CMR 1.00.

(c) The Special Education Appeals hearing officer shall have the power and the duty to conduct a fair hearing; to ensure that the rights of all parties are protected; to define issues; to receive and consider all relevant and reliable evidence; to ensure an orderly presentation of the evidence and issues; to order additional evaluations by the school district or independent education evaluations at public expense when necessary in order to determine the appropriate special education for the student; to reconvene the hearing at any time prior to the issuance of a decision; to take such other steps as are appropriate to assure the orderly presentation of evidence and protection of the parties' rights at the hearing; to ensure a record is made of the proceedings; and to reach a fair, independent, and impartial decision based on the issues and evidence presented at the hearing and in accordance with applicable law.

(6) *Hearing Decision*. The decision of the hearing officer of the Bureau of Special Education Appeals shall be implemented immediately and shall not be subject to reconsideration by the Bureau of Special Education Appeals or the Department, but may be appealed to a court of competent jurisdiction.

(a) The written findings of fact and decision of the hearing officer along with notification of the procedures to be followed with respect to appeal and enforcement of the decision shall be sent to the parties and their representatives.

(b) A party contending that a Bureau of Special Education Appeals decision is not being implemented may file a motion with the Bureau of Special Education Appeals contending that the decision is not being implemented and setting out the areas of non-compliance. The hearing officer may convene a hearing at which the scope of the inquiry shall be limited to the facts on the issue of compliance, facts of such a nature as to excuse performance, and facts bearing on a remedy. Upon a finding of non-compliance, the hearing officer may fashion appropriate relief, including referral of the matter to the Legal Office of the Department or other office for appropriate enforcement action. The possibility of enforcement action does not make the Department a necessary party in matters pending before the Bureau of Special Education Appeals.

(7) *Student's Right to IEP Services and Placement*. In accordance with state and federal law, during the pendency of any dispute regarding placement or services, the eligible student shall remain in his or her then current education program and placement unless the parents and the school district agree otherwise.

(a) If the parents are seeking initial placement in the public school, and the child is at least five years old, however, the child shall be placed in the public school program.

(b) For children three and four years of age, rights to services from the public school district are limited to children who have been found eligible for special education and have an IEP and placement proposed by the public school district and accepted by the parent.

(c) A hearing officer may order a temporary change in placement of an eligible student for reasons consistent with federal law, including but not limited to when maintaining such student in the current placement is substantially likely to result in injury to the student or others.

(d) Except as provided in 603 CMR 28.08(7)(a through c) above, any party seeking to change the eligible student's placement during the pendency of proceedings before the Bureau of Special Education Appeals or in subsequent judicial proceedings shall seek a preliminary injunction from a state or federal court of competent jurisdiction, ordering such a change in placement.

603 CMR 28.09. Approval of Public and Private Day and Residential Special Education School Programs

(1) *Approval from the Department*. The Department may grant approval to public and private day and residential schools providing special education services (special education schools) in Massachusetts in order to ensure that a continuum of special education programs is available to Massachusetts students with disabilities. Approval shall be granted by the Department in accordance with the provisions of 603 CMR 28.09. Upon receipt of approval special education schools are eligible to enroll publicly funded Massachusetts eligible students. Approval does not relieve special education schools of their obligation to comply with other applicable state or federal statutory or regulatory requirements or requirements set forth in their contracts with referral sources.

(a) *Limited Approval for Out-of-state Programs*. The Department may grant approval to public and private day and residential schools providing special education services (special education schools) in states other than Massachusetts in the following circumstances.

6

1. An out-of-state program, in cooperation with a Massachusetts school district, seeks approval from the Department. The following documentation is required.

(i) Written verification by the Massachusetts school district of its intent to place an eligible Massachusetts student in the out-of-state program.

(ii) Documentation from the program that the host state has approved the program to provide services to students with disabilities. If the host state does not have an approval process, then the program must provide documentation of reputable accreditation.

(iii) Documentation of tuition rate approved by the host state. If the host state does not approve or otherwise regulate tuition rates, then the program shall provide documentation meeting the requirements of the Massachusetts agency responsible for setting rates for special education schools and showing that the proposed rate is the lowest rate charged to any enrolled student for similar services.

2. Upon receipt of required documentation, the Department may grant approval for a period of time not to exceed three years from the date of application. The Department may withhold such approval if it deems that circumstances warrant such action. In such case, the Department will notify the Massachusetts school district and the out-of-state program of its actions and the reason for such actions.

3. Once approved by the Department, out-of-state programs may accept Massachusetts students without additional documentation during the three-year period of approval. It is the responsibility of the out-of-state program, in cooperation with a Massachusetts school district, to reinitiate the three-year approval status.

(b) *Approval for Massachusetts Special Education Schools*. Approval for schools operating in Massachusetts includes meeting all of the requirements of 603 CMR 28.09 and 603 CMR 18.00. The Department reserves the right to withhold or deny approval if, in its discretion, circumstances warrant such action.

6

(2) *Eligibility*. Any individual, not-for-profit corporation or agency, or proprietary corporation or public educational collaborative or school district may file an application to establish and/or operate a special education school in Massachusetts to serve eligible students with disabilities. The Department shall require justification of the need for such program and may establish standards for approval eligibility, including but not limited to, standards for minimum or maximum size of such program.

(a) Residential programs shall demonstrate initiation of a request for a license with the state agency responsible for licensing programs providing residential childcare. Such state agency shall be responsible for licensing the residential non-educational component of the program.

1. The Department of Elementary and Secondary Education shall not grant final approval of the educational component of the residential school until all licensing activity for the residential component has been completed and a license has been awarded.

2. The educational component of a residential program must reflect the 24-hour nature of the service and indicate how residential services and educational services will be fully coordinated.

(b) The Department shall develop approval standards that shall specify the types of information, policies, procedures, and assurances to be included in any application for approval. The application shall include, but not be limited to:

1. A demonstration of the need for such a program;

2. The population to be served. Such population shall, at a minimum, consist of a majority of students who have been determined eligible for special education services.

3. The anticipated special education and related services that the program will provide;

4. The legal and financial stability of the program;

5. The safety and appropriateness of the physical plant for the student population that the school will serve;

6. Documentation of qualified staff; and

7. Procedures detailing how the school will provide education services for the identified population of students.

(c) For public special education school programs, the public school or educational collaborative must demonstrate that the program is developed for programmatic reasons and not because of lack of space at an in-district location.

(3) *Department Review and Approval*. The Department shall review for approval each application submitted and shall consult with other state agencies as necessary. The Department may, at its discretion, schedule site visits, interviews, or other inspection of the proposed program. The Department may deny approval; grant temporary, provisional, or full approval; or grant probationary approval. The Department shall provide the applicant with a written notice of its actions and the reasons for such actions.

(a) *Temporary Approval/Program Pricing*. The Department, upon granting temporary approval to private special education schools, shall forward such approval, together with a description of approved program elements for the educational component of the program, and applicable pricing elements for the residential component of the program, if any, to the state agency responsible for program pricing.

(b) *Provisional Approval*. If provisional approval is granted, the Department shall indicate the specific conditions that shall be met and shall establish a time limit not to exceed six months within which the program shall meet those conditions. In no case shall approval be given unless the applicant can demonstrate to the satisfaction of the Department that the health and safety of the students is protected and the school is able to carry out the provisions of each student's IEP.

(4) *Probationary Approval*. The Department may place the program on probationary status if it becomes aware of conditions at the school that, in the Department's judgment, compromise the program's ability to provide a safe, healthy and appropriate educational environment. In such circumstances, the Department shall provide written notice of the probationary status, the circumstances that caused the Department to take such action, and the actions necessary to correct the problem.

(a) *Health and Safety Issues*. When, in the Department's judgment, conditions at the school threaten the health or safety of the students in the program, acceptance of any additional eligible students (intake) may be prohibited and the Department shall establish a time not to exceed 14 days within which the program shall correct the problem.

(b) *Educational Issues*. When, in the Department's judgment, conditions at the school compromise the program's ability to provide an appropriate education but do not threaten the health and safety of the students, the Department shall establish a time limit up to 90 days during which the program shall correct the problem. The Department shall determine if it is necessary to close intake during this period. The Department shall not close intake for more than 60 days in any 12-month period without a full review of the approval status of the school.

(c) *Notification Requirements*. Within two school days of receipt of notice from the Department placing the program's approval on probation, the program shall provide notification to the parents of all enrolled Massachusetts students, all Massachusetts school districts with enrolled students, and officials of Massachusetts human service agencies or agencies of other states with responsibility for any students at the school. Notification shall state that the school has been assigned probationary status; that intake is closed, if applicable, and the reasons for such status.

(d) *Completed Corrective Action*. At the end of the time period for corrective action or when the issue giving rise to probationary status is resolved, whichever is sooner, the Department may reinstate the approval status of the program, change the approval status to provisional, or withdraw approval. The Department shall provide written notification of its action to the special education school.

(e) *Request for Reconsideration.* Within one month of receipt of a written request for reconsideration of any Department action in relation to probationary status, the Department shall consider the request and make formal written response. The Department may, at its discretion, hold a hearing on the facts, make site visits, or issue an alternative remedy.

(5) *Disclosure of Information.*

(a) An approved special education school shall make available to the Department, on request, information on all aspects of the school's program(s), the certification or credentials of its staff, and the individual records of enrolled Massachusetts students.

(b) The approved special education school shall also maintain on site and provide, on request, documentation of a safety inspection of all buildings by the Department of Public Safety or the local building inspector, an annual fire safety inspection from the local fire department, and a lead paint inspection, if applicable. More frequent inspections may be required at the discretion of the Department.

(c) Prior to any substantial change in program or physical plant, the special education school shall give written notification of intent to change to the Department. Notice shall be given with sufficient time to allow the Department to assess the need for the proposed change and the effects of such change on the educational program. The Department shall provide response to the approved program within thirty days if such change may affect the approval status of the program.

(6) *Public Information and Postings.* Each approved special education school shall maintain on site and make available for public review the following:

(a) Program information including a statement of purpose, a general description of the educational program, an organizational chart, and tuition information;

(b) Documentation of the current approval and or licensing status;

(c) Documents granting authority to operate the school, including documents that fully identify ownership, and, as applicable, the names of officers, boards, charters, partnership agreements, articles of organization, and by-laws;

(d) All required policies and procedures; and

(e) First aid, medical, and emergency procedures. The special education school shall conspicuously post first aid and emergency procedures, including emergency telephone numbers and location of nearest telephones within each building.

(7) *Educational Staffing Requirements.* An approved special education school program shall meet the requirements of 603 CMR 18.00 related to staffing, staff training, and personnel policies and shall demonstrate that its organizational structure provides for the effective and efficient operation of the school, supervision of school staff, and supervision of students. The school staff shall at all times provide appropriate supervision of students while they are engaged in any school related activity on or off school grounds.

(a) At least one staff member shall be designated as the educational administrator for the program. The educational administrator shall either possess licensure as a special education administrator or as a special educator and shall have a minimum of a master's degree in special education or a related field; and shall have a minimum of one year of administrative experience. Such person shall be assigned to supervise the provision of special education services in the school and ensure that the services specified in each student's IEP are delivered. The educational administrator shall be relicensed pursuant to the requirements of 603 CMR 44.00 and shall be required to obtain supervisor approval of his/her Professional Development Plan pursuant to 603 CMR 44.04.

(b) Teaching staff shall have teaching licensure appropriate to meet the needs of the population served and which is provided pursuant to the licensure requirements under 603 CMR 7.00. Teaching staff shall be relicensed pursuant to the requirements of 603 CMR 44.00. For the purposes of relicensure, teaching staff shall be subject to the same requirements as teachers in Massachusetts public schools and shall be required to obtain supervisor approval of Professional Development Plans pursuant to 603 CMR 44.04. At least half of the teaching staff shall be licensed in special education areas appropriate to the population served at the school; other teaching staff may be licensed in other educational areas, in order to provide for content expertise in the general curriculum.

(c) The Department may require a higher proportion of licensed special educators if, in the opinion of the Department, the population requires more specialized services. To the extent that teaching staff is providing special education services, such services shall be provided, designed, or supervised by a special educator.

(d) Staff providing or supervising the provision of related services shall be appropriately certified or licensed in their professional areas.

(e) Instructional groupings and student/teacher ratios shall not exceed the class size standards set forth at 603 CMR 28.06(6) and (7). The Department may impose additional limits, if, in the opinion of the Department, the population requires more specialized services.

(f) The special education school shall have a written plan for staff orientation and training that is consistent with the needs of the student population and provides, on average, at least two hours per month of relevant training for all staff including non-professional staff. Initial staff orientation shall include provision for training in emergency procedures, behavior management procedures, and requirements related to student protections as provided in 603 CMR 28.09(12). The special education school shall maintain written documentation of training provided and staff attendance at training as well as documentation of training received outside of the school. Upon request, such documentation shall be readily available for review by the Department.

(8) *Educational Facilities and Materials. Approved* special education schools shall provide the facilities, textbooks, equipment, technology, materials, and supplies needed to provide the special education and related services specified on the IEPs of enrolled students. If specialized materials or equipment needed solely for an individual student are necessary, the special education school may enter into an agreement for the provision of such materials or equipment by the school district enrolling the student. Approved schools shall additionally meet all facility requirements of 603 CMR 18.00.

(9) *Educational Program Requirements.*

(a) All approved special education schools shall meet or exceed the student learning time requirements for public school students set forth at 603 CMR 27.00 and shall ensure that such requirements are met for individual students unless the student's IEP requires otherwise. In addition to meeting the student learning time requirements, all ten month programs must run a minimum of 180 school days; 11 month programs a minimum of 198 school days and 12 month programs a minimum of 216 school days exclusive of weekends, holidays, and vacations.

(b) Each approved special education school shall ensure that all teaching staff have an understanding and knowledge of the general curriculum expectations and learning standards of the Massachusetts Curriculum Frameworks and that such knowledge is incorporated into the educational programs of the special education school.

(c) All approved special education schools shall ensure that there are flexible procedures and mechanisms that maximize opportunities for enrolled students to gain the capacity to return to a less restrictive educational program. Such mechanisms may include, but are not limited to, a capacity for part-time attendance at a neighborhood public school or other community program or a period of transition from one program option to a less restrictive program option.

(d) All approved special education schools shall ensure that there are written procedures outlining how such schools will ensure that enrolled students also participate in state assessment programs in accordance with the assessment participation information provided on the student's IEP. Such procedures shall include how the approved school will provide for accommodations or alternate assessments when required.

(10) *Student Records*. Approved special education schools shall keep current and complete files for each publicly funded enrolled student and shall manage such files consistent with 603 CMR 23.00: Student Records and M.G.L. c. 71, § 34H.

(11) *Policies and Procedures*. In addition to the written procedures required for residential schools by the state agency responsible for licensing residential programs providing childcare, and written procedures required by 603 CMR 18.00, all approved special education schools shall maintain on site a policies and procedures manual, and shall provide written notice to parents of enrolled students that copies of such policies or procedures are available on request. Policies and procedures shall additionally include the procedures required in 603 CMR 28.09(9) and emergency procedures, admissions procedures, behavior management procedures, procedures regarding suspension or termination of the student's placement, and orientation procedures for parents and students as required under 603 CMR 18.00 and the following:

(a) Personnel policies, including procedures for hiring, discipline, supervision, evaluation, handling complaints, and dismissal of staff. Procedures on hiring shall include a description of the steps the school will take to obtain, consider, and act upon information related to convictions for criminal offenses for any prospective staff members whose responsibilities bring them into direct contact with students in the school.

(b) If applicable, transportation procedures that ensure that vehicles are safe, insured, and operated by qualified and trained individuals, and that students are transported in a safe manner that is responsive to individual student's needs and provisions of their IEPs.

(12) *Student Protections*. Students shall be entitled to protections and standards in accordance with 603 CMR 18.00. In addition approved special education schools shall observe the following requirements:

(a) *Serious Incidents—Immediate Notification and Reporting*. In the event of serious injury or death of a student, criminal activity on the part of a student or staff member, or other serious incident affecting the well-being of any student, the approved special education school shall immediately notify, by telephone and by letter, the parents, the sending school district(s), any state agency involved in student care or program placement, and the Department of Elementary and Secondary Education.

(b) *Emergency Termination of Enrollment*. The special education school shall not terminate the enrollment of any student, even in emergency circumstances, until the enrolling public school district is informed and assumes responsibility for the student. At the request of the public school district, the special education school shall delay termination of the student for up to two calendar weeks to allow the public school district the opportunity to convene an emergency Team meeting or to conduct other appropriate planning discussions prior to the student's termination from the special education school program. With the mutual agreement of the approved special education school and the public school district, termination of enrollment may be delayed for longer than two calendar weeks.

603 CMR 28.10. School District Responsibility

(1) *General Provisions*. School districts shall be programmatically and financially responsible for eligible students based on residency and enrollment.

(a) With the exception of students who are in the care or custody of a state agency, nothing in 603 CMR 28.10 shall require a school district to provide special education to a student whose parent(s), and legal guardian if any, live outside Massachusetts and have placed the student in an education program in Massachusetts or who maintain contact with the student who remains in Massachusetts.

(b) Nothing in 603 CMR 28.10 shall limit the right of the student to timely evaluation, services and placement in accordance with 603 CMR 28.00.

(c) Nothing in 603 CMR 28.10 shall be interpreted to assign responsibility to school districts for any educational service or program other than services or programs provided under state or federal special education law.

(d) Any school district deemed responsible for a student under 603 CMR 28.10 shall continue responsibility for such student until another school district is deemed responsible under 603 CMR 28.10.

(2) *School District Responsibility Based on Student Residence*. The school district where the student resides shall have both programmatic and financial responsibility under the following circumstances:

(a) When students live with their parent(s) or legal guardian.

1. When a student who requires an in-district placement to implement his or her IEP lives with both of his or her parents during the school year, irrespective of school vacation periods, and the parents live in two different Massachusetts school districts, the school district where the student is enrolled shall be responsible for fulfilling the requirements of 603 CMR 28.00.

2. When a student who requires an out-of-district placement to implement his or her IEP lives with both of his or her parents during the school year, irrespective of school vacation periods, and the parents live in two different Massachusetts school districts, the school districts where the parents reside shall be equally responsible for fulfilling the requirements of 603 CMR 28.00.

(b) When students are eighteen years of age or over and they have established their own residences as adults.

(3) *School District Responsibility Based on Residence of Parent(s) or Legal Guardian*. The school district where the parent(s) or legal guardian resides shall have both programmatic and financial responsibility under the following circumstances:

(a) When a student is in a pediatric nursing home.

(b) When a student whose IEP requires an out of district placement lives and receives special education services at a special education residential school pursuant to a placement by the IEP Team.

(c) When a student lives and receives educational services in an institutional facility operated by or, through contract, authorized by the Department of Mental Health, the Department of Public Health, the Department of Youth Services, or the Department of Correction or County House of Correction, except as provided in 603 CMR 28.10(3)(c)1. and 2.

1. If an eligible student was placed or resided in foster care at the time the student entered the institutional facility, then responsibility shall remain with the district(s) assigned most recently pursuant to 603 CMR 28.10(5)(b).

2. If a student is 18 years of age or older and has established his or her own residence as an adult, the school district where the student resided prior to entering the institutional facility shall remain programmatically and fiscally responsible.

(4) *Shared School District Responsibility*. The school district where the parent(s) or legal guardian resides shall have financial responsibility and the school district where the student resides shall have programmatic responsibility when a student who is not in foster care, as defined in 603 CMR 28.05(b), is in a relative's home or living in a residence, crisis, or respite facility funded or supervised by a state agency other than the Department of Children and Families.

(a) When such a student is served in an in-district program, the school district where the student lives shall provide such services and may bill and shall receive payment for the special education costs (using the procedures of 603 CMR 10.07 to calculate such costs, including transportation expenses where applicable) from the school district where the parent(s) or legal guardian resides, unless such student is over 18 years of age and has established his or her own residence as an adult as described in 603 CMR 28.10(2)(b).

(b) When such a student is served in an out-of-district program, the school district where the parent(s) or legal guardian resides shall pay the tuition costs for the student's IEP program directly to the out-of-district school, and such other payments as may be required to other individuals or entities that provide services required by the student's IEP.

(c) In all cases where financial and programmatic responsibility are shared, the school district where the student resides shall invite the school district where the parent(s) or legal guardian resides to participate as a member of the student's Team, provided that such participation shall not limit the student's right to timely evaluation and placement in accordance with 603 CMR 28.00.

(5) Responsibility for Homeless Students and Students in Foster Care.

(a) Nothing in 603 CMR 28.00 shall limit the educational rights of homeless students and parents afforded under the McKinney-Vento Homeless Assistance Act, 42 U.S.C. § 11431 et seq. (McKinney-Vento). The following provisions apply to these students.

1. Homeless students shall be entitled to either continue to attend their school of origin, as defined by McKinney-Vento, or attend school in the city or town where they temporarily reside. To the extent feasible, homeless students should remain in their school of origin unless doing so is contrary to the wishes of such student's parent(s) or legal guardian or state agency with care or custody of the student.

2. The school district(s) that was programmatically and financially responsible prior to the student becoming homeless shall remain programmatically and financially responsible for a homeless student until the parent(s) or legal guardian or state agency with care or custody of the student chooses to enroll the student in the school district where the shelter or temporary residence is located. When a student whose IEP requires in-district services is enrolled in the school district where the student is temporarily residing, then that school district shall become programmatically and financially responsible upon enrollment. When a student whose IEP requires out-of-district services is enrolled in the school district where the student is temporarily residing, then that school district shall become programmatically responsible upon enrollment and the school district(s) that was. financially responsible prior to the student becoming homeless shall remain financially responsible until the student is no longer homeless.

(b) Nothing in 603 CMR 28.00 shall limit the educational rights afforded under the Every Student Succeeds Act (ESSA) to students who are in foster care, which means 24-hour substitute care for children placed away from their parents or guardians and for whom the Department of Children and Families has placement and care responsibility. This includes, but is not limited to, placements in foster family homes, foster homes of relatives, group homes, emergency shelters, residential facilities, child care institutions, and preadoptive homes. The provisions in 603 CMR 28.10(5)(b)1. through 4. apply to these students:

1. The school district(s) that was programmatically and financially responsible prior to the student's entry into foster care or prior to a subsequent change in the student's foster care setting shall remain responsible for the student's special education program for as long as the student continues to attend the same school.

2. For students in foster care who do not continue to attend the same school, and who enroll in the district in which their foster care setting is located, programmatic responsibility shall be with the district in which the student is enrolled and financial responsibility shall be with the district where the parent(s) or legal guardian resides.

3. When the Department of Children and Families relocates a student to reside in and attend an approved residential school, the school district that was programmatically responsible prior to this relocation shall remain programmatically responsible and the district where the parent(s) or legal guardian resides shall be financially responsible.

4. For all situations in which school districts share responsibility for students in foster care, the following provisions shall apply:

a. When such a student is served in an in-district program, the school district with programmatic responsibility may bill and shall receive payment for the special education costs (using the procedures of 603 CMR 10.07 to calculate such costs, including transportation expenses where applicable) from the school district where the parent(s) or legal guardian resides.

b. When such a student is served in an out-of-district placement, the school district where the parent(s) or legal guardian resides shall pay the tuition costs for the student's IEP placement directly to the out-of-district school, and such other payments as may be required to other individuals or entities that provide services in the student's IEP.

The school district with programmatic responsibility shall invite the school district where the parent(s) or legal guardian resides to participate as a member of the student's Team, providing that such participation shall not limit the student's right to timely evaluation and placement in accordance with 603 CMR 28.00.

(6) *Program Schools.* A program school shall have programmatic and financial responsibility for enrolled students, subject only to specific finance provisions of any pertinent state law related to the program school. Specific provisions for program schools are as follows:

6

(a) For charter schools, Commonwealth of Massachusetts virtual schools, vocational schools, or schools attended under M.G.L. c. 76, § 12A (Metco), when the Team determines that the student may need an out-of-district placement, the Team shall conclude the meeting pursuant to 603 CMR 28.06(2)(e) without identifying a specific placement type, and shall notify the school district where the student resides within two school days.

1. Upon a determination as in 603 CMR 28.10(6)(a) above, the program school shall schedule another meeting to determine placement, and shall invite representatives of the school district where the student resides to participate as a member of the placement team pursuant to 603 CMR 28.06(2)(e)(1).

2. The Team meeting convened by the program school shall first consider if the school district where the student resides has an in-district program that could provide the services recommended by the Team, and if so, the program school shall arrange with the school district where the student resides to deliver such services or develop an appropriate in-district program at the program school for the student.

3. If the placement Team, in accordance with the procedures of 603 CMR 28.06(2)(e), determines that the student requires an out-of-district program to provide the services identified on the student's IEP, then the placement proposed to the parent shall be an out-of district day or residential school, depending on the needs of the student. Upon parental acceptance of the proposed IEP and proposed placement, programmatic and financial responsibility shall return to the school district where the student resides. The school district where the student resides shall implement the placement determination of the Team consistent with the requirements of 603 CMR 28.06(3).

(b) For schools attended pursuant to M.G.L. c. 76, § 12B (school choice), such schools may bill and receive payment from the school district where the student resides for the costs of out-of-district placements made by the program school. The program school shall invite the school district where the student resides to participate as a member of the student's Team and shall provide notice of the Team meeting at least five school days prior to the meeting, provided that such participation shall not limit the student's right to a timely evaluation and placement in accordance with 603 CMR 28.00.

(c) A Vocational school shall not discriminate in the enrollment of students with disabilities.

1. A vocational school may not accept students with disabilities on a conditional basis unless the vocational school has procedures that ensure that the reasons for conditional acceptance are equally applied to students without disabilities.

2. A vocational school may serve as an "evaluation site" for a student requiring an extended evaluation under the provisions of 603 CMR 28.05(2)(b) of 603 CMR 28.00 if the evaluative information that is required is primarily vocational in nature. In such circumstances, the student is not considered enrolled in the vocational school, nor shall an extended evaluation be considered a temporary placement. For the duration of the extended evaluation the student shall be considered enrolled in the public school district in which he or she was enrolled prior to the extended evaluation.

(7) *Temporary Assignments*. The Department reserves the right to assign temporary responsibility in cases where the student is not receiving services or when lack of assignment threatens the student's placement or program. Such temporary assignment shall be made based on the information available to the Department. The temporary district shall have all of the rights and responsibilities assigned to districts under 603 CMR 28.00. The temporary district may bill and shall be eligible to receive payment for the special education costs (using the procedures of 603 CMR 10.07 to calculate such costs, including transportation expenses where applicable) from the district assigned responsibility for that period of time for which a temporary district was identified.

6

(8) *Department Assignment of School District Responsibility*.

(a) The Department may assign or a school district or agency may request the Department's assistance in assigning a city, town, or school district to be responsible for students in living situations described in 603 CMR 28.10(3), (4), or (5) in the following circumstances.

1. Students who are in the care or custody of a state agency and have no parent or legal guardian residing in Massachusetts; or

2. When the residence or residential history of the student's parent(s) or legal guardian is in dispute; or

3. When the student has a legal guardian who has been appointed on a limited basis; or

4. When a student has not yet been determined to be eligible and/or is not receiving services, or

5. When a student is in the care or custody of a state agency and is hospitalized and the agency gives notice to the responsible school district that the student will not return to the residence held prior to hospitalization.

(b) A request for an assignment shall not limit the right of the student to timely evaluation, services, or placement in accordance with 603 CMR 28.00. The school district or state agency requesting assignment shall be responsible for providing to the Department all required documentation to ascertain the legal status or residence(s) of the student or the student's parent(s) or legal guardian.

(c) The Department shall use the following criteria to assign a city, town or school district responsibility for a student in a living situation described in 603 CMR 28.10(3), (4), or (5).

1. If the child has been voluntarily surrendered for adoption or freed for adoption by the Probate Court or the Juvenile Court, the school district(s) where the parent(s) lived at the time that the child was surrendered or freed for adoption or when parental rights were terminated shall be responsible.

2. If the student is in the care or custody of a state agency and such state agency has obtained a legal guardianship for the student when the student has turned 18 years old, the school district(s) where the parent(s) lived at the time the court granted the request for guardianship shall be responsible.

3. If the parents' rights have been terminated and the Probate Court or the Juvenile Court has appointed a legal guardian for a minor student, the school district where the legal guardian resides shall be responsible.

4. If the legal guardian is an agency or organization or the legal guardian has been appointed on a limited basis such as a guardian ad litem, or a guardian appointed solely to monitor medications or finances, the school district where the parent(s) lives or last lived shall be responsible.

5. If the student's parents live in two different school districts, such school districts shall be jointly responsible for fulfilling the requirements of 603 CMR 28.00 except if the student actually resided with either parent immediately prior to going into a living situation described in 603 CMR 28.10(3) or (4) or the parents are divorced or separated and one parent has sole physical custody, then the school district where the student resided with the parent or the school district of the parent who has sole physical custody shall be responsible and shall remain responsible in the event the student goes into the care or custody of a state agency.

6. If the student's parent(s) or legal guardian resides in an institutional setting in Massachusetts, including, but not limited to, a correctional facility, a hospital, a nursing home or hospice, or a mental health facility, a halfway house, a pre-release center or a treatment facility, the school district where the parent(s) or legal guardian lived prior to entering the institutional setting shall be responsible.

7. If the student's parent(s) or legal guardian does not reside in Massachusetts, and the parent's or legal guardian's whereabouts are unknown, the school district of the last known Massachusetts residence of the student's parent(s) or legal guardian who lived in Massachusetts shall be responsible.

(d) Using the above criteria, the Department shall notify in writing the assigned school district(s) of its decision. Upon notification of responsibility for provision of special education to a student under 603 CMR 28.10(8)(d), the school district(s) shall immediately assume responsibility for the student in accordance with the requirements of 603 CMR 28.00. Until such notification, the school district(s) that had been responsible for providing special education to such student under 603 CMR 28.00 shall continue to be responsible.

(e) The school district(s) that had been responsible for providing special education to the student prior to assignment by the Department under 603 CMR 28.10(8)(d) may bill and shall be eligible to receive payment (using the procedures of 603 CMR 10.07 to calculate such costs, including transportation expenses where applicable), from the newly assigned district for the special education costs that were incurred during the period of time in which the newly assigned district should have been responsible.

(f) A school district may seek a review of the Department's assignment under the procedures of 603 CMR 28.10(8) at any time that the district has information that was not available to the Department at the time that the assignment was made. The Department will review the information presented and will confirm or change the assignment of school district responsibility, and notify the districts of this decision under 603 CMR 28.10(8)(d).

(9) *Appeal of Assignment of School District Responsibility*. The assigned district may appeal the Department's assignment of responsibility to the Bureau of Special Education Appeals, subject to the following procedures:

(a) A district may appeal the assignment of school district responsibility within 60 days of the most recent notification of assignment.

(b) The request for appeal shall meet the following standards:

1. A request for appeal shall be based only on the information provided to the Department under 603 CMR 28.10(8)(b) and 603 CMR 28.10(8)(f) if applicable;

2. The request shall state the basis of the appeal;

3. The request for appeal shall identify the district(s) that the appealing district claims should have been assigned responsibility; and

4. The appealing district shall include such district(s) as a party to the appeal.

(c) A party may request a decision without a hearing with the agreement of all parties.

(d) The Bureau of Special Education Appeals shall render a decision within 45 days of receipt of the hearing request. The granting of a postponement shall not extend the 45-day deadline for issuance of a decision unless the postponement is requested by a party and allowed by the hearing officer for good cause.

(e) The Bureau of Special Education Appeals may return the case to the Department of Elementary and Secondary Education based on new information presented at the hearing.

(f) The decision of the Bureau of Special Education Appeals shall be limited to a determination of the assigned school district and the effective date of such assignment.

** Technical changes. State agency names shall be revised throughout 603 CMR 28.00 where necessary to conform to recent statutory name changes.*

Regulatory Authority: M.G.L. c. 69, § 1B; c. 69, §§ 1J and 1K, as amended by St. 2010, c. 12, § 3; c. 71, § 38G.

603 CMR 46.00. Prevention of Physical Restraint and Requirements If Used

[Added effective Jan. 1, 2016.]

Section

603 CMR 46.01. Authority, Scope, Purpose and Construction

(1) Authority. 603 CMR 46.00 is promulgated by the Board of Elementary and Secondary Education pursuant to M.G.L. c. 69, § 1B, and c. 71, § 37G.

(2) Scope. 603 CMR 46.00 governs the use of physical restraint on students in publicly funded elementary and secondary education programs, including all Massachusetts public school districts, charter schools, virtual schools, collaborative education programs, and the school day of special education schools approved under 603 CMR 28.09, as provided in 603 CMR 18.05(5)(h). Educational programs in facilities operated by the Department of Youth Services, the Department of Mental Health, the Department of Public Health, or County Houses of Correction shall be governed by the restraint, seclusion, and time-out requirements of such agencies.

(3) Purpose. The purpose of 603 CMR 46.00 is to ensure that every student participating in a Massachusetts public education program is free from the use of physical restraint that is inconsistent with 603 CMR 46.00. Physical restraint shall be used only in emergency situations of last resort, after other lawful and less intrusive alternatives have failed or been deemed inappropriate, and with extreme caution. School personnel shall use physical restraint with two goals in mind:

(a) To administer a physical restraint only when needed to protect a student and/or a member of the school community from assault or imminent, serious, physical harm; and

(b) To prevent or minimize any harm to the student as a result of the use of physical restraint.

(4) Construction. Nothing in 603 CMR 46.00 shall be construed to limit the protection afforded publicly funded students under other state or federal laws, including those laws that provide for the rights of students who have been found eligible to receive special education services. Nothing in 603 CMR 46.00 precludes any teacher, employee or agent of a public education program from using reasonable force to protect students, other persons or themselves from assault or imminent, serious, physical harm.

603 CMR 46.02. Definitions

As used in 603 CMR 46.00, the following terms shall have the following meanings:

Commissioner shall mean the commissioner of the Department of Elementary and Secondary Education appointed in accordance with G.L. c. 15, § 1F, or his or her designee.

Consent shall mean agreement by a parent who has been fully informed of all information relevant to the activity for which agreement is sought, in his or her native language or other mode of communication, that the parent understands and agrees in writing to carrying out of the activity, and understands that the agreement is voluntary and may be revoked at any time. The agreement describes the activity and lists the records (if any) which will be released and to whom. In seeking parental consent, a public education program shall not condition admission or continued enrollment upon agreement to the proposed use of any restraint.

Department shall mean the Department of Elementary and Secondary Education.

Mechanical restraint shall mean the use of any device or equipment to restrict a student's freedom of movement. The term does not include devices implemented by trained school personnel, or utilized by a student that have been prescribed by an appropriate medical or related services professional, and are used for the specific and approved positioning or protective purposes for which such devices were designed. Examples of such devices include: adaptive devices or mechanical supports used to achieve proper body position, balance, or alignment to allow greater freedom of mobility than would be possible without the use of such devices or mechanical supports; vehicle safety restraints when used as intended during the transport of a student in a moving vehicle; restraints for medical immobilization; or orthopedically prescribed devices that permit a student to participate in activities without risk of harm.

Medication restraint shall mean the administration of medication for the purpose of temporarily controlling behavior. Medication prescribed by a licensed physician and authorized by the parent for administration in the school setting is not medication restraint.

Parent shall mean a student's father, mother, or legal guardian or person or agency legally authorized to act on behalf of the student in place of or in conjunction with the father, mother, or legal guardian.

Physical escort shall mean a temporary touching or holding, without the use of force, of the hand, wrist, arm, shoulder, or back for the purpose of inducing a student who is agitated to walk to a safe location.

Physical restraint shall mean direct physical contact that prevents or significantly restricts a student's freedom of movement. Physical restraint does not include: brief physical contact to promote student safety, providing physical guidance or prompting when teaching a skill, redirecting attention, providing comfort, or a physical escort.

Principal shall mean the instructional leader or headmaster of a public education school program or his or her designee. The board of directors of a charter school or virtual school, or special education school or program approved under 603 CMR 28.09, shall designate in the restraint prevention and behavior support policy who will serve as principal for purposes of 603 CMR 46.00.

Prone restraint shall mean a physical restraint in which a student is placed face down on the floor or another surface, and physical pressure is applied to the student's body to keep the student in the face-down position.

Public education programs shall mean public schools, including charter schools, virtual schools, collaborative education programs, and the school day of special education schools approved under 603 CMR 28.09, as provided in 603 CMR 18.05(5)(h), and school events and activities sponsored by such programs. The term "programs" may be used in 603 CMR 46.00 to refer to "public education programs." For purposes of 603 CMR 46.00, public education programs shall not include the educational services provided within Department of Youth Services, Department of Mental Health, Department of Public Health, and County Houses of Correction operated or contracted facilities.

School Working Day shall mean a day or partial day that students are in attendance at the public education program for instructional purposes.

Seclusion shall mean the involuntary confinement of a student alone in a room or area from which the student is physically prevented from leaving. Seclusion does not include a time-out as defined in 603 CMR 46.02.

Time-out shall mean a behavioral support strategy developed pursuant to 603 CMR 46.04(1) in which a student temporarily separates from the learning activity or the classroom, either by choice or by direction from staff, for the purpose of calming. During time-out, a student must be continuously observed by a staff member. Staff shall be with the student or immediately available to the student at all times. The space used for time-out must be clean, safe, sanitary, and appropriate for the purpose of calming. Time-out shall cease as soon as the student has calmed.

603 CMR 46.03. Use of Restraint

(1) Prohibition.

(a) Mechanical restraint, medication restraint, and seclusion shall be prohibited in public education programs.

(b) Prone restraint shall be prohibited in public education programs except on an individual student basis, and only under the following circumstances:

1. The student has a documented history of repeatedly causing serious self-injuries and/or injuries to other students or staff;

2. All other forms of physical restraints have failed to ensure the safety of the student and/or the safety of others;

3. There are no medical contraindications as documented by a licensed physician;

4. There is psychological or behavioral justification for the use of prone restraint and there are no psychological or behavioral contraindications, as documented by a licensed mental health professional;

5. The program has obtained consent to use prone restraint in an emergency as set out in 603 CMR 46.03(1)(b), and such use has been approved in writing by the principal; and,

6. The program has documented 603 CMR 46.03(1)(b)1–5 in advance of the use of prone restraint and maintains the documentation.

(c) Physical restraint, including prone restraint where permitted, shall be considered an emergency procedure of last resort and shall be prohibited in public education programs except when a student's behavior poses a threat of assault, or imminent, serious, physical harm to self or others and the student is not responsive to verbal directives or other lawful and less intrusive behavior interventions, or such interventions are deemed to be inappropriate under the circumstances.

(d) All physical restraints, including prone restraint where permitted, shall be administered in compliance with 603 CMR 46.05.

(2) Physical restraint shall not be used:

(a) As a means of discipline or punishment;

(b) When the student cannot be safely restrained because it is medically contraindicated for reasons including, but not limited to, asthma, seizures, a cardiac condition, obesity, bronchitis, communication-related disabilities, or risk of vomiting;

(c) As a response to property destruction, disruption of school order, a student's refusal to comply with a public education program rule or staff directive, or verbal threats when those actions do not constitute a threat of assault, or imminent, serious, physical harm; or

(d) As a standard response for any individual student. No written individual behavior plan or individualized education program (IEP) may include use of physical restraint as a standard response to any behavior. Physical restraint is an emergency procedure of last resort.

(3) Limitations on use of restraint. Physical restraint in a public education program shall be limited to the use of such reasonable force as is necessary to protect a student or another member of the school community from assault or imminent, serious, physical harm.

(4) Referral to law enforcement or other state agencies. Nothing in these regulations prohibits:

(a) The right of any individual to report to appropriate authorities a crime committed by a student or other individual;

(b) Law enforcement, judicial authorities or school security personnel from exercising their responsibilities, including the physical detainment of a student or other person alleged to have committed a crime or posing a security risk; or

(c) The exercise of an individual's responsibilities as a mandated reporter pursuant to G.L. c. 119, § 51A. 603 CMR 46.00 shall not be used to deter any individual from reporting neglect or abuse to the appropriate state agency.

603 CMR 46.04. Policy and Procedures; Training

(1) Procedures. Public education programs shall develop and implement written restraint prevention and behavior support policy and procedures consistent with 603 CMR 46.00 regarding appropriate responses to student behavior that may require immediate intervention. Such policy and procedures shall be annually reviewed and provided to program staff and made available to parents of enrolled students. Such policy and procedures shall include, but not be limited to:

(a) Methods for preventing student violence, self-injurious behavior, and suicide, including individual crisis planning and de-escalation of potentially dangerous behavior occurring among groups of students or with an individual student;

(b) Methods for engaging parents in discussions about restraint prevention and the use of restraint solely as an emergency procedure;

(c) A description and explanation of the program's alternatives to physical restraint and method of physical restraint in emergency situations;

(d) A statement prohibiting: medication restraint, mechanical restraint, prone restraint unless permitted pursuant to 603 CMR 46.03(1)(b), seclusion, and the use of physical restraint in a manner inconsistent with 603 CMR 46.00;

(e) A description of the program's training requirements, reporting requirements, and follow-up procedures;

(f) A procedure for receiving and investigating complaints regarding restraint practices;

(g) A procedure for conducting periodic review of data and documentation on the use of physical restraints as described in 603 CMR 46.06(5) and (6);

(h) A procedure for implementing the reporting requirements as described in 603 CMR 46.06;

(i) A procedure for making reasonable efforts to orally notify a parent of the use of restraint on a student within 24 hours of the restraint, and for sending written notification to the parent within three school working days following the use of restraint to an email address provided by the parent for the purpose of communicating about the student, or by regular mail to the parent postmarked within three school working days of the restraint; and,

(j) If the program uses time-out as a behavioral support strategy, a procedure for the use of time-out that includes a process for obtaining principal approval of time-out for more than 30 minutes based on the individual student's continuing agitation.

(2) Required training for all staff. Each principal or director shall determine a time and method to provide all program staff with training regarding the program's restraint prevention and behavior support policy and requirements when restraint is used. Such training shall occur within the first month of each school year and, for employees hired after the school year begins, within a month of their employment. Training shall include information on the following:

(a) The role of the student, family, and staff in preventing restraint;

(b) The program's restraint prevention and behavior support policy and procedures, including use of time-out as a behavior support strategy distinct from seclusion;

(c) Interventions that may preclude the need for restraint, including de-escalation of problematic behaviors and other alternatives to restraint in emergency circumstances;

(d) When behavior presents an emergency that requires physical restraint, the types of permitted physical restraints and related safety considerations, including information regarding the increased risk of injury to a student when any restraint is used, in particular a restraint of extended duration;

(e) Administering physical restraint in accordance with medical or psychological limitations, known or suspected trauma history, and/or behavioral intervention plans applicable to an individual student; and

(f) Identification of program staff who have received in-depth training pursuant to 603 CMR 46.03(3) in the use of physical restraint.

(3) In-depth staff training in the use of physical restraint. At the beginning of each school year, the principal of each public education program or his or her designee shall identify program staff who are authorized to serve as a school-wide resource to assist in ensuring proper administration of physical restraint. Such staff shall participate in in-depth training in the use of physical restraint. The Department recommends that such training be competency-based and be at least sixteen (16) hours in length with at least one refresher training occurring annually thereafter.

(4) Content of in-depth training. In-depth training in the proper administration of physical restraint shall include, but not be limited to:

(a) Appropriate procedures for preventing the use of physical restraint, including the de-escalation of problematic behavior, relationship building and the use of alternatives to restraint;

(b) A description and identification of specific dangerous behaviors on the part of students that may lead to the use of physical restraint and methods for evaluating the risk of harm in individual situations in order to determine whether the use of restraint is warranted;

(c) The simulated experience of administering and receiving physical restraint, instruction regarding the effect(s) on the person restrained, including instruction on monitoring physical signs of distress and obtaining medical assistance;

(d) Instruction regarding documentation and reporting requirements and investigation of injuries and complaints;

(e) Demonstration by participants of proficiency in administering physical restraint; and,

(f) Instruction regarding the impact of physical restraint on the student and family, recognizing the act of restraint has impact, including but not limited to psychological, physiological, and social-emotional effects.

603 CMR 46.05. Proper Administration of Physical Restraint

(1) Trained personnel. Only public education program personnel who have received training pursuant to 603 CMR 46.04(2) or 603 CMR 46.04(3) shall administer physical restraint on students. Whenever possible, the administration of a restraint shall be witnessed by at least one adult who does not participate in the restraint. The training requirements contained in 603 CMR 46.00 shall not preclude a teacher, employee or agent of a public education program from using reasonable force to protect students, other persons or themselves from assault or imminent, serious, physical harm.

(2) Use of force. A person administering a physical restraint shall use only the amount of force necessary to protect the student or others from physical injury or harm.

(3) Safest method. A person administering physical restraint shall use the safest method available and appropriate to the situation subject to the safety requirements set forth in 603 CMR 46.05(5). Floor restraints, including prone restraints otherwise permitted under 603 CMR 46.03(1)(b), shall be prohibited unless the staff members administering the restraint have received in-depth training according to the requirements of 603 CMR 46.04(3) and, in the judgment of the trained staff members, such method is required to provide safety for the student or others present.

(4) Duration of restraint. All physical restraint must be terminated as soon as the student is no longer an immediate danger to himself or others, or the student indicates that he or she cannot breathe, or if the student is observed to be in severe distress, such as having difficulty breathing, or sustained or prolonged crying or coughing.

(5) Safety requirements. Additional requirements for the use of physical restraint:

(a) No restraint shall be administered in such a way that the student is prevented from breathing or speaking. During the administration of a restraint, a staff member shall continuously monitor the physical status of the student, including skin temperature and color, and respiration.

(b) Restraint shall be administered in such a way so as to prevent or minimize physical harm. If, at any time during a physical restraint, the student expresses or demonstrates significant physical distress including, but not limited to, difficulty breathing, the student shall be released from the restraint immediately, and school staff shall take steps to seek medical assistance.

(c) If a student is restrained for a period longer than 20 minutes, program staff shall obtain the approval of the principal. The approval shall be based upon the student's continued agitation during the restraint justifying the need for continued restraint.

(d) Program staff shall review and consider any known medical or psychological limitations, known or suspected trauma history, and/or behavioral intervention plans regarding the use of physical restraint on an individual student.

(e) After the release of a student from a restraint, the public education program shall implement follow-up procedures. These procedures shall include reviewing the incident with the student to address the behavior that precipitated the restraint, reviewing the incident with the staff person(s) who administered the restraint to discuss whether proper restraint procedures were followed, and consideration of whether any follow-up is appropriate for students who witnessed the incident.

603 CMR 46.06. Reporting Requirements

(1) Circumstances under which a physical restraint must be reported. Program staff shall report the use of any physical restraint as specified in 603 CMR 46.06(2).

(2) Informing the principal. The program staff member who administered the restraint shall verbally inform the principal of the restraint as soon as possible, and by written report no later than the next school working day. The written report shall be provided to the principal for review of the use of the restraint. If the principal has administered the restraint, the principal shall prepare the report

and submit it to an individual or team designated by the superintendent or board of trustees for review. The principal or director or his/her designee shall maintain an on-going record of all reported instances of physical restraint, which shall be made available for review by the parent or the Department upon request.

(3) Informing parents. The principal or director of the program or his/her designee shall make reasonable efforts to verbally inform the student's parent of the restraint within 24 hours of the event, and shall notify the parent by written report sent either within three school working days of the restraint to an email address provided by the parent for communications about the student, or by regular mail postmarked no later than three school working days of the restraint. If the school or program customarily provides a parent of a student with report cards and other necessary school-related information in a language other than English, the written restraint report shall be provided to the parent in that language. The principal shall provide the student and the parent an opportunity to comment orally and in writing on the use of the restraint and on information in the written report.

(4) Contents of report. The written report required by 603 CMR 46.06(2) and (3) shall include:

(a) The name of the student; the names and job titles of the staff who administered the restraint, and observers, if any; the date of the restraint; the time the restraint began and ended; and the name of the principal or designee who was verbally informed following the restraint; and, as applicable, the name of the principal or designee who approved continuation of the restraint beyond 20 minutes pursuant to 603 CMR 46.05(5)(c).

6

(b) A description of the activity in which the restrained student and other students and staff in the same room or vicinity were engaged immediately preceding the use of physical restraint; the behavior that prompted the restraint; the efforts made to prevent escalation of behavior, including the specific de-escalation strategies used; alternatives to restraint that were attempted; and the justification for initiating physical restraint.

(c) A description of the administration of the restraint including the holds used and reasons such holds were necessary; the student's behavior and reactions during the restraint; how the restraint ended; and documentation of injury to the student and/or staff, if any, during the restraint and any medical care provided.

(d) Information regarding any further action(s) that the school has taken or may take, including any consequences that may be imposed on the student.

(e) Information regarding opportunities for the student's parents to discuss with school officials the administration of the restraint, any consequences that may be imposed on the student, and any other related matter.

(5) Individual student review. The principal shall conduct a weekly review of restraint data to identify students who have been restrained multiple times during the week. If such students are identified, the principal shall convene one or more review teams as the principal deems appropriate to assess each student's progress and needs. The assessment shall include at least the following:

(a) review and discussion of the written reports submitted in accordance with 603 CMR 46.06 and any comments provided by the student and parent about such reports and the use of the restraints;

(b) analysis of the circumstances leading up to each restraint, including factors such as time of day, day of the week, antecedent events, and individuals involved;

(c) consideration of factors that may have contributed to escalation of behaviors, consideration of alternatives to restraint, including de-escalation techniques and possible interventions, and such other strategies and decisions as appropriate, with the goal of reducing or eliminating the use of restraint in the future;

(d) agreement on a written plan of action by the program.

If the principal directly participated in the restraint, a duly qualified individual designated by the superintendent or board of trustees shall lead the review team's discussion. The principal shall ensure that a record of each individual student review is maintained and made available for review by the Department or the parent, upon request.

(6) Administrative review. The principal shall conduct a monthly review of school-wide restraint data. This review shall consider patterns of use of restraints by similarities in the time of day, day of the week, or individuals involved; the number and duration of physical restraints school-wide and for individual students; the duration of restraints; and the number and type of injuries, if any, resulting from the use of restraint. The principal shall determine whether it is necessary or appropriate to modify the school's restraint prevention and management policy, conduct additional staff training on restraint reduction/prevention strategies, such as training on positive behavioral interventions and supports, or take such other action as necessary or appropriate to reduce or eliminate restraints.

(7) Report all restraint-related injuries to the Department. When a physical restraint has resulted in an injury to a student or program staff member, the program shall send a copy of the written report required by 603 CMR 46.06(4) to the Department postmarked no later than three school working days of the administration of the restraint. The program shall also send the Department a copy of the record of physical restraints maintained by the principal pursuant to 603 CMR 46.06(2) for the 30-day period prior to the date of the reported restraint. The Department shall determine if additional action by the program is warranted and, if so, shall notify the program of any required actions within 30 calendar days of receipt of the required written report(s).

(8) Report all physical restraints to the Department. Every program shall collect and annually report data to the Department regarding the use of physical restraints. Such data shall be reported in a manner and form directed by the Department.

603 CMR 46.07. Effective Date

The effective date of 603 CMR 46.00, as amended, is January 1, 2016.

603 CMR 53.00. Student Discipline

[Effective July 1, 2014.]

Section

603 CMR 53.01. Authority, Scope, and Purpose

(1) 603 CMR 53.00 is promulgated pursuant to the authority of the Department of Elementary and Secondary Education under G.L. c. 69, §§ 1A and 1B, G.L. c. 71, § 37H, and G.L. c. 71, § 37H¾

(2) The purpose of 603 CMR 53.00 is:

(a) for those discipline offenses subject to G.L. 71, § 37H¾, as set forth in 603 CMR 53.01(3)(a), to limit the use of long-term suspension as a consequence for student misconduct until other consequences have been considered and tried as appropriate;

(b) to promote engagement of a student's parent in discussion of the student's misconduct, and options for responding to it;

(c) to assure that every student who is expelled or suspended, regardless of the reason for suspension or expulsion, has the opportunity to receive education services to make academic progress during the period of suspension or expulsion; and,

(d) to keep schools safe and supportive for all students while ensuring fair and effective disciplinary practices.

(3) 603 CMR 53.00 sets forth, for all public preschool, elementary, and secondary schools and programs in Massachusetts, including charter and virtual schools:

(a) at 603 CMR 53.03 through 53.11, the minimum procedural requirements applicable to the suspension of a student for a disciplinary offense other than: a) possession of a dangerous weapon; b) possession of a controlled substance; c) assault on a member of the educational staff; or d) a felony charge or felony delinquency complaint or conviction, or adjudication or admission of guilt with respect to such felony, if a principal determines that the student's continued presence in school would have a substantial detrimental effect on the general welfare of the school, as provided in G.L. c. 71, §§ 37H or 37H½;

(b) the minimum requirements and procedures necessary to ensure that all students who have been suspended, in-school or out-of-school, or expelled, regardless of the type of offense, have an opportunity to make academic progress during their period of suspension, expulsion, or removal from regular classroom activities; and

(c) the requirements pertaining to school discipline data reporting and analysis.

603 CMR 53.02. Definitions

(1) "Commissioner" means the commissioner of the Department of Elementary and Secondary Education appointed in accordance with G.L. c. 15, § 1F, or his or her designee.

(2) "Department" means the Department of Elementary and Secondary Education.

(3) "Disciplinary offense" means any alleged or determined disciplinary infraction by a student, except for: a) possession of a dangerous weapon; b) possession of a controlled substance; c) assault on a member of the educational staff; or d) a felony charge or felony delinquency complaint or conviction, or adjudication or admission of guilt with respect to such felony, if a principal determines that the student's continued presence in school would have a substantial detrimental effect on the general welfare of the school, as provided in G.L. c. 71, §§ 37H or 37H½. A disciplinary offense, as defined, is subject to the provisions of G.L. c. 71, § 37H¾ and these regulations.

(4) "Disciplinary offense under G.L. c. 71, §§ 37H or 37H½" means one or more of the following alleged or determined disciplinary infractions: a) possession of a dangerous weapon; b) possession of a controlled substance; c) assault on a member of the educational staff; and d) a felony charge or felony delinquency complaint or conviction, or adjudication or admission of guilt with respect to such felony, if a principal determines that the student's continued presence in school would have a substantial detrimental effect on the general welfare of the school, as provided in G.L. c. 71, §§ 37H or 37H½.

(5) "Expulsion" means the removal of a student from the school premises, regular classroom activities, and school activities for more than ninety (90) school days, indefinitely, or permanently, as permitted under G.L. c. 71, §§ 37H or 37H½ for: a) possession of a dangerous weapon; b) possession of a controlled substance; c) assault on a member of the educational staff; or d) a felony charge or felony delinquency complaint or conviction, or adjudication or admission of guilt with respect to such felony, if a principal determines that the student's continued presence in school would have a substantial detrimental effect on the general welfare of the school, as provided in G.L. c. 71, §§ 37H or 37H½.

(6) "In-school suspension" means removal of a student from regular classroom activities, but not from the school premises, for no more than (10) consecutive school days, or no more than ten (10) school days cumulatively for multiple infractions during the school year. Removal solely from participation in extracurricular activities or school-sponsored events, or both, shall not count as removal in calculating school days. In-school suspension for ten (10) days or less, consecutively or cumulatively during a school year, shall not be considered a short-term suspension under these regulations. If a student is placed in in-school suspension for more than ten (10) days, consecutively or cumulatively during a school year, such suspension shall be deemed a long-term suspension for due process, appeal, and reporting purposes under 603 CMR 53.00.

(7) "Long-term suspension" means the removal of a student from the school premises and regular classroom activities for more than ten (10) consecutive school days, or for more than ten (10) school days cumulatively for multiple disciplinary offenses in any school year. A principal may, in his or her discretion, allow a student to serve a long-term suspension in school. Removal solely from participation in extracurricular activities or school-sponsored events, or both, shall not count as removal in calculating school days. Except for students who are charged with a disciplinary offense set forth in subsections (a) or (b) of G.L. c. 71, § 37 H, or in section 37H½ of G.L. c. 71, no student may be placed on long-term suspension for one or more disciplinary offenses for more than ninety (90) school days in a school year beginning with the first day that the student is removed from school. No long-term suspension shall extend beyond the end of the school year in which such suspension is imposed.

6

(8) "Parent" means a student's father, mother, or legal guardian, or person or agency legally authorized to act on behalf of the student in place of or in conjunction with the father, mother, or legal guardian.

(9) "Principal" means the instructional leader or headmaster of a public school or his or her designee for purposes of school disciplinary matters. The board of trustees of a charter school or virtual school shall designate in the school discipline code who will serve as the principal for purposes of 603 CMR 53.00.

(10) "School-wide education service plan" means the document developed by a principal, in accordance with G.L. c. 76, § 21, that includes a list of education services available to students who are expelled or suspended from school for more than 10 consecutive days.

(11) "Short-term suspension" means the removal of a student from the school premises and regular classroom activities for ten (10) consecutive school days or less. A principal may, in his or her discretion, allow a student to serve a short-term suspension in school. Removal solely from participation in extracurricular activities or school-sponsored events, or both, shall not count as removal in calculating school days.

(12) "Superintendent" means the chief executive officer employed by a school committee or board of trustees to administer a school system, charter school, or virtual school pursuant to G.L. c. 71, §§ 59, 59A, 89, or 94, or his or her designee appointed for purposes of conducting a student disciplinary hearing. The board of trustees of a charter school or virtual school shall designate in the school's discipline code who will serve as the superintendent for the purposes of 603 CMR 53.00.

(13) "Suspension" means short-term suspension and long-term suspension unless otherwise stated.

603 CMR 53.03. Policies and Procedures

Each school committee and board of trustees shall ensure that policies and procedures are in place in public preschool, elementary, and secondary schools and programs under its jurisdiction that meet, at a minimum, the requirements of G.L. c. 71, § 37H¾, G.L. c. 76, § 21, and 603 CMR 53.00.

603 CMR 53.04. Investigation of Disciplinary Incidents

Nothing in these regulations shall prevent a school administrator from conducting an investigation, including student interviews, of a school-related disciplinary incident.

603 CMR 53.05. Alternatives to Suspension under Section 37H¾

In every case of student misconduct for which suspension may be imposed, a principal shall exercise discretion in deciding the consequence for the offense; consider ways to re-engage the student in learning; and avoid using long-term suspension from school as a consequence until alternatives have been tried. Alternatives may include the use of evidence-based strategies and programs such as mediation, conflict resolution, restorative justice, and positive behavioral interventions and supports.

603 CMR 53.06. Notice of Suspension and Hearing under Section 37H¾

(1) Except as provided in 603 CMR 53.07 and 603 CMR 53.10, a principal may not impose a suspension as a consequence for a disciplinary offense without first providing the student and the parent oral and written notice, and providing the student an opportunity for a hearing on the charge and the parent an opportunity to participate in such hearing.

(2) The principal shall provide oral and written notice to the student and the parent in English and in the primary language of the home if other than English, or other means of communication where appropriate. The notice shall set forth in plain language:

6

(a) the disciplinary offense;

(b) the basis for the charge;

(c) the potential consequences, including the potential length of the student's suspension;

(d) the opportunity for the student to have a hearing with the principal concerning the proposed suspension, including the opportunity to dispute the charges and to present the student's explanation of the alleged incident, and for the parent to attend the hearing;

(e) the date, time, and location of the hearing;

(f) the right of the student and the student's parent to interpreter services at the hearing if needed to participate;

(g) if the student may be placed on long-term suspension following the hearing with the principal:

1. the rights set forth in 603 CMR 53.08 (3)(b); and

2. the right to appeal the principal's decision to the superintendent.

(3) The principal shall make reasonable efforts to notify the parent orally of the opportunity to attend the hearing. To conduct a hearing without the parent present, the principal must be able to document reasonable efforts to include the parent. The principal is presumed to have made reasonable efforts if the principal has sent written notice and has documented at least two (2) attempts to contact the parent in the manner specified by the parent for emergency notification.

(4) Written notice to the parent may be made by hand delivery, first-class mail, certified mail, email to an address provided by the parent for school communications, or any other method of delivery agreed to by the principal and parent.

603 CMR 53.07. Emergency Removal under Section 37H¾

(1) Nothing in these regulations shall prevent a principal from removing a student from school temporarily when a student is charged with a disciplinary offense and the continued presence of the student poses a danger to persons or property, or materially and substantially disrupts the order of the school, and, in the principal's judgment, there is no alternative available to alleviate the danger or disruption. The principal shall immediately notify the superintendent in writing of the removal and the reason for it, and describe the danger presented by the student. The temporary removal shall not exceed two (2) school days following the day of the emergency removal, during which time the principal shall:

(a) Make immediate and reasonable efforts to orally notify the student and the student's parent of the emergency removal, the reason for the need for emergency removal, and the other matters set forth in 603 CMR 53.06(2);

(b) Provide written notice to the student and parent as provided in 603 CMR 53.06(2);

(c) Provide the student an opportunity for a hearing with the principal that complies with 603 CMR 53.08(2) or 53.08(3), as applicable, and the parent an opportunity to attend the hearing, before the expiration of the two (2) school days, unless an extension of time for hearing is otherwise agreed to by the principal, student, and parent.

(d) Render a decision orally on the same day as the hearing, and in writing no later than the following school day, which meets the requirements of 603 CMR 53.08(2)(c) and 53.08(2)(d) or 603 CMR 53.08(3)(c) and 53.08(3)(d), as applicable.

(2) A principal may not remove a student from school on an emergency basis for a disciplinary offense until adequate provisions have been made for the student's safety and transportation.

603 CMR 53.08. Principal's Hearing under Section 37H¾

(1) The principal shall determine the extent of the rights to be afforded the student at a disciplinary hearing based on the anticipated consequences for the disciplinary offense. If the consequence may be long-term suspension from school, the principal shall afford the student, at a minimum, all the rights set forth in 603 CMR 53.08(3) in addition to those rights afforded to students who may face a short-term suspension from school.

(2) Principal Hearing—Short-term Suspension

(a) The purpose of the hearing with the principal is to hear and consider information regarding the alleged incident for which the student may be suspended, provide the student an opportunity to dispute the charges and explain the circumstances surrounding the alleged incident, determine if the student committed the disciplinary offense, and if so, the consequences for the infraction. At a minimum, the principal shall discuss the disciplinary offense, the basis for the charge, and any other pertinent information. The student also shall have an opportunity to present information, including mitigating facts, that the principal should consider in determining whether other remedies and consequences may be appropriate as set forth in 603 CMR 53.05. The principal shall provide the parent, if present, an opportunity to discuss the student's conduct and offer information, including mitigating circumstances, that the principal should consider in determining consequences for the student.

(b) Based on the available information, including mitigating circumstances, the principal shall determine whether the student committed the disciplinary offense, and, if so, what remedy or consequence will be imposed.

(c) The principal shall notify the student and parent of the determination and the reasons for it, and, if the student is suspended, the type and duration of suspension and the opportunity to make up assignments and such other school work as needed to make academic progress during the period of removal, as provided in 603 CMR 53.13(1). The determination shall be in writing and may be in the form of an update to the original written notice.

(d) If the student is in a public preschool program or in grades K through 3, the principal shall send a copy of the written determination to the superintendent and explain the reasons for imposing an out-of-school suspension, before the short-term suspension takes effect.

(3) Principal Hearing—Long-term Suspension

(a) The purpose of the hearing is the same as the purpose of a short-term suspension hearing.

(b) At a minimum, in addition to the rights afforded a student in a short-term suspension hearing, the student shall have the following rights:

1. In advance of the hearing, the opportunity to review the student's record and the documents upon which the principal may rely in making a determination to suspend the student or not;

2. the right to be represented by counsel or a lay person of the student's choice, at the student's/parent's expense;

3. the right to produce witnesses on his or her behalf and to present the student's explanation of the alleged incident, but the student may not be compelled to do so;

4. the right to cross-examine witnesses presented by the school district;

5. the right to request that the hearing be recorded by the principal, and to receive a copy of the audio recording upon request. If the student or parent requests an audio recording, the principal shall inform all participants before the hearing that an audio record will be made and a copy will be provided to the student and parent upon request.

(c) The principal shall provide the parent, if present, an opportunity to discuss the student's conduct and offer information, including mitigating circumstances, that the principal should consider in determining consequences for the student.

(d) Based on the evidence, the principal shall determine whether the student committed the disciplinary offense, and, if so, after considering mitigating circumstances and alternatives to suspension as set forth in 603 CMR 53.05, what remedy or consequence will be imposed, in place of or in addition to a long-term suspension. The principal shall send the written determination to the student and parent by hand-delivery, certified mail, first-class mail, email to an address provided by the parent for school communications, or any other method of delivery agreed to by the principal and the parent. If the principal decides to suspend the student, the written determination shall:

1. Identify the disciplinary offense, the date on which the hearing took place, and the participants at the hearing;

2. Set out the key facts and conclusions reached by the principal;

3. Identify the length and effective date of the suspension, as well as a date of return to school;

4. Include notice of the student's opportunity to receive education services to make academic progress during the period of removal from school as provided in 603 CMR 53.13(4)(a);

5.0Inform the student of the right to appeal the principal's decision to the superintendent or designee, but only if the principal has imposed a long-term suspension. Notice of the right of appeal shall be in English and the primary language of the home if other than English, or other means of communication where appropriate, and shall include the following information stated in plain language:

a) the process for appealing the decision, including that the student or parent must file a written notice of appeal with the superintendent within five (5) calendar days of the effective date of the long-term suspension; provided that within the five (5) calendar days, the student or parent may request and receive from the superintendent an extension of time for filing the written notice for up to seven (7) additional calendar days; and that

b) the long-term suspension will remain in effect unless and until the superintendent decides to reverse the principal's determination on appeal.

(e) If the student is in a public preschool program or in grades K through 3, the principal shall send a copy of the written determination to the superintendent and explain the reasons for imposing an out-of-school suspension, whether short-term or long-term, before the suspension takes effect.

603 CMR 53.09. Superintendent's Hearing under Section 37H¾

(1) A student who is placed on long-term suspension following a hearing with the principal shall have the right to appeal the principal's decision to the superintendent.

(2) The student or parent shall file a notice of appeal with the superintendent within the time period set forth 603 CMR 53.08(3)(c)5.a). If the appeal is not timely filed, the superintendent may deny the appeal, or may allow the appeal in his or her discretion, for good cause.

(3) The superintendent shall hold the hearing within three (3) school days of the student's request, unless the student or parent requests an extension of up to seven (7) additional calendar days, in which case the superintendent shall grant the extension.

(4) The superintendent shall make a good faith effort to include the parent in the hearing. The superintendent shall be presumed to have made a good faith effort if he or she has made efforts to find a day and time for the hearing that would allow the parent and superintendent to participate. The superintendent shall send written notice to the parent of the date, time, and location of the hearing.

(5) The superintendent shall conduct a hearing to determine whether the student committed the disciplinary offense of which the student is accused, and if so, what the consequence shall be. The superintendent shall arrange for an audio recording of the hearing, a copy of which shall be provided to the student or parent upon request. The superintendent shall inform all participants before the hearing that an audio record will be made of the hearing and a copy will be provided to the student and parent upon request.

(6) The student shall have all the rights afforded the student at the principal's hearing for long-term suspension under 603 CMR 53.08(3)(b).

(7) The superintendent shall issue a written decision within five (5) calendar days of the hearing which meets the requirements of 603 CMR 53.08(3)(c) 1 through 5. If the superintendent determines that the student committed the disciplinary offense, the superintendent may impose the same or a lesser consequence than the principal, but shall not impose a suspension greater than that imposed by the principal's decision.

(8) The decision of the superintendent shall be the final decision of the school district, charter school, or virtual school, with regard to the suspension.

603 CMR 53.10. In-School Suspension under Section 37H¾

(1) The principal may use in-school suspension as an alternative to short-term suspension for disciplinary offenses.

(2) The principal may impose an in-school suspension for a disciplinary offense under this provision, provided that the principal follows the process set forth in 603 CMR 53.10(3) through 603 CMR 53.10(5) and the student has the opportunity to make academic progress as set forth in 603 CMR 53.13(1).

(3) The principal shall inform the student of the disciplinary offense charged and the basis for the charge, and provide the student an opportunity to dispute the charges and explain the circumstances surrounding the alleged incident. If the principal determines that the student committed the disciplinary offense, the principal shall inform the student of the length of the student's in-school suspension, which shall not exceed 10 days, cumulatively or consecutively, in a school year.

(4) On the same day as the in-school suspension decision, the principal shall make reasonable efforts to notify the parent orally of the disciplinary offense, the reasons for concluding that the student committed the infraction, and the length of the in-school suspension. The principal shall also invite the parent to a meeting to discuss the student's academic performance and behavior, strategies for student engagement, and possible responses to the behavior. Such meeting shall be scheduled on the day of the suspension if possible, and if not, as soon thereafter as possible. If the principal is unable to reach the parent after making and documenting at least (2) attempts to do so, such attempts shall constitute reasonable efforts for purposes of orally informing the parent of the in-school suspension.

(5) The principal shall send written notice to the student and parent about the in-school suspension, including the reason and the length of the in-school suspension, and inviting the parent to a meeting with the principal for the purpose set forth in 603 CMR 53.10(4), if such meeting has not already occurred. The principal shall deliver such notice on the day of the suspension by hand-delivery, certified mail, first-class mail, email to an address provided by the parent for school communications, or by other method of delivery agreed to by the principal and the parent.

603 CMR 53.11. Emergency Removal under Section 37H¾

The principal may remove a student from privileges, such as extracurricular activities and attendance at school-sponsored events, based on the student's misconduct. Such a removal is not subject to the procedures in G.L. c. 71, § 37H¾ or 603 CMR 53.00.

603 CMR 53.12. Disciplinary Offenses under Section 37H or 37H½

(1) School districts shall adopt disciplinary policies and procedures applicable to a student who is accused of a disciplinary offense under G.L. c. 71, §§ 37H or 37H½. Such policies and procedures shall be consistent with the applicable statute and provide due process of law.

(2) The principal may remove a student who has committed a disciplinary offense under G.L. c. 71, §§ 37H or 37H½ from school for more than ninety (90) days in a school year.

(3) Any student who is removed from school for a disciplinary offense under G.L. c. 71, § 37H or § 37H½ shall have an opportunity to receive education services and make academic progress during the period of removal, as provided in 603 CMR 53.13.

6

603 CMR 53.13. Education Services and Academic Progress under Sections 37H, 37H½, and 37H¾

(1) Any student who is serving an in-school suspension, short-term suspension, long-term suspension, or expulsion shall have the opportunity to earn credits, as applicable, make up assignments, tests, papers, and other school work as needed to make academic progress during the period of his or her removal from the classroom or school. The principal shall inform the student and parent of this opportunity in writing when such suspension or expulsion is imposed.

(2) Any student who is expelled or suspended from school for more than ten (10) consecutive days, whether in school or out of school, shall have an opportunity to receive education services and make academic progress toward meeting state and local requirements, through the school-wide education service plan.

(3) The principal shall develop a school-wide education service plan describing the education services that the school district will make available to students who are expelled or suspended from school for more than ten (10) consecutive days. The plan shall include the process for notifying such students and their parents of the services and arranging such services. Education services shall be based on, and be provided in a manner consistent with, the academic standards and curriculum frameworks established for all students under G.L. c. 69, §§ 1D and 1F.

(4) Notice of Education Services for Students in Long-Term Suspension and Expulsion; Enrollment Reporting.

(a) The principal shall notify the parent and student of the opportunity to receive education services at the time the student is expelled or placed on long-term suspension. Notice shall be provided in English and in the primary language spoken in the student's home if other than English, or other means of communication where appropriate. The notice shall include a list of the specific education services that are available to the student and contact information for a school district staff member who can provide more detailed information.

(b) For each student expelled or suspended from school for more than ten (10) consecutive days, whether in-school or out-of-school, the school district shall document the student's enrollment in education services. For data reporting purposes, the school shall track and report attendance, academic progress, and such other data as directed by the Department.

603 CMR 53.14. Student Suspension and Expulsion Data Collection and Reporting

(1) Every school district, charter school, and virtual school shall collect and annually report data to the Department regarding in-school suspensions, short- and long-term suspensions, expulsions, emergency removals under 603 CMR 53.07, access to education services under 603 CMR 53.13, and such other information as may be required by the Department. Such data shall be reported in a manner and form directed by the Department.

(2) The principal of each school shall periodically review discipline data by selected student populations, including but not limited to race and ethnicity, gender, socioeconomic status, English language learner status, and student with a disability status. In reviewing the data, the principal shall assess the extent of in-school suspensions, short- and long-term suspensions, expulsions, and emergency removals under 603 CMR 53.07, and the impact of such disciplinary action on selected student populations. The principal shall further determine whether it is necessary or appropriate to modify disciplinary practices due to over-reliance on expulsion, in-school or out-of school suspension, or emergency removals, or the impact of such suspensions, removals, and expulsions on selected student populations compared with other students.

(3) In the fall of each year, the Department shall publish an analysis and report of student discipline data disaggregated by district and school, and by selected student populations, included but not limited to race and ethnicity, gender, socioeconomic status, English language learner status, and student with a disability status. The data shall be reported in a manner that protects the identity of each student and shall be made available to the public online in a machine readable format.

(4) The Department shall annually determine the schools with the highest percentage of students expelled or placed on long-term suspension for more than ten (10) cumulative days in a school year. After review of the discipline data described in 603 CMR 53.14(3) and other relevant school and district information, including but not limited to student demographics, student performance, promotion, attendance, attrition, graduation, and dropout rates, the Commissioner shall identify schools that need assistance to reduce over-reliance on long-term suspension or expulsion as a consequence for student misconduct. The Department shall identify models that such schools may use to incorporate intermediate steps before long-term suspension and expulsion and to foster positive school climate.

Through use of statistical analysis, the Commissioner shall identify schools and districts with data that reflect significant disparities in the rate of suspension and expulsion by race and ethnicity, or disability. Such schools and districts shall develop and implement a plan approved by the Department to address such significant disparities.

Regulatory Authority: M.G.L. c. 71 § 38R and Chapter 77 of the Acts of 2013

PART 7
Delinquency

EDITOR'S NOTE
In an effort to as fully, clearly, and succinctly provide an overview of the more common criminal charges found in the Juvenile Court, the model jury instructions for those selected crimes are being utilized. It should be noted that they have been modified in part in some instances in an attempt to clarify and simplify the reader's understanding of the specific criminal statute. Readers should not rely on them when preparing requested jury instructions. Rather, reference should be made to the exact Model Jury Instruction, as found in the *Criminal Model Jury Instructions for Use in the District Court* (MCLE, Inc. 2009 & Supp. 2011, 2013, 2014, 2016, 2017, 2018, 2019), referred to here as "Dist. Ct. Model Jury Instructions" and *Massachusetts Superior Court Criminal Practice Jury Instructions* (MCLE, Inc. 3d ed. 2018), referred to here as "Super. Ct. Model Jury Instructions." Some of the notes in the District Court Jury Instructions refer to District Court jurisdiction. The reader should be mindful that some of these rules do not apply in Juvenile Court and should look to G.L. c. 119 for guidance. (For resources on mental health and clinical issues, please see the Additional Materials in Part 3.)

Affray

Regulatory Authority—G.L. c. 277, § 39
Dist. Ct. Model Jury Instruction 6.100

The defendant is charged with violating the law by engaging in an affray with others.

In order to prove the defendant guilty of this offense, the Commonwealth must prove three things beyond a reasonable doubt:

First: That the defendant fought with one or more other persons;

Second: That the fighting took place in a public place; and

Third: That at least one person who was lawfully present in the public place was put in fear as a result of the fighting that occurred.

With regard to the first element, fighting is the use of physical force or violence or any threat to immediately use such force or violence.

NOTES

1. **Lawful presence.** Affray is a common law offense, but the term "affray" is defined by G.L. c. 277, § 39: "Affray.—Fighting together of two or more persons in a public place to the terror of the persons lawfully there." Lawful presence in the public place of the person placed in fear is a required element of proof of affray. The purpose for which any person is present is irrelevant. *Commonwealth v. Nee*, 83 Mass. App. Ct. 441, 447 (2013) (victims placed in fear were lawfully present). See *District Attorney for Norfolk Dist. v. Quincy Div. of Dist. Court Dep't*, 444 Mass. 176, 180–81 (2005).

2. **Self-defense.** "Nothing in the definition of affray precludes a defendant so charged from asserting self-defense or defense of another in justification of his conduct." *Commonwealth v. Nee*, 83 Mass. App. Ct. at 449 n.8. See "Self-Defense" (Instruction 9.260).

3. **Sentencing.** Since the General Laws do not specify a penalty for common law affray, a convicted defendant should be punished under G.L. c. 279, § 5, which provides for "such sentence, according to the nature of the crime, as conforms to the common usage and practice in the commonwealth." See *Nee*, 83 Mass. App. Ct. at 445 n.4.

4. **Alignment.** The Commonwealth is not required to prove that the defendant and other participants were on the same or opposing sides. *Commonwealth v. Nee*, 83 Mass. App. Ct. at 447.

Assault with Intent to Murder / Assault with Intent to Kill

Regulatory Authority—G.L. c. 265, § 15
Super. Ct. Model Jury Instructions § 3.12

Assault with Intent to Murder Where There Is No Mitigating Circumstances[1]

In this case, the defendant, (defendant/name), is charged with assault with intent to murder. Our state legislature has specifically defined assault with intent to murder in a statute, G.L. c. 265, § 15, which provides in part:

> Whoever assaults another with intent to commit murder . . . shall be punished . . . .

In order to prove assault with intent to murder, the Commonwealth must prove two elements beyond a reasonable doubt:

First Element: that the defendant assaulted a person; and

Second Element: that the defendant possessed a specific or actual intent to cause the death of the person assaulted.[2]

The first element the Commonwealth must prove beyond a reasonable doubt is that the defendant assaulted (the alleged victim/name). An assault may be committed in one of two ways.[3] First, assault is defined as an attempt or offer by one person to do bodily injury to another by force and violence.[4] Alternatively, an assault may consist of putting a person in fear of immediate bodily injury.[5]

The first type of assault consists of an offer or attempt to commit a battery.[6] In this type of assault, the Commonwealth must prove beyond a reasonable doubt that the defendant intended to physically harm (the alleged victim/name). The Commonwealth must also prove that the defendant did an act toward the commission of inflicting physical harm on (the alleged victim/name).[7] In other words, the Commonwealth must show that the defendant did in fact attempt to do bodily harm to (alleged victim/name) and came reasonably close to accomplishing the intended act.[8] Finally, the Commonwealth must prove the defendant had the actual or apparent ability to inflict bodily harm.[9] This means that the Commonwealth need not show the defendant possessed the actual ability to do bodily harm. Apparent ability will suffice.[10] However, the Commonwealth does not have to show that (the alleged victim/name) was apprehensive or fearful.[11] Fear or apprehension on the part of another is not an essential ingredient of this type of assault.

The second type of assault occurs when the defendant engaged in conduct that a reasonable person would recognize to be threatening, the defendant intended to place (the alleged victim/name) in fear of an imminent battery, and (the alleged victim/name) perceived the threat.[12] First, the Commonwealth must prove beyond a reasonable doubt that the defendant possessed the intention to cause apprehension of imminent bodily harm.[13] Second, the Commonwealth must show that the defendant engaged in conduct of the sort that would raise a reasonable apprehension of bodily harm.[14] For example, pointing an unloaded gun at a person may constitute assault.[15] However, where the defendant utters threatening words to a person, unaccompanied by any act, such conduct generally is not sufficient to constitute assault.[16]

Third, the Commonwealth must demonstrate that as a result of the threatened conduct, (the alleged victim/name) perceived the risk of imminent bodily harm. It is not necessary that (the alleged victim/name) actually be in fear; but (the alleged victim/name) must have been aware of the risk of imminent bodily harm.[17] Finally, similar to the first type of assault, the Commonwealth need not demonstrate that the defendant had the actual ability at the time of the alleged assault to carry out the threat. Apparent ability will suffice.[18]

The second element the Commonwealth must prove beyond a reasonable doubt is that the defendant possessed a specific or actual intent to kill the person assaulted.[19] Intent refers to a person's objectives or purposes. By this I mean that the defendant must have had it in (his/her) mind to do the proscribed act.[20] It involves concentrating or focusing the mind for some perceptible period. It is a conscious act, with the determination of the mind to do an act.[21] It is contemplation rather than reflection, and it must precede the act.[22]

Here, the defendant must have specifically intended to kill (the alleged victim/name). This means that the defendant must have been shown to possess an actual, subjective intent to kill—an intent merely to disable or scare off another is not sufficient intent.[23] The intent to inflict bodily injury or to do serious bodily harm is also not sufficient. Specific intent to kill is a matter of fact that may or may not be proven by direct evidence. If it is not proven by direct evidence, then you the jury, in your role as finders of fact, may but are not required to, infer the specific intent to kill from the defendant's conduct.[24] You may consider all of the surrounding facts and circumstances and weigh them in light of your common knowledge and experience in order to determine whether to draw the inference that the defendant committed the assault with specific intent to kill.

Therefore, if after considering all the evidence you determine the Commonwealth has proven beyond a reasonable doubt each of the elements I have just defined, that is, that the defendant assaulted (the alleged victim/name) and that the defendant possessed the specific or actual intent to kill the person assaulted, then you shall find the defendant guilty of assault with intent to murder.

NOTES

[1] This instruction and notes are taken from the chargebook offered as a guide to Superior Court judges in 1995 and updated by the authors.

[2] Malice, for the purposes of assault with intent to murder, is defined as the absence of justification, excuse, or mitigation. Where there is no evidence of justification, excuse, or mitigation, the element of malice is necessarily proved where the Commonwealth has proved a specific intent to kill. Accordingly, where there is no evidence of justification, excuse, or mitigation, the judge need not instruct on malice. *Commonwealth v. Johnston*, 446 Mass. 555, 558–62 (2006); *see also Commonwealth v. Nardone*, 406 Mass. 123, 132 (1989).

[3] *Commonwealth v. Slaney*, 345 Mass. 135, 140–41 (1962).

[4] *Commonwealth v. Burke*, 390 Mass. 480, 482 (1983); *Salemme v. Commonwealth*, 370 Mass. 421, 424 (1976); *Commonwealth v. Shaffer*, 367 Mass. 508, 515 (1975); *Commonwealth v. Slaney*, 345 Mass. 135, 138 (1962).

[5] *Commonwealth v. Richards*, 363 Mass. 299, 303 (1973); *Commonwealth v. Henson*, 357 Mass. 686, 688–91 (1970); *Ross v. Michael*, 246 Mass. 126, 130 (1923); *Commonwealth v. White*, 110 Mass. 407, 409 (1872); *Commonwealth v. Marcotte*, 18 Mass. App. Ct. 391, 395 n.2 (1984).

[6] See note 4.

[7] *Commonwealth v. Boodoosingh*, 85 Mass. App. Ct. 902, 903, *review denied*, 468 Mass. 1105 (2014).

[8] *Commonwealth v. Hagenlock*, 140 Mass. 125, 127 (1885).

[9] *Commonwealth v. Henson*, 357 Mass. 686, 692 (1970); *Commonwealth v. Slaney*, 345 Mass. 135, 138 (1962); *Commonwealth v. White*, 110 Mass. 407, 409 (1872).

[10] *Commonwealth v. White*, 110 Mass. 407, 409 (1872).

[11] *Salemme v. Commonwealth*, 370 Mass. 421, 424 n.2 (1976); *Commonwealth v. Slaney*, 345 Mass. 135, 139 (1962).

[12] *Commonwealth v. Porro*, 458 Mass. 526, 530–31 (2010).

[13] See note 5.

[14] *Commonwealth v. Howard*, 386 Mass. 607, 614 (1982) (O'Connor, J., concurring); *Commonwealth v. Tarrant*, 367 Mass. 411, 414 (1975); *Commonwealth v. Henson*, 357 Mass. 686, 692 (1970); *Commonwealth v. Slaney*, 345 Mass. 135, 140 (1962) (defendant's conduct must be menacing "by objective standards"); *Commonwealth v. Johnson*, 2 Mass. App. Ct. 877, 878 (1974) (rescript).

[15] *Commonwealth v. White*, 110 Mass. 407, 407–09 (1872); *Commonwealth v. Swahn*, 5 Mass. App. Ct. 642, 645 (1977).

[16] *Commonwealth v. Delgado*, 367 Mass. 432, 436 (1975).

[17] *Commonwealth v. Porro*, 458 Mass. 526, 530–31 (2010); *Commonwealth v. Richards*, 363 Mass. 299, 303–04 (1973); *Commonwealth v. Henson*, 357 Mass. 686, 689 (1970); *Commonwealth v. Slaney*, 345 Mass. 135, 140 (1962). The reasonableness of the victim's apprehension is determined by whether the defendant's conduct, judged by an objective standard, was menacing. *See Commonwealth v. Davis*, 70 Mass. App. Ct. 314, 315–16 (2007).

[18] *Commonwealth v. Howard*, 386 Mass. 607, 614 (1982); *Commonwealth v. Richards*, 363 Mass. 299, 303 (1973); *Commonwealth v. White*, 110 Mass. 407, 409 (1872).

[19] *Commonwealth v. Johnston*, 446 Mass. 555, 559–62 (2006); *Commonwealth v. Nardone*, 406 Mass. 123, 132 (1989); *Commonwealth v. Shea*, 398 Mass. 264, 268 (1986); *Commonwealth v. Gabbidon*, 398 Mass. 1, 4 (1986); *Commonwealth v. Burkett*, 396 Mass. 509, 512 (1986); *Commonwealth v. Henson*, 394 Mass. 584, 590–92 (1985).

[20] *Commonwealth v. Richards*, 363 Mass. 299, 305 (1973).

[21] *Commonwealth v. Nickerson*, 388 Mass. 246, 253–54 (1983).

[22] *Commonwealth v. Nickerson*, 388 Mass. 246, 253–54 (1983); *see also Commonwealth v. Gunter*, 427 Mass. 259, 269 & n.12 (1998) (critical requirement in specific intent offense is that defendant must intend that the particular consequences constituting the offense follow from his or her conduct).

[23] See note 19.

[24] *Commonwealth v. Sylvester*, 35 Mass. App. Ct. 906, 907 (1993) (rescript).

Assault with Intent to Murder Where There Is Evidence of Justification, Excuse, or Mitigating Circumstances[1]

In this case, the defendant, (defendant/name), is charged with assault with intent to murder. Our state legislature has specifically defined assault with intent to murder in a statute, G.L. c. 265, § 15, which provides in part:

> Whoever assaults another with the intent to commit murder . . . shall be punished . . . .

In order to prove assault with intent to murder, the Commonwealth must prove three elements beyond a reasonable doubt:

First Element: that the defendant assaulted a person, and

Second Element: that the defendant possessed a specific or actual intent to cause the death of the person assaulted.[2]

Third Element: that the defendant acted with an absence of justification, excuse or mitigation.[3]

The first element the Commonwealth must prove beyond a reasonable doubt is that the defendant assaulted (the alleged victim/name). An assault may be committed in one of two ways.[4] First, assault is defined as an attempt or offer by one person to do bodily injury to another by force and violence.[5] Alternately, an assault may consist of putting a person in fear of immediate bodily injury.[6]

The first type of assault consists of an offer or attempt to commit a battery.[7] In this type of assault, the Commonwealth must prove beyond a reasonable doubt that the defendant intended to physically harm (the alleged victim/name). The Commonwealth must also prove that the defendant did an act toward the commission of inflicting physical harm on (the alleged victim/name) and came reasonably close to accomplishing the intended act.[8] In other words, the Commonwealth must show that the defendant did in fact attempt to do bodily harm to (thealleged victim/name).[9] Finally, the Commonwealth must prove the defendant had the actual or apparent ability to inflict bodily harm.[10] This means that the Commonwealth need not show the defendant possessed the actual ability to do bodily harm. Apparent ability will suffice.[11] However, the Commonwealth does not have to show that (the alleged victim/name) was apprehensive or fearful.[12] Fear or apprehension on the part of another is not an essential ingredient of this type of assault.

The second type of assault occurs when the defendant defendant engaged in conduct that a reasonable person would recognize to be threatening, the defendant intended to place (the alleged victim/name) in fear of an imminent battery, and (the alleged victim/name) perceived the threat.[13] First, the Commonwealth must prove beyond a reasonable doubt that the defendant possessed the intention to cause apprehension of imminent bodily harm.[14] Second, the Commonwealth must show that the defendant engaged in conduct of the sort that would raise a reasonable apprehension of bodily harm.[15] For example, pointing an unloaded gun at a person may constitute assault.[16] However, where the defendant utters threatening words to a person, unaccompanied by any act, such conduct generally is not sufficient to constitute assault.[17]

Third, the Commonwealth must demonstrate that as a result of the threatened conduct, (the alleged victim/name) perceived the risk of imminent bodily harm. It is not necessary that (the alleged victim/name) actually be in fear; but (the alleged victim/name) must have been aware of the risk of imminent bodily harm.[18] Finally, similar to the first type of assault, the Commonwealth need not demonstrate that the defendant had the actual ability at the time of the alleged assault to carry out the threat. Apparent ability will suffice.[19]

The second element the Commonwealth must prove beyond a reasonable doubt is that the defendant possessed a specific or actual intent to kill the person assaulted.[20] Intent refers to a person's objectives or purposes. By this I mean that the defendant must have had it in (his/her) mind to do the proscribed act.[21] It involves concentrating or focusing the mind for some perceptible period. It is a conscious act, with the determination of the mind to do an act.[22] It is contemplation rather than reflection, and it must precede the act.[23]

Here, the defendant must have specifically intended to kill (the alleged victim/name). This means that the defendant must have been shown to possess an actual, subjective intent to kill—an intent merely to disable or scare off another is not sufficient intent.[24] The intent to inflict bodily injury or to do serious bodily harm is also not sufficient. Specific intent to kill is a matter of fact that may or may not be proven by direct evidence. If it is not proven by direct evidence, then you the jury, in your role as finders of fact, may, but are not required to, infer the specific intent to kill from the defendant's conduct.[25] You may consider all of the surrounding facts and circumstances and weigh them in light of your common knowledge and experience in order to determine whether to draw the inference that the defendant committed the assault with specific intent to kill.

The Commonwealth also bears the burden of proving beyond a reasonable doubt that the defendant acted with an absence of justification, excuse, or mitigation.[26] Justification and excuse refer to situations where the act, although intentional, is not unlawful.[27] Examples of justification or excuse include the acts of a soldier in wartime and the proper use of self-defense.[28]

Mitigation is used to describe situations where the assault with intent to kill is unlawful, but the intention to kill arises from the "frailty of human nature, as in instances of sudden passion induced by reasonable provocation, sudden combat or excessive force in self defense."[29] The absence of mitigation in this context means the absence of reasonable provocation, sudden combat or excessive force in self-defense.[30] If there is evidence of mitigation, the Commonwealth must prove beyond a reasonable doubt that the specific intent to kill was not the product of those mitigating circumstances.

Therefore, if after considering all of the evidence you determine the Commonwealth has proven beyond a reasonable doubt each of the elements I have just defined, that is, that the defendant assaulted (the alleged victim/name), that the defendant possessed the specific or actual intent to kill the person assaulted, and that the assault was committed with the absence of justification, excuse, or mitigation, then you shall find the defendant guilty of assault with intent to murder.

NOTES

[1] This instruction and notes are taken from the chargebook offered as a guide to Superior Court judges in 1995 and updated by the authors.

[2] Malice, for the purposes of assault with intent to murder, is defined as the absence of justification, excuse, or mitigation. Where there is no evidence of justification, excuse, or mitigation, the judge need not instruct on malice. *Commonwealth v. Johnston*, 446 Mass. 555 (2006); *see also Commonwealth v. Nardone*, 406 Mass. 123, 132 (1989); *Commonwealth v. Cowie*, 28 Mass. App. Ct. 742, 745 (1990).

[3] The 2018 edition of the *Model Jury Instructions on Homicide* omits the term "malice." This instruction follows that model instruction.

[4] *Commonwealth v. Slaney*, 345 Mass. 135, 140–41 (1962).

[5] *Commonwealth v. Burke*, 390 Mass. 480, 482 (1983); *Salemme v. Commonwealth*, 370 Mass. 421, 424 (1976); *Commonwealth v. Shaffer*, 367 Mass. 508, 515 (1975); *Commonwealth v. Slaney*, 345 Mass. 135, 138 (1962).

[6] *Commonwealth v. Richards*, 363 Mass. 299, 303 (1973); *Commonwealth v. Henson*, 357 Mass. 686, 688–91 (1970); *Ross v. Michael*, 246 Mass. 126, 130 (1923); *Commonwealth v. White*, 110 Mass. 407, 409 (1872); *Commonwealth v. Marcotte*, 18 Mass. App. Ct. 391, 395 n.2 (1984).

[7] See note 5.

[8] *Commonwealth v. Boodoosingh*, 85 Mass. App. Ct. 902, 903, *review denied*, 468 Mass. 1105 (2014).

[9] *Commonwealth v. Hagenlock*, 140 Mass. 125, 127 (1885).

[10] *Commonwealth v. Henson*, 357 Mass. 686, 692 (1970); *Commonwealth v. Slaney*, 345 Mass. 135, 138 (1962); *Commonwealth v. White*, 110 Mass. 407, 409 (1872).

[11] *Commonwealth v. White*, 110 Mass. 407, 409 (1872).

[12] *Salemme v. Commonwealth*, 370 Mass. 421, 424 n.2 (1976); *Commonwealth v. Slaney*, 345 Mass. 135, 139 (1962).

[13] *Commonwealth v. Porro*, 458 Mass. 526, 530–31 (2010).

[14] See note 6.

[15] *Commonwealth v. Howard*, 386 Mass. 607, 614 (1982) (O'Connor, J., concurring); *Commonwealth v. Tarrant*, 367 Mass. 411, 414 (1975); *Commonwealth v. Henson*, 357 Mass. 686, 692 (1970); *Commonwealth v. Slaney*, 345 Mass. 135, 140 (1962) (defendant's conduct must be menacing "by objective standards"); *Commonwealth v. Johnson*, 2 Mass. App. Ct. 877, 878 (1974) (rescript).

[16] *Commonwealth v. White*, 110 Mass. 407, 407–09 (1872); *Commonwealth v. Swahn*, 5 Mass. App. Ct. 642, 645 (1977).

[17] *Commonwealth v. Delgado*, 367 Mass. 432, 435–37 (1975).

[18] *Commonwealth v. Porro*, 458 Mass. 526, 530–31 (2010); *Commonwealth v. Richards*, 363 Mass. 299, 303–04 (1973); *Commonwealth v. Henson*, 357 Mass. 686, 689 (1970); *Commonwealth v. Slaney*, 345 Mass. 135, 140 (1962). The reasonableness of the victim's apprehension is determined by whether the defendant's conduct, judged by an objective standard, was menacing. *See Commonwealth v. Davis*, 70 Mass. App. Ct. 314, 315–16 (2007).

[19] *Commonwealth v. Howard*, 386 Mass. 607, 614 (1982); *Commonwealth v. Richards*, 363 Mass. 299, 303 (1973); *Commonwealth v. White*, 110 Mass. 407, 409 (1872).

[20] *Commonwealth v. Johnston*, 446 Mass. 555, 559–62 (2006); *Commonwealth v. Nardone*, 406 Mass. 123, 132 (1989); *Commonwealth v. Shea*, 398 Mass. 264, 268 (1986); *Commonwealth v. Gabbidon*, 398 Mass. 1, 4 (1986); *Commonwealth v. Burkett*, 396 Mass. 509, 512 (1986); *Commonwealth v. Henson*, 394 Mass. 584, 590–92 (1985).

[21] *Commonwealth v. Richards*, 363 Mass. 299, 305 (1973).

[22] *Commonwealth v. Nickerson*, 388 Mass. 246, 253–54 (1983).

[23] *Commonwealth v. Nickerson*, 388 Mass. 246, 253–54 (1983); *see also Commonwealth v. Gunter*, 427 Mass. 259, 269 & n.12 (1998) (critical requirement in specific intent offense is that defendant must intend that the particular consequences constituting the offense follow from his or her conduct).

[24] See note 20.

[25] *Commonwealth v. Sylvester*, 35 Mass. App. Ct. 906, 907 (1993) (rescript).

[26] *Commonwealth v. Johnston*, 446 Mass. 555, 559–62 (2006); *Commonwealth v. Nardone*, 406 Mass. 123, 131–32 (1989); *Commonwealth v. Shea*, 398 Mass. 264, 268–69 n.1 (1986); *Commonwealth v. Burkett*, 396 Mass. 509, 511 (1986); *Commonwealth v. Henson*, 394 Mass. 584, 591 (1985); *Commonwealth v. Cowie*, 28 Mass. App. Ct. 742, 745 (1990); *Commonwealth v. King*, 23 Mass. App. Ct. 88, 90–91 (1986).

[27] *Commonwealth v. Johnston*, 446 Mass. 555 (2006); *Commonwealth v. Nardone*, 406 Mass. 123, 130 (1989).

[28] *Commonwealth v. Nardone*, 406 Mass. 123, 130 (1989).

[29] *Commonwealth v. Nardone*, 406 Mass. 123, 131–32 (1989).

[30] *Commonwealth v. Nardone*, 406 Mass. 123, 131–32 (1989).

Assault with Intent to Kill[1,2] (Lesser-Included Offense)

If, however, you determine that the Commonwealth has proven that the defendant assaulted [the alleged victim/name] and acted with the specific intent to kill but has not proven an absence of mitigation beyond a reasonable doubt, then you shall consider whether the defendant is guilty of the lesser-included offense of assault with intent to kill.[3] Assault with intent to kill consists of assault, specific intent to kill, and the mitigating factor of heat of passion induced by sudden combat, reasonable provocation, or the excessive use of force in self-defense.[4] If after your consideration of all of the evidence, the Commonwealth has convinced you beyond a reasonable doubt that the defendant assaulted a person with the specific intent to kill (him/her), but has failed to demonstrate beyond a reasonable doubt the absence of mitigating circumstances, then you shall find the defendant guilty of assault with intent to kill.[5] As I previously instructed you, mitigation is used to describe situations where the assault with intent to kill is unlawful, but the intention to kill arises from the frailty of human nature as in instances of reasonable provocation, sudden combat or excessive force in self-defense.[6]

If, however, after your consideration of all of the evidence you find that the Commonwealth has not proven any one of these elements beyond a reasonable doubt, you shall find the defendant not guilty.

NOTES

[1] This instruction and notes are taken from the chargebook offered as a guide to Superior Court judges in 1995 and updated by the authors.

[2] This instruction is to be given when there is evidence of mitigation.

[3] G.L. c. 265, § 29. *See Commonwealth v. Henson*, 394 Mass. 584, 592 (1985); *Commonwealth v. Demboski*, 283 Mass. 315, 322–23 (1933); *Commonwealth v. Olson*, 24 Mass. App. Ct. 539, 540 n.2 (1987). The judge should not charge on the lesser-included offense if it is not suggested by any reasonable view of the evidence. *Commonwealth v. Nardone*, 406 Mass. 123, 132 (1989); *Commonwealth v. Hebert*, 373 Mass. 535, 538 (1977).

[4] *Commonwealth v. Johnston*, 446 Mass. 555, 559–62 (2006); *Commonwealth v. Nardone*, 406 Mass. 123, 131–32 (1989).

[5] *Commonwealth v. Nardone*, 406 Mass. 123, 131–32 (1989).

[6] One may only be convicted of assault with intent to kill upon facts that would support voluntary, not involuntary, manslaughter had death resulted. *Commonwealth v. Henson*, 394 Mass. 584, 591 (1985); *Commonwealth v. King*, 23 Mass. App. Ct. 88, 91 (1986); *Commonwealth v. Alfonso*, 19 Mass. App. Ct. 599, 605 (1985); *Commonwealth v. Parenti*, 14 Mass. App. Ct. 696, 702–03 (1982).

Supplemental Instruction[1]: Effect of Alcohol or Drugs

You have heard evidence that at the time of the crime the defendant had consumed (alcohol/drugs). You may consider the evidence of the effect of the ingestion of (alcohol/drug) on the defendant at the time of the crime in determining whether the Commonwealth has proven the specific intent to kill beyond a reasonable doubt.[2] However, if you are satisfied beyond a reasonable doubt that the defendant had the specific intent to kill, then the defendant's intoxication, if any, is not an excuse or justification for (his/her) actions.[3]

7

NOTES

[1] This instruction and notes are taken from the chargebook offered as a guide to Superior Court judges in 1995 and is updated by the authors.

[2] *Commonwealth v. Moore*, 36 Mass. App. Ct. 455, 460 (1994).

[3] *Commonwealth v. Bowler*, 407 Mass. 304, 308 (1990); *Commonwealth v. Bray*, 407 Mass. 296, 301–02 (1990); *Commonwealth v. Sylvester*, 400 Mass. 334, 336 (1987); *Commonwealth v. Grey*, 399 Mass. 469, 471 (1987); *Commonwealth v. Dunton*, 397 Mass. 101, 104 (1986); *Commonwealth v. Henson*, 394 Mass. 584, 593–94 (1985); *see also Commonwealth v. Johnston*, 446 Mass. 555, 559 (2006) (mental impairment may be relevant to intent but is not mitigating factor).

Arson[1,2]

Regulatory Authority—G.L. c. 266, § 1
Super. Ct. Model Jury Instructions § 2.32.

Arson

In this case, the defendant is charged with arson under G.L. c. 266, § 1. This offense can be proved in two ways.[3]

NOTES

[1] This instruction quotes the chargebook offered as a guide to Superior Court judges in 1995. The notes that follow are from the same source and have been updated for this text.

[2] The following instructions reflect two theories under which the jury may consider whether the defendant committed arson that vary with respect to the role allegedly played by the defendant.

[3] Arson of a building, G.L. c. 266, § 1, is a lesser-included offense of arson of a building with intent to defraud or injure its insurer, G.L. c. 266, § 10. *Commonwealth v. Shuman*, 17 Mass. App. Ct. 441, 449–51 (1984); *see Commonwealth v. Harrison*, 25 Mass. App. Ct. 267 (1988). However, arson of a dwelling house (G.L. c. 266, § 1) is not a lesser-included offense of arson with intent to defraud an insurance company (G.L. c. 266, § 10) because "[i]n the case of burning a dwelling, there is required, in addition to a burning, independent proof that the target property was habitable as a dwelling." *Commonwealth v. Anolik*, 27 Mass. App. Ct. 701, 711–12 (1989); *see Commonwealth v. De Stefano*, 16 Mass. App. Ct. 208, 214 (1983).

General Laws Chapter 266, § 2 uses similar language in reference to the burning of various types of buildings other than a dwelling house.

Arson (I)[1]

Under the first theory of arson, the Commonwealth must prove three elements beyond a reasonable doubt:

First Element: that the defendant set fire to, burned or caused a building to be burned;

Second Element: that the building was a dwelling house, a building adjoining or adjacent to a dwelling house, or a building whose burning resulted in a dwelling house being burned; and

Third Element: that the defendant acted willfully and maliciously.

The *first* element the Commonwealth must prove beyond a reasonable doubt is that the defendant set fire to, burned or caused to be burned the building in question. This requires that some portion of the building must have actually been on fire and burned. There is, however, no requirement that the building be consumed by the fire or destroyed.[2] Even a charring is sufficient evidence of a burning.[3]

The *second* element the Commonwealth must prove beyond a reasonable doubt is that the building burned was a dwelling house, a building adjoining or adjacent to a dwelling house, or any building the burning of which results in a dwelling house being burned. The phrase "dwelling house" means and includes "all buildings used as dwellings, such as apartment houses, tenement houses, hotels, boarding houses, dormitories, hospitals, institutions, sanitoria, or other buildings" where people live or reside.[4] It is not necessary that the building be occupied at the time of the burning, but the Commonwealth must prove that the building is capable of being occupied as a dwelling, is adjoining or adjacent to a dwelling house, or is a building the burning of which results in a dwelling house being burned.[5] Further, it does not matter if the defendant owned the dwelling house or if it was owned by another.

The *third* element the Commonwealth must prove beyond a reasonable doubt is that the defendant willfully and maliciously set fire to or caused the building to be burned.[6]

Willfulness and malice are required to constitute the state of mind necessary to commit arson. The word willfully means that the act was intentional and by design, rather than an act that is thoughtless or accidental. A person acting willfully intends both his or her conduct and the resulting harm.[7] The requirement of willfulness means that accidentally or negligently caused burnings are not arson.[8]

[Supplemental Instruction (a)—Failure to Extinguish or Report a Fire]

The Commonwealth also must prove beyond a reasonable doubt that the defendant acted maliciously or with malice. The terms of "malice" and "maliciously" have a different meaning under this statute than the ordinary definition of those terms. Malice characterizes all acts done with an evil disposition, with a wrong and unlawful motive or purpose or the willful doing of an injurious act without lawful excuse.[9] A burning is malicious if it is done with any wrongful or unlawful motive or purpose and without lawful excuse.

Therefore, if after considering all of the evidence you find that the Commonwealth has proven beyond a reasonable doubt the three elements of arson, then you should find the defendant guilty of arson.

If, however, after considering all of the evidence you find that the Commonwealth has not proven any one of the three elements under the first theory of arson, then you must find the defendant not guilty under the first theory of arson.

NOTES

[1] This instruction quotes the chargebook offered as a guide to Superior Court judges in 1995. The notes that follow are from the same source and have been updated for this text.

[2] *Commonwealth v. Tucker*, 110 Mass. 403, 404 (1872).

[3] *Commonwealth v. McIntosh*, 10 Mass. App. Ct. 924, 925 (1980) (rescript).

[4] G.L. c. 266, § 1.

[5] *Commonwealth v. DeStefano*, 16 Mass. App. Ct. 208, 214 (1983) (insufficient evidence to warrant a finding beyond a reasonable doubt that the house was a "dwelling house" at the time of a second fire). In light of the 1932 amendment that inserted the words "occupied or unoccupied" into G.L. c. 266, § 1, it is no longer necessary for the Commonwealth to prove an intent to return to an unoccupied dwelling house. *Commonwealth v. Murphy*, 1 Mass. App. Ct. 71, 75 (1973).

[6] Note: The jury may consider intoxication on the issue of the intent required for arson. *Commonwealth v. Glenn*, 23 Mass. App. Ct. 440, 444–45 (1987).

[7] *Commonwealth v. Smith*, 17 Mass. App. Ct. 918, 920 (1983).

[8] *Commonwealth v. Ely*, 388 Mass. 69, 74 (1983); cf. G.L. c. 266, § 8.

[9] *Commonwealth v. McLaughlin*, 431 Mass. 506, 512 (2000) (quoting *Commonwealth v. Niziolek*, 380 Mass. 513, 527 (1980)).

Arson (II)[1]

In order to prove the defendant guilty under the second theory of arson the Commonwealth must prove beyond a reasonable doubt:

First Element: that the defendant intentionally aided, counseled or procured

Second Element: a burning

Third Element: of a dwelling house, a building adjoining or adjacent to a dwelling house, or a building whose burning resulted in a dwelling house being burned.

The *first* element the Commonwealth must prove beyond a reasonable doubt is that the defendant aided, counseled or procured the burning of a dwelling house or building.[2] This means that the defendant participated in committing the crime of arson by agreeing to stand by, at, or near the scene of the crime to render aid, assistance or encouragement, if it became necessary, to the person who set fire to or caused the burning of the dwelling house; or by assisting the perpetrator to make an escape from the scene; or by procuring another person to burn a dwelling house.[3]

In order to prove this element of arson, it is not sufficient for the Commonwealth to prove that the defendant merely knew that a crime was going to be committed. Mere association with the person who set the fire is not enough.[4] Mere presence at the scene of the crime is not enough, even when combined with knowledge of the planned act.[5] A mere failure to take appropriate steps to prevent the commission of the crime or mere acquiescence is not sufficient.[6]

The Commonwealth is not required to prove that the defendant actually physically participated in the crime. What the Commonwealth must prove to you beyond a reasonable doubt is that the defendant, by agreement, was at the scene of the crime in a position to render aid, assistance or encouragement, if it became necessary, to the person who set fire to or caused the burning of the dwelling house, or to assist the perpetrator to make an escape from the scene, or that the defendant procured another person to burn a dwelling house.[7]

The *second* element the Commonwealth must prove to you beyond a reasonable doubt is that a burning occurred. This requires that some portion of the building must have actually been on fire and burned. There is, however, no requirement that the building be consumed by the fire or destroyed.[8] Even a charring is sufficient evidence of a burning.[9]

The *third* element the Commonwealth must prove beyond a reasonable doubt is that the building burned was a dwelling house, a building adjoining or adjacent to dwelling house, or a building whose burning resulted in a dwelling house being burned. The phrase "dwelling house" means and includes "all buildings used as dwellings, such as apartment houses, tenement houses, hotels, boarding houses, dormitories, hospitals, institutions, sanitoria, or other buildings" where people live or reside.[10] It is not necessary that the building be occupied at the time of the burning, but the Commonwealth must prove that the building is capable of being occupied as a dwelling.[11] Further, it does not matter if the defendant owned the dwelling house or if it was owned by another.

Therefore, if after considering all of the evidence you find that the Commonwealth has proven beyond a reasonable doubt the three elements of arson, then you shall find the defendant guilty under the second theory of arson.

If, however, after considering all of the evidence you find that the Commonwealth has not proven any one of the three elements of arson, then you must find the defendant not guilty of arson.[12]

NOTES

[1] This instruction quotes the chargebook offered as a guide to Superior Court judges in 1995, but it has been amended to reflect current case law. See note 12, below. Specifically, a fourth element, "that the defendant shared the same intent as the person who actually set fire to or caused the burning of the dwelling house," has been deleted. The notes that follow are from the same source and have been updated for this text.

[2] A conviction of arson may be based on a finding that the defendant either directly participated in the burning or aided, counseled or procured another to do it. The court has stated that "it is enough to support a conviction if it can be determined, beyond a reasonable doubt, that one of these forms of misconduct must have occurred, although the fact finder cannot say with certainty which one." *Commonwealth v. DeStefano*, 16 Mass. App. Ct. 208, 215 (1983).

[3] *Commonwealth v. Pringle*, 22 Mass. App. Ct. 746, 749 (1986); see *Commonwealth v. Bloomberg*, 302 Mass. 349, 352 (1939). There is very little case law on the second theory of arson. *See Commonwealth v. Bloomberg*, 302 Mass. 349 (1939); *Commonwealth v. Jacobson*, 19 Mass. App. Ct. 666, 674–76 (1985) (insufficient evidence of aiding, counseling or procuring); *Commonwealth v. DeStefano*, 16 Mass. App. Ct. 208, 215–17 (1983) (sufficient evidence of aiding, counseling or procuring).

[4] *Commonwealth v. Pringle*, 22 Mass. App. Ct. 746, 749 (1986).

[5] *Commonwealth v. Benders*, 361 Mass. 704, 708 (1972); *Commonwealth v. Pringle*, 22 Mass. App. Ct. 746, 749 (1986).

[6] *Commonwealth v. Whitehead*, 379 Mass. 640, 651 (1980); *Commonwealth v. Pringle*, 22 Mass. App. Ct. 746, 749 (1986); *Commonwealth v. Crowe*, 21 Mass. App. Ct. 456, 483 (1986).

[7] *Commonwealth v. Casale*, 381 Mass. 167, 173 (1980); *Commonwealth v. Whitehead*, 379 Mass. 640, 651 (1980); *Commonwealth v. Soares*, 377 Mass. 461, 471–72 (1979); *Commonwealth v. Pringle*, 22 Mass. App. Ct. 746, 749 (1986).

[8] *Commonwealth v. Tucker*, 110 Mass. 403, 404 (1872).

[9] *Commonwealth v. McIntosh*, 10 Mass. App. Ct. 924, 925 (1980) (rescript).

[10] G.L. c. 266, § 1.

[11] *Commonwealth v. DeStefano*, 16 Mass. App. Ct. 208, 214 (1983) (insufficient evidence to warrant a finding beyond a reasonable doubt that the house was a "dwelling house" at the time of a second fire). In light of the 1932 amendment that inserted the words "occupied or unoccupied" into G.L. c. 266, § 1, it is no longer necessary for the Commonwealth to prove an intent to return to an unoccupied dwelling house. *Commonwealth v. Murphy*, 1 Mass. App. Ct. 71, 75 (1973).

[12] Note: Under the second theory of arson, the Commonwealth does not have to prove that the defendant acted willfully or maliciously. It is sufficient to prove that the principal acted with the requisite degree of malice. The second theory of arson requires the Commonwealth to prove that the defendant assisted, advised or procured the principal to burn a dwelling house and that the principal actually committed the burning. *Commonwealth v. DeCicco*, 44 Mass. App. Ct. 111, 117–18 (1998) (trial judge properly instructed the jury that the Commonwealth does not have to prove the defendant acted willfully or maliciously to establish the second theory of arson). *See Commonwealth v. Bloomberg*, 302 Mass. 349, 355 (1939).

Supplemental Instruction[1]: Failure to Extinguish or Report a Fire

However, a person may have the required intent for arson if he or she negligently or accidentally causes a fire and then willfully and maliciously makes no attempt to extinguish or to report it.[2]

The necessary criminal state of mind for arson may be formed after a fire starts.[3]

NOTES

[1] This instruction quotes the chargebook offered as a guide to Superior Court judges in 1995. The notes that follow are from the same source and have been updated for this text.

[2] *Commonwealth v. Glenn*, 23 Mass. App. Ct. 440, 443–44 (1987).

[3] *Commonwealth v. Glenn*, 23 Mass. App. Ct. 440, 443–44 (1987); Joseph R. Nolan & Bruce R. Henry, "Criminal Law," 32 *Massachusetts Practice Series*, § 424 (West 2d. 1988); *see also Commonwealth v. MacKenzie*, 376 Mass. 148, 150 (1978) (evidence of defendant's failure to make an effort to extinguish or report a fire was admissible on the issue of whether the defendant had a willful and malicious intent).

Assault

Regulatory Authority—G.L. c. 265, § 13A
Dist. Ct. Model Jury Instruction 6.120

The defendant is charged with having committed an assault upon *[alleged victim]*. Section 13A of chapter 265 of our General Laws provides that "Whoever commits an assault . . . upon another shall be punished . . . ."

An assault may be committed in either of two ways. It is *either* an attempted battery *or* an immediately threatened battery. A battery is a harmful or an unpermitted touching of another person. So an assault can be either an attempt to use some degree of physical force on another person—for example, by throwing a punch at someone—or it can be a demonstration of an apparent intent to use immediate force on another person—for example, by coming at someone with fists flying. The defendant may be convicted of assault if the Commonwealth proves *either* form of assault.

In order to establish the first form of assault—an attempted battery—the Commonwealth must prove beyond a reasonable doubt that the defendant intended to commit a battery—that is, a harmful or an unpermitted touching—upon *[alleged victim]*, took some overt step toward accomplishing that intent, and came reasonably close to doing so. With this form of assault, it is not necessary for the Commonwealth to show that *[alleged victim]* was put in fear or was even aware of the attempted battery.

7

In order to prove the second form of assault—an imminently threatened battery—the Commonwealth must prove beyond a reasonable doubt that the defendant intended to put *[alleged victim]* in fear of an imminent battery, and engaged in some conduct toward *[alleged victim]* which *[alleged victim]* reasonably perceived as imminently threatening a battery.

> Here instruct on Intent (Instruction 3.120), since both branches of assault are specific intent offenses. If additional language on the first branch of assault is appropriate, see Instruction 4.120 (Attempt).
>
> *Commonwealth v. Barbosa*, 399 Mass. 841, 845 n.7 (1987) (an assault is "any manifestation, by a person, of that person's present intention to do another immediate bodily harm"); *Commonwealth v. Delgado*, 367 Mass. 432, 435–37 & n.3 (1975) ("an act placing another in reasonable apprehension that force may be used is sufficient for the offense of criminal assault"; words threatening future harm are insufficient to constitute an assault unless "they put the other in reasonable apprehension of an imminent harmful or offensive contact with his person"); *Commonwealth v. Chambers*, 57 Mass. App. Ct. 47, 49 (2003) (threatened-battery branch "requires proof that the defendant has engaged in objectively menacing conduct with the intent of causing apprehension of immediate bodily harm on the part of the target"); *Commonwealth v. Musgrave*, 38 Mass. App. Ct. 519 (1995), *aff'd*, 421 Mass. 610 (1996) (threatened-battery branch of assault requires specific intent to put victim in fear or apprehension of immediate physical harm); *Commonwealth v. Spencer*, 40 Mass. App. Ct. 919, 922 (1996) (same); *Commonwealth v. Enos*, 26 Mass. App. Ct. 1006, 1008 (1988) (necessary intent inferable from defendant's overt act putting another in reasonable fear, irrespective of whether defendant intended actual injury); *Commonwealth v. Domingue*, 18 Mass. App. Ct. 987, 990 (1984) (assault is "an overt act undertaken with the intention of putting another person in fear of bodily harm and reasonably calculated to do so, whether or not the defendant actually intended to harm the victim"). *See Commonwealth v. Hurley*, 99 Mass. 433, 434 (1868) (assault by joint venture by intentionally inciting assault by others); *Commonwealth v. Joyce*, 18 Mass. App. Ct. 417, 421–22, 426–30 (1984) (assault by joint venture).

NOTES

1. **Aggravated forms of offense.** It is an aggravated form of assault if it causes serious bodily injury, or if the defendant knows or has reason to know that the victim is pregnant, or if the defendant knows that the victim has an outstanding abuse restraining order against the defendant. G.L. c. 265, § 13A(b). An additionally-aggravated sentence is provided for subsequent offenses.

2. **Assault with a dangerous weapon.** (G.L. c. 265, § 15B[b]) has one element in addition to those required for simple assault: that the assault was done by means of a dangerous weapon. *Commonwealth v. Burkett*, 5 Mass. App. Ct. 901, 903 (1977). J.R. Nolan, *Criminal Law* § 323 (1976). *See Commonwealth v. Nardi*, 6 Mass. App. Ct. 180, 181–84 (1978). Simple assault is a lesser included offense of assault by means of a dangerous weapon, but assault and battery is not. *A Juvenile v. Commonwealth*, 404 Mass. 1001 (1989).

Assault with a dangerous weapon on a person 60 years or older (G.L. c. 265, § 15B(a)) is an aggravated form of the offense. The Commonwealth must charge and prove that the victim was 60 years of age or older. The jury may consider the victim's physical appearance as one factor in determining age, but appearance alone is not sufficient evidence of age unless the victim is of "a marked extreme" age, since "[e]xcept at the poles, judging age on physical appearance is a guess . . . ." *Commonwealth v. Pittman*, 25 Mass. App. Ct. 25, 28 (1987). Prior to St. 1995, c. 297, § 6 (effective March 17, 1996), the aggravated offense covered persons 65 years or older.

3. **Multiple victims of single assault.** Where the defendant assaults multiple victims in a single act, the defendant may be convicted of multiple counts of assault and, in the judge's discretion, given consecutive sentences. *Commonwealth v. Dello Iacono,* 20 Mass. App. Ct. 83, 89–90 (1985) (firing gun into house with several residents).

4. **Simultaneous assault and property destruction.** A single act may support simultaneous convictions of assault by means of a dangerous weapon upon the victim who was assaulted and of malicious destruction of property (G.L. c. 266, § 127) with respect to the area where the victim was standing. *Domingue, above* (firing gun in order to damage bar and frighten bartender).

5. **Statement of reasons required if imprisonment not imposed.** A jury session judge sentencing for this or one of the other crimes against persons found in G.L. c. 265 who does not impose a sentence of incarceration "shall include in the record of the case specific reasons for not imposing a sentence of imprisonment," which shall be a public record. G.L. c. 265, § 41.

6. **Victim's apprehension or fear.** The first (attempted battery) branch of assault does not require that the victim was aware of or feared the attempted battery. *Commonwealth v. Slaney*, 345 Mass. 135, 138–39 (1962); *Commonwealth v. Richards*, 363 Mass. 299, 303 (1973); *Commonwealth v. Gorassi*, 432 Mass. 244, 248 (2000).

The second (threatened battery) branch of assault requires that the victim was aware of the defendant's objectively menacing conduct. *Chambers*, 57 Mass. App. Ct. at 48–52. Some older decisions seem to suggest that under the second branch of assault the victim must have feared as well as perceived the threatened battery. This may have resulted from the inherent ambiguity of the term "apprehend," which may signify either. *Chambers, supra*, concluded that subjective fear is not an element of either branch. Other recent decisions appear to be in accord. See *Commonwealth v. Melton*, 436 Mass. 291, 295 n.4 (2002); *Gorassi*, 432 Mass. at 248–49; *Commonwealth v. Gordon*, 407 Mass. 340 (1990); *Slaney*, 345 Mass. at 139–41; *Richards*, 363 Mass. at 303–04, See also the extended discussion of this issue in R.G. Stearns, *Massachusetts Criminal Law: A Prosecutor's Guide* (28th ed. 2008). The model instruction requires perception, but not subjective fear, by the victim under the second branch of assault.

7. **Assault with intent to murder & assault with intent to kill.** Assault with intent to murder (G.L. c. 265, § 15) requires assault, specific intent to kill, and malice. The lesser included offense of assault with intent to kill (G.L. c. 265, § 29) requires assault, specific intent to kill, and absence of malice. "[P]erhaps the simplest and most distinct way to describe the difference" is that the lesser offense has an additional element—namely, the presence of mitigation provided by reasonable provocation, sudden combat, or excessive force in self-defense. If there is no evidence of mitigation, the Commonwealth satisfies its burden on the issue of malice simply by proving specific intent to kill. *Commonwealth v. Nardone*, 406 Mass. 123, 130–32 (1989); *Commonwealth v. Bourgeois*, 404 Mass. 61, 65 (1989). Assault with intent to kill is, in effect, an assault with intent to commit manslaughter. *Commonwealth v. Cowie*, 28 Mass. App. Ct. 742, 745 (1990). Neither offense is within the final jurisdiction of the District Court.

8. **Armed assault in a dwelling** (G.L. c. 265, § 18A), which is not within the final jurisdiction of the District Court, requires proof of: (1) entry of a dwelling while armed; (2) an assault on someone in the dwelling; and (3) accompanying the assault, a specific intent to commit a felony. The intended felony may be a compounded assault charge (such as ABDW) and need not be an additional, factually distinct felony. *Commonwealth v. Donoghue*, 23 Mass. App. Ct. 103, 111–13 (1986). Where the Commonwealth alleges that the intended felony is an attack on a second victim, it must prove specific intent to commit that second attack. *Commonwealth v. Smith*, 42 Mass. App. Ct. 906, 907 (1997). Since § 18A does not require that the weapon be used in the assault, it does not have assault by means of a dangerous weapon (G.L. c. 265, § 15B) as a lesser included offense. *Commonwealth v. Flanagan*, 17 Mass. App. Ct. 366, 371–72 (1984).

9. **Verdict slip.** Where the jury is presented with a lesser included offense of assault, and the Commonwealth proceeds upon the alternate theories of an attempted battery or an imminently threatened battery, the jury need not be unanimous as to the theory and a special verdict slip requiring the jury to elect between the theories is not proper. *Commonwealth v. Arias*, 78 Mass. App. Ct. 429, 433 (2010). A verdict slip need not distinguish between a conviction for an attempted battery and a threatened battery even when the Commonwealth proceeds upon both theories. The jury may return a unanimous verdict for assault even if they are split between the two theories. "Because attempted battery and threatened battery 'are closely related,' *Commonwealth v. Santos*, 440 Mass. 281, 289 (2003), we do not require that a jury be unanimous as to which theory of assault forms the basis for their verdict; a jury may find a defendant guilty of assault if some jurors find the defendant committed an attempted battery (because they are convinced the defendant intended to strike the victim and missed) and the remainder find that he committed a threatened battery (because they are convinced that the defendant intended to frighten the victim by threatening an assault). *See id.* at 284, 289 (jury were not required to be unanimous as to which form of assault was relied on to satisfy assault element of armed robbery)." *Commonwealth v. Porro*, 458 Mass. 526 (2010). *See also Commonwealth v. Arias, supra.*

Assault and Battery

Regulatory Authority—G.L. c. 265, § 13A
Dist. Ct. Model Jury Instruction 6.140

The defendant is charged with having committed an assault and battery upon [the *alleged victim*].

I. Intentional Assault and Battery

In order to prove the defendant guilty of committing an intentional assault and battery, the Commonwealth must prove three things beyond a reasonable doubt.

First: That the defendant touched the person of [the *alleged victim*];

Second: That the defendant intended to touch [the *alleged victim*]; and

Third: That the touching was *either* likely to cause bodily harm to [the alleged victim], or was offensive.

To prove the first element, the Commonwealth must prove the defendant touched [the *alleged victim*]. A touching is any physical contact, however slight.

> *If the touching was indirect.* A touching may be direct as when a person strikes another, or it may be indirect as when a person sets in motion some force or instrumentality that strikes another.

To prove the second element, the Commonwealth must prove that the defendant intended to touch [the *alleged victim*], in the sense that the defendant consciously and deliberately intended the touching to occur, and that the touching was not merely accidental or negligent.

> *If additional language on intent is appropriate.* The Commonwealth is not required to prove that the defendant specifically intended to cause injury to [the alleged victim].
>
> Where there is evidence that the touching may be justified by a legally recognized "right" or "excuse," the jury should be instructed with the specific "right" or "excuse" instructions (e.g., accident (9.100); necessity (9.240); self-defense (9.260). See *Commonwealth v. Wood*, 90 Mass. App. Ct. 271, 286–86 (2016) (where evidence did not raise a claim of right or excuse, the jury need not consider whether the touching was without right or excuse); *Commonwealth v. Conley*, 34 Mass. App. Ct. 50, 58 (1993) (where no evidence of self-defense, jury need not be instructed that right or excuse may justify the touching).

To prove the third element, the Commonwealth must prove that the touching was either likely to cause bodily harm to [the *alleged victim*], or was offensive. A touching is offensive when it is without consent.

> *Commonwealth v. Burke*, 390 Mass. 480, 484 (1983) (in a prosecution for a nonharmful battery, the Commonwealth must prove that the touching was nonconsensual); *Commonwealth v. Colon*, 81 Mass. App. Ct. 8 (offensive battery requires proof that the defendant intentionally touched the victim and that the touching, however slight, occurred without the victim's consent); *Commonwealth v. Hartnett*, 72 Mass. App. Ct. 467, 477 (2008) ("what makes the touching offensive is not that it is an affront to the victim's personal integrity as the defendant posits, but only that the victim did not consent to it. Nothing more is required.")

The model instruction does not separately define assault, since "[e]very battery includes an assault" as a lesser included offense. *Commonwealth v. Burke*, 390 Mass. 480, 482 (1983); *see Commonwealth v. Porro*, 458 Mass. 526, 533–35 (2010). If the evidence would also permit a jury finding of simple assault, the jury should be instructed on lesser included offenses (Instruction 2.280), followed by Instruction 6.120 (Assault), beginning with the second paragraph.

> *Commonwealth v. Ford*, 424 Mass. 709, 711 (1997) (assault and battery is a general intent crime and does not require specific intent to injure the victim, but its intentional branch requires an intentional touching, and not merely an intentional act resulting in a touching); *Burke*, 390 Mass. at 482–83, 487 (any touching likely to cause bodily harm is a battery regardless of consent, but an offensive but nonharmful battery requires lack of consent or inability to consent); *Commonwealth v. McCan*, 277 Mass. 199, 203 (1931) ("An assault and battery is the intentional and unjustified use of force upon the person of another, however slight, or the intentional doing of a wanton or grossly negligent act causing personal injury to another"); *accord Commonwealth v. Bianco*, 390 Mass. 254, 263 (1983) (same); *Commonwealth v. Campbell*,

352 Mass. 387, 397 (1967) (same); *Commonwealth v. Musgrave*, 38 Mass. App. Ct. 519, 521 (1995) (approving instruction for threatened-battery branch of assault that "when we say intentionally we mean that [defendant] did so consciously and voluntarily and not by accident, inadvertence or mistake"), *aff'd*, 421 Mass. 610 (1996); *Commonwealth v. Moore*, 36 Mass. App. Ct. 455, 457–60 (1994) (intentional branch of assault and battery requires proof "that the defendant intended that a touching occur" and not merely "proof that the defendant did some intentional act, the result of which was a touching of the victim"); *Commonwealth v. Ferguson*, 30 Mass. App. Ct. 580, 584 (1991) (intentional branch of assault and battery requires proof "that the defendant's conduct was intentional, in the sense that it did not happen accidentally"); *see Commonwealth v. Bianco*, 388 Mass. 358, 366–67 (1983) (assault and battery by joint venture); *Commonwealth v. Collberg*, 119 Mass. 350, 353 (1876) (mutual consent is no defense to cross-complaints of assault and battery; "such license is void, because it is against the law").

II. Reckless Assault and Battery

A. *If intentional assault and battery was already charged on.* There is a second way in which a person may be guilty of an assault and battery. Instead of intentional conduct, it involves reckless conduct that results in bodily injury.

B. *If intentional assault and battery was not already charged on.* The defendant is charged with having committed an assault and battery upon *[the alleged victim]* by reckless conduct.

In order to prove the defendant guilty of having committed an assault and battery by reckless conduct, the Commonwealth must prove two things beyond a reasonable doubt:

7

First: That the defendant intentionally engaged in actions which caused bodily injury to *[the alleged victim]*; and

Second: That the defendant's actions amounted to reckless conduct.

To prove the first element, the Commonwealth must prove that the defendant intended (his) (her) acts which resulted in the touching, in the sense that the defendant consciously and deliberately intended the act or acts to occur and that the act or acts did not happen accidentally.

The Commonwealth must also prove that the defendant's actions caused bodily injury to [the alleged victim]. Under the law, a bodily injury must be sufficiently serious to interfere with the alleged victim's health or comfort. It need not be permanent, but it must be more than trifling. For example, an act that only shakes up a person or causes only momentary discomfort would not be sufficient.

To prove the second element, the Commonwealth must prove the defendant acted recklessly. It is not enough for the Commonwealth to prove that the defendant acted negligently—that is, acted in a way that a reasonably careful person would not. It must be shown that the defendant's actions went beyond mere negligence and amounted to recklessness. The defendant acted recklessly if (he) (she) knew, or should have known, that such actions were very likely to cause substantial harm to someone, but (he) (she) ran that risk and went ahead anyway.

But it is not necessary that (he) (she) intended to injure or strike the alleged victim, or that (he) (she) foresaw the harm that resulted. If the defendant actually realized in advance that (his) (her) conduct was very likely to cause substantial harm and decided to run that risk, such conduct would of course be reckless. But even if (he) (she) was not conscious of the serious danger that was inherent in such conduct, it is still reckless conduct if a reasonable person, under the circumstances as they were known to the defendant, would have recognized that such actions were so dangerous that it was very likely that they would result in substantial injury.

Commonwealth v. Burno, 396 Mass. 622, 625–27 (1986) ("the intentional commission of a wanton or reckless act (something more than gross negligence) causing physical or bodily injury to another"; injury must have "interfered with the health or comfort of the victim. It need not have been permanent, but it must have been more than transient and trifling. For example, if an alleged victim were shaken up but by his own admission not injured, or if an alleged victim were to have a sore wrist for only a few minutes, the 'injury' in each instance would be transient and trifling at most.") (citation omitted); *Commonwealth v. Welch*, 16 Mass. App. Ct. 271, 273–77 (1983), *rev. denied*, 390 Mass. 1102 ("The law recognizes . . . an alternative form of assault and battery in which proof of a wilful, wanton and reckless act which results in personal injury to another substitutes for . . . intentional conduct"; elements are [1] that the act involved a high degree of likelihood that substantial harm would result to another, and [2] that the victim suffered physical injury as a result of that act); *see also Commonwealth v. Grey*, 399 Mass. 469, 472 n.4 (1987) ("'The standard of wanton or reckless conduct is at once subjective and objective' . . . . It depends on what the defendant knew (subjective) and how a reasonable person would have acted (objective) knowing those facts.") (quoting *Commonwealth v. Welansky*, 316 Mass. 383, 398 (1944)); *Commonwealth v. Godin*, 374 Mass. 120, 129 (1977) (standard "is at once both a subjective and objective standard, and is based in part on the knowledge of facts which would cause a reasonable man to know that a danger of serious harm exists. Such knowledge has its roots in experience, logic, and common sense, as well as in formal legal standards"); *Commonwealth v. Welansky*, 316 Mass. 383, 399 (1944) ("Wanton or reckless conduct amounts to what has been variously described as indifference to or disregard of probable consequences").

Supplemental Instructions

Victim Injured While Escaping. The defendant may be convicted of assault and battery if the Commonwealth has proved beyond a reasonable doubt that the defendant caused *[the alleged victim]* reasonably to fear an immediate attack from the defendant, which then led (him) (her) to try to (escape) (*or*) (defend) (himself) (herself) from the defendant, and in doing so injured (himself) (herself).

Commonwealth v. Parker, 25 Mass. App. Ct. 727, 731, 734, *rev. denied*, 402 Mass. 1104 (1988).

NOTES

1. **No verdict slip or specific unanimity instruction required where both intentional and reckless assault and battery are alleged.** Where the evidence warrants instructing on both intentional assault and battery and reckless assault and battery, the jurors need not be unanimous on whether the assault and battery was intentional or reckless. The judge, therefore, need not give a specific unanimity instruction or provide verdict slips for the jury to indicate the basis of its verdict. *Commonwealth v. Mistretta*, 84 Mass. App. Ct. 906, 906–07, *rev. denied*, 466 Mass. 1108 (2013). This is because "the forms of assault and battery are . . . closely related subcategories of the same crime." *Id.* at 907. "Specific unanimity is not required, because they are not 'separate, distinct, and essentially unrelated ways in which the same crime can be committed.'" *Id.* (quoting *Commonwealth v. Santos*, 440 Mass. 281, 288 (2003)).

2. **Medical testimony.** In a prosecution for assault and battery, medical testimony about the victim's injuries is admissible to establish that the

defendant's assault on the victim was intentional and not accidental. *Commonwealth v. Gill*, 37 Mass. App. Ct. 457, 463–64 (1994).

3. **Transferred intent.** An instruction on transferred intent indicates that the Commonwealth need only prove intent as to one of the intended victims and does not have to prove intent specifically directed at each of the actual victims. *Commonwealth v. Melton*, 436 Mass. 291, 299 n.11 (2002). "It is a familiar rule that one who shoots, intending to hit A., and accidentally hits and injures B., is liable for an assault and battery on B." *Commonwealth v. Hawkins*, 157 Mass. 551, 553 (1893); *accord Commonwealth v. Drumgold*, 423 Mass. 230, 259 (1996); *Commonwealth v. Pitts*, 403 Mass. 665, 668–69 (1989); *Commonwealth v. Puleio*, 394 Mass. 101, 109–10 (1985); *Commonwealth v. Ely*, 388 Mass. 69, 76 n.13 (1983).

4. **Statement of reasons required if imprisonment not imposed.** A jury session judge sentencing for this or one of the other crimes against persons found in G.L. c. 265 who does not impose a sentence of incarceration "shall include in the record of the case specific reasons for not imposing a sentence of imprisonment," which shall be a public record. G.L. c. 265, § 41.

Assault and Battery by Means of a Dangerous Weapon

Regulatory Authority—G.L. c. 265, § 15A
Dist. Ct. Model Jury Instruction 6.300

I. Intentional Assault and Battery By Means of a Dangerous Weapon

The defendant is charged with having committed an intentional assault and battery by means of a dangerous weapon.

In order to prove the defendant guilty of this offense, the Commonwealth must prove three things beyond a reasonable doubt:

First: That the defendant touched the person of *[alleged victim]*, however slightly, without having any right or excuse for doing so;

Second: That the defendant intended to touch *[alleged victim]*; and

Third: That the touching was done with a dangerous weapon.

The Commonwealth must prove beyond a reasonable doubt that the defendant *intended* to touch *[alleged victim]* with the dangerous weapon, in the sense that the defendant consciously and deliberately intended the touching to occur, and that the touching was not merely accidental or negligent. The Commonwealth is not required to prove that the defendant specifically intended to cause injury to *[alleged victim]*.

It is not necessary for the Commonwealth to prove that the defendant actually caused injury to *[alleged victim]* with a dangerous weapon. Any slight touching is sufficient, if it was done with a dangerous weapon.

A. A dangerous weapon is an item which is capable of causing serious injury or death. I instruct you, as a matter of law, that a _____ is a dangerous weapon.

B. An item that is normally used for innocent purposes can become a dangerous weapon if it is intentionally used as a weapon in a dangerous or potentially dangerous fashion. The law considers any item to be a dangerous weapon if it is intentionally used in a way that it reasonably appears to be capable of causing serious injury or death to another person.

For example, a brick can be a dangerous weapon if it is thrust against someone's head or a pillow if it is used to suffocate someone. In deciding whether an item was used as a dangerous weapon, you may consider the circumstances surrounding the alleged crime, the nature, size and shape of the item, and the manner in which it was handled or controlled.

G.L. c. § 265, § 15A(b). *Commonwealth v. Ford*, 424 Mass. 709, 711 (1997) (ABDW is a general intent crime and does not require specific intent to injure the victim, but its intentional branch requires an intentional touching, and not merely an intentional act resulting in a touching); *Commonwealth v. Waite*, 422 Mass. 792, 794 n.2 (1996) (ABDW does not require specific intent to do bodily harm with the dangerous weapon); *Quincy Mut. Fire Ins. Co. v. Abernathy*, 393 Mass. 81, 887 n.4 (1984) (ABDW "requires proof only that the defendant intentionally and unjustifiably used force, however slight, upon the person of another, by means of an instrumentality capable of causing bodily harm"); *Commonwealth v. Manning*, 6 Mass. App. Ct. 430, 436–38 (1978) (ABDW must be "by means of" dangerous weapon, that is, weapon must come into contact with victim); *Commonwealth v. Moffett*, 383 Mass. 201, 212 (1981) (same); *Commonwealth v. Liakos*, 12 Mass. App. Ct. 57, 60–61 (1981) (use of dangerous weapon, though not found or testified to, inferable from nature of victim's wounds).

The Appeals Court approved giving "helpful examples to guide the jury's analysis" in *Commonwealth v. Marrero*, 19 Mass. App. Ct. 921, 923 (1984), and much of the wording of the instruction regarding an item that is not inherently dangerous was reviewed in *Commonwealth v. Tevlin*, 433 Mass. 305, 310 (2001).

Where the dangerousness of the object is for the jury to decide, a lesser included instruction on assault and battery should always be given, and must be given on request. *Commonwealth v. Connolly*, 49 Mass. App. Ct. 424, 426 (2000).

II. Reckless Assault and Battery With a Dangerous Weapon

There is a second way in which a person may be guilty of an assault and battery by means of a dangerous weapon. Instead of intentional conduct, it involves a *reckless* touching.

The defendant is charged with having committed a reckless assault and battery by means of a dangerous weapon upon *[alleged victim]*.

In order to prove that the defendant is guilty of this offense, the Commonwealth must prove three things beyond a reasonable doubt:

7

First: That the defendant engaged in actions which caused bodily injury to *[alleged victim]*.

Second: That the bodily injury was done with a dangerous weapon; and

Third: That the defendant's actions amounted to reckless conduct.

With regard to the first element, the bodily injury must be sufficiently serious to interfere with the alleged victim's health or comfort. It need not be permanent, but it must be more than trifling. For example, an act that only shakes up a person or causes only momentary discomfort would not be sufficient.

A dangerous weapon is an item which is capable of causing serious injury or death. I instruct you, as a matter of law, that a _____ is a dangerous weapon.

An item that is normally used for innocent purposes can become a dangerous weapon if it is used as a weapon in a dangerous or potentially dangerous fashion. The law considers an item to be used in a dangerous fashion if it is used in a way that it reasonably appears to be capable of causing serious injury or death to another person.

For example, a brick can be a dangerous weapon if it is thrust against someone's head or a pillow if it is used to suffocate someone. In deciding whether an item was used as a dangerous weapon, you may consider the circumstances surrounding the alleged crime, the nature, size and shape of the item, and the manner in which it was handled or controlled.

With regard to the third element, it is not enough for the Commonwealth to prove that the defendant acted negligently—that is, in a manner that a reasonably careful person would not. It must be shown that the defendant's actions went beyond mere negligence and amounted to recklessness. The defendant acted recklessly if he (she) knew, or should have known, that such actions were very likely to cause substantial harm to someone, but he (she) ran that risk and went ahead anyway.

But it is not necessary that he (she) intended to injure or strike the alleged victim, or that he (she) foresaw the harm that resulted. If the defendant actually realized in advance that his (her) conduct was very likely to cause substantial harm and decided to run that risk, such conduct would of course be reckless. But even if he (she) was not conscious of the serious danger that was inherent in such conduct, it is still reckless conduct if a reasonable person, under the circumstances as they were known to the defendant, would have recognized that such actions were so dangerous that it was very likely that they would result in substantial injury.

> G.L. c. § 265, § 15A(b). *Commonwealth v. Ford*, 424 Mass. at 711 (the recklessness branch of assault and battery with a dangerous weapon requires proof of an "intentional commission of a wanton or reckless act (something more than gross negligence) causing physical or bodily injury to another" by means of a dangerous weapon).
>
> No verdict slip or specific unanimity instruction required where both intentional and reckless assault and battery by means of a dangerous weapon are alleged. Where the evidence warrants instructing on both intentional and reckless branches, the jurors need not be unanimous on whether the ABDW was intentional or reckless. The judge, therefore, need not give a specific unanimity instruction or provide verdict slips for the jury to indicate the basis of its verdict. See *Commonwealth v. Mistretta*, 84 Mass. App. Ct. 906, 906–07, *rev. denied*, 466 Mass. 1108 (2013). This is because "the forms of assault and battery are . . . closely related subcategories of the same crime." *Id.* at 907. "Specific unanimity is not required, because they are not 'separate, distinct, and essentially unrelated ways in which the same crime can be committed.' " *Id.*, quoting *Commonwealth v. Santos*, 440 Mass. 281, 288 (2003).

NOTES

1. **"Dangerous weapon."** A weapon is "an instrument of offensive or defensive combat; . . . anything used, or designed to be used, in destroying, defeating, or injuring an enemy." *Commonwealth v. Sampson*, 383 Mass. 750, 754 (1981). A dangerous weapon is "any instrument or instrumentality so constructed or so used as to be likely to produce death or great bodily harm." *Commonwealth v. Farrell*, 322 Mass. 606, 614–15 (1948).

If a weapon is inherently dangerous, it need not have been used in a dangerous fashion. *Appleby*, 380 Mass. at 307 n.6. For the list of weapons which are considered inherently dangerous, see G.L. c. 269, § 10(a) & (b) and *Commonwealth v. Appleby*, 380 Mass. 296, 303 (1980) (item is inherently dangerous "if designed for the purpose of bodily assault or defense"). *See Commonwealth v. Lord*, 55 Mass. App. Ct. 265, 267 (2002) (mace spraying device dangerous per se).

Usually-innocent items are also considered to be dangerous weapons if used in a dangerous or potentially dangerous fashion. *Id.* at 303–04, 307 (riding crop; and collecting cases on particular items). *See also Commonwealth v. Scott*, 408 Mass. 811, 822–23 (1990) (gag); *Commonwealth v. Gallison*, 383 Mass. 659, 667–68 (1981) (lit cigarette); *Commonwealth v. Barrett*, 386 Mass. 649, 654–56 (1980) (aerosol can sprayed in eyes of operator of moving vehicle); *Commonwealth v. Fettes*, 64 Mass. App. Ct. 917, 918 (2005) (dog). However, the fact that an appellate court previously held that the object was capable of being used as a dangerous weapon does not make it such in all future cases, regardless of circumstances. *Appleby, supra*. "The essential question, when an object which is not dangerous per se is alleged to be a dangerous weapon, is whether the object, as used by the defendant, is capable of producing serious bodily harm." *Marrero*, 19 Mass. App. Ct. at 922. This is determined by how the object's potential for harm would have appeared to a reasonable observer. *Commonwealth v. Tarrant*, 367 Mass. 411, 414 (1975). This determination is normally for the jury, to be decided on the basis of the circumstances surrounding the crime, the nature, size and shape of the object, and the manner in which it was handled or controlled. *Appleby*, 380 Mass. at 307 n.5; *Marrero*, supra; *Commonwealth v. Davis*, 10 Mass. App. Ct. 190, 193 (1980). "That a dangerous weapon was used can be inferred from the victim's injuries." *Commonwealth v. Roman*, 43 Mass. App. Ct. 733, 736, *S.C.*, 427 Mass. 1006 (1998). Whether an item is a dangerous weapon turns on how it is used, and not the subjective intent of the actor. *Commonwealth v. Lefebvre*, 60 Mass. App. Ct. 912, 913 (2004); *Commonwealth v. Connolly* 49 Mass. App. Ct. 424, 425 (2000).

To qualify as a dangerous weapon, an item need not be capable of being wielded, possessed or controlled, and may be stationary. *Commonwealth v. Sexton*, 425 Mass. 146, 152 (1997) (concrete pavement against which victim's head was repeatedly struck; and collecting cases). *See also Commonwealth v. McIntosh*, 56 Mass. App. Ct. 827, 829 (2002) (windowpane). It may not, however, be a human body part. *Davis*, 10 Mass. App. Ct. at 192-193 (teeth and other body parts). The ocean is not a dangerous weapon for purposes of § 15A where the victim is abandoned far from shore, *Commonwealth v. Shea*, 38 Mass. App. Ct. 7, 15–16, (1995), but perhaps it would be if the victim's head were held underwater, *see Sexton*, 425 Mass. at 150 & n.1.

2. **Knives.** Not all knives are dangerous per se. *Commonwealth v. Miller*, 22 Mass. App. Ct. 694, 694 n.1 (1986) (noting Legislature has not designated all knives as dangerous per se, and discussing the definition of "dirk knife"). By statute, "any stiletto, dagger or a device or case which enables a knife with a locking blade to be drawn at a locked position, any ballistic knife, or any knife with a detachable blade capable of being propelled by any mechanism, dirk knife, any knife having a double-edged blade, or a switch knife, or any knife having an automatic spring release device by which the blade is released from the handle, having a blade of over one and one-half inches" is a dangerous weapon per se. G.L. c. 269, § 10(b). *See Commonwealth v. Smith*, 10 Mass. App. Ct. 770, 776–78 (1996) (a "knife having a double-edged blade" need not be double-edged for its entire length); *Miller, supra* (discussing the difficulties in defining a "dirk knife"). Straight knives typically are regarded as dangerous per se while folding knives, at least those without a locking device, typically are not. *Commonwealth v. Turner*, 59 Mass. App. Ct. 825, 828 (2003). *See Commonwealth v. Young*, 461 Mass. 198, 211–12 (2012) (affirming instruction that a nine-inch knife with a five-inch double-edge blade was dangerous per se). Possession of a closed folding knife is a dangerous weapon for purposes of G.L. c. 269, § 10(b) only if used or handled in a manner that made it a dangerous weapon. *Turner*, 59 Mass. App. Ct. at 828–29.

3. **Shod foot.** "Footwear, such as a shoe, when used to kick, can be a dangerous weapon." *Commonwealth v. Tevlin*, 433 Mass. 305, 311 (2001); *Commonwealth v. Fernandez*, 43 Mass. App. Ct. 313, 315 (1997) (sneakers); *Commonwealth v. Marrero*, 19 Mass. App. Ct. 921, 922 (1984) (boots or sneakers); *Commonwealth v. Zawatsky*, 41 Mass. App. Ct. 392, 398–99 (1996) (unnecessary for prosecutor to prove exactly what type of shoes defendant wore where there was evidence that defendant was wearing shoes and gave victim a vicious kick to the head resulting in injury). *Compare Commonwealth v. Charles*, 57 Mass. App. Ct. 595, 599 (2003) (kicking was "not so minimal as to foreclose an inference" that shod feet were being used as dangerous weapons capable of causing serious injury) *with Commonwealth v. Mercado*, 24 Mass. App. Ct. 391, 397 (1987) (jury may infer that foot was shod, but no more than a nudge was insufficient).

4. **Unseen weapon.** A defendant who claimed to have a weapon may be taken at his word, if it is possible that he did have such a weapon. *Commonwealth v. Hastings*, 22 Mass. App. Ct. 930, 930 (1986) (where victim felt sharp object against her, defendant claiming to have unseen knife may be convicted of ABDW).

5. **Specification of dangerous weapon.** The particular type of dangerous weapon with which the offense was committed is not an essential element of ABDW. *Commonwealth v. Salone*, 26 Mass. App. Ct. 926, 929 (1988). It is therefore surplusage in a complaint and, if the defendant is not surprised, its specification in the complaint may be amended at any time to conform to the evidence. See G.L. c. 277, § 21.

6. **Automobile as extension of occupants.** As to whether a battery of an automobile is also a battery of its occupants, see *Commonwealth v. Burno*, 396 Mass. 622, 627–28 (1986) (agreeing that "a battery could occur although no force was applied to a person directly," but reserving decision on whether "a battery could occur even if no force at all, direct or indirect, was applied to a person").

7. **Victim injured while escaping.** A defendant may be convicted of ABDW where the victim was cut with the defendant's knife while trying to grab the knife away from the pursuing defendant. *Commonwealth v.*

Rajotte, 23 Mass. App. Ct. 93, 96 (1986). See the supplemental instruction to Assault and Battery (Instruction 6.140).

8. **Consent not a defense.** *Commonwealth v. Appleby*, 380 Mass. 296, 310 (1980) (consent is not a defense to ABDW). *Commonwealth v. Burke*, 390 Mass. 480, 482–83 (1983); *Commonwealth v. Leonard*, 90 Mass. App. Ct. 187 (2016).

9. **Transferred intent.** An instruction on transferred intent indicates that the Commonwealth need only prove an intent to touch one of the intended victims and does not have to prove intent specifically directed at each of the actual victims. *Commonwealth v. Melton*, 436 Mass. 291, 299 n.11 (2002). "It is a familiar rule that one who shoots, intending to hit A., and accidentally hits and injures B., is liable for an assault and battery on B." *Commonwealth v. Hawkins*, 157 Mass. 551, 553 (1893). *Accord, Commonwealth v. Dung Van Tran*, 463 Mass. 8, 25 & n.19 (2012); *Commonwealth v. Drumgold*, 423 Mass. 230, 259 (1996); *Commonwealth v. Pitts*, 403 Mass. 665, 668–69 & n.6 (1989); *Commonwealth v. Puleio*, 394 Mass. 101, 109–10, (1985); *Commonwealth v. Ely*, 388 Mass. 69, 76 n.13 (1983).

10. **Joint venture.** A conviction of ABDW by joint venture requires knowledge that the co-venturer had a dangerous weapon, but this may be inferred from the circumstances. *Commonwealth v. Ferguson*, 365 Mass. 1, 8–9 (1974); *Commonwealth v. Meadows*, 12 Mass. App. Ct. 639, 644 (1981). See *Commonwealth v. Britt*, 465 Mass. 87, 100 (2013) (where conviction is based on joint venture theory of crime that has as element use or possession of weapon, Commonwealth bears "the burden of proving that [the defendant] had knowledge that a member of the joint venture had a weapon"). However, "there is no need to prove an anticipatory compact between the parties to establish joint venture, if, at the climactic moment the parties consciously acted together in carrying out the criminal endeavor." *Commonwealth v. Sexton*, 425 Mass. 146, 152 (1997) (joint venture liability for ABDW upheld where defendant continuously kicked and punched the victim while his coventurer repeatedly slammed the victim's head into the pavement, and at no time during this conflict did the defendant seek to withdraw).

11. **Aggravated forms of offense.** Assault and battery on a person 60 years or older by means of a dangerous weapon (G.L. c. 265, § 15A[a]) is an aggravated form of ABDW (§ 15A[b]). The Commonwealth must charge and prove that the victim was 60 years of age or older. The jury may consider the victim's physical appearance as one factor in determining age, but appearance alone is not sufficient evidence of age unless the victim is of "a marked extreme" age, since "[e]xcept at the poles, judging age on physical appearance is a guess . . . ." *Commonwealth v. Pittman*, 25 Mass. App. Ct. 25, 28 (1987). A further-aggravated sentence is provided for subsequent offenses.

An ABDW is also aggravated if it causes serious bodily injury, or if the defendant knows or has reason to know that the victim is pregnant, or if the defendant knows that the victim has an outstanding abuse restraining order against the defendant, or if the defendant is 18 years of age or older and the victim is under the age of 14. G.L. c. 265, § 15A(c)).

12. **Lesser included offenses.** ABDW has as lesser included offenses assault with a dangerous weapon, and assault and battery (Instruction 6.140). *Commonwealth v. Beal*, 474 Mass. 341, 347 (2016) (ADW lesser included offense of ABDW); *Commonwealth v. Connolly*, 49 Mass. App. Ct. 424, 426 (2000) (assault and battery lesser included offense of ABDW). Both theories of assault (Instruction 6.120) are lesser included offenses of intentional ABDW; there is still an open question about whether both theories are lesser included offenses of reckless ABDW). See *Commonwealth v. Porro*, 458 Mass. 526, 534 & n.8 (2010). If the evidence would also permit a jury finding of a lesser included offense, the jury should be instructed on lesser included offenses (Instruction 2.280).

13. **Statement of reasons required if imprisonment not imposed.** A jury session judge sentencing for this or one of the other crimes against persons found in G.L. c. 265 who does not impose a sentence of incarceration "shall include in the record of the case specific reasons for not imposing a sentence of imprisonment," which shall be a public record. G.L. c. 265, § 41.

Attaching Plates

Regulatory Authority—G.L. c. 90, § 23
Dist. Ct. Model Jury Instruction 5.100

The defendant is charged with having intentionally attached the wrong license plates to a motor vehicle in order to conceal its identity. Section 23 of chapter 90 of our General Laws provides as follows:

> "Any person who attaches or permits to be attached to a motor vehicle . . . a number plate assigned to another motor vehicle . . . , with intent to conceal the identity of such motor vehicle . . . shall be punished . . . ."

In order to prove the defendant guilty of this offense, the Commonwealth must prove three things beyond a reasonable doubt:

First: That the defendant attached the license plate in question to a motor vehicle, or permitted it to be so attached;

Second: That the license plate in question was not assigned by the Registry of Motor Vehicles to that particular vehicle; and

Third: That the defendant did so with the intent to conceal the identity of that motor vehicle.

Attempt

Regulatory Authority—G.L. c. 274, § 6
Dist. Ct. Model Jury Instruction 4.120

In this Commonwealth, an attempt to commit a crime is itself a crime.

> The defendant is charged with (attempted) (an attempt to) _____. To prove that the defendant is guilty of this offense, the Commonwealth must prove two things beyond a reasonable doubt:

First: That the defendant had a specific intent to commit _____; and

Second: That the defendant took an overt act toward committing that crime, which was part of carrying out the crime, and came reasonably close to actually carrying out the crime.

The essence of the crime of attempt is that a person has a specific intent to commit a crime and takes a specific step toward committing that crime.

Supplement Instruction

Overt Act. An "overt act" is some actual, outward, physical *action*, as opposed to mere talk or plans. It is not enough that someone just intends to commit a crime or talks about doing so.

The overt act must also be a real step toward *carrying out* the crime. Preliminary preparations to commit a crime are not enough. The overt act has to be more of a step toward actually committing the crime, after all the preparations have been made. It must be the sort of act that you could reasonably expect to trigger a natural chain of events that will result in the crime, unless some outside factor intervenes.

It doesn't have to make the crime inevitable. For example, a pickpocket can be guilty of attempted larceny for putting his hand in another person's pocket with the intent to steal, even if it turns out that there is no money in that pocket. And a person can be guilty of attempted murder even if he doesn't hold the pistol straight when he shoots it at someone. But the overt act must be pretty closely linked with actually accomplishing the intended crime. It has to be an act that isn't too remote, and that is reasonably expected to bring about the crime. This is a question of fact that you must determine from all the evidence in the case.

NOTES

1. **District Court jurisdiction.** Since the District Court has final jurisdiction over some attempts but not others, the judge should examine the complaint before trial. An attempt charge brought under the general attempt statute (G.L. c. 274, § 6) is within the District Court's final jurisdiction unless the attempted crime was murder. The District Court also has final jurisdiction over attempted burning to defraud an insurer (G.L. c. 266, § 10), attempted escape (G.L. c. 268, §§ 16–17), and certain attempted bribery offenses (G.L. c. 268, §§ 13, 13B; G.L. c. 268A, § 2; G.L. c. 271, §§ 39[a], 39A). The District Court does not have final jurisdiction over attempted murder (G.L. c. 265, § 16), attempted extortion (G.L. c. 265, § 25), attempted poisoning (G.L. c. 265, § 285A), or attempted safe-breaking (G.L. c. 266, § 16). See G.L. c. 218, § 26.

2. **Intent.** Complaints charging an attempt require proof "that the defendant had a conscious design to achieve the felonious end . . . . If the [underlying] crime as defined includes the element of intent . . . , the prosecution must prove a specific intent on the part of the defendant." *Commonwealth v. Saylor*, 27 Mass. App. Ct. 117, 121 (1989).

3. **Proximity to success.** An attempt requires specific intent to commit the substantive crime, *Commonwealth v. Ware*, 375 Mass. 118, 120

(1978); *Commonwealth v. Hebert,* 373 Mass. 535, 537 (1977), coupled with an overt act which need not inevitably accomplish the crime but "must come pretty near to accomplishing that result . . . . Usually acts which are expected to bring about the end without further interference on the part of the criminal are near enough, unless the expectation is very absurd," *Commonwealth v. Kennedy,* 170 Mass. 18, 20–21 (1897) (shooting at post thought to be a person is not a criminal attempt, but shooting at a person with a pistol not aimed straight is). Mere intent or preparation are not enough; the overt act must lead toward the actual commission of the crime after preparations have been made. *Commonwealth v. Burns,* 8 Mass. App. Ct. 194, 196 (1979). "The most common types of an attempt are either an act which is intended to bring about the substantive crime and which sets in motion natural forces that would bring it about in the expected course of events but for an unforeseen interruption . . . or an act which is intended to bring about the substantive crime and would bring it about but for a mistake in judgment in a matter of nice estimate or experiment . . . . In either case the would-be criminal has done his last act . . . . Obviously new considerations come in when further acts on the part of the person who has taken the first steps are necessary before the substantive crime can come to pass. In this class of cases there is still a chance that the would-be criminal may change his mind. In strictness, such first steps cannot be described as an attempt . . . . [A]n overt act . . . is not punishable if further acts are contemplated as needful . . . . But some preparations may amount to an attempt. It is a question of degree. If the preparation comes very near to the accomplishment of the act, the intent to complete it renders the crime so probable that the act will be a [criminal attempt]." *Commonwealth v. Peaslee,* 177 Mass. 267, 271–72 (1901) (Holmes, C.J.). *See Commonwealth v. Scott,* 408 Mass. 811, 821–22 (1990) (victim's clothes ripped off, and a hair from victim found inside defendant's shorts, sufficient for attempted rape as a predicate for felony murder); *Commonwealth v. Ortiz,* 408 Mass. 463, 472 (1990) (defendant who armed himself and went searching for intended victim, but did not locate him, cannot be convicted of attempted ABDW). *Commonwealth v. Hamel,* 52 Mass. App. Ct. 250, 256 (2001) (furnishing information regarding form of payment, description of victims, and site for killings to solicitee feigning cooperation, not sufficient for attempted murder conviction). Factual impossibility is not a defense if the crime is apparently possible. *Commonwealth v. Jacobs,* 91 Mass. (9 Allen) 274, 275–76 (1864); *Commonwealth v. Starr,* 86 Mass. (4 Allen) 301, 305 (1862); *Commonwealth v. McDonald,* 59 Mass. (5 Cush.) 365, 367–68 (1850) (pickpocketing empty pocket). See discussion in *Commonwealth v. Bell,* 67 Mass. App. Ct. 266 (2006), *further appellate review denied, Commonwealth v. Bell,* 451 Mass. 1101 (2008).

7

4. **Overt act.** An attempt complaint is fatally defective if it does not include an allegation of any specific overt act. *Commonwealth v. Gosselin,* 365 Mass. 116, 121 (1974); *Commonwealth v. Anolik,* 27 Mass. App. Ct. 701, 710–11, *further appellate review denied,* 406 Mass. 1101 (1989); *Burns,* 8 Mass. App. Ct. at 195. But retrial is permissible since such a defective complaint does not put the defendant in jeopardy. *Burns,* 8 Mass. App. Ct. at 198 n.2. Only the overt act or acts alleged in the complaint may be proved to satisfy the requirement of an overt act. *Gosselin,* 365 Mass. at 121; *Peaslee,* 177 Mass. at 274. An attempt complaint is not required to set out the elements of the substantive crime attempted. *McDonald,* 59 Mass. (5 Cush.) at 367.

5. **Two elements of offense.** Appellate courts have repeatedly held that there are two elements to this offense. *Commonwealth v. Sullivan,* 84 Mass. App. Ct. 26, 27 (2013). *See also Commonwealth v. Rivera,* 460 Mass. 139, 142 (2011); *Commonwealth v. Foley,* 24 Mass. App. Ct. 114, 115 (1987).

6. **Lesser included offense of substantive crime.** While it is true that an attempt to commit a crime is a lesser included offense within that substantive crime, *Gosselin,* 365 Mass. at 120–21; *Commonwealth v. Banner,* 13 Mass. App. Ct. 1065, 1066 (1982), a defendant may be convicted of attempt as a lesser included offense only if the complaint alleges some overt act constituting the attempt. It may also be necessary that the complaint allege the defendant's specific intent to commit *every* element of the substantive crime (which would not normally be found in a complaint for a substantive offense, even one requiring specific intent as to *some* elements). If the complaint for the substantive crime does not meet those requirements, the defendant may be charged with attempt in a subsequent prosecution, since he or she was not put in jeopardy as to that charge. *Foley,* 24 Mass. App. Ct. at 115–17 & n.5.

Breaking and Entering

Regulatory Authority—G.L. c. 266, § 16
Dist. Ct. Model Jury Instruction 8.100

The defendant in this case is charged with breaking and entering a (building) (ship) (vessel) (vehicle) in the nighttime, with the intent to commit a felony, in violation of section 16 of chapter 266 of our General Laws.

In order to prove the defendant guilty of this offense, the Commonwealth must prove four things beyond a reasonable doubt:

First: That the defendant broke into a (building) (ship) (vessel) (vehicle) belonging to another person;

Second: That the defendant entered that (building) (ship) (vessel) (vehicle);

Third: That the defendant did so with the intent to commit a felony in that (building) (ship) (vessel) (vehicle); and

Fourth: That this event took place during the nighttime.

As to the first element of the offense, "breaking" has been defined as exerting physical force, even slight physical force, and thereby forcibly removing an obstruction and gaining entry. Another definition would be: moving in a significant manner anything that bars the way into the (building) (ship) (vessel) (vehicle). Some obvious examples would include breaking a window, or forcing open a door or window, or removing a plank from a wall. But there are some less obvious examples that also are considered to be "breakings." Opening a closed door or window is a breaking, even if they are unlocked. Going in through an open window that is not intended for use as an entrance is also a breaking, but going in through an unobstructed entrance—such as an open door—is not.

> *Commonwealth v. Burke,* 392 Mass. 688, 689–90 (1984); *Commonwealth v. Tilley,* 355 Mass. 507, 508–509 (1969); *Commonwealth v. Shedd,* 140 Mass. 451, 453 (1886); *Commonwealth v. Hall,* 48 Mass. App. Ct. 727, 731 (2000) (open window). See *Commonwealth v. Pearson,* 72 Mass. App. Ct. 1101 (No. 07-P-676, June 6, 2008) (unpublished opinion under Appeals Court Rule 1:28), *further appellate review denied, Commonwealth v. Pearson,* 452 Mass. 1102 (2008) (since a car window is not used or intended to enter a car, leaning torso and both arms through open window of parked car sufficient to support finding of breaking and entering).

The second element of this offense is that the defendant in fact entered the (building) (ship) (vessel) (vehicle). "Entry" is the unlawful making of one's way into a (building) (ship) (vessel) (vehicle). Entry occurs if any part of the defendant's body—even a hand or foot—or any instrument or weapon controlled by the defendant physically enters the (building) (ship) (vessel) (vehicle). Breaking an outer storm window and reaching inside between the outer and inner windows with one's hand is an entry.

> *Burke,* 392 Mass. at 691 (reaching between outer and inner window with a tool, but not a hand, insufficient); *Commonwealth v. Lewis,* 346 Mass. 373, 377 (1963).

The third element of the offense is that the defendant broke in with the intent to commit a felony. In this Commonwealth, offenses for which a person may be sentenced to state prison are called "felonies." Other, lesser offenses are called "misdemeanors."

If no specific felony was charged, or the evidence suggests a different felony: The Commonwealth is not required to prove that the defendant intended any particular felony, but it must prove that the defendant intended to commit *some* felony.

I instruct you that _____ (and) _____ (is a felony) (are felonies). The Commonwealth must prove that the defendant intended to commit a felony at the time he (she) broke and entered the (building) (ship) (vessel) (vehicle).

> *Rogan v. Commonwealth,* 415 Mass. 376 (1993) (jury may find intent to commit an unspecified crime); *Commonwealth v. Poff,* 56 Mass. App. Ct. 201, 203 (2002) (felonious intent must be present at the time

of the breaking and entering); *Commonwealth v. Clemente*, 25 Mass. App. Ct. 229, 235 n.10 (1988) (statute apparently does not require an intent to commit a felony in the same building into which the break was made).

Finally, the Commonwealth must prove that the breaking and entering took place in the nighttime. The law is that the "nighttime" begins one hour after sunset and ends one hour before sunrise the next day, measured according to mean, or average, time at that time of the year in the place where the crime was committed.

The Commonwealth may prove that a crime occurred in the nighttime by (presenting evidence that it was completely dark outside at the time of the offense) (offering an almanac or other reference book to show the time of sunset or sunrise on that day) (asking you as jurors to rely on your common knowledge of approximately when the sun rises or sets on *[date]* in this area). Whatever method is used, you must be convinced beyond a reasonable doubt that the crime occurred sometime between one hour after sunset and one hour before sunrise.

Here instruct on "Intent" (Instruction 3.120).

G.L. c. 278, § 10. *Commonwealth v. Kingsbury,* 378 Mass. 751, 752–54 (1979); *Commonwealth v. Bergstrom,* 10 Mass. App. Ct. 838, 838–39 (1980); *Commonwealth v. Servidori,* 6 Mass. App. Ct. 969 (1979).

Supplemental Instructions

1. ***Constructive breaking.*** It is not always necessary that a person physically break into a (building) (ship) (vessel) (vehicle) to be found guilty of this offense. The defendant may be convicted if an accomplice let him (her) into the (building) (ship) (vessel) (vehicle), or if the defendant convinced an innocent person by trick or threat to allow him (her) to enter, if the defendant entered with the intent to commit a felony.

Commonwealth v. Lowrey, 158 Mass. 18, 19–20 (1893) (accomplice); *Commonwealth v. Labare,* 11 Mass. App. Ct. 370, 377 (1981) (phony name).

2. ***Judicial notice of time of sunset or sunrise.*** The law permits me to take notice of certain facts that are not subject to reasonable dispute. In this case, based upon *[reference book]*, I have decided to accept as proved the fact that on *[date]* the sun (set) (rose) at *[time]*. Therefore, you may accept this fact as true, even though no evidence has been introduced about it. You are not required to do so, but you may.

See the notes to the supplemental instruction on "Judicial Notice" in Instruction 2.220 (What Is Evidence; Stipulations; Judicial Notice).

3. ***Breaking and entering in daytime as lesser included offense.*** If it has not been proved to you beyond a reasonable doubt that the defendant committed this offense sometime between one hour after sunset and one hour before sunrise, but all the other elements of the offense have been proved to you beyond a reasonable doubt, you may find the defendant guilty of the lesser included offense of breaking and entering in the daytime.

Commonwealth v. Sitko, 372 Mass. 305, 307–08 (1977) (breaking and entering in the daytime under G.L. c. 266, § 18 is the equivalent of a lesser included offense in breaking and entering in the nighttime).

4. ***Intent to steal.*** When a person breaks and enters in the nighttime, it is ordinarily a fair inference, in the absence of contrary evidence, that he intends to steal. You are permitted to draw such an inference if you think it reasonable. You are not required to draw such a conclusion, but you may.

Commonwealth v. McGovern, 397 Mass. 863, 868 (1986); *Commonwealth v. Hughes,* 380 Mass. 596, 602–04 (1980) (dwelling); *Commonwealth v. Wygrzywalski,* 362 Mass. 790, 792 (1973) (store); *Commonwealth v. Eppich,* 342 Mass. 487, 493 (1961) (same); *Commonwealth v. Ronchetti,* 333 Mass. 78, 81 (1955) (inference permissible even where defendant attacked homeowner, apparently spontaneously).

NOTES

1. **"Another's" property.** The Commonwealth need not allege the building or vehicle owner's name in the complaint, G.L. c. 277, § 25, and if it does, at trial need only prove that the property was owned by someone other than the defendant, *Commonwealth v. Kalinowski,* 360 Mass. 682, 684–85 (1971). At common law, one could not burglarize one's own dwelling, but the issue turned on rights of occupancy rather than ownership. *Commonwealth v. Ricardo,* 26 Mass. App. Ct. 345, 354–57 (1988) (charge of armed assault in dwelling). *But see Commonwealth v. Derome,* 6 Mass. App. Ct. 900, 901 (1978) (directing verdict for defendant where Commonwealth charged the break of one premise but proved the break of another).

2. **"Breaking and entering and stealing therein."** At common law, a compound charge of "breaking and entering and stealing therein" was a variation on "breaking and entering with intent to steal." Since there is no better proof of intent to steal than actual larceny, the "averment of actual stealing is to be regarded as equivalent to alleging the intent to steal." When the offense was charged in such compound form, the actual larceny could not also be charged as a separate count, and no separate sentence could be imposed for the larceny. *Commonwealth v. Hope,* 22 Pick. 1, 5–7 (1839). When the breaking and entering and the larceny are charged in separate counts, rather than merged in a single count, separate convictions and sentences are permissible on both. *Commonwealth v. Ford,* 20 Mass. App. Ct. 575, 580 (1985); *Josslyn v. Commonwealth,* 6 Met. 236, 240 (1843).

3. **One break or several?** As to whether multiple breaks into different units in a single building may be prosecuted and sentenced as separate crimes, see *Clemente,* 25 Mass. App. Ct. at 233–37.

4. **Related offenses.** The model instruction is designed for the specific offenses of breaking and entering a building or a vehicle in the nighttime with the intent to commit a felony. That section also includes the offenses of breaking and entering a ship or vessel, which would require appropriate changes in the instruction. The instruction can also be used for violations of G.L. c. 266, §§ 16A, 17 and 18 with the following changes:

G.L. c. 266, § 16A (Breaking and entering with intent to commit a misdemeanor): Change the third element of the model instruction to require proof of a misdemeanor. Omit the fourth element, since the breaking and entering can occur at any time. This is a lesser included offense in G.L. c. 266, § 16. *Commonwealth v. Murphy,* 31 Mass. App. Ct. 901, 901 n.1 (1991).

G.L. c. 266, § 17 (Entering in nighttime without breaking, or breaking and entering in daytime, owner put in fear): Entering in nighttime does not require breaking, but entering in the daytime does. In either case, the owner or any other person lawfully therein must be put in fear. Otherwise, the model instruction remains unchanged.

G.L. c. 266, § 18 (Entering dwelling house in nighttime, without breaking, or breaking and entering building in daytime, owner not put in fear): The first offense in § 18 requires a change to "dwelling house" in the first three elements of the model instruction. An unoccupied apartment is a "dwelling house" if the tenants have taken possession and have the right to move in, even if they have not in fact done so. *Commonwealth v. Kingsbury,* 378 Mass. 751 (1979). An occupied motel room is a "dwelling." *Commonwealth v. Correia,* 17 Mass. App. Ct. 233, 234–36 (1983). The second offense in § 18 requires a change to "daytime" in the fourth element of the model instruction.

Breaking and entering (G.L. c. 266, § 16) is not duplicitous of larceny in a building (G.L. c. 266, § 20), *Ford, above,* or of possessing burglarious instruments (G.L. c. 266, § 49), *Commonwealth v. Johnson,* 406 Mass. 533, 535 (1990), or receiving stolen property (G.L. c. 266, § 60). *Commonwealth v. Cabrera,* 449 Mass. 825, 874 (2007). Trespass (G.L. c. 266, § 120) is not a lesser included offense of breaking and entering. *Commonwealth v. Vinnicombe,* 28 Mass. App. Ct. 934 (1990).

5. **Variance in intended felony.** The complaint need not specify the intended felony. *Commonwealth v. Porcher,* 26 Mass. App. Ct. 517, 521 (1988); *Commonwealth v. Wainio,* 1 Mass. App. Ct. 866, 867 (1974). Since a complaint's specification of the intended felony is surplusage,

proof of a different felony is permissible if the defendant is not misled or the jury confused. *Commonwealth v. Costello,* 392 Mass. 393, 402–04 (1984); *Commonwealth v. Hobbs,* 385 Mass. 863, 869–71 (1982); *see also Commonwealth v. Randolph,* 415 Mass. 364, 367 (1993). *See also Rogan, above* (jury may find intent to commit an unspecified misdemeanor on charge of breaking and entering in daytime with intent to commit felony).

6. **Evidence of Time.** The Commonwealth's failure to provide direct evidence of the time of the crime is not fatal to the Commonwealth's case because circumstantial evidence is competent evidence to establish guilt. *Commonwealth v. Bennett,* 424 Mass. 64, 67 (1997). Nor is the Commonwealth compelled to provide any evidence of the time of sunrise. *Commonwealth v. Bennett,* 424 Mass. at 68 ("The jury were entitled to rely on their general knowledge of matters commonly known within the community in determining what inferences may be drawn to establish a material fact not proved by direct evidence, such as the time of sunset or sunrise at a particular time of the year.").

Burning Personal Property, Motor Vehicles, etc.

Regulatory Authority—G.L. c. 266, § 5
Dist. Ct. Model Jury Instruction 8.140

The defendant is charged with unlawfully burning a _____. Section 5 of chapter 266 of our General Laws provides as follows:

> "Whoever wilfully and maliciously (sets fire to) (burns) (destroys or injures by burning) (causes to be burned or otherwise so destroyed or injured) (aids, counsels or procures the burning of) . . . (any personal property [belonging to another person and] . . . exceeding a value of twenty-five dollars . . .) (*or*) (any boat, motor vehicle . . . or other conveyance, whether [belonging to] himself or another . . .) shall be punished . . . ."

In order to prove the defendant guilty of this offense, the Commonwealth must prove four things beyond a reasonable doubt:

First: That the property in question was (personal property belonging to another person with a value of more than $25) (a boat belonging to the defendant or another person) (a motor vehicle belonging to the defendant or another person) (a conveyance belonging to the defendant or another person);

7

Second: That the defendant (set fire to or burned the property) (caused the property to be burned) (aided, counseled, or procured the property to be burned);

Third: That the defendant did so wilfully—that is, intentionally and not by accident; and

Fourth: That the defendant did so maliciously—that is, it was done with some wrong and unlawful motive and without excuse.

Supplemental Instructions

1. ***Wilfully.*** "Wilful" means intentionally and by design, and this eliminates accidental or negligent burnings. However, a person who negligently ignites a fire and then makes no attempt to extinguish or report it may be found to have acted wilfully.

> *See Commonwealth v. McKenzie,* 376 Mass. 148, 150 (1978).

2. ***Maliciously.*** The "malice" that must be shown does not require any particular ill will against someone. A burning is malicious if it is done with a wrong and unlawful motive or purpose; if it is the wilful doing of a harmful act without lawful excuse.

> *Commonwealth v. Niziolek,* 380 Mass. 513, 527 (1980), *habeas corpus denied sub nom. Niziolek v. Ashe,* 694 F.2d 282 (1st Cir. 1982); *Commonwealth v. Lamothe,* 343 Mass. 417, 419–20 (1961).

Carrying a Firearm

Regulatory Authority—G.L. c. 269, § 10(a)
Dist. Ct. Model Jury Instruction 7.600

> The offense found in G.L. c. 269, § 10(a) is commonly referred to as "carrying" a firearm, to distinguish it from the offense of "possession" of a firearm without a firearms ID card, found in § 10(h). The name is no longer strictly accurate, since St. 1990, c. 511 (effective January 2, 1991) eliminated movement of the firearm as an element of § 10(a).

I. Firearm with Barrel Under 16 Inches

The defendant is charged under section 10(a) of chapter 269 of our General Laws with knowingly possessing a firearm unlawfully.

In order to prove the defendant guilty of this offense, the Commonwealth must prove the following (three) (four) things beyond a reasonable doubt:

First: That the defendant possessed a firearm (*or*) (that he [she] had a firearm under his [her] control in a vehicle);

Second: That what the defendant (possessed) (*or*) (had under his [her] control in a vehicle) met the legal definition of a "firearm"; (and)

Third: That the defendant *knew* that he (she) (possessed a firearm) (*or*) (had a firearm under his [her] control in a vehicle.

> *If there is evidence of one of the statutory exceptions, use one of the following:*

A. *If there is evidence that it was in the defendant's residence or place of business.* And *Fourth:* that the defendant possessed the firearm outside of his (her) residence or place of business. A person's "residence" or "place of business" does not include common areas of an apartment or office building, but only areas that are under that person's exclusive control.

B. *If there is evidence that the defendant had a license to carry firearms.* And *Fourth:* that the defendant did *not* have a valid license to carry a firearm outside his (her) home or office.

C. *If there is evidence that the defendant was exempt from the licensing requirement.* And *Fourth:* that the defendant did *not* qualify for one of the exemptions in the law that are a substitute for having a license to carry a firearm outside his (her) home or business.

> The statute exempts a defendant who:
>
> "(1) [was] present in or on his residence or place of business; or
>
> (2) [had] in effect a license to carry firearms issued under [G.L. c. 140, § 131]; or
>
> (3) [had] in effect a license to carry firearms issued under [G.L. c. 140, § 131F to a nonresident or alien]; or
>
> (4) [had] complied with the provisions of [G.L. c. 140, §§ 129C and 131G, granting certain categorical exemptions from the requirement of a license to carry]; or
>
> (5) [had] complied as to possession of an air rifle or BB gun with the requirements imposed by [G.L. c. 269, § 12B]."
>
> General Laws c. 278, § 7 places on the defendant the burden of producing evidence of one of these exemptions; the Commonwealth must then disprove beyond a reasonable doubt the applicability of the claimed exemption. Until there is such evidence, the exemptions are not at issue. *See Commonwealth v. Seay,* 376 Mass. 735, 738 (1978) (former statute); *Commonwealth v. Jones,* 372 Mass. 403, 406–07 (1977) (same); *Commonwealth v. Davis,* 359 Mass. 758 (1971) (same); *Commonwealth v. Baker,* 10 Mass. App. Ct. 852, 853 (1980) (lack of license need not be charged in complaint).
>
> A "firearm" is defined in our law as:
>
> "a pistol, revolver or other weapon . . . loaded or unloaded, from which a shot or bullet can be discharged and . . . the length of [whose] barrel is less than sixteen inches . . . ."

That definition can be broken down into three requirements: *First,* it must be a weapon; *Second,* it must be capable of discharging a shot or bullet; and *Third,* it must have a barrel length of less than 16 inches. The term "barrel length" refers to "that portion of a firearm . . . through which a shot or bullet is driven, guided or stabilized, and [includes] the chamber."

G.L. c. 140, § 121. *Commonwealth v. Williams*, 422 Mass. 111, 120 (1996) (not necessary that firearm be loaded); *Commonwealth v. Bartholomew*, 326 Mass. 218, 219 (1950) (same); *Commonwealth v. Tuitt,* 393 Mass. 801, 810 (1985) (jury can determine from inspection that "firearm"); *Commonwealth v. Fancy,* 349 Mass. 196, 204 (1965) (same); *Commonwealth v. Sampson,* 383 Mass. 750, 753 (1981); *Commonwealth v. Sperrazza,* 372 Mass. 667, 670 (1977) (testimony about "revolver" or "handgun" will support inference that barrel was under 16 inches).

If the firearm may have been "under [the defendant's] control in a vehicle". To establish that a firearm was under the defendant's "control" in a vehicle, it is not enough for the Commonwealth just to prove that the defendant was present in the same vehicle as the firearm. The Commonwealth must also prove that the defendant knew that the firearm was there, and that the defendant had power to exercise control over the firearm, although this did not have to be exclusive control.

See Instruction 3.220 (Possession).

Where the issue is constructive possession rather than actual physical possession, the Commonwealth must prove that "in addition to knowledge and the ability to exercise control over the firearm, the defendant must have the intention to do so." *Commonwealth v. Costa,* 65 Mass. App. Ct. 227 (2005); *Commonwealth v. Sann Than,* 442 Mass. 755, 748 (2004).

Commonwealth v. Brown, 401 Mass. 745 (1988); *Commonwealth v. Bailey,* 29 Mass. App. Ct. 1007 (1990); *Commonwealth v. Diaz,* 15 Mass. App. Ct. 469, 471–72 (1983); *Commonwealth v. Gray,* 5 Mass. App. Ct. 296, 299 (1977); *Commonwealth v. Mott,* 2 Mass. App. Ct. 47, 53–54 (1974).

As I mentioned before, the Commonwealth must prove beyond a reasonable doubt that the defendant knew that he (she) (possessed this item) (*or*) (had this item under his [her] control in a vehicle), *and* also knew that the item was a "firearm," within the common meaning of that term. If it was a conventional firearm, with its obvious dangers, the Commonwealth is not required to prove that the defendant knew that the item met the *legal* definition of a firearm.

See Instruction 3.140 (Knowledge).

Commonwealth v. Sampson, 383 Mass. 750, 762 (1981); *Commonwealth v. Bacon,* 374 Mass. 358, 359 (1978) (knowledge need not be alleged in complaint); *Commonwealth v. Jackson,* 369 Mass. 904, 916–17 (1976); *Commonwealth v. Boone,* 356 Mass. 85, 87 (1969) ("control" in vehicle requires knowledge); *Commonwealth v. Papa,* 17 Mass. App. Ct. 987, 987–88 (1984).

II. Rifle or Shotgun

The defendant is charged under section 10(a) of chapter 269 of our General Laws with knowingly possessing a rifle or shotgun unlawfully.

In order to prove the defendant guilty of this offense, the Commonwealth must prove the following (three) (four) things beyond a reasonable doubt:

First: That the defendant possessed a rifle or shotgun (*or*) (that he [she] had a rifle or shotgun under his [her] control in a vehicle);

Second: That what the defendant (possessed) (*or*) (had under his [her] control in a vehicle) met the legal definition of a "rifle" or a "shotgun"; (and)

Third: That the defendant *knew* that he (she) (possessed a rifle or shotgun) (*or*) (had a rifle or shotgun under his [her] control in a vehicle.

If there is evidence of one of the statutory exceptions, use one of the following:

A. *If there is evidence that it was in the defendant's residence or place of business.* And *Fourth:* that the defendant possessed the rifle or shotgun outside of his (her) residence or place of business. A person's "residence" or "place of business" does not include common areas of an apartment or office building, but only areas that are under that person's exclusive control.

B. *If there is evidence that the defendant had a license to carry firearms.* And *Fourth:* that the defendant did not have a valid license to carry a firearm.

C. *If there is evidence that the defendant was exempt from the licensing requirement.* And *Fourth:* that the defendant did *not* qualify for one of the exemptions in the law that are a substitute for having a license to carry a firearm.

The statute exempts a defendant who:

"(1) [was] present in or on his residence or place of business; or

(2) [had] in effect a license to carry firearms issued under [G.L. c. 140, § 131]; or

(3) [had] in effect a license to carry firearms issued under [G.L. c. 140, § 131F to a nonresident or alien]; or

(4) [had] in effect a firearms identification card issued under [G.L. c. 140, § 129B]; or

(5) [had] complied with the requirements imposed by [G.L. c. 140, §§ 129C] upon ownership or possession of rifles and shotguns; or

(6) [had] complied as to possession of an air rifle or BB gun with the requirements imposed by [G.L. c. 269, § 12B]."

General Laws c. 278, § 7 places on the defendant the burden of producing evidence of one of these exemptions; the Commonwealth must then disprove beyond a reasonable doubt the applicability of the claimed exemption. Until there is such evidence, the exemptions are not at issue. *See Commonwealth v. Seay,* 376 Mass. 735, 738 (1978) (former statute); *Commonwealth v. Jones,* 372 Mass. 403, 406–07 (1977) (same); *Commonwealth v. Davis,* 359 Mass. 758 (1971) (same); *Commonwealth v. Baker,* 10 Mass. App. Ct. 852, 853 (1980) (lack of license need not be charged in complaint).

As to the first exemption, see *Commonwealth v. Dunphy,* 377 Mass. 453, 458–60 (1979) (jury issue whether backyard was common area); *Commonwealth v. Morales,* 14 Mass. App. Ct. 1034, 1035 (1982) (jury question whether a common area to which other occupants or owner had access); *Domingue,* 18 Mass. App. Ct. at 990 (defendant privileged to carry at place of business); *Commonwealth v. Samaras,* 10 Mass. App. Ct. 910, 910 (1980) (no privilege to carry on sidewalk in front of defendant's house).

A "rifle" is defined in our law as:

"a weapon having a rifled bore with a barrel length equal to or greater than sixteen inches, capable of discharging a shot or bullet for each pull of the trigger."

7

A "shotgun" is defined as:

"a weapon having a smooth bore with a barrel length equal to or greater than eighteen inches with an overall length equal to or greater than twenty-six inches, capable of discharging a shot or bullet for each pull of the trigger."

The term "barrel length" refers to "that portion of a firearm . . . through which a shot or bullet is driven, guided or stabilized, and [includes] the chamber."

G.L. c. 140, § 121.

If the rifle or shotgun may have been "under [the defendant's] control in a vehicle". To establish that a rifle or shotgun was under the defendant's "control" in a vehicle, it is not enough for the Commonwealth just to prove that the defendant was present in the same vehicle as the rifle or shotgun. The Commonwealth must also prove that the defendant knew that the rifle or shotgun was there, and that the defendant had both the ability and the intention to exercise control over the rifle or shotgun, although this did not have to be exclusive control.

Commonwealth v. Brown, 401 Mass. 745 (1988); *Commonwealth v. Bailey,* 29 Mass. App. Ct. 1007 (1990); *Commonwealth v. Diaz,* 15 Mass. App. Ct. 469, 471–72 (1983); *Commonwealth v. Gray,* 5 Mass. App. Ct. 296, 299 (1977); *Commonwealth v. Mott,* 2 Mass. App. Ct. 47, 53–54 (1974).

As I mentioned before, the Commonwealth must prove beyond a reasonable doubt that the defendant knew that he (she) (possessed this item) (*or*) (had this item under his [her] control in a vehicle), *and* also knew that the item was a "rifle" or "shotgun" within the common meaning of that term. If it was a conventional rifle or shotgun, with its obvious dangers, the Commonwealth is not required to prove that the defendant knew that the item met the *legal* definition of a rifle or shotgun.

7

Commonwealth v. Sampson, 383 Mass. 750, 762 (1981); *Commonwealth v. Bacon,* 374 Mass. 358, 359 (1978) (knowledge need not be alleged in complaint); *Commonwealth v. Jackson,* 369 Mass. 904, 916–17 (1976); *Commonwealth v. Boone,* 356 Mass. 85, 87 (1969) ("control" in vehicle requires knowledge); *Commonwealth v. Papa,* 17 Mass. App. Ct. 987, 987–88 (1984).

Supplement Instructions

1. ***Nonfiring Firearm, Rifle or Shotgun.*** A weapon that was originally a (firearm) (rifle or shotgun) may become so defective or damaged that it will no longer fire a projectile, and then the law no longer considers it to be a (firearm) (rifle or shotgun). But a weapon remains a (firearm) (rifle or shotgun) within the meaning of the law when a slight repair, replacement or adjustment that the defendant is capable of making on the spot will again make it an effective weapon.

Commonwealth v. Colton, 333 Mass. 607, 608398, 398 (1956) (insertion of ammo clip); *Bartholomew,* 326 Mass. at 220 (insertion of firing pin); *Commonwealth v. Raedy,* 24 Mass. App. Ct. 648, 652–56, *fur. app. rev. den.*, 401 Mass. 1101 (1987) (jury question whether gun that could be fired if inverted was "firearm"; judge who distinguishes between "major" and "minor" repairs need not instruct that Commonwealth must prove that this particular defendant had ability and knowledge to repair gun); *Commonwealth v. Rhodes,* 21 Mass. App. Ct. 968, 969–70, *fur. app. rev. den.*, 397 Mass. 1102 (1986) (not a firearm where bent part rendered inoperable until repaired). See *Commonwealth v. Commonwealth v. Gutierrez,* 82 Mass. App. Ct. 1118 (No. 11-P-1612, Oct. 25, 2012) (unpublished opinion under Appeals Ct. Rule 1:28) (noting objective "slight repair" standard for operability of firearm).

2. ***Firearms Identification Card.*** A "firearms identification card" is not the same thing as a "license to carry a firearm." When a person has a valid firearms identification card, that card gives him the right to possess a firearm within his residence or place of business. But it does not give him the right to possess it outside of his (her) home or business, which requires a license to possess a firearm.

G.L. c. 140, §§ 129B–D. A firearms identification card is a defense to a charge of carrying a rifle or shotgun, but not other firearms. G.L. c. 269, § 10(a).

3. ***Passenger in Vehicle.*** Merely being present in a motor vehicle in which a (firearm) (rifle or shotgun) is found is not sufficient by itself to permit an inference that the person knew about the presence of the (firearm) (rifle or shotgun) without other indications of knowledge.

Commonwealth v. Albano, 373 Mass. 132, 134–36 (1977) (gun in plain view; defendant acted suspiciously); *Commonwealth v. Bailey,* 29 Mass. App. Ct. 1007 (1990) (gun in plain view near defendant's feet; car had been broken into; attempted escape); *Commonwealth v. Lucido,* 18 Mass. App. Ct. 941, 943 (1984) (gun in glove compartment with defendant's personal letters); *Commonwealth v. Montgomery,* 23 Mass. App. Ct. 909, 910 (1986) (gun on defendant's side of auto and defendant had appropriate ammo clip); *Commonwealth v. Donovan,* 17 Mass. App. Ct. 83, 85–86 (1983) (gun under seat of borrowed auto surrounded by defendant's acknowledged property); *Diaz, supra* (gun in plain view on floor in front of defendant). *Compare Commonwealth v. Brown*, 401 Mass. 745 (1988) (insufficient to prove defendant drove stolen car, in which guns were found under passenger seat and both occupants bent forward in unison when stopped); *Commonwealth v. Almeida,* 381 Mass. 420, 422–23 (1980) (insufficient to prove gun inside console of borrowed auto); *Commonwealth v. Boone,* 356 Mass. 85, 87 (1969) (insufficient to prove defendant a passenger in an auto with a gun under a seat); *Commonwealth v. Hill,* 15 Mass. App. Ct. 93, 94–97 (1983) (insufficient to prove gun inside woman's purse at male passenger's feet).

4. ***Absence of Evidence of License.*** You have heard some reference to (a license to carry a firearm) (a legal exemption from the requirement of a license to carry a firearm). There was no evidence in this case that the defendant had a license to carry a firearm, and no evidence that the defendant qualified for one of the legal exemptions that are a substitute for having such a license. For that reason, the issue of a license or exemption is not relevant to your deliberations in this case, and therefore you should put it out of your mind.

This instruction is recommended only when, in the jury's presence, there has been some reference to, but not evidence of, such a license or exemption.

5. ***Knowledge of Licensing Requirement.*** You have heard some mention that the defendant did not know that he (she) was required to have a license before carrying a firearm under these circumstances. The Commonwealth is *not* required to prove that the defendant knew that the law required him (her) to have a license before (possessing a firearm) (*or*) (having a firearm under

his [her] control in a vehicle) outside of his (her) home or place of business.

This instruction is recommended only when it is necessary to correct such a misimpression.

NOTES

1. **Elements.** "To sustain a conviction under G.L. c. 269, § 10(a), the Commonwealth must prove that the defendant knowingly possessed a firearm without either being present in his residence or place of business or having in effect a license to carry firearms or [in the case of a rifle or shotgun] a firearm identification card. The Commonwealth must prove that the gun the defendant possessed met the definition of a working firearm set forth in G.L. c. 140, § 121, that is, that it had a barrel less than sixteen inches long [or was a rifle or shotgun] and was capable of discharging a bullet." *Commonwealth v. White*, 452 Mass. 133 (2008).

2. **Air rifles and BB guns.** In decisions under the earlier version of G.L. c. 269, § 10(a), air guns, BB guns and CO_2 guns were held to be regulated solely by G.L. c. 269, § 12B and not by § 10(a). *Commonwealth v. Fenton,* 395 Mass. 92, 94–95 (1985); *Commonwealth v. Rhodes,* 389 Mass. 641, 644 (1983). The current text of § 10(a) applies to anyone who carries "a firearm . . . without . . . having complied as to possession of an air rifle or BB gun with the requirements imposed by [§ 12B]." Thus, compliance with § 12B is a defense to a prosecution under § 10(a), just as the possession of a firearm license would be. *Commonwealth v. Sayers,* 438 Mass. 238, 240 (2002).

3. **Ballistics certificate.** "A certificate by a ballistics expert of the firearms identification section of the department of public safety or of the city of Boston of the result of an examination made by him of an item furnished him by any police officer, signed and sworn to by such expert, shall be prima facie evidence of his findings as to whether or not the item furnished is a firearm, rifle, shotgun, machine gun, sawed off shotgun or ammunition, as defined by [G.L. c. 140, § 121], provided that in order to qualify as an expert under this section he shall have previously qualified as an expert in a court proceeding." G.L. c. 140, § 121A. The certificate's prima facie effect must be put to the jury in permissive terms. *Commonwealth v. Crawford,* 18 Mass. App. Ct. 911, 912 (1984). See Instruction 3.260 (Prima Facie Evidence).

The admission of such a certificate is the "record of a primary fact made by a public officer in the performance of [an] official duty" that raises no Confrontation Clause problem under *Crawford v. Washington*, 541 U.S. 36 (2004). *Commonwealth v. Morales*, 71 Mass. App. Ct. 587 (2008).

4. **Constitutionality.** The one-year mandatory sentencing provision of § 10(a) is constitutional. *Commonwealth v. Jackson,* 369 Mass. 904 (1976).

5. **Flare guns.** A flare gun is not a "firearm" for purposes of G.L. c. 269, § 10(a). *Sampson,* 383 Mass. at 753–61.

6. **Necessity defense.** The Supreme Judicial Court has assumed that a threat of death or serious injury, if it is direct and immediate, may excuse momentary carrying of a firearm. *Commonwealth v. Lindsey,* 396 Mass. 840, 843–45 (1986). *See Commonwealth v. Iglesia*, 403 Mass. 132, 135–36 (1988); *Commonwealth v. Franklin,* 376 Mass. 885, 888 n.2 (1978). See Instruction 9.240 (Necessity).

7. **Notice of affirmative defense.** Massachusetts R. Crim. P. 14(b)(3) requires a defendant who intends to rely upon a defense based upon a license, a claim of authority or ownership, or exemption to file an advance notice of such defense with the prosecutor and the clerk-magistrate. The rule provides that if the defendant does not comply with that requirement, the defendant may not rely upon such a defense. The judge may allow late filing of the notice, order a continuance, or make other appropriate orders.

8. **Notice of license revocation.** See *Police Comm'r of Boston v. Robinson*, 47 Mass. App. Ct. 767, 773, 774 (1999) (proving notice of license revocation by certified mail requires proof of receipt); *Commonwealth v. Hampton*, 26 Mass. App. Ct. 938, 940 (1988) (defendant who purposefully or wilfully evaded notice of license revocation sent by certified mail had constructive notice of license revocation).

9. **Probable cause.** Possession of a firearm, standing alone and without indication that the person was involved in criminal activity, does not provide probable cause to believe that the person was unlicensed to carry that firearm. *Commonwealth v. Couture,* 407 Mass. 178, cert. denied, 498 U.S. 951 (1990). However, additional evidence of criminal activity and flight would provide such probable cause. *Commonwealth v. Brookins,* 416 Mass. 97, 104 (1993).

10. **"Residence."** See *Commonwealth v. Coren*, 437 Mass. 723, 734 (2002) (defining "residence" to include "all areas in and around a defendant's property, including outside areas, over which defendant retains exclusive control," but not including "public streets, sidewalks, and common areas to which occupants of multiple dwellings have access"); *Commonwealth v. Dunphy,* 377 Mass. 453, 458–60 (1979) (jury issue whether backyard was common area); *Commonwealth v. Morales,* 14 Mass. App. Ct. 1034, 1035 (1982) (jury issue whether area was a common area to which other occupants or owner had access); *Commonwealth v. Domingue,* 18 Mass. App. Ct. 987, 990 (1984) (defendant privileged to carry at place of business); *Commonwealth v. Samaras,* 10 Mass. App. Ct. 910, 910 (1980) (no privilege to carry on sidewalk in front of defendant's house).

Carrying Certain Dangerous Weapons

Regulatory Authority—G.L. c. 269, § 10(b)
Dist. Ct. Model Jury Instruction 7.680

The defendant is charged with unlawfully carrying a _____ (on his [her] person) (on his [her] person or under his [her] control in a vehicle).

Section 10(b) of chapter 269 of our General Laws provides as follows:

> "Whoever, except as provided by law, (carries on his person) (carries on his person or under his control in a vehicle) (any stiletto) (any . . . dagger) (any . . . device or case which enables a knife with a locking blade to be drawn at a locked position) (any ballistic knife) (any knife with a detachable blade capable of being propelled by any mechanism) (any . . . dirk knife) (any knife having a double-edged blade) (a switch knife) (any knife having an automatic spring release device by which the blade is released from the handle, having a blade of over one and one-half inches) (a slung shot) (a . . . blowgun) (a . . . blackjack) (metallic knuckles or knuckles of any substance which could be put to the same use with the same or similar effect as metallic knuckles) (nunchaku, zoobow, also known as klackers or kung fu sticks, or any similar weapon consisting of two sticks of wood, plastic or metal connected at one end by a length of rope, chain, wire or leather) (a shuriken or any similar pointed starlike object intended to injure a person when thrown) (any armband, made with leather which has metallic spikes, points or studs or any similar device made from any other substance) (a cestus or similar material weighted with metal or other substance and worn on the hand) (a manrikigusari or similar length of chain having weighted ends) . . . shall be punished . . . ."

To prove that the defendant is guilty of this offense, the Commonwealth must prove three things beyond a reasonable doubt:

First: That the item involved is a _____;

Second: That the defendant carried the item (on his [her] person) (under his [her] control in a vehicle); and

Third: That the defendant knew that he (she) was carrying the item (on his [her] person) (under his [her] control in a vehicle).

This model instruction covers the offense set out in the first clause of G.L. c. 269, § 10(b). See Instruction 5.603 (Carrying a Dangerous Weapon When Arrested) for the offense set out in the second clause of § 10(b).

See Commonwealth v. Miller, 22 Mass. App. Ct. 694 (1986) (definition of dirk knife).

NOTE

Advance notice of defense based on exemption. A defendant may not rely on a defense based on a license, exemption, or claim of authority or ownership unless he or she has filed an advance notice of such defense with the court and the prosecutor. For cause shown, the judge may allow late filing or a continuance, or may make other appropriate orders. Mass. R. Crim. P. 14(b)(3).

Civil Rights Violations

Regulatory Authority—G.L. c. 265, § 37
Dist. Ct. Model Jury Instruction 6.620

The defendant is charged with having violated the Massachusetts Civil Rights Act, which is found as section 37 of chapter 265 of our General Laws. It provides that:

> "No person . . . shall by force or threat of force, willfully injure, intimidate or interfere with, *or* attempt to injure, intimidate or interfere with, *or* oppress or threaten any other person in the free exercise or enjoyment of any right or privilege secured to him by the constitution or laws of the commonwealth *or* by the constitution or laws of the United States."

In order to prove the defendant guilty of this offense, the Commonwealth must prove four things beyond a reasonable doubt:

First: That *[alleged victim]* was exercising a right or privilege protected by the Constitution or laws of the Commonwealth of Massachusetts or of the United States;

Second: That the defendant either injured, intimidated, interfered with, oppressed or threatened the exercise or enjoyment of that legally protected right by *[alleged victim]*, or attempted to do so;

Third: That the defendant did so by using force or by threatening to use force; and

Fourth: That the defendant did so wilfully.

> The foregoing instruction, and the notes below, are based upon a model instruction developed by the Department of the Attorney General. *See also* A. Sager, "Rights Protected by the Massachusetts Civil Rights Act Against Interference on Account of Race or Color," 17 *Suffolk U. L. Rev.* 53 (1983); Sherman & Goldman, "The Development of the Massachusetts Civil Rights Act," 29 *Boston Bar. J.* 10 (No. 4 Sept./Oct. 1985).
>
> General Laws c. 265, § 37 offers a scope of protection that is similar in many respects to 42 U.S.C. § 242 (the Federal criminal statute governing civil rights violations), and to 42 U.S.C. § 1983 (the Federal civil statute governing civil rights violations). General Laws c. 265, § 37 differs from both Federal statutes in two significant ways: (1) It applies whether or not a defendant was acting under color of law, and therefore encompasses not only private rights secured against the government but also relations between private parties. *O'Connell v. Chasdi,* 400 Mass. 686, 692 (1987); *Bell v. Mazza,* 394 Mass. 176, 182 (1985) (statutory phrase "whether or not acting under color of law" is superfluous); *Batchelder v. Allied Stores Corp.,* 393 Mass. 819, 822–23 (1985); *United States Jaycees v. Massachusetts Comm'n Against Discrimination,* 391 Mass. 594, 609 n.9 (1984). (2) It requires proof of force or threat of force, and is limited to certain specific prohibited acts (e.g. "injure," "intimidate," etc.). *Commonwealth v. Stephens,* 25 Mass. App. Ct. 117, 122 n.5 (1987). In addition, the Massachusetts statute, unlike 42 U.S.C. § 1983, requires that the violation have been "willful," *Redgrave v. Boston Symphony Orchestra, Inc.,* 399 Mass. 93, 99–100, *S.C.,* 831 F.2d 339 (1st Cir. 1987), 855 F.2d 888 (1st Cir. 1988) (en banc).
>
> The Massachusetts Civil Rights Act (St. 1979, c. 801) also contains civil provisions, which are codified at G.L. c. 12, §§ 11H–I.

7

Supplemental Instructions

1. ***"Exercise or enjoyment" of rights.*** A person is exercising or enjoying a right or privilege secured by the Constitution or laws of the Commonwealth or of the United States whenever that person's behavior or interest is protected by any provision of the Massachusetts or the Federal Constitution, or any Federal or state statute. I instruct you that *[constitutional or statutory provision]* guarantees to *[specify persons protected]* the right to *[specify right]*. Such a person exercises or enjoys that legal right whether or not he knows that the law guarantees him that right.

> *Bell, supra* ("secured" means "created by, arising under or dependent upon" rather than "fully protected"; right can be "secured" against private party although Constitution or statute only prohibits governmental interference).
>
> *See* G.L. c. 233, §§ 70 (judicial notice of Federal law) and 75 (proof of Massachusetts and Federal statutes by printed copy).

2. ***"Injure, intimidate or interfere with . . . or oppose or threaten."*** To injure, intimidate, interfere with, oppress or threaten another person in the free exercise or enjoyment of a right or privilege means in general to impede or prevent the full and free benefit of that right. The alleged victim need not be completely prevented from exercising the right, just hampered in exercising it. To "intimidate" means to put in fear. To "interfere" means to hinder or meddle in the affairs of another. To "oppress" means to use authority or power abusively or excessively. To "threaten" means to express an intention to harm another's person or property. This element is satisfied if it is proven beyond a reasonable doubt that the defendant negatively affected the alleged victim's rights in any one of these ways.

> *Delaney v. Chief of Police of Wareham,* 27 Mass. App. Ct. 398, 409 (1989) ("threat" is "acts or language by which another is placed in fear of injury or damage").

3. ***"Attempt to injure, intimidate or interfere with."*** To prove that the defendant attempted to injure, intimidate or interfere with another person's rights, the Commonwealth must prove two things: that the defendant took a step toward interfering with the alleged victim's rights, and that he (she) did so with the specific intention of interfering with those rights. Neither intent alone nor making preparations is enough by itself to constitute an attempt. You must also find that the defendant took an overt act designed to interfere with the alleged victim's right and came reasonably close to doing so.

> See Instruction 4.120 (Attempt).
>
> *Commonwealth v. Ware,* 375 Mass. 118, 120 (1978); *Commonwealth v. Gosselin,* 365 Mass. 116, 121 (1974); *Commonwealth v. Peaslee,* 177 Mass. 267, 271–74 (1901); *Commonwealth v. Burns,* 8 Mass. App. Ct. 194, 196 (1979).

4. ***"Force."*** "Force" means physical force, directed either against a person or against property. But the amount of physical force used does not matter. Even a minimal amount of force is sufficient.

> *Commonwealth v. Richards,* 363 Mass. 299, 302 (1973) (force against person); *Commonwealth v. Jones,* 362 Mass. 83, 87–90 (1972) (even swift purse snatching involves use of "force").

5. ***"Threat of force."*** A threat of force is an expression of an intention to use force which is communicated to the person threatened. It must also seem to any reasonable person standing in the place of the threatened person that the person making the threat actually had the ability to carry it out.

> *Commonwealth v. Chalifoux,* 362 Mass. 811, 816 (1973) (definition of threat); *Commonwealth v. Cor-*

coran, 252 Mass. 465, 483–84 (1925) (apprehension to be determined objectively).

6. ***"Willfully."*** The defendant's act must have been done wilfully. The defendant's act was wilful if it was done either with the specific purpose of interfering with the alleged victim's enjoyment of the interests protected by the right to *[specify right]*, or it was done because the alleged victim had exercised that right.

It is *not* necessary for the Commonwealth to prove that the defendant knew that he (she) was violating the law, or that he (she) knew that the right to *[specify right]* is specifically protected by the Constitution or laws of Massachusetts or the United States. The Commonwealth is only required to prove that the defendant acted with the particular purpose of interfering with the alleged victim's enjoyment of the interests that are protected by that right. If he (she) did so, then he (she) acted wilfully.

See Instruction 3.120 (Intent).

This is a specific intent crime, which involves two determinations:

"The first is a purely legal determination. Is the . . . right at issue clearly delineated and plainly applicable under the circumstances of the case? If the trial judge concludes that it is, then the jury must make the second, factual, determination. Did the defendant commit the act in question with the particular purpose of depriving the victim of his enjoyment of the interests protected by that . . . right? If both requirements are met, even if the defendant did not in fact recognize the [unlawfulness] of his act, he will be adjudged as a matter of law to have acted 'willfully'—i.e. 'in reckless disregard of constitutional [or statutory] prohibitions or guarantees.'"

Stephens, 25 Mass. App. Ct. at 121 n.4, quoting from and adopting the rule of *United States v. Ehrlichman*, 546 F.2d 910, 921 (D.C. Cir. 1976), *cert. denied*, 429 U.S. 1120 (1977).

It is not necessary to prove that the victim knew that he or she was exercising a right protected by § 37, that the defendant knew that he or she was depriving the victim of a specific right protected by § 37, or that the defendant had "a particularly evil or wicked purpose." It is only necessary to prove that the defendant "'engaged in activity which interferes with rights which as . . . matter of law are clearly and specifically protected.'" *Stephens*, 25 Mass. App. Ct. at 124–25, quoting from *Ehrlichman*, 546 F.2d at 928. *See United States v. Guest*, 383 U.S. 745, 760 (1966) (private purpose—e.g. robbery—unrelated to deprivation of legal right insufficient); *Screws v. United States*, 325 U.S. 91, 101–107 (1945) ("wilfully" means acting with purpose of depriving victim of enjoyment of protected interest or in reckless disregard of legal guarantee). Generally, negligent acts will not rise to level of coercion required to convict under this statute. *See Deas v. Dempsey*, 403 Mass. 468, 470–72 (1988).

NOTES ON SELECTED SECURED RIGHTS

1. **Fourteenth Amendment.** ". . . [N]or shall any State deprive any person of life, liberty, or property, without due process of law; nor deny to any person within its jurisdiction the equal protection of the laws."

2. **Art. 1 of Massachusetts Declaration of Rights.** "All people are born free and equal and have certain natural, essential and unalienable rights; among which may be reckoned the right of enjoying and defending their lives and liberties; that of acquiring, possessing, and protecting property; in fine, that of seeking and obtaining their safety and happiness. Equality under the law shall not be denied or abridged because of sex, race, color, creed or national origin." Massachusetts Declaration of Rights, art. 1, as amended by art. 106 of the Amendments.

3. **Education rights.** Under Federal and state law, public school students have a right to attend school and to be educated without discrimination or segregation on account of race. U.S. Const., Amend. 14. *Brown v. Board of Education,* 347 U.S. 483 (1954). Mass. Const., Pt. 1, art. 1. G.L. c. 76, § 5.

4. **Employment rights.** All persons are guaranteed the same right to make and perform employment contracts as is enjoyed by white citizens. 42 U.S.C. § 1981. *Johnson v. Railway Express Agency,* 421 U.S. 454 (1975). The right to work without discrimination because of race, color, religious creed, national origin or ancestry is a right and privilege of all inhabitants of the Commonwealth. St. 1946, c. 368. It is an unlawful discriminatory practice for any employer or his agent to discriminate against an applicant or employee in compensation, terms, conditions or privileges of employment because of race, color, religious creed, national origin, sex, sexual orientation, genetic information, age or ancestry, or for any person to aid, abet, incite, compel or coerce such discrimination. G.L. c. 151B, § 4. *See Radvilas v. Stop & Shop, Inc.,* 18 Mass. App. Ct. 431 (1984) (employment discrimination because of sex and age).

Sexual harassment in the workplace violates both art. 1 of the Massachusetts Declaration of Rights, *O'Connell,* 400 Mass. at 693, and G.L. c. 151B, § 4(1), *College-Town, Div. of Interco, Inc. v. Massachusetts Comm'n Against Discrimination,* 400 Mass. 156, 162 (1987).

5. **Housing rights.** The right to own, rent and occupy housing without discrimination because of race, color, religion, sex, or national origin is guaranteed by the federal Fair Housing Act of 1968. 42 U.S.C. § 3601 et seq. *Trafficante v. Metropolitan Life Ins. Co.,* 409 U.S. 205 (1972). The right to occupy and enjoy housing is protected against racially motivated interference, whether by the property owners or by third persons unconnected to the property owner. *Metropolitan Hous. Dev. Corp. v. Village of Arlington Heights,* 558 F.2d 1283, 1294 (7th Cir. 1977), cert. denied, 434 U.S. 1025 (1978). Black citizens have the same right to inherit, purchase, lease, sell, hold and convey residential property that white citizens have. 42 U.S.C. § 1982. This means that black persons have the right to live wherever white persons have the right to live, and cannot lawfully be prevented from exercising this right on the grounds of race. *Jones v. Alfred H. Mayer Co.,* 392 U.S. 409 (1968). White persons have the right to associate with black persons and have black guests in their homes without discrimination or interference. *Tillman v. Wheaton-Haven Recreation Ass'n, Inc.,* 410 U.S. 431 (1973).

6. **Mental patients' rights.** A mental patient has a constitutional right to basically safe and humane living conditions, which includes protection from assaults. *Harper v. Cserr,* 544 F.2d 1121, 1123 (1st Cir. 1976). *See Goodman v. Parwatikar,* 570 F.2d 801, 804 (8th Cir. 1978).

7. **Personal security rights.** All persons have the same right to the full and equal benefit of all laws and proceedings for the security of persons and property that is enjoyed by white citizens. 42 U.S.C. § 1981. This right is violated by racially motivated violence. *Mahone v. Waddle,* 564 F.2d 1018 (3d Cir. 1977), *cert. denied,* 438 U.S. 904 (1978).

8. **Prisoners' rights.** While officials such as police or corrections officers may use reasonable force to overcome resistance by a person whom they are taking into custody or holding in custody, the constitutional right to due process includes the right not to be subjected to unreasonable, unnecessary or unprovoked force by such officers. Arresting officers may use only such force as is reasonably necessary to effect an arrest or to defend themselves. It is a violation of the Fourteenth Amendment to hold and physically punish a person and thereby deprive him of liberty without due process of law. *Ingraham v. Wright,* 430 U.S. 651, 674 (1977); *Screws,* 325 U.S. at 106, 111; *United States v. McQueeney,* 674 F.2d 109, 113 (1st Cir. 1982); *Landrigan v. Warwick,* 628 F.2d 736, 741–42 (1st Cir. 1980); *United States v. Villarin Gerena,* 553 F.2d 723, 724 (1st Cir. 1977); *Human Rights Comm'n of Worcester v. Assad,* 370 Mass. 482, 487 (1976). G.L. c. 111B, § 8, sixth par. (protective custody statute); G.L. c. 124, § 1(b), (g). 103 Code Mass. Regs. §§ 505.00 et seq. Reasonable force is that which an ordinary prudent person would deem necessary under the circumstances. *Powers v. Sturtevant,* 199 Mass. 265, 266 (1908). This is a jury question. *Commonwealth v. Young,* 326 Mass. 597, 603 (1950).

The right to inform authorities of a violation of Federal law is a "right or privilege" secured by the Federal Constitution. *Motes v. United States,* 178 U.S. 458, 462–63 (1900).

9. **Private establishments open to the public.** Privately owned facilities (such as stores, restaurants, taverns, gas stations, theaters and arcades) which are open to the public and which solicit or accept the patronage of the general public are also places of public accommodation covered by the Massachusetts Public Accommodations Law, *above. See also* 804 Code Mass. Regs. § 5.01.

10. **Public accommodations rights.** The Massachusetts Public Accommodations Law guarantees to all persons the full and equal use of all places of public accommodation free from any distinction, discrimination

or restriction on account of race, color, religious creed, national origin, sex, deafness, blindness, ancestry, or any physical or mental disability. Public facilities such as parks, playgrounds, government buildings, public beaches, highways, streets and sidewalks are all places of public accommodation covered by the law. G.L. c. 272, §§ 92A, 98.

11. **Religious exercise rights.** The right to free exercise of religion is guaranteed by Articles 2 and 3 of the Declaration of Rights of the Massachusetts Constitution and by the First Amendment to the United States Constitution. This right protects religious worship, religious practices, meetings for those purposes, and ownership and use of buildings and other property for religious purposes. It protects the religious activities of individuals, congregations, and their spiritual leaders. Mass. Const., Pt. 1, arts. 2, 3; U.S. Const., Amends. 1, 14.

12. **Travel rights.** Under the United States Constitution, all persons have a right to travel freely between the states, and to use the highways and other avenues of interstate commerce in doing so. *Griffin v. Breckenridge,* 403 U.S. 88 (1971); *Guest, above.* Public transportation vehicles (such as MBTA buses, subway cars, and streetcars), bus stops, and subway stations and platforms are all places of public accommodation under the Massachusetts Public Accommodations Law, *above.*

13. **Voting rights.** The right to elect public officials and to be elected to public office is guaranteed by the Federal Constitution, *United States v. Classic,* 313 U.S. 299, 314 (1941), and by Article 9 of the Massachusetts Declaration of Rights, *Batchelder v. Allied Stores Int'l,* 388 Mass. 83 (1983).

Conspiracy

Regulatory Authority—G.L. c. 274, § 7
Dist. Ct. Model Jury Instruction 4.160

The defendant is charged with the offense of conspiracy. A conspiracy is an agreement of two or more people to do something that is unlawful.

If raised by the evidence: or to do something by unlawful means. The crime is the *agreement* to do something unlawful. *If raised by the evidence:* or to use unlawful means. It does not matter whether the plan was successful or not, or whether any steps were taken to carry out the plan.

To prove the defendant guilty of the crime of conspiracy, the Commonwealth must prove three things beyond a reasonable doubt:

First: That the defendant joined in an agreement or plan with one or more other persons;

Second: That the purpose of the agreement was to do something unlawful; *If raised by the evidence:* or to do something that was itself lawful, but by unlawful means; and

Third: That the defendant joined the conspiracy knowing of the unlawful plan and intending to help carry it out.

It is not necessary that the conspirators formulated a formal agreement among themselves, or that they agreed on every detail of the conspiracy, or even that they met together. But the Commonwealth must prove that there was a joint plan among them, and that the defendant joined in that plan.

It is not always possible to prove a conspiracy by direct evidence. The law allows you, where it seems reasonable, to infer that there was a conspiracy from all of the circumstances. For example, if people who know each other or have been in communication with each other are shown to have been involved in concerted actions which all seem designed to accomplish a specific purpose, then it may be reasonable to conclude that those actions were not coincidental but were taken pursuant to a joint plan.

However, remember that it is not enough that the defendant knew about the conspiracy or associated with conspirators. To be liable as a conspirator, the defendant must have actually joined in the conspiracy as something that he (she) wished to bring about.

G.L. c. 274, § 7 (punishment for conspiracy); *Commonwealth v. Benson,* 389 Mass. 473, 479–80, *cert. denied,* 464 U.S. 915 (1983) (elements of conspiracy; acquittal on substantive charge does not preclude prosecution for conspiracy); *Commonwealth v. Pero,* 402 Mass. 476, 477–79 (1988) (same); *Commonwealth v. Cerveny,* 387 Mass. 280, 288 (1982) (conviction does not require proof of overt act); *Commonwealth v. Beneficial Fin. Co.,* 360 Mass. 188, 249, 303 (1971), *cert. denied sub nom. Farrell v. Massachusetts* and *sub nom. Beneficial Fin. Co. v. Massachusetts,* 407 U.S. 910 (1972) (same; proof of participation is required since knowledge alone is insufficient; conspiracy provable by circumstantial evidence and "silent acquiescence" can suffice); *Commonwealth v. Beckett,* 373 Mass. 329, 341–42 (1977) (whether knowledge of illegality required where act is only malum prohibitum); *Commonwealth v. Nelson,* 370 Mass. 192, 196–201 (1976) (conspiracy provable by circumstantial evidence; conspirator must be aware of unlawful objective, but not necessarily the detailed means, of conspiracy); *Commonwealth v. Stasiun,* 349 Mass. 38, 47 (1965) (co-conspirator cannot be convicted of substantive offense unless he participated or aided in it); *Commonwealth v. Ries,* 337 Mass. 565, 581–82 (1958) (Commonwealth need not prove every detail of conspiracy plan set out in complaint or bill of particulars, but only "sufficient details of the general plan that makes out a conspiracy"); *Commonwealth v. Beal,* 314 Mass. 210, 221–22 (1943) (knowledge alone is insufficient); *Commonwealth v. Farese,* 265 Mass. 377, 380 (1928) (conspiracy may be shown by conduct and reasonable inferences therefrom); *Attorney General v. Tufts,* 239 Mass. 458, 494 (1921) (common purpose may be inferred from concerted action converging to a definite end); *Commonwealth v. Saia,* 18 Mass. App. Ct. 762, 764–65 (1984) (defendant may be convicted of lesser included conspiracy than charged); *Commonwealth v. Nighelli,* 13 Mass. App. Ct. 590, 593–97 (1982) (no overt act required under Massachusetts law; subsequent withdrawal not a defense); *Commonwealth v. Cook,* 10 Mass. App. Ct. 668, 673–77 (1980) (joint venture requires conscious sharing in criminal act but not necessarily an agreement, while conspiracy requires an agreement to work in concert); *Commonwealth v. Dellinger,* 10 Mass. App. Ct. 549, 555–59 (1980), rev'd on other grounds, 383 Mass. 780 (1981) (unlawful purpose need not be proved precisely as alleged unless defendant prejudiced; imminence is not required; conspiracy can be complete even if details of precise target, time or manner still to be worked out).

A criminal conspiracy may be found where neither its purpose nor intended means was criminal, if the Commonwealth proves beyond a reasonable doubt that: (1) either its purpose or intended means was illegal (as distinguished from criminal); (2) the illegality was seriously contrary to the public interest because it caused a strong probability of significant harm to an individual or the public interest; and (3) if the illegality was not malum in se but only malum prohibitum, the defendant knew that the act was illegal. *Commonwealth v. Kelley,* 359 Mass. 77, 87–88 (1971) (violation of non-criminal public bidding law); *Commonwealth v. Gill,* 5 Mass. App. Ct. 337, 340–44 (1977) (same); *Commonwealth v. Benesch,* 290 Mass. 125, 134–35 (1935) (violation of non-criminal securities law). *See Commonwealth v. Beckett,* 373 Mass. 329, 341–42 & n.7 (1977). An act "malum in se" is one that is by "its very nature wrongful and detrimental to the public interest," *Id.,* and includes "in addition to felonies, all breaches of public order, injuries to person or property, outrages upon public decency or good morals, and breaches of official duty, when done wilfully or corruptly," *Commonwealth v. Adams,* 114 Mass. 323, 324 (1873). By contrast, an act that is "malum prohibitum" is "any matter forbidden or commanded by statute, but not otherwise wrong." *Id.* The model instruction, which is phrased in terms of an intended crime, may be modified as appropriate if the intended object or means is illegal but non-criminal.

Supplemental Instruction

Co-conspirator hearsay exception. You may consider against an individual defendant any statement made by another (defendant) (participant in the alleged conspiracy) only if three things have been proved to you about that statement: *First,* that other evidence apart from that statement shows that there was a conspiracy between the speaker and the defendant; *Second,* that the statement was made during the conspiracy; and *Third,* that the statement was made in order to further or help along the conspiracy.

Only if those three things have been proved are you allowed to consider the statement of another (defendant) (alleged conspirator) when you are considering the charges against (a defendant other than the speaker) (the defendant). If those three things have not been proved, then you may not consider the alleged statement in any way when you consider the evidence against *[defendant]*, and he (she) is entitled to have his (her) case determined solely from the evidence about his (her) own acts and statements.

The statement of one co-conspirator during and in furtherance of the conspiracy is admissible against other co-conspirators. Such cases are normally tried by admitting such evidence only as to the speaker. When the judge determines, based on evidence other than the statement, that there is a fair inference that the conspiracy existed, the limitation is removed and the statement becomes subject to "humane practice." The jury should be instructed that they may consider the evidence against a defendant other than the speaker only if they find sufficient evidence apart from the statement to support a fair inference that the conspiracy existed, that the defendant had joined in it, and that the statement was uttered in the course of, and in furtherance of it. *Commonwealth v. Soares*, 384 Mass. 149, 159–60 (1981); *Beckett*, 373 Mass. at 335–41; *Commonwealth v. White*, 370 Mass. 703, 709 (1976) (discussing whether conspiracy to commit crime necessarily includes conspiracy to escape, if necessary); *Commonwealth v. Pleasant*, 366 Mass. 100, 103–04 (1974); *Beneficial Fin. Co.*, 360 Mass. at 231 n.12, 364–65 (statement may be written rather than oral); *Id.*, 360 Mass. at 222–23 (presence of such evidence does not automatically require severance); *Kelley*, 359 Mass. at 85–86. The rule applies even in severed trials. *Commonwealth v. Florentino*, 381 Mass. 193, 194 (1980).

NOTES

1. **District Court jurisdiction.** The general conspiracy statute (G.L. c. 274, § 7) provides different penalties for four groupings of conspiracies, depending on the maximum penalty of the crime which was the object of the conspiracy. Under G.L. c. 218, § 26, it appears that the District Court has final jurisdiction over any conspiracy charged under the third and fourth clauses of § 7, i.e., any conspiracy to commit an offense that is not itself punishable by more than 10 years in state prison.

The specialized drug conspiracy statute (G.L. c. 94C, § 40) does not group intended offenses for penalty purposes, but instead provides that the conspiracy penalty is identical to that for the particular crime which was the object of the conspiracy. Under G.L. c. 218, § 16, it appears that the District Court has final jurisdiction over any drug conspiracy charged under § 40 if the District Court would have final jurisdiction over the conspired offense.

Commonwealth v. Grace, 43 Mass. App. Ct. 905, 907 (1997), created confusion about the District Court's jurisdiction over conspiracy charges. Grace held that the District Court lacked final jurisdiction over a charge of conspiracy to distribute heroin (G.L. c. 94C, § 32[a]) brought under the drug conspiracy statute. On appeal the defense argued that heroin distribution is a 10-year felony and therefore outside the District Court's final jurisdiction. (That argument is erroneous since first-offense heroin distribution [§ 32(a)] is within the District Court's final jurisdiction because it is listed in G.L. c. 218, § 26, as amended by St. 1987, c. 266.) In the Appeals Court the Commonwealth confessed error, apparently adopting a broader view that the District Court lacks final jurisdiction over all conspiracies, and citing *Berlandi v. Commonwealth*, 314 Mass. 424, 441 (1943), *Commonwealth v. Garcia*, 34 Mass. App. Ct. 386, 388 n.3 (1993), and *Commonwealth v. New York Cent. & H. R. R.*, 206 Mass. 417, 418 (1910). However, *Berlandi* and *New York Cent.* were both premised on a statutory exclusion in G.L. c. 218, § 26 ("all misdemeanors, except conspiracies and libels") that was subsequently repealed by St. 1958, c. 138 and replaced with the current wording ("all misdemeanors, except libels"). The one-sentence reference to the issue in the Garcia footnote was dicta, since in that case the conspiracy charge had been dismissed and was not before the Appeals Court. The Appeals Court's opinion in *Grace* cited the *Berlandi* and *Garcia* cases and thus appeared to cast doubt on the District Court's jurisdiction over any conspiracy charge.

The confusion was partly resolved by *Commonwealth v. Stoico*, 45 Mass. App. Ct. 559, 565–566 (1998), which held that the District Court does have final jurisdiction over a charge under the drug conspiracy statute of conspiring to distribute marihuana (G.L. c. 94C, § 32C[a]), which has a 2-year maximum sentence, noting that "[n]othing in [*Garcia*] is to the contrary." *See also Commonwealth v. John R. Kuhn*, 48 Mass. App. Ct. 1106 (No. 98-P-489, Oct. 29, 1999) (unpublished opinion under Appeals Court Rule 1:28) (District Court has jurisdiction over conspiracy to distribute marihuana because it has a maximum penalty of two years).

2. **Acquittal of all other conspirators.** The acquittal of all other co-conspirators at the same trial bars conviction of the defendant, *Benesch,* 290 Mass. at 135–36; *Nighelli,* 13 Mass. App. Ct. at 595, but the rule does not apply if the co-conspirators were tried separately, *Cerveny,* 387 Mass. at 285–86.

3. **Feigned agreement.** Massachusetts probably subscribes to the "bilateral" theory of conspiracy, under which there is no conspiracy if one of two conspirators only feigns agreement but never intends to carry out the unlawful purpose. The jury must resolve any factual dispute about whether the disavowing conspirator intended to join the conspiracy. *Commonwealth v. Abdul-Kareem*, 56 Mass. App. Ct. 78, 80 n.3 (2002) (police informant); *Commonwealth v. Themelis,* 22 Mass. App. Ct. 754, 757–61 (1986) (claim of intent to "rip off" proffered fee without carrying out murder-for-hire).

4. **Multiple conspiracies.** Sub-agreements in pursuit of a common illegal objective are not separate conspiracies. *Commonwealth v. Winter,* 9 Mass. App. Ct. 512, 522–28 (1980). The Commonwealth has the burden of proving multiple conspiracies. *Cerveny,* 387 Mass. at 287–89.

5 **Specification of object of conspiracy.** The intended unlawful purpose, or lawful purpose by unlawful means, must be alleged in the complaint, but need not be described with great particularity. *Commonwealth v. Cantres,* 405 Mass. 238, 240–41 (1989) (allegation of conspiracy to violate the Controlled Substances Act was adequate identification of object of conspiracy).

6. **Trial with substantive offense prohibited.** A conspiracy charge may not be tried simultaneously with a charge for the substantive offense unless the defendant moves for such joinder. Mass. R. Crim. P. 9(e). *Angiulo v. Commonwealth,* 401 Mass. 71, 80 n.10 (1987).

7. **Venue.** Venue for a conspiracy prosecution lies in any county in which an overt act is committed by any one of the conspirators in execution of the plan. *Stasiun,* 349 Mass. at 54.

8. **Wharton's rule.** It is undecided whether Wharton's rule (holding that an agreement by two persons to commit a crime cannot be prosecuted as a conspiracy if the substantive crime requires two persons to commit) applies generally in Massachusetts, but if it does, it is inapplicable to prosecutions for conspiracy to distribute controlled substances because G.L. c. 94C, § 40 indicates a legislative intent to permit such conspiracy prosecutions. *Cantres, above.*

Criminal Harassment; Punishment

Regulatory Authority—G.L. c. 265, § 43A
Dist. Ct. Model Jury Instruction 6.640

The defendant is charged with criminal harassment of section 43A of chapter 265 of our General Laws.

7

In order to prove the defendant guilty of this offense, the Commonwealth must prove five things beyond a reasonable doubt:

First: That the defendant engaged in a knowing pattern of conduct or speech, or series of acts, on at least three separate occasions;

Second: That the defendant intended to target *[the alleged victim]* with the harassing conduct or speech, or series of acts, on each occasion;

Third: That the conduct or speech, or series of acts, were of such a nature that they seriously alarmed *[the alleged victim]*;

Fourth: That the conduct or speech, or series of acts, were of such a nature that they would cause a reasonable person to suffer substantial emotional distress; and

Fifth: That the defendant committed the conduct or speech, or series of acts, willfully and maliciously.

> *Commonwealth v. McDonald*, 462 Mass. 236, 240 (2012) (listing elements).

To satisfy the first element of the offense, the Commonwealth must prove a pattern of conduct which includes a minimum of three incidents of harassment.

To satisfy the second element, the Commonwealth must prove that each incident was directed at *[the alleged victim]*, and that the defendant intended that *[the alleged victim]* know that each incident was directed at (him) (her).

To satisfy the third element, the Commonwealth must prove that *[the alleged victim]* was seriously alarmed by this conduct.

To satisfy the fourth element, the Commonwealth must prove that a reasonable person would suffer substantial emotional distress if confronted with those acts, conduct or speech. By substantial emotional distress, I mean distress that is considerable, of importance, solid and real. The offending conduct must be such as would produce a considerable or significant amount of emotional distress in a reasonable person; something markedly greater than the level of uneasiness, nervousness, unhappiness or the like which is commonly experienced in day to day living.

7

To satisfy the fifth element, the Commonwealth must prove that the defendant acted willfully and maliciously. An act is "willful" if it is done intentionally and by design, and not out of mistake or accident. The defendant acted willfully if the defendant intended the conduct.

An act is done with "malice" if the defendant's conduct was intentional and without justification or mitigation, and any reasonably prudent person would have foreseen the actual harm that resulted to *[the alleged victim]*.

If you find that the Commonwealth has proved each of these elements beyond a reasonable doubt, you should return a verdict of guilty on this charge. If you find that the Commonwealth has not proved one or more of these five elements beyond a reasonable doubt, you must return a verdict of not guilty of this charge.

Supplemental Instruction

Communications covered by statute. The conduct, acts or threats may be communicated by any means including, but not limited to (mail) (telephone) (facsimile transmission) (e-mail) (internet communications) (telecommunications device) (electronic instant messages) (any electronic communication device including any device that transfers [signs] [signals] [writing] [images] [sounds] [data] or [intelligence of any nature] transmitted in whole or in part by a [wire] [radio] [electromagnetic system] [photoelectronic system] [photooptical system]).

NOTES

1. **Wilful conduct.** Wilful conduct must be intentional (as opposed to negligent), but does not require that the defendant intend its harmful consequences as well. *Commonwealth v. O'Neil*, 67 Mass. App. Ct. 284, 290–93 (2006).

2. **Malicious conduct.** The requirement of malice does not require a showing of cruelty, hostility, or revenge, nor does it require an actual intent to cause the required harm, but merely that the conduct be "intentional and without justification or mitigation, and any reasonable prudent person would have foreseen the actual harm that resulted." *Commonwealth v. O'Neil*, 67 Mass. App. Ct. 284, 290–93 (2006). Accord, *Commonwealth v. Paton*, 63 Mass. App. Ct. 215, 219, (2005); *Commonwealth v. Giavazzi*, 60 Mass. App. Ct. 374, 375–76 (2004). Prior to the *O'Neil* decision, the instruction included language that: "An act is 'wilful' if it is done intentionally and by design, in contrast to an act which is done thoughtlessly or accidentally. The defendant acted wilfully if the defendant intended both the conduct and its harmful consequences. An act is done with 'malice' if it is done out of cruelty, hostility or revenge. To act with malice, one must act not only deliberately, but out of hostility toward [the alleged victim]."

3 **Three or more harassing incidents required.** "The phrase 'pattern of conduct or series of acts' requires the Commonwealth to prove three or more incidents of harassment." *Commonwealth v. Welch*, 444 Mass. 80 (2005).

4. **Substantial emotional distress.** The term "substantial emotional distress" is defined as considerable in amount, or of real worth and importance. *Commonwealth v. Robinson*, 444 Mass. 102 (2005); *Commonwealth v. Paton*, 63 Mass. App. Ct. 215 (2005).

5. **Harassing conduct does not encompass protected speech.** Although the statute reaches harassing speech, it does not reach protected speech. Specifically, it reaches only "fighting words." *Commonwealth v. Welch*, 444 Mass. 80 (2005).

Disorderly Conduct

Regulatory Authority—G.L. c. 272, § 53
Dist. Ct. Model Jury Instruction 7.160

In order to prove the defendant guilty of this offense, the Commonwealth must prove three things beyond a reasonable doubt:

First: The Commonwealth must prove that the defendant involved himself (herself) in at least one of the following actions: he (she) *either* engaged in fighting or threatening, *or* engaged in violent or tumultuous behavior *or* created a hazardous or physically offensive condition by an act that served no legitimate purpose of the defendant's;

Second: The Commonwealth must prove beyond a reasonable doubt that the defendant's actions were reasonably likely to affect the public; and

Third: The Commonwealth must prove beyond a reasonable doubt that the defendant *either* intended to cause public inconvenience, annoyance or alarm, *or* recklessly created a risk of public inconvenience, annoyance or alarm.

> See Instruction 3.120 (Intent).

NOTES

1. **G.L. c. 272, § 53.** *Commonwealth v. Feigenbaum*, 404 Mass. 471 (1989) (the "hazardous or physically offensive condition" branch of the statute cannot be applied to political protesters who block passage); *Commonwealth v. A Juvenile*, 368 Mass. 580, 595–99 (1975); *Alegata v. Commonwealth*, 353 Mass. 287, 302–04 (1967), adopting Model Penal Code § 250.2(a) & (c) (1962); *Commonwealth v. Lopiano*, 60 Mass. App. Ct. 723, 725–26 (2004) (finding no violent or tumultuous behavior where defendant, upon being told by police that he would be summoned to court for assault and battery, began to flail his arms and shout at police); *Commonwealth v. Sinai*, 47 Mass. App. Ct. 544, 546 (1999) (affirming first element of crime); *Commonwealth v. Bosk*, 29 Mass. App. Ct. 904, 906–07 (1990) (statute applicable to motorist who stood in traffic lane, forcing vehicles to pass around him, while debating with police officer and refusing to return to his car).

2. **Prohibited conduct.** Our disorderly conduct law seeks to control intentional conduct which tends to disturb the public tranquility, or to alarm or provoke others. It prohibits four separate and distinct acts: It forbids conduct that involves the use of force or violence. It also prohibits making threats that involve the immediate use of force or violence. It forbids tumultuous and highly agitated behavior, which may not involve physical violence, but which causes riotous commotion and excessively unreasonable noise, and so constitutes a public nuisance. Finally, the law prohibits any conduct that creates a hazard to public safety or a physically offensive condition by an act that serves no legitimate purpose of the defendant's. *Commonwealth v. Feigenbaum*, 404 Mass. 471 (1989); *Alegata v. Commonwealth*, 353 Mass. 287, 302–04 (1967); *Commonwealth v. Molligi*, 70 Mass. App. Ct. 108, 111 (holding that "the defendant's conduct—openly carrying a knife on a public street with pedestrian traffic, refusing Officer Fenlon's order, and fleeing across a public street and down a side street—created a hazardous or physically

offensive condition affecting the public"), *review denied*, 450 Mass. 1102 (2007); *Commonwealth v. Blavackas*, 11 Mass. App. Ct. 746, 749 (1981).

3. **Public.** For the defendant to be found guilty, his (her) actions must have been reasonably likely to affect the public, that is, persons in a place to which the public or a substantial group has access. *Alegata v. Commonwealth*, 353 Mass. 287, 302–04 (1967). *See Commonwealth v. Templeman*, 376 Mass. 533, 537 (1978).

4. **Recklessness.** A person acts recklessly when he consciously ignores, or is indifferent to, the probable outcome of his actions. The defendant was reckless if he (she) knew, or must have known, that such actions would create a substantial and unjustifiable risk of public inconvenience, annoyance or alarm, but he (she) chose, nevertheless, to run the risk and go ahead. *Commonwealth v. Welansky*, 316 Mass. 383, 397–401 (1944); *Commonwealth v. Papadinis*, 23 Mass. App. Ct. 570, 574–75 (1987), *rev'd on other grounds*, 402 Mass. 73 (1988).

5. **Offensive language.** General Laws c. 272, § 53 cannot constitutionally be applied to language and expressive conduct, even if it is offensive and abusive, unless it falls outside the scope of First Amendment protections, i.e. it constitutes "fighting words which by their very utterance tend to incite an immediate breach of the peace." *Commonwealth v. Richards*, 369 Mass. 443, 445–50 (1976); *A Juvenile*, 368 Mass. at 587–95. *See Lewis v. New Orleans*, 415 U.S. 130 (1974); *Rosenfeld v. New Jersey*, 408 U.S. 901 (1972); *Chaplinsky v. New Hampshire*, 315 U.S. 568 (1942); *Blavackas*, 11 Mass. App. Ct. at 748–52 (doubtful that public solicitation for sexual activity is "disorderly conduct," which seems to require proof at least of significant risk of violence or serious disturbance). However, non-expressive disorderly conduct is punishable even if accompanied by constitutionally protected speech or expressive conduct. *Richards, above; Commonwealth v. Carson*, 10 Mass. App. Ct. 921, 921–22 (1980).

6. **Offensive and disorderly conduct against persons of opposite sex.** Regarding that portion of G.L. c. 272, § 53 dealing with offensive and disorderly conduct against persons of the opposite sex, see Instruction 6.600.

7. **Political protesters.** The acts that may constitute disorderly conduct fall into two branches: (i) "engag[ing] in fighting or threatening, or in violent or tumultuous behavior," and (ii) "creat[ing] a hazardous or physically offensive condition by any act which serves no legitimate purpose of the actor." Model Penal Code § 250.2(a) & (c) (Proposed Official Draft, 1962). A disorderly conduct prosecution of political protesters is maintainable only under the first of the two branches. "[A]lthough conduct that is designed to call attention to a political cause, and may therefore have a legitimate purpose, may nevertheless be criminal under the common law or by some statute, it does not constitute disorderly conduct under [the second branch of] G.L. c. 272, § 53" because it does serve a legitimate purpose of the actor. *Feigenbaum, above.*

8. **First Amendment.** As to the burden of proof when there is an assertion that the defendant's acts were protected by the First Amendment to the United State Constitution, see *Commonwealth v. Manzelli*, 68 Mass. App. Ct. 691 (2007).

Distribution of a Controlled Substance; Possession with Intent to Distribute a Controlled Substance

Regulatory Authority—G.L. c. 94C, § 1 et seq.
Dist. Ct. Model Jury Instruction 7.800

The defendant is charged with having unlawfully (distributed) (possessed with the intent to distribute) a Class _____ controlled substance, namely _____.

Section _____ of chapter 94C of our General Laws provides as follows:

> "Any person who knowingly or intentionally . . . (distributes) (possesses with intent to . . . distribute) a controlled substance [categorized by the law] in Class _____ . . . shall be punished . . . ."

In order to prove the defendant guilty of this offense, the Commonwealth must prove three things beyond a reasonable doubt:

First: That the substance in question is a Class _____ controlled substance, namely _____;

Second: That the defendant (distributed some perceptible amount of that substance to another person or persons) (possessed some perceptible amount of that substance with the intent to distribute it to another person or persons); and

Third: That the defendant did so knowingly or intentionally.

> The relevant statutory sections (G.L. c. 94C, §§ 32 [Class A], 32A [Class B], 32B [Class C], 32C [Class D], and 32D [Class E]) also penalize manufacturing, dispensing, cultivating, or possession with intent to manufacture, dispense or cultivate a controlled substance. Where such alternatives are charged, the model instruction may be adapted as necessary. Definitions of "manufacture" and "dispense" may be found in G.L. c. 94C, § 1.
>
> Since the enactment of St. 1987, c. 266, the District Court has final jurisdiction only over first offenses involving distribution of Class A, B or C controlled substances, but has final jurisdiction over both first and subsequent offenses involving distribution of Class D or E controlled substances.
>
> See G.L. c. 94C, § 31 for the statutory schedule of controlled substances.

As to the first element, I instruct you that as a matter of law _____ is defined as a Class _____ controlled substance by our statutes. It is your duty to determine whether or not the material in question is in fact _____. In doing so, you may consider all the relevant evidence in the case, including the testimony of any witness who may have testified either to support or to dispute the allegation that the material in question was _____.

As to the second element, (distribution) (possession with intent to distribute), the term "distribute" means to actually deliver a controlled substance to another person. It is irrelevant whether any money or other compensation was involved.

> *If the charge is possession with intent to distribute. First define "possession" from Instruction 3.220.*

If it has been proved that the defendant did possess a controlled substance, you will have to determine whether it was held solely for his (her) own use, or whether it was intended for distribution to others. Among the factors you may consider in making that determination are (how large a quantity of drugs were possessed) (how pure in quality the drugs were) (what the street value of the drugs was) (what the defendant's financial resources were) (how the drugs were packaged) (whether other items were found along with the drugs which might suggest drug sales, such as cutting powder or packaging materials, scales, or large amounts of cash) (whether there is any evidence suggesting that a sale was in progress) (whether there is any evidence that these drugs were part of a larger stash of drugs) (whether there is any evidence that the defendant repeatedly traveled at short intervals to known drug centers).

7

> A number of relevant but complex definitions are given in G.L. c. 94C, § 1. To "distribute" is to "deliver other than by administering or dispensing." To "deliver" is defined in turn as "to transfer, whether by actual or constructive transfer, a controlled substance from one person to another, whether or not there is an agency relationship." "Administer" is defined as "the direct application of a controlled substance whether by injection, inhalation, ingestion, or any other means . . . by . . . a practitioner, or . . . a nurse at the direction of a practitioner in the course of his professional practice, or . . . an ultimate user or research subject at the direction of a practitioner in the course of his professional practice." To "dispense" is defined as "to deliver a controlled substance to an ultimate user or . . . [his] agent . . . by a practitioner or pursuant to the order of a practitioner, including the prescribing and administering of a controlled substance and the packaging, labeling, or compounding necessary for such delivery." Because of their complexity, it is recommended that the jury

be given these definitions in full only where there is an issue as to whether the drugs were possessed or distributed lawfully.

The third thing the Commonwealth must prove beyond a reasonable doubt is that the defendant not only (distributed a Class _____ controlled substance) (possessed a Class _____ controlled substance with the intent to distribute it), but did so knowingly or intentionally. You may find that the defendant acted knowingly or intentionally if he (she) did so consciously, voluntarily and purposely, and not because of ignorance, mistake or accident.

See Instructions 3.120 (Intent) and 3.140 (Knowledge).

The Commonwealth is required to prove only that the defendant knew that she possessed a controlled substance, but not necessarily that she knew she possessed any particular drug. *Commonwealth v. DePalma*, 41 Mass. App. Ct. 798, 802 (1996) (cocaine).

Where it is charged that the violation occurred within 1,000 feet of school property or within 100 feet of a public park or playground, here give Instruction 7.860.

NOTES

1. **DPH, State Police or U. Mass. Medical School certificate of analysis.** See the supplemental instruction to Instruction 5.52. For the statutory pretrial procedure for destroying all but a sample of large quantities of controlled substances, see G.L. c. 94C, § 47A.

2. **Forfeiture motions to forfeit drug proceeds** can be filed in a criminal case pursuant to G.L. c. 94C, § 47(b), without the need for a separate civil action pursuant to § 47(d). As to time and hearing requirements, see *Commonwealth v. Goldman,* 398 Mass. 201, 203–04 (1986). While § 47(b) contains no dispositional provisions, the funds should be distributed in the same manner as specified in § 47(d)—i.e., half to the prosecuting district attorney, and half to the involved police department(s). *District Attorney for the Northwestern Dist. v. Eastern Hampshire Div. of Dist. Court Dep't,* 452 Mass. 199 (2008).

As to whether a judge has discretion to exclude questions at trial to prosecution witnesses about potential forfeitures, allegedly probative of bias, see *Sendele,* 18 Mass. App. Ct. at 760–61.

7

3. **Possession a lesser included offense.** Possession of a controlled substance is a lesser included offense of a charge of distribution or possession with intent to distribute that controlled substance. *Commonwealth v. Perry,* 391 Mass. 808, 813–14 (1984); *Commonwealth v. Ruggerio,* 32 Mass. App. Ct. 964, 966 (1992). Knowingly being present where heroin is kept (G.L. c. 94C, § 35) is not a lesser included offense of a charge of distribution or possession with intent to distribute a Class A controlled substance, which does not require presence. *Commonwealth v. Saez,* 21 Mass. App. Ct. 408, 412 n.3 (1986); *Commonwealth v. Rodriguez,* 11 Mass. App. Ct. 379, 381 (1981).

A defendant cannot be convicted and sentenced both for possession of and for possession with intent to distribute the same quantity of drugs. *Commonwealth v. Amendola,* 26 Mass. App Ct. 713, 713 n.1 (1988). *See Kuklis v. Commonwealth,* 361 Mass. 302, 307 (1976). Such separate convictions for distributing and for possession with intent to distribute are not duplicitous where separate quantities of a controlled substance are involved. *Commonwealth v. Diaz,* 383 Mass. 73, 82–85 (1981).

4. **Sufficiency of evidence of intent to distribute.** *See Commonwealth v. Clermy,* 421 Mass. 325, 331 (1995) (packaging of drugs in many small packets as well as possession of telephone pager, a traditional accouterment of illegal drug trade); *Commonwealth v. Roman,* 414 Mass. 642, 645 (1993) (possession of large amount of illegal drugs raises inference of intent to distribute); *Commonwealth v. Johnson,* 413 Mass. 598 (1992) (purchase with another's money intending to transfer drugs to such person constitutes distribution); *Commonwealth v. Scala,* 380 Mass. 500, 511 (1980) (relevant factors include quantity possessed); *Commonwealth v. Rugaber,* 369 Mass. 765, 770 (1976) (same); *Commonwealth v. Ellis,* 356 Mass. 574, 578–79 (1970) (inference from large quantities of one drug not applicable to small quantities of another drug); *Commonwealth v. Martin,* 48 Mass. App. Ct. 391, 392–93 (1999) (manner of packaging, area of high drug activity, vigorous attempt to avoid apprehension); *Commonwealth v. Pena,* 40 Mass. App. Ct. 905–06 (1996) (area of high drug dealing). *But see Commonwealth v. Reid,* 29 Mass. App. Ct. 537, 538–39 (1990) (despite arrest in "area of high drug activity," court held that "[o]n the scanty evidence of the defendant's actions . . . it was equally as likely that the defendant was the purchaser as that he was the seller"). *See Commonwealth v. Watson,* 36 Mass. App. Ct. 252, 259–60 (1994) ("[S]parse furnishings of the apartment indicated that it was a stash house, used solely for storing and selling drugs."); *Commonwealth v. Monterosso,* 33 Mass. App. Ct. 765, 770–71 (1992) (several persons making short visits to defendant's apartment shortly before the search supported inference of drug distribution as opposed to possession for personal use). *Commonwealth v. Poole,* 29 Mass. App. Ct. 1003, 1004 (1990) (possession as bailee with intent to retransfer to its owner constitutes distribution); *Commonwealth v. LaPerle,* 19 Mass. App. Ct. 424, 428 (1985) (where other indicia of distribution, minute quantity can suffice, since defendant not required to have intended to distribute the precise quantity possessed); *Sendele,* 18 Mass. App. Ct. at 758–59 (relevant factors include quantity, purity, packaging, separation from personal quantity, cash, price list, repeated travel to notorious drug centers); *Commonwealth v. Miller,* 17 Mass. App. Ct. 991, 991 (1984) (relevant factors include apparent prior drug sales); *Commonwealth v. Woodon,* 13 Mass. App. Ct. 417, 422–24 (1982) (relevant factors include cash, whether sale in progress, whether part of larger stash; separate packages relevant only if more consistent with distribution than personal use); *Commonwealth v. Fiore,* 9 Mass. App. Ct. 618, 624, *cert. denied,* 449 U.S. 938 (1980) (relevant factors include street value of drugs). *See also Commonwealth v. Marchese,* 54 Mass. App. Ct. 916, 918 (2002) (prosecutor's comment that there was no evidence of defendant's personal use of drugs improper because it could be construed as "asking the jury to infer the defendant's guilt from his failure to produce direct evidence of his use of cocaine"); *Commonwealth v. McShan,* 15 Mass. App. Ct. 921, 922 (1983) (reversible error to exclude question to police witness whether quantity consistent with personal use); *Commonwealth v. Huffman,* 11 Mass. App. Ct. 185, 190 (1981) (reversible error to exclude defendant's testimony that drugs intended solely for personal use), *aff'd on other grounds,* 385 Mass. 122 (1982).

Disturbing the Peace

Regulatory Authority—G.L. c. 272, § 53
Dist. Ct. Model Jury Instruction 7.200

The defendant is charged with disturbing the peace. In order to prove the defendant guilty of this offense, the Commonwealth must prove three things beyond a reasonable doubt:

First: That the defendant engaged in conduct which most people would find to be unreasonably disruptive, such as (making loud and disturbing noise) (tumultuous or offensive conduct) (hurling objects in a populated area) (threatening, quarreling, fighting, or challenging others to fight) (uttering personal insults that amount to fighting words, that is, are so offensive that they are inherently likely to provoke an immediate violent reaction);

Second: That the defendant's actions were done intentionally, and not by accident or mistake; and

Third: That the defendant did in fact annoy or disturb at least one person.

To amount to disturbing the peace, the defendant's acts must have been voluntary, unnecessary, and contrary to normal standards of conduct. You should consider all the circumstances, including such important factors as time and location, in determining whether the defendant disturbed the tranquility of at least one person in that area, or interfered with at least one person's normal activity.

See Instruction 3.120 (Intent).

G.L. c. 272, § 53. *Commonwealth v. Orlando,* 371 Mass. 732, 733–36 (1977) (definition; statute not unconstitutionally vague or overbroad); *Commonwealth v. Jarrett,* 359 Mass. 491 (1971); Commonwealth v. Oaks, 113 Mass. 8, 9 (1847); *Commonwealth v. Piscopo,* 11 Mass. App. Ct. 905, 905 (1981) (fact that police were called will support inference that citizens of neighborhood were disturbed).

NOTE

Offensive language. General Laws c. 272, § 53 cannot be applied to offensive and abusive language unless it falls outside the scope of First Amendment protection, i.e. it constitutes "profane, libelous, and insulting or fighting words which by their very utterance tend to incite an immediate breach of the peace." However, it is not a defense that proscribed behavior was accompanied by protected speech. *Common-*

wealth v. Bohmer, 374 Mass. 368, 373–77 (1974) (disturbing a school or assembly [G.L. c. 272, § 40]); *Commonwealth v. Richards,* 369 Mass. 443, 448–49 (1976) (disorderly conduct); *Commonwealth v. A Juvenile,* 368 Mass. 580, 584–98 (1975) (same). *See Houston v. Hill,* 482 U.S. 451 (1987) (ordinance forbidding "abuse" of police is unconstitutionally overbroad); *Lewis v. New Orleans,* 415 U.S. 130 (1974) (statute forbidding cursing or using "obscene or opprobrious language" toward police is unconstitutionally overbroad); *Rosenfeld v. New Jersey,* 408 U.S. 901 (1972); *Chaplinsky v. New Hampshire,* 315 U.S. 568 (1942) ("fighting words" can be constitutionally proscribed). Loud speech may be constitutionally proscribed when uttered late at night in a residential neighborhood, so that people are disturbed in their homes by the noise. *Orlando,* 371 Mass. at 735 (disturbing the peace).

Escape

Regulatory Authority—G.L. c. 268, § 16
Dist. Ct. Model Jury Instruction 7.220

The defendant is charged with escaping from lawful custody.

In order to prove the defendant guilty of this offense, the Commonwealth must prove three things:

First: That the defendant was a prisoner who had been committed by legal procedures to the custody of a penal institution or correctional institution, or a jail;

Second: That the defendant (escaped from) (failed to return from any temporary release from) (that [institution] [jail]) (the grounds of that [institution] [jail]) (a courthouse) (the grounds of a courthouse) (the custody of an officer of that [institution] [jail] [courthouse] while being conveyed to or from that [institution] [jail]); and

Third: That the defendant intentionally left custody without permission, in the sense that it was not done by accident or mistake.

See Instruction 3.120 (Intent).

The statute was broadened by St. 1989, c. 313, § 2 to include escapes from a jail or correctional institution, and St. 1993, c. 376 to include escapes from a courthouse. The statute also penalizes attempts to escape; in such cases the model instruction (including its statutory quotation) should be appropriately adapted, and the required fourth element (an overt act) added. *Commonwealth v. Gosselin,* 365 Mass. 116, 121–22 (1974). See Instruction 4.120 (Attempt). The model instruction (and its statutory quotation) may also be appropriately adapted for escapes by persons committed pursuant to G.L. c. 123A as sexually dangerous.

Commonwealth v. Best, 381 Mass. 60, 61–64 (1980) (escape from work release program in violation of G.L. c. 127, § 86F can also be prosecuted under G.L. c. 268, § 16); *Lynch, petitioner,* 379 Mass. 757, 760–61 (1980) (statute applicable to defendant who should have been paroled but had not been); *Commonwealth v. Reed,* 364 Mass. 545, 546–48 (1974) (because of G.L. c. 127, § 119, statute is applicable to prisoners temporarily transferred to a hospital); *Commonwealth v. Antonelli,* 345 Mass. 518, 520–21 (1963) (guard supervising prisoners is "officer" for purposes of statute); *Commonwealth v. Curley,* 101 Mass. 24, 25 (1869) ("land appurtenant thereto" is to be understood broadly to include all grounds "entirely devoted to the purpose, sufficiently secure and suitably protected from all persons without"); *Commonwealth v. Porter,* 87 Mass. App. Ct. 676, 678–82 (failure to return to serve a weekend sentence constitutes escape), *rev. denied,* 473 Mass. 1103 (2015); *Commonwealth v. Clark,* 20 Mass. App. Ct. 962, 962–63 (1985) (lawfulness of custody is an element of offense, but Commonwealth need not demonstrate that original conviction was free of legal error); *Commonwealth v. Faulkner,* 8 Mass. App. Ct. 936, 937 (1979) (statute encompasses escape of pretrial detainee); *Commonwealth v. Giordano,* 8 Mass. App. Ct. 590, 592 (1979) (Commonwealth can demonstrate lawful pretrial custody of defendant obtained pursuant to interstate detainer by relying on presumption of regularity), *rev. denied,* 379 Mass. 927, and *cert. denied,* 446 U.S. 968 (1980); *Commonwealth v. Pettijohn,* 4 Mass. App. Ct. 847, 847–48 (1976) (statute encompasses escape from county jail or house of correction, and therefore deputy sheriff transporting sentenced prisoner from county jail to court); *Commonwealth v. Meranda,* 2 Mass. App. Ct. 890, 891 (1974) (wrongful intent is necessary element, but inferable from unlawful departure in absence of satisfactory explanation); *Commonwealth v. Gosselin,* 1 Mass. App. Ct. 849, 849–50 (1973) (prison librarian was not "officer"; offense requires proof that defendant left prison grounds, not just that whereabouts were unknown for a time), *aff'd on other grounds,* 365 Mass. 116 (1974).

Supplemental Instructions

1. *"Prisoner."* A "prisoner" is defined as a person who is placed in custody in a penal institution or correctional institution or a jail, in accordance with law.

See G.L. c. 125, § 1(k) & (m).

2. *"Escape."* Escape means "absenting oneself from confinement without permission."

United States v. Bailey, 444 U.S. 394, 407 (1980).

3. *"Penal institution" or "correctional institution."* A "penal institution" or a "correctional institution" is defined as any building, enclosure, space or structure used for the custody, control and rehabilitation of committed offenders and of such other persons as may be placed in custody therein in accordance with law.

G.L. c. 125, § 1(d), (e) & (k). A police station cell block is not a penal institution. *Commonwealth v. Clay,* 65 Mass. App. Ct. 215, 216–17 (2005). Nor does the statute seem to apply to persons who, in the absence of criminal charges, have been civilly committed under G.L. c. 123, §§ 7, 8. *Cf. Commonwealth v. Shaheed,* 76 Mass. App. Ct. 598, 601 (an inmate committed under G.L. c. 123, §§ 7, 8 may not be convicted of assault and battery on a correctional officer), *rev. denied,* 457 Mass. 1103 (2010).

4. "Jail." A "jail" is a facility that is used for the detention of persons who are charged with a crime and committed by a court until they are tried.

G.L. c. 126, § 4. "Jails may also be used for the detention of persons arrested without a warrant and not admitted to bail pending appearance before the district court" instead of a local lock-up. G.L. c. 126, § 4.

NOTES

1. **Common law escape.** In Massachusetts an escape by a convicted criminal that is not encompassed by one of the various escape statutes may still be punished as an offense at common law. *Commonwealth v. Farrell,* 87 Mass. (5 Allen) 130, 131–32 (1862).

2. **Necessity defense.** Necessity may be a defense to an escape charge. *Commonwealth v. Thurber,* 383 Mass. 328, 330–33 (1981); *Commonwealth v. Mandile,* 17 Mass. App. Ct. 657, 659–61, *rev. denied,* 391 Mass. 1105 (1984); *Commonwealth v. O'Malley,* 14 Mass. App. Ct. 314, 319–22, *rev. denied,* 387 Mass. 1102 (1982). See Instruction 9.240 (Necessity).

Forgery

Regulatory Authority—G.L. c. 267, § 1 et seq.
Dist. Ct. Model Jury Instruction 8.160

The defendant is charged with forgery of a *[type of docu-*

7

ment]. Section _____ of chapter 267 of our General Laws provides as follows:

> "Whoever, with intent to injure or defraud, falsely makes, alters, forges or counterfeits a *[type of document]*, shall be punished . . . ."

In order to prove the defendant guilty of this offense, the Commonwealth must prove two things beyond a reasonable doubt:

First: That the defendant (falsified one or more significant parts of the document in question) (altered one or more significant parts of the document in question) (counterfeited the document in question to make it appear to be genuine); and

Second: That the defendant did so with the intent to injure or to defraud someone.

To have a forgery, something relating to a legal document *itself,* as distinguished from its contents, must be false. Making a false statement *in* a document is a separate crime under some circumstances, but it is not the offense of forgery, which is concerned with the genuineness of the document itself, rather than the truth of its contents.

Forgery can be committed in three ways: The *first* is to counterfeit or produce what appears to be a genuine legal document, but which is in fact a phony document. The *second* way is to falsely make out one or more important parts of a genuine document—for example, by forging someone else's signature on a check or a bill of sale. The *third* way is closely related to the second: altering in a significant way one or more parts of a genuine document that has already been made out—for example, changing the amount on a check.

Besides proving that the defendant (counterfeited) (falsified) (altered) the document in question, the Commonwealth must also prove beyond a reasonable doubt that the defendant acted with the specific intention of defrauding someone.

> See Instruction 3.120 (Intent).
>
> *Commonwealth v. O'Connell,* 438 Mass. 658, 664 n.9 (2003) (elements of forgery); *Commonwealth v. Apalakis,* 396 Mass. 292 (1985); *Commonwealth v. Segee,* 218 Mass. 501, 504 (1914); *Commonwealth v. Baldwin,* 11 Gray 197, 198 (1858).

7

NOTES

1. **District Court jurisdiction over forgery offenses.** General Laws c. 218, § 26 gives the District Court final jurisdiction over "all felonies punishable by imprisonment in the state prison for not more than five years . . . [and] forgery of a promissory note, or of an order for money or other property." That grant of jurisdiction encompasses some (but not all) of the documents listed in G.L. c. 267, §§ 1–8. It includes forgery of a "promissory note; or an order . . . for money or other property" (G.L. c. 267, § 1), or an admission ticket (§ 2), a railroad ticket or pass (§ 2), a railroad stamp (§ 4), or "a bank bill or promissory note payable to the bearer thereof or to the order of any person, issued by any incorporated banking company" (§ 8). The District Court does not have final jurisdiction over forgery of the Land Court's seal (§ 3), a Commonwealth note (§ 7), or a bank bill or traveller's check (§ 8).

The District Court also has final jurisdiction over a number of forgery offenses found in other chapters of the General Laws, including forgery of historical objects (G.L. c. 9, § 27C), birth, marriage or death certificates (G.L. c. 46, § 30), motor vehicle licenses, permits, certificates or inspector stickers (G.L. c. 90, § 24B), motorboat number certificates (G.L. c. 90B, § 4A), firearms licenses (G.L. c. 140, § 131I), and hunting or fishing licenses (G.L. c. 131, § 33).

2. **Claim of authority.** Lack of authority is not an element of the offense of forgery, but if a claim of authority is properly raised, the Commonwealth must prove the absence of authority beyond a reasonable doubt in order to prove the element of fraudulent intent. Such a claim must [be] raised by timely written notice pursuant to Mass. R. Crim. P. 14(b)(3) or is waived. Lack of authority and fraudulent intent may be proved by circumstantial evidence as well as by testimony from the purported maker. *O'Connell,* 438 Mass. at 664–65. See Instruction 3.160 (License or Authority).

Harassing or Obscene Telephone Calls

Regulatory Authority—G.L. c. 269, § 14A
Dist. Ct. Model Jury Instruction 6.660

I. Harassing Telephone Calls or Electronic Communications

The defendant is charged with making harassing (telephone calls) (or) (electronic communications). Section 14A of chapter 269 of our General Laws provides as follows:

> "Whoever (telephones another person. . . or causes a person to be telephoned,) (contacts another person by electronic communication, or causes a person to be contacted by electronic communication) repeatedly, for the sole purpose of harassing, annoying, or molesting the person or the person's family, whether or not conversation ensues . . . shall be punished."

In order to prove the defendant guilty of this offense, the Commonwealth must prove two things beyond a reasonable doubt:

First: That the defendant (made telephone calls to) (caused telephone calls to be made to) (contacted by electronic communication) (caused to be contacted by electronic communication) *[name of person]* repeatedly, which means three or more times; and

Second: That the defendant's sole purpose in (making the telephone calls) (having the telephone calls made) (making the contacts by electronic communication) (causing the contacts by electronic communication to be made), was either to harass, annoy or molest *[name of person]* or his (her) family.

The Commonwealth is not required to show that the defendant had a conversation or actual contact with *[name of person]*, only that he (she) (made the telephone calls) (had the telephone calls made) (made the contacts by electronic communication) (had the contacts made by electronic communication).

As I indicated, the Commonwealth must prove that the defendant's *only* purpose was to annoy, harass or molest *[name of person]*. For example, your favorite charity might call you repeatedly to ask for donations and that might annoy or even harass you, but it would not violate the law if the intent was not to annoy, harass or molest. If the defendant called repeatedly but not for the *sole* purpose of harassment, he (she) is entitled to be acquitted.

The defendant's intent or purpose cannot be proved directly because there is no way to look into the human mind. But you may determine the defendant's purpose from the surrounding circumstances. You may consider any of the defendant's statements and acts, and any other facts and circumstances shown by the evidence, which help to indicate his (her) state of mind. You may infer that a person ordinarily intends the natural and probable consequences of acts that he (she) does knowingly. For example, if a person makes repeated telephone calls in a short period of time, or in the middle of the night, and hangs up when someone answers the phone, it might be reasonable to infer that the calls were made for the purpose of harassment. However, you should consider all the circumstances in evidence that you deem relevant in determining whether the Commonwealth has proved beyond a reasonable doubt that the defendant acted with the required intent.

> *Commonwealth v. Roberts*, 442 Mass. 1034 (2004) ("The jury could infer the requisite intent from the number of calls, the tenor of the calls, their sequence and timing, and the defendant's persistence in placing the calls despite repeatedly being asked to cease. . . ."); *Commonwealth v. Wotan*, 37 Mass. App. Ct. 727, 728–30 (1994), *rev'd on other grounds*, 422 Mass. 740 (1996) (hundreds of calls are "so obviously vexatious to the receiver that the requisite sole purpose of harassing, annoying and molesting may be inferred; even if getting the receiver's goat is at bottom stimulated by an obsessive desire to get the receiver's attention"). *Compare Commonwealth v.*

Strahan, 30 Mass. App. Ct. 947, 949 (1991) (calling 11 times in 7 minutes, while perhaps partially motivated by a desire to harass, does not support conviction of § 14A where evidence suggests at least a partial motive was to reestablish a prior relationship with victim), *with Commonwealth v. Roberts*, 442 Mass. 1034 (2004) (holding that "certain statements made during some of the calls were, at least superficially, phrased as concern for the [victim] did not make it impermissible for the jury to infer that the actual and sole purpose of the calls was to annoy or harass"). *Commonwealth v. Voight,* 28 Mass. App. Ct. 769 (1990) (government unit cannot be a harassed "person," but calls "could take on a tone so directed at the recipient [employee] as an individual as to constitute harassment under the statute").

Supplemental Instructions

1. *"Electronic communications."* The term "electronic communications" includes but is not limited to any transfer of (signs) (signals) (writing) (images) (sounds) (data) (or) (intelligence of any nature), transmitted in whole or in part by a (wire) (radio) (electromagnetic) (photo-electronic) (or) (photo-optical) system.

2. *When there was no conversation or the communication was not read.* The Commonwealth is not required to show that (the defendant had a telephone conversation with) (the defendant's electronic communication was received by) *[name]*, but only that the defendant (made the telephone calls or had them made) (sent the electronic communications or had them sent) and that they could have been received by *[name]*.

Commonwealth v. Roberts, 426 Mass. 689 (1998) ("to telephone is to place a telephone call that might result in an oral communication").

II. Obscene Telephone Calls

The defendant is (also) charged with making repeated and obscene (telephone calls) (or) (electronic communications). Section 14A of chapter 269 of our General Laws (also) provides as follows:

"[W]hoever (telephones . . . a person repeatedly) (or) (contacts a person repeatedly by electronic communication) and uses indecent or obscene language to the person, shall be punished . . . ."

In order to prove the defendant guilty of this offense, the Commonwealth must prove two things beyond a reasonable doubt:

First: That the defendant (made telephone calls to) (or) (contacted by electronic communication) *[name]* repeatedly, which means three or more times; and

Second: That in making those (calls) (electronic communications), the defendant used indecent or obscene language.

For a definition of "obscene," see Instruction 7.180 (Dissemination of Obscene Matter). For a definition of "indecent," see Instruction 6.500 (Indecent Assault and Battery). *See also F.C.C. v. Pacifica Found.*, 438 U.S. 726, 740 (1978) (in statute banning "obscene, indecent or profane language" over the radio, the word "indecent" should be given its normal dictionary meaning of "nonconformance with accepted standards of morality").

NOTES

1. "Repeatedly." The statutory term "repeatedly" in the first element of each of the above offenses requires three or more such telephone calls. *Commonwealth v. Wotan,* 422 Mass. 740 (1996).

2. Anonymous telephone calls. "[A]nonymous telephone calls and acts . . . are, by their nature, not perceptibly linked to a particular individual. They are anonymous. Yet connections may be inferred through timing, mode of communication, content of the communication, similarity to identified conduct, and interpersonal relationships, particularly those involving grievances against the recipient of the unwanted communication." Where, in addition to evidence of specific calls traced to the defendant, there is evidence of other, anonymous telephone calls, the judge has discretion to permit the jury to consider such evidence as probative of the defendant's intent to harass, annoy or molest if such evidence would permit (even if it would not compel) an inference that the defendant was the source of such anonymous calls. The judge should instruct the jury that they must first consider whether the anonymous calls were in fact made by the defendant and, if so, they are to consider that evidence only on the issue of whether the defendant's sole purpose in making the calls traced to him was to harass, annoy or molest. *Commonwealth v. Wotan,* 37 Mass. App. Ct. 727, 730–34 (1994), *rev'd on other grounds,* 422 Mass. 740 (1996).

Homicide

Super. Ct. Model Jury Instructions §§ 2.2–2.10; Supreme Judicial Court Model Jury Instructions on Homicide (Mar. 2018)

Criminal Responsibility

[Note to Judge: Where there is evidence of lack of criminal responsibility, this instruction, at the discretion of the judge, may be given as a standalone instruction prior to the murder instruction or inserted within the murder instruction. In deciding when to give this instruction, a judge may wish to consider whether the defendant has conceded that he committed the crime and whether the only live issue for the jury to decide is the defendant's criminal responsibility.]

To prove the defendant guilty of any crime, the Commonwealth must prove beyond a reasonable doubt that the defendant was criminally responsible at the time the alleged crime was committed.[1] The burden is not on the defendant to prove a lack of criminal responsibility.[2] Under the law, the Commonwealth bears the burden of proving beyond a reasonable doubt that the defendant committed the crime with which he[3] is charged and also that the defendant is criminally responsible for his conduct.[4]

Criminal responsibility is a legal term. A person is not criminally responsible for his conduct if he has a mental disease or defect, and, as a result of that mental disease or defect, lacks substantial capacity either to appreciate the criminality or wrongfulness of his conduct or to conform his conduct to the requirements of the law.[5]

7

The phrase "mental disease or defect" is a legal term, not a medical term; it need not fit into a formal medical diagnosis. The phrase "mental disease or defect" does not include an abnormality characterized only by repeated criminal conduct.[6] It is for you to determine in light of all the evidence whether the defendant had a mental disease or defect.[7] If the Commonwealth has proved to you beyond a reasonable doubt that the defendant was not suffering from a mental disease or defect at the time of the killing, the Commonwealth has satisfied its burden of proving that the defendant was criminally responsible.

If you have a reasonable doubt whether the defendant had a mental disease or defect at the time of the killing, then you must determine whether, as a result of a mental disease or defect, he lacked substantial capacity either to appreciate the criminality or wrongfulness of his conduct or to conform his conduct to the requirements of the law. To establish that the defendant had substantial capacity to conform his conduct to the requirements of the law, the Commonwealth must prove beyond a reasonable doubt that any mental disease or defect that may have existed did not deprive the defendant of his ability to behave as the law requires, that is, to obey the law.[8]

The word "appreciate" means to understand rather than merely to know. "Criminality" means the legal significance of conduct; "wrongfulness" means the moral significance.[9]

The Commonwealth must prove that the defendant knew and understood that his conduct was illegal or that it was wrong. It is not enough for the Commonwealth to show that the defendant merely knew or was intellectually aware that his conduct was illegal or wrong; rather, the Commonwealth must prove beyond a reasonable doubt that a mental disease or defect did not deprive the defendant of a meaningful understanding of the legal or moral significance of his conduct. The defendant must have been able to realize, in some meaningful way, that his conduct was illegal or wrong.[10]

In considering whether the Commonwealth has met its burden of proof, you may consider all the evidence that has been presented at this trial. You may consider the facts underlying the crime and evidence of the defendant's actions before and after the crime. You may consider the opinions of any experts who testified, and give those opinions whatever weight you think they deserve.[11]

[Where there is evidence that a defendant had a mental disease or defect and consumed drugs or alcohol]

A defendant's lack of criminal responsibility must be due to a mental disease or defect. Intoxication caused by the voluntary consumption of alcohol or drugs, by itself, is not a mental disease or defect. Where a defendant lacked substantial capacity to appreciate the criminality or wrongfulness of his conduct or to conform his conduct to the law solely as a result of voluntary intoxication, then he is criminally responsible for his conduct.[12] However, the consumption of alcohol or drugs may trigger or intensify (make worse) a defendant's preexisting mental disease or defect. If it did so here, and the mental disease or defect then caused the defendant to lose substantial capacity to appreciate the criminality or wrongfulness of his conduct or to conform his conduct to the requirements of the law, the defendant is not criminally responsible for his conduct.[13]

[Where there is evidence the defendant knew that consumption of drugs or alcohol would trigger or intensify a mental disease or defect]

There is one exception to the principle just stated. A defendant who lost the substantial capacity I have just described after he consumed drugs or alcohol, and who knew or had reason to know that his consumption would trigger or intensify in him a mental disease or defect that could cause him to lack that capacity, is criminally responsible for his resulting conduct.[14] In deciding whether the defendant had reason to know about the consequences of his consumption of drugs or alcohol, you should consider the question solely from the defendant's point of view, including his mental capacity and his past experience with drugs or alcohol. But you must keep in mind that where a defendant, at the time the crime is committed, had a mental disease or defect that by itself caused him to lack the required substantial capacity, he is not criminally responsible for his conduct regardless of whether he used or did not use alcohol or drugs. That is true even if he did use alcohol or drugs and the alcohol or drug use made the symptoms of his mental disease or defect worse, and even if he knew they would make his symptoms worse.[15]

[Where there is no evidence the defendant knew that consumption of drugs or alcohol would trigger or intensify a mental disease or defect]

You must also keep in mind that where a defendant, at the time the crime is committed, had a mental disease or defect that by itself caused him to lack the substantial capacity that I have just described, he is not criminally responsible for his conduct regardless of whether he used or did not use alcohol or drugs. That is true even if he did use alcohol or drugs and the alcohol or drug use made the symptoms of his mental disease or defect worse.[16]

[The following paragraphs finish the charge on the criminal responsibility instruction and should be given whether or not the case involves the consumption of drugs or alcohol]

In a moment, I will instruct you on the elements of the offense[s] that the Commonwealth alleges the defendant has committed. Remember that the Commonwealth must prove to you beyond a reasonable doubt that the defendant was criminally responsible at the time the crime was committed, that is, that the defendant did not lack criminal responsibility at that time. Therefore, it is the Commonwealth's burden to prove at least one of the following beyond a reasonable doubt:[17]

1. That at the time of the alleged crime the defendant did not suffer from a mental disease or defect; or

2. That if the defendant did suffer from a mental disease or defect, he nonetheless retained the substantial capacity to appreciate the wrongfulness or criminality of his conduct and to conform his conduct to the requirements of the law; or

3. *[Where there is evidence the defendant consumed drugs or alcohol]* That, if the defendant lacked the substantial capacity to appreciate the wrongfulness or criminality of his conduct or to conform his conduct to the requirements of the law, his lack of such capacity was solely the result of voluntary intoxication by alcohol or other drugs; or

4. *[Where there is evidence the defendant knew that consumption of drugs or alcohol would trigger or intensify a mental disease or defect]* That, if the defendant lacked the substantial capacity I have just described due to a combination of a mental disease or defect and his voluntary consumption of alcohol or other drugs, he knew or should have known that his use of the substance[s] would interact with his mental disease or defect and cause him to lose such capacity.[18]

[Consequences of Verdict of Not Guilty by Reason of Lack of Criminal Responsibility. Note to Judge: Give at the defendant's request or on the judge's own initiative, absent a defense objection.[19]]

As I have previously instructed, your decision should be based solely on the evidence and the law of this case. In any case that raises an issue of lack of criminal responsibility, you are entitled to know what happens to a defendant if he is found not guilty by reason of lack of criminal responsibility.

If a defendant is found not guilty by reason of lack of criminal responsibility, the district attorney or another appropriate authority may, and generally does, petition the court to commit the defendant to a mental health facility or to Bridgewater State Hospital. If the court concludes that the defendant is mentally ill and that his discharge would create a substantial likelihood of serious harm to himself or others, then the court will grant the petition and commit the defendant to a proper mental facility or to Bridgewater State Hospital, initially for a period of six months. At the end of the six months and every year thereafter, the court reviews the order of commitment. If the defendant is still suffering from a mental disease or defect and is still dangerous, then the court will order the defendant to continue to be committed to the mental facility or to Bridgewater State Hospital. There is no limit to the number of such renewed orders of commitment as long as the defendant continues to be mentally ill and dangerous; if these conditions do continue, the defendant may remain committed for the duration of his life.

If at some point the defendant is no longer mentally ill and dangerous, the court will order him discharged from the mental health facility or from Bridgewater State Hospital after a hearing. The district attorney must be notified of any hearing concerning whether the person may be released, and the district attorney may be heard at any such hearing. However, the final decision on whether to recommit or release the defendant is always made by the court.[20]

NOTES

1 *Commonwealth v. Berry*, 457 Mass. 602, 612 (2010) (quoting *Commonwealth v. McHoul*, 352 Mass. 544, 546–47 (1967)).

2 *Commonwealth v. Berry*, 457 Mass. 602, 612 (2010) (quoting *Commonwealth v. McHoul*, 352 Mass. 544, 546–47 (1967)).

3 We use the pronoun "he" through the instructions. Of course, the judge should insert the appropriate gender pronoun, and, where there are multiple defendants who identify with different genders, the judge should use the appropriate pronouns in referring to the defendants.

4 This sentence tracks the language approved in *Commonwealth v. Goudreau*, 422 Mass. 731, 737 ¶ 4 (1996) (promulgating model instruction on criminal responsibility). *See Commonwealth v. Berry*, 457 Mass. 602, 612 (2010) (quoting *Commonwealth v. McHoul*, 352 Mass. 544, 546–47

(1967) ("once a defendant raises the issue of criminal responsibility, the Commonwealth has the burden to prove, beyond a reasonable doubt, that the defendant did not lack the substantial capacity to appreciate the wrongfulness of her conduct or to conform her conduct to the requirements of the law, as a result of a mental disease or defect. In order to prove that a defendant can 'conform [her] conduct to the requirements of the law,' the prosecution must show that the defendant had a 'substantial ability to behave as the law requires; that is, to obey the law'")).

5 This paragraph tracks the language approved in *Commonwealth v. Goudreau*, 422 Mass. 731, 737 ¶ 5 (1996) (promulgating model instruction on criminal responsibility). *See Commonwealth v. Berry*, 457 Mass. 602, 612 (2010) (quoting *Commonwealth v. McHoul*, 352 Mass. 544, 546–47 (1967) ("that the defendant did not lack the substantial capacity to appreciate the wrongfulness of her conduct or to conform her conduct to the requirements of the law, as a result of a mental disease or defect")).

6 This sentence tracks the language approved in *Commonwealth v. Goudreau*, 422 Mass. 731, 737 ¶ 7 (1996) (promulgating model instruction on criminal responsibility).

7 *See Commonwealth v. Sliech-Brodeur*, 457 Mass. 300, 328 (2010) ("We have previously indicated that a judge is not required to define 'mental disease or defect' but has discretion to provide the instructions that are appropriate to the context"); *Commonwealth v. Fuller*, 421 Mass. 400, 411 (1995) ("This court has declined to impose any obligation on a trial judge to provide a further explanation of the terms in issue here. . . . Our unwillingness to impose a mandatory instruction arises not because the term 'mental disease or defect' is so clear on its face that such an explanation would be superfluous. The reason may well be the opposite; the subject is so complex and obscure that any general explanatory formula is likely to mislead and confuse"); *cf. Commonwealth v. Mulica*, 401 Mass. 812, 816–20 (1988) (mental disease and defect instruction focusing jury on one particular type of mental disease or defect may have limited jury's consideration of other types of mental disease or defects and improperly reduced Commonwealth's burden).

8 This sentence tracks the language approved in *Commonwealth v. Goudreau*, 422 Mass. 731, 738 ¶ 5 (1996) (promulgating model instruction on criminal responsibility).

9 This sentence tracks, with modifications, the language approved in *Commonwealth v. Goudreau*, 422 Mass. 731, 736, 738 ¶ 3 (1996).

10 This paragraph tracks, with modifications, the language approved in *Commonwealth v. Goudreau*, 422 Mass. 731, 736, 738 ¶¶ 3–4 (1996).

11 This paragraph tracks, with modifications, the language approved in Commonwealth v. Goudreau, 422 Mass. 731, 736, 739 ¶ 3 (1996).

12 This paragraph comes from *Commonwealth v. DiPadova*, 460 Mass. 424, 439 (2011) (appendix providing model jury instruction). *See Commonwealth v. Berry*, 457 Mass. 602, 617–18 (2010) (citing *Commonwealth v. Sheehan*, 376 Mass. 765, 770 (1978)).

13 This paragraph comes from *Commonwealth v. DiPadova*, 460 Mass. 424, 439 (2011) (appendix providing model jury instruction). *See Commonwealth v. Berry*, 457 Mass. 602, 612–13 (2010) (quoting *Commonwealth v. Brennan*, 399 Mass. 358, 363 (1987) ("if the jury find that the 'defendant had a latent mental disease or defect which caused the defendant to lose the capacity . . . to conform his conduct to the requirements of the law, lack of criminal responsibility is established even if voluntary consumption of alcohol activated the illness,' as long as the defendant did not know or have reason to know that the activation would occur")).

14 This paragraph comes from *Commonwealth v. DiPadova*, 460 Mass. 424, 439–40 (2011) (appendix providing model jury instruction). *See Commonwealth v. DiPadova*, 460 Mass. at 436 ("where a defendant's substance abuse interacts with a mental disease or defect, that defendant is criminally responsible only if two conditions are true: (1) his mental condition alone, prior to the consumption of the drugs, did not render him criminally irresponsible; and (2) he knew or reasonably should have known that this consumption would cause him to lose substantial capacity to appreciate wrongfulness of conduct or to conform his conduct to the law—that is, would cause him to become criminally irresponsible"); *Commonwealth v. Berry*, 457 Mass. 602, 612–13 (2010) (quoting *Commonwealth v. Brennan*, 399 Mass. 358, 363 (1987) (foreknowledge or reason to know that consumption of drugs or alcohol will trigger latent mental defect nullifies defense of lack of capacity)).

15 This paragraph comes from *Commonwealth v. DiPadova*, 460 Mass. 424, 439–40 (2011) (appendix providing model jury instruction). See *Commonwealth v. DiPadova*, 460 Mass. at 437 (jury should be instructed that "(1) if the defendant's mental illness did not reach the level of a lack of criminal responsibility until he consumed drugs, he was criminally responsible if he knew [or should have known] that the consumption would have the effect of intensifying or exacerbating his mental condition; and, in contrast, (2) if the defendant's mental illness did reach the level of lack of criminal responsibility even in the absence of his consumption of drugs, it was irrelevant whether he took drugs knowing that they would exacerbate that condition" [emphasis in original]); *Commonwealth v. Berry*, 457 Mass. 602, 616–18 (2010) ("defense of lack of criminal responsibility is not defeated where the defendant also consumed alcohol or drugs, as long as the mental disease or defect was the cause of the lack of criminal responsibility . . . . Where a defendant has an active mental disease or defect that caused her to lose the substantial capacity to appreciate the wrongfulness of her conduct or the substantial capacity to conform her conduct to the requirements of the law, the defendant's consumption of alcohol or another drug cannot preclude the defense of lack of criminal responsibility").

16 *Commonwealth v. DiPadova*, 460 Mass. 424, 439–40 (2011) (appendix providing model jury instruction). *See Commonwealth v. DiPadova*, 460 Mass. at 437 (jury should be instructed that "(1) if the defendant's mental illness did not reach the level of a lack of criminal responsibility until he consumed drugs, he was criminally responsible if he knew [or should have known] that the consumption would have the effect of intensifying or exacerbating his mental condition; and, in contrast, (2) if the defendant's mental illness did reach the level of lack of criminal responsibility even in the absence of his consumption of drugs, it was irrelevant whether he took drugs knowing that they would exacerbate that condition" [emphasis in original]); *Commonwealth v. Berry*, 457 Mass. 602, 616–18 (2010) ("defense of lack of criminal responsibility is not defeated where the defendant also consumed alcohol or drugs, as long as the mental disease or defect was the cause of the lack of criminal responsibility . . . . Where a defendant has an active mental disease or defect that caused her to lose the substantial capacity to appreciate the wrongfulness of her conduct or the substantial capacity to conform her conduct to the requirements of the law, the defendant's consumption of alcohol or another drug cannot preclude the defense of lack of criminal responsibility").

17 This paragraph and the factors that follow are taken from *Commonwealth v. DiPadova*, 460 Mass. 424, 439–40 (2011) (appendix providing model jury instruction).

18 *Commonwealth v. DiPadova*, 460 Mass. 424, 439–40 (2011) (appendix providing model jury instruction).

19 *Commonwealth v. Biancardi*, 421 Mass. 251, 251–52 (1995) (quoting *Commonwealth v. Mutina*, 366 Mass. 810, 823 n.12 (1975) ("where the defense of insanity [lack of criminal responsibility] is fairly raised, the defendant, on his timely request, is entitled to an instruction regarding the consequences of a verdict of not guilty by reason of insanity")); *see Commonwealth v. Callahan*, 380 Mass. 821, 827 (1980) (judge may give instruction on his or her own initiative where defendant does not object).

20 *Commonwealth v. Chappell*, 473 Mass. 191, 206, 209 (2015) (appendix).

Joint Venture

[Where there is evidence of joint venture]

The Commonwealth is not required to prove that the defendant himself performed the act that caused the victim's death.[1] However, to establish that a defendant is guilty of murder [or voluntary manslaughter or involuntary manslaughter], the Commonwealth must prove two things beyond a reasonable doubt. First, the Commonwealth must prove that the defendant knowingly participated in the commission of the crime [identify the crime if needed to avoid confusion]. Second, the Commonwealth must prove that he did so with the intent required to commit the crime.[2]

A defendant may knowingly participate in a crime in several ways. He may personally commit the acts that constitute the crime. He may aid or assist another in those acts.[3] He may ask or encourage another person to commit the crime, or help to plan the commission of the crime.[4] Alternatively, the defendant may knowingly participate by agreeing to stand by at or near the scene of the crime to act as a lookout, or by providing aid or assistance in committing the crime, or in escaping, if such help becomes necessary.[5] An agreement to help if needed does not need to be made through a formal or explicit written or oral advance plan or agreement; it is enough if the defendant and at least one other person consciously acted together before or during the crime with the intent of making the crime succeed.[6]

The Commonwealth must also prove beyond a reasonable doubt that, at the time the defendant knowingly participated in the commission of the crime [identify the crime if needed to avoid confusion], he had the intent required for that crime.[7] You are permitted, but not required, to infer the defendant's mental state or intent from his knowledge of the circumstances or any subsequent participation in the crime.[8] The inferences you draw must be reasonable, and you may rely on your experience and common sense in determining the defendant's knowledge and intent.[9]

Mere knowledge that a crime is to be committed is not sufficient to convict the defendant.[10] The Commonwealth must also prove more than mere association with the perpetrator of the crime, either before or after its commission.[11] It must also prove more than a failure to take appropriate steps to prevent the commission of the crime.[12]

Mere presence at the scene of the crime is not enough to find a defendant guilty. Presence alone does not establish a defendant's knowing participation in the crime, even if a person knew about the intended crime in advance and took no steps to prevent it. To find a defendant guilty, there must be proof that the defendant intentionally participated in some fashion in committing that particular crime and that he had or shared the intent required to commit the crime. It is not enough to show that the defendant simply was present when the crime was committed or that he knew about it in advance.[13]

[Where felony-murder is charged]

Where a defendant is charged with felony-murder, the Commonwealth must prove beyond a reasonable doubt that the defendant knowingly participated in the commission of the underlying crime [identify the life felony to avoid confusion], that he did so with the intent required to commit the underlying crime, and that he had or shared the intent to kill, the intent to cause grievous bodily harm, or the intent to do an act which, in the circumstances known to him, a reasonable person would have known created a plain and strong likelihood that death would result.[14]

[Where felony-murder is charged and an underlying offense has as one of its elements the use or possession of a weapon]

Where an element of an offense is that a person who committed the crime possessed, carried, or used a weapon, the Commonwealth must prove beyond a reasonable doubt either that the defendant himself possessed a weapon, or that the defendant knew that a person with whom he participated in the commission of the crime was armed with a weapon.[15] However, mere knowledge that a participant in the crime was armed is not sufficient to hold the defendant liable for the acts of that participant. The Commonwealth must also prove that the defendant knowingly participated in the commission of the crime, with the intent required to commit the crime.[16]

[Note to Judge: Where the defendant claims withdrawal from knowing participation in the commission of the crime and there is evidence supporting this claim, the judge should give the following instruction.[17]]

The defendant is not guilty of knowingly participating in the commission of the crime if there is a reasonable doubt whether he withdrew from the planned crime in an effective and timely manner.[18] A defendant withdraws from a planned crime by clearly communicating his intent not to be involved in the crime and ending his involvement.[19] A withdrawal is effective and timely only if: (1) the defendant withdraws from the planned crime before the commission of the crime has begun; (2) the defendant, by words or conduct, clearly communicates his withdrawal to the other participant[s] in the planned crime; and (3) the communication of the withdrawal is done early enough that the other participant[s] has [have] a reasonable opportunity to abandon the crime.[20] A withdrawal is not timely and effective if it comes so late that the crime cannot reasonably be stopped.[21]

[Note to Judge: Where there is evidence of multiple crimes and that the defendant withdrew from knowing participation in the commission of a subsequent crime after knowingly participating in one or more earlier crimes, the judge should give the following instruction after the withdrawal instruction.[22]]

The defendant is charged with having committed a number of crimes with other participants. For each such crime, the Commonwealth must prove that the defendant was a knowing participant during that crime and did not withdraw in a timely and effective manner. For example, a defendant may knowingly participate in one crime, and thus may be guilty of that offense, but then may withdraw from any later planned crime, and, if the withdrawal is timely and effective, the defendant is not guilty of the later offense.[23]

NOTES

1 *Commonwealth v. Deane*, 458 Mass. 43, 50–51 (2010) ("Commonwealth is not required to prove exactly how a joint venturer participated in the murders . . . or which of the two did the actual killing"); *see Commonwealth v. Zanetti*, 454 Mass. 449, 467, 470–71 (2009) (promulgating model jury instruction); *cf. Commonwealth v. Echavarria*, 428 Mass. 593, 598 & n.3 (1998) (giving "exemplary" example, but one that uses obsolete joint venture language).

2 *Commonwealth v. Deane*, 458 Mass. 43, 50–51 (2010); *Commonwealth v. Zanetti*, 454 Mass. 449, 467–68, 470–71 (2009) (promulgating model jury instruction); *see Commonwealth v. Marrero*, 459 Mass. 235, 247 (2011); *Commonwealth v. Housen*, 458 Mass. 702, 706–07 (2010); G.L. c. 274, § 2.

3 *Commonwealth v. Zanetti*, 454 Mass. 449, 462–64 (2009); *Commonwealth v. Santos*, 440 Mass. 281, 290 (2003); *Commonwealth v. Soares*, 377 Mass. 461, 470, *cert. denied*, 444 U.S. 881 (1979).

4 *Commonwealth v. Zanetti*, 454 Mass. 449, 462–63 (2009); *Commonwealth v. Soares*, 377 Mass. 461, 470, *cert. denied*, 444 U.S. 881 (1979).

5 *Commonwealth v. Mavredakis*, 430 Mass. 848, 863–64 (2000) (quoting *Commonwealth v. Colon–Cruz*, 408 Mass. 533, 545 (1990) (escape)); *Commonwealth v. Miranda*, 441 Mass. 783, 791–92 (2004) (quoting *Commonwealth v. James*, 30 Mass. App. Ct. 490, 499 n.10 (1991) (lookout)).

6 *Commonwealth v. Zanetti*, 454 Mass. 449, 466–67 (2009); *Commonwealth v. Deane*, 458 Mass. 43, 50–51 (2010); *Commonwealth v. Echavarria*, 428 Mass. 593, 598 n.3 (1998).

7 A joint venturer need not be proved to have committed the murder with extreme atrocity or cruelty, as long as one joint venturer committed the killing with extreme atrocity or cruelty. *See Commonwealth v. Chaleumphong*, 434 Mass. 70, 79–80 (2001) (quoting *Commonwealth v. Cunneen*, 389 Mass. 216, 227 (1983) (finding no error in instruction that "[i]t is not necessary for the Commonwealth to prove that [the defendants] had a conscious awareness that the acts were being committed with extreme atrocity or cruelty or that either of them desired the acts to be carried out in that manner. . . . We have consistently held that 'proof of malice aforethought is the only requisite mental intent for a conviction of murder in the first degree based on murder committed with extreme atrocity or cruelty'")).

8 *Commonwealth v. Carnes*, 457 Mass. 812, 823 (2010) (citing *Commonwealth v. Soares*, 377 Mass. 461, 470, *cert. denied*, 444 U.S. 881 (1979)).

9 *See Commonwealth v. Carnes*, 457 Mass. 812, 837 (2010) ("reasonable"); *see Commonwealth v. Zanetti*, 454 Mass. 449, 470 (2009).

10 *Commonwealth v. Soares*, 377 Mass. 461, 471, *cert. denied*, 444 U.S. 881 (1979); *Commonwealth v. Perry*, 357 Mass. 149, 151 (1970).

11 *Commonwealth v. Echavarria*, 428 Mass. 593, 598 n.3 (1998).

12 *Commonwealth v. Zanetti*, 454 Mass. 449, 470–71 (2009) (appendix providing model jury instruction); *Commonwealth v. Maynard*, 436 Mass. 558, 564–65 (2002) (quoting *Commonwealth v. Ortiz*, 424 Mass. 853, 859 (1997)).

13 *Commonwealth v. Deane*, 458 Mass. 43, 58 (2010) (citing *Commonwealth v. Ortiz*, 424 Mass. 853, 859 (1997)); *Commonwealth v. Zanetti*, 454 Mass. 449, 470–71 (2009) (appendix providing model jury instruction).

14 *Commonwealth v. Brown*, 477 Mass. 805, 832 (2017).

15 *Commonwealth v. Britt*, 465 Mass. 87, 100 (2013) ("The Commonwealth should only bear the burden of proving that a joint venturer had knowledge that a member of the joint venture had a weapon where the conviction on a joint venture theory is for a crime that has use or possession of a weapon as an element."). Therefore, "the requirement of knowledge of a weapon in the context of murder in the first degree on a joint venture theory applies only where the conviction is for felony-murder and the underlying felony has as one of its elements the use or possession of a weapon." *Commonwealth v. Britt*, 465 Mass. at 100. Neither possession nor use of a firearm is an element of murder in the first degree based on deliberate premeditation or extreme atrocity or cruelty. *See Commonwealth v. Britt*, 465 Mass. at 100.

16 *Commonwealth v. Akara*, 465 Mass. 245, 254 (2013); *Commonwealth v. Zanetti*, 454 Mass. 449, 467–68 (2009).

17 *Commonwealth v. Rivera*, 464 Mass. 56, 74 (2013) (quoting *Commonwealth v. Miranda*, 458 Mass. 100, 118 (2010) (defendant entitled to withdrawal instruction only where there is evidence of "an appreciable interval between the alleged termination and [the commission of the crime], a detachment from the enterprise before the [crime] has become so probable that it cannot reasonably be stayed, and such notice or definite act of detachment that other principals in the attempted crime have opportunity also to abandon it")).

18 *Commonwealth v. Fickett*, 403 Mass. 194, 201 n.7 (1988).

19 *Commonwealth v. Miranda*, 458 Mass. 100, 118 (2010); *Commonwealth v. Fickett*, 403 Mass. 194, 201 (1988).

20 *See Commonwealth v. Rivera*, 464 Mass. 56, 74 (2013) (quoting *Commonwealth v. Miranda*, 458 Mass. 100, 118 (2010)); *Commonwealth v. Pucillo*, 427 Mass. 108, 116 (1998) (no error where judge instructed jury that "the withdrawal and abandonment must be 'in a timely and effective manner,'" that "if [the] withdrawal comes so late that the crime cannot be stopped, then it is too late and it is not effective," and "that 'a withdrawal is effective only if it is communicated to the other persons in the joint venture'").

21 *Commonwealth v. Pucillo*, 427 Mass. 108, 116 (1998).

22 *Commonwealth v. Hogan*, 426 Mass. 424, 434 (1998).

23 *Commonwealth v. Hogan*, 426 Mass. 424, 434 (1998).

Self-Defense and Defense of Another

Self-Defense

[Note to Judge: This instruction, at the discretion of the judge, may be given as a standalone instruction prior to the murder instruction or inserted within the murder instruction.[1] The instruction is to be used where the evidence, viewed in the light most favorable to the defendant,[2] raises an issue of deadly force in self-defense.[3] An instruction on self-defense is generally not warranted where the theory of murder is felony-murder alone, but might be warranted where the killing occurred during the defendant's escape or attempted escape, or where the defendant was unarmed and the victim was the first to use deadly force.[4] If the Commonwealth is entitled to an instruction on murder and felony-murder, the judge should generally instruct the jury that this instruction does not apply to felony-murder because the Commonwealth is not required to prove the absence of self-defense to prove felony-murder.]

Since this case raises a question as to whether the defendant properly used force to defend himself from an attack, I will provide you with instructions concerning the law governing the use of deadly force in self-defense before discussing the elements of the crime of murder.

A person is not guilty of any crime if he acted in proper self-defense.[5] When I use the term "proper self-defense," I am distinguishing self-defense that is both justified and proportional and therefore a complete defense to the crime, from self-defense that is justified, but where excessive force is used. It is the Commonwealth's burden to prove beyond a reasonable doubt that the defendant did not act in proper self-defense.[6] The defendant does not have the burden to prove that he acted in proper self-defense. If the Commonwealth fails to prove beyond a reasonable doubt that the defendant did not act in proper self-defense, then you must find the defendant not guilty.[7]

The law does not permit retaliation or revenge.[8] The proper exercise of self-defense arises from necessity of the moment and ends when the necessity ends.[9] An individual may only use sufficient force to prevent occurrence or reoccurrence of the attack.[10] The question of what force is needed in self-defense, however, is to be considered with due regard for human impulses and passions, and is not to be judged too strictly.[11]

The Commonwealth satisfies its burden of proving that the defendant did not act in proper self-defense if it proves any one of the following four [or five] propositions beyond a reasonable doubt:[12]

1. The defendant did not actually believe that he was in immediate danger of death or serious bodily harm from which he could save himself only by using deadly force.[13] Deadly force is force that is intended or likely to cause death or serious bodily harm.[14]

2. A reasonable person in the same circumstances as the defendant would not reasonably have believed that he was in immediate danger of death or serious bodily harm from which he could save himself only by using deadly force.[15]

3. The defendant did not use or attempt to use all proper and reasonable means under the circumstances to avoid physical combat before resorting to the use of deadly force.[16]

4. The defendant used more force than was reasonably necessary under all the circumstances.[17]

5. *[Where there is evidence the defendant was the initial aggressor]* The defendant was the first to use or threaten deadly force, and did not withdraw in good faith from the conflict and clearly communicate by words or conduct to the person (or persons) he provoked his intention to withdraw and end the confrontation without any use of, or additional use of, force.[18]

I will now discuss each of these four [or five] propositions in more detail, and remind you that the Commonwealth may satisfy its burden of proving that the defendant did not act in proper self-defense by proving any one of these propositions beyond a reasonable doubt:

The first proposition is that the defendant did not actually believe that he was in immediate danger of death or serious bodily harm from which he could save himself only by using deadly force.[19]

The second proposition is that a reasonable person in the same circumstances as the defendant would not reasonably have believed that he was in immediate danger of death or serious bodily harm from which he could save himself only by using deadly force.[20]

In considering whether or not the defendant actually believed that he was in immediate danger of death or serious bodily harm, and the reasonableness of that belief that he was in such danger, you may consider all the circumstances bearing on the defendant's state of mind at the time.[21, 22] Moreover, in determining whether the defendant was reasonably in fear of death or serious bodily harm, you may consider any or all of the following:

- evidence of the deceased's reputation as a violent or quarrelsome person, but only if that reputation was known to the defendant;[23]
- evidence of other instances of the deceased's violent conduct, but only if the defendant knew of such conduct;[24] and
- evidence of threats of violence made by the deceased against the defendant, but again, only if the defendant was aware of such threats.[25]

[Where there is evidence the defendant at the time of the offense had a mental impairment or was under the influence of alcohol or drugs] You may consider the defendant's mental condition at the time of the killing, including any credible evidence of mental impairment or the effect on the defendant of his consumption of alcohol or drugs, in determining whether the defendant actually believed that he was in immediate danger of serious bodily harm or death, but not in determining whether a reasonable person in those circumstances would have believed he was in immediate danger.[26]

[Where the evidence raises an issue of mistaken belief] A person may use deadly force to defend himself even if he had a mistaken belief that he was in immediate danger of serious bodily harm or death, provided that the defendant's mistaken belief was reasonable based on all of the circumstances presented in the case.[27]

The third proposition is that the defendant did not use or attempt to use all proper and reasonable means under the circumstances to avoid physical combat before resorting to the use of deadly force.[28] Whether a defendant used all reasonable means to avoid physical combat before resorting to the use of deadly force depends on all of the circumstances, including the relative physical capabilities of the combatants, the weapons used, the availability of room to maneuver or escape from the area, and the location of the assault.[29]

[For self-defense cases not under the "castle law," G.L. c. 278, § 8A] A person must retreat unless he reasonably believes that he cannot safely do so. A person need not place himself in danger or use every means of escape short of death before resorting to self-defense.[30]

[For self-defense cases under the "castle law," G.L. c. 278, § 8A] A person who is lawfully residing in his house, apartment or some other dwelling is not required to retreat before using reasonable force against an unlawful intruder, if the resident reasonably believes that the intruder is about to kill or seriously injure him or another person lawfully in the dwelling, and also reasonably believes that such force is necessary to protect himself or the other person lawfully in the dwelling.[31]

The fourth proposition is that the defendant used more force than was reasonably necessary under all the circumstances.[32] In considering whether the force used by a person was reasonable under the circumstances, you may consider evidence of the relative physical capabilities of the combatants, the number of persons who were involved on each side, the characteristics of any weapons used, the availability of room to maneuver, the manner in which the deadly force was used, the scope of the threat presented, or any other factor you deem relevant to the reasonableness of the person's conduct under the circumstances.[33]

[Where there is evidence the defendant was the initial aggressor] The fifth proposition is that the defendant was the first to use or threaten deadly force, and did not withdraw in good faith from the conflict and announce to the person (or persons) he provoked his intention to withdraw and end the confrontation without any use of or additional use of force.[34]

Self-defense cannot be claimed by a defendant who was the first to use or threaten deadly force, because a defendant must have used or attempted to use all proper and reasonable means under the circumstances to avoid physical combat before resorting to the use of deadly force.[35] A defendant who was the first to use or threaten deadly force, in order to claim self-defense, must withdraw in good faith from the conflict and announce to the person (or persons) he provoked his intention to withdraw and end the confrontation without the use of force or additional force.[36]

[Note to Judge: In appropriate cases, add the following instruction: However, if the defendant was the first to use nondeadly force but the deceased [or a third party acting together with the deceased] was the first to use deadly force, such as by escalating a simple fist-fight into a knife fight, the defendant may claim self-defense where he responded to the escalation with deadly force.[37]]

For the purpose of determining who attacked whom first in the altercation, you may consider evidence of the deceased's [and a third party acting together with the deceased's] past violent conduct, whether or not the defendant knew of it.[38]

[Note to Judge: Where the evidence, viewed in the light most favorable to the defendant, would permit the jury to find that the force used by the defendant in killing the victim was either deadly or nondeadly force, the defendant is entitled to instructions on the use of both deadly and non-deadly force in self-defense and the jury shall decide on the type of force used.[39]]

NOTES

1 *Commonwealth v. Santiago*, 425 Mass. 491, 506 (1997) ("Although it is generally preferable to instruct on the elements of a defense to a crime after describing the elements of the crime, a specific order in jury instructions is not required").

2 *Commonwealth v. Espada*, 450 Mass. 687, 692 (2008) ("A defendant is entitled to have the jury . . . instructed on the law relating to self-defense if the evidence, viewed in its light most favorable to him, is sufficient to raise the issue." [citation omitted]).

3 *See Commonwealth v. Gonzalez*, 465 Mass. 672, 682–85 (2013) (discussing evidence required for self-defense instruction).

4 An instruction on self-defense is generally not available to a defendant where the defendant committed a felony punishable by life imprisonment that provoked a victim to respond with deadly force. *See Commonwealth v. Rogers*, 459 Mass. 249, 260 (2011) ("Generally, in Massachusetts, one who commits an armed robbery cannot assert a claim of self-defense"); *Commonwealth v. Vives*, 447 Mass. 537, 544 n.6 (2006) ("The right to claim self-defense is forfeited by one who commits armed robbery"); *Commonwealth v. Maguire*, 375 Mass. 768, 773 (1978) ("it has been held that the right to claim self-defense may be forfeited by one who commits an armed robbery, even if excessive force is used by the intended victim"). The rationale for this rule is that the nature of the underlying felony marks the defendant as the "initiating and dangerous aggressor." *Commonwealth v. Rogers*, 459 Mass. at 260 (quoting *Commonwealth v. Garner*, 59 Mass. App. Ct. 350, 363 n.14 (2003)). However, a self-defense instruction might be appropriate where the killing occurred during the defendant's escape or attempted escape, *see Commonwealth v. Rogers*, 459 Mass. at 260–61, or where the defendant was unarmed and the victim was the first to use deadly force. *See Commonwealth v. Chambers*, 465 Mass. 520, 530 (2013) ("critical question in determining whether the Commonwealth proved that the defendant did not act in self-defense when he killed the victim was who first grabbed the kitchen knife that ultimately was the instrument of death, not who shouted first or who struck the first punch"). *See generally Commonwealth v. Chambers*, 465 Mass. at 528 ("in the context of homicide, a defendant may lose the right to claim self-defense only if he was the first to use or threaten deadly force").

5 *Commonwealth v. Rogers*, 459 Mass. 249, 269–70 (2011) ("if the defendant acted with reasonable force in self-defense, he was entitled . . . to a verdict of not guilty").

6 *Commonwealth v. King*, 460 Mass. 80, 83 (2011) ("Commonwealth bears the burden of proving, beyond a reasonable doubt, that the defendant did not act in self-defense"); *Commonwealth v. Glacken*, 451 Mass. 163, 166–67 (2008) (quoting *Commonwealth v. Williams*, 450 Mass. 879, 882 (2008) ("To obtain a conviction of murder '[w]here the evidence raises a question of self-defense, the burden is on the government to prove beyond a reasonable doubt that the defendant did not act in self-defense'")).

7 *See Commonwealth v. Glacken*, 451 Mass. 163, 166–67 (2008).

8 *See Commonwealth v. Pike*, 428 Mass. 393, 398 (1998) (self-defense theory not submitted to jury where evidence showed defendant used force out of "anger or revenge").

9 *Commonwealth v. Santos*, 454 Mass. 770, 782–83 (approving of prior jury instruction); Commonwealth v. Kendrick, 351 Mass. 203, 212 (1966) ("right of self-defense arises from necessity, and ends when the necessity ends").

10 *Commonwealth v. King*, 460 Mass. 80, 83 (2011) ("force that was used was greater than necessary in all the circumstances of the case"); *Commonwealth v. Kendrick*, 351 Mass. 203, 211–12 (1966).

11 *Commonwealth v. Kendrick*, 351 Mass. 203, 211 (quoting *Monize v. Begaso*, 190 Mass. 87, 89 (1906)).

12 *See Commonwealth v. Glacken*, 451 Mass. 163, 167 (2008) (enumerating required factors for self-defense).

13 *Commonwealth v. Wallace*, 460 Mass. 118, 124–25 (2011) (quoting *Commonwealth v. Hart*, 428 Mass. 614, 615 (1999) ("If deadly force is used, a self-defense instruction must be given only if the evidence permits at least a reasonable doubt that the defendant reasonably and actually believed that he was in imminent danger of death or serious bodily harm, from which he could save himself only by using deadly force")); *see Commonwealth v. Santos*, 454 Mass. 770, 773 (2009); *Commonwealth v. Diaz*, 453 Mass. 266, 280 (2009) (quoting *Commonwealth v. Harrington*, 379 Mass. 446, 450 (1980)).

14 *Commonwealth v. Noble*, 429 Mass. 44, 46 (1999) ("force intended or likely to cause death or serious bodily harm"); *Commonwealth v. Cataldo*, 423 Mass. 318, 321 (1996) (quoting *Commonwealth v. Klein*, 372 Mass. 823, 827 (1977)).

15 *Commonwealth v. Wallace*, 460 Mass. 118, 124–25 (2011); *Commonwealth v. Santos*, 454 Mass. 770, 773 (2009).

16 *Commonwealth v. Mercado*, 456 Mass. 198, 209 (2010) (citing *Commonwealth v. Benoit*, 452 Mass. 212, 226 (2008) ("privilege to use self-defense arises only in circumstances in which the defendant uses all proper means to avoid physical combat")).

17 *Commonwealth v. Glacken*, 451 Mass. 163, 167 (2008) ("defendant used more force than was reasonably necessary in all the circumstances of the case").

18 *Commonwealth v. Chambers*, 465 Mass. 520, 528 (2013) (quoting *Commonwealth v. Maguire*, 375 Mass. 768, 772 (1978) ("a criminal defendant who is found to have been the first aggressor loses the right to claim self-defense unless he 'withdraws in good faith from the conflict and announces his intention to retire'")).

19 *Commonwealth v. Hart*, 428 Mass. 614, 615 (1999) (quoting *Commonwealth v. Wallace*, 460 Mass. 118, 124–25 (2011) ("If deadly force is used, a self-defense instruction must be given only if the evidence permits at least a reasonable doubt that the defendant reasonably and actually believed that he was in imminent danger of death or serious bodily harm, from which he could save himself only by using deadly force")); *see Commonwealth v. Santos*, 454 Mass. 770, 773 (2009); *Commonwealth v. Diaz*, 453 Mass. 266, 280 (2009).

20 *Commonwealth v. Wallace*, 460 Mass. 118, 124–25 (2011); *Commonwealth v. Santos*, 454 Mass. 770, 773 (2009).

21 *See Commonwealth v. Santos*, 454 Mass. 770, 773 (2009) ("person using a dangerous weapon [or deadly force] in self-defense must also have actually believed that he was in imminent danger of serious harm or death"); *Commonwealth v. Little*, 431 Mass. 782, 787 (2000).

22 In deciding whether the evidence in the case, viewed in the light most favorable to the defendant, raises a question of self-defense, a judge may consider, among other evidence:

"(a) evidence that the defendant is or has been the victim of acts of physical, sexual or psychological harm or abuse;

"(b) evidence by expert testimony regarding the common pattern in abusive relationships; the nature and effects of physical, sexual or psychological abuse and typical responses thereto, including how those effects relate to the perception of the imminent nature of the threat of death or serious bodily harm; the relevant facts and circumstances which form the basis for such opinion; and evidence whether the defendant displayed characteristics common to victims of abuse."

G.L. c. 233, § 23F; *see Commonwealth v. Anestal*, 463 Mass. 655, 676 (2012) ("psychological consequences of a history of abuse are relevant to the consideration whether the defendant was in fear of serious injury or death").

23 *Commonwealth v. Clemente*, 452 Mass. 295, 308 (2008) (citing *Commonwealth v. Fontes*, 396 Mass. 733, 734–35 (1986) ("The judge instructed in regard to the reputation evidence that the jury could consider whether the victim had a reputation as a 'violent or quarrelsome person that was known to the defendant before the alleged incident.' That instruction was and is a correct statement of the law")).

24 *Commonwealth v. Adjutant*, 443 Mass. 649, 654 (2005) (quoting *Commonwealth v. Fontes*, 396 Mass. 733, 735, 737 (1986) ("Massachusetts has long followed the evidentiary rule that permits the introduction of evidence of the victim's violent character, if known to the defendant, as it bears on the defendant's state of mind and the reasonableness of his actions in claiming to have acted in self-defense")); *Commonwealth v. Rodriquez*, 418 Mass. 1, 5 (1994) (quoting *Commonwealth v. Fontes*, 396 Mass. 733, 735 (1986), and *Commonwealth v. Pidge*, 400 Mass. 350, 353 (1987) ("It is well established that a defendant asserting self-defense is allowed to introduce evidence showing 'that at the time of the killing [she] knew of specific violent acts recently committed by the victim'" because such evidence is relevant in determining "whether the defendant acted justifiably in reasonable apprehension of bodily harm")).

25 *Commonwealth v. Pidge*, 400 Mass. 350, 353 (1987); *Commonwealth v. Edmonds*, 365 Mass. 496, 502 (1974). Where a defendant has been the victim of abuse, evidence of abuse and expert testimony regarding the consequences of abuse are admissible and may be considered by the jury with respect to the reasonableness of a defendant's apprehension that death or serious bodily injury was imminent, the reasonableness of a defendant's belief that he had used all available means to avoid physical combat, and the reasonableness of a defendant's perception of the amount of force needed to deal with the threat. *See* G.L. c. 233, § 23F.

26 *Cf. Commonwealth v. Barros*, 425 Mass. 572, 576 (1997) ("determination as to whether a defendant's belief concerning his exposure to danger was reasonable may not take into account his intoxication").

27 *Commonwealth v. Pike*, 428 Mass. 393, 396–97 (1998) ("If the defendant's apprehension of grievous bodily harm or death, though mistaken, was reasonable, his actions in self-defense may be justifiable").

28 *Commonwealth v. Mercado*, 456 Mass. 198, 209 (2010) (citing Commonwealth v. Benoit, 452 Mass. 212, 226 (2008) ("privilege to use self-defense arises only in circumstances in which the defendant uses all proper means to avoid physical combat")).

29 *Commonwealth v. Pike*, 428 Mass. 393, 399 (1998) ("Whether a defendant used all reasonable means of escape before acting in self-defense is a factual question dependent on a variety of circumstances, including the relative physical capabilities of the combatants, the weapons used, the availability of maneuver room in, or means of escape from, the area, and the location of the assault").

30 *Commonwealth v. Benoit*, 452 Mass. 212, 226–27 (2008) (quoting *Commonwealth v. Pike*, 428 Mass. 393, 398 (1998) ("A self-defense instruction is not required unless there is some evidence that the defendant availed himself of all means, proper and reasonable in the circumstances, of retreating from the conflict before resorting to the use of deadly force. 'This rule does not impose an absolute duty to retreat regardless of personal safety considerations; an individual need not place himself in danger nor use every means of escape short of death before resorting to self-defense. . . . He must, however, use every reasonable avenue of escape available to him'" [citations omitted])); cf. *Commonwealth v. Peloquin*, 437 Mass. 204, 212 (2002) (noting in dicta that set of jury "instructions, taken as a whole, explained that a defendant need not retreat unless he can do so in safety, and need not do so when he would increase the danger to his own life").

31 This instruction is required by G.L. c. 278, § 8A, which provides that, where "an occupant of a dwelling . . . was in his dwelling at the time of the offense and . . . acted in the reasonable belief that the person unlawfully in [the] dwelling was about to inflict great bodily injury or death upon [the] occupant or upon another person lawfully in [the] dwelling, and that [the] occupant used reasonable means to defend himself or such other person lawfully in [the] dwelling[, that] [t]here shall be no duty on [the] occupant to retreat from [the] person unlawfully in [the] dwelling." This instruction is not appropriate where the occupant of a dwelling uses force on another person lawfully in the dwelling. *See Commonwealth v. Peloquin*, 437 Mass. 204, 208 (2002) ("Nothing in G.L. c. 278, § 8A, . . . eliminates the duty on the part of the occupant of the dwelling to retreat from a confrontation with a person who is lawfully on the premises"); *see also Commonwealth v. Carlino*, 449 Mass. 71, 76 (2007) (instruction not warranted where fatal encounter occurs outside of dwelling, in driveway); *Commonwealth v. McKinnon*, 446 Mass. 263, 267–68 (2006) (same; outside stairs and porch).

32 *Commonwealth v. Glacken*, 451 Mass. 163, 167 (2008) ("defendant used more force than was reasonably necessary in all the circumstances of the case").

33 *Commonwealth v. Walker*, 443 Mass. 213, 218 (2005); *Commonwealth v. King*, 460 Mass. 80, 83 & n.2, 87 (2011), affirming the factors given in *Commonwealth v. Kendrick*, 351 Mass. 203, 212 (1966) ("jury should consider evidence of the relative physical capabilities of the combatants, the characteristics of the weapons used, and the availability of maneuver room in, or means of escape from, the . . . area").

34 *Commonwealth v. Chambers*, 465 Mass. 520, 528 (2013) (quoting *Commonwealth v. Maguire*, 375 Mass. 768, 772 (1978) ("a criminal defendant who is found to have been the first aggressor loses the right to claim self-defense unless he 'withdraws in good faith from the conflict and announces his intention to retire'")).

35 *See Commonwealth v. Barbosa*, 463 Mass. 116, 136 (2012) (quoting *Commonwealth v. Maguire*, 375 Mass. 768, 772 (1978) ("right of self-defense ordinarily cannot be claimed by a person who provokes or initiates an assault")); *see also Commonwealth v. Harris*, 464 Mass. 425, 435–36 & n.11 (2013) (noting that instruction that "[a] person who provokes or initiates an assault ordinarily cannot claim the right of self-defense" is "potentially overbroad because it does not define what constitutes provocation of the type that results in the forfeiture of a self-defense claim" and advising judges to "make clear that conduct involving only the use of nonthreatening words will not be sufficient to qualify a defendant as a first aggressor").

36 *Commonwealth v. Pring-Wilson*, 448 Mass. 718, 733 (2007) (quoting *Commonwealth v. Maguire*, 375 Mass. 768, 772 (1978) ("right of self-defense ordinarily cannot be claimed by a person who provokes or initiates an assault unless that person withdraws in good faith from the conflict and announces his intention to retire")).

37 *Commonwealth v. Chambers*, 465 Mass. 520, 528 (2013) ("in the context of homicide, a defendant may lose the right to claim self-defense only if he was the first to use or threaten deadly force"); *see Commonwealth v. Harris*, 464 Mass. 425, 436 n.12 (2013) ("when a first aggressor or initial aggressor instruction is given in the context of self-defense we advise that the judge make clear that conduct involving only the use of nonthreatening words will not be sufficient to qualify a defendant as a first aggressor").

38 *Commonwealth v. Pring-Wilson*, 448 Mass. 718, 736–38 (2007) (quoting *Commonwealth v. Adjutant*, 443 Mass. 649, 664 (2005) (evidence of violent conduct, even when defendant did not know of such conduct, admissible to resolve contested identity of likely first attacker; "where the identity of the first aggressor is in dispute and the victim has a history of violence . . . trial judge has the discretion to admit evidence of specific acts of prior violent conduct that the victim is reasonably alleged to have initiated, to support the defendant's claim of self-defense")).

39 *Commonwealth v. King*, 460 Mass. 80, 83 (2011).

Deadly or Nondeadly Force

Deadly force is force that is intended to or likely to cause death or serious bodily harm. Nondeadly force, by contrast, is

7

force that is not intended to or likely to cause death or serious bodily harm.[1] You must determine whether the Commonwealth has proved beyond a reasonable doubt that the defendant used deadly force. If you have a reasonable doubt whether the defendant used deadly force, but are convinced that he used some force, then you must consider whether the defendant used nondeadly force in self-defense. If the defendant had reasonable grounds to believe that he was in immediate danger of harm from which he could save himself only by using nondeadly force, and had availed himself of all reasonable means to avoid physical combat before resorting to nondeadly force, then the defendant had the right to use the nondeadly force reasonably necessary to avert the threatened harm, but he could use no more force than was reasonable and proper under the circumstances. You must consider the proportionality of the force used to the threat of immediate harm in assessing the reasonableness of non-deadly force.[2]

1 *Commonwealth v. Cataldo*, 423 Mass. 318, 325 (1996) ("force neither intended nor likely to cause death or great bodily harm"); *Commonwealth v. Lopes*, 440 Mass. 731, 739 (2004) (using one's fists is non-deadly force).

2 *Commonwealth v. King*, 460 Mass. 80, 83 (2011) (quoting *Commonwealth v. Franchino*, 61 Mass. App. Ct. 367, 368–69 (2004) ("(1) the defendant had reasonable concern for his personal safety; (2) he used all reasonable means to avoid physical combat; and (3) 'the degree of force used was reasonable in the circumstances, with proportionality being the touchstone for assessing reasonableness'")); *Commonwealth v. Adams*, 458 Mass. 766, 774 (2011); *Commonwealth v. Lopes*, 440 Mass. 731, 739 (2004) (quoting *Commonwealth v. Baseler*, 419 Mass. 500, 502–03 (1995) ("use of nondeadly force is justified at a lower level of danger, in circumstances giving rise to a 'reasonable concern over his personal safety'")); *Commonwealth v. Noble*, 429 Mass. 44, 46 (1999).

Defense of Another

[Note to Judge: As with self-defense, this instruction may be given, in the discretion of the judge, as a standalone instruction prior to the murder instruction or inserted within the murder instruction.[1] The instruction is to be used where the evidence, viewed in the light most favorable to the defendant,[2] raises an issue of deadly force in defense of another.[3] An instruction on defense of another is generally not warranted where the theory of murder is felony-murder alone, but might be warranted where the killing occurred during the defendant's escape or attempted escape or where the defendant and the third person were unarmed and the victim was the first to use deadly force.[4] If the Commonwealth is entitled to an instruction on murder and felony-murder, the judge should generally instruct the jury that this instruction does not apply to felony-murder because the Commonwealth is not generally required to prove the absence of defense of another to prove felony-murder.[5]

Because the issue of defense of another generally arises where there is also an issue of self-defense, the instruction below is premised on the jury having earlier been instructed as to the law of self-defense. Where an issue of defense of another arises without an issue of self-defense, the judge may still need to explain the law of self-defense to assist the jury in understanding the law of defense of another, because the jury are required to determine whether, based on the circumstances known to the defendant, a reasonable person would believe that the other person was justified in using deadly force to protect himself.]

7

A person is not guilty of any crime if he acted in proper defense of another. It is the Commonwealth's burden to prove beyond a reasonable doubt that the defendant did not act in proper defense of another. The defendant does not have the burden to prove that he acted in proper defense of another. If the Commonwealth fails to prove beyond a reasonable doubt that the defendant did not act in proper defense of another, then you must find the defendant not guilty.[6]

The Commonwealth may satisfy its burden of proving that the defendant did not act in proper defense of another by proving any one of the following three propositions beyond a reasonable doubt:[7]

1. The defendant did not actually believe that the other person was in immediate danger of death or serious bodily harm from which the other person could save himself only by using deadly force. You need not determine whether the other person actually believed himself to be in immediate danger of death or serious bodily harm; you must focus instead on whether the defendant actually had that belief.[8]

2. A reasonable person in the circumstances known to the defendant would not have believed that the other person was in immediate danger of death or serious bodily harm from which the other person could save himself only by using deadly force. You need not determine whether a reasonable person in the circumstances known to the other person would have believed himself to be in immediate danger of death or serious bodily harm; you must focus instead on what a reasonable person in the circumstances known to the defendant would have believed.[9]

3. A reasonable person in the circumstances known to the defendant would not have believed that the other person was justified in using deadly force to protect himself.[10]

[Note to Judge: Where the evidence, viewed in the light most favorable to the defendant, would permit the jury to find that the force used by the defendant in killing the victim was either deadly or nondeadly force, the defendant is entitled to instructions on the use of both deadly and non-deadly force in defense of another and the jury shall decide on the type of force used.[11]]

NOTES

1 *Commonwealth v. Santiago*, 425 Mass. 491, 506 (1997) ("Although it is generally preferable to instruct on the elements of a defense to a crime after describing the elements of the crime, a specific order in jury instructions is not required").

2 *Commonwealth v. Okoro*, 471 Mass. 51, 68 (2015) ("A judge must instruct the jury on defense of another where the evidence when viewed in the light most favorable to the defendant could support a finding that the use of force was justified on this basis").

3 *Commonwealth v. Barbosa*, 463 Mass. 116, 135–36 (2012).

4 The law governing self-defense is generally instructive regarding defense of another. An instruction on self-defense is generally not available to a defendant where the defendant committed a felony punishable by life imprisonment that provoked a victim to respond with deadly force. *See Commonwealth v. Rogers*, 459 Mass. 249, 260 (2011) ("Generally, in Massachusetts, one who commits an armed robbery cannot assert a claim of self-defense."); *Commonwealth v. Vives*, 447 Mass. 537, 544 n.6 (2006) ("The right to claim self-defense is forfeited by one who commits armed robbery"); *Commonwealth v. Maguire*, 375 Mass. 768, 773 (1978) ("it has been held that the right to claim self-defense may be forfeited by one who commits an armed robbery, even if excessive force is used by the intended victim"). The rationale for this rule is that the nature of the underlying felony marks the defendant as the "initiating and dangerous aggressor." *Commonwealth v. Rogers*, 459 Mass. at 260 (quoting *Commonwealth v. Garner*, 59 Mass. App. Ct. 350, 363 n.14 (2003)). However, a self-defense instruction might be appropriate where the killing occurred during the defendant's escape or attempted escape, *see Commonwealth v. Rogers*, 459 Mass. at 260–61, or where the defendant was unarmed and the victim was the first to use deadly force. *See Commonwealth v. Chambers*, 465 Mass. 520, 530 (2013) ("critical question in determining whether the Commonwealth proved that the defendant did not act in self-defense when he killed the victim was who first grabbed the kitchen knife that ultimately was the instrument of death, not who shouted first or who struck the first punch"). *See generally Commonwealth v. Chambers*, 465 Mass. at 528 ("in the context of homicide, a defendant may lose the right to claim self-defense only if he was the first to use or threaten deadly force").

5 If the evidence, viewed in the light most favorable to the defendant, supports a finding that the defendant acted in proper defense of another, the court must instruct the jury on defense of another, including cases where the Commonwealth is proceeding on a theory of felony-murder. *See generally Commonwealth v. Brown*, 477 Mass. 805 (2017); *Commonwealth v. Fantauzzi*, 91 Mass. App. Ct. 194 (2017) (where underlying felony is the unlawful possession of a firearm, Commonwealth in some circumstances may need to prove the absence of self-defense). If the Commonwealth is proceeding on a theory of felony-murder, a separate instruction regarding proper defense of another may be re-

quired where defense of another is raised in connection with the underlying felony.

6 *See Commonwealth v. Glacken*, 451 Mass. 163, 166–67 (2008).

7 *See Commonwealth v. Young*, 461 Mass. 198, 208 (2012) (enumerating required factors for defense of another); *Commonwealth v. Martin*, 369 Mass. 640, 649 (1976) (same).

8 *See Commonwealth v. Barbosa*, 463 Mass. 116, 135–36 (2012); *Commonwealth v. Young*, 461 Mass. 198, 209 & n.19 (2012); *Commonwealth v. Martin*, 369 Mass. 640, 649 (1976).

9 *See Commonwealth v. Young*, 461 Mass. 198, 209 & n.19 (2012) (circumstances must be viewed from perspective of intervening defendant, not third party; "whether the third party was, in retrospect, actually entitled to use self-defense is not a consideration"); *see also Commonwealth v. Barbosa*, 463 Mass. 116, 135–36 (2012).

10 *See Commonwealth v. Young*, 461 Mass. 198, 208 (2012) (quoting *Commonwealth v. Martin*, 369 Mass. 640, 649 (1976)); *see also Commonwealth v. Barbosa*, 463 Mass. 116, 135–36 (2012).

11 *Commonwealth v. King*, 460 Mass. 80, 83 (2011).

Deadly or Nondeadly Force

Deadly force is force that is intended to or likely to cause death or serious bodily harm. Nondeadly force, by contrast, is force that is not intended to or likely to cause death or serious bodily harm.[1] If the defendant, based on the circumstances known to the defendant, had reasonable grounds to believe (1) that the other person was in immediate danger of harm from which the other person could save himself only by using nondeadly force, and (2) that the other person was justified in using nondeadly force to protect himself, then the defendant had the right to use whatever nondeadly means were reasonably necessary to avert the threatened harm, but he could use no more force than was reasonable and proper under the circumstances. You must consider the proportionality of the force used to the threat of immediate harm in assessing the reasonableness of nondeadly force.[2]

NOTES

1 *Commonwealth v. Cataldo*, 423 Mass. 318, 325 (1996) ("force neither intended nor likely to cause death or great bodily harm"); *see Commonwealth v. Lopes*, 440 Mass. 731, 739 (2004) (using one's fists is nondeadly force).

2 *See Commonwealth v. King*, 460 Mass. 80, 83 (2011) ("(1) the defendant had reasonable concern for his personal safety; (2) he used all reasonable means to avoid physical combat; and (3) 'the degree of force used was reasonable in the circumstances, with proportionality being the touchstone for assessing reasonableness'"); *Commonwealth v. Adams*, 458 Mass. 766, 774 (2011); *Commonwealth v. Lopes*, 440 Mass. 731, 739 ("use of nondeadly force is justified at a lower level of danger, in circumstances giving rise to a 'reasonable concern over his personal safety'"); *Commonwealth v. Noble*, 429 Mass. 44, 46 (1999).

Murder in the First Degree

There are two different degrees of murder: murder in the first degree and murder in the second degree. If you find the defendant guilty of murder, you shall decide the degree of murder.

The Commonwealth alleges that the defendant committed murder in the first degree on the following theories: *[list theory or theories as follows: murder with deliberate premeditation, murder with extreme atrocity or cruelty, and/or murder in the commission or attempted commission of a felony punishable by a maximum sentence of life.]*

To find the defendant guilty on this theory [any of these theories] of murder, you must be unanimous, that is, all the deliberating jurors must agree that the Commonwealth has met its burden of proving every required element of that theory beyond a reasonable doubt. You should check the appropriate box or boxes on the verdict slip as to each theory on which you agree unanimously.

If you are unable to agree unanimously that the Commonwealth has met its burden to prove beyond a reasonable doubt any [either] of these theories of first degree murder, you shall consider whether the Commonwealth has proved the defendant guilty beyond a reasonable doubt of murder in the second degree.

[Where the jury are to be instructed on voluntary and/or involuntary manslaughter] If you are unable to agree unanimously that the Commonwealth has met its burden to prove beyond a reasonable doubt that the defendant is guilty of murder in the first degree or murder in the second degree, you shall consider whether the Commonwealth has proved the defendant guilty beyond a reasonable doubt of the lesser offenses of voluntary manslaughter or involuntary manslaughter.[1]

I will begin by instructing you on the elements *[and additional requirements of proof]* for each of these theories of murder in the first degree. I will next instruct you on murder in the second degree. *[I will then instruct you on voluntary manslaughter and involuntary manslaughter.]* I will then review the verdict slip with you.

NOTE

1 *Commonwealth v. Figueroa*, 468 Mass. 204, 229 n.11 (2014).

Murder with Deliberate Premeditation

I will first define the elements of murder in the first degree with deliberate premeditation. To prove the defendant guilty of murder in the first degree with deliberate premeditation, the Commonwealth must prove beyond a reasonable doubt the following elements:

1. The defendant caused the death of [victim's name].
2. The defendant intended to kill [victim's name], that is, the defendant consciously and purposefully intended to cause [victim's name] death.
3. The defendant committed the killing with deliberate premeditation, that is, he decided to kill after a period of reflection.
4. [Where there is evidence of self-defense or defense of another] The defendant did not act in proper self-defense or in the proper defense of another.
5. *[Where there is evidence of mitigating circumstances]* In addition to these elements, the Commonwealth must also prove that there were no mitigating circumstances.

I will now discuss each of these requirements in more detail. The first element is that the defendant caused the death of [victim's name]. A defendant's act is the cause of death where the act, in a natural and continuous sequence, results in death, and without which death would not have occurred.[1]

7

The second element is that the defendant intended to kill [the victim], that is, the defendant consciously and purposefully intended to cause [the victim's] death.[2]

[Where there is evidence of accident] If you have a reasonable doubt as to whether the victim's death was accidental, because the death was caused by a negligent, careless, or mistaken act of the defendant, or resulted from a cause separate from the defendant's conduct, you may not find that the Commonwealth has proved this element of intent to kill the victim.[3]

[Where there is evidence of transferred intent] If the defendant intends to kill a person and, in attempting to do so, mistakenly kills another person, such as a bystander, the defendant is treated under the law as if he intended to kill the actual victim. This is referred to as transferred intent under the law. For example, if I aim and fire a gun at one person intending to kill him but instead mistakenly kill another person, the law treats me as if I intended to kill the actual victim. My intent to kill the intended victim is transferred to the actual victim.[4]

The third element is that the defendant committed the killing with deliberate premeditation, that is, he decided to kill after a period of reflection. Deliberate premeditation does not require any particular length of time of reflection. A decision to kill may be formed over a period of days, hours, or even a few seconds.[5] The key is the sequence of the thought process: first the consideration whether to kill; second, the decision to kill; and third, the killing arising from the decision.[6] There is no deliberate premeditation where the action is taken so quickly that a defendant takes no time to reflect on the action and then decides to do it.[7]

[Where there is evidence of mental impairment or consumption of alcohol or drugs] In deciding whether the defendant intended to

kill the victim and whether he formed that intent with deliberate premeditation, you may consider any credible evidence that the defendant suffered from a mental impairment[8] or was affected by his consumption of alcohol or drugs. A defendant may form the required intent and act with deliberate premeditation even if he suffered from a mental impairment or consumed alcohol or drugs,[9] but you may consider such evidence in determining whether the Commonwealth has proved these elements.[10]

[Where there is evidence of self-defense or defense of another] The next element is that the defendant did not act in proper self-defense or in the proper defense of another. I have already instructed you as to the circumstances under which a person properly may act in self-defense or in the defense of another.

[Where there is evidence of mitigating circumstances] Finally, the Commonwealth is also required to prove beyond a reasonable doubt that there were no mitigating circumstances. The law recognizes that in certain circumstances, which we refer to as mitigating circumstances, the crime is a lesser offense than it would have been in the absence of a mitigating circumstance. A killing that would otherwise be murder in the first or second degree is reduced to the lesser offense of voluntary manslaughter if the defendant killed someone under mitigating circumstances.

Not every circumstance you may think to be mitigating is recognized as mitigating under the law. In this case, the mitigating circumstance[s] that you must consider is/are:

1. heat of passion on a reasonable provocation;
2. heat of passion induced by sudden combat;
3. excessive use of force in self-defense or in defense of another.

To prove the defendant guilty of murder in the first degree with deliberate premeditation, the Commonwealth must prove beyond a reasonable doubt that there were no mitigating circumstances. [I will instruct you on this (each of these) mitigating circumstance(s) in more detail later, when I discuss voluntary manslaughter.]

7

NOTES

1 *See Commonwealth v. Rhoades*, 379 Mass. 810, 825 (1980).

2 *See Commonwealth v. Zanetti*, 454 Mass. 449, 455 (2009) ("mental state or intent for deliberately premeditated murder [is] an intent to kill"); *Commonwealth v. Jenks*, 426 Mass. 582, 585 (1998) ("Where only deliberate premeditation is offered to the jury as a basis for murder in the first degree, the inclusion of instructions on second and third prong malice, even if justified for other reasons, could be confusing . . .").

3 *See Commonwealth v. Palmariello*, 392 Mass. 126, 145 & n.4 (1984) (Commonwealth has burden of proof to show beyond a reasonable doubt that death was not accident).

4 *Commonwealth v. Taylor*, 463 Mass. 857, 863 (2012) ("A transferred intent instruction provides that if a defendant intends to kill a person and in attempting to do so mistakenly kills another person, such as a bystander, the defendant is treated under the law as if he intended to kill the bystander"); *Commonwealth v. Shea*, 460 Mass. 163, 172–74 (2011) (discussing proper jury instructions on transferred intent); *Commonwealth v. Castro*, 438 Mass. 160, 165–66 (2002) (quoting *Commonwealth v. Fisher*, 433 Mass. 340, 344–45 (2001) ("to find murder based on a theory of transferred intent, the jury need only find that the defendant 'intended to kill one person and, in the course of an attempt to do so, killed another'")).

5 *See, e.g., Commonwealth v. Gambora*, 457 Mass. 715, 733 (2010) (quoting *Commonwealth v. Coleman*, 434 Mass. 165, 168 (2001) ("no particular period of reflection is required, and . . . a plan to murder may be formed in seconds")); *see Commonwealth v. Tucker*, 189 Mass. 457, 487 (1905) (including extracts from instructions to jury on this subject in numerous earlier trials).

6 *See Commonwealth v. McMahon*, 443 Mass. 409, 418 (2005) (correct instruction explains that sequence of events began with "deliberation and premeditation, then the decision to kill, and lastly, the killing in furtherance of the decision").

7 *See Commonwealth v. Stewart*, 460 Mass. 817, 826 (2012) (proper to instruct "that the defendant's resolution to kill resulted from reflection over some span of time; and that the act could not have been undertaken so quickly as to preclude such reflection"); *Commonwealth v. McInerney*, 373 Mass. 136, 153–54 (1977).

8 *Commonwealth v. The Ngoc Tran*, 471 Mass. 179, 187 (2015) ("[W]e cannot say that the term 'mental impairment' is so obscure that a reasonable jury would be unable to rely on the usual and accepted meanings of these words to determine whether the defendant was capable of forming the required intent.").

9 *Commonwealth v. Figueroa*, 468 Mass. 204, 222 (2014) ("Where a defendant claims diminished capacity because of intoxication, the Commonwealth is required to prove only that the defendant was not so intoxicated that he was incapable of forming the requisite intent.").

10 *Commonwealth v. Mercado*, 456 Mass. 198, 207 (2010) (quoting *Commonwealth v. Sires*, 413 Mass. 292, 300 (1992) ("'All that we have ever required' be said to juries about the effect of mental impairment on a defendant's intent or knowledge is 'satisfied by a simple instruction that the jury may consider credible evidence' of the mental impairment 'in deciding whether the Commonwealth had met its burden of proving the defendant's state of mind beyond a reasonable doubt'")); *see Commonwealth v. Herbert*, 421 Mass. 307, 316 (1995) (instruction regarding intoxication warranted where "evidence raised a reasonable doubt whether the defendant was so intoxicated at the time of the incident that he was incapable of forming the intent that is a necessary element of the crimes charged"); *cf. Commonwealth v. Johnson*, 435 Mass. 113, 121–22 (2001) (reversal due to erroneous instruction on premeditation where mental impairment was live issue).

Murder with Extreme Atrocity or Cruelty

Next I will define the elements of murder in the first degree with extreme atrocity or cruelty.

[Where the Commonwealth has also charged murder in the first degree with deliberate premeditation] You shall consider this theory of murder in the first degree regardless of whether or not you find that the Commonwealth has proved murder in the first degree with deliberate premeditation.[1]

To prove the defendant guilty of murder with extreme atrocity or cruelty, the Commonwealth must prove the following elements beyond a reasonable doubt:

1. The defendant caused the death of [victim's name];
2. The defendant either:
 a. intended to kill [victim's name]; or
 b. intended to cause grievous bodily harm to [victim's name]; or
 c. intended to do an act which, in the circumstances known to the defendant, a reasonable person would have known created a plain and strong likelihood that death would result.
3. The killing was committed with extreme atrocity or cruelty.
4. *[Where there is evidence of self-defense or defense of another]* The defendant did not act in proper self-defense or in the proper defense of another.
5. *[Where there is evidence of mitigating circumstances]* In addition to these elements, the Commonwealth must also prove that there were no mitigating circumstances.

I will now discuss each of these requirements in more detail. The first element is that the defendant caused the death of [victim's name]. A defendant's act is the cause of death where the act, in a natural and continuous sequence, results in death, and without which death would not have occurred.[2]

The second element is that the defendant:

a. intended to kill [victim's name]; or
b. intended to cause grievous bodily harm to [victim's name]; or
c. intended to do an act which, in the circumstances known to the defendant, a reasonable person would have known created a plain and strong likelihood that death would result.

As you can see, this second element has three sub-elements, which I shall call prongs, and the Commonwealth satisfies its burden of proof if it proves any one of the three prongs beyond a reasonable doubt.[3]

The first prong—the defendant intended to kill—is the same as the second element of murder in the first degree with deliberate premeditation. The second and third prongs are different from any element of murder in the first degree with deliberate premeditation.

The second prong is that the defendant intended to cause grievous bodily harm to [victim's name]. Grievous bodily harm means severe injury to the body.[4]

The third prong is that the defendant intended to do an act which, in the circumstances known to the defendant, a reasonable person would have known created a plain and strong likelihood that death would result. Let me help you understand how to analyze this third prong. You must first determine whether the defendant intended to perform the act that caused the victim's death. If you find that he intended to perform the act, you must then determine what the defendant himself actually knew about the relevant circumstances at the time he acted. Then you must determine whether, under the circumstances known to the defendant, a reasonable person would have known that the act intended by the defendant created a plain and strong likelihood that death would result.[5]

[Where there is evidence of accident] If you have a reasonable doubt as to whether the victim's death was accidental, because the death was caused by a negligent, careless, or mistaken act of the defendant, or resulted from a cause separate from the defendant's conduct, you may not find that the Commonwealth has proved that the defendant intended to kill, intended to cause grievous bodily harm, or intended to do an act which, in the circumstances known to the defendant, a reasonable person would have known created a plain and strong likelihood that death would result.[6]

[Where there is evidence of transferred intent] If the defendant intends to kill a person or cause him grievous bodily harm and in attempting to do so mistakenly kills another person, such as a bystander, the defendant is treated under the law as if he intended to kill or cause grievous bodily harm to the actual victim. This is referred to as transferred intent under the law. For example, if I aim and fire a gun at one person intending to kill him but instead mistakenly kill another person, the law treats me as if I intended to kill the actual victim. My intent to kill or cause grievous bodily harm to the intended victim is transferred to the actual victim.[7]

[Where there is evidence of mental impairment or consumption of alcohol or drugs] In deciding whether the defendant intended to kill, intended to cause grievous bodily harm, or intended to do an act which, in the circumstances known to the defendant, a reasonable person would have known created a plain and strong likelihood that death would result, you may consider any credible evidence that the defendant suffered from a mental impairment or was affected by his consumption of alcohol or drugs.[8]

The third element is that the killing was committed with extreme atrocity or cruelty. Extreme atrocity means an act that is extremely wicked or brutal, appalling, horrifying, or utterly revolting.[9] Extreme cruelty means that the defendant caused the person's death by a method that surpassed the cruelty inherent in any taking of a human life.[10] You must determine whether the method or mode of a killing is so shocking as to amount to murder with extreme atrocity or cruelty.[11] The inquiry focuses on the defendant's action in terms of the manner and means of inflicting death, and on the resulting effect on the victim.[12]

In deciding whether the Commonwealth has proved beyond a reasonable doubt that the defendant caused the death of the deceased with extreme atrocity or cruelty, you must consider the following factors:[13]

1. whether the defendant was indifferent to or took pleasure in the suffering of the deceased;[14]
2. the consciousness and degree of suffering of the deceased;[15]
3. the extent of the injuries to the deceased;[16]
4. the number of blows delivered;[17]
5. the manner, degree, and severity of the force used;[18]
6. the nature of the weapon, instrument, or method used;[19] and
7. the disproportion between the means needed to cause death and those employed.[20] This seventh factor refers to whether the means used were excessive and out of proportion to what would be needed to kill a person.

You cannot make a finding of extreme atrocity or cruelty unless it is based on one or more of the factors I have just listed.[21]

[Where there is evidence the defendant at the time of the offense had a mental impairment or was under the influence of alcohol or drugs] You may consider the defendant's mental condition at the time of the killing, including any credible evidence of mental impairment or the effect on the defendant of his consumption of alcohol or drugs, in determining whether the Commonwealth has proved beyond a reasonable doubt that the defendant committed the killing with extreme atrocity or cruelty.[22]

[Where there is evidence of self-defense or defense of another] The fourth element is that the defendant did not act in proper self-defense or in the proper defense of another. I have already instructed you about when a person properly may act in self-defense or in the defense of another.

[Where there is evidence of mitigating circumstances] In addition to these elements, the Commonwealth must also prove that there were no mitigating circumstances. I have already mentioned that I will instruct you on mitigating circumstances later, when I discuss voluntary manslaughter.

NOTES

1 *See Commonwealth v. Candelario*, 446 Mass. 847, 859–60 (2006) (citing *Commonwealth v. Caputo*, 439 Mass. 153, 168 (2003) (jury may find defendant guilty on any theory of murder in first degree advanced by Commonwealth)).

2 *See Commonwealth v. Rhoades*, 379 Mass. 810, 825 (1980).

3 *See Commonwealth v. Townsend*, 453 Mass. 413, 428–29 (2009) (under extreme atrocity or cruelty theory the second element may be satisfied by any one of three prongs).

4 *See Commonwealth v. Reed*, 427 Mass. 100, 105 (1998).

5 *See Commonwealth v. Robidoux*, 450 Mass. 144, 162 nn.8 & 9 (2007).

6 *See Commonwealth v. Palmariello*, 392 Mass. 126, 145 & n.4 (1984) (Commonwealth has burden of proof to show beyond a reasonable doubt that death was not accident).

7 *Commonwealth v. Taylor*, 463 Mass. 857, 863 (2012) ("A transferred intent instruction provides that if a defendant intends to kill a person and in attempting to do so mistakenly kills another person, such as a bystander, the defendant is treated under the law as if he intended to kill the bystander."); *Commonwealth v. Shea*, 460 Mass. 163, 172–74 (2011) (discussing proper jury instructions on transferred intent); *Commonwealth v. Castro*, 438 Mass. 160, 165–66 (2002) (quoting *Commonwealth v. Fisher*, 433 Mass. 340, 344–45 (2001) ("to find murder based on a theory of transferred intent, the jury need only find that the defendant 'intended to kill one person and, in the course of an attempt to do so, killed another'")).

8 *See generally Commonwealth v. Mercado*, 456 Mass. 198, 207–08 (2010); *Commonwealth v. Herbert*, 421 Mass. 307, 316 (1995); *Commonwealth v. Sires*, 413 Mass. 292, 300 (1992).

9 *See, e.g., Commonwealth v. Linton*, 456 Mass. 534, 546–47 (2010); *Commonwealth v. Perry*, 432 Mass. 214, 219–20, 224–27 (2000).

10 *See Commonwealth v. Sok*, 439 Mass. 428, 437 (2003) ("judge correctly impressed on the jury that '[e]xtreme cruelty means that the defendant caused the person's death by a method that surpassed the cruelty inherent in any taking of human life'" [emphasis in original]).

11 *See, e.g., Commonwealth v. Hunter*, 416 Mass. 831, 837 (1994) (quoting *Commonwealth v. Connolly*, 356 Mass. 617, 628, *cert. denied*, 400 U.S. 843 (1970) ("mode")).

12 *See, e.g., Commonwealth v. Barros*, 425 Mass. 572, 581 (1997) (quoting *Commonwealth v. Gould*, 380 Mass. 672, 684 (1980) ("inquiry focuses both on the defendant's actions, in terms of the manner and means of inflicting death, and on the resulting effect on the victim")).

13 *Commonwealth v. Linton*, 456 Mass. 534, 536 n.10 (2010) (approving these factors as defined in *Commonwealth v. Cunneen*, 389 Mass. 216, 227 [1983]); *see Commonwealth v. Akara*, 465 Mass. 245, 259–60 (2013); *Commonwealth v. Stroyny*, 435 Mass. 635, 651 (2002).

14 *See, e.g., Commonwealth v. Roy*, 464 Mass. 818, 825 (2013) (defendant mimicked victim's pleading while describing how he "choked her out"); *Commonwealth v. Anderson*, 445 Mass. 195, 202 (2005) (defendant bragged about brutal murder after crime); *Commonwealth v. Sok*, 439 Mass. 428, 431 (2003).

7

15 *See, e.g., Commonwealth v. Linton*, 456 Mass. 534, 546–47 (2010) (victim consciously suffered as she was strangled to death); *Choy v. Commonwealth*, 456 Mass. 146, 151 (2010).

16 *See, e.g., Commonwealth v. Barbosa*, 457 Mass. 773, 802–03 (2010) (photograph depicting depressed skull fracture highly probative on extent of injury victim sustained).

17 *See, e.g., Commonwealth v. Miller*, 457 Mass. 69, 71 (2010) (evidence consistent with twenty-five blows from hammer to victim's head).

18 *See, e.g., Commonwealth v. Roy*, 464 Mass. 818, 825 (2013) (victim was hit in back of head with hard, flat object); *Commonwealth v. Carlson*, 448 Mass. 501, 502–03 (2007) (defendant "stomped on [victim's] abdomen, kicked her in the groin, and slammed her head on the floor ten times"; autopsy revealed "'massive contusions' in the abdomen and genitalia that required a degree of force that might occur in an automobile accident").

19 *See, e.g., Commonwealth v. Garuti*, 454 Mass. 48, 55 (2009) (defendant used special utility vehicle to strike former wife and then drive back over her).

20 *See, e.g., Commonwealth v. Moses*, 436 Mass. 598, 601 (2002) (after victim raised arms in act of surrender, defendant shot at victim seven times, hitting him four times; two wounds were potentially fatal).

21 *See Commonwealth v. Akara*, 465 Mass. 245, 259–60 (2013) (quoting *Commonwealth v. Whitaker*, 460 Mass. 409, 417–18 (2011) and *Commonwealth v. Szlachta*, 463 Mass. 37, 46 (2012) ("Although no single *Cunneen* factor is 'indispensible' to a determination of extreme atrocity or cruelty . . . , conviction of murder in the first degree on a theory of extreme atrocity or cruelty must be based on evidence of at least one of the [*Cunneen*] factors")); *Commonwealth v. Stroyny*, 435 Mass. 635, 651 (2002) ("reasonable juror would have understood that the Commonwealth bore the burden of proving at least one of the Cunneen factors beyond a reasonable doubt"); *see also Commonwealth v. Smith*, 460 Mass. 318, 323 (2011) (citing *Commonwealth v. Hunter*, 416 Mass. 831, 836–37 (1994) (error to instruct that extreme atrocity or cruelty is not limited to factors defined in *Commonwealth v. Cunneen*, 389 Mass. 216, 227 (1983))).

22 *See Commonwealth v. Gonzalez*, 469 Mass. 410, 421–22 (2014); *Commonwealth v. Rutkowski*, 459 Mass. 794, 798 (2011) (citing *Commonwealth v. Rosenthal*, 432 Mass. 124, 130 (2000) and *Commonwealth v. Gould*, 380 Mass. 672, 683–86 (1980)).

Felony-Murder in the First Degree

Next, I will define the elements of felony-murder in the first degree.

[Where other theories of murder in the first degree are charged] You shall consider this theory of murder in the first degree regardless whether or not you find that the Commonwealth has proved murder in the first degree with deliberate premeditation, or with extreme atrocity or cruelty, or both.

To prove the defendant guilty of felony-murder in the first degree, the Commonwealth must prove the following elements beyond a reasonable doubt:

1. The defendant committed or attempted to commit a felony with a maximum sentence of imprisonment for life.[1]

2. The death was caused by an act of the defendant [or a person participating with him] in the commission or attempted commission of the underlying felony.[2]

3. The act that caused the death occurred during the commission or attempted commission of the underlying felony.[3,4]

4. The defendant:

a. intended to kill [victim's name]; or

b. intended to cause grievous bodily harm to [victim's name]; or

c. intended to do an act which, in the circumstances known to the defendant, a reasonable person would have known created a plain and strong likelihood that death would result.[5]

5. *[Where there is evidence of self-defense or defense of another]* The defendant did not act in proper self-defense or in the proper defense of another.

[Note to Judge: An instruction on self-defense is generally not warranted where the theory of murder is felony-murder alone, but might be warranted where the killing occurred during the defendant's escape or attempted escape, or where the defendant was unarmed and the victim was the first to use deadly force.[6]]

6. *[Where there is evidence of mitigating circumstances]* In addition to these elements, the Commonwealth must also prove that there were no mitigating circumstances.

[Note to Judge: We can imagine few circumstances where an instruction regarding the absence of mitigating circumstances would be warranted by the evidence where the killing occurred during the alleged commission of a felony punishable by life imprisonment.]

I will now explain each element in more detail. The first element is that the defendant committed or attempted to commit a felony with a maximum sentence of imprisonment for life. The Commonwealth alleges that the defendant committed [or attempted to commit] [name of crime[s]]. I instruct you that this crime is a felony with a maximum sentence of life imprisonment.

In order for you to decide whether [name of the crime[s]] actually occurred in this case, I must instruct you on all elements of this [these] underlying offense[s].

[Note to Judge: Define all the elements of the substantive felonies alleged. In appropriate cases, a definition of "attempt" must be included. If more than one felony is alleged, the jury must be instructed that they must be unanimous with regard to the underlying felony in order to return a verdict of guilty of felony-murder in the first degree.[7] Where an underlying felony has as one of its elements the use or possession of a weapon, the jury must be instructed that the defendant must have possessed a weapon or known that a joint venturer possessed a weapon, see the instruction under "[Where felony-murder is charged and an underlying offense has as one of its elements the use or possession of a weapon]" in § 2.3, Joint Venture, above.]

[Where there is evidence the defendant at the time of the offense had a mental impairment or was under the influence of alcohol or drugs] You may consider the defendant's mental condition at the time of the killing, including any credible evidence of mental impairment or the effect on the defendant of his consumption of alcohol or drugs, in determining whether the defendant had the intent required in the underlying offense or the intent to kill, cause grievous bodily harm, or to do an act which, in the circumstances known to the defendant, a reasonable person would have known created a plain and strong likelihood that death would result.[8]

[Merger instruction where (1) the underlying felony contains an element of assault and (2) the underlying felony, by its nature, does not have an intent or purpose separate and distinct from the act causing physical injury or death. The crimes of robbery, rape, and kidnapping are examples of crimes that do not implicate the merger doctrine because each felony has an underlying intent that is independent from the act resulting in death: robbery (intent to steal),[9] rape (intent to engage in sexual intercourse, without consent),[10] and kidnapping (intent to forcibly confine or imprison).[11,12]]

The act of violence that is an element of the underlying felony may not be the same act that caused the victim's death.[13] Where an act of violence is an element of the underlying felony, you may find felony-murder only if you find an act that is separate and distinct from the violent act that resulted in the victim's death.[14] In this case, the Commonwealth alleges the following separate and distinct acts: [list qualifying underlying acts]. You may find felony-murder only if you find that the Commonwealth has proved beyond a reasonable doubt one of these separate and distinct acts. *[If there was more than one separate and distinct act that may satisfy an element of the underlying felony, you may find the underlying felony only if you unanimously find the Commonwealth has proved the same act beyond a reasonable doubt.[15]]*

If you find the defendant guilty of felony-murder, I require you to answer the following question[s]. *[Recite special question or questions specific to the case.]*

The second element is that the killing was caused by an act of the defendant or a person participating with him in the commission or attempted commission of the underlying felony.[16]

The third element is that the act that caused the death occurred during the commission or attempted commission of the felony.[17] The Commonwealth must prove beyond a reasonable doubt that the act that caused the death occurred during the commission of the felony and at substantially the same time and place.[18] *[A killing may be found to occur during the commission of the felony if the killing occurred as part of the defendant's effort to escape responsibility for the felony.]*[19]

The fourth element is that the defendant:

a. intended to kill [victim's name]; or

b. intended to cause grievous bodily harm to [victim's name]; or

c. intended to do an act which, in the circumstances known to the defendant, a reasonable person would have known created a plain and strong likelihood that death would result.

[If murder with extreme atrocity or cruelty is also charged, then the judge should explain the three prongs of malice in the following manner.]

As you can see, this fourth element is the same as the second element of murder with extreme atrocity or cruelty, which I explained earlier. Just as for murder with extreme atrocity or cruelty, the Commonwealth satisfies its burden of proof if it proves any one of the three prongs beyond a reasonable doubt.[20]

[If murder with extreme atrocity or cruelty is not also charged, then the judge should explain the three prongs of malice in the following manner.]

As you can see, this fourth element has three sub-elements, which I shall call prongs, and the Commonwealth satisfies its burden of proof if it proves any one of the three prongs beyond a reasonable doubt.[21]

The first prong—the defendant intended to kill—is the same as the second element of murder in the first degree with deliberate premeditation. The second and third prongs are different from any element of murder in the first degree with deliberate premeditation.

The second prong is that the defendant intended to cause grievous bodily harm to [victim's name]. Grievous bodily harm means severe injury to the body.[22]

The third prong is that the defendant intended to do an act which, in the circumstances known to the defendant, a reasonable person would have known created a plain and strong likelihood that death would result. Let me help you understand how to analyze this third prong. You must first determine whether the defendant intended to perform the act that caused the victim's death. If you find that he intended to perform the act, you must then determine what the defendant himself actually knew about the relevant circumstances at the time he acted. Then you must determine whether, under the circumstances known to the defendant, a reasonable person would have known that the act intended by the defendant created a plain and strong likelihood that death would result.[23]

[Where there is evidence of mental impairment or consumption of alcohol or drugs] In deciding whether the defendant intended to kill, intended to cause grievous bodily harm, or intended to do an act which, in the circumstances known to the defendant, a reasonable person would have known created a plain and strong likelihood that death would result, you may consider any credible evidence that the defendant suffered from a mental impairment or was affected by his consumption of alcohol or drugs.[24]

[Where there is evidence of self-defense or defense of another] The fifth element is that the defendant did not act in proper self-defense or in the proper defense of another. I have already instructed you about when a person properly may act in self-defense or in the proper defense of another.

[Where there is evidence of mitigating circumstances] In addition to these elements, the Commonwealth must also prove that there were no mitigating circumstances. I will instruct you on mitigating circumstances later, when I discuss voluntary manslaughter.

[Note to Judge: As a consequence of the Supreme Judicial Court's decision in Commonwealth v. Brown, 477 Mass. 805, 832 (2017), there is no longer a crime of second degree felony-murder. However, a defendant charged with murder in the first degree on a theory of felony-murder is likely to be entitled to an instruction on second degree murder as a lesser included offense to first degree murder based upon evidence that the defendant caused the victim's death with an intent that satisfied one or more of the three prongs of malice. The defendant may also be entitled to an instruction on voluntary manslaughter or involuntary manslaughter if any view of the evidence supports these lesser included offenses.]

NOTES

1 G.L. c. 265, § 1; *see, e.g., Commonwealth v. Cannon*, 449 Mass. 462, 471 (2007).

2 *See Commonwealth v. Tejeda*, 473 Mass. 269, 269–70, 279 (2015) (defendant not guilty of felony-murder where accomplice was killed by robbery victim who was seeking to thwart commission of underlying felony).

3 G.L. c. 265, § 1; *see, e.g., Commonwealth v. Cannon*, 449 Mass. 462, 471 (2007).

4 Previously, it was described as an element of felony-murder, both in the first and second degrees, that the killing must have been a "natural and probable consequence" of the felony. *See, e.g., Commonwealth v. Matchett*, 386 Mass. 492, 505 (1982). Since 1999, however, the Supreme Judicial Court has recommended that the language not be used "as it is superfluous to the other elements of felony-murder." *Commonwealth v. Rolon*, 438 Mass. 808, 818 n.11 (2003). *See* Model Jury Instructions on Homicide at 67–68 n.8 (1999).

5 *Commonwealth v. Brown*, 477 Mass. 805, 825 (2017).

6 An instruction on self-defense is generally not available to a defendant where the defendant committed a felony punishable by life imprisonment that provoked a victim to respond with deadly force. *See Commonwealth v. Rogers*, 459 Mass. 249, 260 (2011) ("Generally, in Massachusetts, one who commits an armed robbery cannot assert a claim of self-defense"); *Commonwealth v. Vives*, 447 Mass. 537, 544 n.6 (2006) ("The right to claim self-defense is forfeited by one who commits armed robbery"); *Commonwealth v. Maguire*, 375 Mass. 768, 773 (1978) ("it has been held that the right to claim self-defense may be forfeited by one who commits an armed robbery, even if excessive force is used by the intended victim"). The rationale for this rule is that the nature of the underlying felony marks the defendant as the "initiating and dangerous aggressor." *Commonwealth v. Rogers*, 459 Mass. at 260 (quoting *Commonwealth v. Garner*, 59 Mass. App. Ct. 350, 363 n.14 (2003)). However, a self-defense instruction might be appropriate where the killing occurred during the defendant's escape or attempted escape, see *Commonwealth v. Rogers*, 459 Mass. at 260–61, or where the defendant was unarmed and the victim was the first to use deadly force. *See Commonwealth v. Chambers*, 465 Mass. 520, 530 (2013) ("critical question in determining whether the Commonwealth proved that the defendant did not act in self-defense when he killed the victim was who first grabbed the kitchen knife that ultimately was the instrument of death, not who shouted first or who struck the first punch"). *See generally Commonwealth v. Chambers*, 465 Mass. at 528 ("in the context of homicide, a defendant may lose the right to claim self-defense only if he was the first to use or threaten deadly force").

7 *Commonwealth v. Wadlington*, 467 Mass. 192, 208 n.14 (2014) ("[w]here a required element of felony-murder in the first degree is that the defendant committed or attempted to commit a felony with a maximum sentence of imprisonment for life . . . the jury must agree as to the felony committed, even if each of the alternative underlying felonies are life felonies").

8 *Commonwealth v. Herbert*, 421 Mass. 307, 316 (1995) (instruction regarding intoxication warranted where "evidence raised a reasonable doubt whether the defendant was so intoxicated at the time of the incident that he was incapable of forming the intent that is a necessary element of the crimes charged"); *see, e.g., Commonwealth v. Rasmusen*, 444 Mass. 657, 665–66 (2005).

9 *See Commonwealth v. Christian*, 430 Mass. 552, 556 (2000) ("[w]e can envision no situation in which an armed robbery would not support a conviction of [felony-murder]"); *see also Commonwealth v. Morin*, 478 Mass. 415, 430–31 (2017) (merger instruction was not required where underlying felony in felony murder was unarmed robbery).

10 *See Commonwealth v. Wade*, 428 Mass. 147, 152 (1998) ("[T]he

intent to commit the rape, not the intent to inflict serious bodily harm, was the substitute for the malice requirement of murder.").

11 *See Commonwealth v. Oberle*, 476 Mass. 539, 548 (2017) ("[T]he essential element of kidnapping is not the [assaultive element] but rather the defendant's forcible or secret confinement or imprisonment of the victim against [her] will").

12 Under the merger doctrine, if the only felony committed was the assault upon the victim which resulted in the victim's death, the assault merges with the killing and cannot be relied on by the Commonwealth to support felony-murder. In *Commonwealth v. Morin*, 478 Mass. 415, 430–31 (2017), the Supreme Judicial Court declared:

We have relied upon the merger doctrine to ensure that "not every assault that results in death will serve as a basis for murder in the first degree on the theory of felony murder." *Commonwealth v. Scott*, 472 Mass. 815, 819 (2015). The Commonwealth therefore is required to prove that "the conduct which constitutes the felony be 'separate from the acts of personal violence which constitute a necessary part of the homicide itself.'" *Commonwealth v. Gunter*, 427 Mass. 259, 272 (1998), *S.C.*, 459 Mass. 480 (1998), *cert. denied*, 565 U.S. 868 (2011), quoting *Commonwealth v. Quigley*, 391 Mass. 461, 466 (1984), *cert. denied*, 471 U.S. 1115 (1985). *See Commonwealth v. Bell*, 460 Mass. 294, 301 (2011) (no merger between homicide and predicate felony of armed assault in dwelling where defendant assaulted multiple occupants in dwelling in addition to homicide victim); *Commonwealth v. Kilburn*, 438 Mass. 356, 362 (2003) (no merger between fatal shooting and predicate felony of armed assault in dwelling based on evidence of earlier assault on victim).

The merger doctrine does not apply "where the predicate felony has an intent or purpose separate and distinct from the act causing physical injury or death." *Commonwealth v. Morin*, 478 Mass. at 431. Thus, the felony of armed robbery may serve as the underlying felony for felony-murder and is not barred by the merger doctrine because stealing or taking the property of another is an element of armed robbery. *See Commonwealth v. Christian*, 430 Mass. 552, 556 (2000). A robber who kills the victim may be found guilty of felony-murder regardless of whether he shot the victim before or after taking the victim's property. *See Commonwealth v. Christian*, 430 Mass. at 556; *Commonwealth v. Holley*, 478 Mass. 508 (2017). Similarly, the merger doctrine does not apply where the underlying felony is robbery, rape, or kidnapping. *See Commonwealth v. Morin*, 478 Mass. at 431.

Where the underlying felony contains an element of assault, the judge must ensure that the felony found by the jury is independent of the act that resulted in the death of the victim. Where the murder indictment does not specify an independent felonious assault and there is a risk that the jury may find the underlying felony to include the assault that resulted in the victim's death, the Commonwealth, in advance of trial, should identify the independent felonious assault or assaults that it intends to rely on at trial to prove felony-murder. For instance, if the underlying felony is armed assault in a dwelling, and two other persons apart from the homicide victim were in the dwelling at the time of the armed assault, the judge must explain that, to prove this first element of felony-murder, the Commonwealth must prove beyond a reasonable doubt the felony of armed assault in a dwelling of a person other than the homicide victim.

To diminish the risk of confusion, the verdict form may require the jury to specify the person (or persons) other than the homicide victim that they concluded was (or were) assaulted. *See Commonwealth v. Gunter*, 427 Mass. 259, 274 (1998) ("Absent specification of an independent felonious assault in the murder indictment or absent a separate indictment on an independent assault, however, it is advisable in the future that the prosecution seek jury questions specifying the independent felonious assault pursuant to G.L. c. 265, § 18A, that it contends supports a felony-murder conviction").

If the underlying felony is armed assault in a dwelling or armed home invasion and the homicide victim was alone in the dwelling, but the Commonwealth contends that there was an earlier assault of the homicide victim in the dwelling that did not cause his death prior to the assault that did cause his death, the judge in instructing the jury must explain that, to satisfy the first element of felony murder, the Commonwealth must prove beyond a reasonable doubt the felony of armed assault in a dwelling or armed home invasion, with the assault being the first alleged assault of the victim, not the assault that allegedly resulted in the victim's death. *See Commonwealth v. Kilburn*, 438 Mass. 356, 359–60 (2003).

13 *See, e.g., Commonwealth v. Kilburn*, 438 Mass. 356, 359–60 (2003); *Commonwealth v. Gunter*, 427 Mass. 259, 272–74 (1998).

14 *See, e.g., Commonwealth v. Morin*, 478 Mass. 415, 430–31 (2017); *Commonwealth v. Holley*, 478 Mass. 508, 519–20 (2017).

15 *Commonwealth v. Morin*, 478 Mass. 415, 430–31 (2017); *Commonwealth v. Holley*, 478 Mass. 508, 519 (2017).

16 *Commonwealth v. Tejeda*, 473 Mass. 269, 269–70, 279 (2015) (defendant not guilty of felony-murder where accomplice was killed by robbery victim who was seeking to thwart commission of underlying felony).

17 *See, e.g., Commonwealth v. Roderick*, 429 Mass. 271, 277 (1999) (felony murder applies where killing occurred during commission of or attempt to commit felony).

18 *See Commonwealth v. Gunter*, 459 Mass. 480, 488 (2011) (quoting *Commonwealth v. Ortiz*, 408 Mass. 463, 466 (1990)).

19 *See Commonwealth v. Gordon*, 422 Mass. 816, 850 (1996).

20 *See Commonwealth v. Townsend*, 453 Mass. 413, 428–29 (2009) (under extreme atrocity or cruelty theory the fourth element may be satisfied by any one of three prongs).

21 *See Commonwealth v. Townsend*, 453 Mass. 413, 428–29 (2009) (under extreme atrocity or cruelty theory the fourth element may be satisfied by any one of three prongs).

22 *See Commonwealth v. Reed*, 427 Mass. 100, 105 (1998).

23 *See Commonwealth v. Robidoux*, 450 Mass. 144, 162 nn.8 & 9 (2007).

24 *See generally Commonwealth v. Mercado*, 456 Mass. 198, 207–08 (2010); *Commonwealth v. Herbert*, 421 Mass. 307, 316 (1995); *Commonwealth v. Sires*, 413 Mass. 292, 300 (1992).

Murder in the Second Degree

In order to prove murder in the second degree, the Commonwealth must prove the following elements:[1]

1. The defendant caused the death of [victim's name].

2. The defendant:

a. intended to kill [victim's name]; or

b. intended to cause grievous bodily harm to [victim's name]; or

c. intended to do an act which, in the circumstances known to the defendant, a reasonable person would have known created a plain and strong likelihood that death would result.[2]

[Note to Judge: There is no longer a separate theory of felony murder in the second degree. See Commonwealth v. Brown, 477 Mass. 805, 832 (2017).]

3. *[Where there is evidence of self-defense or defense of another]* The defendant did not act in proper self-defense or in the proper defense of another.

4. *[Where there is evidence of mitigating circumstances]* In addition to these elements, the Commonwealth must also prove that there were no mitigating circumstances. If the Commonwealth proves all the required elements, but fails to prove beyond a reasonable doubt that there were no mitigating circumstances, you must find the defendant not guilty of murder, but you shall return a verdict of voluntary manslaughter.

[Where the defendant is charged with murder in the first degree with extreme atrocity or cruelty] The requirements of proof for murder in the second degree are the same as for murder in the first degree with extreme atrocity or cruelty, but without the element that the killing was committed with extreme atrocity or cruelty.

[Note to Judge: Where the defendant is not charged with murder in the first degree with extreme atrocity, the judge must give the detailed instructions for each element of murder in the second degree that are set forth in the instructions for murder in the first degree with extreme atrocity or cruelty.]

NOTES

1 *Commonwealth v. Berry*, 466 Mass. 763, 772 n.16 (2014) ("[t]he intent necessary to be proved for a conviction of murder in the first degree committed with extreme atrocity or cruelty, defined by three alternate prongs, is the same as the intent necessary for murder in the second degree").

2 *See Commonwealth v. Earle*, 458 Mass. 341, 346–47 & n.9, 350 (2010) (finding evidence legally insufficient to support conviction for murder in second degree under theory that parent's intentional failure to act, in circumstances known to parent, created "plain and strong likelihood" of child's death); *Commonwealth v. Grey*, 399 Mass. 469, 470 n.1, 472 n.4 (1987) (in instructing jury regarding whether, in circumstances known to defendant, reasonably prudent person would have known of plain and strong likelihood of death, judge erred in instructing jury that malice was determined by objective standard, as objective reasonable person test is applied to circumstances defendant

knew); *see also Commonwealth v. Lyons*, 444 Mass. 289, 293–94 (2005) (discussing distinction between murder in second degree based on "plain and strong likelihood of death" and involuntary manslaughter based on "high degree of likelihood of substantial harm"; concluding judge erred in reducing conviction to involuntary manslaughter).

Voluntary Manslaughter (Lesser Included Offense to Murder)[1]

To prove the defendant guilty of murder in the first or second degree, the Commonwealth is required to prove beyond a reasonable doubt that there were no mitigating circumstances that reduce the defendant's culpability. A mitigating circumstance is a circumstance that reduces the seriousness of the offense in the eyes of the law. A killing that would otherwise be murder in the first or second degree is reduced to the lesser offense of voluntary manslaughter where the Commonwealth has failed to prove that there were no mitigating circumstances. Therefore, if the Commonwealth proves all the required elements of murder, but fails to prove beyond a reasonable doubt that there were no mitigating circumstances, you must not find the defendant guilty of murder, but you shall find the defendant guilty of voluntary manslaughter.

I will now instruct you on this (each of these) mitigating circumstance(s).

1. Heat of passion on reasonable provocation. Heat of passion includes the states of mind of passion, anger, fear, fright, and nervous excitement.[2]

Reasonable provocation is provocation by the person killed[3] that would be likely to produce such a state of passion, anger, fear, fright, or nervous excitement in a reasonable person as would overwhelm his capacity for reflection or restraint and did actually produce such a state of mind in the defendant.[4] The provocation must be such that a reasonable person would have become incapable of reflection or restraint and would not have cooled off by the time of the killing, and that the defendant himself was so provoked and did not cool off at the time of the killing.[5] In addition, there must be a causal connection between the provocation, the heat of passion, and the killing.[6] The killing must occur after the provocation and before there is sufficient time for the emotion to cool, and must be the result of the state of mind induced by the provocation rather than by a preexisting intent to kill or grievously injure, or an intent to kill formed after the capacity for reflection or restraint has returned.[7]

Mere words, no matter how insulting or abusive, do not ordinarily by themselves constitute reasonable provocation.[8] *[But there may be reasonable provocation where the person killed discloses information that would cause a reasonable person to lose his self-control and learning of the matter disclosed did actually cause the defendant to do so.]*[9]

Reasonable provocation does not require physical contact.[10] But physical contact, even a single blow, may amount to reasonable provocation. Whether the contact is sufficient will depend on whether a reasonable person under similar circumstances would have been provoked to act out of emotion rather than reasoned reflection and on whether the defendant was in fact so provoked.[11] The heat of passion must also be sudden; that is, the killing must have occurred before a reasonable person would have regained control of his emotions and the defendant must have acted in the heat of passion before he regained control of his emotions.[12]

If the Commonwealth has not proved beyond a reasonable doubt the absence of heat of passion on reasonable provocation, the Commonwealth has not proved that the defendant committed the crime of murder.

2. Heat of passion induced by sudden combat. Sudden combat involves a sudden assault by the person killed and the defendant upon each other. In sudden combat, physical contact, even a single blow, may amount to reasonable provocation.[13] Whether the contact is sufficient will depend on whether a reasonable person under similar circumstances would have been provoked to act out of emotion rather than reasoned reflection and on whether the defendant was in fact so provoked.[14] The heat of passion induced by sudden combat must also be sudden; that is, the killing must have occurred before a reasonable person would have regained control of his emotions and the defendant must have acted in the heat of passion without cooling off at the time of the killing.[15] If the Commonwealth has not proved beyond a reasonable doubt the absence of heat of passion induced by sudden combat, the Commonwealth has not proved that the defendant committed the crime of murder.

In summary, a killing that would otherwise be murder is reduced to the lesser offense of voluntary manslaughter if the defendant killed someone because of heat of passion on reasonable provocation or heat of passion induced by sudden combat. The Commonwealth has the burden of proving beyond a reasonable doubt that the defendant did not kill as a result of heat of passion on reasonable provocation or heat of passion induced by sudden combat. If the Commonwealth fails to meet this burden, the defendant is not guilty of murder, but you shall find the defendant guilty of voluntary manslaughter if the Commonwealth has proved the other required elements.

3. Excessive use of force in self-defense or defense of another. As I have explained to you earlier, a person is not guilty of any crime if he acted in proper self-defense [or defense of another]. The Commonwealth must prove beyond a reasonable doubt that the defendant did not act in the proper exercise of self-defense [or defense of another]. If the Commonwealth fails to do so, then you must find the defendant not guilty because an element of the crime that the Commonwealth must prove beyond a reasonable doubt is that the defendant did not act in the proper exercise of self-defense [or defense of another].[16]

In this case, you must consider whether the defendant used excessive force in defending himself [or another]. The term excessive force in self-defense means that, considering all the circumstances, the defendant used more force than was reasonably necessary to defend himself [or another]. In considering the reasonableness of any force used by the defendant, you may consider any factors you deem relevant to the reasonableness of the defendant's conduct under the circumstances, including evidence of the relative physical capabilities of the combatants, the number of persons who were involved on each side, the characteristics of any weapons used, the availability of room to maneuver, the manner in which the deadly force was used, the scope of the threat presented, or any other factor you deem relevant to the reasonableness of the defendant's conduct under the circumstances.[17]

I have already told you that to prove the defendant guilty of murder, the Commonwealth is required to prove beyond a reasonable doubt that the defendant did not act in the proper exercise of self-defense [or the defense of another]. If the Commonwealth proves that the defendant did not act in proper self-defense [or in the proper defense of another] solely because the defendant used more force than was reasonably necessary, then the Commonwealth has not proved that the defendant committed the crime of murder but, if the Commonwealth has proved the other required elements, you shall find the defendant guilty of voluntary manslaughter.[18]

NOTES

1 "If any view of the evidence . . . would permit a verdict of manslaughter rather than murder, a manslaughter charge should be given." *Commonwealth v. Brooks*, 422 Mass. 574, 578 (1996); *see Commonwealth v. Glover*, 459 Mass. 836, 842 (2011) ("Because the theories [of reasonable provocation and excessive use of force in self-defense] are distinct, a defendant is entitled to jury instructions on voluntary manslaughter based on both theories where the evidence supports them"). "If the question whether to give a manslaughter instruction is at all close, especially . . . where the defendant testifies, prudence favors giving the instruction." *Commonwealth v. Felix*, 476 Mass. 750, 757 (2017).

2 *Commonwealth v. Walden*, 380 Mass. 724, 728 (1980) ("in an ordinary person such a state of passion, anger, fear, fright, or nervous excitement as would eclipse his capacity for reflection or restraint, and . . . actually . . . produce such a state of mind in the defendant").

7

3 *Commonwealth v. Hinds*, 457 Mass. 83, 90–91 (2010) (quoting *Commonwealth v. Ruiz*, 442 Mass. 826, 838–39 (2004) ("provocation must come from the victim")). Note, however, that the doctrine of transferred intent can apply where the evidence raises the possibility of reasonable provocation, in which case the provocation could arise from someone other than the victim. *See Commonwealth v. Camacho*, 472 Mass. 587, 603 (2015) (noting, in dicta, "agree[ment] with th[e] general proposition" that, "in circumstances where one (A) who is reasonably and actually provoked by another person (B) into a passion to kill B, shoots at B but accidentally hits and kills an innocent bystander, A's crime is voluntary manslaughter") (quoting *Commonwealth v. LeClair*, 445 Mass. 734, 743 n.3 (2006)).

4 *Commonwealth v. Burgess*, 450 Mass. 422, 439 (2008) (quoting *Commonwealth v. Walden*, 380 Mass. 724, 728 (1980) ("in an ordinary person such a state of passion, anger, fear, fright, or nervous excitement as would eclipse his capacity for reflection or restraint, and . . . actually . . . produce such a state of mind in the defendant")); *Commonwealth v. Colon*, 449 Mass. 207, 220 (2007) (provocation must be sufficient to cause accused to "lose his self-control in the heat of passion"); *Commonwealth v. Lacava*, 438 Mass. 708, 721 n.15 (2003) (quoting *Commonwealth v. Walden*, 380 Mass. 724, 728 (1980) (provocation must "eclipse . . . capacity for reflection or restraint")).

5 *Commonwealth v. Glover*, 459 Mass. 836, 841 (2011) (quoting *Commonwealth v. Acevedo*, 446 Mass. 435, 443 (2006) ("defendant's actions must be both objectively and subjectively reasonable. That is, the jury must be able to infer that a reasonable person would have become sufficiently provoked and would not have 'cooled off' by the time of the homicide, and that in fact a defendant was provoked and did not cool off" [internal quotation omitted])); *Commonwealth v. Garabedian*, 399 Mass. 304, 313 (1987) ("reasonable person would have become sufficiently provoked and that, in fact, the defendant was provoked").

6 *Commonwealth v. Burgess*, 450 Mass. 422, 437–38 (2008) (quoting *Commonwealth v. Garabedian*, 399 Mass. 304, 313 (1987) ("voluntary manslaughter requires the trier of fact to conclude that there is a causal connection between the provocation, the heat of passion, and the killing")).

7 *Commonwealth v. Anderson*, 408 Mass. 803, 805 n.1 (1990) (judge's instructions to this effect upheld).

8 *Commonwealth v. Tu Trinh*, 458 Mass. 776, 783 (2011) (quoting *Commonwealth v. Vick*, 454 Mass. 418, 429 (2009)); *Commonwealth v. Mercado*, 452 Mass. 662, 672 (2008) (proper instruction explained "the distinction between mere words, which 'no matter how insulting or abusive, standing alone do not constitute reasonable provocation,' and statements that convey information 'of the nature to cause a reasonable person to lose his or her self-control and did actually cause the defendant to do so . . .'").

7

9 *Commonwealth v. Schnopps*, 383 Mass. 178, 180–81 (1981) (wife's sudden admission of ongoing adultery sufficient provocation to warrant instruction on voluntary manslaughter); *Commonwealth v. Bermudez*, 370 Mass. 438, 441–42 (1976) ("A reasonable man can be expected to control the feelings aroused by an insult or an argument, but certain incidents may be as provocative when disclosed by words as when witnessed personally"). Generally, for words or statements to incite heat of passion, they must contain new information as distinct from mere insults, taunts, or previously known, if inflammatory, information. *See Commonwealth v. Ruiz*, 442 Mass. 826, 839–40 (2004).

10 *Commonwealth v. Morales*, 70 Mass. App. Ct. 526, 532–33 (2007).

11 *Commonwealth v. Felix*, 476 Mass. 750, 757 (2017) (physical contact between defendant and victim not always sufficient to warrant manslaughter instruction, especially "where the defendant outweighs the victim and is physically far more powerful").

12 *Commonwealth v. Smith*, 460 Mass. 318, 325 (2011) (quoting *Commonwealth v. Colon*, 449 Mass. 207, 220 (2007) ("Provocation and 'cooling off' time must meet both a subjective and an objective standard."); *Commonwealth v. Acevedo*, 446 Mass. 435, 444–45 (2006); *cf. id.* at 444 n.14 (citing *Commonwealth v. Ruiz*, 442 Mass. 826, 839 (2004) (where victim's slaps and physical contact never posed threat of serious harm to defendant, this did not "warrant a manslaughter instruction, even when the victim initiated the contact")).

13 *Commonwealth v. Espada*, 450 Mass. 687, 696–97 (2008) (sudden combat as basis for voluntary manslaughter requires that "victim . . . attack the defendant or at least strike a blow against the defendant").

14 *Commonwealth v. Espada*, 450 Mass. 687, 697 (2008) (assault must pose real threat of serious harm).

15 *See, e.g., Commonwealth v. Vick*, 454 Mass. 418, 429 (2009); *Commonwealth v. Amaral*, 389 Mass. 184, 188 (1983) (quoting *Commonwealth v. Webster*, 59 Mass. 295, 307 (1850) ("whenever . . . the blood has had reasonable time or opportunity to cool . . . it will be murder [rather than manslaughter]")); *Commonwealth v. Acevedo*, 446 Mass. 435, 443 (2006) ("jury must be able to infer that a reasonable person would have become sufficiently provoked and would not have 'cooled off' by the time of the homicide, and that in fact a defendant was provoked and did not cool off").

16 *Commonwealth v. Santos*, 454 Mass. 770, 772–77 (2009) (extensive discussion of murder instructions regarding self-defense); *Commonwealth v. Silva*, 455 Mass. 503, 525–26 (2009) ("One of the elements of self-defense is the reasonableness of the force used to defend oneself, and if the Commonwealth fails to disprove all the elements of self-defense except the element of reasonableness of the force used, i.e., that the defendant used excessive force in self-defense, then self-defense does not lie, but excessive force in self-defense will mitigate murder to voluntary manslaughter"); *Commonwealth v. Glacken*, 451 Mass. 163, 167 (2008) ("To establish that the defendant did not act in proper self-defense, the Commonwealth must prove at least one of the following propositions beyond a reasonable doubt: (1) the defendant did not have a reasonable ground to believe, and did not believe, that he was in imminent danger of death or serious bodily harm, from which he could save himself only by using deadly force; or (2) the defendant had not availed himself of all proper means to avoid physical combat before resorting to the use of deadly force; or (3) the defendant used more force than was reasonably necessary in all the circumstances of the case. If the Commonwealth fails to prove either (1) or (2), but does prove (3)—that is, does prove beyond a reasonable doubt that in his exercise of self-defense the defendant used excessive force—then the jury must return a verdict of not guilty of murder and would be warranted in returning a verdict of guilty of voluntary manslaughter").

17 *Commonwealth v. Kendrick*, 351 Mass. 203, 212 (1966).

18 *Commonwealth v. Santos*, 454 Mass. 770, 776 (2009) ("permissive language should not be used where mandatory language is required . . . . If the defendant killed the victim by the use of excessive force in self-defense, the defendant must be found guilty of manslaughter; the jury cannot be given the option of considering that a murder has been committed"); *Commonwealth v. Torres*, 420 Mass. 479, 491–92 (1995) (in comparable charge, "judge should have used the mandatory word 'shall' rather than the permissive 'may'").

Voluntary Manslaughter (Absent a Murder Charge)

In this case, the defendant is charged with voluntary manslaughter. To prove the defendant guilty of voluntary manslaughter, the Commonwealth must prove beyond a reasonable doubt the following elements:[1]

1. The defendant intentionally inflicted an injury or injuries on the victim likely to cause death.

2. The defendant caused the death of the victim.

3. *[Where there is evidence of self-defense or defense of another]* The defendant did not act in proper self-defense or in the proper defense of another.

NOTE

1 *See Commonwealth v. Ware*, 438 Mass. 1014, 1015 (2003).

Involuntary Manslaughter

[Where the Commonwealth has proceeded on the theory of involuntary manslaughter caused by wanton or reckless conduct][1]

Involuntary manslaughter is an unlawful killing unintentionally caused by wanton or reckless conduct.[2]

[Where the Commonwealth has proceeded on the theory of involuntary manslaughter as an unlawful killing unintentionally caused by a battery]

Involuntary manslaughter is [also] an unlawful killing unintentionally caused by a battery that the defendant knew or should have known created a high degree of likelihood that substantial harm will result to another.[3]

[Note to Judge: If a defendant is charged with felony-murder in the first degree, but the evidence would support a finding of involuntary manslaughter rather than murder, the judge must instruct the jury that they can find the defendant guilty of involuntary manslaughter.[4]]

NOTES

1 An instruction on involuntary manslaughter is required where any reasonable view of the evidence will permit the jury to find that the defendant engaged in wanton or reckless conduct resulting in death.

Commonwealth v. Tavares, 471 Mass. 430, 438 (2015); *Commonwealth v. Braley*, 449 Mass. 316, 331 (2007).

2 The Supreme Judicial Court "has described conduct amounting to involuntary manslaughter as both 'wanton or reckless' and 'wanton and reckless.'" *Commonwealth v. Pagan*, 471 Mass. 537, 547 n.18 (2015) (quoting *Commonwealth v. Tavares*, 471 Mass. 430, 437 n.13 (2015). But expressed either way, "[t]he standard . . . is one standard, not two, and describes intentional conduct where 'there is a high degree of likelihood that substantial harm will result to another.'" *Commonwealth v. Chase*, 433 Mass. 293, 301 (2001) (quoting *Commonwealth v. Cruz*, 430 Mass. 182, 186 (1999)); *see Commonwealth v. Welansky*, 316 Mass. 383, 398 (1944) ("[I]ntentional conduct to which either word applies is followed by the same legal consequences as though both words applied" [emphasis added]). Because a jury may understand wanton to mean something slightly different than reckless, we describe the standard as "wanton or reckless" in these instructions. *See Commonwealth v. Welansky*, 316 Mass. at 398 ("The words 'wanton' and 'reckless' are practically synonymous in this connection, although the word 'wanton' may contain a suggestion of arrogance or insolence or heartlessness that is lacking in the word 'reckless.'").

3 *Commonwealth v. Sneed*, 413 Mass. 387, 393–94 (1992) ("each type of involuntary manslaughter requires a showing that the defendant knew, or should have known, that his conduct created a high degree of likelihood that substantial harm would result to another"); *Commonwealth v. Braley*, 449 Mass. 316, 331 (2007).

4 *Commonwealth v. Sires*, 413 Mass. 292, 301 (1992) ("An instruction on [involuntary] manslaughter is required where any view of the evidence will permit a finding of manslaughter and not murder"); *see Commonwealth v. Brown*, 477 Mass. 805, 832–33 (2017).

Alternative Instruction—Involuntary Manslaughter Caused by Wanton or Reckless Conduct[1]

Wanton or reckless conduct is intentional conduct that created a high degree of likelihood that substantial harm will result to another person. Wanton or reckless conduct usually involves an affirmative act.[2] An omission or failure to act may constitute wanton or reckless conduct where the defendant has a duty to act.[3]

[Where the Commonwealth alleges that the defendant committed an affirmative act that was wanton or reckless]

To prove that the defendant is guilty of involuntary manslaughter because of wanton or reckless conduct, the Commonwealth must prove the following elements beyond a reasonable doubt:

1. The defendant caused the victim's death;[4]
2. The defendant intended the conduct that caused the victim's death;[5]
3. The defendant's conduct was wanton or reckless;[6]
4. *[Where there is evidence of self-defense or defense of another]* The defendant did not act in proper self-defense or in the proper defense of another.

I will now discuss each element in more detail. The first element is that the defendant caused the death of [victim's name]. A defendant's act is the cause of death where the act, in a natural and continuous sequence, results in death, and without which death would not have occurred.[7]

The second element is that the defendant intended the conduct that caused the death.[8] The Commonwealth is not required to prove that the defendant intended to cause the death.[9]

The third element is that the defendant's conduct was wanton or reckless.[10] Wanton or reckless conduct is conduct that creates a high degree of likelihood that substantial harm will result to another.[11] It is conduct involving a grave risk of harm to another that a person undertakes with indifference to or disregard of the consequences of such conduct.[12] Whether conduct is wanton or reckless depends either on what the defendant knew or how a reasonable person would have acted knowing what the defendant knew.[13] If the defendant realized the grave risk created by his conduct, his subsequent act amounts to wanton or reckless conduct whether or not a reasonable person would have realized the risk of grave danger.[14] Even if the defendant himself did not realize the grave risk of harm to another, the act would constitute wanton or reckless conduct if a reasonable person, knowing what the defendant knew, would have realized the act posed a risk of grave danger to another.[15]

It is not enough for the Commonwealth to prove the defendant acted negligently, that is, in a manner that a reasonably careful person would not have acted.[16] The Commonwealth must prove that the defendant's actions went beyond negligence and amounted to wanton or reckless conduct as I have defined that term.

[Where there is evidence of self-defense or defense of another] The fourth element is that the defendant did not act in proper self-defense or in the proper defense of another. I have already instructed you as to when a person properly may act in self-defense or in the defense of another.

[Where there is evidence of mental impairment or consumption of alcohol or drugs] In deciding whether the defendant knew, or should have known, his conduct created a high degree of likelihood that substantial harm would result to another, you may consider any credible evidence that the defendant suffered from a mental impairment or was affected by his consumption of alcohol or drugs.[17] A defendant may have the requisite knowledge even if he suffered from a mental impairment or consumed alcohol or drugs, but you may consider such evidence in determining whether the Commonwealth has proved this element.

[Where the Commonwealth alleges that the defendant's failure to act was wanton or reckless]

An intentional omission or failure to act that creates a high degree of likelihood that substantial harm will result to another may constitute involuntary manslaughter where the defendant has a duty to act.[18] Such a duty may arise out of a special relationship.[19] A duty may also arise where a person creates a situation that poses a grave risk of death or serious injury to another.[20] When such a duty is owed, a failure to act that creates a high degree of likelihood that substantial harm will result to another is wanton or reckless.[21] To prove that the defendant is guilty of involuntary manslaughter by reason of a wanton or reckless failure to act, the Commonwealth must prove beyond a reasonable doubt the following elements:

1. There was a special relationship between the defendant and the victim that gave rise to a duty of care,[22] or the defendant created a situation that posed a grave risk of death or serious injury to another;[23]
2. The defendant's failure to act caused the victim's death;[24]
3. The defendant intentionally failed to act;[25]
4. The defendant's failure to act was wanton or reckless.[26]

I will now discuss each element in more detail.

The first element is that there was a special relationship between the defendant and the victim that gave rise to a duty of care[27] or the defendant created a situation that posed a grave risk of death or serious injury to another.[28] I instruct you that the relationship between [identify specific relationship, e.g., parent and minor child] is a special relationship that gives rise to a duty of care.[29] If you find that the defendant had this relationship with the victim, then you shall find that the defendant had a special relationship with the victim that gave rise to a duty of care.

The second element is that the defendant's failure to act caused the death of [victim's name]. A defendant's failure to act is the cause of death where the failure to act, in a natural and continuous sequence, results in death, and without which death would not have occurred.[30]

The third element is that the defendant intentionally failed to act.[31] The Commonwealth is not required to prove that the defendant intended to cause the death.[32]

The fourth element is that the defendant's failure to act was wanton or reckless.[33] A failure to act is wanton or reckless where there is a duty to prevent probable harm to another, and the defendant could have taken reasonable steps to minimize the risk to the person to whom the duty is owed.[34] A failure to act that is wanton or

7

reckless involves a high degree of likelihood that substantial harm will result to the person to whom the duty is owed.[35] It is a failure to act that amounts to indifference to or disregard of the consequences to the person to whom the duty is owed.[36] Whether the defendant's failure to act was wanton or reckless depends on the circumstances and the steps that a person could reasonably be expected to take to minimize the risk to the person to whom the duty is owed.[37]

Wanton or reckless conduct depends either on what the defendant knew, or how a reasonable person would have acted knowing what the defendant knew.[38] If the defendant realized the grave danger and could have taken reasonable steps to minimize the risk, his subsequent failure to act is wanton or reckless whether or not a reasonable person would have realized the risk of grave danger.[39] Even if the defendant himself did not realize the grave danger of harm to another, his failure to act would be wanton or reckless if a reasonable person in like circumstances would have realized the grave danger and taken steps to minimize the risk.[40]

It is not enough for the Commonwealth to prove the defendant was negligent in failing to act, that is, that a reasonably careful person would have acted.[41] The Commonwealth must prove that the defendant's failure to act went beyond negligence, and was wanton or reckless as I have defined that term.

[Where there is evidence of mental impairment or consumption of alcohol or drugs] In deciding whether the defendant knew, or should have known, his conduct created a high degree of likelihood that substantial harm would result to another, you may consider any credible evidence that the defendant suffered from a mental impairment or was affected by his consumption of alcohol or drugs.[42] A defendant may have the requisite knowledge even if he suffered from a mental impairment or consumed alcohol or drugs, but you may consider such evidence in determining whether the Commonwealth has proved this element.

NOTES

7

1 *Commonwealth v. Earle*, 458 Mass. 341, 347 (2010); *Commonwealth v. Walker*, 442 Mass. 185, 191–92 (2004).

2 *Commonwealth v. Life Care Ctrs. of Am., Inc.*, 456 Mass. 826, 832 (2010) ("Wanton or reckless conduct generally involves a wilful act that is undertaken in disregard of the probable harm to others that may result"); *Commonwealth v. Welansky*, 316 Mass. 383, 397 (1944) ("Usually wanton or reckless conduct consists of an affirmative act . . .").

3 *Commonwealth v. Levesque*, 436 Mass. 443, 451 (2002) ("defendant's omission when there is a duty to act can constitute manslaughter if the omission is wanton or reckless"); *Commonwealth v. Twitchell*, 416 Mass. 114, 117–18 (1993); *Commonwealth v. Welansky*, 316 Mass. 383, 397 (1944) ("But where . . . there is a duty of care . . . wanton or reckless conduct may consist of intentional failure to take such care . . .").

4 *Commonwealth v. Life Care Ctrs. of Am., Inc.*, 456 Mass. 826, 832 (2010) ("Involuntary manslaughter is 'an unlawful homicide unintentionally caused by an act which constitutes such a disregard of probable harmful consequences to another as to amount to wanton or reckless conduct'" [citations omitted]).

5 *Commonwealth v. Life Care Ctrs. of Am., Inc.*, 456 Mass. 826, 832 (2010) ("when we refer to the intent required to support a conviction of involuntary manslaughter, we refer to the intent to perform the act that causes death and not the intent that a death occur").

6 *Commonwealth v. Life Care Ctrs. of Am., Inc.*, 456 Mass. 826, 832 (2010); *Commonwealth v. Welansky*, 316 Mass. 383, 397 (1944) ("[Commonwealth] based its case on involuntary manslaughter through wanton or reckless conduct. . . . Usually wanton or reckless conduct consists of an affirmative act").

7 *See Commonwealth v. Rhoades*, 379 Mass. 810, 825 (1980).

8 *Commonwealth v. Life Care Ctrs. of Am., Inc.*, 456 Mass. 826, 832 (2010) ("when we refer to the intent required to support a conviction of involuntary manslaughter, we refer to the intent to perform the act that causes death and not the intent that a death occur"); *see Commonwealth v. Earle*, 458 Mass. 341, 347 (2010); *Commonwealth v. Walker*, 442 Mass. 185, 191–92 (2004); *Commonwealth v. Catalina*, 407 Mass. 779, 789 (1990); *Commonwealth v. Welansky*, 316 Mass. 383, 398 (1944).

9 *Commonwealth v. Life Care Ctrs. of Am., Inc.*, 456 Mass. 826, 832 (2010) ("reckless conduct does not require that the actor intend the specific result of his or her conduct, but only that he or she intended to do the reckless act"); *Commonwealth v. Walker*, 442 Mass. 185, 192–93 (2004).

10 *Commonwealth v. Welansky*, 316 Mass. 383, 396–97 (1944).

11 *Commonwealth v. Earle*, 458 Mass. 341, 347 (2010) (quoting *Commonwealth v. Welansky*, 316 Mass. 383, 399 (1944) ("'conduct [that] involves a high degree of likelihood that substantial harm will result to another'")); *Commonwealth v. Tolan*, 453 Mass. 634, 648–49 (2009) ("wanton or reckless conduct that creates a high degree of likelihood that substantial harm will result to another"); *Commonwealth v. Walker*, 442 Mass. 185, 192 (2004).

12 *Commonwealth v. Life Care Ctrs. of Am., Inc.*, 456 Mass. 826, 832 (2010) ("act causing death must be undertaken in disregard of probable harm to others in circumstances where there is a high likelihood that such harm will result"); *Commonwealth v. Godin*, 374 Mass. 120, 129 (1977) (quoting *Commonwealth v. Welansky*, 316 Mass. 383, 399 (1944) ("'Wanton or reckless conduct amounts to what has been variously described as indifference to or disregard of probable consequences.'")); *Commonwealth v. Welansky*, 316 Mass. 383, 398 (1944) ("judge charged the jury correctly when he said, 'To constitute wanton or reckless conduct . . . grave danger to others must have been apparent, and the defendant must have chosen to run the risk rather than alter his conduct so as to avoid the act or omission which caused the harm'").

13 *Commonwealth v. Earle*, 458 Mass. 341, 347 n.9 (2010) (citing *Commonwealth v. Welansky*, 316 Mass. 383, 398 (1944) (Welansky) ("relevant inquiry is whether a defendant knew of facts that would cause a reasonable person to know of the relevant danger, or whether the defendant in fact knew of the danger"; "judge charged the jury correctly when he said . . . 'If the grave danger was in fact realized by the defendant, his subsequent voluntary act or omission which caused the harm amounts to wanton or reckless conduct, no matter whether the ordinary man would have realized the gravity of the danger or not. But even if a particular defendant is so stupid [or] so heedless . . . that in fact he did not realize the grave danger, he cannot escape the imputation of wanton or reckless conduct . . . if an ordinary man under the same circumstances would have realized the gravity of the danger'")); *Commonwealth v. Catalina*, 407 Mass. 779, 789 (1990) (citing *Commonwealth v. Welansky*, 316 Mass. at 398–99 ("defendant's subjective awareness of the reckless nature of his conduct is sufficient, but not necessary, to convict him of involuntary manslaughter. Conduct which a reasonable person, in similar circumstances, would recognize as reckless will suffice as well")); *Commonwealth v. Godin*, 374 Mass. 120, 129 (1977) ("standard necessary for a conviction is at once both a subjective and objective standard, and is based in part on the knowledge of facts which would cause a reasonable man to know that a danger of serious harm exists. Such knowledge has its roots in experience, logic, and common sense, as well as in formal legal standards").

14 *Commonwealth v. Chapman*, 433 Mass. 481, 490 (2001) (citing *Commonwealth v. Welansky*, 316 Mass. 383, 398 (1944) ("judge charged the jury correctly when he said, . . . 'If the grave danger was in fact realized by the defendant, his subsequent voluntary act or omission which caused the harm amounts to wanton or reckless conduct, no matter whether the ordinary man would have realized the gravity of the danger or not")).

15 *Commonwealth v. Walker*, 442 Mass. 185, 192 (2004) (citing *Commonwealth v. Catalina*, 407 Mass. 779, 789 (1990) ("Conduct which a reasonable person, in similar circumstances, would recognize as reckless will suffice . . ."), and citing *Commonwealth v. Welansky*, 316 Mass. 383, 398–99 (1944) ("judge charged the jury correctly when he said . . . 'But even if a particular defendant is so stupid [or] so heedless . . . that in fact he did not realize the grave danger, he cannot escape the imputation of wanton or reckless conduct . . . if an ordinary man under the same circumstances would have realized the gravity of the danger'")).

16 *Commonwealth v. Life Care Ctrs. of Am., Inc.*, 456 Mass. 826, 832 (2010) (citing *Commonwealth v. Welansky*, 316 Mass. 383, 397–401 (1944) ("Conviction of involuntary manslaughter requires more than negligence or gross negligence")); *Commonwealth v. Chapman*, 433 Mass. 481, 489–90 (2001); *Commonwealth v. Godin*, 374 Mass. 120, 127, 129 (1977); *Commonwealth v. Bouvier*, 316 Mass. 489, 495–96 (1944) (defendant's actions in negligently discharging gun that killed husband did not "approach[] in character the wanton or reckless conduct essential to a finding of involuntary manslaughter"). When given, this instruction need not include a definition of negligence or gross negligence. *See Commonwealth v. Chapman*, 433 Mass. 481, 489–90 (2001) ("judge's instruction on wanton or reckless conduct incorporated [but did not define] the concepts of ordinary and gross negligence to illustrate the placement of wanton or reckless conduct on a spectrum of fault. The jury can be presumed to have a sufficient understanding of negligence and gross negligence from their collective experience for purposes of this instruction").

17 *Commonwealth v. Iacoviello*, 90 Mass. App. Ct. 231, 243–45 (2016).

18 *Commonwealth v. Levesque*, 436 Mass. 443, 451 (2002) ("defendant's omission when there is a duty to act can constitute manslaughter if the omission is wanton or reckless"); *Commonwealth v. Twitchell*, 416 Mass. 114, 117–18 (1993); *Commonwealth v. Welansky*, 316 Mass. 383, 397 (1944) ("But where . . . there is a duty of care . . . wanton or reckless conduct may consist of intentional failure to take such care . . .").

19 *Commonwealth v. Twitchell*, 416 Mass. 114, 117 (1993) (parent and minor child); *Commonwealth v. Welansky*, 316 Mass. 383, 397 (1944) (nightclub owner and patrons); *Commonwealth v. Godin*, 374 Mass. 120, 125–28 (1977) (discussing duty with regard to employer/employee relationship).

20 *Commonwealth v. Levesque*, 436 Mass. 443, 448–51 (2002) (discussing duty in context of negligently started fire); *Commonwealth v. Life Care Ctrs. of Am., Inc.*, 456 Mass. 826, 832–33 (2010) (discussing duty where one creates "life-threatening condition"); *Commonwealth v. Godin*, 374 Mass. 120, 126–30 (1977) (discussing duty in context of alleged improper storage of fireworks); *Commonwealth v. Atencio*, 345 Mass. 627, 629–30 (1963) (discussing duty in context of playing "Russian roulette").

21 *Commonwealth v. Welansky*, 316 Mass. 383, 397 (1944) ("But where . . . there is a duty of care . . . wanton or reckless conduct may consist of intentional failure to take such care in disregard of the probable harmful consequences . . .").

22 *Commonwealth v. Twitchell*, 416 Mass. 114, 117 (1993) (parent and minor child); *Commonwealth v. Michaud*, 389 Mass. 491, 496 (1983) (same); *Commonwealth v. Welansky*, 316 Mass. 383, 397 (1944) (nightclub owner and patrons). The existence of a relationship giving rise to a duty is a question of fact for the jury although the duty arising from a relationship is a matter of law. *See, e.g., Commonwealth v. Twitchell*, 416 Mass. 114, 117 (1993) ("We shall conclude that parents have a duty . . .").

23 *Commonwealth v. Levesque*, 436 Mass. 443, 449 (2002) (evidence presented to grand jury sufficient to support indictment for involuntary manslaughter where defendant negligently started fire and intentionally failed to report fire causing death of firefighters); *Commonwealth v. Life Care Ctrs. of Am., Inc.*, 456 Mass. 826, 832–33 (2010) (discussing duty where omission creates "life-threatening condition"); *Commonwealth v. Godin*, 374 Mass. 120, 126–30 (1977) (discussing duty in context of alleged improper storage of fireworks); *Commonwealth v. Atencio*, 345 Mass. 627, 629–30 (1963) (discussing duty in context of playing "Russian roulette").

24 *Commonwealth v. Levesque*, 436 Mass. 443, 447–48, 454 (2002) (causation through omission); *Commonwealth v. Life Care Ctrs. of Am., Inc.*, 456 Mass. 826, 832 (2010) ("Involuntary manslaughter is 'an unlawful homicide unintentionally caused by an act which constitutes such a disregard of probable harmful consequences to another as to amount to wanton or reckless conduct'" [citations omitted]); *Commonwealth v. Rhoades*, 379 Mass. 810, 825 (1980) (discussing causation of death in murder case).

25 *Commonwealth v. Levesque*, 436 Mass. 443, 451–53 (2002) (intentional failure to report negligently started fire causing death of responding firefighters would constitute wanton and reckless conduct); *Commonwealth v. Twitchell*, 416 Mass. 114, 117–18 (1993) (intentional failure to provide medical care leading to child's death constituted wanton and reckless conduct).

26 *Commonwealth v. Life Care Ctrs. of Am., Inc.*, 456 Mass. 826, 832 (2010); *Commonwealth v. Levesque*, 436 Mass. 443, 451–53 (2002); *Commonwealth v. Welansky*, 316 Mass. 383, 397 (1944) ("[Commonwealth] based its case on involuntary manslaughter through wanton or reckless conduct [which] may consist of intentional failure to take such care . . .").

27 *Commonwealth v. Twitchell*, 416 Mass. 114, 117 (1993) (parent and minor child); *Commonwealth v. Michaud*, 389 Mass. 491, 496 (1983) (same); *Commonwealth v. Welansky*, 316 Mass. 383, 397 (1944) (nightclub owner and patrons).

28 *Commonwealth v. Levesque*, 436 Mass. 443, 449 (2002) (evidence presented to grand jury sufficient to support indictment for involuntary manslaughter where defendant negligently started fire and intentionally failed to report fire causing death of firefighters); *Commonwealth v. Life Care Ctrs. of Am., Inc.*, 456 Mass. 826, 832–33 (2010) (discussing duty where omission creates "life-threatening condition"); *Commonwealth v. Godin*, 374 Mass. 120, 126–30 (1977) (discussing duty in context of alleged improper storage of fireworks); *Commonwealth v. Atencio*, 345 Mass. 627, 629–30 (1963) (discussing duty in context of playing "Russian roulette").

29 The existence of a relationship giving rise to a duty is a question of fact for the jury although the duty arising from a relationship is a matter of law. *See, e.g., Commonwealth v. Twitchell*, 416 Mass. 114, 117 (1993) ("We shall conclude that parents have a duty . . .").

30 *See Commonwealth v. Rhoades*, 379 Mass. 810, 825 (1980).

31 *Commonwealth v. Levesque*, 436 Mass. 443, 451–53 (2002) (intentional failure to report negligently started fire causing death of responding firefighters would constitute wanton and reckless conduct); *Commonwealth v. Twitchell*, 416 Mass. 114, 117–18 (1993) (intentional failure to provide medical care leading to child's death constituted wanton and reckless conduct).

32 *Commonwealth v. Life Care Ctrs. of Am., Inc.*, 456 Mass. 826, 832 (2010) ("[R]eckless conduct does not require that the actor intend the specific result of his or her conduct, but only that he or she intended to do the reckless act").

33 *Commonwealth v. Life Care Ctrs. of Am., Inc.*, 456 Mass. 826, 832 (2010); *Commonwealth v. Levesque*, 436 Mass. 443, 451–53 (2002); *Commonwealth v. Welansky*, 316 Mass. 383, 397 (1944) ("[Commonwealth] based its case on involuntary manslaughter through wanton or reckless conduct [which] may consist of intentional failure to take such care . . .").

34 *Commonwealth v. Life Care Ctrs. of Am., Inc.*, 456 Mass. 826, 832 (2010) ("Wanton or reckless conduct generally involves a wilful act that is undertaken in disregard of the probable harm to others that may result. . . . If an individual's actions create a lifethreatening condition, there is a duty to take reasonable steps to alleviate the risk created, and the failure to do so may rise to the level of recklessness necessary for involuntary manslaughter"); *Commonwealth v. Levesque*, 436 Mass. 443, 450–51 (2002); *see Commonwealth v. Michaud*, 389 Mass. 491, 495–96, 499 (1983).

35 *Commonwealth v. Levesque*, 436 Mass. 443, 451–52 (2002) (quoting *Commonwealth v. Welansky*, 316 Mass. 383, 399 (1944) ("words 'wanton' and 'reckless' constitute conduct that is . . . 'intentional conduct . . . involv[ing] a high degree of likelihood that substantial harm will result to another'")).

36 *Commonwealth v. Life Care Ctrs. of Am., Inc.*, 456 Mass. 826, 832–33 (2010); *Commonwealth v. Levesque*, 436 Mass. 443, 448 (2002).

37 *Commonwealth v. Levesque*, 436 Mass. 443, 450–51 (2002) ("Whether a defendant has satisfied this duty will depend on the circumstances of the particular case and the steps that the defendant can reasonably be expected to take to minimize the risk"); *Commonwealth v. Welansky*, 316 Mass. 383, 397–401 (1944). *Compare Commonwealth v. Twitchell*, 416 Mass. 114, 117–18 (1993) (failure to provide medical care for child for religious reasons could sustain involuntary manslaughter conviction), *with Commonwealth v. Michaud*, 389 Mass. 491, 495–99 (1983) (failure to provide medical care for child in circumstances where child was doing well shortly before child's death insufficient to sustain involuntary manslaughter conviction).

38 *Commonwealth v. Welansky*, 316 Mass. 383, 398 (1944) ("judge charged the jury correctly when he said . . . '[i]f the grave danger was in fact realized by the defendant, his subsequent voluntary act or omission which caused the harm amounts to wanton or reckless conduct, no matter whether the ordinary man would have realized the gravity of the danger or not. But even if a particular defendant is so stupid [or] so heedless . . . that in fact he did not realize the grave danger, he cannot escape the imputation of wanton or reckless conduct . . . if an ordinary man under the same circumstances would have realized the gravity of the danger'").

39 *Commonwealth v. Welansky*, 316 Mass. 383, 398 (1944) ("judge charged the jury correctly when he said . . . '[i]f the grave danger was in fact realized by the defendant, his subsequent voluntary act or omission which caused the harm amounts to wanton or reckless conduct, no matter whether the ordinary man would have realized the gravity of the danger or not'"); *Commonwealth v. Levesque*, 436 Mass. 443, 451 (2002) ("Whether a defendant has satisfied this duty will depend on the circumstances of the particular case and the steps that the defendant can reasonably be expected to take to minimize the risk").

40 *Commonwealth v. Welansky*, 316 Mass. 383, 398 (1944) ("judge charged the jury correctly when he said . . . '[b]ut even if a particular defendant is so stupid [or] so heedless . . . that in fact he did not realize the grave danger, he cannot escape the imputation of wanton or reckless conduct . . . if an ordinary man under the same circumstances would have realized the gravity of the danger'"); *Commonwealth v. Levesque*, 436 Mass. 443, 451 (2002) ("Although, in this case, the defendants apparently could not have successfully put out the fire, they could have given reasonable notice of the danger they created"); *Commonwealth v. Michaud*, 389 Mass. 491, 495–99 (1983).

41 *Commonwealth v. Levesque*, 436 Mass. 443, 451–52 (2002) ("words 'wanton' and 'reckless' constitute conduct that is 'different in kind' than negligence or gross negligence"); *Commonwealth v. Welansky*, 316

7

Mass. 383, 400 (1944) ("conduct does not become criminal until it passes the borders of negligence and gross negligence and enters into the domain of wanton or reckless conduct"). *Compare Commonwealth v. Twitchell*, 416 Mass. 114, 115–17, 122 (1993) (parental failure to seek medical treatment for child for religious reasons could sustain involuntary manslaughter conviction), *with Commonwealth v. Michaud*, 389 Mass. 491, 498–99 (1983) (parental failure to feed adequately and to seek proper medical treatment for child who appeared to be in good health shortly prior to child's death, even if negligent, insufficient to establish reckless culpability for involuntary manslaughter).

42 *Commonwealth v. Iacoviello*, 90 Mass. App. Ct. 231, 243–45 (2016).

Involuntary Manslaughter Unintentionally Caused by a Battery

[Note to Judge: Our case law limits this instruction to a battery that is not a felony.[1]]

Involuntary manslaughter is [also] an unlawful killing unintentionally caused by a battery[2] that the defendant knew or should have known endangered human life.[3] To prove the defendant is guilty of involuntary manslaughter by reason of a battery, the Commonwealth must prove beyond a reasonable doubt the following elements:

1. The defendant caused the victim's death.[4]
2. The defendant intentionally committed a battery upon the victim that endangered human life.[5]
3. The defendant knew or reasonably should have known that the battery endangered human life.[6]
4. *[Where there is evidence of self-defense or defense of another]* The defendant did not act in proper self-defense or in the proper defense of another.

I will now discuss each element in more detail. The first element is that the defendant caused the death of [victim's name]. A defendant's act is the cause of death where the act, in a natural and continuous sequence, results in death, and without which death would not have occurred.[7]

The second element is that the defendant intentionally committed a battery on the victim that endangered human life.[8] A battery is the intentional or unjustified use of force upon the person of another. To satisfy this element, the Commonwealth must prove that the battery created a high degree of likelihood that substantial harm would result to the victim.[9] Because the essence of manslaughter is an unintentional killing, the Commonwealth need not prove that the defendant intended the death that resulted from the battery.

The third element is that the defendant knew or reasonably should have known that the battery endangered human life in that it created a high degree of likelihood that substantial harm would result to the victim.[10] In determining whether the defendant reasonably should have known that the battery created a high degree of likelihood that substantial harm would result to another, you must consider the nature and extent of the defendant's knowledge at the time he acted and whether, in the circumstances known by the defendant, a reasonable person would have recognized that the battery created a high degree of likelihood that substantial harm would result to another.[11]

[Where there is evidence of self-defense or defense of another] The fourth element is that the defendant did not act in proper self-defense or in the proper defense of another. I have already instructed you about when a person properly may act in self-defense or in the defense of another.

NOTES

1 *See Commonwealth v. Simpson*, 434 Mass. 570, 590 (2001) ("battery not amounting to a felony which the defendant knew or should have known endangered human life"); *Commonwealth v. Catalina*, 407 Mass. 779, 784, 788–89 (1990).

2 *Commonwealth v. Catalina*, 407 Mass. 779, 784, 788–89 (1990) (citing *Commonwealth v. Sheppard*, 404 Mass. 774, 775–76 (1989)); *Commonwealth v. Welansky*, 316 Mass. 383, 401 (1944).

3 *Commonwealth v. Fitzmeyer*, 414 Mass. 540, 547 (1993) ("knew or should have known that the battery he was committing endangered human life"); *Commonwealth v. Sneed*, 413 Mass. 387, 394 (1992) (quoting *Commonwealth v. Welansky*, 316 Mass. 383, 399, 401 (1944) ("high degree of likelihood that substantial harm will result to another")).

4 *Commonwealth v. Catalina*, 407 Mass. 779, 789 (1990) ("person henceforth may be prosecuted for involuntary manslaughter only for causing an unintentional death . . ."); *Commonwealth v. Sheppard*, 404 Mass. 774, 776 (1989).

5 *Commonwealth v. Braley*, 449 Mass. 316, 331 (2007); *Commonwealth v. Reed*, 427 Mass. 100, 104 (1998); *Commonwealth v. Fitzmeyer*, 414 Mass. 540, 547 (1993); *Commonwealth v. Sires*, 413 Mass. 292, 302 n.10 (1992).

6 *Commonwealth v. Linton*, 456 Mass. 534, 552 (2010); *Commonwealth v. Braley*, 449 Mass. 316, 331 (2007) (quoting *Commonwealth v. Simpson*, 434 Mass. 570, 590 (2001) ("battery not amounting to a felony which the defendant knew or should have known endangered human life")); *Commonwealth v. Sires*, 413 Mass. 292, 302 n.10, 303 n.14 (1992) ("defendant knew or should have known that the battery he was committing endangered human life").

7 *See Commonwealth v. Rhoades*, 379 Mass. 810, 825 (1980).

8 *Commonwealth v. Braley*, 449 Mass. 316, 331 (2007); *Commonwealth v. Fitzmeyer*, 414 Mass. 540, 547 (1993) (citing *Commonwealth v. Sires*, 413 Mass. 292, 302 n.10 (1992)); *Commonwealth v. Catalina*, 407 Mass. 779, 783–84, 788–89 (1990); *Commonwealth v. Sheppard*, 404 Mass. 774, 776 (1989); *Commonwealth v. Welansky*, 316 Mass. 383, 401 (1944).

9 *Commonwealth v. Sneed*, 413 Mass. 387, 394 (1992) (quoting *Commonwealth v. Welansky*, 316 Mass. 383, 399 (1944) ("level of the risk of physical harm that the evidence must show to warrant an instruction on involuntary manslaughter battery causing death is . . . 'a high degree of likelihood that substantial harm will result to another'")). The model instruction harmonizes the line of cases that defined this element in terms of endangering human life with cases that focused on the likelihood of substantial harm. *Compare, e.g., Commonwealth v. Fitzmeyer*, 414 Mass. 540, 547 (1993) ("knew or should have known that the battery he was committing endangered human life"), *with Commonwealth v. Sneed*, 413 Mass. 387, 394 & n.5 (1992). The model instruction retains the "endangered human life" element and explains the element in terms of whether the defendant created "a high degree of likelihood that substantial harm will result to another."

10 *Commonwealth v. Braley*, 449 Mass. 316, 331 (2007) (quoting *Commonwealth v. Simpson*, 434 Mass. 570, 590 (2001) ("battery not amounting to a felony which the defendant knew or should have known endangered human life")); *Commonwealth v. Sneed*, 413 Mass. 387, 394 (1992) (quoting *Commonwealth v. Welansky*, 316 Mass. 383, 399 (1944) ("level of the risk of physical harm that the evidence must show to warrant an instruction on involuntary manslaughter battery causing death is . . . 'a high degree of likelihood that substantial harm will result to another'")); *Commonwealth v. Sires*, 413 Mass. 292, 302 n.10, 303 n.14 (1992) ("defendant knew or should have known that the battery he was committing endangered human life").

11 *See Commonwealth v. Sires*, 413 Mass. 292, 302 n.10, 303 n.14 (1992) ("degree of risk of physical harm that a reasonable person would recognize was created by particular conduct, based on what the defendant knew").

Supplemental Instructions

Charging a Minor with Murder

The Massachusetts Legislature has determined that all persons fourteen years of age or older who are charged with murder are to be tried as adults. That the defendant is being tried as an adult has nothing to do with this individual defendant, his alleged role in this case, or the strength of the evidence.

Definition of Death

Death occurs when the heart has stopped long enough to result in complete and permanent loss of brain function. This complete and permanent loss of brain function occurs when, in the opinion of a licensed physician based on ordinary and accepted standards of medical practice, there has been a total and irreversible cessation of spontaneous brain functions and further attempts at resuscitation or continued supportive maintenance would not be successful in restoring such functions.[1]

NOTE

1 *Commonwealth v. Golston*, 373 Mass. 249, 252–55 (1977) (affirming instruction on "brain death" that "occurs when, in the opinion of a li-

censed physician, based on ordinary and accepted standards of medical practice, there has been a total and irreversible cessation of spontaneous brain functions and further attempts at resuscitation or continued supportive maintenance would not be successful in restoring such functions").

Object of Killing Must Be a Human Being

A killing is not murder unless a human being has been killed. A viable fetus is a human being under the common law of homicide.[1]

NOTES

1 *Commonwealth v. Crawford*, 430 Mass. 683, 689 (2000) ("killing a 'viable fetus,' as defined in the common law, is a punishable offense"); *Commonwealth v. Lawrence*, 404 Mass. 378, 383–84 (1989) (viable fetus is human being for purposes of crime of murder); *Commonwealth v. Cass*, 392 Mass. 799, 807 (1984) ("We think that the better rule is that infliction of prenatal injuries resulting in the death of a viable fetus, before or after it is born, is homicide").

Use of Dangerous Weapon

[Where the judge determines from the evidence at trial that the nature of the dangerous weapon used and the manner of its use reasonably supports the following inference, the judge may give the following instruction.]

As a general rule, you are permitted (but not required) to infer that a person who intentionally uses a dangerous weapon on another person intends to kill that person, or cause him grievous bodily harm, or intends to do an act which, in the circumstances known to him, a reasonable person would know creates a plain and strong likelihood that death would result.[1]

[Note to Judge: It may not in all circumstances be reasonable to infer the intent required for murder in the first or second degree merely from the intentional use of a dangerous weapon. Before giving this instruction, a judge should consider the type of dangerous weapon and the manner in which it was used in the circumstances of the case, and should only give this instruction where the nature of the weapon and the manner of its use reasonably supports the inference.]

NOTE

1 *See Commonwealth v. Tu Trinh*, 458 Mass. 776, 784 & nn.12, 13 (2011) (instruction that "[a]s a general rule you are permitted to infer that a person who intentionally uses a dangerous weapon on another person is acting with malice" was "proper," but noting that "[b]ecause a firearm is inherently dangerous, we do not need to decide whether such an instruction permitting an inference of malice to be drawn would be proper if the weapon at issue were less dangerous—a shod foot, for example").

Questions from Jury

Before Supplemental Instructions

Members of the jury, I am about to give you some additional instructions. In response to your question, I am going to further clarify some areas of the law for you. These new instruction(s) are no more or less important than the other instructions I gave you originally. When you [begin/resume] deliberations, you are to consider all of my instructions together as a whole.[1]

NOTE

1 *Commonwealth v. Hicks*, 22 Mass. App. Ct. 139, 144–45 (1986) ("At the beginning and again at the end of the supplemental instructions, the judge should advise the jurors that all of the instructions are to be considered as a whole and that the supplemental instructions are to be considered along with the main charge, unless, of course, the supplemental instructions are given to correct an error in the main charge"); *Commonwealth v. Green*, 55 Mass. App. Ct. 376, 383 (2002).

After Supplemental Instructions

Remember in your deliberations you are to consider all of my instructions together as a whole—those I gave you before and those I have just given you.

Jury's Obligation on Guilt or Innocence

If the evidence convinces you beyond a reasonable doubt that the defendant is guilty of a criminal offense, you have a duty to find the defendant guilty of the most serious offense that the Commonwealth has proved beyond a reasonable doubt.[1] If the evidence does not prove beyond a reasonable doubt that the defendant is guilty of any offense charged, you must find him not guilty.

NOTE

1 *Commonwealth v. Rivera*, 445 Mass. 119, 131 (2013) (jury required by law to return verdict of highest degree of murder proved beyond a reasonable doubt); *Commonwealth v. Anderson*, 408 Mass. 803, 808 (1990) (judge entitled to inform jury of duty to return guilty verdict for highest crime proved beyond a reasonable doubt); *Commonwealth v. Nelson*, 468 Mass. 1, 16–17 (2014) (no error where judge reinstructed jury on duty to find defendant guilty of most serious offense proved beyond reasonable doubt).

After Jury Reports Deadlock on Murder in the First Degree

[Note to Judge: This instruction should only be given when the jury explicitly reports that they are deadlocked on murder in the first degree, and not, for instance, when they simply state that they are deadlocked.]

Your present inability to reach agreement as to murder in the first degree does not mean that you are a hung jury. If, after all reasonable efforts, you are unable to reach agreement as to murder in the first degree, or if you reach agreement that the defendant is not guilty of murder in the first degree, you should move on to consider murder in the second degree.[1]

NOTE

1 *Commonwealth v. Figueroa*, 468 Mass. 204, 228–29 (2014) (upon receiving note that jury was deadlocked as to murder in first degree, "the judge should have instructed the jury that they were not a hung jury and that if, after all reasonable efforts, they were unable to reach agreement as to murder in the first degree [or if they reached agreement that the defendant was not guilty of murder in the first degree], they should move on to consider murder in the second degree").

Supreme Judicial Court Chalk: Requirements of Proof for Homicide

I. MURDER IN THE FIRST DEGREE

A. Murder with Deliberate Premeditation

1. The defendant caused the death of [name of victim].

2. The defendant intended to kill.

3. The defendant committed the killing with deliberate premeditation.

4. *[Where there is evidence of self-defense or defense of another]* The defendant did not act in proper self-defense or in the proper defense of another.

5. *[Where there is evidence of mitigating circumstances]* There were no mitigating circumstances.

B. Murder with Extreme Atrocity or Cruelty

1. The defendant caused the death of [name of victim].

2. The defendant either:

a. intended to kill; or

b. intended to cause grievous bodily harm; or

c. intended to do an act which, in the circumstances known to him, a reasonable person would have known created a plain and strong likelihood that death would result.

3. The killing was committed with extreme atrocity or cruelty.

4. *[Where there is evidence of self-defense or defense of another]* The defendant did not act in proper self-defense or in the proper defense of another.

5. *[Where there is evidence of mitigating circumstances]* There were no mitigating circumstances.

C. Felony-Murder

1. The defendant committed or attempted to commit [name of crime], a felony with a maximum sentence of life imprisonment.

2. The killing was caused by an act of the defendant [or a person participating with the defendant] in the commission or attempted commission of the underlying felony.

3. The act that caused the killing occurred during the commission or attempted commission of the felony.

4. The defendant either:

a. intended to kill; or

b. intended to cause grievous bodily harm; or

c. intended to do an act which, in the circumstances known to him, a reasonable person would have known created a plain and strong likelihood that death would result.

5. *[Where there is evidence of self-defense or defense of another]* The defendant did not act in proper self-defense or in the proper defense of another.

6. [Where there is evidence of mitigating circumstances] There were no mitigating circumstances.

II. MURDER IN THE SECOND DEGREE

A. Murder

1. The defendant caused the death of [name of victim].

2. The defendant either:

a. intended to kill; or

b. intended to cause grievous bodily harm; or

c. intended to do an act which, in the circumstances known to him, a reasonable person would have known created a plain and strong likelihood that death would result.

3. *[Where there is evidence of self-defense or defense of another]* The defendant did not act in proper self-defense or in the proper defense of another.

4. *[Where there is evidence of mitigating circumstances]* There were no mitigating circumstances.

III. VOLUNTARY MANSLAUGHTER

A. Voluntary Manslaughter as a Lesser Included Offense

1. The defendant caused the death of [name of victim].

2. The defendant either:

a. intended to kill; or

b. intended to cause grievous bodily harm; or

c. intended to do an act which, in the circumstances known to him, a reasonable person would have known created a plain and strong likelihood that death would result.

3. *[Where there is evidence of self-defense or defense of another]* The defendant did not act in proper self-defense or in the proper defense of another.

B. Voluntary Manslaughter Absent a Murder Charge

1. The defendant intentionally inflicted an injury or injuries on [name of victim] likely to cause death.

2. The defendant caused the death of [name of victim].

3. *[Where there is evidence of self-defense or defense of another]* The defendant did not act in proper self-defense or in the proper defense of another.

IV. INVOLUNTARY MANSLAUGHTER

A. Death Caused by Wanton or Reckless Conduct

1. The defendant caused the death of [name of victim].

2. The defendant intended the conduct that caused the death of [name of victim].

3. The defendant's conduct was wanton or reckless.

4. *[Where there is evidence of self-defense or defense of another]* The defendant did not act in proper self-defense or in the proper defense of another.

B. Death Caused by Wanton or Reckless Failure to Act

1. There was a special relationship between the defendant and [name of victim] which gave rise to a duty of care, or the defendant created a situation that posed a grave risk of death or serious injury to another.

2. The defendant's failure to act caused the death of [name of victim].

3. The defendant intentionally failed to act.

4. The defendant's failure to act was wanton or reckless.

C. Death Unintentionally Caused by a Battery

1. The defendant caused the death of [name of victim].

2. The defendant intentionally committed a battery upon [name of victim] that endangered human life.

3. The defendant knew or reasonably should have known that the battery endangered human life.

4. *[Where there is evidence of self-defense or defense of another]* The defendant did not act in proper self-defense or in the proper defense of another.

Immunity

As to the question of whether, in authorizing judges presiding over jury sessions in the Juvenile Court to have and exercise all the powers and duties that a justice in the Superior Court may exercise in the trial and disposition of criminal cases, the legislature "intended to confer on the Juvenile Court the Superior Court's power to grant immunity to a witness[, w]e conclude that the legislature did not so intend." *Commonwealth v. Russ R.*, 433 Mass. 515 (2001).

Although G.L. c. 233, § 20E lists only three courts which can *grant* witness immunity, the Supreme Judicial Court recently held that an immunity order granted in Superior Court protects the witness from risk of incrimination in any proceeding in any court in the Commonwealth. *Commonwealth v. Austin A.*, 450 Mass. 665, 668 (2008).

Indecent Assault and Battery

Regulatory Authority—G.L. c. 265, § 13H
Dist. Ct. Model Jury Instruction 6.500

The defendant is charged with indecent assault and battery.

To prove the defendant guilty of this offense, the Commonwealth must prove three things beyond a reasonable doubt:

First: That the defendant committed an assault and battery on the alleged victim. Assault and battery is the intentional touching of another person, without legal justification or excuse.

Second: That the assault and battery was "indecent."

and *Third:* That the alleged victim did not consent to the alleged indecent assault and battery.

An indecent act is commonly understood as measured by common understanding and practices. It is one that is fundamentally offensive to contemporary standards of decency. An assault and battery may be "indecent" if it involves touching portions of the anatomy commonly thought private.

> See Instruction 6.140 (Assault and Battery) for additional language defining assault and battery. If the alleged victim was under the age of 14, see Instruction 6.520 (Indecent Assault and Battery on a Child under 14).

> "A touching is indecent when, judged by the normative standard of societal mores, it is violative of social and behavioral expectations in a manner which [is] fundamentally offensive to contemporary moral values . . . [and] which the common sense of society would regard as immodest, immoral and improper." *Commonwealth v. Vasquez,* 65 Mass. App. Ct. 305, 306 (2005) (internal quotations omitted). "It has been held that the intentional, unjustified touching of private areas such as 'the breasts, abdomen, buttocks, thighs, and pubic area of a female' constitutes an indecent assault and battery." *Commonwealth v. Mosby*, 30 Mass. App. Ct. 181, 184–185 (1991) (quoting *Commonwealth v. De La Cruz,* 15 Mass. App. Ct. 52, 59 (1982)).

> The above list of private anatomical parts and areas "has never been declared to be exhaustive . . . [and may] include other parts of the body—whether clothed or unclothed—that, if intentionally and unjustifiably touched, would violate our contemporary views of personal integrity and privacy." *Commonwealth v. Castillo*, 55 Mass. App. Ct. 563, 566 (2002) (internal quotations omitted).

Supplemental Instruction

Where victim touches the defendant's private part An indecent act includes those acts where the defendant directs or commands the alleged victim to touch a private part of the defendant (or another person).

Where the defendant touches the victim with his or her private part An indecent act includes those acts where a defendant touches the alleged victim with his (her) own private part (or that of another person).

Where capacity of victim over 14 to consent is at issue. I have instructed you that one element of this offense is that [alleged victim] did not consent to the touching.

In some cases, you may also have to consider a related question: whether the alleged victim was *able* to consent. If a person is so impaired because of the consumption of drugs or alcohol or for some other reason (for example, sleep, unconsciousness, intellectual disability, or physical helplessness) that he (she) is incapable of consenting, then it automatically follows that he (she) did not consent.

In such cases, the Commonwealth may prove that *[alleged victim]* did not consent by proving beyond a reasonable doubt:

First, that *[alleged victim]* was so impaired because of (consumption of alcohol or drugs) (intellectual disability) (injury) (physical helplessness) (sleep) (*[other reason]*) that he (she) was incapable of freely giving consent; and

Second, that the defendant knew, or reasonably should have known, that *[alleged victim's]* condition rendered him (her) incapable of consenting.

It is a question of fact in each case as to whether a particular person was or was not able to consent on a particular occasion. How do you determine this?

Where drugs or alcohol were involved: (Consumption or intoxication with alcohol or drugs, by itself, does not necessarily mean that an individual is incapable of deciding whether to consent . It is a matter of common knowledge that there are many levels of intoxication. The question is whether, as a result of a person's consumption of drugs, alcohol, or both, that person was unable to give or to refuse consent.)

If intoxication is not involved: (The crucial factors are often the person's intelligence or physical condition, but you may also consider other factors, such as the person's maturity and experience. The question comes down to whether the person was intelligent and aware enough to understand and evaluate what was happening, and to make a decision whether or not to consent based on that understanding.)

If the Commonwealth has proved beyond a reasonable doubt that *[alleged victim]* did not have enough understanding and awareness on that occasion to be able to consent, and that the defendant knew or reasonably should have known this, then it automatically follows that he (she) did not consent.

If the Commonwealth has failed to prove beyond a reasonable doubt that *[alleged victim]* was incapable of consenting and that the defendant knew or reasonably should have known this, then the Commonwealth must prove beyond a reasonable doubt that *[alleged victim]* did not in fact give consent.

In a case where the complainant's capacity to consent is at issue, the judge should instruct that if "because of the consumption of drugs or alcohol or for some other reason (for example, sleep, unconsciousness, mental retardation, or helplessness), a person is so impaired as to be incapable of consenting to sexual intercourse, then intercourse occurring during such incapacity is without that person's consent .... This formulation ... is intended to communicate to the jury that intoxication must be extreme before it can render a complainant incapable of consenting." However, the judge should not suggest that the alleged victim must be "wholly insensible" or "unconscious or nearly so .... The issue is whether, as a result of such intoxication, the complainant was unable to give or refuse consent." *Commonwealth v. Blache*, 450 Mass. 583, 592 & n.14, 595 n.19 (2008).

Blache also held that a defendant's reasonable mistake as to the complainant's ability to consent is a defense to a rape charge that is premised on the complainant's inability to consent. When a complainant is able to give or refuse consent, mistake about consent is not a defense because the need to prove the use or threat of force should negate any such mistake. But where the complainant is incapable of consenting, the Commonwealth need only prove the force necessary for penetration, and this increases the possibility of a reasonable mistake about consent. In rape cases tried after the *Blache* rescript (February 21, 2008) that are premised on inability to consent, the Commonwealth must prove that the defendant knew or reasonably should have known that the complainant was incapable of consenting. *Id.*, 450 Mass. at 592–597.

This supplemental instruction assumes that *Blache* is to be applied also in indecent assault and battery cases, and incorporates the contents of the suggested model instruction set out in *Blache*, 450 Mass. at 595 n.19.

NOTES

1. **Accidental touching.** If there is evidence, no matter how incredible, that the touching may have been accidental, the judge must charge on request that the Commonwealth has the burden of proving beyond a reasonable doubt that the touching was not accidental. *Commonwealth v. Maloney*, 23 Mass. App. Ct. 1016, 1016–17 (1987). See Instruction 9.100 (Accident).

2. **Aggravated forms of offense if victim 60 or older or disabled, or after prior sex offense.** General Laws c. 265, § 13H provides for an aggravated form of this offense if the victim is 60 or older or disabled. The District Court lacks final jurisdiction over that aggravated offense.

3. **First complaint.** Testimony concerning "first complaint" (see Instruction 3.660) is not limited to rape prosecutions, but may be received in other cases of sexual assault. *Commonwealth v. King*, 445 Mass. 217, 237–48 (2005) (replacing fresh complaint doctrine with first complaint rule for "sexual assaults"); *Commonwealth v. Brenner*, 18 Mass. App. Ct. 930, 931–32 (1984) (fresh complaint doctrine applicable to indecent assault and battery).

7

4. **Intent.** Indecent assault and battery does not require a specific intent, but only "the general criminal intent to do that which the law prohibits." *Commonwealth v. Egerton*, 396 Mass. 499, 504 (1986). "The intent element [of indecent assault and battery] is satisfied upon proof that 'the defendant intended—had a conscious purpose . . . —to commit an indecent or offensive touching without [the victim's] consent.'" *Commonwealth v. Kennedy*, 478 Mass. 804, 810 (2018), quoting *Commonwealth v. Marzilli*, 457 Mass. 64, 67 (2010). *See also Commonwealth v. Confrey*, 37 Mass. App. Ct. 290, 299–301 (1994) (indecent assault and battery on a child under G.L. c. 265, § 13B is not a specific in-tent crime, and therefore need not have been done for the purpose of sexual gratification or arousal).

5. **Kissing, hugging, and touching of clothing.** The mouth and its interior are an intimate part of the body. *Commonwealth v. Rosa*, 62 Mass. App. Ct. 622, 623–24 (2004) (insertion of thumb into mouth, coupled with other suggestive circumstances, found indecent). "[A]n unwanted kiss on the mouth has been held to constitute indecent conduct, at least in circumstances involving the forced insertion of the tongue, when coupled with surreptitiousness and a considerable disparity in age and authority between the perpetrator and the victim. We do not read our cases, however, as requiring that there always be tongue involvement for an act that might be characterized as a kiss to be found indecent, as other facts and circumstances may allow the trier of fact rationally to determine that the kiss was an indecent act . . . . [I]n most situations it would not be appropriate to criminalize a brief kiss on the mouth that did not involve the insertion or attempted insertion of the tongue [except where] the kiss could be viewed as having improper, sexual overtones, violative of social and behavioral expectations." *Commonwealth v. Vasquez*, 65 Mass. App. Ct. 305, 307, 309 (2005) (internal quotations omitted). See *Commonwealth v. Castillo*, 55 Mass. App. Ct. 563, 566–67 (2002) (kiss with forced insertion of tongue).

6. **Lesser included offenses.** Indecent assault and battery is a lesser included offense of forcible rape (G.L. c. 265, § 22). *Commonwealth v. Thomas*, 401 Mass. 109, 119–20 (1987); *Egerton*, 396 Mass. at 503 n.3. Assault and battery is a lesser included offense of indecent assault and battery; there is no lesser included offense of "indecent assault." *Com-*

monwealth v. Eaton, 2 Mass. App. Ct. 113, 116–18 (1974). See *Commonwealth v. Niels* N., 73 Mass. App. Ct. 689, 694 (2009) (assault and battery not a lesser included offense of indecent assault and battery on a child). Indecent assault and battery on a person over the age of fourteen is not a lesser included offense of indecent assault and battery on a child under the age of fourteen. See *Commonwealth v. Farrell*, 31 Mass. App. Ct. 267, 268–69 (1991).

7. **Parental Activity.** There is no risk that a jury could consider "normal parental activity" indecent where the judge instructed that an indecent act is to be "measured by common understanding and practices." *Commonwealth v. Trowbridge*, 419 Mass. 750, 758 (1995).

8. **Prior uncharged sexual contacts with same victim.** Evidence of the defendant's prior illicit sexual acts with the same victim, not charged in the complaint, may be admissible to show inclination to commit the acts charged in the complaint if sufficiently similar and not too remote in time. *Commonwealth v. Sosnowski*, 43 Mass. App. Ct. 367, 371 (1997) (two months not too remote); *Commonwealth v. Calcagno*, 31 Mass. App. Ct. 25, 26–27 (1991) (court properly admitted two acts of uncharged sexual conduct, one of which was one year prior to charged act and the other four months prior to the charged act); *Commonwealth v. King*, 387 Mass. 464, 469–70 (1982) (prior uncharged acts were contemporaneous to the charged acts).

9. **Privileged records.** In a prosecution for a sexual offense, the defense may seek pretrial access to statutorily privileged records of the alleged victim (e.g., psychological records) by a motion under Mass. R. Crim. 17(a)(2). The prosecutor must notify the subject and the record holder that they may, but are not required to, appear and be heard. After hearing, the judge must determine (1) whether the records are presumptively privileged, i.e., prepared in circumstances suggesting that some or all are likely to be privileged, and (2) whether the four requirements of *Commonwealth v. Lampron*, 441 Mass. 265 (2004), have been satisfied: that the documents are evidentiary and relevant, that they are not otherwise procurable by due diligence, that the defense cannot properly prepare for trial without them, and that the application is made in good faith and is not a general fishing expedition. If so, the judge is to order the clerk-magistrate to issue a summons for the records along with written instructions to the record keeper, who is then to deliver them under seal to the clerk-magistrate. Defense counsel is to be permitted to inspect them after signing a protective order with "stringent provisions" against disclosure (including to the defendant). Defense counsel must seek court authorization to disclose the privileged records to others, and must file a motion in limine no later than the final pretrial conference in order to use privileged content at trial. *Commonwealth v. Dwyer*, 448 Mass. 122 (2006).

10. **Rape shield law.** The admission of evidence concerning the prior sexual conduct of the victim is limited by the rape shield law, G.L. c. 233, § 21B. *Commonwealth v. Ruffen*, 399 Mass. 811, 816 (1987). In some circumstances, the statute may have to yield to the defendant's right to demonstrate bias on the part of the victim, but only if evidence of bias cannot otherwise be elicited. *Commonwealth v. Elder*, 389 Mass. 743, 750-751 (1983); *Commonwealth v. Joyce*, 382 Mass. 222, 224–32 (1981). See *Jury Trial Manual for Criminal Offenses Tried in the District Court* § 4.13.

11. **Rape trauma syndrome.** It is within a judge's discretion to permit expert testimony regarding post-assault behavior and symptoms of adult or child victims of sexual abuse. Such testimony is for the limited purpose of helping the jury to assess the alleged victim's credibility, and is not admissible as affirmative evidence that sexual abuse did occur. *Commonwealth v. Hudson*, 417 Mass. 536, 540–43 (1994) (child victims); *Commonwealth v. Dockham*, 405 Mass. 618, 629 (1989) (same); *Commonwealth v. Mamay*, 407 Mass. 412, 421–22 (1990) (adult victims).

However, it is reversible error to permit such an expert witness to offer an opinion that the alleged victim was in fact sexually assaulted. *Commonwealth v. Colin C.*, 419 Mass. 54, 59–61 (1994). If the expert witness has interviewed or evaluated the alleged victim in the case, particular care must be taken to prevent the expert from implicitly rendering an opinion as to the alleged victim's truthfulness. *Trowbridge*, 419 Mass. at 759 (expert testimony that child's behavior was consistent with that of sexually abused children, and that child's physical condition was consistent with type of abuse alleged in the case, was impermissible endorsement of child's credibility). In such cases, the judge should conduct a voir dire at which the expert answers the proposed questions. If the judge allows the testimony, the witness should be cautioned in advance not to opine on the credibility of the particular victim or that of sexual abuse victims in general. The judge should charge the jury after the expert's testimony and again during final instructions on the role of experts, and also charge on request that expert testimony is not affirmative evidence of sexual abuse and that the expert did not assess the credibility of the particular alleged victim. Counsel too should be very careful in closing argument not to imply that the expert vouched for the credibility of the particular alleged victim. *Commonwealth v. Rather*, 37 Mass. App. Ct. 140 (1984).

12. **Self-defense claim.** In a prosecution for indecent assault and battery involving a scuffle between the complainant and the defendant, the defendant is not entitled to a self-defense charge if the evidence would only permit the jury to find that the defendant initiated an indecent touching of the complainant, which triggered her physical response. The defendant is entitled to a self-defense charge if the evidence would permit the jury to find that the complainant initiated the scuffle and that any contact between the defendant and a sexually private area of the complainant occurred only when he tried to push her away in justifiable self-defense. *Commonwealth v. Lyons*, 71 Mass. App. Ct. 671 (2008).

13. **Statement of reasons required if imprisonment not imposed.** A jury session judge sentencing for this or one of the other crimes against persons found in G.L. c. 265 who does not impose a sentence of incarceration "shall include in the record of the case specific reasons for not imposing a sentence of imprisonment," which shall be a public record. G.L. c. 265, § 41.

14. **Consent.** It appears that absence of consent may not be an element of an indecent assault and battery upon a victim who is 14 or older if the touching was "physically harmful" or "potentially physically harmful." See *Commonwealth v. Burke*, 390 Mass. 480, 487 (1983).

15. **Defendant does not perform touching.** The case law supports a conclusion that forcing a victim to take off his or her clothing, or forcing the victim to commit an indecent touching, may constitute indecent assault and battery. *A.P. v M.T.*, 92 Mass. App. Ct. 156, 164 (2017).

Indecent Assault and Battery on a Child Under Fourteen

Regulatory Authority—G.L. c. 265, § § 13B, 13B½, 13B¾
Dist. Ct. Model Jury Instruction 6.520

The defendant is charged with indecent assault and battery on a child less than 14 years of age.

To prove the defendant guilty of this offense, the Commonwealth must prove three things beyond a reasonable doubt:

First: That the child was not yet 14 years of age at the time of the alleged offense;

Second: That the defendant committed an assault and battery on that child. Assault and battery is essentially the intentional touching of another person without legal justification or excuse.

and *Third:* The Commonwealth must prove beyond a reasonable doubt that the assault and battery was "indecent" as that word is commonly understood, measured by common understanding and practices.

An indecent act is one that is fundamentally offensive to contemporary standards of decency. An assault and battery may be "indecent" if it involves touching portions of the anatomy commonly thought private.

If the alleged victim is under 14 years of age, it is irrelevant whether or not (he) (she) consented to any touching.

The model instruction reflects the law on the issue of consent applicable to such offenses committed on and after October 6, 1986, when St. 1986, c. 187 amended G.L. c. 265, § 13B to provide that "[i]n a prosecution under this section, a child under the age of fourteen years shall be deemed incapable of consenting to any conduct of the defendant for which said defendant is being prosecuted."

For such an offense committed before October 6, 1986, the judge must charge that absence of consent is a fourth required element of the crime; the judge should also give the supplemental instruction to Instruction 6.500 (Indecent Assault and Battery), appropriately modified to discuss "maturity," concerning the child-victim's ability to consent. See *Commonwealth v. Reid*, 400 Mass. 534, 541 (1987) (prior to 1986 amendment, lack of consent was element of offense of indecent assault and battery on a child under the age of fourteen years); *Commonwealth v. Burke*, 390 Mass. 480, 487 (1983); *Commonwealth v. Maloney*, 23 Mass. App. Ct. 1016, 1016 (1987) (lack of consent inferable from age and verbal reluctance of witness).

See also the citations and notes under Instruction 6.500 (Indecent assault and battery)

Where victim touches the defendant's private part An indecent act includes those acts where the defendant directs or commands the alleged victim to touch a private part of the defendant (or that of another person).

Where the defendant touches the victim with his or her private part An indecent act includes those acts where a defendant touches the alleged victim with his (her) own private part (or that of another person).

NOTES

1. **Age of victim.** The age of the victim is an essential element of this offense. *Commonwealth v. Rockwood,* 27 Mass. App. Ct. 1137, 1139 (1989).

2. **Aggravated forms of offense.** Statute 2008, c. 205 (effective October 22, 2008), created two new aggravated forms of this offense:

Aggravated indecent assault and battery on a child under 14 (G.L. c. 265, § 13B½) provides for enhanced punishment if the offense was committed (1) by a person who was a mandated reporter of child abuse or neglect, or (2) if it was committed during the commission or attempted commission of twelve specified offenses: armed burglary (G.L. c. 266, § 14); unarmed burglary (G.L. c. 266, § 15); breaking and entering (G.L. c. 266, § 16); entering without breaking (G.L. c. 266, § 17); breaking and entering in a dwelling (G.L. c. 266, § 18); kidnapping (G.L. c. 265, § 26); armed robbery (G.L. c. 265, § 17); unarmed robbery (G.L. c. 265, § 19); assault and battery with a dangerous weapon (G.L. c. 265, § 15A); assault with a dangerous weapon (G.L. c. 265, § 15B); home invasion (G.L. c. 265, § 18C); or exhibiting a child in a state of nudity or sexual conduct (G.L. c. 272, § 29A).

Indecent assault and battery on a child under 14 after prior sex offense (G.L. c. 265, § 13B¾) provides for enhanced punishment if the offense was committed after a prior conviction or juvenile adjudication for any of ten sex offenses: indecent assault and battery on a child under 14 (G.L. c. 265, § 13B); aggravated indecent assault and battery on a child under 14 (G.L. c. 265, § 13B½); indecent assault and battery on a person 14 or older (G.L. c. 265, § 13H); assault to rape a child (G.L. c. 265, § 24B); rape of a child (G.L. c. 265, § 22A); aggravated rape of a child (G.L. c. 265, § 22B); statutory rape (G.L. c. 265, § 23); aggravated statutory rape (G.L. c. 265, § 23A); rape (G.L. c. 265, § 22); or "a like violation of the laws of another state, the United States or a military, territorial or Indian tribal authority."

Under G.L. c. 218, § 26, the District Court has jurisdiction over violations of G.L. c. 265, § 13B but does not have final jurisdiction over these aggravated forms (§§ 13B½ and 13B¾) of the offense.

The same statute also repealed the prior enhanced penalty for a subsequent conviction of § 13B.

3. **Hearsay statement by child victim.** General Laws c. 233, § 81 permits, under certain limited circumstances, the admission of hearsay statements by sexual abuse victims under 10 years of age. The Supreme Judicial Court has assumed without deciding that § 81 is facially constitutional. However, the judge "must strictly adhere" to the requirements of § 81 and in addition: (1) the Commonwealth must give the defense advance notice that it will seek to use such hearsay statements; (2) the Commonwealth must show its compelling need to do so "by more than a mere preponderance of evidence"; (3) any separate hearing regarding the reliability of the statement must be on the record, and the defendant and defense counsel must be permitted to attend "[w]here possible without causing severe emotional trauma to the child witness"; (4) the judge's finding of reliability must be supported by specific findings on the record; (5) if the child is presently unavailable because incompetent to testify, that incompetence must not call into question the reliability of the hearsay statement; and (6) there must be other, independently-admissible evidence that corroborates the child's hearsay statement. *Commonwealth v. Colin C.,* 419 Mass. 54, 61–66 & n.8 (1994). The judge should also consider the impact of *Crawford v. Washington,* 541 U.S. 36 (2004), on the viability of this statute. See *Commonwealth v. DeOliveira,* 447 Mass. 56, 64–65 (2006) (six year old child's statement to doctor not testimonial, as it was made for medical treatment, not in anticipation of litigation).

4. **Individual voir dire required on request.** For the trial of any sexual offense against a minor, the judge must, on request, question prospective jurors individually as to whether they are the victim of a childhood sexual offense. *Commonwealth v. Flebotte,* 417 Mass. 348, 353–56 (1994).

5. **Inflammatory evidence.** In a trial based on the defendant having touched the breast of a 12-year-old girl, the judge correctly admitted in evidence items taken from the defendant's car which included photographs of fully-clothed young girls in outdoors play, small-sized underwear, and pornographic magazines showing pictures of teenage girls and of sexual activity between adults. As evidence of the defendant's voyeuristic interest in sexual matters and young females, they were probative as to whether the defendant had intentionally or accidentally touched the victim's breast. The Appeals Court assumed that a second group of items from the car (consisting of a knife, rope, duct tape, and personal lubricant) should have been excluded as irrelevant and perhaps suggestive that the defendant intended to kidnap and rape the victim. *Commonwealth v. Wallace,* 70 Mass. App. Ct. 757, 764–66 (2007).

6. **Lesser included offenses.** Since simple assault and battery (G.L. c. 265, § 13A) requires *either* an actually or potentially physically harmful touching *or* an unconsented touching, it is not a lesser included offense of indecent assault and battery on a child under 14, since lack of consent is no longer an element of the latter offense. *Commonwealth v. Farrell,* 31 Mass. App. Ct. 268–69 (1991). Indecent assault and battery on a child under 14 is a lesser included offense of forcible rape of a child (G.L. c. 265, § 22A). *Commonwealth v. Cobb,* 26 Mass. App. Ct. 283, 284 (1988). Indecent assault and battery on a person over the age of fourteen is not a lesser included offense of indecent assault and battery on a child under the age of fourteen. See *Commonwealth v. Farrell,* 31 Mass. App. Ct. 267, 268–69 (1991). For offenses committed prior to October 6, 1986, indecent assault and battery on a child under 14 is not a lesser included offense of statutory rape (G.L. c. 265, § 23). *Reid,* 400 Mass. at 541.

7. **Contact with non-sexual parts of the body.** In *Commonwealth v. Cruz,* 93 Mass. App. Ct. 136, 139–40 (2017), the Appeals Court held that the almost-sixty year old defendant's hugging of the thirteen year old complainant "like a hug her parents would give her" was not indecent, nor was his lifting of her shirt at the hip where no part of her body was exposed.

Indecent Exposure

Regulatory Authority—G.L. c. 272, § 53
Dist. Ct. Model Jury Instruction 7.340

The defendant is charged with indecent exposure. In order to prove the defendant guilty of this offense, the Commonwealth must prove three things beyond a reasonable doubt:

First: That the defendant exposed his (her) (genitals) to one or more persons;

Second: That the defendant did so intentionally; and

Third: That one or more persons were offended by the defendant's thus exposing himself (herself).

> G.L. c. 272, § 53. See Instruction 3.120 (Intent). See also Instruction 7.400 (Open and Gross Lewdness and Lascivious Behavior, G.L. c. 272, § 16); Instruction 7.500 (Unnatural and Lascivious Act, G.L. c. 272, § 35); and Instruction 7.380 (Lewd, Wanton and Lascivious Act, G.L. c. 272, § 35).

NOTE

Limited to exposure of genitalia. The misdemeanor of indecent exposure (G.L. c. 272, § 53) is applicable only to exposure of the genitalia, and not to exposure of the genital area, pubic hair, buttocks, or female breasts. *Commonwealth v. Arthur,* 420 Mass. 535 (1995). By contrast, the separate felony offense of open and gross lewdness and lascivious behavior (G.L. c. 272, § 16), includes the intentional exposure of genitalia, buttocks, or female breasts, but has the additional element that it must be done in such a way as to produce actual alarm or shock. *See Commonwealth v. Quinn,* 439 Mass 492 (2003); *Commonwealth v. Fitta,* 391 Mass. 394, 396 (1984) (unlike open and gross lewdness, the crime of indecent exposure does not require that it be done in such a way as to produce alarm or shock); *Commonwealth v. Broadland,* 315 Mass. 20, 21–22 (1943) (indecent exposure involves "an intentional act of lewd exposure, offensive to one or more persons"); *Commonwealth v. Bishop,* 296 Mass. 459, 462 (1937) (offense need not be in public place or involve exposure to more than one person).

Intimidating a Witness, Juror, Court Official or Law Enforcement Officer

Regulatory Authority—G.L. c. 268, § 13B
Dist. Ct. Model Jury Instruction 7.360

Note: Instruction 7.365 is a stand-alone instruction on intentionally misleading an investigator in a criminal investigation.

The defendant is charged with intimidation of a *[insert statutory class of person alleged to have been intimidated]*. In order to prove the defendant guilty of this offense, the Commonwealth must prove three things beyond a reasonable doubt:

First: The defendant willfully, either directly or indirectly:

- (threatened)
- (attempted to cause physical injury to) (caused physical injury to)
- (attempted to cause emotional injury to) (caused emotional injury to)
- (attempted to cause economic injury to) (caused economic injury to)
- (attempted to cause property damage to) (caused property damage to)
- (conveyed a gift, offer, or promise of anything of value to)
- (misled)[1]
- (intimidated)
- (harassed)

another person;

Second: The other person was:

- a witness or potential witness
- a person who was aware of information, records, documents, or objects related to a violation of (a criminal statute) (conditions of (probation) (parole) (bail)
- a (judge) (juror) (grand juror) (attorney) (police officer) (federal agent) (investigator) (clerk) (court officer) (probation officer) (parole officer)
- a person (who is or was attending) (who made known an intention to attend) a (criminal proceeding of any type) (civil proceeding of any type), namely _____)[2], (grand jury proceeding) (juvenile proceeding)

[or]

If the alleged act was committed on or after April 13, 2018:

- (victim witness advocate) (correction officer) (court reporter) (court interpreter);
- a person who is or was aware of information, records, documents or objects that relate to a violation of a court order;
- a family member of a person described in this section, namely _____;

If the alleged act was committed before April 13, 2018:

- a person who was furthering a (criminal proceeding of any type) (civil proceeding of any type), namely _____), (grand jury proceeding) (juvenile proceeding).

Third element when intentional conduct is alleged.

and *Third:* That the defendant did so with the specific intent to: (impede, obstruct, delay, prevent or otherwise interfere with a (criminal investigation at any stage) ((criminal proceeding of any type) (civil proceeding of any type), namely _____)[3], (grand jury proceeding) (juvenile proceeding);

If the alleged act was committed on or after April 13, 2018:

[or]

punish, harm or otherwise retaliate against any such persons which I previously defined or such person's family member for participating in a (criminal investigation at any stage) ((criminal proceeding of any type) (civil proceeding of any type), namely_____)[4], (grand jury proceeding) (juvenile proceeding).

Further instruction on specific intent. To prove the third element, the Commonwealth must prove that the defendant specifically intended to: impede, obstruct, delay, prevent, or otherwise interfere with a (criminal investigation at any stage) ((criminal proceeding of any type) (civil proceeding of any type, namely _____)[5] (grand jury proceeding) (juvenile proceeding);

If the alleged act was committed on or after April 13, 2018:

[or]

(punish, harm or otherwise retaliate against any such person which I previously defined or such person's family member for participating in a (criminal investigation at any stage) (criminal proceeding of any type) (civil proceeding of any type), namely _____)[6], (grand jury proceeding) (juvenile proceeding)).

That is, it must prove the purpose or objective of any behavior of the defendant. Obviously, it is impossible to look directly into the defendant's mind. But in our everyday affairs, we often decide from the actions of other what their state of mind is. In this case, you may examine the defendant's actions and words, and all of the surrounding circumstances, to help you determine what (his) (her) intent was at the time.

Third element when reckless conduct is alleged. And *Third*: [or] That the defendant acted in reckless disregard that (his) (her) conduct may impede, obstruct, delay, prevent, or otherwise interfere with a (criminal investigation at any stage) ((criminal proceeding of any type) (civil proceeding of any type), namely _____)[7], (grand jury proceeding), (juvenile proceeding)).

Further instruction on reckless conduct. To prove the third element, it is not enough for the Commonwealth to prove that the defendant acted negligently—that is, acted in a way that a reasonably careful person would not. It must be shown that the defendant's actions went beyond mere negligence and amounted to recklessness. The defendant acted recklessly if (he) (she) knew, or should have known, that such actions were very likely to impede, obstruct, delay, prevent, or otherwise interfere with a (criminal investigation at any stage) ((criminal proceeding of any type) (civil proceeding of any type), namely _____) (grand jury proceeding)[8] (juvenile proceeding), but (he) (she) ran that risk and went ahead anyway.

But it is not necessary that (he) (she) intended to interfere with the proceeding. If the defendant actually realized in advance that (his) (her) conduct was very likely to interfere with the proceeding and decided to run that risk, such conduct would of course be reckless. But even if (he) (she) was not conscious of the result that was inherent in such conduct, it is still reckless conduct if a reasonable person, under the circumstances as they were known to the defendant, would have recognized that such actions were very likely to interfere with the proceeding.

If the Commonwealth has proved each of the three elements of the crime beyond a reasonable doubt, you should return a verdict of guilty. If any element of the crime has not been proved beyond a reasonable doubt, you must find the defendant not guilty.

FOOTNOTES

1 For a definition of what constitutes "misleading" conduct, see Instruction 7.365—Intentionally misleading an investigator in a criminal investigation.

2 G.L. c. 268, § 13B, as amended by st. 2018, c. 69, § 155, specifically references the following proceedings in addition to identifying criminal proceedings of any type and civil proceedings of any type: grand jury proceeding, dangerousness hearing, motion hearing, trial, any type of a parole hearing, parole violation proceeding, probation violation proceeding, administrative hearing, probate or family court proceeding, juvenile proceeding, housing proceeding, land proceeding, clerk's hearing, and court-ordered mediation.

3 See fn. 1, *supra.*

4 See fn. 1, *supra.*

5 See fn. 1, *supra.*

6 See fn. 1, *supra.*

7 See fn. 1, *supra.*

8 See fn. 1, *supra.*

Supplemental Instructions

1. *"Investigator."* An "investigator" is defined by our law to mean an individual or group of individuals lawfully authorized by (a department or agency of the federal government, or any political subdivision thereof) (a department or agency of the Commonwealth) (a political subdivision of the Commonwealth, such as a city or town) to conduct or engage in an investigation of, prosecution

7

for, or defense of an alleged violation of law in the course of his or her official duties.

G.L. c. 268, § 13B(2).

2. *"Criminal investigation."* Where a person is charged with intimidation in connection with a criminal investigation, the Commonwealth does not have to prove that a crime had actually occurred or that a criminal investigation was in progress when the alleged intimidation occurred. Rather it must prove beyond a reasonable doubt that a possible criminal violation occurred that would lead to a criminal investigation or proceeding.

Commonwealth v. Fragata, 480 Mass. 121, 127 (2018).

3. *"Harass."* To "harass" means to engage in any act directed at a specific person or group of persons, which act seriously alarms or annoys such person or group of persons and would cause a reasonable person or group of persons to suffer substantial emotional distress.

Such act shall include, but not be limited to, an act conducted by mail, electronic mail, internet communications, facsimile communications, or other telephonic or telecommunications device.

Devices include, among others, those that transfer signs, signals, writing, images, sounds, data, or intelligence of any nature transmitted in whole or in part by a wire, radio, electromagnetic, photo-electronic, or photo-optical system. This includes transfers by electronic mail, internet communications, instant messages, or facsimile communications.

G.L. c. 268, § 13B(3).

NOTES

1. **Effective date.** On April 13, 2018, G.L. c. 268, § 13B was amended by St. 2018, c. 69, § 155, so that an act committed in retaliation for past participation in a criminal investigation or court proceeding can now be charged as a crime under § 13B. As a result, the holding in *Commonwealth v. Hamilton*, 459 Mass. 422, 435–37 (2011), that § 13B did not cover retaliation for past participation in a criminal investigation or court proceeding, has been superseded. In addition, the amendment eliminated the category of persons protected by the statute who "further[ed] a civil or criminal proceeding . . . of any type," and added the following additional categories of persons protected by the statute: a person who is or was aware of information, records, documents, or objects that relate to a violation of a court order; victim witness advocate; correction officer; court reporter; court interpreter; and family member of a person described in the section.

This model instruction applies to acts committed both prior to, and after, the April 13, 2018, amendment to § 13B.

2. **Related statutes.** See G.L. c. 268, §§ 13 (bribing or attempting to bribe juror), 13A (picketing court to obstruct or influence), 13C (disrupting court proceedings), 14 (juror accepting bribe).

3. **Attempt to intimidate need not succeed.** In a prosecution for attempted intimidation it is immaterial that the witness had already recanted her testimony against the defendant before receiving his threatening telephone calls. *Commonwealth v. Pagels*, 69 Mass. App. Ct. 607, 614-615 (2007). *See also Commonwealth v. Robinson*, 444 Mass. 102, 109 (2005).

4. **"Criminal proceeding."** The trial does not end when the verdict is announced. *Commonwealth v. Cathy C.*, 64 Mass. App. Ct. 471, 474 (2005). When a show cause hearing was held and the application was either allowed or no decision had yet been announced, the proceeding was still ongoing. *Robinson*, 444 Mass. at 109-110.

5. **"Intimidation"** in G.L. c. 268, § 13B does not require that the victim be placed in fear or apprehension of actual harm. *Commonwealth v. Gordon*, 44 Mass. App. Ct. 233, 235 (1998). It is not necessary that the defendant's statement or conduct refer directly to a pending court case in order to constitute intimidation. *Commonwealth v. Drumgoole*, 49 Mass. App. Ct. 87, 91 (2000). The jury may infer that the act of pointing a cellular telephone camera at a witness waiting to testify in a criminal proceeding, and making a physical gesture consistent with taking a photograph of the witness, while not overtly threatening, falls within the meaning of intimidation. *Commonwealth v. Casiano*, 70 Mass. App. Ct. 705, 708-709 (2007). Photographing the victim's family near the victim's home on the day of a court hearing is sufficient for the jury to infer intent to intimidate. *Commonwealth v. Robinson*, 444 Mass. 102, 110 (2005). Intent to intimidate is inferable from the defendant's bizarre telephone call during stalking trial, though its content was similar to earlier calls. *Commonwealth v. Potter*, 39 Mass. App. Ct. 924, 926 (1995). It is not required that the defendant specifically articulated a warning against speaking to the police or other criminal investigator. The fact finder may evaluate the circumstances in which a statement was made, including its timing, to determine whether the defendant in fact intended to intimidate the victim. *Commonwealth v. King*, 69 Mass. App. Ct. 113, 120 (2007) (inferable that defendant's statement that "[i]f he saw [the victim] on [TV] News he was going to come back and kill [him]" was a shorthand warning against reporting a robbery to the police).

6. **Future cooperation with police.** There is no requirement that the victim must be furnishing information on the day that the intimidating action is taken or statement made. *King*, 69 Mass. App. Ct. at 121. "It is enough that the jury reasonably conclude from the surrounding circumstances that it was likely that the victim would furnish to an official investigating authority information pertaining to the crime and that the defendant intended to discourage such communication." *Id.*

7. **Separate threats or inducements in same communication.** Separate and distinct threats or inducements may be charged as separate offenses even if they are contained within a single telephone call, letter or personal confrontation. *Commonwealth v. Lester*, 70 Mass. App. Ct. 55, 68 (2007) (a "person seeking to influence a witness may, in one telephone call, threaten physical harm to the witness, threaten to kill a family member, or offer varying inducements").

Kidnapping[1,2]

Regulatory Authority—G.L. c. 265, § 26
Super. Ct. Model Jury Instructions § 3.14

In this case, the defendant, (defendant/name), is charged with kidnapping. The state legislature has specifically defined kidnapping in G.L. c. 265, § 26. The relevant portions of the statute read as follows:

> Whoever, without lawful authority, forcibly or secretly confines or imprisons another person within this Commonwealth against his will, or forcibly carries or sends such person out of this Commonwealth, or forcibly seizes and confines (or inveigles) another person, with intent either to cause him to be secretly confined or imprisoned in this Commonwealth against his will, or to cause him to be sent out of this Commonwealth against his will or in any way held to service against his will, shall be punished. . . .[3]

NOTES

[1] This instruction and notes are taken from the chargebook offered as a guide to Superior Court judges in 1995 and updated by the authors.

[2] *Note:* The judge should read the elements for the theory that is appropriate to the facts of the case and for which the defendant is indicted. There are three separate theories under which a person may be convicted of kidnapping. The statute itself breaks down into three parts:

> Whoever, without lawful authority, [1] forcibly or secretly confines, or imprisons another person within this Commonwealth against his will, or [2] forcibly carries or sends such person out of this commonwealth, or [3] forcibly seizes and confines or inveigles or kidnaps another person, with intent either to cause him to be secretly confined or imprisoned within this commonwealth against his will, or to cause him to be sent out of this commonwealth against his will or in any way held to service against his will. . . .

G.L. c. 265, § 26.

[3] *Commonwealth v. Ware*, 375 Mass. 118, 119 n.1 (1978).

Kidnapping (I)[1,2]

General Laws c. 265, § 26, states:

> Whoever, without lawful authority, forcibly or secretly confines, or imprisons another person within this Commonwealth against his will . . . shall be punished.

In order to establish the defendant's guilt on this charge, the Commonwealth must prove each of the following three elements beyond a reasonable doubt.

First Element: that the defendant was without lawful authority;

Second Element: that the defendant forcibly or secretly confined or imprisoned another person within the Commonwealth against (his/her) will; and

Third Element: that the defendant committed the offense against the other person's will.

I will now further define each of these three elements.

The first element the Commonwealth must prove beyond a reasonable doubt is that the defendant was acting without lawful authority. An act taken under lawful authority means that it was authorized, sanctioned or allowed by law. An act is taken without lawful authority if it is not authorized by law.[3]

The second element the Commonwealth must prove beyond a reasonable doubt is that the defendant forcibly or secretly confined or imprisoned (the alleged victim/name) in Massachusetts.[4] The word "forcibly" means carried out through the use of force. One acts "forcibly" toward another if one compels, constrains or obliges (him/her) to do something against (his/her) will.[5] Force may be either actual or constructive, so there need not be actual physical force applied against (the alleged victim/name); it is sufficient that (the alleged victim/name) is subdued by a display of potential force.[6] "Secretly" means to do something without the knowledge of others. "Confine" means to enclose within bounds or limit, to restrict, to shut up or keep in.[7] "Imprison" means to detain in custody or to hold in restraint. Any restraint of a person's liberty is a confinement or an imprisonment.[8]

The third element the Commonwealth must prove beyond a reasonable doubt is that the defendant committed the offense against the person's will. "Against his/her will" means that (the alleged victim/name) did not consent to be seized, confined, imprisoned, carried, sent, inveigled or kidnapped by the defendant.[9] A person's submitting because of fear is not consent.[10] If on the evidence the Commonwealth has failed to prove beyond a reasonable doubt one or more of the three elements I have described, you must return a verdict of not guilty on the charge of kidnapping. However, if the Commonwealth did prove beyond a reasonable doubt *all* of the elements I have described, you must return a verdict of guilty on the charges of kidnapping.

[The fourth element the Commonwealth must prove beyond a reasonable doubt is that the defendant committed the offense of kidnapping, as described above, with the specific intent to extort money or some other valuable thing.

Intent refers to a person's objective or purpose.[11] Specific intent, which is required in this case, is the act of concentrating or focusing the mind for some perceptible period. It is a conscious act, with the determination of the mind to do an act.[12] It is contemplation rather than reflex, and it must precede that act.[13] The Commonwealth must prove specific intent on the part of the defendant; this requires you to make a decision about the defendant's state of mind at the time of the crime. In this case, you may or may not infer the defendant's intent by considering all of the facts, as well as evidence, of defendant's conduct offered during the trial.[14] To "extort" means to obtain property, coerce payment of money, secure a pecuniary advantage for oneself, or compel another to do an act against his or her will as a result of a threat. "The emphasis in the crime of extortion is on the wrongful use of fear to compel (the alleged victim/name) to surrender something of value to the extortionist."[15]][16]

NOTES

[1] This instruction and notes are taken from the chargebook offered as a guide to Superior Court judges in 1995 and updated by the authors.

[2] General Laws Chapter 265, § 26, provides that the crime of kidnapping can be committed by alternate means.

[3] *Commonwealth v. Wilkinson*, 415 Mass. 402, 408 (1993) (Formerly, a bail bondsman could seize a bailed individual for surrender at any time and remove that individual from the Commonwealth. The Uniform Criminal Extradition Act, G.L. c. 276, § 11-20R, requires the bondsman to comply with certain procedures prior to removing a bailed individual.) Under 2018 Mass. Acts c. 69, § 179, the legislative prohibited the practice of compensation for acting as surety.

[4] *Commonwealth v. Jackson*, 417 Mass. 830, 844 (1994) (Conviction for kidnapping upheld where there was evidence that the victim "was transported, that he was alive at the time that he was bound, and that the manner in which he was bound would have rendered him incapacitated.").

[5] *Commonwealth v. Ware*, 375 Mass. 118, 119 n.1 (1978).

[6] *Commonwealth v. LaPlante*, 73 Mass. App. Ct. 199, 202–03 (2008); *Commonwealth v. Titus*, 32 Mass. App. Ct. 216, 221 (1992) (quoting *Commonwealth v. Caracciola*, 409 Mass. 648, 652 (1991)).

[7] *Commonwealth v. Rivera*, 460 Mass. 139, 142–44 (2011) (to secretly confine someone is to isolate or insulate them from meaningful contact or communication with the public, where the confinement is in a place or manner that makes it unlikely that members of the public will know or learn of the victim's unwilling confinement within a reasonable period of time), (citing 3 W.R. LaFave, *Substantive Criminal Law* § 18.1(c), at 17 (3rd ed. 2003)).

[8] *Commonwealth v. Oberle*, 476 Mass. 539, 548 (2017); *Commonwealth v. Nickerson*, 87 Mass. (5 Allen) 518, 525–26 (1862).

[9] *Commonwealth v. Edgerly*, 13 Mass. App. Ct. 562, 580 (1982) (the phrase "against her will" is equal to "without her consent"), *review denied*, 386 Mass. 1104 (1982); *see Commonwealth v. Travis*, 408 Mass. 1, 8 (1990) (preventing victim from leaving car "by pushing against her body with his hand" can support inference of nonconsensual conduct in the context of kidnapping). A twelve-year-old child falls within the tender years doctrine and, as a matter of law, cannot consent to leaving or being taken from the custody of his or her parents or legal guardians. *Commonwealth v. Colon*, 431 Mass. 188 (2000).

[10] *Commonwealth v. Caracciola*, 409 Mass. 648 (1991).

[11] *Commonwealth v. Nickerson*, 388 Mass. 246, 253–54 (1983).

[12] *Commonwealth v. Nickerson*, 388 Mass. 246, 254 (1983).

[13] *Commonwealth v. Nickerson*, 388 Mass. 246, 254 (1983); *see also Commonwealth v. Gunter*, 427 Mass. 259, 269 & n.12 (1998) (critical requirement in specific intent offense is that defendant must intend that the particular consequences constituting the offense follow from his or her conduct).

[14] *Commonwealth v. Niziolek*, 380 Mass. 513, 528 (1980).

[15] *Commonwealth v. Miller*, 385 Mass. 521, 526 (1982).

[16] Use only if kidnapping with intent to extort is alleged.

Kidnapping (II)[1,2]

General Laws c. 265, § 26, states:

> Whoever, without lawful authority . . . forcibly carries or sends such person out of this commonwealth . . . shall be punished.

In order to establish the defendant's guilt on this charge, the Commonwealth must prove each of the following two elements beyond a reasonable doubt:

First Element: that the defendant was without lawful authority and

Second Element: that the defendant forcibly carried or sent another person out of this Commonwealth.

I will now further define each of these two elements.

The first element the Commonwealth must prove beyond a reasonable doubt is that the defendant was acting without lawful authority. An act taken under lawful authority means that it was authorized, sanctioned or allowed by law. An act is taken without lawful authority if it is not authorized by law.

The second element the Commonwealth must prove beyond a reasonable doubt is that the defendant forcibly carried or sent (the alleged victim/name) out of Massachusetts. The word "forcibly" means carried out through the use of force. One acts "forcibly" toward another if one compels, constrains or obliges (him/her) to do something against (his/her) will.[3] Force may be either actual or constructive, so there need not be actual physical force applied against (the alleged victim/name); it is sufficient that (the alleged victim/name) is subdued by a display of potential force.[4] "Out of the Commonwealth" means outside of the state of Massachusetts. If based on the evidence the Commonwealth has failed to prove beyond a reasonable doubt any one of the two elements I have described, then you must return a verdict of not guilty on the charge of kidnapping. However, if the Commonwealth does prove beyond a reasonable doubt *each* of the two elements I have described, you must return a verdict of guilty on the charges of kidnapping.

[The third element the Commonwealth must prove beyond a reasonable doubt is that the defendant committed the offense of kidnapping, as described above, with the specific intent to extort money or some other valuable thing. Intent refers to a person's objective or purpose.[5] Specific intent, which is required in this case, is the act of concentrating or focusing the mind for some perceptible period. It is a conscious act, with the determination of the mind to do an act.[6] It is contemplation rather than reflex, and it must precede that act.[7] The Commonwealth must prove specific intent on the part of the defendant. This requires you to make a decision about the defendant's state of mind at the time of the crime. In this case, you may or may not infer the defendant's intent by considering all of the facts, as well as evidence of defendant's conduct, offered during the trial.[8] To "extort" means to obtain property, coerce payment of money, secure a pecuniary advantage for oneself, or compel another to do an act against his or her will as a result of a threat. "The emphasis in the crime of extortion is on the wrongful use of fear to compel (the alleged victim/name) to surrender something of value to the extortionist."[9]][10]

NOTES

[1] This instruction and notes are taken from the chargebook offered as a guide to Superior Court judges in 1995 and updated by the authors.

[2] General Laws Chapter 265, § 26, provides that the crime of kidnapping can be committed by alternate means.

[3] *Commonwealth v. Ware*, 375 Mass. 118, 119 n.1 (1978). A twelve-year-old child falls within the tender years doctrine and, as a matter of law, cannot consent to leaving or being taken from the custody of his or her parents or legal guardians. *Commonwealth v. Colon*, 431 Mass. 188 (2000).

[4] *Commonwealth v. Titus*, 32 Mass. App. Ct. 216, 221 (1992).

[5] *Commonwealth v. Nickerson*, 388 Mass. 246, 253–54 (1983).

[6] *Commonwealth v. Nickerson*, 388 Mass. 246, 253–54 (1983).

[7] *Commonwealth v. Nickerson*, 388 Mass. 246, 253–54 (1983); *see also Commonwealth v. Gunter*, 427 Mass. 259, 269 & n.12 (1998) (critical requirement in specific intent offense is that defendant must intend that the particular consequences constituting the offense follow from his or her conduct).

[8] *Commonwealth v. Niziolek*, 380 Mass. 513, 528 (1980).

[9] *Commonwealth v. Miller*, 385 Mass. 521, 527 (1982).

[10] Use this paragraph only if kidnapping with intent to extort is alleged.

Kidnapping (III)[1,2]

General Laws c. 265, § 26, states:

> Whoever, without lawful authority . . . forcibly seizes and confines or inveigles or kidnaps another person, with intent either to cause him to be secretly confined or imprisoned within this commonwealth against his will, or to cause him to be sent out of this commonwealth against his will or in any way held to service against his will . . . shall be punished.

In order to establish the defendant's guilt on this charge, the Commonwealth must prove each of the following three elements beyond a reasonable doubt:

First Element: that the defendant was without lawful authority;

Second Element: that the defendant forcibly seized and confined, or inveigled or kidnapped another person; and

Third Element: that the defendant did so with intent to cause the other person to be secretly confined or imprisoned in the Commonwealth against (his/her) will or to cause (him/her) to be sent out of this Commonwealth against (his/her) will or to cause (him/her) to be in any way held to service against (his/her) will.

I will now further define each of these three elements.

The first element the Commonwealth must prove beyond a reasonable doubt is that the defendant was acting without lawful authority. An act taken under lawful authority means that it was authorized, sanctioned or allowed by law. An act is taken without lawful authority if it is not authorized by law.

The second element the Commonwealth must prove beyond a reasonable doubt is that the defendant forcibly seized and confined or inveigled (the alleged victim/name). The word forcibly means carried out through the use of force. One acts forcibly toward another if one compels, constrains or obliges him or her to do something against his or her will.[3] Force may be either actual or constructive, so there need not be actual physical force applied against (the alleged victim/name); it is sufficient that (the alleged victim/name) is subdued by a display of potential force.[4]

"Confine" means to enclose within bounds, limit, restrict or shut up or keep in.[5] Any restraint of a person's liberty is a confinement or an imprisonment.[6]

[To "inveigle" means to lure or entice through deceit or insincerity.[7]][8]

"Against his/her will" means that (the alleged victim/name) did not consent to be seized, confined, imprisoned, carried, sent, inveigled or kidnapped by the defendant.[9] A person's submitting because of fear is not consent.[10] A forcible act is necessary for a conviction under this section of the law.

The third element the Commonwealth must prove beyond a reasonable doubt is that the defendant acted with the specific intent to cause (the alleged victim/name) to be secretly confined or imprisoned in Massachusetts against (his/her) will. Alternately, the Commonwealth must prove beyond a reasonable doubt that the defendant acted with the specific intent to cause (the alleged victim/name) to be sent out of the state of Massachusetts, or that the defendant acted with the specific intent to cause, in any way, (the alleged victim/name) to be held to service against (his/her) will.[11]

Intent refers to a person's objective or purpose.[12] Specific intent, which is required in this case, is the act of concentrating or focusing the mind for some perceptible period. It is a conscious act, with the determination of the mind to do an act.[13] It is contemplation rather than reflex, and it must precede that act.[14] The Commonwealth must prove specific intent on the part of the defendant. This requires you to make a decision about the defendant's state of mind at the time of the crime. In this case, you may or may not infer the defendant's intent by considering all of the facts, as well as evidence of defendant's conduct, offered during the trial.[15] If, based on the evidence, the Commonwealth has failed to prove beyond a reasonable doubt each of the elements I have described, then you must return a verdict of not guilty on the charge of kidnapping. However, if the Commonwealth does prove beyond a reasonable doubt *all* of the elements I have described, you must return a verdict of guilty on the charges of kidnapping.

[The fourth element the Commonwealth must prove be-yond a reasonable doubt is that the defendant committed the offense or kidnapping, as described above, with the specific intent to extort money or some other valuable thing. The words specific intent have the same meaning that I gave them previously. To "extort" means to obtain property, coerce payment of money, secure a pecuniary advantage for oneself, or compel another to do an act against his or her will as a result of a threat. "The emphasis in the crime of extortion is on the wrongful use of fear to compel (the alleged victim/name) to surrender something of value to the extortionist."[16]][17]

NOTES

[1] This instruction and notes are taken from the chargebook offered as a guide to Superior Court judges in 1995 and updated by the authors.

[2] General Laws c. 265, § 26, provides that the crime of kidnapping can be committed by alternate means.

[3] *Commonwealth v. Ware*, 375 Mass. 118, 119 n.1 (1978). A twelve-year-old child falls within the tender years doctrine and, as a matter of law, cannot consent to leaving or being taken from the custody of his or her parents or legal guardians. *Commonwealth v. Colon*, 431 Mass. 188 (2000).

[4] *Commonwealth v. Titus*, 32 Mass. App. Ct. 216, 221 (1992).

[5] *Commonwealth v. Rivera*, 460 Mass. 139, 142–44 (2011) (to secretly confine someone is to isolate or insulate them from meaningful contact or communication with the public, where the confinement is in a place or manner that makes it unlikely that members of the public will know or learn of the victim's unwilling confinement within a reasonable period of time) (citing 3 W.R. LaFave, *Substantive Criminal Law* § 18.1(c), at 17 (3rd ed. 2003)).

[6] *Commonwealth v. Oberle*, 476 Mass. 539, 548 (2017); *Commonwealth v. Nickerson*, 388 Mass. 246, 253–54 (1983).

[7] *Black's Law Dictionary* 739 (5th ed. 1979).

[8] Use this paragraph if applicable.

[9] *Commonwealth v. Travis*, 408 Mass. 1, 8 (1990).

[10] *Commonwealth v. Caracciola*, 409 Mass. 648, 652–53.

[11] *Commonwealth v. Ware*, 375 Mass. 118, 119 n.1 (1978).

[12] *Commonwealth v. Ware*, 375 Mass. 118, 119 n.1 (1978).

[13] *Commonwealth v. Ware*, 375 Mass. 118, 119 n.1 (1978).

[14] *Commonwealth v. Ware*, 375 Mass. 118, 119 n.1 (1978).

[15] *Commonwealth v. Niziolek*, 380 Mass. 513, 528 (1980).

[16] *Commonwealth v. Miller*, 385 Mass. 521, 527 (1982).

[17] Use this paragraph only if kidnapping with intent to extort is alleged.

Larceny

Regulatory Authority—G.L. c. 266, § 30
Dist. Ct. Model Jury Instruction 8.520

The defendant is charged with larceny. Section 30 of chapter 266 of our General Laws provides as follows:

> "Whoever steals . . . the property of another . . . shall be guilty of larceny . . . ."

Stealing is the wrongful taking of the personal property of another person, with the intent to deprive that person of such property permanently.

In order to prove the defendant guilty of larceny, the Commonwealth must prove three things beyond a reasonable doubt:

First: That the defendant took and carried away property;

Second: That the property was owned or possessed by someone other than the defendant; and

Third: That the defendant did so with the intent to deprive that person of the property permanently.

> G.L. c. 277, § 39. *Commonwealth v. Donovan*, 395 Mass. 20, 25–26 (1985); *Commonwealth v. Johnson*, 379 Mass. 177, 181 (1979).

7

Supplemental Instructions

1. *"Took and carried away."* "Taking and carrying away" was accomplished if the defendant physically transferred the property from the other person's control to his (her) own. It does not matter if the transfer involved only slight movement, or if it lasted only for a short time.

> *Commonwealth v. Fielding*, 371 Mass. 97, 117 (1976) (any separation of property from victim's dominion, even if brief in space and time, sufficient); *Commonwealth v. Salerno*, 356 Mass. 642, 648 (1970) (taking can be proved by circumstantial evidence); *Commonwealth v. Luckis*, 99 Mass. 431, 433 (1868) (wallet need not be removed from victim's pocket, but defendant "must for an instant at least have had perfect control of the property"); *Commonwealth v. Stephens*, 14 Mass. App. Ct. 994, 994–95 (1982) (sufficient that victim put property in bag at defendant's orders, though defendant never touched it); *Commonwealth v. Bradley*, 2 Mass. App. Ct. 804, 805 (1974) (momentary transfer sufficient); *Commonwealth v. Flowers*, 1 Mass. App. Ct. 415, 418–19 (1973) (transfer of property from victim's control to thief's sufficient, since literal "carrying away" not required; transfer may be through agent or victim).

2. *"Property."* The term "property" includes (money) (movable items of personal property) (bank notes) (public records) (anything that is part of or attached to real estate) (apartment security deposits) (electronically processed or stored data, either tangible or intangible) (domesticated animals, including dogs, birds and other animals ordinarily kept in confinement).

> This is only a partial list. See G.L. c. 266, § 30(2) for the complete list of items, in addition to those at common law, that may be the subject of larceny. *See also Commonwealth v. Yourawski*, 384 Mass. 386, 388 (1981) (intellectual property, such as taped performance, not subject to larceny statute); *Commonwealth v. Beckett*, 373 Mass. 329, 341–43 (1977) (intent to commit larceny from welfare department inferable from circumstances).

3. *"Of Another."* The Commonwealth must prove that the property was owned or possessed by a person other than the defendant. This can be proved by direct evidence that someone else owned or possessed the property. Or, in some cases, it may be reasonable for you to infer this from the surrounding circumstances. The Commonwealth is not required to prove *who* owned or held the property, as long as it proves that the defendant did *not*.

> G.L. c. 277, § 25 (identity of owner need not be alleged if property described with sufficient certainty); G.L. c. 278, § 9 ("owner" includes anyone in actual or constructive possession). *Commonwealth v. Souza*, 397 Mass. 236, 238–39 (1986) (identity of owner need not be proved, only that it was not defendant; because of G.L. c. 277, § 35, misnomer of owner is immaterial if defendant not misled); *Commonwealth v. Kiernan*, 348 Mass. 29, 50–51 (1964), *cert. denied sub nom. Gordon v. Mass.*, 380 U.S. 913 (1965) ("owner" includes anyone with a possessory or property interest); *Commonwealth v. Binkiewicz*, 342 Mass. 740, 748 (1961) (because of G.L. c. 278, § 9, complaint about "the property of *x*" in effect reads "the property of *x*, or of another but in *x*'s actual or constructive possession"; driver with shared dominion over auto registered in spouse's name is "owner"); *Commonwealth v. Finn*, 108 Mass. 466, 467 (1871) (one may steal from thief); *Commonwealth v. Sullivan*, 104 Mass. 552, 554–55 (1870) (person who orders goods is in constructive possession of them once delivered to a common carrier, absent a shipping agreement to the contrary); *Commonwealth v. Arrance*, 5 Allen 517, 517–18 (1862) (because of G.L. c. 278, § 9, permissible to allege and prove only one co-owner). *Commonwealth v. Pimental*, 54 Mass. App. Ct. 325, 328 (2002) ("Direct proof of ownership, although preferable, is not essential. . . .").

4. *Intent to deprive permanently.* The Commonwealth must prove that the defendant intended to deprive the owner of the property permanently. This may be proved by direct evidence or by inference from the surrounding circumstances. For example, if a person takes the property of another and disposes of it with utter indifference to whether the owner recovers its possession, you might infer from that an intent to deprive the owner of it permanently.

> See Instruction 3.120 (Intent).
>
> *Salerno, supra; Commonwealth v. Weston*, 241 Mass. 131, 141–43 (1922); *Commonwealth v. Moore*, 36 Mass. App. Ct. 455, 456–57 (1994); *Commonwealth v. Coyle*, 17 Mass. App. Ct. 982, 984 (1984); *Commonwealth v. Ellison*, 5 Mass. App. Ct.

862, 862–63 (1977) (intent to make restitution later is not a defense).

5. *Larceny over $250.* If you determine that the Commonwealth has proved beyond a reasonable doubt that the defendant is guilty of larceny, you must also go on to determine whether

(*If more than one item stolen:* all) the property that was stolen was worth more than $250 or less than $250. You need to consider that question only if you find the defendant guilty, so that I will know which range of sentences the law permits in this case.

So if your verdict is guilty, you must also indicate on your verdict slip whether or not the Commonwealth has also proved beyond a reasonable doubt that the property was worth more than $250.

You may use your general knowledge in evaluating the value of a piece of property; it is not required that you have any expert evidence of its value.

For a sample verdict slip, see the appendix (Instruction 8.521). [*Editors' Note*: Verdict slip not included in this publication. It is available in the online version of the jury instructions at http://www.mass.gov/courts/court-info/trial-court/dc/dc-crim-model-jury-inst-gen.html.]

General Laws c. 266, § 30(1) provides for aggravated punishment "if the property stolen is a firearm . . . or if the value of the property stolen exceeds two hundred and fifty dollars. . . ." The supplemental instruction may be appropriately adapted if the theft is of a firearm.

Commonwealth v. Kelly, 24 Mass. App. Ct. 181, 183–85 & n.4, *fur. app. rev. den.*, 400 Mass. 1103 (1987) held that whether or not the value of the property stolen is alleged in the complaint, "the judge should instruct the jury that if they convict, they must determine by their verdict whether the value did or did not exceed [$250] so that the judge will know what range of punishments is available. Otherwise the judge will be required to sentence as if the value did not exceed [$250]." *Kelly* also indicated that the value of the stolen property need not be alleged in the complaint, since "the value of the property . . . is an element of the punishment but not an element of the offense of larceny. . . ." Compare, *Commonwealth v. Pyburn*, 26 Mass. App. Ct. 967 (1988) (in prosecution for wanton destruction of property under G.L. c. 266, § 127, "if there is an allegation in a complaint . . . that the value of the property so destroyed or injured exceeded" $250 then jury must determine that issue, but instruction need not present that factor as an essential element of the offense since it is not such) with *Commonwealth v. Beale*, 434 Mass. 1024, 1025 & n.2 (2001) ("the value of the property must be treated as an element of the felony of malicious destruction of property" but "the focus of the constitutional inquiry is not a formalistic examination of whether a finding is labeled an 'element' or a 'sentencing factor,' but whether the finding is made by a jury on proof beyond a reasonable doubt"). *See also Commonwealth v. Harrington*, 130 Mass. 35, 36 (1880) (statutory attempt to dispense with need to charge that crime is subsequent offense, where an element of enhanced sentencing, violated art. 12 of Massachusetts Declaration of Rights).

The jury may use its common knowledge, and does not require expert evidence, in evaluating value. *Commonwealth v. Hosman*, 257 Mass. 379, 386 (1926); *Commonwealth v. McCann*, 16 Mass. App. Ct. 990, 991 (1983).

6. *Single scheme*. The complaint in this case charges the defendant with stealing property between two dates pursuant to a single scheme. Therefore, in addition to the three elements of larceny that I have just instructed you about, the Commonwealth must also prove beyond a reasonable doubt that during that period of time the defendant acted out of a single, continuing intent to steal; that even though time elapsed between incidents, they were not separately motivated but were part of one general scheme or plan to steal.

If relevant to evidence: If this is proved beyond a reasonable doubt, you may consider the total value of all property obtained on all of those occasions cumulatively in deciding whether the value of the property stolen was in excess of $250.

Commonwealth v. John G. Grant & Sons Co., 403 Mass. 151, 157 (1988) (statutory language making each day of a continuing violation a separate offense prevents charging as single, continuous offense); *Commonwealth v. Murray*, 401 Mass. 771 (1988) (where several acts of a defendant are involved, successive takings in a single, continuing larcenous scheme may, but need not, be charged as a single scheme); *Commonwealth v. England*, 350 Mass. 83, 86–87 (1966) (value of successive larcenies in single scheme may aggregate to grand larceny); *Commonwealth v. Stasiun,* 349 Mass. 38, 45 (1965) (same); *Commonwealth v. Peretz*, 212 Mass. 253, 254 (1912) (same); *Slater v. United States Fidelity & Guar. Co.*, 7 Mass. App. Ct. 281, 285 (1979), *rev'd on other grounds*, 379 Mass. 801 (1980) (same); *Donovan*, 395 Mass. at 27–31 (where a single act of a defendant is involved, successive takings in a single, continuing larcenous scheme must be charged as a single offense); *Commonwealth v. Pina*, 1 Mass. App. Ct. 411, 412 n.2 (1973). Compare G.L. c. 277, § 32 (charging a continuing offense); *Sullivan*, 104 Mass. at 553 (distinct larcenies may be presented in multiple counts; stealing at one time of articles belonging to several owners may be charged either as one larceny or as distinct larcenies). But see *Commonwealth v. Donovan*, 395 Mass. 20, 29 (1985) (only one count of larceny, not seven, where defendant mounted imitation deposit lock box over the real one at a bank, obtaining seven bank deposits from different depositors). See also *Commonwealth v. Baldwin*, 52 Mass. App. Ct. 404, 407 (2001) (*Donovan* inapplicable where circumstances involve more than one discrete offense, such that different property is taken at different times and from different locations).

7. *Claim of Right.* If the defendant took another person's property in an honest and reasonable belief that (he) (she) (another person on whose behalf he [she] was acting) had a legal right to it, then you must find the defendant not guilty, even if that belief was in fact mistaken, because he (she) lacked the intent to steal.

Commonwealth v. Garrity, 43 Mass. App. Ct. 349, 358 n.7 (1997); *Commonwealth v. Larmey*, 14 Mass. App. Ct. 281, 283–85 (1982); *Commonwealth v. Anslono*, 9 Mass. App. Ct. 867, 868 (1980); *Ellison*, *supra*; *Commonwealth v. White*, 5 Mass. App. Ct. 483, 485–88 (1977).

NOTES

1. **"Breaking and entering and stealing therein."** See notes to Instruction 8.100 (Breaking and Entering).

2. **Merger of offenses.** "In a [complaint] for criminal dealing with personal property with intent to steal, an allegation that the defendant stole said property shall be sufficient; and such [complaint] may be supported by proof that the defendant committed larceny of the property, or embezzled it, or obtained it by false pretences." G.L. c. 277, § 41. "Stealing. Larceny.—The criminal taking, obtaining or converting of personal property, with intent to defraud or deprive the owner permanently of the use of it; including all forms of larceny, criminal embezzlement and obtaining by criminal false pretences." G.L. c. 277, § 39.

"[T]he purpose of the assimilation of offenses was to reduce, if not eliminate, the opportunities for a fatal variance which existed whenever an indictment charged one offence and the proof disclosed a different one." *Commonwealth v. Kelly*, 24 Mass. App. Ct. at 184. Proof of any one of the three alternatives will support a conviction for larceny. *Commonwealth v. Leland*, 311 Mass. 447, 448 (1942); *Commonwealth v. Kelley*, 184 Mass. 320, 324 (1883). The Commonwealth cannot be required to elect which of the three alternatives it intends to prove. *Commonwealth v. Corcoran*, 348 Mass. 437, 440–42 (1965); *Commonwealth v. King*, 202 Mass. 379, 386–89 (1909). A bill of particulars is a limitation only as to the proof to be offered; the judge may charge on any of the three alternatives warranted by the evidence. *Corcoran, above*; *Commonwealth v. Kenneally*, 10 Mass. App. Ct. 162, 176 (1980), *aff'd on other grounds*, 383 Mass. 269, *cert. denied*, 454 U.S. 849 (1981). Precise instructions to the jury on the Commonwealth's theory of how the defendant stole are critical because traditional larceny, embezzlement, and larceny by false pretenses have different required elements. *Commonwealth v. Mills*, 436 Mass. 387, 399 (2002).

3. **Related offenses.** For instructions for other larceny offenses, see:

- Instruction 8.200 (Theft, etc. of Motor Vehicle, G.L. c. 266, § 28)
- Instruction 8.400 (Fraudulent Insurance Claim, G.L. c. 266, § 111A)
- Instruction 8.420 (Identity Fraud by Posing as Another, G.L. c. 266, § 37E [b])
- Instruction 8.440 (Identity Fraud by Obtaining Personal Information, G.L. c. 266, § 37E [c])
- Instruction 8.460 (Larceny by Check, G.L. c. 266, § 37)
- Instruction 8.480 (Larceny by Embezzlement, G.L. c. 266, § 30)
- Instruction 8.500 (Larceny by False Pretenses, G.L. c. 266, § 30)
- Instruction 8.540 (Larceny by Stealing in a Building, G.L. c. 266, § 20)
- Instruction 8.560 (Larceny from the Person, G.L. c. 266, § 25 [b])
- Instruction 8.580 (Larceny of Leased or Rented Personal Property, G.L. c. 266, § 87)
- Instruction 8.600 (Receiving Stolen Property, G.L. c. 266, § 60)
- Instruction 8.620 (Shoplifting, G.L. c. 266, § 30A)
- Instruction 8.640 (Unauthorized Transfer of Sound Recordings, G.L. c. 266, § 143A).

7

For other specialized larceny offenses, see also G.L. c. 266, §§ 37B–37C (Credit Card Fraud), 33A (Larceny of Commercial Computer Service) and 120F (Unauthorized Access to Computer System).

4. **Stealing and receiving same property.** A defendant cannot be convicted both of stealing and receiving the same goods. *Commonwealth v. Dellamano*, 393 Mass. 132, 134 (1984); *Commonwealth v. Haskins*, 128 Mass. 60, 61 (1880). A defendant may be charged with both crimes; if the evidence would support either, it is for the jury to decide "under clear and precise instructions" of which to convict. *Commonwealth v. Ross*, 339 Mass. 428 (1959); *Commonwealth v. Kelley*, 333 Mass. at 195, 129; *Commonwealth v. Obshatkin*, 2 Mass. App. Ct. 1, 4-5 (1974). See Instruction 5.41 (Larceny by Stealing). Each crime should be charged in a separate count or complaint. *Commonwealth v. Dellamano*, 393 Mass. at 134 n.7, If the jury incorrectly convicts on both charges, the judge should reinstruct the jury and send them out again. If the jury persists, the charge of receiving stolen property should be dismissed. *Commonwealth v. Nascimento*, 421 Mass. 677, 684–85 (1996).

Larceny in a Building

Regulatory Authority—G.L. c. 266, § 20
Dist. Ct. Model Jury Instruction 8.540

The defendant is charged with stealing in a building. Section 20 of chapter 266 of our General Laws provides as follows: "Whoever steals in a building . . . shall be punished . . . ."

Stealing is the wrongful taking of personal property from the possession of another person, with the intent to deprive that person of such property permanently.

In order to prove the defendant guilty of stealing in a building, the Commonwealth must prove four things beyond a reasonable doubt:

First: That the defendant took and carried away property;

Second: That at the time the property was being kept safe by virtue of being in a building;

Third: That the property belonged to someone other than the defendant; *and*

Fourth: That the defendant took the property with the intent to deprive the owner of it permanently.

> *Commonwealth v. Sollivan*, 40 Mass. App. Ct. 284, 287 (1996) (approving model instruction).

"Taking and carrying away" was accomplished if the property was physically transferred from the place where it was being kept. It does not matter if the transfer involved only slight movement, or if it lasted for only a short time.

> *Commonwealth v. Fielding*, 371 Mass. 97, 117 (1976) (any separation of property from victim's dominion, even if brief in space and time, sufficient); *Commonwealth v. Salerno*, 356 Mass. 642, 648 (1970) (taking can be proved by circumstantial evidence); *Commonwealth v. Luckis*, 99 Mass. 431, 433 (1868) (wallet need not be removed from victim's pocket, but defendant "must for an instant at least have had perfect control of the property"); *Commonwealth v. Stephens*, 14 Mass. App. Ct. 994, 994–95 (1982) (sufficient that victim put property in bag at defendant's orders, though defendant never touched it); *Commonwealth v. Bradley*, 2 Mass. App. Ct. 804, 805 (1974) (momentary transfer sufficient); *Commonwealth v. Flowers*, 1 Mass. App. Ct. 415, 418–19 (1973) (transfer of property from victim's control to thief's sufficient, since literal "carrying away" not required; transfer may be through agent or victim).

The Commonwealth must prove that the property was being protected and kept safe by virtue of being in the building rather than being under the watchful eye or personal care of someone in the building.

The Commonwealth must prove that the property was owned or possessed by a person other than the defendant. This can be proved by direct evidence that someone else owned or possessed the property. Or, in some cases, it may be reasonable for you to infer this from the surrounding circumstances. The Commonwealth is not required to prove who owned or held the property, as long as it proves that the defendant did not.

> G.L. c. 277, § 25 (identity of owner need not be alleged if property described with sufficient certainty); G.L. c. 278, § 9 ("owner" includes anyone in actual or constructive possession). *Commonwealth v. Souza*, 397 Mass. 236, 238–39 (1986) (identity of owner need not be proved, only that it was not defendant; because of G.L. c. 277, § 35, misnomer of owner is immaterial if defendant not misled); *Commonwealth v. Kiernan*, 348 Mass. 29, 50–51 (1964), *cert. denied sub nom. Gordon v. Mass.*, 380 U.S. 913 (1965) ("owner" includes anyone with a possessory or property interest); *Commonwealth v. Binkiewicz*, 342 Mass. 740, 748 (1961) (because of G.L. c. 278, § 9, complaint about "the property of x" in effect reads "the property of x, or of another but in x's actual or constructive possession"; driver with shared dominion over auto registered in spouse's name is "owner"); *Commonwealth v. Finn*, 108 Mass. 466, 467 (1871) (one may steal from thief); *Commonwealth v. Sullivan*, 104 Mass. 552, 554–55 (1870) (person who orders goods is in constructive possession of them once delivered to a common carrier, absent a shipping agreement to the contrary); *Commonwealth v.*

Arrance, 5 Allen 517, 517–18 (1862) (because of G.L. c. 278, § 9, permissible to allege and prove only one co-owner).

Supplemental Instructions

1. ***"Property."*** The term "property" includes (money) (movable items of personal property) (bank notes) (public records) (anything that is part of or attached to real estate) (apartment security deposits) (electronically processed or stored data, either tangible or intangible) (domesticated animals, including dogs, birds and other animals ordinarily kept in confinement).

This is only a partial list. See G.L. c. 266, § 30(2) for the complete list of items, in addition to those at common law, that may be the subject of larceny. See also *Commonwealth v. Youraski*, 384 Mass. 386, 388 (1981) (intellectual property, such as taped performance, not subject to larceny statute); *Commonwealth v. Beckett*, 373 Mass. 329, 341–343 (1977) (intent to commit larceny from welfare department inferable from circumstances).

2. ***Intent to deprive permanently***. The Commonwealth must prove that the defendant intended to deprive the owner of the property permanently. This may be proved by direct evidence or by inference from the surrounding circumstances. For example, if a person takes the property of another and disposes of it with utter indifference to whether the owner recovers its possession, you might infer from that an intent to deprive the owner of it permanently.

See Instruction 3.120 (Intent) and the supplemental instructions and note to Instruction 8.520 (Larceny by Stealing).

Salerno, supra; *Commonwealth v. Cabot*, 241 Mass. 131, 141–43 (1922); *Commonwealth v. Moore*, 36 Mass. App. Ct. 455, 456–57 (1994); *Commonwealth v. Coyle*, 17 Mass. App. Ct. 982, 984 (1984); *Commonwealth v. Ellison*, 5 Mass. App. Ct. 862, 862–63 (1977) (intent to make restitution later is not a defense). It is not enough that the theft be committed within a building. The building—rather than a particular person—must be protecting the property. *See Commonwealth v. Willard*, 53 Mass. App. Ct. 650 (2002).

General Laws c. 266, § 20 also applies to stealing in a ship, vessel or railroad car. The model instruction may be adapted as necessary.

NOTE

Value of property stolen immaterial. Larceny in a building is a felony regardless of the value of the property stolen. *Commonwealth v. Graham*, 62 Mass. App. Ct. 642, 647 (2004).

Larceny from the Person

Regulatory Authority—G.L. c. 266, § 25(b)
Dist. Ct. Model Jury Instruction 8.560

The defendant is charged with larceny from the person. Section 25(b) of chapter 266 of our General Laws provides as follows:

"Whoever commits larceny by stealing from the person of another shall be punished . . . ."

Larceny from the person is the wrongful taking of personal property from the person of another, or from the immediate area of control of another, with the intent to deprive that person of such property permanently.

In order to prove the defendant guilty of this offense, the Commonwealth must prove four things beyond a reasonable doubt:

First: That the defendant took and carried away property;

Second: That the property was owned or possessed by someone other than the defendant;

Third: That the defendant took the property from the person of someone who owned or possessed it

If relevant: or from such a person's area of control in his presence;

and *Fourth:* That the defendant did so with the intent to deprive that person of the property permanently.

See the definitions of "took and carried away," "property," "of another," and "intent to deprive permanently" in the supplemental instructions to Instruction 8.520 (Larceny by Stealing). See also Instruction 3.120 (Intent).

Commonwealth v. Glowacki, 398 Mass. 507, 514 (1986) (larceny from the person is lesser included offense of robbery); *Commonwealth v. Stewart,* 365 Mass. 99, 108 (1974) (in robbery prosecution, element of larceny "from the person" includes the common law concept of larceny in the victim's presence); *Commonwealth v. Jones,* 362 Mass. 83, 86–87 (1972) (same; offense distinguished from robbery by absence of use or threat of force); *Commonwealth v. Subilosky,* 352 Mass. 153, 166 (1967) (property need only be taken from victim's area of control in his presence; here, theft from cash drawers supervised by bank manager); *Commonwealth v. Cline,* 213 Mass. 225, 225–26 (1913) (unnecessary to allege victim's name or to allege description or value of property); *Commonwealth v. Luckis,* 99 Mass. 431, 433 (1868) (wallet need not be removed from victim's pocket, but defendant "must for an instant at least have had perfect control of the property"); *Commonwealth v. Burke,* 12 Allen 182, 183 (1866) (value of property is not an element); *Commonwealth v. McDonald,* 5 Cush. 365, 367 (1850) (putting hand into empty pocket will support conviction for attempted larceny from person); *Commonwealth v. Diamond,* 5 Cush. 235, 237–38 (1849) (offense may be committed by fraud rather than stealth). *See Commonwealth v. Acevedo,* 25 Mass. App. Ct. 1114 (No. 87-628, March 2, 1988) (unpublished opinion under Appeals Court Rule 1:28) (theft of package set on ground while victim opened auto trunk is "from the *person*").

NOTES

1. **Pickpocketing and purse snatching.** An ordinary pickpocketing usually is a larceny from the person rather than an unarmed robbery, even if the victim realizes what is happening, because no intimidation is involved and the "force" utilized is not the kind of violence necessary for robbery. *Commonwealth v. Davis*, 7 Mass. App. Ct. 9, 11 (1979). But a purse snatching of which the victim is aware involves sufficient force to constitute robbery, even if done so quickly as to deny the victim any opportunity to resist. *Jones,* 362 Mass. at 88–89. The same is true of rolling a drunk. *Commonwealth v. Smith*, 21 Mass. App. Ct. 619, 623–24 (1986), *aff'd*, 400 Mass. 1002 (1987).

2. **Value of property.** Note that, unlike larceny offenses prosecuted under G.L. c. 266, § 30, whether the stolen property is worth more or less than $250 is irrelevant to punishment in a prosecution under G.L. c. 266, § 25.

3. **Victim 65 years or older.** Larceny from the person of a victim who is 65 years or older (G.L. c. 266, § 25[a]) is an aggravated form of this offense. The model instruction may be adapted by adding as a fifth element that the victim was 65 years of age or older. The jury may consider the victim's physical appearance as one factor in determining age, but appearance alone is not sufficient evidence of age unless the victim is of "a marked extreme" age, since "[e]xcept at the poles, judging age on physical appearance is a guess . . . ." *Commonwealth v. Pittman,* 25 Mass. App. Ct. 25, 28 (1987).

Leaving the Scene of an Accident Involving Property Damage

Regulatory Authority—G.L. c. 90, § 24(2)(a)
Dist. Ct. Model Jury Instruction 5.180

The defendant is charged with knowingly leaving the scene of an accident involving property damage. In order to prove the defendant guilty of this offense, the Commonwealth must prove four things beyond a reasonable doubt:

First: That the defendant operated a motor vehicle;

Second: That while the defendant was operating the vehicle, (he) (she) caused damage to another vehicle or property either by colliding with it or in some other way;

Third: That the defendant *knew* (he) (she) (had collided with another's property) (or) (had in some way caused damage to the property of another)); and

Fourth: That after causing such collision or damage, the defendant did not stop and make known (his) (her) name, home address, and the registration number of (his) (her) motor vehicle.

A person "operates" a motor vehicle not only while doing all of the well-known things that drivers do as they travel on a street or highway, but also when doing any act which directly tends to set the vehicle in motion. The law is that a person is "operating" a motor vehicle whenever he or she is in the vehicle and intentionally manipulates some mechanical or electrical part of the vehicle—like the gear shift or the ignition—which, alone or in sequence, will set the vehicle in motion.

For the complete definitions of "Operation of a Motor Vehicle," see instruction 3.200.

A driver has a duty to immediately stop at the scene and offer the specific information required: name, home address and motor vehicle registration number. This duty is not satisfied by stopping at some remote place or by being passively willing to answer inquiries.

Commonwealth v. Martinez, 87 Mass. App. Ct. 582, 584–86 (2015); *Commonwealth v. Horsfall*, 213 Mass. 232, 236 (1913).

Supplemental Instructions

7

The law defines what a "motor vehicle" is as follows: "all vehicles constructed and designed for propulsion by power other than muscular power."

(See G.L. c. 90, § 1 for the statutory definition of a "motor vehicle.")

To "operate" a motor vehicle within the meaning of the law, it is not necessary that the engine be running. A driver continues to operate his or her motor vehicle when it is stopped in the ordinary course of its operation for some reason that is fairly incidental to the vehicle's operation. A person is also considered to be "operating" a stationary vehicle when he or she manipulates some part of it, like the gear shift, so that it moves forward of its own weight.

You may find that the defendant was the operator of the motor vehicle even if no witness saw him (her) driving the vehicle, if there is enough circumstantial evidence to prove to you beyond a reasonable doubt that the vehicle was operated and that the defendant, and no one else, was the operator of that vehicle.

The statute requires that the specified information must be given to the person whose property has been damaged, if reasonably possible, and if not, to someone acting in their interest or to some public officer or other person at or near the place at the time of the injury.

Commonwealth v. Horsfall, 213 Mass. 232, 236 (1913); *Commonwealth v. Donohue*, 41 Mass. App. Ct. 91, 94 (1996).

The extent of the damage is not relevant except to the extent that it may be circumstantial evidence of whether or not the defendant knew that there had been a collision.

NOTES

1. **Circumstantial evidence.** Circumstantial evidence may support an inference that the defendant did not make himself known, *Commonwealth v. LaVoie*, 9 Mass. App. Ct. 918–19 (1980), or that the defendant was the operator, *Commonwealth v. Smith*, 368 Mass. 126, 128 (1975); *Commonwealth v. Rand*, 363 Mass. 554, 561–62 (1973); *Commonwealth v. Swartz*, 343 Mass. 709, 712 (1962); *Commonwealth v. Henry*, 338 Mass. 786 (1958). *But see Commonwealth v. Shea*, 324 Mass. 710, 712–14 (1949) (defendant not shown to be driver where unknown person had been driving vehicle three hours earlier, and no evidence that defendant operated vehicle on that date).

2. **Collision.** "Collide" means to strike together. The statute applies whenever the defendant is in some way an actor, a partial cause in the collision, but not where the defendant is merely a passive participant (e.g. where a pedestrian falls or walks into the defendant's stopped vehicle). *Commonwealth v. Bleakney*, 278 Mass. 198, 201–02 (1932). An owner-passenger can be found guilty if he or she retained control over his chauffeur's operation of the vehicle. *Saltman, petitioner*, 289 Mass. 554, 561 (1935).

3. **Constitutionality.** The statutory obligation does not violate the privilege against self-incrimination. *California v. Byers*, 402 U.S. 424 (1971); *Commonwealth v. Joyce*, 326 Mass. 751, 753–57 (1961).

4. **Fault.** The statute applies whether or not the defendant was at fault, since the statute "focuses on causation, not fault." *Commonwealth v. Robbins*, 414 Mass. 444, 446–48 (1993).

5. **Good faith mistake.** It is not a defense that the defendant believed that he or she was known to persons at the scene. *Commonwealth v. Joyce*, 326 Mass. 751, 752–53 (1951); *Commonwealth v. Lewis*, 286 Mass. 256 (1934). *Commonwealth v. Horsfall*, 213 Mass. 232, 237 (1913), held that the defendant's good faith belief that he had taken the necessary steps to make himself known was a defense, but the statute was subsequently amended and that defense is no longer available, *Commonwealth v. Coleman*, 252 Mass. 241, 243–44 (1925).

6. **Not a continuing offense.** For purposes of the statute of limitations, the crime of leaving the scene of an accident is not a continuing offense. *Commonwealth v. Valchuis*, 40 Mass. App. Ct. 556, 561–62 (1996) (offense involving personal injury).

7. **Causal Relationship.** The Commonwealth must prove that the accident caused property damage. *Commonwealth v. Velasquez*, 76 Mass. App. Ct. 697, 699–701 (2010).

8. **Offering information without more violates statute.** A motorist must actually provide the required information. Merely offering to provide it is not sufficient to avoid liablity under G.L. c. 90, § 24(2)(a). It remains undecided whether an emergency or event such as road rage would excuse a motorist from compliance. *Commonwealth v. Martinez*, 87 Mass. App. Ct. 582, 585–86 & n.12, *rev. denied*, 473 Mass. 1101 (2015).

9. **Unit of prosecution is incident-based.** The offense is defined by the act of leaving the scene of the accident, not by the number of people injured. *See Commonwealth v. Constantino*, 443 Mass. 521, 524–27 (2005); *see also Commonwealth v. Henderson*, 89 Mass. App. Ct. 205, 209–11 (2016) (leaving scene of multi-vehicle crash constitutes a single offense).

10. **Only one penalty may be assessed.** "Only one penalty may be assessed . . . for a single act of leaving the scene . . . because 'the proscribed act is scene related, not victim related.'" *Commonwealth v. Henderson*, 89 Mass. App. Ct. 205, 210 (2016) (quoting *Commonwealth v. Constantino*, 443 Mass. 521, 524 (2005)).

Leaving the Scene of an Accident Involving Personal Injury Not Resulting in Death

Regulatory Authority—G.L. c. 90, § 24(2)(a½)(1)
Dist. Ct. Model Jury Instruction 5.190

The defendant is charged with knowingly leaving the scene of an accident involving personal injury. In order to prove the defendant guilty of this offense, the Commonwealth must prove four things beyond a reasonable doubt:

First: That the defendant operated a motor vehicle;

Second: That (he) (she) operated it (on a way) (or) (in a place where the public has a right of access) (or) (upon a way or in a place where members of the public have access as invitees or licensees);

Third: That the defendant knowingly collided with or otherwise injured another person;

Fourth: That after such collision or injury, the defendant did not stop and make known (his) (her) name, home address, and the registration number of (his) (her) motor vehicle.

At this point, the jury must be instructed on the definitions of "Operation of a Motor Vehicle" (Instruction

3.200) and "Public Way" (Instruction 3.280).

1991 Mass. Acts c. 460 (effective January 30, 1992) removed the offense of leaving the scene of personal injury from G.L. c. 90, § 24(2)(A) and bifurcated the two offenses: (1) the misdemeanor of leaving the scene of personal injury "not resulting in the death of any person" (G.L. c. 90, § 24(2)(a½)(1), and (2) the felony of leaving the scene of personal injury resulting in a death in order "to avoid prosecution or evade apprehension" (G.L. c. 90, § 24(2)(a½)(2)). The District Court lacks final jurisdiction over the felony branch.

Supplemental Instructions

1. ***Duty to provide means of identification.*** The purpose of this statute is to enable anyone who has been injured by a motor vehicle to obtain immediate and accurate information about the person in charge of that motor vehicle. It imposes an active and positive duty on the driver to immediately stop at the scene and offer the specific information required by the statute, in order to identify (him) (her) and to make it simple to find (him) (her) later. The statute is not satisfied by stopping at some remote place or by being passively willing to answer inquiries.

Commonwealth v. Horsfall, 213 Mass. 232, 236 (1913).

2. ***To whom information must be given.*** By plain implication, the statute requires that the specified information must be given to the person who has been injured, if reasonably possible, and if not, to someone acting in their interest or to some public officer or other person at or near the place at the time of the injury.

Horsfall, 213 Mass. at 236.

3. ***Extent of injury.*** The extent of the injury is not relevant except to the extent that it may be circumstantial evidence of whether or not the defendant knew that there had been a collision.

NOTES

1. **Circumstantial evidence.** Circumstantial evidence may support an inference that the defendant did not make himself known, *Commonwealth v. LaVoie*, 9 Mass. App. Ct. 918, 918–19 (1980), or that the defendant was the operator, *Commonwealth v. Smith*, 368 Mass. 126, 128 (1975); *Commonwealth v. Rand*, 363 Mass. 554, 561–62 (1973); *Commonwealth v. Swartz*, 343 Mass. 709, 712 (1962); *Commonwealth v. Henry*, 338 Mass. 786 (1958). *But see Commonwealth v. Shea*, 324 Mass. 710, 712–14 (1949) (defendant not shown to be driver where unknown person had been driving vehicle three hours earlier, and no evidence that defendant operated vehicle on that date).

2. **Collision.** "Collide" means to strike together. The statute applies whenever the defendant is in some way an actor, a partial cause in the collision, but not where the defendant is merely a passive participant (e.g. where a pedestrian falls or walks into the defendant's stopped vehicle). *Commonwealth v. Bleakney*, 278 Mass. 198, 201–02 (1932). An owner-passenger can be found guilty if he or she retained control over his chauffeur's operation of the vehicle. *Saltman, petitioner*, 289 Mass. 554, 561 (1935).

3. **Constitutionality.** The statutory obligation does not violate the privilege against self-incrimination. *California v. Byers*, 402 U.S. 424 (1971); *Commonwealth v. Joyce*, 326 Mass. 751, 753–57 (1951).

4. **Fault.** The statute applies whether or not the defendant was at fault, since the statute "focuses on causation, not fault." *Commonwealth v. Robbins*, 414 Mass. 444, 446–48 (1993).

5. **Good faith mistake.** It is not a defense that the defendant believed that he or she was known to persons at the scene. *Commonwealth v. Joyce*, 326 Mass. 751, 752–53 (1951); *Commonwealth v. Lewis*, 286 Mass. 256 (1934). *Commonwealth v. Horsfall*, 213 Mass. 232, 237 (1913), held that the defendant's good faith belief that he had taken the necessary steps to make himself known was a defense, but the statute was subsequently amended and that defense is no longer available, *Commonwealth v. Coleman*, 252 Mass. 241, 243–44 (1925).

6. **Not a continuing offense.** For purposes of the statute of limitations, the crime of leaving the scene of an accident is not a continuing offense. *Commonwealth v. Valchuis*, 40 Mass. App. Ct. 556, 561–62 (1996).

7. **Causal Relationship.** The Commonwealth must prove that the accident caused the injury (where that is the basis of criminal liability). *Commonwealth v. Velasquez*, 76 Mass. App. Ct. 697, 699–701 (2010) (property damage case).

8. **Offering information without more violates statute.** A motorist must actually provide the required information. Merely offering to provide it is not sufficient to avoid liability under G.L. c. 90, § 24(2)(a). It remains undecided whether an emergency or event such as road rage would excuse a motorist from compliance. *Commonwealth v. Martinez*, 87 Mass. App. Ct. 582, 585–86 & n.12, *rev. denied*, 473 Mass. 1101 (2015).

9. **Unit of prosecution is incident-based.** The offense is defined by the act of leaving the scene of the accident, not by the number of people injured. *See Commonwealth v. Constantino*, 443 Mass. 521, 524–27 (2005); *see also Commonwealth v. Henderson*, 89 Mass. App. Ct. 205, 209–11 (2016) (leaving scene of multi-vehicle crash constitutes a single offense).

10. **Only one penalty may be assessed.** "Only one penalty may be assessed . . . for a single act of leaving the scene . . . because 'the proscribed act is scene related, not victim related.'" *Commonwealth v. Henderson*, 89 Mass. App. Ct. 205, 210 (2016) (quoting *Commonwealth v. Constantino*, 443 Mass. 521, 524 (2005)).

11. **Statutory language "not resulting in death" is not element of offense.** See *Commonwealth v. Muir*, 84 Mass. App. Ct. 635, 639 (2013). This offense is a lesser included offense of leaving the scene of personal injury causing death. *Muir*, 84 Mass. App. Ct. at 639. See G.L. c. 90, § 24(2)(a½)(2). The District Court does not have jurisdiction over the latter offense. G.L. c. 218, § 26.

Lewd, Wanton and Lascivious Act

Regulatory Authority—G.L. c. 272, § 53
Dist. Ct. Model Jury Instruction 7.380

The defendant is charged with having committed a lewd, wanton and lascivious act. Section 53 of chapter 272 of our General Laws provides that:

> "lewd, wanton and lascivious persons in speech or behavior . . . may be punished . . . ."

This provision of our law is intended to punish the performance or solicitation of a sexual touching which does not rise to the level of a completed sexual act, and which is performed or intended to be performed in a public place where others may be offended by it.

In order to prove the defendant guilty of this offense, the Commonwealth must prove four things beyond a reasonable doubt:

First: That the defendant (committed) (publicly solicited another person to commit) a sexual act;

Second: That the sexual act involved touching the genitals or buttocks, or the female breasts;

Third: That the defendant did this either for the purpose of sexual arousal or gratification, or for the purpose of offending other people; and

Fourth: That the sexual act (was) (was to be) committed in a public place; that is, a place where the defendant either intended public exposure, or recklessly disregarded a substantial risk of public exposure at that time and under those circumstances, to others who might be offended by such conduct.

The defendant cannot be found guilty of this offense if he (she) desired privacy for a sexual act

If relevant to evidence: with another consenting adult

and took reasonable measures in order to secure that privacy. Therefore the Commonwealth must prove that in choosing that particular locale, the defendant either intended public exposure or recklessly disregarded a substantial risk of public exposure at that place and time.

Commonwealth v. Roy, 420 Mass. 1 (1995) (statute cannot be applied to solicitation for sexual conduct where unclear whether it was to occur in a public or private place); *Commonwealth v. Beauchemin*, 410 Mass. 181, 183–84 (1991) (statute cannot be applied to sexual conduct in location where little likelihood of being observed by casual passersby); *Commonwealth*

7

v. Sefranka, 382 Mass. 108, 117–18 (1980) (provision "prohibits only the commission of conduct in a public place, or the public solicitation of conduct to be performed in a public place . . . involving the touching of the genitals, buttocks, or female breasts, for purposes of sexual arousal, gratification, or offense, by a person who knows or should know of the presence of a person or persons who may be offended by the conduct," and can be applied to speech only if it solicits particular public sexual conduct which is itself criminal); *Commonwealth v. Templeman*, 376 Mass. 533, 537–38 (1978) (provision cannot be applied to protected speech or expressive conduct); *Commonwealth v. Kelley*, 25 Mass. App. Ct. 180 (1987) (masturbation) (place need not be one "to which the public or a substantial group has access," but "judges, in the interest of caution, would be well advised to charge that the offense requires either that the defendant 'intended public exposure or recklessly disregarded a substantial risk of exposure to one or more persons'"); *Commonwealth v. A Juvenile (No. 2)*, 6 Mass. App. Ct. 194, 197 n.1 (1978) (the terms "lewd, wanton and lascivious" appear "to be redundant rather than disjunctive").

NOTE

Private acts of prostitution. Prior to *Sefranka, above,* evidence of prostitution in a non-public place would also support a conviction of this offense, and therefore dual prosecutions were duplicitous. *A Juvenile (No. 2)*, 6 Mass. App. Ct. at 196–97. The *Sefranka* opinion notes that it addressed only noncommercial sexual acts or solicitation, 382 Mass. at 118 n.10, and it is unclear to what extent the *Sefranka* redefinition of this offense is applicable to commercial but private sexual acts or solicitation.

Open and Gross Lewdness and Lascivious Behavior

Regulatory Authority—G.L. c. 272, § 16
Dist. Ct. Model Jury Instruction 7.400

7

The defendant is charged with open and gross lewdness and lascivious behavior.

In order to prove the defendant guilty of this offense, the Commonwealth must prove five things beyond a reasonable doubt:

First: That the defendant exposed his (her) (genitals) (buttocks) (*or*) (female breasts) to one or more persons;

Second: That the defendant did so intentionally;

In a prosecution for intentional exposure to a single person in a private setting, the following element may be rephrased by deleting the word "public" and replacing the word "others" with "another person."

Third: That the defendant did so "openly," that is, either he (she) intended public exposure, or he (she) recklessly disregarded a substantial risk of public exposure, to others who might be offended by such conduct;

Fourth: That the defendant's act was done in such a way as would alarm or shock a reasonable person; and

Fifth: That at least one person was alarmed or shocked.

Alarm or shock means the defendant's conduct created a serious, negative emotional experience. Alarm or shock requires more than proof of mere nervousness or offense.

Commonwealth v. Maguire, 476 Mass. 156, 158, 161 (2017); *Commonwealth v. Kessler*, 442 Mass. 125, 127 (2008).

NOTES

1. **Constitutionality.** The criminal prohibition of open and gross lewdness (G.L. c. 272, § 16), as limited by prior decisions, is facially constitutional. *Commonwealth v. Ora*, 451 Mass. 125, 128 (2008). The statute prohibits the imposition of lewdness or nudity on an unsuspecting or unwilling person, and cannot be applied to expressive conduct that falls within the ambit of the First Amendment (which does not include legally obscene acts) and is offered to a willing audience. *Mendoza v. Licensing Bd. of Fall River*, 444 Mass. 188, 197 (2005) (nude dancing enjoys constitutional protection as a form of expression under both the First Amendment to the U.S. Constitution as well as art. 16 of the Massachusetts Declaration of Rights); *Revere v. Aucella*, 369 Mass. 138, 142–43, *appeal dismissed sub nom* (statute does not apply to nude go-go dancing where there is no imposition of the lewdness or nudity on an unsuspecting or unwilling person).

2. **Degree and nature of shock clarified.** The display of nudity must be intentional, done in a manner to produce alarm or shock, and must actually produce alarm or shock that is a "serious negative emotional experience," and not just "nervousness and offense." *Commonwealth v. Kessler*, 442 Mass. 770, 774 (2004). Vicarious concern for other people or even disgust does not "convert any ordinary indecent exposure case into one for open and gross lewdness." *Commonwealth v. Maguire*, 476 Mass. 156, 160 (2016) (insufficient where detective was "disgusted", not for himself, but rather out of concern for the women seated nearby and no evidence that the women sustained a "serious negative emotional experience" stronger than "mere nervousness and offense"). *See Commonwealth v. Ora*, 451 Mass. 125, 127 (2008) (as a felony, it "is thus a much more serious offense than the misdemeanor of indecent exposure, G.L. c. 272, § 53, and consequently requires a substantially more serious and negative impact as a result of the behavior").

The fourth element has an objective standard which is satisfied only if the factfinder determines that the subjective response was reasonable. *Commonwealth v. Maguire*, 476 Mass. 156, 161(2016).

3. **"Buttocks" or "female breasts."** Open and gross lewdness is not limited to exposure of the genitals, and may include exposure of the "buttocks" or "female breasts." *Commonwealth v. Quinn*, 439 Mass. 492 (2003) (exposure of thong-clad buttocks); *Commonwealth v. Ora*, 451 Mass. 125, 127 (2008).

4. **Open.** Requirement that act be "open" refers to defendant's intent that act be seen by one or more unwilling persons present and does not require that it be done in a public place. *Commonwealth v. Kelley*, 25 Mass. App. Ct. 180, 184–85 (1987). *See Commonwealth v. Wardell*, 128 Mass. 52, 53–54 (1880) (salesman exposed himself in private home to minor children); *Com-monwealth v. Guy G.*, 53 Mass. App. Ct. 271, 273 (2001) (student defendant exposed penis to female student in shared cubicle); *Commonwealth v. Montez*, 45 Mass. App. Ct. 802, 806, (1997) (standing in window of apartment and masturbating); *Commonwealth v. Gray*, 40 Mass. App. Ct. 901, 901 (1996) (fellatio in public bathroom). *Compare Commonwealth v. Ferguson*, 384 Mass. 13, 14–15 (1981) (statute inapplicable to sexual acts in car parked in dark parking lot reasonably expected to be private) *with Commonwealth v. Adams*, 389 Mass. 265, 272 (1983) (masturbating in a public place "certainly falls within the common understanding" of the offense).

5. **Eyewitness testimony.** There is no requirement that the Commonwealth must prove the exposure element solely through the victim's eyewitness testimony. *Commonwealth v. Poillucci*, 46 Mass. App. Ct. 300, 303 n.3 (1999).

Operating Negligently so as to Endanger

Regulatory Authority—G.L. c. 90, § 24(2)(a)
Dist. Ct. Model Jury Instruction 5.240

The defendant is charged with operating a motor vehicle negligently in a manner that might endanger the public. Section 24(2)(a) of chapter 90 of our General Laws provides as follows:

"Whoever, upon any way *or* in any place to which the public has a right of access, *or* [in] any place to which members of the public have access as invitees or licensees, operates a motor vehicle . . . negligently so that the lives or safety of the public might be endangered . . . shall be punished . . . ."

In order to prove the defendant guilty of this offense, the Commonwealth must prove three things beyond a reasonable doubt:

First: That the defendant operated a motor vehicle;

Second: That he (she) did so (on a way) (*or*) (in a place where the public has a right of access) (*or*) (in a place where members of the public have access as invitees or licensees); and

Third: That he (she) did so in a negligent manner so that the lives or safety of the public might have been endangered.

At this point, the jury must be instructed on the definitions of "Operation of a Motor Vehicle" (Instruction 3.200) and "Public Way" (Instruction 3.280).

The third thing the Commonwealth must prove beyond a reasonable doubt is that the defendant drove negligently in a manner that might have endangered the lives or safety of other people.

A person acts negligently when he fails to use due care, that is, when he acts in a way that a reasonable person would not act. This can happen either by doing something that a reasonably prudent person would not do under those circumstances, or by failing to do something that a reasonably prudent person would do. The defendant acted negligently if he (she) drove in a way that a reasonable person would not have, and by doing so created an unnecessary danger to other people, a danger that he (she) could have avoided by driving more carefully.

A. ***If there was no accident.*** A person can be found to have driven negligently even if no accident resulted, and even if there was no one else actually on the road to be put in danger. A person is negligent if he drives in a way that has the potential to cause an accident or to endanger anyone who might be on the road.

B. ***If there was an accident.*** The fact that an accident occurred is not by itself evidence that the defendant was negligent. You must examine all the evidence about how the accident happened in order to determine whether any negligence was involved, and if so, whether that negligence was the defendant's.

In determining whether the defendant drove negligently in a manner that might have endangered the public, you should take into account all the facts of the situation: the defendant's rate of speed and manner of operation, the defendant's physical condition and how well he (she) could see and could control his (her) vehicle, the condition of the defendant's vehicle, what kind of a road it was and who else was on the road, what the time of day, the weather and the condition of the road were, what any other vehicles or pedestrians were doing, and any other factors that you think are relevant.

If you find that the defendant acted negligently, the defendant's intent is not relevant. You are not required to find that the defendant intended to act negligently or unlawfully. This is in that category of situations where public safety requires each driver to determine and to adhere to an objective standard of reasonable behavior. Therefore the defendant's subjective intent is irrelevant; the issue is whether or not he (she) drove as a reasonable person would have under the circumstances.

> See also Instruction 3.180 (Negligence). For a supplemental instruction on violation of the law as evidence of negligence, see supplemental instruction to Instruction 3.180. If the violation is speeding, see supplemental instruction 5.640 (Road Racing).
>
> *Commonwealth v. Burno*, 396 Mass. 622, 624 (1986) (potential danger to public is relevant factor for jury consideration); *Commonwealth v. Campbell*, 394 Mass. 77, 87 (1985) (victim's contributory negligence is not defense); *Commonwealth v. Jones*, 382 Mass. 387, 389–92 (1981) (finding of ordinary negligence satisfies vehicular homicide statute [G.L. c. 90, § 24G], which was taken almost verbatim from driving so as to endanger statute); *Commonwealth v. Charland*, 338 Mass. 742, 744 (1959) (speed is relevant factor); *Commonwealth v. Gurney*, 261 Mass. 309, 312 (1927) (relevant jury factors); *Commonwealth v. Vartanian*, 251 Mass. 355, 358 (1925) (same); *Commonwealth v. Horsfall*, 213 Mass. 232, 235 (1913) (reckless operation can occur even on deserted street); *Commonwealth v. Gordon*, 15 Mass. App. Ct. 901 (1982), *aff'd*, 389 Mass. 351 (1983) (negligent inattention to driving plus glassy eyes and slurred speech will support conviction); *Commonwealth v. A Juvenile*, 383 Mass. 877, 878 (1981) (offense is one for which juvenile may be transferred for trial as adult).
>
> Prior to St. 1928, c. 281, this was a strict liability offense that did not include any requirement of negligence. That fact must be kept in mind when reviewing early decisions involving the former statute.

Supplemental Instructions

1. ***Negligence or intoxication of other driver.*** You have heard testimony suggesting that the driver of the other vehicle involved in this matter, *[name]*, was (negligent) (or) (intoxicated). It is up to you to decide whether or not to accept that testimony as accurate.

If you *do* conclude that the other driver was (negligent) (or) (intoxicated), then you must determine what role that driver's (negligence) (or) (intoxication) played in this matter.

The other driver's driving is irrelevant to the defendant's guilt or innocence on this charge unless the other driver was the sole cause of what happened. The defendant is not excused merely because the other driver was (negligent) (or) (intoxicated), if the defendant's negligence was the direct cause of what happened, and the other driver's (negligence) (or) (intoxication) merely aggravated the result. On the other hand, if the other driver's (negligence) (or) (intoxication) was the sole cause of what happened and the defendant was not negligent, then the defendant must be found not guilty.

> *Commonwealth v. Galluzzo*, 25 Mass. App. Ct. 568, *fur. app. rev. den.*, 402 Mass. 1104 (1988) (judge must allow evidence of other driver's negligence if it would warrant a finding that the sole negligence was that of the other driver, but careful instructions are required to make clear that contributory negligence is not a defense). If additional language on supplemental and superseding causes is appropriate, the supplemental instruction to Instruction 5.160 (Homicide by a Motor Vehicle [Misdemeanor]) may be appropriately adapted.

2. ***Emergency situation.*** In determining whether the defendant's conduct was negligent, you may consider whether there was a sudden emergency which required rapid decision. If there was, you must determine whether the defendant acted as a reasonable person would under similar emergency circumstances.

> *Newman v. Redstone*, 354 Mass. 379, 383 (1968).

NOTE

Victim's injuries. The alleged victim of a defendant charged with operating so as to endanger may be permitted to testify as to physical injuries sustained in the accident, since the nature and extent of such injuries are relevant to the issue of negligence. The judge must determine whether their prejudice outweighs their relevance. *Commonwealth v. Cohen,* 27 Mass. App. Ct. 1210, 1211 (1989).

Operating Recklessly

Regulatory Authority—G.L. c. 90, § 24(2)(a)
Dist. Ct. Model Jury Instruction 5.260

The defendant is charged with operating a motor vehicle recklessly. Section 24(2)(a) of chapter 90 of our General Laws provides as follows:

> "Whoever, upon any way *or* in any place to which the public has a right of access, *or* [in] any place to which members of the public have access as invitees or licensees, operates a motor vehicle recklessly . . . shall be punished . . . ."

In order to prove the defendant guilty of this offense, the Commonwealth must prove three things beyond a reasonable doubt:

First: That the defendant operated a motor vehicle;

7

Second: That he (she) did so (on a way) (or) (in a place where the public has a right of access) (or) (in a place where members of the public have access as invitees or licensees); and

Third: That he (she) did so in a reckless manner.

At this point, the jury must be instructed on the definitions of "Public Way" (Instruction 3.280) and "Operation of a Motor Vehicle" (Instruction 3.200).

The third thing the Commonwealth must prove beyond a reasonable doubt is that the defendant drove recklessly. A person drives recklessly when he ignores the fact that his manner of driving is very likely to result in death or serious injury to someone, or he is indifferent to whether someone is killed or seriously injured.

It is not enough for the Commonwealth to prove that the defendant acted negligently—that is, acted in a way that a reasonably careful person would not. It must be shown that the defendant's actions went beyond mere negligence and amounted to recklessness. The defendant was reckless if he (she) knew, or should have known, that such actions would pose a grave danger of death or serious injury to others, but he (she) chose, nevertheless, to run the risk and go ahead.

A. ***If there was no accident.*** A person can be found to have driven recklessly even if no accident resulted, and even if there was no one else actually on the road near him. A person is reckless if he consciously disregards, or is indifferent to, a significant possibility of serious injury to anyone else who might be on the road.

B. ***If there was an accident.*** The fact that an accident occurred is not by itself evidence that the defendant was reckless. You must examine all the evidence about how the accident happened in order to determine whether the defendant was at fault, and if so, whether the defendant's actions rose to the level of recklessness.

In determining whether the defendant drove recklessly, you should take into account all the facts of the situation: the defendant's rate of speed and manner of operation, the defendant's physical condition and how well he (she) could see and could control his (her) vehicle, the condition of the defendant's vehicle, what kind of a road it was and who else was on the road, what the time of day, the weather and the condition of the road were, what any other vehicles or pedestrians were doing, and any other factors that you think are relevant.

7

The defendant must have intended his (her) acts, in the sense that they were not accidental. But it is not necessary that the defendant intended or foresaw the consequences of those acts, as long as a reasonable person would know that they were so dangerous that death or serious injury would probably result. This is in that category of cases where public safety requires each driver, once he knows what the situation is, to determine and to adhere to an objective standard of behavior.

"[B]y custom and usage the element of 'recklessness' has been of little or no significance in the application of the operating to endanger statute," *Commonwealth v. Jones,* 382 Mass. 387, 392 (1981), because of the availability of the negligence branch of the statute, see *Commonwealth v. Guillemette,* 243 Mass. 346, 346 (1923). See Instruction 5.240 (Operating Negligently so as to Endanger).

Commonwealth v. Catalina, 407 Mass. 779, 789 (1990) (subjective awareness of reckless nature of conduct unnecessary; conduct which a reasonable person in similar circumstances would recognize as reckless suffices); *Commonwealth v. Olivo,* 369 Mass. 62, 67 (1975) (recklessness depends on facts of case); *Commonwealth v. Horsfall,* 213 Mass. 232, 235 (1913) (reckless operation can occur even on deserted street); *Commonwealth v. Welansky,* 316 Mass. 383, 397–401 (1944) (definition of recklessness); *Commonwealth v. Sullivan,* 29 Mass. App. Ct. 93, 96 (1990) (same); *Commonwealth v. Papadinis,* 23 Mass. App. Ct. 570, 574–75 (1987), *rev'd on other grounds*, 402 Mass. 73 (1988) (same). Proposed Criminal Code of Massachusetts c. 263, § 16(d) (1972) (same).

Operating With a Blood Alcohol Level of .08% or Greater

Regulatory Authority—G.L. c. 90, § 24
Dist. Ct. Model Jury Instruction 5.300

The defendant is charged with operating a motor vehicle while having a blood alcohol level of .08 percent or greater (and with operating a motor vehicle while under the influence of alcohol).

In order to prove the defendant guilty of operating a motor vehicle while having a blood alcohol level of .08 percent or greater, the Commonwealth must prove three things beyond a reasonable doubt:

First: That the defendant operated a motor vehicle;

Second: That the defendant did so (on a public way) (or) (in a place where the public has a right of access) (or) (in a place where members of the public have access as invitees or licensees); and

Third: That at the time of operation, the percent of alcohol in the defendant's blood was .08 or greater.

At this point, the jury must be instructed on the definitions of "Operation of a Motor Vehicle" (Instruction 3.200), "Public Way" (Instruction 3.280), and percentage of alcohol in the defendant's blood (which follows), unless these are stipulated. See instruction below regarding stipulations.

The third element that the Commonwealth must prove beyond a reasonable doubt is that at the time of operation the percent of alcohol in the defendant's (breath) (blood) was .08 or greater. The law allows a defendant's blood alcohol level to be shown by a chemical test or analysis of his (her) breath or blood.

If there is a challenge whether the breath test was properly administered, see Supplemental Instruction 2.

If any elements are stipulated. Because the parties have stipulated (that the defendant was operating a motor vehicle) (and) (that the location was a public way) (that the location was one to which the public had a right of access) (and) (that the percent of alcohol in the defendant's blood was .08 or greater), the only element(s) the Commonwealth must prove beyond a reasonable doubt is (are) that the defendant *(elements)*. If the Commonwealth has proved (that) (those) element(s) beyond a reasonable doubt, you should return a verdict of guilty. If it has not, you must find the defendant not guilty.

If there are no stipulations. So there are three things that the Commonwealth must prove beyond a reasonable doubt:

First: That the defendant operated a motor vehicle;

Second: That the defendant did so (on a public way) (or) (in a place where the public has a right of access) (or) (in a place where members of the public have access as invitees or licensees); and

Third: That at the time he (she) operated the vehicle, the percent of alcohol in the defendant's blood was .08 or greater.

If the Commonwealth has proven all three elements beyond a reasonable doubt, you should return a verdict of guilty. If the Commonwealth has failed to prove one or more of these elements beyond a reasonable doubt, you must return a verdict of not guilty.

Supplemental Instructions

1. ***If the defendant is permitted to introduce additional test samples.*** (You have heard testimony) (A document has been introduced in evidence reporting) that the defendant gave more than one breath sample, and that the results were [*results of each sample*]. By regulation, the result of the defendant's test is the lower

reading. You may consider the additional sample(s) only on the issue of whether the test result was accurate.

The Commonwealth may not introduce more than one test result. *Commonwealth v. Steele*, 455 Mass. 209, 213 (2009). See 501 CMR 2.15(2)(b).

2. ***If there is a challenge regarding the administration of the breath test.*** In deciding whether the Commonwealth has proved the defendant's blood alcohol level beyond a reasonable doubt, you may consider evidence, if any, about:

- when the test was given;
- the qualifications of the person who gave the test, and your assessment of his (her) credibility;
- the pre-test procedures that were employed;
- whether the testing device was in good working order at the time the test was administered;
- whether the test was administered properly;
- and any other evidence pertaining to the administration of the test.

NOTES

1. **Statute now bifurcated.** Statute 2003, c. 28, § 1 (effective June 30, 2003) amended G.L. c. 90, § 24(1) so that it now punishes anyone who "operates a motor vehicle with a percentage, by weight, of alcohol in their blood of eight one-hundredths or greater, or while under the influence of intoxicating liquor" or specified drugs. The two alternatives comprise a single offense that may be committed in two different ways. *Commonwealth v. Colturi*, 448 Mass. 809 (2007). The "operating under the influence" alternative requires proof of operation "with a diminished capacity to operate safely," *Commonwealth v. Connolly*, 394 Mass. 169, 173 (1985), but not proof of any specific blood alcohol level, while the "per se" alternative requires proof of operation with a blood alcohol level of .08% or greater but not proof of diminished capacity. Consequently, evidence pertaining to impairment is not relevant to the offense of operating a motor vehicle with a blood alcohol level of .08 or greater.

2. **Model instruction.** The model instruction is based on *Colturi, supra* and *Commonwealth v. Zeininger*, 459 Mass. 775 (2011).

3. **Evidence in a per se case.** If the Commonwealth proceeds only on the per se offense, evidence about the defendant's behavior and appearance may not be relevant. The legislature has defined the crime in terms of the alcohol content of one's blood.

4. **Breath tests: challenges to particular test result.** Before the result of a breath test may be admitted, the Commonwealth must establish the existence of and compliance with the requirements of a periodic testing program for breath testing machines in accordance with G.L. c. 90, § 24K and regulations promulgated thereunder. *Commonwealth v. Barbeau*, 411 Mass. 782, 784–86 (1992). Those requirements of § 24K are met by the provision of 501 Code Mass. Regs. § 2.00 et seq. (effective April 30, 2010).

A breath test result is admissible only if the Commonwealth has introduced evidence that the machine was working properly. *Commonwealth v. Cochran*, 25 Mass. App. Ct. 260, 264 (1988). Beyond that minimum level, generally any delay in administering a blood alcohol test, *Commonwealth v. Marley*, 396 Mass. 433, 438–39 (1985), any weaknesses in the test operator's knowledge and skill, *Commonwealth v. Shea*, 356 Mass. 358, 361 (1969), or any procedural weaknesses in the administration of a particular test, *Commonwealth v. Malloy*, 15 Mass. App. Ct. 958 (1983); *Commonwealth v. Hazelton*, 11 Mass. App. Ct. 899, 900 (1980), are matters of weight for the jury and do not affect the admissibility of the test result.

The requirement that an arrestee "should be observed by the breath testing operator for at least 15 minutes prior to the administration of the test" (501 Code Mass. Regs. § 2.13(3)) does not require that such observation be done at the testing location or room. If the arresting officer is also the breathalyzer operator, the requirement could be satisfied by the officer's being continuously with the arrestee from the traffic stop until the test provided there is actual observation consistent with the regulation. Normally, compliance issues go to weight rather than admissibility, but if the prosecution fails to make a sufficient showing of compliance with the letter and purpose of the regulation, the test results must be suppressed. *Commonwealth v. Pierre*, 72 Mass. App. Ct. 230 (2008).

5. **Breath tests: expert testimony.** The Commonwealth may introduce a breath or blood test result to establish the level of alcohol in the defendant's blood at the time of operation without offering expert testimony to provide "retrograde extrapolation" (calculating what the defendant's blood alcohol level must have been at the time of the offense based on his or her subsequent blood alcohol level), provided the test was taken within a "reasonable time" after operation. This is usually up to three hours, although particular facts and circumstances may establish that a greater or lesser time period should be applied by the judge in his or her discretion. *Colturi*, 448 Mass. at 816–17. If expert testimony on retrograde extrapolation is proffered, it should be evaluated by the usual criteria of whether its methodology is scientifically valid, in general, and in the particular instance. *Commonwealth v. Senior*, 433 Mass. 453, 458–62 (2001); *Commonwealth v. Smith*, 35 Mass. App. Ct. 655, 662–64 (1993).

The defendant has the right to present a qualified expert to challenge the accuracy of the breath test result in the defendant's particular case. *Connolly*, 394 Mass. at 175; *Marley, supra*; *Smythe*, 23 Mass. App. Ct. at 351–55. If there is expert testimony, see Instruction 3.640 ("Expert Witness").

6. **§ 24O notice.** While the requirement of G.L. c. 90, § 24O that defendants convicted of motor vehicle offenses should be given a written statement of the statutory provisions applicable to any subsequent violation "should be observed by the District Courts," failure to give a defendant such notice is not a defense against a subsequent charge as a second offender. *Commonwealth v. Dowler*, 414 Mass. 212 (1993).

7. **Admissibility of breathalyzer records.** Certified copies of breathalyzer records are admissible under the business records exception to the hearsay rule. *Zeininger, supra.*

8. **Possible effect on breath test results of a required finding.** If the Commonwealth initially proceeds under both portions of the statute and the judge subsequently allows a motion for directed verdict on the per-se portion of the offense, the judge must determine whether or not to strike any breath test evidence, absent expert testimony. See *Colturi, supra* ("if the per se and impaired ability theories of criminal liability are charged in the alternative . . . and so tried, we see no prejudice in the admission of breathalyzer test results without expert testimony . . . . If, however, the Commonwealth were to proceed only on a theory of impaired operation and offered a breathalyzer test result of .08 or greater, . . . it must present expert testimony establishing a relationship between the test result and intoxication as a foundational requirement of the admissibility of such tests" since otherwise "the jury would be left to guess at its meaning"). If the breath test results are allowed to remain in evidence, the box entitled "Limited use of a breath test result of .08 or greater" in Instruction 5.310 ("Operating under the Influence of Intoxicating Liquor") should be incorporated at the point indicated.

Operating Under the Influence of Intoxicating Liquor

Regulatory Authority—G.L. c. 90, § 24
Dist. Ct. Model Jury Instruction 5.310

The defendant is charged with operating a motor vehicle while under the influence of intoxicating liquor (in the same complaint that charges the defendant with operating a motor vehicle with a blood alcohol level of .08% or greater).

In order to prove the defendant guilty of this offense, the Commonwealth must prove the following three things beyond a reasonable doubt:

First: That the defendant operated a motor vehicle;

Second: That the defendant did so (on a public way) (or) (in a place where the public has a right of access) (or) (in a place where members of the public have access as invitees or licensees); (and)

Third: That while operating the vehicle, the defendant was under the influence of intoxicating liquor.

At this point, the jury must be instructed on the definitions of "Operation of a Motor Vehicle" (Instruction 3.200), "Public Way" (Instruction 3.280), and under the influence of intoxicating liquor (which follows), unless the defendant has stipulated to these elements. See instruction below regarding stipulations.

The third element which the Commonwealth must prove beyond a reasonable doubt is that the defendant was under the influence of intoxicating liquor while operating a motor vehicle. What does it mean to be "under the influence" of alcohol? It is not illegal to drive after consuming alcohol as long as the operator is not under the influence of alcohol. However, neither does someone have to be drunk to be under the influence of alcohol. A person is under the influence of alcohol if he (she) has consumed enough alcohol to reduce his (her) ability to operate a motor vehicle safely, by decreasing his (her) alertness, judgment, and ability to respond promptly. It means that a person has consumed enough alcohol to reduce his (her) mental clarity, self-control and reflexes, and thereby left him (her) with a reduced ability to drive safely.

The Commonwealth is not required to prove that the defendant actually drove in an unsafe or erratic manner, but it is required to prove that his (her) *ability* to drive safely was diminished by alcohol. The amount of alcohol necessary to do this may vary from person to person. You may rely on your experience and common sense about the effects of alcohol. You should consider any believable evidence about the defendant's alleged consumption of alcohol, as well as the defendant's appearance, condition, and behavior at the time.

Limited use of breath test result of .08 or greater. You may also consider whether a (breath) (blood) test showed that the defendant had consumed any alcohol. However, no matter what the reading is, the (breath) (blood) test is not sufficient by itself to prove that the defendant was under the influence of alcohol.

> A result of .08 or greater is not admissible on the issue of impairment without "expert testimony establishing a relationship between the test results and intoxication as a foundational requirement of the admissibility of such results." *Commonwealth v. Colturi,* 448 Mass. 809, 818 (2007); *Commonwealth v. Hubert*, 71 Mass. App. Ct. 661, 663, *aff'd*, 453 Mass. 1109 (2009). The evidence of a breath test is admissible only on the issue of whether the defendant consumed alcohol.
>
> If the Commonwealth initially proceeds under both portions of the statute and the judge subsequently allows a motion for required finding on the per-se portion of the offense, the judge must determine whether or not to strike any breath test evidence, absent expert testimony. *See Colturi, supra* ("if the per se and impaired ability theories of criminal liability are charged in the alternative . . . and so tried, we see no prejudice in the admission of breathalyzer test results without expert testimony . . . . If, however, the Commonwealth were to proceed only on a theory of impaired operation and offered a breathalyzer test result of .08 or greater, . . . it must present expert testimony establishing a relationship between the test result and intoxication as a foundational requirement of the admissibility of such tests" since otherwise "the jury would be left to guess at its meaning"). If the breath test results are allowed to remain in evidence, the above insertion should be incorporated.

If there are stipulations. Because the parties have stipulated (that the defendant was operating a motor vehicle) (and) (that the location was a public way) (that the location was one to which the public had a right of access) (that the defendant was under the influence of intoxicating liquor), the only element(s) the Commonwealth must prove beyond a reasonable doubt is (are) that the defendant *(elements)*. If the Commonwealth has proved (that) (those) element(s) beyond a reasonable doubt, you should return a verdict of guilty. If it has not, you must find the defendant not guilty.

If there are no stipulations. So there are three things that the Commonwealth must prove beyond a reasonable doubt:

First: That the defendant operated a motor vehicle;

Second: That the defendant did so (on a public way) (or) (in a place where the public has a right of access) (or) (in a place where members of the public have access as invitees or licensees); and

Third: That while the defendant was operating the vehicle, he (she) was under the influence of intoxicating liquor.

7

If the Commonwealth has proven all three elements beyond a reasonable doubt, you should return a verdict of guilty. If the Commonwealth has failed to prove one or more of these elements beyond a reasonable doubt, you must return a verdict of not guilty.

Supplemental Instructions

1. ***If there is opinion evidence about the defendant's sobriety (optional).*** You have heard testimony of (an opinion) (opinions) about the defendant's sobriety. Ultimately, it is for you as the jury to determine whether the defendant was under the influence of alcohol according to the definition I have provided. You may consider any opinion you have heard and accept it or reject it. In the end, you and you alone must decide whether the defendant was under the influence of intoxicating liquor.

2. ***"Downs" instruction only where requested by the defendant.*** You are not to consider in anyway whatsoever, either for or against either side, that there is no evidence of a breathalyzer. You may not speculate or guess about it because there is no evidence of it. Do not consider that in any way. Do not mention it. And put it completely out of your mind.

3. ***If there is evidence of field sobriety tests or roadside assessments.*** You have heard evidence in this case that the defendant performed (field sobriety tests) (roadside assessments). It is for you to decide if those (tests) (assessments) demonstrate the defendant's ability to operate a motor vehicle safely was diminished. It is for you to decide whether to rely on this evidence. You may accept it or reject and you may give it such weight as you think it deserves. In evaluating the evidence, you may consider the nature of the tests, the circumstances under which they were given and performed, and all of the other evidence in this case.

4. ***If there is evidence the defendant was not offered a field sobriety test.*** There is evidence that there were no (field sobriety tests) (roadside assessments). This is a factor you may consider in evaluating the evidence presented in this case. With respect to this factor, you should consider three questions:

First: Whether the omitted tests were standard procedure or steps that would otherwise normally be taken under the circumstances;

Second: Whether the omitted tests could reasonably have been expected to lead to significant evidence of the defendant's guilt or innocence; and

Third: Whether the evidence provides a reasonable and adequate explanation for the omission of the tests or other actions.

If you find that any omissions in the investigation were significant and not adequately explained, you may consider whether the omissions tend to affect the quality, reliability, or credibility of the evidence presented by the Commonwealth.

All of these considerations involve factual determinations that are entirely up to you, and you are free to give this matter whatever weight, if any, you deem appropriate based on all the circumstances.

> A motorist's *refusal* to perform sobriety tests when requested to do so by the police may not be admitted in evidence, since such evidence violates the privilege against self-incrimination under art. 12 of the Massachusetts Declaration of Rights. *Commonwealth v. McGrail*, 419 Mass. 774 (1995).
>
> This supplemental instruction is available in the different situation where the police did *not* offer the defendant an opportunity to perform field sobriety tests, and the defendant argues to the jury that this deprived the defendant of an opportunity to generate exculpatory evidence. *See Commonwealth v. Ames*, 410 Mass. 603, 609 (1991). The judge may also wish to consider leaving the matter to the parties to argue, see *Commonwealth v. Ly*, 19 Mass. App. Ct. 901, 901–02 (1984), unless an instruction is necessary to

correct a suggestion that such tests are legally required. This instruction is based upon Instruction 3.740 ("Omissions in Police Investigation").

In instructing that such tests are not legally mandatory, the judge must avoid negating the defendant's right to build a defense on the grounds that available, probative testing was not performed by police. See *Commonwealth v. Bowden*, 379 Mass. 472, 485–86 (1980).

5. ***If there is evidence both of alcohol and drug use.***

If the Commonwealth has proved beyond a reasonable doubt that the defendant's ability to operate safely was diminished by alcohol, then he (she) has violated the law even if some other factor tended to magnify the effect of the alcohol or contributed to his (her) diminished capacity to operate a vehicle safely. Alcohol need not be the only exclusive cause. It is not a defense that there was a second contributing cause so long as alcohol was *one* of the causes of the defendant's diminished capacity [to] operate safely.

Commonwealth v. Bishop, 78 Mass. App. Ct. 70, 74–75 (2010).

6. ***If breath test result of .05 or less is in evidence.*** If the percentage of alcohol by weight in the defendant's blood was .05 percent or less, that is evidence from which you may infer that the defendant was *not* under the influence of intoxicating liquor. You are not required to reach that conclusion. You may consider the test result along with all the other evidence in the case to determine whether the Commonwealth has met its burden of proving beyond a reasonable doubt that the defendant was under the influence of intoxicating liquor.

7. ***If breath test result of .06 or .07 is in evidence.*** If the percentage of alcohol by weight in the defendant's blood was .06 percent or .07 percent, that is evidence which you may consider in determining whether the defendant had consumed any alcohol. However, you may not draw any inference from those results as to whether or not the defendant was under the influence of alcohol. To determine that issue, you must look to all the evidence in the case.

"In any prosecution for a violation of [G.L. c. 90, § 24(a)], evidence of the percentage, by weight, of alcohol in the defendant's blood at the time of the alleged offense, as shown by chemical test or analysis of his blood or as indicated by a chemical test or analysis of his breath, shall be admissible and deemed relevant to the determination of the question of whether such defendant was at such time under the influence of intoxicating liquor . . . . If such evidence is that such percentage was five one-hundredths or less, there shall be a permissible inference that such defendant was not under the influence of intoxicating liquor . . . . [;] if such evidence is that such percentage was more than five one-hundredths but less than eight one-hundredths there shall be no permissible inference." G.L. c. 90, § 24(1)(e).

See *Colturi*, 448 Mass. at 817, as to instructing the jury on these statutory inferences.

NOTES

1. **Statute now bifurcated.** Statute 2003, c. 28, § 1 (effective June 30, 2003) amended G.L. c. 90, § 24(1) so that it now punishes anyone who "operates a motor vehicle with a percentage, by weight, of alcohol in their blood of eight one-hundredths or greater, or while under the influence of intoxicating liquor" or specified drugs. The two alternatives comprise a single offense that may be committed in two different ways. *Commonwealth v. Colturi*, 448 Mass. 809 (2007). The "operating under the influence" alternative requires proof of operation "with a diminished capacity to operate safely," *Commonwealth v. Connolly*, 394 Mass. 169, 173 (1985), but not proof of any specific blood alcohol level, while the "per se" alternative requires proof of operation with a blood alcohol level of .08% or greater but not proof of diminished capacity.

2. **Model instruction.** The model instruction is based on *Commonwealth v. Colturi*, 448 Mass. 809 (2007); *Commonwealth v. Tynes*, 400 Mass. 369, 374–75 (1987); *Connolly*, 394 Mass. 169 (1985); *Commonwealth v. Bernier*, 366 Mass. 717, 720 (1975); and *Commonwealth v. Lyseth*, 250 Mass. 555 (1925).

It is correct to charge that a person need not be drunk to be under the influence of liquor, but it is error to instruct that the defendant need only be "influenced in some perceptible degree" by liquor, *Connolly*, 394 Mass. at 172, since "a conviction may rest only on proof that alcohol affected him in a particular way, i.e., by diminishing his capacity to drive safely" (emphasis in original). *Tynes*, 400 Mass. at 375. "[T]he Commonwealth must prove beyond a reasonable doubt that the defendant's consumption of alcohol diminished the defendant's ability to operate a motor vehicle safely. The Commonwealth need not prove that the defendant actually drove in an unsafe or erratic manner, but it must prove a diminished capacity to operate safely" (emphasis in original). *Connolly*, 394 Mass. at 173. A non-conforming charge is reversible error unless there is no objection and there is substantial evidence of unsafe operation. *Contrast Commonwealth v. Marley*, 396 Mass. 433 (1985) (reversible error); *Commonwealth v. Luiz*, 28 Mass. App. Ct. 973 (1990) (same); *Commonwealth v. Laurino*, 23 Mass. App. Ct. 983 (1987) (same); *Commonwealth v. Brochu*, 23 Mass. App. Ct. 937 (1986) (same), *with Commonwealth v. Bryer*, 398 Mass. 9 (1986) (harmless error); *Commonwealth v. Ranahan*, 23 Mass. App. Ct. 201 (1986) (same); *Commonwealth v. Haley*, 23 Mass. App. Ct. 10 (1986) (same); *Commonwealth v. Riley*, 22 Mass. App. Ct. 698 (1986) (same).

The model instruction appropriately uses the phrase "mental clarity, self-control, and reflexes" as examples or factors that the jury may use in determining whether the defendant's capacity to operate safely was impaired. The Commonwealth must prove such impairment beyond a reasonable doubt, but is not required to prove any of those particular three factors. *Commonwealth v. Riley*, 48 Mass. App. Ct. 463 (2000).

3. **Absence of breath test.** Where there has been no breath test, a judge may give the instruction approved in *Commonwealth v. Downs*, 53 Mass. App. Ct. 195, 198 (2001), if and only if the defendant requests the instruction (or if there is "some rare set of facts that specifically directs the jury's attention to the absence of alcohol-test evidence"). *Commonwealth v. Wolfe*, 478 Mass. 142, 149–50 (2017). It should not be given even when a jury inquires about a missing breath test unless assented to by the defendant. The judge may instruct only that the jury must not speculate about matters about which there is no evidence.

4. **Refusal of breath test.** "Evidence that the defendant failed or refused to consent to [a blood alcohol] test shall not be admissible against him in a civil or criminal proceeding . . . ." G.L. c. 90, § 24(1)(e). Admission of such evidence would violate the privilege against self-incrimination under art. 12 of the Massachusetts Declaration of Rights. *Opinion of the Justices*, 412 Mass. 1201 (1992). The jury instruction that was formerly required by § 24(1)(e) whenever there is no evidence of blood alcohol level "tend[ed] to have the same effect as the admission of refusal evidence," and violated art. 12. *Commonwealth v. Zevitas*, 418 Mass. 677 (1994). That statutory requirement has now been repealed. *See* St. 2003, c. 28 (effective June 30, 2003).

5. **Breath tests: statutory inferences.** In charging the jury as to the significance of blood or alcohol tests for the "under the influence" alternative, note that the third part of the former statutory inference in G.L. c. 90, § 24(1)(e) ("and if such evidence is that such percentage was eight one hundredths or more, there shall be a permissible inference that such defendant was under the influence of intoxicating liquor") has been deleted. Therefore, the jury may no longer be instructed in such terms. On the other hand, § 24(1)(e) continues to provide that "evidence of the percentage, by weight, of alcohol in the defendant's blood at the time of the alleged offense, as shown by chemical test or analysis of his blood or as indicated by a chemical test or analysis of his breath, shall be admissible and deemed relevant to the determination of the question of whether such defendant was at such time under the influence of intoxicating liquor."

6. **Testimony about actions of defendant who agreed to a breath test.** Once a defendant consents to a breath test, testimony about the defendant's performance or non-performance is admissible without a preliminary ruling of admissibility by the court. *Commonwealth v. Adonsoto*, 475 Mass. 497, 501 (2016).

7. **Drugs as a contributing cause.** Supplemental Instruction 4, *supra*, is closely modeled on the language of, and the recommended instruction in, *Commonwealth v. Stathopoulos*, 401 Mass. 453, 456–57 & n.4 (1988) and *Commonwealth v. Bishop*, 78 Mass. App. Ct. 70 (2010). This situation, where both alcohol and illegal or prescription drugs are concurrent causes of the defendant's intoxication, must be distinguished from that where a defendant's intoxication was caused solely by prescription medication taken as prescribed. In cases in which there is evidence that the defendant's impairment was caused solely by prescription

medication, "the jury should be instructed that a defendant is entitled to an acquittal if [the defendant's] intoxication was caused solely by [the defendant's] prescription medication, taken as prescribed, and [that the defendant] did not know or have 'reason to know of the possible effects of the drug on [the defendant's] driving abilities.'" *Commonwealth v. Bishop*, 78 Mass. App. Ct. at 75 (emphasis in original) (quoting *Commonwealth v. Wallace*, 14 Mass. App. Ct. 358, 365 (1982)). If, however, alcohol contributed to a defendant's diminished ability to operate a motor vehicle safely, the defendant is not entitled to an instruction that she should be acquitted if she did not know of the potential effects of mixing her medication with alcohol. *Commonwealth v. Bishop*, 78 Mass. App. Ct. at 74–75. No reported case has yet discussed whether the same rule applies to involuntary intoxication from legal but non-prescription drugs.

For an instruction on the effect of alcohol or prescription medication on a defendant's criminal responsibility, see *Commonwealth v. Darch*, 54 Mass. App. Ct. 713, 715–16 (2002) (discussing interaction of prescription medication and alcohol on a person with a mental disease or defect).

8. **Subsequent offenses.** See Instruction 2.540 ("Subsequent Offenses"). To be convicted of a second offense OUI, the first conviction must have preceded the date of the second offense (and not merely the date of the second conviction). *Commonwealth v. Hernandez*, 60 Mass. App. Ct. 416 (2004).

9. **Videotapes.** Videotapes are admissible if they are relevant, they provide a fair representation of what they purport to depict, and they are not otherwise barred by an exclusionary rule. A videotape of the defendant being booked in an open area of a station house does not offend the Fourth Amendment (because no "search" is involved), does not violate the Sixth Amendment (where the right to counsel has not attached at the time of arrest), and its video portion does not violate the Fifth Amendment (since the defendant's condition and actions are not "testimonial"). With respect to the audio portion, the defendant's responses to standard booking questions do not require a valid *Miranda* waiver to be admissible, since they do not involve "custodial interrogation," but any answers to questions about the defendant's drinking must be excised from the videotape unless there was a valid *Miranda* waiver. *Commonwealth v. Mahoney*, 400 Mass. 524, 526–30 (1987); *Commonwealth v. Carey*, 26 Mass. App. Ct. 339, 340–42 (1988). See *Commonwealth v. Harvey*, 397 Mass. 351, 357–59 (1986) (videotape of protective custody); *Commonwealth v. Cameron*, 25 Mass. App. Ct. 538 (1988) (lost police videotape).

7

10. **§ 24O notice.** While the requirement of G.L. c. 90, § 24O that defendants convicted of motor vehicle offenses should be given a written statement of the statutory provisions applicable to any subsequent violation "should be observed by the District Courts," failure to give a defendant such notice is not a defense against a subsequent charge as a second offender. *Commonwealth v. Dowler*, 414 Mass. 212 (1993).

Operating without Being Licensed

Regulatory Authority—G.L. c. 90, § 10
Dist. Ct. Model Jury Instruction 5.600

The defendant is charged with operating a motor vehicle without being licensed to do so. Section 10 of chapter 90 of our General Laws provides as follows:

> "No person . . . shall operate a motor vehicle upon any way . . . . unless licensed by the registrar [of motor vehicles] [with certain exceptions that are not relevant here]."

In order to prove the defendant guilty of this offense, the Commonwealth must prove three things beyond a reasonable doubt:

First: That the defendant operated a motor vehicle;

Second: That the defendant did so on a way; and

Third: That the defendant did so without having a valid license to operate a motor vehicle, issued by the Registrar of Motor Vehicles.

> At this point, the jury must be instructed on the definition of "Operation of a Motor Vehicle" (Instruction 3.200) and the definition of "way" in G.L. c. 90, § 1, which may be excerpted from Instruction 3.280.
>
> *Watson v. Forbes*, 307 Mass. 383, 384–85 (1940) (not a defense that defendant was never notified of expiration of license); *Santa Maria v. Trotto*, 297 Mass. 442, 446 (1937) (license is required only for operation on "way"); *but see Desmarais v. Standard Acc. Ins. Co.*, 331 Mass, 199 (1954), limiting the application of *Santa Maria v. Trotto.*; *Commonwealth v. Magarosian*, 261 Mass. 228 (1927) (defendant licensed to operate one category of vehicle is unlicensed with respect to other categories of vehicles).

NOTES

1. **Burden of proof as to unlicensed status.** In a prosecution for operating an uninsured auto (G.L. c. 90, § 34J), the Commonwealth has the burden of proving that the defendant's vehicle is uninsured, and cannot utilize G.L. c. 278, § 7 to shift this burden to the defendant, since lack of "insurance is an element of the crime charged, not a mere license or authority [and] cannot be viewed as an affirmative defense . . ." *Commonwealth v. Munoz*, 384 Mass. 503, 507 (1981). It appears that the same rationale would apply to the issue of license in a prosecution under G.L. c. 90, § 10.

The Commonwealth will normally prove the defendant's unlicensed status by means of a certificate from the Registry of Motor Vehicles. *See* G.L. c. 90, § 30; G.L. c. 233, § 76.

2. **Not a civil motor vehicle infraction.** Operating without being licensed (G.L. c. 90, § 10) is a criminal offense and not a civil motor vehicle infraction. G.L. c. 90C, § 3(A), par. 1.

3. **Statutory exceptions.** General Laws c. 90, § 10 contains seven exceptions to the requirement of a Massachusetts license: (1) a person who is licensed in another state or country, has applied for a Massachusetts license but has not yet been given a drivers test, and has been issued a 60-day temporary permit by the Registry of Motor Vehicles; (2) a person who possesses a valid Massachusetts learner's permit; (3) a person who is licensed in another state and who is accompanying a spouse who is a member of the armed forces on assignment to Massachusetts; (4) a member of the armed forces on active duty who has a license issued by the state of his or her domicile; (5) a member of the armed forces within 45 days of returning from active duty outside the United States who has a license issued by the armed forces in a foreign country; (6) a nonresident who is licensed in the state or country where the vehicle is registered, but for not more than 30 days in the aggregate annually or beyond 30 days after acquiring a regular abode or place of business within Massachusetts unless Massachusetts liability insurance requirements are met; and (7) a nonresident who is licensed in the state or country of his or her domicile, if it grants reciprocal privileges to Massachusetts residents, but for not more than 30 days in the aggregate annually or beyond 30 days after acquiring a regular abode or place of business within Massachusetts unless Massachusetts liability insurance requirements are met.

Perjury

Regulatory Authority—G.L. c. 268, § 1
Former Model Jury Instruction 5.65

The defendant is charged with having committed perjury. The crime of perjury has been defined by our state legislature in G.L. c. 268, § 1. The statute states:

> Whoever being lawfully required to depose the truth in a judicial proceeding or in a proceeding in a course of justice, wilfully swears or affirms falsely in a matter material to the issue or point in question, or whoever being required by law to take an oath or affirmation wilfully swears or affirms falsely in a matter relative to which such oath or affirmation is required, shall be guilty of perjury.

To prove the defendant guilty of perjury, the Commonwealth must prove each of the following four elements beyond a reasonable doubt:[1]

First Element: that the defendant made a statement under oath in a judicial proceeding, in a proceeding in a course of justice, or when required by law to take an oath or affirmation to tell the truth;

Second Element: that the statement was false;

Third Element: that at the defendant knew the statement was false at the time (he/she) made the statement and that (he/she) made the statement willfully; and

Fourth Element: that the statement was material to the issue or point in question. Each of these elements will now be further explained.

The first element the Commonwealth must prove beyond a reasonable doubt is that the defendant did in fact make the statement[2] in question and did so in a judicial proceeding while under oath.[3]

The second element the Commonwealth must prove beyond a reasonable doubt is that the statement was in fact false.[4] The Commonwealth may or may not prove this through the means of direct evidence. If the falsity of the statement is not proved by direct evidence, then you, in your role as finders of fact, may or may not infer the falsity of the statement based on your consideration of all of the facts and circumstances in this case.

[Here the defendant claims that (his/her) statement was not false when considered together with the rest of (his/her) testimony. You should determine what the defendant meant by (his/her) words from all of (his/her) testimony at the proceeding. You may use other answers that the defendant gave and also the overall context of the statement to determine the meaning that the defendant intended at the time of the alleged false statement.[5]][6]

[Here the defendant claims (his/her) statement was unclear, uncertain or capable of more than one meaning, and therefore cannot be labeled false. A perjury charge must be based on a definite falsehood. As you saw during this trial, a witness can only answer the questions posed, and cannot talk freely or volunteer explanations on the witness stand. If the defendant gave an answer at the earlier proceeding that you find uncertain or ambiguous, and the answer was not later explained, you cannot find such a statement to be perjury, and you must find the defendant not guilty.[7]][8]

The third element the Commonwealth must prove beyond a reasonable doubt is that the defendant knew that the statement was false at the time (he/she) made it. In other words, you must be convinced beyond a reasonable doubt that the defendant made the statement with wilful, deliberate and intentional falsity.[9] You may or may not infer knowledge from circumstantial evidence that reasonably tends to show that knowledge existed.[10] Such knowledge may or may not be inferred from the falsity of the statement itself, at least if considered in relation to the facts relating to the defendant's opportunity to have knowledge.[11]

[In deciding whether the defendant *knew* (his/her) statement was false when (he/she) made it, you can draw reasonable inferences from all the circumstances about what the defendant knew at the time. However, remember that the Commonwealth must show beyond a reasonable doubt that the defendant *did in fact* know (his/her) statement was false at the time (he/she) made it. Here, the defendant asserts that (he/she) made an honest mistake because (he/she) (believed the statement was true when made/spoke out of confusion, haste or nervousness). In deciding whether the defendant made an honest mistake or instead told an intentional falsehood, you should consider all the evidence before you, particularly any other statements the defendant made during the original proceeding to determine what the defendant actually meant by the statement that is claimed to be false.[12] If the defendant later retracted or withdrew the statement, you may also take that into account in deciding whether the defendant had previously made an honest mistake. However, if the defendant knew (his/her) statement was false when (he/she) made it, the fact that the defendant later retracted or withdrew the false statement will not excuse (him/her.)[13]][14]

The fourth and final element the Commonwealth must prove beyond a reasonable doubt is that the defendant's false statement was material. That is, it was significant to the proceeding in which it was made.[15] The statement was material if it tends to affect, in reasonable degree, some aspect or result of the inquiry.[16] It is not necessary that the defendant's statement did in fact influence the outcome or affect an important aspect of the proceeding. It is only necessary that it had a reasonable and natural tendency to do so.[17] Therefore, even if the defendant intentionally made a false statement under oath, it is not perjury unless it had a reasonable tendency to affect the determination of what was at issue.

[It sometimes happens in the trial of a personal charge, as here, that the jury's decision involves a decision about whom to believe—the defendant or a single, accusing witness. As jurors, you must work through such contradiction by weighing all the credible evidence and the reasonable inferences that you can draw from the evidence in light of your common sense and experience in life. In such cases, it is important to realize that accusations of perjury are easily made, but that you as the jury are sworn to return a guilty verdict only if every element of the crime is proved beyond a reasonable doubt. You may convict a person of perjury based on the testimony of a single witness only if there is also evidence of a direct or clear and compelling character that will support no explanation that is consistent with the innocence of the defendant.[18]][19]

[In a case such as this, where the prosecution has presented a single accusing witness who says that the defendant's statement was a lie, it is important to realize that accusations of perjury are easily made, but that you as the jury are sworn to return a guilty verdict only if every element of the crime is proved beyond a reasonable doubt. You may convict a person of perjury based on the testimony of a single witness only if there is also evidence of a direct or clear and compelling character that will support no explanation that is consistent with innocence of the defendant.[20]][21]

[In a case such as this where the prosecution has not presented a live witness who says the defendant's statement was a lie, you may convict the defendant of perjury only if the prosecution has presented direct or clear and compelling circumstantial evidence that is objectively inconsistent with the innocence of the defendant.[22] It is important to realize that accusations of perjury are easily made, but that you as the jury are sworn to bring in a guilty verdict only if every element of the crime is proved beyond a reasonable doubt.][23]

Therefore, if after considering all the evidence you find that the Commonwealth has proved beyond a reasonable doubt each of the elements just defined for you, that is, that the defendant made a statement under oath in a judicial proceeding, a proceeding in the course of justice, or when required by law to take an oath or affirmation; that the statement was false; that defendant knew at the time (he/she) made the statement that it was false, and that the statement was material to some aspect of the proceeding, then you shall find the defendant guilty of perjury.

If however, after your consideration of all of the evidence you find that the Commonwealth has not proved any of these four elements beyond a reasonable doubt, you shall find the defendant not guilty.

NOTES

[1] *See Commonwealth v. Geromini*, 357 Mass. 61, 63–64 (1970).

[2] If several counts are involved there may be a question as to whether each count constitutes a separate offense. "Insofar as each count is based on a separate act, i.e., a false answer to a question concerning a different material fact or point, then each count is a distinct offense of perjury." *Commonwealth v. Gurney*, 13 Mass. App. Ct. 391, 402 (1982). However, if the statements comprising the separate counts are "substantially identical," only one perjury can be committed. *Commonwealth v. Gurney*, 13 Mass. App. Ct. at 402.

[3] Grand jury proceedings are judicial proceedings. *Commonwealth v. Leavitt*, 17 Mass. App. Ct. 585, 590 (1984), *review denied*, 391 Mass. 1105 (1984), *cert. denied*, 460 U.S. 1060 (1984). The words "proceeding in the course of justice" deal only with adjudicatory and not investigatory proceedings. *Commonwealth v. Dawson*, 399 Mass. 465, 468 (1987). Therefore, this clause does not apply to sworn statements given in the course of prosecutorial investigations. *Commonwealth v. Dawson*, 399 Mass. at 468.

The second clause of the statute ("whoever, being required by law to take an oath or affirmation . . .) applies to hearings before investigative and legislative bodies. *Commonwealth v. Giles*, 350 Mass. 102, 108 (1966) (*Giles I*). What is material to such proceedings will frequently cover a much wider range. *Commonwealth v. Giles*, 350 Mass. at 111.

7

An agency's authority to require oaths may be implicitly granted in the agency's enabling statute. This is a question of statutory construction for the judge to determine and to so inform the jury. *Commonwealth v. McDuffee*, 379 Mass. 353, 366 (1979).

[4] *Commonwealth v. Geromini*, 357 Mass. 61, 64 (1970).

[5] *Commonwealth v. Borans*, 379 Mass. 117, 137 (1979); *Commonwealth v. Giles*, 353 Mass. 1, 11–12 (1967) (*Giles II*).

[6] Use this paragraph when defendant asserts statement was true in context given.

[7] *Commonwealth v. Giles*, 353 Mass. 1, 15 (1967) (*Giles II*); *Commonwealth v. Brady*, 71 Mass. (5 Gray) 78, 79 (1855); *Commonwealth v. Pollard*, 53 Mass. (12 Met.) 225, 227 (1847); *Commonwealth v. Coleman*, 20 Mass. App. Ct. 541, 550 (1985), *aff'd*, 397 Mass. 1001 (1986) (rescript).

[8] Use this paragraph when defendant asserts statement was uncertain or ambiguous.

[9] *Commonwealth v. Giles*, 353 Mass. 1, 14 (1967) (*Giles II*).

[10] *Commonwealth v. Giles*, 350 Mass. 102, 112 (1966) (*Giles I*).

[11] *Commonwealth v. Giles*, 350 Mass. 102, 112 (1966) (*Giles I*).

[12] *Commonwealth v. Giles*, 353 Mass. 1, 13–14 (1967) (*Giles II*).

[13] *Commonwealth v. Geromini*, 357 Mass. 61, 65 (1970).

[14] Use this paragraph when the defendant asserts honest mistake.

[15] *Commonwealth v. McDuffee*, 379 Mass. 353, 365 (1979) (materiality is a question of fact for the jury).

[16] *Commonwealth v. D'Amour*, 428 Mass. 725, 745 (1999); *Commonwealth v. Giles*, 350 Mass. 102, 110 (1966) (*Giles I*); *Commonwealth v. Pollard*, 53 Mass. (12 Met.) 225, 230 (1847) (statement need only be circumstantially material; it need not directly establish the issue in question).

[17] *Commonwealth v. Giles*, 350 Mass. 102, 111 (1966) (*Giles I*).

[18] *Commonwealth v. Coleman*, 20 Mass. App. Ct. 541, 558 (1985), *aff'd*, 397 Mass. 1001 (1986). The common law rule in Massachusetts had been that a defendant may be convicted of perjury only on the direct testimony of two witnesses, or one witness plus "independent evidence of strong corroborating circumstances, of such a character as clearly to turn the scale and overcome the oath of the defendant and the legal presumption of his innocence." *Commonwealth v. Coleman*, 20 Mass. App. Ct. at 553–57. This rule has been modified to eliminate the requirement that the Commonwealth introduce direct testimony of a live witness in every perjury prosecution. *Commonwealth v. Silva*, 401 Mass. 318, 323 (1987). However, this modification does not change the requirement of strong corroborating evidence when only one witness testifies. *Commonwealth v. Knowlton*, 50 Mass. App. Ct. 266, 268-70 (2000) (Commonwealth must introduce corroborating evidence of a direct or clear or compelling character).

7

[19] Use when there is a single prosecution witness and the defendant testifies.

[20] *Commonwealth v. Coleman*, 20 Mass. App. Ct. 541, 558 (1985), *aff'd*, 397 Mass. 1001 (1986).

[21] Use when there is a single prosecution witness and the defendant does not testify.

[22] *Commonwealth v. Silva*, 401 Mass. 318, 324 (1987).

[23] Use when the prosecution presents no direct testimony.

Possession of a Controlled Substance

Regulatory Authority—G.L. c. 94C, § 34
Dist. Ct. Model Jury Instruction 7.820

The defendant is charged with unlawful possession of _____. Section 34 of chapter 94C of our General Laws provides as follows:

> "No person knowingly or intentionally shall possess a controlled substance unless such substance was obtained directly [from], or pursuant to a valid prescription or order from, a [licensed] practitioner [who was] acting in the course of his professional practice, or except as otherwise authorized [by law]."

In order to prove the defendant guilty of this offense, the Commonwealth must prove three things beyond a reasonable doubt:

First: That the substance in question is a controlled substance, namely: _____;

Second: That the defendant possessed some perceptible amount of that substance; and

Third: That the defendant did so knowingly or intentionally.

As to the first element, I instruct you that as a matter of law _____ is defined as a controlled substance by our statute. It is your duty to determine whether or not the material in question is in fact _____. In doing so, you may consider all the relevant evidence in the case, including the testimony of any witness who may have testified either to support or to dispute the allegation that the material in question was _____.

> *Commonwealth v. Dawson,* 399 Mass. 465, 466–67 (1987) (since offense may be proven by circumstantial evidence, it is not mandatory that drug be introduced or chemically analyzed, although sight identification alone would rarely be sufficient); *Commonwealth v. Cantres,* 405 Mass. 238, 245–46 (1989) (same; familiarity can be based on prior use or sale coupled with observation of present substance); *Commonwealth v. LaPerle,* 19 Mass. App. Ct. 424, 428, *fur. app. rev. den.*, 394 Mass. 1104 (1985) (a quantity visible to the naked eye but measurable only on an analytical balance will support a possession conviction); *United States v. Drougas,* 748 F.2d 8, 15 (1st Cir. 1984) (same). See G.L. c. 94C, § 31 for the schedule of controlled substances.
>
> Here instruct on the definition of "Possession" (Instruction 3.220).

Finally, the Commonwealth must prove beyond a reasonable doubt that the defendant not only possessed _____, but did so knowingly or intentionally. You may find that the defendant knowingly or intentionally possessed _____ if he (she) did so consciously, voluntarily and purposely, and not because of ignorance, mistake or accident.

> See Instructions 3.120 (Intent) and 3.140 (Knowledge).
>
> If the defendant maintains that the controlled substance was lawfully possessed pursuant to a prescription, see Instruction 3.160 (License or Authority).

Supplemental Instruction

DPH, State Police, or U. Mass. Medical Center Certificate of Analysis. You may consider a properly executed certificate from (an analyst employed by the Department of Public Health) (a chemist employed by the Department of State Police) (an analyst employed by the University of Massachusetts Medical School) as evidence of the chemical composition, purity and weight of the substance tested. You are not required to accept such evidence, but you may.

> See Instruction 3.260 (Prima Facie Evidence).
>
> G.L. c. 22C, § 39 (State Police chemist's certificate of drug analysis); G.L. c. 111, § 13 (D.P.H. or U.Mass. Medical School chemist's certificate of drug analysis). *See also* G.L. c. 94C, § 47A (in misdemeanor cases, officer's testimony that he or she sent drugs by registered mail for analysis, together with return receipt, is prima facie evidence that drugs are those seized). *Commonwealth v. Chappee,* 397 Mass. 508, 520 (1986) (certificate remains probative evidence throughout trial even if contradicted); *Commonwealth v. Sheline,* 391 Mass. 279, 285–86 (1984) (certificate should be sanitized of any aliases); *Commonwealth v. Claudio*, 405 Mass. 481 (1989) (erroneous to charge that certificate creates a "presumption" that must be followed "unless there is any evidence to the contrary to rebut that presumption"); *Commonwealth v. Reynolds,* 36 Mass. App. Ct. 963 (1994) (immaterial that certificate of analysis lacked notary public's seal).

Commonwealth v. Verde, 444 [Mass.] 279 (2005), held that the admission of a drug analysis certificate under G.L. c. 111, § 13 raises no Confrontation Clause problem under *Crawford v. Washington*, 541 U.S. 36 (2004). *See also Commonwealth v. Melendez-Diaz*, 69 Mass. App. Ct. 1114 (No. 05-P-1213, July 31, 2007) (unpublished opinion under Appeals Court Rule 1:28) (following *Verde*), *further app. review denied*, 449 Mass. 1113 (2007), *cert. granted*, 557 U.S. 305 (2008)[, *rev'd and remanded*, 557 U.S. 305 (2009), *on remand*, 76 Mass. App. Ct. 229 (2010)].

A certificate of analysis is not a prerequisite to proving that a substance is a controlled substance. *Commonwealth v. Alisha A.*, 56 Mass. App. Ct. 311 (2002); *see also Commonwealth v. Dawson*, 399 Mass. 465, 467 (1987) ("Proof that a substance is a particular drug need not be made by chemical analysis and may be made by circumstantial evidence").

EDITORS' NOTE

Impact of *Melendez-Diaz*. The U.S. Supreme Court held in *Melendez-Diaz v. Massachusetts*, 557 U.S. 305 (2009), that the Sixth Amendment's Confrontation Clause "does not permit the prosecution to prove its case via ex parte out-of-court affidavits," and thus, the admission of drug analysis certificates under G.L. c. 111, § 13 is unconstitutional without the analyst testifying at trial. *Melendez-Diaz v. Massachusetts*, 557 U.S. at 329 (reversing and remanding *Commonwealth v. Melendez-Diaz*, 69 Mass. App. Ct. 1114 (2007)). *See Commonwealth v. Vasquez*, 456 Mass. 350 (2010) (where drug certificate identifying substance as cocaine was only evidence at trial pertaining to substance's chemical nature, reversal required under *Melendez-Diaz*); *Commonwealth v. Charles*, 456 Mass. 378 (2010) (although "[p]roof that a substance is a particular drug 'may be made by circumstantial evidence'" the conclusory and largely equivocal testimony regarding substances' composition given by arresting police officers who were not qualified as experts was insufficient to nullify effect of drug certificates' admission without analyst's testimony at trial (quoting *Commonwealth v. Dawson*, 339 Mass. 465, 467 (1987))). Note that the District Court model jury instruction regarding drug analysis certificates has not been updated to account for *Melendez-Diaz v. Massachusetts*.

NOTES

1. **Medical necessity defense unavailable for marihuana.** A defendant may not offer as a defense to marihuana possession that it provides the only effective alleviation of the side effects of scleroderma, a disease resulting in the painful buildup of scar tissue throughout the body. Any benefit resulting from alleviation of the defendant's medical symptoms would not outweigh the possible negative impact on the enforcement of the drug laws. *Commonwealth v. Hutchins*, 410 Mass. 726 (1991).

2. **Constructive possession.** In the case of constructive possession, possession implies "knowledge coupled with the ability and intention to exercise dominion and control." *Commonwealth v. Brzezinski*, 405 Mass. 401 (1989); *Commonwealth v. Amparo*, 43 Mass. App. Ct. 922, 923 (1997) (setting aside verdict where no evidence that defendant "rented, occupied, spent a great deal of time or exercised control over the apartment or its contents"). Behavior tending to show that defendant knew of the presence of drugs is not sufficient, by itself, to prove that he had the ability and intent to control the drugs. *Commonwealth v. Cruz*, 34 Mass. App. Ct. 619, 623 (1993); *Commonwealth v. Amparo*, 43 Mass. App. Ct. at 924 (evidence that defendant attempted to flee out back door and possessed beeper insufficient).

3. **Joint possession.** To be a joint possessor, one must actively and personally participate in the procurement of the drugs. *Commonwealth v. Minor*, 47 Mass. App. Ct. 928, 928 (1999) (holding insufficient evidence that defendant contributed to pool of money with which codefendant bought rugs).

Possession of Burglarious Tools

Regulatory Authority—G.L. c. 266, § 49
Dist. Ct. Model Jury Instruction 8.180

The defendant is charged with an offense that is commonly referred to as "possessing burglarious tools." Section 49 of chapter 266 of our General Laws provides as follows:

"Whoever knowingly has in his possession . . . [a] tool or implement [that is] adapted and designed for cutting through, forcing or breaking open a building, room, vault, safe or other depository, in order to steal therefrom money or other property, or to commit any other crime, knowing [the tool or implement] to be adapted and designed for [that] purpose . . . shall be punished . . . ."

In order to prove the defendant guilty of this offense, the Commonwealth must prove five things beyond a reasonable doubt:

First: That the defendant knowingly possessed a tool or implement, specifically a _____;

Second: That such tool or implement could reasonably be used to break into a (building) (room) (vault or safe) (place for keeping valuables);

Third: That the defendant knew that the tool or implement could reasonably be used for that purpose;

Fourth: That the defendant intended to use the tool or implement for that purpose; and

Fifth: That the defendant had the specific intention of (stealing from) (committing a crime in) that place.

Here the jury must be instructed on "Possession" (Instruction 3.220).

"The gist of the offense lies in the possession of the tools, the purpose for which they are possessed and, their suitability for that purpose." *Commonwealth v. Aleo*, 18 Mass. App. Ct. 916, 917 (1984). The defendant must have intended to use the tool to effectuate the breaking and entering. *Commonwealth v. Redmond*, 53 Mass. App. Ct. 1, 6 (2001).

The model instruction is structured to address the most common variety of the offense defined in G.L. c. 266, § 49, which also punishes "mak[ing] or mend[ing], or begin[ning] to make or mend" such items, and bans burglarious "engine[s]" and "machine[s]" as well as tools and instruments. The instruction may be adapted as necessary.

Supplemental Instruction

Licit implements. To qualify as a "burglarious tool," it is not necessary that a tool or implement be designed or usable only for unlawful purposes. Items which are commonly used for lawful purposes, such as screwdrivers or chisels or kitchen knives, are considered to be "burglarious tools" if they can be used to break into a (building) (room) (vault or safe) (place for keeping valuables), and are possessed for that reason.

While burglarious intent can be inferred from mere possession of tools uniquely or very highly adapted to burglarious purposes, common items can be burglarious tools if they can be used and are possessed for burglarious purposes. *Commonwealth v. Dellinger*, 10 Mass. App. Ct. 549, 561 (1980), *aff'd in part and rev'd in part on other grounds*, 383 Mass. 780 (1981). *See Commonwealth v. Jones*, 355 Mass. 170, 176–77 (1969) (screwdriver and kitchen knife); *Commonwealth v. Tivnon*, 8 Gray 375, 380–81 (1857) (chisel). *But see Commonwealth v. Purcell*, 19 Mass. 1031, 1031 (1985) (even if worn to facilitate burglary, gloves cannot be burglarious instruments). A burglarious instrument does not lose its character as such because it needs repair. *Aleo, supra.* Innocent tools are admissible in evidence when mixed with burglarious tools. *Commonwealth v. Williams*, 2 Cush. 582, 586 (1849).

NOTES

1. **Attempted break-in unnecessary.** An attempted break-in is not a required element of this offense, since the offense is complete when

tools are procured with a burglarious intent. *Commonwealth v. Tivnon,* 8 Gray 375, 380–81 (1857).

2. **Breaking and entering is distinct offense.** Possession of burglarious tools and breaking and entering (G.L. c. 266, § 18) are separate offenses, and neither is a lesser included offense of the other. *Commonwealth v. Johnson,* 406 Mass. 533, 535 (1990).

3. **"Depository".** It is not necessary to prove that a depository was located within a building, *Commonwealth v. Tilley,* 306 Mass.412, 416 (1940), or that the defendant intended to break into any particular depository, *Commonwealth v. Tivnon,* 8 Gray 375, 380–81 (1857). A boat storage area open on one side is not a depository. *Commonwealth v. Schultz,* 17 Mass. App. Ct. 958 (1983). An auto trunk is a depository. *Tilley, above.* A locked passenger automobile reasonably can be inferred to be a depository, even without proof that the particular vehicle was used to store valuables. *Commonwealth v. Dreyer,* 18 Mass. App. Ct. 562, 564–65 (1984). A bolt cutter used to cut through a bicycle chain attaching a bicycle to a bicycle rack is not a burglarious tool, since it is not "adapted and designed for cutting through, forcing or breaking open a . . . depository." The chain itself cannot be a depository "as it has no capacity to hold property for safekeeping." Even if the rack is considered a depository, it is "highly implausible that a small pair of bolt cutters could be used to cut open the metal frames of a bicycle rack" and therefore the cutters were probably not intended for use on the rack. And "because the bicyclist furnishes the chain, . . . it requires a strained interpretation of the statute to conclude that the chain and rack together" constitute a depository. *Commonwealth v. Antonio Ortiz,* 38 Mass. App. Ct. 1107 (1995) (unpublished opinion under Appeals Court Rule 1:28). Such unpublished opinions have no precedential value in other cases. *Lyons v. Labor Relations Comm'n,* 19 Mass. App. Ct. 562, 566 & n.7 (1985), *rev'd on other grounds,* 397 Mass. 498 (1986).

4. **Intended crimes.** It is not necessary that burglary or theft be the intended crime. *Commonwealth v. Krasner,* 358 Mass. 727, 729–31, *S.C.* 360 Mass. 848 (1971) (trespass); *Commonwealth v. Tilley,* 306 Mass. at 414–15 (stealing from auto trunk). However, if the complaint charges the defendant only with the first of the two intent alternatives in the statute ("to steal therefrom such money and other property as might be found therein") the Commonwealth is so limited in its proof, and may not convict upon proof of the second intent alternative ("to commit any other crime"). *Commonwealth v. Graud,* 8 Mass. App. Ct. 915, 915–16 (1979); *Commonwealth v. Armenia,* 4 Mass. App. Ct. 33, 38 (1976). *See Commonwealth v. Aldrich,* 23 Mass. App. Ct. 157, 165 (1985). To satisfy the second intent alternative, the "any other crime" must be intended to be committed in the "building, room, vault, safe or other depository." *Krasner, above; Schultz, above.*

5. **Motor vehicle master keys.** Since the enactment of St. 1966, c. 269, the statute has also included a separate branch punishing possession of a motor vehicle master key, the effect of which is that possession of motor vehicle master keys can no longer be prosecuted under the generic branch of the statute. *Commonwealth v. Collardo,* 13 Mass. App. Ct. 1013, 1014 (1982).

Possessing a Firearm

Regulatory Authority—G.L. c. 269, § 10(h)
Dist. Ct. Model Jury Instruction 7.620

The defendant is charged with unlawfully possessing a firearm. Section 10(h) of chapter 269 of our General Laws provides as follows:

> "Whoever . . . possesses . . . a firearm . . . without complying with the requirements [of law] relating to [a] firearm identification card . . . shall be punished . . . ."

In order to prove the defendant guilty of this offense, the Commonwealth must prove (three) (four) things beyond a reasonable doubt:

First: That the defendant possessed an item;

Second: That the item meets the legal definition of a "firearm"; (and)

Third: That the defendant knew that he (she) possessed that firearm.

> *If there is evidence of one of the statutory exceptions, use one of the following:*

A. *If there is evidence that the defendant had a firearm ID card.* And Fourth: that the defendant did not have a valid firearm ID card.

B. *If there is evidence that the defendant was exempt from the firearm ID card requirement.* And Fourth: that the defendant did not qualify for one of the exemptions in the law that are a substitute for having a valid firearm ID card.

> See Instruction 3.160 (License or Authority).
>
> G.L. c. 278, § 7; *Commonwealth v. Jones,* 372 Mass. 403, 406–07 (1977). The issuance of firearm identification cards is governed by G.L. c. 140, §§ 129B–D. Section 129C also lists a number of exemptions from the requirement of a firearms identification card. *See also* Op. A.G. No. 86/87-4 (October 31, 1986) (18 U.S.C. § 926A provides a defense to a charge under § 10[h] for a non-resident traveling through the Commonwealth with an unloaded and inaccessible handgun who is in compliance with the firearms laws of the states of origin and destination).
>
> Here define "possession" (Instruction 3.220).

A "firearm" is defined in our law as:

> "a pistol, revolver or other weapon . . . loaded or unloaded, from which a shot or bullet can be discharged and . . . the length of [whose] barrel is less than sixteen inches."

That definition can be broken down into three requirements: *First,* it must be a weapon; *Second,* it must be capable of discharging a shot or bullet; and *Third,* it must have a barrel length of less than 16 inches. The term "barrel length" refers to "that portion of a firearm . . . through which a shot or bullet is driven, guided or stabilized, and [includes] the chamber."

> G.L. c. 140, § 121. *Commonwealth v. Tuitt,* 393 Mass. 801 (1985), *cert. denied,* 484 U.S. 945 (1987) (jury can determine from inspection that "firearm"); *Commonwealth v. Fancy,* 349 Mass. 196, 204 (1965) (same); *Commonwealth v. Sampson,* 383 Mass. 750, 753 (1981); *Commonwealth v. Sperrazza,* 372 Mass. 667, 6701977) (testimony about "revolver" or "handgun" will support inference that barrel was under 16 inches); *Commonwealth v. Bartholomew,* 326 Mass. 218, 219 (1950) (not necessary that firearm be loaded).

As I mentioned before, the Commonwealth must prove beyond a reasonable doubt that the defendant knew that he (she) (possessed this item) (*or*) (had this item under his [her] control in a vehicle), *and* also knew that the item was a "firearm," within the common meaning of that term. If it was a conventional firearm, with its obvious dangers, the Commonwealth is not required to prove that the defendant knew that the item met the *legal* definition of a firearm.

> See Instruction 3.140 (Knowledge).
>
> General Laws c. 269, § 10(h) punishes "own[ing]" or "transfer[ring] possession" as well as possession, and is applicable to a "rifle, shotgun or ammunition" as well as a firearm. In cases with such fact patterns, the model instruction may be adapted accordingly. See G.L. c. 140, § 121 for definitions of "rifle," "shotgun" and "ammunition."
>
> *Commonwealth v. Sampson,* 383 Mass. 750, 762 (1981); *Commonwealth v. Bacon,* 374 Mass. 358, 359 (1978) (knowledge need not be alleged in complaint); *Commonwealth v. Jackson,* 369 Mass. 904, 916–17 (1976); *Commonwealth v. Boone,* 356 Mass. 85, 87 (1969); *Commonwealth v. Papa,* 17 Mass. App. Ct. 987, 987 (1984).

Supplemental Instructions

1. ***Absence of evidence of firearm ID card.*** You have heard some reference to (a firearm ID card) (a legal exemption from the requirement of a firearm ID card). There was no evidence in this case that the defendant had a firearm ID, and no evidence that the defendant qualified for one of the legal exemptions that are a substitute for having a firearm ID card. For that reason, the issue of a firearm ID card or exemption is not relevant to your deliberations in this case, and therefore you should put it out of your mind.

> This instruction is recommended only when, in the jury's presence, there has been some reference to, but not evidence of, a firearm ID card or exemption.

2. ***Knowledge of firearm ID card requirement.*** You have heard some mention that the defendant did not know that he (she) was required to have a firearm ID card before possessing a firearm. The Commonwealth is *not* required to prove that the defendant knew that the law required him (her) to have a firearm ID card before (possessing a firearm) (*or*) (having a firearm under his [her] control in a vehicle).

> This instruction is recommended only when it is necessary to correct such a misimpression.

NOTES

1. **Possession of a firearm (§ 10[h]) as a lesser included offense of carrying a firearm (§ 10[a]).** Prior to 1991, possession of a firearm (§ 10[h]) was a lesser included offense of carrying a firearm (§ 10[a]). See *Commonwealth v. Nessolini,* 19 Mass. App. Ct. 1016, 1016 (1985). Statute 1990, c. 511 (effective January 2, 1991) amended § 10(h) to provide that "[a] violation of this subsection shall not be considered a lesser included offense to a violation of subsection (a) . . ." and that no one shall "prosecute as a violation of [§ 10(h)] the mere possession of a firearm, rifle, or shotgun by an unlicensed person not being present in or on his residence or place of business, nor shall the court allow an attempt to so prosecute." However, both 1991 amendments were repealed by St. 1998, c. 180, § 69 (effective October 21, 1998).
2. **Non-firing firearm.** See the first supplemental instruction to Instruction 7.600 (Carrying a Firearm).
3. **Passenger in vehicle.** See the third supplemental instruction to Instruction 7.600 (Carrying a Firearm).

Rape (G.L. c. 265, § 22)

Regulatory Authority—G.L. c. 265, §§ 22, 22A, 23.
Super. Ct. Model Jury Instructions § 3.1

In this case, the defendant, (defendant/name), is charged with rape.[2] Our state legislature has specifically defined this crime in a statute, G.L. c. 265, § 22, which provides in relevant part:

> Whoever has sexual intercourse or unnatural sexual intercourse with a person, and compels such person to submit by force and against his will, or compels such person to submit by threat of bodily injury . . . shall be punished.[3]

First, I will define rape for you. Rape is natural or unnatural sexual intercourse with another person by force and against that person's will, or that compels such person to submit to such act by threat of bodily force or violence.[4]

In order to prove the defendant guilty of rape, the Commonwealth must prove the following two elements beyond a reasonable doubt:

First Element. the Commonwealth must prove beyond a reasonable doubt that the defendant engaged in sexual intercourse, either natural or unnatural with (the complainant/name); and

Second Element: the Commonwealth must prove beyond a reasonable doubt that the sexual intercourse was accomplished by compelling (the complainant/name) to submit by force or threat of bodily injury and against (his/her) will.

The first element the Commonwealth must prove beyond a reasonable doubt is that the defendant engaged in either natural or unnatural sexual intercourse with (the complainant/name). Natural intercourse consists of inserting the penis into the female sex organ.[5] Unnatural sexual intercourse includes oral and anal intercourse, including fellatio and cunnilingus,[6] and other intrusions of a part of a person's body[7] or other object[8] into the genital or anal opening of another's body.[9] Either natural or unnatural sexual intercourse is complete on penetration, no matter how slight, of a person's genital or anal opening.[10] In addition to the vagina, the female genital opening includes the anterior parts known as the vulva and labia. Penetration into the vagina itself is not required.[11,12]

The second element the Commonwealth must prove beyond a reasonable doubt is that the natural or unnatural sexual intercourse was accomplished by force or by threat of bodily injury and against (the complainant's/name's) will.[13] The force needed for rape may, depending on the circumstances, be constructive force,[14] as well as physical force, violence or threat of bodily harm.[15]

[Supplemental Instruction (a)—Constructive Force]

The Commonwealth must also prove beyond a reasonable doubt that the defendant performed the sexual intercourse "against the person's will." The Commonwealth must prove that at the time of penetration (the complainant/name) did not consent, or in other words, that the intercourse was against (the complainant's/name's) will.[16] If a person submits because of fear it is not consent. The person must be free to exercise (his/her) will without restraint. You may consider evidence of (the complainant's/name's) state of mind at the time of the alleged incident on the issue of consent.[17]

(The complainant/name) is not required to use physical force to resist.[18] However, you may consider evidence of any attempt to restrain or confine (the complainant/name), of violence by the defendant, or of struggle or outcry by (the complainant/name) on the issues of force and consent.[19] However, lack of such evidence does not necessarily imply consent or the absence of force, because in certain circumstances physical resistance may not be possible.[20] You may consider all of the circumstances and the entire sequence of events in determining whether the intercourse was without (the complainant/name)'s consent and (his/her) ability to resist.[21]

[Supplemental Instruction (c)—Complainant Unconscious or in a Stupor]

[Supplemental Instructions (d)—Aggravated Rape]

Therefore, if after considering all of the evidence you determine that the Commonwealth has proven beyond a reasonable doubt each of the two elements I have just defined, that is, that the defendant engaged in either natural or unnatural sexual intercourse with (the complainant/name), and that the sexual intercourse was accomplished by compelling (the complainant/name) to submit by force or threat of bodily injury and against (the complainant/name)'s will, then you shall find the defendant guilty of rape.

If, however, after your consideration of all of the evidence you find that the Commonwealth has not proven either of these two elements beyond a reasonable doubt, you shall find the defendant not guilty of rape.

ENDNOTES

[1] This instruction and notes are taken from the chargebook offered as a guide to Superior Court judges in 1995 and updated by the authors.

[2] It is no defense to a charge of rape that the complainant is the spouse of the accused. *Commonwealth v. Chretien,* 383 Mass. 123, 127–32 (1981). While natural sexual intercourse as defined by law may only be accomplished between a male and a female, the law prohibits forcible unnatural intercourse regardless of the sex of either or any of the persons involved. *Commonwealth v. Chretien,* 383 Mass. at 127–32. In *Commonwealth v. Whitehead,* 379 Mass. 640, 646–50 (1980), female defendants were put on notice that forcible female to female intercourse would be prosecuted by the Commonwealth. The Court also noted that accomplices of either sex may be liable as principles in the rape of persons of either sex, and that penetration by an accomplice need not be proven to establish his or her guilt.

In *Commonwealth v. Guy,* 24 Mass. App. Ct. 783, 785–87 (1987), the Appeals Court held that where two male defendants forced a female to perform cunnilingus on two other (consenting) females, such sexual act constituted rape of the first female by the defendants within the meaning

7

of G.L. c. 265, § 22(a). *See Commonwealth v. Nuby*, 32 Mass. App. Ct. 360, 362 (1992) (defendant guilty of rape by forcing victim to perform oral sex on other nonconsenting party); *see also Commonwealth v. Davidson*, 68 Mass. App. Ct. 72, 74–76 (2007) (physical conduct does not have to be committed by the defendant); *Commonwealth v. Portonova*, 69 Mass. App. Ct. 905, 905–06 (2007) (same).

[3] G.L. c. 265, § 22(b). General Laws Chapter 265, § 22(a), provides for punishment for a joint enterprise. Section 22(a) also provides additional penalty for such offense which "results in or is committed with acts resulting in serious bodily injury."

[4] The crime of rape is codified at G.L. c. 265, § 22(b). In *Commonwealth v. Gallant*, 373 Mass. 577, 590 (1977), the Supreme Judicial Court held that the term "unnatural sexual intercourse" as used in G.L. c. 265, § 23, is not void for vagueness. *See Commonwealth v. Gonzales*, 5 Mass. App. Ct. 705, 707 (1977) (words "unnatural sexual intercourse" have the same meaning in both G.L. c. 265, § 22 and G.L. c. 265, § 23).

[5] *See Commonwealth v. Gallant*, 373 Mass. 577, 584 (1977); *Commonwealth v. Cobb*, 26 Mass. App. Ct. 283, 286 (1988). Emission of semen, either before, during, or after the penetration of the vagina is not necessary. *Commonwealth v. Gallant*, 373 Mass. at 584; *Commonwealth v. Horn*, 23 Mass. App. Ct. 319, 325 (1987).

[6] In *Commonwealth v. Edward*, 34 Mass. App. Ct. 521, 523 (1993), the court instructed that rape could be found if defendant's lips came in contact with the victim's vagina, vulva, or labia.

[7] *Commonwealth v. Mamay*, 5 Mass. App. Ct. 708 (1977) (penetration of victim's genital opening by hand or fingers).

[8] *Commonwealth v. Cifizzari*, 397 Mass. 560, 576–77 (1986) (rape by a mop handle); *Commonwealth v. Gallant*, 373 Mass. 577, 584–85 (1977).

[9] The term unnatural sexual intercourse is a broad term and encompasses a variety of acts. *Commonwealth v. Nuby*, 32 Mass. App. Ct. 360, 362 (1992). In *Nuby*, the Appeals Court found that the defendant's act of forcing one party to perform oral sex on another party constituted unnatural sexual intercourse. *Commonwealth v. Nuby*, 32 Mass. App. Ct. at 362. Thus, actual penetration by the defendant is not necessary; the "outrage of compelled sex" marks the offense. *Commonwealth v. Nuby*, 32 Mass. App. Ct. at 362.

[10] *Commonwealth v. Sherman*, 451 Mass. 332, 335–37 (2008); *Commonwealth v. McJunkin*, 11 Mass. App. Ct. 609, 613 (1981). Sexual intercourse is defined as penetration of the victim, regardless of degree. *Commonwealth v. Lopez*, 433 Mass. 722, 726–27 (2001). It is not necessary to prove that the vagina itself was intruded to constitute rape. It is sufficient if the Commonwealth proves beyond a reasonable doubt that the defendant intruded the vulva or labia of the victim by his penis, some other body part (such as the finger) or another object to constitute the penetration required for rape. *Commonwealth v. Aviles*, 58 Mass. App. Ct. 459, 468 (2003); *Commonwealth v. Nylander*, 26 Mass. App. Ct. 784, 788 (1989); *Commonwealth v. Baldwin*, 24 Mass. App. Ct. 200, 204–05 (1987). It is also sufficient if the Commonwealth proves beyond a reasonable doubt that the defendant intruded the anal opening of the victim by his penis, some other body part, or another object. *Commonwealth v. Nylander*, 26 Mass. App. Ct. at 788–92; *see Commonwealth v. Caracino*, 33 Mass. App. Ct. 787, 792 (1993). In *Commonwealth v. Vega*, 36 Mass. App. Ct. 635, 636–37 (1994), the victim's testimony that defendant sodomized her was sufficient to infer anal penetration.

[11] *Commonwealth v. Nylander*, 26 Mass. App. Ct. 784, 788 (1989).

[12] The following supplemental instruction is recommended when appropriate: "The phrase 'anal opening' is intended in its strict anatomical sense. It refers to the opening at the end of the digestive tract (or alimentary canal). The penetration must be of the anal opening itself, not simply the groove between the buttocks." *See Commonwealth v. Nylander*, 26 Mass. App. Ct. 784, 788–89 (1989).

[13] *Commonwealth v. Lopez*, 433 Mass. 722, 727 (2001). Rape is not a specific intent crime. *Commonwealth v. Troy*, 405 Mass. 253, 260 (1989); *Commonwealth v. Cordeiro*, 401 Mass. 843, 850–51 n.11 (1988); *Commonwealth v. Grant*, 391 Mass. 645, 649–51 (1984); *Commonwealth v. Blair*, 21 Mass. App. Ct. 625, 631 (1986); *Commonwealth v. Lefkowitz*, 20 Mass. App. Ct. 513, 518 (1985). "The elements necessary for rape do not require that the defendant intend the intercourse be without consent." *Commonwealth v. Lopez*, 433 Mass. at 727; *Commonwealth v. Grant*, 391 Mass. at 650. "The essence of the crime of rape, whether aggravated or unaggravated, is sexual intercourse with another compelled by force and against the victim's will or compelled by threat of bodily injury." *Commonwealth v. Grant*, 391 Mass. at 650 (citing *Commonwealth v. Sherry*, 386 Mass. 682, 687 (1982)). There is no "special emphasis on the defendant's state of mind." *Commonwealth v. Lefkowitz*, 20 Mass. App. Ct. at 519. "The scienter element of the offense thus equates with the scienter sufficient to convict of most crimes, a general intent. That element is not usually explained to the jury in the enumeration of the elements of the crime, being left to be inferred from all the evidence in the case. (See the language in the *Grant* decision 391 Mass. at 651, which speaks in terms of 'the defendant intend[ing] intercourse' as sufficient intent.)" *Commonwealth v. Lefkowitz*, 20 Mass. App. Ct. at 519 (parenthetical sentence included in original). For a discussion of other jurisdictions' treatments of the mistake-of-fact defense in a rape case, *see Commonwealth v. Lopez*, 433 Mass. 722, 728–32 (2001) (court declined to recognize, as a mistake-of-fact defense to the crime of rape, defendant's asserted honest and reasonable belief as to complainant's consent). However, in a case where the jury must find the victim lacked capacity to consent, the Commonwealth must prove the defendant knew or reasonably should have known the complainant's condition rendered her incapable of consenting. *Commonwealth v. Blache*, 450 Mass. 583, 593–94 (2008).

Furthermore, a defendant is not entitled to an instruction allowing the jury to consider the effect of intoxication on a defendant's ability to form general intent. *Commonwealth v. Blake*, 409 Mass. 146, 155 (1991); *see Commonwealth v. Henson*, 394 Mass. 584, 592 (1985); *Commonwealth v. Blair*, 21 Mass. App. Ct. at 631. However, in cases where the Commonwealth must prove that the defendant knew or reasonably should have known that a victim's condition rendered him or her incapable of consenting, a defendant is entitled to have the jury consider his mental condition as it relates to his ability to possess the requisite knowledge if there is credible evidence of such impairment. For the purposes of meriting a voluntary intoxication instruction, there must be credible evidence of debilitating intoxication that that would hinder the defendant's ability to have the requisite knowledge. *Commonwealth v. Mountry*, 463 Mass. 80, 90–93 (2012).

[14] Constructive force constitutes threatening words or gestures that operate on the mind and requires proof that the victim was afraid or submitted to the defendant because his conduct intimidated her. *Commonwealth v. Vasquez*, 462 Mass. 827, 846 (2012); *Commonwealth v. Caracciola*, 409 Mass. 648, 652 (1991); *Commonwealth v. Newcomb*, 80 Mass. App. Ct. 519, 521–26, *review denied*, 461 Mass. 1101 (2011) (where defendant charged with rape, jury entitled to look at whole picture of relationship between defendant and victim in analyzing element of force); *Commonwealth v. Wallace*, 76 Mass. App. Ct. 411, 417–18 (2010) (where defendant charged with statutory rape and rape, events that took place after victim turned sixteen must be viewed in light of history of relationship and defendant's predatory behavior). In cases where it relies on constructive force, the Commonwealth must also prove that the sexual intercourse was against the will of the victim. *Commonwealth v. Caracciola*, 409 Mass. at 653. However, fraudulent acts or statements do not constitute force if there are no threats or conduct calculated to instill fear in the victim. *Commonwealth v. Caracciola*, 409 Mass. at 653.

[15] *Commonwealth v. Caracciola*, 409 Mass. 648, 653 (1991); *Commonwealth v. Sherry*, 386 Mass. 682, 696 (1982). Threats of bodily harm may be expressed or implied, as long as it is reasonable in the circumstances for the victim to be in fear and not resist. *Felix F. v. Commonwealth*, 471 Mass. 513, 518 (2015). Furthermore, proof of lack of capacity may permit a jury, with proper instruction, to conclude that the force necessary to affect the intercourse is sufficient to constitute the force element of rape. *Commonwealth v. Eldridge*, 28 Mass. App. Ct. 936, 937 (1990).

In *Commonwealth v. Goldenberg*, 338 Mass. 377, 384 (1959), the Supreme Judicial Court held that "[f]raud cannot be allowed to supply the place of force which the statute makes mandatory." While the validity of this holding has been questioned, *Commonwealth v. Keevan*, 400 Mass. 557, 571 (1987) (Abrams, J. concurring), the Supreme Judicial Court has explicitly declined to overrule *Goldenberg*. *See Suliveres v. Commonwealth*, 449 Mass. 112 (2007). However, in *Commonwealth v. Caracciola*, the court found that the defendant's activities, albeit fraudulent, also constituted force or threats. Justice O'Connor's dissent noted that the defendant's activities constituted fraud, and thus warranted dismissal. *Commonwealth v. Caracciola*, 409 Mass. at 664.

[16] The phrase "without her consent" may be submitted for "against her will." *Commonwealth v. Roosnell*, 143 Mass. 32, 40 (1886) (citing *Commonwealth v. Burke*, 105 Mass. 376 (1870)); *see Commonwealth v. Edgerly*, 13 Mass. App. Ct. 562, 580 (1982); *Commonwealth v. Goldenberg*, 338 Mass. 377, 383 (1959); *see also Commonwealth v. Guisti*, 434 Mass. 245 (2001) (to prove a charge of rape, Commonwealth need not prove lack of consent; sufficient to prove victim's fear of harm if he or she did not submit); *Commonwealth v. Eminpah*, 81 Mass. App. Ct. 657, 660–61, *review denied*, 462 Mass. 1109 (2012) (instruction adequately covered situation where evidence suggested victim withdrew consent after initiation of intercourse).

[17] *Commonwealth v. Dies*, 248 Mass. 482, 489 (1924). In this case the questions, "Did either of these men have relations with you by your

consent?" and "Were you willing or unwilling for these men to do what they did?" were deemed proper to establish the victim's state of mind.

[18] *Commonwealth v. Caracciola*, 409 Mass. 648, 651 (1991); *Commonwealth v. Sherry*, 386 Mass. 682, 688 (1982).

[19] In *Commonwealth v. Merrill*, 80 Mass. (14 Gray) 415, 417 (1860), these factors were called "the usual, proper and essential evidence in support of a charge of intent to accomplish a felonious purpose on the body of a female by force and against her will." *See Commonwealth v. Goldenberg*, 338 Mass. 377, 383 (1959) (fact that none of these indicators were found "negatived the use of force").

[20] *See, e.g., Commonwealth v. Kerr*, 36 Mass. App. Ct. 505, 507–08 (1994).

[21] *Commonwealth v. Caracciola*, 409 Mass. 648, 652 (1991); *Commonwealth v. Slattery*, 147 Mass. 423 (1888) (the victim cannot condone or ratify the crime of rape by later excusing or forgiving the perpetrator); *Commonwealth v. Sherry*, 386 Mass. 682, 688 (1982).

Supplemental Instructions

Constructive Force[2]

Constructive force may be by threatening words or gestures and operates on the mind to instill fear in (the complainant/name) in order for the defendant to achieve his goal. There must be proof that (the complainant/name) was afraid or that (the complainant/name) submitted to the defendant because his conduct intimidated her [or him].[3]

You may consider all of the circumstances, including the respective age and size of the parties, and the overall relationship between the parties, including whether the defendant was an authority figure in determining whether the rape was by force and against (the complainant's/name's) will.[4]

ENDNOTES

[1] Unless noted, these instructions and notes are taken from the chargebook offered as a guide to Superior Court judges in 1995 and updated by the authors.

[2] This instruction was written by previous authors of this chapter and is updated for this text.

[3] *Commonwealth v. Vasquez*, 462 Mass. 827, 846 (2012); *Commonwealth v. Caracciola*, 409 Mass. 648, 652 (1991); *Commonwealth v. Newcomb*, 80 Mass. App. Ct. 519, 521 (2011).

[4] *Commonwealth v. Moniz*, 87 Mass. App. Ct. 532, 535–36, *review denied*, 472 Mass. 1108 (2015); *Commonwealth v. Newcomb*, 80 Mass. App. Ct. 519, 522–25 (2011); *Commonwealth v. Wallace*, 76 Mass. App. Ct. 411, 418 n.11 (2010). What is important is that "the defendant's 'course of conduct . . . was designed to instill fear in order to achieve his goal.'" *Commonwealth v. Dumas*, 83 Mass. App. Ct. 536, 539, *review denied*, 466 Mass. 1106 (2013) (quoting *Commonwealth v. Wallace*, 76 Mass. App. Ct. at 418 n.11).

Use of Force by a Third Person

The force or threat of bodily injury does not have to come directly from the defendant. It may be the result of a third person's use of force or threat of bodily injury against (the complainant/name) if the defendant is aware of it and takes advantage of it.[1]

ENDNOTES

[1] *Commonwealth v. Therrien*, 383 Mass. 529, 538–39 (1981); *see Commonwealth v. Coleman*, 30 Mass. App. Ct. 229, 233 (1991) (finding victim submitted to second perpetrator unwillingly and as a result of threats delivered by first perpetrator).

Complainant Unconscious or in a Stupor[1]

In this case, there has been evidence that (the complainant/name) [had consumed alcohol; had consumed drugs; was unconscious; etc.]. If, because of the consumption of drugs or alcohol or for some other reason (for example, sleep, unconsciousness, intellectual disability, or helplessness), a person is so impaired as to be incapable of consenting to sexual intercourse, then intercourse occurring during such incapacity is without that person's consent.[2]

If you find that the Commonwealth has proved beyond a reasonable doubt that (the complainant/name) was so impaired as to be incapable of consenting as I have just described, and if you further find that the Commonwealth has proved beyond a reasonable doubt that the defendant knew, or reasonably should have known, that (the complainant's/name's) condition rendered her [or him] incapable of consenting, then the Commonwealth has proved the element of lack of consent, and, on the element of force, the Commonwealth need only prove that the defendant used the degree of force necessary to accomplish the sexual intercourse—that is, to effect penetration.[3] In determining whether the Commonwealth has proven beyond a reasonable doubt that the defendant should have reasonably known that (the complainant/name) was incapable of consenting, you should examine whether a reasonable person, in the circumstances known to the defendant, would have known (the complainant/name) was incapable of consent.[4]

However, if the Commonwealth has not proved that (the complainant/name) lacked the capacity to consent, or if the Commonwealth has not proved that the defendant knew or reasonably should have known of such incapacity, then in order to find the defendant guilty of rape, you must find that the Commonwealth has proved the elements of lack of consent and force as I have defined these elements for you earlier.

ENDNOTES

[1] Taken from *Commonwealth v. Blache*, 450 Mass. 583, 595 n.19 (2008) and *Commonwealth v. Mountry*, 463 Mass. 80, 90–92 (2012). This instruction should be given whenever "the evidence would support a finding that because of the consumption of drugs or alcohol or for some other reason (for example, sleep, unconsciousness, mental retardation, or helplessness), the complainant was so impaired as to be incapable of consenting to intercourse." *Commonwealth v. Blache*, 450 Mass. at 591–92; *see also Commonwealth v. St. Hilaire*, 470 Mass. 338, 346 (2015) (consent vitiated by mental incapacity).

[2] *Commonwealth v. Blache*, 450 Mass. 583, 591–92 (2008); *Commonwealth v. Urban*, 450 Mass. 608, 612–14 (2008).

[3] *Commonwealth v. Blache*, 450 Mass. 583 (2008) (Where the complainant is so incapacitated as to be incapable of consenting, the force necessary to sustain a conviction for rape is only the force necessary to obtain penetration. In this case, the defendant must know, or reasonably should have known that the complainant was incapable of consenting); *see also Commonwealth v. LeBlanc*, 456 Mass. 135, 138 (2010).

[4] In a rape prosecution where the Commonwealth must prove that the defendant knew or reasonably should have known that a victim's condition rendered him or her incapable of consenting, a defendant is entitled to have the jury consider his mental impairment as it relates to his ability to possess the requisite knowledge if there is credible evidence of such impairment. *See Commonwealth v. Mountry*, 463 Mass. 80, 81 (2012); *see also Commonwealth v. Jones*, 472 Mass. 707, 731–32 (2015) (element of knowledge is not purely objective; Commonwealth must prove what the defendant reasonably should have known). For the purposes of meriting a voluntary intoxication instruction, there must be credible evidence of debilitating intoxication that that would hinder the defendant's ability to have the requisite knowledge. *See Commonwealth v. Mountry*, 463 Mass. at 91–92.

Aggravated Rape

The defendant is also charged with aggravated rape.[1] Aggravated rape is a more serious offense than rape, and it requires the Commonwealth to prove one additional element beyond a reasonable doubt.[2] In order to prove the defendant guilty of aggravated rape, the Commonwealth must prove beyond a reasonable doubt that the rape resulted in or was committed with acts resulting in serious bodily injury, was committed by a joint venture, or was committed during the commission or attempted commission of the crime of (offense).[3]

[It is for you to determine whether (the complainant/name) was raped with acts resulting in serious bodily injury.][4]

[See Joint-Venture Charge.][5]

[See Jury Charge of Relevant Crimes.][6]

Therefore, if after considering all of the evidence you determine that the Commonwealth has proven beyond a reasonable doubt that the defendant raped (the complainant/name) and that the rape resulted in or was committed with acts resulting in serious bodily injury, was committed by a joint venture, or was committed during the commission or attempted commission of the crime of (offense), then you shall find the defendant guilty of aggravated rape.

7

If, however, after your consideration of all of the evidence, you determine that the Commonwealth has proven beyond a reasonable doubt that the defendant raped (the complainant/name), but has not proven beyond a reasonable doubt that the rape resulted in or was committed with acts resulting in serious bodily injury, was committed by a joint venture, or was committed during the commission or attempted commission of the crime of (offense), then you shall return a verdict of guilty to only the lesser-included offense of rape.

If, however, after your consideration of all of the evidence, you determine that the Commonwealth has not proven beyond a reasonable doubt that the defendant raped (the complainant/name), then you shall find the defendant not guilty.

ENDNOTES

[1] Aggravated rape is defined by G.L. c. 265, § 22(a).

[2] Rape is a lesser-included offense of aggravated rape. *Commonwealth v. Sherry*, 386 Mass. 682, 695 (1982). A charge on the lesser-included offense of rape should be given when the evidence provides a rational basis for acquitting the defendant of the crime charged and convicting him or her of the lesser-included offense. *Commonwealth v. Henry*, 37 Mass. App. Ct. 429, 439 (1994). Accordingly, where the aggravating element is sufficiently in dispute, the jury should also be instructed on rape. *Commonwealth v. Henry*, 37 Mass. App. Ct. at 439–41.

[3] The following is a list of offenses that elevate rape to aggravated rape as provided in G.L. c. 265, § 22(a):

a. Assault and battery upon a person sixty years or older by means of a dangerous weapon (G.L. c. 265, § 15A(a)).

b. Assault and battery by means of a dangerous weapon (G.L. c. 265, § 15A(b)).

c. Assault upon a person sixty years or older by means of a dangerous weapon (G.L. c. 265, § 15B(a)).

d. Assault by means of a dangerous weapon (G.L. c. 265, § 15B(b)).

e. Armed robbery (G.L. c. 265, § 17).

f. Unarmed robbery from a person sixty years or older (G.L. c. 265, § 19(a)).

g. Unarmed robbery (G.L. c. 265, § 19(b)).

h. Kidnapping (G.L. c. 265, § 26).

i. Armed or assaultive burglary (G.L. c. 266, § 14).

j. Unarmed burglary (G.L. c. 266, § 15).

k. Breaking and entering in the nighttime with intent to commit a felony (G.L. c. 266, § 16).

l. Entering without breaking in the nighttime with intent to commit a felony, the owner or other person lawfully therein being put in fear (G.L. c. 266, § 17).

m. Breaking and entering in the daytime with intent to commit a felony, the owner or other person lawfully therein being put in fear (G.L. c. 266, § 17).

n. Entering without breaking a dwelling house in the nighttime with intent to commit a felony, no person lawfully therein being put in fear (G.L. c. 266, § 18).

o. Breaking and entering in the daytime with intent to commit a felony, no person lawfully therein being put in fear (G.L. c. 266, § 18).

p. Carrying a firearm (G.L. c. 269, § 10(a)).

q. Carrying certain dangerous weapons (G.L. c. 269, § 10(b)).

r. Possession of a machine gun or sawed-off shot gun (G.L. c. 269, § 10(c)).

s. Possession of a firearm (G.L. c. 269, § 10(h)).

t. Carrying a firearm in any building or grounds of any secondary school, college or university without written authorization (G.L. c. 269, § 10(j)).

[4] There are no Massachusetts cases that define serious bodily injury as an aggravating factor of rape. In *Commonwealth v. Sumner*, 18 Mass. App. Ct. 349, 351–52 (1984), the Court of Appeals of Massachusetts held that the following evidence was sufficient to warrant a denial of the defendant's motion for a required finding of not guilty of aggravated rape based on serious bodily injury to the victim: Testimony by the victim, a doctor and others, as well as photographs of the victim that indicated the victim was forced to engage repeatedly in various sexual acts for an hour and half, was choked until she was gasping for air, was bruised, had scrapes on her throat and back, and was in an emotionally disturbed condition. *See Commonwealth v. Robinson*, 78 Mass. App. Ct. 1110, *2 (2010) (unpublished); *Butler v. O'Brien*, 2010 WL 607295, at *5–6 (D. Mass. Feb. 18, 2010).

[5] In 2010 the Supreme Judicial Court reformulated the joint venture jury charge. *See Commonwealth v. Zanetti*, 454 Mass. 449, 467–68 (2009) (when there is evidence that more than one person may have participated in the offense, judge should instruct the jury that the defendant is guilty if the Commonwealth has proved beyond a reasonable doubt "that the defendant knowingly participated in the commission of the crime charged, alone or with others, with the intent required for that offense"). See § 2.3 in chapter 2 of this book for an instruction on joint venture.

[6] It is not necessary that the aggravating factor be used to facilitate the unlawful sexual intercourse as long as the aggravating factor and the rape "constituted one continuous episode and course of conduct." *See Commonwealth v. McCourt*, 438 Mass. App. Ct. 486, 492, 496 (2003) (quoting *Commonwealth v. Moreschi*, 38 Mass. App. Ct. 562, 569–70 (1995)); *see also Commonwealth v. Thomas*, 89 Mass. App. Ct. 422, *review denied*, 475 Mass. 1104 (2016); *Commonwealth v. Brown*, 66 Mass. App. Ct. 237, 243–44 (2006).

Rape of a Child: Use of Force (G.L. c. 265, § 22A)

Regulatory Authority—G.L. c. 265, § 22A
Super. Ct. Model Jury Instructions § 3.3

In this case, the defendant is charged with rape of a child with force. Our state legislature has specifically defined this crime in a statute—G.L. c. 265, § 22A. The relevant portions of the statute read as follows:

> Whoever has sexual intercourse or unnatural sexual intercourse with a child under sixteen, and compels said child to submit by force and against his will or compels said child to submit by threat of bodily injury, shall be punished.

In order for you the jury to find the defendant guilty of rape of a child under 16, the Commonwealth must prove the following three elements beyond a reasonable doubt:

First Element: that the defendant engaged in sexual intercourse, either natural or unnatural, with (the complainant/name);

Second Element: that the sexual intercourse was accomplished by compelling (the complainant/name) to submit by force or by threat of bodily injury and against (his/her) will; and

Third Element: that (the complainant/name) was a child under sixteen years of age at the time of the alleged offense.

I will now further define each of these three elements.[2]

The first element the Commonwealth must prove beyond a reasonable doubt is that the defendant engaged in either natural or unnatural sexual intercourse with (the complainant/name). Natural intercourse consists of insertion of the penis into the female sex organ. Unnatural sexual intercourse includes oral and anal intercourse, including fellatio or cunnilingus, and other intrusions of a part of a person's body or other object into the genital or anal opening of another's body. Either natural or unnatural sexual intercourse is complete on penetration, no matter how slight, of a person's genital or anal opening.[3] In addition to the vagina, the female genital opening includes the anterior parts known as the vulva and labia. Penetration into the vagina itself is not required.[4,5]

The second element the Commonwealth must prove beyond a doubt is that the natural or unnatural sexual intercourse was accomplished by force or by threat of bodily injury and against (the complainant's/name's) will.[6] The force needed for rape may, depending on the circumstances, be constructive force[7] as well as physical force, violence or threat of bodily harm.[8]

In determining whether force was used and whether the alleged acts were against (the complainant's/name's) will, you may consider (the complainant's/name's) age, the time of the acts, the relationship between the defendant and (the complainant/name), the circumstances of the acts, including where they occurred and whether (the complainant/name) was alone with the adult, and whether (the complainant/name) would have been in a position to resist or complain under the circumstances given the child's age, size, degree of sophistication and other factors. It need not necessarily be physical force in and of itself, but can be constructive force under the circumstances.[9] You may consider all these circumstances in considering whether the Commonwealth has proven beyond a reasonable doubt that the rape was by force and against (the complainant's/name's) will.

The third element the Commonwealth must prove beyond a reasonable doubt is that the defendant engaged in sexual intercourse with a child who was under sixteen years of age at the time of the alleged offense.[10]

Therefore, if after considering all of the evidence you find that the Commonwealth has proven beyond a reasonable doubt each of the three elements I have just defined, that is, that the defendant engaged in either natural or unnatural sexual intercourse with a child under sixteen years of age, and that the sexual intercourse was accomplished by compelling (the complainant/name) to submit by force or by threat of bodily injury, and against (his/her) will, then you shall find the defendant guilty of rape of a child under sixteen. However, if after your consideration of all of the evidence you find that the Commonwealth has not proven each and every one of these three elements beyond a reasonable doubt, you shall find the defendant not guilty of rape of a child under sixteen.

ENDNOTES

[1] This instruction was written by previous authors of this chapter and is updated for this text.

[2] Where the indictment was filed more than twenty-seven years after the date of the offense, there must be independent evidence that corroborates the complainant's allegation. G.L. c. 277, § 63; *Commonwealth v. White*, 475 Mass. 724, 734–40 (2016).

[3] *Commonwealth v. Lopez*, 433 Mass. 722, 726–27 (2001). In *Commonwealth v. Edward*, 34 Mass. App. Ct. 521, 524 (1993), the court instructed that rape could be found if defendant's lips came into contact with the victim's vagina, vulva, or labia. In *Commonwealth v. King*, 445 Mass. 217, 223 (2005), the element of penetration was established where the minor victim's tongue came into contact with the defendant's penis.

[4] *Commonwealth v. Nylander*, 26 Mass. App. Ct. 784, 788 (1989).

[5] The following supplemental instruction is recommended when appropriate: "The phrase 'anal opening' is intended in its strict anatomical sense. It refers to the opening at the end of the digestive tract (or alimentary canal). The penetration must be of the anal opening itself, not simply the groove between the buttocks." *See Commonwealth v. Nylander*, 26 Mass. App. Ct. 784, 788–89 (1989).

[6] *Commonwealth v. Lopez*, 433 Mass. 722, 727 (2001).

[7] *Commonwealth v. Caracciola*, 409 Mass. 648, 652 (1991).

[8] *Commonwealth v. Caracciola*, 409 Mass. 648, 653 (1991).

[9] *Commonwealth v. Moniz*, 87 Mass. 532, 535–36, *review denied*, 472 Mass. 1108 (2015); *Commonwealth v. Moniz*, 43 Mass. App. Ct. 913–14 (1997) (rescript); *see Commonwealth v. Wallace*, 76 Mass. App. Ct. 411, 417 n.9 (2010); *Commonwealth v. Armstrong*, 73 Mass. App. Ct. 245, 255–56 (2008); *Commonwealth v. Lewandowski*, 22 Mass. App. Ct. 148, 150 (1986).

[10] The defendant's honest belief that the victim was sixteen years of age or older is not a defense to this charge. *Commonwealth v. Moore*, 359 Mass. 509, 514 (1971).

Supplemental Instructions

Rape of a Child Under Sixteen with Force; Subsequent Offense

The defendant is also charged with rape of a child under sixteen with force as a subsequent offense.[1] Rape of a child under sixteen with force as a subsequent offense requires the Commonwealth to prove one additional element beyond a reasonable doubt. In order to prove the defendant guilty of rape of a child under sixteen with force as a subsequent offense, the Commonwealth must prove beyond a reasonable doubt that the defendant committed a rape of a child under sixteen with force and has been previously convicted of or adjudicated delinquent or as a youthful offender for (enumerated offense).[2]

ENDNOTES

[1] Rape of a child under sixteen, use of force, as a subsequent offense is defined by G.L. c. 265, § 22C. Where the indictment was filed more than twenty-seven years after the date of the offense, there must be independent evidence that corroborates the complainant's allegation. G.L. c. 277, § 63; *Commonwealth v. White*, 475 Mass. 724, 734–40 (2016).

[2] The following is a list of the previous convictions that elevate a rape of a child under sixteen with force to aggravated rape of a child under sixteen with force as a subsequent offense:

(a) Indecent assault and battery on a child under fourteen (G.L. c. 265, § 13B);

(b) Aggravated indecent assault and battery on a child under fourteen (G.L. c. 265, § 13B½);

(c) Indecent assault and battery on a person fourteen or older (G.L. c. 265, § 13H);

(d) Assault of a child with intent to commit rape (G.L. c. 265, § 24B);

(e) Rape of a child with force (G.L. c. 265, § 22A);

(f) Aggravated rape of a child with force (G.L. c. 265, § 22B);

(g) Rape and abuse of a child (G.L. c. 265, § 23);

(h) Aggravated rape and abuse of a child (G.L. c. 265, § 23A);

(i) Rape (G.L. c. 265, § 22); or

(j) A like violation of the laws of another state, the United States, or a military, territorial, or Indian tribal authority.

Supplemental Instructions

Aggravated Rape of a Child Under Sixteen with Force

The defendant is also charged with aggravated rape of a child under sixteen with force.[1] Aggravated rape of a child under sixteen with force requires the Commonwealth to prove one additional element beyond a reasonable doubt. In order to prove the defendant guilty of aggravated rape of a child under sixteen with force, the Commonwealth must prove beyond a reasonable doubt that the defendant committed a rape of a child under sixteen with force and

the sexual intercourse or unnatural sexual intercourse is committed during the commission or attempted commission of (enumerated offense),[2] or

the sexual intercourse or unnatural sexual intercourse results in, or is committed by means of an act or acts resulting in, substantial bodily injury. Substantial bodily injury, for the purposes of this indictment, is substantial impairment of the physical condition including any burn, fracture of any bone, subdural hematoma, injury to any organ, any injury which occurs as the result of repeated harm to any bodily function or organ including human skin or any physical condition which substantially imperils a child's health or welfare, which creates a permanent disfigurement, protracted loss or impairment of a function of a body member, limb or organ, or substantial risk of death,[3] or

the sexual intercourse or unnatural sexual intercourse is committed while (the complainant/name) is tied, bound or gagged, or

the sexual intercourse or unnatural sexual intercourse is committed after the defendant administered, or caused to be administered, alcohol or a controlled substance by injection, inhalation, ingestion, or any other means to (the complainant/name) without (the complainant's/name's) consent, or

the sexual intercourse or unnatural sexual intercourse is committed by joint enterprise, or

the sexual intercourse or unnatural sexual intercourse was committed in a manner in which (the complainant/name) could contract a sexually transmitted disease or infection of which the defendant knew or should have known he was a carrier.

Therefore, if after considering all of the evidence you determine that the Commonwealth has proven beyond a reasonable doubt that the defendant committed rape of a child under sixteen with force and that the sexual intercourse or unnatural sexual intercourse was committed during the commission or attempted commission of (enumerated offense), resulted in or was committed by means of an act or acts resulting in substantial bodily injury, was committed while (the complainant/name) was tied, bound, or gagged, was committed after the defendant administered or caused to be administered alcohol or a controlled substance by injection, inhalation, ingestion, or any other means to (the complainant/name) without (the complainant's/name's) consent, was committed by joint enterprise, or was committed in a manner in which (the

7

complainant/name) could contract a sexually transmitted disease or infection of which the defendant knew or should have known he was a carrier, you shall find the defendant guilty of aggravated rape of a child under sixteen with force.

If, however, after your consideration of all of the evidence, you determine that the Commonwealth has proven beyond a reasonable doubt that the defendant committed rape of a child by force, but has not proven beyond a reasonable doubt that the sexual intercourse or unnatural sexual intercourse was committed during the commission or attempted commission of (enumerated offense), resulted in or was committed by means of an act or acts resulting in substantial bodily injury, was committed while (the complainant/name) was tied, bound, or gagged, was committed after the defendant administered or caused to be administered alcohol or a controlled substance by injection, inhalation, ingestion, or any other means to (the complainant/name) without (the complainant's/name's) consent, was committed by joint enterprise, or was committed in a manner in which (the complainant/name) could contract a sexually transmitted disease or infection of which the defendant knew or should have known he was a carrier, then you shall return a verdict of guilty to only the lesser-included offense of rape of a child under sixteen by force.

If, however, after your consideration of all of the evidence, you determine that the Commonwealth has not proven beyond a reasonable doubt that the defendant committed rape of a child by force, then you shall find the defendant not guilty.

ENDNOTES

[1] Aggravated rape of a child under sixteen with force is defined by G.L. c. 265, § 22B. Where the indictment was filed more than twenty-seven years after the date of the offense, there must be independent evidence that corroborates the complainant's allegation. G.L. c. 277, § 63; *Commonwealth v. White*, 475 Mass. 724, 734–40 (2016).

[2] The following is a list of convictions that elevate a rape of a child under sixteen with force to aggravated rape of a child under sixteen with force:

(a) Armed burglary (G.L. c. 266, § 14);
(b) Unarmed burglary (G.L. c. 266, § 15);
(c) Breaking and entering (G.L. c. 266, § 16);
(d) Entering without breaking (G.L. c. 266, § 17);
(e) Breaking and entering into a dwelling house (G.L. c. 266, § 18);
(f) Kidnapping (G.L. c. 265, § 26);
(g) Armed robbery (G.L. c. 265, § 17);
(h) Unarmed robbery (G.L. c. 265, § 19);
(i) Assault and battery with a dangerous weapon or assault with a dangerous weapon (G.L. c. 265, §§ 15A and 15B;
(j) Home invasion (G.L. c. 265, § 18C); or
(k) Posing or exhibiting child in state of nudity or sexual conduct (G.L. c. 272, § 29A).

[3] Substantial bodily injury, for a conviction of aggravated rape of a child by force, is statutorily defined by reference to the definition for substantial bodily injury in the statute for assault and battery on a child. *See* G.L. c. 265, 13J; G.L. c. 265, § 22B.

7

Supplemental Instructions

Statute of Limitations for Indictments Filed More Than Twenty-Seven Years After Date of Offense[1]

The Commonwealth has the burden to prove beyond a reasonable doubt that the offense occurred within the statute of limitations.[2] A statute of limitations sets forth the time period within which a criminal charge must be brought. General Laws Chapter 277 section 63 provides that an indictment for [offense][3] may be brought at any time after the date of the offense; however, if the indictment is filed more than twenty-seven years after the date of the commission of the offense the indictment must be supported by independent evidence that corroborates the complainant's allegation.[4] This independent corroboration must not consist solely of the opinions of mental health professionals.[5]

The indictment in this case was filed on [date]. If you find that the offense took place more than twenty-seven years prior to the date of the indictment, you must find that the indictment is supported by independent evidence that corroborates the complainant's allegation.[6]

ENDNOTES

[1] This instruction is to be given where an indictment for one of the following enumerated offenses, or for a conspiracy or accessory thereto, is filed more than twenty-seven years after the offense.

(a) indecent assault and battery on a child under the age of fourteen (G.L. c. 265, § 13B);
(b) aggravated indecent assault and battery on a child under the age of fourteen (G.L. c. 265, § 13B½);
(c) indecent assault and battery on a child under the age of fourteen, subsequent offense (G.L. c. 265, § 13B¾);
(d) indecent assault and battery on a person with an intellectual disability (G.L. c. 265, § 13F);
(e) assault and battery on a person with an intellectual disability, in violation (G.L. c. 265, § 13F);
(f) reckless endangerment of a child (G.L. c. 265, § 13L);
(g) rape of a child with force (G.L. c. 265, § 22A);
(h) aggravated rape of a child with force (G.L. c. 265, § 22B);
(i) rape of a child with force, subsequent offense (G.L. c. 265, § 22C);
(j) rape and abuse of a child (G.L. c. 265, § 23);
(k) aggravated rape and abuse of a child (G.L. c. 265, § 23A);
(l) rape and abuse of a child, subsequent offense (G.L. c. 265, § 23B);
(m) assault of a child with intent to commit rape (G.L. c. 265, § 24B);
(n) trafficking a person for sexual servitude under the age of eighteen, in violation of G.L. c. 265, § 50(b).

[2] The statute of limitations is an affirmative defense. When the evidence permits an inference rising to the level of an affirmative defense, the Commonwealth must prove the offense occurred within the statute of limitations beyond a reasonable doubt. *Commonwealth v. Shelley*, 477 Mass. 642, 648 (2017); *Commonwealth v. Shanley*, 455 Mass. 752, 780–81 & nn. 36 & 37 (2010).

[3] See note 1.

[4] G.L. c. 277, § 63.

[5] G.L. c. 277, § 63; *Commonwealth v. White*, 475 Mass. 724, 742 n.30 (2016).

[6] *Commonwealth v. White*, 475 Mass. 724, 741–42 & n.29 (2016). G.L. c. 277, § 63 contains tolling provisions for where a defendant is not usually and publicly a resident of Massachusetts and, for indictments charging a violation of sections 13B, 13F, 13H, 22, 22A, 23, 24B, 26A, or 50 of 265, or sections 1, 2, 3, 4, 4A, 4B, 5, 6, 7, 8, 12, 13, 17, 26, 28, 29A, 29B, 33, 34, 35, or 35A of chapter 272, provides that the statute of limitations shall not commence until the age of sixteen or the violation is reported to a law enforcement agency. In *White*, the court, without specifically addressing issues of tolling or commencement of the statute of limitations as to the twenty-seven-year independent corroboration provision, treated the independent corroboration requirement as taking effect twenty-seven years from the date of the commission of the offense.

Rape and Abuse of a Child (G.L. c. 265, § 23)

Regulatory Authority—G.L. c. 265, § 23
Super. Ct. Model Jury Instructions § 3.4

In this case, the defendant is charged with rape of a child. Our state legislature has specifically defined this crime in a statute—G.L. c. 265, § 23. The relevant portions of the statute read as follows:

> Whoever unlawfully has sexual intercourse or unnatural sexual intercourse, and abuses a child under sixteen years of age shall . . . be punished. . . .

In order for you the jury to find the defendant guilty of rape of a child under 16, the Commonwealth must prove the following three elements beyond a reasonable doubt:

First Element: that the defendant engaged in sexual intercourse, either natural or unnatural, with (the complainant/name);

Second Element: that (the complainant/name) was a child under sixteen years of age at the time of the alleged offense; and

Third Element: that the sexual intercourse was unlawful.

I will now further define each of these three elements.[2]

The first element the Commonwealth must prove beyond a reasonable doubt is that the defendant engaged in either natural or unnatural sexual intercourse with (the complainant/name). Natural intercourse consists of insertion of the penis into the female sex organ. Unnatural sexual intercourse includes oral and anal intercourse, including fellatio or cunnilingus, and other intrusions of a part of a person's body or other object into the genital or anal opening of another's body. Either natural or unnatural sexual intercourse is complete on penetration, no matter how slight, of a person's genital or anal opening.[3] In addition to the vagina, the female genital opening includes the anterior parts known as the vulva and labia. Penetration into the vagina itself is not required.[4,5]

The second element is that the defendant engaged in sexual intercourse with a child who was under sixteen years of age at the time of the alleged offense.[6]

The third element the Commonwealth must prove beyond a reasonable doubt is that the sexual intercourse was unlawful. Unlawful sexual intercourse is intercourse outside of a marital relationship.

Therefore, if after considering all of the evidence you find that the Commonwealth has proven beyond a reasonable doubt each of the three elements I have just defined, that is, that the defendant engaged in either natural or unnatural sexual intercourse, with a child under sixteen years of age, and that the sexual intercourse was unlawful, then you shall find the defendant guilty of rape of a child. However, if after your consideration of all of the evidence you find that the Commonwealth has not proven each and every one of these three elements beyond a reasonable doubt, you shall find the defendant not guilty of rape of a child.

ENDNOTES

[1] This instruction was written by previous authors of this chapter and is updated for this text.

[2] Where the indictment was filed more than twenty-seven years after the date of the offense, there must be independent evidence that corroborates the complainant's allegation. G.L. c. 277, § 63; *Commonwealth v. White*, 475 Mass. 724, 734–40 (2016).

[3] *Commonwealth v. Lopez*, 433 Mass. 722 (2001). In *Commonwealth v. Edward*, 34 Mass. App. Ct. 521, 524 (1993), the court instructed that rape could be found if defendant's lips came into contact with the victim's vagina, vulva, or labia. *See also Commonwealth v. Rodriguez*, 76 Mass. App. Ct. 59, 62 (2009). In *Commonwealth v. King*, 445 Mass. 217, 223 (2005), the element of penetration was established where the minor victim's tongue came into contact with the defendant's penis.

[4] *Commonwealth v. Nylander*, 26 Mass. App. Ct. 784, 788 (1989).

[5] The following supplemental instruction is recommended when appropriate: "The phrase 'anal opening' is intended in its strict anatomical sense. It refers to the opening at the end of the digestive tract (or alimentary canal). The penetration must be of the anal opening itself, not simply the groove between the buttocks." *See Commonwealth v. Nylander*, 26 Mass. App. Ct. 784, 788–89 (1989).

[6] The defendant's honest belief that the victim was sixteen years of age or older is not a defense to this charge. *Commonwealth v. Miller*, 385 Mass. 521, 522–25 (1982); *Commonwealth v. Harris*, 74 Mass. App. Ct. 105, 112–13 (2009) (knowledge of the child's age is not required for conviction on a "presence" joint venture theory, court left open possibility that where prosecution rests on "nonpresence" theory that "avoidance of injustice may in some cases require proof that the joint venture had more specific knowledge about the victim's age than would be required for conviction of the principle"); *Commonwealth v. Bernardo B.*, 453 Mass. 158, 171–72 (2009) (statutory rape in Massachusetts is a strict liability felony). "Rape is a violent invasion of personal integrity and dignity committed in a sexual manner, an essential element of which is the absence of the victim's consent. . . . In the case of rape of a child under the age of sixteen years committed without the use of force or threat, such lack of consent is, nevertheless, conclusively presumed by law." *Commonwealth v. Smith*, 431 Mass. 417, 420 (2000); *see also Commonwealth v. Dineen*, 70 Mass. App. Ct. 1, 6 n.5 (2007).

Supplemental Instructions

Rape of a Child; Subsequent Offense

The defendant is also charged with rape of a child as a subsequent offense.[1] Rape of a child as a subsequent offense requires the Commonwealth to prove one additional element beyond a reasonable doubt. In order to prove the defendant guilty of rape of a child as a subsequent offense, the Commonwealth must prove beyond a reasonable doubt that the defendant committed a rape of a child and has been previously convicted of or adjudicated delinquent or as a youthful offender for (enumerated offense).[2]

ENDNOTES

[1] Rape of a child as a subsequent offense is defined by G.L. c. 265, § 23B. Where the indictment was filed more than twenty-seven years after the date of the offense, there must be independent evidence that corroborates the complainant's allegation. G.L. c. 277, § 63; *Commonwealth v. White*, 475 Mass. 724, 734–40 (2016).

[2] The following is a list of the previous convictions that elevate a rape of a child to rape of a child as a subsequent offense:

(a) Indecent assault and battery on a child under fourteen (G.L. c. 265, § 13B);

(b) Aggravated indecent assault and battery on a child under fourteen (G.L. c. 265, § 13B½);

(c) Indecent assault and battery on a person fourteen or older (G.L. c. 265, § 13H);

(d) Assault of a child with intent to commit rape (G.L. c. 265, § 24B);

(e) Rape of a child with force (G.L. c. 265, § 22A);

(f) Aggravated rape of a child with force (G.L. c. 265, § 22B);

(g) Rape and abuse of a child (G.L. c. 265, § 23);

(h) Aggravated rape and abuse of a child (G.L. c. 265, § 23A);

(i) Rape (G.L. c. 265, § 22); or

(j) A like violation of the laws of another state, the United States, or a military, territorial, or Indian tribal authority.

Supplemental Instructions

Aggravated Statutory Rape of a Child Under Sixteen

The defendant is also charged with aggravated statutory rape of a child under sixteen.[1] Aggravated statutory rape of a child requires the Commonwealth to prove additional elements beyond a reasonable doubt. In order to prove the defendant guilty of aggravated statutory rape of a child, the Commonwealth must prove beyond a reasonable doubt that the defendant committed a statutory rape of a child under sixteen and

(i) there exists more than a five-year age difference between the defendant and (the complainant/name) and (the complainant/name) is under twelve years of age; or

(ii) there exists more than a ten-year age difference between the defendant and (the complainant/name) where (the complainant/name) is between the age of twelve and sixteen years of age; or

(iii) at the time of such intercourse, was a mandated reporter as defined in G.L. c. 119, § 21.[2]

ENDNOTES

[1] Aggravated statutory rape of a child under sixteen is defined by G.L. c. 265, § 23A. Where the indictment was filed more than twenty-seven years after the date of the offense, there must be independent evidence that corroborates the complainant's allegation. G.L. c. 277, § 63; *Commonwealth v. White*, 475 Mass. 724, 734–40 (2016).

[2] Under G.L. c. 119, § 21, a "mandated reporter" is defined as "a person who is: (i) a physician, medical intern, hospital personnel engaged in the examination, care or treatment of persons, medical examiner, psychologist, emergency medical technician, dentist, nurse, chiropractor, podiatrist, optometrist, osteopath, allied mental health and human services professional licensed under section 165 of chapter 112, drug and alcoholism counselor, psychiatrist or clinical social worker; (ii) a public or private school teacher, educational administrator, guidance or family counselor, child care worker, person paid to care for or work with a child in any public or private facility, or home or program funded by the commonwealth or licensed under chapter 15D that provides child care or residential services to children or that provides the services of child care resource and referral agencies, voucher management agencies or family child care systems or child care food programs, licensor of the department of early education and care or school attendance officer; (iii) a probation officer, clerk-magistrate of a district court, parole officer, social worker, foster parent, firefighter, police officer; (iv) a priest, rabbi, clergy member, ordained or licensed minister, leader of any church or religious body, accredited Christian Science practitioner, person performing official duties on behalf of a church or religious body that are recognized as the duties of a priest, rabbi, clergy, ordained or licensed minister, leader of any church or religious body, accredited Christian Science practitioner, or person employed by a church or religious body to supervise, educate, coach, train or counsel a child on a regular basis; (v) in charge of a medical or other public or private institution, school or facility or that person's designated agent; or (vi) the child advocate."

Receiving Stolen Property

Regulatory Authority—G.L. c. 266, § 60

Dist. Ct. Model Jury Instruction 8.600

The defendant is charged with knowingly receiving stolen property.

In order to prove the defendant guilty of this offense, the Commonwealth must prove the following three things beyond a reasonable doubt:

First: That the property in question was stolen;

Second: That the defendant knew that the property had been stolen; and

Third: That the defendant knowingly (had the stolen property in his [her] possession) (bought the stolen property) (aided in concealing the stolen property).

To prove the first element, the Commonwealth must prove beyond a reasonable doubt that the property was stolen—that is, that someone had taken and carried it away without right and without the consent of the owner, while intending to deprive the owner of it permanently. The Commonwealth is not required to prove who it was who stole the property.

The Commonwealth must also prove that the defendant knew or believed that the property was stolen. This is a question of the defendant's actual knowledge or belief at the time. Even if you find that, under the circumstances, a prudent person would have known or believed that the property was stolen, the defendant cannot be found guilty unless the Commonwealth has proved that he (she) actually knew that the property was stolen, or at least believed that it was stolen.

A person's knowledge is a question of fact. Because you cannot look directly into someone's mind, a person's knowledge is normally shown by inferences from all the facts and circumstances surrounding the event. You may infer that the defendant knew that the goods were stolen if the Commonwealth has proved beyond a reasonable doubt that the defendant possessed) (bought) (helped to conceal) recently stolen goods, and if the facts and circumstances in this case support an inference that the defendant knew that those goods were stolen. You should consider all the facts and circumstances surrounding the defendant's alleged (possession) (purchase) (concealment) of stolen goods in deciding whether or not it is reasonable for you to draw such an inference, and in determining whether the Commonwealth has proved beyond a reasonable doubt that the defendant knew that the goods he (she) possessed (bought) (concealed) were stolen. Remember: under such circumstances you may, but you are not required to, draw an inference that the defendant knew that the goods were stolen.

Commonwealth v. Burns, 388 Mass. 178, 183 n.11 (1983).

If the case involves receipt rather than purchase or concealment: Finally, the Commonwealth must show that the defendant knowingly "received" the property. A person "receives" property by knowingly taking custody or control of it. It is not necessary that the defendant personally possessed the stolen property, as long as it is proved that he (she) knowingly exerted control over it in some way.

The Commonwealth does not have to show that the defendant made any personal profit from receiving or disposing of the stolen property.

Supplemental Instructions

1. ***"Recently" Stolen Goods.*** The term "recently" is a relative term, and has no fixed meaning. Whether property should be considered to be recently stolen depends on the type of property it is, its size and appearance, its marketability, the circumstances of its recovery, and all the other circumstances of the situation. The longer the period of time since the theft, the less likely it is that you can draw any reasonable inference simply from the defendant's possession of stolen goods.

Commonwealth v. Kirkpatrick, 26 Mass. App. Ct. 595, 600–01 (1988); *United States v. Redd*, 438 F.2d 335, 336 (9th Cir. 1971). A judge must initially determine as a matter of law whether the facts would warrant the jury in inferring that the theft was recent. *Kirkpatrick, supra* (collecting cases). Whether or not it was recent then becomes a fact issue for the jury unless the theft was so remote or so recent as to render it a question of law. *Commonwealth v. Sandler*, 368 Mass. 729, 744 (1975).

2. ***Stolen Property Worth More Than $1,200.*** If you determine that the Commonwealth has proved beyond a reasonable doubt that the defendant is guilty of receiving stolen property, you must also go on to determine whether the stolen property (was) (*If there were multiple items:* all together were) worth more than $1,200. You may use your general knowledge in evaluating the value of a piece of property; it is not required that you have any expert evidence of its value.

So if your verdict is guilty, you must also indicate on your verdict slip whether or not the Commonwealth has also proved beyond a reasonable doubt that the stolen property (was) (all together were) worth more than $1,200.

Effective April 13, 2018, St. 2018, c. 69 increased from $250 to $1,200 the felony threshold for the offenses of receiving stolen property (G.L. c. 266, § 60), larceny (§ 30) and wilful or wanton destruction of property (§ 127). For offenses committed prior to April 13, 2018, this instruction can be utilized, just inserting $250 wherever it refers to $1,200.

Commonwealth v. Kelly, 24 Mass. App. Ct. 181, 183–86 & n.4 (1987), held that, whether or not the value of the property stolen is alleged in the complaint, in a prosecution for larceny "the judge should instruct the jury that if they convict, they must determine by their verdict whether the value did or did not exceed [$1,200] so that the judge will know what range of punishments is available. Otherwise the judge will be required to sentence as if the value did not exceed" $1,200. *Kelly* also indicated that the value of the stolen property need not be alleged in the complaint, since "the value of the property . . . is an element of the punishment but not an element of the offense of larceny. . . ." *Commonwealth v. Tracy*, 27 Mass. App. Ct. 455, 467 (1989) cited *Kelly* approvingly in seemingly applying the same rule to receiving stolen property cases. Since the language of G.L. c. 266, § 60 is similar to that of § 30, it appears that a similar approach to instructing the jury should be utilized in prosecutions for receiving stolen property when the evidence indicates a possible value of more than $250 but the complaint does not so allege.

Compare *Commonwealth v. Pyburn*, 26 Mass. App. Ct. 967 (1988) (in prosecution for wanton destruction of property under G.L. c. 266, § 127, "if there is an allegation in a complaint . . . that the value of the property so destroyed or injured exceeded" $250 then jury must determine that issue, but instruction need not present that factor as an essential element of the offense since it is not such) with *Commonwealth v. Beale*, 434 Mass. 1024, 1025 & n.2 (2001) ("the value of the property must be treated as an element of the felony of malicious destruction of property" but "the focus of the constitutional inquiry is not a formalistic examination of whether a finding is labeled an 'element' or a 'sentencing factor,' but whether the finding is made by a jury on proof beyond a reasonable doubt").

The jury may use its common knowledge, and does not require expert evidence, in evaluating value. *Commonwealth v. Hosman*, 257 Mass. 379, 386 (1926); *Commonwealth v. McCann*, 16 Mass. App. Ct. 990, 991 (1983).

3. ***Subsequently learning property stolen.*** Even if the defendant did not know that the property was stolen at the time when he (she) received it, the defendant is still guilty of receiving stolen property if he (she) subsequently learned that the property had been stolen, and at that point decided to keep it and to deprive the owner of its use.

Sandler, 368 Mass. at 740–41; *Commissioner of Pub. Safety v. Treadway*, 368 Mass. 155, 160 (1975); *Kirkpatrick*, 26 Mass. App. Ct. at 599.

NOTES

1. **Model instruction.** The model instruction has been prepared for instructing a jury relative to a charge of receiving stolen property under G.L. c. 266, § 60. The fact patterns of particular cases may require additional definitions of the three main elements (stolen property, knowledge and possession). See Instructions 3.140 (Knowledge) and 3.220 (Possession).

2. **Inference of knowledge from possession of recently stolen goods.** The jury may draw a permissive inference that the defendant knew the property was stolen from his or her possession of recently stolen property where the facts of the case do not show that the possession was innocent. Such an inference is constitutionally permissible. *Barnes v. United States*, 412 U.S. 837, 841–47 (1973). *See Sandler*, 368 Mass. at 741–42. Such an inference may itself support a finding of knowledge beyond a reasonable doubt. *See Commonwealth v. Sala*, 18 Mass. App. Ct. 762, 766 (1984); *Commonwealth v. Taylor*, 10 Mass. App. Ct. 452, 458 n.8, *aff'd on other grounds*, 383 Mass. 272 (1981). "However, '[c]autious vigilance must be maintained against the employment of a naked legal principle in a factual setting which provides no reasonable basis for the principle's application'" (citation omitted). *Kirkpatrick*, 26 Mass. App. Ct. at 600.

It is reversible error for the judge to suggest that there is some "burden of explanation" on the defendant with regard to possession of recently stolen property, since the jury is likely to confuse this "burden of explanation" with the burden of proof. *Burns*, 388 Mass. at 180–83. If the defendant does offer an innocent explanation, the Commonwealth is not required to disprove that explanation beyond a reasonable doubt; evidence rebutting a permissible inference is to be weighed by the jury. *Id.*, 388 Mass. at 182 n.8.

3. **Knowledge.** The defendant's subjective knowledge that the property was stolen is required; a negligent or reckless failure to inquire is not enough. *Commonwealth v. Boris*, 317 Mass. 309, 315–17 (1944); *Commonwealth v. May*, 26 Mass. App. Ct. 801, 806–08 (1989). The knowledge requirement is satisfied if the defendant either knew or believed that the property was stolen, or later discovered that it was stolen and undertook to deprive the owner of its use. *Commonwealth v. Dellamano*, 393 Mass. 132, 138 (1984); *Sandler, supra*; *Treadway, supra*; *Kirkpatrick, supra*.

The defendant's knowledge can be inferred from circumstantial evidence. *See, e.g. Commonwealth v. Imbruglia*, 377 Mass. 682, 693–94 (1979) (recent fencing of similar goods); *Commonwealth v. Kelley*, 333 Mass. 191, 194 (1955) (improbable explanation); *Commonwealth v. Matheson*, 328 Mass. 371, 373–74 (1952) (joint occupancy of apartment where goods trafficked openly); *Boris*, 317 Mass. at 316 (suspicious circumstances of sale which would satisfy a reasonable person that goods were stolen); *Commonwealth v. Billings*, 167 Mass. 283, 285–86 (1897) (possession of unusually large quantity of goods in defendant's home); *Commonwealth v. Leonard*, 140 Mass. 473 (1886) (failure to keep records in ordinary course of business); *Commonwealth v. Dias*, 14 Mass. App. Ct. 560, 562 (1982) (same); *Commonwealth v. McGann*, 20 Mass. App. Ct. 59, 66–67 (1985) (price; circumstances of receipt; type of seller; location and circumstances of storage); *Commonwealth v. Santucci*, 13 Mass. 933, 934 (1982) (improbable explanation; steeply discounted price; cash payment required); *Commonwealth v. Segal*, 3 Mass. App. Ct. 732, 733 (1975) (prior course of dealings with thief); *Commonwealth v. Smith*, 3 Mass. App. Ct. 144, 147 (1975) (possession of many stolen items, whether recently stolen or not). *Compare Commonwealth v. Scarborough*, 5 Mass. App. Ct. 302 (1977) (merely riding as passenger in auto with stolen goods in trunk is insufficient to infer possession and knowledge). For the same reason, the defendant may introduce evidence of his reputation as an honest merchant to disprove his knowledge that the goods were stolen. *Commonwealth v. Gazzolo*, 123 Mass. 220, 221 (1877).

It is irrelevant whether the defendant intended to derive personal benefit from receiving the goods, *Commonwealth v. Bean*, 117 Mass. 141, 142 (1875) (receiver doing personal favor for another equally guilty), or thought the actions justified, *Commonwealth v. Weston*, 241 Mass. 131, 143–44 (1922) (knowing use of stolen papers in bar discipline investigation).

4. **Possession.** Buying, receiving, or aiding in the concealment of stolen property are disjunctive, alternate ways of violating the statute. *Commonwealth v. Ciesla*, 380 Mass. 346, 347 (1980). A complaint drawn in the language of G.L. c. 277, § 79 (that the defendant did "buy, receive, and aid in the concealment of" stolen property) is sufficient, even though G.L. c. 266, § 60 is phrased in the disjunctive, and the defendant may be convicted upon proof of any one of the three branches. *Commonwealth v. Valleca*, 358 Mass. 242, 244–45 (1970). The Commonwealth is not required to elect among them before trial. *Commonwealth v. Colella*, 2 Mass. App. Ct. 706, 708 (1974).

Constructive possession is enough. *Commonwealth v. Carroll*, 360 Mass. 580, 586 (1971) (items held by others in a joint criminal enterprise); *Commonwealth v. Settipane*, 5 Mass. App. Ct. 648, 652 (1977) (same); *Commonwealth v. Kuperstein*, 207 Mass. 25, 27 (1910) (offering to sell goods to undercover agent); *Smith*, 3 Mass. App. Ct. at 146 (dominion and control is equivalent of possession). A prosecution based upon concealment can be made out by any purposeful action to withhold the property from its owner or to make it more difficult for the owner to discover. *Ciesla*, 380 Mass. at 349; *Commissioner of Pub. Safety, supra*; *Matheson, supra.*

5. **Severance of multiple charges.** As to whether severance of multiple charges of receiving stolen property is required, see *McGann*, 20 Mass. App. Ct. at 63.

6. **"Stolen" property.** The Commonwealth must prove that the property was in fact stolen. *Commonwealth v. Budreau*, 372 Mass. 641, 643–44 (1977). The stolen property must either be such as could be the subject of larceny at common law, or be listed in G.L. c. 266, § 30(2). *Commonwealth v. Yourawski*, 384 Mass. 386, 387 (1981). It is not necessary to prove who the thief was, or that the defendant received the goods directly from the thief. *Commonwealth v. Grossman*, 261 Mass. 68, 70–71 (1927).

Circumstantial evidence can suffice to demonstrate that the goods were stolen. *Commonwealth v. Ryan*, 11 Mass. App. Ct. 906 (1981). It is insufficient merely to prove that the defendant was found with common, fungible goods without identifying marks, which are similar to goods previously stolen. *Budreau, supra*; *Billings*, 167 Mass. at 286. However, "[t]he law does not require the impossible. Not every exemplar of every kind of property can be individually recognized, and the closer to fungibility the property comes the less possible is accuracy of identification. Likelihood plays a part . . . . Time is a factor too . . ." (citation omitted). Often this is a jury issue. *Commonwealth v. Rossi*, 15 Mass. App. Ct. 950, 952 (1983).

7

7. **Statute of limitations.** Concealing stolen property is not a continuing offense if the defendant took no further actions after the initial concealment, and the statute of limitations runs from the initial concealment date. However the limitations period begins to run anew from the date of any specific, subsequent affirmative act in aid of the continued purposeful concealment. *Ciesla, supra.*

8. **Stealing and receiving same property.** A defendant cannot be convicted both of stealing and receiving the same goods, since receipt of stolen property requires that the property already be stolen at the time of receipt. *Commonwealth v. Dellamano*, 393 Mass. at 134; *Commonwealth v. Haskins*, 128 Mass. 60, 61 (1880); *Commonwealth v. Corcoran*, 69 Mass. App. Ct. 123, 127 n.6 (2007). A defendant may be charged with both crimes; if the evidence would support either, it is for the jury to decide "under clear and precise instructions" of which to convict. *Commonwealth v. Ross*, 339 Mass. 428, 430–32 (1959); *Commonwealth v. Kelley*, 333 Mass. at 195; *Commonwealth v. Obshatkin*, 2 Mass. App. Ct. 1, 4–5 (1974). See Instruction 8.520 (Larceny by Stealing). Each crime should be charged in a separate count or complaint. *Commonwealth v. Dellamano*, 393 Mass. at 134 n.7. If the jury incorrectly convicts on both charges, the judge should reinstruct the jury and send them out again. If the jury persists, the charge of receiving stolen property should be dismissed. *Commonwealth v. Nascimento*, 421 Mass. 677, 684–85 (1996).

However, a conviction for receipt of stolen property does not require the Commonwealth to preclude the possibility that the defendant was the thief. If there is sufficient evidence to support a conviction for receipt of stolen property, such a conviction may stand even if there is also evidence that the defendant may be, or is in fact, the thief, since the jury is free to reject the evidence tending to prove theft and to infer receipt from the fact of possession. *Commonwealth v. Corcoran*, 69 Mass. App. Ct. at 127 (defendant charged only with receipt of stolen property), overruling *Commonwealth v. Janvrin*, 44 Mass. App. Ct. 917 (1998).

9. **Receiving stolen property not duplicative of breaking and entering.** While a defendant cannot be convicted both of larceny and of receiving the same stolen property, a defendant may be convicted both of breaking and entering in the nighttime to commit larceny (G.L. c. 266, § 16) and of receiving (G.L. c. 266, § 60) the same stolen property. *Commonwealth v. Cabrera*, 449 Mass. 825 (2007).

10. **Venue.** Venue lies either where the goods were stolen or where they were received. G.L. c. 277, § 58A. The place of receipt can be established by circumstantial evidence. *Commonwealth v. Obshatkin*, 2 Mass. App. Ct. at 3. The Commonwealth is not required to allege or prove either the place of the theft or the place of receipt. *Commonwealth v. Parrotta*, 316 Mass. 307, 308–09 (1944).

Refusal to Obey Police Officer

Regulatory Authority—G.L. c. 90, § 25
Dist. Ct. Model Jury Instruction 5.620

The defendant is charged with the offense that is commonly referred to a refusing to obey a police officer. Section 25 of chapter 90 of our General Laws provides as follows:

> "Any person who, while operating or in charge of a motor vehicle, (shall refuse, when requested by a police officer, to give his name and address or the name and address of the owner of such motor vehicle, or who shall give a false name or address,) (*or*) (. . . shall refuse or neglect to stop when signaled to stop by any police officer who is in uniform or who displays his badge conspicuously on the outside of his outer coat or garment,) (*or*) (. . . refuses, on demand of [any police] officer [who is in uniform or who displays his badge conspicuously on the outside of his outer coat or garment], to produce his license to operate such vehicle or his certificate of registration . . .) (*or*) (. . . refuses, on demand of [any police] officer [who is in uniform or who displays his badge conspicuously on the outside of his outer coat or garment], to sign his name in the presence of such officer . . .) shall be punished . . . ."

7

In order to prove that the defendant is guilty of this offense, the Commonwealth must prove four things beyond a reasonable doubt:

First: That the defendant was operating or in charge of a motor vehicle;

Second: That the police officer was either in uniform or had his (her) badge conspicuously displayed on the outside of his clothing;

Third: That the defendant (refused to give his [her] name and address to the officer upon request) (refused to give the name and address of the owner of the motor vehicle to the officer upon request) (gave the officer a false name and address) (refused or neglected to stop when signaled to do so by the officer) (refused to produce his [her] license and registration upon the officer's request) (refused to sign his [her] name in the presence of the officer); and

Fourth: That the defendant realized that the police officer had made such a command, and the defendant intentionally disobeyed it.

NOTES

1. *Commonwealth v. Schiller*, 377 Mass. 10, 12 (1979) (statute applies only to person in active control of a vehicle, either in it or in physical proximity to it); *Commonwealth v. Materia*, 350 Mass. 785, 785 (1966); *Commonwealth v. Sullivan*, 311 Mass. 177, 178 (1942) (badge requirement is to inform driver that person making demand has authority to do so). For the definition of "police officer," see G.L. c. 90, § 1; for a definition of "operation," see Instruction 3.200. A violation of G.L. c. 90, § 25 is a criminal offense and not a civil motor vehicle infraction. See G.L. c. 90C, § 3(A), first par.

Despite the statute's literal requirement that the police officer either be in uniform or "display[ ] his badge conspicuously on the outside of his outer coat or garment," it is sufficient if in some other manner "the defendant was effectively notified that he was being told to stop by a police officer." *Commonwealth v. Gray*, 423 Mass. 293, 295 (1996) (sufficient for officer in unmarked cruiser pulling alongside motorist to flash strobe lights and hold up badge); *Commonwealth v. Ross*, 73 Mass. App. Ct. 181 (2008) (where motorist was attempting to hit unmarked cruiser pulling alongside, sufficient for officer to use siren, blue lights and strobe lights and shout "pull over," without displaying badge).

2. The statute also penalizes anyone who refuses "to permit such officer to take the license or certificate in hand for the purpose of examination," anyone who without reasonable excuse fails to surrender his license, registration or number plate on demand, and anyone who "refuses to or neglects to produce his license when requested by a court . . . ." The model instruction may be appropriately adapted for such situations.

Robbery

Regulatory Authority—G.L. c. 265, §§ 17, 19(b)
Super. Ct. Model Jury Instructions § 3.16

Armed Robbery (G.L. c. 265, § 17)[1]

In this case the defendant, (defendant/name), is charged with the crime of armed robbery. Our state legislature specifically defines armed robbery in G.L. c. 265, § 17, which provides that

> [w]hoever, being armed with a dangerous weapon, assaults another and robs, steals or takes from his person money or other property . . . shall be punished . . . .

In order to prove the defendant guilty of armed robbery, the Commonwealth must prove four elements beyond a reasonable doubt:

First Element: that the defendant was armed with a dangerous weapon;

Second Element: that the defendant either applied actual force and violence to the body of (the alleged victim/name), or put (the alleged victim/name) in fear by threatening words or gestures;

Third Element: that the defendant took the money or other property with the intent to steal it; and

Fourth Element: that the defendant took the money or other property from the person or immediate control of (the alleged victim/name).

The first element the Commonwealth must prove beyond a reasonable doubt is that the defendant was armed with a dangerous weapon. This means that the Commonwealth must prove that the defendant had a dangerous weapon in (his/her) possession. The crime of armed robbery is based on the potential for injury. That potential for injury does not depend on the precise moment at which the defendant becomes armed, so long as (he/she) becomes armed at a point directly related to the commission and completion of the robbery.[2] A dangerous weapon is any instrument that by the nature of its construction or the manner of its use is capable of causing grievous bodily injury or death, or could be perceived by a reasonable person as capable of such injury.[3]

[Supplemental Instruction (a)—Dangerous Weapon Further Defined]

[Supplemental Instruction (b)—Apparent Ability to Cause Serious Bodily Injury]

[Supplemental Instruction (c)—Toy Gun or other Fake Weapon]

[Supplemental Instruction (d)—Possession of a Dangerous Weapon Inferred]

The law of armed robbery does not require the Commonwealth to show that the instrument was actually used. It is sufficient if the Commonwealth proves beyond a reasonable doubt that the defendant was actually armed with a dangerous weapon.[4]

The second element the Commonwealth must prove beyond a reasonable doubt is that the defendant either applied actual force and violence to the body of (the alleged victim/name), or by threatening words or gestures put (the alleged victim/name) in fear.

[Supplemental Instruction (e)—Force and Violence Further Defined]

[Supplemental Instruction (f)—Threatened Force Further Defined]

The actual force and violence, or assault and putting (the alleged victim/name) in fear, must be the cause of the defendant obtaining possession of the property.[5]

The third element the Commonwealth must prove beyond a reasonable doubt is that the defendant took the money or other property with the intent to steal it. This means that the Commonwealth must prove that the defendant took and carried away property, against (the alleged victim's/name's) will, with the intent to deprive (the alleged victim/name) of (his/her) possessions permanently.[6]

[Supplemental Instruction (g)—Asportation Defined]

[Supplemental Instruction (h)—Specific Intent Defined]

[Supplemental Instruction (i)—Intent Inferred][7]

[Supplemental Instruction (j)—Intent Must Coincide with the Crime]

The fourth element the Commonwealth must prove beyond a reasonable doubt is that the defendant took the money or other property from the possession or control of (the alleged victim/name).[8]

(The alleged victim/name) need not have actual physical possession of the property.[9] It is sufficient if the property is within (the alleged victim's/name's) area of control.[10] Property is considered under the control of (the alleged victim/name) when it is within his or her reach, inspection, observation or control so that he or she can readily obtain possession of it if not overcome by violence or fear.[11] The property need not have been owned by the person from whom it was taken, so long as it was in his or her possession or control at the time it was taken.[12] The value of the property does not matter, and the Commonwealth is not required to prove the property's value as alleged in the indictment as long as the Commonwealth proves it has some value.

[Joint Venture Charge][13]

Therefore, if after considering all of the evidence you find that the Commonwealth has proven beyond a reasonable doubt each of the four elements I have just defined, that is: (1) that the defendant was armed with a dangerous weapon; (2) that the defendant either applied actual force and violence on (the alleged victim/name), or by threatening words or gestures put (the alleged victim/name) in fear; (3) that the defendant took the money or other property with the intent to steal it; and (4) that the defendant took the money or other property from the person or immediate control of (the alleged victim/name) then you must find the defendant guilty of armed robbery.

If, however, after your consideration of all of the evidence you find that the Commonwealth has not proven any one of these four elements beyond a reasonable doubt, you must find the defendant not guilty of armed robbery.

[If the Commonwealth has failed to prove beyond a reasonable doubt that the defendant was armed with a dangerous weapon, but has proven each of the other three elements beyond a reasonable doubt, then you may find the defendant guilty of unarmed robbery.][14]

ENDNOTES

[1] This instruction and notes are taken from the chargebook offered as a guide to Superior Court judges in 1995 and updated by the authors.

[2] *Commonwealth v. Davis*, 70 Mass. App. Ct. 314 (2007) (teller turned over money due to teller's reasonable fear for the safety of customer standing near defendant sufficient proof for conviction of unarmed robbery); *Commonwealth v. King*, 69 Mass. App. Ct. 113, 115–19 (2007); *Commonwealth v. Dedrick*, 33 Mass. App. Ct. 161, 167 (1992) (defendant picked up gun on street and fled, then used gun to shoot a state trooper in an attempt to complete the theft). *But see Commonwealth v. Garrett*, 473 Mass. 257 (2015) (where indictment charges the defendant with being armed with a handgun or firearm, it was error in instructing the jury in a manner that "permit[ted] [them] to find that a replica or toy firearm met the statutory requirement of being armed with a firearm" and the court explained that such an instruction might have been appropriate if the defendant had been charged with the more broadly defined offense of armed robbery while armed with a dangerous weapon).

[3] *Commonwealth v. Farrell*, 322 Mass. 606, 614–15 (1948).

[4] *Commonwealth v. Nickologines*, 322 Mass. 274, 277 (1948); *Commonwealth v. Goldman*, 5 Mass. App. Ct. 635, 637 (1977).

[5] *Commonwealth v. Jones*, 362 Mass. 83, 87 (1972). In *Commonwealth v. Anderson*, 461 Mass. 616, 633–34 (2012), the court overruled its contrary conclusion reached in *Commonwealth v. Santos*, 440 Mass. 281 (2003), that had determined assault by means of a dangerous weapon was a lesser-included offense of armed robbery.

[6] *Commonwealth v. Subilosky*, 352 Mass. 153, 166 (1967). Note: Where specific intent is an element of the crime and there is evidence of mental impairment, intoxication or the use of drugs, the judge should instruct the jury that they may consider evidence of the defendant's mental impairment, intoxication, or use of drugs with regard to whether the prosecution has proven specific intent beyond a reasonable doubt. *Commonwealth v. Parker*, 402 Mass. 333, 335 (1988) (applies *Henson* to unarmed robbery also); *Commonwealth v. Sylvester*, 400 Mass. 334, 336 (1987); *Commonwealth v. Grey*, 399 Mass. 469, 470–71, 474 (1987); *Commonwealth v. Henson*, 394 Mass. 584, 593–94 (1985). If there is sufficient evidence of intoxication and lack of mental capacity, the judge should, sua sponte, instruct on the effect of voluntary intoxication. *Commonwealth v. Fano*, 400 Mass. 296, 307–08 (1987).

[7] If the defendant presents some evidence that he or she believed the property was his or hers, then instruct: "There is no intent to steal if the defendant honestly and reasonably believes that the property is his/hers."

If defendant presents some evidence that he or she believed the property belonged to another, and he or she intended to return the property, then instruct: "If he/she honestly and reasonably believes the property belongs to another and he/she intends to return the property to that person, no intent to steal exists."

[8] *Commonwealth v. Weiner*, 255 Mass. 506, 509 (1926).

[9] *Commonwealth v. Jones*, 362 Mass. 83, 90 (1972).

[10] *Commonwealth v. Jones*, 362 Mass. 83, 87 (1972).

[11] *Commonwealth v. Homer*, 235 Mass. 526, 533–34 (1920).

[12] *Commonwealth v. Weiner*, 255 Mass. 506, 509 (1926).

[13] In 2010, the Supreme Judicial Court put forth a new formulation of the joint venture jury charge. *See Commonwealth v. Zanetti*, 454 Mass. 449, 467–68 (2009) (when there is evidence that more than one person may have participated in the offense, judge should instruct the jury that the defendant is guilty if the Commonwealth has proved beyond a reasonable doubt "that the defendant knowingly participated in the commission of the crime charged, alone or with others, with the intent required for that offense"); *Commonwealth v. Williams*, 475 Mass. 705 (2016) (to prove joint venture where there is no proof the defendant himself or herself was armed, proof that the defendant knew that his or her coventurer was so armed would satisfy the element of armed robbery requiring the presence of a dangerous weapon).

[14] Unarmed robbery, as well as assault and larceny, are lesser-included offenses of armed robbery. *Commonwealth v. Novicki*, 324 Mass. 461, 466 (1949). Pocketknives, razors, hammers, wrenches, and cutting tools are not considered per se dangerous as those listed above. *Commonwealth v. Novicki*, 324 Mass. 461, 466 (1949).

Armed Robbery While Masked[1] (G.L. c. 265, § 17)

The defendant, (defendant/name), is charged with armed robbery while masked. Our state legislature has specifically defined armed robbery while masked in G.L. c. 265, § 17, which provides, in part:

> Whoever, being armed with a dangerous weapon, assaults another and robs, steals or takes from his person money or other property . . . provided, however, that any person who commits any offense described herein while masked or disguised or while having his features artificially distorted shall [be punished].

7

In order to prove the defendant guilty of armed robbery while masked, the Commonwealth must prove five elements beyond a reasonable doubt:

First Element: that the defendant was armed with a dangerous weapon;

Second Element: that the defendant either applied actual force and violence to the body of (the alleged victim/name), or put (the alleged victim/name) in fear by threatening words or gestures;

Third Element: that the defendant took the money or other property with the intent to steal it;

Fourth Element: that the defendant took the money or other property from the person or immediate control of (the alleged victim/name); and

Fifth Element: that the defendant committed the armed robbery while masked or disguised or while having his or her features artificially distorted.

The first element the Commonwealth must prove beyond a reasonable doubt is that the defendant was armed with a dangerous weapon. This means that the Commonwealth must prove that the defendant had a dangerous weapon in (his/her) possession. The crime of armed robbery is based on the potential for injury. That potential for injury does not depend on the precise moment at which the defendant becomes armed, so long as (he/she) becomes armed at a point directly related to the commission and completion of the robbery.[2] A dangerous weapon is any instrument that by the nature of its construction or the manner of its use is capable of causing grievous bodily injury or death, or could be perceived by a reasonable person as capable of such injury.[3]

[Supplemental Instruction (a)—Dangerous Weapon Further Defined]

[Supplemental Instruction (b)—Apparent Ability to Cause Serious Bodily Injury]

[Supplemental Instruction (c)—Toy Gun or Other Fake Weapon]

7

[Supplemental Instruction (d)—Possession of a Dangerous Weapon Inferred]

The law of armed robbery does not require the Commonwealth to show that the instrument was actually used. It is sufficient if the Commonwealth proves beyond a reasonable doubt that the defendant was actually armed with a dangerous weapon.[4]

The second element the Commonwealth must prove beyond a reasonable doubt is that the defendant either applied actual force and violence to the body of (the alleged victim/name), or by threatening words or gestures put (the alleged victim/name) in fear.

[Supplemental Instruction (e)—Force and Violence Further Defined]

[Supplemental Instruction (f)—Threatened Force Further Defined]

The actual force and violence, or assault and putting (the alleged victim/name) in fear, must be the cause of the defendant obtaining possession of the property.[5]

The third element the Commonwealth must prove beyond a reasonable doubt is that the defendant took the money or other property with the intent to steal it. This means that the Commonwealth must prove that the defendant took and carried away property, against (the alleged victim's/name's) will, with the intent to deprive (the alleged victim/name) of (his/her) possessions permanently.[6]

[Supplemental Instruction (g)—Asportation Defined]

[Supplemental Instruction (h)—Specific Intent Defined]

[Supplemental Instruction (i)—Intent Inferred][7]

[Supplemental Instruction (j)—Intent Must Coincide with the Crime]

The fourth element the Commonwealth must prove beyond a reasonable doubt is that the defendant took the money or other property from the possession or control of (the alleged victim/name).[8]

(The alleged victim/name) need not have actual physical possession of the property.[9] It is sufficient if the property is within (the alleged victim's/name's) area of control.[10] Property is considered under the control of (the alleged victim/name) when it is within his or her reach, inspection, observation or control so that he or she can readily obtain possession of it if not overcome by violence or fear.[11] The property need not have been owned by the person from whom it was taken, so long as it was in his or her possession or control at the time it was taken.[12] The value of the property does not matter, and the Commonwealth is not required to prove the property's value as alleged in the indictment as long as the Commonwealth proves it has some value.

[Joint Enterprise Charge][13]

The fifth element the Commonwealth must prove beyond a reasonable doubt is that the defendant committed the armed robbery while masked or disguised, or while having (his/her) features artificially distorted.[14] The word masked has no peculiar technical meaning in law, but is to be taken in its common usage. It means that a person's face is covered or partially covered so that the face is screened or concealed from view. The face need not be totally concealed. It is enough if it is materially and substantially obstructed. Recognition need not be wholly obstructed. Thus, the mask need not be one that so totally covers or conceals the facial features that the wearer cannot be identified or recognized. The statute applies equally to the inept or bungling masker as it does to the skillful one.[15]

Therefore, if after considering all of the evidence you find that the Commonwealth has proven beyond a reasonable doubt each of the five elements I have just defined, that is: (1) that the defendant was armed with a dangerous weapon; (2) that the defendant either applied actual force and violence or put (the alleged victim/name) in fear by threatening words or gestures; (3) that the defendant took the money or other property with the intent to steal it; (4) that the defendant took the money or other property from the person or immediate control of (the alleged victim/name); and (5) that the defendant committed the armed robbery while masked or disguised, or while having (his/her) features artificially distorted, then you must find the defendant guilty of armed robbery while masked.

If, however, after your consideration of all of the evidence you find that the Commonwealth has not proven any one of these five elements, you must find the defendant not guilty of armed robbery while masked.

ENDNOTES

[1] This instruction and notes are taken from the chargebook offered as a guide to Superior Court judges in 1995 and updated by the authors.

[2] *Commonwealth v. Dedrick*, 33 Mass. App. Ct. 161, 167 (1992) (defendant picked up gun on street and fled, then used gun to shoot a state trooper in an attempt to complete the theft). *But see Commonwealth v. Garrett*, 473 Mass. 257 (2015) (where indictment charges the defendant with being armed with a handgun or firearm, it was error in instructing the jury in a manner that "permit[ted] [them] to find that a replica or toy firearm met the statutory requirement of being armed with a firearm" and the court explained that such an instruction might have been appropriate if the defendant had been charged with the more broadly defined offense of armed robbery while armed with a dangerous weapon).

[3] *Commonwealth v. Farrell*, 322 Mass. 606, 614–15 (1948).

[4] *Commonwealth v. Nickologines*, 322 Mass. 274, 277 (1948); *Commonwealth v. Goldman*, 5 Mass. App. Ct. 635, 637 (1977).

[5] *Commonwealth v. Jones*, 362 Mass. 83, 87 (1972).

[6] *Commonwealth v. Subilosky*, 352 Mass. 153, 166 (1967).

Note: Where specific intent is an element of the crime and there is evidence of mental impairment, intoxication or the use of drugs, the judge should instruct the jury that they may consider evidence of the defendant's mental impairment, intoxication, or use of drugs with regard to whether the prosecution has proven specific intent beyond a reasonable doubt. *Commonwealth v. Parker*, 402 Mass. 333, 335 (1988) (applies *Henson* to unarmed robbery also); *Commonwealth v. Sylvester*,

400 Mass. 334, 336 (1987); *Commonwealth v. Grey*, 399 Mass. 469, 470–71, 474 (1987); *Commonwealth v. Henson*, 394 Mass. 584, 593–94 (1985). If there is sufficient evidence of intoxication and lack of mental capacity, the judge should, sua sponte, instruct on the effect of voluntary intoxication. *Commonwealth v. Fano*, 400 Mass. 296, 307–08 (1987).

[7] If the defendant presents some evidence that he or she believed the property was his or hers, then instruct: "There is no intent to steal if the defendant honestly and reasonably believes that the property is his/hers." If defendant presents some evidence that he or she believed the property belonged to another, and he or she intended to return the property, then instruct: "If he/she honestly and reasonably believes the property belongs to another and he/she intends to return the property to that person, no intent to steal exists."

[8] *Commonwealth v. Weiner*, 255 Mass. 506, 509 (1926).

[9] *Commonwealth v. Jones*, 362 Mass. 83, 90 (1972).

[10] *Commonwealth v. Jones*, 362 Mass. 83, 87 (1972).

[11] *Commonwealth v. Homer*, 235 Mass. 526, 533–34 (1920).

[12] *Commonwealth v. Weiner*, 255 Mass. 506, 509 (1926).

[13] In 2010, the Supreme Judicial Court reformulated the joint venture jury charge. *See Commonwealth v. Zanetti*, 454 Mass. 449, 467–68 (2009) (when there is evidence that more than one person may have participated in the offense, judge should instruct the jury that the defendant is guilty if the Commonwealth has proved beyond a reasonable doubt "that the defendant knowingly participated in the commission of the crime charged, alone or with others, with the intent required for that offense"); *Commonwealth v. Williams*, 475 Mass. 705 (2016) (to prove joint venture where there is no proof the defendant himself or herself was armed, proof that the defendant knew that his or her coventurer was so armed would satisfy the element of armed robbery requiring the presence of a dangerous weapon).

[14] G.L. c. 265, § 17.

[15] *Commonwealth v. Flynn*, 362 Mass. 455, 477–78 (1972). Use of a black substance to obscure facial features would support a finding that the robbery was done with distorted facial features. *Commonwealth v. Flynn*, 362 Mass. at 477–78; *Commonwealth v. Quinones*, 78 Mass. App. Ct. 215, 219–20 (2010); *Commonwealth v. Cincotta*, 6 Mass. App. Ct. 812, 821 (1979), *aff'd on other grounds*, 379 Mass. 391 (1979).

Unarmed Robbery (G.L. c. 265, § 19(b))[1]

The defendant, (defendant/name), is charged with unarmed robbery. Our state legislature has specifically defined unarmed robbery in G.L. c. 265, § 19(b), which provides in part:

> [W]hoever, not being armed with a dangerous weapon, by force and violence, or by assault and putting in fear robs, steals or takes from the person of another, or from his immediate control, money or other property . . . shall be punished . . . .

In order to prove the defendant guilty of unarmed robbery, the Commonwealth must prove three elements beyond a reasonable doubt:

First Element: that the defendant either applied actual force and violence to the body of (the alleged victim/name) or put (the alleged victim/name) in fear by threatening words or gestures;

Second Element: that the defendant took the money or other property with the intent to steal it; and

Third Element: that the defendant took the money or other property from the immediate control of (the alleged victim/name).

The first element the Commonwealth must prove beyond a reasonable doubt is that the defendant either applied actual force and violence to the body of (the alleged victim/name), or by threatening words or gestures put (the alleged victim/name) in fear.

[Supplemental Instruction (e)—Force and Violence Further Defined]

[Supplemental Instruction (f)—Threatened Force Further Defined]

The actual force and violence, or assault and putting (the alleged victim/name) in fear, must be the cause of the defendant obtaining possession of the property.[2]

The second element the Commonwealth must prove beyond a reasonable doubt is that the defendant took the money or other property with the intent to steal it. This means that the Commonwealth must prove that the defendant took and carried away property, against (the alleged victim's/name's) will, with the intent to deprive (the alleged victim/name) of (his/her) possessions permanently.[3]

[Supplemental Instruction (g)—Asportation Defined]

[Supplemental Instruction (h)—Specific Intent Defined]

[Supplemental Instruction (i)—Intent Inferred][4]

[Supplemental Instruction (j)—Intent Must Coincide with the Crime]

The third element the Commonwealth must prove beyond a reasonable doubt is that the defendant took the money or other property from the possession or control of (the alleged victim/name).[5]

(The alleged victim/name) need not have actual physical possession of the property.[6] It is sufficient if the property is within (the alleged victim's/name's) area of control.[7] Property is considered under the control of (the alleged victim/name) when it is within his or her reach, inspection, observation or control so that he or she can readily obtain possession of it if not overcome by violence or fear.[8] The property need not have been owned by the person from whom it was taken, so long as it was in his or her possession or control at the time it was taken.[9] The value of the property does not matter, and the Commonwealth is not required to prove the property's value as alleged in the indictment as long as the Commonwealth proves it has some value.

[Joint Enterprise Charge][10]

Therefore, if after considering all of the evidence you find that the Commonwealth has proved beyond a reasonable doubt each of the three elements I have just defined, that is, that the defendant either applied actual force and violence or put (the alleged victim/name) in fear by threatening words or gestures, that the defendant took the money or other property with the intent to steal it, and that the defendant took the money or other property from the person or immediate control of (the alleged victim/name), then you must find the defendant guilty of unarmed robbery.

If, however, after your consideration of all of the evidence you find that the Commonwealth has not proven any one of these three elements, you must find the defendant not guilty of unarmed robbery.

7

ENDNOTES

[1] This instruction quotes the chargebook offered as a guide to Superior Court judges in 1995. The notes that follow are from the same source and have been updated for this text.

[2] *Commonwealth v. Davis*, 70 Mass. App. Ct. 314 (2007) (teller turned over money due to teller's reasonable fear for the safety of customer standing near defendant sufficient proof for conviction of unarmed robbery); *Commonwealth v. Jones*, 362 Mass. 83, 87 (1972).

[3] *Commonwealth v. Subilosky*, 352 Mass. 153, 166 (1967).

Note: Where specific intent is an element of the crime and there is evidence of mental impairment, intoxication, or the use of drugs, the judge should instruct the jury that they may consider evidence of the defendant's mental impairment, intoxication, or use of drugs with regard to whether the prosecution has proven specific intent beyond a reasonable doubt. *Commonwealth v. Parker*, 402 Mass. 333, 335 (1988) (applies *Henson* to unarmed robbery also); *Commonwealth v. Sylvester*, 400 Mass. 334, 336 (1987); *Commonwealth v. Grey*, 399 Mass. 469, 470–71, 474 (1987) (1987); *Commonwealth v. Henson*, 394 Mass. 584, 593–94 (1985). If there is sufficient evidence of intoxication and lack of mental capacity, the judge should, sua sponte, instruct on the effect of voluntary intoxication. *Commonwealth v. Fano*, 400 Mass. 296, 307–08 (1987).

[4] If the defendant presents some evidence that he or she believed the property was his or hers, then instruct: "There is no intent to steal if the defendant honestly and reasonably believes that the property is his/hers." If defendant presents some evidence that he or she believed the property belonged to another, and he or she intended to return the property, then instruct: "If he/she honestly and reasonably believes the property belongs to another and he/she intends to return the property to that person, no intent to steal exists."

[5] *Commonwealth v. Weiner*, 255 Mass. 506, 509 (1926).

[6] *Commonwealth v. Jones*, 362 Mass. 83, 90 (1972).

[7] *Commonwealth v. Jones*, 362 Mass. 83, 87 (1972).

[8] *Commonwealth v. Homer*, 235 Mass. 526, 533–34 (1920).

[9] *Commonwealth v. Weiner*, 255 Mass. 506, 509 (1926).

[10] In 2010, the Supreme Judicial Court reformulated the joint venture jury charge. *See Commonwealth v. Zanetti*, 454 Mass. 449, 467–68 (2009) (when there is evidence that more than one person may have participated in the offense, judge should instruct the jury that the defendant is guilty if the Commonwealth has proved beyond a reasonable doubt "that the defendant knowingly participated in the commission of the crime charged, alone or with others, with the intent required for that offense").

Supplemental Instructions[1]

Dangerous Weapon Further Defined

Firearms, daggers, stilettos and brass knuckles are usually considered dangerous weapons because they were designed or constructed with the purpose of producing death or great bodily harm.[2]

The definition of a dangerous weapon also includes any instrument or instrumentality which, because of the manner in which it is used or attempted to be used, endangers the life or inflicts great bodily injury, or is reasonably capable of causing death or serious bodily injury.[3] Thus, even if an instrument in its ordinary use is not designed to produce death or serious bodily injury, it may qualify as a dangerous weapon if it is so used as to be likely to produce death or great bodily harm.[4]

It is for you to decide whether the instrument in this case was used in a dangerous manner so as to endanger the life or to inflict bodily injury.[5] When making your decision, you may consider the circumstances surrounding the alleged crime, the nature and size of the object, and the manner in which it was handled or used.[6] You should consider "whether, based on the objective conditions existing at the time of the assault, the exhibition of the instrument could *reasonably* engender (the alleged victim's/name's) fear, and whether the perpetrator of the robbery intended to provoke such fear in order to facilitate the theft."[7] You may consider (the alleged victim's/name's) apprehension and subjective state. However, it is not necessary that (the alleged victim/name) be shown to have, in fact, experienced fear.[8]

7

ENDNOTES

[1] These instructions quote the chargebook offered as a guide to Superior Court judges in 1995. The notes that follow are from the same source and have been updated for this text.

[2] *Commonwealth v. Appleby*, 380 Mass. 296, 303 (1980).

[3] *Commonwealth v. Appleby*, 380 Mass. 296, 304 (1980).

[4] *Commonwealth v. Tarrant*, 367 Mass. 411, 416 n.4 (1975). However, in deciding whether an instrument is a dangerous weapon, you should consider whether the instrument presented an objective threat of danger to a person of reasonable and average sensibility. *Commonwealth v. Tarrant*, 367 Mass. 411, 416 n.4 (1975). Where a neutral object is involved, the issue turns on whether the instrumentality under the control of the perpetrator has the apparent ability to inflict harm, whether the victim reasonably so perceived it, and whether the perpetrator by use of the instrumentality intended to elicit fear in order to further the robbery. *Commonwealth v. Tevlin*, 433 Mass. 305, 311 (2001) (sneakers). For example, a pencil is not a dangerous weapon if used to write, but may be a dangerous weapon if directed toward a vulnerable portion of the human body such as the eye. A shoe is not a dangerous weapon if used to walk, but may be a dangerous weapon if used to kick or jump on someone. *Commonwealth v. Appleby*, 380 Mass. 296, 303–04 (1980); *Commonwealth v. Fettes*, 64 Mass. App. Ct. 917, 918 (2005) (a dog may be a dangerous weapon); *Commonwealth v. Davis*, 10 Mass. App. Ct. 190, 192–98 (1980) (teeth, hands, fingers, feet, and other unadorned parts of the body are not dangerous weapons).

[5] *Commonwealth v. Farrell*, 322 Mass. 606, 615 (1948).

[6] *Commonwealth v. Appleby*, 380 Mass. 296, 304–05 (1980); *Commonwealth v. Tarrant*, 367 Mass. 411, 416 (1975); *Commonwealth v. Farrell*, 322 Mass. 606, 614–15 (1948); *Commonwealth v. Davis*, 10 Mass. App. Ct. 190, 193 (1980).

[7] *Commonwealth v. Tarrant*, 367 Mass. 411, 417 (1975). See note 5.

[8] *Commonwealth v. Tarrant*, 367 Mass. 411, 417 (1975). See note 5.

Apparent Ability to Cause Serious Bodily Injury

Additionally, you may consider whether, at the time of the alleged offense, the exhibition of the object could reasonably have engendered fear in (the alleged victim/name), and whether the defendant intended to provoke fear in order to facilitate the robbery.[1] This means that it is not necessary that the instrument be actually capable of causing serious bodily harm or death so long as it appears to a reasonable person that it is capable.[2] For example, for the purposes of establishing this element of armed robbery, an unloaded gun (or a gun that can't fire bullets) can be a dangerous weapon if the gun appears capable of causing serious bodily harm to (the alleged victim/name).[3]

ENDNOTES

[1] *Commonwealth v. Tarrant*, 367 Mass. 411, 416–17 (1975) (whether an instrument is dangerous is measured by objective standards and not by the victim's subjective apprehension).

[2] *Commonwealth v. Tarrant*, 367 Mass. 411, 417–18 (1975).

[3] *Commonwealth v. Nickologines*, 322 Mass. 274, 277 (1948); *Commonwealth v. Goldman*, 5 Mass. App. Ct. 635, 637 (1977); *see Commonwealth v. Mattei*, 455 Mass. 840, 844 (2010).

Toy Gun or Other Fake Weapon

A person who uses a toy gun or other fake weapon to commit a robbery may be convicted of armed robbery if (the alleged victim/name) reasonably took it to be a real weapon capable of inflicting bodily injury.[1]

ENDNOTES

[1] *Commonwealth v. Powell*, 433 Mass. 399 (2001); *Commonwealth v. Nicholson*, 20 Mass. App. Ct. 9, 17 (1985); *Commonwealth v. Perry*, 6 Mass. App. Ct. 531, 534 (1978). *But see Commonwealth v. Garrett*, 473 Mass. 257 (2015) (where indictment charges the defendant with being armed with a handgun or firearm, it was error in instructing the jury in a manner that "permit[ted] [them] to find that a replica or toy firearm met the statutory requirement of being armed with a firearm" and the court explained that such an instruction might have been appropriate if the defendant had been charged with the more broadly defined offense of armed robbery while armed with a dangerous weapon).

Possession of a Dangerous Weapon Inferred

You may consider that the defendant was armed with a dangerous weapon even if no weapon was seen by (the alleged victim/name), provided it is reasonable for you to infer that the defendant possessed a weapon.[1]

For example, if the Commonwealth proves beyond a reasonable doubt that the defendant had spoken words implying (he/she) possessed a dangerous weapon, and the circumstances indicate that sometime afterwards the defendant had an opportunity to dispose of it, you may infer that the defendant did have a dangerous weapon at the time (he/she) made (his/her) statement.[2] However, a defendant cannot be found to be apparently armed with a dangerous weapon when in fact (he/she) was unarmed.[3]

Finally, (the alleged victim/name) does not have to be aware that the defendant was in possession of a weapon in order for you to find that the defendant was armed.[4]

ENDNOTES

[1] *Commonwealth v. Howard*, 386 Mass. 607, 608 (1982).

[2] *Commonwealth v. Jackson*, 419 Mass. 716, 724–25 (1995); *Commonwealth v. Howard*, 386 Mass. 607, 610 (1982); *Commonwealth v. Delgado*, 367 Mass. 432, 437 (1975).

[3] *Commonwealth v. Howard*, 386 Mass. 607, 608 (1982). *But see Commonwealth v. Johnson*, 27 Mass. App. Ct. 746, 748–49 (1989) (concealed hairbrush reasonably represented an objective threat of danger).

[4] *Commonwealth v. Goldman*, 5 Mass. App. Ct. 635, 637 (1977).

Force and Violence Further Defined

When actual force is used, it must be applied to or exerted on the body of (the alleged victim/name).[1] The degree of force used by the defendant does not matter so long as it is sufficient for the defendant to obtain (the alleged victim's/name's) property against (his/her) will.[2] (The alleged victim/name) must be aware of the application of such force.[3] However, an opportunity to resist or actual resistance is not necessary on the part of (the alleged victim/name).[4] Where the Commonwealth proves that the defendant has exerted actual force and violence, no fear need be instilled in (the alleged victim/name).[5]

ENDNOTES

[1] *Commonwealth v. Richards*, 363 Mass. 299, 302 (1973); *Commonwealth v. Novicki*, 324 Mass. 461, 465 (1949).

[2] *Commonwealth v. Santos*, 440 Mass. 281 (2003) (defendant's having snatched an envelope of money from one victim constituted "sufficient force"); *Commonwealth v. Jones*, 362 Mass. 83, 87 (1972); *see also Commonwealth v. Brown*, 2 Mass. App. Ct. 883 (1974) (defendant purse-snatcher convicted of robbery although victim had no prior awareness of impending act). *But see Commonwealth v. Davis*, 7 Mass. App. Ct. 9 (1979) (pickpocketing, even if not artfully performed, will not support robbery conviction based on force and violence, but may be sufficient if based on assault and putting in fear).

[3] *Commonwealth v. Jones*, 362 Mass. 83, 87 (1972); *Commonwealth v. Novicki*, 324 Mass. 461, 465 (1949).

[4] *Commonwealth v. Jones*, 362 Mass. 83, 89 (1972).

[5] *Commonwealth v. Jones*, 362 Mass. 83, 87 (1972).

Threatened Force Further Defined

When force is not actually used but only threatened by words or gestures, (the alleged victim/name) must be aware of the threat and be put in fear.[1] The force or threat of force need not be directed at (the alleged victim/name) if (the alleged victim/name) is aware of force or threat of force directed at another and is thereby put in fear.[2]

ENDNOTES

[1] *Commonwealth v. Novicki*, 324 Mass. 461, 466 (1949).

[2] *Commonwealth v. Davis*, 70 Mass. App. Ct. 314 (2007) (teller turned over money due to teller's reasonable fear for the safety of customer standing near defendant sufficient proof for conviction of unarmed robbery); *Commonwealth v. Richards*, 363 Mass. 299, 304 (1973); *Commonwealth v. Novicki*, 324 Mass. 461, 465–66 (1949).

Asportation Defined

The carrying away is accomplished when the defendant transfers the property from (the alleged victim's/name's) control to (his/her) own.[1] The transfer of property may be made by the defendant or by another, or may even be made by (the alleged victim/name), so long as it is done under the defendant's direction.[2] The distance the property is carried is immaterial so long as possession or control is transferred from (the alleged victim/name) to the defendant.[3]

ENDNOTES

[1] *Commonwealth v. Luckis*, 99 Mass. 431, 431–32 (1868); *Commonwealth v. Flowers*, 1 Mass. App. Ct. 415, 418 (1973).

[2] *Commonwealth v. Flowers*, 1 Mass. App. Ct. 415, 418–19 (1973).

[3] *Commonwealth v. Flowers*, 1 Mass. App. Ct. 415, 418–19 (1973).

Specific Intent Defined

The word intent refers to a person's objectives or purposes. The Commonwealth must prove beyond a reasonable doubt that the defendant possessed the specific intent to steal. Specific intent requires a conscious decision. It involves concentrating or focusing the mind before the desired act is committed. In other words, an act performed with specific intent is a conscious one done with the determination of the mind to commit the act.[1]

ENDNOTES

[1] *Commonwealth v. Nickerson*, 388 Mass. 246, 253–54 (1983).

Intent Inferred

The intent to permanently deprive the owner of his or her property can be inferred from the defendant's words or conduct. For example, an intent to steal may be inferred where a person takes property without the owner's permission and then uses or disposes of it in a way that shows indifference as to whether the owner recovers possession.[1]

There is no intent to steal if the defendant honestly and reasonably believes that the property is (his/hers).[2] Also, if the defendant honestly and reasonably believes the property belongs to another, and (he/she) intends to return the property to that person, no intent to steal exists.[3]

ENDNOTES

[1] *Commonwealth v. Salerno*, 356 Mass. 642, 648 (1970). *But see Commonwealth v. Van Winkle*, 443 Mass. 230, 241–42 (2005) (indifference concerning whether an owner recovers possession of his or her property does not automatically prove specific intent to steal).

[2] *Commonwealth v. Newhook*, 34 Mass. App. Ct. 960, 961 (1993); *Commonwealth v. Anslono*, 9 Mass. App. Ct. 867, 867–68 (1980). This instruction should be given whenever the defendant presents some evidence that he or she believed the property was his or hers. *Commonwealth v. Anslono*, 9 Mass. App. Ct. at 867–68.

[3] *Commonwealth v. Larmey*, 14 Mass. App. Ct. 281, 285 (1982). This instruction should be given whenever the defendant presents some evidence that he or she believes the property belongs to another and he or she intends to return the property to that person. *Commonwealth v. Larmey*, 14 Mass. App. Ct. at 285 (1982); *Commonwealth v. Vives*, 447 Mass. 537, 541–42 (2006) (defendant entitled to a jury instruction on the defense of honest and reasonable belief he was collecting a valid debt where no sufficient evidence that debt was the result of illegal transaction).

Intent Must Coincide with the Crime

The intent to steal must coincide with the force or threats against (the alleged victim/name).

Therefore, it is not robbery if a person sets out to commit an assault, and then as an afterthought commits a theft.[1] In the same way, if a person has committed a theft that is over and done with, and then afterwards displays force or threats, that is not a robbery unless the thief has a continuing intent to steal.[2]

ENDNOTES

[1] *Commonwealth v. Moran*, 387 Mass. 644, 646 (1982).

[2] *Commonwealth v. Rajotte*, 23 Mass. App. Ct. 93, 94–95 (1986); *Commonwealth v. Assad*, 19 Mass. App. Ct. 1007, 1008–09 (1985) (rescript); *see Commonwealth v. Correia*, 17 Mass. App. Ct. 233, 236–37 (1983).

School Zone Drug Violation

Regulatory Authority—G.L. c. 94C, § 32J
Dist. Ct. Model Jury Instruction 7.860

> Effective August 2, 2012, St. 2012, c. 192, §§ 30–31 amended G.L. c. 94C, § 32J by reducing the size of the school zone area from 1,000 feet to 300 feet and by limiting the scope of the statute to offenses that occur between the hours of 5:00 AM and midnight. These changes apply to school zone drug violations committed on or after August 2, 2012.
>
> For use with Instruction 7.800 (Distribution of, or Possession with Intent to Distribute, a Controlled Substance) or Instruction 7.840 (Sale of, or Possession with Intent to Sell, Drug Paraphernalia) where the complaint alleges that the violation occurred within 300 feet of school property.
>
> First instruct on underlying offense.

If you find the defendant guilty of _____, you must go on to consider whether the Commonwealth has proven beyond a reasonable doubt:

First: That the offense was committed within 300 feet of the real property comprising (a public preschool, headstart facility, elementary, vocational or secondary school) (a private accredited preschool or private accredited headstart facility) (a private elementary, vocational or secondary school); and

Second: That the offense was committed between five o'clock in the morning and twelve o'clock midnight. It does not matter whether or not the school, preschool or headstart facility was in session, but the Commonwealth must prove beyond a reasonable doubt that the offense occurred between five o'clock in the morning and twelve o'clock midnight.

It is not necessary for the Commonwealth to prove that the defendant knew that he (she) was within 300 feet of the real property of a school, preschool, or headstart facility.

> *Commonwealth v. Bell*, 442 Mass. 118, 125–26 (2004) ("secondary school" does not require Department of Education accreditation); *Commonwealth v. Roucoulet*, 413 Mass. 647 (1992) (defendant need not intend to distribute drugs within the school zone; sufficient to have possessed drugs within the school zone with intent to distribute them anywhere); *Commonwealth v. Taylor*, 413 Mass. 243 (1992) (§ 32J creates a distinct offense which can be charged separately from the underlying drug offense, although § 32J seems to contemplate that it will normally be tried together with the underlying charge); *Commonwealth v. Labitue*, 49 Mass. App. Ct. 913, 914 (2000) (same); *Commonwealth v. Gonzales*, 33 Mass. App. Ct. 728, 730 (1992) (Commonwealth must prove that school is one of the types enumerated in the statute; subject is not appropriate for judicial notice).

NOTES

1. **Additional sentence.** General Laws c. 94C, § 32J provides a mandatory minimum term of imprisonment for violations of G.L. c. 94C, §§ 32, 32A–F or 32I committed within 300 feet of the grounds of a school, with the sentence to run from and after the expiration of the sentence for the predicate offense. For cases arising prior to August 2, 2012, the distance was 1000 feet.

2. **Constitutionality.** General Laws c. 94C, § 32J does not violate due process in providing that lack of knowledge that the defendant's drug-dealing was within 1,000 feet (300 feet as of August 2, 2012) of a school is not a defense, and does not violate double jeopardy principles by requiring a separate mandatory sentence on and after that for the underlying drug offense.

7

3. **Measuring boundaries.** General Laws c. 94C, § 32J does not specify any particular method for establishing the boundaries of a school. See *Commonwealth v. Spano,* 414 Mass. 178, 181 (1993) (under § 32J, distance from school should be measured in straight line from school's boundary line to site of illegal drug activity); *Commonwealth v. Johnson,* 53 Mass. App. Ct. 732 (2002) (Commonwealth need not establish exact point of school boundary, if measurement taken from point that is reasonably inferable to be located on property used for school purposes); *Commonwealth v. Cintron,* 59 Mass. App. Ct. 905, 907 (2003) (under dictionary definitions of the word "site," front door of apartment building should suffice); *Commonwealth v. Rodriguez,* 40 Mass. App. Ct. 1117 (No. 94-P-1438, Apr. 23, 1996) (unpublished opinion under Appeals Ct. Rule 1:28) ("just as a principal of a school or an arresting officer may testify as to the type of school specified in the school zone statute based on his or her personal knowledge, a principal of a school or a police officer . . . may testify as to the boundaries of the school from their personal knowledge"); *Commonwealth v. Wayne Wilson,* 49 Mass. App. Ct. 1114 (No. 99-P-1482, June 26, 2000) (unpublished opinion under Appeals Ct. Rule 1:28) ("site" of illegal drug activity in a building is the building rather than any particular room).

5. **Surrounding land.** For purposes of G.L. c. 94C, § 32J, the "real property comprising a . . . school" may include undeveloped and unused land that is within the boundaries of the school's property and contiguous to the school's developed real estate. When "a boundary line circumscribes a public elementary school building together with adjacent school land areas which are contiguous, and not separated by intervening land under different jurisdiction, . . . § 32J is violated where the proscribed activity occurs within one thousand feet [300 feet as of August 2, 2012] of such boundary line." Section 32J does not require that the property be owned by the school department or used for school purposes. *Commonwealth v. Paige,* 54 Mass. App. Ct. 840 (2002).

6. **Preschool or headstart facilities.** Public preschools or headstart facilities do not need to be accredited to fall within § 32J, but private preschools and headstart facilities fall within § 32J only if they are accredited. *Commonwealth v. Thomas,* 71 Mass. App. Ct. 323 (2008).

7. **Kindergarten.** A school consisting only of a kindergarten is not an "elementary school" for purposes of § 32J, since the dictionary definition of an elementary school is a school for the first six or eight grades. *Commonwealth v. Burke,* 44 Mass. App. Ct. 76 (1997).

Sexual Conduct for a Fee (Prostitution)

Regulatory Authority—G.L. c. 272, § 53A
Dist. Ct. Model Jury Instruction 7.480

I. Prostitute

The defendant is charged with either engaging in sexual conduct for a fee, or agreeing to engage in sexual conduct for a fee, or offering to engage in sexual conduct for a fee—the activity that is commonly referred to as prostitution.

Section 53A of chapter 272 of our General Laws provides as follows:

> "Any person who engages, agrees to engage, or offers to engage in sexual conduct with another person in return for a fee . . . shall be punished . . . ."

In order to prove the defendant guilty of this offense, the Commonwealth must prove two things beyond a reasonable doubt:

First: That the defendant either engaged, or agreed to engage, or offered to engage, in sexual conduct with another person; and

Second: That the sexual conduct (was) (was to be) done in return for a fee.

The defendant may be convicted only if the sexual conduct (was) (was to be) in exchange for a fee—that is, if the transaction was of a commercial nature.

> From the passage of St. 1959, c. 304 until the enactment of St. 1983, c. 66, the punishment of "prostitutes" was provided for in G.L. c. 272, § 53. Prostitution was defined as "common indiscriminate sexual activity for hire, in distinction from sexual activity confined exclusively to one person." *Commonwealth v. King*, 374 Mass. 5, 12 (1977). See *Commonwealth v. Walter*, 388 Mass. 460, 463 (1983); *Commonwealth v. United Food Corp.*, 374 Mass. 765, 767 (1978); *Commonwealth v. Cook*, 12 Met. 93, 97 (1846); *Commonwealth v. A Juvenile (No. 2)*, 6 Mass. App. Ct. 194, 196 (1978) (prostitution comprises both "the performance of indiscriminate sexual acts for hire and the indiscriminate solicitation or agreement to perform sexual acts for hire"). Acts of prostitution are not constitutionally protected, since "[c]ommercial sex is performed for profit and the sexual contact involved is incidental to that profit. . . . The decision to engage in the business of sex for money is not the type of intimate, personal decision which is protected by the right to privacy" under either Federal or Massachusetts law. *Walter*, 388 Mass. at 465. Statute 1983, c. 66 removed the word "prostitutes" from G.L. c. 272, § 53, and created a new statutory offense (§ 53A) which punishes both the prostitute and the prostitute's client. *Commonwealth v. An Unnamed Defendant*, 22 Mass. App. Ct. 230, 234 (1986). Therefore, it is no longer necessary to define prostitution in terms of the *King* case.

II. Customer or Procurer of Prostitute

The defendant is charged with (paying) (agreeing to pay) (offering to pay) another person to engage in sexual conduct with (him) (her) (some third person).

Section 53A of chapter 272 of our General Laws provides as follows:

> "Any person who pays, agrees to pay or offers to pay another person to engage in sexual conduct or to agree to engage in sexual conduct with another natural person may be punished . . . ."

In order to prove the defendant guilty of this offense, the Commonwealth must prove two things beyond a reasonable doubt:

First: That the defendant (paid) (agreed to pay) (or) (offered to pay) another person; and

Second: That the payment was in exchange (for that person's engaging in sexual conduct) (or) (for that person's agreeing to engage in sexual conduct) with (the defendant) (or) (another person).

The defendant may be convicted only if the sexual conduct (was) (was to be) in exchange for a fee, that is, if the transaction was of a commercial nature.

See also G.L. c. 272, § 8 (soliciting for a prostitute).

Supplemental Instruction

"Sexual conduct." The term "sexual conduct" includes (sexual intercourse) (anal intercourse) (fellatio, or oral sex involving contact between the mouth of one person and the penis of another person) (cunnilingus, or oral sex involving contact between the mouth of one person and the female sex organs—the vagina, vulva or labia—of another person) (masturbation of another person) (or) (any other intrusion of a part of one person's body or some other object into the genital or anal opening of another person's body).

> The term "'sexual activity' . . . encompass[es] all acts commonly understood to be described by the term, including masturbation" of another as well as sexual intercourse and deviate sexual intercourse, and is not unconstitutionally vague. *Walter,* 388 Mass. at 463, 465–66. *See, e.g., Commonwealth v. Gallant,* 373 Mass. 577, 584 (1977) (in rape prosecution, "unnatural sexual intercourse" includes "oral and anal intercourse, including fellatio, cunnilingus, and other intrusions of a part of a person's body or other object into the genital or anal opening of another person's body"); *Commonwealth v. Guy,* 24 Mass. App. Ct. 783, 785–87 (1987) (in rape prosecution, "unnatural sexual intercourse" includes female-to-female cunnilingus); *Commonwealth v. Baldwin,* 24 Mass. App. Ct. 200, 204–05, *further appellate review denied,* 400 Mass. 1102 (1987); *overruled in part on other grounds; Commonwealth v. Pagan,* 445 Mass. 161 (2005) (in rape prosecution, "unnatural sexual intercourse" includes digital penetration of vagina, vulva or labia).

NOTE

Selective prosecution of females. The Massachusetts Equal Rights Amendment (art. 106 of the Articles of Amendment to the Massachusetts Constitution) requires that a § 53A charge against a female defendant be dismissed with prejudice upon an appropriate showing that the particular police department or prosecutor's office consistently prosecutes female prostitutes but not their male customers. *An Unnamed Defendant,* 22 Mass. App. Ct. at 233–36. *See Commonwealth v. Hackett,* 383 Mass. 888, 888–89 (1981); *King,* 374 Mass. at 17–22.

Shoplifting

Regulatory Authority—G.L. c. 266, § 30A
Dist. Ct. Model Jury Instruction 8.620

> [If the value is alleged to be $250 or more, include supplemental instruction 3.]

The defendant is charged with (shoplifting) (shoplifting by concealing merchandise) (shoplifting by switching a price tag) (shoplifting by ringing up a false price) (removing a shopping cart). Section 30A of chapter 266 of our General Laws provides in substance:

> *Instruct on one or more of the following alternatives, as applicable:*

A. *Shoplifting.*

In order to prove the defendant guilty of shoplifting, the Commonwealth must prove the following three things beyond a reasonable doubt:

First: That the defendant intentionally (took possession of, carried away, or transferred) (or) (caused to be carried away or transferred) retail merchandise;

Second: That the merchandise was owned or possessed by someone other than the defendant; and

Third: That the defendant (took possession of, carried away, or transferred) (or) (caused to be carried away or transferred) that merchandise and did so (with an intent to deprive the merchant of its possession, use or benefit) (or) (with an intent to convert it to his [her] own use without having paid full value for it).

B. *Shoplifting by concealing merchandise.*

In order to prove the defendant guilty of shoplifting by concealing merchandise, the Commonwealth must prove the following three things beyond a reasonable doubt:

First: That the defendant concealed retail merchandise on his (her) person or elsewhere under his (her) control;

Second: That the merchandise was owned or possessed by someone other than the defendant; and

Third: That the defendant concealed that merchandise (with an intent to deprive the merchant of its possession, use or benefit) (or) (with an intent of converting it to his [her] own use without having paid full value for it).

C. *Shoplifting by switching a price tag.* In order to prove the defendant guilty of shoplifting by switching (a) price tag(s), the Commonwealth must prove the following four things beyond a reasonable doubt:

First: That the price of retail merchandise owned or possessed by someone other than the defendant was contained on a label, price tag or other marking;

Second: That the defendant intentionally (altered) (transferred) (removed) that label, price tag or marking from the merchandise;

Third: That the defendant, personally or by agreement with another person, then attempted to purchase that merchandise at less than the full retail price; and

Fourth: That the defendant did so with the intent to deprive the merchant of all or some part of its retail value.

D. *Shoplifting by switching containers.*

In order to prove the defendant guilty of shoplifting by switching containers, the Commonwealth must prove the following four things beyond a reasonable doubt:

First: That retail merchandise was displayed in or on a container;

Second: That the merchandise was owned or possessed by someone other than the defendant;

Third: That the defendant intentionally transferred the merchandise to some other container; and

Fourth: That the defendant did so with an intent to deprive the merchant of its full price.

E. *Shoplifting by ringing up a false price.*

In order to prove the defendant guilty of shoplifting by ringing up a false price, the Commonwealth must prove the following four things beyond a reasonable doubt:

First: That the defendant intentionally rang up or recorded a price for merchandise;

Second: That the price rung up was less than the actual retail price;

Third: That the defendant knew that the price rung up was less than the actual retail price; and

Fourth: That the defendant acted with the intent to deprive the merchant of the full price.

F. *Removing a shopping cart.*

In order to prove the defendant guilty of removing a shopping card, the Commonwealth must prove the following four things beyond a reasonable doubt:

First: That the defendant intentionally removed a shopping cart from the premises of a retail merchant;

Second: That the cart was owned by someone other than the defendant;

Third: That the defendant removed the cart without the consent of that merchant; and

Fourth: That the defendant did so with an intent to deprive the merchant of the possession or use of the cart permanently.

Supplemental Instructions

1. ***"Retail merchandise."*** "Retail Merchandise" means products or goods that are offered for sale in relatively small quantities directly to consumers. It refers to the type of merchandise sold in an ordinary store open to the public, as opposed to sold in bulk to merchants but not directly to the public.

2. ***"Conceal."*** *To "conceal"* means to cover an object to keep it from being seen or to withdraw an object from view to prevent its discovery. To conceal is to take an action that makes it more difficult for the owner to discover the property or that makes discovery or identification of the property more difficult.

> *Commonwealth v. Balboni*, 26 Mass. App. Ct. 750 (1989).

3. ***Shoplifting $250 or more.*** If you determine that the Commonwealth has proved beyond a reasonable doubt that the defendant is guilty of shoplifting, you must also go on to determine whether (if more than one item stolen: all) the property that was shoplifted was worth $250 or more. You may use your general knowledge in evaluating the value of the property; it is not required that you have any expert evidence of its value.

> Effective April 13, 2018, the aggravated form of this offense was increased from $100 to $250. St. 2018, c. 69, § 139. For offenses committed prior to April 13, 2018, this instruction can be utilized, just inserting $100 wherever it refers to $250.

> The jury may use its common knowledge, and does not require expert evidence, in evaluating value. *Commonwealth v. Hosman*, 257 Mass. 379, 386 (1925); *Commonwealth v. McCann*, 16 Mass. App. Ct. 990, 991 (1983).

NOTES

1. **Larceny prosecution is alternative only for goods with value of $250 or over.** Where the retail value of the goods obtained is less than $250, § 30A shall apply to the exclusion of § 30. G.L. c. 266, § 30A, para. 7.

Stalking

Regulatory Authority—G.L. c. 265, § 43
Dist. Ct. Model Jury Instruction 6.680

The defendant is charged with stalking *[alleged victim]*. Section 43 of chapter 265 of our General Laws provides as follows:

> "Whoever . . . willfully and maliciously engages in a knowing pattern of conduct or series of acts over a period of time directed at a specific person which seriously alarms or annoys that person and would cause a reasonable person to suffer substantial emotional distress, *and* makes a threat with the intent to place the person in imminent fear of death or bodily injury, shall be guilty of the crime of stalking and shall be punished . . . ."

In order to prove the defendant guilty of stalking, the Commonwealth must prove five things beyond a reasonable doubt:

First: That over a period of time the defendant knowingly engaged in a pattern of conduct or series of acts, involving at least three incidents, directed at *[alleged victim]*;

Second: That those acts were of a kind that would cause a reasonable person to suffer substantial emotional distress;

Third: That those acts did cause *[alleged victim]* to become seriously alarmed or annoyed;

Fourth: That the defendant took those actions wilfully and maliciously.

An act is "willful" if it is done intentionally and by design, and not out of mistake or accident.

An act is done with "malice" if the defendant's conduct was intentional and without justification or mitigation, and any reasonable prudent person would have foreseen the actual effect on *[the alleged victim]*.

And *Fifth:* The Commonwealth must prove beyond a reasonable doubt that the defendant also made a threat with the intention of placing *[alleged victim]* in imminent fear of death or bodily injury.

> See Instructions 3.120 (Intent) and 2.240 (Direct and Circumstantial Evidence).

> The model instruction incorporates the definition of stalking found in G.L. c. 265, § 43, as amended by St. 1996, c. 298, § 11 (effective November 7, 1996), which eliminated the two-pronged definition (stalking by harassing or stalking by following) found in the earlier version of § 43, as enacted by St. 1992, c. 31 (effective May 18, 1992). The "threat" element "closely approximates the common law definition of the crime of assault" and is to be so interpreted. *Commonwealth v. Matsos,* 421 Mass. 391, 394 (1995).

> The statutory phrase "pattern of conduct or series of acts" appears to require three or more incidents. *See Kwiatkowski*, 418 Mass. at 548 n.6 (identical phrase in definition of "harasses" in prior version of § 43, coupled with phrase "repeatedly harasses," requires proof of three or more incidents); *Commonwealth v. Martinez*, 43 Mass. App. Ct. 408, 410–11 (1997) (phrase "repeatedly follows" in prior version of § 43 requires proof of three or more incidents). *See also Commonwealth v. Wotan*, 422 Mass. 740, 742 (1996) ("repeatedly" in G.L. c. 269, § 14A requires three rather than two harassing telephone calls because defendant entitled to benefit of plausible ambiguity in statute).

Supplemental Instruction

Communications covered by statute. The conduct, acts or threats may be communicated by any means including, but not limited to (mail) (telephone) (facsimile transmission) (e-mail) (internet communications) (telecommunications device) (electronic instant messages) (any electronic communication device including any device that transfers [signs] [signals] [writing] [images] [sounds] [data] or [intelligence of any nature] transmitted in whole or in part by a [wire] [radio] [electromagnetic system] [photoelectronic system] [photooptical system]).

NOTES

1. **Stalking in violation of a court order.** General Laws c. 265, § 43(b) establishes an aggravated form of this offense with a mandatory minimum penalty if it is committed in violation of a temporary or permanent vacate, restraining or no-contact order or judgment issued pursuant to G.L. c. 208, §§ 18, 34B or 34C, G.L. c. 209, § 32, G.L. c. 209A, §§ 3–5, or G.L. c. 209C, §§ 15 or 20, or a protection order issued by another jurisdiction, or a temporary restraining order or preliminary or permanent injunction issued by the Superior Court. The model instruction should be modified by adding as additional elements the existence and violation of such a court order.

2. **Subsequent offenses not within District Court jurisdiction.** General Laws c. 265, § 43(c) establishes a mandatory minimum penalty for repeat offenders. Subsequent offenses are not within the final jurisdiction of the District Court.

3. **Violation of c. 209A order is lesser included offense.** Violation of a 209A order (G.L. c. 209A, § 7) is a lesser included offense of stalking (G.L. c. 265, § 43), and therefore a defendant who has been convicted of violating a Chapter 209A order may not be convicted of stalking based upon the same conduct. *Edge v. Commonwealth*, 451 Mass. 74, 76–77 (2008).

4. **Harassing letters.** In a prosecution under § 43, a judge should not exclude otherwise-admissible harassing letters sent by the defendant to the complainant, because they are repetitive or unduly prejudicial. The Commonwealth is entitled to present to the jury the totality of the defendant's conduct, since it must prove the victim's alarm or annoyance, and the likelihood that a reasonable person in the victim's position would suffer substantial emotional distress. *Commonwealth v. Matsos,* 421 Mass. at 392 n.3

5. **Willful and malicious conduct.** Willful conduct must be intentional (as opposed to negligent) but does not require that the defendant intend its harmful consequences as well. *Commonwealth v. O'Neil,* 67 Mass. App. Ct. 284, 290–93 (2006) (criminal harassment). The modern definition of "malice" does not require any showing of "cruelty, hostility or revenge, nor does it require an actual intent to cause the required harm, but merely that the conduct be "intentional and without justification or mitigation, and any reasonable prudent person would have foreseen the actual harm that resulted." *Commonwealth v. O'Neil,* 67 Mass. App. Ct. 284, 290–93 (2006). Prior to the *O'Neil* decision, this instruction included language that: "An act is done maliciously if it is done out of cruelty or hostility or revenge, or other wrongful motive."

6. **Pre-1996 incidents.** The model instruction's description of the elements of the offense may also be used for incidents between August 3, 1994 and November 6, 1996 prosecuted under the "harassing" prong of the prior version of § 43. See *Commonwealth v. Kwiatkowski,* 418 Mass. 543 (1994). *Kwiatkowski's* invalidation of pre-August 3, 1994 "harassing" convictions is to be applied retroactively in cases that were on direct appeal when it was decided if the defendant raised the constitutional validity of the statute at trial; if not, the defendant is entitled to have the conviction set aside only if there is a substantial risk of a miscarriage of justice. *Commonwealth v. Matsos,* 421 Mass. at 396–99.

7. **Statement of reasons required if imprisonment not imposed.** A jury session judge sentencing for this or one of the other crimes against persons found in G.L. c. 265 who does not impose a sentence of incarceration "shall include in the record of the case specific reasons for not imposing a sentence of imprisonment," which shall be a public record. G.L. c. 265, § 41.

8. **Venue.** Violations of § 43 may be prosecuted wherever "an act constituting an element of the crime was committed." G.L. c. 277, § 62B.

Theft, Purchase, Receipt, Possession or Concealment of Stolen Motor Vehicle; Malicious Damage to Motor Vehicle; Stealing Parts from Motor Vehicle Taken without Authority; Concealing Motor Vehicle Thief

Regulatory Authority—G.L. c. 266, § 28
Dist. Ct. Model Jury Instruction 8.200

The defendant is charged with (stealing a motor vehicle) (malicious damage to a motor vehicle) (possessing a stolen motor vehicle) (receiving a stolen motor vehicle) (stealing motor vehicle parts) (concealing motor vehicle theft).

In order to prove the defendant guilty of this offense, the Commonwealth must prove beyond a reasonable doubt:

First, that the defendant took the motor vehicle;

Second, that the motor vehicle was owned or possessed by someone other than the defendant; and

Third, that the defendant did so with the intent to deprive that person of the motor vehicle permanently.

> This instruction is modeled after Instruction 8.520, Larceny by Stealing.
>
> The value of the stolen vehicle is not an element of the offense. *Commonwealth. v. Casserly,* 23 Mass. App. Ct. 947, 948 (1986).

To prove the first element, the Commonwealth must prove beyond a reasonable doubt that the defendant physically transferred the motor vehicle to his (her) own control. It does not matter if the transfer involved only slight movement, or if it lasted only for a short time.

> *Commonwealth v. Fielding,* 371 Mass. 97, 117 (1976) (any separation of property from victim's dominion, even if brief in space and time, sufficient); *Commonwealth v. Salerno,* 356 Mass. 642, 648, (1970) (taking can be proved by circumstantial evidence); *Commonwealth v. Bradley,* 2 Mass. App. Ct. 804, 805 (1974) (momentary transfer sufficient); *Commonwealth v. Flowers,* 1 Mass. App. Ct. 415, 418–19 (1973) (immaterial whether the transfer is done by the robber himself or by another person, even by the victim, acting at the robber's direction).

To prove the second element, the Commonwealth must prove beyond a reasonable doubt that the motor vehicle was owned or possessed by a person other than the defendant. This may be proved by direct evidence that someone else owned or possessed the motor vehicle. The Commonwealth is not required to prove who owned or possessed the motor vehicle as long as it proves that the defendant did not.

> G.L. c. 277, § 25 (identity of owner need not be alleged if property described with sufficient certainty); G.L. c. 278, § 9 ("owner" includes anyone in actual or constructive possession). *Commonwealth v. Souza,* 397 Mass. 236, 238–39 (1986) (identity of owner need not be proved, only that it was not defendant; because of G.L. c. 277, § 35, misnomer of owner is immaterial if defendant not misled); *Commonwealth v. Kiernan,* 348 Mass. 29, 50–51 (1964), cert. denied sub nom. *Gordon v. Mass.,* 380 U.S. 913 (1965) ("owner" includes anyone with a possessory or property interest); *Commonwealth v. Binkiewicz,* 342 Mass. 740, 748 (1961) (because of G.L. c. 278, § 9, complaint about "the property of *x*" in effect reads "the property of *x*, or of another but in *x*'s actual or constructive possession"; driver with shared dominion over auto registered in spouse's name is "owner"); *Commonwealth v. Finn,* 108 Mass. 466, 467 (1871) (one may steal from thief); *Commonwealth v. Sullivan,* 104 Mass. 552, 554–55 (1870) (person who orders goods is in constructive possession of them once delivered to a common carrier, absent a shipping agreement to the contrary); *Commonwealth v. Arrance,* 5 Allen 517, 517–18 (1862) (because of G.L. c. 278, § 9, permissible to allege and prove only one co-owner)

To prove the third element, the Commonwealth must prove beyond a reasonable doubt that the defendant intended to deprive the owner or possessor of (his) (her) (its) vehicle permanently. You may, but are not required, to find such intent if the defendant's conduct showed utter indifference as to whether the vehicle would be recovered.

> See Instruction 3.120 (Intent).
>
> *Commonwealth v. Salerno,* 356 Mass. 642, 648, (1970); *Commonwealth v. Cabot,* 241 Mass. 131, 141–43 (1922); *Commonwealth v. Olivera,* 48 Mass. App. Ct. 907, 909 (1999) (difference between larceny of motor vehicle and use without authority is intent to deprive permanently; the latter assumes returning stolen vehicle to its owner or abandoning it where it might be recovered); *Commonwealth v. Moore,* 36 Mass. App. Ct. 455, 456–57 (1994); *Commonwealth v. Coyle,* 17 Mass. App. Ct. 982, 984 (1984); *Commonwealth v. Ellison,* 5 Mass. App. Ct. 862, 862–63 (1977) (intent to make restitution later is not a defense).

If the defendant took another person's motor vehicle in an honest belief that (he) (she) (another person on whose behalf he (she) was acting) had a legal right to it, then you must find the defendant not guilty, even if that belief was in fact mistaken, because he (she) lacked the intent to steal.

Commonwealth v. Liebenow, 470 Mass. 151, 157 (2014) (the specific intent to steal is negated by a finding that a defendant held an honest, albeit mistaken, belief that he was entitled to the property he took).

In order to prove the defendant guilty of this offense, the Commonwealth must prove beyond a reasonable doubt:

First: That the defendant injured or destroyed a motor vehicle

Second: That the vehicle belonged to another person, and

Third: The defendant acted with malice.

The term "malice" refers to a state of mind of cruelty, hostility or revenge. To prove that an act was malicious, the Commonwealth must prove beyond a reasonable doubt not only that it was done deliberately, but also that it was done out of cruelty, hostility or revenge toward another.

Commonwealth v. Chambers, 90 Mass. App. Ct. 137, 143–44 & n.7 (2016).

In order to prove the defendant guilty of this offense, the Commonwealth must prove beyond a reasonable doubt:

First: That the defendant intentionally took a motor vehicle

Second: That he (she) did so without authority of the owner, and

Third: That he (she) stole from it one or more of its parts or accessories.

Here instruct on Intent (Instruction 3.120) and the definition of stealing from Larceny by Stealing (Instruction 8.520).

In order to prove the defendant guilty of this offense, the Commonwealth must prove beyond a reasonable doubt:

First: That the defendant (bought) (received) (possessed) (concealed) (obtained control of) a motor vehicle,

Second: That the motor vehicle had been stolen, and

Third: That the defendant knew or believed it had been stolen.

7

See supplemental instruction on knowledge, below. Where applicable, see instruction on possession (Instruction 3.220)

A person "receives" property by knowingly taking custody or control of it. It is not necessary that the defendant personally possessed the stolen property, as long as it is proved that he (she) knowingly exerted control over it in some way.

Mere presence in a stolen car is insufficient to support an inference of knowledge that the car was stolen, but "presence supplemented by other incriminating evidence will serve to tip the scales." *Commonwealth v. Johnson,* 6 Mass. App. Ct. 956, 957 (1978). *See Commonwealth v. Boone,* 356 Mass. 85, 87 (1969); *Commonwealth v. Johnson,* 7 Mass. App. Ct. 191, 193 (1979). *See also Commonwealth v. Hunt,* 50 Mass. App. Ct. 565, 568–69 (2000).

If defendant learns property was stolen after receiving it. Even if the defendant did not know that the property was stolen at the time when he (she) received it, the defendant is still guilty of receiving stolen property if he (she) subsequently learned that the property had been stolen, and at that point decided to keep it and to deprive the owner of its use.

Commonwealth v. *Sandler*, 368 Mass. 729, 740–41 (1975); *Commissioner of Pub. Safety v.Treadway*, 368 Mass. 155, 160 (1975); *Kirkpatrick*, 26 Mass. App. Ct. 595, 599 (1988).

In order to prove the defendant guilty of this offense, the Commonwealth must prove beyond a reasonable doubt:

First: That a person stole a motor vehicle,

Second: That the defendant knew or believed the person had stolen a motor vehicle, and

Third: That the defendant intentionally concealed that person.

A motor vehicle has been stolen if a person took it away from the person who owned or possessed it with the intent to deprive that person of the vehicle permanently.

See supplemental instruction on knowledge below. Where necessary, see instruction on Larceny by Stealing (Instruction 8.520).

Supplemental Instruction

The Commonwealth must prove beyond a reasonable doubt that the defendant actually knew or believed that (the motor vehicle had been stolen) (the person concealed had stolen a motor vehicle). Mere negligence or failure to exercise a reasonable level of care is not enough. Personal knowledge or belief is required, and our law allows for no substitute.

It is obviously impossible to look directly into a person's mind. But in our everyday affairs, we often look to the actions of others in order to decide what their state of mind is. In this case, you may examine the defendant's actions and words, and all of the surrounding circumstances, to help you determine the extent of the defendant's knowledge.

You should consider all of the evidence, and any reasonable inferences you draw from the evidence, in determining whether the Commonwealth has proved beyond a reasonable doubt, as it must, that the defendant acted with the knowledge that the person he (she) concealed had stolen the motor vehicle in question.

Commonwealth v. Dellamano, 393 Mass. 132, 138 (1984); *Commonwealth v. Boris*, 317 Mass. 309, 315–17 (1944).

NOTES

1. **Altered vehicle identification number as prima facie evidence of knowledge.** "Evidence that an identifying number or numbers of a motor vehicle or trailer or part thereof has been intentionally and maliciously removed, defaced, altered, changed, destroyed, obliterated, or mutilated, shall be prima facie evidence that the defendant knew or had reason to know that the motor vehicle, or trailer or part thereof had been stolen." G.L. c. 266, § 28(a), second par. See Instruction 3.260 (Prima Facie Evidence). *See Commonwealth v. Gonsalves,* 56 Mass. App. Ct. 506, 512 (2002) (emphasizing that "the use of prima facie evidence, sufficient to establish a presumption in favor of the scienter, carries no particular presumption of validity" and that "the presumed fact [scienter] must be proven beyond a reasonable doubt."

2. **Certificate of title as evidence of unauthorized use.** "[C]ertified copies of any motor vehicle or trailer ownership records, including computer records, in the possession of the registrar of motor vehicles, attested by the registrar or his designee or, if the motor vehicle or trailer is registered or titled in another state, such records similarly certified by the keeper of records of the appropriate motor vehicle department, shall be admissible as proof of ownership of a motor vehicle or trailer and shall be prima facie evidence that the use of the motor vehicle or trailer was unauthorized. If the defendant rebuts such evidence, the commonwealth may be granted a reasonable continuance to enable the owner of the vehicle to be brought into court to testify." G.L. c. 22C, § 42. This statutory provision should be presented to the jury only as a permissive inference. See Instruction 3.240 (Presumption). Since its language may imply that the effect of the provision disappears if "rebutt[ed]," it is not clear whether it rises to the level of prima facie evidence, which remains evidence even though contrary evidence is introduced. See the notes to Instruction 3.260 (Prima Facie Evidence).

A defendant's reliance on a title certificate in his or her name is not itself a defense to a charge of receiving a stolen motor vehicle, but merely one factor to be weighed in determining whether the Commonwealth has proven that the defendant knew that the vehicle was stolen. *Casserly,* 23 Mass. App. Ct. at 948.

3. **Charging both theft and receiving.** A defendant may be charged both with theft of a motor vehicle and receiving that stolen motor vehicle, but may not be convicted of both. *Dellamano,* 393 Mass. at 134 n.4.

4. **Restitution is mandatory.** Upon conviction under this section, in addition to any other punishment, a restitution order is mandatory for any financial loss (including, but not limited to, loss of earnings, out-of-

pocket expenses, and replacement costs) sustained by the victim, his dependents or insurer. G.L. c. 266, § 29; G.L. c. 276, § 92A.

Threat to Commit Crime

Regulatory Authority—G.L. c. 275, §§ 2, 4
Dist. Ct. Model Jury Instruction 6.700

The defendant is charged with having threatened to commit a crime against the person or property of another. Threatening [a person with a crime against his or her person or property] [a person by threatening a crime against someone else or their property] is itself a crime.

In order to prove the defendant guilty of this offense, the Commonwealth must prove four things beyond a reasonable doubt:

First: That the defendant expressed an intent to injure a person, or property of another, now or in the future;

Second: That the defendant intended that his (her) threat be conveyed to a particular person;

Third: That the injury that was threatened, if carried out, would constitute a crime; and

Fourth: That the defendant made the threat under circumstances which could reasonably have caused the person to whom it was conveyed to fear that the defendant had both the intention and the ability to carry out the threat.

> G.L. c. 275, §§ 2–4. *Commonwealth v. Chalifoux*, 362 Mass. 811, 816–17 (1973) (victim's testimony of prior assault relevant to issue of apprehension); *Commonwealth v. DeVincent*, 358 Mass. 592, 594–95 (1971); *Commonwealth v. Maiden*, 61 Mass. App. Ct. 433, 436 (2004) (actual receipt by victim of threat not a necessary element; intent that threat be conveyed to target is sufficient, whether or not it was successfully communicated); *Commonwealth v. Hughes*, 59 Mass. App. Ct. 280, 283 (2003); *Commonwealth v. Ditsch*, 19 Mass. App. Ct. 1005 (1985) (immediate or personal ability to carry out threat unnecessary, only "intention and ability in circumstances which would justify apprehension on the part of the recipient"); *Commonwealth v. Daly*, 12 Mass. App. Ct. 338 (1981) (under Mass. R. Crim. P. 4[b], others beside victim may bring complaint). *See also Wagenmann v. Adams*, 829 F.2d 196, 207 (1st Cir. 1987); *Robinson v. Bradley*, 300 F. Supp. 665, 668 (D. Mass. 1969) (3-judge court); *Commonwealth v. Kerns*, 449 Mass. 641 (2007).

Supplemental Instructions

1. ***Victim's apprehension.*** It is not required that *[alleged victim]* actually became apprehensive because of any threat that was made. But you may consider whether or not he (she) *was* apprehensive in determining whether the Commonwealth has proved the fourth thing that it must prove—namely, that the defendant made the threat under circumstances which *could* reasonably have caused *[alleged victim]* to fear that the defendant had both the intention and the ability to carry out the threat.

> *Chalifoux, supra*; *Commonwealth v. Winter*, 9 Mass. App. Ct. 512, 528 (1980). The test for victim apprehension is objective: "Whether the threat by its contents in the circumstances was such as would cause the target of the threat to fear that the threatened crime and injury might be inflicted." *Maiden*, 61 Mass. App. Ct. at 436.

2. ***Threat made indirectly.*** The Commonwealth is not required to prove that the threat was communicated directly to *[alleged victim]*. This element is satisfied if it is proved beyond a reasonable doubt that the defendant *intended* the threat to be conveyed to *[alleged victim]*. This can be done directly or indirectly through a third party or by some other means. The proof may be by direct or circumstantial evidence.

> See Instruction 2.240 (Direct and Circumstantial Evidence). *Commonwealth* v. *Hughes*, 59 Mass. App. Ct. 280, 283 (2003); *Maiden*, 61 Mass. App. Ct. at 435 ("the legal definition of threat requires 'communication' of the threat in the sense that it must be uttered, not idly, but to the target, to one who the defendant intends to pass it on to the target, or to one who the defendant should know will probably pass it on to the target"); *Commonwealth* v. *Furst*, 56 Mass. App. Ct. 283 (2002); *Commonwealth* v. *Meier*, 56 Mass. App. Ct. 278 (2002).

3. ***Unsuccessful communication.*** The Commonwealth is not required to prove that the threat was successfully communicated to *[alleged victim]*. It must prove beyond a reasonable doubt that the defendant made a communication that he intended would reach the *[alleged victim]*, even if he (she) was unsuccessful in doing so. That proof may be by direct or circumstantial evidence.

> See Instruction 2.240 (Direct and Circumstantial Evidence). *Commonwealth* v. *Kerns*, 449 Mass. 641 (2007); *Commonwealth v. Maiden*, 61 Mass. App. Ct. 433, 436 (2004); *Commonwealth* v. *Hughes*, 59 Mass. App. Ct. 280, 283 (2003); *Commonwealth v. Furst*, 56 Mass. App. Ct. 283 (2002); *Commonwealth* v. *Meier*, 56 Mass. App. Ct. 278 (2002).

NOTES

1. **Warrantless arrest.** General Laws c. 275, §§ 2–6 does not authorize warrantless arrest for threats. *Commonwealth v. Jacobsen*, 419 Mass. 269 (1995).

2. **First Amendment.** The offense of threatening to commit a crime only reaches cases of "true threats," which do not qualify as protected speech. *Commonwealth v. Sholley*, 432 Mass. 721, 727 (2000). The term "true threat" distinguishes between words that literally threaten but have an expressive purpose such as political hyperbole, and words that are intended to place the target of the threat in fear. *Commonwealth v. Chou*, 433 Mass. 229, 236 (2001). *Compare Watts v. United States*, 394 U.S. 705, 706, 708 (1969) (per curiam) (statement at political rally that, if inducted into Army and made to carry rifle, "the first man I want to get in my sights is L.B.J.," was, given its conditional nature and context in which it was made, political hyperbole and, therefore, not a "true threat" under 18 U.S.C. § 871[a]), with *United States v. Fulmer*, 108 F.3d 1486, 1490, 1492 (1st Cir. 1997) (voicemail message to Federal agent that "[t]he silver bullets are coming. . . . Enjoy the intriguing unraveling of what I said to you" was, given defendant's history of threats against the agent, reasonably understood as a "true threat" under 18 U.S.C. § 875[c]). *See also Chou*, 433 Mass. at 237 (2001) (missing person flyer describing ex-girlfriend in sexually offensive and abusive language was a "true threat").

3. **Length of probationary sentence.** General Laws c. 275, § 4 authorizes a maximum sentence of six months imprisonment or, alternatively, a peace bond for a maximum period of six months. There is no six-month limitation on any probationary period. *Commonwealth v. Powers*, 73 Mass. App. Ct. 186 (2008).

Trespass

Regulatory Authority—G.L. c. 266, § 120
Dist. Ct. Model Jury Instruction 8.220

The defendant is charged with trespass.

In order to prove the defendant guilty of trespass, the Commonwealth must prove two things beyond a reasonable doubt:

First: That, without right, the defendant entered or remained (in a dwelling house) (in a building) (on a boat) (on improved or enclosed land) of another; and

Second: That the defendant was forbidden both to enter or to remain there by the person in lawful control of the premises, either directly or by means of a posted notice.

> *Commonwealth v. Richardson*, 313 Mass. 632, 637 (1943) (the two forbidden acts are phrased disjunctively); *Commonwealth v. Einarson*, 6 Mass. App.

Ct. 835 (1978) (municipal ordinance or regulation forbidding trespass after dark must be introduced in evidence).

The first requirement is satisfied by proof that the defendant either entered on the premises without permission, or failed to leave after being requested to do so. To satisfy the second element, the Commonwealth is not required to prove that the defendant actually saw a notice forbidding trespassing. The Commonwealth is only required to prove that there was a reasonably distinct notice forbidding trespass, and that it was posted in a reasonably suitable place so that a reasonably careful trespasser would see it.

Fitzgerald v. Lewis, 164 Mass. 495, 500–01 (1895) (notice need not be signed or indicate the basis of its authority).

To satisfy the second element by proving that the owner "directly" forbade entry to the defendant, the law does not require a person having control of unposted premises to be on the premises at all times of the day or night to personally warn off intruders. Such a person may also bar entry by securing the premises with secure fences or walls and with locked gates or doors, and this is considered to be "directly" forbidding entry to the premises.

Commonwealth v. A Juvenile (No. 1), 6 Mass. App. Ct. 106, 108 (1978).

NOTES

1. **"Another's" property.** Evidence supporting an inference that the property did not belong to the defendant is sufficient to establish that the property belonged to another. *Commonwealth v. Averill,* 12 Mass. App. Ct. 260, 263 (1981).

2. **Without right.** "A belief on the part of the person entering upon land not in his control that the land is his" is still an entry without right. *Fitzgerald v. Lewis,* 164 Mass. 495, 501 (1895).

3. **External deck, porch, steps.** An external deck or porch, or steps leading to the front door, are properly regarded as part of a building for purposes of the trespass statute. *Commonwealth v. Wolf,* 34 Mass. App. Ct. 949, 949 (1993).

7

4. **Holdover tenants.** A trespass charge may not be brought against holdover tenants; instead the owner must resort to civil proceedings. G.L. c. 266, § 120. As to a foreclosing mortgagee's rights, see *Attorney General v. Dime Savings Bank of New York, FSB,* 413 Mass. 284 (1992).

5. **Implied license.** Under some circumstances, a person may be privileged to enter onto another's property to determine whether the person in control wishes to deal with him, and for passage off upon receiving a negative answer. *See Commonwealth v. Hood,* 389 Mass. 581, 589–90 (1983); *Commonwealth v. Krasner,* 360 Mass. 848, 848 (1971) (such implied license may extend to some parts of property but not others); *Richardson,* 313 Mass. at 638–41.

6. **Not lesser included offense of breaking and entering.** Trespass is not a lesser included offense of breaking and entering. *Commonwealth v. Vinnicombe,* 28 Mass. App. Ct. 934 (1990).

7. **Public property.** General Laws c. 266, § 120 may be applied to state or municipal property as well as to privately owned property. *Commonwealth v. Egleson,* 355 Mass. 259, 262 (1969). The model instruction may be adapted for a complaint brought under G.L. c. 266, § 123 (trespass on certain public property).

8. **Necessity defense.** In determining whether a defendant has satisfied the foundational requirements to claim necessity (see Instruction 9.240), the requirement that a defendant must present enough evidence to demonstrate at least a reasonable doubt that there were no effective legal alternatives available does not require a defendant "to rebut every alternative that is conceivable; rather, a defendant is required to rebut alternatives that likely would have been considered by a reasonable person in a similar situation." *Commonwealth v. Magadini,* 474 Mass. 593, 601 (2016) (defendant's testimony that he had been denied entry to the local homeless shelter, that he was unable to rent an apartment despite repeated attempts, and that he had no place else to stay was sufficient for the issue to go to the jury; whether it is an effective legal alternative for a homeless person to seek shelter outside of his or her home town is a question of fact for the jury to decide).

9. **Related statutes.** *See* G.L. c. 266, §§ 121 (trespass with firearms), 121A (trespass with vehicle), 120A (owner of trespassing parked vehicle is prima facie the trespasser), 120D (disposal of trespassing parked vehicle), 120B (abutter's privilege), 120C (surveyor's privilege).

Unnatural and Lascivious Act

Regulatory Authority—G.L. c. 272, § 35
Dist. Ct. Model Jury Instruction 7.500

The defendant is accused of having committed an unnatural and lascivious act. Section 35 of chapter 272 of our General Laws provides as follows: "Whoever commits any unnatural and lascivious act with another person shall be punished . . . ."

The purpose of the statute is to prevent public sexual conduct that might give offense to persons present in a place that is frequented by members of the public.

In order to prove the defendant guilty of this offense, the Commonwealth must prove three things beyond a reasonable doubt:

First: That the defendant committed an unnatural and lascivious act with another person. The term "unnatural and lascivious act" includes (anal intercourse) (fellatio, or oral sex involving contact between the mouth of one person and the penis of another person) (cunnilingus, or oral sex involving contact between the mouth of one person and the female sex organs—the vagina, vulva or labia—of another person) (masturbation of another person) (or) (any other intrusion of a part of one person's body or some other object into the genital or anal opening of another person's body);

Second: That the defendant committed that act intentionally; and

Third: That the sexual act was done in a public place; that is, a place where the defendant either intended public exposure, or recklessly disregarded a substantial risk of public exposure at that time and under those circumstances, to others who might be offended by such conduct.

The defendant cannot be found guilty of this charge if he (she) desired privacy for a sexual act

If relevant: with another consenting adult

and took reasonable measures in order to secure that privacy. Therefore the Commonwealth must prove that in choosing that particular locale, the defendant either intended public exposure or recklessly disregarded a substantial risk of public exposure at that place and time.

See Instructions 3.120 (Intent) and 3.140 (Knowledge).

G.L. c. 277, § 45 ("allegation that the defendant committed an unnatural and lascivious act with the person named or referred to in the indictment shall be sufficient"). *Commonwealth v. Ferguson*, 384 Mass. 13, 16 (1981) (in circumstances, parking lot was not a public place) (statutory objective is to prevent possibility of offense to persons present in a place frequented by the public; theoretical right of public access is insufficient, since a "place may be public at some times and under some circumstances and not public at others"; statute cannot be applied to the consensual acts of "persons who desire privacy and who take reasonable measures to secure it," but only to persons who "intended . . . or recklessly disregarded a substantial risk of exposure . . . . The Commonwealth must prove that the likelihood of being observed by casual passersby must have been reasonably foreseeable to the defendant, or stated otherwise, that the defendant acted upon an unreasonable expectation that his conduct would remain secret"); *Commonwealth v. Scagliotti*, 373 Mass. 626, 628 (1977) (private cubicle in motion picture theatre) (statute cannot be applied to private places removed from public view which eliminate the possibility of offending persons in place frequented by the public); *Commonwealth v. Balthazar*, 366 Mass. 298, 302 (1974), *habeas corpus granted sub nom. Balthazar v. Superior Court*, 428 F. Supp. 425 (D. Mass. 1977) (statute inapplicable to consensual conduct of adults unless committed in a public place); *Commonwealth v. Morrill*, 68 Mass. App. Ct. 812 (2007) (holding cell and basement hallway of courthouse were public places under G.L. c. 272, § 35); *Commonwealth v. Bloom*, 18 Mass. App. Ct. 951, 952 (1984) (open area of public toilet, as distinguished from inside of stall, is a public place).

The definition of what constitutes "unnatural" sexual intercourse is drawn from *Commonwealth v. Gallant*, 373 Mass. 577, 584 (1977) (in rape prosecution, "unnatural sexual intercourse" includes "oral and anal intercourse, including fellatio, cunnilingus, and other intrusions of a part of a person's body or other object into the genital or anal opening of another person's body"). *See also Commonwealth v. Sefranka*, 382 Mass. 108, 116 (1980) (statute includes public fellatio and oral-anal contact); *Commonwealth v. Delano*, 197 Mass. 166, 166–67 (1908) (statute is applicable to "any and all unnatural and lascivious acts with another person," but not copulation, i.e. "the natural act of coition"); *Commonwealth v. Dill*, 160 Mass. 536, 536–37 (1894) (statute was enacted to apply to a broader range of sexual acts than the common law definition of sodomy); *Commonwealth v. Benoit*, 26 Mass. App. Ct. 641, 646–48 (1988) (cunnilingus is an "unnatural and lascivious act" and, except in a rape prosecution, does not require proof of penetration of the genital opening); *Commonwealth v. Guy*, 24 Mass. App. Ct. 783, 785–87 (1987) (in rape prosecution, "unnatural sexual intercourse" includes female-to-female cunnilingus); *Commonwealth v. Baldwin*, 24 Mass. App. Ct. 200, 204–05, *further appellate review denied*, 400 Mass. 1102 (1987); *overruled in part; Commonwealth v. Pagan*, 445 Mass. 161 (2005) (in rape prosecution, "unnatural sexual intercourse" includes digital contact with vagina, vulva or labia). *Jaquith v. Commonwealth*, 331 Mass. 439, 442 (1954) held that "unnatural and lascivious" are words of common usage meaning "irregular indulgence in sexual behavior, illicit sexual relations, and infamous conduct which is lustful, obscene and in deviation of accepted customs and manners," but *Benoit*, 26 Mass. App. Ct. at 649, has cautioned that "the broad language of *Jaquith* . . . would be inappropriate standing alone in jury instructions today [without being] promptly pinned down by specific instructions" (citation omitted).

NOTES

1. **Nonconsensual conduct.** The statute may be applied to nonconsensual conduct, in which case the public nature of the act is not an element of the offense, but absence of consent is. *Balthazar*, 366 Mass. at 302–03. In such prosecutions, absence of consent is an element of the offense that must be proved as part of the Commonwealth's case-in-chief, not a matter of defense to be raised by the defendant. *Commonwealth v. Reilly*, 5 Mass. App. Ct. 435, 437 (1977). The third element of the model instruction may be appropriately adapted in such cases.

2. **Unnatural and lascivious act with child under 16 (G.L. c. 272, § 35A).** Nonconsent is not an element of a violation of § 35. Unlike prosecutions under § 35 involving consent adults, § 35A may be applied to private as well as public sexual acts. *Benoit*, 26 Mass. App. Ct. at 643–46.

Use of Vehicle without Authority

Regulatory Authority—G.L. c. 90, § 24(2)(a)
Dist. Ct. Model Jury Instruction 5.660

The defendant is charged with knowingly using a motor vehicle without authority. Section 24(2)(a) of chapter 90 of our General Laws provides that ". . . whoever uses a motor vehicle without authority knowing that such use is unauthorized . . ." shall be punished.

In order to prove the defendant guilty of this offense, the Commonwealth must prove three things beyond a reasonable doubt:

First: That the defendant used a motor vehicle;

Second: That at the time he (she) used that motor vehicle, he (she) did so without the permission of the owner, or the permission of some other person who possessed the legal right of control ordinarily exercised by the owner; and

Third: That at the time he (she) used the motor vehicle, the defendant *knew* that he (she) was not authorized to use that vehicle.

A person "uses" a motor vehicle within the meaning of the law if he rides in it, either as the driver or as a passenger. It is not necessary that the defendant personally drove or controlled the vehicle, only that he (she) rode in it while it moved.

The Commonwealth may prove that the defendant was not authorized to use the vehicle either by testimony from the owner or other person in charge of the vehicle, or through inferences that you are reasonably able to draw from all the circumstances.

Finally, the defendant must have *known* that his (her) use of the motor vehicle was unauthorized. If it has been proved that the defendant was a passenger in the vehicle, that fact alone does not establish that he (she) *knew* that he (she) was not authorized to use it. You should consider all of the circumstances, and any reasonable inferences which you can draw from the evidence, in determining whether the defendant had actual knowledge that his (her) use of the vehicle was unauthorized. If the defendant did *not* know that his (her) use was unauthorized, you must find him (her) not guilty.

NOTES

1. **Knowledge.** Mere presence is not enough to support an inference of guilty knowledge, and therefore the owner's testimony that he had not authorized use of the vehicle is not enough, without more, to convict a defendant-passenger of knowledge that the use was unauthorized. *Commonwealth v. Boone,* 356 Mass. 85, 87 (1969); *Commonwealth v. Conway,* 2 Mass. App. Ct. 547, 554 (1974). Mere presence plus consciousness-of-guilt evidence is similarly insufficient. *Commonwealth v. Butler,* 7 Mass. App. Ct. 918 (1979); *Commonwealth v. Johnson,* 6 Mass. App. Ct. 956 (1978). However, presence coupled with other incriminating evidence can be sufficient to permit an inference of knowledge. *Id.; Commonwealth v. Porter,* 15 Mass. App. Ct. 331 (1983) (inference of knowledge from unexplained, or incredible explanation of, possession of recently stolen vehicle).

2. **Lack of authority.** Authorization apparently may be given either by the owner or "by one who in law possesses the right of control ordinarily vested in the owner." *Commonwealth v. Coleman,* 252 Mass. 241, 243 (1925). *See Commonwealth v. Campbell,* 352 Mass. 387, 402 (1967). The owner or controller's testimony is not always essential; lack of authority can be inferred from circumstantial evidence (e.g., of stealth). *See Commonwealth v. Patti,* 10 Mass. App. Ct. 857, 857–58 (1980).

3. **Larceny of motor vehicle as lesser included offense.** Use of a motor vehicle without authority is a lesser included offense of larceny of a motor vehicle (G.L. c. 266, § 28), without the element of intending to deprive the owner of possession permanently. *Commonwealth v. Giannino,* 371 Mass. 700, 703 (1977); *Commonwealth v. Linder,* 17 Mass. App. Ct. 967, 967 (1983).

4. **Public way.** "Public way" is not an element of the crime of use of a motor vehicle without authority. *Commonwealth v. Morris M.,* 70 Mass. App. Ct. 688, 693 (2007), *review denied,* 450 Mass. 1110 (2008) (rejecting dictum in *Commonwealth v. Giannino,* 371 Mass. at 702, suggesting that "in a public way" is a fourth element of offense).

5. **Use.** The statutory term "use" includes use as a passenger. *Coleman, above.* However, "use" requires some movement of the vehicle; merely sitting on the passenger side of a stationary motor vehicle in a parking lot is insufficient. *Linder, above.*

6. **Not lesser included offense of receiving stolen motor vehicle.** Use without authority is not a lesser included offense of the crime of receiving a stolen motor vehicle. *Commonwealth v. Bynoe,* 49 Mass. App. Ct. 687, 691 (2000). Consequently, an acquittal on the latter would not bar a prosecution on the former. *Commonwealth v. Bynoe,* 49 Mass. App. Ct. 687, 691 (2000).

Uttering

Regulatory Authority—G.L. c. 267, § 28. See also G.L. c. 267, § 5 et seq.
Dist. Ct. Model Jury Instruction 8.240

The defendant is charged with the offense of uttering a false, forged or altered (check) (promissory Note) (order for other property). "Uttering" means attempting to pass a worthless legal document in circulation as genuine. Section 5 of chapter 267 of our General Laws provides as follows:

> "Whoever with intent to injure or defraud, utters and publishes as true a false, forged or altered [order for money, which is commonly called a "check"] [or] [promissory note] [or] [order for other property], knowing the same to be false, forged or altered, shall be punished . . . ."

In order to prove the defendant guilty of this offense, the Commonwealth must prove four things beyond a reasonable doubt:

First: That the defendant passed or attempted to pass as true and genuine (a check or other order for money) (a promissory note) (an order for other property);

Second: That the (check) (promissory note) (order for property) was (falsely made) (forged) (altered);

Third: That the defendant knew it was (falsely made) (forged) (altered); and

Fourth: That the defendant passed or attempted to pass it with the specific intent to injure or defraud someone.

To prove the first element, the Commonwealth need not prove that the (check) (promissory note) (order for property) was successfully passed to someone. It is sufficient if the Commonwealth proves beyond a reasonable doubt that the defendant attempted to pass it to someone, even if (he) (she) was unsuccessful in doing so.

To establish the second element, the Commonwealth need not prove that the whole (check) (promissory note) (order for property) was (falsified) (forged) (altered), but only that one or more significant parts of it were (falsified) (forged) (altered).

To prove the fourth element—that the defendant intended to defraud someone—the Commonwealth need not prove the identity of the person whom the defendant intended to defraud, but it must prove that the defendant intended to defraud someone.

> See Instructions 3.120 (Intent), 3.140 (Knowledge) and 8.160 (Forgery).
>
> *Commonwealth v. O'Connell,* 438 Mass. 658, 664 n.9 (2003) (elements of uttering); *Commonwealth v. Analetto,* 326 Mass. 115, 118 (1950) (defendant must have intended to defraud someone, but not necessarily any particular person); *Commonwealth v. Segee,* 218 Mass. 501, 504 (1914) (forgery requires only some material change in document); *Commonwealth v. Bond,* 188 Mass. 91 (1905) (not necessary that intended victim have been misled by forgery). *See Commonwealth v. Crocker,* 384 Mass. 353, 358 (1981) (uttering not a lesser included offense of larceny by false pretenses); *Commonwealth v. Russell,* 156 Mass. 196, 196–97 (1861) (prior acts of uttering admissible as to knowledge and intent); *Commonwealth v. Hill,* 11 Mass. 136, 136–37 (1814) (uttering may be accomplished through innocent agent).

NOTES

1. **District Court jurisdiction over uttering offenses.** General Laws c. 267, § 5 is a 10-year felony that punishes anyone who "with intent to injure or defraud, utters and publishes as true a false, forged or altered record, deed, instrument or other writing mentioned in [G.L. c. 267, §§ 1–4], knowing the same to be false, forged or altered." The District Court does not have final jurisdiction over uttering most of the items referenced in § 5 and listed in §§ 1–4, but only over "uttering as true . . . a forged [promissory] note or order [for money or other property], knowing the same to be forged." G.L. c. 218, § 26. The District Court also has final jurisdiction over the 3-year felony of uttering a false "railroad ticket, railroad mileage book or railroad pass, or a ticket, badge, pass or any written or printed license purporting to entitle the holder or owner thereof to admission to any exhibition, entertainment, performance, match or contest" (G.L. c. 271, § 6) and the 5-year felony of uttering a false "bank bill or promissory note payable to the bearer thereof or to the order of any person" or a traveler's check (G.L. c. 267, § 10). The instruction may be adapted appropriately to cover such items.

2. **Checks.** Uttering a false, forged or altered check may be prosecuted under G.L. c. 267, § 5 because a check is "an order . . . for money" (G.L. c. 267, § 1). *See O'Connell, supra, passim; Bond, supra;* G.L. c. 106, § 3-104 (a check is "a draft, other than a documentary draft, payable on demand and drawn on a bank" and is an order if, among other things, it is "an unconditional promise or order to pay a fixed amount of money"). Uttering a false check is not within the scope of G.L. c. 267, § 10 (uttering a false note) or 12 (possession with intent to utter a false note) because a check is not a "note," "promissory note," "bank bill" or "bank note" within the meaning of those sections. An attempt to negotiate a false check will support a conviction for attempted larceny (G.L. c. 266, § 30). *Commonwealth v. Green,* 66 Mass. App. Ct. 901 (2006).

3. **Claim of authority.** Lack of authority is not an element of the offense of uttering, but if a claim of authority is properly raised, the Commonwealth must prove the absence of authority beyond a reasonable doubt in order to prove the element of fraudulent intent. Such a claim must be raised by timely written notice pursuant to Mass. R. Crim. P. 14(b)(3) or is waived. Lack of authority and fraudulent intent may be proved by circumstantial evidence as well as by testimony from the purported maker. *O'Connell,* 438 Mass. at 664–65. See Instruction 3.160 (License or Authority).

Vandalism

Regulatory Authority—G.L. c. 266, § 126A
Dist. Ct. Model Jury Instruction 8.250

The defendant is charged with having committed vandalism. In order to prove that the defendant is guilty of having committed the offense of vandalism, the Commonwealth must prove four things beyond a reasonable doubt:

First: That the defendant (painted) (marked) (scratched) (etched) (injured) (marred) (defaced) (or) (destroyed) property;

Second: That the defendant did so intentionally;

Third: That the defendant did so (wilfully with malice) (wantonly); and

Fourth: That the property was owned or possessed by someone other than the defendant.

To prove the second element, the Commonwealth must prove the defendant acted consciously and deliberately, rather than by accident or as the result of negligence.

To prove the third element, the Commonwealth must prove that the defendant acted (wilfully with malice) (or) (wantonly).

If willful and malicious conduct is alleged:

A person acts wilfully if (he) (she) intends both the conduct and its harmful consequences. The act must be done with the intent that it have harmful consequences.

An act is done with "malice" if it is done out of cruelty, hostility or revenge. To act with malice, one must act not only deliberately, but out of cruelty, hostility or revenge toward another.

> *Commonwealth v. Chambers*, 90 Mass. App. Ct. 137, 144–45 (2016).

If wanton conduct is alleged:

A person acts wantonly by acting recklessly or with indifference to the fact that (his) (her) conduct would probably cause substantial injury to, or destruction of, another's property. The Commonwealth must prove that the defendant consciously disregarded, or was indifferent to this probability.

Conduct is wanton if (1) the defendant knew it would create a risk of substantial injury or destruction to an-other's property, or (2) a reasonable person—knowing what the defendant knew—would have realized the act posed a risk of substantial injury to or destruction of another's property.

It is not enough for the Commonwealth to prove that the defendant acted negligently—that is, acted in a way that a reasonably careful person would not. To prove the defendant acted wantonly, the Commonwealth must prove that the defendant's actions went beyond mere negligence and amounted to to wanton conduct as I have defined that term.

The defendant must have intended his (her) act, in the sense that it did not happen accidentally.

If relevant to evidence: If you find that the defendant's act occurred by accident, then you must find the defendant not guilty.

Supplemental Instructions

A person cannot be convicted of wanton injury to property unless it was likely that his actions would result in substantial damage to others or their property. It is not enough that some slight or insignificant injury was likely to result. A person acts "wantonly" only if it is likely that his actions will result in substantial harm.

However, it is not necessary that the damage actually was substantial, only that such actions were likely to cause substantial damage. The actual outcome of someone's actions is sometimes a matter of luck, and here the law measures the nature of the actions, not the outcome.

> *Commonwealth v. Ruddock*, 25 Mass. App. Ct. 508, 512–14 (1988).

NOTES

1. Malicious act must be wilful; wanton act requires only general intent. The offense in G.L. c. 266, § 126A, includes two distinct theories with distinct elements. In order to prove malicious conduct, a specific intent must be proved and the act must be wilful and the defendant must have a specific intent to engage in the conduct and to achieve its harmful consequences. In order to prove wanton conduct, a general intent is all that is required. *Commonwealth v. McDowell*, 62 Mass. App. Ct. 15, 18–24, *rev. denied*, 442 Mass. 1113 (2004).

Wilful and malicious property destruction is a specific intent crime requiring proof that the defendant intended both the conduct and its harmful consequences, while wanton property destruction requires only a showing that the actor's conduct was indifferent to, or in disregard of, the probable consequences. *Commonwealth v. Armand*, 411 Mass. 167, 170–71 (1991); *Commonwealth v. Redmond*, 53 Mass. App. Ct. 1, 5, *rev. denied*, 435 Mass. 1107 (2001). "The forcible entry into an office will, without doubt, result in some destruction of property, but a messy thief is not necessarily malicious within the meaning of the statute." *Redmond*, 53 Mass. App. Ct. at 5. "The essence of the distinction appears to lie in the fact that a wilful actor intends both his conduct and the resulting harm whereas a wanton or reckless actor intends his conduct but not necessarily the resulting harm." *Commonwealth v. Smith*, 17 Mass. App. Ct. 918, 920 (1983). As an example, if youths throw rocks from a bridge and one strikes a car passing below, the act is wanton if the rocks were thrown casually, without thought of striking any cars, but the act is wilful and malicious if the rocks were aimed at passing cars. *Commonwealth v. Cimino*, 34 Mass. App. Ct. 925, 927 (1993). "It is worth noting that destruction of property which accompanies even violent crime may not by that token alone qualify as wilful and malicious." *Id.*

Violation of an Abuse Prevention Order under G.L. c. 209A

Regulatory Authority—G.L. c. 209A, § 7
Dist. Ct. Model Jury Instruction 6.720

The defendant is charged with knowingly violating an abuse prevention order issued by a court. Section 7 of chapter 209A of our General Laws provides in substance that: It is unlawful to violate an order issued pursuant to that chapter which orders the defendant:

(to refrain from abusing the person who requested the order) (or that person's child); (or) (to refrain from contacting the person who requested the order) (or that person's child) unless authorized by a court; (or) (to stay a particular distance away from the person who requested the order) (or that person's child); (or) (to vacate and remain away from the [household] [multiple family dwelling] of the person who requested the order); (or) (to vacate and remain away from the work place of the person who requested the order).

In order to prove the defendant guilty of this offense, the Commonwealth must prove four things beyond a reasonable doubt:

First: That a court had issued an order pursuant to chapter 209A of our General Laws which ordered the defendant (to refrain from abusing [*name of plaintiff or child*]); (or) (to refrain from contacting [*name of plaintiff or child*] (directly or indirectly) unless authorized by a court); (or) (to stay a particular distance away from the person who requested the order [or that person's child]); (or) (to vacate and remain away from the household or multiple family dwelling of [name of plaintiff or child]); (or) (to remain away from the workplace of [*name of plaintiff or child*] [located at [*address*]).

Second: That such order was in effect on the date that this violation of the order allegedly occurred;

Third: That the defendant knew that the pertinent term(s) of the order (was) (were) in effect, either by having received a copy of the order or by having learned of them in some other way; and

Fourth: That the defendant violated the order by (abusing [*name of plaintiff or child*]) (or) (contacting [*name of plaintiff or child*] [directly or indirectly] unless authorized by a court); (or) (failing to stay a particular distance away from the person who requested the order [or that person's child]); (or) (failing to vacate and remain away from the household or multiple family dwelling of [*name of plaintiff or child*]) (or) (failing to remain away from the workplace of [*name of plaintiff or child*] [located at [*address*]).

> Here the jury must be instructed on "Knowledge" (Instruction 3.140). *Commonwealth v. Gordon*, 407 Mass. 340 (1990).

Supplemental Instructions

1. ***"Abuse."***

By "abuse" the law means: (causing or attempting to cause another person physical harm); (or) (placing another person in fear of immediate serious physical harm); (or) (causing another person by force or threat or duress to engage involuntarily in sexual relations).

> G.L. c. 209A, § 1.

2. ***"Accidental contact."***

If there is evidence suggesting that the alleged (contact) (encounter) may have occurred by accident, the Commonwealth must prove one of two things beyond a reasonable doubt: either that the alleged (contact) (encounter) did not occur by accident or, if it did occur by accident, that the defendant failed to take reasonable steps to end the accidental (contact) (encounter).

An accident is an unexpected happening that occurs without intention or design on a person's part. A (contact) (encounter) was accidental if the defendant did not have reason to know or believe that [*name of plaintiff or child*] would be present at that time or place.

If a (contact) (encounter) occurred by accident, the defendant was required to take reasonable steps to end the (contact) (encounter). The defendant must be found not guilty unless the Commonwealth proves beyond a reasonable doubt that he (she) could have taken steps to terminate the accidental (contact) (encounter) but unreasonably delayed or failed to do so.

The Commonwealth is not required to prove that the defendant intended to violate the abuse prevention order. It must prove only that he (she) intended the act which would constitute a violation.

So if the evidence raises the possibility that the defendant did not know or could not reasonably have known that [*name of plaintiff or child*] would be present at the time and place alleged, then the Commonwealth must prove beyond a reasonable doubt either that the (contact) (encounter) was *not* accidental or, if it was accidental, that the defendant failed to take reasonable steps to end it.

If the Commonwealth has proved beyond a reasonable doubt each element of the offense and also proved beyond a reasonable doubt either that the (contact) (encounter) was *not* accidental or that the defendant did not take reasonable steps to end an accidental encounter, you should return a verdict of guilty.

If the Commonwealth failed to prove beyond a reasonable doubt any element of the offense, you must return a verdict of not guilty. In addition, if the Commonwealth failed to prove beyond a reasonable doubt either that the (contact) (encounter) was *not* accidental or that the defendant unreasonably delayed in ending an accidental (contact) (encounter), you must return a verdict of not guilty.

If a person subject to a restraining order happens upon a protected person whom he or she did not and could not reasonably know to be present at that time and place, the party subject to the order must make reasonable efforts to terminate the accidental encounter. *Commonwealth v. Stoltz,* 73 Mass. App. Ct. 642 (2009). When there is evidence that fairly raises the issue of accident, the burden falls on the Commonwealth to disprove it. See *Commonwealth v. Zezima,* 387 Mass. 748, 756 (1982); *Commonwealth v. Ferguson,* 30 Mass. App. Ct. 580, 583 (1991) ("Where the evidence raises the possibility of accident, the defendant is, as matter of due process, entitled upon request to a jury instruction that the Commonwealth has the burden of proving beyond a reasonable doubt that the act was not accidental").

See notes to Instruction 9.100 (Accident).

3. ***"Incidental Contact."*** If there is evidence before you that suggests that the alleged contact may have been incidental to a legitimate, lawful activity such as *(e.g., contacting a child, going to work, going to school)*, then the Commonwealth must prove beyond a reasonable doubt that the alleged violation was not incidental to that permitted activity. Conduct that is incidental to legitimate, lawful activity is conduct which is connected to that activity—conduct which is purely or naturally a reasonable outgrowth or necessary part of that legitimate, lawful activity.

7

So, for example, if a person subject to an abuse prevention order waited in the only public hallway of a courthouse for the start of a hearing, and the person protected by that order was waiting somewhere else in that same public hallway, that conduct would be incidental to a legitimate, lawful activity—attending the court hearing. Although there might be a stay away order in effect, there would be no violation of that order because the conduct was purely a natural and reasonable outgrowth of the scheduling of the hearing.

On the other hand, if the subject entered the public hallway and intentionally stood directly next to the plaintiff when the subject could have stood elsewhere, that would violate the order because it was not incidental or necessary to the lawful activity.

The Commonwealth may prove that the defendant's conduct was not incidental to a lawful activity by proving that the alleged violation was not purely or naturally a reasonable outgrowth or necessary part of that legitimate, lawful activity.

Put another way, the Commonwealth must prove that the defendant's conduct was not a good faith attempt by the defendant to do that which was permitted.

In deciding whether there was any contact which violated the abuse prevention order, you may consider any evidence bearing upon: (1) the nature and purpose of any contact; (2) the number of contacts over time; (3) the length of any contact; and (4) the substance and tenor of any statements made during any contact.

You should consider all the evidence in the case to decide whether any contact was made in good faith for a legitimate reason or whether that reason was merely a pretext or excuse for contacting the protected party, *[name of plaintiff or child]*. If the Commonwealth has proved beyond a reasonable doubt each of the elements of the offense and also that the violation was not committed incidental to a legitimate, lawful activity, you should return a verdict of guilty. If the Commonwealth has failed to prove beyond a reasonable doubt any of the elements of the offense or that the contact(s) was (were) not incidental to a legitimate, lawful activity, you must return a verdict of not guilty.

Commonwealth v. *Silva*, 431 Mass. 194 (2000); *Commonwealth v. Consoli,* 58 Mass. App. Ct. 734, 738 (2003); *Commonwealth v. Stewart,* 52 Mass. App. Ct. 755 (2001); *Commonwealth v. Leger,* 52 Mass. App. Ct. 232 (2001); *Commonwealth v. Mendonca,* 50 Mass. App. Ct. 684, 687 n.8 (2001).

4. ***Violation through third party.*** If there is evidence that the conduct by which the defendant is alleged to have violated the abuse prevention order resulted from the action of a third person, the Commonwealth must prove beyond a reasonable doubt that the defendant had an intent, or shared an intent with the third person, to do an act that could result in a violation of the protective order. The defendant is not guilty unless he (she) had such an intent or shared intent. The defendant cannot be found guilty for an act of another person which he (she) did not intend and over which he (she) had no control.

The Commonwealth is not required to prove that the defendant specifically intended to violate the abuse prevention order. It is required only to prove that the defendant intended, or shared an intent with the third party, that an act be done which violated the order.

If the Commonwealth has proved beyond a reasonable doubt each of the elements of the offense and also that the defendant had an intent or shared intent with a third person to do an act that could result in a violation of a protective order, you should return a verdict of guilty. If the Commonwealth failed to prove beyond a reasonable doubt any element of the offense or failed to prove beyond a reasonable doubt that the defendant intended or shared the intent of a third party to commit such an act, you must return a verdict of not guilty.

If appropriate, here instruct on inferences (Instruction 3.100).

Commonwealth v. *Collier,* 427 Mass. 385, 389 (1998) (where act constituting violation was committed by third party, Commonwealth must prove act was intended by defendant but not that defendant intended to violate order). *See also Commonwealth* v. *Russell,* 46 Mass. App. Ct. 307 (1999).

NOTES

1. **Related violations of abuse restraining orders.** In appropriate cases, the model instruction may be adapted to indicate that it is now a criminal offense under G.L. c. 209A to violate an order to surrender any firearm, firearms license or firearms identification card, or to violate an abuse prevention order issued by another state.

The model instruction may also be modified as appropriate for violations of restraining, vacate or no-contact orders entered under G.L. c. 208, §§ 18, 34B, or 34C, G.L. c. 209, § 32, or G.L. c. 209C, §§ 15 or 20. The model instruction should also be adapted in a case involving the aggravated offense of violating an abuse prevention order in retaliation for the plaintiff's having reported the defendant to the Department of Revenue for failing to pay child support or for the establishment of paternity.

2. **Attempted physical harm requires overt act.** The nature of an attempt to cause a person physical harm, "like criminal attempt, is predicated on an unsuccessful but affirmative effort at commission of the underlying offense." *Commonwealth v. Fortier,* 56 Mass. App. Ct. 116 (2002). "Usually acts which are expected to bring about the end without further interference on the part of the criminal are near enough, unless the expectation is very absurd." *Commonwealth v. Fortier,* 56 Mass. App. Ct. at 122 (citing *Commonwealth v. Kennedy,* 170 Mass. 18, 20–21 (1897)).

3. **Service or knowledge of extended order.** A defendant may be prosecuted for violating an order that was extended unchanged after a "10-day" hearing, despite not being served with the extended order, if he had been served with the prior ex parte temporary order, which provided sufficient notice that his failure to attend the scheduled hearing would

result in the continuation of the temporary order by operation of law. *Commonwealth v. Delaney*, 425 Mass. 587 (1997). However, the same is not true of successive annual extensions of the order; failure to serve a copy of the current extended order is fatal where there have been successive annual extensions unless the Commonwealth proves constructive knowledge of the extension. *Commonwealth v. Molloy,* 44 Mass. App. Ct. 306 (1998).

4. **Intent to violate order.** The statute does not require any specific mens rea or intent to violate the order, merely knowledge of and violation of the order. *Commonwealth v. Delaney,* 425 Mass. 587 (1997).

5. **Stalking.** Violating a G.L. c. 209A order (G.L. c. 209A, § 7) is a lesser included offense of stalking in violation of that same 209A order (G.L. c. 265, § 43[b]). As a result, a defendant may not be prosecuted for the latter offense based on incidents already prosecuted as violations of the 209A order. *Edge v. Commonwealth*, 451 Mass. 74, 76–77, (2008).

Wanton Destruction of Property

Regulatory Authority—G.L. c. 266, § 127
Dist. Ct. Model Jury Instruction 8.260

The defendant is charged with wanton destruction of property (of a value over $1,200).

In order to prove the defendant guilty of this offense, the Commonwealth must prove (two) (three) things beyond a reasonable doubt:

First: That the defendant injured or destroyed the (personal property) (dwelling house) (building) of another; (and)

Second: That the defendant did so wantonly.

If value of property is alleged to be greater than $1,200, add third element.

(and) *Third:* That the amount of damage inflicted to the property was more than $1.

> Effective April 13, 2018, St. 2018, c. 69, increased the felony threshold for this offense from $250 to $1,200. For offenses committed prior to April 13, 2018, insert "$250" in place of "$1,200."

An act of destruction is "wanton" if the person was reckless or indifferent to the fact that his (her) conduct would probably cause substantial damage. Someone acts "wantonly" when he (she) consciously disregards, or is indifferent to, this probability.

Conduct is wanton if (1) the defendant knew it would create a risk of substantial damage or destruction to another's property, or (2) a reasonable person—knowing what the defendant knew—would have realized the act posed a risk of substantial damage to or destruction of another's property.

It is not enough for the Commonwealth to prove that the defendant acted negligently—that is, acted in a way that a reasonably careful person would not. The Commonwealth must prove that the defendant's actions went beyond mere negligence and amounted to wanton conduct as I have defined that term.

The defendant must have intended his (her) act, in the sense that it did not happen accidentally.

> *If relevant to evidence.* If you find that the defendant's act occurred by accident, then you must find the defendant not guilty.
>
> *Commonwealth v. McGovern*, 397 Mass. 863, 868 (1987); *Commonwealth v. Dellamano*, 393 Mass. 132, 137 (1984); *Commonwealth v. Welansky*, 316 Mass. 383, 398–99 (1944); *Commonwealth v. Ruddock*, 25 Mass. App. Ct. 508, 512–14 (1988); *Commonwealth v. Peruzzi*, 15 Mass. App. Ct. 437, 440–44 (1983).

If value of property is alleged to be greater than $1,200. If you determine that the Commonwealth has proved beyond a reasonable doubt that the defendant is guilty of wanton destruction of property, you must go on to determine whether the Commonwealth also proved beyond a reasonable doubt that the reasonable cost of repair of the damaged property—or the reasonable cost of replacement if it cannot be repaired—was in excess of $1,200.

> See *Commonwealth v. Kirker*, 441 Mass. 226, 228–29 (2004); *Commonwealth v. Deberry*, 441 Mass. 211, 221–22 (2004).

Supplemental Instruction

Likelihood of Substantial Damage. A person cannot be convicted of wanton injury to property unless it was likely that his actions would result in substantial damage to others or their property. It is not enough that some slight or insignificant injury was likely to result. A person acts "wantonly" only if it is likely that his actions will result in substantial harm.

However, it is not necessary that the damage actually was substantial, only that such actions were likely to cause substantial damage. The actual outcome of someone's actions is sometimes a matter of luck, and here the law measures the nature of the actions, not the outcome.

> *Commonwealth v. Ruddock*, 25 Mass. App. Ct. 508, 512–14 (1988)

NOTES

1. **Distinction between "willful and malicious" and "wanton" destruction.** Wilful and malicious property destruction is a specific intent crime requiring proof that the defendant intended both the conduct and its harmful consequences, while wanton property destruction requires only a showing that the actor's conduct was indifferent to, or in disregard of, the probable consequences. *Commonwealth v. Armand,* 411 Mass. 167, 170–71 (1991). The essence of the distinction "appears to lie in the fact that a wilful actor intends both his conduct and the resulting harm, whereas a wanton or reckless actor intends his conduct but not necessarily the resulting harm." *Commonwealth v. Smith*, 17 Mass. App. Ct. 918, 920 (1983). As an example, if youths throw rocks from a bridge and one strikes a car passing below, the act is wanton if the rocks were thrown casually, without thought of striking any cars, but the act is wilful and malicious if the rocks were aimed at passing cars. *Commonwealth v. Cimino,* 34 Mass. App. Ct. 925, 927 (1993).

2. **"Wanton" destruction is not lesser included offense of "willful and malicious" destruction.** Wanton property destruction is not a lesser included offense of wilful and malicious property destruction (see Instruction 8.280), since wanton conduct requires proof that the likely effect of the defendant's conduct was substantial harm, but wilful and malicious conduct does not. *Commonwealth v. Schuchardt,* 408 Mass. 347, 352 (1990).

3. **Value.** The value of the property destroyed or injured is a question for the jury and must be established beyond a reasonable doubt before it may be relied on to increase the range of punishment. *Commonwealth v. Beale,* 434 Mass. 1024, 1025 (2001); *Commonwealth v. Lauzier,* 53 Mass. App. Ct. 626, 633 n.10 (2002). Where the damage is repairable, the value of the property is to be measured by the pecuniary loss (usually the reasonable repair or replacement cost), and not by the fair market value of the whole property or of the damaged portion. *Commonwealth v. Deberry,* 441 Mass. 211, 221–22 (2004), *rev'g* 57 Mass. App. Ct. 93 (2003). "Of course, in certain circumstances a seemingly minor type of damage may effectively destroy the value of an entire property, such as a tear in a valuable painting or a chip in an antique cup." *Commonwealth v. Deberry,* 441 Mass. at 222 n.20.

Willful and Malicious Destruction of Property

Regulatory Authority—G.L. c. 266, § 127
Dist. Ct. Model Jury Instruction 8.280

The defendant is charged with willful and malicious destruction of property (of a value over $1,200).

In order to prove the defendant guilty of this offense, the Commonwealth must prove (three) (four) things beyond a reasonable doubt:

First: That the defendant injured or destroyed the (personal property) (dwelling house) (building) of another;

Second: That the defendant did so willfully; (and)

Third: That the defendant did so with malice;

If value of property is alleged to be greater than $1,200, add third element

and *Fourth:* That the amount of damage inflicted to the property was more than $1,200.

Effective April 13, 2018, St. 2018, c. 69, increased the felony threshold for this offense from $250 to $1,200. For offenses committed prior to April 13, 2018, insert "$250" in place of "$1,200."

An act is "willful" if it is done intentionally and by design, in contrast to an act which is done thoughtlessly or accidentally. A person acts willfully if he (she) intends both the conduct and its harmful consequences.

An act is done with "malice" if it is done out of cruelty, hostility or revenge. To act with malice, one must act not only deliberately, but out of hostility toward another.

If value of property is alleged to be greater than $1,200. If you determine that the Commonwealth has proved beyond a reasonable doubt that the defendant is guilty of willful and malicious destruction of property, you must go on to determine whether the Commonwealth also proved beyond a reasonable doubt that the reasonable cost of repair of the damaged property—or the reasonable cost of replacement if it cannot be repaired—was in excess of $1,200.

Commonwealth v. Deberry, 441 Mass. 211, 215 n.7 (2004) (citing model instruction approvingly); *Commonwealth v. McGovern*, 397 Mass. 863, 868 (1986); *Commonwealth v. Hosman*, 257 Mass. 379 (1926); *Commonwealth v. Chambers*, 90 Mass. App. Ct. 137, 144 n.7 (2016) (malice need not be directed toward owner of the property, just toward someone); *Commonwealth v. O'Neil,* 67 Mass. App. Ct. 284, 291 (2006) (offense requires proof of cruel, hostile or vengeful intent in addition to intentional doing of the unlawful act); *Commonwealth v. Peruzzi*, 15 Mass. App. Ct. 437, 440–44, (1983) (malice requires a showing that defendant was motivated by "cruelty, hostility or revenge"). Destruction incidental to some other venture or purpose is insufficient. *Commonwealth v. Morris M.*, 70 Mass. App. Ct. 688, 692–93 (2007) (it is not reasonably inferable that defendant purposefully destroyed the fence and turf motivated by hostility, cruelty, or vengeance as opposed to the resulting damage being occasioned by, or incidental to, his desire to escape his circumstances).

7

Supplemental Instruction

Where "willful and malicious" and "wanton" destruction are charged in separate counts. If you find that it has been proved beyond a reasonable doubt that the defendant did commit the property damage as alleged, you must then go on to determine whether it was done "willfully and maliciously" as alleged in Count _____, or "wantonly" as alleged in Count _____. As I have informed you, such conduct would be "willful and malicious" if the defendant acted out of cruelty, hostility or revenge toward another, and intended both the conduct and the harmful consequences.

Such conduct would instead be "wanton" if the defendant intended the conduct but not the harmful consequences, and was reckless or indifferent to the substantial damage that such conduct would probably cause. Since the required intent is different for the two counts, if you find the defendant guilty on one of those counts, you are to return a not guilty verdict on the other count.

See Instruction 8.260, Wanton Destruction of Property.

NOTES

1. **Distinction between "willful and malicious" and "wanton" destruction.** Wilful and malicious property destruction is a specific intent crime requiring proof that the defendant intended both the conduct and its harmful consequences, while wanton property destruction requires only a showing that the actor's conduct was indifferent to, or in disregard of, the probable consequences. *Commonwealth v. Armand,* 411 Mass. 167, 170–71 (1991). The essence of the distinction "appears to lie in the fact that a wilful actor intends both his conduct and the resulting harm, whereas a wanton or reckless actor intends his conduct but not necessarily the resulting harm." *Commonwealth v. Smith,* 17 Mass. App. Ct. 918, 920 (1983). As an example, if youths throw rocks from a bridge and one strikes a car passing below, the act is wanton if the rocks were thrown casually, without thought of striking any cars, but the act is wilful and malicious if the rocks were aimed at passing cars. *Commonwealth v. Cimino,* 34 Mass. App. Ct. 925, 927 (1993). "It is worth noting that destruction of property which accompanies even violent crime may not by that token alone qualify as wilful and malicious." *Commonwealth v. Cimino,* 34 Mass. App. Ct. at 927.

2. **"Wanton" destruction not lesser included offense of "wilful and malicious" destruction.** Wanton property destruction (see Instruction 8.260) is *not* a lesser included offense of wilful and malicious property destruction, since wanton conduct requires proof that the likely effect of the defendant's conduct was substantial harm, but wilful and malicious conduct does not. *Commonwealth v. Schuchardt,* 408 Mass. 347, 352 (1990).

3. **Value.** To prove the felony branch of this offense, the Commonwealth must additionally prove that "the value of the property so destroyed or injured" is over $1,200. *Commonwealth v. Beale,* 434 Mass. 1024 (2001); *Commonwealth v. Lauzier,* 53 Mass. App. Ct. 626, 633 n.10 (2002). Where the damage is repairable, the value of the property is to be measured by the pecuniary loss (usually the reasonable repair or replacement cost), and not by the fair market value of the whole property or of the damaged portion. *Commonwealth* v. *Deberry,* 441 Mass. 211, 221–22 (2004), *rev'g* 57 Mass. App. Ct. 93 (2003); *Commonwealth v. Kirker,* 441 Mass. 226, 228–29 (2004). "Of course, in certain circumstances a seemingly minor type of damage may effectively destroy the value of an entire property, such as a tear in a valuable painting or a chip in an antique cup." *Commonwealth* v. *Deberry,* 441 Mass. at 222 n.20.

PART 8

Department of Youth Services Regulations

109 CMR 1.00. Reserved

109 CMR 2.00. General Conditions

[Dated Dec. 16, 2016.]

109 CMR 2.01. Introduction

The Department of Youth Services (Department) was created by St. 1969, c. 838, as codified in M.G.L. c. 18A, § 1, with the mandate to provide a comprehensive and coordinated program of services to delinquent children and youth referred or committed to the Department by the courts; community services for the prevention of juvenile delinquency; and services and facilities for the study, diagnosis, care, treatment, including medical and behavioral health and social services, education training and rehabilitation of all youth referred or committed.

As the juvenile justice agency for the Commonwealth of Massachusetts, the Department promotes positive change in the youth in the Department's care and custody. The Department's mission is to make communities safer by improving the life outcomes for youth in its care. The Department achieves its mission through investing in highly qualified staff and a service continuum that engages youth, families and communities in strategies which are fair and promote positive youth development.

109 CMR 2.02. Definitions

Throughout 109 CMR, the following terms shall have the following meanings unless otherwise specified:

Commissioner. The Commissioner of the Department of Youth Services.

Commitment. The order of a youth to the physical custody of the Department by a court in resolution of a delinquency complaint, youthful offender indictment or probation violation.

Community Based Placement. A non-residential program designed to provide services to youth in the community, which may include, but is not limited to foster care, independent living, and placement at home with community supervision.

Department or DYS. The Department of Youth Services.

Deputy Commissioner. A Deputy Commissioner of the Department of Youth Services.

Detention. The temporary physical custody ordered by a court in lieu of posted bail of a youth awaiting resolution of a pending delinquency complaint, youthful offender indictment or probation violation.

Discharge. The termination of a youth's commitment to the Department of Youth Services.

Hardware-secure Placement. Placement in a Department or Provider operated residential program characterized by locked entrances and exits and other physically restrictive construction and procedures designed to prevent a youth from physically leaving the program without the Department's approval.

Provider. An individual or entity the Department contracts with to access services which include, but are not limited to, medical, behavioral health and social services, education, training and rehabilitation for youth detained by or committed to the Department as required by M.G.L. c. 18A, § 2.

Regional Review Team (RRT). Regional body composed of senior Department of Youth Services' regional managers which is responsible for determining the length and type of treatment and placement for a youth.

Residential Placement. Placement in any DYS or Provider operated program where a youth resides until approval is granted by the Department to move to a Community-Based placement.

Secure Placement. Any Department or Provider operated residential program which may use hardware or staff security; also known as a "facility".

Staff-secure Placement. Placement in a Department or Provider operated residential program that is characterized by unlocked entrances and exits where staff personnel provide the primary security to prevent a youth from physically leaving the program without the approval of the Department.

109 CMR 2.03. Applicability

109 CMR is binding on all personnel of the Department, and the Providers that are under contract to the Department. Failure to comply may result in actions against the employees of the Department or the Provider.

109 CMR 2.04. Administrative Relief

Anyone aggrieved by actions of a Departmental or Provider employee(s) who has violated the requirements of 109 CMR may request an administrative review by the Commissioner or designee, unless the aggrieved party is already pursuing or has pursued his or her grievance in another forum. The aggrieved person must present allegations in writing to the Commissioner's office either in person or by mail. Upon receipt of such allegations, the Commissioner or designee will review the allegations and any relevant documents, and may conduct interviews before issuing a decision. The Commissioner or designee's decision shall be issued within 20 business days from receipt of the request for review. The decision of the Commissioner, or his or her designee, shall be final.

109 CMR 2.05. Sanctions

As provided in M.G.L. c. 214, § 3B, employees of the Department, and other persons who violate the requirements of 109 CMR, and M.G.L. c. 66A, may be subject to the sanctions provided therein including but not limited to reprimand, suspension, or dismissal, or other sanctions as provided by law.

109 CMR 2.06. Severability

The provisions of 109 CMR are severable. If any provision of 109 CMR is declared unconstitutional or invalid by a court of competent jurisdiction, the validity of the remaining portions shall not be affected.

Regulatory Authority—109 CMR 2.00: M.G.L. c. 18A

109 CMR 3.00. Access to All Records of Youth Detained by or Committed to the Department of Youth Services

[Dated Aug. 25, 2017]

Section

109 CMR 3.01. Purpose and Scope

109 CMR 3.00 establishes rules for the management of and access to all Youth Records maintained by the Department of Youth Services (Department). The provisions of 109 CMR 3.00 shall apply to the following persons:

(1) Each current or former Department employee;

(2) Current or former Providers and their employees;

(3) All Youth served by the Department;

(4) Each person or entity to whom Department representatives disclose confidential Youth Records information; and

(5) Each person or entity that requests Youth Records from the Department.

109 CMR 3.02. Applicability

109 CMR 3.00 is applicable to all records maintained by the Department of Youth Services regarding Youth, whether currently or previously detained by or committed to the Department. 109 CMR 3.00 does not apply to access to records sought in conjunction with Research as defined in 109 CMR 10.00: Social Science Research by Outside Agencies or Persons.

109 CMR 3.03. Definitions

Data Sharing Agreement. An agreement between the Department and another Executive Office of Health and Human Services Agency pursuant to 101 CMR 16.00: Personal Data Use and Permitted Disclosures by and among the Executive Office of Health and Human Services and its Agencies for the purposes of sharing data to assist assessment; service development, coordination, or provision; eligibility for or determinations of benefit amounts; or quality assurance activities.

Keeper of the Records. A person designated by the Department to administer all rules and regulations governing access to Youth Records.

8

Legal Unit. Those employees who report to the Department's general counsel, including any assistant general counsels, paralegals or administrative support staff.

Memorandum of Understanding or Agreement. A documented agreement between the Department and another agency or entity which may include agreements regarding the sharing of certain Youth Records.

Personal Data. As defined by M.G.L. c. 66A, § 1, information in any form which, because of name, identifying number, mark or description can be readily associated with a particular individual; provided, however, that such information is not contained in a public record, as defined in M.G.L. c. 4, § 7, clause 26 and shall not include intelligence information, evaluative information or criminal offender record information as defined in M.G.L. c. 6, § 167.

Youth. Any person who is or has at any time been referred to, detained by or committed to the Department.

Youth Records. Any information maintained by the Department regarding the referral, detention or commitment of a Youth including, but not limited to, Personal Data as defined in 109 CMR 3.03.

109 CMR 3.04. Records of Youth Served by the Department of Youth Services

No Youth Records shall be disseminated to anyone other than an authorized Department employee or contracted Provider except as specifically authorized by the Commissioner pursuant to M.G.L. c. 120, § 21, or as follows:

(1) A Youth may obtain a copy of his or her own records by submitting a written request to the Keeper of the Records.

(2) A parent or guardian of a Youth who is currently younger than 18 years old may obtain a copy of the Youth's records by submitting a written request to the Keeper of the Records.

(3) An attorney representing a Youth may obtain a copy of the Youth's records by submitting a written request to the Keeper of the Records, accompanied by authorization from the Youth.

(4) Any person, agency or entity providing services to a Youth may obtain a copy of the Youth's records by submitting a request in writing to the Keeper of the Records, accompanied by authorization from the Client and the Client's legal guardian, if the Client is younger than 18 years old at the time of the request.

(5) Any person, agency or entity empowered by statute, regulation or other applicable law to have access to Personal Data may obtain a copy of a Youth's records by submitting a written request to the Keeper of the Records that sets forth the legal bases and the scope of the authorization permitting the Department to release the records requested.

(6) Any person who presents a written order from a court compelling release of Youth Records to that person may have access to Youth Records subject to the requirements set forth in 109 CMR 3.05.

(7) Any agency authorized by law or ordered by a court to complete a presentence report may have access to Youth Records upon submission of a written request and a copy of any order to the Keeper of the Records.

(8) Law Enforcement agencies, including the District Attorney's Offices may have access to portions of Youth Records where the information sought is related to the investigation of a crime, or subject to the requirements set forth in 109 CMR 3.05, or as otherwise authorized by law.

(9) Victims of crime may obtain access to such Personal Data of Youth as provided by M.G.L. c. 258B, § 3(t) and c. 6, § 178A.

(10) In the case of a Youth's psychiatric or medical emergency that precludes Youth consent, a physician treating a Youth may obtain medical or psychiatric data in client records if necessary to treat the Youth. As soon as reasonably practical after said emergency, a Youth shall receive notice that his or her information was released for treatment purposes.

(11) As provided for by law, any investigative agent of the Attorney General, State Auditor or the State Ethics Commission acting in furtherance of his or her duties may have access to Youth records to the extent necessary.

(12) Nothing in 109 CMR 3.00 shall preclude the Department from entering into a Memorandum of Understanding or Data Sharing Agreement to allow the sharing of Youth Records pursuant to 101 CMR 16.00: Personal Data Use and Permitted Disclosures by and among the Executive Office of Health and Human Services and its Agencies with any other agency or provider regarding:

(a) Eligibility determinations;

(b) Determination of benefit amounts;

(c) Assessment of Youth needs or the provision of services, insofar as the use or disclosure of Personal Data will assist the individual who is the subject of the Personal Data to access needed medical, social, educational, or other services, or will improve the coordination or management of services provided to the individual(s); and

(d) Quality assurance activities.

109 CMR 3.05. Response to Compulsory Legal Process

Youth Records may be released in response to compulsory legal process; however, no Personal Data shall be made available in response to a demand under compulsory legal process unless the Client is reasonably notified so that he or she may seek to have the process quashed as provided in M.G.L. c. 66A, § 2(k), unless such notice may be withheld by law pursuant to M.G.L. c. 66A, § 2(i).

(1) A subpoena for Youth Records can be accepted by an employee other than the one named on the subpoena. Employees eligible to accept service include employees of the Department's Legal Unit, regional administration, and program administration. Such an acceptance of service still creates an obligation to comply on the part of the person named in the subpoena.

(2) Upon accepting any subpoena for Youth Records, the person receiving the subpoena shall immediately notify the Department's Legal Unit.

(3) The Department's efforts to notify the Youth may be written or oral, including notice by telephone. The Department shall document in writing the efforts made to contact the Youth and if said contact is made. If the Department is unable to contact the Youth after multiple attempts, the Department shall release the records sought, after redacting Personal Data.

109 CMR 3.06. Audit Trails

The Department is required by M.G.L. c. 66A, § 2(f) to maintain records of every access to a Youth's Records by anyone other than Departmental employees or Providers acting within their official duties. All Department and Provider offices and facilities, where Youth Records are maintained shall keep a log which shows access to Youth Records by anyone other than Department or Provider employees and contain the following information in an audit trail:

(1) the name of the person or entity granted access to the Youth's Records;

(2) the purpose and date of the access; and

(3) the name of the person who authorized inspection.

109 CMR 3.07. Training of Staff

The Legal Unit of the Department shall alert all Department personnel and Providers of 109 CMR 3.00 and shall conduct training sessions to acquaint staff with the requirements of 109 CMR 3.00 and M.G.L. c. 66A.

Regulatory Authority—109 CMR 3.00: M.G.L. c. 120, § 4; 101 CMR 8.01(4).

109 CMR 4.00. Classification of Youth Committed to the Department of Youth Services

[Dated July 28, 2017.]

Section

109 CMR 4.01. Purpose and Scope

109 CMR 4.00 describes the Classification process required for each youth committed to the Department of Youth Services (Department). The Classification process is designed to ensure that each youth receives the services he or she needs to transition safely and successfully back to the community, through the use of effective risk assessment, meaningful family and community engagement, and a continuum of services based on the science of adolescent development and proven and promising practices in juvenile justice, consistent with positive youth development and the promotion of public safety.

109 CMR 4.02. Applicability

109 CMR 4.00 applies to all youth committed to the Department of Youth Services as well as Department and Provider employees.

109 CMR 4.03. Definitions

Assessment. The comprehensive review of a youth's strengths, treatment needs, risk areas and history of offending behavior, mental status, medical and behavioral health history, developmental history, family relationships, functioning in and ties to the community, educational needs, history of compliance with probation or other supervised release, and history of compliance while detained pre-trial, where applicable, completed by regional clinical, medical, and educational staff, and a youth's caseworker.

Case History. A document completed in conjunction with a youth's initial Assessment and updated on a regular basis by a youth's caseworker or other authorized staff, regarding the youth's personal and family history.

Classification. The process by which a youth's treatment plan and placement are determined following commitment.

Classification Grid. Offense based guidelines used by a youth's Treatment Team and the Regional Review Team when determining the length of time a youth may spend in residential treatment.

Extension. The term used when the treatment assignment given to a youth by the RRT is increased to provide additional time for the youth to meet treatment goals or address emergent treatment issues, to enable the youth to transition to a less restrictive placement or the community.

Pass Eligibility. The determination by the RRT that a youth has met sufficient treatment milestones to merit his or her eligibility for structured, supervised and unsupervised access to the community.

Staffing. A meeting of a youth's Treatment Team first held within 45 days of a youth's commitment to the Department to review the Assessment and other information relevant to the youth's strengths, needs, history of offending behavior and level of risk, to develop the treatment plan that will be recommended to the RRT. Staffing also used to refer to subsequent meetings of the Treatment Team following the youth's initial classification to discuss changes in placement or emergent treatment needs and determine whether the youth should be presented to the RRT for a review of his or her placement and/or treatment plan.

Treatment Team. Regional body assembled to assist in the Assessment, Classification, placement and treatment of a youth upon the youth's commitment to the Department. The Treatment Team may include, but is not limited to, the youth, the youth's parent or guardian, the youth's Caseworker, the District Manager, the Program Clinical Director, the Program Advocate, the Program Educational Coordinator, and where applicable, the youth's attorney, Department of Children and Families and/or Department of Mental Health caseworker, probation officer, school personnel and other community partners.

8

109 CMR 4.04. Classification Process

(1) All youth committed to the Department of Youth Services shall undergo an Assessment within 30 through 45 days of commitment.

(2) Within two weeks of commitment, the Departmental members of a youth's Treatment Team shall determine an anticipated date for completion of a youth's Assessment and set a date for the youth's initial Staffing to take place following the date of anticipated completion. The Treatment Team shall make reasonable efforts to schedule the Staffing at a time and location that is facilitates participation by the youth's parent or legal guardian, attorney and other relevant community partners.

(3) The youth's Staffing shall include, but not be limited to, a review of the Assessment and any other information relevant to the youth's treatment needs, personal history, history of offending behavior, and risk of re-offense. The Staffing shall afford all Treatment Team members an opportunity to be heard regarding the information presented.

(4) Within five business days of the youth's staffing, the as-

signed caseworker shall update the youth's case file to reflect the outcome of the Staffing and any other information relevant to the youth's Classification. This information, including a copy of the youth's Assessment and Case History shall be made available to authorized Treatment Team members, for review prior to the presentation of the Treatment Team's recommendations to the RRT.

(5) Within ten business days of the youth's Staffing, the RRT shall convene to review the recommendations of the youth's Treatment Team and classify the youth. The Caseworker or his or her designee shall present the recommendations of the Treatment Team and contextual information. The youth shall be afforded the opportunity to be heard by the RRT regarding this recommendation.

(6) Within five business days of the RRT meeting, the RRT shall issue a Classification decision. The Regional Review Team will consider all information presented at the RRT meeting and render a Classification decision consistent with the Classification Factors outlined in 109 CMR 4.06. This decision shall be in writing and shall reference the information considered by the RRT and provide the rationale for the RRT's decision. The RRT shall provide the decision to the youth, his or her guardian, and attorney of record. Accompanying this decision shall be information regarding the youth's right to appeal and the requirements regarding appeals outlined in 109 CMR 4.07.

(7) Nothing in 109 CMR 4.00 shall preclude a youth's Treatment Team from presenting a youth's case to the RRT for review of the youth's Classification at any time; however, the youth shall be notified of any request for extension of his or her treatment beyond the upper limit of the treatment time for the Grid level approved at his or her Classification. The youth shall be afforded an opportunity to be heard by the RRT and to appeal the RRT's decision. Any such appeal shall follow the requirements outlined in 109 CMR 4.07.

109 CMR 4.05. Classification Grid

The Classification Grid, as defined in 109 CMR 4.03, shall be available to the public and subject to annual review by the Department.

109 CMR 4.06. Classification Factors

(1) The Classification decision shall be based on the risks and needs identified in the Assessment completed by the youth's Treatment Team, the youth's history of offending behavior, and the recommended amount of treatment in the Classification Grid for the youth's most serious commitment offense.

(2) In making a Classification decision, the RRT shall give due consideration to any mitigating or aggravating circumstances concerning the youth's commitment offense(s). Such factors include, but are not limited to:

(a) The youth's role in the offense; and

(b) The harm caused to the victim and/or the community by the youth's actions.

(3) When the Treatment Team requests that the RRT review a youth's Classification for the purposes of extending his or her treatment or adjusting his or her placement, the RRT shall also consider the following factors:

(a) The youth's adjustment to and progress in treatment;

(b) Any serious incidents the youth has been involved in, as defined by policy, relevant to previously identified treatment issues or which relate to the management of the youth's risk to self or others; and

(c) Any emergent treatment issues not identified at the youth's Staffing or initial Classification.

(4) No youth younger than 14 years old shall be classified to receive treatment in a Hardware-secure Placement.

109 CMR 4.07. Appeal Procedure

(1) A youth may appeal the Classification time assignment, determined by the RRT, by submitting a written request to the Commissioner or Commissioner's Designee within seven business days of receiving the RRT's decision. The appeal may be submitted by the youth and/or the youth's attorney.

(2) The assigned Caseworker shall advise the youth of his or her right to appeal and the procedures for an appeal, within one business day of the RRT's issuance of its written decision.

(3) A written response to the appeal shall be provided to the youth, legal guardian, and the youth's attorney, if applicable, within 14 business days of receipt of the request for appeal. The decision of the Commissioner or the Commissioner's Designee shall be final.

Regulatory Authority—109 CMR 4.00: M.G.L. c. 120, § 26.

109 CMR 5.00. Involuntary Room Confinement of Youth Detained by or Committed to the Department of Youth Services

[Dated May 6, 2016.]

Section

109 CMR 5.01. Purpose and Scope

109 CMR 5.00 establishes the rules and procedures for involuntary room confinement of youth detained by or committed to the Department of Youth Services, while placed at hardware secure programs.

(1) Youth may be kept involuntarily in a room during non-sleep hours for the following reasons:

(a) to calm a youth who is exhibiting seriously disruptive or dangerous behavior;

(b) for population management;

(c) for the safety and security of a youth; and

(d) for the investigation of an incident.

(2) Involuntary room confinement to calm a youth who is exhibiting seriously disruptive or dangerous behavior or for the safety and security of a youth may only be used when less restrictive interventions have failed and for the least amount of time required for the youth to regain self-control.

(3) Involuntary room confinement shall never be used as a sanction for non-compliance or punishment.

(4) Involuntary room confinement for population management or for the investigation of an incident may only be used when less restrictive alternatives are not available and only for the amount of time reasonably necessary to resolve the population issue or investigation.

(5) Involuntary room confinement shall not be used with any youth who is on any suicide watch status.

(6) DYS shall have a policy detailing the use of involuntary room confinement. This policy shall be approved by the Commissioner and shall be reviewed by the Department annually in light of best practices.

109 CMR 5.02. Applicability

109 CMR 5.00 is applicable to all Department or Provider operated hardware secure programs housing youth committed to or detained by the Department of Youth Services.

109 CMR 5.03. Authorization, Documentation and Reporting of Involuntary Room Confinement

Each use of involuntary room confinement shall be authorized, documented and reported in accordance with the policy referenced in 109 CMR 5.01(6).

(1) The Program Director, Assistant Program Director, Clinical Director and Shift Administrator or their equivalents shall review each use of involuntary room confinement and complete a program level Room Confinement Report.

(2) Any failure to comply with 109 CMR 5.00 or the Department of Youth Services' policy regarding involuntary room confinement shall be reported using the applicable reporting policy for serious incidents.

(3) Failure to comply with 109 CMR 5.00 or the Department's policy regarding involuntary room confinement may result in disciplinary or corrective action.

(4) Data regarding involuntary room confinement shall be collected and reviewed by the Department on an annual basis.

109 CMR 5.04. Visual Observation

Staff shall monitor all youth who are involuntarily confined at regular intervals in accordance with policy. Such policy shall set the time frames within which youth must be viewed, provided that such time frames shall be set at a minimum frequency of 15 minute increments.

Regulatory Authority—109 CMR 5.00: M.G.L. c. 120, §§ 6A and 10.

109 CMR 6.00. Restraints and Use of Force with Youth Detained by or Committed to the Department of Youth Services

[Dated May 6, 2016.]

Section

109 CMR 6.01. Purpose and Scope

109 CMR 6.00 describes the rules and procedures governing the use of restraints, including mechanical restraints, and the use of force in DYS operated or Provider programs.

(1) Restraints and use of force shall be limited to those situations where a youth demonstrates by his or her actions that he or she is dangerous to him or herself or others, and no other intervention has been or is likely to be effective in averting the danger posed by the youth's behavior.

(2) Reasonable efforts shall be made to verbally deescalate and disengage youth from volatile situations prior to the use of force or restraint.

(3) DYS shall have policies detailing the use of restraints and use of force in situations involving individual youth as well as group disturbances. These policies shall be approved by the Commissioner and reviewed annually by the Department to ensure consistency with best practices.

(4) DYS shall train its employees, and providers where applicable, to address situations with youth in a manner that minimizes the use of restraints and force, consistent with 109 CMR 6.00 and the policies described in 109 CMR 6.04(3).

(5) Only employees specifically trained in the use of force and restraints are permitted to use such techniques or the devices associated with restraints.

(6) 109 CMR 6.00 pertains only to the use of restraints to address programmatic safety and security and does not cover the use of mechanical restraints by Department employees, Providers, the Department of Correction or the various sheriffs during transportation of youth detained by or committed to the Department.

109 CMR 6.02. Applicability

109 CMR 6.00 is applicable to all programs operated by the Department of Youth Services as well as Provider programs that are co-located with Department programs. Provider programs that are not co-located with Department programs shall comply with the restraint requirements of the Department of Early Education and Care or the equivalent licensing body.

109 CMR 6.03. Documentation and Reporting

All restraints shall be documented and reported in accordance with the policies described in 109 CMR 6.01(3).

(1) The Program Director, Assistant Program Director, Clinical Director and Shift Administrator, or their equivalents shall review each restraint conducted in their program in accordance with the requirements established by the relevant policy. Restraint data shall be collected and reviewed by the Department at least annually.

(2) Any employee who witnesses a violation of 109 CMR 6.00 or the Department of Youth Services' policy on restraints and use of force shall report such violation using the applicable reporting process for serious incidents.

(3) Violations of 109 CMR 6.03 or the Department of Youth Services1 policy regarding restraints and use of force, or a failure to report violations of this policy may result in disciplinary or corrective action.

Regulatory Authority—109 CMR 6.00: M.G.L. c. 120, § 6.

8

109 CMR 7.00. The Granting of Passes for Youth Committed to the Department of Youth Services

[Dated May 6, 2016.]

Section

109 CMR 7.01. Purpose and Scope

109 CMR 7.00 establishes regulations governing the granting of passes for youth committed to the Department of Youth Services who are placed in secure programs.

(1) Passes are to be utilized to support graduated re-entry to the community consistent with the youth's treatment plan, to allow the youth increasing levels of self-management and aid in the youth's successful transition to the community.

(2) DYS shall have a policy that sets forth the eligibility criteria for passes and outlines the approval processes required for the granting of passes.

(3) DYS may authorize passes when youth committed to the Department are eligible and approved for passes in accordance with the policy in 109 CMR 7.01(2).

(4) The policy in 109 CMR 7.01(2) shall be approved by the Commissioner and reviewed annually by the Department in light of best practices.

109 CMR 7.02. Applicability

109 CMR 7.00 is applicable to all youth committed to the Department of Youth Services who are in secure placements.

109 CMR 7.03. Emergency Pass Procedures

(1) An emergency pass may be granted for a youth committed to the Department of Youth Services by the Department in the event of medical emergency or death in the youth's immediate family.

(2) All requests for emergency passes and available relevant documentation shall be reviewed by Regional Administration on an expedited basis and then submitted to the Commissioner or his or her designee for final approval prior to any release of the youth on a pass. An emergency pass must be approved by the Facility Administrator and the appropriate Regional Director or their designee. This

approval may be made by telephone; it must be followed by a written request for approval and written confirmation.

109 CMR 7.04. Behavior Expected of Youth on Pass

A youth granted a pass must agree to abide by the rules established for the pass. Any violation of 109 CMR 7.00, the policy referenced in 109 CMR 7.01(2), or the terms of a pass, may result in the immediate return of the youth to a secure placement.

Failure to return from an unsupervised pass at the time specified may be grounds for the issuance of a warrant of apprehension.

Regulatory Authority—109 CMR 7.00: M.G.L. c. 120, §§ 6 and 6A.

109 CMR 8.00. The Granting and Revocation of Conditional Liberty for Youth Committed to the Department of Youth Services

[Dated Dec. 30, 2016.]

Section

109 CMR 8.01. Purpose and Scope

To establish rules and regulations for the granting and revocation of conditional liberty for youth committed to the Department of Youth Services. The granting of conditional liberty shall be used to enhance the healthy development of the committed youth and enable the youth to return to and succeed as a valued and contributing member of the community.

A youth's conditional liberty may only be revoked after the consideration of reasonable alternatives, including graduated responses for the least amount of time necessary to effectuate the goals of the revocation. The Department will prioritize, explore and promote positive youth interventions in the community as an alternative to placement in a secure placement. Where revocation is necessary, the process will be conducted in a manner that promotes both actual, and the experience of, fairness for a committed youth.

109 CMR 8.02. Applicability

109 CMR 8.00 shall apply to all Department and Provider employees as well as to youth committed to the Department who face revocation of conditional liberty. 109 CMR 8.00 shall not apply to any youth otherwise committed to the Department who is held on bail by a court pending the disposition of a new charge or without bail pending the disposition of a probation violation.

109 CMR 8.03. Definitions

Conditional Liberty. The placement of a youth in any community-based setting (including home), contingent upon the youth's agreement to abide by certain predetermined rules.

Conditional Liberty Agreement. Also known as Grant of Conditional Liberty. A written agreement between a youth and the Department that defines rules of conduct a committed youth must comply with in order to remain at liberty in the community.

Emergency. A situation requiring placement or retention of a youth in a secure placement because:

(a) the youth is at imminent risk for taking actions that will endanger him or herself or other persons; or

(b) the youth's planned Community Placement becomes unavailable without adequate notice to the Department and the Department has no other reasonable community placement options.

Hearing Officer. An employee of the Department designated by the Commissioner to hold revocation hearings for youth alleged to have violated the terms of their Conditional Liberty Agreement.

Revocation. The process used, pending a hearing, to remove a youth who has allegedly violated his or her Conditional Liberty Agreement from a Community Based Placement, and place him or her in a secure placement where he or she may remain after a determination at the hearing that the youth violated his or her Conditional Liberty Agreement.

Treatment Plan. A plan detailing the resources, opportunities, services and goals for each youth, designed to meet his or her developmental and rehabilitative needs and aligned with his or her assessed level of risk, to promote his or her success in the community and public safety.

109 CMR 8.04. Procedure

Whenever a youth is released to a community setting as part of a treatment plan, such release is conditional upon the youth's agreement to the specified conditions within his or her Conditional Liberty Agreement. The violation of any condition of the youth's Conditional Liberty Agreement may result in the issuance of a warrant of apprehension and placement of the youth in a secure placement. In cases where treatment longer than 120 days or a specialized placement is indicated for a youth found to have violated his or her Conditional Liberty Agreement, he or she shall be referred to the classification process. See 109 CMR 4.00: Classification of Youth Committed to the Department of Youth Services.

109 CMR 8.05. Conditional Liberty Agreement

Prior to any placement in a community-based setting, including home, a youth must agree in writing to abide by specific conditions. Such conditions shall be memorialized in the youth's Conditional Liberty Agreement, which shall meet the following criteria:

(1) The terms set forth in the Conditional Liberty Agreement shall be in accordance with the standards established by the Department. In developing the standards, the Department shall take into account adolescent brain development, and normative adolescent behavior and reflect best practices for juvenile re-entry and Positive Youth Development.

(2) The Conditional Liberty Agreement shall be written in clear and developmentally appropriate language, and be customized to accommodate the cognitive, social-emotional and cultural circumstances of the youth to whom it applies and public safety concerns.

(3) The Department shall afford a youth and his or her legal guardian the opportunity to review and provide input into any Conditional Liberty Agreement prior to its finalization.

(4) The Conditional Liberty Agreement shall be signed by the youth and the youth's Caseworker and/or the relevant District Manager or designee.

(5) A youth's Conditional Liberty Agreement shall be reviewed at least once every four months and updated to remain consistent with the youth's circumstances, capabilities, goals and treatment plan, as well as any emergent public safety concerns.

109 CMR 8.06. Violation of Conditional Liberty Agreement

(1) If a Department or Provider employee believes that a youth has not abided by the terms of the Conditional Liberty Agreement, the allegation(s) must be put in writing and submitted to the District Manager for review.

(2) The District Manager or designee, after review of the allegations, may make a preliminary decision to have the youth placed in a Secure Placement pending a hearing, if there is probable cause to believe that the youth has violated one or more of the terms of his or her Conditional Liberty Agreement.

(3) In deciding whether to pursue revocation, the District Manager or designee shall consider factors including, but not limited to:

(a) the youth's committing charge, level of community supervision and assessed risk;

(b) the potential disruption of community services and supports that the youth is engaged in; and

(c) the purpose of the return to a Secure Placement and whether the goals for the youth can be accomplished in a community setting without compromising public safety.

(4) Where a District Manager or designee determines there is probable cause to believe the youth has violated one or more of the terms of his or her Conditional Liberty Agreement, and the youth must be placed in a Secure Placement pending a hearing, the District Manager may seek the issuance of a warrant for the youth's apprehension.

(5) If a youth is arrested on a new offense and held on bail by either a bail commissioner or after arraignment, the Department shall recall any warrant of apprehension lodged against the youth and in its place, may lodge a detainer to prevent the youth's release if bail is posted or the youth is otherwise released.

109 CMR 8.07. Notice of Violation and Right to Hearing

(1) Upon being placed in a secure placement, a youth shall be promptly informed of the alleged violations of his or her Conditional Liberty Agreement and all rights available to him or her by either District Office or Program Staff. Youth shall be afforded access to counsel, either appointed by the Committee for Public Counsel Services or privately retained, and shall be provided the following documentation directly or through counsel:

(a) Documentation of and regarding the alleged violations;

(b) Copies of his or her treatment and service delivery plans;

(c) Documentation regarding his or her history of prior revocation violations and dispositions;

(d) Any other documents or evidence the Department intends to rely on in support of the revocation;

(e) Any additional documentation the youth requests from his or her Department case file in order to assist in his or her defense.

(2) The documentation and evidence described in 109 CMR 8.07 shall be provided at least two business days prior to the scheduled hearing.

(3) In the event that a youth engages in actions that harm or are intended to harm persons or property while awaiting his or her revocation hearing that demonstrate an emergent treatment concern, such that the actions will be offered for consideration in disposition of the revocation, the Caseworker shall provide the youth directly, or through counsel, any evidence, including documents and video footage, to be offered at the hearing regarding the youth's actions, as soon as reasonably practicable, prior to the hearing.

109 CMR 8.08. Waiver

A youth may waive the right to a revocation hearing. Such waiver shall be after consultation with an attorney, where one has been appointed or retained; however, nothing in 109 CMR 8.08 shall preclude a youth from declining to accept an offer of assistance of counsel. Where a youth chooses to waive his or her right to a revocation hearing, liberty is revoked provided the youth has endorsed his or her intent to waive in writing. In any case where a youth has waived a hearing, the Hearing Officer shall review the revocation documents to determine the adequacy of the grounds for revocation, as well as evaluate the effectiveness of the waiver prior to affirming the youth's revocation of conditional liberty. The disposition of a youth who has waived a hearing shall be subject to the provisions of 109 CMR 8.11.

In the event there is a question as to the continued validity of the waiver of a revocation hearing based on factors including, but not limited to, a change in the Department's requested disposition or the youth's reconsideration of the waiver, the Department shall promptly notify the attorney, if any, who counseled the youth regarding the waiver.

109 CMR 8.09. Revocation Hearing

A hearing shall be conducted by a Hearing Officer within seven working days after the return of a youth from a Community Placement to a Secure Placement, unless the youth or the Department requests and is granted a continuance by the Hearing Officer. Continuances may only be granted where a youth has not received proper notice of the alleged violations and additional time is necessary for the youth to obtain or review relevant evidence. This hearing will follow procedural requirements including:

(a) Written notice of the allegations against the youth within one business day of the youth's return to custody;

(b) Disclosure of evidence against the youth two business days prior to the hearing, or where emergent events arise while the youth is awaiting hearing, as soon as reasonably practicable prior to the hearing;

(c) Notice of all witnesses one business day prior to the hearing;

(d) Opportunity to be heard by the Hearing Officer;

(e) Right to confront and cross-examine adverse witnesses;

(f) Access to counsel, either appointed by the Committee for Public Counsel Services or privately retained;

(g) Right to call witnesses on his or her own behalf;

(h) Receipt of the Hearing Officer's decision within two business days of the hearing; and

(i) Right to appeal the Hearing Officer's decision as outlined in 109 CMR 8.12. The rules of evidence used in judicial proceedings shall not apply.

109 CMR 8.10. Role of the Hearing Officer

(1) The Hearing Officer shall have the duty to conduct a hearing in a fair and impartial manner.

(2) The Hearing Officer shall consider all evidence presented, ensure an orderly presentation of the evidence and reach a decision based upon the issues and evidence presented at the hearing, and in accordance with the law.

(3) The Hearing Officer shall not engage in ex parte communication with any party to a hearing, either prior to, during, or after the resolution of the case, or conduct an independent investigation into any facts or circumstances.

(4) The Hearing Officer shall not be bound by common law or statutory rules of evidence.

(5) The Hearing Officer may continue or adjourn the hearing with or without the consent of the parties, if, in his or her judgement, a fair and impartial hearing requires such a delay.

(6) The Hearing Officer is vested with all the power and authority granted to the Department to revoke and modify any previous order granting liberty subject to the appeal process and subject to the statutory authority vested in the Commissioner.

(7) The Hearing Officer may weigh the relevancy of all evidence offered and exclude irrelevant or repetitious evidence.

(8) The Hearing Officer's decision must be based upon a preponderance of the evidence offered.

(9) The Hearing Officer shall issue a written decision no later than two business days after the hearing. This decision shall set forth the evidence upon which it is based.

(10) Notwithstanding the provisions of 109 CMR 8.10, the Hearing Officer may take a case under advisement for any reasonable length of time.

109 CMR 8.11. Disposition Options

(1) Where a Hearing Officer finds, by a preponderance of the evidence, that a youth has violated his or her Conditional Liberty Agreement, the Officer shall order revocation of the youth's conditional liberty.

(2) Where a Hearing Officer finds that the evidence does not support a finding that the youth has violated his or her Conditional Liberty Agreement, the Officer shall order the youth released from a Secure Placement and returned to the District or Regional Office for further placement and/or planning.

(3) When Hearing Officer finds that a violation has been substantiated, the Hearing Officer may order any of the following:

(a) Immediate return of the youth to the community under continued supervision.

(b) Placement of the youth in a Secure Placement for a period of time between one and 120 days.

(c) Referral of the matter to the Regional Review Team for consideration of treatment longer than 120 days.

(d) Other reasonable alternatives in the best interest of the youth.

(4) In determining the appropriate disposition, the Hearing Officer shall consider:

(a) The youth's committing charge, level of community supervision and assessed risk;

(b) The potential disruption of community services and supports the youth is demonstrably engaged in; and

(c) The purpose of the return to secure placement and whether such goals for the youth can be accomplished in community setting.

(5) Where the disposition entered is referral to the RRT for consideration, the youth shall be afforded an opportunity to be heard by the RRT regarding the appropriate length of treatment. The RRT shall issue a written decision referencing the information considered by the RRT and providing the rationale for the RRT's decision, within two business days of hearing the youth's case, which is to be provided to the youth, his or her legal guardian, and his or her attorney of record. Accompanying the decision shall be information regarding the youth's right to appeal and the requirements regarding appeals outlined in 109 CMR 8.12.

(6) Notwithstanding the provisions of 109 CMR 4.00: Classification of Youth Committed to the Department of Youth Services and 8.00, any youth whose conditional liberty has been revoked, who assaults a Department or Provider staff or another resident, or otherwise engages in behavior that jeopardizes his or her safety or that of any other person, may be brought before the Hearing Officer who revoked his or her conditional liberty for reconsideration of the disposition imposed. A youth facing reconsideration of his or her revocation disposition shall be afforded the following:

8

(a) Prompt notice of the request for reconsideration, including notice to the revocation counsel of record;

(b) Disclosure of, and a meaningful opportunity to review, evidence relied upon by the Department in seeking reconsideration.

(c) An opportunity to be heard regarding this evidence by the Hearing Officer who issued the disposition;

(7) Should the Hearing Officer find, by a preponderance of the evidence, that the circumstances warrant a reconsideration of a change of disposition, the Hearing Officer shall enter a new disposition consistent with the options outlined in 109 CMR 8.11(3) and provide a decision consistent with 109 CMR 8.11(4).

(8) Such reconsideration and new disposition shall be subject to appeal as outlined in 109 CMR 8.12.

109 CMR 8.12. Appeals

(1) Decisions by the Hearing Officer can be appealed by the youth or the Department. If either party wishes to file an appeal, they may do so, in writing, within seven days of receipt of the decision to the Commissioner, or designee.

(2) The Commissioner, or designee, will review the case record and render a decision within 14 calendar days of receipt of the appeal.

(3) The Commissioner, or designee, may grant an expedited review of a youth's appeal upon request, where the request is timely filed and he or she determines that the circumstances put forth to justify the request warrant such review.

(4) In deciding an appeal, the Commissioner or designee's review shall be confined to the submitted appeal, any response by the non-moving party, and materials or evidence submitted for consideration at the hearing. The Commissioner, or designee, will review appeals to determine whether the Hearing Officer or RRT's decision was:

(a) Beyond the authority of the Hearing Officer or RRT;

(b) Based on an error of law or procedure;

(c) Unsupported by the weight of the evidence; or

(d) Arbitrary and/or capricious.

(3) The decision of the Commissioner, or designee, shall be final.

109 CMR 8.13. Emergency Provision

Notwithstanding the provisions of 109 CMR 8.00, the Commissioner may, for emergency reasons as defined in 109 CMR 8.03, order a youth to be placed or remain in a secure placement past his or her anticipated date of return to the community.

A youth facing placement or retention in a secure placement for emergency reasons shall be afforded the following:

(a) Prompt notice of the Emergency Provision request;

(b) Access to counsel where the request is to place or retain a youth in a secure placement beyond seven days; and

(c) Disclosure of and an opportunity to submit a written response to the information relied upon by the Department.

Regulatory Authority—109 CMR 8.00: M.G.L. c. 120, §§ 6, 12.

109 CMR 9.00. Discharge of Youth Committed to the Department of Youth Services

[Dated Aug. 29, 2016.]

109 CMR 9.01. Purpose and Scope

109 CMR 9.00 establishes the criteria and requirements for discharging youth committed to the Department of Youth Services. The Department is committed to working toward long-term positive outcomes for the youth committed to its custody and considers discharge planning and the implementation of services necessary for youth to maintain gains made during commitment a critical component of its mission.

109 CMR 9.02. Applicability

109 CMR 9.00 shall apply to all departmental personnel who are responsible for case management of youth committed to the Department of Youth Services.

109 CMR 9.03. Definitions

Discretionary Discharge. The termination of a youth's commitment to the Department of Youth Services following a decision by the Department that the youth meets the criteria established in 9.05 for discharge prior to his or her mandatory age for discharge.

Mandatory Discharge. The termination of a youth's commitment to the Department of Youth Services because the youth has reached 18, 19, 20 or 21 years of age as dictated by M.G.L. c. 119, §§ 58 and 72.

Voluntary Services. The services provided to a youth after the youth has attained the age of discharge. The services are provided pursuant to a voluntary agreement between the Department and the youth which is terminable by either the Department or the youth.

109 CMR 9.04. Procedures for Discharge

(1) Each Regional Director shall ensure the cases of all youth under the jurisdiction of a Region are reviewed no less than monthly to determine each youth's eligibility for discharge under criteria established in 109 CMR 9.05.

(2) In any case where a discharge is mandatory, or the Regional Director believes discharge is appropriate, the Regional Director shall ensure that appropriate service planning has taken place prior to such discharge.

(3) The discharge of any youth who resides outside the Commonwealth of Massachusetts will be subject to approval under the Interstate Compact Regulations, M.G.L. c. 119: Appendix.

(4) The Department shall offer to youth, prior to discharge, the option of participating in Voluntary Services as defined in 109 CMR 9.03.

(5) Any agreement between the Department and a youth for voluntary services shall be terminable by either the Department or the youth, upon notice by either of their intent to terminate services. Where the Department is seeking to terminate services, the Department must provide the youth with the opportunity to be heard regarding the termination of services before the services the youth has been receiving are terminated.

(6) The Department's offer of voluntary services shall remain open for 90 days, even where the youth may have initially declined services or has terminated voluntary services within the 90 day period.

109 CMR 9.05. Criteria for Discharge

(1) A youth meeting any of the following criteria shall be discharged from commitment to the Department:

(a) Death of the juvenile;

(b) Revocation of such commitment by a court of competent jurisdiction;

(c) Expiration of commitment by reason of the youth's reaching 18, 19, or 20 years of age as dictated by M.G.L. c. 119, §§ 58 and 72, or 21 years of age in the case of commitment as a youthful offender pursuant to M.G.L. c. 119, § 58.

(d) Enlistment of the youth in the Armed Forces.

(2) A Regional Director may recommend a youth for consideration for discharge if the youth meets any of the following criteria:

(a) The youth is eligible for consideration for a good adjustment discharge because a minimum of one year has passed since the date of the youth's last commitment and the youth has not been arrested within a year of the youth's placement in the community or returned to custody for any violation of the youth's conditional liberty within the six months preceding the request;

(b) The youth becomes legally married;

(c) The youth is committed to another state agency or sentenced to adult probation;

(d) There are exceptional circumstances in the case presenting compelling reasons for discharge. Such circumstances must be fully documented.

109 CMR 9.06. Notice Upon Discharge

The Department shall provide notice in a timely manner to anyone eligible by law to receive notice of a youth's discharge.

Regulatory Authority—109 CMR 9.00: M.G.L. c. 120A, §§ 16 and 17.

109 CMR 10.00. Social Science Research by Outside Agencies or Persons

[Dated Dec. 16, 2016.]

Section

109 CMR 10.01. Purpose and Scope

109 CMR 10.00 establishes the rules governing research conducted by outside persons or agencies, within programs regarding youth detained by or committed to the Department.

(1) The Department supports research by qualified persons or agencies which will contribute to a better understanding of various aspects and activities of the Department and to understanding the causes and prevention of delinquency.

(2) The Department does not support and will not allow research to be conducted with youth detained by or committed to the Department that exposes research subjects to the possibility of physical, psychological, or other harm as a consequence of their participation in the study.

(3) The Department shall have a formal application process for any person seeking to complete science research within the Department's programs or regarding youth detained by or committed to the Department.

(4) 109 CMR 10.00 shall not apply to requests for de-identified aggregate data or other information that would otherwise be considered a public record pursuant to M.G.L. c. 4, § 7(26).

(5) The Department shall publish a procedural handbook setting forth the requirements and expectations for researchers and their projects. This procedural handbook will be approved by the Commissioner and reviewed annually by the Department to ensure such procedures reflect best practices and the requirements set forth in 109 CMR 10.03.

109 CMR 10.02. Applicability

109 CMR 10.00 applies to all persons and/or entities that conduct research within or relating to the Department of Youth Services and the youth who are or who have been detained by or committed to the Department.

109 CMR 10.03. Definitions

Internal Review Board. The board created by the Department to oversee and approve the direction and implementation of research by outside entities or persons.

Research. Scientific, educational or other studies for a public purpose involving the use of interviews, questionnaires, and reviews of case records of youth who are or who have been detained by or committed to the Department.

109 CMR 10.04. Application to Conduct Research

Any individual(s) or agency wishing to conduct research involving youth detained by or committed to the Department shall provide the following information to the Internal Review Board (IRB).

(1) The name, address and telephone number of the principal researcher and of all research staff;

(2) An endorsement by a recognized research organization such as a university, private foundation, non-profit agency, consulting firm or public agency certifying that the research is for scientific, educational or other public purposes;

(3) A summary of the goals of the research, including how research requiring direct contact with youth will have demonstrable benefits for the youth involved with the Department or youth generally;

(4) A description of the research design, including procedures for data collection, procedures to protect the privacy of the youth and confidentiality of any Youth Records as defined in 109 CMR 3.03: Definitions to which the researcher may have access, details of any compensation to be paid to the youth;

(5) Written assurance the researcher assumes all financial liability for the expenses of carrying out the research;

(6) Written assurance the researcher will submit all research and findings to the Department's IRB for review prior to releasing any research or findings in any form, including but not limited to presentation, publication, news release or paper submission;

(7) Written assurance the researcher will include a written statement issued by the Department regarding the Department's disagreement with the research and/or its findings in any presentation, publication, news release or paper submission;

(8) Written assurance no files, documents or photos will be copied or removed from the premises where they are furnished to the researcher, unless prior written approval is obtained from the Department;

(9) Written assurance any evidence of improper care, child abuse, neglect, or any unanticipated problems involving risk to youth or others uncovered by the researcher will be reported immediately to the Department;

(10) Written assurance the researcher will provide written reports regarding the progress of the research and of any preliminary and final findings to the Department.

(11) Written assurance no publication will identify any youth by name or other recognizable characteristic.

(12) Written assurance the researcher shall promptly report to the IRB any proposed changes to the approved research activity and agrees that any such proposed changes to the approved research activity will not be initiated without IRB review and written approval.

109 CMR 10.05. Conduct of Research

(1) The principal investigator shall provide a clear and comprehensive explanation of the study to all potential subjects and obtain informed consent from all participants, including that of a legal guardian for any youth younger than 18 years old.

(2) All youth shall be informed that their participation in the research is purely voluntary and that participation or non-participation will not affect any of the terms of their detention or commitment.

(3) The Department reserves the right to terminate any research activity that jeopardizes the health, safety or welfare of any individual participant or program.

109 CMR 10.06. Compensation of Subjects

(1) No compensation, remuneration or payment of any kind shall be given to any youth in connection with a research study without the express written approval of the Department.

(2) No employee of the Department shall receive compensation, remuneration or payment of any kind from any research project conducted in accordance with 109 CMR 10.00.

Regulatory Authority—109 CMR 10.00: M.G.L. c. 18A, § 2.

109 CMR 11.00. Rescinded

109 CMR 12.00. Rescinded

[Superseded by 101 CMR 15.00: Executive Office of Health and Human Services—Criminal Offender Record Checks. See below.]

101 CMR 15.00. Executive Office of Health and Human Services Criminal Offender Record Checks

[Dated June 30, 2017.]

Section

8

101 CMR 15.01. Purpose

The purpose of 101 CMR 15.00 is to establish a core standardized policy and procedure for the Executive Office of Health and Human Services (EOHHS), its agencies, and vendor programs regarding the review of criminal records of candidates for employment.

101 CMR 15.02. Policy

It is the policy of EOHHS that an individual's background, including any Criminal Offender Record Information (CORI) and other relevant information, be carefully considered so that the vulnerable populations served by EOHHS and its agencies are protected. It is also the policy of EOHHS that qualified rehabilitated offenders are given a fair opportunity to be employed and reintegrate successfully into the workforce. Further, a criminal background check should only occur, and its results considered, in those instances where a current or prospective employee shall have been deemed otherwise qualified and the content of a criminal record is relevant to the duties and qualifications of the position.

101 CMR 15.03. Scope

(1) Upon completion of registration with the Department of Criminal Justice Information Services (DCJIS), criminal history information shall be required and only considered with respect to the following categories of applicants and employees of EOHHS, its agencies, and vendor programs:

(a) applicants and employees seeking a position that entails the potential for unsupervised contact with program clients;

(b) applicants and employees for whom a CORI is necessary to comply with other legal requirements, or for whom a CORI is otherwise deemed by EOHHS, its agencies, or vendor programs to be relevant to the duties and qualifications of the position; and

(c) employees who apply for a new position that falls within the scope of 101 CMR 15.03(1)(a) or (b).

(2) Current employees in positions where a CORI is required may be subject to a criminal record review at other times in the hiring authority's discretion. Notwithstanding the foregoing, the hiring authority shall not take any action based on the CORI unless the CORI reveals criminal activity that did not appear on the prior CORI.

(3) Neither MassHealth providers nor entities or persons who are licensed by an EOHHS agency or who receive a grant from EOHHS or an EOHHS agency are subject to 101 CMR 15.00 solely by virtue of their status as MassHealth providers, EOHHS licensees, or grant recipients. Notwithstanding the foregoing, nothing in 101 CMR 15.00 should be construed to limit the MassHealth program or an EOHHS agency from considering a person's CORI or other criminal record information when determining if he or she may participate as a provider in the MassHealth program, be licensed, or receive a grant.

(4) Notwithstanding anything in 101 CMR 15.00, a CORI is not required for EOHHS and EOHHS agency employees who, as of May 1, 2009, and for vendor program employees, who, as of July 1, 2009, hold a position where a CORI would otherwise be required, but who were not previously the subject of a CORI nor required to have been so under the EOHHS or EOHHS agency regulations applicable when the employee was hired.

(5) Notwithstanding anything in 101 CMR 15.00, EOHHS, EOHHS agencies, and vendor programs, at their expense, may use convictions and pending criminal matters in other states in addition to CORI. Such information shall be reviewed in accordance with 101 CMR 15.00 and as if the crime had occurred in Massachusetts.

(6) Notwithstanding anything in 101 CMR 15.00, 101 CMR 15.00 shall not apply to applicants for positions in or employees of vendor programs licensed by the Department of Early Education and Care. Such vendor programs shall be subject to 606 CMR 14.00: Criminal Offender and Other Background Record Checks.

(7) The procedures under 101 CMR 15.06 through 15.09 shall be followed for all positions that fall within the scope of 101 CMR 15.03.

101 CMR 15.04. Definitions

Applicant. Any person seeking employment with EOHHS or an EOHHS agency or their vendor programs, including current employees seeking new positions.

Candidate. Any person who is first determined otherwise qualified for the position and has received a conditional offer of employment subject to consideration of any criminal record information.

Client. Any person applying for or receiving EOHHS or EOHHS agency or their vendor program services.

Community Service Worker. Any individual who, as a condition of probation, is applying for a position.

CORI Cleared Employee. Any candidate hired as an employee after the hiring authority completed all requirements of 101 CMR 15.00.

CORI Coordinator. The person designated by the hiring authority to send requests and receive responses from the Department of Criminal Justice Information Services (DCJIS).

CORI Investigation. The process of requesting, receiving, and evaluating CORI related to candidates for employment.

Criminal Justice Official. Either the candidate's probation officer, parole officer, or correctional facility superintendent (or designee), depending upon whomever had the most recent responsibility for supervision of the candidate. Candidates last supervised in a correctional facility may advise the hiring authority of any employee of the correctional facility who may have specific information about the candidate that would assist the superintendent in his or her assessment process.

Criminal Offender Record Information (CORI). Information recorded as a result of criminal proceedings or any consequent related proceedings and regulated by the Department of Criminal Justice Information Services under 803 CMR 2.00: Criminal Offender Record Information (CORI).

Department of Criminal Justice Information Services (DCJIS). The Commonwealth agency statutorily designated to, among other things, provide a public safety information system and network to support data collection, information sharing, and interoperability for the Commonwealth's criminal justice and law enforcement community and to oversee the authorized provision of Criminal Offender Record Information (CORI) to the non-criminal justice community.

Employees. Individuals holding full and part-time positions, including state employees, contract employees, individual consultants, temporary employees, volunteers, trainees, interns, or students, regardless of whether the individuals receive compensation and the source of funding for the positions. For the purposes of 101 CMR 15.04, a current client of a facility or program who provides services at that facility or program will not be considered an employee at that facility or program.

Employment. Full and part-time positions held by any person, including state employees, contract employees, individual consultants, temporary employees, volunteers, trainees, interns, or students, regardless of whether the person receives compensation and the source of funding for the positions.

EOHHS. The Executive Office of Health and Human Services.

EOHHS Agency. Any agency, department, commission, office, board, division, or other body within and subject to EOHHS under M.G.L. c. 6A, § 16, including the Office of Elder Affairs.

EOHHS Funded or Operated Program. Any program operated by EOHHS or an EOHHS agency or their vendor programs that provides health and human services for or on behalf of EOHHS or EOHHS agency clients in accordance with a contract under 808 CMR 1.00: Compliance, Reporting and Auditing for Human and Social Services.

Hiring Authority. The person or persons legally authorized or designated to make hiring decisions within EOHHS or an EOHHS agency or their vendor programs. Different persons may be authorized or designated as responsible for specific parts of the process in making a hiring decision.

No Record. The conclusion from a CORI search that shows no information relating to the candidate is available for release to EOHHS, an EOHHS agency, or their vendor programs. A finding of "no record" does not necessarily mean, however, that criminal information is not present in the CORI database.

Otherwise Qualified. An applicant who meets all other employment criteria and consideration for a position.

Pending. A criminal matter is considered pending if the CORI report indicates that the matter remains open and without final resolution, including that the case has been continued without a finding.

Potential Unsupervised Contact. Potential for contact with a client when no other CORI cleared employee is present. A person having only the potential for incidental unsupervised contact with clients in commonly used areas such as elevators, hallways, and waiting rooms, will not be considered to have the potential for unsupervised contact for purposes of 101 CMR 15.03. The term "commonly used areas" does not include bathrooms or other isolated areas that are separated by sight and sound from other staff.

Qualified Mental Health Professional. A psychiatrist licensed to practice medicine under M.G.L. c. 112, § 2, a psychologist licensed under M.G.L. c. 112, § 118 through 121, or an independent clinical social worker licensed under M.G.L. c. 112, § 130 through 132; provided that he or she has at least 1,000 hours of experience over a minimum of two years involving assessment, treatment, and consultation concerning individuals with behavior that presents a risk of harm to others in the community, in the workplace, in treatment settings, or in correctional facilities; provided further that he or she has not provided treatment to the candidate.

Trainee. Any person enrolled in an academic program or participating in a pre- or post-doctoral training program that is affiliated with an accredited educational institution or hospital, who receives a placement within EOHHS or an EOHHS agency or their vendor programs.

Vendor Program. A program, administered by an individual, corporation, partnership, organization, trust, association, or other entity, that provides services to EOHHS or EOHHS agency clients under a contract issued by EOHHS or an EOHHS agency in accordance with 808 CMR 1.00: Compliance, Reporting and Auditing for Human and Social Services. An individual or entity will not be considered a vendor program solely because they participate as a MassHealth provider or are licensed by an EOHHS agency or receive a grant from EOHHS or an EOHHS agency.

Volunteer. Any person who works in an unpaid capacity for EOHHS, an EOHHS agency, or vendor program. For the purposes of 101 CMR 15.04, a current client of a facility or program who provides unpaid services at that facility or program will not be considered a volunteer at that facility or program.

Work Release Program. A program of unpaid work performed by an individual under the custody of the state or county correctional system.

101 CMR 15.05. Community Service and Work Release Workers

(1) Notwithstanding anything in 101 CMR 15.00, EOHHS or any EOHHS agency or their vendor programs that participate in either a criminal justice related community service program or a work release program must require all individuals who participate to disclose his or her criminal record on a form signed by the candidate's criminal justice official. No inquiry, however, may be made inconsistent with M.G.L. c. 151B, § 4, para 9 which prohibits the disclosure of:

(a) an arrest, detention, or disposition regarding any violation of law in which no conviction resulted; or

(b) a first conviction for any of the following misdemeanors: drunkenness, simple assault, speeding, minor traffic violations, affray, or disturbance of the peace; or

(c) any conviction of a misdemeanor where the date of such conviction or the completion of any period of incarceration resulting there from, whichever date is later, occurred five or more years prior to the date of such application for employment or such request for information, unless such person has been convicted of any offense within five years immediately preceding the date of such application for employment or such request for information.

(2) In addition, as a condition of participation, the candidate's criminal justice official must conclude in writing that the candidate will not pose an unacceptable risk of harm to clients, or the community service program or work release program will take responsibility for providing physical supervision for the candidate at all times.

101 CMR 15.06. Application Forms

(1) Disclosure of Criminal Records.

(a) No initial employment application form may ask whether an applicant has a criminal record. Only a candidate who has been first determined otherwise eligible for a position subject to a CORI and given a conditional offer of employment subject to consideration of any criminal record, may be asked to complete a supplemental form requiring the disclosure of the candidate's criminal record. No inquiry may be made inconsistent with M.G.L. c. 151B, § 4, para 9, referenced under 101 CMR 15.05(1).

(b) Any other criminal record information will be obtained in accordance with 101 CMR 15.06(2).

(2) CORI Authorization Forms and Consent.

(a) The hiring authority will ensure that a candidate provides consent to a CORI investigation and, where applicable, to the periodic conduct of further CORI investigations during the course of employment.

(b) All candidates must complete an appropriate CORI Acknowledgement Form and in accordance with 803 CMR 2.00: Criminal Offender Record Information (CORI), the hiring authority shall verify the candidate's identity by forms of documentation as determined by DCJIS. If the hiring authority is unable to verify a subject's identity and signature in person, the subject may submit a completed CORI Acknowledgment Form acknowledged by the candidate before a notary public.

(c) The hiring authority will also inform the candidate that his or her CORI may be utilized by qualified mental-health professionals conducting themselves in conformance with 101 CMR 15.09 and by EOHHS, EOHHS agency, or vendor program personnel responsible for carrying out the provisions of 101 CMR 15.00.

101 CMR 15.07. CORI Investigations

(1) A hiring authority will complete a CORI investigation only after determining that the person is otherwise qualified for employment and making a conditional offer of employment to a candidate, subject to consideration of any criminal record.

(2) The hiring authority will confirm an offer only after the hiring authority receives written confirmation that the criminal record investigation has resulted in a finding of "no record" or the hiring authority has complied with the requirements of 101 CMR 15.07, 15.08, and 15.09. The hiring authority will not permit any candidate to commence employment until after the candidate is cleared as a result of the CORI investigation in accordance with 101 CMR 15.00. Notwithstanding the foregoing, pending the candidate being cleared, the hiring authority may permit the candidate to commence employment on a temporary basis in a position outside the scope of 101CMR 15.03(1).

(3) All CORI investigations that result in a finding of "no record" are transmitted back to the hiring authority and provide sufficient evidence of suitability for hire for 60 business days. A "no record" finding may be valid for consideration for other positions during such 60 days.

(4) All CORI investigations that show findings of criminal records are sent immediately to the hiring authority for review and action consistent with 101 CMR 15.00.

101 CMR 15.08. Findings from CORI Investigations—No Further Review—Outstanding Warrants

(1) If the CORI investigation reveals a conviction of a 101 CMR 15.15: Table B crime that is a felony more than ten years old, or a 101 CMR 15.15: Table B crime that is a misdemeanor more than five years old, and there are no subsequent convictions or pending cases of any kind, the hiring authority will not consider such crime. For purposes of computing the five and ten-year time periods, the time period will run from the date any court supervision, probation, or sentence was terminated.

(2) If the CORI investigation reveals an outstanding warrant for any offense, the hiring authority will inform the candidate that he or she is ineligible for employment unless the warrant is removed.

(3) Storage, retention, and destruction of all CORI reports, including those with a finding of "no record", shall be in accordance with 803 CMR 2.00: Criminal Offender Record Information (CORI).

101 CMR 15.09. Findings from CORI Investigation—Crimes Subject to Review

(1) If the CORI investigation reveals a conviction of a 101 CMR 15.15: Table A crime, regardless of when it occurred, or a pending 101 CMR 15.15: Table A crime, or a conviction of a 101 CMR 15.15: Table B crime within the five- and ten-year time periods referenced under 101 CMR 15.08(1), or a pending 101 CMR 15.15: Table B crime, the hiring authority will give careful consideration to the following factors in its decision to hire or not hire the candidate:

(a) time since the conviction or pending offense;

(b) age of the candidate at the time of the offense;

(c) nature and specific circumstances of the offense;

(d) sentence imposed and length of any period of incarceration;

(e) relationship of the criminal act to the nature of the work to be performed;

(f) number of offenses;

(g) whether offenses were committed in association with a dependence on drugs or alcohol, from which the candidate has since recovered;

(h) any relevant evidence of rehabilitation or lack thereof, such as information about compliance with conditions of parole or probation, including orders of no contact with victims and witnesses; and the individual's conduct and experience since the time of the offense, including but not limited to educational or professional certifications obtained; and

(i) any other relevant information, including information submitted by the candidate, or requested by the hiring authority.

(2) The hiring authority, using a form prescribed by EOHHS, will also make a written determination of its decision to hire or not hire such candidate. This form will document the factors considered and the rationale for the hiring authority's decision. A copy of such written determination will be maintained by the hiring authority in a secure location, together with the CORI and criminal record disclosure information that may have been requested under 101 CMR 15.06(1)(a). Completion of the written determination form will serve to confirm that the hiring authority has carefully reviewed the CORI and other relevant information, including information provided by the candidate, so that the vulnerable populations served by EOHHS agencies are protected and candidates with criminal histories are given a fair opportunity to be employed and to reintegrate successfully into the workforce.

(3) (a) In addition, if the hiring authority decides to hire a candidate with a CORI showing a conviction of, or pending Table A crime, the hiring authority will submit the prescribed form to the EOHHS Secretary or the EOHHS agency Commissioner or their designees. The hiring authority will not proceed to hire the candidate for five business days from the date the EOHHS Secretary or the EOHHS agency Commissioner or their designees receive the form. During such time, the EOHHS Secretary or EOHHS agency Commissioner or their designees may disapprove the hire or request additional information. Notwithstanding the foregoing, a hiring authority may proceed to hire the candidate before the expiration of the five-day period if the EOHHS Secretary or EOHHS agency Commissioner or designee, after receiving the prescribed form, informs the hiring authority that he or she does not intend to disapprove the hire or request additional information.

(b) EOHHS or an EOHHS agency may require that the hiring authority's review include the following:

1. a review by the candidate's criminal justice official, including a determination in writing that the candidate, within the position sought, does not pose an unacceptable risk of harm to the clients; or

2. if the criminal justice official has been determined by the hiring authority to be unavailable or has indicated he or she has insufficient information to render an assessment, a written determination from a qualified mental-health professional that the candidate, within the position sought, does not pose an unacceptable risk of harm to the clients. The EOHHS agency or EOHHS, if EOHHS makes the request, will bear the cost of an assessment by a qualified mental-health professional of the candidate's risk of harm.

(4) If the hiring authority does not wish to hire a candidate with a 101 CMR 15.15: Table A crime, or a 101 CMR 15.15: Table B crime within the five- and ten-year time periods referenced under 101 CMR 15.08(2), the prescribed form will be completed as outlined in 101 CMR

15.09(2) and will be maintained on file in a secure location.

(5) Before any determination or hiring decision is made on the basis of the CORI, the hiring authority will comply with all requirements of the DCJIS under 803 CMR 2.00: Criminal Offender Record Information (CORI) including:

(a) providing a candidate with a copy of his or her CORI, EOHHS CORI regulations, and DCJIS information concerning the process for correcting a criminal record;

(b) notifying the candidate of the potential adverse decision based on the CORI;

(c) informing the candidate what part of the criminal record appears to make him or her ineligible for the position;

(d) providing the candidate with an opportunity to dispute the accuracy and relevancy of the CORI; and

(e) upon receipt of any additional documentation received from the candidate or DCJIS, reviewing the information with the candidate and informing him or her of the decision.

101 CMR 15.10. Post Audit and Compliance Review

(1) EOHHS or an EOHHS agency may conduct a periodic review of all documentation of compliance with 101 CMR 15.00, including written determinations of hiring decisions of candidates as required under 101 CMR 15.09(2).

(2) If such review or other relevant information obtained by EOHHS or an EOHHS agency raises concerns about the hiring authority's compliance, EOHHS or an EOHHS agency may require the hiring authority to submit documentation for all hiring decisions and provide EOHHS or an EOHHS agency five business days to disapprove any decision to hire. EOHHS or an EOHHS agency may require the hiring authority to follow such prior review process for as long a period as it determines is necessary to ensure that the hiring authority is complying.

(3) Notwithstanding 101 CMR 15.10(2), in the event of noncompliance by a vendor program with any provision under 101 CMR 15.00, EOHHS may terminate the vendor's contract or take such other action it determines appropriate

101 CMR 15.11. Dissemination

CORI records may be disseminated only to individuals, such as the hiring authority or CORI Coordinator, designated by the agency or vendor program to receive such information, and included in the agency or vendor's need to know list. The hiring authority will maintain a listing of persons so designated. Any further dissemination shall be accordance with 803 CMR 2.00: Criminal Offender Record Information (CORI), and a log of such secondary dissemination shall be maintained in accordance with DCJIS regulations. Willful dissemination of CORI to unauthorized individuals is punishable by a jail sentence of up to one year and/or a fine of $5,000, or in the case of dissemination by an entity that is not a natural person, a fine of up to $50,000. Further in the case of dissemination of juvenile delinquency records such fine may be up to $7,500 and if by an entity not a natural person, up to $75,000.

101 CMR 15.12. Incidents

If any hiring authority receives an allegation that an EOHHS, an EOHHS agency, or vendor program employee whose CORI contained a record has harmed a client, the hiring authority will immediately report the allegation to the EOHHS or EOHHS agency General Counsel. Notification will include documentation of the hiring decision of the hiring authority.

8

101 CMR 15.13. Agency Regulations

101 CMR 15.00 is intended to supersede any EOHHS agency regulations on the use of CORI for employment purposes. To the extent that any agency regulation may conflict, 101 CMR 15.00 will take precedence.

101 CMR 15.14. Severability

If any provisions of 101 CMR 15.01 through 15.15, or the applications of such provisions to any person or circumstance are held invalid or unconstitutional, the other provisions of said 101 CMR 15.01 through 15.15, or the application of such provisions to any person or circumstance other than that as to which it is held invalid or unconstitutional, shall not be affected thereby.

101 CMR 15.15. Tables of Offenses

The offenses included in 101 CMR 15.15 are to be construed as including similar violations of the law of Massachusetts, another state, the United States, or a military, territorial, or Native American tribal authority. If an offense is determined to be similar, the hiring authority will consider the offense as if it were on the same table as the included offense.

Table A	M.G.L.
Abandon Child Younger than ten Years Old, Resulting in Death	c. 119, § 39
Abuse of Patient in Long Term Care Facility	c. 265, § 38
Animals, Cruelty to	c. 272, § 77
Armed Career Criminal	c. 269, § 10G
Arson of Dwelling House	c. 266, § 1
Assault, Aggrevated	c. 265, § 13A(b)
Assault & Battery, Dangerous Weapon, Aggravated	c. 265, § 15A(c)
Assault & Battery, Dangerous Weapon, Victim 60 Years of Age or Older	c. 265, § 15A(a)
Assault & Battery on Child	c. 265, § 13J
Assault & Battery on Elder or Person with Disability	c. 265, § 13K
Assault & Battery, Intimidation, Race/Color/Religion	c. 265, §§ 39(a) and 39(b)
Assault & Battery on Person With Intellectual Disability	c. 265, § 13F
Assault with Intent to Murder or Rob, Armed	c. 265, § 18(b)
Assault with Intent to Murder or Rob, Victim 60 Years of Age or Older, Armed	c. 265, § 18(a)
Assault in Dwelling, Armed	c. 265, § 18A
Assault by Dangerous Weapon, Victim 60 Years of Age or Older	c. 265, § 15B(a)
Assault with Intent to Murder or Maim	c. 265, § 15
Assault with Intent to Rape	c. 265, § 24
Assault with Intent to Rape Child Younger than 16 Years Old	c. 265, § 24B
Breaking and Entering Night, Bldg/Ship/Motor Vehicle, Intent to Commit Felony	c. 266, § 16
Carjacking, Armed	c. 265, § 21A
Child in Nude or Sexual Act, Pose/Exhibit or Distribute Material	c. 272, §§ 29A and 29B
Child Enticement	c. 265, § 26C
Civil Rights Violation, Bodily Injury	c. 265, § 37
Criminal Harassment, Subsequent Offense	c. 265, § 43A(b)
Drugs, Distribute to Minor	c. 94C, § 32F
Drugs, Trafficking in Cocaine	c. 94C, § 32E(b)(1)-(b)(4)
Drugs, Trafficking in Heroin	c. 94C, § 32E(c)(4)
Drugs, Trafficking in Marijuana	c. 94C, § 32E(a)(4)
Elder/Disabled, Permit Abuse on	c. 265, § 13K(a ½)
Explosion, Malicious	c. 266, § 102(B) (c. 266, § 101 prior to July 15, 2010)
Extortion	c. 265, § 25
Firearm, Armed Career Criminal	c. 269, § 10G
Home Invasion	c. 265, § 18C
Identity Fraud	c. 266, § 37E
Incest	c. 272, § 17
Indecent Assault & Battery on Person 14 Years of Age or Older	c. 265, § 13H
Indecent Assault & Battery on Child Younger than 14 Years Old	c. 265, § 13B
Indecent Assault & Battery on Child Younger than 14 Years Old, Aggravated	c. 265, § 13B½
Indecent Assault & Battery on Child Younger than 14 Years Old, Aggravated, Subsequent Event	c. 265, § 13B¾

8

Table A	M.G.L.
Indecent Assault & Battery on Disabled/Person 60 Years of Age or Older	c. 265, § 13K
Indecent Assault & Battery on Retarded Person	c. 265, § 13F
Kidnapping	c. 265, § 26
Kidnapping Minor by Relative, Endanger Safety	c. 265, § 26A
Manslaughter (Voluntary or Involuntary)	c. 265, § 13
Mayhem	c. 265, § 14
Murder	c. 265, §§ 1 and 2
Obscene Pictures, Distributing	c. 272, §§ 28 and 29
Obscene Materials Harmful to Minor, Distribute or Possess with Intent to Distribute	c. 272, § 28
Photograph Unsuspecting Nude Person/Photograph of Unsuspecting Nude Person, Disseminate	c. 272, §§ 105(b) and (c) (c. 272, §§ 104(b) and (c) prior to March 7, 2014)
Prescription; Forgery, Alter, Subsequent Offense	c. 94C, § 33(c)
Prostitution, Derive Support from	c. 272, § 7
Prostitution, Derive Support from Child	c. 272, § 4B
Prostitution, Induce Minor to	c. 272, § 4A
Prostitution, Maintain House of	c. 272, § 6
Prostitution/Unlawful Sex/Abduct Person for	c. 272, § 2
Prostitution/Solicitation (with Person Younger than 18 Years Old)	c. 272, § 53A(b)
Prostitution/Solicitation (with Person Younger than 14 Years Old); Prior to February 19, 2012	c. 272, § 53A(b)
Rape	c. 265, § 22(b)
Rape, Aggravated	c. 265, § 22(a)
Rape & Abuse of a Child, Aggravated	c. 265, § 23A
Rape & Abuse of a Child, Aggravated, Subsequent Event	c. 265, § 23B
Rape of Child with Force	c. 265, § 22A
Rape of Child with Force, Aggravated	c. 265, § 22B
Rape of Child with Force, Aggravated, Subsequent Event	c. 265, § 22C
Rape of Child (Statutory)	c. 265, § 23
Reckless Endangerment to Children	c. 265, § 13L
Robbery, Armed	c. 265, § 17
Sex Offender, Failure to Register	c. 6, § 178H(a)
Sexual Conduct with Child Younger than 18 Years Old, Pay for or for Fee	c. 272, § 53A(b)
Sexual Conduct with Child Younger than 14 Years Old, Pay for or for fee; Prior to February 19, 2012	c. 272, § 53A(b)
Sexual Intercourse, Administer Drugs for	c. 272, § 3
Sexual Intercourse, Induce Minor	c. 272, § 4
Stalking	c. 265, § 43(a)
Stalking in Violation of Restraining Order	c. 265, § 43(b)
Unnatural Acts with Child Younger than 16 Years Old	c. 272, § 35A
Violate Domestic Protective Order	c. 208, § 34C
Violation of Protective Order (209A)	c. 209A, § 7
Weapon of Mass Destruction	c. 266, § 102C
Conspiracy to Commit any of the above Table A Crimes	c. 274, § 7
Accessory Before the Fact of any of the above Table A Crimes	c. 274, § 2
Attempt to Commit any of the above Table A Crimes	c. 274, § 6

Table B

Crime Name	M.G.L.	Felony or Misdemeanor
Abandon Child Younger than ten Years Old	c. 119, § 39	M
Accessory after Fact (Variable)	c. 272, § 4	F
Accosting; Lewd & Lascivious Conduct; Indecent Exposure	c. 272, § 53	M
Affray, Subsequent Offense Affray (Prior to August 1, 2009)	c. 272, § 53	M
Aid Escape from Custody	c. 268, § 17	M
Alcoholic Beverages, Sell/Deliver to Person Younger than 21 Years Old	c. 138, § 34	M
Alien in Possess of Firearm	c. 140, § 131H	M
Assault	c. 265, § 13A(a)	M
Assault with Intent to Rob, Unarmed	c. 265, § 20	F
Assault & Battery	c. 265, § 13A(a)	M
Assault & Battery on Public Servant/Police Officer	c. 265, § 13D	M
Assault & Battery on Correctional Officer	c. 127, § 38B	F
Assault & Battery Dangerous Weapon	c. 265, § 15A(b)	F
Assault by Dangerous Weapon	c. 265, § 15B(b)	F
Assault with Hypodermic Needle, Syringe	c. 265, § 15C(a)	F
Assault & Battery with Hypodermic Needle, Syringe	c. 265, § 15C(b)	F
Attempt to Injure Depository of Valuables	c. 266, § 16	F
Betting; Taking, Allowing	c. 271, § 17	M
Body Armor, Use of in Commission of Felony	c. 269, § 10D	F
Bomb Scare /Hijack Threat	c. 269, § 14	F
Bomb/Explosives, Unlawful Possession	c. 148, § 35	M
Breaking and Entering Day, Intent to Commit Felony, Person in Fear	c. 266, § 17	F
Breaking and Entering Day, Intent to Commit Felony	c. 266, § 18	F
Breaking and Entering Railroad Car	c. 266, § 19	F
Breaking and Entering Truck, Intent to Commit Felony	c. 266, § 20A	F
Breaking and Entering, Intent to Commit Misdemeanor	c. 266, § 16A	M
Bribery of a Police Officer (State/Local Official or Member of the Judiciary)	c. 268A, § 2	F
Bribery/Gifts to Influence Business Affairs	c. 271, § 39	F
Burglarious Tools, Make or Possess	c. 266, § 49	F
Burglarious Tools, Motor Vehicle Master Key, Make or Possess	c. 266, § 49	F
Burglary, Armed	c. 266, § 14	F
Burglary, Unarmed	c. 266, § 15	F
Burning Building	c. 266, § 2	F
Burning Motor Vehicle or Personal Property	c. 266, § 5	F
Burning to Defraud Insurance Co.	c. 266, § 10	F
Burn Motor Vehicle, Willful & Malicious	c. 266, § 127	F
Civil Rights Violation, No Bodily Injury	c. 265, § 37	M
Compounding or Concealing Felony	c. 268, § 3	F
Contribute to Delinquency of Child	c. 119, § 63	M
Confine or Put in Fear to Steal or Attempt to Steal	c. 265, § 21	F
Credit Card, Larceny or Misuse of	c. 266, § 37B	M
Credit Card, Unauthorized Use, over $250	c. 266, § 37C	F
Criminal Harassment	c. 265, § 43A(a)	M
Dangerous Weapon, Carrying	c. 269, §§ 10(b) and 10(d)	F
Dangerous Weapon, Unlawful Possession	c. 269, § 10(b)	F
Defacement of Real or Personal Property	c. 266, § 126A	F
Destruction of Property over $250, Malicious	c. 266, § 127	F
Disorderly Conduct	c. 272, § 53	M
Drugs, Larceny from Authorized Person	c. 94C, § 37	F
Drugs, Failure to Keep Records	c. 94C, § 15	M
Drugs, Illegal Possession Class C Substance	c. 94C, § 34	M
Drugs, Illegal Possession Class D Substance	c. 94C, § 34	M
Drugs, Illegal Possession Class E Substance	c. 94C, § 34	M
Drugs, Dispense Without Prescription or When Not Registered	c. 94C, § 25	M
Drug Paraphernalia, Distribute or Intend to Distribute	c. 94C, § 32I(a)	M
Drug Paraphernalia, Sell to Minor	c. 94C, § 32I(b)	F
Drugs, Manufacture/Distribute Class A Substance	c. 94C, § 32	F
Drugs, Manufacture/Distribute Class B Substance	c. 94C, § 32A	F
Drugs, Manufacture/Distribute Class C Substance	c. 94C, § 32B	F
Drugs, Manufacture/Distribute Class D Substance	c. 94C, § 32C	F
Drugs, Manufacture/Distribute Class E Substance	c. 94C, § 32d(a)	M
Drugs, Manufacture/Distribute/ Dispense Class B Substance	c. 94C, § 32A	F
Drugs, Manufacture/Distribute/ Dispense Class A Substance in, on or near School/Park	c. 94C, § 32J	F
Drugs, Manufacture/Distribute/ Dispense Class B Substance in, on or near School/Park	c. 94C, § 32J	F

8

Crime Name	M.G.L.	Felony or Misdemeanor
Drugs, Motor Vehicle Homicide, Negligent Operation	c. 90, § 24G(b)	F
Drugs, Possess Class A Substance	c. 94C, § 34	M
Drugs, Possess Class A Substance, Intent to Distribute	c. 94C, § 32(a)	F
Drugs, Possess Class B Substance	c. 94C, § 34	M
Drugs, Possess Class B Substance, Intent to Distribute	c. 94C, § 32A(a)	F
Drugs, Possess Class C Substance, Intent to Distribute	c. 94C, § 32B(a)	F
Drugs, Possess Class C Substance, Subsequent Offense	c. 94C, § 34	M
Drugs, Possess Class D Substance, Intent to Distribute	c. 94C, § 32C(a)	F
Drugs, Possess Class D Substance, Subsequent Offense	c. 94C, § 34	M
Drugs, Possess Class E Substance, Intent to Distribute	c. 94C, § 32D	M
Drugs, Possess Controlled Substance with Intent to Distribute, Subsequent Offense	c. 94C, § 32(b)	F
Drugs, Possess Counterfeit Substances with Intent to Distribute	c. 94C, § 32G	F
Drugs, Possess Class A Substance with Intent to Distribute in, on or near School/Park	c. 94C, § 32J	F
Drugs, Possess Class B Substance with Intent to Distribute in, on or near School/Park	c. 94C, § 32J	F
Drugs, Possess Class D Substance with Intent to Distribute in, on or near School/Park	c. 94C, § 32J	F
Drugs, Trafficking in Cocaine in, on or near School/Park	c. 94C, § 32J	F
Drugs, Trafficking in Heroin in, on or near School/Park	c. 94C, § 32J	F
Drugs, Trafficking in Marijuana in, on or near School/Park	c. 94C, § 32J	F
Drugs, Unlawfully Obtaining Controlled Substance; False Prescription, Fraud, False Registration	c. 94C, § 33	F
Embezzlement	c. 266, §§ 51-52, 55-59	F
Enter Without Breaking, Bldg/Ship/Motor Vehicle, Intent to Commit a Felony, Person in Fear	c. 266, § 17	F
Enter Without Breaking a Dwelling in Night, Intent to Commit Felony	c. 266, § 18	F
Enter Without Breaking, Truck, with Intent to Commit Felony	c. 266, § 20A	F
Escape by Prisoner	c. 268, § 16	F
Escape, Furlough	c. 268, § 16	F
Explosives, Throwing	c. 266, § 102	F
Explosives, Throw/Place/Explode or Possess with Intent to Injure	c. 266, § 102	F
Firearm, Carrying Loaded Rifle/Shotgun	c. 269, § 12D(a)	M
Firearm, Carrying Loaded or Unloaded Firearm on a Public Way; Unenclosed Case	c. 269, § 12D(b)	F

Crime Name	M.G.L.	Felony or Misdemeanor
Firearm, Discharge Within 500 Ft. of a Building	c. 269, § 12E	M
Firearm, Discharge Within 500 Ft. of a Dwelling or near Highway	c. 131, § 58	M
Firearm License/ID Card, False	c. 140, § 131I	F
Firearm, Possess Without Fire Arms ID	c. 269, § 10(h)	M
Firearm, Possess of, Serial/ID Number Obliterated	c. 269, § 11C	F
Firearm, Possess of, Serial/ID Number Obliterated, Used in Commission or Attempted Commission of a Felony	c. 269, § 11B	F
Firearm, Sell Without License	c. 140, § 128	F
Firearm, Shotgun, Barrel Und 18 "Sawed Off", Possess, Subsequent Offense	c. 269, § 10(d)	F
Firearm, Shotgun, Barrel Und 18 " Sawed Off", Possess	c. 269, § 10(c)	F
Firearm Unattended	c. 269, § 10(h)	F
Firearm, Unlawful Possession, Commission Felony	c. 265, § 18B	F
Firearm, Shotgun, Unlawful Possession	c. 140, § 129	M
Firearm Violation, Carry with Ammunition	c. 269, § 10(n)	M
Forged Instrument, Utter	c. 267, § 5	F
Fugitive from Justice	c. 276, § 20A	M
Gun Permit, False Information for	c. 140, § 129	M
Hoax Device/Substance, Possess/Transport/Use	c. 266, § 102A½	F
Indecent Exposure	c. 272, § 53	M
Infernal Machine, Possess	c. 266, § 102A	F
Kidnapping Minor by Relative	c. 265, § 26A	M
Kill Beast, Willful & Malicious	c. 266, § 112	F
Larceny, Motor Vehicle or Trailer	c. 266, § 28	F
Larceny, Person	c. 266, § 25	F
Larceny, Person 65 Years of Age or Older	c. 266, § 25	F
Larceny by Check under $250	c. 266, § 37	M
Larceny by Check over $250	c. 266, § 37	F
Larceny, Firearm	c. 266, § 30	F
Larceny in Bldg, Ship, Vessel, or RR Car	c. 266, § 20	F
Larceny in Truck/Trailer	c. 266, § 20B	F
Larceny over $250	c. 266, § 30	F
Larceny under $250	c. 266, § 30	M
Larceny, Bank Employee or Officer	c. 266, § 52	F
Leave Scene after Personal Injury, Motor Vehicle	c. 90, § 24(2)(a½)(1)	M
Lewd & Lascivious Conduct	c. 272, § 53	M
Lewdness, Open & G ross	c. 272, § 16	F
Liquor, Procure for Minor	c. 138, § 34	M
Machine or Sawed off Shot Gun, Possession of	c. 269, § 10(c)	F
Machine Gun, Possession of Without License	c. 269, § 10(c)	F
Manslaughter by Operating under the Influence	c. 265, § 13½	F
Medical Assistance (Medicaid) Fraud	c. 118E, § 40	F

8

Crime Name	M.G.L.	Felony or Misdemeanor
Medical Assistance (Medicaid) Kickback	c. 118E, § 41	F
Motor Vehicle Homicide, Reckless Operation	c. 90, § 24G(b)	F
Motor Vehicle Homicide, under Influence Drugs, Negligent or Reckless	c. 90, § 24G(a)	F
Motor Vehicle, Use of in Commission of Felony	c. 90, § 24(2)(a)	F
Motor Vehicle Homicide, under Influence Liquor	c. 90, § 24G(b)	F
Motor Vehicle Homicide, under Influence Liquor, Negligent or Reckless	c. 90, § 24G(b)	F
Motor Vehicle, Operating after License Revoked for Drunk Driving	c. 90, § 23	M
Motor Vehicle, Operating under Influence of Drugs, Alcohol	c. 90, § 24(1)(a)(1)	M
Motor Vehicle, Operating under Influence of Drugs, Alcohol, 3rd and Subsequent Offense	c. 90, § 24(1)(a)(1)	F
Motor Vehicle, Operating under Influence of Drugs, Liquor, 3rd and Subsequent Offense	c. 90, § 24	F
Motor Vehicle, Take Without Authority, Steal Parts	c. 266, § 28	F
Obscene Materials, Possess with Intent to Distribute	c. 272, § 29	F
Obscene Literature, Sell to Minor	c. 272, § 28	M
Obstruction of Justice	Common Law	M [See c. 279, § 5 Re: Penalty for Common Law Crimes.]
Perjury	c. 268, § 1	F
Prescription; Forgery, Alter	c. 94C, § 33(b)	F
Prescription, Utter False	c. 94C, § 33	F
Prisoner, Deliver Articles to or from Inmate	c. 268, § 31	F
Prisoner, Deliver Drugs to	c. 268, § 28	F
Prostitution/solicitation	c. 272, § 53A	M
Prostitution, Engaging in Sex "John"	c. 272, § 53A	M
Prostitution, Keep House of	c. 272, § 24	M
Prostitute, Solicit for	c. 272, § 8	M
Resisting Arrest	c. 268, § 32B	M
Riot	c. 269, § 1	M
Robbery, Unarmed	c. 265, § 19(b)	F
Robbery, Unarmed, Victim 60+	c. 265, § 19(a)	F
Shoplifting, 3rd or Subsequent Offense	c. 266, § 30A	M
Stolen Property, Receive, over $250	c. 266, § 60	F
Stolen Motor Vehicle, Receive/ buy	c. 266, § 28(a)	F
Telecommunications Fraud	c. 166, § 42A	M
Telephone Calls, Annoying or Obscene	c. 269, § 14A	M
Unnatural Acts	c. 272, § 35	F
Vandalize Church/Synagogue/ Cemetery	c. 266, § 127A	F
Vandalize School/Church/ Educational Bldg	c. 266, § 98	F
Witness, Intimidate or Retaliate Against	c. 268, § 13B	F
Conspiracy to Commit any of above Table B Crimes		
Attempts to Commit any of the above Table B Crimes		
Accessory Before any of the above Table B Crimes		

Regulatory Authority—101 CMR 15.00: M.G.L. c. 6A, § 16 and c. 71B, § 12C.

8

Additional Materials: Department of Youth Services Policies

Note 1: The following materials are available in the eBook version of this Sourcebook. See the Electronic Download page at the front of this book for instructions on downloading a copy of the eBook.

Note 2: Department of Youth Services policies are available on the department's website at https://www.mass.gov/lists/dys-policies-regulations.

Policy

Chapter 01. *Department Policies*
01.01.01(c) Policy Administration
01.01.02(b) Repealed
01.01.03(a) Repeal of Policies
01.01.04(a) Policy Definitions
01.01.09(b) On-Call System
01.02.01(b) Fiscal Control
01.02.02(b) Signatory Authority
01.02.03(b) State Budget Preparation
01.02.04(b) Receipt of Cash
01.02.05(c) Financial Compliance of Contracted Services
01.02.06(b) Encumbrances
01.02.07(b) Client Service Payments
01.02.08(b) Vendor Payments (Goods)
01.02.09(b) Repealed
01.02.10(b) Inventory Control
01.02.11(b) Supplies and Inventory
01.02.12(b) MMARS Security
01.02.13(b) Segregation of Duties
01.02.14(b) MMARS Document Coding
01.02.15(c) Competitive Procurement of Client Services
01.02.16(b) Vehicle Maintenance
01.02.17(b) Use of Fuel Cards
01.02.18(b) Client Travel
01.02.19(b) Personal Use of Cellular Telephone
01.02.20(b) Vendor File Maintenance
01.02.21(b) Client Social Security Benefits
01.02.22(b) Budget Review
01.02.23(b) Travel Reimbursement Process
01.02.24(b) Federal Funds
01.02.25 Repealed
01.02.26(a) Gift Card Use for Youth and Families
01.03.01 Compulsory Legal Process
01.03.02(b) Repealed
01.03.03(d) Youth Committed for Firearm Offenses
01.03.04(a) Sex Offender Registration
01.03.05(f) Serious Incident Reporting
01.04.06 Special Placement Management
01.05.01(b) Employee Handbook
01.05.02(b) Personnel Records
01.05.03(b) Employee Identification Cards
01.05.04(d) Code of Employee Conduct
01.05.05(a) Employee Dress Code
01.05.06(a) Hiring of Staff
01.05.07(b) Prevention of Sexual Abuse and Sexual Harassment of Youth
01.05.08 Prohibition of Sexual Harassment in the Workplace
01.05.09(b) Tardiness and Failure to Report to Work
01.05.10(b) Sick Leave
01.05.11 Self Service Time and Attendance

01.05.12(b)	Tobacco Free Campus
01.05.19(b)	Extended Client and Family Contact
01.05.20	Separation from Employment
01.05.21	Overtime for Work at Residential Programs
01.05.22	Social Media
01.06.01	Workplace Violence Prevention
01.07.01(a)	Zero Tolerance for Sexual Assault, Domestic Violence and Stalking
01.07.02	Confidentiality of Client Records
01.07.03(b)	Client Photographs
01.08.01(a)	General Technology Procedures
01.08.02	Information Security Policy
01.08.05(b)	Electronic Mail
01.08.06(a)	Use of Internet and the World Wide Web
01.08.07(a)	Repealed
01.10.01(a)	Volunteer and Intern Services
01.11.01(a)	Victim Notification
Chapter 02.	*Continuum of Care Policies*
02.01.01(c)	Intake Procedures
02.01.02(b)	Transportation
02.01.03	Security and Safety Procedures for Transportation
02.02.01(b)	Treatment Plans
02.02.02(c)	Individual Support Plan
02.02.03(b)	Advocate System
02.02.04(b)	Progress Reports
02.02.05(c)	Suicide Assessment in Secure Facilities
02.02.06(a)	Suicide Assessment in Residential Facilities
02.02.07	Fee-for-Service Providers
02.02.07(a)	Suicide Assessment at Community Placements
02.03.01(b)	Repealed
02.03.02	Client and Staff Interaction
02.03.06(b)	Youth Substance Abuse Assessment, Prevention and Treatment
02.04.02(b)	Repealed
02.04.03(b)	Repealed
02.04.04(b)	Repealed
02.04.06(d)	Education of Youth Through High School Equivalency
02.05.01(a)	Standard Precautions
02.05.02	Medical Waste Management in Residential Locations
02.05.04	Authorization for Medical Care
02.05.06	Access to Diagnostic Services, Consultants, and Continuity of Care
02.05.07	Continuity of Care
02.05.08	Use of Over the Counter Medications
02.05.09	Narcan Use in Response to Overdose
02.05.14(b)	HIV Awareness
02.05.15(c)	Client-Centered Medication Administration
02.05.16(b)	Use of Psychotropic Medication
02.05.17	Tuberculosis Control and Prevention
02.08.05(b)	Caseworker Visits
02.10.01(a)	Access to Counsel in DYS Revocation Proceedings
Chapter 03.	*Daily Living Policies*
03.01.01(a)	Contraband
03.01.01(b)	Rated Capacity
03.01.02(a)	Searches in Secure Facilities
03.01.03(a)	Searches in Residential Facilities
03.01.04(a)	Searches in Community Programs
03.02.01(b)	Logs
03.02.02(d)	Security Checks and Inspections within Residential Locations
03.02.04(b)	Client Counts
03.02.05(b)	Client Movement
03.02.07(d)	Weapons
03.02.08(e)	Restraints and Use of Force in Residential and Community Placement
03.02.09(b)	Position Assignments
03.02.11(b)	Key Control
03.02.13(b)	Audio Communications Equipment
03.02.14(b)	Law-Enforcement Assistance
03.02.15(d)	Fire Prevention Program
03.02.16(b)	Hazardous Materials
03.02.17(b)	Bomb Threats
03.02.18(b)	Severe Weather
03.02.19(b)	Evacuation Procedures
03.02.20(c)	Response to Residential Group Disturbances
03.02.22(b)	Hunger Strikes
03.02.23(b)	Hostage Situations
03.02.24(c)	Escapes and Parole Violations
03.02.25(b)	Passes
03.02.28(b)	Water Activities
03.03.01(a)	Involuntary Room Confinement
03.04.01	Youth Grievance Process
03.04.02(b)	Mail
03.04.03(b)	Telephone Use
03.04.04(c)	Visitation
03.04.05(b)	Voting
03.04.06(b)	Foreign Languages in Facilities
03.04.07(b)	Movies
03.04.08(b)	Religious Services
03.04.09	Prohibition of Harassment and Discrimination Against Youth
03.04.10	Youth Residential Wellness Program
03.05.05	Storage and Disposal of Personal Property and Funds
Chapter 04.	*Departure Policies*
04.02.01(a)	Inter-Regional Transfers, Temporary Transfers, and Emergency Placements
04.04.02	Repealed

PART 9

Department of Youth Services Classification Grid

DYS Classification Grid

[Amended as of June 26, 2012.]

GRID LEVELS & TIME RECOMMENDATIONS									PENALTY TYPES
GRID LEVEL:	1	2	3	4	5	6	U	U-1	F = Felony M = Misdemeanor V = Varies CL = Common Law CIV = Civil Infraction
RANGE (MONTHS):	1–4	3–5	5–8	8–12	12–24	24–36	grid level of the underlying offense	one grid level below the underlying	
DYS commitments are indeterminate until discharge at 18 or 21 years. DYS has the right to determine placement within the DYS system and the length of time a youth will remain in residential treatment. These Grid time recommendations, therefore, are only one factor in DYS' analysis and are merely a guideline.									

Mass. General Law Chapter & Section	Offense Description	Grid Level	Penalty Type	Notes
G.L. c. 90 § 9	Motor vehicle, operate without registration	2	M	
G.L. c. 90 § 10	Motor vehicle, operate without license	1	M	
G.L. c. 90 § 24(1)(a)(1)	Motor vehicle, OUI liquor or drugs	2	M	
G.L. c. 90 § 24(2)(a)	Motor vehicle, leave scene after causing property damage	2	M	
G.L. c. 90 § 24(2)(a)	Motor vehicle, negligent operation of	2	M	
G.L. c. 90 § 24(2)(a)	Motor vehicle, use without authority	2	M	
G.L. c. 90 § 24(2)(a½)(1)	Motor vehicle, leave scene after causing personal injury	3	M	
G.L. c. 94C § 32(a)	Drug, distribute or possess with intent, class A	3	F	Drug classes defined in G.L. c. 94C § 31.
G.L. c. 94C § 32A(a)	Drug, distribute or possess with intent, class B	3	F	Drug classes defined in G.L. c. 94C § 31.
G.L. c. 94C § 32A(c)	Cocaine, distribute or possess with intent	3	F	
G.L. c. 94C § 32B(a)	Drug, distribute or possess with intent, class C	3	F	Drug classes defined in G.L. c. 94C § 31.
G.L. c. 94C § 32C(a)	Drug, distribute or possess with intent, class D	2	M	Drug classes defined in G.L. c. 94C § 31.
G.L. c. 94C § 32D(a)	Drug, distribute or possess with intent, class E	2	M	Drug classes defined in G.L. c. 94C § 31.
G.L. c. 94C § 32F(a)	Drug, distribute or possess with intent, to minor, class A	4	F	Drug classes defined in G.L. c. 94C § 31.
G.L. c. 94C § 32F(b)	Drug, distribute or possess with intent, to minor, class B	3	F	Drug classes defined in G.L. c. 94C § 31.
G.L. c. 94C § 32F(c)	Drug, distribute or possess with intent, to minor, class C	3	F	Drug classes defined in G.L. c. 94C § 31.
G.L. c. 94C § 32F(d)	Cocaine, distribute or possess with intent, to minor	4	F	
G.L. c. 94C § 32J	Drug violation within 1000 feet of school zone	3	F	
G.L. c. 94C § 34	Drug, possess, class A	2	M	Drug classes defined in G.L. c. 94C § 31.
G.L. c. 94C § 34	Drug, possess, class B	2	M	Drug classes defined in G.L. c. 94C § 31.
G.L. c. 94C § 34	Drug, possess, class C	2	M	Drug classes defined in G.L. c. 94C § 31.
G.L. c. 94C § 34	Drug, possess, class D	1	M	Drug classes defined in G.L. c. 94C § 31.
G.L. c. 94C § 34	Drug, possess, class E	1	M	Drug classes defined in G.L. c. 94C § 31
G.L. c. 94C § 34	Heroin, possess	2	M	
G.L. c. 94C § 34	Marijuana over 1 oz, possess	1	M	Must be more than one ounce.
G.L. c. 94C § 40	Conspiracy to violate drug law	U	V	
G.L. c. 127 § 38B	A&B on correction officer	3	F	This section also applies to other employees, volunteers, and contractors. It does not apply to police officers—see G.L. c. 265 § 13D.
G.L. c. 138 § 34C	Alcohol, possession by minor	1	M	Includes transporting or carrying.

Mass. General Law Chapter & Section	Offense Description	Grid Level	Penalty Type	Notes
G.L. c. 138 § 34C	Alcohol, transportation by minor	1	M	Includes possessing or carrying.
G.L. c. 209A § 7	Abuse prevention order violation	2	M	
G.L. c. 265 § 13A(a)	A&B	2	M	
G.L. c. 265 § 13A(a)	Assault	2	M	
G.L. c. 265 § 13B	Indecent A&B on child under 14	4	F	
G.L. c. 265 § 13D	A&B on public employee	2	M	Applies to police officers. See G.L. c. 127 § 38B for A&B on correction officers.
G.L. c. 265 § 13H	Indecent A&B on elder 60 or over/disabled	4	F	
G.L. c. 265 § 13H	Indecent A&B on person 14 or over	3	F	
G.L. c. 265 § 15	Assault to murder or maim	4	F	
G.L. c. 265 § 15A(a)	ABDW on elder 60 or over, no/minor injury	2	F	
G.L. c. 265 § 15A(a)	ABDW on elder 60 or over, moderate injury	3	F	
G.L. c. 265 § 15A(a)	ABDW on elder 60 or over, significant injury	4	F	
G.L. c. 265 § 15A(b)	ABDW, no/minor injury	2	F	
G.L. c. 265 § 15A(b)	ABDW, moderate injury	3	F	
G.L. c. 265 § 15A(b)	ABDW, significant injury	4	F	
G.L. c. 265 § 15B(a)	Assault with dangerous weapon on elder 60 or over	2	F	
G.L. c. 265 § 15B(b)	Assault with dangerous weapon	2	F	
G.L. c. 265 § 17	Robbery, armed, no display of gun	4	F	
G.L. c. 265 § 17	Robbery, armed, display of gun	5	F	
G.L. c. 265 § 17	Robbery, armed, with firearm, subsequent	6	F	
G.L. c. 265 § 17	Robbery, armed & masked, no display of gun	5	F	
G.L. c. 265 § 17	Robbery, armed & masked, display of gun	6	F	
G.L. c. 265 § 17	Robbery, armed & masked, with firearm, subsequent	6	F	
G.L. c. 265 § 18(a)	Assault to rob elder 60 or over, armed	4	F	
G.L. c. 265 § 18(a)	Assault to rob elder 60 or over, armed, with firearm, subsequent	6	F	
G.L. c. 265 § 18(a)	Assault to murder elder 60 or over, armed	5	F	
G.L. c. 265 § 18(a)	Assault to murder elder 60 or over, armed, with firearm, subsequent	6	F	
G.L. c. 265 § 18(b)	Assault to rob, armed	4	F	
G.L. c. 265 § 18(b)	Assault to murder, armed	5	F	
G.L. c. 265 § 18C	Home invasion	6	F	
G.L. c. 265 § 19(a)	Robbery of elder 60 or over, unarmed	4	F	
G.L. c. 265 § 19(b)	Robbery, unarmed	3	F	
G.L. c. 265 § 20	Assault to rob, unarmed	3	F	
G.L. c. 265 § 21A	Carjacking	4	F	
G.L. c. 265 § 21A	Carjacking, armed	5	F	
G.L. c. 265 § 21A	Carjacking, armed, with firearm	6	F	
G.L. c. 265 § 22(b)	Rape	5	F	
G.L. c. 265 § 22A	Rape of child under 16 with force	6	F	
G.L. c. 265 § 23	Rape of child under 16, statutory	4	F	
G.L. c. 266 § 2	Burn building/contents	3	F	
G.L. c. 266 § 14	B&E dwelling at night (burglary), for felony, armed or assault on occupants	6	F	
G.L. c. 266 § 14	B&E dwelling at night (burglary), for felony, with firearm	6	F	
G.L. c. 266 § 15	B&E dwelling at night (burglary), for felony, unarmed, no assault on occupants	3	F	

Mass. General Law Chapter & Section	Offense Description	Grid Level	Penalty Type	Notes
G.L. c. 266 § 16	B&E building, ship, or vehicle at night, for felony, non-dwelling	2	F	
G.L. c. 266 § 16	B&E building, ship, or vehicle at night, for felony, dwelling	3	F	
G.L. c. 266 § 16	Break safe or vault, for larceny or felony, or attempt, non-dwelling	2	F	
G.L. c. 266 § 16	Break safe or vault, for larceny or felony, or attempt, dwelling	3	F	
G.L. c. 266 § 16A	B&E building, ship, or vehicle, for misdemeanor	2	M	
G.L. c. 266 § 17	B&E daytime or enter at night, for felony, person in fear, non-dwelling	4	F	
G.L. c. 266 § 17	B&E daytime or enter at night, for felony, person in fear, dwelling	4	F	
G.L. c. 266 § 17	B&E daytime or enter at night, for felony, with firearm, person in fear, non-dwelling	5	F	
G.L. c. 266 § 17	B&E daytime or enter at night, for felony, with firearm, person in fear, dwelling	5	F	
G.L. c. 266 § 18	B&E daytime, for felony, non-dwelling	2	F	
G.L. c. 266 § 18	B&E daytime, for felony, dwelling	3	F	
G.L. c. 266 § 18	B&E daytime, for felony, with firearm, non-dwelling	5	F	
G.L. c. 266 § 18	B&E daytime, for felony, with firearm, dwelling	5	F	
G.L. c. 266 § 18	Enter dwelling at night, for felony	4	F	
G.L. c. 266 § 18	Enter dwelling at night, for felony, with firearm	5	F	
G.L. c. 266 § 18A	Entering dwelling by false pretense, for felony or with larceny, no person in fear	3	F	
G.L. c. 266 § 20	Larceny from boat, building, railroad car, under $10,000	2	F	
G.L. c. 266 § 20	Larceny from boat, building, railroad car, $50,000 and over	3	F	
G.L. c. 266 § 25	Larceny from person	2	F	Pickpocketing, purse-snatching.
G.L. c. 266 § 25	Larceny from person 65 or older	3	F	
G.L. c. 266 § 28(a)	Motor vehicle, larceny/malicious damage/receive stolen/steal parts	2	F	
G.L. c. 266 § 30(1)	Larceny under $250	2	M	
G.L. c. 266 § 30(1)	Larceny over $250, under $10,000	3	F	
G.L. c. 266 § 30(1)	Larceny of firearm	4	F	
G.L. c. 266 § 30(5)	Larceny from elder/disabled person, $250 or under	2	M	This section includes fraud.
G.L. c. 266 § 30A	Shoplifting	1	M	
G.L. c. 266 § 49	Burglarious instrument/MV master key, make or possess	2	F	
G.L. c. 266 § 60	Receive stolen or falsely traded property, under $250	2	M	
G.L. c. 266 § 60	Receive stolen or falsely traded property, over $250, under $10,000	2	F	
G.L. c. 266 § 120	Trespass	1	M	
G.L. c. 266 § 126B	Tagging property	2	M	
G.L. c. 266 § 127	Destruction of property under $250, wanton or malicious	1	M	
G.L. c. 266 § 127	Destruction of property over $250, malicious	2	F	
G.L. c. 266 § 127	Destruction of property over $250, wanton	2	M	
G.L. c. 268 § 13B(1)	Intimidate juror/witness, or retaliate against	4	F	
G.L. c. 268 § 32B	Resist arrest	2	M	

Mass. General Law Chapter & Section	Offense Description	Grid Level	Penalty Type	Notes
G.L. c. 269 § 10(a)	Firearm, carry without license	4	F	Possession/carrying of a firearm, when not at home or work, without a license to carry. Distinct from G.L. c. 269 § 10(h)(1): possession w/o FID card. Bartley-Fox: 6-month minimum in a facility.
G.L. c. 269 § 10(b)	Dangerous weapon, carry, no prior felonies	2	M	See statute for examples of dangerous weapons.
G.L. c. 269 § 10(b)	Dangerous weapon, carry, with prior felonies	3	F	See statute for examples of dangerous weapons.
G.L. c. 269 § 10(c)	Machine gun/sawed-off shotgun, possess	5	F	Bartley-Fox: 6-month minimum in a facility.
G.L. c. 269 § 10(h)(1)	Firearm or ammunition without FID card, possess	3	M	Ownership, possession, or transfer of firearm / shotgun / rifle / ammunition without an FID card (per G.L. c. 140 § 129C). Distinct from G.L. c. 269 § 10(a)—possession/carrying of a firearm, when not at home or work, without a license to carry.
G.L. c. 269 § 10(j)	Dangerous weapon, carry on school grounds, non-firearm	2	M	
G.L. c. 269 § 10(j)	Dangerous weapon, carry on school grounds, firearm	4	M	
G.L. c. 269 § 11C	Firearm serial number, deface or receive with defaced number	3	M	
G.L. c. 269 § 14(b)	Bomb threat, false	3	F	This section also specifies other kinds of threats.
G.L. c. 272 § 16	Open and gross lewdness	2	F	1st offense doesn't trigger SORB notification or registration.
G.L. c. 272 § 40	School or public assembly, disturb	1	M	
G.L. c. 272 § 53	Disorderly conduct	1	M	
G.L. c. 272 § 53	Disturbing the peace	1	M	
G.L. c. 272 § 53	Indecent Exposure	1	M	
G.L. c. 272 § 53	Lewd, wanton & lascivious conduct	1	M	
G.L. c. 272 § 53	Nightwalker, common	1	M	Equivalent to "Streetwalker, common". Involves not a fee but conduct (including accosting, annoying, lewd and lascivious behavior). Distinct from § 53A "Sexual conduct, pay for or for fee".
G.L. c. 272 § 53A(a)	Sexual conduct, pay for or for fee	2	M	This section addresses prostitution.
G.L. c. 274 § 6	Attempt to commit crime, Larceny	U-1	M	
G.L. c. 274 § 6	Attempt to commit crime, under 5-year felony or misdemeanor	U-1	V	Underlying offense may trigger SORB or SDP protocols.
G.L. c. 274 § 6	Attempt to commit crime, 5-year felony or greater	U-1	F	Underlying offense may trigger SORB or SDP protocols.
G.L. c. 275 § 2	Threat to commit crime	1	M	Penalty found in G.L. c. 275 § 4.
	Prostitution			See G.L. c. 272 § 53A "Sexual conduct, pay for or for fee" or G.L. c. 272 § 53 "Nightwalker, common" if no fee.
G.L. c. 265 § 13A(a)	A&B	2	M	
G.L. c. 127 § 38B	A&B on correction officer	3	F	This section also applies to other employees, volunteers, and contractors. It does not apply to police officers—see G.L. c. 265 § 13D.
G.L. c. 265 § 13D	A&B on public employee	2	M	Applies to police officers. See G.L. c. 127 § 38B for A&B on correction officers.
G.L. c. 265 § 15A(a)	ABDW on elder 60 or over, moderate injury	3	F	
G.L. c. 265 § 15A(a)	ABDW on elder 60 or over, no/minor injury	2	F	
G.L. c. 265 § 15A(a)	ABDW on elder 60 or over, significant injury	4	F	
G.L. c. 265 § 15A(b)	ABDW, moderate injury	3	F	
G.L. c. 265 § 15A(b)	ABDW, no/minor injury	2	F	

Mass. General Law Chapter & Section	Offense Description	Grid Level	Penalty Type	Notes
G.L. c. 265 § 15A(b)	ABDW, significant injury	4	F	
G.L. c. 209A § 7	Abuse prevention order violation	2	M	
G.L. c. 138 § 34C	Alcohol, possession by minor	1	M	Includes transporting or carrying.
G.L. c. 138 § 34C	Alcohol, transportation by minor	1	M	Includes possessing or carrying.
G.L. c. 265 § 13A(a)	Assault	2	M	
G.L. c. 265 § 18(a)	Assault to murder elder 60 or over, armed	5	F	
G.L. c. 265 § 18(a)	Assault to murder elder 60 or over, armed, with firearm, subsequent	6	F	
G.L. c. 265 § 15	Assault to murder or maim	4	F	
G.L. c. 265 § 18(b)	Assault to murder, armed	5	F	
G.L. c. 265 § 18(a)	Assault to rob elder 60 or over, armed	4	F	
G.L. c. 265 § 18(a)	Assault to rob elder 60 or over, armed, with firearm, subsequent	6	F	
G.L. c. 265 § 18(b)	Assault to rob, armed	4	F	
G.L. c. 265 § 20	Assault to rob, unarmed	3	F	
G.L. c. 265 § 15B(b)	Assault with dangerous weapon	2	F	
G.L. c. 265 § 15B(a)	Assault with dangerous weapon on elder 60 or over	2	F	
G.L. c. 274 § 6	Attempt to commit crime, 5-year felony or greater	U-1	F	Underlying offense may trigger SORB or SDP protocols.
G.L. c. 274 § 6	Attempt to commit crime, Larceny	U-1	M	
G.L. c. 274 § 6	Attempt to commit crime, under 5-year felony or misdemeanor	U-1	V	Underlying offense may trigger SORB or SDP protocols.
G.L. c. 266 § 16	B&E building, ship, or vehicle at night, for felony, dwelling	3	F	
G.L. c. 266 § 16	B&E building, ship, or vehicle at night, for felony, non-dwelling	2	F	
G.L. c. 266 § 16A	B&E building, ship, or vehicle, for misdemeanor	2	M	
G.L. c. 266 § 17	B&E daytime or enter at night, for felony, person in fear, dwelling	4	F	
G.L. c. 266 § 17	B&E daytime or enter at night, for felony, person in fear, non-dwelling	4	F	
G.L. c. 266 § 17	B&E daytime or enter at night, for felony, with firearm, person in fear, dwelling	5	F	
G.L. c. 266 § 17	B&E daytime or enter at night, for felony, with firearm, person in fear, non-dwelling	5	F	
G.L. c. 266 § 18	B&E daytime, for felony, dwelling	3	F	
G.L. c. 266 § 18	B&E daytime, for felony, non-dwelling	2	F	
G.L. c. 266 § 18	B&E daytime, for felony, with firearm, dwelling	5	F	
G.L. c. 266 § 18	B&E daytime, for felony, with firearm, non-dwelling	5	F	
G.L. c. 266 § 14	B&E dwelling at night (burglary), for felony, armed or assault on occupants	6	F	
G.L. c. 266 § 15	B&E dwelling at night (burglary), for felony, unarmed, no assault on occupants	3	F	
G.L. c. 266 § 14	B&E dwelling at night (burglary), for felony, with firearm	6	F	
G.L. c. 269 § 14(b)	Bomb threat, false	3	F	This section also specifies other kinds of threats.
G.L. c. 266 § 16	Break safe or vault, for larceny or felony, or attempt, dwelling	3	F	
G.L. c. 266 § 16	Break safe or vault, for larceny or felony, or attempt, non-dwelling	2	F	
G.L. c. 266 § 49	Burglarious instrument/MV master key, make or possess	2	F	

Mass. General Law Chapter & Section	Offense Description	Grid Level	Penalty Type	Notes
G.L. c. 266 § 2	Burn building/contents	3	F	
G.L. c. 265 § 21A	Carjacking	4	F	
G.L. c. 265 § 21A	Carjacking, armed	5	F	
G.L. c. 265 § 21A	Carjacking, armed, with firearm	6	F	
G.L. c. 94C § 32A(c)	Cocaine, distribute or possess with intent	3	F	
G.L. c. 94C § 32F(d)	Cocaine, distribute or possess with intent, to minor	4	F	
G.L. c. 94C § 40	Conspiracy to violate drug law	U	V	
G.L. c. 269 § 10(j)	Dangerous weapon, carry on school grounds, firearm	4	M	
G.L. c. 269 § 10(j)	Dangerous weapon, carry on school grounds, non-firearm	2	M	
G.L. c. 269 § 10(b)	Dangerous weapon, carry, no prior felonies	2	M	See statute for examples of dangerous weapons.
G.L. c. 269 § 10(b)	Dangerous weapon, carry, with prior felonies	3	F	See statute for examples of dangerous weapons.
G.L. c. 266 § 127	Destruction of property over $250, malicious	2	F	
G.L. c. 266 § 127	Destruction of property over $250, wanton	2	M	
G.L. c. 266 § 127	Destruction of property under $250, wanton or malicious	1	M	
G.L. c. 272 § 53	Disorderly conduct	1	M	
G.L. c. 272 § 53	Disturbing the peace	1	M	
G.L. c. 94C § 32J	Drug violation within 1000 feet of school zone	3	F	
G.L. c. 94C § 32(a)	Drug, distribute or possess with intent, class A	3	F	Drug classes defined in G.L. c. 94C § 31.
G.L. c. 94C § 32A(a)	Drug, distribute or possess with intent, class B	3	F	Drug classes defined in G.L. c. 94C § 31.
G.L. c. 94C § 32B(a)	Drug, distribute or possess with intent, class C	3	F	Drug classes defined in G.L. c. 94C § 31.
G.L. c. 94C § 32C(a)	Drug, distribute or possess with intent, class D	2	M	Drug classes defined in G.L. c. 94C § 31.
G.L. c. 94C § 32D(a)	Drug, distribute or possess with intent, class E	2	M	Drug classes defined in G.L. c. 94C § 31.
G.L. c. 94C § 32F(a)	Drug, distribute or possess with intent, to minor, class A	4	F	Drug classes defined in G.L. c. 94C § 31.
G.L. c. 94C § 32F(b)	Drug, distribute or possess with intent, to minor, class B	3	F	Drug classes defined in G.L. c. 94C § 31.
G.L. c. 94C § 32F(c)	Drug, distribute or possess with intent, to minor, class C	3	F	Drug classes defined in G.L. c. 94C § 31.
G.L. c. 94C § 34	Drug, possess, class A	2	M	Drug classes defined in G.L. c. 94C § 31.
G.L. c. 94C § 34	Drug, possess, class B	2	M	Drug classes defined in G.L. c. 94C § 31.
G.L. c. 94C § 34	Drug, possess, class C	2	M	Drug classes defined in G.L. c. 94C § 31.
G.L. c. 94C § 34	Drug, possess, class D	1	M	Drug classes defined in G.L. c. 94C § 31.
G.L. c. 94C § 34	Drug, possess, class E	1	M	Drug classes defined in G.L. c. 94C § 31
G.L. c. 266 § 18	Enter dwelling at night, for felony	4	F	
G.L. c. 266 § 18	Enter dwelling at night, for felony, with firearm	5	F	
G.L. c. 266 § 18A	Entering dwelling by false pretense, for felony or with larceny, no person in fear	3	F	
G.L. c. 269 § 10(h)(1)	Firearm or ammunition without FID card, possess	3	M	Ownership, possession, or transfer of firearm / shotgun / rifle / ammunition without an FID card (per G.L. c. 140 § 129C). Distinct from G.L. c. 269 § 10(a)—possession/carrying of a firearm, when not at home or work, without a license to carry.
G.L. c. 269 § 11C	Firearm serial number, deface or receive with defaced number	3	M	
G.L. c. 269 § 10(a)	Firearm, carry without license	4	F	Possession/carrying of a firearm, when not at home or work, without a license to carry. Distinct from G.L. c. 269 § 10(h)(1): possession w/o FID card. Bartley-Fox: 6-month minimum in a facility.
G.L. c. 94C § 34	Heroin, possess	2	M	

Mass. General Law Chapter & Section	Offense Description	Grid Level	Penalty Type	Notes
G.L. c. 265 § 18C	Home invasion	6	F	
G.L. c. 265 § 13B	Indecent A&B on child under 14	4	F	
G.L. c. 265 § 13H	Indecent A&B on elder 60 or over/disabled	4	F	
G.L. c. 265 § 13H	Indecent A&B on person 14 or over	3	F	
G.L. c. 272 § 53	Indecent Exposure	1	M	
G.L. c. 268 § 13B(1)	Intimidate juror/witness, or retaliate against	4	F	
G.L. c. 266 § 20	Larceny from boat, building, railroad car, $50,000 and over	3	F	
G.L. c. 266 § 20	Larceny from boat, building, railroad car, under $10,000	2	F	
G.L. c. 266 § 30(5)	Larceny from elder/disabled person, $250 or under	2	M	This section includes fraud.
G.L. c. 266 § 25	Larceny from person	2	F	Pickpocketing, purse-snatching.
G.L. c. 266 § 25	Larceny from person 65 or older	3	F	
G.L. c. 266 § 30(1)	Larceny of firearm	4	F	
G.L. c. 266 § 30(1)	Larceny over $250, under $10,000	3	F	
G.L. c. 266 § 30(1)	Larceny under $250	2	M	
G.L. c. 272 § 53	Lewd, wanton & lascivious conduct	1	M	
G.L. c. 269 § 10(c)	Machine gun/sawed-off shotgun, possess	5	F	Bartley-Fox: 6-month minimum in a facility.
G.L. c. 94C § 34	Marijuana over 1 oz, possess	1	M	Must be more than one ounce.
G.L. c. 266 § 28(a)	Motor vehicle, larceny/malicious damage/receive stolen/steal parts	2	F	
G.L. c. 90 § 24(2)(a½)(1)	Motor vehicle, leave scene after causing personal injury	3	M	
G.L. c. 90 § 24(2)(a)	Motor vehicle, leave scene after causing property damage	2	M	
G.L. c. 90 § 24(2)(a)	Motor vehicle, negligent operation of	2	M	
G.L. c. 90 § 10	Motor vehicle, operate without license	1	M	
G.L. c. 90 § 9	Motor vehicle, operate without registration	2	M	
G.L. c. 90 § 24(1)(a)(1)	Motor vehicle, OUI liquor or drugs	2	M	
G.L. c. 90 § 24(2)(a)	Motor vehicle, use without authority	2	M	
G.L. c. 272 § 53	Nightwalker, common	1	M	Equivalent to "Streetwalker, common". Involves not a fee but conduct (including accosting, annoying, lewd and lascivious behavior). Distinct from § 53A "Sexual conduct, pay for or for fee".
G.L. c. 272 § 16	Open and gross lewdness	2	F	1st offense doesn't trigger SORB notification or registration.
	Prostitution			See G.L. c. 272 § 53A "Sexual conduct, pay for or for fee" or G.L. c. 272 § 53 "Nightwalker, common" if no fee.
G.L. c. 265 § 22(b)	Rape	5	F	
G.L. c. 265 § 22A	Rape of child under 16 with force	6	F	
G.L. c. 265 § 23	Rape of child under 16, statutory	4	F	
G.L. c. 266 § 60	Receive stolen or falsely traded property, over $250, under $10,000	2	F	
G.L. c. 266 § 60	Receive stolen or falsely traded property, under $250	2	M	
G.L. c. 268 § 32B	Resist arrest	2	M	
G.L. c. 265 § 19(a)	Robbery of elder 60 or over, unarmed	4	F	
G.L. c. 265 § 17	Robbery, armed & masked, display of gun	6	F	
G.L. c. 265 § 17	Robbery, armed & masked, no display of gun	5	F	
G.L. c. 265 § 17	Robbery, armed & masked, with firearm, subsequent	6	F	

Mass. General Law Chapter & Section	Offense Description	Grid Level	Penalty Type	Notes
G.L. c. 265 § 17	Robbery, armed, display of gun	5	F	
G.L. c. 265 § 17	Robbery, armed, no display of gun	4	F	
G.L. c. 265 § 17	Robbery, armed, with firearm, subsequent	6	F	
G.L. c. 265 § 19(b)	Robbery, unarmed	3	F	
G.L. c. 272 § 40	School or public assembly, disturb	1	M	
G.L. c. 272 § 53A(a)	Sexual conduct, pay for or for fee	2	M	This section addresses prostitution.
G.L. c. 266 § 30A	Shoplifting	1	M	
G.L. c. 266 § 126B	Tagging property	2	M	
G.L. c. 275 § 2	Threat to commit crime	1	M	Penalty found in G.L. c. 275 § 4.
G.L. c. 266 § 120	Trespass	1	M	
G.L. c. 6 § 178	CORI, disseminate/seek unlawfully, falsify	2	M	
G.L. c. 6 § 178H(a)(1)	Failure to register or verify registration info by sex offender	3	F	
G.L. c. 6 § 178H(a)(2)	Failure to register or verify registration info by sex offender, subsequent	4	F	
G.L. c. 6 § 178N	Sex Offender Registry information, illegal use of	2	M	
G.L. c. 12 § 11J	Civil rights order violation	2	M	This involves violation of a court order, distinct from G.L. c. 265 § 37 "Civil rights violation or attempt".
G.L. c. 12 § 11J	Civil rights order violation with injury	4	F	This involves violation of a court order, distinct from G.L. c. 265 § 37 "Civil rights violation with bodily injury or attempt".
G.L. c. 18 § 5B	Public Assistance fraud	2	M	
G.L. c. 22E § 11	DNA sample, refuse to provide	1	M	
G.L. c. 33 § 65	National Guard encampment, trespass on	1	M	Penalty found in G.L. c. 33 § 66.
G.L. c. 40 § 21D	Violation of state, town, city, or MDC ordinance, non-criminal disposition	1	M	
G.L. c. 40 § 37A	Curfew, violate	1	M	
G.L. c. 48 § 13	Fire in open, set	1	M	
G.L. c. 56 § 46	Disorderly conduct at poll	1	M	
G.L. c. 90 § 1A	Motor vehicle, registration without liability insurance	1	CIV	Penalty found in G.L. c. 90 § 20.
G.L. c. 90 § 9	Motor vehicle, operate without registration	2	M	
G.L. c. 90 § 10	Motor vehicle, operate without license	1	M	
G.L. c. 90 § 12(b)	Motor vehicle, permit operation with suspended/no license	1	M	
G.L. c. 90 § 12(b)	Motor vehicle, permit operation with suspended/no license, subsequent	2	M	
G.L. c. 90 § 13	Motor vehicle, violate safety precautions	1	CIV	Penalty found in G.L. c. 90 § 20.
G.L. c. 90 § 16	Motor vehicle, operate offensively or illegally	1	M	
G.L. c. 90 § 17	Motor vehicle, operate with excessive speed	1	M	
G.L. c. 90 § 17B	Motor vehicle, racing by licensed operator	2	M	
G.L. c. 90 § 23	Motor vehicle license, exhibit another's	1	M	
G.L. c. 90 § 23	Motor vehicle license, exhibit another's, subsequent	2	M	
G.L. c. 90 § 23	Motor vehicle number plate violation to conceal ID	1	M	
G.L. c. 90 § 23	Motor vehicle, operate with license revoked as HTO	2	M	HTO = Habitual Traffic Offender.
G.L. c. 90 § 23	Motor vehicle, operate with license suspended	1	M	
G.L. c. 90 § 23	Motor vehicle, operate with license suspended, subsequent	2	M	

Mass. General Law Chapter & Section	Offense Description	Grid Level	Penalty Type	Notes
G.L. c. 90 § 23	Motor vehicle, operate with license suspended for OUI	2	M	
G.L. c. 90 § 23	Motor vehicle, operate with registration suspended	1	M	
G.L. c. 90 § 23	Motor vehicle, operate with registration suspended, subsequent	2	M	
G.L. c. 90 § 23	Motor vehicle, OUI while license suspended for OUI	2	M	
G.L. c. 90 § 24(1)(a)(1)	Motor vehicle, OUI liquor or drugs	2	M	
G.L. c. 90 § 24(1)(a)(1)	Motor vehicle, OUI liquor or drugs, 2nd off.	2	M	
G.L. c. 90 § 24(1)(a)(1)	Motor vehicle, OUI liquor or drugs, 3rd off.	3	F	
G.L. c. 90 § 24(1)(a)(1)	Motor vehicle, OUI liquor or drugs, 4th off.	3	F	
G.L. c. 90 § 24(2)(a)	Motor vehicle license, allow another to use	2	M	
G.L. c. 90 § 24(2)(a)	Motor vehicle license, false statement in application for	2	M	
G.L. c. 90 § 24(2)(a)	Motor vehicle registration, false statement in application for	2	M	
G.L. c. 90 § 24(2)(a)	Motor vehicle, leave scene after causing property damage	2	M	
G.L. c. 90 § 24(2)(a)	Motor vehicle, negligent operation of	2	M	
G.L. c. 90 § 24(2)(a)	Motor vehicle, racing	2	M	See also G.L. c. 90 § 17B.
G.L. c. 90 § 24(2)(a)	Motor vehicle, reckless operation of	2	M	
G.L. c. 90 § 24(2)(a)	Motor vehicle, speeding to make record	2	M	See also G.L. c. 90 § 17B.
G.L. c. 90 § 24(2)(a)	Motor vehicle, use without authority	2	M	
G.L. c. 90 § 24(2)(a)	Motor vehicle, use without authority, 2nd off.	2	F	
G.L. c. 90 § 24(2)(a)	Motor vehicle, use without authority, 3rd and subsequent	3	F	
G.L. c. 90 § 24(2)(a½)(1)	Motor vehicle, leave scene after causing personal injury	3	M	
G.L. c. 90 § 24(2)(a½)(2)	Motor vehicle, leave scene after causing personal injury resulting in death	3	F	
G.L. c. 90 § 24B	Motor vehicle license, false application for	3	F	
G.L. c. 90 § 24B	RMV document or signature, possess false/stolen, misuse/forge	3	F	
G.L. c. 90 § 24G(a)	Motor vehicle homicide OUI liquor or drugs, with negligent operation	5	F	
G.L. c. 90 § 24G(a)	Motor vehicle homicide OUI liquor or drugs, with reckless operation	6	F	
G.L. c. 90 § 24G(b)	Motor vehicle homicide by negligent operation	4	M	
G.L. c. 90 § 24G(b)	Motor vehicle homicide by reckless operation	5	M	
G.L. c. 90 § 24G(b)	Motor vehicle homicide OUI liquor or drugs	5	M	
G.L. c. 90 § 24H	Motor vehicle, improper removal of abandoned/stolen/crushed	2	M	
G.L. c. 90 § 24I	Motor vehicle, possess alcohol open container	1	M	Statute addresses possession, not drinking, and doesn't specify locations other than a motor vehicle.
G.L. c. 90 § 24L(1)	Motor vehicle, OUI liquor or drugs, with negligent operation, causing serious injury	3	F	
G.L. c. 90 § 24L(1)	Motor vehicle, OUI liquor or drugs, with reckless operation, causing serious injury	4	F	
G.L. c. 90 § 24L(2)	Motor vehicle, OUI liquor or drugs, causing serious injury	3	M	
G.L. c. 90 § 24U(a)(1)	Motor vehicle ignition interlock, bypass for another	2	M	
G.L. c. 90 § 24U(a)(1)	Motor vehicle ignition interlock, bypass for another, subsequent	3	F	

Mass. General Law Chapter & Section	Offense Description	Grid Level	Penalty Type	Notes
G.L. c. 90 § 25	Motor vehicle, refuse to comply with police officer	1	M	
G.L. c. 90 § 34J	Motor vehicle, operate without insurance	1	M	
G.L. c. 90B § 8(a)(1)(A)	Boat, OUI liquor or drugs	2	M	
G.L. c. 90B § 8(a)(1)(A)	Boat, OUI liquor or drugs, 2nd off.	2	M	
G.L. c. 90B § 8(a)(1)(A)	Boat, OUI liquor or drugs, 3rd off.	3	M	
G.L. c. 90B § 8(a)(1)(A)	Boat, OUI liquor or drugs, 4th off.	3	F	
G.L. c. 90B § 8(e)(1)	Boat, operate recklessly/negligently	2	M	
G.L. c. 90B § 8(e)(1)	Boat, use without authority, 1st off.	2	M	
G.L. c. 90B § 8(e)(1)	Boat, use without authority, 2nd off.	2	F	
G.L. c. 90B § 8(e)(1)	Boat, use without authority, 3rd and subsequent	3	F	
G.L. c. 90B § 8A(1)	Boat, OUI liquor or drugs, reckless/ negligent operation, causing serious injury	3	F	
G.L. c. 90B § 8A(2)	Boat, OUI liquor or drugs, causing serious injury	3	M	
G.L. c. 90B § 8B(1)	Boat, OUI liquor or drugs, reckless/ negligent operation, causing death	5	F	
G.L. c. 90B § 8B(2)	Boat, operate negligently, causing death	3	M	
G.L. c. 90B § 8B(2)	Boat, operate recklessly, causing death	4	M	
G.L. c. 90B § 8B(2)	Boat, OUI liquor or drugs, causing death	4	M	
G.L. c. 90B § 25	Operating snow/recreational vehicle on public way	1	M	Penalty found in G.L. c. 90B § 34.
G.L. c. 90C § 10	Motor vehicle citation, attempt to falsify or dispose of	1	M	
G.L. c. 90D § 32(a)	Motor vehicle, alter, forge, or counterfeit certificate of title or salvage title	3	F	
G.L. c. 92 App. § 1-8	Destruction of property held by the MA Water Resource Authority	2	M	
G.L. c. 94C § 22(b)	Drug, practitioner fail to label	1	M	Penalty found in G.L. c. 94C § 39.
G.L. c. 94C § 22(b)	Drug, practitioner fail to label, subsequent	2	M	Penalty found in G.L. c. 94C § 39.
G.L. c. 94C § 25(1)	Drug, dispense without prescription	2	M	Penalty found in G.L. c. 94C § 38.
G.L. c. 94C § 25(1)	Drug, dispense without prescription, subsequent	3	M	Penalty found in G.L. c. 94C § 38.
G.L. c. 94C § 26(1)	Drug, registrant distribute without order, class I	2	M	Penalty found in G.L. c. 94C § 38.
G.L. c. 94C § 26(1)	Drug, registrant distribute without order, class II	3	M	Penalty found in G.L. c. 94C § 38.
G.L. c. 94C § 27	Hypodermic for drugs, sell to minor	1	M	Penalty found in G.L. c. 94C § 38.
G.L. c. 94C § 27	Hypodermic for drugs, sell to minor, subsequent	2	M	Penalty found in G.L. c. 94C § 38.
G.L. c. 94C § 27	Hypodermic for drugs, unlicensed sale of	1	M	Penalty found in G.L. c. 94C § 38.
G.L. c. 94C § 27	Hypodermic for drugs, unlicensed sale of, subsequent	2	M	Penalty found in G.L. c. 94C § 38.
G.L. c. 94C § 32(a)	Drug, distribute or possess with intent, class A	3	F	Drug classes defined in G.L. c. 94C § 31.
G.L. c. 94C § 32(b)	Drug, distribute or possess with intent, class A, subsequent	4	F	Drug classes defined in G.L. c. 94C § 31.
G.L. c. 94C § 32A(a)	Drug, distribute or possess with intent, class B	3	F	Drug classes defined in G.L. c. 94C § 31.
G.L. c. 94C § 32A(b)	Drug, distribute or possess with intent, class B, subsequent	3	F	Drug classes defined in G.L. c. 94C § 31.
G.L. c. 94C § 32A(c)	Cocaine, distribute or possess with intent	3	F	
G.L. c. 94C § 32A(d)	Cocaine, distribute or possess with intent, subsequent	4	F	
G.L. c. 94C § 32A(c)	Methamphetamine, distribute or possess with intent	3	F	
G.L. c. 94C § 32A(d)	Methamphetamine, distribute or possess with intent, subsequent	4	F	

9

Mass. General Law Chapter & Section	Offense Description	Grid Level	Penalty Type	Notes
G.L. c. 94C § 32A(c)	Phencyclidine, distribute or possess with intent	3	F	
G.L. c. 94C § 32A(d)	Phencyclidine, distribute or possess with intent, subsequent	4	F	
G.L. c. 94C § 32B(a)	Drug, distribute or possess with intent, class C	3	F	Drug classes defined in G.L. c. 94C § 31.
G.L. c. 94C § 32B(b)	Drug, distribute or possess with intent, class C, subsequent	3	F	Drug classes defined in G.L. c. 94C § 31.
G.L. c. 94C § 32C(a)	Drug, distribute or possess with intent, class D	2	M	Drug classes defined in G.L. c. 94C § 31.
G.L. c. 94C § 32C(b)	Drug, distribute or possess with intent, class D, subsequent	3	M	Drug classes defined in G.L. c. 94C § 31.
G.L. c. 94C § 32D(a)	Drug, distribute or possess with intent, class E	2	M	Drug classes defined in G.L. c. 94C § 31.
G.L. c. 94C § 32D(b)	Drug, distribute or possess with intent, class E, subsequent	3	M	Drug classes defined in G.L. c. 94C § 31.
G.L. c. 94C § 32E(a)(1)	Marijuana, trafficking in, 50 to 100 lbs.	3	F	
G.L. c. 94C § 32E(a)(2)	Marijuana, trafficking in, 100 to 2000 lbs.	3	F	
G.L. c. 94C § 32E(a)(3)	Marijuana, trafficking in, 2000 to 10,000 lbs.	4	F	
G.L. c. 94C § 32E(a)(4)	Marijuana, trafficking in, 10,000 lbs or more	5	F	
G.L. c. 94C § 32E(b)(1)	Cocaine, trafficking in, 14 to 28 g	3	F	
G.L. c. 94C § 32E(b)(2)	Cocaine, trafficking in, 28 to 100 g	4	F	
G.L. c. 94C § 32E(b)(3)	Cocaine, trafficking in, 100 to 200 g	5	F	
G.L. c. 94C § 32E(b)(4)	Cocaine, trafficking in, 200 g or more	5	F	
G.L. c. 94C § 32E(b)(1)	Phenmetrazine, trafficking in, 14 to 28 g	3	F	
G.L. c. 94C § 32E(b)(2)	Phenmetrazine, trafficking in, 28 to 100 g	4	F	
G.L. c. 94C § 32E(b)(3)	Phenmetrazine, trafficking in, 100 to 200 g	5	F	
G.L. c. 94C § 32E(b)(4)	Phenmetrazine, trafficking in, 200 g or more	6	F	
G.L. c. 94C § 32E(c)(1)	Heroin/morphine/opium, trafficking in, 14 to 28 g	3	F	
G.L. c. 94C § 32E(c)(2)	Heroin/morphine/opium, trafficking in, 28 to 100 g	4	F	
G.L. c. 94C § 32E(c)(3)	Heroin/morphine/opium, trafficking in, 100 to 200 g	5	F	
G.L. c. 94C § 32E(c)(4)	Heroin/morphine/opium, trafficking in, 200 g or more	6	F	
G.L. c. 94C § 32F(a)	Drug, distribute or possess with intent, to minor, class A	4	F	Drug classes defined in G.L. c. 94C § 31.
G.L. c. 94C § 32F(b)	Drug, distribute or possess with intent, to minor, class B	3	F	Drug classes defined in G.L. c. 94C § 31.
G.L. c. 94C § 32F(c)	Drug, distribute or possess with intent, to minor, class C	3	F	Drug classes defined in G.L. c. 94C § 31.
G.L. c. 94C § 32F(d)	Cocaine, distribute or possess with intent, to minor	4	F	
G.L. c. 94C § 32G	Counterfeit drug; create, distribute, or possess with intent	1	M	
G.L. c. 94C § 32I(a)	Drug paraphernalia, distribute or possess with intent	2	M	
G.L. c. 94C § 32I(b)	Drug paraphernalia, sell to person under 18	3	F	
G.L. c. 94C § 32J	Drug violation within 100 feet of park/playground	3	F	
G.L. c. 94C § 32J	Drug violation within 1000 feet of school zone	3	F	
G.L. c. 94C § 32K	Drug, induce minor to distribute	5	F	
G.L. c. 94C § 32K	Drug, induce minor to possess funds of	5	F	
G.L. c. 94C § 33(a)	Drug, false registration number for	3	F	Penalty found in G.L. c. 94C § 33(c).
G.L. c. 94C § 33(b)	Drug, obtain by fraud	3	F	Penalty found in G.L. c. 94C § 33(c).
G.L. c. 94C § 33(b)	Prescription, utter false	3	F	Penalty found in G.L. c. 94C § 33(c).
G.L. c. 94C § 34	Drug, possess, class A	2	M	Drug classes defined in G.L. c. 94C § 31.
G.L. c. 94C § 34	Drug, possess, class A, subsequent	2	M	Drug classes defined in G.L. c. 94C § 31.

Mass. General Law Chapter & Section	Offense Description	Grid Level	Penalty Type	Notes
G.L. c. 94C § 34	Drug, possess, class B	2	M	Drug classes defined in G.L. c. 94C § 31.
G.L. c. 94C § 34	Drug, possess, class B, subsequent	2	M	Drug classes defined in G.L. c. 94C § 31.
G.L. c. 94C § 34	Drug, possess, class C	2	M	Drug classes defined in G.L. c. 94C § 31.
G.L. c. 94C § 34	Drug, possess, class C, subsequent	2	M	Drug classes defined in G.L. c. 94C § 31.
G.L. c. 94C § 34	Drug, possess, class D	1	M	Drug classes defined in G.L. c. 94C § 31.
G.L. c. 94C § 34	Drug, possess, class D, subsequent	2	M	Drug classes defined in G.L. c. 94C § 31.
G.L. c. 94C § 34	Drug, possess, class E	1	M	Drug classes defined in G.L. c. 94C § 31.
G.L. c. 94C § 34	Heroin, possess	2	M	
G.L. c. 94C § 34	Heroin, possess, subsequent	2	F	
G.L. c. 94C § 34	Marijuana over 1 oz, possess	1	M	Must be more than one ounce.
G.L. c. 94C § 34	Marijuana over 1 oz, possess, subsequent	2	M	Must be more than one ounce.
G.L. c. 94C § 35	Heroin, being present where kept	2	M	
G.L. c. 94C § 37	Drug, larceny of	3	F	
G.L. c. 94C § 40	Conspiracy to violate drug law	U	V	
G.L. c. 119 § 1	Interstate Compact for Juveniles (ICJ) - IN	0	V	For youth committed in another state, held by DYS.
G.L. c. 119 § 1	Interstate Compact for Juveniles (ICJ) - OUT	0	V	For youth committed to DYS, held by another state.
G.L. c. 119 § 1	Interstate Compact for Juveniles (ICJ) - OTHER	0	V	For "courtesy holds," such as out-of-state runaways held by DYS due to court order.
G.L. c. 119 § 39	Child under 10, abandon	2	M	
G.L. c. 119 § 63	Contribute to delinquency of child	2	M	
G.L. c. 120 § 26	Escape from DYS, or aiding child to escape	2	M	Applies to escape or attempt; but, per DYS policy, not flight from a non-hardware secure program.
G.L. c. 127 § 38B	A&B on correction officer	3	F	This section also applies to other employees, volunteers, and contractors. It does not apply to police officers—see G.L. c. 265 § 13D.
G.L. c. 131 § 43	Poison mammal/bird	2	M	Penalty found in G.L. c. 131 § 90.
G.L. c. 131 § 58	Firearm, discharge within 500 feet of dwelling/highway	3	M	Penalty found in G.L. c. 131 § 90.
G.L. c. 131 § 66	Shotgun shells in closed season	2	M	Penalty found in G.L. c. 131 § 90.
G.L. c. 131 § 67	Rifle/revolver/pistol of unlawful caliber, use or possess	2	M	A Fisheries & Game offense. Penalty found in G.L. c. 131 § 90.
G.L. c. 138 § 2	Alcohol, sell/make/store unlawfully	1	M	
G.L. c. 138 § 22	Alcohol, transport unlawfully	1	M	
G.L. c. 138 § 34	Alcohol, sell/deliver to person under 21	1	M	
G.L. c. 138 § 34B	Liquor ID card/license, false/misuse	1	M	
G.L. c. 138 § 34C	Alcohol, possession by minor	1	M	Includes transporting or carrying.
G.L. c. 138 § 34C	Alcohol, transportation by minor	1	M	Includes possessing or carrying.
G.L. c. 140 § 122B	Ammunition, unlicensed sale of	2	M	
G.L. c. 140 § 128	Firearm sale, violation	3	F	
G.L. c. 140 § 129	Firearm application, false statement on	2	M	
G.L. c. 140 § 129	Firearm application, false statement on, subsequent	3	F	
G.L. c. 140 § 130	Firearm sale to minor/alien	3	F	
G.L. c. 140 § 131(h)	Firearm license violation, false information on application	2	M	
G.L. c. 140 § 131C	Firearm, carry improperly in a motor vehicle	2	M	Applies to a licensed person carrying improperly in a motor vehicle.
G.L. c. 140 § 131E	Firearm, purchase for another	3	F	
G.L. c. 140 § 131H	Firearm, non-resident of Commonwealth owns/possesses without license	2	M	

Mass. General Law Chapter & Section	Offense Description	Grid Level	Penalty Type	Notes
G.L. c. 140 § 131I	Firearm license/FID card, false	3	F	
G.L. c. 140 § 131J	Electric stun gun, sell/possess	2	M	
G.L. c. 140 § 131M	Assault weapon, sell/possess	4	F	
G.L. c. 140 § 131M	Assault weapon, sell/possess, subsequent	4	F	
G.L. c. 140D § 27	Unauthorized use of credit cards	2	F	
G.L. c. 148 § 16	Explosives/flammables, improperly make/store	1	M	
G.L. c. 148 § 35	Bomb/explosives, possess in violation	3	M	
G.L. c. 148 § 39	Fireworks, sell or possess unlawful	2	M	
G.L. c. 159 § 104	Bus/railroad car, throwing missile or assaulting	2	M	
G.L. c. 159A § 31	Bus/driver, interfere with	4	F	
G.L. c. 160 § 220	Railroad fare, evade	1	M	
G.L. c. 162 § 18	Railroad track (electric), walking or standing on	1	M	
G.L. c. 166 § 42A	Cable TV/telephone service, obtain by fraud, or attempt, under $5,000	2	M	
G.L. c. 169A § 2-13	Check cashing violation	2	M	Penalty found in G.L. c. 169A § 13.
G.L. c. 208 § 34C	Abuse prevention order violation, probate act	2	M	
G.L. c. 209A § 3B	Abuse prevention order violation, failure to surrender firearms	2	M	
G.L. c. 209A § 7	Abuse prevention order violation	2	M	
G.L. c. 209A § 7	Abuse prevention order violation, retaliation	3	M	Perpetrator retaliates against victim for establishing his paternity or reporting his failure to pay child support.
G.L. c. 233 § 5	Witness fail to appear in criminal case	1	M	
G.L. c. 233 § 20H	Witness fail to testify, immunized	2	M	
G.L. c. 258E § 9	Harassment, criminal, prevention order violation	2	M	This involves violation of a court order, distinct from G.L. c. 265 § 43A(a) "Criminal harassment".
G.L. c. 264 § 2	Treason	6	F	
G.L. c. 264 § 3	Misprision of treason	3	F	
G.L. c. 264 § 11	Riot, incite	2	F	
G.L. c. 265 § 1	Murder	7	F	Penalty found in G.L. c. 265 § 2.
G.L. c. 265 § 9	Fight by arrangement	2	F	
G.L. c. 265 § 10	Fight by arrangement, aid/promote	2	F	
G.L. c. 265 § 11	Fight by arrangement, out-of-state	2	F	
G.L. c. 265 § 13	Manslaughter, involuntary	5	F	
G.L. c. 265 § 13	Manslaughter, voluntary	6	F	
G.L. c. 265 § 13	Manslaughter involving explosives	6	F	
G.L. c. 265 § 13A(a)	A&B	2	M	
G.L. c. 265 § 13A(a)	Assault	2	M	
G.L. c. 265 § 13A(b)	Assault, aggravated	3	F	
G.L. c. 265 § 13A(b)(i)	A&B, aggravated, serious bodily injury	3	F	
G.L. c. 265 § 13A(b)(ii)	A&B, aggravated, pregnant victim	3	F	
G.L. c. 265 § 13A(b)(iii)	A&B, aggravated, restraining order	3	F	
G.L. c. 265 § 13B	Indecent A&B on child under 14	4	F	
G.L. c. 265 § 13B	Indecent A&B on child under 14, subsequent	5	F	
G.L. c. 265 § 13B½	Indecent A&B on child under 14, aggravated	6	F	
G.L. c. 265 § 13C	A&B to collect loan	3	F	
G.L. c. 265 § 13C	A&B to collect loan, subsequent	3	F	
G.L. c. 265 § 13D	A&B on public employee	2	M	Applies to police officers. See G.L. c. 127 § 38B for A&B on correction officers.
G.L. c. 265 § 13D½	Firefighter, injure by setting fires	4	F	

9

Mass. General Law Chapter & Section	Offense Description	Grid Level	Penalty Type	Notes
G.L. c. 265 § 13F	A&B on retarded person	3	F	
G.L. c. 265 § 13F	A&B on retarded person, subsequent	3	F	
G.L. c. 265 § 13F	Indecent A&B on retarded person	4	F	
G.L. c. 265 § 13F	Indecent A&B on retarded person, subsequent	5	F	
G.L. c. 265 § 13G	Felony for hire	3	F	The "for hire" penalty is in addition to the penalty for the underlying felony.
G.L. c. 265 § 13H	Indecent A&B on elder 60 or over/disabled	4	F	
G.L. c. 265 § 13H	Indecent A&B on person 14 or over	3	F	
G.L. c. 265 § 13I	A&B/Assault on ambulance personnel	2	M	
G.L. c. 265 § 13J	A&B on child under 14, bodily injury	4	F	
G.L. c. 265 § 13J	A&B on child under 14, substantial bodily injury	5	F	
G.L. c. 265 § 13J	Child, permit injury to	3	M	
G.L. c. 265 § 13K(a½)	A&B on elder 60 or over/disabled person	2	F	
G.L. c. 265 § 13K(b)	A&B on elder 60 or over/disabled person, bodily injury	3	F	
G.L. c. 265 § 13K(c)	A&B on elder 60 or over/disabled person, serious bodily injury	4	F	
G.L. c. 265 § 13K(d½)	Caretaker permits abuse on elder/disabled person	2	F	
G.L. c. 265 § 13L	Reckless endangerment to children	2	M	
G.L. c. 265 § 13M	A&B on family member, subsequent	2	F	
G.L. c. 265 § 13M	Assault on family member, subsequent	2	F	
G.L. c. 265 § 14	Mayhem	5	F	
G.L. c. 265 § 15	Assault to murder or maim	4	F	
G.L. c. 265 § 15A(a)	ABDW on elder 60 or over, no/minor injury	2	F	
G.L. c. 265 § 15A(a)	ABDW on elder 60 or over, no/minor injury, subsequent	3	F	
G.L. c. 265 § 15A(a)	ABDW on elder 60 or over, moderate injury	3	F	
G.L. c. 265 § 15A(a)	ABDW on elder 60 or over, moderate injury, subsequent	3	F	
G.L. c. 265 § 15A(a)	ABDW on elder 60 or over, significant injury	4	F	
G.L. c. 265 § 15A(a)	ABDW on elder 60 or over, significant injury, subsequent	5	F	
G.L. c. 265 § 15A(b)	ABDW, no/minor injury	2	F	
G.L. c. 265 § 15A(b)	ABDW, moderate injury	3	F	
G.L. c. 265 § 15A(b)	ABDW, significant injury	4	F	
G.L. c. 265 § 15A(c)(i)	ABDW, aggravated, serious bodily injury	5	F	
G.L. c. 265 § 15A(c)(ii)	ABDW, aggravated, no serious bodily injury, pregnant victim	4	F	
G.L. c. 265 § 15A(c)(iii)	ABDW, aggravated, no serious bodily injury, restraining order	4	F	
G.L. c. 265 § 15A(c)(iv)	ABDW, aggravated, no serious bodily injury, victim under 14	4	F	
G.L. c. 265 § 15B(a)	Assault with dangerous weapon on elder 60 or over	2	F	
G.L. c. 265 § 15B(a)	Assault with dangerous weapon on elder 60 or over, subsequent	3	F	
G.L. c. 265 § 15B(b)	Assault with dangerous weapon	2	F	
G.L. c. 265 § 16	Murder, attempted	5	F	
G.L. c. 265 § 17	Robbery, armed, no display of gun	4	F	
G.L. c. 265 § 17	Robbery, armed, display of gun	5	F	
G.L. c. 265 § 17	Robbery, armed, with firearm	5	F	
G.L. c. 265 § 17	Robbery, armed, with firearm, subsequent	6	F	

Mass. General Law Chapter & Section	Offense Description	Grid Level	Penalty Type	Notes
G.L. c. 265 § 17	Robbery, armed & masked, no display of gun	5	F	
G.L. c. 265 § 17	Robbery, armed & masked, no display of gun, subsequent	5	F	
G.L. c. 265 § 17	Robbery, armed & masked, display of gun	6	F	
G.L. c. 265 § 17	Robbery, armed & masked, display of gun, subsequent	6	F	
G.L. c. 265 § 17	Robbery, armed & masked, with firearm	5	F	
G.L. c. 265 § 17	Robbery, armed & masked, with firearm, subsequent	6	F	
G.L. c. 265 § 18(a)	Assault to rob elder 60 or over, armed	4	F	
G.L. c. 265 § 18(a)	Assault to rob elder 60 or over, armed, subsequent	5	F	
G.L. c. 265 § 18(a)	Assault to rob elder 60 or over, armed, with firearm	4	F	
G.L. c. 265 § 18(a)	Assault to rob elder 60 or over, armed, with firearm, subsequent	6	F	
G.L. c. 265 § 18(a)	Assault to murder elder 60 or over, armed	5	F	
G.L. c. 265 § 18(a)	Assault to murder elder 60 or over, armed, subsequent	5	F	
G.L. c. 265 § 18(a)	Assault to murder elder 60 or over, armed, with firearm	5	F	
G.L. c. 265 § 18(a)	Assault to murder elder 60 or over, armed, with firearm, subsequent	6	F	
G.L. c. 265 § 18(b)	Assault to rob, armed	4	F	
G.L. c. 265 § 18(b)	Assault to rob, armed, with firearm	4	F	
G.L. c. 265 § 18(b)	Assault to murder, armed	5	F	
G.L. c. 265 § 18(b)	Assault to murder, armed, with firearm	5	F	
G.L. c. 265 § 18A	Assault in dwelling, armed	6	F	
G.L. c. 265 § 18A	Assault in dwelling, armed, with firearm	6	F	
G.L. c. 265 § 18B	Firearm, possess in felony	4	F	
G.L. c. 265 § 18B	Firearm, possess in felony, subsequent	5	F	
G.L. c. 265 § 18B	Firearm, possess in felony, large capacity	5	F	Definition of "Large capacity": http://www.mass.gov/legis/laws/mgl/140-121.htm.
G.L. c. 265 § 18C	Home invasion	6	F	
G.L. c. 265 § 18C	Home invasion, subsequent	6	F	
G.L. c. 265 § 19(a)	Robbery of elder 60 or over, unarmed	4	F	
G.L. c. 265 § 19(a)	Robbery of elder 60 or over, unarmed, subsequent	5	F	
G.L. c. 265 § 19(b)	Robbery, unarmed	3	F	
G.L. c. 265 § 20	Assault to rob, unarmed	3	F	
G.L. c. 265 § 21A	Carjacking	4	F	
G.L. c. 265 § 21A	Carjacking, armed	5	F	
G.L. c. 265 § 21A	Carjacking, armed, with firearm	6	F	
G.L. c. 265 § 22(a)	Rape, aggravated	6	F	
G.L. c. 265 § 22(a)	Rape, aggravated, subsequent	6	F	
G.L. c. 265 § 22(a)	Rape, aggravated, armed, with firearm	6	F	
G.L. c. 265 § 22(a)	Rape, aggravated, armed, with firearm, subsequent	6	F	
G.L. c. 265 § 22(b)	Rape	5	F	
G.L. c. 265 § 22(b)	Rape, subsequent	6	F	
G.L. c. 265 § 22(b)	Rape, armed, with firearm	5	F	
G.L. c. 265 § 22A	Rape of child under 16 with force	6	F	
G.L. c. 265 § 22A	Rape of child under 16 with force, subsequent	6	F	
G.L. c. 265 § 22B	Rape of child under 16 with force, aggravated	6	F	

Mass. General Law Chapter & Section	Offense Description	Grid Level	Penalty Type	Notes
G.L. c. 265 § 22C	Rape of child under 16 with force, after certain sex offenses	6	F	
G.L. c. 265 § 23	Rape of child under 16, statutory	4	F	
G.L. c. 265 § 23	Rape of child under 16, statutory, subsequent	5	F	
G.L. c. 265 § 23A	Rape of child under 16, statutory, aggravated	6	F	Aggravating factors: age difference, commission by mandated reporter.
G.L. c. 265 § 23B	Rape of child under 16, statutory, after certain sex offenses	6	F	
G.L. c. 265 § 24	Assault to rape	4	F	
G.L. c. 265 § 24	Assault to rape, subsequent	5	F	
G.L. c. 265 § 24	Assault to rape, armed, with firearm	4	F	
G.L. c. 265 § 24	Assault to rape, armed, with firearm, subsequent	6	F	
G.L. c. 265 § 24B	Assault to rape child under 16	5	F	
G.L. c. 265 § 24B	Assault to rape child under 16, subsequent	6	F	
G.L. c. 265 § 24B	Assault to rape child under 16, armed, with firearm	6	F	
G.L. c. 265 § 24B	Assault to rape child under 16, armed, with firearm, subsequent	6	F	
G.L. c. 265 § 25	Extortion or attempt	3	F	
G.L. c. 265 § 26	Kidnapping	4	F	
G.L. c. 265 § 26	Kidnapping, armed with firearm	6	F	
G.L. c. 265 § 26	Kidnapping for extortion	6	F	
G.L. c. 265 § 26	Kidnapping for extortion, armed with firearm	6	F	
G.L. c. 265 § 26	Kidnapping, with sexual assault, armed with dangerous weapon	6	F	
G.L. c. 265 § 26	Kidnapping, with serious bodily injury, armed with dangerous weapon	6	F	
G.L. c. 265 § 26	Kidnapping child under age 16	5	F	
G.L. c. 265 § 26A	Kidnapping incompetent or child by relative	2	M	
G.L. c. 265 § 26A	Kidnapping & endangering incompetent or child by relative	3	F	
G.L. c. 265 § 26C	Enticement of child under age 16	3	F	
G.L. c. 265 § 28	Poisoning with intent to kill or injure person	5	F	
G.L. c. 265 § 29	Assault to commit felony	3	F	
G.L. c. 265 § 34	Tattooing	1	M	
G.L. c. 265 § 35	Public way, throw object on	1	M	
G.L. c. 265 § 37	Civil rights violation or attempt	2	M	Distinct from G.L. c. 12 § 11J "Civil rights order violation".
G.L. c. 265 § 37	Civil rights violation with bodily injury or attempt	4	F	Distinct from G.L. c. 12 § 11J "Civil rights order violation with injury".
G.L. c. 265 § 39(a)	A&B or property damage to intimidate for race/religion	2	M	
G.L. c. 265 § 39(b)	A&B or property damage to intimidate for race/religion, bodily injury	3	F	
G.L. c. 265 § 39(b)	A&B or property damage to intimidate for race/religion, bodily injury, armed	4	F	
G.L. c. 265 § 43(a)	Stalking	3	F	
G.L. c. 265 § 43(c)	Stalking, subsequent	3	F	
G.L. c. 265 § 43(b)	Stalking in violation of restraining order	3	F	
G.L. c. 265 § 43A(a)	Harassment, criminal	2	M	Distinct from G.L. c. 258E § 9 "Harassment, criminal, prevention order violation".
G.L. c. 265 § 43A(b)	Harassment, criminal, subsequent	3	F	
G.L. c. 265 § 44	A&B on child to coerce criminal conspiracy	3	F	Includes actions by criminal street gangs.

Mass. General Law Chapter & Section	Offense Description	Grid Level	Penalty Type	Notes
G.L. c. 265 § 44	A&B on child to coerce criminal conspiracy, subsequent	3	F	Includes actions by criminal street gangs.
G.L. c. 265 § 48	Sex Offender engaging in ice cream truck vending	2	M	
G.L. c. 266 § 1	Burn dwelling house (arson)	4	F	
G.L. c. 266 § 2	Burn building/contents	3	F	
G.L. c. 266 § 5	Burn boat/MV/personalty	3	F	Personalty = personal property.
G.L. c. 266 § 5A	Burn boat/MV/personalty, attempt to	2	F	Personalty = personal property.
G.L. c. 266 § 5A	Burn dwelling house (arson), attempt to	3	F	
G.L. c. 266 § 5A	Burn public building, attempt to	3	F	
G.L. c. 266 § 7	Burn woods	2	M	
G.L. c. 266 § 8	Fire on land, set	2	M	Requires the property of another to be injured.
G.L. c. 266 § 9	Fire on land, fail to extinguish/control	1	M	
G.L. c. 266 § 10	Burn building/MV/personalty to defraud insurer, or attempt to do so	3	F	Personalty = personal property.
G.L. c. 266 § 11	Fire alarm, disable	2	M	
G.L. c. 266 § 14	B&E dwelling at night (burglary), for felony, armed or assault on occupants	6	F	
G.L. c. 266 § 14	B&E dwelling at night (burglary), for felony, armed or assault on occupants, subsequent	6	F	
G.L. c. 266 § 14	B&E dwelling at night (burglary), for felony, with firearm	6	F	
G.L. c. 266 § 14	B&E dwelling at night (burglary), for felony, with firearm, subsequent	6	F	
G.L. c. 266 § 15	B&E dwelling at night (burglary), for felony, unarmed, no assault on occupants	3	F	
G.L. c. 266 § 15	B&E dwelling at night (burglary), for felony, unarmed, no assault on occupants, subsequent	4	F	
G.L. c. 266 § 16	B&E building, ship, or vehicle at night, for felony, non-dwelling	2	F	
G.L. c. 266 § 16	B&E building, ship, or vehicle at night, for felony, dwelling	3	F	
G.L. c. 266 § 16	Break safe or vault, for larceny or felony, or attempt, non-dwelling	2	F	
G.L. c. 266 § 16	Break safe or vault, for larceny or felony, or attempt, dwelling	3	F	
G.L. c. 266 § 16A	B&E building, ship, or vehicle, for misdemeanor	2	M	
G.L. c. 266 § 17	B&E daytime or enter at night, for felony, person in fear, non-dwelling	4	F	
G.L. c. 266 § 17	B&E daytime or enter at night, for felony, person in fear, dwelling	4	F	
G.L. c. 266 § 17	B&E daytime or enter at night, for felony, with firearm, person in fear, non-dwelling	5	F	
G.L. c. 266 § 17	B&E daytime or enter at night, for felony, with firearm, person in fear, dwelling	5	F	
G.L. c. 266 § 18	B&E daytime, for felony, non-dwelling	2	F	
G.L. c. 266 § 18	B&E daytime, for felony, dwelling	3	F	
G.L. c. 266 § 18	B&E daytime, for felony, with firearm, non-dwelling	5	F	
G.L. c. 266 § 18	B&E daytime, for felony, with firearm, dwelling	5	F	
G.L. c. 266 § 18	Enter dwelling at night, for felony	4	F	
G.L. c. 266 § 18	Enter dwelling at night, for felony, with firearm	5	F	
G.L. c. 266 § 18A	Entering dwelling by false pretense, for felony or with larceny, no person in fear	3	F	

Mass. General Law Chapter & Section	Offense Description	Grid Level	Penalty Type	Notes
G.L. c. 266 § 19	B&E or enter at night railroad car, for felony	3	F	
G.L. c. 266 § 20	Larceny from boat, building, railroad car, under $10,000	2	F	
G.L. c. 266 § 20	Larceny from boat, building, railroad car, $10,000 to $50,000	3	F	
G.L. c. 266 § 20	Larceny from boat, building, railroad car, $50,000 and over	3	F	
G.L. c. 266 § 20A	B&E or enter truck, trailer, or freight container, for felony	2	F	
G.L. c. 266 § 20B	Larceny from truck, trailer, or freight container, under $10,000	2	F	
G.L. c. 266 § 20B	Larceny from truck, trailer, or freight container, $10,000 to $50,000	3	F	
G.L. c. 266 § 20B	Larceny from truck, trailer, or freight container, $50,000 and over	3	F	
G.L. c. 266 § 23	Larceny at fire, under $10,000	2	F	Penalty found in G.L. c. 266 § 24.
G.L. c. 266 § 23	Larceny at fire, $10,000 to $50,000	3	F	Penalty found in G.L. c. 266 § 24.
G.L. c. 266 § 23	Larceny at fire, $50,000 and over	3	F	Penalty found in G.L. c. 266 § 24.
G.L. c. 266 § 25	Larceny from person	2	F	Pickpocketing, purse-snatching.
G.L. c. 266 § 25	Larceny from person 65 or older	3	F	
G.L. c. 266 § 25	Larceny from person 65 or older, subsequent	3	F	
G.L. c. 266 § 27	Larceny of construction tools	1	M	
G.L. c. 266 § 27	Larceny of construction tools, subsequent	1	M	
G.L. c. 266 § 28(a)	Motor vehicle, larceny/malicious damage/receive stolen/steal parts	2	F	
G.L. c. 266 § 28(a)	Motor vehicle, larceny/malicious damage/receive stolen/steal parts, subsequent	3	F	
G.L. c. 266 § 28(b)	Motor vehicle, conceal thief of	3	F	
G.L. c. 266 § 30(1)	Larceny under $250	2	M	
G.L. c. 266 § 30(1)	Larceny over $250, under $10,000	3	F	
G.L. c. 266 § 30(1)	Larceny over $250, $10,000 to $50,000	3	F	
G.L. c. 266 § 30(1)	Larceny over $250, $50,000 and over	3	F	
G.L. c. 266 § 30(1)	Larceny by single scheme, under $250	1	M	
G.L. c. 266 § 30(1)	Larceny from common carrier	3	M	
G.L. c. 266 § 30(1)	Larceny of firearm	4	F	
G.L. c. 266 § 30(5)	Larceny from elder/disabled person, $250 or under	2	M	This section includes fraud.
G.L. c. 266 § 30(5)	Larceny from elder/disabled person, over $250, under $10,000	3	F	This section includes fraud.
G.L. c. 266 § 30(5)	Larceny from elder/disabled person, over $250, $10,000 to $50,000	3	F	This section includes fraud.
G.L. c. 266 § 30(5)	Larceny from elder/disabled person, over $250, $50,000 and over	3	F	This section includes fraud.
G.L. c. 266 § 30A	Shoplifting	1	M	
G.L. c. 266 § 30A	Shoplifting, 3rd and subsequent	2	M	
G.L. c. 266 § 33(1)	False pretense in commercial transaction, under $250	2	M	Penalty found in G.L. c. 266 § 30.
G.L. c. 266 § 33(1)	False pretense in commercial transaction, over $250, under $10,000	2	F	Penalty found in G.L. c. 266 § 30.
G.L. c. 266 § 33(1)	False pretense in commercial transaction, over $250, $10,000 to $50,000	3	F	Penalty found in G.L. c. 266 § 30.
G.L. c. 266 § 33(1)	False pretense in commercial transaction, over $250, $50,000 and over	3	F	Penalty found in G.L. c. 266 § 30.
G.L. c. 266 § 34	Larceny by false pretense, under $250	1	M	Penalty found in G.L. c. 266 § 30.

Mass. General Law Chapter & Section	Offense Description	Grid Level	Penalty Type	Notes
G.L. c. 266 § 34	Larceny by false pretense, over $250, under $10,000	2	F	Penalty found in G.L. c. 266 § 30.
G.L. c. 266 § 34	Larceny by false pretense, over $250, $10,000 to $50,000	3	F	Penalty found in G.L. c. 266 § 30.
G.L. c. 266 § 34	Larceny by false pretense, over $250, $50,000 and over	3	F	Penalty found in G.L. c. 266 § 30.
G.L. c. 266 § 37	Larceny by check, under $250	2	M	Distinct from G.L. c. 267 § 1 "Check, forgery of". Penalty found in G.L. c. 266 § 30.
G.L. c. 266 § 37	Larceny by check, over $250, under $10,000	2	F	Distinct from G.L. c. 267 § 1 "Check, forgery of". Penalty found in G.L. c. 266 § 30.
G.L. c. 266 § 37	Larceny by check, over $250, $10,000 to $50,000	3	F	Distinct from G.L. c. 267 § 1 "Check, forgery of". Penalty found in G.L. c. 266 § 30.
G.L. c. 266 § 37	Larceny by check, over $250, $50,000 and over	3	F	Distinct from G.L. c. 267 § 1 "Check, forgery of". Penalty found in G.L. c. 266 § 30.
G.L. c. 266 § 37B	Credit card violations, $250 or less	1	M	
G.L. c. 266 § 37C	Credit card fraud over $250, under $10,000	2	F	
G.L. c. 266 § 37C	Credit card fraud over $250, $10,000 to $50,000	3	F	
G.L. c. 266 § 37C	Credit card fraud over $250, $50,000 and over	3	F	
G.L. c. 266 § 37E(b)	Identity fraud, pose	2	M	
G.L. c. 266 § 37E(c)	Identity fraud, intent to pose	2	M	
G.L. c. 266 § 49	Burglarious instrument/MV master key, make or possess	2	F	
G.L. c. 266 § 60	Receive stolen or falsely traded property, under $250	2	M	
G.L. c. 266 § 60	Receive stolen or falsely traded property, under $250, subsequent	2	F	
G.L. c. 266 § 60	Receive stolen or falsely traded property, over $250, under $10,000	2	F	
G.L. c. 266 § 60	Receive stolen or falsely traded property, over $250, $10,000 to $50,000	3	F	
G.L. c. 266 § 60	Receive stolen or falsely traded property, over $250, $50,000 and over	3	F	
G.L. c. 266 § 63	Boat, use without authority	1	M	
G.L. c. 266 § 73	False pretense of trade, obtain goods by	2	F	
G.L. c. 266 § 76	Fraud/cheat, gross	3	F	
G.L. c. 266 § 98	Church or school, damage	2	M	
G.L. c. 266 § 101	Explosion, malicious	5	F	
G.L. c. 266 § 102	Explosives, throw/place/explode or possess to injure	5	F	
G.L. c. 266 § 102A	Infernal machine, possess	4	F	
G.L. c. 266 § 102B	Molotov cocktail, make/sell/use/possess	3	F	
G.L. c. 266 § 104	Building, damage to	1	M	
G.L. c. 266 § 112	Poison/kill/maim domestic animal	2	F	
G.L. c. 266 § 114	Trees and fences, malicious injury	1	M	
G.L. c. 266 § 117	Trespass for tree/plant/fruit	1	M	
G.L. c. 266 § 117	Trespass for tree/plant/fruit, Sunday/disguised/ nighttime	1	M	
G.L. c. 266 § 120	Trespass	1	M	
G.L. c. 266 § 120F	Computer system, unauthorized access to	1	M	
G.L. c. 266 § 121	Trespass with firearm	3	M	
G.L. c. 266 § 123	Trespass on state/county property	1	M	
G.L. c. 266 § 126A	Defacement of real or personal property	2	F	
G.L. c. 266 § 126B	Tagging property	2	M	

Mass. General Law Chapter & Section	Offense Description	Grid Level	Penalty Type	Notes
G.L. c. 266 § 127	Destruction of property under $250, wanton or malicious	1	M	
G.L. c. 266 § 127	Destruction of property over $250, malicious	2	F	
G.L. c. 266 § 127	Destruction of property over $250, wanton	2	M	
G.L. c. 266 § 127A	Church, threat to injure	2	M	
G.L. c. 266 § 127A	Church/synagogue, injury to, under $5000	2	M	Includes $5000 and under.
G.L. c. 266 § 127A	Church/synagogue, injury to, over $5000	3	F	
G.L. c. 266 § 139(a)	Motor vehicle VIN, remove/alter	2	F	
G.L. c. 266 § 139(b)	Motor vehicle, sell with defaced VIN, or attempt	2	F	
G.L. c. 266 § 139(c)	Motor vehicle, possess or receive with defaced VIN	2	M	
G.L. c. 267 § 1	Check, forgery of	2	F	Distinct from G.L. c. 266 § 37, "Larceny by check under $250".
G.L. c. 267 § 1	Forgery, check forgery, promissory note forgery	3	F	Distinct from G.L. c. 266 § 37, "Larceny by check under $250".
G.L. c. 267 § 5	Utter false check, instrument, or promissory note	3	F	
G.L. c. 267 § 9	Counterfeit notes, possess	3	F	This section applies to possession of 10 or more notes/bills; for fewer than 10, apply G.L. c. 267 § 12.
G.L. c. 267 § 12	Counterfeit note or traveler's check, possess	2	F	This section applies to possession of fewer than 10 notes/bills; for 10 or more, apply G.L. c. 267 § 9.
G.L. c. 268 § 1	Perjury	3	F	
G.L. c. 268 § 1	Perjury in trial of capital case	5	F	
G.L. c. 268 § 2	Perjury, suborn	3	F	Penalty found in G.L. c. 268 § 1.
G.L. c. 268 § 3	Perjury, attempt to suborn	2	F	
G.L. c. 268 § 13B(1)	Intimidate juror/witness, or retaliate against	4	F	
G.L. c. 268 § 13C	Court proceedings, disrupt	1	M	
G.L. c. 268 § 15	Escape, aid accused misdemeanant to	2	V	Penalty type (F/Misd.) depends on the prisoner's status (F/Misd.) and escape location (prison/HOC).
G.L. c. 268 § 15	Escape, aid convicted misdemeanant or convicted HOC felon to	3	F	
G.L. c. 268 § 15	Escape, aid accused felon or convicted state prison felon to	3	F	
G.L. c. 268 § 15A	Escape from municipal lockup	2	M	
G.L. c. 268 § 16	Escape from penal institution/court/SDP center, or attempt	4	F	
G.L. c. 268 § 17	Escape from officer, aid	2	M	
G.L. c. 268 § 19	Escape from penal institution, permit	3	F	
G.L. c. 268 § 24	Police officer, fail to assist	1	M	
G.L. c. 268 § 28	Prisoner, deliver drugs or article to	3	F	
G.L. c. 268 § 32	False alarm from police call box or tamper with police/fire call box	2	M	
G.L. c. 268 § 32A	Firefighter, interfere with	2	F	
G.L. c. 268 § 32B	Resist arrest	2	M	
G.L. c. 268 § 33	Police officer or public official, impersonate	2	M	
G.L. c. 268 § 34A	False name or Social Security number, furnish to police	1	M	
G.L. c. 269 § 2	Riot, fail to disperse or fail to assist in dispersing	2	M	
G.L. c. 269 § 7	Riot, destroy building/boat in	2	F	

Mass. General Law Chapter & Section	Offense Description	Grid Level	Penalty Type	Notes
G.L. c. 269 § 10(a)	Firearm, carry without license	4	F	Possession/carrying of a firearm, when not at home or work, without a license to carry. Distinct from G.L. c. 269 § 10(h)(1): possession w/o FID card. Bartley-Fox: 6-month minimum in a facility.
G.L. c. 269 § 10(a)	Firearm, carry without license, 1 prior violent/drug crime	4	F	Possession/carrying of a firearm, when not at home or work, without a license to carry. Distinct from G.L. c. 269 § 10(h)(1): possession w/o FID card. Bartley-Fox: 12-month minimum in a facility. Penalty found in G.L. c. 269 § 10G(a).
G.L. c. 269 § 10(b)	Dangerous weapon, carry, no prior felonies	2	M	See statute for examples of dangerous weapons.
G.L. c. 269 § 10(b)	Dangerous weapon, carry, with prior felonies	3	F	See statute for examples of dangerous weapons.
G.L. c. 269 § 10(c)	Machine gun/sawed-off shotgun, possess	5	F	Bartley-Fox: 6-month minimum in a facility.
G.L. c. 269 § 10(c)	Machine gun/sawed-off shotgun, possess, with 1 prior violent/drug crime	5	F	Bartley-Fox: 12-month minimum in a facility. Penalty found in G.L. c. 269 § 10G(a).
G.L. c. 269 § 10(d)	Dangerous weapon, carry, 2nd off.	4	F	Bartley-Fox: 12-month minimum in a facility.
G.L. c. 269 § 10(d)	Dangerous weapon, carry, 3rd off.	4	F	Bartley-Fox: 12-month minimum in a facility.
G.L. c. 269 § 10(d)	Dangerous weapon, carry, 4th off.	5	F	Bartley-Fox: 12-month minimum in a facility.
G.L. c. 269 § 10(d)	Firearm, carry without license, 2nd off.	5	F	Bartley-Fox: 12-month minimum in a facility.
G.L. c. 269 § 10(d)	Firearm, carry without license, 3rd off.	5	F	Bartley-Fox: 12-month minimum in a facility.
G.L. c. 269 § 10(d)	Firearm, carry without license, 4th off.	6	F	Bartley-Fox: 12-month minimum in a facility.
G.L. c. 269 § 10(d)	Machine gun/sawed-off shotgun, possess, 2nd off.	5	F	Bartley-Fox: 12-month minimum in a facility.
G.L. c. 269 § 10(d)	Machine gun/sawed-off shotgun, possess, 3rd off.	6	F	Bartley-Fox: 12-month minimum in a facility.
G.L. c. 269 § 10(g)	Rifle/shotgun without serial number, sell	3	M	
G.L. c. 269 § 10(h)(1)	Firearm or ammunition without FID card, possess	3	M	Ownership, possession, or transfer of firearm / shotgun / rifle / ammunition without an FID card (per G.L. c. 140 § 129C). Distinct from G.L. c. 269 § 10(a)—possession/carrying of a firearm, when not at home or work, without a license to carry .
G.L. c. 269 § 10(h)(1)	Firearm or ammunition without FID card, possess, subsequent	2	M	
G.L. c. 269 § 10(h)(2)	Firearm, leave unattended with intent to transfer possession	3	F	
G.L. c. 269 § 10(i)	Firearm license/FID card, fail to surrender	2	M	
G.L. c. 269 § 10(j)	Dangerous weapon, carry on school grounds, non-firearm	2	M	
G.L. c. 269 § 10(j)	Dangerous weapon, carry on school grounds, firearm	4	M	
G.L. c. 269 § 10(m)	Firearm, possess large capacity	4	F	Definition of "Large capacity": http://www.mass.gov/legis/laws/mgl/140-121.htm.
G.L. c. 269 § 10(m)	Firearm, possess large capacity, with valid FID	3	F	Definition of "Large capacity": http://www.mass.gov/legis/laws/mgl/140-121.htm.
G.L. c. 269 § 10(n)	Firearm, carry without license, loaded	3	M	This offense is a "from & after" penalty. That is, "sentence shall begin from and after the expiration of the sentence for the violation of paragraph (a) or paragraph (c)".
G.L. c. 269 § 10(n)	Machine gun/sawed-off shotgun, carry, loaded	3	M	This offense is a "from & after" penalty. That is, "sentence shall begin from and after the expiration of the sentence for the violation of paragraph (a) or paragraph (c)".
G.L. c. 269 § 10D	Body armor, use in felony	2	F	
G.L. c. 269 § 10E	Firearms, trafficking in, 3-9 weapons, 6-8 months	4	F	Bartley-Fox: 6-month minimum in a facility.

Mass. General Law Chapter & Section	Offense Description	Grid Level	Penalty Type	Notes
G.L. c. 269 § 10E	Firearms, trafficking in, 10-19 weapons, 8-12 months	5	F	Bartley-Fox: 6-month minimum in a facility.
G.L. c. 269 § 10E	Firearms, trafficking in, 20 or more weapons, 12 month min.	6	F	Bartley-Fox: 6-month minimum in a facility.
G.L. c. 269 § 11B	Firearm, possess in felony, with defaced serial number	4	F	Judge has discretion over 6-month minimum—not a true mandatory minimum.
G.L. c. 269 § 11C	Firearm serial number, deface or receive with defaced number	3	M	
G.L. c. 269 § 12	Dangerous weapon, manufacture/sell certain	1	M	
G.L. c. 269 § 12A	BB gun/air rifle, sell/give to minor	1	M	
G.L. c. 269 § 12B	BB gun/air rifle, possess or shoot in public place	2	M	
G.L. c. 269 § 12D(a)	Rifle/shotgun on way, carry loaded	4	M	
G.L. c. 269 § 12D(a)	Rifle/shotgun on way, carry loaded, large capacity	4	V	Definition of "Large capacity": http://www.mass.gov/legis/laws/mgl/140-121.htm.
G.L. c. 269 § 12D(b)	Firearm, carry on way, unloaded, large capacity	4	F	Definition of "Large capacity": http://www.mass.gov/legis/laws/mgl/140-121.htm.
G.L. c. 269 § 12E	Firearm, discharge within 500 feet of building	3	M	
G.L. c. 269 § 13	Fire alarm, false	2	M	
G.L. c. 269 § 13A	Crime report, false	2	M	
G.L. c. 269 § 14(b)	Bomb threat, false	3	F	This section also specifies other kinds of threats.
G.L. c. 269 § 14(c)	Bomb/hijack threat with serious public alarm	4	F	
G.L. c. 269 § 14A	Telephone calls, annoying or obscene	1	M	
G.L. c. 269 § 14B	False/silent 911 call	2	M	
G.L. c. 269 § 17	Hazing	2	M	
G.L. c. 270 § 18	Inhale toxic fumes for stupefaction, glue or other	1	M	
G.L. c. 271 § 12	False lottery tickets: creation, sale, or possession	2	F	
G.L. c. 271 § 39(a)	Bribe, business	3	F	
G.L. c. 271 § 39A	Bribe, offer or accept/solicit sports	2	M	
G.L. c. 271 § 49(a)	Usury	3	F	
G.L. c. 272 § 2	Prostitution/unlawful sex, abduct or entice person for	2	F	
G.L. c. 272 § 3	Sexual intercourse, drug for	3	F	
G.L. c. 272 § 4	Sexual intercourse, induce chaste minor	2	F	
G.L. c. 272 § 4A	Prostitution, induce minor to	3	F	
G.L. c. 272 § 4B	Prostitute, derive support from child	4	F	
G.L. c. 272 § 7	Prostitute, derive support from	3	F	
G.L. c. 272 § 8	Prostitute, solicit for	1	M	
G.L. c. 272 § 12	Prostitution, procure person to practice	2	M	
G.L. c. 272 § 16	Open and gross lewdness	2	F	1st offense doesn't trigger SORB notification or registration.
G.L. c. 272 § 16	Open and gross lewdness, with previous sex offense	3	F	Triggers SORB notification & registration.
G.L. c. 272 § 17	Incest	5	F	
G.L. c. 272 § 17	Incest with person under 21	5	F	
G.L. c. 272 § 18	Fornication	1	M	
G.L. c. 272 § 22	Fetal death out of wedlock, conceal cause	2	M	
G.L. c. 272 § 28	Obscene matter, distribute to minor	2	F	
G.L. c. 272 § 28	Obscene matter, distribute to minor, 2nd and subsequent	3	F	
G.L. c. 272 § 29	Obscene matter, distribute	2	F	
G.L. c. 272 § 29	Obscene matter, distribute, 2nd and subsequent	3	F	

Mass. General Law Chapter & Section	Offense Description	Grid Level	Penalty Type	Notes
G.L. c. 272 § 29A(a)	Child in nude, pose/exhibit for visual material, with lascivious intent	4	F	
G.L. c. 272 § 29B(a)	Child in nude, disseminate visual material of, with lascivious intent	4	F	
G.L. c. 272 § 29A(b)	Child in sexual act, pose/exhibit for visual material, with lascivious intent	4	F	
G.L. c. 272 § 29B(b)	Child in sexual act, disseminate visual material of, with lascivious intent	4	F	
G.L. c. 272 § 29C	Child pornography, possession of	3	F	
G.L. c. 272 § 34	Crime against nature (sodomy)	3	F	
G.L. c. 272 § 35	Unnatural & lascivious act	2	F	
G.L. c. 272 § 35A	Unnatural & lascivious act with child under 16	3	F	
G.L. c. 272 § 35A	Unnatural & lascivious act with child under 16, subsequent	4	F	
G.L. c. 272 § 40	School or public assembly, disturb	1	M	
G.L. c. 272 § 40	School or public assembly, disturb, 3rd and subsequent	2	M	
G.L. c. 272 § 40A	Alcohol, possess in school	1	M	
G.L. c. 272 § 43	Disorderly conduct on public conveyance	1	M	Penalty found in G.L. c. 272 § 40.
G.L. c. 272 § 43	Disorderly conduct on public conveyance, 3rd and subsequent	2	M	Penalty found in G.L. c. 272 § 40.
G.L. c. 272 § 43A	Smoking on MBTA	1	M	
G.L. c. 272 § 53	Accost/annoy person of opposite sex	1	M	
G.L. c. 272 § 53	Disorderly conduct	1	M	
G.L. c. 272 § 53	Disorderly house, keep	1	M	
G.L. c. 272 § 53	Disturbing the peace	1	M	
G.L. c. 272 § 53	Indecent Exposure	1	M	
G.L. c. 272 § 53	Lewd, wanton & lascivious conduct	1	M	
G.L. c. 272 § 53	Nightwalker, common	1	M	Equivalent to "Streetwalker, common". Involves not a fee but conduct (including accosting, annoying, lewd and lascivious behavior). Distinct from § 53A "Sexual conduct, pay for or for fee".
G.L. c. 272 § 53A(a)	Sexual conduct, pay for or for fee	2	M	This section addresses prostitution.
G.L. c. 272 § 53A(b)	Sexual conduct, pay for or for fee, with child under 14	4	F	This section addresses prostitution.
G.L. c. 272 § 59	Municipal ordinance violation: loitering, trespassing, drinking, accosting	1	V	
G.L. c. 272 § 66	Vagrancy	1	M	
G.L. c. 272 § 68	Vagabond	1	M	
G.L. c. 272 § 77	Animal, cruelty to	2	F	
G.L. c. 272 § 77A	Police horse/dog, mistreat/interfere with	2	M	
G.L. c. 272 § 94	Animal fight, keep/promote	2	F	
G.L. c. 272 § 95	Animal fight, presence at	1	F	
G.L. c. 272 § 105(b)	Photograph unsuspecting nude person	2	M	
G.L. c. 272 § 105(c)	Photograph of unsuspecting nude person, disseminate	2	F	
G.L. c. 273 § 15	Support child out of wedlock, enter Commonwealth without	2	F	Penalty found in G.L. c. 273 § 15A(3).
G.L. c. 273 § 15	Support child out of wedlock, fail to	2	F	Penalty found in G.L. c. 273 § 15A(2).
G.L. c. 274 § 2	Accessory to felony before the fact	U	F	
G.L. c. 274 § 4	Accessory to felony after the fact	U-1	F	
G.L. c. 274 § 6	Attempt to commit crime, Larceny	U-1	M	

Mass. General Law Chapter & Section	Offense Description	Grid Level	Penalty Type	Notes
G.L. c. 274 § 6	Attempt to commit crime, under 5-year felony or misdemeanor	U-1	V	Underlying offense may trigger SORB or SDP protocols.
G.L. c. 274 § 6	Attempt to commit crime, 5-year felony or greater	U-1	F	Underlying offense may trigger SORB or SDP protocols.
G.L. c. 274 § 6	Attempt to commit crime, punishable by death	U-1	F	Underlying offense may trigger SORB or SDP protocols.
G.L. c. 274 § 7(4)	Conspiracy for misdemeanor	U	M	
G.L. c. 274 § 7(3)	Conspiracy for felony, not more than 10 years	U	F	
G.L. c. 274 § 7(2)	Conspiracy for felony, more than 10 years	U	F	
G.L. c. 274 § 7(1)	Conspiracy for felony, death penalty or life imprisonment	U	F	
G.L. c. 275 § 2	Threat to commit crime	1	M	Penalty found in G.L. c. 275 § 4.
G.L. c. 276 App. § 1-5	Detainers, escape or attempt	2	F	
G.L. c. 276 § 19	Fugitive, fail bring before court	1	M	
G.L. c. 276 § 82A	Failure to appear, recognizance or bail, misdemeanor	2	M	
G.L. c. 276 § 82A	Failure to appear, recognizance or bail, felony	2	F	
Common Law	Affray [Grid 2012]	1	CL	Penalty found in G.L. c. 279 § 5.
Common Law	Contempt, criminal [Grid 2012]	2	CL	Penalty found in G.L. c. 279 § 5.
Common Law	Escape from police officer [Grid 2012]	2	CL	Penalty found in G.L. c. 279 § 5.
Common Law	Police officer, interfere with [Grid 2012]	2	CL	Penalty found in G.L. c. 279 § 5.
G.L. c. 265 § 13A(a)	A&B	2	M	
G.L. c. 265 § 44	A&B on child to coerce criminal conspiracy	3	F	Includes actions by criminal street gangs.
G.L. c. 265 § 44	A&B on child to coerce criminal conspiracy, subsequent	3	F	Includes actions by criminal street gangs.
G.L. c. 265 § 13J	A&B on child under 14, bodily injury	4	F	
G.L. c. 265 § 13J	A&B on child under 14, substantial bodily injury	5	F	
G.L. c. 127 § 38B	A&B on correction officer	3	F	This section also applies to other employees, volunteers, and contractors. It does not apply to police officers—see G.L. c. 265 § 13D.
G.L. c. 265 § 13K(a½)	A&B on elder 60 or over/disabled person	2	F	
G.L. c. 265 § 13K(b)	A&B on elder 60 or over/disabled person, bodily injury	3	F	
G.L. c. 265 § 13K(c)	A&B on elder 60 or over/disabled person, serious bodily injury	4	F	
G.L. c. 265 § 13M	A&B on family member, subsequent	2	F	
G.L. c. 265 § 13D	A&B on public employee	2	M	Applies to police officers. See G.L. c. 127 § 38B for A&B on correction officers.
G.L. c. 265 § 13F	A&B on retarded person	3	F	
G.L. c. 265 § 13F	A&B on retarded person, subsequent	3	F	
G.L. c. 265 § 39(a)	A&B or property damage to intimidate for race/religion	2	M	
G.L. c. 265 § 39(b)	A&B or property damage to intimidate for race/religion, bodily injury	3	F	
G.L. c. 265 § 39(b)	A&B or property damage to intimidate for race/religion, bodily injury, armed	4	F	
G.L. c. 265 § 13C	A&B to collect loan	3	F	
G.L. c. 265 § 13C	A&B to collect loan, subsequent	3	F	
G.L. c. 265 § 13A(b)(ii)	A&B, aggravated, pregnant victim	3	F	
G.L. c. 265 § 13A(b)(iii)	A&B, aggravated, restraining order	3	F	
G.L. c. 265 § 13A(b)(i)	A&B, aggravated, serious bodily injury	3	F	
G.L. c. 265 § 13I	A&B/Assault on ambulance personnel	2	M	

Mass. General Law Chapter & Section	Offense Description	Grid Level	Penalty Type	Notes
G.L. c. 265 § 15A(a)	ABDW on elder 60 or over, moderate injury	3	F	
G.L. c. 265 § 15A(a)	ABDW on elder 60 or over, moderate injury, subsequent	3	F	
G.L. c. 265 § 15A(a)	ABDW on elder 60 or over, no/minor injury	2	F	
G.L. c. 265 § 15A(a)	ABDW on elder 60 or over, no/minor injury, subsequent	3	F	
G.L. c. 265 § 15A(a)	ABDW on elder 60 or over, significant injury	4	F	
G.L. c. 265 § 15A(a)	ABDW on elder 60 or over, significant injury, subsequent	5	F	
G.L. c. 265 § 15A(c)(ii)	ABDW, aggravated, no serious bodily injury, pregnant victim	4	F	
G.L. c. 265 § 15A(c)(iii)	ABDW, aggravated, no serious bodily injury, restraining order	4	F	
G.L. c. 265 § 15A(c)(iv)	ABDW, aggravated, no serious bodily injury, victim under 14	4	F	
G.L. c. 265 § 15A(c)(i)	ABDW, aggravated, serious bodily injury	5	F	
G.L. c. 265 § 15A(b)	ABDW, moderate injury	3	F	
G.L. c. 265 § 15A(b)	ABDW, no/minor injury	2	F	
G.L. c. 265 § 15A(b)	ABDW, significant injury	4	F	
G.L. c. 209A § 7	Abuse prevention order violation	2	M	
G.L. c. 209A § 3B	Abuse prevention order violation, failure to surrender firearms	2	M	
G.L. c. 208 § 34C	Abuse prevention order violation, probate act	2	M	
G.L. c. 209A § 7	Abuse prevention order violation, retaliation	3	M	Perpetrator retaliates against victim for establishing his paternity or reporting his failure to pay child support.
G.L. c. 274 § 4	Accessory to felony after the fact	U-1	F	
G.L. c. 274 § 2	Accessory to felony before the fact	U	F	
G.L. c. 272 § 53	Accost/annoy person of opposite sex	1	M	
Common Law	Affray [Grid 2012]	1	CL	Penalty found in G.L. c. 279 § 5.
G.L. c. 272 § 40A	Alcohol, possess in school	1	M	
G.L. c. 138 § 34C	Alcohol, possession by minor	1	M	Includes transporting or carrying.
G.L. c. 138 § 34	Alcohol, sell/deliver to person under 21	1	M	
G.L. c. 138 § 2	Alcohol, sell/make/store unlawfully	1	M	
G.L. c. 138 § 22	Alcohol, transport unlawfully	1	M	
G.L. c. 138 § 34C	Alcohol, transportation by minor	1	M	Includes possessing or carrying.
G.L. c. 140 § 122B	Ammunition, unlicensed sale of	2	M	
G.L. c. 272 § 94	Animal fight, keep/promote	2	F	
G.L. c. 272 § 95	Animal fight, presence at	1	F	
G.L. c. 272 § 77	Animal, cruelty to	2	F	
G.L. c. 265 § 13A(a)	Assault	2	M	
G.L. c. 265 § 18A	Assault in dwelling, armed	6	F	
G.L. c. 265 § 18A	Assault in dwelling, armed, with firearm	6	F	
G.L. c. 265 § 13M	Assault on family member, subsequent	2	F	
G.L. c. 265 § 29	Assault to commit felony	3	F	
G.L. c. 265 § 18(a)	Assault to murder elder 60 or over, armed	5	F	
G.L. c. 265 § 18(a)	Assault to murder elder 60 or over, armed, subsequent	5	F	
G.L. c. 265 § 18(a)	Assault to murder elder 60 or over, armed, with firearm	5	F	
G.L. c. 265 § 18(a)	Assault to murder elder 60 or over, armed, with firearm, subsequent	6	F	
G.L. c. 265 § 15	Assault to murder or maim	4	F	

9

Mass. General Law Chapter & Section	Offense Description	Grid Level	Penalty Type	Notes
G.L. c. 265 § 18(b)	Assault to murder, armed	5	F	
G.L. c. 265 § 18(b)	Assault to murder, armed, with firearm	5	F	
G.L. c. 265 § 24	Assault to rape	4	F	
G.L. c. 265 § 24B	Assault to rape child under 16	5	F	
G.L. c. 265 § 24B	Assault to rape child under 16, armed, with firearm	6	F	
G.L. c. 265 § 24B	Assault to rape child under 16, armed, with firearm, subsequent	6	F	
G.L. c. 265 § 24B	Assault to rape child under 16, subsequent	6	F	
G.L. c. 265 § 24	Assault to rape, armed, with firearm	4	F	
G.L. c. 265 § 24	Assault to rape, armed, with firearm, subsequent	6	F	
G.L. c. 265 § 24	Assault to rape, subsequent	5	F	
G.L. c. 265 § 18(a)	Assault to rob elder 60 or over, armed	4	F	
G.L. c. 265 § 18(a)	Assault to rob elder 60 or over, armed, subsequent	5	F	
G.L. c. 265 § 18(a)	Assault to rob elder 60 or over, armed, with firearm	4	F	
G.L. c. 265 § 18(a)	Assault to rob elder 60 or over, armed, with firearm, subsequent	6	F	
G.L. c. 265 § 18(b)	Assault to rob, armed	4	F	
G.L. c. 265 § 18(b)	Assault to rob, armed, with firearm	4	F	
G.L. c. 265 § 20	Assault to rob, unarmed	3	F	
G.L. c. 140 § 131M	Assault weapon, sell/possess	4	F	
G.L. c. 140 § 131M	Assault weapon, sell/possess, subsequent	4	F	
G.L. c. 265 § 15B(b)	Assault with dangerous weapon	2	F	
G.L. c. 265 § 15B(a)	Assault with dangerous weapon on elder 60 or over	2	F	
G.L. c. 265 § 15B(a)	Assault with dangerous weapon on elder 60 or over, subsequent	3	F	
G.L. c. 265 § 13A(b)	Assault, aggravated	3	F	
G.L. c. 274 § 6	Attempt to commit crime, 5-year felony or greater	U-1	F	Underlying offense may trigger SORB or SDP protocols.
G.L. c. 274 § 6	Attempt to commit crime, Larceny	U-1	M	
G.L. c. 274 § 6	Attempt to commit crime, punishable by death	U-1	F	Underlying offense may trigger SORB or SDP protocols.
G.L. c. 274 § 6	Attempt to commit crime, under 5-year felony or misdemeanor	U-1	V	Underlying offense may trigger SORB or SDP protocols.
G.L. c. 266 § 16	B&E building, ship, or vehicle at night, for felony, dwelling	3	F	
G.L. c. 266 § 16	B&E building, ship, or vehicle at night, for felony, non-dwelling	2	F	
G.L. c. 266 § 16A	B&E building, ship, or vehicle, for misdemeanor	2	M	
G.L. c. 266 § 17	B&E daytime or enter at night, for felony, person in fear, dwelling	4	F	
G.L. c. 266 § 17	B&E daytime or enter at night, for felony, person in fear, non-dwelling	4	F	
G.L. c. 266 § 17	B&E daytime or enter at night, for felony, with firearm, person in fear, dwelling	5	F	
G.L. c. 266 § 17	B&E daytime or enter at night, for felony, with firearm, person in fear, non-dwelling	5	F	
G.L. c. 266 § 18	B&E daytime, for felony, dwelling	3	F	
G.L. c. 266 § 18	B&E daytime, for felony, non-dwelling	2	F	
G.L. c. 266 § 18	B&E daytime, for felony, with firearm, dwelling	5	F	

Mass. General Law Chapter & Section	Offense Description	Grid Level	Penalty Type	Notes
G.L. c. 266 § 18	B&E daytime, for felony, with firearm, non-dwelling	5	F	
G.L. c. 266 § 14	B&E dwelling at night (burglary), for felony, armed or assault on occupants	6	F	
G.L. c. 266 § 14	B&E dwelling at night (burglary), for felony, armed or assault on occupants, subsequent	6	F	
G.L. c. 266 § 15	B&E dwelling at night (burglary), for felony, unarmed, no assault on occupants	3	F	
G.L. c. 266 § 15	B&E dwelling at night (burglary), for felony, unarmed, no assault on occupants, subsequent	4	F	
G.L. c. 266 § 14	B&E dwelling at night (burglary), for felony, with firearm	6	F	
G.L. c. 266 § 14	B&E dwelling at night (burglary), for felony, with firearm, subsequent	6	F	
G.L. c. 266 § 19	B&E or enter at night railroad car, for felony	3	F	
G.L. c. 266 § 20A	B&E or enter truck, trailer, or freight container, for felony	2	F	
G.L. c. 269 § 12B	BB gun/air rifle, possess or shoot in public place	2	M	
G.L. c. 269 § 12A	BB gun/air rifle, sell/give to minor	1	M	
G.L. c. 90B § 8B(2)	Boat, operate negligently, causing death	3	M	
G.L. c. 90B § 8B(2)	Boat, operate recklessly, causing death	4	M	
G.L. c. 90B § 8(e)(1)	Boat, operate recklessly/negligently	2	M	
G.L. c. 90B § 8(a)(1)(A)	Boat, OUI liquor or drugs	2	M	
G.L. c. 90B § 8(a)(1)(A)	Boat, OUI liquor or drugs, 2nd off.	2	M	
G.L. c. 90B § 8(a)(1)(A)	Boat, OUI liquor or drugs, 3rd off.	3	M	
G.L. c. 90B § 8(a)(1)(A)	Boat, OUI liquor or drugs, 4th off.	3	F	
G.L. c. 90B § 8B(2)	Boat, OUI liquor or drugs, causing death	4	M	
G.L. c. 90B § 8A(2)	Boat, OUI liquor or drugs, causing serious injury	3	M	
G.L. c. 90B § 8B(1)	Boat, OUI liquor or drugs, reckless/ negligent operation, causing death	5	F	
G.L. c. 90B § 8A(1)	Boat, OUI liquor or drugs, reckless/ negligent operation, causing serious injury	3	F	
G.L. c. 266 § 63	Boat, use without authority	1	M	
G.L. c. 90B § 8(e)(1)	Boat, use without authority, 1st off.	2	M	
G.L. c. 90B § 8(e)(1)	Boat, use without authority, 2nd off.	2	F	
G.L. c. 90B § 8(e)(1)	Boat, use without authority, 3rd and subsequent	3	F	
G.L. c. 269 § 10D	Body armor, use in felony	2	F	
G.L. c. 269 § 14(b)	Bomb threat, false	3	F	This section also specifies other kinds of threats.
G.L. c. 148 § 35	Bomb/explosives, possess in violation	3	M	
G.L. c. 269 § 14(c)	Bomb/hijack threat with serious public alarm	4	F	
G.L. c. 266 § 16	Break safe or vault, for larceny or felony, or attempt, dwelling	3	F	
G.L. c. 266 § 16	Break safe or vault, for larceny or felony, or attempt, non-dwelling	2	F	
G.L. c. 271 § 39(a)	Bribe, business	3	F	
G.L. c. 271 § 39A	Bribe, offer or accept/solicit sports	2	M	
G.L. c. 266 § 104	Building, damage to	1	M	
G.L. c. 266 § 49	Burglarious instrument/MV master key, make or possess	2	F	
G.L. c. 266 § 5	Burn boat/MV/personalty	3	F	Personalty = personal property.

9

Mass. General Law Chapter & Section	Offense Description	Grid Level	Penalty Type	Notes
G.L. c. 266 § 5A	Burn boat/MV/personalty, attempt to	2	F	Personalty = personal property.
G.L. c. 266 § 2	Burn building/contents	3	F	
G.L. c. 266 § 10	Burn building/MV/personalty to defraud insurer, or attempt to do so	3	F	Personalty = personal property.
G.L. c. 266 § 1	Burn dwelling house (arson)	4	F	
G.L. c. 266 § 5A	Burn dwelling house (arson), attempt to	3	F	
G.L. c. 266 § 5A	Burn public building, attempt to	3	F	
G.L. c. 266 § 7	Burn woods	2	M	
G.L. c. 159A § 31	Bus/driver, interfere with	4	F	
G.L. c. 159 § 104	Bus/railroad car, throwing missile or assaulting	2	M	
G.L. c. 166 § 42A	Cable TV/telephone service, obtain by fraud, or attempt, under $5,000	2	M	
G.L. c. 265 § 13K(d½)	Caretaker permits abuse on elder/disabled person	2	F	
G.L. c. 265 § 21A	Carjacking	4	F	
G.L. c. 265 § 21A	Carjacking, armed	5	F	
G.L. c. 265 § 21A	Carjacking, armed, with firearm	6	F	
G.L. c. 169A § 2-13	Check cashing violation	2	M	Penalty found in G.L. c. 169A § 13.
G.L. c. 267 § 1	Check, forgery of	2	F	Distinct from G.L. c. 266 § 37, "Larceny by check under $250".
G.L. c. 272 § 29B(a)	Child in nude, disseminate visual material of, with lascivious intent	4	F	
G.L. c. 272 § 29A(a)	Child in nude, pose/exhibit for visual material, with lascivious intent	4	F	
G.L. c. 272 § 29B(b)	Child in sexual act, disseminate visual material of, with lascivious intent	4	F	
G.L. c. 272 § 29A(b)	Child in sexual act, pose/exhibit for visual material, with lascivious intent	4	F	
G.L. c. 272 § 29C	Child pornography, possession of	3	F	
G.L. c. 119 § 39	Child under 10, abandon	2	M	
G.L. c. 265 § 13J	Child, permit injury to	3	M	
G.L. c. 266 § 98	Church or school, damage	2	M	
G.L. c. 266 § 127A	Church, threat to injure	2	M	
G.L. c. 266 § 127A	Church/synagogue, injury to, over $5000	3	F	
G.L. c. 266 § 127A	Church/synagogue, injury to, under $5000	2	M	Includes $5000 and under.
G.L. c. 12 § 11J	Civil rights order violation	2	M	This involves violation of a court order, distinct from G.L. c. 265 § 37 "Civil rights violation or attempt".
G.L. c. 12 § 11J	Civil rights order violation with injury	4	F	This involves violation of a court order, distinct from G.L. c. 265 § 37 "Civil rights violation with bodily injury or attempt".
G.L. c. 265 § 37	Civil rights violation or attempt	2	M	Distinct from G.L. c. 12 § 11J "Civil rights order violation".
G.L. c. 265 § 37	Civil rights violation with bodily injury or attempt	4	F	Distinct from G.L. c. 12 § 11J "Civil rights order violation with injury".
G.L. c. 94C § 32A(c)	Cocaine, distribute or possess with intent	3	F	
G.L. c. 94C § 32A(d)	Cocaine, distribute or possess with intent, subsequent	4	F	
G.L. c. 94C § 32F(d)	Cocaine, distribute or possess with intent, to minor	4	F	
G.L. c. 94C 32E(b)(3)	Cocaine, trafficking in, 100 to 200 g	5	F	
G.L. c. 94C § 32E(b)(1)	Cocaine, trafficking in, 14 to 28 g	3	F	
G.L. c. 94C § 32E(b)(4)	Cocaine, trafficking in, 200 g or more	5	F	
G.L. c. 94C § 32E(b)(2)	Cocaine, trafficking in, 28 to 100 g	4	F	

9

Mass. General Law Chapter & Section	Offense Description	Grid Level	Penalty Type	Notes
G.L. c. 266 § 120F	Computer system, unauthorized access to	1	M	
G.L. c. 274 § 7(1)	Conspiracy for felony, death penalty or life imprisonment	U	F	
G.L. c. 274 § 7(2)	Conspiracy for felony, more than 10 years	U	F	
G.L. c. 274 § 7(3)	Conspiracy for felony, not more than 10 years	U	F	
G.L. c. 274 § 7(4)	Conspiracy for misdemeanor	U	M	
G.L. c. 94C § 40	Conspiracy to violate drug law	U	V	
Common Law	Contempt, criminal [Grid 2012]	2	CL	Penalty found in G.L. c. 279 § 5.
G.L. c. 119 § 63	Contribute to delinquency of child	2	M	
G.L. c. 6 § 178	CORI, disseminate/seek unlawfully, falsify	2	M	
G.L. c. 94C § 32G	Counterfeit drug; create, distribute, or possess with intent	1	M	
G.L. c. 267 § 12	Counterfeit note or traveler's check, possess	2	F	This section applies to possession of fewer than 10 notes/bills; for 10 or more, apply G.L. c. 267 § 9.
G.L. c. 267 § 9	Counterfeit notes, possess	3	F	This section applies to possession of 10 or more notes/bills; for fewer than 10, apply G.L. c. 267 § 12.
G.L. c. 268 § 13C	Court proceedings, disrupt	1	M	
G.L. c. 266 § 37C	Credit card fraud over $250, $10,000 to $50,000	3	F	
G.L. c. 266 § 37C	Credit card fraud over $250, $50,000 and over	3	F	
G.L. c. 266 § 37C	Credit card fraud over $250, under $10,000	2	F	
G.L. c. 266 § 37B	Credit card violations, $250 or less	1	M	
G.L. c. 272 § 34	Crime against nature (sodomy)	3	F	
G.L. c. 269 § 13A	Crime report, false	2	M	
G.L. c. 40 § 37A	Curfew, violate	1	M	
G.L. c. 269 § 10(j)	Dangerous weapon, carry on school grounds, firearm	4	M	
G.L. c. 269 § 10(j)	Dangerous weapon, carry on school grounds, non-firearm	2	M	
G.L. c. 269 § 10(d)	Dangerous weapon, carry, 2nd off.	4	F	Bartley-Fox: 12-month minimum in a facility.
G.L. c. 269 § 10(d)	Dangerous weapon, carry, 3rd off.	4	F	Bartley-Fox: 12-month minimum in a facility.
G.L. c. 269 § 10(d)	Dangerous weapon, carry, 4th off.	5	F	Bartley-Fox: 12-month minimum in a facility.
G.L. c. 269 § 10(b)	Dangerous weapon, carry, no prior felonies	2	M	See statute for examples of dangerous weapons.
G.L. c. 269 § 10(b)	Dangerous weapon, carry, with prior felonies	3	F	See statute for examples of dangerous weapons.
G.L. c. 269 § 12	Dangerous weapon, manufacture/sell certain	1	M	
G.L. c. 266 § 126A	Defacement of real or personal property	2	F	
G.L. c. 92 App. § 1-8	Destruction of property held by the MA Water Resource Authority	2	M	
G.L. c. 266 § 127	Destruction of property over $250, malicious	2	F	
G.L. c. 266 § 127	Destruction of property over $250, wanton	2	M	
G.L. c. 266 § 127	Destruction of property under $250, wanton or malicious	1	M	
G.L. c. 276 App. § 1-5	Detainers, escape or attempt	2	F	
G.L. c. 272 § 53	Disorderly conduct	1	M	
G.L. c. 56 § 46	Disorderly conduct at poll	1	M	
G.L. c. 272 § 43	Disorderly conduct on public conveyance	1	M	Penalty found in G.L. c. 272 § 40.
G.L. c. 272 § 43	Disorderly conduct on public conveyance, 3rd and subsequent	2	M	Penalty found in G.L. c. 272 § 40.
G.L. c. 272 § 53	Disorderly house, keep	1	M	
G.L. c. 272 § 53	Disturbing the peace	1	M	
G.L. c. 22E § 11	DNA sample, refuse to provide	1	M	

9

Mass. General Law Chapter & Section	Offense Description	Grid Level	Penalty Type	Notes
G.L. c. 94C § 32I(a)	Drug paraphernalia, distribute or possess with intent	2	M	
G.L. c. 94C § 32I(b)	Drug paraphernalia, sell to person under 18	3	F	
G.L. c. 94C § 32J	Drug violation within 100 feet of park/ playground	3	F	
G.L. c. 94C § 32J	Drug violation within 1000 feet of school zone	3	F	
G.L. c. 94C § 25(1)	Drug, dispense without prescription	2	M	Penalty found in G.L. c. 94C § 38.
G.L. c. 94C § 25(1)	Drug, dispense without prescription, subsequent	3	M	Penalty found in G.L. c. 94C § 38.
G.L. c. 94C § 32(a)	Drug, distribute or possess with intent, class A	3	F	Drug classes defined in G.L. c. 94C § 31.
G.L. c. 94C § 32(b)	Drug, distribute or possess with intent, class A, subsequent	4	F	Drug classes defined in G.L. c. 94C § 31.
G.L. c. 94C § 32A(a)	Drug, distribute or possess with intent, class B	3	F	Drug classes defined in G.L. c. 94C § 31.
G.L. c. 94C § 32A(b)	Drug, distribute or possess with intent, class B, subsequent	3	F	Drug classes defined in G.L. c. 94C § 31.
G.L. c. 94C § 32B(a)	Drug, distribute or possess with intent, class C	3	F	Drug classes defined in G.L. c. 94C § 31.
G.L. c. 94C § 32B(b)	Drug, distribute or possess with intent, class C, subsequent	3	F	Drug classes defined in G.L. c. 94C § 31.
G.L. c. 94C § 32C(a)	Drug, distribute or possess with intent, class D	2	M	Drug classes defined in G.L. c. 94C § 31.
G.L. c. 94C § 32C(b)	Drug, distribute or possess with intent, class D, subsequent	3	M	Drug classes defined in G.L. c. 94C § 31.
G.L. c. 94C § 32D(a)	Drug, distribute or possess with intent, class E	2	M	Drug classes defined in G.L. c. 94C § 31.
G.L. c. 94C § 32D(b)	Drug, distribute or possess with intent, class E, subsequent	3	M	Drug classes defined in G.L. c. 94C § 31.
G.L. c. 94C § 32F(a)	Drug, distribute or possess with intent, to minor, class A	4	F	Drug classes defined in G.L. c. 94C § 31.
G.L. c. 94C § 32F(b)	Drug, distribute or possess with intent, to minor, class B	3	F	Drug classes defined in G.L. c. 94C § 31.
G.L. c. 94C § 32F(c)	Drug, distribute or possess with intent, to minor, class C	3	F	Drug classes defined in G.L. c. 94C § 31.
G.L. c. 94C § 33(a)	Drug, false registration number for	3	F	Penalty found in G.L. c. 94C § 33(c).
G.L. c. 94C § 32K	Drug, induce minor to distribute	5	F	
G.L. c. 94C § 32K	Drug, induce minor to possess funds of	5	F	
G.L. c. 94C § 37	Drug, larceny of	3	F	
G.L. c. 94C § 33(b)	Drug, obtain by fraud	3	F	Penalty found in G.L. c. 94C § 33(c).
G.L. c. 94C § 34	Drug, possess, class A	2	M	Drug classes defined in G.L. c. 94C § 31.
G.L. c. 94C § 34	Drug, possess, class A, subsequent	2	M	Drug classes defined in G.L. c. 94C § 31.
G.L. c. 94C § 34	Drug, possess, class B	2	M	Drug classes defined in G.L. c. 94C § 31.
G.L. c. 94C § 34	Drug, possess, class B, subsequent	2	M	Drug classes defined in G.L. c. 94C § 31.
G.L. c. 94C § 34	Drug, possess, class C	2	M	Drug classes defined in G.L. c. 94C § 31.
G.L. c. 94C § 34	Drug, possess, class C, subsequent	2	M	Drug classes defined in G.L. c. 94C § 31.
G.L. c. 94C § 34	Drug, possess, class D	1	M	Drug classes defined in G.L. c. 94C § 31.
G.L. c. 94C § 34	Drug, possess, class D, subsequent	2	M	Drug classes defined in G.L. c. 94C § 31.
G.L. c. 94C § 34	Drug, possess, class E	1	M	Drug classes defined in G.L. c. 94C § 31
G.L. c. 94C § 22(b)	Drug, practitioner fail to label	1	M	Penalty found in G.L. c. 94C § 39.
G.L. c. 94C § 22(b)	Drug, practitioner fail to label, subsequent	2	M	Penalty found in G.L. c. 94C § 39.
G.L. c. 94C § 26(1)	Drug, registrant distribute without order, class I	2	M	Penalty found in G.L. c. 94C § 38.
G.L. c. 94C § 26(1)	Drug, registrant distribute without order, class II	3	M	Penalty found in G.L. c. 94C § 38.
G.L. c. 140 § 131J	Electric stun gun, sell/possess	2	M	
G.L. c. 266 § 18	Enter dwelling at night, for felony	4	F	
G.L. c. 266 § 18	Enter dwelling at night, for felony, with firearm	5	F	
G.L. c. 266 § 18A	Entering dwelling by false pretense, for felony or with larceny, no person in fear	3	F	

Mass. General Law Chapter & Section	Offense Description	Grid Level	Penalty Type	Notes
G.L. c. 265 § 26C	Enticement of child under age 16	3	F	
G.L. c. 120 § 26	Escape from DYS, or aiding child to escape	2	M	Applies to escape or attempt; but, per DYS policy, not flight from a non-hardware secure program.
G.L. c. 268 § 15A	Escape from municipal lockup	2	M	
G.L. c. 268 § 17	Escape from officer, aid	2	M	
G.L. c. 268 § 19	Escape from penal institution, permit	3	F	
G.L. c. 268 § 16	Escape from penal institution/court/SDP center, or attempt	4	F	
Common Law	Escape from police officer [Grid 2012]	2	CL	Penalty found in G.L. c. 279 § 5.
G.L. c. 268 § 15	Escape, aid accused felon or convicted state prison felon to	3	F	
G.L. c. 268 § 15	Escape, aid accused misdemeanant to	2	V	Penalty type (F/Misd.) depends on the prisoner's status (F/Misd.) and escape location (prison/HOC).
G.L. c. 268 § 15	Escape, aid convicted misdemeanant or convicted HOC felon to	3	F	
G.L. c. 266 § 101	Explosion, malicious	5	F	
G.L. c. 266 § 102	Explosives, throw/place/explode or possess to injure	5	F	
G.L. c. 148 § 16	Explosives/flammables, improperly make/store	1	M	
G.L. c. 265 § 25	Extortion or attempt	3	F	
G.L. c. 276 § 82A	Failure to appear, recognizance or bail, felony	2	F	
G.L. c. 276 § 82A	Failure to appear, recognizance or bail, misdemeanor	2	M	
G.L. c. 6 § 178H(a)(1)	Failure to register or verify registration info by sex offender	3	F	
G.L. c. 6 § 178H(a)(2)	Failure to register or verify registration info by sex offender, subsequent	4	F	
G.L. c. 268 § 32	False alarm from police call box or tamper with police/fire call box	2	M	
G.L. c. 271 § 12	False lottery tickets: creation, sale, or possession	2	F	
G.L. c. 268 § 34A	False name or Social Security number, furnish to police	1	M	
G.L. c. 266 § 33(1)	False pretense in commercial transaction, over $250, $10,000 to $50,000	3	F	Penalty found in G.L. c. 266 § 30.
G.L. c. 266 § 33(1)	False pretense in commercial transaction, over $250, $50,000 and over	3	F	Penalty found in G.L. c. 266 § 30.
G.L. c. 266 § 33(1)	False pretense in commercial transaction, over $250, under $10,000	2	F	Penalty found in G.L. c. 266 § 30.
G.L. c. 266 § 33(1)	False pretense in commercial transaction, under $250	2	M	Penalty found in G.L. c. 266 § 30.
G.L. c. 266 § 73	False pretense of trade, obtain goods by	2	F	
G.L. c. 269 § 14B	False/silent 911 call	2	M	
G.L. c. 265 § 13G	Felony for hire	3	F	The "for hire" penalty is in addition to the penalty for the underlying felony
G.L. c. 272 § 22	Fetal death out of wedlock, conceal cause	2	M	
G.L. c. 265 § 9	Fight by arrangement	2	F	
G.L. c. 265 § 10	Fight by arrangement, aid/promote	2	F	
G.L. c. 265 § 11	Fight by arrangement, out-of-state	2	F	
G.L. c. 266 § 11	Fire alarm, disable	2	M	
G.L. c. 269 § 13	Fire alarm, false	2	M	
G.L. c. 48 § 13	Fire in open, set	1	M	
G.L. c. 266 § 9	Fire on land, fail to extinguish/control	1	M	

9

Mass. General Law Chapter & Section	Offense Description	Grid Level	Penalty Type	Notes
G.L. c. 266 § 8	Fire on land, set	2	M	Requires the property of another to be injured.
G.L. c. 140 § 129	Firearm application, false statement on	2	M	
G.L. c. 140 § 129	Firearm application, false statement on, subsequent	3	F	
G.L. c. 140 § 131(h)	Firearm license violation, false information on application	2	M	
G.L. c. 269 § 10(i)	Firearm license/FID card, fail to surrender	2	M	
G.L. c. 140 § 131I	Firearm license/FID card, false	3	F	
G.L. c. 269 § 10(h)(1)	Firearm or ammunition without FID card, possess	3	M	Ownership, possession, or transfer of firearm / shotgun / rifle / ammunition without an FID card (per G.L. c. 140 § 129C). Distinct from G.L. c. 269 § 10(a)—possession/carrying of a firearm, when not at home or work, without a license to carry.
G.L. c. 269 § 10(h)(1)	Firearm or ammunition without FID card, possess, subsequent	2	M	
G.L. c. 140 § 130	Firearm sale to minor/alien	3	F	
G.L. c. 140 § 128	Firearm sale, violation	3	F	
G.L. c. 269 § 11C	Firearm serial number, deface or receive with defaced number	3	M	
G.L. c. 140 § 131C	Firearm, carry improperly in a motor vehicle	2	M	Applies to a licensed person carrying improperly in a motor vehicle.
G.L. c. 269 § 12D(b)	Firearm, carry on way, unloaded, large capacity	4	F	Definition of "Large capacity": http://www.mass.gov/legis/laws/mgl/140-121.htm.
G.L. c. 269 § 10(a)	Firearm, carry without license	4	F	Possession/carrying of a firearm, when not at home or work, without a license to carry. Distinct from G.L. c. 269 § 10(h)(1): possession w/o FID card. Bartley-Fox: 6-month minimum in a facility.
G.L. c. 269 § 10(a)	Firearm, carry without license, 1 prior violent/drug crime	4	F	Possession/carrying of a firearm, when not at home or work, without a license to carry. Distinct from G.L. c. 269 § 10(h)(1): possession w/o FID card. Bartley-Fox: 12-month minimum in a facility. Penalty found in G.L. c. 269 § 10G(a).
G.L. c. 269 § 10(d)	Firearm, carry without license, 2nd off.	5	F	Bartley-Fox: 12-month minimum in a facility.
G.L. c. 269 § 10(d)	Firearm, carry without license, 3rd off.	5	F	Bartley-Fox: 12-month minimum in a facility.
G.L. c. 269 § 10(d)	Firearm, carry without license, 4th off.	6	F	Bartley-Fox: 12-month minimum in a facility.
G.L. c. 269 § 10(n)	Firearm, carry without license, loaded	3	M	This offense is a "from & after" penalty. That is, "sentence shall begin from and after the expiration of the sentence for the violation of paragraph (a) or paragraph (c)".
G.L. c. 269 § 12E	Firearm, discharge within 500 feet of building	3	M	
G.L. c. 131 § 58	Firearm, discharge within 500 feet of dwelling/highway	3	M	Penalty found in G.L. c. 131 § 90.
G.L. c. 269 § 10(h)(2)	Firearm, leave unattended with intent to transfer possession	3	F	
G.L. c. 140 § 131H	Firearm, non-resident of Commonwealth owns/possesses without license	2	M	
G.L. c. 265 § 18B	Firearm, possess in felony	4	F	
G.L. c. 265 § 18B	Firearm, possess in felony, large capacity	5	F	Definition of "Large capacity": http://www.mass.gov/legis/laws/mgl/140-121.htm.
G.L. c. 265 § 18B	Firearm, possess in felony, subsequent	5	F	
G.L. c. 269 § 11B	Firearm, possess in felony, with defaced serial number	4	F	Judge has discretion over 6-month minimum—not a true mandatory minimum.

Mass. General Law Chapter & Section	Offense Description	Grid Level	Penalty Type	Notes
G.L. c. 269 § 10(m)	Firearm, possess large capacity	4	F	Definition of "Large capacity": http://www.mass.gov/legis/laws/mgl/140-121.htm.
G.L. c. 269 § 10(m)	Firearm, possess large capacity, with valid FID	3	F	Definition of "Large capacity": http://www.mass.gov/legis/laws/mgl/140-121.htm.
G.L. c. 140 § 131E	Firearm, purchase for another	3	F	
G.L. c. 269 § 10E	Firearms, trafficking in, 10-19 weapons, 8-12 months	5	F	Bartley-Fox: 6-month minimum in a facility.
G.L. c. 269 § 10E	Firearms, trafficking in, 20 or more weapons, 12 month min.	6	F	Bartley-Fox: 6-month minimum in a facility.
G.L. c. 269 § 10E	Firearms, trafficking in, 3-9 weapons, 6-8 months	4	F	Bartley-Fox: 6-month minimum in a facility.
G.L. c. 265 § 13D½	Firefighter, injure by setting fires	4	F	
G.L. c. 268 § 32A	Firefighter, interfere with	2	F	
G.L. c. 148 § 39	Fireworks, sell or possess unlawful	2	M	
G.L. c. 267 § 1	Forgery, check forgery, promissory note forgery	3	F	Distinct from G.L. c. 266 § 37, "Larceny by check under $250".
G.L. c. 272 § 18	Fornication	1	M	
G.L. c. 266 § 76	Fraud/cheat, gross	3	F	
G.L. c. 276 § 19	Fugitive, fail bring before court	1	M	
G.L. c. 265 § 43A(a)	Harassment, criminal	2	M	Distinct from G.L. c. 258E § 9 "Harassment, criminal, prevention order violation".
G.L. c. 258E § 9	Harassment, criminal, prevention order violation	2	M	This involves violation of a court order, distinct from G.L. c. 265 § 43A(a) "Criminal harassment".
G.L. c. 265 § 43A(b)	Harassment, criminal, subsequent	3	F	
G.L. c. 269 § 17	Hazing	2	M	
G.L. c. 94C § 35	Heroin, being present where kept	2	M	
G.L. c. 94C § 34	Heroin, possess	2	M	
G.L. c. 94C § 34	Heroin, possess, subsequent	2	F	
G.L. c. 94C § 32E(c)(3)	Heroin/morphine/opium, trafficking in, 100 to 200 g	5	F	
G.L. c. 94C § 32E(c)(1)	Heroin/morphine/opium, trafficking in, 14 to 28 g	3	F	
G.L. c. 94C § 32E(c)(4)	Heroin/morphine/opium, trafficking in, 200 g or more	6	F	
G.L. c. 94C § 32E(c)(2)	Heroin/morphine/opium, trafficking in, 28 to 100 g	4	F	
G.L. c. 265 § 18C	Home invasion	6	F	
G.L. c. 265 § 18C	Home invasion, subsequent	6	F	
G.L. c. 94C § 27	Hypodermic for drugs, sell to minor	1	M	Penalty found in G.L. c. 94C § 38.
G.L. c. 94C § 27	Hypodermic for drugs, sell to minor, subsequent	2	M	Penalty found in G.L. c. 94C § 38.
G.L. c. 94C § 27	Hypodermic for drugs, unlicensed sale of	1	M	Penalty found in G.L. c. 94C § 38.
G.L. c. 94C § 27	Hypodermic for drugs, unlicensed sale of, subsequent	2	M	Penalty found in G.L. c. 94C § 38.
G.L. c. 266 § 37E(c)	Identity fraud, intent to pose	2	M	
G.L. c. 266 § 37E(b)	Identity fraud, pose	2	M	
G.L. c. 272 § 17	Incest	5	F	
G.L. c. 272 § 17	Incest with person under 21	5	F	
G.L. c. 265 § 13B	Indecent A&B on child under 14	4	F	
G.L. c. 265 § 13B½	Indecent A&B on child under 14, aggravated	6	F	
G.L. c. 265 § 13B	Indecent A&B on child under 14, subsequent	5	F	
G.L. c. 265 § 13H	Indecent A&B on elder 60 or over/disabled	4	F	
G.L. c. 265 § 13H	Indecent A&B on person 14 or over	3	F	
G.L. c. 265 § 13F	Indecent A&B on retarded person	4	F	

9

Mass. General Law Chapter & Section	Offense Description	Grid Level	Penalty Type	Notes
G.L. c. 265 § 13F	Indecent A&B on retarded person, subsequent	5	F	
G.L. c. 272 § 53	Indecent Exposure	1	M	
G.L. c. 266 § 102A	Infernal machine, possess	4	F	
G.L. c. 270 § 18	Inhale toxic fumes for stupefaction, glue or other	1	M	
G.L. c. 119 § 1	Interstate Compact for Juveniles (ICJ) - IN	0	V	For youth committed in another state, held by DYS.
G.L. c. 119 § 1	Interstate Compact for Juveniles (ICJ) - OTHER	0	V	For "courtesy holds," such as out-of-state runaways held by DYS due to court order.
G.L. c. 119 § 1	Interstate Compact for Juveniles (ICJ) - OUT	0	V	For youth committed to DYS, held by another state.
G.L. c. 268 § 13B(1)	Intimidate juror/witness, or retaliate against	4	F	
G.L. c. 265 § 26	Kidnapping	4	F	
G.L. c. 265 § 26A	Kidnapping & endangering incompetent or child by relative	3	F	
G.L. c. 265 § 26	Kidnapping child under age 16	5	F	
G.L. c. 265 § 26	Kidnapping for extortion	6	F	
G.L. c. 265 § 26	Kidnapping for extortion, armed with firearm	6	F	
G.L. c. 265 § 26A	Kidnapping incompetent or child by relative	2	M	
G.L. c. 265 § 26	Kidnapping, armed with firearm	6	F	
G.L. c. 265 § 26	Kidnapping, with serious bodily injury, armed with dangerous weapon	6	F	
G.L. c. 265 § 26	Kidnapping, with sexual assault, armed with dangerous weapon	6	F	
G.L. c. 266 § 23	Larceny at fire, $10,000 to $50,000	3	F	Penalty found in G.L. c. 266 § 24.
G.L. c. 266 § 23	Larceny at fire, $50,000 and over	3	F	Penalty found in G.L. c. 266 § 24.
G.L. c. 266 § 23	Larceny at fire, under $10,000	2	F	Penalty found in G.L. c. 266 § 24.
G.L. c. 266 § 37	Larceny by check, over $250, $10,000 to $50,000	3	F	Distinct from G.L. c. 267 § 1 "Check, forgery of". Penalty found in G.L. c. 266 § 30.
G.L. c. 266 § 37	Larceny by check, over $250, $50,000 and over	3	F	Distinct from G.L. c. 267 § 1 "Check, forgery of". Penalty found in G.L. c. 266 § 30.
G.L. c. 266 § 37	Larceny by check, over $250, under $10,000	2	F	Distinct from G.L. c. 267 § 1 "Check, forgery of". Penalty found in G.L. c. 266 § 30.
G.L. c. 266 § 37	Larceny by check, under $250	2	M	Distinct from G.L. c. 267 § 1 "Check, forgery of". Penalty found in G.L. c. 266 § 30.
G.L. c. 266 § 34	Larceny by false pretense, over $250, $10,000 to $50,000	3	F	Penalty found in G.L. c. 266 § 30.
G.L. c. 266 § 34	Larceny by false pretense, over $250, $50,000 and over	3	F	Penalty found in G.L. c. 266 § 30.
G.L. c. 266 § 34	Larceny by false pretense, over $250, under $10,000	2	F	Penalty found in G.L. c. 266 § 30.
G.L. c. 266 § 34	Larceny by false pretense, under $250	1	M	Penalty found in G.L. c. 266 § 30.
G.L. c. 266 § 30(1)	Larceny by single scheme, under $250	1	M	
G.L. c. 266 § 20	Larceny from boat, building, railroad car, $10,000 to $50,000	3	F	
G.L. c. 266 § 20	Larceny from boat, building, railroad car, $50,000 and over	3	F	
G.L. c. 266 § 20	Larceny from boat, building, railroad car, under $10,000	2	F	
G.L. c. 266 § 30(1)	Larceny from common carrier	3	M	
G.L. c. 266 § 30(5)	Larceny from elder/disabled person, $250 or under	2	M	This section includes fraud.
G.L. c. 266 § 30(5)	Larceny from elder/disabled person, over $250, $10,000 to $50,000	3	F	This section includes fraud.

Mass. General Law Chapter & Section	Offense Description	Grid Level	Penalty Type	Notes
G.L. c. 266 § 30(5)	Larceny from elder/disabled person, over $250, $50,000 and over	3	F	This section includes fraud.
G.L. c. 266 § 30(5)	Larceny from elder/disabled person, over $250, under $10,000	3	F	This section includes fraud.
G.L. c. 266 § 25	Larceny from person	2	F	Pickpocketing, purse-snatching.
G.L. c. 266 § 25	Larceny from person 65 or older	3	F	
G.L. c. 266 § 25	Larceny from person 65 or older, subsequent	3	F	
G.L. c. 266 § 20B	Larceny from truck, trailer, or freight container, $10,000 to $50,000	3	F	
G.L. c. 266 § 20B	Larceny from truck, trailer, or freight container, $50,000 and over	3	F	
G.L. c. 266 § 20B	Larceny from truck, trailer, or freight container, under $10,000	2	F	
G.L. c. 266 § 27	Larceny of construction tools	1	M	
G.L. c. 266 § 27	Larceny of construction tools, subsequent	1	M	
G.L. c. 266 § 30(1)	Larceny of firearm	4	F	
G.L. c. 266 § 30(1)	Larceny over $250, $10,000 to $50,000	3	F	
G.L. c. 266 § 30(1)	Larceny over $250, $50,000 and over	3	F	
G.L. c. 266 § 30(1)	Larceny over $250, under $10,000	3	F	
G.L. c. 266 § 30(1)	Larceny under $250	2	M	
G.L. c. 272 § 53	Lewd, wanton & lascivious conduct	1	M	
G.L. c. 138 § 34B	Liquor ID card/license, false/misuse	1	M	
G.L. c. 269 § 10(n)	Machine gun/sawed-off shotgun, carry, loaded	3	M	This offense is a "from & after" penalty. That is, "sentence shall begin from and after the expiration of the sentence for the violation of paragraph (a) or paragraph (c)".
G.L. c. 269 § 10(c)	Machine gun/sawed-off shotgun, possess	5	F	Bartley-Fox: 6-month minimum in a facility.
G.L. c. 269 § 10(d)	Machine gun/sawed-off shotgun, possess, 2nd off.	5	F	Bartley-Fox: 12-month minimum in a facility.
G.L. c. 269 § 10(d)	Machine gun/sawed-off shotgun, possess, 3rd off.	6	F	Bartley-Fox: 12-month minimum in a facility.
G.L. c. 269 § 10(c)	Machine gun/sawed-off shotgun, possess, with 1 prior violent/drug crime	5	F	Bartley-Fox: 12-month minimum in a facility. Penalty found in G.L. c. 269 § 10G(a).
G.L. c. 265 § 13	Manslaughter involving explosives	6	F	
G.L. c. 265 § 13	Manslaughter, involuntary	5	F	
G.L. c. 265 § 13	Manslaughter, voluntary	6	F	
G.L. c. 94C § 34	Marijuana over 1 oz, possess	1	M	Must be more than one ounce.
G.L. c. 94C § 34	Marijuana over 1 oz, possess, subsequent	2	M	Must be more than one ounce.
G.L. c. 94C § 32E(a)(4)	Marijuana, trafficking in, 10,000 lbs or more	5	F	
G.L. c. 94C § 32E(a)(2)	Marijuana, trafficking in, 100 to 2000 lbs.	3	F	
G.L. c. 94C § 32E(a)(3)	Marijuana, trafficking in, 2000 to 10,000 lbs.	4	F	
G.L. c. 94C § 32E(a)(1)	Marijuana, trafficking in, 50 to 100 lbs.	3	F	
G.L. c. 265 § 14	Mayhem	5	F	
G.L. c. 94C § 32A(c)	Methamphetamine, distribute or possess with intent	3	F	
G.L. c. 94C § 32A(d)	Methamphetamine, distribute or possess with intent, subsequent	4	F	
G.L. c. 264 § 3	Misprision of treason	3	F	
G.L. c. 266 § 102B	Molotov cocktail, make/sell/use/possess	3	F	
G.L. c. 90C § 10	Motor vehicle citation, attempt to falsify or dispose of	1	M	
G.L. c. 90 § 24G(b)	Motor vehicle homicide by negligent operation	4	M	
G.L. c. 90 § 24G(b)	Motor vehicle homicide by reckless operation	5	M	
G.L. c. 90 § 24G(b)	Motor vehicle homicide OUI liquor or drugs	5	M	

Mass. General Law Chapter & Section	Offense Description	Grid Level	Penalty Type	Notes
G.L. c. 90 § 24G(a)	Motor vehicle homicide OUI liquor or drugs, with negligent operation	5	F	
G.L. c. 90 § 24G(a)	Motor vehicle homicide OUI liquor or drugs, with reckless operation	6	F	
G.L. c. 90 § 24U(a)(1)	Motor vehicle ignition interlock, bypass for another	2	M	
G.L. c. 90 § 24U(a)(1)	Motor vehicle ignition interlock, bypass for another, subsequent	3	F	
G.L. c. 90 § 24(2)(a)	Motor vehicle license, allow another to use	2	M	
G.L. c. 90 § 23	Motor vehicle license, exhibit another's	1	M	
G.L. c. 90 § 23	Motor vehicle license, exhibit another's, subsequent	2	M	
G.L. c. 90 § 24B	Motor vehicle license, false application for	3	F	
G.L. c. 90 § 24(2)(a)	Motor vehicle license, false statement in application for	2	M	
G.L. c. 90 § 23	Motor vehicle number plate violation to conceal ID	1	M	
G.L. c. 90 § 24(2)(a)	Motor vehicle registration, false statement in application for	2	M	
G.L. c. 266 § 139(a)	Motor vehicle VIN, remove/alter	2	F	
G.L. c. 90D § 32(a)	Motor vehicle, alter, forge, or counterfeit certificate of title or salvage title	3	F	
G.L. c. 266 § 28(b)	Motor vehicle, conceal thief of	3	F	
G.L. c. 90 § 24H	Motor vehicle, improper removal of abandoned/stolen/crushed	2	M	
G.L. c. 266 § 28(a)	Motor vehicle, larceny/malicious damage/ receive stolen/steal parts	2	F	
G.L. c. 266 § 28(a)	Motor vehicle, larceny/malicious damage/ receive stolen/steal parts, subsequent	3	F	
G.L. c. 90 § 24(2)(a½)(1)	Motor vehicle, leave scene after causing personal injury	3	M	
G.L. c. 90 § 24(2)(a½)(2)	Motor vehicle, leave scene after causing personal injury resulting in death	3	F	
G.L. c. 90 § 24(2)(a)	Motor vehicle, leave scene after causing property damage	2	M	
G.L. c. 90 § 24(2)(a)	Motor vehicle, negligent operation of	2	M	
G.L. c. 90 § 16	Motor vehicle, operate offensively or illegally	1	M	
G.L. c. 90 § 17	Motor vehicle, operate with excessive speed	1	M	
G.L. c. 90 § 23	Motor vehicle, operate with license revoked as HTO	2	M	HTO = Habitual Traffic Offender.
G.L. c. 90 § 23	Motor vehicle, operate with license suspended	1	M	
G.L. c. 90 § 23	Motor vehicle, operate with license suspended for OUI	2	M	
G.L. c. 90 § 23	Motor vehicle, operate with license suspended, subsequent	2	M	
G.L. c. 90 § 23	Motor vehicle, operate with registration suspended	1	M	
G.L. c. 90 § 23	Motor vehicle, operate with registration suspended, subsequent	2	M	
G.L. c. 90 § 34J	Motor vehicle, operate without insurance	1	M	
G.L. c. 90 § 10	Motor vehicle, operate without license	1	M	
G.L. c. 90 § 9	Motor vehicle, operate without registration	2	M	
G.L. c. 90 § 24(1)(a)(1)	Motor vehicle, OUI liquor or drugs	2	M	
G.L. c. 90 § 24(1)(a)(1)	Motor vehicle, OUI liquor or drugs, 2nd off.	2	M	

Mass. General Law Chapter & Section	Offense Description	Grid Level	Penalty Type	Notes
G.L. c. 90 § 24(1)(a)(1)	Motor vehicle, OUI liquor or drugs, 3rd off.	3	F	
G.L. c. 90 § 24(1)(a)(1)	Motor vehicle, OUI liquor or drugs, 4th off.	3	F	
G.L. c. 90 § 24L(2)	Motor vehicle, OUI liquor or drugs, causing serious injury	3	M	
G.L. c. 90 § 24L(1)	Motor vehicle, OUI liquor or drugs, with negligent operation, causing serious injury	3	F	
G.L. c. 90 § 24L(1)	Motor vehicle, OUI liquor or drugs, with reckless operation, causing serious injury	4	F	
G.L. c. 90 § 23	Motor vehicle, OUI while license suspended for OUI	2	M	
G.L. c. 90 § 12(b)	Motor vehicle, permit operation with suspended/no license	1	M	
G.L. c. 90 § 12(b)	Motor vehicle, permit operation with suspended/no license, subsequent	2	M	
G.L. c. 90 § 24I	Motor vehicle, possess alcohol open container	1	M	Statute addresses possession, not drinking, and doesn't specify locations other than a motor vehicle.
G.L. c. 266 § 139(c)	Motor vehicle, possess or receive with defaced VIN	2	M	
G.L. c. 90 § 24(2)(a)	Motor vehicle, racing	2	M	See also G.L. c. 90 § 17B.
G.L. c. 90 § 17B	Motor vehicle, racing by licensed operator	2	M	
G.L. c. 90 § 24(2)(a)	Motor vehicle, reckless operation of	2	M	
G.L. c. 90 § 25	Motor vehicle, refuse to comply with police officer	1	M	
G.L. c. 90 § 1A	Motor vehicle, registration without liability insurance	1	CIV	Penalty found in G.L. c. 90 §20.
G.L. c. 266 § 139(b)	Motor vehicle, sell with defaced VIN, or attempt	2	F	
G.L. c. 90 § 24(2)(a)	Motor vehicle, speeding to make record	2	M	See also G.L. c. 90 § 17B.
G.L. c. 90 § 24(2)(a)	Motor vehicle, use without authority	2	M	
G.L. c. 90 § 24(2)(a)	Motor vehicle, use without authority, 2nd off.	2	F	
G.L. c. 90 § 24(2)(a)	Motor vehicle, use without authority, 3rd and subsequent	3	F	
G.L. c. 90 § 13	Motor vehicle, violate safety precautions	1	CIV	Penalty found in G.L. c. 90 §20.
G.L. c. 272 § 59	Municipal ordinance violation: loitering, trespassing, drinking, accosting	1	V	
G.L. c. 265 § 1	Murder	7	F	Penalty found in G.L. c. 265 § 2.
G.L. c. 265 § 16	Murder, attempted	5	F	
G.L. c. 33 § 65	National Guard encampment, trespass on	1	M	Penalty found in G.L. c. 33 § 66.
G.L. c. 272 § 53	Nightwalker, common	1	M	Equivalent to "Streetwalker, common". Involves not a fee but conduct (including accosting, annoying, lewd and lascivious behavior). Distinct from § 53A "Sexual conduct, pay for or for fee".
G.L. c. 272 § 29	Obscene matter, distribute	2	F	
G.L. c. 272 § 28	Obscene matter, distribute to minor	2	F	
G.L. c. 272 § 28	Obscene matter, distribute to minor, 2nd and subsequent	3	F	
G.L. c. 272 § 29	Obscene matter, distribute, 2nd and subsequent	3	F	
G.L. c. 272 § 16	Open and gross lewdness	2	F	1st offense doesn't trigger SORB notification or registration.
G.L. c. 272 § 16	Open and gross lewdness, with previous sex offense	3	F	Triggers SORB notification & registration.
G.L. c. 90B § 25	Operating snow/recreational vehicle on public way	1	M	Penalty found in G.L. c. 90B § 34.

Mass. General Law Chapter & Section	Offense Description	Grid Level	Penalty Type	Notes
G.L. c. 268 § 1	Perjury	3	F	
G.L. c. 268 § 1	Perjury in trial of capital case	5	F	
G.L. c. 268 § 3	Perjury, attempt to suborn	2	F	
G.L. c. 268 § 2	Perjury, suborn	3	F	Penalty found in G.L. c. 268 § 1.
G.L. c. 94C § 32A(c)	Phencyclidine, distribute or possess with intent	3	F	
G.L. c. 94C § 32A(d)	Phencyclidine, distribute or possess with intent, subsequent	4	F	
G.L. c. 94C § 32E(b)(3)	Phenmetrazine, trafficking in, 100 to 200 g	5	F	
G.L. c. 94C § 32E(b)(1)	Phenmetrazine, trafficking in, 14 to 28 g	3	F	
G.L. c. 94C § 32E(b)(4)	Phenmetrazine, trafficking in, 200 g or more	6	F	
G.L. c. 94C § 32E(b)(2)	Phenmetrazine, trafficking in, 28 to 100 g	4	F	
G.L. c. 272 § 105(c)	Photograph of unsuspecting nude person, disseminate	2	F	
G.L. c. 272 § 105(b)	Photograph unsuspecting nude person	2	M	
G.L. c. 131 § 43	Poison mammal/bird	2	M	Penalty found in G.L. c. 131 § 90.
G.L. c. 266 § 112	Poison/kill/maim domestic animal	2	F	
G.L. c. 265 § 28	Poisoning with intent to kill or injure person	5	F	
G.L. c. 272 § 77A	Police horse/dog, mistreat/interfere with	2	M	
G.L. c. 268 § 33	Police officer or public official, impersonate	2	M	
G.L. c. 268 § 24	Police officer, fail to assist	1	M	
Common Law	Police officer, interfere with [Grid 2012]	2	CL	Penalty found in G.L. c. 279 § 5.
G.L. c. 94C § 33(b)	Prescription, utter false	3	F	Penalty found in G.L. c. 94C § 33(c).
G.L. c. 268 § 28	Prisoner, deliver drugs or article to	3	F	
G.L. c. 272 § 7	Prostitute, derive support from	3	F	
G.L. c. 272 § 4B	Prostitute, derive support from child	4	F	
G.L. c. 272 § 8	Prostitute, solicit for	1	M	
	Prostitution			See G.L. c. 272 § 53A "Sexual conduct, pay for or for fee" or G.L. c. 272 § 53 "Nightwalker, common" if no fee.
G.L. c. 272 § 4A	Prostitution, induce minor to	3	F	
G.L. c. 272 § 12	Prostitution, procure person to practice	2	M	
G.L. c. 272 § 2	Prostitution/unlawful sex, abduct or entice person for	2	F	
G.L. c. 18 § 5B	Public Assistance fraud	2	M	
G.L. c. 265 § 35	Public way, throw object on	1	M	
G.L. c. 160 § 220	Railroad fare, evade	1	M	
G.L. c. 162 § 18	Railroad track (electric), walking or standing on	1	M	
G.L. c. 265 § 22(b)	Rape	5	F	
G.L. c. 265 § 22A	Rape of child under 16 with force	6	F	
G.L. c. 265 § 22C	Rape of child under 16 with force, after certain sex offenses	6	F	
G.L. c. 265 § 22B	Rape of child under 16 with force, aggravated	6	F	
G.L. c. 265 § 22A	Rape of child under 16 with force, subsequent	6	F	
G.L. c. 265 § 23	Rape of child under 16, statutory	4	F	
G.L. c. 265 § 23B	Rape of child under 16, statutory, after certain sex offenses	6	F	
G.L. c. 265 § 23A	Rape of child under 16, statutory, aggravated	6	F	Aggravating factors: age difference, commission by mandated reporter.
G.L. c. 265 § 23	Rape of child under 16, statutory, subsequent	5	F	
G.L. c. 265 § 22(a)	Rape, aggravated	6	F	
G.L. c. 265 § 22(a)	Rape, aggravated, armed, with firearm	6	F	

Mass. General Law Chapter & Section	Offense Description	Grid Level	Penalty Type	Notes
G.L. c. 265 § 22(a)	Rape, aggravated, armed, with firearm, subsequent	6	F	
G.L. c. 265 § 22(a)	Rape, aggravated, subsequent	6	F	
G.L. c. 265 § 22(b)	Rape, armed, with firearm	5	F	
G.L. c. 265 § 22(b)	Rape, subsequent	6	F	
G.L. c. 266 § 60	Receive stolen or falsely traded property, over $250, $10,000 to $50,000	3	F	
G.L. c. 266 § 60	Receive stolen or falsely traded property, over $250, $50,000 and over	3	F	
G.L. c. 266 § 60	Receive stolen or falsely traded property, over $250, under $10,000	2	F	
G.L. c. 266 § 60	Receive stolen or falsely traded property, under $250	2	M	
G.L. c. 266 § 60	Receive stolen or falsely traded property, under $250, subsequent	2	F	
G.L. c. 265 § 13L	Reckless endangerment to children	2	M	
G.L. c. 268 § 32B	Resist arrest	2	M	
G.L. c. 131 § 67	Rifle/revolver/pistol of unlawful caliber, use or possess	2	M	A Fisheries & Game offense. Penalty found in G.L. c. 131 § 90.
G.L. c. 269 § 12D(a)	Rifle/shotgun on way, carry loaded	4	M	
G.L. c. 269 § 12D(a)	Rifle/shotgun on way, carry loaded, large capacity	4	V	Definition of "Large capacity": http://www.mass.gov/legis/laws/mgl/140-121.htm.
G.L. c. 269 § 10(g)	Rifle/shotgun without serial number, sell	3	M	
G.L. c. 269 § 7	Riot, destroy building/boat in	2	F	
G.L. c. 269 § 2	Riot, fail to disperse or fail to assist in dispersing	2	M	
G.L. c. 264 § 11	Riot, incite	2	F	
G.L. c. 90 § 24B	RMV document or signature, possess false/stolen, misuse/forge	3	F	
G.L. c. 265 § 19(a)	Robbery of elder 60 or over, unarmed	4	F	
G.L. c. 265 § 19(a)	Robbery of elder 60 or over, unarmed, subsequent	5	F	
G.L. c. 265 § 17	Robbery, armed & masked, display of gun	6	F	
G.L. c. 265 § 17	Robbery, armed & masked, display of gun, subsequent	6	F	
G.L. c. 265 § 17	Robbery, armed & masked, no display of gun	5	F	
G.L. c. 265 § 17	Robbery, armed & masked, no display of gun, subsequent	5	F	
G.L. c. 265 § 17	Robbery, armed & masked, with firearm	5	F	
G.L. c. 265 § 17	Robbery, armed & masked, with firearm, subsequent	6	F	
G.L. c. 265 § 17	Robbery, armed, display of gun	5	F	
G.L. c. 265 § 17	Robbery, armed, no display of gun	4	F	
G.L. c. 265 § 17	Robbery, armed, with firearm	5	F	
G.L. c. 265 § 17	Robbery, armed, with firearm, subsequent	6	F	
G.L. c. 265 § 19(b)	Robbery, unarmed	3	F	
G.L. c. 272 § 40	School or public assembly, disturb	1	M	
G.L. c. 272 § 40	School or public assembly, disturb, 3rd and subsequent	2	M	
G.L. c. 265 § 48	Sex Offender engaging in ice cream truck vending	2	M	
G.L. c. 6 § 178N	Sex Offender Registry information, illegal use of	2	M	
G.L. c. 272 § 53A(a)	Sexual conduct, pay for or for fee	2	M	This section addresses prostitution.
G.L. c. 272 § 53A(b)	Sexual conduct, pay for or for fee, with child under 14	4	F	This section addresses prostitution.

Mass. General Law Chapter & Section	Offense Description	Grid Level	Penalty Type	Notes
G.L. c. 272 § 3	Sexual intercourse, drug for	3	F	
G.L. c. 272 § 4	Sexual intercourse, induce chaste minor	2	F	
G.L. c. 266 § 30A	Shoplifting	1	M	
G.L. c. 266 § 30A	Shoplifting, 3rd and subsequent	2	M	
G.L. c. 131 § 66	Shotgun shells in closed season	2	M	Penalty found in G.L. c. 131 § 90.
G.L. c. 272 § 43A	Smoking on MBTA	1	M	
G.L. c. 265 § 43(a)	Stalking	3	F	
G.L. c. 265 § 43(b)	Stalking in violation of restraining order	3	F	
G.L. c. 265 § 43(c)	Stalking, subsequent	3	F	
G.L. c. 273 § 15	Support child out of wedlock, enter Commonwealth without	2	F	Penalty found in G.L. c. 273 § 15A(3).
G.L. c. 273 § 15	Support child out of wedlock, fail to	2	F	Penalty found in G.L. c. 273 § 15A(2).
G.L. c. 266 § 126B	Tagging property	2	M	
G.L. c. 265 § 34	Tattooing	1	M	
G.L. c. 269 § 14A	Telephone calls, annoying or obscene	1	M	
G.L. c. 275 § 2	Threat to commit crime	1	M	Penalty found in G.L. c. 275 § 4.
G.L. c. 264 § 2	Treason	6	F	
G.L. c. 266 § 114	Trees and fences, malicious injury	1	M	
G.L. c. 266 § 120	Trespass	1	M	
G.L. c. 266 § 117	Trespass for tree/plant/fruit	1	M	
G.L. c. 266 § 117	Trespass for tree/plant/fruit, Sunday/disguised/nighttime	1	M	
G.L. c. 266 § 123	Trespass on state/county property	1	M	
G.L. c. 266 § 121	Trespass with firearm	3	M	
G.L. c. 140D § 27	Unauthorized use of credit cards	2	F	
G.L. c. 272 § 35	Unnatural & lascivious act	2	F	
G.L. c. 272 § 35A	Unnatural & lascivious act with child under 16	3	F	
G.L. c. 272 § 35A	Unnatural & lascivious act with child under 16, subsequent	4	F	
G.L. c. 271 § 49(a)	Usury	3	F	
G.L. c. 267 § 5	Utter false check, instrument, or promissory note	3	F	
G.L. c. 272 § 68	Vagabond	1	M	
G.L. c. 272 § 66	Vagrancy	1	M	
G.L. c. 40 § 21D	Violation of state, town, city, or MDC ordinance, non-criminal disposition	1	M	
G.L. c. 233 § 5	Witness fail to appear in criminal case	1	M	
G.L. c. 233 § 20H	Witness fail to testify, immunized	2	M	

PART 10

Sex Offender Registration Requirements

Sex Offenses Which Require Registration

Sex offenses which require registration, pursuant to G.L. c. 6, §§ 178C–178Q, inclusive:

Sex Offense:	
c. 265 § 13B:	Indecent assault and battery on a child under 14
c. 265 § 13B½:	Aggravated indecent assault and battery on a child under 14
c. 265 § 13B¾:	Indecent assault and battery on a child under 14 by certain repeat offenders
c. 265 § 13F:	Indecent assault and battery on a mentally retarded person
c. 265 § 13H:	Indecent assault and battery on a person age 14 or over; indecent assault and battery on elder or person with disability
c. 265 § 22:	Rape
c. 265 § 22A:	Rape of a child under 16 with force
c. 265 § 22B:	Aggravated rape of a child under 16 with force
c. 265 § 22C:	Rape of a child under 16 with force by certain repeat offenders
c. 265 § 23:	Rape and abuse of a child
c. 265 § 23A:	Aggravated rape and abuse of a child
c. 265 § 23B:	Rape and abuse of child by certain repeat offenders
c. 265 § 24:	Assault with intent to commit rape
c. 265 § 24B:	Assault of a child with intent to commit rape
c. 265 § 26:	Kidnapping of a child under 16, fourth paragraph
c. 265 § 26C:	Enticing a child under the age of 16
c. 265 § 26D:	Enticing a child under 18 via electronic communications to engage in prostitution, human trafficking or sexual servitude
c. 265 § 50:	Trafficking of persons for sexual servitude
c. 265 § 52:	Second or subsequent violation of human trafficking for sexual servitude
c. 272 § 2:	Enticing away a person for prostitution or sexual intercourse
c. 272 § 3:	Drugging persons for sexual intercourse
c. 272 § 4A:	Inducing a minor into prostitution
c. 272 § 4B:	Living off/sharing earnings of a minor prostitute
c. 272 § 16:	Second and subsequent adjudication or conviction for open and gross lewdness and lascivious behavior, but excluding a first or single adjudication as a juvenile delinquent before August 1, 1992
c. 272 § 17:	Incestuous marriage or intercourse
c. 272 § 28:	Disseminating to a minor matter harmful to a minor
c. 272 § 29A:	Posing or exhibiting a child in a state of nudity
c. 272 § 29B:	Dissemination of visual material of a child in a state of nudity or sexual conduct
c. 272 § 29C:	Possession of child pornography
c. 272 § 35A:	Unnatural and lascivious acts with a child under 16
c. 272 § 77C	Engaging in sexual contact with an animal
c. 272 § 39:	Aggravated rape
c. 274 § 6:	Any attempt to commit a violation of any of the aforementioned sections; or a like Violation of the Laws of another State, the United States, or a military, territorial or Indian tribal authority

803 CMR 1.00. Sex Offender Registry Board: Registration, Classification and Dissemination

(Dated Mar. 11, 2016.)

Section

803 CMR 1.01. Purpose

803 CMR 1.00 sets forth guidelines pertaining to the registration and classification of sex offenders, and the resulting dissemination of sex offender registry information in accordance with the law based on the offender's level of risk of reoffense and degree of

dangerousness posed to the public. 803 CMR 1.00 additionally provides a process for the removal from the sex offender registry of those individuals not required to register. The Sex Offender Registry Board (the "Board") may from time to time and in its discretion develop, implement, and/or amend its policies, procedures, and protocols to this end. The Board will exercise sound judgment and apply its expertise when making any registration or classification determination as required in 803 CMR 1.00.

803 CMR 1.00 sets forth the registration and classification procedures and guidelines the Board uses to determine whether a convicted or adjudicated sex offender may be required to register as a sex offender and, if so, the offender's level of risk of reoffense and degree of dangerousness posed to the public.

803 CMR 1.02. Regulations Do Not Limit Statutory Authority, Cancellation

Nothing contained in 803 CMR 1.00 shall be interpreted to limit, contradict or override the authority granted to the Sex Offender Registry Board or others pursuant to M.G.L. c. 6, §§ 178C through 178Q and any other applicable provisions of the Massachusetts General Laws. 803 CMR 1.00 cancels all previous Sex Offender Registry Board policy statements, rules or regulations to the extent they are inconsistent with 803 CMR 1.00. The recommended classification of any offender who has not been finally classified prior to the effective date of 803 CMR 1.00 shall remain valid. Likewise, the Final Classification of any offender issued prior to the effective date of 803 CMR 1.00 shall also be deemed to remain valid.

803 CMR 1.03. Definitions

All words and phrases not defined in 803 CMR 1.00 shall be defined by M.G.L. c. 6, § 178C. Unless otherwise indicated in a specific factor enumerated in 803 CMR 1.33, the use of the male gender in 803 CMR 1.00 shall be deemed to include the female or neutral gender. The use of the singular includes the plural and vice versa where the context so permits.

As used in 803 CMR 1.00, the following words and phrases shall have the following meanings:

Authorized Representative. An appointed or privately retained attorney, legal guardian or any other person authorized by the sex offender to represent him or her during the hearing process. For appointment of counsel, see 803 CMR 1.09. If the authorized representative is not an attorney, he or she shall submit to the Board a written authorization signed and dated by the sex offender at least ten business days prior to the scheduled hearing date. The written authorization shall state the relationship between the authorized representative and the sex offender.

Classification File. The part of the sex offender's file maintained by the Board that contains the documentary evidence compiled by the Board to complete the recommendation process.

Classification Worksheet. A form developed and approved by the Board that reflects the recommendation process, shows the foundation for and indicates the Board's recommended registration and classification determination for each offender. The worksheet shall include a review of the factors enumerated in M.G.L. c. 6, § 178K(1)(a) through (l) and explained further in 803 CMR 1.33. The Board shall make a blank copy of the Classification Worksheet and related policies, procedures, protocols, and objective standards generally available and available upon request. The Hearing Examiner presiding over a classification hearing is not bound by the recommended classification or the means by which it was adduced.

Clear and Convincing Evidence. The standard applied at administrative hearings where the Hearing Examiner determines, based upon all of the evidence, there is a high degree of probability that the sex offender meets the standards specified for the duty to register and to be classified at a designated level. The Board shall bear the burden of proof at such hearings.

Documentary Evidence. Clear and legible records, data, reports, or letters submitted to the Board by the sex offender or on behalf of the sex offender relative to his or her risk of reoffense and the degree of dangerousness he or she poses to the public and his or her duty to register.

Employment. Any work that is full-time or part-time for a period of time exceeding 14 days or for an aggregate period of time exceeding 30 days during any calendar year, whether compensated or uncompensated, self-employed or working for an entity. To "work" shall mean to perform employment or work defined in 803 CMR 1.00.

Expert Witness. A licensed medical doctor or mental health professional, excluding employees of the Sex Offender Registry Board, whose testimony and report offering an opinion as to a sex offender's risk of reoffense and degree of dangerousness were prepared expressly for reliance by a Party at a hearing conducted pursuant to 803 CMR 1.10 through 1.20. Reports prepared by licensed mental health professionals that contain an opinion as to a sex offender's risk of reoffense and degree of dangerousness that were prepared for any other purpose will not qualify as Expert Witness opinions for a hearing conducted pursuant to 803 CMR 1.10 through 1.20.

Factor(s). The descriptions and definitions as well as the principles and authorities enumerated in 803 CMR 1.33 which the Board uses in its registration and classification determinations.

Final Classification. A sex offender shall be deemed finally classified when the presiding Hearing Examiner determines that he or she is a Level 1, Level 2 or Level 3 Offender, except where a sex offender has declined to request a hearing, in which case the recommended classification accomplished pursuant to 803 CMR 1.06 will become the Final Classification.

Full Board. At least four members of the Sex Offender Registry Board. The full board may establish policies and procedures to implement the provisions of M.G.L. c. 6, §§ 178C through 178Q and 803 CMR 1.00.

Hearing Examiner. An individual employed by the Sex Offender Registry Board, a single member of the Sex Offender Registry Board, or a hearing panel, or the Chair's designee to conduct administrative hearings to determine by clear and convincing evidence a sex offender's duty to register and final classification level.

Jurisdiction. The Board has jurisdiction over a person who resides, has secondary addresses, works or attends an institution of higher learning in the Commonwealth and who has been convicted of a sex offense or who has been adjudicated as a youthful offender or as a delinquent juvenile by reason of a sex offense or a person released from incarceration or parole or probation supervision or custody with the department of youth services for such a conviction or adjudication or a person who has been adjudicated a sexually dangerous person under M.G.L. c. 123A, § 14 as in force at the time of adjudication, or a person released from civil commitment pursuant to M.G.L. c. 123A, § 9, whichever last occurs, on or after August 1, 1981.

Juvenile. An individual younger than 18 years old at the time of committing a sex offense. If the sex offender is a juvenile, all written notifications from the Board shall also be mailed to:

(a) his or her legal guardian;

(b) the Department of Children and Families or the Department of Youth Services if the Juvenile is receiving services from, or subject to proceedings initiated by, one or more of these agencies; and

(c) his or her most recent attorney of record.

Level 1 Offender. The designation given to a sex offender when it has been determined his or her risk of reoffense is low and the degree of dangerousness posed to the public is not such that a public safety interest is served by public access to information pertaining to the offender.

Level 2 Offender. The designation given to a sex offender when it has been determined his or her risk of reoffense is moderate and the degree of dangerousness posed to the public is such that a public safety interest is served by public access to sex offender registry information.

Level 3 Offender. The designation given to a sex offender when it has been determined his or her risk of reoffense is high and the degree of dangerousness posed to the public is such that a substantial public safety interest is served by active dissemination (community notification) of sex offender registry information.

Party. The sex offender and the Sex Offender Registry Board. At the hearing, the sex offender may represent himself or herself or have an authorized representative. For representation at hearing see 803 CMR 1.09. The Board may have a representative responsible for presenting evidence and argument regarding the offender at any hearing held under 803 CMR 1.00. The Sex Offender Registry Board shall be identified by its name and not by its individual representatives' names.

Receipt. The delivery of mail. There shall be a rebuttable presumption that any notice or letter mailed by the Sex Offender Registry Board to the offender at the address(es) at which he or she is currently registered was received by the offender within three days of mailing.

Recommendation. The Board's recommended classification, also referred to as preliminary classification level, made pursuant to the policies, procedures, protocols, and objective standards set forth in M.G.L. c. 6, § 178K(1)(a) through (l) and explained in 803 CMR 1.33 to base its recommended classifications. The Board shall make its policies, procedures, protocols, and objective standards for the recommendation process generally available and available upon request.

School. Any public or private educational institution, including any secondary school, trade, vocational or professional institution, or a post-secondary institution of higher learning.

Second and Subsequent Adjudication or Conviction for Open and Gross Lewdness and Lascivious Behavior. The later of two or more separate convictions pursuant to M.G.L. c. 272, § 16. Multiple convictions resulting from a single act shall be treated as a single conviction, but arraignments occurring on the same date and resulting in multiple convictions shall be presumed to be the result of separate acts and treated as separate convictions.

Sex Offender Number (SON). The unique identification number assigned to every sex offender by the Sex Offender Registry Board. The offender must include his or her SON on all written communications with the Sex Offender Registry Board.

Sex Offender Registry. The central computerized database of all sex offenders required to register pursuant to M.G.L. c. 6, §§ 178C through 178Q.

Sex Offender Registry Board (Board or SORB). The administrative agency of the Commonwealth consisting of the members, as set forth in M.G.L. c. 6, § 178K, and its staff.

Student. Any person who is enrolled on a full-time or part-time basis, in any school.

803 CMR 1.04. Registration and Classification Process

(1) **Preamble**. Pursuant to M.G.L. c. 6, § 178K(1), the Board is required to publish guidelines for determining each sex offender's level of risk of reoffense and degree of dangerousness posed to the public, or for relief from the obligation of registration. Pursuant to M.G.L. c. 6, § 178K(1) and (2), these guidelines shall provide for three levels of notification based on a sex offender's risk of reoffense and degree of dangerousness. The offender's final classification level determines the amount of information that can be disseminated about him or her to the public through the notification procedures, pursuant to M.G.L. c. 6, §§ 178C through 178Q. The registration and classification process is a two stage process.

(2) In the first stage, the Board makes a recommendation regarding each sex offender's duty to register and classification level pursuant to M.G.L. c. 6, § 178L. During the recommendation process, the sex offender is entitled to present documentary evidence for the Board to consider. The sex offender will be notified in writing of the Board's recommendation. The sex offender may either accept or reject the recommendation. The recommendation process is set forth at 803 CMR 1.06 through 1.08. If the sex offender accepts the Board's recommendation, then the recommended classification level shall become final and is not subject to judicial review, pursuant to M.G.L. c. 30A.

(3) If the sex offender rejects the Board's recommendation, the process moves into the second stage which is set forth at 803 CMR 1.09 through 1.22. The sex offender is provided with a de novo hearing at which all relevant evidence is evaluated by a Hearing Examiner to reach a final decision regarding the sex offender's duty to register and final classification level. The Hearing Examiner shall base his or her decision on the totality of all the relevant evidence introduced at the sex offender's individualized hearing. The final agency decision issued by the Hearing Examiner is subject to judicial review in the Superior Court, pursuant to M.G.L. c. 30A.

(4) **Factors**. M.G.L. c. 6, §§ 178K(2) and 178L(1), sets forth criteria to be considered by the Board in determining risk of reoffense and degree of dangerousness and authorize the Board to identify and utilize additional risk factors and criteria not specifically listed in the statute. Based on this statutory authority, the Board created 803 CMR 1.33 which describes and defines the factors that the Board shall consider in making all registration and classification decisions. In determining the final classification, the Hearing Examiner shall be guided by the definitions, explanations, principles, and authorities contained in the Factors set forth in 803 CMR 1.33 and shall not be bound by the Board's recommendations.

803 CMR 1.05. Registration

(1) A sex offender, as defined in M.G.L. c. 6, § 178C, shall register with the Sex Offender Registry Board, by mail, on a registration form provided by the Board. Additionally, the Board shall accept the registration form it receives from any nonresident person who has employment or is enrolled in school in the Commonwealth if such person is required to register as a sex offender in the state in which he or she resides.

(2) **Registration Form**. The registration form shall require the sex offender to provide the following information:

(a) name of the sex offender;

(b) date of birth;

(c) Social Security number (optional);

(d) home address or intended home address;

(e) secondary address or intended secondary address;

(f) location for homeless offenders;

(g) work address or intended work address;

(h) name and address of any school at which the offender works, intends to work, is enrolled as a student, and/or intends to enroll as a student; and

(i) signature of the sex offender, signed under the pains and penalties of perjury.

(3) The information obtained from the registration form shall be used by the Board to notify the sex offender of his or her right to submit documentary evidence during the recommendation process, as set forth in 803 CMR 1.06 through 1.08, as well as to offer him or her the opportunity to request a hearing in accordance with the procedures established in 803 CMR 1.00. It is the sex offender's obligation to provide the Board with accurate information during the recommendation process.

(4) **Sex Offenders in the Community**.

(a) For sex offenders who have been released from all custody and supervision, the Board shall mail the registration form and notification of the requirements of M.G.L. c. 6, §§ 178C through 178Q to the last known address of all sex offenders residing in the Commonwealth. The registration form must be completed by the offender and mailed to the Board within ten calendar days of receipt.

(b) For sex offenders who have been convicted or adjudicated for a sex offense but have not been sentenced to confinement for 90 days or more to be served immediately, the registration form must be completed by the sex offender and mailed to the Board within two calendar days of receiving notification by the court of the duty to register or within two calendar days of release from confinement, whichever is later.

(5) **Sex Offenders Subject to Community Supervision**. For sex offenders who are currently on probation or parole, the registration form must be completed by the offender and mailed to the Board within two calendar days of receiving notification of the duty to register.

(6) **Incarcerated Sex Offenders**. For sex offenders who are currently incarcerated, the registration form must be completed by the sex offender and mailed to the Board not later than two calendar days before release from custody. No sex offender shall be released from custody unless such registration form has been filled out, signed and mailed to the Board.

If the Board finally classified an incarcerated sex offender as either a Level 2 or Level 3 Offender before or during the sex offender's incarceration:

(a) not later than two days before his or her release, the offender shall complete and mail the registration form to the Board; and

(b) the Board shall notify the local police department in the city or town in which the offender intends to live, or if he or she does not intend to reside in the Commonwealth, in the city or town in which he or she intends to work or in which he or she intends to attend a school in the Commonwealth.

(7) For sex offenders who have been afforded the opportunity for a hearing and who have been finally classified, registration shall be in accordance with M.G.L. c. 6, §§ 178F through 178F½. Registration information shall be available to the public on those offenders finally classified as a Level 2 or a Level 3 Offender.

(8) Sex offenders are responsible for complying with all of the registration duties and obligations as set forth in M.G.L. c. 6, §§ 178C through 178Q. These registration duties and obligations shall be enforced to the extent permissible pursuant to the law.

(9) Upon receiving a sex offender's registration information or change in registration information, the Board shall transmit the registration information to:

(a) police departments in municipalities where the sex offender lives and works, or where the sex offender intends to live and work upon release and where the offense was committed;

(b) police departments in municipalities, including campus police departments or other state recognized law enforcement agencies at a school, where the sex offender works and/or attends a school or where the sex offender intends to work and/or attend a school upon release; and

(c) the Federal Bureau of Investigation.

Registration information received by the Board and disseminated to law enforcement pursuant to 803 CMR 1.05(9) shall not be disseminated to the public except in accordance with M.G.L. c. 6, §§ 178I, 178J and 178K.

803 CMR 1.06. Duty to Register and Recommended Classification Level

(1) **Duty to Register**. Pursuant to M.G.L. c. 6, §§ 178C, 178K(2) and 178L(1), the Board shall determine whether a sex offender has a duty to register and, if so, shall then prepare a recommended classification of the sex offender as a Level 1, Level 2, or Level 3 offender.

(2) **No Duty to Register**. If the Board determines that the offender does not have a duty to register, it shall notify the offender in writing. The Board shall promptly remove information pertaining to the offender from the sex offender registry.

(3) **Recommended Classification**. If the Board determines that the offender does have a duty to register, the Board shall prepare a recommended classification level based on the factors enumerated in M.G.L. c. 6, § 178K(1)(a) through (l) and further explained at 803 CMR 1.33. Pursuant to M.G.L. c. 6, § 178L(1), in preparing the recommended classification level, the Board shall consider any relevant materials, including documentary evidence submitted by the sex offender. A staff member of the Board shall complete the classification worksheet based on this information.

(4) **Written Approval by Board Member**. Pursuant to M.G.L. c. 6, § 178L(1), the classification worksheet shall be reviewed by one Board member, who shall enter written findings and determine the recommended classification level. The Board member who made the recommendation shall not be subject to a subpoena nor shall his or her mental process in reaching the recommended classification level be otherwise probed, as the recommendation may be appealed at a de novo hearing.

(5) **Juvenile Recommendations**.

(a) If the sex offender was a juvenile at the time of the sex offense, the written findings and recommended classification level made pursuant to 803 CMR 1.06(4) shall be completed by the Board member who is a licensed psychologist or psychiatrist with special expertise in the assessment and evaluation of juvenile sex offenders.

(b) To prepare a recommended classification for a juvenile or an adult whose only sex offense(s) was committed as a juvenile, the Board may meet with the juvenile sex offender. If the Board chooses to meet with the juvenile sex offender, he or she is permitted to be represented by his or her authorized representative. The Board shall not draw any adverse inferences from an offender's refusal or failure to meet with the Board.

(6) A Board member shall not preside at the classification hearing in a case where he or she made written findings and determined the recommended classification level pursuant to 803 CMR 1.06(4), except in the case of a juvenile sex offender or an adult sex offender whose only sex offense(s) was committed as a juvenile. In these circumstances, the Board member who is a licensed psychologist or psychiatrist with expertise in juvenile sex offenders may complete the recommended classification pursuant to 803 CMR 1.06(4) and also preside at the classification hearing with the consent of the juvenile.

(7) The Board member who made the written findings and determined the recommended classification level pursuant to 803 CMR 1.06(4) shall not be prohibited from participating in any sexually violent predator recommendation made pursuant to M.G.L. c. 6, § 178K(2)(c), or any motion to terminate registration obligation pursuant to 803 CMR 1.30, or any request to reclassify pursuant to 803 CMR 1.31.

803 CMR 1.07. Right to Submit Documentary Evidence During the Recommendation Process

(1) **Notification**. Pursuant to M.G.L. c. 6, § 178L(1)(a), the Board shall notify the sex offender of his or her right to submit documentary evidence relative to his or her duty to register, risk of reoffense, and degree of dangerousness posed to the public. Any documents submitted by the offender shall become part of his or her classification file. The offender shall submit any documentary evidence to the Board within 30 calendar days of receiving his or her notification.

(2) **Extending the Time to Respond**. Pursuant to M.G.L. c. 6, § 178L(1)(a), the Board may extend the timeframe for a sex offender to submit documentary evidence. The sex offender shall send a written request to the Board seeking an extension. In evaluating the request, the Board may consider such claims as insufficient notification, the offender's inability to secure records or documents from a sex offender treatment provider, or other unforeseen circumstances.

803 CMR 1.08. Right to Request a Hearing to Challenge Recommendations

(1) **Notification**. Pursuant to M.G.L. c. 6, § 178L(1)(a), upon completion of the process set forth in 803 CMR 1.06 and 1.07, the Board shall notify the sex offender, in writing, of his or her duty to register, the recommended classification level, and his or her right to request a hearing to challenge the Board's recommendations.

(2) **Request for a Classification Hearing**. At the same time the Board provides the notification pursuant to 803 CMR 1.08(1), the Board shall also provide each sex offender with a form to request a hearing. The completed form must be returned to the Board within 20 calendar days of receipt of the notice sent pursuant to 803 CMR 1.08(1). By requesting a hearing, the sex offender shall be deemed to have expressly rejected the Board's recommendation, and will have thereby agreed to be finally classified pursuant to 803 CMR 1.20 and 1.21.

(3) **Failure to Request a Classification Hearing**. Pursuant to M.G.L. c. 6, § 178L(1)(a), the failure to timely request a hearing shall result in a waiver of the right to a hearing. The recommended registration and classification level shall become the final decision of the Sex Offender Registry Board and shall not be subject to judicial review pursuant to M.G.L. c. 30A. Notification of this final decision shall be accomplished in accordance with 803 CMR 1.23. In addition, law enforcement shall be notified in accordance with 803 CMR 1.25.

(4) **Sex Offender's Withdrawal of Request for Hearing**. A sex offender who has requested a hearing may withdraw his or her request by:

(a) providing written notice to the Board at any time prior to the date of his or her scheduled classification hearing; or

(b) stating his or her intent to withdraw on the record at the classification hearing prior to any testimony being presented. An offender may not thereafter withdraw his or her request for a hearing except upon approval by the presiding Hearing Examiner.

Any withdrawal by the sex offender will be deemed an acceptance of the Board's recommended classification and shall result in a waiver of the right to a hearing. The registration determination and the recommended classification level shall become the final classification of the Sex Offender Registry Board and shall not be subject to judicial review pursuant to M.G.L. c. 30A. Notification of the sex offender's final classification level shall be accomplished in accordance with 803 CMR 1.23. In addition, law enforcement shall be notified in accordance with 803 CMR 1.25.

(5) **Board's Withdrawal of Recommended Classification**. At any time prior to the date of the scheduled classification hearing, the Board may withdraw its recommended classification of a sex offender upon the receipt of new information of a significant event that occurred after the initial recommended classification that may change the recommended classification level. A "significant event" includes, but is not limited to, such things as:

(a) the sex offender was charged or convicted of a new sex offense;

(b) the sex offender was charged or convicted of a violent crime;

(c) the sex offender violated the terms or conditions of community supervision;

(d) the sex offender becomes the subject of a sexually dangerous person petition or has been adjudicated a sexually dangerous person, pursuant to M.G.L. c. 123A; or

(e) any judicial determinations that may affect the nature of his or her sex offense history.

If the Board withdraws its recommended classification, it must provide written notification to the sex offender that the recommended classification will be re-evaluated based on the new information. The Board shall follow the procedures set forth in 803 CMR 1.06 through 1.08.

803 CMR 1.09. Representation at Classification Hearing

(1) **Notification**. Pursuant to M.G.L. c. 6, § 178L(1)(a), the Board shall notify the sex offender that at the classification hearing he or she has the right to represent himself or herself; the right to retain private counsel to represent him or her at his or her hearing; the right to have an authorized representative, other than an attorney, represent him or her at the hearing; and the right to have counsel appointed for him or her if he or she is found indigent, as determined by the Board pursuant to M.G.L. c. 211D.

(2) **Right to Counsel if Indigent**. At the same time the Board provides notice pursuant to 803 CMR 1.09(1), the Board shall also provide the sex offender with the requisite forms to be completed if the sex offender claims to be indigent and requests the appointment of counsel. All forms must be completed and mailed to the Board within 20 calendar days of receipt.

(a) If the Board has determined that the sex offender is indigent and thus entitled to the appointment of counsel pursuant to M.G.L. c. 211D, the sex offender and CPCS shall be notified in writing that he or she has satisfied the requirements to have an attorney represent him or her at the hearing.

(b) If the Board has determined that the sex offender is not entitled to the appointment of counsel pursuant to M.G.L. c. 211D, the sex offender shall be notified in writing that he or she will not have an attorney appointed to represent him or her. The sex offender shall further be notified that he or she may retain private counsel; that he or she may have an authorized representative; or he or she may represent himself or herself at the hearing.

(3) **Juvenile Offenders**. All sex offenders who are juveniles at the time of notification of the hearing shall be represented by counsel at the hearing. Any offender who is a juvenile at the time of the notification and who has not retained counsel is entitled to appointment of counsel.

(4) **Notice of Appearance**. A written notice of appearance must be submitted to the Board at least ten calendar days prior to the scheduled hearing date. The notice must include the name, address, telephone number, Board of Bar Overseers number, if applicable, and signature of the authorized representative, as well as the name and sex offender number of the offender he or she will be representing. If the authorized representative is not an attorney, he or she shall also submit a written authorization signed and dated by the sex offender.

(5) **Self-representation**. The sex offender may represent himself or herself at the hearing. The Hearing Examiner shall require the offender to sign a statement, or affirm under oath in the case of video-conference hearings, that he or she has been informed of his or her right to have representation and that he or she has knowingly and voluntarily waived that right. The sex offender representing himself or herself shall be placed under oath by the Hearing Examiner at the beginning of the hearing.

(6) **Notice of Withdrawal**. If an authorized representative is no longer representing the sex offender, the authorized representative must file a written notice of withdrawal with the Board. An authorized representative who is an attorney shall not be permitted to withdraw his or her appearance on the day of the scheduled hearing unless successor counsel is present and prepared to proceed

with the hearing or the offender is prepared to proceed by representing himself or herself, or another authorized representative is present and prepared to proceed with the hearing.

(7) An authorized representative may not testify as a witness at the hearing.

(8) The Board may have a staff person or an attorney represent it at the hearing. These individuals shall have the status of a party.

803 CMR 1.10. Scheduling of the Classification Hearing

(1) **In General**. The Board shall arrange the date, time and place of the classification hearing.

(2) **Notification**. Not less than 30 calendar days prior to the date of the classification hearing, the Board shall notify the sex offender or his or her representative, if a notice of appearance has been filed pursuant to 803 CMR 1.09(4), of the date, time and place of the hearing. At such time, the sex offender or his or her authorized representative shall also be provided with a copy of his or her classification file.

803 CMR 1.11. Rescheduling the Classification Hearing

(1) **Rescheduling by the Board**. The Board may change the date, time, or place of the classification hearing. The Board shall send written notification of any changes to the parties.

(2) **Sex Offender's Request to Reschedule Prior to the Hearing Date**.

(a) No later than three business days before a scheduled hearing, the offender may request, in writing, that his or her hearing be rescheduled. The written request must include an affidavit and supporting documentation explaining the reason(s) for the request to reschedule the hearing. A request to reschedule a hearing filed without a supporting affidavit or documentation will be denied.

(b) The Director of the Hearings Unit, or his or her designee, shall rule on all requests to reschedule hearings.

(c) In evaluating a sex offender's request to reschedule the hearing, the Board may consider such reasons as the following:

1. The amount of advance notice the sex offender had of the hearing date;

2. The reasons or circumstances provided in the affidavit;

3. The sex offender or his or her authorized representative's ability to anticipate the circumstances which resulted in the request to reschedule his or her hearing;

4. Delay by the sex offender in notifying the Board of his or her inability to attend the hearing; and

5. The number of previous requests to reschedule the hearing and the reasons provided in those previous requests.

(d) A request to reschedule a hearing based on a scheduling conflict of the sex offender's attorney will not be granted unless the attorney provides an affidavit identifying the following: case name, court and docket number, and the date the court issued its order requiring the attorney to appear.

(e) A request to reschedule a hearing based on the unavailability of a witness will not be granted unless the witness's absence was unforeseeable and the offender or his or her authorized representative demonstrates that his testimony is necessary for a fair hearing. Except as provided for in 803 CMR 1.17, the Hearing Examiner may grant leave to allow the witness, within a reasonable time, to submit written documents in lieu of live testimony.

(3) **Incarcerated and Civilly Committed Sex Offenders**. In addition to the reasons provided in 803 CMR 1.11(2) in evaluating the sex offender's request to reschedule hearing, the Board shall also consider the following:

(a) The sex offender's anticipated release date;

(b) Whether the sex offender has sought parole and status of his or her parole hearing;

(c) Whether the sex offender has filed a petition for discharge pursuant to M.G.L. c. 123A, § 9 and status of that petition; or

(d) Any other information relevant to the sex offender's anticipated release.

(4) **Allowance of the Request to Reschedule the Hearing**. If the Board approves the request to reschedule the hearing, the sex offender shall be notified in writing of the new date, time, and location of the hearing. The Board may provide this notice less than 30 calendar days before the rescheduled hearing date.

(5) **Denial of the Request to Reschedule the Hearing**. In denying the sex offender's request to reschedule, the Board shall provide, in writing, its reason for denying the motion. The hearing will go forward as scheduled pursuant to 803 CMR. 1.10.

803 CMR 1.12. Failure of Sex Offender to Appear at the Classification Hearing

(1) **Voluntary Waiver**. Failure of the sex offender to appear at the scheduled hearing without good cause shown will be deemed a voluntary waiver of his or her attendance at the hearing. The hearing shall proceed as scheduled, without the offender present. The Hearing Examiner shall make a final classification decision, pursuant to 803 CMR 1.20.

(2) **Good Cause to Reschedule Hearing**. If the sex offender fails to appear at the scheduled hearing, he or she shall have ten calendar days following the close of the hearing to file a request to reschedule the hearing for good cause. The written request must include an affidavit and supporting documentation explaining the reason(s) for the request to reschedule the hearing. A request to reschedule a hearing filed without a supporting affidavit or documentation will be denied.

To determine good cause, the presiding Hearing Examiner may consider such things as:

(a) The amount of advance notice the sex offender had of the hearing date;

(b) The reasons or circumstances that resulted in his or her inability to appear at the hearing; and

(c) The timing of the sex offender's notification to the Board that he or she was unable to appear at the scheduled hearing.

(3) If the Hearing Examiner determines that the offender has provided good cause for failing to appear at the scheduled hearing, the Board shall reschedule the hearing to the earliest possible date. The sex offender shall be notified in writing of the new date, time, and location of the hearing. The Board may provide this notice less than 30 calendar days before the rescheduled hearing date.

(4) If the Hearing Examiner does not find that the sex offender had good cause for failing to appear at the hearing, the Hearing Examiner shall make a final classification decision pursuant to 803 CMR 1.20 and include, as part of the final decision, an order with his or her reasoning for denying the request to reschedule the hearing.

803 CMR 1.13. *Ex Parte* Communications

(1) **General Provisions**.

(a) No party to a classification proceeding before the Board shall submit to the Hearing Examiner or any employee of the agency who is or may reasonably be expected to be involved in the final decision making process any information, evidence, argument or advice, whether written or oral, regarding any matter at issue, unless such submission is offered openly during the course of the hearing or in writing after the hearing, if allowed pursuant to 803 CMR 1.18. A copy of any written submissions shall be offered immediately to all parties.

(b) 803 CMR 1.13(1) will apply from the time the sex offender requests a hearing to challenge his or her recommended classification under 803 CMR 1.08 until the final classification is issued pursuant to 803 CMR 1.20.

(2) **Exceptions**.

(a) 803 CMR 1.13(1) does not apply to the process set forth in 803 CMR 1.06(5) for juvenile sex offenders and adult sex offenders whose only sex offense(s) was committed as a juvenile.

(b) 803 CMR 1.13(1) does not apply to consultation among Board employees concerning the internal administrative functions or procedures of the Board.

803 CMR 1.14. Classification Hearings

(1) **Scope of the Classification Hearing**. The hearing shall be a de novo review of the evidence and be limited to determining, by clear and convincing evidence, the sex offender's duty to register and, if applicable, his or her final classification level. The Board shall bear the burden of proof.

(2) **Closed to Public**. Hearings held by the Board are not open to the public. For purposes of 803 CMR 1.14(2), correctional staff required by the facility to be present at the hearing shall not be considered members of the public.

(3) The hearing may be conducted via video conference.

(4) **Conduct of the Hearing**. The Hearing Examiner shall govern the conduct of every phase of the hearing, including, but not limited to, the interpretation and construction of 803 CMR 1.00 and the conduct of all parties. All parties, authorized representatives, witnesses and other persons present shall conduct themselves in a professional manner consistent with the standards of decorum commonly observed in the courts of the Commonwealth. If a party's conduct interferes with the orderly presentation of the evidence, the Hearing Examiner may take any appropriate action, including, but not limited to, continuing the hearing in the absence of the offending participant and rendering a decision based on the evidence admitted.

(5) **Order of Presentation**. Unless otherwise determined by the Hearing Examiner, the Board proceeds first at all stages in the hearing, except that the Board proceeds last with its closing argument.

(6) **Swearing in of Witnesses**. A witness's testimony shall be under oath or affirmation, administered by the Hearing Examiner.

803 CMR 1.15. Subpoenas

(1) Any party to the classification hearing shall have the right to subpoena witnesses and documents in accordance with M.G.L. c. 30A, § 12.

(2) **Petition to Modify or Vacate Subpoena**. Pursuant to M.G.L. c. 30A, § 12(3) and (4), a subpoena may be modified or vacated by the presiding Hearing Examiner at the request of the subpoenaed witness. If a witness petitions the Board to modify or vacate a subpoena, the presiding Hearing Examiner shall promptly notify the parties.

In acting upon such a request, the presiding Hearing Examiner may grant a petition, in whole or in part, after considering whether:

(a) the testimony or evidence sought is relevant or reasonably related to the classification hearing;

(b) the subpoena adequately describes the evidence required;

(c) compliance with the subpoena poses an unreasonable burden on the witness; or

(d) the testimony or documents requested fall within a constitutional or statutory privilege.

(3) **Failure to Comply with Subpoena**. Pursuant to M.G.L. c. 30A, § 12(6), if a witness fails to comply with a subpoena issued in the name of the Board that has not been revoked or modified pursuant to 803 CMR 1.15(2), the Board or the party who requested the subpoena be issued may apply to the Superior Court for an order directing the witness to comply.

(4) **Timing to Request Subpoena from the Board**. A subpoena request must be made in writing and directed to the presiding Hearing Examiner. The written request must set forth the name, address and date of birth of the witness and additionally, the substance of the witness's expected testimony. All subpoena requests must be filed no later than 21 business days prior to the hearing date.

803 CMR 1.16. Motions

(1) **General Provisions**. All motions, unless made during the classification hearing, shall be in writing. All motions and rulings will be included in the administrative record of the hearing. The Hearing Examiner shall have the discretion to rule on any motion at the time it is made or to reserve ruling until a later time, including as part of the final decision issued pursuant to 803 CMR 1.20.

Motions to reschedule hearings are addressed exclusively in 803 CMR 1.11.

(2) **Written Motions**.

(a) **Grounds and Affidavit**. All written motions shall state the specific grounds for the motion and shall set forth the action or order that is sought. Affidavits and other documents in support of the motion must be attached to the motion upon filing.

(b) **Oral Argument**. The Hearing Examiner may hear oral argument on motions at the hearing.

(c) **Timely Filing**. Parties shall file all written motions no later than ten calendar days prior to the scheduled hearing date.

(d) **Service and Notice**. A copy of any motion, including all supporting affidavits and documents, must be served on the other party at the same time the originals are filed with the Board's Hearings Unit.

(e) **Opposition to Motion**. Oppositions to any motion may be submitted in writing or argued orally at the hearing.

(f) **Record**. All written motions and rulings will be included in the administrative record of the hearing.

(3) **Oral Motions**. If a motion is made orally at the hearing, the Hearing Examiner may request that the motion and any opposition be reduced to writing.

(4) **Motion for Expert Funds**. An offender who has been deemed indigent pursuant to 803 CMR 1.09 may file a written motion for expert funds at least ten calendar days before the scheduled hearing.

(a) The written motion for expert funds must:

1. identify a condition or circumstance special to the sex offender and explain how that condition is connected to his or her risk of reoffense or level of dangerousness;

2. identify the particular type of Expert Witness who would provide testimony to assist the Hearing Examiner in his or her understanding and analysis; and

3. include supporting documentation or affidavits verifying the specific condition or circumstance that the offender suffers from.

Any motion that fails to meet the criteria in 803 CMR 1.16(4) may be denied prior to the hearing.

(b) Motions for funds for the purpose of an expert to provide a general opinion on the sex offender's risk to reoffend and degree of dangerousness will be deemed insufficient and denied prior to the hearing.

(c) When a motion for expert funds is allowed, the presiding Hearing Examiner shall issue an order requiring the sex offender to provide an affidavit from the proposed Expert Witness. At minimum, the affidavit must include the following:

1. identification of the expert's area of expertise, including a copy of the expert's curriculum vitae;

2. summary of the anticipated opinion and testimony of the Expert Witness paying particular attention to the condition or circumstance identified by the sex offender in his or her motion for expert funds with an explanation as to how that condition or circumstance correlates to the sex offender's risk to reoffend or degree of dangerousness; and

3. the Expert Witness's hourly fee and estimated number of hours that the Expert Witness expects will be required to conduct an evaluation, prepare a written report to be admitted as evidence at the hearing, and testify at the hearing.

(d) As part of the order allowing the motion for expert funds, the Hearing Examiner shall include deadlines for:

1. the sex offender to submit to the Board the Expert Witness's affidavit and a copy of the expert's written report that will be submitted as evidence at the hearing; and

2. scheduling the hearing for the expert testimony.

(e) If the sex offender fails to comply with the Hearing Examiner's order, the Hearing Examiner may withdraw the order and deny the motion for expert funds.

(5) **Motion to Reopen the Record**. At any time after the close of evidence and prior to the issuance of the final decision pursuant to 803 CMR 1.20, a party may move to reopen the record to submit new evidence.

(a) For purposes of this motion, "new evidence" consists of newly discovered evidence which, by due diligence, could not have been discovered prior to the close of the evidence at the hearing by the party seeking to offer it.

(b) The moving party shall include a copy of the newly discovered evidence and provide the reason(s) explaining why the evidence was not discovered prior to the close of evidence at the hearing and how the evidence is relevant to the Hearing Examiner's analysis.

(c) The non-moving party shall have ten calendar days to oppose the motion.

(d) The presiding Hearing Examiner may rule on this motion as part of the written final classification decision.

(6) **Motion for Reconsideration**. After the final decision has been issued pursuant to 803 CMR 1.20 and before the expiration of the time for filing a complaint for judicial review pursuant to M.G.L. c. 30A, a party may move for reconsideration. The motion must clearly identify at least one of the following criteria:

(a) a clerical or mechanical error in the final decision;

(b) a significant factor that the Hearing Examiner overlooked in making the final classification level; or

(c) a material change in the sex offender's circumstances that was not foreseeable at the time of the hearing.

A properly filed motion for reconsideration shall be deemed a motion for rehearing pursuant to M.G.L. c. 30A, § 14(1) for the purposes of tolling the time to file a complaint for judicial review. The filing of this motion will not alter the final classification level or stay dissemination of registration information.

803 CMR 1.17. Discovery Obligations and Witness Disclosures

(1) **Board's Discovery Obligations**.

(a) At the same time the Board notifies the sex offender of the arrangements for his or her classification hearing pursuant to 803 CMR 1.10, the Board shall also provide him or her with a copy of his or her classification file.

(b) No later than ten calendar days before the scheduled hearing, the Board shall send to the sex offender, or his or her authorized representative, a copy of any additional documents the Board intends to introduce into evidence at the classification hearing.

(c) A Board employee shall redact data from Board's discovery documents that are deemed to be privileged, confidential, investigatory, intelligence information, or information that identifies a victim. Such redacted data shall not: be introduced into evidence; be communicated to the Hearing Examiner; or become part of the record.

(2) **Sex Offender's Discovery Obligations**. No later than ten calendar days before the scheduled hearing, the offender shall provide the Board with copies of all documents he or she intends to introduce as evidence at the classification hearing.

(3) **Witnesses**. No later than ten calendar days before the scheduled hearing, each party shall provide the Board's Hearings Unit with a complete witness list. A witness list is not complete unless it includes all of the following information for each witness: the name, address, date of birth, and relationship to the offender (e.g., family member, therapist, Expert Witness, etc.). The Hearing Examiner shall exclude the testimony of any witness not properly identified on the witness list. The failure to provide sufficient information may result in a witness being denied entry into correctional facilities.

(4) The Hearing Examiner may permit a party to supplement or amend a witness list no later than five calendar days prior to the scheduled hearing date only if the moving party provides good cause for the additional time.

(5) **Expert Witnesses**.

(a) If a party intends to rely on the opinion of an Expert Witness at the classification hearing, a report or a written substantive summary of the Expert Witness's anticipated testimony must be provided to the other party at least ten calendar days prior to the scheduled hearing date. This report or summary must include the name of each Expert Witness who is anticipated to testify, the subject matter of such testimony, and the substance of the facts and opinions of the anticipated testimony. The party intending to rely on an Expert Witness shall also provide the curriculum vitae of the Expert Witness.

(b) Failure to comply with 803 CMR 1.17(5)(a) will result in the exclusion of an Expert Witness's report and testimony from evidence.

(c) At the classification hearing, a party shall be permitted to introduce into evidence an Expert Witness's written report, including his or her opinion as to the offender's risk of reoffense and/or dangerousness, only if the author of the report is called to testify at the hearing and is otherwise qualified as an expert in the area that he or she is being called to testify. The failure to call the Expert Witness to testify at the hearing will result in the exclusion of so much of the report as expresses the Expert Witness's opinion as to the sex offender's risk of reoffense or degree of dangerousness.

(d) **Board's Intention to Rely on Expert Witness at Hearing**. Pursuant to M.G.L. c. 6, § 178L, in any case where the Board intends to rely on the testimony or report of an Expert Witness, as defined in 803 CMR 1.03, the Board shall notify the sex offender or his or her authorized representative of this intention. In the event that the Board intends to rely on an Expert Witness and the sex offender has been found to be indigent, the Board shall notify the offender or his or her authorized representative that he or she may apply for and the Board may grant the payment of fees for an Expert Witness.

803 CMR 1.18. Evidence

(1) **General**. Pursuant to M.G.L. c. 30A, § 11(2), the rules of evidence observed by courts shall not apply to classification hearings, but the rules of privilege recognized by law shall be observed. Evidence may be admitted and given probative effect only if it is the kind of evidence on which reasonable persons are accustomed to rely on in the conduct of serious affairs. The Hearing Examiner may exclude irrelevant, unreliable, and repetitive evidence.

(2) **Presentation at Hearing**. Evidence will not be considered unless it is presented at the hearing or accepted by the Hearing Examiner in conjunction with a motion to reopen the record under 803 CMR 1.16(5). The Hearing Examiner may, upon request of a party for good cause shown, hold the record open to receive additional evidence for a specified period of time after the hearing. When additional evidence is admitted post-hearing, the other party must be granted a specific period of time to review the evidence and submit a written response.

(3) **Oral Testimony**. Each witness shall testify under oath or affirmation. Each witness shall be available for direct examination and cross-examination.

(4) **Stipulations**. The parties may, by written stipulation filed with the Hearing Examiner at any stage of the proceeding or by oral stipulation made at the hearing, agree as to the truth of any fact pertinent to the proceedings.

803 CMR 1.19. Duties and Powers of the Hearing Examiner

(1) The duties of a presiding Hearing Examiner shall include, but are not limited to, the following:

(a) to maintain a list of the names and addresses of all individuals who are in attendance at the hearing;

(b) to administer the oath or affirmation to each witness prior to his or her testimony;

(c) to assist all witnesses in making a full and free statement of the facts in order to bring out all the information necessary to decide the issues involved;

(d) to ensure orderly presentation of the evidence;

(e) to ensure that all parties have a full opportunity to present their claims at the scheduled hearing;

(f) to receive, rule on, exclude, or limit evidence;

(g) to receive and rule on all motions; and

(h) to assess the reliability of the exhibits introduced into evidence and credibility of witnesses; draw all reasonable inferences therefrom; and render a fair, independent and impartial decision based on the issues and evidence presented and in accordance with the law.

(2) The powers of the presiding Hearing Examiner shall include, but are not limited to, the following:

(a) to limit attendance or assign seating, or both, at the hearing in consideration of security, space availability, privacy and confidentiality;

(b) to request that parties produce additional evidence;

(c) to examine witnesses;

(d) to rule on any motions or requests made during the hearing;

(e) to regulate the presentation of evidence and the participation of the parties for the purposes of ensuring an adequate and comprehensive record of the hearing;

(f) to change the date, time or place of the hearing on his or her own motion or at the request of any Party, upon due notice to all parties;

(g) to continue a hearing that is in progress. All parties shall be notified of the date, time and place of the continued hearing;

(h) to request that parties submit post-hearing briefs and/or proposed findings; and

(i) to take notice of any fact which may be judicially noticed by courts, as well as general, technical or scientific facts within the Board's specialized knowledge, pursuant to M.G.L. c. 30A, § 11(5).

803 CMR 1.20. Hearing Examiner's Final Decision

(1) **Written Decision**. Pursuant to M.G.L. c. 30A, § 11(7) and (8), after the classification hearing the Hearing Examiner shall issue a final written decision containing the following:

(a) statement of the issues involved in the hearing;

(b) summary and analysis of the evidence, including credibility and reliability determinations, as needed;

(c) specific findings of fact on all relevant disputed factual matters;

(d) rulings of law on all relevant disputed legal issues;

(e) conclusions drawn from the findings of fact and rulings of law which form the basis of the final registration determination and classification level; and

(f) final registration determination and classification level.

For purposes of judicial review, pursuant to M.G.L. c. 30A and M.G.L. c. 6, § 178M, the Hearing Examiner's final written decision shall be considered the final agency action.

(2) The Hearing Examiner may maintain, decrease, or increase the Board's recommended classification level in reaching his or her final decision. The Hearing Examiner shall consider the relevant and credible evidence and reasonable inferences derived therefrom to determine:

(a) the offender's risk of reoffense;

(b) the offender's dangerousness as a function of the severity and extent of harm the offender would present to the public in the event of reoffense; and

(c) in consideration of the foregoing, whether and to what degree public access to the offender's personal and sex offender information, pursuant to M.G.L. c. 6, § 178K, is in the interest of public safety.

(3) **Relief from Registration**. In a manner consistent with M.G.L. c. 6, § 178K(2)(d) and 803 CMR 1.29, the Hearing Examiner may find that the offender has no obligation to register as a sex offender. The Hearing Examiner shall make written findings providing reasons for relieving the sex offender from his or her duty to register.

(4) **Unavailable Hearing Examiner**. If the Hearing Examiner becomes unavailable before completing his or her decision, the Chair or the Chair's designee shall appoint a successor to assume the case and render the decision. If the presentation of evidence has been completed and the record is closed, the successor shall decide the case on the basis of the record, unless testimony was taken. In those cases, the hearing shall be reconvened before the successor examiner for taking of the testimony again. If the evidence portion of the hearing has not been completed when the successor is assigned, the successor may either proceed with the hearing where it left off or require the presentation of evidence from the beginning. If the successor proceeds with the hearing where it left off, the Board shall provide the successor and the parties with a copy of the transcript, or completed portions thereof, without cost.

803 CMR 1.21. Hearing Examiner's Decision as the Final Sex Offender Registry Board Decision

(1) The Hearing Examiner's decision shall be the final Sex Offender Registry Board decision, except as expressly provided in 803 CMR 1.16(6) and (7) and 1.21.

(2) Judicial review, pursuant to M.G.L. c. 30A, § 14, is not available to the Board to correct errors in a Hearing Examiner's decision. Pursuant to 803 CMR 1.21, the Board shall be authorized to review a Hearing Examiner's final decision or any finding or ruling within the final decision on its own initiative or upon request by the Board's General Counsel, when any of the following grounds are presented:

(a) the decision is based upon an error of law;

(b) the decision is not in conformity with procedural due process standards;

(c) the decision is unsupported by substantial evidence;

(d) the decision is the result of arbitrary or capricious conduct;

(e) the decision is the result of an abuse of discretion; or

(f) the decision is not in conformity with the law.

(3) To request a review of a Hearing Examiner's decision, the Board's General Counsel or the General Counsel's designee shall file a written request for review.

(a) The written request shall state the grounds for seeking review, as outlined in 803 CMR 1.21(2)(a) through (f), and the reason that review is appropriate, and cite to the information from the hearing record which supports the review requested. The written request for review shall be filed with the Chair or the Chair's designee within ten days of the issuance date of the Hearing Examiner's decision. Notice of the submission of a written request for review shall be made pursuant to 803 CMR 1.23(1). The offender or his or her authorized representative may file a response to the written request for review within ten days of receipt, addressing any of the matters contained in the request. The filing of a written request for review shall stay the effect of the Hearing Examiner's decision for purposes of judicial review, registration and dissemination.

(b) The majority of the Board's sitting members shall determine whether to grant the written request for review. Notice of the

Board's determination on whether to grant the written request for review shall be made pursuant to 803 CMR 1.23(1). If the Board grants the written request for review, the Hearing Examiner's decision shall continue to be stayed for purposes of judicial review, registration and dissemination.

(4) If the Board grants review, the classification hearing shall be deemed re-opened. The Board may decide the issue based solely on the written request for review and the offender's response, if any, or may direct the parties to file additional memoranda of law before deciding the issue or issues before it. The majority of the Board's sitting members shall determine whether the Hearing Examiner's final decision was in error. The Board shall issue a written decision and shall notify the parties of its decision pursuant to 803 CMR 1.23(1). If the Board finds no error, the Hearing Examiner's decision shall become final. Notice of the Board's finding shall be made pursuant to 803 CMR 1.23(1). The date that the notice is received by the offender or his or her authorized representative shall govern the time for filing a petition for judicial review, the time for registration and the dissemination of offender information as mandated by the sex offender registry laws.

(5) If the Board determines that the Hearing Examiner's decision was in error, in whole or in part, the Board shall proceed in one of two ways:

(a) The Board may issue a decision setting aside a portion or portions of the Hearing Examiner's decision. In such cases, the Board shall issue a decision stating with specificity the portion or portions that it is setting aside and its reasons for setting them aside. The Board's decision shall incorporate by reference the portions of the original Hearing Examiner's decision that it intends to uphold. The Board's revised decision shall be the final agency decision. Notice of the Board's revised decision shall be made pursuant to 803 CMR 1.23(1). The date that the revised decision is received by the offender or his or her authorized representative, shall govern the time for filing a petition for judicial review, the time for registration and the dissemination of offender information as mandated by the sex offender registry laws.

(b) The Board may issue a decision setting aside the Hearing Examiner's decision in its entirety. In such cases, the Board shall issue a decision stating with specificity the reasons for its action and remand the case back to the Hearing Examiner. Notice of the Board's decision shall be made pursuant to 803 CMR 1.23 (1). The Hearing Examiner's new decision shall be the final agency decision. Notice of the Hearing Examiner's new decision shall be made pursuant to 803 CMR 1.23(1). The date that the new decision is received by the offender or his or her authorized representative, shall govern the time for filing a petition for judicial review, the time for registration and the dissemination of offender information as mandated by the sex offender registry laws.

(6) The Board's General Counsel or General Counsel's designee may file a written request for Board review of the Hearing Examiner's new decision if, in the opinion of the General Counsel or the General Counsel's designee, the Hearing Examiner's new decision fails to correct the error or errors that caused the decision to be remanded or if the new decision contains additional errors that meet the criteria of 803 CMR 1.21(2). The same process set forth in 803 CMR 1.21(3) shall apply if a written request for review is submitted by the General Counsel or General Counsel's designee at this stage.

(7) All documents considered by the Board during the review process described in 803 CMR 1.20 shall be included in the record that is filed by the Board's attorney in any judicial review case initiated pursuant to M.G.L. c. 30A, § 14.

803 CMR 1.22. Administrative Record

(1) **General Principles**. Pursuant to M.G.L. c. 30A, § 11(4), all documents, testimony and other evidence offered and accepted into evidence by the Hearing Examiner shall become part of the administrative record. For purposes of judicial review, the record shall include the Hearing Examiner's final decision issued pursuant to 803 CMR 1.20.

(2) **Excluded Evidence**. Any evidence offered at the hearing, but not accepted by the Hearing Examiner will be marked for identification purposes only and be included in the record.

(3) **Transcript of Hearing**.

(a) All evidence and testimony at the hearing will be recorded electronically, digitally, stenographically, or by any other recording device deemed necessary or appropriate by the Board, in its discretion. The Board shall incur the cost of recording. Pursuant to M.G.L. c. 30A, § 11(6), transcripts will be made and supplied to the sex offender or his or her authorized representative, upon written request, at the offender's expense, and in accordance with any procedures the Board may establish. Upon written request, a sex offender who has been determined to be indigent for the classification hearing shall receive a transcript at no cost.

(b) Corrections to the transcript are permitted at the discretion of the Hearing Examiner. The Hearing Examiner may accept corrections by agreement of the parties, or if the parties cannot agree, the Hearing Examiner may accept recommended corrections from each party to determine what corrections, if any, are necessary.

(4) The administrative record is not available to the public.

803 CMR 1.23. Notification of the Final Decision

(1) Notification of the final decision made pursuant to 803 CMR 1.20 will be mailed to the sex offender and his or her authorized representative as soon as practicable. The sex offender or his or her authorized representative may request in writing, at the time of his or her administrative hearing, that the final decision made pursuant to 803 CMR 1.20 be sent to him or her via facsimile.

(2) **Relief from Registration**. If the final decision is to relieve the sex offender from his or her obligation to register as set forth in M.G.L. c. 6, § 178K and 803 CMR 1.20(3), the Board shall promptly remove information pertaining to the offender from the Sex Offender Registry.

(3) **Duty to Register and Final Classification Level**. If the final decision requires the sex offender to register and a final classification level is assigned, pursuant to M.G.L. c. 6, §§ 178K and 178L, the notification shall also inform the sex offender of his or her registration obligations as set forth in M.G.L. c. 6, §§ 178F or 178F½, and 178Q.

803 CMR 1.24. Judicial Review

(1) **Notification**. The written notifications of the final decision sent pursuant to 803 CMR 1.23 must inform the sex offender or his or her authorized representative of his or her right to seek judicial review of the final decision, pursuant to M.G.L c. 30A and M.G.L. c. 6, § 178M.

(2) Pursuant to M.G.L. c. 30A, § 14, the sex offender has the right to pursue judicial review within 30 calendar days from the date of receipt of the final Sex Offender Registry Board decision.

(3) Pursuant to M.G.L. c. 6, § 178M and M.G.L. c. 30A, § 14, the filing of a complaint for judicial review will not alter the final classification level or stay the sex offender's registration requirements or the dissemination of registration information.

803 CMR 1.25. Transmission of the Final Decision to Law Enforcement

(1) **General Principles**. Pursuant to M.G.L. c. 6, § 178K(2)(a) through (c), the Board shall transmit all final registration and classification information to law enforcement.

(2) **No Duty to Register**. If the Board's final decision is to relieve or terminate a sex offender's duty to register, the Board shall promptly remove the sex offender's information from the sex offender registry and notify:

(a) police departments in municipalities where such sex offender lives and works, or where the sex offender intends to live and work upon release and where the offense was committed;

(b) police departments in municipalities, including campus police departments or other state recognized law enforcement agencies at any school, where the sex offender works and/or attends an Institution of Higher Learning or where the sex offender intends to work and/or attend an Institution of Higher Learning upon release; and

(c) the Federal Bureau of Investigation.

(3) **Duty to Register and Final Classification**. If the Board's final decision is that the sex offender has a duty to register and a final classification level is assigned, the Board shall, within three business days of reaching the decision, transmit the final registration and classification information to:

(a) police departments in municipalities where such sex offender lives and works, or where the sex offender intends to live and work upon release and where the offense was committed;

(b) police departments in municipalities, including campus police departments or other state recognized law enforcement agencies at an Institution of Higher Learning, where the sex offender works and/or attends an Institution of Higher Learning or where the sex offender intends to work and/or attend an Institution of Higher Learning upon release; and

(c) the Federal Bureau of Investigation.

803 CMR 1.26. Registration Requirements and Dissemination of Information

(1) A sex offender who has not been finally classified or is finally classified as a Level 1 sex offender shall register annually in accordance with the requirements in M.G.L. c. 6, §§ 178E, 178F and 178Q. The general public shall not have access to this sex offender information, pursuant to M.G.L. c. 6, §§ 178D, 178I, 178J and 178K(2)(a).

(2) A sex offender who is finally classified as a Level 2 or Level 3 sex offender shall register in accordance with the requirements in M.G.L. c. 6, §§ 178E, 178F½ and 178Q. The public shall have access to this sex offender information, pursuant to M.G.L. c. 6, §§ 178D, 178I, 178J and 178K(2)(b) and (c).

(3) A Level 3 sex offender designated as a sexually violent predator, pursuant to M.G.L. c. 6, § 178K(1)(c) shall register in accordance with the requirements in M.G.L. c. 6, §§ 178E, 178F½ and 178Q. The public shall have access to this sex offender information, pursuant to M.G.L. c. 6, §§ 178D, 178I, 178J and 178K(2)(b) and (c),

(4) **Dissemination of Information to Victims**. Upon the request of a victim who has enrolled with the Board's Victim Services Unit, the Board may inform that victim of the sex offender's final registration and classification determination.

(5) **Updating Information**. Pursuant to M.G.L. c. 6, § 178D, the Board is required to keep the registry up-to-date and accurate. Pursuant to M.G.L. c. 6, §§ 178E, 178F and 178F½, the sex offender is required to verify that his or her registration data is current and accurate. Upon verifying registration data or giving notice of a change of address or intended change of address, the sex offender shall provide independent written verification of the address at which he or she is registered or, if changing address, will be registered. For purposes of 803 CMR 1.26(5), independent written verification shall include:

Any two types of the following five types of unaltered original documents bearing the name of the sex offender and his or her present address:

(a) rent or mortgage receipt;

(b) utility bill;

(c) bank or credit card statement;

(d) passport, driver's license or official photo identification issued by the Registry of Motor Vehicles; and

(e) any other current written document the Sex Offender Registry Board deems sufficient.

With the exception of a passport, driver's license or official photo identification issued by the Registry of Motor Vehicles, all other documentation must be dated within 45 days of presentation to the Sex Offender Registry Board or the police department.

(6) **Sex Offender Registration Fee.**

(a) Pursuant to M.G.L. c. 6, § 178Q, the sex offender shall pay an annual sex offender registration fee to the Board.

(b) **Waiver**. The sex offender may request that the Board waive payment of the sex offender registry fee. The request must be made on a form approved by the Board and submitted to the Board at the time the sex offender submits his or her registration form to the Board. The Board may waive the fee if it determines that payment would constitute an undue hardship on the offender or his or her family due to limited income, employment status, or any other relevant factor. The Board shall use the indigency standards developed pursuant to M.G.L. c. 211D to determine whether the payment of the fee constitutes an undue hardship on the offender. If the Board determines that payment of the fee is not an undue hardship, the Board shall notify the offender informing the offender that he or she must pay the fee within ten days of receiving the notice. If the Board determines that payment of the fee is an undue hardship, it shall waive the fee for the offender for one year. The offender may renew his or her request for a waiver when payment of his next annual fee is due.

803 CMR 1.27. Sex Offender Internet Database

(1) The information contained in the Sex Offender Internet Database, or website, pursuant to M.G.L. c. 6 §§ 178D and 178K(2), will be created and updated on a regular basis from the Sex Offender Registry, but must be kept physically separate from the Sex Offender Registry.

(2) The information contained in the Sex Offender Internet Database must not include the following information:

(a) pertaining to unclassified or Level 1 sex offenders and any Level 2 sex offender finally classified prior to July 12, 2013;

(b) identifying victims' names, addresses or relation to Level 2 and Level 3 sex offenders; and

(c) relating to requests for registration data under sections M.G.L. c. 6, §§ 178I and 178J.

(3) Pursuant to M.G.L. c. 6, § 178N, the Sex Offender Internet Database shall include a warning explaining the criminal penalties for use of sex offender registry information to commit a crime or to engage in illegal discrimination or harassment of a sex offender and the punishment for threatening to commit a crime under M.G.L. c. 275, § 4.

(4) The Board shall develop and implement policies, procedures, and protocols to update and maintain the Sex Offender Internet Database in order to:

(a) validate the accuracy, integrity, and security of information contained in the Sex Offender Internet Database;

(b) ensure the prompt and complete removal from the Sex Offender Internet Database of registration data for sex offenders whose duty to register has terminated or expired under M.G.L. c. 6, §§ 178G, 178L, or 178M or any other law or order of any Court; and

(c) protect against the inaccurate, improper, or inadvertent publication of registration information on the Internet.

803 CMR 1.28. Community Notification

(1) Pursuant to M.G.L. c. 6, § 178K(2)(c), the police department shall actively notify organizations and individual members of the public in the community that are likely to encounter a finally classified Level 3 sex offender or a sexually violent predator through a community notification plan. The community notification

plan shall require notification by the police department to all schools in the community. The chief of the police department may notify day care centers, youth programs, recreational programs, organizations providing elder services, and other organizations as deemed necessary to protect the public safety.

(2) The method of community notification may include, but is not limited to:

(a) publication of the information in local newspapers;

(b) public announcement via local cable television; and

(c) posting the information in the local town or city hall, libraries, and similar publicly accessible areas, as determined by the chief of police.

(3) As part of a community notification plan, the chief of the police department may put the registration information for Level 3 sex offenders who live, work, or attend school in the community on the police department's website. The police department's website must comply with M.G.L. c. 6, § 178D and 803 CMR 1.27 and must be regularly updated with information from the Sex Offender Registry. The chief shall develop and implement policies, procedures, and protocols such as those described in 803 CMR 1.27 for the department's website. The chief may include, on the department's website, a link to the Sex Offender Internet Database as described in 803 CMR 1.27.

(4) Police departments shall, at least once annually, actively disseminate Level 3 sex offender information. If a Level 3 offender has been designated a sexually violent predator, community notification shall occur every 90 calendar days. Community notification shall also occur each time a Level 3 sex offender changes his or her home address, secondary address, or work address, or enrolls as a student. Pursuant to M.G.L. c. 6, § 178K(c)(2), the Board and police may require or facilitate additional active dissemination if deemed necessary to protect the public.

803 CMR 1.29. Motion for Relief from Registration Obligation Prior to Final Classification

(1) **General Principles.** Pursuant to M.G.L. c. 6, § 178K(2)(d), a sex offender may submit to the Board a written motion seeking relief from a registration obligation. The burden of proof will be on the sex offender to show that he or she does not qualify as a sex offender as defined by M.G.L. c. 6, § 178C or does not pose a risk to reoffend or a danger to the public.

(2) **Filing.** A motion for relief from registration may be in the form of a letter or petition and must be filed with the Board:

(a) prior to or upon submitting the registration form pursuant to 803 CMR 1.05;

(b) upon submitting documentary evidence pursuant to 803 CMR 1.06 and 1.07; or

(c) at least ten business days before the date of a scheduled classification hearing, pursuant to 803 CMR 1.10.

(3) Any motion for relief from registration filed after the Board makes a final decision pursuant to 803 CMR 1.20 will be treated as a motion for termination pursuant to 803 CMR 1.30 or as a motion for reclassification pursuant to 803 CMR 1.31.

(4) Pursuant to M.G.L. c. 6, § 178K(2)(d), a sex offender is not eligible for relief from his or her duty to register if the offender:

(a) has been determined to be a sexually violent predator pursuant to M.G.L. c. 6, § 178K(2)(c);

(b) has been convicted of two or more sex offenses involving a child, as defined by M.G.L. c. 6, § 178C, committed on different occasions;

(c) has been convicted of a sexually violent offense, as defined by M.G.L. c. 6, § 178C; or

(d) has been convicted of a sex offense involving a child, and has not already registered for at least ten years.

(5) **Motions Filed During Recommendation Process.**

(a) If the Board allows the motion for relief from registration during the recommendation process pursuant to 803 CMR 1.06 through 1.08, the Board shall make specific findings and provide written notification to the sex offender. The Board shall promptly remove information pertaining to the offender from the sex offender registry.

(b) If the Board notifies the sex offender that he or she has a duty to register pursuant to 803 CMR 1.08, the motion for relief shall be deemed denied. The sex offender may file a new motion for relief prior to the hearing, pursuant to 803 CMR 1.29(2)(c), to be decided as part of the classification process, pursuant to 803 CMR 1.29(6).

(6) **Motions Filed During Classification Process.**

(a) If the Board denies the sex offender's motion for relief during the recommendation process and the offender has requested a hearing, or if the sex offender has applied for relief pursuant to 803 CMR 1.29(2)(c) the classification hearing shall proceed.

(b) At the hearing, the sex offender shall have the burden to prove by clear and convincing evidence that he or she is eligible for relief and that the circumstances of the sex offender's offense in conjunction with the offender's criminal history do not indicate a risk of reoffense or a danger to the public.

(c) If the Hearing Examiner allows the motion for relief from registration after the classification hearing, the Hearing Examiner shall make specific findings and provide written notification to the sex offender, pursuant to M.G.L. c. 6, § 178K(2)(d) and 803 CMR 1.20. The Board shall promptly remove information pertaining to the offender from the sex offender registry.

803 CMR 1.30. Motion to Terminate Registration Obligation

(1) **General Principles.** Pursuant to M.G.L. c. 6, § 178G, a sex offender whose registration and classification determination has become final pursuant to M.G.L. c. 6, § 178L(2) and 803 CMR 1.08 and 1.20, may file a written motion with the Board to terminate his or her obligation to register. The burden of proof will be on the sex offender to show by clear and convincing evidence that he or she has not committed a sex offense within ten years following conviction, adjudication or release from all custody or supervision, whichever last occurs, and that he or she does not pose a risk to reoffend or a danger to the public.

(2) **Filing and Form of the Motion.**

(a) In his or her motion, the sex offender shall include his full name, date of birth, address, sex offender number (SON), name and address of legal representative (if applicable), and name and address of legal guardian (if applicable).

(b) In his or her motion, the sex offender shall include proof, by clear and convincing evidence, that he or she has not committed a sex offense within ten years following the date of conviction, adjudication or release from all custody or supervision, whichever last occurs. In addition, the sex offender shall provide clear and convincing evidence that he or she is not likely to pose a risk to reoffend or a danger to the safety of others.

(c) Any motion for termination filed before a sex offender's registration and classification determination has become final will be treated as motion for relief from registration pursuant to 803 CMR 1.29.

(d) The Board may summarily deny, without a hearing, an offenders motion for termination if:

1. the offender is incarcerated;

2. the offender has pending criminal charges;

3. the offender's last classification decision is currently under Judicial Review pursuant to M.G.L. c. 30A, § 14 or on appeal, or on review by the Board as a result of an order by a court of the Commonwealth or a federal court.

The Board will notify the offender, in writing, the substantive reasons for summarily denying the motion for termination. The denial of a motion for termination under 803 CMR 1.30(2) is not subject to Judicial Review. 803 CMR 1.30(2)(d) does not apply to offenders whose only sex offense was a result of an adjudication as a youthful offender or as a delinquent juvenile.

(3) Pursuant to M.G.L. c. 6, § 178G, a sex offender is not eligible for termination if the offender:

(a) has been determined to be a sexually violent predator pursuant to M.G.L. c. 6, § 178K(2)(c);

(b) has been convicted of two or more sex offenses involving a child, as defined by M.G.L. c. 6, § 178C, committed on different occasions;

(c) has been convicted of a sexually violent offense, as defined by M.G.L. c. 6, § 178C; or

(d) has been convicted of a sex offense involving a child and has not already registered for at least ten years.

(4) A sex offender whose only sex offense was the result of an adjudication as a youthful offender or as a delinquent juvenile may file a motion to terminate at any time after he or she is finally classified notwithstanding the provisions in 803 CMR 1.30(1).

(5) By filing a motion for termination, the offender authorizes the Board to obtain any information accessible under M.G.L. c. 6, §§ 178E and 178K(3) to assist in its review of the offender's motion.

(6) **Termination Hearing Process**. The Chair may appoint a panel of Hearing Examiners or a single Hearing Examiner to conduct the hearing on the sex offender's motion for termination.

(a) The Board will notify the sex offender in writing of the date, time and location of the termination hearing. An offender may waive his or her right to appear at the hearing before the Board. If an offender does not appear at his or her hearing, the Board shall treat the offender's failure to appear as a waiver of his or her appearance and shall proceed to rule on the offender's motion, unless the offender presents good cause within three calendar days of the hearing.

(b) No later than five calendar days before the scheduled hearing date, the sex offender may submit a written request to reschedule the hearing for good cause.

(c) No later than 20 calendar days before the scheduled hearing date, the Board and offender shall exchange all additional information intended to be submitted to the panel or Hearing Examiner.

(d) The sex offender may be represented at the hearing by privately retained counsel or an authorized representative.

(e) Motions for termination shall be decided on new and updated information not available at the time of the original classification. This does not foreclose the panel or Hearing Examiner from considering the information relied on by the Board to determine the sex offender's classification levels, including any prior written decisions issued by the Board.

(7) **Decision on Motion for Termination**. The panel or Hearing Examiner shall determine whether the sex offender has met his or her burden by clear and convincing evidence that he or she is not likely to pose a risk to reoffend or a danger to the safety of others. Pursuant to M.G.L. c. 30A, § 11(7) and (8), the panel or Hearing Examiner shall make specific written findings detailing the reasons for its decision after the hearing. For purposes of judicial review, pursuant to M.G.L. c. 30A, § 14 and M.G.L. c. 6, § 178M, these written findings shall be considered the final agency action.

(8) **Notification of Decision**.

(a) Notification of the decision on a motion for termination made pursuant to 803 CMR 1.30(7) will be mailed to the sex offender and his or her authorized representative, if applicable, as soon as practicable. The sex offender or his or her authorized representative may request in writing, at the time of his administrative hearing, that the final decision made pursuant to 803 CMR 1.20 be sent to him or her via facsimile.

(b) The decision will inform the sex offender of his or her right to seek judicial review of the final decision, pursuant to M.G.L c. 30A § 14 and M.G.L. c. 6, § 178M. Pursuant to M.G.L. c. 30A, § 14, the sex offender has right to pursue judicial review within 30 calendar days from the date of receipt of the final Sex Offender Registry Board decision. The filing of a complaint for judicial review will not alter the final agency decision or stay the sex offender's registration requirements or the dissemination of registration information.

(9) A sex offender may re-apply for termination, following the same procedures, three years after the date the Board denied the motion or after the final disposition in court, whichever is later.

803 CMR 1.31. Sex Offender's Request for Reclassification

(1) **General Principles**. The Board recognizes the risk to reoffend and the degree of dangerousness posed by a sex offender may decrease over time. The burden of proof shall be on the sex offender to show that his or her risk of reoffense and degree of dangerousness posed to the public have decreased following his or her final classification.

(2) **Requirements for Motion for Reclassification**.

(a) No sooner than three years after the date of his final classification pursuant to 803 CMR 1.08, or 803 CMR 1.20, a sex offender who is finally classified as a Level 2 or 3 sex offender may file a written motion with the Board to re-examine his or her classification level. Sex offenders who have been convicted of a new sex offense may not seek reclassification sooner than ten years from the date of the last classification decision.

(b) In his or her motion, the sex offender shall include his or her full name, date of birth, address, sex offender number (SON), name and address of legal representative (if applicable), name and address of legal guardian (if applicable), the classification level sought, and grounds for seeking reclassification.

(c) In his or her motion, the sex offender shall include proof, by clear and convincing evidence, that his or her risk of reoffense and the degree of dangerousness he or she poses to the public have decreased since his or her final classification. In support of his or her motion, the sex offender shall attach documentation that supports his or her request for reclassification, including information pertaining to:

1. participation or completion of sex offender treatment (Factor 32);

2. stability of current environment and support systems (Factors 33 and 34);

3. successful completion of probation (Factor 28);

4. physical condition (Factor 31);

5. psychological or psychiatric profiles indicating his or her risk to reoffend (Factor 35); and

6. substance-free and offense-free lifestyle in the community (Factors 9 and 29).

The offender may include with his or her motion any other additional information that may be relevant to his or her request.

(d) The sex offender shall also include an affidavit that provides an overview of his or her behavior and lifestyle during the three years prior to the filing of his or her motion for reclassification.

(e) The Board may summarily deny, without a hearing, an offenders motion for reclassification if:

1. the offender is incarcerated;

2. the offender has pending criminal charges;

3. the offender has not remained offense free for more than three continuous years since his or her last classification; or

4. the offender's last classification decision is currently under Judicial Review pursuant to M.G.L. c. 30A, § 14 or on appeal, or on review by the Board as a result of an order by a court of the Commonwealth or a federal court.

The Board will notify the offender, in writing, the substantive reasons for summarily denying the motion for reclassification. The denial of a motion for reclassification under 803 CMR 1.31(2)(e) is not subject to Judicial Review.

(3) **Material Change in Medical Circumstances**. If a sex offender has experienced a material change in circumstances related to a medical condition, he or she may file a motion for reclassification sooner than three years after the date of his or her prior classification. In addition to the requirements listed in 803 CMR 1.31(2), the sex offender shall also include an affidavit from the treating medical provider for his or her stated condition. The affidavit, at a minimum, shall identify and include the following information:

(a) the type of medical condition;

(b) the onset or date of diagnosis of the medical condition;

(c) a detailed description of the limitations the medical condition has caused; and

(d) a summary of the offender's treatment and prognosis.

(4) By filing a motion for reclassification, the offender authorizes the Board to obtain any information accessible under M.G.L. c. 6, §§ 178E and 178K(3) to assist in its review of the offender's motion.

(5) **Reclassification Hearing Process**. The Chair may appoint a panel of Hearing Examiners or a single Hearing Examiner to conduct the hearing on the sex offender's motion for reclassification.

(a) The Board will notify the sex offender in writing of the date, time and location of the reclassification hearing. An offender may waive his or her right to appear at the hearing before the Board. If an offender does not appear at his or her hearing, the Board shall treat the offender's failure to appear as a waiver of his or her appearance and shall proceed to rule on the offender's motion for reclassification, unless the offender presents good cause within three calendar days of the hearing.

(b) No later than five calendar days before the scheduled hearing date, the sex offender may submit a written request to reschedule the hearing for good cause.

(c) No later than 20 calendar days before the scheduled hearing date, the Board and offender shall exchange all additional information intended to be submitted to the panel or Hearing Examiner.

(d) The sex offender may be represented at the hearing by privately retained counsel or an authorized representative.

(e) Motions for reclassification shall be decided on new and updated information not available at the time of the original classification. This does not foreclose the panel or Hearing Examiner from considering the information relied on by the Board to determine the sex offender's prior classification levels, including any prior written decisions issued by the Board.

(6) **Reclassification Decision**. The panel or Hearing Examiner shall determine whether the sex offender has met his or her burden to reduce his or her classification level. Pursuant to M.G.L. c. 30A, § 11(7) and (8), the panel or Hearing Examiner shall make specific written findings detailing the reasons for its decision after the reclassification hearing. For purposes of judicial review, pursuant to M.G.L. c. 30A, § 14 and M.G.L. c. 6, § 178M, these written findings shall be considered the final agency action.

(7) **Notification of Reclassification Decision**.

10

(a) Notification of the final reclassification decision made pursuant to 803 CMR 1.31(6) will be mailed to the sex offender and his or her authorized representative, if applicable, as soon as practicable. The sex offender or his or her authorized representative may request in writing, at the time of his or her administrative hearing, that the final decision made pursuant to 803 CMR 1.20 be sent to him via facsimile.

(b) The Board will notify the sex offender of his or her new classification level and the offender shall be required to comply with registration requirements as set forth in M.G.L. c. 6, §§ 178E, 178F, 178F½ and 178Q. In addition, the Board shall update the information pertaining to the offender in the sex offender registry.

(c) The decision will inform the sex offender of his or her right to seek judicial review of the final decision, pursuant to M.G.L c. 30A, § 14 and M.G.L. c. 6, § 178M. Pursuant to M.G.L. c. 30A, § 14, the sex offender has the right to pursue judicial review within 30 calendar days from the date of receipt of the final Sex Offender Registry Board decision. The filing of a complaint for judicial review will not alter the final reclassification level or stay the sex offender's registration requirements or the dissemination of registration information.

(8) A sex offender may re-apply for reclassification no sooner than three years from the date of the last classification decision. Subsequent motions for reclassification shall be based on additional information not available during prior classifications.

803 CMR 1.32. Board's Reclassification of Sex Offender

(1) **General Principles**. Pursuant to M.G.L. c. 6, § 178L(3), the Board may reclassify any finally classified sex offender upon receipt of information that indicates the offender may present an increased risk to reoffend or degree of dangerousness.

(2) Reclassification may be based on, but is not limited to, information indicating the sex offender has:

(a) Been investigated for or charged with committing a new sex offense;

(b) Been convicted of a new sex offense;

(c) Been adjudicated a sexually dangerous person, pursuant to M.G.L. c. 123A;

(d) Been terminated from a sex offender treatment program;

(e) Violated the terms or conditions of community supervision;

(f) Been incarcerated for more than 60 consecutive days at any time following final classification by the Board;

(g) Failed to comply with the provisions of M.G.L. c. 6, §§ 178C through 178Q; or

(h) Demonstrated a lack of stability in the community.

(3) If a majority of the Full Board determines that the offender may present an increased risk to reoffend or increased degree of dangerousness, it shall authorize a review of the offender's current classification level. The Board shall notify the offender that his or her classification level is being reevaluated.

(4) During the reclassification process, the Board shall follow the same procedures as used in the classification process as set forth in M.G.L. c. 6, §§ 178C through 178Q and 803 CMR 1.06 through 1.24.

803 CMR 1.33. Risk Factors

Pursuant to M.G.L. c. 6, §§ 178K(1)(a) through (l) and 178L, the Board shall use the following factors to determine each sex offender's level of risk of reoffense and degree of dangerousness posed to the public in reaching a final classification decision.

Research supports that the strongest predictors of sexual recidivism for all sex offenders are variables related to antisocial orientation and sexual deviance. (Cortoni, 2010; Hanson and Morton-Bourgon, 2004; Prescott 2006)

These factors may be present to varying degrees in any individual case. The final classification level is not based on a cumulative analysis of the applicable factors, but rather a qualitative analysis of the individual sex offender's history and personal circumstances. Factors that are not specifically referenced in a final classification decision are deemed inapplicable.

Some factors apply to adult male offenders, adult female offenders and juvenile offenders in different ways. These differences are reflected in each factor. Juvenile females are classified using juvenile factors. (Frey, 2010; Hunter et al., 2006; Kubick et al. 2002; Matthews et al., 1997; Van deer Put, 2013)

The Board recognizes that adult female sex offenders generally have lower recidivism rates than adult male sex offenders. (Cortoni et al., 2010). The Board shall apply mitigating weight to this lower recidivism rate, along with the other relevant regulatory factors, in determining the final classification level.

HIGH-RISK FACTORS:

Pursuant to M.G.L. c. 6, § 178K(1)(a)(i) through (vi), the

presence of Factors 1 through 6, is indicative of a high risk of reoffense and degree of dangerousness. The absence of Factors 1 through 6 does not reduce an offender's risk of reoffense or lower his degree of dangerousness.

(1) **Factor 1: Mental Abnormality**.

(a) **Adult Male**. The presence of a statutorily defined mental abnormality specifically related to sexual deviance is significantly associated with an increased risk of reoffense.

The Board shall consider documentation from a licensed mental health professional that indicates that the offender has been diagnosed with a paraphilic disorder related to sexual fantasies, urges, and behaviors.

In the case of pedophilic disorder, this would only be applicable to offenders who are 16 years of age or older at the time of diagnosis. (Doren, 2002; Hanson and Morton-Bourgon, 2004; Hanson and Morton-Bourgon, 2005; and Mann et al. 2010)

(b) **Adult Female**. Factor 1 applies in the same manner to female offenders. (Ford and Cortoni, 2008; Hart et al., 2003; Rousseau and Cortoni, 2010)

(c) **Juvenile**. Factor 1 applies in the same manner to juvenile offenders. (Prescott, 2006; Worling and Curwen, 2001; Worling and Langstrom, 2006)

(2) **Factor 2: Repetitive and Compulsive Behavior**.

(a) **Adult Male**. Repetitive and compulsive behavior is associated with a high risk of reoffense. Factor 2 is applied when a sex offender engages in two or more separate episodes of sexual misconduct. To be considered separate episodes there must be time or opportunity, between the episodes, for the offender to reflect on the wrongfulness of his conduct.

The Board may give increased weight to offenders who have been discovered and confronted (by someone other than the victim) or investigated by an authority for sexual misconduct and, nonetheless, commit a subsequent act of sexual misconduct. The most weight shall be given to an offender who engages in sexual misconduct after having been charged with or convicted of a sex offense. (Harris et al., 2003; Harris and Hanson, 2004)

(b) **Adult Female**. Factor 2 applies in the same manner to female offenders. (Cortoni, et al., 2010; Vandiver and Kercher, 2004)

(c) **Juvenile**. Factor 2 applies only to juvenile offenders who continue to commit sex offenses after they have been detected for prior sexual misconduct. Detection includes: being cautioned, warned, disciplined, criminally charged, or otherwise sanctioned by an adult authority (e.g. police, parent, or teacher).

An offender who engages in sexual misconduct after having been charged with or convicted of a prior sex offense presents an even higher risk to reoffend.

803 CMR 1.33(2)(c) includes adults whose only sex offense(s) were committed as a juvenile. (ATSA, 2012; Curwen and Costin, 2007; Epperson et al., 2009; Nisbet, et al., 2004; Powers-Sawyer and Miner, 2009; Prentky and Righthand, 2003; Stetson School, 2012; Worling and Curwen, 2001; Worling and Langstrom, 2003 and 2006)

(3) **Factor 3: Adult Offender with a Child Victim**.

(a) **Adult Male**. Adult offenders who target children pose a heightened risk to public safety because children normally lack the physical and mental strength to resist an offender. In addition, children can be lured into dangerous situations more easily than most adults. For purposes of factor 3, the Board shall consider any victim younger than 16 years old as a "child victim".

Offenders who target prepubescent children, generally younger than 13 years old, are more likely to have a deviant sexual interest and, therefore, pose an even higher risk of reoffense and degree of dangerousness and are given greater weight.

If the difference in age between the offender and the victim is five years or less and there is evidence of a consensual, although statutorily criminal, sexual act, the Board shall give limited weight to factor 3. (Hanson & Bourgon, 2005; Hanson et al. 2007, Levinson et al., 2008; Mann et al., 2010)

(b) **Adult Female**. Factor 3 will apply in the same manner to adult female offenders.

(c) **Juvenile**. Factor 3 does not apply to juvenile offenders. Factor 27 addresses juvenile offenders who target child victims, including adults whose only sex offense(s) were committed as a juvenile.

(4) **Factor 4: Age at First Offense**.

(a) **Adult Male**. Age at first offense is an important variable related to risk of reoffense and degree of sexual deviance. Offenders who manifest an early onset and persistence of deviant sexual interests or behaviors are at a higher risk to reoffend sexually.

Factor 4 applies to offenders convicted as adults who committed their first detected sexual misconduct as a juvenile and continued to engage in sexual misconduct after the age of 21. (Hanson and Harris, 2000; Skelton and Vess, 2008)

(b) **Adult Female**. Factor 4 will apply in the same manner to adult female offenders.

(c) **Juvenile**. Factor 4 applies to juvenile offenders who committed their first act of sexual misconduct when they were younger than 13 years old, were detected, and then continued to engage in sexual misconduct after 14 years of age or older.

803 CMR 1.33(4)(c) includes adults whose only sex offense(s) were committed as juveniles. (Prentky, et al., 2010; Prescott, 2006)

(5) **Factor 5: Adjudicated Sexually Dangerous Person or Released from Civil Commitment**.

(a) **Adult Male**. Pursuant to M.G.L. c. 6, § 178K(1)(a)(v), the Board views any offender who has been adjudicated as a sexually dangerous person, pursuant to M.G.L. c. 123A or the equivalent in another state, whether he has been released or not, to present a substantial risk to reoffend and degree of dangerousness.

Because of the statutory differences between the criteria and legal process for civilly committing sexually dangerous persons and classifying sex offenders living in the community, the Board uses criteria to determine an offender's risk of reoffending and degree of dangerousness that are different from those used by the courts in a sexually dangerous person proceeding.

(b) **Adult Female**. Factor 5 applies in the same manner to adult female offenders.

(c) **Juvenile**. Factor 5 applies in the same manner to juvenile offenders.

(6) **Factor 6: Maximum Term of Incarceration**.

(a) **Adult Male**. Pursuant to M.G.L. c. 6, § 178K(1)(a)(vi), the Board considers the offender who declines early release, specifically to avoid community supervision or due to his own concerns of reoffending, to present an increased risk of reoffense and degree of dangerousness.

803 CMR 1.33(6)(a) includes adults whose only sex offense(s) were committed as a juvenile, but who were incarcerated for other offenses as an adult.

(b) **Adult Female**. Factor 6 applies in the same manner to adult female offenders.

(c) **Juvenile**. Factor 6 does not apply to juvenile offenders.

RISK-ELEVATING FACTORS:

(7) **Factor 7: Relationship between Offender and Victim**. The relationship between an offender and the victim is an important variable in determining risk of reoffense and degree of dangerousness.

(a) **Adult Male**. For purposes of Factor 7, the following relationship categories are relevant:

1. **Intrafamilial Victim** includes the following:

a. Any persons whose marriage to the offender would be prohibited pursuant to M.G.L., c. 207, §§ 1 through 3;

b. Legally married spouses;

c. Adoptive children, first cousins, brothers- and sisters-in-law; and

d. Any persons who are family member substitutes (e.g., foster, step-relatives, or any other type of familial household "live-in" relationship) who lived in the same household with the offender for two or more years prior to the offending behavior.

Offenders who only target intrafamilial victims may be at a lower risk to reoffend as compared to offenders who target unrelated victims. However, having an intrafamilial victim is not a risk mitigating, nor a risk elevating, factor. It is included for definitional purposes only.

2. **Extrafamilial Victim** includes the following:

a. Any person who has a recognizable non-intrafamilial relationship with the offender, such as a friend, co-worker, or acquaintance; and

b. Any persons who are family member substitutes (e.g. foster, step-relatives, or any other type of familial household "live-in" relationship) who lived in the same household with the offender for less than two years prior to the offending behavior.

Having victims outside the family relationship is empirically related to an increased risk of reoffense. The number of potential victims substantially increases when offenders choose to sexually offend against extrafamilial victims.

Position of Trust. The Board gives special consideration to offenders who commit a sex offense while in a position of trust as established by their profession or role with the victim. These offenders present an increased degree of dangerousness because they violate the victim's and the public's sense of trust, safety, and security.

3. **Stranger Victim** includes the following:

a. Any person who has known the offender for less than 24 hours prior to the offense;

b. Any person who has had no memorable interaction with the offender prior to the offense;

c. There are cases where the offender and victim relationship is established via electronic communications. To consider an adult victim a stranger, the contact sex offense would have to occur within 24 hours of the initial contact. To consider a child victim a stranger, the offender would have to transmit sexually explicit materials or make sexually explicit comments within 24 hours of first electronic contact.

Sex offenders who have sexually offended against a stranger victim have a higher risk of reoffense then offenders who target victims known to them. (Hanson and Bussiere, 1998; Hanson and Harris, 2000; Harris et al., 2003; Knight and Thornton, 2007)

(b) **Adult Female**. Factor 7 applies in the same manner to adult female offenders. (Poels, 2007; Williams and Nicholaichuk, 2001)

(c) **Juvenile**. Factor 7 applies in the following manner for juvenile offenders:

1. **Intrafamilial Victim** includes the following:

a. Any persons whose marriage to the offender would be prohibited pursuant to M.G.L., c. 207, §§ 1 through 3;

b. Any other siblings or cousins, whether biological, step or adoptive; and

c. Any persons who are family member substitutes (e.g., foster, or any other type of familial household "live-in" relationship) and who lived in the same household with the offender for more than one year prior to the offending behavior.

Offenders who only target intrafamilial victims may be at a lower risk to reoffend as compared to offenders who target unrelated victims. However, having an intrafamilial victim is not a risk mitigating, nor a risk elevating, factor. It is included for definitional purposes only.

2. **Extrafamilial Victim** includes the following:

a. Any person who has a relationship with the offender, but is not related, such as: friends, schoolmates, co-workers, neighbors, family friends; and

b. Any persons who are family member substitutes (e.g. foster or any other type of familial household "live-in" relationship) and who lived in the same household with the offender for less than one year prior to the offending behavior.

Juvenile offenders who target extrafamilial victims pose an increased danger to the community.

Position of Trust: The Board gives special consideration to offenders who commit a sex offense while in a position of trust as established by their jobs. These offenders may present an increased level of dangerousness because they violate the victim's and the public's sense of trust, safety, and security.

3. **Stranger Victim** includes the following:

a. Any person who has known the offender for less than 24 hours prior to the offense;

b. Any person who has had no memorable interaction with the offender prior to the offense;

c. There are cases where the offender and victim relationship is established within electronic communications. If the offender transmits sexually explicit materials or makes sexually explicit communication within 24 hours of first electronic contact, this counts as a stranger relationship, even if the actual offense occurred on a later date.

Juvenile offenders who have sexually offended against a stranger victim have an increased risk of reoffense and present a greater degree of dangerousness to the safety and welfare of the public than offenders who target victims known to them.

803 CMR 1.33(7)(c) includes adults whose only sex offense(s) were committed as a juvenile. (Gerhold, et al., 2007; Heilbrun, et al., 2005; Hendriks and Bijlevild, 2008; McCann and Lussier, 2008; Miccio-Fonseca and Rasmusen, 2009; Powers-Sawyer and Miner, 2009; Stetson School, 2012; Worling and Curwen, 2001; Worling and Langstrom, 2006)

(8) **Factor 8: Weapon, Violence or Infliction of Bodily Injury**.

(a) **Adult Male**. All sex offenses are inherently violent, but not necessarily in a physical sense. Offenders who use or threaten to use violence or weapons or cause bodily injury during the commission of a sexual assault are more likely to reoffend and present an increased degree of dangerousness. These behaviors may be indicative of sexual arousal to violence or an antisocial orientation.

Any force or threat of force beyond that necessary to commit the sexual offense shall constitute violence. Any object used to injure, incapacitate, penetrate, force, or threaten the victim during the course of the sexual assault shall be considered a weapon. Any injury, including but not limited to bruises, abrasions, and cuts, or any injury requiring medical attention other than for investigative purposes that is sustained by the victim during a sexual offense shall be deemed bodily injury. (Boer et al., 1997; Epperson et al., 1998; Harris et al., 2003; Knight and Thornton, 2007; Mann et al., 2010; Mokres et al., 2012)

(b) **Adult Female**. Factor 8 applies in the same manner to adult female offenders. (Poels, 2007)

(c) **Juvenile**. Factor 8 applies in the same manner to juvenile offenders. (ATSA, 2012; Curwen and Costin, 2007; McCann and Lussier, 2008; Prentky and Righthand, 2003; Stetson School, 2012; Worling and Curwen, 2001; Worling and Langstrom, 2006)

(9) **Factor 9: Alcohol and Substance Abuse**.

(a) **Adult Male**. Drugs and alcohol are behavioral disinhibitors. Substance abuse may increase an offender's risk of reoffense. Factor 9 applies when the sex offender has a history of substance abuse, demonstrates active substance abuse, or when the offender's substance use was a contributing factor in the sexual misconduct. An offender's history of drug and alcohol use and history of treatment, abstinence and relapse should be considered in determining the weight given to factor 9.

803 CMR 1.33(9)(a) includes adults whose only sex offense(s) were committed as a juvenile, unless the substance misuse was time-limited experimentation during adolescence. (Bonta and Andrews, 2007; Douglas and Skeem, 2005; Hanson and Harris, 2000; Hanson et al., 2007)

(b) **Adult Female**. Factor 9 applies in the same manner to adult female offenders. (Cortoni, 2010; Ford, 2010; Giguere and Bumby, 2007; Hanson et al., 2007; Hart et al., 2003; Rousseau and Cortoni, 2010; Sandler and Freeman, 2009; Vandiver and Kercher, 2004).

(c) **Juvenile**. Factor 9 applies in the same manner to juvenile offenders. (Heilbrun, et al., 2005; Stetson School, 2012)

(10) **Factor 10: Contact with Criminal Justice System**.

(a) **Adult Male**. Individuals are expected to comply with the law. Lawlessness and antisocial behavior correlate with risk of reoffense and degree of dangerousness. For the purposes of factor 10, the Board shall consider evidence of a persistent disregard for rules, laws, and the violation of the rights of others.

Ongoing criminal behavior weighs heavily in the application of factor 10. Analysis under factor 10 shall include the consideration of the number and type of criminal charges, dispositions on the charges, dates of the criminal conduct, and number of abuse prevention or harassment prevention orders.

When classifying adults whose only sex offense(s) were committed as a juvenile, the Board shall consider their entire criminal history. (Duwe and Freske, 2012; Hanson and Bussière, 1998; Hanson and Bourgon, 2005; and Harris et al., 2003)

(b) **Adult Female**. Factor 10 applies in the same manner to adult female offenders. (Cortoni, 2010; Hanson et al., 2007; Hart et al., 2003; Sandler and Freeman, 2007, 2009; Vandiver and Kercher, 2004; Vandiver, 2006)

(c) **Juvenile**. Juveniles with a history of multiple charges or adjudications, including non-sexual crimes, are at increased risk of reoffense. Analysis under factor 10 shall include consideration of the number and severity of criminal charges, abuse prevention orders, harassment prevention orders, and Child Requiring Assistance proceedings, dispositions on the charges, and dates of the criminal conduct. (Carpentier et al., 2011; Epperson et al., 2009; Gerhold et al. 2007; McCann & Lussier, 2008; Nisbet et al,. 2004; Prentky and Righthand, 2003; Zimring et al., 2007; Zimring et al., 2009).

(11) **Factor 11: Violence Unrelated to Sexual Assaults**.

(a) **Adult Male**. An offender is more likely to reoffend and present a greater danger if he has previously demonstrated that he can act violently and with no regard to the safety of others. Analysis under factor 11 shall include the consideration of the severity and frequency of violence towards other persons or animals. (Harris et al., 2003; Hanson & Bourgon, 2005)

(b) **Adult Female**. Factor 11 applies in the same manner to adult female offenders. (Hanson and Cortoni, 2005; Poels, 2007)

(c) **Juvenile**. Factor 11 applies in the same manner to juvenile offenders. (Curwen and Costin, 2007; Knight et al., 2009; Prentky and Righthand, 2003; Stetson School, 2012; Worling and Curwen, 2001, and Worling et al., 2012)

(12) **Factor 12: Behavior While Incarcerated or Civilly Committed**.

(a) **Adult Male**. Offenders are expected to comply with the rules of the institutional setting. Poor behavior while incarcerated or civilly committed is an indicator of antisocial behavior. An offender who unsatisfactorily adjusts to the rigors of confinement by violating rules in a highly structured environment presents an increased degree of dangerousness. Unsatisfactory adjustment is evidenced by violations of the rules. In determining the potential risk of reoffense and dangerousness of an offender, the Board may consider such elements as:

1. the number of poor behavioral reports or disciplinary reports the offender received while confined;

2. the seriousness of the violation; and

3. the length of time that has elapsed between the offender's last report and his release.

803 CMR 1.33(12)(a) includes adults whose only sex offense(s) were committed as a juvenile and who also have a history of adult incarcerations or commitment. (Doren, 2002; and Epperson et al., 2003)

(b) **Adult Female**. Factor 12 applies in the same manner to adult female offenders.

(c) **Juvenile**. Factor 12 does not apply to juvenile offenders. Factor 13 addresses juvenile offenders in custody.

(13) **Factor 13: Non-compliance with Community Supervision**.

(a) **Adult Male**. Offenders are expected to comply with the terms of community supervision. Non-compliance with the rules of community supervision is an indicator of antisocial behavior. An offender who unsatisfactorily adjusts to the external controls inherent to community supervision poses a significant risk when those controls are removed. Unsatisfactory adjustment is evidenced by violations of the rules of the supervising agency or the conditions of release. In determining the potential risk and dangerousness of an offender, the Board may consider such elements as:

1. the number of violations the offender received during his period of supervision;

2. the seriousness of the violation reported in the violation notice or report; and

3. the length of time that has elapsed between the offender's last violation notice or report and his release from supervision.

The Board shall consider the offender who engages in sexual misconduct while on community supervision to pose a greater risk of reoffense and a greater degree of danger to the public.

When classifying adults whose only sex offense(s) were committed as a juvenile, the Board shall consider the offender's entire history of community supervision. (Hanson and Harris, 2000; Knight and Thornton, 2007; Mann et al., 2010).

(b) **Adult Female**. Factor 13 applies in the same manner to adult female offenders. (Hanson et al., 2007; Hart et al., 2003; Stuart and Brice-Baker, 2004)

(c) **Juvenile**. For purposes of factor 13, juvenile offenders are considered to be under "community supervision" when they are supervised in the community by probation or the Department of Youth Services (DYS), or when they are in a residential treatment program or a DYS detention center or program.

A juvenile who unsatisfactorily adjusts to the external controls inherent to supervision may pose a significant risk when those controls are removed. Unsatisfactory adjustment is evidenced by a pattern of violations of rules and regulations of the supervising agency or program. In determining the potential risk and dangerousness of an offender, the Board may consider such elements as:

1. the number of disciplinary issues or rule violations;

2. their seriousness; and

3. the length of time that has elapsed since the offender's last disciplinary issue or violation.

While not sufficient by itself to invoke factor 13, a juvenile's history of suspension and expulsion from school may be considered in assessing a pattern of behavior while in a supervised setting.

The Board shall consider juvenile offenders who engage in sexual misconduct while under community supervision to pose a heightened risk of reoffense and a greater degree of danger to the public. (Epperson et al., 2009; Prentky and Righthand, 2003)

(14) **Factor 14: Recent Threats**.

(a) **Adult Male**. The Board shall consider the offender who expresses threats or intent to sexually assault another person to be at an increased risk of reoffense and degree of dangerousness.

803 CMR 1.33(14)(a) includes adults whose only sex offense(s) were committed as a juvenile. (Hanson and Harris, 2000; Hanson et al., 2007; Harris et al., 2003)

(b) **Adult Female**. Factor 14 applies in the same manner to adult female offenders.

(c) **Juvenile**. Factor 14 applies in the same manner to juvenile offenders.

(15) **Factor 15: Hostility Towards Women**.

(a) **Adult Male**. Hostile attitudes and behavior towards women are predictive of sexual reoffense and increased dangerousness. Factor 15 is applied when an offender has a pervasive pattern of conflicts with women, physical aggression toward women, and using derogatory and demeaning language towards women, or has multiple abuse prevention orders or harassment prevention orders taken out by different women at different times.

803 CMR 1.33(15)(a) includes adults whose only sex offense(s) were committed as a juvenile and who evidence a recent pattern of hostility toward women. (Allan et al. 2000; Hanson et al., 2007; Mann et al., 2010)

(b) **Adult Female**. Factor 15 does not apply to adult female offenders.

(c) **Juvenile**. Factor 15 does not apply to juvenile offenders.

(16) **Factor 16: Public Place**.

(a) **Adult Male**. The commission of a sex offense or engaging in sexual misconduct in a place where detection is likely reflects the offender's lack of impulse control. The Board may apply less weight to factor 16 if there is evidence that the offender made a clear and concerted effort to conceal his offending behavior from others. For purposes of factor 16, a "public place" includes any area maintained for or used by the public and any place that is open to the scrutiny of others or where there is no expectation of privacy. (Epperson et al., 2000)

(b) **Adult Female**. Factor 16 applies in the same manner to adult female offenders.

(c) **Juvenile**. Factor 16 applies in the same manner to juvenile offenders. (Langstrom, 2001)

(17) **Factor 17: Male Offender against Male Victim**.

(a) **Adult Male**. Male offenders who have engaged in sexual misconduct against a male victim reoffend at a higher rate. Factor 17 applies when a male offender commits any sexual misconduct against a non-consenting male or a male child younger than 16 years old. (Hanson et al., 2003; Harris et al., 2003; Harris and Hanson, 2004; Knight and Thornton, 2007)

(b) **Adult Female**. Factor 17 does not apply to adult female offenders.

(c) **Juvenile**. Factor 17 applies only to juvenile offenders who were 13 years of age or older at the time of the sexual misconduct.

There are two circumstances when juvenile sex offenders who have male victims are at a higher risk to reoffend. Factor 17 only applies:

1. when the male victim is younger than 13 years old and is at least five years younger than the offender at the time of the sexual misconduct; or

2. if there is penetration and physical force in the sexual assault, regardless of the age of the victim.

803 CMR 1.33(17)(c) includes adults whose only sex offense(s) were committed as a juvenile. (McCann and Lussier, 2008; Prescott, 2006; Prentky and Righthand, 2003; Worling and Curwen, 2001).

(18) **Factor 18: Extravulnerable Victim**.

(a) **Adult Male**. Offenders who engage in sexual misconduct against an extravulnerable victim pose a greater danger to public safety. For purposes of factor 18 "extravulnerable" includes any condition or circumstance that:

1. renders a victim more susceptible to sexual assault or unable to effectively defend himself or herself; or

2. compromises his or her ability to effectively report the abuse or provide testimony in court.

The Board considers victims who are younger than eight years old or 60 years of age or older to be extravulnerable by virtue of their age. (Levinson, et al., 2001; McGrath, 1991)

(b) **Adult Female**. Factor 18 applies in the same manner to adult female offenders.

(c) **Juvenile**. Factor 18 applies in the same manner to juvenile offenders.

(19) **Factor 19: Level of Physical Contact**.

(a) **Adult Male**. Sexual assault involving penetration has been shown to cause increased psychological harm to the victim. The offender who engages in penetration, especially penile penetration, as part of the sexual assault poses an increased degree of dangerousness. In the case of an adult with a child victim, if the difference in age between the offender and the victim is five years or less and there is evidence of a consensual, although statutorily criminal sexual act, the Board shall give limited weight to factor 19. (Lesserman et al., 1997)

(b) **Adult Female**. Factor 19 applies in the same manner to adult female offenders.

(c) **Juvenile**. Factor 19 applies in the same manner to juvenile offenders. However, when determining the weight to apply to factor 19, the Board should consider: age difference between offender and victim; whether there is evidence of an ongoing dating type relationship; whether the victim consented; and whether there was force or coercion.

803 CMR 1.33(19)(c) includes adults whose only sex offense(s) were committed as a juvenile. (Stetson School, 2012)

(20) **Factor 20: Diverse Sexual Behavior**.

(a) **Adult Male**. Diverse sexual behavior may reflect sexual preoccupation, elevated sex drive, or sexual deviance. Offenders who have a history of engaging in different types of inappropriate sexual behaviors, in separate episodes, are at an increased risk to reoffend. Diverse sexual behaviors include, but are not limited to: voyeurism, exhibitionism, possession of pornography, contact sexual assaults, stealing of a person's belongings for sexual arousal, frottage, stalking, photographing or videotaping a partially nude or nude person or the intimate parts of a person without their consent, and engaging in sexual harassment. In determining the weight applied to factor 20, the Board shall consider the number, types, and frequency of the diverse sexual behaviors. (Hanson and Harris, 2000; Hanson et al., 2007; Harris et al., 2003; and Mann et al., 2010)

(b) **Adult Female**. Factor 20 applies in the same manner to adult female offenders. (Hart et al., 2003)

(c) **Juvenile**. Factor 20 applies in the same manner to juvenile offenders. (Curwen and Costin, 2007; Prentky and Righthand, 2003; Worling and Curwen, 2001)

(21) **Factor 21: Diverse Victim Type**.

(a) **Adult Male**. Offenders whose acts of sexual misconduct traverse victim types, such as multiple ages, gender, or relationship categories, present a greater risk of reoffense and danger to public safety because they have a broader victim pool. (Hanson and Harris 2000; Heil et al., 2003; Kleban et al., 2012)

(b) **Adult Female**. Factor 21 applies in the same manner to adult female offenders.

(c) **Juvenile**. Factor 21 applies in the same manner to juvenile offenders. (Curwen and Costin, 2007; Epperson et al., 2009; Stetson School, 2012; Worling and Curwen, 2001; Parks and Bard, 2006)

(22) **Factor 22: Number of Victims**.

(a) **Adult Male**. Offenders who have committed acts of sexual misconduct against two or more victims present an increased risk of reoffense and degree of dangerousness.

(b) **Adult Female**. Factor 22 applies in the same manner to adult female offenders.

(c) **Juvenile**. Factor 22 applies in the same manner to juvenile offenders. (Epperson et al., 2009; Gerhold et al., 2007; Miccio-Fonseca, 2009; Prentky and Righthand, 2003; Powers-Sawyer and Miner, 2009; Stetson School, 2012; Worling and Curwen, 2001; Worling and Langstrom, 2006)

(23) **Factor 23: Victim Access**.

(a) **Adult Male**. An offender's risk of reoffense increases when he has frequent and easy access to potential victims from his preferred victim pool.

The Board may consider such things as:

1. whether the offender has regular and ongoing opportunities for interaction with potential victims through such things as coaching, teaching, or volunteering, or through his living, employment, or relationship settings; or

2. whether the offender appears to be intentionally seeking circumstances that put him in contact with his preferred victims.

For offenders who target stranger victims, factor 23 applies when the offender's conduct suggests an intentional seeking out of circumstances similar to his prior offending behavior.

803 CMR 1.33(23)(a) includes adults whose only sex offense(s) were committed as juveniles. (Hanson and Harris, 2000; Hanson et al., 2007)

(b) **Adult Female**. Factor 23 applies in the same manner to adult female offenders.

(c) **Juvenile**. The risk of reoffense increases when juveniles have frequent, unsupervised access to potential victims from their preferred victim pool or appear to be intentionally seeking circumstances that allow such access. (Carpentier and Proulx, 2011; Spice, et al., 2013; Worling and Langstrom, 2006)

(24) **Factor 24: Less than Satisfactory Participation in Sex Offender Treatment**.

(a) **Adult Male**. Offenders who refuse to participate in, dropped out of, or are terminated by their treatment provider from sex offender treatment present an increased risk of reoffense.

The Board shall consider the offender who, during his most recent opportunity to participate in treatment while in custody or when required by community supervision, refused to participate in a sex offender treatment program or dropped out or was involuntarily terminated to be at an increased risk of reoffense and degree of dangerousness. (Hanson and Harris, 2000; Hanson et al., 2002; Lösel and Schmucker, 2005)

(b) **Adult Female**. Factor 24 applies in the same manner to adult female offenders.

(c) **Juvenile**. Factor 24 applies in the same manner to juvenile offenders. (Curwen and Costin, 2007; Epperson et al., 2009; Gerhold, et al., 2007; Powers-Sawyer and Miner, 2009; Vitacco et al., 2009; Worling and Curwen, 2001; Worling and Langstrom, 2006)

(25) **Factor 25: Prostitution of Children**.

(a) **Adult Male**. Factor 25 does not apply to male offenders.

(b) **Adult Female**. Female offenders convicted of offenses related to either promoting or patronizing prostitution of a child have an increased risk of reoffense. (Sandler and Freeman, 2009)

(c) **Juvenile**. Factor 25 does not apply to juvenile offenders.

(26) **Factor 26: History of Abusing Children**.

(a) **Adult Male**. Factor 26 does not apply to male offenders.

(b) **Adult Female**. Female offenders with a history of engaging in any type of non-sexual child abuse have an increased risk of reoffense. The Board shall consider evidence of prior child abuse, including charges, investigations, and convictions. (Cortoni and Gannon, 2011; Sandler and Freeman, 2009; Wijkman and Bijleveld, 2013)

(c) **Juvenile**. Factor 26 does not apply to juvenile offenders.

(27) **Factor 27: Age of Victim**.

(a) **Adult Male**. Factor 27 does not apply to male offenders.

(b) **Adult Female**. Factor 27 does not apply to female offenders.

(c) **Juvenile**. Factor 27 only applies to juvenile offenders who were 13 years of age or older at the time of the sex offense.

1. **Child Victims**. Juvenile offenders who target younger child victims outside of their peer age group present an increased risk of reoffense and degree of dangerousness. For purposes of factor 27, the Board shall consider "child victim" as younger than 13 years old and at least five years younger than the offender at the time of the offense.

2. **Adult Victims**. Juvenile offenders who target adult victims present an increased risk of reoffense and degree of dangerousness. For purposes of factor 27, the Board shall consider "adult victim" as 18 years of age or older and at least five years older than the offender at the time of offense.

803 CMR 1.33(27)(c) includes adults whose only sex offense(s) were committed as a juvenile. (ATSA, 2012; McCann and Lussier, 2008; Nisbet, et al, 2004; Stetson School, 2012; Worling and Curwen, 2001; Worling and Langstrom, 2006)

RISK-MITIGATING FACTORS:

(28) **Factor 28: Supervision by Probation or Parole**.

(a) **Adult Male**. Supervision of sex offenders released into the community increases public safety. An offender's risk of reoffense and degree of dangerousness are reduced while he is serving a term of community supervision. Factor 28 also applies to offenders who are incarcerated at the time of the classification hearing and will be under community supervision upon release. Factor 28 may be given less weight if there is a history of probation violations.

803 CMR 1.33(28)(a) includes adults whose only sex offense(s) were committed as a juvenile. (English et al., 1995; Vries Robbé and Vogel, 2013)

(b) **Adult Female**. Factor 28 applies in the same manner to female offenders.

(c) **Juvenile**. Community supervision reduces a juvenile sex offender's risk of reoffense and degree of dangerousness. For purposes of factor 28, juvenile offenders are under "community supervision" when they are serving a probation sentence or are being monitored by DYS while in the community. (Stetson School, 2012)

(29) **Factor 29: Offense-Free Time in the Community**.

(a) **Adult Male**. The likelihood of sexual recidivism decreases the longer the sex offender has had access to the community without committing any new sex offense or non-sexual violent offense. The risk of reoffense decreases for most offenders after living in the community offense-free for five to ten years. The risk of reoffense lowers substantially after ten years of offense-free time in the community.

For purposes of factor 29, the offense-free time begins on the date of an offender's most recent release from custody for a sex offense or non-sexual violent offense. In the case of an offender who was not committed, the offense-free time begins on the most recent date of conviction or adjudication of a sex offense or non-sexual violent offense.

803 CMR 1.33(29)(a) includes adults whose only sex offense(s) were committed as a juvenile. (Hanson et al., 2013; Harris & Hanson, 2004)

(b) **Adult Female**. Factor 29 applies in the same manner to female offenders.

(c) **Juvenile**. Adolescence is a time of rapid social, sexual, physical, cognitive, and emotional developmental changes. The likelihood of recidivism decreases for most juvenile sexual offenders after living in the community offense-free for three years. The risk of re-offense continues to lower over time and by ten years of offense-free time the risk of reoffense has substantially decreased.

For purposes of factor 29, the offense-free time begins on the most recent date the juvenile offender is released from DYS detention for a sex offense or non-sexual violent offense. In the case of an offender who is not in detention, the offense-free time begins on the most recent date of adjudication in the juvenile court for a sex offense or non-sexual violent offense. (Prentky et al., 2010; Worling and Langstrom, 2006; Worling, et al., 2010)

(30) **Factor 30: Advanced Age**.

(a) **Adult Male**. Recidivism rates incrementally decline as sex offenders get older, especially as offenders move into their later years. While advanced age alone does not outweigh other risk-elevating factors present in an individual offender, advancing age has a mitigating effect on risk of reoffense.

Factor 30 does not apply uniformly to all sex offenders. Although risk of reoffense gradually declines when an offender is in his forties, the Board considers advanced age to have a significant mitigating effect when the offender is 50 years of age or older or, for those with child victims, when the offender is 60 years of age or older. For purposes of factor 30, the Board will consider the offender's age at the time of the classification hearing.

Factor 30 should be given less weight when an offender continues to demonstrate an active sex drive or general criminality.

803 CMR 1.33(30)(a) includes adults whose only sex offense(s) were committed as a juvenile. (Barbaree and Blanchard, 2008; Hanson, 2002; Hanson, 2006; Fazel et al., 2006; Lussier and Healy, 2009; Nicholaichuk et al., 2014; Prentky and Lee, 2007; Skelton and Vess, 2008; Thornton, 2006)

(b) **Adult Female**. Factor 30 applies in the same manner to adult female offenders.

(c) **Juvenile**. Factor 30 does not apply to juvenile offenders.

(31) **Factor 31: Physical Condition**.

(a) **Adult Male**. Pursuant to M.G.L. c. 6, § 178K(1)(d), the Board shall give consideration to the offender who has a physical condition that is documented by a treating medical provider. Factor 31 seeks to identify those offenders who have a decreased risk of reoffense or degree of dangerousness due to a physical condition, including a debilitating illness. At minimum, the medical documentation must:

1. Identify the physical condition;

2. Indicate the onset or date of diagnosis of the physical condition;

3. Provide a detailed description of the offender's limitations connected to the physical condition; and

4. Provide a summary of the offender's treatment and prognosis relative to the physical condition.

(b) **Adult Female**. Factor 31 applies in the same manner to adult female offenders.

(c) **Juvenile**. Factor 31 applies in the same manner to juvenile offenders.

(32) **Factor 32: Sex Offender Treatment**. In order for factor 32 to apply, it shall be the responsibility of the offender to provide documentation from a treatment provider verifying his treatment participation or completion. This documentation must, at minimum, include: the name and license number of the offender's treatment provider; the treatment provider's description of the treatment program's milieu, methodology, goals, and objectives; and a record of the offender's attendance, level of participation, and degree of progress.

(a) **Adult Male**. The Board has determined that participation in or successful completion of sex offense-specific treatment, specifically in a program utilizing a cognitive-behavioral modality, such as Relapse Prevention, Risk-Needs-Responsivity, or Good Lives, is a risk-reducing factor. The Board may also consider pharmacological treatment for paraphilic disorders as risk reducing.

The risk-mitigating weight applied to factor 32 varies in degrees based on the following:

1. **Completion of Treatment**. In general, offenders who have successfully completed a treatment program have lower rates of reoffense than those who have not. Participation in treatment through the end of a term of incarceration or community supervision is not considered "completion of treatment" unless there is documentation that the offender met all the goals of the program.

2. **Currently Participating in Treatment**. The Legislature has identified current participation in treatment as a risk mitigating factor. Offenders who voluntarily participate in treatment in the community, not solely as a condition of supervised release, and offenders who continue to participate in treatment after their treatment providers have determined that they have completed the program, may receive more weight under factor 32.

3. **Past Participation in Treatment**. The Board shall consider an offender's past participation in treatment. Offenders who participated in treatment while incarcerated or under community supervision, but did not complete the sex offender treatment program, may receive less weight under factor 32.

4. **Denial**. One of the primary goals of successful sex offender treatment is accepting responsibility for engaging in harmful sexual offending behavior. While some individuals who deny committing their sex offense can benefit from treatment, their lack of responsibility or degree of minimization for their behaviors may diminish the weight assigned to factor 32.

When classifying adults whose only sex offense(s) were committed as a juvenile, the Board shall consider their past participation in treatment as a juvenile and participation in sex offender treatment as an adult. (Hanson et al., 2009; Levenson, 2011; Lösel and Schmucker, 2005; Marques, 2005; Olver et al., 2013; Saleh and Guidry, 2003)

(b) **Adult Female**. Many female sex offenders have treatment needs that may not be addressed in traditional treatment programs created for male sex offenders. The Board shall give mitigating weight to participation in or successful completion in a program utilizing a cognitive-behavioral modality such as Relapse Prevention, Risk-Needs-Responsivity, and Good Lives or general psychological therapy. The Board shall consider the degree of participation in treatment and denial in the same manner as adult males. (Blanchette and Brown, 2006; Blanchette and Taylor, 2010; Ford, 2010)

(c) **Juvenile**. Juvenile offenders may have broader treatment needs than their adult counterparts. Because juveniles are still maturing and developing, they may be more amenable to treatment.

The Board has determined that participation in any psychological therapy that addresses various areas of the offender's life, including family, school, emotional, and social domains, or sex offense specific treatment is a risk-reducing factor. The amount of weight assigned to factor 32 increases with the offender's progress and level of participation, family involvement, level of accountability, amount of focus on sex offending behavior, or whether the offender completed a treatment program. (ATSA, 2012; Borduin et al., 2009; Reitzel and Carbonell, 2006; Worling et al., 2010)

(33) **Factor 33: Home Situation and Support Systems**.

(a) **Adult Male**. Factor 33 is applied to an offender who is currently residing in a positive and supportive environment. The likelihood of reoffense is reduced when an offender is supported by family, friends, and acquaintances.

The Board shall give greater mitigating consideration to evidence of a support network that is aware of the offender's sex offense history and provides guidance, supervision, and support of rehabilitation.

803 CMR 1.33(33)(a) includes adults whose only sex offense(s) were committed as a juvenile. (Tabachnick and Klein, 2011; de Vries Robbé and Vogel, 2013; de Vries Robbé et al., 2014)

(b) **Adult Female**. Factor 33 applies in the same manner to adult female offenders. (Gannon and Rose, 2008)

(c) **Juvenile**. A juvenile who is currently residing in a positive and supportive environment is less likely to reoffend. Factor 33 is applied when there is evidence of stable relationships with family, stable and therapeutically supportive family, pro-social friends and acquaintances, or positive engagement with social services, teachers or other adults.

The Board shall give greater mitigating consideration to evidence of a positive support network that is aware of the offender's sex offense history and provides guidance, supervision, and support of rehabilitation. (Bremer, 2006; Prentky and Righthand, 2003; Prentky et al., 2010; Worling and Curwen, 2001)

(34) **Factor 34: Materials Submitted by the Sex Offender Regarding Stability in the Community**.

(a) **Adult Male**. Pursuant to M.G.L. c. 6, § 178K(1)(l), the Board shall give mitigating consideration to materials submitted by the offender that demonstrate stability in the community. The Board shall consider evidence that directly addresses the offender's recent behavior and lifestyle including, but not limited to: his residential stability, sustained sobriety, education or employment stability, type of employment, and non-work related activities. (Tabachnick and Klein, 2011; de Vries Robbé and Vogel, 2013; de Vries Robbé et al., 2014)

(b) **Adult Female**. Factor 34 applies in the same manner to adult female offenders. (Gannon and Rose, 2008)

(c) **Juvenile**. Factor 34 applies in the same manner to juvenile offenders. (Bremer, 2006; Prentky et al., 2010)

ADDITIONAL FACTORS:

(35) **Factor 35: Psychological or Psychiatric Profiles Indicating Risk to Reoffend**.

(a) **Adult Male**. The Board shall consider evaluative reports, empirically-based risk assessment instruments, or testimony from a licensed mental health professional that discuss psychological and psychiatric issues, including major mental illness, as they relate to the offender's risk of reoffense.

The Board may give appropriate evidentiary weight to documentary reports and risk assessment, but the ultimate risk opinion, if any, will be excluded from consideration unless the mental health professional testifies as an expert witness at the classification hearing. (Abracen and Looman, 2012; Fazel et. al. 2007; Hanson and Bussière, 1998; Hanson and Harris, 2000; Kafka, 2012)

(b) **Adult Female**. Factor 35 applies in the same manner to adult female offenders. (Cortoni, 2010; Gannon, et al., 2014; Hart et al., 2003; Rousseau and Cortoni, 2010; Vandiver and Kercher, 2004)

(c) **Juvenile**. Factor 35 applies in the same manner to juvenile offenders. (Kafka, 2012).

(36) **Factor 36: Online Offending Behavior**.

(a) **Adult Male**. The presence of other regulatory factors must also be considered in assessing the risk of reoffense and degree of dangerousness posed by online offenders. The Board categorizes online offending behavior in the following ways:

1. **Child Pornography**. Sex offenders who limit their offending to possessing child pornography, in the absence of other factors, generally pose a lower risk of reoffense and degree of dangerousness than sex offenders who commit contact offenses.

Evidence of sexual deviance may demonstrate an increase in risk to commit contact sex offenses. Useful indicators of sexual deviance include, but are not limited to: evidence of actively searching for images of prepubescent children; collecting larger amounts of prepubescent pornography relative to adolescent or adult pornography; collecting larger amounts of child pornography relative to adult pornography; sorting and organizing files versus random downloading; and primarily focusing on child pornography depicting boys or a higher boy to girl ratio in a collection. (Kim, 2004; Seto et al., 2011; Seto & Eke, 2015)

2. **Online Communicating**. Sex offenders who engage in sexually explicit communications or exchange pornographic photos with minors or persons they believe to be minors by any electronic means present a danger to the public.

These offenders generally pose a higher degree of dangerousness than those who limit their offending behavior to child pornography as described in 803 CMR 1.33(36)(a)1.

3. **Solicitation Offending**. Sex offenders who communicate with minors or persons they believe to be minors by any electronic means for the purpose of enticing or meeting in-person to engage in sexual misconduct present the greatest danger among online offenders. (Seto & Eke, 2005; Babchishin et al., 2011; Briggs et al, 2011; Seto et al., 2011; Eke et al., 2011)

(b) **Adult Female**. Factor 36 applies in the same manner to adult female offenders.

(c) **Juvenile**. The categories of online offending apply to juveniles in the same manner as adults.

Juveniles whose online offending targets similarly aged peers may present a lower degree of risk and dangerousness than adults who target juveniles. (Saleh et al., 2014)

(37) **Factor 37: Other Information Related to the Nature of the Sexual Behavior**.

(a) **Adult Male**. Pursuant to M.G.L. c. 6, § 178L(1), the Board shall consider any information that it deems useful in determining risk of reoffense and degree of dangerousness posed by any offender.

(b) **Adult Female**. Factor 37 applies in the same manner to adult female offenders.

(c) **Juvenile**. Factor 37 applies in the same manner to juvenile offenders.

(38) **Factor 38: Victim Impact Statement**.

(a) **Adult Male**. The Board recognizes the substantial impact sex offenses have on victims. Pursuant to M.G.L. c. 6, § 178K(1)(k), the Board shall consider any written statement authored by the victim, the parent or guardian of a minor victim or a deceased victim, or the guardian of an adult victim of a sex offense that resulted in a conviction or adjudication.

(b) **Adult Female**. Factor 38 applies in the same manner to adult female offenders.

(c) **Juveniles**. Factor 38 applies in the same manner to juvenile offenders.

803 CMR 1.34. Information Sharing

(1) Pursuant to M.G.L. c. 6, § 178K(4) any agency as defined by M.G.L. c. 6, § 178C, shall provide to the Board, within 15 business days of request, any information that is relevant to the Board's classification and/or reclassification of a sex offender's level. Such information includes but is not limited to:

(a) Any information associated with a conviction for a sex offense, including but not limited to, any narratives describing the offending behavior, victim statements and all investigative reports;

(b) Any documentation demonstrating the offender has been investigated for or charged with committing a new sex offense;

(c) Any documentation demonstrating the offender has been non-compliant with community supervision along with any reports generated as a result of non-compliance;

(d) Any documentation demonstrating the offender has been non-compliant with required programing;

(e) Any evaluation, risk assessment or discharge summary;

(f) Any documentation demonstrating the offender has received any disciplinary reports for non-compliance with institutional rules and regulations;

(g) Any restraining or harassment orders that have been issued;

(h) Any new arrest or report generated as a result of violent or assaultive behavior; and

(i) Any new arrest or report involving drugs or alcohol.

(2) Upon receipt and review of the information that has been provided to the Board, if the Board determines that additional information is necessary such agencies shall comply with the

Board's request for additional information within ten business days.

803 CMR 1.35. Severability

If any regulation or section, sub-section, sentence, phrase or portion thereof is found to be invalid by a court of competent jurisdiction for any reason, said portion shall be deemed a separate, distinct, and independent provision, and the validity of the other regulations shall not be affected.

REGULATORY AUTHORITY

803 CMR 1.00: M.G.L. c. 6, §§ 178C through 178Q and St. 2003, c. 77, § 23.

PART 11
Selected Federal Laws

25 U.S.C. c. 21. Indian Child Welfare

§ 1901. Congressional findings

Recognizing the special relationship between the United States and the Indian tribes and their members and the Federal responsibility to Indian people, the Congress finds—

(1) that clause 3, section 8, article I of the United States Constitution provides that "The Congress shall have Power * * * To regulate Commerce * * * with Indian tribes" and, through this and other constitutional authority, Congress has plenary power over Indian affairs;

(2) that Congress, through statutes, treaties, and the general course of dealing with Indian tribes, has assumed the responsibility for the protection and preservation of Indian tribes and their resources;

(3) that there is no resource that is more vital to the continued existence and integrity of Indian tribes than their children and that the United States has a direct interest, as trustee, in protecting Indian children who are members of or are eligible for membership in an Indian tribe;

(4) that an alarmingly high percentage of Indian families are broken up by the removal, often unwarranted, of their children from them by nontribal public and private agencies and that an alarmingly high percentage of such children are placed in non-Indian foster and adoptive homes and institutions; and

(5) that the States, exercising their recognized jurisdiction over Indian child custody proceedings through administrative and judicial bodies, have often failed to recognize the essential tribal relations of Indian people and the cultural and social standards prevailing in Indian communities and families.

§ 1902. Congressional declaration of policy

The Congress hereby declares that it is the policy of this Nation to protect the best interests of Indian children and to promote the stability and security of Indian tribes and families by the establishment of minimum Federal standards for the removal of Indian children from their families and the placement of such children in foster or adoptive homes which will reflect the unique values of Indian culture, and by providing for assistance to Indian tribes in the operation of child and family service programs.

§ 1903. Definitions

For the purposes of this chapter, except as may be specifically provided otherwise, the term—

(1) "child custody proceeding" shall mean and include—

(i) "foster care placement" which shall mean any action removing an Indian child from its parent or Indian custodian for temporary placement in a foster home or institution or the home of a guardian or conservator where the parent or Indian custodian cannot have the child returned upon demand, but where parental rights have not been terminated;

(ii) "termination of parental rights" which shall mean any action resulting in the termination of the parent-child relationship;

(iii) "preadoptive placement" which shall mean the temporary placement of an Indian child in a foster home or institution after the termination of parental rights, but prior to or in lieu of adoptive placement; and

(iv) "adoptive placement" which shall mean the permanent placement of an Indian child for adoption, including any action resulting in a final decree of adoption.

Such term or terms shall not include a placement based upon an act which, if committed by an adult, would be deemed a crime or upon an award, in a divorce proceeding, of custody to one of the parents.

(2) "extended family member" shall be as defined by the law or custom of the Indian child's tribe or, in the absence of such law or custom, shall be a person who has reached the age of eighteen and who is the Indian child's grandparent, aunt or uncle, brother or sister, brother-in-law or sister-in-law, niece or nephew, first or second cousin, or stepparent;

(3) "Indian" means any person who is a member of an Indian tribe, or who is an Alaska Native and a member of a Regional Corporation as defined in 1606 of title 43;

(4) "Indian child" means any unmarried person who is under age eighteen and is either (a) a member of an Indian tribe or (b) is eligible for membership in an Indian tribe and is the biological child of a member of an Indian tribe;

(5) "Indian child's tribe" means (a) the Indian tribe in which an Indian child is a member or eligible for membership or (b), in the case of an Indian child who is a member of or eligible for membership in more than one tribe, the Indian tribe with which the Indian child has the more significant contacts;

(6) "Indian custodian" means any Indian person who has legal custody of an Indian child under tribal law or custom or under State law or to whom temporary physical care, custody, and control has been transferred by the parent of such child;

(7) "Indian organization" means any group, association, partnership, corporation, or other legal entity owned or controlled by Indians, or a majority of whose members are Indians;

(8) "Indian tribe" means any Indian tribe, band, nation, or other organized group or community of Indians recognized as eligible for the services provided to Indians by the Secretary because of their status as Indians, including any Alaska Native village as defined in section 1602(c) of title 43;

(9) "parent" means any biological parent or parents of an Indian child or any Indian person who has lawfully adopted an Indian child, including adoptions under tribal law or custom. It does not include the unwed father where paternity has not been acknowledged or established;

(10) "reservation" means Indian country as defined in section 1151 of title 18 and any lands, not covered under such section, title to which is either held by the United States in trust for the benefit of any Indian tribe or individual or held by any Indian tribe or individual subject to a restriction by the United States against alienation;

(11) "Secretary" means the Secretary of the Interior; and

(12) "tribal court" means a court with jurisdiction over child custody proceedings and which is either a Court of Indian Offenses, a court established and operated under the code or custom of an Indian tribe, or any other administrative body of a tribe which is vested with authority over child custody proceedings.

Subchapter I: Child Custody Proceedings

§ 1911. Indian tribe jurisdiction over Indian child custody proceedings

(a) Exclusive jurisdiction

An Indian tribe shall have jurisdiction exclusive as to any State over any child custody proceeding involving an Indian child who resides or is domiciled within the reservation of such tribe, except where such jurisdiction is otherwise vested in the State by existing Federal law. Where an Indian child is a ward of a tribal court, the Indian tribe shall retain exclusive jurisdiction, notwithstanding the residence or domicile of the child.

(b) Transfer of proceedings; declination by tribal court

In any State court proceeding for the foster care placement of, or termination of parental rights to, an Indian child not domiciled or residing within the reservation of the Indian child's tribe, the court, in the absence of good cause to the contrary, shall transfer such proceeding to the jurisdiction of the tribe, absent objection by either parent, upon the petition of either parent or the Indian custodian or the Indian child's tribe: Provided, That such transfer shall be subject to declination by the tribal court of such tribe.

(c) State court proceedings; intervention

In any State court proceeding for the foster care placement of, or termination of parental rights to, an Indian child, the Indian custodian of the child and the Indian child's tribe shall have a right to intervene at any point in the proceeding.

(d) Full faith and credit to public acts, records, and judicial proceedings of Indian tribes

The United States, every State, every territory or possession of the United States, and every Indian tribe shall give full faith and credit to the public acts, records, and judicial proceedings of any Indian tribe applicable to Indian child custody proceedings to the same extent that such entities give full faith and credit to the public acts, records, and judicial proceedings of any other entity.

§ 1912. Pending court proceedings

(a) Notice; time for commencement of proceedings; additional time for preparation

In any involuntary proceeding in a State court, where the court knows or has reason to know that an Indian child is involved, the party seeking the foster care placement of, or termination of parental rights to, an Indian child shall notify the parent or Indian custodian and the Indian child's tribe, by registered mail with return receipt requested, of the pending proceedings and of their right of intervention. If the identity or location of the parent or Indian custodian and the tribe cannot be determined, such notice shall be given to the Secretary in like manner, who shall have fifteen days after receipt to provide the requisite notice to the parent or Indian custodian and the tribe. No foster care placement or termination of parental rights proceeding shall be held until at least ten days after receipt of notice by the parent or Indian custodian and the tribe or the Secretary: Provided, That the parent or Indian custodian or the tribe shall, upon request, be granted up to twenty additional days to prepare for such proceeding.

(b) Appointment of counsel

In any case in which the court determines indigency, the parent or Indian custodian shall have the right to court-appointed counsel in any removal, placement, or termination proceeding. The court may, in its discretion, appoint counsel for the child upon a finding that such appointment is in the best interest of the child. Where State law makes no provision for appointment of counsel in such proceedings, the court shall promptly notify the Secretary upon appointment of counsel, and the Secretary, upon certification of the presiding judge, shall pay reasonable fees and expenses out of funds which may be appropriated pursuant to section 13 of this title.

(c) Examination of reports or other documents

Each party to a foster care placement or termination of parental rights proceeding under State law involving an Indian child shall have the right to examine all reports or other documents filed with the court upon which any decision with respect to such action may be based.

(d) Remedial services and rehabilitative programs; preventive measures

Any party seeking to effect a foster care placement of, or termination of parental rights to, an Indian child under State law shall satisfy the court that active efforts have been made to provide remedial services and rehabilitative programs designed to prevent the breakup of the Indian family and that these efforts have proved unsuccessful.

(e) Foster care placement orders; evidence; determination of damage to child

No foster care placement may be ordered in such proceeding in the absence of a determination, supported by clear and convincing evidence, including testimony of qualified expert witnesses, that the continued custody of the child by the parent or Indian custodian is likely to result in serious emotional or physical damage to the child.

(f) Parental rights termination orders; evidence; determination of damage to child

No termination of parental rights may be ordered in such proceeding in the absence of a determination, supported by evidence beyond a reasonable doubt, including testimony of qualified expert witnesses, that the continued custody of the child by the parent or Indian custodian is likely to result in serious emotional or physical damage to the child.

§ 1913. Parental rights; voluntary termination

(a) Consent; record; certification matters; invalid consents

Where any parent or Indian custodian voluntarily consents to a foster care placement or to termination of parental rights, such consent shall not be valid unless executed in writing and recorded before a judge of a court of competent jurisdiction and accompanied by the presiding judge's certificate that the terms and consequences of the consent were fully explained in detail and were fully understood by the parent or Indian custodian. The court shall also certify that either the parent or Indian custodian fully understood the explanation in English or that it was interpreted into a language that the parent or Indian custodian understood. Any consent given prior to, or within ten days after, birth of the Indian child shall not be valid.

(b) Foster care placement; withdrawal of consent

Any parent or Indian custodian may withdraw consent to a foster care placement under State law at any time and, upon such withdrawal, the child shall be returned to the parent or Indian custodian.

(c) Voluntary termination of parental rights or adoptive placement; withdrawal of consent; return of custody

In any voluntary proceeding for termination of parental rights to, or adoptive placement of, an Indian child, the consent of the parent may be withdrawn for any reason at any time prior to the entry of a final decree of termination or adoption, as the case may be, and the child shall be returned to the parent.

(d) Collateral attack; vacation of decree and return of custody; limitations

After the entry of a final decree of adoption of an Indian child in any State court, the parent may withdraw consent thereto upon the grounds that consent was obtained through fraud or duress and may petition the court to vacate such decree. Upon a finding that such consent was obtained through fraud or duress, the court shall vacate such decree and return the child to the parent. No adoption which has been effective for at least two years may be invalidated under the provisions of this subsection unless otherwise permitted under State law.

§ 1914. Petition to court of competent jurisdiction to invalidate action upon showing of certain violations

Any Indian child who is the subject of any action for foster care placement or termination of parental rights under State law, any parent or Indian custodian from whose custody such child was removed, and the Indian child's tribe may petition any court of competent jurisdiction to invalidate such action upon a showing that such action violated any provision of sections 1911, 1912, and 1913 of this title.

§ 1915. Placement of Indian children

(a) Adoptive placements; preferences

In any adoptive placement of an Indian child under State law, a preference shall be given, in the absence of good cause to the contrary, to a placement with (1) a member of the child's extended family; (2) other members of the Indian child's tribe; or (3) other Indian families.

(b) Foster care or preadoptive placements; criteria; preferences

Any child accepted for foster care or preadoptive placement shall be placed in the least restrictive setting which most approximates a family and in which his special needs, if any, may be met. The child shall also be placed within reasonable proximity to his or her home, taking into account any special needs of the child. In any foster care or preadoptive placement, a preference shall be given, in the absence of good cause to the contrary, to a placement with—

(i) a member of the Indian child's extended family;

(ii) a foster home licensed, approved, or specified by the Indian child's tribe;

(iii) an Indian foster home licensed or approved by an authorized non-Indian licensing authority; or

(iv) an institution for children approved by an Indian tribe or operated by an Indian organization which has a program suitable to meet the Indian child's needs.

(c) Tribal resolution for different order of preference; personal preference considered; anonymity in application of preferences

In the case of a placement under subsection (a) or (b) of this section, if the Indian child's tribe shall establish a different order of preference by resolution, the agency or court effecting the placement shall follow such order so long as the placement is the least restrictive setting appropriate to the particular needs of the child, as provided in subsection (b) of this section. Where appropriate, the preference of the Indian child or parent shall be considered: Provided, That where a consenting parent evidences a desire for anonymity, the court or agency shall give weight to such desire in applying the preferences.

(d) Social and cultural standards applicable

The standards to be applied in meeting the preference requirements of this section shall be the prevailing social and cultural standards of the Indian community in which the parent or extended family resides or with which the parent or extended family members maintain social and cultural ties.

(e) Record of placement; availability

A record of each such placement, under State law, of an Indian child shall be maintained by the State in which the placement was made, evidencing the efforts to comply with the order of preference specified in this section. Such record shall be made available at any time upon the request of the Secretary or the Indian child's tribe.

§ 1916. Return of custody

(a) Petition; best interests of child

Notwithstanding State law to the contrary, whenever a final decree of adoption of an Indian child has been vacated or set aside or the adoptive parents voluntarily consent to the termination of their parental rights to the child, a biological parent or prior Indian custodian may petition for return of custody and the court shall grant such petition unless there is a showing, in a proceeding subject to the provisions of section 1912 of this title, that such return of custody is not in the best interests of the child.

(b) Removal from foster care home; placement procedure

Whenever an Indian child is removed from a foster care home or institution for the purpose of further foster care, preadoptive, or adoptive placement, such placement shall be in accordance with the provisions of this chapter, except in the case where an Indian child is being returned to the parent or Indian custodian from whose custody the child was originally removed.

§ 1917. Tribal affiliation information and other information for protection of rights from tribal relationship; application of subject of adoptive placement; disclosure by court

Upon application by an Indian individual who has reached the age of eighteen and who was the subject of an adoptive placement, the court which entered the final decree shall inform such individual of the tribal affiliation, if any, of the individual's biological parents and provide such other information as may be necessary to protect any rights flowing from the individual's tribal relationship.

§ 1918. Reassumption of jurisdiction over child custody proceedings

(a) Petition; suitable plan; approval by Secretary

Any Indian tribe which became subject to State jurisdiction pursuant to the provisions of the Act of August 15, 1953 (67 Stat. 588), as amended by title IV of the Act of April 11, 1968 (82 Stat. 73, 78), or pursuant to any other Federal law, may reassume jurisdiction over child custody proceedings. Before any Indian tribe may reassume jurisdiction over Indian child custody proceedings, such tribe shall present to the Secretary for approval a petition to reassume such jurisdiction which includes a suitable plan to exercise such jurisdiction.

(b) Criteria applicable to consideration by Secretary; partial retrocession

(1) In considering the petition and feasibility of the plan of a tribe under subsection (a) of this section, the Secretary may consider, among other things:

(i) whether or not the tribe maintains a membership roll or alternative provision for clearly identifying the persons who will be affected by the reassumption of jurisdiction by the tribe;

(ii) the size of the reservation or former reservation area which will be affected by retrocession and reassumption of jurisdiction by the tribe;

(iii) the population base of the tribe, or distribution of the population in homogeneous communities or geographic areas; and

(iv) the feasibility of the plan in cases of multitribal occupation of a single reservation or geographic area.

(2) In those cases where the Secretary determines that the jurisdictional provisions of section 1911(a) of this title are not feasible, he is authorized to accept partial retrocession which will enable tribes to exercise referral jurisdiction as provided in section 1911(b) of this title, or, where appropriate, will allow them to exercise exclusive jurisdiction as provided in section 1911(a) of this title over limited community or geographic areas without regard for the reservation status of the area affected.

(c) Approval of petition; publication in Federal Register; notice; reassumption period; correction of causes for disapproval

If the Secretary approves any petition under subsection (a) of this section, the Secretary shall publish notice of such approval in the Federal Register and shall notify the affected State or States of such approval. The Indian tribe concerned shall reassume jurisdiction sixty days after publication in the Federal Register of notice of approval. If the Secretary disapproves any petition under subsection (a) of this section, the Secretary shall provide such technical assistance as may be necessary to enable the tribe to correct any deficiency which the Secretary identified as a cause for disapproval.

(d) Pending actions or proceedings unaffected

Assumption of jurisdiction under this section shall not affect any action or proceeding over which a court has already assumed jurisdiction, except as may be provided pursuant to any agreement under section 1919 of this title.

§ 1919. Agreements between states and Indian tribes

(a) Subject coverage

States and Indian tribes are authorized to enter into agreements with each other respecting care and custody of Indian children and jurisdiction over child custody proceedings, including agreements which may provide for orderly transfer of jurisdiction on a case-by-case basis and agreements which provide for concurrent jurisdiction between States and Indian tribes.

(b) Revocation; notice; actions or proceedings unaffected

Such agreements may be revoked by either party upon one hundred and eighty days' written notice to the other party. Such revocation shall not affect any action or proceeding over which a court has already assumed jurisdiction, unless the agreement provides otherwise.

§ 1920. Improper removal of child from custody; declination of jurisdiction; forthwith return of child: danger exception

Where any petitioner in an Indian child custody proceeding before a State court has improperly removed the child from custody of the parent or Indian custodian or has improperly retained custody after a visit or other temporary relinquishment of custody, the court shall decline jurisdiction over such petition and shall forthwith return the child to his parent or Indian custodian unless returning the child to his parent or custodian would subject the child to a substantial and immediate danger or threat of such danger.

§ 1921. Higher state or federal standard applicable to protect rights of parent or Indian custodian of Indian child

In any case where State or Federal law applicable to a child custody proceeding under State or Federal law provides a higher standard of protection to the rights of the parent or Indian custodian of an Indian child than the rights provided under this subchapter, the State or Federal court shall apply the State or Federal standard.

§ 1922. Emergency removal or placement of child; termination; appropriate action

Nothing in this subchapter shall be construed to prevent the emergency removal of an Indian child who is a resident of or is domiciled on a reservation, but temporarily located off the reservation, from his parent or Indian custodian or the emergency placement of such child in a foster home or institution, under applicable State law, in order to prevent imminent physical damage or harm to the child. The State authority, official, or agency involved shall insure that the emergency removal or placement terminates immediately when such removal or placement is no longer necessary to prevent imminent physical damage or harm to the child and shall expeditiously initiate a child custody proceeding subject to the provisions of this subchapter, transfer the child to the jurisdiction of the appropriate Indian tribe, or restore the child to the parent or Indian custodian, as may be appropriate.

§ 1923. Effective date

None of the provisions of this subchapter, except sections 1911(a), 1918, and 1919 of this title, shall affect a proceeding under State law for foster care placement, termination of parental rights, preadoptive placement, or adoptive placement which was initiated or completed prior to one hundred and eighty days after November 8, 1978, but shall apply to any subsequent proceeding in the same matter or subsequent proceedings affecting the custody or placement of the same child.

25 C.F.R. 23.101–23.144. Indian Child Welfare Act Proceedings

[Effective Dec. 12, 2016. See 81 Fed. Reg. 38777, June 14, 2016.]

Subsection

§ 23.101. What is the purpose of this subpart?

The regulations in this subpart clarify the minimum Federal standards governing implementation of the Indian Child Welfare Act (ICWA) to ensure that ICWA is applied in all States consistent with the Act's express language, Congress's intent in enacting the statute, and to promote the stability and security of Indian tribes and families.

§ 23.102. What terms do I need to know?

The following terms and their definitions apply to this subpart. All other terms have the meanings assigned in § 23.2.

Agency means a nonprofit, for-profit, or governmental organization and its employees, agents, or officials that performs, or provides services to biological parents, foster parents, or adoptive parents to assist in the administrative and social work necessary for foster, preadoptive, or adoptive placements.

Indian organization means any group, association, partnership, corporation, or other legal entity owned or controlled by Indians or a Tribe, or a majority of whose members are Indians.

§ 23.103. When does ICWA apply?

(a) ICWA includes requirements that apply whenever an Indian child is the subject of:

(1) A child-custody proceeding, including:

(i) An involuntary proceeding;

(ii) A voluntary proceeding that could prohibit the parent or Indian custodian from regaining custody of the child upon demand; and

(iii) A proceeding involving status offenses if any part of the proceeding results in the need for out-of-home placement of the child, including a foster-care, preadoptive, or adoptive placement, or termination of parental rights.

(2) An emergency proceeding.

(b) ICWA does not apply to:

(1) A Tribal court proceeding;

(2) A proceeding regarding a criminal act that is not a status offense;

(3) An award of custody of the Indian child to one of the parents including, but not limited to, an award in a divorce proceeding; or

(4) A voluntary placement that either parent, both parents, or the Indian custodian has, of his or her or their free will, without a threat of removal by a State agency, chosen for the Indian child and that does not operate to prohibit the child's parent or Indian custodian from regaining custody of the child upon demand.

(c) If a proceeding listed in paragraph (a) of this section concerns a child who meets the statutory definition of "Indian child," then ICWA will apply to that proceeding. In determining whether ICWA applies to a proceeding, the State court may not consider factors such as the participation of the parents or the Indian child in Tribal cultural, social, religious, or political activities, the relationship between the Indian child and his or her parents, whether the parent ever had custody of the child, or the Indian child's blood quantum.

(d) If ICWA applies at the commencement of a proceeding, it will not cease to apply simply because the child reaches age 18 during the pendency of the proceeding.

§ 23.104. What provisions of this subpart apply to each type of child-custody proceeding?

The following table lists what sections of this subpart apply to each type of child-custody proceeding identified in § 23.103(a):

Section	Type of proceeding
23.101–23.106 (General Provisions)	Emergency, Involuntary, Voluntary.
Pretrial Requirements:	
23.107 (How should a State court determine if there is reason to know the child is an Indian child?)	Emergency, Involuntary, Voluntary.
23.108 (Who makes the determination as to whether a child is a member whether a child is eligible for membership, or whether a biological parent is a member of a Tribe?)	Emergency, Involuntary, Voluntary.
23.109 (How should a State court determine an Indian child's Tribe when the child may be a member or eligible for membership in more than one Tribe?)	Emergency, Involuntary, Voluntary.
23.110 (When must a State court dismiss an action?)	Involuntary, Voluntary.
23.111 (What are the notice requirements for a child-custody proceeding involving an Indian child?)	Involuntary (foster-care placement and termination of parental rights).
23.112 (What time limits and extensions apply?)	Involuntary (foster-care placement and termination of parental rights).
23.113 (What are the standards for emergency proceedings involving an Indian child?)	Emergency.
23.114 (What are the requirements for determining improper removal?)	Involuntary.
Petitions to Transfer to Tribal Court:	
23.115 (How are petitions for transfer of a proceeding made?)	Involuntary, Voluntary (foster-care placement and termination of parental rights).
23.116 (What happens after a petition for transfer is made?)	Involuntary, Voluntary (foster-care placement and termination of parental rights).
23.117 (What are the criteria for ruling on transfer petitions?)	Involuntary, Voluntary (foster-care placement and termination of parental rights).
23.118 (How is a determination of "good cause" to deny transfer made?)	Involuntary, Voluntary (foster-care placement and termination of parental rights).
23.119 (What happens after a petition for transfer is granted?)	Involuntary, Voluntary (foster-care placement and termination of parental rights).
Adjudication of Involuntary Proceedings:	
23.120 (How does the State court ensure that active efforts have been made?)	Involuntary (foster-care placement and termination of parental rights).
23.121 (What are the applicable standards of evidence?)	Involuntary (foster-care placement and termination of parental rights).
23.122 (Who may serve as a qualified expert witness?)	Involuntary (foster-care placement and termination of parental rights).
23.123 Reserved	N/A.
Voluntary Proceedings:	
23.124 (What actions must a State court undertake in voluntary proceedings?)	Voluntary.
23.125 (How is consent obtained?)	Voluntary.

Section	Type of proceeding
23.126 (What information must a consent document contain?)	Voluntary.
23.127 (How is withdrawal of consent to a foster-care placement achieved?)	Voluntary.
23.128 (How is withdrawal of consent to a termination of parental rights or adoption achieved?)	Voluntary.
Dispositions:	
23.129 (When do the placement preferences apply?)	Involuntary, Voluntary.
23.130 (What placement preferences apply in adoptive placements?)	Involuntary, Voluntary.
23.131 (What placement preferences apply in foster-care or preadoptive placements?)	Involuntary, Voluntary.
23.132 (How is a determination of "good cause" to depart from the placement preferences made?)	Involuntary, Voluntary.
Access:	
23.133 (Should courts allow participation by alternative methods?)	Emergency, Involuntary.
23.134 (Who has access to reports and records during a proceeding?)	Emergency, Involuntary.
23.135 Reserved.	N/A.
Post-Trial Rights & Responsibilities:	
23.136 (What are the requirements for vacating an adoption based on consent having been obtained through fraud or duress?)	Involuntary (if consent given under threat of removal), voluntary.
23.137 (Who can petition to invalidate an action for certain ICWA violations?)	Emergency (to extent it involved a specified violation), involuntary, voluntary.
23.138 (What are the rights to information about adoptees' Tribal affiliations?)	Emergency, Involuntary, Voluntary.
23.139 (Must notice be given of a change in an adopted Indian child's status?)	Involuntary, Voluntary.
Recordkeeping:	
23.140 (What information must States furnish to the Bureau of Indian Affairs?)	Involuntary, Voluntary.
23.141 (What records must the State maintain?)	Involuntary, Voluntary.
23.142 (How does the Paperwork Reduction Act affect this subpart?)	Emergency, Involuntary, Voluntary.
Effective Date:	
23.143 (How does this subpart apply to pending proceedings?)	Emergency, Involuntary, Voluntary.
Severability:	
23.144 (What happens if some portion of part is held to be invalid by a court of competent jurisdiction?)	Emergency, Involuntary, Voluntary.

Note: For purposes of this table, status-offense child-custody proceedings are included as a type of involuntary proceeding.

§ 23.105. How do I contact a Tribe under the regulations in this subpart?

To contact a Tribe to provide notice or obtain information or verification under the regulations in this subpart, you should direct the notice or inquiry as follows:

(a) Many Tribes designate an agent for receipt of ICWA notices. The BIA publishes a list of Tribes' designated Tribal agents for service of ICWA notice in the Federal Register each year and makes the list available on its Web site at www.bia.gov.

(b) For a Tribe without a designated Tribal agent for service of ICWA notice, contact the Tribe to be directed to the appropriate office or individual.

(c) If you do not have accurate contact information for a Tribe, or the Tribe contacted fails to respond to written inquiries, you should seek assistance in contacting the Indian Tribe from the BIA local or regional office or the BIA's Central Office in Washington, DC (see www.bia.gov).

§ 23.106. How does this subpart interact with State and Federal laws?

(a) The regulations in this subpart provide minimum Federal standards to ensure compliance with ICWA.

(b) Under section 1921 of ICWA, where applicable State or other Federal law provides a higher standard of protection to the rights of the parent or Indian custodian than the protection accorded under the Act, ICWA requires the State or Federal court to apply the higher State or Federal standard.

§ 23.107. How should a State court determine if there is reason to know the child is an Indian child?

(a) State courts must ask each participant in an emergency or voluntary or involuntary child-custody proceeding whether the participant knows or has reason to know that the child is an Indian child. The inquiry is made at the commencement of the proceeding and all responses should be on the record. State courts must instruct the parties to inform the court if they subsequently receive information that provides reason to know the child is an Indian child.

(b) If there is reason to know the child is an Indian child, but the court does not have sufficient evidence to determine that the child is or is not an "Indian child," the court must:

(1) Confirm, by way of a report, declaration, or testimony included in the record that the agency or other party used due diligence to identify and work with all of the Tribes of which there is reason to know the child may be a member (or eligible for membership), to verify whether the child is in fact a member (or a biological parent is a member and the child is eligible for membership); and

(2) Treat the child as an Indian child, unless and until it is determined on the record that the child does not meet the definition of an "Indian child" in this part.

(c) A court, upon conducting the inquiry required in paragraph (a) of this section, has reason to know that a child involved in an emergency or child-custody proceeding is an Indian child if:

(1) Any participant in the proceeding, officer of the court involved in the proceeding, Indian Tribe, Indian organization, or agency informs the court that the child is an Indian child;

(2) Any participant in the proceeding, officer of the court involved in the proceeding, Indian Tribe, Indian organization, or agency informs the court that it has discovered information indicating that the child is an Indian child;

(3) The child who is the subject of the proceeding gives the court reason to know he or she is an Indian child;

(4) The court is informed that the domicile or residence of the child, the child's parent, or the child's Indian custodian is on a reservation or in an Alaska Native village;

(5) The court is informed that the child is or has been a ward of a Tribal court; or

(6) The court is informed that either parent or the child possesses an identification card indicating membership in an Indian Tribe.

(d) In seeking verification of the child's status in a voluntary proceeding where a consenting parent evidences, by written request or statement in the record, a desire for anonymity, the court must keep relevant documents pertaining to the inquiry required under this section confidential and under seal. A request for anonymity does not relieve the court, agency, or other party from any duty of compliance with ICWA, including the obligation to verify whether the child is an "Indian child." A Tribe receiving information related to this inquiry must keep documents and information confidential.

§ 23.108. Who makes the determination as to whether a child is a member, whether a child is eligible for membership, or whether a biological parent is a member of a Tribe?

(a) The Indian Tribe of which it is believed the child is a member (or eligible for membership and of which the biological parent is a member) determines whether the child is a member of the Tribe, or whether the child is eligible for membership in the Tribe and a biological parent of the child is a member of the Tribe, except as otherwise provided by Federal or Tribal law.

(b) The determination by a Tribe of whether a child is a member, whether a child is eligible for membership, or whether a biological parent is a member, is solely within the jurisdiction and authority of the Tribe, except as otherwise provided by Federal or Tribal law. The State court may not substitute its own determination regarding a child's membership in a Tribe, a child's eligibility for membership in a Tribe, or a parent's membership in a Tribe.

(c) The State court may rely on facts or documentation indicating a Tribal determination of membership or eligibility for membership in making a judicial determination as to whether the child is an "Indian child." An example of documentation indicating membership is a document issued by the Tribe, such as Tribal enrollment documentation.

§ 23.109. How should a State court determine an Indian child's Tribe when the child may be a member or eligible for membership in more than one Tribe?

(a) If the Indian child is a member or eligible for membership in only one Tribe, that Tribe must be designated as the Indian child's Tribe.

(b) If the Indian child meets the definition of "Indian child" through more than one Tribe, deference should be given to the Tribe in which the Indian child is already a member, unless otherwise agreed to by the Tribes.

(c) If an Indian child meets the definition of "Indian child" through more than one Tribe because the child is a member in more than one Tribe or the child is not a member of but is eligible for membership in more than one Tribe, the court must provide the opportunity in any involuntary child-custody proceeding for the Tribes to determine which should be designated as the Indian child's Tribe.

(1) If the Tribes are able to reach an agreement, the agreed-upon Tribe should be designated as the Indian child's Tribe.

(2) If the Tribes are unable to reach an agreement, the State court designates, for the purposes of ICWA, the Indian Tribe with which the Indian child has the more significant contacts as the Indian child's Tribe, taking into consideration:

(i) Preference of the parents for membership of the child;

(ii) Length of past domicile or residence on or near the reservation of each Tribe;

(iii) Tribal membership of the child's custodial parent or Indian custodian; and

(iv) Interest asserted by each Tribe in the child-custody proceeding;

(v) Whether there has been a previous adjudication with respect to the child by a court of one of the Tribes; and

(vi) Self-identification by the child, if the child is of sufficient age and capacity to meaningfully self-identify.

(3) A determination of the Indian child's Tribe for purposes of ICWA and the regulations in this subpart do not constitute a determination for any other purpose.

§ 23.110. When must a State court dismiss an action?

Subject to 25 U.S.C. 1919 (Agreements between States and Indian Tribes) and § 23.113 (emergency proceedings), the following limitations on a State court's jurisdiction apply:

(a) The court in any voluntary or involuntary child-custody proceeding involving an Indian child must determine the residence and domicile of the Indian child. If either the residence or domicile is on a reservation where the Tribe exercises exclusive jurisdiction over child-custody proceedings, the State court must expeditiously notify the Tribal court of the pending dismissal based on the Tribe's exclusive jurisdiction, dismiss the State-court child-custody proceeding, and ensure that the Tribal court is sent all information regarding the Indian child-custody proceeding, including, but not limited to, the pleadings and any court record.

(b) If the child is a ward of a Tribal court, the State court must expeditiously notify the Tribal court of the pending dismissal, dismiss the State-court child-custody proceeding, and ensure that the Tribal court is sent all information regarding the Indian child-custody proceeding, including, but not limited to, the pleadings and any court record.

§ 23.111. What are the notice requirements for a child-custody proceeding involving an Indian child?

(a) When a court knows or has reason to know that the subject of an involuntary foster-care-placement or termination-of-parental-rights proceeding is an Indian child, the court must ensure that:

(1) The party seeking placement promptly sends notice of each such child-custody proceeding (including, but not limited to, any foster-care placement or any termination of parental or custodial rights) in accordance with this section; and

(2) An original or a copy of each notice sent under this section is filed with the court together with any return receipts or other proof of service.

(b) Notice must be sent to:

(1) Each Tribe where the child may be a member (or eligible for membership if a biological parent is a member) (see § 23.105 for information on how to contact a Tribe);

(2) The child's parents; and

(3) If applicable, the child's Indian custodian.

(c) Notice must be sent by registered or certified mail with return receipt requested. Notice may also be sent via personal service or electronically, but such alternative methods do not replace the requirement for notice to be sent by registered or certified mail with return receipt requested.

(d) Notice must be in clear and understandable language and include the following:

(1) The child's name, birthdate, and birthplace;

(2) All names known (including maiden, married, and former names or aliases) of the parents, the parents' birthdates and birthplaces, and Tribal enrollment numbers if known;

(3) If known, the names, birthdates, birthplaces, and Tribal enrollment information of other direct lineal ancestors of the child, such as grandparents;

(4) The name of each Indian Tribe in which the child is a member (or may be eligible for membership if a biological parent is a member);

(5) A copy of the petition, complaint, or other document by which the child-custody proceeding was initiated and, if a hearing has been scheduled, information on the date, time, and location of the hearing;

(6) Statements setting out:

(i) The name of the petitioner and the name and address of petitioner's attorney;

(ii) The right of any parent or Indian custodian of the child, if not already a party to the child-custody proceeding, to intervene in the proceedings.

(iii) The Indian Tribe's right to intervene at any time in a State-court proceeding for the foster-care placement of or termination of parental rights to an Indian child.

(iv) That, if the child's parent or Indian custodian is unable to afford counsel based on a determination of indigency by the court, the parent or Indian custodian has the right to court-appointed counsel.

(v) The right to be granted, upon request, up to 20 additional days to prepare for the child-custody proceedings.

(vi) The right of the parent or Indian custodian and the Indian child's Tribe to petition the court for transfer of the foster-care-placement or termination-of-parental-rights proceeding to Tribal court as provided by 25 U.S.C. 1911 and § 23.115.

(vii) The mailing addresses and telephone numbers of the court and information related to all parties to the child-custody proceeding and individuals notified under this section.

(viii) The potential legal consequences of the child-custody proceedings on the future parental and custodial rights of the parent or Indian custodian.

(ix) That all parties notified must keep confidential the information contained in the notice and the notice should not be handled by anyone not needing the information to exercise rights under ICWA.

(e) If the identity or location of the child's parents, the child's Indian custodian, or the Tribes in which the Indian child is a member or eligible for membership cannot be ascertained, but there is reason to know the child is an Indian child, notice of the child-custody proceeding must be sent to the appropriate Bureau of Indian Affairs Regional Director (see www.bia.gov). To establish Tribal identity, as much information as is known regarding the child's direct lineal ancestors should be provided. The Bureau of Indian Affairs will not make a determination of Tribal membership but may, in some instances, be able to identify Tribes to contact.

(f) If there is a reason to know that a parent or Indian custodian possesses limited English proficiency and is therefore not likely to understand the contents of the notice, the court must provide language access services as required by Title VI of the Civil Rights Act and other Federal laws. To secure such translation or interpretation support, a court may contact or direct a party to contact the Indian child's Tribe or the local BIA office for assistance in locating and obtaining the name of a qualified translator or interpreter.

(g) If a parent or Indian custodian of an Indian child appears in court without an attorney, the court must inform him or her of his or her rights, including any applicable right to appointed counsel, right to request that the child-custody proceeding be transferred to Tribal court, right to object to such transfer, right to request additional time to prepare for the child-custody proceeding as provided in § 23.112, and right (if the parent or Indian custodian is not already a party) to intervene in the child-custody proceedings.

§ 23.112. What time limits and extensions apply?

(a) No foster-care-placement or termination-of-parental-rights proceeding may be held until at least 10 days after receipt of the notice by the parent (or Indian custodian) and by the Tribe (or the Secretary). The parent, Indian custodian, and Tribe each have a right, upon request, to be granted up to 20 additional days from the date upon which notice was received to prepare for participation in the proceeding.

(b) Except as provided in 25 U.S.C. 1922 and § 23.113, no child-custody proceeding for foster-care placement or termination of parental rights may be held until the waiting periods to which the parents or Indian custodians and to which the Indian child's Tribe are entitled have expired, as follows:

(1) 10 days after each parent or Indian custodian (or Secretary where the parent or Indian custodian is unknown to the petitioner) has received notice of that particular child-custody proceeding in accordance with 25 U.S.C. 1912(a) and § 23.111;

(2) 10 days after the Indian child's Tribe (or the Secretary if the Indian child's Tribe is unknown to the party seeking placement) has received notice of that particular child-custody proceeding in accordance with 25 U.S.C. 1912(a) and § 23.111;

(3) Up to 30 days after the parent or Indian custodian has received notice of that particular child-custody proceeding in accordance with 25 U.S.C. 1912(a) and § 23.111, if the parent or Indian custodian has requested up to 20 additional days to prepare for the child-custody proceeding as provided in 25 U.S.C. 1912(a) and § 23.111; and

(4) Up to 30 days after the Indian child's Tribe has received notice of that particular child-custody proceeding in accordance with 25 U.S.C. 1912(a) and § 23.111, if the Indian child's Tribe has requested up to 20 additional days to prepare for the child-custody proceeding.

(c) Additional time beyond the minimum required by 25 U.S.C. 1912 and § 23.111 may also be available under State law or pursuant to extensions granted by the court.

§ 23.113. What are the standards for emergency proceedings involving an Indian child?

(a) Any emergency removal or placement of an Indian child under State law must terminate immediately when the removal or placement is no longer necessary to prevent imminent physical damage or harm to the child.

(b) The State court must:

(1) Make a finding on the record that the emergency removal or placement is necessary to prevent imminent physical damage or harm to the child;

(2) Promptly hold a hearing on whether the emergency removal or placement continues to be necessary whenever new information indicates that the emergency situation has ended; and

(3) At any court hearing during the emergency proceeding, determine whether the emergency removal or placement is no longer necessary to prevent imminent physical damage or harm to the child.

(4) Immediately terminate (or ensure that the agency immediately terminates) the emergency proceeding once the court or agency possesses sufficient evidence to determine that the emergency removal or placement is no longer necessary to prevent imminent physical damage or harm to the child.

(c) An emergency proceeding can be terminated by one or more of the following actions:

(1) Initiation of a child-custody proceeding subject to the provisions of ICWA;

(2) Transfer of the child to the jurisdiction of the appropriate Indian Tribe; or

(3) Restoring the child to the parent or Indian custodian.

(d) A petition for a court order authorizing the emergency removal or continued emergency placement, or its accompanying documents, should contain a statement of the risk of imminent physical damage or harm to the Indian child and any evidence that the emergency removal or placement continues to be necessary to prevent such imminent physical damage or harm to the child. The petition or its accompanying documents should also contain the following information:

(1) The name, age, and last known address of the Indian child;

(2) The name and address of the child's parents and Indian custodians, if any;

(3) The steps taken to provide notice to the child's parents, custodians, and Tribe about the emergency proceeding;

(4) If the child's parents and Indian custodians are unknown, a detailed explanation of what efforts have been made to locate and contact them, including contact with the appropriate BIA Regional Director (see www.bia.gov);

(5) The residence and the domicile of the Indian child;

(6) If either the residence or the domicile of the Indian child is believed to be on a reservation or in an Alaska Native village, the name of the Tribe affiliated with that reservation or village;

(7) The Tribal affiliation of the child and of the parents or Indian custodians;

(8) A specific and detailed account of the circumstances that led the agency responsible for the emergency removal of the child to take that action;

(9) If the child is believed to reside or be domiciled on a reservation where the Tribe exercises exclusive jurisdiction over child-custody matters, a statement of efforts that have been made and are being made to contact the Tribe and transfer the child to the Tribe's jurisdiction; and

(10) A statement of the efforts that have been taken to assist the parents or Indian custodians so the Indian child may safely be returned to their custody.

(e) An emergency proceeding regarding an Indian child should not be continued for more than 30 days unless the court makes the following determinations:

(1) Restoring the child to the parent or Indian custodian would subject the child to imminent physical damage or harm;

(2) The court has been unable to transfer the proceeding to the jurisdiction of the appropriate Indian Tribe; and

(3) It has not been possible to initiate a "child-custody proceeding" as defined in § 23.2.

§ 23.114. What are the requirements for determining improper removal?

(a) If, in the course of any child-custody proceeding, any party asserts or the court has reason to believe that the Indian child may have been improperly removed from the custody of his or her parent or Indian custodian, or that the Indian child has been improperly retained (such as after a visit or other temporary relinquishment of custody), the court must expeditiously determine whether there was improper removal or retention.

(b) If the court finds that the Indian child was improperly removed or retained, the court must terminate the proceeding and the child must be returned immediately to his or her parent or Indian custodian, unless returning the child to his parent or Indian custodian would subject the child to substantial and immediate danger or threat of such danger.

§ 23.115. How are petitions for transfer of a proceeding made?

(a) Either parent, the Indian custodian, or the Indian child's Tribe may request, at any time, orally on the record or in writing, that the State court transfer a foster-care or termination-of-parental-rights proceeding to the jurisdiction of the child's Tribe.

(b) The right to request a transfer is available at any stage in each foster-care or termination-of-parental-rights proceeding.

§ 23.116. What happens after a petition for transfer is made?

Upon receipt of a transfer petition, the State court must ensure that the Tribal court is promptly notified in writing of the transfer petition. This notification may request a timely response regarding whether the Tribal court wishes to decline the transfer.

§ 23.117. What are the criteria for ruling on transfer petitions?

Upon receipt of a transfer petition from an Indian child's parent, Indian custodian, or Tribe, the State court must transfer the child-custody proceeding unless the court determines that transfer is not appropriate because one or more of the following criteria are met:

(a) Either parent objects to such transfer;

(b) The Tribal court declines the transfer; or

(c) Good cause exists for denying the transfer.

§ 23.118. How is a determination of "good cause" to deny transfer made?

(a) If the State court believes, or any party asserts, that good cause to deny transfer exists, the reasons for that belief or assertion must be stated orally on the record or provided in writing on the record and to the parties to the child-custody proceeding.

(b) Any party to the child-custody proceeding must have the opportunity to provide the court with views regarding whether good cause to deny transfer exists.

(c) In determining whether good cause exists, the court must not consider:

(1) Whether the foster-care or termination-of-parental-rights proceeding is at an advanced stage if the Indian child's parent, Indian custodian, or Tribe did not receive notice of the child-custody proceeding until an advanced stage;

(2) Whether there have been prior proceedings involving the child for which no petition to transfer was filed;

(3) Whether transfer could affect the placement of the child;

(4) The Indian child's cultural connections with the Tribe or its reservation; or

(5) Socioeconomic conditions or any negative perception of Tribal or BIA social services or judicial systems.

(d) The basis for any State-court decision to deny transfer should be stated orally on the record or in a written order.

§ 23.119. What happens after a petition for transfer is granted?

(a) If the Tribal court accepts the transfer, the State court should expeditiously provide the Tribal court with all records related to the proceeding, including, but not limited to, the pleadings and any court record.

(b) The State court should work with the Tribal court to ensure that the transfer of the custody of the Indian child and of the proceeding is accomplished smoothly and in a way that minimizes the disruption of services to the family.

§ 23.120. How does the State court ensure that active efforts have been made?

(a) Prior to ordering an involuntary foster-care placement or termination of parental rights, the court must conclude that active efforts have been made to prevent the breakup of the Indian family and that those efforts have been unsuccessful.

(b) Active efforts must be documented in detail in the record.

§ 23.121. What are the applicable standards of evidence?

(a) The court must not order a foster-care placement of an Indian child unless clear and convincing evidence is presented, including the testimony of one or more qualified expert witnesses, demonstrating that the child's continued custody by the child's parent or Indian custodian is likely to result in serious emotional or physical damage to the child.

(b) The court must not order a termination of parental rights for an Indian child unless evidence beyond a reasonable doubt is presented, including the testimony of one or more qualified expert witnesses, demonstrating that the child's continued custody by the child's parent or Indian custodian is likely to result in serious emotional or physical damage to the child.

(c) For a foster-care placement or termination of parental rights, the evidence must show a causal relationship between the particular conditions in the home and the likelihood that continued custody of the child will result in serious emotional or physical damage to the particular child who is the subject of the child-custody proceeding.

(d) Without a causal relationship identified in paragraph (c) of this section, evidence that shows only the existence of community or family poverty, isolation, single parenthood, custodian age, crowded or inadequate housing, substance abuse, or nonconforming social behavior does not by itself constitute clear and convincing evidence or evidence beyond a reasonable doubt that continued custody is likely to result in serious emotional or physical damage to the child.

§ 23.122. Who may serve as a qualified expert witness?

(a) A qualified expert witness must be qualified to testify regarding whether the child's continued custody by the parent or

Indian custodian is likely to result in serious emotional or physical damage to the child and should be qualified to testify as to the prevailing social and cultural standards of the Indian child's Tribe. A person may be designated by the Indian child's Tribe as being qualified to testify to the prevailing social and cultural standards of the Indian child's Tribe.

(b) The court or any party may request the assistance of the Indian child's Tribe or the BIA office serving the Indian child's Tribe in locating persons qualified to serve as expert witnesses.

(c) The social worker regularly assigned to the Indian child may not serve as a qualified expert witness in child-custody proceedings concerning the child.

§ 23.123. [Reserved]

§ 23.124. What actions must a State court undertake in voluntary proceedings?

(a) The State court must require the participants in a voluntary proceeding to state on the record whether the child is an Indian child, or whether there is reason to believe the child is an Indian child, as provided in § 23.107.

(b) If there is reason to believe the child is an Indian child, the State court must ensure that the party seeking placement has taken all reasonable steps to verify the child's status. This may include contacting the Tribe of which it is believed the child is a member (or eligible for membership and of which the biological parent is a member) to verify the child's status. As described in § 23.107, where a consenting parent requests anonymity, a Tribe receiving such information must keep relevant documents and information confidential.

(c) State courts must ensure that the placement for the Indian child complies with §§ 23.129–23.132.

§ 23.125. How is consent obtained?

(a) A parent's or Indian custodian's consent to a voluntary termination of parental rights or to a foster-care, preadoptive, or adoptive placement must be executed in writing and recorded before a court of competent jurisdiction.

(b) Prior to accepting the consent, the court must explain to the parent or Indian custodian:

(1) The terms and consequences of the consent in detail; and

(2) The following limitations, applicable to the type of child-custody proceeding for which consent is given, on withdrawal of consent:

(i) For consent to foster-care placement, the parent or Indian custodian may withdraw consent for any reason, at any time, and have the child returned; or

(ii) For consent to termination of parental rights, the parent or Indian custodian may withdraw consent for any reason, at any time prior to the entry of the final decree of termination and have the child returned; or

(iii) For consent to an adoptive placement, the parent or Indian custodian may withdraw consent for any reason, at any time prior to the entry of the final decree of adoption, and have the child returned.

(c) The court must certify that the terms and consequences of the consent were explained on the record in detail in English (or the language of the parent or Indian custodian, if English is not the primary language) and were fully understood by the parent or Indian custodian.

11

(d) Where confidentiality is requested or indicated, execution of consent need not be made in a session of court open to the public but still must be made before a court of competent jurisdiction in compliance with this section.

(e) A consent given prior to, or within 10 days after, the birth of an Indian child is not valid.

§ 23.126. What information must a consent document contain?

(a) If there are any conditions to the consent, the written consent must clearly set out the conditions.

(b) A written consent to foster-care placement should contain, in addition to the information specified in paragraph (a) of this section, the name and birthdate of the Indian child; the name of the Indian child's Tribe; the Tribal enrollment number for the parent and for the Indian child, where known, or some other indication of the child's membership in the Tribe; the name, address, and other identifying information of the consenting parent or Indian custodian; the name and address of the person or entity, if any, who arranged the placement; and the name and address of the prospective foster parents, if known at the time.

§ 23.127. How is withdrawal of consent to a foster-care placement achieved?

(a) The parent or Indian custodian may withdraw consent to voluntary foster-care placement at any time.

(b) To withdraw consent, the parent or Indian custodian must file a written document with the court or otherwise testify before the court. Additional methods of withdrawing consent may be available under State law.

(c) When a parent or Indian custodian withdraws consent to a voluntary foster-care placement, the court must ensure that the Indian child is returned to that parent or Indian custodian as soon as practicable.

§ 23.128. How is withdrawal of consent to a termination of parental rights or adoption achieved?

(a) A parent may withdraw consent to voluntary termination of parental rights at any time prior to the entry of a final decree of termination.

(b) A parent or Indian custodian may withdraw consent to voluntary adoption at any time prior to the entry of a final decree of adoption.

(c) To withdraw consent prior to the entry of a final decree of adoption, the parent or Indian custodian must file a written document with the court or otherwise testify before the court. Additional methods of withdrawing consent may be available under State law.

(d) The court in which the withdrawal of consent is filed must promptly notify the person or entity who arranged any voluntary preadoptive or adoptive placement of such filing, and the Indian child must be returned to the parent or Indian custodian as soon as practicable.

§ 23.129. When do the placement preferences apply?

(a) In any preadoptive, adoptive, or foster-care placement of an Indian child, the placement preferences specified in § 23.130 and § 23.131 apply.

(b) Where a consenting parent requests anonymity in a voluntary proceeding, the court must give weight to the request in applying the preferences.

(c) The placement preferences must be applied in any foster-care, preadoptive, or adoptive placement unless there is a determination on the record that good cause under § 23.132 exists to not apply those placement preferences.

§ 23.130. What placement preferences apply in adoptive placements?

(a) In any adoptive placement of an Indian child under State law, where the Indian child's Tribe has not established a different order of preference under paragraph (b) of this section, preference must be given in descending order, as listed below, to placement of the child with:

(1) A member of the Indian child's extended family;

(2) Other members of the Indian child's Tribe; or

(3) Other Indian families.

(b) If the Indian child's Tribe has established by resolution a different order of preference than that specified in ICWA, the Tribe's placement preferences apply.

(c) The court must, where appropriate, also consider the placement preference of the Indian child or Indian child's parent.

§ 23.131. What placement preferences apply in foster-care or preadoptive placements?

(a) In any foster-care or preadoptive placement of an Indian child under State law, including changes in foster-care or preadoptive placements, the child must be placed in the least-restrictive setting that:

(1) Most approximates a family, taking into consideration sibling attachment;

(2) Allows the Indian child's special needs (if any) to be met; and

(3) Is in reasonable proximity to the Indian child's home, extended family, or siblings.

(b) In any foster-care or preadoptive placement of an Indian child under State law, where the Indian child's Tribe has not established a different order of preference under paragraph (c) of this section, preference must be given, in descending order as listed below, to placement of the child with:

(1) A member of the Indian child's extended family;

(2) A foster home that is licensed, approved, or specified by the Indian child's Tribe;

(3) An Indian foster home licensed or approved by an authorized non-Indian licensing authority; or

(4) An institution for children approved by an Indian Tribe or operated by an Indian organization which has a program suitable to meet the child's needs.

(c) If the Indian child's Tribe has established by resolution a different order of preference than that specified in ICWA, the Tribe's placement preferences apply, so long as the placement is the least-restrictive setting appropriate to the particular needs of the Indian child, as provided in paragraph (a) of this section.

(d) The court must, where appropriate, also consider the preference of the Indian child or the Indian child's parent.

§ 23.132. How is a determination of "good cause" to depart from the placement preferences made?

(a) If any party asserts that good cause not to follow the placement preferences exists, the reasons for that belief or assertion must be stated orally on the record or provided in writing to the parties to the child-custody proceeding and the court.

(b) The party seeking departure from the placement preferences should bear the burden of proving by clear and convincing evidence that there is "good cause" to depart from the placement preferences.

(c) A court's determination of good cause to depart from the placement preferences must be made on the record or in writing and should be based on one or more of the following considerations:

(1) The request of one or both of the Indian child's parents, if they attest that they have reviewed the placement options, if any, that comply with the order of preference;

(2) The request of the child, if the child is of sufficient age and capacity to understand the decision that is being made;

(3) The presence of a sibling attachment that can be maintained only through a particular placement;

(4) The extraordinary physical, mental, or emotional needs of the Indian child, such as specialized treatment services that may be unavailable in the community where families who meet the placement preferences live;

(5) The unavailability of a suitable placement after a determination by the court that a diligent search was conducted to find suitable placements meeting the preference criteria, but none has been located. For purposes of this analysis, the standards for determining whether a placement is unavailable must conform to the prevailing social and cultural standards of the Indian community in which the Indian child's parent or extended family resides or with which the Indian child's parent or extended family members maintain social and cultural ties.

(d) A placement may not depart from the preferences based on the socioeconomic status of any placement relative to another placement.

(e) A placement may not depart from the preferences based solely on ordinary bonding or attachment that flowed from time spent in a non-preferred placement that was made in violation of ICWA.

§ 23.133. Should courts allow participation by alternative methods?

If it possesses the capability, the court should allow alternative methods of participation in State-court child-custody proceedings involving an Indian child, such as participation by telephone, videoconferencing, or other methods.

§ 23.134. Who has access to reports and records during a proceeding?

Each party to an emergency proceeding or a foster-care-placement or termination-of-parental-rights proceeding under State law involving an Indian child has a right to timely examine all reports and other documents filed or lodged with the court upon which any decision with respect to such action may be based.

§ 23.135. [Reserved]

§ 23.136. What are the requirements for vacating an adoption based on consent having been obtained through fraud or duress?

(a) Within two years after a final decree of adoption of any Indian child by a State court, or within any longer period of time permitted by the law of the State, the State court may invalidate the voluntary adoption upon finding that the parent's consent was obtained by fraud or duress.

(b) Upon the parent's filing of a petition to vacate the final decree of adoption of the parent's Indian child, the court must give notice to all parties to the adoption proceedings and the Indian child's Tribe and must hold a hearing on the petition.

(c) Where the court finds that the parent's consent was obtained through fraud or duress, the court must vacate the final decree of adoption, order the consent revoked, and order that the child be returned to the parent.

§ 23.137. Who can petition to invalidate an action for certain ICWA violations?

(a) Any of the following may petition any court of competent jurisdiction to invalidate an action for foster-care placement or termination of parental rights under state law where it is alleged that 25 U.S.C. 1911, 1912, or 1913 has been violated:

(1) An Indian child who is or was the subject of any action for foster-care placement or termination of parental rights;

(2) A parent or Indian custodian from whose custody such child was removed; and

(3) The Indian child's Tribe.

(b) Upon a showing that an action for foster-care placement or termination of parental rights violated any provision of 25 U.S.C. 1911, 1912, or 1913, the court must determine whether it is appropriate to invalidate the action.

(c) To petition for invalidation, there is no requirement that the petitioner's rights under ICWA were violated; rather, a petitioner may challenge the action based on any violations of 25 U.S.C. 1911, 1912, or 1913 during the course of the child-custody proceeding.

§ 23.138. What are the rights to information about adoptees' Tribal affiliations?

Upon application by an Indian who has reached age 18 who was the subject of an adoptive placement, the court that entered the final decree of adoption must inform such individual of the Tribal affiliations, if any, of the individual's biological parents and provide such other information necessary to protect any rights, which may include Tribal membership, resulting from the individual's Tribal relationship.

§ 23.139. Must notice be given of a change in an adopted Indian child's status?

(a) If an Indian child has been adopted, the court must notify, by registered or certified mail with return receipt requested, the child's biological parent or prior Indian custodian and the Indian child's Tribe whenever:

(1) A final decree of adoption of the Indian child has been vacated or set aside; or

(2) The adoptive parent has voluntarily consented to the termination of his or her parental rights to the child.

(b) The notice must state the current name, and any former name, of the Indian child, inform the recipient of the right to petition for return of custody of the child, and provide sufficient information to allow the recipient to participate in any scheduled hearings.

(c) A parent or Indian custodian may waive his or her right to such notice by executing a written waiver of notice and filing the waiver with the court.

(1) Prior to accepting the waiver, the court must explain the consequences of the waiver and explain how the waiver may be revoked.

(2) The court must certify that the terms and consequences of the waiver and how the waiver may be revoked were explained in detail in English (or the language of the parent or Indian custodian, if English is not the primary language), and were fully understood by the parent or Indian custodian.

(3) Where confidentiality is requested or indicated, execution of the waiver need not be made in a session of court open to the public but still must be made before a court of competent jurisdiction in compliance with this section.

(4) The biological parent or Indian custodian may revoke the waiver at any time by filing with the court a written notice of revocation.

(5) A revocation of the right to receive notice does not affect any child-custody proceeding that was completed before the filing of the notice of revocation.

§ 23.140. What information must States furnish to the Bureau of Indian Affairs?

[Amended effective Nov. 5, 2018.]

(a) Any State court entering a final adoption decree or order in any voluntary or involuntary Indian-child adoptive placement must furnish a copy of the decree or order within 30 days to the Bureau of Indian Affairs, Chief, Division of Human Services, 1849 C Street NW, Mail Stop 3645 MIB, Washington, DC 20240, along with the following information, in an envelope marked "Confidential":

(1) Birth name and birthdate of the Indian child, and Tribal affiliation and name of the Indian child after adoption;

(2) Names and addresses of the biological parents;

(3) Names and addresses of the adoptive parents;

(4) Name and contact information for any agency having files or information relating to the adoption;

(5) Any affidavit signed by the biological parent or parents asking that their identity remain confidential; and

(6) Any information relating to Tribal membership or eligibility for Tribal membership of the adopted child.

(b) If a State agency has been designated as the repository for all State-court adoption information and is fulfilling the duties described in paragraph (a) of this section, the State courts in that State need not fulfill those same duties.

§ 23.141. What records must the State maintain?

(a) The State must maintain a record of every voluntary or involuntary foster-care, preadoptive, and adoptive placement of an Indian child and make the record available within 14 days of a request by an Indian child's Tribe or the Secretary.

(b) The record must contain, at a minimum, the petition or complaint, all substantive orders entered in the child-custody proceeding, the complete record of the placement determination (including, but not limited to, the findings in the court record and the social worker's statement), and, if the placement departs from the placement preferences, detailed documentation of the efforts to comply with the placement preferences.

(c) A State agency or agencies may be designated to be the repository for this information. The State court or agency should notify the BIA whether these records are maintained within the court system or by a State agency.

§ 23.142. How does the Paperwork Reduction Act affect this subpart?

The collections of information contained in this part have been approved by the Office of Management and Budget under 44 U.S.C. 3501 et seq. and assigned OMB Control Number 1076-0186. Response is required to obtain a benefit. A Federal agency may not conduct or sponsor, and you are not required to respond to, a collection of information unless the form or regulation requesting the information displays a currently valid OMB Control Number. Send comments regarding this collection of information, including suggestions for reducing the burden, to the Information Collection Clearance Officer—Indian Affairs, 1849 C Street NW., Washington, DC 20240.

§ 23.143. How does this subpart apply to pending proceedings?

None of the provisions of this subpart affects a proceeding under State law for foster-care placement, termination of parental rights, preadoptive placement, or adoptive placement that was initiated prior to December 12, 2016, but the provisions of this subpart apply to any subsequent proceeding in the same matter or subsequent proceedings affecting the custody or placement of the same child.

§ 23.144. What happens if some portion of this part is held to be invalid by a court of competent jurisdiction?

If any portion of this part is determined to be invalid by a court of competent jurisdiction, the other portions of the part remain in effect. For example, the Department has considered separately whether the provisions of this part apply to involuntary and voluntary proceedings; thus, if a particular provision is held to be invalid as to one type of proceeding, it is the Department's intent that it remains valid as to the other type of proceeding.

42 U.S.C. § 290dd-2. Substance Abuse and Mental Health Services Administration; Confidentiality of Records

Subsection

(a) Requirement

Records of the identity, diagnosis, prognosis, or treatment of any patient which are maintained in connection with the performance of any program or activity relating to substance abuse education, prevention, training, treatment, rehabilitation, or research, which is conducted, regulated, or directly or indirectly assisted by any department or agency of the United States shall, except as provided in subsection (e) of this section, be confidential and be disclosed only for the purposes and under the circumstances expressly authorized under subsection (b) of this section.

(b) Permitted disclosure

(1) Consent.

The content of any record referred to in subsection (a) of this section may be disclosed in accordance with the prior written consent of the patient with respect to whom such record is maintained, but only to such extent, under such circumstances, and for such purposes as may be allowed under regulations prescribed pursuant to subsection (g) of this section.

(2) Method for disclosure.

Whether or not the patient, with respect to whom any given record referred to in subsection (a) of this section is maintained, gives written consent, the content of such record may be disclosed as follows:

(A) To medical personnel to the extent necessary to meet a bona fide medical emergency.

(B) To qualified personnel for the purpose of conducting scientific research, management audits, financial audits, or program evaluation, but such personnel may not identify, directly or indirectly, any individual patient in any report of such research, audit, or evaluation, or otherwise disclose patient identities in any manner.

(C) If authorized by an appropriate order of a court of competent jurisdiction granted after application showing good cause therefor, including the need to avert a substantial risk of death or serious bodily harm. In assessing good cause the court shall weigh the public interest and the need for disclosure against the injury to the patient, to the physician-patient relationship, and to the treatment services. Upon the granting of such order, the court, in determining the extent to which any disclosure of all or any part of any record is necessary, shall impose appropriate safeguards against unauthorized disclosure.

(c) Use of records in criminal proceedings

Except as authorized by a court order granted under subsection (b)(2)(C) of this section, no record referred to in subsection (a) of this section may be used to initiate or substantiate any criminal charges against a patient or to conduct any investigation of a patient.

(d) Application

The prohibitions of this section continue to apply to records concerning any individual who has been a patient, irrespective of whether or when such individual ceases to be a patient.

(e) Nonapplicability

The prohibitions of this section do not apply to any interchange of records—

(1) within the Uniformed Services or within those components of the Department of Veterans Affairs furnishing health care to veterans; or

(2) between such components and the Uniformed Services.

The prohibitions of this section do not apply to the reporting under State law of incidents of suspected child abuse and neglect to the appropriate State or local authorities.

(f) Penalties

Any person who violates any provision of this section or any regulation issued pursuant to this section shall be fined in accordance with title 18.

(g) Regulations

Except as provided in subsection (h) of this section, the Secretary shall prescribe regulations to carry out the purposes of this section. Such regulations may contain such definitions, and may provide for such safeguards and procedures, including procedures and criteria for the issuance and scope of orders under subsection (b)(2)(C) of this section, as in the judgment of the Secretary are necessary or proper to effectuate the purposes of this section, to prevent circumvention or evasion thereof, or to facilitate compliance therewith.

(h) Application to Department of Veterans Affairs

The Secretary of Veterans Affairs, acting through the Under Secretary for Health, shall, to the maximum feasible extent consistent with their responsibilities under title 38, prescribe regulations making applicable the regulations prescribed by the Secretary of Health and Human Services under subsection (g) of this section to records maintained in connection with the provision of hospital care, nursing home care, domiciliary care, and medical services under such title 38 to veterans suffering from substance abuse. In prescribing and implementing regulations pursuant to this subsection, the Secretary of Veterans Affairs shall, from time to time, consult with the Secretary of Health and Human Services in order to achieve the maximum possible coordination of the regulations, and the implementation thereof, which they each prescribe.

42 C.F.R. §§ 2.61, 2.62, and 2.64. Selected Federal Regulations: Confidentiality of Alcohol and Drug Abuse Patient Records

Part 2—Confidentiality of Alcohol and Drug Abuse Patient Records

§ 2.61. Legal effect of order

[Amended effective Mar. 1, 2017.]

(a) Effect. An order of a court of competent jurisdiction entered under this subpart is a unique kind of court order. Its only purpose is to authorize a disclosure or use of patient information which would otherwise be prohibited by 42 U.S.C. 290dd-3 and the regulations in this part. Such an order does not compel disclosure. A subpoena or a similar legal mandate must be issued in order to compel disclosure. This mandate may be entered at the same time as and accompany an authorizing court order entered under the regulations in this part.

(b) Examples.

(1) A person holding records subject to the regulations in this part receives a subpoena for those records. The person may not disclose the records in response to the subpoena unless a court of competent jurisdiction enters an authorizing order under the regulations in this part.

(2) An authorizing court order is entered under the regulations in this part, but the person holding the records does not want to make the disclosure. If there is no subpoena or other compulsory process or a subpoena for the records has expired or been quashed, that person may refuse to make the disclosure. Upon the entry of a valid subpoena or other compulsory process the person holding the records must disclose, unless there is a valid legal defense to the process other than the confidentiality restrictions of the regulations in this part.

§ 2.62. Order not applicable to records disclosed without consent to researchers, auditors and evaluators

[Amended effective Mar. 1, 2017.]

A court order under the regulations in this part may not authorize qualified personnel, who have received patient identifying information without consent for the purpose of conducting research, audit or evaluation, to disclose that information or use it to conduct any criminal investigation or prosecution of a patient. However, a court order under § 2.66 may authorize disclosure and use of records to investigate or prosecute qualified personnel holding the records.

§ 2.64. Procedures and criteria for orders authorizing disclosures for noncriminal purposes

[Amended effective Mar. 1, 2017.]

(a) Application. An order authorizing the disclosure of patient records for purposes other than criminal investigation or prosecution may be applied for by any person having a legally recognized interest in the disclosure which is sought. The application may be filed separately or as part of a pending civil action in which the applicant asserts that the patient records are needed to provide evidence. An application must use a fictitious name, such as John Doe, to refer to any patient and may not contain or otherwise disclose any patient identifying information unless the patient is the applicant or has given written consent (meeting the requirements of the regulations in this part) to disclosure or the court has ordered the record of the proceeding sealed from public scrutiny.

(b) Notice. The patient and the person holding the records from whom disclosure is sought must be provided:

(1) Adequate notice in a manner which does not disclose patient identifying information to other persons; and

(2) An opportunity to file a written response to the application, or to appear in person, for the limited purpose of providing evidence on the statutory and regulatory criteria for the issuance of the court order as described in § 2.64(d).

(c) Review of evidence: Conduct of hearing. Any oral argument, review of evidence, or hearing on the application must be held in the judge's chambers or in some manner which ensures that patient identifying information is not disclosed to anyone other than a party to the proceeding, the patient, or the person holding the record, unless the patient requests an open hearing in a manner which meets the written consent requirements of the regulations in this part. The proceeding may include an examination by the judge of the patient records referred to in the application.

(d) Criteria for entry of order. An order under this section may be entered only if the court determines that good cause exists. To make this determination the court must find that:

(1) Other ways of obtaining the information are not available or would not be effective; and

(2) The public interest and need for the disclosure outweigh the potential injury to the patient, the physician-patient relationship and the treatment services.

(e) Content of order. An order authorizing a disclosure must:

(1) Limit disclosure to those parts of the patient's record which are essential to fulfill the objective of the order;

(2) Limit disclosure to those persons whose need for information is the basis for the order; and

(3) Include such other measures as are necessary to limit disclosure for the protection of the patient, the physician-patient relationship and the treatment services; for example, sealing from public scrutiny the record of any proceeding for which disclosure of a patient's record has been ordered.

45 C.F.R. Parts 1355 and 1356. Selected Federal Regulations Implementing ASFA and MEPA

§ 1355.20. Definitions

(a) * * *

Child care institution means a private child care institution, or a public child care institution which accommodates no more than twenty-five children, and is licensed by the licensing authority responsible for licensing or approval of institutions of this type as meeting the standards established for such licensing. The licensing authority must be a State authority in the State in which the child care institution is located, a Tribal authority with respect to a child care institution on or near an Indian Reservation, or a Tribal authority of a Tribal title IV–E agency with respect to a child care institution in the Tribal title IV–E agency's service area. This definition must not include detention facilities, forestry camps, training schools, or any other facility operated primarily for the detention of children who are determined to be delinquent.

* * * * *

Date a child is considered to have entered foster care means the earlier of: The date of the first judicial finding that the child has been subjected to child abuse or neglect; or, the date that is 60 calendar days after the date on which the child is removed from the home pursuant to § 1356.21(k). A title IV–E agency may use a date earlier than that required in this definition, such as the date the child is physically removed from the home. This definition determines the date used in calculating all time period requirements for the periodic reviews, permanency hearings, and termination of parental rights provision in section 475(5) of the Act and for providing time-limited reunification services described at section 431(a)(7) of the Act. The definition has no relationship to establishing initial title IV–E eligibility.

* * * * *

Entity, as used in § 1355.38, means any organization or agency (e.g., a private child placing agency) that is separate and independent of the title IV–E agency; performs title IV–E functions pursuant to a contract or subcontract with the title IV–E agency; and, receives title IV–E funds. A State or Tribal court is not an "entity" for the purposes of § 1355.38 except if an administrative arm of the State or Trial court carries out title IV–E administrative functions pursuant to a contract with the title IV–E agency.

Foster care means 24-hour substitute care for children placed away from their parents or guardians and for whom the title IV–E agency has placement and care responsibility. This includes, but is not limited to, placements in foster family homes, foster homes of relatives, group homes, emergency shelters, residential facilities, child care institutions, and preadoptive homes. A child is in foster care in accordance with this definition regardless of whether the foster care facility is licensed and payments are made by the State, Tribal or local agency for the care of the child, whether adoption subsidy payments are being made prior to the finalization of an adoption, or whether there is Federal matching of any payments that are made.

Foster care maintenance payments are payments made on behalf of a child eligible for title IV–E foster care to cover the cost of (and the cost of providing) food, clothing, shelter, daily supervision, school supplies, a child's personal incidentals, liability insurance with respect to a child, and reasonable travel for a child's visitation with family, or other caretakers. Local travel associated with providing the items listed above is also an allowable expense. In the case of child care institutions, such term must include the reasonable costs of administration and operation of such institutions as are necessarily required to provide the items described in the preceding sentences. "Daily supervision" for which foster care maintenance payments may be made includes:

(1) *Foster family care*—licensed child care, when work responsibilities preclude foster parents from being at home when the child for whom they have care and responsibility in foster care is not in school, licensed child care when the foster parent is required to participate, without the child, in activities associated with parenting a child in foster care that are beyond the scope of ordinary parental duties, such as attendance at administrative or judicial reviews, case conferences, or foster parent training. Payments to cover these costs may be: included in the basic foster care maintenance payment; a separate payment to the foster parent, or a separate payment to the child care provider; and

(2) *Child care institutions*—routine day-to-day direction and arrangements to ensure the well-being and safety of the child.

Foster family home means, for the purpose of title IV–E eligibility, the home of an individual or family licensed or approved as meeting the standards established by the licensing or approval authority(ies), that provides 24-hour out-of-home care for children. The licensing authority must be a State authority in the State in which the foster family home is located, a Tribal authority with respect to a foster family home on or near an Indian Reservation, or a Tribal authority of a Tribal title IV–E agency with respect to a foster family home in the Tribal title IV–E agency's service area. The term may include group homes, agency-operated boarding homes or other facilities licensed or approved for the purpose of providing foster care by the State or Tribal agency responsible for approval or licensing of such facilities. Foster family homes that are approved must be held to the same standards as foster family homes that are licensed. Anything less than full licensure or approval is insufficient for meeting title IV–E eligibility requirements. Title IV–E agencies may, however, claim title IV–E reimbursement during the period of time between the date a prospective foster family home satisfies all requirements for licensure or approval and the date the actual license is issued, not to exceed 60 days.

Full review means the joint Federal and title IV–E agency review of all federally-assisted child and family services programs, including family preservation and support services, child protective services, foster care, adoption, and independent living services, for the purpose of determining the title IV–E agency's substantial conformity with the plan requirements of titles IV–B and IV–E as listed in § 1355.34 of this part. A full review consists of two phases, the statewide assessment (or for a Tribal title IV–E agency, an assessment of the service area) and a subsequent on-site review, as described in § 1355.33 of this part.

* * * * *

Legal guardianship means a judicially-created relationship between child and caretaker which is intended to be permanent and self-sustaining as evidenced by the transfer to the caretaker of the following parental rights with respect to the child: protection, education, care and control of the person, custody of the person, and decision-making. The term legal guardian means the caretaker in such a relationship.

National Child Abuse and Neglect Data System (NCANDS) means the voluntary national data collection and analysis system established by the Administration for Children and Families in response to a requirement in the Child Abuse Prevention and Treatment Act (Pub. L. 93-247), as amended.

Partial review means:

(1) For the purpose of the child and family services review, the joint Federal and State/Tribal review of one or more federally-assisted child and family services program(s), including family preservation and support services, child protective services, foster care, adoption, and independent living services. A partial review may consist of any of the components of the full review, as mutually agreed upon by the title IV–E agency and the Administration for Children and Families as being sufficient to determine substantial conformity of the reviewed components with the plan requirements of titles IV–B and IV–E as listed in § 1355.34 of this part; and

(2) For the purpose of title IV–B and title IV–E State plan compliance issues that are outside the prescribed child and family services review format, e.g., compliance with AFCARS requirements, a review of State laws, policies, regulations, or other information appropriate to the nature of the concern, to determine State plan compliance; or

(3) For the purpose of title IV–E plan compliance issues for a Tribal title IV–E agency which are outside of the prescribed child and family services review format, a review of Tribal laws, policies, regulations, or other information appropriate to the nature of the concern, to determine plan compliance.

Permanency hearing means:

(1) The hearing required by section 475(5)(C) of the Act to determine the permanency plan for a child in foster care. Within this context, the court (including a Tribal court) or administrative body determines whether and, if applicable, when the child will be:

(i) Returned to the parent;

(ii) Placed for adoption, with the title IV–E agency filing a petition for termination of parental rights;

(iii) Referred for legal guardianship;

(iv) Placed permanently with a fit and willing relative; or

(v) Placed in another planned permanent living arrangement, but only in cases where the title IV–E agency has documented to the State or Tribal court a compelling reason for determining that it would not be in the best interests of the child to follow one of the four specified options above.

(2) The permanency hearing must be held no later than 12 months after the date the child is considered to have entered foster care in accordance with the definition at § 1355.20 of this part or within 30 days of a judicial determination that reasonable efforts to reunify the child and family are not required. After the initial permanency hearing, subsequent permanency hearings must be held not less frequently than every 12 months during the continuation of foster care. The permanency hearing must be conducted by a family or juvenile court or another court of competent jurisdiction or by an administrative body appointed or approved by the court which is not a part of or under the supervision or direction of the title IV–E agency. Paper reviews, ex parte hearings, agreed orders, or other actions or hearings which are not open to the participation of the parents of the child, the child (if of appropriate age), and foster parents or preadoptive parents (if any) are not permanency hearings.

* * * * *

Statewide assessment (or Tribal assessment) means the initial phase of a full review of all federally-assisted child and family services programs in the States (or for a Tribal title IV–E agency, in the service area), including family preservation and support services, child protective services, foster care, adoption, and independent living services as described in § 1355.33(b) of this part, for the purpose of determining substantial conformity with the plan requirements of titles IV–B and IV–E as listed in § 1355.34 of this part.

§ 1355.38. Enforcement of section 471(a)(18) of the Act regarding the removal of barriers to interethnic adoption

(a) Determination that a violation has occurred in the absence of a court finding.

(1) If ACF becomes aware of a possible section 471(a)(18) violation, whether in the course of a child and family services review, the filing of a complaint, or through some other mechanism, it will refer such a case to the Department's Office for Civil Rights (OCR) for investigation.

(2) Based on the findings of the OCR investigation, ACF will determine if a violation of section 471(a)(18) has occurred. A section 471(a)(18) violation occurs if a title IV–E agency or an entity in the State/Tribe:

(i) Has denied to any person the opportunity to become an adoptive or foster parent on the basis of the race, color, or national origin of the person, or of the child, involved;

(ii) Has delayed or denied the placement of a child for adoption or into foster care on the basis of the race, color, or national origin of the adoptive or foster parent, or the child involved; or,

(iii) With respect to a title IV–E agency, maintains any statute, regulation, policy, procedure, or practice that on its face, is a violation as defined in paragraphs (a)(2)(i) and (2)(ii) of this section.

(3) ACF will provide the title IV–E agency or entity with written notification of its determination.

(4) If there has been no violation, there will be no further action. If ACF determines that there has been a violation of section 471(a)(18), it will take enforcement action as described in this section.

(5) Compliance with the Indian Child Welfare Act of 1978 (Pub. L. 95–608) does not constitute a violation of section 471(a)(18).

(b) Corrective action and penalties for violations with respect to a person or based on a court finding.

(1) A title IV–E agency or entity found to be in violation of section 471(a)(18) of the Act with respect to a person, as described in paragraphs (a)(2)(i) and (a)(2)(ii) of this section, will be penalized in accordance with paragraph (g)(2) of this section. A title IV–E agency or entity determined to be in violation of section 471(a)(18) of the Act as a result of a court finding will be penalized in accordance with paragraph (g)(4) of this section. The title IV–E agency may develop, obtain approval of, and implement a plan of corrective action any time after it receives written notification from ACF that it is in violation of section 471(a)(18) of the Act.

(2) Corrective action plans are subject to ACF approval.

(3) If the corrective action plan does not meet the provisions of paragraph (d) of this section, the title IV–E agency must revise and resubmit the plan for approval until it has an approved plan.

(4) A title IV–E agency or entity found to be in violation of section 471(a)(18) of the Act by a court must notify ACF within 30 days from the date of entry of the final judgment once all appeals have been exhausted, declined, or the appeal period has expired.

(c) Corrective action for violations resulting from a title IV–E agency's statute, regulation, policy, procedure, or practice.

(1) A title IV–E agency found to have committed a violation of the type described in paragraph (a)(2)(iii) of this section must develop and submit a corrective action plan within 30 days of receiving written notification from ACF that it is in violation of section 471(a)(18). Once the plan is approved the title IV–E agency will have to complete the corrective action and come into compliance. If the title IV–E agency fails to complete the corrective action plan within six months and come into compliance, a penalty will be imposed in accordance with paragraph (g)(3) of this section.

(2) Corrective action plans are subject to ACF approval.

(3) If the corrective action plan does not meet the provisions of paragraph (d) of this section, the title IV–E agency must revise and resubmit the plan within 30 days from the date it receives a written notice from ACF that the plan has not been approved. If the title IV–E agency does not submit a revised corrective action plan according to the provisions of paragraph (d) of this section, withholding of funds pursuant to the provisions of paragraph (g) of this section will apply.

(d) Contents of a corrective action plan. A corrective action plan must:

(1) Identify the issues to be addressed;

(2) Set forth the steps for taking corrective action;

(3) Identify any technical assistance needs and Federal and non–Federal sources of technical assistance which will be used to complete the action steps; and,

(4) Specify the completion date. This date will be no later than 6 months from the date ACF approves the corrective action plan.

(e) Evaluation of corrective action plan. ACF will evaluate corrective action plans and notify the title IV–E agency (in writing) of its success or failure to complete the plan within 30 calendar days. If the title IV–E agency has failed to complete the corrective action plan, ACF will calculate the amount of reduction in the title IV–E agency's title IV–E payment and include this information in the written notification of failure to complete the plan.

11

(f) Funds to be withheld. The term "title IV–E funds" refers to the amount of Federal funds advanced or paid to the title IV–E agency for allowable costs incurred by a title IV–E agency for: foster care maintenance payments, adoption assistance payments, administrative costs, and training costs under title IV–E and includes the title IV–E agency's allotment for the Chafee Foster Care Independence Program under section 477 of the Act.

(g) Reduction of title IV–E funds.

(1) Title IV–E funds shall be reduced in specified amounts in accordance with paragraph (h) of this section under the following circumstances:

(i) A determination that a title IV–E agency or entity is in violation of section 471(a)(18) of the Act with respect to a person as described in paragraphs (a)(2)(i) and (a)(2)(ii) of this section, or:

(ii) After a title IV–E agency's failure to implement and complete a corrective action plan and come into compliance as described in paragraph (c) of this section.

(2) Once ACF notifies a title IV–E agency (in writing) that it has committed a section 471(a)(18) violation with respect to a person, the title IV–E agency's title IV–E funds will be reduced for the fiscal quarter in which the title IV–E agency received written notification and for each succeeding quarter within that fiscal year or until the title IV–E agency completes a corrective action plan and comes into compliance, whichever is earlier. Once ACF notifies an entity (in writing) that it has committed a section 471(a)(18) violation with respect to a person, the entity must remit to the Secretary all title IV–E funds paid to it by the title IV–E agency during the quarter in which the entity is notified of the violation.

(3) For title IV–E agencies that fail to complete a corrective action plan within 6 months, title IV–E funds will be reduced by ACF for the fiscal quarter in which the title IV–E agency received notification of its violation. The reduction will continue for each succeeding quarter within that fiscal year or until the title IV–E agency completes the corrective action plan and comes into compliance, whichever is earlier.

(4) If, as a result of a court finding, a title IV–E agency or entity is determined to be in violation of section 471(a)(18) of the Act, ACF will assess a penalty without further investigation. Once the title IV–E agency is notified (in writing) of the violation, its title IV–E funds will be reduced for the fiscal quarter in which the court finding was made and for each succeeding quarter within that fiscal year or until the title IV–E agency completes a corrective action plan and comes into compliance, whichever is sooner. Once an entity is notified (in writing) of the violation, the entity must remit to the Secretary all title IV–E funds paid to it by the title IV–E agency during the quarter in which the court finding was made.

(5) The maximum number of quarters that a title IV–E agency will have its title IV–E funds reduced due to a finding of a title IV–E agency's failure to conform to section 471(a)(18) of the Act is limited to the number of quarters within the fiscal year in which a determination of nonconformity was made. However, an uncorrected violation may result in a subsequent review, another finding, and additional penalties.

(6) No penalty will be imposed for a court finding of a violation of section 471(a)(18) until the judgement is final and all appeals have been exhausted, declined, or the appeal period has expired.

(h) Determination of the amount of reduction of Federal funds. ACF will determine the reduction in title IV–E funds due to a section 471(a)(18) violation in accordance with section 474(d)(1) and (2) of the Act.

(1) Title IV–E agencies that violate section 471(a)(18) with respect to a person or fail to implement or complete a corrective action plan as described in paragraph (c) of this section will be subject to a penalty. The penalty structure will follow section 474(d)(1) of the Act. Penalties will be levied for the quarter of the fiscal year in which the title IV–E agency is notified of its section 471(a)(18) violation, and for each succeeding quarter within that fiscal year until the title IV–E agency comes into compliance with section 471(a)(18). The reduction in title IV–E funds will be computed as follows:

(i) 2 percent of the title IV–E agency's title IV–E funds for the fiscal year quarter, as defined in paragraph (f) of this section, for the first finding of noncompliance in that fiscal year;

(ii) 3 percent of the title IV–E agency's title IV–E funds for the fiscal year quarter, as defined in paragraph (f) of this section, for the second finding of noncompliance in that fiscal year;

(iii) 5 percent of the title IV–E agency's title IV–E funds for the fiscal year quarter, as defined in paragraph (f) of this section, for the third or subsequent finding of noncompliance in that fiscal year.

(2) Any entity (other than the title IV–E agency) which violates section 471(a)(18) of the Act during a fiscal quarter must remit to the Secretary all title IV–E funds paid to it by the title IV–E agency in accordance with the procedures in paragraphs (g)(2) or (g)(4) of this section.

(3) No fiscal year payment to a title IV–E agency will be reduced by more than 5 percent of its title IV–E funds, as defined in paragraph (f) of this section, where the title IV–E agency has been determined to be out of compliance with section 471(a)(18) of the Act.

(4) The title IV–E agency or an entity, as applicable, will be liable for interest on the amount of funds reduced by the Department, in accordance with the provisions of 45 CFR 30.18.

§ 1355.39. Administrative and judicial review

A title IV–E agency determined not to be in substantial conformity with titles IV–B and IV–E plan requirements, or a title IV–E agency or an entity in violation of section 471(a)(18) of the Act:

(a) May appeal, pursuant to 45 CFR part 16, the final determination and any subsequent withholding of, or reduction in, funds to the HHS Departmental Appeals Board within 60 days after receipt of a notice of nonconformity described in § 1355.36(e)(1) of this part, or receipt of a notice of noncompliance by ACF as described in § 1355.38(a)(3) of this part; and

(b) Will have the opportunity to obtain judicial review of an adverse decision of the Departmental Appeals Board within 60 days after the title IV–E agency or entity receives notice of the decision by the Board. Appeals of adverse Department Appeals Board decisions must be made to the district court of the United States for the judicial district in which the principal or headquarters office of the agency responsible for administering the program is located.

(c) The procedure described in paragraphs (a) and (b) of this section will not apply to a finding that a title IV–E agency or an entity has been determined to be in violation of section 471(a)(18) which is based on a judicial decision.

§ 1356.20. Title IV-E plan document and submission requirements

(a) To be in compliance with the title IV–E plan requirements and to be eligible to receive Federal financial participation (FFP) in the costs of foster care maintenance payments and adoption assistance under this part, a title IV–E agency must have a plan approved by the Secretary that meets the requirements of this part, part 1355 section 471(a) of the Act and for Tribal IV–E agencies, section 479B(c) of the Act. The title IV-E plan must be submitted to the appropriate Regional Office, ACYF, in a form determined by the title IV–E agency.

(b) Failure by a title IV–E agency to comply with the requirements and standards for the data reporting system for foster care and adoption (§ 1355.40 of this chapter) shall be considered a substantial failure by the title–IV-E agency in complying with the plan.

(c) The following procedures for approval of plans and amendments apply to the title IV–E program:

(1) Plan. The plan consists of written documents furnished by the title IV–E agency to cover its program under part E of title IV. After approval of the original plan by the Commissioner, ACYF, all relevant changes, required by new statutes, rules, regulations, interpretations, and court decisions, are required to be submitted currently so that ACYF may determine whether the plan continues to meet Federal requirements and policies.

(2) Submittal. Plans and revisions of the plans are submitted first to the State governor or his/her designee, or the Tribal leader or his/her designee for review and then to the regional office, ACYF. Title IV–E agencies are encouraged to obtain consultation of the regional staff when a plan is in process of preparation or revision.

(3) Review. Staff in the regional offices are responsible for review of plans and amendments. They also initiate discussion with the title IV–E agency on clarification of significant aspects of the plan which come to their attention in the course of this review. Plan material on which the regional staff has questions concerning the application of Federal policy is referred with recommendations as required to the central office for technical assistance. Comments and suggestions, including those of consultants in specified areas, may be prepared by the central office for use by the regional staff in negotiations with the title IV–E agency.

(4) Action. ACYF has the authority to approve plans and amendments thereto which provide for the administration of foster care maintenance payments and adoption assistance programs under section 471 of the Act. The Commissioner, ACYF, retains the authority to determine that proposed plan material is not approvable, or that a previously approved plan no longer meets the requirements for approval. The Regional Office, ACYF, formally notifies the title IV–E agency of the actions taken on plans or revisions.

(5) Basis for approval. Determinations as to whether plans (including plan amendments and administrative practice under the plans) originally meet or continue to meet, the requirements for approval are based on relevant Federal statutes and regulations.

(6) Prompt approval of plans. The determination as to whether a plan submitted for approval conforms to the requirements for approval under the Act and regulations issued pursuant thereto shall be made promptly and not later than the 45th day following the date on which the plan submittal is received in the regional office, unless the Regional Office, ACYF, has secured from the title IV–E agency a written agreement to extend that period.

(7) Prompt approval of plan amendments. Any amendment of an approved plan may, at the option of the title IV–E agency, be considered as a submission of a new plan. If the title IV–E agency requests that such amendment be so considered, the determination as to its conformity with the requirements for approval shall be made promptly and not later than the 45th day following the date on which such a request is received in the regional office with respect to an amendment that has been received in such office, unless the Regional Office, ACYF, has secured from the title IV–E agency a written agreement to extend that period. In absence of request by a title IV–E agency that an amendment of an approved plan shall be considered as a submission of a new plan, the procedures under § 201.6(a) and (b) shall be applicable.

(8) Effective date. The effective date of a new plan may not be earlier than the first day of the calendar quarter in which an approvable plan is submitted, and with respect to expenditures for assistance under such plan, may not be earlier than the first day on which the plan is in operation on a statewide basis or, in the case of a Tribal title IV–E agency, in operation in the Tribal title IV–E agency's entire service area. The same applies with respect to plan amendments.

(d) Once the title IV–E plan has been submitted and approved, it shall remain in effect until amendments are required. An amendment is required if there is any significant and relevant change in the information or assurances in the plan, or the organization, policies or operations described in the plan.

§ 1356.21. Foster care maintenance payments program implementation requirements.

(a) Statutory and regulatory requirements of the Federal foster care program. To implement the foster care maintenance payments program provisions of the title IV–E plan and to be eligible to receive Federal financial participation (FFP) for foster care maintenance payments under this part, a title IV–E agency must meet the requirements of this section, 45 CFR 1356.22, 45 CFR 1356.30, and sections 472, 475(1), 475(4), 475(5), 475(6), and for a Tribal title IV–E agency section 479(B)(c)(1)(C)(ii)(II) of the Act.

(b) Reasonable efforts. The title IV–E agency must make reasonable efforts to maintain the family unit and prevent the unnecessary removal of a child from his/her home, as long as the child's safety is assured; to effect the safe reunification of the child and family (if temporary out-of-home placement is necessary to ensure the immediate safety of the child); and to make and finalize alternate permanency plans in a timely manner when reunification is not appropriate or possible. In order to satisfy the "reasonable efforts" requirements of section 471(a)(15) (as implemented through section 472(a)(2) of the Act), the title IV–E agency must meet the requirements of paragraphs (b) and (d) of this section. In determining reasonable efforts to be made with respect to a child and in making such reasonable efforts, the child's health and safety must be the paramount concern.

(1) Judicial determination of reasonable efforts to prevent a child's removal from the home.

(i) When a child is removed from his/her home, the judicial determination as to whether reasonable efforts were made, or were not required to prevent the removal, in accordance with paragraph (b)(3) of this section, must be made no later than 60 days from the date the child is removed from the home pursuant to paragraph (k)(1)(ii) of this section.

(ii) If the determination concerning reasonable efforts to prevent the removal is not made as specified in paragraph (b)(1)(i) of this section, the child is not eligible under the title IV–E foster care maintenance payments program for the duration of that stay in foster care.

(2) Judicial determination of reasonable efforts to finalize a permanency plan.

(i) The title IV–E agency must obtain a judicial determination that it has made reasonable efforts to finalize the permanency plan that is in effect (whether the plan is reunification, adoption, legal guardianship, placement with a fit and willing relative, or placement in another planned permanent living arrangement) within twelve months of the date the child is considered to have entered foster care in accordance with the definition at § 1355.20 of this part, and at least once every twelve months thereafter while the child is in foster care.

(ii) If such a judicial determination regarding reasonable efforts to finalize a permanency plan is not made in accordance with the schedule prescribed in paragraph (b)(2)(i) of this section, the child becomes ineligible under title IV–E at the end of the month in which the judicial determination was required to have been made, and remains ineligible until such a determination is made.

(3) Circumstances in which reasonable efforts are not required to prevent a child's removal from home or to reunify the child and family. Reasonable efforts to prevent a child's removal from home or to reunify the child and family are not required if the title IV–E agency obtains a judicial determination that such efforts are not required because:

(i) A court of competent jurisdiction has determined that the parent has subjected the child to aggravated circumstances (as defined in State, or for a Tribal title IV–E agency, Tribal law, which definition may include but need not be limited to abandonment, torture, chronic abuse, and sexual abuse);

(ii) A court of competent jurisdiction has determined that the parent has been convicted of:

(A) Murder (which would have been an offense under section 1111(a) of title 18, United States Code, if the offense had occurred in the special maritime or territorial jurisdiction of the United States) of another child of the parent;

(B) Voluntary manslaughter (which would have been an offense under section 1112(a) of title 18, United States Code, if the offense had occurred in the special maritime or territorial jurisdiction of the United States) of another child of the parent;

(C) Aiding or abetting, attempting, conspiring, or soliciting to commit such a murder or such a voluntary manslaughter; or

(D) A felony assault that results in serious bodily injury to the child or another child of the parent; or,

(iii) The parental rights of the parent with respect to a sibling have been terminated involuntarily.

(4) Concurrent planning. Reasonable efforts to finalize an alternate permanency plan may be made concurrently with reasonable efforts to reunify the child and family.

(5) Use of the Federal Parent Locator Service. The State agency may seek the services of the Federal Parent Locator Service to search for absent parents at any point in order to facilitate a permanency plan.

(c) Contrary to the welfare determination. Under section 472(a)(2) of the Act, a child's removal from the home must have been the result of a judicial determination (unless the child was removed pursuant to a voluntary placement agreement) to the effect that continuation of residence in the home would be contrary to the welfare, or that placement would be in the best interest, of the child. The contrary to the welfare determination must be made in the first court ruling that sanctions (even temporarily) the removal of a child from home. If the determination regarding contrary to the welfare is not made in the first court ruling pertaining to removal from the home, the child is not eligible for title IV–E foster care maintenance payments for the duration of that stay in foster care.

(d) Documentation of judicial determinations. The judicial determinations regarding contrary to the welfare, reasonable efforts to prevent removal, and reasonable efforts to finalize the permanency plan in effect, including judicial determinations that reasonable efforts are not required, must be explicitly documented and must be made on a case-by-case basis and so stated in the court order.

(1) If the reasonable efforts and contrary to the welfare judicial determinations are not included as required in the court orders identified in paragraphs (b) and (c) of this section, a transcript of the court proceedings is the only other documentation that will be accepted to verify that these required determinations have been made.

(2) Neither affidavits nor nunc pro tunc orders will be accepted as verification documentation in support of reasonable efforts and contrary to the welfare judicial determinations except for a Tribal title IV–E agency for the first 12 months that agency's title IV–E plan is in effect as provided for in section 479B(c)(1)(C)(ii)(I) of the Act.

(3) Court orders that reference State or Tribal law to substantiate judicial determinations are not acceptable, even if such law provides that a removal must be based on a judicial determination that remaining in the home would be contrary to the child's welfare or that removal can only be ordered after reasonable efforts have been made.

(e) Trial home visits. A trial home visit may not exceed six months in duration, unless a court orders a longer trial home visit. If a trial home visit extends beyond six months and has not been authorized by the court, or exceeds the time period the court has deemed appropriate, and the child is subsequently returned to foster care, that placement must then be considered a new placement and title IV–E eligibility must be newly established. Under these circumstances the judicial determinations regarding contrary to the welfare and reasonable efforts to prevent removal are required.

(f) Case review system. In order to satisfy the provisions of section 471(a)(16) of the Act regarding a case review system, each title IV–E agency's case review system must meet the requirements of sections 475(5) and 475(6) of the Act.

(g) Case plan requirements. In order to satisfy the case plan requirements of sections 471(a)(16), 475(1) and 475(5)(A) and (D) of the Act, the title IV–E agency must promulgate policy materials and instructions for use by staff to determine the appropriateness of and necessity for the foster care placement of the child. The case plan for each child must:

(1) Be a written document, which is a discrete part of the case record, in a format determined by the title IV–E agency, which is developed jointly with the parent(s) or guardian of the child in foster care; and

(2) Be developed within a reasonable period, to be established by the title IV–E agency, but in no event later than 60 days from the child's removal from the home pursuant to paragraph (k) of this section;

(3) Include a discussion of how the case plan is designed to achieve a safe placement for the child in the least restrictive (most family-like) setting available and in close proximity to the home of the parent(s) when the case plan goal is reunification and a discussion of how the placement is consistent with the best interests and special needs of the child. (FFP is not available when a court orders a placement with a specific foster care provider);

(4) Include a description of the services offered and provided to prevent removal of the child from the home and to reunify the family; and

(5) Document the steps to finalize a placement when the case plan goal is or becomes adoption or placement in another permanent home in accordance with sections 475(1)(E) and (5)(E) of the Act. When the case plan goal is adoption, at a minimum, such documentation shall include child-specific recruitment efforts such as the use of State, Tribal, regional, and national adoption exchanges including electronic exchange systems

(h) Application of the permanency hearing requirements.

(1) To meet the requirements of the permanency hearing, the title IV–E agency must, among other requirements, comply with section 475(5)(C) of the Act.

(2) In accordance with paragraph (b)(3) of this section, when a court determines that reasonable efforts to return the child home are not required, a permanency hearing must be held within 30 days of that determination, unless the requirements of the permanency hearing are fulfilled at the hearing in which the court determines that reasonable efforts to reunify the child and family are not required.

(3) If the title IV–E agency concludes, after considering reunification, adoption, legal guardianship, or permanent placement with a fit and willing relative, that the most appropriate permanency plan for a child is placement in another planned permanent living arrangement, the title IV–E agency must document to the court the compelling reason for the alternate plan. Examples of a compelling reason for establishing such a permanency plan may include:

(i) The case of an older teen who specifically requests that emancipation be established as his/her permanency plan;

(ii) The case of a parent and child who have a significant bond but the parent is unable to care for the child because of an emotional or physical disability and the child's foster parents have committed to raising him/her to the age of majority and to facilitate visitation with the disabled parent; or,

(iii) the Tribe has identified another planned permanent living arrangement for the child.

(4) When an administrative body, appointed or approved by the court, conducts the permanency hearing, the procedural safeguards set forth in the definition of permanency hearing must be so extended by the administrative body.

(i) Application of the requirements for filing a petition to terminate parental rights at section 475(5)(E) of the Social Security Act.

(1) Subject to the exceptions in paragraph (i)(2) of this section, the title IV–E agency must file a petition (or, if such a petition has been filed by another party, seek to be joined as a party to the petition) to terminate the parental rights of a parent(s):

(i) Whose child has been in foster care under the responsibility of the title IV–E agency for 15 of the most recent 22 months. The petition must be filed by the end of the child's fifteenth month in foster care. In calculating when to file a petition for termination of parental rights, the title IV–E agency:

(A) Must calculate the 15 out of the most recent 22 month period from the date the child is considered to have entered foster care as defined at section 475(5)(F) of the Act and § 1355.20 of this part;

(B) Must use a cumulative method of calculation when a child experiences multiple exits from and entries into foster care during the 22 month period;

(C) Must not include trial home visits or runaway episodes in calculating 15 months in foster care; and,

(D) Need only apply section 475(5)(E) of the Act to a child once if the title IV–E agency does not file a petition because one of the exceptions at paragraph (i)(2) of this section applies;

(ii) Whose child has been determined by a court of competent jurisdiction to be an abandoned infant (as defined under State or for a Tribal title IV–E agency, Tribal law). The petition to terminate parental rights must be filed within 60 days of the judicial determination that the child is an abandoned infant; or,

(iii) Who has been convicted of one of the felonies listed at paragraph (b)(3)(ii) of this section. Under such circumstances, the petition to terminate parental rights must be filed within 60 days of a judicial determination that reasonable efforts to reunify the child and parent are not required.

(2) The title IV–E agency may elect not to file or join a petition to terminate the parental rights of a parent per paragraph (i)(1) of this section if:

(i) At the option of the title IV–E agency, the child is being cared for by a relative;

(ii) The title IV–E agency has documented in the case plan (which must be available for court review) a compelling reason for determining that filing such a petition would not be in the best interests of the individual child. Compelling reasons for not filing a petition to terminate parental rights include, but are not limited to:

(A) Adoption is not the appropriate permanency goal for the child; or,

(B) No grounds to file a petition to terminate parental rights exist; or,

(C) The child is an unaccompanied refugee minor as defined in 45 CFR 400.111; or

(D) There are international legal obligations or compelling foreign policy reasons that would preclude terminating parental rights; or

(iii) The title IV–E agency has not provided to the family, consistent with the time period in the case plan, services that the title IV–E agency deems necessary for the safe return of the child to the home, when reasonable efforts to reunify the family are required.

(3) When the title IV–E agency files or joins a petition to terminate parental rights in accordance with paragraph (i)(1) of this section, it must concurrently begin to identify, recruit, process, and approve a qualified adoptive family for the child.

(j) Child of a minor parent in foster care. Foster care maintenance payments made on behalf of a child placed in a foster family home or child care institution, who is the parent of a son or daughter in the same home or institution, must include amounts which are necessary to cover costs incurred on behalf of the child's son or daughter. Said costs must be limited to funds expended on items listed in the definition of foster care maintenance payments in § 1355.20 of this part.

(k) Removal from the home of a specified relative.

(1) For the purposes of meeting the requirements of section 472(a)(1) of the Act, a removal from the home must occur pursuant to:

(i) A voluntary placement agreement entered into by a parent or guardian which leads to a physical or constructive removal (i.e., a non-physical or paper removal of custody) of the child from the home; or

(ii) A judicial order for a physical or constructive removal of the child from a parent or specified relative.

(2) A removal has not occurred in situations where legal custody is removed from the parent or relative and the child remains with the same relative in that home under supervision by the title IV–E agency.

(3) A child is considered constructively removed on the date of the first judicial order removing custody, even temporarily, from the appropriate specified relative or the date that the voluntary placement agreement is signed by all relevant parties.

(l) Living with a specified relative. For purposes of meeting the requirements for living with a specified relative prior to removal from the home under section 472(a)(1) of the Act, all of the conditions under section 472(a)(3), and for Tribal title IV–E agencies section 479B(c)(1)(C)(ii)(II) of the Act, one of the two following situations must apply:

(1) The child was living with the parent or specified relative, and was AFDC eligible in that home in the month of the voluntary placement agreement or initiation of court proceedings; or

(2) The child had been living with the parent or specified relative within six months of the month of the voluntary placement agreement or the initiation of court proceedings, and the child would have been AFDC eligible in that month if s/he had still been living in that home.

(m) Review of payments and licensing standards. In meeting the requirements of section 471(a)(11) of the Act, the title IV–E agency must review at reasonable, specific, time-limited periods to be established by the agency:

(1) The amount of the payments made for foster care maintenance and adoption assistance to assure their continued appropriateness; and

(2) The licensing or approval standards for child care institutions and foster family homes.

(n) Foster care goals. The specific foster care goals required under section 471(a)(14) of the Act must be incorporated into State law or Tribal law by statute, code, resolution, Tribal proceedings or administrative regulation with the force of law.

(o) Notice and right to be heard. The title IV–E agency must provide the foster parent(s) of a child and any preadoptive parent or relative providing care for the child with timely notice of and the opportunity to be heard in any proceedings held with respect to the child during the time the child is in the care of such foster parent, preadoptive parent, or relative caregiver. Notice of and opportunity to be heard does not include the right to standing as a party to the case.

§ 1356.22. Implementation requirements for children voluntarily placed in foster care

11

(a) As a condition of receipt of Federal financial participation (FFP) in foster care maintenance payments for a dependent child removed from his home under a voluntary placement agreement, the title IV–E agency must meet the requirements of:

(1) Section 472 of the Act, as amended;

(2) Sections 422(b)(8) and 475(5) of the Act;

(3) 45 CFR 1356.21 (e), (f), (g), (h), and (i); and

(4) The requirements of this section.

(b) Federal financial participation is available only for voluntary foster care maintenance expenditures made within the first 180 days of the child's placement in foster care unless there has been a judicial determination by a court of competent jurisdiction, within the first 180 days of such placement, to the effect that the continued voluntary placement is in the best interests of the child.

(c) The title IV–E agency must establish and maintain a uniform procedure or system, consistent with State or Tribal law, for revocation by the parent(s) of a voluntary placement agreement and return of the child.

§ 1356.30. Safety requirements for foster care and adoptive home providers.

(a) The title IV–E agency must provide documentation that criminal records checks have been conducted with respect to prospective foster and adoptive parents.

(b) The title IV–E agency may not approve or license any prospective foster or adoptive parent, nor may the title IV–E agency claim FFP for any foster care maintenance or adoption assistance payment made on behalf of a child placed in a foster home operated under the auspices of a child placing agency or on behalf of a child placed in an adoptive home through a private adoption agency, if the title IV–E finds that, based on a criminal records check conducted in accordance with paragraph (a) of this section, a court of competent jurisdiction has determined that the prospective foster or adoptive parent has been convicted of a felony involving:

(1) Child abuse or neglect;

(2) Spousal abuse;

(3) A crime against a child or children (including child pornography); or,

(4) A crime involving violence, including rape, sexual assault, or homicide, but not including other physical assault or battery.

(c) The title IV–E agency may not approve or license any prospective foster or adoptive parent, nor may the title IV–E agency claim FFP for any foster care maintenance or adoption assistance payment made on behalf of a child placed in a foster home operated under the auspices of a child placing agency or on behalf of a child placed in an adoptive home through a private adoption agency, if the title IV–E agency finds, based on a criminal records check conducted in accordance with paragraph (a) of this section, that a court of competent jurisdiction has determined that the prospective foster or adoptive parent has, within the last five years, been convicted of a felony involving: (1) Physical assault;

(2) Battery; or,

(3) A drug-related offense.

(d) [Reserved by 77 FR 949]

(e) In all cases where the State opted out of the criminal records check requirement, as permitted prior to the amendments made by section 152 of Public Law 109-248, the licensing file for that foster or adoptive family must contain documentation which verifies that safety considerations with respect to the caretaker(s) have been addressed.

(f) In order for a child care institution to be eligible for title IV–E funding, the licensing file for the institution must contain documentation which verifies that safety considerations with respect to the staff of the institution have been addressed.

Additional Materials

Note: The following materials are available in the eBook version of this Sourcebook. See the Electronic Download page at the front of this book for instructions on downloading a copy of the eBook.

Prison Rape Elimination Act, 42 U.S.C. §§ 30301–30309

United States Sentencing Commission Guidelines Manual, Chapter 4: Criminal History and Criminal Livelihood

PART 12

Table of Authorities and Index

Cases

D

Federal Statutes, Rules, and Regulations

12

Massachusetts Statutes, Rules, and Regulations

12

Massachusetts General Laws (G.L. c.)
Massachusetts General Laws (G.L. c.)

12

Additional References and Resources

Index

12

12

12

12

12

12

12

12

12

12

12

12

12

12